The Cambridge Dictionary of

Classical Civilization

The Cambridge Dictionary of
Classical Civilization

edited by

GRAHAM SHIPLEY
JOHN VANDERSPOEL
DAVID MATTINGLY
LIN FOXHALL

Advisory Editors

SUSANNA BRAUND
AVERIL CAMERON
HELENE FOLEY
DAVID FURLEY
NATALIE BOYMEL KAMPEN
BERYL RAWSON
DAVID SEDLEY
RICHARD SORABJI
ROGER WILSON

CAMBRIDGE UNIVERSITY PRESS
Cambridge, New York, Melbourne, Madrid, Cape Town, Singapore, São Paulo

Cambridge University Press
The Edinburgh Building, Cambridge CB2 2RU, UK

Published in the United States of America by Cambridge University Press, New York

www.cambridge.org
Information on this title: www.cambridge.org/9780521483131

First published 2006

Printed in the United Kingdom at the University Press, Cambridge

A catalogue record for this book is available from the British Library

ISBN-13 978-0-521-48313-1 hardback
ISBN-10 0-521-48313-1 hardback

Contents

List of contributors *page vi*
Editors' preface *xv*
Acknowledgements *xvii*
How to use this book *xviii*
Classified list of headwords *xxi*
Headwords not covered in the *Oxford Classical Dictionary* *xxxii*
Some technical terms *xxxv*
List of abbreviations *xliii*

Dictionary entries A–Z *1*

Sources and acknowledgements for figures *963*

Contributors

To enable the reader to identify authors from the initials appended to entries, names are here ordered, first by *final initial*, then by first initial, second initial, and so on. Authors with hyphenated surnames are therefore ordered by final initial, not by the first letter of their surname.

CA Catherine Atherton
University of California Los Angeles

CEPA Colin E. P. Adams
University of Liverpool

GSA Gregory S. Aldrete
University of Wisconsin, Green Bay

JJA Jean-Jacques Aubert
Université de Neuchâtel

JKA J. K. Aitken
University of Reading

KWA K.W. Arafat
King's College London

SEA Susan E. Alcock
Brown University

TJA Tana J. Allen
Memorial University of Newfoundland

AB Andrew Barker
University of Birmingham

AJLB Alastair J. L. Blanshard
University of Sydney

CGB Christopher G. Brown
University of Western Ontario

CK-B Clare F. Kelly-Blazeby
University of Leicester

DJB D. J. Blackman
Oxford

HB Hugh Bowden
King's College London

KB Kai Brodersen
Universität Mannheim

MB Maria Brosius
University of Newcastle upon Tyne

PAB Patricia A. Baker
University of Kent at Canterbury

PMB Philip Beagon
Hulme Grammar School for Girls, Manchester

RSB	ROGER S. BAGNALL *Columbia University*
SB	SUSANNA BRAUND *Stanford University*
SMB	STANLEY M. BURSTEIN *California State University, Los Angeles*
ASEC	SIMON ESMONDE CLEARY *University of Birmingham*
CC	CRAIG COOPER *University of Winnipeg*
GC	GILLIAN CLARK *University of Bristol*
GLC	GORDON CAMPBELL *National University of Ireland, Maynooth*
JBC	BRIAN CAMPBELL *The Queen's University of Belfast*
JCNC	JON COULSTON *University of St Andrews*
JDC	DUNCAN CLOUD *University of Leicester*
JRCC	ROBERT COUSLAND *University of British Columbia*
KMC	KATHLEEN COLEMAN *Harvard University*
MJC	MICHAEL J. CARTER *Brock University*
NJC	NEIL CHRISTIE *University of Leicester*
PAC	PAUL CARTLEDGE *University of Cambridge*
RBC	R. BERTOLÍN CEBRIÁN *University of Calgary*
RIC	ROBERT I. CURTIS *University of Georgia*
SC	SARAH CURRIE *Ashtead, UK*
AD	ANDREW DALBY *St. Coutant, Deux-Sèvres, France*
DD	DAVID DUNGWORTH *English Heritage*
ED	EMMA DENCH *Birkbeck College, University of London*
HD	HAZEL DODGE *Trinity College Dublin*
JDD	JOHN DILLERY *University of Virginia*
JKD	JOHN K. DAVIES *University of Liverpool*

SD SUZANNE DIXON
Brisbane, Australia

SLD STEPHEN DYSON
State University of New York at Buffalo

HE HELLA ECKARDT
University of Reading

HWE HUGH ELTON
British Institute at Ankara

MJE MICHAEL J. EDWARDS
Queen Mary, University of London

BWF BRUCE W. FRIER
University of Michigan

CMF COLIN FORCEY
Portsmouth

DJF DAVID FURLEY
Princeton University

GF GEORGE FERZOCO
University of Leicester

HAF HAMISH FORBES
University of Nottingham

HPF HELENE P. FOLEY
Barnard College, Columbia University

LF LIN FOXHALL
University of Leicester

PWF PEDAR W. FOSS
DePauw University

REF REBECCA FLEMMING
King's College London

AG ALAN M. GREAVES
University of Liverpool

DWJG DAVID GILL
University of Wales Swansea

KG KEVIN GREENE
University of Newcastle upon Tyne

MDG MARTIN GOODMAN
University of Oxford

MG MONICA GALE
Trinity College Dublin

MJG MARTIN GOALEN
Academy Projects LLP, London

PMG PETER GREEN
University of Texas at Austin

AMH ANGELA M. HEAP
Cambridge

CH CHRISTOPHER HOWGEGO
Ashmolean Museum, University of Oxford

JH JANET HUSKINSON
The Open University

JRH	J. R. Hume *University of Calgary*
KH	Kenneth W. Harl *Tulane University*
LAH	Lisa A. Hughes *University of Calgary*
MDH	Mark Humphries *National University of Ireland, Maynooth*
MEH	Mary Harlow *University of Birmingham*
MHH	Mogens Herman Hansen *Copenhagen Polis Centre*
PRH	Philip Hardie *Corpus Christi College, Oxford*
RBH	R. Bruce Hitchner *Tufts University, Medford, Mass.*
RJH	Jim Hankinson *University of Texas at Austin*
TH	Tamar Hodos *University of Bristol*
TNH	Thomas Habinek *University of Southern California*
VDH	Victor Davis Hanson *The Hoover Institute, Stanford University*
WH	Waldemar Heckel *University of Calgary*
AJ	Anton G. Jansen *Brock University*
LL-J	Lloyd Llewellyn-Jones *University of Edinburgh*
MHJ	†M. H. Jameson *Stanford University*
MJ	Mark Joyal *University of Manitoba*
RLJ	R. L. Judson *Christ Church, Oxford*
RPD-J	R. P. Duncan-Jones *Gonville and Caius College, Cambridge*
CSK	C. S. Kraus *Yale University*
DLK	David Kennedy *University of Western Australia*
DPK	Dennis Kehoe *Tulane University*
HK	Helen King *University of Reading*
IK	Ioanna Kralli *Hellenic Open University*

LK	LAWRENCE KEPPIE *Hunterian Museum, University of Glasgow*
MK	MARC KLEIJWEGT *University of Wisconsin–Madison*
NBK	NATALIE BOYMEL KAMPEN *Barnard College, Columbia University*
BML	B. M. LEVICK *St Hilda's College, Oxford*
JDeL	JANET DELAINE *University of Reading*
KL	KATHRYN LOMAS *Institute of Archaeology, University College London*
RJL	ROGER LING *University of Manchester*
RL	RAY LAURENCE *University of Birmingham*
DJM	DAVID J. MATTINGLY *University of Leicester*
EACM	EIREANN MARSHALL *Open University*
FMM	FIONA MCHARDY *University of Roehampton*
HBM	HAROLD MATTINGLY *Cambridge*
IM	IAN MORRIS *Stanford University*
JDM	J. D. MUHLY *University of Pennsylvania*
JM	JUSTIN J. MEGGITT *University of Cambridge*
KM	KIERAN MCGROARTY *National University of Ireland, Maynooth*
LGM	LYNETTE G. MITCHELL *University of Exeter*
MDM	MARK MONAGHAN *Glasgow*
MLM	MICHELLE L. MANN *University of Leicester*
MM	MARK MUNN *Pennsylvania State University*
PJEM	PHILIP J. E. MILLS *University of Leicester*
WHM	W. H. MANNING *Cardiff University*
WMM	WILLIAM M. MURRAY *University of South Florida*
HSN	HANNE SIGISMUND NIELSEN *University of Calgary*

LCN LISA C. NEVETT
University of Michigan

OVN ONNO M. VAN NIJF
University of Groningen

GJO G. J. OLIVER
University of Liverpool

JO JOSIAH OBER
Princeton University

DP DOMINIC PERRING
University College London

DSP DAVID POTTER
University of Michigan

EP EVA PARISINOU
Open University, London

JJP JEREMY PATERSON
University of Newcastle upon Tyne

JP J. R. PORTER
University of Saskatchewan

JRP JOHN R. PATTERSON
Magdalene College, Cambridge

JRWP JONATHAN R. W. PRAG
Merton College, Oxford

NDP NIGEL POLLARD
University of Wales Swansea

TGP TIM G. PARKIN
University of Queensland

TWP †TIM POTTER
British Museum

BR BERYL RAWSON
Australian National University

CLNR CLIVE RUGGLES
University of Leicester

DR DAVID RIDGWAY
Institute of Classical Studies, London

EER E. E. RICE
Wolfson College, Oxford

GR GARY REGER
Trinity College (Hartford, Connecticut)

JBR J. B. RIVES
York University, Toronto

JSR JOHN S. RICHARDSON
University of Edinburgh

JWR JOHN RICH
University of Nottingham

LR LYN RODLEY
The Queen's University of Belfast/Open University

TER T. E. RIHLL
University of Wales Swansea

BAS B. A. SPARKES
University of Southampton

CJS CHRISTOPHER SMITH
University of St Andrews

DGJS D. GRAHAM J. SHIPLEY
University of Leicester

DLS DAVID L. STONE
Florida State University

DNS DAVID SEDLEY
University of Cambridge

EJS E. J. STAFFORD
University of Leeds

GB-S G. R. BOYS-STONES
University of Durham

JBS J. B. SALMON
University of Nottingham

LFS LOUISE STEEL
University of Wales Lampeter

NS NIGEL SPENCER
London

PDeS PHILIP DE SOUZA
University College Dublin

RWBS R. W. BENET SALWAY
University College London

RWS ROBERT W. SHARPLES
University College London

SAS SARAH SCOTT
University of Leicester

SS SUZANNE SAÏD
Columbia University

GRT G. R. TSETSKHLADZE
University of Melbourne

MBT MICHAEL TRAPP
King's College London

PGT PETER TOOHEY
University of Calgary

RBT ROBERT B. TODD
University of British Columbia

RJAT RICHARD J. A. TALBERT
University of North Carolina, Chapel Hill

RST ROBERTA TOMBER
London

JV JOHN VANDERSPOEL
University of Calgary

AIW ANDREW WILSON
University of Oxford

CMW COLIN M. WELLS
Trinity University, San Antonio

FWW FRANK W. WALBANK
Peterhouse, Cambridge

HVW HANS VAN WEES
University College London

JIW JAMES WARREN
Corpus Christi College, Cambridge

JW JANE WEBSTER
University of Newcastle upon Tyne

MRW M. R. WRIGHT
University of Wales Lampeter

NJW NICOLA WAUGH
Edinburgh

RJAW R. J. A. WILSON
University of British Columbia

RW RICHARD WALLACE
Keele

Editors' preface

The present volume has its origin in a suggestion by our first CUP editor, Caroline Bundy, in 1993. In planning the work over the following months, we identified a need for an encyclopedia of antiquity that combined the maturity and depth of classical subjects – some of the oldest university disciplines in the West – with new approaches emphasizing social issues in the ancient world, as well as new sources of information such as archaeology. We, with our 166 expert contributors from a dozen countries, have attempted to produce a volume that is not only authoritative but also accessible and attractive to the widest possible range of users. We have used illustrations, tables and sometimes boxes to explain and exemplify points made in the entries. To enable readers to pursue their interest beyond this volume, we have provided most entries with a short bibliography (usually in English). We intend this book to attract non-specialists into deepening their knowledge of classical antiquity. We hope it will help readers appreciate the fascination of the ancient world, enriching their understanding of how its richly varied cultures and institutions related to one another.

This book is about classical civilization in its broadest sense. The chronological core ranges from the mid-8th century BC to the end of the 5th century AD, covering the period from the beginnings of the Greek city-states through to the hellenistic world, the Roman empire, and the transformation into the later Roman world and Byzantium. The bulk of the material, deliberately, is drawn from the heyday of the classical Greek city-state, the Roman Republic and the Roman imperial period. But we have widened our remit to set this 'classical' world, spatially and temporally, in its – and our – cultural contexts. We have tried to do justice to civilizations beyond the Mediterranean world with which classical cultures were in contact (e.g. China, India, Persia), and to non-Greco-Roman cultures within the ambit of classical civilization (e.g. Africans, Celts, Ethiopia, Garamantes, Jews, Phoenicians, Scythians).

With about 1,630 main entries (including about 100 that represent a Greek and Roman pair), the present volume is somewhat smaller than another authoritative classical encyclopedia, the *Oxford Classical Dictionary*, to which we acknowledge our immense debt as editors and as scholars. We do not aim to compete with it in the number of entries and depth of scholarly detail, but we believe our volume breaks new ground in accessibility, and in the amount of space devoted to social, economic and cultural features of Greek and Roman society. While attempting to give full coverage, as far as space allowed, to literature, philosophy and conventional military–political aspects (e.g. through entries on particular events and people), we have consciously tried to emphasize defining features (both general and particular) of ancient economies, geography, religion, science and technology. Entries on theory and method (e.g. critical theory, ethnoarchaeology, textual criticism) stand alongside thematic discussions of the environment (including animals and plants), and general features of societies (e.g. assemblies, bestiality, civil strife, diplomacy, disability, fraternity, legacies, matriarchy). We have been more selective in commissioning entries on men than of women, who are under-represented in the ancient evidence. The reader will find a classified list of headwords near the start of the volume, together with a list of headwords in this encyclopedia that do not appear in the *Oxford Classical Dictionary*.

More significant still, we believe, is our policy of stressing the classical heritage of modern societies. 'Heritage' has two senses. The first is that of the pathways along which classical learning has come down to us (see the entries on e.g. Elgin, Islamic scholarship, Renaissance). The second, and more important, is the emphasis on similarities and differences between ancient and modern ways of doing things, and the innumerable things in modern life that we owe to Greece and Rome.

Acknowledgements

The editors' greatest debt is to Caroline Bundy, who has combined the patience of Job with the determination of Sisyphos throughout the long gestation of this project. We thank her for nurturing the book, and for her gracious responses to our sometimes ill-informed queries and suggestions. Her classical colleague Pauline Hire made many helpful suggestions. Pauline's successor at Cambridge University Press, Dr Michael Sharp, his assistant, Sinéad Moloney, and our project controller, Alison Powell, have given timely and constructive aid in the later stages of production. Our copy-editor, Nancy-Jane Rucker, made substantial improvements to the internal consistency and appearance of the book.

To Dr Samantha Burke, our research assistant for four years, we express our deepest gratitude for her painstaking and accurate work in maintaining both hard-copy records and a headword database that at times approached 2,000 items. We had not sufficiently appreciated the complexity of attempting to commission entries from large numbers of authors, which required complex records of the stage negotiations had reached with each one, and of their progress. Samantha set very high standards, which we hope we have lived up to.

Additional thanks are due to Debbie Miles-Williams for help with illustrations; to Dr Mark Monaghan and Alun Salt for assistance with the database at crucial stages; and to our respective departments and colleagues at Calgary and Leicester for providing supportive environments in which to work.

Our nine-member editorial board has been ready with helpful advice at key stages, such as when we were devising headword lists in subject areas outside our core competencies. We thank particularly Helene Foley, David Sedley and Roger Wilson, who read final drafts of several hundred entries at short notice.

To those contributors who signed up early, we apologize for the delay in bringing the volume to a satisfactory conclusion, and we were especially saddened to learn of the deaths of Tim Potter and Michael Jameson, who will not be able to see the publication of their work. To all our contributors, who are responsible for 85 per cent of the text, we extend thanks for their excellent and often timely submissions and their readiness to respond positively to suggestions. To allow them to map their own territory and speak in their own voices, we have not resolved all instances of repetition or differences of opinion. We are grateful to those authors who agreed to write entries at a late stage, to fill gaps in our coverage.

All four editors have collective responsibility for the volume, and each of us has been glad of the scrutiny and suggestions offered by the others. In the later stages, David Mattingly and Lin Foxhall took the lead in assembling the illustrations, while Graham Shipley and John Vanderspoel focused on commissioning and editing the 740,000-word text. The three original editors would like to offer special thanks to John, whom we welcomed to the team during his visiting professorship at Leicester in 2002 and who shouldered a large proportion of the work in the final two years.

September 2004

Leicester	D. G. J. S.
Calgary	J.V.
Leicester	D. J. M.
Leicester	L. F.

How to use this book

Finding related and additional information

Various tools are provided to enable readers to use this book most effectively.

To allow readers to see at a glance the overall coverage, and look for entries on related topics, a **classified list of headwords** (pp. xxi–xxxi) lists all the main entries, selectively brought together under broad headings.

Most entries include **cross-references** to other entries. These are indicated by text in SMALL CAPITALS. We have given them selectively, where we believe readers will find relevant information in the entry referred to. The words in small capitals may not be exactly in the same form as the relevant headword, but should enable the reader to locate the relevant entry: e.g. under ACADEMY the cross-reference SCEPTICAL is intended to guide the reader to SCEPTICISM, RELIGIOUS (where there is a further cross-reference to SCEPTICS). Sometimes an additional list of cross-references follows the end of the entry. Most often, pairs of entries have been brought under a single headword, with the Greek and Roman portions distinguished by the Athenian owl (🦉) and the Roman arch (🏛). The additional cross-references sometimes appear at the end of each segment, sometimes at the end of the full entry. On some occasions, cross-references of all types, whether in an entry, at the end of an entry, in the List of Technical Terms, or following the additional headwords (see below), refer to the Greek or Roman portion of a paired entry, but the form of the cross-reference may be confusing initially. For example, a phrase such as 'in the Roman economy' may appear in the text as 'in the ROMAN ECONOMY' or 'in the Roman ECONOMY', but the cross-reference in either case is to the Roman portion of the entry on 'ECONOMY'. There is no entry under 'Roman economy, nor 'economy, Roman' in the alphabetical sequence of headwords. For a name like 'SEPTIMIUS SEVERUS', readers may need to look under both names to find the correct entry: inthis case, the entry is 'SEVERUS, SEPTIMIUS', but the 'the consul JULIUS CAESAR' is a cross-reference to 'JULIUS CAESAR'. Readers will also find phrases such as 'the EPIC POET HOMER' or 'AGRICULTURAL EMPLOYMENT'. There is no entry 'epic poet Homer' or 'agricultural employment'; rather, the cross-references are to separate entries, 'EPIC', 'POET' and 'HOMER', and similarly, 'AGRICULTURE' and 'EMPLOYMENT'. After some experience with this volume, readers will be able to interpret the different forms of cross-references with relative ease. Many entries also direct readers to additional illustrative material. These cross-references, usually placed at the ends of entries (at the very end of a paired entry), are preceded by an 'eye' symbol (👁) and refer to maps, family trees, tables and illustrations elsewhere in the volume. On occasion, readers will need to turn a page to find relevant illustrations; most often this is noted at the end of the entry in question.

Most entries are accompanied by a short **bibliography** of translated ancient sources and/ or modern literature. We have consciously selected works in English, bearing in mind the probable readership of this volume, but have occasionally cited works in other languages (French, German, Italian) where no English work seemed adequate. (In the bibliographies, editions of volumes of *Inscriptiones Graecae* are distinguished by the conventional superscript numerals: thus *IG* II^2 = *Inscriptiones Graecae*, vol. 2, 2nd edn. For all other works, the edition number is not generally given, and the date given is usually that of the most recent edition. Titles of modern works are sometimes abbreviated, and subtitles generally omitted.)

In addition to the main entries, we have added several hundred headwords that direct readers to locations where they may discover relevant material. Some of these represent alternate spellings, especially when the headword for the main entry appears in a form closer to the Greek spelling, but one that may be unfamiliar to some readers (e.g. BOEOTIA directs readers to BOIOTIA). Others refer to entries that address topics where space limitations precluded full treatment (e.g. DIVINATION); because this latter group of headwords depends entirely on the content of the main entries, the number of cross-references and the level of coverage inevitably varies from topic to topic.

Finally, the **List of technical terms** located later in the preliminary material (pp. xxxv–lxii) gives selected Greek and Latin words, with cross-references to entries in the main text where further information or brief explanations may be found. Inclusion of specific terms again depends on the content of the main entries.

Dates and periods

We have retained the abbreviations BC and AD only because they are still current in most anglophone scholarship. We do not mean to enforce a hegemony of christianized cultures over others, but considered that other abbreviations, such as BCE and CE, would be unfamiliar to many readers. We hope that readers with a different view will not be inconvenienced.

In this book, period terms are generally used in the following senses:

Greece and eastern Mediterranean

'Dark Age(s)'	1100–900 BC
Geometric	c.900–c.700 BC
archaic	c.700–c.500 or 480 BC
classical	for historical events, 480–323 BC; archaeologically c.500 (or 480)–c.300 BC. Also used generally for the period of ancient Greco-Roman antiquity.
hellenistic	historically 323–30 BC; archaeologically the last three centuries BC
Roman (or imperial)	historically 30 BC to c. AD 300; archaeologically the first three centuries AD
late Roman or early Byzantine	c. AD 300–c.600

Rome and Italy

regal period	c.753–510 BC
Republic	510–31 BC
principate or imperial	31 BC–AD 284
late Roman	AD 284–565

Further information about standard period names, etc., will be found in the entry on CHRONOLOGY.

Quantities

Distances, dimensions, capacities and weights are usually in metric units, with UK equivalents in parentheses. Gallons are, as always indicated, UK gallons (1 US gallon = 0.83 UK gallons). Tonnes (metric tons) are assumed to be equal to avoirdupois tons, and are not converted (1 ton = 2,200 lb = 0.984 tonnes).

Transliteration of ancient names and Greek words

Where there is a modern English form of an ancient name that is different from the ancient name, it is generally used if it is likely to be familiar to readers (e.g. Aeneas, Aeschylus, Ajax, Athens, Carthage, Corinth, Cyrus, Porphyrogenitus, Rome, Thucydides, Virgil). We have, however, modified some of these to bring them closer to Greek originals (e.g. Achaia, Aitolia, Antiochos, Lakedaimon, Perikles, Peisistratos, Seleukos).

Where there is no such familiar form of a Greek name, it is given in a Greek-like form (e.g. Keos rather than Ceos). Where a Greek name occurs in a Roman context, however, it sometimes retains a latinized form.

Both ancient and modern forms are usually given. Where they differ markedly, particularly in the first few letters, there is usually a headword for each form (one being a cross-reference only). Many illustrations were originally published when it was not standard procedure to transliterate Greek names into Greek-like forms. Consequently, some place-names will appear differently in figures than they do in the text of this book. The alternate forms included among the headwords will assist readers in these instances as well.

In transliterating Greek common nouns – but usually not names – *ê* and *ô* represent the Greek vowels eta (long *e*) and omega (long *o*) respectively.

A diaeresis (¨) over the second of two or more adjacent vowels indicates that the preceding vowel is pronounced separately (e.g. Arsinoë, Boëthius, *poiëô*, Soloëis – the last two words each have three syllables).

Classified list of headwords

Most headwords appear only once. Readers are advised to search in several sections, as many headwords are relevant to a number of headings.

Headings and sub-headings employed

Approaches
methodologies
theories and analytical tools

Archaeology
general
cities
other sites and monuments

Belief systems
Christianity
deities
mythology
philosophers
philosophies
religion

Classical heritage
legacy and reception
scholarship and transmission

Environment, economy
economy
environment
food and foodstuffs

Geography and ethnography
general
Greece and adjacent areas
Italy
other regions and peoples

History and institutions
battles
empires
justice, law, administration
military organization
politics
wars

Literature
general
drama
history, biography, letters
languages, literate culture
oratory
poetry
technical writing
other prose

Persons
families, dynasties
men, Greek
men, Roman
men, other
women, Greek
women, Roman
women, other

Science and technology
medicine
science, measurement
substances, products, commodities
technologies

Social relations
family, sex, gender
personal life
practices, institutions
professions, status groups

Approaches

METHODOLOGIES

Annales school
archaeology
demography
epigraphy
excavation
field survey
forensic archaeology
philology, comparative
papyrology
textual criticism

THEORIES AND ANALYTICAL TOOLS

acculturation
anthropology
class
colonialism
consumer city
core–periphery
critical theory
culture
ethnicity and identity
ethnoarchaeology
feminism
imperialism, modern
literary criticism
Marx, Karl
marxism
nationalism
orientalism, modern
other, the
peer polity interaction
post-colonialism
post-modernism
racism
semiotics
sociology
structuralism and post-structuralism

Archaeology

GENERAL

agora
akropolis
amphitheatres
amphoras
apartment buildings
aqueducts
archaeology
arches, monumental
architecture
Arretine ware
art
basilicas
baths
bridges
burial
catacombs
choregic monuments
circus buildings

caryatids
colonization
columns, monumental
couches
dining rooms
domes
figurines, bronze
figurines, terracotta
fishponds
forums
fountains and fountain houses
granaries
harbours
gymnasia
Hallstatt
hoards
houses
instrumentum domesticum
kitchens and kitchen utensils
kouroi and *korai*
lamps
La Tène
lighthouses
Lysippos
market buildings
masonry styles
migrations
Minoans
mosaics
mummy portraits
musical instruments
Mycenaeans
nuraghi
orders, architectural
painting
palaces
palaestras
Pheidias
Polykleitos
portraiture
Praxiteles
rural settlement
samian ware
sarcophagi
sculpture
Seven Wonders
silverware
shipwrecks
space
stoa
temples
theatres
tholoi
toilets
tombs
town planning
urbanization
vase-painting
villages
villas
wall-painting
warehouses
water mills
workshops

CITIES

Ai Khanum
Al Mina
Alexandria
Antioch
Apameia
Aphrodisias
Aquileia
Arsinoë (city)
Athens
Augst
Baalbek
Babylon
Bath
Brundisium
Caesarea (Mauretania)
Caesarea Maritima
Camulodunum
Capua
Carthage and Carthaginians
Carthago Nova
Constantinople
Corinth
Cosa
Cremona
Cumae
Dura Europus
Edessa
Ephesos
Euesperides
Fishbourne
Gades
Halieis
Halikarnassos
Herculaneum
Jerash
Jerusalem
Karanis
Knidos
Lambaesis
Lepcis Magna
Leptiminus
Ligures Baebiani
Lixus
London
Lyon
Marseilles
Megara
Metapontum
Milan
Miletos
Motya
Naukratis
Nicomedia
Nisibis
Numantia
Olynthos
Oplontis
Ostia and Portus
Oxyrhynchos
Palmyra
Pella
Pergamon
Persepolis
Petra
Piraeus
Pithekoussai
Pompeii (city)
Praeneste
Puteoli
Pydna
Ravenna
Rome
Saguntum
Samosata
Sardis
Satricum
Sinope
Smyrna
Sparta
Syracuse
Tarquinia
Tarracina
Tarraco
Thapsus
Thebes
Thessalonike
Thugga
Timgad
Trier
Troy
Utica
Veii
Veleia
Xanthos
York
Zeugma

OTHER SITES AND MONUMENTS

Acropolis, Athenian
Adamklissi
Agora, Athenian
Antonine wall
Ara Pacis
Ara Pietatis
Barbegal
Boscoreale
Boscotrecase
Brauron
Capitolium
Capri
Carrara
Cerveteri
Circus Maximus
Curia

Delphi
Didyma
Dodona
Dokimeion
Eleusis
Hadrian's wall
Hatra
Kerameikos
Knossos
Laurion
Lefkandí
Lyceum
Marzabotto
Masada
Mons Claudianus
Mons Graupius
Monte Testaccio
Mycenae
Olympia
Pantheon
Parthenon
pomerium
Sperlonga
Spina
Thermon
Tivoli
Trajan's column
Vergína
Vindolanda

Belief systems

CHRISTIANITY

Ambrose
apocryphal gospels
Arianism
ascetics
Athanasius
Augustine (1)
Augustine (2)
Basil
Bible
bishops
Boëthius
Catholicism
celibacy
Christian philosophy
Christianity
church councils
church, Christian
churches
Cyprian
Eusebios
Gnosticism
Gregory of Nazianzus
hermits
Jerome
Jesus
Lactantius
Manichaeism
Martin, St
martyrs
monasteries
New Testament
Orosius
Paul, St
persecutions
saints
schism
Synesius
Tertullian

DEITIES

Ahura-Mazda
Amon-Ra
Aphrodite
Apollo
Artemis
Asklepios
Athena
Baal Hammon
Bacchus
Capitoline triad
Ceres
Cocidius
concord and Concordia
Cybele
Demeter
demons
Diana
Dionysos
Dioscuri
Epona
Eros
Fortuna
Furies
Ge
gods and goddesses
Hades
Hera
Herakles
Hercules
Hermes
Isis
Janus
Juno
Jupiter
Mars
Medusa
Mercury
Minerva
Mithras and Mithraism
mother goddesses
Neptune
Nike
Pan
Poseidon
Priapus
Roma
Saturn
Silvanus
Sulis
Tanit
Venus
Vesta
Yahweh
Zeus

MYTHOLOGY

Achilles
Aeneas
Agamemnon
Ajax
Amazons
Andromache
Antigone
Atalanta
Atlantis
Clytemnestra
Eurydike (1)
giants
golden age
Hektor
Helen of Troy
Iphigeneia
Lucretia
myth
Narcissus
Odysseus
Oedipus
Oresteia
Orpheus
Pelasgians
Romulus and Remus
Theseus
Trojan war

PHILOSOPHERS

Aelian
Apollonios of Tyana
Aristotle
Demokritos
Dio Chrysostom
Diogenes Laërtius
Epicurus
Herakleitos
Hipparchia
Macrobius
Parmenides
Philo Judaeus
Philodemos
Philostratos
Plato
Plotinus
Posidonius
Protagoras
Pythagoras and Pythagoreanism
Seneca the Younger
Socrates
Theophrastos
Xenophanes
Zeno of Citium
Zeno the Eleatic

PHILOSOPHY

Academy
Aristotelianism
atomism
causes
cosmology
Cynicism
dialectic
diatribe
divisibility
emotion
Epicureanism
ethics
evil
fate
fear
free will
future
God
grief
immortality
inquiry
knowledge
kosmos
logic
matter
metaphysics
mind and body
morality
motion
Neoplatonism
Neopythagoreanism
paradoxes
past
Peripatetics
philosophical schools
philosophy
Platonism
political theory
Presocratic philosophy
progress
questions and answers
Sceptics
sophists
soul, the
Stoicism
utopias and utopianism
vegetarianism
virtue
wisdom

RELIGION

afterlife
ancestor worship
Apocrypha
Arval brethren
augury
curses
Dead Sea scrolls
dreams
Druids and druidism
Eleusis and Eleusinian mysteries
Essenes
fanaticism
festivals
funeral rites
herms
hero-cult
heroes
human sacrifice
imperial cult
Judaism
magic
monotheism
mystery religions
numen
Old Testament
oracles
orphism
paganism
personification
phallus
pollution, ritual
prayer
priests and priestesses
processions
prophecy
purification
religion
rites of passage
ritual
ruler-cult
sacrifice
satyrs
scepticism, religious
Septuagint
Serapeum
Sibylline oracles
Sol Invictus
superstition
syncretism
Vestal virgins
vows
Zoroaster

Classical heritage

LEGACY AND RECEPTION

architecture, modern
Asterix
comic strips
film
Greece, modern
heritage, classical
museums
novels, historical
Renaissance
Shakespeare
theatre, modern

SCHOLARSHIP AND TRANSMISSION

antiquities and antiquarianism
archaeology
collectors and collecting
commentators, textual
Cyriac of Ancona
Elgin, Lord
Erasmus
encyclopedias
Hesychios
historians and historiography, modern
Petrarch
Pollux
scholarship, ancient
scholarship, Byzantine
scholarship, classical
scholarship, Islamic
scholia
Suda
transmission

Environment, economy

ECONOMY

accounting
advertising
agriculture
Attic *stêlai*
aviaries
banking
coinage
consumers and consumption
customs duties
debt
debt-bondage
economy
employment
exchange
fish sauces
food supply
growth, economic
industry
insurance
investment
labour
land and property
loans
managers
manufacturing
markets
modes of production
mina
money
money supply
moneylending
pastoralism
poverty
prices

production and surplus
rationality, economic
subsistence
taxation
tenants and tenancy
trade
transhumants
unemployment
wealth

ENVIRONMENT

animals
birds
bulls
camels
cattle
cereals
climate
climatic change
donkeys and mules
draught animals
earthquakes
ecology
elephants
figs
flowers
forests and forestry
fruit
gardens and gardening
goats
insects
landscape
nature
pets
pigs
plants
pollution
poultry
rivers
sheep
silphium
spices
trees, cultivated
vegetables
volcanoes
wetlands
wind
zoos

FOOD AND FOODSTUFFS

baking
beer
bread
cheese
honey
ice and icehouses
bees and beekeeping
butchery
diet
fish and fishing
food preservation
meat
olive, olive oil
salt
sweets and sweeteners
vine
wine

Geography and ethnography

GENERAL

Adriatic sea
Alps
Atlantic
Black sea
Danube
exploration
geography
islands
maps
Mediterranean sea
mountains
Nile
Rhine
Rhône
travellers

GREECE AND ADJACENT AREAS

Achaia, Roman
Aegean sea
Aigina
Aitolia and Aitolian league
Argos and Argolid
Arkadia
Attica
Boiotia
Chalkidike
Chios
Crete
Delos
East Greece
Elis
Epirus
Euboia
Greece
Hellespont and Propontis
Illyria and Illyrians
Ionian islands
Kopaïs, Lake
Laconia
Lesbos
Lokris
Macedonia, ancient
Melos
Messenia
Naxos
Paros
Peloponnese
Phokis
Rhodes
Samos
Thasos
Thera
Thessaly
Thrace and Thracians

ITALY

Clitumnus
Etruria and Etruscans
Gallia Cisalpina
Italy, Roman
Latins
Magna Graecia
Sabines
Samnites
Tiber
Umbrians

OTHER REGIONS AND PEOPLES

Afghanistan
Africa and Africans
Africa, Roman
Alani
Anatolia
Arabia and Arabs
Armenia and Armenians
Asia, Roman
Baetica
Baleares
Belgae
Britannia
British Isles and Britons
Cappadocia
Caria
Celts
China and Chinese empire
Cilicia
Commagene
Corsica
Cyprus
Cyrene and Cyrenaica
Dalmatia
Egypt
Elam
Ethiopia and Ethiopians
Fayûm
Franks
Garamantes
Gaul
Germany and Germans
Goths
Hispania
Huns
Iberia (1), (2)
India
Jews
Judaea
Levant

Libya
Lombards
Lusitania
Lycia
Lydia
Meroë
Mesopotamia
Nabataea
Noricum
Oscans
Pakistan
Pannonia
Parthia and Parthians
Persia and Persians
Persian empire
Phoenicia and Phoenicians
Phrygia and Phrygians
Raetia
Sardinia
Sassanian empire
Scythia and Scythians
Sicily
Syria, Roman
Vandals

History and institutions (*see also* 'LITERATURE: historiography')

BATTLES

Actium
Adrianople
Aigospotamoi
Alalia
Arginousai
Cannae
Carrhae
Caudine Forks
Chaironeia
Ctesiphon
Gaugamela
Granikos
Himera
Hysiai
Ilipa
Ipsos
Issos
Koroneia
Kynoskephalai
Lake Regillus
Leuktra
Magnesia
Mantineia
Marathon
Milvian bridge
Munda
Mylai
Oinophyta
Pharsalus
Philippi
Plataea
Salamis
Sellasia
Teutoburgian forest
Thermopylai
Zama

EMPIRES

Athenian
Bosporan kingdom
Chinese
imperialism
Persian
provinces and provincial government, Roman
Roman
Sassanian
Seleukid

JUSTICE, LAW, ADMINISTRATION

adoption
adultery
alimenta
archives
banishment and exile
bureaucracy
crime and criminals
ephetai
Gaius (lawyer)
Gortyn code
guardianship
inheritance
Irni
justice
Justinian, works of
law
law-codes
lawcourts
legacies
manumission
murder
Notitia Dignitatum
oaths
post (mail)
prisons
punishment
secrecy
secret police
spies and spying
Theodosian Code
torture
treaties
Twelve Tables
Ulpian
wills

MILITARY ORGANIZATION

archery
armies, organization of
arms and armour
artillery
auxiliaries
battles
cavalry
fortification
forts and fortresses
generalissimos (late antique)
generals
hoplites
horses and horsemanship
legions
mercenaries
naval tactics and weapons
naval warfare, Greek
navies
officers, military
peace
praetorian guard
rams, battering
sieges and siege warfare
soldiers
strategy, military
supply, military
tactics, military
trireme
trophies, military
veterans
war

POLITICS

Achaian league
aediles
alliances
ambassadors and embassies
Areiopagos
aristocracy
assemblies
Augustus (title)
Caesar (title)
careers
censors
censuses
cities
citizenship
city-states
civil strife
cleruchs, cleruchy
client rulers
consuls
councils
demes
democracy
dictators
diplomacy
elections
emperors, Roman
ephebes
ephors
federalism
Four Hundred, the

frontiers
honours
international relations
kings and kingship
liturgies
magistrates
oligarchy
ostracism
ovations
peasant uprisings
phratries
plebs
polis
political participation
political systems
power
praetors
princeps and principate
procurators
prytany
public order
quaestors
records, public
Republic, Roman
republics
revolution
riots
senate and senators, Roman
senatus consulta
state, the
Tabula Banasitana
theoric fund
third-century crisis
Thirty, the
tribes
tribunes
triumphs, Roman
triumvirates
tyranny
voting

WARS

Celtiberian
Chremonidean
civil, Roman
Corinthian
Dacian
Gallic
Germanic
Gothic
Hannibalic
Ionian revolt
Jugurthan
Lamian
Macedonian
Marcomannic
Messenian
Pannonian
Parthian
Peloponnesian
Persian, Greek
Persian, Roman
Punic
sacred, Greek
Samnite
Sicilian expedition
social wars
Syrian wars, of Ptolemies

Literature (*see also* 'BELIEF SYSTEMS: philosophers')

GENERAL

biography and biographers
chorus
comedy 1: Old Comedy
comedy 2: New Comedy
declamation
didactic poetry
drama
elegy
epic
epigrams
fables
genre
historians and historiography, ancient
lyric poetry
masks
metre
mime
novels
oral tradition
orators
oratory
panegyrists
pantomime
parables
pastoral poetry
poetry
poetesses
prose
recitations
Res Gestae
rhetoric
satire
Second Sophistic
scholia
songs and singing
tragedy

DRAMA

Aeschylus
Aristophanes
Euripides
Herodas
Menander
Plautus
Seneca the Younger
Sophokles
Terence

HISTORY, BIOGRAPHY, LETTERS

Alexander Romance
Ammianus Marcellinus
Appian
Arrian
Berossos
Cassius Dio
Diodorus Siculus
Dionysios of Halikarnassos
Douris of Samos
Ephoros
Herodian
Herodotos
Hieronymos of Kardia
Historia Augusta
Ion of Chios
Josephus
Livy
Manetho
Nepos
Old Oligarch
Oxyrhynchos historian
Pliny the Younger
Plutarch
Polybios
Procopius
Sallust
Suetonius
Tacitus
Theopompos
Thucydides
Timaios
Valerius Maximus
Velleius Paterculus
Xenophon

LANGUAGES, LITERATE CULTURE

alphabets
bilingualism
cuneiform
Eteocretan
language and languages
letters
libraries
literacy
writing

ORATORY

Aelius Aristides
Aischines
Apollodoros the orator
Demosthenes
Fronto
Gorgias
Isaios

Isokrates
Libanius
Lysias
Second Sophistic
Seneca the Elder
Symmachus
Themistius

POETRY

Alkaios
Alkman
Apollonios of Rhodes
Aratos of Soloi
Archilochos
Asklepiades
Ausonius
Bacchylides
Catullus
Claudian
Corinna
Corippus
Ennius
Erinna
Gallus
Greek Anthology
Hesiod
Homer
Horace
hymns
Juvenal
Kallimachos
Lucan
Lucretius
Lykophron
Martial
Nonnos
Ovid
Persius
Philetas
Pindar
Propertius
Prudentius
Sappho
Semonides
Sidonius Apollinaris
Silius Italicus
Simonides
Solon
Statius
Theognis and the *Theognidae*
Theokritos
Tibullus
Virgil

TECHNICAL WRITING

Aeneas Tacticus
Agatharchides
Antonine Itinerary
Apicius
Apollonios of Perge
Archimedes
Aristarchos of Samos
Celsus
Columella
Eratosthenes
Euclid
Frontinus
Galen
Gellius, Aulus
Heron of Alexandria
Hipparchos of Nikaia
Hippocratic corpus
Hippokrates
Longinus
Mago
Mela
Pappos of Alexandria
Pausanias
Peutinger Table
Philon of Byzantion
Pliny the Elder
Polyainos
Ptolemy of Alexandria
Quintilian
Ravenna cosmographer
Rufus
Soranus
Strabo
Varro
Vegetius
Vitruvius

OTHER PROSE

Aesop
Apollodoros the mythographer
Apuleius
Athenaeus
Longus
Lucian
Petronius

Persons

FAMILIES, DYNASTIES

Aemilii
Alkmaionidai
Antigonids
Claudii
Clodii
Cornelii
Domitii
Fabii
Flaminii
Julii
Junii
Licinii
Livii
Marcelli
Marcii
Metelli
Minucii
Mucii
Opimii
Pompeii (family)
Ptolemies
Seleukids
Successors of Alexander
Sulpicii

MEN, GREEK

Agathokles and Sosibios
Agathokles of Syracuse
Agesilaos
Agiatis
Agis II
Agis IV
Alcibiades
Alexander III ('the Great')
Antiochos III ('the Great')
Apollonios the *dioikêtês*
Aratos of Sikyon
Archidamos II
Areus I
Aristeides 'the Just'
Brasidas
Demades
Demetrios I Poliorketes
Demetrios of Phaleron
Dion of Syracuse
Dionysios I of Syracuse
Epameinondas
Herodes Atticus
Heroninos
Iphikrates
Kallikrates
Kimon
Kleisthenes of Athens
Kleomenes I
Kleomenes III
Kleon
Konon of Athens
Kritias
Leonidas
Lykourgos of Athens
Lykourgos of Sparta
Lysander
Lysimachos
Nabis
Nikias
Pausanias (king of Sparta)
Pausanias the regent
Peisistratos
Pelopidas
Perikles
Philip II
Philip V
Philopoimen
Phokion
Pleistoanax
Ptolemy I
Pyrrhos

Seleukos I
Themistokles
Thrasyboulos
Timoleon
Timotheos

MEN, ROMAN

Aemilius Paullus
Agricola
Agrippa
Annobal Tapapius Rufus
Antinous
Antoninus Pius
Antony, Mark
Atticus
Augustus
Aurelian
Brutus
Caligula (Gaius)
Caracalla
Catiline
Cato the Elder
Cato the Younger
Cicero
Claudius
Clodius
Commodus
Constantine
Corbulo
Coriolanus
Crassus
Decebalus
Diocletian
Domitian
Ducetius
Elagabalus
Fabius Pictor
Flamininus
Flaminius
Flavius Cerialis
Galerius
Gallienus
Gordian III
Gracchi
Hadrian
Honorius
Hostilius, Tullus
Julian
Julius Caesar
Justinian
Lars Porsenna
Licinius
Maecenas
Marcellus
Marcus Aurelius
Marius
Maximian
Maximinus Thrax
Nero
Numa
Otho
Pescennius Niger
Philip the Arab
Pompey
Pontius Pilate
Scipio Aemilianus
Scipio Africanus
Sejanus
Sertorius
Servius Tullius
Severus, Alexander
Severus, Septimius
Stilicho
Sulla
Tarquinius Priscus
Tarquinius Superbus
Tetrarchs
Theodosius I
Tiberius
Titus
Trajan
Valentinian I
Valerian
Verres
Vespasian

MEN, OTHER

Alaric
Artaxerxes I, II, III
Bar Kochba
Barcids
Cunobelinus
Cyrus I ('the Great')
Cyrus the Younger
Darius I
Datames
Hannibal
Herod the Great
Jugurtha
Maccabees, revolt of
Masinissa
Mausolus
Mithradates
Shapur I
Spartacus
Theoderic
Vercingetorix
Viriathus
Xerxes

WOMEN, GREEK

Arsinoë II Philadelphos
Aspasia
Berenike I
Cleopatra
Corinna
Diotima
Erinna
Eurydike (1), (2), (3)
Hipparchia
Neaira
Oinanthe
Olympias
Sappho
Stratonike

WOMEN, ROMAN

Aemilia Pudentilla
Agrippinae, the
Clodia
Cornelia
Egeria
Eumachia
Faustina
Galla Placidia
Helena (empress)
Hypatia
Julia
Julia Domna
Julia Mammaea
Livia
Lucilla
Melania, Elder and Younger
Messalina
Monica
Perpetua
Plancia Magna
Poppaea Sabina
Proba
Pulcheria
Sulpicia Lepidina
Tullia
Verginia

WOMEN, OTHER

Boudica
Cartimandua
Zenobia

Science and technology

MEDICINE (*SEE ALSO* 'LITERATURE: TECHNICAL WRITING')

contraception
disease
doctors
drugs
epidemics
health
hygiene
illness
insomnia
madness
mental illness
medicine
pregnancy and childbirth

SCIENCE, MEASUREMENT

alchemy
astrology
astronomy
calendars
chronology
colour
counting
energy
experiments and experimentation
geography, ancient
mathematicians
mathematics
measurement
mechanics
moon
natural history
numeracy
Parian Marble
physics
science
sound and acoustics
sun
sundials
time
time-keeping
weights and measures
zodiac

SUBSTANCES, PRODUCTS, COMMODITIES (*SEE ALSO* 'ENVIRONMENT: FOOD AND FOODSTUFFS')

alum
amber
bone
books
carpentry
catapults
charcoal
chariots
concrete
copper
copper alloys
coral
dyes and dyeing
electrum
fastening
fire
flint and chert
footwear
fuel
fur
furniture
gems and gem-cutting
glass and glass-making
glues
gold
iron
ivory
lead
leather and leatherworking
lime
locks
manure
marble
mummies
nails
obsidian
oils
ores
papyrus
perfume
petroleum products
pewter
pigments
plaster and plastering
poisons
pottery
purple
resin
rope
screws
shell
silk
silver
soap
stone
string
stucco
sulphur
textiles
tiles
timber
tin

TECHNOLOGIES

agrimensores
architects
brick and tile making
canals
carpentry
chemistry
communications
dentists and dentistry
engineering
fire-fighting
fulling
heating
inventions
knitting
land surveying
lighting
lime-kilns
machines
metallurgy
mills and milling
mines
mining
navigation
pests and pest control
plumbing
presses
quarries and quarrying
roads
roofs and roofing materials
sanitation
scientific instruments
ships and shipbuilding
spinning
storage
technology
tools
transport
waste disposal
water supply
waterproofing
weather forecasting
weaving
wheeled vehicles

Social relations

FAMILY, SEX, GENDER

age organization
bestiality
divorce
family
femininity
gender
fraternity
friendship
homosexuality
households
incest
kinship
marriage
masculinity
matriarchy
pornography
rape
sex
sexuality
virginity

PERSONAL LIFE (*SEE ALSO* 'SCIENCE AND TECHNOLOGY: MEDICINE')

body, the
chitôn
cosmetics
dance
death
disability
dress
drugs and drug addiction
etiquette
fashion
hair and hairstyling
honour
identity
immorality

jewellery
love
nudity
old age
shoes
suicide
toga
veiling
worry

PRACTICES, INSTITUTIONS

alcohol and alcoholism
ball games
banditry
bathing
beds
board games and other games
chariot racing
child abuse
clubs
competition
cooking and cuisine
dining
games
education
funeral clubs
gambling
holidays
housework
hunting
inns
leisure
meals
music
names and naming
Olympic games
patronage
scandals
schools
shops and shopping
sport
swimming
symposia
tourism
toys
violence
washing

PROFESSIONS, STATUS GROUPS

actors and actresses
artists
athletes and athletics
bakers
barbarians
benefactors and benefaction
blacks
childhood
coloni and colonate
curial class and *curiales*
élites
equestrians
eunuchs
freedmen and freedwomen
gladiators
gourmets
helots
heralds
masons
men
metics
midwives
musicians
nomads
nurses and nursing
patricians
peasants
pirates and piracy
plebeians
poets
prostitutes and prostitution
publicani
pygmies
queens
race
refugees
sailors
shepherds
singers
slavery
society
Trimalchio
wetnurses
women

Headwords not covered in the *Oxford Classical Dictionary*, 3rd edition

As a further aid to readers, we list headwords for which there is no direct equivalent in the 3rd edition of the *Oxford Classical Dictionary*. (Some of the material covered here appears under different headings in *OCD*.)

acculturation
Adrianople, battle of
advertising
Aemilia Pudentilla
Afghanistan
Agathokles and Sosibios
Agiatis
agora, Athenian
agrimensores
Aigospotamoi, battle of
akropolis
Alalia
alum
ambassadors and embassies
Amon-Ra
ancestor worship
Annales school
Annobal Tapapius Rufus
antiquities and antiquarianism
Antonine Itinerary
Antonine wall
apartment buildings
Apocrypha
apocryphal gospels
Ara Pietatis
architecture, modern
Aristotelianism
Arretine ware
Asterix
Atlantic, the
Attic stelai
Augustine (2)
aviaries
Baal Hammon
Baalbek
bakers
baking
banditry
Barbegal
Barcids
bathing
battles
beds
beer
bestiality
Bible
bishops
blacks
board games and other games
bone
Boscotrecase
bread
brick and tile making
bulls
burial
butchery
Caesar (title)
Capitoline triad
carpentry
Catholicism
cattle
causes
celibacy
Cerveteri
charcoal
cheese
child abuse
chitôn
chorus
church councils
church, Christian
Circus Maximus
city-states
Cocidius
collectors and collecting
colonialism
columns, monumental
comic strips
commentators, textual
communications
concrete
consumer city
consumers and consumption
copper
coral
core–periphery
Corippus
cosmology
couches
counting
crime and criminals
critical theory
culture
customs duties
Cyriac of Ancona
debt-bondage
dining
disability
divisibility
doctors
domes
donkeys and mules
draught animals
drugs
drugs and drug addiction
East Greece
electrum
Elgin, Lord
emotion
emperors, Roman
employment
encyclopedias
energy
engineering
epidemics
Erasmus
Eteocretan
ethics
ethnoarchaeology
etiquette
Eumachia
evil
excavation
exploration
fanaticism
fashion
fastening
fear
femininity
figurines, bronze
figurines, terracotta
film
fire-fighting
fish sauces
Fishbourne
fishponds
Flavius Cerialis
flint and chert
flowers
food preservation
footwear
forensic archaeology
forests and forestry
fraternity

free will
frontiers
fruit
fuel
funeral clubs
fur
future
gambling
generalissimos
geography (modern)
glues
God
gourmets
Greece, modern
grief
growth, economic
hair and hairstyling
Hallstatt
health
Helena (empress)
heritage, classical
hermits
Heroninos
Hipparchia
Hispania
hoards
holidays
honours
human sacrifice
hygiene
ice and icehouses
identity
Ilipa
illness
immorality
immortality
imperialism, modern
inquiry
insects
insomnia
instrumentum domesticum
insurance
international relations
inventions
investment
Ionian islands
Irni
Jerash
Jesus
jewellery
Judaism
Karanis
kitchens and kitchen utensils
knitting
knowledge
kosmos
land and property
landscape
leather and leatherworking
legacies
leisure
Leptiminus
Levant
Ligures Baebiani
lime
lime-kilns
Lixus
locks
machines
madness
managers
manufacturing
manure
Martin, St
martyrs
Marx, Karl
masculinity
masonry styles
masons
mathematicians
matter
meat
Melania, Elder and Younger
men
mental illness
metaphysics
Milvian bridge, battle of
mina
mind and body
modes of production
monasteries
money supply
moneylending
Monica
Mons Graupius
moon
morality
mother goddesses
motion
mummies
mummy portraits
Munda
Mylai
nails
natural history
naval tactics and weapons
naval warfare, Greek
Neaira
New Testament
novels, historical
nudity
numeracy
nuraghi
nurses and nursing
obsidian
officers, military
oils
Oinanthe
old age
Old Testament
ores
other, the
Pakistan
parables
Parthian wars
past
peasant uprisings
peer polity interaction
perfume
Perpetua
Persian wars, Roman
personification
pests and pest control
Petrarch
petroleum products
pewter
Philip the Arab
pigments
pigs
Plancia Magna
plaster and plastering
plebeians
Pleistoanax
plumbing
poetesses
poetry
poets
poisons
pollution
post-colonialism
post-modernism
poultry
power
presses
prices
production and surplus
prose
public order
Pulcheria
queens
questions and answers
rams, battering
rationality, economic
Ravenna cosmographer
Renaissance
Republic, Roman
republics
resin
revolution
riots
Roma
roofs and roofing materials
rope
sailors
saints
salt
scandals
schism
scholarship, Byzantine
scholarship, Islamic
schools
scientific instruments
screws

secrecy
secret police
Sellasia, battle of
semiotics
Serapeum
sex
Shakespeare
Shapur I
shell
shepherds
shoes
shops and shopping
singers
soap
society
sociology
soldiers
songs and singing
space
spies and spying
sport
stone
storage
strategy, military
string
stucco
subsistence
Successors of Alexander
Sulis
sulphur
Sulpicia Lepidina
supply, military
sweets and sweeteners
swimming
Tabula Banasitana
tactics, military
tenants and tenancy
Thapsus
theatre, modern
third-century crisis
tiles
time
toilets
tombs
tools
transmission
Trimalchio
unemployment
vegetables
veiling
villages
Vindolanda
virtue
volcanoes
warehouses
washing
waste disposal
water mills
waterproofing
weather forecasting
wetlands
wetnurses
wheeled vehicles
wills
workshops
worry
Yahweh
zoos

Some technical terms

The words in the first column represent some of the technical terms employed in the *Cambridge Dictionary of Classical Civilization*. The second column lists entries that readers may consult for information. Many terms appear more often than the entries listed here, but the goal has been to list places where these terms are defined or where enough information is provided to allow an understanding of the basic meaning.

Term	Entries
aerarium	records, public, Roman; taxation, Roman
ager publicus	Africa, Roman; Ligures Baebiani
agôgê	education, Greek; society, Greek
agôn, agônes	competition; festivals, Greek; sport; tragedy
ala	armies, organization of, Roman; auxiliaries
amici Caesaris	lawcourts, Roman
amicitia	friendship, Roman; patronage
anachôrein, anachôrêsis	hermits; peasant uprisings; taxation, Roman
andrôn	dining rooms, Greek; houses, Greek; men; *symposia*
angchisteia	family, Greek
annona	food supply, Roman; supply, military
aparchai	ritual, Greek
apoikia	colonization
archê	Athenian empire; imperialism, ancient
architektôn	engineering
aretê	morality; virtue
argyraspides	arms and armour, Greek; veterans
arx	*akropolis*; Capitolium
auctoritas	Augustus (title); councils; *Res Gestae*
augur, augures	augury; clubs, Roman
aulêtai, aulêtrides	music; musicians
auspicium, auspicia	kingship, Roman
basileus	kingship, Greece
basilica Ulpia	forum; Trajan's column
boulê	assemblies, Greek
bouleutêrion	agora, Athenian
boustrophêdon	epigraphy, Greek; literacy
caldarium	bath-houses; bathing
capite censi	armies, organization of, Roman; censuses; legions
capitolia	athletes and athletics, Roman; Lyon
cavea	theatres, Roman
cella	Capitoline triad; Capitolium; temples
centuria	elections; society, Roman; *see also* land surveying, Roman
choê, choai	children; toys

choinix, choinikes	weights and measures, Greek
chôra	*polis*
chorêgos, choregia	benefactors and benefaction, Greek; choregic monuments; chorus; drama, Greek; liturgies
chthôn	gods and goddesses; religion
civitas sine suffragio	Caere
classis	class; society, Roman
clientes	manumission, Roman; society, Roman
cognomen	names and naming, Roman
cohors	legions
collegia	clubs, Roman
colonia	colonization
comitia centuriata	assemblies, Roman; kingship, Roman; political participation, Roman
comitia curiata	assemblies, Roman; political participation, Roman
concilium plebis	assemblies, Roman; plebeians; plebs; political participation, Roman
conductor	land and property, Roman; supply, military; taxation, Roman
consilium	family, Roman; senate and senators
consilium principis	Cassius Dio; *Tabula Banasitana*
consules ordinarii	consuls
consules suffecti	consuls
controversia	education, Roman
contubernium	family, Roman; marriage, Roman; *see also* armies, organization of, Roman; forts and fortresses, Roman
conubium	citizenship, Roman
cuniculus	Etruria and Etruscans
curator	family, Roman; guardianship, Roman
curator aquarum	Frontinus; Rome
curatores viarum	roads, Roman
cursus honorum	careers; magistrates, Roman
cursus publicus	*Antonine Itinerary*; communications; horses and horsemanship
daimôn	demons; mind and body
damnatio memoriae	Maximian
decreta	law-codes
dekarchia, dekarchiai	imperialism, ancient
dekêrês, dekēreis	ships and shipbuilding
dêmarchos	demes; villages
dêmos	demes; democracy; villages
diekplous	tactics, military, Greek
dikastês, dikastai	lawcourts
dikê	crime and criminals, Greek; justice
dioptra	scientific instruments
disciplina Etrusca	Etruria and Etruscans
dokimasia	elections
domus Augusta	Augustus

domus Augustana	houses, Roman; palaces
domus aurea	domes; palaces
doulos, doulê	slavery, Greek
drachmê	money
duumvir	voting
dux	generals, Roman
eisphora	benefactors and benefaction, Greek; metics; taxation, Greek
ekklêsia	assemblies, Greek
elenchos	logic; Socrates
enômotia, enômotiai	armies, organization of, Greek
epiklêros	family, Greek; incest; wills; women, Greek
epistatês	prytany
epistulae	letters, Roman
epiteichismos	forts and fortresses, Greek
erastês	homosexuality; sexuality
ergastêrion, ergastêria	manufacturing
erômenos	homosexuality; sexuality
ethnos, ethnê	federalism; tribes, Greek
euchê	prayer; vows
euergetês	honours
familia	family, Roman; slavery, Roman; society, Roman
fasces	consuls; magistrates, Roman; political systems, Roman; punishment
fasti	records, public, Roman
fasti consulares	chronology
fasti triumphales	ovations; triumphs
fiscus	taxation, Roman
flamen	priests and priestesses, Roman
foedus	peace
forum Romanum	forum
frigidarium	bath-houses; bathing
genos	family, Greek; fraternities
gerousia	councils; elections; political participation; Sparta
gês periodos	maps
graphê, graphê paranomôn	assemblies, Greek; crime and criminals, Greek; Solon
groma	*agrimensores*; cities, Roman; land surveying; scientific instruments
gynaikôn	houses, Greek
harmostai	imperialism, Greek
haruspex	Etruria and Etruscans
hêgemôn, hêgemonia	Athenian empire; imperialism, ancient; international relations
hêliaia	lawcourts
hellênotamiai	imperialism, ancient, Greek; Sophokles
hetaira	love; prostitutes and prostitution
hetaireia	clubs, Greek

hetairos	Aristeides 'the Just'; Philip II
hippeis	Solon
historiê (historia)	historians and historiography, ancient
honestiores	society, Roman
horos, horoi	land and property, Greek; *polis*
horreum	warehouses
humiliores	society, Roman
hypaspists	arms and armour, Greek
hypokritês	tragedy
imbrex	tiles
imperator	Augustus; generals, Roman
imperium	imperialism, Roman; magistrates, Roman; political systems, Roman
imperium, maius	Augustus; power
impluvium	houses, Roman
insula	apartment buildings
isonomia	political theory
itinerarium	maps
iugerum	weights and measures, Roman
ius gentium	international relations
ius Italicum	taxation, Roman
kitharistai, kitharôdoi	education; music
klêros, klêroi	Sparta
klêrouchia, klêrouchos	cleruchy
koinê	language and languages; prose
kômê	villages; Syria, Roman
kômos	comedy; dance
kybernêtês	sailors
kyrios	family, Greek; guardianship, Greek; households, Greek; marriage, Greek; Yahweh
laconicum	bathing
lararium	furniture
latus clavus	senate and senators, Roman
leges Iuliae	clubs, Roman; freedmen and freedwomen, Roman; immorality; morality
legio	legions
liberti	slavery, Roman
limitanei	armies, organization of, Roman; imperialism, ancient, Roman
locatio, conductio	tenants
lochos	armies, organization of, Greek
logographos, logographoi	Demosthenes; Isaios; Isokrates; law; Lysias; oratory; prose; rhetoric, Greek
logos	body; childhood; Christian philosophy; cosmology; fables; Herakleitos; monotheism
ludi plebeii	games, Roman; Jupiter
lustratio	childhood; names and naming, Roman
magister	education, Roman
magister equitum	dictators; *Notitia Dignitatum*; magistrates, Roman

maiestas	banishment and exile; crime and criminals, Roman; lawcourts, Roman
manes	afterlife; death; funerals, Roman
manus	marriage, Roman; society, Roman
medimnos	weights and measures, Greek
metoikos, metoikoi	metics
monachos	hermits
mora	armies, organization of, Greek
mos maiorum	morality
municipium	Hispania
murex	purple; shell
naos	Parthenon; temples, Greek
nauarchos	naval warfare, Greek
nauklêros	sailors
nautês (Gk), *nauta* (Lat.)	sailors
navicularius	sailors
neodamôdeis	imperialism, ancient
nexum	debt-bondage
nomos	Arsinoë (city); music; nature; nomads
novus homo	careers
nundinae	calendars
oikos	family, Greek; households, Greek
opus africanum	masonry styles
opus incertum	concrete
opus mixtum	masonry styles
opus quadratum	masonry styles
opus reticulatum	concrete
opus sectile	churches
opus signinum	waterproofing
opus testaceum	concrete
orchêstra	drama; theatres, Greek
pagus	paganism; village
paidagôgos, paidagôgoi	education
paidotribês	education
pankration	athletes and athletics, Greek
parapêgmata	sun
pater patriae	Cicero
paterfamilias	family, Roman; masculinity; men
patria potestas	family, Roman; households, Roman; power
patrimonium	taxation, Roman
peculium	manumission
pentakosiomedimnoi	Solon
pentathlon	athletes and athletics, Greek
pentêrês, pentêreis	navies, Roman; ships and shipbuilding
peplos	dress, Greek
peregrinus, peregrini	citizenship, Roman
periodos gês	geography
perioikoi	helots; Laconia; Sparta

periplous, periploi	maps; Mela; navigation; *see also* tactics, military, Greek; travellers
philia	friendship; love
phoros	imperialism, ancient, Greek
phylê, phylai	tribes, Greek
pietas	households, Roman
plebiscitum, plebiscita	political systems, Roman
polemarchos	armies, organization of, Greek; generals, Greek
pôlêtai	accounting
politês	citizenship, Greek; *polis*
pompê, pompai	processions; ritual, Greek
pontifex	priests and priestesses, Roman
pontifex maximus	priests and priestesses, Roman; ritual, Roman
pornê	prostitutes and prostitution
portoria	taxation, Roman
praefectus annonae	Rome
praenomen	names and naming, Roman
praetorium	forts and fortresses, Roman
pragmatikê historia	Polybios
principia	forts and fortresses, Roman
prorogatio	generals, Roman
proskynêsis	Alexander III ('the Great')
provincia	Augustus
proxenos	benefactors and benefaction, Greek; *polis*
prytaneion	cities, Greek; *polis*; prytany
psêphisma	assemblies, Greek
psiloi	armies, organization of, Greek
psychê	mind and body; soul
quaestio	lawcourts, Roman; murder
regia	Carrara; Mars; Numa
religio	philosophy, Roman
rex	kingship, Roman
rostrum	Cicero; trophies, military, Roman
Salii	priests and priestesses, Roman; songs and singing
salutationes	houses, Roman; patronage
saris(s)a	arms and armour, Greek; battles, Roman; cavalry; Philip II; Sellasia; tactics, military, Roman
scholê	literacy
seisachtheia	Solon
skênê	drama, Greek; theatres, Greek
societates	money lending; *publicani*
socius	social wars
sodales	fraternity
stadion	athletes and athletics, Greek; games, Greek; gymnasia, Greek; measurement; Olympic games; weights and measures
stasis	civil wars, Greek
statêr	electrum
stichomythia	tragedy

stoichêdon	epigraphy, Greek
stratêgos, stratêgia	generals, Greek; strategy
suovetaurilia	cattle; Mars; sacrifice
sylê	pirates and piracy
symmachia	alliances
syssition	homosexuality; men; Sparta
taberna	cities, Roman
tablinum	houses, Roman
tabularium	records, public, Roman
tagos	Thessaly
taurobolium	bulls; Cybele; sacrifice
taxiarchos, taxiarchoi	armies, organization of, Greek
technê, technai	art; rhetoric, Greek; technology
tegula	tiles
temenos	agora, Athenian; Olympia
terra sigillata	manufacturing, Roman; samian ware; trade, Roman
terracotta	figurines, terracotta; waterproofing
theôros, theôroi	travellers
theôrodokos, theôrodokoi	travellers
thermae	baths
thêtes	cleruchs, cleruchy; naval warfare, Greek; political participation, Greek; Solon
timê	honour
tria nomina	names and naming, Roman
tribuni militum	tribunes
tribuni plebis	tribunes
tribunicia potestas	emperors, Roman; power
tributum	taxation, Roman
tributum capitis	taxation, Roman
tributum soli	taxation, Roman
triclinium	dining; dining rooms
triêmiolion, triêmiolionia	naval tactics and weapons
triêrarchia	benefactors and benefaction; Demetrios of Phaleron; liturgies
triêrês	trireme
trittys	demes
vectigal	taxation, Roman
vellum	libraries
venationes	games; hunting
vexillatio	legion
vicesima hereditatum	taxation, Roman
vicus	cities, Roman; villages; Vindolanda
vigiles	cities, Roman; crime; fire-fighting; public order, Roman; Rome
xenêlasia	society, Greek
xenia	barbarians, Greek; communications; diplomacy; friendship, Greek; *polis*; society, Greek

xenos	barbarians, Greek; benefactors and benefaction, Greek; diplomacy; friendship, Greek; honours; metics; *polis*; society, Greek
zeugitai	cleruchs, cleruchy; Solon

Abbreviations

ABSA	*Annual of the British School at Athens*
AE	*L'Année épigraphique*
AJA	*American Journal of Archaeology*
AJP	*American Journal of Philology*
ANRW	*Aufstieg und Niedergang des römischen Welt*
AntAf	*Antiquités africaines*
BASP	*Bulletin of the American Society of Papyrologists*
BCH	*Bulletin de correspondance hellénique*
BICS	*Bulletin of the Institute of Classical Studies*
CAH	*Cambridge Ancient History* (followed by volume numbers; sometimes with chapter or page numbers)
CIL	*Corpus Inscriptionum Latinarum*
CJ	*Classical Journal*
CM	*Classica et Mediaevalia*
CP	*Classical Philology*
CQ	*Classical Quarterly*
CW	*Classical World*
EHR	*Economic History Review*
FGrH	F. Jacoby (1923–58) *Die Fragmente der griechischen Historiker*
G&R	*Greece and Rome*
GRBS	*Greek, Roman and Byzantine Studies*
Hansen and Nielsen, *Inventory*	M. H. Hansen and T. H. Nielsen, eds. (2004) *An Inventory of Greek Poleis in the Archaic and Classical Periods*
HSCP	*Harvard Studies in Classical Philology*
HTR	*Harvard Theological Review*
IG	*Inscriptiones Graecae*
ILS	*Inscriptiones Latinae selectae*
JAS	*Journal of Archaeological Science*
JECS	*Journal of Early Christian Studies*
JHS	*Journal of Hellenic Studies*
JRS	*Journal of Roman Studies*
LIMC	*Lexicon iconographicum mythologiae classicae* (with volume and page numbers)
Mattingly and Salmon, *Economies beyond Agriculture*	D. J. Mattingly and J. Salmon, eds. (2001) *Economies beyond Agriculture in the Classical World*

ML	R. Meiggs and D. Lewis (1988) *A Selection of Greek Historical Inscriptions to the End of the Fifth Century* BC, rev. edn [references are to document nos.]
OJA	*Oxford Journal of Archaeology*
P&P	*Past & Present*
PBSR	*Papers of the British School at Rome*
PCPS	*Proceedings of the Cambridge Philological Society*
PP	*Parola del passato*
PSAS	*Proceedings of the Society of Antiquaries of Scotland*
RE	Pauly, A. F. von and Wissowa, G. (1894–1972) *Realencyclopädie der classischen Altertumswissenschaft*, 83 vols., including supplements.
REA	*Revue des études anciennes*
SEG	*Supplementum epigraphicum Graecum*
Tod	M. N. Tod (1946–8) *A Selection of Greek Historical Inscriptions*, 2 vols. [references are to document nos.]
YCS	*Yale Classical Studies*
ZPE	*Zeitschrift für Papyrologie und Epigraphik*

abacus see COUNTING; EDUCATION, ROMAN.

Academy The philosophical school founded by PLATO, named after the GYMNASIUM near Athens in which it was located. Three stages in the history of the school are conventionally distinguished. The Old Academy developed Plato's dogmatic teachings, including his interest in MATHEMATICS. Beginning with Arkesilaos (316/15–242/1 BC) the Middle Academy emphasized rather the sceptical aspect of Plato's writings, rejecting the STOIC account of KNOWLEDGE and showing that, as there were arguments against every position, it was wise to suspend judgement. The New Academy of Karneades (214/13–129/8 BC) similarly rejected dogmatism. While Kleitomachos interpreted Karneades as holding that it was wise not to assent, Philo of Larisa (159/8–84/3 BC) took his view to be that the wise person could hold opinions while being aware that they might be false and went so far as to claim that this had been the consistent doctrine of the school throughout. In the confusion following SULLA's sack of Athens in 86 BC the school seems to have disintegrated, Antiochos of Askalon (b. c.130 BC) rejecting Philo's position and claiming to restore the dogmatic position of the Old Academy, asserting that the views of the Old Academy, ARISTOTLE and the Stoics had been essentially similar. Whether the Academy continued as an institution is uncertain, as is the relation to it of the later NEOPLATONIST 'School of Athens'. In the first two centuries AD 'Academic' was increasingly used to indicate SCEPTICAL followers of Plato, 'Platonist' those who adopted a more dogmatic position – the 'Middle Platonists' (not to be confused with the earlier Middle Academy). RWS

See Dillon, J. (1996) *The Middle Platonists*; Glucker, J. (1978) *Antiochus and the Late Academy*; Ostwald, M. and Lynch, J.P. (1994) Plato's academy, in *CAH* 6, 602–16; Schofield, M. (1999) Academic epistemology, in K. Algra et al., eds., *The Cambridge History of Hellenistic Philosophy* 323–51.

Acarnania see AKARNANIA.

accounting It has been argued that the absence of double-entry book-keeping was a crucial factor limiting the evolution of rational ECONOMIC management in the ancient world. The non-survival of the vast majority of financial accounts limits our ability to challenge this assertion, but there is ample evidence as early as the classical period of a concern for accurate financial recording. In Athens, for example, public accounts were displayed in the city. The income and expenditure for a series of 5th-century BC buildings (e.g. the PARTHENON and the Propylaia) and sculptural projects (e.g. the statues of Athena Parthenos and Athena Promachos) were cut onto marble slabs and displayed in public areas such as the ACROPOLIS. These accounts are usually at the macro-scale, suggesting that they summarize payments made elsewhere. For example, quarrying of marble is entered as a block entry. However, in the Erechtheion accounts from the end of the 5th century there are entries for named sculptors working on specific figures in the frieze. Records of the *pôlêtai*, the officials responsible for public finances, have been recovered during excavations in the Agora. Records of commercial transactions can be found scratched onto the bases of exported Athenian pottery. These can list the size of consignments and their value in *drachmai* and obols (and occasionally in other currencies such as Persic obols on Cyprus).

Work on estate records from Ptolemaic and Roman Egypt has revealed some sophistication in accounting practices. For example, the HERONINOS archive of the Appianus estate in the Fayûm (3rd century AD) consists of monthly accounts compiled by a series of managers. They record cash receipts and offset them with total disbursements, including cash salaries and food payments for estate employees and casual payments for specified tasks, along with other cash expenses and lists of tools and foodstuffs held in the granaries of the estate. These detailed records could have had a primary function of limiting the scope of managers for defrauding absentee landowners. However, the records also indicate a more advanced economic understanding, for instance in the ability of managers to deal with internal transfers of produce and labour between separate units of the estate, and in the arrangement of transactions by type, not by date. The conclusion is that Greek and Roman accounting, though primitive by modern standards, could nonetheless have allowed the profitability of larger economic enterprises to be assessed. DJM, DWJG

See Johnston, A.W. (1981) *Trademarks on Greek Vases*; Langdon, M.K. (1991) Poletai records, in G.V. Lalonde et al., *Inscriptions: horoi, poletai records, leases of public lands* (Athenian Agora, 19) 53–143; Macve, R.H. (1985) Some glosses on 'Greek and Roman accounting', in P.A. Cartledge and F.D. Harvey, eds., *Crux* 233–64; Rathbone, D. (1991) *Economic Rationalism and Rural Society in Third-century AD Egypt*.

acculturation The term acculturation signifies all the phenomena of interaction resulting from the contact of two distinct 'cultures'. It denotes the process and mechanisms of interaction and also its outcome. In theory, such interaction is bilateral, though in most cases studied one 'culture' is dominant and the other is subordinate. Thus the usage is somewhat euphemistic and serves to conceal the term's political implication in the discourse and practice of colonial domination. In these contexts, acculturation is often accompanied by an active 'destructuration' of those aspects of native culture inimical to the ruling power. This feature, its association with the discredited notion of 'diffusion' and the ambiguities of the concept of culture itself have cast doubt on its utility as an explanatory concept among modern social scientists. If, however, in a 'POST-COLONIAL' context, notions of power and domination are added, it may be

ACCULTURATION: an asymmetric cultural relationship? Cartoon by Simon James.

possible to rehabilitate the use of the concept of acculturation as a tool of analysis.

Ancient historians and archaeologists often hide the notion of acculturation under the formulations 'romanization' and 'hellenization'. These terms carry their own hidden agenda and are frequently linked to the traditional colonialist dichotomy of 'civilization' versus 'barbarism'. In the classical context, it is helpful to realize that acculturation was often the outcome of an unequal negotiation of power between a dominant imperial authority and the subordinated native communities it had conquered. This is true of the 'romanization' of the north-west provinces of the Roman empire, which can be used as a paradigmatic case for attempts to explain and analyse the processes of social change involved. Acculturation was made manifest by the adoption by Britons and GAULS of (among other things) the Latin language, town life and new forms of habitation, a market economy, new material culture and dress, new cuisines and new forms of RELIGION. The classic statement of the mechanisms and outcome of acculturation is provided by Tacitus, referring to the social policy of the Roman governor AGRICOLA in the province of Britain (AD 77–84).

Clearly, the mechanisms of acculturation were bilateral: pro-active efforts by Roman governors such as Agricola were matched by a quest for status and by emulation on the part of the native élite, who saw Roman culture as a new arena for social competition and advancement. The last sentence reveals that acculturation was regarded by the Romans as eminently a method of control. The domination ensured by the Roman army was reinforced by 'hegemony' or 'manufacturing consent'. This programme is not exclusive to the Roman empire: the history of colonialism demonstrates that limited acculturation (usually of native élites) has been a tool of domination by imperial powers throughout history, as it ensured the governability of the colonized. It was to this end that the education of the sons of the native élite was directed. The progressive acquisition of ROMAN CITIZENSHIP by native élites, promoted by EMPERORS such as CLAUDIUS, facilitated their allegiance. The IMPERIAL CULT was another remarkable method of promoting social solidarity within the empire.

Although many aspects of Roman culture were adopted by native élites, it seems clear that further down the social scale there was less inducement or need to 'romanize', so much so that some have claimed (for the province of Britain) that romanization was a mere (élite) veneer over an underlying and continuing native social structure and culture. Implicit in this hypothesis is the assumption of the continuity of a primordial 'Celtic' culture. Recent historical research on 'ethnogenesis', however, suggests that ETHNICITY and culture are active historical constructions and are subject to constant reinvention as a response to outside pressure. It seems probable that 'Celtic' ethnicity and culture were reinvented in response to the Roman presence and promoted new forms of IDENTITY, rather than remaining as some unchanging, primordial substrate.

Although acculturation was regarded by the Roman authorities as a useful tool of hegemony, it was potentially a double-edged weapon. Such an 'antagonistic acculturation' is evident in the 'conspiracy of Civilis' in Roman Gaul and the Rhineland (AD 69–70). Here the acquisition of Roman military and organizational skills (marshalled by Civilis) and classical rhetorical culture (deployed by the orator Valentinus against the Romans) in combination with certain aspects of native culture (Civilis dyed his hair red as a symbolic gesture of cultural defiance) was used against the Romans and made the insurrection of Civilis all the more formidable (Tacitus, *Histories* 4–5). CMF

See Jones, S. (1997) *The Archaeology of Ethnicity*; Millett, M. (1990) *The Romanization of Britain*; Wachtel, N. (1978) *The Vision of the Vanquished*.

Achaea (Achaia) see PELOPONNESE.

Achaean league see ACHAIAN LEAGUE; PELOPONNESE.

Achaemenids see PERSIA AND PERSIANS.

Achaia, Roman (Achaea, Roman) This small PROVINCE, encompassing the heart of 'Old Greece', was probably created early in the reign of AUGUSTUS, following his victory off the Greek coast at ACTIUM. Achaia's territory was roughly coterminous with the boundaries of modern Greece (minus CRETE, THESSALY and MACEDONIA); a separate province of EPIRUS was formed later. Roman colonies or foundations in the province were relatively few: Augustus established Nikopolis ('Victory City') to commemorate his triumph at Actium; the Julian colony at CORINTH probably acted as provincial capital.

For much of its history, Achaia was a senatorial province. Its most dramatic departure from that status came when NERO declared the Greeks 'free' (AD 67) – a gift almost immediately revoked by VESPASIAN. *POLEIS* and league structures served as the province's dominant political and administrative structures, as local ÉLITE families took charge of the IMPERIAL CULT, tax collection, public order and other basic liturgies. Dozens of cities continued to dot the Achaian landscape; chief among these were ancient centres such as Athens, SPARTA and ARGOS. The antique panhellenic sanctuaries also continued, now attracting participants from Rome and elsewhere in the empire; existing FESTIVALS in the province were frequently expanded to embrace worship of the imperial family.

Achaia's position within the Roman world was complicated by civic myths and histories, the hellenic heritage so often admired by philhellenic Roman authorities. This could lead to great benefits, as when ANTONINUS PIUS awarded freedom to the Arkadian village of Pallantion on the grounds that it had been the home of Evander, an early founder of Rome. Athens, Sparta and other venerable sights became tourist attractions. The PAST, especially the memory of the classical era, was carefully cultivated in a 'nostalgic' Achaia, not out of sycophancy or inertia, but as a strategy for negotiating the new position of Greek cities, and their leading families, within the empire.

This emphasis on the classical past has often resulted in the province being viewed as a kind of academic haven or an isolated, passive backwater. The cultural significance of Achaia has tended to discourage investigation into other dimensions of life within the province, a reluctance abetted by scholarly bias against studying 'the glory that was Greece' in periods of dependence or of submission. The late 20th century witnessed the passing of such attitudes; for example, the ARCHAEOLOGY of Roman Greece has received much more attention in recent years. A good number of regional survey projects now attest to significant changes in settlement and landholding patterns in the province; centuriation systems have been traced around Roman colonies such as Corinth; alterations in the Greek ritual landscape have been observed. 'Greece, the captive, took her savage victor captive', wrote HORACE (*Epistles* 2.1.156), but it is increasingly clear that Roman annexation in its turn had a deep impact on Achaia, the 'homeland' of the Greeks. (see p. 4) SEA

See Alcock, S.E. (1993) *Graecia Capta*; Cartledge, P. and Spawforth, A. (1989) *Hellenistic and Roman Sparta*; Hoff, M. C. and Rotroff, S., eds. (1997) *The Romanization of Athens*.

 ROMAN EMPIRE: (b).

Achaian league (Achaean league) POLYBIOS implies that the Achaians had a federal state early on (2.41.4–6); since their colonies lack named *mêtropoleis* (mother-cities), this may be true. The Achaians were certainly divided into 12 regions by the 5th century BC (HERODOTOS 1.145), and the league's existence can be inferred from Achaian relations with the ATHENIAN EMPIRE.

The league's heyday was the 3rd century. Having added new members in the 280s and 270s, it became an important power under the leadership of ARATOS OF SIKYON (general for the first time in 245), who united his Dorian *polis* to the federation. Frequently at odds with the AITOLIANS, Sparta and MACEDONIA, the Achaians over time drew closer to Macedonia, beginning in the 220s when they together inflicted on Sparta its great defeat at Sellasia (222/1). This entente ended when the Achaians were forced to side with Rome in 198. Under the leadership of PHILOPOIMEN, the league controlled almost all of the Peloponnese. Growing tensions with Rome led to the removal to Italy of 1,000 hostages (including Polybios), and eventually war in 146/5. Once defeated, the league permanently lost its independence.

Centred on a shrine of ZEUS at Aigion, the government of the league was composed of an ASSEMBLY, council and elected MAGISTRATES: a GENERAL (originally two), ten *damiorgoi*, secretary, a hipparch, an admiral and a *hypostratêgos*. Cities were autonomous, but there were also league laws, as well as uniform weights, measures, COINAGE and common courts, though Polybios (2.37–8) exaggerates the degree of harmonization and the league's democratic credentials. JDD

See Larsen, J. A. O. (1968) *Greek Federal States*; Walbank, F.W. (1984) Aratus of Sicyon and the Achaean league, in *CAH* 7.1, 243–6; Macedonia and the Greek leagues, in *CAH* 7.1, 446–81.

Achilles Greek HERO, son of Peleus and Thetis, a sea nymph. Mythology revolves around two major phases of the life of Achilles: his education under Cheiron, the wise and friendly centaur in THESSALY, and his adult life as the prince of the Myrmidons in the ACHAIAN camp during the siege of Troy. HOMER, PINDAR and to a lesser extent EURIPIDES (*Iphigeneia at Aulis*) shaped ancient traditions about Achilles' childhood alongside later authors, notably PAUSANIAS, APOLLODOROS and PHILOSTRATOS. Thetis unsuccessfully attempted to render her son immortal by dipping him in the river Styx; he was held by his heel, preventing complete immersion (hence the phrase 'Achilles heel'). Subsequently the boy was committed to Cheiron who taught him hunting, as well as healing, music and other arts.

Homer's *Iliad* presents full insights into the hero's *ethos*, psychology and relationships in the Achaian camp, particularly through his conflict with AGAMEMNON, the leader of the Achaians, and his fatal choice to avenge the death of his friend Patroklos by pursuing and killing the Trojan prince HEKTOR. Achilles was renowned for his outstanding military skill and prowess, and his natural beauty, but also for excessive emotions which often proved destructive for the Achaians and ultimately himself.

A less famous phase in Achilles' life, generated by his mother's concerns to protect him, is his mythical sojourn, disguised as a woman, at the palace of Lykomedes on Skyros during the preparation for

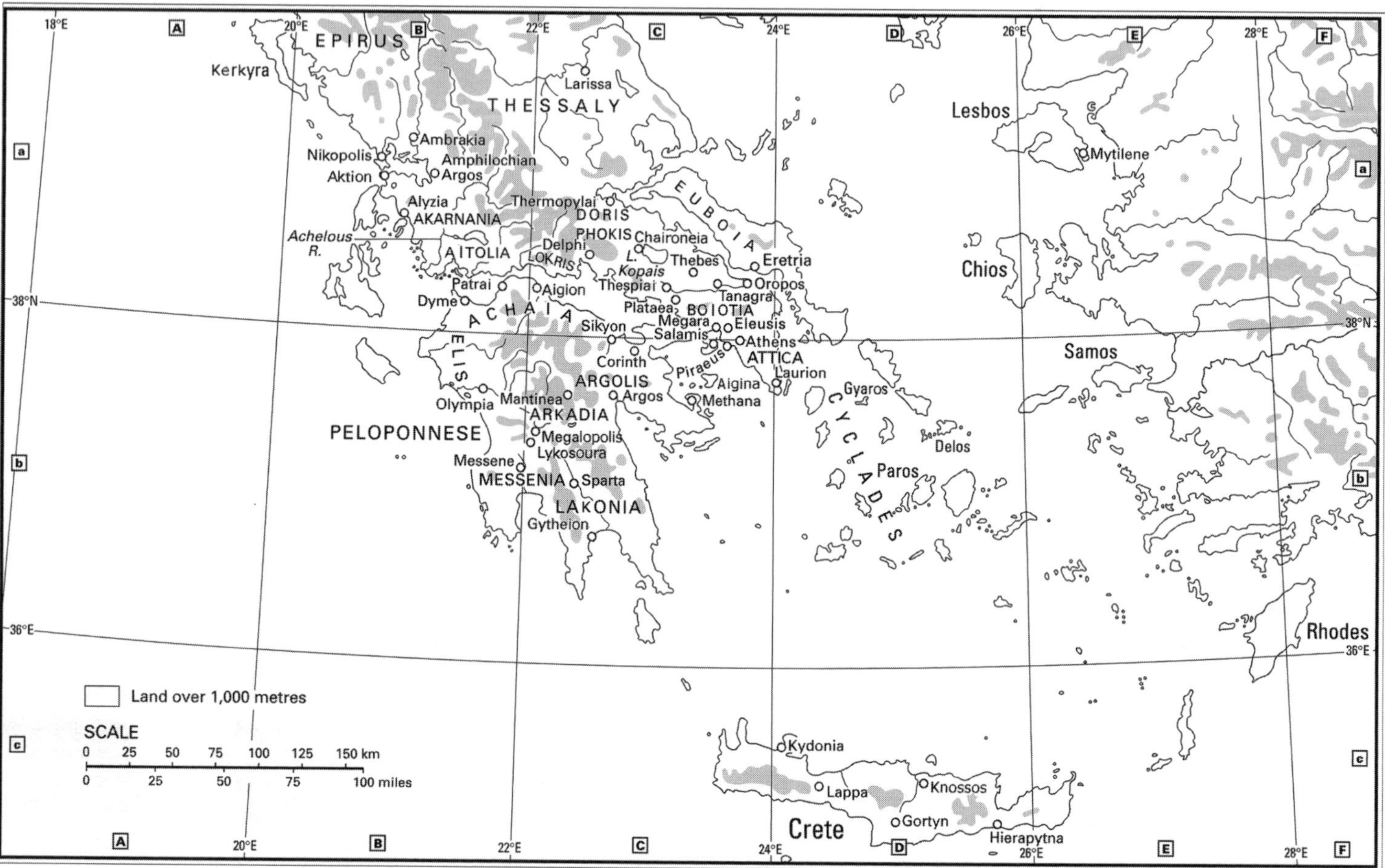

Achaia, Roman: map of mainland Greece and the Aegean under Roman rule.

Achilles: defeats the female Amazon warrior Penthesileia, exemplifying the triumph of masculine Greek values over Others.

the Trojan expedition. Only through a trick did Odysseus and his Achaian companions manage to approach him and lure him into joining the campaign. EP

See Kossatz-Deissman, A. (1981) Akhilleus, in *LIMC* vol. 1, 37–200; Schein, S. L. (1984) *The Mortal Hero*; Zanker, G. (1994) *The Heart of Achilles.*

acropolis see *AKROPOLIS*.

Acropolis, Athenian The term literally means 'upper (*akron*) town (*polis*)'. It occupied the summit of one of the three major rocky hills of Athens, the other two being the Areiopagos and Lykabettos. The name of the Acropolis is often synonymous with the sanctuary of the goddess Athena which rose to panhellenic prominence from the 5th century BC onwards.

The origins of the site go back to the Neolithic period. Although the archaeological evidence for life on the Acropolis at that time is meagre, it has been possible to associate several pottery pit-deposits on the north-western and south slopes of the hill with areas of habitation at the site. Further support for this hypothesis has been offered by the presence of a fountain (known as Klepsydra) on the north-western slopes and traces of a structure identified as a hut on the south slope. The latter area was probably occupied in the succeeding period, while from the 13th century the first attempts of a more substantial development appear, including terraces and high, neatly built walls. This must have transformed the site into a fortified citadel, as happened elsewhere in Greece during this period. Isolated architectural pieces have often been taken to belong to a system of political and social organization of some sophistication. Whether there was a palace or the home of a local ruler is hard to infer from the surviving architectural remains.

The beginnings of the historical age on the Acropolis are not marked by any noteworthy developments in terms of building remains. It is, however, likely that the sacred character of the place, which is undoubted from the early 6th century onwards, began to emerge by that time. This is shown by the type and level of investment in prestigious artefacts from 750 BC, including bronze objects of types that are found dedicated at other major Greek sanctuaries

Acropolis, Athenian: (a) general view from Hill of the Muses.

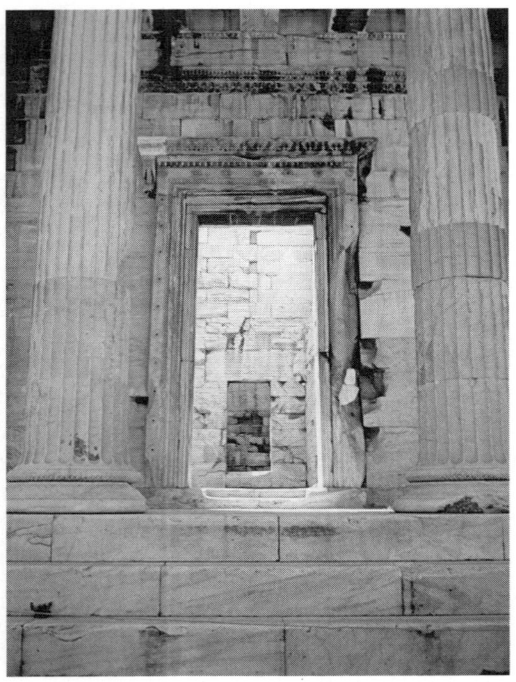

ACROPOLIS, ATHENIAN: (b) entrance to Erechtheion.

at the time, notably fragments of tripod cauldrons and FIGURINES.

The Acropolis acquired the first definite features of a major sanctuary around 575 BC, a period coinciding with a sudden burst of building activity and display of wealth through the treasures dedicated to the goddess worshipped there. Following a modest 7th-century TEMPLE which housed the ancient image of the goddess Athena Polias, a monumental STONE temple, surrounded by a colonnade and adorned with SCULPTURE, was built in about the 560s, perhaps early in the TYRANNY of PEISISTRATOS (561/0–528/7 BC). Although the exact location remains a problem, it seems fairly clear that another temple of the goddess, known as the Old Temple (*archaios neôs*), replaced or co-existed with the earlier Peisistratid one from c.525 BC. The entrance to the site was remodelled under Peisistratos and next to it, an old MYCENAEAN bastion was transformed into a temple dedicated to Athena NIKE (the goddess of Victory). Furthermore, a number of sacred buildings (*hiera oikêmata*) are mentioned in inscriptions from the site, testifying to the intensification of religious activity on the summit of the Acropolis. The latter is confirmed by the range of luxurious dedications to the city goddess, most notably in the form of MARBLE sculpture and bronzes.

Life on the Acropolis continued to prosper after Peisistratos and particularly under democratic rule. Plans for redevelopment of the site began with the construction of a new temple to Athena and a monumental gateway at the entrance to the site. The temple was a thanksgiving to the goddess for her continuous support in Athens' sweeping military victory at MARATHON against its oriental enemies, the PERSIANS, in 490 BC. The temple would have stood at the site of its Periklean successor, the PARTHENON, had it not been left unfinished because of a second Persian invasion led by XERXES. Like other sacred buildings on the Acropolis, including the Old Temple, the pre-Parthenon fell victim to the Persians when they gained access to the city in 480. After the Persians were repelled at PLATAEA in 479, it took about 30 years for the Athenians to undertake substantial rebuilding work on the destroyed temples. Instead, work focused on the fortification of the Acropolis, the building of the Long Walls which linked the city with PIRAEUS, and the rebuilding of the AGORA and the lower city; some essential sacred structures of the upper city were temporarily fixed. When a more extensive operation began in 447 BC, the Parthenon rose out of the former unfinished temple of Athena and was dedicated to Athena Parthenos. It was a grand and unusual building, designed to honour the city goddess and to promote the glory of her city to the world. The iconographic programme of its sculptural decoration constituted a powerful message of the superiority of the culture and lifestyle of Athens and their contribution to the Greek struggle for independence from the oriental enemy. The rebuilding extended to other temples in the 5th century, such as that of Athena Nike and the former old temple of Athena Polias, known as the Erechtheion.

The turbulent history of the Acropolis did not stop there. It lasted through hellenistic and Roman times until the conversion of the Parthenon and other temples into CHRISTIAN CHURCHES. Subsequently the Parthenon was turned into a Turkish mosque, while other buildings, like the Erechtheion, were used for habitation after the occupation of Greece by the Turks in the 15th century. The Parthenon was finally turned into a ruin after it was blown up by the Venetians while they were besieging the Turks on the Acropolis in 1687. The stripping of the monuments' architectural and sculptural parts by foreign visitors to the site continued, and artworks were often transported away to be displayed in museums or antiquities markets abroad. The scene changed with the outbreak of the Greek movement for independence from Ottoman rule in 1821, which finally succeeded in driving the Turks off the Acropolis 12 years later. Since then, substantial EXCAVATION and restoration work has been carried out on the buildings, which are still regarded as the most prominent parts of the Greek heritage. Controversially, this work has also involved the removal of post-Roman structures such as the medieval tower at the west end, in an attempt to restore the 'original' appearance of the citadel. EP

See Hurwit, J. M. (1999) *The Athenian Acropolis.*

ATHENS: (a); PARTHENON: (a)–(b).

Actium, battle of A defining moment in the transition between the Roman REPUBLIC and PRINCIPATE was the defeat of Mark ANTONY and CLEOPATRA by Octavian (soon to be AUGUSTUS) at Actium, on the west coast of Greece, on 2 September 31 BC. The NAVAL battle, involving over 600 ships, took place at the opening of the Ambrakian gulf, where Antony's forces were blockaded by Octavian's superior fleet and army. Cleopatra's panic and flight apparently

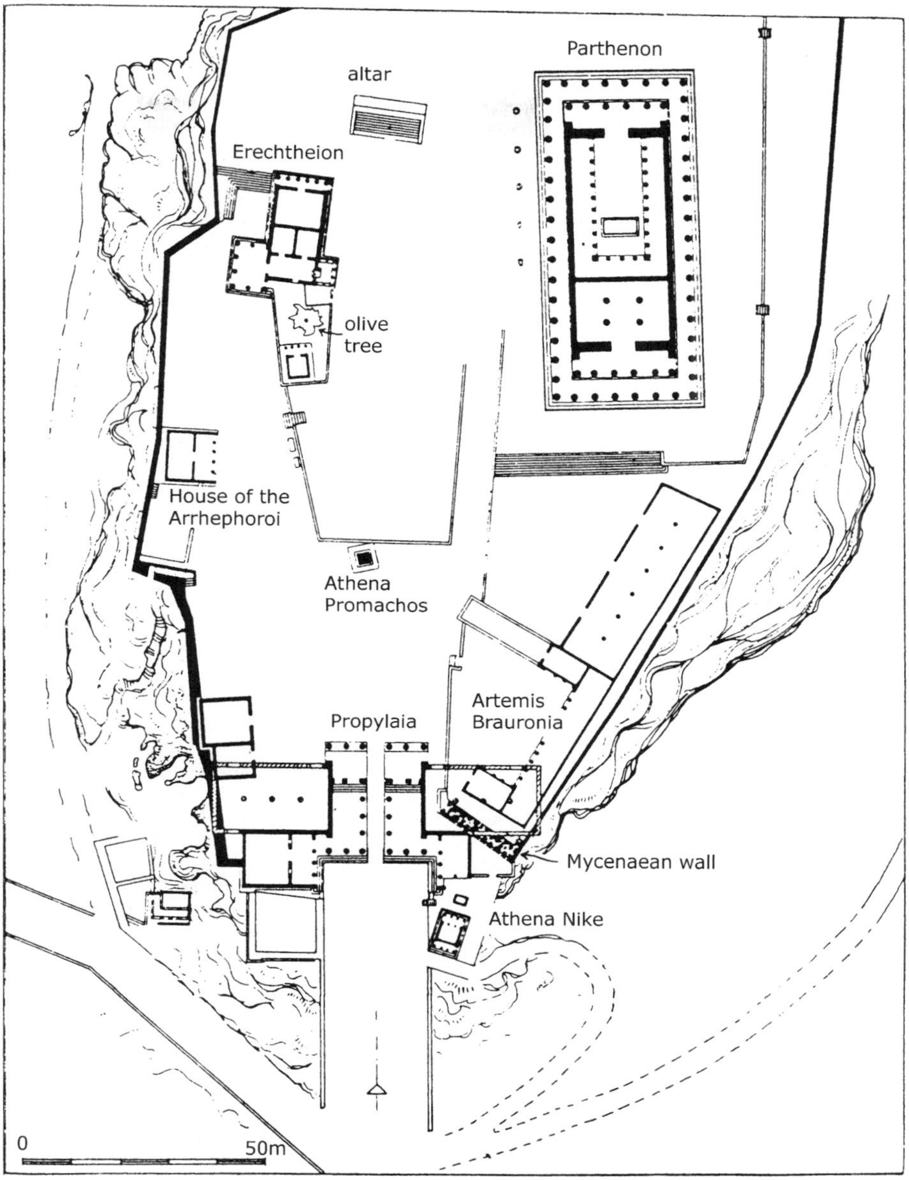

ACROPOLIS, ATHENIAN: (c) overall plan.

led to an overwhelming victory for Octavian. This was the last major action of the prolonged civil wars, leaving him the acknowledged master of a MEDITERRANEAN empire. Although both Antony and Cleopatra escaped, they committed suicide when Octavian's army reached Egypt. The cape of Actium overlooking the battle already contained a temple of APOLLO, and Augustus later developed the site further in honour of his victory and his special relationship with the god. A colony called Nikopolis ('Victory City') was also established on the opposite side of the gulf, and traditional Greek GAMES (*Actia*) were initiated. STRABO mentions that Augustus dedicated a series of ten captured warships in the enlarged sanctuary of Apollo (7.7.6) and elements of a substantial victory monument have been found. The rams (*rostra*) from other ships were placed in front of the temple erected to the deified CAESAR in the Republican FORUM at Rome. Contemporary Roman sources hailed Actium as the triumph of Roman traditional virtues over a decadent eastern monarchy. In truth it marked the effective start of Rome's own monarchical principate. DJM

ACHAIA: (a).

actors and actresses The early history of the acting profession in the Greek world is beyond recovery, and simply to repeat ARISTOTLE's story of the evolution from a single actor, or *hypokritês*, to three in TRAGEDY would be misleading (*Poetics* 1449a 2–25). Most likely, the institution of a competition for actors in 449 BC at the Athenian Dionysia canonized the number three for tragedy. The apparent lack of this limitation on the number in contemporary Attic COMEDY (as many as five are needed for some ARISTOPHANIC comedies) supports the view that the number was fluid into the middle of the 5th century. After that, the limitation on actors for tragedy appears to have influenced comedy; by the end of the 4th century, three became standard in that genre as well.

ACTORS AND ACTRESSES: (a) comic actors on stage in costume wearing masks. The actor dressed as a woman (on the right) is actually a man.

ACTORS AND ACTRESSES: (b) mosaic from the House of the Tragic Poet at Pompeii showing actors backstage preparing for a satyr play.

Actors in tragedies and comedies performed at city FESTIVALS at Athens and elsewhere were all free men of good standing and could become significant public figures. Their 'star power' made them people of importance throughout the Greek world; actors were even sent on embassies from Athens to PHILIP II of MACEDONIA, evidently to appeal to his well-known interest in the stage. In the late 4th century, actors began to form professional associations to negotiate the terms under which they would appear at festivals. These associations, which appear to have coalesced into the 'artisans of Dionysos' in the course of the 3rd century, probably served to protect the interests of all members of the profession, including performers of lesser status than the stars of the tragic and comic stage, who contended for prizes.

All performers who could contend for prizes in the Greek world were men. In other forms of drama, such as MIME, regarded as an inferior form of comedy, women too played roles. This was also true at Rome, where all stage performers were considered to be of low status – a result of the very different tradition of entertainment in the Italic world, where performers were regarded as clients of great ARISTOCRATS, and were often of servile origin. Despite this prejudice, substantial fortunes could be made by actors and actresses on the Roman stage. In the early period of Greek-influenced Roman drama in the 3rd and 2nd centuries, there is evidence for an association of professional actors, associated with playwrights, who would often appear in their works. In the 1st century AD, we find another association, this time for actors in mime and the popular form of DANCE known as PANTOMIME, the 'parasites of Apollo', providing evidence for leading mime actors (*archimimi*) and actresses (*archimimae*).

Under the Roman empire the contradiction between the Greek tradition of high-status individuals who acted in traditional forms and the Roman tendency to declare all stage performers as being of low status, subject to *infamia*, continued to be observed. The most significant development was that the performance of new tragedies and comedies gave way, in the course of the first three centuries AD, to solo performances by actors of tragedy. At the same time, the evident preference for risqué performances by mime actors and actresses led to the domination of the stage by these art forms. DSP

See Easterling, P. and Hall, E., eds. (2002) *Greek and Roman Actors.*

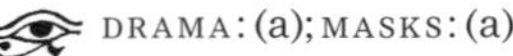 DRAMA: (a); MASKS: (a).

Adamklissi (ancient Tropaeum Traiani) Location of one of most spectacular Roman victory TROPHIES. It lies at the southern end of the main north–south route down the Dobrudja plain (south-east Romania), the strategic corridor between the DANUBE and the BLACK SEA. Adamklissi marks a crucial cross-roads of routes, at a point where invaders advancing down the Dobrudja can chose to move south towards

Greece or west towards MOESIA. The complex of monuments commemorate both Roman defeat and victory and at least one of the battles must have taken place close to this spot. There are three main structures within 100 m or so of each other – reflecting several different aspects of the poorly known story that lies behind their erection. The first is a large 'altar' (c.16 m square, 6 m high) engraved with details of significant legionary and auxiliary casualties in a battle that probably took place in the reign of DOMITIAN or in the initial stages of the first DACIAN WAR (AD 101). Close by lies a large, circular cenotaph structure (40 m in diameter), erected over a pit filled with sacrificed oxen. To the south, the third component was another circular drum (30 m in diameter), evidently erected after the first two monuments and decorated with relief metopes celebrating Trajan's victory in the second Dacian war and the death of DECEBALUS. On top of the drum was placed a series of statues of chained prisoners around a representation in stone of a lopped tree draped with arms and armour. The entire monument was at least 10 m high. The dedication of the *tropaeum* c.AD 108 to MARS Ultor provides the link between the three monuments, which thus commemorate the avenging of an earlier defeat. The Roman town below the hill took its name from the *tropaeum*. DJM

See Richmond, I. (1967) Adamklissi, *PBSR* 35: 29–39.

adhesives see GLUES.

admirals see NAVAL WARFARE.

Adonis see MOTHER GODDESSES; POETESSES.

adoption

In ancient Greece, adoption provided someone to inherit property in the absence of sons. People did not adopt simply because they wanted a FAMILY, or to give orphaned children a home. In Athens it was illegal to adopt foundlings, since they might not be of citizen birth. Childless men usually adopted male adults, who were frequently close relatives. Women and children were only rarely adopted (Isaios 11). In Athens a man who had daughters, but no sons, might adopt a son to marry his daughter (Demosthenes 41). Alternatively, a grandfather might adopt his daughter's son, sometimes posthumously. An adopted son inherited the estate of his adoptive father, but forfeited the right to inherit from his biological father.

Provisional adoption was sometimes incorporated in WILLS, so that the adoption only happened if the testator died childless. Men about to go off to fight in battle regularly made such wills, since they could not be certain of returning alive. A large estate with no obvious heir was likely to become the subject of dispute. Even the rights of an adopted son might be contested, and the lawsuits could last many years.

Our main sources for adoption are the courtroom speeches of 4th-century BC Athens and the Great Law Code of GORTYN, CRETE (early 5th century BC). Despite differences of detail, the general principles are similar in both, suggesting that Greek concepts of adoption were deeply rooted and closely linked to INHERITANCE. LF

See Rubinstein, L. (1993) *Adoption in IV. Century Athens.*

For the childless man – married or unmarried – adoption provided a means of perpetuating his family name and cult. It was possible to adopt someone posthumously, in a WILL (e.g. the younger PLINY). The law distinguished between *adoptio* of a boy or man still in his father's power and *adrogatio* of a man with a family in his own power, whose whole family would transfer legally to that of the adopter. The middle (gentile) Roman name was changed to that of the adoptive father but the original gentile name, in extended form, replaced the third name (*cognomen*) – thus Publius Aemilius Paullus, adopted by Publius Cornelius SCIPIO AFRICANUS, became Publius Cornelius Aemilianus. Adoptees, who were usually adults and often relatives, relinquished legal claims (such as INHERITANCE) to the family of their birth but still maintained relations with them. Many adoptions transferred the son of a daughter or sister from the female to the male line. A female Roman citizen could be adopted but could not adopt. She could establish quasi-maternal relations by naming a favourite as heir in her will, or by rearing a poor relative or social inferior (an *alumnus* or *alumna*) who would care for her in old age and perform her funeral rites. Romans could therefore extend kinship and emotional relationships without fictions of biological parenthood or secrecy. SD

See Crook, J. A. (1967) *Law and Life of Rome.*

Adrianople, battle of Gothic victory over the Romans, 9 August AD 378. In 376 the emperor Valens allowed a large group of GOTHS, who were trying to escape the HUNS, to cross the DANUBE into the empire, hoping to recruit troops from them. Mistreatment by Roman officers while the Goths were still in THRACE led them to revolt under the leadership of Fritigern. After two years of inconclusive campaigning, Valens took the field himself in 378, marching from CONSTANTINOPLE. Informed by his scouts that there were only 10,000 Goths in the region, he determined to attack. In an acrimonious council meeting at Adrianople, Valens refused to wait for assistance from his Western colleague Gratian. Leaving behind his administrative staff, he led the Eastern field army against the Gothic groups in their wagon laager (circle) nearby. The attack was hurried, and the Roman left wing was still deploying when fighting began in the centre. When the main forces were engaged, the Gothic CAVALRY returned, attacking the Romans in the still undeployed left flank. As the Roman left wing collapsed, the reserve regiment of the Batavi could not be found. The Roman army dissolved, and Valens was caught in a farmhouse and burnt to death with his bodyguard. Roman losses were large, but the sources provide no figures for the size of either army. This battle is often described as a triumph of cavalry over infantry, but would be better seen as a result of poor scouting and Valens' impatience. HWE

See Ammianus Marcellinus, book 31; Heather, P. J. (1991) *Goths and Romans 332–489.*

Adriatic sea Body of water between Italy and the Greek peninsula. From very early on, the Greeks established colonies and trading posts along the north-east coast of the Adriatic; they also maintained, where possible, friendly ties with the natives of the region and traded with Italy, for example with

ETRUSCAN SPINA, sometimes thought to be a Greek foundation. Throughout the Greek and hellenistic periods, the Adriatic was afflicted with PIRACY, an activity particularly associated with ILLYRIANS. Rome's later attempts to eradicate this were not completely successful, at least initially. Rome's conquest of Italy provided it with access to the Adriatic across land; several roads directly from Rome ended at Italy's eastern coast, for example, the Via Appia at Brundisium (the main port for travel to Greece), the Via Flaminia at Fanum Fortunae, and the Via Salaria near Picenum.

Rome's first military foray across the Adriatic occurred in 229 BC, to protect Greek cities against the expansionist aims of the Illyrian queen Teuta. Subsequently, Roman military involvement was regular, if not necessarily continuous, until the PANNONIAN WARS of AUGUSTUS brought Illyrian territory under Roman control. From the early years of the HANNIBALIC WAR, Rome maintained a fleet in the Adriatic, initially to guard against MACEDONIAN (and Illyrian) expansion but also to protect TRADE and hinder piracy. By late antiquity, naval units were stationed at various points on the Adriatic coasts; their importance increased when RAVENNA became the residence of the Western emperors. JV

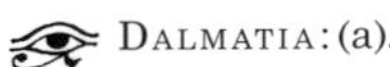 DALMATIA: (a).

adultery In Greek and Roman society, adultery was defined by the status of the woman. Married men could freely have sex with SLAVES and PROSTITUTES. In Greece, adultery was seen as a threat to the purity of the citizen line. In Athens, a wronged husband could demand monetary damages from his wife's lover or kill him if he caught him in the act (Lysias, *On the Killing of Eratosthenes* 30). He was obliged to DIVORCE his wife. The sources are silent on her fate, which must have been grim. It is uncertain whether she retained her dowry, but we know she could be attacked if she tried to attend religious ceremonies – the main social outlet for Athenian women (Pseudo-Demosthenes, *Against Neaira* 85). The stigma on herself and her children was considerable. In SPARTA the small but dominant Spartiate group, also preoccupied with civic purity, practised selective polyandry. It was not adultery if a respectable woman could have children with a worthy man approved by her husband for the good of the state (Xenophon, *Spartan Society = Lakedaimonion politeia* 1).

Like their Greek equivalents, wronged husbands at Rome sometimes adopted vicious and colourful self-help measures against their rivals, but apparently stopped short of the 'homicide of honour'. The emperor AUGUSTUS' legislation of 18 BC imposed severe penalties (loss of property, exile) on adulterers of both sexes. SD

See Lacey, W.K. (1968) *The Family in Classical Greece*; Richlin, A. (1981) Approaches to the sources on adultery at Rome, *Women's Studies* 8.1–2: 225–50.

advertising In the ancient world, advertising was done through images and the written word. In a world where the majority of the people were illiterate or semi-literate, the former may have been more important than the latter. A painting on the outside of the WORKSHOP or SHOP owned by Marcus Caecilius

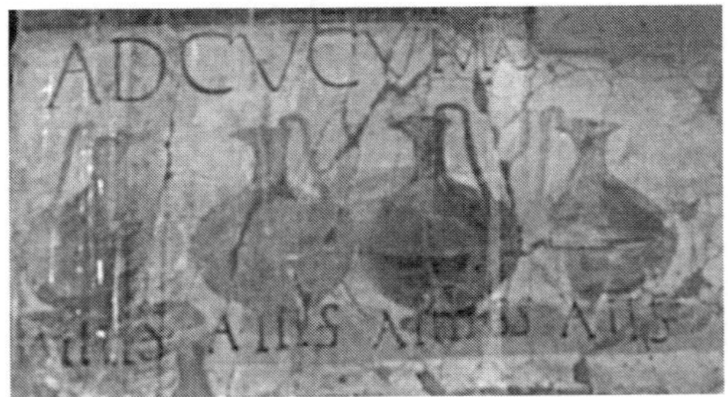

ADVERTISING: painted Roman sign from a street wall in Herculaneum, advertising the prices of different wines.

Verecundus at POMPEII, a dealer in clothes, shows his labourers combing wool and engaging in fulling activities, and the owner himself proudly displaying the finished product. Further examples come from an inn and a FULLERY, also from Pompeii. Some commercial establishments targeted a more literate audience and used written advertisements. The poet MARTIAL writes that the doorposts of the bookshop owned by one Atrectus were painted with advertisements for the books on sale. SLAVES who were offered for sale carried a placard advertising their skills, age and other details that might be of relevance to potential buyers. Non-commercial advertising extended to electoral slogans, announcements of GLADIATORIAL and other GAMES, and a few notices aimed at the recovery of runaway slaves or HORSES. In the area of classifieds, notices of property up for rent were painted on the walls of houses in Pompeii, and the same phenomenon is described in PETRONIUS' novel *Satyrica*. Occasionally, other materials such as wood may have been used for these purposes. Besides making use of the written word and images, people could also advertise a simple message, such as a theft or the disappearance of a slave, by hiring a street-crier. MK

See Cicero, *Letters to his Brother Quintus* 9.3; *Digest* 21.1.1; Dio Chrysostom, *Orations* 7.123; Martial 1, 117.11; Petronius 29.3, 38.10, 16, 97.1–2.

aediles Originally (494 BC), two PLEBEIAN MAGISTRATES in charge of the TEMPLE (*aedis*) where ARCHIVES recording concessions made by PATRICIANS were kept. By the time plebeians had access to the highest magistracies (367 BC), two new 'curule' aediles were created to take over some of the CONSULS' powers, especially aspects of municipal administration (FIRE-FIGHTING, SANITATION, law and order, public morality), the organization of public GAMES (often the cause of their subsequent popularity) and the FOOD SUPPLY. Each was assigned to one of the city neighbourhoods (*regiones*); he was vested with police powers and had limited civil and criminal jurisdiction (*potestas*) in connection with public works, MARKETS, and public establishments. Aediles issued edicts outlining their policies, co-operated with the CENSORS in letting out public contracts, and were assisted by junior magistrates, public servants and their own private staffs. Six in number since AUGUSTUS, they gradually lost their powers to newly created officials. They are known to have acted forcefully on occasion, like Pythias, who had his assistant trample some fish whose freshness was in doubt at Hypata in THESSALY (APULEIUS, *Golden Ass* 1.24–5). They could be held personally responsible for poor performance: while aedile, the future EMPEROR VESPASIAN was publicly humiliated by CALIGULA's soldiers upon the emperor's order, having mud stuffed down his garment in retribution for allowing dirty streets (SUETONIUS, *Vespasian* 5). Not long before the magistracy ceased to exist in the 3rd century AD, the Severan jurist Callistratus suggests that aediles had lost much of their impact: he reports that shopkeepers shamelessly beaten up by the officials once regarded as protectors of the urban PLEBS experienced no socio-political demotion as a result. JJA

See Robinson, O. F. (1992) *Ancient Rome*.

Aegean sea The body of water between ASIA Minor and Greece on the east–west axis, and THRACE and CRETE on the north–south. It seems to have formed as a result of tectonic processes in the Miocene period. Continuing tectonic activity renders the region subject to EARTHQUAKES, reported repeatedly in ancient sources, and was responsible for volcanic activity, notably at the islands of THERA, MELOS, and Nisyros (all now apparently dormant). Ranging from about 611 km (380 miles) north–south and 299 km (186 miles) west–east (maximum) and covering approximately 214,000 sq km (83,000 sq miles), the Aegean is littered with thousands of ISLANDS, hundreds of which are large enough to have sustained permanent human population. Some fall into more or less coherent groups, of which the most important are the northern Sporades, Cyclades (or Kyklades) centred on DELOS, and southern Sporades (mod. Dodecanese), the most important of which was RHODES. Various derivations were offered in antiquity for the name: the mythical Athenian king Aigeus; a rock in the sea called Aix lying between Tenos and CHIOS; a mountain on the coast of Asia Minor; or the town of Aigai on EUBOIA, a view that was perhaps predominant. The Aegean was 'closed' to navigation in winter, when the wind blows often from the south and brings stormy, unpredictable conditions. In summer the Etesian ('annual') winds, which blow steadily from the north or north-east, combined with land and sea breezes and fair weather, make for usually reliable sailing, but in one summer CICERO needed 16 days to cross from Athens to EPHESOS. The currents are erratic and depend often on the direction and strength of the winds. In general, the Aegean presents a relatively impoverished environment for FISH and other sea life. But the notion that the islands were poor in antiquity is mistaken. They supported human populations from the Neolithic period onwards, and some, particularly Melos and Thera, preserve important Bronze Age remains. During the archaic period the central Cycladic islands of NAXOS and PAROS played an important role in history, and Delos always held a vital place as a centre of cult. It has become increasingly evident that many islands supported their largest ever historical populations in the 5th to early 3rd centuries BC, when intensive AGRICULTURAL exploitation may have been facilitated by the construction of terraces. Control of the sea was a main objective of Athenian policy in the 5th and 4th centuries BC, and the Aegean was a stage on which the PTOLEMIES and the MACEDONIANS competed in the early hellenistic period. Its many little islands with hidden coves offered cover for PIRACY, which flourished in many periods, sometimes with the connivance of seafaring powers. After Pompey eliminated piracy in 67–66 BC the sea seems to have remained relatively safe for much of the time. Recent archaeological work has increasingly revealed the implantation of CHRISTIANITY and the appearance of CHURCHES in late antiquity. The Aegean was always a crucial link between the Greek peninsula and Asia Minor. (see also ECOLOGY) (see pp. 12–14) GR

See Brun, P. (1996) *Les Archipels égéens dans l'antiquité grecque*; Gorur, N. et al. (1995) Rift formation in the Gokova region, southwest Anatolia: implications for the opening of the Aegean sea, *Geological Magazine* 132: 637–51; Koder, J. (1998) *Tabula Imperii Byzantini* 10; Morton, J. (2001) *The Role of the Physical Environment in Ancient Greek Seafaring*; Talbert, R., ed. (2000) *Barrington Atlas of the Greek and Roman World*, map 57.

 GREECE: (a); CHALKIDIKE: (a).

Aegina see AIGINA.

Aegospotami see AIGOSPOTAMOI.

Aelian (Claudius Aelianus) c.AD 175–235 A FREEDMAN, born in PRAENESTE (Palestrina), about 30 km (20 miles) east of Rome. His native tongue was Latin, but his literary production was entirely in Greek, which he wrote in a simple, unadorned style. According to the ancient biography by PHILOSTRATOS, he learned the language from the SOPHIST (RHETORICIAN) Pausanias of Caesarea, a student of HERODES ATTICUS. Although his writings clearly reflect the influence of the Second Sophistic, it is not as a sophist that Aelian made his name. His two main works, *Miscellaneous Stories* and *Characteristics of Animals*, demonstrate a 2nd- and 3rd-century attraction to compilations – collections of short accounts and anecdotes on a wide variety of topics – of the kind that FAVORINUS, AULUS GELLIUS, and ATHENAEUS also composed. Aelian apparently selected the material for his compilations more for its ability to astonish the reader than for its inherent unity. But STOIC influence is evident in the way that he portrays divine reason as informing the natural world, both ANIMAL and human. This theme also seems to have been prominent in the fragmentary works *On Providence* and *On Divine Manifestations*. It is clear from the range of authors whom he quotes, paraphrases and cites as sources of information that he read widely. His knowledge of these sources, however, often seems superficial; this suggests that he relied heavily on literary compilations rather than profound study at first hand. MJ

See Aelian, *On the Characteristics of Animals*, 3 vols., trs. A. L. Scholfield (1958–9); *Letters* (with those of Alkiphron and Philostratos), trs. A. R. Benner and F. H. Fobes (1949); *Historical Miscellany*, trs. N. G. Wilson (1997).

Aelius Aristides (Publius Aelius Aristides) AD 117–c.181 One of the most famous sophists of the 2nd century AD, when 'sophist' was not a term of abuse – it was said by a near-contemporary (HERODES ATTICUS) that 'he conversed with cities as his

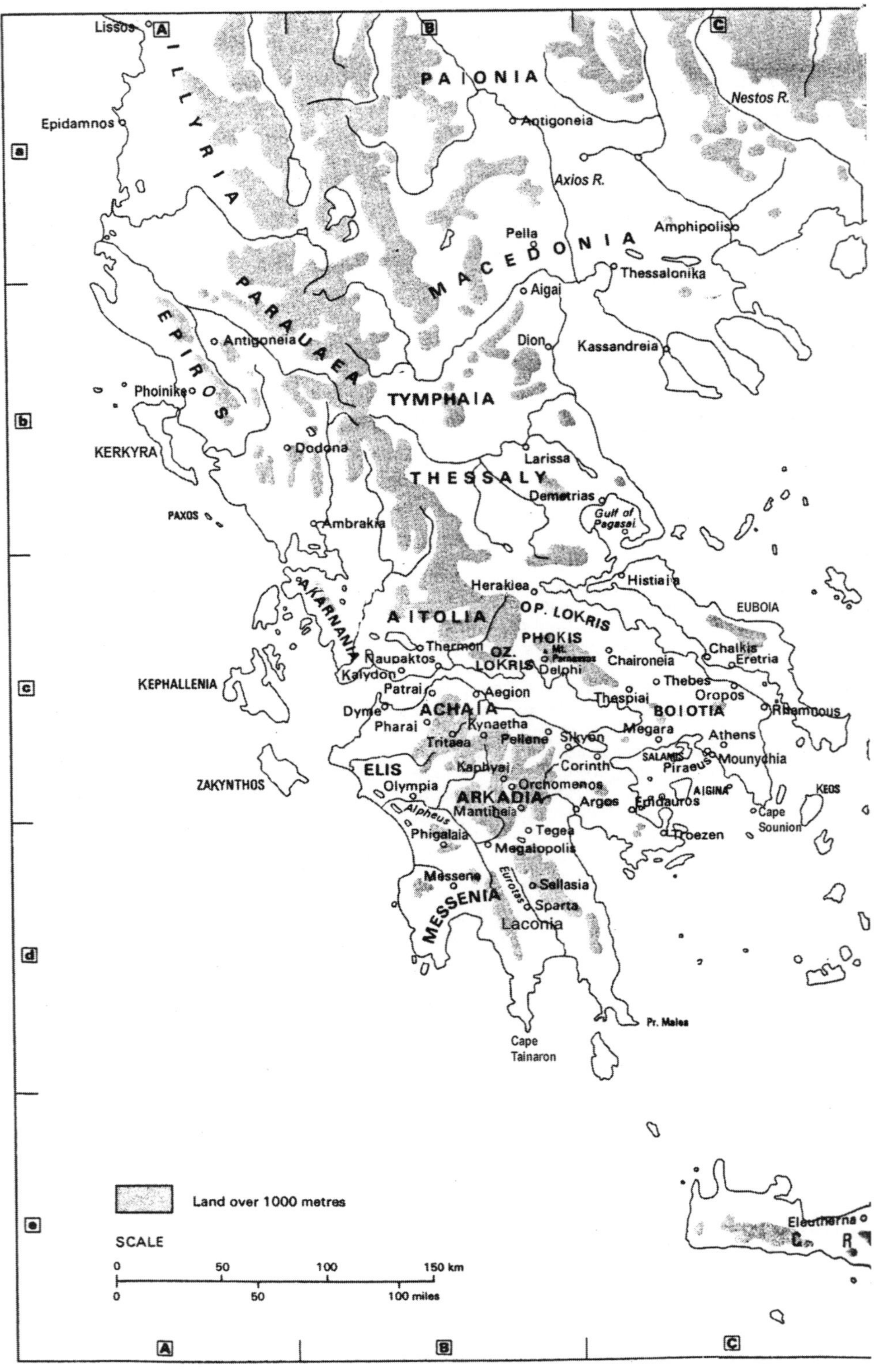

AEGEAN SEA: (a) general map.

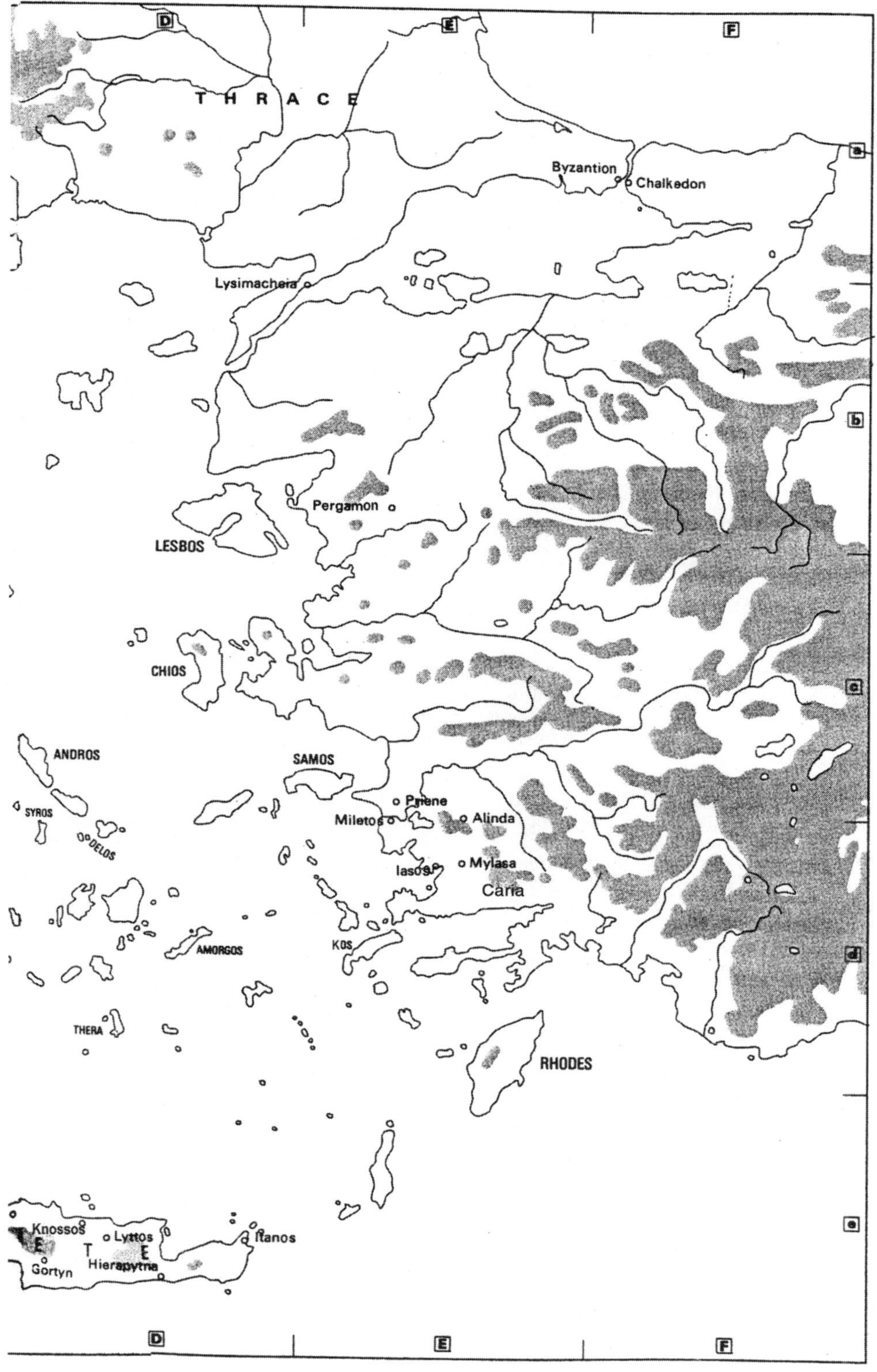
D
E
F
THRACE
Byzantion
Chalkedon
Lysimacheia
Pergamon
LESBOS
CHIOS
ANDROS
SAMOS
SYROS
DELOS
Priene
Miletos
Alinda
Iasos
Mylasa
Caria
AMORGOS
KOS
THERA
RHODES
Knossos
Lyttos
Itanos
Gortyn
Hierapytna
a
b
c
d
e

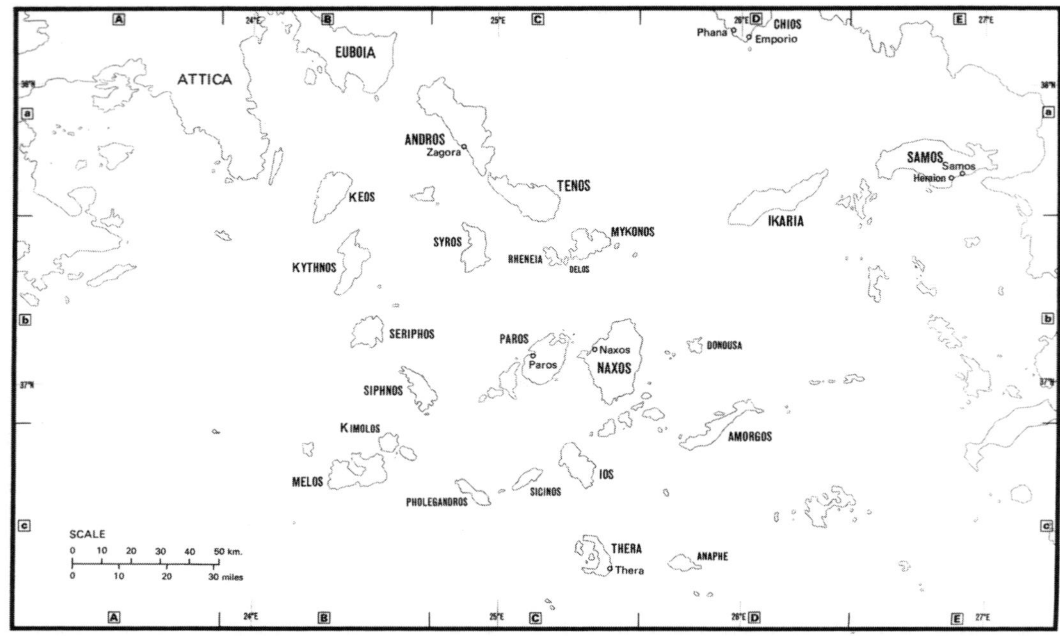

AEGEAN SEA: (b) detail of Cycladic islands in the central Aegean.

inferiors, emperors as not his superiors, and the gods as his equals'. The cities of the Greek East vied to have such men represent their interests to the ruling power in Rome. Aristides' family was wealthy, owning estates near SMYRNA, and he was to champion that city. PHILOSTRATOS, who includes a BIOGRAPHY of Aristides in his *Lives of the Sophists*, says that he could quite literally claim to be the founder of Smyrna, since his eloquence swayed MARCUS AURELIUS to provide funds for the reconstruction of the city following a devastating EARTHQUAKE in 177.

More than 50 of Aristides' works survive. The range is wide: treatises against PLATO and on the river NILE; PANEGYRICS in praise of cities, most notably Rome and Athens; speeches on RHETORIC and RELIGION (10 extant works, *Orations* 37–46, are usually designated HYMNS); the *Sacred Tales*; and DECLAMATIONS based on situations from Greek history. His work is very much the product of the Second Sophistic, as Greek intellectuals looked back to the glorious past of their culture, in part at least to compensate for their prosaic (albeit relatively prosperous) present as citizens of the Roman empire.

The two panegyrics on Rome (*Oration* 26) and Athens (*Oration* 1, the Panathenaic oration) are especially significant in this respect. The former was probably delivered during a visit to Rome in 143. In it, Rome is quite literally the city of the world, its constitution optimistically described as a universal DEMOCRACY under the one man who can rule and govern best; good government means that the whole civilized world can behave as if on HOLIDAY. In the Panathenaic oration the role of Rome remains unchanged as the guarantor of PEACE and security, but Athens takes centre stage as the source of EDUCATION and civilization. The value and importance of the Greek cultural inheritance is reasserted, in response to the fact of Roman political power. Aristides will also have been aware of the challenge to hellenic values posed by emergent CHRISTIANITY. Smyrna had a considerable Christian population and the martyrdom of its BISHOP, Polycarp, took place within a few years of the composition of the speech.

Aristides' visit to Rome was curtailed by ill-health. For the next ten years and more he was a frequent patient at the TEMPLE of ASKLEPIOS at PERGAMON, where GALEN met him. Aristides' illness provided a convenient excuse to avoid various liturgies and also resulted in his most fascinating work, the *Sacred Tales*. Here, he records 130 dreams in which the god instructed him about his health. They are important for what they tell us both about medical practice and about personal pagan belief. PMB

See Behr, C.A. (1968) *Aelius Aristides and the Sacred Tales*; Oliver, J.H. (1953) *The Ruling Power*; (1968) *The Civilizing Power*.

Aemilia see ITALY, ROMAN.

Aemilia Pudentilla A wealthy widow of Oea (Tripoli) wooed and married by the AFRICAN writer APULEIUS in the mid-2nd century AD. She was the mother of a young friend of Apuleius, Sicinius Pontianus, who initially encouraged the match. The union caused a local scandal and led (AD 158) to the unsuccessful prosecution of Apuleius for witchcraft at the instigation of her FAMILY and disappointed local suitors. Evocatively recalled by Apuleius in his *Apologia*, the case reveals a number of interesting aspects of Roman provincial society. First, the WEALTH and independence of Aemilia Pudentilla are notable features (her personal fortune was worth

4 million *sestertii*). As a widowed woman with grown-up children, and whose own father had died, she had a legal right to take control of her own financial affairs. Second, it is clear that she had been subjected to concerted, though unsuccessful, efforts by the Aemilii and Sicinii clans (two of the leading *gentes* of Oea) to coerce her into a MARRIAGE that would have been more favourable for them. This indicates the social pressures that could be brought to bear even on women who were notionally free of male control. Pudentilla's ability to marry for love was achieved at a high cost, with the death of one of her grown-up sons (having fallen ill on a journey occasioned by the case) and her estrangement from the other. She appears to have left Oea subsequently, to live with Apuleius at CARTHAGE. DJM

See Mattingly, D. J. (1995) *Tripolitania*.

Aemilianus see SCIPIO AEMILIANUS.

Aemilianus (emperor)

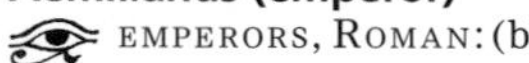 EMPERORS, ROMAN: (b).

Aemilii One of the oldest PATRICIAN families of the REPUBLIC (a *maior gens*), giving its name to the TRIBE Aemilia. It first appears, like several others, in the mid-480s BC, subsequently splitting into several branches (Barbulae, Lepidi, Mamerci or Mamercini, Papi, Paulli, Regilli, Scauri). Later traditions variously linked the family to a son of PYTHAGORAS or NUMA, to Amulius, king of Alba, or to a child of AENEAS (Emylos or Aemilia). Although the family was dominant in the period of the PYRRHIC war, only the Paulli held consulships during the PUNIC WARS (Lucius Aemilius Paullus dying a hero's death at CANNAE). The Paulli died out with Lucius AEMILIUS PAULLUS, victor at PYDNA in the third MACEDONIAN WAR (d. c.160 BC) – his surviving sons were adopted into the FABII and CORNELII Scipiones. The Lepidi endured to the time of CALIGULA, the most distinguished being Marcus Aemilius Lepidus, *pontifex maximus* and *princeps senatus* between 179 and his death in 152 BC. The Via Aemilia, which he built from Placentia to Ariminum, transmitted his name to the Italian region of Emilia Romagna. Of the same line and name was the fellow TRIUMVIR of Mark ANTONY and OCTAVIAN. The family was responsible for the first stone BRIDGE over the Tiber, the *Pons Aemilius* (Ponte Rotto). JRWP

Aemilius Paullus (Lucius Aemilius Paullus) c.228–160 BC Conqueror of Macedonia and biological father of Africanus the Younger (SCIPIO AEMILIANUS). Aged 12 when his father was killed at the battle of CANNAE, Paullus carved out an impressive military career of his own. A three-year praetorian command in Spain (191–189) ended with a TRIUMPH; consular command in Liguria (182–181) saw him acclaimed *imperator* by his troops for the second time (thrice in all); as CONSUL for the second time he defeated Perseus at PYDNA (168), ending the third MACEDONIAN WAR and winning a second triumph. He was 46 when he first reached the consulship, after several failed attempts, but went on to be CENSOR (164). He had two sons by his first wife, Papiria, whom he divorced after a long marriage. With two more sons by his (unknown) second wife, he gave the first two up for adoption (one to his childless sister Aemilia Tertia, daughter-in-law of SCIPIO AFRICANUS); his Macedonian triumph was marred by the death of his two younger sons. Paullus' traditional image as a philhellene is belied by his actions in EPIRUS after Pydna: PLUTARCH (*Aemilius* 29) records that within the space of an hour 150,000 people were enslaved and 70 towns sacked. In part this reflects a difference between Roman and modern notions of 'philhellene': he gave his sons a Greek EDUCATION and flooded Italy with (plundered) Greek art. But it is also a consequence of POLYBIOS' admiration and close links with his sons. JRWP

See Plutarch, *Aemilius Paullus*, trs. R. Waterfield (1999); Reiter, W. (1988) *Aemilius Paullus*.

Aeneas (Aineias) Trojan HERO and ancestor of the Romans. He is the son of Anchises and APHRODITE (VENUS), and a member of the junior branch of the Trojan royal family. Already in the *Iliad* an important warrior, but one who has to be rescued from Diomedes by APOLLO and from ACHILLES by POSEIDON, he is more famous for the story of his adventures after the capture of Troy, which exists in several versions. The tradition that he migrated to Italy goes back to Stesichoros; it was taken up by the ETRURIANS and then the Romans, for whom it became a central part of their foundation legend. In the version immortalized in VIRGIL'S *Aeneid*, the pious Aeneas leaves Troy carrying his father on his shoulders and bearing the sacred objects of Troy. He then wanders around the MEDITERRANEAN like ODYSSEUS, loves and leaves Dido in CARTHAGE (the episode may be a Virgilian invention), and eventually arrives in Italy. There, after a fierce war, he kills Turnus, marries Lavinia, daughter of the Latin king, and founds the city of Lavinium. On his death he became a GOD. He was said to be the ancestor of JULIUS CAESAR and hence of Caesar's adoptive son AUGUSTUS; the Julian family (Iulii) were named after Aeneas' son Iulus (also known as Ascanius), who founded the city of Alba Longa, from whose royal family would come ROMULUS, founder of Rome. PRH

See Galinsky, G. K. (1969) *Aeneas, Sicily and Rome*.

AENEAS: vase painting from Nola showing the legend of Aeneas' flight from Troy carrying his father Anchises.

Aeneas Tacticus (Aineias Taktikos) Perhaps the energetic Stymphalian who served as GENERAL of the Arkadian federation in 367 BC. His sole surviving work, *Siegecraft* (*Poliorkêtika*), was one of several treatises on military preparations (the rest are now lost), and composed somewhere around 355–350 BC. Unlike later ancient tactical authors, Aeneas writes from personal observation and apparent battle experience. Comparison with his contemporary XENOPHON, who also combined a practical life with more abstract research, reflects a growing interest of the times in pragmatic military literature. Most of the *Siegecraft* involves mundane problems of defending, rather than attacking, cities. There are technical discussions of passwords, signals, coded messages, counter-measures against siege, and so on. But more importantly, Aeneas is also a rich source for the political, economic and social confusion of the 4th-century *polis*.

Aeneas does not really distinguish between enemies outside or inside the walls, but rather in the chaotic conditions of the mid-4th century sees social unrest as the logical twin to foreign assault; attackers are often viewed as deliverers by political malcontents. Thus defence is a holistic – even at times near-paranoid – idea, and involves everything from the choice of guards, passwords, and propaganda to rooting out plots and smugglers.

While Aeneas clearly writes from the vantage-point of an ARISTOCRACY worried about the dangerous propensities of a restive citizenry, his interests are more professional than political. Throughout his work, great emphasis is placed on the responsibilities of the general, whose job is to provide paid, skilled resistance on behalf of the status quo. In that sense, his didactic treatise most likely is directed at a small audience of city fathers and a growing professional military class who are hired to serve them. VDH

See Whitehead, D. (2001) *Aineias the Tactician* (trs. and commentary).

Aeolis see AIOLIS.

Aequi see IMPERIALISM, ROMAN; PRAENESTE.

Aeschines see AISCHINES.

Aeschylus (Aischylos) c.525/4–456/5 BC The earliest of the Athenian tragedians for whom we have complete plays, he was born into a well-established family at ELEUSIS and fought against the PERSIANS at MARATHON and (probably) SALAMIS. There is evidence that he visited the court of Hieron, tyrant of SYRACUSE, in the mid- to late 470s, where he produced the lost *Women of Aetna*; a later visit to SICILY ended with his death at Gela in 456/5.

Aeschylus' dramatic career began c.499, his first victory coming in 484. Tradition ascribes as many as 90 plays to him; this suggests participation in some 22 dramatic FESTIVALS at Athens, in 13 of which he is said to have been victorious. Six of his TRAGEDIES survive, along with the *Prometheus Bound*, either a work of the poet's old age or, perhaps more likely, the work of an unknown author composed in the manner of Aeschylus. There are also interesting portions of a SATYR play (*Net-fishers*, on the rescue of Danaë and the infant Perseus) as well as numerous isolated fragments. The surviving plays date to the latter half of the playwright's career: *Persians* (472), *Seven Against Thebes* (467), *Suppliant Women* (c.466–459), and the *ORESTEIA* trilogy (*Agamemnon*, *Choêphoroi* [*Libation Bearers*], *Eumenides*, [*Furies*] 458). All the preserved works, with the exception of *Persians* and perhaps *Prometheus Bound*, were produced as part of coherent tetralogies dedicated to a set of related MYTHS, a practice that seems to have been largely abandoned in later tragedy. After his death, Aeschylus was awarded the singular honour of having revivals of his plays entered in the dramatic festivals. Such later reproductions may account for the engagement with Aeschylean tragedy in some works of SOPHOKLES and EURIPIDES.

The works of Aeschylus reflect the ancient Greeks' belief in the power of the spoken and sung word. The typical Aeschylean play has little stage action and relatively little in the way of plot development, at least as modern audiences tend to understand the concept. *Persians*, for example, deals with the catastrophic defeat of XERXES' forces at the battle of Salamis, but the outcome is announced at lines 249–55, leaving the play's final 800 lines to describe the battle and ponder its significance; Xerxes himself, the nominal tragic hero, does not appear until the concluding scene. In no case do we find the dynamic plot development that marks Sophokles' works, where interaction between the characters drives the course of the play. Instead, the heart of Aeschylus' productions lies in the choral odes. It is there that the significance of the limited stage action is teased out, as the CHORUS struggles to make sense of events around it and meditates upon the broader context that informs those events.

The result is far from static. Through the chorus' meditations, Aeschylus' characters are presented as operating within a highly charged atmosphere, where past events and the brooding presence of inscrutable GODS burden their every action and cause their decisions to be fraught with danger. The central characters are vividly presented, but are not rounded individuals so much as focal points for a matrix of themes with which the playwright wishes his audience to engage. On-stage events often focus the audience's attention upon a pivotal decision taken by the principal character. This decision may be practical in nature (Pelasgos on the question of whether to aid the Danaids in *Suppliant Women*; Orestes' decision to kill his mother in *Libation Bearers*) or symbolic (AGAMEMNON's decision to tread on the tapestry in *Agamemnon*), but in each case serves to crystallize key issues and draw together themes developed elsewhere in the play. Much of the texture and dramatic tension of the typical Aeschylean production lies in the elaboration and interweaving of the imagery through which these themes are conveyed: climactic moments are often attended by the tangible manifestation on stage of one or more of the play's principal metaphors. Equally important is the archaic grandeur of Aeschylus' diction: the vivid yet often darkly allusive language of the plays is integral to their overall effect.

Aeschylus' works offer perhaps the most profound exploration of a view of the gods' relation to human affairs, first articulated for us in the poems of SOLON. Aeschylus presents a troubled world governed by divine forces whose justice is both violent and mysterious, where the actions of one's ancestors and the dictates of an obscurely defined fate act in combination with one's own deeds to bring about one's downfall. His ZEUS is a particularly ominous figure; his retribution takes the transgressor altogether by surprise, frequently after enticing him to his doom, and can only be perceived clearly once the blow has fallen. This conception of the workings of the gods informs the essential structure of many of the plays, which generally includes four elements: (1) an opening note of brooding anxiety and uncertainty; (2) the realization of the feared disaster; (3) a revelatory scene (often mantic in nature) which locates events within a larger context and provides some broader understanding of their significance; (4) a concluding scene of reflection, lamentation or (in the first two plays of a connected tetralogy) further anxiety and uncertainty. In no case is Aeschylus' vision altogether straightforward. Even *Persians*, with its celebration of the Greek victory at Salamis, raises troubling questions about the dangers of empire and human ambition, matters of some relevance to an era that witnessed increasing Athenian domination of the Delian League.

As *Persians* demonstrates, Aeschylus' plays also highlight themes relevant to contemporary Athens: the proper relationship between ruler and governed (*Suppliant Women*), the administration of justice (*Oresteia*), sophistic analyses of TYRANNY, and the origins of human culture (*Prometheus Bound*, if written by Aeschylus). A useful impression of the reception of his poetry is offered by the comic portrayal of the poet and his works in ARISTOPHANES' *Frogs* (405 BC). JP

See Herington, J. (1986) *Aeschylus*; Rosenmeyer, T. G. (1982) *The Art of Aeschylus*. There are many translations.

Aesculapius see ASKLEPIOS.

Aesop The putative author of a large body of Greek FABLES that survive in several collections. Aesop did not invent the genre, but he was its best-known exponent, a byword to Greeks, who cite his fables from the 5th century BC onward. HERODOTOS calls him the 'storyteller', naming him and Rhodopis, the famous courtesan, as fellow SLAVES of Iadmon from SAMOS (2.134). This would place Aesop in the 6th century. Perhaps, like Rhodopis, he was THRACIAN by origin. Like ORPHEUS, another legendary Thracian, Aesop gave voice to the natural world, but in prose rather than poetry. The majority of his extant fables involve talking ANIMALS and plants; almost inevitably he draws a sententious moral.

We are told by ARISTOTLE that Aesop, while defending a Samian demagogue on trial for his life, quoted his own story of the fox and the hedgehog. The Samians, Aesop concluded, were represented by the fox and the wealthy tyrant was like the fleas infesting it (*Rhetoric* 2.20). Aesop, then, recognized the forensic utility of his own fables. He was no stranger to political or legal controversy, if we may believe Herodotos' only other biographical point: the DELPHIANS killed him (we are not told why) and were then commanded by an ORACLE to pay compensation; only the grandson of Iadmon came forward to accept it (2.134). Other details about Aesop's life derive from later legendary tradition. JRH

See Aesop, *The Complete Fables*, trs. O. Temple and R. Temple (1988); Perry, B. (1952) *Aesopica*.

Afghanistan The territory of modern Afghanistan includes, in the south, Sakastane, parts of Drangiane and Areia in the west, and western Gedrosia in the south-east. The mountainous bulk of the country comprises ancient Paropamisadai and the extensive area of Baktria in the north-east. The Oxus river (mod. Amu Darya), the Pamir mountains, the Hindu Kush and the Indus river formed the natural borders of ancient Afghanistan. Its landscape is dominated by high mountain ranges, deserts and steppes. In antiquity it was renowned for its fertile

AFGHANISTAN: rulers of Baktria.

Dates (BC)	Ruler	Relationship to other rulers
256–248	Diodotos I	
248–235	Diodotos II	s. Diodotos I
(henceforward, all dates are approximate)		
235–200	Euthydemos I	
200–190	Euthydemos II	
200–185	Demetrios I	
195–185	Antimachos I	
185–180	Pantaleon	
185–175	Demetrios II	
180–165	Agathokles	
171–155	Eukratides I (usurper?)	
155–130	Agathokleia and Menandros	
...		
75–55	Kalliope and Hermaios (last known rulers)	

Key: s. = son of. Some 20 other names are known. For details, see tables in *CAH* vol. 8, 420–1.

soil and rich oases. Afghanistan's geographic position made it a vital link for overland trade between MESOPOTAMIA and INDIA. From the 2nd millennium BC onwards it was inhabited by Iranian-speaking peoples. Historical accounts begin in the mid-6th century BC, when CYRUS the Great made Baktria a PERSIAN province with Baktra (mod. Balkh) as its satrapal centre. The Persian satrap was chosen from among the close relatives of the king, emphasizing the importance of the province. After GAUGAMELA Darius III intended to raise a new army in Baktria, and the satrap Bessos contested ALEXANDER's power in Persia, proclaiming himself Darius' successor as Artaxerxes IV. Later, Baktria was a province of the SELEUKID empire, but between 250 and 230 BC the governor Diodotos claimed independence from Seleukid rule and founded the Greco-Baktrian empire. In the early decades of the 2nd century AD it succumbed to invasions of NOMADIC tribes from the north, including the Tocharians and Asiani, or Kushans, who then founded the Kushan empire which extended from central Asia to parts of northern India. When the SASSANIANS incorporated the territories of the Kushan empire into their own empire, Baktria ceased to exist as an independent province. MB

See Bosworth, A. B. (1988) *Conquest and Empire*; Sherwin-White, S. and Kuhrt, A. (1993) *From Samarkhand to Sardis*.

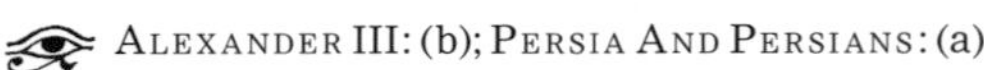
ALEXANDER III: (b); PERSIA AND PERSIANS: (a).

Africa and Africans The term 'Africa' may originally have referred to the territory of the Afer, a tribe located near Uzalitana in north-west Tunisia. It was applied by Rome to the immediate territory of CARTHAGE and more specifically to the PROVINCE that incorporated the lands formerly under Carthaginian control in what is now northern Tunisia. The term eventually came to designate the African provinces generally. The indigenous inhabitants of ancient North Africa comprised numerous tribes and sub-tribes. Of these, the most noteworthy are the Numidians who inhabited the region to the west of the territory of Carthage, which in the hellenistic period became the kingdom of Numidia.

AFRICA AND AFRICANS: Roman coin showing personification of Africa with attributes (elephant head-dress, scorpion, bushel of wheat, cornucopia).

The mixed PHOENICIAN and indigenous population along the eastern Tunisian coast was referred to as Libyophoenician. The Mauri, a term originally applied to the peoples of what is now modern Morocco and western Algeria, gave their name to the kingdom and later Roman provinces of Mauretania Caesariensis and Mauretania Tingitana. By late antiquity, Mauri was used generically to refer to all the indigenous tribes more or less outside Roman and later VANDAL and Byzantine control. RBH

See Brett, M. and Fentress, E. (1996) *The Berbers*; Mattingly, D. J. (1994) *Tripolitania*.

GARAMANTES: (a)–(b).

Africa, Roman One of the richest and most important of Rome's overseas territories was created along the southern shore of the MEDITERRANEAN following the final defeat of the Romans' bitterest enemy, CARTHAGE, by SCIPIO AEMILIANUS in 146 BC. The initial Roman territory was focused on the Carthaginian heartlands in north-east Tunisia and ruled from Utica (Carthage having been completely destroyed). It was bordered by the Numidian kingdom, ruled by the descendants of MASINISSA. Widespread centuriation in northern Tunisia attests to the scale of land confiscation involved with the annexation of Carthaginian territory. The original limits of Roman territory appear to have been demarcated by a continuous ditch, the *fossa regia*.

Expansion of the initial province followed problems with the Numidian prince JUGURTHA, who seized power in 112 BC, and the final annexation of the Numidian kingdom in 46 BC, after Juba I backed the wrong party in the civil war. Africa Vetus and Africa Nova were soon amalgamated into Africa Proconsularis (covering western Libya to eastern Algeria), though by AD 40 the proconsular governor was no longer in charge of the army, which was under the control of a separate imperial legate. The CYRENAICAN territory of eastern Libya had been added to the empire in 96 BC and early in the reign of CLAUDIUS, the annexation of the Mauretanian kingdom of Juba II led to the creation of two new provinces, Mauretania Caesariensis (western Algeria) and Mauretania Tingitana (Morocco). By the early 3rd century, the frontier region of Africa Proconsularis was recognized as a separate province of Numidia, and Tetrarchic reorganizations saw the creation of further provinces from Proconsularis: Tripolitana in north-west Libya, Byzacena in central and eastern Tunisia, Zeugitana in northern Tunisia.

The Roman military garrison of North Africa appears to have always been small relative to its area. There was a single legion, the III Augusta, for most of the PRINCIPATE (though it was temporarily cashiered in the 3rd century), supported by a larger number of AUXILIARIES. The total garrison may have amounted to c.20,000–30,000 troops. Several significant excavations have been carried out on military sites, most notably at the long-term legionary fortress at LAMBAESIS in Algeria and at a Libyan desert outpost fort at Bu Njem (anc. Gholaia). At the latter site, a cache of OSTRAKA has been discovered, shedding light on the daily life of the garrison. The African FRONTIER was embellished with a series of discontinuous linear earthworks

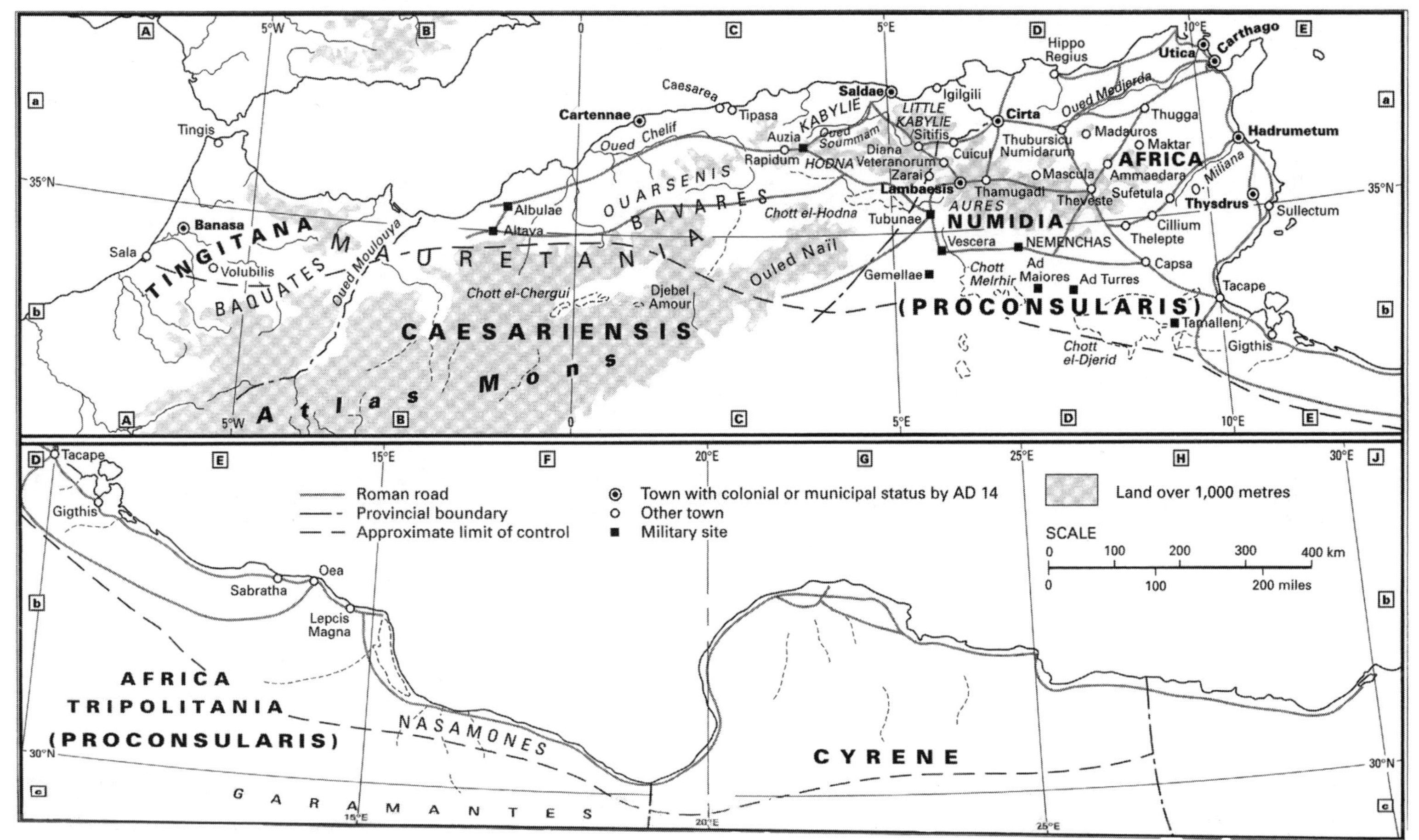

Africa, Roman: map.

(collectively referred to as the *fossatum Africae*, though some of the shorter sections are known by the term *clausurae*). These seem to have been constructed across the line of the major TRANSHUMANCE routes from the desert to the steppe lands and upland pastures within the province; the provision of gates through these barriers suggests that they were an attempt to control and regulate these movements, rather than to debar pastoral groups from access.

The African provinces were among the most densely URBANIZED of the Roman world, though the process was far from uniform and built on four separate traditions. In Cyrenaica (eastern Libya) the towns originated as Greek colonies, and many of the coastal cities in western Libya and Tunisia (with a few outliers further west, such as LIXUS) were PHOENICIAN entrepôts. The inland areas of Tunisia and Algeria had seen some urban development on a Punic model during the time of the Numidian kingdom and similar development can be traced at Volubilis in Mauretania. Finally, overlain on this was a significant level of Roman foundations, of both *coloniae* and *municipia*, in part related to the large amount of *ager publicus* (public land) available there for VETERAN settlement (with large numbers of foundations in the aftermath of the civil wars, as AUGUSTUS sought to halve the number of legions). The total number of urban centres with a status of at least *civitas* level is calculated at over 600, and through further promotion a high percentage eventually attained *municipium* or *colonia* status. Carthage was refounded by CAESAR (after an earlier failed attempt) and when reinforced under Augustus, this became not only the provincial capital, but the largest city of the Western empire after Rome. Several decades of excavations (initially sponsored by UNESCO) have transformed knowledge of the site's Roman (and Punic) occupation, making this one of the best-explored and most extensively published urban centres. Large-scale excavations of other well-preserved sites in the late 19th and early 20th centuries have revealed substantially complete urban plans and spectacular monuments that reflect the wealth of the African provinces. Thamugadi (TIMGAD) is the classic example of a Roman military colony, laid out on a rigid grid plan that evokes the legionary FORTRESSES of the soldiers responsible for its construction. But other sites, such as the small town of THUGGA (mod. Tébessa), retain aspects of their Numidian origins in the maze of winding streets that interconnect the very Roman-style monuments. Phoenician coastal emporia are represented by sites such as LEPCIS MAGNA or LEPTIMINUS, the former embellished by Libyphoenician citizens such as ANNOBAL TAPAPIUS RUFUS. Some individual monuments stand out, such as the magnificent AMPHITHEATRE at Thysdrus (mod. El Djem) or the extraordinary subterranean suites of rooms in the ÉLITE houses at Bulla Regia. The embellishment of public buildings, especially BATHHOUSES, with MARBLE and MOSAICS, reflects the prosperity of many communities, and private houses of the urban élite were frequently ornamented with fine examples of the mosaicist's craft.

Rural life in Africa is evoked in literary works, INSCRIPTIONS and artworks such as mosaics, but most emphatically in the archaeological traces in the landscape itself (from traces of centuriation systems covering tens of thousands of sq km, to well-preserved farms and OLIVE PRESSES). Indeed the Roman era represents the apogee of exploitation in scale and extent of the cultivated area in many parts of the Maghreb, and traces of Roman-period farming extend far beyond the modern limits. The reputation of Africa as the 'breadbasket of Rome' related to a comparatively restricted area of north-eastern Tunisia, but the more marginal lands of southern Tunisia, Libya and Algeria were developed increasingly from the 1st century AD to supply another essential commodity of Mediterranean trade, OLIVE OIL. Survey work in the Tunisian high steppe near Sufetula and in the pre-desert zone of Tripolitana has revealed high numbers of olive presses. The wealth that could be made from farming is illustrated by the inscribed autobiography of the so-called 'Mactar reaper', whose social standing as urban MAGISTRATE and property owner belied his origins as a leader of itinerant harvest teams across the wheat belt of Africa (*CIL* 8.11824).

The economic impact of Africa's agricultural production was considerable and the range and scale of its exports is hinted at by the distribution of African transport AMPHORAS and *terra sigillata* (African Red Slip ware). Grain and olive oil were exported in significant quantities (though in part at least in the context of the *annona* arrangements of the city of Rome), but wine was also exported. FISH SAUCES and other preserved marine products were another major export and many coastal sites have revealed traces of the distinctive *garum* vats and of production of transport amphoras. Purple DYE production is attested at a number of sites (Mogador, Gerba), and TEXTILES appear to have been important in the economy of a number of inland towns, such as Thamugadi. Another lucrative and specialized item of trade for the African provinces consisted in supplying many wild ANIMALS for the arenas of the Roman world.

Religion in Roman Africa was affected by the import of a number of Roman innovations (the CAPITOLINE TRIAD, the IMPERIAL CULT) but, as in other provinces, the dominant trend appears to have been the SYNCRETISM of pre-existing local cults with deities from the Roman pantheon. For example, the most popular cult was that of SATURN, or BAAL HAMMON, to recognize his pre-Roman pedigree. CHRISTIANITY made early inroads in Africa and the region was influential in the consolidation of the church when it became accepted as the predominant religion of the late empire. TERTULLIAN, CYPRIAN and AUGUSTINE (1) were among the most prominent early Christian writers.

The end of Roman Africa is sometimes presented as a sudden *caesura*, but an alternative view of late antiquity is one of prolonged and gradual change. The conquest of the North African provinces by the VANDALS in the early 5th century, by the Byzantine empire in the early 6th century and by ARAB invaders in the 7th century clearly wrought huge changes on the organization of land, production, trade and urban life. But it is now much clearer that the proverbial wealth of North Africa was still a potent image through late antiquity and a motivating factor in the Arab conquests. DJM

See Mattingly, D. J. and Hitchner, R. B. (1995) Roman Africa: an archaeological review, *JRS* 85: 165–213; Whittaker, C. R.

(1996) Roman Africa, in *CAH* 10, 586–618; (2000) Africa, in *CAH* 11, 514–46.

 LEPCIS MAGNA: (a)–(b); TIMGAD: (a).

Africanus see SCIPIO AFRICANUS.

afterlife At the prospect of death, Greeks and Romans resorted to MYTHS, MYSTERIES and METAPHYSICS to explain what lay beyond the grave. Funerary rituals, too, helped shape implicit attitudes about the afterlife. As *thnêtoi* ('mortals') by very nature, the ancients met death and its sequel with resignation. Only gradually did the afterlife become an article of either consolation or fear.

The first, bleakest literary references to the afterlife occur in HOMER and HESIOD, who supplied an eschatological vocabulary well into the classical period. The 'damp house of chill Hades' had been the destiny of humans since the time of the bronze race (Hesiod, *Works and Days* 152–5). This fate is not explicitly punitive; rather, it is the undifferentiated destiny of all mortals, with few exceptions. Heroism and virtue merit no special treatment; likewise, only extraordinary wickedness (*hybris* against the gods) receives hellish punishment. Not until VIRGIL (*Aeneid* 6) are social and domestic crimes requited in the HADES of EPIC tradition. For most tragedians, too, retribution must be accomplished this side of the grave. Vengeance on behalf of the dead (as in AESCHYLUS' *ORESTEIA*) was only an extreme instance of the network of needs and duties binding this world to the next. The living were also piously obliged to provide the deceased with food and libations at their burial sites for at least a month after the funeral, indicating a popular belief in ghosts. The SOULS of SUICIDES, the untimely dead and the unburied could linger for longer periods. The underworld was, at least, a preferable fate to such rootlessness.

Mystery cults, by contrast, promised post-mortem rewards for membership. DEMETER's and ORPHEUS' devotees could expect the transfer of their souls to Elysium, as the instructions on gold plates (*lamellae*) buried with the Orphic dead indicate: they directed the deceased through the labyrinth of Hades to the Elysian fields. It is possible that a doctrine of rebirth, perhaps the *metempsychôsis* associated with the PYTHAGOREAN sect, was also a tenet of the mystery cults. PLATO, though inimical to ORPHISM himself, spells out this hope of reincarnation most clearly in his Myth of Er (*Republic* 10), in which the threat of punishment for ethical misconduct and the promise of reward for merit (and not merely for cultic membership) are specified for the first time in Greek literature.

Plato's anthropology, which regarded the living body as the soul's tomb, naturally perceived death optimistically. Other philosophical schools, notably EPICUREANISM and STOICISM, also recommended a fearlessness of death, though for opposite reasons. The Epicureans denied the afterlife altogether; the Stoics weighed death favourably against the suffering of this present life. Both attitudes are most fully expressed in Latin (rather than Greek), by LUCRETIUS and SENECA THE YOUNGER respectively. This is, perhaps, no surprise: the ancient Romans usually concerned themselves with the fate of the dead in this world (their memory among the living) rather than in the next. The Roman dead were generally thought to belong to the community of *di manes* ('divine spirits'), or alternatively of the *maiores* ('majority', i.e. our ancestors) whose commemoration figured large in the CALENDAR. CHRISTIANITY, which would succeed these PHILOSOPHIES and practices, owes some elements of its doctrine of the afterlife to most of them. JRH

See Davies, J. (1999) *Death, Burial and Rebirth in the Religions of Antiquity*; Garland, R. (1985) *The Greek Way of Death*; Johnston, S. I. (1999) *Restless Dead*; Toynbee, J. M. C. (1971) *Death and Burial in the Roman World*.

Agamemnon Greek hero and leader of the Achaian forces during the TROJAN WAR (HOMER, *Iliad*). Epic tradition portrays Agamemnon as the king of 'golden MYCENAE'. As a young man he struggled to regain the throne of his father, Atreus, whose murderers had kept him and his brother Menelaos in exile in Sikyon. Eventually, he restored himself to power with the aid of Tyndareos and his daughter, CLYTEMNESTRA, whom he later married. She gave Agamemnon at least three children, IPHIGENEIA, Orestes and Elektra. After Agamemnon's (attempted?) sacrifice of Iphigeneia, their eldest daughter, at the outset of the Trojan expedition, Clytemnestra fostered an enmity toward her husband that she would act upon ten years later when he returned to Greece.

Agamemnon was the chief organizer and military commander of the Achaian (Greek) forces during the Trojan war. His decision to begin this risky undertaking was triggered by desire to take vengeance on the Trojan prince, Paris, who had dared to seduce HELEN away from her legitimate husband, Menelaos. These themes are explored by 5th-century Athenian dramatists, notably EURIPIDES in *Helen* and *Trojan Women*.

The *Iliad* portrays Agamemnon's questionable leadership of the Achaian army as well as his military *ethos*, and offers substantial insights into his rivalries with other Achaians such as ACHILLES and AJAX. The Achaian triumph at Troy was the highest military achievement for Agamemnon as a commander. Yet, on the personal front, his victorious homecoming marked the beginning of an inglorious fall. Agamemnon was trapped in a treacherous plan devised by Clytemnestra and his cousin and rival Aigisthos, who became her lover during Agamemnon's absence. This final act in a turbulent life inspired Athenian playwrights and artists, as is illustrated in AESCHYLUS' *Oresteia*. EP

See Touchefeu, O. and Karuskopf, I. (1981) Agamemnon, in *LIMC* vol. 1, 256–77.

Agatharchides b. c.200 BC Grammarian and historian from KNIDOS. Raised in the household of Herakleides Lembos (an important official under Ptolemy VI and a minor PERIPATETIC philosopher), Agatharchides became Herakleides' secretary and reader. Nothing else is known about his life except that he, too, was a Peripatetic and lived for some time in Athens, probably being exiled by Ptolemy VIII in 145 BC. The principal source for his life, Photios, credits him with seven works including an epitome of Antimachos of Kolophon's *Lyde*, a book on friendship, and a collection of excerpts from writers on remarkable natural and human phenomena. Agatharchides was best known in antiquity, however, for three large historical works: *On Affairs in Asia* in 10 books, *On Affairs in Europe* in 49 books, and *On the Erythraian Sea* in 5 books. Thanks to the survival of an epitome of books 1 and 5 of the third work (by Photios), it is clear that Agatharchides based his account of the Red sea and its hinterlands on the reports of 3rd-century BC Ptolemaic EXPLORERS. The book was the main source for Greek accounts of the geography and ethnology of ancient Nubia and Arabia. Besides Photios' epitome, extensive excerpts are preserved in DIODORUS SICULUS, STRABO, and AELIAN's *On the Nature of Animals*. SMB

See Burstein, S. M. (1989) *Agatharchides of Cnidus, On the Erythraean Sea*.

Agathokles and Sosibios PTOLEMAIC courtiers. Sosibios, son of Dioskourides, had advised Ptolemy III. Agathokles, son of the courtesan OINANTHE, became minister to Ptolemy IV Philopator (r.222–205 BC) and allegedly the king's lover. Together they guided the young Philopator's policy throughout his reign, first disposing of potential threats from the royal family and neutralizing KLEOMENES III of Sparta after he took refuge in Alexandria. They are the subject of adverse comment by Polybios, but successfully repulsed ANTIOCHOS III's invasion of Egypt by mobilizing native troops (battle of Rhaphia, 217) – a necessary move whose destabilizing consequences POLYBIOS perhaps exaggerates. Agathokles wielded extra influence through his sister Agathokleia, the king's mistress. The sources portray Philopator as relying too much upon these men and living a life of indulgence; they may reflect anti-Ptolemaic propaganda and the rewriting of history after the events. Philopator's premature death was kept secret; Agathokles may even have murdered the king and his queen (and sister), Arsinoë III. (Sosibios disappears from the story about now.) Agathokles' debauchery while regent allegedly provoked a revolt in 202; but he may have been the victim of political intrigues. His fall and death are a case study in the methods of Polybios, who describes at length how Agathokles and his family were lynched by the Alexandrians. Whether or not their influence was malign, Agathokles and Sosibios are examples of the advisers upon whom hellenistic monarchs relied heavily, and illustrate the tangled workings of dynastic power. DGJS

See Polybios, esp. 15.25–36.

Agathokles of Syracuse 361–289 BC The son of Karkinos, an exile from Rhegion, who had received SYRACUSAN citizenship in the time of TIMOLEON. Agathokles served as a mercenary in the 320s and helped to oust the Syracusan OLIGARCHY, only to find himself expelled from the city on the suspicion that he was aiming at supreme power. In 317 he returned and was elected *stratêgos autokratôr*, but his subsequent attempts at conquest in SICILY brought him into conflict with the CARTHAGINIANS, who defeated his army in the battle of Likata in 311 and proceeded to besiege Syracuse. Agathokles entrusted the city to his brother Antander (Antandros) and made a bold invasion of Africa, where he enlisted the aid of Ophellas of CYRENE. The latter was, however, assassinated and many of his troops joined Agathokles. In a dramatic move (imitated by Cortés in 1519) he burned the SHIPS and left the army with no means of salvation except through victory. He himself contrived to return to Syracuse in 307, and peace was made with Carthage in the following year. In 305/4 he proclaimed himself king, following the example of ALEXANDER's successors, with whom he entered into alliances by marrying a daughter of PTOLEMY I and giving his own daughter Lanassa to the EPIROTE king PYRRHOS. In 289 he died, apparently of POISON. Despite his claims to have returned freedom to the Syracusans, his was a cruel and brutal TYRANNY of 28 years (317–289). WH

age organization The organization of society according to the division of the human life span into sequential stages (e.g. childhood, adulthood, old age). In Greek and Roman antiquity, as in any society, the concept of dividing the life cycle into different stages responded to biological processes such as physical development and puberty. However, it could also reflect preconceptions rooted in society's experiences of, for example, life expectancy, and in cultural values attached to physical strength, gender and social status. Furthermore, there could be imprecision in the use of terminology for different stages. In Greece, for example, children under 15 were known as *paides* (singular *pais*), but the same term could be applied to older youths, young men and SLAVES. In some societies, progress through the stages of life was marked not only by rites of passage but also by the organization of particular age groups into sets. In classical SPARTA it seems that organization of the army occurred according to age groups, and this may reflect the use of such age sets in the organization of other Spartiate social institutions (Thucydides 5.64.2–3). Dionysios of Halikarnassos describes a similar phenomenon at Rome, where males on the verge of adulthood marched in a separate group in religious processions; however, they were distinguished also by social rank (*Roman Antiquities* 7.72.1). MDH

See Harlow, M. and Laurence, R. (2002) *Growing Up and Growing Old in Ancient Rome*; Singor, H.W. (1999) Admission to the *syssitia* in fifth-century Sparta, in S. Hodkinson and A. Powell, eds., *Sparta: new perspectives* 67–89.

agentes in rebus see SECRECY; SECRET POLICE.

Agesilaos c.445–360 BC Eurypontid king of Spa-rta (r. c.400–360), son of king Archidamos II by a second marriage. Since he was not born the heir apparent, and anyway was born lame in one leg, Agesilaos was brought up like any other Spartan boy, enduring the rigours of the famous state education system (*agôgê*) from the age of seven. That he did in fact succeed his half-brother Agis II as king was largely due to the political machinations of the war hero LYSANDER, who had formerly been his lover. Sparta in 400 appeared to be at the peak of its power. By the time of Agesilaos' death in his mid-eighties, when he was returning from campaigning in North Africa to raise funds for Sparta's impoverished treasury, his city was bankrupt politically as well as economically. Since Agesilaos was for most of his reign Sparta's chief power-broker and policy-maker, the question must be asked whether he was personally, directly and culpably responsible for Sparta's decline.

In 396 Agesilaos became the first Spartan king to command land forces on the Asiatic mainland, in pursuit of the liberation of Greeks from the control of PERSIA. Ten years later he was complicit with a Persian-dictated peace settlement, the so-called King's Peace. This left Persia in control of those cities, but also gave Sparta a free hand to impose on the cities of its Greek allies and enemies alike the kind of control that Agesilaos, following Lysander's lead, favoured – through narrow oligarchical regimes. MANTINEIA in 385, THEBES in 382, and Olynthos and Phleious in 379 were all subjected to the brutal control formula of Agesilaos. Sparta's intervention in Thebes, however, breached the peace of 386 and paved the way for co-operation between Thebes and Athens. Its intervention in Olynthos opened the way for the rise of MACEDONIA, a kingdom which was eventually to conquer all Greece. From 378 Agesilaos (by then in his late sixties) devoted most of his energies to unremitting assaults on Thebes, but the outcome was the decisive defeat of Sparta at LEUKTRA in 371.

Agesilaos was not himself in command at Leuktra, but the chief responsibility for this catastrophe was his. Within a couple of years, Sparta's home territory had been invaded for the first time and part of it liberated from Spartan control, together with the MESSENIAN ex-HELOTS who now founded their own city of Messene. A few years later the PELOPONNESIAN LEAGUE, too, dissolved. Sparta, whose citizen body had by then shrunk to less than 1,000, was condemned to the status of a local Peloponnesian wrangler. Agesilaos nevertheless retained most of his old authority at home, largely because of his exemplary Spartan lifestyle and unswerving patriotism. Abroad, his career and his life ended in bathos. XENOPHON, client and friend, wrote an encomium of him as a 'thoroughly good man'. PLUTARCH also composed a largely laudatory BIOGRAPHY. But few today would take him as a model of either political acumen or moral virtue. PAC

See Cartledge, P. A. (1987) *Agesilaos and the Crisis of Sparta*; Shipley, D. R. (1997) *A Commentary on Plutarch's Life of Agesilaos*.

Agiatis d. c.224 BC Wealthy Spartan woman, reputedly beautiful. As widow of the executed reformer AGIS IV (the representative of the Eurypontid royal house), she was forced by the Agiad king, the elderly Leonidas II, to marry his son, the future KLEOMENES III. Her infant son by Agis, Eudamidas III, was the new Eurypontid king in name only; we know of no regent being appointed, so Leonidas and then Kleomenes effectively wielded sole authority. According to PLUTARCH, Kleomenes was devoted to Agiatis and often asked her about her first husband's ideas. Although scholars often assume that she persuaded him to be a reformer, Plutarch does not say so. Agiatis is, rather, one of those assertive Spartan women depicted by Plutarch whose apparent liberation is in reality circumscribed by the patriarchal society in which they live. Agiatis died of natural causes not long before Kleomenes' defeat at SELLASIA. DGJS

See Plutarch, *Agis and Kleomenes*, trs. in R. J. A. Talbert (1988) *Plutarch on Sparta*; Powell, A. (1999) Spartan women assertive in politics? in S. Hodkinson and A. Powell, eds., *Sparta: new perspectives* 393–419.

Agis II Spartan king of the Eurypontid family (r. c.427–400 BC), son of the powerful ARCHIDAMOS II; the junior king until the death of PLEISTOANAX in 409. After leading the Spartan army to victory at MANTINEIA in 418, Agis was the main Spartan commander in the later PELOPONNESIAN WAR and set up the Spartans' FORT at Dekeleia within Attica. His death was followed by the controversial accession of AGESILAOS. DGJS

See Thucydides 5.54–74, 7.19–20, 27, 8.70–1, and *passim*.

Agis IV Spartan king of the Agiad family (r. c.244–241 BC), famous for attempting radical reform of the state. Far junior to the elderly Leonidas II, he forced his fellow king into exile and deposed the EPHORS in order to enact his reform programme. Since only c.700 citizens now had enough land to qualify as citizens, he planned to cancel debts and redistribute land among able-bodied Spartans, augmenting their numbers with *perioikoi* (citizens of Sparta's dependent towns) and foreigners. While the abolition of debts was welcomed, the rich (led, says PLUTARCH, by the women, who were able to inherit property under Spartan law) opposed his land reform. Leonidas returned and Agis was executed; but his widow, AGIATIS, was married off to Leonidas' son KLEOMENES III. Plutarch's main historical source for Agis was Phylarchos (now lost), later a sympathetic eye-witness of Kleomenes' career. DGJS

See Plutarch, *Agis and Cleomenes*, trs. in R. J. A. Talbert (1988) *Plutarch on Sparta*; Cartledge, P. and Spawforth, A. (2002) *Hellenistic and Roman Sparta*.

agora All Greek towns had an open space in which the people gathered (*agora* comes from *ageirô*, 'I bring together'). The earliest uses of the word, in HOMER, refer to actual meetings (e.g. *Iliad* 7.345, *Odyssey* 9.112) as well as to gathering places (*Odyssey* 7.44) where political or judicial decisions were made. As states grew in size and complexity, civic bodies had their own particular places to meet, often in or near the *agora*. The classical *agora* was a setting for sacred spaces, ranging from major TEMPLES to small hero shrines and altars. The whole area was sometimes regarded as sacred. In Athens boundary markers were set up at its edges and persons accused of pollution, such as homicides, were prohibited from entering.

Commercial activity in and near the *agora* was usual, so that the PERSIAN king Cyrus could be quoted as expressing his scorn for a people who had a special place set aside in their towns for deceiving each other under oath (HERODOTOS 1.153). Although urban examples are best known, there were also areas designated as *agorai* in the countryside (cf. STRABO 9.1.10) and in border areas (e.g. DEMOSTHENES 23.29). The *genos* of the Salaminioi possessed one in south ATTICA near Sounion which presumably was used as a market and generated income. Temporary *agorai* were set up outside towns for supplying military forces on campaign (e.g. THUCYDIDES 1.62).

The earliest archaeological evidence for an *agora* is at Megara Hyblaia in eastern SICILY in the late 8th century BC. It is a trapezoidal space at the juncture of two slightly different grids in the plan of the city. Well-preserved *agorai* from the 4th and 3rd centuries respectively are at THASOS and Kassope. Before the hellenistic period, the location of most *agorai* cannot be predicted from what is known of the rest of the town plans of these cities. Unlike the central

PALACES, temples or CHURCHES of Near Eastern or medieval civilizations, the *agora* was not the point on which the whole plan focused; in port towns it might lie near a HARBOUR. Nor was there a standard plan for the buildings surrounding the usually quadrilateral open space (occupying one or more blocks in the grids of planned cities). By the hellenistic period, long STOAS often occupied two or more sides of the *agora* in large, carefully planned cities such as MILETOS and Magnesia on the Maeander, both in ASIA Minor. MHJ

See Hoepfner, W. and Schwandner, E. (1986) *Haus und Stadt im klassischen Griechenland*; Martin, R. (1951) *Recherches sur l'agora grecque*; (1959) *Thasos, l'agora*; (1974) *L'Urbanisme dans la Grèce antique*; Vallet, F. et al. (1976) *Fouilles de Mégara Hyblaea*, vol. 1: *Le Quartier de l'agora archaïque*; Wycherley, R. E. (1962) *How the Greeks Built Cities*.

Agora, Athenian *Agora* literally means 'gathering place', but the *agora* of a classical town fulfilled many and varied functions. Nestling at the foot of the ACROPOLIS, the Athenian Agora housed such important buildings as the council house (*bouleutêrion*), the office of the generals (*stratêgeion*), the mint, the office for standard weights and measures, the LAWCOURTS, and prominent monuments such as the Eponymous Heroes. The 500 legislators of the Athenian council (*boulê*) met every day in the *bouleutêrion*, and buildings such as the South STOA and Royal Stoa gave shelter from sun and rain. The *Metroön* (shrine of the Mother of the Gods) housed the central ARCHIVES, and the Tholos served as the headquarters of the *prytaneis*, the executive committee of the *boulê*. The Tholos also served as the dining room of the *prytaneis* where those on duty were fed at public expense.

The administration of the city, however, took up a fairly small part of the agora, the rest being given over to housing, SHOPS, MARKETS, WORKSHOPS and taverns. Commercial activity took place every day in

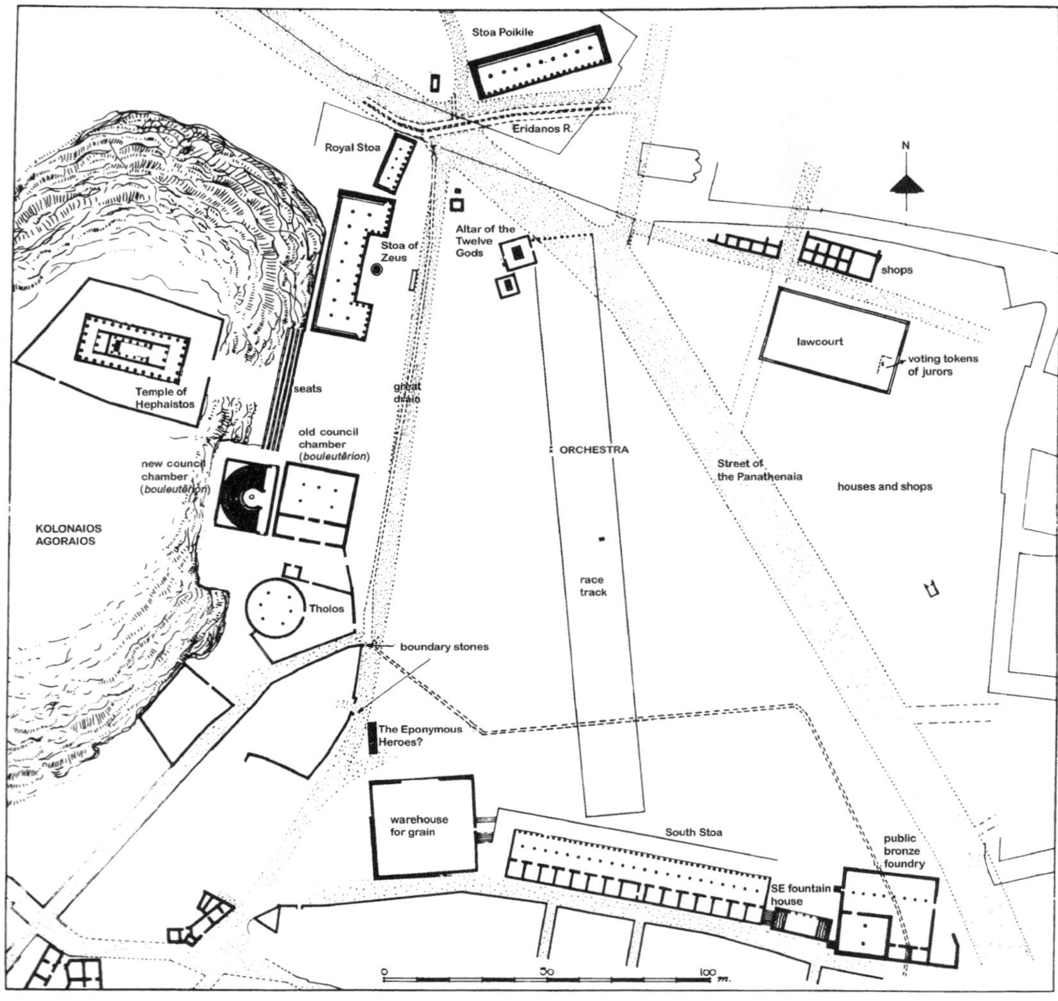

AGORA, ATHENIAN: (a) plan of the agora in the 5th century BC.

AGORA, ATHENIAN: (b) general view of central sector of the Agora, looking towards the Acropolis.

AGORA, ATHENIAN: (c) from the 2nd century BC the stoa of Attalos (reconstructed in modern times) closed off the east side of the Agora.

large market buildings such as stoas (e.g. in the hellenistic period, the stoa of Attalos), in small private shops, and on temporary wooden stalls or *skênai*. POLLUX tells us that the Attic orators named places in the Agora after the goods sold there; for instance, they might say 'I went off to the WINE, the OLIVE OIL, the pots.' XENOPHON in his *Oikonomikos* states that 'Whatever servant you order to buy something for you from the Agora, and bring it, not one of them will have any difficulty; everyone will plainly know where he must go to get each class of goods. The reason for this, I said, is simply that they are kept in their appointed places.'

The Agora also served as a major religious centre. In addition to the extremely well-preserved Hephaisteion, crowning the hill of Kolonos Agoraios ('Agora Hill') to the west, numerous altars and small sanctuaries were scattered throughout the buildings, many of them dedicated to demigods or heroes. These shrines, set right at the heart of daily life, would have received far more everyday recognition than the great cult buildings on the Acropolis. HERODOTOS (2.7) may imply that distances from Athens were measured from the altar of the Twelve Gods in the Agora. Boundary stones demarcated the Agora's *temenos*, and convicted felons could be barred from entering its confines.

The great street known as the Panathenaic Way traversed the Agora on its way up to the Acropolis, and was the setting for religious processions and ATHLETIC contests. Wooden seating (known to have collapsed at least once) was erected for spectators on these occasions.

The museum housed in the restored stoa of Attalos displays material from the Agora's earliest beginnings in the prehistoric period, its use as a cemetery from the 15th to the 7th centuries BC, its decline during the hellenistic period, and its revival under the Roman emperor HADRIAN. CK-B

See Camp, J.M. (1986) *The Athenian Agora*; (1993) *The Athenian Agora: an ancient shopping center.*

 ATHENS: (a).

Agricola (Gnaeus Iulius Agricola) AD 40–93 Born in Provence to a wealthy family of Gallic descent, Agricola's upbringing was typical for the son of a senator and included a classical education in Massalia (MARSEILLES) prior to his apprenticeship in Rome.

Agricola's first military post as aide to the governor of BRITAIN (AD 60–2) involved the rebellion of BOUDICA and the Roman annihilation of the DRUIDS on Anglesey. From AD 63 onwards, Agricola served as financial secretary in the PROVINCE of ASIA and held the PRAETORSHIP in Rome. In 69 Agricola returned to Britain as GENERAL of Legion XX. With this post, Agricola earned the respect of the emperor VESPASIAN. A promotion to PATRICIAN rank, control of the province of Aquitaine (74–7) and the CONSULSHIP in Rome (77) followed shortly thereafter.

It was as governor of Britain (78–84), however, that Agricola excelled. His campaigns in the north enabled the extension of the military frontier to the Forth–Clyde isthmus. Agricola also won acclaim with his victory over the northern tribes of Scotland. When not on campaign, he was a just administrator who encouraged the spread of LITERACY and the civilized trappings of Roman culture. His recall from Britain in 84 was rumoured to precede a transfer to SYRIA. Despite his triumphant return to Rome, military prowess was no longer required by the emperor DOMITIAN. Agricola lived out the remainder of his years in relative obscurity. Fortunately, his career was recorded in the BIOGRAPHY by his son-in-law, TACITUS (*Agricola*). MLM

 BRITANNIA: (a); BRITISH ISLES: (a).

agriculture

The livelihood for most people in the ancient Greek world, including those living in cities. Ideally, a *POLIS* consisted of an urban centre within a rural territory in which the citizens grew the food to sustain the city. Normally only citizens could own

AGRICULTURE: (a) ploughing and sowing scene on a Greek black-figure vase in the British Museum collection.

land within the territory of a *polis*, and in most *poleis* only landowners could claim full citizen rights. Although landholdings were unequally divided, with many small landholdings and a few large ones, Greek countrysides were not characterized by the kinds of huge estates found in Roman Italy. Athens is the city whose agricultural economy is best documented in the literary, epigraphical and archaeological records, though archaeological survey has dramatically enhanced our knowledge of other Greek countrysides in recent years.

Athenian literary sources stress the ideal of self-sufficiency (*autarkeia*) in food supplies for both individual HOUSEHOLDS and for the city itself. Most farmers were probably owner-occupiers who aimed at subsistence (or better). Although farmers may regularly have rented land, our only surviving leases relate to land belonging to TEMPLES or public bodies, rented out in large parcels to rich people. There may have been a private market in land rental, but we know next to nothing about it.

The normal INHERITANCE practice in use throughout ancient Greece was to divide land equally among the heirs (usually only sons). The impact of this on landholding was that 'farms' did not consist of a single, contiguous plot of land, but of many small parcels scattered throughout the landscape. Hence, most 'farms' included land of different types and quality, located at different altitudes, and with different soils, exposures and aspects. Such differences mean that any one plot would have been better for some crops than others, and that some plots would perform better or worse than others in any particular year depending on weather. So, for example, wheat planted on a dry, south-facing plot might grow poorly in a year with little rainfall, but produce a bumper crop in a year of excessive rainfall when wheat on plots in damp locations would suffer from fungal rusts.

Farmers did not necessarily work their own land. Larger landowners used SLAVE labour, and this is well documented in literary sources such as XENOPHON's treatise on household management, the *Oikonomikos*. How far down the socio-economic scale the use of slaves for agricultural labour went has been much debated. There are occasional references to casual, seasonal hired labourers used at busy times of the year such as the harvest or the vintage (Demosthenes 57.45, 53.21), but the extent to which such casual labour was used is uncertain, and such workers might be of either free or slave status.

Much of Greece is hilly and rugged, with only relatively small areas of flat land, though there are extensive plains in some parts of central Greece such as BOIOTIA and THESSALY. In many parts of Greece areas of deep, fertile soils are limited, and thin, limey soils are common. Much of the Greek world (though not all) has a MEDITERRANEAN type climate characterized by hot dry summers and mild, rainy winters. Rainfall is often limited and can be highly variable from month to month and from year to year, adding considerable unpredictability to farming for a livelihood.

Agricultural technology was limited, and basic by modern standards, though this does not mean that Greeks were primitive or ignorant farmers. They were well aware of the nuances of their climate and countryside, and were able to exploit it effectively. Tools were simple and made of wood and stone with relatively small amounts of expensive metal. Ploughs, for example, were simple ard ploughs, quite appropriate for the shallow cultivation suitable for Greek soils. The only metal element would have been a ploughshare, and even this was not essential since it could be made entirely of wood (Hesiod, *Works and Days* 429–33). Traction and TRANSPORT were provided by CATTLE, mules, and, most commonly, DONKEYS.

The main crops grown in these environmental conditions were cereals (the main food staple), OLIVES, vines and other tree crops. A range of cereals was cultivated, among which barley was the most reliable, though less desirable for food than wheat. The olive and vine are the most famous Mediterranean tree crops, but FIGS, almonds and other fruit trees were also important. In addition, other products were grown including legumes (broad beans, chick peas, lentils, vetch), sesame, and VEGETABLES. Flax and hemp were cultivated for making linen and ROPE. Most agrarian regimes also included small-scale animal husbandry, especially SHEEP and GOATS kept for milk, MEAT, wool and manure. Winter vegetables such as onions, lettuce, spinach and cabbages were planted at this time of year. Ideally, arable land would be sown with crops one year, then left fallow the next year, in a two-year cycle of rotation. Fallow land was also ploughed, if possible two or three times, which prevented weeds from consuming soil nutrients and moisture and allowed two years' rainfall to be conserved in the soil for arable crops. However, other more complex rotation systems are also known from classical antiquity, and Greek farmers were aware of the soil-enriching properties of leguminous crops.

The agricultural year began in October, with the first rains initiating the busiest period of the cycle. It is significant that there is only one known Athenian religious FESTIVAL (and that a minor one) between the beginning of November and mid-December, probably because most people were so busy with farm work. Once the soil was moistened after the drought of summer, manure could be spread on fields and ploughing could start to break up the soil for the sowing. Barley was sown first, followed by wheat, then beans and other legumes. Work started with fields at lower altitudes, moving up into the hills and mountains as the sowing progressed. Depending on the weather and the location, sowing might continue until January.

Most ancient sources suggest that farmers pruned their vines in the autumn, another time-consuming task. This also entailed ploughing around the vines and, ideally, digging trenches around each vine to create a basin. In modern Greece, many slopes are terraced before planting with vines or trees, but it is likely that terracing was less common in classical times. The practice of digging around vines and other fruit trees enabled winter rains to reach the roots most effectively, cut down competition for moisture and soil nutrients from weeds, and slowed down the rate at which water ran down slopes and channelled it, thus limiting the effects of erosion. This was also the best time of year to plant new vines and fruit trees.

Another autumn job was the olive harvest, which peaked in November. Olives produce large crops only once every two years, so in a year when there were many olives farmers with limited labour resources may have planted fewer cereals and other arable crops. Once picked, olives were processed for table olives or pressed for oil. During the olive picking, farmers often pruned the trees, whose leafy branches provided valuable fodder for sheep and goats. As for vines, olive trees were often grown on sloping land without terraces, and farmers would have ploughed and dug around them at this time of year.

During the coldest part of the winter, from about mid-December through the end of January, sowing and ploughing ground to a halt. Farmers spent their time on other jobs such as wood-cutting and repairs, weather permitting. By February it was possible to begin planting spring-sown crops such as spring wheat (called 'three-month wheat' in many ancient sources), chick peas and sesame. Any unfinished vine and tree pruning could resume, cereal fields had to be weeded by hand, and fallow fields were ploughed. This was also the lambing season, and the surplus milk produced by sheep and goats had to be made into CHEESE. During March and April, as the weather warmed up, all of these jobs continued and young trees could be grafted.

From early May the trenches which had been dug around vines and trees had to be earthed up around the trunks, to kill weeds and to protect trees from the summer heat, a particularly arduous task. The cereal harvest, another busy period of the agricultural year, began in May and continued into July, depending on the year and the location. Barley ripened earlier than wheat, and fields at low altitudes were reaped earlier than those at higher altitudes. Once cereals were harvested, they had to be threshed and cleaned (weed seeds and rocks picked out) for storage, and this might continue until the end of July or later. Threshing was the process of separating cereal grains from the straw and husks (chaff). This was done by driving draught animals over the harvested grain spread out on a threshing floor, or by dragging over it a threshing-sledge (a heavy plank of wood with stone teeth set in the underside). If possible, fallow fields were also ploughed in June or July to create a layer of dry, crumbly earth on the surface, in order to minimize the amount of moisture lost through evaporation over the hot summer.

Once the main work of the harvest was out of the way, summer was a relatively relaxed period of the agricultural year. In later July and August fruit picking and processing, especially of figs and almonds, was the most important activity. However, garden crops and any vines or trees newly planted the previous autumn had to be watered to survive the summer. Vines might need tying up, and grape clusters were thinned. This was a good time of year to clean out yards and animal stabling, and to heap manure on the fields, not least because at this time of year manure was dry, lightweight and not too smelly.

September was the month of the vintage and wine-pressing. Although the work was heavy, it was fun, and warm weather provided the last pleasure of summer before the hard work of autumn started all over again. LF

See Isager, S. and Skydsgaard, J.E. (1992) *Ancient Greek Agriculture.*

For the Mediterranean region, the basics of Roman agriculture were similar to those of the Greek world. The triad of cereals, grape–vine and OLIVE predominated and in most areas agriculture

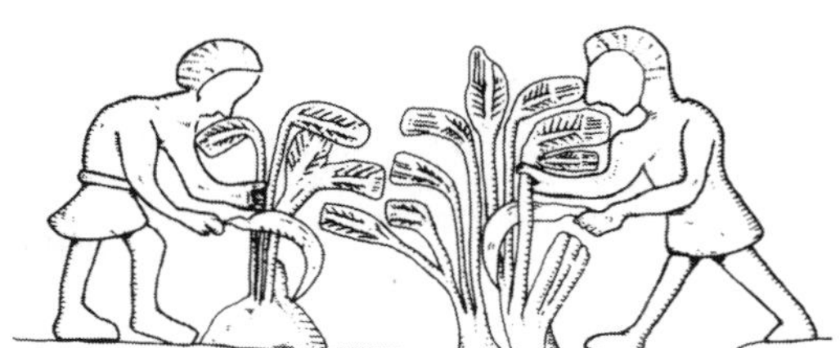

AGRICULTURE: (b) harvesting of cereals with sickles, as portrayed on a late Roman tomb from Ghirza in the Libyan pre-desert.

outweighed PASTORALISM (though even in Italy there were regions that were renowned for stock-raising, such as the Apennine valleys). The combination of the relatively arid Mediterranean climate, simple technology and variable soils imposed constraints on productivity, but the overall extent of cultivated land during the Roman period was probably not surpassed until recent centuries.

There was a well-developed tradition of writing agricultural manuals, though these were more works on estate management than on the practical detail of farming methods. The most influential surviving works are by Roman aristocrats such as CATO THE ELDER, VARRO and COLUMELLA. These dealt unequally with the various components of farming: viticulture is generally given the most space (reflecting an age-old ARISTOCRATIC interest in the production of WINE), then cereals, then olives. In Varro's account stock-raising features prominently, as does market-gardening, and in general terms the 'ideal' Roman agricultural estate seems to have been conceived as a self-sufficient mixed-farming unit. All the writers describe the management of slave labour (showing the Italian context of their experience – rural slaves were far less common in the provinces) and the construction of estate buildings (VILLAS). The most spectacular archaeological example of an Italian aristocratic estate is the Settefinestre villa near COSA.

From other Roman sources, we know that one result of Roman expansionism was the creation of large numbers of smallholders, in part through land allocations to time-expired soldiers. However, they do not feature in the works of the agronomists, and archaeological evidence suggests that in many areas there was a tendency towards the consolidation of larger estates (described as *latifundia* in Italy) out of the early, smaller distributions. Many small farmers ended up serving as tenants rather than as freeholders and, particularly outside Italy, the importance of this sort of dependent labour in supporting large estates cannot be over-emphasized.

The reality of Roman farming in the provinces was in many respects rather different from the picture we derive from the literary sources about Italy. Although we can detect the formation of large estates in many regions, coupled with the emergence of a 'villa economy', there are several clear instances of crop specialization. Papyrological evidence from the HERONINOS ARCHIVE, relating to an estate in the Egyptian FAYÛM, reveals a complex infrastructure linking several production units. Although producing a variety of crops, the main cash crop was wine, which was produced and traded on quite a large scale. Similar regional specializations in farming can be detected in southern Spain, several regions in North AFRICA (olive oil), and southern GAUL (wine). These economic success stories stand in contrast to regions such as Greece, where the early Roman period appears to have been one of contraction and under-development (though renewed development occurred in late Roman times). In North Africa, two regions were crucial for the production of cereals needed to feed the city of Rome: the NILE delta in Egypt, and northern Tunisia. Both were regions of large imperial estates with a complex infrastructure for gathering the *annona* grain from other producers. As noted, lands less suitable for cereals were strongly developed for other crops, notably the olive, making North Africa a far more dynamic region economically than its modern agriculture would indicate.

Outside the Mediterranean zone in temperate Europe, the existence of heavier soils was offset by more reliable and abundant rainfall. Cereal cultivation became well developed, and viticulture gradually extended far to the north of its previous limits, even reaching the BRITISH ISLES and GERMANY. The olive, on the hand, remained restricted to the Mediterranean climatic zone, because of its vulnerability to cold. Stock-raising for MEAT and secondary products was in general a more important element in north-western Europe, exploiting the abundant pasture lands. BEER produced from barley malt, and animal fats in cooking and for LIGHTING, remained key cultural markers of the north, despite the partial inroads by wine-makers and the imports of olive oil. DJM

See Carandini, A. et al. (1984) *Settefinestre: una villa schiavistica nell'Etruria romana*; Frayn, J. (1979) *Subsistence Farming in Roman Italy*; Mattingly, D. (1996) First fruit? The olive in the Roman world, in G. Shipley and J. Salmon, eds., *Human Landscapes in Classical Antiquity* 213–53; Rathbone, D.W. (1991) *Economic Rationalism and Rural Society in Third-century AD Egypt*; Spurr, M. S. (1986) *Arable Cultivation in Roman Italy*; White, K. D. (1970) *Roman Farming*.

agrimensores Roman land surveyors were called *mensores* or *agrimensores* ('land measurers'), or in the later empire *gromatici* (from *groma*, their surveying instrument). By the late Republic, when they were in great demand for colonial foundations, surveyors had acquired some professional status, though they generally remained men of low degree; indeed, some were SLAVES or FREEDMEN. There were also military surveyors attached to the legions and praetorian guard, who were responsible for laying out camps and FORTS and could be seconded to work on civilian projects.

There is a substantial technical literature on surveying, and several treatises dating from the late 1st to 5th centuries AD were collected in the 6th century. Some manuscripts contain diagrams and coloured illustrations, which are probably later additions. The most important authors are FRONTINUS (possibly the distinguished SENATOR and author of *The Aqueducts of Rome*), Agennius Urbicus, Siculus Flaccus and Hyginus (there are two treatises under this name, probably by different authors). An anonymous work, the *Liber coloniarum*, describes settlements, mainly in Italy, from the GRACCHI to the 2nd century AD. These works are partly didactic, containing many references to the personal investigations of practising surveyors. They illustrate methods of land division, land categories, boundary marking, MAP designations, record-keeping, the role of surveyors in land disputes, the development of landholding patterns in the Roman world, and the layout of many Italian rural communities. Archaeological investigation of Roman field systems has confirmed the accuracy of much of the information in the surveying treatises. JBC

Campbell, B. (2000) *The Writings of the Roman Land Surveyors*.

Agrippa (Marcus Vipsanius Agrippa) b.64/3 BC Principal associate of Octavian (later AUGUSTUS). Agrippa's family was undistinguished, but his friendship with Octavian went back to their schooldays. He was at Octavian's side throughout the period after CAESAR's death and commanded forces for him from the Perusine war (41–40) on. He held early office (PRAETOR 40, CONSUL 37), campaigned successfully in GAUL (39–38), and was principally responsible for the victory over Sextus Pompeius, commanding the fleet at Mylae and Naulochus (36). As AEDILE in 33 (the only ex-consul ever to hold the post), he enhanced the popularity of Octavian by lavish welfare spending at Rome, and took permanent responsibility for the upkeep of the AQUEDUCTS. At ACTIUM (31) he commanded the fleet's left wing and played a decisive part in Mark ANTONY's defeat. After the victory, he assisted Octavian in the political settlement, holding a CENSUS with him (29–28) and sharing the consulship in 28–27. He then remained at Rome, where he constructed BATHS and other public buildings on the Campus Martius. By 23, Augustus' promotion of his nephew MARCELLUS led to tension, resolved by Marcellus' death later in that year. Agrippa now became Augustus' effective partner in rule and successor, marrying his daughter Julia (21) and receiving grants of independent *imperium* (23, 18, 13) and tribunician power (18, 13). He was employed on a series of overseas commands, in Gaul and Spain (20–19), twice in the eastern provinces (23–22, 17–13), and in Pannonia (13–12). Agrippa's talents and loyalty made an enormous contribution to Augustus' success in establishing his rule. His death in March 12 BC seriously weakened the regime. JWR

See Reinhold, M. (1933) *Marcus Agrippa*; Roddaz, J.-M. (1984) *Marcus Agrippa*.

Agrippinae, the Vipsania Agrippina (1) is known by her *gens* name Vipsania. Daughter of Marcus

AGRIPPINAE, THE: coin portrait of Agrippina the Younger (3).

AGRIPPA, granddaughter of CICERO's ATTICUS, she was wife of TIBERIUS c.19–12 BC and mother of Drusus Caesar, then married Gaius Asinius Gallus, bearing five or six sons including the consuls of 23, 25 and 38. She died in 20.

Her half-sister Agrippina the Elder (2) was born to AUGUSTUS' daughter Julia in 14 BC. Uniting the ruling family, she married Germanicus, Tiberius' adopted son, in about AD 5. Her role gave her, as it had her mother, exceptional prominence (as monuments attest) – more than Tiberius liked. After a Roman setback in GERMANY (AD 15), she stood at the RHINE bridge, preventing it being demolished. She accompanied Germanicus to the East (17) and brought his ashes to Rome (19–20). She worked for her sons Nero Caesar and Drusus Caesar, causing further offence to Tiberius and his minister SEJANUS, was imprisoned with Nero in 29, and starved to death on Pandateria in 33. Her youngest son, GAIUS, survived to become emperor (37).

The eldest of her three daughters, (Julia) Agrippina the Younger (3) (AD 15–59), was honoured by her brother Gaius but fell under suspicion and was exiled after the death of her husband Lepidus (39). CLAUDIUS recalled her, and when he had to destroy his wife Messalina in 48 his only way to recover prestige was to marry Germanicus' daughter – his niece! – and make her Augusta. Her birthplace, Colonia Claudia Ara Agrippinensium (Cologne), was named after her in 50, and in 51 she presided at a parade of BRITISH prisoners. Claudius adopted Agrippina's son by her first marriage as an older partner for his own son Britannicus, but when he died (in 54, not without suspicion falling on Agrippina) NERO alone succeeded. At first Agrippina enjoyed honours hardly paralleled for a woman, but her power was restricted and she looked for other protégés, of whom Britannicus was the first. Nero had her murdered at Baiae, so escaping from the control of all his mentors. This was the first of the crimes that made deposing Nero seem legitimate. Agrippina's memoirs, used by TACITUS, are lost. BML

See Barrett, A. (1996) *Agrippina*.

AUGUSTUS: (a).

Ahura-Mazda 'Wise Lord', the Old PERSIAN name of an Iranian deity. Ahura-Mazda is evoked in Persian royal inscriptions as the creator of the earth and the sky, of man and of human happiness. According to the inscriptions the follower of Ahura-Mazda is praised as a follower of the Truth (*arta* in Old Persian) and an opponent of the Lie (*drauga*). As the principal god of the Achaemenid dynasty, he bestows the kingship on the Persian kings and guides them in their striving for just rule. The inscriptions mention him alongside 'the other gods', including Mithra, the god of light and of treaties, and Anahita, the goddess of water and fertility.

It is difficult to determine whether Ahura-Mazda was worshipped by the early Persian kings, or whether his cult was established by Darius I, to be observed by the Achaemenid kings and the nobility. There is much debate as to whether the god of the Achaemenid period represents Ahura-Mazda, the god of ZOROASTRIAN religion. The main difficulties are the lack of factual evidence about ZOROASTER, and the dependency of the spread of his religion on oral tradition; consequently, the earliest written evidence, the *Avesta*, dates from the 9th or 10th centuries AD. It seems historically more accurate to regard the Achaemenid cult of Ahura-Mazda as a form of Mazdaism, and to suggest that the religion of Ahura-Mazda, as preached in the *Avesta*, was established in the SASSANIAN period. MB

See Wiesehöfer, J. (2001) *Ancient Persia*.

Ai Khanum Greco-Baktrian city in Baktria (north Afghanistan), founded c.300 BC on the site of an Achaemenid fortification at the confluence of the Amu Darya (anc. Oxus) and Kokcha rivers; excavated by French archaeologists in the 1960s and 1970s. The founder was presumably Seleukos I or Antiochos I. The ancient name is uncertain, but the level of architectural investment indicates it was important to Seleukid economic planning and frontier defence. Within a basically Greek town plan, there are both Greek-style buildings (theatre, sanctuary, GYMNASIUM, FORTIFICATIONS, public spaces defined by STOAS) and others reminiscent of Achaemenid styles, including TEMPLES. There is no evidence of racial segregation, to judge by the HOUSES. Excavation revealed the reversed imprint of a papyrus text in the soil, and a stone inscription containing inscribed DELPHIC maxims a PHILOSOPHER had brought from Greece. The Greek population was evidently anxious to maintain links with its homeland. Ai Khanum is an important case study for the interaction of Greek and non-Greek cultures, at least at the ÉLITE level, under the patronage of the SELEUKIDS, who were concerned to maintain secure control. Baktria broke away to form an independent Greek kingdom in the mid-3rd century, and Ai Khanum was destroyed by invaders from the east around 150 BC. DGJS

See Bernard, P. (1967) Aï Khanum on the Oxus, *Proceedings of the British Academy* 53: 71–95; Bernard, P. et al. (1973–92), *Fouilles d' Aï Khanoum*, vols. 1–8; Sherwin-White, S. and Kuhrt, A. (1993) *From Samarkhand to Sardis*.

ALEXANDER III: (b).

Aias see AJAX.

Aigai see VERGINA.

Aigina (Aegina) Island (83 sq km, 32 sq miles) in the Saronic gulf. According to legend, it was originally uninhabited and named Oinone, but renamed after the daughter of Asopos, carried there by ZEUS. Their union produced Aiakos, ancestor of ACHILLES and AJAX. Aigina was inhabited from late Neolithic, with extensive activity from the early Bronze Age. The mid-2nd millennium shows CRETAN connections, such as MINOAN GOLD redeposited in a MYCENAEAN tomb. A late Bronze Age shrine underlies the sanctuary of Aphaia, the Cretan Britomartis, taken there by fishermen who saved her after she fell into the sea escaping Minos. HERODOTOS mentions resettlement by Epidaurians c.1000 BC; THUCYDIDES says the Argive TYRANT Pheidon ruled Aigina (probably early 7th century). Remains include the TEMPLE of APOLLO (c.520–510), built on 6th-century predecessors. In the sanctuary of Aphaia, an 8th-century open-air shrine was enclosed in the early 6th. The first stone temple is c.575, the present one probably also archaic. The west pediment shows the Homeric capture of TROY, the east the first capture, by the older Aiakids.

Aigina prospered throughout the archaic period by shipping and transport of, for example, corn (XERXES saw Aiginetan corn ships in the HELLESPONT), METALS, TIMBER and wool. The city helped found Naukratis c.570, and trade in ETRURIA is attested. Aigina distinguished itself at the battle of SALAMIS, the island of Ajax, but lost a long conflict with Athens in 457, paying severe penalties. Expelled by Athens in 431, the Aiginetans were restored by the Spartan LYSANDER in 404. The later history of the island follows each dominant power in Greece until bequeathed to Rome by Attalos III in 133 BC; his ancestor Attalos I had bought the island from the Aitolians. KWA

See Figueira, T. (1991) *Athens and Aigina in the Age of Imperial Colonization*; Ohly, D. (1978) *Ägina: Tempel und Heligtum der Aphaia*.

 AEGEAN: (a).

Aigospotamoi (Aegospotami) A small beach on the northern side of the HELLESPONT, where the Spartan admiral LYSANDER and his large armada defeated the last surviving fleet of the ATHENIAN EMPIRE, and so brought the PELOPONNESIAN WAR to a close. The Athenian-led forces were huge, 180 triremes with about 36,000 combatants, and outnumbered their opponents. But the crews were in political turmoil, the command uneven and rotating, and their bivouac hard to supply with food and water.

The sound advice of the mercurial ALCIBIADES, now a civilian who resided nearby, to ensure better logistical support, obtain land troops to protect the ships, and find sheltered waters was rejected. The Athenians, after five days of careless patrolling, were surprised by Lysander, who chased a small Athenian patrol squadron right onto the beach, where he then caught the remaining crews and nearly destroyed all the triremes. Only nine ships managed to escape.

The destruction of the fleet, the butchery of some 3,000 Athenian prisoners, and the rumour that Lysander intended to force his way into the PIRAEUS created near-panic at Athens. Growing hunger, a right-wing coup, the loss of the century-old navy, and the sudden revolt of tributary allies forced Athens to sue for surrender.

Astute contemporaries saw Aigospotamoi almost as divine retribution for the past *hybris* of the imperial Athenians. Timid generalship was due to the prior execution of the victorious admirals of ARGINOUSAI; massacred prisoners were the payback for past Athenian atrocities; and careful rejection of the sound advice of Alcibiades was as injurious as blindly accepting his previous foolhardy schemes. VDH

See Kagan, D. (1987) *The Fall of the Athenian Empire*.

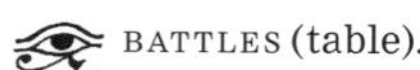 BATTLES (table).

Aiolis see CUMAE; ERINNA.

Aischines (Aeschines) c.397–c.322 BC Athenian orator. Aischines came from a family impoverished by the PELOPONNESIAN WAR, but both he and his two brothers achieved some distinction. Aischines was decorated for valour at the battle of Tamynai (348), trained as a tragic ACTOR, and was the secretary to the Athenian ASSEMBLY. He came to the fore politically as a supporter of Euboulos. A member of the Council in 347/6, when his hostility to DEMOSTHENES began, Aischines was sent on an embassy to Megalopolis as part of Euboulos' unsuccessful attempt to secure united Greek support against the threat of PHILIP II of MACEDONIA. He and Demosthenes were then members of the embassy which negotiated the peace of Philokrates in 346. But Philip was soon threatening PHOKIS, and Demosthenes quickly tried to dissociate himself from the treaty; Aischines realized the reality of the situation and continued to speak in Philip's favour. Demosthenes interpreted this as indicating bribery and in 346/5 initiated a prosecution of Aischines for his role in negotiating the peace, but did so through the alleged former male prostitute Timarchos, whom Aischines immediately and successfully counter-prosecuted (by the *Against Timarchos*) for speaking in the Assembly when debarred by his IMMORALITY. Demosthenes had to wait until 343 for the chance to attack Aischines again, as being entirely responsible for the Assembly's acceptance of the peace. *On the Embassy* secured a narrow acquittal, but his reputation was tarnished. In 340/39 he served as one of Athens' representatives on the Amphiktionic council of Delphi, where he foolishly provoked a SACRED WAR against Amphissa, so giving Philip the excuse to intervene. This culminated in the Greek defeat at CHAIRONEIA (338), after which Aischines negotiated the peace terms. He went on the offensive against Demosthenes in 336, when he indicted Ktesiphon for illegally proposing that Demosthenes be crowned for his services to Athens in the THEATRE at the Dionysia, though the political situation delayed the prosecution until 330. *Against Ktesiphon* is a competent speech, selectively reviewing Demosthenes' career, but Demosthenes' reply as an advocate (*synêgoros*) for Ktesiphon was his masterpiece, *On the Crown*. Aischines failed to secure the requisite one-fifth of the votes and was fined, after which he retired to RHODES to teach RHETORIC.

There is no evidence that Aischines formally learned rhetoric or worked as a logographer; only the three speeches mentioned above, plus a spurious fourth concerning DELOS, were known to the Augustan critics. He spoke naturally and forcefully, using simple vocabulary, and in a dignified manner, without extravagant gestures, despite his earlier acting career. He was fond of quoting POETRY and showing off his learning, and the speeches contain vivid narrative passages. Aischines' method was to concentrate on the legalities of the case, and he clearly was an effective speaker. But his vision was far narrower than Demosthenes' and he has inevitably suffered by comparison with him. Nevertheless, PHILOSTRATOS later credited Aischines with being the founder of the Second Sophistic movement. MJE

See Adams, C. D., trs. (1919) *The Speeches of Aeschines*; Harris, E. M. (1995) *Aeschines and Athenian Politics*; Fisher, N. R. E. (2001) *Aeschines, Against Timarchos*.

Aischylos see AESCHYLUS.

Aitolia and Aitolian league A mountainous region occupying the hinterland north and west of the

Corinthian gulf, Aitolia had the reputation of being the home of a semi-barbarous people given to brigandage. The Aitolian league was the federal state of this region, wielding considerable power in the hellenistic period, especially the 3rd century BC.

A loose, tribal structure based on a common *ethnos* no doubt existed in the archaic and classical periods. There were three major subgroups: Apodotoi, Eurytaneis, and Ophioneis. The gods APOLLO and ARTEMIS were especially important, with a cult to the former located at THERMOS. The region was formally organized into a federation, with its centre at Thermos, by the early 4th century BC. Tod 137 (367) refers to the *koinon* ('community', roughly 'federation') of the Aitolians. Its ASSEMBLY was the sovereign body of the league, and was unusual in that it consisted of all male citizens; other leagues preferred representative assemblies. It met twice a year; at the second meeting (the *panaitôlika*) it elected MAGISTRATES. There was also a large council of 1,000, with member states sending representatives in proportion to the military strength they contributed. Additionally, there was an elected committee of the council (the *apoklètoi*), no doubt responsible for the running of day-to-day affairs; it also probably had significant influence over the assembly. The government was led by the elected magistrates: the GENERAL (*stratêgos*), secretary, hipparch, *agônothetês* (who oversaw the Soteria festival at DELPHI) and treasurer (*tamias*). A person could be chosen general more than once, but could not serve in consecutive years. Though very DEMOCRATIC in organization, the government of the league became more OLIGARCHIC over time.

With THEBES in decline from the mid-4th century, the Aitolian league became the leading power in central Greece. The Athenian HYMN to DEMETRIOS POLIORKETES mentions the league's occupation of Delphi c.300 (*FGrH* 76 F 13); it gained lasting control of the shrine shortly after the defeat of the Gallic invaders of 280/79, assuming leadership of the Delphic amphiktiony (governing council). The league became an ally of Rome against PHILIP V in 212 or 211; worn down by the conflict, it reached a separate peace with Philip in 206. When hostilities in the region were resumed, the league again joined Rome, and its forces played an important role in the preliminaries to the decisive defeat of Philip at KYNOSKEPHALAI in 197. However, relations between the league and Rome immediately deteriorated, with matters developing eventually into serious differences. These culminated with the league joining forces with ANTIOCHOS III in 192. In 189 it was forced to become a subject ally of Rome, and while the league continued in name it had lost its power to influence other states. (see also DELPHI; FEDERALISM) JDD

See Livy, esp. book 39; Polybios, esp. book 18; Larsen, J. A. O. (1968) *Greek Federal States*; Walbank, F.W. (1984) The rise of Aetolia, in *CAH* 7.1, 232–6.

 AEGEAN: (a).

Ajax (Aias, Aiax) Two Greek HEROES from the Trojan saga are known by this name: 'greater' Ajax, son of Telamon the king of SALAMIS, and 'lesser' Ajax, prince of the Lokrians and son of Oileus. Both characters appear in HOMER, with the second presented in a less favourable light, as is reflected by his name Ajax the Lesser. This is probably due to his involvement in the rape of APOLLO's virgin prophetess, the Trojan princess Kassandra.

Ajax the Greater's reputation as one of the best Achaian fighters in the TROJAN WAR has its beginnings in myths surrounding his birth. He is associated with the Dorian hero HERAKLES, a close friend of his father, who even attempted to render the newborn baby immortal. Very little else is known about his childhood from the myth. His adult life is marked by participation in the Trojan war along with his paternal half-brother, Teukros. Because of his great military exploits, but also his enormous size and his full-body shield, he was known as 'the bulwark of the Achaians' (*Iliad* 3.226–9). He was a front-line warrior during the years of the siege of Troy, and one of the most valiant Achaian leaders. Less glorious is his suicide, a result of his humiliating loss of the arms of ACHILLES to the consummate strategist ODYSSEUS. Ajax was worshipped as local hero in his homeland, Salamis (Pindar, *Nemean Odes* 4.58), and celebrations known as 'Aianteia' were held in his honour (Pausanias 1.35.2). EP

See Touchefeu, O. (1981) Aias I and Aias II, in *LIMC* vol. 1, 312–51.

Akarnania see EPIRUS; GREECE; TRIBES, GREEK.

***akropolis* (acropolis)** The 'high city,' or citadel, the *akropolis* was the defensive and ceremonial centre of a Greek city (*arx* has the identical meaning in Latin). In the *Iliad*, the 'summit of the city' (*akrê polios*) at TROY is where the temple of ATHENA is located, and where ZEUS is invoked. In the *Odyssey*, *akropolis* describes fortified Troy as a whole. The legendary citadel of Priam exemplifies strongholds remembered as the fortified residences of ancient kings, their chief dependants, and patron deities. Sometimes, as with the ATHENIAN ACROPOLIS and the Kadmeia at THEBES, a substantial Bronze Age citadel became the focus of important civic cults in the core of a growing town. Other *akropoleis*, like Akrokorinthos at Corinth and the Larisa of ARGOS, were peripheral to the town below, but vital to its defence and cultic traditions. At PERGAMON in ASIA Minor in the hellenistic period, the massive *akropolis* was both town and royal citadel. The term could describe an abandoned ancient stronghold employed as a temporary FORTRESS (Pylos in MESSENIA, THUCYDIDES 4.26.2), a venerable place that became a new civic *akropolis* (Mt Ithome, PAUSANIAS 4.33.1), a new foundation symbolizing power (DIONYSIOS I's personal fortress on the island of Ortygia at SYRACUSE, DIODORUS 14.7.3), or a metaphor for authority (Lakedaimon is called 'the *akropolis* of Greece' after the Spartan victory over Athens in 405 BC, ML 95). *Akropoleis* were vital defensive strongholds during civil war or when a foreign garrison was introduced to protect a town or enforce its submission. MM

Al Mina Iron Age port near the mouth of the Orontes river, today in the Hatay province of Turkey. It was excavated by Leonard Woolley over two seasons in 1936 and 1937. He identified nine continuous occupation levels dating from 750 to c.300 BC with a medieval reoccupation at the uppermost level. The nature of the foundation of Al Mina has been the subject of much debate, with interpretations making it variously the first Greek trading post of the Iron Age, a Greek MERCENARY settlement, and a LEVANTINE site with Greek contact. The site has been noted most for its quantity of 8th-century BC (levels 10–9) imported Greek Geometric POTTERY, which surpasses relative proportions at contemporary, neighbouring settlements (e.g. Tarsus and Tell Soukas) when compared with the areas excavated.

Architecturally, the fragmentary remains of these early levels conform to standard local building methods using stone foundations with mudbrick superstructures, though such a small area was excavated that it is difficult to obtain an understanding of the layout of the earliest settlement. In addition to the imported Geometric wares, ceramics were locally produced at an early date in the site's history.

The town seems to have been reconstructed along new lines at the beginning of the 7th century (levels 8–7). Ceramic imports from CYPRUS begin to appear at this time, with increasing imports from East Greece by the middle of the century. During the 6th century (levels 6–5), buildings were constructed that can be identified as offices and magazines. CORINTHIAN ceramics supplemented the East Greek and Cypriot wares, alongside Cypriot terracottas and limestone figures.

The settlement was rebuilt in the late 6th century (level 4). Uniform, rectangular structures with courtyards and chambers were constructed along orthogonal lanes. These buildings served as storerooms for the imports and exports that passed through the port, and also as retail SHOPS, as attested by pottery remains and small finds such as weights and silver coins. Imports from Athens seem to dominate ceramic trade at this time, while scarabs from Egypt and GLASS, perhaps from PHOENICIA, were also imported. Athens continued to dominate the ceramic market during the 5th and 4th centuries (levels 3–2) with local wares closely imitating the Greek imports. That some of the merchants lived at their place of business is suggested by stone coffins dug into the floors of several buildings of otherwise mercantile function, or adjacent to them. The site continued in use only briefly after ALEXANDER's conquest of the region, until SELEUKOS I Nikator founded the nearby port of Seleukeia in 301 BC. Since its medieval reoccupation (level 1), the mound has been levelled and is currently an orange grove. TH

See Boardman, J. (1999) *The Greeks Overseas*; Woolley, L. (1938) The excavations at Al Mina, Sueidia, I–II, *JHS* 58: 1–30, 133–70.

 PHOENICIA AND PHOENICIANS: (a).

Alalia Phokaian colony on eastern coast of CORSICA, founded c.565 BC. Persian subjugation of Ionia resulted in waves of colonists leaving Asia Minor for prospects elsewhere. Corsica was rich in minerals, wood, wax and honey, and was known to the Phokaians from their other western Mediterranean colonial and commercial enterprises.

In c.535 BC, Alalia was involved in a battle against an alliance between CARTHAGE and the ETRUSCANS, who were hostile to Greek activity in the region. Known as the battle of Alalia, it can be considered the first great NAVAL BATTLE of recorded history. Outnumbered two to one by alliance ships, the Phokaians won the battle but lost almost the entire fleet that had been sent out. HERODOTOS reports that the survivors and their families then abandoned Corsica in favour of the Italian mainland at Rhegion, where they founded a new colony in Oenotria called Elea (Castellamare di Bruca, Lucania).

Subsequently, Carthage held the balance of power, becoming the dominant political force by the end of the 6th century. Carthage lost Alalia to the Romans in 259 BC during the first PUNIC WAR. The settlement then became known as Aleria and remained under Roman control until AD 456, when it was annexed by the VANDAL Gaiseric. In AD 552, it was reconquered by JUSTINIAN I to become a province. Fieldwork in and around the town has been carried out since 1955. TH

See Herodotos 1.165–7; Jehasse, J. and Jehasse, L. (1997) *Aléria ressuscitée = Aleria rediviva.*

Alamanni (Alemanni) see CONSTANTINE; MAXIMINUS THRAX; RAETIA; VALENTINIAN I; VALERIAN.

Alani Nomadic tribes, descended from the Sarmatians, who lived in the mountains of northern Caucasus. They were very active from the 2nd to the early 5th century AD, and were a strong threat to the Romans. One of the chief purposes of the province of CAPPADOCIA and the Caucasian frontier was to protect the rest of the empire against these tribes. ARRIAN withstood one such attack while governor. Later, the Dariel and Derbend passes were fortified against them. As well as playing an important role as a buffer state between Rome and PARTHIA, the Iberian kingdom in Transcaucasia had a function in stopping the Alani. In the 4th century AD the HUNS conquered the lands of the Alani, killing some and driving others westward where they reached Spain and GAUL. Archaeologically, the Alani are known thanks to their extensive burial grounds. Many aspects of their life are subject to scholarly debate. GRT

See Bosworth, A.B. (1977) Arrian and the Alani, *HSCP* 81: 217–55.

 GERMANY AND GERMANS: (b).

Alaric (Alaricus) c.AD 365/70–410 GOTHIC warlord and leader from c.391. Alaric's most famous act was the sack of Rome in 410: on this single event has rested his reputation as the first barbarian leader in eight centuries to infiltrate and pillage the city. Yet the reality of Alaric's role in the events still sometimes described as 'the decline and fall of the Roman empire' was more complex than it appears to be.

He emerged as a leader of Gothic troops settled in the empire, whom he commanded in the war against the Western usurper Eugenius in 394. He felt that Gothic units were treated with disdain by Roman commanders, a complaint justified by the large numbers of Gothic casualties sustained in the conflict. Thereafter, he sought to extract favourable terms for the Goths, first from the Eastern emperor Arcadius in CONSTANTINOPLE and then from his Western counterpart HONORIUS in RAVENNA. Part of the deal was a position in the military high command for Alaric himself, which would provide recognition of the Goths' contribution to the Roman army. Repeatedly, however, he was rebuffed, and it was these circumstances that led to the sack of Rome. Having tried numerous schemes (including sponsoring a usurper of his own) to force Honorius to come to terms, Alaric, exasperated at the emperor's intransigence, turned his troops on the city. Far from being a barbarian conqueror, then, Alaric was a disaffected partner in the empire.

The sack of Rome was a failure, since Honorius still refused to deal with the Goths. Alaric died soon afterwards, but his successor Athaulf eventually secured terms from the empire, leading to the establishment of the Visigothic kingdom in southern GAUL. MDH

See Heather, P. (1991) *Goths and Romans 332–489*; Liebeschuetz, J. H. W. G. (1990) *Barbarians and Bishops*.

Alcaeus see ALKAIOS.

alchemy A combination of technology, PHILOSOPHY, mystic religion and ASTROLOGY. Different strands came together at ALEXANDRIA in the 2nd and 3rd centuries AD to form a phenomenon eventually called alchemy, but 'the work' or 'the sacred art' in antiquity. Attempts to turn base metals into gold and the search for the 'philosopher's stone' were not initial developments. Specialized practitioners had developed an ability, kept secret, to give GLASS and METALWORK the appearance of gold and silver. Concepts drawn from ARISTOTLE, the ATOMISTS and the STOICS – including the four elements, the essential unity of all things animate and inanimate, and a *pneuma* (spirit) flowing through the universe – added their influence, and the idea eventually developed that metals might be transformed. Religious ingredients joined the mix, already primed for the addition of mystical components by the initial secrecy of the crafts. The accretion of astrology occasions no surprise. It appears in many mysticisms, whose cosmologies incorporated seven heavenly bodies. In alchemy, they were linked with seven metals. The most important surviving writings, which often attribute later concepts to prominent earlier figures, were authored by Zosimus of Panopolis about AD 300. The Egyptian Hermetic Corpus offers additional material, while Firmicus Maternus, among others, refers to the link between secret arts, astrology and workers in metal. JV

See Zosimus of Panopolis (1995) *Les Alchimistes grecs*, text and translation, ed. M. Mertens; Copenhaver, B. P. (1992) *Hermetica: the Greek Corpus Hermeticum and the Latin Asclepius* (introduction, translation); Lindsay, J. (1970) *The Origins of Alchemy in Graeco-Roman Egypt*.

Alcibiades (Alkibiades) 451/0–404 BC Athenian politician and general, the most colourful and controversial public figure of his generation, vividly portrayed throughout THUCYDIDES 5–8 and in PLUTARCH's *Life*. Aristocratic, arrogant and ambitious, he showed exceptional abilities, but could not consistently subordinate them to current Athenian political correctness. After projecting himself through the 420s as soldier, SOCRATIC and rake, he gained early office as GENERAL for 420/19, influencing Athenian policy in the Peloponnese till 416 via close ties with ARGOS. Extravagance (notably by CHARIOT RACING, winning at OLYMPIA in 416) bought success for his advocacy of the SICILIAN EXPEDITION in 415. However, alleged involvement in two blasphemous scandals terminated his generalship, lost him his property, and exiled him to Sparta itself. After rapid acculturation there, giving well-directed advice on how best to damage Athens, and committing ADULTERY with king Agis' wife, he shifted allegiance briefly in 412 to the PERSIAN satrap Tissaphernes in order to regain Athenian favour. Eventually, in 411, he was recognized as general by the Athenian fleet based at SAMOS. Several naval successes, and the recovery of many AEGEAN allies, gave him a triumphal return to Athens in 407: in symbolic annulment of scandal, he escorted the procession of would-be initiates to the Eleusinian mysteries. However, on returning to the Aegean, a naval defeat precipitated renewed voluntary exile in THRACE, from which, as ARISTOPHANES' *Frogs* reveals, the Athenians could not decide whether to recall him. The THIRTY had him killed in 404, but debate about him continued for another 20 years. (see also ELEUSIS) JKD

See Forde, S. (1989) *The Ambition to Rule*; Gribble, D. (1999) *Alcibiades and Athens*.

Alcmaeonidae see ALKMAIONIDAI.

Alcman see ALKMAN.

alcohol and alcoholism WINE-drinking was a fundamental feature of the culture of the Greco-Roman world, though beer remained popular in both Egypt and the CELTIC regions of the Roman empire. The ambivalent nature of the effects of the consumption of alcohol were well known. As the Greek medical writer Mnesitheos stated, 'the gods had revealed wine to mortals to be the greatest blessing for those who use it aright, but for those who use it without restraint, the reverse' (Athenaeus 2.36). Alcoholism, as such, was not recognized in the ancient world – indeed, there is a case for asserting that it is a disease only discovered or invented in the modern world. But the classical medical writers were fascinated with the physical and mental effects of wine consumption. Further, SENECA THE YOUNGER (*Letter* 83.9) makes the careful distinction between a man who is *ebrius* (drunk) and one who is *ebriosus* (a drunkard). It was the enervating effects of alcohol that were stressed in the ancient world; a tendency to drink too much made people 'careless' and 'idle'. This, however, was to be contrasted with the beneficial effects of drink in moderation. This was considered to aid socializing (see the Falstaffian passage in ARISTOPHANES, *Knights* 85ff.), to promote frank conversation (*in vino veritas*), and to provide a sort of test of character, which is why PLATO devoted so much attention to wine in his *Laws* (books 1–2). All this was to be seen at its most formal and ritualistic in the Greek social institution of the *SYMPOSION* and, in a rather different way, in the Roman *convivium*. The drinking at the *symposion* was regulated, most notably by the practice of mixing the wine with water. On occasion, however – particularly, it seems, among groups of wealthy young 'hooray Henries' – it could spill over into public riot and even VIOLENCE (DEMOSTHENES 54, against Konon for drunken assault, vividly illustrates the phenomenon).

The misuse of drink was bound to become a fruitful topic for invective. Hence it is no surprise to find many leading public figures accused of being drunkards, from KIMON and KLEON in Athens and ALEXANDER of Macedonia to CATO the YOUNGER, MARK ANTONY, and EMPERORS such as TIBERIUS and

Nero in Rome. The truth of such accusations is probably irrecoverable now. There were those who were abstainers (see the examples collected by Athenaeus 2.44b–f). But 'water-drinking' could itself be the subject of criticism, as being anti-social behaviour. JJP
See Davidson, J. (1997) *Courtesans and Fishcakes*; Murray, O., ed. (1990) *Sympotica*; Murray, O. and Tecuşan, M., eds. (1995) *In Vino Veritas*; Sournia, J.-C. (1990) *A History of Alcoholism*, trs. N. Hindley; Walton, S. (2001) *Out of It*.

Alemanni (Alamanni) see Constantine; Maximinus Thrax; Raetia; Valentinian I; Valerian.

Alesia see Gallic wars; Vercingetorix.

Alexander III ('the Great') King of Macedonia (r.336–323 BC) and conqueror of the Persian empire, who came to power when his father, Philip II, was assassinated. Ancient sources are divided between a more reliable tradition (culminating in Arrian and some of Plutarch's work), a less reliable one (Diodorus and Quintus Curtius Rufus), and a popular (the *Alexander Romance*).

Alexander may have had Aristotle as his tutor. Like his royal forebears, he believed he was fully Hellenic, carrying a copy of the *Iliad* everywhere for inspiration. He put down a revolt of the southern Greeks, punishing the city of Thebes by razing it to the ground in 334, and then carried out his father's planned invasion of the Persian empire. Landing in Asia Minor, he visited the reputed tomb of Achilles, the Homeric hero from whom he apparently believed he was descended. Rapid conquest of Asia Minor followed, with key victories over Darius III at the river Granikos (334) and at Issos (333). During the next two years he conquered Phoenicia and Egypt, where he founded Alexandria and was hailed as the son of Zeus by the priest of Ammon (Amon-Ra). In 331–330 he took the war into the Persian heartland, defeating Darius at Gaugamela and capturing Babylon and Sousa, where he recovered statues looted from Athens by Xerxes in 480 BC. The burning of the palace at Persepolis in 330, whether deliberate or accidental, served his propaganda purposes, allowing him to claim revenge for Xerxes' invasion on behalf of all Greeks. In 329, he exacted justice from Darius' murderer, Bessos, making clear his wish to be seen as Darius' heir and the new king of Persia.

By now, what others would forever identify as his autocratic traits were manifest. He fell out with some of his closest advisers and had them executed (Philotas, Parmenion, and later the court historian Kallisthenes), killed another in a drunken rage (Kleitos), and demanded *proskynêsis* (Persian-style obeisance) from Greeks. At the same time, he pressed ever further east, conquering Baktria (north Afghanistan) and penetrating Punjab (326), until his troops mutinied for a return home. His unwise crossing of the Gedrosian desert (325), the execution of Persian satraps, and the alienation of his treasurer, Harpalos (who fled to Greece with a fortune), have all fuelled the image of a man who had lost his power of judgement. He may have had visions of a unified Greco-Persian ruling class – he arranged a mass marriage of his soldiers to non-Greek wives – and probably intended to invade Arabia and the western Mediterranean. The death in 324 of his lover, Hephaistion, depressed him and in 323 he died at Ekbatana, perhaps of pneumonia exacerbated by excessive drinking. He had failed to provide clearly for the royal succession, and decades of combat between his generals (Successors of Alexander) ensued.

Alexander inspired fanatical devotion, and was without doubt a brilliant general and politician. He created a Hellenic regime in western Asia and Egypt that would endure for centuries. Plutarch thought that those he conquered were lucky to have been civilized. Generals from Pompey to Napoleon have emulated him, and modern idealists have seen in his grand plans a precedent for the League of Nations. Sceptics now question his sanity or posit alcoholism. Balanced assessments point to the ground already prepared by Philip, the massive demographic effort by Greeks and Macedonians that his campaigns entailed, and an ideological climate in which barbarians were seen as fit to be ruled. While the desire for conquest and wealth was normal in ancient societies, Alexander's heroic insatiability reached new heights and cost the lives of many innocent people. (see pp. 36–7) DGJS
See Arrian, *Anabasis of Alexander*; Quintus Curtius Rufus, *The History of Alexander*, trs. J. Yardley; Plutarch, *Alexander*; Bosworth, A. B. (1998) *Alexander the Great*; Bosworth, A. B. and Baynham, E. J., eds. (2000) *Alexander the Great in Fact and Fiction*; *Greece & Rome* 12.2 (1965) (collection of articles); Green, P. (1991) *Alexander of Macedon*; Worthington, I., ed. (2002) *Alexander: a reader*.

Amon-Ra: (a); elephants: (a); Macedonia: (b); Persia and Persians: (a).

Alexander III ('the Great'): (a) an Alexandrian silver tetradrachm, depicting the head of Alexander as Hercules and the seated figure of Zeus.

Alexander of Troy see Paris.

Alexander Romance A group of Greek, Roman, and medieval tales about Alexander the Great in verse and prose, also known as Pseudo-Kallisthenes or by their Latin title, *Historia Alexandri Magni*. Versions survive in most medieval languages: from Hebrew to Magyar, from Scots to Syriac. Western versions derive from Latin ones. Elements of the Eastern accounts are found in Ethiopian, Iranian, and Arabic texts including the Koran. (Folk-tales about Alexander, still told in the Mediterranean and Near East, originate partly from the same tradition.) There is a general unity of plot, though details vary and no composite text can be considered the true one. Alexander is fathered on Olympias by Nectanebo, last pharaoh of Egypt, disguised as the god Ammon. The narrative of the Persian expedition includes what purport to be real letters from Alexander, but is enlivened with extraordinary and often magical places, events, people, and animals. He explores the ocean depths in a diving bell, visits the Land of Darkness and the Land of the Blessed, and attempts to explore the sky in a leather bag carried by giant birds. After conquering INDIA, he visits the trees of the Sun and Moon, the palace of queen Semiramis, and the dwellings of the gods. Antipatros murders him with poison. The tales are evidence of popular tradition in the generations after Alexander, and of how different cultures reacted to and reshaped Alexander's image over many centuries. DGJS

See Stoneman, R., trs. (1991) *The Greek Alexander Romance*; trs. (1994) *Legends of Alexander the Great* (medieval texts).

Alexander Severus see SEVERUS, ALEXANDER.

Alexandria Chief city of hellenistic and Roman Egypt, situated at the west edge of the Nile delta. Alexandria was founded by ALEXANDER the Great in spring 331 BC after his return from the ORACLE at Siwa, but probably grew to significance only under PTOLEMY I, who moved the court there from Memphis. It was eventually the largest city of the hellenistic world and second only to Rome under the empire, with a population of perhaps half a million, fed by Egypt's abundant wheat production.

Though a Greek city, it was never given much autonomy by KINGS or EMPERORS and lacked a council for much of its history. Its LAWS, of which extracts survive in a PAPYRUS, were modelled on those of Athens. The population was cosmopolitan, with large Egyptian and JEWISH elements. Famously turbulent RIOTS repeatedly shook governments, and violent anti-Jewish pogroms in AD 38 were only a prelude to a bloody revolt in 66 and the uprising of 115–17, in which most of the Jewish population of Egypt was exterminated. Outside criticism (as by DIO CHRYSOSTOM) made no dent in Alexandrian self-confidence, and a bloody confrontation with CARACALLA in 216 caused enormous damage. CHRISTIAN violence destroyed the SERAPEUM in 391.

The early PTOLEMIES strove to make Alexandria the cultural capital of the Greek world, with scholars, scientists and writers attracted to the Mouseion and to the first great Greek LIBRARY. Their early success set a standard of greatness from which subsequent work inevitably seemed a decline. In the Roman period the Mouseion and library were apparently less central to the city's cultural life; the destruction of the library remains obscure, with claimants ranging from JULIUS CAESAR to the Arabs. But Alexandria was both the most vital cultural centre of hellenistic JUDAISM (where the scriptures were translated into the Greek of the SEPTUAGINT) and more generally an intellectual stronghold throughout the Roman period. From the 3rd century AD on, it naturally served as a major base of Christian teaching, polemic and scholarship.

The city's size and wealth rested in part on its function as royal court, then prefect's seat, as administrative capital, and as location of part of Egypt's military forces. VILLA and GARDEN districts, with extensive vineyards and associated POTTERY works, extended in both directions along the coast. It was also a large commercial city with two good HARBOURS on the sea, a port connected to the NILE on Lake Mareotis, and the Pharos, its famous LIGHTHOUSE. It was the main entrepôt for TRADE with the east, and its productive capacity in a variety of industries was sizeable. The ancient city lies mainly under the modern one; the tangible reality of ancient Alexandria can thus only be recovered piecemeal. Noteworthy

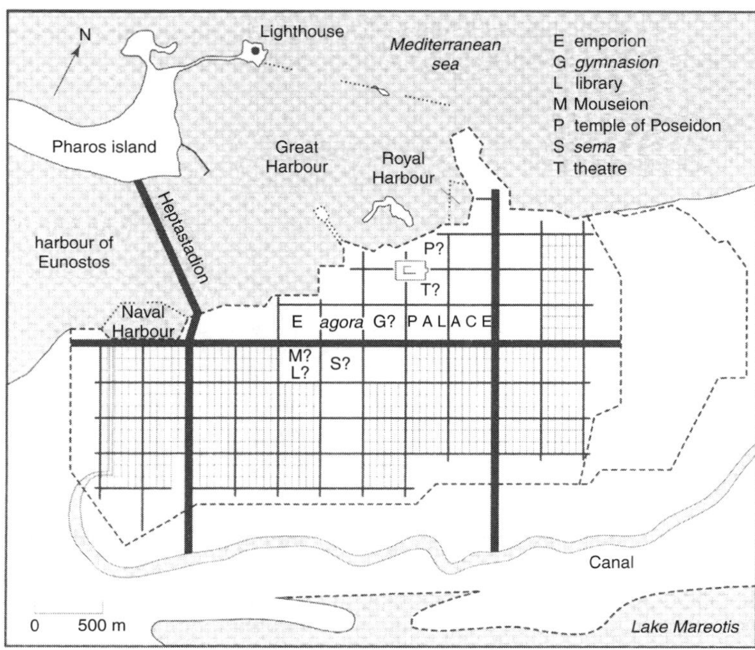

ALEXANDRIA: plan.

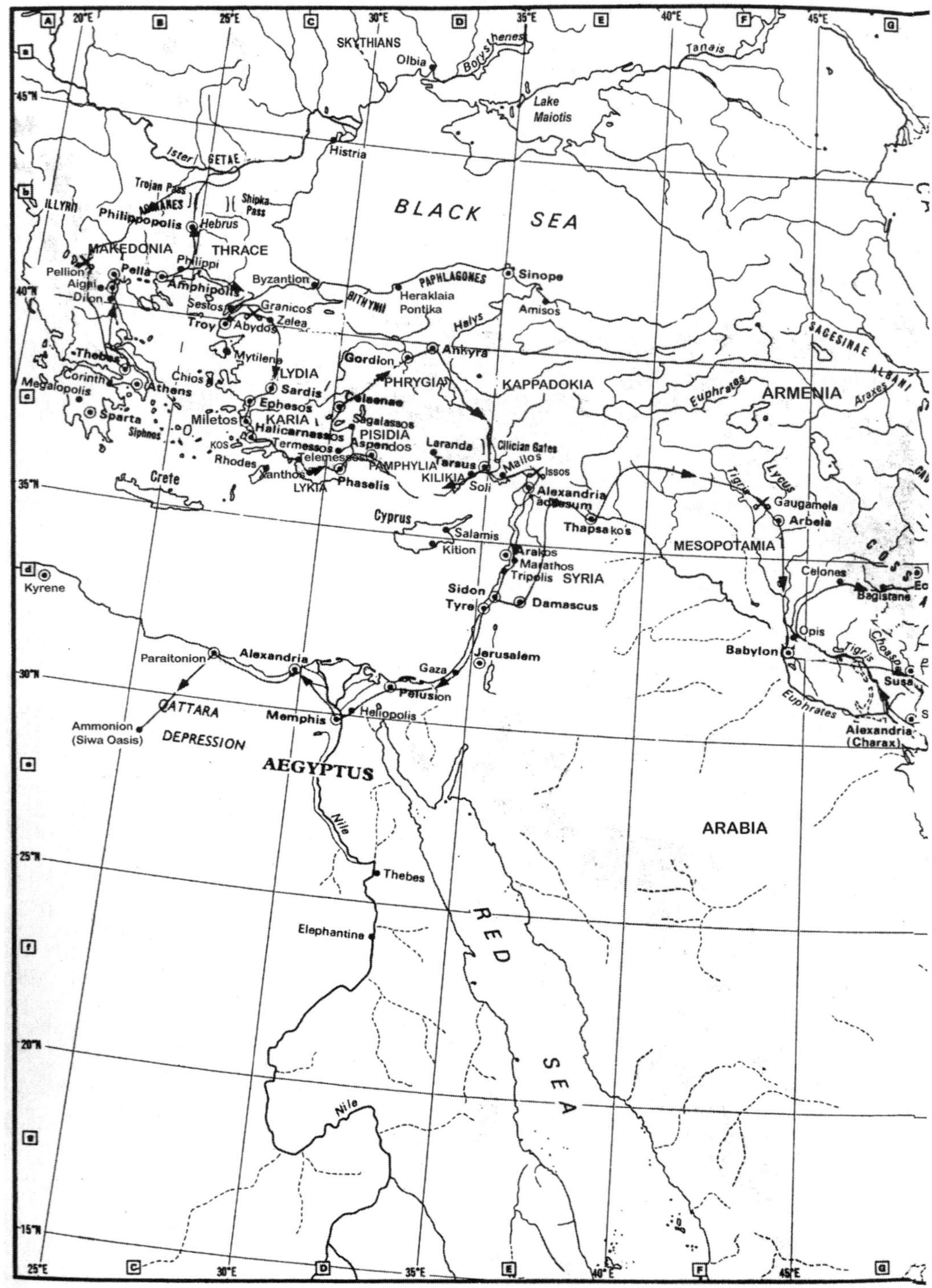

Alexander III ('the Great'): (b) map of campaigns of Alexander.

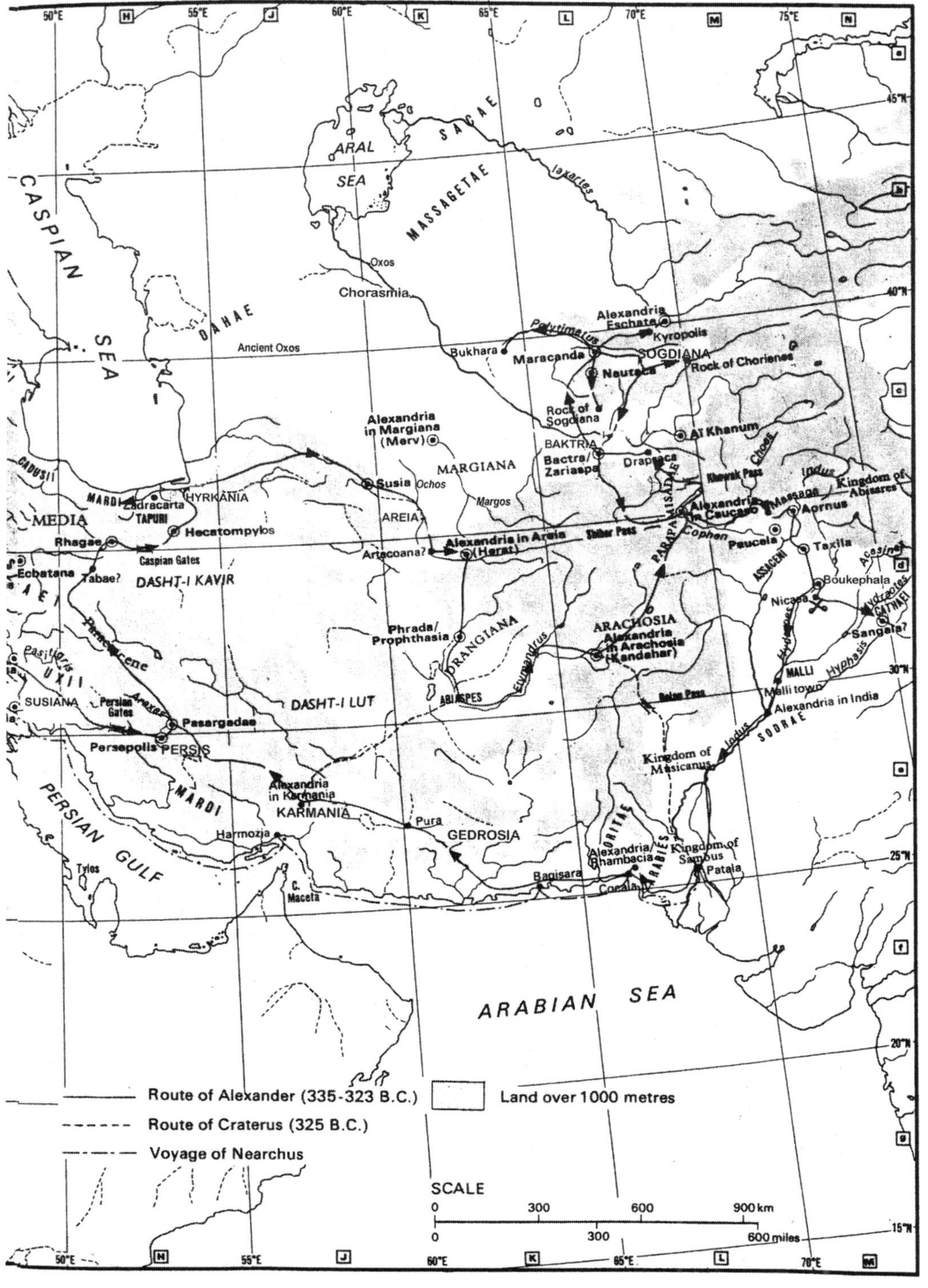
ARAL SEA
CASPIAN SEA
PERSIAN GULF
ARABIAN SEA
SACAE
MASSAGETAE
DAHAE
Oxos
Chorasmia
Ancient Oxos
Iaxartes
Alexandria Eschate
Kyropolis
Polytimetus
Bukhara
Maracanda
SOGDIANA
Nautaca
Rock of Chorienes
Rock of Sogdiana
Ai Khanum
BAKTRIA
Bactra/ Zariaspa
Drapsaca
Alexandria in Margiana (Merv)
MARGIANA
Susia
Ochos
Margos
AREIA
Alexandria in Areia (Herat)
Artacoana?
Alexandria in Caucaso
Massaga
Aornus
Cophen
Peucela
Taxila
Boukephala
Nicaea
Sangala?
CATHAEI
Hydraotes
Acesines
Hyphasis
MALLI
Malli town
Alexandria in India
SODRAE
Indus
Kingdom of Abisares
Khawak Pass
Shibar Pass
PARAPAMISADAE
ARACHOSIA
Alexandria in Arachosia (Kandahar)
Bolan Pass
Phrada/ Prophthasia
DRANGIANA
ARIASPES
Etymandrus
Kingdom of Musicanus
Kingdom of Sambus
Patala
ORITAE
ARABIES
Alexandria/ Rhambacia
Bagisara
Cocala
GEDROSIA
Pura
KARMANIA
Alexandria in Karmania
Harmozia
C. Maceta
Tylos
MARDI
PERSIS
Persepolis
Pasargadae
Persian Gates
SUSIANA
UXII
Pasitigris
Pareitacene
Araxes
DASHT-I LUT
DASHT-I KAVIR
Ecbatana
Tabae?
Rhagae
Caspian Gates
Hecatompylos
MEDIA
TAPURI
Zadracarta
HYRKANIA
MARDI
CADUSII
Choes
Route of Alexander (335-323 B.C.)
Route of Craterus (325 B.C.)
Voyage of Nearchus
Land over 1000 metres
SCALE
0 300 600 900 km
0 300 600 miles
50°E
55°E
60°E
65°E
70°E
75°E
45°N
40°N
30°N
25°N
20°N
15°N

are the housing blocks, the suburban cemeteries, the vast system of underground cisterns, and the recent underwater discoveries near the site of the Pharos and in the PALACE quarter. RSB

See Strabo 17.1.6–10; Cameron, A. (1995) *Callimachus and his Critics*; Fraser, P. M. (1972) *Ptolemaic Alexandria*; Haas, C. (1997) *Alexandria in Late Antiquity*.

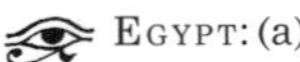 EGYPT: (a).

alimenta During the Roman empire, various programmes both public and private were established to provide food for children. Most extensive of these was the imperial *alimenta*, begun by Nerva and TRAJAN. In this scheme, the state gave loans to Italian landowners; they in turn paid annual interest, which was used to give allowances to selected children of their town. Details are preserved by tablets describing the arrangements in the towns of LIGURES BAEBIANI and Veleia. The loans were about 8 per cent of the value of the estates pledged, and the landowners paid annual interest of c.5 per cent of the amount loaned. Boys were supported until age 18, girls until 14, with the following monthly allowances: legitimate boys, 16 HS (*sestertii*); legitimate girls, 12 HS; illegitimate boys, 12 HS; illegitimate girls, 10 HS.

At least 50 Italian towns were part of this system, which lasted at least until AURELIAN but ended by the time of CONSTANTINE. One source cites the motivation for these efforts as being poor relief, but the status of the recipients is unclear, and certainly the *alimenta* were exploited for their propaganda value as imperial patronage in media such as COINAGE.

A variety of private alimentary schemes are also attested, such as PLINY THE YOUNGER's foundation for the town of Comum. GSA

See Duncan-Jones, R. (1964) The purpose and organisation of the alimenta, *PBSR* 32: 123–46; (1982) *The Economy of the Roman Empire* 288–322; Woolf, G. (1990) Food, poverty and patronage, *PBSR* 58: 197–228.

Alkaios (Alcaeus) A contemporary of SAPPHO at the end of the 7th century BC and, like her, a poet from LESBOS, and a citizen of Mytilene. These two poets wrote solo songs sung to the accompaniment of the lyre, composed in stanzas of four verses in complex metres that were later largely imitated by Roman poets. Alkaios and Sappho shared their metres and dialect, but their subject matter was very different. As in Sappho's case, Alkaios' topics often reflected his life and his political activities, marked by WAR and EXILE. Many of these poems may have been performed in *SYMPOSIA*, ritualized drinking parties hosted and attended by wealthy men, often political 'friends'. Many of Alkaios' poems are drinking songs. However, in the archaic period poetry and song were regularly used as vehicles for political discourse. His poetry also treats mythological themes, including the characters of the Trojan war (Priam, AJAX, ACHILLES, Helen) and gods (the DIOSCURI, APHRODITE), and it is not clear that these poems were symposiastic.

Many cities in archaic times saw the struggle for power of ÉLITE factions, and rivalry (*stasis*) between these rich men and the often self-proclaimed TYRANTS. This is the world in which Alkaios grew up and took active part. In his poems, he represents civic dissensions as storms at sea in which the winds blow in different directions; hence the perils of the sea become a metaphor for the evils menacing the state. The image of the state as a ship, used extensively in later classical literature, perhaps derives from Alkaios, though it is common in archaic poetry.

The contemporaries whom Alkaios mentions in his poetry, notably Pittakos and Myrsilos, were important figures in the politics of Mytilene. Alkaios had been a friend of Pittakos (later considered one of the Seven Sages), who was a former ally of Alkaios' older brother in the fight against the tyrant Myrsilos. However, according to Alkaios' vicious political invective, Pittakos assumed power and became a tyrant, in part by marrying into a prominent family. Alkaios' opposition to him resulted in his unhappy EXILE (or perhaps asylum) in a sanctuary relatively close to the city but outside the walls. The image of the cunning fox, depicting the treachery and volatility of political friendship, appears in Alkaios' works, as it does in the elegiac verse of Solon. Another poetic topic shared by many archaic poets is the fear of POVERTY, which Alkaios makes the sister of helplessness. RBC, LF

See Campbell, D. A., trs. (1982) *Greek Lyric*, vol. 1; Fränkel, H. (1973) *Early Greek Poetry and Philosophy*; Gerber, D. E., ed. (1991) *A Companion to the Greek Lyric Poets*; Page, D. L. (1959) *Sappho and Alcaeus*; West, M. L., trs. (1994) *Greek Lyric Poetry*.

 LYRIC POETRY: (a).

Alkibiades see ALCIBIADES.

Alkmaionidai (Alcmaeonidae) An aristocratic Athenian family that included several political leaders of the archaic and classical periods. In the 7th century BC the earliest known Alkmaionid, Megakles, incurred a curse that was often recalled later (see ATHENS). His grandson, another Megakles, married Kleisthenes tyrant of Sikyon and was a rival of PEISISTRATOS. The family's most famous member, Megakles' son KLEISTHENES, was probably archon in the 520s but the family was later in exile, from which he returned to oust the TYRANTS and set up the Athenian DEMOCRACY. The family was accused of pro-Persian sympathies during the invasion of XERXES, and although both PERIKLES and ALCIBIADES had Alkmaionid mothers the male line of the family produced no leading politicians after the Persian wars. DGJS

Alkman Poet at SPARTA in the second half of the 7th century BC, whose work is extant only in a fragmentary state. In one fragment, he claims descent from a family of SARDIS, but it may not be appropriate to take this too literally. Some later writers claimed he was LACONIAN in origin, and the testimony that he was a slave granted freedom because of his art is probably fictitious. Wherever Alkman was from, he resided in Sparta and composed in the Doric dialect with HOMERIC resonances, which remained the language of CHORAL poetry.

A PAPYRUS has provided a large fragment of a choral song (*partheneion*), the genre for which Alkman was best known, performed by adolescent girls at a Spartan religious festival to 'Orthria' (possibly ARTEMIS Ortheia). These songs allow us to glimpse

Sparta's rich ritual life, in which music, song and dance played a major part. In his *partheneia*, Alkman takes on the voices of these teenage girls as they show off their elaborate clothing and JEWELLERY, admire each other, and vie with one another in their beauty. The poems also seem to reflect their homoerotic infatuations and relationships with each other, similar to the love between women and girls that emerges in SAPPHO's poems. Alkman also draws imagery from local myths and the natural world. His poems offer no reference to contemporary events. RBC, LF

See Campbell, D. A., ed. (1988) *Greek Lyric*, vol. 2; Fränkel, H. (1973) *Early Greek Poetry and Philosophy*; Gerber, D. E., ed. (1991) *A Companion to the Greek Lyric Poets*; West, M. L., trs. (1994) *Greek Lyric Poetry*.

Allectus see CARAUSIUS; LONDON.

Allia see BATTLES, ROMAN; FABIUS MAXIMUS.

alliances Greek alliances were usually agreements to fight together, *symmachiai*. Frequently one member had more power than others: the Peloponnesian league was centred around SPARTA in the 6th century BC, and the Delian league around Athens early in the 5th century. Alliances were often sworn for all time; lumps of metal might be thrown into the water, and the oath taken to be binding until they floated, as at the foundation of the Delian league. Breaking an oath was considered a grave offence, though not in fact uncommon.

Roman alliances developed into a very complex network of relationships between individual states and Rome, thus reinforcing the centre's control. Alliances (*foedera*) could be 'equal' or 'unequal' depending on the extent of Roman demands and the status of the other party, and required the acknowledgement of Roman *maiestas*. Although they could be concluded by Roman commanders, they had to be ratified by the centuriate ASSEMBLY; religious aspects were supervised by the *fetiales*, and the terms were published on bronze tablets at Rome.

Alliances were an important aspect of the negotiation of power and influence in the ancient world. They were often clear indicators of power relationships; for it has been said of the Greeks, and is equally true for the Romans of the REPUBLIC, that they were unable to create institutions above the level of the city-state that were not instruments of hegemony. (see also FEDERALISM; TREATIES) CJS

alloys see COPPER ALLOYS; ELECTRUM; LEAD; METALLURGY; PEWTER; TIN.

Alpes see ALPS.

alphabets The Greek alphabet was one of the most significant innovations of the 1st millennium BC. Its development and diffusion had an impact on the introduction of the alphabet to other regions of the MEDITERRANEAN, and ultimately facilitated the transmission of classical literature from antiquity to the present.

The creation of alphabets in the Mediterranean allowed sounds and combinations of sounds to be expressed in letters. The earliest surviving evidence for the Greek alphabet dates to the third quarter of the 8th century, for the ETRUSCAN alphabet around 700 BC, and for Latin soon after. In its infancy, the Greek alphabet consisted of a related set of local or

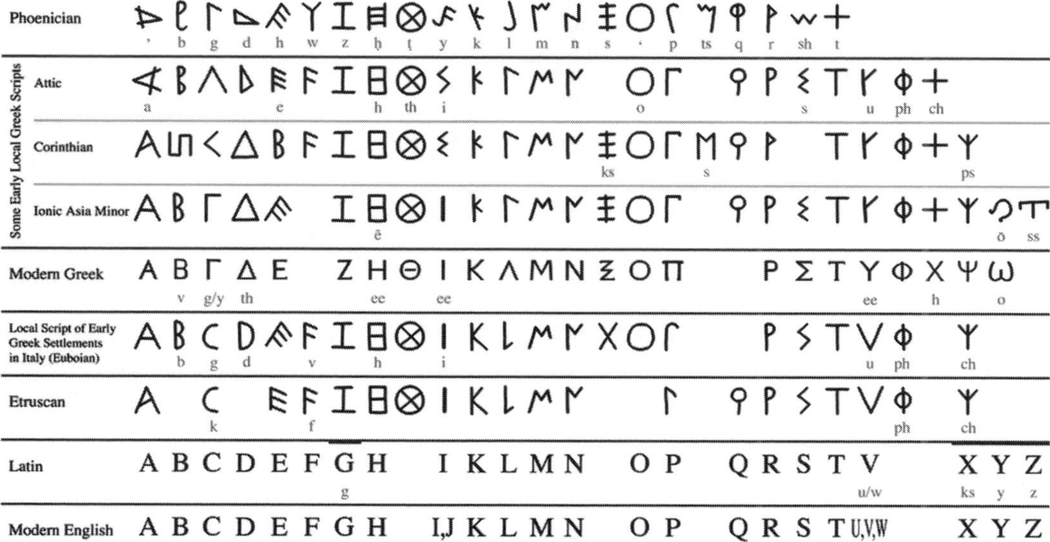

ALPHABETS: comparative chart of various Greek, Phoenician and Latin alphabets. Greeks learned alphabetic writing in Phoenicia (mod. Lebanon), using many local variations of their alphabet between the 8th and 6th centuries BC. The Etruscans and the Romans based their alphabets on those used by Euboean Greeks living in southern Italy. Our modern alphabets are based on the Roman one.

epichoric alphabets. Greek communities had slightly different versions of an alphabet that had clearly grown out of the script of 22 characters used by PHOENICIAN communities. The variations may well have reflected in some way the different TRADE movements of the Mediterranean in the archaic period.

The Greeks borrowed how the letters were written, the direction of writing (initially from right to left) and the order of letters from the Phoenicians. The term used by HERODOTOS for letters, *phoinikeia* (Phoenician things), reflects these origins; but his story that the alphabet derived from Phoenician settlers in BOIOTIA (5.58) may be mistaken. The Greeks transformed Phoenician consonants into vowel sounds (some regions used symbols for sounds not required by other parts of the Greek world) and added new letters after tau (T) for combinations of sounds not represented in the Phoenician alphabet. The Greeks translated the sound of the initial letter of each Phoenician alphabetical word into a Greek letter, and so retained the form of much of the Phoenician alphabet: aleph became alpha (A) and so forth.

The alphabet used by the Greeks from the 8th century onwards differed greatly from the earliest Greek scripts such as Linear B. That script was preserved by chance on clay tablets baked in conflagrations at MYCENAEAN towns such as Pylos, Mycenae and KNOSSOS (15th–12th centuries BC). Linear B employed a system of characters representing symbols, numbers and syllables, but not letters. No evidence at present survives to link it to the alphabet of early Greece, though the language it recorded was a form of Greek. Classical Cypriot, a syllabic script of the local Greek dialect on CYPRUS from c.600 to 300 BC, relates in some way to Cypro-MINOAN, a script known from Bronze Age Cyprus (15th–12th centuries).

Over time, the regional variety of the Greek alphabet gradually diminished but never completely disappeared. One form came to dominate the Greek world from the early 4th century: the Ionic alphabet. This was adopted at Athens as the official civic alphabet in 403/2 BC (though it appears on inscriptions well before this date). Further developments in the Greek alphabet took place in the late 4th and 3rd centuries, when more rounded letters were used. These letters, which we call cursives, were probably influenced by the widespread use of writing in ink.

Not all areas of the Greek world took up the Greek alphabet. An inscription of the late 6th century BC shows that the Lemnians retained their native language, which is still only partly understood though it is that used by the Etruscans of Italy. This may confirm the story in Herodotos (1.94) that the Etruscans originated from LYDIA. The earliest Greek inscriptions appear on Lemnos c.500.

No alphabet was known in Italy until the Greeks arrived and established colonies during the later 8th century BC. The Etruscans had borrowed their alphabet from the local script used by the Euboians who had established colonies at PITHEKOUSSAI and then at CUMAE. Etruscan, like Phoenician, was usually written from right to left. A number of the letters used in the Etruscan alphabet never appear on their inscriptions; some new ones were introduced, while further changes around 400 BC saw several letters disappear. Latin developed in Italy, borrowing from the Etruscan-influenced Faliscans. Three new letters were added to the alphabet by the emperor CLAUDIUS for sounds made by Greek letters that were not successfully reflected by the Latin alphabet; though they appear in some inscriptions during his reign, they quickly fell out of use (TACITUS, *Histories* 2.13–14).

Our knowledge of early forms of alphabets is gained largely from inscriptions. A number of early examples take the form of names on objects, statements that '*X* wrote, or made, or dedicated this', and abecedaria (where the alphabet, or part of it, has been written out). The earliest uses of the alphabet depend very much on the nature of the objects that have survived and the context in which they may have been used or placed. Graffiti continue to appear throughout antiquity and provide important evidence, particularly abecedaria. In Italy, OSCAN originated in Campania towards the end of the 5th century BC; by piecing together fragments of abecedaria, scholars have established the Oscan alphabet.

It is difficult not to underestimate the importance of the alphabetic traditions of Greece and Italy. The simplicity of the Greek alphabet allowed one character to be used for each sound. Combinations of those characters represented more complex sounds. Our modern ABC embraces a history that can be traced back through Latin and Etruscan, to the Greeks and ultimately the Phoenicians. GJO

See Easterling, P. and Handley, C., eds. (2001) *Greek Scripts*; Hooker, J.T. (1990) *Reading the Past*.

Alpheios see ARKADIA; OLYMPIC GAMES.

Alps While Rome expanded into the MEDITERRANEAN from the 3rd century BC, the Alps long remained outside direct Roman control; hence the failure to counteract the progress of HANNIBAL'S CARTHAGINIAN army in the later 3rd century, and the problems encountered by CAESAR in his Gallic campaigns beyond the Alps in the mid-1st century BC. The Italian Alps were only formally integrated by Rome after AUGUSTUS' defeat of numerous tribes in 25 BC, as recorded in his Tropaeum above Monaco and on the ARCH at Susa. Subsequently a full network of roads was established, notably the Via Claudia Augusta, enhancing the prehistoric system of trackways, leading to the major Alpine passes and linking Italy with the provinces of Gallia, RAETIA and PANNONIA. Three formal Alpine PROVINCES were created: the Alpes Maritimae (from 14 BC), the Alpes Cottiae (from the reign of NERO) and the Alpes Atrectianae (later Graiae) et Poeninae (from the 2nd century AD). Key centres such as Aosta and Susa oversaw the movement of trans-Alpine traffic into the Po valley, while sizeable settlements were established at the passes. Following the crises of the 3rd century AD, a defensive network was installed across the main routes of the eastern, Julian Alps, comprising FORTS, watchposts and barrier walls. This system, the *Claustra Alpium Iuliarum*, is depicted in the *NOTITIA DIGNITATUM* and formed part of the broader defence, the *Tractus Italiae circa Alpes*, under the command of the *comes Italiae*. The *Claustra* appear defunct by 395, however, and subsequent invasions by Visigoths, HUNS, Ostrogoths and Lombards exploited this weak north-east corridor in particular. NJC

See Pauli, L. (1984) *The Alps*.

GAUL: (a)–(b).

alum (potash) A whitish mineral salt (chemically a double salt of aluminium and potassium, or potassium aluminium sulphate), widely used in antiquity as a mordant (or fixer) in DYEING, for medicinal uses and in tanning. It was both rare and highly valued in the ancient world, particularly in TEXTILE manufacturing. In Egypt, both its production at the oases of Kharga and Daklah and its export seem to have been controlled as an imperial monopoly by the Romans. Another major source is known to have been the island of Lipara off the coast of southern Italy, and DIODORUS says that the trade enriched both the local inhabitants and the Roman state (5.10.2; cf. PLINY, *Natural History* 35.184–90). While it is difficult to trace the distribution of alum within the Roman world, AMPHORAS produced within the Lipari archipelago are widespread in the western MEDITERRANEAN. It is possible that alum powder was transported in some of these amphoras, or that these jars (perhaps produced for WINE or marine products) stand in as proxies for a traffic in the valued mineral salt. DJM

See Frank, T. (1933–40) *Economic History of the Roman World*, *s.v.* alum.

Amazons Women warriors who lived in a faraway place without men. Greek writers were never consistent about where that place was, and said the women came from PHRYGIA or LYDIA (both in Asia Minor) or even from Libya. According to 5th-century BC Greek writers such as HERODOTOS, the Amazons killed their male enemies and the sons they bore after promiscuous sex, and raised their daughters to become warriors. As opposites of the way real (Greek) women should be, refusing to stay at home and care for children, riding HORSES and fighting men, they marked out what Greeks thought barbarous. In Greek ART, from their 6th-century representation on vases through their popularity as subjects for SCULPTURE of the 5th century (e.g. on the PARTHENON) and later, the Amazons are represented as exotic, wild and fierce. Nevertheless they always lose their battles with Greeks. In this way they help to show the victory of Greek civilization over barbarism, and at the same time they suggest real victories by Greeks over such foreign enemies as the PERSIANS. The battle with the Amazons continued to be popular in ETRUSCAN and Roman art, though mainly for funerary monuments where its specific meanings have never been clear. NBK

AMAZONS: Amazons, women dressed as barbaric Scythian warriors, from an Attic vase painting.

See Herodotos 4.114; Lysias, *Funeral Oration* 2.4–6; Bothmer, D. von (1957) *Amazons in Greek Art*; duBois, P. (1982) *Centaurs and Amazons*; Tyrell, W. B. (1984) *Amazons*.

 ACHILLES: (a).

ambassadors and embassies

There were a number of criteria by which Greek ambassadors could be selected. In Athens it was by popular election in the assembly (which tended to favour the most prominent, and so the upper classes). In Sparta, though the method of selection is less clear, ambassadors still came from among the most privileged Spartan families. Connected with this, ambassadors were expected to be men of repute, and wealth was a desirable attribute (though at Athens ambassadors were among the best-paid public magistrates). PLUTARCH advises that one include a good orator among one's number on an embassy. Ambassadors could be selected because of their personal connections with the state to which they were being sent. The ambassadors on the Argive embassy sent to Sparta in 420 BC were chosen because they seemed 'most friendly' to the Spartans, and in 346 the THEBANS sent an embassy to PHILIP of Macedonia comprising his ritualized FRIENDS. Nevertheless political affiliation could also be an important factor, and the three Athenian ambassadors sent to Sparta in 372/1 possibly represented different political groups within Athens.

In Athens and Sparta, our two best-attested states, embassies generally seem to have been made up of one, two, three, five or ten men, though four-man embassies in either state are not unknown. At Athens the first step was to decide the number of envoys to be appointed, then how nominations were to be taken: whether candidates were to be drawn from all citizens, or whether there were to be limitations such as age restrictions or selection from a particular board. As a passage from AISCHINES shows, nominations could be taken from the assembly floor, and the election was conducted by a show of hands in the assembly. This process favoured the competing influences of political groups, so the pattern of appointment can show the strength of different groups at any particular time according to the number of ambassadors they managed to get appointed.

In Sparta, on the other hand, in most cases the assembly probably ratified a list of ambassadors drawn up by the EPHORS. There was evidently an attempt to maintain continuity of service between a particular ambassador and a state, so that, for example, Endios the son of ALCIBIADES is known to have represented Sparta in Athens on at least three separate missions, and Antalkidas was sent to PERSIA on four occasions. There was a clear bias towards selecting men because of their personal association with a state.

As part of the diplomatic procedure it was customary for the ambassadors to speak in order of age – as the youngest member of the Athenian embassy to

Philip in 346, Demosthenes spoke last – and each presented his own pre-prepared speech. LGM

See Mosley, D. J. (1973) *Envoys and Diplomacy in Ancient Greece.*

In the Roman, as in the Greek, world, ambassadors and embassies are not necessarily to be equated with contemporary individuals and institutions of the same name. Both ambassadors and embassies comprised individuals who were official messengers or agents sent on official missions to foreign city-states or countries. Typically these missions were set up to calm relations between discordant parties. Ambassadors were not professionally groomed for their roles, nor did they receive salaries. They may have received a small compensation to take care of any expenses that could arise. The establishment of a permanent ambassador in a given country or city-state was not the norm. More often than not, individuals were chosen because of their stature in the community rather than for their ability to negotiate. Such was the case in the famous philosophical embassy sent from Athens to Rome in 155 BC. At Rome, the SENATE was responsible for both receiving and sending out an embassy (*legatio*). The Athenian philosophical embassy, however, went beyond the regular procedure of issuing a formal plea to the senate. Instead, they pleaded their case at formal lectures.

When carrying out diplomatic missions, individuals did not act of their own accord but rather represented the wishes of their governing rulers. Embassies could be subject to unethical behaviour, namely taking bribes. To skirt such activities, individuals in the diplomatic party were not allowed to accept gifts from the host country or city; doing so could result in death. No evidence exists for ambassadors or embassies filing for immunity or inviolability. Since they were under the protection of the GODS, envoys were obligated to perform rites in honour of the host city. Often their invocations would include HEROES and gods native to both the home and host cities in the effort to achieve their goals. For example, Quintus Fabius Pictor was sent as a Roman ambassador to Delphi after the catastrophic Roman loss at Cannae in 216 BC. There, he was entrusted with finding out what measures the Romans had to take to appease the gods for their loss. He returned to Rome with instructions that if SACRIFICES were performed in honour of certain gods, battles would be won. In return, ambassadors were required to send the spoils from a victorious battle back to Delphi in honor of Apollo. The obligation was fulfilled with the victory at Mentaurus in 205 BC.

Under the empire, if problems arose in the provinces, embassies would not necessarily be sent to the governor in charge but rather directed to the EMPEROR. For example, Philo Judaeus came to Rome from Alexandria to plead a case for exempting Jews from the worship of the IMPERIAL CULT. His work, entitled *Legatio ad Gaium*, records this famous embassy before the emperor Caligula. LAH

See Gruen, E. S. (1990) *Studies in Greek Culture and Roman Policy*; Jones, C. P. (1999) *Kinship Diplomacy in the Ancient World.*

amber The fossilized resin of extinct coniferous trees. A Greek myth, recounted by Ovid (*Metamorphoses* 2.364), tells how the tears wept by the sisters of Phaeton were hardened by the sun and turned into lumps of amber. Despite the popularity of such stories, the processes by which amber was formed and its geographical distribution were known by the 4th century BC. Both the ancient sources and modern chemical analysis demonstrate that most of the amber used in antiquity came from the Baltic coast. Pliny the Elder (*Natural History* 37.45) refers to the exploration of the amber route during the reign of Nero, and Roman coins found in the area of Gdańsk show that this trade flourished well into the late 2nd century AD. The scale of the trade in amber is demonstrated by a series of three hoards found along the amber route, which have a combined weight of 2,750 kg.

Amber was valued for its magical and amuletic as well as its medicinal properties, and in the Roman period it was regarded as a high-status luxury. It was used mainly for items of personal adornment, in particular necklaces and rings, but could also be used to produce small decorative carvings as well as vases and even portrait busts. It is thought that the Italian town of Aquileia was one of the main centres of amber carving. HE

See Strong, D. E. (1966) *Catalogue of the Carved Amber in the Department of Greek and Roman Antiquities.*

Ambrose AD 339–397 Born in Trier, where his father was praetorian prefect of Gaul, Ambrose had a conventional EDUCATION and training as a lawyer that led him to become *consularis Liguriae et Aemiliae*. In 374 he became involved, in his official capacity, in the dispute between Arians and Catholics over the vacant see of Milan, and found himself proclaimed BISHOP despite not yet being a baptized Christian. Ambrose learnt quickly in his new role and established himself as a figure who awed Augustine (1) during his sojourn in Milan. The proverbial 'when in Rome, do as the Romans' has its origin in a brusque rejoinder of Ambrose to Augustine's mother, Monica, when pestered on a point of liturgical detail. In Milan things were done Ambrose's way.

Ambrose produced important religious works, such as his *Hexaëmeron* (owing much to Basil of Caesarea) and the *De spiritu sancto* (*On the Holy Spirit*), but consummate political ability defines his episcopate. Championing catholic orthodoxy, he was invariably successful in disputes with EMPERORS. In 386, adeptly mobilizing popular support, he defied an imperial attempt to dedicate one CHURCH in Milan for the use of Arians. He built a new church in celebration, endowing it with conveniently discovered relics. He also thwarted attempts to have the PAGAN altar of Victory restored to the senate house in Rome. Even that most catholic of emperors, Theodosius I, was forced to do public penance, following a massacre of some thousands of civilians in Thessalonike. Ambrose died in 397. (see also Symmachus) PMB

See McLynn, N. (1994) *Ambrose of Milan.*

Ammianus Marcellinus Late 4th-century AD Latin historian. He probably came from the local ARISTOCRACY of Antioch in Syria, though recently it has been argued that he may have come from Phoenicia. He served as an officer in the Roman army under the emperor Constantius II (337–61), and later accompanied Julian (361–3) on his ill-fated invasion of Persia. After retiring from active service, he travelled to research his *History* (*Res gestae*), ending up in Rome where he completed the work around 390. Though a Greek-speaker by origin, Ammianus wrote in Latin. Moreover, at a time when the empire was edging towards intolerant espousal of CHRISTIANITY, Ammianus was a PAGAN. Such experiences form the background to his *History*.

In its original form, the *History* covered the period from the accession of the emperor Nerva in AD 96 to the defeat of the emperor Valens by the GOTHS at the battle of Hadrianople in 378. Ammianus' decision to commence his *History* with Nerva has suggested to some that he was consciously imitating TACITUS (whose *Histories* concluded at that point). For his own part, Ammianus was emphatic that he was writing a historical narrative of an elaborate and sophisticated variety: as he laid down his pen, he enjoined any would-be successors to write 'in the grand style' (31.16.9). The work has not survived complete, however: approximately half of it is entirely lost, and the remaining 18 books begin with events in 353. This suggests that the scope of Ammianus' narrative was unbalanced, with the period of his own lifetime covered in great detail while the 2nd and 3rd centuries were given more cursory treatment. Moreover, within the surviving books the short career of Julian, particularly his Persian war, is narrated at disproportionate length.

Ammianus' narrative is the only surviving source for the 4th century AD that approaches the scope and scale of great classical historians such as THUCYDIDES and Tacitus. As such, it contrasts sharply with the blatantly partisan ecclesiastical histories which also narrate the period. Consequently, it has attracted many accolades, particularly in terms of its objectivity. More recent studies have argued, however, that Ammianus was no detached observer of his times. His writing could be vivid and exciting, such as in the account of his own experiences inside the besieged Eastern frontier town of Amida in 359 (19.1–9). Moreover, he was prone to bias, particularly in his favourable analysis of the last pagan emperor, Julian, who was his hero, and his damning portrait of the Roman aristocracy, where personal resentments may be detected. MDH

See Ammianus, trs. J. C. Rolfe (1935–40), 3 vols.; Barnes, T. D. (1998) *Ammianus Marcellinus and the Representation of Historical Reality*; Drijvers, J. W. and Hunt, D. (1999) *The Late Roman World and its Historian*; Matthews, J. (1989) *The Roman Empire of Ammianus*.

Amon-Ra (Amun, Ammon) The manifestation of the sun god Ra in Egyptian Thebes, Amun was one of the most important gods of pharaonic Egypt, the principal member of the triad of gods of the Theban region. He is first mentioned in texts of the 5th Dynasty (2494–2345 BC), but became much more important in later periods as a primeval creator god. He is portrayed in various forms, most notably as the creator Amun Kematef in Hermopolis Magna and in ithyphallic form in Thebes, closely related to Min (later associated with the Greek god PAN). His power was augmented by the fact that he was often combined with other powerful deities such as Ra. The centre of his cult was the great temple complex of Karnak.

In later periods he was known as 'king of the gods', and thus he came to be associated, under the name Ammon, with the Greek god ZEUS by the Greco-Roman period. His most notable sanctuary in this period was at the oasis of Siwa in the western desert, first mentioned by HERODOTOS. Archaeological remains within the oasis include a number of VILLAGES and cemeteries as well as several major Greek or Egyptian style monumental temples. The major oracular centre is identified with that at Aghurmi, close to an important sacred spring. In 331 BC Alexander paid his famous visit to the oasis, as reported by Quintus Curtius Rufus and ARRIAN. The visit saw his confirmation as the son of Ammon, affording him not only semi-divine status but also legitimate rule as pharaoh in Egypt. The link with Alexander added greatly to the cult's popularity and repute.

AMON-RA: Ammon, the ram-horned Libyan god of the desert, as depicted on a coin of Cyrene.

The cult of Amun had earlier spread to CYRENE, according to HERODOTOS, where Ammon represents the hellenized form of the chief god of the desert, corresponding to Amon-Ra and equated with JUPITER as well as ZEUS. From there it apparently spread to Greece, especially to Sparta, BOIOTIA and OLYMPIA. There was a tradition that the famous oracle at DODONA had a common origin with that of Siwa. Typical of the Libyan and Egyptian animalistic tradition, Ammon generally appears in anthropomorphic depictions as a ram-horned god, featuring on the coinage of CYRENE and other cities in the 5th century BC, and later on the coins of Alexander.

In the Roman period, smaller temples of Ammon (*ammonia*) are attested at Aujila and other desert locations in Libya. The cult evidently remained strong and its oracle active until late antiquity, when it is mentioned by PROCOPIUS and CORIPPUS. DJM, CEPA

See Talbert, R., ed. (2000) *The Barrington Atlas of the Greek and Roman World*; Watterson, B. (1984) *The Gods of Ancient Egypt*.

amphiktiony, amphiktyony see DELOS.

Amphiktyony, Delphic see DELPHI.

amphitheatre A building usually elliptical rather than circular in plan with an oval arena, completely surrounded by seating, a structure almost exclusively associated with the Romans. GLADIATORIAL

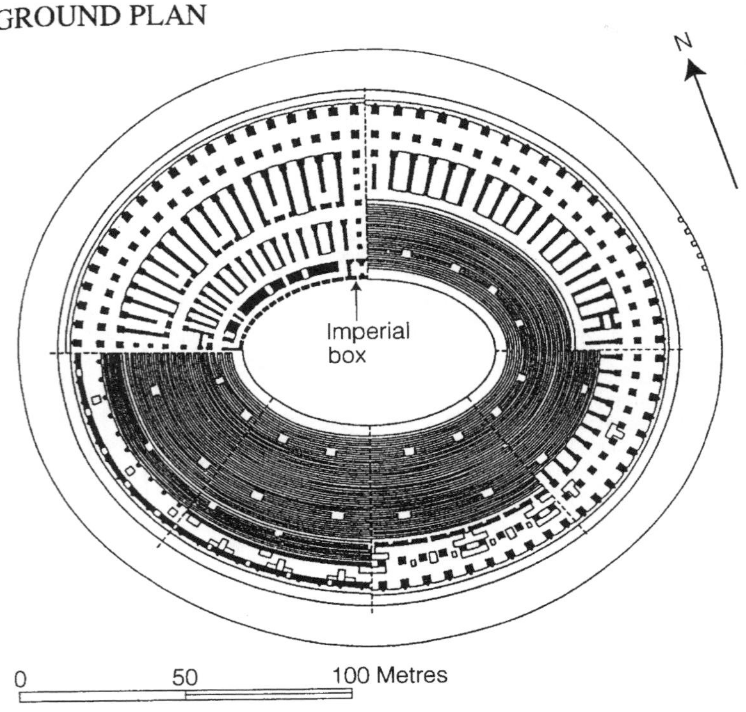

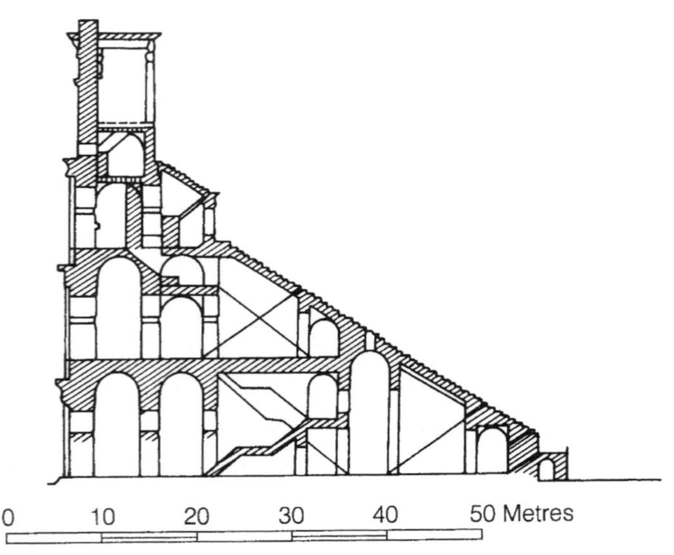

AMPHITHEATRE: (a) plan and cross-section of the largest Roman amphitheatre, the Colosseum in Rome.

GAMES, ANIMAL fights, and sometimes aquatic displays involving the introduction of water into the arena were held in the amphitheatre. In the Republic, amphitheatres were temporary and of wood. The earliest closely datable, permanent amphitheatre was built at POMPEII soon after 78 BC, but other amphitheatres in Campania, which survive in only a fragmentary state, are likely to be as early as c.120 BC. In Republican Rome, temporary wooden seating was erected in the FORUM Romanum, and the first permanent amphitheatre was constructed by Titus Statilius Taurus, dedicated in 30 or 29 BC and destroyed in the fire of AD 64. The Flavian amphitheatre, or Colosseum, was dedicated in AD 80 and was the largest in the Roman world. This structure influenced the construction of many others (e.g. El Djem,

AMPHITHEATRE: (b) the Colosseum, as depicted on contemporary coinage.

Nîmes, Italica), built up on substructures of radial and annular vaulted corridors to facilitate access and circulation. Many smaller amphitheatres were either cut into the natural rock (e.g. Sutri, Cagliari) or formed from simple earth mounds with a MASONRY retaining wall. Surviving evidence indicates that many amphitheatres were provided with awnings (*velaria*) over all or part of the audience (e.g. the Colosseum and those at Pula, Nîmes and Arles).

Amphitheatres were particularly common in AFRICA and the Western PROVINCES. A development particularly characteristic of the north-western provinces is a combined amphitheatre and THEATRE (e.g. Les Arènes, Paris). In the East, there are far fewer amphitheatres (e.g. CORINTH, Pergamon, CAESAREA MARITIMA and Scythopolis), but other entertainment buildings were either adapted to accommodate gladiatorial and HUNTING displays or built with a joint function in mind (e.g. the theatre at ARGOS and the stadium at APHRODISIAS). HD

See Bomgardner, D.L. (2000) *The Story of the Roman Amphitheatre*; Golvin, C. (1988) *L'Amphithéâtre romain*; Welch, K. (2004) *The Roman Amphitheatre from its Origins to the Colosseum*.

 GAMES: (a); GARAMANTES: (a); GLADIATORS: (a)–(b); HUNTING: (a); RIOTS: (a).

amphora A large, two-handled jar was called *amphoreus* by the Greeks, *amphora* by the Romans. The majority of amphoras were made for the transport and storage of WINE, though in the classical Greek world many were used for OIL, preserved FISH and pitch. XENOPHON in his *Anabasis* relates how the Mossynoikians kept 'slices of dolphin salted away in jars' (5.4.28). Roman traders imported and exported amphoras filled with perishable products like olive oil, wine, fruit, fish sauce (*garum*), tuna, olives, honey, lard, eggs and spring water, as well as inedible commodities such as paint, unguents, pitch and COSMETICS. The shapes of these Roman amphoras indicated what was in them: tall and slim for wine, globular or round-bellied for olive oil, and hollow-toed for fish sauce.

Amphoras came in many variations of the standard two-handled shape, but all had a mouth narrow enough to be corked, two opposite vertical handles, and a knob or tapering end on the bottom half which served as a third handle, most useful when pouring out liquid. A more practical flat bottom, which would have allowed the amphora to stand, would have given no leverage when pouring. When the jar needed to be held upright, wooden, ceramic or metal stands could be used, or the amphora inserted into a hole in the ground. For storage and transport, amphoras would have been stacked together, and images of ordered rows of amphoras are familiar from Mediterranean SHIPWRECKS.

Under normal circumstances amphoras would have tended to accumulate, so the problem was solved by reuse. Some became funerary urns; others, with a section cut from the side, served as coffins for infants. HERODOTOS tells us (8.28) how during a military campaign the PHOKIANS dug a massive pit across a mountain pass and filled it with empty amphoras before covering it up and disguising their efforts. When the enemy CAVALRY charged, their unsuspecting HORSES smashed through the empty jars and broke their legs. During the Roman period, the chief secondary use of amphoras was in construction. Broken fragments were cemented together and used in walls, foundations, piers and breakwaters. The Romans also discovered that empty amphoras, when embedded in ceilings or placed under THEATRE stages or speaker's platforms, improved acoustics.

In classical Greece, each wine-producing region manufactured its own unique and distinctive shape of amphora for transporting wine to distant markets (local wines would have been delivered in skins). Many of the handles were stamped with the name of the producer or licensed manufacturer – something like today's *Dénomination d'Origine Contrôlée* – some mark of standard capacity and most likely a price. Dates on stamps may have served to identify the age of a special vintage.

The shaping and marking of these jars make them valuable evidence for classical trade and the routes travelled by merchants. Large numbers of stamped handles are excavated annually from ancient dumps and fills as, being the most resilient part of the jar, they are virtually indestructible. The dated stamps provide invaluable evidence for the dating of archaeological contexts. John Camp, in his 1986 book on the ATHENIAN AGORA, was able to say that over 20,000 amphora handles had so far been catalogued from the site, and that 870 whole jars were held in the excavation storerooms. A standard amphora carried approximately 32 litres (7 gallons), and according to the orator Hypereides (*Against Philippides*) an amphora's worth of water in the water clock was specified as an agreed time limit for a speech in the LAWCOURT. (see pp. 46–7) CK-B

See Garlan, Y. (1983) Greek amphorae and trade, in P. Garnsey et al., eds., *Trade in the Ancient Economy* 27–35; Peacock, D. P. S. and Williams, D. F. (1982) *Amphorae and the Roman Economy*; Whitbread, I. K. (1995) *Greek Transport Amphorae*.

 POTTERY, ROMAN: (b).

Ampurias (Emporion; Empúries) see ARTILLERY; IBERIA (2); SCULPTURE.

Amun see AMON-RA.

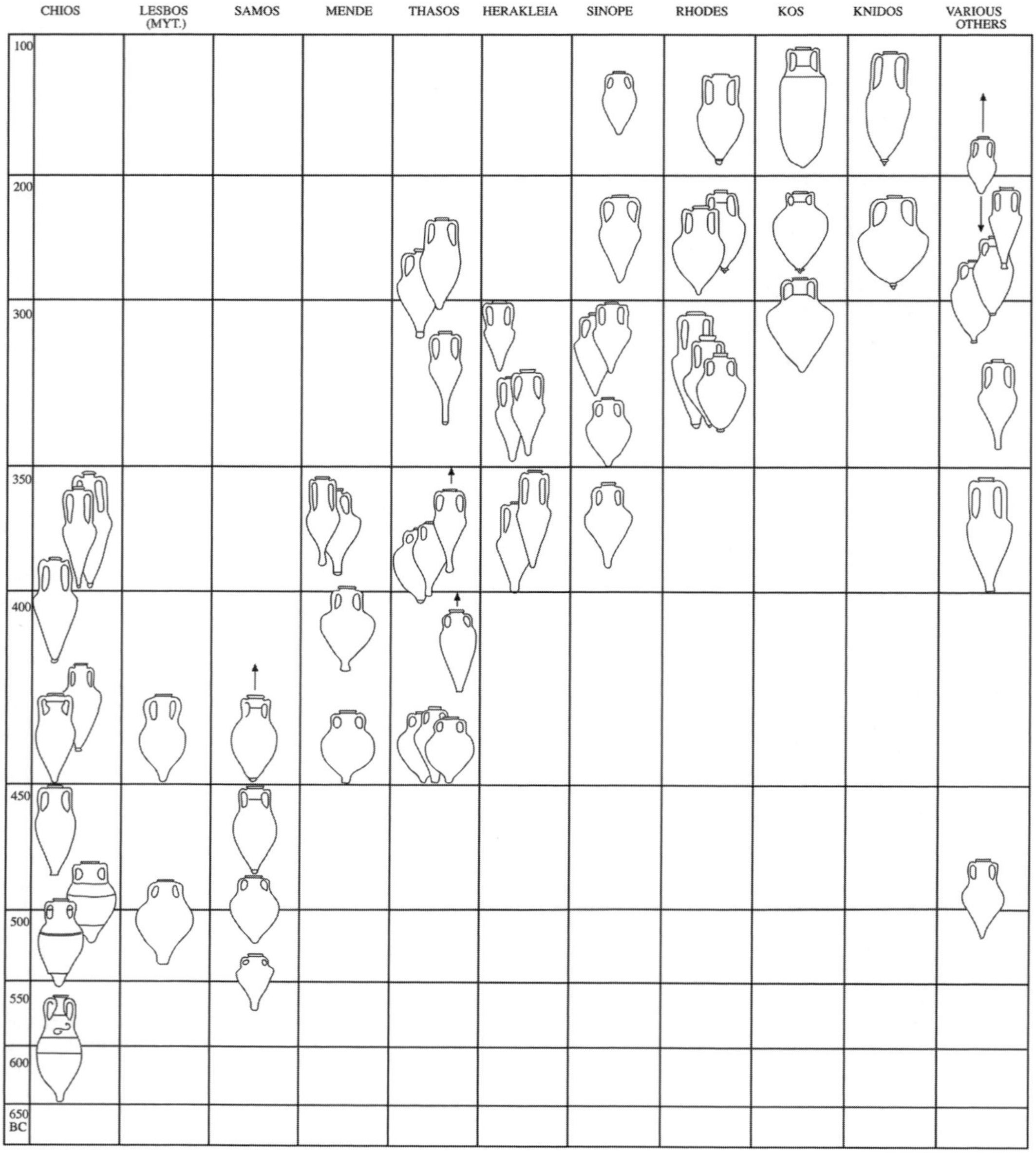

CHIOS LESBOS (MYT.) SAMOS MENDE THASOS HERAKLEIA SINOPE RHODES KOS KNIDOS VARIOUS OTHERS

100 200 300 350 400 450 500 550 600 650 BC

AMPHORA: (a) some common Greek amphora types arranged by area of origin and date (all dates are BC).

Anakreon and Anacreontea see ELEGY; LYRIC POETRY, GREEK; POETRY, GREEK.

Anatolia A land mass comprising the northern part of the eastern MEDITERRANEAN world, ancient Anatolia is roughly equivalent to modern Asiatic Turkey. The predominant vegetation is deciduous FORESTS, with subtropical woodlands on the alluvial plains of IONIA and CILICIA, grasslands on the inner plateau, and coniferous forests in the north-east. Much of Anatolia has a Mediterranean CLIMATE, with hot dry summers and a winter rainy season. It was inhabited by humans at least as early as the 7th millennium BC, as is evident from many sites, including the Neolithic Çatal Höyük. The dominant RIVER in central Anatolia was known to Greeks as the Halys ('Salt River'). The Hittites called it Marassanta or Marassantiya, which means the 'Red River' (as does Kizil Irmak, the modern Turkish name). The heartland of the Bronze Age Hittite empire was located within the great bend of this river. The Taurus mountains separated Anatolia, except for Cilicia, from SYRIA and the Amanus mountains.

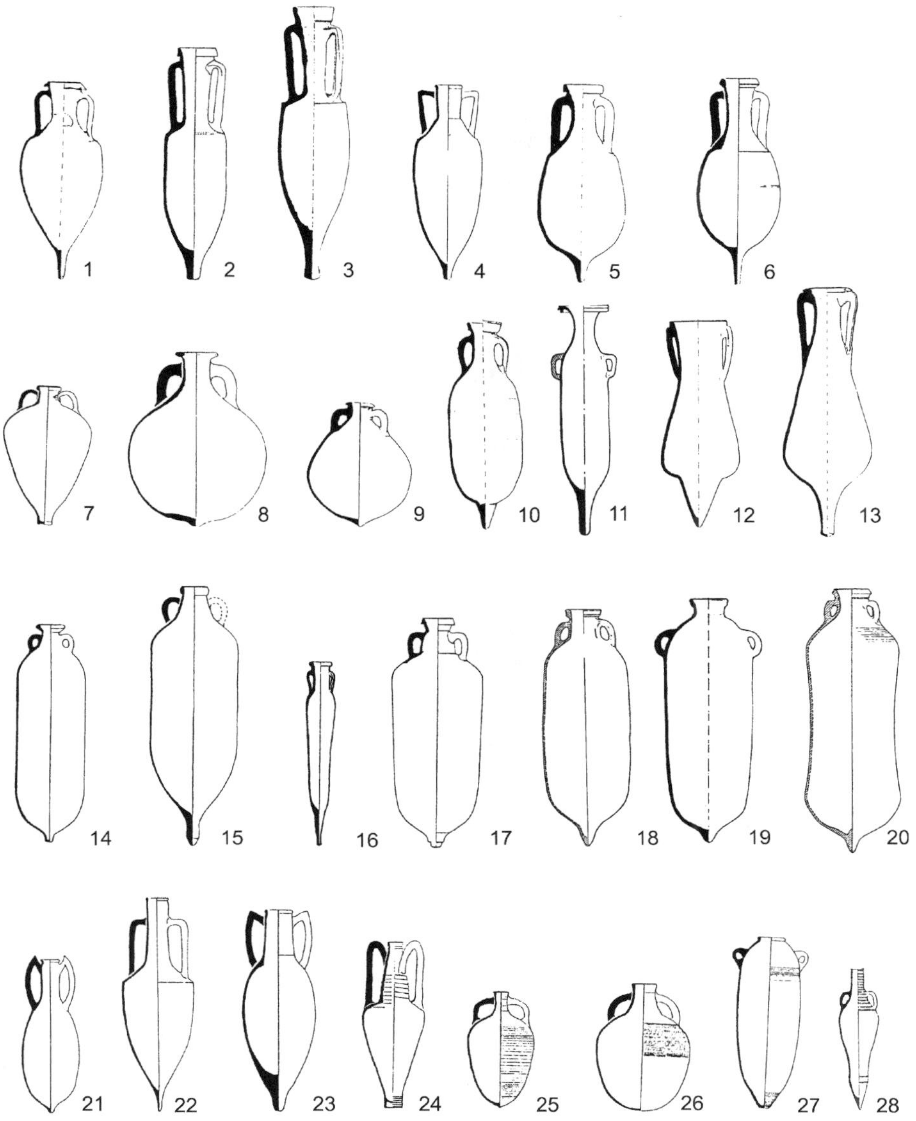

AMPHORA: (b) some common Roman amphora types. 1. Greco-Italic; 2. Dressel 1A; 3. Dressel 1B; 4. Dressel 2–4; 5. Lamboglia 2; 6. Dressel 6 (1–6 all Italy); 7. Gauloise IV (France); 8. Dressel 20; 9. Dressel 23; 10. Haltern 70; 11. Dressel 18; 12. Beltran IIA; 13. Beltran IIB (8–10, 12–13 Spain); 14. Africana 1; 15. Africana 2; 16. 'Spatheion'; 17. Keay 62; 18. Tripolitania 1; 19. Tripolitania 2; 20. Tripolitania 3 (11, 14–20 Africa); 21. Cretan; 22. Chian; 23. Rhodian; 24. Kapitan 2; 25. Late Roman 1; 26. Late Roman 2; 27. Late Roman 4; 28. Late Roman 7 (21–8 Aegean and Eastern Mediterranean).

The geographical term Anatolia was not used by early Greeks and Romans, and is no earlier than the 3rd century AD. ASIA Minor, essentially equivalent to Anatolia, is first used as a geographical term by PTOLEMY OF ALEXANDRIA in the mid-2nd century AD. HERODOTOS has no name for this specific area. For him the inhabited world consists of Europe, Asia and LIBYA (4.36–45), with Asia extending much further east than Anatolia proper. He distinguishes between Upper (1.95) and Lower (1.72) Asia, divided by the Halys river. To the river's west were Upper Asia and the Lydian kingdom, while to the east were Lower Asia and the kingdom of the Medes. (see p. 48) JDM

See Georgacas, D. J. (1971) *The Names for the Asia Minor Peninsula*; Yakar, J. (1991) *Prehistoric Anatolia*.

ASIA, ROMAN.

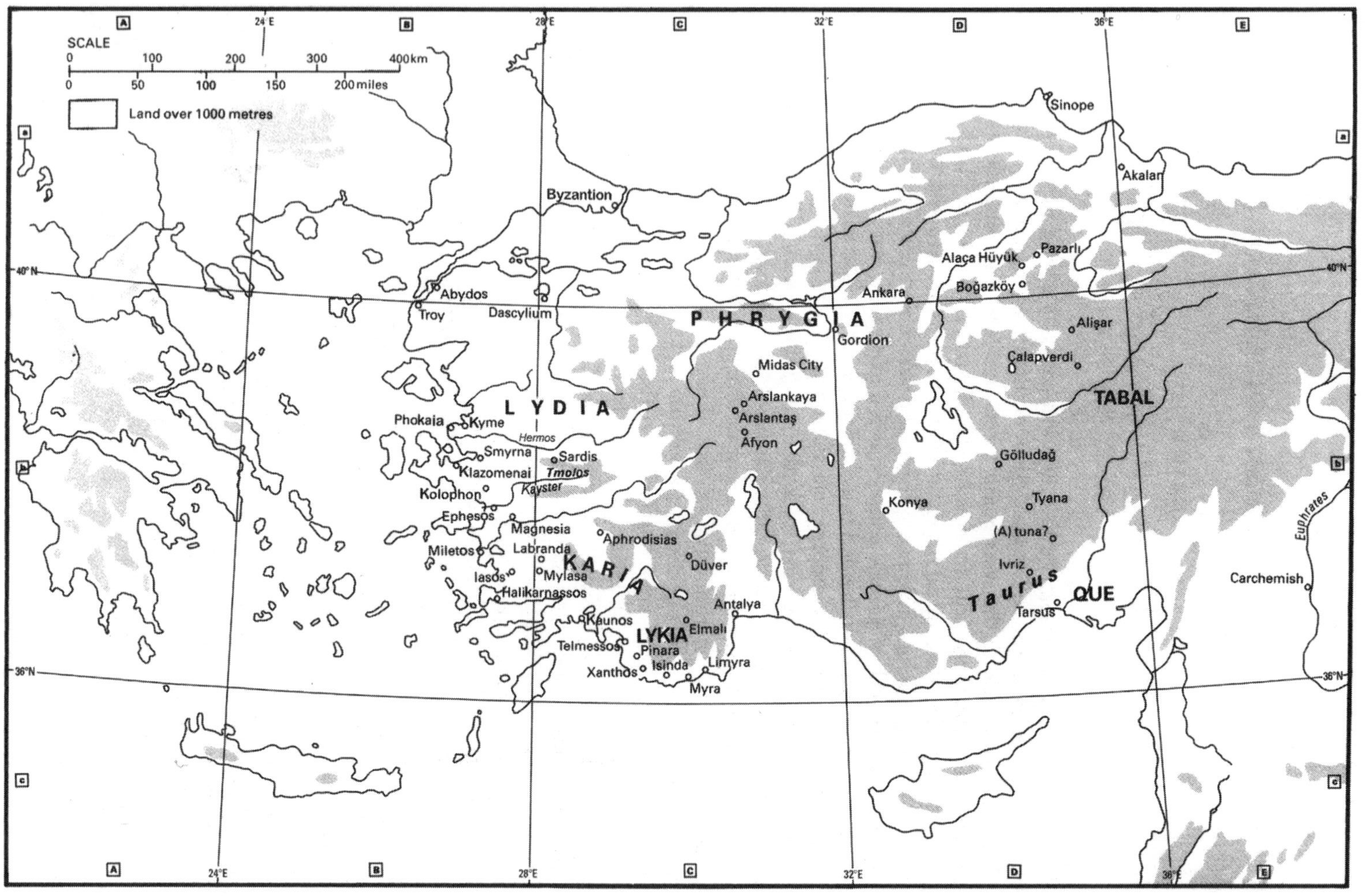

Anatolia: map.

Anaxagoras see PRESOCRATIC PHILOSOPHY.

Anaximander see PRESOCRATIC PHILOSOPHY.

Anaximenes see PRESOCRATIC PHILOSOPHY.

ancestor worship A feature of many ancient societies and incorporated into formal aspects of Greco-Roman RITUALS and FESTIVALS. Two basic tendencies can be identified: superstitious fear of malevolent ghosts who needed propitiating, and solicitous remembrance of ancestors to ensure their continued support for the living. In the Roman period, the former tendency was represented by the festival of Lemuria (held on three non-consecutive days in mid-May) and involving the *paterfamilias* in midnight wanderings through the house, spitting beans from his mouth and mumbling incantations in order to quiet the restless souls of malevolent spirits. Happy remembrance and honouring the dead were most closely associated with the Parentalia and Feralia between 13 and 21 February. This was the time for visiting FAMILY tombs outside the towns and for placing offerings at graves – often specifically linked to direct appeals for the continued support of the 'parent god'. Ancestor worship was taken even further in some other ancient societies. The LIBYANS, for instance, were known to sleep at the tombs of their ancestors in order to receive revelatory dreams (Herodotos 4.172; Mela 1.8.45). The presence of 'incubation' chambers attached to some tombs reflects this divinatory aspect of ancestor cult. DJM

See Scullard, H.H. (1981) *Festivals and Ceremonies of the Roman Republic.*

Andromache Wife of the Trojan prince HEKTOR and daughter of the CILICIAN king Eëtion from the city of Thebes. Her whole family perished by the hand of ACHILLES when he captured Trojan Thebes during the first years of the TROJAN WAR (*Iliad* 6). Yet her sufferings at the hands of the Achaians, and particularly the family of Achilles, did not stop there. Her husband, Hektor, meets a cruel death in a duel with Achilles (*Iliad* 22); her infant son, Astyanax, is hurled from the walls of Troy by Neoptolemos, Achilles' son, soon after the fall of the city. She is then carried to the Achaian ships as the war booty of Neoptolemos, who takes her home to Phthia as his slave and concubine.

The unfortunate fate of Andromache as mother and wife is illustrated in high emotional overtones by the tragedian EURIPIDES in his play *The Trojan Women*. There her virtues as a loyal and sensible wife are dramatically exploited to the full, particularly by contrast with HELEN, her anti-ideal counterpart. Andromache attracts the admiration of Trojan women, notably Hekabe (Hecuba), her mother-in-law. The latter part of her life in Neoptolemos' court is related in Euripides' *Andromache*, which tells how the heroine, who bore Neoptolemos a son, aroused the rage of his childless wife Hermione who threatened her with death. After Neoptolemos' death Andromache was returned to Hektor's brother, Helenos, in EPIRUS, later ending her wanderings in Mysia (Pausanias 1.11.1). EP

See Touchefeu-Meynier, O. (1981) Andromache I, in *LIMC* vol. 1, 767–74.

animals In the classical world, animals feature prominently in life, culture, literature and the visual arts. Naturally, many species provided food, as well as other products and by-products including clothing and adornment, for the human population. Some varieties were put to service as beasts of burden and TRANSPORT for military, commercial and agricultural purposes. Others were hunted or provided entertainment: in the wild, on game reserves, at private parks and ZOOS maintained by wealthy individuals including many Roman EMPERORS, and in the arenas – the last especially during the Roman imperial period. Specific animals were associated with particular deities, and not a few served religion in a quite different form, as SACRIFICIAL victims. More fortunate members of many species were kept as PETS, including dogs, which were used to guard houses and livestock and were bred for HUNTING.

The earliest detailed classification of animals is in several works of ARISTOTLE, including *Researches into Animals*, *Parts of Animals*, and *Generation of Animals* (also known by their Latin titles *Historia animalium*, *De partibus animalium* and *De generatione animalium*). His work remains highly important for zoologists, because his classifications remain the basis for modern work. Naturally, the availability of a wider range of specimens and scientific equipment, among other factors, has led to modifications and addition of detail. To some considerable extent, the tenacity of Aristotle's classifications is the result of his thorough and solid research; in part, however, the static nature of scientific thought in

ANIMALS: realistic depiction in a Roman mosaic from Tunisia of non-ferocious beasts being hunted in the arena.

Western Europe through the medieval period, evident in other areas of SCIENCE, contributed to the permanence of Aristotelian research as the basis for subsequent study. PLINY THE ELDER, in his *Natural History*, devotes much attention to different categories of animals, but in general terms his work is more descriptive, less scientific, and significantly less accurate. He presumably had opportunities to view animals not indigenous to Italy in shows at Rome, and was thus able to report from first-hand experience. AELIAN relates many stories in his treatise *On the Nature of Animals*, but in essence he does so to draw philosophical morals; his treatments are not without science, but are not truly scientific.

The archaeological record preserves many parts of ancient animals, but complete specimens are rare except in unusual circumstances. Numerous sites yield discarded BONES and to a lesser extent other body parts. While earlier archaeologists often ignored animal remains, modern excavators carefully collect bone and other remnants. Study of these permits conclusions about DIET and other features of ancient life not always so easily obtained from literature and art even when they survive. To take a single example: careful study of animal remains can illuminate the relative proportions of different animal products used as food, whereas written descriptions of elaborate dinners usually reveal only that specific animals were served, and can sometimes mislead since they tend to record the more luxurious activities of an upper class at its most outlandish, as in PETRONIUS' *Trimalchio's Dinner*. Where soil and other conditions permit, combs and other utensils of bone or horn, as well as hides and external coverings like wool or hair, used as raw materials for a myriad of uses, are preserved. In addition to data about the products themselves, these remains reveal much about the animal life in and around human populations.

Most information about animals, however, derives from literature and art, where they appear with great frequency. A few written works are devoted almost entirely to an animal or animals, like funerary poems commemorating pets or FABLES employing animals to draw particular morals. Authors also mention animals often. A description of a military campaign, for example, will reveal the presence of horses and pack animals, while NOVELS and other works may mention pets, describe hunts, or refer to the animals and animal products served as food. The moving encounter between the returning Odysseus and his old dog, Argos (*Odyssey* 17.290–327), confirms that real affection could exist between humans and working animals. Frequently, historians and other writers of the Roman imperial period mention the number and variety of animals slaughtered in the arenas during celebrations and games. The count is sometimes immense: TRAJAN celebrated his victories with 70 days of games and shows, at which some 11,000 animals were killed. On such occasions, the success and renown of the games were partly measured by the presence of exotic beasts; writers mention rhinoceroses, hippopotamuses, giraffes, ELEPHANTS, lions, tigers, leopards, cheetahs, bears (including in one instance, it seems, a polar bear) and many others. Generally, the appearances of animals in written works are not designed to provide scientific information, but are most often casual notices in the course of a narrative, simply part of the development of a story both in fiction and non-fiction. These notices allow modern observers to glean much information about animals and attitudes to them in the ancient world.

The visual arts devoted much attention to animals. Sculptors, whether in relief or in the round, fashioned likenesses of many species in terracotta, bronze and marble among other media. Some images were employed as religious votives; many were purely decorative, sometimes recalling a favourite pet. Similarly, VASE-PAINTERS depicted a rich variety of fauna, real or mythical, on decorative and functional pottery. WALL-PAINTINGS and MOSAICS abound with animal life; while scenes from mythology are frequent, so too are vignettes of nature, images of hunting, and many other activities that include animals, domestic and wild.

Animals were equally, or even more, important to the human population of classical times than in the modern world. Most information derives from evidence that was not specifically designed to provide data to future generations. Nevertheless, much is known, and further study will no doubt reveal more. (see also AGRICULTURE; BUTCHERY; IVORY; PASTORALISM; SHEPHERDS) JV

See Green, M. (1992) *Animals in Celtic Life and Myth*; Pellegrin, P. (1986; trs. A. Preus) *Aristotle's Classification of Animals*; Toynbee, J. M. C. (1973) *Animals in Roman Life and Art*; White, K. D. (1970) *Roman Farming*.

 MILLS AND MILLING: (a); PETS: (a).

***Annales* Maximi** see FABIUS PICTOR; MUCII; PROSE.

***Annales* school** This 20th-century French historical movement sought to turn attention away from the conventional approaches that emphasized above all the political dimension of history ('great events and great men'). The *Annales* historians (named after their journal *Annales: économies, sociétés, cultures* or *Annales ESC*) aspired to 'total history', utilizing a wide range of sources and integrating the approaches of historical geographers, sociologists and economic historians. They have stressed the importance of *la longue durée* (long-term structures of society and landscape) as opposed to *conjonctures* (medium-term structural changes) and *évènements* (short-term changes and events). One of the most notable exponent of these approaches was Fernand Braudel, and overall the influence of the *Annales* school has been profound, though narrative political history still remains a vital part of historical enquiry in France and elsewhere. The approaches of the *Annales* tradition have been found to be particularly suited to the nature and chronological coarseness of much archaeological data, especially that from FIELD SURVEY, where long-term trends in rural settlement, economy and society are investigated. DJM

See Bintliff, J., ed. (1991) *The Annales School and Archaeology*; Braudel, F. (1973) *The Mediterranean and the Mediterranean World in the Age of Philip II* [of Spain]; Knapp, A. B. (1992) *Archaeology, Annales and Ethnohistory*.

Annobal Tapapius Rufus A prominent citizen of LEPCIS MAGNA in the reign of AUGUSTUS, illustrative

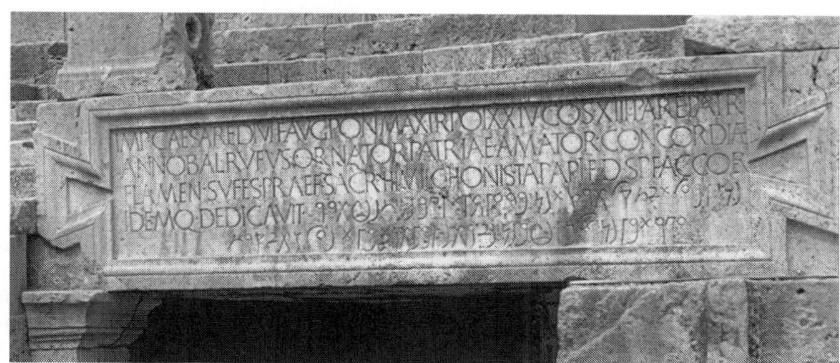

ANNOBAL TAPAPIUS RUFUS: bilingual inscription in Latin and neo-Punic recording his donation of the theatre at Lepcis Magna (AD 1–2).

of the role of Libyphoenician aristocrats in the acculturation of the province of Roman AFRICA. Annobal's Roman-style *tria nomina* and his togate statue from the city's FORUM both attest to his close affinity with Rome. They cannot, however, disguise his Punic cultural roots, a point emphasized by the fact that his building activity at Lepcis Magna was recorded in both Latin and neo-Punic texts. Annobal paid for the erection of the town's MARKET in 8 BC and its THEATRE in AD 1–2, and he was a *flamen* (priest) of the IMPERIAL CULT. It may seem ironic to find a man called 'Hannibal' at the forefront of promoting the integration of a Punic town into the Roman world, but his inscriptions stress his role as a patriot and benefactor of his home city (*amator patriae, ornator patriae*). Other members of the Tapapii family were also active in dedicating buildings and serving as urban MAGISTRATES and PRIESTS during the 1st century AD, though the family name disappeared by the end of this period with the acquisition of Roman CITIZENSHIP. What we glimpse here is the strongly pragmatic convergence of interests of provincial ÉLITES with those of the Roman state. DJM

 LEPCIS MAGNA: (a); MARKETS: (b).

anthropology From its origins in the late 19th and early 20th centuries, anthropology, the study of human cultures and their diversity, has been inspired by the classical world. At this time the educated élite of Europe came face to face with societies in Africa, Latin America and Asia completely different from their own, through the colonial and imperial policies of European governments. As part of the process of trying to understand them, they looked to their classical training and found that many of the 'strange' institutions and practices they met appeared to have parallels in the ancient world. Henry Maine (*Ancient Law*, 1861) believed that he found some features of the earliest Roman laws, the TWELVE TABLES, in the indigenous legal systems of Africa. James Frazer (*The Golden Bough*, 1890) attempted to link religious rituals from a wide array of world cultures, including Greece and Rome. The inspiration was not entirely one-way: early 20th-century classicists such as Jane Harrison (*Themis*, 1912) and A. B. Cook (*Zeus*, 1914–40), studying Greek and Roman religion, embraced the work of Frazer. Familiarity with the classics influenced the perspective even of those anthropologists who were not explicitly trying to draw such parallels, as demonstrated by the title of the classic 'ethnography' (detailed anthropological account based on the experience of living in another society) *Argonauts of the Western Pacific* by B. Malinowski (1922).

From these origins, a long tradition has developed in classical scholarship of drawing upon the ethnography and social theory generated by anthropologists to find useful analogies for explaining how the societies of classical antiquity worked. *The Black Hunter* by P. Vidal-Naquet (1981) explains the rituals and rites of passage associated with young men in ancient Athens through the structuralist anthropological theories originating with C. Levi-Strauss. S. Price in *Rituals and Power* (1984) draws upon the post-structuralist thought of P. Bourdieu (*Outline of a Theory of Practice*, 1977) to explain why the cities of Asia Minor seem, at least in their public inscriptions, to have embraced Roman rule so enthusiastically. L. Llewellyn-Jones, in *Aphrodite's Tortoise* (2003), compares the situation and lifestyles of women in classical Greece to those of women in traditional Islamic societies, arguing that in ancient Greece women were regularly fully veiled, especially in public. Academic fashions change, and it is all too easy to 'borrow' out-of-date elements from another discipline, or to use analogies in an uncritical or inappropriate manner. The world of classical antiquity was in many ways very different from the kinds of societies from which most classicists draw their anthropological parallels, and no societies exist in the modern world that are quite like ancient Greece and Rome. However, the critical use of anthropology is now well-established practice in classical scholarship. When, as in the examples cited above, scholars use the theories and insights drawn from ethnography to construct carefully controlled analogies, they offer an effective tool for creating new perspectives on the classical world. LF

See Humphreys, S. C. (1978) *Anthropology and the Greeks*.

Antigone Mythic daughter of OEDIPUS and Jocasta; sister of Ismene, Eteokles and Polyneikes. She is best known from the eponymous TRAGEDY by SOPHOKLES. The play traces the activities following the Theban war, in which both of Antigone's brothers have died in sibling combat. Her uncle, Kreon, the new Theban king, has proclaimed that Polyneikes' body should remain unburied, but Antigone is absorbed with giving her brother a proper burial and flaunts the edict. She is arrested, but proudly defends her loyalty to her brother. Despite the protestations of Haimon, Kreon's son and Antigone's prospective husband, she is condemned to death by being confined in a sealed-up tomb. Finally the prophet Teiresias declares that the GODS are angry at the sight of Polyneikes' exposed corpse, which is subsequently interred. Unfortunately this news arrives too late for Antigone; she is discovered hanging by her waist-sash from the roof of the TOMB. In despair, Haimon kills himself, as does Kreon's wife, Eurydike.

Antigone also appears in Sophokles' *Oedipus at Colonus*, leading her blind father into exile, and in EURIPIDES' *Phoenician Women*, though her mythology predates her appearances in Athenian tragedy. The strength of character she displays in Sophokles' play has made her a popular heroine in subsequent reworkings of her story since the Roman period. Among many later versions of this play, she is the heroine of Traetta's opera *Antigona* (1772) and Anouilh's *Antigone* (1944). Sophokles' *Antigone* is still one of the most regularly performed plays of the Greek canon. LL-J

See Steiner, G. (1984) *Antigones*.

Antigonids Macedonian royal dynasty (294–168 BC), founded by Antigonos I Monophthalmos; the first SUCCESSOR to assume the royal title (in 306 BC; along with his son DEMETRIOS POLIORKETES), he exercised a decisive impact on the development of hellenistic KINGSHIP. He and his son undertook an ultimately futile struggle to rule Asia and the eastern MEDITERRANEAN. In 294 BC Demetrios Poliorketes ascended to the Macedonian throne, taking advantage of dynastic struggle. He died in 283, in the course of his final bid for Asia. Under Antigonos II Gonatas (277–239) and his successors, Antigonid foreign policy largely focused on control of Greece proper through garrisons and favourable regimes; two naval victories over Egypt secured Macedonian control of the AEGEAN.

Demetrios II's reign (239–229) was marked by continuous warfare both in southern Greece as well as in Macedonia. Antigonos III Doson (229–221) restored peace and established a Hellenic league that operated successfully first against Sparta and later, under PHILIP V, against AITOLIA and its allies (SOCIAL WAR, 220–217). Philip V's (221–179) operations in the ADRIATIC and his alliance with HANNIBAL led to an indecisive war with the Romans (215–205). His subsequent operations against PERGAMON and RHODES, allies of Rome, led the latter to declare war (200–197); as a result Philip was confined to Macedonia, and Rome assumed the role of protector of the Greeks. Philip's successor, Perseus, claimed this role for himself and a third war broke out. The dynasty, as well as Macedonian independence, came to an end with Perseus' defeat at the battle of PYDNA in 168 BC. IK

See Shipley, G. (2000) *The Greek World after Alexander*.

 MACEDONIA: (b).

antimony see COSMETICS; GLASS AND GLASS-MAKING.

Antinous According to CASSIUS DIO, Antinous was born in Bithynium in Bithynia-Pontus, probably in AD 110–12. His charm and good looks made him Hadrian's boy-favourite (*paidika*). In 130, he accompanied HADRIAN to Egypt, where the emperor and his entourage visited many important sites and cities. After they had reached the city of Hermopolis in Middle Egypt, Antinous drowned in the river NILE. Popular rumours surrounded his death, holding that it was a simple accident, that he gave his life for Hadrian, or even that he was offered as a SACRIFICE. Whatever the truth, Hadrian was devastated and sought to honour him. He founded the city of Antinoöpolis, based on a Greek constitution but with many Roman features. According to Dio, Hadrian set up statues of Antinous throughout the empire. The emperor also claimed to have seen a star which represented him. Perhaps it was this mystery, and Hadrian's interest in mystical arts, that persuaded him to encourage a cult devoted to his favourite, along with FESTIVALS and other honours. A continuing fascination with Antinous resulted in the production of a huge amount of statuary celebrating his beauty and divinity, much of it in an Egyptianizing style. CEPA

See Lambert, R. (1984) *Beloved and God: the story of Hadrian and Antinous*.

 TRAJAN (stemma).

Antioch (Antiocheia; mod. Antakya) Hellenistic and Roman city in the north-west of ancient SYRIA (mod. south-east Turkey). A SELEUKID royal capital and a principal city of the Roman MEDITERRANEAN, Antioch was founded as a royal capital (in 300 BC according to the 6th-century historian Malalas) by SELEUKOS I Nikator and named after his father Antiochos. Its importance ensures that much of its history and topography are known from ancient literature. Excavations were conducted there by Princeton University (1932–9). However, the depth of fill over the site hampered excavation, and much of the work was on suburban VILLAS and their MOSAICS rather than the heart of the ancient city. Antioch was established on the left bank of the Orontes, under Mt Silpius, where the fortified *akropolis* lay. The site was an important intersection of land and water routes close to MOUNTAINS and to the fertile plain around the Orontes and its lake. The city expanded in the hellenistic period to incorporate new quarters, on a nearby island in the Orontes and on the lower slopes of Silpius. Its wealth and importance meant that it became equipped with a full range of elaborate Greek and Roman public buildings, some known from fragmentary archaeological recovery (for example, the CIRCUS on the island) as well as from literature.

The political importance of the city continued after POMPEY's acquisition of Syria as a Roman PROVINCE in 64 BC. It was the seat of the provincial governor and a base for campaigns on the Eastern frontier, visited regularly by the EMPEROR. There are vivid descriptions, for example, of TRAJAN's time in the city in AD 115, when it was devastated by an EARTHQUAKE (CASSIUS DIO 68.24–5) and of JULIAN's difficulties there in AD 362–3 (AMMIANUS MARCELLINUS 22.10–14; Julian's own *Misopogon* or *Beard-Hater*). Antioch survived temporary demotion at the hands of SEPTIMIUS SEVERUS and at least one sack by the PERSIANS in the mid-3rd century AD to remain not only one of the greatest cities of the late Roman world, but also one of the best documented, thanks in particular to the details of municipal life preserved in the speeches of the rhetorician LIBANIUS. Its role in the Persian wars of the 6th century AD, including another sack in 540, is described by PROCOPIUS.

The city was always cosmopolitan. In Libanius' day the city was visited by the Syriac-speaking PEASANTS of the rural hinterland. A substantial JEWISH community existed in the hellenistic and Roman periods, and there was an important early CHRISTIAN community. As in other major cities of the ancient world, religious, doctrinal and political disputes regularly led to well-documented PERSECUTIONS of one group or another, rioting and clashes between circus factions.

Antioch came under Arab control in AD 637–8 and had a long subsequent history. It had declined drastically by the 18th century, but has grown again since then. NDP

See Downey, G. (1961) *A History of Antioch in Syria*; Grainger, G. (1990) *The Cities of Seleukid Syria*; Liebeschuetz, J. (1972) *Antioch*.

 CITIES: (b); SYRIA, ROMAN: (a).

Antiochos I of Commagene see COMMAGENE.

Antiochos I, II, IV see SELEUKIDS; SELEUKOS I; STRATONIKE; SYRIAN WARS, OF PTOLEMIES; see also JEWS, JUDAEA; MACCABEES, REVOLT OF.

Antiochos III ('the Great') c.252–187 BC Hellenistic king. Antiochos acceded to the throne of his father, Seleukos II Kallinikos (r.241–226), when his own elder brother Seleukos III Soter Keraunos was murdered in 222 after a brief reign. His military success against the insurrections of Achaios in Asia Minor and Molon in Media established his rule, while the fourth Syrian war against Ptolemy IV led to a defeat at Raphia in 217 and the loss of southern Syria. However, in a great *anabasis* ('march inland') from 212 to 205, Antiochos reconquered most of what the SELEUKID kings had once owned in the East (the so-called 'upper satrapies'), including Commagene, ARMENIA, PARTHIA and Baktria. Diplomatic links with INDIA, now under the Maurya dynasty, were renewed. Success in the fifth Syrian war against Ptolemy V added Koile Syria, PHOENICIA and JUDAEA to the empire. Antiochos' conquests and his successful reorganization of the territories, his economic policy and his establishment of a RULER CULT for the empire justify the contemporary title 'the Great'.

From 196 Antiochos won over many Greek cities in southern and western Asia Minor, refounded Lysimacheia on the European side of the HELLESPONT, and established links to mainland Greece. In 192, encouraged by the AITOLIANS and HANNIBAL, he invaded Greece in spite of the inevitable clash with the Romans and their allies, notably PERGAMON and RHODES. He was defeated by them in 191 at THERMOPYLAI and in 190 at Magnesia in Asia Minor. The peace of APAMEIA in 188 forced him to give up the western parts of the Seleukid empire in Asia Minor to the west and north of the Tauros range, and stipulated a massive reduction of military power as well as heavy indemnities. Antiochos is said to have been killed when trying to rob a temple in Elymais. However, he stands out as one of the great conquerors and organizers of the hellenistic world. KB

See Ma, J. (1999) *Antiochos III and the Cities of Western Asia Minor*; Shipley, G. (2000) *The Greek World after Alexander*.

antiquities and antiquarianism Antiquities are monuments or artefacts dating before the Middle Ages and belonging geographically to Greece and Rome. An antiquarian was an individual who used an unscientific or pre-scientific approach to digging up antiquities, and typically paid out heavy sums of money from his own pocket to do so. Antiquarianism prevailed between the 16th and 19th centuries, yet it can be argued that there is still a strong interest in it today. In its early stages during the RENAISSANCE, travellers interested in antiquities set out to Greece and Italy in the hope of recovering fine *objets d'art*. This recovery took the form of either the EXCAVATION or acquisition of classical art. In 1738, thanks to the findings of the Spanish military engineer Rocque Joaquin de Alcubierre, the interest in antiquities magnified. Commissioned by king Charles III of Naples to excavate HERCULANEUM, he blasted tunnels that led into the ancient city. De Alcubierre and his men picked artworks that would later become the core collection of the Museo Archeologico, Naples. Later, antiquarians emphasized the cataloguing of material evidence and the creation of typologies to establish relative dates. Antiquarianism conceptually set out to examine both the progression of natural history as well as the role of ETHNICITY in material culture. Gradually the focus began to shift to include non-Western peoples. LAH

See Fagan, B. M. (1999) *Archaeology: a brief introduction*; Trigger, B. G. (1989) *A History of Archeological Thought*.

Antonine Itinerary (*Itinerarium Antoninianum*) A series of itineraries covering all regions of the Roman empire at it stood at the end of the 3rd century AD. Divided into regional subdivisions, which are often titled, the itinerary lists named stations along routes, giving distances between them in Roman miles. Such organization of information was widespread in the Roman world: the so-called *Elogium* of Polla and an inscription from Tongres record similar information. The itinerary begins at the Pillars of HERCULES (Straits of Gibraltar) and proceeds in a counter-clockwise direction, beginning from Mauretania, including a single itinerary from Rome to Hiera-Sykaminos in Egypt, and finishes with a section devoted to BRITAIN.

The structure of the work is not uniform. Rather than being a general itinerary, some sections seem to record specific journeys, with more detailed local information. The route from Rome to Hiera-Sykaminos is often considered to be the centrepiece onto which other routes are pegged, and is perhaps related to a journey made by CARACALLA in AD 214–15. But the origin and development of the work are difficult to ascertain, as this route also contains information of TETRARCHIC date. Most likely the work is the final version of an itinerary tradition that had developed over time; this may explain the complicated conflation of information. The *Antonine Itinerary* is probably based on publicly displayed lists of stages and distances, but interesting questions surround its relationship to the *cursus publicus* and to later annotated and pictorial itineraries. Its origins probably lie not in theories of GEOGRAPHY, but in the experience of TRAVEL. CEPA

See Adams, C. E. P. and Laurence, R., eds. (2001) *Travel and Geography in the Roman Empire.*

Antonine wall Constructed in AD 142–3, and named after ANTONINUS PIUS, the wall runs east–west over a distance of 60 km (37 miles) across the island of BRITAIN from the river Forth at Bo'ness to the river Clyde at Old Kilpatrick. It consisted of a stone foundation course 4.2 m (15 Roman ft) wide, topped by a rampart of laid turf. In front, on the north side, was a broad V-shaped ditch measuring up to 12 m wide and 3.5 m deep, with an upcast mound beyond. Construction work was shared by detachments of the LEGIONS II Augusta, VI Victrix and XX Valeria Victrix. A series of FORTS, ranging in size from 0.5 to 2.6 ha (1.2–6.4 acres), built in two phases, together with mile-fortlets and some lesser structures, held the resident garrisons. A metalled ROAD, the Military Way, linked the forts. The occupational history of the wall is imperfectly understood: many of the forts saw only a single phase of occupation, and may have passed out of use c.AD 155. Less certainly, a second phase, beginning c.158, saw reduced garrisons in fewer forts until the early 160s AD, with limited coin evidence suggesting some later activity on the Forth–Clyde line up to c.AD 180, by which date Roman forces had withdrawn from Scotland to the line of the Cheviots. LK

See Glasgow Archaeological Society (1899) *The Antonine Wall Report*; Hanson, W. S. and Maxwell, G. S. (1983) *Rome's North-west Frontier*; Macdonald, G. (1934) *The Roman Wall in Scotland*; Robertson, A. S. (2001) *The Antonine Wall.*

 BRITANNIA: (a).

Antoninus Pius (Titus Aurelius Fulvius Boionius Arrius Antoninus) Born on 19 September AD 86 and ADOPTED by HADRIAN after the death of his intended successor, Lucius Aelius Caesar, Antoninus was given tribunician power on 25 February 138, and succeeded Hadrian on 10 July. He ruled until his death on 7 March 161. Before AD 120 he had married Annia Galeria FAUSTINA, who bore him four children, two sons and two daughters, three of whom (both sons and one daughter) died before Antoninus' adoption. Prior to Hadrian's death, and at his bidding, he adopted two more sons, who would become the emperors MARCUS AURELIUS and Lucius Verus. He was accorded the title Pius by the SENATE for his insistence upon the deification of Hadrian.

Antoninus was in many ways the polar opposite of his predecessor. Whereas Hadrian wandered the empire, Antoninus did not leave ITALY in the course of his reign. While Hadrian had a fearsome temper and a difficult relationship with the senate, Antoninus was noted for his mild disposition and was well liked in senatorial circles. Although the garrison of BRITAIN extended its zone of control north of HADRIAN'S WALL (constructing the ANTONINE WALL), he otherwise appears to have pursued a passive foreign policy. He is said to have resisted offers from neighbouring peoples who wished to place themselves under Roman rule, on the grounds that they could not afford the garrisons he would have to deploy. The long peace that obtained in most of the empire during his reign promoted the extension of imperial culture and prosperity, and in provinces such as ACHAIA he was honoured with countless altars. DSP

See Birley, A. (2000) *Marcus Aurelius.*

 EMPERORS, ROMAN: (a); TRAJAN (stemma).

Antony, Mark b.83 BC Roman statesman and GENERAL, Mark Antony is one of the most famous and romantic figures of antiquity. In his youth he served in the CAVALRY in Palestine and Egypt before joining JULIUS CAESAR in GAUL. He fought at Caesar's side at PHARSALUS in 48, and in 44 enacted an important role at the Lupercalia when he offered Caesar the diadem of rulership. Following Caesar's assassination, Antony became part of the TRIUMVIRATE with Lepidus and OCTAVIAN. He defeated Cassius and BRUTUS at PHILIPPI in 42, and took over the governance of Rome's Eastern empire.

In 41 he met CLEOPATRA VII at Tarsus and began his romantic and political liaison with the queen. She bore him twins, Alexander Helios and Cleopatra Selene, before political tensions in Rome forced Antony to marry Octavian's sister Octavia who bore him two daughters, both named Antonia (the Elder and Younger). By 36 he was back in Egypt, having scorned Octavia and roused her brother's anger. A hostile propaganda campaign at Rome was further fuelled by the defeat of Antony's expedition against PARTHIA in 36. Cleopatra, who married Antony according to Egyptian rites, bore him another son, Ptolemy Philadelphos, in 36, and together the couple began a campaign to expand Cleopatra's territories. At the 'Donations of Alexandria' in 34, Antony ceded Roman territories to Cleopatra and her children. Open hostilities between Antony and Octavian came to a head at the NAVAL BATTLE of ACTIUM in September 31, resulting in a defeat for Antony's forces. He fled back to Egypt and finally committed SUICIDE in August 30, shortly before Octavian arrived in ALEXANDRIA.

Handsome and strong, Antony had a reputation for hard drinking and riotous living. He was immortalized by Shakespeare in *Julius Caesar* and *Antony*

ANTONY, MARK: coin portrait of Antonia, daughter of Mark Antony.

and Cleopatra and by Richard Burton's portrayal of him on film in *Cleopatra* (1963). LL-J
See Southern, P. (1998) *Mark Antony*.

AUGUSTUS: (a).

Antony, St see ATHANASIUS.

anxiety see WORRY.

Apameia (Apamea) Hellenistic and Roman city in SYRIA, founded by SELEUKOS I Nikator c.301–299 BC on the site of an existing MACEDONIAN settlement, Pella. The site is eminently defensible, just north of Seleukos' frontier with the PTOLEMAIC kingdom. Strabo records it as a Seleukid military headquarters, with the royal stud and war ELEPHANTS.

After the Roman annexation of Syria, Apameia retained its military importance, as a fortress during the civil wars of the 40s BC. Though some distance west of the Roman–PERSIAN frontier in later centuries, it was the winter quarters of the Legion II Parthia through the first half of the 3rd century AD. Vivid evidence for this and for the Roman army in general is provided by the many inscribed and sculpted military tombstones incorporated into later fortifications of the city. Apameia was sacked by the Persians in the mid-3rd century AD, revived somewhat later, but depopulated after the Arab conquest.

Much of the ancient (particularly Roman) topography and ARCHITECTURE remains visible or has been revealed by ongoing Belgian excavations. Notable discoveries include the (restored) great colonnade flanking the main north–south street, remains of CHRISTIAN CHURCHES and a THEATRE, and elaborate Roman private houses. Impressive polychrome MOSAICS are a particular feature of the later Roman city. NDP
See Balty, J.-C. (1988) Apamea in Syria in the second and third centuries AD, *JRS* 78: 91–104; Grainger, J. D. (1990) *The Cities of Seleukid Syria*.

SYRIA, ROMAN: (a).

Apameia-on-the-Euphrates see ZEUGMA.

apartment buildings Among the portents for 218/17 BC, LIVY (21.62) records that an ox climbed up to the third floor of a tenement before plunging from a window to its death. This is the earliest mention of the multi-storey apartment buildings (*insulae*) which became the hallmark of Rome, though they are also recorded for other major cities of the MEDITERRANEAN such as Tyre and CARTHAGE. The best-preserved examples are found at OSTIA,

APARTMENT BUILDINGS: massive vaulted structures of a Roman apartment block at Ostia – parts of three storeys still survive here.

while upstairs apartments (*cenacula*) can also be identified at POMPEII and HERCULANEUM. When first discovered in the 1920s, the Ostian *insulae* appeared surprisingly modern and were much admired as the direct forerunners of the contemporary Italian apartment building.

In Rome, the pressure on space to accommodate the vast urban population was exacerbated from the late REPUBLIC by the large amount of land occupied by public buildings and the pleasure GARDENS of the ÉLITE. The often shoddily built apartment buildings became taller, and tales of threatened or actual collapse are frequent in the sources of the 1st century BC and 1st century AD. Both AUGUSTUS and TRAJAN imposed height restrictions of 70 and 60 Roman feet respectively (20 and 18 m), and standards improved with the widespread use of CONCRETE construction after the mid-1st century AD. By the 4th century, the 200-year-old Insula of Felicula was a major landmark in Rome, famous for its extreme height and size.

A multi-storey apartment building usually offered a mixture of different types of accommodation, mostly for rent. Commercial units, typically one or two-roomed SHOPS sometimes with additional living accommodation above, occupied the main street frontages. The ground floor often also contained one or more independent residential units, while external staircases leading directly from the street gave access to separate upper-floor apartments. Large buildings were organized around an internal courtyard which provided light and ventilation to all floors. Although the evidence is limited, some *insulae* at Ostia have their own communal WATER SUPPLY and LATRINES (e.g. House of Diana).

The standard of apartments varied enormously. A typical midrange unit at Ostia might consist of four to six rooms, including a reception room, grouped around a broad hall (*medianum*). While presumably designed for a single family, this was also adaptable to shared accommodation. In some *insulae*, spacious high-class apartments occupied the ground and first floors (e.g. Insula of the Muses at Ostia). Though lacking the traditional atrium or peristyle, these had large vestibules and richly decorated reception rooms suitable for the entertainment of CLIENTS and friends. They were available for long-term rent or were owner-occupied. In the absence of lifts (elevators) and piped water, the space at the top of the *insula* served the lower end of the market, usually single small rooms rented by the day or week, with a communal *medianum* for eating. The use of space, however, changed frequently over time, and most Ostian *insulae* show extensive signs of restructuring. JDeL

See Frier, B.W. (1980) *Landlords and Tenants in Imperial Rome*; Hermansen, G. (1982) *Ostia*.

Aphrodisias Hellenistic and Roman city in Caria (mod. Geyre in Turkey), founded as a sympolity (combined foundation) from a community of that name and nearby Plarasa. This probably took place in the later 2nd century BC, and recent resistivity survey has shown that a unified orthogonal grid plan existed from early in the city's history. Aphrodisias was the location of an important cult of APHRODITE-VENUS. In part because of JULIUS CAESAR and OCTAVIAN's family connection with Venus, Aphrodisias remained loyal to them through the civil wars. The subsequent favour shown by Octavian is demonstrated by an important series of inscriptions set up in the city, particularly in the THEATRE, emphasizing the role of Zoilos, a former SLAVE of Octavian and a citizen and benefactor of Aphrodisias. The epigraphic record from Aphrodisias is particularly rich, and extends into the Byzantine period, providing evidence for the administration of the city, its relations with Rome, provincial administration, public entertainment, and its JEWISH and CHRISTIAN communities. Excavations in recent decades have uncovered and shed more light on civic and entertainment buildings, including the temple of Aphrodite (converted into a Christian church c. AD 500), two *AGORAI*, a BASILICA, a *bouleutêrion* (council house) and a stadium. There is also the *Sebasteion*, an IMPERIAL CULT centre, decorated with spectacular SCULPTURE including imperial PORTRAITS and allegorical depictions of Roman PROVINCES. Sculpture produced by Aphrodisians is attested from Rome and elsewhere in the empire, and investigation of the sculptural 'school' of Aphrodisias has included study of a sculptors' workshop in the city itself. NDP

See Erim, K.T. (1986) *Aphrodisias*; Reynolds, J. (1982) *Aphrodisias and Rome*.

Aphrodite Greek GODDESS of beauty and erotic love. According to Hesiod's *Theogony*, she was born out of the sea-foam (*aphros*) that surrounded the genitals of the sky-god, Ouranos, after his son Kronos castrated him and threw his member into the sea. Aphrodite first emerged in the area of Paphos on the coast of CYPRUS. Another mythical tradition mentions ZEUS and Dione as her parents.

Her beauty surpassed that of any other goddess, and it was precisely this feature of her persona that shaped her divine realm. Beauty as a means of erotic seduction would eventually lead her protégés to MARRIAGE, even though Aphrodite was not a goddess of marriage, strictly speaking. Related divinities included the personifications of EROS (erotic desire), Harmonia (harmony), Peitho (persuasion) and Pothos (longing), as well as Himeros (yearning) and the divine group Hôrai (the hours).

The cult of the goddess enjoyed wide popularity at different periods in the east, notably in Cyprus (hence her Homeric epithet Kypris), Ionia and Greece proper. Her worship in coastal towns and ports reflects a further capacity of the goddess as protectress of NAVIGATION, confirmed by her epithet Euploia, 'of good sailing' (e.g. at KNIDOS and CORINTH). During hellenistic and Roman times, she came to be associated with the underworld, as PLUTARCH and DIODOROS attest, at places such as CRETE and Kenchreai near Corinth. EP

See Delivorrias, A. et al. (1984) Aphrodite, in *LIMC* vol. 2, 2–151; Pirenne-Delforge, V. (1994) *L'Aphrodite grecque*.

Apicius Several Romans bore this name, which is also applied as a title to the surviving late Roman recipe book. The most famous of the historical figures was Marcus Gavius Apicius, a contemporary of the EMPERORS AUGUSTUS and TIBERIUS. As a notorious

GOURMET he presumably took his *cognomen* from the earliest known Apicius, also famous for gluttony, who lived in Rome around 90 BC. A later Apicius, an imperial cook, devised a method for packing fresh oysters to despatch to the emperor TRAJAN while on campaign in MESOPOTAMIA in about AD 115.

According to Tacitus, Marcus Gavius Apicius had been the lover of the young SEJANUS, later infamous as minister to the emperor Tiberius. Among the legends that gathered round him was that of his journey across stormy seas to the Libyan coast in search of large and succulent prawns; as he neared the coast, the fishermen offered him nothing better than he had seen in Italy, so he sailed back without landing. According to SENECA, after calculating that his assets had fallen to 10 million *sestertii*, inadequate to sustain his luxurious way of life, he committed SUICIDE. Certain expensive dishes and techniques were named after him. He is said to have been admired by the emperors Lucius Verus and ELAGABALUS.

The only contemporary reference to a recipe book named *Apicius* occurs about AD 400. The recipe collection that is known to us may well date from that time, though dating it is difficult because in recipe books each recipe may have its own history. Some recipes are named 'Apician', others after the imperial gourmet VITELLIUS. The two early manuscripts, in the Vatican and the New York Academy of Medicine, are both 9th-century.

Apicius is written in Vulgar (colloquial) Latin and contains a high proportion of Greek loan-words. These features suggest the book's origin and readership was among literate but not fully educated people, such as staff in wealthy households. It contains some familiar Latin words in colloquial forms ancestral to those of the Romance languages, such as *amindala* (almond) and *gingiber* (ginger).

The historical importance of *Apicius* is as a clue to the elaborate cuisine of the Roman empire. It supplies recipes for certain dishes mentioned in historical texts. It confirms the importance of MEAT and meat sauces, and the use of a wide range of exotic and costly SPICES. FISH SAUCE (*liquamen, garum*) is called for in practically every recipe; this was evidently the preferred way of adding SALT to food, since salt in other forms is practically never required. Usual sweeteners are HONEY, concentrated must and dates. Other common ingredients are pepper, lovage, cumin, rue, coriander, vinegar and OLIVE OIL. Scarcely any recipes in *Apicius* specify quantities; methods are stated with extreme brevity if at all. These features suggest its use as an aide-memoire rather than a book from which one learned to cook. AD

See Flower, B. and Rosenbaum, E., trs. (1958) *Apicius*; Grainger, S. and Grocock, C., trs. (2004) *Apicius*.

Apocrypha JEWISH and CHRISTIAN texts which purport to be scripture but which are not included in the canon of the OLD and NEW TESTAMENTS. While the existence of apocryphal texts might suggest some deliberate dissimulation by their authors, it is crucial to remember that the selection of canonical books for both testaments was a surprisingly late development. As is clear from the 2nd-century BC Greek translation of the Hebrew BIBLE known as the SEPTUAGINT, the Jews had long used the texts which form the Christian Old Testament. The Jews' decision to establish a canonical list of biblical books did not come, however, until the late 1st century AD. Likewise, the formation of the New Testament was a gradual and variable process, since groups of Christians scattered across the MEDITERRANEAN disagreed (sometimes vehemently) as to what was canonical. Even today, Christian churches differ as to whether certain texts belong in the canon.

Apocryphal texts range across a wide variety of genres, reflecting trends in ancient historiography, the NOVEL, didactic manuals and apocalypses. For example, the second book of Maccabees, a polemical account of Jewish resistance to the SELEUKIDS, states that it is an epitome of a historical work by Jason of CYRENE (2 Maccabees 2.23). Thus the *Apocrypha* reflect the interaction of Judaism and early Christianity with the polyglot culture of the eastern Mediterranean in the hellenistic and Roman periods. (see also APOCRYPHAL GOSPELS) MDH

See Elliott, J. K. (1993) *The Apocryphal New Testament*; Metzger, B. M. (1977) *The Oxford Annotated Apocrypha*.

apocryphal gospels Accounts of the life of Christ other than the canonical NEW TESTAMENT gospels attributed to Matthew, Mark, Luke and John. Among the many apocryphal texts to survive are various gospels. Some are supplementary to the established canon, generally narrating events passed over in those texts, such as Christ's childhood or the mystical events which occurred between his crucifixion and resurrection. There are also apocryphal narratives, such as *The Gospel of the Birth of Mary*, concerned with personalities found in the canonical gospels. Other apocryphal gospels were meant as alternatives to their canonical counterparts. Among these are GNOSTIC versions, such as the *Gospel of Truth* and *Gospel of Thomas*. These texts are reminders that the biblical canon of four gospels was only arrived at gradually, often through acrimonious debate.

The existence of rival versions of the gospels was a central concern in Irenaeus of LYON's tirade against the Gnostics. Irenaeus also accused the Gnostics of deriving much of their material from classical POETRY and PHILOSOPHY rather than Christian scripture. Although this point is made as polemic, it demonstrates the vibrant literary culture in which the apocryphal gospels were produced. As well as drawing material from those texts later recognized as canonical, the apocryphal gospels show strong affinities with a variety of literary genres, such as ancient BIOGRAPHY and the NOVEL. (see also *APOCRYPHA*) MDH

See Elliott, J. K. (1993) *The Apocryphal New Testament*; Metzger, B. M. (1987) *The Canon of the New Testament*.

Apollo Greek GOD, son of ZEUS and Leto, daughter of a Titan. Ancient literature presents the god in a range of capacities, often conflicting with each other. Apollo is sensitive to mortal arrogance and quick to deliver justice to disrespectful mortals, such as the satyr Marsyas and the children of Niobe (OVID, *Metamorphoses* 6.385–400 and 148–315). The god can both cause plagues (as in *Iliad* 1) and be deliverer. He is also strongly linked to MUSIC and the Muses, and is frequently allied with his virgin sister ARTEMIS and his mother Leto.

Apollo appears as a well-established figure of the early Greek pantheon in HOMER, notably in the *Iliad*. In the latter, he is presented as the patron god of the Trojans with substantial oracular capacity, served by his prophetess the Trojan princess Kassandra. Divination was practised at various sanctuaries of the god in Greece, most notably at DELPHI. The appeal of the Delphic ORACLE was on a panhellenic (inter-state) scale covering Greece and beyond, and played a prominent role during the period of Greek COLONIZATION.

Apollo's other major panhellenic sanctuary on the AEGEAN island of DELOS assumed political significance during the early classical period as the centre of the defensive alliance formed by Greek states against PERSIAN threat. Further mythical associations of Apollo with Delos go back to the god's birth and early childhood on the island, recounted by three major sources, notably Homer, PINDAR and KALLIMACHOS. EP

See Lambrinoudakis, V., et al. (1984) Apollon, in *LIMC* vol. 2, 183–327.

 ARCHITECTURE: (a); DELPHI: (a); GODS AND GODDESSES: (a).

Apollodoros the mythographer Author of a work called the *Library* (*Bibliothêkê*), which may be dated, on account of its language, anywhere between the 1st and the 3rd centuries AD. The work is wrongly attributed by Photius and the *SUDA* to Apollodoros of Athens, the famous grammarian active at ALEXANDRIA in the 2nd century BC who wrote *On the Gods*.

Designed as an aid to anyone with pretensions to a culture that also indicated status, the *Library* is the most substantial handbook of MYTHOLOGY that survives from antiquity, in a single incomplete manuscript supplemented by an epitome and fragments. It presents a coherent narrative of the history of the GODS (from Ouranos to the victory of ZEUS over Typhoios) and heroic times, including the TROJAN WAR and the homecomings of the HEROES, and concludes with the death of ODYSSEUS. Like the HESIODIC *Catalogue of Women* and the *Genealogies* of Hekataios, it puts the Greek myths into chronological order by means of genealogies. According to an EPIGRAM that prefaced it in Photius' copy, it aimed to replace EPIC, LYRIC and tragic POETRY as a source for 'the tales of ancient culture'. But its author, who was no doubt familiar with HOMER, HESIOD and Attic TRAGEDY, seems to derive most of his information from existing mythographic compendia. SS

See Apollodorus, *The Library*, 2 vols., trs. J. G. Frazer (1921).

Apollodoros the orator 4th-century BC Athenian orator. Seven of the speeches included among the works of DEMOSTHENES were delivered by Apollodoros, and it is now widely thought that they were composed by him. Apollodoros was born in 394 BC, the elder son of Pasion and Archippe. Pasion started out in Athens as a SLAVE, but later rose to prominence as a banker and was awarded Athenian CITIZENSHIP. Despite his father's lowly background, Apollodoros took a central role on the Athenian political stage and was very active in performing his civic duties. He was trierarch several times and chorus producer once. He also served once on the city council (349–348 BC), where he made a proposal to use surplus funds for military purposes. Stephanos prosecuted him for making an illegal proposal, and he was convicted and fined. This marked the beginning of his feud with Stephanos, which lasted throughout the 340s. Apollodoros' wife, by whom he had two daughters, was the daughter of Deinias. One of his own daughters married her mother's brother Theomnestos, who appears as the main prosecutor in Apollodoros' most famous speech, *Against Neaira*. With this prosecution, Apollodoros aimed at a combination of personal and political revenge against Stephanos, whom he accused of being married to a non-Athenian wife, Neaira, against the laws. We know nothing of Apollodoros' activities after 340 and it is uncertain when he died. FMM

See Carey, C. (1992) *Apollodoros, Against Neaira [Demosthenes] 59*; Trevett, J. (1992) *Apollodoros the Son of Pasion*.

Apollonios of Perge late 3rd century BC Apollonios is the last MATHEMATICIAN of the great creative period of Greek geometry whose work survives to any extent. He was born in Perge in Pamphylia, but also spent some time at EPHESOS and PERGAMON (presumably at the court of the kings of Pergamon, in whose territory Perge lay). Although a number of works on MATHEMATICS and ASTRONOMY are attributed to him, his major contribution to geometry is the *Kônika* (*Conics*). Of its eight books, four survive in Greek, three are preserved in Arabic translation, and one is lost. The subject of the treatise is the geometry of the parabola, the ellipse, and the hyperbola. These figures had been regarded by previous geometers as sections of different kinds of right circular cones (hence they are called 'conic sections'). Apollonios' achievement (and, despite his unwillingness to claim any degree of originality for his work, it is a substantial one) was to generate all of the conic sections from the double oblique circular cone, gaining a greater degree of generality. In its approach and conception the work closely resembles the *Elements* of EUCLID, and became for conic sections what the *Elements* was for the rest of geometry. It was the basis for all future work, and much of the terminology still used by mathematicians in connection with conic sections is derived from it. Of Apollonios' other works, only *On the Cutting off of a Ratio* survives, in Arabic translation. RW

See Heath, T. L. (1896) *Apollonius of Perga*; (1921) *A History of Greek Mathematics*.

Apollonios of Rhodes c.305–c.235 BC EPIC poet, author of the *Argonautika*, Apollonios was (from c.265) head of the Alexandrian LIBRARY under Ptolemy II Philadelphos, and tutor to his son and successor, Ptolemy III Euergetes. Other details of both his life and his career are fiercely debated. A native of either ALEXANDRIA or NAUKRATIS, he came under the influence of KALLIMACHOS, whose student he may have been. According to our ancient sources, he spent some formative years early in his career on the island of RHODES, where he taught and engaged in public affairs. The statement that this self-exile was because his first attempts at epic had met with ridicule in Alexandria tends to be discounted – perhaps wrongly – by modern scholarship. On the accession of Ptolemy III in 246, Apollonios retired and was replaced as chief librarian by the great mathematician ERATOSTHENES. The claim (made by the late Byzantine ENCYCLOPEDIA the *SUDA*, and still sometimes argued) that Apollonios succeeded Eratosthenes rather than preceding him rests on a confusion with a later Apollonios who also became chief librarian.

The *Argonautika* retells the story of Jason and the Argonauts in four books averaging 1,500 lines of hexameters – the metre of Homer. Books 1–2 cover Jason's voyage to the Black sea to recover the Golden Fleece from king Aietes, including (in book 2) the famous episode where the ship *Argo* successfully negotiates the Symplegades (Clashing Rocks). In book 3 Jason passes Aietes' tests, rounding up fire-breathing bulls to plough a field, sowing the teeth of dragons, and killing the 'earth-born' warriors that spring from the soil. To do so, Jason requires the aid of the king's daughter, Medea, and her magical powers – the more easily gained since she falls violently in love with him. In book 4 (the longest book) the Argonauts and Medea escape with the fleece, Jason and Medea are married, and make their way to Jason's home in Thessaly via Crete, where they defeat the bronze giant Talos, again with the help of Medea's magic. The poem combines an interest in the exotic and in individual (especially erotic) psychology that are characteristic of the hellenistic age.

The *Argonautika* is the only ancient epic between Homer and Virgil to survive intact. Since it owes a vast and complex debt to the first, and had a pervasive influence on the second, it occupies a crucial point in Greco-Roman literary history. Until comparatively recent times it was systematically underrated as an inferior imitation of Homer. However, contemporary studies not only of hellenistic poetics, but also of the way in which hellenistic authors such as Kallimachos and Apollonios – rather than the earlier (and in modern times more highly regarded) dramatists or lyric poets – tended to provide the models for late Republican and Augustan Rome, have radically revised critical estimates of their intrinsic value. Nor was it only young 'Neoterics' of the 1st century BC, such as Calvus or Catullus, who aspired to emulate them: Ptolemy II's court poets found their natural successors in the Augustan circle of Maecenas. The *Aeneid* owes a huge debt to Apollonios, of which Virgil's Dido, as a development of the *Argonautika*'s Medea, is only the most obvious example.

Ancient tradition reports a quarrel, probably literary, between Apollonios and Kallimachos. This is most often dismissed today as fiction, on the grounds that Apollonios in fact shares, rather than opposes, his mentor's characteristics of experimentalism, allusiveness, aetiologizing and conscious intertextuality (e.g. in the foreshadowing of the tragic end of Jason's marriage to Medea as delineated by Euripides). Yet however Kallimachean the four long books of the *Argonautika* may be in technique and language, the genre in which they are cast is still that of the cyclic epic which Kallimachos rejected. Their approach to myth in particular, with its acceptance of marvels and magic, is far closer to that of Pindar (on whose *Pythian* 4 Apollonios drew heavily) than to the fashionable rationalizing allegorical version of the Argonaut myth by a contemporary such as Dionysios Skytobrachion (summary in Diodorus Siculus 4.40–56) – one reason for its immediate, and continuing, popularity. PMG

See Green, P., trs. (1997) *The Argonautika by Apollonios Rhodios* (with commentary); Apollonius of Rhodes, *Jason and the Golden Fleece*, trs. R. Hunter (1995).

Apollonios of Tyana (usually Apollonius) A sage of the 1st century AD, much glorified by his biographer Philostratos. Few details about Apollonius are known with certainty, and even his existence is sometimes doubted. In the tradition, Apollonius was a Neopythagorean miracle-worker of prodigious activity who came into conflict with the emperors Nero, Domitian and Nerva, and encountered others. He travelled widely through the Roman empire and beyond, delivering speeches in the manner of itinerant sophists while gaining familiarity with different philosophies and religions, including Brahmanism. Like others, he was accused of misconduct and was expelled from Rome, perhaps twice. The biography is a collection of themes that usually appear in accounts of similar figures, except that the accumulation of stories, miracles and more is greater. A group of letters is of doubtful authenticity, at least in its current form, and the historicity of other writings has been questioned. He is named by Lucian, Origen and Cassius Dio among others. Julia Domna, wife of Septimius Severus, commissioned Philostratos to write the biography.

Whether he was real, imagined or something in between, Apollonius represents a common type, especially in the early empire. Later, in the reign of Diocletian (284–305), Sossianus Hierocles, an exponent of the persecution of Christians, transformed him into a pagan Jesus, to counter the growing importance of Christianity by providing a similar figure for non-Christians to revere. The attempt was neither successful nor enduring. JV

See Philostratos, *Life of Apollonius*, trs. F. C. Conybeare (1912); Anderson, G. (1986) *Philostratus*.

Apollonios the *dioikêtês* Minister in charge of the economy of Egypt, including agriculture, taxation, coinage, monopolies and commerce, under Ptolemy II Philadelphos. Apollonios is the earliest *dioikêtês* known from the Ptolemaic period, but the office, a virtual vizierate (*senti* in Egyptian), is older, perhaps a Saite innovation. Nothing is known with certainty of Apollonios' origin, patronymic, early career, wife or children, but he has been plausibly identified as the father of Aëtos (eponymous priest in 253/2) and grandfather of the Thraseas who founded Arsinoë at Nagidos; if so, he was from Aspendos. He was in office by c.261 and remained there at least until the death of Philadelphos in 246, perhaps as late as 243. His end is unknown, but his putative family's later success suggests that he did not fall in disgrace.

Apollonios was, after the king, the most important figure in the Ptolemaic government of his time, his power extending to the possessions outside Egypt and missing little of significance except the military. He was *dioikêtês* when the famous 'Revenue Laws' of Philadelphos, with taxation and monopoly ordinances, were drawn up in the form we have them (259). He accompanied Berenike and her dowry from Pelousion to the Seleukid border when she married Antiochos II Theos in 253. He is known mainly from the papers of Zenon of Kaunos, the largest surviving archive of Ptolemaic Egypt. Zenon served Apollonios' business interests, first in Palestine, then (from 258) in Egypt, setting out (spring 256) as manager of Apollonios' estate of 10,000 arouras (2,756 ha, 6,807 acres) near Philadelphia in the Fayûm until 248. It is therefore Apollonios' private dealings that are best documented: estates also in the Memphite nome, craft production, SHIPPING, and domestic and international trade. He was much interested in vines, fruit-trees and livestock. His numerous letters show an energetic, tough administrator, far-ranging but in command of every detail. He seems to have been devoted to the cult of Arsinoë II. RSB

See Edgar, C.C. (1931) *Zenon Papyri in the University of Michigan Collection.*

Appian Born in Alexandria at the end of the 1st century AD, Appian moved to Rome to pursue advocacy, gaining the rank of procurator under ANTONINUS PIUS. His life is known partly from the letters of his PATRON, FRONTO; his autobiography is lost. The structure of his extant historical work is unusual. He begins with the kings of Rome and moves through the various peoples as Rome conquered them, from the Italians to the campaigns of TRAJAN and his commanders in DACIA and ARABIA. Egypt, his home country, plays a prominent part towards the end. The result is a remarkably wide-ranging work. The accounts of the Iberian, HANNIBALIC and MACEDONIAN WARS, the wars with the SELEUKIDS, and the CIVIL WARS from the GRACCHI to the triumviral period survive.

Out of necessity Appian had to abridge, and he is not necessarily an accurate guide to what his sources wrote. In particular, he is prone to transpose his experience of his own time back into the past. His choice of material suits his own narrative and artistic interests. He does use speeches, which are clearly invented, at various points. This gives him the opportunity to show off his own RHETORICAL skills, but they are usually well motivated. More conscious and insidious manipulation is to be found in the emphasis on Egypt, and also in Appian's own obsession with the dangers of civil war. A loyal subject of the Roman empire, he laments both the Roman collapse in the late Republic and the failures in Egypt to avoid internal unrest. Interestingly, he may have been involved somehow in the great Jewish revolt of AD 115–17 when he escaped from some JEWS into the reeds of the NILE.

Good counsel, good luck and providence combine with virtue to ensure the Roman success. Fate may make the better side the loser on occasion, but for Appian the Romans were both consciously aiming for an empire and destined to emerge from the civil wars into harmony. He was far too pragmatic to believe that the monarchy of the first century AD was by definition the best constitution; his interest is in the systems that work best, and the qualities that preserve leaders from bloodshed.

Appian's audience was similar to himself, the well-to-do élite of the Greek-speaking PROVINCES who sought to understand the reasons behind Rome's rise to power. It should not be assumed that this interest was equivalent to uncritical devotion. Appian's real loyalties may well have lain with Egypt (it is a pity that those books of his history are not extant), and he is clear-eyed about the merits of the present situation and the mistakes Rome has made. CJS

See White, H., trs. (1912–13) *Appian's Roman History*; Appian, *The Civil Wars*, trs. J. Carter (1996); Swain, S. (1996) *Hellenism and Empire.*

Appii Claudii see CLAUDII; CLODIA; ROADS, ROMAN; ROME; VERGINIA.

Apuleius Orator, philosopher and novelist. Born at Madauros in AFRICA c.AD 123–5, Apuleius was educated at CARTHAGE, Athens and Rome, and followed the career of a rhetorician. About 156, on a journey to ALEXANDRIA, he rested at OEA, where Sicinius Pontianus persuaded him to marry his widowed mother. After Pontianus died, relatives brought Apuleius to court for using MAGIC to seduce AEMILIA PUDENTILLA into the marriage; their true concern was her estate, which was of considerable value. Apuleius answered the charge with his *Apology.* He appeals to the governor Claudius Maximus as a man of his own ÉLITE literate class and frequently denigrates, with obvious relish, the rusticity of his accusers. His central argument is that apparent magic was simply the knowledge and research interests of an educated man. Subsequently, Apuleius lived at Carthage and was revered as a philosopher and orator; he became the chief priest of the province, and received many public honours, including a statue 'To the Platonic philosopher' (the base survives). Nothing certain is known of his life after the 160s, but he may have lived into the 180s or 190s.

Apuleius is best known for *The Golden Ass* (or *Metamorphoses*), the only complete Latin NOVEL extant. Based (like the Greek *Lucius or the Ass* sometimes ascribed to LUCIAN) on a non-extant Greek work called *Metamorphoses*, Apuleius tells the adventures of a Lucius who became a donkey because of a mistake in a magical procedure. The central portion of the narrative is the story of Cupid and Psyche, told to Lucius by an old woman. From jealousy of Psyche, Venus commanded Cupid to inflame her with passion for someone insignificant. He fell in love with her himself, but visited her only after dark and forbade her to see him. One night, she lit a candle while he was sleeping, but spilled a drop of wax, waking him and causing him to disappear in anger. Subsequently, Psyche experienced a wide range of trials and tribulations, until Jupiter took pity and brought her to the heavens, where she was reunited with Cupid. The story's source remains obscure; neither Greek version has it or the concluding portion about ISIS. Though Lucius' adventures are unusual and often bawdy, the novel is a vibrant characterization of everyday life in the Roman world of the 2nd century AD.

His *Florida* (lit. 'flowers': an anthology of rhetorical excerpts) and *On the God of Socrates* are extant; the authorship of other surviving works credited to him is disputed. Lost works, on fish, trees, agriculture, astronomy, mathematics, the state, proverbs and other subjects, reveal a typical educated man of the 2nd century AD, the period of the SECOND SOPHISTIC. JV

See Apuleius, *The Golden Ass*, trs. E.J. Kenney (1998); Apuleius, *Rhetorical Works* (includes *Apology, Florida, On the god of Socrates*), trs. S. Harrison, J. Hilton and V. Hunink (1994); Millar, F. (1981) The World of the *Golden Ass*, *JRS* 71: 63–75; Tatum, J. (1979) *Apuleius and the Golden Ass.*

Apulia see ITALY, ROMAN.

Aquae Sextiae see BATTLES, ROMAN.

aqueducts Long-distance artificial conduits for WATER SUPPLY. Aqueducts were used by the Assyrians in the 8th century BC, and appear to be one of the technological legacies of the ancient Near East to the

AQUEDUCTS: (a) massive arcaded structures carrying the water channel of the 135 km Carthage aqueduct.

AQUEDUCTS: (b) preserved channel of a ground-level aqueduct, Mont St-Victoire, Aix-en-Provence.

archaic Greek world. The earliest known Greek aqueducts, both of the second half of the 6th century BC, are the pipeline to the Enneakrounos FOUNTAIN at Athens, built under PEISISTRATOS, and the aqueduct of SAMOS which included the famous mile-long tunnel of Eupalinos. Greek aqueducts tended to run along the contours of the landscape, in rock-cut channels or terracotta pipelines; the latter technique, in which water could cross slight depressions under low pressure, removed the need for exact levelling. In the hellenistic period more ambitious ENGINEERING works were introduced, such as the 'inverted siphon' or U-shaped pipeline to cross deep valleys. A 2nd-century BC example on the Madra Dağ aqueduct at PERGAMON crosses a 200 m deep valley before rising up to the ACROPOLIS.

Roman aqueducts took more liberties with the terrain, as CONCRETE and arcaded construction allowed the cost-effective shortening of some routes by bridging wide and deep valleys, or carrying the aqueduct for miles on arcading, instead of always following the contours. Nevertheless, most of an aqueduct's length would consist of a channel at or just below ground level, with arcades, BRIDGES, inverted siphons and tunnels accounting for a relatively small percentage of the total. Aqueducts might vary in length from a few hundred metres to over 100 km (98 km, 61 miles, in the case of the 2nd-century aqueduct for CARTHAGE, later increased to 132 km, 82 miles, by the addition of new sources). Conduit construction varied. When not rock-cut, the sides were usually in masonry or concrete and the ROOF vaulted, if the conduit was large enough to walk through, or, if smaller, covered with flat stone slabs that could be removed for maintenance.

Greek aqueducts had delivered water to public fountains but not, in general, to private houses. Roman aqueducts distributed water not only to fountains and nymphaea but also, from the late Republic onwards, to public BATHS, private individuals who could afford to pay for water, and occasionally to commercial establishments. They engendered a culture of urban public bathing and conspicuous water consumption, and their monumental arcades striding across the landscape are a potent symbol of Roman dominion. By diversifying means of water supply, however, they also facilitated the growth of urban populations; in the more arid PROVINCES of the empire such as North AFRICA, aqueduct construction accompanies or even precedes urban expansion. Numerous cities had more than one aqueduct, and Rome eventually acquired 11, operated by a numerous staff, as described by FRONTINUS in his *De aquis urbis Romae*. AIW

See Hodge, A. T. (1992) *Roman Aqueducts and Water Supply*; Lewis, M. J. T. (1999) Vitruvius and Greek aqueducts, *PBSR* 67: 145–72; Wikander, Ö., ed. (2000) *Handbook of Ancient Water Technology*; Wilson, A. I. (1999) Deliveries extra urbem: aqueducts and the countryside, *JRA* 12: 314–30.

Aquileia Founded as a Latin colony in 181 BC, Aquileia was located 10 km (6 miles) from the north ADRIATIC coast, but communicated with it through the river CANALS of the Natiso and Alsa. Raised to *municipium* status in 90 BC, it was later claimed as the ninth biggest town in the empire (AUSONIUS, *Ordo nobilium urbium* 9). Its growth owed much to its location on the crossroads of major trade routes through the Julian ALPS, linking with the DANUBE via NORICUM and PANNONIA. A series of defensive works are known here, probably responses to documented sacks and sieges of the city by the Marcomanni in the 160s AD, by MAXIMINUS in 238 and later by Attila's HUNS in 452. Though elevated to the seat of a patriarch, Aquileia appears to have been in decline in the 5th century, with a heightened role going to its former port of Grado. With the Lombard invasions of 568, the patriarch withdrew here. The Lombards later established their own patriarch, but Aquileia itself shrank to a small village by the Middle Ages. Extensive remains are visible of the FORUM and commercial zones. The 5th-century cathedral and baptistery are still intact; the cathedral features its original MOSAIC floor with dedicatory panel of bishop Theodore (d.320). Much of the early CHRISTIAN fabric of Grado also survives, its CHURCHES likewise presenting fine late antique mosaics and marble-work. NJC

See Bertacci, L. (1994) *Basilica, museo e scavi: Aquileia.*

 ITALY: (b).

Aquitania see GAUL; GENERALISSIMOS; GERMANY AND GERMANS.

Ara Pacis Set up in the Campus Martius at Rome, 13–9 BC, the Ara Pacis Augustae is a high MARBLE enclosure with an altar inside, all with relief SCULPTURE, celebrating the emperor AUGUSTUS as bringer of peace. Its emphasis on fertility, family and piety communicates a sense of the stability of the regime, the dynasty, and Rome itself.

The graceful style evokes 5th-century Athenian art in its use of a measured pace for the processions of the imperial family and PRIESTS and officials on the north and south sides. The processions move toward the eastern entrance, as if about to make a SACRIFICE to Peace. On the front, panels show the arrival of AENEAS, ancestor of Augustus, in Italy, and (badly damaged) ROMULUS AND REMUS, founders of Rome, suckled by the wolf. On the back is a damaged panel apparently representing the goddess Roma along with the well-preserved panel of a female divinity or personification (Tellus, Pax, Italia, or VENUS?) holding two infants and surrounded by lush nature. Beneath the panels and friezes of the exterior, a profusion of delicate plant life reminds the viewer of the fecundity of nature that Augustus' peace guarantees. Sculpted garlands and ox skulls decorated the inner walls, and reliefs showing the ritual procession with ANIMALS, priests and priestesses, and celebrants, ornamented the altar itself. NBK

See Castriota, D. (1995) *The Ara Pacis Augustae and the Imagery of Abundance*; Simon, E. (1967) *Ara Pacis Augustae*; Zanker, P. (1988) *The Power of Images in the Age of Augustus.*

 ROME: (a).

ARA PACIS: (a) detail of a well-preserved end panel of the enclosure, showing a seated goddess amidst a scene of pastoral harmony.

ARA PACIS: (b) procession including members of the family of Augustus from the side of the outer enclosure.

Ara Pietatis In AD 22 the emperor TIBERIUS and the Roman SENATE planned an altar to honour Tiberius' mother, LIVIA, who was gravely ill at the time (TACITUS, *Annals* 3.64). This altar of filial piety came to be associated with an Ara Pietatis Augustae, supposedly dedicated in 43–4; the inscription on which this information is based has, however, been questioned recently, because of its medieval date.

Whether the Ara Pietatis Augustae was ever built, and whether it had anything to do with the altar Tacitus mentions, remains unclear. Two groups of relief fragments have been associated with the supposed altar because of their Claudian style. One group (Villa Medici, Rome) was found during the RENAISSANCE; a second set (Museo Capitolino, Rome) was excavated between 1923 and 1933. A few comparable reliefs in the Louvre in Paris have similar styles and subjects. All these reliefs are historical in the sense that they show PROCESSIONS and SACRIFICES before buildings known from Rome, events that seem connected with the altar and perhaps also with ceremonies carried out by the VESTAL VIRGINS with whom Livia was closely associated. NBK

See Torelli, M. (1982) *Typology and Structure of Roman Historical Reliefs.*

Arabia and Arabs As early as the 9th century BC, Arabs are recorded as a distinct people by Assyrian and biblical sources, appearing initially as nomadic PASTORALIST inhabitants in the Syrian desert. In Greek and Roman geographical terms, Arabia referred to the steppe and desert areas bordering EGYPT and the fertile crescent as well as the Arabian peninsula. These areas were not necessarily contiguous, and included to the north the part of MESOPOTAMIA that became the Roman province of Osrhoene. Initially authors such as HERODOTOS were most familiar with the western parts of this region, but by the time of ERATOSTHENES (cited by STRABO and PLINY THE ELDER) they were well aware of the limits of the Arabian peninsula, which was explored by sea and to a lesser extent by land. The Romans knew the Arabian peninsula as Arabia Felix (the southern coastal part) and Arabia Deserta (the desert interior). Aelius Gallus led an unsuccessful expedition to Arabia Felix in the reign of AUGUSTUS. Subsequently (AD 106) the name Arabia was applied to a Roman province derived from the NABATAEAN kingdom, centred on modern Jordan. Later Roman contacts with the rich civilization of the Sabaeans of southern Arabia were as traders and TRAVELLERS, both by sea and overland, with other Arab peoples such as PALMYRENES and Nabataeans controlling caravan routes across the desert regions.

The two major cities of the Roman province were PETRA, the former royal capital, and Bostra, the provincial capital and the base of the single Legion III Cyrenaica throughout the 2nd century AD. The so-called Babatha archive of documents, found in a cave near the Dead Sea, sheds fascinating light on legal, economic and social matters in the south of the province in the late Nabataean–HADRIANIC period. Intensive archaeological work in the pre-desert areas of the province has provided much information on economic relationships between nomadic and sedentary peoples, and on AGRICULTURE and water management in these marginal areas. Major administrative changes came in the reign of DIOCLETIAN, when the southern part of the province, including Petra and the Negev, was detached to form part of Palestine (subsequently Palaestina Salutaris) while the northern part retained the name Arabia.

To Greeks and Romans, Arabs, broadly speaking, were inhabitants of Arabia. The definition is more complicated than that, as not all the inhabitants of that region were Arabs and many groups within that area (Nabataeans, Palmyrenes and Sabaeans, for example), who are legitimately regarded as Arabs, had distinctive local identities. Living in the desert, and pastoral nomadism, were key defining characteristics, while other factors often used to define ethnicity (such as language and material culture) show diversity. Not all Arab groups primarily used the Arabic language: dialects of Aramaic predominated in Nabataea and Palmyra, certainly in written form. Especially from the 4th century onwards, Arabs (often called Saracens) were prominent as both allies and enemies of Rome on the desert frontiers of Arabia and SYRIA. (see p. 64) NDP

See Bowersock, G.W. (1983) *Roman Arabia*; Hoyland, R.G. (2001) *Arabia and the Arabs*; Millar, F. (1983) *The Roman Near East 31 BC–AD 337.*

 ROMAN EMPIRE: (b).

Aratos of Sikyon 271–213 BC Head of the ACHAIAN LEAGUE in the second half of the 3rd century BC, Aratos was one of the ablest leaders of his day. Born in 271, he was brought up in ARGOS following the murder of his father, Kleinias, a former tyrant of his city. As a young man Aratos engineered the expulsion of a later tyrant of Sikyon, and brought the city into the Achaian league. In 245 he was elected GENERAL for the first time. Often at odds with Macedonia, in 243 he scored a signal victory with the capture of Acrocorinth, and thus gave the league control of the isthmus. Shortly afterwards, he arranged an alliance with Ptolemy III and oversaw an increase in league membership. With the Macedonians and AITOLIANS united against the Achaians, Aratos defeated the Aitolians at Pellene and made peace with both powers in 241. In 239 he brought about the alliance of the Achaian and Aitolian leagues against Macedonia. The rise of Sparta under KLEOMENES III, however, forced him to seek help from Macedonia. Kleomenes was defeated at Sellasia (222/1), and shortly afterwards Aratos was compelled to seek Macedonian aid against the Aitolians. Remaining loyal to Macedonia during the SOCIAL WAR, Aratos kept the league out of conflict with Rome despite PHILIP V. He died of natural causes in 213, though it was said that Philip was responsible. JDD

See Walbank, F.W. (1933) *Aratos of Sikyon*; (1984) Macedonia and Greece, in *CAH* 7.1, 221–56; Macedonia and the Greek leagues, in *CAH* 7.1, 446–81.

Aratos of Soloi c.305–c.240 BC Greek poet and scholar who studied at Athens with ZENO OF KITION and later enjoyed the patronage of Antigonos II Gonatas of Macedonia and Antiochos I of Syria. His chief surviving work, *Phainomena*, was written for Gonatas and deals with ASTRONOMY. Its first part (lines 19–732), based on Eudoxos, enumerates 45 constellations, relating each to its mythological counterpart. Aratos recognizes the 12 ZODIACAL

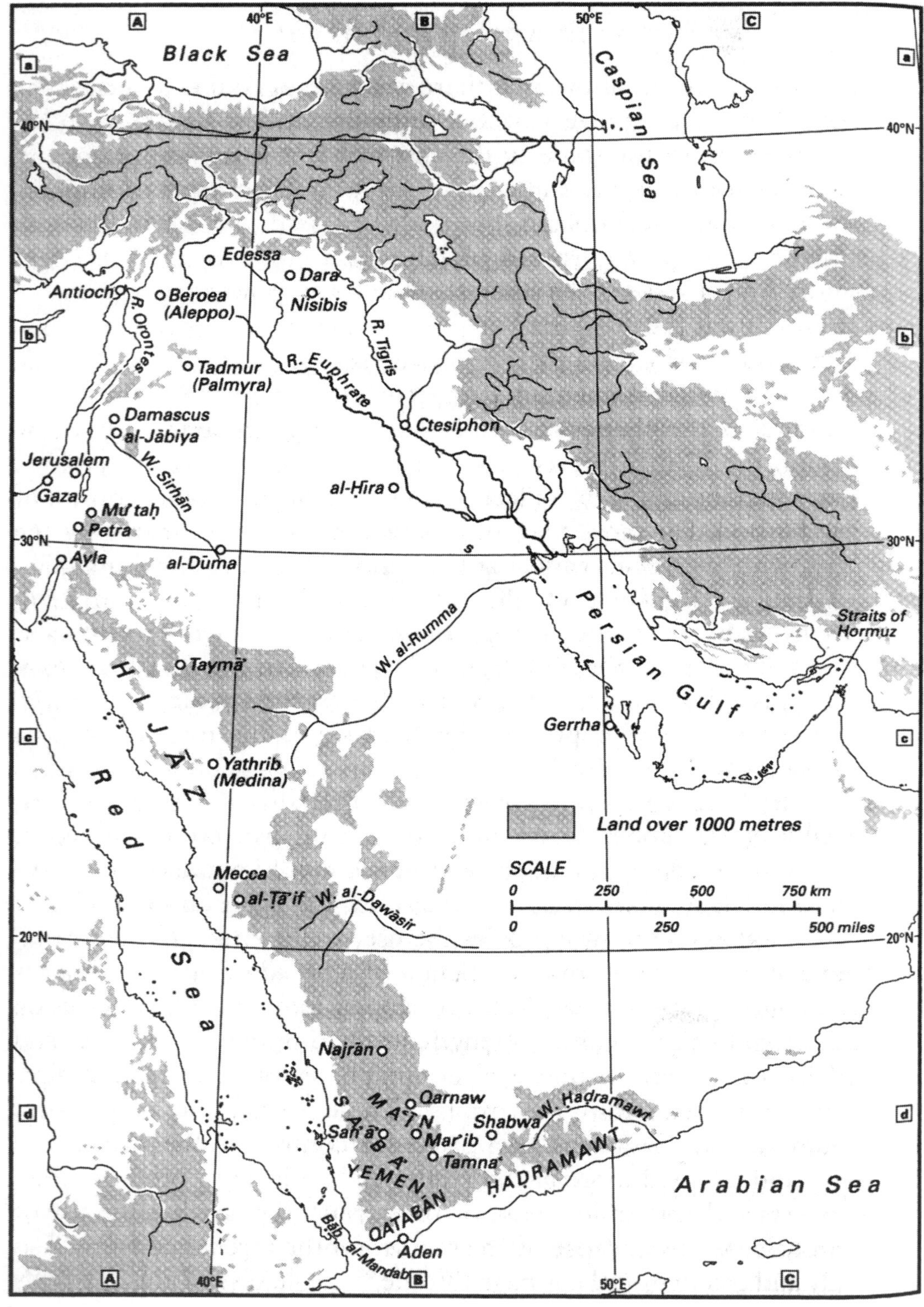

Arabia and Arabs: map of pre-Islamic sites.

constellations as a group, but uses no single term corresponding to 'zodiac'. He deals with the great circles of the sky (including the Milky Way) and the risings and settings of constellations, but not the planets. The second part (733–1154), reworking THEOPHRASTOS, alludes to the 19-year Metonic cycle, then covers weather signs, chiefly changes in the sun and moon and the behaviour of animals. Despite its recherché subject matter and technical inaccuracies, *Phainomena* became the most widely read work of Greek literature after Homer. It was translated into Latin by CICERO and others, and later into Arabic. Although it stems from a hellenistic fashion for disseminating science in verse, given its poetic diction it is a literary rather than a scientific work, doubtless meant for élite readers, not persons involved in the realities of AGRICULTURE or navigation. DGJS, CLNR

See Mair, G. R., trs. (1921) (with Callimachus, etc.).

Arausia see LAND SURVEYING, ROMAN; MAPS.

Arcadia see ARKADIA; GOLDEN AGE.

Arcadius see HONORIUS.

 THEODOSIUS (stemma).

arch, the see ARCHITECTURE; ARCHES, MONUMENTAL.

archaeology The archaeology of Greece and Rome centres on classical civilizations located in Greece and Italy and other parts of the Greek and Roman cultural area, especially the Mediterranean, the Black sea, and north-western Europe. Time periods covered range from the end of the Bronze Age to the fall of the Roman empire. More than most branches of the discipline, it is a complex combination of field and museum archaeology.

Classical archaeology started in the Italian RENAISSANCE, when artists and ANTIQUARIANS began to record standing ruins and collect ancient objects such as SCULPTURE, coins and gems for private and public collections. Antiquarian studies of Greek and Roman material culture accelerated in the 17th and 18th centuries, focused on remains in Italy and north-western Europe.

The German scholar Johann Joachim Winckelmann, who developed a chronological and stylistic framework for the study of Greek and Roman art, is regarded as the founder of classical archaeology. In his ideological interpretation of classical civilization, Greece was seen as the primary creative force. That led to a shift in emphasis from Roman to Greek archaeology that is still dominant today, for example in North America, where teaching positions are focused in Greek archaeology and more major excavations are conducted on Greek than Roman sites. In Europe, by contrast, Roman archaeology tends to dominate, at least quantitatively, because most of Europe was within the Roman empire.

The early 19th century saw an increased emphasis on topographical investigations in classical archaeology. Scholars combined the study of classical texts, modern topography and standing remains to examine ancient cities and reconstruct ancient landscapes. Rome and its environs became one important area of study, with topographers such as Antonio Nibby and William Gell making important contributions to our understanding of the ancient city and its countryside.

Classical archaeology in Greece received a major impetus in the mid-18th century from the architectural studies of the English architects James Stuart and Nicolas Revett. In the early 19th century topographical research in Greece also increased. Using information provided by authors such as PAUSANIAS, investigators such as William Leake began reconstructing the GEOGRAPHY of ancient Greece and the topography of cities and religious centres. In 1875 the Germans under Ernst Curtius initiated the excavation at OLYMPIA and began the emphasis on excavation at major Greek sites that continues today. Important examples have been the French excavations at DELPHI and the American excavations in the Athenian Agora. ARCHITECTURAL remains and urban planning have received special attention.

After 1870 the Italian government prohibited foreign excavations, which meant that after this date most fieldwork was done by national archaeologists. The city of Rome received special attention, especially during the fascist period when archaeology was used as a propaganda tool. Again the emphasis was on the recovery of monumental remains and works of ART.

During this time, museum archaeology went in its own directions. Antiquarian investigations and such phenomena as the 18th-century Grand Tour led to the development of large collections of antiquities, especially sculpture (mainly Roman copies of Greek originals). In the 19th century several important collections of SCULPTURE, for example the Elgin Marbles from the PARTHENON, or those from PERGAMON and HALIKARNASSOS in Turkey, were acquired by European museums. By the late 19th century most countries prohibited the export of antiquities and museums turned increasingly to the antiquities market. This history has meant that museum archaeology has focused mainly on questions of dating, stylistic analysis and aesthetic presentation, with less effort to relate objects in their archaeological context. Such research has not been without its uses for field archaeologists. John Beazley undertook detailed stylistic analyses of Athenian POTTERY, producing a precise chronology of certain types of widely used ceramics. That provided an important chronological tool for excavators. The Beazley aesthetic approach has been increasingly complemented by scientific analyses that provide information on clay sources and MANUFACTURING techniques.

The archaeology of Greece and Rome has remained focused on towns, sanctuaries and élites through much of its history. The countryside was little studied, and except at special sites like POMPEII little attention was paid to non-high-status aspects of Greek and Roman society. Systematic survey in the countryside of Greece and Italy only began after the Second World War, with American research in MESSENIA in the south-west PELOPONNESE and British work around VEII north of Rome. Both demonstrated the ability of survey archaeology to reconstruct long-term rural histories. Survey archaeology has now become more common, but only a small portion of the Greek and Roman countryside has been systematically researched. Information from underwater archaeology has increased our knowledge of the Greek and Roman ECONOMY and shipping, and has led to the scientific study of objects of daily use like transport AMPHORAS.

Italy opened up to foreign expeditions after the Second World War. The emphasis remained on urban archaeology, with excavations like those of the Americans at Cosa and Morgantina. In the same period more archaeology was undertaken in Turkey, but again was focused on major classical centres such as SARDIS and APHRODISIAS. As even more countries prohibited the export of antiquities, museums have become more dependent on the antiquities market. This has led to increased illegal excavation and exportation of archaeological objects.

Although the archaeology of Greece and Rome has focused on the central Mediterranean, the Greek diaspora in the western Mediterranean and Black sea, and the Roman conquest of north-west Europe, have encouraged classical archaeologists to extend their activities into those areas. Countries like Britain and France have long histories of antiquarian studies of Roman as well as indigenous antiquities. Such research has often represented a combination of nationalistic archaeology and identification with Roman civilization. This can be seen in the 19th-century research sponsored by Napoleon III of France on sites associated with CAESAR's conquest of GAUL. In all European countries, rescue archaeology and problems associated with the preservation of archaeological heritage are placing new demands on classical as well as prehistoric archaeologists.

Intellectually, many classical archaeologists are still focused on questions and approaches derived from the 18th and 19th centuries. The theoretical debates that have forced changes in many other branches of archaeology beginning in the 1960s have had relatively little impact on classical archaeology, which has remained intellectually conservative while maintaining a tradition of high-quality scholarship and fieldwork. Some change is now evident in Greek archaeology and the archaeology of the Western Roman PROVINCES, where post-processual archaeology is having an impact on both field strategies and interpretations of the archaeological data. SLD

See Millett, M. (1990) *The Romanization of Britain*; Morris, I. (2000) *Archaeology as Cultural History*; Shanks, M. (1996) *Classical Archaeology of Greece*; Snodgrass, A. M. (1987) *An Archaeology of Greece*; Sauer, E.W., ed. (2004) *Archaeology and Ancient History*.

archery In Greece, Egypt and the LEVANT archery was dominated by the use of 'composite' bows from the Bronze Age onwards. These were constructed with a wooden core, a back (the face away from the archer) of ANIMAL sinew, and a belly (towards the archer) of horn. Components were stuck together using animal glue, and often covered and painted or lacquered for weather protection. Staves were constructed in a reversed 'C' so that the limbs had to be pulled back to be strung and greater energy was stored for the full draw.

The dimensions of bows evolved over time, but a small weapon (length c.0.75–1.00 m along the side) with a set-back handle, probably introduced from central Asia by Scythian NOMADS, was used in Greece from the archaic period (the 'Cupid's bow' of Greco-Roman art). This was also employed by Achaemenid PERSIAN armies and CRETAN MERCENARY archers. Scythian horsemen used a combination bow-case and quiver (*gorytos*) slung from the archer's waist, the cased bow being left strung. Persian and other infantry carried a sheath quiver on their backs.

Larger central Asian bows were introduced during the 2nd to 1st centuries BC by the PARTHIANS and spread throughout the Levant and into Roman use. These were longer than the 'Scythian' bows (length c.1.50 m) and had angled end-sections ('ears'), each stiffened by a pair of BONE or antler laths so that they could act as levers to pull back the limbs when the weapon was drawn. Laths survive archaeologically after all the other organic components have perished; thus the 'Parthian' bow can be traced on sites right across the Roman empire from DURA EUROPUS in SYRIA to the ANTONINE WALL in northern BRITAIN.

On horseback, either a combination unstrung bow-case and quiver was worn at the side, or a separate unstrung bow-case was slung on the left and a cylindrical quiver on the right. During the later REPUBLIC, Roman infantry armies were badly defeated in Syria–MESOPOTAMIA by Parthian horse-archery; under the EMPERORS, care was taken to recruit specialist archer regiments from Levantine areas with a long cultural tradition of archery. The absence of laths from Sarmatian graves suggests that these steppe nomads continued to use 'Scythian' bows until the 4th century. At that time, a new design was introduced by the HUNS with different dimensions (length c.1.50–1.60 m) and additional laths on the belly and sides of the handle. The latter are attested in graves as far west as Austria and Germany. The bow form is reflected in funerary finds of gold-foil sheathing from full-size model bows, used as symbols of leadership in the Hunnic empire. 'Hunnic' bows entered Roman use, and in the 6th century were still superior to SASSANIAN Persian weapons.

Simple wooden bows were used by northern peoples such as the GAULS and GERMANS, and composite bows were only occasionally adopted through steppe nomad contacts. JCNC

See Coulston, J. C. (1985) Roman archery equipment, in M. C. Bishop, ed., *The Production and Distribution of Roman Military Equipment* 220–366; Rausing, G. (1967) *The Bow*.

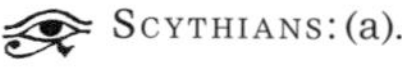 SCYTHIANS: (a).

arches, monumental Honorific or monumental arches (*fornices*) are a particularly characteristic feature of the ROMAN EMPIRE, with over 100 known in Italy (50 in Rome alone) and large numbers in other provinces, generally built as free-standing structures spanning roads within towns. They are sometimes described as 'triumphal arches', since a common theme in their ornamentation was the celebration of military victory, but were dedicated for a range of other reasons as well. The promotion of an urban centre to higher status (e.g. from *civitas* to *municipium*) was a frequent motivation. Originating in the 2nd century BC, arches become more frequent from the reign of AUGUSTUS onwards, when their potential as huge billboards to advertise the power of Rome and the loyalty of its subjects was realized. From an initial form as simple, single masonry arches, the form became progressively more elaborate. By the 3rd century AD they commonly comprised

ARCHES, MONUMENTAL: reconstruction drawing of the arch of Constantine, Rome, showing the surmounting chariot group.

massive, triple-arched structures bearing large inscriptions; the arch of CONSTANTINE was a colossal 21 m high, 25.6 m wide and 10 m deep. The arch of TITUS in Rome is an excellent example of the triumphal type, with a vivid depiction in relief panels of the victory parade in Rome after the capture of Jerusalem, in which we see the procession disappearing through an arch – perfectly illustrating the role such monuments played in the ceremonial street theatre. The masonry core of arches was normally decorated by columns, other architectural devices and relief panels, and frequently topped off by flamboyant statue groups or TROPHIES. Four-way arches (*tetrapyla*) placed at major crossroads are a particularly grandiose variant, of which one of the most florid examples has been reconstructed at LEPCIS MAGNA. DJM

See Claridge, A. (1998) *Rome*.

 EPIGRAPHY, ROMAN: (a); ROME: (e); SENATE: (a); TRIUMPHS: (a)–(b).

Archidamian war see PELOPONNESIAN WAR.

Archidamos II Spartan king of the Eurypontid family (r. c.469–427 BC). He succeeded his grandfather, Leotychidas II, at age 16 and enjoyed one of the longest reigns of any king. He quelled the HELOT revolt of the 460s and is best known for his speech in 432, reported by Thucydides, urging caution in the face of Athenian imperialism. Despite his seniority, the Spartans voted that Athens had broken its treaty, leading to a vote for war by Sparta's allies. Archidamos invaded Attica several times after the outbreak of the PELOPONNESIAN WAR, and despite his early death its first decade is named the 'Archidamian war'. Two of his sons became kings: his successor, AGIS II, son of his first wife, and 27 years later AGESILAOS, offspring of his second marriage. DGJS

See Thucydides, *passim*, esp. 1.79–85.

Archilochos LYRIC POET of the second half of the 7th century BC. Archilochos was born on the AEGEAN island of PAROS. His father Telesikles was sent, c.680 BC, to colonize THASOS, an island contested as well by NAXIAN colonists and native THRACIANS. Paros was an important centre for the cult of DEMETER, and Archilochos' family was apparently closely connected to it. Ancient writers also associate him with the cult of DIONYSOS. Archilochos is one of three archaic poets (the others are SEMONIDES and Hipponax) whom ALEXANDRIAN scholars included in the canon of iambographers, writers of *iambos* or burlesque poems associated with these cult festivals. Archilochos doubtless derived many invectives and lampoons from his religious associations. His attacks on Lykambes and his daughters may originate in actual experience, since Lykambes broke Archilochos' engagement to one of his daughters, Neoboule, or may reflect the conventions of iambic poetry. One large fragment of Archilochos' erotic poetry, preserved on a papyrus dating to the 2nd century AD (now in Cologne: *P.Colon*. inv. 7511), graphically (indeed, almost pornographically) describes a sexual encounter with a beautiful young woman and his taunting rejection of Neoboule, represented as an ugly, sex-mad old woman.

Archilochos is the earliest lyric personality known to us and, like other poets of the time, appears to derive his topics from the range of his personal experiences of life in an archaic *polis*. He was a soldier who subverted the heroic ideology expressed in the HOMERIC poems, conscious of his own meagre chances of survival as a soldier. In one poem, he boasts about abandoning his shield beside a bush in order to save his life. In others, he describes the harsh life of the MERCENARY and a preference for a courageous, but ugly, general to a handsome one. Some of his poetry seems to be intended for the *symposion*, some takes up mythological themes. Other poems are political, and feature his friends, exploits and campaigns, but the image of the ship struggling to stay afloat on the stormy sea may be a metaphor for the turmoil of political factionalism. Archilochos also wrote ELEGIES; a poem on sorrow experienced after the death at sea of his brother-in-law is the most well known. RBC

See West, M. L., trs. (1993) *Greek Lyric Poetry*; Fränkel, H. (1975) *Early Greek Poetry and Philosophy*; Podlecki, A. J. (1984) *The Early Greek Poets and their Times*.

Archimedes His death in the Roman sack of his native city, SYRACUSE, in 212 or 211 BC both firmly dates Archimedes' life and guaranteed his fame in antiquity. He was popularly known exclusively as an ENGINEER and inventor. The SIEGE engines he allegedly constructed to defend Syracuse in the siege, mechanical devices like the Archimedean SCREW used to raise water, a system of pulleys supposedly used to launch the monstrous ship *Syrakousia*, and his famous planetarium are the sort of things which impressed ancient authors. His mathematical achievements are rarely mentioned. But his reputation as one of the greatest mathematical thinkers of all times rests on a series of treatises on pure MATHEMATICS (e.g. *On the Sphere and Cylinder*, *On Conoids and Spheroids* and *On Spirals*), on theoretical MECHANICS (*On the Equilibrium of Planes*) and on hydrostatics, a subject he appears to have invented himself (*On Floating Bodies*).

Archimedes pushed the fields in which he worked almost as far as they could be advanced until the invention of calculus. In most of his surviving works the method of exposition is the one standard in Greek mathematics, which is exemplified by EUCLID's *Elements*. However, the discovery by Heiberg in 1908 of a manuscript of the *Method* (the parchment of which had been reused) revealed for the first time that he worked out his proofs initially by quite different methods, treating figures as combinations of strips, infinitely thin, to which mechanical methods could be applied. He did not, however, regard this method as sufficiently rigorous, and so in publishing his results he used more conventional proofs. RW

See Dijksterhuis, E. J. (1987) *Archimedes*.

architects Nearly all buildings from the ancient world are the work of anonymous architects, though names are sometimes revealed by inscriptions, such as the name of Gaius Julius Lacer on the bridge at Alcantara in Spain. Many other architects' names are recorded, but little can be said about their work. They prepared plans to scale, presumably on PAPYRUS, and provided specifications before a project could start; they also performed the role of the modern quantity surveyor, preparing estimates of materials and their cost. Sometimes sketches were incised in stone to aid construction.

Among Greek engineers and architects, a few stand out: Rhoikos and Theodoros (third TEMPLE of HERA on SAMOS), Chersiphon and his son Megasthenes (temple of ARTEMIS at EPHESOS), Eupalinos (underground AQUEDUCT for Polykrates of Samos), Hippodamos (street layouts of the PIRAEUS, RHODES and possibly Thourioi in south Italy), Iktinos (the PARTHENON, assisted by Kallikrates; hall of the Mysteries at ELEUSIS; temple of APOLLO at Bassai), Mnesikles (Athenian Propylaia) and Deinokrates, ALEXANDER the Great's court architect (ALEXANDRIA). Major hellenistic architects include Sostratos (the Pharos LIGHTHOUSE at Alexandria), Paionius and Daphnis (temple of Apollo at DIDYMA) and Hermogenes (temples of Artemis at Magnesia and ATHENA Polias at Priene). Worth including for novelty is Andronikos (water-clock known as the Tower of the Winds in Athens). Hellenistic Greek architects like Hermodoros also worked in Rome (temple of JUPITER Stator).

Vitruvius, who worked for JULIUS CAESAR and AUGUSTUS, owes his fame to his ten books *On Architecture* and was a Roman CITIZEN. Architects who signed work in the THEATRE at Pompeii (Marcus Artorius Primus) and at the temple of Augustus in Pozzuoli (Lucius Cocceius Auctus, also HARBOUR works at Lake Avernus and road tunnels at Cumae and Naples–Pozzuoli) were FREEDMEN. We know the names of architects responsible for NERO's Golden

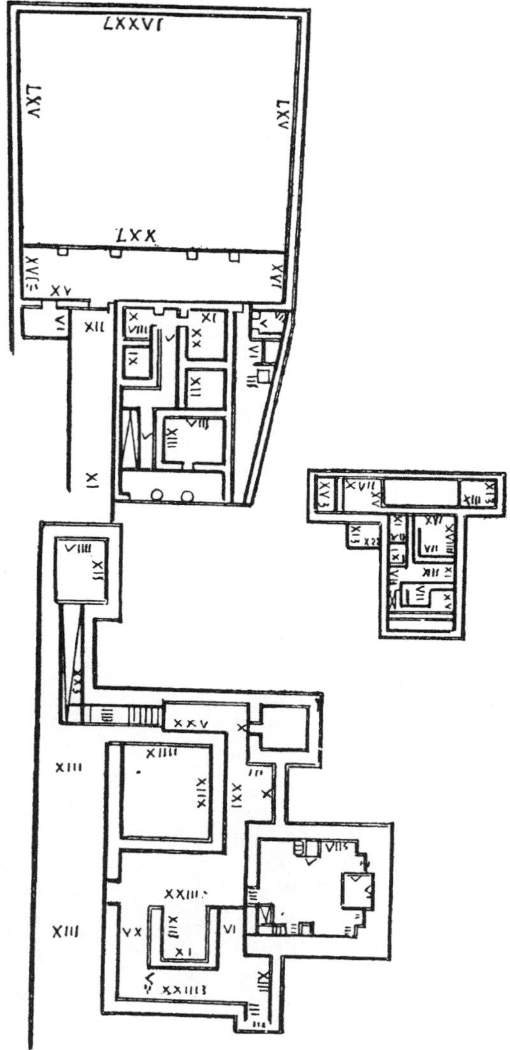

ARCHITECTS: architectural plan of a Roman tomb complex (relief on a marble slab from Via Labicana cemetery). The Roman numerals indicate the ancient measurements of rooms as shown on the plan.

House (Domus Aurea), Severus and Celer, and for DOMITIAN'S PALACE on the Palatine in Rome, Rabirius, but little else can be gleaned about them. The greatest known Roman architect is Apollodorus. A provincial from Damascus, he was responsible for TRAJAN'S BRIDGE over the DANUBE, an *odeion* in Rome and the great FORUM of Trajan and its MARKET complex. He presumably developed the novel idea of using a giant COLUMN as a vehicle for propaganda. Whether he also designed HADRIAN'S PANTHEON is unrecorded but entirely plausible. Hadrian had architectural aspirations of his own, designing the temple of VENUS and Rome and inventing the 'pumpkin' dome seen occasionally in his palaces (Serapeum at TIVOLI, pavilion in the Gardens of Sallust). (see also TOWN PLANNING) RJAW

See Anderson, J. C. (1997) *Roman Architecture and Society*; Coulton, J. J. (1977) *Greek Architects at Work*; Wilson Jones, M. (2000) *Principles of Roman Architecture*.

architecture

The first identifiable TEMPLES in the Greek world, datable to the 8th century BC, are small-scale hut-like buildings with posts in front to support a porch. They derive from contemporary house plans, and reflect the function of the temple as the house of a divinity represented by its cult-image. The change to monumentality occurred c.700–675 BC, with early temples of peripteral type (with columns all the way round the exterior) at CORINTH, Isthmia and Eretria. The ORDER may have been Doric, but the superstructure was of timber throughout the 7th century, and the details are therefore lost. Temples with stone COLUMNS and entablatures occur in mainland Greece from c.600–550; at first the columns were monoliths (well seen at the temple of APOLLO at CORINTH, c.540), but for convenience were made up of drums soon after. Archaic Doric temples tend to be elongated (a layout of 6 × 16, or 6 × 15, columns is not unusual), but the main elements of the Doric entablature had settled down to canonical form by c.530. In the more elaborate examples, sculptural compositions were placed in pediments and some or all of the metopes could be carved. The use of paint in such SCULPTURE (ubiquitous in the ancient world), also employed to highlight other elements of architectural detail, lent an element of brilliant colour to such buildings that is hard to appreciate today. The material in mainland Greece for Doric is local limestone and sandstone, liberally covered with STUCCO. By contrast, the island communities of the AEGEAN and the western seaboard of Asia Minor often used showy white MARBLE (NAXOS was a notable early source) and built huge temples by comparison with mainland Greece, as in the temples of ARTEMIS at EPHESOS and HERA at SAMOS. The Ionic order was preferred here, as it was in mainland Greece, for those smaller buildings such as treasuries which were built by Eastern city-states at the panhellenic sanctuaries (e.g. the treasury of Siphnos at DELPHI, c.525).

By the beginning of the classical period, the Doric temple had become standardized as having a plan of 6 × 13 columns, with matching porch (*pronaos*) and rear false porch (*opisthodomos*). The type is well epitomized by the temple of ZEUS at OLYMPIA (between 469 and 457) but there were exceptions, especially in SICILY and south Italy where the standard rules were not closely obeyed. With the opening up of the Pentelic quarries, Athens adopted marble for its finest temples from c.450, such as the Hephaisteion (449–440) and the revolutionary PARTHENON (447–432). These were probably the first temples in mainland Greece to combine the Doric order with elements of Ionic (a combination foreshadowed, however, in the temple of ATHENA ('CERES') at Paestum in Italy 50 years earlier). The Parthenon is also the most complex illustration of the Greek obsession with detail in order to achieve architectural harmony. This can be seen both in the balance of proportions (a ratio of 4:9 is used for several fundamental elements of its design) and in optical 'refinements' such as the *entasis* (slight

ARCHITECTURE: (a) temple of Apollo, Corinth, Doric order, 6th century BC.

ARCHITECTURE: (b) temple of Athena Nike, Athenian Acropolis, Ionic order, 5th century BC.

ARCHITECTURE: (c) temple of Fortuna Virilis, Rome, Corinthian order, 1st century AD.

outward bulging) of columns and the upward curvature of the stylobate platform. (These features had first appeared in relatively crude form as early as 540.) Purely Ionic buildings were also now built in Athens, such as the temple on the Ilissos (c.450), its later copy the temple of Athena Nike (c.425), and the elaborate and unconventional Erechtheion (421–405), the last two located on the ACROPOLIS. Iktinos, ARCHITECT of the Parthenon, went one step further at Bassai, where the newly invented Corinthian order was used alongside Ionic inside the temple of Apollo, whose exterior order is Doric. Such mixing of orders became commonplace in 4th-century temples (such as those of Athena Alea at Tegea and Zeus at Nemea), when the standard rectangular temple was joined more commonly by circular temples (*tholoi*) also employing a mixture of orders (in the sanctuaries of Athena at DELPHI and of ASKLEPIOS at Epidauros, for example).

The 4th and 3rd centuries saw the monumentalization in stone of other building types on a more substantial scale than hitherto, notably the THEATRE (such as at Epidauros, c.340) and STOA. Courtyard buildings for public use, such as the Pompeion at Athens beside the Sacred gate (an assembly point for processions to ELEUSIS), used an inner peristyle of columns. This was soon transferred to the inner courts of MACEDONIAN royal PALACES, and thence to the architecture of the well-to-do private house in later hellenistic and Roman times. The ARCH made an appearance in the 4th century BC, both in city gateways (as at Velia in south Italy) and for entrance tunnels in stadia and the like (at Nemea, Epidauros and Olympia). The first barrel vaults in cut stone appeared in the grandiose chamber TOMBS of the

ARCHITECTURE: (d) columnar *aediculae* and internal façade, Pantheon, Rome, 2nd century AD.

ARCHITECTURE: (e) arched and vaulted construction, market hall at Ferentinum, c.100 BC.

Macedonian royal family at VERGINA and elsewhere. Another hellenistic development is the use of two superimposed orders in a single façade, seen on the Great Tomb at Lefkadia in the early 3rd century BC and later adopted in two-storey stoas, such as the now rebuilt stoa of Attalos at Athens.

The earliest monumental structure at Rome, the huge temple of Capitoline JUPITER of c.509 BC, of which little now survives, set the tone for later Roman temple building. Both the lofty platform (*podium*) on which it is built and the frontal aspect (with a deep porch) are elements which distinguish the developed Roman temple in stone from its Greek counterpart. Well-preserved examples are the temple of Portunus (FORTUNA Virilis) in Rome of c.80 BC and the Maison Carrée at Nîmes in the south of France (AD 2/3). With increasing Greek influence during the later Republic, the architectural detail of such buildings was often modelled on that of Greek architecture; but alongside the Greek orders was the use of an indigenous Tuscan order, a Roman version of Doric, and, from the Augustan period onwards, the fresh invention of the Composite.

The real revolution in Roman architecture came not, however, from subtle manipulations of standard Greek approaches to 'trabeated' architecture (architecture using beams), but with the introduction of a wholly new material, CONCRETE. Its experimental stage probably occurred in the second half of the 3rd century BC, at the same time as Rome was first trying out the arch. Combination of the two led to the invention of the concrete barrel vault, which not only revolutionized the ROOFING of interior space but also allowed the creation of artificial terracing as a part of building design. This made possible such grandiose, cliffside-clinging sanctuaries as those of Fortuna at PRAENESTE (Palestrina), Feronia (Jupiter Anxur) at TERRACINA, and HERCULES at TIVOLI (all c.120–80 BC).

Concrete also facilitated the introduction of new building-types during the late Republic. One was the BATH-house, where the concrete barrel vaults of heated rooms provided a long-term solution to dealing with the damp and steamy atmosphere which no conventional roof could have long withstood. Another was the theatre, where the type chosen was the D-shaped form of the hellenistic Greek theatre of southern Italy and Sicily rather than the one that was normal in mainland Greece (where the seating embraced two-thirds of a circle). More significantly, concrete provided the possibility of raising the seating on artificial barrel-vaulted substructures, so that theatres could now be erected on flat ground (as was Rome's first permanent theatre, that of POMPEY in 55 BC) rather than on a hillside. A third, quintessentially Roman, building type first introduced during the Republic was the AMPHITHEATRE. The earliest permanent examples in stone come from Campania (c.120 BC; Pompeii's of c.70 BC is a well-preserved early example) – another structure which could be wholly free-standing if necessary, thanks to the invention of concrete. A fourth new building type of the late Republic was the civilian BASILICA.

Although a handful of buildings in Rome during the Republic had been built of imported Greek marble (the round temple by the TIBER of c.120–100 BC is the only one extant), the opening up of white marble quarries at CARRARA (Luna) in the mid-1st century BC was an important step. It was seized upon first by JULIUS CAESAR, then by AUGUSTUS, as a means by which the visual appearance of Rome could be immeasurably enhanced. Alongside Carrara white, a wide range of polychrome marbles from Greece, Asia Minor, Egypt and Tunisia were imported from Augustan times onwards, for use as wall and floor veneers as well as for columns. Much of the Augustan programme was essentially conservative, and the heritage of Greece was openly acknowledged (in such details as the caryatids in the FORUM of Augustus, dedicated in 2 BC, directly imitating those of the Erechtheion in Athens). Much else, however, pointed to the future. Brick-faced concrete, soon to be a standard construction method throughout central Italy, was tentatively tried for the first time. The monumental arch, articulated with decorative columns and sculpture, made its first appearance in its developed form (the type had a long and distinguished history after Augustus, down into the 20th century). Finally, it was probably under Augustus that the first hemispherical DOMES in concrete were constructed (the oldest surviving is the 'temple of MERCURY' at Baiae, C.AD 25).

MARBLE, BRICK and experiments in roofing, including the dome, were all essential ingredients in the architectural developments of the early empire. They were well exploited, for example, in Nero's Golden House (Domus Aurea) (AD 64–8), where the earliest tentative cross-vaults occur (as well as the first standing dome in Rome). Here, too, NERO's architects experimented with endlessly changing room-shapes to provide a surprise and a variety in the architecture of interior space that had not been attempted before. The symmetrical plan of the great imperial bath-building, of which there was to be a succession in Rome down to the early 4th century (those of CARACALLA and DIOCLETIAN are the best surviving), not to mention imitations in the PROVINCES, was also first tried out in Nero's baths in Rome. Bath-buildings, too, were essays in dazzling interior space, full of light and colour: columns were now decorative adornments rather than serving the essentially structural function of an earlier age. Quite apart from these, and the floor and wall veneers of marble, a further blaze of colour was provided by the MOSAICS and coloured stuccoes that adorned the soaring vaults and domes. The Hadrianic PANTHEON remains a supremely eloquent statement of the same visual language of the architecture of interior space, not least because the building can still be experienced in something close to its original state. Later generations of Roman architects were essentially still expressing the same ideas in a multitude of different building types, to which the architecture of the early CHRISTIAN CHURCH was a new addition in the early 4th century. Their legacy in turn influenced not only the further developments of Byzantine architecture but also the whole shape of subsequent architectural thought, especially from the RENAISSANCE down into modern times. RJAW

See Adam, J.-P. (1994) *Roman Building: materials and techniques*; Anderson, J. C. (1997) *Roman Architecture and Society*; Boethius, A. (1978) *Etruscan and Early Roman Architecture*; Dinsmoor, W. B. (1950) *The Architecture of Ancient Greece*; Lawrence, A.W. (1996) *Greek Architecture*; MacDonald, W. L. (1982–6) *The Architecture of the Roman Empire*; Summerson, J. (1980) *The Classical Language of Architecture*; Ward-Perkins, J. B. (1981) *Roman Imperial Architecture*; Wilson Jones, M. (2000) *Principles of Roman Architecture*.

 ORDERS, ARCHITECTURAL: (a).

architecture, modern Edward Gibbon (1737–1794) famously announced in the final sentence of his *Decline and Fall* that it was among the ruins of the Capitol at Rome that he had conceived his study of the ROMAN EMPIRE. His final chapter began with a parallel scene: Poggio Brancolini (1380–1459) inspecting those same ruins some three and a quarter centuries earlier (in 1430). Poggio studied the vicissitudes of fortune amid gardens and fallen columns where once Rome had stood. Gibbon, after offering reasons for the ruin of the city of Rome, sees that, in the years between Poggio's presence on the CAPITOLINE hill and his own, Rome had become once again the goal 'of a new race of pilgrims from the remote and once savage countries of the North'. The aim of these new pilgrims was not only antiquarian and literary; it was artistic.

Poggio's meditation on the ruins of Rome had been preceded, 25 years earlier, by the architect Filippo Brunelleschi's more urgent activity. Brunelleschi (1377–1446) was described by Vasari as 'like one out of his mind ... sparing neither time nor expense' in working to measure the ancient buildings of Rome, 'until he was able to see in imagination Rome as she was before she fell into ruins'. Brunelleschi returned to Florence in 1407 to work on the Duomo, a building recognized by its contemporaries as being one that regained the spirit and technique of the Roman world.

Brunelleschi's imaginary reconstruction of the form of ancient Rome became a recurring theme in the architecture of the RENAISSANCE, in James Ackermann's phrase 'each architect finding his own antiquity in turn'. The art-historical categories of Early and High Renaissance, Mannerism and Baroque might be replaced by a categorization based on changing images of antiquity created through its study. Added to the measurement and drawing of the ruins was a study of the only architectural text surviving from antiquity, VITRUVIUS' *De architectura*. Both Leon Battista Alberti (1404–1472) and Andrea Palladio (1508–1580) wrote architectural treatises that combined a study of the ruins with an interpretation of Vitruvius' text. Palladio's *Quattro libri dell'architettura* (1570) presents this combination visually. Modelled on the structure of Vitruvius' work, it describes the vaults, columns, streets, TEMPLES and public buildings of ancient Rome, but, in the case of domestic architecture, 'as we have but very few examples from the ancients ... I shall insert the plans and elevations of many buildings I have erected'. Thus Palladio presents his own buildings as forming a single body of work with the remains of the ancient world – a provoking notion, and one that, because of the graphic qualities of his treatise, had a powerful influence in northern Europe. An influential stream in English architecture, for instance, was introduced through Inigo Jones's study of Palladio in the early 17th century: his St Paul's, Covent Garden (1631–8) is a built version of Vitruvius' description of the ETRUSCAN temple as interpreted by Palladio.

Architectural study and interpretation of the ruins had not ceased when Gibbon reached in Rome in 1764. The Académie de France à Rome had been founded in 1666; it admitted architects from 1720. British architects, too, had studied the ruins as well as the modern architecture of Rome: George Dance the Younger (1741–1825) and James Wyatt (1747–1813) were both in Rome at the time of Gibbon's visit. But Gibbon's critical history was now paralleled by a critical study of the ancient buildings and greater precision in delineating them. New models were also sought. Gibbon gained his knowledge of Athens (which he did not visit) not only from the 17th-century

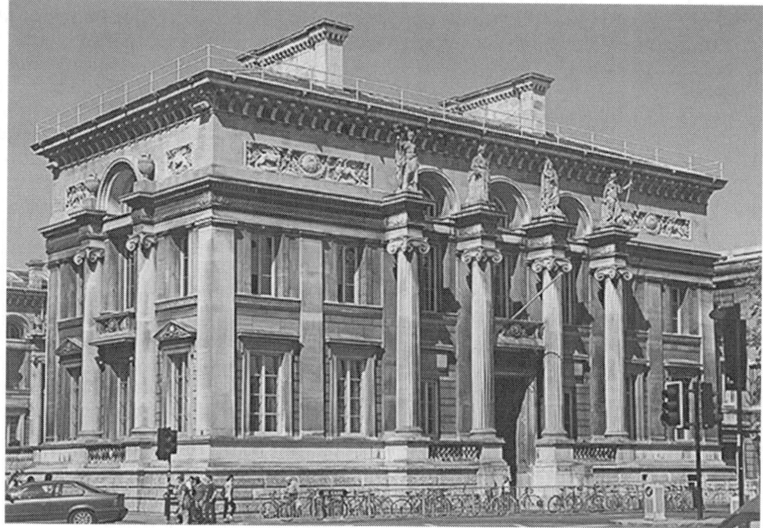

ARCHITECTURE, MODERN: Taylorian Institute, Oxford (designed 1839–40) view from the south-east. The architect, C. R. Cockerell (1788–1863), had made his name in the discovery of the architectural sculpture of the temples at Aigina and Bassai. The engaged (and freestanding) Ionic order show the unique capitals of the inner order at Bassai. The upper windows – framed by piers after the manner of the Choregic Monument of Thrasyllos – are linked by a meander frieze: a carved version of that painted on the inner architrave of the Parthenon. The main architrave has a frieze carved with intertwining bands of the guilloche, following those carved on the base mouldings at the north porch of the Erechtheion at Athens. Where the frieze steps forward over the projecting capitals the outline of the earliest Corinthian capital discovered at Bassai, is carved in shallow relief. But while the detail is Greek, the composition reflects Cockerell's admiration of Palladio's adaptation of ancient Roman architectural models to modern needs: the Taylorian is a variation on the triumphal arch theme of Palladio's Loggia del Capitaniato in Vicenza (1571).

travellers Jacob Spon and George Wheler, but also from contemporary British architects, sponsored by the Society of Dilettanti, who were measuring and drawing the architecture of ancient Greece. Gibbon acknowledges James 'Athenian' Stuart and Nicholas Revett's *The Antiquities of Athens* (vol. 1, 1762), and the work of Richard Chandler (*The Antiquities of Ionia*, vol. 1, 1767). Rome's equivocal acknowledgement of the artistic primacy of Greece was now paralleled by a critical search for origins, combined with a belief in the superiority of the original. However improved the accuracy of delineation and the inherent quality of what was delineated, it cannot be said that the imaginary recreation of ancient Greece through its architecture reaches the emotional intensity of Brunelleschi. Paradoxically, a search for origins leads to a multiplicity of models; Egypt is added to the canon, then the architecture of medieval Europe. Scholarship and architecture separate.

The 240 years that separate Gibbon's presence on the Capitol from our own day present a more bewildering variety of relations to the past in our architecture. A. E. Richardson's *Monumental Classical Architecture of Great Britain and Northern Ireland* (1914) identifies an eclectic mixture: the 'Roman Palladian' (1730–80), the 'Graeco-Roman' (1780–1820), the 'Greek' (1820–40), and the 'Neo-Grec and Italian' (with, as its hero, C. R. Cockerell (1788–1863), the explorer of AIGINA and Bassai). This is confusion indeed – and Richardson was writing about only one stream of 19th-century architecture.

In the 20th century such confusion of models has tended to become more internalized. To take just one example, one of the most influential architects of the century, Le Corbusier (Charles Édouard Jeanneret (1887–1965)), in making his 'Grand Tour' of the classical sites – Athens, POMPEII, Rome – also studied sites which he labelled in his itinerary as 'industry' and 'folklore'. It was a melding of forms and ideas from these three worlds that created his mature architecture, but a melding where the individual elements have become so intertwined that it has taken a generation of scholars to identify them; a situation not unlike that of the study of James Joyce. It is no accident perhaps that for Le Corbusier one of the great discoveries of his life was his reading of Joyce's *Ulysses*. MJG

See Ackerman, J. S. (1992) *Distance Points: essays in theory and Renaissance art and architecture*; Curtis, W. J. R. (1986) *Le Corbusier: ideas and form*; Goalen, M. J. (forthcoming) *Ideal or Model: ancient Greece and modern architecture 1758–1958*; Middleton, R. and Watkin, D. (1980) *Neoclassical and 19th-century Architecture*; Summerson, J. (1963) *The Classical Language of Architecture*.

archives In PAPYROLOGY, the term 'archive' is used to describe a collection of documents concerning an individual, family, institution or office, which were kept together in antiquity and in some cases pasted together to form long rolls. They should be distinguished from a 'dossier', which is used to describe a group of documents that may relate to an individual or institution, but which are grouped together by a modern scholar from diverse sources. Both provide valuable information to the historian: unlike isolated documents, archives and dossiers often provide context. Of these, archives can be particularly informative simply because they have been kept together for a purpose and can thus offer valuable information about ancient documentary practice. This is especially true for official archives, such as that of the *grapheion* (registry office) at Tebtunis in Egypt, dating to the reign of Claudius, which preserves tax registers and legal contracts. But it is often difficult to distinguish boundaries between public and private in archives, as state officials seem often to have kept public documents which have become mixed up with their private correspondence. So far, some 250 archives have been identified, some small, some very large. Small ones allow snapshots of the lives of individuals or families, but often these can be fitted into a broader context. This is certainly the case with larger archives (the best examples are those of Zenon and Heroninos, from the 3rd century BC and 3rd century AD respectively), and it affords the historian the opportunity to fit particular evidence into a more generally valid context. (see also RECORDS, PUBLIC) CEPA

See Bagnall, R. S. (1995) *Reading Papyri, Writing Ancient History.*

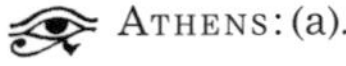 BOOKS: (a).

archon see AREIOPAGOS; POLITICAL PARTICIPATION, GREEK.

Areiopagos (Areopagus; Hill of Ares) The site of the Athenian council of elders, whose composition and role changed alongside developments in Athens' political system, in early times the Areiopagos was a body of ARISTOCRATS, which advised the KING and subsequently the archons. By the time of SOLON its membership of about 150 was made up of ex-archons, and it had taken on the role of guardian of the state and its laws. It had also assumed powers of jurisdiction, notably in homicide cases. Solon's reforms restricted the political influence of the Areiopagos, and the nature of its membership was radically modified as the archons were elected on the basis of wealth instead of family background. The decline in their power during the 5th century further detracted from the Areiopagos' political position, and the crucial blow to this anachronistic remnant from Athens' non-democratic past was delivered in 462/1 BC by the reforms of Ephialtes. But the Areiopagos retained its jurisdiction in cases of homicide (an ancient role celebrated in AESCHYLUS' *Eumenides*), wounding and arson, and in religious cases; and this judicial function continued at least until the 4th century AD. MJE

See Wallace, R. W. (1989) *The Areopagus Council to 307 BC.*

ATHENS: (a).

aretê see MORALITY.

Areus I SPARTAN king of the Agiad house (r.309–265), who succeeded his aged grandfather, the little-known Kleomenes II (king since 370), and reigned himself for a further 40 years, mostly as senior king. He introduced Sparta to COINAGE, minting Alexander-style coins with the legend 'of king Areus' – no co-king is named. He seems to have introduced some of the style of early hellenistic monarchy to Sparta, such as through royal portrait sculpture, and cultivated diplomatic links with kings abroad as well as the JEWS (correspondence in the first book of MACCABEES). After a quiet period since Agis III was killed fighting the Macedonians in 331, Sparta was militarily active again. Areus campaigned in Italy (helping Sparta's colony Taras (Tarentum) against its enemies, 303) and central Greece (attempting to free Delphi from the Aitolians, 281), and repelled invasions by DEMETRIOS I and PYRRHOS. The Athenian decree of c.268 documenting the southern Greek alliance against Macedonia at the outset of the CHREMONIDEAN WAR names Areus alongside 'the Lakedaimonians', again without his co-king. He was killed attempting to liberate Corinth. If there were opportunities to modernize the social structure during his reign, he did not take them. Some 20 years after his death Sparta's fortunes reached their nadir, prompting the radical reforms of AGIS IV and KLEOMENES III. DGJS

See Cartledge, P. and Spawforth, A. (2002) *Hellenistic and Roman Sparta.*

Arginousai (Arginusae) The small islands off LESBOS near the coast of Asia Minor, where the Athenians won a decisive naval victory over the Spartan alliance (406 BC) in the greatest sea-battle of the PELOPONNESIAN WAR. The fleet of 150 triremes under Athenian leadership faced 120 more skilfully manned ships of the Spartan alliance. The death of the gifted young Spartan admiral Kallikratidas (another LYSANDER in the making) and innovative outflanking tactics by the Athenians led the Spartans to withdraw after hard fighting and caused the loss of more than half their armada. As many as 20,000 Greeks may have died from the fighting and subsequent rough weather.

The Athenian strategic advantages from the battle were reversed two years later at the catastrophe at AIGOSPOTAMOI (404). Arginousai, however, became infamous because of the subsequent Athenian indictment of the victorious admirals, who were unable to bring home safely the surviving Athenian crews of the disabled and sunken ships – purportedly because of miscommunications and rough seas. Nearly 1,000 survivors, clinging to at least 12 wrecked triremes, drowned; hundreds of corpses disappeared beneath the waves.

Two of the returning ship-captains, Theramenes and THRASYBOULOS, avoided punishment but added to the hysteria whipped up by demagogues and the families of the lost. Six of the admirals who obeyed the summons were quite illegally tried in mass and then executed – among them the late PERIKLES' son. SOCRATES' refusal as a member of the *prytaneis* to take part in the illicit action became legendary – a commentary both on his own personal integrity and the destructive tendency of the Athenian *dêmos* to devour its own at its greatest moment of success. VDH

See Kagan, D. (1987) *The Fall of the Athenian Empire.*

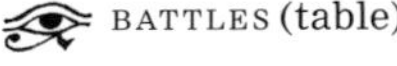 BATTLES (table).

Argonauts see APOLLONIOS OF RHODES.

Argos and the Argolid In historical times Argos was the principal settlement in the Argive plain, the largest on the east coast of the PELOPONNESE and home to sizeable populations in the Bronze Age and later. 'Argolis' and 'Argeia' are used of the plain and its surrounding valleys, and sometimes of the mountainous peninsula stretching 50 km (30 miles) to the south-east, also known as the Argolic Akte, which followed largely an independent course and had three to five small city-states.

In the Bronze Age, Mycenae, Tiryns and Midea all had fortified citadels with PALACES. The relationship of the different settlements is obscure but the area was clearly the richest and most dynamic in Greece, with wide-ranging and productive maritime contacts. After the collapse of MYCENAEAN civilization, Argos emerged by the 8th century as a prosperous town, probably second to none in mainland Greece. The sanctuary of HERA 9 km ($5\frac{1}{2}$ miles) to the north, the arena for the display of Argos' leadership in the whole area, may only gradually have come completely under Argive control. Agreement on a *modus vivendi* between the leading settlements, all Doric in dialect and tradition, explains why the outermost settlements, at Asine and then Nauplia, were the first to be subjugated (c.700 and c.600 BC, respectively).

Interpretation of the early historical period is controversial, as are the date and character of Pheidon, KING or TYRANT, and dated variously late 8th to early 6th century. In periods when Sparta dominated the Peloponnese from the south and CORINTH was active in trade and COLONIZATION on the north coast, Argos and its neighbouring settlements remained relatively isolated and turned inwards. A stable and conservative regime of substantial landowners controlling a dependent serf-like labour force, and understandings between the major communities of such landowners, sustained a prosperous society and a HOPLITE army that was potentially, though rarely in fact, a serious rival to Spartan power. On recovery from a crushing defeat by Sparta early in the 5th century BC (battle of Sepeia), the Argives put an end to the autonomy of the other communities (notably Mycenae and Tiryns), probably to the benefit of their own growing, free lower class. Alliances with Athens and, more rarely, Corinth (which briefly, early in the 4th century BC, took the form of a union of the two cities) were to keep Sparta at bay. In the hellenistic era, when not under the control of tyrants, Argos was an important member of the ACHAIAN LEAGUE. In the Roman period, freed of political pressures, the town flourished as a provincial centre.

Reports of extensive excavations in the town of Argos and some specialized studies have been issued, but there is no comprehensive publication. MHJ

See Foley, A. (1988) *The Argolid 800–600 BC*; Jameson, M. H. et al. (1994) *A Greek Countryside: the southern Argolid from prehistory to the present day*; Kelly, T. (1976) *A History of Argos to 500 BC*; Mee, C. B. and Forbes, H., eds. (1997) *A Rough and Rocky Place* [Methana survey]; Tomlinson, R. (1972) *Argos and the Argolid*; Wells, B., ed. (1996) *The Berbati–Limnes Archaeological Survey.*

GREECE; PELOPONNESE.

Ariadne see BACCHUS; THESEUS.

Arianism A doctrine named after Arius (c.AD 260–336), a presbyter from ALEXANDRIA, which questioned the relationship of the persons of the Trinity, claiming that the Son could not be consubstantial with the Father. This maintained the MONOTHEISTIC supreme power of the Father, but threw doubt on the validity of the sacrifice of Christ, if he were less than God. The controversy was dealt with by CONSTANTINE at the council of Nicaea (325). The emperor, whose main interest was in political unity rather than theological orthodoxy, presided over a decision that the Son was *homoöusios* (of the same substance) with the Father. The Nicene Creed stressed the unity of the Father and the Son but did not settle the question of Arianism.

Various forms of Arianism developed in the aftermath of Nicaea, the most radical group being the *Anomoians* or neo-Arians (claiming that Father and Son were completely unlike, *anomoios*, each other), the more conciliatory known as the *Homoians* (from *homoios*, 'similar'). Arianism also had political repercussions. It created power rivalries between the sees of Rome, CONSTANTINOPLE and Alexandria. Constantius II and Valens both held anti-Nicene views. JULIAN allowed the controversy to continue in the hope that it would damage the CHRISTIAN CHURCH, but orthodoxy was finally victorious in the East under THEODOSIUS I at the council of Constantinople (381). In the West Arianism continued to be problematic with the conversion of many GOTHS by the Arian Ulfila. (see also CHURCH COUNCILS) MEH

See Barnes, T. D. (1993) *Athanasius and Constantius*; Hanson, R. P. C. (1988) *The Search for the Christian Doctrine of God*; Williams, R. (1987) Arianism, in E. Ferguson, ed., *Encyclopedia of Early Christianity.*

Aricia see DIANA; DICTATORS; LARS PORSENNA.

Aristarchos of Samos c.310–230 BC Greek ASTRONOMER who worked in Alexandria. He was the first to advance the heliocentric hypothesis (quoted by Archimedes, *Sand-reckoner* 4–5): that the earth is not the centre of everything, but revolves around the sun. Yet in calculating (in his only preserved work) the sun's distance from the earth, he used the orthodox model. It has been suggested that his hypothesis was an exercise rather than a serious description of reality, since he assumes the apparent diameter of the moon to be 2 degrees, four times what it should be. But although PLUTARCH says Aristarchos 'only hypothesized' the heliocentric idea, he probably did offer it as a mathematically true account of the movements of the heavenly bodies. It was perhaps too much at odds with accepted COSMOLOGY to find favour; Plutarch says only one later astronomer stated it as a fact. Aristarchos also invented a type of SUNDIAL and calculated accurately the length of the year, probably from Babylonian data. He exemplifies the extent to which early hellenistic scientists, while not eschewing practical applications, were more interested in model-building than testing hypotheses against data. DGJS, CLNR

See Irby-Massie, G. L. and Keyser, P. T. (2002) *Greek Science of the Hellenistic Era*; Thomas, I., trs. (1941) *Greek Mathematical Works*, vol. 1.

Aristarchos of Samothrace see COMMENTATORS, TEXTUAL; HESYCHIOS; PHILETAS; SCHOLARSHIP, ANCIENT.

Aristeides ('the Just') c.520–467 BC Athenian statesman and general. About his family we know only that he was related to Kallias son of Hipponikos, one of the richest men in Athens. Popular tradition remarked on the extreme poverty of Aristeides, who was buried at public expense, but in the early 5th century he must have had sufficient wealth to qualify for the office of archon.

According to PLUTARCH, Aristeides was a *hetairos* (associate) of KLEISTHENES, which may suggest that his family was closely associated with the Alkmaionids and the democratic reforms of 508/7. In 490/89 he was elected *stratêgos* and served as general at MARATHON. In 489/8 he was chosen archon, and in the decade that followed he earned such a reputation for integrity that his popularity rivalled that of THEMISTOKLES. This may have led to his OSTRACISM in 482. Later tradition presented Aristeides as the honest conservative opposed to the wily demagogue, Themistokles. In 480, under a general amnesty, Aristeides returned to Athens, and at the battle of SALAMIS he led Athenian troops against PERSIAN forces stationed on the islet of Psyttaleia. In 479/8 he was again elected *stratêgos* and commanded the Athenian contingent at PLATAEA. As *stratêgos* in 478/7 he led the Athenian arm of the allied Greek NAVY and was instrumental in securing the transfer of leadership from Sparta to Athens. When the Delian league was formed in the same year, he was chosen to draw up the assessment of contributing members. After this date, his career falls into obscurity. CC

See Plutarch, *Life of Aristeides*; Davies, J. K. (1971) *Athenian Propertied Families*; Develin, R. (1989) *Athenian Officials: 684–321 BC*.

 OSTRACISM.

aristocracy The Greek word *aristokratia* ('rule of the best') appears to have been coined in the 5th century BC as a balance to *dêmokratia* ('rule of the people'). It was used by PLATO in the *Republic* to denote the ideal form of constitution. But the English word aristocracy is used primarily to denote the government of archaic Greece, the key to which was birth: power was in the hands of hereditary nobilities of wealthy landowners. Archaic Greek aristocracies, particularly of the 6th century, are characterized by the aspiration to refined culture, seen for example in their cultivation of sculpture, LYRIC POETRY and athleticism. At Athens the aristocrats were called the Eupatridai ('well-born'), members of some 60 families (*genê*) who ruled through the AREIOPAGOS council. The aristocrats' supremacy was in time challenged by a new class of rich citizens whose WEALTH was based on non-landed property and who served as HOPLITES in the army. As they demanded a share in government, wealth gradually superseded birth as the basis of power, a process legitimated at Athens by SOLON's reforms. Democracy was never universal, however, and aristocracy persisted in states such as Sparta.

The term aristocracy is also applicable at Rome, where the Republic was in practice governed by a restricted group of about 50 aristocratic families (*nobiles*), who dominated the CONSULSHIP. A class of wealthy, non-noble Romans developed as in Greece, but while entry to the SENATE was achievable through the QUAESTORSHIP, relatively few reached the highest levels so jealously guarded by the old aristocracy. MJE

See Gabrielsen, V. (1997) *The Naval Aristocracy of Hellenistic Rhodes*; Gardner, J. F., ed. (1974) *Leadership and the Cult of the Personality*; Gelzer, M. (1969) *The Roman Nobility*, trs. R. Seager; Malkin, I. and Rubinsohn, Z.W., eds. (1995) *Leaders and Masses in the Roman World*; Ober, J. (1989) *Mass and Elite in Democratic Athens*; Starr, C. G. (1992) *The Aristocratic Temper of Greek Civilization*.

Aristophanes The most successful writer of OLD COMEDY, who wrote at least 40 plays, 11 of which survive, and won several first prizes. He was born (probably) some time between 460 and 450 BC and died in, or shortly before, 386. Aristophanes is the only playwright from this period whose plays have come down to us complete, and for this reason is frequently considered synonymous with ancient Greek comedy as a whole. There were, however, other great comic writers after him, like MENANDER, as well as before and contemporary with him – Epicharmos, Kratinos and Eupolis, for example. The Aristophanes that we have may not necessarily be typical either of his work or of his genre. Fantastic situations are a favourite of his – a speaking dog (*Wasps*), a city in the sky (*Birds*), a giant beetle (*Peace*) and a visit to the underworld (*Frogs*). MYTH and RITUAL are, it has been argued, important elements; several titles of lost plays suggest mythological burlesque.

Aristophanes liked to indulge in vicious political satire, targeting real individuals. Among the latter are KLEON (in *Knights*), EURIPIDES (*Frogs* and *Women at the Thesmophoria* or *Thesmophoriazousai*) and SOCRATES (*Clouds*). He tackles with vigour current political issues, such as the need for peace and friendship with SPARTA (*Acharnians*, *Lysistrata*). Allusions which could be obscure are sometimes brought up to date in modern productions, an intellectual challenge for any translator or producer, but worth the effort to convey something of the impact of the original jokes. Aristophanes' wit tends to be abusive. This is also true of the ORATORS, however, whose audience in the LAWCOURTS may have been essentially the same people. Sex and excretion are frequent and acceptable sources of humour for Aristophanes.

Scholars continue to debate whether Aristophanes is ever being serious. Some argue that the 'carnival' atmosphere of the FESTIVALS at which Old Comedy was presented did give a certain freedom to insult powerful but foolish individuals. The competitions were, though, very much civic events at which the *dêmos* itself could hardly be criticized. Kleon was provoked to prosecute Aristophanes (unsuccessfully) for abusing the Athenians in a play, the *Babylonians* of 426, but Aristophanes' response was a whole play, the *Knights*, making fun of him. The Athenians voted this play first prize; soon afterwards, however, they elected Kleon a GENERAL. PLATO claimed in his *Apology* that *Clouds* helped to create the prejudice against Socrates that led to his death: in his *Symposium*, however, the playwright and the PHILOSOPHER are portrayed as friendly drinking companions.

There are lyrical passages in Aristophanes which seem to express genuine sentiments, such as praise for the farmer's way of life, untroubled by WAR. Vulgarity and farce are otherwise characteristic of the plays, and Aristophanes exploits this incongruity. Sometimes the very last word of a 'serious' piece will have a surprising comic twist. Aristophanes also enjoys making up ridiculously long words.

ORACLES and technical language lent themselves to extensive parody. Often parodies are grounded in a thorough acquaintance with actual tragic passages. In *Frogs*, for instance, AESCHYLUS and Euripides imitate each other's lyrics. Sometimes the play selected for such treatment had only recently been performed and been a success – take the parody of Euripides' *Andromeda* in *Thesmophoriazousai*, with the Old Man, in the role of Andromeda, being rescued by Euripides as Perseus.

Many of Aristophanes' plays take their names from the CHORUS, a band of 24 people who sang and danced elaborately symmetrical routines, wearing MASKS and brightly coloured costumes. This is the case with *Wasps*, *Birds* (which alludes to many different kinds of birds) and *Frogs* (if the chorus in that play were seen). The chorus' entry onto the stage (the *parodos*) would have been spectacular, and in what is known as the *parabasis* they would address the audience directly. Bridging the transition between Old and New Comedy are *Women at the Assembly* and *Wealth*, two later comedies (c.391 and 388 BC respectively), in which the role of the chorus is diminished. Interludes of some kind, however, are indicated in the texts by the word *chorou*, 'song of the chorus'.

It is said of Aristophanes that he is happy to sacrifice consistency of character to the particular demands of the plot or the joke, but there are some extremely memorable characters in the plays. Xanthias, for instance (*Frogs*), is the forerunner of some New Comedy SLAVES, cheekily playing tricks on the unsuspecting DIONYSOS. (To make fun of the god of the THEATRE himself and characterize him as cowardly was not, apparently, forbidden.) There is the powerful Lysistrata in the play of that name, a woman (possibly recalling a real PRIESTESS, Lysimache) taking over the man's world of the Athenian assembly.

Aristophanes was representing Athenian men's worst nightmares in comic form, this being emphasized, it has been argued, by the fact that all the women's parts were in fact performed by male ACTORS (as in most ancient DRAMA). As a character, Lysistrata may have been seen as more ridiculous than admirable to Aristophanes' original audiences – or is some serious point being made about women? What is certain is that Aristophanes remains, despite his specific topical references and his age, fresh, appealing and hilarious – fun to watch and fun to perform. AMH

See Henderson, J., trs. (1998–2002) *Aristophanes*, 4 vols.; Sommerstein, A.H., trs. and commentary (1980–2002) *The Comedies of Aristophanes*, 12 vols.; Bowie, A.M. (1993) *Aristophanes*; Cartledge, P. (1990) *Aristophanes and his Theatre of the Absurd*; Dover, K. J. (1972) *Aristophanic Comedy*; MacDowell, D. M. (1995) *Aristophanes and Athens*.

 DRAMA: (a).

Aristotelianism The body of philosophical doctrines associated with ARISTOTLE and with subsequent attempts to interpret and develop his views. Among the doctrines most characteristic of Aristotelianism (though not all were accepted by all of Aristotle's followers) can be included the following. KNOWLEDGE and enquiry are valuable for their own sake. PLATO's doctrine that material objects derive their being from immaterial exemplars of each type of thing (the Platonic 'Forms') is to be rejected. Individual things ('substances', such as human beings) are the primary existents on the earth and the region surrounding it as far as the moon; qualities, quantities and the like are attributes of substances. The SOUL cannot exist independently of the BODY. There is only one world-system, with our earth at its centre, and it is everlasting. There is a distinction between the heavens, which undergo movement but no other type of change, and the sublunary region, where individual things come to be and pass away. Things in the sublunary region are made up of four 'elements', fire, air, water and earth, which can however change into each other; the heavens are made of a distinct, fifth element. MATTER is essentially continuous, even if small temporary pockets of void exist. Teleological explanation, explanation in terms of purpose, is appropriate for at least some of the things in the universe. Virtue on its own is not sufficient for happiness, though it is necessary for it. EMOTIONS (such as anger) should be felt to the appropriate extent; absence of proper emotion, as well as excess, is a fault. (see also PERIPATETICS) RWS

See Caston, V. (1997) Epiphenomenalisms: ancient and modern, *Philosophical Review* 106: 309–63; Gottschalk, H. B. (1987) Aristotelian philosophy in the Roman world, in H. Temporini and W. Haase, eds., *ANRW* 2.36.2, 1079–174; Sharples, R.W. (1999) The Peripatetic school, in D.J. Furley, ed., *From Aristotle to Augustine* 147–87.

Aristotle (Aristotelês) 384–322 BC Although a MACEDONIAN, Aristotle lived most of his life in Athens, where he associated with PLATO for 20 years, writing dialogues in the manner of his master. None of these survives: we possess virtually nothing of Aristotle's published ('exoteric') work. Rather we have notes, made either for or from his private ('esoteric') lectures, edited two centuries after his death; this accounts for the unliterary roughness of Aristotle's style as we have it. But what we do possess amounts to the largest surviving philosophical *oeuvre* from classical antiquity, and the most important and influential. It is a body of work staggering in its intellectual range and grasp. Aristotle wrote and lectured on LOGIC, LANGUAGE, RHETORIC, poetics, the theory of KNOWLEDGE, the nature of SCIENCE, METAPHYSICS and PHYSICS, biology, COSMOLOGY, psychology, ETHICS and POLITICS. He made important contributions to all of these fields, and founded several of them.

In logic, he pioneered the systematic treatment of argument (*Prior Analytics*), distinguishing valid patterns (those yielding true conclusions from true premises in virtue of their form) from invalid, and investigating the nature of possibility and necessity. This gave logic a fundamental form it was to retain until the late 19th century. In line with this, he elaborated an account of the nature of science in which sciences were to be presented as rigorous deductions from necessarily true general premises about the domain in question (*Posterior Analytics*), the fundamental axioms of which are taken to impress themselves directly upon the faithful, observant and intellectually capable investigator.

In *De anima* (*On the Soul*) he developed a psychology to support this. Perception, he holds, is a fundamentally causal process, in which ANIMALS who are so suited by nature take on in their sensoria the form of the things perceived without their MATTER. From these formal imprints are developed general concepts in the form of physical mental traces which are then used (at least by those animals, paradigmatically humans, capable of so using them) as the foundations for discursive thought. Minds are not separate Cartesian stuffs, on Aristotle's view, but rather simply locuses of psychological capacities. Those capacities cannot be exhaustively described in material terms, but equally they cannot be instantiated other than in matter (with the possible and controversial exception of pure intellect, and of the pure thinking being, God).

Aristotle's psychology is linked both with his general biology and his metaphysics, as well as with his ethics and politics. The idea that what distinguishes animal species from each other is what they are capable of doing informs his general understanding of the hierarchical organization of nature. The universe is a universe of ends: things are directed towards their particular goals, the fulfilment of their specific capacities.

This drives the 'function argument' of his ethics. If we want to know what is the best human life, we must first determine what it is that humans do characteristically (or best) as humans. The good human life will then consist in fulfilling these 'functions' to the highest degree possible. These functions turn out to be, in the *Nicomachean Ethics*, the capacity for deliberation about the future, and (relatedly) the capacity for complex social organization. The distinctively human 'virtues' just are the abilities (and the dispositions) to carry out these functions, and thus Aristotelian virtues divide into intellectual (broadly speaking those having to do with rational deliberation) and moral (having to do with social organization).

Thus the moral virtues (courage, benevolence and wittiness, among others) are those dispositions in virtue of which we are good at living together. But they are also, for Aristotle, integral to the expression of humanity – in a genuine sense, a recluse or a misanthrope is not properly a human being at all. Aristotle's answer to the question 'why should I be good' is, simply, that if I am not I am subhuman, a poor representative of my species.

Politics, which for Aristotle was continuous with ethics, is thus the study of what types of political organization are most conducive to the realization of these goals. But crucially Aristotle saw individual human beings as necessarily (at least in their fulfilled condition) part of a larger social whole. The state is a natural, organic growth in a very literal sense – and, as with all natural things, its parts exist for the sake of the whole. Notoriously, some parts are better than others, and the worse exist for the sake of the better. Thus Aristotle seeks to justify the subordination of women (in whom reason is not in control) to men, and of 'natural SLAVES' to the naturally free. Political power should be given to those who are by nature fitted to exercise it. Aristotle's politics is less authoritarian (and more practical) than Plato's, but it is hardly more democratic.

Here Aristotle's biological researches, which were of an unprecedentedly detailed and incisive nature, feed into the picture. His great study of animal morphology, *Parts of Animals*, is designed to bring out the functional well-adaptedness of animals' bodies, as well as noting the intricate relations of generic similarities and differences which they manifest. In general, Aristotle thought, animals are only provided with organs they can make use of. This relates back to the psychology: only creatures capable of locomotion are endowed with senses, since it is only if you have the power to reposition yourself within your environment that there is much point in knowing what that environment is like. Nature, in Aristotle's famous teleological slogan, does nothing in vain.

But it is important not to misunderstand the nature of this teleology. Although Aristotle's universe contains a God, a pure thinking being untainted by physical weariness, that God has nothing (at any rate directly) to do with the organization of the world. Aristotle's God, unlike Plato's, is not a creator. Rather, to say that nature does nothing in vain is simply to state in its most general terms a fact about the irreducibly purposive nature of the physical world. It is a structure of wholes and their parts directed intrinsically towards ends.

Another way of putting that is to say that merely analysing the furniture of the world in terms of the matter of which it is composed, plus various dynamic properties, will not be enough to account for the emergence of complex self-regulating and self-replicating structures. Aristotle is implacably opposed to those, pre-eminently the ATOMISTS, who did indeed think exactly that complex worlds simply arise from time to time out of the random buzz of atoms in the void. For Aristotle, such an explanation cannot remotely account for the incredible complexity and well-adaptedness of the biosphere, as well as its stability and self-regulation. Hence the introduction of the irreducible teleological component into natural explanation, the final cause.

The final cause is one of Aristotle's four fundamental categories of explanation (outlined in *Physics* 2.3 and put to work throughout his works). The others are the formal, the material and the efficient causes. Form and matter are among Aristotle's basic metaphysical categories. The form is, roughly, what the thing is, its causal structure and what is captured in its definition; the matter is what underlies or supports the form. The form–matter distinction is closely related to another Aristotelian duo, that of actuality and potentiality: matter is what is (something or other) potentially, but not as such actually, the fully formed individual. Equally, matter is assimilated to the generic, form to the specific: form is a restriction of a more general class. But form, too, is in a sense general. All of us share a single universal human form; still, it may have particular instantiations in distinct parcels of matter, with different spatio-temporal histories, and in that sense your form is numerically distinct from mine though specifically identical with it. Aristotle struggles to elucidate these difficult notions in the central books of his *Metaphysics*.

Change, a metaphysical problem since PARMENIDES, is also analysed in these terms. Change consists of a materially persisting substrate taking on a new form. This may be of a substantial nature, making a new thing (as when a human being is created by the sperm's inducing a certain form in the menstrual matter), or it may be merely an incidental change, leaving the overall identity of the object intact (as when a fair skin becomes tanned). In the latter case, the object itself, considered as a substantial form, is what persists through the change. But in the case of the coming into existence of substances (particular individual entities), what persists is the matter which makes them up, then unformed, now formed. All such changes are induced by some agent, or efficient cause, which in Aristotle's view shares the form which it induces; man begets man, as he puts it. It is this formal identity between efficient causes and what they produce that accounts for the stability of the natural world which Aristotle thinks inexplicable in purely mechanistic, material terms. Typically (though not invariably), too, these natural processes are directed towards some end (indeed, the end may be conceived as the working-out of the formal blueprint: thus efficient, formal, and final causes are closely linked). And thus all four of the Aristotelian causes are invoked in paradigmatic cases of change.

Also relevant here is the distinction between essence and accident. A thing's essence (expressed in its definition) is its form – it cannot cease to have it and remain the same thing. By contrast, its various accidental properties (e.g. size, colour) may alter without affecting its identity as such. If a thing genuinely does possess an essence, then it is in Aristotle's terms a substance, an ontologically free-standing item, the proper subject of predicates. In his early essay in logical grammar, the *Categories*, Aristotle unequivocally accepts that substance is primarily individual: species terms such as 'human' indicate secondary substances. This is one expression of one of Aristotle's fundamental disagreements with Plato, who made form separable, and individual. For Aristotle, form is always the form of something. And yet by the *Metaphysics*, he found himself pulled in the direction of the generality of form, since he was convinced that, *qua* human, no individual human differs from any other: all essence (and hence all definition, for definitions are accounts of essences) is general.

This brief survey has done no more than scratch the surface of a few central Aristotelian concerns. Nothing has been said of his zoological researches, his detailed investigation and account of the *Generation of Animals*, his elaboration of an elemental theory of the universe in *De Caelo*, *On Generation and Corruption*, and *Meteorology* (essentially the study of the intermediate elements between heaven and earth, and thus broader than its title suggests). His *Rhetoric* included a seminal discussion of the nature of emotion. His enormously influential (if incomplete) *Poetics* introduced the world to such concepts as catharsis, the tragic error, and reversal of fortune. Aristotle truly was, as Dante said, 'the master of those who know'. RJH

See Barnes, J., ed. (1984) *The Complete Works of Aristotle* (trs.); note also Aristotle, *Politics*, trs. E. Barker (1995); Barnes, J. (1982) *Aristotle*; Lear, J. (1988) *Aristotle: the desire to understand*.

Arkadia The heartland of the PELOPONNESE, and the largest of its regions apart from LACONIA. It corresponds roughly to modern Arkadía (c.4,300 sq km, 1,660 sq miles), though it had no coastline. The two largest cultivable plains are separated by hill-land. The eastern plain contained the important city-states of Tegea and MANTINEIA with a less prominent city-state, Orchomenos. Its altitude (c.650 m) precludes the growing of OLIVES or FIGS, while a lack of good drainage gave rise to marshes, necessitating careful water management. The lower, western plain (c.430 m), through which runs the river Alpheios, supported no major towns before the mid-4th century. By far the largest part of Arkadia, however, is mountain land, separating these plains from the north coast of the Peloponnese and containing most of the 40-odd classical Arkadian city-states (as well as sizeable lakes at Stymphalos and Pheneos). Land communications were easiest in the south, to and from LACONIA and MESSENIA (the western plain being essentially a continuation of the Eurotas furrow), though its position makes Arkadia a nodal point in the road system of the entire Peloponnese.

XENOPHON says the Arkadians are the most numerous people in Greece, the only indigenous inhabitants of the Peloponnese, and highly regarded as MERCENARY soldiers. Regional identities were strong, and local groups of smaller towns joined together to form larger organizations. In archaic times Tegea, the *polis* closest to SPARTA, offered stern resistance which may have led Sparta to adopt a less aggressive, alliance-based strategy for dominating the Peloponnese. Rivalries between major towns determined much of Arkadian history; Mantineia, Tegea's neighbour, was often anti-Spartan because Tegea was loyal to Sparta. After Sparta's defeat by Thebes in 371, Megalopolis (more correctly Megalêpolis), 'Bigtown', was founded as a safeguard against Spartan power, absorbing many smaller communities in western Arkadia. The short-lived, markedly democratic Arkadian FEDERAL league of the 360s offered the possibility of strength through unity, but soon split into Megalopolitan and Mantineian camps, perhaps permanently. In the early hellenistic period, emigration, a permanent feature of Arkadian life, was high. Sparta again threatened the towns, and many joined the ACHAIAN LEAGUE heyday. Excavation at city sites such as Gortys and Stymphalos reveals the development of advanced amenities in late classical and hellenistic times, while urban and rural cults also underwent architectural development. Reports of depopulation under Roman rule may reflect conditions in the countryside, but many towns remained prosperous and survived into medieval times. The idealized, PASTORAL Arkadia of hellenistic and Roman poetry reflects life in the smaller mountain *poleis* rather than those of the plain. It captures, however, the importance of urban and rural cult places for local identities, exemplified by the excavated sanctuaries at Lousoi, Lykosoura and Tegea (Athena Alea) and the well-preserved temple at Bassai. (see also GOLDEN AGE) DGJS

See Pausanias, book 8; Jost, M. (1985) *Sanctuaires et cultes d'Arcadie*; Nielsen, T. H. and Roy, J., eds. (1999) *Defining Ancient Arkadia*; Nielsen, T. H. (2002) *Arkadia and its Poleis in the Archaic and Classical Periods*.

Arles see AMPHITHEATRES; BARBEGAL; CHURCH COUNCILS; CIRCUS BUILDINGS; MARSEILLES; RHÔNE.

Armenia and Armenians A hilly area situated in Transcaucasia, east of ANATOLIA, in ancient times bounded by Atropatene, CAPPADOCIA and COMMAGENE. Armenians are an Indo-European people, successors to the Urartu in the region around Lake Van, the river Araxes and Lake Sevan. Between 530 and 331 BC the territory was a satrapy of the Achaemenid empire; later it became SELEUKID territory; then it was subject to MITHRADATES. After followers of POMPEY colonized Asia Minor it became known as Greater Armenia, reaching as far as the upper Euphrates in the east. The first local Armenian dynasty, the Orontids, ruled from c.330–c.190 BC; their successors, the house of Artaxias, ruled to AD 14. The most famous and ambitious king of this dynasty, Tigranes II (the Great), allied himself with MITHRADATES VI and was thereby brought into conflict with Rome. After half a century of confusion, the Arsakid dynasty came to power in AD 63 and reigned until 428, latterly as Roman clients.

Armenia had been proclaimed a Roman PROVINCE during TRAJAN's Eastern campaign and remained under Roman control until the end of the 3rd century. From the 3rd century the SASSANIDS coveted it, and in 296 Narses concluded a treaty with DIOCLETIAN, recognizing all Armenia as Roman, but only as a protectorate. In 387 the PERSIANS occupied half the country. The early conversion to CHRISTIANITY of Armenia, straddling the trade routes to the East, benefited Rome. From the 6th century Armenia established close links with the Byzantine empire. It was conquered by the Arabs in 653.

Culturally, three main periods can be distinguished, coinciding with political developments and influence. The first, known as the ACHAEMENID and dating from the 6th to the 4th century BC, shows not just a very strong Achaemenid influence on all aspects of life but the probable existence in Armenia of one of the satrapal production centres. The second, covering the hellenistic period, shows very strong Greek influence brought here by the rule of ALEXANDER the Great (Strabo 11.14.1–16). The 1st to 3rd centuries AD are noticeable for the Roman features in Armenian culture; this was when the most famous royal residential complex was built in Garni, with a wonderful Greek-style TEMPLE (completely restored at the beginning of the 20th century). GRT

See Chahin, M. (1987) *The Kingdom of Armenia*; Burney, C. and Lang, D. M. (1971) *The Peoples of the Hills*.

SYRIA, ROMAN: (b).

armies, organization of

Greek states often hired MERCENARIES and sometimes maintained small standing forces of citizens, but the bulk of their armies always consisted of amateur soldiers, recruited *ad hoc* from the citizen body. The core of such armies were the HOPLITES (*hoplitai*), heavy armed infantrymen, supported by a numerous but apparently disorganized crowd of light-armed troops (*psiloi*). The communities of northern Greece maintained large CAVALRY forces and troops of specialist javelin throwers (*peltastai*). These often lent their services, as allies or mercenaries, to those cities (including ATHENS and SPARTA) that regarded horsemen and javelin-throwers as inferior in courage to hoplites, and therefore trained no peltasts of their own and did not begin to raise their own cavalry until the late 5th century BC.

In early Greece, mobilization for communal warfare (as opposed to private raiding) was probably largely enforced by the pressure of public opinion (Homer, *Odyssey* 14.237–9), but fines may have been imposed (*Iliad* 13.669). By c.600 BC, service in the heavy infantry was a legal obligation in Athens for all who had an annual income of 200 *medimnoi* (8 tonnes) of AGRICULTURAL produce, and in Sparta for all who were able to make a fixed contribution in kind to the common messes. The level of these property requirements was high – many below this level could and did buy their own ARMS AND ARMOUR – and the obligation to serve thus extended only to a rather small ÉLITE. The less well-off were free to serve, as hoplites or light-armed men, but were under no compulsion to do so. At the root of this arrangement lay a close link between military duty and political privilege: only those liable to hoplite service had the right to hold office in Athens, and the right to vote in Sparta.

Most campaigns involved the mobilization of no more than a few thousand men from among those obliged to serve, selected on an individual basis (in 5th-century Athens, lists of names were posted in the Agora) or by year-groups (as in Sparta, and later in Athens). By contrast, mobilization in self-defence, and for large-scale campaigns against neighbours, was 'by general levy' (*pandêmei*), including not only the entire hoplite census class but everyone in possession of any kind of weapon. The presence in the general levy of light-armed soldiers – citizens, resident aliens and SLAVE attendants – was taken for granted and is rarely mentioned. A 'large crowd of light-armed' joined the Athenian hoplites in their invasions of MEGARA, for example, and more than 10,000 light-armed took part in the Athenian invasion of BOIOTIA in 424 BC (Thucydides 1.106, 2.31, 4.72, 93–4).

In the Homeric epics, armies are crowds of small warrior bands, each consisting of a leader and his personal followers; they are loosely connected by personal ties between leaders, and ranked by their leader's personal status. Developments during the archaic period are poorly attested, but it is clear that they resulted in the formalization and centralization of armies, with the creation of fixed hierarchies of units commanded by publicly appointed officers.

The classical Spartan army consisted of 'sworn bands' (*enômotiai*) of between 30 and 40 men, two or more of which formed a 'fifty' (*pentêkostys*). Two or more 'fifties' formed a 'company' (*lochos*) or 'regiment' (*mora*) – or first a 'company' and then a 'regiment' at the next level – commanded by a *polemarchos*. Several regiments made up an army, under the supreme command of a Spartan king or general and his staff. The sources are inconsistent, and Spartan military organization probably changed repeatedly, but its comparatively elaborate hierarchy always stood out: 'almost the entire Spartan army consists of officers above officers' (Thucydides 5.66). Even so, there were spectacular examples of insubordination and of commanders taking advice from common soldiers in the midst of battle (Herodotos 9.53–7; Thucydides 5.65, 71–2; Xenophon, *Hellenika* 4.2.22).

The Athenian army had only three levels of command: the board of GENERALS (*stratêgoi*), with their staff, who were in charge of the army as a whole; the *taxiarchoi*, who led each of the ten 'tribal' regiments, introduced in 501 BC; and the commanders of an unspecified number of companies into which each tribe was divided (Aristotle, *Athenian Constitution* 61.3).

The main form of training was exercise in the GYMNASIA, which primarily consisted of wrestling, running, jumping and throwing the javelin and discus. It may have included weapons training, but apparently no formation drill. DANCING was seen as

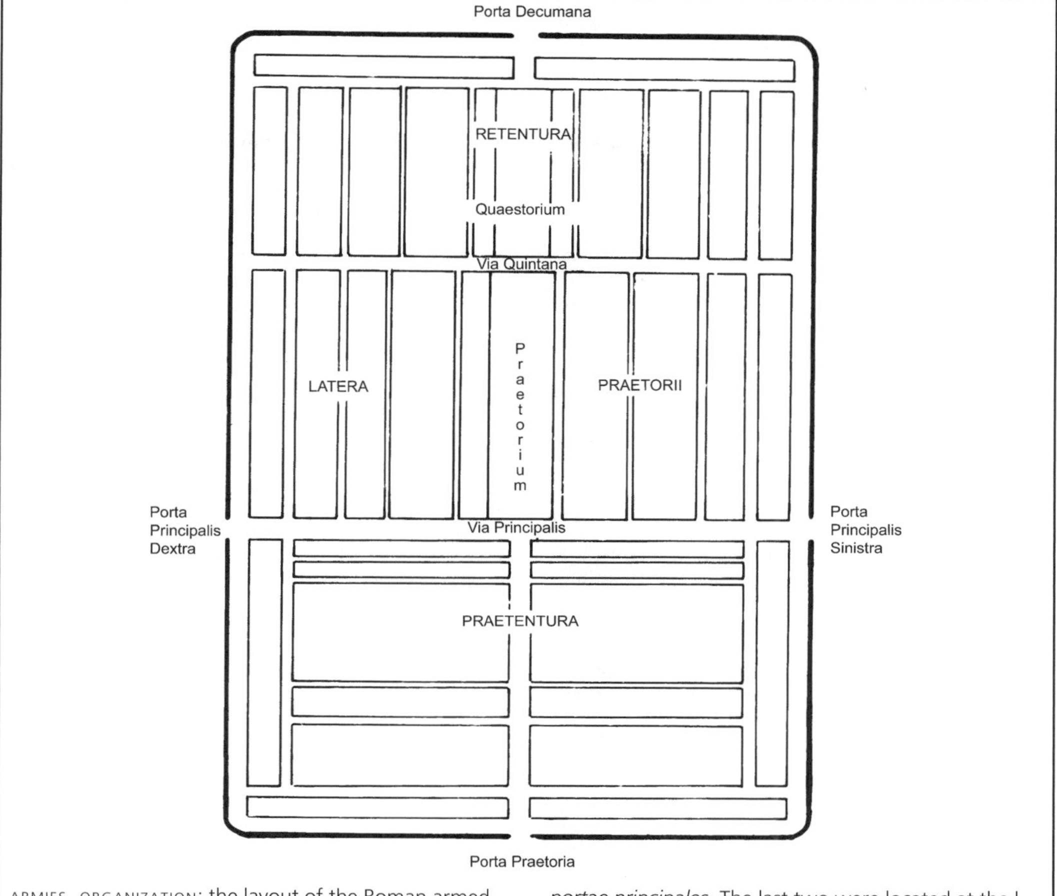

ARMIES, ORGANIZATION: the layout of the Roman armed camp was as follows. There were four gates: the *porta praetoria* (located in front of the commander's headquarters or *praetorium*, to the rear of which we find the *quaestorium*); the *porta decumana*; and two *portae principales*. The last two were located at the l. and r. ends of the *via principalis*, which ran through the camp between the *praetorium* and the tents of the troops, and were known as the *porta principalis sinistra* and *porta principalis dextra*.

a means of improving co-ordination in battle, and there was indeed a war-dance, the *pyrrichê*, which mimicked combat movements. It was left to private initiative how often and how hard a man trained, and whether he took additional instruction in the use of weapons from a private tutor (Plato, *Laches* 178a–184c).

Some cities maintained more rigorously trained crack units, such as ARGOS' Thousand (Thucydides 5.67.2, 72.3–4) or Thebes' Sacred Band of 300 men, organized in homoerotically linked pairs (Diodorus 12.70.1; Plutarch, *Pelopidas* 18–19). Only in Sparta was training regimented for all male citizens, who exercised on a regular basis and in organized groups from the age of seven. On campaign, soldiers continued to exercise twice a day, before breakfast and before the evening meal (Xenophon, *Spartan Constitution* 12). As elsewhere, the main goal was general fitness, strength and agility rather than specific combat skills.

Both Sparta and Athens ensured that 18- and 19-year-old youths gained military experience through patrolling the countryside before joining the regular army. In Sparta, this took the form of the notorious *krypteia*, covert patrols which terrorized the serf population. Athens employed regular patrols (*peripoloi*), best known as EPHEBES. A reform of the 330s instituted a full year of training in hoplite fighting, archery, javelin-throwing and catapult-firing for ephebes (Aristotle, *Athenian Constitution* 42.2–5). At the same time, training and the attendant obligation to serve were extended well beyond the traditional hoplite census class. This move away from the old military system represented a doomed attempt by Athens to create a larger, more professional army and catch up with its new rival, MACEDONIA. HvW

See Hanson, V. D., ed. (1991) *Hoplites*; Lazenby, J. F. (1985) *The Spartan Army*; Wees, H. van (1992) *Status Warriors: war, violence and society in Homer and history*.

The Roman army of the regal period was small and based on social standing. ROMULUS' forces were said to have comprised 3,000 infantry (*pedites*) and 300 aristocratic horsemen (*celeres*), all drawn from the 30 *curiae*. The SERVIAN reforms made it possible to levy a larger number of troops, with the heavy infantry coming from the highest property classes (omitting the super-class of *equites*) and the lighter troops (then called *rorarii*) from the lower property classes. By the 4th century BC, the basic and best-known unit in the Roman army was the LEGION (*legio*,'levy'), whose strength in the early Republican period was generally 4,200, comprising 1,200 *hastati*, 1,200 *principes*, 600 *triarii* and 1,200 *velites* (or light-armed troops). Legions of greater size are attested: LIVY mentions legions of 6,000 and 6,200, and although a single legion could contain 2,000 or more *hastati*, the number of *triarii* remained fixed at 600. The *velites* were the light-armed troops (and presumably the poorest legionaries). The *principes* fought originally in the front line, using the sword (*gladius*), whereas the *hastati* were named after their chief weapon, the spear (*hasta*). Both units were later rearmed with the *pilum* (a heavy javelin c.2 m long), and the *hastati* moved into the front line of fighting. The *triarii*, as their name suggests, formed the third rank, a reserve of veterans. Added to each legion were 300 CAVALRY (*equites*), organized into 30 squadrons called *turmae*.

The early Roman army was thus a rigid phalanx. The troops carried the *clipeus*, a round shield later replaced by the oval *scutum*. To achieve greater flexibility, the Romans turned to smaller units called maniples (*manipuli*, literally 'handfuls'), which could act independently and give the formerly rigid lines an elasticity they had hitherto lacked. During the MACEDONIAN WARS these maniples effectively exploited the gaps that invariably formed in the Macedonian phalanx, especially when it fought on uneven terrain.

Recruitment was based on property qualifications, but numerous wars and lengthy terms of service, combined with the land problems that came to a head in the GRACCHAN period, reduced the pool of eligible recruits. Hence MARIUS, during his first CONSULSHIP in the JUGURTHINE WAR, drew heavily on the poor (the *capite censi*,'counted by head'), who signed on for 20 years. For reasons of economy and military efficiency they carried their own gear and came to be known as 'Marius' Mules' (*muli Mariani*). In the process the Romans acquired a professional army, but also one in which soldiers increasingly looked to commanders for pay and for land settlements at the end of their service. Devotion to the GENERAL soon replaced loyalty to the state. The Marian reforms also saw the integration of the *principes*, *hastati* and *triarii* (or *pilani*), though the terms continued to be used in reverse order to designate the rankings among the centurions, of whom there were six per cohort. In Marius' time, too, the *aquilae*, 'eagles' or legionary standards, were introduced.

By the late Republic the cohort (480 men) had replaced the maniple as the basic unit, though the maniple continued to exist and comprised two 'centuries' (i.e. 160 men). The system carried over into imperial times. Cohorts were divided into six centuries of 80, each commanded by a centurion. The smallest groupings were the *contubernia*, ten groups of 8 men who lived and ate together. The legion itself was made up of ten cohorts, but the first cohort comprised five 'double centuries', that is, 800 men; in addition, each legion contained 120 cavalrymen.

In addition to the legionary soldiers there were allied forces known as *auxilia*. They supplemented the Roman heavy infantry both in numbers and style of fighting. *Auxilia* appear in the Republican period and were used effectively by CAESAR, but their organization and terms of service were firmly established in the PRINCIPATE. The three main units of the *auxilia* – cavalry 'wings' (*alae*, so called presumably because they were stationed on the wings), infantrymen and combinations of infantry and cavalry (*cohortes equitatae*) – were organized into cohorts and *alae* of 500 with their own commanders, though often they served in conjunction with certain legions of heavy infantry. One benefit of service was ROMAN CITIZENSHIP upon honourable discharge. In late antiquity, large units of AUXILIARIES, drawn from FRANKS, GOTHS, HUNS and others, were major elements of the military, and the native commanders often held high positions in the command structure.

In the Republican period, commanders were authorized to draft legions by senatorial authority, though some generals acted on their own initiative when permission was lacking. From the time of AUGUSTUS, most legions were under the authority of the EMPERORS; the senate retained supremacy in some regions. The regular standing army, with legions posted to PROVINCES permanently, also dates from this period. While units were shifted as circumstances required, the bulk of Rome's imperial military was in permanent quarters, with recruits added as necessary. On rare occasions, a new legion was inscribed to replace a defeated one or to augment forces for specific campaigns.

CONSTANTINE reformed this structure to a considerable degree. Essentially he divided the military into stationary troops at the frontier (*limes*, hence *limitanei*) and mobile troops that accompanied emperors on campaigns (*comitanenses*) or marched to areas where additional troops were required. Other changes included a revised command structure, in particular, the *magistri* (*peditum*, *equitum*, *militum*: masters of infantry, cavalry, soldiers) and a greater percentage of cavalry, often native units attached to the regular army. By the 5th century, when recruitment had become very difficult, especially in the West, armies were often almost entirely aggregations of 'barbarian' units assembled by such GENERALISSIMOS as STILICHO, Aëtius and others. WH

See Campbell, J. B. (1994) *The Roman Army: a sourcebook*; Elton, H. (1996) *Warfare in Roman Europe AD 350–425*; Keppie, L. (1984) *The Making of the Roman Army*; Le Bohec, Y. (1994) *The Imperial Roman Army*.

DACIAN WARS: (a); LEGIONS (table).

Arminius see BATTLES, ROMAN; GERMAN WARS; TEUTOBURGIAN FOREST.

arms and armour

The study of Greek military equipment relies upon historical sources (XENOPHON, THUCYDIDES, POLYBIOS) and some more technical works (AENEAS TACTICUS, AELIAN, ARRIAN). Sculptures and other media provide iconographic evidence. Artefacts come predominantly from sanctuaries, battlefield burials, siege sites and SHIPWRECKS. Funerary deposition is the most important survival mechanism on the margins of the Greek world. Small-scale, city-based craftsmen were the main producers of equipment, and these could be co-ordinated for specific projects, as was done by DIONYSIOS of SYRACUSE.

ARMS AND ARMOUR: (a) the classic Greek panoply was that of the heavily armed infantryman (hoplite), typically comprising helmet, cuirass, large shield, greaves and spear.

POLIS warfare from the mid-7th century BC involved the development of a specific panoply to equip HOPLITE citizen infantry. Bronze plate cuirass, greaves and helmet were combined with a shield (*hoplon* or *aspis*). The latter was circular and concave, made of wood with a sheet bronze cover and painted geometric or figural decoration. Motifs were individual to the hoplite in most cities, but perhaps uniform for the élite troops of SPARTA and THEBES. At 80–100 cm in diameter, it protected the user from chin to knee, and was carried by a central sleeve (*porpax*) and handle (*antilabê*) near the rim. It projected out to half-protect the man to the user's left, while the user was half-shielded by the man to his right. Thus the hoplite could only stand in a line of similarly equipped men. Helmets were predominantly of the enclosed Corinthian form, which gave good protection and allowed display through crests and plumes. Although it rendered the wearer deaf, the phalanx did not perform subtle evolutions requiring reaction to vocal orders. The primary weapon of the hoplite was a leaf-bladed spear (*dory*) 2–$2\frac{1}{2}$ m long, generally used for thrusting overarm in the front ranks of the phalanx. Rear ranks used the square, cross-sectioned, iron or bronze butt (*saurotêr*) to thrust down and punch through the armour of fallen enemies. A short single- or double-edged slashing sword was the secondary armament.

In the late archaic and classical periods, cuirasses made up of multiple layers of glued linen became dominant. They were constructed so as to wrap around the torso in four sections, laced at side or back, with two stiff flaps (*epômides*) pulled down over the shoulders and fastened on the chest. Integral, slitted flaps (*pteryges*) formed a flexible skirt which protected the legs above the knees. Thus a full panoply was economically achieved with just the helmet and greaves as metal elements. A greater range of helmet forms also developed, allowing for improved hearing (the modern Attic, Pilos, Phrygian and Boiotian types), and often these were translations of non-metal hat shapes. The classical period also saw a diversification of infantry functions with un-armoured light troops (*psiloi*) using a variety of weapons (javelins, bows, slings, staff-slings) to support the phalanx. In the developing MERCENARY market of the later 5th to 4th centuries, javelin- and shield-armed barbarian light infantry, principally THRACIANS, became a dominant model. They were initially characterized by a flat, lobate, semicircular shield (*pelta*) from which the term 'peltast' was derived. A ribbed, flat, oval shield (*thyreos*) was current in the hellenistic period. Other troops in Greek employ, such as Galatians, used their native forms of equipment.

During the 4th century BC there was experimentation with lighter hoplite armour and deeper phalanx formations, but the crucial innovation came in the reign of PHILIP II of MACEDONIA. To make a large number of less wealthy, thus lightly armoured, royal infantry (*pezetairoi*) effective against hoplites, a much longer spear was developed, the Macedonian pike (*sarisa*). This was a 5–6 m long shaft in two parts joined by a metal sleeve, with a large counter-weight butt-spike and a small head. Its weight and length necessitated that it be carried underarm with both hands, so a smaller shield, 0.6 m in diameter, was suspended from a shoulder-strap and worn over the left arm. Protection from missiles provided by helmets, greaves, shields and body armour for the front ranks was supplemented by the forest of *sarisa* shafts above. Some, if not all, Macedonian troops carried the sunburst badge of the Argead royal family on their shields; élite sections of the phalanx derived titles from their shields (*hypaspistai*, 'under-shield-men'; *argyraspides*, 'silver-shields'). The hellenistic *sarisa* phalanx would always have been a slow, deep and primarily defensive formation.

The single-edged, short, heavy slashing-sword (*kopis*) was favoured for use on horseback. Archaic and classical Greek CAVALRY wore cuirasses and carried short spears and javelins, but not shields. Other types of horsemen developed under barbarian influences on the fringes of the Greek world. SCYTHIAN horse-archers served as mercenaries in Athens and elsewhere as purely skirmishing troops, as did some Western javelin cavalry. Scythia and the Eastern Achaemenid satrapies where archery was dominant saw the concomitant development of scale armour for horse and rider. Under Thracian and Scythian influence, the Macedonian mounted élite (*hetairikê hippos*) used the steppe bow for hunting, and a 4.8–5.0 m long cavalry lance (*xyston*) for war. All these cavalry rode without saddles until the CELTIC horned saddle spread across the MEDITERRANEAN world, perhaps from the 3rd century BC onwards. Cavalry armed with spears and javelins (but not bows or lances) started to use round or oval shields in the hellenistic period.

The SUCCESSOR kings employed any exotically equipped troops and equipment that their cultural and economic contacts could command, including very heavily armoured cavalry, horse-archers, scythed CHARIOTS, ELEPHANTS, siege-machines and ARTILLERY. They also created strategic reserves of materiel in magazines such as those at PERGAMON, APAMEIA and AÏ KHANUM.

Evidence for the earlier periods of Roman military equipment comes from élite funerary deposits, artworks and literary notices, informed by comparative study of contemporary neighbours and reconstruction ARCHAEOLOGY. SIEGE sites have proved rich in artefacts, and a mass of newly published Republican material comes from Spain and the Balkans. Equipment production was generally based on urban craft industries, as was the case after SCIPIO took Carthago Nova (Polybios 10.16), but finds from NUMANTIA make it clear that the army could manufacture its own equipment when necessary.

Wealthy regal and early Republican period Romans were equipped after the Greek hoplite fashion, while the very richest served as cavalry. The long spear (*hasta*) was the primary weapon though light javelins may have had some currency with Italian hoplites, and Italic variations on Greek helmets forms were also current. Equipment and degree of armour provision depended upon wealth. The hoplite order of the SERVIAN constitution was too monolithic for the expanding Roman state with its new Italian and Gallic adversaries, so citizen troops became more flexibly organized and their equipment evolved to conform. The *hoplon* gave way to the long Italic body shield which curved on its horizontal axis and was held by a single, horizontal hand-grip in the Celtic manner. Spears were progressively replaced by javelins (*pila*) so that by the mid-2nd century BC (Polybios) only the third-line *triarii* retained the *hasta*. The wealthy soldiers now wore the Celtic ring-mail cuirass (*lorica hamata*), less well-off men wore a square or circular chest-plate (*pectorale*). WARS in the West had introduced the Spanish form of short sword (*gladius Hispaniensis*). Celtic 'Montefortino' type helmets predominated, though a great range of forms presumably came into Roman use through victories over hellenistic armies. By the time of MARIUS the *pilum* was universal and mail was widely worn because relaxed property qualifications for service necessitated state supply of equipment. Thus in the course of four centuries the legionary had become an armoured swordsman with missiles, designed to face down both northern barbarian and Eastern hellenistic armies. Light infantry (*velites*) with round shields and javelins were integral to Polybios' LEGION, but they disappeared, perhaps during the transition from manipular to cohort organization. Legionary cavalry was equipped in Greek fashion (Polybios) but increasingly with Celtic features such as mail and horse-harness. The allies (*socii*) were drawn up in equivalent legionary formations and were presumably similarly equipped. After the SOCIAL WAR the new model will have been current for all legionary troops including those raised irregularly by CAESAR and others. Roman armies usually employed a variety of mercenaries who were armed according to their own specialisms such as Italian light cavalry, Spanish, Gallic and Thracian aristocratic cavalry, Moorish javelin-cavalry, and Cretan, Numidian or oriental archers.

Sources for Roman imperial period equipment are far more plentiful than before. The development of installations and their orderly abandonment at times when frontiers expanded or contracted provide rich contexts for artefactual finds. Weapons continued to be deposited in ritual contexts (graves, shrines, water features). Sculpted state monuments, particularly in Rome (TRAJAN'S COLUMN), formed a traditional source of iconographic evidence, though direct artefactual studies now take priority in most respects. Private figural military gravestones were erected as a regional funerary practice at different times and on these equipment was often well observed. Incidental references in the works of ancient historians may be supplemented with notices in sub-literary sources and some supposedly technical treatises (e.g. Arrian, Pseudo-Hyginus, VEGETIUS). In the West equipment was manufactured almost exclusively by the army in legionary FORTRESSES and other military installations. In the Eastern provinces there may have been more use of urban craftsmen but the army probably only resorted to them when new formations were raised or during major campaign preparations. From the late 3rd century a series of *fabricae* were established to supply mobile units and newly raised formations, and to manufacture high value bullion equipment.

Legionary infantry continued to be heavily armoured, close-order swordsmen with javelins. In addition to mail and scale armour, from at least the Augustan period through to the second half of the 3rd century AD articulated plate cuirasses (modern *lorica segmentata*) were worn. Helmets derived from Gallic forms predominated. Greaves and articulated arm-defences were widespread in infantry use. Shields remained large and curving, the overall shape varying. Short swords developed through the 'Mainz' (Augustan) and 'Pompeii' (Flavian) types, and some *pila* became heavier. Imperial legions seem also to have possessed integral skirmishing infantry armed with bunches of light javelins (*lanceae*). The auxiliary troops were also all armoured in mail or scale, but generally carried flat shields of varying shape (rectangular, oval, hexagonal). The short sword was used by infantry, the long Celtic *spatha* by cavalry. The latter used Celtic forms of harness, especially the horned saddle, and specialized 'sports' helmets and chamfrons for training and display exercises (Arrian). Auxiliary infantry and cavalry were armed with spears or javelins and shield, bow and no shield, or, in the case of specialist DANUBIAN cavalry (*contarii*) under Sarmatian influence, a two-handed lance. From the time of HADRIAN more heavily armoured cavalry appear, designated *catafracti* or *clibanarii*. Finds of stone, clay and lead sling-missiles suggest that this weapon, like the bow, was widely employed.

Legionary and auxiliary equipment converged during the 3rd century AD so that most now carried the large, dished oval shields found at DURA EUROPUS and depicted on gravestones. Plate cuirasses dwindled in use but infantry armour remained heavy. Helmets with deep neck-guards, first developed for cavalry ('Heddernheim' type) spread to the infantry. *Spathae* came to be increasingly used by infantry, though short swords survived through into the 4th century. A much greater range of spears and javelins were used by legionaries alongside the *pilum*. Thus equipment specific to close-order fighting (*lorica segmentata*, curved shields) gave way to arms which could be employed in series of contexts. Late Roman infantry continued to be armoured, but from the late 3rd century new forms of 'Ridge' and segmental (*spangenhelm*) helmets came into use. Many extant examples consist of the gilded silver helmet

ARMS AND ARMOUR: (b) the Roman legionary of the high empire was a heavily armed and armour-clad infantryman, expected to carry all his kit – including his entrenching tool for constructing camps on the march.

ARMS AND ARMOUR: (c) detail of reconstructed legionary body armour (*lorica segmentata*) of the early principate.

ARMS AND ARMOUR: (d) tombstone of a Roman auxiliary cavalry trooper (note the oval shield, long sword and elaborate horse gear).

ARMS AND ARMOUR: (e) reconstruction painting of late Roman soldiers.

sheath for an iron helmet (Deurne, Netherlands; Berkasovo, Serbia). Shield-bosses, spear-heads and brooches were similarly rich, decorated items, 'gifting' the soldiers with valuable equipment as part of their reward for service. Germanic round, flat shields were in Roman use alongside oval boards during the 4th century. Late shield blazons may be studied in a range of artefactual and iconographic sources: for example leather facings from Egypt and the manuscript illuminations of the *NOTITIA DIGNITATUM*. JCNC

See Bishop, M. C. and Coulston, J. C. N. (1993) *Roman Military Equipment from the Punic Wars to the Fall of Rome*; *Journal of Roman Military Equipment Studies*; Connolly, P. (1998) *Greece and Rome at War*; Snodgrass, A. M. (1991) *Arms and Armour of the Greeks.*

 ACHILLES: (a); AUXILIARIES: (a); CAVALRY: (a)–(b); HOPLITES: (a).

Arretine ware Italian red-gloss tableware, deriving its name from the large workshops at Arretium (Arezzo) in Tuscany. Other production sites are now known in the region, including Rome and Torrita di Sienna, but also as far north as the Po valley and south to the bay of Naples; it is therefore now best described by the umbrella term 'Italian sigillata'. Outside the province, Arezzo potters are responsible for the production of Italian-style sigillata at La Muette, LYON.

Its origins can be traced to the shapes of Campanian black-gloss vessels, with the red colour inspired by that seen on sigillata vessels imported into Italy from the East. The earliest Italian potters date between c.40–20 BC and production continued into the 2nd century AD, the latest phase being distinguished as 'Tardo Italico', primarily from Pisa. Its height of export was during the Augustan period. Beyond the empire, rare sherds occur as distantly as INDIA.

Standardized vessel shapes are platters for serving and cups for drinking, along with mould-decorated chalices or pedestal bowls. It was generally manufactured using techniques and decorative motifs similar to those described for Gaulish SAMIAN, though with applied decoration more common, and less densely arranged moulded motifs. The stamping of vessels indicates diversity in the scale and organization of production, sometimes involving SLAVES. Stamps enclosed in footprints (*in planta pedis*) are characteristic and are post-Augustan in date. RST

See Oxé, A., Comfort, H. and Kenrick, P.M. (2000) *Corpus Vasorum Arretinorum*.

 POTTERY, ROMAN: (a).

Arrian (Lucius Flavius Arrianus 'Xenophon') Greek PHILOSOPHER, HISTORIAN and statesman born c.AD 85–92 in NICOMEDIA, Bithynia. His family was wealthy and held Roman CITIZENSHIP. Arrian's importance in his own city is attested by the fact that he held the priesthood of DEMETER and Kore, the most significant in the city.

In his youth, Arrian went to Nikopolis in EPIRUS to study philosophy with Epiktetos (c.108). He preserved Epiktetos' teaching in eight books of *Diatribes* (four survive) and a summarized 'Handbook' (*Encheiridion*, also extant). These were possibly published early in his career, though there can be no certainty on this issue. Arrian may well have written other philosophical works recording his own thoughts, since his reputation in antiquity was first and foremost as a philosopher.

In the years following his studies, Arrian probably performed military service. Epigraphical evidence suggests that he was praetorian proconsul at Baetica (c.125), and he probably held a CONSULSHIP (c.129) before taking up the governorship of CAPPADOCIA (c.131). This position recognized his capabilities as a general and administrator. In 131/2 he led a tour of inspection around the BLACK SEA which is recorded in his extant *Periplus of the Black Sea*. Other works known to have been composed at this time were about military TACTICS. One based on the invasion of the Alans, which Arrian was responsible for beating back in 135, describes the formation of Arrian's troops in this campaign. His term in Cappadocia finished in 137, shortly before the death of HADRIAN.

At this time, Arrian took up residence in Athens where he held the eponymous archonship in 145/6. His activities at this point in his career are a matter for debate. It was earlier thought that Arrian wrote all of his major works during his retirement in Athens. However, recently it has been maintained that he probably continued in his political career at Rome during this time. Moreover, scholars now agree that his historical works were composed throughout his career, not only during his time at Athens. It is not known when he died.

The most important of Arrian's extant works is the *Anabasis of Alexander*, an account of the campaigns of ALEXANDER the Great in seven books. Some scholars maintain that this was written early in Arrian's career, perhaps when he was in his thirties. He used sources close to Alexander (Ptolemy, Aristoboulos) when composing this work, and this has led to criticism of Arrian for being too flattering in his portrayal of the monarch. Other lost historical works include *Events after Alexander*, *Parthica* and *Bithynia*.

In his writings, Arrian was much influenced by XENOPHON, whose name he sometimes used. He claimed to share the interests of Xenophon – namely tactics, hunting and philosophy. In particular his work *On Hunting* (*Kynêgetikos*) aimed to emulate the earlier writer. FMM

See Arrian, *History of Alexander, Indica*, 2 vols., trs. P. A. Brunt (1983); Bosworth, A. B. (1980) *A Historical Commentary on Arrian's History of Alexander*; Stadter, P. A. (1980) *Arrian of Nicomedia*.

Arsinoë (city) The chief town (*mêtropolis*) of the Arsinoïte nome (*nomos*, province) in the FAYÛM basin in Middle Egypt. The Greeks rendered its Egyptian name (S*dt) as Krokodilonpolis (City of Crocodiles); after the death of Ptolemy VIII it was renamed Ptolemaïs Euergetis, which long remained its denomination as a place for official acts. In the Roman period Arsinoïton Polis comes to prevail as the official name for the citizens corporately. Arsinoë, its common name in modern usage, was only an informal usage until late antiquity. From a modest town in the Ptolemaic period (with a population probably not exceeding 5,000), Arsinoë grew into a sizeable Roman city; its surviving mounds earlier this century were, at well over 200 ha (500 acres), the largest known site of a nome capital. From them in the 19th century came large numbers of PAPYRI, mainly from late antiquity. The destruction and building over of the remains, already underway 80 years ago, is now virtually complete. The PTOLEMIES settled thousands of Greek and MACEDONIAN soldiers in the Fayûm, for whom Arsinoë was the main urban centre. Their self-conscious descendants dominated the local élite through the Roman period, and probably commissioned most of the MUMMY PORTRAITS found at Hawara and other cemeteries in the vicinity of Arsinoë. RSB

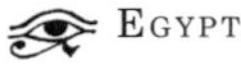 EGYPT.

Arsinoë II Philadelphos b. c.316 BC The daughter of PTOLEMY I of Egypt and his mistress BERENIKE I, Arsinoë was married c.300 BC to LYSIMACHOS of MACEDONIA. Allegedly under her influence, Lysimachos killed Agathokles, his eldest son by

another wife, Nikaia. Following Lysimachos' death Arsinoë married her half-brother, Ptolemy Keraunos, but when he murdered her sons by Lysimachos she fled to Samothrace and then to Egypt. In c.276 she married her full-brother Ptolemy II, ousting his first wife, Arsinoë I, from her position as Great Wife. Ptolemy used the notion of brother–sister marriage to define the divine status of the Ptolemaic monarchy; the title Philadelphos ('brother-loving') adopted by Arsinoë strengthened the message. Ptolemy II and Arsinoë II thus established a matrimonial precedent for all later PTOLEMIES. In her lifetime Arsinoë was honoured as a priestess of the cult of monarchy in ALEXANDRIA. Later the royal couple became the focus of a dynastic cult as Theoi Adelphoi ('sibling gods'). With her death in 270 or 268, Arsinoë became the first Ptolemaic queen to be worshipped in a temple cult. Her death was memorialized by KALLIMACHOS. The Egyptian-style iconography invented for Arsinoë after her death knows no precedent; she is depicted wearing a hybrid combination of pharaonic crowns indicating her cultic and political significance. She exerted considerable political influence over her brother-husband during her lifetime. A district of Egypt was called after her, and the city of Philadelphia was named in her honour. LL-J

See Hölbl, G. (2001) *A History of the Ptolemaic Empire*.

art The concept of art articulated in Greek and Roman written sources differs significantly from that which most modern Westerners take for granted. No clear definition remains in the scattered texts of the ancient MEDITERRANEAN, though the most consistent definition for the terms used (Greek *technê*, Latin *ars*) seems to be 'skill' or 'craftsmanship'. Even this, however, varies according to the writer and his purposes as well as to the period. In the hellenistic period, for example, the artist's creative inspiration or wisdom (Greek *phantasia* or *sophia*) begins to be cited by writers (e.g. ARISTOTLE, *On the Soul* 428a) at just the moment when the artist is making important works increasingly for private and royal as well as for civic patrons. The one thing that seems to emerge from an investigation of monuments, objects and texts is that the ontological category of art used in the West post-c.1700 is generally missing from classical antiquity. Neither the primacy of originality nor the centrality of commodity fetishism appears consistently in antiquity.

Greek and Roman texts on art do not survive in large numbers, but Roman writers tend to make use of lost Greek sources and thus preserve the stories, theories and literary genres of earlier generations. In addition to texts, documents on stone and inscriptions on vases provide information about art and its makers. Stone inscriptions tell how much individual workmen received for their labours, for example on the ACROPOLIS in Athens. Similarly, vases often preserve the names of potters and painters among the Greeks, just as Roman clay table-ware with relief decoration often names the owner of the POTTERY-making establishment. Far more rarely one finds signatures on SCULPTURE, as on the ODYSSEY sculptures that decorated the grotto of Tiberius' VILLA at SPERLONGA; no WALL-PAINTINGS have such identifications. These bits and pieces of archaeological evidence contribute to our understanding of the nature of production in antiquity, but this is seldom the focus of writers (VITRUVIUS is a partial exception), most of whom were men of the literate citizen stratum to whom production was often of as little interest as the actual workers. Those workers were generally regarded as lowly in status, especially in early Greece and during Roman times. However, some authors give evidence of respect for individual achievement, as is the case with PHEIDIAS, director of the sculpture programme for the PARTHENON (e.g. PLUTARCH, *Perikles* 13), or Apollodorus of Damascus, the reputed creator of the forum of TRAJAN (CASSIUS DIO 64.9). Despite the general literary presentation of the low status of the artist, one of the most important categories of textual evidence is the anecdote about his life and contributions (rarely hers, though PLINY, *Natural History* 35.40.147–8, and others do mention some hellenistic women painters). For example, we know from texts that the mid-5th-century sculptor POLYKLEITOS wrote a book about ideal systems of proportion for statues, and that his *Doryphoros* (*Spear-bearer*) stood as an example of the 'canon' or system he described (Pliny 34.55).

Of the remaining texts, then, there are artist stories and bits of biographical information. Much of this may be apocryphal, as when ALEXANDER the Great presents the painter Apelles with Pankaspe; the woman was Alexander's mistress, and Apelles, painting her, fell in love with her. The story is as much about Alexander's generosity as it is about the artist, but the element of sexual desire that haunts ancient views of art is certainly present as well (Pliny 35.86). In addition, critical theories can be found, as in PLATO's concern with the way mimetic art endangers the viewer by acting as a seduction, 'an imitation of an imitation' that moves the viewer from understanding of the ideal forms of natural phenomena to imitations of those phenomena (*Republic* 10.596e–597e). Here, as in the stories whose punch-lines end 'it was so real that ...', mimesis is central (*Greek Anthology* 1.104.9: Aphrodite sees the Knidian statue by PRAXITELES and exclaims, 'Where did Praxiteles see me naked?'). The *ars*, the skill to make something that can stand in for the real, seems to be what ancient writers are thinking about when they discuss Art. The interchange between objects and the 'ecphrastic' description of them in texts, where the writer demonstrates his *ars*, his mimetic skill, by making the work of art seem real, continues the centrality of mimesis into the 2nd and 3rd centuries AD, in the work of authors such as MARTIAL (*Epigram* 9) or PHILOSTRATOS (*Eikones*, describing art collections). Both in the texts and in the monuments, superb craftsmanship matters far more than originality, since the latter may violate tradition while at the same time endangering the commitment to the 'reality effect'.

A number of texts modify this rather rigid notion of art. Aesthetic pleasure, visual desire and greed for highly valued things all play a part in ancient attitudes toward art, despite the absence of a theory of art as rooted specifically in aesthetic pleasure or financial value beyond that inherent in the thing's materials. The uplifting character of art works is cited by DIO CHRYSOSTOM in his discussion of Pheidias (*Olympian Oration* 12.50–2). The loveliness of a scene in a painting, the depiction of a 'place of pleasure' (*locus amoenus*), is often the focus of an ecphrastic description too, though here the mimetic character of the text's goals are clear (e.g. Kallistratos,

Descriptions 8.1–3). More than aesthetic pleasure, some combination of appreciation for a thing's skilful making, its closeness to the thing it represents, and its appropriateness to its site or function contribute to the viewer's enjoyment of it. Thus, the many famous statues replicated around the reflecting pool at HADRIAN's villa at TIVOLI gain some of their value from their fame or antiquity, some from the fineness of their craftsmanship (and thus, like the Nile crocodile, their convincing qualities), and some from the playful grace of their installation in an open arcade of columns around the pool. Similarly, at a house in Rome a pair of statues stands at the entrance; they had been installed in such way as to allow the viewer to study the subtle differences in their poses and details. All these cases attest to a sophisticated sense of aesthetic interest and pleasure that rarely receives notice or documentation in ancient texts.

The texts do attest to the existence of visual desire when they tell stories, often satiric or scandalous, about objects. In some cases, as when Pliny the Elder speaks of the youth whose desire for the statue of Aphrodite at KNIDOS led him to hide in the sanctuary and during the night to give way to his lust for her, the confusion of statue and real woman stands at the heart of the story (*Natural History* 36.20; cf. Pseudo-Lucian, *Amores* 13). NARCISSUS' confusion of his own face with his reflection demonstrates that the story is less about the nature of art than about the dilemma of mimesis; the story of Pygmalion's love for his statue and her ability to come to life through divine intervention gives us something comparable (OVID, *Metamorphoses* 3.342ff. and 10.243ff.). The way that aesthetic appreciation and sexual desire merge is attested in these texts with considerable vigour, and a moralizing element always lurks under the surface. It comes up for air in stories of greed, as with the accusations by CICERO against his enemy VERRES who looted tons of valuable objects during his administration in SICILY (Cicero, *Verrine Orations* 2). Greed as a moral EVIL is closely related in Greek and Roman culture with other forms of excess, including lust. Thus the work of art is consistently entangled in a web of moral conflicts, and becomes a vehicle for accusation and invective as well as for the demonstration of excellence in skill and also in character.

Among the issues in ancient art about which many questions remain is the status of individual GENRES and categories of objects. Virtually nothing exists to tell us whether Greeks and Romans ever thought of funerary monuments as having a status comparable to, for example, GOLD and SILVER statues or the paintings of Parrhasios. It seems likely that neither Greek VASE-PAINTING nor Roman wall-painting and floor MOSAICS were of this stature, though the great Alexander mosaic from the House of the Faun in POMPEII may replicate a famous painting of the past and thus take on some of the value of its model. The same could be said of Roman replicas of famous statues from TEMPLES in Greece; they too become a kind of Art by virtue of their ability to bring the valuable past into the present. But whether this was the case with wall-paintings in private HOUSES, as in Pompeii or EPHESOS, is unclear. Certainly the great public paintings of Athens received admiring comment from writers (Pausanias 1.15.1), but the same cannot be said of wall-paintings in Roman private houses, about which writers are generally silent.

Greeks and Romans displayed objects, both as ideologically fraught war booty and as objects of moral and visual pleasure, in public (as well as private) venues such as gardens and public buildings on a regular basis (Strabo 8.6.23). How such collections were received, who saw them and under what circumstances is not known, nor is the extent of such public display in places other than the major metropolitan centres around the Mediterranean. Whether there was ever a consciousness of a distinction between utilitarian objects and those we might call Art among provincial populations outside metropolitan centres, and among people of non-élite status, one does not know. Military camps along the northern frontier offer a wide range of religious, funerary and documentary monuments as well as bronze statuettes, and these often make use of famous Greek and Roman metropolitan statues and painted or sculpted compositions as models for representation in a range of local styles. Whether the use of these models hints at an interest in the historically or morally valued object remains an open question. NBK

See Bartman, E. (1988) Decor et duplicatio: pendants in Roman sculptural display, *AJA* 92: 211–25; Boersma, J. (1970) *Athenian Building Policy from 561/0 to 405/4 BC*; Elsner, J. (1995) *Art and the Roman Viewer*; Pollitt, J. J. (1965) *The Art of Ancient Greece: sources and documents*; (1974) *The Ancient View of Greek Art: criticism, history, and terminology*; (1983) *The Art of Ancient Rome, c.753 BC–AD 337: sources and documents*; Staniszewski, M. A. (1995) *Believing is Seeing: creating the culture of art*; Steiner, D. (2001) *Images in Mind*.

MOSAICS: (a)–(c); PAINTING: (a); SCULPTURE: (a)–(c); WALL-PAINTING: (a)–(c).

Artaxerxes I, II, III The son of XERXES and Amestris, Artaxerxes I (465–424 BC) succeeded to the PERSIAN throne after Xerxes and the designated heir to the throne, Darius, were killed in a palace coup. His accession triggered a brief revolt in Baktria, followed in 460 BC by a revolt in Egypt led by the LIBYAN king Inaros, which was quashed in 455/4. Artaxerxes I offered asylum to the ostracized THEMISTOKLES, probably in 465. In c.449 he may have agreed to a peace with Greece (peace of Kallias). During his reign, building work in PERSEPOLIS continued with the completion of the One-hundred-column Hall and the construction of a third private palace.

Artaxerxes II (404–359 BC) was the throne-name of Arsakes, son of Darius II and Parysatis. After his accession he defended his kingship against his brother CYRUS THE YOUNGER, who was killed in the battle of Kounaxa (Cunaxa) in 401. Parysatis was sent into exile in Babylonia for having supported Cyrus. In 386 Artaxerxes II concluded the King's Peace with Sparta, which brought the Greek cities of Asia Minor back under Persian control. He was unable to regain control of Egypt, in full rebellion since 400, allowing Egypt to remain independent for 65 years. While unsuccessfully campaigning against the Cadusians, he quashed the rebellions of Euagoras of Salamis and western Asiatic satraps.

Artaxerxes III Ochos (359–338 BC) was a son of Artaxerxes II and Stateira. Depicted in Greek sources as a ruthless king, having killed most of his siblings in order to secure his kingship, his reign is marked by considerable political and military success. He re-conquered Egypt in 343, and quashed a revolt of

Phoenicia, Syria and Cyprus led by king Tennes of Sidon. In 342 he provided military support for the Greek defence of Byzantion and Perinthos, forcing the Macedonian army to withdraw from the Hellespont. In continuation of Achaemenid practice, he built a palace in Persepolis, restored Darius' palace at Susa, and constructed a new Apadana (throne hall) on the site of Darius' palace in Babylon. MB

Artemis Greek goddess, one of the most fascinating figures in the pantheon. She displays a complex interplay of the characteristics of virgin, huntress, nurturer, destroyer, protector and punisher, and was one of the most popular deities among worshippers. Pious devotion to her was displayed across a wide range of social strata and age groups by both male and female adherents. Daughter of Zeus and Leto and twin sister of Apollo, Artemis was most importantly a goddess of transitions who oversaw the processes of birth and coming of age in both sexes. She was instrumental in bringing about the deaths of women through illness ('a lion to women' is how Homer describes her), particularly of unmarried girls. As an eternal virgin, she rejected sex and demanded virginity of her most loyal devotees (usually nymphs, including the ill-fated Kallisto). Tantalizingly beautiful, she nevertheless punished those who viewed or responded to her sexuality (such as Actaeon). Mortal worshippers entering into a life of marriage and procreation needed to ensure that the jealous goddess was sufficiently propitiated before taking that momentous life-changing step. Artemis was also the mistress of wild animals and is often shown in the iconography carefully rearing a young deer. Yet she was in addition the goddess of hunting who destroyed the game she best loved. She inhabited woodlands and pastures, but was also a goddess of cities (most famously Ephesos; note also rich finds from the sanctuary of Artemis Ortheia, located by the river in Sparta). All in all, Artemis was a goddess of baffling contradictions. LL-J

See Bannister, N. and Waugh, N. J., eds. (2005) *Essence of the Huntress: the worlds of Artemis and Diana*; Burkert, W. (1985) *Greek Religion*; Dawkins, R. M., ed. (1929) *The Sanctuary of Artemis Orthia at Sparta*.

 Brauron; gods and goddesses: (a).

Artemision, battle of see Themistokles; Xerxes.

artillery

Warfare as practised by the classical city-states put great reliance on collisions of hoplite infantry. There was a long-standing Hellenic prejudice against missiles of all types, which were felt to be both unfair and unheroic. In addition, because of an ethical reluctance to employ capital and technology to create engines that might replace infantry nerve and muscle, military technology was retarded, lagging far behind the general Greek scientific and mathematical renaissance. It is no accident that the rather late discovery of artillery was made possible largely through sponsorship by tyrants and kings. They possessed the necessary capital to subsidize research and construction, cared little for the old military protocols of the *polis*, and had the constant need to storm recalcitrant fortified cities.

Spring-loaded artillery of complex mechanical designs was not seen in Greece until Dionysios I employed non-torsion catapults against Motya in 399 BC. Blowtorches had been used earlier, during the upheaval of the Peloponnesian war, by the Thebans at Delion (424) and the Spartans at Lekythos (423); but such primitive engines blew flames with the aid of bellows and incendiaries, rather than heaving projectiles as true artillery. Dionysios' machine was essentially a large composition crossbow (*gastraphetês*) with a base and stock, cocked through a slide mechanism, and designed to hurl arrows of greater size and at farther distances than hand-held bows. Very quickly engineers began to mass-produce such non-torsion artillery that were able to fire stones (as the *lithobolos*) and bolts (the *katapeltês oxybelês*) instead of arrows at distances up to 250 m. Classical literature abounds with tales of impaled victims and mutilated corpses, testimony to the lethality of these anti-personnel weapons.

Some time after 350 BC, engineers working for Philip II of Macedonia discovered true torsion artillery. Instead of pulling back and cocking the composite bow, greater propulsive power was achieved by spring-loading the stock through the tension of wound animal sinew, women's or horse's hair. Such catapults could heave much heavier projectiles of up to 40 kg at ranges over 350 m, and were effective against stone fortifications and city gates. In response, city engineers buttressed fortifications, inaugurating an expensive race between offensive and defensive siegecraft. To withstand catapult shot, walls needed to be nearly 5 m thick and have round towers and shuttered windows that might accommodate counter-artillery. The latter, in turn, grew ever larger and more sophisticated.

A technical literature, concerning not just artillery construction but also calibration and propulsion, was far advanced by the mid-3rd century. Greek scientists such as Ktesibos, Philon and Heron wrote *Belopoiika* about the proper use of catapults. The wide dissemination of such scientific knowledge explains the ubiquity of artillery, for by the end of the 3rd century catapults appear in nearly every Greek siege – on land and on sea, by defender and attacker alike – and on inventory lists of municipal armouries. While Onomarchos of Phokis, Alexander the Great and Perseus used field catapults, the absence of mobile models, problems of maintenance, and the weight of ammunition made their rapid and sudden use in pitched battles awkward. VDH

See Marsden, E.W. (1969) *Greek and Roman Artillery: historical development*; Winter, F. (1971) *Greek Fortifications;* Baatz, D. (1980) Introduction to E. Shramm, *Die antiken Geschütze der Saalburg*.

Roman Republican artillery continued to develop from hellenistic weapons which had first derived from large and powerful composite bows. These shot arrows accurately over a long distance, principally in siege contexts. Metal-plated, wooden-framed weapons came into use in the second half of the 4th century BC with their arms powered by twin, vertical torsion coils of sinew or hair. Characteristic toothed washers were used to adjust the tension. The smaller of these weapons (*catapultae* or *scorpiones*) shot arrows, the larger (*ballistae*) projected stone balls. A complete set of plates and

ARTILLERY: Roman field ballista in action during Trajan's Dacian campaigns (from Trajan's column).

washers was found at Ampurias (Spain) dating to the 2nd century BC. Ancient technical treatises, and stone shot found at Republican period sites (e.g. NUMANTIA, Spain), suggest calibres of machines defined by weight of ball at 1, 2, 3 and 10 *minae* (436, 872, 1,308 and 4,360 g). Catapult arrows had characteristic pyramidal heads and are found on many sites (e.g. Entremont in France). *Ballistae* were used particularly to batter away at parapets in order to remove defenders' protection, or to break up besiegers' wooden constructions. *Catapultae* were point-accuracy weapons for hitting specific, individual targets. Artefactual and treatise evidence may be supplemented with artistic depictions of weapons and modern working reconstructions.

Under the Roman emperors, artillery was closely linked with legionary organization: one stone-thrower for each cohort, one arrow-shooter for each century (VEGETIUS). TACITUS reports *ballistae* in use during the AD 68–9 civil war, as does JOSEPHUS in the sieges of the first Jewish war. Metal fittings found at Hatra (Iraq) belonged to 3rd-century wooden-framed *ballistae* which shot stones of c.10 Roman pounds (3,270 g). *Catapulta* washers from CREMONA (Italy) were accompanied by a copper-alloy sheet 'shield' from the front of a frame, its manufacture dated by consular inscription to AD 45. Pyramidal artillery arrowheads are common finds on military installations along the imperial frontiers. At some point in the 1st century AD a new form of small artillery-piece was developed with entirely iron housings (*kambestria*) for the torsion coils, and iron struts for the frame. First depicted on TRAJAN'S COLUMN, it is described in late Roman treatises. Frames and struts have been found at 4th-century Gornea and Orsova (Romania). A much shorter missile was used than earlier arrows; corresponding wooden, vaned 'quarrel' bodies have been found at DURA EUROPUS (Syria). The term *ballista* came to be employed for bolt-shooters, with additional prefixes denoting size and type of weapon (VEGETIUS): *arcuballista* for a composite crossbow shooting arrows; *manuballista* for a small, hand-held torsion weapon (Orsova) shooting bolts; *ballista* for the larger bolt-shooters (Gornea); *carroballista* for cart-mounted mobile weapons (Trajan's column). All these types were in use in the Roman army in defence of FORTIFICATIONS, along the frontiers and with specialist units of *ballistarii*. Larger stone-throwers continued in use, as did one-armed torsion weapons (*onagri*).

After the defeat of CARTHAGE and the hellenistic kingdoms, the use of artillery in open battle and sieges was largely confined to the Roman army, with the occasional exception of captured Roman weapons in the hands of JEWS, DACIANS or BANDITS. Direct evidence for SASSANIAN Persian artillery is lacking. JCNC

See Bishop, M. C. and Coulston, J. C. N. (1993) *Roman Military Equipment from the Punic Wars to the Fall of Rome.*

artists Greek artists are known from the writings of PLINY THE ELDER (*Natural History* books 34–6) and a few other authors, but contemporary Greek textual sources have largely disappeared. What remains is often much later, and describes works and artists' lives minimally. Signatures on Greek vases from the 6th century BC onwards name painters and potters, but SCULPTURE indicates the name of a maker more rarely. The status of artists is uncertain, many apparently living as artisans. The contracts for the men who worked on the PARTHENON, and the living conditions of many potters and painters, indicate that they did not often share the status of the famous few, such as the painters Apelles or Zeuxis or the sculptors PHEIDIAS or POLYKLEITOS, known from later sources as friends of rulers, authors of books, men of authority.

Roman artists seem even more anonymous than Greek, though a few ARCHITECTS' names are known, as are several makers of relief POTTERY and GLASS. Inscriptions identify a small number of SCULPTORS and MOSAICISTS. The low opinion of artists as ungentlemanly manual labourers tended to pervade élite Roman culture. Comments by writers, and names in inscriptions, suggest that some of the prejudice may have resulted from artists sometimes being SLAVES or captives and almost never being members of the Roman élite. Art-making (unlike ARCHITECTURE) was often seen as unappetizingly foreign, as well as being low-status manual labour. NBK

See Burford, A. (1972) *Craftsmen in Greek and Roman Society*; Pollitt, J. J. (1965) *The Art of Greece 1400–31 BC*; (1966) *The Art of Rome ca. 753 BC–AD 337.*

Arval brethren Roman priestly college with 12 members. Roman tradition attributed its foundation to ROMULUS, and its antiquity is confirmed by its cult hymn (*carmen Arvale*), which is known only from a copy inscribed in AD 218 but must date back to the 5th century BC. The college's original function was to celebrate the annual FESTIVAL of Dea Dia, who may have been a celestial deity (cf. *dius*, 'bright', and *divum*,'sky'). Her cult, based in a sacred grove on the TIBER some 8 km (5 miles) west of Rome, was concerned chiefly with AGRICULTURAL fertility, whence the name of the college (from *arvum*,'ploughed field'). By the mid-1st century BC it was perhaps moribund, but AUGUSTUS gave it new prestige and expanded its duties to include rites on behalf of the EMPEROR, such as annual vows for his well-being, regular SACRIFICES on imperial anniversaries, and occasional sacrifices celebrating victories or deliverance from conspiracies and illness. The college recorded its activities in an extensive series of inscriptions, dating from 21 BC to AD 241, with an isolated fragment from AD 304. As a result, more is known about the workings of this cult than of any other and also about the membership of the college, drawn from men of the highest rank. JBR

See Beard, M. (1985) Writing and ritual: a study of diversity and expansion in the Arval Acta, *PBSR* 53: 114–62.

as see COINAGE (tables).

ascetics The Greek term *askêsis* originaly meant the rigours of training for ATHLETES and soldiers. It came to be appropriated metaphorically by philosophical groups, and denoted a concentrated denial of the physical world designed to free up the soul or mind for contemplation of the spiritual and divine. It involved various forms of self-denial: typically fasting, sexual continence, austerity in terms of physical comforts and dress, and often voluntary POVERTY. Ascetic practice played a part in many traditional religions in the ancient world, but it is predominantly associated with the rise of CHRISTIANITYand monasticism in the 3rd and 4th centuries AD. It was influenced by the life of Antony (as told by ATHANASIUS), who forsook his wealthy life to live a solitary one of fasting, prayer and celibacy in the deserts of EGYPT. Over time, different types of ascetic life developed: solitary (eremetic), in communities (cenobitic) and domestic (within the household); most extreme were the stylites who lived on top of pillars (*styloi*). By the later 4th century, some ascetic holy men and women came to acquire a spiritual kudos which translated into social power, often enhanced by the performance of miracles. The idea that ascetic practice and extreme denial of the physical body and its needs could return human beings to a pre-lapsarian state underlies the writings of many churchmen, such as JEROME, AUGUSTINE (1), AMBROSE, Gregory of Nyssa and John Chrysostom, and was highly influential in the development of Christian teaching. MEH

See Brown, P. (1988) *The Body and Society*; Edwards, M. (2000) Development of office in the early Church, in P. F. Esler, ed., *The Early Christian World*.

Asclepiades see ASKLEPIADES.

Asclepius see ASKLEPIOS.

Asia, Greek and hellenistic see ALEXANDER III; ANTIOCHOS III; CARIA; EAST GREECE; IONIAN REVOLT; SELEUKIDS; SUCCESSORS OF ALEXANDER.

Asia, Roman An important and wealthy Roman province occupying the western (AEGEAN) coastal region of modern Turkey, its hinterland and ISLANDS. It included such famous, culturally Greek cities as EPHESOS, SMYRNA, SARDIS, Kyzikos, MILETOS and PERGAMON and islands such as LESBOS, CHIOS and SAMOS in the regions of Ionia, LYDIA, PHRYGIA, CARIA and the HELLESPONT. Asia is known through references in the works of Roman writers and through the archaeological remains of its cities. However, of particular importance is the province's exceptionally rich legacy of (mostly Greek) inscriptions, which shed detailed light on all aspects of the government of the cities and their place in the Roman empire.

The province of Asia came into Roman possession through the will of king Attalos III of Pergamon (d.133 BC), which provided for his royal lands to become the property of the Roman people. Acceptance of this bequest was urged by Tiberius GRACCHUS, who saw revenues from the new territories as a way to fund agrarian reform. Establishment of the province came c.126 BC at the hands of Manius Aquillius, after Gracchus' death and following conflict in the region with Aristonikos. Subsequently Gaius Gracchus enacted legislation that the rights to collect direct and indirect taxes in the province should be auctioned in Rome among *societates* (companies) of EQUESTRIAN *publicani* (contractors or tax farmers) to raise revenue for the state. The apparently unpopular Roman administration disintegrated in 89–88 BC in the face of an invasion by MITHRADATES VI of Pontos after he defeated Rome's Bithynian allies. In response to Rome's declaration of war, Mithradates instigated the massacre of Roman and other Italian residents of the cities of Asia. The Romans regained control in 85–84 BC, and SULLA imposed a savage financial settlement on the cities which was subsequently moderated by Lucullus.

Asia was on the wrong side in each of the CIVIL WARS of the middle of the 1st century BC, and suffered accordingly. First BRUTUS and Cassius, then ANTONY, each demanded the equivalent of ten years' tribute from the province in order to raise and support their military forces, and the presence of inflated armies as well as actual campaigning inflicted considerable damage. In 40–38 BC Quintus Labienus even led a PARTHIAN army into Asia Minor and advanced as far as Caria, where APHRODISIAS was plundered.

Because of its wealth and important cities, Asia was always one of the most prestigious provinces to govern. From the reign of AUGUSTUS it was a 'senatorial' province, governed by proconsuls of ex-consular rank appointed by the SENATE rather than by imperial legates. Governing Asia was the climax of many prestigious senatorial careers; famous proconsuls

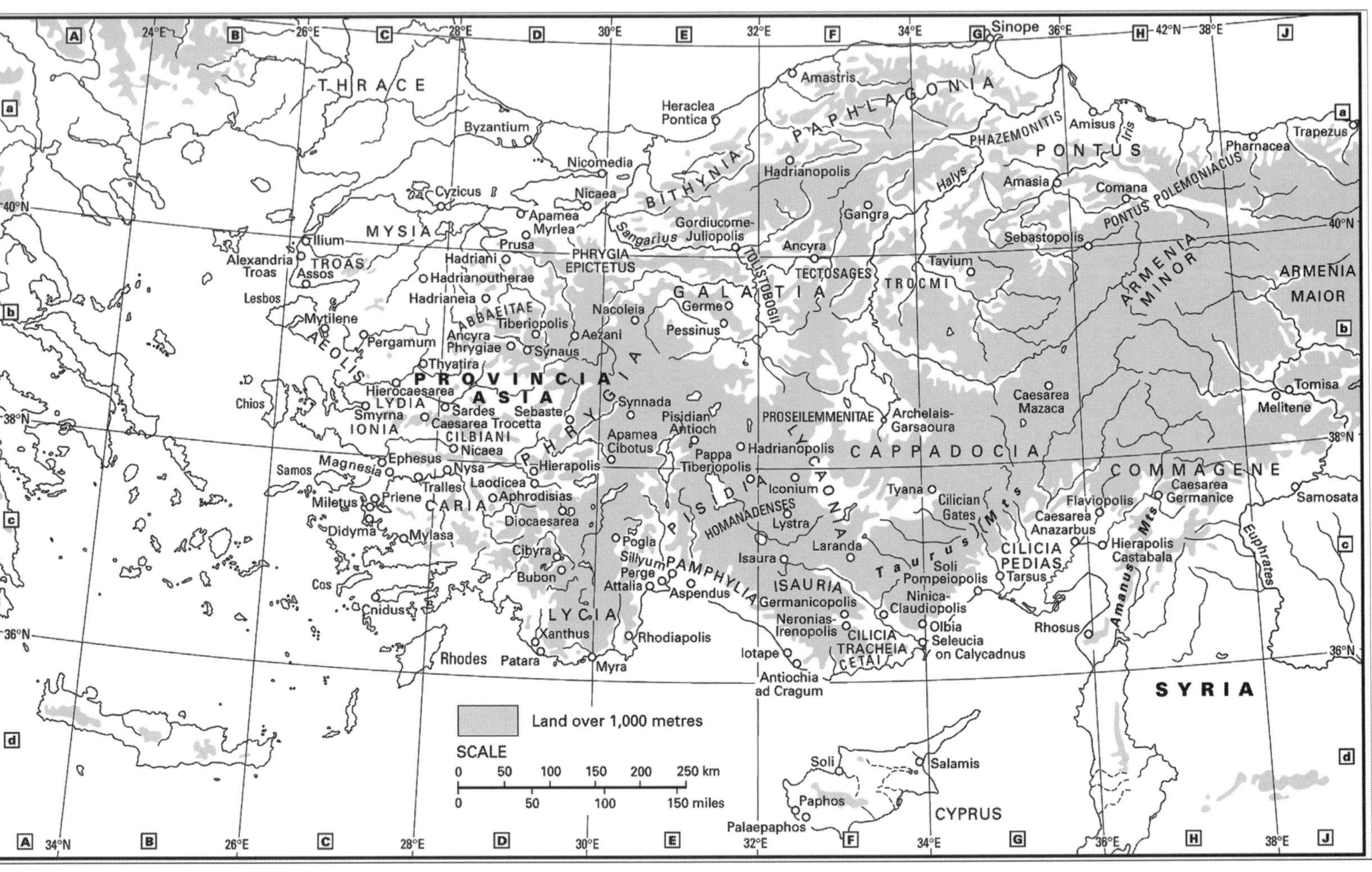

Asia, Roman: map of Roman province of Asia.

include FRONTINUS (the curator of the water supply of Rome), Marcus Ulpius Traianus (father of the emperor TRAJAN) and the historian TACITUS.

In common with most 'senatorial' provinces the administration of Asia was not a significant military post, as it had no legionary garrison. However, EPIGRAPHIC evidence confirms the presence of a small auxiliary garrison, of value for keeping internal order. As in many other Roman provinces, the bulk of the governor's work was juridical. While Ephesos served as the provincial capital, the governor and his entourage travelled regularly between major cities to hear lawsuits. The circuit of assize centres in Asia can be reconstructed from a number of sources, including STRABO and an inscription from Ephesos. The principal cities included MILETOS, EPHESOS, Alabanda, HALIKARNASSOS, SMYRNA, PERGAMON, SARDIS, Adramytteion, Apameia, Kibyra, Synnada, Philomelion and Kyzikos (Cyzicus). The fact that Asia was governed by proconsuls, however, did not stop emperors from intervening in its internal affairs; as early as 20 BC Augustus himself was active in the province (CASSIUS DIO 54.7). The importance of the province meant that it received visits from later emperors too, especially the philhellene HADRIAN (AD 123–4 and 129–31), whose extensive travels and BENEFACTIONS there were commemorated by the construction of TEMPLES (at Kyzikos, for example) and by FESTIVALS.

Imperial procurators were also involved in the administration, including Gnaeus Lucilius Capito, whose prosecution in AD 23 for over-reaching his authority is recorded by Tacitus (*Annals* 4.15). By the 2nd century AD the regular Roman administrators were sometimes supplemented by temporary imperial appointees (*curatores*) dealing with misgovernment (especially financial) of individual cities. They are attested from inscriptions in various places, including Ephesos (auditing civic finances) in the mid-2nd century AD, and Aphrodisias (authorizing the use of civic funds for a festival) later in the same century.

The Greek cities of Asia (along with those of neighbouring Bithynia) were important in the development of the IMPERIAL CULT. Cassius Dio (51.20) describes how they took the initiative in setting up a cult of the living emperor for the Greek inhabitants of the province, centred on Pergamon, in 29 BC. This provincial imperial cult was administered by a *koinon* or 'commonwealth' of the Greeks of Asia. A collective body, representing the Greek cities as a whole, had existed in some form through the 1st century BC, but overseeing the imperial cult for the province as a whole gave it a regular focus. Initially, representatives met annually at the cult centre at Pergamon and elected the high priest. Later meetings were also held at other cities, including Smyrna shortly before 9 BC and then other major centres such as Ephesos, Sardis and Kyzikos. Similarly, the single focus of the provincial cult at Pergamon changed with the addition of further provincial temples at Sardis and Ephesos. Cities were granted the title 'temple-warden' (*neôkoros*), which at first indicated the presence of a temple of the provincial imperial cult. Subsequently the title spread beyond these cities to include many others that did not have such temples. Some major cities took the title more than once; Ephesos is described as 'three times temple-warden' by the reign of CARACALLA. In addition to involvement in the province-wide provincial cult, individual cities maintained their own temples and temples dedicated to the worship of the emperor.

The office of asiarch, held by more than one individual simultaneously and well documented in the imperial period, probably relates to the province as a whole and the *koinon* in some sense. However, it is still debated whether it referred (at first, at least) solely to priests of the provincial cult or was related to other duties such as that of delegate to the *koinon*, or even was used in purely civic contexts.

The *koinon* also took on a political or administrative aspect, as the only body capable of representing the cities of the province as a whole to Roman authority. It brought prosecutions in Rome against governors and other officials accused of offences during their time in office. The best-known examples are the prosecutions in the reign of TIBERIUS recorded by Tacitus, including the condemnation of Gaius Junius Silanus for extortion in AD 22 (*Annals* 3.66), the accusers being 'assisted by the best public ORATORS from the whole province of Asia'.

The unity of the province represented by the *koinon* in fact belied the tremendous rivalries between and within individual cities. These rivalries took the form of competitive public building, funded by civic resources and benefaction, and also of competition for honours and titles. Besides the title of 'temple warden', Ephesos, Smyrna and Pergamon competed over the status of 'First and Greatest Metropolis of Asia', an issue that was referred as high as the emperor, as shown by a rescript sent to Ephesos by ANTONINUS PIUS.

The unpopular Republican system whereby direct taxes (*tributa* – poll and land taxes) were collected by *publicani* was abandoned by JULIUS CAESAR. It was replaced by a process whereby individual cities were responsible for collecting taxes from their territories and passing them on to Roman authorities. However, the collection of indirect taxes such as customs dues remained the prerogative of the *publicani*. One of the most interesting pieces of evidence for Roman administration discovered in recent decades is a 1st-century AD inscription excavated at Ephesos that details the law on the collection of customs dues in Asia (*AE* 1989, 681). This sets out where taxes are to be collected on goods crossing provincial boundaries, over land and by sea, and records the procedures and rates of tax to be exacted by the *publicani*.

The wealth of Asia was famous, and the remains of lavish public buildings still visible in the ruins of the cities confirm it. The cities have traditionally remained the focus of archaeological fieldwork, and relatively little attention has been paid to the sources of their wealth, particularly their rural territories. VILLAGES were an important form of settlement throughout the region, and interesting evidence for settlement hierarchies is provided by an inscription of AD 125 (*SEG* 38. 1462). This relates to the city of Oinoanda in the adjacent province of LYCIA, but probably is relevant to Asia too. It shows the city's rural territory divided up into villages (*kômai*) and smaller units, perhaps scattered single farms or isolated holdings of agricultural land farmed from the cities or villages. Sporadic literary sources mention the fertility of much agricultural land, including the river valleys of the Maeander and Hermos. Ionia and

Lydia were particularly famous for their WINES. TEXTILE production is also recorded as an important source of wealth in many cities. Miletos, for example, was particularly well known for wool production and processing.

Much of the evidence for these economic activities is purely anecdotal, but the export of MARBLE from Ionia and Phrygia is well attested archaeologically. In general, economic activity has not been a primary focus of archaeological study in the region, but there is non-literary evidence for exports. The hellenistic–early Roman red-slipped tableware conventionally known as 'Pergamene' in fact has nothing to do with Pergamon. But similar red-slipped pottery was produced at Çandarlı near Pergamon and was widely exported in the eastern MEDITERRANEAN in the 1st–3rd centuries AD, as was the later red-slipped fineware produced at Phokaia. The AMPHORAS that transported wine from KNIDOS and Kos to (among other places) Roman Italy are well known, but other widely distributed types (such as the long-lived form Riley Carthage late Roman amphora 3, Peacock and Williams 45, probably produced in western Asia Minor, whose contents are unknown) are less well understood, and further study might increase our knowledge of the economy of the province.

While our knowledge of the cultures of Roman Asia is dominated by the Greek cities and their written records, this Greek culture overlay a range of local cultures (particularly in remoter and rural areas) that sometimes can be glimpsed through written sources and archaeological evidence. Occasionally, even local languages are attested in written form. For example, a hundred or so inscriptions in Phrygian, written in Greek characters, are known, most of them dating to the 3rd century AD.

While both civil wars and destructive EARTHQUAKES had an impact on the province, Roman Asia remained relatively safe from external enemies until the mid-3rd century AD. At that time it was raided (particularly in coastal areas) by GOTHS and Herulians. One raid (perhaps AD 262) even resulted in the burning of the temple of ARTEMIS at Ephesos. Nevertheless, Asia remained a prosperous and important part of the Roman empire down to late antiquity. Provincial reforms under DIOCLETIAN saw the extent of the province of Asia reduced, so that by c.315 the new administrative unit (*dioikêsis*, 'directorate' or 'diocese') of Asiana approximated to the old province of Asia. This was composed of the new, smaller province of Asia proper alongside other, smaller units such as Hellespont, the islands, Phrygia I and II, Lydia and Caria, governed by equestrian officials. NDP

See Magie, D. (1950) *Roman Rule in Asia Minor*; Price, S. (1984) *Rituals and Power: the Roman imperial cult in Asia Minor.*

EAST GREECE; ROMAN EMPIRE: (b).

Asklepiades c.330–c.260 BC Early hellenistic epigrammatist from Samos. (Why he was sometimes referred to as 'Sikelidas', implying a Sicilian origin, and how his name came to be given to the 'Asclepiadean' metre familiar to Aiolic poets of the archaic age such as ALKAIOS, remain unsolved mysteries.) Over 40 of his EPIGRAMS (some disputed) survive: they reveal a youthful ARISTOCRATIC hedonism sharply tempered by an acute sense of life's mayfly brevity. The ideal of mutual love remains bittersweet but elusive, repeatedly collapsing into a series of pursuits and rejections: it seems likely that CATULLUS knew Asklepiades' work well. Several epigrams are early examples of the *paraklausithyron*, the shut-out lover's lament before his mistress' closed door, in the cold wind or rain. The Erotes, already well on their way to becoming pretty *putti*, play dice, indifferent to their victims' distress. There is an unmistakable sense of *Weltschmerz* in the air. Like Alkaios, when erotic idealism founders on the harsh rocks of sexual reality, Asklepiades can (as a friend and drinking companion recommends) find relief in the wine-bowl.

THEOKRITOS (7.40) acknowledged Asklepiades' influence, and he also left his mark on KALLIMACHOS who nevertheless, in the *Aitia*, regarded him as one of the 'malignant gnomes' – perhaps for praising Antimachos. He was a pioneer in extending the epigram as a literary genre far beyond its monumental and, in particular, its funerary conventions to embrace the themes of sympotic ELEGY and LYRIC. But he also imparted to the form a highly original and personal flavour: passionate introspection tempered by ironic wit. PMG

See Gow, A. S. F. and Page, D. L (1965) *The Greek Anthology: hellenistic epigrams*, 2 vols. (text, trs., commentary); Clack, J. (1999) *Asclepiades of Samos and Leonidas of Tarentum: the poems*; Gutzwiller, K. (1998) *Poetic Garlands: hellenistic epigrams in context* 122–50.

Asklepios (Aesculapius) Greek HERO and god of healing; in HOMER the 'blameless physician', father of the healing heroes Machaon and Podaleirios (*Iliad* 2.729–33). Details of his life story vary, but most make him son of APOLLO and Koronis, taught the secrets of MEDICINE by the centaur Cheiron. His healing career ended when he attempted to bring a dead man back to life, for which presumption ZEUS struck him dead with a thunderbolt. Over the 5th century he acquired several divine daughters personifying aspects of his work: Hygieia, Akeso, Iaso, Panakeia ('Health, Cure, Healing, Cure-all'). From the late archaic period he was worshipped as a god at a number of centres, the major sanctuary at Epidauros providing a centre for later expansion, especially to Athens and Rome, the latter in response to a plague (293 BC). Medicine was practised at his sanctuaries, no conflict of interest apparently being felt: at the Asklepieion on Kos a school of physicians called themselves 'descendants of Asklepios', and the HIPPOCRATIC oath was sworn to Asklepios among others. Accounts of many more or less miraculous cures appear in inscriptions from Epidauros and the *Sacred Discourses* of Aelius ARISTIDES (frequenter of the PERGAMON Asklepieion). Asklepios is usually depicted as a mature man with a *himation* over one shoulder, the other bare, carrying a snake-entwined staff. EJS

See Edelstein, E. J. and Edelstein, L. (1945) *Asclepius: a collection and interpretation of the testimonies*; Garland, R. (1992) Asklepios and his sacred snake, in *Introducing New Gods* 116–35.

Aspasia A *hetaira* (courtesan), born c.460 BC in MILETOS, who achieved notoriety as the mistress of PERIKLES. Her name, meaning 'Gladly Welcomed', was probably her professional nickname. She was reputedly skilled in RHETORIC and a friend of SOCRATES (PLATO acknowledges her role as an intellectual). As a *hetaira* and Perikles' mistress she was abused by his political enemies. After his DIVORCE, c.445, Perikles began to cohabit with her. They had one son, Perikles, later legitimized and made an Athenian citizen. The relationship between Aspasia and Perikles was allegedly a happy one (PLUTARCH, *Perikles* 24), though her exact status is much debated. Some maintain that she was his concubine, while others suggest she was his legitimate wife. Plutarch portrays her as an influential courtesan and blames her for Perikles' decision to start the war against SAMOS. Several ancient authors state that she operated a brothel (Plutarch, *Perikles* 24.3); ARISTOPHANES refers to 'Aspasia's whores', and in a comic setting, blames the start of the PELOPONNESIAN WAR on the abduction of two of her *hetairai* (*Acharnians* 527–30). Following the death of Perikles in 429 she married Lysikles, who became a successful politician in Athens through her assistance. No more is heard of her after this. Accurate information about Aspasia is difficult to find in the ancient sources, as authors tend to use her to illustrate their views on PHILOSOPHY, rhetoric and Periklean government. LL-J

See Henry, M. M. (1995) *Prisoner of History.*

Aspendos see FORUMS; THEATRES, ROMAN; THRASYBOULOS.

assemblies

The Greek assembly (*ekklêsia*) comprised adult male citizens with an equal voice and vote. Details vary in different constitutions, but in classical Athens, where there was no property qualification as in OLIGARCHIC states, the assembly was the sovereign body and met on the Pnyx hill four times in each of the year's ten prytanies, with extraordinary meetings when required. The quorum for certain measures was 6,000, but not all meetings will have had this level of attendance and pay was introduced as an inducement in 403 BC. Voting was by a majority show of hands (roughly estimated by the presiding officers). The assembly sat as a court and elected the GENERALS, but its primary function was legislative, covering all spheres. By the 4th century it passed decrees (*psêphismata*), less permanent measures than laws (*nomoi*), for which special procedures were developed. The assembly's business, much of which was routine, was subject to prior discussion by the council (*boulê*), which prepared the agenda and put forward formal resolutions (*probouleumata*) with or without specific proposals. Any citizen could propose a motion or amendment to the assembly, though in practice policy was dictated by influential politicians; and proposals had to be within the compass of the laws, or the proposer was liable to prosecution for illegality (*graphê paranomôn*). The assembly lost most of its importance to the council in the hellenistic age.

The Roman assembly met in three different groupings, hence its plural title *comitia*. Unlike Greek assemblies, the *comitia* could only vote on MAGISTRATES' proposals, without emendation, and their decisions had to be ratified by the SENATE. The earliest, the *comitia curiata*, in which the people were divided into 30 wards (*curiae*), had a purely formal role in the REPUBLIC, its functions being mostly taken over by the *comitia centuriata*. This assembly, traditionally instituted by SERVIUS TULLIUS in the mid-6th century, was loosely based on the army centuries and so met on the Campus Martius outside the *POMERIUM*. Its complex voting system, of 193 centuries divided into five property classes, favoured wealthy citizens aged over 46; it elected CONSULS, PRAETORS and CENSORS, declared war, legislated and acted as a court of appeal. The wealthy similarly dominated the *comitia tributa*, in which the voting groups were the 35 tribes, with the urban PLEBS concentrated in only four of these. There were two tribal *comitia*, the more important being the assembly of PLEBEIANS, traditionally founded by Publilius Volero in 471 BC and strictly called the *concilium plebis*, since PATRICIANS were excluded. Summoned by TRIBUNES, it passed plebiscites which were binding on all citizens after 287 BC, elected tribunes and plebeian AEDILES, and sat as a court for non-capital offences. The *comitia populi tributa*, founded soon after, included patricians and was convoked by the consuls or praetors; it elected quaestors, curule aediles and military tribunes. The *comitia* lost their powers in the early PRINCIPATE, but still formally existed in the 3rd century AD. MJE

See Hansen, M. H. (1987) *The Athenian Assembly in the Age of Demosthenes*; Ste Croix, G. E. M. de (1972) *The Origins of the Peloponnesian War*, appendix 23 (on Sparta); Taylor, L. R. (1966) *Roman Voting Assemblies.*

associations see CLUBS; *PUBLICANI*.

Astarte see CYPRUS; TANIT.

Asterix The hero of a comic series invented by Albert Uderzo and René Goscinny in 1959. The son of Astronomix and his wife Sarsaparilla, Asterix is a small Gallic warrior who never hesitates to undertake dangerous missions in the quest to keep his village free from Roman domination. He always triumphs over his adversaries, usually with the help of a magic potion brewed by the DRUID Getafix, which gives him the strength of ten men. Asterix's name is made up of *aster* (star) and *rix* (king, in CELTIC dialect). He was born on the same day as his friend, the oafish but lovable Obelix. Asterix is both an excellent warrior and an able mediator; he is also a firm believer in the values of DEMOCRACY. He has a complex personality: sometimes grumpy, sometimes mischievous, diplomatic and a go-getter, he is always an excellent companion. His adventures, recounted in 30 volumes, have taken him to Rome, Greece, Egypt, BRITAIN, CORSICA, SICILY and many other ancient locations. He wears a feathered helmet (the direction of the two feathers helps us tell what kind of mood he is in). He has blond hair and a blond handlebar moustache. He is a tough little guy. The popularity of the *Asterix* comics has seen the hero's adventures translated into many languages. There have been seven animated feature films and two live action movies: *Asterix and Obelix against Caesar* (1999) and *Mission Cleopatra* (2002). LL-J

See Uderzo, A. and Goscinny, R. (1973) *Asterix the Gaul.*

astrology The technique of using the positions of stars and planets to predict the future. Once humans noticed that motions of heavenly bodies in the night sky were regular, farmers and others employed them to record the progress of seasons and to guide their agricultural and other planning. From this rose the belief that the positions of heavenly bodies at a given time had important consequences for the future, whether for individuals or for communities. The earliest evidence comes from MESOPOTAMIA c.2100 BC, when king Gudea built a temple in line with the stars. Not much later, lists of stars and manuals of celestial omens appear. In the 7th century at Nineveh, scholars inscribed some 70 tablets, known as the *Enuma Anu Enlil*, which list c.7,000 omens and predictions gathered over the course of a millennium or more and include the first detailed accounts of planet movements. By that time, the concept of the celestial equator had developed, and other documents name constellations in relation to the ecliptic (the sun's apparent path through the sky), offering a rudimentary version of what became the ZODIAC. Charts of the risings and settings of the sun and stars and the movements of the moon and planets were kept, along with accounts of eclipses and other celestial omens. Monthly summaries, known as 'Diaries' and intended to aid the construction of a scientific calendar, soon appeared. By the late 6th century, the ecliptic was divided into 12 segments of 30 degrees, creating the zodiac, which first appears in a Diary in 464 BC. By the late 5th century BC, horoscopes recording planet positions at an individual's birth appear in Mesopotamia, simple at first but with increasing complexity. Interpretative texts, describing the meaning of birth within a particular sign or portion of a sign, were also composed.

Unlike BABYLONIANS who developed and employed MATHEMATICS, the Greeks, though aware of Mesopotamian scholarship, studied the sky in terms of geometry and kinetics. Egypt, meanwhile, offered a simple calendar, including the concept of decans, groups of ten days, later incorporated into the zodiac. Although the details are obscure, astrology as practised in the classical world apparently developed in Egypt, regarded as the origin of astrology by writers as early as the 1st century BC. At ALEXANDRIA, Greek COSMOLOGY and spatial geometry, the Egyptian calendar, and Babylonian ASTRONOMY, astrology and celestial data met, and the conjunction spawned theoretical astrological texts in the Hermetic tradition, horoscopic astrology and Greek philosophical interest in both. With Rome's conquest of Greece and the Roman ÉLITE's taste for Greek learning, astrology entered the Roman world.

From the late 1st century BC, astrology was popular at Rome, even among the élite, but most practitioners were Greek. The first Roman of note to practise and write on astrology was Nigidius Figulus, a Roman SENATOR whose learning CICERO regarded highly. Cicero himself, like many others, was sceptical of astrology. Opponents might point to the different fates of twins (whose horoscopes should be identical) as an argument, but the disdain resulted primarily from a disinclination to believe that the stars and planets influenced human activity. Later, religions like CHRISTIANITY opposed astrology on mainly religious grounds and Christian EMPERORS legislated against it. Even earlier, emperors tried to curtail the practice, defining as treason any attempt to inquire about the length of a emperor's life or one's own prospects of becoming emperor. SEPTIMIUS SEVERUS used his horoscope for propaganda, built a Septizonium at Rome, and had his palace painted with depictions of the heavens, but never divulged the exact moment of his birth. TIBERIUS too was given to astrology and tested several candidates before choosing Thrasyllus as his personal astrologer. Many other emperors regularly consulted astrologers.

At least eight times between 33 BC and AD 180 and several times before that, usually in times of crisis like food shortages, astrologers, philosophers or ACTORS, and sometimes all three groups, were temporarily expelled from Rome or Italy, for they possessed an ability to spark disturbances. Despite such setbacks, astrologers, often called Chaldaeans or *mathematici* in the texts, remained popular at all levels of society throughout the empire. Quite naturally, opportunists and charlatans with meagre training operated alongside professionals. PLINY THE YOUNGER (*Letters* 2.20) derides a certain Regulus, who employed astrology and haruspicy to convince a wealthy woman on her deathbed that she would recover: she did, just long enough to write him into her will.

In general terms, astrology can be divided into native and horary. The first is based on the birth of individuals, while the second relates to a prediction at a specific point in time in the life of an individual or an institution like a city. In native astrology, the planets, the Sun, Moon, Saturn, Jupiter, Mars, Venus and Mercury, are placed into the zodiac in the positions occupied at the birth of an individual. Charts, which stipulated allowances for geographic latitude, were available for this purpose. The life of the subject was predicted on the basis of these positions with the aid of interpretative works. The interpretations became more detailed as techniques developed, while the zodiac itself was defined into smaller segments to permit greater precision, and areas in it were held to govern different aspects of life. Horary astrology involved similar techniques, but the questions, and thus the answers, were of a different nature. Astrologers were asked to predict the likely success of a military campaign, the advisability of a MARRIAGE, and the best time to take medicine, among many other requests.

Many horoscopes (the precise zodiac at birth) survive on PAPYRI and in other writings. Interpretation is usually not included, but handbooks for this are extant in the *Mathesis* of Firmicus Maternus (4th century AD) and the *Pentateuchos* of Dorotheos of Sidon (originally 1st century AD), in an Arabic translation. Other works of various date include Manilius, *Astronomica*, Manetho, *Prognostics*, and Vettius Valens, *Anthologies*. ARATOS' *Phainomena* was translated by Cicero and survives in a Latin version attributed to Germanicus Caesar. JV

See Barton, T. (1994) *Ancient Astrology*.

ZODIAC: (a)–(b).

astronomy The origins of the modern analytical and predictive science of astronomy are generally acknowledged to lie in the fusion, in the hellenistic era, of earlier BABYLONIAN and Greek traditions. As a result, ancient Greek astronomy has been intensively studied by historians of astronomy, though the historical sources are fragmentary. The Babylonian tradition had been empirically based and arithmetical. Since the 8th century BC the SUN, MOON, planets and stars had been systematically observed and their

ASTRONOMY: astronomical graffito on a fragment of a mixing bowl (*krater*) from Pithekoussai, Italy dating to the late 8th century BC (Late Geometric). The information may have been used for navigation. The graffito probably depicts a constellation, possibly that known to the Romans as the 'Keystone of Hercules' or earlier to Greeks as the 'Kneeling Man'. The two bright stars may be Vega and Arcturus and the B might stand for either Boötes (the constellation of which Arcturus is a part) or Boreas (the north star).

positions recorded, with remarkable accuracy, on clay tablets. The regularities that became apparent led, for example, to the discovery around the 5th century BC of the 'Metonic cycle'. This provided a means by which lunar calendars could be kept in step with the solar year by adding a 13th month in 7 out of every 19 years. The Greek tradition was more theoretical in the sense that it relied upon the use of models to explain what was observed. By the 4th century BC, PHILOSOPHERS of the PYTHAGOREAN school, as well as influential figures such as PLATO and ARISTOTLE, were developing broad visions of the nature of the COSMOS. They invoked intuitive concepts of beauty and harmony, and attempted to provide logical explanations of particular phenomena. Plato and Aristotle agreed that the structure of the cosmos as a whole (macrocosm) paralleled that of the human body (microcosm), with direct links between celestial bodies or phenomena and human organs. This was a conviction that led to the extensive use of ASTROLOGY in MEDICINE. At the same time, Aristotle argued that since the earth always casts a circular shadow on the moon during a lunar eclipse, it must be spherical.

Hellenistic astronomers, combining these traditions, applied quantitative geometrical models to problems such as the observed motions of the sun, moon and planets. Aristarchos famously anticipated Copernicus by more than 17 centuries by suggesting that the earth moved in a circle around a stationary sun, but mainstream thought retained a stationary earth. Around 200 BC, APOLLONIOS OF PERGE developed the idea of epicycles and deferents to explain the apparent motions of the planets. By the mid-2nd century BC, Hipparchos had discovered the precession of the equinoxes and provided elegant models to explain the apparent motions of the sun and moon. Our knowledge of these and subsequent ideas is almost exclusively due to the writings of PTOLEMY three centuries later, and to their preservation and development in turn by the astronomers of the Islamic world. Although over a dozen astronomical and/or astrological texts in Latin survive from the Greco-Roman world in the 1st to 5th centuries AD, they are mainly textbooks presenting existing ideas, and for this reason historians of science have tended to pay relatively little attention to them.

Another aspect of astronomy in the classical world, just as in a great many different human societies stretching back into prehistory, is the use made of observations of celestial phenomena by common people. An obvious example of this is in regulating farming activities through the seasons. HESIOD's poem *Works and Days* bears witness to the detailed knowledge passed down orally in central Greece in the 8th century BC. For example, the heliacal rising of the Pleiades (their first appearance in the pre-dawn sky after a 40-day period of invisibility) indicated the time of year to start harvesting, while 'when Orion and Seirios are come to the middle of the sky, and the rosy-fingered Dawn confronts Arcturus, then, Perses, cut off all your grapes, and bring them home with you' (609–11; trs. Lattimore). The *Works* part of *Works and Days* contains many seasonal astronomical indicators of this nature that are, on the whole, readily explicable. The *Days* part, on the other hand, contains prognostications associated with the phase of the moon which, from a modern scientific perspective, seem no more than irrational superstition.

Some evidence of the nature of 'folk astronomy' in classical Greece and Rome has been obtained from archaeoastronomical investigations of the location and orientation of graves, TEMPLES and PALACES. It is clear that the practice of deliberately orientating graves in relation to the sun or moon extends back to MINOAN times. A cemetery at Armenoi in western CRETE is located near a mountain with a peak sanctuary dedicated to a moon goddess, and its 224 tombs are consistently oriented upon moonrise. It has been suggested that elements of both MYCENAEAN and Minoan orientation practices survived to influence archaic and classical Greek temples. Studies of temple orientations were pioneered by Heinrich Nissen in the later 19th century, and in the 1930s William Dinsmoor concluded that the majority (73 per cent) were oriented eastwards within the limits of sunrise. In particular, the PARTHENON was aligned upon Mt Hymettos where the sun rose on the day of the feast of ATHENA, the goddess to whom the temple was dedicated. An obvious question is whether it was common practice to orient temples towards sunrise on the FESTIVAL day of the deity in question. Unfortunately, matters are often complicated by uncertainties in the original dedication and changes in the orientation between different phases of construction. In addition, written sources such as Vitruvius (*De architectura* 4.5) suggest that a variety of other considerations may often have exerted an influence, such as a preference for facing nearby cities, RIVERS or ROADS. There has been a recent revival of interest in this question and new detailed and systematic studies of temple locations and orientations are currently being undertaken.

Roman astronomy has tended to be neglected by historians of science, owing to the perceived lack of innovative developments in philosophical cosmology or mathematical astronomy in the Roman world. It has also been neglected by archaeoastronomers, since there is no clear overall consistency among Roman temple orientations, in stark contrast to the Greek case. Yet there is ample evidence, both historical and ARCHAEOLOGICAL, of the practical use of astronomy in the Roman world. Instruction books attest to the knowledge of astronomy needed by the navigators of commercial ships, and by surveyors setting out all over the empire. SUNDIALS were commonplace: some three dozen are known in POMPEII alone. Regarding RELIGION and beliefs, astrology certainly played a hugely significant role in many aspects of Roman life, and indigenous solar rituals strongly influenced the development of the Roman and, subsequently, of the CHRISTIAN CALENDAR. CLNR

See Aveni, A. (1989) *Empires of Time*; Dinsmoor, W. (1939) Archaeology and astronomy, *Proceedings of the American Philosophical Society* 80: 95–173; Hoskin, M. (1997) *The Cambridge Illustrated History of Astronomy*; (2001) *Tombs, Temples and their Orientations*; Shank, M., ed. (2000) *The Scientific Enterprise in Antiquity and the Middle Ages.*

Atalanta (Atalantê) Mythical HUNTRESS and ATHLETE from ARKADIA or BOIOTIA. Details about her family are not clear in myth, but her childhood is associated with the wild countryside where she was raised by hunters and suckled by a bear (APOLLODOROS 3.9.2). She is known for a range of virtues and skills which were normally mastered by male HEROES in Greek mythology. These included swiftness in running and outstanding ability in wrestling and archery. Atalanta is the only female among a group of young male hunters during the mythical hunt of the Kalydonian boar and the first one to hit the beast, as attested by Apollodoros. In the funeral games in honour of Pelias, Atalanta won a wrestling contest with Peleus. Atalanta rejects erotic union with men (THEOGNIS 1291–4) and kills whoever violates this wish. Apollodoros relates how one of her male companions, Melanion, eventually wins her for life, having defeated her in the footrace by trickery. Stories told by Apollodoros, OVID and others describe Atalanta's and Melanion's transformation into lions by divine hand for having transgressed sacred rules in a shrine of ZEUS or CYBELE.

ATALANTA: as depicted on a 5th-century BC vase in the Louvre (Paris), dressed as a female athlete.

In ART, Atalanta is portrayed in hunting or athletic outfit and action from as early as the late 7th century. She typically wears a short garment or trunks and exercise cap and is often depicted topless. EP

See Boardman, J. (1984) Atalante, in *LIMC* vol. 2, 940–50.

Atellan farces see DRAMA, ROMAN; GAMES, ROMAN; OSCANS.

Athanasius Bishop of ALEXANDRIA, AD 328–73. Born to humble parents c.AD 299, Athanasius was educated in the household of Alexander, his predecessor as BISHOP, and became a deacon at an early age. In 325, he attended the council of Nicaea, summoned by CONSTANTINE to treat doctrinal and other issues, including ARIANISM. As deacon and bishop, Athanasius led the opposition to Arianism and suffered as a result. Church councils expelled him in 335, 338/9 and 356; he was condemned by councils in the late 340s and early 350s, but avoided expulsion. Athanasius wrote to EMPERORS, officials and bishops defending himself against charges of heresy, mismanagement of church property and violence against consecrated virgins – all stock charges in religious disputes. He travelled to Rome in 339, seeking assistance from that city's bishop. Athanasius met the emperor Constantius several times, and, during the 340s had audiences with Constans; these generated accusations of stirring the Western emperor against his brother. His writings on his own behalf, including *Defence against the Arians*, *Defence before Constantius*, *Defence of his Flight*, and *History of the Arians*, are masterpieces of self-interest and often misrepresent the truth. He returned to Alexandria in 362, after JULIAN permitted religious exiles to return, but withdrew after the emperor excluded him from the amnesty. In 365, he retired again, but was restored in 366. He authored numerous works on theological issues and maintained contact with Egypt, even from exile.

Athanasius had strong support from Egyptian monks, especially Pachomius, who founded a chain of monasteries, and Antony, a hermit and the first monk to enjoy political influence. In 336, Antony wrote to Constantine on behalf of Athanasius; two years later, he visited Alexandria, castigated Arians, and performed a miracle, demonstrating his support for Athanasius. The *Life of Antony*, long ascribed to Athanasius, is now generally regarded as the work of another or the bishop's revision of an earlier biography. JV

See Barnes, T. D. (1993) *Athanasius and Constantius*; Brakke, D. (1995) *Athanasius and the Politics of Asceticism*; Robinson, A. (1891) *St Athanasius, Select Works and Letters* (translation, in P. Schaff and H. Wade, eds., *A Select Library of Nicene and Post-Nicene Fathers*, series II, vol. 4).

atheism see SCEPTICISM, RELIGIOUS.

Athena The Athenian GODDESS *par excellence*. The Homeric Hymn relates how Athena was born in

Athena: vase-painting of Athena's dramatic birth from the head of Zeus; the other gods and goddesses are, from l. to r., Hebe or Iris, Poseidon, Hephaistos (who has just split open Zeus' head to release Athena), Eileithyia and Artemis.

full armour from the head of her father Zeus. Her role as a warrior goddess shaped her persona as early as Homer. She takes an active part in the Trojan war in favour of the Achaians (*Iliad*), and in connection with heroes, such as Odysseus, Achilles, Agamemnon and others. Together with Zeus, Athena was a major contributor to the triumphal victory of the Olympian gods over the old divine regime of the Titans, as Hesiod narrates in the *Theogony*. Major Greek heroes, notably Herakles, Perseus and Jason with the Argonauts, would have never accomplished their god-sent tasks without Athena's precious help.

Her excellence in arms did not, however, supersede Athena's feminine side. In her capacity as *Ergane*, Athena presided over arts and crafts, and particularly weaving. She famously punished the mortal woman Arachne for daring to compete with her, turning her into a spider. The offering of a newly woven garment to the goddess marked the culmination of the procession at the Panathenaia, the major religious festival in her honour at Athens. Craftsmen and artists paid their respects to the goddess and to the smith god Hephaistos in another Athenian festival known as Chalkeia. A further prominent aspect of the personality of Athena is her virginity, as shown by her cult titles Parthenos and also probably Pallas. An attempt to violate her sexual purity was made by Hephaistos the smith god, but without success. This attempt led to the birth of Erichthonios, the first king of Athens, from the earth.

The cult of Athena enjoyed wide popularity throughout Greece and particularly in Athens, as is attested by the myth of her dispute with Poseidon over the patronage of the city. Athena's offer of the olive tree was chosen by the Athenians over Poseidon's gift of a spring of saltwater. A sacred olive tree stood near the oldest temple of Athena on the Acropolis and was described, together with the contents of the temple, by the Roman traveller Pausanias in his first book. The particular link of Athena with civic space is highlighted by her cult title Polias (goddess of the *polis*) in Athens and elsewhere, but also by the epithet Promachos, reflecting her role as defender of territory. EP

See Deacy, S. and Villing, A., eds. (2001) *Athena in the Classical World*; Demargne, P. (1984) Athena, in *LIMC* vol. 2, 955–1044.

 architecture: (b); gods and goddesses: (a); Parthenon: (a)–(b).

Athenaeus From Naukratis in Egypt, Athenaeus was a Greek rhetorician and grammarian at the end of the 2nd and the beginning of the 3rd century AD. His great work, *Deipnosophistae* (*Philosophers at Dinner*), is of vital importance for understanding ancient cultural and literary history. This extensive work (15 books) contains about 1,000 quotations from hundreds of ancient authors. The quotations range in date from Homer through classical Athens to Athenaeus' own time and in many cases are only found in this work. The first two books and parts of books 3, 10 and 15 are only extant in 'epitome' (summary), but otherwise we seem to possess the work in its entirety. Without a doubt, if this collection of miscellany and anecdotes about the ancient world had not survived, modern scholarship would lack an indescribable wealth of material. Nearly 800 writers and 2,500 separate writings are referred to by Athenaeus; and he boasts of having read 800 plays of Middle Comedy alone.

The work recounts the imagined discussions among prominent Greco-Roman intellectuals attending a fictitious banquet. It professes to be an account given by the author to Athenaeus' friend Timokrates of a banquet held at the house of Laurentius, a scholar and wealthy patron of art. It is thus a dialogue within a dialogue, after the manner of PLATO, but also a conversation of sufficient length to occupy several dialogues. The conversation ranges from the dishes set before the guests to literary matters, including points of grammar and criticism. The guests discuss PHILOSOPHY, WOMEN, courtesans, Oriental monarchs, TYRANTS, parody, FISH, dancing, drinking and much more. The guests are expected to bring with them extracts from the POETS, who are read aloud and discussed at the dining table. The whole work is an effective, if clumsy, apparatus for displaying the author's varied and extensive reading. As a work of art it is often considered unimportant, but as a repertory of fragments and morsels of information it is extremely valuable, indeed, unique. LL-J

See Athenaeus, *The Deipnosophists*, 7 vols., trs. G. B. Gulick (1927–41); Braund, D. and Wilkins, J., eds. (2000) *Athenaeus and his World*.

Athenian empire In 480–479 BC a handful of Greek cities successfully resisted a massive invasion of Greece by land and sea commanded by king XERXES of PERSIA. Naval resistance was led by the democratic city of Athens, especially at the battle of SALAMIS. Under Athens' direction, and with the crucial support of important island states (especially SAMOS, CHIOS and the cities of LESBOS), a new anti-Persian alliance was established in 478/7. The alliance was to be both offensive and defensive, aiming to ravage Persian territory, liberate Greeks still under Persian domination in the northern AEGEAN and western Asia Minor, and guarantee permanent security against the likelihood of a renewed Persian invasion. Some allies were required to contribute SHIPS and their crews, others (far more in number) to contribute collectively the large sums of money needed to pay for these. Oaths of perpetual alliance were sworn on the Cycladic island of DELOS, an important religious centre sacred to APOLLO; here the alliance's war-chest was to be kept and meetings of the allies held. Hence the alliance's modern name, the Delian league. This organization constituted the basis of the Athenians' 5th-century empire (*archê*).

Strictly speaking, however, the Greeks had no word for 'empire'. *Archê* meant legitimate rule within a Greek city, as well as international and possibly illegitimate rule over another city. Moreover, *archê* and its cognates were not used, so far as we know, by either the Athenians or their allies to describe their mutual relations until about 450 BC. Nevertheless some modern scholars, taking 'empire' to mean a striking disparity of power in favour of the alliance's 'leader' (*hêgemôn*), have considered that Athens was in an imperial position from very early in the alliance's history. Certainly, it was Athens that from the start contributed by far the largest number of trireme warships and sailors. The admirals and the treasurers of the alliance were always Athenians, appointed by and responsible to the people of Athens rather than to the alliance as a whole. The early campaigns did further the aims of the alliance generally, but they also disproportionately benefited Athens. When NAXOS, the largest Cycladic island-state, wished to withdraw from the alliance in c.470 but was compelled by allied military force to remain a member, there was the first obvious sign that the alliance might already be regarded as an Athenian empire.

THUCYDIDES, our main narrative source for the empire's history, wrote that Naxos had been not merely disciplined but 'enslaved contrary to established usage'. This is strong language, widely echoed in the closing stages of the PELOPONNESIAN WAR. But during the first two to three decades of the alliance's existence revolts were very rare, and the general impression is that the Athenians were popular for carrying out the alliance's aims with success. Indeed, so successful were the alliance's campaigns against Persia that in about 450 or soon afterwards Athens concluded some kind of formal peace, or informal non-aggression pact, with Persia – the so-called 'peace of Kallias'. At any rate, hostilities between the alliance and the Persian empire ceased for more than three decades.

By 450 the number of allies had risen to about 200, extending all round the Aegean basin. Almost all contributed cash rather than the much more expensive ships, and few paid really large money contributions. But by then the treasury was no longer kept on Delos. Partly for security reasons, but also as a reflection of Athens' *de facto* imperial position within the alliance, it had been transferred in 454 to the ATHENIAN ACROPOLIS. The change is visible concretely in the inscribed tribute quota lists set up on the Acropolis, recording the quota (one-sixtieth) of the tribute monies that was now paid to the patron goddess of Athens, ATHENA Polias. After 450, with the cessation of hostilities against Persia, a significant part of the large surplus balance began to be devoted to causes not envisaged under the original terms of the alliance: war against Sparta, and a massive programme of religious and secular building in Athens.

Relations between Athens and Sparta had become seriously strained in the later 460s, and in about 460 war broke out between Athens and Sparta, together with their respective allies. That conflict, sometimes known as the first Peloponnesian war, was finally concluded in 446/5, on terms very much in favour of Athens. Construction had meanwhile begun in 447 on the PARTHENON, a kind of cathedral to the Athenian empire, and over the next half-century many other large and expensive structures, both rebuilt and entirely new ones, graced the Acropolis and the AGORA (civic centre) of the city.

Shortly after the Parthenon was completed, the Peloponnesian war broke out in 431. Athens' eventual defeat in 404, by a Sparta backed by massive Persian financial aid, meant the end of the empire. Samos alone remained loyal to Athens to the end, and shortly before 404 these two cities entered into a unique mutual-citizenship ('isopolity') agreement: Samians could become Athenians should they take up residence in Athens, and vice versa. That agreement, however, not only was very short-lived but also highlighted the normal exclusivity of the Athenians' attitude to their CITIZENSHIP, the privileges of which they jealously guarded.

Long before 404 Athens had become the target of widespread criticism for behaving like a 'tyrant' city: that is, treating its allies as servile subjects rather than

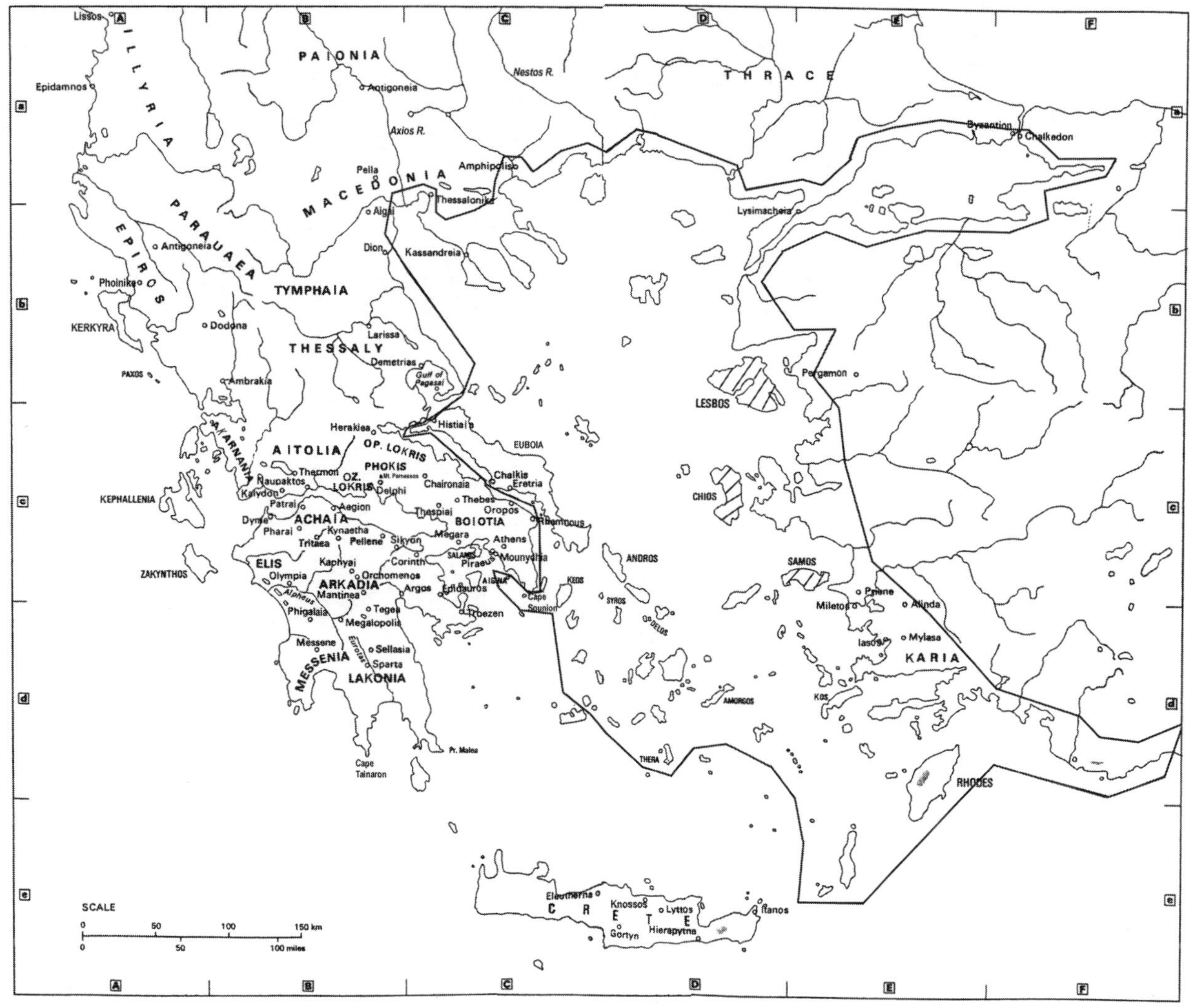

ATHENIAN EMPIRE: (a) the outlined area denotes the extent of the Athenian 'empire', the cities which paid tribute to Athens during the 5th century BC. The islands of Chios, Samos and Lesbos (hatched) contributed ships to the fleet rather than paying money.

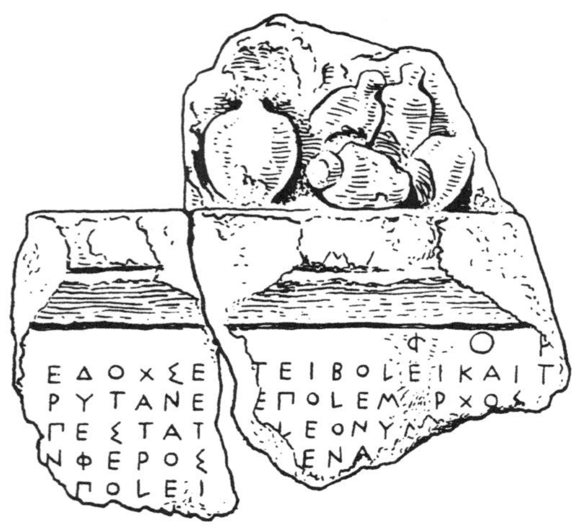

Athenian empire: (b) fragment from the Athenian 'Tribute Lists' recording the donations to the goddess Athena in Athens of $\frac{1}{60}$ of the tribute paid. The relief at the top shows the payments as jars of coins.

co-operating with them as partners in a common and mutually beneficial enterprise. Specific grievances included judicial interference in allied autonomy, and economic exploitation through expropriation of allied land and excessive tribute demands. The criticism was not all entirely fair; and the sharpest critics were wealthy, upper-class Athenians and allies who intensely disliked the fact that the empire as they saw it promoted the political and economic interests of the lower classes at their own expense.

Yet even the Athenians publicly and officially recognized – in retrospect – that some aspects of the charges against them were valid. When they developed a new naval alliance in the 370s – against Sparta this time – the published 'charter' of the Second Athenian confederacy spelled out that neither collectively nor individually were Athenians permitted to acquire property rights in the territory of the allies. The allies for their part were granted a separate council chamber in which league policy was formally determined and grievances against the Athenians might be legally heard. Too soon, however, the Athenians were again accused of going down the same imperialist path as their 5th-century forebears, and the league ceased to be an effective power-unit long before its formal disbandment, by Macedonia, in 338/7. PAC

See Meiggs, R. (1972) *The Athenian Empire*; Osborne, R., ed. and trs. (2000) *The Athenian Empire* (documents); Rhodes, P. J. (1993) *The Athenian Empire*.

Athenian imperialism see Athenian empire; Athens; imperialism, Greek; Konon of Athens; Peloponnesian war; Perikles; Thucydides.

Athens The chief town of Attica. Athens grew up around the foot of the Acropolis which, among other functions, served as a fortified refuge in times of danger. There was a Mycenaean fortification and probably palatial centre on the citadel, but most early remains were swept away when later monumental buildings were erected. The growth of the city as a settlement can be traced through the locations of cemeteries. Just as many institutions still thriving in today's world have their origin in classical Athens (5th and 4th centuries BC), so philosophy, theatre, politics and law have all left their mark on the city's archaeology.

The myth of Theseus 'synoikizing' Attica (bringing it together into a single settlement) was a convenient charter myth. In the late Geometric and early archaic periods, the population of the central settlement may have grown through immigration from Attica and outside; there was no need to export population overseas. By the 6th century BC Attica seems to have been organized as a single *polis*, so that in a political sense 'Athens' refers not only to the city but to the rest of the Attic peninsula as well, particularly after the codifications of law by Drakon (late 7th century) and Solon (early 6th).

Land was the foundation of political power in early Athens, and remained so. Early politics was driven by aristocrats with power-bases in different regions. In c.632/1 Kylon was stopped from making himself tyrant only by being killed at an altar, an impiety that placed an ancestral curse on the Alkmaionid family. The 6th-century tyranny of Peisistratos (561–527) and his son Hippias (527–510), whose homeland was in eastern Attica, accelerated the political unification of Attica, which was completed by the reforms of the Alkmaionid Kleisthenes (508 BC). The largely rural territory was settled with numerous 'demes' (*dêmoi*, literally 'peoples') whose occupants enjoyed full citizenship of Athens. Each was a miniature *polis*, with its own temples and assemblies. After Kleisthenes, a man's civic identity was expressed through the use of given name, father's name (patronymic) and, crucially, his deme name (demotic): for example, *Themistoklês Neokleous Phrearrhios*, 'Themistokles son of Neokles, from the deme Phrearrhioi'. It was probably as a result of its long history of regional competition that Athenians from all districts awarded themselves full rights in the city's decisions.

The sufferings of the Athenians and their city in the Persian wars, and their contribution to the victory over Xerxes, provided a justification for their leadership of Greeks dissatisfied with Spartan leadership. This 'Delian league' gradually became the Athenian empire. Allied tribute, and the burgeoning wealth of the Piraeus, were the economic base for extensions of democracy sponsored by the shadowy Ephialtes and by Perikles, a leader of Churchillian stature and partly Alkmaionid ancestry. The late 5th century saw the most radical democracy, with landless men paid for rowing warships and exercising their political privileges enthusiastically, and for the most part intelligently. Athens was now a cosmopolitan place, with trade flowing through the Piraeus and thousands of metics (resident aliens from other Greek and foreign states) contributing to economic growth and paying for the privilege of living in Athens or Piraeus, as well as fighting in Athens' armed forces.

From the time of Themistokles' stalling embassy to Sparta in the early 470s, the city was encircled by a 6.5 km (4 miles) fortification wall punctuated by gates at the junctions of main roads. Outside the

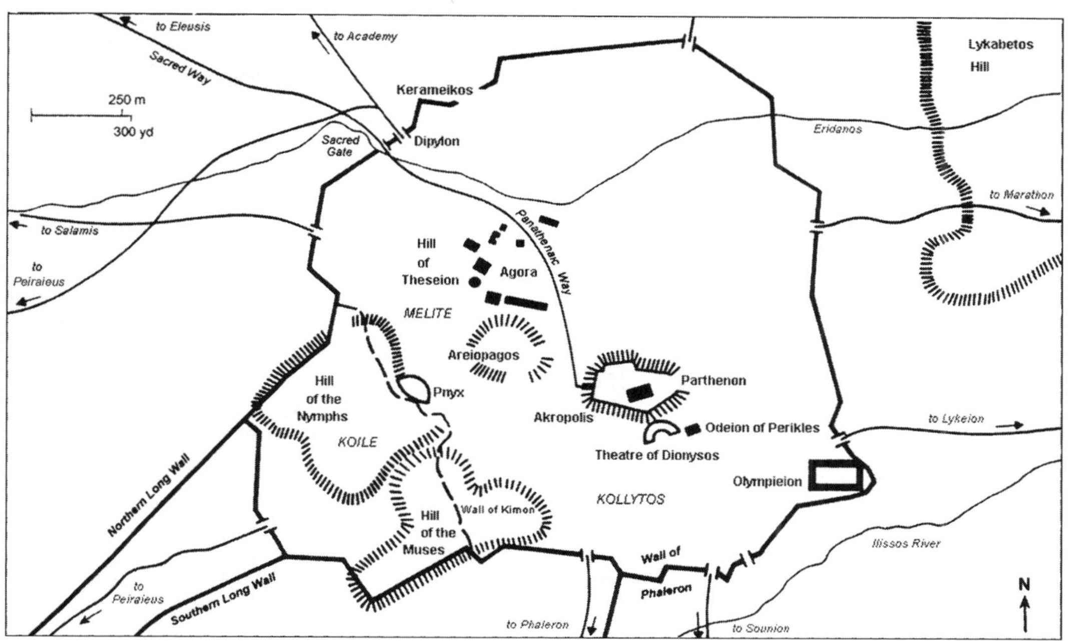

ATHENS: (a) general plan of classical period.

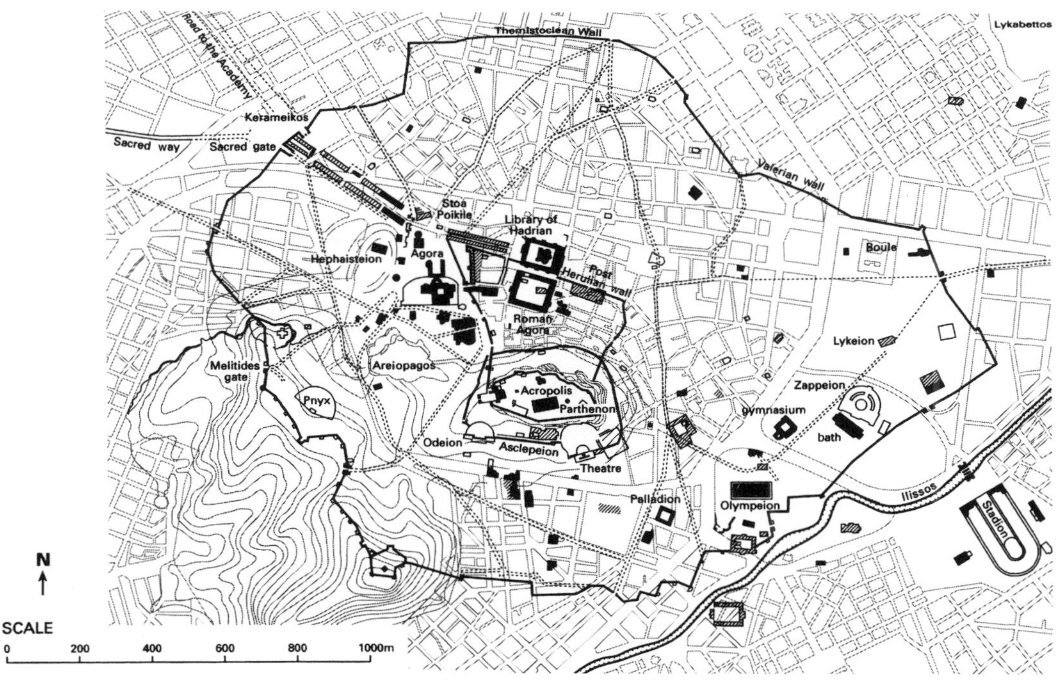

ATHENS: (b) plan in the late Roman period.

gates these roads were lined with graves and tombs. Some can still be seen, clustered around the Dipylon and Sacred gates in the Kerameikos (potters' quarter). From the former a road led to the Academy (originally a sacred grove of the Attic hero Akademos); from the latter the Sacred way led, as it still does, to Eleusis. The river Eridanos, into which the great drain emptied, exited the city through the Sacred gate, which also provided the starting-point for the inward-bound Panathenaic procession up to the Acropolis.

When a formal peace was (probably) concluded with Persia around 450, Perikles proposed an ambitious programme of public works to replace the destroyed temples on the Acropolis. The Parthenon (447–432), Propylaia (437–432), temple of Athena Nike (430–425), and Erechtheion (421–406) were all constructed during this age of Athenian political, economic and military dominance. Several important sanctuaries in the outlying Attic demes also enjoyed the attention of Perikles: Eleusis, Sounion, and Rhamnous all had new temples erected over the ruins of pre-sack predecessors. Piraeus, Athens' port and home to its fabled navy, was connected to the city via the 'long walls'. First laid out under Kimon and completed by Perikles, these two parallel walls ran from the city wall of Athens to join with that of Piraeus, ensuring that Athens could receive essential seaborne imports during times of danger.

Armed conflict with Sparta and its allies began sporadically around 460 and culminated in the so-called Peloponnesian war of 431–404 (really a series of wars). Athens held its own in the first decade of the war (the 'Archidamian war'), but some of the monumental buildings were interrupted; lifting-bosses on the unfinished east wall of the Propylaia testify to this. Religious monuments continued to be built, but not as lavishly as before. The reason for this continued cult interest may have been the devastating outbreaks of plague that swept the city in 429 and 427/6, the latter claiming Perikles among its victims. The shrine of Asklepios, the healing son of Apollo, one of the most important shrines of the lower city (beneath the Acropolis), was founded at this point. Aside from cult installations, the Athenians also continued to build within the city, albeit on a more modest scale, with mudbrick walls and packed earth floors. Beyond its magnificent marble edifices, Athens was not noted for its beauty or cleanliness – slaves had to be employed to keep the streets free of dung and corpses! To the period of the war we can also attribute the new Bouleuterion (council house) and South stoa in the *agora* as well as the fortification of the demes of Sounion, Thorikos and Rhamnous. These were presumably to protect the Athenian grain route from the Black sea. It is often overlooked that, almost continuously from the early 6th century to the Roman period, Athens owned several northern Aegean islands (usually Skyros, Imbros and Lemnos) as naval bases ensuring access to the Hellespont.

Later in the Peloponnesian war, the Athenians rashly launched the Sicilian expedition (415–413), alienated their major allies, suffered a suspension of democracy under the regime of the Four Hundred (411), and finally succumbed in the Ionian war (411–404). What turned the scales was Persian financial aid to the Peloponnesians. A Spartan-sponsored extreme oligarchy of the Thirty (404–403), however, did not last, and within a few years Athens was again a major power. After the confusing inter-state warfare of the early 4th century, Athens was in a position to rebuild a wide-ranging alliance, the second Athenian confederacy (from 378). This was curtailed by Athens' renewed unpopularity in the 350s, and by the rise of Philip II of Macedonia. His victory over the southern Greeks at Chaironeia (338) was followed by a programme of reforms to Athens' finances and administration under politicians such as Euboulos and Lykourgos, as well as a renewal of grand monumentalization. Lykourgos relined Piraeus' three harbours with ramped shipsheds to house the city's triremes. The theatre of Dionysos on the south slope of the Acropolis, the arsenal in the harbour of Zea at Piraeus, and the completion of the Panathenaic stadium are all attributed to Lykourgos. The assembly-place, known as the Pnyx, was rebuilt around 345–335 (its third phase), and a large stepped speakers' platform (*bêma*) was added. An important landmark, the monument of the Eponymous Heroes, was erected in the *agora* as well as lawcourts, fountain houses, and a *klepsydra* or water-clock.

Until the construction of the new Athens metro (completed in 2000), most of the extant information about classical Athens came from the Acropolis and the surrounding *agora*. However, as new railway tunnels were dug, large sections of hitherto unknown archaeology were brought to light everywhere under the modern city. Some 32,000 objects adding greatly to our knowledge of the lives of ordinary, everyday Athenians were catalogued during four years of intense archaeological investigation. This has led to permanent exhibitions in several stations, most notably Syntagma, Evangelismos and Panepistimio.

Democracy survived under Alexander and his successors, but periodic interruptions resulted from changes of overlord. The Macedonian-sponsored tyrant Demetrios of Phaleron (317–307) restricted voting rights to those with a certain amount of property, as would happen on more than one occasion, and banned lavish funerals; the plain, inverted-cone gravestones introduced now remained standard thereafter. Macedonia exercised direct rule over Piraeus from 295, and over Athens from 262 following the disastrous Chremonidean war in which the southern Greeks attempted to drive out the Macedonians. The liberation of both Athens and Piraeus in 229 led to close ties with Ptolemaic Egypt, but the democratic leaders Eurykleides and Mikion successfully pursued a policy of neutrality which was maintained during the Macedonian–Roman wars of the late 3rd century.

After Philip V's Akarnanian allies devastated Attica (201), the Athenians firmly aligned themselves with Rome for over a century. In 167 the Romans awarded them the island of Delos, with its prestigious sanctuary and rich trading community. The 3rd and 2nd centuries produced some of the most important buildings still visible today. Kings such as Eumenes II (197–159/8) and Attalos II (159/8–139/8) of Pergamon were permitted to endow the city with sculptures and colonnades. The enormous stoa of Attalos, reconstructed in the 1950s, houses the Agora Museum. Attalos also attempted to complete the gigantic temple of Olympian Zeus, begun by the Peisistratids. The new Middle Stoa and second South stoa created a distinct 'south square'. The *agora* became less open and more formal, a process that continued in the Roman period. Although Athens was no longer a major power, a king could gain prestige by attaching his name to its monuments. The so-called Tower of the Winds, or Horologion (water-clock) of Andronikos of Kyrrhestos (later 2nd century?) may have been such a benefaction.

Only when MITHRADATES VI of Pontos massacred all Italians in Asia Minor (88) did an anti-Roman party gain the upper hand in Athens, with disastrous results. SULLA besieged the city (87–85); it was sacked and looted of many works of art which were shipped to Italy. The Romans brought about the effective end of democracy, though Athens remained officially democratic and free until Octavian created the province of Achaia (27). By now JULIUS CAESAR had begun work on a new *agora*, east of the old one, which Octavian (as Augustus) completed. It was left to the emperor HADRIAN (AD 117–38) to finish the temple of Olympian Zeus, and to mark the entry from the old 'city of Theseus' to his new suburb with the arch that bears his name. A few years later the Athenian HERODES ATTICUS rebuilt the Stadium and built the splendid Odeion (concert hall) that is once more in use today.

Medieval and Ottoman modifications, such as the Frankish castle with its huge tower and a mosque inside the Parthenon, created a composite Acropolis. Its appearance was very different from what we see today, after the 19th-century demolition of such reminders of foreign occupation. Yet a glance at the spectacular post-classical buildings still surviving around the Acropolis reminds the visitor that the contributions of these periods to Athens' urban fabric was at least as important as those of the two 'classical' centuries. CK-B, DGJS

See Boatwright, M. T. (1992) *Hadrian and the Cities of the Roman Empire*; Camp, J. M. (1986) *The Athenian Agora*; (2001) *The Archaeology of Athens*; Coulson, W. D. E. et al., eds. (1994) *The Archaeology of Athens and Attica under the Democracy*; Habicht, C. (1997) *Athens from Alexander to Antony*; Hansen, M. H. (1999) *The Athenian Democracy in the Age of Demosthenes*; Hoff, M. C. and Rotroff, S. I., eds. (1997) *The Romanization of Athens*; Garland, R. (1987) *The Piraeus*; Parlama, L. and Stampolidis, N. C., eds. (2000) *The City Beneath the City* [Metro excavations]; Stockton, D. (1990) *The Classical Athenian Democracy*; Thompson, H. A. and Wycherley, R. E. (1972) *The Agora of Athens*; Travlos, J. (1971) *Pictorial Dictionary of Ancient Athens*; Wycherley, R. E. (1978) *The Stones of Athens*.

ACROPOLIS, ATHENIAN: (a), (c); AGORA, ATHENIAN: (a)–(b); PARTHENON: (a); PIRAEUS: (a).

athletes and athletics

At no point in their history can Greek athletics be considered amateur events, if 'amateur' implies that the contestants did not expect some tangible reward for triumph. The modern concept of amateur athletics is a product of the 19th century, retrojected into the Greek world to support a contemporary ideology. The earliest record of athletic competition, in book 23 of the *Iliad*, involves heroes competing for prizes of considerable value, and makes it clear that such competitions were an extension of an ARISTOCRATIC society where status was marked by gift exchange. While it is true that the official prizes offered at the great panhellenic festivals were crowns of olive, laurel or celery leaves, the winners expected substantial rewards from their home communities.

The early evolution of the panhellenic festivals is shrouded in mystery. The traditional date for the foundation of the OLYMPIC games, 776 BC, is nearly two centuries earlier than the date for the next festival, the Pythian. This was founded in 582, followed by the Isthmian festival in 581 and the Nemean in 573. The Olympic and Pythian games took place every four years, with the Pythian falling in the third year of an Olympiad; the Isthmian and Nemean were held every two years, in the second and fourth years of each Olympiad. The early date for the Olympics, ostensibly supported by a list of victors reflecting the addition of new events in the course of the next century, is not plainly attested before the 3rd century BC; it is not certain that the 3rd-century list actually derives from Hippias of Elis' list of Olympic victors, composed in the late 5th century, as we know nothing of that work's contents.

According to tradition, the introduction of events at Olympia was dated as follows: in 776 BC the *stadion* race (one stade); in 724 the *diaulos* (a double *stadion* race); in 720 the *dolichos* (a long-distance running event); in 708 the *pentathlon* (running, long jump, discus, javelin and wrestling); in 688 boxing; in 680 CHARIOT RACING; in 648 HORSE racing and *pankration* (a combination of boxing and wrestling but considerably more violent than either). The Homeric poems, datable to the later 8th century, already reflect a rather more sophisticated array of events than the records of Olympic victors. They also point to a different context for the evolution of these contests: the funeral games of wealthy aristocrats. It is probably better to see the organization of the Olympic games as somewhat later in time than the tradition allows, and as an epiphenomenon of the transformation of Greek society in the later 8th century that saw the formation of *POLIS* communities.

In the later 6th century, the evolution of Greek athletic festivals seems to have been very rapid, establishing a format that remained constant until the decline of athletic competition in the 4th century AD. The principal features were the division of contestants by age group, and competition in the nude. The age classifications were 'boys' (under 18 years), 'young men' (18–20) and 'men' (older than 20). The category of 'young men' is not attested for all festivals, and occasionally a successful competitor in the 'boys' category would try to move directly into the 'men's' division, sometimes in the course of a festival. Some athletes would also compete in more than one event. This was especially common in foot races, but is also well attested for the 'heavy' events of boxing, wrestling and *pankration*, which was the most prestigious of all the competitions.

Another feature of Greek athletics, though only significant for the 'heavy' events, was a lack of weight classes. One reason for the longevity of the great Milo of Kroton, winner of six Olympic wrestling crowns during the later 6th century BC and the most successful athlete in Greek history, may well have been his enormous physical size. Literary accounts of boxing matches, as in book 6 of VIRGIL's *Aeneid*, suggest that matches pitting a very large, strong fighter against a smaller, faster man were of great interest. In all the heavy events the emphasis was upon both skill and endurance. There were no rounds

ATHLETES AND ATHLETICS: (a) typical scene of Greek field sports including, at far left and right, long jumpers with distinctive jumping weights, javelin and discus throwers.

ATHLETES AND ATHLETICS: (b) *pankration* represents the violent extreme of Greek athletics, a no-holds-barred style of fighting.

or time limits. Wrestling matches were decided by the best two out of three falls, while boxing and *pankration* matches were fought until one competitor conceded or, in very rare circumstances, until the sun went down. Matches could also end with the disqualification of one or both contestants, or because they were thought to be so bad that neither deserved a prize. If there was no winner, the crown of victory was placed on the altar of the GOD in whose honour the festival was being held.

Athletics were an important feature of general male education. They were felt to inculcate important civic virtues such as discipline, obedience and determination. Cities founded and supported GYMNASIA, where young men were expected to go virtually every day to work out under the supervision of professional trainers. With the rise of the gymnasium as an educational institution, we find a growing distinction between athletes who were able to contend at the 'international' level and those who simply remained in the contests of the local gymnasium. In the classical and hellenistic periods, cities would support associations of victors at the international events. In the 1st century BC, we find the earliest evidence for international synods of victors and competitors at the great festivals (which had expanded in number, even though the four festivals of the classical 'cycle' remained the most prestigious). These synods, or as it became under the Roman rule, the synod, were self-governing associations that set conditions for membership, fought for and obtained significant privileges for their members, and oversaw the organization of what were, by this period, thoroughly professional athletic events throughout the empire. By the 2nd century AD, Greek athletics, supported and encouraged by the Roman imperial government, were common throughout the MEDITERRANEAN world and the Roman Near East. In the 4th century, with the decline of the institutions that had supported athletics, their prestige diminished and athletes are often found competing as a form of entertainment between chariot races. DSP

Despite the fact that athletic competition was never as important to Roman society as it was to Greek, the Romans seem to have practised and appreciated it from the very beginning. The ETRUSCANS, perhaps themselves influenced by the Greeks, introduced running, boxing and wrestling to pre-REPUBLICAN Rome. According to LIVY, the first *ludi Romani* held by the Etruscan king TARQUINIUS PRISCUS included HORSE races and Etruscan boxers (Livy 1.35). These events seem to have been spectacles rather than proper competitions, for Livy later records that Marcus Fulvius Nobilior in 186 BC was the first to present an athletic contest (*athletarum certamen*) in Rome (Livy 39.22). This *certamen* was apparently a Greek-style athletics competition (*agôn*), though it was part of games vowed to JUPITER Optimus Maximus. In 167 BC, Lucius AEMILIUS PAULLUS celebrated his momentous victory over MACEDONIA at PYDNA the previous year with a great festival at Amphipolis, featuring athletes from all over the Greek world (Livy 45.32). Although ambassadors from all the Greek cities and hellenistic kingdoms were there to observe, the majority of the spectators will have been Paullus' own soldiers. At any rate, CICERO implies that athletic spectacles or competitions had become a regular feature of the Roman *ludi* (state games) by the late Republic (*On the Laws* 2.38). AUGUSTUS was a known aficionado of boxing, and his concern for the fitness of the youth of Rome led to the revival of the Troy Game, though this was more paramilitary than athletic. At Nikopolis, the city founded at ACTIUM to commemorate his victory over CLEOPATRA and MARK ANTONY, Augustus established the Actian games, sacred games on the model of Greek sacred agonistic festivals.

A regularly occurring competition (*certamen, agôn*) was not introduced to Rome until the 1st century AD. In 60, Nero, a great admirer of Greek culture, introduced a Greek-style competitive festival, the Neronia, intended to be held every five years and comprising musical, equestrian and athletic contests. This should be seen as part of a larger hellenizing programme by Nero, which included the establishment of a GYMNASIUM in Rome. The Neronia did not survive his reign, due in part to the scandal that this programme caused. DOMITIAN's Capitolia, in honour of Jupiter Capitolinus (in the same way that the OLYMPICS were in honour of ZEUS Olympios) was also a Greek-style sacred *agôn*, consisting of MUSICAL, equestrian and athletic competitions. The Capitolia were more enduring, and the shape of his stadium can still be seen in the Piazza Navona in Rome. Other cities in the Western empire, such as CARTHAGE, established Greek-style sacred *agônes*, and under the emperors Greek athletic competitions experienced a growth in popularity as many emperors, especially HADRIAN, encouraged and offered them PATRONAGE. Greek athletics under Roman domination must be seen, however, as a continuation of earlier FESTIVALS. Because they were essentially celebrations in the context of traditional religion, athletic contests around the Roman world were gradually abandoned or abolished under the CHRISTIAN empire.

In contrast to its fundamental position in Greece, sport in Roman society was not viewed as integral to the EDUCATION of a young man. Indeed, athletics were seen by conservatives as degenerate and unsuitable for the youth, since the exercises provided little in the way of military training. Traditionally, upper-class Roman youth practised military and equestrian exercises in the Campus Martius. Although strength, agility and physical fitness were important aspects of Greek athletics, so were grace and rhythm, which seemed to traditionally minded Romans too effeminate. Beyond the frivolity of Greek athletics, old-fashioned Romans were especially suspicious of athletic nudity and the associated liberal application of OLIVE OIL. HOMOSEXUALITY was thought a characteristic of the gymnasium and PALAESTRA. Archaeological and literary evidence, however, supports the contention that Roman WOMEN could participate in athletic exercise. Both MARTIAL and JUVENAL mention, with disdain, female athletes, whom they saw as rather too masculine.

Of the different athletic events, the Romans tended to prefer combat sports, especially boxing. This contest may have been indigenous, but was certainly influenced by Greek traditions. The Romans, however, preferred a more violent spectacle and it was then that the terrifying *caestus* (gloves studded with iron) were introduced. In general, the Roman attitude to sport was as a spectacle to be observed. This is different from the Greek attitude, which held that sport was participatory: citizens exercised and competed against one another.

Many individual athletes and athletic associations (or guilds) from the time of the Roman empire are known from literature and especially inscriptions. DIO CHRYSOSTOM, for example, provides us with a lengthy portrait of the boxer Melancomas of CARIA, whom he described as the strongest and most beautiful of all humanity. MJC

See Potter, D. S. and Mattingly, D. J., eds. (1999) *Life, Death and Entertainment in the Roman Empire*; Thuillier, J.-P. (1996) *Le Sport dans la Rome antique.*

 GYMNASIA.

ATHLETES AND ATHLETICS: (c) the Greek author PLUTARCH summarizes the Roman attitude to Greek athletics: 'The Romans were exceedingly suspicious of rubbing down with oil, and believe that nothing has been so much the cause of the enslavement and effeminacy of the Greeks as their gymnasia and palaestras, which engender listlessness and idleness in the cities and wasted time, as well as pederasty and the destruction of the bodies of the young through sleep and walks and rhythmic movements and strict regiments, because of which they have not noticed that they have pulled back from the practice of arms and have become fond of being called nimble and beautiful wrestlers instead of good men-at-arms and horsemen' (*Roman Questions* 40).

Atlantic, the HERODOTOS (1.202) first used the term Atlantic ('sea of Atlas', according to PLATO the eponymous king of ATLANTIS) to denote the body of water variously called Outer sea (as opposed to the MEDITERRANEAN or Inner sea), Great sea, Western ocean or OCEAN (*Ôkeanos*). Early Greeks knew it as a RIVER flowing around the earth, but later Greek and Roman writers saw it as the great body of water beyond the Pillars of HERCULES which surrounded the inhabited world. HOMER's knowledge of the western Mediterranean beyond SICILY was vague, and PHOENICIAN colonization on the Atlantic coast of Spain is unsubstantiated before the 8th century BC. Phokaians may have reached the area by the later part of the following century, but CARTHAGINIANS prevented further Greek travel westward. Around 500 BC the Carthaginian Hanno explored the Atlantic coast of Africa, while Himilco sailed north of Gibraltar to Brittany in northern France. Pytheas from Massalia (MARSEILLES) coasted Spain and Gaul and reached the northern part of BRITAIN c.300 BC. The Romans explored much of the Atlantic coast of Africa and Europe. In the imperial period the Atlantic supplied Roman fisheries and probably served as a TRADE route from the Mediterranean to northern Europe and Britain. The Atlantic figures strongly in Roman imperial literature, being linked to the AUGUSTAN

ideal of a boundless empire (VIRGIL), to the promise of a UTOPIAN society (HORACE), or, pessimistically, to moral decline (SENECA). (see also EXPLORATION) RIC
See Carpenter, R. (1966) *Beyond the Pillars of Hercules*; Romm, J. S. (1992) *The Edges of the Earth in Ancient Thought*.

 ROMAN EMPIRE: (a).

Atlantis The creation of POSEIDON, god of the sea. When he fell in love with a mortal woman, Kleito, he created for her security the island where she gave birth to five sets of twin boys, the first rulers of Atlantis. The island was divided among the brothers with the eldest, Atlas, crowned the first king. At the top of the island a TEMPLE was built to honour Poseidon. Here the Atlanteans would come to discuss laws, pass judgements and pay tribute to the god. For generations they lived virtuous lives, but slowly greed and power began to corrupt them. When ZEUS saw their IMMORALITY he gathered the other GODS together to determine a suitable punishment. Soon, in one violent tidal wave, it was gone; Atlantis, its people and its memory were swallowed by the sea.

The story is found in two of PLATO's dialogues, *Timaios* and *Kritias*. They are the only known written records which refer specifically to a lost civilization called Atlantis. Many people believe the tale to be complete fiction, the creation of a PHILOSOPHER's imagination used to illustrate an argument. Others believe that the story was inspired by catastrophic events which may have destroyed the MINOAN civilization on CRETE and THERA. Still others maintain that the story is an accurate representation of a long-lost and almost completely forgotten land. LL-J
See Joseph, F. (2002) *The Destruction of Atlantis*.

atomism Leukippos and DEMOKRITOS in the 5th century were the founders of atomism, the theory that the cosmos consists of an infinite number of solid, eternal and immutable bodies of minimum size that cannot be further divided (hence *a-toma*, 'uncuttable things'), moving through an infinite extent of void. EPICURUS later adapted the theory for the basis of his ETHICAL system, which valued tranquillity and freedom from fear; his materialism was expounded for the Romans in the poem of LUCRETIUS, *On the Nature of the Universe*. The atomic theory does not allow absolute generation or destruction, but explains the present world order as arising from an initial rotation in a group of atoms (started, according to Epicurus, by a 'swerve' in their linear movement), with the heavier moving towards the centre and the lighter outwards. Other world orders are similarly supposed to be forming and disintegrating throughout the limitless universe. Individual atoms, too small to be seen, are distinguishable only by size, shape and weight – the variety of phenomena to be explained as arrangements and rearrangements of these basic units and the intervening spaces. The movements and groupings of atoms in the void are mechanistic, with no divine intelligence involved in the workings of physical laws. The human SOUL is an atomic construct, brought together, maturing and destined to disintegrate along with the body, of which it is as much a physical part as hand or foot. The classical atomists anticipated the distinction between primary and secondary qualities which was important for the advance of CHEMISTRY from the 17th century onwards, and in modern times much of their theory is still relevant to the understanding of the function and movement of the 'electric atoms' or electrons of contemporary physics. MRW

atrium see HOUSES, ROMAN; VILLAS.

Attalids see PERGAMON.

Attalos I, II, III see PERGAMON.

Attic *stêlai* The name given to a group of late 5th-century Athenian inscriptions (*IG* I³ 421–30) listing the property of a notorious group of wealthy men. The late Roman scholar POLLUX discussed these inscriptions and bestowed the name.

One night in 415 BC, as the Athenian fleet prepared to leave for the SICILIAN EXPEDITION, rowdy drunks (or perhaps political activists) defaced the street-corner images of HERMES (herms) by breaking off their erect phalluses (Thucydides 6.27–9). The Athenians were horrified, and interpreted it as a disastrous omen for their military campaign. Investigations produced reports of more shocking acts of impiety: the ELEUSINIAN MYSTERIES had been parodied at private parties. Eminent Athenians, including the general ALCIBIADES and a number of METICS, were implicated, and many fled into exile. Their property was seized by the state and sold to the highest bidder by MAGISTRATES known as *pôlêtai* ('sellers'). Because the criminals were rich and the trials were politicized, a complete inventory of the auction was inscribed on stone for public display, in the interests of democratic accountability. There are large gaps in the text, and the *pôlêtai* probably did not get their hands on all that these men owned, so the considerable wealth documented is not a full list of their property. These documents, however, are our best records of the HOUSEHOLD possessions of wealthy Greeks, and critical for our understanding of the economy of classical Athens. LF
See Amyx, D. A. (1958) Attic stelae III, *Hesperia* 27: 163–310; Pritchett, W. K. (1956) Attic stelae II, *Hesperia* 25: 178–329.

Attica Large peninsula (c.2,400 sq km, 920 sq miles) in south-eastern Greece, the territory of ancient ATHENS. It is one of the driest parts of Greece, though with water-management it was possible to grow cereals and vines in the coastal and inland plains. The most important plains were that of Athens itself; the Thriasian coastal plain with the town of ELEUSIS, beyond Mt Aigaleos to the west of Athens; and the inland Mesogaia plain, behind Mt Hymettos east of the city. Attica's role as a communications node for sea and land travel, and its proximity to the Cyclades as stepping-stones to Asia, played a large part in its development.

Although much of Attica was mountainous, the total area of arable land was large. Land was the basis of élite wealth, which acted strongly upon society and politics at all periods. The resources that arguably contributed most to Athens' historical prominence, however, were non-agricultural. The silver-bearing lead ores of the LAURION district, exploited since the Bronze Age, were redeveloped in the early 5th century BC when rich veins of ore were found. In the 480s, THEMISTOKLES persuaded the Athenians to use the revenues earned by leasing out state silver-mines to build a fleet of warships, in anticipation of a Persian invasion. With the growth of the Athenian empire in the mid-5th century, the PIRAEUS, one of the safest and deepest natural harbours in the Mediterranean, rose to prominence as a commercial centre. Another important resource was high-grade white and grey MARBLE, particularly from Mts Pentelikon, north of Athens, and Hymettos to the south-east. These mountains and Aigaleos ringed the city, dividing its immediate territory (sometimes known simply as the Plain) from the rest of Attica (officially the Coast and the Hills). A fourth, much larger mountain range, Parnes, bounded Attica on the north and north-west.

In the classical period, Athens was remarkable for being a single *POLIS* embracing a whole region, with men from every subordinate settlement having an equal say in the city's affairs. Athens the *polis* was thus co-extensive with Attica. The mythical hero THESEUS was believed to have unified the region. Its Bronze Age organization is unclear; but there was probably a palace-like centre at Athens, where occupation continued through the so-called Dark Ages. Archaeology suggests that Athens gradually extended its authority until, by the 8th century or earlier, it was the central settlement for the region, perhaps both colonizing the rural landscape and attracting new settlers from inside and outside Attica. Henceforth Attica's history is that of Athens.

In the archaic period the three geographical regions acted as power-bases supporting different aristocratic factions, and exacerbated the rivalries that led to the 6th-century TYRANNY. DEMOCRACY was introduced in 508 by KLEISTHENES. He arranged the institutional map to minimize the possibility of renewed tyranny by creating ten new tribes, each made up of DEMES (*dêmoi*, 'peoples': constituent villages of the *polis*) from all three regions of Attica. This diluted the influence of men from any given region. Indeed, it was probably the demand by outlying settlements to be included that created and maintained the unity of Attica, rather than any centre-out process. (LACONIA, in contrast, had a network of dependent *poleis*, and only citizens of the central settlement, SPARTA, took decisions for the whole region.) Flourishing demes embellished with sculptural monuments in the 5th and 4th centuries include Acharnai north of the city, Eleusis, Rhamnous on the far north-east coast, BRAURON on the east coast, and Sounion at the far southern tip of Attica. These were not the only demes with large populations, but they had particularly important temples. Demes both inside and outside the city centre of Athens commanded fierce local pride, while those at a distance played a full part in the political life of the *polis*. The strength of local culture, as well as the ties between centre and countryside, are illustrated by the high level of investment in deme cults during the classical period, and by periodic festivals involving PROCESSIONS to or from Athens.

From the 4th century, the defence of Attica was reorganized around a ring of border and coastal FORTS, with garrisons at Eleusis, Eleutherai, Panakton, Phyle, Rhamnous, Sounion and elsewhere. In the hellenistic period, investment in deme sites appears to decline, as does the number of civic documents from outlying demes. Field survey has not progressed far enough to reveal changes in rural habitation clearly, but does indicate a wide variety of settlement forms. The 3rd and 2nd centuries may have witnessed a fall in rural population, and many Athenians (like people from all over the Greek world) emigrated to ALEXANDRIA. Falling numbers of inscriptions from rural demes, however, may indicate a lack of funds or changed preferences in élite display, rather than a drop in population. The Athenians at this time had no problem recruiting COUNCILLORS from all of Attica. In the Roman period, while élite estates appear to have become larger, there was renewed investment in the network of cult sites across the landscape. DGJS

See Barber, R. L. N. (1999) *A Guide to Rural Attika* (privately published); Goette, H. R. (2001) *Athens, Attica and the Megarid*; Lohmann, H. (1992) Agriculture and country life in classical Attica, in B. Wells, ed., *Agriculture in Ancient Greece* 29–60; Ober, J. (1985) *Fortress Attica*; Osborne, R. (1985) *Demos*; Traill, J. S. (1975) *The Political Organization of Attica*; Whitehead, D. (1986) *The Demes of Attica*.

 BOIOTIA; GREECE: (a).

Atticus (Titus Pomponius Atticus) 110–32 BC Wealthy and cultured Roman *eques* (member of the élite equestrian class), best known as lifelong friend and frequent correspondent of CICERO and the subject of a biography by NEPOS. He showed remarkable facility in negotiating a financially prosperous, but politically neutral, path through the turbulent politics of the late Republic. The more than 400 extant letters between Cicero and Atticus range from trivial anecdotes to eye-witness accounts of pivotal events, and collectively represent one of the most important sources of information about the personality and actions of Cicero and the events and culture of the late Republic. Atticus was a friend or acquaintance of nearly all the prominent figures of his time including SULLA, Hortensius, CAESAR, BRUTUS, POMPEY, and, simultaneously, OCTAVIAN and MARK ANTONY. He gave financial assistance to many (MARIUS, Brutus, Fulvia) and forged familial ties with others (his sister married Cicero's brother, his daughter married AGRIPPA, his granddaughter married TIBERIUS). Atticus was born into a rich family and further benefited by ADOPTION and an accompanying INHERITANCE from a wealthy uncle (Quintus Caecilius). From 85 to the mid-60s, he took refuge from the civil unrest in Italy in philosophical (especially EPICUREAN) studies at Athens. He was the author of numerous works now lost, including genealogical studies, MAGISTRATE lists and chronological histories. When stricken with an intestinal ailment, he committed SUICIDE by starvation. GSA

See Horsfall, N., trs. (1989) *Cornelius Nepos* (with commentary); Perlwitz, O. (1992) *Titus Pomponius Atticus*; Shackleton Bailey, D. R. (1965–70) *Cicero's Letters to Atticus*.

 AUGUSTUS: (b).

Attis see CYBELE; EUNUCHS.

Augst The *colonia* of Augusta Raurica (mod. Augst in Switzerland, 10 km or 6 miles east of Basel) founded in 44 BC in the territory of the Raurici by Lucius Munatius Plancus (who also founded LYON). The site lay on a well-watered terrace just south of the RHINE, intended to control not only the upper Rhine valley but also the route from Italy across the ALPS.

Archaeological evidence suggests that substantial building activity did not start until c.15 BC, at first in TIMBER; public buildings in stone started appearing between c.AD 40 and c.70. Its forum–basilica complex is a good example of the double FORUM, with a free-standing TEMPLE in honour of Rome and the emperor in the open piazza at one end, and a BASILICA and the local senate house (*curia*) at the other. This type of forum was especially favoured in GAUL. Temples of both classical and Romano-Celtic type have been excavated, as well as an impressive THEATRE, an AMPHITHEATRE, two public BATHS and several houses. Much is known about industrial production, including bronze- and GLASS-working and POTTERY kilns.

Decline set in from the mid-3rd century, but a new FORTRESS bordering the Rhine at mod. Castrum Rauracense (Kaiseraugst) was established c.AD 300 on the northern outskirts of Augusta Raurica. An excellent example of a late Roman military fortification, the fortress had powerful walls and projecting towers; a bath-house and an early Christian CHURCH have also been excavated and preserved. The hoard of mid-4th-century SILVER plate found here in 1961 ranks among the more important such treasures from the late Roman world.

Excavations, regular since 1878 and continuous since 1957, have made Augst one of the best known examples of Roman urban planning and development in the north-west provinces. RJAW

See Furger, A. R. (1995) *Augusta Raurica*.

augury The body of lore maintained by the Roman college of augurs. Its purpose was not to reveal the future, but to determine whether the GODS approved or disapproved of a particular action. Augural learning dated back to the earliest days of the city, but was steadily augmented by new rulings of the augurs. It encompassed two classes of RITUAL. One was that of auguries proper, rituals whereby an augur would establish for all time the gods' approval of a particular person (in the case of state PRIESTS) or place. The other was that of auspices, the interpretation of natural events as signs of divine will. These signs were either encountered by chance or deliberately sought. The latter included the feeding pattern of sacred chickens: it was a good sign if they ate so greedily that they dropped grain from their bills. The most well-known signs, which could be either sought or noted by chance, were those observed in the sky, particularly thunder and lightning, and from BIRDS, based on their number, position and behaviour. All public action in Republican Rome occurred in spaces and at times marked off by augural ritual. Ascertaining divine approval through auspices was a necessary preliminary to the ELECTION of MAGISTRATES, the passing of LAWS, meetings of the SENATE and military campaigns. Since mistakes in procedure might invalidate the results, expertise in augural lore could be of considerable political importance. JBR

See Linderski, J. (1986) Cicero and Roman divination, *P&P* 36: 12–38.

Augusta Trevorum see TRIER.

Augustales see HERCULANEUM; IMPERIAL CULT.

Augustine (1) (Aurelius Augustinus) AD 354–430 Theologian and father of the church; bishop of Hippo Regius (Bône in Algeria) from 395. Born into an impoverished family at Thagaste (Souk-Ahras in Algeria), Augustine was first destined for a career as a teacher, for which he received his education at the African centres of Madaurus (Mdaourouch) and CARTHAGE. After a brief spell as a teacher at home in Thagaste, he returned to Carthage, where his talents soon came to the attention of the proconsular governor. In such circumstances, a move to Rome was perhaps inevitable, and Augustine took up residence there in 383. In the capital, he attracted the patronage of SYMMACHUS, through whose influence he was appointed professor of RHETORIC at MILAN in 384. By this stage, Augustine was suffering much spiritual turmoil. Though born a Christian, he had sought solace in PHILOSOPHY, MANICHAEISM, and NEOPLATONISM. At Milan, however, he fell under the spell of the dynamic BISHOP, AMBROSE, under whose auspices he converted back to CHRISTIANITY and was baptized.

From the moment of his conversion, Augustine had responded to a strong ASCETIC impulse, and on his return to AFRICA he began establishing monastic communities. It was with this intention that he went to Hippo in 391. His growing reputation for ascetic spirituality went before him, and he was seized by the populace and forcibly ordained a priest of their church. In 395, he was consecrated coadjutor-bishop to Valerius of Hippo, whom he succeeded the following year. During his episcopate he was active in the struggle against the Donatists, whose schism had divided the African church for a century. This prompted Augustine to meditate on the nature of episcopal authority. At his behest, his friend Paulinus wrote a life of Augustine's episcopal hero, Ambrose of Milan. Later, in imitation of this, another friend, Possidius, wrote a *Life of Augustine*.

The struggle against Donatism also made Augustine ponder the role of the state in ecclesiastical affairs. At first he was an enthusiastic supporter of the use of coercion by secular authorities against religious miscreants. Yet his views changed. Even after the GOTHIC sack of Rome in 410, his friend OROSIUS could still subscribe to the positive view of the role played by the Roman empire in Christian history, as formulated by EUSEBIOS of Caesarea in the early 4th century AD. For Augustine, however, such optimism was misplaced in view of his doubts about the human race's chances of salvation. In *The City of God*, Augustine expounded his views, producing a subtle interpretation of Christian history which moved away from the simplistic triumphalism of earlier authors. The last years of Augustine's life can only have fuelled his pessimism; indeed, as he lay dying in August 430, a VANDAL army sat outside the walls of Hippo.

Augustine was a prolific writer and surely the most original thinker produced by Latin Christianity. Through his writings, much of the classical heritage was systematically assimilated to the CHURCH, and he was an important transmitter of ancient ideals to the medieval world. This was done most explicitly in his *De doctrina Christiana* (*On Christian Teaching*), in which Augustine provided Christians with a blueprint of how to read PAGAN literature. A similar endeavour underpinned those books of *The City of God* in which Augustine examined the pagan Roman past. Augustine's interest in the classical heritage reflects a lifelong interest in ancient philosophy, especially PLATONISM and Neoplatonism. His great spiritual autobiography, the *Confessions*, is richly embroidered with the language of Neoplatonic mysticism, much of it derived from PLOTINUS. Augustine's reliance is particularly remarkable, bearing in mind his self-confessed failure to learn adequate Greek. Yet even in the last, sad days at besieged Hippo, he continued to quote and draw comfort from Plotinus' writings.

Augustine's Platonism was infused by a profound spirituality, and in the course of his career he participated in several theological debates. He brought his immense intellect to bear in disputes with heretics, such as the ARIAN bishop Maximinus. His most celebrated conflict, however, was that with the Pelagians, especially bishop Julian of Eclanum. The Pelagians had sought to reform moral laxity through a programme in which human choices about behaviour were of paramount importance. In his critique of Manichaeism, Augustine had put forward similar arguments on human determination in human actions ('FREE WILL'), but he had to redefine his stance in response to the Pelagians. For Augustine it was inconceivable that human action should occur without external divine direction, which he termed God's Grace. The Fall from Eden was central to Augustine's doctrine of Grace and his arguments against Pelagius' supporters. Through the Fall, he argued, humankind had become tainted with original sin. This severely limited free will, since humanity could not achieve salvation without the action of God's Grace. This Grace was mediated to humankind through the rite of baptism, by which God chose a special group, 'the elect', who would be saved. How God chose the elect was inscrutable to humankind in its fallen condition, but it would become apparent at the last judgement. In his disputes with the Pelagians, Augustine had clearly formulated a doctrine of predestination. In so doing, he provide a source of controversy which was to divide Western Christendom in the centuries after his death. MDH

See Augustine, *Confessions*, trs. H. Chadwick (1991); *The City of God*, trs. H. Bettenson (1972); *De doctrina Christiana*, trs. R. P. H. Green (1995); *Select Letters*, trs. H. H. Baxter (1930); Possidius, *Life of Augustine*, trs. F. H. Hoare (1954) in *The Western Fathers*; Bonner, G. (1986) *St Augustine of Hippo*; Brown, P. (1967) *Augustine of Hippo*; Chadwick, H. (1986) *Augustine*; Harrison, C. (2000) *Augustine*; Lawless, G. (1987) *Augustine of Hippo and his Monastic Rule*; Markus, R. (1988) *Saeculum*; Rist, J. M. (1994) *Augustine*.

Augustine (2) First archbishop of Canterbury (AD 597–604). In 596, pope Gregory I sent Augustine to establish CHRISTIANITY among the Anglo-Saxons. When he and his 40 monks reached Britain in 597, king Ethelbert permitted them to remain in his lands and to preach, and provided lodgings and supplies at Canterbury. Christianity was familiar to him, for his FRANKISH wife Bertha worshipped in a late Roman church, perhaps rebuilt and dedicated to St MARTIN after her arrival in 560. After ordination as BISHOP at Arles in 597, Augustine continued his mission by establishing a monastery and (re)building churches. Many Anglo-Saxons converted and were baptized. Ethelbert himself became Christian by mid-601 and granted Augustine land to establish a metropolitan see. In 601, Gregory sent priests to broaden the mission within southern England, delegated Augustine to appoint an archbishop at YORK (Christianity had survived in northern England), and established the priority of an archbishopric of LONDON over that of York (the old Roman capitals). Instead, given his land at Canterbury and because Ethelbert did not rule at London, Augustine retained his metropolitan see at Canterbury and began to build an appropriate church there. In his remaining years, Augustine continued to organize the church in southern England and appointed bishops at various places, including London, as the need arose. He died on 26 May 604 and is generally regarded as the founder of the church in England. JV

Augustus (Gaius Octavius; Gaius Julius Caesar Octavianus) 63 BC–AD 14 The future emperor Augustus was born in Rome on 23 September 63 BC. The son of Gaius Octavius and Atia, niece of JULIUS CAESAR, he was the youngest of three children, his father having one daughter by a previous marriage and a second daughter with Atia. After the sudden death of the elder Octavius in 58, Atia married Marcius Philippus (the consul of 56), in whose household Octavian grew to maturity. His great-uncle Caesar, who had no son he could acknowledge as legitimate, was impressed by the young Octavius' abilities, marking him out for preferment at the age of 16. In 45, Octavius accompanied Caesar to Spain. Apparently as a result of this contact, Caesar decided to ADOPT him by testament, whereby Octavius would become his son and heir upon his death. In 44 he sent Octavius to Apollonia, planning to have him join the campaign against PARTHIA that he intended to initiate later that year.

When he learned of the assassination of Caesar on 15 March 44, Octavius returned to Rome to take up his inheritance as Gaius Julius Caesar Octavianus, whom we call 'Octavian'. In the course of the summer, he united a group of Caesar's former supporters and opponents to drive MARK ANTONY from power in the city. In 43, given the rank of PRAETOR by the SENATE, he joined with the consuls Hirtius and Pansa, who were assigned the command in the war against Mark Antony. After the deaths of Hirtius and Pansa in successive victories over Antony at Mutina in Cisalpine GAUL, Octavian assumed command. He then changed sides, to ally with Antony and Marcus Lepidus against the forces of the assassins. Entering Rome in November, Octavian, Antony and Lepidus were appointed TRIUMVIRS 'for the restoration of the Republic' by the *lex Titia*. They used this power to institute a wide-ranging series of proscriptions to eliminate perceived political enemies and to confiscate large estates. These measures, combined with heavy taxes imposed upon ITALY, enabled them to finance the war against the assassins of Caesar.

In the later 40s Octavian first secured his position in Italy and Gaul, taking over the latter from Antony, and suppressed a revolt led by Antony's wife and brother at Perugia. Antony acquiesced in Octavian's assertion of control through the treaties of Brundisium and Misenum in 40 and 39. At the end of 37, the powers of the triumvirs were retroactively renewed for a further five-year term, beginning at the end of 38. Shortly after this agreement and the defeat in 36 of Sextus Pompey, who controlled the seas around Italy with a large fleet, Octavian relieved Lepidus of his army in SICILY, sending him into internal exile for the rest of his life. In 33, as the second term of their triumviral

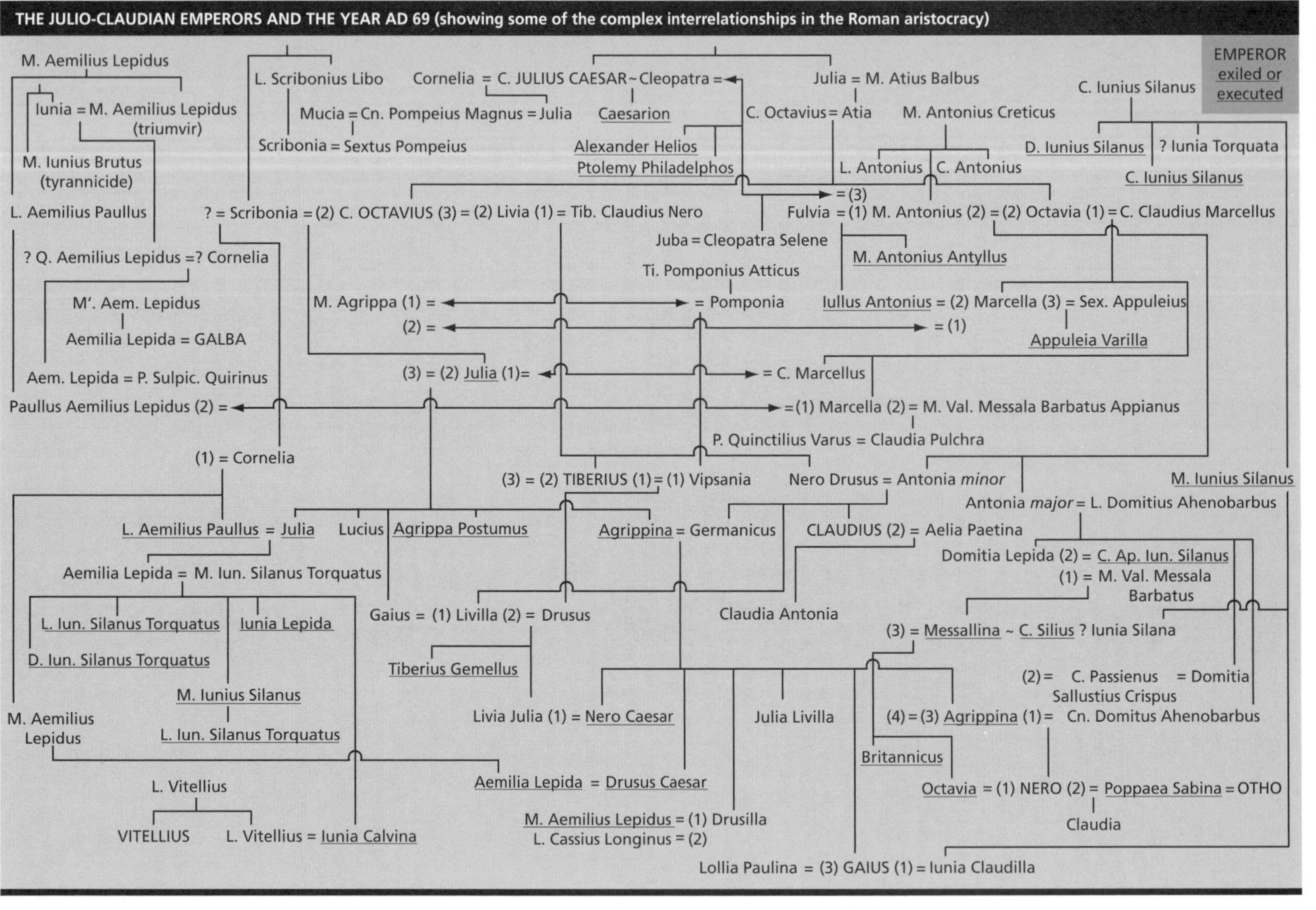

AUGUSTUS: (a) Stemma of the Julio-Claudian dynasty.

AUGUSTUS: (b) the forum of Augustus, dominated by the temple of Mars Ultor ('the Avenger'), was one of the most impressive architectural achievements of his reign.

powers expired, Octavian and Antony declared war on each other. Octavian defeated Antony at the battle of ACTIUM on 2 September 31.

Octavian returned to Italy in 28, where he began to lay the foundations of a new regime. In January 27 he received the *cognomen* Augustus, 'Venerable', from the senate. Since he had changed his *praenomen* to Imperator after the defeat of Sextus Pompey, and his patronymic had been transformed with the declaration of Julius Caesar's divinity in 42, he would henceforth be known as *Imperator Caesar divi filius* ('son of the god') *Augustus*. The new name represented a break with the revolutionary past, but carried no constitutional authority. He continued to hold the office of consul and governed the bulk of the garrisoned PROVINCES, which were his *provincia*, through legates. He was also granted *imperium maius* (greater *imperium*) over all governors. In 23 this system was altered when he laid down the consulship, supplementing *imperium maius* with *tribunicia potestas* (the powers of a tribune of the plebs). In 19 he was given the power of a magistrate within Rome and Italy. These diverse powers, conferred by separate laws, came to define the legal position of the *princeps* in later generations.

In the ten years after 27 BC, Augustus established the administrative foundations of the imperial system of government. The Augustan reform of government paid close attention to the traditions of the REPUBLIC, respecting the traditional division between civic and provincial administration and employing senators in their traditional administrative roles. At the same time, the evolution of a palace administration began in Augustus' household and through the governance of his vast estates throughout the empire. In AD 5, he completed the transformation of the Roman army into a long-serving, professional force by instituting clear terms of service and retirement benefits.

The development of the administration took place against the background of a continuous series of military operations that brought Spain more firmly under Roman control, solidified the frontier on the RHINE and established a new relationship with the Parthian kingdom. The eastern campaign of 23–19 BC did not involve serious fighting, but the Parthian decision to surrender the standards taken from CRASSUS and Antony enabled Augustus to claim that he had avenged the most embarrassing defeats of the previous generation. In the last two decades of the 1st century BC, armies commanded by Augustus' generals, and family members whom he was attempting to promote as potential successors, occupied GERMANY as far as the Elbe and stabilized the Roman frontier in the Balkans along the DANUBE. In the last decade of Augustus' life, expansion ceased; the Western European frontier was withdrawn to the Rhine after the massacre of three legions under Varus in AD 9 at the battle of TEUTOBERGER Wald.

Almost immediately after the defeat of Antony, Augustus attempted to create a system of dynastic succession, elevating the *domus Augusta* to a unique position in the Roman world as the home of future rulers. His plans for succession, which involved advancing pairs of potential successors, were thwarted by his own longevity. It was only in AD 4, after the deaths of his grandsons, Gaius and Lucius Caesar, that he adopted his stepson, TIBERIUS, who would ultimately succeed him after his death on 19 August AD 14.

Augustus catalogued his achievements in his *Res gestae*, published and inscribed across the empire after his death. Recent work has emphasized the ideological and cultural programme by which the ideology of the new regime was disseminated in Rome and across the empire. Architecture, sculpture, coinage, and even fashion reflected the autocracy veiled in a republican form. Augustus' long reign, with the whole Mediterranean world now under one command, also witnessed the culmination of Greco-Roman intellectual programmes, for example in the form of compendious technical literature (Vitruvius), world histories (Diodorus, Livy) and universal geographies (Strabo). (see also Augustus (title)) DSP

See Cassius Dio; Suetonius, *Augustus*; Brunt, P. A. and Moore, J. M., eds. and trs. (1989) *Res Gestae Divi Augusti*; Sherk, R. K. (1988) *The Roman Empire: Augustus to Hadrian* (translated documents); Eck, W. (2002) *The Age of Augustus*; Raaflaub, K. A. and Toher, M., eds. (1990) *Between Republic and Empire*; Rowe, G. (2002) *Princes and Political Cultures: the new Tiberian senatorial decrees*; Syme, R. (1939) *The Roman Revolution*; (1986) *The Augustan Aristocracy*; Zanker, P. (1988) *The Power of Images in the Age of Augustus*.

Ara Pacis: (b); emperors, Roman: (a); *Res Gestae*; Rome: (b).

Augustus (as title) The name conferred on Octavian in 27 BC and subsequently used by all emperors was originally part of religious vocabulary with connotations of being worthy of honour, of being august and venerable. Cassius Dio states that it signified some divine potential, as sacred objects are referred to as *augusta* (53.16). Various authors implied other connotations: of authority (*auctoritas*) (Dio), of augury (Suetonius), and of sacred (*sanctus*) status (Ovid). It became both the name and the title that designated the holder of supreme power; other members of imperial families were not allowed to use it. Under the Tetrarchy the two senior emperors were designated by the title Augustus while their junior partners were Caesar.

The female equivalent, Augusta, was first conferred on Livia in AD 14 by Augustus' will. It was granted selectively to other imperial women, often wives or mothers of emperors. MEH

Aurelian (Lucius Domitius Aurelianus) Roman emperor AD 270–5. He was a soldier of Balkan origins, born c.215. He was involved in the coup against Gallienus in 268 and rose to become Claudius II's cavalry commander. After Claudius' death and the brief reign of Quintillus, Aurelian was acclaimed emperor by the army in 270. At his accession he controlled the central portion of the empire, while Gaul, Spain and Britain were held by the Gallic empire and Asia Minor, Syria and Egypt by Palmyra. Aurelian began by securing his northern borders with campaigns on the Rhine and Danube. He also initiated the construction of walls around Rome (finally completed under Probus). In 272 Aurelian marched against the Palmyrans under their queen Zenobia and defeated them in battles at Immae and Antioch. Before reaching Rome, he fought on the Danube again and suppressed a further Palmyran and an Egyptian revolt. On his return to Rome he built a temple to Sol Invictus and set in motion currency reforms. He then defeated the Gallic emperor Tetricus at Châlons in 274. In the same year, he abandoned the Transdanubian province of Dacia. He celebrated his victories at Rome, with Tetricus and Zenobia led in triumph. He was killed at Perinthus in 275 by the praetorian guard, during preparations for a Persian war. Aurelian's efforts to deal with the crises he faced were similar to those of Diocletian. Although he was ultimately unsuccessful, his reign paved the way for Diocletian's success. HWE

See Watson, A. (1999) *Aurelian and the Third Century*.

 emperors, Roman: (b).

Aurelius Victor see biography and biographers.

aureus see coinage (Table).

Auruncians see Oscans.

Ausonius (Decimus Magnus Ausonius) c.AD 310–c.395 Gallic poet, professor and sometime politician. A native of Burdigala (Bordeaux), Ausonius came from a distinguished line of professors (his uncle Arborius had spent a short spell as tutor to imperial princes in Constantinople). The family is well documented, largely through Ausonius' own writings, and seems to have been quite wealthy and well connected among the provincial aristocracy of 4th-century Aquitaine. Ausonius' prominence among the Gallic élite was enhanced considerably when, sometime in the mid-360s, he was summoned to the imperial court to tutor Gratian, son of the Western emperor Valentinian I. Ausonius was now well placed to foster connections with other Western aristocrats, such as the Roman senator Symmachus, who visited the Western court in 369–70, and with whom he corresponded. Following Valentinian's sudden death (17 November 375) and Gratian's accession as Western Roman emperor, the political importance of Ausonius and his family increased. Ausonius himself became praetorian prefect of Gaul, Italy and Africa, and similar honours were bestowed on his father, Julius Ausonius, and son, Decimus Hilarianus Hesperius. How much of a hand he took in Gratian's administration is open to question, but his influence has been postulated in some of the new emperor's legislation, such as the decree that professorial salaries be paid by the state (*Theodosian Code* 13.3.11). The summit of Ausonius' career came in 379 when Gratian appointed him consul, which prompted one of Ausonius' most important works, the eulogy of Gratian known as the *Gratiarum actio* (*Speech of Thanks*). Thereafter he seems to have retired from an active political career, though other members of his family remained in high office. With Gratian's death at the hands of the usurper Magnus Maximus in 383, however, the family's political fortunes came to an abrupt halt. Ausonius seems to have retired to the family estates round Bordeaux, where he lived long enough to hear of Maximus' death in 388 and to exchange letters with Gratian's avenger, the emperor Theodosius I. He is last heard of corresponding with Paulinus of Nola in the early or mid-390s. Thereafter he disappears from the record, presumably dead, but having enjoyed an unusually long life by the standards of the time.

Ausonius was a prolific writer across a variety of poetic genres. Among his most important works are the above-mentioned *Speech of Thanks* to Gratian; the *Professors of Bordeaux* and *Parentalia*, both giving fascinating insights into Ausonius' background; the *Mosella*, a classicizing account of a journey along the river Mosel; and the *Order of the Famous Cities*, a series of verse portraits of 20 urban centres. Though famously excoriated by Edward Gibbon, who remarked that 'the poetical fame of Ausonius condemns the taste of his age', Ausonius has gained a more sympathetic audience in recent years. In particular, his poetry is seen as an important window onto the cultural horizons of a significant provincial aristocracy in the later Roman empire. MDH

See Green, R. P. H. (1991) *The Works of Ausonius*; Sivan, H. (1993) *Ausonius of Bordeaux*.

auxiliaries Non-Roman troops (*auxilia*), are attested in the Republican armies but they were employed as supplementary forces – CAVALRY, slingers and archers – in conjunction with the heavy infantry of the Roman legions, on an *ad hoc* basis without consistent organization or fixed terms of service. They were either allies or foreigners who served as MERCENARIES. JULIUS CAESAR, for example, made extensive use of Gallic cavalry.

Under the PRINCIPATE the *auxilia* were given consistent organization, training and uniforms. Auxiliaries were not organized into LEGIONS but rather formed independent cohorts of roughly 500, comprising either infantry or cavalry, or in some cases mixed units with a 4:1 ratio of infantry to cavalry. A cavalry wing (*ala*) comprised 480 men organized in 16 *turmae* of 30 each; in addition, each *turma* had two junior OFFICERS, bringing the total size of the *ala* to 512 men. Mixed units combined 480 infantrymen with 120 cavalry. In addition to these cohorts and *alae*, there were the so-called milliary units, which had a nominal strength of 1,000 but ranged from 800 to 1,000; these may have been intended to balance the double strength of the first cohort of the Roman legion, which comprised five double centuries.

Recruitment of *auxilia* was normally from non-Romans within the empire, though there were some from outside and others who were Roman citizens. Pay appears to have been five-sixths of the regular pay for legionaries, and the period of service was 25 years, at the end of which the auxiliaries were entitled to Roman CITIZENSHIP for themselves and their children. Hence the children of auxiliaries could serve in the Roman legions. The allocations of land and the rewards paid upon discharge (*praemia*) to legionary troops were apparently not given to auxiliaries. The number of cohorts, both regular and milliary, seems to have varied, but the number of auxiliary soldiers in the 2nd century AD was about a quarter of a million, more than the grand total of legionary troops at the same time.

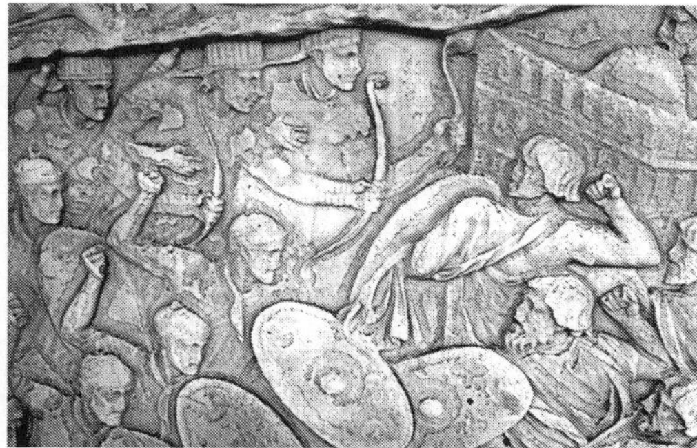

AUXILIARIES: non-citizen troops fighting in the Dacian wars – Syrian archers supporting possibly Gallic infantry.

Especially from the 4th century AD onwards, various peoples, GOTHS, HUNS, Alans and others, provided contingents to supplement the Roman army. Technically not auxiliaries but allied units, these troops, often heavily weighted toward cavalry, typically fulfilled obligations required by treaties, for example by CONSTANTINE's treaty with the Goths in AD 332, in a manner similar to that in which Rome had used Italian allies as auxiliaries in the Republic. They tended to serve under native commanders, who frequently received positions within the regular command structure. WH

See Keppie, L. (1984) *The Making of the Roman Army*; Le Bohec, Y. (1994) *The Imperial Roman Army*.

 ARMS AND ARMOUR: (d); FORTS AND FORTRESSES, ROMAN: (a).

Averroes see SCHOLARSHIP, ISLAMIC.

aviaries Pigeon lofts and dovecotes were ubiquitous on Greek and Roman farmsteads, and, indeed, were to be found on the ROOFS of many townhouses in cities such as Rome. The creation of larger-scale aviaries for the keeping and rearing of birds, either for pleasure or for profit, was developed in the hellenistic period, and this is reflected in the fact that most of the technical terms used are Greek. In the 2nd century BC, for example, king Ptolemy VIII bred pheasants and guinea-fowl in his PALACE in ALEXANDRIA. This fashionable addition to the country VILLA reached new heights in Roman Italy in the 1st century BC. Lucullus, the contemporary of CICERO, tried the idea of including his dining space (*triclinium*) within an aviary, where he and his guests could gain an added frisson from eating birds while their companions fluttered overhead; the experiment was a failure because it took no account of the stench caused by the bird-droppings (VARRO, *On Agriculture* 3.4.3). Aviaries could be STONE or BRICK buildings, often around or turret-shaped with small latticed windows and with perches and nest-boxes on the walls. They were also constructed by enclosing the peristyles round courtyards, or colonnades, with netting made of hemp or gut. In addition to pigeons and doves, thrushes and blackbirds were favourite birds to be kept and fattened in aviaries. Varro makes great claims for the profitability of such aviaries, but this depended on occasional times of exceptional demand for birds for the table, such as public feasts and TRIUMPHS in Rome. The late agronomist Palladius emphasizes aviaries as a vital source of fertilizer from bird-droppings. JJP

See Columella book 8; Palladius 1.23–31; Varro, *On Agriculture* book 3.

 BIRDS: (a)–(b).

awards see ATHLETES AND ATHLETICS; CHARIOT RACING; GAMES; HONOURS; OLYMPIC GAMES.

B

Baal Hammon Primary male deity of CARTHAGE and the surrounding regions, worshipped under the name SATURN in Roman times. Baal Hammon came to Carthage with the PHOENICIAN founders of the city, but the precise meaning of his name and many of his attributes, which include solar imagery, are matters of considerable disagreement. The expansion of the Carthaginian empire extended his worship to SICILY, SARDINIA and Malta. He was the consort of TANIT, the enigmatic Carthaginian goddess, who is more often attested than her partner and takes precedence on thousands of texts, as 'the face of' or 'facing' Baal. Consequently, Baal Hammon is sometimes regarded as the silent deity. He was the recipient, at the *tophet* of Salammbô (a sacred area at Carthage) of HUMAN SACRIFICE, primarily of children under the age of four (the only securely attested human sacrifice in the ancient world). According to TERTULLIAN (*Apologeticus* 9.2–4), this practice continued to his own time (end of the 2nd century AD), but the deity was now Saturn, and sacrifices no longer took place at Salammbô but elsewhere.

Baal Hammon remained part of popular religion after 146 BC (when Carthage was destroyed) as the AFRICAN Saturn, who differs from the Roman deity in several respects, since he was god of both the sky and the underworld, and protector of harvests. He was thus an all-encompassing male deity, who was sometimes confused with JUPITER. JV

See Hughes, D. (1991) *Human Sacrifice in Ancient Greece*; Lancel, S. (1995) *Carthage*.

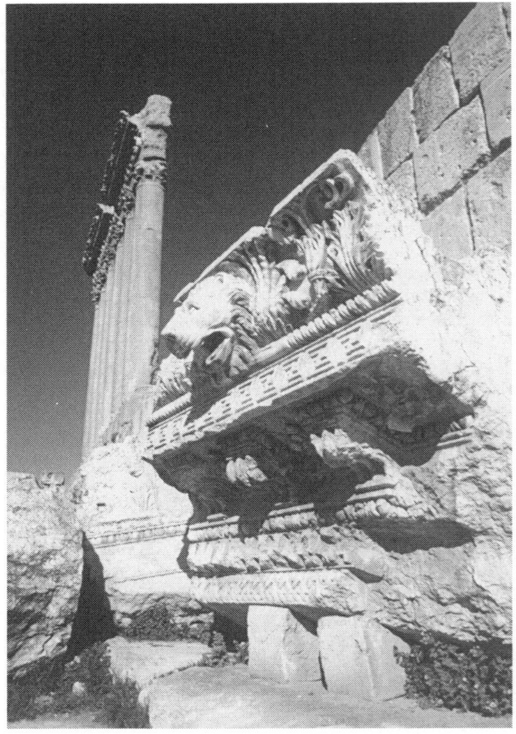

BAALBEK: the massive colonnade of the temple of Jupiter Heliopolitanus, still standing c.20 m high.

Baalbek (anc. Heliopolis) Hellenistic and Roman religious centre and city in SYRIA (mod. Lebanon). Located in the Bekaa between the Lebanon and Antilebanon mountain ranges, Baalbek lies about 70 km (40 miles) east of Beirut. It became important as a religious sanctuary (dedicated to, among others, the local semitic GOD Baal, hence Baalbek) for the independent kings of Ituraea, who ruled southern Syria from the decline of SELEUKID power in the late 2nd century BC until its conquest by the Romans. It gained greater importance in 15 BC, when Roman legionary VETERANS were settled at the colony of Berytus (Beirut). Heliopolis lay within its territory, attracting the attention of settlers, and hence the attention and favour of emperors. The principal deity was worshipped in Roman form as JUPITER Optimus Maximus Heliopolitanus. Heliopolis was made a colony independent of Berytus by SEPTIMIUS SEVERUS to punish Berytus for its support of his rival PESCENNIUS NIGER. It remained a centre of PAGAN worship into the late empire.

The site is best known for the remains of the gigantic and sumptuous sanctuary, with its great TEMPLE dedicated principally to Jupiter. The temple may be AUGUSTAN in origin, and epigraphic evidence suggests it was nearing completion in AD 60. Its ARCHITECTURE and decoration are primarily western Roman in form, though there is debate over whether the plan of the complex as a whole, which continued to develop into the 3rd century AD, was influenced by Syrian religious architecture. This architectural debate parallels a historical one regarding the nature of the cults themselves and whether they retained any 'oriental' character in the Roman period. NDP

See Ess, M. van and Weber, T., eds. (1999) *Baalbek*; Ragette, F. (1980) *Baalbek*.

Babylon The capital city of ancient Babylonia on the Euphrates. In 539 BC Babylonia was conquered by CYRUS the Great, and Babylon became a satrapal centre and one of the royal residences of the Persian kings. In 516 DARIUS I divided the province of Babylonia and Across-the-River (i.e. Syria-Palestine and Phoenicia) into two satrapies.

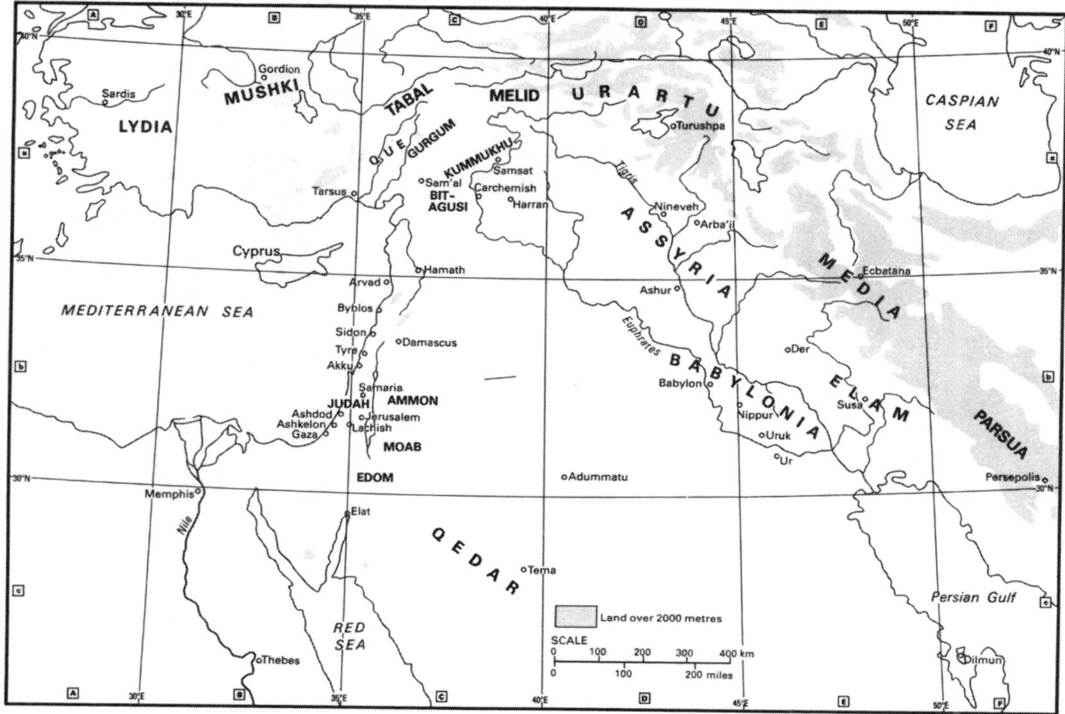

Babylon: map of Babylonia and the Near East the 1st millennium BC.

After the flight of the Babylonian king Nabonidus, Cyrus accepted the surrender of Babylon in October 539. In a demonstration of a peaceful takeover, achieved through the divine support of the city god Marduk, Cyrus entered Babylon in a ceremonious procession. At the same time his son Kambyses was made regent of Babylon for one year. Later king Xerxes quashed two revolts in Babylon, those of Bel-shimani in 484 and Shamash-eriba in 482. The long-held view that Xerxes removed the statue of Marduk from the temple in Babylon has been convincingly disproved. Herodotos does not reveal the name of the figure whose statue is removed, and clearly states that it was removed from the temple precinct, not from the interior where Marduk's statue was placed.

Both Darius I and Artaxerxes III (359–338) carried out building work in Babylon, constructing throne-halls in the royal residence. In 321 the Persian satrap Mazaios surrendered the city to Alexander the Great without a battle. Alexander's plans to make Babylon the royal centre of his empire were never realized. With the foundation of Seleukeia-on-the-Tigris by Seleukos I, Babylon lost its significance as a royal residence and provincial centre. MB

See Kuhrt, A. and Sherwin-White, S. (1987) Xerxes' destruction of Babylonian temples, in H. Sancisi-Weerdenburg and A. Kuhrt, eds., *Achaemenid History* 2, 69–78; Kuhrt, A. (1988) Babylonia from Cyrus to Xerxes, in *CAH* 4, 112–38; Kuhrt, A. (1995) *The Ancient Near East*, vol. 2.

Bacchus *Bakchos* was a cult title of the Greek god Dionysos, whose Roman manifestation, Bacchus, also assimilated the Italian fertility god Liber Pater. No other god in the classical pantheon is so multi-faceted, or has such a varied mythology or rich iconography.

The main tradition (there are numerous variants) has him as the 'twice-born' offspring of Zeus and Semele; snatched early from his dying mother's womb, he was brought to term sewn up in the thigh of Zeus. The best-known aspect of Dionysos–Bacchus was as the god who gave wine to humans. As such, he was associated with numerous wine festivals throughout the ancient world, such as the Anthesteria in Attica, which celebrated the opening of the new wine in the spring, and the Liberalia in Rome. His role as the god of wine was just a part of his manifestation as a god of nature, vegetation and fertility (the phallus plays an important part in some of the cults to him). Distinct from this, Dionysos–Bacchus was the centre of an ecstatic cult primarily for women. Bands of celebrants (*bakchai* or *mainades*, 'maenads'), left their communities every other year to go to the mountains. There they celebrated the god with dancing and ecstatic behaviour (*bakcheuein*), though they did not recreate literally the myth, so vividly portrayed in Euripides' tragedy *Bacchae*, of tearing apart wild animals and eating the raw flesh. At some point in the classical Greek or hellenistic period, a full-blown mystery cult developed around Dionysos–Bacchus, which took on aspects of an Orphic cult, using the myth of Dionysos being torn to pieces, devoured by the Titans, and resurrected.

BACCHUS: Maenads (the female attendants of the god) were infamous for their wild revels.

The myths of Dionysos–Bacchus are ambiguous. On the one hand, he is the god who brings the great blessing of wine to mankind; on the other, he is the subverter of order, just as wine can produce drunkenness. When the Dionysiac cult reached southern Italy in the early 2nd century BC, the Roman SENATE in 186 took the unusual step of seeking to regulate it closely and almost suppress it, because of the social disruption to FAMILY and community allegedly caused by its followers. It revived to receive official sponsorship from JULIUS CAESAR and favours from MARK ANTONY, who was styled in the East as the 'New Dionysos'.

The iconography of Dionysos–Bacchus is as varied as the mythology. He was sometimes represented as a bearded man wearing an ivy wreath and frequently an animal skin, but more often as a young boy wreathed in ivy, nude or semi-nude. The scenes from his story which most attracted artists included his capture by Tyrrhenian PIRATES, whom he turned into dolphins while their ship's mast became a vine; Bacchus' conquest of INDIA and his exotic TRIUMPH surrounded by tigers, panthers and ELEPHANTS; and the god's marriage on NAXOS to Ariadne, the jilted lover of THESEUS. The myth has continued to exert its spell over artists throughout history: consider the disturbing representations of the young Bacchus by Caravaggio, Titian's vivid representation of Bacchus and Ariadne, and Richard Strauss's opera *Ariadne auf Naxos*. JJP

See Euripides, *Bacchae*; Livy 39.8ff.; Bremmer, J. N. (1994) *Greek Religion*; Otto, W. F. (1965) *Dionysus*.

GODS AND GODDESSES: (a).

Bacchylides Born on the island of Keos at the end of the 6th century, Bacchylides was a nephew of SIMONIDES and a contemporary and rival of PINDAR. Merely a hundred lines of his poetry were known until 1896, when a new PAPYRUS came to light, offering fragments of 14 victory odes and 6 dithyrambs (choral songs with a mythical narration, sung at the FESTIVAL of a god). The dithyrambs were mostly written for the Athenians.

Until recently, critics considered him a poet inferior to Pindar, an assessment universal since antiquity. However, new studies have allowed Bacchylides to emerge as a poet in his own right. He is best regarded for his 'epinician' poetry, poems composed in honour of the victors at the periodic games (OLYMPIC, Nemean, Isthmian and Pythian). His odes, like Pindar's, present a triadic structure: brief mentions of the victor and victory being celebrated at the beginning and the end, a central mythic narration, and general maxims derived from these. Bacchylides does not narrate a complete myth but selects passages that are symbolic and evocative. His language is not as obscure as Pindar's; perhaps for this reason, Hieron, tyrant of SYRACUSE, appointed him to celebrate his most important victory, won in the chariot race at the Olympic games of 468 BC. In this ode composed for an ill Hieron, he narrates the story of Croesus, who was spared by APOLLO from a death on the pyre. Pindar, too, had compared Hieron to Croesus, in his first Pythian ode in 470; evidently, the rivals paid careful attention to each other's production. Bacchylides' ode for Hieron's previous victory in the horse race at the Olympic games in 476 is considered his masterpiece. In it, the myth of HERAKLES' descent to the underworld is employed to remind the audience of the limits of mortal existence, and that 'no mortal is fortunate in every way' (54–5). RBC

See Slavitt, D. R., trs. (1998) *Epinician Odes and Dithyrambs of Bacchylides*; Fränkel, H. (1975) *Early Greek Poetry and*

Philosophy; Pippin Burnett, A. (1985) *The Art of Bacchylides*; Podlecki, A. J. (1984) *The Early Greek Poets and their Times*.

Bactria see BAKTRIA.

Baecula see HISPANIA; SCIPIO AFRICANUS.

Baetica One of the three Roman PROVINCES in Spain in the imperial period. It comprised that part of the peninsula to the south of the river Anas (Guadiana), and was based on the valley of the river Baetis (mod. Guadalquivir). It was formed from the subdivision of the large republican province of HISPANIA Ulterior after the wars against the Cantabri and the Astures (27–16 BC), the remainder becoming the province of LUSITANIA. The governor was a proconsul, appointed by the SENATE. The capital of the province was at Corduba (mod. Córdoba), established in the mid-2nd century BC, which was also the centre of one of the four judicial regions (*conventus*), the other centres being Gades (mod. Cadiz), Hispalis (mod. Seville) and Astigi (mod. Ecija). It was rich in minerals (especially SILVER and GOLD in the Sierra Morena), OLIVE OIL, fish and fish products (especially FISH SAUCES). The Baetis valley in particular was heavily settled by the Romans at an early date, the first settlement being at Italica (mod. Santiponce, near Seville), established by SCIPIO AFRICANUS in 206 BC for wounded VETERANS; it was the home town of the emperors TRAJAN and HADRIAN. At the end of the 1st century AD, many towns became *municipia* as a result of the grant by VESPASIAN. Following the collapse of Roman control of the peninsula, Baetica was for a short time held by the VANDALS before being taken by the Visigoths. (see also GOTHS) JSR

See Fear, A. T. (1996) *Rome and Baetica*; Richardson, J. S. (1996) *The Romans in Spain*.

 HISPANIA; ROMAN EMPIRE: (a).

bakers According to PLINY THE ELDER, bakers first appeared in Rome around 171–168 BC. Prior to this time, BAKING was carried out at home, presumably by women. The need for bakers came about through a rise in population and the consequent dearth of baking facilities, as well as the fact that people no longer grew their own grain. Bakers were known as *pistores* (literally 'crushers') in Rome because they crushed and husked grain before milling it. Bakers carried out the whole process of making BREAD. They had grain delivered, milled the grain, kneaded the dough, baked the bread, weighed it and sold it on the premises. This process is illuminated by the many *pistrina* still found in POMPEII, as well as by the frieze carved on the TOMB of Eurysaces in Rome. While the size of *pistrina* varied, their layouts were similar. Bakeries were often fronted by a counter from which the bread was sold; behind this lay the *furni* or ovens. The mills lay at the back of the establishments, while smaller bakeries typically had mezzanine floors that served as living quarters. Larger bakeries boasted an enormous SLAVE force as well as a number of DONKEYS used both for milling the grain and for kneading the dough. Some bakers, such as Modestus in Pompeii and, above all, Eurysaces, became wealthy, not only because bread was a staple food but because the state contracted bakers to supply bread for the dole. EACM

baking In early Rome, people carried out much of their baking at home. However, with the population expansion of the mid- to late REPUBLIC, people tended to buy their BREAD directly from a BAKER. They could also bake some of their food at the bakers. Larger establishments, particularly farmsteads, continued to bake at home. These used *furni*, or ovens, which resembled modern pizza ovens in that they were dome-shaped and did not have chimneys. Food was placed into ovens after the embers were removed. Some smaller establishments used portable ovens, which were miniature versions of *furni*. They had the same shape, were made of either metal or earthenware, and were placed on top of hearths. A more economical and common way of baking involved a *tesum* or *testus*, apparently identical to the Greek *klibanos*. These were round earthenware covers which were placed on top of dough and were, in turn, both covered and surrounded by embers. Baking tiles and bricks were used in a similar way. Typically, dough was placed on top of tiles, and was then covered by bricks which were surrounded and surmounted by ashes. This is a method of baking described in the Virgilian *Moretum*. A simpler way of baking involved placing dough or cake mixture on top of hearths and burying it in ashes and coals. CATO gives a recipe for Picentine bread in which the dough was placed in

BAKERS: tomb of Eurysaces, a baker at Rome. The monument is thought to evoke ovens with its multiple round holes and has a frieze illustrating different stages in the process of bread making.

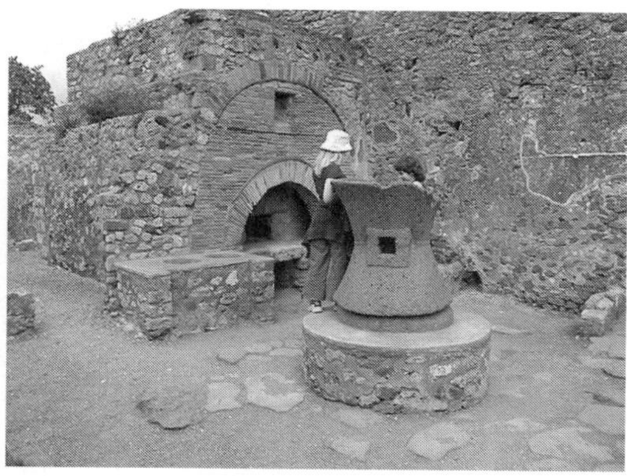

BAKING: donkey mill and oven of a Roman bakery at Pompeii.

earthenware pots that broke in the process of baking. EACM

See Brumfield, A. (1997) Cakes in the Liknon votives from the sanctuary of Demeter and Kore on Acrocorinth, *Hesperia* 66: 147–72; Cubberley, A. (1995) Bread baking in ancient Italy, in J. Wilkins, et al., eds., *Food in Antiquity* 55–68; Curtis, R. I. (2001) *Ancient Food Technology*.

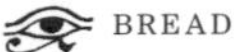 BREAD.

Baktria see AFGHANISTAN; ALEXANDER; INDIA; PAKISTAN; SELEUKID EMPIRE; SUCCESSORS.

Balbinus

EMPERORS, ROMAN: (a).

Baleares The Balearic islands were known to the Greeks as the Gymnêsiai ('islands of the naked'), either because the inhabitants were reputed to go naked on summer nights or (perhaps more likely) because they made good light-armed troops. During the Bronze Age, megaliths (*talayots*) were constructed; these continued to be built down to the Roman period. In the 7th century BC, PHOENICIANS settled on Ibiza, and the islands were a base for Phoenician and CARTHAGINIAN trade with Greek colonies in the western MEDITERRANEAN as well as with the Iberians of eastern Spain. Although Ibiza played some part in the second PUNIC WAR in the late 3rd century, the Romans only secured their position in the islands after the campaigns in 123 and 122 BC of Quintus Metellus Balearicus, who founded two settlements at Palma and Pollentia on Mallorca. Under the empire, the islands were part of the judicial *conventus Carthaginensis*, centred on Carthago Nova (Cartagena) within the province of HISPANIA Citerior. They were used as a place of exile by emperors in the 1st century AD. The inhabitants were used within Roman armies as specialists with the sling-shot, and in JULIUS CAESAR's army in GAUL they appear to have formed a separate unit. The islands were seized by the VANDALS in AD 411 and became part of the Visigothic kingdom in 467. JSR

 ROMAN EMPIRE: (a).

ball games Games with balls are attested in both the Greek and Roman worlds. Various forms of 'catch' were by far the most common, and could be played by both men and women. The ball game played by Nausikaa and her handmaidens in the *Odyssey* is the earliest literary reference to this sort of play. By the hellenistic period, as ball games were used to enhance co-ordination and conditioning, *sphairistêria* (purpose-built areas for ball games) were constructed in some GYMNASIA and team games, apparently similar to the modern children's game of dodge-ball, were developed for young men. In the Roman period they were also recommended, along with juggling, as forms of exercise to preserve health.

A ball game involving sticks is illustrated on a 5th-century BC Attic relief; while the sticks used by the players evoke comparison with modern field hockey, it appears that the game involved one-on-one competition between the players. There is no literary description of the game, which may have been rare.

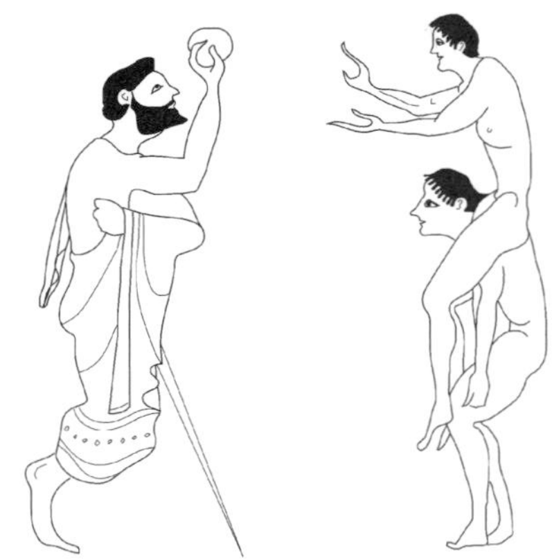

BALL GAMES: part of a gymnasium scene from an Attic vase-painting showing a teacher throwing a ball to a boy sitting on another's shoulders as part of a game or exercise.

In SPARTA, a team game involved groups of young men who apparently tried to control a ball and were allowed to tackle members of the opposing team. This game, too, appears to have been rare. That such games should seem anomalous is perhaps best explained by the usual context of ball play as a form of training and conditioning. DSP

banditry Groups of armed robbers or bandits were a widespread hazard in the classical world. Greek words for bandit include *lêistês*, *peiratês* and the rarer *kixallês*. In Latin the commonest word is *latro*, but *praedo* may also be used. Banditry is usually referred to as *lêisteia* in Greek and *latrocinium* in Latin. Mythical stories like the exploits of THESEUS, the founder of Athens, who defeated several bandits on his journey from Troizen (Plutarch, *Theseus* 6–11), suggest that banditry was widespread in early Greece before the development of the *POLIS* (city-state). Similarly, the foundation myth of Rome features the transformation of the twins ROMULUS AND REMUS from central Italian SHEPHERDS into bandit leaders and then city founders (Livy 1.4–10). Such myths can be interpreted as symbolizing the transition from a socio-political hierarchy dominated by predatory warrior bands to one in which a more peaceable, co-operative community of citizens is the norm. This transition was also marked by the abandonment of the habitual carrying of arms in public and the creation of citizen armies whose use of violence was gradually limited to formal wars, which required specific legitimization. Classical political and legal theorists distinguished the primitive exercise of personal authority, as characterized by bandits, from the sophisticated city or nation state where authority was exercised through officials and institutions, within constitutional and judicial frameworks (e.g. Cicero, *Laws* 2.13; Augustine, *City of God* 4.4).

Bandits were most common in places where centralized authorities were either weak or non-existent. Thucydides (1.5) claimed that banditry was a respectable way of life in the uplands of AITOLIA, Akarnania and western Lokris in the 5th century BC, and it remained endemic in many mountainous regions, such as Isauria and Rough CILICIA, even when the Roman empire was at its most powerful and stable. It was generally expected that rulers and their representatives would take measures to suppress banditry, but Greek and Roman writers present it as a routine danger on journeys through the open countryside. Bandits are regularly encountered by the protagonists of Greek and Latin NOVELS of the imperial period, skulking around the fringes of towns and cities or occupying uncivilized mountains and wetlands (e.g. Heliodoros, *Aithiopika*; Apuleius, *Metamorphoses*).

Accusations of banditry were often made for political purposes. Polybios (4.3) calls the Aitolian Dorimachos in 222 BC a leader of bandits. MARK ANTONY is called 'the bandit' by CICERO (*Letters to his Friends* 10.5–6, 12.12). Opponents of Roman power were often characterized in this way, such as the Lusitanian Viriathus (APPIAN, *Iberian War* 60–75). The equation of resistance to Rome with banditry helped to justify the ruthless suppression of Rome's enemies, as bandits and PIRATES did not have to be treated with the same respect and honour as legitimate foes (*Digest of Roman Law* 50.16.118). Some bandits became popular heroes, as in the cases of Maternus (Herodian, *Histories* 1.10) and Bulla Felix (CASSIUS DIO, *Roman History* 77.10) in the 2nd century AD. PDeS

See MacMullen, R. (1966) *Enemies of the Roman Order*, appendix B; Shaw, B. (1993) The bandit, in A. Giardina, ed., *The Romans* 300–41; Winkler, J. J. (1980) Lollianos and the desperadoes, *JHS* 100: 155–81.

banishment and exile (Greek *phygê*, Latin *exsilium*) Banishment and exile were often employed as sanctions or punishments in the ancient world. Entire communities might become exiles when cities were captured. Exile could also be a means of avoiding retribution for serious crimes. Formal banishment from a Greek city-state was usually accompanied by loss of citizen rights and property. Democratic Athens developed a form of temporary exile without loss of property, known as OSTRACISM. Civil strife frequently resulted in exile for those on the losing side, who might plot with external forces to achieve their restoration (as did ALCIBIADES of Athens). The restoration of exiles might gain political support, but it also caused disputes over status and property, as with ALEXANDER the Great's decree restoring exiles in 324 BC.

Exile became a way of avoiding capital punishment for the Roman Republican ARISTOCRACY, confirmed by an annually renewed prohibition of water and fire (*interdictio aquae et ignis*). Gradually it became the formal penalty for SENATORS convicted of political VIOLENCE (*vis*), treason (*maiestas*) and extortion in a province (*repetundae*). Although interdicted Romans lost their CITIZENSHIP, they retained their wealth, until in 49 BC JULIUS CAESAR introduced confiscation of half the exile's property. Under the principate many aristocrats were executed, but a form of internal exile to an island (*deportatio*) was introduced for crimes like ADULTERY (e.g. AGRIPPINA the Younger). Banishment from specific cities or PROVINCES (*relegatio*) was employed by Roman emperors against political agitators (e.g. DIO CHRYSOSTOM). PDeS

See McKechnie, P. (1989) *Outsiders in the Greek Cities in the Fourth Century BC*.

banking In the ancient world, a wide variety of institutions and individuals performed the functions that are traditionally associated with a bank. In classical Greece, loans were available from TEMPLES and individuals; some of these would also take deposits for safe keeping. Moneychangers were available to facilitate the exchange of the numerous currencies in circulation. Although we can determine the range of financial services available in the classical Greek world, their scale remains debatable. It was certainly possible for individuals to make tremendous profits through banking activity. However, it is important not to lose sight of the fact that an entrenched system of social transactions, regulated by ties of friendship and familial obligation, provided a substantial supplement to the financial services provided by these groups. The person looking for banking services had a wide variety of options.

The best evidence for banking in the hellenistic world comes from Egypt. Here we see a complex arrangement of private and state institutions that offered a wide variety of services to customers. Branch offices, letters of credit and bills of exchange are all attested.

In Rome, loans were available to clients from wealthy patrons, while professional money dealers (*argentarii*) were available to receive deposits and also lend money. Money changing was performed by a *nummularius* who would also check coins to see whether they were forgeries. AJLB

See Andreau, J. (1999) *Banking and Business in the Roman World*; Bogaert, R. (1994) *Trapezitica Aegyptiaca*; Cohen, E. (1992) *Athenian Economy and Society*; Millett, P. (1991) *Lending and Borrowing in Ancient Athens*.

Bar Kochba Leader of a Jewish revolt in JUDAEA against Rome, AD 132–5. The precise causes of the revolt are unclear, but it was not the first time JEWS had resisted Roman rule, and probably older animosities continued. Bar Kochba's name, meaning 'son of the star', alludes to the messianic prediction of a ruler arising like a star in the Book of Numbers (24.17). This may indicate national independence as one factor in the causes, though it is uncertain whether he initiated the revolt or later became its protagonist. Certainly, coins from the period bear such legends as 'liberation', 'the liberation of JERUSALEM' and 'the redemption of Israel'. The consequences were devastating for Jews. The emperor HADRIAN, after quelling the revolt, rebuilt Jerusalem as the Roman city of Aelia Capitolina, banned all Jews from entering the territory of the city, and renamed the province of Judaea as Syria Palaestina. Although the earlier destruction of the Jerusalem temple in AD 70 could be said to have been formative for later JUDAISM, the Bar Kochba revolt shows that many Jews did not see the fall of the Temple as the end, but hoped for a re-establishment of the Jewish state. It was probably only after Hadrian's imperial decree excluding them from Jerusalem that it became clear that the Temple would not be rebuilt, and that religious and organizational structures were changed forever. JKA

See Hayes, J. H. and Mandell, S. R. (1998) *The Jewish People in Classical Antiquity*.

barbarians

The Greek term *barbaros* originated in an attempt to characterize the sound of the meaningless babble of foreign peoples. The pejorative use of the term 'barbarian' in the sense of the political, cultural and above all ethical antithesis of 'Greek' is visible in the aftermath of the Persian wars. It should be understood within the context of Athenian claims for hegemony, and ultimately the building of the Athenian empire, in the 5th century BC. In contrast, in the archaic period, foreigners tended rather to be referred to as *xenoi*: the term suggests the ritualized guest–host relationship of *xenia*, and does not distinguish between Greeks and non-Greeks. Athenian ideology in the 5th century made much of Athens' role in driving back the Persians during and immediately after the Persian wars, while it was against the figure of the barbarian, a slave to despotism, that the self-image of the 5th-century Athenian democracy was formed. The category of barbarian swiftly came to encompass all non-Greeks, and the Eastern barbarian, blurring together numerous different ethnic groups, became a stock figure, the antecedent of the modern 'oriental'. There was some enlightened interest in the later 5th century in the idea of good barbarians and bad Greeks. The stock barbarian, however, was a remarkably persistent figure in ancient thought, thriving in a number of very different environments – including non-Greek ones – as a means to express social, cultural or military superiority. ED

See Hall, E. (1989) *Inventing the Barbarian*.

The figure of the barbarian remained important throughout Roman history, despite the fact that the Romans themselves were sometimes considered to be barbarians by the Greeks. In the Republic, the Romans themselves made much of this irony: while on the one hand they were keen to assimilate themselves to Greeks in their superiority over barbarians, they were also keen to distinguish themselves from Greeks. In Roman literature, we hear most about Roman views of northern barbarians, such as Celts, Germans and Britons, reflecting Roman imperialist activity in northern Europe in the Republic and empire. The Romans tended to characterize the behaviour of such peoples as prone to drunkenness, brutish, uncivilized and environmentally determined by the cold, wet climate. Nevertheless, Roman authors such as Tacitus were ambivalent about the supposed primitivism of northern barbarians. The Romans had appropriated and developed classical and hellenistic anxieties about the connection between luxury and empire, and the primitivism of northern barbarians could recall Rome's supposedly morally upright past, in contrast with the debauched contemporary capital of empire. Importantly, the Roman tendency to incorporate foreign peoples within the army or the citizenship on an individual or group basis meant that the line between Roman and barbarian was sometimes fluid. The slur of 'barbarian' is thus sometimes a rhetorical point of view rather than a reflection on the realities of cultural or juridical difference. ED

See Tacitus, *Germania*; Dench, E. (1995) *From Barbarians to New Men*.

Garamantes: (a); Germany and Germans: (b); Huns; Scythia and Scythians; trophies, military: (a).

Barbegal Perhaps the best known and one of the largest water mills of the ancient world, the Barbegal mill is located 7 km (4 miles) west of Arles on a steep ridge at the entrance to the Vallée des Baux. The mill, 61 by 20 m, is divided into two parts separated by a limestone stairway. Water was provided by an aqueduct cut through the top of the ridge, and channelled into two descending mill-races constructed against the interior face of the building's exterior walls. Within the mill-races were spaces for 16 wheels. The rooms between the races and the stairway housed the grinding mills turned by the wheels. The entire complex was enclosed by a wall.

Originally dated by F. Benoit to the late 3rd century AD, the construction of the mill is now, following recent excavations by P. Leveau, placed in the early 2nd century. Once thought to be an imperial monument, and a symbol of the Christianization of the

Barbegal: the two parallel series of Roman flour mills were driven by water wheels powered by a flow of water delivered to the top of the slope by an aqueduct.

Roman world and the end of ancient slavery, the mill is now interpreted as a municipal structure supplying Arles with flour. The grain for the mill was provided by a series of villas recently identified by archaeological survey in the Vallée des Baux. Both the villas and recent geomorphological study of the valley indicate that it was at least partially drained and cultivated in the Roman period. The mill continued in use through the 4th century, though the chronology of its final closure is uncertain. (see also mills and milling) RBH

See Bellamy, P. and Hitchner, R.B. (1996) The villas of the Vallée des Baux and the excavations at la Mérindole villa and cemetery, *JRA* 9: 154–76.

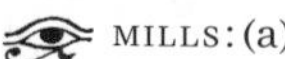 mills: (a).

Barca see Barcids.

Barcids Ruling family of Carthage, which rose to prominence in the 3rd century BC. Silius Italicus is the sole ancient author to comment on the origin of the Barcids; he identifies them as descendants of a Tyrian who came to Carthage with Dido (*Punica* 1.72). Members of the family included Hamilcar Barca, Hasdrubal Barca and Hannibal Barca. These three generals successively led the Carthaginians against Rome during the first and second Punic wars (264–241, 218–202 BC).

Hamilcar came close to defeating the Romans in Sicily at the end of the first war, and was regarded by Polybios (1.64) as the best naval commander of the conflict. After the war, he suppressed an uprising of Carthaginian mercenaries and led his army to establish a new territorial base for Carthage between Alicante and Cadiz, south of the river Guadalquivir in Spain. Coins here arguably depict the Barcids as hellenistic rulers, and some modern historians have referred to the region between as the 'Barcid kingdom', though these issues are debated among scholars. Hamilcar was succeeded in 229 by his son-in-law Hasdrubal and then in 221 by his son Hannibal, one of the legendary figures of antiquity whose exploits defy the imagination. DLS

See Cornelius Nepos, *Life of Hannibal*; Lancel, S. (1995) *Hannibal*.

 Carthage and Carthaginians: (a).

barley see beer; cereals.

Basil c. AD 330–79? One of the Cappadocian Fathers, along with his brother Gregory of Nyssa and his friend Gregory of Nazianzus. Basil of Caesarea had a considerable influence in defining Christian 'orthodoxy' by the end of the 4th century AD, and was a leading figure in the development of communal monastic institutions. He was born into a wealthy aristocratic family of Pontus and Cappadocia. The family had Christian traditions stretching back to Gregory Thaumaturgus. Two brothers of Basil also became bishops, while his sister Macrina was a founder of female asceticism.

Basil studied at Constantinople and Athens before returning to a rhetorical chair at Caesarea. In the late 350s, he toured monastic settlements in Syria and Egypt before retiring to the family estate in Pontus to live the ascetic life with Gregory of Nazianzus. He became bishop of Caesarea in 370, and soon found himself dealing with the Arian emperor Valens. The confrontation has been over-dramatized by the panegyrical sources. His episcopate was marked by a series of struggles to maintain unity in the church. Gregory of Nazianzus never really forgave him for making him bishop of Sasima, a benighted village in the Cappadocian wilderness. Some also suspected Basil's own theological orthodoxy, in respect of his views on the Holy Spirit. Basil was dogged by ill-health, which can be chronicled from his letters, a major source for the period. The council of Constantinople in 381 essentially vindicated the theological positions he had upheld. (see also church councils) PMB

See St Basil, *Letters*, 4 vols., trs. R.J. Deferrari (1926–34); Rousseau, P. (1994) *Basil of Caesarea*.

basilica Name for a variety of structures in the Roman world. The most common is the rectangular hall used as a market, as a meeting place, and probably for the administration of justice in a Roman town, especially in the central and Western empire. Most typically the roof is supported on columns forming a wider central space and two aisles; alternatively, columns form a rectangle parallel to the outer walls. When not a separate building, a town's senate house is usually set in a side chamber of the basilica. In Italy the basilica is generally a separate building off the forum or close to it, but in the provinces it was often integrated with the forum; the type almost certainly derives from the headquarters building of military forts. Also found, especially in larger cities of Gaul, is a double forum type, with a temple in the middle of one half and the basilica at the opposite end of the other. Basilicas are less common in the Greek east; when not adopting Italian models, the basilica there often resembles an enlarged stoa.

The word basilica was used for similar structures with different functions: the covered exercise hall of legionary and civilian bath-buildings, market halls, religious shrines and the hall in palaces where emperors dispensed justice. This last type inspired Christian churches in the early 4th century AD. The earliest basilicas, including the Basilica Porcia at Rome and those at Pompeii and Cosa, belong to the 2nd century BC. The word means 'royal' in Greek, suggesting that palaces of hellenistic kings contained halls for justice. None has been found in Macedonia, but one is inferred from the pleasure barge of Ptolemy IV (222–204 BC). Archaeologically, such halls are attested in the 'Palace of the Columns' at Ptolemais in Libya, and in Herod's palaces. Vitruvius calls such columnar halls in Roman houses 'Egyptian rooms'. The basilica may originate in Alexandrian palaces, but how and why the type came to Italy to be used as a public building is a matter for conjecture. (see p. 124) RJAW

churches: (a)–(c).

Bath (Aquae Sulis) The Roman town of Bath originated around three hot springs sacred to the local goddess Sulis. The recovery of Celtic coins dating to the late Iron Age suggests that the springs were

BASILICA: the Severan basilica at Lepcis Magna, early 3rd century AD, later converted into a church.

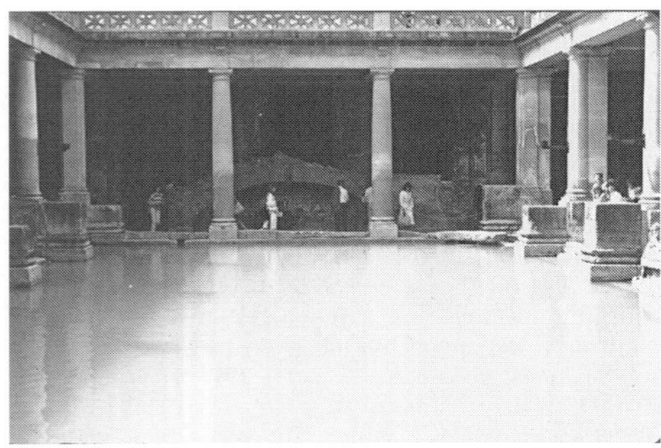

BATH: the large bathing pool fed by thermal springs at Aquae Sulis.

once the focus of pre-Roman ritual. It was not until the construction of the BATH and TEMPLE complex in Flavian times, however, that the curative properties, as well as the religious aspects, of the springs were fully developed. After 300 years of use, the baths were left to decline around AD 350.

Limited excavations have revealed five phases of construction, each successive phase designed to enhance the bathing facilities. The religious significance of the site is apparent in the magnificence of the classical temple, its architectural embellishment and the remains of a sacrificial altar. Finds recovered from the sacred spring suggest the extent to which the local GODDESS, later conflated with the Roman MINERVA, was appropriated.

The extent to which the town of Bath served an administrative function remains unknown. The remains of other Roman buildings have been noted, including the possible existence of a THEATRE adjacent to the temple precinct. The existence of numerous VILLAS in the fertile lands surrounding the town, in addition to a wealth of mineral resources, suggest that Bath was a significant nucleus for retired VETERANS and craftspeople, in addition to housing the numerous PRIESTS and employees of the baths and temple precinct. It also attracted a wide range of pilgrims from within the empire. MLM

See Cunliffe, B. (2000) *Roman Bath Discovered.*

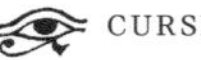 CURSES: (a)–(b).

bathing Bathing was a key component of Greek and Roman culture. In the earliest Greek literature, bathing features as a primary element of a civilized household. Nestor and Menelaos provide Telemachos with a bath when he arrives at their palaces in HOMER's *Odyssey*, while the uncivilized barbarians whom ODYSSEUS encounters make no similar offers (3.465, 4.48).

The first public bath-houses were built in classical Greece. A 5th-century BC bath at OLYMPIA contained a large open-air pool, a sauna building and a structure with semicircular tubs for washing. Greek vases depict two bathers taking a shower from spouts shaped like panthers' heads. These are presumably public BATHS, but private bathing may have been more common, as depicted on other vases showing naked bathers standing adjacent to oval washbasins resting on a stand. In this discussion, 'public' and 'private' designate clientele rather than ownership.

The Roman bath was an adaptation of the Greek GYMNASIUM, and contained baths in conjunction with exercise courts and porticoes for discussion. Among the Romans, baths performed many of the functions of a modern health club and more. There were pools of hot and cold water for bathing, courtyards for sports and recreation, LIBRARIES, lecture halls, promenades and small business establishments. Latin authors used multiple terms to refer to baths: *balneum*, *balneae* and *thermae*. The first two generally referred to small public or private baths. The last literally meant 'hot springs' but was applied to the monumental public baths.

Residents of Rome had their choice of baths. According to ancient sources, in the late 1st century BC there were at least 170 baths in the city; by the 5th century AD there were as many as 856. Marcus AGRIPPA built the first of the monumental imperial baths during AUGUSTUS' reign. He was followed by NERO, TITUS, TRAJAN, CARACALLA, DIOCLETIAN and CONSTANTINE. The baths of Caracalla and Diocletian are well preserved today; the former could accommodate 2,500 bathers at a time, the latter 4,000. Such gigantic establishments served as popular advertisements for the emperor who built them: 'what is worse than Nero, what is better than Nero's baths?' quipped MARTIAL (7.34). The popularity of baths extended throughout the empire. Well-preserved luxurious baths can today be visited in Paris, CARTHAGE, SARDIS and BATH, England – a town named after its famous spa – to cite just four examples. Even in the countryside, wealthy estates frequently contained baths (PLINY THE YOUNGER, *Letters* 2.17, 5.6; SIDONIUS APOLLINARIS, *Letter* 2.2).

BATHING: (a) Greek women showering at a fountain (possibly located in a sanctuary?).

Public baths were open during daylight hours. Men and women bathed separately for the most part, though the topic of mixed bathing provided fodder for critiques directed at specific individuals or general licentiousness. Some baths offered women's hours in the morning and men's in the afternoon; others (like the Stabian baths in POMPEII) had separate facilities for men and women. Preferred bathing hours for men appear to have been in the early afternoon, once the business of the day was complete and before the main meal. Bathing was inexpensive: at Vipascum, Portugal, a detailed inscription recorded the entrance fees as 1 *as* (a small coin) for women, half an *as* for men. Children, soldiers and certain others were admitted free of charge. The main expenses for proprietors of the baths were labour and heating. They met these by selling drinks, OIL, perfumes, towels and massages, or leasing space to tradesmen who provided these services. Additionally, wealthy citizens might be convinced to donate funds. The younger Pliny, for example,

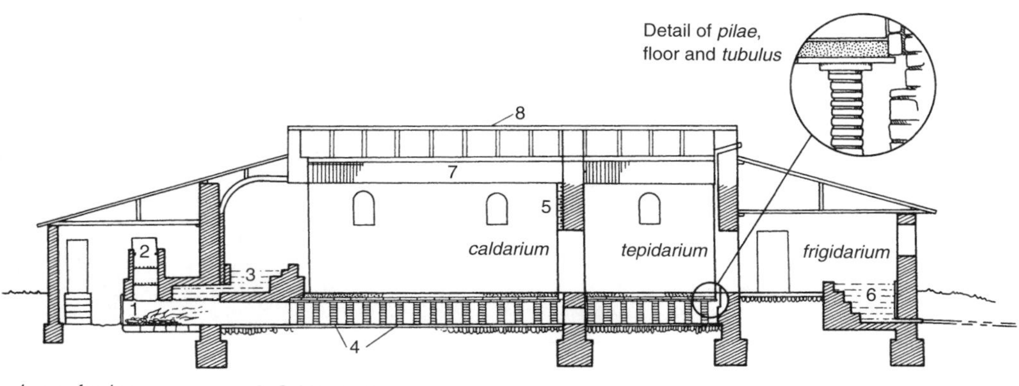

BATHING: (b) cross-section of a Roman hypocaust system. The warmest room was the *caldarium* adjacent to the furnace (which also furnished the hottest water for the plunge baths in this area), with the cold room or *frigidarium* essentially unheated.

provided 300,000 *sestertii* for the decoration and 200,000 *sestertii* for the maintenance of baths in his home town, Comum.

AQUEDUCTS provided water to large public baths; smaller establishments used cisterns to collect and store rainwater. Public latrines featured in larger baths, probably because the volume of waste water was sufficient to flush the sewers. PLINY THE ELDER credited Sergius Orata with the invention of the hypocaust early in the 1st century BC (*Natural History* 9.168).

Upon arrival, the first stop for patrons of the baths was the changing room (*apodyterium*). This contained wooden cabinets or niches built in the walls which served as 'lockers'. Theft of one's clothes was a concern; slaves or bath attendants were charged with guarding them. Ancient DOCTORS recommended exercise before bathing. The large courtyards, or PALAESTRAS, in bath-buildings were designed for a variety of sports: BALL GAMES, running, wrestling, and weight-training among others. Bathers probably progressed from the exercise area to the warm rooms. They may have begun in a warm sweating-room (*laconicum*, *sudatorium*, *tepidarium*), moved to the hot pool (*caldarium*) and finished by plunging into the cold pool (*frigidarium*). Several ancient sources describe this general order, but bathers could follow their own regimen. Massage, anointing with oil or perfume, and cleansing with a metal strigil or sponge were other steps in the bathing routine.

Critics of public baths in Greece and Rome abounded. Some claimed that their patrons wasted their lives in baths by indulging in their luxurious atmosphere. But a popular saying responded 'baths, wine and women corrupt our bodies, but these things make life itself'. Others disapproved of the disturbance baths brought to the neighbourhood. SENECA wrote that the sound of ball-players, masseurs, sausage-sellers, depilators – and their clients – and other visitors to the baths disrupted the peace and quiet of his nearby apartment (*Letter* 51). Such complaints nevertheless offer a clear picture of activities in the baths. DLS

See Lucian, *Hippias*; Martial, 6.42; Pliny the Younger, *Letters* 2.17, 5.6; Seneca, *Letters* 51, 56, 86; Sidonius Apollinaris, *Letter* 2.2; Statius, *Silvae* 1.5; Vitruvius, *On Architecture* 5.10; Cunliffe, B. (1996) *Roman Bath*; Fagan, G. (1999) *Bathing in Public in the Roman World*; Yegül, F. (1992) *Baths and Bathing in Classical Antiquity*.

bathrooms see TOILETS.

baths While the origins of public bathing in the Greek world lie in the cold pools and showers of the GYMNASIUM, heated public baths had become established as a normal community facility in urban centres and sanctuaries by the 4th century BC. The central feature comprised a number of hip baths arranged in individual niches around the often circular main room (*tholos*), with heated water poured over the seated bather by an attendant. The furnace for heating the water was sometimes adapted to provide heat for the bathing room, but usually a simple brazier sufficed. Single hip baths are also found in private houses. Such baths were adopted all over the hellenistic world, and in a few areas, such as Egypt,

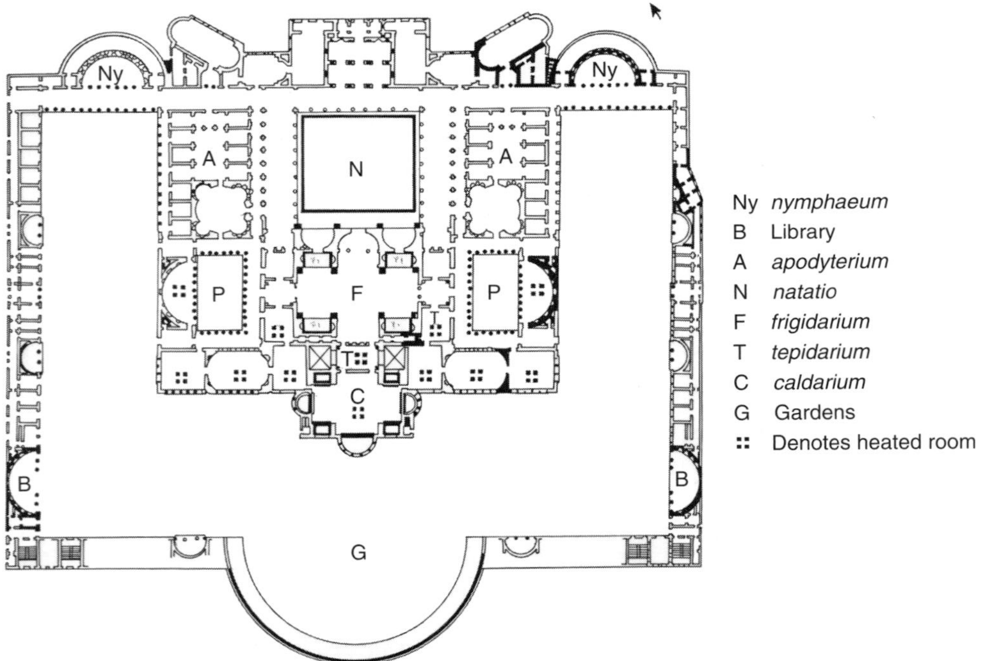

BATHS: (a) the baths of Trajan, Rome, an example of the largest scale public *thermae*, covers a total area of approximately 4 ha (10 acres).

BATHS: (b) interior of the baths of Diocletian at Rome (converted into the church of Santa Maria dei Angeli) showing the lavishly decorated interior and the high ceiling vaults of the largest public *thermae*.

Greek bathing practices continued well into the Roman period with little change.

The transition to Roman-style baths (*balneum, balneae, thermae*), characterized by the substitution of communal immersion pools for the hip baths and the development of under-floor heating systems (hypocausts), took place during the 2nd to 1st centuries BC in central Italy, perhaps under the influence of VOLCANIC springs and fumaroles. A system gradually developed of venting the hot gases from the hypocaust through hollow wall-coverings to create radiating surfaces, thus permitting wide variation in the degree of heat and humidity in different rooms. In the absence of thermostats, controlling the heating system was a skilled task, and the SLAVE who operated the furnace (the *fornacator*) was sold with the building and other apparatus if the baths changed hands.

The basic features of the developed Roman baths included a changing-room (*apodyterium*), an unheated *frigidarium* with a cold water pool (or pools), a moderately warm room (*tepidarium*) sometimes containing a tepid pool, dry (*laconica*) and/or moist (*sudatoria*) sweating rooms, and a hot room with one or more highly heated pools (*caldarium*). Many public baths also boasted a PALAESTRA and an open-air swimming pool (*natatio*). The essential rooms, found even in the smallest baths, were the *apodyterium*, which might contain a cold pool or basin and act also as a *frigidarium*, and the *caldarium*.

By the 1st century BC, public baths in Italy were often located centrally near the FORUM, reflecting their important if pragmatic role in urban life. Under the influence of the vast and luxurious baths

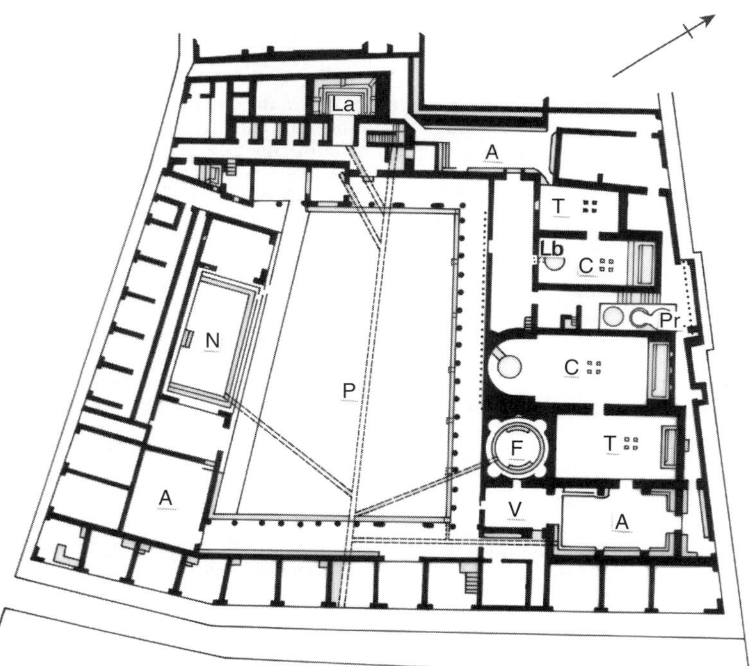

BATHS: (c) plan of the forum baths at Pompeii, a typical example of the smaller style of facility and at approximately 0.2 ha (0.5 acres) a fraction of the size of the imperial *thermae* at Rome. The baths are surrounded by arcades of shops and other commercial premises.

BATHS: (d) domed and vaulted roofs of a typical small Roman bath-building – the so-called Hunting Baths at Lepcis Magna.

built by the EMPERORS in Rome (particularly the *thermae* of NERO and TRAJAN), provincial baths increased in size and elaboration and took over the role of the forum as the focus of social life. No self-respecting community was without at least one set of baths and most towns had several; OSTIA had at least 17 by the early 3rd century AD. While some served specific groups, such as members of a *collegium*, and others the everyday needs of local residents, the most lavish were built as a civic embellishment by wealthy benefactors for the whole community, including women and slaves. JDeL

See Fagan, G. G. (1999) *Bathing in Public in the Roman World*; Yegül, F. K. (1992) *Baths and Bathing in Classical Antiquity*.

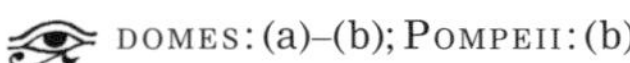

DOMES: (a)–(b); POMPEII: (b).

battles

The nature of the Greek world in the archaic and classical periods, divided as it was into a large number of small independent city-states, meant that small-scale conflicts were a regular feature of life. On land, the HOPLITE phalanx, developed in the 7th century, remained the basic fighting formation of the cities into the 4th century. Greek cities had no standing armies, and the phalanx was made up of landowning citizens, wearing heavy armour and fighting at close quarters behind a wall of shields. If the phalanx broke, the soldiers would turn and run immediately. This meant that casualties in battle were often comparatively light, an important consideration when the same men who fought in the battle-line had to work the land to support the population. Sparta was unusual in that its small, wealthy citizen body (the Spartiates) did not work the land themselves and could devote most of their time to military training. However, it is likely that the richer members of other cities had enough leisure to take part in the necessary training for hoplite fighting, and even Sparta had to rely on non-Spartiates in battle. The hoplite phalanx was eventually superseded by the Macedonian phalanx, which made use of long pikes. The Roman legions proved more effective still.

At sea, the trireme became the key fighting instrument from the 6th century onwards. These were rowed in battle and carried a small contingent of marines. The main tactic was to ram the enemy vessel, though skilful manoeuvring could also cause enemy ships to become entangled with each other, making it easier to deal with them. Cities with a large urban population, especially Athens, had a ready supply of oarsmen, who were available for training during much of the year.

There are a number of traditions about major wars between Greek states in the early archaic period, but although a number of significant battles are mentioned the evidence is usually very slight. For the classical period, it has been suggested that the various wars covering most of the period 479–338 BC are effectively one continuous state of war. Thus individual battles take on a greater significance in showing the relative strengths and weaknesses of the different states. Apart from colonial foundations on the edges of the Greek world, the Greek states encountered only two significant external military threats in the period before they became absorbed into the ROMAN EMPIRE: from the PERSIANS in the early 5th century BC, and from the Romans in the 2nd. For most Greeks, most of the time, their experience of battle was against other Greeks. HB

See Hanson, V. D. (1989) *The Western Way of War*; Pritchett, W. K. (1971–91) *The Greek State at War*, 5 vols.

War, whether against external enemies or fellow-citizens, was an almost permanent condition for the Romans. Very few periods of Roman history, from the founding of the REPUBLIC in 509 BC to the fall of the Western empire in AD 476, were free of warfare on some front. Hence battles (the clearest manifestations of war) fill the annals of the HISTORIANS and constitute one of the defining images of Roman POWER.

The importance of victory in battle is nowhere more obvious than in the institution of the TRIUMPH, in which the victorious commander conducted a

BATTLES, GREEK: principal battles of the Greek world.

Battle	Date	Victor	Vanquished
Hysiai (land)	669/8	Argives	Spartans
'Battle of the Champions' (land)	mid-6th century	Spartans	Argives
Lade (sea)	494	Persians	Ionians
Marathon (land)	490	Athenians and Plataians	Persians
Thermopylai (land)	480	Persians	Spartans and Phokians
Artemision (sea)	480	Greeks	Persians
Salamis (sea)	479	Greeks	Persians
Plataia (land)	479	Greeks	Persians
Mykale (sea)	479	Greeks	Persians
Eurymedon (land and sea)	c.466	Athenians and allies	Persians
Tanagra (land)	457	Spartans and allies	Athenians, Argives and allies
Oinophyta (land)	457	Athenians	Boiotians
Koroneia (land)	446	Boiotians	Athenians
Delion (land)	424	Boiotians	Athenians
Amphipolis (land)	422	Spartans and allies	Athenians
Mantineia (land)	417	Spartans and allies	Argives, Athenians and allies
Kyzikos (sea)	410	Athenians	Peloponnesians
Notion (sea)	407	Peloponnesians	Athenians
Arginousai (sea)	406	Athenians	Peloponnesians
Aigospotamoi (sea)	405	Peloponnesians	Athenians
Haliartos (land)	395	Thebans	Spartans
Leuktra (land)	371	Thebans	Spartans
Mantineia (land)	362	Thebans	Spartans
Chaironeia (land)	338	Macedonians	Athenians and Thebans
Granikos (land)	334	Macedonians	Persians
Issos (land)	333	Macedonians	Persians
Gaugamela (land)	331	Macedonians	Persians
Ipsos (land)	301	Demetrios Poliorchetes and Antigonos Monophthalmos	Lysimachos, Seleukos, Kassandros
Lade (sea)	201	Philip V and Macedonians	Rhodians
Kynoskephalai (land)	197	Romans	Philip V and Macedonians
Thermopylai (land)	191	Romans	Antiochos III
Pydna (land)	168	Romans	Perseus and Macedonians
Pydna (land)	148	Romans	Andriskos and Macedonians

procession from the Campus Martius to the CAPITOLINE displaying the captured standards of the enemy, the booty and the prisoners of war. But triumphs were reserved for GENERALS whose victories met certain criteria, including a minimum of 5,000 enemy dead. Lesser victories could be voted an 'ovation'. Furthermore, since CONSULS and PRAETORS were awarded areas of operation (*provinciae*) which normally required the securing of borders or the subjugation of Rome's enemies, leadership in battle was a basic function of virtually every man elected to high office. Indeed, in the mid-Republic at least 10 years' military service was a prerequisite for the higher MAGISTRACIES. Nevertheless, many were elected to the consulship who lacked military competence, as MARIUS noted in an address to the Roman people, and consequently many of Rome's most memorable battles were in fact defeats.

One of the noteworthy early defeats, at the river Allia (c.386 BC), led to the sack of the city; a subsequent victory under the leadership of Camillus appears to be a Roman fiction. Against the SAMNITES, too, the Roman army was defeated at the Caudine Forks and forced to go under the yoke (321 BC). But it was the tenacity of the Roman people and the stability of its constitution – to say nothing of abundant sources of manpower – that allowed the Romans to suffer serious defeats on the battlefield without losing wars. Likewise the Romans prevailed over Pyrrhos after two initial defeats at Heraclea (280) and Asculum (279).

The classic example of Roman resilience was the second Punic war. After crossing the Alps in 218 and winning relatively minor victories over the Romans at the rivers Ticinus and Trebia, Hannibal in the following year lured the Roman consul Gaius Flaminius into an ambush on the north shore of lake Trasimene. Placing the bulk of his army at the eastern end of the lake, Hannibal planted others in the hills alongside the route Flaminius was taking as he approached his enemy's camp. These descended upon the marching column and drove the Romans into the sea. Escape was virtually impossible and the disaster complete. This defeat was followed in 216 by an even greater disaster at Cannae, where Hannibal's deliberately weakened centre allowed the Roman forces to push forward so that it gradually became enveloped by the Carthaginian wings. Hannibal's Numidian cavalry had routed their Roman counterparts, leaving the infantry to be slaughtered in numbers that some contemporaries estimated as high as 70,000. Rome rebounded from this defeat, in part by accepting the wisdom of Quintus Fabius Maximus, whose delaying tactics in the period between Trasimene and Cannae had been dismissed as cowardly and unnecessary. Successes in battle at the Metaurus river (207) and finally in Africa, at Zama (202), secured the Roman victory in the Hannibalic war.

In the subsequent battles against hellenistic kings, Rome's armies were regularly victorious: at Kynoskephalai (197) against Philip V of Macedonia, at Thermopylai (191) and Magnesia (189) against Antiochos III, and against Perseus of Macedonia at Pydna in 168 BC. Victories against hellenistic opponents were due in no small part to the organization of the Roman army into smaller units known as maniples (literally 'handfuls') which were able to exploit gaps in the more rigid Macedonian phalanx that was ill-suited to wage battle on uneven ground. Roman legionaries, armed with the larger protective shield (*scutum*) and the short thrusting sword (*gladius*), wreaked havoc among the phalangites whose shield offered limited protection and who used both hands to wield their sarissas, which ranged in length from 5.5 to 7.3 m (18 to 24 ft).

Gaius Marius – who, after his election to the consulship, fought successful minor engagements in North Africa only to have his enemy, Jugurtha, captured through treachery by Sulla – defeated the Teutones in 102 in the battle of Aquae Sextiae (Aix-en-Provence). But Roman generals soon began to turn their armies against one another in a bitter series of civil wars. Among the most famous of these battles were Caesar's victory over the senatorial forces of Pompey at Pharsalus in 48 BC. (Of all Caesar's victories, it was the relatively insignificant one over Pharnaces at Zela in 47 that evoked the famous words '*veni, vidi, vici*', a testament to the ease with which it was won.) Others were Mark Antony and Octavian's defeat of Cassius and Brutus at Philippi (42), and Octavian's victory over Antony (and Cleopatra VII) at Actium in 31. The last battle brought the combined naval and land forces of the rivals into play, but the issue was decided by sea before the land armies could even engage. In the sea battle, Antony's fleet found itself blockaded and attempted a break-through. The action resulted in heavy losses (some 350 ships were lost out of 480) but a portion of the fleet escaped to Egypt, something the pro-Augustan historians depicted as cowardice and flight. However one interprets the action, the outcome was the same: defeat at sea, surrender on land, supremacy for Octavian.

The imperial age again saw its share of Roman disasters on the battlefield, one of the most famous occurring in AD 9, where Publius Quinctilius Varus lost three legions against the Germans under Arminius in the Teutoburg forest. The battle of the Milvian bridge (AD 312) witnessed the victory of Constantine the Great over his rival Maxentius, and is noteworthy for the claim that before the battle Constantine saw the sign of the cross in the sky and instructed his soldiers to paint this sign (or rather the Greek letter chi, X) on their shields. The story is probably apocryphal but worthy of the great christianizing emperor. Two other battles deserve mention. In 378 the emperor Valens suffered a crushing defeat at the hands of the Visigoths at Adrianople, a battle that opened the door for barbarian invaders who now ravaged the empire and in 410, under the leadership of Alaric, sacked Rome. In 451 in the battle of Châlons, Fl. Aëtius defeated the ferocious army of Attila the Hun, but, whatever the consequences of the victory for Western Europe, it produced only a short respite for Rome. In 476 the Western empire came to an end, during the reign of the emperor named (fittingly) Romulus Augustulus. WH

See Fuller, J. F. C. (1965) *Julius Caesar* (1965); Goldworthy, A. (2000) *Roman Warfare*; (2001) *Cannae*; Heather, P. (1991) *Goths and Romans 332–489* (1991); Lazenby, J. F. (1978) *Hannibal's War*.

 war (table).

beds The Latin word *lectus* and the Greek *klinê* incorporate the meaning of both the modern terms 'bed' and 'couch' to describe a piece of furniture which in the ancient world was used for sleeping, dining and working. The focus here is on its use for sleeping; the term couch best describes the other functions of this versatile and important piece of furniture.

In their simplest form, beds consisted of a wooden frame with a mattress resting on an arrangement of leather straps and ropes. More commonly, ancient beds had high, lathe-turned legs and curved foot- and head-rests. The mattress and cushions were filled with straw or hay (Pliny the Elder, *Natural History* 18.193), though wool and feathers were popular luxury alternatives. Beds were usually made from wood held together with dowels, tenons, metal nails and glue. They could be decorated with gold plating, inlays of ivory and tortoise shell and silver or ivory feet. Strongly defined mouldings on the legs and the presence of a high back are both Roman innovations. Roman and Greek beds were quite high and necessitated the use of footstools. Most beds were quite narrow, though double beds are known in the Roman period.

The bed (*lectus cubicularis*) could also be associated with illness and DEATH (*lectus funebris*). In the Greek world, the deceased would lie in state (*prothesis*) before being taken in a solemn procession (*ekphora*) to the cemetery. Such scenes are commonly depicted on Greek vases and Roman tombstones. HE

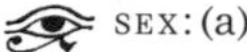 SEX: (a).

beer To the Greeks and Romans, drinking beer (as opposed to WINE) was the real mark of the BARBARIAN, and it was generally consumed in the outer, colder fringes of the classical world where grapes were difficult to cultivate. DIONYSOS was the Greek GOD of drinking and is most often associated with wine, but there are two stories linking him with beer. Diodorus Siculus (1.20.4, 3.73.6, 4.2.5) relates that Dionysos generously taught the art of beer-making in those places where the vine would not grow. Julius Africanus (*Cesti* 1.19) tells us how Dionysos punished the barbarians by neglecting to teach them how to make wine, leaving them only with beer.

Aristotle noted that people drunk on wine fall down on their faces, whereas those drunk on beer lie flat on their backs – wine makes one top-heavy but beer stupefies (Athenaeus 1.34b). Xenophon mentions that ARMENIAN beer is strong and good once a person became accustomed to it (*Anabasis* 4.5.27), while Diodorus regards beer as pretty much like wine in terms of its strength and smell (1.20.4, 1.34.10, 3.73.6, 4.2.5). That is about the extent of positive appraisals by classical authors.

Barley beer was first brewed in the ancient Near East, and hops have only relatively recently become an integral part of the process. Since ancient times other plants and herbs have been used to flavour beer: parsley, pomegranate, sesame, cinnamon, anise, date, coriander, mint and lemon leaf, to name but a few. CK-B

bees and beekeeping Bees were highly valued in the Greek and Roman world, as HONEY was the main sweetener in antiquity. Honey was used for sweet cakes (CATO, *On Agriculture* 76.3.77) and added to WINE (PLINY THE ELDER, *Natural History* 14.20). It was also thought to have medicinal qualities (7.57.6). Due to the importance of honey, the practicalities of beekeeping were well understood though some anatomical misunderstandings persisted. Thus ARISTOTLE suggests that bees do not breathe and that they have tongues for the collection of nectar (*History of Animals* 1.1.7, 5.22.5).

In antiquity, beekeeping was not a separate profession but part of good AGRICULTURAL practice. As such, it is covered in some detail by a number of Roman writers such as VARRO, COLUMELLA, Pliny and VIRGIL. Bees were kept in hives, usually made from wood, bark or wicker. Beehives were carefully sited away from unpleasant smells but close to clear water and suitable plants. Varro (*On Agriculture* 3.16.14) specifically mentions the high-quality honey produced from the flowers of beans, lentils and peas. Smoke was used to clear out pests and infestations, and when removing the honey. In contrast to modern beekeepers, no special clothing appears to have been worn, but Columella (9.14.3) specifies that beekeepers should be clean and when handling bees should abstain from intercourse, ALCOHOL and strong-smelling foods such as garlic and onions. Honey was collected two or, more usually, three times a year, with the spring honey being more highly valued than that produced in late autumn (Pliny 11.34). The habits of wild bees and the location of beehives in hollow trees (Virgil, *Georgics* 2.452) and caves (Homer, *Iliad* 2.87) were also known from earliest times. In contrast to honey, which could yield profits of 10,000 *sestertii* per year (Varro 3.16.10), wax was considered to be a less profitable by-product (Columella 9.16.1). It is likely that tallow was used for most candles and open LAMPS. It is only in late antiquity that beeswax was especially valued for use in altar candles.

Bees played an important part in ancient folklore and MYTHOLOGY and were regarded as having social and symbolic attributes such as industriousness, cleanliness and bravery (Varro 3.16.4, 7; SENECA, *Letters to Lucilius* 121.22). Beehives are described as communities akin to those of humans (CICERO, *On Duties* 1.157). On the other hand, swarms of bees were usually interpreted as a bad omen (CASSIUS DIO 41.61, 42.26; LIVY 21.46.2). Honey was thought to have dripped from trees in the GOLDEN AGE (OVID, *Metamorphoses* 1.111–12) and was used in some funerary rites and the cult of MITHRAS. HE

See Crane, E. (1999) *The World History of Beekeeping and Honey Hunting*; Forbes, R. J. (1966) *Studies in Ancient Technology*, vol. 5, 80–111; Fraser, H. M. (1931) *Beekeeping in Antiquity*.

Bel see BAAL HAMMON; BEROSSOS; PALMYRA.

Belgae One of the three 'parts' or major ethnic groupings into which CAESAR famously divided GAUL (*Gallic War* 1.1), saying (at 2.4) that they were of GERMAN descent and had been attracted across the RHINE by the quality of the land. STRABO (4.196) placed them between the Rhine and the Loire, though the 15 tribes identified by Caesar as Belgae (Ambiani, Aduatuci, Atrebates, Bellovaci, Caerosi, Caleti, Condrusi, Eburones, Menapii, Morini, Nervii, Remi, Suessiones, Veliocasses and Viromandui) lay well to the north of the Loire. He occasionally refers to part of this region as *Belgium*, and his mention (2.4) of a 'general council' of the Belgae suggests that they were aware of their separate identity. He also relates (5.12) that Belgae had invaded the 'maritime area' of BRITAIN; after the Roman conquest there was a *civitas* of the Belgae in central southern Britain.

The archaeology of the areas covered by the Belgae shows considerable variation in settlement type, material culture and socio-political structures between the southern tribes and those of the north and the coastal areas. The COINAGE suggests a pre-eminent role for the peoples of the Somme region. Most of the changes in late Iron Age south-eastern Britain postdate Caesar's alleged Belgic settlement. ASEC

See Haselgrove, C. C. (1990) The romanization of Belgic Gaul: some archaeological perspectives, in T. Blagg and M. Millett, *The Early Roman Empire in the West* 45–71; Wightman, E. M. (1985) *Gallia Belgica* 1–52.

 GAUL AND GAULS: (a).

Bellona see MOTHER GODDESSES.

benefactors and benefaction

Benefactors (*euergetai*, sing. *euergetês*) in Greece were individuals, almost always very wealthy, who performed actions that brought some benefit upon others, usually among the wider community and often within the context of the POLIS (city). Benefaction became institutionalized within some *poleis* during the classical period, and by the 4th century the role of the benefactor as an individual giver of gifts came to have much more prominence. Benefaction is a significant theme in the hellenistic and Roman periods, but its role in earlier Greek history must not be underestimated.

In the society depicted in the HOMERIC poems, the *Iliad* and the *Odyssey*, generosity and extravagance (*megaloprepeia*) among the HEROES received considerable praise. Gift exchange was fundamental to Homeric culture. Such gifts held great value and created a reciprocal bond between giver and receiver. The relationship between gift-giver and the wider social group was deeply embedded in the value systems of the Greek world.

In the archaic period, many Greek cities were ruled by TYRANTS who lavished considerable wealth on luxurious lifestyles. Some financed large public projects for the benefit of civic, commercial and religious life. Polykrates of SAMOS is thought to have been the author of the three greatest constructions in Greece, listed by HERODOTOS (3.60): a mainly underground AQUEDUCT, the HARBOUR mole, and the TEMPLE of HERA. Periandros of CORINTH constructed the dragway for SHIPS, the *diolkos*, across the isthmus of Corinth and built the harbour at Lechaion. The PEISISTRATIDS of Athens extended the sanctuary of DEMETER at ELEUSIS, and built aqueducts and the 'Nine Spouts' FOUNTAIN (Enneakrounos) at Athens (Thucydides, *Histories* 2.15.3).

In the classical period, the *polis* exerted greater control over the expenditure of personal wealth, especially in DEMOCRATIC Athens where the wealthy were restrained from public munificence. The people rejected PERIKLES' gesture to fund the care of the WATER SUPPLY and decided to pay for improvements from the tribute of the empire (*IG* I^3 49 = Fornara 117). The rich in Athens spent their own wealth in other forms, notably LITURGIES. They paid for DRAMATIC productions (through the *chorêgia*), TRIREMES (through the *triêrarchia*), made financial payments (the *eisphora*), and served in the CAVALRY. Such institutionalization of personal expenditure slowed down the growth of benefaction from citizens within the city but still allowed the wealthy a means of expressing their civic virtue.

Foreign benefactors, however, were encouraged; many were made *proxenos*, a citizen of one community representing in his own city the interests of another city. At Athens, *proxenoi* (civic guest-friends) were honoured from the mid-5th century and often declared to be benefactors. But in the 4th century *proxenoi* were eclipsed by those individuals sought by *poleis* as political benefactors and providers of raw materials – in particular grain, a commodity that was heavily dependent on good inter-personal overseas contacts. The dynasty of KINGS on the BOSPOROS, the Spartokids, was rewarded for their aid in supplying grain to Athens in both the 4th and 3rd centuries BC (Rhodes and Osborne, no. 64).

The campaigns of ALEXANDER the Great and the subsequent disintegration of his empire into the hellenistic kingdoms hastened the growth in benefaction that had been accelerating in the 4th century. Individuals acquired great wealth. Some could boast important political contacts as 'friends' of the kings, potentially the greatest benefactors of all. A super-benefaction economy developed. A king, or friend of a king, ready to spend money and resources could exert important political muscle in securing the loyalty of cities. For liberating Athens from DEMETRIOS OF PHALERON and Kassandros (Cassander) in 307 (Plutarch, *Demetrios* 8–10), the hellenistic kings ANTIGONOS and DEMETRIOS I Poliorketes received numerous honours from the Athenians, such the creation of two new civic TRIBES, Antigonis and Demetrias.

At some cities, such as Athens again, the internal organization of the expenditure of wealth had changed by the early 3rd century; the system of liturgies had gradually disappeared towards the end of the 4th century. The appeal for donation of money (*epidosis*) for specific purposes became an important tool to fund urgent projects or emergencies. In the mid-3rd century at Athens, among those who gave money for the defence of the countryside were the philosopher Lykon and the poet KALLIMACHOS. More usually, civic benefactors came to serve as MAGISTRATES or DIPLOMATS. At Istria, Agathokles performed magistracies and embassies and negotiated the safety

BENEFACTORS AND BENEFACTION: the emperor was expected to be the greatest individual benefactor in the Roman world, a role that was semi-formalized in public handouts called *congiaria*, as illustrated here in a relief carving from the arch of Constantine.

of the *polis* against external threats from the Thracians in the first half of the 2nd century BC (Austin no. 100).

Benefactors received all kinds of honours: crowns of myrtle, olive, ivy or GOLD; various civic privileges, such as the right to own property; for some, CITIZENSHIP; exceptionally, statues or paintings; occasionally, the renaming of civic institutions or the creation of FESTIVALS. EPIGRAPHY provides most of the evidence in the hellenistic period. The recording of such privileges on stone inscriptions was an honour but also served a further purpose in advertising to other potential benefactors that a city rewards those who perform such services. For a benefactor, desire for honours (*philotimia*), political power or civic pride motivated the expenditure of time and money.

In the later hellenistic and Roman periods, cities were almost exclusively dependent on wealthy benefactors for the provision of civic amenities. At MILETOS, for example, Eirenias negotiated an increase in the benefaction given by Eumenes II of PERGAMON for the construction of a GYMNASIUM. The wealthy ÉLITE within Greek cities was of considerable importance to the wider community, but the hellenistic kings found much greater levels of wealth at their disposal. GJO

See Austin, M. M. (1981) *The Hellenistic World*; Bringmann, K. (2001) Grain, timber and money: hellenistic kings, finance, buildings and foundation in Greek cities, in Z.H. Archibald et al., eds., *Hellenistic Economies* 205–14; Rhodes, P. J. and Osborne, R. G. (2003) *Greek Historical Inscriptions, 404–323 BC*; Veyne, P. (1990) *Bread and Circuses*, ed. O. Murray, trs. B. Pearce.

The offering of benefactions to the community was as much a trademark of Roman society as it was of the hellenistic world. The essential difference from benefactors in the modern world is that ancient benefactors never targeted a specific category of the poor or destitute. While distributing cash or food, higher-status groups of citizens received more money and better food than those of lower status. It was not charity, but part of the profession of being a politician and a member of the leisured classes. Politicians were rarely paid for holding office, and in addition it was expected of them to provide the community and its citizens with amenities, entertainment and basic necessities such as grain. From the surviving evidence, it would appear that the benefactor was the more powerful party in the social relationship; but based on the ancestral reputation, wealth and political success of the family the recipients could manipulate the politician's ambitions to meet their expectations. It was difficult to ignore the shouts of a crowd of thousands assembled in the THEATRE urging the benefactor to be even more generous. The returns for benefaction took the form of social kudos made visible and tangible in statues, acclamations and other ceremonies of gratitude. Apart from engaging in compulsory benefactions that arose from the holding of office, benefactors occasionally stepped in of their own free will to solve an economic crisis, erect a building, or provide GAMES. These private initiatives gained them additional honour and prestige. Some did even better by paying for the statues that had been voted in their honour.

Thanks to the considerable extent of their resources, the EMPERORS were the largest benefactors in the Roman world, even though the main focus of their benefactions was Rome and Italy. Even small communities of fewer than 2,000 inhabitants had benefactors willing to trade their wealth for an increase in honour and prestige. The level of expenditure engaged in by some benefactors in rural communities is impressive, and raises the question of how such wealth was generated. One gets the impression that a fortune carefully built up over some generations was spent out of a sense of urgency in order to make a permanent mark on the community. What is even more amazing is that some families managed to maintain a reputation for generosity over several generations.

The RHETORIC of honorific inscriptions presents a harmonious relationship between benefactor and recipients. Occasionally, however, we are allowed a different view on the matter. One benefactor from a small town in northern Italy complains that he was not properly thanked for his efforts and that his fellow-citizens were jealous of him, ultimately driving him into exile. Other cases show that there could be a considerable lapse of time between the promise of a benefaction and its fulfilment. This could be due to unwillingness or to financial constraints. With deteriorating economic circumstances in the later Roman empire, there was a decrease in the preparedness of politicians to hold office and consequently to provide benefactions. MK

See Lomas, K. and Cornell, T., eds. (2003) *'Bread and Circuses': euergetism and municipal patronage in Roman Italy*; Veyne, P. (1990) *Bread and Circuses*.

Berbers see AFRICA AND AFRICANS; CORIPPUS; ROMAN EMPIRE; TIMGAD.

Berenice see BERENIKE I; see also TITUS.

Berenike I Mistress, and later wife, of PTOLEMY I Soter of Egypt. She was the daughter of a MACEDONIAN named Magos and was initially married to a commoner named Philip. She was the niece or cousin of Eurydike, Ptolemy's wife, whom she followed to the Egyptian court and finally supplanted in Ptolemy's affections. In c.316 BC she gave birth to a daughter, Arsinoë II; in 308 BC she delivered a son, the future Ptolemy II Philadelphos. She had at least one more child, a daughter named Philotera. Berenike contrived to have Ptolemy Keraunos, her husband's eldest son by Eurydike (who bore Ptolemy at least six children), removed from the succession. In c.287 BC it appears that Eurydike and her son left Egypt; certainly Ptolemy Keraunos is next attested at the courts of LYSIMACHOS and SELEUKOS. Little else about Berenike's life is known, but when she died in 279 she was included in the dynastic cult and worshipped in the TEMPLE of the Theoi Soteres ('Saviour Gods') at ALEXANDRIA. It is also highly likely that she received personal cult, as there is evidence for a temple to Berenike, the Berenikeion, in Alexandria c.275. According to THEOKRITOS (*Idyll* 15.22–4), it was none other than APHRODITE herself who elevated Berenike I to the status of a goddess. LL-J

See Odgen, D. (1999) *Polygamy, Prostitutes and Death*.

Bernal, M. see RACISM.

Berossos Babylonian historian (late 4th–early 3rd centuries BC). Berossos was a Chaldaean and a priest of Bel (Marduk). His life spanned the period from the reign of ALEXANDER the Great to that of Antiochos I Soter, and he ended his life in exile teaching ASTROLOGY on Kos. His only known work is *Babyloniaka*, a history in three books, intended to correct Greek misconceptions about BABYLON. It was dedicated to Antiochos.

The work was organized according to traditional Babylonian views of man and his place in the world. Book 1 dealt with the origins of Babylon and the communication of culture to the first men by the demigod Oannes. Book 2 treated the history of Babylon from Oannes' appearance, 432,000 years before the Flood, to the reign of Nabunasir in the 8th century BC. Book 3 dealt with the Neo-Babylonian and PERSIAN periods.

Berossos' claim that his history was based on CUNEIFORM sources preserved in the temple of Bel at Babylon is confirmed by the fragments of his work, which reveal the use of a version of the Babylonian creation epic in book 1, a flood story and a king-list related to the *Sumerian King-list* in book 2, and various chronicle texts in book 3. Unfortunately, Berossos failed to supplant Ktesias as the principal Greek authority for Mesopotamian history. As a result, the *Babyloniaka* is known only through fragments preserved by JOSEPHUS and EUSEBIOS. SMB

See Burstein, S. M. (1978) *The Babyloniaca of Berossus.*

bestiality Images of bestiality, that is, sexual coition between a human and an ANIMAL, occur sporadically in Greco-Roman ART, predominantly in the genre we now regard as pornography, though the ancients may have regarded them as 'fantasy' images. This is emphasized by the use of SATYRS in such scenes; these half-men are sometimes shown coupling with animals – DONKEYS, deer and even a sphinx. One cup shows a naked maenad reclining against a large AMPHORA and preparing to have sex with an ithyphallic donkey. Scenes of bestiality usually have a mythic setting. There is a large corpus of myth wherein a god rapes a mortal female in the guise of a beast. These stories often incorporate the theme of HUNTING, as the rape takes place in the wilds. Some examples of bestial rape include Kanake, raped by POSEIDON in the form of a BULL; he also uses the shape of a dolphin to ravish Melantho. ZEUS takes several animal forms; most famous, perhaps, is his metamorphosis into a swan to rape Leda. Most bizarre is APOLLO's transformation into a tortoise in his rape of Dryope. Sometimes the raped female is transformed into an animal while the divine rapist keeps his human shape: thus Taygete is changed into a deer as Zeus defiles her. The theme of bestial rape being degrading to the girl is a familiar one in Greco-Roman myth. LL-J

See Robson, J. E. (1997) Bestiality and bestial rape in Greek myth, in S. Deacy and K. F. Pearce, eds., *Rape in Antiquity* 65–96.

Bible As a term denoting a collection of a particular set of books in both JUDAISM and CHRISTIANITY, 'Bible' (Greek *biblia*, 'books') derives no earlier than the 2nd or 3rd century AD. The Christian Bible differs from the Jewish in its number and order of books of the OLD TESTAMENT, as well as the addition of the NEW TESTAMENT. Nevertheless, we already find from the 2nd century BC onwards a priority and importance given to some books in Judaism that were later to form the canonical Bible. References are also found to collections of books, most notably to the Law and the Prophets, divisions familiar in later Jewish writings. At the same time the designation of 'sacred books' comes to be used of the Jewish Law (the first five books of the Old Testament), and the term continues into Christianity. Greek and Roman authors also began in the hellenistic period to develop the concept of sacred books, something only occasionally formulated before (e.g. in ORPHIC circles). One aspect of a sacred book is its use for divination or ORACULAR prediction, and for this purpose Jews sometimes used their Law, consulting it before a battle to learn what the outcome might be (1 Maccabees 3.48). Thus, the role of the PROPHET came to be replaced by the Bible itself. JKA

See Rutgers, L.V. et al., eds. (1988) *The Use of Sacred Books in the Ancient World.*

bilingualism In antiquity bilingualism was widespread, but for many Greeks their mother tongue was superior and all other languages were barbarous. THEMISTOKLES, the famous Athenian GENERAL of the 5th century, was exceptional in learning PERSIAN (Thucydides 2.138). The story that PYTHAGORAS learnt Egyptian underlines how unusual it was to have acquired such linguistic ability (Diogenes Laërtios 2.8.3). Many Greeks, therefore, did not learn other languages. HERODOTOS, a visitor to Egypt, suffered from his dependence on an interpreter: he was told that an inscription in Egyptian hieroglyphs recorded the enormous sum of 1,600 talents as the amount spent on radishes, onions and leeks for the LABOURERS constructing the pyramids (2.125).

Clearly, significant groups of people were able to benefit from bilingualism. Interpreters were of considerable importance, particularly on military campaign. For XENOPHON and the 10,000 Greek MERCENARIES returning home through enemy territory in Asia Minor at the end of the 5th century BC, their Persian–Greek interpreter had to be more reliable than Herodotos' (*Anabasis* 4.5). Armies in the Greek world, right back to the Trojan army of HOMER (*Iliad*, 4.437–8), contained soldiers speaking different languages. Greek- and MACEDONIAN-speaking soldiers served in ALEXANDER's armies and met many different peoples who used a variety of languages. But conservatism still dominated. Peukestas, Alexander's bodyguard, appointed as satrap of the PERSIANS, became the only Macedonian to dress like a Persian and learn the Persian language (Arrian, *Anabasis* 6.30.2). The other Macedonians, however, resented his particular form of bilingualism, despite this being a practice which Alexander approved (Arrian 7.6.3).

It was not only military circumstances that encouraged bilingualism. Financial gain often drove the acquisition of another language. In 2nd-century BC Egypt we hear of a Greek man learning Egyptian in order to teach young SLAVES medical knowledge and thereby earn a living (Bagnall and Derow, no. 116). In Greek cities it was more likely that foreigners and slaves were bilingual and used both their native language and Greek. A number of private inscriptions – most often tombstones or religious dedications – put up by members of PHOENICIAN communities in DELOS and Athens illustrate the simultaneous use of Greek and Phoenician.

The Roman empire embraced an even greater linguistic polyculture. Latin was the official language of the empire but was also used in private letters. Ennius, the epic poet, knew three languages: Oscan (his native tongue), Latin and Greek. Bilingualism was common among the élite of Rome, for the senators in the Republic understood visiting embassies from Greece who spoke in their own language (Cicero, *De finibus* 5.29). Service in the Roman army encouraged bilingualism, possibly even trilingualism among some soldiers. The writing tablets found at Vindolanda on Hadrian's wall show that soldiers from non-Latin-speaking northern Europe were writing Latin.

The movement and integration of different peoples in antiquity produced a richly diverse linguistic culture in which bilingualism was not unusual. GJO

See Bagnall, R. S. and Derow, P. (1981) *Greek Historical Documents: the hellenistic period.*

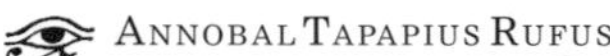
Annobal Tapapius Rufus.

biography and biographers Ancient biography is an elusive and anonymous genre. The word *biographia* appears only in the 6th century AD. Its ancient counterparts, Greek *bios* and Latin *vita* (both meaning 'life'), were used not only for biographies but also for cultural histories by Dikaiarchos and Varro. One has to choose between modern definitions: either too narrow ('an account of the life of a man from birth to death', Momigliano) or too broad ('a description of the nature of a personality considered in the unity of his actions and words', Gentili–Cerri). Moreover, the boundaries between 'biography' and neighbouring genres are not clearly drawn. It is obviously close to history: many historians, from Herodotos to Eusebios, have included biographies in their works, organized their description of contemporary events around a person (e.g. Theopompos, *Philippics*), or written biographies (Polybios, Nikolaos of Damascus, Tacitus). Hence the many attempts of modern scholars and ancient biographers, from Polybios to Cornelius Nepos and Plutarch, to distinguish between the two, emphasizing either the content (deeds versus character, true versus exaggerated accounts) or the form (dignified versus plain). It is also difficult to distinguish biography from rhetoric, from encomiums including biographical elements (Socrates' *Apologies*, Greek eulogies of Evagoras and Agesilaos, the *Panegyric* of Julian), and from the biographies with encomiastic function (Polybios' *Philopoimen*, Tacitus' *Agricola*, Eusebios' *Constantine*). Collection of exempla, anecdotes or conversations may also be included in a broad definition of the genre.

That explains the on-going disagreement among scholars about the beginnings of biography. Leo emphasized the 4th century BC and the decisive role of Aristotle's school. There are now attempts to move the antecedents of Greek biography back to the 5th century – to the *Visits* of Ion of Chios, who recounted his meetings with the great men of his day, the sketches of Themistokles, Thucydides and Perikles by Stesimbrotos of Thasos, and the first biography of Homer by the rhapsode Theagenes of Rhegion – or even to the archaic period (to the epics about Herakles, and the collection of anecdotes about Aesop and the Seven Wise Men). There is a tendency to find additional causes for the rise of biographical writings in Greece in the impact of the exemplary life of Socrates in philosophy and the new centrality of leading individuals in politics.

In the 4th century, Isokrates' *Evagoras* and Xenophon's *Agesilaos* combine a systematic review of their subjects' virtues and a chronological survey of their deeds, which make them into the first examples of political biographies. This is also the case with the *Cyropaedia*, where Xenophon concentrates on the family, character and education of Cyrus the Great to draw the portrait of an exemplary ruler. On the other hand, the *Apologies* of Socrates by Plato and Xenophon, together with the *Memoirs* (*Memorabilia*) in which Xenophon relates all he remembers about him (1.2.1), inaugurate the philosophical biography.

With the exception of the *Life of Euripides* by Satyros, preserved by a substantial papyrus and characterized by dialogical form, thematic structure and ample use of literary sources, hellenistic biography remains a ghost. The Peripatetic *Lives* of philosophers (by Aristoxenos of Tarentum, Dikaiarchos, etc.), poets (by Chamaileon), legislators (by Hermippos) or tyrants (by Phanias of Eresos), as well as the *Lives of Philosophers* by Antigonos of Karystos and the works centred around Alexander and Polybios' *Philopoimen*, are only known through summaries, indirect tradition or meagre papyrus fragments.

It is only with the late Roman Republic and the imperial period that we gain an acquaintance with complete texts. These can be roughly divided into two categories: on the one hand, statesmen and generals; on the other, intellectuals, philosophers and saints.

The earliest extant biographer in Latin is Cornelius Nepos (c.110–24 BC). He wrote at least 16 books *On Famous Men*, both Romans and foreigners, grouped into series. The extant part (a book on eminent foreign leaders and two lives of historians) betrays an unusual sense of cultural relativism, but pales in comparison with Plutarch (c.AD 45–120). His justly famous *Parallel Lives*, which confront Greek and Roman statesmen, portray them through their words and deeds, narrated in roughly chronological order, and provide the reader with an image of virtue. They had no posterity. But his eight *Lives of the Caesars* (Augustus to Vitellius), which break the history into successive reigns, inaugurated a popular genre first adopted and transformed by Suetonius (born c.AD 70). His *Lives of the Twelve Caesars* (Caesar to Domitian) exemplified the virtues and vices of the emperors by actions and anecdotes, documented with scholarly impartiality. They were followed by the works of Marius Maximus (Nerva to Elagabalus), Aurelius Victor (Augustus to Constantius II), and the *Historia Augusta* (Hadrian to the sons of Carus), written under Theodosius with a wealth of details on imperial eccentricities. There were also individual biographies of political figures with laudatory bias. Such were Nikolaos of Damascus' *Life of Augustus* (known through extensive fragments), Plutarch's *Aratos* and *Artaxerxes*, and above all Tacitus' *Agricola*, a panegyric integrated with historical and ethnographical material. Likewise Eusebios' *Constantine* is a portrait of a model of pious life supported by a series of documents.

Suetonius' *Illustrious Men*, packed with recondite information, covers the literary culture of Rome. It is segmented into categories exemplified by individuals disposed in chronological order, as demonstrated by the surviving book on teachers of grammar and rhetoric. The *Lives and Opinions of Famous Philosophers* (first half of 3rd century) by DIOGENES LAËRTIOS, a blend of biography and doxography structured according to schools, surveys the history of Greek philosophy from Thales. They are almost contemporary with PHILOSTRATOS' *Lives of the Sophists*, a vivid portrait of the masters of epideictic rhetoric from the time of NERO to the Severans. In contrast, Eunapius' *Lives of the Philosophers and the Sophists* (covering PLOTINUS to Chrysanthios) is a proselytizing work written for the pagan literati. Besides these, there were individual biographies proposing models of philosophical life. LUCIAN chose to portray Demonax, 'the best of the contemporary philosophers'. Philostratos' *In Honour of Apollonios of Tyana* helped to promote the myth of the holy man, also exemplified by the lives of PYTHAGORAS by Porphyry and Iamblichos that advertise the Pythagorean way of life, and by the lives in which NEOPLATONIST philosophers celebrated the divine virtues of their teachers Plotinus, Proclus and Isidoros. Those narratives competed with the CHRISTIAN hagiographies, which fused the life and teachings of the saints. The most popular was the *Life of Antony*, a chronicle of his ascent to perfection and an illustration of his glory; it paved the way for the most prolific medieval genre. SS

See Cox, P. (1983) *Biography in Late Antiquity*; Geiger, J. (1985) *Cornelius Nepos and Ancient Political Biography*; Gentili, B. and Cerri, G. (1988) *History and Biography in Ancient Thought*; Hägg, T. and Rousseau, P., eds. (2000) *Greek Biography and Panegyric in Late Antiquity*; Momigliano, A. (1971) *The Development of Greek Biography*.

Bion see EURYDIKE (1); LYRIC POETRY, GREEK; THEOKRITOS.

birds From AVIARIES on the estates of the wealthy to frequent appearances in literature and visual arts, birds were everywhere in the classical world. As with ANIMALS and INSECTS, initial attempts to classify birds occur in works of ARISTOTLE. PLINY THE ELDER and AELIAN discuss birds in some detail, but are less scientific and more given to narrating stories of interest, intended to amuse, to cause wonder or sometimes to edify. The FABLES of AESOP include some moralistic tales about birds.

In literature, birds appear in many contexts. Because they inhabited the landscape as well as the cities of the ancient world, authors often include birds in the settings they describe. On occasion, the subject of an entire literary work is a bird or birds; perhaps the best-known is ARISTOPHANES' *Birds*, where the comic playwright imagines a human-like world peopled by birds. Elsewhere, a poem might be devoted to a favourite bird, particularly at its death, like CATULLUS' treatment of the death of Lesbia's pet sparrow (*Poems* 2) or the series of EPIGRAMS where a poet first mourns the loss of a pet partridge to a cat – which had bitten its head off, but the remainder was rescued – and promises to execute the cat in a second

BIRDS: (a) mosaic of different birds from Italica, Spain.

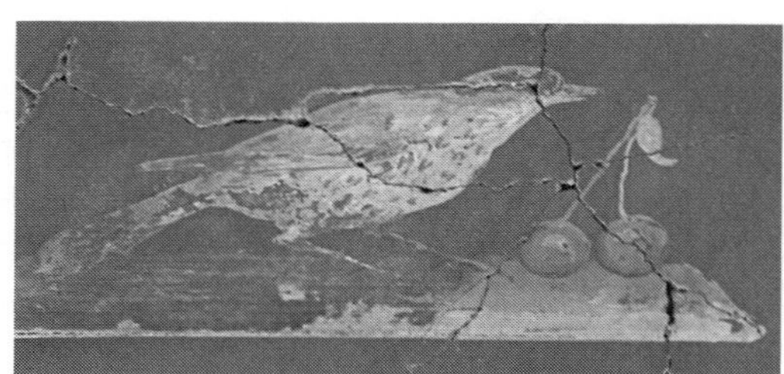

BIRDS: (b) wall-painting showing a mistle thrush (*Turdus viscivorus*) after cherries.

poem, while his friend reprimands the cat in a third effort (*Palatine Anthology* 7.204–6). Similarly, birds appear regularly in the naturalistic scenes painted on walls. Examples from POMPEII are well known, but the skies and trees in WALL-PAINTINGS and MOSAICS devoted to different subjects offer a bird or two. POTTERY provides numerous examples, and birds of many types were sculpted in various media.

In addition to association of particular birds with deities, like the eagle with ZEUS and JUPITER, the owl with ATHENA, and the ibis with ISIS, birds were the source of AUGURY and divination. Birds and bird-like creatures, like Sirens, were also the subject of folklore and MYTH, and at times the human SOUL was portrayed in the shape, completely or partially, of a bird. The reappearance of birds from their migrations heralded the return of spring, and observations of bird behaviour might be employed to forecast weather.

Birds of different types were kept as pets, some for singing, some, including parrots and ravens, for an ability to mimic human speech. On 28 March AD 36, a funeral was held outside Rome along the Via Appia for a cobbler's parrot slain by a neighbouring shopkeeper; it had flown to the FORUM each day to greet the emperor TIBERIUS, and Germanicus and Drusus Caesar, by name (Pliny the Elder, *Natural History* 10.60). Other birds, like cocks and birds of prey, were kept for fighting, sport and falconry. Most varieties of birds, snared or caught with bird lime, were consumed as food, sometimes after they had been fed to fatten them. JV

See Pollard, J. (1977) *Birds in Greek Life and Myth*; Thompson, D'A.W. (1936) *A Glossary of Greek Birds*; Toynbee, J. M. C. (1973) *Animals in Roman Life and Art.*

bishops The origin of the episcopacy in the Christian CHURCH has, historically, been the subject of sectarian controversy. At issue has been the true nature of the 'pure' early CHURCH. The word bishop (*episkopos*, 'overseer') is first found in NEW TESTAMENT texts (Acts 20.28, Philippians 1.1) as a synonym for presbyter, in contexts which imply a twofold ministry of bishops or presbyters and deacons. A similar situation may be observed in the first letter attributed to Clement of Rome, addressed to the church in CORINTH, dated to the 90s AD. The first generation of Christian churches saw bishops or presbyters co-existing as sources of authority alongside apostles and prophets. The *Didache*, a text usually dated to the 1st century, envisages such a situation. However, as the first apostolic generation of Christians passed away, local structures of church authority inevitably became more important. The idea of the monarchical bishop is prominent in the letters of Ignatius of ANTIOCH (c.AD 35–c.107). He thought that the best way for each community to avoid the snares of heresy was to have a single focus of unity and authority. By the mid-2nd century a threefold ministry of bishop, presbyters and deacons had emerged, and with it the idea of bishops as successors of the apostles.

As the church became institutionalized, administrative ability as much as holiness was required of a bishop. In the mid-3rd century the bishop of Rome was responsible for the care of more than 1,500 widows and needy folk, and his clerical staff included 46 priests (EUSEBIOS, *Ecclesiastical History* 6.46). The bishop's powers were wide-ranging: he held office for life, controlled all revenues and was responsible for all ordinations. He judged who should be admitted and expelled from the church community. A judicial role also developed. Such power and autonomy meant that it was difficult to control 'rogue' bishops, even through councils. The appointment of bishops was theoretically a matter in which the local clergy and laity had a voice, though a bishop was actually consecrated by fellow-bishops. The 4th-century councils of Arles and Nicaea laid down that consecration should be carried out by at least three bishops from the same PROVINCE, with the approval of the metropolitan, and a bishop was not meant to move from one see to another. The emergence of metropolitan sees, with wider spheres of authority, is connected with the church's practice of modelling its organization along the lines of the civil administration. By the same token, bishops of the major cities of the empire came to exercise influence and authority far beyond the boundaries of their own diocese.

Constantine granted bishops extensive secular jurisdiction (restricted by later EMPERORS), and his generous donations to the church made some bishoprics extremely wealthy. 'Make me bishop of Rome,' a PAGAN SENATOR said, ironically, 'and I will become a Christian tomorrow.' In the 4th century, some men of high social status became bishops and acted as effective patrons for their congregations in dealings with government. PMB

See Chadwick, H. (1967) *The Early Church*; Lane Fox, R. (1986) *Pagans and Christians*; Telfer, W. (1962) *The Office of a Bishop.*

Bithynia and Pontos see ANTINOUS; NICOMEDIA; PLINY THE YOUNGER.

Black sea AEGEAN Greeks had a definite image of the Black sea. They imagined it as far distant, having no islands, its dangerous shores inhabited by piratical shipwreckers. In MYTHS it was a distant area of legends, famous for its riches, the land of Medea and the Golden Fleece. The Greeks first called it 'Inhospitable' (*Axeinos*) and only placated it with the title 'Hospitable' (*Euxeinos*) once it had become more familiar to them. Its Latin name is *Pontus Euxinus*. Its maximum length is 1,130 km (700 miles), its breadth 610 km (380 miles). The climate in ancient times was colder than now, and the sea level has undergone six major changes in the last 6,000 years. It last rose (by 3–5 m) in the 1st–2nd centuries AD.

Although the question of the first Greek penetration of the Black sea continues to be debated, ARCHAEOLOGICAL material proves that the first COLONIES were founded by Milesians from Ionia in the last third of the 7th century BC. These colonies were small and situated on peninsulas (Berezan settlement, now an island, Histria, Apollonia Pontica, the Taganrog settlement, SINOPE and Amisos). The vast majority of colonies were established in the 6th century, the number reaching 75–90 by the beginning of the 5th century. MEGARIANS and BOIOTIANS established Herakleia Pontica in 554, which in its turn established Chersonesos in the Crimea (422/1) and Kallatis in the western Pontos (early 4th century). If Ionian colonization was characteristically peaceful, Dorian was hostile. During the establishment of Herakleia the local population was either slaughtered or enslaved; at Chersonesos an earlier Ionian settlement was destroyed.

The Black sea region was populated by natives with a variety of ways of life. In the west were the agricultural THRACIANS; in the steppes behind the northern Black sea, NOMADIC SCYTHIANS; in the western Crimea, the Tauroi; on the Taman peninsula, Maiotians and Sindians; to the east, Kolchians, Heniochoi and Zygoi; to the south, Chalybes, Makrones, Mosynoikoi, Tibarenoi and Mariandynoi. The relations between these tribes and the Greek colonies were mostly pacific; only the Tauroi, Zygoi and Heniochoi attacked the Greeks and engaged in PIRACY.

The Black sea was of considerable importance to the Greeks and Romans because of its location and natural resources (including SLAVES, honey, wax, fish and grain, Polybios 4.38.4–6). Although the Romans' first knowledge of the sea dates to the 2nd century BC (through their encounter with the kingdom of Pontos), their real interest developed only after POMPEY's expedition to the Caucasus in 65 BC. Only from the time of the emperors CLAUDIUS and NERO did Roman garrisons arrive, resulting in the creation of the Pontic *limes* (frontier). Several

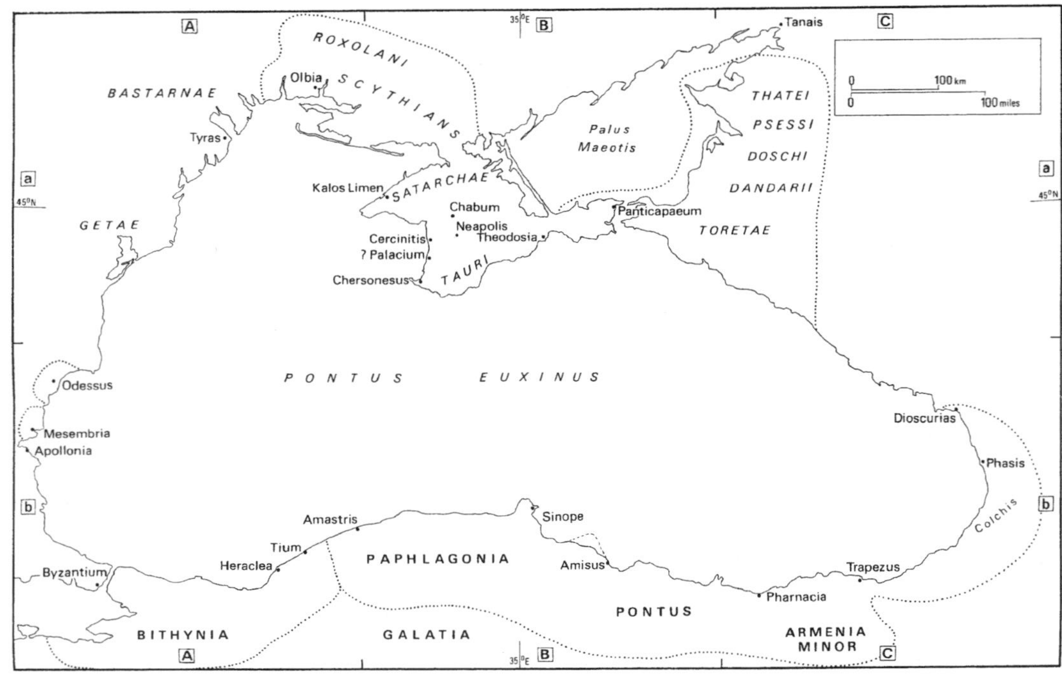

Black sea: map showing the Black sea region in Roman times.

provinces were situated around the sea. The area was famous for local hostility to Roman rule. Goths and Huns passed through the northern and western regions, destroying everything in their paths. From the 6th century AD the whole sea fell under Byzantine influence. GRT

See Ascherson, N. (1995) *Black Sea*; Isaac, B. (1992) *The Limits of Empire*; Millar, F. (1981) *The Roman Empire and its Neighbours*; Tsetskhladze, G. R. and De Angelis, F., eds. (1994) *The Archaeology of Greek Colonization*.

 colonization: (c).

blacks In general, Greek and Roman assessment of other peoples was based on cultural and environmental factors rather than on physical appearance. Nevertheless, they commented unfavourably on skin colours – both very pale and very dark – and other physical features different from their own. The Greeks and Romans had several terms for dark skin colour, and tended to distinguish between different shades of black. The 'Ethiopian', the Greco-Roman term for individuals with the darkest skin, curliest hair and fullest lips, has a narrower application than the broader modern usage of 'black' that has different historical roots both in racist ideologies and the civil rights movement. Greeks and Romans judged very dark skin colour in aesthetic and symbolic terms: they associated the colour black with dirt and the demons of the underworld. Their assessment of human character was, however, more usually based on environmental considerations rather than on skin colour: thus southern peoples in general were considered to be cowardly and over-interested in sex. Dark skin colour was explained in various ways: sunburn from a hot sun was one theory, and another was that the mother had seen a black person while pregnant. 'Ethiopians' were thought to be exotic, and thus we find them employed as jugglers and performers, while faces with exaggerated 'Ethiopian' features were a popular decoration for jugs and other domestic objects. ED

blacks: Phoenician glass bead depicting a negroid face.

See Snowden, F. (1983) *Before Color Prejudice*; Thompson, L. (1989) *Romans and Blacks*.

blindness see DISABILITY.

board games and other games Board games were popular from Egyptian times through to the late Roman period. The British Museum has a game board marked with the cartouche of queen Hatshepsut c.1500 BC, which was found with several lion-headed playing pieces in light and dark wood. The Romans were fond of a board and dice game called *ludus duodecim scriptorum* ('game of the 12 writers'). Hundreds of variations of the board have been found in Rome, decorated with various circles, squares, letters and even erotic symbols. In the 1st century AD it was replaced in fashionable circles by *tabula*. According to SUETONIUS (*Claudius* 33) the emperor CLAUDIUS liked the game so much that he wrote a book on the subject, and even had a board attached to his chariot so he could play while travelling.

We know less about Greek board games, though they appear in the visual record, such as the Attic black-figure amphora by Exekias dating to c.540–530 BC and depicting AJAX and ACHILLES hunched over a board game. Knucklebones was a popular game with Greek children, and appears to have also been played in Egypt since they were found in Tutankhamen's tomb. Other children's games included those with balls (which could also have erotic connotations), *ephidrismos* (a piggyback game), *ostrakinda* (a chasing game), and less structured play such as juggling, balancing sticks or handstands. Adult games include the Greek wine-flicking game of *kottabos*, and dicing was universally popular. (see also BALL GAMES; TOYS) NJW

See Kurke, L. (1999) Ancient Greek board games and how to play them, *CP* 94.3: 247–68; Purcell, N. (1995) Literate games: Roman urban society and the game of alea, *P&P* 147: 3–37.

body, the In pre-classical Greece we find little of the distinction between body and IDENTITY upon which modern, 'scientific' readings of the body are based. The HOMERIC epics assume that a heroic, beautiful body houses a heroic, beautiful soul. Classical Greece adopted an increasingly objective view of the body, constructing it in relation to the SOUL. A proper identity resided in their harmonious interaction. This could be achieved through regimen (Greek *diaita*, Latin *regimen*), described in the works attributed to HIPPOKRATES of Kos. Regimen was an art of living, a system of checks and balances, consumption and expenditure. Its components – deportment, exercise and DIET – were operations upon the body, yet they affected the soul. Attitudes to *aphrodisia* (sexual matters) are regulatory; SEX should be managed according to the body's requirements.

Not all bodies were equal. Deformity was treated as inauspicious throughout antiquity and was a criterion for the exposure of infants. Healthy, male, citizen bodies, celebrated in ART and ATHLETICS, were the standard. Hippokrates testifies to women's bodies as alien, with tubes susceptible to blockages hindering fertility. Lack of DOCTORS' examination suggests women may have participated in these ideas. Suspicion, yet implicit advocacy, of female adornment is common in antiquity; in the *Art of Love*, OVID asserts that the process is repulsive, yet without it women are unworked stone. According to humoural theory children were hot and wet, hence their unruly temperament. Their perceived softness necessitated swaddling, though the practice was less widespread and severe than doctors of Greece and Rome prescribed.

In the classical binarism of body and soul, the soul was superior. Women and children were identified with the body. Most corporeal of all were SLAVES, who lacked *logos* (reason). This led to a disturbing aspect of the Athenian and Roman judicial systems, the use of torture to extract evidence from slaves. Slaves, it was assumed, would lie under normal conditions, but under torture, since they were just bodies, they could only tell the truth, unlike citizens whose *logos* permitted them to lie even in extreme pain. Slaves' bodies were a means of accessing the truth.

In the Roman empire the body appears even more intensely as an externalized object in philosophy and medicine. Roman imperial society before CHRISTIANITY was receptive to bodily austerity, including the restriction of sex to marriage. PLUTARCH urged caution in the marital bed. SORANUS of EPHESOS extolled virginity's benefits. There was fear of any excess which threatened the body and through it the soul. Modern responses to SEXUALITY tend to trace their lineage to this period, when the body's desires were scrutinized; the shift from pleasure to desire permitted the stigmatizing of sexual acts such as pederasty, and of sexuality altogether. Christian MARTYRS and monks paraded indifference to the body. Some heretics, however, notably the GNOSTICS, held that the body was evil; CATHOLICS saw Christ's flesh as evidence of the body's sanctity and espoused bodily resurrection after death. SC

See Brown, P. (1988) *The Body and Society*; Foucault, M. (1985) *The Use of Pleasure*.

Boeotia see BOIOTIA.

Boëthius (Anicius Manlius Severinus Boëthius) Rather like AUGUSTINE (1), he forms a crucial link between the classical world and the Middle Ages. This is due in particular to his most famous work, *On the Consolation of Philosophy*, written in prison while he awaited execution. He has been termed 'the last of the Romans; the first of the scholastics'. He was born into a Roman senatorial family of high rank in the early 480s AD, shortly after the traditional 'end' of the Roman empire in the West. In fact, his life and career bear eloquent testimony to the enduring values of the Roman ARISTOCRACY as it came to terms with its new GOTHIC masters in power at RAVENNA. As a child, Boëthius came under the protection of one of the grandees of the Roman SENATE, Symmachus, who epitomized the continuity of Roman tradition. Boëthius married his daughter, and became CONSUL in 510 and *magister officiorum* in 522. His true home was the library rather than the FORUM; he believed, however, in the Platonic ideal of the philosopher-ruler.

His early works on MUSIC and arithmetic established his reputation, but it was in LOGIC and DIALECTIC that his main interests lay. He determined to translate PLATO and ARISTOTLE into Latin, though the project was not completed and relatively little survives. He was greatly influenced by NEOPLATONISM; a translation and commentary on one of PORPHYRY's works on Aristotle survives.

Boëthius' main philosophical merit is as a compiler and translator rather than as an original thinker. The true significance of his work was that, for many centuries, his translations provided the only knowledge of Aristotle in the west. Boëthius was a Catholic Christian, though the degree and quality of his commitment have been the subject of scholarly debate. He wrote five theological *Tractates*, which attempted to apply philosophical techniques to issues of faith and revelation. However, it was the shifting sands of the complex religious politics of the time that provided the context for his tragic downfall.

The Gothic king Theoderic had successfully operated a policy of toleration and co-operation, if not of integration, between Romans and Goths in Italy. Ironically, religious rapprochement between Rome and Constantinople, initiated in 518 by the emperor Justin (r.518–27), led to the disintegration of this harmony. The Goths were Arian Christians, and Theoderic became alarmed at moves against his co-religionists in the East, as well as suspicious that many in the Roman senate, Boëthius among them, owed their true allegiance to the emperor in Constantinople. Court intrigue played a part also. Boëthius had made enemies in office and was arrested on a charge of treasonable negotiation with Justin. Though imprisoned for some time near Pavia and subjected to torture, he wrote his *Consolation of Philosophy*, a mixture of prose and verse (a Menippean satire). The work demonstrates the depth of Boëthius' immersion in classical culture. The exact date of his execution is not known, probably 525 or early 526. PMB

See Boethius, *Tracts and De Consolatione Philosophiae*, trs. H.F. Stewart and E.K. Rand (1918); Chadwick, H. (1981) *Boethius: the consolations of music, theology and philosophy.*

Boiotia (Boeotia) The most populous region north of Attica and south of Thessaly. Never as unified as Attica or Laconia, the Boiotian league was nevertheless often a rival to Athens and Sparta. All the major towns were in inland basins containing the best farmland in central Greece. Around the Kopaïc basin lay Orchomenos, Lebadeia, Koroneia, Haliartos, Akraiphnion and several smaller towns; Thebes overlooked the Teneric plain; in the Asopos valley, Plataea and Hysiai dominated the upland and Tanagra the lowland portions.

Minyan Orchomenos and Kadmean Thebes were the most famous Boiotian towns of legend. Mycenaean remains confirm the early importance of both, and they remained great rivals in historical times. Various traditions report non-Greek elements in the Boiotian population (among them Phoenician settlers under Kadmos, and Hyantes, Pelasgians and Thracians expelled after the Trojan war). The *Boiôtoi* of the classical period recalled their migration from Thessaly, and observed cults also found in Thessaly (notably Athena Itonia). The Boiotian dialect contained elements of Aiolic (Thessalian) and north-west Greek.

Boiotia was famous for its horse-rearing aristocracy (*Homeric Hymn 3 To Apollo* 222–76), who usually held political power. Hesiod's picture (*Works and Days*) of life at Askra (near Thespiai) at the beginning of the 7th century represents the voice of the freehold farmer calling for justice from the ruling élite. Land ownership was a prerequisite for citizenship in most periods. Boiotia's agrarian orientation gave rise to the image of Boiotians as a tough but dull-witted lot. Exceptions to this invidious stereotype include the early poets Hesiod, Pindar, and Corinna, the Socratic and Pythagorean

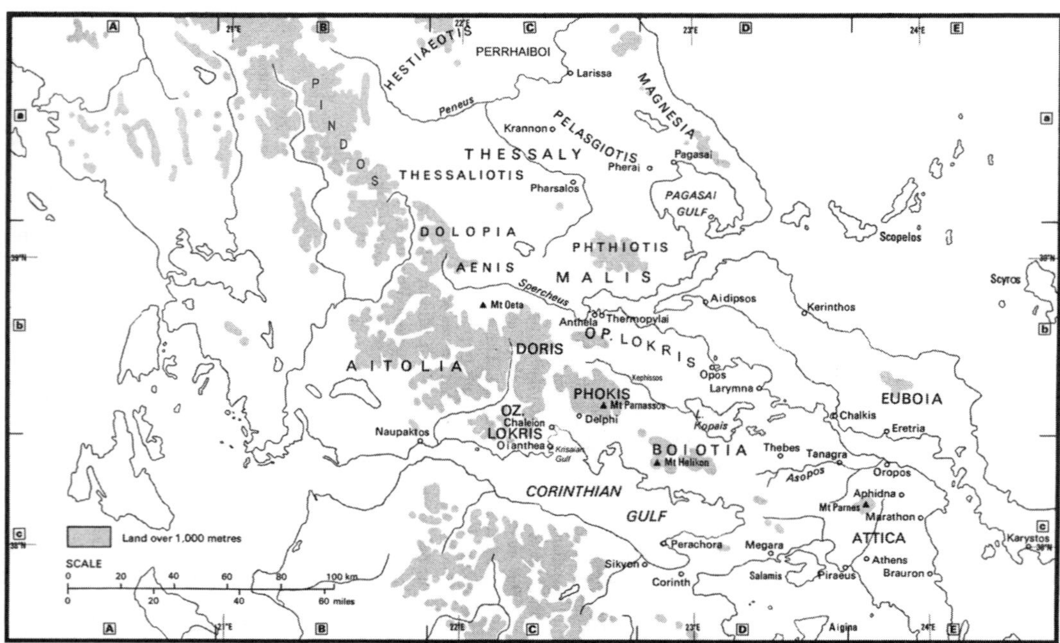

BOIOTIA: map showing cities of classical Boiotia and Central Greece.

PHILOSOPHERS Kebes and Simmias (and reportedly EPAMEINONDAS) and later Krates the CYNIC, and in the Roman period PLUTARCH of CHAIRONEIA.

A coherent historical picture emerges in the later 6th century BC, when Thebes became the leader of a unified Boiotian league and contended with Athens over Plataea. Boiotia medized during the PERSIAN WARS (excepting Thespiai and Plataea), and allied with Sparta during the PELOPONNESIAN WAR. The Boiotian federal constitution is best attested at the beginning of the 4th century in the OXYRHYNCHOS HISTORIAN (16.2–4). Eleven districts each provided 1,000 HOPLITES and 100 CAVALRY, and elected one Boiotarch and 60 councillors as representatives in a federal government usually convening at Thebes. Usually constituted as an OLIGARCHY, the Boiotians embraced DEMOCRACY under Athenian domination between the battles of Tanagra and Oinophyta in 458 and Koroneia in 446, and again under the Theban hegemony of the 4th century, when a popular assembly replaced the federal council as sovereign body. Following the destruction of Thebes by ALEXANDER (335), the Boiotian assembly met on neutral ground at the sanctuary of POSEIDON at Onchestos.

Because of its strategic location, Boiotia saw more than its share of decisive battles: Plataea (479), LEUKTRA (371), Chaironeia (338 and 86). Epameinondas aptly called his homeland 'the dancing-floor of Ares' (Plutarch, *Marcellus* 21.2). MM

See Bintliff, J. L. and Snodgrass, A. M. (1985) The Cambridge/Bradford Boeotian expedition: the first four years, *Journal of Field Archaeology* 12: 123–61; Bintliff, J., ed. (1997) *Recent Developments in the History and Archaeology of Central Greece*; Buck, R. J. (1979) *A History of Boeotia*; (1994) *Boiotia and the Boiotian League*; Fossey, J. M. (1988) *Topography and Population of Ancient Boiotia*; Schachter, A. (1981–94) *Cults of Boeotia*, 4 vols.

 GREECE: (a).

bolts see FURNITURE; LOCKS; WAREHOUSES.

bone ANIMAL bone was a widely available resource in antiquity. Even unworked animal bone can provide important insights into daily life, as it is the refuse from BUTCHERY and food consumption and therefore relates to diets and husbandry practice. Bones were also a source of GLUE and for grease used for candles, OILS and lubricants. Once stripped of meat and marrow, bones had little value but could be carved into a wide range of artefacts. The majority of the bone used in the Greek and Roman world came from domesticated animals, though objects could also be made from deer antlers. Long bones were usually preferred for ease of working. Bone could serve as a cheap alternative to IVORY, and in this capacity was often used for FURNITURE inlay. Thus many Roman COUCHES are decorated with elaborately carved bone. Bone could also be used to copy metal artefacts such as hairpins. The value of these objects would lie in their elaborately carved decoration rather than their raw material. Bone could also be worked into objects of entertainment and play, such as simple dolls or dice, or into functional objects such as knife and sword handles or furniture hinges. HE

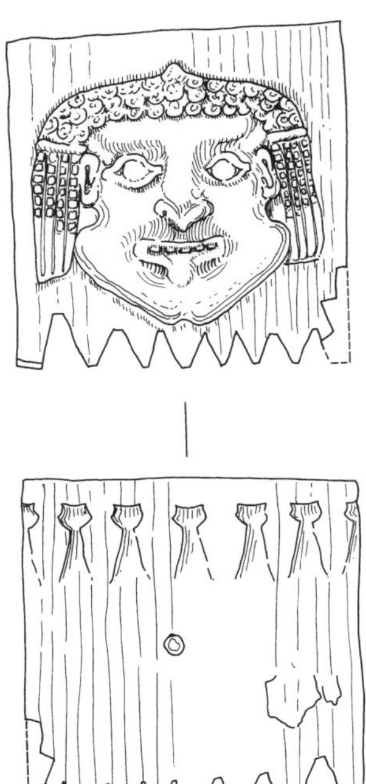

BONE: a bone weaving comb from the temple of Artemis Ortheia near Sparta.

See MacGregor, A. (1985) *Bone, Antler, Ivory and Horn: the technology of skeletal materials since the Roman period*; Reitz, E. J. and Wing, E. S. (1999) *Zooarchaeology*.

books Not until the 5th century BC (coinciding with the SOPHISTS) do we have evidence for books functioning as we would understand them – copies of literary works being circulated, bought and collected. Before this, they had either been recited or written down as aides-memoire for recital. HOMER was certainly the most popular book, and was to remain so throughout the Greek and Roman periods. Major developments took place in the 4th century BC. ISOKRATES is the first author we know of to write specifically for reading (aloud), the earliest literary PAPYRUS from Egypt dates to the late 4th century, and the creation of the ALEXANDRIAN LIBRARY in the early 3rd century not only made a repository for written works but influenced style and documentary practice.

The principal medium for ancient books was papyrus, though parchment or vellum, wooden tablets and (early on) animal skin were probably in common use. But papyrus came to be the norm. Writing papyrus was formed by placing two layers of cut papyrus reed on a flat surface (the second perpendicular to the first), applying pressure, which had the effect of gluing the layers together. Once dry, the result was a very robust writing material. The size of papyrus sheets was restricted, and it is rare to find texts much more than 30 cm high. However, by pasting lengths together it was possible to form substantial rolls, often as much as 10 m wide. In their finest form, these were often supplied with rollers, might

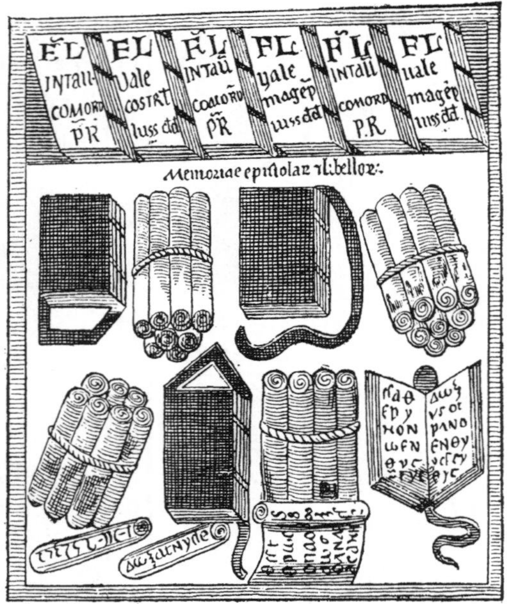

books: illustration from the *Notitia Dignitatum* depicting both scrolls (*volumina*) and flat books (*codices*).

be covered with a protective vellum sheath, and frequently had a label for identification.

Writing on papyrus rolls is not for the faint-hearted reader; there are few concessions. There was no standard column length or width (apart from poetry, where the metre dictated it), margins were small, divisions between words was rare (scribes preferring *scripta continua*), and punctuation, accents and breathings were rarer still.

By the Roman period, the production and trade of books was well established. Cicero, for example, wrote his work for publication. Unfortunately, few Roman books survive. Most ancient texts have been preserved on papyrus from Egypt, where Greek was the spoken and written language and Greek literature seems to have been preferred. This almost certainly skews our knowledge of ancient literature, though in rare cases we have a glimpse of what might have been contained in a personal library. What we know of Latin books suggests that in them, unlike in Greek, words were divided. Romans developed the use of tablets, often made up of a number of leaves, but their purpose seems to have been for business accounts and memoranda rather than literature.

The papyrus codex was the logical progression in book design, possibly developing from earlier forms of notebook in parchment or wood. The codex was formed by folding a papyrus sheet in two to form leaves of equal size. Additional sheets could be pasted into the middle, which made up a codex. Gradually parchment replaced papyrus, and thus the parchment codex became the most widely used medium throughout the late antique world. cepa

See Gavrilov, A. K. (1997) Techniques of reading in classical antiquity, *CQ* 91: 56–73 (with postscript by M. Burnyeat, 74–6); Johnson, W. A. (2000) Towards a sociology of reading in antiquity, *AJP* 121: 593–627; Kenyon, F. G. (1951) *Books and Readers*; Lewis, N. (1974) *Papyrus in Classical Antiquity*; Turner, E. G., 2nd edn, P. J. Parsons (1987) *Greek Manuscripts of the Ancient World*.

boots see Caligula (Gaius); drama; dress, Greek; shoes.

Boscoreale An area c.1–2 km (1 mile) north-north-west of Pompeii. Over a dozen *villae rusticae* (country houses with working farms) were partially excavated there following the 1894 discovery of a decorated silver table setting and other valuables at the 'Pisanella' villa. Among the paintings removed from the 'Villa of P. Fannius Synistor' were a megalographic frieze depicting Macedonian royalty, and fantastic architectural vistas from a *cubiculum* (bedroom or sitting-room) now in the Metropolitan Museum in New York. These murals, the apex of Second Style painting (c.60–40 bc), break down conceptual boundaries between reality and illusion, and evoke almost mythical settings of regal luxury and leisure.

More recently, excavations in 1977–83 at the 'Villa Regina' site revealed the economic, architectural and agricultural layout of a small farm. The main building included work rooms, storerooms and living quarters set around a colonnaded courtyard containing 18 sunken wine *dolia* (storage jars). Palaeobotanical work around the villa has reconstructed orderly, dense rows of vines interspersed with olive, fig, walnut, apricot, peach and almond trees. Grains, vegetables and livestock were also raised. The farm pursued a diversified production strategy centred around wine-making. (see also Boscotrecase; gardens) pwf

See Ling, R. (1996) *Villae rusticae* at Boscoreale, *JRA* 9: 344–50.

villas: (c); wine: (a).

Boscotrecase This territory just west of Boscoreale has revealed several villas. Most important is the 'Villa of Agrippa Postumus' (12 bc–ad 14), identified with the son of Agrippa, Augustus' general, through epigraphic evidence found during the 1903–5 excavations. The elder Agrippa probably began the villa c.21–16 bc; it was finished and decorated posthumously. Its murals, now split between the Metropolitan Museum in New York and the Museo Archeologico, Naples, are the finest examples of early Third Style painting. They were found in the western, residential portion of the villa, in rooms along a terrace with an extensive southern view to the Bay of Naples. Their varied painted landscapes reflect the country outside, filtered through Roman concepts of nature and culture. The Black and Red Rooms feature sacro-idyllic landscape vignettes that idealize the piety and peace of country living, themes popular in the pastoral poems of Virgil and Horace. Two panels survive from the Mythological Room: the respectively tragic and heroic love stories of Polyphemos and Galatea, and Perseus and Andromeda. Slave quarters (nine small cells) and facilities for agricultural production were located in the eastern part of the villa. The villa was destroyed in a 1906 eruption of Vesuvius. pwf

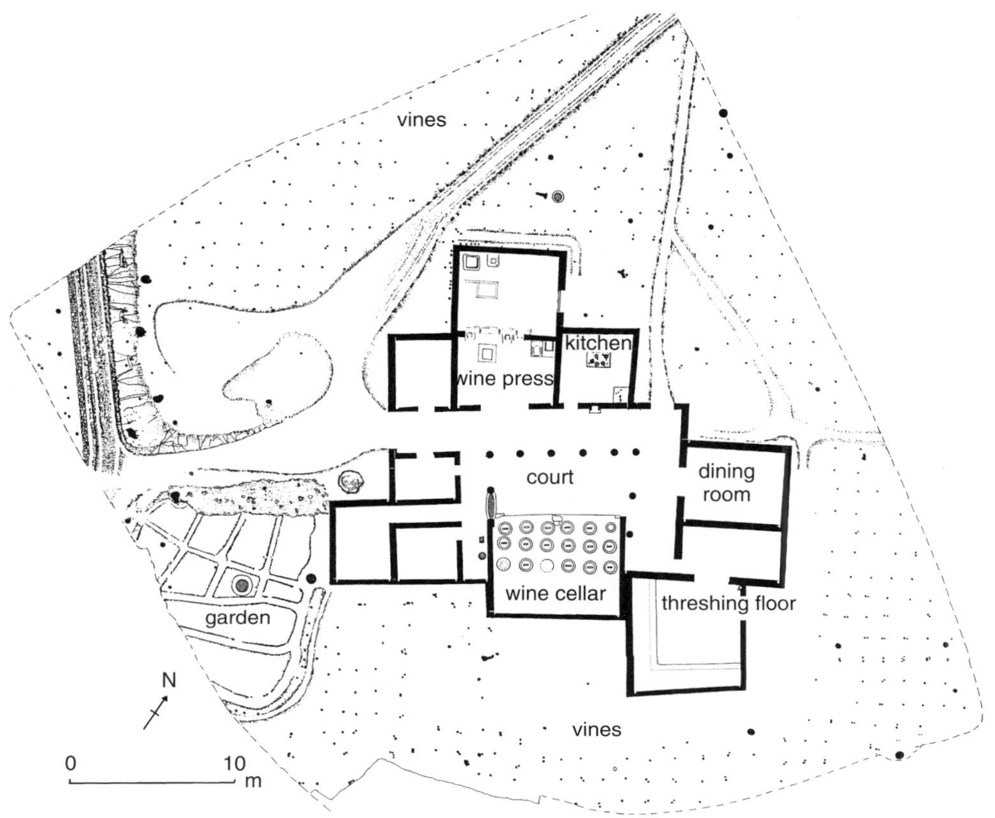

Boscoreale: plan of the La Regina villa showing the attribution of the main rooms and its location within vineyards.

See Blanckenhagen, P. H. von and Alexander, C. (1990) *The Augustan Villa at Boscotrecase.*

Bosporan kingdom Situated on the northern Black sea littoral, the Bosporan kingdom was divided into two parts, European and Asian, by the Bosporos (Kerch strait), which connects the Black sea with the Propontis (sea of Marmara). The European part encompassed the eastern Crimea, where the capital, Pantikapaion (mod. Kerch), was situated. The Asian part covered the whole of the Taman peninsula, which was an archipelago in ancient times. The kingdom was established in about 480 BC as a union of Greek cities against the threat of Scythian encroachment. The first dynasty, the Archaianaktidai (of Milesian origin), a clan of tyrants, stayed in power for 42 years until 438/7 when the Spartokids (of Thracian origin) succeeded them, ruling until 109. In inscriptions they were often styled 'archons'. During the 4th century BC this was a prosperous state. It incorporated the remaining Greek cities, Theodosia and Nymphaion, by force, and the numerous local peoples of the Taman peninsula peacefully. Close links with Athens were established and grain exported there. From the 3rd century BC Sarmatians migrated and settled on its territory. After the death of the last Spartokid, the area became part of the Pontic empire of Mithradates VI. During the first three centuries AD the kingdom fell under the influence of the Roman empire, its kings becoming Roman clients.

The Bosporan kingdom is known as a Greco-barbarian state, not only for having a dynasty of Thracian origin but also from a cultural perspective. In the 5th century BC the culture of its Greek cities was almost entirely Hellenic; from the 4th or 3rd century, by the incorporation of local tribes and Sarmatian migration, it was heavily influenced by the native cultures of these peoples. At the same time the native élites were hellenized. (see also Hellespont and Propontis) GRT

See Hind, J. (1994) The Bosporan kingdom, in *CAH* 6, 476–511 (4th century BC).

Bosporus see Bosporan kingdom; Mediterranean sea.

Boudica (Boudicca) Wife of king Prasutagus, and queen of the Iceni (East Anglia), who led the Britons in revolt against the Romans in AD 60. When Prasutagus died he willed half his kingdom to the Roman empire and half to Boudica and their two daughters, Camorra and Tasca. British law allowed royal inheritance to be passed to daughters; Roman did not. The Roman administrator ignored the will and proceeded to take over the entire kingdom. Enraged, Boudica joined the Iceni forces with those of the Trinobantes, and together they fought back. They attacked and conquered the Roman colony CAMULODUNUM (Colchester) and burned the temple dedicated to CLAUDIUS. The few Roman troops sent from LONDON (Londinium) were not enough, and Camulodunum was quickly overrun and sacked. The procurator fled to GAUL, and Boudica marched on London. Suetonius Paullinus, the governor of BRITANNIA, rushed to London but realized that there were too few troops to defend it and abandoned it, together with nearby Verulamium (St Albans). Paullinus marshalled 10,000 men including AUXILIARIES from local garrisons, and met the enemy at Mancetter. With her daughters in front of her, Boudica drove her chariot among the tribes, shouting encouragement at the BRITONS. But the Romans were victorious and slaughtered the rebel troops. Boudica and her daughters poisoned themselves rather than suffer capture. Today her legacy lives on in the Welsh name 'Buddug' and its English translation, 'Victoria'. LL-J

See Fraser, A. (1988) *The Warrior Queens*; Sealey, P. R. (1997) *The Boudiccan Revolt against Rome*.

 BRITANNIA: (a).

boundaries see FRONTIERS; GEOGRAPHY, ANCIENT; LAND SURVEYING, ROMAN; see also IDENTITY; OTHER, THE; SPACE.

Bourdieu, P. see ANTHROPOLOGY.

Brasidas d.422 BC The most innovative Spartan infantry commander of the PELOPONNESIAN WAR. Following distinguished service in saving the town of Methone at the beginning of the Peloponnesian war, and after holding various political and military appointments, he achieved a series of tactical and strategic successes between 424 and 422 BC at the northern Greek cities of Amphipolis, Torone, Skione and Mende. By encouraging local independence from Athens and establishing garrisons in the region, he was for a time able to deny the Athenians both the human and material capital of the Thraceward districts. He is singled out by THUCYDIDES as a military mind of the first order, in part because of his own successful role against Thucydides in capturing Amphipolis in 424. He was later killed near that town in a successful defence against the Athenians. His death, along with the demise of the Athenian demagogue KLEON at the same battle, helped to bring the ARCHIDAMIAN war (431–421) to a close.

Brasidas' close association with corps of freed HELOTS suggests a military pragmatism rare at Sparta. His genius lay in recognizing and overcoming the inherent weakness of Spartan military doctrine. His enlistment of helots, the free use of light-armed troops, and a willingness to campaign far from LACONIA signalled a radical departure from the traditional Spartan reliance on numerically inferior heavy infantry close to home. His generous character ('showing himself so noble a person in every respect as to leave the firm impression that the others behind were like him') was feltby contemporaries like Thucydides to be integral to his success. He is notable as a rare recipient of divine honours while alive (from the people of Amphipolis, Thucydides 5.11). VDH

See Westlake, H. D. (1968) *Individuals in Thucydides*.

brass see COPPER ALLOYS.

Braudel, F. see *ANNALES* SCHOOL.

Brauron According to a legend, one of the 12 communities that joined together to form the Athenian state. The settlement is located on the east coast of ATTICA in the Erasinos valley, in marshy land near the mouth of the river. The region shows evidence of habitation from the Neolithic period. Its most distinguishing feature is the sanctuary to ARTEMIS Brauronia, one of three separate Artemis cults found on the coast of Attica. Three main buildings have been excavated. The main temple is set on a terrace cut into the hillside. To its south-east, set into a cleft in the rock, is a smaller temple associated with Iphigeneia (cf. Euripides, *Iphigenia in Tauris* 1462–7). The temples date from the late 6th or early 5th century BC. To the north is a pi-shaped stoa built some time in the final quarter of the 5th century.

Ritual use at Brauron is attested from the Geometric period. Dedications associated with childbirth are particularly prevalent. Like the sanctuary of Artemis Mounichia, it was a site for the performance of the *arkteia*, a ritual in which young girls became 'bears'. An ancient explanation of the ritual suggests that all Athenian girls were required to perform this rite before marriage to atone for the killing of a sacred bear. In addition, there was a four-yearly festival, the Brauronia, involving a procession to the shrine. The festival was administered by a board of officials selected in Athens. Our sources also include a reference to a sacred hunt. The sanctuary ceased to function in the 3rd century BC, perhaps because of local flooding. AJLB

See Camp, J. M. (2001) *The Archaeology of Athens* 277–80; Osborne, R. (1985) *Demos: the discovery of classical Attika* 154–72; Papademetriou, J. (1963) The sanctuary of Artemis at Brauron, *Scientific American*, June, 110–20.

 BOIOTIA.

BRAURON: the sanctuary of Artemis at Brauron is set in a marshy, low-lying area (note the hills in the distance). This photograph shows the stoa with its dining rooms used by worshippers making dedications or celebrating festivals.

BREAD: painting of a bread-seller from Pompeii.

bread A central part of the Greek and Roman diet. Due to their climate and generally poor soil, Greeks tended to make bread from barley. Although barley bread tends to be heavy, it was eaten by poor and rich alike. Conversely, Romans principally made bread from wheat and only gave barley bread to soldiers, GLADIATORS and ANIMALS.

Bread was made with or without leavens. CATO describes a bread made without a leaven which was lightened through the process of kneading. PLINY THE ELDER describes a kind of brewer's yeast obtained by skimming froth from grain which had been left to soak. Similarly, Picentian bread was leavened by using flour left to ferment in water for a period of days.

Breads were seasoned with a variety of herbs. Cato gives a recipe for *libum* in which the dough is placed on bay leaves and baked. Other herbs were used, including anise. Breads were also topped with seeds such as poppy and coriander, and could be flavoured by salt, which was either put into the dough or sprinkled on top of the bread after it was baked. Loaves of bread, such as those commonly found in POMPEII, were often divided into different sections before being baked; this served as decoration and allowed the bread to be broken up more easily. Greeks and Romans sometimes flavoured bread by dipping it into milk or WINE, thereby making dry bread more palatable. EACM

See Wilkins, J. M., et al., eds. (1995) *Food in Antiquity.*

 BAKERS: (a).

brick and tile making Sun-dried mudbrick was used for millennia before the classical period. Fired brick and clay, too, were widespread on the Greek mainland by the 7th century BC. Both traditions continue alongside each other throughout the classical period.

The manufacture of sun-dried bricks required the preparation of clay from suitable sources, often strengthened with straw. This was shaped, usually in a mould, and then left to bake hard before use.

For fired brick and tile, clay was dug and prepared. Temper was often added to increase the strength and stability of the final product. Pieces could be shaped by a variety of methods – by moulds, by frames or by hand – and could then be finished and trimmed with a knife or wire. Occasionally stamps were cut into the moulds; alternatively, the products were marked using a metal or wooden stamp. These stamps can indicate military or imperial production. Brick stamps suggest complex webs between landowners, tile makers, WORKSHOP owners and clay sources in private and state control. Other marks could also be made on the material at this point: simple signatures of the tile maker, graffiti, tally marks to keep track of the amount made, keying marks for adherence to mortar, and plaster and ANIMAL prints. They were then left to dry to 'leather' hardness; at that stage, a slip could be applied by brush or hand. The product was then fired. While control over the final product was apparently not as tight as for POTTERY, with examples of green, over-fired tiles often being used in buildings, the external colours were often controlled using oxidizing or reducing conditions within the kiln. This technique could be used to make roofs or walls showing polychromatic designs.

Firing was accomplished at its simplest by a clamp kiln built around the stacked material, but remains of specialized tile and brick kilns are known from the archaeological record. Kilns themselves are found in a variety of shapes and sizes. The different levels of production reflected the variety of requirements for different projects or areas.

The lowest level of production of brick and tile was that made for a single commission, perhaps with future sporadic requirements for repairs or extensions to the original building. These commissions could be carried out by semi-skilled local LABOUR, or by itinerant tile and brick makers. Where the combination of suitable raw materials (clay, water and wood), good communications and demand allowed, permanent centres of brick production existed. These could produce a large quantity of material that was distributed to a surprisingly large area (e.g. Italian tiles are found in North Africa; tiles from southern Turkey are found along the LEVANTINE coast). SHIPWRECK evidence suggests that the TRANSPORT of tiles over long distances is not uncommon. These brick-producing centres were under the control of private individuals, the military or the state. The existence of animal prints (such as those of cattle and GOATS) indicates that even these centres were also involved in other AGRICULTURAL activities. PJEM

See Brodribb, G. (1987) *Roman Brick and Tile*; Le Ny, F. (1988) *Les Fours de tuiliers gallo-romains*; McWhirr, A., ed. (1979) *Roman Brick and Tile.*

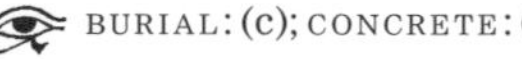 BURIAL: (c); CONCRETE: (a).

bricks see BRICK AND TILE MAKING; *INSTRUMENTUM DOMESTICUM.*

bridges

When classical Greek authors mention bridges, they usually give no details of their construction. More than a few are the work of Persian kings, like DARIUS' bridge over the Danube (built by an architect from SAMOS) or XERXES' pontoon bridge over the HELLESPONT. Southern Greece has few large or perennial rivers, so a bridge (*gephyra*) tended to be constructed only where a stream or ravine had to be crossed for ceremonial or religious purposes. A few stone examples survive, but short bridges and causeways may usually have been made of timber. The early classical bridge over the stream at the sanctuary of Artemis at BRAURON consists of rectangular piles with massive blocks laid across them. From a bridge over the river Kephisos on the Sacred way from Athens to ELEUSIS, people shouted ritual insults (*gephyrismoi*, 'bridgings') at those in the procession. Strabo refers to the bridge joining the island to the mainland of Ortygia at SYRACUSE (also mentioned by THUCYDIDES) as an example of how geography can be changed. By 400 BC a bridge 2 *plethra* in length (according to Strabo; c.60 m long) joined EUBOIA to mainland Greece at Chalkis. PAUSANIAS mentions a similar bridge at KNIDOS, perhaps the fine hellenistic example that partly survives. The hellenistic period saw longer road bridges built with royal funding.

Surviving remains are hard to date. At SPARTA, sources, inscriptions, and archaeology identify more than one bridge but their chronological relationships are not always clear. At Xirokámbi, a few km south of Sparta, is a famous arched road bridge, possibly late hellenistic, spanning the mouth of a ravine. Given its location adjoining the plain, where movement should have been easy, it is uncertain whether it had a practical or ceremonial purpose.

Situated on the banks of the TIBER river, Rome needed bridges from early in its history. According to LIVY (1.33.6), the first bridge, on wooden piles, was built in the reign of Ancus Martius (traditionally 642–617 BC); it caught fire during a battle between the Romans and SABINES not many years later (Livy 1.37.1). On another occasion, Horatius Cocles single-handedly held up the ETRUSCANS at one end of the (wooden) bridge while his fellow-soldiers (successfully) did their utmost to destroy the structure to thwart the enemy's advance (Livy 2.10).

BRIDGES: well-preserved Roman bridge at Merida in southern Spain.

These legendary stories point to the significance of bridges. The development of stone structures reduced the possibility of FIRE, but bridges remained important in military campaigns. To take a single example, CONSTANTINE defeated Maxentius at MILVIAN BRIDGE in AD 312, with immediate consequences for the empire. During the accumulation and history of Rome's empire, military ENGINEERS designed and constructed many bridges, along with a ROAD system, to facilitate troop movement and SUPPLY, both within Roman territory and across the FRONTIER. TRAJAN's bridge over the DANUBE was notable for its length and difficulty of construction (only scant remains survive). The use of the ARCH and the development of CONCRETE were key factors contributing to their permanency.

In times of peace, bridges at the frontier were often locations to collect CUSTOMS DUTIES and to control travel across the frontier. Within the empire, bridges contributed to the economy by easing the TRANSPORT of goods and the travels of officials and inhabitants generally. DGJS, JV

See Hammond, N. G. L. and Roseman, L. J. (1996) The construction of Xerxes' bridge over the Hellespont, *JHS* 116: 88–107; O'Connor, C. (1993) *Roman Bridges*.

Brindisi see BRUNDISIUM.

Britannia One of the last PROVINCES to be added to the ROMAN EMPIRE, following the invasion launched by CLAUDIUS in AD 43 (the earlier campaigns of JULIUS CAESAR had been little more than reconnaissance in force). The subsequent history of the British provinces, until their abandonment c.410, reflects in part the island's marginal position with respect to the empire. Its separation from the continent by a narrow strip of the much-feared ATLANTIC gave the island considerable mystique in Rome, but also posed constraints on TRADE and integration with the core territories. The major part of Britain lies at a more northerly latitude than any other province and was not only surrounded by sea to east, north and west, but was in the same directions bordered by enemies (real or potential). Rather as with DACIA, the province thus had a peculiar character as a geographical salient beyond the main land mass of the empire.

For much of the 1st century AD, Roman intentions appear to have been total conquest of the main island of Britain. This was most nearly achieved by AGRICOLA, governor c.77–83, but troop withdrawals for use elsewhere necessitated a withdrawal to northern England. Thereafter the Romans maintained a frontier within Britain, initially on the Tyne–Solway isthmus (HADRIAN'S WALL) and for a time also further north, on the Forth–Clyde line (ANTONINE WALL). The military garrison comprised around 50,000 troops (about 10 per cent of the empire-wide total). Three LEGIONS were based at Caerleon, Chester and YORK and a large AUXILIARY component was distributed through Wales, northern England and Scotland in smaller FORTS, of which VINDOLANDA is an important example. From the 3rd century, increasing threats by sea led to the construction of additional forts along the south and east coasts of Britain (the 'Saxon Shore' command). Discontent sometimes led to revolts (in 367, for example)

BRITANNIA: map.

and usurpers (Carausius and Allectus in c.286–96; Constantine III in c.407–11).

The British peoples before the conquest appear to have been organized in a series of regional tribal societies, some coalescing in the decades before the invasion into kingdoms. Resistance to the Roman invasion was sustained but mostly disunited. Dramatic evidence of Roman SIEGE assaults on traditional British hillforts has been found at Hod hill and Maiden castle in Dorset, and can be linked with the activities of the future emperor VESPASIAN, who commanded one of the legions of the invasion force. The revolt of queen BOUDICA in AD 60–1 briefly threatened Roman military power, but was cruelly repressed. In consequence, Britannia never lost its military character, necessitating a heavy garrison presence.

Archaeologically, the province is one of the most thoroughly investigated in the empire, with a particular wealth of information on military FORTIFICATIONS, towns, RURAL SETTLEMENT and the material culture of the region. A major distinction can be made between the south and south-east of Britain on the one hand, and the north and west on the other. The former was gradually released from military control and developed urban-based local government. It is also the region where almost all the so-called VILLAS are to be found. The rest of Britain experienced little urban development and mostly retained military garrisons for much of the Roman period, suggesting that a large part of the province may not have been released from military government to civil.

The province was governed in the 1st and 2nd centuries by an imperial legate of senior consular status, often with prior military experience. In common with other parts of the empire, the province was subdivided into two in the early 3rd century, and again into four provinces around AD 300 (with a possible further subdivision added later in the 4th century). Although this will have added to the BUREAUCRACY, the imperial administration of Britain was always based on a small core of people, backed up by the army. The initial capital was based at LONDON, which may eventually have been granted the status of *colonia*, joining at this rank three legionary COLONIES (Colchester, Lincoln and Gloucester) and another of the provincial capitals, York. With the exception of Verulamium (St Albans) there is no certain evidence that other British towns achieved promotion to *municipium* rank, and urban development appears to have been slow and decline early in the remaining towns. The most extensively excavated sites are the 'greenfield' locations, such as Silchester, Caerwent and Verulamium, where the Roman towns are not overlain by medieval and modern successors. With only about 22 main towns, urban density is low compared with some regions, but there were something like 100 minor towns, road stations and substantial agglomerations (most closely linked to the Roman road systems). Recent research has shown that these may have played an important economic role in the province, while a few can be shown to have served a specialized role as spa towns and religious centres (as did BATH).

'Villas' are commonly believed to have been typical of Roman rural settlement, but the class shows huge internal variety, from simple rectangular cottage-style ranges to palatial structures covering several hectares and with more than 20 separate rooms (as at FISHBOURNE). In numerical terms, villas were by no means the norm: c.2,000 examples known must be set against c.70,000 other rural sites recorded for England alone (the latter including 'villages', farmsteads of traditional Iron Age type, including roundhouses and other timber buildings). The picture now emerging is of a countryside that was far less influenced by Roman fashions than was once imagined.

The ECONOMY appears to have been dominated by farming, building on a strong Iron Age tradition. There is also evidence to suggest that Britain's substantial mineral reserves were exploited by the Romans, especially in the early phases of the conquest. Overall, the economic integration of Britain with the rest of the empire appears to have been constrained by distance and the heavy military presence, which through its supply needs may have inhibited economic development of the north and west in particular. DJM

See Jones, B. and Mattingly, D. (2002) *An Atlas of Roman Britain*; Millett, M. (1990) *The Romanization of Britain*; Salway, P. (1980) *The Oxford History of Roman Britain*.

British Isles and Britons The Romans referred to the peoples of the southern part of the British Isles as *Britanni* (Britons) and those of the northern part as *Britones*. After the conquest of AD 41, they named their new civil province *Britannia*. Greek EXPLORERS first drew the attention of the MEDITERRANEAN world to what is now Britain. The earliest known voyager was the 6th-century BC mariner whose account of a journey along the ATLANTIC coasts (a document known as the Massiliote Periplus) was later utilized in Avienus' *Ora Maritima* (*Shores of the Sea*). In c.300 BC, another Greek SAILOR, Pytheas, travelled through the straits of Gibraltar into the Atlantic and recorded his experiences in *On the Ocean*. From these and other accounts, we glimpse something of the ARCHAEOLOGICALLY attested TRADE networks binding communities along the Atlantic coastlines of Spain, Brittany and the British Isles in the centuries before JULIUS CAESAR's two expeditions to the south-east tip of England (55 and 54 BC) brought the Britons more firmly into classical view.

Caesar's account of his dealing with the Trinovantes and other peoples of the south-east forms one of the many strands of evidence enabling archaeologists to build up a detailed picture of the polities ('tribes') of the British Isles in the later Iron Age. Other important strands include archaeological and numismatic data, the *Annals* and *Agricola* of TACITUS, and the administrative structure of the subsequent Roman province, which 'froze' many earlier political boundaries.

In the south-east (the part of pre-conquest Britain about which the Romans knew by far the best), the most powerful pre-conquest peoples were the Trinovantes of Essex and the Catuvellauni, whose 'capital' lay at Verulamium (St Albans) in Hertfordshire. By the time of the CLAUDIAN conquest, these two peoples had united as a single power block, and in terms of numismatic data, at least, they are indistinguishable. To the south of the Thames lay the Cantii (or Cantiaci) of Kent and the Atrebates of Sussex, Surrey and Hampshire. East Anglia was dominated by the Iceni, northern England by the Parisi and Brigantes. Further to the north, in lowland Scotland, lay the Votadini, and beyond these the Maeatae and Caledones, about whom information remained sketchy long after the conquest. The first detailed references to the northernmost peoples appear in the work of CASSIUS DIO at the very end of the 2nd century (*Epitome* 76).

Were the Britons CELTS? It has long been believed that there were 'Celtic' invasions of the British Isles. Caesar recorded that Belgae from northern GAUL had settled in southern Britain, and some tribal names are found both on the continent and in Britain (Atrebates, Parisi). Modern linguistic studies have shown that the indigenous tongues of the British and the Irish were closely related to those of the continental Gauls, and that all were members of the Celtic family of languages. There is also evidence that certain institutions (such as DRUIDISM) were common to Britons and Gauls. On the other hand, not a single classical writer referred to the Britons as Celts, and many archaeologists today would question whether the Britons ever identified themselves as such. JW

British Isles and Britons: map showing approximate locations of principal indigenous peoples both within and outside the province.

bronze see copper alloys; figurines, bronze; metallurgy; sculpture.

Brundisium (mod. Brindisi) An important port city of the Messapians on the north-east coast of Italy, at which a Latin colony was founded in 244 BC. It was strategically important in the wars with Hannibal and in the conquest of Macedonia and Greece. Its location at the end of the Via Appia allowed the city to become an important port linking the sea crossing to Greece with land communications to Rome. Cicero, returning from exile in 57 BC, arrived in the city on the anniversary not only of his daughter's birth but also that of the city itself. It was the entry point for all those crossing from Greece. The strategic importance of Brundisium is confirmed by Caesar's attempt in 49 BC to cut off Pompey's access to the port. The linkage of a sea crossing and the transport of armies by land caused the continued importance of the city; for example, Trajan set out for his Dacian campaigns from here in AD 105. Communications were also enhanced by Trajan's construction of a new road from Beneventum to Brundisium in AD 109. Standing remains of the city walls and other parts of the city can be seen today, alongside a museum displaying recent investigations of underwater archaeology and other finds. RL

Italy: (a).

Brutus The Roman name Brutus, meaning something like 'stupid', is mainly associated with two men who helped to end tyranny. According to Livy, Lucius

Junius Brutus pretended to be mentally deficient to avoid suspicion before the murder of TARQUINIUS SUPERBUS. He established the Roman REPUBLIC and was one of its first CONSULS in 509 BC. The date is suspect, but Brutus was probably a historical person who advanced Republican principles.

Marcus Junius Brutus was an assassin of JULIUS CAESAR. Born c.85 BC, he was not advanced in his career when Caesar defeated POMPEY, whose side Brutus had joined. Nevertheless, Caesar made him governor of Cisalpine GAUL in 46 and favoured him. Brutus joined the conspiracy for patriotic reasons, and soon left Rome to become a leader of forces against ANTONY and Octavian. He minted coins glorifying the Ides of March, but after defeat at PHILIPPI on 23 October 42 he committed SUICIDE. Son-in-law of CATO, he professed STOIC philosophy, and CICERO dedicated works to him. Beyond letters to Cicero, little survives, but he wrote books on philosophical topics, epitomes of histories, and POETRY. He notoriously charged 48 per cent interest on a loan to inhabitants of Cyprus. SHAKESPEARE's Antony calls him the 'noblest Roman', and the dying Caesar exclaims, 'you too, Brutus?' SUETONIUS and CASSIUS DIO report that the words, in Greek, were 'you too, my son?' – an expression of surprise, not of paternity, if actually spoken. JV

See Livy, book 1; Plutarch, *Julius Caesar, Brutus*; Clarke, M. L. (1981) *The Noblest Roman*; William Shakespeare, *Julius Caesar*.

 AUGUSTUS: (a).

bucchero see ETRURIA AND ETRUSCANS.

bulls Bulls were more important for their symbolic than for their economic value in classical antiquity. In the more arid parts of the MEDITERRANEAN region fewer CATTLE were kept than SHEEP and GOATS. A single bull can serve many cows, so it was not necessary for every farmer to own a bull. Since they are comparatively useless animals, which need large amounts of food and water, require secure housing, and were often too dangerous and unpredictable to use for traction, it is likely that only relatively wealthy farmers bothered to keep them.

In contrast, the significance of bulls as symbols of masculine power and VIOLENCE, especially divine power, was widespread in ancient religion and MYTH. They were a core element of the MINOAN religion of Bronze Age CRETE, though we do not now understand what bulls meant to Minoans. Bulls were regularly represented together with figures who seem to be divinities, particularly on seal-stones. Most famous are the images of 'bull-leapers': acrobats leaping over the horns of charging long-horned bulls and onto their backs. The most famous of these is a fresco in the PALACE at KNOSSOS, but bull-leapers appear on GEMS and seals as well. The significance of the practice is not clear, though it is generally agreed to be ritual in inspiration. The so-called 'Horns of Consecration' which feature regularly in Minoan art and architecture are often thought to be symbolic representations of bulls' horns. Bulls also appear as a symbolic element in MYCENAEAN art.

Later Greek mythology 'remembered' the Cretan fixation with bulls in the story of the Minotaur, a fierce monster who lived in the Labyrinth, a huge maze at Knossos. He was the illicit offspring of queen Pasiphaë's sexual encounter with a bull. He was defeated by the Athenian hero THESEUS, who broke the Minotaur's bad habit of eating seven young men and maidens every year. Another of Theseus' legendary exploits was the capture of a vicious bull from the well-watered plain of MARATHON, north of Athens. In Greek myth the bull was often associated with the god ZEUS. In the story of the rape of Europa, Zeus disguises himself as a bull and carries her off.

Extraordinarily, there is no evidence in Greek cult practice for the SACRIFICE of bulls. The Athenian FESTIVAL of the Bouphonia, the 'ox-killing', to Zeus Polieus (guardian of the city), featured the sacrifice of a plough-ox, not a bull. Athenian VASE-PAINTINGS occasionally depict ploughing with bulls. Given the potential dangers of this practice, these scenes are normally interpreted as ritual, though it is not clear with what ritual they were associated.

The bull maintained considerable symbolic significance in Roman religion. In the cult of MITHRAS, popular among Roman soldiers, Mithras' slaughter of a bull as a sacrifice was the central myth. This was regularly, and violently, depicted in painting and sculpture in his sanctuaries. The 'bull killing' (*taurobolium*) for the well-being of the EMPEROR was a key element in the cult of Magna Mater at OSTIA. Stylized bulls' skulls with horns, *boukrania*, were often used as a decorative element in Roman art and appear regularly on SARCOPHAGI. LF

See Beard, M. et al. (1998) *Religions of Rome*.

bureaucracy The bureaucratic practice of the Greek and Roman worlds is difficult to reconstruct because of poor evidence. From literary and EPIGRAPHIC sources we know that the sovereign assemblies of Greek *poleis* had committees or *boulai* that prepared their agenda, but the exact nature of their role, and the roles of officials, remains obscure. It is reasonable to assume that records or minutes of meetings and other business were kept (if only because inscriptions record details that would be difficult to remember otherwise). By the 4th century, not only cities but also important persons had staff who kept copies of outgoing correspondence. When Alexander's secretary, Eumenes, lost his papers in a fire he was able to replace them by writing to Alexander's other subordinates and requesting copies. The inscribed letters of hellenistic rulers sometimes quote directly from preceding correspondence, showing that files were kept. In the ROMAN REPUBLIC, similarly, records of business must have been kept. In the imperial period we see the development of more complicated bureaucracy, most notably imperial secretaries (fully developed under CLAUDIUS) and a more structured officialdom. More centralized government developed, and by the reign of TRAJAN it appears that provincial governors were increasingly directed from the office of the EMPEROR.

But for evidence of Greek PAPYRI from Ptolemaic and Roman Egypt, we would be largely ignorant of how invasive ancient bureaucracy was. An extraordinary number of state-generated documents are testament to a highly developed and centralized bureaucracy and system of record-keeping. Letters exchanged between officials, tax registers, CENSUS documents, and memoranda (and copies of each, in duplicate and triplicate) all served either to extend the state's power over individuals, or to provide some vestige of protection for an individual against that power. Literacy was not required for either purpose.

It is not clear how far this culture of documentation and bureaucracy extended throughout the Roman world, though with finds of similar documents beginning to appear in countries such as Britain (e.g. Vindolanda), Syria and Libya, it is beginning to look as though documentary practices attested in Egypt were common to Roman provinces. At least we can be sure that, in its usual manner, bureaucracy certainly increased over time. CEPA

See Beard, M. et al. (1993) *Literacy in the Roman World*; Welles, C. B. (1934) *Royal Correspondence in the Hellenistic Period*.

 equestrians: (b).

burial

A burial is part of a funeral, which is part of a larger set of rituals by which the living separate a deceased person from themselves. Ancient burials therefore tell us most about ritual practices and representations of the social order. Religious beliefs determined much in the burial rituals, but it is difficult to infer such beliefs directly from the material remains, except in unusual cases like a late 4th-century BC grave at Derveni in Macedonia, which contained a papyrus text describing the afterlife. Grave goods buried with the dead are also a major source of information about material culture, and the physical remains of the dead are one of the most important sources for economic historians (though classical archaeologists have been slow to exploit this evidence). Burials are important because they are the most visible part of ancient death-rituals. Hundreds of thousands of graves have been excavated and published from the Greco-Roman world.

Burial was normally performed by the deceased's family, often (at least in theory) by those kin who inherited from the deceased. Burial at public expense was normally a great honour, reserved in classical Athens for the war dead (see especially Thucydides 2.34–46) and ambassadors. Some communities passed laws limiting the scale of burials in order to control aristocratic competition, but the actual form of burials was usually left to individual and family wishes. In some periods there was much consistency in burial types across large areas (e.g. the Roman empire after the 3rd century AD); at other times there was huge variation within even a single community (e.g. Athens in the 8th century BC). Sometimes age, sex and wealth differences were given strong expression in burial, while at other times a single burial type might be favoured for all members of the community. In most periods, burials were grouped in cemeteries outside settlements (most often on the roads leading away from towns), organized according to kinship. However, in a few periods (especially early Iron Age Greece and late antiquity) the dead might be buried within the settlement or even under house floors. These locations were particularly favoured for those dying in childhood.

Given such variation, there are many exceptions to any general statement about ancient burial, but a few general trends can be discerned. In the late Bronze Age Aegean, inhumation dominated, in chamber tombs containing two or three skeletons. Grave goods were generally poor, but a few more sumptuous burials are known, and the royal shaft graves at Mycenae had spectacular offerings. A handful of sites have enormous tholos ('beehive') tombs, which were robbed in antiquity.

After 1100 BC there was a shift toward individual inhumation, often in stone-lined 'cist' graves, sometimes contracted and sometimes supine. At Athens cremation was preferred, the ashes being put in clay urns. Grave goods were very poor in most regions, and child burials are generally rare. Within any particular area of Greece burials were homogeneous, but variation between regions was very high across the early Iron Age. The great exception to any generalization are the hero burials at Lefkandí, c.1000–950 BC, which were marked by an enormous mound and contained rich heirlooms. Variability increased in the late 8th century, but by 700 large, homogeneous, poor inhumation cemeteries were the norm, and warrior burials were very rare. A few archaic aristocratic tombs with mounds and sculptures are known (particularly from Attica), but grave goods were nearly always poor. The trend toward simplicity peaked in the 5th century, when even gravestones were rare. Regional variability also declined; from the 5th century onward, extended inhumations were the norm all over Greece. Cremations continued to occur, but burning the dead seems to have had links to masculinity, heroic status and war.

The simplicity of archaic–classical graves and the absence of strong ritual distinctions may have been linked to egalitarianism and democracy. But beginning around 425, this long-lived trend was reversed. Private monuments, almost absent through most of the 5th century, returned. Funerary spending escalated through the 4th century, and after 336 Macedonian vaulted tombs, some with painted walls, caught on, along with burial mounds and other heroizing imagery. Warrior burials and rich grave goods also returned, and gold-leaf diadems were quite common.

Greeks and Macedonians exported hellenistic burial styles to the Near East in the 3rd century BC, where they were mixed with indigenous customs. After the incorporation of the Greek East into the Roman empire, there was a broad division in the first two centuries AD between Latin-speaking cremating provinces and Greek-speaking inhuming provinces. Between AD 170 and 200 the highest social circles at Rome switched to inhumation, which took over the whole Western empire in the 3rd century, in the biggest change of rituals in ancient history. There is no good evidence that Christianity caused the shift to inhumation – élite imitation of Greek behaviour, followed by the poor emulating the rich, seems more likely – but the new rite worked well for the Christian communities of the 4th and 5th centuries. Christian burials were often laid out east–west, with such simple grave goods that it can be hard to date graves between AD 200 and 600.

In the later Roman empire the use of space became the primary means of marking rank in burial. The graves of saints might be commemorated with basilicas, and high-status individuals then sought burial as close as possible to the saints. IM

See Kurtz, D. and Boardman, J. (1971) *Greek Burial Customs*; Morris, I. (1992) *Death-ritual and Social Structure in Classical Antiquity*; Sourvinou-Inwood, C. (1995) *'Reading' Greek Death*.

Roman burials could be either cremations or inhumations. During the REPUBLIC cremation seems to have been the most widespread. Certain families, however, traditionally adhered to inhumation burial: the CORNELII did not change their habit of inhuming their dead until 78 BC. Before about 100 BC Roman burials were simple and have not left many archaeological traces. Neither are there many epitaphs from this period. Subsequently, TOMBS became more spectacular. Burials were not allowed within the city limits (*POMERIUM*) for hygienic and religious reasons. Therefore the ROADS leading out of any Roman town or city were lined with tombs, many still visible today. Death and burial in ROME were – just like in all other societies – surrounded by a number of RITUALS depending on the status of the deceased and his or her family. Members of the ARISTOCRACY would be followed to their grave by a huge procession, including previously deceased family members represented by actors wearing MASKS. Those without relatives or means were unceremoniously thrown in pits, the so-called *puticuli* (literally 'places to rot'), together with all kinds of waste. When they were excavated in the late 19th century, their contents and stench were still appalling after nearly 2,000 years.

Burial and commemoration were important to the Romans, and even very poor people would obtain a tomb, provided they had relatives left to take care of it. Often these burials did not have an inscribed tombstone but only the neck of an AMPHORA to mark the tomb's location, so that relatives could perform the annual rituals in connection with the festivals for the dead. Examples of this type of burial can be found at Isola Sacra between OSTIA and PORTUS, close to Rome. People with few or no relatives, but with enough funds, could become members of a FUNERAL CLUB (*collegium funeraticum*) that would see to their burial. Membership was open to all who could pay the entrance fee, including SLAVES. As their burial places, these clubs usually used *columbaria*, which means 'dovecots'; contrary to the frequent statements of modern scholars, the word is not a modern invention but was used by the ancients to denote this particular structure. *Columbaria* were frequently underground and could contain as many as 3,000 burials, but usually would only hold a few hundred. Urns with the remains of the deceased were placed in little niches – hence the name – in several rows quite close to each other. Underneath the niche a small plaque

BURIAL, ROMAN: (a) *columbarium* or tomb with multiple cremation burials (each arched *loculus* contains space for a pair of urns), Ostia.

BURIAL, ROMAN: (b) child inhumation inside an amphora (the upper half removed during excavation to expose the skeleton), Leptiminus.

BURIAL, ROMAN: (c) tile cover over an adult inhumation from Leptiminus (ancient ground level was c.1 m above the top of the tile structure).

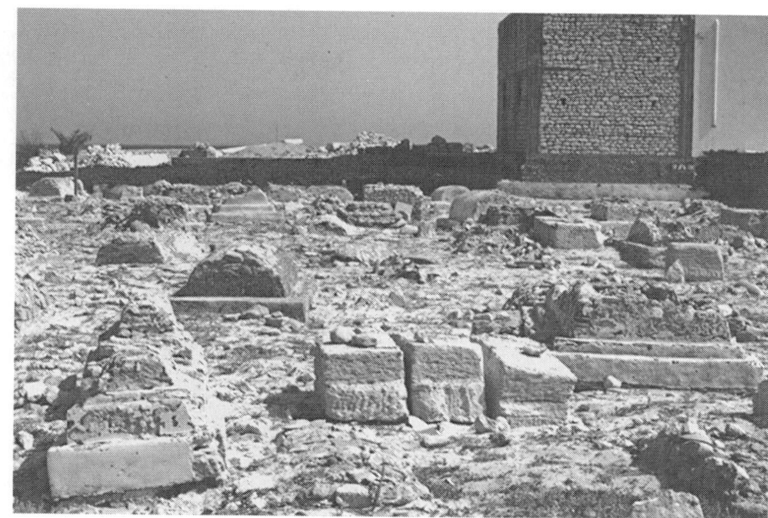

BURIAL, ROMAN: (d) dense surface markers over burials at Sullechtum.

BURIAL, ROMAN: (e) funerary stele and offering tables marked many graves, as here at Timgad.

might be inscribed with the name of the deceased, his or her age at death and perhaps a characterizing epithet. *Columbaria* were not used only by burial clubs; many were owned by the imperial and other aristocratic families in Rome as burial places for their dependants. In some *columbaria*, niches could be bought and sold freely by individuals. *Columbaria* are primarily found in the city of Rome, where people lived their lives in densely populated APARTMENT BUILDINGS and after their death were deposited in rows of niches on top of each other. This type of burial was an inexpensive but decent way of obtaining a personal burial. *Columbaria* were meant for cremation burials, and no new *columbaria* were built after the Romans changed their habit from cremation to predominantly inhumation. Secondary burials in SARCOPHAGI are, however, found in *columbaria*.

The tombs lining the roads outside the city were meant as burial places either for an entire HOUSEHOLD or for single persons commemorated by one or two relatives. In the late Republican and early imperial periods (c.100 BC–AD 100), most were cremation tombs. The tombs designed to contain the burials of an entire household are sometimes called family tombs, but this term is somewhat misleading since these tombs were meant as burial places for the masters of the household, their children, slaves and FREEDMEN and FREEDWOMEN, and all their descendants. A more appropriate name would thus be household tombs. The more modest examples were small plots of land with an inscription defining the size of the plot and who was entitled to be buried there. Frequently, however, household tombs were big buildings, richly decorated with frescoes and MOSAICS, showing that the owners of these mausolea were wealthy people with many dependants. Good examples can be seen at Isola Sacra. The tombs at this cemetery were built c.AD 100, that is, in the period of transition from cremation to inhumation in Roman society. This means that some of the tombs originally were built with niches for funerary urns like those in *columbaria*, but later modified with *arcosolia* for sarcophagus burials. It is not known why the Romans changed their burial habits about this time. Nothing indicates that religious considerations lie behind the transition. Possibly, the increased concern for the individual discernible in many areas of life at this time played a role.

Both JEWS and CHRISTIANS were opposed to cremation and preferred inhumation for religious reasons. The Jewish CATACOMBS in Rome have been excavated, but are inaccessible because of their poor condition, but the epitaphs from Jewish burials throw considerable light on the lives of Jews in Rome. The earliest Christian burials are impossible to distinguish from contemporary PAGAN ones. Not until the Christians had developed an EPIGRAPHICAL language of their own, together with specifically Christian burial places, do they become discernible. Like Jews, Christians buried their dead in catacombs, with the earliest Christian catacombs dating from about AD 300. Initially, catacombs were dug out under properties owned by wealthy members of the CHURCH, frequently in connection with earlier pagan *columbaria*

BURIAL, ROMAN: (f) impressive monuments and mausolea often flanked the main approach roads to a city, as here at Pompeii.

BUTCHERY: (a) 'pig's head anybody?' – relief of Roman butcher's shop.

BUTCHERY: (b) young pigs and game hanging outside a butcher's shop from the Villa Albani.

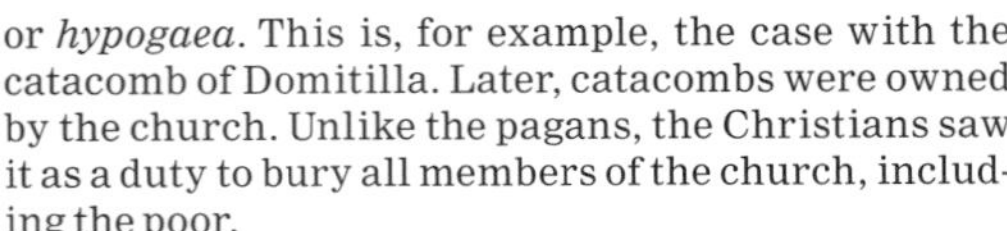

or *hypogaea*. This is, for example, the case with the catacomb of Domitilla. Later, catacombs were owned by the church. Unlike the pagans, the Christians saw it as a duty to bury all members of the church, including the poor.

The thousands of tombstones put up to commemorate the deceased on pagan, Jewish and Christian tombs remain the most important written source for our understanding of family structure and private morals of the huge majority of people who are not mentioned in literature because they did not belong to the ruling classes. HSN

See Toynbee, J. M. C. (1971) *Death and Burial in the Roman World*.

 TOMBS: (a)–(b).

butchery In the Greek world, butchery was mostly done by PRIESTS, since almost all MEAT eaten came from ritually slaughtered, sacrificial ANIMALS. Priests were normally paid for their work as butchers with the skins of sacrificed animals and sometimes a portion of the meat as well. Surplus meat from private or state SACRIFICES was then sold in the marketplace by retailers. Abundant finds of animal BONES with butchery marks found in sanctuary sites suggest that this was where most butchery was done. In contrast, only very small numbers of animal bones are found in or near Greek private houses, suggesting that people rarely cooked or ate meat on the bone at home. The evidence of VASE-PAINTING also suggests that butchers worked out of doors: one depiction shows the joint of meat hanging from a tree.

In the Roman world there is evidence for larger-scale, specialist trade in meat. Most Roman towns in Italy appear to have had livestock MARKETS, which according to VARRO (*On Agriculture* 2.1.20) sold animals for sacrificial victims to specific standards. Not all meat animals were ritually slaughtered. Specialist butchers (*lanii*) killed the animals, but market traders (*macelli*) also appear to have sold butchered meat. Roman butchery was developed into a fine art, and wealthy customers bought the choicest cuts. Many parts of PIGS, SHEEP and CATTLE were processed before selling (head, feet, offal). Much pork, in particular, was salted and made into hams and sausages. LF

See Frayn, J. (1995) The Roman meat trade, in J. Wilkins, D. Harvey and M. Dobson, eds., *Food in Antiquity* 107–14; Jameson, M. H. (1988) Sacrifice and animal husbandry in classical Greece, in C. R. Whittaker, ed., *Pastoral Economies in Classical Antiquity* 87–119.

 SACRIFICE: (a), (c).

Byblos see LEVANT; LITERACY, GREEK; PHOENICIA AND PHOENICIANS.

Byzacena see AFRICA, ROMAN; LEPTIMINUS; THAPSUS.

Byzantion (Byzantium) see CONSTANTINOPLE.

Cadiz see GADES.

Caecilii Metelli see METELLI.

Caelestis see TANIT; THUGGA.

Caere see CERVETERI.

Caesar (as title) Originally a *cognomen* of the IULII, of whom the most famous was Gaius JULIUS CAESAR, assassinated in 44 BC. Octavian, his heir, took his name, and subsequently all emperors took the name Caesar with the title AUGUSTUS. According to the *HISTORIA AUGUSTA* (*Verus* 1–2), Verus was the first, as he did not become emperor, to take the name Caesar without ever receiving any of the other titles. From this period Caesar became the title of the emperor-designate, who, until the establishment of the TETRARCHY, was preferably the son of the reigning emperor. Under the Tetrarchy DIOCLETIAN attempted to bypass the tradition of blood inheritance by establishing two senior rulers, Augusti, who each had a named junior partner, a Caesar. The Tetrarchic system did not long survive Diocletian's retirement in 305, but the tradition of naming an heir or heirs by appointing them Caesar persisted throughout the later empire. MEH

Caesar, Julius see JULIUS CAESAR.

Caesarea in Mauretania (mod. Cherchel) Caesarea lay on the coast of Algeria, where its HARBOUR was a matter of note. Originating as a Punic trading station, known as Iol, there is archaeological evidence of occupation from the 6th century BC. During the 2nd century BC, Iol became a Numidian royal centre, and its most illustrious king was Juba II, who ruled from 25 BC to AD 23. Educated in Rome, and a friend of AUGUSTUS, Juba sought to convert his city (which he renamed Caesarea) into a Greco-Roman showpiece. Surviving buildings include a THEATRE and AMPHITHEATRE, and there is a remarkable collection of SCULPTURE. His son Ptolemy was murdered in AD 40, at which time Caesarea became capital of the new province of Mauretania Caesariensis. Administered by a procurator, it soon prospered. The walls enclosed 370 ha (910 acres), and there were at least three sets of BATHS and a CIRCUS. Much wealth came from OLIVE OIL production in the hinterland, an AGRICULTURAL bounty illustrated in the site's famous MOSAICS. The Severan period saw considerable refurbishment of the city, especially through Publius Aelius Peregrinus Rogatus, procurator in 201; the FORUM was also enlarged. Taken in the revolt led by Firmus but recaptured in 373, in 429 it fell to the VANDALS. Around this time, the civic centre was remodelled, with the construction of one or two CHURCHES and a MARKET. Decay set in about 500, and the Byzantine reconquest of 533–4 is so far unmarked archaeologically. TWP

See Leveau, P. (1984) *Caesarea de Maurétanie*; Potter, T.W. (195) *Towns in Late Antiquity*.

 AFRICA, ROMAN: (a).

Caesarea Maritima Herodian-period and Roman city located in modern Israel. Caesarea developed on the site of a minor hellenistic settlement called Strato's Tower that formed part of the Roman province of SYRIA as settled by POMPEY. Assigned to the kingdom of HEROD (Herodes) the Great by OCTAVIAN and rebuilt extensively as a fortified city between 22 and 10/9 BC, it was renamed Caesarea in honour of the emperor. After serving as Herod's residence, it became the seat of the Roman procuratorial administration of JUDAEA from AD 6 to 41. The city saw severe conflict between the JEWISH and Greek–Syrian elements of its population from the later 50s, with a constitutional dispute resolved in the favour of the Greek–Syrians after an appeal to NERO. Conflict continued, and in AD 66 a massacre of the Jewish population (20,000 individuals in one hour according to Josephus, *Jewish War* 2.18.1) provoked the first Jewish revolt. After serving as the Roman headquarters, Caesarea was made a *colonia* by VESPASIAN. With the destruction of JERUSALEM, it became the main city and provincial capital of Roman Judaea and subsequently (under SEVERUS ALEXANDER) the *metropolis* of Syria Palaestina.

Caesarea has seen extensive archaeological study on land and underwater in recent decades. Perhaps the most impressive result has been increased knowledge of the great artificial harbour (built up from concrete breakwaters) that formed a major element in Herod's reconstruction of the city. NDP

See Holum, K. G. et al. (1988) *King Herod's Dream*; Levine, L. I. (1975) *Caesarea under Roman Rule*.

 JUDAEA.

calendars

Most Greek communities had calendars, which were developed very early in Greek history. However, since Greece was a multiplicity of different states there was no single common calendar, and different names were regularly used for different months. Typically the name of a god or a festival was used as the month's name. In Athens, for example, Poseideon was a month named after the god POSEIDON, while Anthesterion was named after the festival of Anthesteria, held in honour of DIONYSOS and to celebrate the new WINE.

Calendars were an integral part of time-reckoning, but the inherent discrepancy between the lunar and solar years required the Greeks to intercalate – to add, every few years, a 13th month to the normal 12.

CALENDARS: (a) names of Athenian months.

Athenian festival month name	Equivalent modern month
Hekatombaion	July/August
Metageitnion	August/September
Boedromion	September/October
Pyanopsion	October/November
Maimakterion	November/December
Posideon	December/January
Gamelion	January/February
Anthesterion	February/March
Elaphebolion	March/April
Mounychion	April/May
Thargelion	May/June
Skirophorion	June/July

A month was usually reckoned as the time taken for the passing of one phase of the MOON, which alternates between 29 and 30 days since the moon takes on average c.29.53 days to orbit the earth (with considerable variations). Twelve phases or lunations (c.354.4 days) are about 11 days short of a solar year (the time the earth takes to complete one orbit of the sun, c.365.24 days). A normal year thus had 354 (±1) days, a leap year 384 (±1) days. The use of leap years was a way of making sure that the moon-based calendar did not fall out of step with the passing of the seasons and the AGRICULTURAL year. The practice of intercalation, however, was subject to local decision and thus inconsistent.

ASTRONOMERS in antiquity devised various schemes to harmonize the solar and lunar years. The 'Metonic cycle' is the name now given to the system devised by the Athenian astronomer Meton, whereby a 19-year solar cycle lasted almost exactly 235 lunar months (just under 6,940 days). During each 19-year cycle, seven intercalary or leap years were required in which an extra (13th) lunar month would be added. This Metonic cycle was initiated in 432/1 BC and probably continued in use throughout much of Athenian history. The extra month was usually inserted after Poseideon (the sixth month).

The organization of the calendar is best known at Athens. The beginning of each month was meant to coincide with the new moon (PLATO, *Laws* 767c), and the new year was signalled by the first new moon after the summer solstice. The months do not coincide with, but overlap, those used in the modern (Gregorian) calendar, and the Table is therefore only a rough guide for a normal year.

In Greek communities, the calendar provided the basis for festivals based on the agricultural activities of the year, such as the sowing and harvesting of specific crops. In the pre-CHRISTIAN period, Greeks did not have weekends. HOLIDAYS were therefore restricted to festival days, and these were carefully observed. Examples of surviving religious calendars dictate sacrificial details such as the type of offering, its cost and size, and the date and deity to whom a SACRIFICE should be made.

Alongside the religious or festival calendar at Athens was the civic calendar. The official year of the Athenian state was marked not only by the sequence of months starting with Hekatombaion, but was also divided into ten prytanies (*prytaneiai*) or civic months. A prytany was the portion of the year when one prytany (a subgroup of the Athenian council) served. Before 307/6 there were ten prytanies in each year (one for each of the ten tribes) and the succession of prytanies did not coincide exactly with each of the 12 months. Decrees of the Athenian state were dated by the prytany calendar until the second quarter of the 4th century, and thereafter were usually dated by both the civic (prytany) and the religious or festival calendar. The correspondence between these two calendars has allowed considerable advances in the understanding of the civic calendars of Athens.

Detailed knowledge of how other Greek cities controlled their calendars barely exists. Inscriptions provide precious but incomplete information about the organization of such calendars. The names of the months are known for many Greek communities, but well over 200 different month names were in use in ancient Greece. The Linear B tablets from Pylos and KNOSSOS reveal that month names in the MYCENAEAN period had little in common with those of the classical era.

The days of each month did not follow a simple pattern. There was no repetition of, for example, Monday, Tuesday, Wednesday and so on. At Athens the last day of the month was called the 'old and the new', elsewhere it was 'the 30th'. The count of days in a month depended on the moon. Days 2–10 were the 2nd to the 10th of the 'rising' or 'waxing' month. Days 11–20 were the 11th to the 20th of the month. The final 9 or 10 days were counted backwards from the end of the month or the waning of the moon (e.g. the 25th was the '6th of the waning moon' in a 30-day month).

Dates were important in the Greek world, but the translation of dates from different Greek calendars was as much a problem in antiquity as it has proved for subsequent historians of the ancient world. THUCYDIDES, famous for dividing his years into summer and winter, avoided cross-referring the variety of month-names used in different parts of the Greek world, and counted years in terms of Athenian archons and OLYMPIADS. The complexity of the calendar in the Greek world was not lost on those who had to endure the many variations from city to city. But some communities may never have quite grasped the problem, for one comic writer suggested that at Ioulis on Keos some confusion existed about what day it was and whether a festival was taking place or not. GJO

See Bickerman, E. J. (1980) *Chronology of the Ancient World*; Mikalson, J. D. (1975) *The Sacred and Civil Calendar of the Athenian Year.*

The Roman calendar remains one of the most enduring aspects of the classical legacy. Two of our months, July and August, are named after JULIUS CAESAR and AUGUSTUS, and the structure of the year remains much as it was devised by Caesar himself. The original Roman calendar appears to have had only ten months, from March to December, with the winter months January and February added at a later date. Our evidence for the calendar comes from surviving inscribed calendars found at a number of

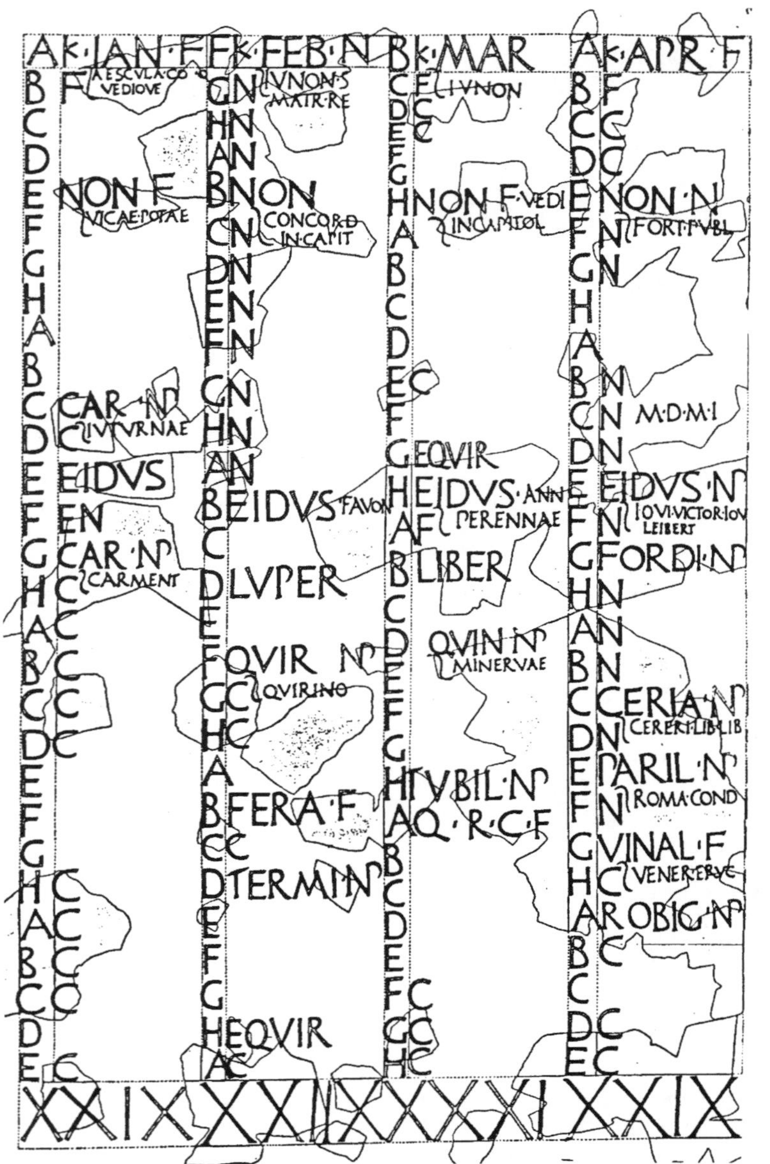

CALENDARS: (b) reconstructed Roman calendar detailing the sequence of local markets in central Italy.

sites in central Italy, with the most important at Antium and PRAENESTE. The more elaborate calendars contain annotations, which are attributed to the Augustan scholar Verrius Flaccus.

The calendars divide the year into the 12 months, each between 28 and 31 days long. Each day is classed with regard to various categories. Every 9th day is a market day (*nundinae*); some days are *comitiales*, on which one can do business; others are *nefasti*, ill-omened and not available for business, because of a FESTIVAL or anniversary. The *Kalendae* (Kalends in English; always the 1st of the month), *Nonae* (Nones; the 5th, or the 7th in months of 31 days, originally March, May, July, and October), and *Idus* (Ides; 13th, or 15th in a 31-day month) are specified, as are the festivals for each day. Some festivals are marked in some calendars in large red letters (hence 'red-letter day'). The collection of these festivals may well represent the cycle of festivals which dates back to the archaic period, and may thus be used to reconstruct some part of the early religious history of Rome. Festivals were constantly added thereafter.

The calendar of the Republic contained 355 days, less than the $365\frac{1}{4}$ days of the solar year. It was necessary, therefore, to devise a process of intercalation, the insertion of extra days into the calendar. Every other year (the even years BC), 22 or 23 days were inserted after 23 February. How early this practice began and how the Romans came to use it is unclear, though the practice is analogous to some Greek examples.

One crucial aspect of the calendar is that it was controlled by the *pontifices* (PRIESTS). A *pontifex* together with the *rex sacrificulus* proclaimed each month when the Nones and Ides would fall, and the *pontifices* arranged the intercalation. In this they were not always successful – in the 190s the month of March was coming round in late autumn, and something similar happened in the late Republic – but it is plausible that this reflected the exceptionally disturbed conditions rather than a chronic failure to reconcile the calendar with the seasons. In 304 BC, pontifical control was challenged when a curule AEDILE and scribe of the CENSOR Appius Claudius Caecus called Gnaeus Flavius published the calendar for the first time. The regulation of time was a matter of political control as well as practical interest.

By the late Republic the flaws in the calendar in terms of its relationship to the solar year were clear, and Julius Caesar, relying on Egyptian advice, began a new calendar in 45 BC. It had an average of $365\frac{1}{4}$ days, with ten extra days inserted at the end of months and an extra day added after 24 February every fourth year – essentially the same as our own calendar. Unfortunately the *pontifices* failed to follow the proper method and added the leap day every three years; Augustus then omitted it for 16 years, and the Julian calendar operated properly from AD 8 until the reforms of pope Gregory the Great in 1582. It is still used by the Greek and Russian Orthodox churches. The use of this calendar spread through the Roman empire.

The Roman calendar was not the only way of measuring time. Outside Rome, local calendars continued to exist, and both at Rome and elsewhere the method of counting years changed from time to time and place to place. To designate a year it was common to use the regnal year of the EMPEROR or the names of local MAGISTRATES, or to think in terms of the number of years from a certain event. Moreover, festivals of the emperors were inserted into provincial calendars; a calendar of religious holidays celebrated by a military garrison that survives from DURA EUROPUS in the 3rd century AD contains festivals of emperors from Julius Caesar onwards. Again it is evident that the organization of the calendar was a political concern, but that the calendar in itself provided a conspectus of Roman history.

The calendar was the subject of learned debate in the late empire. MACROBIUS discussed it, and John Lydus and Censorinus wrote learned accounts of the evolution and nature of the Roman calendar, largely based on earlier but now lost sources. One of the major changes was the move towards a seven-day week, a result of Judaeo-Christian influence, which we begin to see in the 4th century. Despite 5th-century attempts to expurgate PAGANISM, the old festivals survive tenaciously on calendars. Hence we find both CHRISTIAN and pagan elements on the Codex Calendar of AD 354, and even in the calendar of Polemius Silvius of AD 448–9, written in GAUL and dedicated to the BISHOP of LYON, pagan elements remain as necessary explanatory items or purely cultural events. Roman calendars still decorated the walls of Christian churches in medieval times. CJS

See Bickerman, E. J. (1980) *Chronology of the Ancient World*; Michels, A. K. (1967) *The Calendar of the Roman Republic*; Salzman, M. R. (1990) *On Roman Time*.

Caligula (Gaius; Gaius Iulius Caesar Germanicus) AD 12–41 Roman emperor 37–41, son of the popular general Germanicus and AGRIPPINA the Elder. Caligula ('Little Boot') was a nickname acquired as a boy while living in army camps because he habitually wore miniature versions of soldiers' boots. Caligula and his adoptive brother Gemellus were named co-heirs in TIBERIUS' will, but the will was set aside and Caligula declared sole heir. Caligula was married four times (to Junia Claudilla, Livia Orestilla, Lollia Paulina and Milonia Caesonia) and additionally was accused of incest with his posthumously deified sister, Drusilla. He planned the invasion of BRITAIN later carried out by CLAUDIUS, and raised two new legions. The first serious friction between Rome and the JEWS occurred during his rule. Caligula had a number of SENATORS executed, many of whom do appear to have been plotting against him. His actions became increasingly bizarre and despotic, and he accepted extravagant honours approaching deification. Caligula has acquired the reputation of being one of the archetypal mad emperors, though whether this was literally true is uncertain. The main ancient sources are hostile but not contemporary: CASSIUS DIO (book 59) and SUETONIUS (*Caligula*), who pointedly divided his biography of Caligula into accounts of 'the *PRINCEPS*' and 'the monster'. Caligula, his last wife and his daughter were murdered by Cassius Chaerea and other disaffected officers of the praetorian guard. GSA

See Barrett, A. (1989) *Caligula*; Ferrill, A. (1991) *Caligula Emperor of Rome*.

 AUGUSTUS: (a); EMPERORS, ROMAN: (a).

Callicrates see KALLIKRATES.

Callimachus see KALLIMACHOS.

Callinus see KALLINOS.

Callisthenes see KALLISTHENES.

Cambyses see KAMBYSES.

camels Domesticated pack animals, common in Egypt, Africa and the Near East in the Roman period. Camels are not indigenous to Egypt or Africa, and the date of their introduction is a matter of controversy. Despite a tradition that they were brought to Egypt in the PTOLEMAIC period, there is clear ARCHAEOLOGICAL evidence for their presence in southern Egypt in the early 1st millennium BC. They are mentioned in Ptolemaic PAPYRI, but it seems that their use did not become widespread until the Roman period. At that point, apart from their usual role in TRADE, they appear often in military contexts as pack animals, and their remains have been found as far west as Vindonissa in Switzerland. Camels are mentioned by Roman writers from the time of STRABO, and most particularly by PLINY THE ELDER.

Pliny noted that there were two types, the dromedary and the Bactrian, and that they were used as beasts of burden and sometimes in WAR. Although ancient writers did not understand the physiology of camels, their ability to travel without water was remarked upon, as well as their notorious obstinacy – apparently they often refused to travel beyond their customary march or carry heavy loads. The odder habits, reported by ancient writers, such as their refusal to drink clean water, can be put down to their remarkable methods of survival in an arid environment. It is clear that the camel became an important TRANSPORT animal in the Roman world, especially in long-distance desert travel. CEPA

See Gauthier-Pilters, H. and Dagg, A. I. (1981) *The Camel*.

DRAUGHT ANIMALS.

Campania see CAPUA; CUMAE; ITALY, ROMAN; LATINS; OSCANS; PUTEOLI; SAMNITE WARS.

Camulodunum (mod. Colchester) Occupying more than 16 sq km (6 sq miles), and comprising a complex of sites bounded by massive earthworks, Camulodunum was one of the new 'territorial *oppida*' that emerged in south-eastern BRITAIN c.100 BC. Other sites in this category include Verulamium (St Albans) and Noviomagus (Chichester). Camulodunum – 'the *dun* (fortified site) of the god Camulos' – was almost certainly the central place of the Trinovantes, a powerful people of late pre-Roman Iron Age southern Britain. The complex was later associated with the Catuvellauni. The date of the transfer is unclear, but by c.AD 10 the Colchester area was certainly under the control of the Catuvellaunian king CUNOBELINUS. The strategic and political importance of Iron Age Camulodunum is underscored by the fact that a legionary FORTRESS was erected here immediately after the Roman conquest of AD 43. This subsequently became the VETERAN settlement of *Colonia Victricensis*, one of the most important towns in Roman Britain.

A number of important pre-conquest sites have been identified within the Camulodunum complex. These include a settlement at Sheepen (which may have been the home of Cunobelinus), a religious complex at Gosbecks Farm, and several funerary sites including a possible 'kingly' tumulus at Lexden. In 1997 an important new group of ÉLITE cremations was identified at Stanway, just outside the later Iron Age boundaries of Camulodunum. Some of the well-preserved 'satellite' cremations surrounding the central chambers at Stanway have excited special interest. The so-called 'doctor's grave' (dating to c.AD 50–60) has produced the earliest identifiable set of surgical instruments from Britain, and indeed one of the earliest from the ancient world as a whole. JW

See Crummy, P. (1997) *City of Victory*.

BRITANNIA: (a).

canals Manmade waterways for the purpose of irrigation, drainage or transport were well known in the ancient world. Complex systems of canals and dikes for irrigation were common in Mesopotamia and Egypt until the Roman period, but not elsewhere. Canals were built for the drainage of Lake Kopaïs in Boiotia in the 4th century BC. A canal was built through the Pomptine marshes, south-east of Rome, but a drainage project failed.

Many ancient stories about canals were designed to highlight the megalomania of rulers. When XERXES decided to dig a canal through Mt Athos to facilitate the passage of his troops in 480 BC, it was perceived as yet another example of the *hybris* that led to his ultimate downfall (Herodotos 7.23–4). An attempt by the Egyptian pharaoh Nechos (610–595 BC) to link the Nile to the Red sea by a canal 'wide enough for two triremes to pass each other' took the lives of more than 120,000 Egyptians, but failed to reach the Red sea. It was finished by Ptolemy II (285–246 BC). Attempts to cut a way through the Isthmus of CORINTH are known from the reign of Periandros (6th century BC), but the most spectacular attempt was made by NERO, who famously was the first 'to break ground with a mattock and to carry off a basketful of earth' (Suetonius, *Nero* 19). The attempt failed, and the PELOPONNESE remained connected to the mainland until the 19th century.

Yet, Roman authorities could move the earth if they wanted to. The conquest of the northern PROVINCES involved large-scale operations of the Roman fleet, and where nature had not provided a safe waterway Roman GENERALS, such as Drusus and Corbulo, were prepared to interfere. Thus successful canal building projects often depended on military expedience. Considerations of public health may have lain behind the construction of an industrial canal for the refuse water of the FULLERS of ANTIOCH (*SEG* 35.1483). When far-sighted officials acknowledged commercial advantages, their projects did not always succeed. As governor of Bithynia, PLINY THE YOUNGER suggested a link from a lake near Nicomedia to the sea, citing the high cost and slowness of land transport among his reasons (*Letters* 10.41–2), but the canal was never built. A passage in TACITUS indicates why such projects often failed: when in AD 55 the Roman governor of Germania Superior planned a canal between the Mosel and the Saône, he was dissuaded by a colleague who suggested that the plan might curry favour with the local populations, but was certain to arouse the jealousy of the emperor (*Annals* 13.53). When EMPERORS were personally involved, such projects had better chances of succeeding. A 4th-century commercial geography mentions that the emperor Constantius II (324–61) had a canal dug through a mountain to Syrian Antioch, thus providing the city with a safe HARBOUR (*Expositio totius mundi* 28). OvN

See Moore, F. G. (1950) Three canal projects: Roman and Byzantine, *AJA* 54: 97–111; White, K. D. (1984) *Greek and Roman Technology*.

candles see BEES AND BEEKEEPING; BONE; LIGHTING.

Cannae 216 BC Rome's worst military defeat. After defeating Roman armies at the river Trebia (in 218) and at lake Trasimene (217), HANNIBAL continued to advance through Italy. Rome combined both consular armies, creating an unprecedented force of eight legions, and on 2 August the two sides engaged near Cannae in Apulia, beside the Ofanto (Aufidus) river. Outnumbered 2 to 1, but with a significant CAVALRY advantage, Hannibal displayed his tactical genius to devastating effect. Deliberately weakening his centre, he drew the main Roman force forward. With his cavalry victorious on both flanks, Hannibal turned both wings of his army inwards, enveloping the main Roman force; his cavalry attacked the Roman rear. Roman losses were catastrophic, greater than on the first day of the Somme: c. 50,000 died. Tradition blames the surviving consul Marcus Terentius Varro, but this owes much to POLYBIOS' association with the family of the fallen consul Lucius Aemilius Paullus. The survivors were exiled to fight in SICILY for the rest of the war. Because Hannibal did not immediately march on Rome (though some believe Rome's destruction was never his aim), and because he ultimately lost the war, many have agreed with his officer Marhabal: 'You know how to win a victory, Hannibal, but you don't know how to use one.' JRWP

See Livy 22.36–61; Polybios 3.107–18; Daly, G. (2002) *Cannae*.

capitalism see HISTORIANS AND HISTORIOGRAPHY, MODERN; MARXISM; SOCIOLOGY.

Capitoline hill see CAPITOLIUM; ROME.

Capitoline triad From the 6th century BC, when Rome's last kings, the TARQUINS, constructed a large TEMPLE on the CAPITOLIUM, a triad of deities was worshipped on the site. The shrine was dedicated to JUPITER Capitolinus (or Optimus Maximus, 'Best and Greatest'), whose imposing statue occupied the central *cella* (chamber); the goddesses JUNO Regina ('queen') and MINERVA received homage in separate *cellae*. Dumézil suggests that this group supplanted a more primitive Roman triad consisting of Jupiter, MARS and Quirinus. The Capitolium itself had originally been associated with SATURN.

The Capitoline triad may have been of ETRUSCAN inspiration, for Juno and Minerva were probably non-Roman in origin, and both Tarquins were of Etruscan background. The triad's roots in the regal period are, at any rate, solid: Jupiter was the pre-eminent guarantor of monarchical power. But the triple cult continued with force into the Republican era, after the temple was dedicated by the first CONSULS in 509 BC (LIVY 2.8). Henceforth Capitoline ritual dominated the city like the citadel itself. Supported by his consorts, Jupiter presided over auspices and received the laurels of military victory. On the Kalends (1st) of January new consuls presented themselves to him; on the Ides of September a procession ascended the hill during the *ludi Romani* (Roman GAMES). In imperial times, the Capitoline cult flourished as the symbol of centralized power. JRH

See Beard, M. et al. (1998) *Religions of Rome*; Bonnefoy, Y., ed. (1991) *Roman and European Mythologies*; Dumézil, G. (1987) *Archaic Roman Religion*.

Capitolium The smallest of Rome's seven hills. It consisted of two promontories, the Arx to the north and the Capitolium proper to the south, with a saddle (the 'asylum') joining the two. Ringed about by cliffs (including the famed Tarpeian rock), it formed a natural FORTRESS. There is evidence for Bronze Age settlements there, but according to tradition, ROMULUS fortified the citadel, founded a TEMPLE to JUPITER Feretrius, and established an 'asylum' for incoming refugees. Tradition further relates that the TARQUINS chose the lower promontory as the site for the temple of Jupiter Optimus Maximus, the most important of the Roman temples. It contained three cellas: one each for Jupiter, MINERVA and JUNO, who together constituted the CAPITOLINE TRIAD. During the temple's construction, a human skull of exceptional size was discovered on the hill and interpreted as a sign of Rome's future greatness. This head (*caput*) is said to have given the hill its name.

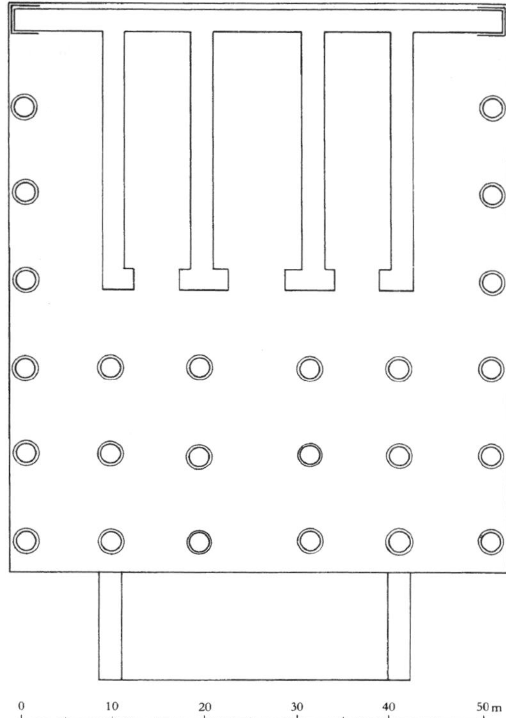

CAPITOLIUM: (a) plan of the original Capitoline temple, of Etruscan form – though on a very large scale – and dating to the late 6th century BC.

In historical times, the temple housed the SIBYLLINE ORACLES, and served as the locus for the inauguration of CONSULS and the ultimate destination for TRIUMPHAL processions. The temple burnt several times: in 83 BC, AD 69 and 80. The first two rebuilt temples retained the ETRUSCAN features of the original – a platform base, widely spaced columns and a spreading roof – but the last, constructed by DOMITIAN (c. AD 82), was a far more elaborate structure.

The Arx served as the site for the augur's observation post (the *auguraculum*) and temples dedicated to Juno Moneta (344 BC) and CONCORDIA (216 BC). (see p. 162) JRCC

 SACRIFICE: (c).

Cappadocia A sparsely populated region of central ASIA Minor, north of the Taurus mountains, east of the Salt Lake and south of the river Halys. Cappadocia was one of the Persian satrapies created by DARIUS in the 6th century BC, and part of the hellenistic empire of ALEXANDER the Great in the 4th century BC. It was an independent kingdom from c. 260 BC

CAPITOLIUM: (b) detail of a relief carving depicting the pedimental sculpture of the 4th Capitoline temple of the late 1st century AD.

until it was brought into the Roman empire in the 1st century BC. In the 3rd century AD DIOCLETIAN made the easternmost area part of ARMENIA. The chief town was Mazaka (mod. Kayseri), renamed Caesarea after Caesar AUGUSTUS. Further north, Sebasteia (Sivas) was the place where, in AD 320, 40 Roman soldiers were MARTYRED for their CHRISTIAN faith by being made to stand all night in a freezing lake.

The ancient world seems to have valued the HORSES of Cappadocia more than its people, who are spoken of with scorn. Nonetheless, the region did produce the 1st-century geographer STRABO and, in the 4th century AD, three pillars of the Byzantine church, the Cappadocian Fathers: BASIL the Great (BISHOP of Caesarea), his brother Gregory of Nyssa, and his friend GREGORY OF NAZIANZUS. Popularly associated with these three, or even with persecuted Christians of the 2nd and 3rd centuries AD, are the numerous rock-cut chapels in the region around Mt Argaios (Erciyas Dağ) – but erroneously so, for most are of Middle Byzantine or later date though a few rock-cut TOMB façades may be hellenistic or Roman. CHURCHES of the 4th and 5th centuries are found in the Aksaray–Niğde–Kayseri region. LR

See Giovannini, L. (1971) *Arts of Cappadocia*.

ROMAN EMPIRE: (b).

Capri Island in the bay of Naples; the name (Capreae) comes from Greek *kapros*, 'boar'. Insignificant until AUGUSTUS fell in love with it in 29 BC, Capri was a favourite haunt of TIBERIUS, who lived there between AD 27 and 37. TACITUS says that these EMPERORS constructed 12 VILLAS; substantial remains survive of three. Augustus' favoured residence was the one now called 'Palazzo a Mare' on the north coast, situated on a series of terraces. The main residential block with its own bath-suite lies at the east end; an adjacent artificial harbour provided access. A second villa (Damaceuta) lies on another site at the north-west corner of Capri: a block of rooms, one with a projecting semi-circular bay (probably the main dining room), is linked by a corridor to what were perhaps the emperor's private quarters further east. Best-preserved, and Tiberius' favourite, was the Villa of Jupiter (Villa Iovis) recorded by PLINY and SUETONIUS, on a stunning site at the north-east corner of the island, with precipitous drops to the sea 300 m below. This villa (some 7,000 sq m in area) is arranged around a central square courtyard. BATHS occupy much of the south wing, and the west wing contains service quarters and a kitchen. The emperor's private quarters were in the north wing, and a main reception hall or dining room (again with projecting semi-circular bay) is situated in the middle of the east wing, on the cliff edge. Staircases and ramps link various parts of a complicated split-level building into a cohesive, tight-knit unit. To the north of the main villa a staircase leads down to a long corridor ending at a series of small rooms. Despite extensive robbing of statuary and MARBLE and MOSAIC decoration, these villas provide an insight into the private lifestyle of Rome's first two emperors and demonstrate the skill of Roman architects at adapting mountain-top sites. RJAW

See Maiuri, A. (1956) *Capri: its history and its monuments.*

 ITALY: (a).

Capua (mod. Santa Maria di Capua Vetere, in Campania in central Italy) One of the most prosperous cities of Italy throughout the classical period, at the centre of an outstandingly fertile territory, the *ager Campanus*. Founded c.800 BC, it emerged as an ETRUSCAN city, which was conquered by the OSCANS in 424 BC. Connections with Rome were always going to be important. In 338, after the LATIN WAR, Capua received 'Roman citizenship without the vote', and in 312 it was linked to Rome by the Via Appia. In 216, during the second PUNIC WAR, an anti-Roman faction handed Capua over to HANNIBAL. In 211 Rome recaptured the city, executed its political leaders and deprived it of its political rights and territory. The *ager Campanus* was rented out for profit by the Roman CENSORS. In 83 a Roman colony was established at Capua, and in 59 the city had its full rights restored so that it could act as the centre for large-scale settlement of colonists in its territory by JULIUS CAESAR. The prosperity of the new settlements in the imperial period is shown not least by the AMPHITHEATRE, second only to the Colosseum at Rome. The community survived to the 9th century AD.

Apart from its AGRICULTURAL output, Capua was famous for the production of bronze vessels and for its PERFUME industry, which helped to make its FORUM for perfume-sellers, called Seplasia, a byword for luxury. JJP

See Frederiksen, M. (1984) *Campania.*

 ITALY: (a).

Caracalla Roman emperor, the son of SEPTIMIUS SEVERUS and JULIA DOMNA. His name at birth – at LYON on 4 April AD 186 or 188 – was Lucius Septimius Bassianus. After Severus adopted his family into that of MARCUS AURELIUS, he became Marcus Aurelius Antoninus. The *cognomen* Caracalla (perhaps more accurately Caracallus) was derived from a Gallic cloak that he favoured.

Caracalla was named CAESAR in 195 or 196, and marked out from that time as Severus' heir designate. In 205 he was probably the driving force behind the assassination of Plautianus, the long-term praetorian prefect, whose daughter was Caracalla's wife. In the later years of Severus' reign, Caracalla's role as presumptive heir was challenged by his brother Geta. When Septimius died on 4 February 211, he left his sons with equal titles and authority. The joint reign lasted until December, when Caracalla assassinated Geta and instituted a thorough, and bloody, purge of the palace staff.

Caracalla left Rome in 213, first for the northern frontier, then for the East. After a journey through ASIA Minor, where he indulged his fascination for ALEXANDER the Great, he reached ALEXANDRIA at the end of 215 and, because of a misunderstanding, ordered a massacre of many of its inhabitants. He spent the next year in SYRIA, preparing to invade PARTHIA. The invasion never took place: Caracalla was murdered while answering a call of nature outside CARRHAE in April 217.

Caracalla's most celebrated act was the *constitutio Antoniniana*, issued in early 212, which granted citizenship to most inhabitants of the empire. Said by CASSIUS DIO to reflect Caracalla's need for hard currency, the edict's preamble, preserved on PAPYRUS, implies a celebration of Geta's death. It was not an act of policy motivated by philosophic concerns. Despite his short reign, Caracalla is a significant figure. He consciously rejected the Antonine style of government, appearing on coins without the philosopher's beard. His brutality led to a reaction among officials who were satisfied, for the next two decades, with very young emperors easily dominated by the court. DSP

See Sherwin-White, A. N. (1973) *The Roman Citizenship.*

EMPERORS, ROMAN: (a); SEVERUS, SEPTIMIUS: (a).

Carausius Usurper in BRITAIN, c.AD 286–93, succeeded by Allectus, c. 293–6, both poorly documented in the sources. Marcus Aurelius Maus(aeus?) Carausius was a native of Menapia, the coastal region of Gallia Belgica. After service under MAXIMIAN against the Bagaudae in 285/6, he commanded a fleet to secure the Gallic coast. Accused of keeping booty, he assumed imperial power and fled to Britain, though he seems to have retained some foothold in northern GAUL. Maximian defeated enemy forces on the continent before his (failed) attempt in 289 to regain Britain. In spring 293, Constantius I besieged Boulogne and defeated the usurper's forces. About the same time, Carausius was assassinated at the instigation of Allectus, his treasurer. Allectus' reign was prosecuted mainly in Britain, and he is associated with several buildings in LONDON. He died in battle c.296 against Asclepiodotus, the praetorian prefect; heavy seas had delayed Constantius' own crossing.

Carausius' usurpation testifies to early discontent in Britain and north-western Gaul with an empire that no longer provided adequate security, and other usurpers with varying goals followed. Magnentius, of Frankish and British ancestry, and Silvanus, a

CARAUSIUS: (a) coin portrait of the usurper Carausius.

Carausius: (b) coin portrait of Allectus the right hand man, assassin and successor of Carausius as 'emperor' in Britain. The two issues are typical of the coinage minted by pretenders in claiming legitimacy.

Frank, usurped against Constantius II, and the Frankish general Arbogast propped up Eugenius in the 390s. Other usurpers emanating from Britain (but not necessarily British) are Magnus Maximus and Constantine III, who essentially abandoned Britain in 409. JV

See Casey, P. J. (1994) *Carausius and Allectus: the British usurpers.*

careers There is no exact Latin equivalent for the modern notion of advancement in a profession, nor anything like the same degree of structured professions as in modern Europe. This owes much to the nature of Roman society, where the significant divisions are not between, for example, amateur and professional, but between élites and (urban) trades or professions. The ideology of our sources (written by the élites) reflects this. Cicero (*On Duties* 1.150–2) discusses which types of *artificia* ('trades') and *quaestus* ('means of livelihood') are more or less respectable: craftsmen (*opifices*), traders (*mercatores*), tax collectors and money-lenders are base (*sordidi*). Trade on a grand scale, however, is more reputable! Those professions (*artes*) with higher levels of social usefulness (*utilitas*) or good sense (*prudentia*), such as medicine, architecture or teaching, are better but belong to a certain social stratum (*ordo*). Much the most respectable (*liberalis*) is *agricultura* (again, on a grand scale). The overlap is weak between the occupation by which one makes a living and the idea of a career: those, such as Cicero, who pursue a 'political career', derive their livelihood from elsewhere. For those engaged in trades, crafts and professions there were clubs (*collegia*), often linked to specific occupations, but these did not exist for the improvement of social or economic position: rather they were religious organizations at heart, acting as social clubs and often providing for a member's burial.

The *cursus honorum*, the increasingly structured ladder of public office in the Republic, comes closest to the idea of a 'career', but it was not a full-time or salaried occupation, nor a 'specialism', as it combined political, administrative and military roles. Sulla established a compulsory *cursus*, but many elements were already law (e.g. by the *lex Villia Annalis* of 180 BC). After 10 years' military service (beginning usually at 17), one could stand for quaestor (compulsory by 80 BC). Election to the *curule* magistracies followed: aedile (from age 36; not compulsory), praetor (from 39; compulsory) and consul (from 42). Tribuneships, military and popular, could be held at any point, but usually early. Re-election to an office within 10 years was normally prohibited. From Cicero it is clear that birth and patronage were crucial in winning elections. Cicero won the consulship as a *novus homo*, 'new man', meaning the first of his family to achieve high office – a considerable achievement. Military skills, statesmanship and oratory (in that order) were the keys to success.

The other area in which one might speak of a career is the army. As Rome's military campaigns extended ever further afield, the annually levied citizen army necessarily became increasingly professional. Every citizen was liable for military service: 10 years for the cavalry, 16 for infantry. Although this service could be spread across both time and space according to the variable requirements of Rome's wars, it is clear that already by the 2nd century BC there were men who volunteered and could be described as 'career soldiers' (Livy 42.34.5–11). With Marius' opening of the army to the lowest property classes and the development of rewards on retirement for veterans in the 1st century BC, this tendency increased further. JRWP

See Cicero, *On Duties*, trs. M.T. Griffin and E.M. Atkins (1991); Astin, A.E. (1958) *The Lex Annalis before Sulla*; Keppie, L. (1984) *The Making of the Roman Army*; Taylor, D.W. and Murrell, J., trs. (1968) *Quintus Cicero, A Short Guide to Electioneering*, or Shackleton Bailey, D.R., trs., (2002) *A Guide to Electioneering* (both = *Commentariolum petitionis*).

 equestrians (table); senate and senators (table).

Caria (Karia) An arid yet relatively populous region of south-west Asia Minor, seen as on the edge of the Greek world. Contact with Greece came early, and the Greek settlers of Miletos are said to have intermarried with the local women. Carian mercenaries were widespread in the ancient world; they served alongside Ionians in Egypt. This is held to explain the proverbially low esteem in which Carians were held, as in 'Let the risk be for the Carian and not the general' (Polybios 10.32.11). Knidos and Kaunos were Greek colonies on the coast, but the hellenization of Caria was most rapid under the Hekatomnid dynasts of the 4th century. Towns in Caria included Mylasa, Pedasa and Iasos, the most important being Halikarnassos (Herodotos' birthplace).

Caria was annexed by Lydia under Croesus and then for Persia by Harpagos in 546 BC. Persian rule was from Sardis in the 6th and 5th centuries. The Carians sided with the Greeks in the Ionian revolt (499–494) but went on to assist the Persians in the subsequent invasion of Greece (albeit half-heartedly). Carian towns joined the Delian league from the beginning; Halikarnassos was a wealthy and loyal member. In the early 4th century, Caria became a Persian satrapy under the Hekatomnids, who though officially ruling for Persia were effectively independent. Caria's most famous ruler, Mausolus (377–353), greatly expanded his territory, causing conflict with Athens. He synoikized several towns into a single settlement at Halikarnassos, creating an impressive capital, where his widow Artemisia erected one of the SEVEN WONDERS of the world, the Mausoleum, in his memory. In 334 Halikarnassos was besieged and Caria taken by ALEXANDER, after whose death it fell to PTOLEMY. It remained a free city and flourished again in the imperial period. (see also APHRODISIAS) AG

See Hornblower, S. (1982) *Mausolus.*

 ANATOLIA: (a).

Carinus see DIOCLETIAN.

 EMPERORS, ROMAN: (b).

carmen saeculare see HORACE.

Carneades see KARNEADES.

Carnuntum see CONSTANTINE; DIOCLETIAN; GALERIUS; MARCUS AURELIUS; MAXIMIAN; PANNONIA; TETRARCHS.

carpentry An essential craft, especially in urban and military contexts where TIMBER constructions were widely employed. Even cities built largely in STONE relied on carpenters for ROOFS, fixtures and fittings. Wooden objects are perishable, and their importance is therefore easy to underestimate. In unusual circumstances, however, ancient wood has survived. Waterlogged urban deposits like those of Roman Carlisle and LONDON, MEDITERRANEAN SHIPWRECKS, the desiccated sites of ancient Egypt and the carbonized remains of POMPEII and HERCULANEUM have preserved a wide range of carpentered objects.

The remains of timber houses bear witness to a wide range of regional traditions of structural carpentry. These skills were also applied to major ENGINEERING projects such as wooden BRIDGES, quays, MILLS and water-lifting devices, as well as the vast timber scaffoldings employed in the construction of MASONRY buildings. Other specialist skills were adopted by SHIPBUILDERS and wheelwrights, in the fabrication of the wooden barrels used in the shipment of WINE, and by wood-turners. Further evidence is found in WALL-PAINTINGS that show carpenters at work, and on carved tombstones depicting these craftsmen with the tools of their trade. Carpenters' tools have also been found in EXCAVATIONS. These sources of information permit a detailed description of the technologies involved.

CARPENTRY: detail of a late Roman gold inlaid glass vessel base, showing a range of carpentry tools in use (saws, adzes, chisels, drills).

The first stages of preparation took place where the trees were felled and prepared for TRANSPORT. Hatchets, axes and wedges were used in this process. Felling usually took place in the autumn, at the end of the growth season. The timbers were squared by axe and converted to beams, boards and battens in the timber yard. The splitting of large timbers and boards with the use of wedges is a characteristic of using straight-grained wildwood timber, but this ancient technology was widely replaced by sawing on trestles. Planks were prepared by cutting from both ends of a square-hewn baulk. Bow-saws, with a blade fitted into the end of a piece of wood bent into a semicircle, were still used, but by the Roman period iron frame-saws had been found to offer significant advantages. Straight iron blades were held in a saw-frame made of wooden uprights connected by a cross-bar above or below. Dampened cord tied to each end of the wooden frame kept the blade taut. The teeth could be set so that they projected alternately to right and left. Double-handled saws allowed two men to prepare the planks. These technologies allowed for sawing both along and across the grain. Other important tools within the carpenter's kit included the plane with cutting-irons, bow-drills, gouges, tanged and socketed chisels, punches and augurs. Woodworkers also made use of the lathe.

Roman joinery involved the tightly cut mortise and tenon joint, lap dovetails, and complex scarf joints. Nails were also used to reinforce timber joints, though this was not standard practice. Timber-framed buildings have been studied in detail at the Roman FORT of Valkenburg in Holland and in excavations in LONDON. These structures of the 1st century AD were built of timber uprights (studs) with projecting tenons slotted into mortises cut into base-plates (ground beams). Top-plates were inserted over the uprights, and reinforced by diagonal bracing. Tie beams braced the buildings at ceiling level. These frames were of 'normal assembly', in which the top-plates were laid before the tie beams. The nature of the joints and the lack of pegs suggest that the walls were not pre-assembled but built piecemeal on site. Wattle-and-daub panels were inserted between the uprights. These panels were made of circular-sectioned sails, woven vertically around square-sectioned horizontal rods slotted into vertical notches cut in the sides of the studs. They were probably pre-assembled and dropped into place.

One 2nd-century building in London, however, may have been prefabricated in an assembly yard before being brought to site. The cut timbers had dried and warped before use, no woodworking debris was found on site, and the building had been laid out in a regular fashion to standard measures. Wall posts with tenons were set into a ground beam; lesser uprights alternated with larger timbers, with more substantial corner posts. There was no evidence of cross-bracing, but the external face of the walls was reinforced with horizontal square-edged boards set on edge. These were chamfered at the ends to improve the join and housed by a rebate in the corner posts.

Cruck construction may have been employed in Roman houses, though the evidence is inconclusive. This alternative to timber-framed construction involved curved or angled timbers arranged so that the rafters supporting the roof effectively sprang from, rather than rested on, the load-bearing uprights. Possible instances of cruck building are confined to small AGRICULTURAL buildings in and beyond the GERMAN borders.

Our knowledge of roof carpentry involves a degree of conjecture. In simple structures, paired timber supports are likely to have taken coupled principal rafters, braced by collar beams to form A-frames. A more complex form of roof, sometimes known as the double roof, involved the use of horizontal timbers or purlins to support the rafters. Simple roofs at Pompeii consisted of short rafters slotted onto large axial purlins resting on walls and struts from below. More sophisticated carpentry was employed to span larger interiors. The king-post roof was possibly a hellenistic innovation, but is first positively attested by a bronze copy in the 2nd-century AD porch of the PANTHEON at Rome. In this form of roof, large principal rafters supported lesser purlins and rafters. These rafters were prevented from lateral movement by tie beams across the width of the covered area. These were in turn prevented from bowing by a king post suspended from the apex of the roof. Constructions of this type are found in early CHRISTIAN CHURCH architecture, and the Constantinian roof of Old St Peter's, Rome, would appear to have rested on double trusses with a scarfed tie beam and pendant king posts. VITRUVIUS offers a description of roof carpentry broadly consistent with this evidence. DP

See Perring, D. (2002) *The Roman House in Britain*; Strong, D. and Brown, D. (1976) *Roman Crafts*.

FURNITURE: (a).

Carrara (Roman Luna) Quarries in northern Italy, which in the first two centuries AD provided Rome with a large proportion of its white MARBLE, were probably worked from the early 2nd century BC. The earliest recorded use of Carrara (*marmor Lunense*) in Rome was in 48 BC (Pliny the Elder, *Natural History* 36.48) when Mamurra used it for columns in his house. The earliest use in a public building was in the rebuilding of the Regia in 36 BC. It was used extensively by AUGUSTUS in his building programme in Rome, including his FORUM, the ARA PACIS and the temple of APOLLO Palatinus. It continued to be used as the major white marble for ARCHITECTURE in Rome, and was one of the major SCULPTURAL marbles used in Italy and the Western empire. In the early 2nd century AD it was most famously used for the COLUMN of TRAJAN and in Trajan's forum. However, from the time of HADRIAN white marbles from Greece and ASIA Minor became more commonly used in Rome. The quarries continued to be worked into the later Roman period. Exploitation of the quarries since the RENAISSANCE has obliterated virtually all ancient traces of quarrying. HD

See Dolci, E., ed. (1982) *Mostra 'Marmo lunense': cave romane e materiali archeologiche*; Mannoni, L. and Mannoni, T. (1985) *Marble: the history of a culture*, ch. 4, 199–245.

MARBLE: (a).

Carrhae Harran (the original name for Carrhae) was founded c.2000 BC where water irrigated one of the rich pockets of alluvial soil in north-western MESOPOTAMIA. Later it acquired a wider significance because of its location on natural east–west and north–south routes. The original Akkadian name means 'crossroads', and it flourished as a trading, administrative and military centre of the Assyrian empire. It was from here that Abraham migrated to Canaan.

The insertion of MACEDONIAN colonists c.300 BC brought a hellenization of its name, but the old form re-emerged a thousand years later and survives still. After two centuries of SELEUKID rule, it was part of the PARTHIAN empire for two centuries more before passing to Rome in the AD 160s for almost 400 years. Although CHRISTIANITY took root in Roman times and the city had its own BISHOP, it remained an extensively pagan community until the moment of its final seizure by the Muslim Arabs in AD 639. The focus of this paganism was the very ancient cult of the moon goddess, Sin.

Location and cult were what allowed the city a significant role in imperial events. After centuries of seizure, damage and restoration by warring armies, the neo-Babylonian king Nabonidus rebuilt the TEMPLE and made his mother the high priestess. When the Roman GENERAL Marcus Licinius CRASSUS led his army across the Euphrates on his invasion of Parthian Mesopotamia, his route inevitably led him to Harran. His army was destroyed near here in 53 BC, one of the most devastating disasters in Roman military history and a turning-point in Rome's advances in the East. The emperor CARACALLA was assassinated nearby in AD 217 while breaking from his Parthian WAR to sacrifice to Sin. JULIAN also sacrificed to her in 363 when his army passed. It was frequently on the lines of advance of Roman and Parthian and Persian armies.

The foundation of EDESSA (Sanliurfa) on a new site 40 km (25 miles) to the north-east c.300 BC offered an alternative centre which slowly eclipsed Carrhae. It remained an important FORTRESS, but the small medieval and modern Turkish town is a backwater sitting amidst the ruins of the CHURCHES and ancient city wall. DLK

SYRIA, ROMAN: (b).

Cartagena see CARTHAGO NOVA.

Carthage and Carthaginians According to legend, queen Dido fled the LEVANTINE city of Tyre with fellow PHOENICIANS to found Carthage after the murder of her husband. Upon arrival in North AFRICA, Dido (also known as Elissa) negotiated with the LIBYAN king Iarbas for the amount of territory that she could cover with an oxhide. Cutting the hide into thin strips, she stretched it around a prominent hill

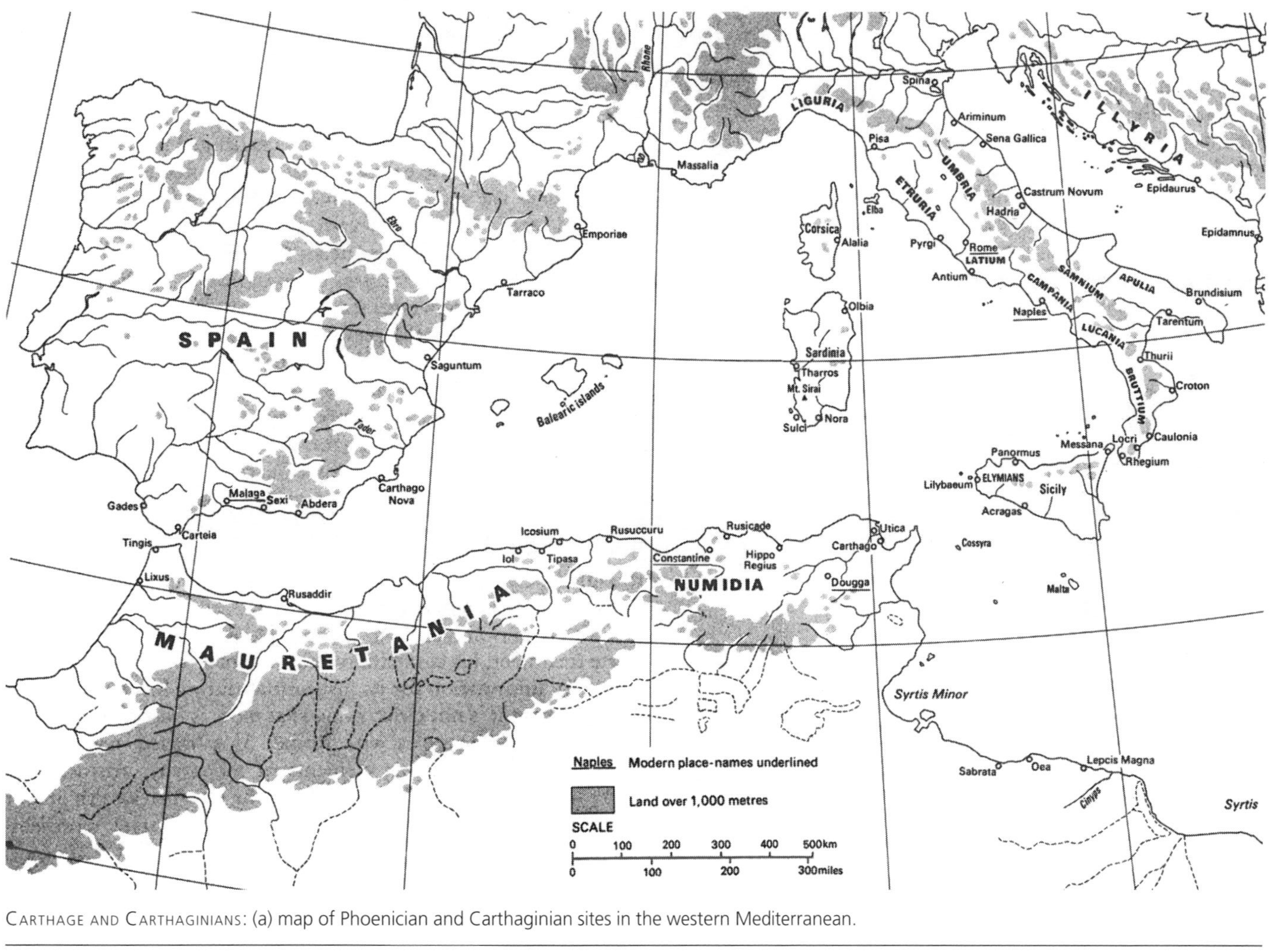

Carthage and Carthaginians: (a) map of Phoenician and Carthaginian sites in the western Mediterranean.

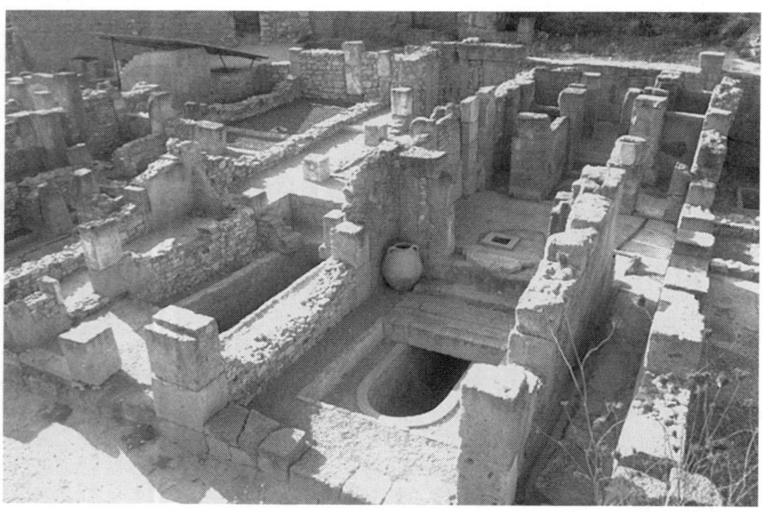

Carthage and Carthaginians: (b) houses from hellenistic Carthage destroyed in the Roman sack of 146 BC. Note the large sub-floor cisterns.

(the Byrsa, which served as the citadel of Carthage throughout antiquity). Literary sources propose different dates for Dido's foundation: 1215 BC in the high chronology, 814 in the low. Most scholars adhere to the latter date, or shortly thereafter, as the earliest pottery found at the site dates to around 725. The existence of this myth signals something of the status of Carthage in antiquity. While foundation myths pertaining to all other Phoenician cities either did not exist or have not survived, the tale of Dido indicates that ancient peoples regarded Carthage in the same league as important Greek and Italian cities with similar fabled origins.

Carthage (Qart Hadasht in Phoenician) translates as 'new town', compared with the earlier foundation at Utica. Situated approximately in the centre of North Africa, Carthage acquired its significance as the key node in east–west trade along the southern shore of the Mediterranean. By the 5th century BC it exercised dominance over towns all along this route as well as in western Sicily and Sardinia. It also controlled a hinterland that extended to much of modern Tunisia. Early Carthage was a Phoenician settlement, but the city's subsequent empire is known as the Punic civilization.

Although Carthaginian literature has not survived, Greek and Roman authors commented on the city's political organization. Aristotle praised the Carthaginian government's mixture of aristocracy and oligarchy (*Politics* 1272b). One person, generally from a group of ruling families, was appointed 'king', apparently by election rather than inheritance. Other members of the leading families, the best known of whom were the Magonids, Hannonids and Barcids, formed the senate. Annually elected magistrates, *sufetes*, were responsible for civil administration. The popular assembly appears to have been endowed with limited powers of arbitrating disputes among the aristocracy. Carthaginians worshipped divinities brought from Phoenicia: Tanit, Baal Hammon and Melqart were the most prominent.

The city itself lay on a defensible peninsula within the sheltered gulf of Tunis, a large bay between the arm of Cap Bon and the North African mainland. Archaeological evidence for Punic Carthage indicates two main public districts, one on the Byrsa hill and the other on flat ground between the hill and the sea. To the south lay two ports, one commercial and the other military, whose reconstruction indicates their sophisticated organization in the 2nd century BC. Nearby, several archaeological teams have excavated the Tophet, a cemetery for children. Archaeologists tend to regard the burials as containing the bones of children sacrificed to Tanit and Baal Hammon, though there is no universal agreement about this conclusion. More elaborate cemeteries with rock-cut tombs of the 7th and 6th centuries lay to the north on the hill of Juno and Borj Jedid. Prestige goods such as hatchets, razors, worked ivories, amphoras from the Levant, perfume jars and drinking cups from Greece were found in these tombs. Private houses occupied the central area of the city; one can see their pier-and-rubble walls, courtyards paved with pebbles and oval-shaped subterranean cisterns on the south slope of the Byrsa hill today. Punic culture proved to be durable. Well after the fall of Carthage, the inhabitants of North Africa still spoke Punic, elected *sufetes* to run their cities, offered dedications to Punic gods (later syncretized with Roman ones), and employed the Punic cubit as the unit of measurement for their buildings.

Disputes with Rome over territory in Sicily led Carthage to enter the first Punic war (264–241 BC) which it lost. The second (218–202) presented Carthage with its best chance to defeat Rome when its greatest general Hannibal led the Carthaginian army from Spain over the Alps and into Italy. After 15 years of fighting in Italy, Hannibal retreated to Africa, where he was defeated by Scipio Africanus at Zama. The third Punic war, inspired by Cato's proclamation before the Roman senate *Carthago delenda est* ('Carthage must be destroyed'), was by contrast a brief contest (149–146).

Modern scholars invented the idea that Romans poured salt on the fields of Carthage, but the city was destroyed in 146 and remained unoccupied for a century until, around the time of his death, Julius Caesar established a Roman colony there. The refounded city, known as Colonia Iulia Concordia Carthago, became the capital of the Roman province of Africa in 40 BC and received additional colonists in 29. Romans rapidly constructed a grid plan and major public buildings such as a theatre, a harbour, a forum and temples. In the 2nd century AD an amphitheatre, a circus, one of the longest aqueducts and one of the largest bath buildings in the Roman world were erected. The city was the seat of the provincial governor and the main conduit through which African tribute and commerce (mainly grain, olive oil and fish products) were exported to Rome and numerous other destinations. It attained a position of prominence in the empire, ranking in importance with Athens, Alexandria and Antioch among provincial cities. Some of the best known Christian writers (Tertullian and Augustine (1)) and martyrs (Cyprian, Perpetua and Felicitas) emerged in the city during the later 2nd, 3rd and 4th centuries. The city had important churches and church councils. Under the Vandals, who conquered the city in 439, commerce and Christian activities appear to have been relatively uninterrupted. Justinian's army reconquered the city for Byzantium in 533, but when it fell to Arab invaders in 698 many inhabitants fled. The Arab commander, Hassan ibn en-Noman, made his capital in nearby Tunis.

Although Carthage's buildings served as a stone quarry for Tunis and other cities during the Middle Ages, modern archaeological projects have excavated many of its structures and have built museums. Today the city is one of UNESCO's World Heritage sites. DLS

See Lancel, S. (1995) *Carthage*; Raven, S. (1993) *Rome in Africa*.

aqueducts: (a); cities: (b); colonization: (a)–(c).

Carthago Nova Hasdrubal, Hamilcar Barca's son-in-law, founded the city (mod. Cartagena) during his period of command in Spain (229–221 BC), and called it Carthago (Qart Hadasht), meaning 'New Town'. Carthago Nova (New Carthage) is the Roman name for the city. It was ideally placed for contact with Carthage proper, and was said by some ancient authors to have been intended by Hasdrubal as the royal capital for a Spanish empire, dominated by the Barcids. It has an excellent harbour, and was close to important silver mines. In 209 it was captured from the Carthaginians by Scipio Africanus in a rapid and brilliant attack, which began his campaigns in the peninsula. Polybios (10.15–16) dwells on its capture to exemplify the Romans' brutality on such occasions.

Carthago Nova remained an important base for the Romans throughout the late Republican period, though the capital of the province of Hispania Citerior was always at Tarraco (Tarragona). Under Julius Caesar or Augustus it became a *colonia*, with the name Colonia Urbs Iulia Nova Carthago, and minted coins down to the reign of Caligula. It was the centre of the juridical *conventus* that bore its name, and became a provincial capital under the boundary changes instituted by Diocletian. Excavations have revealed public and private buildings and late Roman walls. In addition to the silver mines, Carthago Nova was renowned for the esparto grass which grew in the district and was used for ropes and basketwork. JSR

See Richardson, J. S. (1996) *The Romans in Spain*.

 Hispania: (a).

Cartimandua Queen of the Brigantes (d. AD 69), a loosely unified tribal federation in northern Britain which remained loyal to Rome during Cartimandua's reign. Historical documentation for Cartimandua is limited to scant references in Tacitus (*Annals*, *Histories*), few of which are complimentary to her character. In particular, Tacitus portrays her as an impetuous and immoral ruler easily swayed by her emotions, an estimation that may owe more to his Romanocentric view of women rulers than to specific examples of her conduct.

A case in point is Cartimandua's betrayal of Caratacus, the Catuvellaunian leader of the native rebellion and son of Cunobelinus, who sought her aid in AD 51. Rather than offer him sanctuary, she delivered the rebel to the Roman authorities, an action consistent with her status as a Roman ally. Tacitus' treatment of this incident, however, stresses the native queen's moral depravity, since her servitude to Rome surpassed her support for native resistance to the empire. Her reluctance to champion the native cause was also evident in 60 when the Brigantes failed to join the Boudican revolt.

Additional examples of Cartimandua's turbulent reign include an adulterous liaison with Vellocatus, the armour-bearer of her husband Venutius, in 57. This change of consort resulted in a lengthy period of intra-tribal warfare, in which Venutius was the ultimate victor in 69. Roman forces were needed to extricate Cartimandua from Venutius' wrath; they were unable, however, to salvage her sovereignty. MLM

See Braund, D. (1996) *Ruling Roman Britain*.

Carus see Ctesiphon

emperors, Roman: (b).

caryatids (*karyatides*) In architecture, female figures used in place of columns. The earliest preserved occurrence of the word is as the title of a work by Pratinas (c.500 BC), cited by Athenaeus (9.329f.). Elsewhere (6.241) Athenaeus suggests that the word properly applied to supporting figures with one arm raised, perhaps indicating derivation from dancers in the service of Artemis of Karyai (Plutarch, *Artaxerxes* 18; cf. Pausanias 3.10.7, 4.16.9).

Vitruvius (1.1.5) derives the term from representations of the captive women of Karyai after the Persian wars. However, the type occurs earlier, originating in the Near East and used from the mid- to later 6th century onwards. Early examples include the Knidian and Siphnian treasuries at Delphi, and the throne of Apollo at Amyklai in Laconia (Pausanias 3.18.10). On a smaller scale, female figures as supports occur on an early 7th-century Attic vase, on sculpted *perirrhantêria* from the mid-7th century, and on mirrors from c.600. It is possible that some archaic *korai* were used as caryatids, and the possibility of caryatids on the archaic Acropolis of Athens

CARYATIDS: (a) drawing of caryatid from the Athenian Erechtheion.

CARYATIDS: (b) caryatids from the sculptural collection of the emperor Hadrian at his villa near Tivoli.

may be reflected in the archaizing elements of the most famous examples, those on the Erechtheion (c.420–415 BC), though inscriptions refer to these only as *korai* or 'girls'. The Erechtheion caryatids were copied in Hadrian's villa at Tivoli and in the forum of Augustus. Other Roman examples include those in the collection of Asinius Pollio (made by Praxiteles), on the pantheon of Agrippa, and on the Hadrianic Velletri sarcophagus. KWA

See Congdon, L. (1981) *Caryatid Mirrors of Ancient Greece*; Schmidt, E. (1982) *Geschichte der Karyatide*.

Cassander see KASSANDROS.

Cassandra see KASSANDRA.

Cassius see ANTONY, MARK; ASIA, ROMAN; BATTLES, ROMAN; CIVIL WARS, ROMAN; PHILIPPI.

Cassius Dio (Cassius Dio Cocceianus; less correctly Dio Cassius) The historian was born c.AD 163 at Nicaea in Bithynia, son of Cassius Apronianus, a CONSUL and provincial governor of Lycia-Pamphylia, CILICIA and DALMATIA. He travelled to Rome in c.AD 180 at the beginning of COMMODUS' reign and began his public career as a QUAESTOR, thereby becoming a SENATOR. Subsequently he held a PRAETORSHIP in 194 or 195, a provincial governorship, a suffect CONSULSHIP in 205 or 206, membership in SEPTIMIUS SEVERUS' *consilium* and other provincial commands. He achieved a second consulship in 229, with SEVERUS ALEXANDER as his colleague.

Of his three works, which included a BIOGRAPHY of ARRIAN and a memoir on the dreams and portents of Septimius Severus, only his *History of Rome* survives. Dio himself (73.23.1–3) claims that a divine power commanded him to write the history. This incorporated earlier material, covering the wars of the late 2nd century and presented to Septimius Severus, into a work spanning Roman history from its beginning to the death of Severus. (Treatments of Caracalla and Elagabalus were added later.) He claims it took 10 years to collect his information and 12 to write his history, but is unclear when it was completed. The history, written in an annalistic style, is not completely extant. Fully preserved are books 36–54 (on 68–10 BC), but substantial fragments of 55–60 (9 BC–AD 46) and parts of 79–80 (the death of CARACALLA and half the reign of ELAGABALUS) survive. Otherwise the work is preserved in excerpt and epitome (summary) by Byzantine historians: Xiphilinos of Trapezous, writing in the 11th century (books 36–80 of Dio), and the more coherent Zonaras some half a century later, who summarized books 1–20.

As a historian, Dio has his moments. His importance is not in doubt, not least because his is the only surviving narrative history of the reign of AUGUSTUS. But we are largely ignorant of how he used his sources. Some chronological displacement is certain. He offers static views of certain administrative practices, and reflections not only of Dio's experiences of his own times but of his class and background are evident, though all these are important in their own right. He certainly was willing and able to be truthful, though he famously notes the difficulties of so doing under an imperial regime. He is largely favourable to the imperial system (if not to all its emperors) and paints Augustus in a very favourable light, a valuable portrait because it sets out a different picture from other sources, especially TACITUS. But Augustus is portrayed as the ideal emperor very much in order to project Dio's own view of what an emperor should be like, and of how the empire should be governed in his own time. His traditional support for his peers in the senate is strong, alongside the usual distrust of the soldiery. But such perspectives make Dio's history all the more important to an understanding of the Roman empire. CEPA

See Dio Cassius, *Roman History*, 9 vols., trs. E. Cary (1914–27); Millar, F. G. B. (1964) *A Study of Cassius Dio*.

Castor see DIOSCURI.

catacombs Places of burial usually associated with CHRISTIANS and JEWS at Rome, but also found at Naples, SYRACUSE, Malta, ALEXANDRIA, Hasdrumetum, Emesa and elsewhere. Their generic name probably derives from directions to a cemetery (now San Sebastiano) on the Via Appia, using Greek words for 'at the hollows' (*kata kumbas*). Often built near MARTYRS' TOMBS, catacombs are complex passageways dug underground or into hillsides; their length at Rome totals more than 550 km (340 miles). Bodies were wrapped in shrouds and placed into rows of niches (*loculi*, 'little places'). Many of the thousands of burials are identified, and these inscriptions and graffiti, as well as the painted walls, allow scholars to study aspects of the Christian community, mainly Greek-speaking in early phases, in some detail. Catacombs reflect the status of Christians, because they were less expensive than individual tombs, but desire for communal burial near martyrs contributed to their development and use. The period of greatest activity was the 3rd and 4th centuries, as the Christian community grew larger. In the 4th century and later, churches were built at many Christian cemeteries, with bodies often placed under their floors near the relics, but burial in catacombs continued until the 6th century.

Contrary to popular belief, catacombs were known to officials and were not widely used for refuge during PERSECUTIONS or for secret worship, though martyrs might be celebrated at their tombs. During the Valerianic persecution (AD 253–9), Christians were forbidden to visit catacombs. JV

See Stevenson, J. (1978) *Catacombs*; Webb, M. (2001) *The Churches and Catacombs of Early Christian Rome*.

 CHURCHES: (b).

catapults Using the term loosely, catapults were torsion and non-torsion machines, either bolt-firing (e.g. a *katapeltês oxybelês*) or stone-throwing (a *lithobolos* or *petrobolos*). They were used primarily in siege-craft to destroy FORTIFICATION walls. The original 'catapult' was the crossbow, and the goal was for its arrow to pierce the shield (*peltê*). Limited mobility made their use on the battlefield uncommon, not only because of difficulties in deploying them during battle but also because of the problems associated with transport from one battlefield to another. Catapults are, at any rate, a relatively late invention, the so-called *gastraphetês* ('belly-bow') being first employed c.399 BC by DIONYSIOS OF SYRACUSE and becoming more common in the mid-4th century. The first torsion catapult appears to have been used by ALEXANDER at Tyre, the work of a certain Diades, who may have picked up the idea in PHOENICIA. The torsion device employed the power of uncoiling cables that had been twisted tightly by means of levers. The skeins themselves were often made of hair – poorer women regularly sold their hair for such machines, and the well-to-do women of CARTHAGE were famous for donating their locks during the third PUNIC WAR – or animal sinews. An arrow fired by a *katapeltês* could inflict damage at a range of 200 m, though elevated machines could launch a missile up to 500 m. The *lithobolos* could hurl stones weighing up to 18 kg, probably for a distance of 200 m; modern tests have yielded different results. WH

See Marsden, E.W. (1969) *Greek and Roman Artillery*; Tarn, W.W. (1930) *Hellenistic Military and Naval Developments* (1930).

 ARTILLERY: (a).

catholicism From the Greek *katholikos* meaning 'universal', this term appears to be first used of the CHURCH by Ignatius of Antioch in AD 110: 'Where the bishop is, there let the people be, there is the catholic (*katholikê*) church' (*Smyrnaeans* 8). Clement of Alexandria further defines it as 'the ancient and catholic church which stands alone in essence, idea, principle and pre-eminence' (*Stromata* 7.17). Both use the term to signify the universal church in the face of perceived heretical beliefs, and of the unity of the church in the face of schism. The idea of unity and universality was enhanced by the imperial need for a united church. In 380 a law of THEODOSIUS stated that those who followed the religion of the BISHOPS of Rome and ALEXANDRIA were to be called catholic Christians (*Theodosian Code* 16.1.2). In the east the council of CONSTANTINOPLE (381) produced a creed that declared the 'one holy catholic and apostolic church'. In the West it also appears in the creed by the 4th century. Since the Reformation, the term catholic has normally been used in contrast to protestant, often without qualification. (see also CHURCH COUNCILS) MEH

See Halton, T. (1997) Catholic church, in E. Ferguson ed., *Encyclopedia of Early Christianity*; Stevenson, J. (1989) *Creeds, Councils and Controversies*.

Catiline (Lucius Sergius Catilina) A revolutionary put to death in 63 BC, Lucius Sergius Catilina was a young man of good family whose success did not match his ambition. His quest for the CONSULSHIP, delayed because of indictments in previous years, came up against his own wild talk and the popularity of CICERO, who defeated him. He spoke disparagingly of Cicero, who openly wore body armour to exaggerate his personal danger at the elections for 62, when Catiline lost again. From this point, Catiline's words escalated to action, partly goaded by Cicero, who raised the stakes with his own ORATORY. Catiline found support among a variety of desperadoes, unsuccessful farmers among SULLA's veterans, the indebted, and even Sempronia (wife of Decimus Brutus, consul in 77), whose unmatronly skill in cultural pursuits drew SALLUST's ire. Cicero's spy was Fulvia, mistress of Quintus Curius, a gambler whose sudden promises of expensive gifts aroused her curiosity and awoke her patriotism. A letter from the conspirators to envoys of the Gallic Allobroges at Rome provided the necessary written evidence of Catiline's plans. Leaders at Rome were quickly arrested and executed, and Catiline was defeated and killed.

To glorify his uneventful consulship, Cicero considers the conspiracy more dangerous than it was and portrays himself as a new ROMULUS for stopping it. Catiline is more accurately to be seen as a symptom of chaos attending the fragile stability of the late REPUBLIC than as its cause. JV

See Cicero, *Orations against Catiline*; Sallust, *Catiline*; Stockton, D. (1971) *Cicero*; Wilkins, A.T. (1994) *Villain or Hero: Sallust's portrayal of Catiline.*

Cato the Elder (Marcus Porcius Cato) 234–149 BC Occupant of a special position in the history of the Roman REPUBLIC, as one of the most vivid figures of the 2nd century. Undoubtedly he is responsible for some of the stereotypes of Romanness that became current in antiquity and subsequently. Born at Tusculum to a family without Roman political experience, his own career was fostered by his PATRICIAN patron Lucius Valerius Flaccus. As QUAESTOR in 204 he served under SCIPIO AFRICANUS in SICILY and Spain. He was PLEBEIAN AEDILE in 199, PRAETOR in 198 and CONSUL in 195, when he was involved with the suppression of revolt in Spain, for which he won a TRIUMPH. In 191 he fought against ANTIOCHOS III at THERMOPYLAI; in 184 he and Flaccus were elected CENSORS on the ticket of reforming public MORALITY.

After this extraordinarily successful career, the censorship marked something of a watershed. Rigorous application of the rules that governed membership of the senatorial and equestrian orders, large-scale public building works, and high TAXATION on luxuries meant that Cato gained many enemies in the SENATE (though many friends among the people). While he retained his influence through his large bulk of ORATORICAL work, he never held political office again. Apart from remaining a scourge of certain individuals, particularly Scipio and his friends, he vehemently opposed Rome's involvement in the East, fearing perhaps the adoption of oriental manners foreign to the Roman way of life. Equally vehemently, however, he demanded the destruction of CARTHAGE (famously ending all his speeches, whatever the topic, with the words 'Carthage must be destroyed').

Cato's speeches survived to CICERO's day at least; he was also the founder of Latin PROSE writing. The *Origines*, which survive in fragments, collected stories on the foundations and customs of various Italian towns, and moved on to Roman military success from the first PUNIC WAR. His *De agricultura* is the first Latin technical manual. It describes how to run successfully a small VILLA farm with SLAVES, practising a mixed economy including the production of WINE and OLIVE OIL, and covers everything from relations with the bailiff (*vilicus*) to appropriate prayers.

Cato was a complicated and enigmatic figure. He lauded and to some extent embodied the virtuous and thrifty citizen, but pursued wealth through farming with enthusiasm. He appears to have grown steadily more cruel towards his slaves while acknowledging their usefulness in AGRICULTURE, and showed an unusual tenderness towards his son, whom he taught himself, not entrusting him to slaves or Greeks. Although he knew Greek, he was bitter in his criticism of Greeks and their culture, despite the fact that the *Origines* is in some ways indebted to Greek traditions of scholarship and research. His final legacy may have been to provide a model for his grandson CATO THE YOUNGER, who prized inflexibility and a disregard for political realities, and thereby contributed to the descent into CIVIL WAR at the end of the Republic. CJS

See Cato, *On Agriculture* (with Varro), trs. H.B. Ash and W.D. Hooper (1935); *Origines* (Budé edition); Plutarch, *Life of Cato*; Astin, A. (1978) *Cato the Censor.*

Cato the Younger (Marcus Porcius Cato Uticensis) 95–46 BC A great-grandson of CATO THE ELDER, he grew up in the Livian household of his mother, a sister of Marcus Livius Drusus (tribune 91 BC). He served as QUAESTOR (64), TRIBUNE (62) and PRAETOR (54), but never held the CONSULSHIP. Throughout his career, he inevitably insisted on the maintenance of the old Republican principles. Consequently, he opposed CAESAR vociferously in 59 and was briefly imprisoned. As the political situation deteriorated, Cato supported POMPEY and was a GENERAL of Republican forces. Upon the defeat of Pompey, he held Utica for the Pompeians. Its inhabitants honoured him when he and his wife committed SUICIDE, a few days after Caesar's defeat of the Pompeians at Thapsus on 6 April 46.

Cato was well connected within the aristocracy, where he was more respected than liked. His second wife, daughter of Lucius Marcius Philippus, consul in 56, was Marcia, whom he lent to Quintus Hortensius Hortalus. Cato's daughter Porcia was first married to Marcus Calpurnius Bibulus, Julius Caesar's colleague as consul in 59, then to Marcus Junius BRUTUS the tyrannicide.

His attempt to hold to ancient Roman principles was genuine and admirable, but even CICERO complained of a utopianism that sacrificed practicality to idealism: '[Cato] speaks as if he were living in the Republic of PLATO, not the sewer of ROMULUS' (*Letters to Atticus* 2.1.8). Nonetheless, he wrote a *Cato* that Caesar was compelled to answer with an *Anti-Cato*, which so distorted Cato's morality that it generated sympathetic views. JV

See Plutarch, *Lives*, vol. 8, trs. B. Perrin (1921).

cattle In the ancient world, cattle played many different roles. Faunal evidence suggests that ancient cattle were considerably smaller than their modern descendants. They were commonly used as traction animals, prized for their reliability and capacity for pulling large loads. Cows, BULLS and oxen are all represented as plough animals. Though slow, they were effective on areas of flat ground, but not as useful on steep or narrow fields: cattle need far more room to turn a plough than do mules or DONKEYS. In the hot and dry parts of the MEDITERRANEAN region they are more difficult to keep in good condition over the rainless summer and early autumn months than SHEEP and GOATS, because they need better grazing and more water. For this reason, the use of cow's milk, CHEESE and butter was rare in many parts of the classical world. Nor did every farming family necessarily own a team of plough cattle, since they were expensive to buy and to maintain.

Cattle were used for MEAT, and were the required animals for some Greek (e.g. the Athenian Bouphonia) and Roman (e.g. the Suovetaurilia) SACRIFICES. These were generally quite special rituals, since cattle were valuable animals and produced large quantities of meat – much more than a single family could eat fresh. Other important products of the BUTCHERY of cattle included hides, horn and BONE. LF

See Isager, S. and Skydsgaard, J. E. (1992) *Ancient Greek Agriculture* 89–91; Whittaker, C. R., ed. (1988) *Pastoral Economies in Classical Antiquity.*

Catullus (Gaius Valerius Catullus) c.84–54 BC POET, born in Verona (then part of the province of Cisalpine GAUL), who appears to have spent most of his adult life in Rome. He was a leading figure in the so-called Neoteric movement, a loose association of self-consciously innovative writers adhering above all to the poetic ideals associated with the name of KALLIMACHOS. Poem 1, which takes the form of a dedication to the BIOGRAPHER and HISTORIAN Cornelius NEPOS, offers a concise statement of these ideals. The poet describes his 'little book' as 'new', 'charming' and 'polished', and refers to the poems contained in it as 'trifles'. The qualities hinted at in this opening manifesto (wit, panache, stylistic elegance, conciseness and a preference for themes considered trivial by traditional Roman standards) are amply documented in the remaining poems, many of which are concerned directly or indirectly with poetic composition. These include broadsides against fellow poets whom Catullus regards as old-fashioned (e.g. poem 36) or incompetent (14, 22), and elegant compliments addressed to other members of the coterie (35, 95). Several poems allude more or less explicitly to Kallimachos (7, 70, 116). Poem 66 is a translation from book 4 of Kallimachos' *Aitia*. Other prominent themes include friendship, the death of the poet's brother, and the corrupt social and sexual mores of eminent politicians (especially JULIUS CAESAR, attacked in poems 29, 54, 57 and 93) and other public figures. Catullus has been most widely admired since antiquity, however, for the series of passionate love poems addressed to a (married) woman whom he calls by the pseudonym Lesbia.

The so-called Lesbia-cycle – made up of some 26 poems, approximately a quarter of the surviving collection – has been the focus of intense controversy for more than a century. Nineteenth- and early 20th-century criticism revolved around attempts to establish a chronology for the relationship (regarded essentially as a historical event) and to determine the identity of Lesbia. The name is apparently an allusion to SAPPHO of Lesbos, to whom – like Kallimachos – Catullus pays tribute through the medium of translation (poem 51 is a loose version of Sappho fragment 31). The NOVELIST Apuleius, writing some 150 years after the poet's death, asserts that Lesbia's real name was CLODIA. She is commonly identified with the Clodia who is memorably depicted by Cicero (*Pro Caelio*) as a passionate, manipulative and sexually promiscuous socialite. Some critics have questioned whether the identification can be made with certainty, and there has been a tendency in more recent scholarship to reject the romantic interpretation of the poems as a direct reflection of an actual, historical love affair. An alternative approach is to recognize that many of Lesbia's qualities – both good and bad – reflect contemporary stereotypes, and to see her as essentially a creation of the poet. In this sense, she acts as a vehicle or focus for the expression of his erotic ideals, and as a target for his more misogynistic impulses. The poems addressed to or concerned with Lesbia are particularly characterized by a striking and systematic inversion of gender roles, and by the poet's appropriation of vocabulary normally confined to the public, male sphere. Thus, Lesbia is from the outset the dominant force in the relationship: Catullus plays JUNO to her JUPITER (68.138–40), and complains that she has destroyed his love like a fragile flower (11.21–4; for the flower as a symbol of female virginity, see e.g. 62.39–47). At the same time, the poet makes much of his longing for an equal, reciprocal relationship, described in terms of the system of mutual, aristocratic obligation (*officium, amicitia*) which underpinned Roman public and social life (see especially poems 75, 76, 109). Many of the best-known poems in the collection are framed as introspective reflections on the poet's incompatible feelings of desire and distaste (e.g. 8, 75, 85); others address Lesbia in pathetic tones comparable to those used to upbraid faithless friends (cf. especially poems 76–7) or take the form of virulent invectives in which she is condemned as a depraved, insatiable whore (11, 37, 58). Viewed in this light, the love poems do not stand out as distinctly from the rest of the collection as has sometimes been supposed. Rather, the Lesbia cycle can be seen to develop themes (gender roles and masculinity; the nature of friendship in the public and private spheres; social and poetic ideals) that are characteristic of Catullus' poetry as a whole.

In addition to the short poems in a variety of metres (1–60) and the EPIGRAMS (69–116), the collection which has come down to us contains a central group of longer poems, including two *epithalamia* or wedding songs (61–2), two poems on mythological subjects (63–4) and a highly innovative elegiac poem (68) which weaves together the themes of love, death and loss and is centred on an extended comparison between Catullus and Lesbia and the mythical lovers Laudamia and Protesilaus. Poem 64 – which has been described as Catullus' masterpiece – is an *epyllion* or 'mini-epic' of some 400 lines, dealing with the marriage of ACHILLES' parents Peleus and Thetis. The 'inset tale' of Ariadne and THESEUS contrasts with the (apparently) happy marriage in the frame narrative, and contains intriguing echoes of the language employed in the Lesbia poems. Both stories are told in an elliptical and allusive manner, which points, once again, to the influence of Kallimachos and his Alexandrian contemporaries. The poem was clearly widely admired, and is frequently echoed by the poets of the next generation, notably VIRGIL, who draws on Catullus' Ariadne as a model for the speeches of Dido in *Aeneid* 4.

Catullus' shorter poems, too, had a profound impact on both Augustan and Silver Latin poets, notably the elegists PROPERTIUS, TIBULLUS and OVID (who elaborated on the earlier poet's inversion of gender roles and other conventional hierarchies of values, particularly the privilege traditionally accorded to the public over the private sphere). The epigrams of MARTIAL also engage frequently with Catullus' poetic and social ideals. In modern times, Catullus has continued to fascinate readers and writers, and has been the subject of several novels as well as reworkings and translations of the poems. MG

See Lee, G., trs. (1991) *The Poems of Catullus*; Martin, C. (1992) *Catullus*.

Caudine Forks The second SAMNITE WAR began in 326 BC with a prolonged Roman offensive. This came to an end in 321, when the advancing Roman army was trapped in the Caudine Forks (Caudinae Furculae), a narrow defile, and forced to surrender. The location is uncertain: LIVY's account is not to be considered entirely accurate, and the traditional site, the Arienzo–Arpaia valley between CAPUA and Beneventum, is as good as any. According to some versions a battle took place. The Roman army was disarmed and sent under the 'yoke' by the Samnite commander, Gavius Pontius (from whom Gaius Pontius Telesinus, the Samnite commander in the SOCIAL WAR, defeated by SULLA at the Colline Gate in 82 BC, claimed descent). When the army returned to Rome, the SENATE repudiated the agreement (on the basis that any such agreement must be ratified by the people) and handed over to the Samnites the CONSULS responsible (Titus Veturius Calvinus and Spurius Postumius Albinus). Livy records Roman victories in the following two years, including the story that after the siege of Luceria 7,000 Samnites under Gavius Pontius were, in their turn, sent under the yoke. The fact that otherwise there was peace until 316 rather suggests that this may be a justificatory fiction, in response to one of the more humiliating episodes in Roman history. JRWP

See Livy 9.1–7, trs. B. Radice (1982); Cornell, T. J. (1995) *The Beginnings of Rome*.

causes ARISTOTLE himself distinguished four sorts of causal factor: MATTER, form, agent and end. In the case of a SCULPTURE, the material cause is the bronze, the formal cause is what makes it a sculpture (its structure), the efficient cause is the sculptor (or the art of sculpture) and the end, or final cause, what it was made for (fame, money, satisfaction). Aristotle produced the first formal analysis of types of explanatory factor, but a concern with cause and explanation appeared early in GREEK PHILOSOPHY, as Aristotle himself knew – he complains, with some justice, that the early PRESOCRATICS were only interested in material explanation. In the 5th century BC, the growth of political and legal institutions engendered a corresponding interest in matters of legal and social responsibility. Such debates were couched in terms of what was to be the appropriate causal analysis of events. In a famous case, a bystander was transfixed by a javelin at the GAMES. It was subject of forensic debate whether the thrower, the victim, the games organizer or the javelin itself was really guilty. In parallel, the rise of rational MEDICINE at the same time generated an interest in causal analysis, prompting the HIPPOCRATICS to distinguish between genuine causes, background conditions, prerequisites and occasions. This debate continued throughout the long history of Greek medicine. Some doctors (e.g. Erasistratos, fl. c.260 BC) refused to consider any non-necessitating factor a cause, and held that causes must be coeval with their effects (PLATO had already claimed that causes must be invariably associated with their effects). Their opponents, pre-eminently GALEN (AD 129–c. 215), replied that causing involved a complex of factors, all of which could be relevant to the outcome even if none of them (individually) necessitated it. SCEPTICAL philosophers, influenced by Erasistratos and other doctors, sought to show that the very concept of a cause was incoherent – causes must both precede and be coeval with their effects – but that is impossible. Again, counterattacks were mounted by philosophically sophisticated doctors like Galen and by philosophers committed to causal explanation such as the STOICS. But the most profound debate of all pitted those, like Aristotle and Plato (in their different ways), who thought that purposive explanation was appropriate, indeed essential, even in the case of the natural world, and those, pre-eminently the ATOMISTS, who thought that all natural explanation should be mechanical in form. For Aristotle (and the Stoics, and Galen), the natural world is simply too structured, too endowed with self-maintaining and regenerating form, to be accounted for solely in terms of the haphazard dynamic interaction of fundamental physical stuffs. For the atomists, and those influenced by them, material and dynamical principles ought to suffice. The debate reverberated through antiquity and beyond. Indeed, in some forms it is with us still. RJH

See Hankinson, R. J. (1998) *Cause and Explanation in the Ancient Greek World*; Sorabji, R. R. K. (1980) *Necessity, Cause and Blame*.

cavalry Although the HORSE has a long history of domestication, the early armies of the MEDITERRANEAN world and Near East tended to use them for CHARIOT warfare, adding speed and mobility to wheeled devices previously drawn by oxen and DONKEYS. Difficulties of training, and the lack of essential items such as the saddle, stirrup and horseshoe, retarded the development of the war-horse and the mounted warrior. In the Iron Age, cavalry emerged in the empires of Assyria and PERSIA, as well as among the SCYTHIANS and even the Greeks.

CAVALRY: (a) Macedonian cavalryman with two long lances.

CAVALRY: (b) dreadlocked Moorish auxiliary cavalry serving with the Roman army in Dacia.

But the difficulties of mounting and keeping an armed warrior on horseback, even with the development of the 'treed saddle', bridle and bit, and spurs, were considerable until the introduction of the stirrup in the Middle Ages. In Greece, topography and the preference for HOPLITE battle limited the role of cavalry until the 4th century BC. The expense of maintaining a horse and the often ostentatious gear of the horseman meant that numbers of cavalry were generally low and their functions limited to protecting the flanks of the infantry, reconnaissance and pursuit. Horses in antiquity were, at any rate, not large by modern standards: rather they were ponies that stood about 1.35 m ($4\frac{1}{2}$ ft) at the withers (1.50 m, 5 ft, was considered substantial) and were ill suited to carry heavily armed warriors.

Not surprisingly, the best cavalry developed in THESSALY and lowland MACEDONIA, where more extensive range-land was to found. By contrast, Thucydides (7.27.5) reports that during the Dekeleian war (the later phase of the PELOPONNESIAN WAR) horses, because they were not shod, frequently went lame as a result of patrolling the rocky terrain of ATTICA. PHILIP II and ALEXANDER made much greater use of various specialized forces, particularly light-armed (*psiloi*) infantry and cavalry. Whereas the early Greek cavalryman fought with the spear, the Macedonians armed many of their horsemen with the short *sarissa* (about 4.25 m, 14 ft, in length, including spearhead and butt-spike) and organized entire units of *sarissophoroi* to go along with mounted javelin-men (*hippakontistai*). In the later stages of his campaign, Alexander began to employ Scythian horse-archers (*hippotoxotai*) for his campaigns in INDIA. Greek armies of the classical age had attempted to reach a quick decision on the battlefield by means of colliding hoplite armies. Alexander began instead to use his cavalry on the wings (particularly the right, where he personally led the 'Companions') as shock troops, leaving the infantry phalanx in the centre, and the Thessalian horse on the left, to assume a more defensive role.

The hellenistic period also witnessed the numerous and deadly horsemen of the PARTHIANS, who fought either with the asymmetrical bow, which allowed them to discharge arrows as they fled (whether in real or feigned retreat: the famous 'Parthian shot'), or as heavily armed *kataphraktoi*. In the West, the Romans were confronted with the skilful Numidian horsemen during their struggle with HANNIBAL. Although in many Greek and Roman armies cavalry scarcely exceeded 10 per cent of the total forces, foreign armies often fielded cavalry in much larger proportions. (For example, about 20 per cent of Hannibal's army of 50,000 at CANNAE consisted of cavalry, whereas the Romans fielded some 6,000 cavalry to support their 80,000 infantry.) Indeed, as the power of the Romans grew, they came to rely more heavily on foreign (allied) cavalry – CELTS, Numidians, DALMATIANS and GERMANS – who employed just such tactics as the Parthians, Sarmatians and Numidians had used effectively against Roman armies, serving as both light-armed skirmishers and shock troops. WH

See Bugh, G. (1988) *The Horsemen of Athens*; Goldsworthy, A. (1996) *The Roman Army at War, 100 BC–AD 200*; Spence, I. (1993) *The Cavalry of Classical Greece*; Worley, L. J. (1994) *The Cavalry of Ancient Greece*.

 ARMS AND ARMOUR: (d).

celibacy Defined as abstention from marriage, in the CHRISTIAN context this also included sexual continence but not, initially, lifelong virginity. Celibacy was not considered a prerequisite for ordination in the early CHURCH, though according to TERTULLIAN it was an aspirational ideal. While MARRIAGE was not prohibited, remarriage after widowhood was frowned upon. The rise of the ascetic movement in the 4th century AD brought ideas about the place of SEXUALITY and sexual relations in religious life to the fore. The council of Elvira (c.300) had stated that clergy who entered the priesthood unmarried should remain so but did not prohibit those who had married before ordination. The matter of clerical celibacy was also debated at the council of Nicaea (325). Throughout the 4th and 5th centuries it continued to be a subject of debate, and regional councils passed a variety of rulings. For example, the councils of Toledo (400) and Turin (401) extended the rule of celibacy to the lower orders of clergy, and SYNESIUS of CYRENE, elected BISHOP against his will, knew this meant the dissolution of his marriage. In 528 JUSTINIAN excluded married men from the clergy and ruled that clergy could only bequeath property to the church, not their families. The council at Trullo (692) allowed lower orders to marry after ordination; priests and deacons could remain married if they already were before ordination; bishops were expected to practice sexual continence, and wives to go into a convent. Clearly, clerical celibacy was not universally regulated throughout antiquity. (see also CHURCH COUNCILS) MEH

Celsus (Aulus Cornelius Celsus) fl. c.AD 10–30 The author of a six-part Latin ENCYCLOPEDIA entitled *The Arts*, encompassing AGRICULTURE, MEDICINE, warfare, RHETORIC, PHILOSOPHY and probably also law. Only the eight books *On Medicine* survive. This attempt to summarize what men of the Roman élite should know about these technical subjects follows the precedent set by VARRO's *The Disciplines*, but Celsus parts company with his predecessor in his attitude to Greek learning. He engages not in polemic against, but dialogue with, Greek intellectualism and its products, using them for his own, distinctly but not antagonistically Roman, purposes. The position he adopts in relation to the essentially Greek past and present of the medical art, as set out in the *prooemium* (prologue) to *On Medicine*, is therefore that of an independent seeker after truth: someone able to steer a sensible middle course between competing medical models and factions, to take the best from all of them in order to forge an art that is both rational and practical. Applying these principles, Celsus proceeds to provide prescriptions for the preservation of HEALTH, and then an ordered description of types of DISEASES, and their treatment by regimen, pharmacology and surgery. He thus furnishes the Roman *paterfamilias* with the knowledge necessary to act properly as guardian not only of his own health, but also that of those under his authority; that is, not only directly but also indirectly as the ultimate arbiter of medical care received by those in his household. REF

See Celsus, *De medicina*, 3 vols., trs. W. G. Spencer (1935–8).

Celtiberian wars The name Celtiberian is given by Greek and Roman writers to a group of peoples living in the area of the Ebro valley and the north-eastern sector of the great central plateau (*meseta*) of Spain. Inscriptions from sites in this area reveal that they used a CELTIC language, but wrote it using an Iberian script. After the arrival of the Romans, they were involved in the sporadic wars which marked the first 30 years of the 2nd century BC; but Tiberius Sempronius Gracchus, proconsular PRAETOR in HISPANIA Citerior from 180 to 178, concluded treaties with them. War began again in 153 in a dispute over the town of Segeda, which led to the formation of a Celtiberian coalition, made up of the Arevaci, Belli and Titthi, centred on NUMANTIA. This war continued for 20 years, with a pause between 149 and 145, and resulted in a series of Roman defeats. The most spectacular of these, in 137, led to the surrender by the CONSUL, Gaius Hostilius Mancinus, of himself and his entire army. In the later 140s an alliance was struck between the Arevaci and their allies and the LUSITANIAN forces under VIRIATHUS, who was also fighting the Romans in the west of the peninsula. In 134, Publius SCIPIO AEMILIANUS was elected consul to fight the Celtiberians. After a long siege, he captured Numantia. JSR

See Richardson, J. S. (1986) *Hispaniae*.

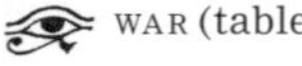 WAR (table).

Celts The term Celt comes to us via the Greeks, who first wrote of them as living in certain parts of north-western Europe c.500 BC. Hekataios in the early 5th century was the first to mention *Keltoi*, referring probably to communities living near Massalia (MARSEILLES) in France. HERODOTOS later states that the DANUBE rises in the territory of the *Keltoi*, and he implies the presence of Celtic peoples on the Iberian peninsula. It is reasonable to infer, then, that from c.500 BC (the start of the LA TÈNE period) there were peoples in western Europe whom the Greeks recognized as being ethnically similar, and that some of these probably called themselves something like *Keltoi*.

Since the 19th century, the second (or La Tène) Iron Age of western and central Europe (approximately 5th to 1st centuries BC) has been firmly associated with the Celts, whose 'homeland' is thought to have been centred on the RHINE and Danube. The traditional view has been that, from c.400, Celtic peoples migrated from their homelands, coming to occupy vast territories including Britain, Ireland, Spain, the ALPS, GERMANY, Bohemia, northern Italy, the Balkans and ANATOLIA. Throughout the 'migration' period (c.400–200), Celtic peoples came into contact with the Romans (who called them *Galli*, our 'Gauls'), fighting a protracted series of wars well documented by POLYBIOS, LIVY and other Roman historians.

In support of the traditional view, ARCHAEOLOGISTS can point to the emergence of shared BURIAL practices and artefact styles (particularly METALWORKING styles) across much of Europe after 400 BC. There is also linguistic evidence (mostly of the Roman period) for the use of Celtic languages in Western European countries. In the last 20 years, however, the traditional view of a 'Celtic Europe' has come under scrutiny. Many archaeologists now believe that it is impossible to regard Europe as home to a single group of people with a shared ethnicity – that is, with one name and a common sense of belonging. For a variety of reasons, archaeologists seem willing to acknowledge the weaknesses inherent in each of the three main categories of evidence used to assign 'Celtic' identity to Iron Age communities: material culture, classical textual sources and the Celtic languages.

It is undeniable that from c.400 BC a 'shared' later Iron Age European material culture emerged. Some of the most widespread phenomena include the flat grave inhumation rite, the use of Waldalgesheim style decoration (named after the site in Germany associated with it) and the use of 'dragon-pair' swords. But many question whether these shared characteristics point to a shared identity. Many communities using Waldalgesheim decorative items, for example, may have acquired them through TRADE or as prestige goods. It is also possible (as has been argued for dragon-pair swords) that certain motifs were seen as having magical or protective properties, and were sought out for this reason by peoples who would not necessarily have regarded themselves as Celts.

With reference to classical accounts of *Keltoi*, one must remember that early Greek writers knew little indeed about those to the north and west of the MEDITERRANEAN, and wittingly or unwittingly undoubtedly ignored a myriad of ethnic nuances in the belief that western and central Europe as far as Russia belonged to *Keltoi*, and the lands further east to the SCYTHIANS. The term *Keltoi* is no more useful an ethnic marker than the generic term 'Indian', employed by European settlers in North America. In this context it is interesting to note that in the 50s BC, when JULIUS CAESAR provides the first classical reference to an Iron Age people calling themselves Celts (as opposed to being given that name by outsiders), he clearly indicates that by that date, at least, the word had a very limited geographic applicability. 'Gaul is divided into three parts inhabited

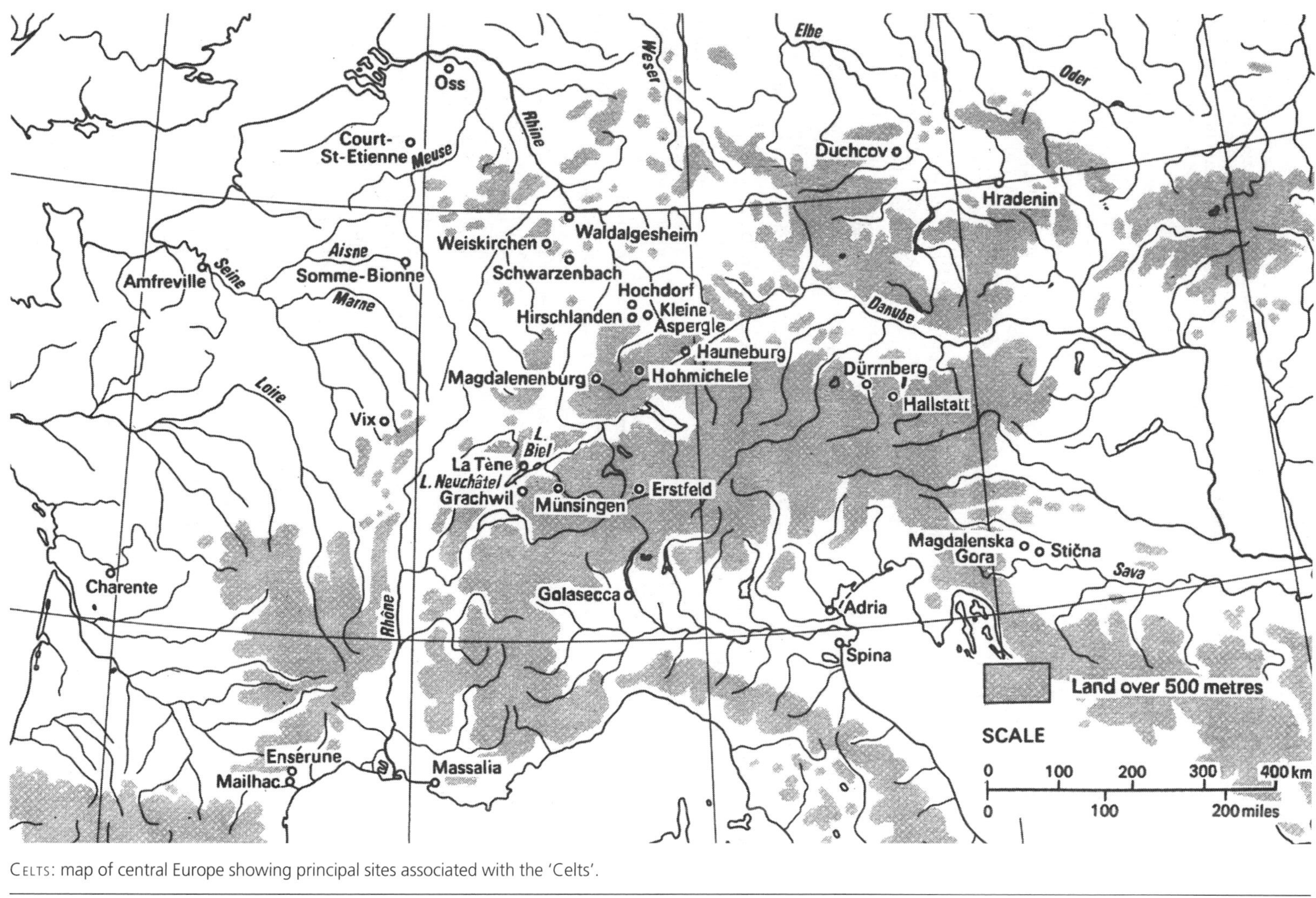

Celts: map of central Europe showing principal sites associated with the 'Celts'.

respectively by the Belgae, the Aquitani and the people who call themselves Celts, though we call them Gauls. All of these have different languages, customs, and laws. The Celts are separated from the Aquitani by the river Garonne, from the Belgae by the Marne and the Seine' (*Gallic War* 1.1). According to Caesar then, the Celts were not a Europe-wide phenomenon, but simply the people who lived in central France.

Linguistic evidence has shown that modern peoples bordering on the ATLANTIC speak (or have recently spoken) languages with a common ancestry. These 'Celtic' languages (a group name first used in the 16th century) include Scots Gaelic, Irish Gaelic, Welsh, Cornish Celtiberian and Breton. But it does not necessarily follow from this that the peoples who lived in these areas in the Iron Age were Celtic-speakers too. Certainly, we cannot assume an unbroken 'ancestral' link between modern speakers of Celtic languages and the ancient peoples we now refer to as Celts. Nevertheless, the recognition of 'Celtic' languages has had a fundamental impact on archaeologists. As it developed into a discipline during the 19th century, Iron Age archaeology grew up in the context of a widespread belief that 'the Celts' had at some point occupied much of Western Europe. At the end of the century, archaeologists began to unearth a distinctive range of artefacts, all making use of a similar art style, that appeared to be used by many different communities across Europe. In the mid-19th century, the British scholar Sir Augustus Franks made an explicit equation between this new 'La Tène' material culture and the Celts of both classical literature and linguistic theory. From that time, 'La Tène' has been thought of not simply as a series of metalwork styles (which is essentially what it is) but as a synonym for a people, 'the Celts'.

In Britain (and to a lesser extent in continental Europe, where the Celts largely continue to be regarded as an ancestral 'European' people), many archaeologists now question the concept of a 'Celtic' Iron Age. Heterogeneous, regionalized Iron Ages are emerging from this process, and this is now beginning to have an impact upon the study of the later, supposedly 'Romano-Celtic' peoples of Roman BRITAIN, Spain and Gaul. JW

See James, S. (1993) *Exploring the World of the Celts*; (1999) *The Atlantic Celts.*

 GAUL: (a).

cement see CONCRETE; HOUSES; LAURION; OSTIA; WATER SUPPLY; WATERPROOFING; see also GLUES.

cemetery see BURIALS; CATACOMBS; FUNERARY RITES.

censors The *censores* were a pair of Roman MAGISTRATES, usually elected every five years for an 18-month term by the *comitia centuriata* and possessing broad powers to review the list of citizens. Until 339 BC censors were exclusively PATRICIAN. They did not possess *imperium* and were not assigned lictors, but the censorship was the highest step on the *cursus honorum*, and by the mid-Republic it was normally reserved for ex-CONSULS. The intervals between the elections of censors could often be erratic, particularly in times of political turbulence such as the late Republic. During the imperial period, the office was often assumed by the EMPEROR himself.

The censors' primary duty was to conduct the CENSUS of the Roman people, which included not merely the counting of citizens and registration of property, but also a review of the morality of individual citizens. Those who were found lacking for whatever reason could be removed from the membership rolls of their tribe and consigned to the category of *aerarii*, which still seems to have implied a tax-paying obligation. In addition to the considerable odium accruing to such a demotion, if the person was a SENATOR he was expelled from the senate. The duties of the censors extended well beyond the revision of citizenship, as they were responsible for auctioning contracts for tax collection, letting contracts for public works projects, and leasing public property for purposes such as MINING. GSA

See Lintott, A. (1999) *The Constitution of the Roman Republic*; Suolahti, J. (1963) *The Roman Censors.*

censuses Enumerations of CITIZENS. At Rome, its origin was credited to SERVIUS TULLIUS. In office normally every five years, Roman CENSORS counted citizens, probably only adult males, and allocated them to voting units. The lists were the basis for military service. Registration was compulsory but compliance could vary, especially from the poorest classes, who were 'counted by head' (*capite censi*) and drew little benefit from inclusion. Many census figures survive, but some are corrupt. The earliest records 80,000 citizens at the time of Servius Tullius (Livy 1.44); the number for AD 14 is 4,937,000 (Augustus, *Res Gestae* 8.4). Large grants of Roman citizenship in the 1st century BC contributed extensively to the later figures. Little is known of censuses during the imperial period, but evidence from the early 4th century AD reveals that they continued, mainly for TAXATION purposes.

Fewer enumerations are known from the Greek world. Most cities registered citizens when they reached adulthood, but DIONYSIOS I conducted a formal census while TYRANT at SYRACUSE (406–367 BC) as a basis for taxation. As early as the 7th century BC, pharaohs had counted the citizens of Egypt, women and children included, for tax reasons; the cycle was 14 years (the indiction), with ongoing registration of births. HERODOTOS (7.60) reports that XERXES counted his army by packing 10,000 men tightly in a circle, building a low wall around them, and refilling the circle until all the men had passed through; strictly speaking, this was not a census. JV

See Brunt, P. A. (1971) *Italian Manpower, 225 BC–AD 14.*

centre-periphery see CORE-PERIPHERY.

centuriation see GALLIA CISALPINA; LANDSCAPE; SPACE.

cereals The main dietary staple in classical antiquity. Although many different types of cereals were grown, in most parts of the ancient world varieties of barley and wheat were the most important, and different places had their preferred local varieties.

Barley (*Hordeum* spp., Greek *krithê*, Latin *hordeum*) is more tolerant of drought and of saline conditions than wheat, and therefore was more reliable in arid parts of the MEDITERRANEAN region and the Near East. The two main types of barley were two-rowed barley (*Hordeum distichum*) and six-rowed

CENSUSES: population figures from the Roman census.

Date	Population	Source
6th century BC	80,000	Livy 1.44.2
508	130,000	Dion. Hal. 5.20
503	120,000	Jerome, Ol.69.1
498	150,700	Dion. Hal. 5.75.3
493	110,000+	Dion. Hal. 6.96.4
474	103,000+ (or 133,000)	Dion. Hal. 9.36.3
465	104,714	Livy 3.3.9
459	117,319	Livy 3.24.10
393/2	152,573	Pliny, *NH* 33.16
340/339	165,000	Eusebios, Ol. 110.1
323	150,000	Orosius 5.22.2
294/3	262,321	Livy 10.47.2
290–287	272,000	Livy, *Epit.* 11
280/79	287,222	Livy, *Epit.* 13
276/5	271,224	Livy, *Epit.* 14
265/4	292,324	Eutropius 2.18
252/1	297,797	Livy, *Epit.* 18
247/6	241,212	Livy, *Epit.* 19
241/0	260,000	Jerome, Ol. 134.1
234/3	270,212	Livy, *Epit.* 20
209/8	137,108 or 237,108	Livy 26.36
204/3	214,000	Livy 29.37
194/3	147,704 or 243,704	Livy 35.9
189/8	258,318	Livy 38.36
179/8	258,794	Livy, *Epit.* 41
174/3	269,015	Livy 42.10
169/8	312,805	Livy, *Epit.* 45
164/3	337,022	Livy, *Epit.* 46
159/8	328,316	Livy, *Epit.* 47
154/3	324,000	Livy, *Epit.* 48
147/6	322,000	Eusebios, Ol. 158.3
142/1	327,442	Livy, *Epit.* 54
136/5	317,933	Livy, *Epit.* 56
131/0	318,823	Livy, *Epit.* 59
125/4	394,736	Livy, *Epit.* 60
115/4	394,336	Livy, *Epit.* 63
86/5	463,000	Jerome, Ol. 173.4
70/69	910,000	Phlegon F.12.6
28	4,063,000	*Res Gestae* 8.2
8	4,233,000	*Res Gestae* 8.3
AD 14	4,937,000	*Res Gestae* 8.4

After P. Brunt (1971) *Italian Manpower* 13–14; *CAH*, 7.2, 137; Ol. = Olympiads, employed in the chronologies of Eusebios and Jerome (Hieronymus).

CEREALS: principal cereal types in the classical world.

Cereal	Latin name	Season	Special properties	Weaknesses
bread wheat	*Triticum aestivum*	autumn sown, late spring/ early summer harvest	good for bread	less drought tolerant than barley
durum wheat	*Triticum durum*	autumn sown, late spring/ early summer harvest	high in protein, very good for bread	less drought tolerant than barley, needs good soil
emmer	*Triticum dicoccum*	autumn sown, late spring harvest	good storage properties	hulled
spelt	*Triticum spelta*	autumn sown, late spring harvest	high in protein, good storage properties	hulled
einkorn	*Triticum monococcum*	autumn sown, late spring harvest	good storage properties, tolerant of cooler conditions	hulled, relatively low yields
barley	*Hordeum distichum, H. hexastichum*	autumn sown, late spring harvest	tolerant of drought, saline and alkaline conditions, higher yields than wheat	generally hulled, makes poor quality bread, less cold tolerant than wheat and rye
millet	*Panicum miliaceum*	late winter/spring sown, summer harvest	very high yields	needs rich soil and moisture
oats	*Avena sativa*	winter or spring sown, early or late summer harvest	tolerant of cold, wet and acid conditions	sensitive to heat, not useful for bread
rye	*Secale cereale*	winter or spring sown, early or late summer harvest	tolerant of cool, damp conditions	sensitive to heat, not adapted to Mediterranean conditions

barley (*Hordeum hexastichum*). The varieties most widely grown were not free-threshing; that is, the grains were tightly secured in their inedible husks, and had to be released by violent pounding in a large mortar and pestle. Although this created more work in processing the grain for human consumption, the protective husks enhanced their keeping qualities in storage and they were less prone to attack by INSECTS. Barley bread is dense, hard and very nasty to eat. Because of this, ancient medical writers mistakenly believed that barley was less nutritious than wheat. Barley was often made into other products such as thin, unleavened bread or porridge. If more desirable cereals were readily available, barley was used for ANIMAL fodder.

Several kinds of wheat were known and widely grown in classical antiquity. Emmer (*Triticum diccocum*, Greek *zeia*, Latin *far*), a husked wheat, was a particularly important staple used for bread and porridge in early Rome. It was well suited to the relatively moist conditions of central and northern Italy though it was also grown in Greece, particularly as a spring-sown wheat. Spelt (*Triticum spelta*; Greek *olyra*, Latin *spelta*), another husked wheat, was widely used by the Roman army for making BREAD, again because of its excellent keeping qualities. Like barley, both of these wheats were processed by arduous pounding. The most desirable wheats were durum wheat (*Triticum durum*, Greek *pyros*, Latin *triticum*) – best known today for making spaghetti and pasta – and bread wheat (*Triticum aestivum*, Greek *pyros*, Latin *triticum*). These are both 'naked', free-threshing wheats, that is the grain falls freely out of the husk when trampled, beaten or shaken. These wheats are easiest to process and make by far the nicest bread. Bread made with durum wheat has an elastic quality and is often slightly yellow. They were considered by far the most desirable cereals in classical antiquity.

Less common, though important as a summer crop, especially in damp and marshy areas, was millet (*Panicum miliaceum*, Greek *kenchros*, Latin *panicum*). The round, hard seeds could be made into bread or porridge, and could be stored for longer than either wheat or barley. It was also used for animal fodder.

Oats (*Avena sativa*) and rye (*Secale cereale*) were alien curiosities to the Greeks and Romans. Though known, they are not cereals which grow successfully in Mediterranean countries, though they are well suited to the temperate climates of northern Europe. LF

See Pliny, *Natural History*, book 18; Spurr, S. (1986) *Arable Cultivation in Roman Italy*.

 AGRICULTURE: (a)–(b).

Ceres Roman goddess of growth; her name derives from the root **ker*–, 'grow', found in Latin *crescere*, 'to increase'. We know that her cult, also attested in OSCAN-speaking regions, was very old, because one of the archaic PRIESTS known as *flamines* was dedicated to her and her festival on 19 April was in the original Roman religious calendar. She also shared with Tellus ('Earth') the sowing festivals in January. By the early 5th century BC she was identified with the Greek DEMETER, when a TEMPLE on the Aventine was dedicated to Ceres, Liber and Libera, a triad reflecting the Eleusinian group of Demeter, Kore (Persephone) and DIONYSOS. The temple soon became a focus of activity by PLEBEIANS: it housed their ARCHIVES and was managed by new plebeian MAGISTRATES, the AEDILES. The plebeian aediles in Republican times were also responsible for the games of Ceres, traditionally the time for plebeian socializing. By the AUGUSTAN period these games extended from 12 to 19 April and took the form of CHARIOT RACES. In addition to the old Roman FESTIVALS and the archaic *flamen* (priest), there were more recent 'Greek' rites, apparently involving initiations like those at ELEUSIS, but limited to women, and also Greek priestesses from southern Italy. The cult of Ceres was in imperial times especially popular in AFRICA, where dedications to 'the Cereses' probably indicate continuity with the cult of Demeter and Kore brought from SYRACUSE to CARTHAGE in the early 4th century BC. JBR

See Spaeth, B. S. (1996) *The Roman Goddess Ceres.*

 GODS AND GODDESSES: (a).

Cerveteri Modern name, derived from *Caere vetus*, for a wealthy ETRUSCAN city a few miles from the coast, about 50 km (30 miles) north of Rome. The Romans knew it as Caere, the Etruscans as Cisna or Chaire, the Greeks as Agylla. The site was a plateau with evidence of previous Villanovan settlement. A centre of METALWORKING, Caere was active in MEDITERRANEAN trade with Greece and CARTHAGE during the 7th to 5th centuries BC from several ports, including Pyrgi, Punicum, Alsium and Fregenae. Excavations at Pyrgi have yielded a bilingual inscription on gold leaf in Etruscan and PHOENICIAN; the latter is only a paraphrase, but the document provides valuable evidence for the Etruscan language. Caere itself was a site of c.150 ha (375 acres), but its two main cemeteries, Banditaccia and Monte Abatone, covered more than 400 ha (1,000 acres). Chamber TOMBS, including some elaborate examples, were laid out in streets in the cemeteries from the 7th century.

Caere suffered a decline from the late 5th century BC, in the context of Roman expansion. The city is associated with the *civitas sine suffragio* ('citizenship without voting rights') status, often granted by Rome to *municipia* (originally, allied communities not given Latin status). Ancient sources differ on the reason, citing the city's protection of the VESTAL VIRGINS during the Gallic invasions of the 4th century or punishment for a revolt in the 3rd century. The negative associations of the status favour the latter. JV

See Haynes, S. (2000) *Etruscan Civilization*; Scullard, H. H. (1967) *The Etruscan Cities and Rome.*

 ETRURIA AND ETRUSCANS.

Chaironeia A leading city of the BOIOTIAN confederacy, situated in the Kephisos plain that borders PHOKIS. In 447 BC, when Boiotia was under Athenian control, it was seized by exiled oligarchs, but recaptured by the Athenians under Tolmides, who subsequently was defeated at Koroneia. It was later the setting for one of the most momentous battles in Greek history, when in 338 BC PHILIP II of Macedonia routed the Greek army led by the THEBANS and Athenians. This defeat signalled the end of freedom in general for the Greek city-states. Philip's tactics appear to have been a feigned retreat of the right end of his phalanx, which sucked in the pursuing Athenians (among whom fought DEMOSTHENES); this created a gap in the Greek line that was exploited by the Macedonian CAVALRY under the command of ALEXANDER. The battle was commemorated by a huge stone lion, which was damaged during the Greek war of independence (1821–2) but subsequently restored. The monument is thought to have marked the burial place (*polyandreion*) of the Theban Sacred Band, which fought to the last on the right of the Greek line; the bones of 254 men were discovered in its vicinity.

Another major battle was fought at Chaironeia in 86 BC, when SULLA defeated the army of MITHRADATES VI, under the command of the Greek general Archelaos. Chaironeia afterwards became famous as the birthplace of PLUTARCH. MJE

See Cawkwell, G. L. (1978) *Philip of Macedon*; Fossey, J. (1988) *Topography and Population of Ancient Boeotia.*

 BATTLES (table).

Chalkidike A peninsula in the north-west AEGEAN, jutting out from the mainland of MACEDONIA in a trident shape with three promontories. Pallene is the westernmost, Sithonia the central, and Akte (also Mt Athos) the easternmost, where a mighty storm in 492 BC destroyed DARIUS' PERSIAN fleet as he attempted to invade Greece. The EUBOIAN city of Chalkis colonized here in the archaic period, giving the region its name. CORINTH also had colonies and influence here, most notably at Poteidaia, which played an important part in the PELOPONNESIAN WAR. In 480 BC Darius' successor XERXES by-passed the hazards of Akte with a canal across the isthmus. Many cities in the peninsula helped Xerxes but some later revolted; Poteidaia (sited on Pallene) was besieged, the inhabitants of Olynthos (the Bottiaians) were killed, and the town given to the Chalkidians.

Cities of Chalkidike joined the Delian league early, but Poteidaia, the Bottiaians and the Chalkidians revolted in 432 BC, encouraged by the Macedonian king, Perdikkas. At this time the Chalkidian towns were resettled at a single inland site, OLYNTHOS, a formidable planned city (a process known as the *anoikismos*). Now (or some time afterwards) the Chalkidian league was organized by Olynthos, in which all member states were equal with common laws, CITIZENSHIP and commerce. During the 4th century the league covered most of the peninsula; it joined the SECOND ATHENIAN CONFEDERACY early (378–377 BC) but broke away (367) to ally with Amphipolis. PHILIP II of Macedonia destroyed Olynthos and the league was dissolved c.348. (see p. 182) AG

See Zahrnt, M. (1971) *Olynth und die Chalkidier.*

GREECE: (a).

Chalkis see EUBOIA.

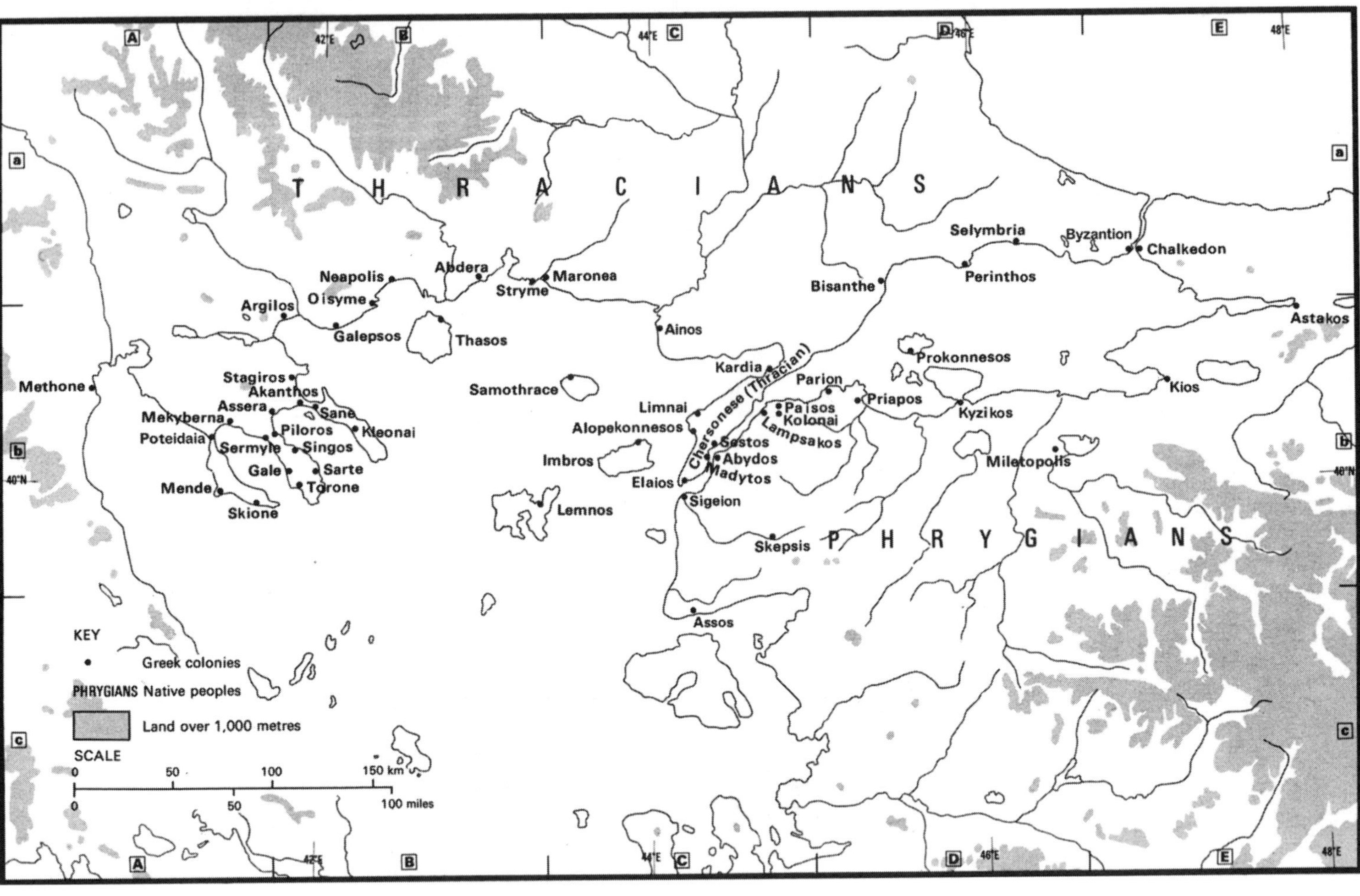

CHALKIDIKE: map of Chalkidike and the northern Aegean.

charcoal (Greek *anthrax*, Latin *carbo*) One of the most important FUELS in antiquity. It was prepared, as it is today in the Mediterranean countryside, by slowly 'cooking' lengths of wood in a close-laid stack covered in earth to create a reducing (oxygen-poor) atmosphere. Charcoal was widely used for HEATING and COOKING, and was a particularly efficient and effective fuel for burning in portable braziers. Because it burns slowly with little smoke and an intense heat that can easily be controlled with blowpipes or bellows, it is especially suitable for METALLURGY. Theophrastos (*Enquiry into Plants* 5.9) describes how a charcoal-heap is constructed and discusses the best charcoal for different purposes, noting, for example, that charcoal from close-grained wood is best for silver-smelting. Weight for weight, charcoal when burnt produces less energy than wood, but its storability and lightness made it an article of commerce, at least over short distances. The men of the Attic deme of Acharnai, as well as being stalwart democrats, were proverbial charcoal-makers, no doubt supplying a good proportion of Athens' need for fuel. DGJS

See Olsen, S. D. (1991) Firewood and charcoal in classical Athens, *Hesperia* 60: 411–20.

CHARCOAL: a charcoal burner in the 1980s in the southern Argolid, Greece, standing in front of his carefully stacked heap of wood ready for burning. In antiquity charcoal was a major fuel, important for both domestic and industrial purposes because of its capacity to produce steady heat at high temperatures.

chariot racing

The earliest description of a chariot race in the Greek world is found in the funeral games for Patroklos (HOMER, *Iliad* 23.262–538). The competitors raced two-horse chariots over an improvised track, around a turning-post (here a dead tree) and back across a predetermined finish line. The most difficult and exciting manoeuvre was the turn, evident from the advice that Nestor gives to his son. SOPHOKLES perhaps provides the most vivid account of the dangers in his description of the race in which Orestes supposedly competed (*Elektra* 681–763). According to PAUSANIAS (5.8.7–8), the four-horse chariot (*tethrippon*) race was introduced into the programme at OLYMPIA during the 25th Olympiad (680 BC). Other equestrian events were added later, including the *synôris* for two horses (408 BC), and the *apênê* or mule-cart race (500 to 444 BC). At Olympia, as at other competitive FESTIVALS, the chariot race was held on a hippodrome, a specially constructed, elongated racetrack about 1,050 metres long. The teams (as many as 48 apparently were able to take part), made 12 laps around the course. As in the *Iliad*, the most thrilling and dangerous parts of the event were the turns. The competitors were deemed to be the owners of the team of horses rather than their drivers, and victory was awarded to the owner, almost always a different person. Thus chariot racing and other equestrian events were primarily open only to the wealthy. Even women could compete, most famously Kyniska, a SPARTAN princess who won at Olympia. MJC

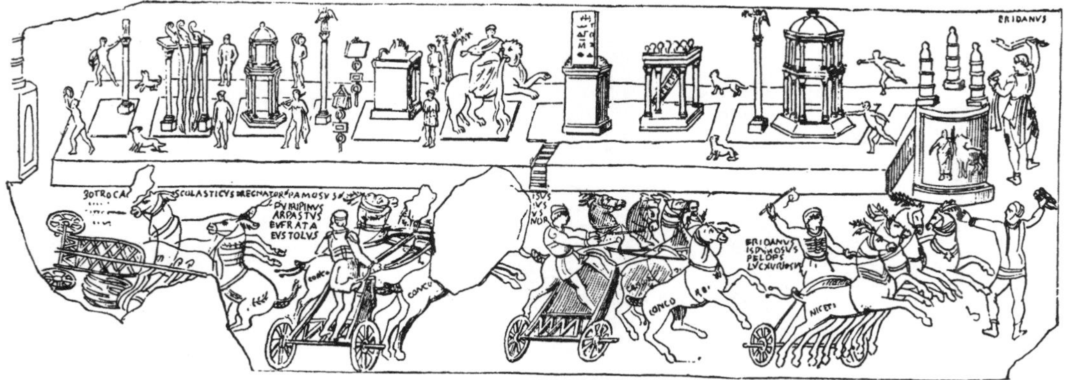

CHARIOT RACING: drawing from a Roman mosaic found in Barcelona depicting the thrills and spills (to l.) of the race around the architecturally elaborate central barrier of the Circus Maximus.

See Golden, M. (1998) *Sport and Society in Ancient Greece*; Raschke, W. J., ed. (1988) *The Archaeology of the Olympics*.

The form and content of Roman chariot racing derived from the CIRCUS MAXIMUS, and the evolution of this space offers the best evidence for the sport's history. The essential elements of a race were: competitors in multiples of four; a sprint from the starting gate to the end of a long, low barrier that extended for two-thirds of the length of the race track; and seven laps around this barrier, ending in the middle of the track. The course's form appears to have been fixed by the mid-4th century BC, when the first permanent gates were constructed. Although this point remains controversial, the four factions (Red, Green, Blue and White) which provided the racing teams and drivers probably also existed at this time.

These factions separate Roman chariot racing from other forms. Elsewhere, chariot racing was the quintessential aristocratic sport. In contrast to the Greek world, where the owner took credit for the victory, in Rome the victory went to the faction. The drivers, born into the lower socio-economic classes, were heroes, as were the horses. No aristocrat was sole patron of a faction; factions were administered by members of the EQUESTRIAN order, usually several men for each faction. At the end of the 3rd century AD, former charioteers (who may well have become extraordinarily wealthy from prizes) began to take over as faction administrators (*domini*, 'masters').

Evidence suggests that the level of competition was extraordinarily high. The most successful charioteers won most of their prizes in 'races of champions', with one team from each faction rather than the usual three. The relatively small number of races that such champions won in competition with a full field, and the regular mention of second and third prizes in honorific inscriptions, suggest that the distance dividing the great charioteer from the average was small. The key to a race was the start. The charioteer in the lead after the opening sprint won a disproportionate number of races. To come from second place or further back at this point was extraordinary, because a position on the inside, in a very even field, conferred a great advantage.

It may be that the enormous cost involved in the construction of CIRCUS BUILDINGS retarded the spread of Roman-style racing. Only in the 3rd century AD do circuses begin to become more common in large provincial cities, but by the 4th century chariot racing was clearly the dominant form of entertainment in the empire. Supported by EMPERORS, and not regularly condemned by the CHRISTIAN church, circus races became a focal point for urban life. Attachment to one or another faction appears to have been one of the few things that most urban inhabitants had in common. Consequently, the circus was a forum for political activity as well as amusement. The sport faded as the sophisticated urban society necessary to support it declined with the collapse of Roman authority. By the 10th century AD, CONSTANTINOPLE may have been the only city where races were still run. DSP

chariots Light horse-drawn vehicles with two spoked wheels, designed for rapid transportation of one or more people in a standing position. They had a range of uses in classical society: WARFARE, HUNTING, ÉLITE display, religious and civic ritual processions, CHARIOT RACING as sport and entertainment. The origins of the chariot were in the Bronze Age, where the Egyptians and Hittites both made considerable use of them in war – though they were at all times primarily an élite conveyance in battle and dependent on suitable terrain. From the East the technology and iconography of the chariot spread through Europe and North AFRICA (its image appears even in remote corners of the Sahara). In MEDITERRANEAN warfare the chariot was supplanted quite early by the development of heavy armoured infantry, though it endured longer in north-west Europe and was still encountered by CAESAR in BRITAIN. From the archaic period onwards, other uses became more significant in the Mediterranean, notably the dangerous art of racing these flimsy vehicles. Races were already well represented in Greek and ETRUSCAN art before the sport reached an altogether different level in the CIRCUS arenas of the Roman world. Early CHARIOT RACING was essentially an ARISTOCRATIC competition, but Roman charioteers were often of servile or humble status. Nonetheless, the prestige nature of the chariot endured, as indicated by its status as the vehicle of choice at Rome for PROCESSIONS

CHARIOTS: (a) detail of a Greek chariot.

CHARIOTS: (b) detail of Roman racing chariots, emphasizing the very insubstantial nature of these vehicles.

and in representations of EMPERORS and TRIUMPHAL victors. DJM

See Crouwel, J. (1992) *Chariots and other Wheeled Vehicles in Iron Age Greece.*

charisma see CHRISTIANITY; CLEOPATRA; JESUS.

charity see *ALIMENTA*; BENEFACTORS AND BENEFACTION; CHURCH, THE; FAUSTINA; VIRTUE.

cheese Many of the nutritional qualities of milk remain in cheese, which improves its digestibility. In ancient conditions fresh milk, butter and cream were only available in proximity to the producing ANIMAL; cheese was the best way to store the nourishment offered by milk. The milk of several animals might be used, including cows, HORSES, asses and CAMELS. GOAT's and SHEEP's milk cheeses were the best known. Cheese-making requires the addition of a small quantity of rennet to the milk to make it curdle. The rennet was usually taken from a deer's or cow's stomach; alternatively, FIG sap could be used. Young cheeses were placed in a cheese-basket to let the whey run off, or were shaped in a mould (Latin *forma*).

ARCHAEOLOGY suggests that cheese-making skills existed in Greece by 3,000 BC. The monstrous Kyklops in HOMER's *Odyssey* is an expert cheese-maker. In classical Greece, SICILY, Italy and the Roman PROVINCES cheese was widely available. In both Athens and Rome, there was a market for young cheese fresh from the farm. Cheese was also matured (often in brine) and some was smoked: the smoke of apple-wood was used for the purpose. Several local specialities are mentioned in literary sources, many of them being small, shaped cheeses of the type still popular in Europe; they include the *trophalis* of Kythnos in the AEGEAN, and the *meta* or pyramid of Sassina in Italy.

Cheese was eaten at the end of a meal, among desserts, served with HONEY. It was also sufficiently nourishing to be eaten with bread as the chief relish of a modest meal. AD

chemistry In strictly scientific terms, specific work on chemistry, at either the practical or theoretical level, was limited in antiquity. The word *chêmia* or *chêmeia* (meaning 'alchemy') appears only in very late Greek. The ancient Greeks and Romans were aware of chemical reactions, but these emerged mainly from practical experience, either by trial and error or simply by accident, rather than through work in laboratories. Thus, medical practitioners might discover haphazardly that certain substances cured diseases or alleviated symptoms; they did not usually know the specific chemicals, nor were they generally able to extract them as individual substances. Similarly, the mix of components in CONCRETE produced a high-quality building material, but the Romans did not understand the chemical properties that caused the effect.

Chemistry in the ancient world was thus almost entirely a matter of observation: people saw the results of chemical reactions but did not understand the processes involved. Theoretical considerations were the preserve of PHILOSOPHERS. They devised, for example, the theory that each substance was made up of a unique mixture of the four elements (fire, air, water, earth). This view was more likely to inhibit than encourage attempts to discover new chemicals or devise further theory. Attempts to alter substances, either in appearance or in actuality, are more properly the realm of ALCHEMY, which developed in Egypt, than chemistry. Both words ultimately derive from *Chemia*, the Egyptian name for their own land (Plutarch, *On Isis and Osiris* 33). JV

Chersonese, Thracian see CLERUCHS, CLERUCHY; FORTIFICATION, GREEK; PHILIP II.

chert see FLINT.

child abuse This concept certainly existed in classical antiquity, though defined differently from today. First, the gender and legal status of the child were critical in determining what counted as abuse. A SLAVE child could be starved, whipped or prostituted, but that was the concern of no one, not even the state. For example, in Xenophon's *Symposion*, the owner of two performing slaves, a girl and a boy, takes it for granted that he can command their sexual favours. However, a freeborn child could not be treated in the same way, and the abuser would be liable to both moral censure and legal penalties. Even among free children, boys might be fed, clothed and treated better than unwanted girls or disabled children. Girls were not thought to remain children as long as boys, and there is good evidence from Roman tombstones that prepubescent girls were sometimes married off and expected to engage in full sexual relationships with their husbands. Second, the borderline between discipline and maltreatment was drawn in a different place. In the setting of a more violent society, harsh corporal punishment was regularly meted out by parents and teachers. Greek fathers were certainly expected to be authoritarian, and the Roman father, in his role as *paterfamilias*, had the power of life and death over his children. What they deemed good discipline might often be considered abuse by modern standards. LF

CHILD ABUSE: corporal punishment was a regular feature of Greek and Roman life. It is unlikely that they saw this as abusive or abnormal behaviour.

childhood Greek children, who lacked *logos* (reason), strength and morality, comprised boys not yet citizens – in Athens, citizenship meant enrolment in the DEME at 17 or 18 – and girls before MARRIAGE. Yet the vocabulary for childhood distinguishes between younger children (*brephos*, *nepios*, *paidion*), older children (*pais*) and youth (*meirakion*). Infants were accepted or exposed as the father wished. The *amphidromia*, when fathers carried them around the hearth and made a SACRIFICE, purified babies on their fifth or seventh day; front doors were decorated with wool for girls, OLIVE wreaths for boys. There followed the *dekatê*, on the tenth day, at which children were named. The delay in naming may be because many infants died within their first week, as ARISTOTLE asserts. Children were distinguished by gender, class and status. Poor free children and SLAVE children alike tended livestock and harvested from the age of five.

Children had ritual roles, for example at the Anthesteria on the day called (in English) the Choës – jugs (*choai*, singular *choê*) have been found depicting children playing – or at the Aiora, when they sat in swings. Children had responsibilities at the ELEUSINIAN MYSTERIES. On the PARTHENON frieze, a child delivers ATHENA's robe. The linguistic link between childhood, play and culture suggests that Greece valued play, including singing, guessing and physical games. TOYS, including rattles, hoops and dolls, were dedicated to the GODS in Greece and Rome, by boys at manhood and girls at MARRIAGE.

Republican Rome was arguably insensitive to children. The child 'emerged' in the late Republic, influenced by hellenistic culture where putti enhanced children's visibility. Children entered ART dramatically on Augustus' ARA PACIS, tugging at TOGAS. The former boy–young man–old man divisions of life succumbed to Greek models and added little ones: *infans*, *parvus*, *parvulus*. Childhood as depicted on SARCOPHAGI includes birth, BATHING, cradling, playing in animal-drawn chariots and recitation. Various rituals surrounded childhood. At birth, three men struck the threshold with a pestle and broom to keep evil away. Fathers decided

CHILDHOOD: (a) Greek high-chair/potty depicted on a red-figure pot.

CHILDHOOD: (b) simple wheeled toys.

whether to keep children (and exercised power of life and death over even adult offspring). There followed the *levana*, when children were raised up, and the ninth-day *lustratio*, for naming and purification. CITIZEN children wore a *bulla*, a protective necklace. Rich Roman boys, identifiable by their bordered TOGAS, donned white togas at maturity. Girls could marry at 12, boys at 14.

Children's purity was valued in SACRIFICE and the worship of the Lares (spirits of the ancestors). They were adored, according to QUINTILIAN, PLUTARCH and epitaphs. After Augustus, children were cultivated by EMPERORS in ALIMENTARY schemes. This attitude co-existed with beatings, exposure, infanticide, slaves in child-rearing and WETNURSING who weakened parent–offspring bonds, child labour and slave children, who were also vulnerable to CHILD ABUSE. In late antiquity, Christian baptism eclipsed age distinctions and innocent childhood was to be emulated. SC

See Golden, M. (1990) *Children and Childhood in Classical Athens*; Wiedemann, T. (1989) *Children and Adults in the Roman Empire.*

China and Chinese empire Organized settlement in China dates back to at least 5000 BC, but the first attested dynasty, the Hsia (Xia), emerged at the end of the 3rd millennium. ARCHAEOLOGY provides little to verify the literary tradition, which dates the Hsia to a 500-year period beginning in either the late 23rd or late 21st century BC. The relative sophistication of the Shang period (1523–1028 BC), however, presupposes earlier centuries of organized development. The Shang were supplanted by the Chou (Zhou), whose period of 'rule' can be divided into Western Chou (ending in 771 BC), Eastern Zhou and that of the Warring States. The middle period has been called that of Spring and Autumn; the philosopher Confucius (Kongfuze; 551–479) belongs to this era. The loss of military authority by the Chou rulers began already in the 8th century, as a feudal system (similar to that of Europe later) resulted in a proliferation of smaller political entities. At one point during the Warring States period, these units numbered as many as 170. In the final years of nominal Chou authority, they had been reduced to about seven, of which the Ch'in were to emerge as dominant. In 221 BC the prince Cheng established himself as 'august sovereign' (*huang-ti*) and created a centralized government with standard measures and coinage. The round copper coin with a square hole in the centre, which survived into modern times, was first used by the Ch'in. Destroying the defensive walls of formerly independent states, the Ch'in emperor built instead a long wall intended (without success) to keep out the nomadic Hsiung-nu, who lived to the north. (The Great Wall, which attracts tourists today, is the product of the Ming dynasty, dating to the 15th century of our era.)

Ch'in power did not long outlive the death of the founding emperor in 209 BC. By 202 a new dynasty, the Early Han, had established itself; in the 1st century BC it was exercising its authority as far north as Korea and as far south as Vietnam. In the west, Han military expeditions advanced into Ferghana and Sogdiana (SELEUKID territory). During this period Chinese SILKS made their way through PARTHIAN-dominated central Asia to the eastern Roman provinces. The Roman name for the Chinese was *Seres* or 'silk people', though the term was also used of INDIANS and east Asians in general. In turn, Roman luxury items reached the Han court. The first Roman TRADE embassy to China is attested in AD 166, and these merchants appear to have come by sea as far as Indo-China. A brief *interregnum* under the usurper Wang Mang (AD 9–23, also called the Hsiu era) separates Early Han from the Later period (AD 25–220).

The collapse of the Later Han dynasty, with the forced abdication of its last ruler, was followed by three and a half centuries of great political complexity and rich intellectual activity. After a brief reign by the Hsiu, the long-lived Tang dynasty brought long-term stability to China, well into the time of the European high Middle Ages.

The cultures of systematic enquiry that developed in Greece and China around the same (c.400 BC–AD 200) offer interesting parallels as well as important differences, and illuminate the origins of modern science. The similarities, however, have to do with the social location of enquirers within those societies, not with any common origin or mutual influence. WH

See Carrington Goodrich, L. (1969) *A Short History of the Chinese People*; Gernet, J. (1996) *A History of Chinese*

Civilization; Lloyd, G. E. R. (2002) *The Ambitions of Curiosity: understanding the world in ancient Greece and China*.

Chios Large AEGEAN island, close to the coast of Asia Minor, with a city of the same name. In antiquity, Chios was particularly renowned for its WINE, and its prosperity was such that 'Chian luxury' was proverbial. It was claimed as the birthplace of HOMER, and the guild of bards known as the 'sons of Homer' were active there. Other famous Chians include the tragic poet Ion, the historian THEOPOMPOS and the sophist Theokritos.

Chios was colonized by Ionian settlers c.1000 BC. Early political regimes appear to have been monarchies, and archaeologists have discovered remains of a megaron on the *AKROPOLIS* of the ancient city. In c.560, there is EPIGRAPHICAL evidence for a broader form of government, possibly a DEMOCRACY. Chios fell to CYRUS in c.545 and later took part in the IONIAN REVOLT (499) with 100 ships. After defeat at the battle of Lade (494), the island was devastated by the PERSIANS. It was finally liberated after the Persian defeat in 479. Chios then joined the Delian league, and was a steadfast ally of Athens until 411 when it revolted and joined the Spartans. After the PELOPONNESIAN WAR, the Chians drove out the Spartan garrison (394); later they joined the SECOND ATHENIAN CONFEDERACY before revolting again in 354. Chios was briefly under Macedonian rule during the time of ALEXANDER. Later it had excellent relations with Rome and for this reason it was sacked in 86 by Zenobios, general of Mithradates. VESPASIAN abolished Chian autonomy in AD 70. FMM

See Boardman, J. and Vaphopoulou-Richardson, C. E., eds. (1986) *Chios*.

AEGEAN: (a)–(b).

chitôn Generically a term for a male or female tunic, but mostly associated with Greek women. Made from one or two lengths of pleated linen, the *chitôn* was fastened on the body by means of pins or buttons running from the shoulders and down the arms. It was held in place by a waist sash. This fashionable dress is known as the 'Ionic' *chitôn*, since it is said to have been introduced into Greece from CARIA in Asia Minor. Generally the female *chitôn* reached to the ground, but it could be shortened to knee-length by hitching up the excess fabric. In its shortened state the *chitôn* becomes known as the *chitôniskos* ('little *chitôn*') and was worn by women in ATHLETIC pursuits and religious rituals – girls in the cult of ARTEMIS Brauronia wear yellow-red *chitôniskoi*. The well-known statue of the wounded AMAZON by POLYKLEITOS wears an Ionic *chitôn* fastened only on one shoulder and thus exposing a breast; it is frequently seen in this way in Greek representations of Amazons. The *chitôn* could be made of very fine, semi-transparent linen; its diaphanous quality is often exaggeratedly depicted in Greek vase-painting. In daily life, however, and certainly when out of doors, women were required to cover themselves in extra layers of clothing, including a *himation* or cloak, which was pulled over the head as a veil. Effeminate men or, on occasions, gods like DIONYSOS are said to wear yellow-red *chitônes*. LL-J

See Llewellyn-Jones, L., ed. (2002) *Women's Dress in the Ancient Greek World*.

 DRESS, GREEK: (a).

choregic monuments Monuments erected by victorious *chorêgoi* following victory in a public festival during the 5th and 4th centuries BC, particularly at Athens. The wealthiest citizens or residents of Athens were required each year to perform special services for the state, liturgies (*leitourgiai*). Many of these could be very expensive. *Chorêgoi* paid for the costs of one of the DRAMATIC productions, and victorious *chorêgoi* in the dithyrambic competition were able to erect their prize, a tripod, in the city at their own expense. Many elaborate structures were designed to support and display these tripods. Victors in the TRAGEDY and COMEDY competitions or at the Panathenaia tended to commemorate success with simpler inscribed monuments. The majority of choregic monuments were located either in or close to the sanctuary of DIONYSOS on the south-east slope of the ACROPOLIS, or along the street leading from the sanctuary to the site of the Prytaneion (almost the route followed today by Tripods Street, Ódos Tripódon, in the Pláka district of Athens). The monument of Lysikrates is perhaps the most well-known choregic monument, surviving almost intact. It was paid for by Lysikrates, son of Lysitheides, of the deme Kikynna, who served as *chorêgos* for the winning tribe of Akamantis in the boys' dithyramb for the year 335/4 BC. DEMETRIOS OF PHALERON, however, put a

CHOREGIC MONUMENTS: the well-preserved choregic monument of Lysikrates in Athens, 335 BC.

CHORUS: tomb painting from Cyrene, evidently showing a theatrical scene with chorus.

stop to the annual liturgies sometime between 317 and 307 BC, and the creation of new monuments halted. GJO

See Wilson, P. (2000) *The Athenian Institution of the Khoregia.*

chorus The Greek word *choros* can have three different meanings: a group of singer-dancers, their activity (choral DANCE), or the place where they dance. The chorus was composed of the participants and a leader (*chorêgos*) who organized and led the singing and dancing. Choruses are found in LYRIC POETRY, TRAGEDY and COMEDY. The number of persons in a chorus was fixed in tragedy (AESCHYLUS used 12, SOPHOKLES and EURIPIDES 15) and in comedy (24), whereas it varied in lyric performances and could be anywhere between 2 and 17. There were choruses of boys, girls, adult men and adult women, depending on the gender and character of the god or hero being celebrated. On some occasions choruses were mixed, with the *chorêgos* male and other participants female.

Participation in the lyric chorus was seen as both an honour and a place of EDUCATION which prepared girls to be adult women of charm and beauty, and boys to be citizens. Many choral lyric performances were associated with rites of passage. Choral dance was a channel of communication with the GODS, whose protection was sought for the next stage in the participants' lives.

According to ARISTOTLE, tragedy developed from the leader-singers of choral songs for DIONYSOS (dithyrambs). Comedy, likewise, will have developed from a previous choral lyric genre. RBC

See Calame, C. (1997) *Choruses of Young Women in Ancient Greece*; Mullen, W. (1982) *Choreia: Pindar and dance*; Webster, T. B. L. (1970) *The Greek Chorus.*

 DRAMA: (a).

Chremonidean war The chief combatants were, on the one side, PTOLEMY II and his allies, especially Athens and Sparta; on the other, ANTIGONOS II Gonatas. The war, which broke out in 268/7 BC, takes its name from the Athenian general Chremonides who proposed the decree creating an alliance between Athens and Sparta and their allies, and declaring war (*IG* II^2 687). The pact embraced Ptolemy, the ACHAIANS, a number of PELOPONNESIAN cities and some CRETANS. Ptolemy sent a fleet to ATTICA and occupied several fortified points in Athenian territory, but never committed his full forces or energies to the campaign. Antigonos besieged Athens. An attempt by the Spartan king Areus to bring an army in support of the allies failed when he could not get past the Antigonid garrison at CORINTH. A MERCENARY revolt at MEGARA forced Antigonos to raise the SIEGE briefly, but he reinstated it soon. Another attempt by Areus to bring relief ended in his death, and Athens surrendered in early 261 BC. Antigonos installed a garrison and arranged for Athens to be governed by men he trusted. The Ptolemaic fleet evidently withdrew. There was additional conflict on the coast of Ionia, around MILETOS, EPHESOS and LESBOS (the latter two now coming under Ptolemaic control). Ptolemaic garrisons were installed or strengthened on a number of strategic islands in the AEGEAN. The war may have ended with the battle of Kos, a naval engagement between Ptolemy's and Antigonos' forces which the latter won, though some historians prefer a later date. The main issue in the war seems to have been competition in the Aegean between Ptolemy and Antigonos. Although Ptolemy can be said to have 'lost' the war, he emerged from it with his position in the Aegean well strengthened. GR

See Gabbert, J. A. (1997) *Antigonus II Gonatas* 45–53; Hölbl, G. (2001) *A History of the Ptolemaic Empire* 40–3.

 WAR (table).

Christian philosophy 'What has Athens to do with Jerusalem?' asked TERTULLIAN. The question cannot be answered as simply as his RHETORIC implies. Tertullian himself, who also famously declared 'I believe because it is absurd', was a well-educated man. From its inception, the Christian CHURCH had grappled with the relationship between faith and reason. St PAUL debated with EPICUREANS and STOICS at Athens (Acts 17.18), while at the same time urging the Colossians to beware of philosophy. The prologue of the gospel of John, with its emphasis on the *logos* ('word' or 'reason') of God, indicates Christian engagement in what was both a JEWISH and a Greek philosophical tradition. Philosophical debate was not foremost in the minds of the earliest Christians, who initially were more preoccupied with the imminence of the end of the world. However, by the mid-2nd century the church had a double incentive to produce rational accounts of its faith. First, there was a need to combat the various, heretical GNOSTIC sects. Second, intelligent Christians desired to establish the rationality of their faith, both to themselves and non-believers. A series of Greek writers rose to the challenge.

The most significant is Justin, a PLATONIST until a chance meeting with an old man by the sea set him towards Christianity. In his *Apology* and *Dialogue with Trypho* he is optimistic that Christianity and philosophy may be reconciled. There was much that was amenable to him, both in Stoic ETHICS and Platonic METAPHYSICS. Like many other Christian writers who followed, Justin argued that Greek philosophy was derived from the OLD TESTAMENT. He even felt able to call HERAKLEITOS and SOCRATES Christians. His writing on the Trinity is influenced by the work of his middle-Platonist contemporary, Numenius.

Clement of Alexandria, writing towards the end of the 2nd century AD, may have been taught by Justin's pupil Tatian, but his main teacher was a converted Egyptian Stoic, Pantainos. Clement saw both the Old Testament and Greek philosophy as tributaries of the great river of Christianity. Philosophy had been God's providential gift to the Greeks. His writings, *Protrepticus*, *Paedagogus* and *Stromateis*, show that he was well acquainted with Platonic and Stoic philosophers. ORIGEN's *Contra Celsum* (c.248) crystallizes the nature of the PAGAN–Christian philosophical debate. Christ himself was silent in the face of his accusers, so why bother, Origen wonders, to refute Celsus. But refute him he does, in the process showing a detailed knowledge of Platonism and Stoicism. Origen does not mind borrowing an argument from one hellenistic philosophy to combat another, in the cause of defending Christianity.

Little of significance to Christian philosophy was written in Latin until the 4th century. Then the massive figure of AUGUSTINE (1) looms. His synthesis of Christian theology and Platonic philosophy, especially evident in the *Confessions*, has been immensely influential. PMB

See Augustine, *Confessions*; Brown, P. (1967) *Augustine of Hippo*; Chadwick, H. (1980) *Origen, Contra Celsum*; (1984) *Early Christian Thought and the Classical Tradition*; Grant, R. (1988) *Greek Apologists of the Second Century.*

Christianity Having begun as a messianic movement within 1st-century AD JUDAISM, Christianity focused upon the figure of Jesus of Nazareth (Christ). This charismatic teacher and miracle-worker, according to Christian and non-Christian testimony, was executed by order of the Roman prefect of Judaea, PONTIUS PILATE, during the reign of TIBERIUS. The details of Jesus' life are difficult to determine with certainty, not least because most relevant sources were composed by those whose chief concern was to instil or confirm faith in him, not to provide posterity with an impartial historical record (though see Luke 1.1–4). Nonetheless, it is reasonably certain that Jesus' proclamation of the imminent reign of God, and his claims about his own role in how this would occur, appeared a threat to imperial authority and resulted in his crucifixion, despite the fact that he evidently espoused non-violent ETHICS (Matthew 5.43ff., Luke 6.27). It is telling in this regard that, at least initially, only he was put to death, not his followers.

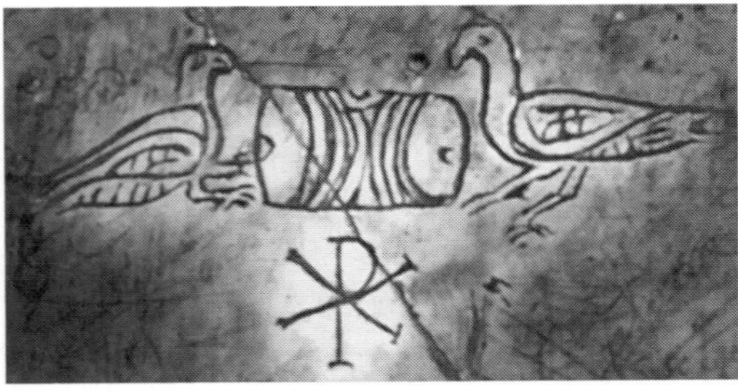

CHRISTIANITY: Christian symbolism (here doves and the chi-rho symbol) is particularly common in late antique art and material culture.

Within a few decades of Jesus' execution, the movement associated with him claimed adherents throughout the empire and beyond. It had also, rather surprisingly, become predominantly non-Jewish, and most members did not observe Jewish law. Followers affirmed the revelation of God to the people of Israel but believed that this God had now acted definitively in Jesus, in raising him from the dead (Romans 10.9) for the benefit of the universe and all its inhabitants (Colossians 1.15–20). Despite the staunch MONOTHEISM of its Jewish origins (1 Corinthians 8.4), its followers soon began to equate Jesus with God (Philippians 2.5–11, John 1.1; PLINY THE YOUNGER, *Letters* 10.96–7) – another striking development.

Christianity was originally an obscure movement emerging from a marginal area. It encountered PERSECUTION, often *ad hoc* but sometimes intense, particularly under NERO, Decius and DIOCLETIAN. It was based upon a perplexing and vulnerable historical claim. How it became the empire's established religion and, perhaps even more remarkably, remained so is one of the most puzzling issues facing students of antiquity. To what extent it both transformed and was transformed by the classical world is also a subject worthy of analysis.

To make sense of Christianity's growth and influence, it is necessary to recognize that its actual attributes were not always clear to those inside or outside the movement. Its identity was inchoate for much of its early history; the term 'Christian' is used only three times in the NEW TESTAMENT (Acts 11.26, 26.28; 1 Peter 4.16). From the outset, protagonists were often in fierce dispute with one another over defining characteristics of the new faith (e.g. Galatians 2.11–14), as later Christians were happy to admit. The reasons for disagreements varied. In the 1st century, one of the most pressing concerned the significance of Jewish law, as the movement became increasingly gentile in membership. In the 4th century, the most adequate way to describe the relationship between Christ and God was the main cause of dissension, a dispute that owed much to the attempt to reconcile fundamental convictions about the significance of Jesus with the presuppositions of Greek PHILOSOPHY. These disputes happened despite (or perhaps because of) recurrent attempts to articulate and enforce normative verbal definitions of the faith through the promulgation and defence of doctrine (e.g. 2 Timothy 2.14–17) and, most visibly, doctrine in its most distilled form: creeds. Some disputes were between discernible factions or theological positions, such as Donatists and CATHOLICS, or Nicaeans and ARIANS. To understand the history of Christianity, however, rather than the history of the formation of Christian doctrine, it is important to recognize that divisions, even over significant aspects of belief and practice, were not always formal and visible. For example, leaders in the CHURCH were regularly appalled at the level of SYNCRETISM or heterodoxy that constituted 'Christianity' for many believers. In the 5th century, for example, pope Leo complained of Christians SACRIFICING to a statue of CONSTANTINE and praying to him as to a PAGAN god.

We must also be wary of interpreting the growth of Christianity teleologically. Although Christianity (or a particular form of it) became the religion of the empire, we must be careful not to assume this was inevitable from the outset. Indeed, the key event, the 'conversion' of Constantine, without which Christianity might well have remained historically inconsequential, was impossible to predict: central to it was the religious experience of one man. Following a vision, he credited the Christian god with ensuring his victory against Maxentius in 312 at the battle of the MILVIAN BRIDGE. From then on he encouraged his worship and favoured the cause of the movement's followers (though he himself was not baptized until his deathbed). Some have maintained that this decision was an expedient response to the prominence of the new faith. This seems unlikely, as most writers of this period do not think Christianity worthy of mention – an indication that it had made little impact, despite the picture that Christian sources paint. Before Constantine's decision to champion the new god, Christianity was widely dispersed geographically (though predominantly urban) and had a membership drawn from most groups within Greco-Roman society (though the poverty of many remained prominent: ORIGEN, *Contra Celsum* 3.55). It does not yet seem to have attracted large numbers. Belief in visions had featured from at least the time of HOMER, and it seems best to recognize its importance in Constantine's decision. Other factors, such as a predisposition towards MONOTHEISM as a consequence of developments within popular paganism and in particular the paganism of his father Constantius, no doubt contributed.

Imperial patronage clearly encouraged individuals to join, as Christianity became a respectable rather than deviant way of life. But other factors played a part before and after Constantine. From the Christian perspective (see e.g. Acts), the growth of the new religion owed itself to the providence and activity of God through the action of the Holy Spirit, manifest in the inspired preaching and miracles of its advocates. Christian writers also believed in the intellectual superiority of their religious claims, and often presupposed that by reason and persuasion converts could be made, as can be seen in Minucius Felix's Christian novel *Octavius*.

Rather more prosaic explanations for conversion are possible and necessary. The ethos of the community may have appealed, particularly to the socially marginalized. Distinctions of ethnicity, enslavement and gender were apparently dissolved in the baptismal rites (e.g. Galatians 3.28). The practical concern early Christians showed for one another, and for those outside their fold, was a distinguishing feature that may also have proved attractive. It was distinctive enough to be lampooned by the satirist LUCIAN (*Flight of Peregrinus*) and regarded with envy by the emperor JULIAN (*Letter to Arsacius*). Attending to the needs of widows and the sick was regarded as a necessary part of a Christian's religious instruction (St Hippolytus, *Apostolic Tradition* 20). Indeed, it may have had a dramatic effect on the number of such people who survived among the Christians relative to the rest of the population. However, it is important not to exaggerate the attractiveness or effectiveness of the apparently egalitarian ideology of the movement. For all the prominence of women such as Phoebe, Priscilla or Lydia in the first church, emerging traditions quickly curtailed women's authority (e.g. 1 Timothy 2.12–15). Although slaves may well have found something empowering about their new faith, SLAVERY *per se* was never questioned.

Pride of place should be given to the importance of vital social networks in the process of conversion and maintaining membership. Most people who were associated with the movement before Constantine did so as a result of contact with friends and family already associated with it (*Apostolic Traditions* 15–16; Minucius Felix, *Octavius* 3.1). Indeed, from the outset it was stressed that all believers had the potential to recruit new members, something that appeared insufferably audacious and arrogant to its cultured critics (such as Celsus). Indeed, in the early period exogamous MARRIAGE was tolerated on this confident assumption (e.g. 1 Peter 3.1–2; 1 Corinthians 7.12–16).

The promotion of Christianity by Constantine and his successors did not mark a complete rupture with what had gone before. Earlier, for example, courts could not sit during specific pagan FESTIVALS. Afterwards, the festivals treated in this manner were Christian. Indeed, 'christianization' of the empire was not a quick process. It was not until 382 that emperors ceased holding the office of *pontifex maximus* – the high priest of traditional Roman religion – and not until 392 that THEODOSIUS I outlawed traditional Roman religious practices in private and public. Even then, it is important to note that paganism as such was not outlawed, and many forms of worship and belief remained unchanged. Indeed, dynamic forms of paganism developed in the changed context, such as the Euphemitai in Lebanon.

With the notable exception of the prominence given to almsgiving (also characteristic of Judaism), the ethical life of the empire was remarkably little altered in any practical way by the adoption of Christianity, in which ETHICS occupied a central place. Many rigourist groups who espoused the sectarian ethic of the early church found themselves marginalized or persecuted. The ASCETIC movement (from which monasticism developed) which emerged under the influence of Antony and others in the 4th century did preserve Christianity's ethical radicalism, and managed (often with difficulty) to stay within the authorized church.

But some changes were profound. The form of Christianity which came to dominate the empire was concerned not just with right worship but also with right belief. All worshippers were expected to be able to expound and understand creeds and scripture and, more importantly, agree upon their meaning. This was a significant innovation. Rational reflection on the divine predated Christianity, but had been largely the preserve of the philosophical few who were under no compulsion to agree. For most pagans, religion was a matter of correct and appropriate observance. As a result of this 'democratization of theological reflection' (Garnsey and Humfress), even the most arcane points of theology could motivate popular passions. Gregory of Nyssa complained that one could not take a bath in 5th-century Constantinople without the threat of Christological debate. Emperors, naturally concerned with unity, found the potential for conflict extremely problematic. Indeed, following the council of Chalcedon in 451, the emperor Marcian passed a law forbidding all public theological discussion – a vain hope.

This characteristic of Christianity resulted in the attempt to demarcate between licit and illicit religious belief, previously of little interest. Far more laws were passed and enforced against heretical groups such as the MANICHAEANS or the Marcionites than against pagans, though heresy itself was an unstable category and shaped by the vicissitudes of political history. For example, ARIANS were 'heretics' from the perspective of Nicaean orthodoxy, but some emperors, such as Constantius II (317–61) and Valens (328–78), supported this position, making the Nicaeans themselves heretics.

There were obvious aesthetic consequences of the triumph of the new faith, including considerable adaptation and innovation in the imagery and iconography produced by believers. Through construction and destruction, the empire was remodelled as a Christian empire. Vast edifices were erected (e.g. St Peter's, built by Constantine on the Vatican hill), vast edifices were torn down (e.g. the SERAPEUM in ALEXANDRIA), and many pre-existing buildings were completely transformed.

In a number of respects, the adoption of Christianity led to the transformation not just of the empire but of the religion. The hierarchical structures of the church had emerged before Constantine; indeed, by the 3rd century the authority of BISHOPS made them special targets of persecution. However, secular power soon began to influence the institutions of the church, as emperors became adjudicators between episcopal rivals and even took a hand in the formulation of central beliefs: Constantine intervened in the writing of the Nicene creed in 325. The relationship between church and state was a complex one, and we can see church leaders influencing emperors in a very direct way: AMBROSE of MILAN excommunicated Theodosius I after a particularly bloody act by the emperor, forcing him to make public penance. But by the 5th century Christianity, the religion whose founder had been ridiculed and killed by representatives of the empire, had become synonymous with it. (see also CHURCH COUNCILS; ASCETICS; MONASTERIES; NEW TESTAMENT) JM

See Brown, P. (1996) *The Rise of Western Christendom*; Garnsey, P. and Humfress, C. (2001) *The Evolution of the Late Antique World*; Lane Fox, R. (1986) *Pagans and Christians*; Stark, R. (1996) *The Rise of Christianity*; Theissen, G. and Merz, A. (1998) *The Historical Jesus*.

chronology While some ancient authors strove to establish accurate dates, ordinary people were not used to thinking in terms of absolute time, as we are. Since there was no numbering of calendar years, expressions for spans of time were variable and relative.

Herodotos, writing of the distant past, thinks in generations: 'in Thasos I found a sanctuary of Herakles founded by the Phoenicians who . . . founded Thasos, and this was five generations of men before Herakles the son of Amphitryon arrived in Greece' (2.44). Chronological exactitude, however, is not his prime concern. When he equates 300 generations with 10,000 years (2.142), he may really be stressing Egypt's great age. Although we may use his lists of Leonidas' and Leotychidas' ancestors (7.204, 8.131) for dating purposes, his purpose is rather to highlight these men's distinguished ancestry. He uses other measures of time too, giving Darius' reign as 36 years (7.4) and assigning important events to the year of office of an Athenian archon (e.g. 8.51).

Around 260 BC, an unknown scholar drew up a list of dated events which was inscribed on a stone known as the 'Parian Marble' (Austin 1980, no. 1). A typical entry runs: 'From the time when Philip died and Alexander came to the throne, 72 years, and Pythodelos was archon at Athens'. This is interpreted as 336/5 BC and exemplifies the synchronization that is the bedrock of chronology. Some fixed points come from Near Eastern documents (such as Egyptian or Babylonian records) or the computed dates of eclipses (e.g. that on 27 August 413 BC which terrified the Athenians in Sicily). Given the fluidity of Greek and Roman history before the 5th century BC, it is not surprising that some scholars question the accuracy of earlier dates. Archaeological tests, such as carbon-14 and dendrochronology, can confirm or revise traditional dating, but are used less in the Mediterranean, where organic remains are preserved less often.

Greek coinage often bears written legends or images referring to military events or monarchs' reigns, but rarely a date. Detailed study of sculpture, pottery, and other items produces fairly firm chronologies for some kinds of art (e.g. Attic painted pottery, late archaic and early classical sculpture) and for the letter-forms of inscriptions (from places with plenty of material). Particularly helpful are 'sealed' deposits like the broken sculptures on the Athenian Acropolis, buried after the Persian sack of 480 BC. Such a fixed point, not just in archaeology, may yield a *terminus ante quem* ('point before which', i.e. latest possible date) or *terminus post quem* ('point after which', earliest possible). Where these are lacking, it is doubtful how accurate stylistic chronology can be. An artist may work in one style throughout a long career. New fashions are imitated at different times in different places.

Thucydides imposed greater rigour than Herodotos, organizing his narrative around summers and winters, related to fixed points by naming magistrates' years. Thus the Peloponnesian war broke out in the 15th year of the Thirty Years' Peace, 'in the 48th year of office of the priestess Chrysis at Argos, when Ainesias was ephor at Sparta and Pythodoros still had two months left of his archonship at Athens, in the 6th month after the battle of Poteidaia, at the start of spring' (2.2.1; cf. 5.20). For Sicily, he gives relative dates for the foundations of Greek colonies (e.g. '108 years, as near as can be reckoned, after their own foundation the people Gela founded Akragas', 6.4) which may derive from local tradition but are probably unreliable.

Around 400 BC, Hippias of Elis compiled a list of Olympic victors which, though it cannot have been totally accurate, appeared to supply fixed points but did not immediately become a normal way of dating events. A century later, Timaios compiled parallel lists of Olympic victors, Athenian archons, Spartan kings and ephors, and Argive priestesses. Dating by numbered 'Olympiad' (the four-yearly festival) became standard with Eratosthenes and remained so in Roman times and beyond. The first Olympics are conventionally placed in 776 BC; the 101st Olympiad is thus 376–373 BC. New research, however, suggests that well-known contradictions between dates for certain events, and puzzling synchronisms, reflect different versions of the list that placed the first Olympiad up to 128 years apart! The implications are serious, perhaps entailing a down-dating of many events in early Greek history.

Athenian democracy dated its public inscriptions by archon year and the name of the secretary to the council. In hellenistic kingdoms, documents were dated by the year of a reign, with synchronizations: 'In the reign of Ptolemy (II) son of Ptolemy Soter (I), year 34 [252 BC], in the time of the priest of Alexander and the Sibling Gods named Neoptolemos son of Kraisis, and in the time of the basket-bearer of Arsinoë named Arsinoë daughter of Nikolaos' (*Hibeh Papyrus* 98). In 181 BC, Eumenes II of Pergamon exempted a village from tax unpaid 'for the 16th year' of his reign, dating his order 'year 17, 4th day from the end of Dios', i.e. 181 BC (Austin 1980, no. 202).

The notion of counting years from the founding of a state reappears in Roman contexts, though reckoning *ab urbe condita* (AUC, 'from the foundation of the city', i.e. Rome) was not a habitual way of dating an event, which was usually done by giving the name of one or both consuls of a year. The inscribed consular *fasti* (annals) list key events: '*Imperator* Caesar, son of the god, grandson of Gaius, Augustus, (consul) for the 11th (time), abdicated; in his place was elected Lucius Sestius' (entry for 23 BC). Rome's foundation was not always dated to 753 BC; that is simply the date calculated by Cicero's friend Atticus and popularized by the scholar Varro. It became orthodox only later; in the 19th century 'Varronian' dating was still standard in textbooks. Thus AUC 710 is the year of Julius Caesar's death, 44 BC.

Sextus Julius Africanus appears to have been the first to calculate Jesus' birth in relation to the Creation, which he put 5,500 years earlier. In late antiquity, there developed chronologies 'from the time of Abraham', 'from Adam' (referring to the Creation), or 'from Moses', which were initially more popular than dating from Christ's birth. Eusebios and Jerome are among the authors who correlated different systems. The Christian era was standardized by Dionysius Exiguus in the 6th century (Jesus is now generally thought to have been born around 4 BC) but first used in a historical context by the Venerable Bede in 8th-century Northumbria. The practice of dating earlier events by counting back from Jesus' birth, occasionally used by Bede, became standard only in the 17th century. It should be noted that, in dealing with the distant past, archaeologists of pre-literate societies often count back from the present time. Thus 5100 BP ('before present') equals approximately 3100 BC; the fact that, strictly speaking, the date referred to changes continually as our own time moves forwards is ignored because the error thus introduced would be insignificant in the context.

The abbreviations BC ('before Christ') and AD (*anno Domini*, 'in the year of the Lord') are traditionally used in British and related cultures, and have their equivalents in other European languages (Italian a.C./d.C., French av. J.-C./ap. J.-C., German v.Chr./n.Chr., etc.). Some writers of English prefer the less overtly Christian BCE ('before the common era') and CE ('common era'). When calculating spans of time, it is important to remember that there was no year zero: 1 BC is followed by AD 1.

The division of prehistory into the Stone, Bronze and Iron ages was developed and verified in Denmark in the late 18th and early 19th centuries, though it partly recalls chronological sequences of ages such as gold–silver–bronze–heroic–iron, found as early as HESIOD (*Works and Days* 109–201). The division between prehistory and history is to some extent arbitrary but could be placed either at the end of the Late Bronze Age (c.1100 BC in Greece) or at the point where writing is reintroduced to Greece (second half of 8th century). Within the Greek historical period, the conventional divisions owe much to the classification of art by earlier archaeologists. Geometric (c.900–700 BC) refers to a pottery style, archaic (c.700–c.500 or 480) to a sculptural style, classical (c.500 or 480 to 323 or c.300) to what was regarded as the best art. (Within the late Geometric and archaic periods, an 'orientalizing' phase is often identified, based on the adoption of motifs from Near Eastern styles. The definition of this phase varies, but for mainland Greek pottery it can be called c.725–625 BC.) Hellenistic (323 or 300–146 or 30), however, is both political (marking the transition to Macedonian dynasties) and a culture label embodying the (now discredited) notion that Alexander's empire 'became Greek' (hellenized).

Roman periods tends to be divided politically: first the kingly period (753–510 BC), then the Republic (510–31 BC) and principate (31 BC–AD 284). The late Roman period, or 'late antiquity', is sometimes called the Dominate and may be defined as AD 284–565; in a Greek context, it approximates to 'early Byzantine'. 'Byzantine' refers to the division of the Roman empire into Eastern and Western halves. Roman is also sometimes divided into early, middle, and late, particularly in archaeological discussion; but the meaning of these terms varies according to the date when Rome conquered a region, or simply personal usage.

While periods are always conventional and sometimes fluid, disavowing them is an almost equally conventional gesture. They remain useful for describing processes of change, as long as they are not elevated into absolute dividing-lines. (see also ASTRONOMY; BUREAUCRACY; CALENDARS; TIME; TIME-KEEPING) DGJS

See Austin, M. M. (1980) *The Hellenistic World*; Bickerman, E. J. (1980) *Chronology of the Ancient World*; Biers, W. R. (1992) *Art, Artefacts, and Chronology in Classical Archaeology*; Croke, B. (1983) The origins of the Christian world chronicle, in B. Croke and A. Emmett, eds., *History and Historians in Late Antiquity* 116–31; Rhodes, P. J. (2003) Herodotean chronology revisited, in P. Derow and R. Parker, eds., *Herodotus and his World* 58–72; Samuel, A.E. (1972) *Greek and Roman Chronology*; Shaw, P.-J. (2003) *Discrepancies in Olympiad Dating*; Whitrow, G. J. (1988) *Time in History*.

chryselephantine see POLYKLEITOS; PHEIDIAS.

church, the Christians defined themselves as those who believed in the teachings of Jesus Christ, and initially considered themselves, and were considered by the Roman authorities, to be a JEWISH sect. The early church (Greek *ekklêsia*, 'assembly') developed as a result of the mission of Peter and PAUL (1st century AD) to the wider community of gentiles. CHRISTIANITY existed initially within the power structure of the Roman empire, and spread first around the MEDITERRANEAN. The first converts were centred around individuals within a city, often the most prominent convert within the community (e.g. Stephanos at CORINTH) whose household served as a meeting-place. In the letters of Paul it is clear that some communities already had presbyters and deacons. By the beginning of the 2nd century the hierarchical system of BISHOPS, priests, deacons and laity was established, though its development across the empire was somewhat haphazard. By the mid-1st century, the writings of Christians suggest a common (CATHOLIC) identity that stressed notions of unity, coming together for liturgy, acts of charity and obedience to the bishop in matters of doctrine and discipline. It is unclear when bishops emerged as the arbiters of faith and as the power of the church, but their authority was recognized by the mid-2nd century. One factor was that the nascent church was also establishing its identity in the face of perceived heresies. The spread of movements such as GNOSTICISM and Marcionism, which produced their own documents, required the church to define those books it considered authoritative, which eventually came to make up the accepted canon. Bishops became the local voice of authority on doctrinal matters. Christian apologists of the same period were producing writings that addressed the place of Christians in the Roman world. Works such as those of TERTULLIAN and Clement of Alexandria offer a wealth of detail of social life, while trying to explain Christian practice to the communities in which they lived. Christians understood from the NEW TESTAMENT that they should obey the power of the state and were subject to the usual demands of TAXATION, civic responsibility and military service. However, the exclusivity of MONOTHEISM was bound to clash with the Roman authorities.

The earliest reported PERSECUTIONS were sporadic, and the motivations behind them are often unclear. NERO used Christians as scapegoats for the fire at Rome in 64 AD, but thereafter persecution was not pursued consistently. There were sporadic episodes in the next century, but the attitude of the authorities is best summed up by the correspondence between PLINY THE YOUNGER and TRAJAN (c.AD 112). Pliny regarded Christianity as a *superstitio* whose refusal to engage in IMPERIAL CULT rendered its followers traitorous. He had executed some who persistently refused to give up their allegiance, but was now unsure how to deal with a larger number, of all classes, who had been anonymously denounced but claimed they were no longer Christians. Trajan advised that people should be punished only if obstinate, that anonymous accusations should be discounted, and that Christians should not be sought out (Pliny the Younger, *Letters* 10.96).

Persecution could range from confiscation of property and imprisonment to TORTURE and death in the arena. Until the mid-3rd century, however, it remained an inconsistent policy on the part of emperors. Under MARCUS AURELIUS, Polycarp of Smyrna, Justin (Martyr) (in 165) and 48 members of the church at LYON (in 177) were martyred. SEPTIMIUS SEVERUS banned conversion to JUDAISM or Christianity in 202, which resulted in the first empire-wide action against Christians. The persecutions under Decius (249–52) and those of DIOCLETIAN (303–5) and GALERIUS (305–11) were by far the most aggressive and marked a new phase in church–state relations. Decius began his reign with an attack on bishops, whom the authorities now recognized as the key to the coherence and unity of the church. By the beginning of the 4th century, Christians were found in high positions in the army and the imperial administration. The notion that this might undermine the state's relationship with the traditional gods and their goodwill may have motivated the edict of Diocletian in 303 ordering the destruction of church buildings, the burning of scriptures and enforced performance of SACRIFICE by clergy. While this action was short-lived in the West, it was pursued by Galerius in the East until he issued an Edict of Toleration in 311 while, according to LACTANTIUS, suffering a very painful illness which soon led to his death.

Persecution provoked a variety of different reactions among Christians. Some suffered, indeed sought, MARTYRDOM while others recanted. Still others retreated to the countryside and waited until the crisis abated. As most periods of persecution were short-lived, the aftermath presented a problem to more zealous Christians. Novatianism and Donatism were influential schismatic movements which resented the acceptance back into the church of those who had recanted during a period of persecution. Both groups persisted into the 7th century.

When the so-called Edict of MILAN (313) extended religious freedom to Christians, the situation radically changed. CONSTANTINE, the emperor in the West, was Christian. For the first time, Christians were permitted freedom of worship, and church property previously confiscated was returned. Constantine's successors were also Christian (though Constantius II was of ARIAN persuasion) with the exception of JULIAN (361–3). During a brief reign Julian attempted to reinstate traditional Roman religion, though his writings on the subject suggest that official PAGANISM should aspire to many of the moral teachings associated with Christianity. Even when accepted, the church was not united, and 4th- and 5th-century emperors saw it as part of their role to call church councils, implement their decisions and push for unity. Relations between church and state fluctuated throughout the 4th century. EUSEBIOS had presented an image of congruity between the heavenly kingdom and the Christian Roman empire, with responsibility for the church lying with the emperor. At the end of the 4th century the relationship between emperor and church came to a head with a confrontation between THEODOSIUS I and AMBROSE, bishop of

Milan. Ambrose insisted on the supremacy of the church over matters spiritual and that the church could not submit to the state. Under Theodosius pagan ritual was banned and TEMPLES closed, though in reality it took several decades for paganism to die out. MEH

See Halton, T. (1990) Church, in E. Ferguson, ed., *Encyclopedia of Early Christianity*; McManners, J., ed. (1990) *The Oxford Illustrated History of Christianity.*

church councils Formal assemblies of the clergy and certain secular dignitaries, particularly the emperor in the early period, to discuss and legislate on matters of doctrine ('symbols'), liturgy, discipline and organization (*acta*). The form of councils varied throughout the imperial period. They could be ecumenical (called by EMPERORS and intended to represent the whole church, though geographical limitations sometimes prevented representation from certain areas), patriarchal (synods of Rome, CARTHAGE, CONSTANTINOPLE, ALEXANDRIA and ANTIOCH), provincial (BISHOPS of a region assembling twice a year), or diocesan (bishops and local clergy).

The earliest councils date from the mid-2nd century, when bishops in ASIA Minor met to discuss Montanism and those in SYRIA and Palestine decided on the date of Easter. By the mid-3rd century it became the custom of regional clergy to meet with some regularity, and councils became institutionalized in the church establishment. They were given increased impetus with the accession of CONSTANTINE, who saw church unity as the key to concord throughout the empire, and viewed the instigation of rulings on church matters as part of his imperial role. His first council was called at Arles (314) to discuss the question of the Donatists in North AFRICA.

There were seven great ecumenical councils in antiquity. Their major doctrinal decisions, which concerned primarily Trinitarian and Christological matters, are listed here by date. It should be noted that they all ruled on clerical behaviour and liturgical matters as well. Such canons ranged from the regulation of MARRIAGE, civic responsibilities and dress of clergy to organizational matters and the selling of ecclesiastical office for gain. (1) The council of Nicaea in 325 was instigated by the debate raised by Arius over the nature of the relationship of the persons in the Trinity; it agreed on a formulation of *homoöusios* ('of the same substance') and produced the Nicene creed declaring this. It also decided the date of Easter. (2) The first council of Constantinople in 381 saw major debates over the teachings of Maximus, who questioned the divinity of the Holy Ghost. Additions were made to the Nicene creed, to include the Holy Spirit. (3) The council of Ephesus in 431 declared Mary to be the Mother of God (*theotokos*) against Nestorius of Constantinople. (4) The council of Chalcedon in 451 retrospectively granted the previous three councils authority in doctrinal matters, and defined the two natures of Christ. (5) The second council of Constantinople in 553 reconfirmed the rulings of Chalcedon against continuing Christological controversy, and condemned the writings of ORIGEN and others. (6) The third council of Constantinople in 680–1 defined the divine and human will of Christ as two distinct principles. (7) The second council of Nicaea in 787 dealt with the issue of the veneration of images that had arisen from c.730 (the first preserved ruling against them being made in 754); it ended the first Iconoclasm and restored the use of images.

The regional councils of antiquity (Ancyra 314; Neocaesarea 314–25; Gangra c.340; Antioch c.341; Laodica c.380) were focused on codifying clerical and church discipline. (see also ARIANISM) MEH

See Hefele, J. K. and Leclercq, H. (1883–96) *A History of the Councils of the Church from the Original Documents*, 5 vols.; Stevenson, J. (1989) *Creeds, Councils and Controversies.*

churches Surviving evidence for churches provides a tangible and living link with the late Roman and late antique past. Although in the vast majority of cases their spaces and ornamentations have been expanded and modified, various examples of early Christian and early Byzantine churches survive to document design and decorative and liturgical schemes. Written sources, such as Paulinus of Nola for early 5th-century Italy and the *Liber Pontificalis* for early papal Rome and its environs, offer detailed information regarding numerous aspects of form (such as internal decoration, external approaches) and of furniture and portable wealth (LAMPS, candles, chalices, altar covers, hangings, etc.). In other contexts, archaeological EXCAVATION is vital for recognizing the impact of churches on town space (e.g. 5th-century churches in CARTHAGE or Cherchel) or within or over VILLAS. Excavation can also clarify the origins of standing buildings (e.g. the early abbey church at Montecassino), and it is essential for investigating the deceased congregations of churches (including élite BURIALS in SARCOPHAGI).

Well before the formal state acceptance of CHRISTIANITY under CONSTANTINE I in AD 313, places of worship and BISHOPS had been established in many urban centres within the empire. These early congregational points, or *domus ecclesiae* ('houses of assembly'), were in many cases provided or donated by Christian or sympathetic nobility. The names of such donors or founders often appear as the dedication when these emerge as documented *tituli* (community or parish centres). These house churches often comprised merely a large room within an APARTMENT block, as at San Clemente, Rome, where excavations have identified the presence of a MITHRAEUM within the same *insula*. At DURA EUROPUS on the Euphrates a house church of the first half of the 3rd century consisted of a meeting-room and font with walls decorated by paintings. Excavations of many palaeochristian churches (e.g. Santa Maria at Luni in north-west Italy) reveal primary, secular, domestic phases. In 5th-century metropoleis like Rome, many aristocratic *domus* (mansions) with distinctive audience rooms were donated to the CHURCH or made into MONASTERIES.

Most early urban church building was concentrated outside the walls, over existing cemeteries and over the graves of MARTYRS, victims of 2nd- and 3rd-century PERSECUTIONS. As with St Peter's (Vatican), churches were located so as to site their altar over the burial spot of key martyrs. Subsequent burials around these cemeterial churches would congregate particularly around the apse in order to be 'by the martyr(s)', *ad martyrem* or *ad martyres*, so that some of the holiness of the saint(s) could pass on to the deceased. From the 6th century, and particularly from the 9th, the bones of such martyrs were translated inside

CHURCHES: (a) interior of the church of Santa Sabina at Rome, 5th century AD.

churches and often dispersed, wholesale or as parts, to intramural churches and even to monasteries within the West as relics. Paulinus of Nola attests relics as protectors and miracle workers already by the early 5th century.

Intramural church building developed only from the 5th century, and in part reflected the growing insecurity beyond the walls as well as more, or wholly, christianized populations inside them. Conversion saw donations of structures and property, and stimulated the input of private wealth into churches, which until the 5th century was primarily a state concern. The level of PAGAN resistance to accept or convert to Christianity is in part reflected in the slow take-up of church building in towns. In the frontier province of BRITAIN (quitted by Rome already in the early 5th century), excavated examples of late Roman churches are minimal, the best known being Lincoln's St Paul in the Bail and Silchester; their sizes are small overall, reflecting limited congregations. In the case of Lincoln, the church is strikingly located within the old heart of the Roman city, the FORUM, presumably signifying the redundancy of surrounding secular and pagan buildings. With this inward expression, pressure grew for intramural burial to be permitted, though this is not well attested before the early 6th century. After Roman rule in the West, GERMANIC nobles were often interred close to or even inside intramural churches (e.g. Tours, Cologne).

Generally the church sought to create new structures, distinct from the pagan TEMPLES, though *spolia* (reused pieces) from these were often employed in church construction. The conversion into churches of pagan structures (such as the Pantheon in 608) or of former secular civic buildings (such as the senate-house in Rome, converted into San Adriano in the 620s) emerged only once residual pagan connotations had long since gone, or was prompted by major financial deficiencies and by the logic of reuse. The predominant plan of the early Christian church was based on the Roman LAWCOURT or BASILICA, comprising nave, aisles and apse with occasional forecourt, offering spaces for assembly and procession. Arguably the adoption of this plan by Constantine for both St Peter's and St John's at Rome created the architectural template. Nonetheless, Constantinian works at CONSTANTINOPLE and particularly in the Holy Land reveal an architectural diversity, with cruciform and circular churches also prominent. The 'circiform' cemeterial church, however, known in Rome's suburbs, was short-lived.

The designs and decoration of these complexes were charged with implicit and explicit symbolism, perhaps best understood in the baptisteries (fonts, inscriptions, columned canopies, paintings or mosaics of Christ's baptism) but brought out also in the descriptions by Paulinus of paintings in his St Felix shrine at Nola. A key contrast with the former pagan temples was the emphasis on the buildings' interior and apse. For JERUSALEM's church of the Holy Sepulchre, the historian EUSEBIOS highlights the mass of polychrome MARBLE panelling, the carvings and the gold of the ceiling. Surviving churches house

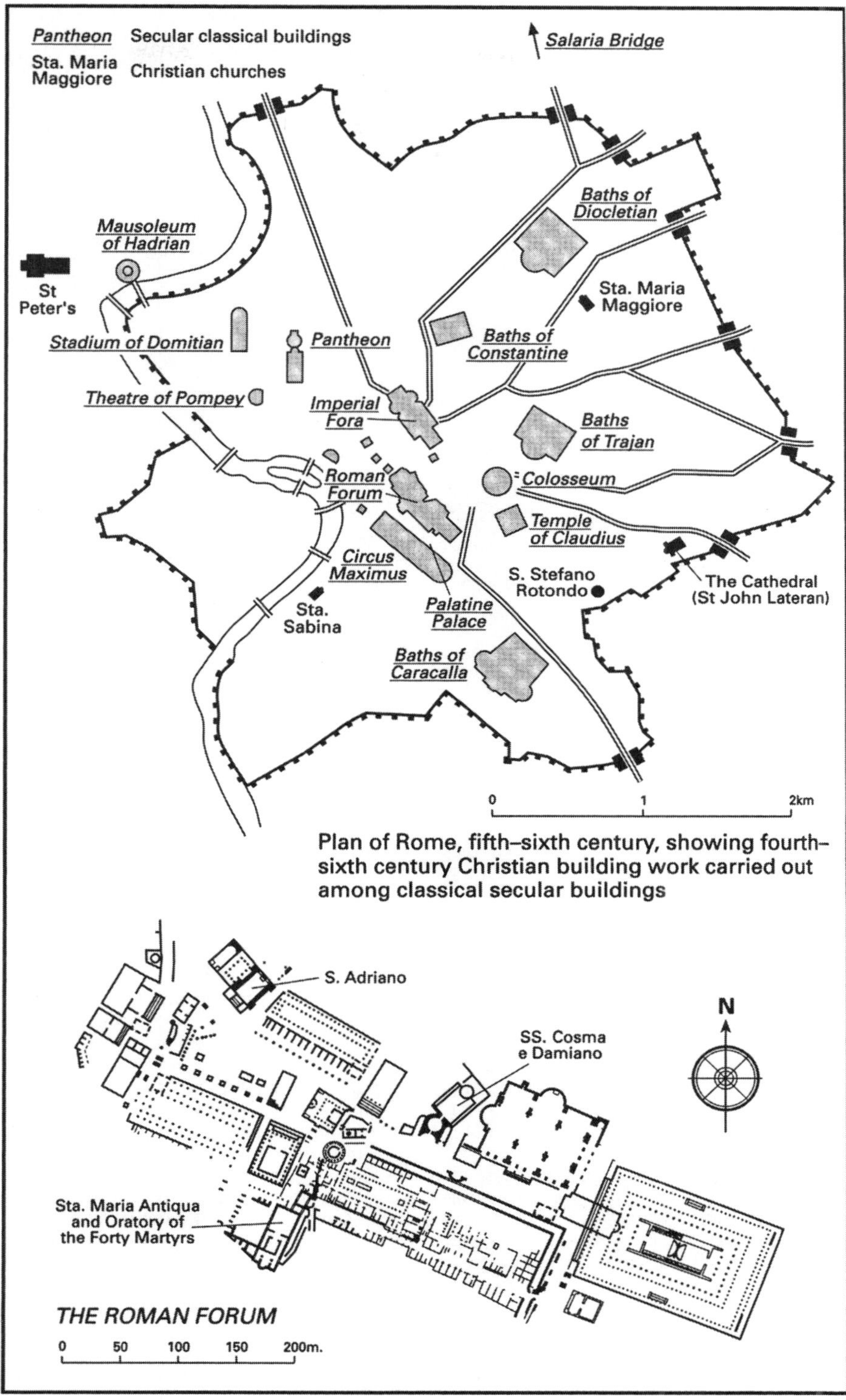

CHURCHES: (b) location of some of the major churches in late antique Rome.

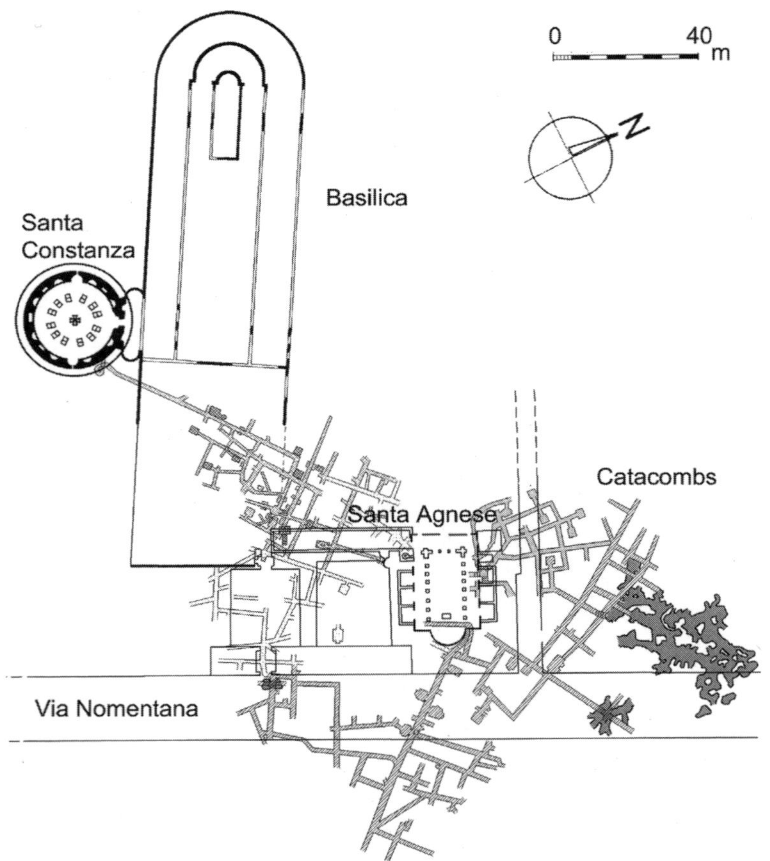

CHURCHES: (c) the Christian complex on the Via Nomentana, comprising mausoleum and basilica of Santa Constanza, the church of Sant'Agnese and associated catacombs.

many early Christian and later artistic treasures. The 5th-century Santa Sabina in Rome features mosaic images and an inscription above the door; marble panelling in *opus sectile* ran around the top of the arcades beneath the clerestory; marble screens framed the presbytery surrounding the altar; and panelled wooden doors with carvings of scenes from the OLD and NEW TESTAMENT still adorn the façade. Mosaics particularly featured in the apses of churches from the mid-5th century. Stunning examples of 6th-century mosaic work appear in the Ostrogothic period churches at RAVENNA. In Byzantine Grado, floor panels inform us of contributions by soldiers, lay people and clerics. A revival of such mosaic work – and of wider early Christian artistic and architectural themes – came in the context of the 'Carolingian Renaissance' of the late 8th and 9th centuries. NJC

See Deichmann, F.W. (1993) *Archeologia Cristiana*; Krautheimer, R. (1986) *Early Christian and Byzantine Architecture*; Milburn, R. (1988) *Early Christian Art and Architecture*.

Cicero (Marcus Tullius Cicero) 106–43 BC ORATOR, statesman, PHILOSOPHER, and best-known figure of the Roman REPUBLIC, Cicero was born into an equestrian family in the Italian town of Arpinum (which received Roman citizenship in 188 BC). MARIUS came from the same town, and the two families had connections. Cicero's EDUCATION at Rome, in both Greek and Latin, included time spent in the circles of leading statesmen and jurists. It was during this period that he met Titus Pomponius ATTICUS, his lifelong friend and principal correspondent.

Although he served under POMPEY's father in the SOCIAL WAR, he built his reputation in public life as an orator. He made his first forensic speech in 81 (*Pro Quinctio*) but established his name with the speech *Pro Roscio Amerino* in the following year, daring to attack elements of SULLA's administration. Worries about his health prompted a period abroad (79–77), when he studied in both Athens and RHODES, encountering POSIDONIUS. His health was never again a major problem. On his return he won election to a QUAESTORSHIP for 75, which he served in SICILY. By his own account (*Pro Plancio* 64–6), this experience made him resolve to remain in the public eye at Rome. His only other provincial office, performed scrupulously but without enthusiasm, was the governorship of CILICIA (51–50).

Cicero only ever undertook one prosecution. His demolition in 70 of Gaius Verres, corrupt governor of Sicily (73–71), was total. Verres went into exile after the first speech, leaving Cicero to publish another five. In winning the case Cicero supplanted Quintus Hortensius, Verres' counsel, as the leading Roman advocate. Aedile in 69, he won the praetorship of 66 at his first eligibility (aged 39). His first surviving political speeches date from this year, expressing support for Pompey (*De imperio Gnaei Pompei*; see Mithradates).

In the face of weak opposition, assisted by his oratorical reputation and a broad support base among *equites* and Italians, Cicero won election to the consulship of 63 BC – the first year possible. As a *novus homo* ('new man') he was the first of his family to stand so high. His consulship was dominated by the 'Catilinarian conspiracy', a revolt instigated by one of his defeated opponents, Lucius Sergius Catilina. With the passing of the ultimate decree of the senate, Cicero briefly united Rome and secured the capture of the leading conspirators, executing five of them. For Cicero it was his greatest moment, and he saw himself as the saviour of his country, acclaimed *pater patriae*, 'father of the fatherland'. His excessive pride antagonized contemporaries and continues to antagonize many. Ultimately it was to lead to his downfall. In 61 he incurred the hostility of Publius Clodius Pulcher by giving evidence against him in the Bona Dea scandal. Subsequently, in 58, having declined the support of Caesar, he found himself exiled at the hand of Clodius (now tribune), for executing citizens without trial. He was recalled a year later with the support of Pompey, and returned through Italy to a considerable popular welcome.

On his return he re-engaged in political activity, attempting to separate Pompey from his association with Caesar (dating back to the so-called 'first triumvirate' of 60 BC) and continuing to clash with Clodius. Cicero was undone by the renewal of the 'triumvirate' at Luca in 56 and forced into an embarrassing climb-down, declaring his support for Caesar. He now largely withdrew from politics, playing little part in the spiral towards civil war. Between 55 and 51 he wrote a number of philosophical works, including *De oratore* (*On the Orator*), *De re publica* (*On the Republic*, or *On the State*) and the unpublished *De legibus* (*On Laws*). The last two were in conscious imitation of Plato's *Republic* and *Laws* and suggestive of the conservative reform Cicero felt the state required. He continued to undertake forensic cases, not always with success.

Cicero remained on the sidelines in the civil war. He hesitated long in Italy, resisting Caesar's overtures, before finally crossing the Adriatic to join the Pompeians, with whom he was not on good terms. He was absent from the battle of Pharsalus and subsequently returned to Italy with a pardon from Caesar, but did not approve of Caesar's dictatorship and remained outside political life. As in the 50s, he resorted to philosophical and rhetorical writing, producing the *Brutus* and the *Orator* by 46.

This period saw considerable upheaval in his family life. He fell out with his hot-tempered younger brother Quintus, though they were later reconciled. In 46 he divorced his wife of some 30 years, Terentia, by whom he had had a daughter, Tullia, and a son, Marcus. A second marriage, to his young ward Publilia, in late 46, did not last long. The death of his daughter in February 45 struck him particularly hard. He even wrote himself a *Consolatio*, admired in antiquity, but not extant. Writing became his consolation, and between her death and November 44 he produced the *Academica* (partially surviving), *On Ends* (usually known as *De finibus*), *Tusculan Disputations*, *On the Nature of the Gods*, *On Divination*, *On Fate* (fragmentary), *On Old Age*, *On Friendship*, *On Duties* (*De officiis*) and several other works now lost.

On Caesar's death, Cicero experienced a renaissance of his political career (he welcomed the murder, but was not part of the plot). As the senior surviving statesman he took the lead against Mark Antony, seeking, perhaps naively, to unite the young Octavian (Augustus) to the senate and the Republican cause. Beginning on 2 September 44 he delivered or published the famous series of speeches known as the *Philippics*, in which he violently attacked Antony (so-called after the *Philippics* of Demosthenes; 14 survive; at least three are lost). But when, in 43, Octavian sided with Antony and the new triumvirate was formed, Cicero (and his brother) fell victim to Antony's hatred in the proscriptions which followed. He was caught and killed on 7 December 43; his head and hand(s) were displayed on the *rostra* (speaker's platform) in the Roman forum.

Apart from Cicero's importance in the last generation of the Republic, his great significance lies in the writings and speeches he left behind. Some 58 speeches, political and forensic, out of a known 88, survive in whole or in part. As an orator he traditionally takes the Latin crown, Demosthenes the Greek. His writings on rhetoric and philosophy (most of which are mentioned above) constitute a contribution of the first order to the Latin language, as well as to Latin rhetorical theory and philosophy; he effectively created a Latin philosophical vocabulary. Stylistically he has often been taken as the Latin ideal. He also wrote poetry, of which little survives, perhaps fortunately: Tacitus (*Dialogue* 21) was to comment 'Caesar and Brutus also wrote poetry, not better than Cicero, but with better luck, for fewer know that they did so.' His philosophical treatises underlay much of the writing of the early Christians: the lost *Hortensius* inspired Augustine (1). Known principally for his philosophical work during the Middle Ages, in Renaissance Europe Cicero, and his works such as *De officiis* and *De oratore*, epitomized the 'whole man'. His influence was equally strong in 18th-century France and England.

But the real reason we know Cicero so well is his surviving correspondence, largely rediscovered by Petrarch and others in the 14th century: 16 books of letters to Atticus (*Ad Atticum*), 16 books of letters *To his Friends* (*Ad familiares*, actually to and from a variety of persons), and smaller collections written to his brother Quintus and to Brutus. Not, as far as we know, written for publication, they range from official letters to the senate to highly informal and allusive letters to his closest friend, Atticus. They cast an unparalleled light upon the man and his times. If it is not possible always to like him, then it is Cicero's misfortune that we know one so great so well. JRWP

See Cicero, 29 vols., trs. E. O. Winstedt et al. (1912–99); *Letters*, ed. and trs. D. R. Shackleton Bailey, various edns; Plutarch, *Lives*, vol. 7, trs. B. Perrin (1921); Rawson, E. (1975) *Cicero*.

Cilicia Area in south-east ANATOLIA between the Taurus and Amanus mountains, in two distinct parts: Rough Cilicia (Greek *Kilikia tracheia*, Latin *Cilicia aspera*) and Cilicia of the Plain (*pedias, campestris*). The Taurus and Antitaurus, accessible through the Cilician gates, possessed rich mineral resources which were exploited as early as the 3rd millennium BC. The Taurus remained an important source of SILVER and LEAD throughout the Greek, Roman, Byzantine and Ottoman periods. The well-watered alluvial plain produced grapes, cereals, grains and flax.

Human settlement in Cilicia went back to Neolithic and Chalcolithic times (c. 6300–4500 BC). In the 2nd millennium BC Cilicia came under the influence of the newly formed Hittite empire, centred on the uplands of inland Anatolia. Prominent architectural remains include the Hittite fortress at Mersin and the Hittite 'temple' at Tarsus. After Sennacherib's great campaign in 696 BC, resulting in the destruction of Tarsus, Cilicia remained loyal to Assyria. In Neo-Babylonian times Cilicia was ruled by a dynast (*syennesis*) who had his palace at Tarsus (Xenophon, *Anabasis* 1.2.26) and took orders from BABYLON. This system was continued by the Achaemenids. A separate dynastic power-centre lay at Olba in Rough Cilicia.

Following the death of ALEXANDER the Great, the PTOLEMIES and the SELEUKIDS fought for control of this strategically located region. The city of Soloi was home to the poet ARATOS; Tarsus was later the birthplace of St PAUL. As the powers of the hellenistic dynasts waned, the Cilicians became increasingly independent and took up PIRACY, eventually forcing the Romans to create in 78–77 a command called the PROVINCE of Cilicia, which did not, however, include the area normally considered Cilicia. Granted a special command by the SENATE in 67 BC, POMPEY eliminated the pirates and added parts of Cilicia to this province, which was eventually divided between SYRIA and Galatia. Pompey revived some run-down cities, and Soloi was renamed Pompeiopolis. CICERO exercised the governorship of Cilicia (a wider area) in 51/50. In the early empire, dynasts controlled the region, but in AD 72 Cilicia again became a Roman province with its capital at Tarsus. After various readjustments of frontiers, Cilicia remained strategically important for its control of coastal and overland travel, notably during CARACALLA's Eastern expedition of 216. JDM

See Treggiari, S. trs. (1996) *Cicero's Cilician Letters.*

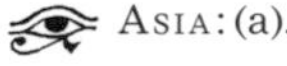 ASIA: (a).

Cimon see KIMON.

Cinna see CAESAR, JULIUS; CORNELII; SERTORIUS; SOCIAL WAR, ROMAN.

circus buildings The Roman circus (*hippodromus*) was the large entertainment building used primarily for CHARIOT RACES. By the imperial period the circus had taken the form of a hairpin, but earlier it was far less formalized. Along the central axis of the structure was a long barrier (the *euripus*). The racers travelled anti-clockwise, normally circling seven times around this barrier; a typical race in the CIRCUS MAXIMUS at Rome was just over 5 km (3 miles). The starting-gates were usually placed along a shallow arc so that all competitors had the same distance to the beginning of the *euripus*, where the track narrowed considerably. The *euripus* was often adorned with statues and other monuments. AUGUSTUS re-erected an Egyptian red granite obelisk 24 m high (dated to Rameses II, 13th century BC) on the *euripus* of the Circus Maximus. Similar obelisks were erected in the circus at CAESAREA MARITIMA in Israel. Also on the central barrier and near the finishing line was a device to count down the laps, in the form of seven movable eggs or seven dolphins. At either end were the turning posts (*metae*), cone-shaped markers in bronze or stone.

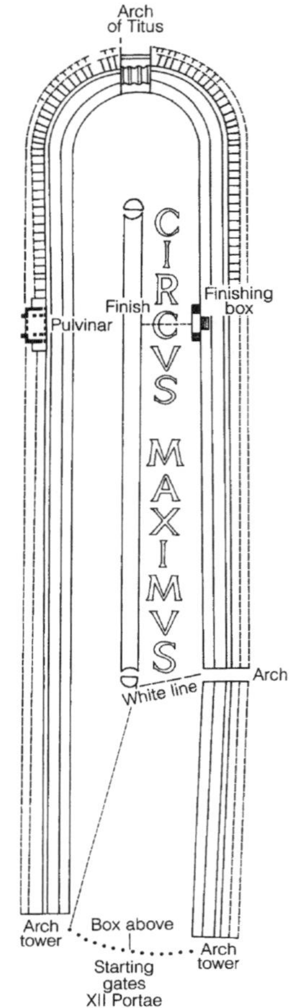

CIRCUS BUILDINGS: schematic plan of the Circus Maximus, the largest of the Roman chariot-racing arenas.

Monumental circuses are more common in the Western empire. One of the best-preserved and most thoroughly investigated is at LEPCIS MAGNA in modern Libya. Other circuses in the west include Dougga (THUGGA), CARTHAGE, Merida and Arles. In the East, monumental circuses are rarer; they are attested at ANTIOCH on the Orontes, Bostra, Gerasa and CYRENE. Interestingly, there are no attested monumental

circuses in Greece, apart from the TETRARCHIC circus at THESSALONIKE. HD
See Humphrey, J. (1986) *Roman Circuses.*

 GAMES: (a).

Circus Maximus The only location in early Rome where chariots were raced, the Circus Maximus is located on the flat plain between the Palatine and Aventine hills. Roman tradition put the earliest construction of a race-track in that area in the age of the TARQUINS. An early date appears to be confirmed by the statement that a permanent seat at the races was reserved for Manius Valerius Maximus in 494 BC near the shrine of Murcia. In 329 BC, permanent starting-gates were built; there is no reason to doubt that subsequent starting-gates were constructed in the same location, just to the south-east of the Ara Maxima or Greatest Altar (of HERCULES). On race days, wooden stands were constructed to accommodate spectators.

From the 2nd century BC onwards the circus was used as a venue for other forms of entertainment (principally beast hunts and ATHLETIC contests); the arena of the circus was open to other uses when entertainments were not in progress. Shortly before his death, JULIUS CAESAR began work on a dedicated circus building, completed and extended by AUGUSTUS. Central to the Caesarian–Augustan design were the elaboration of the decoration of the central barrier, canals around the outside of the track (for drainage and the protection of spectators from wild beasts) and the construction of stone seats surrounding the arena. The upper courses continued to be built of wood until the reign of TRAJAN, who decided to rebuild all the seats out of MARBLE, though even then there was additional wooden seating for the poorest spectators. The Circus Maximus provided the model for other circus buildings throughout the Roman empire, and prescribed the essential features of Roman CHARIOT RACING. DSP
See Humphrey, J. (1986) *Roman Circuses.*

 CHARIOT RACING; CIRCUS BUILDINGS.

Cisalpine Gaul see GALLIA CISALPINA.

cisterns see GARDENS, GREEK; HOUSES, GREEK; LAURION; LEAD; PLUMBING; WASHING; WATER SUPPLY.

cities

An examination of classical writings shows that, in the classical period, Greek writers did not (other than metaphorically) apply the term 'CITY-STATE' (*POLIS*, plural *poleis*) to any URBAN entity that was not politically organized (having citizens and public decision-making) or to any which lacked a built-up centre of some sort (however small). This principle has been humorously termed (by M. H. Hansen) the *lex Hafniensis de civitate* or 'Copenhagen law of the *polis*'. Even the smallest places called *poleis*, with a few hundred citizens and a total population of a few thousand, qualified as city-states, no less than the largest metropolitan entities like Athens and Corinth.

The inscription on the bronze Serpent column, dedicated at Delphi to celebrate the Greek victory over Xerxes in 480–479, lists the peoples who contributed to the war effort. Tellingly, it lists them by their city. Under the heading 'These fought in the war' are 31 *ethnika* (ethnic or civic group names), beginning 'Lakedaimonians' (Spartans and their dependants), 'Athenians, Corinthians, Tegeates, Sikyonians, Aiginetans, Megarians, Epidaurians', and so on. This could equally be translated 'the men of Lakedaimon, Athens, Corinth, Tegea, Sikyon, Aigina, Megara, Epidauros'. All are in the same size of lettering, and they are in no particular order except that the first three are the cities agreed to have made the largest contributions to victory.

In Greek eyes, a *polis* remained a city-state even when it was a 'dependent *polis*'. Examples of dependent *poleis* include the perioikic *poleis* of SPARTA (one of the 70-odd subordinate communities of free Lakedaimonians) and members of FEDERAL alliances (such as the ACHAIAN LEAGUE of the 3rd century BC). Nor did a *polis* cease to be a *polis* when it lost 'independence', *autonomia* (a stronger concept in the classical period than the English word 'autonomy'); it was simply a dependent *polis*. We need not worry about whether a small, dependent *polis* was 'really' (whatever that means) a city. Clearly it was not a city in terms a modern geographer would recognize (though even today the Italian term *città* extends to large VILLAGES of a certain administrative status). Equally clearly, it was a city as far as the Greeks were concerned.

There were c.1,500 *poleis* (city-states) in the classical Greek world. The rest of the text on the Serpent column exemplifies their variety (here translated as a list of cities rather than *ethnika*): 'Orchomenos, Phleious, Troizen, Hermione, Tiryns, Plataiai, Thespiai, Mykenai, Keos, Melos, Tenos, Naxos, Eretria, Chalkis, Styra, Elis, Poteidaia, Leukas, Anaktoron, Kythnos, Siphnos, Amprakia, Lepreon'. Most of those towns were small; many will be unfamiliar to modern readers. Some are tiny islands with one *polis*; some are middle-sized mainland *poleis*. Two are on the Adriatic coast, far from the Greek heartland. These small places were the 'real' Greece, if by 'real' one means typical – what Hans-Joachim Gehrke calls 'the third Greece'. The places we know most about, like Athens and Sparta, were decidedly unusual.

A large proportion of Greek *poleis* were COLONIES, new settlements scattered along the coasts of the Mediterranean and Black sea. Rectilinear TOWN PLANNING began in colonies in the early archaic period, and was adopted widely in Old Greece whenever cities were built or rebuilt. Although older cities such as Athens retained irregular street layouts, they adopted the types of monumental political ARCHITECTURE that came to be hallmarks of a civilized state, such as TEMPLES, COUNCIL houses, an *AGORA*, THEATRES, LAWCOURTS, *prytaneia* (buildings for the group holding the PRYTANY), sometimes ASSEMBLY buildings, and (particularly in the hellenistic period) STOAS. FORTIFICATION walls became increasingly common for defence, and were normal by the 4th century BC. Amenities making use of the water supply, such as FOUNTAIN HOUSES, public TOILETS and later BATH-HOUSES, were a feature especially of the late classical, hellenistic and Roman periods. The town and its physical amenities were for the benefit not only of the town-dwellers but also of citizens resident in dependent settlements, as well as visitors from elsewhere. Attic COMEDIES, such as

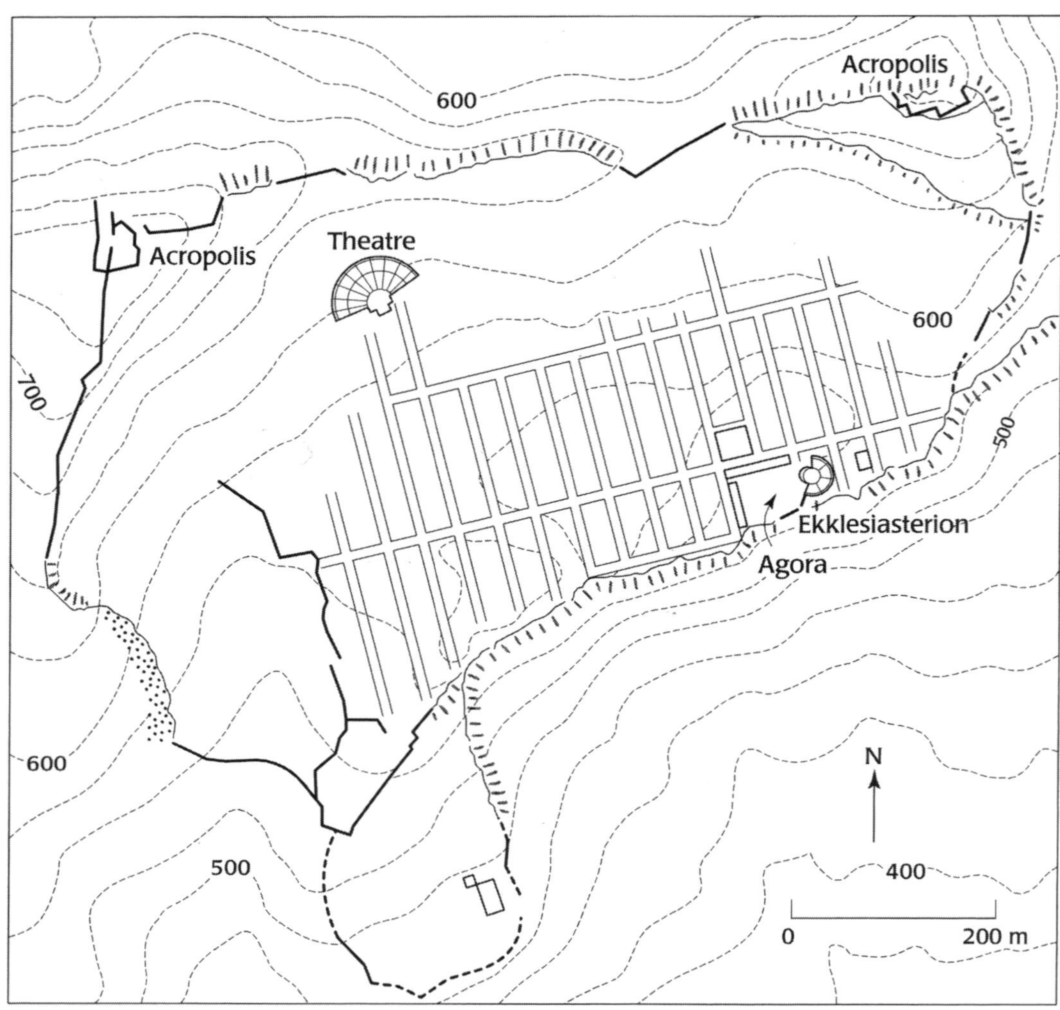

CITIES: (a) plan of Kassope, showing many typical features of the Greek polis (*agora*, street grid with long rectangular insulae, walls and acropolis, theatre and assembly building (*ekklêsiastêrion*).

those of ARISTOPHANES and MENANDER, paint a lively picture of everyday hustle and bustle in the streets and open spaces of a city.

Despite their political primacy, Greek cities were surrounded by networks of smaller settlements. To understand Greece from the viewpoint of a human geographer we can use a definition based on size or population, provided we do not imagine that it conforms to Greek ways of thinking about social life, administration and politics. Horden and Purcell even propose that we abandon the notion of the town in Mediterranean history, dissolve the town–country boundary, and consider all the LANDSCAPE as a continuum with varying uses and forms of settlement. For them, towns are rather 'loci of contact or overlap between different ecologies'. While this approach may be appropriate to an ecological–historical inquiry, it obscures the fact that Greek identity was closely bound up with urban entities. For most purposes, historians should adopt the Greeks' own terminology. DGJS

See Damgaard Andersen, H. et al., eds. (1997) *Urbanization in the Mediterranean in the 9th to 6th Centuries BC*; Gehrke, H.-J. (1986) *Jenseits von Athen und Sparta: das dritte Griechenland*; Hansen, M. H. (1998) *Polis and City-state*; Horden, P. and Purcell, N. (2000) *The Corrupting Sea*; Jones, A. H. M. (1937) *The Cities of the Eastern Roman Provinces*; (1940) *The Greek City: from Alexander to Justinian*; Mitchell, L. G. and Rhodes, P. J., eds. (1997) *The Development of the Polis in Archaic Greece*; Murray, O. and Price, S., eds. (1990) *The Greek City: from Homer to Alexander*; Owens, E. J. (1990) *The City in the Greek and Roman World*; Polignac, F. de (1995) *Cults, Territory, and the Origins of the Greek City-state*; Rhodes, P. J. (1986) *The Greek City States: a source book*; Wycherley, R. E. (1962) *How the Greeks Built Cities*.

Cities in the Roman empire, apart from the already urbanized East, came to play a somewhat

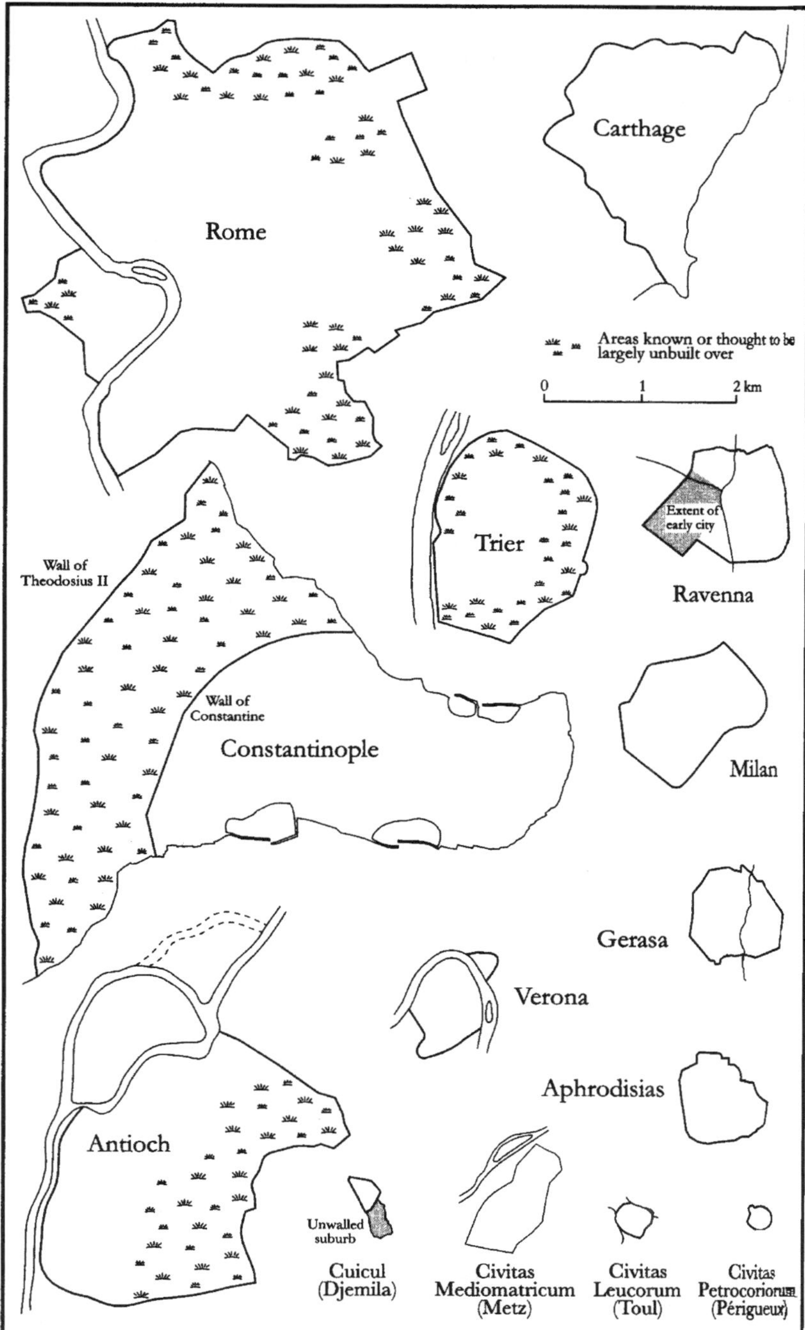

CITIES: (b) comparative plans of some Roman cities illustrating the exceptional size of the two imperial capitals, Rome and Constantinople, along with a handful of still unusually large cities such as Trier, Carthage and Antioch. The vast majority of all Roman cities were far smaller, equivalent to the examples in the bottom r. corner of the figure.

different conceptual role compared with their role in the Greek world. Greece and large parts of the eastern Mediterranean, and indeed Italy before its unification under Rome, were landscapes of city-states. In Italy and the West, however, the city (*urbs*), whether located in Italy or in the PROVINCES, was generally part of a larger administrative structure. In form and organization, it was to a greater or lesser extent a reflection of the capital, ROME.

Roman cities were made up of component parts, namely buildings used for administration, entertainment, RELIGION and habitation. Variations from the capital in style and layout reflected differences in topographical features as well as local customs and resources. During the foundation ceremony of a town, an augur would RITUALLY mark out the *cardo maximus* (main north–south road) and *decumanus maximus* (main east–west road). The LAND SURVEYOR would then place the *groma* on the intersecting point of these two roads and map out the main gates that would be placed on the outer edges of the rectangular site. The town would also be ritually ploughed to delineate the perimeter for a defensive wall, and the *POMERIUM* or sacred boundary would encircle the wall from the outside.

Roman TOWN PLANNING had its roots in the Greek and ETRUSCAN grid plan systems. The focal point of the grid plan was the intersection between the *cardo* and *decumanus maximus*. Typically, the FORUM or main square was built at this junction in the developing city's centre (e.g. OSTIA and POMPEII). Grid plans in northern Italy, however, as well as in the northern provinces, differ from this pattern. There a building usually blocks the *cardo* from intersecting the *decumanus maximus*: the result was a formation of a T-junction. In turn, this offset the forum as the central focal point or core of the city (e.g. MILAN and Verona). Other streets ran parallel to the main axes, dividing the territory into square or rectangular parcels of land called *insulae* ('islands', i.e. blocks). Major streets were usually made of stone paving-blocks, and were sometimes bisected by stepping-stones to enable pedestrians to avoid any litter, faecal matter and rainwater that might have accumulated on the street. Smaller streets or alleyways running behind buildings were narrower and made of pounded dirt or cobblestones. Often ARCHES erected by prominent local benefactors or commemorating a military TRIUMPH would line a city's major roadways. Cities were usually surrounded by defensive FORTIFICATION walls, and traffic coming in or out was regulated by entrances and gateways into the city. Narrow passages were reserved for pedestrians, with wider ones for livestock and vehicles. During the early empire walls did not frequently appear in urban planning, but their appearance revived during the 2nd and 3rd centuries AD.

Several types of ARCHITECTURE corresponded to the city's administrative, religious and social composition. The forum or square constituted the city's central political, commercial, religious and social area. Covered walkways and buildings could demarcate the open air enclosure. The administration buildings comprised the *CURIA* (the civic meeting hall) and the BASILICA (public meeting hall or LAWCOURT). TEMPLES for worship of local and state deities were also present. Statuary and inscriptions prevailed in the centre of the forum or among its covered walkways. Statues included those of honorary citizens, BENEFACTORS and members of the imperial family. If needed, one could also find additional fora used for commercial purposes (e.g., FISH MARKETS, CATTLE markets, VEGETABLE markets) in larger urban centres. New fora were built, as at Rome, to meet the administrative needs of the city's growing population. Rome's leaders between 54 BC and AD 114 left behind a legacy symbolizing their rule by constructing five new fora to the north and north-east of the original Forum Romanum. The grandest of all was the forum of TRAJAN, which provided new lawcourts, LIBRARIES and a market.

Places for entertainment were a main feature of the city. THEATRES would house dramatic performances, *odea* (from the Greek term *ôdeia*) were for musical performances, and in AMPHITHEATRES one could watch GLADIATORIAL combats and wild-beast hunts. Equestrian events such as CHARIOT and HORSE RACES were held in the CIRCUS. If necessary, foot races and gladiatorial combats were staged here as well. Around the 1st century AD in the eastern regions of the Roman empire, *stadia* (singular *stadium*) made their appearance, modelled on Greek designs and used for foot races. Typically the entertainment venues, situated near city gates and away from the forum, were planned strategically to regulate public activities. For example, if a crowd got out of hand its speedy removal could be facilitated by the close proximity of the city gates. INNS, restaurants and SHOPS figured prominently in these areas, catering for travellers and revellers taking part in the spectacles. Some inns (e.g. *cauponae*) would offer meals, rooms and, in some instances, PROSTITUTES. More respectable establishments included *hospitia* and *deversoria*.

RELIGION also played a significant role in the urban domain. The TEMPLE (*templum*) was not merely the temple building proper. The sacred SPACE consisted of the *area* or open viewing space bound by some form of enclosure, an altar for SACRIFICE and the *aedes* or temple building housing the cult statue. Worshippers did not congregate inside the *aedes*. One could find temples in the fora or in other areas of the city deemed sacred (e.g. shrines dedicated to local deities). Temples were also venues for political administration. MAGISTRATES at Rome, such as the CONSULS, met at the temple of Castor, QUAESTORS at the temple of Saturnus. Specific religious groups had their own houses of worship. Those devoted to MITHRAISM worshipped inside temples designed like caves. JEWS and CHRISTIANS also performed rituals in an interior setting. Jewish synagogues were built for EDUCATION, administration and PRAYER. Christians in the early stages congregated in HOUSES, then gradually adapted the BASILICA plan for public worship.

Neighbourhoods within cities were called *vici* and were named after specific landmarks or professions known in the neighbourhood (e.g. Vicus Frumentarius in Rome, from the grain market). Within these neighbourhoods were diverse living quarters and commercial centres. In Rome several generations of the imperial family resided in PALACES located on or near the Palatine hill. Most individuals lived in a *domus* (home, household), the most common design being in the atrium style. APARTMENT blocks or *insulae* made their appearance in heavily populated areas. Residential and commercial activities often went hand in hand in these dwellings. Facing onto the street, BAKERIES, SHOPS (*tabernae*), WORKSHOPS and the ancient counterpart of the fast-food emporium figured in these buildings. Food markets or *macella* were also present in the city, built either in or near the forum; they were prevalent during the imperial period. Originally sellers hawked MEAT in these markets, but gradually other foodstuffs were sold. To store goods imported into the city, large-scale WAREHOUSES and GRANARIES were built.

Habitation for the dead also had a distinctive form of urban planning. Areas designated for BURIAL were typically, but not always, found outside the city walls, in order not to pollute the areas inside. Cemeteries were arranged much like houses with tomb façades facing the passer-by.

Many public and private services were available for the inhabitants of a city. There were several options available for policing. The military could assume certain roles. For instance, FIRES were always a great risk, and cohorts of the *vigiles* (guards) both prevented and fought fires. AEDILES, for the most part, kept public order when it came to managing roads, BATHS and inns, but on the whole responsibility fell to the private citizen. EDUCATION typically took place in the HOUSEHOLD, but some SCHOOLS could be held in open spaces such as the forum or simply on street corners.

WATER SUPPLY and SANITATION were also available to a city's inhabitants. In most cities, the distribution of drinking water came via the AQUEDUCT. The water flowed into a *castellum* or distribution tower and then could be channelled to various neighbourhoods via pipes and conduits. Water from aqueducts was not only potable but was available for use in public and private baths. Public bath-houses were major social institutions. Not only did they provide a place to maintain personal hygiene, but they also were venues where ATHLETES could train and PHILOSOPHERS could meet. Waste water from the baths was put to good use. Public TOILETS made their appearance in most cities, and the water from the baths was used to flush sewage. Fresh running water was also channelled into the lavatories for washing.

The amenities of the Roman city, which developed from those of the Greek and hellenistic worlds, set a standard which later urban communities aspired to match. LAH

See Grimal, P. (1983) *Roman Cities*; MacDonald, W. L. (1986) *The Architecture of the Roman Empire*, vol. 2; Perring, D. (1991) Spatial organization and social change, in J. Rich and A. Wallace-Hadrill, eds., *City and Country in the Ancient World* 273–93; Stambaugh, J. E. (1988) *The Ancient Roman City*; Ward-Perkins, J. B. (1974) *Cities of Ancient Greece and Italy: planning in classical antiquity*.

citizenship

The English word 'citizenship' is derived from Latin *civitas* (citizenship; state); the equivalent Greek term, *politeia*, is derived from *POLIS*. A Greek citizen was literally a '*POLIS*-man' (*politês*), and such men collectively were the *polis* in its concrete actuality. Different Greek cities operated different positive rules for CITIZENSHIP, but all agreed negatively that WOMEN and SLAVES as well as children should not count as citizens in the sense of being actively involved in the public sphere of decision-making.

ARISTOTLE in the *Politics* spent considerable time worrying how best to define the (free adult male Greek) citizen. In the end he decided it was the free adult Greek male who participated in legal judgement (*krisis*) and office-holding (*archê*), though he confessed that in practice that definition better suited the citizen of a DEMOCRACY than of an OLIGARCHY. In other words, in an oligarchy, a distinction was drawn, on grounds of WEALTH, between two different classes of citizen: full and partial, active and passive, first- and second-class. Only the former might qualify to hold office and pass formal legal judgement. In a democracy, a citizen was a citizen was a citizen. All citizens of a democracy were – ideally – as equal in practice as they were in theory.

The normal minimal qualification for citizenship of a Greek *polis* was birth. One had to be the legitimate son of one or two citizen-status parents. The Athenian democracy operated the double-descent rule with unusual rigour and vigour: to qualify eventually as an Athenian citizen after 451/0 BC one had to be born of a lawfully married Athenian father and his Athenian wife. Then, at the age of 18, one had to be formally enrolled on the register of one's local DEME (village, ward, parish), supported by the appropriate witnesses (relatives, friends, neighbours). In other states it was enough to have a citizen father; in CRETE one's mother might even be unfree.

In Sparta, by contrast – and uniquely in Greece – there was added to the birth qualification an educational criterion. Entry to the adult citizen body was conditional upon a boy's having passed successfully through a gruelling system of public education between the ages of 7 and 18, and being elected to a military-style dining group (*syssition*). There was, furthermore, an economic criterion for retaining citizenship: one had to provide each month a specified minimum quantity of natural produce to one's dining group. Correspondingly, hardly any outsiders were ever admitted to Spartan citizenship for honorific reasons. The reason for this uniquely severe policing of citizenship in Sparta was that the citizen body was also the people in arms, a standing army of HOPLITE infantrymen. (see also POLITICAL SYSTEMS; STATE, THE) PAC

See Hansen, M. H. (1993) Introduction: the polis as a citizen-state, in M. H. Hansen, ed., *The Ancient Greek City-state* 7–29; Manville, P. B. (1990) *The Origins of Citizenship in Ancient Athens*.

At no time did the population of the Roman world solely comprise Roman citizens; rather there existed a patchwork of statuses: Roman, LATIN, free foreigner (*peregrinus*) and SLAVE. Individual status dictated relations with other members of society and the Roman state. In addition to the vote, membership of the citizen body (*civitas*) generally gave one the rights to marry (*conubium*) and transact business (*commercium*), as well as affording access to the legal system. However, citizenship did not mean equality. Female citizens lacked the right to vote or stand for office and the organization of ELECTIONS effectively gave greater weight to the votes of the wealthy. In the REPUBLIC, the membership roll of the citizen body was revised in a CENSUS every five years.

Most citizens inherited their status from their parents, but a principle of awarding it for proven service either to an individual Roman or to the Roman state in general allowed a continual flow of new blood into the citizen body. During the conquest of Italy the Romans extended their citizenship to many communities, though in the early 1st century BC it was only the SOCIAL WAR that secured it for their remaining Italian allies. It was most astonishing to Greek commentators that slaves MANUMITTED by a living master, or granted freedom in a master's WILL, could themselves gain Roman citizenship. Legislation by AUGUSTUS imposed various restrictions and regularized the position of those informally manumitted. These were deemed 'Latins' and could upgrade to full citizenship if they produced a child surviving beyond one year. Although they could vote, FREEDMEN were unable to stand for election to MAGISTRACIES or hold various public offices. Under the empire, tenure of magistracies in provincial communities with the 'Latin right' conferred citizenship, while large numbers earned citizenship for themselves, their first wife and their children through 25 years' service in the armed forces. VETERANS who felt they might need proof of this new status could get certified copies, issued in bronze, of the original grant displayed in Rome. Additionally individuals might petition for citizenship, though this required the sponsorship of powerful PATRONS which might come at a price, as the tribune who arrested St PAUL complained (Acts 22.28). Despite a gradual whittling away of fiscal and judicial privileges under the empire, the access citizenship gave to official positions remained valuable.

In the Western provinces, possession of citizenship was generally accompanied by a familiarity with Roman culture and the Latin language. However, the latter was not always the case in the East, though the pedantic CLAUDIUS chose to deprive a Lycian ambassador of his Roman citizenship because he could not understand Latin (Cassius Dio 60.17.3). Although citizenship was extended to all free subjects by the emperor CARACALLA in AD 212 (the so-called *constitutio Antoniniana*), the continued creation of new Latins, the immigration of foreigners, and the sizeable slave population meant that the distinction of citizen remained meaningful. Roman status even lived on outside the empire, in the law codes of the barbarian successor kingdoms. RWBS

See Gardner, J. F. (1993) *Being a Roman Citizen*; Sherwin-White, A. N. (1973) *The Roman Citizenship*.

city-states Small political units with an urban centre and associated AGRICULTURAL hinterland, city-states were the most common form of organization in the ancient MEDITERRANEAN and surrounding lands, from early Bronze Age Sumer to the Roman conquests. They typically controlled areas of a few hundred to a few thousand sq km, with populations ranging from a few thousand to a few hundred thousand. PLATO (*Laws* 737d–738e) thought that the ideal city-state would have 5,040 adult male CITIZENS (perhaps meaning a total population of 40,000 to 50,000), while ARISTOTLE (*Politics* 1267b31) suggested 10,000. Normally no more than about 10 per cent of the residents would live in the urban centre. City-states normally developed in clusters united by culture, LANGUAGE, RELIGION and often a sense of ETHNICITY. They tended to compete fiercely for resources and power, with regional leadership passing rapidly from one city-state to another.

Sociologically, city-states were typically organized around a citizen community, which possessed political and legal rights. The citizen body was normally a subset of the resident adult males. The citizen–non-citizen boundary might be based on property, military participation or urban residence. In some cities the whole citizen community had a voice of some kind in political decisions, while in others a king or narrow ARISTOCRACY might monopolize most important functions. The definition of the citizen was crucially important, and the major difference between Greek and Italian city-states on the one hand and Near Eastern cities like BABYLON was that the former saw much more urban–rural unity than the latter, allowing countrymen as well as town-dwellers to be citizens. Greek citizen bodies were also unusually egalitarian, developing the first male DEMOCRACIES and generally rejecting kingship. Even OLIGARCHY, a widespread constitutional form in Greece, embodied principles of equality and public decision-making, though within a narrower group.

All city-states developed systems of dependent LABOUR. Most based these on urban versus rural legal divisions, or on DEBT-BONDAGE. Others (particularly in COLONIAL settings) depended on conquest and the creation of subject populations of serfs, or on importing foreign chattel SLAVES. There were substantial inequalities in wealth, though usually less than in ancient empires.

All these factors combined to make it very difficult for any one city-state to subdue the entire network of states to which it belonged. Already in the 3rd millennium BC Agade and Ur came close, but both empires fragmented within two centuries. The major 1st-millennium BC empires in the east Mediterranean region – Assyria, PERSIA and MACEDONIA – all developed out of non-city-state backgrounds. In the AEGEAN, Athens came close to overwhelming all rivals in the 5th century, but after its failure in 404 no other city managed this. ROME was the most important exception, developing uniquely flexible institutions in the 4th century BC that allowed it to harness the manpower and resources of Italy and to use them to conquer the whole Mediterranean basin. IM

See Hansen, M., ed. (2000) *A Comparative Study of Thirty City-state Cultures*; (2002) *A Comparative Study of Six City-state Cultures*; Molho, M. et al., eds. (1991) *City-states in Classical Antiquity and Medieval Italy*; Nichols, D. and Charlton, T., eds. (1997) *The Archaeology of City-states*.

civil strife Conflict or contention between or among different segments or factions within a state, with the goal of altering the government or the law. The Greeks regarded the division of the populace into contending factions as one of the greatest threats facing a state. The term for this phenomenon was *stasis*. THUCYDIDES offers a classic account in his analysis of discord at Kerkyra (Corcyra; 3.69–85; see also ARISTOTLE, *Politics* 4.9.8–10, 5.2.1–4.8). In early Greece, these conflicts centred around different constitutions and forms of government, including rule by TYRANTS and competition among the OLIGARCHS for POWER. Some struggles took on the nature of class warfare, the rich against the poor, with concern over DEBT and LAND ownership driving the dissension.

At Athens, some of these tensions were defused peacefully through the actions of reformers such as SOLON and KLEISTHENES. In the early Roman REPUBLIC, the 'Conflict of the Orders' was a series of disputes between PATRICIANS and PLEBEIANS which resulted in expanded political rights and the establishment of the TRIBUNATE of the PLEBS. The late Republic saw another round of intense civil strife, with the attempt at debt and land reform by the GRACCHI brothers (133 and 123 BC), the destructive SOCIAL WAR fought over granting full CITIZENSHIP to Rome's Italian allies and partial citizens (91–87 BC), and eventually the CIVIL WARS which ended in the destruction of the Republic and the establishment of the PRINCIPATE. (see also REVOLUTION; VIOLENCE) GSA

See Brunt, P. A. (1971) *Social Conflicts in the Roman Republic*; Lintott, A. (1982) *Violence, Civil Strife, and Revolution in the Classical City 750–330 BC*.

civil wars, Roman Political conflicts at Rome had led to intermittent urban VIOLENCE since 133 BC, but the conditions for civil war were created by the SOCIAL WAR which broke out between the Romans and their Italian allies in 91 (fighting began in 90) and led to a huge mobilization of troops in Italy. In 88 the tribune Sulpicius transferred the prestigious command against MITHRADATES from the consul SULLA to his associate MARIUS. Sulla responded by marching on Rome with his army. His justification, repeatedly echoed in subsequent civil wars, was that he was freeing the REPUBLIC from a faction which had seized power, but the prospect of the lucrative Asian campaign impelled his troops to act. After his departure for the East in 87, conflict broke out again and the armies in Italy were drawn in, Sulla's opponents emerging victorious. Sulla's return in 83 was followed by civil war throughout Italy and the Western PROVINCES. Except in Spain, Sulla's side was victorious by 81. His opponents were proscribed, his troops settled on confiscated land. In Spain SERTORIUS held out until 72.

Stability of a kind now returned, and CATILINE's uprising was swiftly crushed in 63–2. However, the rise first of POMPEY and then CAESAR to exceptional prominence led to war between them in 49. Each claimed to be in the right. Their troops were swayed partly by personal and political loyalties, but also by promises of cash and land. Caesar beat Pompey at PHARSALUS (48) and the remnants of his party at THAPSUS (46) and Munda (45). He amazed all by treating the defeated with clemency. The campaigns were succinctly chronicled by Caesar and his continuators, and a century later became the subject of LUCAN's epic.

Caesar's assassination in 44 unleashed another series of civil wars. His heir Octavian (the future AUGUSTUS) first fought with the SENATE against MARK ANTONY, but then switched sides to form the TRIUMVIRATE with Antony and Lepidus. The triumvirs proscribed their opponents, defeated BRUTUS and Cassius at PHILIPPI (42), and confiscated land for their troops. Octavian fought further wars against Antony's brother at Perusia (41–40) and Sextus Pompeius off Sicily (38–36). His relationship with Antony broke down in 32, and his victories at ACTIUM (31) and ALEXANDRIA (30) made him sole ruler of the Roman world.

The fear of renewed civil war helped to ensure general support for the rule of Octavian, and he contrived to take the army out of politics by establishing fixed terms of service and rewards on discharge. Minor uprisings apart, civil war did not recur until the fall of NERO ended the Julio-Claudian dynasty (AD 68). Various senators, mostly army commanders, declared their candidature, and the wars of the 'Year of the Four Emperors' (69), vividly recounted in TACITUS' *Histories*, ended in the victory of VESPASIAN. After that it was not until 193–7 that conflict over the imperial succession again led to warfare. WAR between imperial contenders was endemic in the anarchic conditions of the mid-3rd century, and recurred from time to time in the late empire. JWR

See Henderson, J. (1998) *Fighting for Rome*.

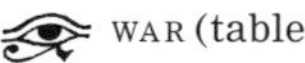 WAR (table).

class The *Communist Manifesto* of MARX and Engels (1848) opens with the bold declaration 'The history of all hitherto existing society is the history of class struggles.' Yet they never gave a coherent definition of 'class', which remains a fiercely controversial term in historical and sociological studies. Any application of 'class' to classical civilization involves therefore a certain amount of conscious stipulation and manipulation of terminology.

For example, economic class might be defined as a relationship between persons similarly placed in an economic system. Classes so composed would usually stand in a relationship of subordination or superiority to other such classes. A further ingredient, of self-consciousness in belonging to a particular class, might be considered crucially necessary to influence behaviour on grounds of class in economic or non-economic contexts. Suppose further that people are classified according to their relationship to the means and LABOUR of economic production, between those who do and do not own such means, and therefore do or do not have to work for a living. Granted all that, one might try to interpret the familiar Greek and Roman political and sociological distinction between the few 'rich' and the many 'poor' citizens as a distinction of class. That indeed seems to have been what Marx himself did – citing in different contexts ARISTOTLE (whom he considered a 'giant thinker') and the Greek-speaking Roman historian APPIAN.

But closer analysis causes difficulties. Are the richest Roman SENATOR and the non-working owner of a relatively modest pottery WORKSHOP to be placed in the same class? Or consider wealthy metics in a Greek city: debarred from land ownership on legal grounds, they were thus debarred from the safest as well as most respectable form of economic investment, except in so far as they might lease land and work it with unfree or hired labour. Are they to be placed in the same economic class with rich citizen landowners? Perhaps, but then what is the explanatory power of 'class' in so far as class, on a Marxian view, necessarily gives rise to class struggles?

Likewise problematic in class terms are the relations of Greek and Roman SLAVES to their masters. In so far as slaves were deracinated, rightless and wholly owned chattels, they were liable to almost unlimited exploitation by their masters, who could perhaps be said to have struggled to maintain this – to them – satisfying economic relationship. But the slaves for their part were ill equipped actively to struggle back, least of all collectively and consciously as a class, and mass slave revolts are almost unheard of. The one exception to that rule is the Spartans' HELOTS, but they, crucially, were not chattel slaves but a form of collective serfs. Equally importantly, they were of Greek, indeed local Greek, origin. Again, pure economic class was cut across by legal status and subjective consciousness.

This is all a long way from the etymological root of class. That lies in the Latin term *classis*, a collective noun designating all those Roman citizens who were judged by the CENSORS to be in possession of a certain minimum amount of property and therefore eligible for (compulsory) military service. (see also CITIZENSHIP; MARXISM) PAC

See Ste Croix, G. E. M. de (1983) *The Class Struggle in the Ancient Greek World.*

classical scholarship see SCHOLARSHIP, CLASSICAL.

Claudian The Egyptian poet Claudius Claudianus was born in the late 4th century AD, possibly in ALEXANDRIA. Like many Egyptian contemporaries, he studied RHETORIC and POETRY in both Greek and Latin. After publishing some minor Greek works, he travelled to Rome where he gave a PANEGYRIC on the consuls of 395, Probinus and Olybrius. The successful reception of this work led to commissions from the court at MILAN from 396 for the emperor HONORIUS and the *magister militum* STILICHO. Numerous poems provided interpretations of Stilicho's policies against ALARIC, Rufinus, Eutropius and Gildo. Stilicho rewarded Claudian with the position of *tribunus et notarius* in 397 and a rich bride. He died c.404.

His extant Latin works include epic poems, invectives, panegyrics (to Stilicho, Honorius and other consuls) and *epithalamia* (wedding songs), almost all written in compact hexameters. They are structured following traditional practice, yet are highly innovative, combining many motifs from poetry (PERSONIFICATION and similes) with forms (panegyrics) often associated with prose. Claudian's descriptions are intensely visual. Though himself a PAGAN, he worked for CHRISTIAN patrons using classically inspired themes. Claudian's stylistic innovations were followed by many Western poets, such as SIDONIUS APOLLINARIS. The availability of several datable works over a short period allows historians to observe small shifts in Stilicho's public image, especially with respect to Alaric's GOTHS and the Eastern court of Arcadius. HWE

See Platnauer, M., trs. (1922) 2 vols.; Cameron, A. (1970) *Claudian*; Long, J. (1996) *Claudian's In Eutropium.*

Claudianus, Mons see MONS CLAUDIANUS.

Claudii One of the great PATRICIAN clans of the Roman Republic (the Claudii Marcelli are a distinct PLEBEIAN *gens*). The principal tradition traces the family back to the migration to Rome by the SABINE aristocrat Attus Clausus (latinized to Appius Claudius) c.504 BC. The existence of the TRIBE Claudia by 495 is presumably closely linked to this event, though later members of the family seem to belong to the Quirina or Palatina tribes. The distinctive *praenomen* Appius is generally retained.

The first great historical figure of the family and, it is often said, of the Republic, was Appius Claudius Caecus ('the blind'), censor in 312. He built the Via Appia and Rome's first AQUEDUCT, the Aqua Appia. Caecus' political activities, which included widening the political influence of the people, are most plausibly assessed as those of a PATRICIAN who made some use of demagogic methods. Tradition considers the Claudii the prime examples of patrician *superbia* ('arrogance'), but this is more fiction than fact. Caecus is important also in the history of Latin prose; to him is attributed the saying, *faber est suae quisque fortunae* ('each man is the architect of his own fortune').

Several of Caecus' descendants were active in the PUNIC WARS (Caudex led the army across to SICILY in 264). The principal line adopted the *cognomen* Pulcher in the 3rd century. The most famous was Publius CLODIUS Pulcher, the demagogic tribune and enemy of CICERO – 'Clodius' is an alternative spelling which only gained significance, as supposedly more 'popular', in this later period. Clodius' sister CLODIA is believed to be the Lesbia of CATULLUS' poetry. The Claudii Nerones, belonging to the Arnensis tribe, are difficult to trace through the Republican period but ultimately emerged to prominence through Tiberius Claudius Nero, first husband of LIVIA. AUGUSTUS adopted their son TIBERIUS, who became his successor; Tiberius' grand-nephew Gaius (CALIGULA) and nephew CLAUDIUS were in turn emperors; NERO was adopted into the family. The name became increasingly commonplace in the imperial period as a result of the many acts of enfranchisement carried out by Claudius and Nero, with many Claudii from the Eastern part of the empire subsequently entering the senate. JRWP

Claudius (Tiberius Claudius Nero; Germanicus after his brother's death) 10 BC–54 AD The second son of the war-hero Nero Drusus and of Antonia Minor, daughter of MARK ANTONY, Claudius was born on 1 August 10 BC. Defects of HEALTH and demeanour (perhaps due to cerebral palsy) meant that he wrote rather than made history until his CONSULSHIP with his nephew Gaius CALIGULA (37). Whether he colluded in Gaius' assassination (41) is unclear; the story has him being picked up by marauding guardsmen. His accession was briefly resisted, and Claudius gained prestige by invading BRITAIN (43). In the East, however, his dealings ended with a PARTHIAN occupying the throne of ARMENIA. At home he proved concerned and active, busy with jurisdiction, AQUEDUCTS, a HARBOUR at OSTIA, and draining the Fucine lake. Grants of CITIZENSHIP (sometimes bought) and further privileges aroused resentment. Struggles at court forced Claudius to destroy his wife Messalina (48), and he had to bolster his position by marrying Germanicus' daughter AGRIPPINA. She brought with her her son, NERO after his adoption, to take first place from Claudius' own son Britannicus (b.41). When Claudius died (13 October 54, allegedly from Agrippina's poison), Nero was saluted. Claudius was deified (for Nero's advantage); despite mockery (see SENECA THE YOUNGER), his services to the people were genuine and his transmission of power to an heir, though not his own son, preserved peace in the empire. BML

See Levick, B. (1990) *Claudius.*

 AUGUSTUS: (a); EMPERORS, ROMAN: (a).

Claudius II Gothicus see Constantine.

emperors, Roman: (b).

Claudius Ptolemy see Ptolemy of Alexandria.

Cleanthes see Kleanthes.

Cleisthenes see Kleisthenes.

Cleomenes I see Kleomenes I.

Cleomenes III see Kleomenes III.

Cleon see Kleon.

Cleopatra (Kleopatra VII) b.69 BC The last Ptolemaic ruler of Egypt (51–30 BC), Cleopatra VII was the daughter of Ptolemy XII Auletes and bore a name common to many queens of the Ptolemies. Following Auletes' death, she married her brother Ptolemy XIII and acceded jointly with him to the throne. In the third year of their reign, however, Ptolemy drove her into exile in Syria. She gathered an army but was unable to assert her claim until the arrival of Julius Caesar into Alexandria. He became her lover. He triumphed over Ptolemy's forces in the Alexandrian war, and in 47 Ptolemy was killed. Caesar then proclaimed Cleopatra as queen and her younger brother, Ptolemy XIV, as her husband and king. Cleopatra went to Rome, where she lived as Caesar's mistress. She gave birth to a son, Caesarion (Ptolemy XV Caesar); it is believed that Caesar was his father. After Caesar's assassination in 44, Cleopatra is said to have murdered Ptolemy XIV. She returned to Egypt and made Caesarion her co-regent.

Because she hesitated to take sides in the civil war that followed Caesar's death, Mark Antony summoned her to meet him and explain her conduct. She put on a show of vulgar ostentation for him when they met at Tarsus; he quickly fell in love with her and returned with her to Egypt. Antony was compelled to return to Rome, where he married Octavia, sister of Octavian Caesar (the future Augustus). After Antony's departure from Egypt, however, Cleopatra bore him twins, Alexander Helios and Cleopatra Selene. In 36 Antony went to the East to lead an expedition against the Parthians. He sent for Cleopatra, who joined him at Antioch. They were married, and a third child, Ptolemy Philadelphos, was born. In 34, after a successful campaign against the Parthians, he celebrated his triumph at Alexandria and doled out vast tracts of land to Cleopatra.

In 32 Octavian declared war against Cleopatra when Antony divorced Octavia. A naval engagement at Actium in 31 was disastrous; Cleopatra and Antony fled to Alexandria. On the approach of Octavian, Antony committed suicide. Hearing that Octavian intended to exhibit her in his triumph at Rome, Cleopatra killed herself, probably by the bite of an asp (or a cobra, a symbol of pharaonic majesty). Caesarion was put to death by Octavian, and Egypt subsequently became Roman territory.

Cleopatra's life has formed the basis for many literary works, the most notable of which are the plays *Antony and Cleopatra* by Shakespeare, Dryden and Shaw. She has inspired artists and opera and ballet composers, and has appeared many times on screen. There her legendary beauty (which is actually highly debatable) has been immortalized by Theda Bara (1917), Claudette Colbert (1932), Vivien Leigh (1945) and, most famously, Elizabeth Taylor (1963). Coin portraits of Cleopatra are not very flattering. Her powers of seduction were probably due to her charisma, intelligence and personality rather than to physical beauty. LL-J

See Llewellyn-Jones, L. (2002) Celluloid Cleopatras, in D. Ogden, ed., *The Hellenistic World*; Walker, S. and Higgs, P., eds. (2001) *Cleopatra of Egypt*.

 Augustus: (a).

cleruchs, cleruchy (*klêrouchia*) A colony in which the settlers retained citizenship in the mother-city and continued to have military and financial obligations to that city. It was particularly associated with the expansion of the Athenian empire. Cleruchies were often established on land confiscated from allied cities, and became a means by which Athens could monitor the activities of its allies and help the poor of Athens. In 450 BC cleruchs (*klêrouchoi*, literally 'allotment holders') were settled on Naxos, Andros and in Karystos on Euboia, perhaps in response to trouble in the Cyclades. In 447 Perikles led 1,000 colonists to the Thracian Chersonesos, and in the same year cleruchies were established on Lemnos and Imbros. Disturbances in the Thracian region prompted the establishment of the colony of Brea around the same time. The decree calling for its foundation (*IG* i^3 46; ML 49) gave preference to thetes and *zeugitai*, and the measure should be seen as part of the Periklean policy to 'turn thetes into hoplites' (Antiphon fr. 61) by granting plots of land to the poor. After the revolt of Euboia had been crushed (446), the whole population of the city of Hestiaia was removed and 1,000 Athenians settled in its territory. Similar fates awaited Aigina (431) and Melos (416). In other cases only a portion of the land was confiscated. After the surrender of Mytilene (427), the island of Lesbos was divided up into 3,000 plots (*klêroi*), which were leased back by the Athenian cleruchs to the Mytilenaeans. The income supported the cleruchs as a garrison. CC

See Graham, A. J. (1964) *Colony and Mother City in Ancient Greece*.

client see banking; elections; friendship, Roman; houses, Roman; law, Roman; manumission; patronage; society, Roman.

client rulers Kings and, less frequently, queens of areas allied to Rome. Roman sources rarely use the word 'client' to describe the relationship, but employ the terminology of friendship and alliance. These rulers governed territory beyond the Roman empire's boundaries and formed alliances with Rome, which often provided assistance against a friendly ruler's enemies, external or internal. Client rulers appear from the 2nd century BC to the end of the empire, and were particularly prominent in Asia Minor in the early period.

Although client kingdoms provided a buffer zone against enemies, a more important goal was the stability of Rome's own frontier regions and the availability of allied military resources. Occasionally, an allied king without heirs bequeathed his kingdom to Rome, which also sometimes annexed a troublesome kingdom or one in a strategic location. Many client rulers obtained their thrones with Roman assistance or as a grant; rival claimants might seek audiences with influential Romans in the provinces or at Rome for this purpose. Thrones were offered on Roman terms, and disloyalty resulted in dethronement or even a trial at the capital. Many allied rulers became Roman CITIZENS and part of the governing ÉLITE. Their children often lived at Rome and were educated there, sometimes as hostages, sometimes as guests, especially of emperors. Frequently, gift-giving consolidated these friendships. The arrangement usually suited both parties, though the resources of the Roman empire gave it the upper hand. JV

See Braund, D. (1983) *Rome and the Friendly King*.

climate Situated on the MEDITERRANEAN sea, Greece and Italy are part of its climatic zone. While it has been suggested that the climate was significantly different in ancient times, this is not supported by pollen analysis. The majority of scholars agree that the climate then was much the same as now (despite recent global warming), though it would appear that it was somewhat wetter prior to the Neolithic period. If anything, the climate in the classical to Roman periods may have been slightly cooler and less arid than today.

The Mediterranean climate was made up of two main seasons, summer and winter (though the interstices of spring and autumn were recognized). Winter was typically a time of strong winds and heavy rainstorms coming in from the west. The storms were normally short-lived and intense, and there was no fog or general gloom as experienced in, for example, northwest Europe. Summer was a time of clear skies, dazzling sunshine and dry heat, though brief torrential downpours and even hailstorms occurred, which could be damaging to soils and crops. While excellent for ripening FRUIT such as grapes and FIGS, the heat and the scarcity of rainfall meant a risk of drought and vegetation loss.

A preoccupation with WATER SUPPLIES is reflected in the literary sources and various aspects of ancient culture and TECHNOLOGY. Odysseus, in describing his island home of Ithaca, emphasizes that rain and dew were not lacking (*Odyssey* 13.245–6). CORINTH, though among the driest places in Greece, is blessed with many springs. In winter it experiences very heavy storms, which deliver water into the porous rock below the clay and act to feed the numerous springs. Water scarcity was also addressed by irrigation. The Romans turned this into an art form with their monumental AQUEDUCTS, which also served urban populations. The Greeks made frequent use of underground cisterns to store water long-term, and a concern with the public WATER SUPPLY is reflected in the creation of monumental FOUNTAIN HOUSES.

Within the general climate, regional variations existed that were due to geography. Most of the PELOPONNESE, for example, has a typical southern Greek climate, but subregions such as eastern Arkadia are differentiated by altitude, and in some places there were no OLIVES or figs. In many parts of the Mediterranean, hot northerly winds are experienced during the summer, often contributing to soil erosion and drying out the crops. In GREECE these are known as the *meltémi*, while western ITALY is exposed to the *sirocco*. MACEDONIA, and the areas of Italy north of the Apennines, were more continental in climate, with colder winters and less harsh summers. Though not always gathering as much snow as some regions of Greece, in general Macedonia drops to a lower temperature in winter. This is obviously reflected in the AGRICULTURE of the region; it was better suited to raising CEREAL crops, HORSES, SHEEP and CATTLE than peninsular Greece, but the olive could not survive the region's frosts. THESSALY, also famous for horse-rearing, is in a transitional zone between the two climate types. Local micro-climates, particularly in densely contoured landscapes such as southern Greece and the ISLANDS of the AEGEAN, influenced farming strategies; fragmented landholding was one way to spread risk. Variation between years ('inter-annual variability') was also an important factor and could lead to local or regional famine.

STRABO was well aware of the particular Mediterranean climate, and also of the regional variations determined by geography. He viewed this as a favourable factor, as it allowed a diversity in agriculture that ensured the survival of the community in times of catastrophe. This diversity is also reflected in Virgil's *Georgics* (2.110ff.), where the poet discusses the varieties of soils that allow many different plants to be grown.

The Mediterranean climate affected not just agriculture but all aspects of daily life, from clothing to housing to religion. The violence of winter storms may be reflected in the thunderbolt-wielding GODS (Virgil, *Georgics* 1.328–9). TRADE and travel were affected – winter snow made the Apennines impassable, and in summer the Mediterranean was a busy pond with SHIPS from all around its edges taking advantage of the trade winds; it became deserted from October to April when winter storms raged. NJW

See Grove, A.T., and Rackham, O. (2001) *The Nature of Mediterranean Europe*, ch. 9.

climatic change Occasionally invoked as an explanation for major changes in ancient societies, the relevance of climatic change for the classical world is now widely doubted. There was undeniably a major incident about 5,000 years ago, the Aridization, leading to the drying out of the Sahara and affecting lands bordering the MEDITERRANEAN. The emergence of complex states in Egypt and the Near East at this time may in part have been a human response to the new conditions. There is no evidence to suggest further climatic change of high magnitude in historical times, though Vita-Finzi's much-debated model of pan-Mediterranean alluviation in late antiquity has highlighted that there are regional sequences of higher erosion and soil deposition in Mediterranean valleys. These do not seem to be synchronous events, and some may have been caused by factors other than climatic variation (such as abandonment of agricultural lands or over-grazing). Although there may have been minor oscillations in climate in the period 500 BC to AD 500, the general view is that the CLIMATE was broadly similar to that of the present day. DJM

See Grove, A.T., and Rackham, O. (2001) *The Nature of Mediterranean Europe*, chs. 7–9; Sallares, R. (1991) *The Ecology of the Ancient Greek World*; Vita-Finzi, C. (1969) *The Mediterranean Valleys*.

Clitumnus RIVER near Trebiae in Umbria, most famous for the white cattle raised on its banks, often used in SACRIFICES (e.g. Virgil, *Georgics* 2.146–8). The personified river was worshipped as a god in a shrine near its source, described by the younger PLINY (*Letter* 8.8). Pliny indicates that the shrine functioned as an ORACLE, in which *sortes*, inscribed lots or slips of wood, were used in divination; he also describes it as filled with the laudatory inscriptions of the god's worshippers. JBR

Cloaca Maxima see POLLUTION; ROME; TARQUINIUS SUPERBUS.

clocks see LAWCOURTS, GREEK; MEASUREMENT; SUNDIALS; TIME-KEEPING.

Clodia b. c.95 BC The second of three daughters of Appius Claudius Pulcher, scion of the patrician CLAUDII, CONSUL 79 BC and pillar of the SULLAN restoration. Her MARRIAGE to her cousin Quintus Metellus Celer fits that background, but like her youngest brother CLODIUS she affected the SABINE vowel in her name. She was one of the most notorious women of the late REPUBLIC. Her lovers included CATULLUS, in whose POEMS she appears as 'Lesbia'; Marcus Caelius Rufus, against whom she contrived charges that CICERO rebutted in the *Pro Caelio* (56); and even, Cicero hints, her brother. The accusation that she poisoned her husband (59) made her 'the Clytemnestra you can have for a copper'. Modern views, however, are revisionist. BML

See Edwards, C. (1993) *The Politics of Immorality in Ancient Rome.*

Clodii Some Republican Clodii were members of the SABINE CLAUDII who affected PLEBEIAN sympathy by adopting the Sabine spelling of the name. Under the empire there are distinguished but unconnected Italians and provincials. Publius Clodius Thrasea Paetus of Padua, suffect (replacement) CONSUL in AD 56, died in 66 after outspoken opposition to NERO. His accuser was the low-born Capuan Titus Clodius Eprius Marcellus, suffect consul in 62, who clashed with Thrasea's son-in-law in 70 and became suffect again in 74 after three years governing ASIA. He perished in a 'conspiracy' 'discovered' by TITUS towards the end of VESPASIAN's reign. Lucius Clodius Macer, commander of the Legion III Augusta in AFRICA, revolted against Nero in 68, issuing COINAGE and raising a Legion Macriana Liberatrix; Galba had him killed. Decimus Clodius Albinus of Hadrumetum, governor of BRITAIN when SEPTIMIUS SEVERUS seized power (193), became Septimius and CAESAR, invaded GAUL as AUGUSTUS in 195 on CARACALLA's elevation to the rank of Caesar, and was killed at LYON (197). Marcus Clodius Pupienus Maximus, emperor with Decimus Caelius Balbinus in 238, was assassinated by PRAETORIANS. BML

See Birley, A. R. (1981) *The Fasti of Roman Britain*; Griffin, M. T. (1984) *Nero*; Wiseman, T. P. (1971) *New Men in the Roman Senate 139 BC–14 AD.*

Clodius (Publius Clodius Pulcher) b. c.92 BC Youngest child of the CONSUL of 79, and most famous member of a maverick PATRICIAN family, the CLAUDII, he is unfortunately known mainly from CICERO. His career began conventionally on the staff of Lucullus in the war against Mithradates VI (c.73–67), though he was accused of encouraging mutiny; he engaged in DIPLOMACY in an area where he had family ties. A conventional prosecution of CATILINE (65) was collusive. In 62–1 Clodius, QUAESTOR designate, was tried by special court for violating the rites of the Bona Dea, and his alibi was broken by Cicero. For *optimates* (including Lucullus) Clodius was a scapegoat distracting the people from the end of Catiline and from hopes of reform. Friends secured his acquittal, and when he returned from his province (SICILY) in 60 he sought transfer to PLEBEIAN status, which he achieved through POMPEY and CAESAR (59). Elected TRIBUNE with a radical programme (58), he exiled Cicero for illegally executing the Catilinarians, began free grain distributions, restored *collegia*, and checked SENATORIAL obstruction of legislation and the CENSORS' *nota* (their mark of censure). Clodius followed this return to old-fashioned *popularis* politics in face of domination by big men with the intimidation of Pompey by VIOLENCE. This ended during Clodius' AEDILESHIP (56) after Pompey and Caesar met at Luca: Clodius' brother was to receive the consulship of 54. Canvassing for the PRAETORSHIP (52), Clodius was killed at Bovillae on 20 January by his rival Titus Annius Milo. His marriage to Fulvia, descendant of Gaius GRACCHUS' ally, fitted his politics; their daughter was AUGUSTUS' first wife. BML

See Gruen, E. S. (1975) *The Last Generation of the Roman Republic;* Rawson, E. (1991) *Roman Culture and Society.*

Clodius Albinus see CLODII; SEVERUS, SEPTIMIUS.

EMPERORS, ROMAN: (a).

clothing see DRESS.

clubs

In many Greek states, political activity was conducted through political groups, or political clubs as they are sometimes known: groups of men clustering around political leaders. These were often amorphous, bound together as much by personal ties of friendship and relationship as by policy, and had at their heart small gatherings of companions (*hetaireiai*) of the same age and status. The *hetaireia* formed the nucleus for the policy, direction and shape of the group, and was the basis of the networks of personal connections which held the group together.

The *hetaireiai* themselves originated in drinking clubs which met together to discuss matters of philosophical or common interest (in PLATO's *Symposium* the participants are each called upon to give their account of the nature of love). Although many of these sympotic clubs would have remained social gatherings, they could easily become politicized. HERODOTOS tells us how in 6th-century Athens the young aristocrat Kylon tried to seize the Acropolis with the help of his *hetaireia*. THUCYDIDES says that in Athens the *synômosiai* (similar to *hetaireiai*) were useful in the LAWCOURTS and for appointments, and describes how the *hetaireiai* were instrumental in the oligarchic coups of 411 and 404. Both XENOPHON and the Oxyrhynchos Historian attest to the activity of *hetaireiai* in THEBES in the first quarter of the 4th century, and Thucydides says they played an important role in the civil war in Kerkyra in the 420s.

Political groups had a reputation for being OLIGARCHIC because of their involvement in revolutions in Athens. It was perhaps natural that they should be so, given that *hetaireiai* were often made up of young aristocrats. Yet the political groups were not oligarchic by nature. PERIKLES, who led the move with Ephialtes for more radical DEMOCRACY at Athens in the 460s, came from an aristocratic family. Birth did not dictate political persuasion: NIKIAS, the statesman and GENERAL, was the leader of one of the more conservative groups in Athens, though his family had only recently come into great wealth through his father's interests in the SILVER MINES.

Indeed, the political groups were not parties in the modern sense with a rigid party line. Although groups may have been generally democratic or oligarchic, it is wrong to think of them as having a set membership or as strictly adhering to a consistent policy. They generally acted according to what the group thought was best for the state (and for themselves). In 424, when MEGARA was under pressure from both an invading Athenian army and Megarian oligarchic exiles who had set themselves up outside the city, political groups within the city were divided in their response. One group supported the exiles (who were also supported by the Spartan commander BRASIDAS); the other invited the Athenian generals to take the city. Neither group was interested so much in oligarchy or democracy as in what was best for the city and the group, which they probably saw as being the same thing.

In 5th-century Athens the political groups were usually large. Although the story has sometimes been doubted, PLUTARCH tells how, probably in 416 when ALCIBIADES and Nikias both faced the risk of being OSTRACIZED, they united their political groups and turned the vote away from themselves and onto Hyperbolos, a less influential politician.

At Athens, however, a number of changes in the structures of the political experience meant that by the beginning of the 4th century the shape of the political group had altered. There was a shift away from personal connections towards mass alliances in the body of the political group: now leaders tried to attract the popular vote through public rather than private benefactions, such as Perikles' building programme and the establishment of jury pay. This was taken a stage further by men like KLEON, known as demagogues, who attached the people to themselves through ORATORY. This does not mean that Perikles and Kleon did not belong to a *hetaireia* as has sometimes been suggested: Plutarch, while emphasizing their new political style, makes clear that they did. But their links with the political group at large, outside the *hetaireia*, were by that time less strong. In addition, the levelling effects of WAR meant that Athenian society became more homogeneous economically, while more men from non-traditional backgrounds aspired to become politically important. As a result of the fear and distrust engendered by the role of *hetaireiai* and political groups in the oligarchic revolutions, a law was passed, probably upon the restoration of the democracy in 403, banning *hetaireiai* which aimed to overthrow the democracy.

All of these changes did not mean the end of the *hetaireia* or the political group. But they did mean that political groups tended to become smaller, more numerous, and less stable, so that the political 'voice' became more fragmented. As a result, in the face of the Macedonian threat of the 350s and 340s, it was difficult to attain a united response to a crisis. Although all agreed to peace with PHILIP in 346 BC, this consensus lasted barely long enough for the oaths to be sworn before DEMOSTHENES and his group broke away and stirred up the people against it. LGM

See Calhoun, G. M. (1913) *Athenian Clubs in Politics and Litigation*; Connor, W. R. (1971) *The New Politicians of Fifth-century Athens*; Mitchell, L. G. (1997) *Greeks Bearing Gifts*.

The inhabitants of Roman cities routinely organized themselves into clubs and societies, usually known as *collegia*. These groups had a long history at Rome, some supposedly founded by the semi-mythical king NUMA. Many organizations were composed of people who shared the same trade or profession, while others consisted of members of similar backgrounds or interests, such as VETERANS' groups or sport clubs. Still others had worship as their central purpose or were mutual aid societies, such as BURIAL clubs.

Whatever their primary function, nearly all clubs included an element of religion, and the veneration of one or several tutelary GODS was an important component of ritual, with the deities frequently included in the name of the club. Other characteristics of *collegia* in general were regular meetings, which routinely included some form of feasting, and complex internal hierarchies with positions whose titles were often drawn from those of civic officials, such as *curatores* or *decuriones*. These clubs had elaborate charters specifying membership requirements, procedure at meetings, and members, as well as responsibilities and obligations. They ranged in size from less than a dozen individuals to many hundreds, and the more prosperous owned a clubhouse known as a *schola*.

Collegia fulfilled an important social role by providing a sense of comradeship to their members as well as lending them a certain degree of status both within society as a whole and among their peers. A lowly porter might be a titled official within his *collegium*. Knowledge of *collegia* comes primarily from the monuments they erected in great numbers, listing their members and frequently commemorating gifts to the society by wealthy patrons. Many inscriptions, even of humble *collegia*, identified patrons of very high status, often of SENATORIAL or EQUESTRIAN rank. They serve as testimony to the central role of PATRONAGE as one of the powerful vertical links which bound together different strata of Roman SOCIETY.

The activities of *collegia* transcended their primary purpose. The members express a collective political opinion, as attested by numerous graffiti at POMPEII in which a *collegium* announces its support for a candidate. They repeatedly fell under suspicion of being breeding grounds for rebellion or other anti-government agitation. Such fears intensified in the late REPUBLIC, and in 64 BC there was a general suppression of most *collegia*. In 58 BC, CLODIUS revived them to use as rallying points for his supporters. JULIUS CAESAR again curbed them; finally, in AD 7, a law, the *lex Iulia*, was passed stipulating that every club required official sanction from the EMPEROR or senate. Although restrictions eventually were loosened, emperors continued to fear that clubs could turn into flash-points for sedition, as evidenced by an exchange of letters between the emperor TRAJAN and one of his governors. Trajan rejects his request for the formation of a FIRE brigade at NICOMEDIA on the grounds that sooner or later any gathering of men will develop a political purpose (PLINY THE YOUNGER, *Letters* 10.33–4; similarly 10.92–3). In a similar vein, the meetings of CHRISTIANS were sometimes regarded as gatherings of non-sanctioned *collegia*.

Large Roman cities supported an astounding number of highly specialized occupations. These artisans, craftsmen, artists, merchants and labourers formed themselves into trade associations with their fellows of the same profession. These were not guilds in the medieval sense. The surviving evidence offers little proof that they sought to gain privileges or monopolies for their profession, nor do they appear to have played a role in training apprentices. Rather, they seem to have been primarily social clubs whose members gathered on a regular basis to dine together and to participate in cult activities. *Collegia* were egalitarian in that their ranks contained a mixture of FREEDMEN and freeborn. The *collegia* of OSTIA are particularly well attested in inscriptions; as befits a port city, many associations were concerned with the transportation of goods and shipping and SHIPBUILDING activities. Ostia also preserves the archaeological remains of several *scholae*. Trade *collegia* formed natural units for interaction with state officials and for participation in civic spectacles.

One of the more important types of *collegia* for urban inhabitants, many of whom probably lacked the social safety net of family, were burial clubs (*collegia tenuiorum*). Membership ensured a decent burial, and the wealthier clubs built structures called *columbaria* to hold their burial urns. Romans seem to have accepted social intermingling in death at least, since the membership of several burial clubs included the freeborn alongside SLAVES and ex-slaves. The elaborate rules for a burial club from the town of Lanuvium reveal that there was an entry fee of 100 sesterces along with an AMPHORA of good WINE, followed by modest monthly dues of five *asses* (*CIL* 14.2112). Burial clubs were social clubs as well, and Lanuvium charter spells out precisely how much food should be provided to members at feasts – down to the precise number of sardines – as well as listing fines for unruly behaviour at their gatherings. The distinction between burial clubs and other types is hazy, since trade associations often looked after the funerals of their members and *collegia* usually conducted formal cult activities. The major Roman colleges of priests responsible for state worship, including the *pontifices* and the *augures*, were also formally known as *collegia*. GSA

See Dill, S. (1956) *Roman Society from Nero to Marcus Aurelius*; La Piana, G. (1927) Foreign groups in Rome during the first centuries of the empire, *HTR* 20: 225–81; MacMullen, R. (1974) *Roman Social Relations 50 BC to AD 284*; Meiggs, R. (1973) *Roman Ostia*.

Clytemnestra (Klytaimnestra) Wife of AGAMEMNON and eldest daughter of Tyndareos and Leda. She is the mother of up to four daughters and a son, Orestes. Her portrait is painted in tragic DRAMA by EURIPIDES (*Iphigeneia at Aulis*). The play relates how she is deceived by Agamemnon into bringing their daughter IPHIGENEIA to the Achaian camp at Aulis, on the pretext that the girl is to be given to ACHILLES as a bride. Instead Iphigeneia is sacrificed at the altar of ARTEMIS to appease the goddess's anger towards Agamemnon, and in this way to obtain a favourable wind for the departure of the Achaian fleet to Troy.

Clytemnestra serves as a foil to the virtuous Penelope in Homer's *Odyssey*, but plays a far more dominant role in Aeschylus' *Agamemnon*. During Agamemnon's absence at Troy she establishes an adulterous relationship with his cousin Aigisthos, and plots with his support to murder her husband and his war-prize, the Trojan prophetess Kassandra, in order to avenge her daughter. Her son, with the help of his sister Elektra, takes revenge for their father's death by killing the now tyrannical Clytemnestra and Aigisthos. Aeschylus (*Libation-bearers*), Sophokles (*Elektra*) and Euripides (*Elektra*) have all left us versions of this story. Clytemnestra is killed by Orestes, who thus in turn avenges his father's death. (see also *ORESTEIA*) EP

See Morizot, Y. (1992) Klytaimnestra, in *LIMC* vol. 6, 72–81.

Cocidius Northern British male deity from the region of HADRIAN'S WALL, who was variously equated with the Roman gods MARS and SILVANUS in imperial times. Dedications to Cocidius place his centre of worship in the Irthing valley, the probable location of the *fanum Cocidi* cited in the *RAVENNA COSMOGRAPHY*. From Bewcastle, in particular, two silver repoussée plaques bearing inscriptions 'to the god Cocidius' suggest the existence of a shrine in the vicinity. That Cocidius was embraced by the Roman forces stationed at Hadrian's wall is noted in 16 inscriptions, a few of which bestow on the native god the epithet 'god of soldiers'.

Cocidius' equation with the Roman god of WAR, as well as his martial appearance on the plaques from Bewcastle, suggest that Cocidius was primarily worshipped by the population of the western portion of Hadrian's wall in his protective role as warrior. Interestingly, this martial aspect is absent in the east, where dedications to Cocidius name Silvanus, the Roman god of the woodland, as his epigraphic counterpart. An altar to Cocidius and Silvanus at Risingham, for example, depicts the god in the peaceful role of a hunter flanked by his hound and a stag. MLM

See Ross, A. (1967) *Pagan Celtic Britain*.

cognomen see NAMES AND NAMING, ROMAN.

coinage A coin is a piece of money, made of metal, which conforms to a standard and bears a design. The earliest coinage was made of ELECTRUM, and was

COINAGE: (a) relative values of the Attic standard.

	Drachmai	Silver (g)
talent	6000	unit of account
mina	100	unit of account
tetradrachm	4	17.2
drachm	1	4.3
obol	$\frac{1}{6}$	0.72

COINAGE: (b) Roman imperial denominations under Augustus.

Denomination	Value		Metal	approximate weight (g)
	asses	sestertii		
aureus	400	100	gold	7.9
denarius	16	4	silver	3.9
sestertius	4	1	brass	26
dupondius	2	$\frac{1}{2}$	brass	13
as	1	$\frac{1}{4}$	copper	12
quadrans	$\frac{1}{4}$	$\frac{1}{16}$	copper	3

struck in Lydia and Ionia around 600 BC. The CHINESE independently introduced a coinage a century or so later, but all other coinages are ultimately derived from the Greco-Roman tradition. Coins were mass-produced, the vast majority being struck between engraved dies, and survive in very substantial quantities. They carry an immense range of images and inscriptions, with a more even geographical and chronological coverage of the ancient world than can be claimed for literary sources, inscriptions and PAPYRI.

Around the middle of the 6th century BC electrum was displaced as the principal metal for coinage by SILVER, and coin production spread rapidly over the Greek world. Except in hellenized areas, non-Greek peoples were slow to adopt coinages. The conquests of ALEXANDER were the main stimulus for the spread of coinage to the east, and although Iron Age coinages antedate the expansion of Rome in many areas, the ROMAN EMPIRE performed a similar role in extending coin use to the north and west.

Silver was struck in a variety of denominations, on standards that varied between regions. For example, Athens in the 5th century BC was supplied with coins ranging from a tetradrachm down to half an obol, and smaller coins were produced intermittently. (*see* Table: COINAGE (a)) Although we now know that silver fractional coinage was more common than we thought a few decades ago, the introduction of a token base metal currency for small denominations was clearly important for the use of coinage in low-value transactions. Base metal coinage, most usually of bronze, was first struck before 425 BC in some mints in Italy and SICILY, and during the 4th century its production spread widely. At the top end of the denominational scale, GOLD coinage was much less ubiquitous in the Greek world than one might have supposed. There were some substantial series, much the most important of which was the gold in the names of PHILIP II and Alexander the Great. Rome issued gold in quantity only from 46 BC onwards, but it rapidly became important and played a major role in the economy of the later Roman empire.

Roman coinage began under Greek influence not long before 300 BC. It was on a large scale from the time of the second PUNIC WAR, during which the denominational system based on the silver *denarius* was introduced. This system lasted with some modifications for nearly 500 years. (*see* Table: COINAGE (b)) As Rome expanded, it took over a wide variety of local coinage systems. Such Roman provincial coinages, as they are now called, continued alongside the imperial issues until the second half of the 3rd century AD. After that, a standardized imperial coinage was struck for the whole of the empire at mints distributed throughout the PROVINCES. The Roman model of coinage was thus the only one available after the fall of the Roman empire to be copied by the 'barbarian' kingdoms in the West, and it was continued in the East under the Byzantine empire.

Ancient coins can be of considerable art historical interest. In this connection many would think first of the splendid silver of SICILY in the 5th and 4th centuries BC, and of the portraits of hellenistic kings and of Romans from JULIUS CAESAR onwards. The iconography of coinage has much to offer the study of RELIGION and MYTHOLOGY, ARCHITECTURE, and cultural and narrative history, as well as many other areas. Particularly notable is the high incidence of political and imperial themes on Roman coinage from the late Republic onwards. But the contribution of coinage to our knowledge of the ancient world is not confined to the images and inscriptions they bear. Coins were economic objects. Since a major reason for coin production in the ancient world was to facilitate state expenditure, patterns of output may offer insights into state finance. Debasements or weight reductions may be revealing about fiscal crises, and may in some cases be linked with episodes of inflation. Patterns of circulation may be defined and explanations sought (of which TRADE is only one), and used to inform or test our understanding of how the ancient ECONOMY worked. CH

See Burnett, A. (1987) *Coinage in the Roman World*; Crawford, M. H. (1985) *Coinage and Money under the Roman Republic*; Howgego, C. (1995) *Ancient History from Coins*; Kraay, C. M. (1976) *Archaic and Classical Greek Coins*; Meadows, A. and Shipton, K., eds. (2001) *Money and its Uses in the Ancient Greek World*; Mørkholm, O. (1991) *Early Hellenistic Coinage*.

 EMPERORS, ROMAN: (a)–(b).

Colchester see CAMULODUNUM.

collectors and collecting The reasons why public and private collectors wish to possess pieces of the classical past have always been many and complex. Nevertheless, it is clear enough that the genuine interest in the classical world which was the prevailing stimulus from the RENAISSANCE until the end of the Enlightenment has largely been replaced in modern times by the need (perceived far beyond classical lands) to demonstrate some kind of prestige.

This change has taken place at the same time as the development of legislation designed to protect the cultural heritage of modern Greece, Italy and Turkey. Interest everywhere in the past is now reflected in the scholarly conviction that no artefact can be properly informative in social, economic and historical terms if its ancient context has not been reliably recorded and published. The commercial value of 'new' classical art objects outside their countries of origin has accordingly soared to the point where collections can be assembled primarily for investment purposes. Not surprisingly, it is only rarely that the erudition routinely paraded in the resulting exhibition and auction catalogues can shed light on the ancient societies which produced and distributed the artefacts themselves. The ethos of modern collecting thus has little in common with the authentic passion for ancient sculpture that inspired the paintings of Mantegna, and still less with the lively intellectual debate occasioned by the subsequent recognition that the ancient cemeteries of Campania were full of classical art.

From the early 18th century onwards, in fact, classical antiquities were nowhere more eagerly and learnedly discussed than in Naples, by local savants and by foreign connoisseurs (among them Winckelmann) and other cultured visitors from north of the ALPS. Many of the latter acquired pieces for their collections while on the Grand Tour, which is why some anonymous Attic vase-painters have since been named after European cities (e.g. Berlin, Edinburgh). Foremost among the foreign collectors of the later 18th century was Sir William Hamilton, British envoy extraordinary to the court at Naples from 1764 until 1800. The publication of his first vase collection exercised a powerful influence not only on subsequent Hyperborean collectors but also on the early industrial production of master craftsmen such as the British potter Josiah Wedgwood of Etruria in Staffordshire. This is what Hamilton intended: 'Our aim has certainly been to shew a considerable collection of exquisite Models, but we likewise have proposed to ourselves to hasten the progress of the Arts, by discussing their true and first principles.' Hamilton sold his first collection in 1772 to the British Museum, where it constitutes the nucleus of the present Greek and Roman department.

The initial study of the material record of the classical world undoubtedly owes much to the culture of collecting that reached its peak during the European Enlightenment. It is equally true that the study of classical civilization no longer has any use for unprovenanced antiquities, the continuing and necessarily discreet supply of which to collectors is increasingly seen as nothing more than a disreputable and irrelevant side-show. DR

See Haskell, F. and Penny, N. (1981) *Taste and the Antique*; Jenkins, I. and Sloan, K. (1996) *Vases and Volcanoes*.

***coloni* and colonate** The Latin term for 'farmers', *coloni* is used to refer to farm tenants in the ROMAN EMPIRE. Leasing to farm tenants was a characteristic method by which Roman landowners could exploit their estates. *Coloni* occupied their land under a variety of regimes, including leasing for fixed cash rents in Italy, sharecropping in AFRICA, and leasing for fixed amounts of crops in Egypt. Likewise *coloni* represented a range of economic statuses, from wealthy middlemen to small farmers economically dependent on their landlords. The importance of *coloni* to the economic interests of Roman landowners led in the later Roman empire to the colonate, that is, the institutionalized binding of *coloni* to the land that they cultivated. In its effort to systematize the collection of taxes, the imperial government often imposed this task on landowners, who were responsible for paying the taxes on behalf of *coloni* registered on their estates. *Coloni* thus became tied to their land as a result of imperial fiscal policy, and the status of *colonus* refers primarily to a farmer's tax liability, not to his or her economic situation. But the restriction of movement imposed on *coloni* certainly had long-term effects on the conditions under which they cultivated their land. With less freedom of movement than their counterparts in the early empire, late imperial *coloni* tended to become more economically and socially dependent on larger landowners. (see also LABOUR) DPK

See Jones, A. H. M. (1964) *The Later Roman Empire 284–602*; (1974) The Roman colonate, in M. I. Finley, ed., *Studies in Ancient Society* 288–303; Whittaker, C. R. and Garnsey, P. (1997) Rural life in the later Roman empire, in *CAH* 13, 277–311.

colonialism Most simply, colonialism can be defined as foreign domination over local communities. The term implies unequal relations, whether social, political or economic, for an extended period, between an intrusive foreign group and the population already living in a particular locale. Colonialism involves the establishment and maintenance of settlements in a territory at some distance from the colonists' place of origin, with the result that the indigenous residents become subordinate to the settlers in one capacity or another. The term intimates a binary imbalance of colonizers over colonized, with no regard for hybrid development. It was used originally in association with the colonial experiences of European capitalist economies. ARCHAEOLOGY and ethnography were utilized to document the inability of native cultures to change, serving to highlight European cultural advancement and superiority and to justify European domination of indigenous territories. Post-1945 decolonization, and the post-modernist movement in the second half of the 20th century, inspired reassessment of the term, resulting in acknowledgement of its biases, limitations and ensuing interpretations. In turn, these have given rise to the notion of POST-COLONIALISM, which contests colonial domination and seeks to redress interpretative imbalances by analysis of plural media of representation, reflective of the varieties and complexities of culture contact. TH

See Lyons, C. L. and Papadopoulos, J. K., eds. (2002) *The Archaeology of Colonialism*; Trigger, B. (1989) *A History of Archaeological Thought*.

colonization The process of establishing and maintaining settlements in foreign territory. Reasons often cited for colonization include TRADE, overpopulation, natural disaster and political or socio-economic advancement. Most colonies had a good natural HARBOUR and/or good communication routes, were easy to defend, and possessed natural water and fertile land resources. Different terms distinguish between types of colonies. The Greek term *apoikia* (an 'away-home') is often used to describe a

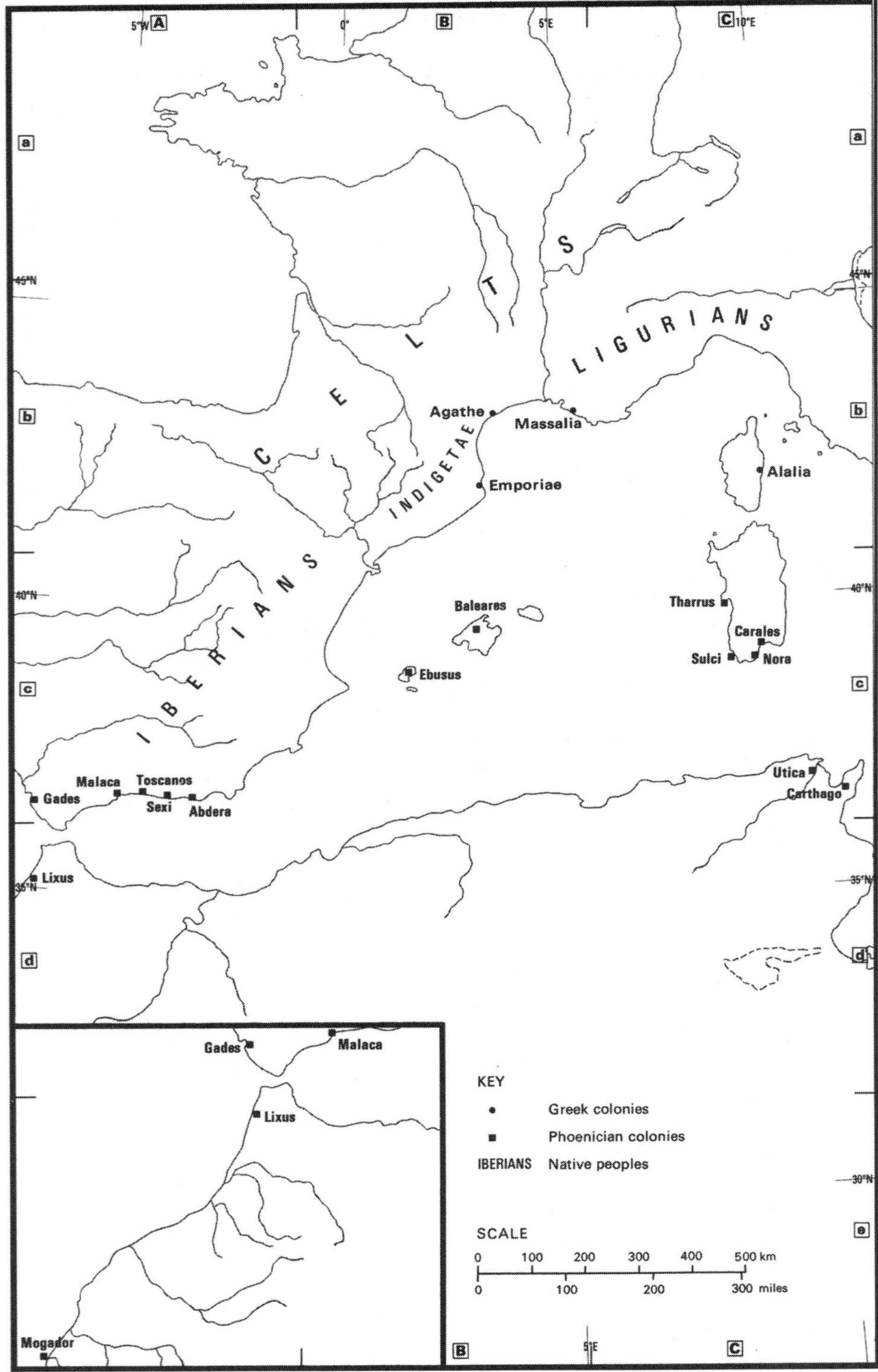

COLONIZATION: (a) Greek and Phoenician colonies in the western Mediterranean.

COLONIZATION: (b) Greek mother cities and Greek and Phoenician colonies in the central Mediterranean.

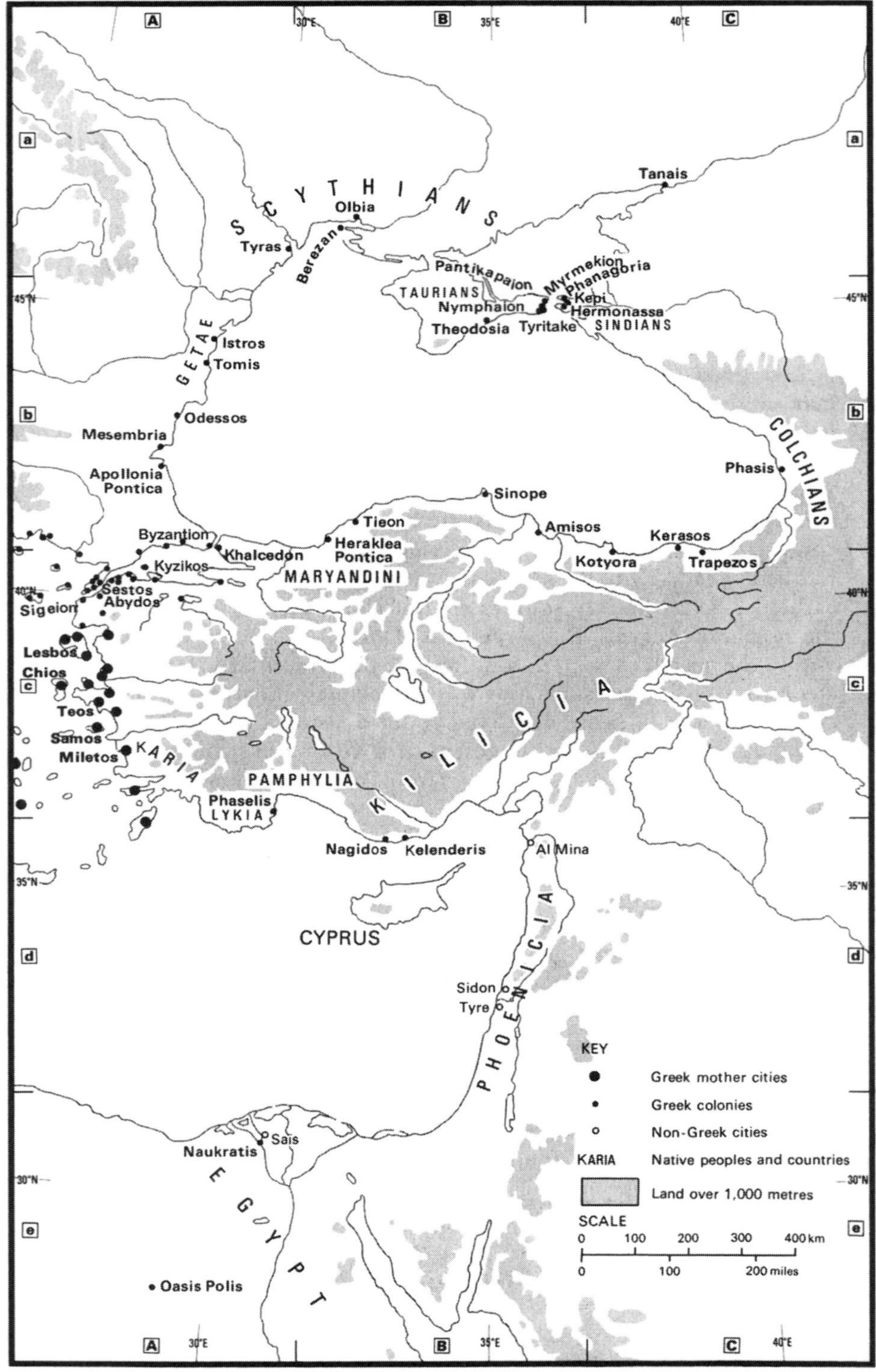

COLONIZATION: (c) Phoenician and East Greek mother cities and Greek colonies in the Black sea area.

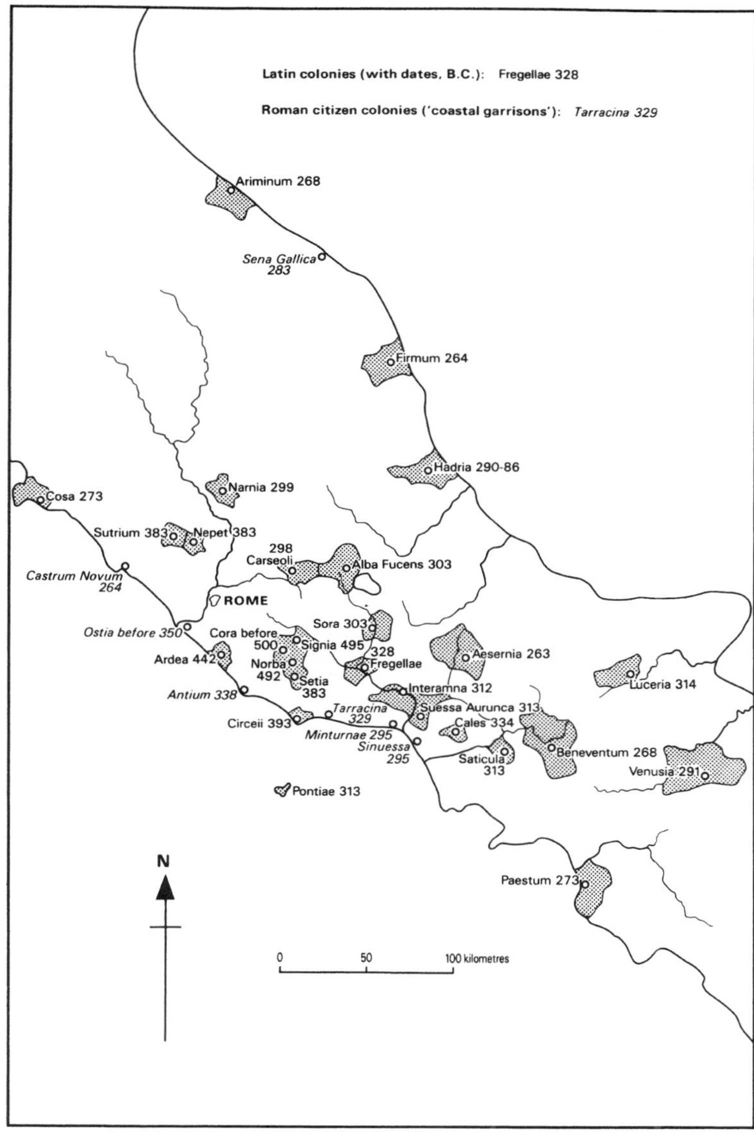

COLONIZATION: (d) Roman and Latin colonies in central Italy to the mid-3rd century BC.

settlement with a hinterland, presumably for self-sufficiency purposes, as opposed to an *emporion* ('trade-place'), which had no interest in territory beyond the city limits. Other terms, such as CLERUCHY or *colonia*, relate to degrees of political independence and CITIZENSHIP. Yet there is evidence that some terms were used interchangeably, at least by ancient Greek authors. This has led to debate among modern scholars about the intended nature of many of these foreign settlements.

The MINOANS of the middle and late Bronze Age seem to have exercised some sort of maritime trade route control through a number of AEGEAN island and ANATOLIAN coastal settlements. After the Thera eruption, Minoan power waned. The MYCENAEANS exploited this, replacing the Minoans and expanding horizons to Italy, SICILY and SARDINIA until their twilight in the 12th century BC.

The Greek colonial movement of the Iron Age began in the 8th century, when EUBOIANS established Pithekoussai off the coast of Italy c.770. Mainland settlement began during the second half of the 8th century, when Greeks from Euboia, CORINTH and MEGARA established settlements along the coast of south-central Italy and eastern Sicily. It is more likely that PHOENICIANS shared knowledge of suitable sites, rather than that Greeks recalled previous Mycenaean links. Towards the end of the 8th century, Achaians settled around the instep of Italy and to the south of CUMAE to secure the land routes between the Ionian and Tyrrhenian seas, bypassing the Euboian-controlled straits of Messina. Many of the original settlements quickly established subcolonies to enhance territorial control.

By the end of the 8th century, Greeks, particularly Corinthians, had begun to settle along the ADRIATIC islands and mainland side of Italy. Euboians moved into the north Aegean region, while East Greek colonists established themselves along the THRACIAN coast. Milesians founded a series of settlements on the shores of the BLACK SEA. By the end of the 7th century, the foreign settlement movement had expanded to North Africa, France and Spain. The Theraians had begun a movement to CYRENAICA, while colonists from Phokaia had settled at the mouth of the RHÔNE and further along the coast in Spain. By this time, a number of Greek *poleis* had joined together at the Egyptian trading port of NAUKRATIS.

Many of these expeditions were led by an oikist, who assumed leadership responsibility for the expedition, the foundation of the settlement and the distribution of land. Sometimes he was commemorated through BURIAL within the city walls, where a cult developed. It was not uncommon for the oikist to consult the DELPHIC ORACLE before departure. Foundation narratives come from later authors, however, who may have mythologized colonial foundations as justification for foreign occupation and manipulated metaphors with regard to current events.

These settlements often came into conflict with the indigenous populations, and native responses to colonization are as varied as the number of Greek city-states establishing them. There were hostile and co-operative interactions, and native and Greek cultures adopted selective aspects of their new neighbours' social and material cultures.

Colonization during the 5th century was led by Athens, and took a more direct political form. One of Athens' more blatant means of controlling its allies was through the establishment of cleruchies, such as on NAXOS and Andros, and in Thrace. These settlements were made up of lower-class Athenians who were sent out to take over land confiscated from suspect or subdued allies, in order to make the locals fearful of rebelling. The cleruchs retained their Athenian citizenship and lived alongside the citizens of the subject ally. The term may also be applied to those who took over the land of a tributary ally, as at Skyros. Athens also established settlements with a military purpose to protect Athenian interests, such as at Brea in Thrace; residents of these *poleis* gave up their Athenian citizenship.

Rome's establishment of settlements can be traced back to the earliest days of the REPUBLIC, and possibly even to the monarchy in the cases of Fidenae, Cora and Signia, when Rome worked in alliance with neighbouring LATIN communities for the general defence of Latium. Settlers in these so-called Latin colonies (*coloniae Latinae*), such as Velitrae, Ardea and SATRICUM, were not granted Roman citizenship but citizenship of the new civic community. Through this method, by 380 BC Latin-speakers had secured territorial control of the Tyrrhenian side of central Italy. After the Latin war (340–338), other towns were incorporated into the Republic, usually as *municipia*, whose members were granted full or partial Roman citizenship. Rome continued to establish settlements that pushed the boundaries of its territory as it expanded its regional control during the 4th and 3rd centuries BC.

To protect its territory initially from external attack, and with the specific intent of territorial expansion and control after the second PUNIC WAR and during the empire, Rome established citizen colonies (*coloniae civium Romanorum*). Members of such settlements did retain Roman citizenship alongside citizenship of the colony, and consequently these sites acted as extensions of Rome. From their foundation, these communities were of a self-administering civic nature. Often three commissioners were appointed by the SENATE or emperor to supervise all aspects of the foundation, from SURVEYING and parcelling of land to construction of the urban centre. OSTIA and Antium are the first examples of this type of settlement, and begin a pattern of foundation in pairs. During the Gracchan period, colonization took on a political–economic function. Sulla and AUGUSTUS began intensive overseas settlement, and under the empire colonies were founded ostensibly to provide discharged LEGIONARIES with land and a means of civilian life. TH

See Boardman, J. (1999) *The Greeks Overseas*; Salmon, E.T. (1969) *Roman Colonization under the Republic*.

colour There is no direct correlation between modern and ancient terms for colour, because colours in antiquity were categorized according to the amount of light emitted rather than their hue. As such, Greeks and Romans use the same words for colours we find very different, such as blue and yellow. Similarly, the Greek term *ȍchron* (from which we derive 'ochre') comprises a variety of colours including red, yellow and green, because these have a similar lightness. The Latin *purpura* and Greek *porphyrios* are equally indistinct, in that they are used for both purple and red. It is because of this conception of colour that HOMER only refers to a few different colours and classical Greeks did not use terms for a wide spectrum of colours.

Partly because of ancient conceptions of colour, some colours had very symbolic meanings. Civilizations from all over the MEDITERRANEAN associated purple with power. The PHOENICIANS, in particular, were famed for their fabrication of purple dye from murex SHELLS. They were so famous for this that their name was inextricably linked with it. In Rome, purple distinguished high officials from the rest of the population. SENATORS wore the *latus clavus*, a toga with a broad purple stripe, while GENERALS celebrating TRIUMPHS wore special purple and gold robes. Developing this symbolic use of the colour purple further, EMPERORS wore purple garments and gradually claimed the exclusive right to wear the colour. Theoretically anyone caught wearing purple could be prosecuted, which necessitated the passing of laws which defined true, imperial purple. Emperors also wore *calcei mulli*, purple shoes. To an extent, purple was prestigious because it was so difficult and expensive to produce. Other dyes, however, appear to have been equally difficult to make, though they were not so highly valued. This suggests that purple was prized for its qualities, in particular its lustre and ability to reflect light.

Gold was similarly linked with power and opulence. In his *Persians*, AESCHYLUS frequently associates PERSIANS with gold because of their famed wealth. Although it was clearly prized for economic reasons, gold was associated with power for symbolic reasons as well. Like purple, gold was associated with lightness, and this explains its prestige. Red, often conflated with purple, was again associated with light. Since light was sometimes equated with life, it is not surprising that red is associated with important stages in life. Just as MARRIAGE and DEATH are often linked in literary works, so red was the colour of both weddings and funerals. Lastly, some vivid colours were associated with exotic countries. Aeschylus describes king DARIUS' shoes as being of the colour of saffron. Centuries later, the Galli, exotic PRIESTS of CYBELE, wore orange robes that marked them as foreign. In these instances, colours helped not only to define people as foreign but as decadent. EACM

Columella Very little is known about Columella apart from incidental information gleaned from his work. He was a native of GADES and a contemporary of SENECA THE YOUNGER, who lived in the early 1st century AD. He was a military tribune and probably served in CILICIA and SYRIA, but spent most of his life in Rome, though he retired and probably died in Tarentum. Two of his works survive, both of which probably date to the mid-1st century AD. The larger, *De re rustica* (*On the Countryside*), is concerned with all aspects of AGRICULTURE, while *De arboribus* (*On Trees*) is focused on the cultivation and maintenance of trees and vines.

In his own preface to the *De re rustica*, Columella lays out the need and purpose of his work. In common with his contemporaries, he bemoans the unproductiveness of Italian land. Unlike them, he attributes poor returns to ignorance rather than overuse of the soil. In his view, ignorance about agriculture stems from the fact that there are no agricultural teachers and pupils, and from the general disdain of farmers. He complains that, while there is no more honest and genteel way to generate income than farming, people would rather leave their estates in charge of SLAVES than take an active interest themselves.

De re rustica was written serially and dedicated to Publius Silvinus. It is a handbook on agriculture which gives technical expertise to those who own large estates. Columella covers a wide variety of topics, including fundamental aspects such as where to put farms, which buildings are necessary and how to erect them. He also discusses staffing, namely the jobs to be allotted to slaves. In addition, he covers both how to till the land and animal husbandry. In the final two books he writes about the duties of a farm bailiff (*vilicus*) and his wife (*vilica*). Book 10 is interesting because it consciously takes up VIRGIL's suggestion to write about GARDENING in verse.

The work gives very detailed and practical advice about many things, such as how to make a chicken coop and what name to give a dog. Columella advises that when one builds on a slope one must start at the lower end. Finally, he gives practical advice about preserving and making WINES; among other things, he says storage jars should be equally wide from top to bottom.

Mixed in with this practical advice are moral messages. Like other Roman writers, he advocates a return to past ideals. He rants against his contemporaries for being too steeped in luxury and afraid of honest toil. He accuses the young of being flabby and licentious, while women of his day are said to ruin their husbands by spending all their money on clothes. He compares them unfavourably with women of previous times who ran their farms. Patriotically, Columella also rails against the importation of foreign grain. EACM

See Lucius Junius Moderatus Columella, *On Agriculture*, 3 vols. (*De re rustica* and *De arboribus*), trs. H. B. Ash et al. (1941).

columns see ORDERS, ARCHITECTURAL.

columns, monumental Drawing on hellenistic practice, columns bearing statues were raised to honour prominent Romans, usually victors in war. Those with naval connections bore ships' prows (*columnae rostratae*, Gaius Duilius, AEMILIUS PAULLUS and AUGUSTUS in Rome). Columns erected for EMPERORS are still standing at CONSTANTINOPLE (Istanbul) and Ankara. The column of ANTONINUS PIUS in Rome had a white MARBLE base, bearing an inscription, and funeral reliefs. A 50-foot monolithic shaft of red Egyptian granite supported a capital and statue, as depicted on commemorative coins. The latest in this series was erected in the FORUM Romanum to Phocas in AD 608, and had a 50-foot shaft of reused drums. TRAJAN'S COLUMN set a related precedent with its 100-foot shaft of drums (*columna centenaria*), internal staircase, viewing balcony and helical relief frieze running up the outside. This was closely emulated by the surviving column of MARCUS AURELIUS in Rome, and by the demolished columns of THEODOSIUS I and Arcadius in Constantinople. Modern versions, with or without helical friezes, have been erected in London, Newcastle upon Tyne, Paris and Vienna. JCNC

See Jordan-Ruwe, M. (1995) *Das Säulenmonument*; Vogel, L. (1973) *The Column of Antoninus Pius*.

DACIAN WARS; MARCOMANNIC WARS.

comedy 1: Old Comedy The term for comedies produced at Athens during the 5th century BC. For 4th-century plays, 'Middle Comedy' and NEW COMEDY are used. These terms are misleading, in that they suggest clearer divisions between historical periods and comic genres than can actually be established.

COLUMNS, MONUMENTAL: Trajan's column as depicted on a contemporary coin.

There is little evidence for how Greek comedy began. ARISTOTLE saw two possible influences – 'PHALLIC' SONGS and SICILIAN drama. In ARISTOPHANES' *Acharnians* a phallus was carried onto the stage and addressed in song. Songs accompanied the (sometimes masked) carrying of the phallus at FESTIVALS of DIONYSOS at Athens, as did mocking words. The ACTORS in Old Comedy wore grotesque masks, padded stomachs and buttocks, and exaggerated *phalloi*; choral costumes could be more fantastic and variable. Costumes like all these are sometimes to be seen on Greek vases, with which may be compared the many terracotta figurines of Old Comedy actors that have been found.

Forty or more titles of lost works by Epicharmos (active in the 470s BC) are known, about half suggesting subjects from MYTH. The royal circle of Hieron I at SYRACUSE in Sicily included, besides Epicharmos, such visitors as PINDAR and AESCHYLUS. It cannot be deduced, however, from plurals like *Persians* and *Sirens* that these plays contained CHORUSES like those in Aristophanes and other Old Comedy. Nothing survives of the MUSIC and the DANCING which were such an important part of those performances. Early choruses are perhaps depicted on vases: on one Attic black-figure AMPHORA of the mid-6th century BC, some men are disguised as HORSES with others riding on their backs. Aristophanes' *Knights* had not yet been written.

Other influences on the development of Old Comedy have been put forward, although much is yet more speculation. The word 'comedy' itself could derive from *kômos*, a village 'revel' involving singing, dancing and joking. During the 5th century, Attic DRAMA became pre-eminent: in 486 a competition for comedies was introduced at Athens.

The earliest Old Comedy play in existence is the *Acharnians* of Aristophanes (425 BC). Eleven of his plays survive complete, the rest of the genre only as titles, citations or fragments. Of the Old Comedy poets who competed, antiquity judged Aristophanes to be the best. There were, however, other famous names such as Chionides, Kratinos, Magnes, Krates, Pherekrates, Eupolis and Ameipsias. Some wrote plays that were judged better at the time than Aristophanes, whose *Wasps*, *Peace* and *Birds* all came second (*Peace* to Eupolis' *Kolakes* in 421). Eupolis was a serious rival, as was Kratinos, who won first prize at the City Dionysia six times, beating *Clouds* with *Pytine* in 423 (as did Ameipsias with *Konnos*). In *Pytine*, Kratinos joked about his own drunkenness, coming on stage to argue with his wife and his mistress Alcohol. The year before, in *Knights*, Aristophanes had spoken affectionately of Krates and dismissed Kratinos as a has-been whose songs were once all the rage at parties. Nearly 30 titles by Kratinos are known (to Eupolis' 19), over 500 citations (as for Eupolis), and PAPYRUS fragments survive of one play, *Ploutoi*. Kratinos' *Dionysalexandros* demonstrates that Aristophanes' *Frogs* was not alone in portraying Dionysos as foolish, cowardly, ingenious and dishonest (Eupolis did, too, in *Taxiarchoi*). Eupolis was still being read in Egypt in the 4th century AD, Kratinos in the 2nd or 3rd.

The parasites of Eupolis' *Kolakes* (another was to be found in Epicharmos' *Hope or Wealth*) turn up again in the Middle and New Comedy which developed after Old Comedy. Characteristic of Old Comedy, though, were attacks on real individuals. In Kratinos' *Cheirones*, PERIKLES' head is compared to a dome. Aristophanes mocked KLEON, EURIPIDES and SOCRATES, among others. Eupolis ridiculed Kallias and Hyperbolos. Any legislation to restrict personal attacks (there was such a decree in 440/39) cannot have been very effective.

Epicharmos also afforded examples of literary allusion of the kind found in Aristophanes, both to HOMER and to TRAGEDY. Kratinos' *Cheirones* provided a kind of theogony (recalling HESIOD) in lyric, which satirized mythical genealogies, as well as abusing Perikles and his *hetaira* ASPASIA (the *hetaira* was another favourite of Middle and New Comedy).

A papyrus summary of Kratinos' *Dionysalexandros* shows what some lost plays by Aristophanes may have been like, to judge from their titles. A story from mythology receives comic treatment, but still admits contemporary allusions (Kratinos' story of the TROJAN WAR was a veiled attack on Perikles). Some Old Comedy may have centred more around scenes from everyday life, such as Pherekrates' *Korianno* (another *hetaira*?). Like Pherekrates, Krates may have been gentler than Aristophanes, Kratinos and Eupolis, though Kratinos' *Odysses* and Aristophanes' *Aiolosikon* are mentioned together in one source as if they were both lacking in abuse. Aristophanes' *Kokalos* is even referred to as introducing RAPE, recognition and other elements familiar from MENANDER. These kinds of Old Comedy may have paved the way for Middle and New.

The Old Comedy of Aristophanes has an enduring appeal, despite its age and topical references. It is lively and liberating, frequently hilarious, imaginative and fun to perform, naughty but thought-provoking – a colourful and amazing spectacle. AMH

See Csapo, E. and Slater, W. J. (1994) *The Context of Ancient Drama*; Green, J. R. (1994) *Theatre in Ancient Greek Society*; Green, R. and Handley, E. (1995) *Images of the Greek Theatre*; Handley, E.W. (1989) Comedy, in P.E. Easterling and B.M.W. Knox, eds., *The Cambridge History of Classical Literature* vol. 1, 355–425; Pickard-Cambridge, A. (1988) *The Dramatic Festivals of Athens*; Sandbach, F. H. (1985) *The Comic Theatre of Greece and Rome*; Simon, E. (1982) *The Ancient Theatre*; Winkler, J. J. and Zeitlin, F. I., eds. (1990) *Nothing to do with Dionysos*.

 DRAMA: (a); MASKS.

comedy 2: Middle and New Comedy New Comedy is the term used for plays from the last quarter of the 4th century BC by MENANDER (c.342–292) and his contemporaries Philemon of SYRACUSE (368/60–267/6), Diphilos of Sinope (b. c.360–350), Philippides, Poseidippos, Apollodoros and others. Philemon and Menander had statues erected in their honour, as did Poseidippos – it survives – but Menander, was soon the most admired, though not until after his death.

PAPYRUS discoveries during the 20th century and subsequently have increased our knowledge of the genre, which previously depended largely on studying Roman comedies: adaptations rather than translations, and produced for Roman audiences. To embrace these too with the term 'New Comedy' is therefore misleading. Common features between the Greek and the Roman comedies can be identified, but

COMEDY 2: NEW COMEDY: scene from a Greek comedy depicted on a relief sculpture found at Pompeii.

so far the papyri have mostly produced Menander rather than other authors, and only one parallel passage (indicating significant changes), from Menander's *Dis exapaton* (*The Twice Deceiver*), the model for PLAUTUS' *Bacchides*.

In ARISTOPHANES' *Women at the Assembly* (*Ekklesiazousai*, c.391 BC) and *Wealth* (*Ploutos*, 388), the role of the CHORUS is reduced and there are fewer topical references (though with some emphasis on social and economic problems). These two plays, with fragments from other contemporary playwrights (404–321), have come to be known as Middle Comedy. Some scholars, however, would dispense altogether with the latter term, finding it, like Old and New Comedy, too rigid in what it implies – a sudden change of direction. The constraints on touring companies may have made a chorus, at any rate a full chorus, optional. There were interludes, which could have been, if not the work of the same playwright, superior musically and choreographically to those of the 5th century. Other evidence, such as a plural play title, *Garland-sellers* by Euboulos (active c.380–c.355), with a fragment to match, suggests that the traditional chorus continued in existence for some time.

For unknown reasons, Middle Comedy is very fragmentary and therefore difficult to study. Myth, probably in various forms, remained an important subject until about the 350s: the titles of Aristophanes' last, lost plays suggest mythological subjects, though Aiolos in one was a cook. Plautus' *Amphitruo* may reflect one kind of treatment.

Alexis (c.375–c.275 BC) may have taught Menander. Stock characters of a stereotyped nature, reflected in terracotta statuettes and their replicas, and forerunners of those in New Comedy, seem to have become established in this period. These include the cook, the boastful soldier, the mercenary *hetaira* and the parasite. They may have helped to make comedy more universal and marketable outside Athens, though TRAGEDY had already been exported in the days of AESCHYLUS, and PINDAR wrote both for home and abroad. (Many Middle Comedy poets, like Diphilos and Philemon, were non-Athenian.) Figurines have been found in places as far apart as Spain and southern Russia.

The quotations of Middle Comedy that we have are too short and without sufficient context to allow a sustained study of the characterization. Many extracts are to be found in ATHENAEUS (fl. c.AD 200), who claims to know of 57 poets and 800 plays; he also quotes New Comedy, but was mainly interested in references to food and drink.

There is little political satire surviving, though some comedy of the period was described by ISOKRATES in 355 BC as irresponsible, a sentiment echoed by PLATO in his *Laws*. Menander has a few digs at established targets, DEMOSTHENES is a target for the pro-Macedonian Timokles, and Philippides attacks king DEMETRIOS I POLIORKETES. Perhaps most political comment had become unwise or even illegal now that MACEDONIA had dominated Athens since 338, though a drastic decline in the practical effects of Athenian power after 404 is now disputed.

There were some political and social changes. Between 322 and 317 CITIZENSHIP was limited to the wealthier classes and the THEORIC FUND, a grant which had enabled poorer people to attend the THEATRE, was withdrawn. Menander's audience, unlike that of Aristophanes, would have been largely from the upper strata of society, with the exception, perhaps, of SLAVES accompanying their masters. The CHORUS was no longer paid for by a private individual.

The costume in New Comedy had no padding or *phalloi*. MASKS were still worn, but were stylized and, in the case of slaves, somewhat grotesque. Archaeological finds of replica masks and figurines in terracotta on the Aiolian island of Lipari, dating from the time of Menander and preserved when the town was destroyed by the Romans in 252, bring the costumes and gestures of actual New Comedy performances to life.

In Aristophanes' Old Comedy the dramatic illusion was often hilariously broken, with actors even being rude to the audience. Menander's characters, by contrast, share their private feelings with the audience, but without speaking any more directly to them than saying 'gentlemen' at the beginning of, or during, what is essentially a soliloquy. At some point it became usual in New Comedy to have a prologue, five acts and a choral interlude (announced more than once in Menander as a band of tipsy revellers).

In Menander, situations and characters could appear stereotyped, but are realistic enough to offer interesting insights into life at the time. Romantic love is not the only theme; family relationships, including those between slaves and masters, friendships, the position of women and many kinds of misunderstandings receive sympathetic treatment. Philemon, on the other hand, may have written some mythological burlesques, perhaps with a satirical tone. Plautus adapted some of his plays as well as Menander's, as he did Diphilos; in this way different styles may be distinguished. Diphilos was also a model for TERENCE, as was Apollodoros; the latter was apparently influenced by Menander. It may, however, be just as dangerous to speculate about the nature of lost New Comedy as it is about some Old and Middle Comedy.

Much of New Comedy seems to have centred around the family or *oikos* (the action taking place over a single day). Three doors represented, typically, two different urban HOUSEHOLDS with a shrine or

TEMPLE in between. Painted panels could represent ARCHITECTURE or suggest trees and GARDENS, or possibly wilder surroundings. In the *Dyskolos* of Menander the setting is the cave of PAN (a real place) near Athens, and in his *Leukadia* the backdrop is the temple of APOLLO on the cliffs of the island of Leukas.

Evidence exists that many of these New Comedy plays were performed outside Athens. (There are VASE-PAINTINGS which suggest that Aristophanes, too, was performed elsewhere, in southern Italy.) Theatres were built all over the 'new' Greek world conquered by ALEXANDER. Dramatic contests continued to take place, including revivals of 5th-century TRAGEDIES and comedies. With touring plays came the development of touring companies of ACTORS who organized themselves into ultimately powerful guilds; there were now prizes for acting. By this date New Comedy was being read as well as performed. Though gentler than Old Comedy, New Comedy continued to entertain, going on to inspire Plautus and Terence and, through them, much of European comedy. AMH

See Dobrov, G.W., ed. (1995) *Beyond Aristophanes*; Green, R. and Handley, E. (1995) *Images of the Greek Theatre*; Konstan, D. (1995) *Greek Comedy and Ideology*; Sidwell, K. (2000) From Old to Middle to New? Aristotle's *Poetics* and the history of Athenian comedy, in D. Harvey and J. Wilkins, eds., *The Rivals of Aristophanes* 247–58; Simon, E. (1982) *The Ancient Theatre*.

 ACTORS AND ACTRESSES: (a)–(b); DRAMA: (b)–(c).

comic strips The most famous comic books set in the ancient world are, without doubt, the ASTERIX stories created by René Goscinny (text) and Albert Uderzo (drawings). They were first published on 29 October 1959 in the weekly magazine *Pilote*, but 30 years later *Asterix* remains a symbol of quality entertainment literature, and the international popularity of the comic strip has never waned. To date, the 34 stories have been translated into 40 languages, and more than 220 million books have been sold worldwide. The success of the books is largely due to the immaculate research into GAULISH and Roman life undertaken by the authors, even though the adventures themselves are uproariously zany.

A learned approach to ancient history is also taken by Larry Gonick, a San Francisco-based cartoonist. His most famous work is a monumental eight-volume cartoon strip, covering from the dinosaur age to the end of the Roman empire in 650 illustrated pages. His thorough immersion in ancient history, and his accurate sense of narrative, allow Gonick to lampoon ancient attitudes by juxtaposing them with modern viewpoints and some very funny images. Not only is Gonick's work a wickedly funny read, it is also an effective educational tool. LL-J

See Gonick, L. (1990) *The Cartoon History of the Universe 1–7: from the Big Bang to Alexander the Great*; (1994) *The Cartoon History of the Universe 8–13: from the springtime of China to the fall of Rome*; Goscinny, R. and. Uderzo, A. (1999) *Le Livre d'Astérix le gaulois.*

Commagene The kingdom of Commagene (Greek Kommagênê) lay on the west bank of the Euphrates in northern SYRIA, extending from the Taurus mountains through a relatively well-watered plateau before descending to the arid steppe below ZEUGMA. Much of the territory was hilly, but the valleys where

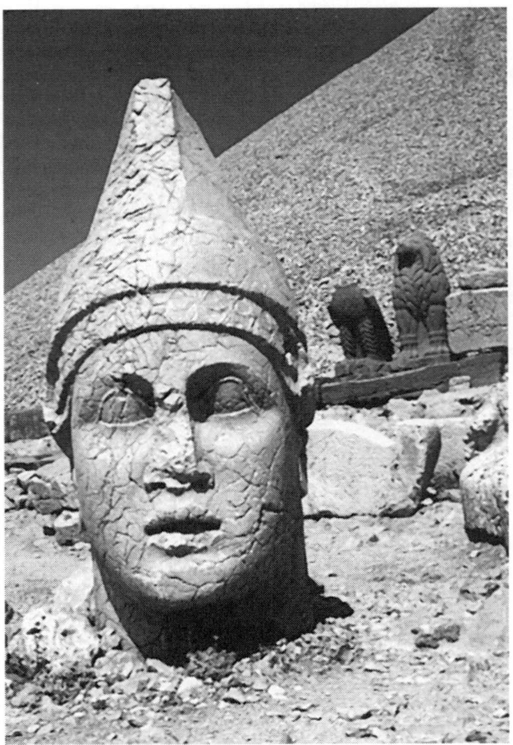

COMMAGENE: head of colossal statue from the mountain-top burial sanctuary at Nemrud Dağı (in the rear the tumulus of Antiochos I, ruler of Commagene in the late 1st century BC).

the four major towns arose – SAMOSATA, Caesarea Germaniceia, Perrhe and Doliche – are fertile. It was 'an exceedingly fertile, though small, territory' according to STRABO (16.2.3); TACITUS (*Annals* 2.81.1) speaks of its final ruler as enjoying 'the highest prosperity'. Wealth also came from a major trade route from Iran and BABYLONIA. From Samosata routes ran north to Melitene (mod. Malatya) and west to Caesarea Germaniceia (Maras). These routes were strategic, and the region was often the prey of regional powers. Hittites left relief-decorated stele, and 'Kummuh' appears in Assyrian records of the 10th to 7th centuries BC.

Kummuh evidently passed to Babylon in the late 7th century, and we can infer PERSIAN satraps there in the 4th and 3rd centuries. Subsequently, the SELEUKIDS dominated the region; the name Commagene appears at this time. The decline of Seleukid power saw the emergence of an independent dynasty. These KINGS, from Ptolemy (Ptolemaios, c.163–c.130 BC) onwards, created a prosperous and brilliant kingdom balanced between powerful neighbours. They claimed descent from DARIUS, ALEXANDER, the Seleukids and the PTOLEMIES. Samosata was named after, and perhaps founded by, Ptolemy's successor Samos (c.130–100). Mithradates I (c.100–c.70) displayed in his name the Persian affiliation of this dynasty, which fell to Tigranes the Great (c.86). In 63 POMPEY recognized the kingdom, giving it control of Zeugma. Antiochos I (c.70–c.36) supplied troops for Pompey at PHARSALUS but was caught in the Roman–PARTHIAN WARS. Suspecting assistance to the PARTHIANS, Mark ANTONY invaded in 38 but failed to capture Samosata. Mithradates II (c.36–20) supported Antony at ACTIUM, but AUGUSTUS recognized him and his son, Mithradates III (king from c.20 BC, date of death uncertain).

The death of Antiochos III in AD 17 led the emperor TIBERIUS to the first of three annexations. Gaius CALIGULA briefly restored the dynasty under Antiochos IV in 38; CLAUDIUS reinstated him fully in 41. In 54 NERO mobilized Antiochos for a Parthian war, and the dynast supplied troops in the Jewish war. In 70 the king's son Antiochos was wounded in the Flavian cause, but two years later VESPASIAN believed that his ally was conspiring with the Parthians and sanctioned his removal. Commagene was now joined to Syria.

The dynasty lived on, its descendants prominent in the imperial entourage (Balbilla's name was inscribed alongside HADRIAN's on the statue of Memnon in EGYPT) and serving as CONSULS at Rome. Gaius Julius Antiochos Philopappos, suffect consul in 109, was also archon at Athens and a benefactor of the city; his grand tomb still stands atop the Hill of the Muses in Athens. By the 4th century AD Commagene was part of a new province, Euphratensis, at the heart of the Roman interface with Persia.

The dynasty created a fascinating fusion of cultures. They used Greek and Parthian names, took Roman ones when granted CITIZENSHIP (visible in the name of the last ruler, Gaius Julius Antiochos Epiphanes), and employed Greek for coin legends and honorific inscriptions. Rulers, often depicted with Seleukid, Parthian and ARMENIAN tiaras, were buried under striking tumuli, including one 50 m high above the temple tomb of Antiochos I on the summit of Nemrud Dağı. His cult links him to the Hittite past, hellenistic Syria, Parthia and emergent MITHRAISM. Parallels are found at Arsameia, and the Hittite iconography evident in the cult depictions of the Jupiter of Doliche is notable. In architecture, what strikes the visitor to Samosata is the unexpected Roman *opus reticulatum* in the walls of the PALACE and the city.

The region boasts some remarkable monuments, including the well-known ones of the regal period but also impressive Roman tower-tombs. The Roman BRIDGES across the Chabina Su and the Goksu are among the best-preserved anywhere. (see also PERSIAN WARS, ROMAN) DLK

See Millar, F. G. B. (1993) *The Roman Near East, 31 BC–AD 337.*

 ASIA; SAMOSATA.

commanders see CONSULS; GENERALS; MAGISTRATES; OFFICERS, MILITARY.

commentators, textual In scholarship, textual commentators perform a key role, that of restoring as far as possible an author's original text. The beginnings of this activity lie in ALEXANDRIA in the 3rd century BC, where scholars in the Mouseion and LIBRARY edited and preserved texts dating back to the Homeric EPICS. That classical Greek literature survives today is in no small measure due to the efforts of men such as Zenodotos, KALLIMACHOS, ERATOSTHENES, Aristophanes of Byzantion, and Aristarchos of Samothrace. The Alexandrians recognized that the manuscripts they were working on were corrupt through scribal error, giving rise to the expression *graphikon hamartêma* ('mistake in writing'), and they undertook the tasks of TEXTUAL CRITICISM, classification and exposition in the form of full commentaries or marginal notes (*scholia*). Principles of interpretation were developed, most notably the one usually attributed to Aristarchos, that we should 'clarify HOMER through Homer', i.e. interpret a doubtful passage in an author in the light of his usage elsewhere. But their editing difficulties were immediately exacerbated by problems of convention, including local spelling variations and faulty transliteration into the Ionic alphabet which predominated after 403 BC. More than that, there was the problem of interpreting texts written without word division, a practice that persisted for centuries. Again, the hellenistic invention of accentuation was not applied consistently until the Middle Ages, while punctuation was erratic and POETRY was written continuously like prose (Aristophanes of Byzantion is credited with the invention of colometry (the division of verse into metrical units), which in turn led to the writing of poetry in lines).

In their efforts to standardize texts, the Alexandrians strove in particular to detect interpolations and were very ready to reject lines of Homer as being unworthy of the poet or out of context. These spurious lines were not deleted, but were indicated in the left-hand margin by a horizontal stroke (*obelos*) and so are preserved for us. They would also compare different versions of texts and suggest conjectural readings; and they produced a rudimentary form of *apparatus criticus*, using a range of critical signs which they wrote in the margins of their manuscripts. The *asteriskos* (※) was used to indicate a repeated line and the sigma, and antisigma (C, Ɔ) to indicate successive lines which might be swapped round.

Another, less well-known centre of textual industry was PERGAMON, from where Krates visited Rome (c.159 BC) and helped to spark an interest among the Romans for accurate texts of their earlier writers. But work on the dramatists (e. g. VARRO on PLAUTUS) led to a demand for modern, more accessible versions of the plays, and when popularized versions of later writers also began circulating, a renewed need was felt for revision of the Latin classics. A notable figure in this field from the late 1st century AD is Marcus Valerius Probus, who edited the texts of LUCRETIUS, Virgil and HORACE using the Alexandrian signs system. MJE

See Reynolds, L. D. and Wilson, N. G. (1991) *Scribes and Scholars*; Zetzel, J. E. G. (1984) *Latin Textual Criticism in Antiquity*.

Commodus (Lucius Aurelius Commodus) AD 161–192 Born at Lanuvium on 31 August AD 161, Commodus was the only son of MARCUS AURELIUS and FAUSTINA to survive early childhood (six other sons died before reaching the age of five). In 177 he was given imperial power by his father, and he succeeded as sole emperor on 17 March 180. He swiftly brought to an end the ongoing campaigns against tribes north of the DANUBE, and returned to Rome, where he celebrated a TRIUMPH over the GERMANS on

22 October. In 182 he survived an assassination attempt spearheaded by men in the entourage of his older sister, LUCILLA. From that point onwards his reign was dominated by a series of powerful favourites. These included Perennis, the praetorian prefect, murdered in 185; Cleander, a freedman who also became praetorian prefect and was overthrown after a riot in 190; and then, it appears, his concubine, Marcia. By 192 Commodus was showing signs of dangerously erratic tendencies. He renamed Rome as Colonia Commodiana, renamed the months of the year after himself, appeared as HERCULES in the AMPHITHEATRE, and trained as a GLADIATOR. On 31 December 192 he was murdered by the palace staff at the instigation of Marcia. DSP

 EMPERORS, ROMAN: (a); TRAJAN (stemma).

communications Efficient communications were essential to the ability of an ancient community, city or state to interact, pursue a foreign policy or dominate others. In early Greek communities, communication was effected through the development of protocols surrounding the reception and treatment of guests (guest-FRIENDSHIP or *xenia*). Later this extended to include citizens of one *POLIS* who resided in another and represented the interests of their home *polis* (*proxenoi*). On matters of great importance, embassies extended the interests of one state or group of states. The best examples are the many embassies and speeches of AMBASSADORS related by THUCYDIDES in his account of the PELOPONNESIAN WAR – good evidence for communication between Athens and its imperial subjects. In addition, recent research has found a complex ROAD network in the PELOPONNESE, which must have facilitated communication. With the domination of the Greek world by hellenistic kings, states were more restricted in their ability to pursue independent foreign policy. WAR ceased to be the ultimate method for settling disputes; not only fuller international relations but also an early form of international law, primarily based on arbitration, developed.

More rigidly organized systems of communications existed. HERODOTOS (5.52–3) details the organization and infrastructure of the post service of the PERSIAN EMPIRE, based on a system of relays, with fresh HORSES at regularly spaced rest-houses. This 'Royal Road' could be used by all, and supported WHEELED TRANSPORT. Upon this system the PTOLEMAIC kings modelled their service, for which we have important evidence (*P. Hib.* I. 110). A close link exists between the heavily centralized governments of the Persians and Ptolemies, where efficient organization and speed were important, and communication.

Under the Romans, efficient communication found its greatest expression. According to Suetonius, AUGUSTUS created the Roman post service (*cursus publicus*). It was founded upon earlier systems, not least that of the newly annexed province of Egypt, and was not a relay system: messengers travelled the full length of their journey so that they could be questioned personally. Increasingly drawn from the army, they were issued with a warrant (*diplôma*), signed by an emperor or provincial governor, to enable them to use the facilities. The service was closely monitored but frequently abused. Considerable evidence for illegal use and requisition of transport services exists on inscriptions, in PAPYRI and in legal sources. The state was naturally concerned with its own interests, not those of provincial communities, which were often expected to provide hospitality or transport ANIMALS.

Significant changes to the system were made by SEPTIMIUS SEVERUS in the early 3rd century AD. He established a service for transporting provisions to the army (*cursus clabularis*), and the systems further developed into the 4th century (to which most of our evidence relates). Resting stops (*mansiones* or *stationes*) were placed at strategic intervals on roads; Roman roads were central to the system. ANIMALS, food, fodder and even blankets were requisitioned from local citizens, as detailed in recently published papyri from OXYRHYNCHOS. Considerable bureaucracy was involved – this is evident from a small number of itineraries preserved on papyrus – but it is unclear to what extent this bureaucracy lay behind the development of formal itineraries or maps, such as the *ANTONINE ITINERARY* or *PEUTINGER TABLE*. Nevertheless, communication and its infrastructure were vital not only to Rome's control of its empire, but also to the development of provincial landscapes. (see also POST (MAIL)) CEPA

See Adams, C. E. P. and Laurence, R., eds. (2001) *Travel and Geography in the Roman Empire*; Casson, L. (1994) *Travel in the Ancient World*.

 ROADS: (a)–(b).

competition The idea of competition (Greek *agôn*, Latin *certamen*) held a central place in both the Greek and Roman value system. That the ancient Greeks were competitive people cannot be doubted, given the evidence for competitions, large and small, not only in a variety of ATHLETIC and equestrian events but also in MUSIC and POETRY. Even dramatic FESTIVALS, such as the Dionysia in ATHENS, were typically staged as competitive celebrations. Thus, the idea of competition reached beyond its obvious expression in athletics and affected all aspects of Greek life. The fundamental importance of the agonistic ethos in Greek society has led some scholars to suggest that in this the ancient Greeks were in some way unique. This view does tend to discount the various competitive impulses in other ancient societies.

Roman society was competitive, too; not simply in that Romans, like Greeks, celebrated competitive festivals and games, but also because social pressures among the urban ÉLITE compelled them to compete with each other and with their predecessors. Thus the magnitude of the GAMES (*ludi, munera*) given by Roman MAGISTRATES tended to grow in splendour and included ever more spectacular refinements. In both the Greek and Roman worlds, the wealthy élite competed for office and public recognition through a variety of civic BENEFACTIONS (a process known as euergetism). Indeed, this expensive impulse may be seen as a mark of the spread of romanized culture throughout the Roman empire. MJC

See Golden, M. (1998) *Sport and Society in Ancient Greece*; Kyle, D. G. (1987) *Athletics in Ancient Athens*; Poliakoff, M. (1987) *Combat Sports in the Ancient World*.

concord and Concordia The ideal of social and political accord (Greek *homonoia*, Latin *concordia*), sometimes personified as a GODDESS. The idea first appears in Greek texts of the later 5th century BC. The goddess first appears in the 4th; her cult was popular in SICILY and Magna Graecia. The latter may have influenced the cult of Concordia in Rome, which according to tradition originated in 367 BC, when Marcus Furius Camillus built her a TEMPLE in the midst of PATRICIAN–PLEBEIAN strife. Other shrines followed, similarly dedicated in times of conflict. The SENATE rebuilt Camillus' shrine in 121 BC after the suppression of Gaius GRACCHUS, and in the turmoil of the late Republic CICERO made the notion of a 'concord of orders', the senate and the *EQUITES*, into a cornerstone of his political programme. With the advent of the imperial system, concord between different social factions became less important, but Concordia was evoked in new contexts which ensured her continued importance. One was the idea of concord within the imperial house, an idea first expressed in the reign of AUGUSTUS when TIBERIUS rebuilt the old temple of Concordia. In this context the goddess frequently appears on coins, especially in the reigns of joint EMPERORS. The second context is the 'concord of the armies', advertising military support for the emperor. This motif is first found on coins of the late 1st century AD and soon becomes commonplace. JBR

See Levick, B. (1978) Concordia at Rome, in R. A. G. Carson and C. M. Kraay, eds., *Scripta Nummaria Romana* 217–33.

concrete A major contribution to ARCHITECTURE made by the Romans was the perfection and exploitation of concrete, known as *opus caementicium*. This was a material initially developed on the bay of Naples in the later 3rd or early 2nd century BC. It was made from a mortar which derived its unique strength from the use of the local volcanic sand, *pozzolana* (*pulvis puteolanus*). This sand, derived from volcanic rocks, had active ingredients of amorphous and vitreous silicates and aluminates. When combined with LIME and water, the resulting chemical reaction meant that the mortar did not need to lose water by evaporation during the setting process, thus enabling it to set in damp conditions, or indeed underwater, properties noted by VITRUVIUS (2.6.1). This mortar was laid with aggregate which was often skilfully graded by weight; the supreme example is the DOME of the PANTHEON.

Roman concrete is usually defined according to the type of facing used. The three main facings are *opus incertum*, a facing of small stones roughly uniform in size but irregular in shape; *opus reticulatum*, comprising small, squared facing-stones set on the diagonal; and *opus testaceum*, fired BRICK or TILE facing. The facing was purely superficial, as the strength of the structure lay in the concrete core. By the imperial period, concrete was the standard basic building material for wall and vault construction in both public and private buildings. HD

See Lamprecht, H. O. (1987) *Opus Caementicium*.

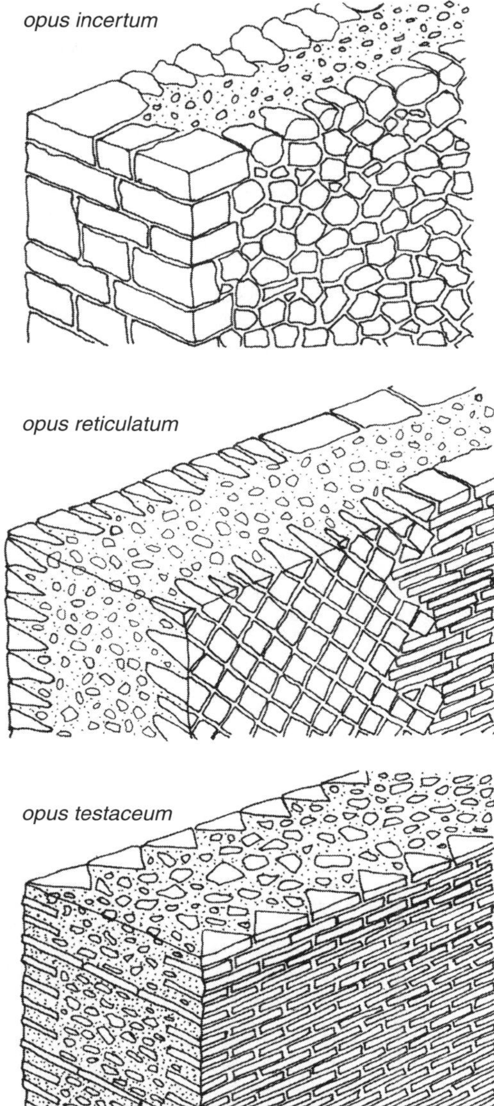

CONCRETE: the main styles of facing in Roman concrete construction.

Conon see KONON.

Constans see ATHANASIUS; CONSTANTINE I.

 EMPERORS, ROMAN: (b); TETRARCHS: (b).

Constantine I ('the Great') c. AD 272/3–337; emperor 306–37 (Flavius Valerius Constantinus) The son of Constantius I (Chlorus) and HELENA, born at Naïssus (Niš in Yugoslavia). His father was CAESAR to MAXIMIAN in 293 and raised to AUGUSTUS in 305. Constantine himself served on campaign under both DIOCLETIAN and GALERIUS. In 305/6 he joined his father, upon whose death in YORK he was proclaimed Augustus by the troops (July 306).

The period that follows is confused. Galerius recognized him as Caesar while elevating Severus to Augustus in the Western empire. Meanwhile, Maxentius, supported by his father Maximian, who had come out of retirement, had also been acclaimed Augustus. In 307 Maximian raised Constantine to Augustus, while Constantine married his daughter

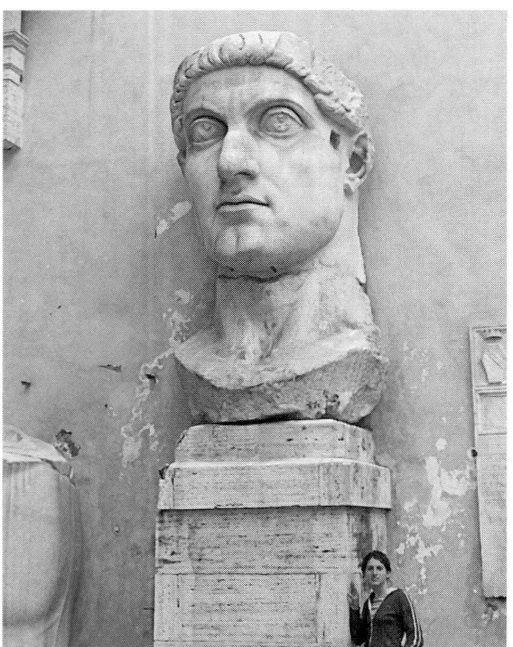

CONSTANTINE I ('THE GREAT'): early 4th-century AD head of Constantine from a colossal statue erected in the Basilica Nova in Rome.

Fausta. After the death of Severus, Galerius raised LICINIUS to Augustus at a conference at Carnuntum in 308, expecting Constantine to serve as his Caesar. Both Constantine and Maximin Daia refused to resign their ranks and retained the full title of Augusti. During this time, Constantine was successful on the RHINE frontier against the FRANKS and the Alamanni. While he was absent on campaign, Maximian seized MARSEILLES, whereupon Constantine forced him to surrender and commit SUICIDE (310). The *Latin Panegyric* of 310 stressed his descent from the 3rd-century emperor Claudius Gothicus (268–70), and from this period Constantine seems to have abandoned his father's epithet of Herculius; his coins bore the SOL INVICTUS ('Unconquered Sun'). Both actions aligned him with AURELIAN (emperor 270–5) and stressed a dynastic right to power rather than legitimacy through the TETRARCHY. Constantine now needed to protect his position. In 312 he invaded ITALY, and after successes at Turin and Verona he marched on Rome. He defeated Maxentius outside Rome near the MILVIAN BRIDGE, and gained control of the West.

In the following year Constantine and Licinius met at MILAN and issued the 'Edict' that granted CHRISTIANS the right to worship and returned confiscated property to the CHURCH. The alliance, cemented by Licinius' marriage to Constantine's sister Constantina, was uneasy even after Licinius' victory over Maximin Daia left only himself and Constantine as emperors. A conflict in 316 resulted in the sons of the Augusti (Crispus, Constantine II and Licinius) becoming Caesars in an attempt to maintain the truce, but tension remained. In 323 Licinius accused Constantine of usurping his function when Constantine fought off a GOTHIC incursion, and war was inevitable. After two defeats (Adrianople and Chrysopolis) Licinius was forced to abdicate. He and his son were soon murdered. Constantine was now sole emperor but did not stop campaigning: on the Rhine (328/9), against Goths (332) and Sarmatians (334), and north of the DANUBE (336). A Persian war was imminent at the time of his death.

Constantine consolidated most of the provincial and administrative reforms begun by Diocletian. Praetorian prefects became purely administrative and judicial offices, losing their military functions. Central government was reorganized with a *magister officiorum* to control imperial offices, and the chief treasury officer (*comes sacrarum largitionum*) is attested by the reign's end. While the inflation endemic in the previous century seems to have continued, Constantine did issue a GOLD coin, the *solidus*, which remained in use until the later Byzantine period; it was probably paid for initially by confiscation of treasures from pagan TEMPLES and taxes in gold and SILVER. SENATORS were brought back into official posts, particularly as provincial governors and prefects of the city of Rome, but these posts, like the largely honorific CONSULSHIP, did not have the power they had had in the earlier empire. Constantine's enlargement of the senatorial order led to the eventual decline of the EQUESTRIAN class. As for lower orders, Constantine restricted the movement of the decurion class to force them to fulfil civic obligations. *COLONI* were likewise forbidden to leave estates. He also continued Diocletain's military reforms, pursuing a two-tier army of field and frontier troops. Zosimus accused Constantine of weakening the frontiers by taking the better troops for his field army.

Also following Diocletian, Constantine saw the strategic importance of an imperial centre in the East. He decided on Byzantium, renamed CONSTANTINOPLE. Major work was begun in 326 and a *dedicatio* performed in 330 with both pagan and Christian rites. Assumptions that he was moving the capital to the East or creating a Christian capital are misguided. Rome was already partially superseded in the West by other tetrarchic cities such as Milan and TRIER. Moreover, while Constantine was committed to Constantinople, the ARCHAEOLOGY does not support EUSEBIOS' claim that no PAGANISM was allowed within the city. Constantine did not ignore Rome; with his mother he was responsible for many building schemes, particularly CHURCHES, including the first St Peter's. He celebrated his *decennalia* there in 315, commemorated by the ARCH of Constantine.

Constantine is remembered as the first Christian emperor, but his version of Christianity is still disputed. In the early stages of his life he saw his divine protection as coming from Sol Invictus, and he may have viewed the Christian god in the same way. Christian apologists depict him defeating Maxentius under the banner of the Christian symbol (chi–rho). His legislation was certainly tolerant of Christian practice from 313 onwards. From 324 he actively set about returning church property, allowed church courts the power of law, and granted clergy dispensation from the duties of the decurionate. He saw it as part of his imperial role (as 'bishop outside the church') to regulate church affairs, both organizational and theological. He summoned CHURCH COUNCILS in 313 (Rome) and 314 (Arles) to settle the Donatist controversy in North Africa, and in 325 convened the council of Nicaea to discuss, among other issues, the doctrines of Arius. The resulting decision was very much influenced by Constantine's need for compromise and unity within the church and thus the empire, but the Arian controversy was not settled. In 335 Constantine called the council of Tyre to banish Athanasius, the defender of Nicene orthodoxy.

In 336 he celebrated his *tricennalia* (the 30th anniversary of his accession) in Constantinople, where Eusebios delivered the *De laudibus Constantini*. He soon fell ill and was baptized by Eusebios of Nicomedia. After his death in May 337, he was buried in his mausoleum in Constantinople. Constantine's first wife, Minerva, was the mother of his son Crispus. By Fausta he had five more children: Constantine, Constantius and Constans, who all became Augusti, and two daughters, Constantina (who married Gallus, Caesar 351–4) and Helena (m. Julian, Augustus 361–3). Crispus and Fausta died in mysterious circumstances in 326. On his death the empire was divided between his surviving sons. MEH

See Barnes, T. D. (1982) *The New Empire of Diocletian and Constantine*; Cameron, A. and Hall, S. (1999) *Eusebius' Life of Constantine*; Lieu, S. N. C. and Montserrat, D., eds. (1998) *Constantine*.

 ARCHES, MONUMENTAL; EMPERORS, ROMAN: (b); TETRARCHS: (b).

Constantine II see CONSTANTINE.

 EMPERORS, ROMAN: (b); TETRARCHS: (b).

Constantine III see HISPANIA; STILICHO.

Constantine Porphyrogenitus see SCHOLARSHIP, BYZANTINE.

Constantinople The name *Kônstantinoupolis* was given to the town of Byzantion by the Roman emperor Constantine I, when he inaugurated it in AD 330. According to legend, it had been founded at least 1,000 years earlier, in the 7th century BC, by the

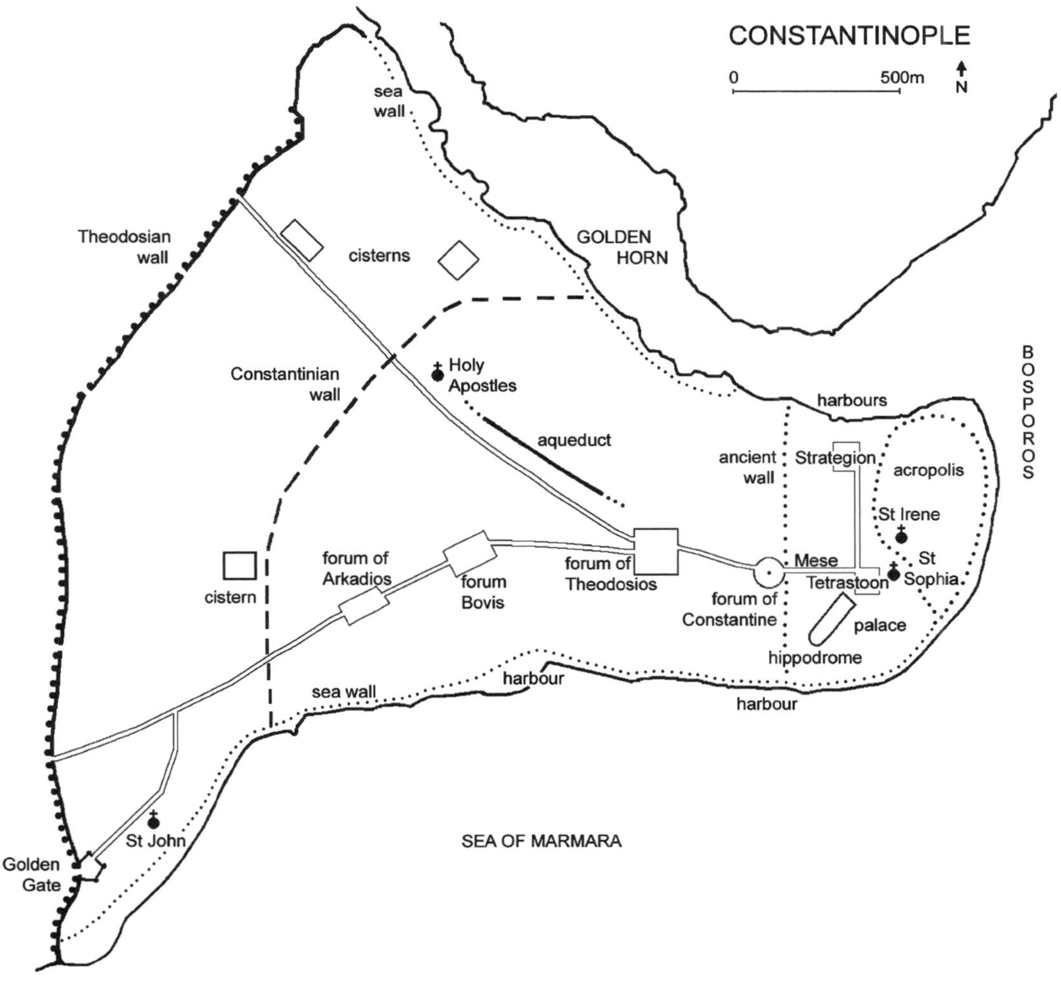

Constantinople: simplified plan of the city.

MEGARIAN king Byzas (hence the original name and, from Constantine onwards, the 'Byzantine' empire). The city occupies a promontory on the western side of the Bosporos, the narrow stretch of water connecting the BLACK SEA with the sea of Marmara, which in turn opens into the AEGEAN and finally the MEDITERRANEAN. In times when it was easier to travel by water than by land, the strategic and commercial advantages of such a site doubtless governed both the initial settlement there and its increasing importance as a city of antiquity. Most of the great powers of the ancient world controlled it for a time. DARIUS of Persia took it in 512 BC, PAUSANIAS restored it to the Greeks in 479, ALEXANDER the Great captured it in 334, and by the late 2nd century it had become part of the Roman empire. In c.79 BC it was fought over by the Romans and MITHRADATES. Just over two centuries later (AD 196) it was attacked and severely damaged by SEPTIMIUS SEVERUS for harbouring his rival, PESCENNIUS NIGER. By the time of DIOCLETIAN in the 3rd century AD it was one of several important administrative bases in the Eastern PROVINCES. A further thousand years beyond Constantine, in 1453, Constantinople was the last part of the Byzantine empire to fall to the Ottoman Turks, and in modern times it acquired the name Istanbul (from the Turkish pronunciation of Greek *stên poli*, '(at) the city'). To modern Greeks it is often simply *I Póli*, 'The City'.

With such a history, and given the continuous occupation of the city to the present day, the many phases of Constantinople's physical appearance are inevitably obscure. Little now remains that is earlier than the 6th century AD, and archaeological investigation has been scant and episodic. The ancient town seems to have occupied just the tip of the promontory, where there was a fortified *AKROPOLIS* overlooking the Bosporos and the Marmara. Below this, to the north, were HARBOURS just inside an inlet from the Bosporos known as the Golden Horn – an important area of calm water where both military and commercial shipping could escape the fierce currents of the Bosporos. A sea wall extended from this harbour area around the promontory to the beginning of the Marmara shore, its two extremities linked by a land wall, so that the end of the promontory was defensible on all sides. Within the walls were TEMPLES on the *akropolis* (of ZEUS, ATHENA and DIONYSOS), an AMPHITHEATRE, possibly a hippodrome, and the public BATHS of Zeuxippos.

Constantine extended the sea walls and built a new land wall, more than doubling the enclosed area and accommodating a new harbour on the Marmara shore. He is also credited with considerable rebuilding in the enlarged city, including work on the hippodrome, public baths, and SENATE house and the construction of an imperial PALACE. He embellished his 'new Rome' with fine SCULPTURE. A few pieces survive, including the Serpent column, a bronze column in the form of three intertwined snakes (originally dedicated 800 years earlier at DELPHI to mark the Greek victory in the PERSIAN WARS), which still stands (minus the heads) on the spine of the hippodrome. Also from the hippodrome are the four bronze horses that formed part of the loot of the Fourth Crusade of AD 1204 and were later placed on the façade of San Marco in Venice.

The site of the FORUM of Constantine is still marked by a great column of porphyry (a STONE of imperial purple) which once carried a statue of the emperor as APOLLO. Just inside the land wall, to the north-west, was Constantine's large circular mausoleum, alongside which his son Constantius built a CHURCH of the Holy Apostles (rebuilt in the 6th century by JUSTINIAN). The whole mausoleum complex was razed in the 15th century to provide a site for the mosque of Mehmet the Conqueror, but the Istanbul Archaeological Museum has a number of huge porphyry SARCOPHAGI which probably came from it.

Constantine apparently did not build a major church in his capital. The BISHOP of Constantinople officiated from the pre-Constantinian Hagia Eirene (St Irene), and the Great Church (Hagia Sophia; St Sophia) was not built until 360, by Constantius. (The Hagia Sophia now standing is another Justinianic replacement – the dearth of early structures in the city may owe something to Justinian's enthusiasm for rebuilding.)

In the early 5th century, Theodosius II extended the city still further westwards, building a new land wall and a further harbour on the Marmara shore. Traditionally explained as a response to increasing population, this second enlargement of the city is now thought to have been undertaken to accommodate the large open cisterns needed to ensure a regular supply of fresh water. The Theodosian land wall still stands, albeit incorporating substantial later Byzantine and Ottoman rebuilding. It is a massive structure, consisting of inner and outer walls, each with 96 towers, and a moat beyond the outer wall. Of the ten gateways, the most splendid is the Golden Gate, near to the Marmara shore, through which TRIUMPHAL entrances were made. From this gate, and another towards the north, run two main ROADS which join before they reach the Mese, the principal street of the town centre. Forums on these roads had columns bearing statues of 5th-century emperors; that of Marcian still stands, but without its statue.

Some of the most famous churches of Constantinople were 5th-century foundations, such as the church of the Virgin in the Blachernai district (at the north end of the Theodosian wall) which housed the *maphorion* (veil or robe) of the Virgin Mary, and the church of the Virgin in Chalkoprateia (near Hagia Sophia), where her girdle was kept. These buildings are lost, but the large basilican church of St John, near the Theodosian wall and the Marmara, endures as a magnificent ruin. LR

See Mango, C. (1985) *Le Développement urbain de Constantinople (IVe–VIIe siècles).*

CITIES: (b); FORTIFICATIONS: (d); ROMAN EMPIRE: (b).

Constantius I ('Chlorus') see CONSTANTINE; GALERIUS; HELENA; MAXIMIAN; TETRARCHS; YORK.

EMPERORS, ROMAN: (b); TETRARCHS: (b).

Constantius II see ARIANISM; ATHANASIUS; CHRISTIANITY; CONSTANTINE; CONSTANTINOPLE; JULIAN; LIBRARIES; PROBA; THEMISTIUS.

EMPERORS, ROMAN: (b); TETRARCHS: (b).

Constantius III

 Theodosius I.

constitutio Antoniniana see Caracalla; citizenship, Roman; Ulpian.

consuls A pair of Roman magistrates elected annually by the *comitia centuriata*. In the Republic, they served as the chief executive and military officers of the state. The exact title of the earliest holders of this office is unclear (possibly *praetor maximus*), but by 367 BC these magistrates were known as the *consules*. The office seems to have been intended to replace the kingship and possessed similarly broad powers, with the important restrictions of one-year term limits and collegiality. Eventually some of the consuls' powers and duties were assigned to other magistrates, chiefly the censors and praetors. The system of dual chief magistrates holding equal power was typical of the Romans' unease with granting exclusive authority to individuals. The principle of collegiality was on the whole successful, but could be cumbersome when there was discord between the consuls, as during the famously antagonistic consulship of Julius Caesar and Marcus Calpurnius Bibulus in 59 BC.

The consuls' primary duties were to command Rome's armies in the field, to preside over meetings of the senate, and to enforce its policies. As holders of full *imperium*, when outside Rome, consuls were entitled to *fasces* complete with axes, representing their power to mete out punishment up to and including execution. During the Republic, the consuls were elected from a list of candidates proposed by the senate, but in the imperial period the emperor often put forward candidates or held one of the consulships himself. Until 153 BC consuls took office on 15 March, afterwards on 1 January. After 367 BC it was mandated that at least one of the consuls be plebeian. By the late Republic, the minimum age required to hold the consulship was set by law at 42, but there were exceptions, and in the imperial period this rule was frequently ignored.

The pair of consuls who took office at the beginning of the year were known as the *consules ordinarii*. The year was dated by both their names. Any additional consuls appointed as replacements in the same year (e.g. when an *ordinarius* died) were termed *consules suffecti* ('suffect consuls'). Particularly in the imperial period, it became standard practice for the emperor to appoint a number of suffect consuls each year as a form of reward or honour, or as a means of widening the pool of available magistracies and ex-magistrates. In AD 190 there were no fewer than 25 *suffecti*, and by the late empire this practice had substantially reduced the prestige of the suffect consulship, though the ordinary consulship remained notable. Even in its diluted form, the institution of the consulship lasted in the Western empire until AD 534 (in the East until 541). GSA

See Bagnall, R. et al. (1987) *Consuls of the Later Roman Empire*; Broughton, T. (1960) *The Magistrates of the Roman Republic*; Lintott, A. (1999) *The Constitution of the Roman Republic*.

consumer city Originally developed by Max Weber as one in a series of ideal types of city, and subsequently enlarged on by Moses Finley, this model seeks to characterize the ancient city. A 'consumer city' is one where the major income for the urban consumers comes from rural rents, the products of local rural labour supply the subsistence needs of the urban population, and manufacturing and inter-regional commerce are 'essentially petty'. Many ancient historians have found the model very attractive, in that it seems to fit well with literary testimony of the ruling classes on their economic outlook and urban-centred lifestyle. Finley, in particular, argued that the parasitical relationship between consumer city and its rural hinterland operated in favour of highly localized, small-scale economies and against economic development, urban manufacturing and inter-regional trade. In recent times, opposition to the model has increased, in part because Weber's ideal types were essentially designed to model the economic characteristics of pre-industrial cities, whereas the 'consumer city' has become a leitmotif for the ancient city as a political and social centre. In addition, the growth in archaeological evidence has shown that the urban economy was far less uniform than is sometimes assumed and that some towns, notably harbour cities, had a much greater manufacturing and commercial engagement. (see Leptiminus for instance) DJM

See Hansen, M. H. (2004) The concept of the consumption city applied to the Greek polis, in T. H. Nielsen, ed., *Once Again: studies in the ancient Greek polis* 9–47; Mattingly and Salmon, *Economies beyond Agriculture*; Parkins, H., ed. (1997) *Ancient Urbanism: beyond the consumer city*.

 Leptiminus.

consumers and consumption The classical world could be called a 'consumer society', in that the consumption of goods was a factor in creating personal and social identity. This is not surprising in societies where wealth, and thus the power to consume, were closely connected with power and status. Consuming particular kinds of goods, including special foods, clothing (see dress) and perfumes, signalled a person's aspirations.

Much of the long-distance and large-scale trade in classical antiquity documented by archaeological remains consisted of products such as wine, olive oil, fish sauce, perfume and spices and other condiments. Quality was of major importance: good-quality wine or oil was far more desirable than poor, and quality was a factor in the amount of prestige that could be derived from the consumption of such products. Many of these products were consumed in large amounts by the richest people, but even quite poor people were able to consume them on special occasions (such as religious festivals). The fictional, social-climbing eponymous freedman in Petronius' *Trimalchio's Dinner* insists that his dinner guests know the exotic origin and splendid quality of everything he is serving. The foreign origin of commodities such as perfume or textiles might also enhance their value. For example, the poets Sappho and Alkman, writing in the late 7th and early 6th centuries in different parts of the Greek world, both mention the desirability of Lydian headgear.

One form of conspicuous consumption was the habit of burying the dead with many expensive goods (see BURIAL), literally disposing of highly desirable goods. This practice is particularly common in (though not restricted to) earlier periods. A good example is the 9th-century BC graves from ATHENS, filled with pottery, jewellery, imported faience, perfume and metal items. This kind of consumption presumably enhanced the status and prestige of the living on the occasion of a FUNERAL. However, even the less well-off had aspirations to bury their dead with objects that conferred respect and identity: 193 of the 584 archaic (8th–6th century BC) graves at Pithekoussai (32 per cent) contained metal pins. Most graves had only one or two, but one grave contained 22 pins. This suggests that the consumption and disposal of goods as part of the construction of identity was not restricted to the wealthiest. LF

See Foxhall, L. (1998) Cargoes of the heart's desire, in N. Fisher and H. van Wees, eds, *Archaic Greece* 295–309.

Consus see GAMES, ROMAN.

contraception Because conception was seen as a very gradual process in which the seed 'set' and was slowly 'cooked' in the womb, little distinction was generally made in the ancient world between contraception and abortion; DRUGS which were taken as abortives were usually presented as multi-purpose expulsives, meaning that 'bringing on a late period' could be a euphemism for an early abortion, while even infanticide could be seen as a particularly late abortion. The medical writer SORANUS, whose *Gynaecology* was produced during the reigns of TRAJAN and HADRIAN, was unusual in recommending contraception, which prevented the male and female seeds from uniting, in preference to abortion, because it was a safer form of birth control.

Ways of preventing conception included the use of non-fertile sexual positions, *coitus interruptus*, and attempts to expel the seed from the womb immediately after intercourse by jumping up and down or inducing sneezing. The belief that the fertile period was immediately after a menstrual period meant that the ancient 'safe period' would have overlapped with our 'fertile period'. Amulets and charms were also used; one that survives on a 4th-century PAPYRUS involves making a frog swallow the seeds of bitter vetch soaked in menstrual blood, and claims that one year of contraception is ensured by each seed swallowed. In the HIPPOCRATIC medical texts of the 5th and late 4th centuries BC, the emphasis is on fertility rather than its suppression, so that only one contraceptive recipe is given, using a substance called *misy*, which may be COPPER ore. In contrast, in the Roman world, medical writers listed substances that could be applied to the vagina, or inserted on sponges as pessaries, to prevent conception. These included OLIVE OIL, vinegar and various resins, which may have altered the pH balance of the vagina, making it hostile to sperm.

The motivation for using contraception varied. It has been argued that the repository for contraceptive knowledge was PROSTITUTES, with medical men then learning from them. Certainly someone whose value depended on it would be more likely to have an interest in contraception. Soranus condemns those whose interest in contraception is solely the preservation of their beauty, or the protection of secrecy in an ADULTEROUS relationship, but accepts that sometimes it is necessary if the womb is small and the woman's health would be endangered by PREGNANCY.

The problem with all ancient contraceptives lay in the fact that polypharmacy was the norm in ancient medicine. Since people would be using several different remedies at once, and possibly also using charms and amulets, in the event of successful prevention of pregnancy it would be very difficult to know what had worked and to transmit this information to others. It is not possible to know whether the majority of people in the ancient world were even interested in contraception; with high infant mortality, there may have been more concern with improving one's chances of conception. Furthermore, infanticide – unlike contraception and abortion – meant that it was possible to discover the sex of a child before deciding whether or not to rear it. (see also MEDICINE) HK

cooking and cuisine Our understanding of ancient diet and tastes comes from texts (medical, AGRICULTURAL, philosophic and gastronomic), palaeobotanical investigation (the EXCAVATION and identification of seeds and food remains), and continuity in traditional food-ways. Classical cuisine relied primarily on the MEDITERRANEAN triad of CEREALS, OLIVES and the VINE, each associated with a deity: DEMETER, ATHENA and DIONYSOS respectively. This edible triad provided a basic complement of proteins, carbohydrates, fats and vitamins.

In the HOMERIC poems, meaty feasts are intricately wrapped in a RITUAL context. Portions of CATTLE, SHEEP, GOATS and PIGS were distributed after public sacrifices, but these ANIMALS were too valuable (for their labour and other renewable by-products) for everyday slaughter. Sausages were more common, supplementing occasional wild game, FISH, and other marine fauna as protein sources. The chicken, or 'Persian bird', was introduced to Greece by the 6th century BC, though eggs were not commonly consumed until the Roman period. In an essentially meatless diet, olive oil was an essential source of lipids. Vegetables included beans, lentils, turnips, onions, radishes, cabbage, cucumbers and lettuces. Followers of the philosopher PYTHAGORAS refused to eat broad beans, probably because they believed that beans housed transmigrating human souls. Carrots and asparagus were used in medicines; Romans would later grow carrots just for their tasty tops. Cheese, honey, nuts and FRUIT (largely figs, apples and pears) filled out a basic menu, washed down with WINE. Alexander's army, in its conquest of the PERSIAN EMPIRE, encountered new fruits such as the apricot, peach, cherry, lemon, orange and citron. For SPICES, Greeks could rely on the naturally abundant sage, rosemary, thyme, bay, fennel, basil, coriander and anise. They also imported cinnamon, myrrh, cardamom and the mysterious SILPHIUM, such a potent and valuable plant that it was featured on the coins of its source-city, CYRENE (in Libya), and was practically extinct by the 1st century AD.

Cereals supplied most calories for most people. Barley, ill-suited to leavening, was hearty fare when roasted or made into unleavened cakes or porridge. Wheat was increasingly used during the 6th to 4th centuries BC; most was imported from the BLACK SEA regions and Egypt. In fact, protecting foreign grain became a major factor in Athens' military policy during the PELOPONNESIAN WAR. BREAD-making required a quern and grinder, ideally of volcanic stone. The flour, mixed with water and sometimes leaven, was kneaded and then baked in an upright terracotta oven. One could also use a large terracotta dome-shaped lid: build a fire underneath, remove the coals when hot, place the dough underneath and heap the coals over the top. Baking takes about half an hour.

The existence of KITCHENS in houses excavated at OLYNTHOS has been inferred from the presence of permanent hearths and probable openings to the sky. Whether or not this is so, terracotta braziers (still used in North Africa) were more common. Cooking stands and tripods held pots over the charcoal-fed flame for warming, stewing, steaming or boiling. There were also grills, frying-pans, graters, strainers, funnels, mixing bowls, knives, ladles and numerous storage jars from small jugs to *pithoi* more than 1m tall. Cooking was done by WOMEN in most HOUSEHOLDS that were unable to afford SLAVES. The slave-cook became a stock comic figure in NEW COMEDY, ridiculed for their cost and their bragging, scheming and pinching. Slaves, however, created the sort of cuisine described in the late 2nd-century AD *Deipnosophistai* (*Philosophers at Dinner*) of ATHENAEUS, our main source for Greek cookery.

Roman authors often idealized the simple and rustic food-ways of their ancestors, but with the Republic's expansion into the hellenistic world during the 3rd–1st centuries BC, new foods, techniques and cooks flooded into Rome. This influx sparked a conservative counter-reaction every 20 years or so: sumptuary laws limited the type, amount and cost of food. For instance, the *lex Fannia* forbade the consumption of fattened hens (to save grain); clever farmers castrated roosters and produced fattened capons instead. Never very successful, such legislation was abandoned by the late 1st century AD, a time known for its GOURMETS. To one such celebrity, Marcus Gavius APICIUS, was attributed the lone surviving cookbook from antiquity, though it is actually a later compilation containing many Greek recipes. Among the named concoctions of Apicius is his riceless version of *paella*: cook a leek bulb, some mint, tiny fish, meatballs, rooster testicles and piglet sweetbreads together in olive oil, *garum*, wine, honey and spices, thicken with crumbled dough, and top with pepper.

Garum (*liquamen*) owes its fame to its ubiquity in Roman cooking. Prized not only for its potent aroma and taste, *garum* was concentrated protein and added SALT as well – similar FISH SAUCE is still made in south-east Asia. In the early 19th century, a variant purée from southern France (where by the 5th century BC Greek colonists were producing *garum*) was smeared on flat bread and topped with olives, onions and tomatoes – an ancestor of modern pizza.

Roman kitchens, originally consisting of a hearth in the atrium, eventually gained their own space (often shared with a latrine, with all its health hazards) by the early 2nd century BC. A well-equipped kitchen would have a stove built of a tiled platform supported by arched supports 60–90 cm above the floor. Small fires fed by CHARCOAL and wood would be built on the platform, with cooking wares set on tripods set over the flame. Other pots and implements were hung on the wall or stacked in a corner. Slave-cooks would prepare food on a wooden work-table (known from artistic representations but not found in excavations). A sink and drain allowed cleaning afterwards, but the room was generally undecorated, dark and smelly. PWF

See Giacosa, I. G. (1992) *A Taste of Ancient Rome*; Toussaint-Samat, M. (1994) *A History of Food*; Wilkins, J., Harvey, D. and Dobson, M., eds. (1995) *Food in Antiquity*.

 KITCHENS AND KITCHEN UTENSILS.

copper The use of copper had been widespread in Europe for many centuries before the rise of the classical civilizations. The advent of IRON, however, resulted in copper and COPPER ALLOYS being used for less utilitarian purposes. The alloys were now used primarily in the manufacture of small items of JEWELLERY and HOUSEHOLD fittings, as well as some larger items such as statues and FIGURINES.

Copper ores are found throughout much of Europe and the Near East, and were extensively mined well before the rise of classical civilizations. CYPRUS was an important source at one time and gave the Romans their word for copper (*cuprum*). By the beginning of the imperial period the production of copper at Cyprus had diminished somewhat, but it was still famous for the quality of its product. Other famous sources of copper included Campania and Spain, but archaeological evidence shows that copper was produced in many Roman PROVINCES. The copper was smelted like most other metals and was tapped from the furnace into round ingots. This metal was rarely used on its own, however, but is found in alloys with other metals such as TIN, LEAD and zinc. (see also FIGURINES, BRONZE; METALLURGY; SCULPTURE) DD

 METALLURGY.

copper alloys Pure copper was used rarely in the ancient world. It was more common to alloy the copper with at least one other element. TIN was added to produce bronze, and on occasion LEAD was added, especially where the alloy was to be used in the production of large and complex castings. Brass (an alloy containing zinc) was almost unknown before the last quarter of the 1st century BC. It became an important alloy when it was used to produce some of the coins for AUGUSTUS' new currency.

A wide range of copper alloys was available in the Roman empire, yet many patterns can be detected. The clearest is the link between artefact type and alloy composition. In some cases these links are dictated by the physical properties of the alloys. Roman copper alloy mirrors were made of an alloy containing much higher than usual levels of tin (20–30 per cent) which produced a silvery-white metal with a highly reflective surface. Large and complex castings usually had at least some lead added, which would ensure that the molten metal remained fluid as long as possible and would correctly fill the mould. On the other hand, lead tends to make alloys brittle and so sheet and wire, which must be subjected to repeated hammering, were rarely made from alloys containing more than 1 per cent lead.

Other differences in alloy composition are more subtle and harder to relate to differences in manufacturing TECHNOLOGY. The subtle but distinct differences in the alloys used for many 1st-century AD brooches are consistent across the empire and suggest the use of recipes (PLINY THE ELDER, *Natural History* 34.20.94–8) in the manufacture of different types of brooch. DD

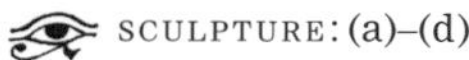 SCULPTURE: (a)–(d).

coral A marine creature, consisting of a tube-like polyp which lives inside a skeleton made from the calcium carbonate secretions of its own body. The ancients believed it to be a marine plant that petrified when taken out of the water. OVID relates that this property was absorbed from the gorgon MEDUSA's severed head when Perseus rested it on the beach (*Metamorphoses* 4.740–53). It lives in warm and temperate waters, including the MEDITERRANEAN, where it is still harvested off the coast of Malta and around SICILY. A pink, tubular variety lives in the Red sea and was popular in pre-dynastic Egypt.

Coral appears in the ARCHAEOLOGICAL record mainly as JEWELLERY, either as inlays or in bead form. Beads, thought to be of fossilized coral, have been found at Çatal Höyük and date to the 6th millennium BC. The colours range from white to reds and oranges, which were the more popular for jewellery, but coral also occurs in black. The most prized variety was the deep red coral from the Mediterranean which is today called 'oxblood'. Examples of this have been found in PTOLEMAIC Egypt, and in the time of the Roman empire it was exported to INDIA. However, coral was never a common ornament, and in Greece it has only been found at the sanctuary of HERA Limenia at Perachóra (anc. Peiraion) near CORINTH, where an intaglio and scaraboid have been excavated, dating to the 6th century BC. NJW

See Ogden, J. (1982) *Jewellery of the Ancient World*.

Corbulo (Gnaeus Domitius Corbulo) A major senatorial figure of the late Julio-Claudian period, connected through numerous siblings and step-siblings to the highest aristocracy. His stepsister Caesonia was the last wife of Gaius CALIGULA and was murdered with him. His daughter Domitia Longina, wife of DOMITIAN, joined the plot that ended the Flavian dynasty in AD 96. Corbulo is well known from literature (partly based on his memoirs) and inscriptions, not least the great CUSTOMS tariff at PALMYRA.

He (rather than his father) is probably the (suffect) CONSUL of 39, and he was governor of Germania Inferior (Lower Germany) under CLAUDIUS (AD 47), being awarded *ornamenta triumphalia*. While in GERMANY Corbulo established a reputation as a man of military action and a stern disciplinarian. He set his troops to dig a CANAL between the RHINE and the Meuse, and was restrained by Claudius from the vigorous campaigns he set in train and planned.

With the collapse of Claudius' arrangements for ARMENIA in late 54, NERO appointed Corbulo to restore Roman prestige; his efforts established him as the leading general of his time. As special governor of Galatia and CAPPADOCIA he restored discipline, then imposed Roman control on ARMENIA, capturing Artaxata (58) and Tigranocerta (59), and crowned a non-Arsakid king (60). He was made governor of SYRIA after Ummidius Quadratus died. When the situation in Armenia collapsed, Corbulo was granted a wider *imperium* once more. In 63 Tiridates, the Arsakid nominee for the Armenian throne, offered his diadem before Nero's image in Corbulo's camp at Rhandeia. A victim of suspicion in 66, Corbulo was called to join Nero in Greece and invited to kill himself. His reputation rests on 'old school' ideas of military discipline and military successes in a difficult sphere of operation. DLK

See Tacitus, *Annals* books 12–15; Cassius Dio, books 60–3.

Corcyra see KERKYRA.

cord see STRING.

Corduba see BAETICA; LUCAN; SENECA THE YOUNGER.

core–periphery Also known as 'centre–periphery' and 'world-systems analysis', 'core–periphery' models have been used by historians and archaeologists to elucidate the mechanisms of long-distance interaction between complex 'core civilizations' and less developed societies. Such models supersede the discredited notion of 'diffusion', and build on a structural–functionalist concept of society. This new theorization was first formulated by the neo-marxist historian Immanuel Wallerstein with respect to the dramatic rise of capitalist economies in the West in the past 500 years. According to Wallerstein, this gave rise to a 'world-system' based on unequal long-distance structural relationships of exchange between dominant core societies of the West and subordinated 'Third World' societies on their periphery. Typically, exchange is mediated through *emporia* or ports-of-trade, and induces inescapable social change within the peripheral nations implicated in this relationship.

Following and modifying Wallerstein's theory, archaeologists and historians have detected the operation of 'world-systems' in the ancient world. For instance, it is claimed that the Roman empire had an indirect role in promoting social differentiation and structural change within neighbouring tribal societies in GAUL and BRITAIN, through competition between native élites to monopolize TRADE within the Roman superpower. Such trade was often mediated through *emporia*. Although such world-system theories tend to be mechanistic, it is suggested that they have a greater power to explain qualitative social change than the traditional culture-history school. CMF

See Champion, T. C., ed. (1989) *Centre and Periphery*; Cunliffe, B. (1988) *Greeks, Romans and Barbarians*; Rowlands, M. et al., eds. (1987) *Centre and Periphery in the Ancient World*; Bilde, P. et al., eds. (1993) *Centre and Periphery in the Hellenistic World*.

Corfu see KERKYRA.

Corinna Poetess born in Tanagra, BOIOTIA. Her poems have arrived to us, in fragmentary state, in the Boiotian dialect of the end of the 3rd century BC; an alternative tradition, however, makes her contemporary with PINDAR. The veracity of this tradition has been doubted, and the later date has become more prevalent, though not certain. Her work was ignored by ALEXANDRIAN scholars, but Corinna was rediscovered and valued in post-Alexandrian times for her poetic abilities and as a source of erudition. The myths in her poems are local, even more so than those in other authors. Her compositions, thought to have been written mainly for local FESTIVALS, are partly choral and focus on 'cultural' myths and HEROES. The best-known fragment narrates a singing competition between Mt Helikon and Mt Kithairon. The fragment contains the final vote and the proclamation of Kithairon as victor. In response, Helikon reacts in rage by flinging rocks or, according to another interpretation, throwing himself down the rocks. RBC

See Bowra, C. M. (1953) The daughters of Asopus, in *Problems in Greek Poetry* 54–65; Kirkwood, G. M. (1974) *Early Greek Monody*; Rayor, D. J. (1991) *Sappho's Lyre: archaic lyric and women poets of ancient Greece*; Segal, C. (1975) Pebbles in golden urns: the date and style of Corinna, *Eranos* 73: 1–8.

Corinth (Korinthos) City whose territory (the Korinthia: c. 900 sq km, 350 sq miles) contained the isthmus which joined the PELOPONNESE to central Greece. The site was among the earliest exploited in

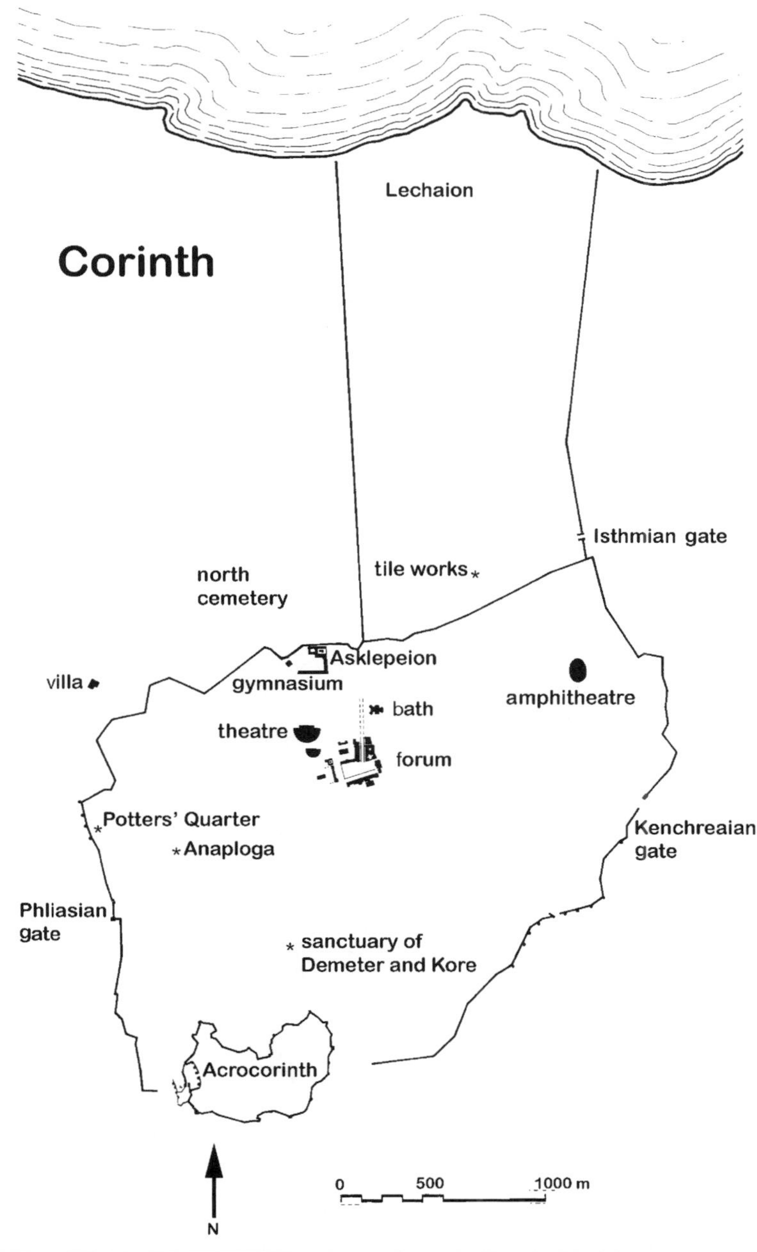

CORINTH: (a) plan of ancient Corinth.

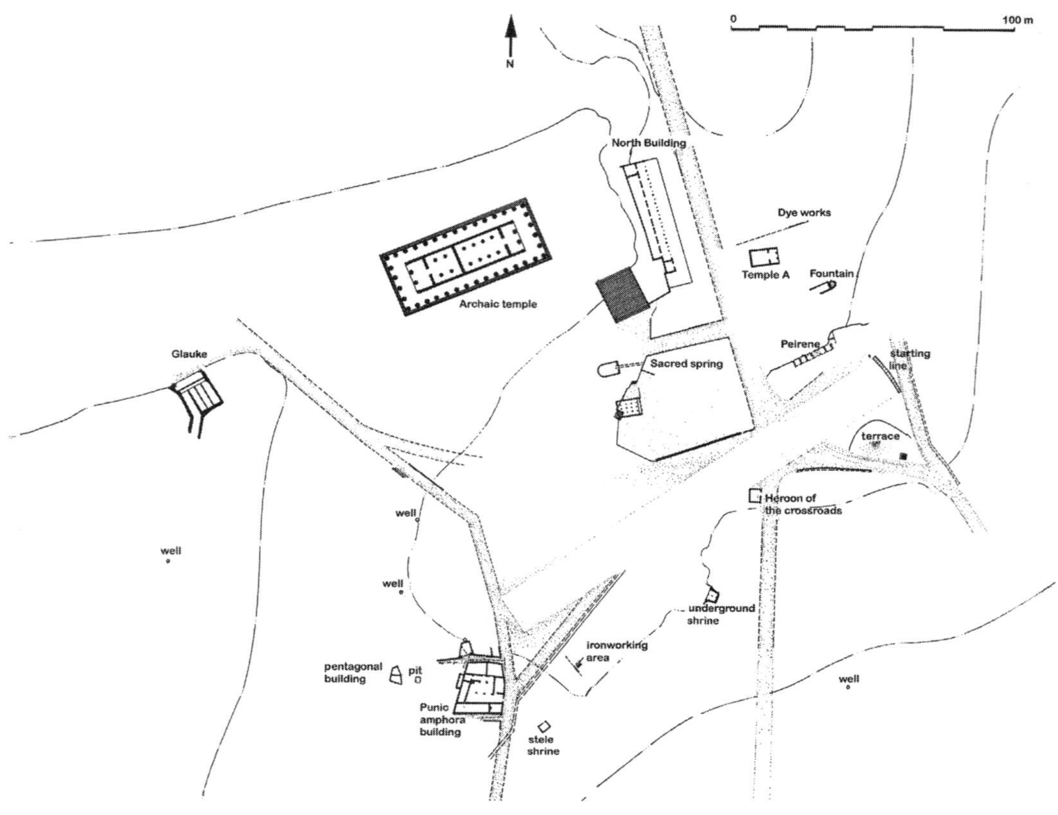

CORINTH: (b) classical Corinth (second half of 5th century BC).

the peninsula. It enjoyed copious springs and access to a rich coastal plain as well as a defensible, if unusually high, citadel (Acrocorinth) and the land route over the isthmus itself. Corinthians helped to lead Greece out of the so-called Dark Age (c.1100–900 BC). Easy access by sea to the west brought them to DELPHI, Ithaca and EPIRUS by the mid-8th century. Colonies were founded at Kerkyra (Corfu in the IONIAN ISLANDS) and SYRACUSE in Sicily, and a regular pattern of westward trade was established. The governing Bacchiad aristocracy was exceptionally exclusive. In 657 BC (a broadly accurate traditional date) it was overthrown by Kypselos, who established the earliest and one of the longest lasting Greek TYRANNIES and passed power to his son Periander (Periandros), who was for ARISTOTLE (and even HERODOTOS) the typical repressive tyrant. He built an artificial HARBOUR at Lechaion and a trackway (*diolkos*) to transport ships across the isthmus. Periander's nephew could not maintain power, and from c.585 a narrow but relatively enlightened OLIGARCHY ruled.

Corinth was among the most advanced cities in archaic Greece. The economy was already remarkably diverse in the 7th century. As always in Greece, AGRICULTURE was central, but there was also MANUFACTURING (including POTTERY, some of which reached exquisitely high standards), trade and public building. Sacred PROSTITUTION at the temple of APHRODITE, probably adopted from the East, was almost unique in the Greek world. Corinth played an important role in the development of the Doric order, and exported stone for 4th-century temples at Delphi and Epidauros; Corinthians 'despised craftsmen least of all the Greeks' (Herodotos 2.167). The tyrants established Corinth's naval interest; when Sparta began to make alliances, Corinth brought it a fleet, and remained an important ally for nearly two centuries. Corinth tried with some success c.500 to limit Spartan primacy, but helped to defend Greece against XERXES and was inscribed with Sparta and Athens at the head of the Serpent column commemorating the victory. Corinth took an active part in the so-called first Peloponnesian war of the 450s, but accepted the Thirty Years' Peace until bitter resentment against Athens over the Kerkyra dispute made it an eager advocate of the PELOPONNESIAN WAR. Subsequent events demonstrated that its naval capacity was outdated. Corinthian agitation against the peace of NIKIAS caused serious difficulties for Sparta. The city joined the anti-Spartan coalition in the Corinthian war of the 390s, during which its territory suffered extensively. Sparta reimposed a favourable regime, and the Corinthians remained loyal until Sparta's decline after LEUKTRA (371). They fought against PHILIP II at CHAIRONEIA, but became the centre of the 'league of Corinth' by which he hoped to exercise control; Acrocorinth was garrisoned by successive Macedonian rulers as one of the 'fetters of Greece'. The city mostly remained under external domination until it was destroyed as an example to the troublesome Greeks by the Roman general Mummius in 146. Refounded by JULIUS CAESAR a century later, it became the seat of the governor of the province of Achaia.

The oracular sanctuary of Hera Akraia at Peiraion (mod. Perachóra), on a peninsula in the gulf of Corinth opposite the city, flourished from Geometric to hellenistic times. JBS

See Pausanias, book 2; American School excavations in *Corinth, Kenchreai* and *Isthmia* volumes (1929–) and in the journal *Hesperia*; Engels, D. (1990) *Roman Corinth*; Gregory, T. E. (1994) *The Corinthia in the Roman Period*; Legon, R. P. (2004) Megaris, Corinthia and Sikyonia, in Hansen and Nielsen, *Inventory* 462–71; Payne, H. G. G., Dunbabin, T. J. et al. (1940–62) *Perachora*, 2 vols.; Salmon, J. B. (1984) *Wealthy Corinth*; Wiseman, J. (1978) *The Land of the Ancient Corinthians*.

 AEGEAN SEA: (a); PELOPONNESE.

Corinthian war 395–386 BC With the Spartans involved in an imperialistic drive in Asia Minor, some states from the Greek mainland – THEBES, Athens, ARGOS and CORINTH – with financial encouragement from PERSIA, formed a quadruple alliance against Sparta. Initially provoked by the Thebans, who supported the Lokrians against Sparta's ally PHOKIS in a border dispute, LYSANDER the Spartan commander was killed in the first battle at Nemea. As a consequence of this war, the Spartans were forced to withdraw their main force from Asia, though fighting continued there until 386 BC. Owing to their lack of success in either the war in Asia or that on the mainland, the Spartans tried to make peace in summer 392 at SARDIS and again the following winter in Sparta. The other Greeks refused, since the terms required that the Greeks in Asia Minor would be given into Persian control. In 387 the Spartans won Persian support, and together they forced the other Greeks to make peace in 386 in the Persian-guaranteed agreement known as the King's Peace. LGM

See Diodorus Siculus 14.81–117; Xenophon, *Hellenica* 3.5–5.1.

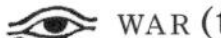 WAR (table).

Coriolanus (Gnaeus or Gaius Marcius Coriolanus) Tragically heroic figure of the early REPUBLIC. A young Roman noble, he received the name Coriolanus for his part in the capture of the town of Corioli from the Volsci in 493 BC. Exiled for tyrannical behaviour (and for opposing a distribution of grain to the people in time of famine), he sought revenge by surrendering himself to the Volscians of Antium. Accepted as their leader, he led the Volscian army to the gates of Rome; he was only turned back by the pleas of his wife Volumnia and mother Veturia (Vergilia and Volumnia in PLUTARCH). According to most versions, he was subsequently killed by the Volsci.

The story's basis in fact is inevitably doubted. None of the main figures appears in the lists (*fasti*) of Roman MAGISTRATES. The MARCII were a PLEBEIAN family, which is problematic since the point of the story lies in Coriolanus' arrogant PATRICIAN behaviour. But the historical context is good. Rome and Latium were threatened by the Volsci in this period; the ARISTOCRATIC 'horizontal social mobility' that the story illustrates characterizes the period and parallels the movement into Rome of the TARQUINS and CLAUDII. As well as being recounted by LIVY, Plutarch and others in antiquity, the story was made famous in English literature by Shakespeare's play of the same name, largely based upon Plutarch. JRWP

See Plutarch, *Coriolanus* (in *Makers of Rome*), trs. I. Scott-Kilvert (1965); Livy 2.33–40.

Corippus (Flavius Cresconius Corippus) AFRICAN POET, who produced two major works. *Johannis* was an epic poem in eight books written c.AD 549, recounting the recent campaign of the Byzantine general John Troglita against the Berbers in Africa. *In laudem Iustini augusti minoris*, a panegyric in four books, was written in honour of Justin II in c.566. Corippus was probably a teacher (*grammaticus*) from a small town in Africa, and later a wandering poet writing PANEGYRICS of cities (*patriae*) for wealthy patrons of cities. Corippus travelled to CONSTANTINOPLE where he produced the accession poem for Justin II and died some time after 567. The *Johannis* provides information on African topography and the names, leaders and customs of many of the Berber tribes and sub-tribes in the provinces of Zeugitan Africa, Byzacene, Tripolitania and even Numidia in the early 6th century. The panegyric for Justin II is valuable as a source for the ceremonial aspects of the Byzantine court in the 6th century. RBH

See Cameron, A. (1983) Corippus' *Iohannis*: epic of Byzantine Africa, in F. Cairns, ed., *Papers of the Liverpool Latin Seminar*, vol. 4, 167–80.

corn see CEREALS.

Cornelia b. c.190 BC, d. before 100 Mother of the GRACCHI, daughter of SCIPIO AFRICANUS, and wife of Tiberius Sempronius Gracchus. Of her 12 children by Sempronius, only three survived to adulthood: a daughter, Sempronia, who married Scipio Africanus the younger (SCIPIO AEMILIANUS), and the famous TRIBUNES Tiberius and Gaius Sempronius Gracchus. Her husband died c.153, around the time of Gaius' birth, and her devotion to the upbringing of her sons was often remarked upon in antiquity. A highly educated woman, the EDUCATION she ensured for them (largely Greek) was considered a formative influence, as was her own desire for their glory. PLUTARCH relates her complaint that she was known as Scipio's mother-in-law, not the mother of the Gracchi. A surviving statue base demonstrates that she got her wish: 'Cornelia, daughter of Africanus, mother of the Gracchi'. She refused to remarry despite offers from, among others, Ptolemy VIII Physkon of Egypt – an illustration of the cultured and philhellene circles in which she moved. Part of what is probably a contemporary, if not actually genuine, letter from her to Gaius survives in the writings of Cornelius NEPOS. CICERO read and praised her letters. She was famous for her stoicism at her sons' deaths. A more negative tradition accused her of assisting and encouraging their disruptive politicking, and even of the death of her son-in-law in 129, after he opposed Tiberius. JRWP

See Plutarch, *Tiberius* and *Gaius Gracchus*; Bernstein, A. H. (1978) *Tiberius Sempronius Gracchus*; Horsfall, N. (1989) *Cornelius Nepos*.

Cornelii Greatest of the Republican clans of Rome. PATRICIAN, and a *maior gens*, the family gave its name to the TRIBE Cornelia and is the most frequent name in the lists *(fasti)* of Republican MAGISTRATES. A quarter of all *principes senatus* (heads of the senate) and *pontifices maximi* (chief priests of Rome) were Cornelii.

The first Cornelius shared the consulship with the first FABIUS in 485 BC. Several branches soon developed, distinguished by *cognomina*, but the links between them are often untraceable. The two greatest branches were the Scipiones and the Lentuli. Some, such as the Cinnae and Sisennae, may not belong to the patrician house. The Scipiones are forever associated with the PUNIC WARS. CORNELIA, daughter of SCIPIO AFRICANUS and mother of the GRACCHI, is one of the few women of the period to appear in our sources. The disgraced CONSUL of 71 BC, Publius Cornelius Lentulus Sura, led CATILINE's conspirators in Rome, encouraged by an ORACLE that three Cornelii would rule Rome; Lucius Cornelius Cinna (consul 86–84) and Lucius Cornelius SULLA Felix (DICTATOR 82–79) were the others. He was executed, along with other conspirators, on the orders of CICERO in 63. By the end of the Republic the name had spread phenomenally, and many later bearers of the name are unrelated. JRWP

Coronea see KORONEIA.

Corsica (Greek *Kyrnos*, Latin *Cyrnus*) The island receives scant notice in ancient sources. A short-lived Phokaian Greek colony at Alaia, founded c.565 BC, was abandoned after intervention by the ETRUSCANS 30 years later. The Etruscans controlled much of the island until it came under the dominance of CARTHAGE during the 4th century. Caught up in the 3rd-century power struggle for MEDITERRANEAN supremacy between Carthage and Rome, Corsica fell to the latter in 238. Organized with SARDINIA as a joint PROVINCE in 227, Corsica became a separate *provincia* in the early empire.

STRABO calls it a wild land, its inhabitants wilder than animals: its fertile eastern plains were plague-ridden in summer and subject to BANDIT raids. SENECA gives an equally dismal assessment, hardly surprising since he was exiled there. Festus adds that its people were untrustworthy. Aleria, the provincial capital founded by SULLA (on the site of Alaia), and Mariana, settled by MARIUS, were the only two significant towns. Itineraries list a single trunk ROAD, linking these with the southern port of Pallae (Bonifacio?). A detachment of the Misenum fleet was stationed in the lagoon at Portus Dianae, north of Aleria. PTOLEMY lists 14 other places in the rugged interior, but all are likely to have been *oppida*, like the excavated example at Lurinum, rather than fully fledged towns. Yet even the Vanacini tribe possessed the trappings of the IMPERIAL CULT with *sacerdotes Augusti* (priests of Augustus) by the Flavian period. DIODORUS mentions Corsican HONEY, milk and meat, but the sole significant export was probably TIMBER. Corsican pine and fir were especially prized, and THEOPHRASTOS reports that in height and girth the Corsican trees surpassed those of Latium and southern Italy. RJAW

 SARDINIA and CORSICA.

Cos see KOS.

Cosa Latin colony of Rome, founded in 273 BC on a hill overlooking the Tyrrhenian coast of Italy 140 km (90 miles) north-west of Rome. Located in territory Rome had recently taken from the ETRUSCAN town of Vulci, Cosa was probably founded to serve as a stronghold. The earliest structure, a massive polygonal wall enclosing the colony's c.13 ha site (32 acres), attests to its defensive purpose. Excavations conducted by the American Academy in Rome since the late 1940s have revealed the features of a traditional Roman town into which the colony developed over the next two centuries.

Cosa's two summits contained TEMPLES; the higher was the location of the *capitolium*. Main streets on a grid plan led to the temples and FORUM; narrower streets divided blocks of houses. One long side of the forum contained a temple, BASILICA, *comitium* and CURIA; a monumental triple ARCH stood at the northern entrance. Recent excavations have revealed SHOPS and houses on the other sides of the forum. At the foot of the hill, a port was constructed with inner and outer HARBOURS, breakwaters, docks and a rock-cut channel designed to prevent silting. Beyond the walls of Cosa, field surveys have located centuriated fields and the remains of farms of the Etruscan, Roman Republican and Roman imperial periods.

A second introduction (*deductio*) of colonists arrived in 197 BC. Cosa suffered a widespread destruction after 71 and was partially rebuilt under AUGUSTUS. A smaller town existed in the imperial period. DLS

See Brown, F. E. (1980) *Cosa*; McCann, A. M. (1987) *The Roman Port and Fishery of Cosa*.

 ITALY, ROMAN: (b).

cosmetics Beautifying oneself through the application of cosmetics was almost as popular in ancient times as today. Egypt was particularly famous for its cosmetics, and CLEOPATRA was considered a connoisseur. The demands on ancient cosmetics were much simpler than in modern times: white skin, red cheeks and dark eyebrows and lashes. White skin could be achieved by a 'proper' Greek or Roman woman remaining at home with her WEAVING, but nature, then as now, often required a little support of the chemical kind. A whitening effect for skin was created (or emphasized) by the application of white LEAD (lead acetate), called *psimythion*. It could be produced by corroding lead in vinegar, then powdering and heating the resulting corrosions. The poisonous qualities of the cosmetic were noted by PLINY THE ELDER (*Natural History* 34.176).

Red cheeks were created with the use of rouge or blusher, which could be made from seaweed, from the plant bugloss or simply from crushed mulberries. Eyes were a focal feature for cosmetic enhancement. Eyebrows and the rims of the eyes could be darkened with kohl (a mixture of antimony sulphide and lead sulphate), or alternatively with soot or lamp-black.

Numerous names for specific items of the cosmetic wardrobe, as listed by ARISTOPHANES (fr. 332), are often difficult to reconcile with objects in the material record. Little vases (*aryballoi*) were used from the archaic period onward to hold PERFUMES in an oil solution, and the dried remains of white lead have been found in vases excavated from women's graves. NJW

See Dayagi-Mendels, M. (1989) *Perfumes and Cosmetics in the Ancient World.*

cosmology The Greek word *KOSMOS* has a primary sense of 'order'. Hence it is the order and arrangement of the universe as a whole that cosmology engages with. Add to this the Greek word *logos*, 'reason', and we get 'cosmology' with two fundamental meanings, either 'a reasoned account of the order of the universe' or 'the study of the reason or mind behind the order of the universe'. Thus cosmology will encompass everything in the universe, and attempt to explain the world from its creation to destruction, the origins of life, the nature of the GODS and especially the place of humans within the world system.

Both ancient Greek mythological and philosophical cosmologies are concerned particularly with the origins of the world. It is through the examination of how things began that the way things are now is proved, legitimated or criticized. Ancient cosmologies were written not as objective scientific or disinterested accounts of the universe, but as underpinnings to crucial assumptions about the world.

The mythological mode of thought is characterized by a tendency to personify gods and draw analogies with human life. In MYTH are found various single principles from which all things originally came forth: from Night perhaps, or Okeanos – sometimes described as the origin of gods and humans – or from a chasm (Chaos) as in HESIOD's *Theogony.* Gods, and parts of the world personified as gods, emerge first, with Eros, god of love and thus clearly necessary for creation, often among the first. The parts of the world separate out to form earth, sea, air and sky. The divine marriage of the Earth-mother and Sky-father – personified as gendered creative opposites – leads to the birth of gods, humans and ANIMALS.

The earliest Greek PHILOSOPHERS, the PRESOCRATICS in the 6th and 5th centuries BC, tended to concentrate more on finding the primordial physical principles from which all things came, and to move away, at least to some degree, from PERSONIFICATION and human analogies. Various single primordial creative principles were put forward (e.g. Thales: water; Anaximenes: air; Heraclitus: fire). Others had two creative principles (e.g. Xenophanes: earth and water), but four principles were established by Empedokles: earth, air, fire and water, a division on the microscopic level that matches the obvious division of the macroscopic world into land, sea, air and the fiery *aithêr* of SUN, MOON and stars. These elements ('roots' in Empedokles) are eternal fundamental particles that create all MATTER by their combination, separation and recombination in different mixtures. Empedokles, then, divided the world into its constituent parts in a way not too different from Hesiod's division of Earth and Sky, whose union and separation were the cause of the birth of all things. But for Empedokles, this creative union and separation occurred on a small rather than a large scale.

Further thematic continuations from mythological cosmologies can be seen in Presocratic philosophy. The myth of the marriage and separation of Earth and Sky is a story of the union and separation of creative opposites, and this is just what we find in the Presocratics. Empedokles' four elements can be seen as pairs of opposites – fire and water, earth and air – but the idea of creation from the union and separation of opposites is explicit in reports of Anaximander and Anaxagoras. For Anaximander the hot and the cold were instrumental in the creation of the world. Anaxagoras posited the dense and the rare, the dry and the moist, the hot and the cold, and the bright and the dark as creative opposites.

Again, the ideas of creation from the formlessness of Okeanos, Night or Hesiod's empty, formless *Chaos* are reflected in Anaximander's theory that the creative opposites emerged from the *apeiron* ('unlimited'), a boundless, indefinite or infinite 'substance'. In this idea we seem to see two sorts of chaos: the emptiness of Hesiod's Chaos and the undifferentiated random chaos of the ATOMISTS. DEMOKRITOS and Leukippos posited a very large variety of different 'uncuttable' elements from which all matter is formed: *atoma*, atoms, the smallest possible units of matter. All that exists is made of atoms and void, and creation takes place by a storm of elements in the infinite void, colliding, combining and separating randomly to form the matter that eventually creates a world. This random, undirected process leads to the creation of an infinite number of worlds in a universe infinite in time and space.

This materialist focus of Presocratic cosmology was challenged most successfully by PLATO's late venture into cosmology, the *Timaeus.* Borrowing physical ideas from the Presocratics, especially Empedokles, he blends them with PYTHAGOREAN MATHEMATICS and psychology, and his own theory of Forms, to produce an account of the creation of the world by a divine craftsman – a demiurge (*dêmiourgos*) – told in the form of a myth, a 'likely story', by the supposedly Pythagorean philosopher Timaeus (Timaios). The phenomenal world, for Plato, is a copy of an ontologically prior ideal model, and is a living divine creature, governed by reason; in contrast to Demokritos' infinity of worlds, it is unique.

This Platonic world-view was in turn challenged by the EPICUREANS, who adapted the atomic theory of Demokritos. The Epicurean world is one of an infinite number of worlds which are constantly coming into being and dying over infinite time in an infinite universe. Worlds are created by the random undirected collision of atoms. If, given infinite time and an infinite number of atoms, an infinite number of atomic collisions take place, then inevitably an infinite number of worlds will be created. Teleology and design are explicitly rebutted. Although the Epicureans insist the gods exist, they are relegated to the spaces between the worlds and take no part in human affairs. Further, to counter the perceived physical determinism of the Demokritean system, Epicurus introduced a random, uncaused swerve among the atoms, thus freeing events from any chain of causation and also granting humans FREE WILL.

The Epicureans' main rivals in hellenistic philosophy, the STOICS, in contrast, held that the world is suffused by an intelligent and divine designing fire which creates and controls all things in the world. Everything, then, comes about in a teleological process in accordance with the divine will: the world is a perfect expression of divine goodness and wisdom. GLC

See Furley, D. J. (1987) *The Greek Cosmologists*; Wright, M. R. (1995) *Cosmology in Antiquity*.

couches The Latin word *lectus* and the Greek *klinê* incorporate the meanings of both the modern terms 'bed' and 'couch' to describe a piece of FURNITURE which in the ancient world was used for sleeping, dining and working. Here the focus is on the use of this important piece of furniture for dining and working. Couches were usually lower than BEDS, and were made of wood with inlays of IVORY, BONE and precious metal. Mattresses and cushions, often brightly coloured, provided the necessary comfort.

The practice of reclining on couches while dining was introduced from the Near East and remained customary throughout the Greek and Roman period. Greek dining couches were arranged along the walls, often on a raised plinth. Roman dining couches (*lecti tricliniares*) were designed for three diners, reclining on their left side with their head facing the centre of the room. 'Respectable' women did not dine with men in the Greek period, and Roman ladies were expected to sit on chairs rather than recline on couches. Roman tombstones showing funerary banquets often show the male deceased reclining on a couch while female relatives are seated nearby. In POMPEII some GARDENS have STONE couches to create outdoor summer *triclinia*. A couch (*lectus lucubratorius*) could also be used for work, in particular reading and writing (PLINY THE YOUNGER, *Letters* 5.5.5). HE

 DINING; SYMPOSIUM.

councils The commonest state-form in the ancient world was the CITY-STATE, even under the ROMAN EMPIRE; and nearly all city-states had a governing council with wider or narrower powers.

The regular Greek word for council was *boulê*, denoting a body of citizens which oversaw the daily running of the state, prepared the business of the ASSEMBLY and implemented its decisions, and had certain judicial functions. Solon probably instituted a council of 400 at Athens (there is a parallel in 6th-century CHIOS). This was superseded in the reforms of KLEISTHENES by one of 500, appointed annually by lot from citizens over 30 pre-selected by the DEMES (and so called *prokritoi*), 50 from each of the ten tribes. Since two terms of office were the maximum, a relatively large percentage of the citizen body served on the council, and PERIKLES introduced payment. The 50 representatives of each tribe acted as presidents (*prytaneis*) for one-tenth of the year (a prytany), sitting daily (except on festivals) in the council house (*bouleutêrion*) and dining in the public hall (*tholos*). A different chairman (*epistatês*) was chosen by lot each day. The *boulê* remained in existence until the Roman period, with brief interruptions during the oligarchic regimes of 411 and 404/3 BC.

At Sparta, the *gerousia* was a council of elders, consisting of the two kings and 28 members over 60, elected for life from a restricted number of aristocratic families by acclamation of the citizens. It prepared business for the assembly and acted as a court in cases involving the kings and the penalties of death, EXILE and disfranchisement.

The Roman SENATE (*senatus*) was perhaps originally the PATRICIAN council (*patres*) advising the kings, but by the early REPUBLIC its size had been increased to 300 by the admission of PLEBEIAN 'enrolled members' (*conscripti*). SULLA increased the senate to 600 and CAESAR to 900, before Augustus reduced it to 600 again. After the *lex Ovinia* (late 4th century) senators effectively served for life, unless expelled by the CENSORS, and were mostly ex-MAGISTRATES; Sulla made the QUAESTORSHIP the qualification for entry. Senators had to be qualified for membership of the equestrian order; membership was largely (though not exclusively) hereditary and mainly comprised members of the noble families. The senators met in the senate house (*curia*) and spoke in a fixed order of seniority, beginning with the censors and CONSULS; the leading senator was called the *princeps senatus*. The senate in practice governed Rome, preparing legislation and issuing its own decrees (*senatus consulta*) which could, however, be vetoed by the TRIBUNES. It administered the state

COUNCILS: (a) reconstruction of the council chamber (*bouleutêrion*) at Miletos.

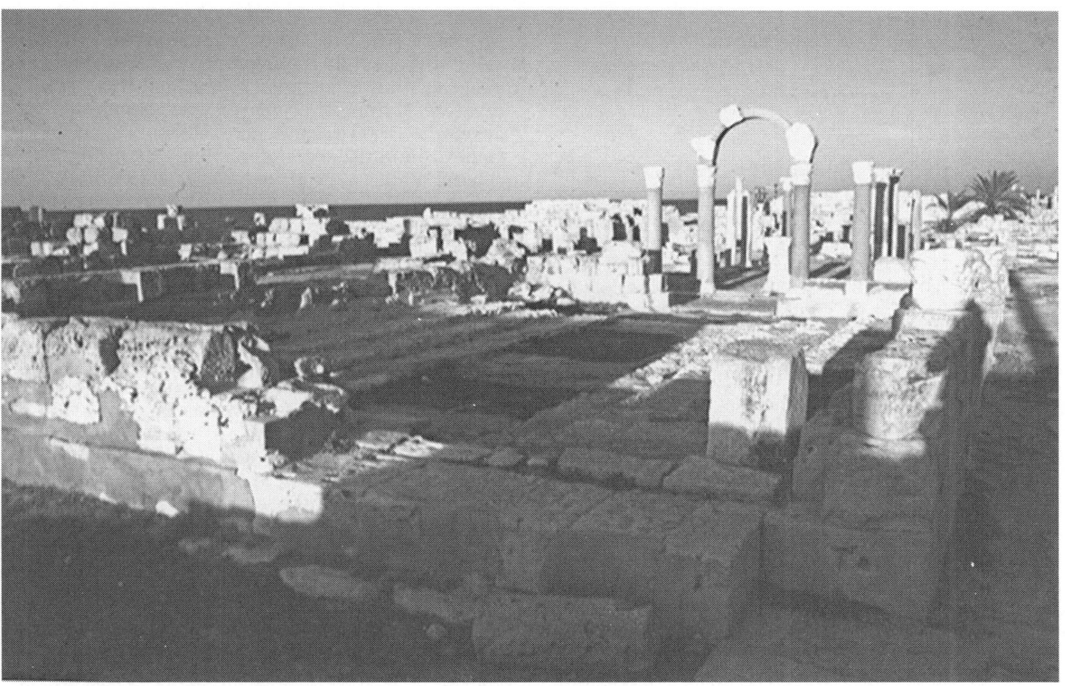

COUNCILS: (b) view of the curia at Sabratha, Libya. Note the raised steps on either side of the chamber for seating.

religion and finances, assigned magistrates to PROVINCES and dictated foreign policy, and set up courts of inquiry; its members served as jurors. But as a body of mainly ex-magistrates it acted not through legal power (*imperium*) but by virtue of its authority (*auctoritas*), a position undermined in the late Republic by the rise of politician GENERALS backed by armies. Under the PRINCIPATE the senate administered the public treasury (*aerarium*) and various provinces, issued binding decrees, and acted as a court. MJE

COUNTING: some principles of Greek and Roman numbers.

GREEK	
'Alphabetic' or 'Milesian'	
αψμζ	1,747
ωη	808
ιδ Μ,γτοβ	143,372
αψμζ ωη	808 1,747
'Herodianic' or 'acrophonic'	
Μ 𐅆𐅅 ΗΔΔΙΙΙ	15,623
ROMAN	
MDCCXXXXVII *or* MDCCXLVII	1,747

See Cartledge, P. A. (2002) *Sparta and Lakonia*; Rhodes, P. J. (1972) *The Athenian Boule*; Wiseman, T. P. (1971) *New Men in the Roman Senate*.

 SENATE: (a)–(b).

counting Practical counting and calculation were done using the fingers or an abacus, a device by which complex calculations can be done quickly and accurately. For writing numbers several systems were used. The most common system in the Greek-speaking world (the 'Milesian' system) used for numbers the usual 24 letters of the ALPHABET plus three others not found in the Attic alphabet. The first nine represent 1–9, the next nine 10–90, the remaining nine 100–900. The sequence begins again with the addition of a stroke below the letter, up to 9,000. 10,000 is represented by M (for *myrioi*), and for multiples a number is written above the M. For unit fractions (e.g. $\frac{1}{2}$), an accent was added to the letter representing the denominator. Complex fractions were combinations of unit fractions, or the numerator and denominator were written separately (usually with the denominator above the numerator). In Athens and elsewhere the 'Herodianic' system, which made up numbers by combining the initial letters of number words, was used up to the 1st century BC. For writing very large numbers ARCHIMEDES in *The Sand-reckoner* proposed using combinations of powers of 10, but this was never used practically. The familiar Roman number system is based on seven signs (for 1, 5, 10, 50, 100, 500, and 1,000). Its origins are obscure. The convention that smaller numbers to the left of

larger numbers are subtracted from them was applied much less commonly than today. RW
See Dilke, O. A.W. (1987) *Mathematics and Measurement.*

cows see CATTLE.

Crassus (Marcus Licinius Crassus) c.115–53 BC Prominent public figure in the late Roman Republic, notorious for his great wealth. After the deaths of his distinguished father, Publius, and his brother in the CIVIL WAR of the mid-80s, Crassus went into hiding in Spain. Along with many of his contemporaries, he returned with SULLA and played a key role in his victory. He subsequently rose steadily through the MAGISTRACIES. After his PRAETORSHIP, he was given a special command in late 72 to end the SLAVE revolt of SPARTACUS. For his success he was awarded an ovation and elected to the consulship of 70 along with POMPEY, a lifelong rival. Later he was an ineffectual censor in 65. Crassus' wealth was criticized because it was accumulated by profiting from the proscription of Sulla's enemies and was invested on a large scale in urban property in Rome rather than in country estates. In politics Crassus was a fickle friend and an uncertain enemy, who preferred to work behind the scenes. In 59, and again in 55, CAESAR brought Crassus and Pompey together to help steamroller through a body of legislation to their mutual benefit. Holding their second consulships in 55, Pompey and Crassus awarded themselves major military commands. Crassus got the province of SYRIA with the controversial intention of attacking the PARTHIANS. In 53 he was defeated and killed near CARRHAE, a disaster which it took another generation of fighting to avenge. JJP
See Plutarch, *Crassus*; Marshall, B. A. (1976) *Crassus*; Ward, A. M. (1977) *Marcus Crassus and the Late Roman Republic.*

Crates see KRATES.

credit see BANKING; LOANS.

Cremona Latin colony on the north bank of the Po, founded in 218 BC, possibly in the territory of the Cenomani. Together with Placentia it was well placed to prevent a renewal of the Gallic uprising that had occupied Rome from 225 to 222 BC. The Via Postumia between Genoa and AQUILEIA was built nearby. The colony was directly affected by HANNIBAL's invasion, and by the rebellion of the Gauls that this inspired, but it held out bravely and was refounded with new settlers in 190. Traces of centuriation are visible from the division of the territory, which was later confiscated for VETERANS of PHILIPPI in 41 BC. In AD 69 the town staunchly supported the short-lived emperor Vitellius, but VESPASIAN's army under Antonius Primus won an important victory outside the town, sacked and burnt it, then restored it (Tacitus, *Histories* 3.1–45). It had a permanent parade ground, still discernible in the street plan today. It retained its important military role, and gained an ecclesiastical one as the seat of a BISHOP from the 5th century. CJS
See Potter, T. (1987) *Roman Italy.*

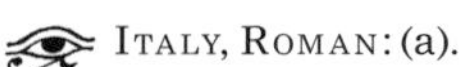

Crete A large island (c.250 × 50 km, 150 × 30 miles) in the south AEGEAN. Crete is mountainous and was originally heavily forested. It had no aboriginal peoples, but was occupied by the Neolithic period by non-Indo-European peoples. It was these people who developed Crete as the centre of Bronze Age civilization. Crete's resources of TIMBER, pasture land and coastal plains were all exploited. These formed the basis of trade for imports of bronze to the metal-poor island. The MINOAN civilization, named after the mythical Minos, was centred at great PALACES like KNOSSOS, Mallia and Phaistos. The legends of later Greeks about Minoan control of the sea ('thalassocracy') and Cretan wealth were perhaps based on extensive maritime trade controlled by the palaces. Minoan Crete was conquered by Mycenaean Greeks c.1400 BC, at which time all palaces except Knossos were destroyed. Further destruction at Knossos marked the end of the Bronze Age.

During the early Iron Age, Crete was dominated by Greeks speaking a Doric dialect, but EPIC poetry mentions other peoples there, including a group called ETEOCRETANS (true Cretans). Other Greeks considered the warrior and serf classes of Crete's archaic cities to be very similar to those of SPARTA. Crete was famous for its early law codes, for example at GORTYN, and any monarchies had been replaced by aristocractic governments of *kosmoi* (annual magistrates) by the 6th century BC.

That Crete was a depressed region in the classical period is shown by references to the warfare among its cities and the ease with which its men could be hired as MERCENARIES. In this Crete was similar to much of 4th-century BC Greece. It was also notorious for PIRACY until it was conquered by the Romans in 68 BC. It was combined with Cyrene as a Roman province in 27 BC. We know little of early Roman Crete, but the island was prosperous in the 4th century AD, as attested by several AQUEDUCTS and CHRISTIAN basilicas. AJ
See Cavanagh, W. G. and Curtis, M., eds. (1998) *Post-Minoan Crete*; Chaniotis, A., ed. (1999) *From Minoan Farmers to Roman Traders*; Whitley, J. (2001) *The Archaeology of Ancient Greece*; Willetts, R. F. (1965) *Ancient Crete*; (1977) *The Civilization of Ancient Crete.*

crime and criminals

In classical ATHENS crimes like homicide or battery were not criminal offences prosecuted by the state, but private offences for which the victim (or in the case of homicide the deceased's family) sought restitution through a private suit (*dikê*). More serious crimes like aggravated assault (*hybris*) or intentional wounding were prosecuted by a public suit (*graphê*), a procedure which allowed a third party to prosecute on behalf of the victim. Again the initiative did not rest with the state but with an individual.

Crimes committed by criminals known as 'wrongdoers' (*kakourgoi*) were covered under a special law which allowed for the arrest of these criminals. Classed as *kakourgoi* were thieves, clothes-snatchers, kidnappers, 'wall-burrowers' (burglars) and cutpurses. If a citizen caught a person in the act of committing such a crime, he could by the

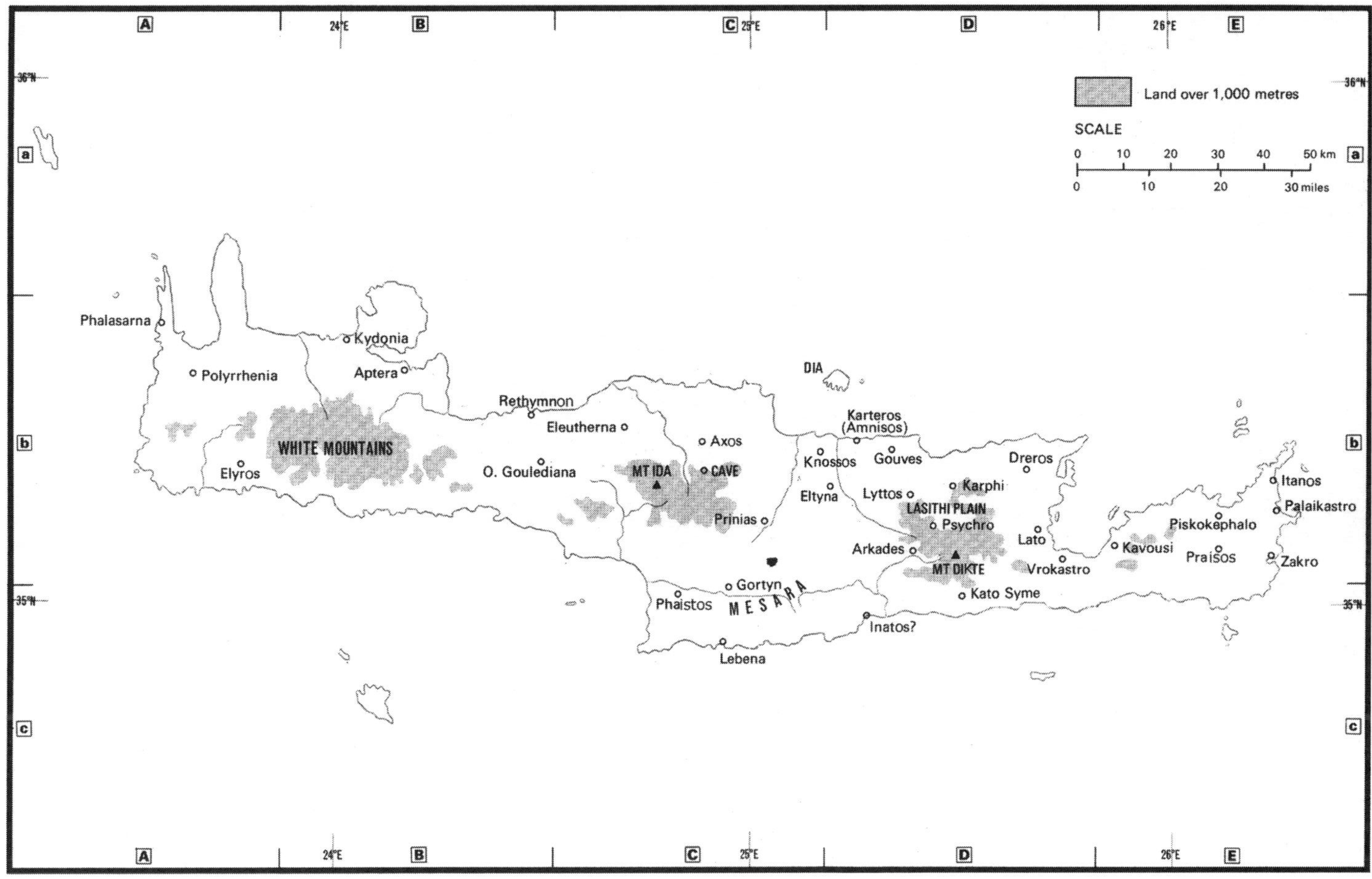

CRETE: map of classical Greek cities of Crete.

procedure known as *apagôgê* arrest the offender and haul him off to the Eleven, the state officials in charge of the PRISON. Optionally the citizen could either report the crime in writing (*endeixis*) to the Eleven, who would authorize the arrest of the accused, or lead the MAGISTRATES (by *ephêgêsis*) to the scene of the crime and have them make the arrest. Once the criminal was arrested, if he confessed he was executed. If he denied the charge, he was prosecuted in the court of the Eleven by the citizen initiating the arrest.

The law on theft, which went back to SOLON, specified the circumstances under which citizen's arrest could be exercised: any theft at night; during the day, any theft from a GYMNASION; in the HARBOUR only theft over the value of 10 drachmas and elsewhere over 50 drachmas. A further condition for arrest was to catch the thief 'in the act', that is in the act of committing the crime or in possession of the stolen goods. In the latter instance, the person making the arrest could pile the stolen goods on the back of alleged thief, bring him before the Eleven and demand that he prove he obtained the goods legitimately. By the 4th century the provision 'in the act' was thus widely interpreted to allow the arrest of a person suspected of theft after the crime had been committed. The law would even allow a victim of theft to search a house for the stolen property, on condition he strip down to his tunic to prevent him from planting goods in the house. For more petty thefts, the victim could sue by *dikê klopês*. If the defendant was convicted, not only did he return the stolen property but he was also required to pay damages equal to twice the value of the stolen goods. If he was unable to return the property, he paid ten times the value. The court could impose an additional penalty of five days and nights in the stocks. CC

See Cohen, D. (1984) *Theft in Athenian Law*; Hansen, M. H. (1976) *Apagoge, Endeixis and Ephegesis against Kakourgoi, Atimoi and Pheugontes*; Harrison, A. R. W. (1998) *The Law of Athens*; MacDowell, D. M. (1978) *The Law in Classical Athens*.

Like other societies before the 18th century, Rome lacked a police force and indeed the concept of one. So, by comparison with modern societies, there was a far greater reliance on self-help, social controls were to a major degree internalized, and a high level of criminal behaviour was taken for granted. Self-help operated at various levels. The élite, even in the imperial period, surrounded themselves with bodyguards to protect themselves and support their clients. Private prosecution was the rule in the criminal courts instituted in the late Republic. Even in courts like those of the city prefect under the empire or the provincial governor, private prosecution or at least action by an informer was normally required to trigger a court case. Citizen's arrests are regularly reported in the literature.

None of this would have worked without an impressive level of internalized social controls. In 186 BC the so-called Bacchanalian conspiracy was successfully handled by a small group of MAGISTRATES and their assistants because of the readiness of the inhabitants of Rome to inform against suspected cult members. Acceptance of a hierarchical social structure was vital; hence, for example, the ambivalence of the governing classes towards non-Roman cults like that of Bacchus, and indeed JUDAISM and CHRISTIANITY. A significant aspect of hierarchy at Rome was the dual penalty system. From the 3rd century BC to the 2nd century AD citizens convicted on a capital charge were seldom put to death but were in effect allowed to go into EXILE. The only major exceptions were persons treated as public enemies: under the Republic, most obviously the victims of the proscriptions of 81–80 and 43–42 BC, and under the empire those convicted of treason (*maiestas*). On the other hand, for SLAVES a capital sentence meant death, e.g. by crucifixion. In Rome itself, three minor magistrates (*tresviri capitales*) had some kind of summary jurisdiction over slaves and riff-raff. At some stage a different system of tariffs came into operation, with higher-status citizens (*honestiores*) mainly being exiled or fined while for the same misdeeds citizens of lower status (*humiliores*) were executed or condemned to forced LABOUR in MINES or on public works, much as if they were slaves. Some scholars suppose that the dual system of tariffs was formalized in the 2nd century AD; others argue that it grew up haphazardly according to the crime committed and was not formalized until the 3rd or 4th century, if indeed it ever was.

Crime levels are difficult to quantify, but a description of virtual anarchy in Rome between 60 and 52 BC emerges from CICERO's letters and from references to widespread brigandage in Italy and the PROVINCES. This suggests not only high levels of violent crime but an acceptance of them. This tolerance was not unlimited. In 52 the SENATE empowered POMPEY to bring in troops to end the gang warfare on the streets of Rome. AUGUSTUS stationed permanently a force of urban cohorts at Rome, presumably to deal with civil disorder and to protect himself and the magistrates. The fire brigade (*vigiles*), and the praetorian guards stationed just outside the city, were also available. In the imperial period, there were periodical military sweeps when levels of brigandage became intolerable and local authority measures proved more than usually ineffectual. JDC

See Bauman, R. A. (1996) *Crime and Punishment in Ancient Rome*; Garnsey, P. (1970) *Social Status and Legal Privilege in the Roman Empire*; Lintott, A. W. (1968) *Violence in Republican Rome*; Nippel, W. (1995) *Public Order in Ancient Rome*; Robinson, R. F. (1996) *The Criminal Law of Ancient Rome*.

Critias see KRITIAS.

critical theory The term 'critical theory' is often treated as a synonym for literary theory. The explosion of literary theory and theories is a phenomenon primarily of the late 20th century. In the 1950s, in literary studies, a distinction was usually made between scholars (those who pursued editing, or lexicology) and critics (those interested in explicating the meaning of literary texts). The critics were often 'New Critics' who believed that texts were best studied in isolation from BIOGRAPHY and history, and were best understood through technical components such as imagery, metaphor, themes, authorial voice, point of view and so on. The critic's task was above all to demonstrate unity and meaning. The New Critics seemed to believe that meaning was always recoverable, even across time. This confidence ended in the English-speaking world sometime in the early 1970s. The STRUCTURALISTS and then the SEMIOTICIANS offered new ways of looking at texts. Their successors began to ask, almost like philosophers, 'how do we know?' and 'what is "meaning"?'. The POST-STRUCTURALISTS argued that meaning was controlled by a number of forces outside the author's control (psychology, history and so forth). Subsequently, a myriad brands of theory have developed: DECONSTRUCTION, INTERTEXTUALISM, New Historicism, FEMINIST theory, queer theory, narratology, reader reception theory and so on. Texts for all of these groups, however, are culture-specific. Why, then, critical theory instead of literary theory? These theories of knowing and meaning have increasingly been applied, particularly through the academic study and teaching of communications, to the understanding not just of literary texts but also of non-literary popular culture (e.g. pop music or advertising). (see also POST-MODERNISM) PGT

crop selection see AGRICULTURE; MANURE.

crops see AGRICULTURE.

Ctesiphon For almost seven centuries Ctesiphon served as a winter capital of the PARTHIAN and SASSANIAN empires. Its origins lie soon after 141 BC, when the Parthians seized Babylonia and settled a garrison to watch over the turbulent hellenistic city of Seleukeia-on-the-Tigris. Situated 35 km (22 miles) south of Baghdad, Seleukeia was identified in the 20th century as part of a vast area (30 sq km, 12 sq miles) of urban ruins of the Parthian and Sassanian periods. The circular city just east of it, once the favoured location for Ctesiphon, is now known to be Sassanian. The current preference is for the site called al-Ma'aridh.

About 50 BC Ctesiphon was transformed from an occasional residence for the peripatetic Parthian kings into a formal winter capital. The progressive decline of Seleukeia – the result of the foundation of rival commercial centres, its seven-year rebellion (AD 35–42), and its destruction by the Romans in 165 and 197/8 – was matched by the development of Ctesiphon. At its height, Ctesiphon was a great entrepôt for trade from the east, both overland and from the Persian gulf. Little is known about the sacks by TRAJAN (116), Lucius Verus (165), and Carus (283) or its possible capture by the PALMYRENE ruler Odenathus (261). SEPTIMIUS SEVERUS in 197/8 is reported to have taken 100,000 captives, and Ctesiphon is undoubtedly one of the cities depicted on his victory ARCH.

The Sassanids made Ctesiphon their principal capital, but developed and founded other cities nearby, the basis of the Arabs' claim to have captured the 'seven cities' of Ctesiphon in 636. Excavations on various sites east of Ctesiphon took place in the 1920s, 1960s and 1970s. At al-Ma'aridh, late Sassanian houses have been excavated. DLK

SASSANIAN EMPIRE.

cult see CYBELE; ELEUSIS AND ELEUSINIAN MYSTERIES; GODS AND GODDESSES; ISIS; MITHRAS AND MITHRAISM; MOTHER GODDESSES; RELIGION; RITUAL; see also IMPERIAL CULT; RULER CULT.

culture The English word 'culture' derives from Latin *cultura* ('care', 'cultivation'). In common with Latin usage, it was originally associated with the idea of tending or cultivating crops or ANIMALS (as in 'agriculture'). It is from this usage that we derive one of the central modern meanings of the word culture: the process of human development. Culture is today a complex term, denoting variously the process of human development (the transition from HUNTING and gathering to AGRICULTURE being one such developmental step), civilization, the specific and variable cultures of different nations and peoples (a way of life, or 'lived culture'), and the arts ('high culture', as opposed to popular or lived culture). A good baseline definition of culture, as a social scientist today would understand it, might be 'the system of shared beliefs, values, customs, behaviours, and artefacts that the members of society use to cope with their world and with one another, and that are transmitted from generation to generation through learning' (Bates and Plog).

It is easier to express why we want to study 'culture' (ancient or modern) than to define the term itself. As the ANTHROPOLOGIST Clifford Geertz puts it, 'understanding a people's culture exposes their normalness without reducing their particularity . . . It renders them accessible: setting them in the frame of their own banalities, it dissolves their opacity.' Culture makes us who we are, in other words, and this point is as valid for classical scholars as it is for anthropologists and SOCIOLOGISTS studying living communities.

ARCHAEOLOGISTS commonly refer to the remains left by past peoples as 'material culture'. The meaning of this term has itself changed over time. One of the earliest – and most misguided – archaeological ideas about 'material culture' was the notion that groups of people who shared specific material remains also had a shared ETHNIC identity. This view was most famously articulated by the prehistorian Vere Gordon Childe, who stated, 'We find certain types of remains – pots, implements, ornaments, burial sites, house forms – constantly recurring together. Such a complex of regularly associated traits we shall term a "culture group" or just a "culture". We assume that such a complex is the material expression of what today would be called a "people".' Many archaeologists of Childe's era believed it was possible to write an ethnic prehistory of 'barbarian' Europe, dividing up the continent in terms of culture-specific 'folk' groups. This approach to the past (known as 'culture history') relied heavily on classical texts of the later 1st millennium BC in which 'barbarian' peoples living to the north of the MEDITERRANEAN, such as the Germani (Germans) and the Keltoi or Galli (Celts), were named for the first time. Since Childe's day, archaeologists have come to realize both that it is at best simplistic to 'read off' ethnicity from artefacts, and that group names like Germani and Keltoi mask complex ethnic realities which classical writers either ignored or oversimplified. JW

See Bates, D. G. and Plog, F. (1991) *Human Adaptive Strategies;* Childe, G. (1929) *The Danube in Prehistory*, vols. 5–6; Geertz, C. (1973) *The Interpretation of Cultures* 14.

Cumae (Greek Kyme, mod. Cuma) A Greek COLONY on the mainland of Campania, within sight of PITHEKOUSSAI. Its oikists (founders) are named by STRABO as Megasthenes of Chalkis in Euboia and Hippokles of Kyme (either Kyme in Euboia or Kyme in Aiolis, the native city of the historian EPHOROS, Strabo's source). More important than the names is the clear colonial status that Strabo accords to this, the earliest and most northerly Greek foundation on the Italian mainland. Archaeologically, Cumae appears to have been established c.725 BC. It clearly inherited substantial MANUFACTURING skills from Pithekoussai, and directed them from the early 7th century towards the lucrative markets for 'orientalizing' wares provided by the emerging native ÉLITES elsewhere in Campania, in Latium and especially in ETRURIA. Cumae remained until c.500 BC a major western centre for the dissemination of Greek art, cults, culture (including the ALPHABET, passed to the Etruscans c.700) and manners. The gallery below the *AKROPOLIS*, rightly or wrongly equated with the cave of the Cumaean SIBYL (Virgil, *Aeneid* 6), is probably pre-6th-century Greek work. Cumae's long Greek traditions survived both the Etruscan hegemony in Campania from c.650 and its own capture by the SAMNITES in 421. A prolific WORKSHOP of South Italian red-figured vases was active in the late 4th century. Its excellent HARBOUR facilities were not identified until the late 1960s. Clarification of the history of its FORTIFICATIONS proceeds, together with the identification of public buildings (Samnite and Roman) within them. DR

See Frederiksen, M. (1984) *Campania*.

 ROADS, ROMAN: (a).

Cunaxa, battle of see KOUNAXA.

cuneiform The form of WRITING used in the Near East from c.3300 BC to the 1st century AD. Cuneiform script was first written on moist clay with a pointed reed stylus, forming wedge-shaped impressions, and hence is called cuneiform from the Latin *cuneus*, 'wedge'. Initially cuneiform recorded word signs, but then developed a phonic system with vowels and vowel–consonant combinations.

Cuneiform was used to write a variety of languages, the first being Sumerian, which itself derived from a pictographic script. By c.2500 BC it recorded Semitic languages, especially Eblaite and Akkadian, the latter differentiating between three dialects, Old Akkadian, Babylonian and Assyrian. Indo-European languages such as Hittite, as well as those unrelated to either language family (such as Elamite, Hurrian and Urartaean), were also written in cuneiform.

The earliest cuneiform tablets have been found in MESOPOTAMIA, western Iran and northern SYRIA. Their primary function was to record ECONOMIC transactions of grain, livestock and TEXTILES in the temple and palace economies, but this was extended to record the economic and legal affairs of private and business enterprises. Royal inscriptions, literary texts, ASTRONOMICAL and religious documents also formed important corpora of cuneiform documents.

Clay tablets intended as permanent records were baked, but most tablets were sun-dried and stored in ARCHIVE rooms, where they were placed on wooden shelves, or kept in jars or wooden boxes, until they had served their purpose. The shape and size of the clay tablets varied according to the type of text to be recorded, from palm-sized, pillow-shaped tablets to large rectangular ones. MB

See Daniels, P.T. and Bright, W., eds. (1995) *World's Writing Systems*; Mieroop, M. van de (1999) *Cuneiform Texts and the Writing of History*; Walker, C.B.F. (1990) Cuneiform, in J.T. Hooker, ed., *Reading the Past* 15–73.

Cunobelinus c.AD 10–43 British king of the Catuvellauni or Trinovantes, and the self-styled son of Tasciovanus. The legendary figure of Cunobelinus was the inspiration for Shakespeare's Cymbeline.

Evidence for the historical reign of Cunobelinus is restricted to his coin issues, the majority minted at his tribal capital of Colchester (CAMULODUNUM). Unlike his Catuvellaunian predecessors, Cunobelinus came to exert considerable political influence over most of south-east BRITAIN, as the widespread distribution of his coin types indicates. In the territory of the Cantii (Kent), in particular, his coins displaced earlier tribal issues shortly after his accession to the throne. SUETONIUS' reference (*Caligula* 44) to Cunobelinus as 'king of the Britons', and the frequent use of imperial imagery on his coinage, suggest that his political expansion may have been favoured by Rome. Indeed, a coin issue that depicts the head of TIBERIUS may allude to a political bond between the emperor and the British dynast.

By AD 35, however, the political climate had altered. Adminius, a son of Cunobelinus, fled to GAUL after a disagreement with his father. Epaticcus, another self-styled son of Tasciovanus, encroached upon the territory of the Atrebates–Regni, which eventually led to the dethronement of Verica (CASSIUS DIO's Berikos?) c.AD 42 and his subsequent flight to the continent. Political unrest in southern Britain, the death of Cunobelinus and the dynastic aspirations of his sons Caratacus and Togidubnus may have provoked the CLAUDIAN invasion of 43. MLM

See Braund, D. (1996) *Ruling Roman Britain*.

Cupid see APULEIUS; EROS; LOVE.

Curia The SENATE house of Rome, located in the north-west corner of the Roman FORUM. This site bore a succession of buildings, beginning with the Curia Hostilia erected by Tullus Hostilius, restored and enlarged by SULLA in 80 BC and burnt down in the RIOTS following the death of CLODIUS in 52. It was rebuilt by Sulla's son, then supplanted by the Curia Iulia begun by JULIUS CAESAR in 44 BC. The latter was completed by AUGUSTUS in AD 29, destroyed by FIRE in 283 and restored by DIOCLETIAN. The remains of this structure survive today, having been converted to the CHURCH of San Adriano. It is a rectangle 25.2 m deep and 17.6 m wide, with bronze doors at one end and a dais at the other. The sides were lined by three stepped levels where senators sat or stood.

Originally *curia* was the term for the oldest divisions of the Roman people. Citizens were divided by birth and geography into 30 *curiae*, which played a role in early civil and military organization as well as in religious cults and FESTIVALS. *Curia* also came to be used in a variety of contexts to designate a place of ASSEMBLY or headquarters of various groups, ranging from local municipal senates to the *curia athletarum* ('ATHLETES' clubhouse') at Rome. (see also CURIAL CLASS) GSA

See Bartoli, A. (1963) *Curia Senatus*; Palmer, R. (1970) *The Archaic Community of the Romans*; Talbert, R. (1984) *The Senate of Imperial Rome*.

 SENATE: (a)–(b).

curial class, *curiales* The members of the local councils (*curiae*) which ran most of the network of cities throughout the Roman empire. The councillors, also known as *decuriones* ('decurions'), were co-opted and served for life. Qualifications for membership included origin or domicile in the city, free birth, a minimum age (25, later 18) and a minimum level of property, which varied greatly depending of the prosperity of the community. By the 3rd century AD, membership was a requirement for all suitably qualified persons and in effect became hereditary. The *curiales* enjoyed high status and privileges, but were also faced with considerable obligations. They were expected by their communities to finance and supervise the provision of civic amenities. The imperial administration made them responsible for the collection and underwriting of imperial TAXES, the maintenance of ROADS and the official POSTAL SERVICE, and even the conscription of troops. Not for nothing were they described as 'the sinews of the state and the hearts of the cities'. From the early empire onwards, exemption from these burdens was granted widely to individuals: SENATORS and *EQUITES*, military VETERANS, privileged occupations (such as DOCTORS), and later the CHRISTIAN priesthood. As a result, the wealthiest people were increasingly creamed off from cities. In the late empire, the EMPERORS tried unsuccessfully to reverse the trend. Nevertheless the institution continued until at least the beginning of the 7th century. (see also CURIA) JJP

See Jones, A. H. M. (1964) *The Later Roman Empire 284–602*; Millar, F. (1983) Empire and city, Augustus to Julian: obligations, excuses and status, *JRS* 73: 76–96.

curses The modern generic term for the ancient practice of calling upon deities to bring evil upon an opponent (or opponents), or even upon oneself, if one were to break a promise to the GODS at some stage in the future. In antiquity, the latter kind of 'conditional' curses are frequently part of a public OATH or PRAYER, often expressed through a community's representatives. For the former, a widely used method of such imprecations, from the 6th century BC to late antiquity, was writing a letter, often on a thin sheet of lead, to one or more specific chthonic goddesses or gods and depositing it in a well or grave. The durable writing material and the usual method of deposition have enabled several thousands of such 'curse tablets' to survive. The texts do not name their authors, who may have used the services of scribes or magicians. They aim to 'tie down' the opponent (hence the Greek term *katadesmos* and Latin *defixio* for these tablets). Curses are used against competitors in the LAWCOURTS, in the THEATRE or CIRCUS, in commerce and TRADE, and, notably, in love. The curses often detail the evil which is to afflict the opponent. Over time, they tended to become more elaborate, especially in the lists of deities addressed, and more formulaic. Other forms of curses, again written on tablets, were vindictive prayers to a deity invoking her or him to punish an (unknown and hence unnamed) perpetrator of a theft or slander.

Curses were ubiquitous: 'there is no one who does not fear to be victim of a *defixio*' (Pliny the Elder, *Natural History* 28.19). They were apparently used by all social groups, from SLAVES to the nobility. There is even a genre of poetry known as *arai* (Greek; Latin *dirae*; e.g. Ovid's *Ibis*). Some non-verbal curses (like voodoo dolls) seem to have served the same general purpose as the tablets, and amulets against curses were widely used. KB

See Brodersen, K., ed. (2001) *Gebet und Fluch, Zeichen und Traum*; Ogden, D. (1999) Binding spells, in B. Ankarloo and

(a)

(b)

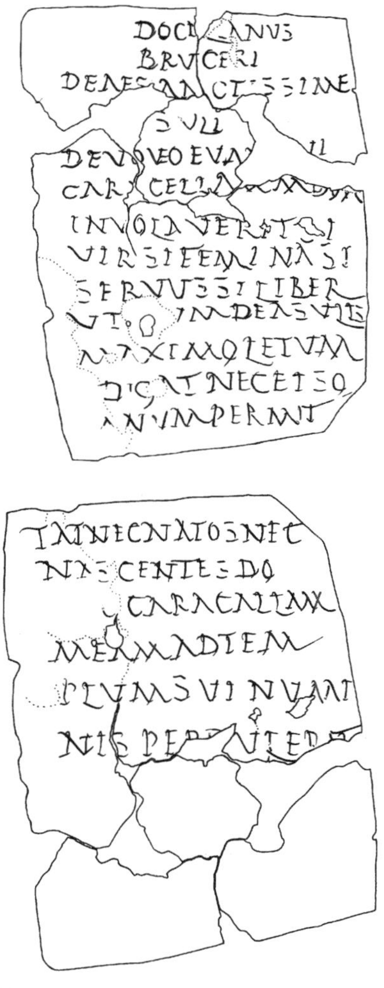

CURSES: (a) and (b) curse tablet (*defixio*) inscribed on both sides of a thin sheet of lead alloy, found in the sacred spring at Bath. The text translates as: 'Docilianus son of Brucerus to the most holy goddess Sulis. I curse him who has stolen my hooded cloak, whether man or woman, whether slave or free. May the goddess Sulis inflict death upon him and not allow him sleep or children now and in the future, until he has brought my hooded cloak to the temple of her divinity.'

S. Clark, eds., *Witchcraft and Magic in Europe: ancient Greece and Rome* 1–90.

 BATH.

Curtius Rufus see ALEXANDER III.

curule aediles see AEDILES; ASSEMBLIES, ROMAN; MAGISTRATES, ROMAN.

customs duties Greek cities usually levied duties of 2 per cent upon goods that were imported, and sometimes also those that were exported. Many states did not collect the duties directly, but leased them out to private tax farmers. This could easily lead to malpractice (Andokides, *On the Mysteries* 133). Although cities passed strict customs laws (as in Kyparissia, cf. *SEG* 9.1026), it was not too difficult to evade paying duties. A place just outside Piraeus was known as the 'Thieves' harbour' because smugglers often landed there (Demosthenes, *Against Lakritos* 28). The purpose of custom duties was not to protect home INDUSTRIES from foreign competitors, but to raise revenues for the state. This could occasionally amount to a substantial income. When the Romans set up Delos as a free port in 166 BC, it was reported that the Rhodian harbour dues dropped from 1 million to 150,000 drachmas; the annual turnover in Rhodes must have run into millions (Polybios 30.31.10–12).

During the Roman REPUBLIC and the early PRINCIPATE, the collection of custom duties was farmed out to private entrepreneurs (*publicani*, 'men in the public service') for periods of five years. The empire was divided into several tax districts or *portoria* for this purpose. The companies of the *publicani* established an empire-wide infrastructure of offices in the cities and harbours where the duties were levied. A recently published inscription from EPHESOS, which contains the regulations for the tax district of ASIA, provides new information about the structure and organization of customs stations. A tax farmer was in charge of running the operation, but much of the work was carried out by his agents, who could be SLAVES. The bad reputation of the tax farmers was proverbial: in the NEW TESTAMENT, publicans are classed with sinners (cf. Matthew 11.19). The 2nd-century AD lexicographer POLLUX provides his readers with a list of useful words to insult a tax farmer (*Onomasticon* 9.30–1). The duties were usually between 2 and 5 per cent, but could rise to 25 per cent for luxury goods imported from beyond the borders of the empire. From the later part of the 2nd century the imperial administration became more closely involved in the collection of custom duties, but the exact details of this development are unclear.

Individual cities also levied taxes that could be farmed out or were taken on as LITURGIES by wealthy citizens. A bilingual inscription from PALMYRA (in Greek and Palmyrene) of AD 138 carries a detailed tax law that was passed by the council of that city. It contains a long list of goods and items that were taxed. Loads of produce that were carried to and from the VILLAGES in the territory were apparently exempt. A temporary exemption, *ateleia*, was sometimes granted at the occasion of FESTIVALS. The main reason was probably to attract TRADERS for a steady FOOD SUPPLY during the festival, but it would also have boosted the status of the city. OvN

See Brunt, P. A. (1990) Publicans in the principate, in *Roman Imperial Themes* 354–432; Matthews, J. F. (1984) The tax-law of Palmyra, *JRS* 74: 157–80.

Cybele ANATOLIAN GODDESS, whose chief shrine was at Pessinos in PHRYGIA. Although she was primarily a goddess of fertility, her worshippers tended to see her as a sovereign deity with wide-ranging powers. Her consort in MYTH, and eventually cult, was the youthful and castrated Attis. By the early 5th century BC Cybele was known in Greece, where she received TEMPLES as the Great Mother. It was under this same name that in 204 BC her worship was introduced into Rome, when her cult symbol, together with her clergy of EUNUCH PRIESTS (Galli) wearing robes of an orange COLOUR, was brought from Pessinos. The SENATE instituted GAMES in her honour, but her cult was otherwise largely confined to the precincts of her temple on the Palatine. Roman citizens were forbidden to join the ranks of the castrated Galli. Under the empire the cult acquired a higher profile. From the reign of CLAUDIUS onwards, we hear of a public FESTIVAL in March lasting several days and involving processions, feasts, a 'Day of Blood' on which some worshippers flogged and even castrated themselves, and a ritual bath of the idol. In the 2nd century AD a new rite appeared, the *taurobolium*. In its developed form, this involved the sacrifice of a bull over a grill-covered pit, thereby drenching with its blood the worshipper below. From Rome the cult spread to much of the Western empire; it retained its importance until the end of the 4th century AD. JBR

See Turcan, R. (1996) *The Cults of the Roman Empire*.

Cyclades see AEGEAN; DELOS; NAXOS; PAROS.

Cymbeline see CUNOBELINUS.

Cynicism A philosophical movement sometimes thought to have been inspired by a particular interpretation of SOCRATES' ethical stance. Perhaps the most famous members of the movement were Antisthenes and Diogenes of Sinope; the latter is said to have lived in a barrel in the Athenian AGORA. There were Cynic influences in some branches of STOICISM (especially that of Ariston of Chios).

The Cynics emphasized the notion that virtue is necessary and sufficient for a good human life, and also the thesis that all other values are merely conventional and to be discarded and debased. But they did not merely recognize the lack of justification for any such values; they sought actively to reveal and ridicule what they saw as unfounded conceit. This attack on conventional mores was famously conducted through very public and provocative acts of unconventional 'shameless' behaviour, notoriously including public masturbation and urination. Such deliberate rejection and criticism of customary practice extended to the Cynics' dealings with figures of (conventional) authority such as ALEXANDER.

This unusual – and sometimes apparently bestial – behaviour earned them the name Cynics, after the Greek word for 'dog'. Much evidence about early Cynicism is in the form of brief anecdotes relating an example of such behaviour or a particular provocative pronouncement. Cynics were also often associated with a distinctive appearance, and are regularly depicted wearing a dishevelled cloak and carrying their only possessions, a staff and pouch, sometimes accompanied by a dog to make the identification clear. JIW

See Bracht Branham, R. and Goulet-Cazé, M.-O., eds. (1996) *The Cynics.*

Cynoscephalae see KYNOSKEPHALAI.

Cyprian (Thascius Caecilius Cyprianus) c.AD 200–58) BISHOP of CARTHAGE from 248 and MARTYR. Cyprian was born a PAGAN into the civic ÉLITE of Carthage, and seemed destined for a career as an imperial administrator until his conversion to CHRISTIANITY and election as bishop. On becoming bishop, he was confronted by the upheavals of the PERSECUTION ordered by the emperor Decius in 250. Unlike any before it, this persecution aimed at a purge of churches across the whole empire, and had a devastating effect on the social cohesion of Christian communities. Cyprian, controversially, had gone into hiding while many of his congregation had suffered imprisonment, torture and death for the faith. Later, when certain Christians who had lapsed during the persecution sought readmission to the CHURCH, it provoked a storm as hard-liners argued that this would compromise the integrity of the church. These challenges led Cyprian to pen his two great treatises, *On the Lapsed* and *On the Unity of the Catholic Church*, in which he argued for a stronger Christian community under the bishop's leadership. Those who opposed his stance he branded as schismatics, a decision that ultimately brought him into conflict with bishop Stephen of Rome, who supported hard-line Christians against the more moderate approach advocated by Cyprian. In 257, under the emperor VALERIAN, another persecution began, and this time Cyprian suffered a martyr's death (258). Yet the responses he had made to Decius' persecution had marked an important stage in the evolution of the role of bishop, while his writings highlight the extent to which imperial action could influence the developing structure of the church. MDH

See Cyprian, *Letters*, trs. G.W. Clarke (1984–9); Cyprian, *The Lapsed; The Unity of the Catholic Church*, trs. M. Bévenot (1957); Rives, J.B. (1995) *Religion and Authority in Roman Carthage from Augustus to Constantine.*

Cyprus (Kypros) Mountainous island (c.9,300 sq km, 3,600 sq miles) in the eastern MEDITERRANEAN. Two MOUNTAIN ranges, Troödos (anc. Trogodos) in the south-west and the Kyrenia (anc. Keryneia) in the north-east, are separated by the Mesaoria plain. The wealth of Cyprus was based on its strategic position with respect to TRADE routes, and on exploitation of its COPPER resources (the word 'copper' derives from *Kypros*). In antiquity it was densely FORESTED (Strabo 14.6.5), and TIMBER was probably another valuable resource.

Cyprus is famed as the birthplace of the goddess APHRODITE. The earliest references linking the goddess with the island are in HOMER. Her sanctuary at Palaipaphos was established in the 12th century BC and remained in use into the Roman period. Other major sanctuaries are the temple of APOLLO Hylates at Kourion, established during the archaic period, a second sanctuary to Aphrodite (Kypria) at Amathous, the PHOENICIAN temple to Astarte at Kition, and the temple to ZEUS at Salamis, built in the 2nd century BC.

Cyprus played an important role in late Bronze Age trading systems (c.1600–1200 BC), exporting copper 'oxhide' ingots and importing luxury exotica from Egypt and the LEVANT and large quantities of MYCENAEAN pottery from the AEGEAN. Wealthy cities, such as Énkomi, grew up along the south coast. The name of Cyprus at this time is unknown, but it is plausible that the island, or one of its cities, should be identified with the Alashiya known from the Amarna letters. A series of destructions afflicted the island c.1200 BC and many sites were abandoned, accompanied by several changes in material culture, in particular the overwhelming adoption of locally made Mycenaean pottery. This is usually attributed to a massive influx of ACHAIANS fleeing the destructions on the Greek mainland. In the Iron Age Cyprus was divided into numerous city kingdoms including Salamis, Kourion, Marion, Paphos, Soloi, Idalion and Tamassos. The first historical references to these kingdoms are in Assyrian texts of Sargon II (709 BC) and Esarhaddon (673/2). EPIGRAPHIC evidence suggests that Cyprus was inhabited by three ethnic groups: Greeks (descendants of the Mycenaean immigrants), Eteocypriots (the indigenous population; this name is a modern coinage) and PHOENICIANS.

In 545 Cyprus was incorporated into the PERSIAN EMPIRE. The island became embroiled in the wars between Greece and Persia, beginning with the Ionian revolt of 499/8 (Herodotos 5.104, 108–16). In 450 the Athenian general KIMON set out to liberate Cyprus, but after his death the Athenians were forced to withdraw and in 449/8 they probably signed a peace treaty, the peace of Kallias, with the Persians. Euagoras became king of Salamis in 411. He officially introduced the Greek alphabet to Cyprus and tried to bring all the kings of the island under his authority, but in 381 he was defeated by the Persians in a sea battle off Kition and forced to renounce his plans.

Cyprus was freed from Persian rule by ALEXANDER the Great in 333 and assimilated into the Ptolemaic kingdom of Egypt by PTOLEMY I in 294. The island was ruled from Paphos by a *stratêgos* (governor-general) who also functioned as high priest. An important Cypriot of the hellenistic period was the philosopher ZENO OF KITION (c.336–264), founder of the STOIC School of PHILOSOPHY. In 30 BC Cyprus became a Roman province. Paphos remained the administrative centre of the island and the site of the Roman garrison. (see p. 250) LFS

See Gjerstad, E. (1948) *Swedish Cyprus Expedition*; Karageorghis, V. (1982) *Cyprus*; Reyes, A. (1994) *Archaic Cyprus*; Tatton-Brown, V. (1997) *Ancient Cyprus.*

 ASIA.

Cyrene and Cyrenaica A city and region in eastern LIBYA, between Egypt and the Syrtic desert. In antiquity, the area was frequently referred to as the Pentapolis since Cyrenaica was a confederation of five cities, including Euesperides (later renamed Berenike), Taucheira, Barka (or Ptolemais), Cyrene and Apollonia. The term Cyrenaica was first used in

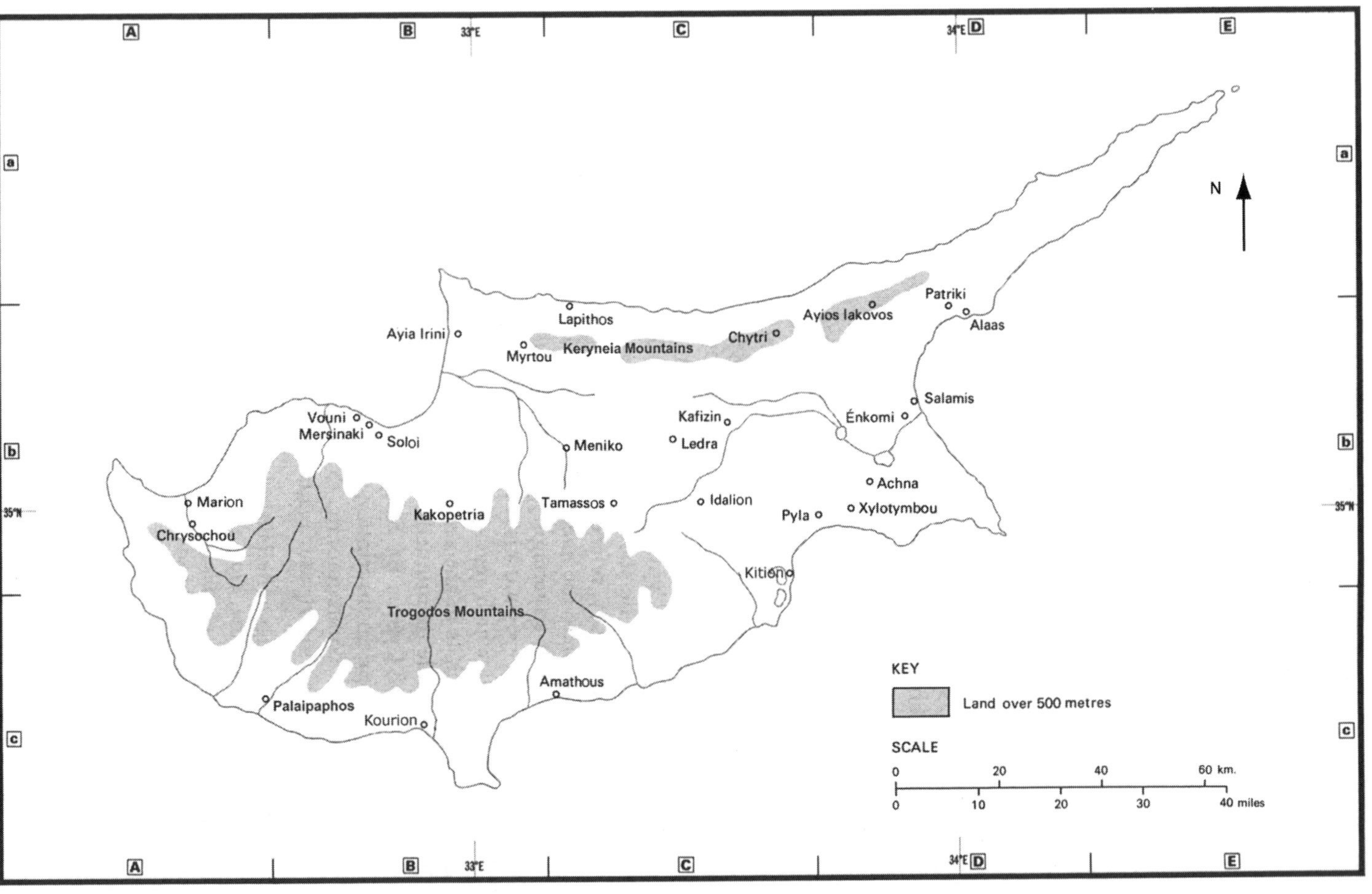

Cyprus: map of Cyprus in the classical period.

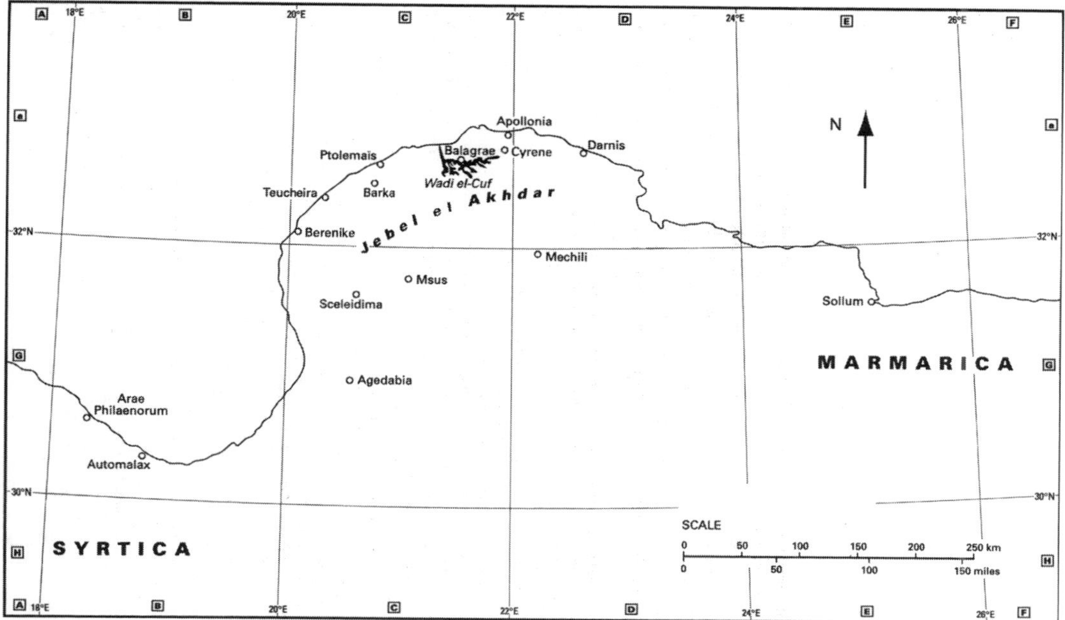

CYRENE AND CYRENAICA: map.

the Roman period; before this time, and even later, Cyrene (Greek Kyrênê, Kyrana) was used for both the city and region. The cities appear to have been largely independent from one another, though Cyrene dominated the region until late antiquity.

According to HERODOTOS, Cyrene was founded by a stammerer named Battos, who led a group of Theraians to Libya. Modern historians generally date the foundation of Cyrene to c. 630 BC. Battos gave his name to a dynasty, the Battiads, who ruled Cyrene until the 5th century BC. Of note is Battos II, who encouraged immigration to the city, issuing land grants to anyone willing to settle in the area. After the Battiads, the history of Cyrene becomes far less clear. Cyrenaica seems to have flourished during the hellenistic period, when the region came under the control of the PTOLEMIES of Egypt and enjoyed close contact with ALEXANDRIA. Cyrenaica became part of the Roman empire in 96 BC when Ptolemy Apion bequeathed it to Rome. Although Cyrenaica suffered from a damaging earthquake in AD 265, as well as incursions from Libyan tribes, it seemed to have remained reasonably prosperous in the late antique period.

Cyrenaica had quite a mixed population. A number of JEWS settled in the area from the hellenistic period onwards; the most famous was Simon of Cyrene, who tried to carry Christ's cross. Relations with Jews in the region were often fraught with difficulties, culminating in the Jewish revolt of AD 115–17 in which many of Cyrene's monuments were destroyed. Cyrenaica's cities also hosted a number of indigenous Libyans, as is evident by the significant number of Libyan names in inscriptions. Cyrenaicans and Libyans intermarried throughout antiquity, and the children of Libyan mothers and Cyrenaican fathers were given citizenship from the hellenistic period. Despite this, Cyrenaicans also fought against Libyans at various intervals, most famously during the Marmaric wars at the time of AUGUSTUS. SYNESIUS, the 5th-century AD BISHOP of Ptolemais, gives a vivid account of battles between Cyrenaicans and Libyans (Ausurians) from the Sahara.

In antiquity, Cyrenaica was famed for its AGRICULTURAL fertility, which was in large part due to its abundant rainfall; the story of Libyans telling Greeks that the sky over Cyrene has a hole in it (Herodotos 4.158) probably refers to this. Cyrenaica also was well known for its export of SILPHIUM, the wild plant used as a luxury food and DRUG. In addition, Cyrenaicans excelled in HORSE breeding and equestrianism, as PINDAR emphasizes in his fourth and fifth *Pythian Odes*.

A number of important intellectuals hailed from the region. In the 4th century BC, Aristippos founded a school of PHILOSOPHY known as the Cyrenaican, which advocated that people should seek the pleasure of the moment. His near contemporary, Theodoros, was a MATHEMATICIAN who taught both PLATO and Theaitetos. In the 3rd century Cyrene produced the poet KALLIMACHOS, a descendant of Battos, and the multi-talented ERATOSTHENES. EACM

See Applebaum, S. (1979) *Jews and Greeks in Ancient Cyrene*; Barker, G.W.W., Lloyd, J.A. and Reynolds, J., eds. (1985) *Cyrenaica in Antiquity*.

 SILPHIUM: (a)–(b).

Cyriac of Ancona (Ciriaco Pizzicolli) c.AD 1391–c.1453 The first great intellectual traveller from the medieval West to devote himself to recovering Greece's classical past. Born into a merchant family, Cyriac enjoyed the patronage of a cardinal and the

support of Italian humanists who collected manuscripts from Byzantine Greece. Between 1425 and his death, he travelled frequently in Greek lands for antiquarian purposes, becoming famous for recording buildings and inscriptions. Many of his notebooks were destroyed, but a copy survives of his journey in 1436–7 to north-west Greece, Attica and Mystras (the medieval city near ancient Sparta), where he met the renowned Neoplatonist Gemistos Plethon. On his voyage of 1444–7 he made observations at Kyzikos and Samothrace that are still of value. He also accompanied the sultan Mehmet as he sacked CONSTANTINOPLE in 1453; this need not astonish us if we appreciate that Cyriac's idealized Greece was at odds with the idea of a Christian empire. He is important not only for the ARCHITECTURE and documents that he recorded and are now lost, but also for his pioneering legacy to ANTIQUARIANISM and ultimately classical ARCHAEOLOGY. DGJS

See Stoneman, R. (1987) *Land of Lost Gods*, ch. 2.

Cyrus ('the Great') (Akkadian *Kurash*, Old Persian *Kuraush*) 559–530 BC Founder of the PERSIAN EMPIRE; son of Kambyses and Mandane (daughter of the Median king Astyages), grandson of Cyrus I, and great-grandson of Teispes. (In recent scholarship he is usually called Cyrus II, in older works often Cyrus I.)

Cyrus rose to power in Persis (the Persian homeland in the southern Zagros mountains of Iran) after the collapse of the ELAMITE kingdom of Susa and Anshan. Regarding himself as successor to the kings of Elam, he took the royal title 'king of Anshan'. He first conquered Media in 549 BC, defeating Astyages in battle in the plain of Murghab in Persis. Here, in commemoration of his victory, he built the first Persian royal residence, Pasargadai (Batrakatash in Old Persian). In the 540s he defeated Croesus of Lydia, and in 539 he conquered BABYLONIA. In September–October 539 he attacked Opis, brutally killing the civilian population, and accepted the surrender of Sippar and Babylon. By allowing JEWISH captives at Babylon to return home and rebuild the temple in JERUSALEM, he gained the reputation of a humane ruler whose tolerance particularly benefited the Jews. Yet the reasons for the seeming 'religious tolerance' of Cyrus and his successors are to be found in their acute sense of *realpolitik*: they calculated that people's resistance to a new regime would be limited if their cultural and religious customs remained undisturbed. With the conquests of eastern Iran and Baktria, Cyrus had established a world empire within three decades. He died during a campaign against the Massagetai on the northern frontier. MB

See Young, T. C. (1988) The early history of the Medes and the Persians and the Achaemenid empire to the death of Cambyses, in *CAH* 4, 1–52.

Cyrus the Younger The second son of the Persian king Darius II and of Parysatis. He is best known as the implacable enemy of Athens in the PELOPONNESIAN WAR, and as the leader of the failed coup against his brother, ARTAXERXES II, that involved the Ten Thousand Greek MERCENARIES of XENOPHON'S *Anabasis*.

Cyrus was sent out as satrap and commander of all the forces mustered in the Kastolos plain by his father in 407 BC. This meant that he had extraordinary authority over the western satrapies, together with broad military and diplomatic powers; his mission was to bring the resources of the PERSIANS squarely against ATHENS. He developed a close relationship with LYSANDER, and helped to finance the SPARTAN forces fighting the Athenians. When Artaxerxes ascended the throne in 405, his command was diminished. In the spring of 401 he mounted an attack on his brother from SARDIS. His army was composed of levies from ASIA Minor and 10,000 Greek mercenaries; he was aided by Parysatis. Cyrus belongs to a long line of Achaemenid princes who disputed the succession. He met Artaxerxes' army at Kounaxa (Cunaxa) near BABYLON in the autumn of 401 and was killed fighting. Xenophon paints an idealized portrait of Cyrus as the perfect leader, similar in spirit to his longer treatment of CYRUS THE GREAT in the *Cyropaedia*. JDD

See Xenophon, *Anabasis* (*Persian Expedition*); Briant, P. (1996) *Histoire de l'empire perse*, ch. 15; Lewis, D. M. (1977) *Sparta and Persia*.

Dacian wars The Dacians, centred on the Carpathian mountains, posed a recurrent threat to Roman Moesia and PANNONIA from the 1st century BC onwards. A Dacian invasion of Moesia which killed the governor Oppius Sabinus (AD 84–5) initiated a decisive series of wars. The emperor DOMITIAN campaigned in person and celebrated a Dacian TRIUMPH in 86. In the same year a Roman army invading Dacia was disastrously defeated and its commander, the praetorian prefect Cornelius Fuscus, was killed. A renewed offensive under Tettius Iulianus won a major victory over the new Dacian king, DECEBALUS, at Tapae on the western route into Dacia (88). The treaty that was then agreed confirmed Decebalus as king and supported him with military aid and subsidies. Thereafter, Roman forces were allowed to pass through Dacian lands in their offensives against other barbarians.

However, the new emperor TRAJAN determined to humble Decebalus, perhaps following renewed attacks on Roman territory. Decebalus was again defeated at Tapae and forced into a humiliating treaty (101–2). After its terms were violated, Trajan's forces crossed his new Drobeta BRIDGE, invaded the Carpathian heartland and assaulted the strong mountain FORTRESSES, including Decebalus' capital at Sarmizegethusa (105–6). Decebalus killed himself, his treasure was captured and his head was displayed in Rome. A new Roman PROVINCE of Dacia was established, rich in metal resources. In Rome a triumph was held after each Trajanic Dacian war, on a lavish scale intended to upstage Domitian's achievements. A stylized narrative of the wars was carved on TRAJAN'S COLUMN, erected as part of a great FORUM complex paid for by Dacian spoils. A TROPHY monument with battle reliefs was also erected at ADAMKLISSI in the Romanian Dobrudja. JCNC

See Lepper, F. and Frere, S. (1988) *Trajan's Column*.

 AUXILIARIES; DALMATIA; WAR (table).

Dalmatia Roman province along the north-east coast of the ADRIATIC SEA, bounded on its north by PANNONIA, on the east by Moesia. The region, which also borders north-east Italy, was known as ILLYRIA in the Greek world. Rome sent its first expedition against the expansionist Illyrian queen Teuta in 229 BC, and their second in 219 against Demetrios and his associate Skerdilaidas. Subsequently, Rome's relations with Illyria depended on the latter's relations with MACEDONIA. After the Illyrian king Gentius, previously accused of PIRACY, threw in his lot with Perseus of Macedonia, Illyria was part of the conquest that ended in Rome's favour in 167 BC. The Illyrian kingdom was dismembered, but did not become a PROVINCE. Instead, Rome maintained alliances and intervened with some regularity, generally against the Delmatae, to ensure stability. These wars were often used as military training exercises and opportunities for glory.

In 59 BC, JULIUS CAESAR gained oversight of Illyricum, the Roman name for the region. Early in the CIVIL WAR, Pompeians used the area as a base, but

DACIAN WARS: the Roman victories were hard fought and depended to some extent on the engineering capability of the army, seen here engaged in construction of a temporary camp.

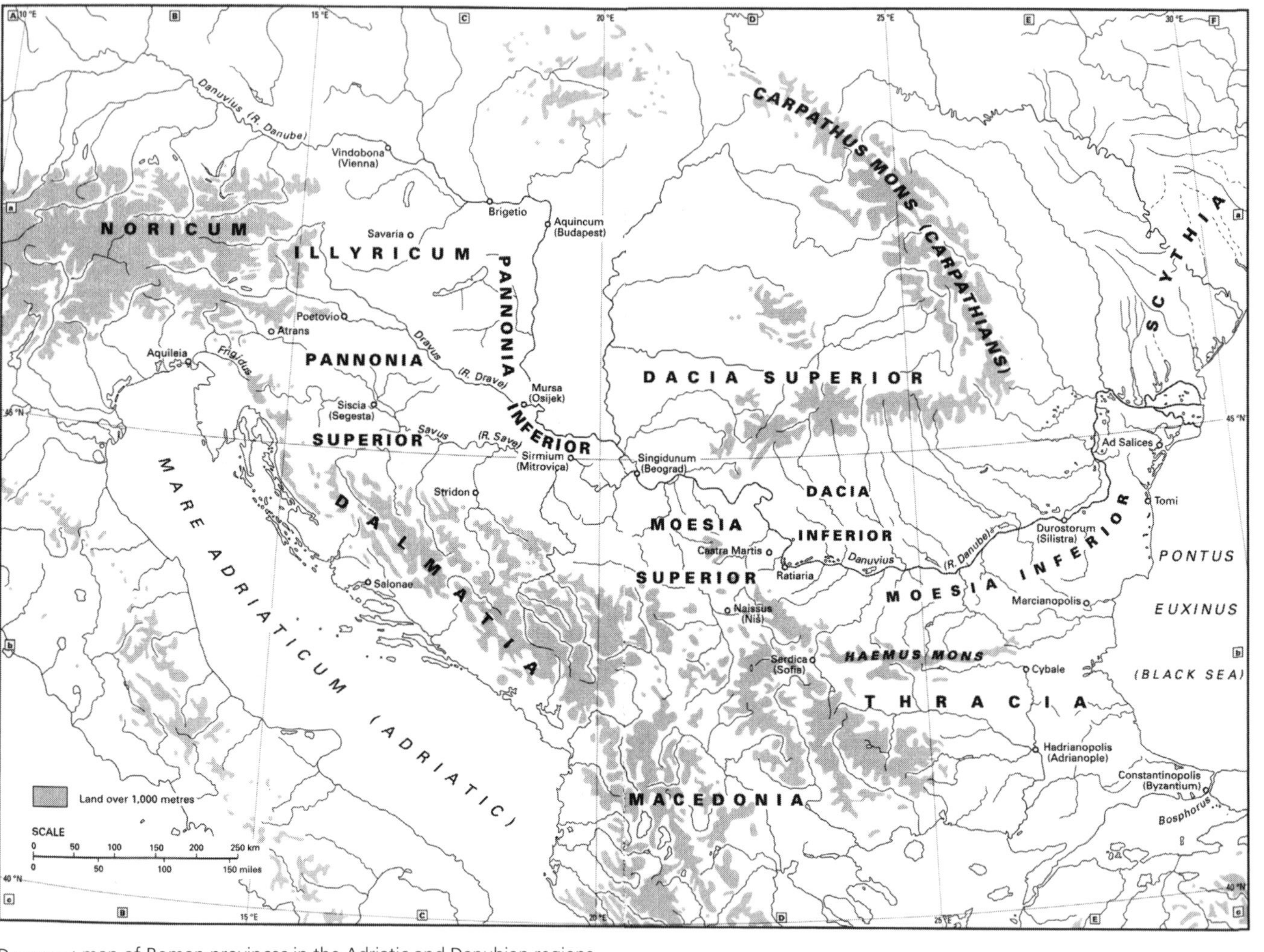

DALMATIA: map of Roman provinces in the Adriatic and Danubian regions.

DANCE: (a) vase painting of a komast dancer, 6th century BC, Corinthian.

Caesar as DICTATOR sent generals to campaign there. As a result of AUGUSTUS' PANNONIAN WARS, by AD 9 the larger region became three provinces, Moesia, PANNONIA and Dalmatia (the last two had briefly been a single province of Illyricum). The province, rich in SILVER and IRON, was of considerable strategic and economic importance, and the empire maintained it accordingly. DIOCLETIAN was almost certainly born in Dalmatia and retired there after his abdication. JV

See Wilkes, J. J. (1969) *Dalmatia*.

 DANUBE.

dance To the Greeks who believed it to have been an art form given to them as a divine gift, dance was of particular importance. Termed *mousikê*, dance was closely assimilated with POETRY and MUSIC as a performance art in which the body was expected to interpret the words and rhythms of a work through the employment of conventional gestures and moves, known as *cheironomia*. Dance was a fundamentally important aspect of religious worship, especially in MYSTERY rites and in the worship of DIONYSOS, who was honoured with a dance derived from wild mountain dances by a select *thiasos* or group of trained dancers. Dionysos was also worshipped in the dance-dramas of the Greek THEATRE. Dance was also used as an element of a youth's EDUCATION and military training, particularly in SPARTA where the discipline of rhythm and movement was held in high regard. Generally, there was a sharp GENDER division in dance performances: men and women rarely danced together communally. Nevertheless, dance was a vital element of daily life, especially at times of family-related events such as weddings, infants' naming-days, harvests and even FUNERALS. In addition, rowdy public dance PROCESSIONS (*kômoi*), like a modern-day conga-line, were a familiar feature of Athenian nightlife; these were often made up of male symposiasts and *hetairai*. The SYMPOSION was the site of more specialized dance performances, as hired professional dancers (often female) entertained the assembled male guests. The occupation of professional dancer was often linked to PROSTITUTION – public performers were, by definition, highly visible and perhaps the majority of public dancing women came from the margins of 'respectable' society.

Professional performers are well attested in hellenistic ALEXANDRIA, where a particular type of veil-dancing (an early form of belly-dancing, perhaps) was performed. ATHENAEUS provides us with many names of popular dances including the *geranos* (a night-time serpentine dance), *pyrrhikê* (performed by armour-clad men and boys), *partheneion* (a song and dance performed by girls) and *hyporchêma* (a kind of pantomime dance).

The Romans took a different attitude to dance and showed more restraint in the way in which they used dance as an expression of their society. Indeed some Romans, including CICERO, were openly hostile to the dance profession and regarded dance as 'oriental' decadence. Nonetheless, dance was used at family events and social occasions, and occasionally to add significance to religious rituals such as the *tripudia* ('three-foot' dances), ceremonies involving the *fratres arvales* (performed by armoured Salii) and the 'rope dances' performed by girls in honour of JUNO. The worship of foreign deities in Rome made abundant use of dance: the rites of CYBELE were often celebrated with noisy ecstatic dances imported from the East. Roman dinner-parties were often enlivened with professional dancers or mimes. Some became notorious and wealthy: Lykoris, for example, was born a slave in c.70 BC but became a celebrated dancer and ultimately the mistress of MARK ANTONY. LL-J

See Lawler, L. B. (1964) *The Dance in Ancient Greece*.

 BACCHUS; PROCESSIONS.

Danube (anc. Danuvius, from CELTIC or THRACIAN) A major river originating in the ALPS and

DANCE: (b) Etruscan dance from Tarquinian tomb painting.

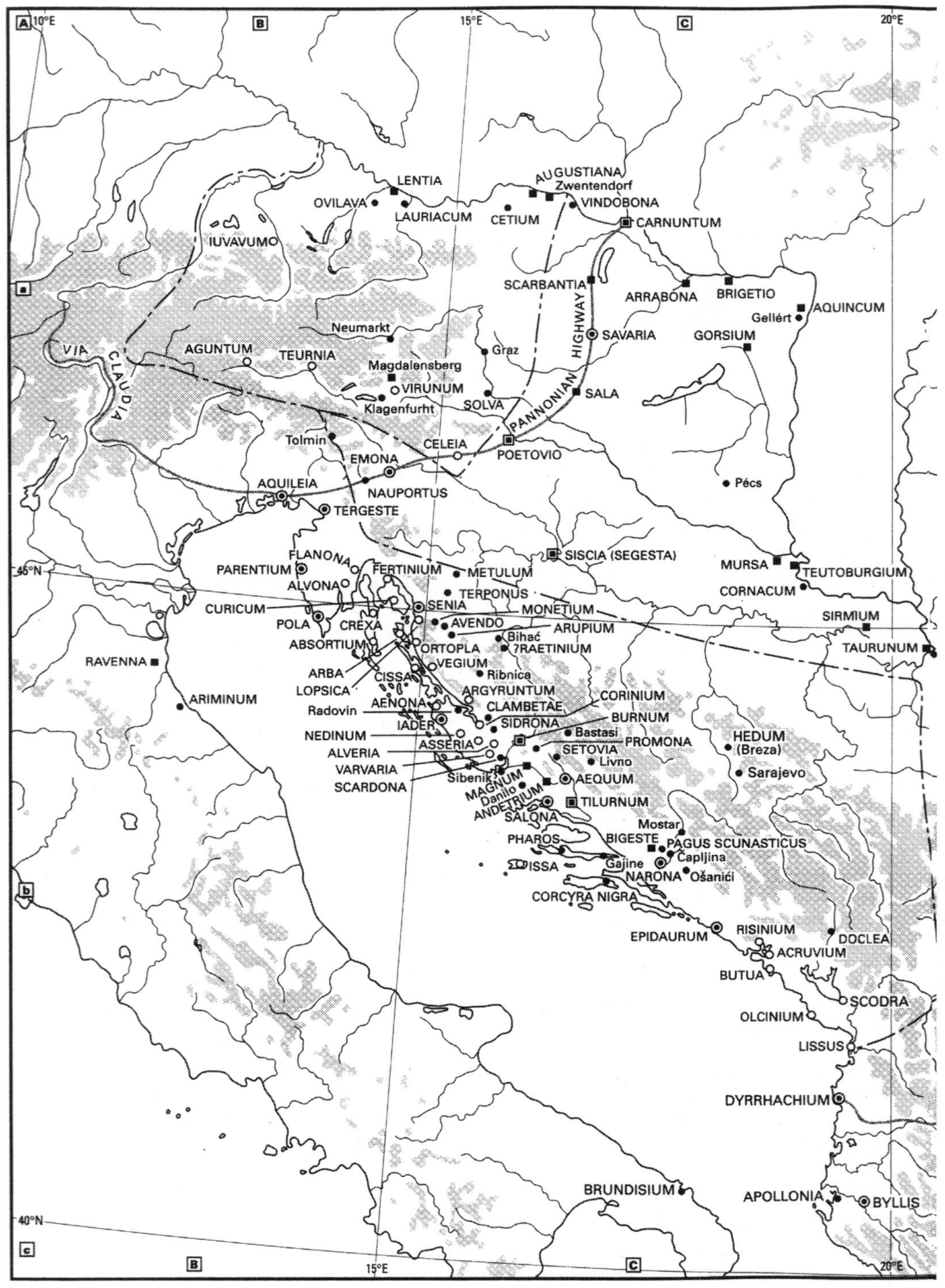

DANUBE: map of principal Roman sites in the Adriatic and Danubian regions.

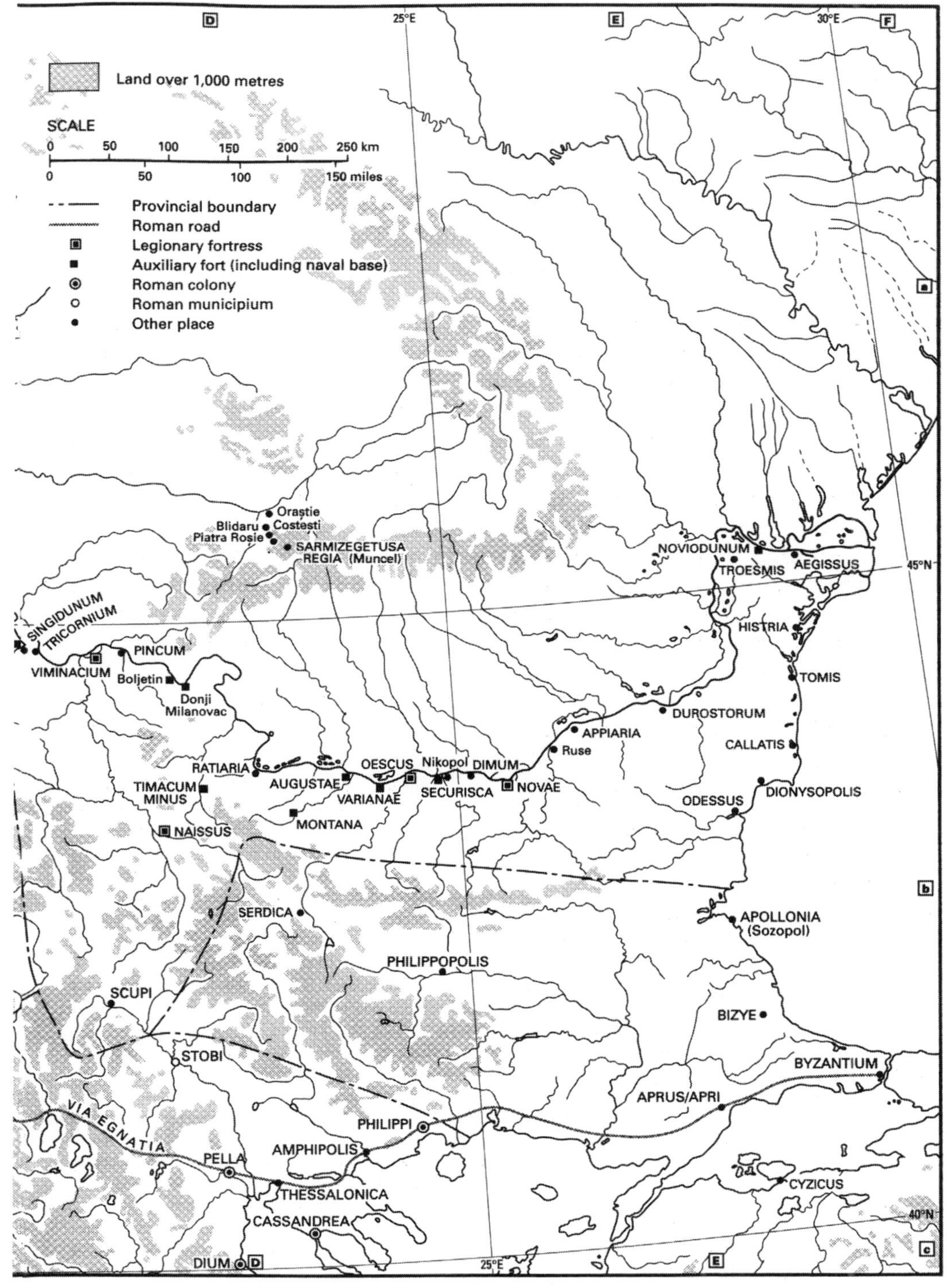

Land over 1,000 metres
SCALE
0 50 100 150 200 250 km
0 50 100 150 miles
Provincial boundary
Roman road
Legionary fortress
Auxiliary fort (including naval base)
Roman colony
Roman municipium
Other place
D
E
F
25°E
30°E
45°N
40°N
a
b
c
Orăştie
Blidaru
Costeşti
Piatra Roşie
SARMIZEGETUSA REGIA (Muncel)
NOVIODUNUM
TROESMIS
AEGISSUS
HISTRIA
TOMIS
DUROSTORUM
CALLATIS
DIONYSOPOLIS
ODESSUS
APPIARIA
Ruse
SINGIDUNUM
TRICORNIUM
PINCUM
VIMINACIUM
Boljetin
Donji Milanovac
RATIARIA
AUGUSTAE
OESCUS
Nikopol
DIMUM
VARIANAE
SECURISCA
NOVAE
TIMACUM MINUS
MONTANA
NAISSUS
SERDICA
APOLLONIA (Sozopol)
PHILIPPOPOLIS
SCUPI
BIZYE
STOBI
BYZANTIUM
APRUS/APRI
VIA EGNATIA
PHILIPPI
AMPHIPOLIS
PELLA
THESSALONICA
CYZICUS
CASSANDREA
DIUM

emptying into the BLACK SEA, the Danube was for most of antiquity the boundary of classical civilization. The lower portion, *Istros* in Greek ('Ister' in English), lay in Thracian and SCYTHIAN territory, beyond which the landscape was desolate and peopled by unknown inhabitants, according to Herodotos (5.9). Except for DACIA north of the river, the Danube marked the limits of the Roman empire after the PANNONIAN WARS of AUGUSTUS. Despite campaigns across it (from both sides), the river was generally recognized as a boundary. In AD 369, the Gothic chieftain Athanaric and the emperor Valens signed a treaty in neutral territory on an island in the river. A few years later, in 376, some of the GOTHS asked permission to cross the Danube and settle in Roman territory. CONSTANTINE's campaigns in the 330s had resulted in positive relations with the Goths, but were not designed to extend the empire.

Despite problems with ice in winter and spring, the Danube was navigable for much of its length and the Romans maintained small fleets to patrol it. Canals and towpaths were built through the Djerdap, a narrow gorge from Olubac to Orsova, and at the Iron Gates, just below Orsova. The most important BRIDGE, whose ruins remain visible, was built at Drobeta under TRAJAN and rebuilt under Constantine. Many FORTS and other military installations were constructed throughout the Roman period, and the boundary was considerably strengthened under VALENTINIAN and Valens in the 360s and 370s. JV

DALMATIA; SACRIFICE: (d).

Darius I 522–486 BC King of Persia, who succeeded to the throne after overthrowing Bardiya (or Gaumata) and quashing several rebellions in the empire. Scholars have expressed doubt as to whether he was the legitimate successor, suspecting him of killing the rightful heir, Bardiya, rather than the impostor Gaumata. It certainly seems to have been necessary for Darius to legitimate his reign through an extensive marriage policy, extending to the female members of the royal family, and by ensuring the support of the nobility through rewards and privileges. In his genealogy he established an Achaemenid clan which enabled him to demonstrate a familial link between his family and that of CYRUS THE GREAT. He completed Cyrus' city Pasargadai and laid claim to the ancient ELAMITE capital, Susa, before founding the Achaemenid royal centre, PERSEPOLIS.

Darius extended Persian power to THRACE, MACEDONIA and INDIAN territory. In a period of consolidation he reassessed tribute payments of the empire, implemented legal reforms, and introduced Persian COINAGE, the *daric*. Maintenance of the Royal ROADS facilitated communication and overland trade, while the completion of a canal between the Red sea and the NILE improved maritime commerce. In 490 Darius ordered a punitive campaign against ATHENS and Eretria for their involvement in the IONIAN REVOLT (499/8–493/2); this ended in the Persian defeat at MARATHON. A rebellion in Egypt delayed his plan for a renewed attack on Athens, and after his death in December 486 it was left to XERXES to carry out his father's plans. MB

See Wiesehöfer, J. (2001) *Ancient Persia*.

Darius III see ALEXANDER III; PERSIAN EMPIRE; PERSIAN WARS, GREEK.

Datames Persian officer and independent ruler of CAPPADOCIA in the late 370s and 360s BC, who played an important part in the revolt of the satraps (372–362/1). Datames' career demonstrates the advantage the Achaemenids gained through reliance on their ÉLITE, as well the danger such reliance entailed. We know him chiefly through his coins and an excellent biography by CORNELIUS NEPOS (1st century BC).

Born c.405, Datames was the son of Kamisares, a sub-satrap in CILICIA. Having won distinction through military service, he was sent by ARTAXERXES II in 373/2 to replace Pharnabazos as commander of the PERSIAN forces occupied with quelling revolt in Egypt. Replaced himself shortly thereafter, Datames returned to Asia Minor and, as his COINAGE attests, controlled at various points territory stretching from Tarsus to Sinope. He eventually carved out a region of northern CAPPADOCIA that was completely detached from Achaemenid control. While our sources do not make it clear, he may have co-ordinated his crossing of the Euphrates with attacks on the Persians launched by other regional rulers (Tachos in Egypt, Orontes in SYRIA, Agesilaos in PHOENICIA). The effort eventually failed and Datames was probably assassinated, though Cappadocia remained independent for some time. He is the only 'barbarian', apart from Hamilcar and HANNIBAL, selected for treatment by Nepos, for whom he is an exemplar of intelligent generalship and good faith. JDD

See Hornblower, S. (1994) Persia, in *CAH* 6, 45–96; Moysey, R. A. (1989) Observations on the numismatic evidence relating to the great satrapal revolt of 362/1, *REA* 91: 107–39; Sekunda, N. V. (1988) Some notes on the life of Datames, *Iran* 26: 35–53.

Dead sea scrolls In 1947 a cache of parchment and leather scrolls was discovered near Qumran, a site in the Judaean desert close to the north-western coast of the Dead sea. The texts had been hidden inside jars in a series of caves. The manuscripts have been dated between 200 BC and AD 100. They were probably deposited during or after the Jewish revolt of AD 66–70. Most of the texts contain excerpts of BIBLICAL books, but some are commentaries on biblical works and a number are sectarian writings, including rules for a distinctive sectarian community.

The biblical manuscripts are of interest primarily as evidence for textual variants and the complex transmission of the Hebrew text. A copy of a distinctive Greek translation of some of the Psalms reflects an early stage in the revision of the SEPTUAGINT. The biblical commentaries in some cases contain the Hebrew originals of texts previously known only from translations (such as *Jubilees*). They also reveal the ancient origins of some motifs in the interpretation of particular biblical passages found otherwise in rabbinic works of later periods. The *pesher* form of commentary, in which a biblical passage is understood as a coded account of an event in the more recent past, seems to have been a technique distinctive of the Dead sea sect.

The other sectarian documents include the Rule of the Community, the War Scroll (a description of the eschatological struggle between the Sons of Light and the Sons of Darkness), the Temple Scroll (an idiosyncratic paraphrase of part of *Deuteronomy*) and Miqsat Maasei-ha Torah (MMT, a letter purporting to have been sent by the leader of the community to the high priest in Jerusalem).

The scrolls derive from different periods, and not all were composed or copied by sectarians. The sectarian texts are probably best interpreted in conjunction with the settlement site at Qumran, which confirms evidence of communal life from the 2nd century BC to the late 1st century AD. According to these texts, the existence of members of the sect was governed by strict rules which were enforced by severe punishments. Religious RITUAL revolved around communal meals. Differences of practice found in the various sectarian rules, in particular with regard to the role of WOMEN, must be accounted for either by the development of the sect over time or by the existence of various branches.

Scholars have identified the Dead sea sect with almost every other type of JUDAISM known to have flourished in this period. The most common and plausible identification is with the ESSENES. However, the sectarian documents do not fit precisely the ancient description of any group. Although the discrepancies can be explained away, it may be better to see the main value of the scrolls as the evidence they provide for a type of Judaism not mentioned in the texts preserved since antiquity by rabbinic Judaism and early CHRISTIANITY. MDG

See Vermes, G. (1997) *The Dead Sea Scrolls in English.*

deafness see DISABILITY.

death HOMER, our earliest literary source, depicts death (*thanatos*) as a miserable state in which the deceased, who dwell in HADES, are merely feeble images (*psychai*) of their living selves. For this reason the ghost of ACHILLES in the *Odyssey* (book 11) claims that life as an unknown serf would have been better than a HERO's death. But Homer is also aware of other views: certain extraordinary CRIMINALS are tried and punished by the judges of the underworld, a picture which suggests a conceptual link between death and MORALITY; on the other hand, some heroes are thought to live a happy afterlife in the 'Islands of the Blessed' or Elysium (HESIOD is another early source for this idea). Optimistic beliefs in a better existence after death for ordinary people are reflected in the popular cults of the mystery religions (e.g. the ELEUSINIAN MYSTERIES). On the basis of all these traditions, PLATO, the PYTHAGOREANS and some other philosophical and religious movements developed elaborate theories about death, the SOUL and the AFTERLIFE.

Roman views are similarly varied. CICERO and CATULLUS speak of death (*mors*) as extinction or an eternal sleep. The belief was nevertheless widespread that the dead continued an existence as shades (*manes*). As such, they received the regular worship and observance of their descendants, notably at the FESTIVAL of Parentalia. Veneration was given especially to the Lares, the spirits of dead ANCESTORS, to whom prayers were offered every day. Like the Greeks, the Romans took disposal of their dead very seriously. The spirits of the unburied and of those improperly interred were thought to be the most malevolent. MJ

See Garland, R. (1985) *The Greek Way of Death*; Toynbee, J. M. C. (1971) *Death and Burial in the Roman World.*

 RITUAL.

debt Ubiquitous at all levels of society in the classical world, debt was a trap for the poor, which tied them to wealthy men by making the former dependent on the willingness of the latter to tide them over hard times with a LOAN. Despite the ideals of self-sufficiency and independence pervading the works of moral writers such as the Greek Hesiod and the Roman Cato, it was probably difficult for the poor to escape debt for long.

In contrast, for the wealthy, loans could provide a way of expanding their networks and pursuing their social ambitions. In classical Athens, for example, the *eranos* ('friendly loan') was a common institution. Wealthy men regularly incurred public obligations to perform services for the state (LITURGIES, e.g. equipping a warship or producing a play), and private duties such as providing a dowry for a daughter or ransoming relatives or FRIENDS captured in war. To raise money for such endeavours, they would ask for part of the sum needed from a range of friends and relations. These loans were 'friendly' because they came from friends and were felt to underpin the sense of obligation between friends. They carried low rates of interest, or occasionally were interest-free.

Generally, debt was not incurred for 'productive' purposes in classical antiquity – that is, to invest in a business venture or other productive enterprise. More commonly, borrowed money was spent by the wealthy on display, and the investment was in enhanced social and/or political prestige. (see also DEBT-BONDAGE; ÉLITE) LF

See Millett, P. C. (1991) *Lending and Borrowing in Ancient Athens.*

debt-bondage This occurs when a person pledges his personal services as security for a DEBT. This institution should be distinguished from cases of enslavement for debt, where the creditor is able to seize the debtor on default of payment of the debt, and either keep him as a SLAVE or sell him to somebody else. It seems most likely that it was this practice, not debt-bondage, that was outlawed by SOLON (fr. 36 West; Aristotle, *Constitution of Athens* 2.2, 6.1). In cases of debt-bondage, the creditor only gains rights to the services of an individual for a limited time until the debt is paid.

The institution of debt-bondage is attested throughout the ancient Mediterranean and Near East. There are references to the institution in the laws of Hammurabi, and in Hebrew scriptures. The GORTYN CODE mentions the institution, and seems to accord the debt-bondsman a position between slave and free man. So, for example, if anybody harmed such a man, half the damages went to the creditor and half to the man himself. In contrast, if anybody harmed a slave, the damages went entirely to the master. Evidence from Athens is thinner. A fragment of ISAIOS seems to refer to the institution. Plots involving debt-bondage can be found in New COMEDY, and there are allusions to the institution in other dramas. The Roman form of debt-bondage was denoted by the term *nexum*, and references to it can be found in the TWELVE TABLES (6.1). It was abolished by the *lex Poetilia* in the early 4th century BC (326 or 313) after a number of abuses, which supposedly included attempted rape and beatings. The precise procedure by which the debtor was bonded, and the terms of his or her indenture, were debated in antiquity and remain unclear today.

Debt-bondage existed because securing a means of livelihood for many in the ancient world was a difficult and unsure enterprise. The victims of debt-bondage are almost always those at the very bottom of society. REFUGEES from war, orphans and those whose meagre farms have been blighted by disease are typical examples of those forced into such agreements. AJLB

See Finley, M. I. (1981) *Economy and Society in Ancient Greece* 150–66; Harris, E. M. (2002) Did Solon abolish debt-bondage? *CQ* 52: 415–30; Watson, W. A. J. (1975) *Rome of the XII Tables* 111–24.

Decebalus King of the DACIANS (late 1st and early 2nd century AD). During the early 80s, the Dacians had been reunited by Decebalus' predecessor, Diurpaneus, who established a capital at Sarmizegethusa c.100 km (60 miles) north of the Danube, opposite the province of Moesia. Unexpectedly, Decebalus attacked Moesia in the winter of 85–6, with initial success despite two visits to the region by DOMITIAN himself. Under the command of Tettius Iulianus at the battle of Tapae in 88, the Roman forces defeated the Dacians. Decebalus asked for peace, not granted until 89 at a conference between Domitian, who had returned following a Roman defeat, and Decebalus' brother Diegis. Decebalus became a CLIENT king, but a troublesome one.

From early in his reign, TRAJAN prepared for a DACIAN campaign, which took place in 101–2. Despite defeat, Decebalus and his people continued to threaten, and Trajan undertook a second campaign in 105–6. Decebalus' SUICIDE to avoid capture is depicted on TRAJAN'S COLUMN. His kingdom became the Roman province of Dacia, while Sarmizegethusa became the colony Ulpia Traiana. Dacian booty provided the funds for a massive triumphal celebration and building programme at Rome. JV

See Bennett, J. (1997) *Trajan: optimus princeps.*

DECEBALUS: detail from Trajan's column of the suicide of Decebalus, enabling him to evade capture by the Roman cavalry whose horses can be seen bearing down on him.

Decius see CHRISTIANITY; CYPRIAN; PERSECUTION; PHILIP THE ARAB; SCHISM; VALERIAN.

 EMPERORS, ROMAN: (b).

declamation A practice speech on a fictional topic. Declamatory exercises include *controversiae*, which deal with conflicting laws or with scenarios in which LAW and equity clash; *suasoriae*, in which the declaimer pretends to advise a legendary or historical figure at a turning-point in his life; and discussions of general issues or theses of the kind 'Should a man marry?' Originally part of RHETORICAL training in Greece and Rome, declamation flourished as an independent activity in the early empire, where it constituted a politically safe venue for the pursuit of glory. Declamation reinforced the privileged position of ÉLITE males by training them to articulate the interests of those without voice in Roman society, namely women, children and former SLAVES. In both style and outlook declamation influenced many literary texts, including OVID'S *Metamorphoses* and the satires of JUVENAL. But it provoked controversy as well, because of the unreality of many of its topics. PETRONIUS parodied it in the *Satyricon*, and QUINTILIAN said that teaching it to free youths was the equivalent of castrating slaves. Besides SENECA THE ELDER, the writing of Sopatros (Greek) and pseudo-Quintilian (Latin) provide the most important evidence for theory and practice of declamation. TNH

deconstructionism see CRITICAL THEORY; POST-MODERNISM; STRUCTURALISM AND POST-STRUCTURALISM.

deification see ALEXANDER III; HERO-CULT; HEROES; IMPERIAL CULT; RULER-CULT.

Deinarchos see ORATORS, GREEK.

deities see GODS AND GODDESSES; RELIGION.

Delos A tiny island (3 sq km, 1 sq mile) which owed its importance in antiquity to its claim to be the birthplace of APOLLO and ARTEMIS. Cult at the site of the sanctuary has been traced back to MYCENAEAN times. During the archaic and classical periods the sanctuary attracted attention from the neighbouring islands of the Cyclades (which took their name from the notion that they 'encircled' Delos), especially NAXOS, which exercised a kind of hegemony over the island in the 6th century. Naxian dedications included a series of MARBLE lions and a colossal statue of Apollo. The island became a centre of cult for the Ionians and a component of the Athenian claim to be the *metropolis* of the Ionian cities. This helps explain its interest to PEISISTRATOS, who conducted a purification there, and the choice under Athenian leadership to house the administrative organs and treasury of the Delian league on the island. For much of the 5th and 4th centuries the island or its sanctuaries were controlled through an amphiktiony under the Athenians. In the late 4th century the Delians regained control of the island, and it later attracted dedications by hellenistic monarchs. The administrators of the sanctuary compiled masses of information about its operation, which was recorded annually on inscriptions; the data they preserve has played an important role in understanding the economy and operation of the sanctuary. In 167 BC, as a way of punishing RHODES, the Romans gave the island back to the Athenians, who expelled the Delians and installed their own government. Thanks to the abolition of harbour dues, the island grew into an important centre of long-distance trade. To this period date most of the remains currently visible, including the spectacular multi-storey private houses with MOSAICS and frescoes. The depredations of 88 and especially 69 BC drastically reduced the population, and although the island continued to have a small population through the rest of antiquity it never recovered its former importance. GR

See Habicht, C. (1997) *Athens from Alexander to Antony*, ch. 10; Hamilton, R. (2000) *Treasure Map: a guide to the Delian inventories*; Reger, G. (2004) Delos, in Hansen and Nielsen, *Inventory* 738–40; (1994) *Regionalism and Change in the Economy of Independent Delos*.

Delphi Situated in PHOKIS in central Greece, Delphi was the home of an oracular sanctuary dedicated to the god APOLLO Pythios. The site was renowned for the ATHLETIC contests organized there, the Pythian games, as part of the Pythia FESTIVAL marking one of the four major panhellenic (national) encounters in antiquity. The fame of the ORACLE extended beyond the boundaries of the Greek world to include colonial Greek populations and foreign rulers. Apollo's cult became prominent at the site in the Geometric period, replacing an earlier cult of a female deity generally identified with Earth. By the 6th century BC the popularity of the Delphic sanctuary was flourishing under the administration of the Amphiktyony (or Amphtiktiony), a league of neighbouring cities who ensured the protection and autonomy of the sanctuary. The latter was maintained after the first (600–590 BC) and second (448 BC) SACRED WARS and proved to be a significant factor contributing to the oracle's prestige and influence on political and religious matters on a panhellenic scale. Of these, COLONIZATION was a vital issue on which the oracle was regularly consulted. The extent of the control and/or manipulation that the Delphic oracle may have exercised in the shaping of inter-state politics in Greece through its regular consultation by states and individuals is still a matter of dispute among scholars.

In the 4th century BC Delphi enjoyed the patronage of PHILIP II of MACEDONIA, whose military intervention in the third (356 BC) and fourth (339 BC) sacred wars saved the sanctuary's land and treasures from the threat of the Phokians and Lokrians. Philip introduced a period of substantial refurbishment and rebuilding in the sanctuary. After a period of dominance by the AITOLIANS, who successfully kept the sanctuary safe from Gallic assaults, the Romans took over in 191 BC. Under Roman rule, the political significance of Delphi declined dramatically while its treasures often fell prey to the plunder of Roman GENERALS (e.g. SULLA in 86 BC) and tribes like the THRACIAN Maides in 83 BC. Revivals of the PAGAN shrine and oracle were short-lived and came as a result of the politics of some Roman EMPERORS, notably HADRIAN (AD 117–38) and later JULIAN the Apostate (AD 360–3). The coming of CHRISTIANITY put an inevitable end to the operations of the oracle through a decree issued by THEODOSIUS I.

EXCAVATIONS at Delphi began in 1893 under the auspices of the French School in Athens. They have uncovered TEMPLES of the major divinities at the site, Apollo Pythios and ATHENA Pronaia, as well as other sacred buildings in the sanctuary including a range of treasuries (*thêsauroi*) for storing valuables. Significant public buildings were found outside the sanctuary, notably the GYMNASIUM and stadium, but also parts of the cemetery and the settlement. EP

See Jacquemin, A., ed. (1992) *Delphes cent ans après la grande fouille*; Morgan, C. A. (1990) *Athletes and Oracles*; Price, S. (1985) Delphi and divination, in P. E. Easterling and J.V. Muir, eds., *Greek Religion and Society* 128–54.

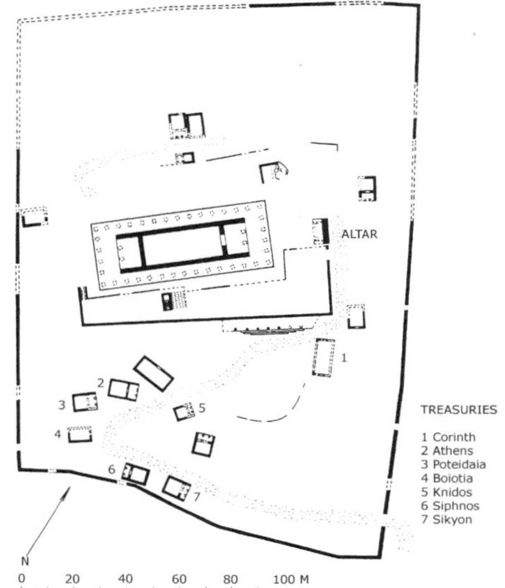

DELPHI: plan of sanctuary of Apollo.

Demades c.380–319 BC Athenian politician. He proved his negotiating skills in 338 BC when he swore to uphold the peace treaty with PHILIP II, and again in 335 when rescuing Athens from ALEXANDER's wrath. He proposed honours for certain leading Macedonians – even divine honours for Alexander – initiating a policy of rapprochement with Macedonia and avoidance of any rush to involvement in military conflict. At the same time Demades saw to military finance and maintenance of the fleet, which indicates that he did have Athens' best interests in mind, contrary to accusations of pro-Macedonian affiliations. His policies should better be described in terms of acceptance of Athens' military weakness and adjustment to the needs of the moment.

After Athens' defeat in the LAMIAN WAR in 322/1, he participated in the peace negotiations with Antipatros which resulted in the establishment of a Macedonian garrison and an OLIGARCHIC regime.

What has harmed his reputation the most is that he proposed the decree condemning to death the orators responsible for the war. However, in order to have the garrison withdrawn Demades tried to take advantage of the struggle between Antipatros and Perdikkas; his activities were discovered, and Kassandros (Antipatros' son) put him to death. IK

See Burtt, J. O., trs. (1954) *Minor Attic Orators*, vol. 2; Brun, P. (2000) *L'Orateur Démade*.

demagogue see KLEON; OSTRACISM.

demes (*dêmos*, pl. *dêmoi*, lit. 'people, peoples') Population centres in the city and countryside of ATTICA, of varying size and complexity. Of the 139 demes in the classical period, some were the size of a small town (ELEUSIS and Acharnai) while others were small VILLAGES, some of which have yet to be identified on the map. Most demes had an identifiable focus, such as an *AGORA* or a place for public meetings. All had a principal MAGISTRATE, the demarch (*dêmarchos*), and celebrated local religious FESTIVALS for which inscribed CALENDARS have survived (e.g. Thorikos and Erchia). Some demes had their own THEATRE: Aixone and Euonymon shared one, located at modern Trachones; Ikarion had one of Dionysos; there were others at PIRAEUS, Rhamnous and Thorikos. Other demes were home to cults of importance to the *POLIS* as a whole (ARTEMIS at Brauron) and even to the Greek world (the Mysteries at ELEUSIS).

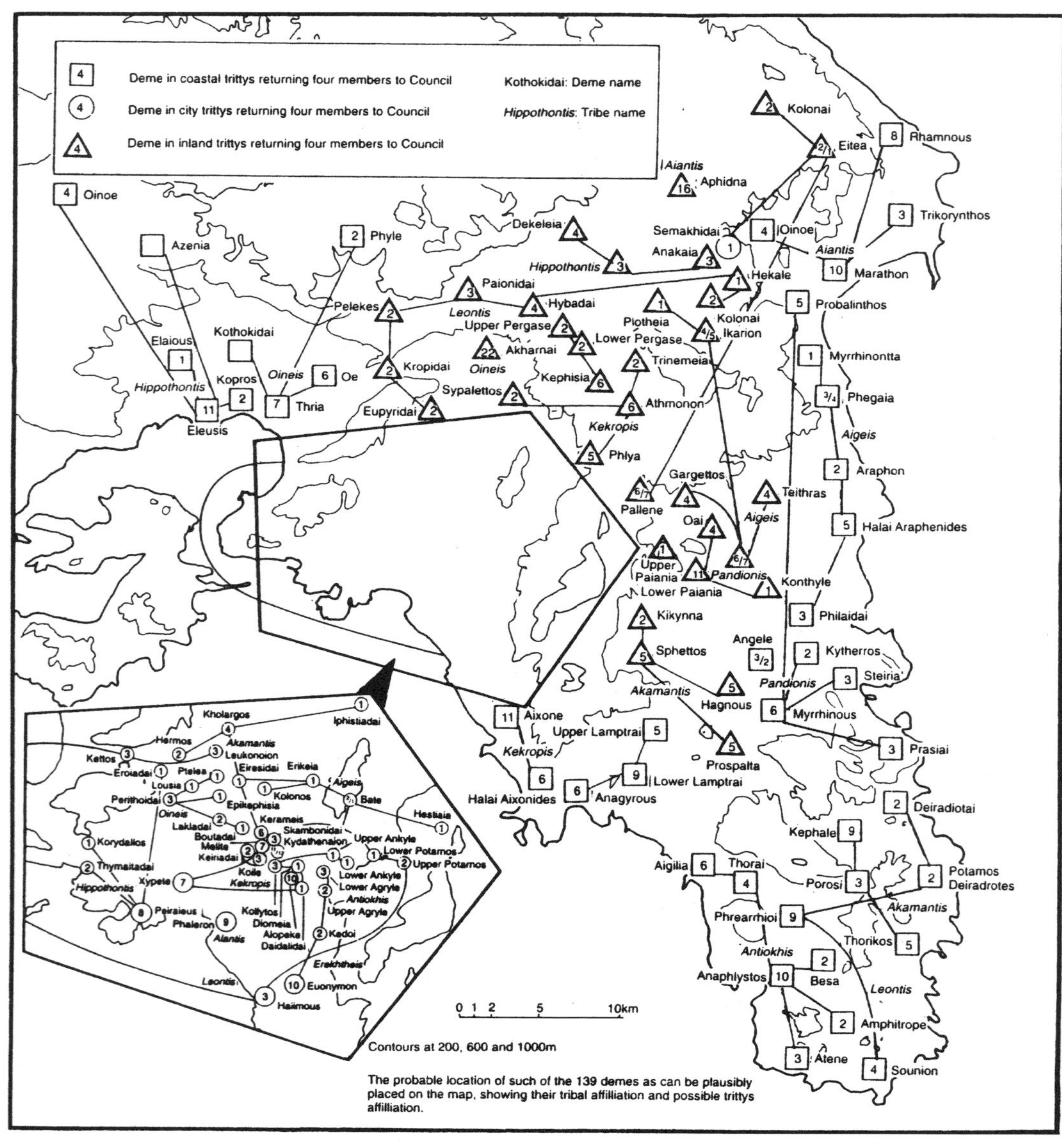

DEMES: (a) map of probable locations of Attic demes.

DEMES: (b) the Demes of Attica, with tribe, *trittys* and number of councillors.

Deme	Tribe	*Trittys*	Councillors
Acharnai (part)	Oineis	city	7 or 6?
Acharnai (part)	Oineis	inland	15 or 16
Acherdous	Hippothontis	inland?	1
Agryle, Lower	Erechtheis	city	3
Agryle, Upper	Erechtheis	city	2
Aigilia	Antiochis	inland	6
Aithalidai	Leontis	inland	2
Aixone	Kekropis	coast	11
Alopeke	Antiochis	city	10
Amphitrope	Antiochis	coast	2
Anagyrous	Erechtheis	coast	6
Anakaia	Hippothontis	inland?	3
Anaphlystos	Antiochis	coast	10
Angele	Pandionis	coast	3 or 2
Ankyle, Lower	Aigeis	city	1
Ankyle, Upper	Aigeis	city	1
Aphidna	Aiantis	inland	16
Araphen	Aigeis	coast	2
Atene	Antiochis	coast	3
Athmonon	Kekropis	inland	6?
Auridai	Hippothontis	coast?	1
Azenia	Hippothontis	inland?	2
Bate	Aigeis	city	2 or 1
Besa	Antiochis	coast	2
Boutadai	Oineis	city	1
Cholargos	Akamantis	city	4
Cholleidai	Leontis	city	2
Daidalidai	Kekropis	city or inland?	1
Deiradiotai	Leontis	coast	2
Dekeleia	Hippothontis	inland	4
Diomeia	Aigeis	coast	1
Eiresidai	Akamantis	city	1
Eitea	Akamantis	city	2
Eitea	Antiochis	city	2 or 1
Elaious	Hippothontis	coast?	1
Eleusis	Hippothontis	coast	11?
Epieikidai	Kekropis	city or inland?	1
Epikephisia	Oineis	city	1
Erchia	Aigeis	inland	6 or 7
Erikeia	Aigeis	city	1
Eroiadai	Hippothontis	city?	1
Eroiadai	Antiochis	city	1
Euonymon	Erechtheis	city	10
Eupyridai	Leontis	inland	2
Gargettos	Aigeis	inland	4

DEMES: (b) the Demes of Attica, with tribe, *trittys* and number of councillors (cont.)

Deme	Tribe	*Trittys*	Councillors
Hagnous	Akamantis	inland	5
Halai Aixonides	Kekropis	coast	6
Halai Araphenides	Aigeis	coast	5
Halimous	Leontis	city	3
Hamaxanteia	Hippothontis	coast?	1
Hekale	Leontis	inland	1
Hermos	Akamantis	city	2
Hestiaia	Aigeis	city	1
Hippotomadai	Oineis	city?	1
Hybadai	Leontis	inland	2
Ikarion	Aigeis	city	4 or 5
Ionidai	Aigeis	inland	2 or 1
Iphistiadai	Akamantis	city	1
Kedoi	Erechtheis	city?	2
Keiriadai	Hippothontis	city	2
Kephale	Akamantis	coast	9
Kephisia	Erechtheis	inland	6
Kerameis	Akamantis	city	6
Kettos	Leontis	city	3
Kikynna	Akamantis	inland	2
Koile	Hippothontis	city	3
Kollytos	Aigeis	city	3
Kolonai	Leontis	inland	2
Kolonai	Antiochis	city	2
Kolonos	Aigeis	city	2
Konthyle	Pandionis	inland	1
Kopros	Hippothontis	coast	2
Korydallos	Hippothontis	city	1
Kothokidai	Oineis	coast	2
Krioa	Antiochis	city	1
Kropidai	Leontis	inland	1
Kydantidai	Aigeis	inland	2 or 1
Kydathenaion	Pandionis	city	11 or 12
Kytherros	Pandionis	coast	2
Lakiadai	Oineis	city	2
Lamptrai, Lower	Erechtheis	coast	9
Lamptrai, Upper	Erechtheis	inland	5
Leukonoion	Leontis	city	3
Lousia	Oineis	city	1
Marathon	Aiantis	coast	10
Melite	Kekropis	city	7
Myrrhinous	Pandionis	coast	6
Myrrhinoutta	Aigeis	coast	1
Oai	Pandionis	inland	4
Oe	Oineis	coast	6

DEMES: (b) the Demes of Attica, with tribe, *trittys* and number of councillors (cont.)

Deme	Tribe	*Trittys*	Councillors
Oinoe	Hippothontis	inland?	4
Oinoe	Aiantis	coast	4
Oion Dekeleikon	Hippothontis	inland	3
Oion Kerameikon	Leontis	inland	1
Otryne	Aigeis	city?	1
Paiania, Lower	Pandionis	inland	11
Paiania, Upper	Pandionis	inland	1
Paionidai	Leontis	inland	3
Pallene	Antiochis	inland	6 or 7
Pambotadai	Erechtheis	coast?	1 or 0*
Peiraieus	Hippothontis	city	8?
Pelekes	Leontis	inland	2
Pergase, Lower	Erechtheis	inland	2
Pergase, Upper	Erechtheis	inland	2
Perithoidai	Oineis	city	3
Phaleron	Aiantis	city	9
Phegaia	Aigeis	coast	3 or 4
Phegous	Erechtheis	inland?	1
Philaidai	Aigeis	inland	3
Phlya	Kekropis	inland	5?
Phrearrhoi	Leontis	coast	9
Phyle	Oineis	coast	2
Pithos	Kekropis	inland or city	2 or 3
Plotheia	Aigeis	city	1
Poros	Akamantis	coast	3
Potamos Deiradiotes	Leontis	coast	2
Potamos, Lower	Leontis	city	1
Potamos, Upper	Leontis	city	2
Prasia	Pandionis	coast	3
Probalinthos	Pandionis	city	5
Prospalta	Akamantis	inland	5
Ptelea	Oineis	city	1
Rhamnous	Aiantis	city	8
Semachidai	Antiochis	city	1
Skambonidai	Leontis	city	3
Sounion	Leontis	coast	4
Sphettos	Akamantis	inland	5
Steria	Pandionis	coast	3
Sybridai	Erechtheis	coast?	1 or 0**
Sypalettos	Kekropis	inland	2
Teithras	Aigeis	coast	4
Themakos	Erechtheis	inland?	1
Thorai	Antiochis	inland	4
Thorikos	Akamantis	coast	5
Thria	Oineis	coast	7

DEMES: (b) the Demes of Attica, with tribe, *trittys* and number of councillors (cont.)

Deme	Tribe	*Trittys*	Councillors
Thymaitadai	Hippothontis	city	2
Trikorynthos	Aiantis	coast	3
Trinemeia	Kekropis	inland	2
Tyrmeidai	Oineis	inland?	1 or 0
Xypete	Kekropis		7

A large deme like Acharnai might be in more than one *trittys*. Each deme's quota of councillors for the Council (*Boulê*) gives a rough indication of the size of the deme. Larger demes were allowed more councillors (e.g. Aphidna), while very small demes would alternate with another small deme to provide one councillor for every year (e.g. * Pambotadai and ** Sybridai).

The demes are important not only as a feature of the human GEOGRAPHY of Attica, but also because they were the fundamental building blocks of the three-tiered structure of the KLEISTHENIC organization of the Athenian *polis* (deme, *trittys*, TRIBE). Every Athenian citizen had to be registered at the age of 18 in the same deme as his father. As subsequent generations of citizens moved away from their familial deme, membership no longer became an indication of residency.

The role of the deme in the military and civic structure of the city meant that membership was not the only feature of an individual's identity. The demes were parcelled into groups called *trittyes*, or 'thirds' of tribes (like the three 'ridings' of Yorkshire in England), identified as coastal, city or inland depending on their geographical location. There were ten *trittyes* in each of these three geographic groups, making 30 *trittyes* in all. Each of the ten tribes was made up of three *trittyes*, taking one from each geographical group: each tribe thus had a *trittys* of coastal demes, one of city demes, and one of inland demes. The armed forces of Athens were organized and mustered on the basis of tribes and *trittyes*, and the distribution of demes into *trittyes* meant that no tribe was dominated by any one particular geographical area.

Each deme provided a number of councillors for the *boulê* (council) each year, the number depending on the deme's population. The larger demes provided the most councillors each year: Eleusis and (Lower) Paiania provided about 11 each, Acharnai about 22. The same structure of *trittyes* and tribes made up the council. Any Athenian citizen was therefore simultaneously a member of a tribe, a *trittys*, and a deme but did not necessarily reside in that deme.

Study of Athenian history has shown that the most active politicians are not known to have cut their teeth in deme politics. But Thucydides (2.16) tells us that for many Athenians their deme felt like their *polis*, and that abandoning the deme (if it lay at a distance from Athens) for the city, for reasons of safety during the PELOPONNESIAN WAR, was particularly traumatic. GJO

See Osborne, R. G. (1985) *Demos*; Traill, J. S. (1975) *The Political Organization of Attica*; (1986) *Demos and Trittys*; Whitehead, D. (1986) *The Demes of Attica*.

Demeter Greek GODDESS whose domain is inseparable from the earth, its natural cycles and cultivation. References in HOMER are rare. She does not live on Mt Olympos as do the rest of the Olympians. In HESIOD's divine genealogies, she is daughter of the Titans Kronos and Rhea, and sister of ZEUS, POSEIDON, Plouton, HERA and Hestia. Her name (*Dê-mêtêr*) reveals her predominant identity as a mother (*mêtêr* in Greek). This is confirmed by both myth and art through her close bonds with her daughter, Persephone. The *Homeric Hymn to Demeter* provides the earliest account of Demeter's wanderings after Persephone is abducted by the king of the underworld, HADES, to become his queen. The image of the mourning mother is a pervasive theme in the hymn, and it eventually leads to the establishment of her cult at ELEUSIS, where the famous MYSTERIES of the two goddesses were enacted. Demeter is said to have introduced AGRICULTURE to mortals, which was then disseminated from Eleusis by Triptolemos.

Demeter's cult was particularly appealing to WOMEN, who took an active role and enjoyed exclusive participation in her FESTIVALS, notably the Thesmophoria and Haloa. The cult's appeal to rural communities deserves emphasis, as well as the usual location of her worship beyond the boundaries of the *POLIS*. EP

See Cole, S. G. (1994) Demeter in the ancient Greek city and its countryside, in S. E. Alcock and R. Osborne, eds., *Placing the Gods* 199–216; Richardson, N. J. (1974) *The Homeric Hymn to Demeter*.

 ELEUSIS AND ELEUSINIAN MYSTERIES; FESTIVALS, GREEK; GODS AND GODDESSES: (a).

Demetrios I Poliorketes ('the Besieger') c.337–283 BC The first ANTIGONID king of MACEDONIA, son of Antigonos I Monophthalmos. The vicissitudes of his fortune made him the ideal 'tragic' hero for PLUTARCH; he is the only SUCCESSOR of Alexander (other than the non-Macedonian Eumenes of Kardia) to whom Plutarch devoted a *Life*.

In the context of his father's struggle for domination in the eastern MEDITERRANEAN, Demetrios freed Athens from Kassandros (ruler of Macedonia) and restored the DEMOCRACY in 307. In return he was awarded divine honours, among others, but his meddling with civic and religious affairs eventually impaired relations with Athens. In 306, after their victory over PTOLEMY I at SALAMIS, Antigonos and Demetrios assumed the royal title. By 302 Demetrios had brought the region round the Isthmus of CORINTH under his control and re-established the league of Corinth – essentially an alliance against

Kassandros. The Antigonids' success, however, was cut short by their defeat at IPSOS in 301.

Internal strife brought Demetrios back to Athens in 295, where he established a regime with oligarchic features. A dynastic struggle between Kassandros' sons gave him the opportunity to ascend to the Macedonian throne in 294. He extended his control to THESSALY and BOIOTIA, but within a few years he lost everything. His plans to campaign in Asia and to capture Egypt led the other Successors to form a coalition against him and deprive him of Macedonia and the ISLANDS. The city of Athens (but not Piraeus) was liberated in 286 BC. Demetrios did pursue his Asiatic campaign, but was imprisoned by SELEUKOS I and died in captivity. IK

See Plutarch, *Demetrios*; Shipley, G. (2000) *The Greek World after Alexander*; Will, É. (1984) The succession to Alexander, in *CAH* 7.1, 23–61, at 55–61; The formation of the hellenistic kingdoms, in *CAH* 7.1, 101–17, at 101–9.

Demetrios of Phaleron c.355–280 BC Athenian politician, a distinguished student of the PERIPATOS and a prolific writer. In 317 BC Kassandros, ruler of MACEDONIA, established an oligarchic regime in Athens and put Demetrios in charge.

His rule brought about financial prosperity but at the expense of the DEMOCRACY – though the ASSEMBLY, council and courts were retained. Demetrios abolished payment for attending the ASSEMBLY and LAWCOURTS as well as subsidies for attending THEATRE performances (*theôrika*). Thus the state budget was reduced but a significant part of the people were excluded from civic life. He introduced sumptuary laws motivated by Athens' financial needs but also influenced, rather indirectly, by his philosophic ideals. The AREIOPAGOS and seven 'controllers of WOMEN' (*gynaikonomoi*) were responsible for enforcing these laws. Furthermore, Demetrios abolished the LITURGY of *chorêgia*, introducing instead the elective office of *agônothetês*; possibly he also abolished the liturgic *triêrarchia*. He either introduced or reinforced the annually elected board of the seven 'guardians of law' (*nomophylakes*) who supervised civic officials and could veto decisions of the assembly and the COUNCIL. The results of a general CENSUS he carried out have been employed in studies of Athenian DEMOGRAPHY.

In 307 he left Athens, forced out by DEMETRIOS I POLIORKETES (Kassandros' rival). He spent his last years in Egypt, where he became adviser to PTOLEMY I Soter and co-operated with him over the foundation of the LIBRARY of ALEXANDRIA. IK

See Fortenbaugh, W.W. and Schütrumpf, E., eds. (2000) *Demetrius of Phalerum*; Habicht, C. (1997) *Athens from Alexander to Antony*.

democracy From the Greek words *dêmos* ('People') and *kratos* ('sovereign power'), the compound noun *dêmokratia* meaning 'people-power' is first attested in (depending on when one dates them) either HERODOTOS or the OLD OLIGARCH. According to Herodotos, it was KLEISTHENES who in 508/7 BC 'introduced the democracy for the Athenians'. But the new regime was controversial, and the pro-democracy speaker in Herodotos' 'Persian debate' (3.80–3) is careful to avoid the term altogether. For the *dêmos* in question could be taken to mean, not the People as a whole, but the common people, the lower classes, the poor majority of the citizen body; so that instead of 'people-power', *dêmokratia* might be understood as masses-power, or (to use a pardonable anachronism) the dictatorship of the proletariat. 'Old Oligarch' is a modern name for the Athenian author of a radically anti-democratic pamphlet, written probably about 425. One of his aims was to show that the Athenian *dêmos* (in the pejorative sense of the lower classes), though morally and socially contemptible, did at any rate know how to work the democratic system cynically to their own political and economic advantage.

Athens was Greece's, indeed the world's, first CITIZEN democracy. It was, moreover, a direct democracy, not a representative system such as is the norm today (as it has been since the American Revolution of 1776). The qualification for full membership of the Athenian citizen body, or *dêmos* in the sense of people, was simply legitimate citizen birth, not WEALTH as prescribed in the main alternative form of Greek political regime, OLIGARCHY. Once enrolled on the citizen register at the age of 18, an Athenian citizen could vote in the ASSEMBLY (*ekklêsia*), the body which, with the assistance of a COUNCIL of 500 (chosen by lot), decided public policy. From the age of 30 he was eligible to be selected, again by lot, for jury-service in the people's court, and for a wide range of collegial offices, most of which were also appointed by lot. Since use of the lottery presumed that all citizens were equally capable of ruling, and maximized the chances of any one citizen's being appointed to office, it was thoroughly egalitarian. But in the interests of efficiency, strict democratic egalitarianism was suspended in the case of the highest military and financial offices. These were filled instead by direct ELECTION and, in the case of the latter, from a restricted pool of only the very wealthiest citizens. All Athenian democratic officials, however, whether elected or selected by lot, were fully and regularly held accountable to the People through the council and the people's court. The decisions of the people's court were, moreover, final.

To enable as many citizens as possible to play their active part in the democracy, political pay was introduced. At first it was for the jurymen of the people's court (6,000 on the roll at any one time, though juries, chosen of course by lot, usually numbered 501). Later it was introduced for holding office, and finally, from the 390s, for attending the assembly. PERIKLES, in the Funeral Speech attributed to him by THUCYDIDES, emphasized that no Athenian citizen should be debarred from doing his political duty by POVERTY alone. Public pay was also made available for military purposes, for both infantrymen (HOPLITES) and the sailors who rowed the city's warfleet. Since the latter were drawn exclusively from the *dêmos* in the sense of the lower classes, there was a close connection between the development of Athens' 5th-century naval empire and the development of democracy at home – a connection naturally deplored by the Old Oligarch and his fellow members of the Athenian upper class. Public funds were also doled out to the poorest Athenians, both in exceptional times of food emergency (so that they could buy the high-quality wheat that was regularly imported, especially from the Ukraine and Crimea) and to enable them to attend the annual religious play-festival of TRAGEDY, SATYR drama and COMEDY. The THEATRE was considered almost as much a democratic political arena as were the assembly and LAWCOURTS.

Athens was only one of the more than 1,000 separate Greek states, and its democracy was exceptionally radical and well developed. ARISTOTLE, the great theorist of Greek political life within the *polis* or citizen-state, analysed four different grades or degrees of democracy in his *Politics* (written in the 330s), and Athens predictably corresponded most closely to his 'last' or most extreme variety. Under the influence of Athens, and sometimes at Athens' direct behest or intervention, democracy had been exported within the ATHENIAN EMPIRE during the second half of the 5th century. But it reached its widest extension during the 4th century, usually in the more moderate forms described – and approved – by Aristotle.

In 322, however, the new ruling power of Greece, MACEDONIA, formally terminated the democracy at Athens, as it had already done elsewhere throughout most of the AEGEAN Greek world. That termination was in the interests of the Greek upper classes, through whom Macedonia intended to rule its empire. Pockets of democracy nevertheless persisted during the 3rd century, most notably at RHODES. But the Romans shared the view of the Macedonians, whom they conquered along with the remainder of the Greek world during the 2nd century, and their empire was run on strictly oligarchic lines. Although the word democracy survived, it became more and more distanced from its original meaning. In the 2nd century AD, indeed, the Roman empire itself could be described by a Greek orator as 'a perfect democracy – under one man'! By the 6th century, in the reign of the Byzantine EMPEROR JUSTINIAN, the process of linguistic degeneration was complete: 'democracy' could now be used to refer merely to an urban riot. When the term finally recovered a wholly positive sense, in the 19th century, it did so only with a quite different content. This was representative not direct democracy, rule of the people and for the people, perhaps, but not (despite Abraham Lincoln) also by the people. (see also POLITICAL SYSTEMS; POLITICAL THEORY; STATE) PAC

See Finley, M. I. (1985) *Democracy Ancient and Modern*; Forrest, W. G. (1966) *The Emergence of Greek Democracy*; Hansen, M. H. (1999) *The Athenian Democracy in the Age of Demosthenes*; Sinclair, R. K. (1988) *Democracy and Participation in Athens.*

Democritus see DEMOKRITOS.

demography The study of the structure and dynamics of human populations. At its most basic level ancient demography concerns itself with the size of populations, a hotly debated topic since we have little information from antiquity and most of that is contradictory or confused, dealing most often with army sizes. Other avenues of enquiry, based on such factors as the carrying capacity of the land or the quantity of food imports, are unpromising. But scholars have reached some conclusions (about none of which, however, there is total consensus), of which the following figures are of general interest. The male citizen population of ancient Athens in the 4th century BC was of the order of 20,000–30,000; the total population of ancient Greece at the same time was probably around 2 million. The population of the city of Rome in the early 1st century AD was close to 1 million, that of the Roman empire as a whole of the order of 50–60 million.

At a more sophisticated level demography concerns itself with the structure of populations. Three factors are crucial: mortality, fertility and migration. Again ancient evidence is sparse and problematical; the demographer has very little in the way of CENSUS material, or records of births, deaths and MARRIAGES, with which to work. Most ancient evidence, such as tombstone inscriptions and skeletons, is unfortunately of very little value. Over 300 census returns from Roman Egypt have survived, and with sophisticated interpretation they can yield important clues. But we are most reliant on comparative evidence, especially 'model life tables', to clarify what is plausible or probable in terms of ancient populations. There is every reason to believe that many demographic variables differed little between the Greek and Roman worlds (despite the difference in population sizes), and so for convenience both will be treated together.

The most striking feature regarding mortality is how high its rate was from an early age. In general terms average life expectancy at birth was between 20 and 30 years. This highlights, more than anything else perhaps, the vast difference between ancient times and our own. In this regard the ancient world is more comparable to so-called Third World countries today than to 'developed' countries. The low figure is mainly reflective of very harsh levels of infant mortality, owing particularly to gastrointestinal illnesses. One in three children died in their first year of life – a great proportion within the first few weeks, depending upon whether or not infants were breastfed immediately. One in two children did not survive beyond the age of 10. After that life looks a little brighter. A 10-year-old might expect on average to live another 35–40 years, a 40-year old at least another 20 years. So some people in the ancient world did survive into OLD AGE, just not as great a proportion as do today. But most older adults would not have parents alive, and would quite likely themselves have lost children. As for mortality differences due to gender, we cannot be certain. It is highly probable that women did not generally live as long as men (maternal mortality is one relevant factor, though its level should not be exaggerated), and that males very slightly outnumbered females in the population.

Such high mortality may be attributed to a combination of low levels of HYGIENE and SANITATION (particularly in urbanized areas) and of low standards of medical care, as well as poor nutrition for poorer people. We hear much in the ancient sources of food shortages, epidemics (infectious diseases must have taken a severe toll), and war – Malthus' positive checks. Modern demographic methods also allow us to glimpse the nature of the living population in terms of age structure, and here another notable difference from our own experience occurs. Ancient populations would have been very young: something like half the population would have been under the age of 25 at any one time, and only about 7 per cent over the age of 60.

To counteract such high mortality, fertility levels also needed to be high. A woman in the ancient world on average gave birth five or six times (we must remember that many of these births resulted in infant death). Some WOMEN produced many more than that; the (alleged) record was 30 births, while one woman in Roman Egypt was said to have given birth to quintuplets on four separate occasions. Other women, especially because of quite high levels of infertility, never gave birth at all – such was a constant complaint of Roman upper-class men (women tending to get the blame). On the other hand, we hear a significant amount about CONTRACEPTION (a mixture of MAGIC and MEDICINE), abortion and exposure and/or infanticide. Poorer families, and even richer families who did not want to spread their wealth too widely, limited their family size by such means. But even with such relatively high fertility levels, mortality rates ensured that the average family size was small.

The Roman emperor AUGUSTUS felt that low fertility levels, at least among the Roman upper classes, were such a problem that he introduced legislation to benefit those married with children and penalize those who were married without children or who never married at all (18 BC and AD 9). But unmarried adults were rare. Greeks and Romans married routinely: females in their mid- to late teens, males some ten years later. Again, however, mortality would have taken its toll. One or other of the spouses would on average have died within some 18 years of married life. And it would seem that DIVORCE rates were high as well.

It is more difficult to generalize about migration; our information is very patchy and impossible to quantify. COLONIZATION, widely practised, is the most obvious indication of MIGRATION in the ancient world, but most people probably moved little, or at most as young males from countryside to city to find a job or a bride. The SLAVE trade was one of the less subtle forms of migration.

In order to calculate levels of population growth or decline, one needs to be able to measure rates of mortality, fertility and migration. We do not have the variables to do this for antiquity. But it is reasonable to assume that at most periods in ancient history levels of growth were close to zero (there are some major probable exceptions, for example 8th-century BC Greece). High mortality rates were balanced by high levels of fertility. For ancient people this was the harsh reality of life. *Carpe diem* was one natural reaction. TGP

See Bagnall, R. S. and Frier, B.W. (1994) *The Demography of Roman Egypt*; Brunt, P. A. (1971) *Italian Manpower*; Hansen, M. H. (1986) *Demography and Democracy*; Parkin, T. G. (1992) *Demography and Roman Society*; Saller, R. P. (1994) *Patriarchy, Property and Death*; Scheidel, W., ed. (2001) *Debating Roman Demography*.

Demokritos b. c.460 BC The earliest ATOMISTIC theory was formulated by Leukippos and his younger colleague Demokritos of Abdera. They thought that the reality of change and of the sensible world could be saved from the attacks of the Eleatics (PARMENIDES, ZENO and Melissos) by supposing it to consist of eternal, indivisible and unchanging bodies, differing from each other in size and shape, which move in a limitless void: change is really the movement and rearrangement of atoms. Demokritos developed the theory in great detail, writing a vast number of books on COSMOLOGY, CHEMISTRY, biology and psychology, all of which are now lost. For Demokritos scientific explanations of macroscopic phenomena do not involve appeal to anything except the void, the atoms and their basic features – size, something like mass or weight, shape, indivisibility, position and velocity. What are now termed 'secondary qualities' (colours, tastes and so on) exist 'by convention' – that is, they are merely mind-dependent. Minds and mental events, too, are just sets of atoms and of atomic events. Demokritos also posed acute questions in epistemology: if atomism is correct, and thus the nature of physical reality is utterly at variance with how the world appears, how can the atomist claim that the senses provide us with reliable data? Demokritos also wrote extensively on ETHICS and political theory, though it is controversial how far his views in these areas were based on his atomism. RLJ

See Cartledge, P. A. (1998) *Democritus and Atomistic Politics*; Hussey, E. (1972) *The Presocratics*; Taylor, C. C.W. (1999) *The Atomists*.

demons Derived from the Greek word *daimôn* (plural *daimones*), demons were considered by HESIOD (*Works and Days* 122–6) to be the men of the GOLDEN AGE, who had been transformed at death by ZEUS to become invisible guardians over mortals. PLATO (*Phaedo* 107d) states that each mortal has a guardian *daimôn* appointed at birth.

In the *Iliad* the GODS could be described as *daimones*. While they could be associated with negative occurrences, as in AESCHYLUS' *Agamemnon*, they were more commonly considered a force providing personal impetus. Mortals could become *daimones* after death. In Aeschylus' *Persians* the deceased king DARIUS is raised as a *daimôn*; in EURIPIDES' *Alkestis* the eponymous heroine is also called a *daimôn*. By the hellenistic period grave inscriptions describe the deceased as *daimones*. The PYTHAGOREANS even claimed to be able to see and hear *daimones*, and were surprised that others could not.

In his *Symposium* PLATO considers *daimones* to be a separate class of being between the gods and humans, acting as messengers for both. It was his follower Xenokrates who suggested that *daimones* were evil. He argued that they brought disease, discord and barrenness and that they were responsible for all the dark and nasty aspects of religion. It is this usage that was employed by CHRISTIAN writers, who turned *daimones* into 'demons' and associated them with the devil. NJW

Demosthenes 384–322 BC Athenian speechwriter, orator and politician. Demosthenes' public career began at the age of 18 when he came of age and brought to trial his guardians (two uncles and a family friend) for embezzling the substantial estate left to him by his father, who had died when Demosthenes was seven. Although his suit was ultimately successful, the young man managed to recover only a portion of his inheritance. Nonetheless he was still wealthy enough to be a member of the class of Athenians expected to perform public BENEFACTIONS for the city.

He began his training in ORATORY as a student of ISAIOS during his adolescence, and was supposed to have been inspired as a boy when taken to hear the orator Kallistratos declaim. Allegedly sickly, weak-voiced, labouring under a speech impediment, and ridiculed for his first attempts at public speaking, Demosthenes, according to PLUTARCH, is said to have built a subterranean room in his house where he could practise voice exercises with a mouth full of pebbles. It is said that he used, 'on going down to the shore at Phaleron, to address himself to the roar of the waves, so that he might not be disconcerted if the people tried to yell him down'.

After successfully prosecuting his guardians, Demosthenes began his career as a professional speechwriter (*logographos*) for private cases. One of the earliest of these speeches is thought to be *Against Spoudias*. As his reputation grew, he was asked to write speeches for cases of public significance. The first was *Against Androtion* in 355 for Diodoros, in which the speaker attacked Androtion for proposing the customary honours for the COUNCIL at the end of their term of office even though they had failed to provide new TRIREMES for the navy. In the same year he wrote, and is said to have delivered himself, the speech *Against Leptines*.

His political career moved up another notch when he began to write and perform speeches in the ASSEMBLY. The first extant speech, *On the Symmories*, was delivered in 354, and advocated conservatism against the PERSIAN threat that was thought to be brewing in the East. However, Demosthenes was soon to find a new and more pressing cause to worry him – PHILIP II of MACEDONIA. Rather than conservatism, he demanded immediate, large-scale action.

Although in his speech *On the Liberty of the Rhodians* (351) Demosthenes seems to have been largely unaware of Philip, later in the same year in the *First Philippic* he warned against the impending danger of Macedonia. By 349 he was urging the Athenians in his *Olynthiacs*, against those who were eager to avoid a distant and expensive war, to sail to their allies in OLYNTHOS and confront Philip there before they found him in their own backyards in southern Greece. A force was finally sent, but too little too late; Olynthos was lost. Nevertheless, in 348 when Philokrates proposed in the assembly that peace be made with Philip, Demosthenes defended him when the motion was attacked as unconstitutional. In 346, too, he supported the peace of Philokrates, agreed between Philip and the Athenians. The peace collapsed almost immediately (perhaps at Demosthenes' instigation), and he tried to distance himself from both it and its author, Philokrates.

The war with Philip simmered on for a further eight years. Philokrates was impeached by Hypereides in 343 for receiving bribes from Philip; he fled and was condemned in his absence. Demosthenes impeached AISCHINES, another of the ambassadors involved in the peace negotiations, on the same charge, attacking him in his speech *On the False Embassy*. Aischines made a spirited reply and was narrowly acquitted. Meanwhile in the *Second Philippic* of 344, and in the speech *On the Chersonese* and the *Third Philippic* of 341, Demosthenes kept up his anti-Macedonian pressure.

In 338 Philip was again in southern Greece. This time Demosthenes called for alliance with the THEBANS to form a common resistance, and got it. The opposing armies met at CHAIRONEIA, and Philip was victorious. Peace was again made, this time through another orator, DEMADES, but Demosthenes was called upon to make the funeral speech for those who died in battle. But by 336 Philip was dead and ALEXANDER was installed as the new king in Macedonia. Thebes, encouraged by Demosthenes, stirred in revolt, but in 335 was swooped on and devastated by Alexander, who demanded the lives of ten prominent Athenians, Demosthenes among them, but later relented.

Alexander then embarked on his Asian campaign. Demosthenes reappears in 324 as one of those who opposed the entry into Athens of Harpalos, Alexander's runaway treasurer. Nevertheless Harpalos was admitted into the city and his money stored on the ACROPOLIS for safe-keeping, under the guardianship of a commission that included Demosthenes. When Harpalos escaped, Demosthenes was accused of receiving bribes, was investigated and impeached, but escaped into exile at AIGINA and Troizen. He remained in exile until after Alexander's death and the outbreak of the LAMIAN WAR, when he joined the Athenian ambassadors urging the Greeks to unite against Macedonia. As a result the Athenians voted for his recall.

However, when the Greek army was crushed at Krannon in 322, Demosthenes was forced to flee Athens again. He was pursued by Antipatros' men to Kalaureia, an island off the coast of the Argolid, where he had taken refuge at the temple of POSEIDON. Here he died, having sucked poison, it was said, from the end of his pen. He was 62 years old. The Athenians later raised a statue in the marketplace in his honour. LGM

See Demosthenes, 7 vols., trs. J.H. Vince et al. (1926–49); Plutarch, *Demosthenes*; Pseudo-Plutarch, *Lives of the Ten Orators*; Kennedy, G. (1963) *The Art of Persuasion in Greece*.

denarius see COINAGE (tables).

dentists and dentistry In Greece and Rome, as now, toothache was seen as one of the more painful things that could befall a person (Celsus 6.9). They ancients developed a variety of means by which they could stave off dental problems, by which they could remedy such afflictions, or even by which they could beautify their teeth. The wife of the Roman emperor CLAUDIUS, the well-known MESSALINA, beautified her teeth with a dentifrice of stag's horn, mastic and sal ammoniac. For the less well-off there were chalk, urine and toothpicks. Physicians could suggest less specific dental care (such as a mixture of dill, aniseed and myrrh in white WINE to preserve the gums) or advise on diet generally. Dental operations were common and seem to have been of a high order: extractions were common and crown work was possible. Technicians, rather than dentists or physicians, could provide false teeth (which curiously seem to have been removed before eating); they were carved from IVORY or made from ANIMALS' teeth. Loose teeth were bound into place with GOLD wire. We learn of this from the TWELVE TABLES (10.8), which specifically forbid the BURIAL or cremation of a person with gold accoutrements. A specific exception is made for teeth. PGT

See Hoffmann-Axthelm, W. (1981) *History of Dentistry*.

Derrida, J. see POST-MODERNISM; STRUCTURALISM AND POST-STRUCTURALISM.

development see GROWTH, ECONOMIC; see also CHILDHOOD; EDUCATION.

Diadochoi see SUCCESSORS OF ALEXANDER.

Diadumenianus

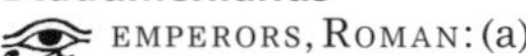 EMPERORS, ROMAN: (a).

dialectic The term 'dialectic' came to acquire a wide range of meanings, but all are connected, conceptually or historically or both, to what was probably the earliest, and certainly always a central, notion: that of PHILOSOPHICAL argument conducted by means of QUESTION AND ANSWER, whether genuinely adversarial, formalized (as in the later ACADEMY) or imaginary. ARISTOTLE is reported to have called ZENO OF ELEIA the founder of dialectic, probably on the basis rather of the precision and concision of his mode of argument (as opposed to the expansiveness of RHETORIC, founded by Empedokles) than of its format. This opposition was later adopted by the founder of the Stoa, ZENO OF CITIUM. But at least the early Stoa remained loyal to the question-and-answer conception of dialectic which has its roots in the SOCRATIC 'elenchus' (testing one's opponent's views by arguments). In PLATO's works there emerges the figure of the expert dialectician able to defend a thesis (say, a definition) under pressure of questioning, without inappropriate concessions or self-contradiction, and to probe effectively another's defence of a position. Dialectic thus conceived usefully permits investigation, at any rate in piecemeal form, of what a given proposition presupposes, implies or rules out. Here, then, are to be found the origins of what we call 'LOGIC', in particular analysis of the concepts of the proposition and its parts, argument, proof, inference, contrariety and contradiction, in both the Aristotelian and the STOIC traditions. Platonic dialectic embraces other methods too, above all that of the 'collection and division' of members of a genus into a hierarchy of species. Aristotle's 'dialectical method' constitutes a necessary complement to the particular sciences, whose basic, undemonstrable principles and concepts it recovers from received or expert wisdom. Stoic dialectic, scorned by EPICUREANS, developed into a branch of knowledge of a wide range of disciplines (parts of psychology and epistemology; linguistics; stylistics; the study of definition and division; formal and philosophical logic; the analysis of ambiguities and fallacies) all ultimately devoted to the detection of falsehood and the preservation of truth by the dialectician, whose skill in defending his commitments in face-to-face argument plainly shows his Socratic pedigree. CA

Diana Italian GODDESS associated with the wilderness and with WOMEN; she was identified at an early date with the Greek ARTEMIS. Diana was worshipped especially in LATIUM, but also in Campania and in SABINE territory. Her shrines were often in the outlying territory of a city, reflecting her associations with the wilderness. One important shrine was on Mt Tifata near Capua. The most famous was in a grove near Aricia, where her PRIEST, the *rex Nemorensis*, 'king of the grove', was a runaway SLAVE who obtained his position by slaying his predecessor. Diana was often invoked in votive dedications as a goddess of ANIMALS and of HUNTING, and she is usually depicted in art as a huntress, in a short tunic with a bow and quiver and sometimes hounds. She had strong connections with women, who invoked her especially during childbirth; numerous dedications to Diana by women are extant, and the votive offerings from Aricia often relate to children and childbirth. Her cult also had a political aspect from an early date. The cult at Aricia was an old cult centre of the Latin league, and her temple on the Aventine, traditionally founded by SERVIUS TULLIUS, was perhaps built in rivalry. Her identification with Artemis led to an association with APOLLO, resulting in an important role in AUGUSTUS' religious revival. Outside Italy, Diana was popular in GAUL and GERMANY, where she was probably identified with local hunting and FOREST goddesses. JBR

See Bannister, N. and Waugh, N. J., eds. (2005) *Essence of the Huntress: the worlds of Artemis and Diana*; Dumézil, G. (1970) *Archaic Roman Religion*.

 GODS AND GODDESSES: (a).

diatribe The essential meaning of the Greek word *diatribê* is 'way of spending time'. The word was used with philosophical application first by PLATO and his contemporaries to describe SOCRATES' conversations. In modern scholarship it is employed in a specialized sense to denote the kind of popular, moralizing exhortations associated in particular with the ancient CYNICS and STOICS, who saw themselves as the true heirs of Socrates. Whether they themselves and their audience recognized 'diatribe' as a distinct class of literature is at least debatable. Certain common features can nevertheless be distinguished in the works of Bion, Teles, Musonius Rufus, Epictetus and others who are most often connected with the composition of diatribes. They utilize a pointed RHETORICAL style, informal colloquial expression and vivid imagery. They assume either the presence of an audience or the participation of an anonymous respondent. They decry vices and rail against conventional values. Above all, they urge people to change their way of life. This kind of speech had a powerful influence on early CHRISTIAN sermons and Western rhetorical literature in general. MJ

See Schenkeveld, D. M. (1997) Philosophical prose, in S. E. Porter, ed., *Handbook of Classical Rhetoric in the Hellenistic Period, 330 BC–AD 400*; Stowers, S. K. (1981) *The Diatribe and Paul's Letter to the Romans*.

dice see BOARD GAMES AND OTHER GAMES; GAMBLING.

dictators Holders of a magistracy, the dictatorship, at Rome, appointed in emergencies. In the early Republic a consul, with the approval of the SENATE and people, appointed a *dictator* to resolve a crisis, usually military. The dictator, also called *magister populi* ('master of the army', not 'master of the populace'), held office for six months or until the emergency ended. He selected an assistant, the *magister equitum* ('master of horsemen'), and thereby controlled both infantry and cavalry. Other MAGISTRATES retained their offices, all subject to the dictator's authority, including CONSULS. On occasion, a dictator was appointed to solve a social or political crisis. The most interesting is the *dictator clavi figendi causa*, appointed 'for the purpose of hammering a nail' into the wall of the TEMPLE of JUPITER on the Ides of

September, appointed when both consuls were away; but the ceremony eventually disappeared. Appeal against a dictator's decisions was possible at some points. The 4th century BC, when Rome was frequently fighting seditious allies, offers many dictators: between 367 and 300 BC more than 40 are attested. Rome employed extended military commands thereafter, and only four more dictators appear, two at critical moments during the PUNIC WARS, in 249 and 217. The others are SULLA and JULIUS CAESAR, appointed *rei publicae constituendae*, 'to re-establish the state'. Sulla was dictator for a year, then abdicated (while consul). Caesar resigned his initial tenure of the dictatorship while consul; his subsequent year-long tenure was renewed, extended to ten years, and finally for life.

Annual magistrates in some other Latin towns, like Alba Longa, Aricia and Lanuvium, bore the title dictator. JV

See Cornell, T. J. (1995) *The Beginnings of Rome.*

 JULIUS CAESAR.

didactic poetry From the Greek *didaskein* ('to teach'), didactic or 'teaching' poetry was generally regarded in the ancient world as a sub-GENRE of EPIC. Virtually all surviving didactic poems employ the dactylic hexameter, the metre of HOMER and his successors (the exceptions are OVID's works, below, which are in elegiac couplets). Other features common to didactic and (heroic) epic are elevated language and the formal extended simile; didactic poets may also indicate their generic affiliation by reference or allusion to Homer and other writers of epic.

HESIOD (fl. c.700 BC) is conventionally regarded as the founder of the genre. His *Works and Days* sets the pattern for subsequent didactic poems in various ways: particularly important for the later development of the genre is Hesiod's characteristic combination of technical subject matter (AGRICULTURE) with moral and religious precept. Hesiod's poem is also concerned, especially in its opening section, to establish (predominantly MYTHOLOGICAL) explanations for the character of the world as it now is; this 'aetiological' element, too, becomes prominent in later didactic.

Hesiod was composing at a time before prose writing was fully developed in Greece, and verse was the natural medium for the communication and dissemination of ideas. This may have been equally true for his successors in the 6th and 5th centuries (notably the PHILOSOPHER poets PARMENIDES and Empedokles); but by the 4th century it was no longer the case, and the didactic genre seems to have declined accordingly. In the hellenistic period, however, it takes on a new lease of life, with such poets as ARATOS OF SOLOI (fl. c.250 BC) and Nicander (Nikandros, fl. c.130 BC), whose surviving works deal respectively with ASTRONOMY and the bites of poisonous ANIMALS. The hellenistic didactic poets were 'metaphrasts', that is, they versified the prose works of others rather than composing original poems from scratch. Their overriding concern seems to have been stylistic elegance, and they apparently relished the challenge presented by such prosaic subjects. We should resist the temptation, however, to dismiss their work as trivial: Aratos, at least, seems concerned to present a coherent and philosophically informed world-view, not merely a dazzling display piece.

With the Roman didactic poets, the genre returns to something like the earnestness of the archaic period. LUCRETIUS' *De rerum natura* (*On the Nature of Things*, c.55 BC) embodies in verse the philosophical system of EPICURUS, and thus has something in common with the work of the hellenistic metaphrasts. At the same time, it has an explicitly missionary purpose, being designed to convert, not just to charm the reader. VIRGIL's *Georgics* (29 BC) responds to the fervent intensity of Lucretius' poem with a multi-layered meditation on the relationship between human beings and the natural world. Like Hesiod, Virgil deals overtly with farming, but exploits his AGRICULTURAL subject matter as a vehicle for reflection on a range of philosophical, ETHICAL and political issues.

Later didactic poets include OVID, whose *Ars amatoria* and *Remedia amoris* (1 BC–AD 2) are in part a kind of joint parody of the didactic and elegiac genres; Manilius (early 1st century AD), the author of a five-book poem on astrology, the *Astronomica*; Grattius (late 1st century BC) and Nemesianus (3rd century AD), both of whom wrote on HUNTING; and Oppian (2nd century AD), who wrote on FISHING. MG

See Dalzell, A. (1996) *The Criticism of Didactic Poetry*; Toohey, P. (1996) *Epic Lessons.*

Didius Julianus see LUCILLA; PERTINAX; SEVERUS, SEPTIMIUS.

 EMPERORS, ROMAN: (a).

Dido see AENEAS; CARTHAGE; VIRGIL.

Didyma An important oracular shrine of APOLLO, located in Asia Minor 16 km (10 miles) south of MILETOS. A spring and sacred grove already marked it as a cultic site before an Ionic temple was built there in the 6th century BC and a sacred way was laid from the nearby harbour of Panormos. The *adyton* (sanctuary) was a roofless courtyard, within which a small *naïskos* (chapel) enclosed the spring. Here Apollo's PRIESTESS sat on an axle and 'received the god' by dipping her feet or the hem of her garment into the water, or perhaps simply breathing upon its surface. (This description is from a late source, Iamblichos.) A second, larger temple on the site was incomplete when DARIUS I destroyed it in 494 BC. The ORACLE revived in the hellenistic period. SELEUKOS I commissioned a third temple of impressive proportions that was never finished, though construction lasted for two centuries. The shrine withstood raids by the GAULS in 278 BC and PIRATES in 70 BC, and served as an important prophetic centre until the 3rd century AD. In the face of a GOTHIC invasion in AD 262, the temple lost its sacred character and became a military FORTRESS. The voice of 'Apollo of Miletos' could still be heard, however, during the reign of DIOCLETIAN, when it pronounced against CHRISTIANITY. JRH

See Bean, G.E. (1989) *Turkey beyond the Maeander*; Stillwell, R. et al., eds. (1976) *The Princeton Encyclopedia of Classical Sites.*

 ASIA, ROMAN.

diet Ancient physicians were more concerned with diet than their modern counterparts. They regarded foodstuffs as effective medicines, whose correct balance, individually prescribed, would promote HEALTH. Equally they advised on lifestyle and routine. Greek *diaita* and the Latin equivalent, *regimen*, denote lifestyle including diet. The oldest discussion of these matters is *Peri diaitês* (*Regimen* or *On Diet*), ascribed to HIPPOKRATES, written around 400 BC. A later study, GALEN's *On the Properties of Foods*, catalogues foodstuffs with much interesting detail. By Galen's time humoural theory was fully elaborated: in his work the humoural effect of each food is specified. Thus, although coincidences between ancient and modern opinions on diet exist, their theoretical bases are wholly different. Greek and Roman diets were potentially close to the modern 'MEDITERRANEAN diet', with more FISH than MEAT, more FRUIT and VEGETABLES than either of these, and a generous supply of WINE and wheat bread. Milk was generally consumed as CHEESE; the usual food oil was OLIVE OIL; sugar sources were HONEY, raisins, dates and FIGS. However, the advice of physicians, if attended to, led to dubious food choices, including avoidance of fresh fruit and salad. Written sources suggest that WOMEN and children, especially girls, would have received relatively poor nourishment; archaeobiology is beginning to give evidence of diseases of malnutrition, supporting such deductions. AD

See Dalby, A. (2003) *Food in the Ancient World from A to Z*; Garnsey, P. (1999) *Food and Society in Classical Antiquity*; Grant, M., trs. (2000) *Galen on Food and Diet.*

Digest see JUSTINIAN, WORKS OF; LAW, ROMAN; LAWCODES; ULPIAN.

Dinarchus see DEINARCHOS.

dining In the political or religious arena, public meals fostered community. Likewise, in Greek and Roman homes, formal dinners both defined and mediated social distinctions between individuals and families. Greeks called the event a *SYMPOSION*, 'drinking together', a drinking-party with food on the side. In contrast, Romans held a food-party with drinking on the side: a *convivium*, or 'living together', where social reunion was the essence of mealtime (CICERO, *On Old Age* 45).

As HOMER portrays in the *Odyssey*, meals were settings for EPIC storytelling and LYRIC POETRY. Meals were also RITUAL occasions. In the 8th and 7th centuries BC, people conducted ritual meals at monumental Bronze Age TOMBS, honouring mythologized HEROES, perhaps in an attempt to connect their own emergent *poleis* with past civilizations. During the archaic and classical periods, *symposia* were increasingly social occasions that displayed *isonomia*, equal rights for citizens under the law. Initiation into the world of WINE and adult behaviour was a coming-of-age ritual for young men. *Symposia* excluded women, however, except as servers, entertainers or courtesans. A social order was designed into the layout of couches, with the host taking the couch left of the door and the guest of honour the couch immediately to the right. Activities, overseen by a guest elected as *symposiarchos*, centred around mixing water with wine, drinking and conversations or competitions. Guests might contest in PHILOSOPHY, SONG, improvised THEATRE, DANCING or *kottabos*, a game involving flicking wine dregs from one's cup at a target. DIONYSOS' gift was ambiguous, like his half-human, half-animal followers, the SATYRS. In a comic fragment, the god remarks that the first three bowls of wine are for the temperate, assisting health, love, pleasure and sleep. Successive bowls, however, belonged to insolence, clamorous processions, black eyes, run-ins with the law, peevishness, MADNESS and throwing objects about (ATHENAEUS 2.36b–c).

ETRUSCANS and Romans, like the Greeks, exchanged sitting for reclining at banquets. However, their men and women ate together. In early afternoon, after a bath, the company would be arranged in the *triclinium*. The guest of honour would

DINING: Pompeian wall-painting illustrating a variant of the normal Roman dining arrangements, involving a curving couch (*sigma*) – with a continuous cushion to support the diners.

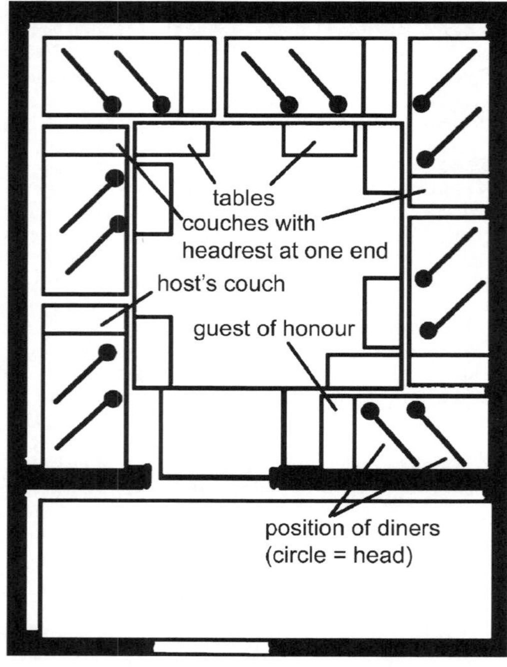

DINING ROOMS: (a) the Greek dining room (*andrôn*), with small vestibule – based on the 4th-century House of the Mosaics at Eretria.

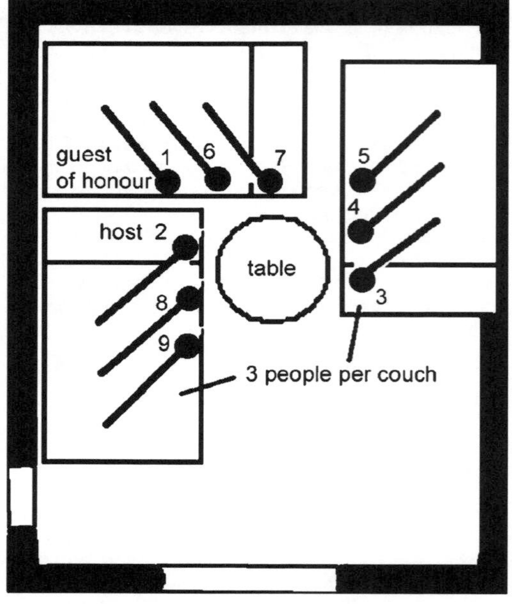

DINING ROOMS: (b) Roman *triclinium* (based on House XI.1.7) at Pompeii. Numbers indicate the social order of the diners, in descending order (1 = guest of honour; 2 = host; 3–7 = other guests; 8–9 = host's family members).

receive third position on the *lectus medius*, close to the host heading the *lectus imus*. The order continued across the *lectus summus*, *medius* and *imus*. A series of appetizers, three main courses and dessert comprised a standard meal, followed by the *commissatio* or drinking-party. Slaves served, cleaned and entertained; besides leftovers, their rewards were praise, promotion, punishment or degrading (including sexual) service. PETRONIUS' *Trimalchio's Dinner* humorously depicts extreme behaviours at the home of a rich ex-slave. In the House of the Moralist at POMPEII (probably owned by FREEDMEN), proper ETIQUETTE was written plainly on the dining room wall: 'Let the slave wash and dry your feet, let him cover the couches with linens (don't soil them!); don't make eyes at another's wife, and speak decently, avoiding quarrels, lest you wish to return home.' Socializing over meals was not limited to the wealthy; inns, clubs and pubs at nearly every corner catered for apartment dwellers and small shopkeepers. Every evening, the company and conditions of dinner reckoned people's social standing throughout the empire. (see also DINING ROOMS) PWF

See Gowers, E. (1993) *The Loaded Table*; Slater, W., ed. (1991) *Dining in a Classical Context*.

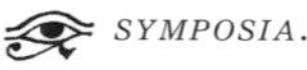 *SYMPOSIA*.

dining rooms Formal dining rooms are among the most easily recognized spaces in the archaeological record, and among the most amply described environments in literary sources. As one of the few domestic areas available to non-family members, they were also well decorated and appointed, allowing the wealth and tastes of families to be prominently displayed.

The classical Greek dining room was the *andrôn* ('men's room'), the location of drinking-parties and meals for male relatives and friends. Sometimes preceded by a vestibule, it was located off the courtyard, as examples at Olynthos and Eretria show. Square in shape, the *andrôn* had an off-centre door that allowed an odd number of dining couches to be placed along a raised strip of undecorated pavement around the perimeter of the room. MOSAICS often adorned floors in the room's central square, entrance and vestibule. The wooden or stone couches measured c.0.9 by 1.8 m and comfortably held one or two individuals reclining on cushions, with food and drink on a table before them. The centre remained open for service and entertainment (DANCERS, pipe-girls or the game of *kottabos*). After a meal, a drain carried away food remains and WINE dregs. Public dining rooms occupied STOAS in *AGORAI* and sanctuaries, even public office buildings such as the circular Tholos in Athens, where 50 men on duty for state business were fed daily at state expense. During the hellenistic period, broader and more elaborate dining rooms suitable for general purposes of reception appeared in HOUSES and PALACES.

Roman dining rooms have several names, including *cenatio* (literally, the eating of the evening meal) and *triclinium*, so called from its three dining-couches (from the Greek word *klinai*). Roman couches (c.1.2 by 2.5 m) were large enough to hold three diners each, for a total of nine. Participants reclined on their left elbows, facing the table at the centre of the couches. Each couch and couch position represented that diner's social position. Additional benches and chairs sometimes seated low-status participants like children or SLAVES. Couches were marked by mosaic floor decoration, and/or by special niches cut into the walls. The ARCHITECT VITRUVIUS (6.3) distinguishes several special types of dining rooms (tetrastyle, Corinthian, Kyzikene and Egyptian) by their lighting and arrangement of decorative columns. Inlaid couches, fine cushions and drapery, and metal and GLASS table-wares completed the ambience. Larger houses invariably had more and varied dining rooms with different views, decorative schemes and seasonality. Those used in winter tended to be placed around the sheltered atrium, while warm-weather dining rooms were placed with clear access to light and air. In the wealthier residences they had views onto GARDENS and peristyles containing FOUNTAINS, greenery and statuary. Outdoor dining rooms had permanent masonry couches and vine-draped bowers to shelter diners from the sun. Although dining rooms and couches were normally rectangular, semicircular ones became popular in late imperial times. (see also DINING) PWF

Dio, Dio Cassius see CASSIUS DIO.

Dio Chrysostom (Dio Cocceianus) Greek ORATOR and PHILOSOPHER whose extensive surviving works are an important source for the social and intellectual history of the late 1st century AD. Dio was born, probably between AD 40 and 50, into a wealthy family owing several estates near Prusa in Bithynia. As a young man, he came under the influence of Musonius Rufus, the STOIC opponent of NERO. He had close connections with the Flavian court, though his appearance in PHILOSTRATUS' *Life of Apollonios of Tyana*, in a debate giving advice to VESPASIAN, is fictional. He was relegated from Italy and Bithynia by DOMITIAN, probably because of his friendship with the EMPEROR's disgraced cousin, Flavius Sabinus. Dio was able to travel widely, from Egypt to the northern shores of the BLACK SEA, gathering material the while for his *Getica*, a work now lost. The accession of Nerva, an old friend, brought his wanderings to an end, and he returned to Prusa to play an active, if controversial, role in civic life. In 100 he conducted an embassy to TRAJAN, and he is mentioned in the younger PLINY's correspondence dating to 110–11 (*Letters* 10.81–2).

There has been much debate, ancient and modern, about how Dio should be categorized. Philostratos awards him a place in his *Lives of the Sophists*, while the early 5th-century Christian writer SYNESIUS thought he detected in Dio a conversion to PHILOSOPHY after his exile. His philosophical position was essentially Stoic, though there are elements of CYNICISM in his work, and he was an admirer of Diogenes. He gained the nickname Chrysostomos ('Golden-mouthed') from his consummate skill in speaking.

Some 80 speeches attributed to Dio survive. Subsequent editors placed his four orations *On Kingship* first in the corpus, a reflection of their influence. They are usually regarded as addressed to Trajan, but the emperor is not mentioned by name. *Orations* 1 and 3 develop the idea of the ideal ruler as one who labours on behalf of his people, illustrated by the philosophic choice of HERAKLES (a popular figure in Trajanic propaganda). *Orations* 2 and 4 are imaginary dialogues featuring ALEXANDER the Great.

The speeches delivered in Bithynia (38–51) provide vivid glimpses of the often turbulent social life in the cities of the PROVINCE. In conjunction with Pliny's letters, they leave us exceptionally well informed about Bithynia. Attempts have been made to exploit the speeches to support a hypothesis of city life in crisis at the end of the 1st century (e.g. *Oration* 46 on a bread shortage at Prusa), but they provide better evidence for the essential robustness of the institutions of the Greek city. Among Dio's other speeches, *Oration* 7, the Euboian oration, is much prized by historians for its vivid account of the author's SHIPWRECK and its romantic picture of rural PEASANT life, set against the duplicity of the city. Its literary motifs, however, render it a problematic source. One should compare *Oration* 36, another description of an ideal community, Olbia on the Black sea. It is a great pity that Dio's work on the ESSENE community in Palestine is lost. PMB

See Cohoon, J.W. et al., trs. (1932–51) 5 vols.; Jones, C. P. (1978) *The Roman World of Dio Chrysostom.*

Diocletian (Gaius Aurelius Valerius Diocletianus) Roman EMPEROR, AD 284–305, born Diocles in DALMATIA in the 230s or 240s. His early career was military, and by 284 he had risen to be commander of the *domestici* (imperial bodyguard). After the death of Numerianus in 284, he was acclaimed AUGUSTUS by the army at NICOMEDIA. In 285 he defeated Carinus, Numerianus' brother, at Margus in the Balkans. In 286 he appointed a CAESAR, MAXIMIAN, to share the burdens of office. This was the beginning of the TETRARCHY, a formal system with a senior emperor (Augustus) and junior colleague (Caesar) in both East and West.

Diocletian is often seen as the founder of the late Roman empire and the man who resolved the 3rd-century crisis. Many reforms are attributed to him, in military, imperial, financial and administrative matters, though in many cases it is not clear whether the reform was his or CONSTANTINE's innovation. Most importantly, he ruled as emperor for over 20 years, giving the empire a chance to pull itself back together, despite problems with usurpers in Egypt and BRITAIN and foreign wars in AFRICA, on the RHINE and DANUBE, and against the PERSIANS. He was also assisted by the earlier efforts of AURELIAN.

Diocletian's great innovation was the creation of the Tetrarchy. A distinct ideology was created, as Diocletian was identified with JUPITER, Maximian with HERCULES, and court protocols developed to make the emperors more remote. There was also an increase in the state infrastructure, with the existence of four PALACE staffs and four small, regional field armies.

In military terms, Diocletian was highly conservative. He raised many new regiments, but placed most of them in border PROVINCES, reversing a 3rd-century trend towards a large, central field army under the emperor. He increased the number of provinces to bring governors closer to their provinces' cities, and created supra-provincial administrative units, the dioceses. Near the end of his reign he began to persecute CHRISTIANS, first expelling them from the army, then closing CHURCHES and demanding holy books to be surrendered, before finally requiring sacrifices by the entire population of the empire.

Diocletian was well aware of the effects of inflation. He attempted COINAGE reforms and issued the famous, though unsuccessful, Price Edict of AD 301, which attempted to dictate the maximum PRICES for all economic transactions in the empire. Diocletian reformed TAXATION, creating the indiction system, under which the taxes required could be levied on a sliding scale in kind, according to annual government estimates of income required, rather than at a fixed rate in cash.

In 305, Diocletian retired to his palace at Split where he lived to c.312, growing cabbages. His retirement was broken only in 308, when he tried to avert the collapse of the Tetrarchy in a conference at Carnuntum. Here he had to reject GALERIUS' attempt to restore him to imperial power. Diocletian was married to Prisca and had a daughter Valeria, but no sons. HWE

See Williams, S. (1985) *Diocletian and the Roman Recovery*.

 BATHS: (b); EMPERORS, ROMAN: (b); TETRARCHS: (a)–(b).

Diodorus Siculus The historian Diodorus of Agyrrhion in SICILY (hence 'Siculus'), author of a 40-book history of the world down to 60 BC, the most extensively preserved history in Greek to survive from antiquity. Diodorus titled his work *Bibliothêkê* ('Library'). The first six books deal with GEOGRAPHY, ethnography and the MYTHOLOGICAL period down to the TROJAN WAR. The remainder deal mainly with Greek history (including that of his native Sicily). Roman history is briefly treated down to the first PUNIC WAR, more fully thereafter. Books 1–5 and 11–20 (covering the period 480–302) survive intact, the others in excerpts. Diodorus tells us that he spent 30 years on his history (probably c.60–30 BC), visited Egypt (c.60) and lived for a long time in Rome. He frequently praises JULIUS CAESAR, but nothing is known of his status or connections.

Where it can be checked, Diodorus' narrative shows a close, often verbatim dependence on his sources, which for the historical period included EPHOROS, HIERONYMOS, TIMAIOS, POLYBIOS and POSIDONIUS. His own contribution seems to have consisted chiefly of general observations, mostly banal, for example on the moral value of history. For the historical period, Diodorus organized his history annalistically (year by year), with much chronological confusion. His work's chief importance is as a repository of the historical tradition. For the reigns of Philip II and of ALEXANDER'S SUCCESSORS it is our principal source. JWR

See Oldfather, C. H. et al. (1933–67) *Diodorus Siculus* (text and translation); Hornblower, J. (1981) *Hieronymus of Cardia*; Sacks, K. S. (1990) *Diodorus Siculus and the First Century*.

Diogenes Laërtius (Diogenes Laërtios) c.AD 200–50 Author of a ten-book collection of 'Lives' of Greek PHILOSOPHERS, as well as some EPIGRAMS. His dates are uncertain, but they can be fixed roughly between the latest philosophers who receive mention in his work (these date from the 2nd century AD) and the prominent movements with which he is apparently unfamiliar (NEOPLATONISM in particular). He was clearly not a philosopher himself, and although he shows some interest in the thought and doctrines of many of his subjects, it is their personalities that especially fascinate him. At times he is purely factual, recording parentage, date and place of birth, formative intellectual influences and his subject's written works. At other times, his style is heavily anecdotal, including the use of pithy apophthegms that enable a subject to demonstrate a quick wit and practical wisdom through exchange with a conversational partner. Diogenes would merit little serious attention if it were not for the fact that he frequently provides philosophical information of a precise, technical kind which derives from sources that would otherwise be lost. Outstanding examples include the long and important account of STOICISM in his *Life of Zeno* (7.38–159), which he probably lifted nearly verbatim from an earlier source; the catalogue of Platonic doctrines in his *Life of Plato* (3.67–80), which derives substantially from an ancient commentary on PLATO's influential *Timaeus*; and EPICURUS' letters to HERODOTOS, Pythokles and Menoikeus (10.35–83, 84–116, 122–35), which are central to our understanding of EPICUREANISM. MJ

See Hicks, R. D., trs. (1925) 2 vols.; Mejer, J. (1978) *Diogenes Laertius and his Hellenistic Background*.

diolkos see BENEFACTORS AND BENEFACTION, GREEK; CORINTH; ROADS, GREEK.

Dion of Syracuse c.408–353 BC A Syracusan with close connections to DIONYSIOS I and Dionysios II, he was the brother-in-law, later also son-in-law, of Dionysios I and was noted both for his wealth and his personal austerity. Although he was a trusted courtier of Dionysios I, he became increasingly distanced from the latter's son Dionysios II (r.367–357) and ambitious for personal power. In 388/7 and 367/6, his close interest in PLATONISM led him to invite PLATO to SYRACUSE, on the second occasion with the specific intention of converting Dionysios II to Platonism. Shortly after this, Dion was discovered to be in contact with the CARTHAGINIANS, enemies of Syracuse. He was exiled but was well received by several mainland Greek cities and in 357, raised a MERCENARY force and landed in western SICILY. Initially successful, he briefly gained control of Syracuse, becoming plenipotentiary general (*stratêgos autokratôr*), but was soon forced out after quarrelling with the leader of a DEMOCRATIC faction. He based himself at Leontinoi, and in 355 regained enough support to retake Syracuse and establish himself as ruler. However, his regime had no stable support and he was personally unpopular. He was assassinated in 353. KL

See Diodorus Siculus 16.5–20; Plato, *Letters* 7 and 8; Plutarch, *Dion*.

Dionysios I TYRANT of SYRACUSE, 406–367 BC. One of the more colourful characters of Greek history, Dionysios gained power during a period of *stasis*, as leader of a popular faction. He based his power on the existing constitution, becoming *stratêgos* (general) and eventually sole *stratêgos*. He consolidated his control of the city by pursuing campaigns against the CARTHAGINIANS in SICILY, and against Greeks in Sicily and southern Italy. In 404–402 he extended Syracusan hegemony northwards, destroying Naxos and Katane and conquering territory from the indigenous Sicels. He moved against the Carthaginian city of MOTYA in 398. Despite military successes in 398–396 and 393–392, which resulted in a treaty recognizing Syracusan domination over much of Sicily, he was forced to cede Selinous and Akragas back to Carthage in 378. He extended citizenship to freed SLAVES and MERCENARIES and rebuilt the Ortygia district of Syracuse as a militarized zone and personal stronghold, establishing FORTIFICATIONS and restricting residence to his own supporters and mercenaries. Once his power was established, he maintained control until his death in 367, relying on a personal *clientela* of friends and family, and on his mercenary army, to maintain power. He was succeeded by his son, Dionysios II. Despite his success as a political and military leader, the source tradition preserved by DIODORUS and in PLATO's letters is mainly hostile to Dionysios, and includes numerous negative *topoi* and scandalous stories emphasizing his supposedly tyrannical nature. (see also DION) KL

See Diodorus Siculus 14.1–15.74; Plato, *Letters* 7; Caven, B. (1990) *Dionysios I*; Sanders, L. J. (1987) *Dionysios I of Syracuse and Greek Tyranny.*

Dionysios of Halikarnassos Greek literary critic and historian of early Rome. Having arrived at Rome c.30 BC, Dionysios taught RHETORIC there and was well established in ÉLITE literary circles. Besides his history, a number of his critical essays survive (some dedicated to prominent Romans). Several discuss historical writing, notably a severely critical study of THUCYDIDES. The treatises on ORATORY champion the classical Attic style and attack 'Asianism'.

The *Roman Antiquities* covered Roman history from Rome's origins to 264 BC (POLYBIOS' starting-point) in 20 books. The first 11 (to 441 BC) survive intact, the rest in excerpts. Dionysios tells us that he worked on his history from his arrival in Rome and published the first book in 7 BC. The work is written from a pro-Roman stance, arguing that the Romans were fit rulers of the world because of their Greek origin and their virtues. The first book deals with the origins of Rome and argues the case for its Greekness, drawing on a wealth of Greek and Roman writers. In the rest, Dionysios used mainly Roman historical writers and paid much attention to political and other institutions. He writes on a very ample scale, introducing numerous, freely composed speeches. Often tediously long-winded, he nonetheless shows considerable powers of historical analysis. JWR

See Dionysius of Halicarnassus, *Roman Antiquities*, 7 vols., trs. E. Cary (1937–50); Usher, S., trs. (1974–85) *Dionysius of Halicarnassus, Critical Essays*, 2 vols.; Gabba, E. (1991) *Dionysius and 'The History of Archaic Rome'.*

Dionysos Although Dionysos was counted as one of the major Olympian deities, he represented a different aspect of the Greeks' religious understanding. In MYTH he was born of ZEUS and Semele, daughter of Kadmos, king of THEBES. When adult, he returned to Greece from the East as a GOD, and the people who rejected him were persecuted for their refusal to recognize his divinity. With his companions, the nymphs and SATYRS, his *thyrsos* (a fennel stalk tipped with ivy) and his gift of WINE, he possessed women with his power and sent them DANCING in ecstasy on the MOUNTAINS, where they tore ANIMALS apart with their bare hands and donned the animals' skins (as in EURIPIDES' *Bacchae*). This suspension of normal behaviour brought about a surrender of IDENTITY and emphasized the irrational side of human beings.

Within the historical period, there were many FESTIVALS in honour of Dionysos, and at some the madness on the mountains was ritually re-enacted. Those celebrated at Athens, such as the Lenaia, rural Dionysia and City Dionysia, developed the hymns and dithyrambs to the gods into DRAMA (TRAGEDY, COMEDY and satyr play), with actors in masks. In art, Dionysos is shown among his followers and taking part in the return of Hephaistos to Mt Olympos, the battle of the gods and giants, and the Theban story. BAS

See Burkert, W. (1985) *Greek Religion*; Carpenter, T. H. (1986) *Dionysian Imagery in Archaic Greek Art*; Carpenter, T. and Faraone, C. (1993) *Masks of Dionysus*; Dodds, E. R. (1960) *Euripides, Bacchae* (esp. introduction).

 GODS AND GODDESSES: (a); RELIGION: (a).

Dioscuri (Greek *Dios kouroi*) Literally, the 'youths of Zeus', the twins Kastor and Polydeukes, or Castor and Pollux in Latin. They are also called the *Tyndaridai* or sons of Tyndareos, husband of Leda. In HOMER they appear as the deceased brothers of Helen, though the story that they divide their time between the underworld and heaven is also very early. SPARTA was the original centre of their cult, but they were popular throughout the Greek world, especially southern Italy. In Homer Kastor is a horseman and Polydeukes a boxer, but later literature and art associate them both very closely with HORSES. PINDAR often invokes their ATHLETIC qualities, and many victors made dedications to them. They were regarded as saviours in times of crisis, especially during storms at sea and in battle.

Their cult reached ETRURIA and LATIUM by the late 6th century BC; a dedication found near Lavinium dates to c.500. According to tradition, their cult was introduced into Rome after the battle of LAKE REGILLUS in 499, in which they aided the Romans. Castor, the horseman, was originally the more important, and their TEMPLE in the FORUM was called 'the temple of Castor' throughout the Republic; the normal Latin term for the two together was *Castores*. In the imperial period they continued to be important as equestrian gods, and in Roman art are overwhelmingly represented with horses. JBR

See Burkert, W. (1985) *Greek Religion*; Dumézil, G. (1970) *Archaic Roman Religion.*

Diotima A woman from MANTINEIA in ARKADIA, introduced by SOCRATES to the discussion portrayed in PLATO's *Symposium*. She is otherwise unknown, and may be a Platonic invention. In the *Symposium* Socrates claims it was she who revealed to him the truth about desire (in Greek, *ERÔS*). After a dialectical section which casts Socrates in the role of the young interlocutor and Diotima in the more usual Socratic role, Socrates reveals Diotima's vision of Eros as the son of Wealth and Poverty, neither mortal nor immortal, neither beautiful nor ugly. (In fact, the description of Eros is very like that of Socrates himself elsewhere in the dialogue.) Then he relates how all of us are pregnant, and are drawn to beauty in order to give birth and attain immortality through producing offspring, whether physical or more valuable intellectual offspring. Perhaps the most famous section of the speech, the 'ascent passage', relates how the lover gradually moves from being drawn to an individual's physical beauty to seeing beauty generally in BODIES, then in SOULS, and eventually moving to a recognition of 'the Beautiful itself', which is described in terms reminiscent of other characterizations of Platonic Forms. JIW

See Halperin, D. M. (1990) Why is Diotima a woman? in D. M. Halperin et al., eds., *Before Sexuality* 257–308.

diplomacy In the public domain, relations between states could be regularized by means of TREATIES and alliances, which took a variety of forms. These could be negotiated by constitutionally elected AMBASSADORS, and were sworn by officials who generally represented a cross-section of the community.

But there was a range of other less formal diplomatic activities and stratagems. Although such arrangements would generally have to be approved by constitutional procedures, private friendships could be utilized in the interests of the state, particularly the traditional aristocratic networks of ritualized friendship or guest-friendship (*xenia* in Greece; *hospitium* in Rome). For example, the Athenian peace with ARGOS in 420 BC was brought about largely by the negotiations of the Athenian ALCIBIADES and his Argive *xenoi*. In addition, *xenia* developed on a civic level into *proxenia*, where states appointed individuals (*proxenoi*) in other states to look after their interests. This could entail entertaining visiting ambassadors, or making representations in the assembly on behalf of the awarding state.

In Rome there was a tendency for these private relationships, like public treaties, to become unequal, so that the relationship of *hospitium* tended to become that of *clientela*. This became particularly important when the relationship was with a foreign king, and the representations of the Roman patron became an important means for securing a hearing in the Roman SENATE. LGM

See Badian, E. (1958) *Foreign Clientelae*; Mosley, D. J. (1973) *Envoys and Diplomacy in Ancient Greece*.

disability The concept of disability is a modern one which embraces conditions as diverse as partial deafness and manic depression, and has problematic connotations. Disability is nowadays a legal, political and even ethical term, with no equivalent in the ancient world. The current scholarly interest in such phantom concepts as disability is also the result of the interest in 'body history' stimulated in the 1980s by the work of Michel Foucault, which asked whether the BODY is contrived in the same way in all cultures, and whether disability is understood the same way in all eras and cultures. When discussing disability in ancient Greece and Rome, we need to speak about specific instances. We should speak of deafness, lameness, speech impediments, blindness and so forth. The term, in fact, is set about with unsolvable conundrums such as: when does a deformity (e.g. lameness) become a disability (probable answer: in the legalese of a social legislation that aims never to give offence)? Is blindness a disability or a deformity? (The answer may depend on the importance of sight for a particular culture.) Niceties of distinction, therefore, can be as perplexing as they may be pointless. There is an additional conceptual problem to be encountered when dealing with ancient representations of what we would term disability. Many of the most famous examples (e.g. OEDIPUS or Teiresias) are to be drawn from a literature (DRAMA or EPIC in this case) which worked in symbols and metaphors (Teiresias is blind but 'sees'; Oedipus' deformity is reflected in his name which in turn puns on the notion of 'knowledge').

To turn to specifics: apparent disability or deformity in the newborn was something that could lead to infanticide (so SENECA THE ELDER, *Controversies* 10.14.16). To judge from the ill treatment received by such figures as Thersites in HOMER's *Iliad* (2.211–20) or the emperor CLAUDIUS in SENECA's *Apocolocyntosis*, disability or deformity, then as now, could be grounds for a lack of popular sympathy. And then as now the deformed possessed a macabre attraction. Wealthy Roman families sometimes kept them as 'pets' (Pliny the Elder, *Natural History* 7.75). Such 'pets' were popular at ancient parties (LUCIAN, *Symposium* 18). No doubt the insistence in a wide variety of ancient texts on the need for control of the body, and for its comparable moulding, did not assist in the extension of a whole-hearted sympathy to the disabled. It comes as a welcome surprise, therefore, to learn that in classical Athens individuals who suffered from disability in body (nicely termed the *adynatoi*, 'powerless') and had property worth less than three *MINAS* received a state pension of one obol a day, subject to a physical examination by city authorities. This Athenian legislation, however, was intended only for CITIZENS. SLAVES, depending on their circumstances, must have run a much higher than average risk of disability or deformation because of their often difficult LABOUR. We can only speculate on their subsequent quality of life. One generalizes over the attitude to and the status of the disabled in antiquity, therefore, at some risk. PGT

See Garland, R. S. J. (1995) *Deformity and Disability in the Ancient World*.

disasters, natural see EARTHQUAKES; VOLCANOES.

disease Like OLD AGE and DEATH, disease was seen as an intrinsic part of human experience, present in the world ever since Pandora opened her box and released them to injure mortals. It could also be sent by the GODS, particularly by ARTEMIS and APOLLO whose arrows were seen as a mode of transmission. In such a situation, disease sent to an individual or a community was a form of punishment for a RITUAL transgression.

In medical writing, in the absence of germ theory, all disease, in the sense of doctors' models of the causes of symptoms experienced by patients, was seen primarily in terms of imbalance. Rather than applying a set of disease labels, such as 'pneumonia' or 'tuberculosis', the doctor was more interested in locating the cause of symptoms in an excess or a deficiency of the fluids which were thought to exist in the body. This meant that disease was seen as a process rather than an entity, and each case had to be treated separately. Instead of giving one specific remedy for each identified and labelled 'disease', the doctor would investigate the way of life of each patient in relation to his or her environment and to the season of the year, and then prescribe DRUGS and dietary changes suitable in that particular case. (see also DIET; MEDICINE) HK

dithyramb see DIONYSOS; DRAMA, GREEK; MUSIC; PINDAR; POETRY, GREEK; THEATRES, GREEK.

divination see APOLLO; AUGURY; BIRDS; DELPHI; DREAMS; DRUIDS AND DRUIDISM; ETRURIA AND ETRUSCANS; ORACLES; PROPHECY; RITUAL, ROMAN; SACRIFICE; TARQUINIA.

divinities see GODS AND GODDESSES; RELIGION.

divisibility Spatial and temporal extensions have parts. This suggests that they are divisible. A day is divisible into morning and afternoon, and then further into smaller units of time. A cake is divisible into slices, each of which can be further divided. Such divisions – so it seems – can be made at any point of the extension.

ZENO OF ELEA challenged this intuitive position by making divisibility central to some of his PARADOXES. We have to reconstruct his arguments from later reports, but one may have been the following dilemma. If an extension can be divided a limitless number of times, what is the size of each of the limitless number of products of such division? Either it has some extension or none. If each has no size then they cannot recombine to produce a positive sum (though we started with a finite extension). If each still has some extension then the process of division has not yet been completed – any such magnitude will itself contain a number of smaller parts and can be further divided. He similarly produced paradoxes of MOTION. For example, if one wants to move from point A to point B one must cross midpoint C. But in crossing from A to C one must cross midpoint D. If this process of division can be continued indefinitely one can never begin to move, since before one can reach any point along the way there is an infinite number of intervening points which have to be crossed beforehand.

Anaxagoras accepted that there is no lower limit to division (fr. 3): of any small part, there can always be some smaller part. It is unclear whether he was writing after Zeno or was acquainted with his works. Even if he was so acquainted, clearly he felt that Zeno's paradoxes posed no real difficulties. Later PHILOSOPHERS offered a number of different solutions to Zeno's problem of division. ARISTOTLE insisted on a distinction between 'potential' and 'actual' division. Any extension is potentially divisible at each and every point, but it cannot actually be so divided. Zeno's puzzles, he claimed, resulted from a confusion of these two.

Perhaps the most radical reaction came from the early ATOMISTS, DEMOKRITOS and Leukippos, who asserted that there was a limit beyond which nothing could be further divided physically. These indivisible units, atoms, are the basis of all other larger bodies, which they form through different atomic combinations. It is a matter of some debate how the atomists explained the indivisibility of atoms. EPICURUS, who revived atomism in the hellenistic period, elaborated on their account by claiming that atoms themselves are composed of smaller units (Greek *elachista*, Latin *minima*) which have extension but no parts. Being partless, *minima* cannot be divided; being extended, they can be parts of larger extensions, atoms. This doctrine had important repercussions for the Epicureans' view of geometry, since it implies that, since they are composed of whole *minima*, all lengths must be commensurable. JIW

See Furley, D. J. (1967) *Two Studies in the Greek Atomists*; Makin, S. (1993) *Indifference Arguments*.

divorce In Greco-Roman cultures, divorce was governed by convention rather than state regulation. Scattered references to Athenian divorce suggest that it generally fell under convention rather than LAW, other than the expectation that an Athenian husband divorce an ADULTEROUS wife. Wives (perhaps assisted by male relatives) could also divorce their husbands. The dowry was probably returned in either case, but children would remain with their father.

Hellenistic MARRIAGE contracts, mostly from PTOLEMAIC Egypt, impose conditions of behaviour on husband and wife – the wife would not absent herself overnight without the husband's agreement; the husband would not maintain a concubine – as well as rules for the return of dowry on the dissolution of the marriage by DEATH or divorce.

Divorce was probably rare and disgraceful in early Rome, but it had become common by the late REPUBLIC. AUGUSTAN legislation formalized procedures and required husbands to divorce adulterous wives. Legal ground-rules for the division of property after divorce were apparently derived from suits (*actiones rei uxoriae*) brought by ex-wives (and their fathers) who had not concluded pre-nuptial dotal pacts; but negotiated agreements were more common than litigation. Children normally stayed with the father after divorce, but arrangements were flexible and there is no trace of bitter disputes about visiting rights and custody in the modern sense. SD

See Lacey, W. K. (1968) *The Family in Classical Greece*; Pomeroy, S. B. (1984) *Women in Hellenistic Egypt*; Rawson, B., ed. (1991) *Marriage, Divorce, and Children in Ancient Rome*.

doctors There was no recognized training in antiquity for those wishing to become doctors. Some learned their craft from family members, or by a form of apprenticeship. A few, particularly in the Roman empire, travelled the world studying with the famous doctors of their day, but there was nothing to prevent any persuasive person attempting to cure others. The best way to gain a reputation as a good doctor was simply to treat a famous patient. GALEN (AD 129–216), the best-known and subsequently most influential doctor in the ancient world, was employed to treat the GLADIATORS in PERGAMON before becoming personal physician to the emperor MARCUS AURELIUS and his family. The son of a rich ARCHITECT, Galen had been able to train for the unusually long period of ten years, including four years in the medical centre of ALEXANDRIA.

In their attempt to claim the authority to give medical treatment, doctors were up against competition from, among others, family members, influential neighbours, root-cutters (medicinal herb-collectors), wandering prophets, temple medicine and magicians. In the Roman world, most doctors were Greeks; hence, though some were CITIZENS, many others were SLAVES or FREEDMEN. Some cities employed 'public physicians', who were given immunity from TAXATION. The status of doctors in the Roman world was not high; like other craftsmen, they could belong to trade guilds which acted as social clubs and arranged FUNERALS.

The ancient doctor was expected to diagnose by studying the external signs in order to determine what was happening inside. Medical texts from the HIPPOCRATIC CORPUS and from the Roman world show how the doctor first needed to gain the patient's trust by his appearance, his demeanour, his cheerful and gentle manner and his general conversation. The Hippocratic texts on medical decorum advise against strong PERFUMES, and recommend that the doctor should not quote from the POETS, while Galen rails against 'flashy SILVER instruments'. A central feature of the medical encounter was prognosis, in which the doctor predicted the likely course of the illness. In Hippocratic medicine this could involve the theory of 'critical days', in which the crisis – the point when symptoms became worse and death or cure hung in the balance – was thought to occur on, for example, the 7th or 9th day after the illness began.

Texts written by doctors give the impression of high standards and considerable knowledge, but the dominant image of the doctor in general literature is of an unreliable person, potentially a poisoner, to be avoided if at all possible. The 'Hippocratic Oath', a document probably representing only a very small group of practitioners, shows that at least some found it necessary to state explicitly that their aim was to help the sick, that they would not give POISONS, that they would not reveal confidences entrusted to them, and that they would refrain from taking sexual advantage of members of the HOUSEHOLD in which they were working. HK

See King, H. (2001) *Greek and Roman Medicine.*

 MEDICINE.

Dodecanese see AEGEAN SEA; RHODES.

Dodona Sanctuary and ORACLE of ZEUS in EPIRUS, north-western Greece. It was believed to have been the oldest Greek oracle, as HERODOTOS attests (2.52), but its greatest prosperity and fame should be placed in the late classical period (4th century BC). The latter coincides with the period of supremacy of the Molossian tribe in Epirus, who took control of the sanctuary from its former masters, the Thesprotians.

References to Dodona and its divine patron Zeus exist in HOMER and particularly in book 14 of the *Odyssey*. Here, explicit mention of the oracle is made in connection with the oracular medium, an old sacred oak tree through which the will of god was revealed. The *Iliad* (book 16) and the HESIODIC *Catalogues* offer further insights into the oracular process with reference to the interpreters of divine omens known as Selloi or Helloi, while a group of PRIESTESSES called 'doves' may have performed a similar role.

Archaeological excavations at the sanctuary revealed buildings that have been identified with the oracular shrine of Zeus and TEMPLES dedicated to Dione, Themis, APHRODITE and HERAKLES. Notable among public buildings are a council house, a house of the *prytaneis*, a THEATRE and a structure interpreted as house for PRIESTS. In addition, a wealth of portable finds came from votive deposits, the earliest dating to the late Bronze Age, including a large number of bronze and POTTERY vessels, FIGURINES, JEWELLERY, weapons and other utensils. EP

See Parke, H.W. (1967) *The Oracles of Zeus.*

dogs see ANIMALS; HUNTING; PASTORALISM; PETS; SACRIFICE; SHEPHERDS; see also CYNICISM.

Dokimeion MARBLE quarries located near modern İscehisar 23 km (14 sq miles) north-east of Afyon, Turkey. These were worked extensively from the later 1st century BC, producing various types of white and grey marbles and the particularly famous *pavonazzetto*, a creamy white marble with purple markings. According to STRABO (12.8.14), Dokimeion marble was a very good commercial stone and was quarried very intensively. The quarries were imperial property by the time of AUGUSTUS, with their administrative headquarters at Synnada. *Pavonazzetto* was used extensively in Rome, e.g. in the FORUM of Augustus and the forum of TRAJAN, where it was employed particularly for the large statues of Dacians. All types of marble were exported: in block form for veneer and SCULPTURE, as columns, and as sarcophagi, the last often in finished form. All quarry products were transported by ROAD to the coast (a distance of nearly 300 km, 190 miles); none of the RIVERS in the area was navigable in the Roman period. This might in part explain the very high price of 250 *denarii* for Dokimeion marble in the Price Edict of DIOCLETIAN. HD

See Fant, J. C. (1989) *Cavum Antrum Phrygiae.*

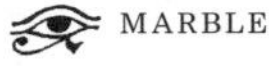 MARBLE.

Doliche see COMMAGENE.

domes Cut stone domes had appeared in the *tholoi* of MYCENAEAN TOMBS, but this method of ROOFING then fell into disuse until Roman times. Twin advances of the second half of the 3rd century BC in Italy – the adoption of the ARCH (borrowed from the Greeks) and the invention of CONCRETE – led to novel forms of roofing, such as the concrete barrel vault to cover rectangular halls. The invention of the dome, a hemispherical envelope of concrete resting on a normally circular or octagonal drum wall, developed from such barrel-vaulted halls; its invention created new possibilities in the architecture of interior space. The earliest surviving dome is the Julio-Claudian structure known as the TEMPLE of MERCURY at Baiae (c.AD 25?), but BATH buildings at Rome of Augustan (and earlier?) date with circular central halls, such as the baths of AGRIPPA, perhaps first experimented with the dome. The earliest surviving example in Rome itself covers the central octagonal pavilion in the Esquiline wing of NERO's

DOMES: (a) concrete construction and the use of vaults and domes allowed the Romans to create remarkable interior spaces, as in this example from a bath complex at Baiae on the bay of Naples.

DOMES: (b) exterior view of same structure.

Domus Aurea (Golden House; between AD 64 and 68). The supreme masterpiece of Roman dome engineering is the PANTHEON, HADRIAN's great temple to all the GODS. Not surprisingly, the building spawned countless imitations in later Roman times. In the middle and late empire, domes occur in a wide range of structures including bath buildings, GARDEN pavilions and mausolea, while one of its greatest legacies was as a central feature in many early Christian churches. RJAW

See Adam, J.-P. (1994) *Roman Building: materials and techniques*; De Fine Licht, K. (1968) *The Rotunda in Rome*.

 PANTHEON: (a)–(c).

Domitian (Titus Flavius Domitianus) 24 October AD 51–18 September 96 Younger son of the Roman emperor VESPASIAN, Domitian succeeded his brother TITUS as emperor, who died suddenly and childless in 81. Modern scholarly attempts to whitewash Domitian's reputation have largely failed in the face of the uniformly negative view in the numerous contemporary sources. They testify to a reign of terror which stemmed from Domitian's battles with a hostile section of the SENATE and led to the suppression of one major military revolt by Lucius Antonius Saturninus (in 89), the execution of at least 12 ex-CONSULS, and the exiling of more. Nor can this be brushed aside by dwelling on the more positive aspects of Domitian's administration. He was remarkable for the extent to which he campaigned successfully in person in a succession of wars against tribal incursions on the RHINE and DANUBE. His recall of the general AGRICOLA from BRITAIN after his success owed less to jealousy than to his low estimation of the value of completing the costly conquest of the island. Domitian increased the pay and privileges of the armies for the first time in almost a century. In Rome he was responsible for the largest public building programme since AUGUSTUS, which included a spectacular new PALACE on the Palatine. He was murdered in a palace coup, which may have involved his wife. JJP

See Cassius Dio, book 67; Juvenal, *Satire* 4; Martial; Pliny, *Panegyric*; Statius; Suetonius, *Domitian*; Tacitus, *Agricola*; Jones, B.W. (1992) *The Emperor Domitian*; Southern, P. (1996) *Domitian*.

 EMPERORS, ROMAN: (a); ROME: (d); VESPASIAN (stemma).

Domitii PLEBEIAN family of the later REPUBLIC, belonging to the Fabia tribe. The main lines were the Ahenobarbi and the Calvini. A late tradition derived the name Ahenobarbus ('redbeard') from an incident involving the appearance of the DIOSCURI in Rome after the battle of LAKE REGILLUS (496 BC), but the family cannot be traced so early. The Calvini held consulships in the wars with the SAMNITES and Tarentines, and again at the end of the Republic. The Ahenobarbi are more significant and unusual. Beginning with Gnaeus Domitius Ahenobarbus, CONSUL in 192 BC, a single male line held consulships in eight successive generations, and culminated in the emperor NERO (Lucius Domitius Ahenobarbus until his adoption by the imperial house). Both lines were involved in the CIVIL WARS, Gnaeus Domitius Ahenobarbus (consul 32 BC, one of CAESAR's assassins) defeating Gnaeus Domitius Calvinus (consul 53) in a NAVAL BATTLE in 42. The former built (or rebuilt) a TEMPLE of NEPTUNE in Rome from the spoils of the battle, and the sculptural friezes of the so-called 'altar of Ahenobarbus' (now in Paris and

Munich) have traditionally (though probably incorrectly) been associated with this. JRWP

Donatism see CHRISTIANITY; CHURCH COUNCILS; CONSTANTINE I.

donkeys and mules Ubiquitous pack animals of the Greco-Roman world. The often harsh and rocky terrain of the MEDITERRANEAN and Near Eastern world in many ways favoured pack animals over WHEELED TRANSPORT. Their ability to cope with such terrain, in cold or arid climates, and to carry substantial loads over long distances (depending on terrain), their robust nature, and their low maintenance requirements in terms of food and water made them indispensable to farmers and transporters. The evidence suggests that mules (produced by a male donkey and a female HORSE, and usually sterile) were more favoured in the western half of the Mediterranean basin and donkeys (a separate species of the horse family, *Equus asinus*) in the east. Their distribution, however, was also determined by the wealth of regions, for mule-breeding demanded the presence of horses. The Roman agricultural writers CATO, VARRO and COLUMELLA all describe the importance of donkeys and mules. In Varro's opinion, the best and largest donkeys came from Reate in Italy and ARKADIA in the PELOPONNESE. Reate was also apparently a centre for mule-breeding. Good stock was essential for breeding, a profitable business in its own right: there was a high demand for such animals, and animal markets were regular features of the ancient world. ARMIES were important consumers, with mules, in particular, bred for military purposes. Although ownership was widespread, donkeys and mules were expensive and strategies for animal management certainly developed; these included hiring extra animals during busy times of the agricultural year to supplement existing stock, and, for poorer farmers, sharing the ownership of animals. CEPA

See Clutton-Brock, J. (1992) *Horse Power: a history of the horse and the donkey in human societies.*

 BAKING.

Dougga see THUGGA.

Doura Europos see DURA EUROPUS.

Douris of Samos c.340–c.260 BC Greek HISTORIAN. His brother Lynkeus, a comic playwright and friend of MENANDER, studied at Athens, as Douris himself may have done. Reportedly tyrant of SAMOS, his role may have been that of governor acting on behalf of king LYSIMACHOS. He was not necessarily unpopular, or was perhaps forgiven, for he outlived Lysimachos. His works, all lost apart from quotations, included *Samian Annals*, *Macedonian History* and a biography of AGATHOKLES of Syracuse. His reputation for sensationalism may be the result of being quoted by authors interested in moral failings, such as ATHENAEUS and PLUTARCH. He praises men martyred while resisting Macedonian power, such as Phokion and Eumenes of Kardia. He lampoons some of ALEXANDER'S SUCCESSORS, but may have treated Lysimachos and SELEUKOS more kindly. Unsurprisingly, given that the Athenians occupied Samos in the 4th century, he criticizes them for servility towards the ANTIGONIDS, and quotes the famous hymn to DEMETRIOS I that is often misread as evidence of Athenian irreligion. He has been partially rehabilitated as, perhaps, one of the great lost writers of his age, and he exemplifies how Greek ARISTOCRATS combined intellectual output with a role in public affairs. DGJS

See Kebric, R. B. (1977) *In the Shadow of Macedon*; Shipley, G. (1987) *A History of Samos.*

drachma see COINAGE (Tables).

drains and drainage see ENGINEERING; PLUMBING; POLLUTION; ROME; SANITATION; TOILETS; WASTE DISPOSAL; see also CANALS; ETRURIA AND ETRUSCANS; KOPAÏS, LAKE; LANDSCAPE; WETLANDS.

drama

Like other Greek poetic genres, drama is best defined by the context in which it was performed. Drama was institutionalized at Athens towards the end of the 6th century BC, perhaps as early as 534, with tragic competitions in honour of the god DIONYSOS. At the FESTIVAL of the City Dionysia, dithyrambic competitions and COMEDIES followed TRAGEDY in c.509 and 486 respectively. Later, plays were performed at other Dionysiac festivals: at the Lenaia in January–February (from 440), where comedy took pride of place, and at the rural Dionysia, performed in local DEMES. Tragedies were performed at Athens from the 6th century until at least the 2nd century AD. From Athens drama spread throughout the Greek and later the Roman world.

The City Dionysia became under the Attic DEMOCRACY the most important annual civic festival and a major source of pride for the city. Held in the ninth month of the calendar year (roughly March), when the seas became passable, the five-day festival brought many visitors to Athens, including (after 454) allies bringing tribute that was displayed in the THEATRE. At least 15,000 people were present to observe a number of non-dramatic ceremonies: SACRIFICE to the god; the pouring of libations by the ten elected GENERALS of that year, the announcement of the names of CITIZENS who had received crowns as BENEFACTORS of the city; and a parade in full ARMOUR of orphans whose fathers had died in action and were now to be supported by the *POLIS*. The state paid for poorer citizens to attend. Whether WOMEN were present remains controversial; most probably citizen wives of child-bearing age were least likely to have been present, and women will certainly have represented a minority of the audience. Two days before the festival, POETS presented previews of the subjects of their plays and introduced their casts at a *proagôn* or preliminary contest. Before the contests, the statue of Dionysos was removed from its precinct next to the theatre, brought to the VILLAGE of Eleutherai, the mythical site of the god's entry into Attica, and returned in a PHALLIC procession to the theatre, where it stood during the festival.

Before the PELOPONNESIAN WAR (431–404) the festival probably opened with dithyrambic contests; each of the ten TRIBES of Athens entered one CHORUS of 50 men and one of 50 boys, who sang and danced choral songs on mythological themes in a circular formation. On successive days, each of the three tragic

DRAMA: (a) the chorus in Aristophanes' comic play *Knights* as depicted on an Attic vase-painting.

DRAMA: (b) vase-painting depicting theatrical scene in which Zeus visits Alkmene.

DRAMA: (c) Pompeian wall-painting illustrating the dramatic possibilities provided by the architectural backdrop (*scaenae frons*) of a Roman theatre, with its three doorways.

poets competing in the contests at the City Dionysia presented three tragedies and one SATYR play. Satyr plays featured a chorus of satyrs or goat-men, often accompanied by their father Silenos. The themes and major characters of satyr plays were mythical GODS or HEROES – our one complete example is Euripides' *Cyclops*, based on the Polyphemos episode of *Odyssey* 9 – but the unheroic, curious and vulgar satyrs undercut the dignity of the heroes. Typical motifs included the captivity and liberation of the chorus, marvellous inventions (WINE, MUSICAL INSTRUMENTS), the nurturing of heroic or divine infants, and ATHLETICS. Five comedies were performed on a separate day. After 431, three comedies were presented, probably following the three tragic performances at a four-day festival. Two days after the City Dionysia, a democratic assembly was held to review the conduct of the festival. While the form of tragedy largely stabilized in the 5th century, satyric drama dropped out of the theatrical festivals in the 4th century BC, and comedy underwent a gradual transformation from what we call Old via Middle to New Comedy.

The City Dionysia was organized by the eponymous archon, a civic MAGISTRATE charged with 'granting a chorus' to the playwrights and appointing a *chorêgos* (producer, literally 'chorus-leader'). The latter financed many aspects of the production, including recruiting, maintaining, training and costuming the chorus. The city was responsible for the leading ACTORS and poets. The *chorêgoi* were wealthy citizens who competed for status by displaying their largesse to the city in the form of such LITURGIES (an indirect tax). We do not know what criteria were used by the archon in selecting the poets. Both the chorus members (12, later 15) and the actors (three for each tragic performance and up to five for comedy, as well as mute extras) were male citizens, who played both male and female parts. The poets and their *chorêgoi* competed for a prize; victorious poets received ivy crowns. Ten judges drawn from each tribe were elected by lot to prevent corruption, but audience applause could play a critical role in their decision.

Dramatic poets were virtuosic artists who composed both text and MUSIC of their plays, designed and rehearsed the choreography and, in the case of AESCHYLUS and earlier playwrights, acted in their own plays. After 449 there was a competition for tragic first actors (*prôtagônistai*), and from 442 for comic actors. By the mid-4th century each protagonist performed in one tragedy of each poet. Because they were masked and performed to a huge audience, actors were especially prized for their command of voice and gesture. Plays were rehearsed for about six months before being performed, and participants were relieved from military service for this period. Normally, each play received only one performance in the major civic festivals; by 386 BC tragic revivals were legally permitted, contributing to the canonization of Aeschylus, SOPHOKLES and Euripides. Revivals of Aeschylus had been permitted following his death in 456. Despite these revivals, however, the competition for new plays continued for many centuries.

In the theatre of Dionysos, spectators probably sat in wedge-shaped sections on the slope of the south side of the ACROPOLIS, with front seats reserved for dignitaries and sections set aside for individual tribes. The focal point was the *orchêstra* or choral dancing space, which may have been circular, rectangular or trapezoidal and about 20 m across. Early tragedy may have been performed without a stage. Once a wooden *skênê* or stage building was added, it initially contained at least one central door and provided two playing spaces, the roof of the building (often called *theologeion*) and (probably) a long, low wooden stage for the actors. Higher stages were a post-classical development. One or two doors were probably added to the stage building in later centuries, which also saw the building of a stone stage and permanent seating. Actors could enter from the *skênê* door, or through two *eisodoi* or entranceways into the *orchêstra* from either side of the stage building. A wheeled platform (*ekkyklêma*) could be used to bring out a set tableau from the interior of the *skênê*, and a crane (*mêchanê*) could be used to suspend gods, or in the case of comedy other characters, above the stage. The costumes were distinctive for each genre, with grotesque masks and phalluses for satyrs and comic figures. Tragic costume became more elaborate throughout the 5th century; at its conclusion, tragic actors typically wore a long-sleeved, richly decorated *chitôn* and soft leather boots. The tragic mask, covering the whole head, was naturalistic until the hellenistic period, when it developed a high forehead and down-turned mouth. Painted scenery, said to have been introduced by Sophokles, was minimal and could probably not be changed in the course of a play.

Greek drama was more operatic than later theatre. Choruses sang and danced their scene-dividing odes (*stasima*) and their entrance and exit songs, accompanied most typically by the double pipe or *aulos*, a reed instrument like the modern oboe. A limited number of props and other instruments (e.g. the *tympanon* or drum) and sound effects (e.g. thunder) could be introduced as needed. Actors spoke largely without musical accompaniment, in iambic trimeters, a poetic metre that sounded closest to ordinary speech; but they could employ other spoken metres, or sing or employ recitative either in exchanges with the chorus (*amoibaion* and *kommos*) or (increasingly) in solo monodies. Our evidence for the music and dance of drama is confined to representations on VASE-PAINTINGS (which probably rarely present an actual performance), much later discussions of Greek music in antiquity, and a few musical notations on fragmentary PAPYRI.

Acting became increasingly professionalized. From the 3rd century BC, actors formed powerful regional guilds. Star performers could command large fees, and enjoyed special protections, immunities and privileges. They were patronized by rulers and cities and prized as ambassadors. These actors occasionally performed excerpts from tragedies rather than complete plays, and attempted to modify or interpolate passages into the plays. In 330 BC, the Attic statesman LYKOURGOS put a stop to this practice by establishing official versions of the plays. As acting flourished, the choral role declined, until in the 4th century BC and later choruses became mere act-dividing interludes (*embolima*) unrelated to the content of the dramas. HPF

Roman drama comprised thousands of performances of many different kinds of entertainments; but little has survived, which limits our picture. Sources of information include a handful of surviving plays (some 26 COMEDIES, 9 TRAGEDIES and the historical drama *Octavia*), together with numerous tiny fragments of comedies, tragedies and other forms of drama, including MIME and farce. Visual records include 'phlyax' vases from south Italy and SICILY depicting farces, and WALL-PAINTINGS from POMPEII showing stage settings and masks. Material remains of THEATRES survive throughout the Roman empire. Written stories about the history and practice of drama include LIVY's account (7.2.3–12), with its marked parallelism with the history of the development of Greek drama, and HORACE's remarks in the *Ars poetica*. There are also anecdotes about particular performances. The MUSICAL aspects of Roman drama are lost to us, though the SONG and DANCE element was clearly lively and perhaps provided the ancient equivalent of a hit parade of popular songs. It is also hard to gauge the continuity from antiquity through the medieval period into the RENAISSANCE. It is possible that mime-actors were the forerunners of the wandering minstrels (jongleurs) of the Middle Ages, and that the Italian *commedia dell'arte* derives, directly or otherwise, from Roman comic entertainment.

Roman drama takes a variety of forms, ranging from relatively highbrow scripted plays to improvisations with a wider appeal. The more sophisticated part of the audience may have preferred Roman tragedy (based on the Greek tragic dramatists), Roman historical drama (*fabula praetexta*), comedies based on Greek New Comedy (*fabula palliata*) and comedies set in Italian towns (*fabula togata*). At the other end of the scale were the improvised, 'subliterary' forms of drama, which were not written down until the end of the REPUBLIC. These include the native Italian Atellan farce (*fabula Atellana*) and the mime, perhaps from Sicily, which had words, and PANTOMIME, which did not. In all these dramatic forms, the words are in POETRY in a variety of metres, some borrowed from Greek drama and others reflecting native Italian traditions.

This range is reflected in the different costumes. Tragic ACTORS wore the high boot (*cothurnus*) and comic actors the low shoe (*soccus*), while mime-actors appeared barefoot and without masks. Moreover, the only type of drama in which WOMEN appeared was the mime. The social status of actors, often SLAVES, and especially of actresses, was generally low despite their popularity. One notable exception was the famous comic and tragic actor Roscius (1st century BC), whom Sulla raised to the rank of *eques* (knight). The mime was the lowest in status, because of exposure of the face without any mask. An anti-Caesar story tells how CAESAR forced the *eques* Laberius to act in his own mimes, which meant that he lost certain civil rights. But not everyone was reluctant to court the fame available through the stage. In AD 19 a senatorial decree (*SENATUS CONSULTUM Larinum*) was passed which forbade members of the ÉLITE to appear on stage. For some, the last straw was the emperor-turned-actor: NERO caused consternation and disgust by his enthusiasm for taking the roles of Orestes and other HEROES and GODS on stage.

In the early Republic, drama was generally performed along with other forms of entertainment, such as GLADIATORIAL fights and tightrope walking, at the public FESTIVALS (holidays, 'holy days') in honour of JUPITER, APOLLO, Magna Mater, Flora and CERES. This perhaps continued earlier ETRUSCAN forms of music and dance entertainments. Other events funded privately by the élite, such as FUNERAL GAMES for important individuals, also included dramatic entertainments. So the funeral of Lucius Aemilius Paullus in 160 BC was the occasion of the performance of TERENCE's comedy *Brothers*. The state officials (MAGISTRATES) had the responsibility for organizing the theatrical entertainments (*ludi scaenici*) at the festivals, and they used the opportunity to impress the crowds. For a long time, entertainments in and around Rome were staged on temporarily erected structures. Although the Greek cities of southern Italy and Sicily had had stone theatres since the 5th century BC, the first stone theatre at Rome was not built until 55 BC.

Of the more highbrow types of drama, tragedies and comedies are among the earliest recorded works of Latin literature, starting with the *ludi Romani* of 240 BC. Only titles and fragments survive of plays by Livius Andronicus and Naevius in the 3rd century BC and by ENNIUS in the late 3rd and early 2nd centuries. The tragedies of this period were adaptations of plays by AESCHYLUS, SOPHOKLES and EURIPIDES. Nearly all our evidence about comedy (*fabula palliata*) comes from the 2nd century BC, with 20 plays by PLAUTUS and six by Terence surviving. Later there were revivals of the most popular early Republican dramatists' plays, and no new names emerged as comic dramatists. The great tragic dramatists, Ennius' nephew Pacuvius and Accius, flourished in the 2nd century BC and their influence lasted though their works did not. Later, OVID wrote a highly praised *Medea*, doubtless indebted to Ennius' play; only tiny fragments survive. Our sole examples of Roman tragedy are by SENECA THE YOUNGER (mid-1st century AD), apparently written for a private élite audience. One example of a Roman historical drama (*fabula praetexta*), *Octavia*, also survives, dating from after Seneca's death.

Farce and mime were the most popular and most lasting forms of Roman dramatic entertainment. Their obscenity and sexual excitement aroused the disapproval of moralists throughout antiquity into Byzantine times. In south Italy and Sicily there had long been a tradition of farce and mime in Greek, centred upon parody of tragedy and mythological burlesque. The Italian Atellan farce from Campania was a form of improvisation by a small troupe of stock characters including a fool, a hunchback, a glutton and the boss, with obscene language and seedy storylines; it may have specialized in parodying tragedies, to judge from titles that survive, such as Pomponius' *False Agamemnon*. The mime, exceedingly popular with the crowds and EMPERORS alike, was still more explicit. At the Floralia festival the mime actresses even appeared naked in a striptease. One favourite through the years was the ADULTERY mime, which the emperor ELAGABALUS insisted should be acted with realistic sex scenes. The pantomime, introduced at Rome late in the 1st century BC, consisted of expressive dancing and gesticulation; its stories, taken from MYTHOLOGY, were mimed by an actor wearing a mask with closed lips, accompanied by music and a CHORUS. This could be a lucrative form of entertainment: in the 1st century AD the court poet STATIUS made money by writing libretti for pantomime choruses.

Roman comedy is based on Greek New Comedy by MENANDER and other Greek playwrights. The surviving plays are by Plautus (late 3rd–early 2nd century BC) and Terence (c.190–159 BC). They generally have Greek settings and names. The character line-up is predictable: fathers and sons, wives and call girls, pimps and rival customers and slaves. So too the plots, which work towards 'boy gets girl' and focus upon the obstacle, whether it be his father, a rival in love or the girl's pimp. Roman comedy is characterized by conflicts between the generations (e.g. Terence, *Brothers*), the sexes (e.g. Plautus, *Casina*) or master and slave (e.g. Plautus, *Haunted House*) which are resolved by the end of the play. Other standard features are mistaken identity, coincidence, repetition and the use of tokens to bring about recognition of long-lost relatives, for example, in Plautus' *The Rope* and in his *Brothers Menaechmi*, the original of SHAKESPEARE's *The Comedy of Errors*.

Into this Greek framework, which Terence reproduces closely, the more innovative Plautus inserts distinctively Italian dramatic elements including rude language and physical VIOLENCE; his characters resemble those of Atellan farce. His introduction of song and dance makes his comedies the obvious forerunner of the Broadway musical. The film based on the Stephen Sondheim musical, *A Funny Thing Happened on the Way to the Forum*, closely replicates the pace and twists of Plautine comedy. Plautus often suspends 'normality', as suits the carnival atmosphere: in his plays, groups of people who in real life have no power over the man of the HOUSEHOLD (*paterfamilias*) – sons, wives, slaves – outmanoeuvre him. The chief Plautine character is the clever slave, above all Pseudolus (in the play of that name), who orchestrates the action and outwits everyone, especially his master.

Roman comedy clearly influenced European comedy significantly, including Shakespeare and Molière. A modern descendant is the TV situation comedy (sitcom), which has the same small family group and the same limited plots, including misunderstandings and mistakes, repetitions and coincidences, with a guaranteed resolution by the end of the episode.

From the beginning, Roman tragic drama appears to have taken plots and stories from Greek tragedy. Titles of plays by Livius Andronicus, the earliest recorded tragedian, indicate his debt to Sophokles and Euripides. The tragedies of Ennius (239–169 BC) include themes from Euripides (*Medea*) and Aeschylus (*Eumenides*). Tragedy on Roman themes (*fabula praetexta*) was an innovation of Naevius (d. c.200 BC): titles include *Romulus* and *The Wolf*. In the 2nd century BC, Pacuvius (220–130) wrote plays based on Sophokles and a Roman tragedy, *Paullus*. His prolific young friend Accius (170–c.90) wrote plays based on Euripides, Sophokles and Aeschylus, including *Atreus*, *Bacchae* and *Phoenissae*; his *fabulae praetextae* include *Brutus* and *Sons of Aeneas*; he also wrote a literary history. VARRO and CICERO considered Pacuvius the greatest Roman tragic poet, but it was Accius whose plays were revived throughout the last years of the Republic and who was considered supreme in the 1st century AD. His *Clytemnestra* was performed in 55 BC to celebrate the opening of POMPEY's stone theatre in Rome. Members of the élite also wrote tragedies: Caesar an *Oedipus* and AUGUSTUS an *Ajax*; Varius Rufus' *Thyestes* was performed at the Actian games in 29 BC.

We know little about the early performances of tragic drama in Latin, beyond that there was a musical accompaniment and that the LYRIC (choral) passages were more developed than in Greek tragedy. Seneca's tragedies, written under CLAUDIUS and/or Nero, seem to be a different phenomenon, designed for an élite audience. A scholarly debate rages over whether they were for performance or for recitation by a single actor. Seneca takes the material of Greek tragedy – the stories of OEDIPUS, AGAMEMNON, Medea and Phaedra – but uses these plots as vehicles to explore the human experience of passion, especially conflicting passion (e.g. *Medea*, *Phaedra*), good and bad models of kingship (*Oedipus*, *Mad Hercules*, *Thyestes*) and other issues which connect with Roman STOICISM and Roman political thought. Seneca's plays, like the late Republican revivals of Accius, may have been designed to deliver political messages, though we are hampered by our ignorance of the dates and circumstances of the plays. Seneca's tragedies are articulated in a highly DECLAMATORY mode which reflects the ubiquitous influence of RHETORIC on Roman literature of the period. There are many gruesome 'set pieces' depicting the supernatural and the macabre, such as the haruspicy and necromancy scenes in *Oedipus* and the reassembling of Hippolytos' dismembered body in *Phaedra*. Seneca's influence on European tragedy, including Shakespeare and Racine, is profound. In Elizabethan and Jacobean times, Jasper Heywood's translations of Seneca were popular, scholars wrote Senecan-style plays in Latin, and Jacobean tragedians such as Webster (c.1580–c.1625, e.g. *The White Devil*) and Massinger (1583–1640, e.g. *The Roman Actor*) incorporated characteristic Senecan features such as long 'rhetorical' speeches, torture and blood-letting. In the 20th century Eugene O'Neill treated the Phaedra story in *Desire under the Elms*, Ted Hughes adapted Seneca's *Oedipus* for performance, and Sarah Kane developed Seneca by including on-stage fellatio and anal rape in her *Phaedra's Love*. The only surviving Roman historical tragedy, *Octavia*, probably of Flavian date, portrays Nero's treatment of his wives Octavia and POPPAEA and even features Seneca as a character. SB

See Beacham, R. C. (1991) *The Roman Theatre and its Audience*; (1987) Staging Roman comedy: Pompeian painting and Plautus (*Ancient Theatre and its Legacy*; video); Bieber, M. (1961) *The History of the Greek and Roman Theater*.

 ACTORS AND ACTRESSES: (a)–(b); CHORUS.

draught animals Almost any agricultural, economic or military task in the ancient world required the use of animals for TRANSPORT. Often the nature of the terrain or the loads carried required pack-animals, but draught animals were necessary for most heavy work – ploughing, drawing CHARIOTS and wagons, or powering machines such as water-wheels. The most common draught animal was the ox, though mules, DONKEYS and even CAMELS were often used (and camels were probably the most capable of animals for these purposes, but were clearly used more commonly in arid climates). HORSES, though used for drawing some forms of carriages and chariots (for racing rather than war), were not used frequently for draught purposes until the early medieval period.

Good draught animals had considerable value, and were expensive to train, maintain and breed. In ancient technical literature, much space is dedicated to the ownership of animals. In the Greek world

DRAUGHT ANIMALS: camel caravan from Ghirza in the Libyan pre-desert.

Hesiod, Aristotle and Palladius, and in the Roman world Columella, Cato, Varro and Vitruvius, all comment on these matters. In Greek papyri from Egypt, the use of animals in the agricultural economy is well documented. Iconographic evidence, for example animals depicted on Trajan's column, show how animals were used in transport but fall short of providing detail on perhaps a most perplexing problem, the nature and efficiency of ancient animal harnessing.

The harnessing system probably originated from a pole-and-yoke system placed between oxen and around their horns or withers (chest). Early equid harnesses, similarly, were placed around the withers, but this is commonly believed to have restricted the horse's breathing and thus its tractive efficiency. Such an argument was vigorously advocated by Lefebvre des Noëttes, who claimed that the inefficient nature of ancient animal harnessing (until the invention of the horse collar in the medieval period) had the effect of stifling economic growth more generally in the ancient world. His arguments are flawed on two main counts: his misunderstanding of harness techniques and efficiency, and his misinterpretation of his principal ancient source, Diocletian's edict on maximum prices. Modern experiments on traction, and reinterpretation of evidence, have shown that good traction could be obtained and that ancient draught animals could haul considerable loads efficiently. There are many good examples, but perhaps the most significant are the hauling of stone blocks in temple building projects in Epidauros and Eleusis, where up to 33 yokes of oxen were harnessed together.

It now seems certain that good traction could be obtained by draught animals in the ancient world. It is likely that terrain and topography, as well as fixed wooden axles (which made steering difficult) and limitations in wheel design, had more limiting effects on transport and its development than did harnessing systems. CEPA

See Clutton-Brock, J. (1992) *Horse Power: a history of the horse and the donkey in human societies*; Raepsaet, G. (2002) *Attelages et techniques de transport dans le monde gréco-romaine*.

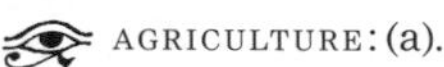 AGRICULTURE: (a).

dreams Although in some ways the ancient concept of dreaming is very similar to our own, in other ways it is very different. Whereas we tend to speak of 'having' a dream, ancients spoke of 'seeing' a dream. In early Greek literature this was often a dream image – a god or ghost – who delivered a message to the sleeper. We also tend to think differently about the meaning of dreams. Whereas we are much influenced by Freud, who interpreted dreams as manifestations of our subconscious desires and fears, the ancients believed that certain dreams were prophetic, sent by the gods in order to help mortals. This is reflected in the use of dreams to provide medical diagnoses in the sanctuaries of Asklepios. Prophetic dreams (*oneiroi*) would often be allegorical and require interpretation by a professional dream-interpreter. The *Oneirokritikon* of Artemidoros, the only dream-book to survive from classical antiquity, provides a wealth of information about how dreams could be interpreted. Nevertheless, there was an acknowledgement that some dreams (known as *en(h)ypnia*) merely reflected the actions of the day. However, many thinkers dismissed the possibility of prophetic dreams altogether. Aristotle argued against the divine origin of dreams and believed that the actions in people's lives and the sounds they heard in their sleep could influence their sleeping imagination. Cicero also rejected dream divination as mere superstition. Hippocratic writers were also sceptical about the prophetic power of dreams, but they did believe that dreams could be used to diagnose a patient's illness. FMM

dress

The warm climate of Greece encourages loose and layered clothing. The main material used was wool, of varying quality and thickness. The spinning and weaving of wool into cloth was one of the main responsibilities of the majority of Greek women. Linen was used from the Mycenaean period onwards, as was hemp and flax. A form of silk, called *bombycina*, was made from the cocoon of moths found on the island of Kos in Roman imperial times. This is differentiated from 'real', Chinese, silk, mentioned by Pausanias (6.26.6–8). Decoration was woven, embroidered or dyed. Excessive decoration was often frowned upon – a woman wearing too sumptuous an outfit could be considered impious or thought to be a *hetaira* (courtesan). Cloth fine enough to be transparent was associated with *pornai* (prostitutes). Flowery dresses were considered gaudy, as were garments of a saffron colour. Animal hides and skins appear in the fashion outfits of heroes (such as Herakles' lion cloak) and appear to have been worn also in the less cosmopolitan areas of Greece.

In the Bronze Age, there was a distinction between clothing in the mainland Mycenaean culture and that of the Cretan Minoans. Minoan men wore a codpiece and a belt, sometimes with a kilt or apron over the top. Mycenaean men generally dressed in a short-sleeved tunic tied at the waist. They can also be seen wearing shorts, and pins have been excavated that may have been for fastening cloaks. Women's clothing was more elaborate, with long, sometimes flounced, skirts and tight bodices. Minoan women are depicted wearing bodices exposing their breasts, though these may have been religious costumes. Mycenaean women are depicted in the elaborate Minoan outfits, but rarely display their breasts and appear more commonly in a longer version of the tunic worn by Mycenaean men. These appear to have been the designer outfits of their day, particularly for Mycenaean women, as we also see them wearing more simple long tunics tied with a belt.

Greek clothing from the archaic period onward is quite different. Homer mentions the *chitôn* as an ankle-length, unbelted tunic for older and wealthier men. It can be seen in the vase-paintings of the time, often covered over with a cloak, generically called a *himation* by scholars. The *himation* was frequently worn by itself, and during the archaic period men of a certain level of wealth demonstrated their leisurely existence in the convoluted and restrictive wrapping of their clothing. The extreme can be seen in the short-lived fashion for saffron-coloured cloth, with accompanying parasols, head-dresses and long

(a) The long, unbelted *chitôn* of archaic times worn with a *himation* (cloak).

(d) *Chitôn* worn under embroidered *chitôn* with decorative borders.

(b) Short belted tunic.

(e) Dionysos and maenad wearing flowing, transparent Ionic *chitônes* with animal skins, hinting at their 'Eastern' origins.

(c) The goddess Artemis wearing a *peplos*. The decorative borders of the cloth are visible along her right leg.

(f) Man wearing *chitôn* and *himation*.

(g) Youth wearing travelling hat (*petasos*), heavy, embroidered cloak (*chlamys*) and boots.

DRESS, GREEK: (a)–(g) selected illustrations.

DRESS, ROMAN: (a) grave monument from the Via Statilia, Rome, showing man and woman, c.75–60 BC.

DRESS, ROMAN: (b) ivory diptych of late Roman *vicarius* of Rome, Rufius Probianus.

boots, associated with the archaic POET Anakreon and considered rather effeminate. Athletic men and youths of the archaic period continued to wear the short-sleeved or sleeveless, thigh-length, belted tunic (similar to the woman's *peplos*). A 'mini-skirt', called a *zôma*, was worn by ATHLETES until it went out of fashion during the 5th century BC, when NUDITY became the general rule. It was also worn under ARMOUR and by craftsmen and labourers.

The main garment for women in the archaic period was the *peplos*, a woollen garment initially of quite a heavy weight. The rectangular length of cloth was folded in half, with the woman standing in the middle. It was fastened at each shoulder with a pin or brooch. They were usually worn ankle-length with the excess material folded over at the top and caught with the belt or girdle around the waist. They were highly decorated in the early archaic period, and some idea of this can be seen on vase paintings and from the traces of paint on *KORAI*. Women also wore cloaks with many variations of draping.

Around 540 the Ionic *chitôn* came into favour. This was made of linen and sewn so the woman was standing in a tube. The sleeves were voluminous, and the dress was either fastened along the top edge with buttons, or was sewn. Like the *peplos*, it was tied at the waist. It appears to have been of a much finer weave – distinguishable in the artistic record by the minute crinkles of its folds – and was sometimes worn under the *peplos*. Its early popularity in Athens is visible in the representations of *korai*, but soon spread throughout Greece, though the *peplos* was never abandoned, returning to popularity in the 5th century in a lighter form. The *peplos* was less highly decorated at this time, with the borders remaining an area for embellishment. The overfold, *apoptygma*, was longer and often caught under the belt. The sides could be sewn closed, or, in the fashion associated with SPARTAN women, it could be left open – sometimes gaping open if no belt was worn. Spartan women were also notable for wearing a short version of the *peplos* similar to that worn by the men, which reflected their more athletic lives. In Greek iconography this outfit became *de rigueur* for the unmarried, athletic or hunting woman. This includes depictions of the goddess ARTEMIS or mythological heroines such as ATALANTA and nymphs. For Athenians, the short *peplos* was also associated with the 'untamed' girls undergoing the female rites of passage at BRAURON.

Men continued to wear the long and short versions of the *peplos* or *chitôn* in the classical period, but the long version became the appropriate dress for older men or was associated with specific roles, such as charioteer, MUSICIAN and PRIEST. The *peplos* was worn with pins at both shoulders or one shoulder. The single-pinned *peplos* (*exômis*) became the general uniform for SLAVES and workers. A smaller cloak, the *chlamys*, thought to originate in MACEDONIA or THESSALY, was typically worn by HUNTERS or athletes and, in the hellenistic period, by soldiers. It was fastened at the throat with a brooch and could be draped around the shoulders or fly back dramatically when in action.

From the 4th century onward, female fashions allowed the belt to rise higher up the body to lie under the breasts. Decoration on clothing came back into vogue, and necklines dropped and were pinned or sewn to allow draping at the front.

The Greeks do not appear to have been particularly fond of hats. Two types, both made of felt, are visible in the artistic record. The *pilos* was a conical shape and could also be made of LEATHER or metal. The *petasos* was wide-brimmed and tied under the chin; it was often part of the male hunting or travelling outfit. Women used the overfold of the back of their *peplos* to cover their heads, and in the hellenistic period they wore a wide-brimmed hat.

The ancient Greeks often went barefoot, particularly when indoors. A variety of SHOES, boots and sandals are mentioned in the literature and it is often not possible to match them with the images we have. They were generally made of leather: cowhide for strength, with softer versions in calfskin or the skin of SHEEP or GOATS. Wood was used for the soles, and felt to make boots warm. We know from the literary record that men and women had stylistically specific footwear, and Xenophon (*Oikonomikos* 9.19.2) mentions 'high shoes' – the ancient equivalent to high heels. NJW

See Llewellyn-Jones, L., ed. (2002) *Women's Dress in the Ancient Greek World*; Symons, D. J. (1987) *Costume of Ancient Greece.*

As in other cultures, dress in Roman society served various functions: cover for decency and warmth, and a means of enhancing (or more often, concealing) physical charms. It also had a particular importance as a way of signifying social status. Essentially the dress for the freeborn Roman man was the TOGA, which was plain (the *toga virilis*) for most adults, while the toga with a broad purple stripe (*toga praetexta*) was worn by boys and MAGISTRATES. A Roman woman wore a *stola*, a full-length tunic, with a *palla* draped over her shoulders and head. Different occasions brought variations on these: for instance, a candidate for public office wore a whitened toga (*candidatus* means 'whitened'), while brides wore a veil (*flammeum*) and a special HAIRSTYLE. SLAVES and working men would wear basic practical and protective garments. Different regions of the Roman empire had their own styles of dress, often with trousers and tunics for the men and, where they were needed, thick hooded cloaks as protection against the elements. Greek dress, which for men meant the wearing of the *pallium* (a long mantle) was frowned on for upper-class Romans abroad during the Republic and early empire. By the later empire, however, many 'un-Roman' garments were to be seen in the capital, such as long-sleeved tunics and leggings, often of vivid colours and adorned with embroidery and jewels.

The primary evidence for all this is vast, varied and often incidental. However, some items of clothing survive as fragments or in their entirety. The best examples of these come from sites where they have been preserved by particular physical conditions; for instance, a large number of shoes, some of exquisite workmanship, was found at VINDOLANDA, a military site on HADRIAN'S WALL. Burial grounds in Egypt have yielded TEXTILES of late imperial date, including complete tunics of linen or wool and individual panels of ornament. In this particular case it is possible to link the dress as preserved with items of costume as depicted in ART, as these ornamental strips and patches can be seen on the tunics and cloaks of figures which appear, for example, in HUNTING MOSAICS from North AFRICA and Piazza Armerina (SICILY). But generally some caution is needed in reference to visual representations as evidence for what was actually worn. Too often they are concerned more with the ideal or aggrandized than with documentation, and they usually relate to the world of the more privileged. Hence characters engaged in practical, everyday tasks are often shown dressed in elaborate clothes which the viewer is meant to interpret as signs of wealth, and, of course, to enjoy for the sumptuous visual effects. Sometimes, too, Roman art clothes humans after the style of the GODS or HEROES of earlier classical art. Thus one Roman Republican businessman from the Greek island of DELOS is depicted nude, like a heroic classical ATHLETE, while many WOMEN and girls are commemorated in their funerary portraits wearing flimsy, off-the-shoulder robes like goddesses.

Yet art also offers many instances where different types of dress are used to signify a particular role or status for their wearer, an approach which had some basis in historical reality. Once again, some allowance must be made for artistic licence. Not all the Roman men shown on their funerary monuments wearing the distinctive *pallium* and holding scrolls could really have been active 'Greek' PHILOSOPHERS. The outfit of the 'PHRYGIAN cap', tunic and trousers which came to denote non-Roman orientals is used sometimes rather indiscriminately as a signifier in art. Yet both these examples are good illustrations of the way in which a certain set of garments had a specific value in a dress code which was apparently generally appreciated. There are many other cases, particularly in official contexts, where this is worked out in the details of costume which articulate niceties of social rank and status. Portraits of AUGUSTUS, for instance, show how dress was used to differentiate his imperial roles: on the ARA PACIS he is in religious mode, with his head covered, while the famous Prima Porta statue shows him as military leader. Not only does his costume there work with his stance and gesture to build up a total image, but the cuirass itself is decorated with relevant imagery. Four centuries later, the same use of dress to differentiate official roles is clearly illustrated in the IVORY diptych of Probianus, dated c.AD 400. One panel shows him and his companions in a public context, the other in the private sphere: the distinction is spelled out through individual items of dress.

Literary sources also indicate the social value of dress. It was often taken to reflect the wearer's wealth and wish for social visibility and power. For instance, garments of gold and purple (restricted to imperial use by CALIGULA), or of particular materials such as SILK, were tokens of luxury which attracted sumptuary legislation from time to time, while ASCETIC discourses (such as the early CHRISTIAN) took dress as a major theme. Many other passages describe or discuss items of dress. Some are informal and anecdotal, such as the letter from a military commander at Vindolanda who writes to order various types of cloaks for his slaves. (This particular example illustrates another aspect of many literary references to dress: it is sometimes impossible to identify what exactly the specific Latin words describe.) Others discuss, often with antiquarian interest, how certain elements in traditional Roman dress came about: why TRIBUNES of the people did not have a stripe in their togas (Plutarch, *Roman Questions* 81), or why followers of PYTHAGORAS wore robes of white linen (Iamblichos, *On the Pythagorean Life* 153). The use of words for clothing to denote a whole class of wearer – *togatus*, for instance, for a Roman as opposed to a non-Roman; the feminine *togata* for PROSTITUTES who could wear the toga – shows how ingrained in Roman culture was the role of dress in signifying status in Roman society. JH

ARMS AND ARMOUR: (a)–(e); FASTENING; TETRARCHS: (a); TEXTILES.

drink/drinking see ALCOHOL AND ALCOHOLISM; BEER; DINING; *SYMPOSIA*; WINE.

drug addiction The understanding of addiction did not, apparently, exist in the ancient world. ALCOHOL addiction was as unclear a concept as drug addiction. Misuse or excess in drinking, as contrasted to addiction, does appear from time to time, but this is mainly related to a lack of decorum or ETIQUETTE. Evidence for the use and misuse of DRUGS for recreational purposes is, however, entirely lacking. The nearest equivalent, but in a RITUAL context, is reported of the SCYTHIANS by Herodotos (4.73–5). To purify themselves after BURIALS, they prepared a steam bath by tossing seeds of the hemp plant (Greek *kannabis*) onto heated stones. The smoke and vapour thus generated induced howls of delight. The subsequent application of a plaster made from various pulped woods mixed with water both cleansed and perfumed their bodies. Similar uses of drugs for religious reasons include, perhaps, the consciousness-altering properties of leaves chewed by the PRIESTESSES at ORACLES, including DELPHI (natural gases emanating from fissures have been suggested), and the drinking of a hallucinogenic substance, possibly derived from mushrooms, in ZOROASTRIAN religion.

Medical writers were aware that drugs could produce consciousness-altering effects, but this represents faulty pharmacology or errant prescription. It was little different from the use of small quantities of what would be POISONS in larger amounts to achieve benefits for HEALTH. In both cases, accidents might occur. Opium was used mainly for medicinal purposes, for example, to counter INSOMNIA. Since addiction generally requires regular, large or potent quantities of a chemical, the lack of the requisite technology to extract suitable chemicals in their purer forms was perhaps responsible for low incidence of recreational drug use and addiction to chemical substances. JV, PGT

See King, H. (2001) *Greek and Roman Medicine*.

drugs In antiquity, drugs were used to treat a range of physical and mental symptoms. There are references to them in MYTH; for example, in the *Iliad* knowledge of drugs is attributed to HELEN. In the HIPPOCRATIC corpus, not only was diet used as therapy, so that foodstuffs could help the BODY return to HEALTH, but also many special combinations of ANIMAL and plant substances were employed. Some drug materials were easily available and cheap, while others – such as Eastern SPICES and aromatics – may have gained something of their efficacy from their rarity. An important principle of drug selection was odour: many substances, such as SILPHIUM (now extinct), were seen as powerful because of their strong smell.

Attempts to systematize knowledge of drugs were made by ARISTOTLE's successor THEOPHRASTOS and, in the 1st century AD, by Dioscorides in his *Materia medica*, a work which served as a textbook on the subject until the RENAISSANCE. Drug manuals do not always specify amounts, because the strength of a substance would vary considerably according to local conditions, such as the soil in which a plant was grown or the time of year when it was harvested. Drug materials were collected by 'root-cutters', according to strict rules about how and when this should be done.

The efficacy of ancient drugs was both chemical and symbolic. The efficacy of opium or pennyroyal can be understood through modern pharmacology, but substances were not necessarily administered to make use of their soporific, analgesic or diuretic qualities. Other materials were tied into wider religious or cultural ideas associating particular plants with particular deities, or assuming by analogy that their specific properties – such as the ability of the squirting cucumber to eject its seeds with great force – could be harnessed for other purposes. (see also DRUG ADDICTION) HK

Druids and druidism A class of PRIESTS, common to GAUL and BRITAIN, who presided over all things pertaining to religion, including divination and RITUAL sacrifice. The Druids were also responsible for the oral history of their people, as well as for training those who flocked to them for instruction in druidic doctrine. Of all the extant sources that make reference to druidism, CAESAR's commentary (*Gallic War* book 6) is generally regarded as the most useful account, because of his friendship with a Druid, Diviciacus.

In addition to noting their function as religious leaders, Caesar alludes to the political power of the Druids in their role as arbitrators in tribal disputes. Their annual meeting in the centre of Gaul (Carnutian territory), as well as the existence of an archdruid, suggests that their judicial power extended to inter-tribal affairs, not simply those at the intra-tribal level.

A primary tenet of druidism was the belief that the SOUL inhabits another BODY after DEATH; this is often equated with the transmigration of souls associated with PYTHAGORAS. The degree to which this doctrine was an inherent philosophy of the Druids is not substantiated. However, the ubiquity of grave goods in native BURIALS, including items associated with status and the daily necessities of life, suggests the extent to which life after death was acknowledged in the CELTIC world.

The practice of HUMAN SACRIFICE was the most nefarious aspect of druidism and was heavily frowned upon by Rome. In the reign of TIBERIUS, it was prohibited for any Roman citizen to partake in this 'barbaric' ritual, while CLAUDIUS attempted to eradicate it entirely. The empire justified the massacre of the Druids on the island of Mona (Anglesey) in AD 60 as the final eradication of this bloodthirsty rite. MLM

See Piggott, S. (1974) *The Druids.*

Ducetius Native Sicel leader, mid-5th century BC. Ducetius successfully led some Sicels against Katane in eastern SICILY in 461–460. He then founded Menainon and captured Morgantina in 459–458. In 453 he founded Palike, making it the capital of a Sicel league with its own COINS and army. He went on to capture MOTYA in 451, which provoked SYRACUSAN intervention; they lost the battle of Motya that year, but were victorious at Nomai in 450. Ducetius surrendered and was exiled to CORINTH, which led to the collapse of the Sicel league. In 446 he returned to Sicily with Syracusan support and founded a Greek–Sicel colony at Kale Akte. Sensing a threat, Akragas attacked but was repelled by Syracuse, allowing Ducetius to continue to support the Sicels. It was only after Ducetius' death in 440 that Syracuse was able to dominate the lowland Sicels effectively. HWE

Dumézil, G. see CAPITOLINE TRIAD; MYTH; RELIGION, ROMAN.

Dura Europus Hellenistic, PARTHIAN and Roman city in the middle Euphrates valley in eastern SYRIA. Founded as a colony (Europos; 'Dura' is Semitic) by SELEUKOS I Nikator c.312 BC, it was under Parthian control from the late 2nd century BC to AD 165, then Roman until its fall to the SASSANIANS in AD 256–7. Abandoned, it is described by Ammianus Marcellinus (23.5.7) as deserted by 363.

Dura was excavated by F. Cumont and then by Yale University (1922–36), but only partially published. It provides unique evidence for life in an ethnically diverse community on the frontiers of three empires, ranging from public buildings to graffiti, including organic materials (like PAPYRUS) preserved by desert aridity. Dura has a hellenistic grid-plan with an irregular wall circuit, the Euphrates to the east and the desert to the west. Public areas included an *AGORA* and TEMPLES, most of MESOPOTAMIAN courtyard plan, dedicated to a range of Greek and non-Greek deities. In the Roman period there was a synagogue with spectacular biblical wall-paintings and a CHRISTIAN baptistery.

Papyrus documents and inscriptions show survival of Greek institutions into the Roman occupation, and reveal a mixed population of Greco-Macedonians, Mesopotamians and PALMYRENES (including soldiers and traders using the Euphrates trade route). They also provide detailed evidence of the composition and activities of the Roman garrison based in the city. NDP

See Millar, F. (1993) *The Roman Near East 31 BC–AD 337.*

 SYRIA, ROMAN: (b).

Duris see DOURIS OF SAMOS.

dyes and dyeing An important part of the TEXTILE industry in the ancient world. There is a great deal of evidence, both historical and ARCHAEOLOGICAL, that coloured textiles were abundant in antiquity. Not only textiles were dyed, but also hides, wood and IVORY, as well as the staining of parts of the BODY by certain peoples.

Dyestuffs were derived from a wide range of sources, from both ANIMALS and plants, and a wide range of colours could be produced. Purple was probably the most sought-after colour available to ancient dyers, as the dye known as 'Tyrian purple' produced from certain species of MEDITERRANEAN shellfish was the most expensive and prestigious of its kind. The kermes INSECT, which lived on the kermes oak, a tree ubiquitous throughout Greece, was made into a red dye, as was the root of the madder plant. Sources of blue included the leaves of the woad plant and indigo. Saffron and safflower were major sources of yellow. Brown was produced from the green rind of the walnut, while black dyes were produced from oak galls and the plant *akantha*.

Another important substance used in the dyeing process was the mordant, which was used as a fixing agent to produce fast colours and would probably have been a soluble SALT of aluminium, chromium, IRON or TIN. Water was a major ingredient in the dyeing process, along with an alkaline substance such as stale urine which helped to dissolve the dyestuffs. The materials which were dyed included wool and linen. Wool could be dyed before spinning or after weaving, while linen was usually dyed as yarn.

The dyeing process usually involved the immersion of the textile in a vat containing the dye solution. This solution may have been heated or used cold. Certain dyes, such as madder, kermes and saffron,

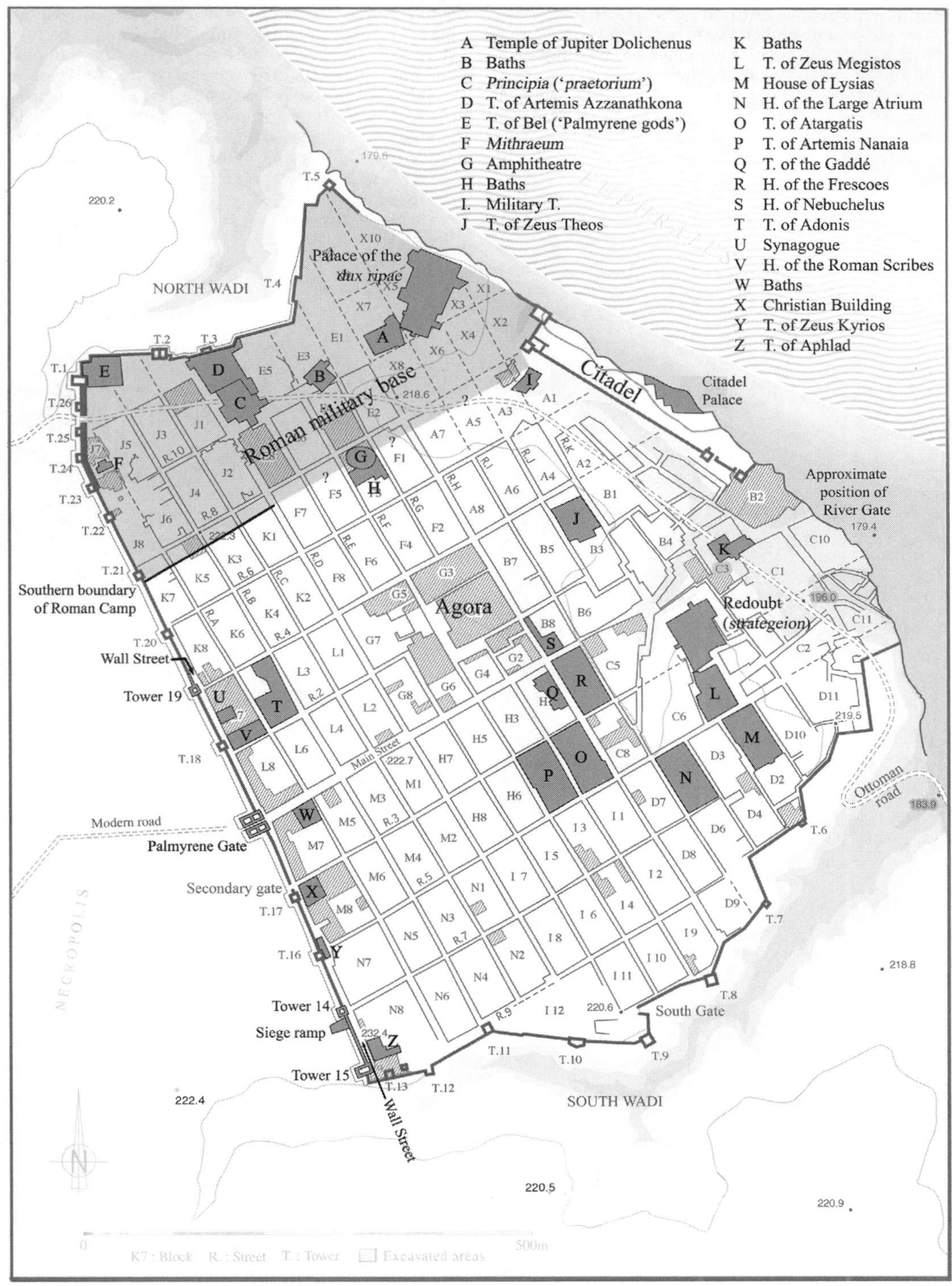

Dura Europus: plan of the city in its final form.

required the use of a mordant to fix them to the fabric, which was either soaked in a separate vat containing the mordant solution or was immersed in a single vat containing the dye and mordant solution together. 'Vat dyes' such as 'Tyrian purple' and indigo did not require the use of a mordant. Once it had reached the required colour, the textile was removed from the dye vat and had the excess liquid squeezed out of it. It was then dried.

Dyeing was done both at a 'HOUSEHOLD' and an 'INDUSTRIAL' level. Textiles whose colour had faded could be dyed at home, as in most cases the equipment needed was fairly simple and easy to acquire. However, the use of some dyes, such as 'Tyrian purple' and woad, required specialist knowledge and could also be extremely unpleasant. As a result, there were a number of 'industrial' dyeing establishments with specialist dyers operating on a large scale. Examples are the hellenistic dyeing complexes at MYCENAE and Isthmia in Greece, and also at POMPEII. MDM

See Forbes, R. J. (1964) *Studies in Ancient Technology*, vol. 4.

E

Earth see GE.

earthquakes Parts of the MEDITERRANEAN are subject to strong earthquakes, owing to the movement of the plates of the earth's crust (Greek thinkers tended to favour explanations in terms of natural elements such as earth, air and water). Although historical records presumably under-report events happening outside inhabited districts, the areas of frequent seismic activity appear to have shifted, so that localities at risk today were not necessarily so in antiquity. STRABO, for example, describes the Sparta area as *euseistos*, 'well shaken', though only a few major earthquakes are attested, the worst being that of c.464 BC which decimated the citizens and may have hastened their decline in numbers. He was perhaps led to this impression by the existence in LACONIA of cults of POSEIDON (the god associated with earthquakes) with titles such as Gaiawochos (Earthholder) and Asphaleios (Steadfast). Nevertheless, several towns of the PELOPONNESE have experienced devastation in modern times, such as Kalamáta in 1986. The local effects of seismic activity are generally intense and are noticed more in architectural, therefore mainly urban, environments. Casual reports can only hint at the real frequency of such events, such as the 'earthquakes' (*seismoi*) mentioned in a 3rd-century inscription from SAMOS, which caused short-term hardship for many citizens. The ACHAIAN city of Helike famously sank below the sea in 373 BC, but its near-neighbour Boura, also destroyed, was soon rebuilt. Long-term effects on the society and economy of a region are hard to prove (as is true of VOLCANOES), and it is unwise to adduce earthquakes as explanations for such developments. Although recent underwater archaeology suggests that in the Roman period parts of ALEXANDRIA sank below the waves, and that one or more nearby cities disappeared, the city survived several major earthquakes known from the sources. POMPEII was revived and renovated after the earthquake of AD 62, only to be destroyed 17 years later by the eruption of Vesuvius. At RHODES in 227/6 BC, an earthquake overthrew the famous Colossus and seriously damaged the dockyards. POLYBIOS (5.88–90) accuses the Rhodians of skilfully turning the calamity to their advantage by soliciting donations from all over the Greek world towards rebuilding their city. He tartly comments that they should have made even better use of the resources, but also notes their 'opportune location'. Given the city's strategic position, it is probable that its mercantile economy would have revived even without outside help.

EARTHQUAKES: temple of Zeus at Olympia, with main colonnade evidently brought down in an earthquake.

The subdiscipline of archaeoseismology examines earthquakes in the archaeological record, identified through physical evidence such as collapsed buildings, cracked walls, and 'offset' (horizontally displaced) column-drums. Specialists, however, are increasingly cautious about the criteria used to identify seismic damage. Linking archaeology to known seismic events involves subjective interpretation, since records are so incomplete. Moreover, the effects of earthquakes may be 'overprinted', so that what we see is the sum of all damage and we cannot distinguish particular events, particularly larger events occurring after lesser ones. Recognition that the characteristics and effects of earthquakes are variable, particularly at a distance from the epicentre, and that 'an' earthquake may consist of a series of shocks lasting months, has fostered still more caution. DGJS

See Guidoboni, E. (1994) *Catalogue of Ancient Earthquakes in the Mediterranean Area*; Noller, J. S. (2001) Archaeoseismology, in P. Goldberg et al., eds., *Earth Sciences and Archaeology* 143–70; Stiros, S. and Jones, R. E., eds. (1996) *Archaeoseismology* (partly superseded); Waldherr, G. H. (1997) *Erdbeben* (collects literary evidence).

East Greece The western coast of Asia Minor and ISLANDS of the east AEGEAN. The mainland was divided into three territorial zones by the Hermos and Maeander (Maiandros) rivers. The northern zone, originally PHRYGIAN territory and under LYDIAN control from the late 8th century, was settled by the Aiolian Greeks. The central zone, around the gulf of Maeander, was settled by the Ionians. This was the birthplace of SCIENCE and PHILOSOPHY and the home of PYTHAGORAS, ZENO and HERAKLEITOS. In the south was CARIA, settled by the Dorians.

The MINOANS established a trade network in the southern part of the east Aegean, incorporating MILETOS, Seraglio on Kos, and Triánda on RHODES. The MYCENAEANS were also active in the area. Their POTTERY has been found as far north as TROY, and important Mycenaean settlements were established at Miletos, and on Rhodes at Ialysos and Triánda. The settlements on Rhodes were abandoned at the end of the Bronze Age, but at Miletos there was continuity of occupation throughout the Submycenaean and Protogeometric periods. A 12th-century refugee settlement may have been established at Emborió on CHIOS.

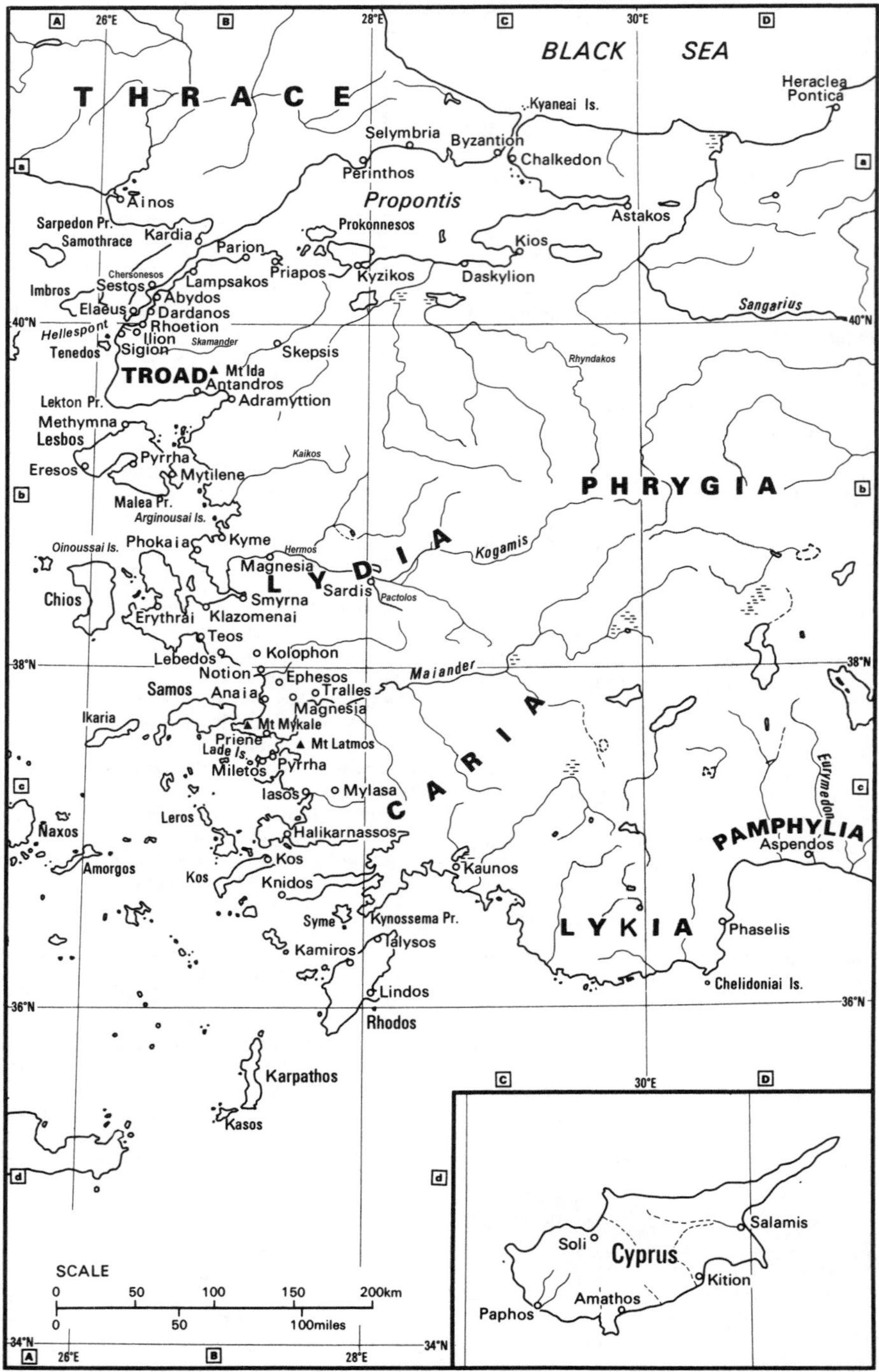

East Greece: map.

In the so-called Dark Age and Geometric period (c.1100–700 BC) there were massive migrations across the Aegean to the east coast of Asia Minor, represented by the appearance of Protogeometric pottery, for example at Miletos and SMYRNA, and on SAMOS, Rhodes and Kos. The main body of migrants were Ionians, but the Aiolians also played a part. The foundation of the Ionic cities is recorded in later literary tradition from the 5th century. There was a second wave of migrations by the Dorians c.900. They settled western Caria and established settlements at KNIDOS and HALIKARNASSOS.

The 12 cities, or 'Dodekapolis', of Ionia are Miletos, Samos, Priene, Myous, EPHESOS, Kolophon, Lebedos, Klazomenai, Teos, Phokaia, Erythrai and Chios. At the end of the 9th century these were organized into a league, the Panionion, headed by Ephesos. The cities were also linked by the Panionia, a FESTIVAL dedicated to POSEIDON Helikonios. Miletos claimed to be the earliest Ionic settlement and was the mother of a number of trading colonies between the HELLESPONT and the Euxine, such as Abydos and Sinope, traditionally founded in the 8th century.

The famous Ionian sanctuaries were among the first Greek TEMPLES to be monumentalized in stone in the 6th century. Early foundation dates are proposed for the Heraion on Samos (8th century) and the temple to APOLLO at DIDYMA (7th century). The third important sanctuary was the Artemision at Ephesos. The Ionian cities had a large territorial hinterland divided into large estates worked by non-Greek slaves or serfs. They were settled as petty kingdoms, and in the 7th and 6th centuries they were ruled by TYRANTS. The conquest of Lydia by CYRUS THE GREAT in 546 brought East Greece under PERSIAN rule. After an abortive revolt in 499 the Ionians were finally freed from the Persian yoke in 479, following the battle of PLATAEA and a second action at Mykale opposite Samos.

The Aiolian cities are less well known. According to HERODOTOS, the Aiolians originally formed a league of 12 cities but this was reduced to 11 by the Ionian capture of Smyrna. Two early foundations are Smyrna and Kyme (*Kymê*), home of HESIOD's father. Excavations at Smyrna give one of the clearest pictures of an early East Greek settlement, including the 9th-century FORTIFICATIONS, remodelled in the 8th century. LFS

See Boardman, J. (1988) *The Greeks Overseas* (rev. edn); Cook, J. M. (1961) Greek settlement in the eastern Aegean and Asia Minor, in *CAH* 2.2, ch. 38; Cook, R. M. and Dupot, P. (1997) *East Greek Pottery*; Cook, J. M. (1962) *The Greeks in Ionia and the East*; Jeffery, L. H. (1976) *Archaic Greece*.

 ASIA, ROMAN.

Eboracum, Eburacum see YORK.

eclipses see ASTRONOMY; CHRONOLOGY.

ecology Defined as 'the study of the relationship between living organisms and their animate and inanimate environment' (Horden and Purcell). (This is different from 'ecological' awareness of environmental issues such as global warming.) The ancients did not have a concept of ecology, though 'NATURE' (Greek *physis*, Latin *natura*) played a central role in their cosmological ideas, sometimes as an active force. THEOPHRASTOS came closest to formulating an interactive model of the relationship between humans and their environment. In modern social science, ecology has progressed beyond older deterministic or systems-based approaches to consider the adaptive strategies which societies use to sustain life, human response to risk, and dynamic evolution. Specifically 'historical ecology', partly inspired by the *Annales* school of geographical history, allows full consideration of change through time and of historical circumstance.

In recent scholarship on the ancient MEDITERRANEAN, ecological thinking has enhanced the understanding of town–country relationships, rural landscapes, land-based and maritime TRADE, and theories of the ECONOMY. The term 'microecologies' has been invented by Horden and Purcell to characterize the network of extremely diverse environments in the Mediterranean world, to which humans respond differently at different times. Microenvironments are thought to gain viability from 'connectivity', dynamic links such as ROADS and sea routes. DGJS

See Grove, A.T. and Rackham, O. (2001) *The Nature of Mediterranean Europe*; Horden, P. and Purcell, N. (2000) *The Corrupting Sea*; Sallares, R. (1991) *The Ecology of the Ancient Greek World*.

economy

There was never a 'Greek economy' in the sense that we can talk about 'the Roman economy', because each city-state had its own independent economic life. Although there were similarities between the economic systems of different Greek *poleis*, and they were to some extent interconnected, there were many local differences.

Sources for Greek economies include incidental references in prose and DRAMA (especially COMEDY), surviving speeches from lawsuits, ARCHAEOLOGICAL sources (POTTERY, MANUFACTURING installations, MARKETPLACES), COINS, and EPIGRAPHY. Most of the

ECONOMY: (a) Roman mosaic from Ostia advertising the shippers (*navicularii*) of Carthage.

ECONOMY: (b) Roman wine barge under tow on tributary of the river Rhône.

important textual sources are from Athens, though inscriptions and coins come from a wide range of cities. For hellenistic Egypt, documents on papyri offer insights into business procedures, ACCOUNTING, credit and finance unmatched elsewhere in the Greek world. Some of the economic practices documented in PAPYROLOGICAL sources were plainly current elsewhere, but often it is difficult to distinguish which were specific to Egypt and which were not.

The extent to which Greek economies were 'primitive' (e.g. based on exchange and reciprocity), or like modern economies, or somewhere in between has been vigorously debated for almost 200 years. Modern studies have been much influenced by the work of M. I. Finley, following Karl Polányi's 'substantivist' position. This approach considers economic activities in ancient Greece to be 'embedded' within political, religious and social activities; 'the economy' was not a free-standing entity or set of specialized institutions (e.g. the stock market) operating according to the 'rational' principles of supply and demand, as it is often perceived to be in modern Western states. The debate about the economies of ancient Greece still rages, and Finley's ideas are still pivotal though rapidly becoming superseded.

From as early as there were CITY-STATES in the Greek world, their economies were founded on AGRICULTURE. Most *POLEIS* consisted of an urban area with its surrounding rural territory, and the inhabitants of the city farmed the countryside as privately owned land holdings. Economy and politics were here entwined, since only citizens could own LAND, and only landowners were CITIZENS in most *poleis*. HOUSEHOLDS and cities generally aimed to be self-sufficient in staple foods (CEREALS), and ensuring a regular supply of grain was one of the few areas of the economy where the state attempted to exert political control. An inscription from 5th-century Teos officially curses people who obstruct the food supply of the city. It is likely that more people made a living from agriculture than from any other activity, though farms were relatively small compared with the huge estates of the Roman world.

MANUFACTURING also operated on a relatively small scale. WORKSHOPS were generally small family businesses: the concept of a 'corporation' was alien to the organization of commerce and industry in the Greek world. The only state-controlled industry in classical Athens was SILVER MINING. Mines were leased out by the state at the leaseholder's risk, and provide one of the few known instances of business partnerships: a number of people each made a small investment, thereby aiming to spread the risks. Generally, workshops and 'factories' were located in towns in ordinary private HOUSES. INDUSTRIAL installations regularly appear in 'DOMESTIC' houses in OLYNTHOS, though their precise function is not always clear. Located among the housing at Locroi Epizephyrioi in south Italy there are several pottery kilns. In ATHENS and CORINTH the pottery industry is particularly well documented by the large-scale survival of its products in the archaeological record, and we know the names of many Athenian potters and VASE-PAINTERS from their signatures on individual pots. Numerous occupations, such as lamp maker, furniture maker, perfume maker, breastplate maker, wheelwright and sandal maker, documented in the inscriptions and literature of classical Athens, testify to considerable economic specialization. However, it is hard to be sure that such 'specialists' were engaged in their craft full-time: they or members of their households may also have been engaged in agriculture for part of the time. Retailers and services are also well documented in town centres. Like workshops they were generally small family businesses, operated wholly or in part by SLAVES. In Athens, METICS (resident aliens, some of whom were certainly freed slaves), who were not allowed to own land, appear to have played a major role in trades, crafts, manufacturing and services. Again, many specialized retail trade and service occupations, such as cloak-seller, donkey or ox driver, salt-seller, fuller, bathhouse-keeper, bookseller, bread-seller, and various kinds of fast-food sellers, are known from classical Athens. In the Athenian AGORA, the marketplace and central business district of the city, market stalls selling all kinds of produce, and businesses, such as cobblers, barbers and wine SHOPS, are well documented (in one case because of the very large number of empty wine jars, mostly from CHIOS, thrown down the well next door!). Less salubrious businesses such as brothels were located further from the Agora (e.g. the KERAMEIKOS), but you might pick up a PROSTITUTE at the Leokorion. WOMEN as well as men worked in both manufacturing and retail trades, and women may have been particularly in businesses such as TEXTILE production. Even though paid work was considered inappropriate for women of citizen status, some women were driven to work by desperation. Many working women may have been metics or slaves.

Greek economies have often been characterized as 'slave economies' by modern scholars, and it is true that slavery in its many forms was a crucial source of LABOUR, essential in the absence of MACHINES. However, the large-scale use of slaves, such as the chain gangs of the American South or Roman mines or *latifundia*, never occurred in ancient Greece. The extent to which slavery was essential for Greek farming is much disputed, because ancient sources provide little information about agricultural slaves. As noted above, slaves were important in manufacturing, retail and service businesses, but within the setting of the household. Frequently they worked independently (their owner simply collected the profits) or alongside free workers, often including their owner himself. This is well documented in the building accounts from the Erechtheion TEMPLE in 5th-century ATHENS, where free citizens and their slaves carry out construction work side by side and are paid the same wages. Frequently workshops were owned by free (often wealthy) citizens but operated by slaves, but it was not unusual for free and slave people to work together, doing the same jobs. This may be why ÉLITE literary sources look down on wage labour: from their point of view it appeared too much like being a slave, the opposite of an autonomous free citizen.

Despite the ideal of self-sufficiency, trade and exchange played a major part in the economies of classical Greek cities. Relatively low-value commodities such as WINE, OLIVE OIL, pickled FISH, PERFUME, dyestuffs, pottery and many other things were widely exported all over the Mediterranean and beyond. For example, the city of Methana in the Saronic gulf imported all of its pottery in the classical period, mostly from the nearby cities of Athens, Corinth and Aigina. This suggests that short-distance TRANSPORT of cheap goods was more expedient than trying to make pottery in a location where decent clay was in short supply because the local soils were volcanic. By the later 5th and 4th centuries BC Athens, probably the largest city in Greece, regularly imported some proportion of its grain supply. Frequently particular cities or regions were known for the production and export of specialist products such as Chian wine (the coins of Chios displayed a wine jar), the SILPHIUM of Cyrene, or cochineal from the central PELOPONNESE.

LOANS, credit and BANKING were all well-developed features of Greek economies, though the details are best known from Athens, in particular from LAWCOURT speeches. Because each city minted its own coinage and many different WEIGHT standards and denominations were used across the Greek world, moneychangers were essential in commercial cities. They regularly served as bankers, performing such functions as making loans at interest, organizing bottomry loans (for shipping), and acting as a repository for cash savings. There were relatively few opportunities for investment in the rather confined economies of Greek cities: buying land, sharing in bottomry loans, and loaning out money at interest were the most common. The wealthy élite of Athens disdained personal involvement with trade, business or financial services, and banks provided a convenient way for wealthy men to engage in these activities without being seen to do so directly. The banking family best known from 4th-century Athens was of slave origin. There is much scholarly debate about the extent to which the economies of classical *poleis* were 'monetized'. Not all may have developed cash economies to the same extent. However, most scholars now agree that Athens' monetary and financial systems were quite sophisticated, and that most of the inhabitants of Athens regularly dealt in cash transactions at some level.

The period after Alexander the Great saw the development of more integrated economic networks throughout the eastern Mediterranean and western Asia, and of more complex financial and commercial institutions. LF

Although it was very large in scale and advanced in some respects by the standards of other pre-industrial societies, the Roman economy was unlike the sophisticated capitalist systems of modern times. In the 1960s and 1970s, Moses Finley led a scholarly reaction against a modernizing tendency in studies of the ancient economy (typified by Rostovtzeff's classic study). Finley stressed the relative primitiveness of the ancient economy, the limited nature of long-distance TRADE and MANUFACTURING, and the minimal economic and TECHNOLOGICAL development over time. The issues are still much debated, but the current consensus is now shifting somewhat away from the extreme position taken by Finley. There is an increasing recognition that economic GROWTH was achieved in some regions of the ROMAN EMPIRE, and that the overall scale of economic activity, increasingly demonstrated by ARCHAEOLOGICAL data, was significantly higher than that achieved in most pre-industrial societies.

While economic concepts and structures were different from modern ones, however, this does not necessarily justify characterizing them as primitive or under-developed. By the standards of the time, the Roman economy was vast in scale and surprisingly sophisticated in many of its practices. There are indications in PAPYRI, for instance, that economic rationalism underlay some complex ACCOUNTING processes. The Roman economy involved the interplay of rural and urban PRODUCTION, the exploitation of LABOUR (including a significant level of slavery within Italy) and the infrastructures of EXCHANGE.

The nature of the evidence relating to the Roman economy is very uneven. Literary sources are few, reflecting the social mores of the time as much as reality. Documentary evidence in the form of papyri and WRITING is limited to a few locations, most notably in Egypt, and its typicality has been much debated. There is a dearth of quantitative data, and our views on the attitudes of Romans are heavily coloured by a small amount of evidence relating to the disparaging remarks of ARISTOCRATS regarding trade. Socially speaking, AGRICULTURE and LAND ownership were the most respectable sources of wealth, and manufacturing and commerce were looked down on. But there is ample evidence to suggest that even SENATORS were loath to overlook non-agrarian money making possibilities altogether, getting round the social stigma by using SLAVES and FREEDMEN to look after their interests in such ventures, or by advancing LOANS. In the PROVINCES there is still less evidence to suggest what were the attitudes of the curial class to manufacturing and commerce, but the active involvement of some dominant local families in a wide portfolio of economic interests seems assured.

Archaeological evidence is increasingly abundant but biased by factors of preservation. Organic commodities, such as foodstuffs, ANIMAL products, wooden artefacts and TEXTILES, are poorly conserved in most archaeological deposits, but are demonstrably key components of TRADE in any age in the past. Certain other valuable items, such as GLASS, METALS and objects made of metal, could be recycled and are disproportionately under-represented in rubbish deposits. The most abundant archaeological materials are ceramics, their numbers reflecting their essential fragility more than their economic value. Yet POTTERY vessels were often containers for other commodities, such as OLIVE OIL, FISH SAUCES or WINE; or were traded alongside long-perished commodities and thus may stand in as proxies for trade in those other goods. Some of the best archaeological evidence for ancient commerce has come from SHIPWRECKS, where the composition and quantification of near-intact cargoes can sometimes be calculated.

It must be accepted, as a starting-point, that the Roman economy was essentially based on farming, primarily agriculture, much of it at or close to subsistence levels. Yet in many regions of the empire there were significant changes in RURAL SETTLEMENT and output following the incorporation of land within the Roman sphere. The conquest of huge territories gave unparalleled opportunities for the reorganization of landholding arrangements. The imposition of the Roman TAXATION system may also have had an impact, but above all it was the organization of LABOUR and production by the local ÉLITES, operating within the new framework, that meant that significant surpluses could be generated at the regional level. The clearest evidence of such changes can be traced in areas like North AFRICA, where several regions developed a clear specialization in olive oil production, with a significant capacity for export.

It is also increasingly recognized that the non-agricultural sector of the Roman economy was of considerable importance at the regional level, and that some cities show a degree of specialization in their commercial and/or manufacturing activity (such as LEPTIMINUS). The image that most cities were passive consumers of localized rural production ('CONSUMER CITIES') is no longer sustainable. One of the major brakes on the development of the economy was the relative difficulty of the empire's COMMUNICATIONS and the constraints of its TRANSPORT systems. However, detailed studies of Roman ROADS, of RIVER transport and maritime traffic all support the view that the period between 200 BC and AD 200 saw substantial growth in the scale and volume of transportation in all these areas.

The geographical, political and social imperatives of the Roman empire contributed a number of peculiarities to its economy. We might conceptualize these in terms of a political economy operating alongside a social economy that was in turn interleaved with a true MARKET economy. The political economy was primarily the product of the need to extract surplus from the empire to support the mechanisms of state. These included securing the FOOD SUPPLY for the city of Rome and for the ARMY (the *annona*), exploiting mineral resources to sustain the COINAGE system, and obtaining and transporting the raw materials to embellish the capital – notably from widespread imperial QUARRIES for a range of decorative stones. Although Rome claimed a monopoly over significant mineral resources and over sources of MARBLE and decorative granites, and had access to substantial volumes of foodstuffs from state lands and imperial estates or as tax in kind, the expense of exploiting these resources and of transporting the commodities huge distances to their chosen destination would have defied normal economic logic. This was a redistributive EXCHANGE system operating on a grand scale. For example, monolithic COLUMNS of granite weighing up to 200 tonnes were quarried at MONS CLAUDIANUS in the eastern Egyptian desert, then transported more than 120 km (75 miles) overland to the NILE and then onwards to Rome. The infrastructure to support this extraordinary operation, involving permanent settlements at the quarries, the requisition of huge numbers of DRAUGHT ANIMALS and the construction of special SHIPS, could only have been undertaken by a state such as Rome. The operation of the political economy of the *annona*, and of the extraction and transport of metals and stone, thus represents a huge anomaly in the economy. It is clear that some of the archaeological evidence of long-distance movement of goods around the Roman world can be related to this political economy, which subsidized or underwrote transport costs.

However, it is also apparent that free market trade also flourished alongside the imperial economy. This can be seen, in part, in the long-distance transport and wide distribution of many goods to centres other than the city of Rome and the main military FRONTIERS. This was a widespread trading economy, sustained by the purchasing power represented in many Roman CITIES. Mercantile relations extended well beyond the imperial frontiers, for instance towards INDIA and CHINA in the East, and sub-Saharan Africa in the south. Several further factors can be highlighted in support of this. The eventual evolution of a coinage system fitted to serve small market transactions is one of the clearest indicators of the role of the market economy. Even more striking is evidence to show that non-cash transactions were often accounted in cash terms to create simple credit systems. Although ancient BANKING was relatively local in operation, there are instances of loans being taken out in one seaport and repaid in another. Other mechanisms of exchange, such as individual gift exchange, élite redistributive mechanisms for moving around the products of their own estates, and barter, are likely to have persisted and played a role at all times. We can discern regional differences in economic activity and success, suggesting that there was not a single integrated economy but rather a series of interlocking regional ones. Nonetheless, the overall volume of manufactures and their distribution patterns are extremely impressive. Above all, one is struck by evidence of large-scale activities, well above the SUBSISTENCE needs of individuals or inward-looking communities. At La Graufesenque in south-west France 1st-century AD KILNS could apparently accommodate tens of thousands of high-quality pots in a single firing, and these pots are found distributed in large numbers across the Western empire. A pottery workshop lease in Egypt specifies the annual production by the potter, for one estate owner, of amphoras (for WINE) with a total capacity of c.300,000 litres.

In late antiquity, the nature of the Roman economy changed considerably, with inter-regional trade shrinking in the West but initially expanding in the East after the foundation of CONSTANTINOPLE. Overall, the transition to the Dark Ages was slower than was once believed to be the case, but the break-up of the empire had undoubted repercussions on its economy. DJM

See Archibald, Z.H. et al., eds. (2001) *Hellenistic Economies*; Anderson Cartledge, P. et al., eds. (2002) *Money, Labour and Land: approaches to the economies of ancient Greece*; Duncan-Jones, R. (1990) *Structure and Scale in the Roman Economy*; Finley, M. (1985) *The Ancient Economy*; Frank, T., ed. (1933–40) *Economic History of the Roman World*, 6 vols.; Garnsey, P. et al., eds. (1983) *Trade in the Ancient Economy*; Greene, K. (1986) *The Archaeology of the Roman Economy*; Harris, W.V. (1993) *The Inscribed Economy: production and distribution in the Roman empire in the light of instrumentum domesticum*; Manning, J. and Morris, I., eds. (2000) *The Ancient Economy: evidence and models*; Mattingly and Salmon, *Economies beyond Agriculture*; Rathbone, D. (1991) *Economic Rationalism and Society in Third-century AD Egypt*; Rostovtzeff, M. (1957) *Social and Economic History of the Roman Empire*.

 AGRICULTURE: (a)–(b); TRADE, ROMAN.

Edessa (mod. Urfa) Hellenistic and Roman city in MESOPOTAMIA, founded (or perhaps refounded) as a colony by SELEUKOS I Nikator, which took its name from Edessa in MACEDONIA. It was also called Orhai in the later Syriac literature of the area, perhaps a local name predating the Macedonian colony. The names Antioch-by-the-Kallirhoë and Justinopolis were also used at various times. The site occupies a strategic position overlooking the plain of Harran (CARRHAE), lying between the important crossing point of the Euphrates at Seleukeia-ZEUGMA and the Tigris, and thence the eastern Seleukid capital of Seleukeia-on-the-Tigris.

With the weakening of Seleukid power, Edessa was the centre of an independent kingdom (Osrhoene), subsequently a Roman CLIENT KINGDOM. CARACALLA brought it under direct Roman control (with a brief restoration of the monarchy in AD 240), and Edessa acquired the title of Roman colony. It retained its strategic importance throughout the wars between the Roman-Byzantine and SASSANIAN empires from the 3rd to the 7th century AD. The trauma Edessa suffered at the hands of PERSIAN invaders and Byzantine garrisons in the 6th century AD are described vividly in the Syriac chronicle popularly attributed to Joshua Stylites.

In the early 4th century, a vigorous CHRISTIAN literary culture in the Syriac language developed at Edessa. It fell to Islamic attack in 639, but remains occupied to the present. A few fragments of the Roman city survive among more modern buildings. NDP

See Millar, F. (1993) *The Roman Near East 31 BC–AD 337*; Segal, J. B. (1970) *Edessa 'The Blessed City'*.

SYRIA, ROMAN: (b).

EDUCATION: (b) Herculaneum painting of an educational Roman whipping, during lessons taking place beneath the shade of a portico!

education

Schools began to appear by the early 5th century in Athens. In the classical period they were not operated or organized by the state, as in some Greek communities of the hellenistic period. They were private enterprises operated out of houses or storefronts by teachers who were hired by the father or guardian of a boy. In most cases the teachers were men of low social standing, whose fees were modest and thus affordable for most Athenians. More respectable schools were available, however, to which the rich could send their children. Although schooling was a private concern and not mandatory, Athenian law did regulate the hours of operation of both schools and *palaistrai* (buildings where athletics was taught), which could not open before sunrise and had to close by sunset. The regulation prevented unwanted pederastic relations from developing between teachers and boys. The law also prescribed the age at which boys were admitted to school and the number of students allowed to attend each school. A MAGISTRATE was assigned to monitor the activities of schools and of *paidagôgoi*, the household slaves who accompanied boys to school.

EDUCATION: (a) school scene from a Greek vase, with lessons in music and writing overseen by the bearded teacher.

Generally Athenian boys started school at the age of 7 and continued until 14, by which time most children of poorer families had already left school to work. Boys from richer families may have started school earlier and attended longer. Before the age of seven boys and girls spent their time together; girls did not receive a formal education. They received training in the domestic arts from older women of the HOUSEHOLD; whatever skill they had in reading and writing they learned at home. Consequently many women remained illiterate, whereas most men, even the poorest, were functionally LITERATE.

The curriculum at school fell into three parts: letters, MUSIC and ATHLETICS. Letters were taught by a grammarian (*grammatistês*), who gave instruction in reading, writing and arithmetic. Boys learned from HOMER and other early poets. Rote learning and memorization were key methods of instruction, and recitations provided a competitive venue for a grammarian to evaluate a student's progress. Strict discipline was enforced by teachers and advocated by parents who insisted that a boy's schooling was as much about instilling good behaviour as about learning. Music was taught by a *kitharistês* from whom boys learned to play the lyre and sing poetry to its accompaniment. Such skill was regarded as the mark of a well-educated gentleman and was essential for participation in religious festivals, like the Dionysia, where CHORAL competitions played a significant part. Moreover, music was thought to affect the mood and character of the listener; wild music could encourage wild behaviour, gentle music calm. So the *kitharistês* taught moderate rhythms that instilled self-control and moderation in the boy (Plato, *Protagoras* 326a). Finally, athletics was taught from age 12 by the *paidotribês* at a *PALAESTRA*, a large, unroofed, square building surrounded by a colonnade. Here boys would learn running, the long jump, discus, javelin and boxing. Such physical conditioning would prepare a boy for later military service and allow him to compete at the Panathenaia, which offered sporting events for boys, youths and men. Between the ages of 18 and 20, Athenians entered mandatory military training as EPHEBES. In the first year they received training in weaponry; in the second they served on garrison duty.

By the second half of the 5th century, a form of post-secondary education was available from SOPHISTS. These specialists taught a wide range of subjects, from MATHEMATICS and ASTRONOMY to ETHICS and RHETORIC and various forms of critical thinking. It was not until the 4th century that actual schools began to appear, like Plato's ACADEMY or ISOKRATES' school, where students were sent to learn PHILOSOPHY or rhetoric. Throughout the hellenistic period these were the two main branches of post-secondary education for the wealthy.

In Sparta, boys went through a mandatory system of public education (the *agôgê*) which aimed at producing well-trained HOPLITE soldiers. It was under the direct supervision of a senior magistrate, the *paidonomos*. At the age of seven, boys were taken from their homes and enrolled with others of their own year into 'herds' (*agelai*) where they lived together in messes. An older boy who had excelled in good judgement and military courage was selected by the *paidonomos* as captain of the 'herd'; to him the younger boys looked for direction, obeying his orders and submitting to his punishments. Thus they instinctively learned obedience. Spartan boys were divided into groups born in the same year, and progressed in these age groups through stages of the education, each lasting six years. From 7 to 12, the first stage, they were taught a limited amount of reading and writing, music and DANCE, and athletics. Though superficially resembling Athenian schooling, Spartan education placed much greater emphasis on physical conditioning and endurance. Boys went barefoot, wore one cloak, slept on bed-mats made of reeds harvested with their bare hands from the Eurotas river, and lived on rations so scarce that they were encouraged to steal extra food. The purpose was to accustom the boy to hunger and teach him resourcefulness. A boy caught stealing, however, was flogged and denied rations. At the age of 12 boys passed to the next stage, which lasted until 18. Each boy of 12 was assigned (under the supervision of the *paidonomos*) a lover, a young man of 20 to act as his mentor. The training at this stage was severe, strict military discipline was enforced, and the adolescent boys were under constant supervision by their elders. Each year-group passed from one class to the next after successfully completing various competitions. At 18, Spartan boys, like Athenian *ephêboi*, underwent two years of militia service to prepare them for adulthood at 20. Spartan girls also underwent some form of communal education, including athletic competitions, something unheard of in Athens. CC

See Plato, *Protagoras*; Cartledge, P. (2001) *Spartan Reflections*; Garland, R. (1990) *The Greek Way of Life*; Golden, M. (1990) *Children and Childhood in Classical Athens*.

The Romans did not have a regulated system of education. As a result, funding was not provided for teaching, nor were there buildings specifically designed for education. In the early years of CHILDHOOD both mothers and fathers taught their children at home, emphasizing basic reading, writing and MATHEMATICS. Children were also taught how to be model Roman CITIZENS. Mothers took the responsibility up to seven years of age; fathers then took their turn, especially when it came to educating sons for roles in public life. More often than not, parents did not have the time to carry out certain responsibilities and brought in nurses and private tutors to teach the basics. For those children who were not from wealthy families, trade apprenticeship was a means of education. After learning basic skills, these children at 11 years of age would engage in the trades of their parents. In the imperial HOUSEHOLD, especially after AUGUSTUS, state-appointed teachers taught family members.

QUINTILIAN is our best source for the Roman curriculum. His 12-book *Institutio oratoria* (*Education of the Orator*) provides information on how the young wealthy Roman was prepared for public life. Students had to learn to read aloud and write, then establish an understanding of specific Greek and Latin authors, grammar, literary criticism, MATHEMATICS, geometry, MUSIC, RHETORIC and PHILOSOPHY. Quintilian's syllabus tends to reflect the Greek model of education, since music and geometry were not part of the Roman model.

Teachers, paid for their services, were categorized according to what they taught. They were typically SLAVES or FREEDMEN. A *litterator* or *ludi magister* taught girls and boys aged 7 to 11 how to read, write and do basic mathematics. Memorization of POETRY, legends and LAWS was the key to learning. If a child misbehaved, verbal abuse or physical discipline was the means of recourse.

Next up in rank was the *grammaticus*, who taught Latin and Greek literature to wealthy male students aged 12 to 15, preparing them for their roles in public life, such as public speaking. Young WOMEN usually stopped their formal education at this point, as MARRIAGE generally then took place, though they could continue their education in philosophy and literature as did CICERO's friend Caerellia (*Letters to Atticus* 13.21a). They were primed chiefly for their role as an ideal *matrona*, improving their WEAVING skills and learning ways of organizing the HOUSEHOLD. Further education at home could include poetry recitations, lyre playing, DANCING and singing.

The *rhetor* handled students who were 16 years old. His role changed considerably in the imperial period, as there was less emphasis on public speaking in the SENATE. His role in later times was to train advocates for the LAWCOURTS. Students followed a regimental routine that emphasized the practice of invention, disposition, elocution and memory work. DECLAMATIONS or rhetorical exercises also featured in the schedule. Here the *rhetor* taught the student the skills of deliberative and legal RHETORIC. In the former, known as *suasoriae*, the student would argue a potential outcome for a historical or MYTHOLOGICAL event. In the latter, known as *controversiae*, students were required to present both sides of a case in a mock court setting. Students of rhetoric did not limit their studies to Rome; *rhetores* often encouraged them to pursue studies in GREECE or ASIA Minor.

Archaeological evidence provides a small amount of information about school supplies and places of learning. Like modern students of ancient languages, pupils in the Roman world wrote out paradigms for various declensions and conjugations in their equivalent of notebooks. They would write in ink on PAPYRI, whitewashed tablets or POTTERY sherds (*ostraca*), or etch with a *stylus* (an instrument of metal or BONE with a pointed end for writing and a flat end for erasing) on wax-covered WRITING tablets. Archaeological finds of Roman notebooks provide information on grammatical and mathematical tables, spelling errors, and poor handwriting. Textbooks of the time include papyri and public inscriptions. For mathematical exercises students used their fingers, an abacus and pebbles.

Archaeological evidence of actual schools, or *ludi*, is scant, but what does exist indicates that where students learned varied greatly. A WALL-PAINTING from POMPEII depicts students with tablets who view the flogging of an individual while seated under a colonnade. The architectural plan of a building in ALEXANDRIA suggests that it could have been used for rehearsing public speeches; it is purely speculative, however, that this building was used for the sole purpose of educating. Students could also be found in PALAESTRAS or GYMNASIA, but the function of these buildings was not restricted to education. Literary sources inform us that APARTMENT buildings and street corners also served as places for learning. Sites which benefited from plenty of sunshine were chosen to capitalize on the open light. Schooling typically took place at daybreak and lasted until mid-afternoon.

Higher forms of education were problematic in outlying Italian towns. PLINY THE YOUNGER wrote of his plans to build a private school run by parents in his hometown of Comum (*Letters* 4.13.3–10). He bids parents invest in this school the money they normally spend on a son's travel, room and board at another institution. In the same letter he remarks that public officials can potentially corrupt schools when parents do not contribute personal funds and consequently exercise oversight of their investments. LAH

See Bonner, S. F. (1977) *Education in Ancient Rome*; Fantham, E. et al., eds. (1994) *Women in the Classical World*; Hemelrijk, E. A. (1999) *Matrona Docta*; Morgan, T. (1998) *Literate Education in the Hellenistic and Roman Worlds.*

 MUSIC.

Egeria Female CHRISTIAN pilgrim, who travelled to the Holy Land and beyond during the reign of THEODOSIUS I (AD 379–95) and wrote an account of her journeys. The manuscripts of *The Itinerary of Egeria* (*Itinerarium Egeriae*) offer no firm evidence for her name and origin, but scholarly consensus holds that she was Egeria from Galicia in north-west Spain, also the origin of Theodosius. Her family was of high status and presumably knew the emperor. Some argue for an ancestry in Aquitaine, because Egeria addresses as 'sisters' (*sorores*) a female religious community often placed in GAUL. Her Latin reveals both Spanish and Gallic elements, and no firm conclusion is possible on that basis; she was perhaps a Spanish devotee of a community in Aquitaine. Since Priscillian attracted a following of ascetic females there in the 380s, Egeria has been linked to this movement, considered heretical or dubious by some contemporaries.

Egeria travelled in the years 381–4. Unlike other pilgrims, she travelled in comfort and was accompanied for part of her journey by a military escort. Her motives are unknown, but a desire to visit the Holy Land was not necessarily the only reason. In 381 Priscillian, with some aristocratic female adherents, sought support in Italy; the reception was not positive, and Egeria, if she belonged to the sect, perhaps hoped to win the favour of Theodosius. In any case, she visited Palestine, the Thebaid in Egypt, Mt Sinai, and, unusually, EDESSA and CARRHAE. From Mt Sinai, she saw the lands of the Saracens (*Itinerary*, ch. 3); curiously, AMMIANUS MARCELLINUS, as a military officer, observed PERSIAN troop movements from a high cliff (18.6.20). Under queen Mavia in the reign of Valens (364–78), the Saracens had created serious problems. Egeria visited monastic communities in the Thebaid during a period of socio-political disturbance in the early 380s. She devotes attention to WATER SUPPLY at Edessa (ch. 19), and was at Carrhae when monks from all over MESOPOTAMIA were present (ch. 20). In the early to mid-380s, the Persian kingship was insecure, with rapid changes and upper-class discontent, creating instability at the borders. Because Egeria viewed these places in times of frontier insecurity and internal disorder, she was possibly also gathering intelligence during her pilgrimages.

Some text is missing at each end of the *Itinerary*. The first part (chs. 1–23) offers an account of the places visited, with more emphasis on monastic communities than main CHURCHES. Egeria does not merely provide a list of sites but writes with a fullness of language not found in other itineraries, draws in biblical material relevant to the sites, and is genuinely emotional, particularly in recollections of her guides, often monks. She ends the section with a request that her 'sisters' remember her, whether or not she ever sees them again. The remainder (chs. 24–49) describes liturgical practices in detail, addressed in the first instance to someone with an interest in liturgy, perhaps Priscillian. JV

See Wilkinson, J. (1971) *Egeria's Travels.*

Egypt To the Greeks and Romans, Egypt was a land of great antiquity. Its days of greatness, however, had passed, and Egypt had for centuries been ruled by foreign dynasties. However, the wealth of Egypt, founded on the rich agricultural base sustained by the river NILE and its annual flood, made it important politically and economically, while the flood provided one of the greatest intellectual conundrums of the ancient world.

There were clear cultural links between Egypt and the Greek world (mentioned by HESIOD and HERODOTOS among others), and Egypt was of intellectual interest to important Greek thinkers: SOLON and Herodotos travelled there. But there were other links: a trading colony was set up by MILETOS at the Delta city of NAUKRATIS under Psammetichos I in the late 7th century BC. It was ALEXANDER the Great who fully incorporated Egypt into the Greek world, when he overthrew unpopular PERSIAN control in 332 BC. He also visited the oracle of AMON at Siwa, where he was recognized as the son of Amon. This strengthened his claim to rule Egypt, and there is a tradition that he was crowned pharaoh at a ceremony in Memphis. His rule was short-lived, and shortly after his death in 323 Egypt was seized by PTOLEMY, son of Lagos, one of Alexander's GENERALS. His descendants, the PTOLEMIES, ruled Egypt until 30 BC, when Egypt was annexed as a Roman province by the future emperor AUGUSTUS. Thus continued what is known as the Greco-Roman period in Egypt, which

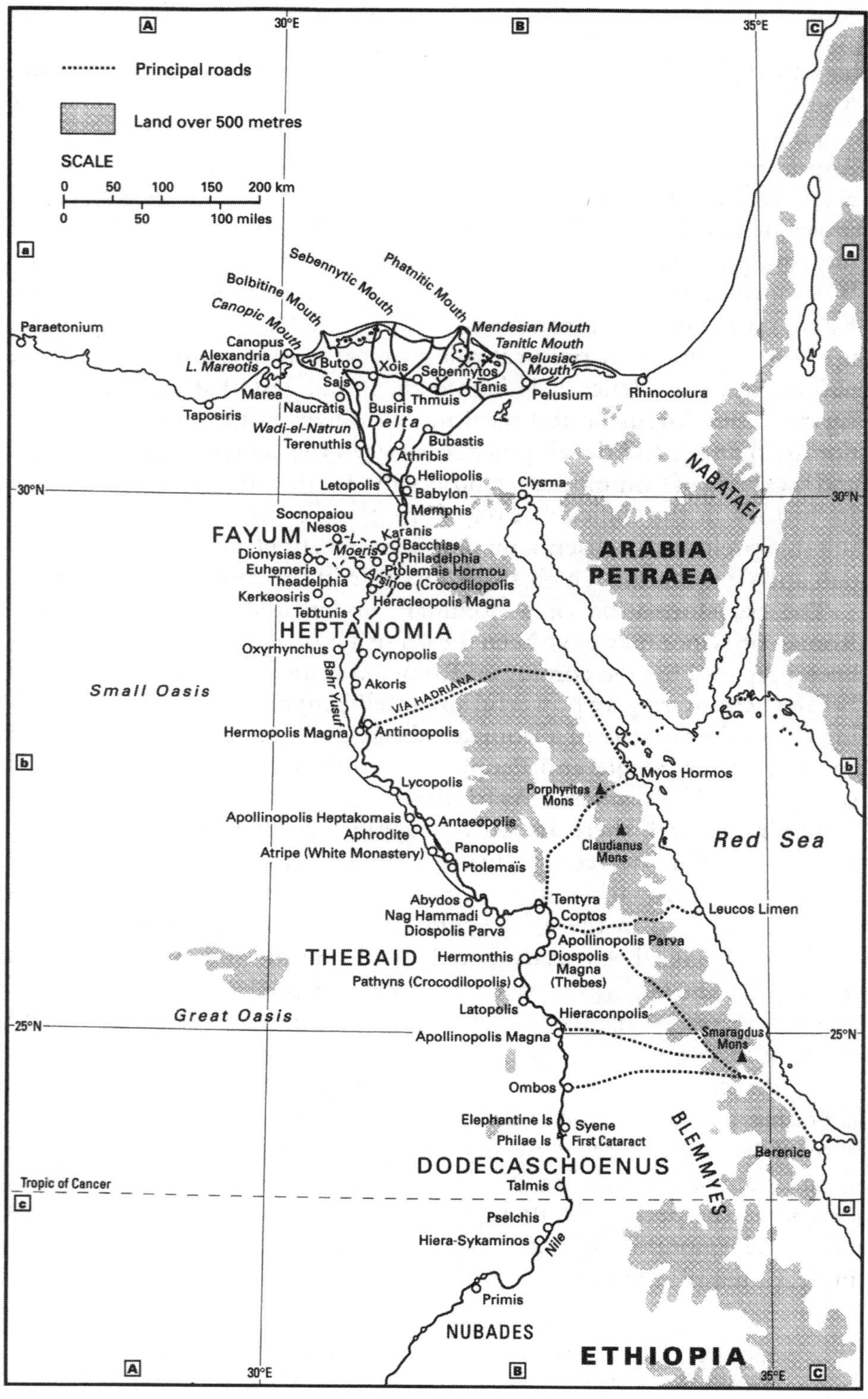

Egypt: map of main Roman sites.

ended in AD 284 when it is traditionally considered to have become part of the Byzantine empire.

Ptolemaic Egypt is characterized by Greek rule: a closed-family of rulers, inter-marriage in the royal family and almost total exclusion of Egyptians, close association of ruler and heir to ensure stability, and a ruling class of Macedonians and Greeks. Many soldiers, mercenaries, artisans and intellectuals came to Egypt, whose administrative and cultural capital became the city of ALEXANDRIA. All land remained the king's, but many Greeks were settled in the countryside (*chôra*) on land allotments (CLERUCHIES), gifts of land (*dôreai*) were given to courtiers, and TEMPLES retained much of their property and privileges (which became a major problem for the Ptolemies). Just how much continuity was retained in administrative systems between the Persian and Ptolemaic periods is unclear for lack of evidence, but it is certain that a highly centralized BUREAUCRACY existed, with tight controls on all aspects of the land economy, TAXATION, documentation and monopolies. So much is clear from the PAPYRI, mainly in Greek but also demotic (cursive Egyptian), which survive from the early 4th century BC onwards. Despite an uneven chronological bunching of evidence, more often than not with the gaps in the periods about which we would like to know most, historians can form a good picture of everyday life. This is especially the case when both Greek and demotic papyri are used together.

Our evidence for the Roman period, though fuller, suffers from similar chronological gaps. Crucially, it is the Augustan period and 1st century AD that are the most under-represented. It was long held that the Romans kept much of the Ptolemaic system of administration in place. This, and a statement of TACITUS (*Histories* 1.11) that Egypt was reserved for special treatment by Augustus, have forced the view that Egypt was somehow different from other Roman PROVINCES. But recently scholars have revealed a significant level of innovation in the administration of Egypt under Augustus, and those features whose absence would make Egypt different, such as city COUNCILS, are still largely present though they may take different forms. No Roman province was typical; all had their differences.

Like any Roman province, Egypt had a small group of Roman officials in charge as governor and staff. The prefect of Egypt, one of the most senior equestrian offices, headed a group of salaried equestrian officials, including three and then four *epistratêgoi* presiding over the administration of the traditional subdivisions of Egypt called nomes (*nomoi*), about 40 in number. Each of these had a *mêtropolis*, and each had a similar group of state officials, the chief of which was the *stratêgos*. Of critical importance were the land economy and systems of taxation, and these formed the core responsibility of state officials. But these men also supervised the selection, appointment and duties of a host of individual LITURGISTS performing a vast array of compulsory public services. This system had the effect of devolving most of the onerous duties and responsibilities of administration onto the local population rather than the Roman state. As time progressed, more of these duties were imposed on MAGISTRATES of the GYMNASIA in the *mêtropoleis* and, after the creation of city councils by SEPTIMIUS SEVERUS, onto them. Significant changes were made in Egypt by and after DIOCLETIAN, which had the effect of regularizing empire-wide systems of administration.

Culturally, Egypt became a melting-pot. Greeks, Romans and Egyptians lived side by side (certainly in the FAYÛM, less so in the more Egyptian Thebaid), not always amicably but certainly borrowing culturally from one another. Many of the great TEMPLES of Egypt date from the Greco-Roman period, Egyptian and Greek GODS became syncretized, worship of Egyptian deities like Sarapis and ISIS became widespread in the Roman world, and Egyptian BURIAL customs were taken on by Greek and Romans. The coming of CHRISTIANITY, earlier in Egypt than in other parts of the empire, and certainly earlier in the countryside, brought further integration of cultures, which found its fullest expression perhaps in the development of Coptic, the Egyptian language in Greek characters. Egypt and Alexandria became important centres of this new faith, and produced many of its greatest writers (such as Clement and ORIGEN) as well as becoming centres of ASCETICISM. Christianity dominated, and the Byzantine emperors ruled Egypt until the Arab conquest in the early 7th century AD. CEPA

See Bowman, A. K. (1996) *Egypt after the Pharaohs*; Lewis, N. (1983) *Life in Egypt under Roman Rule*; Trigger, B. G. et al. (1983) *Ancient Egypt: a social history*.

 ROMAN EMPIRE: (b).

Elagabalus (Varius Avitus Bassianus) C.AD 203–22 Roman emperor (218–22), son of Julia Soaemias and grandson of Julia Maesa (sister of JULIA DOMNA). His accession was organized by his mother and grandmother, who claimed he was the son of CARACALLA, renamed him Marcus Aurelius Antoninus, and brought him to Rome from Emesa at the age of 15. In Emesa he had been the hereditary priest of the Sun-god Heliogabalus, from whom he took his name. He brought the cult to Rome and built two TEMPLES there. He is renowned for outrageous behaviour and for leaving affairs of state to be run by women, even allowing his mother to sit on the CONSUL's bench. Finally, he earned the open hostility of Rome when he planned to have the Sun-god named supreme god of the empire and divorced his wife to marry a VESTAL VIRGIN. Against a background of increasing intrigue, his grandmother persuaded him to adopt his cousin Alexianus, renamed Alexander, to maintain the Severan dynasty. Alexander's mother JULIA MAMMAEA then colluded with the praetorian guard to have Elagabalus murdered. The largely fictional account of his reign in the *HISTORIA AUGUSTA*, however, means that he remains a very enigmatic figure. (see also SEVERUS, ALEXANDER) MEH

See Cassius Dio, books 78–9; Herodian, 5.5–8; *Scriptores historiae Augustae: Elagabalus* (in *Lives of the Later Caesars*, trs. A. R. Birley, 1976).

 EMPERORS, ROMAN: (a); SEVERUS, SEPTIMIUS (stemma).

Elam From the end of the 3rd to the 1st millennium BC Elam comprised a vast area on the Iranian plateau, reaching from Mesopotamia to the borders of the Iranian desert. The kings of Elam bore the royal title 'king of Anshan and Susa', in reference to the two Elamite capitals east and west of the Zagros mountains. During the Neo-Elamite period (1100–539 BC) Elam was in constant conflict with Assyria and Babylon, but suffered a final defeat when Assurbanipal sacked Susa in 646. For a brief period a new Elamite dynasty rose in Susa, while east of the Zagros mountains a Persian dynasty emerged, gradually changing the name of the area to Persis. The Persians had migrated to the Iranian plateau after 1000 BC and, in a process of acculturation, had lived peacefully alongside the indigenous Elamite population. The early Persian kings regarded themselves as successors to the kings of Elam, adapting the Elamite royal title to 'king of Anshan'. The Elamite cuneiform script was used in the Persian administration, while early Persian art reflects Elamite influences. With the reign of Cyrus the Great, Elam, now describing merely the region around Susa, became a Persian satrapy. Eager to lay claim to the Elamite heritage, and in order to prevent a potential resurrection of Elamite power in Susa, Darius I built a palace complex and made it one of the Persian royal capitals. Alongside Media and Babylon, Elam remained a core province of the empire. MB

See Potts, D.T. (1998) *The Archaeology of Elam*.

 BABYLON.

elections A hallmark of Greek and Roman states, even those which were not democratic, was the election to public bodies and offices by a defined group of electors (more or less wide).

In Greece elections were conducted in a variety of ways, with use of the vote (or *psêphos*, literally 'pebble') being by no means the predominant method. DEMOCRACIES in particular made extensive use of sortition, i.e. selection by lot (*klêrôsis*), because it minimized the danger of vote-rigging. The Athenians recognized the desirability of electing certain key officials, in particular the ten GENERALS and some technical MAGISTRATES (especially financial officials). But of their approximately 1,200 officials, some 1,100 were selected by lot, including the 500 members of the council and about 600 other magistrates mainly in boards of ten (to represent each of the ten tribes); the remainder were elected by the assembly of adult male citizens. Elections were held annually between citizens who presented themselves as candidates, and the basic principle was that those appointed by lot could only hold any particular office once (by the 4th century twice in the case of the *boulê*) whereas elected officers could stand for re-election. PERIKLES, for example, built his position of supremacy by repeatedly being elected general. On the other hand, from 487/6 BC the archons at Athens were selected by lot from a previously elected shortlist of candidates (*prokritoi*), and the element of chance (later introduced to both stages of the process) quickly undermined their political status. When VOTING was used, it was not usually conducted by ballot, which mostly was reserved for the lawcourts. (At OSTRACISMS, the peculiar form of election in which the 'winning' candidate was exiled, the Athenians voted on potsherds, *ostraka*.) For example, from 501/0 the assembly elected the generals by a show of hands (*cheirotonia*), the vote being roughly estimated by the presiding officers; similarly, at Sparta members of the *gerousia* were elected by acclamation, a system which ARISTOTLE thought childish. Candidates at Athens had to be aged over 30, and were subjected to preliminary scrutiny (*dokimasia*) and examination after office (*euthynai*).

Election in Athens was by a simple majority vote, but this was not the case at Rome, where again adult male citizens elected magistrates annually. Roman elections were conducted in different groups, depending on which type of ASSEMBLY was in session (centuries or tribes; the curiate assembly did not elect magistrates, though it formally continued to confer their powers throughout the Republic). The majority of votes within a group determined that group's vote, then the majority vote of the groups determined the overall outcome of the election. There has been much debate about the extent to which Roman politics were controlled by the ARISTOCRACY, but there is no doubt that the voting systems were biased towards the wealthy. In the centuriate assembly there were five property classes, but far more centuries were allocated to the rich than the poor, even though they were fewer in number, and the *proletarii* (those below the minimum census qualification) all voted in one century! This gave the votes of the rich proportionately much greater weight – indeed, in the late REPUBLIC, since the 18 equestrian centuries and the 70 centuries of the first class voted first, if they all voted the same way they only needed nine of the remaining 105 centuries to vote with them to secure a majority (97 out of 193) and the voting regularly ended before the *proletarii* had their say. Again, in the tribal assembly the urban PLEBS was concentrated into only four of the 35 tribes, while the rural plebs was clearly at a disadvantage as its members could not afford to go to the city regularly to vote. But on the occasions when they did go, as when Tiberius GRACCHUS was proposing his land reforms in 133 BC, their votes carried great weight, since the number of voters in the rural tribes was far fewer than in the four urban tribes.

Elections in the centuriate and tribal assemblies were preceded by a public meeting (*contio*), at which the candidates were presented, then the presiding magistrate ordered the citizens to disperse into roped-off voting enclosures, each in their appropriate group. They next walked across wooden gangways (*pontes*) to cast their vote, which for much of the Republican period was done orally: they were 'asked' for their vote by *rogatores*, who marked their tablets accordingly. The opportunities afforded by this system for patrons to influence the votes of their clients (or exact reprisals later) are obvious, and between 139 and 107 BC a series of four laws changed it to one by secret ballot on tablets covered in wax. The voter was expected to write the candidate's name himself, dropping his vote into a wickerwork voting-urn (*cista*), but as in the Athenian ostracisms there could be suspicions of foul play, with accusations of pre-prepared votes. Guardians (*custodes*) then gave the urns to the tellers (*diribitores*). In the centuriate assembly, which elected the higher magistracies, the groups voted, and the results were announced, one class after another; in the tribal assembly elections of the lower magistrates the tribes probably voted simultaneously. Elections were held on the Campus Martius; CAESAR began the erection of the Julian Enclosures (*saepta Iulia*) for voting, a project brought to completion by

Agrippa in 26 BC, who also built a tellers' building (the Diribitorium).

The Romans did not appoint officials by sortition, but the lot was nevertheless crucial to the voting system because it was used to select the century (*centuria praerogativa*) which would give the others a lead by voting first. Also, while the tribes voted together, the results were announced in an order chosen by lot: since the vacant places were successively filled by the first candidates to win a majority of the groups, they were not necessarily the ones who had the most votes overall. Roman elections were complicated affairs, with in-built biases and potential for bribery and corruption; but the vast sums of money spent by aspiring politicians on winning popularity (e.g. by putting on extravagant public GAMES) suggests that they were not always a foregone conclusion. MJE

See Staveley, E. S. (1972) *Greek and Roman Voting and Elections*; Taylor, L. R. (1966) *Roman Voting Assemblies.*

electrum An alloy of GOLD and SILVER, known to the Greeks as 'white gold', which was used to make the earliest COINAGE. It was obtained as a natural deposit from some RIVERS in Asia Minor, most notably from the Paktolos, which ran through the LYDIAN capital, SARDIS.

The earliest archaeological context for electrum coinage is under the TEMPLE of ARTEMIS of c.560 BC at EPHESOS. On the basis of associated finds, many scholars believe that the coinage began not long before 600 BC, though some prefer an earlier date on art historical grounds. The material from Ephesos ranges from unmarked lumps through to true coins with a design (and occasionally an inscription) on one side and a punch mark on the other. This range suggests that we are seeing the evolutionary phase of coinage. The coins were struck to a fixed standard, from a stater of 14.1 g down to a 96th weighing 0.15 g. The commonest type of coin, with a lion's head or related design, is generally considered Lydian, but other types may be associated with Greek cities of western Asia Minor. Early electrum coinage is characterized by its wide range of designs, of which a number might be struck at any one place, by its localized circulation within western Asia Minor, and by the prevalence of fractional coinage.

Electrum was replaced by silver as the principal metal for coinage from the mid-6th century BC. It used to be thought that this was because its variable combination of gold and silver made it difficult to value, but it is now known that the TECHNOLOGY for separating the two metals existed at Sardis c.620–550, and that the alloy of some of the early electrum coinage was controlled.

Artificially mixed electrum continued to be used for some significant coinages in western Asia Minor down to the time of ALEXANDER. One group has types that suggest the involvement of a number of cities, and has traditionally been associated with the IONIAN REVOLT. Whether or not this issue belongs to the period of revolt, it is still interesting evidence for the capacity of the cities to co-operate. A later example of such behaviour is known from an inscription of the late 5th or early 4th century recording a monetary agreement whereby Phokaia and Mytilene produced electrum coinage in alternate years.

The most important of the later electrum coinages was that of Kyzikos, which struck a fascinating variety of types and signed its coinage with the badge of a tuna-fish. 'Kyzikenes' were used as an international currency down to c.300 BC, and were of particular importance in northern Greece and the BLACK SEA. CH

See Kraay, C. M. (1976) *Archaic and Classical Greek Coins.*

elegy Best defined as poetry in elegiac metre (a couplet constructed of a dactylic hexameter and a pentameter) which could treat a great variety of topics. A poem is usually directed to a specific addressee, whose actual response to the exhortation expressed in the poem is anticipated. In the view of most scholars, performances of elegies were accompanied by the reed-pipe (*aulos*). Traditionally, political or martial exhortations, epigrams on TOMBS, and varied sympotic poetry have been classified as elegy. Recently, some critics have questioned whether elegy was an actual GENRE during archaic times in Greece. The arguments for denying its existence as a defined genre are the diversity of occasions for performance; in addition, ancient Greeks considered the elegy a lament, but no archaic poem in elegiac metre can be classified with absolute certainty as a dirge. Among early elegists, Kallinos, Tyrtaios, Mimnermos, SOLON, THEOGNIS, Anakreon and SIMONIDES stand out. In the hellenistic period, ALEXANDRIAN poets made ample use of the elegiac metre; chief among them were THEOKRITOS and KALLIMACHOS, who extensively influenced the Roman elegists. Unfortunately, only very few fragments (and not the best ones) have survived.

Roman elegy was composed in elegiac couplets as well, but in all other ways it is independent of Greek elegy. Although it seems earlier poets wrote elegies, the oldest whose elegies survive is CATULLUS; others included TIBULLUS, PROPERTIUS and OVID. A favourite theme of Roman elegies is LOVE; the poet expresses his personal experiences against a mythical background. The inventor of love elegy may have been the hellenistic poet PHILETAS of Kos, whom the Romans deeply admired. At Rome, elegy was considered to represent rebellious attitudes towards traditional values, with such themes as a man willing to become the servant of a woman. RBC

See Fowler, R. L. (1987) *The Nature of Early Greek Lyric*; Harrington, P. K. (1969) *The Roman Elegiac Poets*; Lyne, R. O. A. M. (1980) *The Latin Love Poets*; West, M. (1974) *Studies in Greek Elegy and Iambus.*

elephants The early Greeks knew about IVORY before they knew about its source, the elephant; HERODOTOS and Ktesias mention them. ARISTOTLE wrote about them in various works and knew that there were elephants in INDIA and North AFRICA; the detailed nature of his knowledge suggests that he had seen or read about a dissection. Greeks first fought against elephants when ALEXANDER challenged DARIUS at GAUGAMELA in 331 BC. They met them again at the battle of the Hydaspes against the Indian king Poros in 326, a battle which gave rise to stories of the loyalty of Poros' own elephant and of another which fought at the battle and was still alive in the 2nd century AD, having been dedicated to the SUN by the victorious Alexander.

ELEPHANTS: coin design showing Macedonian cavalryman (Alexander?) attacking Indian elephant of Poros.

The Seleukids in particular continued to use elephants in warfare, but the Romans first met them when Pyrrhos used them at Herakleia and Ausculum. About this time, the elephant first appears in Roman art. Hannibal tried to use them in his invasion, but all except one died in the winter of 218/7; he used them again at the battle of Zama, but by that time the Romans had learnt how to deal with them. The Romans seldom used them in warfare, but they were a constant feature at games and processions (Pompey's four-elephant chariot was too wide for the gate during his triumph), and some were raised and trained in Italy in the imperial period. CJS

See Scullard, H. H. (1974) *The Elephant in the Greek and Roman World.*

Eleusis and Eleusinian mysteries Major cult site in Attica, west of Athens, and centre of the most famed mystery cult in antiquity. The site is mentioned in the *Homeric Hymn to Demeter* as the setting of the final stages of Demeter's wanderings in search of her daughter Persephone, who had been abducted by Hades, the god of the underworld. At Eleusis the goddess accepts the hospitality of the local king, Keleos, and demands that he build a large temple and altar in her honour. Eleusis is associated with the myth justifying the establishment of the mystery cult at the site by Demeter herself.

Landmarks at the sanctuary of Eleusis (for example, the 'mirthless stone', Kallichoron well, and cave of Plouton) make reference to the events related in the hymn, while cult buildings such as the Telesterion (Hall of the Mysteries) offer glimpses of the spatial setting of the mysteries. The Greater Mysteries were celebrated at Eleusis in autumn, during the Attic month Boëdromion, and attracted worshippers from all over the Greek world. The central event of the mysteries was initiation, which appears to have been practised until Theodosius I legislated an end to pagan cult at Eleusis in AD 400. Eleusis was among the places overrun by Alaric in 395. The process of initiation is almost wholly obscure because of the paucity of detail in ancient authors and the inadequacy of material remains to reconstruct the rituals fully. EP

See Clinton, K. (1992) *Myth and Cult*; Mylonas, G. (1961) *Eleusis and the Eleusinian Mysteries.*

 FESTIVALS.

Elgin, Lord 1766–1841 Born Thomas Bruce in Scotland, he became 7th earl of Elgin while a child. He served as ambassador extraordinary and minister plenipotentiary of his Britannic majesty to the sublime porte of Selim III, sultan of Turkey, from 1799 until 1803.

The collection known as the Elgin Marbles (now more commonly Parthenon Marbles) consists of statues, columns, carved reliefs, sculptures and inscriptions from the Athenian Acropolis, all dating to the 5th century BC, collected by Elgin's men between 1801 and 1805. The marbles were acquired by the British Museum in 1816. Elgin also amassed a wider collection of vases, coins and minor antiquities that had been excavated on the Acropolis and around Greece.

ELEUSIS AND ELEUSINIAN MYSTERIES: Demeter and Kore (Persephone) with Triptolemos (holding barley) and Eumolpos, figures associated with the most important of the Greek mystery cults at Eleusis.

Elgin's aim in acquiring the Parthenon sculptures was that they should serve as the best examples of classical ARCHITECTURE and thereby improve artistic appreciation in the United Kingdom, rather than as a collector as such or for purposes of ARCHAEOLOGICAL study. It was not until the publication of Byron's poem *Childe Harold's Pilgrimage* that the Elgin Marbles came to represent the struggle of Greek heritage against European imperialism.

In the 1930s, the British Museum undertook their cleaning, in part because of public expectation that marble be white, as idealized by post-RENAISSANCE art theories. The scraping of the Pentelic marble to expose a white layer in fact removed the original patina, paint remains and tool marks. Thus recent demands for the return of the sculptures to Greece have gained a custodial argument in addition to the cultural. TH

See St Clair, W. (1998) *Lord Elgin and the Marbles.*

Elis City in the north-west PELOPONNESE; its territory was Elis or Eleia. Elis disputed control of the sanctuary of ZEUS at OLYMPIA and its OLYMPIC GAMES with Pisa, whose claim on grounds of proximity was stronger. The temple of Zeus at Olympia was reputedly built from the spoils after the sack of Pisa soon after the PERSIAN WARS; reports of the combination (synoikism) of different communities into the city of Elis c.471 are probably not unconnected. Relations between Elis and Sparta were always doubtful. Eleians served as seers for both the Greeks and the Persians at the battle of PLATAEA, and their troops arrived too late to take part in the battle, though they still figured on the Serpent column at DELPHI. By the second half of the 5th century Elis enjoyed a form of DEMOCRACY; its rejection of the terms of the peace of NIKIAS was more a matter of hostility to Sparta than to Athens. It was a leading member of the quadruple alliance against Sparta soon afterwards; Eleian officials refused Spartans access to the Olympic games of 420. Soon after the end of the PELOPONNESIAN WAR, Sparta invaded Elis. OLIGARCHS helped Sparta, democrats resisted, and Elis was deprived of extensive territory which it claimed to control (the south-western part became the short-lived federation of Triphylia). Much was recovered after LEUKTRA (371), but conflict with ARKADIA over Triphylia brought warfare to Olympia itself during the games of 364. By the end of the hellenistic period, Elis had successfully assimilated the disputed areas. JBS

See Pausanias, books 5–6; Nielsen, T. H. (2004) Triphylia, in Hansen and Nielsen, *Inventory*; Roy, J. (2004) Elis, in Hansen and Nielsen, *Inventory* 489–504; Yalouris, N. (1996) *Ancient Elis.*

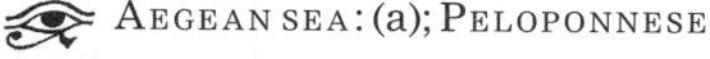
AEGEAN SEA: (a); PELOPONNESE.

élites Generally, the upper segment or segments of the social pyramid. The term is mainly used of individuals or groups who controlled LAND, WEALTH and political power; it is often little more than a synonym for the upper classes. The modern word means, in terms of its linguistic roots, 'the chosen', but ancient concepts focused much more on the qualitative aspects than on the selective. In Greek, the most common term for the wealthy and powerful was *aristoi*, 'the best (men)', whence 'ARISTOCRACY'. Similarly, especially in a context of political factionalism, Romans called some political figures (and their faction) *optimates*, the 'best men' (others were *populares*, 'of the people', though we would regard both groups as élite). Wealth by itself was not sufficient; at Rome, for example, FREEDMEN were not considered élite, but impoverished families of appropriate lineage were.

In both Greek and Roman contexts, the 'best men' tended to be conservative in political and social outlook. Generally, they favoured a political structure that allowed them to exercise most, if not all, of the political power, usually as an aristocracy, and resisted changes that gave a greater voice to other segments of society. Élites held much of the land and preferably derived their income from AGRICULTURE, though they might invest in commercial ventures as well. Directly, quite evidently at Rome through PATRONAGE, and indirectly, the élite controlled the lives and livelihoods of the other social classes. Usually, all groups accepted these differentiations, but from time to time disputes, and even revolts, broke the concord. JV

See Pseudo-Xenophon, *Constitution of Athens* ('The Old Oligarch'); Hopkins, K. (1983) *Death and Renewal*; Ober, J. (1989) *Mass and Elite in Democratic Athens*; Wallace-Hadrill, A. (1991) Elites and trade in Roman towns, in J. Rich and A. Wallace-Hadrill, eds., *City and Country in the Ancient World* 241–72.

embassies see AMBASSADORS AND EMBASSIES.

emotion As part of their discussions of human moral psychology and character, ancient PHILOSOPHERS often turned to investigate the emotions. They concentrated on two central questions. What are emotions? What place (if any) should emotions play in the good human life?

For some philosophers, emotions are produced from non-rational parts or sources in the SOUL. In PLATO's *Republic*, for example, SOCRATES outlines a theory in which fear, sexual desire and the like are produced by the appetitive and spirited parts of the soul. In that case, it is the job of reason to educate and tame these emotions and impose the correct order on the soul. ARISTOTLE similarly conceives of emotions as deriving from non-rational sources. In the *Nicomachean Ethics*, he outlines a picture of the virtuous man as the person who not only understands the right action in a particular circumstance but also feels the appropriate emotion to the right degree at the right time. The courageous man, for example, feels neither too much fear nor too little. This is the core of his 'doctrine of the mean'.

An alternative tradition conceived of emotions as essentially cognitive. They are beliefs, accompanied perhaps with certain physiological effects. For the STOICS, for example, emotions such as anger or fear are caused by the agent believing that he has been slighted or that some harmful future event is imminent. Since the Stoics think that the only things of true value are virtue and vice, these emotions (in Greek, *pathê*) are incorrect value judgements and in order to progress towards virtue we should strive to remove them altogether. JIW

See Nussbaum, M. (1995) *The Therapy of Desire*; Sorabji, R. (2001) *Emotion and Peace of Mind.*

Empedokles (Empedocles) see PRESOCRATICS.

27BC–AD14
Augustus

14–37
Tiberius

37–41
Gaius (Caligula)

41–54
Claudius

54–68
Nero

68–9
Galba

69
Otho

69
Vitellius

69–79
Vespasian

79–81
Titus

81–96
Domitian

96–98
Nerva

98–117
Trajan

117–38
Hadrian

138–61
Antoninus Pius

161–80
Marcus Aurelius

161–9
Lucius Verus

180–92
Commodus

193
Pertinax

193
Didius Julianus

193–4
Pescennius Niger

193–7
Clodius Albinus

193–211
Septimius Severus

198–217
Caracalla

211
Geta

217–18
Macrinus

218
Diadumenianus

218–222
Elagabalus

222–35
Severus Alexander

235–8
Maximinus

238
Gordian I

238
Gordian II

238
Balbinus

238
Pupienus Maximus

238–44
Gordian III

EMPERORS, ROMAN: (a) Augustus to Gordian III. The list omits most usurpers and pretenders. Apart from Augustus all dates are AD.

244–9
Philip

249–51
Decius

251–3
Trebonianus Gallus

251–3
Volusianus

253
Aemilianus

253–60
Valerian

253–68
Gallienus

268–70
Claudius II

270
Quintillus

270–5
Aurelian

275–6
Tacitus

276
Florianus

276–82
Probus

282–3
Carus

283–5
Carinus

283–4
Numerianus

284–305
Diocletian

286–305
Maximian

293–306
Constantius

293–311
Galerius

306–7
Severus

308–13
Maximinus

306–37
Constantine

308–24
Licinius

337–40
Constantine II

337–50
Constans

337–61
Constantius II

351–4
Gallus

361–3
Julian

363–4
Jovian

364–75
Valentinian I

364–8
Valens

367–83
Gratian

375–92
Valentinian II

378–95
Theodosius I

EMPERORS, ROMAN: (b) Philip to Theodosius I. The list omits most usurpers and pretenders.

emperors, Roman The civil unrest and gross mismanagement of the empire which characterized Rome's Republican government in the last century BC inspired a longing among many for some strong man to re-establish order. POMPEY tried to play that role, and JULIUS CAESAR after his victory in the CIVIL WAR was effectively Rome's first emperor. The civil wars which followed his murder were primarily a struggle to find a successor to the position Caesar had created. In 31 BC at the battle of ACTIUM victory went to Octavian, who later, in 27, took the title 'AUGUSTUS'. He and his successors also called themselves CAESAR (drawn from the name of Julius Caesar) and *imperator*, a long-standing title for successful generals, sometimes granted officially by the senate, more often applied as an acclamation by a general's own soldiers.

From the time of Actium, Augustus was in practice a monarch. Nevertheless he proceeded to restore much of the mechanisms of the government of the REPUBLIC. The problem then was how to find a place for the emperor within such a system. After some experimentation, Augustus settled for a bundle of powers and honours which set him above the everyday workings of government and were sufficient to sanction whatever he needed to do. The power of a proconsul with precedence over other proconsuls (*proconsulare imperium maius*) gave him effective control of the empire and its armies, while the power of a TRIBUNE (*tribunicia potestas*) gave what was essential to participate in politics in Rome. He had the right to convene, attend and put proposals to the SENATE. He was also ready to hear appeals from inhabitants of the empire against the actions of other MAGISTRATES – an innovation which was of profound significance to provincials used to the repression of Republican governors. Indeed, in practice all the emperor's statements in letters, replies to requests and speeches in the senate were to have the force of LAW. At the same time, the emperor himself came to be seen as above the law. The nature of these powers mattered because emperors insisted that they were not arbitrary TYRANTS, but 'magistrates of the Roman people' who ruled 'by the consent of all', expressed in the grant of powers and privileges made by the senate and people to each new emperor. We have part of one such grant on a famous inscription, the Law on the Powers of Vespasian (*lex de imperio Vespasiani*, *ILS* 244).

The emperor's powers were granted to him as an individual. The long-term stability of the system was dependent on the transfer of those powers to an acknowledged successor. In Roman law a member of the emperor's family would be the normal heir to his personal wealth and position as head of the family. In any case, in a world dominated by PATRONAGE, people naturally looked to the emperor's family for a legitimate successor. The dynastic principle was all-powerful. Where the emperor had no son, then adopting someone suitable was the obvious option; this became the norm in the 2nd century AD. While the emperor was still alive, his chosen successor was usually invested with many of the powers of an emperor, to ensure that there was continuity on the emperor's death. Indeed, from the 2nd century there were frequent examples of co-rulers (such as MARCUS AURELIUS and Lucius Verus), though normally with the recognition of one partner as senior.

When the succession had not been provided for, as in AD 68 after NERO'S SUICIDE and in 193 after the assassination of COMMODUS, the ultimate arbiters became the ARMIES fighting to put their commander on the throne. In this sense Roman emperors were military autocrats, who ensured the loyalty of the armies by pay and privileges. But it would be wrong to see the emperor as ruling a recalcitrant empire by repressive fear. It is true that the largest single concentration of troops in the Roman world was in the city of Rome, but the armies were mainly scattered along the FRONTIERS and were not well placed to police the heart of the empire. Further, for the first three centuries AD the emperor ran the empire with a group of friends and advisers, along with the SLAVES and FREEDMEN of his household – perhaps no more than a few hundred people. Only in the late empire does an elaborate central bureaucracy emerge. In effect, the empire largely ran itself through self-governing communities. The emperor decided the many matters of contention, provided help in times of distress, and reacted to individual crises. Beyond this it is very difficult to discern any broader policies implemented by emperors.

This system worked for long periods of time, because the vast majority of the inhabitants of the empire wanted it to. Augustus 'seduced everybody with the delights of peace' (Tacitus, *Annals* 1.2). The emperor was the guarantor of the security of the empire, which enabled TRADE to flourish and grow as never before. Beyond that, however, there was for the first time a feeling among the empire's subjects that 'somebody up there loves me'. Whatever the problem, whatever the injustice of the local administrator, if only you could get the emperor to take notice then all would be well. So, for example, at VINDOLANDA, an army camp in the north of England, a soldier, doubtless on hearing of HADRIAN'S impending visit to his new frontier wall, drafted a letter of appeal: 'I implore Your Majesty not to allow me, an innocent man, to have been beaten with rods ... as though I had committed some crime' (*Vindolanda Tablets* 344). No wonder, then, that the emperor became the focus of expressions of loyalty by his subjects, even to the extent of offering RULER-CULT to him similar to that offered to other GODS with TEMPLES, FESTIVALS and SACRIFICES. It was a means for local communities to negotiate getting the goodwill and help of the emperor.

Emperors, of course, played up to the images their subjects had of them. They sought to present themselves as all-seeing, benevolent and sharing the interests of their subjects. As now, the latter were always ready for salacious stories which suggested that their ruler was no better than they were; the truth of these tales of orgies, murder, and deviation is unknowable. Indeed, the true characters of individual emperors are probably irrecoverable. (see pp. 310–11) JJP

See Ando, C. (2000) *Imperial Ideology and Provincial Loyalty in the Roman Empire*; Campbell, J. B. (1984) *The Emperor and the Roman Army 31 BC–AD 235*; Millar, F. (1977) *The Emperor in the Roman World*; (1981) *The Roman Empire and its Neighbours*; Price, S. R. F. (1984) *Rituals and Power*; Wells, C. (1992) *The Roman Empire*.

AUGUSTUS: (b); BENEFACTORS AND BENEFACTION; SEVERUS, SEPTIMIUS; TETRARCHS: (b); TRAJAN (stemma); THEODOSIUS I (stemma); VESPASIAN.

empire see Athenian empire; China; imperialism: ancient, modern; Persian empire; Roman empire; Sassanian empire; Seleukid empire.

employment The ancient world was a predominantly agricultural society and the labour that was required was performed by a variety of workers: slaves, small freeholders and tenants, farmers, craftsmen and wage-labourers. Slaves and independent, small, free craftsmen dominated those branches of the economy in which we now tend to locate wage-labour, that is, in workshops and larger ateliers. Most hired labourers would have found employment in the building industry in the large cities, but peak periods in agriculture may have required a large influx of additional labour. Their numbers, however, are unknowable, for they have left few traces in the surviving evidence. The inscription from North Africa for a man who worked as a harvester for a number of years, then led gangs of hired labourers to the cornfields of Numidia before retiring to Mactar to be elected as one of the leading magistrates of the city, to his own considerable surprise, is a unique document. It is unlikely that many others of his class managed to travel the same route to economic success and social respectability.

The designing of a hierarchical model of employments was a favourite preoccupation of members of the educated upper classes, and they did not need to work to earn a living. The most famous discussion can be found in Cicero's treatise *De officiis* (*On Duties* 1.149–51), which relies heavily on a similar tract by the hellenistic philosopher Panaitios of Rhodes. The employments of all those who work for wages are to be considered illiberal and mean. Of those, the labourers who have no other option but to sell their physical strength rather than their skills, in exchange for wages, receive the lowest appreciation. For them, Cicero asserts, receiving payment for work is the equivalent of slavery.

Providing sufficient employment was not a major concern of ancient governments, but it is self-evident that no ruler could afford to ignore the potential social problems arising from mass unemployment. The one anecdote which illustrates this consciousness has the emperor Vespasian rejecting the introduction of technical devices which would make human labour superfluous, based on the argument that he wanted to feed his people (Suetonius, *Vespasian* 18). It is very likely that he had free hired labour in mind. Unemployment was a phenomenon mainly found in the cities. Dio Chrysostom of Prusa talks about unemployment and poverty as the two great evils of city life, and suggests that the idle and poor be turned into farmers and hired urban labourers (*Euboïkos* 36). As he makes clear, the poverty of the unemployed is a problem which cannot be solved. It was considered to be due either to fate or to personal deficiencies, and from the time of Hesiod onwards it was related to laziness and disgrace. It is only in the later Roman empire that we hear of rudimentary policies against beggars and people without work. Successive emperors ordered those who were healthy but without the means to earn their daily bread to be sent to the public bakeries and factories, so that a life of idleness would be reoriented towards the better things. This is a telling illustration that both employment and unemployment were largely viewed in moral, not economic, terms. MK

Emporion (Empúries; Ampurias) see artillery; Iberia (2); sculpture.

encaustic painting see mummy portraits.

encyclopedias The term is based on the Greek *enkyklios paideia*, 'education in a circle' (or 'the circle of knowledge'). According to Quintilian (1.10.1), the Greeks employed this phrase to describe the complete subject material that boys were to learn – in other words, their general education – before beginning specialized studies in rhetoric; the Latin equivalent is *artes liberales* ('liberal arts'). The Greek phrase *enkyklia paideumata* appears in Pseudo-Plutarch (*On Educating Children* 7c), and *enkyklia agôgê* ('upbringing') in Strabo (1.1.22). In earlier periods, however, *enkyklia* did not necessarily include the full programme, and seems to mean 'ordinary' or 'normal' training given to boys who did not intend to pursue further studies. Quintilian's own *Institutio oratoria* discusses the various subjects that well-educated boys needed to become accomplished orators.

Although its precise nature is disputed, Cato the Elder composed a book or books designed to help in the education of his son; whatever its actual form, this is usually regarded as the earliest Roman encyclopedia. The concept that an encyclopedia was to treat all knowledge, or all knowledge within a particular field, is a more modern concept that can be applied in some sense to various compilations done in antiquity. In the ancient world, these collections were often not arranged alphabetically; for that reason, and simply because of the physical difficulties of handling a large number of scrolls, ancient encyclopedias were not as easy to consult as their modern counterparts.

Much of Aristotle's work, and that of his student and successor Theophrastos, may be regarded as encyclopedic in scope, even though they did not gather into a single place all the knowledge available in the 4th century BC. Among the Romans, Varro and Pliny the Elder must take pride of place among the compilers of information. Pliny's *Natural History* is a massive work compiled from a great variety of sources, and discusses a wide range of topics. Much of Varro's work is no longer extant, but the titles of his books indicate that he gathered a vast storehouse of information. Examples of works designed to offer the full basic knowledge for particular areas of study or occupations include Strabo's *Geography*, Vitruvius' works on architecture and land surveying, and Columella's on agriculture.

In the Byzantine period, compilations of various types continued to be produced. Perhaps the most well-known example is the *Suda*; arranged in more or less alphabetical sequence like a lexicon, it offers some 30,000 entries on a variety of topics designed to provide information. Large portions of the text are quotations and excerpts from classical authors. JV

energy Power sources were almost entirely limited to natural forms – human, animal, water and wind; fire was, of course, used extensively in domestic and industrial contexts, but not as a form of power. Only in exceptional devices associated with religious and social ceremonies, such as those included in

Hero's *Pneumatics*, was there a conversion between forms of energy (e.g. heat to steam or hot air, hydraulic pressure to air pressure). However, forces generated by power sources of any form could be amplified, directed and controlled by levers, gears and pulleys. The practical results were to be found in contexts such as shipping (rigging and bilge-pumps), ARCHITECTURE (cranes), INDUSTRY (MINE drainage), FOOD processing (presses for OLIVES and grapes; animal and water-powered MILLS) and warfare (CATAPULTS and *ballistae*). The emphasis placed by historians of TECHNOLOGY upon devices that appear to be precursors of modern industrial MACHINES (e.g. Hero's aeolipile, a sphere made to rotate by jets of steam in the manner of a turbine, or his organ driven by a windmill) should not be allowed to detract from the fact that most work in the ancient world continued to be carried out by direct application of muscle-power from people and animals, whether in industry, AGRICULTURE or TRANSPORT. (see also ENGINEERING) KG

See Cotterell, B. and Kamminga, J. (1990) *Mechanics of Pre-industrial Technology*; White, K. D. (1984) *Greek and Roman Technology*; Wikander, Ö. (1984) *Exploitation of Water-power or Technological Stagnation?*

engineering It is only in modern times that major distinctions have been drawn between different branches of engineering – e.g. civil, mechanical, electrical; many dictionaries offer military engineering as a separate category. Hill (1984) devised a category called 'fine technology' to describe ASTRONOMICAL instruments, automata and clocks, but excluded military engineering from his account of the subject. The derivation of the modern term from its Latin origins does not clarify matters, since *ingenium* might mean either a talent or a device. The difficulty of definition is compounded by VITRUVIUS' inclusion of many mechanical devices in *De architectura*, in addition to the expected 'architectural' matters. Books 8–9 cover a diverse range of subjects such as WATER SUPPLY, pumps, SUNDIALS and clocks, lifting equipment, and military CATAPULTS. This underlines the overly restrictive nature of our modern understanding, for the original Greek *architektôn* implied an ability to oversee a range of crafts or skills, rather than a specific profession restricted to building construction. The range of devices described by Hill as 'fine technology' underlines the fact that some classical engineering was actually based upon theoretical or observational analyses of forces, such as leverage and pressure. However, experience and 'rule of thumb' remained the dominant design principles until the 18th-century Enlightenment.

Perhaps it is safest simply to note those technical achievements of the classical world that would be considered 'engineering' today, and to deduce from them the range of skills possessed by people we would describe as ARCHITECTS or engineers rather than artisans. The importance attached to different spheres of life should be reflected in the amount of effort devoted to classical engineering. The complexities of urban living were vital for the inhabitants of a MEDITERRANEAN zone characterized by political units based upon CITY-STATES, and this did not change when they were incorporated into an expanding empire. Practical requirements demanded WATER SUPPLIES and drainage, and the range of solutions drawn upon included tunnels, pipes, siphons and arched AQUEDUCTS. Distribution within towns required storage cisterns and water towers, and systems by which private HOUSEHOLDS could access public supplies. Towns were also a focus for adventurous ARCHITECTURE, notably TEMPLES and public buildings, which normally involved large-scale TRANSPORT and lifting devices for heavy STONE blocks, or elaborate scaffolding and BRICK-work for Roman CONCRETE vaulted structures. SIEGE equipment was needed less in Roman imperial times, but the size of the empire demanded extensive FRONTIER works, robust military ROADS, FORTS, and even physical barriers such as HADRIAN'S WALL. These were well within the capabilities of conventional engineering, but increases in their scale demanded sophisticated project management. Urban defences and mechanical ARTILLERY devices became important again as pressure from 'barbarian' invasions rose in the late empire. The role of military engineers underlines the breadth of skills implied by Vitruvius, for they were responsible for everyday aspects of building construction and transport systems, as well as the complexities of operating and maintaining surveying equipment or artillery devices.

Urban populations and military garrisons could not exist without FOOD SUPPLIES, and it is clear from ARCHAEOLOGICAL discoveries that engineering was also present in AGRICULTURAL contexts. Irrigation systems in EGYPT may have prompted the development of many water-lifting devices powered by ANIMALS or humans, but elsewhere in North Africa and the Near East emphasis was placed upon the management of meagre rainfall by means of dams, channels and cisterns. The processing of OLIVES and grapes on an industrial scale required mechanical crushing MILLS and presses operated by leverage or screws, while CEREALS could be turned into flour by means of water-powered mills when required. All of these devices demanded an understanding of varied power sources, and technical aspects such as the design of pulleys, screw threads or gearing to transmit and control the rotation of millstones.

A fundamental contrast with recent centuries is that engineering was not particularly conspicuous in industrial contexts, especially when agricultural enterprises such as olive oil production are excluded. The expansion of QUARRYING and MINING demanded increased muscle-power rather than technical change. Large blocks of stone were moved by designing expanded traction systems involving more oxen, rather than novel methods like the TIMBER trackways of post-medieval Europe. Evidence for the use of water-powered saws to cut stone blocks remains tentative. Metal ores were treated by hand rather than machine, though at some mining sites they were crushed by mills (identical to those used for grinding corn) which could be powered by water or animals. Archaeological discoveries show that mines were drained by pumps and water-wheels whose designs are familiar from Vitruvius, and which probably originated in the work of ARCHIMEDES, Ktesibios and the Alexandrian school. Like rotary mills, they were presumably adopted from their more familiar agricultural functions. None of these devices incorporated standardized components or interchangeable parts, which are considered essential in modern engineering design.

Metal ingots, building materials, grain, olive oil and WINE were transported over long distances in large cargo SHIPS whose designs (like those of the vehicles that carried goods to ports) were scaled up from well-established types. Engineering skills were required for manoeuvring larger, heavier TIMBERS in shipyards, and in fitting out vessels with capstans, pulleys and pumps. Likewise, ports needed moles constructed in deep water, and large FIRE-resistant warehouses with lifting gear. Engineering feats involved in constructing major all-weather roads (tunnels, BRIDGES, cuttings, calculated gradients) for the army and administration benefited all kinds of users. The letters of PLINY THE YOUNGER show that a provincial governor could ask the emperor (in his case, TRAJAN) to send out engineers to advise on problems encountered during building construction, or even to assist in a feasibility study of a CANAL. Military specialists must have been important in spreading all kinds of technical knowledge throughout the Roman empire. (see also ENERGY, MACHINES) KG

See Hill, D. R. (1984) *A History of Engineering in Classical and Medieval Times*; Landels, J. G. (1978) *Engineering in the Ancient World*; Oleson, J. P. (1984) *Greek and Roman Mechanical Water-lifting Devices*; White, K. D. (1984) *Greek and Roman Technology*.

 MACHINES.

Ennius (Quintus Ennius) 239–169 BC Creator of Latin POETRY. Ennius played a crucial role in the history of Latin literature and profoundly influenced later POETS, including LUCRETIUS and VIRGIL. His innovative EPIC poem *Annals* was central to Roman EDUCATION for at least 150 years. In the 3rd century BC Livius Andronicus and Naevius had written DRAMA and epic in the Latin Saturnian metre. But it was Ennius who established the conventions of the poetic genres: epic, TRAGEDY, COMEDY, SATIRE and EPIGRAM. His multicultural origins appear throughout his poems. He came from Calabria where Greek culture was dominant, and spoke Greek, Latin and OSCAN. He lived in Rome and moved in the circle of SCIPIO AFRICANUS. He travelled on military campaigns with his patron Marcus Fulvius Nobilior, who obtained ROMAN CITIZENSHIP for him in 184/3. Only fragments survive, but it is possible to glimpse the characteristics of Ennius' poetry from them. His tragedies handle themes from EURIPIDES and AESCHYLUS, among others. His *Annals* presented the history of Rome from its origins (AENEAS, ROMULUS AND REMUS) down to contemporary times. Similar to the way classical Greeks saw their cultural roots in HOMERIC epic, *Annals* encapsulated Romanness in history, traditions, customs and MORALITY. Ennius actually portrays himself as Homer reincarnate. Adapting the Greek epic metre to the more intractable Latin language was an outstanding achievement. His poetry is vigorous and direct, with striking use of alliteration and assonance, such as characterizes the Anglo-Saxon epic *Beowulf*. AUGUSTAN poets judged that he had talent but lacked technique. While their perspective is understandable, viewed in the setting of his own time, his blend of innovation and skill forged a Latin poetry which expressed the ideology of the rising Roman state. SB

See Warmington, E. H., ed. (1935) *Remains of Old Latin* (text, trs.); Williams, G. and Gratwick, A. S. (1982) Early Republic, in E. J. Kenney and W. V. Clausen, eds., *The Cambridge History of Classical Literature*, vol. 2.

entertainers see ACTORS AND ACTRESSES; ATHLETES AND ATHLETICS; COMEDY; DRAMA; GLADIATORS; MUSICIANS; TRAGEDY.

Epameinondas d.362 BC Theban Boiotarch (leader of the BOIOTIAN confederation). Epameinondas was born into a poor but noble family, studied PHILOSOPHY under the PYTHAGOREAN Lysis of Tarentum, and fought with the SPARTANS against the Athenians at the battle of MANTINEIA in 418. A friend of PELOPIDAS, he had a part in the liberation of the Kadmeia (*ACROPOLIS* of Thebes) from the Spartans in 379, though he is said to have remained in THEBES during the Spartan occupation.

He is first known to have held the position of Boiotarch in 371 when, at the peace conference that year, he opposed the demands of the Spartan king AGESILAOS that the Boiotians swear to the peace city by city. He led the Thebans to victory against Agesilaos at LEUKTRA, where he introduced a new oblique battle formation.

In winter 370/69 he invaded the PELOPONNESE and attacked LACONIA. When the Spartans would not be drawn out to fight, he went on to liberate the MESSENIANS (a devastating blow for Sparta), though on his return home he was accused of illegally retaining his command (he was acquitted). This campaign was followed by further Peloponnesian expeditions in 369 and 366. In 367 Epameinondas became involved in THESSALY (where Pelopidas had been operating), and in 364 he launched a naval campaign to try to break the Athenians' hold in the Aegean, with limited success. He died in battle at Mantineia in 362. (see also TACTICS) LGM

See Diodorus Siculus, book 15; Nepos, *Epaminondas*; Pausanias 9.13–15; Plutarch, *Pelopidas*.

Epeiros see EPIRUS.

ephebes (*ephêbos*, *ephêboi*) Age division of the male citizens in Athens, at the stage before they assumed full political rights. The period of *ephêbeia* came after the young men were registered in the catalogues of their local districts (*dêmoi*) at the age of 18. It lasted two years, and the time was spent on military training. The system appears to have been introduced formally at the end of the 5th century BC and was well in place by the early 4th. After the BATTLE OF CHAIRONEIA in 338, a law was passed to tighten the regulations; this may have coincided with the introduction of a period of service as frontier guards (*peripoloi*) in the rural forts of Attica for those undergoing military training. ARISTOTLE (*Constitution of the Athenians* 42) offers substantial insights into how the system operated. It is not clear whether all classes participated in ephebic training, but at the end of their ephebic period conscripts were entitled to receive a HOPLITE panoply at state expense.

Further involvement of the ephebes in the life of the state included their participation in religious FESTIVALS and ancestral cults. During the Greater Mysteries at ELEUSIS, they paraded in the procession as escorts of the sacred symbols.

Features of the ephebes as a social group at an age of transition are reflected in the mythical tradition that presents them as not yet in control of the ways of hoplite warfare and often resorting to trickery. EP
See Vidal-Naquet, P. (1986) *The Black Hunter.*

Ephesos Greek city of Ionia, on the coast of Asia Minor at the mouth of the Caÿster (Kaÿstros) river, traditionally assumed to have been founded by Androkles, a son of the legendary king Kodros of Athens. Ephesos was one of the key cities in the IONIAN REVOLT against their PERSIAN overlords (499–494 BC). After the defeat of the Persian invasion of Greece it became a member of the Delian league (478/7). The King's Peace of 386 caused it to become part of the PERSIAN EMPIRE again until the conquest of Asia Minor by ALEXANDER the Great. Around 290 LYSIMACHOS compelled the Ephesians to build a new city between Mts Pion and Koressos. In 133 BC the city was part of the Attalid kingdom of PERGAMON which was handed over to Rome under the will of its last king, Attalos III. Under Roman rule Ephesos grew to become a city of 200,000 inhabitants and developed into one of the most important commercial centres in the eastern MEDITERRANEAN. It exported WINE and oil and was an important port of transit for goods from the ANATOLIAN hinterland, such as the dyed items of clothing produced in Hierapolis and Laodikeia. In addition, there was a flourishing SLAVE market. It became the seat of the governor of the province of ASIA Minor and one of the centres for the celebration of the imperial CULT. Ephesos declined as Rome's power waned in late antiquity. It was the seat of two important CHURCH COUNCILS in the 5th century; a century later most of the inhabitants had left the city and moved to the hill of Ayasoluk. The ruins show the hellenistic and Roman city as it was established by Lysimachos and expanded by the Romans. Notable features are the THEATRE, which could seat up to 24,000 spectators, the LIBRARY of Celsus, BATHS and a number of well-preserved terrace HOUSES.

The city was famous for its TEMPLE of ARTEMIS, which dates back to the 8th century BC. It is thought to be an amalgamation of an Artemis cult and a pre-Greek cult of CYBELE. In 356 BC the temple was set alight by a madman and completely destroyed; rebuilding took more than a century. It was considered one of the Seven Wonders of the world. The cult statue is decorated with the signs of the ZODIAC and ANIMALS, and shows the goddess with a great number of oval objects from her neck down to her waist, which some have identified as breasts, others as BULL's testicles. The temple and the goddess feature in the famous episode in the Acts of the Apostles in which the people, under the leadership of a silversmith, come to rally in favour of the goddess against the missionary activities of Paul and his associates. The cult of Artemis Ephesia enjoyed enormous popularity, with a series of PROCESSIONS, FESTIVALS, ATHLETIC GAMES and MARKETS organized in her honour. Apart from attracting huge crowds on these occasions, her cult spread to other cities as well; over 20 cult centres are known from all over the Roman empire. MK
See Bammer, A. (1988), *Ephesos*; Rogers, G.M. (1991) *The Sacred Identity of Ephesos: foundation myths of a Roman city*; Parrish, D., ed. (2001) *Urbanism in Western Asia Minor.*

 ASIA, ROMAN; LIBRARIES.

ephetai An Athenian jury of 51 men who judged cases of homicide. Nothing is known of the origins of the *ephetai*, but the phrasing of Drakon's homicide law makes it clear that even before his time the *ephetai* had jurisdiction over trials for homicide. According to his law, they were also responsible for appointing phratry members to decide upon a pardon in cases of unintentional homicide where the victim had no living relatives.

After the institution of the AREIOPAGOS as the court for intentional homicide, the *ephetai* remained as judges in cases of unintentional homicide (tried at the Palladion), of lawful killing (tried at the Delphinion), and of persons accused of a second homicide when already exiled (tried at the court known as Phreatto in Piraeus). Ancient sources suggest that the *ephetai* were drawn from the ranks of the Areiopagos; not all scholars accept this. Some scholars have argued that large heliastic juries (ordinary juries of the people) replaced the *ephetai* towards the end of the 5th century BC, but the evidence does not support this view. FMM
See Carawan, E. (1991) Ephetai and Athenian courts for homicide in the age of the orators, *CP* 86: 1–16; MacDowell, D.M. (1963) *Athenian Homicide Law in the Age of the Orators.*

Ephoros c.403–330 BC Greek historian. Born in Kyme and said to be a student of Isokrates and contemporary with THEOPOMPOS, Ephoros wrote a 30-book *History*, now mostly lost but known in part through DIODORUS SICULUS, who relied on him heavily. He is said by POLYBIOS to have been the first historian to write a universal history, which according to Diodorus passed over the mythical period and began with the return of the sons of Herakles from the Trojan war. The point at which it ended is not entirely clear: Diodorus says it ended with PHILIP's siege of Perinthos in 340, but elsewhere states that Ephoros' son, Demophilos, wrote about the third SACRED WAR (356–346) since his father had not. Ephoros also wrote other works: a history of Kyme, two books of trivia, and a book on style. His unfinished works were completed by his son.

Although Polybios condemns Ephoros' descriptions of BATTLES (it is as if, Polybios says, he had never seen one), he also had a reputation in antiquity for accuracy. However, he tended to collect detail, and his main interest was with his own time rather than the earlier periods, leading to a lack of balance in his work as a whole. He seems to have written in a generally episodic rather than synchronic style (as THUCYDIDES did), and was probably the first to divide his work into books. For the period after the PELOPONNESIAN WAR, though in general he tended to use more than one source (however uncritically), he probably used the Oxyrhynchos Historian as his principal source, which was more reliable than XENOPHON of whom Ephoros may have been critical. As a result, the value of Diodorus' account is greatly enhanced. On the other hand, Ephoros treated Thucydides' account of the Peloponnesian war badly by supplementing it with 4th-century material. He certainly used HERODOTOS and Hellanikos for the early periods, Kallisthenes for material on

Messenia, and Ktesias' romanticized account of Persian history.

In his history of Kyme he claimed that Homer and Hesiod were from there (though Ephoros was not the first to say this about Homer). His treatise on style is mostly lost, though one important fragment says that 'a speech must have rhythm but not metre'. Other works are attributed to Ephoros which he may not have written. These include two works called *Discoveries* on matters including the origins of Orphism and the alphabet. These belonged to a genre developed by the sophists, and were concerned with science and the arts as the basis of intellectual enquiry. LGM

See FGrH 70 (evidence, fragments); Barber, G. L. (1935) *The Historian Ephorus*; Drews, R. (1963) Ephorus and history written kata genos, *AJP* 84: 244–55.

ephors (*ephoros*, 'overseer') The office is known from a number of Dorian Greek states, but we know most about the Spartan version. There they exercised oversight not only over the community as a whole, but even over the two kings. They could force a king to remarry in order to secure an heir, or exceptionally to abdicate. The post was annual and the five *ephoroi* gave their name to the year. Theoretically any male citizen could stand for the post, and in the 4th century BC some not very rich ephors were tempted to line their pockets to the detriment of policy. If the ephors were united they could temporarily be very influential, especially if the kings were divided or one was a minor. But only very rarely can we explain a sudden lurch in Spartan policy by the advent of new ephors. The kings and the council of elders (Gerousia, with members all over 60) were the real shapers of policy. After defeating Athens in 404, Sparta inherited an empire over other Greeks and this imposed severe strains on the ancestral system, which the ephors defended. For instance, no Spartan was henceforth allowed to own any appreciable amount of coinage, and Sparta issued none of its own. The ephors made an example of Gylippos – himself the son of an ephor – when an informant told them of the nest of owlets (Athenian silver coins) under his rafters. Change was needed, but even when Sparta's invincible military might buckled before Thebes' new model army at Leuktra in 371, Spartan society remained conservative. Nearly a century and a half later, Kleomenes III abolished both the dual monarchy and the office of ephor in a forlorn attempt to modernize the state. HBM

See Cartledge, P. A. (1987) *Agesilaos and the Crisis of Sparta* 125–9; Rhodes, P. J. (1981) The selection of ephors at Sparta, *Historia* 30: 498–502; Richer, N. (1998) *Les Éphores*.

epic The oldest and most central literary genre in classical antiquity, composed in continuous hexameters. Its authority rests on that of Homer, believed to be the author of the *Iliad* and the *Odyssey*, legendary narratives of the deeds of heroes and gods. The former is the pattern for all later epics of warfare, the latter for epics of wandering and adventure. In later antiquity Homer was regarded as an almost divine fountain of literature and culture, and the Homeric epics formed the centre of the Greco-Roman canon; many later genres, such as tragedy and historiography, are significantly indebted to epic. Ancient conceptions of the divine owed much to the picture of the gods in Homer and Hesiod (the first didactic poet; didactic poetry, also in hexameters, was sometimes included in ancient definitions of epic). The Homeric epics were not, however, sacred texts in the sense that the Bible is. Nevertheless their canonical status and the need to make them accessible and relevant to successive centuries ensured that they were subject to scholarly exegesis and allegorization throughout antiquity. The two Homeric epics together with other lost early Greek epics made up the Epic Cycle, covering the whole of history from the birth of the gods to the generation after Odysseus. Later epics were written on historical as well as legendary subjects, but none survives complete before the four-book *Argonautica* of the hellenistic poet Apollonios of Rhodes. The Greek tradition flourished down to the exuberant 5th-century AD *Dionysiaka* of Nonnos.

Roman epic begins with Livius Andronicus' translation of the *Odyssey*, but the main tradition is historical epic, beginning with Naevius' *Bellum Punicum*, in the Saturnian metre. Ennius introduced the hexameter to Rome with his epic on the whole of Roman history, the *Annals*, eventually in 18 books. This was superseded as the national Roman epic by Virgil's *Aeneid*, a legendary epic that appropriates both the *Iliad* and the *Odyssey* for a Roman readership, but at the same time through prophecy and allusion foreshadows the later course of Roman history down to Augustus. The vigorous 1st-century AD tradition of Roman epic, both legendary (Ovid, Statius, Valerius Flaccus) and historical (Lucan, Silius Italicus), displays an intensive engagement with the by now canonical *Aeneid*. There is a late revival of pagan Latin epic in Claudian. The Christian tradition begins with hexameter paraphrases of the Bible by Iuvencus, Sedulius and others. Prudentius' highly Virgilian *Psychomachia* inaugurates the long line of medieval and Renaissance allegorical epics, given further impetus by the late antique allegorical interpretation (e.g. by Fulgentius) of the *Aeneid* as a kind of pilgrim's progress. Epic (and its relative, romance) continued as a vehicle for major nationalist and religious statements down to the Renaissance (e.g. Spenser, Milton). Today its cultural status has been overtaken by that of the novel and the film. PRH

See Feeney, D. C. (1989) *The Gods in Epic*; Quint, D. (1990) *Epic and Empire*; Toohey, P. (1992) *Reading Epic*.

Epicureanism A philosophical movement begun in the hellenistic period and named after its founder, Epicurus. In epistemology, the Epicureans were committed empiricists. They claimed that all sense impressions provide true information about the world and can therefore function as a 'criterion of truth'. The opinions we choose to form, however, may be false and therefore it is important always to check one's opinions against the evidence of the senses. No belief about something perceptible should be accepted unless it is confirmed by sense perception. No belief about something imperceptible (for example, the thesis that the world is composed of atoms) should be accepted until shown to be consistent with the entire range of phenomena.

Epicurean physical theory accepted the Demokritean hypothesis that the world is fundamentally composed of atoms moving in a void. All other bodies are composed from a number of atoms arranged in a certain way. Time and space are both boundless, and there is a limitless number of atoms. Therefore, there is no need to use teleological or theological arguments to explain the coming-to-be of our cosmos; it is merely one among innumerable others, and its constituents are the result of entirely natural processes of trial and error. Only some species survive to reproduce since they happen to be well adapted to their environment. Epicurus was more generous in his ontology than Demokritos, granting reality to properties such as colours and tastes which do not belong to atoms *per se* but rather to their various combinations.

Epicurean ETHICAL theory begins with the assertion that humans naturally aim for pleasure and avoid pain. The goal (*telos*) of human life is then identified as *ataraxia* ('absence of disturbance'), the state of living without mental pain, which is also controversially identified as the highest possible pleasure. In order better to achieve this state, Epicurus advises us to discard any desires which are neither natural nor necessary, since natural and necessary desires – for food, shelter and so on – are most easily satisfied, and unsatisfied desires are a source of pain. Also, a correct Epicurean understanding of the world will serve to remove any anxiety caused by certain conceptions of the GODS or of DEATH. There are gods, but they do not care about human affairs nor do they intervene in the world: being perfectly happy beings, they have no reason to do so. There is no AFTERLIFE and no perception of pleasure or pain after death, and so nothing at all to fear from mortality.

Apart from the writings of Epicurus himself, some of which are quoted in DIOGENES LAËRTIUS' *Life of Epicurus*, two extraordinary Epicurean productions survive from antiquity. LUCRETIUS' Latin hexameter poem in six books *On the Nature of Things* (*De rerum natura*) belongs to the 1st century BC, and a huge inscription was set up in the marketplace of Oinoanda in Asia Minor during the 2nd century AD by an Epicurean named Diogenes. Further texts by Epicurus and other Epicurean writers, such as PHILODEMOS, have been discovered in fragmentary and carbonized form in the LIBRARY of the VILLA of the PAPYRI, just outside HERCULANEUM. JIW

See Inwood, B. et al. (1994) *The Epicurus Reader*; Long, A. A. and Sedley, D. N. (1987) *The Hellenistic Philosophers*.

Epicurus (Epikouros) 341/0–270 BC Athenian citizen and founder of the hellenistic philosophical school that bears his name, now called EPICUREANISM. Epicurus was born on the island of SAMOS to parents who were Athenian CLERUCHS there. He served as an Athenian EPHEBE when he was 18 and, after all the Athenian settlers were expelled from the island by Alexander's SUCCESSOR Perdikkas, the family left Samos for Kolophon on the nearby mainland of Asia Minor. He may have spent some time earning a living as a schoolteacher. Epicurus attended the lectures of Nausiphanes the DEMOKRITEAN while on the island of Teos, and perhaps through them was introduced to Demokritean ATOMISM. Epicurus was later extremely rude about all early influences on his thought, and claimed to be entirely self-taught. This attitude, coupled with his hedonist and materialist doctrines, made him a target for slander and abuse from contemporary and later ancient writers.

He first founded a school at Mytilene on LESBOS, then at Lampsakos in the Troad. In 307/6 he moved with the followers he had already attracted to Athens, where the school met in a plot of land owned by Epicurus just outside the city. The Garden, as the school came to be known, was the focus for a philosophical community organized on strictly hierarchical grounds of teachers and pupils and bound together by shared rituals and communal feasting. Epicurus died in 271/0, perhaps as a result of a kidney disorder, and was succeeded as head of the school by Hermarchos.

Various sculptural portraits of Epicurus survive, generally showing him sitting quietly and displaying the demeanour of someone enjoying absolute tranquillity – the Epicurean ETHICAL ideal. JIW

epidemics In the ancient world, it was the physician rather than the disease that was 'epidemic', in the sense of travelling through a population. Physicians normally wandered from town to town, while the development of disease was thought to be within the person's constitution, rather than being due to an entity passed on from someone else. Hence the title *Epidemics* was used for seven books of case histories in the HIPPOCRATIC tradition, in which the writers describe the effect of different locations and climates on the overall pattern of disease in towns visited in many parts of the Greek world.

It has however been proposed that there is a connection between the Hippocratic *Epidemics* and epidemic diseases in our sense. *Epidemics* 3 describes a condition similar to that described in the most famous plague of antiquity, the Athenian plague of 430 BC known through THUCYDIDES' eye-witness account (2.47–58). The description of the symptoms of this plague, which led to the breakdown of social and religious norms, has acted as a model for many subsequent descriptions of epidemics. The plague has been diagnosed retrospectively as typhus, smallpox, ergotism, mumps or measles, but its identification is made very difficult by the fact that Thucydides' plague is a literary product rather than a medical report. The plague is deliberately placed to contrast with the account of the glory of Athens in the funeral speech by Perikles (2.34–46), making the description of social collapse all the more dramatic. Thucydides also attributes to the plague Athens' subsequent manpower problems and the death of PERIKLES. According to Thucydides, the plague that hit Athens originated in ETHIOPIA, then passed to Egypt and LIBYA. We may speculate that its effects on Athens were more severe because of the overcrowding in the city caused by people moving there for safety while the SPARTAN army was at Dekeleia.

Major epidemics are more common in Roman history. The 'Antonine plague' – possibly smallpox – was first noticed in SMYRNA and NISIBIS in AD 165, and affected the Roman army besieging Seleukeia later that year. From OLD TESTAMENT times onwards, epidemic disease could be seen as a punishment from the gods, and the Antonine plague was thought by some contemporaries to have been sent to punish Rome for its failure to keep an agreement with Seleukeia. The plague was taken back to Rome when the army returned; a series of PURIFICATORY rites had no effect, and it reappeared in 180 when MARCUS AURELIUS contracted it. A further outbreak in 189 had a serious effect on the city of Rome. GALEN, our main source for this epidemic, managed to avoid catching the disease by leaving Rome, claiming that this was for professional reasons. Another epidemic, the 'Cyprian plague', travelled from the NILE valley to affect Italy and Greece by 269. The 'plague of JUSTINIAN' was at its height in 541–4, and may have been bubonic plague.

Whatever their precise identity, the pattern of epidemics in antiquity shows clearly how they were spread along TRADE routes – it is probably significant that the first cases in Athens were in the region of the PIRAEUS – and by armies. HK

See King, H. (2001) *Greek and Roman Medicine.*

epigrams Short poems, functional in origin (from *epigraphô*, 'I write upon'); the earliest epigrams, composed in Greek, dedicated the object upon which they were written, or commemorated the dead upon whose tombstone they appeared. By the hellenistic age the context for epigram had expanded. The dedicatory function was adapted to honour the achievements of monarchs and prominent citizens (as with Posidippos' epigrams on monuments of the PTOLEMIES at ALEXANDRIA), and a sophisticated literary GENRE developed with wide thematic scope: from erotic to insulting, in addition to variations upon dedication and epitaph. The semblance of actuality upon which many literary epigrams are predicated, however, may frequently be fictitious.

The surviving corpus of Greek epigrams is based upon three ancient collections, by Meleager (1st century BC), Philip (1st century AD) and Agathias (6th century AD). Recently the corpus has been substantially increased with the discovery of a papyrus containing 110 hitherto unknown epigrams by Posidippos, arranged under thematic headings. In the late Republic, CATULLUS and his contemporaries enthusiastically composed epigrams in Latin in the hellenistic style. In the late 1st century AD, MARTIAL honed their legacy into the witty and pointed verse that still characterizes epigram today. The *Anthologia Latina*, a post-classical compilation, includes epigrams ascribed to authors ranging from PETRONIUS and SENECA to late antique POETS from North AFRICA. A sub-literary stratum of Latin epigram preserved in graffiti and inscriptions (especially epitaphs) attests the widespread popularity of the genre throughout the Roman world. (see also *GREEK ANTHOLOGY*) KMC

See The Greek Anthology, trs. W. R. Paton, 5 vols. (1916–18); Austin, C. and Bastianini, G., eds. (2002) *Posidippi Pellaei quae supersunt omnia*; Gutzwiller, K. (1998) *Poetic Garlands*; Lattimore, R. (1942) *Themes in Greek and Latin Epitaphs.*

epigraphy

The study of inscriptions – objects, usually of stone or metal, on which Greek letters and/or numbers have been cut or scratched. The study of Greek epigraphy tends to be dominated by specialists ('epigraphers' or 'epigraphists') who devote their time to reading carefully the inscribed stones, transcribing accurately the letters or traces of letters visible on the stone, and then producing a text in Greek with a commentary and (usually) a translation to help the reader understand how the inscription should be interpreted. Epigraphic evidence touches on all areas of ancient civilization, and is therefore relevant to all students of Greece and Rome.

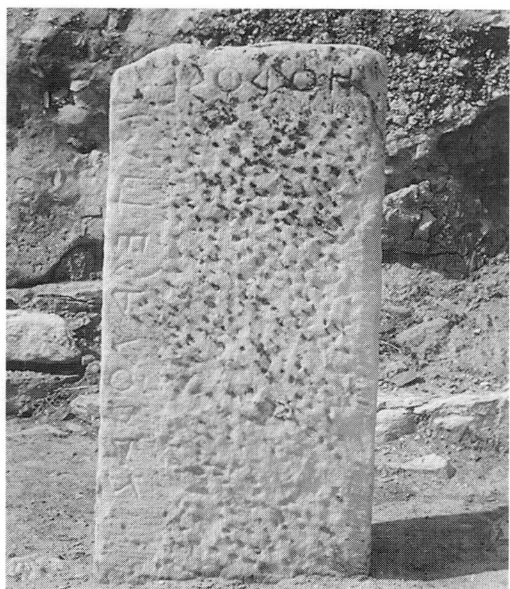

EPIGRAPHY, GREEK: (a) an inscribed boundary stone from the south-west corner of the Athenian Agora, c.490 BC (*Agora* I 5510 = *Agora* XIX H 25).

Epigraphy fascinated even those in antiquity. Krateros made a collection of decrees in the 3rd century AD; Pausanias in the 2nd century gleaned a great deal of information from reading inscriptions. After antiquity, CYRIAC OF ANCONA, in the 14th century, was one of the first to record and make observations about inscriptions, while travellers to Greece since the 16th century have often transcribed inscriptions or removed them to their own countries.

The organized study of Greek epigraphy began during the 19th century with the publication in 1825 of the first volume of *Corpus inscriptionum Graecarum* (*CIG*, 'Corpus of Greek inscriptions') by Augustus Boeckh, under the auspices of what was then the Royal Prussian Academy in Berlin (now the Berlin Academy). *CIG* was intended to collect and publish all Greek inscriptions; four volumes appeared, and publication was completed in 1877, but the ambition was in vain. For during the 19th and even more the 20th centuries, the number of known inscriptions has increased dramatically and *CIG* became out of date even while it was being published. The excavation of major sites, such as the AGORA and ACROPOLIS in Athens, the sanctuaries of DELPHI, DELOS, OLYMPIA, EPHESOS and Priene, have all produced large numbers of inscriptions. A new series of publications, *Inscriptiones Graecae* (*IG*, 'Greek inscriptions'), was begun by the Berlin Academy. It, too, was meant to cover the whole of the Greek world but has suffered from the volume of material. Publication remains incomplete and uneven; while some areas, such as ATTICA, are now in their third edition, others (e.g. MACEDONIA and SAMOS) are appearing now only for the first time.

The organization of Greek epigraphy is very complex. Inscriptions are published not only in series of

EPIGRAPHY, GREEK: (b) law against tyranny, set up in 337/6 BC, shortly after the battle of Chaironeia (*Agora* I 6524 = *Agora* XVI 73).

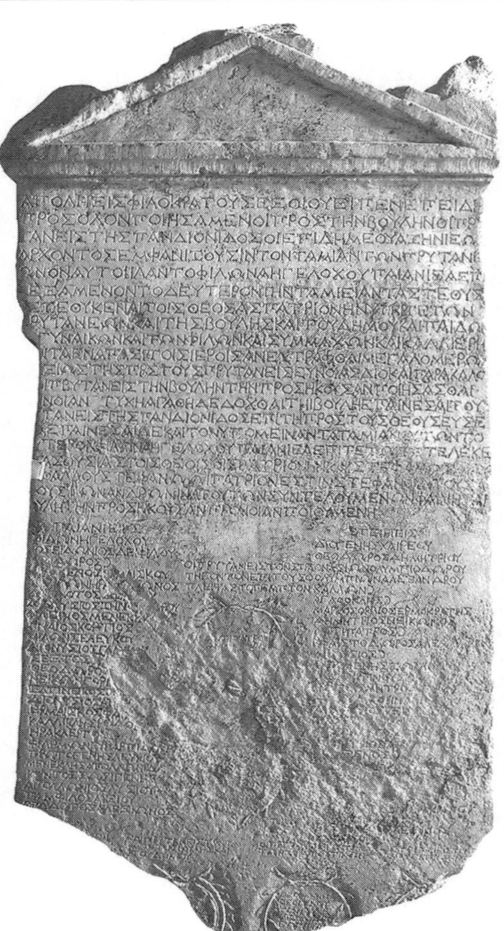

EPIGRAPHY, GREEK: (c) an inscription honouring the treasurer and *prytaneis* of the Athenian *boulê*, c.20 BC, from the *Agora* (*Agora* I 4744 = *Agora* XV 293).

epigraphical publications but also as part of site-based excavations (e.g. from the American excavations of the Agora of Athens and those of the French at Delphi). Individuals have also left their mark. Probably the most influential epigrapher of the 20th century, Louis Robert, published an enormous number of articles and books, an unassailable legacy for all future students of epigraphy. However, the publication of *Supplementum epigraphicum Graecum* (*SEG*, 'Greek epigraphic supplement') now provides an annual record of the most significant epigraphical discoveries and publications. Another resource is the searchable collection of all published Greek inscriptions in digital format, updated on a regular basis and created by an American project, the Packard Humanities Institute. These two tools have eased considerably the work of Greek epigraphers.

The epigrapher now enjoys several ways to assist the transcription and production of a good text. For example, both conventional and digital photographs of inscriptions can help to verify readings made from a stone, though the balance and level of lighting can be critical to image quality. But the most common form of studying inscriptions, apart from the study of the stone itself ('autopsy'), is from a 'squeeze', an impression of the inscribed surface made using water, a purpose-designed brush, and special thick paper. Squeezes are durable (unless they come into contact with water again) and extremely accurate. Collections of squeezes allow epigraphers to build up an archive that can be studied at leisure in a research centre. Special aspects of epigraphy, such as the identification of letter-cutters, individual masons who use a distinctive style or 'hand' when carving, is really only practicable from the careful, time-consuming study and comparison of squeezes.

But why is Greek epigraphy so important? Inscriptions are both a written and a visual record of the ancient world. As monuments, inscriptions existed in a physical context that can sometimes be recovered not only through ARCHAEOLOGY but also from reading the inscriptions themselves. A number of inscriptions specify where the stone is to be set up, often in the most prominent position in a community, an *AGORA* (marketplace) or sanctuary. Occasionally one can gain some impression of what a particularly rich epigraphical ancient site might have looked like. On the Acropolis in Athens, as one approaches the PARTHENON from the west, numerous slots cut into the bedrock indicate where a forest of *STÊLAI* once stood to greet the visitor to the sanctuary.

An inscription should be considered in its entirety: as the dedication on a base for a statue within a TEMPLE or sanctuary, a religious environment, or as an inscribed ARCHITECTURAL form, or as the identification of an individual on a decorated or sculpted tombstone. There are obstacles to seeing epigraphy in this way, because one usually sees an inscription in a museum, where the stone is removed from its original context. More often, inscriptions are read as texts in a book; their visual appearance and archaeological context are rarely considered.

It is as unique documentary evidence of historical events that inscriptions are most commonly used. The most important category of such documents is the LAWS and decrees passed by public bodies. These can be the oaths and terms of alliances, or honorific decrees rewarding individuals whose achievements are related, often in detail. Such evidence is rarely preserved in the work of ancient literary writers. One of the most famous inscriptions, written in both Greek and Latin on the walls of the temple of AUGUSTUS at Ankara, records the emperor's achievements (*RES GESTAE*); another Greek copy has been found at Apollonia, also in Asia Minor. Without these inscriptions, only a brief notice in SUETONIUS attests to the document.

From 5th-century Athens we have the so-called Athenian 'tribute lists', which preserve the contributions by the members of Athens' maritime empire to the goddess ATHENA. The texts record sums which represent one-sixtieth of each member state's total payment to the city; this fraction was deducted and given to the goddess. The lists of the contributions allow historians to reconstruct not only the membership of the Athenian empire, but also the sums of money Athens received from its tribute-paying subjects. All this information has been preserved only in small marble fragments rediscovered over the last 200 years, the remains of massive pillars that once stood on the Acropolis.

But the wealth of epigraphical evidence benefits more than just political history and the illumination of individual events or moments in history. In addition to state laws and decrees, significant categories of inscription include decrees set up by other groups (DEMES, private organizations and religious associations); dedications by individuals, groups and communities to deities; lists of objects, money or contributions dedicated in temples; lists of civic officials or contributors to public funds; records of mortgage arrangements and leases; boundary markers; and the most common form of inscribed document, tombstones. Social, economic and cultural history is illuminated by the study of inscriptions. The study of categories or themes among inscribed material often advances the understanding of the evidence for, and the institutions of, ancient Greece. For example, decrees describing the inviolability of cities and land, the inscribed correspondence of kings and queens, and grants of CITIZENSHIP made by cities to foreigners have all expanded the knowledge of the later classical and hellenistic periods.

Many thousands of inscriptions in Greek, dating from c.750 BC to AD 400, have survived, but they are only a small fraction of the number that existed in antiquity. Not all documents were inscribed: only a small proportion of records were chosen to be recorded on stone or bronze. The preserved epigraphic record is therefore only a sample from the past. Many communities would set up inscriptions, often documents of a civic nature approved by the people. This practice, often called the 'epigraphic habit' or 'epigraphical culture', was most popular at Athens, which has produced the largest amount of epigraphy of any Greek city (c.30,000 inscriptions). A good supply of stone (or metal, usually bronze) was required for the production of inscribed monuments; the mountains of Pentelikon and Hymettos near Athens yielded MARBLE not only for the construction of buildings but also for the cutting of inscriptions.

The masons who cut the long inscribed decrees of the state were skilled craftsmen. In time the style of letter-cutting developed. Letters from the archaic period are distinctive and reflect the diverse local ALPHABETS of early Greek script. The earliest inscriptions were often written from right to left. Some inscriptions were written in lines alternating from right to left, left to right, right to left (*boustrophêdon*, 'like an ox turning' when ploughing). By the classical period at Athens, a chequerboard style of laying out inscriptions had developed where the text was written in grid-like fashion (*stoichêdon*), in rows and columns across the stone's surface. In the classical period it was still unusual to find inscriptions with gaps between words to facilitate reading, though punctuation marks were used sporadically from early times. To ease reading, letters were often painted red. For most inscriptions, it was not their legibility but the LITERACY level of the viewer that might prevent them from being read.

Today it is important to read inscriptions, even in translation. The skills required by students of literature, history and archaeology are all essential to epigraphy, and epigraphy is relevant to all these areas of classical civilization. (see also EPIGRAPHY, ROMAN; WRITING) GJO

See Bodel, J., ed. (2001) *Epigraphic Evidence*; Cook, B. F. (1987) *Greek Inscriptions* (good photographs); Habicht, C. (1998) *Pausanias' Guide to Ancient Greece*; Jeffrey, L.H. with Johnston, A.W. (1990) *Local Scripts of Archaic Greece*; Osborne, M. J. (1981–4) *Naturalization in Athens*; Rhodes, P. J., with Lewis, D.M. (1997) *The Decrees of the Greek States*; Rhodes, P.J. and Osborne, R.G. (2003) *Greek Historical Inscriptions, 404–323 BC*; Rigsby, K.J. (1996) *Asylia*; Sherk, R. K. (1969) *Roman Documents from the Greek East*; Tracy, S.V. (1990) *Attic Letter-cutters of 229 to 86 BC*; (1995) *Athenian*

EPIGRAPHY, ROMAN: (a) public inscriptions – the dedication of the arch of Titus at Rome: 'Senate and People of Rome to the deified Titus Vespasianus Augustus, son of the deified Vespasian'.

EPIGRAPHY, ROMAN: (b) religious dedications – altars from the Carrawburgh Mithraeum, each concluding with the abbreviation *v.s.l.m.* (*votum solvit libens merito*) relating to the willing fulfilment of a vow.

EPIGRAPHY, ROMAN: (c) milestone – main roads were commonly provided with distance markers at mile intervals, in this case erected under Trajan in AD 108–9 on the Via Traiana in southern Italy.

Democracy in Transition: Attic letter-cutters of 340 to 290 BC; (2003) *Athens and Macedon: Attic Letter-cutters of 300–229* BC; Welles, C. B. (1934) *Royal Correspondence in the Hellenistic Period*; Woodhead, A. G. (1992) *The Study of Greek Inscriptions*.

Latin inscriptions constitute a major source of contemporary information about the Roman world, which is increasing constantly with new discoveries. The earliest Latin inscriptions date from the 6th century BC, but there are few before the end of the 1st century BC. Most of the 250,000 or more texts on stone available for study today were inscribed during the first three centuries AD. To this total must be added texts scratched, incised or moulded on a variety of other natural or manmade materials such as wood, GLASS, metals, POTTERY and BONE (generally classed together as *INSTRUMENTUM DOMESTICUM*). Wooden writing tablets have been recovered from the sands of the Middle East and from wet environments in north-west Europe. Upwards of 60,000 inscriptions on stone come from the city of Rome itself, and many thousands from towns such as OSTIA, AQUILEIA, Verona, Salona, Mainz and Köln. Parts of the Roman world, such as BRITAIN (which has yielded a total of some 4,000 texts of all types), are poorly represented. Some provinces, for various reasons, appear never to have acquired the 'epigraphic habit'. Inscriptions bring before us many layers of society: the EMPERORS and the imperial family, SENATORS and EQUESTRIANS, local gentry, tradesmen, PRIESTS, soldiers, ordinary citizens in vast number, less frequently SLAVES.

Inscriptions are an important source of information on the LAWS of the Roman state, decrees and formal responses (rescripts) of the emperors and of city constitutions, inscribed on stone or bronze plaques and erected in a town's FORUM for public viewing. AUGUSTUS' *RES GESTAE* ('achievements'), often considered a literary text, was originally inscribed on bronze pillars after his death in AD 14 at the entrance to his mausoleum in the Campus Martius at Rome (Suetonius, *Augustus* 101), but these do not survive. The text is thus known chiefly from the Latin version, the so-called *Monumentum Ancyranum*, on the walls of the temple of Augustus at Ancyra (mod.

EPIGRAPHY, ROMAN: (d) tombstones – here words combine with images to provide a snapshot of the life of Longinus Biarta, a Roman cavalryman.

EPIGRAPHY, ROMAN: (e) words on things – this curiosity is a copper alloy dice dispenser from a late Roman villa in the Rhineland. The optimistic message round the top and down the front of the object reads: 'Use (me) well. Live life (to the full). Picts beaten. Enemy destroyed. Relax and play.'

Ankara) in Turkey; parts of a Greek version survive here and in another copy at Apollonia.

About three-quarters of all surviving epigraphic texts are funerary. These texts name the deceased and his or her family, and give the age at death and sometimes an occupation such as tradesman or soldier, so providing material for sociological and DEMOGRAPHIC surveys. Many texts are inscribed on upright tombstones of the type familiar today; others are on thin rectangular slabs masking the fronts of niches in communal TOMBS (*columbaria*). Some soldiers' tombstones depict the deceased in military dress; study of military epitaphs illustrates recruitment patterns, changes of posting and the identity of particular garrisons in frontier provinces.

Religious dedications constitute another major category, sometimes taking the form of records of the construction of TEMPLES (such as the PANTHEON, still *in situ*) or attached to votive offerings. Altars, dedicated to a plethora of classical deities and local CELTIC, AFRICAN, oriental and other gods and PERSONIFICATIONS, illustrate the religious practices of the empire's manifold ethnic groups.

Building records are a further category, often commemorating the construction of a major edifice for public or private use. Such texts normally name the benefactor who had paid for the work. In the more prosperous provinces we thus learn of civic life in towns, the names of MAGISTRATES, and the activities of trade guilds. In the less advanced provinces we learn of the construction of frontier works and military installations. Milestones, erected at regular intervals along the Roman roads, testify to the frequency or infrequency of repair work.

Inscriptions on statue bases at Rome and in countless towns throughout Italy and the provinces honour emperors, senators, equestrians and municipal worthies. They provide valuable details of postholding and career progression, and much evidence of family connections and administrative structures, at national and local level. Electoral posters at POMPEII give an insight into municipal politics and the jockeying for power of important local families.

Few texts, even gravestones, bear an exact date for their erection. However, the study of the formulas used, and of spelling, grammar and letter-shapes, may offer some clues, as will any references to historical personages or events. In a few cases, the text can be dated by reference to the CONSULS of the year or by citation of the 'regnal' year, consulships or imperial salutations of an emperor. On tombstones the formula *hic situs est*, 'he lies here' (abbreviated to HSE) is employed frequently in the 1st century AD and occasionally thereafter. The formula *dis manibus*, 'to the spirits of the departed', soon abbreviated to DM, comes into common use by the middle of the 1st century AD and is ubiquitous during the 2nd and 3rd centuries. Often, however, the ARCHAEOLOGICAL or ARCHITECTURAL context of an inscription will date the text, rather than vice versa.

Christian inscriptions are known from the early 2nd century AD onwards, and become more numerous after the adoption of Christianity as the official religion of the empire by CONSTANTINE in 325. Christian texts are, for the most part, instantly identifiable by distinctive wording and associated sculptural detail. Most such texts are funerary, either from the CATACOMBS, especially those on the roads leading from Rome itself, or from the vicinity of CHURCHES. Increasingly they specify the length of life to the nearest day, and a precise date of death.

The majority of inscriptions known from the Roman world are in Latin, but in provinces east of the ADRIATIC Greek is regularly found, and texts in many local scripts, such as Punic and NABATAEAN, are known. For those inscribing the texts, these were the languages they used every day. Some texts are BILINGUAL, even trilingual, as on a dedication erected at Philae in Upper Egypt in 29 BC by Gaius Cornelius GALLUS, the soon to be disgraced prefect of Egypt, inscribed in Egyptian hieroglyphs, Latin and Greek.

The lettering on most texts takes the form of 'Roman' capitals (the *scriptura monumentalis*), sometimes set on lightly incised guidelines; the inscribed letter-shapes were often marked out in red paint. On major public monuments the text may consist of large bronze letters set into the façade of the structure itself (such as on the ARCH of TITUS); these bronze letters rarely survive, but sometimes the text can be reconstructed from traces such as dowel-holes. Other forms of writing were employed. The so-called *scriptura actuaria* was used for public notices such as the electoral posters at Pompeii, and sometimes on stone. 'Cursive script', akin to everyday handwriting, is found chiefly on PAPYRI, writing tablets and ostraca. Texts preserved on pottery, tiles, metal and other materials, and on sealings, WEIGHTS AND MEASURES, provide evidence of MANUFACTURE, TRADING patterns and the economic life of the Roman world. Study of grammar and spelling show the development of the Latin language over many hundreds of years.

The words on an inscribed text are frequently abbreviated, where the full form was obvious or easily understood, to maximize the length of the message imparted in a restricted space. (Abbreviation is commoner in Latin inscriptions than Greek.) Errors can occur, either through ignorance on the part of the stonecutter or his difficulty in transcribing a draft. Letters can be run together (ligatured), either to save space or sometimes as an artistic device to enhance the attractiveness of the monument. Sometimes individual letters (such as 'I') can be lengthened so as to project above the rest of the line, or have accents (*apices*) over them, perhaps an indication of pronunciation. Words can be separated by triangular dots (interpuncts), by ivy-leaf stops or not at all. There were no capital letters at the beginning of sentences.

Inscribed texts are rarely found *in situ*: dismantled tomb monuments and gravestones were frequently reused as building material in late antiquity and after, for example the tomb of Classicianus now in the British Museum. Attention focuses on intact texts, but many inscriptions are incomplete, and only a few letters may survive, which the skilled epigraphist endeavours to restore. On fragmentary stones, the appearance of the letters HSE or DM (see above) will help identify an inscription as a tombstone. The letters VSLLM, abbreviated from the formula *votum solvit laetus libens merito* ('willingly, gladly and deservedly fulfilled his vow'), indicate an altar. The shape of the stone will be a guide to the category to which it belongs. In general, it is important always to remember that the texts are inscribed *on* something, so that they should be studied in conjunction with the overall design and sculptural decoration of the gravestone or monument which they ornament.

The texts of inscriptions have been gathered by scholars from the Middle Ages onwards and studied *en masse* as a separate branch of ancient evidence from RENAISSANCE times. Comprehensive publication was attempted by the editors of the *Corpus inscriptionum Latinarum* (*CIL*), initiated at Berlin in 1847 and still in progress. New material appears annually in the journal *L'Année épigraphique* (*AE*), and individual stones and texts are published in a wide variety of learned journals. An invaluable five-yearly survey is published in the *Journal of Roman Studies*. There are numerous national and regional surveys and publications of museum holdings.

For Britain texts on stone known up to 1954 were published in volume 1 of *The Roman Inscriptions of Britain* (*RIB* I), now supplemented by volume 2 covering *instrumentum domesticum* up to 1986 (*RIB* II). New texts from Britain appear in an annual survey in the journal *Britannia*. Writing tablets from VINDOLANDA and Carlisle have added to our awareness of the realities of life on the northern frontier.

Numerous selections of texts have been made over the years. The general compilations prepared long ago by Dessau (*ILS*), and Diehl (for Christian texts; *ILCV*), remain fundamental tools of research. Other selections cover shorter historical periods or specialized subjects. Handbooks to epigraphy in French, German, Italian, English and Spanish have appeared. Translations from Latin into a wide range of modern European languages have brought inscriptions to a much wider audience. In general, inscriptions, when studied in bulk, serve as raw material for specialist studies and monographs on every aspect of the Roman world, both in Italy and the provinces. (see also EPIGRAPHY, GREEK) LK

See Bérard, F. et al. (2000) *Guide de l'épigraphiste*; Bodel, J. (2001) *Epigraphic Evidence*; Bowman, A. K. and Thomas, J. D. (1983) *Vindolanda: the Latin writing-tablets*; (1994) *The Vindolanda Writing-tablets*; Collingwood, R. G. and Wright, R. P. (1965) *The Roman Inscriptions of Britain*, vol. 1; Degrassi, A. (1965) *Inscriptiones Latinae liberae rei publicae*; Dessau, H. (1892–1916) *Inscriptiones Latinae selectae*; Diehl, E. (1925–31), *Inscriptiones Latinae Christianae veteres*; Ehrenberg, V. and Jones, A. H. M. (1976) *Documents Illustrating the Reigns of Augustus and Tiberius*; Frere, S. S. et al. (1990–5) *The Roman Inscriptions of Britain*, vol. 2; Gordon, A. E. (1983) *Illustrated Introduction to Latin Epigraphy*; Gordon, J. S. and Gordon, A. E. (1957) *Contributions to the Palaeography of Latin Inscriptions*; Ireland, R. (1983) Epigraphy, in M. Henig, ed., *Handbook of Roman Art* 220–33; Keppie, L. (1991) *Understanding Roman Inscriptions;* McCrum, M. and Woodhead, A. G. (1966) *Select Documents of the Principates of the Flavian Emperors*; Millar, F. G. B. (1983) Epigraphy, in M. H. Crawford, ed., *Sources for Ancient History* 80–136; Sandys, J. E. (1927) *Latin Epigraphy*; Sherk, R. K. (1970) *The Municipal Decrees of the Roman West*; Smallwood, E. M. (1966) *Documents Illustrating the Principates of Nerva, Trajan and Hadrian*; (1967) *Documents Illustrating the Principates of Gaius, Claudius and Nero*; Susini, G. (1973) *The Roman Stonecutter*.

ANNOBAL TAPAPIUS RUFUS; ATHENIAN EMPIRE: (b); CURSES: (a)–(b); GORTYN CODE: *RES GESTAE*: SULPICIA LEPIDINA: (a).

Epikouros see EPICURUS.

Epirus (Epeiros) Region of north-western Greece (now divided between Greece and Albania). The name means literally 'the mainland': it was so called by the SAILORS who followed the ADRIATIC coast. Located between Akarnania (at the gulf of Ambrakia) and ILLYRIA, and separated from THESSALY by the Pindos mountains, Epirus comprised at one time at least 14 tribal units, of which the Thesprotians, Chaonians and Molossians emerged as dominant. It remained outside the mainstream of Greek history until the hellenization of the Molossian royal house, which gained control of the sanctuary of Zeus at DODONA. The power of the monarchy was nevertheless limited by MAGISTRATES and a council of tribal representatives. The young king Tharypas received Athenian citizenship during the PELOPONNESIAN WAR – his descent from Molossos, a grandson of ACHILLES, was celebrated by EURIPIDES in *Andromache* – and his son Alketas and grandson Neoptolemos are attested on the decree of Aristoteles as members of the second Athenian confederacy (377 BC). PHILIP II brought Epirus within the MACEDONIAN orbit, marrying the princess OLYMPIAS and soon driving out her uncle Arrhybas (or Arybbas), whom he replaced with Alexander I. His death in Italy in 330 was followed by dynastic instability as Arrhybas' son Aiakides was challenged by rivals. The period after the battle of IPSOS (301) saw Aiakides' son PYRRHOS restored to his ancestral kingdom, which he and his successors ruled from the new capital at Ambrakia until c.232. The Epirote league, which followed the monarchy, supported Macedonia in the third MACEDONIAN WAR and succumbed to Roman power after Perseus' defeat at PYDNA in 168, when some 150,000 Epirotes were taken into captivity. In 31 BC, the battle of ACTIUM in Epirus decided the fate of the Roman world, and Octavian (the future AUGUSTUS) founded Nikopolis here to commemorate his victory over ANTONY. WH

See Cross, G. N. (1932) *Epirus*; Hammond, N. G. L. (1967) *Epirus*.

 AEGEAN SEA: (a).

Epona A native HORSE goddess, worshipped extensively among the northern and eastern tribes of GAUL. Epona is unique in the Romano-Celtic pantheon, since she is never equated with a classical deity. The identification of Epona in the post-conquest period is largely restricted to her figural portrayals with horses, the majority of which depict a female figure either riding side-saddle or standing between a mare and a colt. While inscriptions to Epona exist, the widespread distribution of small cult objects is the primary testimony to her significance in post-conquest RITUAL.

The worship of Epona was not limited to her native homeland. Dedications and iconographic imagery of the goddess are present in BRITAIN and as far afield as North AFRICA, eastern Europe and the stables of Rome. The geographic extent of the cult was primarily due to the widespread deployment of CAVALRY from Gaul, for whom Epona, as a patron deity of horses, had a particular importance. This may explain why a Gallic goddess was accorded an annual festival in Rome on 18 December, a rare honour for a foreign deity.

Epona has many attributes in common with the Welsh Rhiannon of the *Mabinogion*, including her association with horses and chthonic imagery relating to the Otherworld. Another notable aspect of the native goddess is her connection with fertility. Epona quite frequently accompanies dedications to the MOTHER GODDESSES, and is often depicted with the classical accoutrements of fecundity, specifically FRUIT, BREAD and the horn of plenty. MLM

See Green, M. (1997) *The Gods of the Celts*.

equestrians (*equites*) Literally, 'horsemen'. In Rome's legendary past, first 300, then 600 men were chosen to serve as CAVALRY; SERVIUS TULLIUS added 1,200 more. These 1,800 men of aristocratic heritage were allocated 18 centuries in the centuriate assembly, with HORSES provided and maintained by the state. By the late 2nd century BC, when AUXILIARIES had largely replaced the cavalry, the equestrians became a class of wealthy non-senators who served on juries and on the staffs of military commanders, and provided other services like tax collection. In 67 BC, the TRIBUNE Roscius Otho essentially created a new *equites* class, granting the title and privileges of the old equestrians to this group which now included wealthy men from all Italy, with the requisite free birth and a census valuation of 400,000 *sestertii*. With sufficient land and WEALTH, they could choose to join the SENATE, but most preferred not to take an active role in politics.

EQUESTRIANS: (a) sources and types of posts.

Prospective equestrians
Legionary centurions
Chief centurions (*primi pili*)
Wealthy provincial Roman citizens

Equestrian posts	Number c.AD 150
Prefect of 500 man auxiliary unit (*prima militia*)	c.270 units
Tribune of 1000 man auxiliary cohort or legionary tribune (*secunda militia*)	40 units or 141 positions
Prefect of 500 man cavalry *ala* (*tertia militia*)	90 units
Prefect of 1000 man cavalry *ala* (*quarta militia*)	9 units
Junior procuratorial post [LX (60,000 *sestertii*) from Domitian]	See Table (b) below
Medium rank procuratorial posts [C (100,000 *sestertii*) from Domitian]	See Table (b) below
High rank procuratorial posts [CC (200,000 *sestertii*) from Domitian]	See Table (b) below
Special posts, e.g. prefect of Egypt, praetorian prefect, prefect of the Annona	3

Although there was no format career path (*cursus honorum*) like that for senators, some equestrians specialized in one area of administration or military affairs.

EQUESTRIANS: (b) growth in number of posts.

Emperor	Total	LX	C	CC	CCC
Augustus	23				
Tiberius	25				
Caligula	27				
Claudius	38				
Nero	46				
Vespasian	57				
Domitian	64	13	22	29	
Trajan	84	21	29	34	
Hadian	104	35	35	34	
Antoninus Pius	107	35	37	35	
Marcus Aurelius	125	42	49	33	1
Commodus	135	49	49	36	1
Septimius Severus	173	71	56	36	10
Philip	182	77	58	36	11

There was growth in the number of equestrian posts over time, from only 23 under Augustus to 182 by the mid-3rd century. In addition there were about 600 military officers, including chief centurions (*primi pili*). Posts were not necessarily held in order and many appointments were for more than one year, so the number available each year was in reality more restricted.

The early emperors relied heavily on equestrian advisers, who could originate anywhere in the empire. Especially from the reign of HADRIAN, they became an important part of the imperial civil service in place of FREEDMEN, with stipulated salaries and a system of promotion. Over time, more posts were filled with equestrians, even in the military. By the end of the 4th century AD, equestrians were no longer a distinct class. JV

equites see EQUESTRIANS.

Erasmus (Desiderius Erasmus) c.AD 1466–1536 Possibly the most renowned scholar of his time, he was born in Rotterdam and educated by the Brethren of the Common Life, a group of teachers who emphasized the need for self-reflection in CHRISTIAN spirituality. After becoming an Augustinian canon and priest, he taught in the Low Countries, France, Italy, England and Switzerland.

Erasmus wrote voluminously. One important section of his works was didactic, notably the *Enchiridion militis Christiani* (*Handbook of the Christian Soldier*) and the satirical *Moriae encomium* (*Praise of Folly*). Another section dealt with contemporary religious controversy, especially in debate with Martin Luther. Special mention must be made of his many scholarly and philological works, not least of which being his edition of the NEW TESTAMENT in Greek (accompanied by his own Latin translation) in 1516. He also edited, solely or with collaborators, an astonishing range of classical works by ARISTOTLE, CATO, CICERO, LIVY, PTOLEMY, SENECA, SUETONIUS and TERENCE among others, not to mention his editorial work concerning patristic authors. He actively promoted the study of the classics in works such as *De copia*, a manual proposing the best ways to write and speak Latin; its popularity was such that it was reprinted well over 100 times before the end of the 16th century. GF

See Erasmus, *Collected Works* (1974– ; 41 of 86 proposed vols. published to date); Dickens, A. G. and Jones, W. R. D. (1994) *Erasmus the Reformer*; Jardine, L. (1993) *Erasmus, Man of Letters*; Schoek, R. J. (1990) *Erasmus of Europe*.

Eratosthenes c.285–194 BC Greek MATHEMATICIAN, PHILOSOPHER, cosmologist, GEOGRAPHER and chronographer from CYRENE, who worked at Athens and for many years at ALEXANDRIA as head of Ptolemy III's LIBRARY. Like many ancient thinkers, he often published his work in poetic form. He researched classical drama, and may have been the first to call himself a *philologos*, meaning roughly 'literary scholar'. He updated the list of OLYMPIAN victors and revised Greek CHRONOLOGY, starting with the presumed date of the TROJAN WAR. Among his many mathematical works was a calculation of the circumference of the earth, whose remarkable accuracy is less important than the logical method employed, comparing the lengths of noonday shadows in places c.7 degrees apart in latitude. STRABO preserves a summary of this work, and of Eratosthenes' compendious world geography. In other fields, his legacy was equally important. Something of a free-thinker, he believed that people should be judged not by whether they were Greek or BARBARIAN but by their moral worth. He was allegedly nicknamed Beta, 'Number Two', because, while he was expert in more fields than most, someone surpassed him in each. This versatility, however, was a hallmark of hellenistic SCIENCE as an élite pursuit, and Eratosthenes ranks among the most innovative of ancient thinkers. DGJS

See Thomas, I., trs. (1941) *Greek Mathematical Works*, vol. 1; Blomqvist, J. (1992) Alexandrian science: the case of

Eratosthenes, in P. Bilde et al., eds., *Ethnicity in Hellenistic Egypt* 53–75; Irby-Massie, G. L. and Keyser, P.T. (2002) *Greek Science of the Hellenistic Era*.

Erechtheion see ACROPOLIS, ATHENIAN; ARCHITECTURE, GREEK; ATHENS; CARYATIDS; TEMPLES, GREEK.

Eretria see EUBOIA; IONIAN REVOLT; PERSIAN EMPIRE.

Erinna Poetess of the mid-4th century BC who lived on the ISLAND of Telos, near RHODES. According to ancient sources, she died when still very young, probably at the age of 19. She composed in her local Doric dialect, with numerous Aiolisms, a poem of 300 hexameters on the death of her friend Baukis, to whom she also dedicated two EPIGRAMS. Meleager of Gadara (1st century BC) reproduced the epigrams in his *Garland*. Only a few fragments survive of the longer poem to Baukis (*The Distaff*). In it, Erinna lamented the separation that first MARRIAGE, then DEATH brought to the two friends. She remembered their common work and common play in a tender and lively manner, full of small private details. Her thematic stance is very personal, and her style and metre prefigures hellenistic developments, especially the genre of the *epyllion* ('little epic'). RBC

See Arthur, M. B. (1980) The tortoise and the mirror: Erinna PSI 1090, *CW* 74: 53–65.

Eros Greek god, personification of *erôs*, sexual love (Latin *amor*, *cupido*, personified as Amor and Cupid). Eros' nature and origins were much discussed in antiquity (PLATO, *Symposium* and *Phaedrus*; PLUTARCH, *Eroticus*; ATHENAEUS 13.561–3). A philosophical conception of Eros as primitive power, establishing the world's order and binding contrasts together, co-exists with a more anthropomorphic mythology: HESIOD makes Eros both one of the four primordial cosmic principles and 'fairest among the immortal gods' (*Theogony* 120–2). From at least the 6th century BC his mother is usually APHRODITE, his father less regularly Ares. In art he is the constant associate of Aphrodite, inclined to multiply (pl. *Erôtes*), and indistinguishable from other winged youths sometimes identified by inscriptions as Pothos ('Yearning') or Himeros ('Desire'). In SCULPTURE of the classical period he is the ideal youth, embodiment of the desirable. His bow and arrows are first mentioned by EURIPIDES (*Iphigeneia in Aulis* 548–9); these become his regular attributes in hellenistic literature and art, where he has a more playful image as the mischievous child of Aphrodite, frequently punished – hence Eros' later iconography as putto. Despite his ubiquity, his cult is not well documented. Pausanias (9.27.1–5) describes his major sanctuary at Thespiai (BOIOTIA) as 'ancient', with an aniconic cult statue and the Erotidia festival, comparing in importance a sanctuary at Parion in Mysia. At Athens, Eros was worshipped alongside Aphrodite on the north slope of the ACROPOLIS, with an annual festival on 14 Mounychion. We also hear of a cult among the Theban Sacred Band, and private cult in GYMNASIA. EJS

See Hermary, A. et al. (1986) Eros, in *LIMC* vol. 3, 850–942; Thornton, B. S. (1997) *Eros*.

 MARRIAGE: (b).

Erythrai see EAST GREECE.

Essenes Attested in Judaea in the late hellenistic and early Roman period, the Essenes espoused a distinctively ASCETIC type of JUDAISM. The fullest account of their lifestyle and theology is to be found in JOSEPHUS, *Jewish War* 2.119–61. They are also mentioned more briefly by Josephus elsewhere, by PHILO, and by the pagan polymath PLINY THE ELDER, who, however, nowhere called them JEWS. Josephus described the Essenes as adherents of one of three main PHILOSOPHIES in Judaism. If this evaluation was correct, it is curious that the other two, Pharisaism and Sadducaism, are frequently mentioned in the NEW TESTAMENT and rabbinic texts but that Essenes are not. Opinion is divided as to how common Essenism was. According to Josephus and Philo, the Essenes numbered more than 4,000 and were settled in every town in Palestine. If Pliny is correct in his reference to a city of the Essenes located near the Dead Sea, this must have been only one of their communal centres.

Essenes followed a severe regime, wearing a distinctive uniform, holding all property in common, adhering to strict purity rules and a restrictive interpretation of the sabbath laws, and devoting themselves to BIBLE study. The main communal activities seem to have centred on meals. Admission to the group was apparently open only to adult males who prized CELIBACY, though Josephus refers to a second order of Essenes who married. Distinctive teachings included the attribution of a particularly important role to destiny and to angels, and a belief in the immortality of the SOUL. They were thought to have special expertise as healers and as PROPHETS of the future.

Many scholars have considered that the DEAD SEA SCROLLS were produced by Essenes because of the location of the Essene community given by Pliny and because of some parallels between Essene customs and those recorded in some of the sectarian scrolls, but the hypothesis remains uncertain. MDG

See Vermes, G. and Goodman, M. (1989) *The Essenes according to the Classical Sources*.

estates see INHERITANCE; LEGACIES; WILLS; see also ACCOUNTING; AGRICULTURE, ROMAN; APOLLONIOS THE *DIOIKÊTÊS*; HERONINOS; LAND AND PROPERTY; MANAGERS; RURAL SETTLEMENT; VILLAS.

Eteocretans The Homeric term for inhabitants of eastern CRETE, meaning 'true Cretans'. In *Odyssey* book 19 they are noted as one of five peoples on the island together with Kydonians (probably from western Crete), ACHAIANS, Dorians (Greek-speakers) and PELASGIANS. The EPIC reference is supported by some historical and EPIGRAPHICAL evidence. Apparently the people of eastern Crete spoke a different language from Greek. This non-Indo-European language was used in historical times, and inscriptions exist from the city of Praisos in eastern Crete that use Greek letters to write a non-Greek language. The implication of this information is that the Eteocretans were the remnants of the original non-Greek-speaking inhabitants of the island. This would associate them with MINOANS in modern parlance. The conquest of Crete by MYCENAEANS in the 15th century BC may have driven some Minoans into the rugged eastern parts of the island.

Recent archaeological work in eastern Crete has revealed that there was a thriving community around 1300 BC, in the late Minoan period. Architectural remains and cult material show clear links to Minoan culture, but the basic domestic assemblages are also very similar to late Mycenaean ones. VILLAGES and refuge sites from the period are found in various parts of the isthmus of Ierápetra (ancient Hierapytna). The refuge sites seem to be occupied when the island is experiencing troubles around 1200 BC. This hellenized Minoan culture may very well have been labelled by the Greeks as Eteocretan. If so, they remained an identifiable cultural group into the historical period. AJ

See Whitley, J. (1998) From Minoans to Eteocretans: the Praisos region 1200–500 BC, in W. G. Cavanagh and M. Curtis, eds., *Post-Minoan Crete* 27–39.

ethics The area of philosophy which investigates human character and action, values, right and wrong, good and bad. Ancient histories of philosophy often claim that ethical investigation was inaugurated by SOCRATES, who based many of his enquiries around the question 'How should one live?' Certainly, Socrates was the first to concentrate on these issues, but there are signs of similar interests among his predecessors. After Socrates, the investigation of the good human life became a major concern for all thinkers and eventually one of the three canonical parts of philosophy, alongside physics and logic.

Ancient ethical discussions are 'eudaimonist' theories, concerned with providing a recipe for attaining happiness or well-being (Greek *eudaimonia*). As such, they are importantly unlike more modern consequentialist or deontological ethical systems in their concentration on the individual agent and his or her character, motivation, and beliefs and on the creation of a 'good life'. Ancient ethical thinking, therefore, also connects closely with discussions of human psychology and such questions as whether there are incorrigible, irrational sources of motivation within us, and how we can effect moral improvement and changes of character. It also tends to find grounding in some account of 'human nature', what it is to live a human life and, therefore, what it is to live a good human life. Following ARISTOTLE, the hellenistic philosophical schools each promoted a goal (Greek *telos*) which, if achieved, would produce well-being. Each school promoted a different conception of the goal: for the STOICS it was virtue, for the EPICUREANS pleasure. JIW

See Aristotle, *Nicomachean Ethics*; Annas, J. (1993) *The Morality of Happiness*; Irwin, T. (1995) *Plato's Ethics*.

Ethiopia and Ethiopians The Greeks designated the lands south of Egypt as 'Ethiopia', comprising the ancient kingdoms of Kush (Nubia), Meroë and Aksum (modern Ethiopia and Sudan). This area was presumed to contain the source of the NILE. Ethiopia was familiarly known as the land of the 'burnt-skinned people', a title reflected in artistic depictions of Ethiopians. The racial characteristics of black Africans are often depicted in careful detail in Greek ART, where emphasis is placed on the noses, hair and body proportions which, to the Greek mind, render the figures 'Ethiopian'. The images are used to highlight the difference between noble Greeks and barbarian Ethiopians. Thus HERAKLES, the ultimate Greek hero, is shown fighting the Ethiopian priests of Busiris, and Memnon, the white-skinned Greek hero, is shown ruling over dark-skinned Ethiopian subjects. In some artworks Ethiopians, as polar opposites of the Greeks, are depicted in 'PERSIAN' costume. This might have a basis in reality, since Greeks would have seen the Ethiopian mercenaries who made up part of XERXES' army during his invasion of Greece. From the 6th century BC, Greeks made regular visits to Ethiopia, though an expansion in TRADE and cultural interchange occurred during the period of PTOLEMAIC rule in Egypt. It was via Ethiopian Red sea routes that the Greeks began to trade with INDIA.

The contact between the classical world and Ethiopia continued under Roman domination. The Romans routinely applied the term *Aethiopes* to any black (or dark-skinned) people they encountered through their conquests, regardless of true nationality. For the Romans, *Aethiopes* designated a particular physiognomy constituted not only by skin colour, but by a combination of traits including crinkly hair, thick lips and a flat nose. Whether the Romans considered these racial traits attractive is difficult to know. One text (Luxorius 67) extols the features of the black GLADIATOR Olympius as a HERCULES carved from ebony, but another (HELIODORUS' *Aethiopica*) represents the fictional Ethiopian princess Chariklea as white-skinned with blonde hair, rather than as black – despite her black parentage. Heliodorus probably obeys a literary convention whereby heroines uphold the canons of contemporary beauty. In classical literature, particularly late novels, Ethiopia is a quasi-mythical fantasy land of strange sights and topsy-turvy customs. These classical sources betray the fact that the Ethiopian kingdoms were powerful and culturally sophisticated societies. The Meroitic kingdom, in particular, passed successively under Greek and Roman domination while retaining its unique culture. During the height of its power in the 2nd and 3rd centuries AD, Meroë continued a pharaonic tradition, based on Egyptian prototypes, among a line of rulers who raised stelae to record their achievements and erected pyramids as TOMBS. A remarkably large number of reigning queens, known as Kandakes, are recorded in the history of Meroë. This forms a link with the MATRIARCHAL traditions of Africa and the high status accorded to women in Nubian culture. LL-J

See Phillipson, D.W. (1998) *Ancient Ethiopia*; Snowden, F. M. (1970) *Blacks in Antiquity*; Welsby, D. A. (1998) *The Kingdom of Kush*.

ethnicity and identity If an ethnic group is defined as a group of people who can see themselves as different from other groups on the basis of perceived differences in socio-cultural practices, including RELIGION, LANGUAGE, and/or ancestral origins, then ethnicity is all of the shared socio-cultural phenomena that enable an ethnic group to identify themselves as a collective entity. Thus, ethnicity is one form of IDENTITY, since it is dependent on, and propagated by, comparative mechanisms that result from interaction with others.

The discipline of ARCHAEOLOGY has had a significant impact on the concept of ethnicity. This is particularly true of the development of culture-historical archaeology, which emphasizes the correlation between distinct cultural assemblages and the collective groups which produced them. The implicit assumption behind this approach holds that CULTURE was a bounded entity, whose material remains can be identified with distinct ethnic, or racial, groupings. Consequently, the idea that culture was static, with a one-to-one correlation between material remains and ethnic groupings, became a primary tenet in the identification of prehistoric groups through space and time. An obvious example is the identification of 'CELTIC' culture with a 'Celtic' people, suggesting that the two are mutually inclusive. This relationship between ethnicity and culture – the idea that particular races or nations are distinct, objectified entities which can be identified through their cultural artefacts – was further advanced in the rise of nationalist archaeology during the 1940s. This was most notable in countries with a set political agenda.

The archaeological investigation of ethnicity has also had grave consequences in the contemporary world of politics. This is particularly the case in countries with internal divisions regarding land claim disputes and/or threatened minorities. In these instances, the identification of past ethnic groups is projected into the present with the aim of validating modern claims over land ownership and heritage management. The political implication that archaeology can be used to construct and inflame modern identities has led to a critical assessment of both the concept of ethnicity and the discipline's ability to legitimately identify it in the past. MLM

See Jones, S. (1997) *The Archaeology of Ethnicity.*

 BLACKS.

ethnoarchaeology As a term, ethnoarchaeology can be defined as the application of information concerning the lifeways of non-Western societies of the present or recent past for the purpose of interpreting archaeological data. Although archaeologists have always used this approach, it only appeared as a specific concept in the 1960s. The approach has been widely used where there is a direct connection between modern native peoples and their prehistoric past. It has been less commonly used in Europe. Ethnoarchaeological studies in MEDITERRANEAN lands have been concentrated in Greece, partly because of its 'exotic' culture. Studies elsewhere, e.g. North AFRICA and Italy, provide significant exceptions.

The underdevelopment of AGRICULTURE in Mediterranean lands allowed earlier generations of scholars to assume little change between the TECHNOLOGY and culture of 20th-century rural populations they knew and that of ancient societies. But it was only after the Second World War, with the recognition by ANTHROPOLOGISTS that Mediterranean societies were worthy of study, that genuinely ethnographic studies were conducted. Early examples were linked to archaeological research into ancient Greek LANDSCAPES.

Shepherding and crop processing have been two foci of ethnoarchaeology in the Mediterranean. An early example, aimed at interpreting ANIMAL bones, studied shepherding and the teeth of living sheep in Turkey (Payne). More generalized ethnographic information was used in many papers presented at a conference on shepherding in the ancient world (Whittaker). The conference raised a still unresolved question over the relevance of modern data on TRANSHUMANT (migratory) shepherding to classical antiquity.

Studies of primitive CEREALS, and the ways in which crops are grown and processed, have been used to interpret finds of carbonized seeds. Pioneering work was done in Turkey, with subsequent research being conducted in Greece and Spain. Such studies have helped archaeologists understand a variety of aspects of crop processing and storage, for example at the late Bronze Age site of Assiros.

During the 1990s, ethnoarchaeologists began to question the assumption of timelessness and direct continuity from antiquity which underlay a large number of earlier studies. This resulted partly from research into the histories of the communities being studied. Far from being static, these communities have changed, often radically, over the last few centuries. By recognizing the dynamism and fluidity of traditional societies in the Mediterranean region, ethnoarchaeologists are now able to recognize the flexibility of ancient populations and their ability to respond to changing circumstances, just like their modern counterparts (Sutton). HAF

See Aschenbrenner, S. (1972) A contemporary community, in W. A. McDonald and G. R. Rapp, *The Minnesota Messenia Expedition* 47–63; Barker, G. and Grant, A. (1991) Ancient and modern pastoralism in central Italy: an interdisciplinary study in the Ciccolano mountains, *PBSR* 59: 15–88; Jameson, M. H. (1976) A Greek countryside: reports from the Argolid Exploration Project, *Expedition* 19: 2–4; Jones, G. et al. (1986) Crop storage at Assiros, *Scientific American* 254.3: 96–103; Mattingly, D. J. (1985) Olive oil production in Roman Tripolitania, in D. J. Buck and D. J. Mattingly, *Town and Country in Roman Tripolitania* 27–46; Payne, S. (1973) Kill-off patterns in sheep and goats: the mandibles from Aşvan Kale, *Anatolian Studies* 23: 281–303; Whittaker, C. R., ed. (1988) *Pastoral Economies in Classical Antiquity.*

etiquette There is perhaps no more fruitful place to look at etiquette (defined by the *Oxford English Dictionary* as 'conventional rules of personal behaviour in polite society') than at the dinner table. In ancient and modern societies, it has been argued that dining etiquette exists in order to distance human eating from that of ANIMALS. In reality it is designed to make the privileged classes more distinct from the less privileged, and to buttress that privilege. The complexity of etiquette, the demands it makes, and the restraint it enjoins require learning and relative affluence. Greeks and Romans ate while reclining, propped up on one elbow on COUCHES arranged in a semicircular layout. Food was taken from tables in the middle of the room. This mode of ingestion, requiring both surplus capital and affluence, could not have easily been practised by SLAVE classes. At any rate, advice on table etiquette provided by PLUTARCH (*Quaestiones convivales*), ATHENAEUS (*Deipnosophistai*), and Clement of Alexandria (*Christ the Pedagogue*) seems as class-based as we might expect. They stress the need for restraint: one should not thrust one's face towards the food, nor grab and snatch and gouge at it. The same strictures apply to drinking. One should not gulp at WINE, nor spill it on oneself. Spitting, sneezing, nose-blowing and belching are similarly frowned upon. Too much talk during the meal itself seems to have been discouraged. This was saved for the drinks, which were served after the eating. Even here there were rules: the wine was watered to a respectable strength, and talk often centred on pre-agreed topics. Restraint and complex convention, therefore, ruled the table of the ÉLITE, a restraint no doubt irrelevant to the tables of the poor. PGT

See Douglas, M. (1972) Deciphering a meal, *Daedalus* 101: 61–81; Goody, J. (1982) *Cooking, Cuisine and Class*; Leyelle, B. (1995) Clement of Alexandria on the importance of table etiquette, *JECS* 3: 123–41.

Etruria and Etruscans Natural boundaries, formed by the TIBER and Arno RIVERS as well as the Tyrrhenian sea, divide Etruria geographically into three regions. Southern Etruria, known for its volcanic terrain, extends along a major portion of the Tiber at Orvieto and aligns itself along the sea as far as the Tolfa and Ceriti mountains; its major cities include VEII, CERVETERI (Caere), TARQUINIA, Vulci and Volsinii. The Maremma, an area noted for its mineral wealth (IRON, COPPER, SILVER), comprises alluvial plain and tufa outcrops; the region extends along the Tyrrhenian coast from Pyrgi to Populonia. Central Etruria, with its rolling hills, lakes and prime AGRICULTURAL land, branches from the north of Orvieto and inland from the Maremma; Perugia, Cortona, Arezzo, Fiesole, Volterra and Chiusi are its major cities. The Etruscan presence is felt elsewhere in southern Italy in the Campanian settlement at CUMAE. The Etruscans referred to themselves as *Rasenna*, a reference to a prominent leader. The

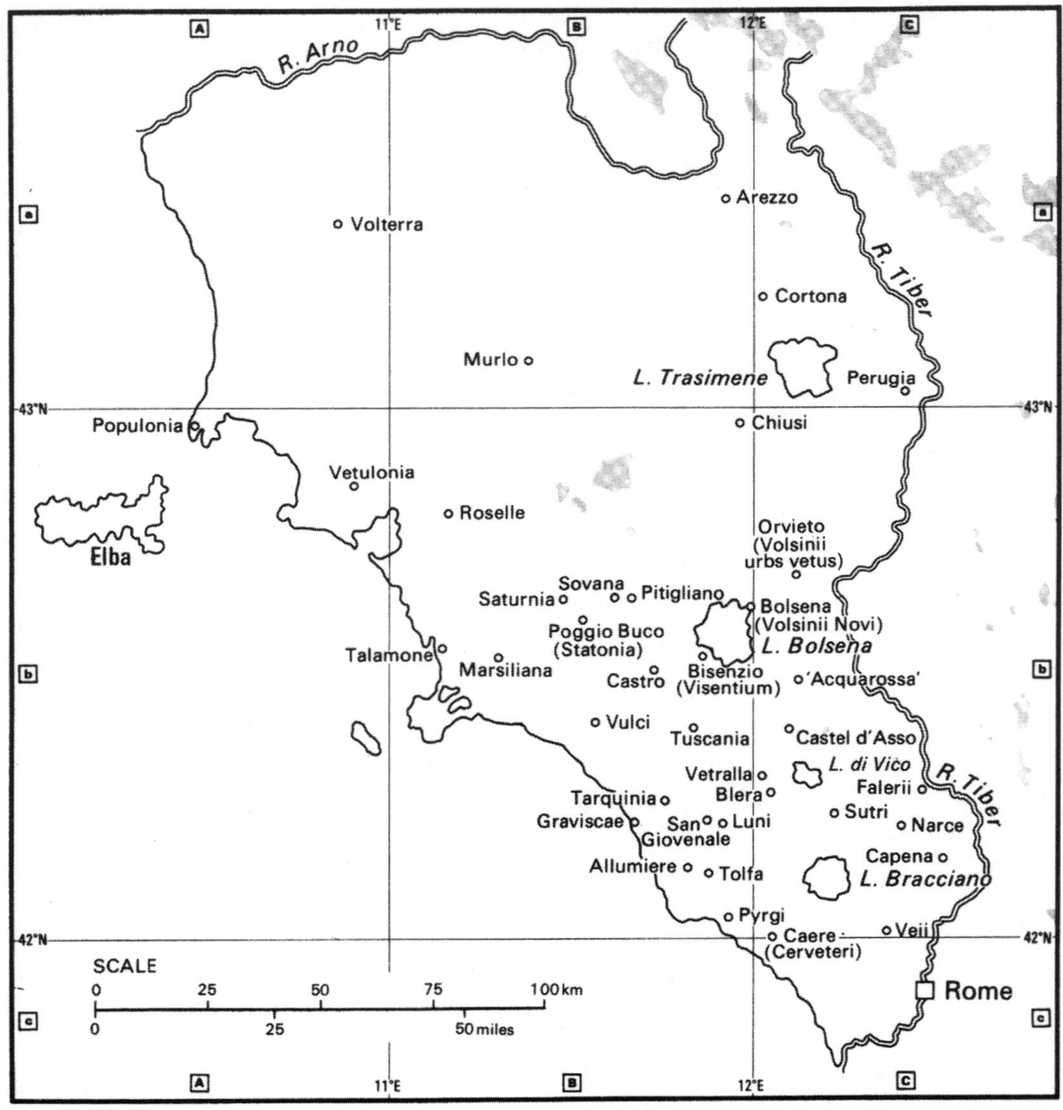

ETRURIA AND ETRUSCANS: map.

Romans named them *Tusci* or *Etrusci*, while the Greeks called them *Tyrrhenoi* or *Tyrsenoi*.

Etruscan civilization developed from the Iron Age Villanovan culture (900–720 BC). Cities began to emerge in the orientalizing period (725–575). Trade relations are manifest with the appearance of foreign cultural influences in the archaeological record. Both PHOENICIANS and Greeks settled and traded in the environs of Etruria because of the rich mineral deposits of iron and copper. The Greeks brought new POTTERY techniques and styles. Refined clay, pottery wheels and geometric styles were introduced, especially in southern Etruria. The Etruscans subsequently developed a ceramic style distinctly their own: bucchero, a shiny black, wheel-made pottery made with purified clay. Bucchero, exported via maritime trade, can be found in Provence and Spain, throughout Italy, in CARTHAGE, in Syria and in parts of Asia Minor.

At this time, Etruscan inscriptions appear more frequently in the archaeological record. The alphabet uses EUBOIAN letters, indicating Etruscan contact with Euboian settlers near Naples. Unfortunately, no major works of literature appear in the archaeological record; rather, inscriptions are the only sources that scholars have to work with. Other foreign influences appear in one of the best-preserved tomb groups from this period, the Regolini Galassi from Cerveteri, currently housed in the Vatican Museum. Weaponry, bucchero statuettes, GOLD, JEWELLERY, IVORY jars, and a gold breastplate all show strong Egyptian and Phoenician traits, but were made locally. In general, new forms of wealth begin to appear in Etruscan TOMBS. Gold and silver jewellery and vessels, CORINTHIAN pottery, faience, and Near Eastern bronzes are some of the luxury items interred with the dead.

In general, tombs can be found outside, or on the slopes of, cities built on hillsides or hilltops for defensive purposes. Tombs vary in architectural style: they can be hewn into a rocky hillside, free-standing and of local limestone, or covered by tumuli and with their foundations carved into the rock. Tombs are typically aligned along streets, and have doors leading into chambers. Decoration on their wall surfaces includes fresco paintings and sculptural relief. Scenes include funerary GAMES and men and women banqueting, complete with DANCERS, MUSICIANS and servants. Types of interment include both cremation and inhumation. Stone stelae or *cippi* could also demarcate tombs. A major agricultural innovation for the production of cereals, olives and grapes is the *cuniculi*, or rock-cut drainage channels, which both irrigated dry soils and drained marshy areas.

In the archaic period (c.575–480 BC) the Etruscan cities flourished. Societal groups were arranged in clans. WOMEN had prominent roles in society and, unlike Greek women, were given honours equal to men at death; they were also permitted to participate in banquets and walk the streets unaccompanied. The aristocracy used a naming system quite different from those of their Roman and Greek counterparts, a double-name system incorporating a first name and family name. In some instances, inscriptions referring to deceased Etruscan males add a father's or mother's name to the double name. From the 4th or 3rd century onwards, a separate name or *cognomen* is given. Etruscan females incorporated the double name, but once married they added their husband's name to their nomenclature. Some prominent aristocratic males became kings at Rome: TARQUINIUS PRISCUS (Tarquin I, 616–579) and TARQUINIUS SUPERBUS (Tarquin the Proud, or Tarquin II, 534–509).

During the classical period, 480–300 BC, Etruria was in the midst of conflict with the Romans, the SAMNITES and the SYRACUSANS. Local artistic production consists of red-figure pottery and bronze mirrors that include domestic and mythological scenes. Traded goods such as Attic pottery begin to diminish in the archaeological record, as does the quality of bronze and sculpture. By 280 the Romans dominated the Etruscan city-states.

Although the Etruscans emulated the Olympian pantheon, the role of the goddess was prevalent, especially in terms of fertility and healing. DEMONS, both male and female, escorted the dead from this world to the afterworld. The *Disciplina Etrusca*, Etruscan religious writings no longer preserved in their entirety, figure highly. For example, books known as the *haruspicini* allowed the *haruspex*, a priest or diviner, to interpret signs found in animal entrails. Bronze statuettes reveal how these priests were dressed: typically they wore mantles over tunics pinned by a fibula, boots and a conical hat. Other parts of the *Disciplina* were books on lightning and books of rituals dealing with the foundation of sanctuaries and cities, as well as the division of land.

Prominent figures who brought Etruscology to the front were George Dennis, a late 19th-century aristocratic traveller who documented the major sites of Etruria (*Cities and Cemeteries of Etruria*, 1883), and the English author D.H. Lawrence, who toured Etruria in 1927 and wrote about his experiences in his book *Etruscan Places*. Massimo Pallottino was responsible for legitimizing the study of the Etruscans in the Italian academy in the 1940s. (see also LAND SURVEYING) LAH

See Bonfante, L., ed. (1986) *Etruscan Life and Afterlife*; Haynes, S. (2000) *Etruscan Civilization*.

 FIELD SURVEY: (a); ITALY: (a); SACRIFICE: (b)–(c).

Etruria, Roman see ITALY, ROMAN.

Etruscans see ETRURIA AND ETRUSCANS.

Euboia (Euboea) Long narrow island along the north-east coast of ATTICA and BOIOTIA (c.3,600 sq km, 1,400 sq miles). The island's strategic position allowed it to dominate TRADE within and beyond the AEGEAN. It was rich in TIMBER resources, and the fertile plain of Lelanton along its south-west coast supported a prosperous agricultural base, growing CEREALS, vines and OLIVES. Euboia also has IRON resources and traditionally COPPER MINES, but the latter were worked out by the classical period. The major prehistoric site was at LEFKANDÍ, and from the archaic period the two main cities were Eretria and Chalkis, governed by horse-breeding ARISTOCRACIES (the Hippeis and Hippobotai respectively). In the late 8th century the two cities went to war for control of the Lelantine plain. The so-called Lelantine war, traditionally won by Chalkis, is extremely shadowy but, if real, may have been the first large-scale war after the Bronze Age.

Eretria was established in the 8th century, and a TEMPLE to APOLLO Daphnephoros was built there between 750 and 700. Eretria was destroyed by the PERSIANS in 490 for aiding the IONIAN REVOLT of 499. Later Eretria was a member of the Delian league. Chalkis is situated on the narrowest part of the straits between Euboia and the Greek mainland, where the famous Euripos current changes direction twice daily. The town dominated Aegean trade. It had a reputation for bronze-working; its name means 'Brazen Town'. Athens defeated Chalkis in 506, confiscating its land and setting up a cleruchy. Chalkis revolted unsuccessfully in 446 and again in 411. In 377 the Euboian cities joined the second Athenian confederacy, but between 371 and 358 they came under THEBAN domination. They formed the Euboian league in 341, but in 338 PHILIP II occupied Chalkis and used the city as a stronghold to control Greece. In the hellenistic period it continued to be a Macedonian strongpoint, one of the 'fetters of Greece'. The Euboian league was revived in 196 but abolished by Rome in 146 because of its support for the ACHAIAN league. In the Roman imperial period, Euboia was incorporated in the province of Achaia.

Euboia played an important role in the resumption of trade between the Aegean and the Near East in the first millennium BC. Some of the earliest oriental imports to the Greek world are found at Lefkandí, dating from the 10th century. From around 800 Euboian pottery is found in large quantities along the Levantine coast and on CYPRUS; a Euboian mercantile presence has been suggested at the Syrian trading post of AL MINA.

Euboia was at the forefront of the COLONIZATION movement in the west, motivated by trade rather than acquiring agricultural land. The earliest Euboian colony at PITHEKOUSSAI, on the island of Ischia, was established c.750 BC. Other Euboian colonies are Kyme, later CUMAE, on the Italian mainland opposite Ischia; Naxos, Leontinoi and Katane (Catana) on SICILY; and Zankle, Mylai and Rhegion (Reggio) on the straits between Sicily and Italy. The main phase of Euboian colonization dates to between 740 and 730. After 700, active Euboian interest in the west dwindles. CHALKIDIKE, in northern Greece, was also colonized by the Euboians in the 8th century and takes its name from Chalkis. LFS

See Boardman, J. (1988) *The Greeks Overseas* (rev. edn); Cahiers du Centre Jean Bérard (1975) *Contribution à l'étude de la société et de la colonisation eubéennes*; Jeffery, L. H. (1976) *Archaic Greece*; Ridgway, D. (1992) *The First Western Greeks*.

 AEGEAN SEA: (a).

Euclid (Eukleides) Although he was the author of perhaps the most important and influential geometrical work written in antiquity, the *Elements* (which continued, in various forms, to be used as an elementary textbook of geometry until the mid-20th century), virtually nothing is known of Euclid's life. Later claims (e.g. by Proclus) that he was a PLATONIST and worked in ALEXANDRIA during the reign of PTOLEMY I are based on no more than guesswork and wishful thinking, and have no independent value. He was sometimes confused with the Socratic philosopher Eukleides of Megara. All that can be said with reasonable certainty is that he preceded ARCHIMEDES (who occasionally alludes to the *Elements*) and came after the geometers of the 4th century whose work he uses.

Euclid was not the first MATHEMATICIAN to whom a systematic compilation and arrangement of geometrical theorems is attributed, and it is hard to be sure to what extent he based his work on that of his predecessors. Certainly he used the work of Theaitetos on irrational lines, and took from Eudoxos his theory of proportion and the so-called 'method of exhaustion' (a technique for handling the relationship between rectilinear figures and figures bounded by curves without involving infinite divisibility). It is not possible to say which parts of the work, if any, are Euclid's own contribution. The *Elements* aims to present geometry as a closely argued system starting from self-evident and undemonstrable axioms (which Euclid divides somewhat arbitrarily into 'postulates' and 'common notions'), several of which were controversial even in antiquity.

The first six books are on plane geometry and cover both rectilinear figures and circles; the treatment of the theory of proportion in book 5 (probably based on the work of Eudoxos) represents one of the most impressive achievements of Greek mathematics. Books 7 and 9 deal with number theory, book 10 is on irrational numbers, and books 11–13 are on solid geometry. The *Elements* became the basis for the development of all later geometry. It rapidly established itself as a fundamental mathematical textbook, and insofar as educated Greeks and Romans acquired any knowledge at all of MATHEMATICS at school, it was of the first few books of Euclid. In the 5th century AD Proclus composed a commentary on the first book of the *Elements*, as an introduction to geometrical method for students of philosophy; in the course of this work he gives us almost all of the information were have on geometry before Euclid.

Other surviving works of Euclid are the *Data* (on what must be 'given' in geometrical construction), the *Phainomena* (on spherical geometry), the *Optics* (on the geometrical aspects of optics), and *On Divisions* (surviving only in Arabic translation). A number of other surviving works are dubiously attributed to him, and the titles of several lost works are recorded in ancient sources. RW

See Heath, T. L. (1926) *Euclid: the thirteen books of the Elements*.

Eudoxos (astronomer) see ARATOS OF SOLOI; EUCLID; HIPPARCHOS OF NIKAIA; KNIDOS; MATHEMATICIANS; MATHEMATICS.

euergetism see BENEFACTORS AND BENEFACTION, GREEK; LITURGIES.

Euesperides Greek city, now in the eastern suburbs of Benghazi (Libya), founded c.600 BC and first mentioned in literature by Herodotos as the easternmost point of the Persian advance in 515. We hear of it again in 414, besieged by LIBYAN tribes and only relieved by the fortuitous arrival of a Spartan fleet under Gylippos en route to Sicily. In 405 the city invited other Greeks to settle and help defend the city against the Libyans, and the population was increased by a contingent of MESSENIANS, who left again in 369. The city government included a COUNCIL (*boulê*), EPHORS and elders (*gerontes*). Euesperides minted its own bronze and silver COINAGE from the last quarter of the 4th century BC onward. The city was abandoned after the death of Magas, governor of CYRENAICA, c.250 BC, when the population was transferred to Berenike.

The site consists of a *tell* mound on a low spur between two lagoons, with a 5th-century extension to the south on flat ground which shows evidence for at least two phases of gridded street plan on slightly different alignments. EXCAVATIONS have uncovered three phases of defences (the latest, it appears, from not long before the city's abandonment) and numerous phases of housing, some with floors in pebble and early tessellated MOSAICS. There is also evidence for purple dye production from *Murex* shellfish, and the pottery indicates extensive TRADE with the AEGEAN, Sicily and the Punic world. AIW

See Buzaian, A.M. and Lloyd, J. A. (1996) Early urbanism in Cyrenaica: new evidence from Euesperides (Benghazi), *Libyan Studies* 27: 129–52.

 CYRENE AND CYRENAICA: (a).

Eukleides see EUCLID.

Eumachia A prominent Pompeian woman in the reign of AUGUSTUS, the details of whose life are vague. She was daughter of a man called Lucius, had a son called Marcus Numistrius Fronto, and may have been married to an eponymously named *duovir* (senior magistrate) of POMPEII of AD 2/3. At any rate she was evidently widowed young, as it was she who dedicated, at her own expense and partly on her son's behalf, a large public building complex at the south-east corner of the FORUM in Pompeii. This incorporates a shrine to CONCORDIA Augusta and Pietas, and has statuary of AENEAS and ROMULUS in niches on the front facing the forum – reminiscent of Augustan monuments in Rome. The overall interpretation of the building has been much debated, not least because a statue of Eumachia in her role as public PRIESTESS was dedicated within it by the town's guild of FULLERS. A religious dimension is clearly present, but utilitarian buildings in Roman towns often incorporated shrines. However, suggestions that this was some sort of a cloth market or a guildhall of the fullers can be dismissed. The more likely possibilities are that it was formally a public space (*porticus*) where a variety of business and social interaction could take place. Through her endowment of this enigmatic building, with its EPIGRAPHIC testimonies to her and her son, Eumachia demonstrates the prominent role that wealthy Roman WOMEN (especially widows) of the curial class could play in their communities. (see also AEMILIA PUDENTILLA) DJM

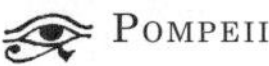 POMPEII: (a).

Eumenes I, II see PERGAMON.

Eumenes of Kardia see SUCCESSORS.

Eumenides see AESCHYLUS

eunuchs Court eunuchs were found in a number of ancient societies, as indeed in the courts of imperial CHINA and the Ottoman empire. Athenians of the 5th and 4th centuries BC were fascinated by the eunuchs of the Near Eastern court: these unmanned men were interpreted as an extreme manifestation of the effeminacy and decadence of the Persians. In the late Roman empire, powerful eunuch imperial chamberlains attended the EMPERORS and controlled access to them. Because of their deformity, lowly social origins and foreign birth, eunuchs did not challenge the power-basis of the ARISTOCRACY and the emperor, while they were also an exotic accessory of the increasingly remote ruler. In the sacred sphere, eunuch PRIESTS served the ecstatic cult of the goddess CYBELE, imported by the Romans from ASIA Minor in 205 BC. These Galli practised self-castration in honour of the mythical Attis, castrated by Cybele, his lover. In the early CHRISTIAN CHURCH, some allegedly took literally the instruction to become eunuchs and had themselves castrated. Whether or not castration in fact resulted in impotence was a matter of confusion in antiquity, as some eunuchs reputedly had intercourse with the women they were supposed to be minding, as well as with men. Castration of a man after puberty may leave him able to get erections and ejaculate. ED

See Hopkins, K. (1978) The political power of eunuchs, in *Conquerors and Slaves* 172–96; Tougher, S., ed. (2002) *Eunuchs in Antiquity and Beyond*.

Eupolis see ARISTOPHANES; COMEDY 1: OLD COMEDY.

Euripides 480–406 BC Pronounced by ARISTOTLE 'the most tragic' of the Greek poets, perhaps because of his searing dramatic representations of suffering. The youngest of the three canonical Greek playwrights of the 5th century BC in Athens, Euripides was the least successful in the dramatic competitions at the City Dionysia (he won only four prizes). By the hellenistic period, however, he had become the most popular, as well as a dominant influence on the Roman tragedies of ENNIUS, OVID and SENECA.

Euripides died in MACEDONIA during what some have argued was a 'voluntary exile' from an Athens torn by the ravages of the final years of the PELOPONNESIAN WAR and a recent OLIGARCHIC revolt against its DEMOCRACY. Euripides' drama reflects the tensions and transitions of this unsettled period. His plays confront the excesses of revenge and the ravages of WAR, with its abuse of helpless victims and its corruption of victors, yet also celebrate the glory of Athens with stirring patriotism. The controversial new PHILOSOPHY and rhetoric promulgated by the SOPHISTS co-exist in his plays with an explosion of MADNESS, erotic passion and irrational violence. Religious SCEPTICISM confronts an abiding hope that private VIRTUES such as FRIENDSHIP and altruism, or the rituals that bind humans to their society and the larger KOSMOS, can offer a fragile structure for salvation.

We have more of Euripides' original 90 plays than of the other playwrights. Ten plays represent a selection such as we have preserved for AESCHYLUS and SOPHOKLES: *Alkestis*, *Medea*, *Hippolytos*, *Andromache*, *Hekabe*, *Troades* (*Trojan Women*), *Phoinissai* (*Phoenician Women*), *Orestes*, *Bacchae* and *Rhesos* (the last perhaps not by Euripides). Of these, *Alkestis*, *Medea*, *Hippolytos* and *Bacchae* retain the most lasting reputation. A single 14th-century AD manuscript, preserving a portion of the poet's complete works in alphabetical order, includes nine additional plays: *Helenê* (*Helen*), *Elektra*, *Herakleidai*, *Herakles*, *Hiketides* (usually known by its Latin name, *Supplices*, or as *Suppliant Women*), *Iphigeneia at Aulis*, *Iphigeneia among the Taurians*, *Ion* and *Kyklops* (*Cyclops*). This random sample of Euripides' work permits us to gain an unusually broad picture of his range as a tragedian. It includes our only complete example of a SATYR play (*Kyklops*), and a number of romances or 'tragicomedies' (*Helen*, *Iphigeneia among the Taurians*, *Ion*) that confirm what we would otherwise have known only from Aristotle: that tragic reversals often achieved a relatively fortunate resolution rather than a fall to disaster.

Euripides' plays reveal how much the boundaries between tragic and comic genres were in the process of evolution in the 5th century, by including much that was later more exclusive to COMEDY: near-parody, domestic disasters, lengthy exchanges of rapid dialogue, and climactic rescues and recognitions. Indeed, one ancient source viewed Euripides for these very reasons as the father of the New Comedy of the 4th century. The comic playwright ARISTOPHANES repeatedly mocks Euripides for his lack of tragic decorum – his eloquent women and SLAVES, his domestic scenarios, his pathetic HEROES in rags – and Aristotle in his *Poetics* remarks that whereas Sophokles represented men as they ought to be, Euripides represented them as they are.

Euripides' sometimes outrageous innovations extend to the formal aspects of tragedy as well. His choral lyrics, often thought to be more tangential to the action than those of his predecessors, heighten the contrast between the greater 'realism' of his plots and characterization and the traditional myths that frame the action. Euripidean CHORUSES may express the view that 'terrible myths are gifts that call mortals to the worship of gods' (*Elektra* 743–4). Yet his characters frequently threaten to throw these myths off the expected course. In *Orestes*, for example, the plot veers entirely from tradition by threatening to condemn Orestes to death for the murder of his father AGAMEMNON and to kill HELEN for her Trojan adultery. Only the last-minute appearance of the god APOLLO on the stage machine (*mêchanê*) rescues the characters for their familiar destinies. These last-minute divine appearances are typically Euripidean, as are his formal prologues (mocked by Aristophanes in *Frogs* for their predictability) and his concluding foundation myths for cults probably still practised in his own day, which serve to tie past to present practice.

Euripides' later plays often include extravagant lyric solos or monodies that serve to define his characters' psychology and social isolation; the poet was also a devotee of the experimental 'new music' of the period. His formal rhetorical debates, which rarely reach resolution and are replete with the latest sophistic arguments and political theories, underline the plays' pessimism about the efficacy of human speech and institutions. The remarks by the historian THUCYDIDES, in his description of the revolution at Kerkyra (3.82–4), that 'war brings men's characters to the level of their fortunes', and that political unrest perverts the traditional meanings of words in the service of violence, revenge and faction, eloquently capture Euripidean drama.

Euripides' scepticism extends to his representation of GODS. On stage they are often petty and excessively anthropomorphic; but his characters seem so uncertain of divine nature that they sometimes question the traditional representation of gods in myth or even a divine concern with a human existence apparently ruled by arbitrary chance (*tychê*).

Euripides' depictions of female characters, for which he was mercilessly mocked by Aristophanes and criticized by Aristotle, range from revengeful heroines like Medea or Hekabe and women helplessly in love to wise mothers and heroic virgins who chose to sacrifice themselves for family, city or nation. The heroine of *Iphigeneia at Aulis*, for example, finally, willingly and heroically accepts her SACRIFICE to permit the Greek expedition to Troy. Aristotle, however, found her sudden change of mind implausible. He also criticizes Euripides' intellectual heroines as out of character. These heroines, like Euripides' two Melanippes, who either defend women against male denigration or have recourse to contemporary SCIENCE to defend their arguments, serve to undercut Euripides' reputation for misogyny that Aristophanes was so influential in creating. Indeed, Euripides' portrayal of women perhaps best sums up the paradoxical drama of this controversial playwright who produced, even in antiquity, so many opposing interpretations of his oeuvre. HPF

See Euripides: many translations, including a series by D. Grene and R. Lattimore (1955–9, 1-vol. edn 1992) and another from Oxford University Press pairing classicists with poets; Conacher, D. J. (1967) *Euripidean Drama*. Michelini, A. (1987) *Euripides and the Tragic Tradition*; Woolf, C. (1982) Euripides, in T. J. Luce, ed., *Ancient Writers*, vol. 1, 233–66.

Eurotas see GREECE; LACONIA; SPARTA.

Eurydike (1) (usually Eurydice) Legendary Greek heroine. The name (literally 'broad-judging') is that of a number of royal WOMEN in legend, but most famously the wife of ORPHEUS, whom he brought back from the dead. The story was known to EURIPIDES (*Alkestis* 357–62; *Iphigeneia at Aulis* 1211–14) and PLATO (*Symposium* 179d). The name is first found in the *Epitaphios for Bion* ascribed to Moschos. That Orpheus lost her for a second time is not certainly attested before the best-known treatment in VIRGIL, *Georgics* 4.453–527, in which Eurydice, pursued by Aristaeus, is bitten by a snake and dies. Orpheus descends to the Underworld and with his music charms the infernal GODS into allowing her to return to the world above, on condition that he does not look back at her on the way. On the point of reaching the light, Orpheus looks back and she disappears back to the underworld. The story was an inspiration for many later poets, including OVID (*Metamorphoses* 10.1–77) and Rilke, and is the subject of operas (including those by Monteverdi and Gluck) and films (e.g. Cocteau's *Orphée*). PRH

See Guthrie, W. K. C. (1935) *Orpheus and Greek Religion*; Linforth, I. M. (1941) *The Arts of Orpheus*; Segal, C. (1989) *The Myth of the Poet*.

Eurydike (2) Macedonian QUEEN, mother of PHILIP II and grandmother of ALEXANDER the Great. Eurydike was born c.410–404 BC, the daughter of Sirr(h)as and granddaughter of Arrhabaios of Lynkestis. She married Amyntas III of MACEDONIA c.390 and bore him three sons, Alexander, Perdikkas and Philip, all of whom became kings of Macedonia. Archaeological evidence shows that she dedicated statues to the cult of Eukleia at VERGINA. It is not known when she died, though it is likely that she was dead before 346.

Ancient literary accounts of Eurydike's involvement in politics at the Macedonian court vary considerably. In the lurid and unreliable account of Justin, she is portrayed as a CLYTEMNESTRA-like wife and mother, who plotted against her husband and murdered her sons Alexander II and Perdikkas III. Justin explains that she did this out of lust for her son-in-law, whom she intended to marry and promote to the throne. Elsewhere Ptolemy is credited with the murder of Alexander, his half-brother, in a dispute over power. Ptolemy became regent to Perdikkas and Philip, and perhaps married Eurydike. In AISCHINES' account, she is represented as a protective mother who took charge of the situation in Macedonia herself. The discrepancy in these accounts is probably related to a combination of Eurydike's marriage to Ptolemy and her active role in Macedonian politics. These factors would have been enough to implicate her in her son's murder in some minds. FMM

See Carney, E. D. (2000) *Women and Monarchy in Macedonia*.

Eurydike (3) c.337–317 BC Macedonian princess, originally named Adeia, a granddaughter of the great king PHILIP II and niece of ALEXANDER the Great. She seems one of the strongest, yet most ill-starred, royal WOMEN of the age of the SUCCESSORS. After Alexander's death in 323, she married one of his two heirs, his half-brother Philip III Arrhidaios, and took a new name which had been that of her great-grandmother EURYDIKE (1), mother of Philip II. Since her husband was thought mentally deficient, she may have been the real wielder of power. Together they sided with Kassandros against Polyperchon, regaining control of MACEDONIA until they were defeated by OLYMPIAS and Polyperchon. Philip was murdered; Eurydike chose suicide. The episode is dramatized by Diodoros (19.11). Eurydike is one of many Macedonian royal women who attempted to exert authority but could only do so, precariously, by attempting to use male relatives as a springboard to power. DGJS

See Renault, M. (1981) *Funeral Games* (novel).

Eurymedon see KIMON; NAVAL WARFARE, GREEK; PERSIAN WARS, GREEK.

Eusebios (of CAESAREA) (c.AD 262–339) Most of what we know about the early CHURCH derives from the 'father of ecclesiastical history'. Eusebios carried on the tradition of CHRISTIAN scholarship in Palestinian Caesarea that had been established by ORIGEN. Together with the future martyr Pamphilus, whose 'son' Eusebios styled himself, he expanded Origen's library, spending the first half of his life in relative scholarly tranquillity. However, in the turbulent opening decades of the 4th century AD he found himself increasingly involved in the major religious and ecclesiastical controversies of the time, as a witness to the DIOCLETIANIC PERSECUTION, a participant in the ARIAN controversy and adviser to the emperor CONSTANTINE. His literary output was prodigious; Jerome comments admiringly upon his *infinita volumina*. The works most important to the secular historian include the *Chronicle*, *Ecclesiastical History*, *Martyrs of Palestine* and *Life of Constantine*.

The *Chronicle* was composed c.303 and consists of synchronized historical accounts of the most significant peoples of the MEDITERRANEAN and MESOPOTAMIAN regions. It is an invaluable tool in the reconstruction of ancient CHRONOLOGY. Eusebios chose as his starting-point the year of Abraham's birth (reckoned to be 2016/5 BC). His intention was to demonstrate that the Hebrew religion was older, and therefore better, than any other. Both in the *Chronicle* and in his major apologetic works, *Praeparatio evangelica* and *Demonstratio evangelica*, he was concerned to show the continuity of the Christian faith with its Old Testament roots. In 380 Jerome both updated and translated the *Chronicle* into Latin, and it became a key historiographical document of the Christian Middle Ages.

Eusebios may have begun his *Ecclesiastical History* before the beginning of the 4th century, but in extant form its ten books cover the period from the foundation of the church to the defeat of LICINIUS in 324. Eusebios does not pretend to write *sine ira et studio*, 'without anger and bias' in Tacitus' famous phrase. He sets out his objectives clearly: to tell of the successors of the Apostles, the BISHOPS, the great teachers of the Christian faith, the dangers posed by heretics, the calamities suffered by the JEWISH race, and finally the Christian persecutions and martyrdoms that paved the way for the divinely ordained victory of the faith with the accession of Constantine. Subsequent generations have found Eusebios' literary style turgid, but the true value of his work lies in the copious selection of documents and sources he quotes.

Though imprisoned in the Great Persecution, Eusebios survived to write the *Martyrs of Palestine* and to become bishop of Caesarea c.314. Constantine regarded him as a close adviser, though they may have met only four times. He confided to Eusebios the famous account of his conversion, found in the *Life of Constantine*. This work is also important for its account of the council of Nicaea. Eusebios' PANEGYRIC on the 30th anniversary of Constantine's accession also survives. He was less than happy with the creed that emerged from Nicaea, having sympathized with Arius. To the end of his life, however, he continued to work for reconciliation in this bitter theological dispute. (see also CHURCH COUNCILS) PMB

See Eusebius, *Ecclesiastical History*, 2 vols., trs. K. Lake, and J. E. L. Oulton (1926–32); Barnes, T. D. (1981) *Constantine and Eusebius*.

evil Relating to both natural disasters and human wrongdoing, the main problem posed by the concept of evil is one of finding an explanation for the suffering of the innocent. The catastrophe of the TROJAN WAR and the events surrounding it were attributed in HOMER's *Iliad* to the fulfilment of the will of ZEUS, and individual fortunes to distributions from the jars of good and evil standing in his hall (*Iliad* 1.1–5, 24.527–33). HESIOD described Pandora (the first woman) opening the jar of troubles and releasing them over the earth. Elsewhere he spoke of natural disasters and criminal activity as innate in the structure of the universe, born of Night at its beginning;

but he also viewed human sorrow and wickedness as characterizing the iron race, the last degeneration from that of gold (*Works and Days* 94–104, 174–201; *Theogony* 211–32). In TRAGEDY the responsibility for present suffering belonged to an ancestral curse on the family or divine vindictiveness, whereas transmigration theories (of the SOUL going through a series of lives in different bodies) viewed suffering as atonement for wrongdoing in a previous existence. For PLATO the world is imperfect because the material of which it is made resists the form which the good creator-god attempts to impose on it, and the individual soul similarly struggles with the hindrance of the body (*Timaeus* 44–51, 69–70). This conflict of good and evil was mythologized as the inner struggle of the divine spark of DIONYSOS with the ashes of the 'old Titan'. STOICS rejected physical disadvantages as indifferent beside the one and only evil of vice, and claimed that Zeus–JUPITER introduced hardship to the human race to stimulate invention (VIRGIL, *Georgics* 1.129–35). The EPICUREANS countered with the incompatibility of divine providence and a world so full of physical and manmade evil (LUCRETIUS 5.156–95). MRW

excavation One of the prime sources of new evidence about the ancient world, which today involves the systematic exploration of material traces of past human settlement and activity, backed up by an array of scientific techniques. A key principle of modern excavation is 'stratigraphy': establishing the sequence of human activity at a site by recording the relative depositional order of all structures and deposits. Palaeoeconomic data on diet, in the form of BONES and botanical remains, are fairly routinely sought by sampling and sieving deposits. Excavation is a destructive process, with evidence being removed as work progresses. This makes careful recording and publication a particular obligation. In its early phases of development in the 18th–19th centuries, however, excavation mostly resembled a method for mining antiquities (as in the tunnelling for statuary from the THEATRE at HERCULANEUM) and was hugely destructive.

Techniques used in the excavation of classical sites have changed considerably over the years. Careful consideration needs to be given to the nature of an excavation in evaluating its results, in much the same way that TEXTUAL CRITICISM directs the literary specialist to consider the reliability of the manuscript tradition. The first excavations resulted from the growing European interest in collecting classical art, and were focused primarily on the extraction of sculptural pieces. The 18th-century rediscovery of Herculaneum and POMPEII initially excited interest because the circumstances of their burial offered the possibility of large numbers of SCULPTURAL and ARCHITECTURAL pieces. The true wealth of the wide range of the material culture preserved – WALL-PAINTINGS, MOSAICS and HOUSEHOLD artefacts reflecting daily life – necessitated that the strategy of excavation evolve.

Though crude and unsatisfactory by today's standards, the methods of excavating and recording at the Vesuvian cities were to be hugely influential in the development of excavation elsewhere during the 19th century. Many early excavations focused on key sites of ancient Greece (notably the sanctuaries) and Italy (notably Rome, Pompeii and Herculaneum, but also the rich ETRUSCAN cemeteries with their abundant Greek vases). Other pioneers who changed public awareness of archaeology by their spectacular discoveries included Heinrich Schliemann, who excavated at MYCENAE, Tiryns and TROY, extending the field of interest back to the Bronze Age civilizations evoked by HOMER, and Arthur (later Sir Arthur) Evans, whose excavations at KNOSSOS brought to light a hitherto unknown Bronze Age civilization, dubbed 'MINOAN'.

The rise of European colonialism in the later 19th and early 20th centuries saw a massive increase in activity in Roman ARCHAEOLOGY, not only at the major sites of MEDITERRANEAN Europe but now also spreading through North Africa, Egypt and the LEVANT and taking root in northern Europe. The archaeology of the Roman ARMY became a particular focus in the latter area. This period saw some of the biggest excavations, employing gangs of workmen to expose, with minimal regard for stratigraphy, large contiguous areas of ancient cities such as OSTIA, TIMGAD or DURA EUROPUS.

By the late 20th and early 21st centuries, such large-scale operations were economically and practically incompatible with the modern emphasis on stratigraphic approaches. While some long-term projects at key sites continue (CORINTH, Athenian AGORA), most excavations are now relatively small-scale or are responsive to modern development (rescue digs). However, the traditional agenda of the 'classical excavation' has not yet been wholly superseded. The targets of excavation remain biased in favour of TOWNS, sanctuaries, ÉLITE residences, cemeteries and military sites, with far less attention paid to humble VILLAGES and minor RURAL SETTLEMENT (where the bulk of the population of the ancient world lived). (see also FIELD SURVEY) DJM

See Joukowsky, M. (1980) *A Complete Manual of Field Archaeology*; Roskams, S.P. (2001) *Excavation*.

exchange A term that describes a range of human activity, sometimes misleadingly summarized as 'trade'. Traditional human societies have operated exchange systems of three main types: reciprocity, redistribution and market exchange. All three mechanisms can be recognized in the ancient world. Reciprocity is the giving of gifts, generally with strings attached (or at least with the implicit understanding that something is due in return). HOMER's world is full of such exchanges, but the same tendencies were still present a millennium later, when Roman aristocrats sent expensive presents to each other across the empire. Redistribution at its simplest involves a chief or big-man gathering in produce from people who are dependent or owe allegiance to him, and then reapportioning it among the various groups, often providing a mechanism for distributing more specialized products across the social units. In the ancient world, states often intervened in the operation of the market to ensure equitable redistribution – especially at times of food shortage or famine. The Romans' massive FOOD SUPPLY system for the city of Rome (the *annona*) is the most spectacular example of a redistributive mechanism from antiquity, though similar things are also attested in the Greek world (notably, though on a smaller scale, in the economic organization of SPARTA). Finally, market exchange is readily identifiable in the Greek and

Roman worlds by a range of evidence, from excavated evidence of MARKETS, SHOPS and WORKSHOPS to literary accounts of commercial activity, graffiti of prices, and the increased production in Roman times of small change to facilitate small market transactions. (see also ECONOMY; TRADE) DJM

exile see BANISHMENT AND EXILE.

experiments and experimentation In contrast to modern scientific practices, experimentation was not often a part of scientific inquiry in the ancient world. Rarely was the evidence gained by experimentation considered relevant to the acquisition of KNOWLEDGE. Moreover, scientists were grappling with new kinds of questions that could not be adequately addressed by experimentation. The experimental method, whereby empirical evidence is used to prove theoretical ideas, was not widely featured in the investigations of the PRESOCRATICS. Instead, the main method of determining the nature of the world focused on thought-modelling. Likewise, ARISTOTLE, who often described test-like procedures, felt that information obtained by experiment could easily lead to inaccurate assumptions. The fault, he believed, lay in the false conditions that needed to be created in order to carry out experiments.

Nevertheless, there is evidence that experimentation did occur, especially among the medical writers. In many HIPPOCRATIC texts, knowledge of anatomy clearly resulted from a hands-on approach, albeit often using ANIMALS. For example, descriptions of dissecting an epileptic GOAT's brain (*On the Sacred Disease*) and severing the throat of a live PIG (*The Heart*) reveal that experiments were indeed conducted. By the hellenistic period, researchers began to ask questions that could be answered by experiments. Erasistratos' attempts to prove weight loss by measuring the weight of a caged BIRD and its excrement show a change in the method of acquiring information. Still later, GALEN, an advocate of animal vivisection, strongly encouraged medical students to conduct frequent experiments in their pursuit of knowledge. Experimentation was featured in other disciplines as well, most notably in PTOLEMY's use of experiments to explain refraction and reflection. (see also ENGINEERING) TJA

exploration The ancient accounts of official exploration or intentional missions of discovery are relatively few in number, perhaps because of preconceptions about the nature of the world. Herodotos tells of PHOENICIAN sailors sent by the pharaoh Necho II (610–585 BC, 26th dynasty) to circumnavigate AFRICA clockwise. Most have doubted the veracity of the story that they re-emerged through the straits of Gibraltar, but their claim to have had the sun on their right while sailing west lends some credence to at least the partial fulfilment of the mission. A later attempt to round the continent by sailing west proved unsuccessful because of the prevailing WINDS and ocean currents, a problem the Portuguese sailors of the 15th century would also encounter. It was not the last attempt to explore Africa from this direction: Hanno the CARTHAGINIAN ventured it c.500 BC, advancing perhaps as far as Sierra Leone before turning back. His account is preserved in a Greek version, the *Periplous of Hanno*. About the same time, DARIUS I commissioned a Greek from CARIA, Skylax of Karyanda, to make a descent of the Indus river-system, thus anticipating by almost 200 years that portion of the voyage of ALEXANDER's admiral Nearchos. Fragments of Skylax's work survive as quotations by later authors, but the curious *Periplous* of the Mediterranean and Black sea preserved under his name is perhaps a NAVIGATIONAL manual by an unknown 4th-century BC author (now called Pseudo-Skylax).

The most famous voyages of exploration in antiquity were doubtless those of Pytheas in the west and Eudoxos in the east. Pytheas set out from MASSALIA (modern Marseilles) c.300 BC and, sailing past Gibraltar (or crossing by land and the Garonne river to the bay of Biscay), reached the British Isles. He circumnavigated the island and discovered Ireland (called Hibernia in antiquity) as well as Ultima Thule – either Iceland or possibly the coast of Norway, which he may have mistaken for an island. Eudoxos of Kyzikos, in the time of Ptolemy VIII Physkon (late 2nd century BC), was enticed by the SPICE trade from the Indies to make two voyages via the Red sea to INDIA. He also explored the easternmost peninsula of Africa. Much else that is written about the outlying regions of the ancient world is little more than fiction on the part of armchair GEOGRAPHERS. WH

See Cary, M. and Warmington, E.H. (1929) *The Ancient Explorers*; Casson, L. (1974) *Travel in the Ancient World*; Cunliffe, B. (2001) *The Extraordinary Voyage of Pytheas the Greek*; Romm, J.S. (1992) *The Edges of the Earth in Ancient Thought*.

F

Fabii Great PATRICIAN clan of the REPUBLIC, a *gens maior*, from which the TRIBE Fabia takes its name. It was said that the family was contemporary with ROMULUS and descended from HERCULES. Fabii first appear in the 480s BC, like several great clans, holding an unparalleled seven consulships in succession, 485–479. Tradition recorded that about 300 Fabii fell at Cremera in 477 (the parallels with THERMOPYLAI in 480 have often been noted). A single survivor maintained the Fabii Vibulani. Fabii Ambusti were partly responsible for the disaster at the Allia and the sack of Rome by the Gauls in 390. The Fabii Maximi emerge onto the historical stage with two of the greatest figures of mid-Republican Rome: Quintus Fabius Maximus Rullianus and Q. Fabius Maximus Verrucosus. Both were five times CONSUL, the former winning the decisive battle of the SAMNITE WARS (Sentinum, 295), the latter nicknamed Cunctator ('the Delayer') for his strategy of refusing pitched battle against HANNIBAL in the second PUNIC WAR. Rullianus, his son Gurges and his grandson Verrucosus were each *princeps senatus*, 'leading man of the senate'. A relative, Q. FABIUS PICTOR, wrote the first history of Rome (in Greek) at the end of the 3rd century BC. In the 2nd century the elder son of AEMILIUS PAULLUS was adopted into the family as Q. Fabius Maximus Aemilianus, and through him the line endured to the time of NERO. JRWP

See Plutarch, *Fabius Maximus*, in I. Scott-Kilvert, trs. (1965) *Makers of Rome*.

Fabius Pictor (Quintus Fabius Pictor) 3rd-century BC Roman HISTORIAN. A participant in the second PUNIC WAR, Fabius wrote a history of Rome from earliest times to his own. Since Latin had not yet developed fully fledged literary PROSE writing, he wrote in Greek, like most Roman writers of this period. He possibly also had a desire to explain Rome to the Greek-speaking world, and was certainly influenced by hellenistic HISTORIOGRAPHY. Previously, only the barest of records had been kept by the priesthoods, recording names of CONSULS and a few notable events each year, mainly prodigies and other items of religious significance, with increasing detail from about 300 BC. Some original documents, like TREATIES, were also available. Additional recollections of the past existed in the family traditions of Rome's *gentes*. From the sources available, including Greek accounts of Roman history, Fabius Pictor constructed a history that was at points not much more than imaginative fabrication, but was clearly discursive rather than annalistic. Some of his dates differ from those of later historians, revealing that the chronology had not yet been established. For example, he placed the founding of Rome in 748 BC, but 753 became the official date. For his achievement, Fabius Pictor is generally considered the first Roman historian. Later historians used his work extensively, but it does not itself survive, except in some fragments. JV

See Peter, H.W. G. (1914) *Historicorum Romanorum reliquiae* (fragments); Alföldi, A. (1963) *Early Rome and the Latins*, ch. 4; Frier, B.W. (1979) *Libri annales pontificum maximorum: the origins of the annalistic tradition*.

fables A short, moralistic tale (Greek *ainos*, *logos*, *mythos*; Latin *fabula*; each of these terms is also of wider application), resembling a PARABLE inasmuch as both are fictional, but differing by being historically impossible (Aristotle, *Rhetoric* 2.20). Most but not all fables feature talking ANIMALS or plants. A moral usually follows the story but sometimes precedes it, as in the Roman author Phaedrus. The lesson tends to be that NATURE cannot be suppressed, or that VIRTUOUS behaviour is the best policy, or that might does not always succeed. The earliest surviving example, however, is of ambiguous morality: HESIOD's *ainos* of the hawk and the nightingale (*Works and Days* 202–12). 'A foolish person', says the hawk, 'strives against the stronger', but Hesiod's lesson is that JUSTICE will triumph over VIOLENCE (213–47).

Greek and Roman fables are akin to similar tales (which do not always draw similar morals) from other ancient cultures. Indeed, a body of Greek fables was called 'Libyan'. The principal Greek collection was, of course, the 'Aesopic', including some of the best known: the hare and the tortoise, the dog in the manger (one of several lacking a moral), the shepherd boy who cried 'wolf', and others. These were attributed to the semi-legendary AESOP.

It is a mark of the intellectual respectability of fables that, during his last days in prison, SOCRATES occupied himself with versifying Aesop's prose (*Phaedo* 60c–61b). Aristotle, moreover, recognized the utility of fables as proofs in RHETORIC. JRH

See Dijk, G.-J. van (1997) *Ainoi, Logoi, Mythoi: fables in archaic, classical and hellenistic Greek literature*; Perry, B. (1952) *Aesopica*.

faience see CONSUMERS AND CONSUMPTION; ETRURIA AND ETRUSCANS; LEFKANDÍ; TARQUINIA.

Faliscans see ALPHABETS; LANGUAGE AND LANGUAGES; MINERVA.

family

A flexible term in ancient Greece, covered by several different Greek words (*oikos*, *genos*, *angchisteia*). Most of our classical sources for understanding Greek families are Athenian, even for information about other city-states, so our viewpoint is skewed towards Athens and towards the wealthier end of the social scale. An important exception is the great code of laws from the Cretan city of GORTYN (early 5th century BC). However, even early Greek sources such as HOMER and HESIOD portray family structures that are remarkably similar to those found later in classical times. For the hellenistic period, Greek PAPYRI from Ptolemaic Egypt provide a wealth of detail about family life unparalleled elsewhere in the Greek world. Despite many similarities to classical Greece, there are also important differences.

For all Greeks, family connections were important both privately and for civic purposes. From the point of view of Athens and Sparta, the notion of family (*genos*, a general word for family, kin or clan; *oikos* or *oikia*, meaning HOUSEHOLD) only applied to people of citizen status. Although people of other statuses, such as Spartan HELOTS, surely had kinship relations and 'families', generally they were irrelevant to the state. Perhaps exceptionally, the Gortyn Code assumes that some families were of mixed status, but it is difficult to determine how common such families were. In all city-states, family connections determined status (e.g. citizen, metic, SLAVE) and were an important criterion for citizenship and political privilege.

The terms *oikos* and *oikia* incorporated our notion of nuclear family. The difference is that Greek households included people who were not related, such as slaves and other dependants. Membership was not fixed or formalized, and changed over time; the main criterion was co-residence. The core of a household was a married couple and their children, but might also include elderly grandparents or unmarried siblings. When a son married he might set up his own household, but not necessarily immediately (as with young Spartans). In one Athenian example (Lysias 32.4), two brothers had divided the liquid assets but not the real estate, so they and their families continued to live in the same HOUSE after the death of their father. WOMEN on MARRIAGE generally moved into the household of their husband, though legally they were not related to their husbands. If the marriage broke down and the family dissolved, or they were widowed, women generally returned to their own original families. In Athens a senior man acted as *kyrios*, head of household, but the position was not fixed by law like that of the Roman *paterfamilias*. The *kyrios*, usually the father, was the main person who transacted economic, political and legal business on behalf of the household; its broker with the outside world.

Family life in Athens was focused on the house and property belonging to the household. Its boundaries formed the limits of trust between the people within its circle. Children were brought up at home, under the care of their mothers and, in rich households, of slave nannies. However, if parents DIVORCED or a mother was widowed, the children generally stayed with their father's family rather than going with their mother to her family (in Athens she had the option of remaining in her husband's household with her children until they were old enough for her to leave). Although boys might be educated outside the family when they were older, they were generally accompanied by a trusted family slave. At least in wealthy families, adult men and women appear to have led quite separate lives. Men spent much of their time outside the house in the fields or the *AGORA*, while women, young children and slaves organized their own lives at home. It is unlikely that men and women regularly ate together in such families. The senior adult man, the *kyrios*, appears to have made most of the major decisions about such domestic matters as entertainment, shopping and home decoration. Domestic violence by men may not have been unusual. However, there is evidence that some wealthy women had business dealings of their own (Demosthenes, *Orations* 27–32 and 41), though these would have been ratified by a *kyrios*.

Wider family networks were also personally and legally significant in Athens. Greek kinship was bilateral, so that a person was related both to their mother's and to their father's family, similarly to most modern, Western kinship systems. However, for many purposes relationships on the father's side were given preferential treatment over those on the mother's side. This is reflected in the NAMING system, where an eldest son was normally named after his paternal grandfather (father's father) and an eldest daughter after her paternal grandmother (father's mother). Subsequent sons and daughters were often named after other relatives, sometimes deceased family members who had not had children of their own.

In legal terms the critical family group was the *angchisteia*, a person's closest relatives, defined by DEMOSTHENES (43.51) as relatedness 'to the children of cousins', though this definition may not have been universally accepted. There was a formal order of succession established by custom and law for determining someone's closest relative. In practical terms, because of the complexity of bilateral kinship and the fact that there were no formal written records of births, marriages and deaths, the further one moved outside the nuclear family the more difficult it was to establish the order of relatedness. In most cases, the system must have disintegrated into confusion at about second cousin. If someone died without sons or grandsons it was the responsibility of the closest male relative (usually the brother or nephew of the deceased) to arrange the funeral and memorial services, and (unless there was a daughter) to inherit his property. Only a man within the *angchisteia* was allowed to initiate a court case if someone were murdered (Demosthenes 47).

If a deceased man had only a daughter, his closest male relative had to marry or arrange for the marriage of any unmarried daughters. In such cases, the daughters with no brothers acquired a special, protected legal status. The name varied from city to city: in Athens she was called an *epiklêros*, in Sparta *patrouchos*, in Gortyn *patroikos*. But, in all cases, this legal protection ensured that she was suitably married, ideally to a close paternal relative, and that her son inherited her father's property, often along with his name. Often this led to an uncle marrying his niece or marriages between cousins. Although many societies would deem such relationships to be forms of INCEST, in classical Greece they were considered highly desirable because they maintained the coherence of family and property from one generation to another.

For all Greek societies, family relationships were considered essential for social stability, though there could be unease that family loyalty might undermine the political coherence of the city-state (Sophokles, *Antigone*). LF

See Cox, C. A. (1998) *Household Interests: property, marriage strategies and family dynamics in ancient Athens*; Patterson, C. B. (1998) *The Family in Greek History*; Pomeroy, S. B. (1997) *Families in Classical and Hellenistic Greece.*

There is no Latin term that corresponds exactly to 'nuclear family'. The *familia*, 'HOUSEHOLD' or 'family property', normally connoted its male head (*paterfamilias*), his children, SLAVES, FREEDMEN AND FREEDWOMEN, and sometimes his wife (if she was married with *manus*); but, as for ourselves, it could have narrower or wider connotations in a person's mind according to circumstances. The residential group comprised all these elements, sometimes spread over different estates (city and country) at different times of the year. The term closest to our family is *mei*, 'my own (people)'.

The triad of father, mother and dependent child(ren), our 'nuclear family', is a central core of any Roman concept of family, but it is not its exclusive element. Examples of co-resident extended families are rare, though individual relatives sometimes lived in the household, as sometimes did lodgers. The frequency of death and DIVORCE meant that remarriage was a common occurrence, with consequent blended families. The absence of state institutions such as orphanages, hospitals and retirement villages made the family the locus of wide social responsibilities – for children, orphans, the ill and the elderly. DEMOGRAPHIC studies show that mortality rates in the newborn and infancy were high, and that by the time children reached the age of first MARRIAGE the probability of their having lost at least one parent was about 50 per cent. Grandparents had a role but were comparatively rare. Uncles and aunts also had a role, and they might come to the rescue of fatherless or parentless children. Foster-children (*alumni*) could include some such children, but they included also abandoned children, often raised as slaves. ADOPTION (usually of adult males, not of infants) was a strategy to provide an heir when natural heirs were lacking. Roman nomenclature is a useful indicator of familial relationships.

Sons and daughters were subject to the legal power (*patria potestas*) of their *paterfamilias*, the eldest ascendant male (e.g. father, grandfather) as long as such a person was alive. The power of the *paterfamilias* was technically absolute, physically and financially, but in fact it was mitigated in various ways: consultation with a family council (*consilium*) was expected before extreme action was taken, public opinion frowned on arbitrary and excessively severe action, the LAW gradually caught up with this and imposed restraints, and the separate residential location of married couples (and sometimes unmarried young men) facilitated considerable personal and financial autonomy. If a *paterfamilias* died before children reached puberty, they required a GUARDIAN (*tutor*) to administer their affairs until the age of 14 (boys) or 12 (girls). After these ages they were legally independent (*sui iuris*) but with restrictions to protect them and their property for some additional years. Males required a *curator* to oversee their financial affairs until aged 25. Females were technically subject to the guardianship of a male for their whole lives, but exemptions could be won (e.g. for childbearing or for financial investment in enterprises of public importance such as the grain trade) and compliant guardians (often dependent ex-slaves) could be obtained.

By the time of the late REPUBLIC, wives did not normally come under their husband's *potestas*. They remained part of their natal family, retaining that family's name and property independent of their husband's. Thus Cicero's daughter remained Tullia through three marriages. Children of a marriage took their father's name; they legally 'belonged' to him after a divorce; and they were automatically his heirs if he died intestate (but not their mother's if she so died). Whether this technical separation of the wife–mother from her husband and children had an impact on affective relationships, on sense of identity, or on family religious rites is unclear. Nevertheless, there is evidence of loving spouses, children remaining resident with a mother after divorce, mothers' financial provision for their children and, in the imperial period, a tendency to add a mother's family name to the father's (or even substitute it). In the 2nd century, through the *senatus consultum Tertullianum* and the *senatus consultum Orfitianum*, there is a legal recognition of the rights of intestate mothers and children to succeed to each other's property.

Children were the explicit reason for marriage. There is much evidence of the high value attached to children and a recognition of CHILDHOOD as a separate stage of life with its own needs and characteristics. This is not inconsistent with the evidence of CONTRACEPTION, abortion, infanticide, exposure, corporal punishment and, in poorer levels of society, early child LABOUR. Slavery was an impediment to family life, in that slaves had no legal rights to marry or to transmit name or property to children resulting from any sexual union. But there is evidence, especially from large urban centres, of enduring marital relationships between slave partners, and some recognition from owners and in the law of such relationships and of consequent children. Funerary inscriptions attest such families, sometimes documenting improved social status (as one or more members won freedom) and eventually the birth of a freeborn child of a legitimate Roman marriage. When at least one partner was still a slave the relationship could only be *contubernium* and not *matrimonium*, and a child took the status of the mother. If a mother were a slave, her child belonged to her owner. If she were free but her partner still slave, a child was freeborn but could claim no legal father. Without *matrimonium* the child was *spurius*, technically 'illegitimate' but a consequence of status, not of irresponsibility or a wilful refusal to marry. Even in *contubernium* much of the language and trappings was borrowed from regular Roman marriage, which remained the ideal.

Slave children (*vernae*) born within the household often had a special place in the owner's affections and received special treatment. Sometimes their mother was a WETNURSE to the owner's child, suckling that child and her own simultaneously. This gave the fellow-nurselings a kind of sibling role to each other. Sometimes the *verna* was a surrogate child for a childless owner. Other child-carers (male and female, usually slave or ex-slave) had important roles in the rearing and education of freeborn children, thus extending the range of the *familia* beyond the nuclear family. For Romans there was no great distinction between public and private space: the constant interaction between various members of a household extended the concept of familial boundaries. This applied in large wealthy households, with retinues of servants and carers, and was inevitable in the crowded APARTMENT dwellings of lower levels of society.

Ex-slaves might become a patron's heir in the absence of surviving sons or daughters. This involved obligations as well as benefits, especially the obligation to see to the patron's BURIAL and proper commemoration. The funerary monuments of the bulk of Rome's population (who could afford commemoration) focus on the family. Although upper-class Roman men who had had public careers preferred to record that career as their memorial, the great mass of epitaphs record family relationships, especially spousal and parent–child(ren). Some of these are very simple, just plaques beneath a niche for the ashes in communal funerary structures called *columbaria* ('dovecotes', not unlike many modern crematorium walls). These structures are often familial in that they bring together in death those who shared the family name (*nomen*), whether received at birth or at manumission. Funerary monuments sometimes carried SCULPTURE. This visual evidence is a rich source for depiction of individuals' self-image or the image of a family, especially for sub-élite classes. When SARCOPHAGI became more frequent with the move to inhumation in the 2nd century AD, their reliefs often showed the life cycle of the deceased in a familial context: birth, learning to walk and play, EDUCATION, death.

Ancient literary sources give some information about upper-class families, though usually incidentally. Representations and records of a much wider range of families are to be found in Roman inscriptions, law and ART. Overall they convey a picture of 'the family' as a central and vital institution for the state and for personal relationships in Roman society, in spite of disruptions and fluidity due to mortality rates, divorce, POVERTY and slavery.

These remarks apply mainly to ROMAN CITIZEN families and those associated with and dependent on them in Rome, Italy and the Roman PROVINCES; in different areas, regional and cultural differences will have modified practice. 'The family' is one of the fastest-growing areas of Roman social history, and the items listed below will point to many other references. (see also NAMES AND NAMING, ROMAN) BR

See Bradley, K. (1991) *Discovering the Roman Family*; Dixon, S. (1992) *The Roman Family*; Kertzer, D. L. and Saller, R. P., eds. (1991) *The Family in Italy from Antiquity to the Present*; Parkin, T. (1992) *Demography and Roman Society*; (2003) *Old Age in the Roman World*; Rawson, B. (1997) *The Roman Family in Italy*; (2003) *Children and Childhood in Roman Italy*; Saller, R. P. (1994) *Patriarchy, Property and Death in the Roman Family*; Treggiari, S. (1991) *Roman Marriage*.

 MARRIAGE: (b) STILICHO.

famine see FOOD SUPPLY.

fanaticism A person who brings religious devotion to frenzied extremes. In origin, the Latin word *fanaticus* simply means something to do with a shrine (*fanum*), and it was used particularly to indicate a priest or devotee of a cult. By the 1st century BC, the word had clearly acquired negative connotations of excessive and frenzied behaviour and was especially associated with foreign cults. CICERO, complaining of the destruction of his house and the building of a shrine on the spot by his enemy CLODIUS, linked fanatical behaviour with SUPERSTITION (*De domo sua* = *On his House* 105). Similarly, TACITUS described as fanatical the wild-looking female adherents of DRUIDIC religion in BRITAIN (*Annals* 14.30). The term was used most frequently, however, of PRIESTS who indulged in the orgiastic rites of Eastern cults. In many cases, the priests whipped themselves up into a frenzied, trance-like state, during which they often mutilated themselves. The most notorious was the cult of CYBELE, introduced to Rome in 204 BC. In the ceremonies of this cult, the priests, known as Galli, became frenzied and castrated themselves in imitation of Attis, Cybele's mythological lover. The activities of the Galli were viewed with contempt by traditionally minded Romans, drawing the opprobrium of authors from JUVENAL (*Satire* 2.112) to the Christian poet PRUDENTIUS (*Crowns of Martyrdom* 10.1061). MDH

See Burkert, W. (1987) *Ancient Mystery Cults*; Vermaseren, M. J. (1977) *Cybele and Attis*.

farmers see AGRICULTURE; *COLONI* AND COLONATE; SUBSISTENCE.

fashion It is clear that a sense of 'fashion' in DRESS existed in the ancient world, even if the fashionable look *per se* developed and changed more slowly than it does today. There were no 'fashion designers', but individuals could be regarded as fashion leaders (like ALCIBIADES and, surprisingly, JULIUS CAESAR). More generally, fashionable styles developed out of new TRADE links or technological developments. Judging from the artistic evidence of the archaic period, Greek men wore elaborately decorated and colourful clothes based on eastern styles. But in the early years of the 5th century BC, these eastern modes were abandoned in favour of a more austere look, which encapsulated new DEMOCRATIC sympathies (THUCYDIDES 1.6). HERODOTOS even tries to find an explanation for the change in female dress that occurred at the same period (5.87). Nevertheless, fashionable caprices continued to exist even in classical Athens: some men preferred a 'SPARTAN' style of dressing, while others adopted a more 'PERSIAN' look. Equally, in Rome fashions changed, dictated by personalities and by increased access to foreign styles and materials. Even the TOGA, the seemingly unchanging symbol of the Roman people, actually altered in style over the centuries. By the late antique period, Roman men, including EMPERORS, were even wearing trousers, the one-time symbol of barbarism. LL-J

See Johnson, M. (1965) *Ancient Greek Dress*; Llewellyn-Jones, L., ed. (2002) *Women's Dress in the Ancient Greek World*; Sebesta, J. L. and Bonfante, L., eds. (1994) *The World of Roman Costume*.

fastening Many of the fastening devices we are used to – obviously zips and Velcro, but even press-studs (snaps) and buttons – are relatively recent inventions. Occasional buttons turn up in the ancient world, but they are unusual and were more often used as decoration than as fastening. One of the more regular uses of buttons as fasteners was to hold sleeves together. Ties and laces were surprisingly little used, and buckles seem to appear mostly on military equipment. The most usual kind of fastening

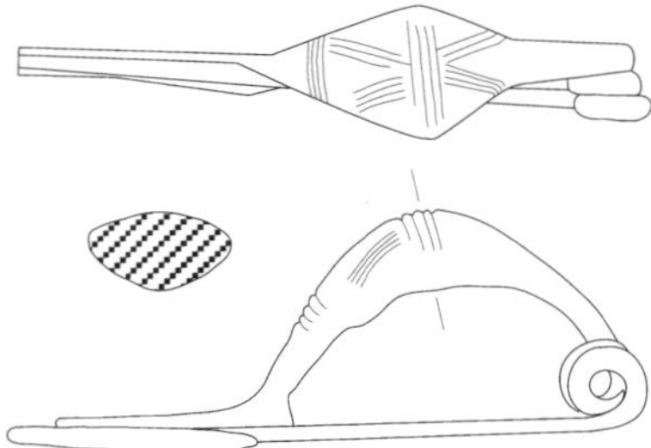

FASTENING: *fibula* ('safety pin') from Pithekoussai, Italy, used to fasten clothing.

was the pin, and both straight pins and safety pins (*fibulae*) were commonly used to hold clothing onto the wearer. Both men and women wore such pins, and they range from the very plain and modest to the precious and beautifully crafted. Sometimes, though not always, they were made in matched sets of two or more. (see also DRESS) LF

fate Derived from *fatum* ('what has been said'), fate was the utterance or prophecy of a god, especially of ZEUS or JUPITER, relating usually to the life-span of an individual or to the doom appointed at its end. More generally the term could cover the destiny of a person or a nation, and by transference the cosmic 'fate' or world-controlling divinity, identified also with the STOIC Providence, responsible for the inevitable processes of natural law. In the plural 'fates' were spoken or written PROPHECIES which might be scratched on leaves and scattered, or inscribed on PAPYRUS and unrolled to reveal the future. The word also indicated what the GODS said or decreed (*fata deum*, '*fata* of the gods') regarding the cosmos and human life within it, decisions often regarded as cruel and irreversible. As personifications, Fates took over the mythology of the three sisters responsible for an individual's destiny, the Moirai – Lachesis, Klotho and Atropos – who allot, spin and cut, respectively, the thread of a person's life. In Rome they were known as Parcae, the birth-goddesses, and statues to them as Tria Fata (the Three Fates) were erected in the Comitium to oversee the voting ASSEMBLIES there. Gods might interpret or implement fate, sometimes postpone it, but not even the greatest could override it. The conflict of human FREE WILL and fate was treated in TRAGEDY (especially in SOPHOKLES' *Oedipus*), in the ethical choices discussed by PLATO and ARISTOTLE, in the EPICUREAN 'swerve' of the soul-atoms, and in the Stoic doctrine of assent to NATURE and reason. (see also FORTUNA; PERSONIFICATION) MRW

Fates see FATE; FUTURE.

Faustina Annia Galeria Faustina 'the Elder' was the daughter of a distinguished SENATOR of consular rank, Marcus Annius Verus, and was related to the imperial family, the future emperor MARCUS AURELIUS being her nephew. She was married to the emperor ANTONINUS PIUS, perhaps in AD 110, and bore him four children: two boys and two girls. Our sources for her life, and for the mid-2nd century

FAUSTINA: (a) coin portrait of Faustina the Elder.

FAUSTINA: (b) coin portrait of Faustina the Younger.

generally, are poorer in the absence of TACITUS or a BIOGRAPHER of SUETONIUS' calibre, but tradition has it that Antoninus and Faustina were happily married, despite later slights on her character. This may be reflected, for example, in the fact that her image on coins and statuary is fairly common, perhaps indicating popularity. She had a reputation for charity, and upon her death in 140/1, Antoninus instituted a new alimentary scheme, the *Puellae Faustinianae*, in her honour. A TEMPLE in her name, with Antoninus, was consecrated in the city of Rome.

One of her daughters, Faustina 'the Younger', married Marcus Aurelius. She also appears regularly on COINAGE, often with a number of children. She gave birth to at least 13, but few survived infancy and early childhood; of the six or seven boys, only COMMODUS, who succeeded his father, survived his parents. Rumour suggested that Faustina colluded with the usurper Avidius Cassius in 175, but this is certainly false. CEPA

See Hemelrijk, E. A. (1999) *Matrona Docta: educated women in the Roman elite from Cornelia to Julia Domna.*

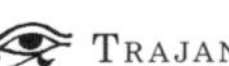 TRAJAN: (stemma).

Favorinus see AELIAN; GELLIUS, AULUS; SECOND SOPHISTIC; WETNURSES.

Fayûm Fertile depression c.100 km (60 miles) southwest of modern Cairo, watered by the Bahr Yusuf. Originally reclaimed in the Middle Kingdom, the Fayûm became an important centre of Greco-Roman culture in EGYPT. It has provided much PAPYROLOGICAL evidence, largely from VILLAGES on the desert fringes. In the Greco-Roman period it was also known as the Arsinoite nome (its metropolis was ARSINOË) and was further split into three subdivisions (*merides*): Herakleides, Polemon and Themistos sectors. The Fayûm was highly fertile, largely because of its complex irrigation system based on CANALS and dykes, which were so impressive that Germanicus Caesar visited in AD 19 to inspect them and to visit the famous labyrinth at Hawara. The region was an important producer of staple crops (wheat, barley and pulses), as well as OLIVE OIL and WINE. Nearly 1,000 customs-house receipts have been preserved from the Roman period; they provide important evidence for the TRADE and TRANSPORT of these products. The villages of the Fayûm have produced large numbers of PAPYRI and ostraca (the most prolific are KARANIS, Tebtunis, Soknopaiou Nesos, Philadelphia and Bakchias), and some have been the sites of EXCAVATION (most notably Karanis), but we know little of the metropolis and centre of administration. Many ARCHIVES of documents have been preserved; the most important are perhaps those of Zenon (3rd century BC) and Heroninos (3rd century AD). The region has also produced the beautiful Fayûm MUMMY PORTRAITS, mainly from Hawara. CEPA

See Rathbone, D. (1993) Villages, land and population in Graeco-Roman Egypt, *PCPS* 36: 103–42.

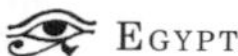 EGYPT.

fear Socrates (in Plato's *Protagoras* and *Laches*) defines fear as 'the expectation of an evil', making clear that it is a future-directed negative emotion. There were no doubt plenty of things to fear in the ancient world. Homer and Hesiod, for example, make a PERSONIFIED Fear (*phobos* in Greek) the son of the god of war, ARES. Philosophical discussions of fear tend to follow the general pattern of discussion of other EMOTIONS. Some philosophers considered fear, like other emotions, to be generated from non-rational psychological sources and therefore to be addressed, and if possible countered, through measures such as habituation and training. Others saw fear as generated by a belief that some future event will be EVIL, and therefore thought that it could be addressed only through rational and persuasive means.

The role of fear in a human life was also debated. ARISTOTLE, for example, insists that it is important, if one is to exhibit the virtue of courage, that one should feel some fear. Too little fear leads to the vice of overconfidence; too much to the vice of timidity. The courageous man will fear appropriately for the particular circumstance. Others, the EPICUREANS, for example, diagnosed certain fears – such as the fear of divine displeasure or the fear of death – as pernicious and irrational impediments to living the good human life. EPICURUS, therefore, sets out to demonstrate that the belief that death is bad is unfounded and that therefore death is not to be feared. JIW

federalism A system of government in which separate states form a unity while retaining their individual autonomy. In the ancient world it is a phenomenon studied chiefly in connection with the Greeks. No one Greek word corresponds to 'federal state' or the concept 'federalism'; the terms that are used to describe this political entity are *koinon* ('a common thing'), *ethnos* ('a people') and *sympoliteia* ('shared citizenship').

In the archaic period, political units, usually *poleis* (CITY-STATES), were connected in leagues for military and/or religious purposes; examples are the DELPHIC Amphiktyony and the Panionion of Ionia (western Asia Minor). Organized around a central shrine and, in the case of the latter, drawing on a sense of shared ETHNICITY, *poleis* came together to maintain the unity of the association, at times expelling members. Even in the formation of what were to become single *poleis*, a process akin to federation took place: synoikism ('uniting of houses'; see e.g. Thucydides 2.15). In several areas of mainland Greece, a sense of shared identity based on the *ethnos* endured from the earliest periods well into historical times, for example in Achaia, AITOLIA, THESSALY and MACEDONIA. These were areas that did not develop large urban centres before the late hellenistic or Roman period. In some instances, this sense of identity no doubt corresponded to a common political structure of some kind.

In origin derived from older *ethnê*, the federal states existed at least by the 5th century BC (e.g. the Achaian). It is not until the 4th century, however, that entities recognizable as such can be documented: an inscription of 367 (Tod 137) refers to the *koinon* of the Aitolians. The Oxyrhynchos Historian (ch. 16) provides a view of how a federal state worked shortly before 387: BOIOTIAN cities were divided into 11 groups, each of which contributed a magistrate to an executive body; in addition, councillors were sent to an assembly; a standing army, jury and tax system were also shared. ARISTOTLE was aware of federal states (*Politics* 1261a), and some were discussed in his catalogue of constitutions. Although it might seem that individual *poleis* lost authority through participation in such federations, especially in foreign relations, in practice federated city-states not only enjoyed significant local autonomy but also prosecuted their own wars and conducted diplomacy. A case in point is Araxa in CARIA, a member of the *koinon* of the LYCIANS (*SEG* 18.570, 2nd century).

Other confederations of note were the Thessalian, ARKADIAN and Achaian. POLYBIOS provides information for the Achaian and Aitolian, though biased in favour of the former and against the latter. They became important in the hellenistic period, at which point common ethnicity was not required (Sikyon, though ethnically Dorian, joined the ACHAIAN LEAGUE). Greek federalism was a way for small states to form political groupings of consequence, and thereby to maintain independence in a world of more powerful states.

Federal states are also found in the Roman world: Dionysios of HALIKARNASSOS describes the Latin league holding a common meeting of their *ethnos* (3.34.3). JDD

See Larsen, J. A. O. (1968) *Greek Federal States*; Walbank, F.W. (1985) Were there Greek federal states? in *Selected Papers* 20–37.

femininity In Greece and Rome, ideal femininity was best expressed by a quiet deportment, with the head bowed and the eyes fixed on the floor. Women were expected to adopt a closed body posture (the 'Pudicitia' pose), which took up as little space as possible. Feminine movements were supposed to be graceful and elegant. When female hands are depicted in Greco-Roman art they are, ideally, shown in aesthetically pleasing ways, delicately touching or elevating items of dress, particularly long skirts, loose sleeves and veils – a gesture of refinement and feminine sensuality: SAPPHO (fragment 67) criticizes the peasant girl who does not know the elegant art of raising the folds of her skirt. Many women in classical art are shown lifting a portion of a veil, a gesture which no doubt finds reflection in the real life practice of VEILING. But the gesture is also enacted for gesture's sake, because it looks pretty – this is the only interpretation that can be offered for depictions where the gesture has no obvious rationale. ARISTOPHANES lampoons such femininity in the character of the playwright Agathon in *Thesmophoriazousai*. LL-J

See Blundell, S. (2002) Clutching at clothes, in L. Llewellyn-Jones, ed., *Women's Dress in the Ancient Greek World* 143–69.

feminism For roughly the past 30 years, feminist theory has contributed much to scholarship in the arts, humanities, and social and natural sciences. The feminist theory that influences scholarship today was initiated in the 1970s, mainly in the field of anthropology, to determine more about WOMEN in other societies, past and present, and to break down androcentric biases in scholarly interpretations and in the workplace. From a historical perspective, feminism has taught us to challenge the belief that women in the past were similar to those living in the time and place of the modern historian. It has also helped initiate studies into GENDER theory, which breaks down the concept that biological SEX and gender are identical. There are no universals in the way gender is defined; each society has its own definition of what makes one male, female or other, and this may not correspond to biological make-up. Moreover, there may be multiple genders that can be dependent upon, for example, age, social status and body type.

Feminism has influenced classical scholarship, as is seen in the growing body of literature on women, children, homosexuality and masculinity in the Greek and Roman worlds. Awareness of ancient constructions of FEMININITY and MASCULINITY is important, because it assists in understanding how interactions occurred between these cultural classifications. Knowing this helps scholars to define social relations and their effects on the organization of the ancient world. PAB

See Foxhall, L. (1994) Pandora unbound: a feminist critique of Foucault's *History of Sexuality*, in A. Cornwall and N. Lindesfarne, eds., *Dislocating Masculinity*; Richlin, A. (1991) Zeus and Metis: Foucault, feminism, classics, *Helios* 18: 160–80.

fertilizer see AVIARIES; FUEL; MANURE; OLIVE, OLIVE OIL.

festivals

The Greeks held celebrations in honour of their GODS at regular intervals all through the year. During these festivals the civic body was enabled publicly to acknowledge their gods, whose support was believed to be indispensable to the smooth functioning of the CITY (*POLIS*). By the 6th century, the notion that gods acted as patrons of the CITY-STATES was widespread, a fact reflected by divine epithets such as Athena Poliouchos (she who holds and protects the *polis*) or Polias (of the *polis*), Zeus Phratrios (protecting the institution of brotherhoods, phratries) and others. Apart from being religious occasions, festivals were beneficial for the civic structure. They enhanced solidarity among people through common activity for the collective good. Citizens and non-citizens, men and women, adults and children, rich and poor, and even SLAVES could generally participate in religious festivities in different ritual roles. Festivals provided unique opportunities for relaxation (Thucydides 2.38) and entertainment, through the consumption of sacrificial MEAT in ritual meals and through DANCES and SONGS. ATHLETIC GAMES and other contests (*agônes*) were popular events at many festivals, particularly those that attracted people from all over Greece and were called 'panhellenic', as at the major sanctuaries of DELPHI and OLYMPIA. Here prominent citizens from various parts of Greece, and often from abroad, met regularly to display their city's or their own wealth through precious offerings and to compete in the games. Panhellenic festivals were instrumental to the preservation of Greek identity among a large number of Greek-speaking communities living in a territory fragmented by natural boundaries. Regional festivals were smaller-scale counterparts

FESTIVALS, GREEK: the rituals connected with the cult of Demeter at Eleusis were the focus of one of the most important of Greek festivals.

of the panhellenic and included many of the same events.

Despite the sacred connotations of Greek festivals, the state took control over their organization and ensured their regularity through the year. EPIGRAPHIC records containing festival dates survive in sacred CALENDARS where festivals are grouped by month, indicating the name of the deity worshipped. Religious and other personnel participating in a festival were also appointed by the state, while state officials played leading roles in festivities and received large portions of public sacrifices. Festivals took place in public SPACES, often but not exclusively within the boundaries of a sanctuary. Among the typical ritual activities in festivals were SACRIFICES, PRAYERS, processions, purifications, ritual meals and merrymaking. Less commonly, and depending on the deity honoured, more specialized ritual acts are found in the programme of festival events, notably initiations and even THEATRE performances. Festival activities usually began early in the day and often extended into the night hours, with the consumption of sacrificial meat, dances and songs enduring until the early morning hours; these events were known as *pannychides*, 'all-nighters'. EP

See Bruit Zaidman, L. and Schmitt Pantel, P. (1989) The festival system: the Athenian case, in *Religion in the Ancient Greek City* 102–11; Connor, W. R. (2000) Tribes, festivals, and processions: civic ceremonial and political manipulation in archaic Greece, in R. Buxton, ed., *Oxford Readings in Greek Religion* 56–75 (= *JHS* 107 (1987) 40–50).

In the modern Western world festivals are occasions for the performing arts. Important religious days are HOLIDAYS, not festivals. The Roman festival is a rich combination of the modern notions of holidays, feasts and festivals.

In the Republic there were 45 regular festivals, occurring each year on the same fixed day. In addition, there were the movable feasts, the dates of whose celebration were fixed and announced each year by the competent authority. Finally, there were a number of festive days which the SENATE voted and for which the CONSULS fixed a day for offerings to be made to the GODS. These were usually thanksgiving days when some public crisis had been surmounted or a sensational victory had been won. The festival day was declared a day on which no official business was allowed to take place. The people generally visited the TEMPLES of the gods and offered their PRAYERS and SACRIFICES. ANIMALS were slaughtered on the altars and then eaten, and WINE was drunk, while libations were made to the gods. The larger the community engaged in the sacrifice, the bigger and better were the sacrificial animals. City-wide festivals were more than mere RITUALS of consumption; they were spectacular entertainments that the community organized for itself and that gave expression to its social cohesion. Festivals usually opened with a procession, with the entire citizen body on parade, arranged on the basis of established social hierarchies. In the PRINCIPATE new festivals, usually in connection with the ruling emperor, were continuously added, so that the calendar became cluttered with days on which no legal business could take place. In the 2nd century the emperor MARCUS AURELIUS set a limit of 135 on the number of days which were marked as festival days.

The Roman year was divided into festival cycles, each celebrating one of the essential Roman activities. There were three cycles concerning living people – work on the land, WAR and politics. In April the corn was in full growth and the vines were sprouting, so festivals were held to encourage fertility and to avert natural disasters. In March and October the god of war, MARS, was the central focal point, the two months marking the beginning and the end of the fighting season. There was another cycle in February concerning the dead, with the main festival, the Parentalia, lasting from the 13th to the 21st.

Festivals enable us to study religious ideas, social rites and ideas of gender, but above all the notion of Roman IDENTITY. At the festival of Anna Perenna in March, Romans would leave the city, cross the river and build primitive huts, resembling those that the earliest Romans built. They would picnic there for the day, and return in the evening to embrace contemporary civilization again. In February, at the Lupercalia naked youths of well-born families ran through the FORUM striking women with leather thongs to induce fertility. Funerary inscriptions from the 1st and 2nd centuries AD proudly advertise that the deceased 'ran at the Lupercalia'. GAMES were staged in connection with festivals, either in the form of theatrical performances or CHARIOT RACES; these could last for a number of days. MK

See Scullard, H. H. (1981) *The Festivals and Ceremonies of the Roman Republic*.

fetiales see ALLIANCES; PRIESTS AND PRIESTESSES, ROMAN.

field survey The systematic investigation of an area to record archaeological remains and landscape features. It involves primarily the investigation of RURAL SETTLEMENT patterns and the elucidation of long-term DEMOGRAPHIC trends. A suite of non-intrusive techniques of investigation is commonly employed, including field walking, monument survey, aerial photography and geophysics. Early practitioners tended to concentrate on major known sites or else selected a broad region to survey in an extensive (non-intensive) manner ('reconnaissance survey'). Field walking nowadays is normally carried out in an intensive manner, with areas of the landscape traversed systematically by archaeologists walking along parallel lines at an equal spacing from one another. POTTERY, TILE and other manufactured or imported materials lying on the ground surface are collected or recorded. Concentrations of such material can indicate the locations of ancient settlements. Intensive survey has proved about 70–100 times more effective than extensive surveys at locating sites, and tends to be more representative of the full settlement hierarchy and all periods of activity. Less dense scatters of material are also now recognized as significant; careful observation of the rise and fall of this 'background noise' has its own story to tell. For instance, some light scatters of pottery and tile may be indicative of MANURE spreading from farmyard dung-heaps onto cultivated land.

Intensive field surveys have revolutionized our knowledge of rural settlement. Densities of up to

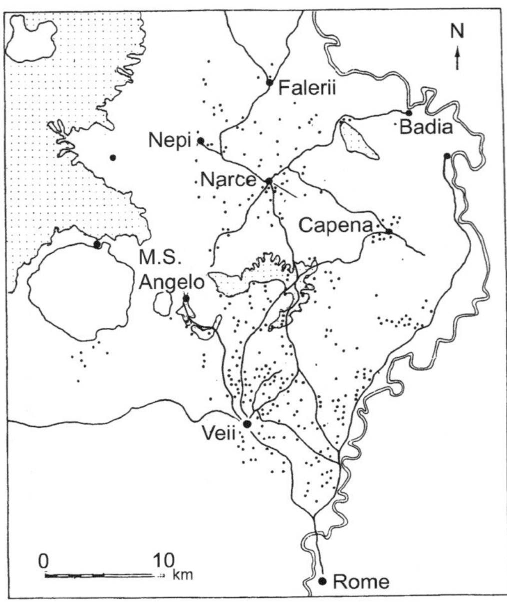

FIELD SURVEY: (a) the South Etruria Survey, settlement and communications of the 7th and 6th centuries BC.

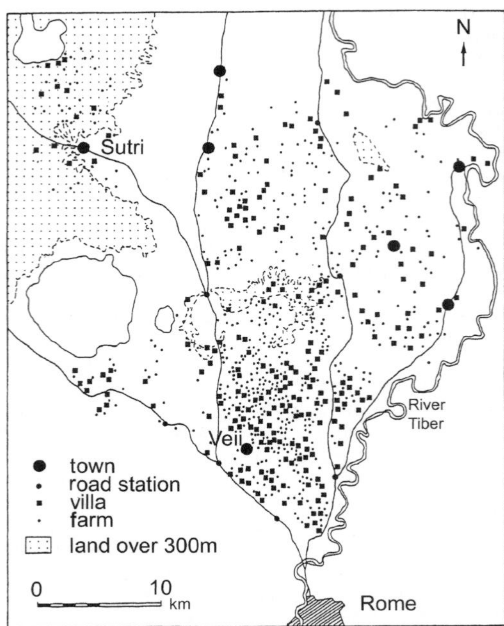

FIELD SURVEY: (b) the South Etruria Survey, settlement and communications of the 1st century AD. The transformation of the rural landscape, political structures and economic orientation of the region is plain.

10 sites per sq km are now commonly attested in the MEDITERRANEAN, something that was entirely unsuspected 30 years ago.

Many areas of Greece and various AEGEAN islands have been sampled through field walking. Methodological development may be seen in a number of surveys whose publication is complete or well advanced, such as BOIOTIA, KEOS, MELOS, Atene in ATTICA, and especially in the PELOPONNESE (LACONIA, around Pylos in MESSENIA, Methana, southern Argolid, Berbati–Limnes, Asea valley, and Nemea). The rural landscapes commonly show a dramatic increase in settlement numbers in the archaic period, with a peak in the classical and a numerical decline by the later hellenistic. The degree of extra-urban activity around cities appears surprising and, though not all sites need have been occupied contemporaneously or all year round, this requires re-evaluation of underlying assumptions about the demographic balance between town and country in classical Greece.

Survey conditions vary from the rich ploughzone archaeology of the Mediterranean littoral to the well-preserved sites and landscapes of the North African pre-desert zone. Pioneering work by the British School at Rome (South Etruria Survey) has been matched by important regional surveys in many provinces, notably in the Western empire. Different regions seem to have experienced highly individual trajectories of growth and decline. Survey also sets the ÉLITE VILLAS (hitherto the focus of attention) in broader relation to other categories of rural site, while offering important evidence for the nature, scale and development of the rural economy and the impact of ROMAN IMPERIALISM. DJM

See Barker, G. and Lloyd, J., eds. (1991) *Roman Landscapes: archaeological survey in the Mediterranean region*; Francovich, R. et al., eds. (2000) *Extracting Meaning from Ploughsoil Assemblages*; Alcock, S. E. and Cherry, J. F., eds. (2004) *Side-by-Side Survey: comparative regional studies in the Mediterranean world*.

LEPTIMINUS; RURAL SETTLEMENT.

figs An unusual fruit, botanically figs are swollen flowering spurs of *Ficus carica*, a species native to the MEDITERRANEAN and Near East. Female trees, on which edible figs grow, have been planted by humans for several thousand years. Most varieties require the presence nearby of male fig trees to permit pollination by the fig wasp; ARISTOTLE, in *History of Animals* (557b25–31), describes the process accurately. Some kinds may bear edible fruit two or three times a year, though not all the crop will ripen.

Fresh figs change markedly at the moment of ripening, becoming sweeter and softer. They can be dried under a hot sun or under low heat, becoming rapidly sweeter still. Figs were a major GARDEN fruit in the classical world, convenient because the tree will grow on an otherwise barren, rocky site. Dried figs were important nutritionally as a stored source of sugar; both fresh and dried figs were also known as a mild laxative. Dried figs were an export from CARIA (particularly the city of Kaunos) and from the neighbouring island of RHODES.

Apart from the fruit, the tree is useful for its bitter, milky sap, which may be used as a rennet in

CHEESE-making. The leaf (Greek *thrion*) sometimes served as a food wrapper. Figs feature in linguistic double entendre: for example, Greek *sykon* ('fig') may stand for the vagina, Greek *ischas* ('dried fig') for the anus, Latin *ficus* ('fig') for haemorrhoids. The fig tree provided two seasonal landmarks to farmers, in mid-spring when the trees came into leaf and in late summer when the first fig of the main crop ripened (Latin *primaficus*). AD

See Condit, I. J. (1947) *The Fig*.

figurines, bronze Small figurines of deities, people and animals were often dedicated in sanctuaries. Some examples were inscribed, recording the name of the person making the dedication and the deity in whose sanctuary the figurine was to be placed; often such texts help with the identification of a particular building. For example, a small bronze (now in Princeton) was found in ARKADIA and carries an inscription, 'Pythodoros, to (the river) Pamisos'. A small bronze runner from OLYMPIA was merely inscribed 'I belong to ZEUS'. Texts can also show the reason why a figurine was dedicated. A bronze youth, now in the Museum of Fine Arts in Boston, had been dedicated to Phoibos APOLLO ('Far Darter of the Silver Bow') as part of the tithe of one Mantiklos; in return, the dedicant had this plea to the god: 'grant gracious recompense'.

Some of the earliest Greek figures date from the Geometric period. Sanctuaries such as Olympia have yielded stylized ANIMALS, especially HORSES. It seems likely that small local WORKSHOPS were set up to meet the demands of those needing to make dedications. These sanctuaries continued to receive small-scale dedications into the classical period. A bronze discus-thrower, said to come from the PELOPONNESE and now in the Metropolitan Museum of Art in New York, may well be a small version of the life-size bronze statues which were erected in major sanctuaries to celebrate victories in contests (agonistic victories).

Many extant bronze figures may have served as attachments on larger objects. In an ARCHAEOLOGICAL context, a cast bronze figure will survive better than the thin-walled vessel to which it was originally attached. For example, a bronze lion from the sanctuary of HERA on SAMOS appears to have been mounted on the rim of a large vessel, probably a krater; an inscription shows that the whole object had been dedicated by a SPARTAN. A bronze HERAKLES from Agrinion in AITOLIA appears to show the hero in a drunken state, until it is realized that the figure was originally one of a pair, or even one of four, mounted next to the vertical handle of a huge bronze vessel.

Sometimes these figurines were made as small copies of full-scale bronzes by famous SCULPTORS (cf. PLINY THE ELDER, *Natural History* 34.49). Thus it is through this medium that glimpses of the genius of figures such as PRAXITELES' APHRODITE or LYSIPPOS' Herakles can be received. Such figures may have been created to satisfy the taste of Roman collectors. (see also COPPER ALLOYS) DWJG

See Lamb, W. (1929) *Greek and Roman Bronzes*; Kozloff, A. P. and Mitten, D. G. (1988) *The God's Delight*; Mattusch, C. C. (1988) *Greek Bronze Statuary*; (1996) *Classical Bronze*; (1996) Bronzes [Greek], in *The Dictionary of Art*, vol. 13, 571–4; Mertens, J. R. (1985) *Greek Bronzes in the Metropolitan Museum of Art*; Nicholls, R.V. (1982) The drunken Herakles, *Hesperia* 51: 321–8; Rolley, C. (1986) *Greek Bronzes*.

figurines, terracotta Small clay figurines were common from the Greek Bronze Age onwards. Examples of this medium were frequently offered in sanctuaries and placed in graves and domestic contexts. Figures were often made for local consumption, and numerous centres of production have been identified. Some of the earliest figures were hand-made, such as the flat standing women from archaic contexts in BOIOTIA. A centaur from 10th-century BC contexts at Lefkandí was wheel-made, perhaps reflecting a continuation of a MYCENAEAN technique. Moulds started to be used by the 7th century BC.

In the East Greek world during the 6th century BC, hollow-moulded terracotta figurines were sometimes used as perfumed-oil containers in the shape of *gorgoneia*, sirens and standing women. This probably explains their widespread distribution. Clay analysis has emphasized the likely role of MILETOS as the centre of production.

Some of these terracotta figurines were probably intended as TOYS. Remains of jointed clay dolls have been discovered during the excavation of HOUSES in the Greek colony of Euesperides in CYRENAICA. Similar figures have been found in ATTICA, though often in funerary contexts. Other Attic figures sometimes have two pierced holes on the underside, which may have allowed the figure to have served as a finger-puppet; one such figure was found in a child's grave on DELOS.

During the hellenistic period, delicately moulded figures of draped women were made in Boiotia; they caused a sensation in 19th-century Europe when they were discovered during digging at Tanagra. Another major centre of terracotta production at this time seems to have been at Myrina in Turkey. Some terracotta figures seem to be copies of famous large-scale bronze sculptures, a phenomenon also observed in small bronzes.

Moulded figurines were produced by the following sequence. The basic figure, known as the archetype or *patrix*, was made and moulds made of it. Detail would then be cut into these moulds; thus, though they are similar in basic form, the finished terracottas might in fact differ in detail. Sometimes the products of the original mould may have been used as a further archetype, giving rise to 'second generation' figures which tend to be smaller than the first, in part through shrinkage of the clay. Up to five 'generations' of figures have been identified, each smaller than the previous one. DWJG

See Higgins, R. A. and Burn, L. (1954, 1959, 2001) *Catalogue of the Terracottas in the British Museum*, vols. 1–3; Higgins, R. A. (1967) *Greek Terracottas*; (1986) *Tanagra and the Figurines*; Jones, R. E. (1986) *Greek and Cypriot Pottery*; Nicholls, R.V. (1952) Type, group and series: a reconsideration of some coroplastic fundamentals, *ABSA* 47: 217–26; Thompson, D. B. (1974) *Miniature Sculpture from the Athenian Agora*; Uhlenbrock, J. (1996) Terracotta, in J. Turner, ed., *The Dictionary of Art*, vol. 13, 577–83; Vafopoulou-Richardson, C. E. (1991) *Ancient Greek Terracottas*.

film From its earliest conception, the genre of film has been fascinated with classical antiquity. Film's ability to capture massive and spectacular events in outdoor locations, with recreations of epic battles, great disasters, miracles and sensational love stories, suited Greco-Roman history; these films became known as 'sword and sandal' epics. Cinema – Hollywood in particular – has played the preponderant role in shaping popular modern perceptions of the classical world. The quality of these films vary considerably from the low-budget *Julius Caesar* (1951) to the opulent but often garish *Cleopatra* (1963). Some offer carefully researched and balanced accounts of their subjects, such as *Alexander the Great* (1955), while others are purely fantastical, *Hercules Against the Moon Men* (1964) being an excellent example of the latter genre. Greek MYTHOLOGY has always formed a staple diet for film-makers, with films like *Helen of Troy* (1956), *Ulysses* (1955), *Jason and the Argonauts* (1963) and *The Clash of the Titans* (1981) making big box-office profits. Foreign art-house films such as Pasolini's *Medea* and Fellini's *Satyricon*, while not necessarily big money-spinners, are regarded as artistic triumphs and offer imaginative and sometimes disturbing retellings of classical literary greats.

Greek history *per se* has until recently only received sporadic filmic attention, chiefly with *Alexander the Great* (1955) and *The 300 Spartans* (1962). Ancient Rome, however, has always been hot box-office property. The popular conception of Rome as decadent and cruel has continuously appealed to movie directors, especially when coupled with CHRISTIAN themes. Numerous films are set in the Roman province of Judaea and follow the life of Christ, using the bigger picture of Rome to provide a socio-political background to the story (for example, the 1961 movie *King of Kings*). Other films use the life of Christ as the background event and allow their heroes to interact with the larger world of Rome in a much more active way: *Salome* (1953), *Barabbas* (1962) and, most famously, *Ben-Hur* (1925, 1959). Some 'Christ movies' operate within Rome itself and are set against the background of Christian PERSECUTION by Roman EMPERORS. The genre started in 1932 with *The Sign of the Cross*, but flourished with *Quo Vadis* (1951), *The Robe* (1953) and its sequel, *Demetrius and the Gladiators* (1954). Other Roman films, however, do not operate in a Christian world: Hollywood alone has made three versions of the CLEOPATRA story (1917, 1934, 1963), while *Spartacus* (1960) tells the story of the famous SLAVE rebellion and is often hailed as a masterpiece of film-making as well as a penetrating social comment. *The Fall of the Roman Empire* (1964) has been seen as the last of the great epic genre, though self-conscious imitations of classical myths and themes are found in modern films like *O Brother, Where Art Thou?* (2000; based on the *Odyssey*). Ridley Scott's *Gladiator* (2000) revived the 'sword and sandal' film to great popular acclaim, and has paved the way for a new trend in epic film-making. Recent films include *Troy* (2004) and *Alexander* (2004), while further treatments of Alexander the Great and Hannibal are (at the time of writing) in production. LL-J

See Solomon, J. (2001) *The Ancient World in the Cinema*; Wyke, M. (1997) *Projecting the Past: ancient Rome, cinema, and history*.

finance see ACCOUNTING; BANKING; COINAGE; ECONOMY; LOANS; RECORDS, PUBLIC; TAXATION.

Finley, M.I. see CONSUMER CITY; ECONOMY; HISTORIANS AND HISTORIOGRAPHY, MODERN; RATIONALITY, ECONOMIC; TECHNOLOGY; TRADE, ROMAN.

fire A natural element and major civilizing force, which forms the basis of TECHNOLOGY and crafts as a strong creative power but can be destructive when used as a weapon or as a means of breaking down organic or other materials. Fire has diverse applications in the practical activities of everyday life, such as COOKING, heating and LIGHTING and is an essential medium for transforming solid materials that would otherwise be impossible to manipulate. The extent and sophistication of how fire is applied for the benefit of human life may be viewed as evidence of the cognitive map of a community in connection with its technological evolution. On another level, fire formed an essential part of human activities to make contact with, or appease, the supernatural. It was employed in ritual practice in many guises and with different functions, most notably in SACRIFICES, the cult of the hearth, FUNERALS, and the keeping and transfer of sacred fire.

In Greek MYTHOLOGY, fire is primarily associated with divinity and the extraordinary power it possesses. The father of the gods, ZEUS, holds the thunderbolt, which emits fire, while other OLYMPIANS such as ARTEMIS and Hekate use torches to kill their victims, in both ART and POETRY. As a powerful weapon, fire not only becomes a means of divine vengeance over arrogant mortals but is also used in divine WARS. In HESIOD's description of the mythical battle between the Olympian gods and their monstrous divine predecessors, the Titans, fire and smoke imagery pervades every aspect of the confrontation. It comes to embody the very essence of VIOLENCE in the most cataclysmic sense, and burns everything or anyone in its way. The gods use fire weapons to confront their opponents, who breathe fire. The destructiveness of fire as a weapon makes it suitable for use in mortal wars too, particularly in cases of torching cities, as during the mythical capture of Troy.

Religious ritual took fire into its service by using it as a means to take living creatures into a new dimension, notably in sacrifices and funerals. Fire was worshipped in the guise of the domestic hearth (Hestia), and assumed symbolic connotations of continuity and security when it burned in the hearths of public institutions or TEMPLES like the *prytaneion*, the temple of Athena Polias in Athens, and that of VESTA at Rome. Its safe-keeping as a valuable force was symbolically enacted in religious events such as torch-races and the rituals underpinning the founding of COLONIES.

The multi-faceted, multi-functional nature of fire, along with its contribution to human life as a civilizing force, was acknowledged in the Greek myths about Prometheus, who stole fire from the gods to offer it to humans as a gift. Furthermore, for a range of smith-gods such as Hephaistos, the Telchines, the Daktyloi and the Kabeiroi, fire was an indispensable ingredient in their artistic miracles. EP

See Furley, W. (1981) *Studies in the Use of Fire in Greek Religion*.

fire-fighting Early efforts at extinguishing fires were doubtless sporadic, reactive attempts at dousing the flames with buckets. Organized fire-fighting dates from the late Roman Republic, when the rapid growth of Rome increased the incidence of urban conflagrations. CRASSUS allegedly made his fortune redeveloping property he had bought from desperate owners as it burnt, ordering his own private fire brigade to put the fire out only when the owner had agreed to sell at a rock-bottom price. In 26 BC Egnatius Rufus organized a private fire brigade during his AEDILESHIP, thereby achieving such popularity that AUGUSTUS felt threatened.

Augustus established the first state fire brigade after the fire of AD 6; these 7,000 *vigiles* were stationed in barracks throughout Rome and patrolled the city at night on the lookout for fires. They were equipped with buckets, axes and hooks to demolish property to create fire-breaks. The large number of men was necessary because they had to fight fires largely by creating a human bucket chain from the nearest water source, usually a public fountain. They also used force-pumps adapted with a swivel nozzle to direct the jet at the blaze (Hero, *Pneumatika* 1.28); it must have been mounted on a cart equipped with a barrel or water reservoir, and was effectively the world's first fire engine. *Vigiles* (and their barracks) are attested also at OSTIA and Aquincum (Budapest). AIW

See Rainbird, J. (1986) Fire stations of imperial Rome, *PBSR* 54: 147–69.

fish and fishing *Halieutica*, or the art of fishing, formed the subject of works by Oppian and OVID, and fish lore and fish cuisine figure prominently in works by ARISTOTLE, ATHENAEUS and others. The importance of fish in the Greco-Roman diet is the focus of recent controversy between a minimalist view (Gallant) and a more optimistic one (Curtis). Greeks and Romans, who preferred sea-fish over freshwater species, caught them in quantity in MEDITERRANEAN areas that tended to concentrate fish populations, such as lagoons or straits (e.g. Gibraltar, Bosporos). Large-scale processing centres operated at these places and elsewhere to produce salt fish and FISH SAUCE for local and long-distance TRADE. Among the most popular fish processed were the tuna, anchovy and pelamyds which were captured in various kinds of nets from the shore or from boats. Other methods used to catch fresh and saltwater fish included hook and line arrangements, weirs, tridents, decoys and POISON. Nets, sinkers and fishhooks appear regularly in EXCAVATION sites near the sea. In art, fishermen, fishing scenes and still-lifes of fish are common motifs. The fisherman was little esteemed in Greek and Roman society, being often presented as the image of POVERTY and frequently the butt of jokes. RIC

See Bekker-Nielsen, T. (2002) Fish in the ancient economy, in K. Ascani et al., eds., *Ancient History Matters* 29–37; Gallant, T. (1985) *A Fisherman's Tale*; Radcliffe, W. (1926) *Fishing from the Earliest Times*.

fish sauces Known from at least the 5th century BC, sauces made from FISH were by-products of salt-fish processing installations located throughout the MEDITERRANEAN and BLACK SEA. *Garum* (a Latin word; Greek *garon*) was the main sauce, while *(h)allec* (or *hallex*) was the solid residue of its production. The term *liquamen*, 'liquid mixture', was synonymous with *garum* by the 3rd century AD. *Muria* was the liquid produced in salting fish-meat. Used

FISH SAUCES: Sullechtum, Tunisia, showing large tanks in which fish sauces could be matured.

FISH AND FISHING: Roman mosaic from Tunisia showing close anatomical familiarity with a huge range of sea creatures and the fishing methods by which these were exploited.

primarily in lieu of SALT as an ingredient in food preparation, fish sauces were nutritious and considered to have medicinal value. Their production, similar to that of modern South-East Asian sauces, involved dissolution of fish innards or small whole fish through autolysis in a solution of varying salinity over a specified period of time. The fermentation process and the strong odour associated with it gave the sauces a bad reputation in literary contexts – PLINY THE ELDER (*Natural History* 31.93), for example, calls *garum* 'that liquid of putrefying matter'. That reputation, however, is contradicted by the evidence of widespread consumption. In reality, the combination of high salt concentration with enzymes of the digestive tract in a solution of low pH value prevented putrefaction and reduced the danger of botulism poisoning. Though affordable by all social classes, particular kinds were expensive. Spain was an important producer and exported its products as far north as HADRIAN'S WALL and as far east as INDIA. Little information can be gathered about individual producers and merchants, except in 1st-century AD POMPEII, where Aulus Umbricius Scaurus dominated the Campanian market. RIC

See Curtis, R. I. (1991) *Garum and Salsamenta*; Lowe, B. (2001) Between colonies and emporia: Iberian hinterlands and the exchange of salted fish in eastern Spain, in Z. H. Archibald et al., eds., *Hellenistic Economies* 175–200.

Fishbourne Roman PALACE, near Chichester, which was one of the most impressive buildings in Roman BRITAIN. It is located near a natural HARBOUR on a site which is believed to have served as a military supply base in the immediate post-conquest period. The early Flavian period saw the construction of a building covering an area of 4 ha (10 acres) and furnished with elegant MOSAIC floors, WALL-PAINTINGS and a BATH suite. The STONE used in the building includes MARBLE imported from eastern France and CARRARA in Italy, and continental craftsmen may have been employed to carve it. EXCAVATION has revealed a large formal GARDEN with bedding trenches for continuous rows of hedges, as well as a sophisticated WATER SUPPLY system. No comparable garden has been discovered west of Italy.

The size and grandeur of the building have led many archaeologists to describe it as a palace. Fishbourne is certainly unusual; it was not the result of gradual growth but was planned and built in a very short time. Its construction also comes very early in the life of the province of Britain, where substantial Roman VILLAS are usually dated to the 3rd and 4th centuries AD. It is often suggested that Fishbourne belonged to Tiberius Claudius Togidubnus, who had been granted CITIZENSHIP under CLAUDIUS and was the CLIENT king governing the area in which the palace was situated. Fishbourne palace was finally destroyed by a disastrous FIRE at the end of the 3rd century AD. HE

See Cunliffe, B. (1998) *Fishbourne Roman Palace*.

fishponds Manmade structures in which to keep live fish (*piscina*) go back to pharaonic Egypt, where representations appear in TOMB paintings. Evidence for Greek pisciculture is sparse. Freshwater ponds appeared in Italy by the 3rd century BC and formed part of mixed intensive farming on *villae rusticae*. Most widespread was the ornamental pool which decorated public, religious and domestic settings and varied according to size, design, location, purpose and type of fish raised. Pools appear prominently in the public PALAESTRA of HERCULANEUM and the sanctuary at Località Santa Venera near Poseidonia (mod. Paestum). Best attested are the saltwater ponds of maritime VILLAS of the 1st centuries BC and AD in which the Roman nobility raised for display rare and expensive species, such as red mullet and lampreys. CICERO (*Letters to Atticus* 1.19) disparagingly refers to them as *piscinarii*; among them was Gaius Sergius Orata, whose *cognomen* (his third name) derived from the name of a fish. Descriptions of artificial fishponds by VARRO (*On Agriculture* 3.17) and COLUMELLA (*On Agriculture* 8.17) can be compared with physical remains found on the shore or jutting out into the sea along the coasts of Latium and Campania, such as at Astura and the imperial grotto at Sperlonga. Roman houses often incorporated ornamental pools into their GARDEN design, such as those in the Praedia of Julia Felix and the house of Decimus Octavius Quartio in POMPEII. Among fishponds outside Italy can be mentioned Khirbet Sabiya and CAESAREA MARITIMA in Israel. RIC

See Higginbotham, F. A. (1997) *Piscinae*.

Five Thousand, the see FOUR HUNDRED, THE.

Flaminii A PLEBEIAN family, prominent in the mid-Republic – not to be confused with the Flaminini (a branch of the PATRICIAN Quinctii). The only members of the family of real significance were Gaius FLAMINIUS and his son of the same name. The elder Gaius achieved the consulship in 223 BC, played a key role in Roman imperial expansion and consolidation between the first and second PUNIC WARS, and is traditionally perceived as an early 'popular' politician, often clashing with the senate. He died in the battle of Lake Trasimene. His son was consul in 187; otherwise the family is largely absent from history. Gaius Flaminius, aedile in 67 BC, may be the Flaminius with whom CATILINE conspired in 63. The Flaminii C(h)ilones (possibly related) are known from the coins they minted. The family name is, however, a prominent part of the Roman landscape, thanks to the monumental works of the elder Gaius. JRWP

Flamininus, Titus Quinctius 229/8–174 BC Not to be confused with Gaius FLAMINIUS. Roman general, first conqueror – and liberator – of the Greeks, who knew him as Titos. His early career is obscure; he governed the Greek city of Tarentum in southern Italy in the later stages of the second PUNIC WAR, and settled Roman VETERANS there. He leapt to prominence when elected CONSUL (for 198) with no previous office other than QUAESTOR and still under 30. He was assigned the command of the war (the 'second MACEDONIAN') in Greece against PHILIP V. Through a mixture of diplomacy and tactical skill he retained the command, defeating Philip at KYNOSKEPHALAI in Thessaly (197). However, it is the subsequent peace settlement for which he is famous. In a spectacular propaganda coup, at the Isthmian games (held near CORINTH) of 196, he declared the 'freedom of the Greeks'. By 194 all Roman troops had been withdrawn from Greece. Flamininus was showered with honours by the grateful Greeks: a rare gold coin (only five examples survive) was minted bearing his portrait – he is the only Roman before Julius Caesar to be so portrayed in his lifetime. In reality, the 'freedom of the Greeks' marked a key development in Roman IMPERIALISM and, as the Greeks were to learn, the absence of Roman presence was not the same as an absence of Roman control. The rest of Flamininus' career (he was censor in 189) was marked by ongoing (often somewhat autocratic) involvement in Greek affairs, consequent upon his huge CLIENT network and experience. On one embassy to Bithynia in 183, he took it upon himself to try to extradite the ageing and exiled HANNIBAL, leading to the latter's suicide. JRWP

See Plutarch, *Flamininus*, in B. Perrin, trs. (1921) *Plutarch's Lives*, vol. 10; Eckstein, A. M. (1987) *Senate and General*.

Flaminius, Gaius Roman general and consul who pursued a radical programme in the last half of the 3rd century BC, for which he was roundly condemned at the time and in subsequent sources starting with FABIUS PICTOR. He came from a family with no political background and was elected TRIBUNE of the people in 232. He immediately set about the distribution of plots of land in northern Italy to the people, which allegedly provoked the Gauls to invade in 225. He was the first annual praetorian governor of SICILY in 227, was elected CONSUL as a *novus homo* in 223, and campaigned against the Gauls. He was elected a second time in 217 but was ambushed by HANNIBAL at Lake Trasimene, where he and 15,000 soldiers were killed; the depth of this disaster has contributed to his unhappy reputation. Flaminius was involved in public building work: the Circus Flaminius (actually a square rather than a true CIRCUS) was begun by him during his censorship in 220. So was the Via Flaminia, the principal ROAD north from Rome, running to Ariminum (Rimini) on the Adriatic coast. One aspect of his career, the consistently negative religious element, is very striking: the omens were always negative at his elections, and he was accused of negligence for his own part in taking the auspices. CJS

See Vishnia, R. F. (1996) *State, Society, and Popular Leaders in Mid-Republican Rome 241–167 BC*.

Flavius Cerialis The EQUESTRIAN commanding officer (prefect) of the 9th Batavian cohort in garrison at the FORT of VINDOLANDA, northern BRITAIN, around AD 100. Although he was a minor player in the overall scheme of Roman military affairs, his life is illuminated through a remarkable dossier of documents, the Vindolanda writing tablets, in which he is the best-represented individual. As commanding officer, Cerialis was the author or recipient of a number of letters in the archive, and there are a number of clues as to his background. It is known that the Batavian units in the Roman army were often commanded by their own nobles, and it is likely that he was from the Batavian homelands in the lower RHINE area. The name Flavius suggests that his family gained Roman citizenship no earlier than AD 70, most likely in the aftermath of the Batavian revolt, presumably because they showed loyalty to Rome. At any event, as a first-generation entrant into the equestrian level of Roman society, he was clearly a man on the rise – his correspondence hints at his seeking preferment with the provincial GOVERNOR. Other letters reflect the power that he already commanded, as fellow officers recommended individuals to him and sought his commendation. His wife, SULPICIA LEPIDINA, was with him at Vindolanda and was very much a part of frontier life. Among their regular correspondents were the commander of a neighbouring fort, Gaius Aelius Brocchus, and his wife, Claudia Severa; military matters are intermixed in their letters with requests for hunting nets and birthday party invitations. DJM

See Bowman, A. (1994) *Life and Letters on the Roman Frontier*.

flint and chert We tend to associate the use of chipped, flaked and ground STONE tools with prehistory (hence terms like Neolithic, 'New Stone Age'). Bronze arrowheads, for example, largely replaced stone in the Bronze Age. But archaeologists increasingly recognize that stone tools played an important role in Mediterranean economies in the historical periods. OBSIDIAN points, for example, may have been embedded in the underside of threshing-sledges to assist in breaking up the grain, as in more recent times. Obsidian occurs only in a few places in the Mediterranean, and locally available flint or chert (collectively referred to as siliceous rocks or 'silex') were often used instead, despite their inferior hardness. Flint was also used for striking a light, as in our own day.

In archaeological FIELD SURVEYS, worked pieces of flint, chert and obsidian are sometimes found on the surface among post-Bronze Age pottery. They typically include blades and scrapers of these materials, flakes and cores left over from their manufacture, and polishing-stones and pounders made from hard, igneous rocks. Many of these stone tools cannot be accurately dated, and their association with pottery of a particular period does not prove their use at that time: they may have been deposited during earlier, prehistoric use of an area, or may even have been found and reused by classical farmers. In excavation of historic-period sites, small stone tools may often be absent because they were normally used in fields and workplaces away from buildings. Sometimes, however, they may fail to be recorded because it is assumed that they are prehistoric and therefore intrusive. Occasionally, however, they are found in stratified deposits of early Iron Age and later date, such as at Halieis in the Argolid, and it is likely that they continued to be used into medieval and early modern times.

Grinding-stones or querns (see MILLS AND MILLING) can often be quite closely dated. These also occur in HOUSES because of their use in or near the KITCHEN, which explains their frequent association with datable pottery in surface survey. (see also FUEL) DGJS

See Humphrey, J. (2003) The utilization and technology of flint in the British Iron Age, in J. Humphrey, ed., *Re-searching the Iron Age* 17–23; Runnels, C. N. (1982) Flaked-stone artifacts in Greece during the historical period, *Journal of Field Archaeology* 9: 363–73; Torrence, R. (1982) The obsidian trade, in C. Renfrew and M. Wagstaff, eds., *An Island Polity* 182–221 (Melos).

Flora see DRAMA, ROMAN.

Florianus

𓂀 EMPERORS, ROMAN: (b).

FLOWERS: garland-making is vividly illustrated by paintings from Pompeii and Herculaneum – situated in a major zone of flower growing for use in perfume manufacture.

flowers One of the greatest splendours of Greece is its wild flowers. Modern Greece alone has a wonderful range of habitats, from snowy mountain and bare rock to lush meadow and sandy shore; it contains over 6,000 species. A similar range existed in antiquity, though many flowers common now are introductions (the weed Bermuda Buttercup, the Hottentot Fig, both from South Africa). Orchids, in particular, are evolving so quickly that there are probably new species.

Ancient Greeks and Romans loved flowers, and used them as pot plants and as cut flowers to decorate living spaces, for special occasions such as weddings, and to wear as wreaths or garlands. Roman sacrificial animals were draped with garlands. People represented on Attic pottery are sometimes shown holding and smelling flowers. Flowers are beautiful but ephemeral, so the use of large numbers of fresh flowers for a wedding, *symposion* or other celebration in Greco-Roman culture was a display of wealth and prestige. ATHENAEUS gives recipes for garlands, and the Roman agricultural writers VARRO and COLUMELLA discuss the cultivation of flowers for the market. Flowers appear regularly in poetry to signify frailty, delicacy and beauty, as in SAPPHO's fragment (132) 'I have a beautiful child who looks like golden flowers, my darling Kleïs, for whom I would not take all Lydia'. This theme is picked up in the poems of CATULLUS.

Flowers appear frequently in myth. For example, in the Homeric hymn to DEMETER, PERSEPHONE is stolen away by HADES while she gathers flowers in a meadow. In most visual representations of PERSEPHONE she is holding flowers, usually poppies, which are weeds of cereal fields. Many flowers were deemed to have mythological origins, such as the hyacinth that sprang from the blood of Hyakinthos when a careless discus throw by his lover, APOLLO, killed him; or NARCISSUS (Narkissos), turned into a flower while falling in love with his own reflection.

ARISTOTLE, and especially THEOPHRASTOS, studied plants and flowers. They were widely exploited, for example for DYES (e.g. saffron, from the stamens of the autumn-flowering *Crocus sativa*) and PERFUMES (in particular the rose and the Madonna lily), as well as for MEDICINAL purposes. The manuscript tradition of Dioskorides (1st century AD) includes both drawings and descriptions, but ancient names do not necessarily refer to a single species in modern terms. (see also ECOLOGY; GARDENS) JBS, LF

See Baumann, H. (1993) *Greek Wild Flowers*; Polunin, O. and Huxley, A. (1987) *Flowers of the Mediterranean*.

food preservation Conserving is a matter of life and death when food supplies are limited to those of local origin. What can be done to prolong the usefulness of a plentiful catch or harvest? Will it last until next year's crop is ripe? Many familiar flavours originate in the necessity to preserve the food value of supplies that cannot be consumed fresh: examples are dried FRUIT, WINE and vinegar, olives and OLIVE OIL, CHEESE, bacon, salt FISH, and FISH SAUCE. All these will keep over many months, and sometimes for several years, when without appropriate treatment the fresh produce from which they are made would rapidly spoil. In the discussion of domestic economy in XENOPHON's *Oikonomikos*, the management of HOUSEHOLD food supplies over a full year is treated as one of the crucial topics. City households were often more improvident than this text implies: many depended on cheap distribution of staple foods. Storage facilities were an essential element in the planning of farm buildings; details varied, but in general cool temperature, low humidity and adequate ventilation were required.

Ancient cookery recipes are brief and vague, but ancient recipes for making conserved foods are detailed and precise, because errors in these processes can spoil large quantities of food and endanger a family's survival. The fullest collection of recipes is in COLUMELLA's manual *On Agriculture* (book 12). AD

See Curtis, R. I. (1991) *Garum and Salsamenta*; (2001) *Ancient Food Technology*.

food supply

The staple food in Greece was CEREALS, especially wheat and barley. The ideal for most city-states was self-sufficiency, which under normal circumstances was no problem. Inclement weather and WARFARE, however, could seriously disrupt the food supply and create a shortfall. If bad conditions

FOOD SUPPLY, ROMAN: mosaic from Ostia, depicting one of the official grain measurers, alongside a *modius* measure, with his levelling stick in his right hand.

continued for a number of years, a food crisis could develop into a famine. Droughts and consequent crop failure are mentioned with alarming frequency by HISTORIANS, and during the archaic period these events – exacerbated by population growth – provided the main stimuli for groups of citizens to leave their mother-cities and establish COLONIES overseas. Maintaining a regular food supply successfully depends on total population figures, AGRICULTURAL potential and CLIMATIC conditions; the precise relative weights of these factors cannot be established for the ancient world, and the only lead is provided by food crises reported in the written evidence.

The city-state about which we are best informed, Athens, is located in one of the driest parts of Greece and the population is thought to have grown at a steady pace from the 6th century onwards. In the early part of the 5th century there is little evidence that the Athenians had to import grain to feed themselves. It is likely that the city managed to intensify agricultural production to meet the rising demands of a growing population. After the outbreak of the PELOPONNESIAN WAR, Athens' capability to feed its own population on locally grown wheat and barley gradually worsened. Even in this period, food crises were rare because of the strong Athenian fleet, which ensured that the grain route from the northeast Aegean was kept open. In the 4th century the Athenians imported grain from Egypt, SICILY, PHOENICIA and the Po region of Italy. By far the most important source of grain, however, was the BOSPORAN KINGDOM, whose king once sent 400,000 *medimnoi* to Athens (enough to keep more than 100,000 people alive), perhaps in connection with an urgent food crisis.

The majority of crises in the food supply were caused, not by natural disasters, but by problems in releasing available grain onto the market. Most of the land on which grain was produced was in the hands of private owners. It was moral outrage and popular protest, rather than governmental pressure, that forced them to release grain onto the market. City-states showed little inclination to take control of the food supply. SAMOS is the only state which is known to have instituted a permanent treasury for the purchase of grain, but the original contributions by the more than 100 sponsors were modest, barely enough to feed 80 people for a year. The best city governments could do was to provide incentives to traders and regulate market operations to combat unfair prices, for example by ensuring that proper WEIGHTS were used and that loaves were of the right size and weight. By the 4th century, Athens had appointed special officials called grain wardens (*sitophylakes*). In the hellenistic and Roman periods it was common for rich citizens to step in to alleviate food crises, but there is a fair suspicion that they did not buy grain but sold their own supplies at a reduced price. MK

See Garnsey, P. (1988) *Famine and Food Supply in the Graeco-Roman World.*

The vast majority of food grown in the Roman world was consumed at the site of production. Much of the remaining marginal surplus was collected and sent towards two destinations: the army and the city of Rome. Food redirected for these purposes created the largest-scale system of long-distance TRADE in antiquity. The population of Rome grew rapidly in the last two centuries of the REPUBLIC until it achieved the unprecedented size of c.1 million inhabitants. The city's nutritional requirements far outstripped local resources and even those of all Italy, necessitating overseas imports on a grand scale. The three staple foods composing the majority of people's diets were grain, olives (usually in the form of OLIVE OIL) and WINE. A minimalist estimate of the annual amount of these staples required by Rome's populace at this time exceeds 400,000 tonnes. During the Republic, the food supply (*annona*) fell under the general duties of the AEDILES, but direct involvement of the state intensified when in 123 BC Gaius GRACCHUS was responsible for a law mandating that CITIZENS in Rome should receive grain at a subsidized price. In 58 CLODIUS transformed this into a free distribution to urban citizens of slightly more than 30 kg of grain per month.

By the early empire, the AGRICULTURAL surpluses of North AFRICA, SICILY, Spain and Egypt were being channelled to Rome. The state took an active role in ensuring an adequate food supply, though at all times private merchants and shippers formed an important part of the system. Much of the food imported from these PROVINCES was collected in the form of TAXES in kind. A steadily growing number of officials, led by the *praefectus annonae*, a position created by AUGUSTUS in AD 7 or 8, oversaw the food supply. A considerable infrastructure developed to store and transport this food. Rome's main port of OSTIA, particularly after expansion projects under the EMPERORS CLAUDIUS and TRAJAN, was a shipping centre with extensive docks and WAREHOUSES. Up-river at Rome, a portion of the city along the banks of the TIBER known as the *emporium* district contained enormous warehouses. A testament to the scale of imports to Rome is Monte Testaccio, a hill several hundred metres long in this district: it is actually a colossal garbage heap of tens of millions of broken olive-oil AMPHORAS.

Although food shortages were common, accounts of actual starvation are extremely rare, so that overall the system seems to have worked fairly well. When CONSTANTINE organized his new capital city at CONSTANTINOPLE, he endowed it with a similar system of grain distributions and associated bureaucracy. The army was fed through a combination of purchased grain and taxes in kind, eventually institutionalized by the later empire as a tax initially called the *annona militaris*. GSA

See Garnsey, P. (1988) *Famine and Food Supply in the Graeco-Roman World*; Rickman, G. (1980) *The Corn Supply of Ancient Rome*; Sirks, B. (1991) *Food for Rome.*

MONTE TESTACCIO; OSTIA AND PORTUS: (a); SHOPS AND SHOPPING: (a)–(b).

footwear In articulating different ranks in society, footwear played an important role. This is particularly the case in Rome, where different classes wore different shoes. Citizens were distinguished from non-citizens by the fact that they wore *calcei* (sing. *calceus*, 'shoe'). In turn, SENATORS wore *calcei* with the letter C affixed to them, while EMPERORS wore purple *calcei*. At the other end of the scale, the very poor probably did not wear shoes at all.

Footwear also helped to gender people. While Greek and Roman men and women frequently wore the same kinds of shoes, they were decorated differently.

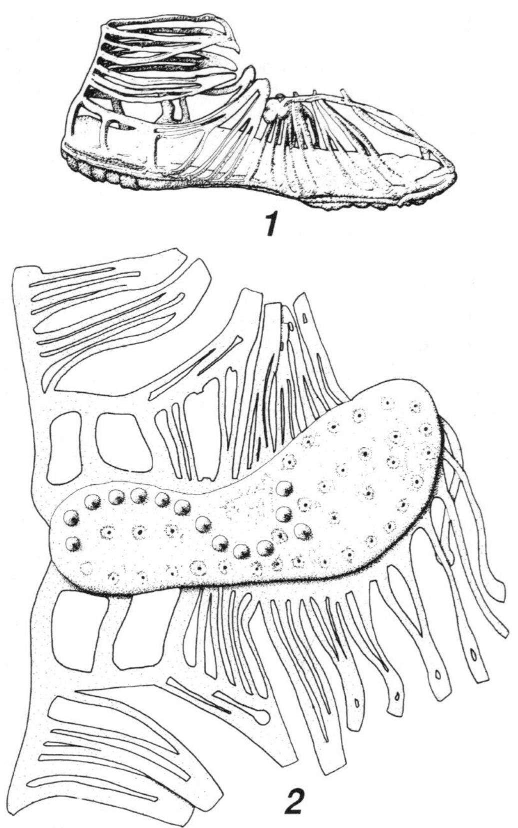

FOOTWEAR: Roman military boots (*caligae*) from Mainz (1 = complete example; 2 = exploded view from below showing hobnail pattern).

For example, *calcei* were dyed black when worn by men, white when worn by women.

Footwear also articulated different activities. Romans wore different footwear depending on whether they were outdoors or indoors. According to the norm, upstanding ROMAN CITIZENS wore closed shoes when they were outside. When they went home, they removed these and wore open shoes such as *sandalia* and *soleae*. The latter were sandals with straps running around the top of the foot and fastening at the heel. *Sandalia* were similar to the house slippers worn in the Greek world. Romans saw this custom of wearing light, open shoes at home as a way of bestowing respect upon their household gods. Romans took off their shoes during mealtimes, a practice so ingrained that the phrase 'removing shoes' came to mean having a repast. SLAVES typically removed the shoes of dinner guests and washed their feet before they reclined to eat. EACM

DRESS, GREEK: (g); LEATHER AND LEATHER-WORKING.

forensic archaeology A comparatively new branch of study, involving both the application of forensic science in archaeology and the adoption of archaeological practices in criminal investigations. An alternative term, 'forensic anthropology', more properly refers simply to the scientific examination of human remains, and is widely used in archaeology. Forensic archaeology is important in modern police investigations, but the techniques are equally relevant to the study of much older burials. For example, the identification of the occupant of the principal tomb at VERGINA in Macedonia as PHILIP II rests largely on forensic reconstruction. This involved not only rebuilding his skull from fragments, but also recreating the actual appearance of the head, complete with facial hair and the unsightly scar from an arrow wound to his right eye. Lindow Man provides a good example of the application of the full range of forensic techniques to a well-preserved body, found in a bog in north-western England. This unfortunate man, of high status to judge by his hair and fingernails, died in grim circumstances – two vicious blows to the head, garrotted, his throat cut and finally his body deposited in the bog. Several factors suggest that this was more than an unsolved murder. The body dates to AD 50–100 (a period of unrest following the Roman invasion), and the analysis of the stomach contents hints that his last meal may have been ritually prepared. The implication is that he was a sacrificial offering to the GODS. DJM

forests and forestry Wildwood, sacred groves and plantations commanded an important place in both the physical and mental landscapes of the ancient world. Forests were common to mountain ranges and remote locations throughout the MEDITERRANEAN, while northern Europe housed extensive deciduous woodland. In most regions the main areas of forest, pasture and cultivation had been established in earlier antiquity. Woods were particularly appreciated for their varied game, and forests most commonly figure in classical art and literature as localities where HUNTING took place. Woodlands were also exploited for a wide range of crops, the most important being fodder, fuel and TIMBER.

Most rural estates had access to their own woodland resources, and these were carefully cultivated. CATO describes the economic value of different kinds of woods, including willow beds, coppice wood and 'mast-wood'. Land grants that accompanied Roman colonial settlements sometimes involved allotting remote woods to farms located elsewhere in the territory. Such woods could be bought and sold for profit, and were subjects of legal disputes. Forests were commonly owned publicly, and in Italy sacred groves were the property of the Roman people. Colonies and municipalities also held woodland, farmed by contractors to supply public buildings with timber and fuel. Specific tracts of woodland were assigned by EMPERORS to fuel the BATHS of Rome.

The exploitation of both wild and managed woodlands is illustrated by the range of structural timbers found in Roman LONDON. Some were split from huge, slow-growing oaks that had lived in high, dark wildwood. Others were taken from small, fast-growing, coppiced trees. Coppicing, in which trees were cut to ground level regularly to promote growth, had been practised from the Neolithic period. COLUMELLA, writing in the 1st century AD, described how the best woods for coppicing were oak and chestnut, with oak cut at 7-year intervals and chestnut on a 5-year cycle. Roundwood found in the Roman fort at Ribchester

(Lancashire) shows short-interval coppicing of hazel and oak, with peaks at 7 and 11 years. Alder was coppiced annually.

Most demands were met from sustainable sources. Shortages of the massive timbers needed for ROOF and ship-timbers are, however, recorded, and some industrial needs could not be met locally. STRABO describes deforestation consequent on COPPER MINING in CYPRUS, and IRON ore from Elba was smelted at Populonia because timber supplies on the island were inadequate. Estimates suggest that the Roman SILVER workings at Rio Tinto in Spain consumed 0.8 ha (2 acres) of woodland daily. Arguments that the ancient world saw periods of catastrophic deforestation, however, are unconvincing. The demand for fuel encouraged the preservation, not the destruction, of woodland. Episodes of forest clearance were more usually a product of agrarian expansion into marginal areas. Pollen diagrams show that the Roman occupation of BRITAIN added impetus to a long-established process of woodland clearance accompanying the extensification of arable land. Deforestation was most marked around HADRIAN'S WALL, where the end of the Roman period was followed by woodland regeneration. DP

See Meiggs, R. (1982) *Trees and Timber in the Ancient Mediterranean World*; Rackham, O. (2001) *Trees, Wood and Timber in Greek History*.

fortification

According to ARISTOTLE (*Politics* 1330b–1331a), fortifications reflect the social and political priorities of their builders. The circuit walls of towns built in the 5th and 4th centuries BC and later represent the most substantial Greek fortifications, and reflect the importance of urbanized centres at that time. Earlier fortifications reflect the development of states out of smaller Dark Age chiefdoms, and responses to the growing scale of land and sea warfare. From the 6th century on, barrier walls were occasionally built to inhibit access to territory. Various walls were built at THERMOPYLAI, and across the THRACIAN Chersonese, the isthmus of Corinth, and the Messapian peninsula in southern Italy. The Dema wall in Attica exemplifies 4th-century refinements.

Over the half-millennium before 500 BC, most fortifications were simple rubble walls, usually reinforcing

FORTIFICATION: (a) view (to north) of the south-eastern tower at the ancient fortified town of Aigosthena (Megarid, Greece). The fort of which this was part may have been built by Demetrios I or another of Alexander's Successors, or perhaps by the Athenians in the 340s BC. It was the tallest surviving Greek fortification until the upper courses were dislodged in a recent earthquake. The square windows indicate that artillery pieces were housed in the uppermost storey. Mt Kithairon is visible in the background.

FORTIFICATION: (b) view (to north) of the eastern range of fortifications at Aigosthena.

FORTIFICATION: (c) view (to east) of the northern range of the classical fortifications at Eleutherai (mod. Gyphtókasto) in north-western Attica (4th century BC).

FORTIFICATION: (d) detail of one of the towers of the land walls of Constantinople.

natural strongholds (e.g. Zagora on Andros, the *akropolis* of Emborió on CHIOS). Occasionally they were repairs to the more massive stone walls of a late Bronze Age citadel (e.g. the ATHENIAN ACROPOLIS). As early as the 9th century BC, more substantial fortifications were built to protect towns on the Ionian coast from raiding Kimmerian horsemen and the forces of the PHRYGIAN and LYDIAN kingdoms. The well-studied fortifications of Old SMYRNA had bastions beside the gates, with walls of mudbrick above a high stone socle forming massive fighting platforms. Such walls were simplified versions of fortifications at SARDIS, Gordion, and PHOENICIAN and SYRIAN cities. By the 6th century, larger Greek settlements in the AEGEAN ISLANDS were fortified on the Ionian pattern.

With the fortification of Athens and PIRAEUS by THEMISTOKLES in 479–478 BC following the PERSIAN occupation, Ionian-style fortifications arrived on the mainland (Thucydides 1.89–93). These assured Athenian independence from the Spartan land power. Once completed by the Long Walls joining Athens to Piraeus by c.457, they secured the Athenian commitment to naval power in the Aegean. By the time of the PELOPONNESIAN WAR, most towns of any size had some manner of defensive circuit. The Spartans' pride in never having walls around their town (until the hellenistic period) is characteristic of their conservatism.

Most walls were built of mudbrick above a stone socle, though on rocky ground they could be entirely of stone. Large circuits and long walls, as at Athens, had towers set at intervals as patrol stations and watchposts. Gates were protected within recessed forecourts or by flanking bastions, and occasional posterns enabled defenders to attack any siege-works. Ditches, placed in front of walls on level ground, impeded rams. By the second quarter of the 4th century, bolt-throwing CATAPULTS were accommodated in towers with enclosed upper chambers and windows, as at Aigosthena in Megarian territory. The stone walls of MESSENE in the south-west Peloponnese and Eleutherai (Gyphtókastro) in north-west ATTICA, are well-preserved examples of 4th-century fortified circuits. More powerful catapults of the late 4th century made covered wall-walks and large ARTILLERY bastions, especially on exposed salients, characteristic of hellenistic defences, but otherwise techniques of fortification remained much as they were in the 4th century. (see also SIEGE AND SIEGE WARFARE; FORTS AND FORTRESSES; *AKROPOLIS*) MM

See Lawrence, A.W. (1979) *Greek Aims in Fortification*; Munn, M.H. (1993) *The Defense of Attica: the Dema wall and the Boiotian war of 378–375 BC*; Winter, F.E. (1971) *Greek Fortifications*.

Roman fortifications functioned both as defence against likely threat and as a prominent and costly civic monument. Rome's ETRUSCAN heritage shows in the attribution of the earliest defences of the city to king SERVIUS TULLIUS (6th century BC), though the earliest surviving elements of the Servian wall are 4th-century, consisting of a stone wall with an earthen rampart or *agger*. The contemporary *castrum* at OSTIA was surrounded by a free-standing stone wall. Republican *coloniae* of the 3rd and 2nd centuries BC in Italy often had walls of careful polygonal masonry (e.g. Alba Fucens, Norba). By the 1st century BC, contact with hellenistic SIEGE warfare and civic ARCHITECTURE led to more impressive defences, as in the new circuit at Ostia or *coloniae* such as Auximum.

In the West and in AFRICA during the PRINCIPATE, grants of fortification were closely linked to status, particularly *coloniae*, and thus defences should be seen as a civic monument. Sometimes walls succeeded military fortifications (e.g. Gloucester) or aped their form (e.g. Aosta, TIMGAD), but sometimes the circuits were impractically long, enclosing much unbuilt-on land (e.g. Cherchel, Nîmes), a display of civic self-regard. Many of these fortifications were of AUGUSTAN date; later examples include TRIER and the unusual series of later 2nd-century earthwork town defences in BRITAIN. Military fortifications were defensively unsophisticated, with internal towers and monumental gateways; they shared an architectural vocabulary with the towns. In the East, towns and cities inherited defensive circuits from the hellenistic period, so few new ones date to the principate, though existing circuits were maintained, embellished and occasionally extended (e.g. Athens, JERUSALEM). Such fortified cities served also as military bases, largely precluding the need for separate FORTS.

The defensive attitude of the late empire is reflected in the (re-)construction of defences. Late Roman defences were characterized by high, thick walls with regularly spaced towers (sometimes for ARTILLERY) and small gateways, and often enclosed much smaller areas than under the principate. Rome was given a new circuit of defences nearly 19 km (12 miles) in length by AURELIAN (AD 270–5). In the West, defences were principally at forts and the main towns. This link with urban status and the careful treatment of visible surfaces (e.g. Le Mans) suggests a function as the defining civic monument of late towns as well as defence and field army bases. Some hilltops (in eastern Gaul) and VILLAS (in the Balkans) were also fortified. Though defensively simple, such walls sufficed against the limited siege capability of the European barbarians. In the East, by contrast, the PERSIANS posed a more serious threat, and towns and fortresses such as Amida and El-Lejjun were heavily fortified, culminating in the massive and monumental triple land-walls of CONSTANTINOPLE under Theodosius II (408–50). ASEC

See Johnson, S. (1983) *Late Roman Fortifications*; Maloney, J. and Hobley, B., eds. (1983) *Roman Urban Defences in the West*; Richmond, I. A. (1930) *The City Walls of Imperial Rome*.

 ACROPOLIS, ATHENIAN: (a).

forts and fortresses

Uncommon in Greek states before the later 5th century, permanent forts reflect a reliance on professional soldiers or a standing citizen levy to protect property against raids. Shortly before the

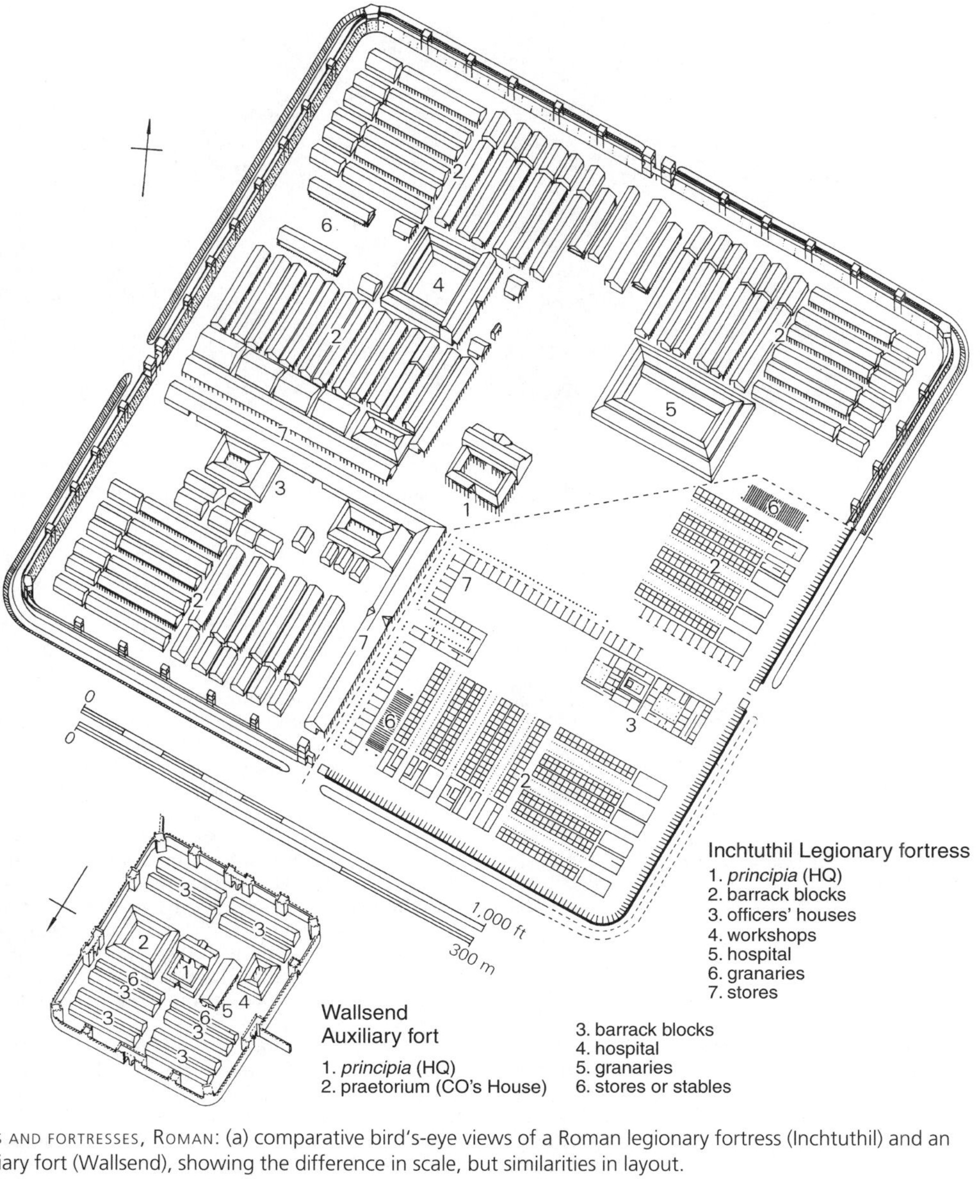

Inchtuthil Legionary fortress
1. *principia* (HQ)
2. barrack blocks
3. officers' houses
4. workshops
5. hospital
6. granaries
7. stores

Wallsend
Auxiliary fort
1. *principia* (HQ)
2. praetorium (CO's House)
3. barrack blocks
4. hospital
5. granaries
6. stores or stables

0 1,000 ft
0 300 m

FORTS AND FORTRESSES, ROMAN: (a) comparative bird's-eye views of a Roman legionary fortress (Inchtuthil) and an auxiliary fort (Wallsend), showing the difference in scale, but similarities in layout.

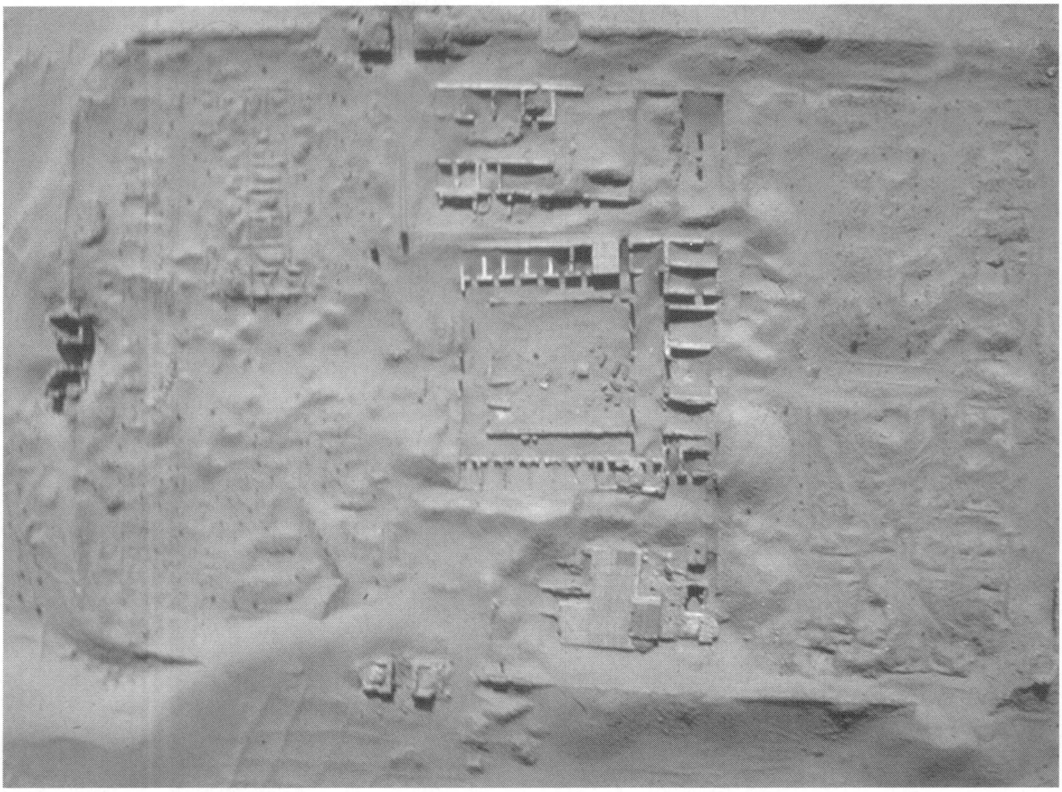

FORTS AND FORTRESSES, ROMAN: (b) aerial photograph of the Roman fort at Bu Njem in the Libyan desert. The central range has been excavated (comprising top to bottom, commandant's house and granary, headquarters building, baths) and the approximate layout of barracks in the *praetentura* and *retentura* can be made out beneath the sand.

FORTS AND FORTRESSES, ROMAN: (c) reconstructed barrack block from South Shields, near Hadrian's Wall.

PELOPONNESIAN WAR, city-states began to establish forts in areas far from urban centres. They were built where garrisons could watch over vital resources, chiefly farmland, sometimes MINES or HARBOURS. In times of war they could shelter portable property and serve as bases for raiding enemy territory, but could not prevent major invasions. Thucydides mentions permanent forts during the Peloponnesian war in ATTICA, southern Italy, SICILY and MACEDONIA. Debates at Athens about garrison strengths during tensions with neighbouring BOIOTIA in the 4th century (Xenophon, *Memorabilia*, *Poroi*; Demosthenes 18–19) reflect the politics of cost versus need. There are substantial remains of Attic forts at Eleusis, Panakton, Eleutherai (Gyphtókastro), Phyle, Rhamnous and Sounion.

Temporary forts built in wartime served similar functions, with an emphasis on offensive strategies. Forts supported siege-works around cities, while *epiteichismos* involved placing a fort in enemy territory as a base for raids (Thucydides 1.142). Other famous examples, both during the Peloponnesian war, are the Athenian fort at Pylos in MESSENIA (4.3–5) and the Peloponnesian fort at Dekeleia in Attica (7.27–8).

Where civic authority was weak or non-existent, forts could be private enterprises, like towers or strong farmsteads. Like the older Macedonian fortresses mentioned by Thucydides, the fortresses controlled by ALCIBIADES in the Thracian Chersonese reflect an old pattern of strongholds belonging to local chieftains (Xenophon, *Hellenika* 1.5, 2.1). MM

See Ober, J. (1985) *Fortress Attica: defense of the Athenian land frontier 404–322 BC*.

A distinctive feature of the Roman army was its construction of purpose-built, defended encampments both on campaign and in garrison. Polybios accounted this one of the reasons for the success of Roman arms, and describes the layout of a camp in book 6 of his *Histories*. Remains of Republican forts are rare, but Renieblas, the earliest of the siege-camps near Numantia (Spain), reflects the Polybian scheme. Later camps in the series (e.g. Castillejo, Peña Redonda) show the transition from manipular to cohortal army.

Forts (for auxiliaries) and fortresses (for legions) of the principate in the European provinces were built to a standardized plan whose origins are obscure. The early 1st-century BC site at Cáceres el Viejo (Spain) may be an early example, the Augustan site at Haltern (Germany) shows the type nearly fully developed, and by the Flavian period it had become standardized. Until the mid-1st century AD in Germany and the end of the 1st century in Britain, forts and fortresses were built of timber, thereafter they were (re-)constructed in stone.

Legionary fortresses were generally c.20 ha (50 acres) in area, built to a rectangular plan with rounded corners, the 'playing-card' shape, and a regular grid of streets. Across the centre of the fortress lay the *principia* (headquarters), *praetorium* (legate's residence) and the barracks of cohort I. Behind these, in the *retentura*, lay the baths, *fabrica* (workshops) and *valetudinarium* (hospital). Across the *via principalis*, in the *praetentura*, lay the tribunes' houses. Most of the rest of the interior was taken up with the barracks of cohorts II–X, with their distinctive plan of pairs of rooms for squads of eight men (*contubernium*), the centurion's quarters lying at the outer end. Near the gates were *horrea* (store buildings). Outside the defences were usually an amphitheatre (*ludus*) and civil settlement (*canabae*). Good examples of fortresses include Inchtuthil (Britain), Neuss (Germany) and Carnuntum (Austria). They are less common in the Eastern provinces, where the army was often brigaded in towns.

Auxiliary forts, both in plan and building-types, were very similar to fortresses but scaled down for the smaller complements of troops; they were usually 2–4 ha (5–10 acres) in size. Not all forts had all the types of building, e.g. *valetudinarium*. Many attempts have been made to deduce unit types and precise unit structures from the number and forms of barrack-blocks, but the variations within unit types and splitting of units suggests this is a vain pursuit. As well as fortresses and forts, there were intermediate-sized 'vexillation fortresses' and temporary 'marching camps' on campaign. Both are particularly well represented in Britain.

In the late empire some sites, such as the Diocletianic fortress at El-Lejjun (Jordan), show descent from the principate, but in general forts varied widely in size, plan and internal buildings, reflecting the more heterogeneous nature of the late Roman army. ASEC

See Johnson, A. (1983) *Roman Forts*; Pamment Salvatore, J. (1996) *Roman Republican Castrametation*.

 ARMIES, ORGANIZATION OF.

Fortuna A Roman goddess, the embodiment of good luck and success. Her name is derived from *fors*, the Latin word for luck. Although she appears to have associations with the Greek goddess Tyche, her origins have also been connected with the Etruscan idea of fate. Fortuna seems not to have belonged to the earliest phase of Roman religion: she does not figure in the earliest festal calendar and had no *flamen* (priest). According to tradition, it was Servius Tullius, the sixth king of Rome, who established the earliest temples to her in Rome. Two further temples were dedicated to her in 293 BC and AD 17.

The number and variety of her cultic titles (cf. Plutarch, *Moralia* 281) make it difficult to specify Fortuna's functions precisely, but especially in the republican period she was considered a benevolent deity. She functioned as a protectress – an image of her watched over the emperors while they slept – and she also had special appeal for slaves and the lower classes, who venerated her as a source of fertility, success and happy coincidences. In the later imperial period, particularly in literature, she is portrayed more negatively. Lucius, the hero of Apuleius' *Metamorphoses*, for instance, celebrates Isis' rescue of him from the capricious realm of blind Fortuna (*Metamorphoses* 11.15).

In iconography, Fortuna resembles figures of Tyche, and is commonly depicted as a standing female figure with a cornucopia in her left hand and a rudder in her right. JRCC

See Plutarch, *Moralia* 316–26; Kajanto, I. (1981) Fortuna, *ANRW* 2.17.1, 502–58.

forums (*fora*) The open square or market place of a Roman town, the equivalent of an *agora* in a Greek city. The term could also be applied to a small settlement, founded along a main road, whose principal purpose was originally a rural market, particularly in the Republic. A number of these developed into towns in their own right, e.g. Forum Api and Forum Novum in Italy, and Forum Iulii in southern France. The forum square over time became the political, judicial and business centre, particularly of towns in the Western Roman empire. The detailed arrangements of these areas varied according to region, but generally such forums often took a regularized form, rectangular rather than square and flanked by a variety of public buildings including temples, a basilica and a council meeting house, as well as shops and colonnades. In the Western provinces, the whole complex was often dominated by the main temple of the town, usually a Capitolium (temple of the Capitoline triad Jupiter, Juno and Minerva), as at Pompeii, or a temple of the imperial cult, as at Tarraco. The forum was also a place for public announcements and display, with honorific statues and monuments. Pre-existing Greek cities in the Eastern provinces often acquired Western types of forum buildings under direct Roman influence, for example at Ephesos and Smyrna. Forum arrangements in Roman-period city foundations in the East, such as colonies, developed a combination of hellenistic and Roman planning and building forms, as at Corinth, Aspendos and Cremna in Pisidia.

The city of Rome was provided with an accumulation of forums over time. The original open area was the Forum Romanum; this became the main area for public business in the Republic after the

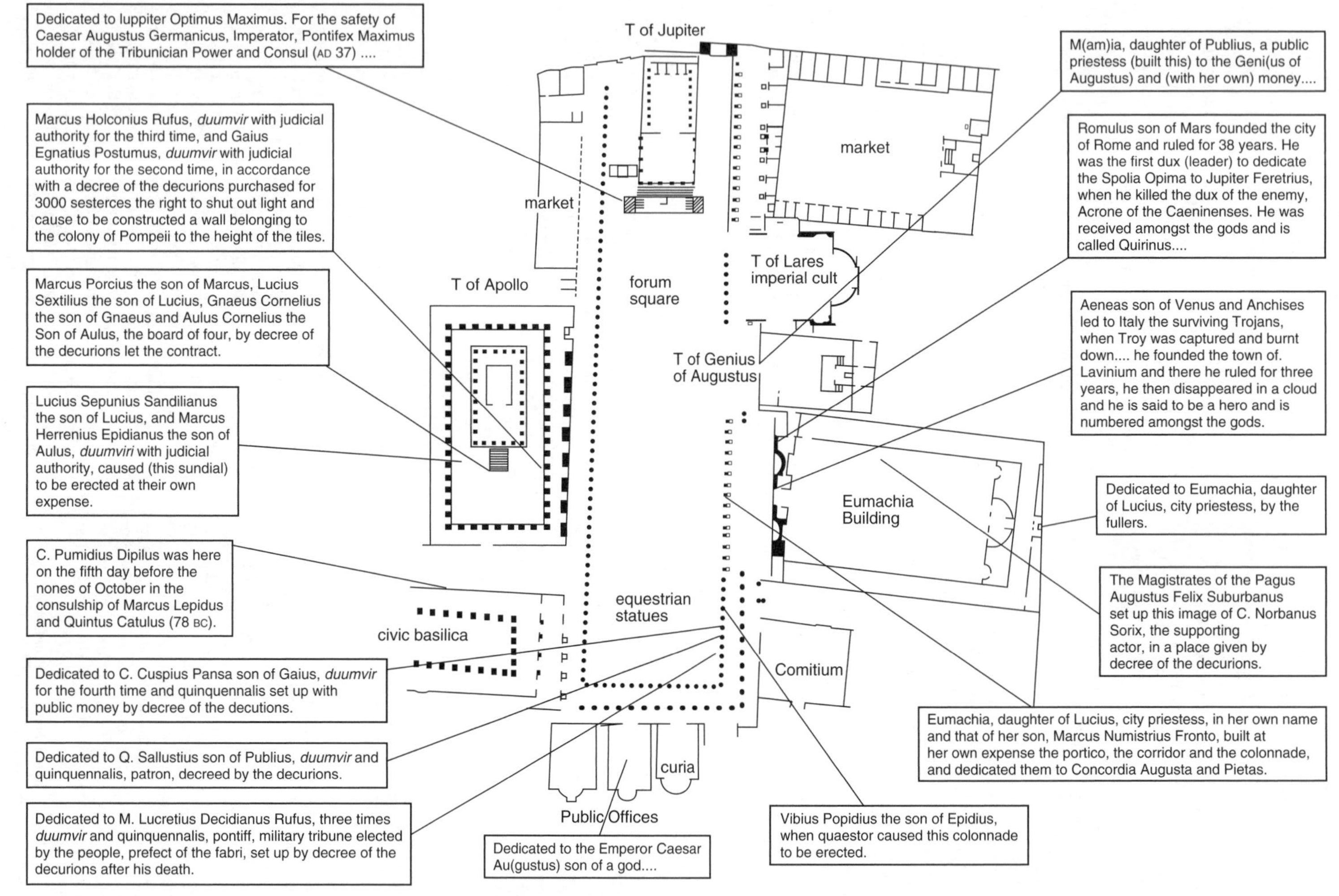

FORUMS: the multiple roles of the forum as public space, political, judicial and religious focus, and for social display are well illustrated by this plan from Pompeii, incorporating just a few of the epigraphic dedications from this area.

development of the Forum Boarium (cattle market) and Forum Holitorium (vegetable market) closer to the Tiber. Five monumental complexes, the 'imperial *fora*', were added to the centre of the capital under Julius Caesar, Augustus, Vespasian, Domitian and Nerva, and Trajan. These were often associated with some aspect of state administration; for example, it was from the forum of Augustus that provincial governors ceremoniously departed and returned. Important lawcourts were convened in the Basilica Ulpia in Trajan's forum; this was also the venue for distributions of imperial largesse and other official acts of generosity, such as the destruction of public debt records and the manumission of slaves. These complexes inspired several monumental forums in the empire, the most elaborate being the great forum built by Septimius Severus at Lepcis Magna in North Africa. HD

See Anderson, J. C. (1984) *The Historical Topography of the Imperial Fora*; Ward-Perkins, J. B. (1974) *Cities of Ancient Greece and Italy*; Grimal, P. (1983) *Roman Cities*, trs. and ed. G. Woloch.

Augustus: (b); markets; Rome: (a).

fostering see adoption; family, Roman; wet-nurses.

Foucault, M. see disability; post-modernism; sexuality.

fountains and fountain houses

An alternative to wells and cisterns for the supply of water. A prerequisite for such structures was the provision for a supply of piped water. In Athens, during the 6th-century BC tyranny of the Peisistratids, a complex series of clay pipes brought water into the heart of the city. One of the outlets was the Enneakrounos, a nine-spouted fountain house drawing water from the spring Kallirhoë (Thucydides 2.15.5). Although the exact location of the fountain has not been identified with certainty, an archaic fountain house dating to c.530–520 has been located in the south-east corner of the Agora (where Pausanias, 1.14.1, believed it to have been located). Late Athenian black-figure pottery is often decorated with scenes of women at a fountain house filling *hydriai*; this may reflect the impact of the new civic amenity.

A large, open-fronted, public fountain house was located just inside the Dipylon Gate at Athens. There are architectural suggestions that the original building, complete with an Ionic colonnade, dated back to the time of Themistokles; but the extant remains, including a floor of Hymettan marble, seem to date from the end of the 4th century when the gate was redesigned. Water was collected in an L-shaped basin. A further 4th-century fountain house was located in the south-west corner of the Agora. Such a public emphasis on fountains is noted with disapproval – along with 'paved streets' – by Demosthenes (*Olynthiacs* 3.29).

In the Roman period, elaborate *nymphaea* became a feature of city life. At Athens, one was located in the south-east corner of the Agora, probably in the Hadrianic period. DWJG

See Crouch, D. P. (1993) *Water Management in Ancient Greek Cities*; Knigge, U. (1991) *The Athenian Kerameikos*; Parlama, L. and Stampolidis, N. C. (2000) *Athens: the city beneath the city*; Tölle-Kastenbein, R. (1990) *Antike Wasserkultur* 130–43.

Public fountains were one of the primary destinations for water in Roman aqueducts, and were sited in streets and squares for public use. At Pompeii, most houses are within a 50 m radius of a street fountain, and fountains must have been vital for the majority in society who could not afford piped water. Frontinus notes that overflow from public fountains was necessary to clean the sewers; originally only fullers, who needed large quantities of water for cleansing cloth, and baths were permitted to use such overflow water (*De aquis* 94, 111).

Fountains varied considerably in design, from simple stone tanks of the street fountains at Pompeii and Herculaneum, with a lead pipe spouting from a gargoyle mask, through more elaborate fountains, such as the conical fountain at Cuicuil (mod. Djemila, Algeria) modelled on the Meta Sudans at Rome, to imposing *nymphaea*. Large *nymphaea*, often semicircular in plan, were decorated with columnar façades and niches housing statues – Herodes Atticus' *nymphaeum* at Olympia included a dynastic monument with statues of his family and the imperial family. An inscription from Cirta (Constantine, Algeria), records that the *nymphaeum* there had (besides bronze and marble statues) chained gilt-inlay drinking

FOUNTAINS AND FOUNTAIN HOUSES: (a) fountain houses were a key source of domestic water supply and scenes of women fetching water appear on many Athenian vases.

FOUNTAINS AND FOUNTAIN HOUSES: (b) Roman fountain from Pompeii, one of more than 30 supplying different neighbourhoods of the city.

goblets and six hand-towels (*ILS* 4921*b*). Such fountains were both ornamental and useful, thronged by people drawing water for household use, refreshing themselves with a drink, or splashing their hands and face; as such, they will have acted as a focus for social interaction and gossip. AIW

See Hodge, A.T. (1992) *Roman Aqueducts and Water Supply*; Gros, P. (1996) *L'Architecture romaine*, vol. 1, 418–44.

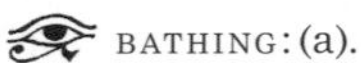 BATHING: (a).

Four Hundred, the The OLIGARCHIC government voted into power at Athens in 411 BC was known as 'the Four Hundred'. Following the disaster in SICILY (413) and revolts of Ionian allies (412), anxieties over dwindling revenues and the progress of the war led the Athenians to adopt radical reforms. In spring 411 they eliminated pay for office and limited citizenship to 5,000 Athenians capable of contributing, in armed service or money, to the safety of the state. The idea originated in a suggestion by ALCIBIADES, then in EXILE, that such a reform could attract PERSIAN support for Athens. This aspiration proved fruitless, and the oligarchic movement came largely under the control of Alcibiades' enemies, notably the demagogue Peisander and the conservative ideologue Antiphon (THERAMENES also rose to prominence in the movement). These men oversaw the abolition of DEMOCRACY and the establishment of a government nominally of the 5,000, but actually under the control of a COUNCIL of 400 men chosen by the oligarchic leaders. The movement was described as a return to the 'ancestral constitution'; the number 400 was probably derived from the size of the pre-KLEISTHENIC council. Never fully implemented, the reforms failed to command the allegiance of the many Athenians then stationed with the fleet at SAMOS. Under Alcibiades' influence the oligarchs became divided in their agenda, and the regime collapsed after four months when it failed to resist the Spartan intervention leading to the revolt of EUBOIA. MM

See Aristotle, *Constitution of Athens*, trs. P. J. Rhodes (1984), chs. 29–33; Thucydides 8.47–98; Munn, M. (2000) *The School of History: Athens in the age of Socrates*; Ostwald, M. (1986) *From Popular Sovereignty to the Sovereignty of Law*.

Franks The collective name for GERMANIC peoples north of the lower RHINE in later sources referring to the 260s AD, first named in a contemporary source in 289. Franks often raided deep into Roman territory in the late 3rd century. In response, EMPERORS exploited divisions between groups to employ Franks to defeat other Franks. From the time of CONSTANTINE (306–37), Frankish units aided the empire, though others continued to harass the Belgic provinces and northern GAUL. After important victories in 358, JULIAN permitted the Salian Franks to settle in Toxandria. Subsequently, the Franks provided many OFFICERS for the Roman army. The most prominent was Bauto in the 380s, whose daughter Eudoxia married the emperor ARCADIUS and was the mother of Theodosius II and PULCHERIA. Governmental and social structure among the Franks was similar to those of other Germanic peoples. Leaders for communal enterprises were chosen when necessary, but had no permanent status.

By the early 5th century, the Salians had begun to assert control over the lower Rhine and extended their territory towards the middle Rhine. Archaeological evidence indicates that some Franks settled in Gaul in this period. After Chlogio brought northern Belgica II into the Frankish domain, Merovechus, founder of the Merovingian dynasty, became the first Frankish king inside Roman territory, with a capital at Tournai. His successor, Childeric, governed in a shared arrangement with Aegidius, a former prefect of Gaul who refused to step down. Both were succeeded by sons, Clovis and Syagrius respectively. After eliminating Syagrius, Clovis established a semi-stable Merovingian domination over all the Franks and much of Gaul by his death in 511. The last Merovingian, Childeric III, was replaced in 751 by the Carolingian Pippin I ('the Short'), son of Charles Martel and grandfather of Charlemagne. France derives its name from the Franks. JV

See James, E. (1988) *The Franks*.

GERMANY AND GERMANS: (b).

fraternity The creation of fictive kinship groups is characteristic of both Greek and Italic peoples in the archaic period. Thus the PHRATRY, a fictive brotherhood linking groups of families, is typical of many Greek states. In HOMER, to be without a phratry is the equivalent of having no home (*Iliad* 9.63–4). In Drakon's homicide law from late 7th-century Athens, the phratry of a victim was responsible for prosecuting a homicide if there were no actual kin (*IG* i^3 104). Under the KLEISTHENIC system of the late 6th century, registration in a DEME and phratry were requirements for CITIZENSHIP. According to Philochoros, membership in a phratry in the archaic period involved admission to a group of *homogalaktes* (those who were suckled on 'the same milk'), later known as *gennêtai* (clansmen) – plainly a further use of biological metaphor to imply unity (*FGrH* 328 F 35). ARISTOTLE (*Politics* 1252b16–18), whose thought may reflect more general Greek practice, defines *homogalaktes* as a subgroup within a *genos* – yet another fictive kinship group. In later Greek, the notion of fraternity could also be expressed through the use of the word *adelphos*, 'brother', which originally signified the biological relationship. Members of an association for the worship of a divinity, a *thiasos*, might thus come to refer to each other as *adelphoi*. This is likely to be the origin of the CHRISTIAN habit of referring to their co-religionists as 'brothers' and 'sisters'.

Fraternitas was a vitally important term in Latin, with a connotation second only to *pietas* in describing mutual obligation, whence derives the Roman habit of describing particularly favoured allies as *fratres*. The archaic system of INHERITANCE known as a *consortium*, in which the sons of a *paterfamilias* would maintain his estate intact by sharing rather than dividing it, survived into the imperial period, providing a theoretical model for close family relationships (AULUS GELLIUS, *Attic Nights* 1.9.12). Outside the family the term *frater*, 'brother', is often used of members of religious groups such as the *fratres* ARVALES or the *Lupercales*. Many organizations in the Roman world could also be described as *sodalitates*, derived from the Latin word *sodalis*, which appears to be connected with an Indo-European root connoting kinship.

Throughout the ancient periods, the notion of brotherhood provided a theoretical model for organizations, secular and sacred, whose members were characterized by affection and homogeneity of purpose. DSP

Frazer, J. G. see ANTHROPOLOGY; SCHOLARSHIP, CLASSICAL; MYTH.

free will Ancient discussions of voluntary action centre around questions of praise and blame. When is it correct to say that someone acted voluntarily and can properly be evaluated for their actions? The answer to such questions often depends upon the underlying theory of human psychology. In PLATO's *Protagoras* (353a–358d), SOCRATES denies the possibility of 'weakness of will' (in Greek, *akrasia*). On his analysis people do not mistakenly pursue closer but lesser goods, rather than more remote but greater goods, because they are 'overcome by pleasure' and compelled to act as they do, but rather because they make an intellectual error in calculating the relative values of the two goods. In the *Republic* (435e–441c), Plato offers a complex view of human psychology which allows people to act on the basis of non-rational impulses derived from distinct 'parts' of the SOUL. It is possible to know the right thing to do but fail to act accordingly because one is driven by some non-rational impulse. Nevertheless, moral evaluation should concern the whole person and it is reasonable to censure someone who, for example, has allowed their appetites to control their reason. In the *Laws* (860c–864c), Plato once again concerns himself with questions about which actions can count as 'voluntary' and the consequences of this analysis for education, punishment and legislation.

ARISTOTLE responds to the Socratic thesis that 'no one does wrong willingly' in *Nicomachean Ethics* 3.1 and 3.5. He claims that voluntary actions, actions for which the agent can be evaluated morally, are those which flow from the agent's character and cannot be traced exclusively to external causes. Individuals are themselves responsible for forming and altering their character through training and habituation.

Only in the later history of ancient philosophy does anything like the modern discussion of 'free will' appear. In the hellenistic period, discussion over the possibility of moral evaluation was provoked by questions of modal logic (in particular Diodoros Kronos' 'Master Argument') and by the different schools' conceptions of causation. The question arose whether agents can be held responsible for their actions if those actions are preordained by the laws of physics, or logic, or god's will. The STOICS believed that, though the world is thoroughly causally determined (by the provident working of divine reason), nevertheless it is possible to evaluate agents morally by considering what contribution is made to the eventual result by their actions. In this sense, they argued, certain actions are 'up to us' and available for moral evaluation. The EPICUREANS thought determinism and moral evaluation incompatible, and attempted to rescue the possibility of free action from the threat of mechanistic determinism offered by their own ATOMIST physics by positing an undetermined atomic motion: the swerve. Exactly how the atomic swerve was supposed to allow voluntary action without introducing purely random events is unclear and the subject of much scholarly disagreement. JIW

See Bobzien, S. (1998) The inadvertent conception and late birth of the free will problem, *Phronesis* 43: 133–75; (1998) *Determinism and Freedom in Stoic Philosophy*; Broadie, S. (1991) *Ethics with Aristotle*.

freedmen and freedwomen

The terms for a freedman in Greek were *exeleutheros* and *apeleutheros*; for a freedwoman, *exeleuthera* and *apeleuthera*. When a male slave was freed he was considered a METIC, a designation that resulted in societal disadvantages. For example, he could not buy land and had legal obligations to his patron. If he failed to perform these duties, his patron had the right to enslave him again. A freed slave was therefore not necessarily considered free immediately after MANUMISSION; there was a period of transition. He was required to sign a contract (*paramenein*) before the gods, which specified his obligations to his former master. Inscriptions attesting to these contracts appear at religious centres such as DELPHI. A woman, for example, may have been expected to provide one of her children as a slave to the ex-master. Some freed slaves remained in this transitional phase as long as their patrons were alive. In the period of the Roman empire, it seems that former Athenian slaves were able to become citizens and serve in local government; the emperor MARCUS AURELIUS, however, banned this practice.

Inscriptions found on funerary monuments, both from Rome and from outside the capital, illustrate the legal status of the freedman. A formulaic inscription included the following: the name of the deceased, their status, the name of their patron, and the slave name. In accordance with the enactment of the *lex Iulia municipalis* of 90 BC, the freedman adopted the *praenomen* (e.g. Gaius) and *nomen* (e.g. Clodius) of his former master, adding them to his original slave name (e.g. Musa) which in turn became his *cognomen*. The following illustrates the standard formula: *C. Clodius C. l. Musa* (*Caius Clodius Cai libertus Musa*), meaning 'Gaius Clodius Musa, freedman of Gaius'. This standardized nomenclature includes the patron's name in the genitive case, followed by 'l.' for *libertus*, 'freedman', or *liberta*, 'freedwoman'. (The word *libertus* may also be complete, or may be abbreviated as 'lib.' or 'libert.') If the patron were female, *Caia*, inscribed as an inverted 'C', would appear in place of *C(aius)* in this example. The terms *libertinus* (masc.) and *libertina* (fem.) often occur in literature, referring to a freedperson's relationship to society.

Slaves took on a wide variety of jobs in the HOUSEHOLD, and these often had a direct relationship to their future occupations as freed slaves. A hierarchy among slaves, based on their relationship with the master, is evident regardless of rural or urban placement. Those who worked in proximity to the master stood a better chance of manumission, and probably maintained a working relationship with him once freed. A freedman, once manumitted, became a Roman citizen and with citizenship came the right to vote. Upon manumission, the censors usually assigned him to one of four specific urban tribes.

The relationship between patron and slave did not end with manumission. According to Roman law, just as the son should honour the father, so the patron 'should always be honoured and held sacred by the freedman' (Justinian, *Digest* 37.15.9). The freedman, therefore, would have some obligations or *operae* (assigned days of labour) to perform in return for his manumission, whether the patron was alive or dead. *Operae* were defined through the concepts of *beneficium* (kindness) and *obsequium* (respectful behaviour).

Factors contributing to a freedman's wealth included his master's economic status, the freedman's personal relationship with him, and the occupation he had engaged in as a slave. In general, when referring to a freedman living in the capital, one can say that he had an important role in society despite certain social and political restrictions. Upon manumission he became a Roman citizen, though with certain restrictions upon his citizenship which, for the most part, reflected societal prejudice rather than legal limitations (e.g. exclusion from public office and the military).

From an economic and social standpoint, freedmen were integral to Rome's prosperity. The occupations they had in daily life formed the basis of the economy, yet the ruling class held these positions in disdain. This is especially true of tradesmen, craftsmen, MUSICIANS and shopkeepers, occupations that reflected freedmen's servile origins. Such occupations, however, ultimately provided freed slaves with the wealth they needed to compete with the lifestyles of their wealthy, freeborn counterparts.

Family was important to a freedman for establishing links with the freeborn élite. For the latter, family was synonymous with a lucrative occupation, namely a life in politics. For a freedman, family was also a component part of a prosperous occupation. In his *familia*, family members, whether blood-kin or slaves freed by the same master (*colliberti*), often worked together. Family and occupation were synonymous with the way wealthy freedmen depicted themselves on their funerary monuments, especially those of the late Republic and early empire. These monuments clearly left their impression on the passer-by. They took the form of either stelae or TOMBS; the decoration on their façades included busts, full-length portraits, or occupational scenes. Inscriptions on the monuments informed the viewer of the names, status and occupations of the individuals memorialized. LAH

See Davies, J. K. (1971) *Athenian Propertied Families 600–300 BC*; Duff, A. M. (1928) *Freedmen in the Early Empire*; Fisher, N. R. E. (1993) *Slavery in Classical Greece*; Joshel, S. (1992) *Work, Identity and Legal Status at Rome*; Kleiner, D. E. E. (1977) *Roman Group Portraiture*; Treggiari, S. (1969) *Roman Freedmen during the Late Republic*; Weaver, P. R. C. (1972) *Familia Caesaris*; Wiedemann, T. (1981) *Greek and Roman Slavery*.

frescoes see PAINTING; PIGMENTS; PLASTER AND PLASTERING; WALL-PAINTING.

Freud, S. see DREAMS; MYTH; OEDIPUS.

friendship

Enmity and friendship (*philia*) were fundamental to the Greeks' view of society, and popular justice was defined by the doctrine that one should help one's friends and harm one's enemies. Consequently the Greeks were very interested in what friendship was and who friends were. Not only do philosophical treatises by PLATO (*Lysis*, *Symposion*) and ARISTOTLE (three chapters of the *Eudemian Ethics* and the *Nicomachean Ethics*) deal with the subject of what friendship is, but friendship became one of the central themes in a number of 5th-century TRAGEDIES (e.g. SOPHOKLES, *Ajax*, *Antigone* and *Philoktetes*; EURIPIDES, *Orestes*).

The Greek concept of friendship was much broader than our own. A Greek man would include among his friends not only those with whom he might be on intimate terms but also his family, relationships of utility such as political associates, and kinds of formalized friends such as ritualized friends or guest-friends (*xenoi*). The last involved relationships between individuals from different states. Consequently, friendship was not a purely private relationship, but a personal relationship that could be used in public situations, and there was a close correspondence between public and private relationships.

Although affection was fundamental to many relationships (Aristotle particularly emphasizes its role in the purest kinds of friendship), reciprocity and exchange were also important features in many relationships, especially those based on utility. This worked on the principle of *quid pro quo*: one gave to others so that they might give in return. The exchange could take the form of either gifts or favours. To make it function properly, friendship was also thought to be based upon equality (though Aristotle recognized that in some relationships, like those between parents and children or between ruler and ruled, equality was qualitative rather than quantitative). This was reflected in the reciprocal nature of the exchange. For this reason, the maintenance of such relationships depended upon trust and the moral force of the exchange.

In the hellenistic period, the SUCCESSORS, following Macedonian tradition, surrounded themselves with recognized 'Friends' (*philoi*) who could act as their advisers. A city would often try to influence a king through his Friends. LGM

See Mitchell, L. G. (1997) *Greeks Bearing Gifts*; Herman, G. (1997) The court society of the hellenistic age, in P. Cartledge et al., eds., *Hellenistic Constructs* 199–224.

Concepts of friendship (*amicitia*) in Rome showed an awareness of Greek notions of friendship, and CICERO in his *De amicitia* knows Aristotle's discussions of *philia* (friendship). As with Greek friendship, the range of relationships encapsulated by *amicitia* was vast, including both private and public. It ranged from those with a high affective content to those that were almost purely instrumental. However, though it could become politicized, *amicitia* could also transcend political boundaries: Cicero could call himself the friend of CAESAR yet not support his policies, a situation more difficult to imagine in Greece. Equality was also less intrinsic to some Roman friendship relationships, and inequalities became institutionalized, such as in the relationship between PATRON and client. In *hospitium*, the Roman equivalent of Greek *xenia*, the foreign partner was reduced to the position of client in relation to his more powerful Roman partner. LGM

See Brunt, P. A. (1988) *Amicitia* in the late Roman republic, in *The Fall of the Roman Republic* 351–81.

friezes see ORDERS, ARCHITECTURAL; PARTHENON; SCULPTURE; TEMPLES.

frontiers

Greek frontiers present a complex set of political, social and economic phenomena. 'Frontier' may carry different meanings. First to consider is that of a boundary between different political units. In this sense the borderland between Athens and THEBES, for example, was a frontier between two independent *poleis*. Such frontiers were often the subject of dispute leading to warfare, as in the territory around Parnassos which had led to war between PHOKIS and Lokris. Frontiers of *poleis* or larger polities like federations might consist of physical features, like the river Acheloös for the AITOLIANS and the Akarnanians, or might be established 'artificially' by the placement of *horoi*, 'boundary markers', as by Ambrakia and Charadros. Sanctuaries were often built on or near political frontiers, and deities like ZEUS Horios bore responsibility for overseeing the security of boundary markers.

In the 4th century and the hellenistic period, disputes over boundaries came more and more to be settled by arbitration rather than open warfare; many documents record third-party arbitrations. When the Romans appeared in the Greek East and became the chief political power, such disputes were often referred to them; they in turn often entrusted their settlement to another party, such as RHODES in the case of a long-standing dispute between SAMOS and Priene. The process of establishing boundaries appears clearly in some documents relating to the foundation of colonies. Pre-existing boundaries were sometimes modified when formerly independent entities were combined in a *sympoliteia* or other forms of political incorporation. But in these cases the former frontiers often continued to exist in a real sense, as demarcators of economic or social boundaries. Frontier zones between polities were often areas with important economic resources, including pasture land, MINES and QUARRIES, and FORESTS. Control of such resources was an important factor in disputes over these zones.

In a larger sense, a political frontier existed between the Greek world and major non-Greek states, most notably the PERSIAN EMPIRE. A major aim of the wars between the Persians and the Greeks of the Delian league, in the second quarter of the 5th century BC, was to settle the boundary between territory in Asia Minor under Greek influence and that controlled by the Persians. Finally, in a broader sense, a 'frontier' could be said to exist between the world of Greek culture and influence and the world outside or beyond. This sense of a 'frontier' (which resembles in some ways the American 'frontier' of the 19th century, and so should be regarded, with due caution to avoid anachronism) comes across most clearly in book 4 of HERODOTOS' *Histories*, devoted to discussion of peoples well beyond the sphere of Greek influence. GR

See Daverio Rocchi, G. (1988) *Frontiera e confini nella Grecia antica*.

The frontier regions of Roman political authority were highly militarized zones of interaction between the Roman state and the local populations, subdivided by a political border. The history of Roman frontiers can be divided into creation and maintenance. During the period of creation, the frontier was extremely fluid, marked by frequent movements of troops and by a strong separation between the agents of the Roman state and the native population. Military requirements created economic opportunity; relationships with the Romans created political opportunity. At the same time, a military presence resulted in improved ROADS and, in areas with little urban development, promoted a change in the settlement pattern. Such frontiers were built over a long period in some areas, as in GAUL, Spain and the Balkans during the last two centuries BC. In other areas the frontier was created rapidly in one place, as in the East against the PARTHIANS by POMPEY's annexation of territory in the 60s BC. Expansion continued until the early 2nd century AD, when the empire had conquered all the surrounding states except the Parthians.

FRONTIERS, ROMAN: (a) earthwork and ditch on the German *limes* near Frankfurt.

FRONTIERS, ROMAN: (b) stone wall controlling a mountain pass in southern Tunisia at Bir Oum Ali.

As expansion ceased on each frontier, frontier regions developed to establish a political separation between the populations within and beyond the empire. On the ground, such borders might be very nebulous. Imperial borders were often marked by linear features such as FORTIFICATIONS (HADRIAN'S WALL in BRITAIN, several palisade systems in GERMANY and RAETIA) or by RIVERS (RHINE, DANUBE, occasionally parts of the Euphrates or Tigris). However, the edges of other parts of the empire were not delimited in a linear fashion and deserts or MOUNTAINS, especially in AFRICA and SYRIA, often served as borders. Since the Romans ruled people and cities rather than territory, such vagueness was acceptable. The ancient terminology used to define these edges varied, including *finis* and *limes* (though *limes* did not have the sense of a fortified frontier until the 4th century AD). Within the established frontier zone an increasing array of fortifications was built and large cities developed, such as TRIER and Singidunum. At the same time, a frontier culture evolved, which benefited immensely from military spending and supply contracts. This culture, though undeniably Roman, was very different from that of peninsular Italy. In many ways, for example, in the provision of MARKETS or of recruits for the army, frontier culture extended on both sides of the political border. This meant that, by the 4th century, many artefacts (such as belt-buckles) appeared indiscriminately within and beyond the border. This pattern began to break down in the Western provinces in the 5th century AD with the collapse of the Western empire, but similar frontiers continued to exist in the Byzantine empire. HWE

See Elton, H. (1996) *Frontiers of the Roman Empire*; Isaac, B. (1997) The eastern frontier, in *CAH* 13, 437–60; Whittaker, C. R. (1994) *Frontiers of the Roman Empire*; (2000) Frontiers, in *CAH* 11, 293–319.

 HADRIAN'S WALL.

Frontinus (Sextus Julius Frontinus) An exemplar of the wide-ranging talents typical of the best of the Roman upper classes, who for 30 years, from VESPASIAN to TRAJAN, was prominent in public life

FRONTIERS, ROMAN: (c) reconstructed Roman watchtower from the German *limes*, emphasizing the surveillance aspect of such frontiers.

and society, as commander, governor, administrator and writer. His friend the younger PLINY described him as one of the two most respected SENATORS of the day. He participated in important military operations, helping in AD 70 to suppress the revolt of Julius Civilis in GAUL, and receiving the surrender of 70,000 Lingones, members of a Gallic tribe. As governor of BRITAIN (73/4–77), he was described by TACITUS as one of the 'great commanders' who extended Roman rule in the province; he led an invasion of south Wales, defeating the Silures and establishing a base for the II Augusta legion at Isca (Caerleon). In 86 he was governor of the wealthy and important province of ASIA, and later served on Nerva's commission to reduce public expenditure. In 97 Nerva appointed him head of the WATER SUPPLY (*curator aquarum*) in Rome. He was three times CONSUL, in 72 or 73, in 98 (with Trajan as colleague) and in 100 (as ordinary consul, again with Trajan). Pliny thought that these signal honours were for 'civic services'. Frontinus perhaps had supported Trajan's elevation to imperial rank.

Frontinus wrote a book (*De aquis*) about his job as *curator aquarum*, partly as a guide for himself and others. The author's pride in a technical achievement that was crucial to the welfare of the Roman people is coupled with a description of his duties and a collection of official documents. This is the only substantial record of how a Roman official went about his task. He also wrote a book on the art of war (now lost) and the *Strategemata*, a collection of anecdotes mainly about the exploits of past commanders, though he mentions with approval tactical ploys of DOMITIAN. Frontinus claims that he intended not merely to entertain, but to guide military commanders by illustrating previous stratagems. Several treatises about LAND SURVEY are ascribed to him: on land categories, on disputes, and on the division and measurement of land. The author expounds much technical detail while giving a sympathetic account of the development and significance of surveying (a subject not usually embraced by the upper classes).

Frontinus enjoyed pleasant times with MARTIAL in literary pursuits and had a VILLA at Formiae, where the Greek writer AELIAN visited him, seeking advice about his work on phalanx tactics. Frontinus died c.103/4. According to Pliny, he disdained a funeral monument, saying that if he had deserved it his life would be monument enough. (see also *AGRIMENSORES*) JBC

See Frontinus, *Stratagems and Aqueducts*, trs. C. E. Bennett and M. B. McElwain (1925); Campbell, B. (2000) *The Writings of the Roman Land Surveyors*; Evans, H. B. (1994) *Water Distribution in Ancient Rome*; Hodge, A.T. (2002) *Roman Aqueducts and Water Supply*.

Fronto (Marcus Cornelius Fronto) ORATOR, who was born in the North African city of Cirta in the last decade of the 1st century AD and died at some point between 165 and 170. He obtained a considerable reputation in the time of HADRIAN and ANTONINUS PIUS, being appointed by the latter as the tutor to his adoptive sons, the future emperors MARCUS AURELIUS and Lucius Verus. He remained on close terms with both men after Pius' death – Marcus thanks him in the *Meditations* for teaching him about 'tyrannical malice, caprice and hypocrisy' and that PATRICIANS were 'without human affections' (1.11). AULUS GELLIUS depicts him favourably in five vignettes of the *Attic Nights*, and his reputation as an orator survived into the 4th century.

A palimpsest containing portions of Fronto's collected works, overwritten by the *Acts of the Council of Chalcedon*, was discovered in 1815. The sections that survive include letters to and from Marcus Aurelius and Lucius Verus, to Antoninus Pius, and to selected friends, as well as some RHETORICAL works in Greek and Latin. Although the initial response on the part of modern readers to these works is often one of distaste, they offer an invaluable insight into the cultural life of the court and confirm the picture of Fronto that appears in Aulus, that of a committed antiquarian in his literary tastes. DSP

See Fronto, *Correspondence*, 2 vols., trs. C. R. Haines (1919–20); Champlin, E. (1980) *Fronto and Antonine Rome*.

fruit Wild fruits and nuts were a major source of food before the beginning of AGRICULTURE. Fruit-growing and storage techniques were gradually elaborated, and useful varieties were developed in the later prehistoric period. An orchard growing OLIVES, pears, apples, FIGS, grapes and pomegranates is carefully described in HOMER's *Odyssey* (7.112–21).

Many fruits and nuts are not only good to eat fresh but can also be stored. The grape is notable for a third pattern of use, equally important nutritionally, as the source of WINE. In ancient conditions, fresh fruits could not be traded over long distances. However, nuts and dried fruits, notably figs and dates, kept well even during TRANSPORTATION. Dates, in fact, will only fruit in the hottest and driest regions of the classical world; they were familiar to people in Greece and Italy as imports. As cities grew, gardeners in their neighbourhood were impelled to develop varieties (of pears and table grapes, for example) that stood up to local transport and the rigours of the market stall.

The MEDITERRANEAN fruit trees best propagated by cuttings and suckers include the olive, vine, fig, date, hazel and pomegranate. Those often propagated by seed include almonds, walnuts, quinces, medlars, sorbs, apples, pears, plums and cherries. With the last four, cultivated varieties soon emerged that can only be maintained by grafting – a technique first recorded by THEOPHRASTOS around 300 BC, but invented at some earlier date now unknown. The pistachio (a central Asian species not yet known by name to Theophrastos) was, soon after his time, spread by grafting on stocks of the terebinth tree (*Pistacia atlantica*).

Apart from the tree fruits, melons, cucumbers, watermelons and gourds were also significant in the ancient DIET. They were annual creeping plants grown in a GARDEN bed. So-called 'soft fruits', such as blackberries and wild strawberries, were unimportant except to poor country people.

Romans were skilled gardeners and fruit-growers. They stand at the end of a tradition to which Assyrians, PERSIANS, classical and hellenistic Greeks and CARTHAGINIANS had all contributed. The Latin agricultural writers, CATO, VARRO, COLUMELLA and Palladius, describe grafting, pruning and other skills in detail; PLINY THE ELDER, in the *Natural History* (books 13–15), lists fruit varieties with a wealth of detail.

Throughout the prehistoric and ancient periods, the range of fruits available around the Mediterranean increased with the transplanting of exotic species. The watermelon, native to southern Africa, and the cucumber, from the Himalayas, had made long, unrecorded journeys in the hands of anonymous gardeners to reach Greece by the beginning of the classical period. Important introductions in hellenistic times include pistachio, peach and apricot. At about the same period the citron, first among the citrus fruits, reached the Mediterranean; the lemon was possibly known by the later classical period. Oranges and aubergines arrived from the east in medieval times. Chillies, sweet peppers, pumpkins (squashes), marrows, tomatoes, garden strawberries and avocados, however, are all native to the Americas and first reached Europe after the voyage of Columbus. AD

See Morgan, J. and Richards, A. (1993) *The Book of Apples*; Zohary, D. and Hopf, M. (1993) *Domestication of Plants in the Old World*.

 BIRDS: (b).

fuel Pliny the Elder (*Natural History* 36.200–1) briefly lists the uses of FIRE in metallurgy and the production of GLASS, PIGMENTS, MEDICINES, and PLASTER – in short, the whole range of manufactured products. Few ancient authors, however, go into detail about fuel technology. Rather than routinely burning coal, and lacking the modern options of mineral oil, gas and electricity, the ancient world relied heavily upon wood, particularly in the form of CHARCOAL. Dung was used in some places (it is documented by archaeobotanical remains in Greco-Roman Egypt), but was a scarce resource that people preferred to use as fertilizer in many parts of the Mediterranean region. PETROLEUM by-products were known to be inflammable, but were regarded as having little practical use (*Natural History* 35.179). Coal and peat were used only where locally available, such as in northern Europe; Theophrastos (*On Stones* 16) mentions sources of lignite in Chios and the Peloponnese. Elsewhere he discusses techniques for starting fires with wooden drills (*Enquiry into Plants* 5.9). Pliny, too, discusses the need for drills and tinder when stones for striking sparks are not available (*Natural History* 16.207–8). (see also MANURE) DGJS

See Humphrey, J.W. et al. (1997) *Greek and Roman Technology: a sourcebook*.

 CHARCOAL.

fulling The activity by which TEXTILE products are cleaned and bleached, removing any impurities from the fibres. These impurities included dirt, as well as naturally occurring substances such as the grease present in large quantities in wool, and the colouring substances, wax and other impurities in flax and hemp. Since these impurities can affect DYEING by preventing the dye from bonding properly with the fibre, it was often necessary to clean fibres before dyeing took place. As fibres could be dyed in a number of different stages of their production, this could be done before spinning (especially in the case of wool) or before weaving (particularly for linen). When white textiles were required, cleaning and bleaching could take place after weaving. Generally, fulling involved washing the fibres or textiles in hot water, to which was usually added a detergent substance. This could include the plant soapwort, 'with which they bleach linen' (THEOPHRASTOS, *Enquiry Into Plants* 9.12.5), as well as urine and a number of minerals. There were a number of so-called 'fuller's earths' available, including natron, or natural soda, and hydrated aluminium silicate, as well as potash, which absorbed grease, removed dirt and gave cloth a heavier and more lustrous appearance. These processes would require similar equipment to dyeing and tanning, namely large watertight vessels, similar ingredients such as large quantities of water and minerals, and similar plants, such as soapwort.

Evidence for fulling in classical and hellenistic Greece is usually provided by references such as that in Theophrastos; archaeological evidence is scarce. The scale of production in classical and hellenistic

FULLING: (a) painting from Pompeii depicting treading of cloth in vats.

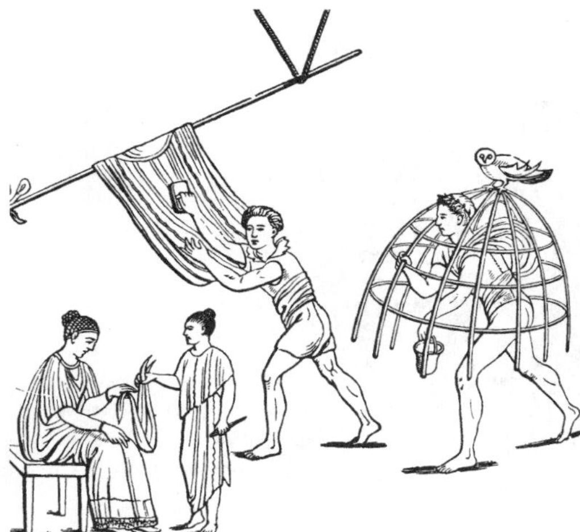

FULLING: (b) painting from Pompeii depicting finishing of cloth in a fullery.

FULLING: (c) detail of vats in fullery of Stephanus at Pompeii.

Greece was relatively small, and elaborate facilities were not required. In some instances, however, production in the Roman period was on a much larger scale, with the result that more fulling establishments have been identified. In Pompeii, depictions of fulling are known from WALL-PAINTINGS in the House of the Vettii and the Fullery of Hypsaeus. As the latter name suggests, the physical remains of a number of fulleries have also been located. Their identification has generally relied on the presence of containers suitable for treading cloth in a solution of water and minerals. The largest Pompeian fullery was that named above, owned by Lucius Veranius Hypsaeus. It consists of two houses. In one of the rooms were four large vats, connected to each other by holes in the walls dividing them. The middle vats were built at a lower level than the end vats. Six 'treading stalls' were situated in this room, as well as a possible storage area for urine consisting of a hole in the floor. A jar containing a white substance, identified as a type of fuller's earth, was found in another room along with a cistern, a shallow vat and a table. This building therefore contained evidence for a well-organized, large-scale fulling operation. MDM

See Forbes, R. J. (1956) *Studies in Ancient Technology*, vol. 4; Moeller, W. O. (1976) *The Wool Trade of Ancient Pompeii*.

funeral clubs Private CLUBS (*collegia*) are a widely attested feature of the Roman world. The lawyers termed some clubs *collegia tenuiorum*, 'associations of the poorer classes'. The clubs themselves used no such terminology but typically named themselves after their patron gods (DIANA and ANTINOUS, for example) or human benefactors. Their ostensible object, for which the state seems to have given them permission to operate in the PRINCIPATE, was to provide BURIAL for their members. They acted in effect as burial-insurance guilds. Membership size varied; 50–100 would have been the norm. Members were mixed: male and female, free and unfree, young and old. Members paid a hefty fee to join and then a modest monthly subscription, and could expect to receive proper burial rites at death, or at least a lump sum payment for their family to perform the burial. With land at a premium, in the city of Rome in particular, the patronless poor generally had only this recourse to avoid anonymous, mass burial. For the very poor, even funeral clubs would have been a luxury.

The clubs provided much more than burial, and were far from morbid bodies. Indeed, burial may have been the pretext rather than their true purpose, for the evidence focuses far more on life than on death. The club met once a month (the maximum allowed by law) to discuss business, and held several banquets every year – a real attraction of the clubs for the living. By all accounts these banquets, held on every possible pretext, were enjoyable and lavish affairs. One imagines that death was not high on the list of topics discussed. TGP

funeral rites

Athenians attached great importance to being properly buried by family in ATTICA. How deeply entrenched this moral sentiment was is reflected in the *dokimasia* (scrutiny) of prospective archons, who were queried about their family TOMBS (Aristotle, *Constitution of the Athenians* 55.3). Any failure to provide for the burial of a parent could be offered as grounds for being denied the right to hold public office (Lysias 31.20–3).

In Greece generally, both inhumation and cremation were practised but the rituals were the same. On the day of death the corpse was prepared for viewing (*prothesis*) in the house of a close relative. Female relatives would wash, anoint with oil, dress and crown with wreaths of FLOWERS the body, which was laid out on a bier. In some cases an obol would be placed in the mouth of the deceased, to pay Charon to ferry the body across the river Styx to HADES. On the second day the body lay in state to be viewed by friends and relatives. Female relatives, dressed in black and with hair cropped, would mourn the deceased by singing a ritual lament and displaying appropriate gestures of grief, such as tearing their hair and striking their breasts. Some richer families even hired professional female mourners to assist in the funeral dirge. On the third day, before dawn, the body, wrapped in a shroud, was carried in procession (*ekphora*) to the graveside. Offerings were made to the dead, consisting of libations, food and various kinds of vessels like lekythoi. Following the funeral, a feast was held. CC

See Garland, R. (1988) *The Greek Way of Death*.

FUNERAL RITES: (a) horse-drawn funerary bier on a Geometric vase, attesting to the existence of large-scale funerary ceremonies.

FUNERAL RITES: (b) Roman relief carving of a funerary cortège from Preturi in northern Italy. Note the musicians in the lead, and the corpse in a large litter followed by mourning women.

The Roman *funus* was a set of rites: closing the eyes; *conclamatio* (calling the deceased's name); washing, anointing, dressing and wreathing the body; placing a coin in the mouth; *collocatio* (lying in state), perhaps for seven days; and the nocturnal procession – the house marked with cypress – accompanied by MUSICIANS and mourners. Some wore ancestors' masks and prominent citizens received public ORATIONS until EMPERORS' funerals, incorporating elaborately attended effigies of the deceased, usurped them.

The dead, considered unclean, were buried outside cities. It was only essential that a little earth be thrown on the remains. From the mid-Republic the deceased were cremated with grave goods, and a libation poured upon the ashes, placed in a casket, urn or pot. A PIG SACRIFICE marked the grave – which it was a crime to disturb – and was followed by the *silicernium* (feast) and the purification of the house and participants. After nine days the latter shared the *cena novendialis* (nine-day feast) at the graveside, an end of mourning. The dead were celebrated in FESTIVALS: the Parentalia for the *di manes* (spirits of the departed), the Lemuria for the unburied.

The pauper's grave might be a pit, the rich man's a splendid TOMB. From the late 1st century BC *columbaria* (dovecote tombs) were built, often by burial CLUBS. In the 2nd century AD inhumation displaced cremation. Other commemorative strategies were posthumous benefaction and tombstones, commemorators that communicated the bond between living and dead. SC

See Toynbee, J. M. C. (1971) *Death and Burial in the Roman World.*

BURIAL, ROMAN: (a)–(f).

funeral speeches see DEMOCRACY; DEMOSTHENES; RHETORIC.

fur The fur trade has an ancient history: the PHOENICIANS and Assyrians certainly traded in exotic furs from Asia and Africa. The Greeks of the

MYCENAEAN era used entire pelts as mantles, and furs are recorded in the *Iliad* as gifts. ANIMAL skins are frequently attested in Greek MYTHOLOGY: ODYSSEUS wears a dog-skin cap, HERAKLES has a lion-skin, ATALANTA and DIONYSOS wear leopard pelts, and maenads wear deer-skins. The Romans used animal pelts as practical clothing and bedding, though from the 2nd century AD a preference began to be expressed for fine furs because of their aesthetic beauty. During the 1st century AD we find Latin inscriptions referring to a *Corpus Pellionum*, 'Corporation of Fur Manufacturers'. Despite the decree of the emperor HONORIUS in AD 397, by which his courtiers were forbidden to wear fur, its use became prevalent not only for protection against the cold but for personal adornment. Standard-bearers in the Roman army were marked out from other soldiers by the animal skins they wore on their heads, usually a bear or wolf without its head, though it is suggested that LEGIONARY standard-bearers used skins with the animal's head still attached. The eagle standard was carried by a special standard-bearer who wore a lion-skin headdress. These skins are perhaps symbolic totems, intended to imbue the wearer with the stealth and strength of the animal from which the pelt was taken. LL-J

See Simkins, M. (1998) *The Roman Army from Caesar to Trajan*.

Furies A group of divinities, also known by the Greek name Erinyes. They belong to the pre-Olympian divine generation, but there appears to be no consistent tradition regarding their origins. HESIOD'S *Theogony* relates how they were born out of the drops of blood shed by Ouranos when he was castrated by his son Kronos. Other traditions associate them with Ge (Mother Earth) and Darkness, Kronos and Eurynome, or Kronos and Night. Tragic DRAMA places the home of the Erinyes underground (AESCHYLUS, *Eumenides* 1026), which recalls their suggested family relations with the Earth, Darkness and Night. The Erinyes are aroused by the blood and anger of victims of MURDER. In Aeschylus' *Eumenides*, the ghost of CLYTEMNESTRA wakes them from sleep, reminding them to avenge her death ruthlessly by pursuing her son and murderer, Orestes. He is then hunted by the Furies and almost driven to madness, until he is purified from pollution (*miasma*) by APOLLO at the DELPHIC sanctuary. The Furies also punished perjury, and their name was often called upon in oaths.

Descriptions of the Erinyes in literature include dark (mainly black) clothing, snakes, wings and swift feet for the pursuit of their victims. Their physical ugliness is reflected in epithets, such as 'dog-faced' and 'black-skinned', in tragic drama. Some of these features, such as their black skin and underworld associations, are transferred to their artistic representations, but they can also be shown as young and sometimes even beautiful females. EP

See Padel, R. (1992) *In and Out of the Mind*; Sarian, H. (1986) Erinys, in *LIMC* vol. 3, 825–43.

furniture Compared to modern houses, both Greek and Roman houses were sparsely furnished. Most had BEDS, COUCHES, chairs and tables as well as chests. Emphasis was placed on portability, as furniture was moved around depending on the season and the occasion. Although the amount of furniture was restricted, Greek and Roman houses would not have appeared bare. Cushions and blankets provided comfort and colour, and the walls and floors were covered by WALL-PAINTINGS and MOSAICS. The wealth of a household was expressed not in the quantity of furniture but in its design and material. It is rare to get a glimpse into furnished ancient houses, but sometimes we do: at POMPEII, for example, the shapes of pieces of furniture, made of now decayed organic material, survive as voids in the surrounding volcanic deposits. The main sources of evidence are depictions on vases, wall-paintings and tombstones. There are also rare finds such as a Roman (2nd century AD) SARCOPHAGUS from Simpelveld (now in the Rijksmuseum, Leiden) which shows the deceased reclining on a couch and surrounded by cherished household possessions.

The bed or couch was probably the most important piece of furniture in Greek and Roman houses, and was used for dining, sleeping and working. Both Greeks and Romans also used simple stools and folding chairs. These usually had a leather seat and iron legs ending in bronze feet, which are often modelled in the shape of ANIMAL paws. More substantial Greek chairs either have a high, elegantly curved back or are barrel-shaped with rounded backs and curving sides. Similar chairs are known in the Roman world, where wooden chairs appear to be associated with men and wicker chairs with women. Women did not normally recline on couches during dining, but used wicker chairs with a high back as well as armrests. As with so much furniture made from organic material, the shape and design of these chairs has to be reconstructed from depictions; wicker chairs are commonly shown on Gaulish clay FIGURINES depicting seated female deities. By contrast, the *solium* was reserved for the use of Roman élite men. This

FURNITURE: (a) carpenter carving a lion-headed table leg.

FURNITURE: (b) similar legs on marble table from Pompeii.

throne-like chair, richly decorated and made from wood or even MARBLE, was used by the *paterfamilias* to receive clients. As with beds, chairs could be decorated with carved figures and often had elaborately turned legs; they were made more comfortable with cushions.

Most ancient tables were round and had three simple curved legs, but elaborate tables made from exotic wood or marble are also known. Citrus wood from AFRICA was especially favoured, and both PLINY THE ELDER and MARTIAL recount the enormous sums paid for such elaborate display tables. While patterning on the table surface was considered important, it was mainly the legs that were decorated. Traditionally the leg ended in a claw foot and the top of the leg showed an animal's head. Lions, antelopes and winged griffins were particularly popular motifs. In BRITAIN, a number of table legs made from Kimmeridge shale, which survives much better than wood in the ground, have been found. Simple tables could be covered by fringed tablecloths.

Clothes and other household goods were traditionally stored in chests, secured with metal fittings and LOCKS. These could also act as strong-boxes for money and documents. In Pompeii, some chests were secured to MASONRY foundations with strong iron bolts. The Romans (in contrast to the Greeks) also used cupboards or wardrobes, which could contain shelves and had either a single or double doors. Such cupboards were used for the storage of book rolls and other household goods, and sometimes even contained the *lararium* or household shrine.

Rooms were lit by LAMPS, which could be placed on elaborate lamp-stands (*candelabra*). These are made of bronze and sometimes SILVER, and can show a wide range of motifs, such as a SLAVE carrying a tray. Soft furnishing added comfort and colour to Greek and Roman homes. Pillows and cushions were made from linen or wool and stuffed with wool, flax, feathers, straw, rushes or other plant materials. Colourful designs, sometimes including GOLD and purple, were preferred, and woven or embroidered fabrics depicting animals as well as floral and geometric motifs are attested in both literary and visual sources. Such soft furnishings rarely survive, but examples are known from Egypt. HE

See Richter, G. M. A. (1966) *The Furniture of the Greeks, Etruscans and Romans.*

 SEX.

future The greater haphazardness of life in antiquity played some role in generating attitudes to the future that differed from a modern perspective. The future was, in terrestrial terms, often short, and people did not plan in the long term for themselves as living human beings. At best, they concerned themselves with remaining in the memory of subsequent generations through children, literary works, tombs and inscriptions, monuments, and other means. The Fates, who measured the span of human life, were arbitrary and capricious, and POETS like HORACE urged readers to 'seize the day' (*carpe diem*). PHILOSOPHERS like HERAKLEITOS and SENECA THE YOUNGER held that a day was equal to an age, and that life should be lived one day at a time.

In general, the ancients knew that time would continue and recognized a future in that sense. Yet they preferred to see a continuation of the PAST expressed through the medium of a constantly regenerating present. Although most families took great care to transfer material wealth to their children or other relatives, that preoccupation was more a preservation of the past than provision for a future, since the primary concern was retention of an accumulated past within a family group. Even dowries returned to a woman's paternal family if no children survived to inherit.

For some religious groups, in particular CHRISTIANS, with a strong sense of salvation and a positive AFTERLIFE, a different sense of the future developed. Yet this perspective tended to encourage a denial of the present (and sometimes the past). JV

G

Gades Reputedly founded by Tyrians c.1100 BC, though archaeological evidence places its origin in the 8th century, Gades (Phoenician Gadir; mod. Cádiz) originally lay on two small offshore islands north-west of the Pillars of HERCULES (Straits of Gibraltar). Under the CARTHAGINIANS it was an important shipping centre, sending its famous brand of salt fish to Athens as early as the 5th century BC. The city surrendered to Publius Cornelius SCIPIO in 206 BC and entered into a treaty alliance with Rome. In 49 BC the Gaditanians rejected the Pompeian governor, Marcus Terentius VARRO, in favour of CAESAR, who in the same year granted them CITIZENSHIP. Within six years the city had obtained the official status of *municipium*. Though never a *colonia*, under AUGUSTUS Gades became one of four *conventus* capitals in BAETICA. It had such Roman amenities as an AMPHITHEATRE, CIRCUS, THEATRE and AQUEDUCT but retained a strong indigenous identity, minting coins with Punic legends into the early empire. Famous for its TEMPLE and ORACLE of Hercules-Melqart and, in the 1st century AD, its DANCING girls (*puellae Gaditanae*), it was also the birthplace of Rome's first non-Italian CONSUL, Lucius Cornelius Balbus (consul 40 BC). His nephew of the same name, later proconsul of AFRICA, enlarged the town, calling it Didyma. Other famous Gaditanians include the agricultural writer COLUMELLA and HADRIAN's mother, Domitia Paulina. Throughout the early empire Gades remained an important port city, but in the 4th century AD Avienus describes it as poor and dilapidated. RIC

See Fear, A. T. (1996) *Rome and Baetica*.

 HISPANIA.

Gaia see GE.

Gaius (emperor) see CALIGULA.

Gaius (legal author) 2nd-century AD writer on legal matters, about whom little is known. Probably born in the reign of TRAJAN, he died no earlier than 178, for he discusses legislation of that year. He lived at Rome for some time, and may have been a teacher in the Sabinian school. He is not cited by contemporaries or the jurists of the Severan age, but was given authority in the Theodosian Law of Citations (AD 426) and is an important figure in the time of JUSTINIAN (AD 527–65).

Gaius wrote (non-extant) commentaries on the TWELVE TABLES, the Praetor's Edict, and the Edict on Provinces, among others. His *Institutes* is the only legal work before the *THEODOSIAN CODE* to survive in substantially original form. Previously known from a few citations and an epitome in Visigothic codes, a more complete text emerged in 1816 from a palimpsest, where Gaius' work is sometimes the earliest of three uses of the parchment. Additional fragments have been found on PAPYRI. Most likely, but not certainly, the *Institutes* represents an original, systematic presentation of Roman private law. Book 1 is a treatment of 'the law relating to persons', books 2 and 3 are devoted to 'the law relating to things', while book 4 covers 'the law relating to actions'. The work became a textbook in law schools and the basis for Justinian's *Institutes*. In consequence, it has had much influence on later legal thought. JV

See Gordon, W. M. and Robinson, O. F., trs. (1988) *The Institutes of Gaius*; Honoré, A. M. (1962) *Gaius*.

Galatia see CILICIA; *RES GESTAE*.

Galba see HISPANIA; NERO; OTHO; SULPICII.

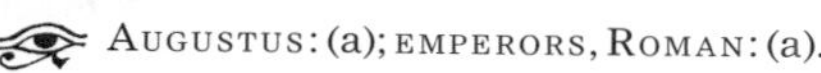 AUGUSTUS: (a); EMPERORS, ROMAN: (a).

Galen AD 129–c.210 The founder of the medical system that was to dominate not only the later centuries of the Roman empire, but also the Islamic, and then Western European, worlds, until the Enlightenment. He was born in PERGAMON and given a sound educational and ethical grounding by his father, the ARCHITECT and landowner Nikon. He began to pursue a more specifically medical learning after a god appeared to Nikon in a dream, telling him that his son was to follow a career in MEDICINE. This pursuit soon took him to SMYRNA, CORINTH and ALEXANDRIA, or so Galen himself tells us in the course of describing the ideal medical training. After a period as physician to the GLADIATORS at Pergamon, he arrived in Rome about AD 162. He was an immediate success in more thoughtful élite circles, with his cures and culture, his demonstrations and disputations. It was in the imperial capital that he lived out almost all the rest of his long and most productive life, providing medical services to successive EMPERORS and their HOUSEHOLDS as well as composing his monumental oeuvre.

Galen wrote LOGICAL, ETHICAL, philosophical and philological, as well as more dedicatedly medical, works of a range of different types, not to mention his autobiographical and bibliographical treatises. *On Demonstration*, *On Morals*, *On the Opinions of Hippokrates and Plato*, and *The Vocabulary of Attic Authors*, as well as *On the Usefulness of the Parts*, *On the Therapeutic Method* and *On the Sects for Beginners* are all titles listed, along with a myriad more, in Galen's work *On the Order of his Own Books*. Fewer texts survive. All, however, are part of a single intellectual project, part of realizing a vision of the medical art that reached into all those fields to take the knowledge and methods it required to attain its goal of health. The best physician was not only a PHILOSOPHER but also a logician. He needed to know about the basic stuff of the KOSMOS as well as the basic distinction between truth and falsehood. He needed to have the proper moral attitude to life, and to know all about words and how to use them. It was these standards against which Galen measured himself; he found himself not wanting.

It was HIPPOKRATES that Galen invoked as his key authority in all this, with PLATO at his side. Hippokrates anchored Galen's remoulding of the medical tradition in his own image. The advances and errors of the intervening period allowed someone as trained and able as Galen himself to bring medicine back to its HIPPOCRATIC starting-point, but at a higher level of elaboration and attainment. It was this process of absorption and rearticulation, this covering of all the previous ground and more in a systematic fashion, that rendered redundant so much of what had been, and paved the way to the development of Galenism as the dominant medical system in the later Roman empire and far beyond. REF

See Galen, *Selected Writings*, trs. P. Singer (1997).

Galerius (Gaius Galerius Valerius Maximianus) c.AD 250–311 Born in Illyricum; after rising through the ranks, Galerius became CAESAR under DIOCLETIAN (293), while Constantius became Caesar to MAXIMIAN, the alliance cemented by marriage of the Caesars to daughters of their respective AUGUSTI. Galerius campaigned on the DANUBE frontier against the Sarmatians and Carpi (294–5) and in SYRIA (296) against Narses the PERSIAN, finally recapturing, after initial setbacks, ARMENIA, MESOPOTAMIA and CTESIPHON (298). He created a TETRARCHIC capital in THESSALONIKE, where the ARCH commemorating his victory can still be seen.

Following Diocletian and Maximian's abdication, Galerius and Constantius became Augusti of the East and West respectively, with Maximin Daia and Severus as Caesars (305). The Tetrarchic system sought to avoid dynasties of blood but this proved impossible. On Constantius' death (306), Galerius raised Severus to Augustus, but the troops chose CONSTANTINE, whom Galerius reluctantly acknowledged as Caesar. At Rome, Maxentius, son of the retired Maximian, was declared emperor and Maximian came out of retirement to support him. Both Severus and Galerius attacked ITALY but failed to displace Maxentius. On Severus' death the conference at Carnuntum (308) attempted to reorganize Tetrarchic rule but failed, and Galerius returned to the East. According to LACTANTIUS he was the driving force behind renewed PERSECUTION of the CHRISTIANS from 303. His final illness, graphically and probably fictionally described by Lactantius, forced him to issue an edict of toleration shortly before his death in 311. MEH

See Lactantius, *De mortibus persecutorum*, trs. J.L. Creed (1984); Williams, S. (1997) *Diocletian and the Roman Recovery*.

 TETRARCHS: (b).

Galla Placidia AD 387/8–450 Daughter of Galla and the emperor THEODOSIUS, born in late 387 or early 388. Her mother died in childbirth in 394, and later that year she and her half-brother HONORIUS travelled from CONSTANTINOPLE to Theodosius at MILAN. On 17 January 395, Theodosius died. Placidia was raised by Serena, wife of STILICHO, until she established her own household. She was expected to marry Stilicho's son Eucherius, but had not done so when he and his father were killed in 408. A few months later, popular opinion held that Serena intended to open Rome's gates to ALARIC, and the SENATE found Placidia willing to share responsibility for her execution. Recourse to Honorius at RAVENNA was difficult, and Placidia perhaps saw a need to calm the fears, or accepted Serena's guilt.

Placidia was captured when Alaric sacked Rome in 410, and remained with the GOTHS for some years. She influenced the Gothic king Athaulf into a desire to support the empire instead of destroying it, and married him in January 414. Their child, named Theodosius, soon died, and Athaulf himself was assassinated in summer 415. Placidia was released and, against her wishes, married Constantius, Honorius' leading general, in 417. She bore him two children, Iusta Grata Honoria (418) and Flavius Placidus Valentinianus (2 July 419). After Constantius was made co-emperor on 8 February 421, she was named AUGUSTA. Following his death on 2 September 421, Placidia survived court intrigue until 423, when she was banished and travelled to Constantinople. On 27 August 423 Honorius died, but Theodosius II named no successor until, to counter the usurper John, he mobilized forces to install Valentinian III and betrothed his baby daughter to him.

As ruler of the West, Placidia was assailed by the intrigues of GENERALS but managed to govern effectively for some years. After Aëtius had eliminated his rivals and gained supremacy, she was astute enough only to nibble at his support when possible. In October 437, Valentinian married Licinia Eudoxia at Constantinople. Subsequently Placidia, who had not accompanied her son, ceded greater independence to him but retained considerable influence. In 449 her daughter Honoria created difficulties: she was caught in illicit sexual relations with her estate manager and had perhaps become pregnant (some sources place a pregnancy in 434). She was expelled from the palace and betrothed to the unambitious Herculanus Bassus, but guarded closely. In response, Honoria appealed to Attila the HUN for help in obtaining her rightful station. Since she had sent a ring, he applied for her hand. Placidia with great difficulty persuaded Valentinian not to execute his sister for treason and to allow the marriage to Bassus. On 27 November 450, Placidia died at Rome and was buried in the family mausoleum near St Peter's. In keeping with her CHRISTIANITY and her station, she had founded CHURCHES at Ravenna and contributed to the adornment of others, at Ravenna and Rome. JV

See Oost, S. I. (1968) *Galla Placidia Augusta*.

 THEODOSIUS I.

Gallia, Gallia Belgica see GAUL.

Gallia Cisalpina POLYBIOS records Gauls as occupying the northern Padane and Alpine regions of Italy c.400 BC. The Gallic peoples later splintered to form a series of distinct tribal groupings such as the Ligures, Insubres and Boii. Overall, their presence was rarely aggressive towards Rome until Rome's northward expansion from the 3rd century BC, commencing with the foundation of Rimini (268) and accelerating after the campaigns of 225–222 before being interrupted by the HANNIBALIC WARS. Revived expansion came from the 180s, and the 2nd and 1st centuries BC witnessed the implementation of road-building (the *viae* Aemilia, Annia, Postumia, and Popillia) and the concomitant foundation of numerous colonies (mainly Latin), notably AQUILEIA, MILAN, Verona and Bologna. These largely gained Roman rights in 49 BC. Although it was a province from c.80 BC, the name Gallia Cisalpina is first documented for 59 BC. LIVY refers to the region variously as *Gallia citerior*, *Gallia*, and *Ligures et Gallia*. The region's main historical significance was as one of JULIUS CAESAR's provinces, signifying its territorial detachment from the rest of Italy. Once the Alpine regions had been finally subjugated, AUGUSTUS' reorganization of Italy marked the division of Gallia Cisalpina into *regiones* VIII, IX, X and XI, in part repeating the likely major Gallic tribal divisions. The region is of great interest archaeologically for the extensive survival of centuriation, which reflects the rapid investment in the northern plains. (see also GAUL; GALLIC WARS) NJC

See Chilver, G. (1941) *Cisalpine Gaul*; Purcell, N. (1990) The creation of a provincial landscape: the Roman impact on Cisalpine Gaul, in T. Blagg and M. Millett, eds., *The Early Roman Empire in the West* 6–29.

 ITALY: (b).

Gallia Lugdunensis, Gallia Narbonensis, Gallia Transalpina see GAUL.

Gallic wars After obtaining Transalpine and Cisalpine GAUL, with ILLYRICUM, as his proconsular province for 58–49 BC, CAESAR began the Gallic wars by punishing the Helvetii for damaging the lands of Rome's allies. When the Suebi under Ariovistus declined to leave the territory they had taken, Caesar defeated them. Next, he took the opportunity to pacify other peoples who threatened the empire's friends, fighting the Belgae and Aquitani among others. In 55, he crossed the RHINE and reconnoitred BRITAIN. His expedition to Britain in 54, however, was unsuccessful, while a revolt, led by Ambiorix of the Eburones, broke out in Gaul. After a difficult winter, Caesar resolved this in 53, but the Arvernian VERCINGETORIX forged ALLIANCES and, with much of Gaul, rebelled in 52. Captured at the siege of Alesia before the year was out, he was kept alive only long enough to grace Caesar's TRIUMPH in 46. Caesar devoted 51 and 50 to consolidation and to the worsening political situation at Rome. In 51 he published *The Gallic War*, each book covering one year from 58 to 52. Aulus Hirtius later added the accounts of 51 and 50.

The conquest of Gaul was a singular accomplishment, in terms of territory conquered (twice) and consolidation achieved, and a tribute to Caesar's preference for using DIPLOMACY unless brutal methods, like his treatment of the Atuatuci, were needed as punishment or useful as deterrent. Later attempts to liberate Gaul from Roman rule were usually on a limited scale, and never enjoyed the full support of the region's inhabitants. JV

See Julius Caesar, *The Gallic War*.

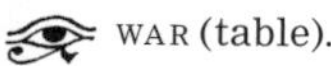 WAR (table).

Gallienus (Publius Licinius Egnatius Gallienus) Roman emperor, AD 253–68, who was appointed AUGUSTUS by his father VALERIAN in September 253. Placed in charge of the Western part of the empire, he was kept busy fighting on the RHINE and DANUBE between 254 and 259. In 257/8 a political split occurred between Gallienus and Valerian, on whose capture by the SASSANIANS in 260 Gallienus began a new series of regnal years. During his reign, 'SC' (*SENATUS CONSULTUM*) disappeared from COINAGE and SENATORS were formally prohibited from holding military commands (only in legal theory; some continued to hold them). A separate CAVALRY army developed, with its own commander, Aureolus, and the creation of a permanent field army allowed problems to be addressed without taking troops from other frontiers. Imperial power was damaged by the emergence of other Roman empires in PALMYRA (under Odenathus) and GAUL (under Postumus). Gallienus' ability to fight either empire was limited by problems in Rome and Egypt. In 263 he campaigned against Postumus, but was wounded and retired to Italy. Subsequently, he accepted the existence of the Gallic and Palmyran empires. New GOTHIC invasions in 268 led to his return to the Danube. After Aureolus, left in command in Italy, deserted to Postumus, Gallienus returned to Italy and besieged Aureolus in MILAN. During the SIEGE, he was murdered in a plot led by his generals Marcus Aurelius Claudius and Lucius Domitius AURELIANUS. HWE

See De Blois, L. (1975) *The Policy of the Emperor Gallienus*.

 EMPERORS, ROMAN: (b).

Gallus (Gaius Cornelius Gallus) 70/69–26 BC Roman POET and statesman. Gallus rose rapidly to political prominence in the 30s BC as an ally of Octavian, the future AUGUSTUS. In 41 he was involved in the confiscations of land from the defeated opponents of the TRIUMVIRS following the battle of PHILIPPI, and he subsequently played a part – probably as *praefectus fabrum* ('prefect of engineers') – in the Egyptian campaign after the battle of ACTIUM. He was appointed by Octavian as the first prefect of Egypt, but subsequently fell from favour and committed SUICIDE.

He is best remembered, however, for his literary rather than his political achievements – despite the fact that almost nothing of his poetry survives. Until the 1970s, only one single-line fragment was preserved. This was supplemented by a further nine (partly damaged) elegiac lines contained in a PAPYRUS discovered at Qasr Ibrîm in Egypt in 1978. Rather more can be conjectured about the style of his poetry from VIRGIL's 10th *Eclogue*, in which Gallus appears as a character and makes a lengthy speech, said by the ancient critic Servius to contain extensive quotation from (or adaptation of) Gallus' own verse. From this meagre evidence – in addition to several references in the work of later poets and prose writers – we can piece together a picture of Gallus as the composer of elegiacs very similar in style to those of the later love elegists. It has been conjectured that he was an extremely influential figure in Latin poetry, as (effectively) the 'inventor' of the genre. MG

See Courtney, E. (1993) *The Fragmentary Latin Poets*.

Gallus (Caesar)

emperors, Roman: (b); Tetrarchs: (b).

gambling Attested in literary texts as early as the *Iliad*, where Homeric heroes bet on the chariot race at the funeral games for Patroklos, gambling was endemic in antiquity. In the *Odyssey*, Penelope's suitors play a form of marbles to determine her presumptive husband. In the classical period, a form of checkers, *pessoi*, was popular, as was *kottabos*, a game played at the end of a drinking bout: contestants tried to throw the dregs of wine in their cups into some target.

Dice games of all sorts were immensely popular at Rome, as were games called 'Twelve lines', *duodecim scripta* (an early form of backgammon), and 'Robbers', *ludus latrunculorum*, similar to chess. Another popular game was *micatio*, in which both players raised fingers on their right hand, calling out as they did so the total number of fingers raised by both. Proverbially, an honest individual was a person with whom one could play *micatio* in the dark.

Aristotle condemned professional gamblers as thieves of a particularly bad sort since they hurt their friends. As early as 204 BC, the Roman state tried to ban professional gambling through the *lex Alearia*, and a *lex Talaria* prohibited dice playing except at mealtimes and during the Saturnalia. Gambling debts were unrecoverable at law. Later laws permitted betting on events contested 'for virtue', presumably including all manner of athletic, circus and amphitheatric events.

Despite the tendency to link dice games with the lower classes (dice tables of various sorts are scratched in public places throughout the empire), members of the upper classes were much attracted to them as well. Augustus wrote to Tiberius about the pleasures of playing, while Julius Caesar allegedly used a phrase derived from the world of gambling when he crossed the Rubicon: *alea iacta est* ('the die has been cast'). DSP

See Friedländer, L. (1907–13) *Roman Life and Manners under the Early Empire*, vol. 1, 218–19; Toner, J. P. (1995) *Leisure and Ancient Rome* 18–101.

epigraphy, Roman: (e).

GAMBLING: dice games were very popular, but could be controversial as in this Pompeian wall-painting: 'I'm out' says player one pugnaciously; 'That's not a three, that's a two' says his opponent.

games

Greek games fall into three categories: those contested for a prize at a festival, those used to train young men and those played for the sake of fitness. Into the latter category fall a variety of ball games and training exercises in the gymnasium. Games used to train young men might include in rare circumstances some team sports, but were ordinarily scaled-down versions of games with lesser prizes at some annual festival connected with the gymnasium. In these cases, prizes were awarded for such accomplishments as hard training and good behaviour, as well as for victories in athletic contests. The games held at civic and international festivals were of the utmost importance in defining both civic and ethnic identity in the Greek world.

The earliest attested Greek games appear to have taken place at aristocratic funerals, with participation limited to men of high standing. They include contests in athletic events such as running, boxing, wrestling, the discus, archery, the javelin and, only in Homer, two armed men fighting to first blood. Equestrian events were apparently limited to chariot races. Contests between bards are of particular interest: these did not necessarily involve people whose status depended upon aristocratic lineage, helping to explain why their prizes were later of lesser value than games exclusively for aristocrats. The association of games with regular religious festivals must date at least to the 6th century; the 8th-century BC date for the Olympic games, if accepted, would obviously push the date much further back. At some festivals, the Brauronia in Attica and the Heraia at Olympia among others, there were races involving girls, though on a shorter track (one-sixth of the 200 m *stadion* used by men).

By the 6th century BC, a clear distinction developed between games attached to a local religious festival (called *agônes thêmatikoi* or *thêmides*), which offered prizes of money or other objects of value, and the great international, sacred games (called *stephanitai*

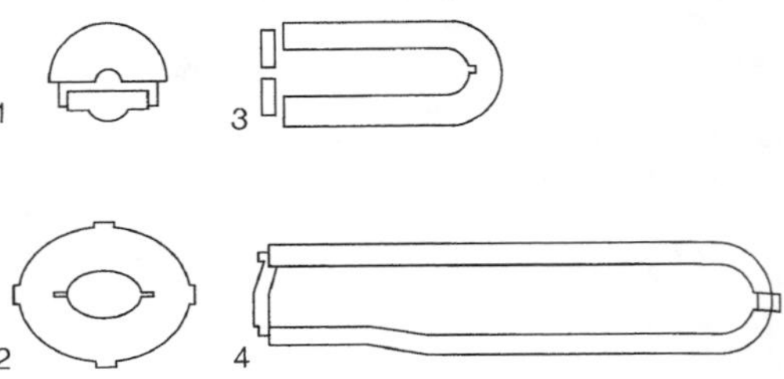

GAMES, ROMAN: comparative plans at a single scale of the main types of buildings used in Roman public entertainments. 1. theatre; 2. amphitheatre; 3. stadium; 4. circus.

'crowned', *hieroi* 'sacred' or, later, *eiselastikoi*), where a crown was the prize. Individual cities determined what further, often substantial, benefits their citizens victorious in these games would receive. The four international, sacred festivals established as a cycle (*periodos*) in the early 6th century were the Olympic games held every four years at the temple of ZEUS at OLYMPIA in Elis, the Pythian games every four years at the temple of APOLLO at DELPHI, the Isthmian games every two years at the temple of POSEIDON at Isthmia, and the Nemean games every two years at the temple of Zeus at Nemea in the Argolid.

The festivals of the *periodos* lasted for a number of days, and the procedure at the Olympics offers an example of what could take place (events might be held in a different order, depending on the festival). The Olympia as a whole lasted for five days. The first day included the swearing of oaths by contestants and their trainers, the inspection of the contestants to ensure that they were competing in the proper category, and the contests for trumpeters and heralds. Equestrian events and the *pentathlon* were held on the second day. The third was reserved for a sacred procession that concluded with a massive sacrifice to Zeus. Boys' contests were held on the morning of the fifth day, while men's contests, concluding with the *pankration*, took place in the afternoon.

The premier events in each category appear to have been the *stadion* race, the four-horse chariot race and the *pankration*. Although the procedure is unknown, a method to limit the number of contestants was necessary. The four-horse chariot race at Olympia could accommodate as many as 48 contestants; given a lack of evidence for preliminary heats, another procedure was employed to ensure that no more than 48 teams were admitted. The same is true of running events, where the number of starting gates limited the number of contestants. For combat events there were several rounds; lots would be drawn to determine pairings when an odd number of contestants was present. A bye in any round was considered to be a major advantage. But here too, the need to compete in all three events on one day must have required preliminary sorting, to eliminate those not qualified to compete on grounds of birth and also (though no direct evidence is available) to ensure that contestants not up to the level of competition were excluded. This is perhaps the reason that athletes were expected to work out under supervision before the games.

The need to ensure the qualifications of contestants may have been a factor contributing to the rise of athletic synods (*synodoi*) in the 1st century BC – though it was certainly not the only factor. Athletes who were members of these self-governing organizations received substantial benefits from the Roman state, including exemption from local tax obligations. While the members of the synods, limited to victors at events in recognized 'international' festivals, certainly benefited from this arrangement, the sponsors of the events benefited as well. Synods helped to organize the enormous number of festivals that came into being during the 1st to 3rd centuries AD, ensuring that festivals would not interfere with each other and thus promoting the ability of first-rate athletes to perform everywhere. Retired athletes were often appointed as supervisors of gymnasia in major cities, and some areas specialized in the training of professionals during the imperial period. This may have regularized the flow of contestants.

The first three centuries AD saw a flowering of Greek-style games and their diffusion throughout much of the Roman empire. There is ample evidence for Greek-style athletics in, for instance, Roman North AFRICA and in Roman Italy, where Greek games had arrived with Greek colonists in the archaic period and been adopted by native Italic peoples. It was, however, only in the imperial period that festivals in Italy, both at Rome and at Naples, acquired international acceptance (largely because they were favoured by emperors). There were equally striking developments in the Semitic world (after a period of significant tension in, for instance, Palestine where, during the 2nd century BC, membership in the gymnasium was regarded as an attack on the fabric of JEWISH life). From the earliest to the latest period of festivals, the production of Greek games would be symbolic of membership in what Greeks regarded as civilized society. DSP

See Golden, M. (1998) *Sport and Society in Ancient Greece*; Miller, S. G. (2004) *Ancient Greek Athletics*; Poliakoff, M. B. (1987) *Combat Sports in the Ancient World*.

The Romans enjoyed a wide variety of public entertainments, and the evolution of these entertainments mirrors the evolution of Roman society itself. At the most basic level, the parallel evolution of the state and its games is evident in the distinction between *ludi* (games) and *munera* (gifts). *Ludi* were festivals instituted by the state, while *munera* were technically presents offered to the people by famous individuals. On a more specific level, *ludi* for a long time excluded some forms of entertainment, chiefly those involving GLADIATORS and the hunting of wild beasts.

As late as the 1st century BC, CICERO wrote that there were two kinds of *ludus*, those of the CIRCUS that involved the exercise of the body (human or equine), and those of the THEATRE that involved the voice or MUSICAL INSTRUMENTS (*Laws* 2.38). The oldest festivals may have been those involving HORSES. Games in the circus date to the end of the regal period, with reasonable evidence for some form of organized horse or CHARIOT RACING in the CIRCUS MAXIMUS from the earliest years of the Republic. The ETRUSCANS also enjoyed ATHLETICS events, and it is unlikely that these were unknown at Rome. Some forms of dramatic performance are mentioned in the context of early Italian entertainment (e.g. Atellan farce, the *ludus talarius*), all predating the arrival of Greek-style DRAMA, which was established at Rome by the second half of the 3rd century BC. Some form of indigenous theatrical entertainment on historical themes probably existed as early as the 4th century. The existence of the earlier forms of drama in the context of *ludi* may explain why Greek-style drama found a place in that context.

GLADIATORS arrived at Rome rather later than drama, athletics and equestrian events. The first recorded gladiatorial exhibition took place in 264 BC, and gladiatorial combat itself appears to have been indigenous to south-central Italy, a region that had only come under Roman control at the end of the previous century. A consequence of this relatively late arrival was that gladiators were not admitted to *ludi* until the imperial period, and those *ludi* were of late foundation. The same is true of beast hunts (*venationes*), which only became common at Rome in the later 2nd century BC, after the establishment of the province of AFRICA.

The earliest *ludi* were probably those administered by colleges of PRIESTS, events such as the Consualia in honour of the god Consus, and the Equirria in honour of MARS. These date from the period of the formation of the Roman community. *Ludi* administered by MAGISTRATES appear to have come into existence from the 6th to the 3rd century, and tended to commemorate the existence of the community and its relationship with the gods. They included the Great Roman games (*ludi Romani magni*) in honour of JUPITER; the Plebeian games (*ludi plebei*), also in honour of Jupiter; the Cerialia (*ludi Ceriales*) in honour of CERES and associated gods; the Floralia, possibly dating to the end of the first PUNIC WAR; the games of Apollo (*ludi Apollinares*), instituted towards the end of the second Punic WAR; and the Megalensian games (*ludi Megalenses*) founded in 202, also in connection with the last stages of the Hannibalic war. The 1st century BC saw a number of changes in the nature of Roman games; *ludi* were directly associated with individuals, first with two short-lived events, in honour of SULLA and JULIUS CAESAR respectively, and then in celebration of events in the life of AUGUSTUS and family members.

The 1st century BC also saw enormous changes in the administration of the games. Under the Republic, we find the circus factions administered by members of the EQUESTRIAN order, associations of ACTORS and athletes administered by members of the associations, and troops of gladiators or beast hunters owned by senators and run by freedmen. Julius Caesar accumulated the largest holding of gladiators of any private citizen and passed these on to Augustus, thus laying the foundation for what would become enormously profitable imperial troupes of gladiators. Under Augustus, the first evidence appears for imperial troupes in the PROVINCES, the first establishment of ZOOS and a training ground for beast hunters. By the time of CLAUDIUS there were three principal zoos around Rome, one for herbivores, another for carnivores and the third for elephants. Exhibitions of carnivores were ordinarily restricted in the provinces to events held by especially favoured individuals, and cost controls were established for gladiatorial combats. At the same time, the professional associations of actors and athletes came under direct imperial patronage. A further change was the rise in the status of PANTOMIME dancers (soloists who performed mythological DANCES to musical and vocal accompaniment).

The tastes of the capital transformed the tastes of Rome's subjects. Greek-style athletic events became commonplace in parts of the Western empire (with particularly important festivals at Rome and Naples), as did all manner of theatrical performances. Gladiators, who had been introduced in the East, became a fundamental feature of celebrations of the IMPERIAL CULT, and an explosion of both athletic and theatrical festivals occurred throughout the Eastern provinces until the 3rd century AD. One event that spread more slowly was circus chariot racing, possibly because of the vast expense of CIRCUS BUILDINGS. They began to be more common in the 3rd century, and in the 4th century chariot racing became the pre-eminent form of entertainment throughout the empire. This was accompanied by a decline in gladiatorial combat, deprecated for doctrinal reasons by CHRISTIAN emperors, and in traditional athletics, which lost their traditional support from civic GYMNASIA as the latter became less significant. Despite the strong disapproval of Christians, theatrical entertainments retained their vigour until the end of the classical city-state, and chariot racing is attested at CONSTANTINOPLE well into the Middle Ages. In Western Europe, Roman forms of entertainment disappeared along with the structures that supported them in the 5th century AD. DSP

See Friedländer, L. (1907–13) *Roman Life and Manners under the Early Empire*, vol. 2, 1–130; Köhne, E. and Ewigleben, C., eds. (2000) *Gladiators and Caesars: the power of spectacle in ancient Rome*; Potter, D. S. and Mattingly, D. J., eds. (1999) *Life, Death, and Entertainment in the Roman Empire*.

Gandhara see INDIA; PAKISTAN.

Garamantes Depicted by classical sources in a predominantly negative light, the Garamantes were viewed as the archetypal BARBARIANS dwelling beyond Rome's southern desert FRONTIERS. Casual reading of this source evidence (5th century BC–6th century AD) would suggest transient PASTORALISTS

GARAMANTES: (a) were they troublesome nomadic brigands, to be executed by exposure to wild beasts in the arenas? (mosaic from Zliten in Libya).

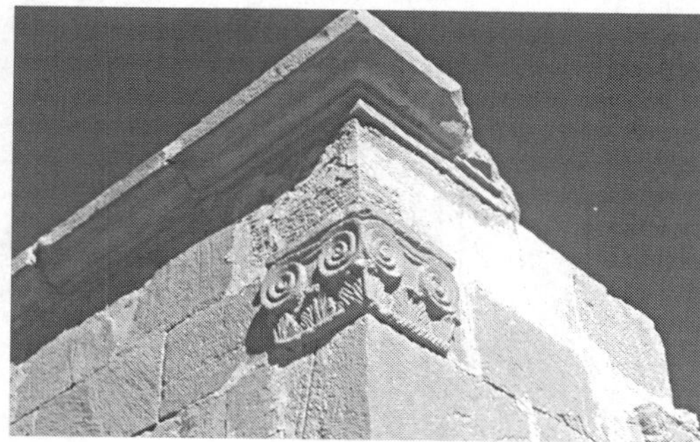

GARAMANTES: (b) or a civilized Saharan state, capable of emulating Mediterranean architecture, practising agriculture and trading peacefully with Rome over a long period?

and brigands with no settled roots and an anarchic social organization. Archaeology reveals a very different picture of sedentary agriculturalists, living in TOWNS and VILLAGES, possessing an ordered and hierarchical social structure and making use of an advanced material culture. They can be associated with the spread of the HORSE, CAMEL and WHEELED VEHICLES in the Sahara, with oasis irrigation using underground water channels, with METALLURGY, with the working of semi-precious GEMSTONES (including carnelian, known in the sources as 'Garamantian carbuncles') and with the development of a written script for the LIBYAN language.

Roman contacts with the Garamantes were initially antagonistic, with campaigning against their desert heartlands recorded on several occasions between c.20 BC–AD 90. Most famously, Cornelius Balbus led a column against them (20 BC), traversing several thousand kilometres of hostile desert terrain and capturing their capital at Garama (Jarma). The Garamantes were ruled by kings, and by the later 1st century more stable relations appear to have been established. This heralded a period of TRADE and peaceful co-existence of the large independent kingdom and the empire. The kingdom dominated the central Sahara for a millennium, and can be recognized as its first true civilization. DJM

See Mattingly, D. J. et al. (2003) *The Archaeology of Fazzan*, vol. 1.

AFRICA, ROMAN.

garbage see WASTE DISPOSAL.

gardens and gardening Growing plants for decorative effect is older than the classical period, and ornamental gardening extends back into Bronze Age Greece and the Near East. The best-documented gardens belonged to the wealthy. Gardens of the pre-Roman period would appear strange to us, and the familiar lawns and borders of the modern English-speaking world were unknown. However, both Greeks and Romans enthusiastically imported and developed ornamental plants, and we are ultimately indebted to them for many which we grow today. The old-fashioned apple variety Court Pendu Plat is thought to have been brought to BRITAIN by the Romans, along with the vines and OLIVES they planted as much for ornament as in hope of profit.

Walking through an ancient Greek town or VILLAGE, we would not recognize the gardens. Houses looked inward onto a courtyard, so from the street only a blank wall was visible, and gardens were not usually attached directly to them. Open spaces between close, cramped blocks of houses were sometimes made into gardens. So, too, plots along the roadside on the outskirts of settlements might be planted ornamentally. Courtyards were important spaces for growing plants, often in containers, though trees and vines on pergolas and peristyles provided welcome summer shade and screened women at work. However, vines are deciduous, so in winter the courtyard caught all available sun. Gardens and similar horticultural areas were also associated with TEMPLES and shrines, and such sites were extensively landscaped and planted in antiquity.

To understand what Greeks thought beautiful and restful in a garden, it is important to remember the 'natural' environment. In contrast to the parched summer lowlands or the dense, even impenetrable, shrubby growth of unfarmed hillsides, a garden should consist of tall trees, preferably ordered in a formal planting pattern. That the trees might have had an economic function did not detract from their ornamental quality. Timber trees such as poplars or fruit trees such as olives or FIGS offered shade, shelter and peace. Planting patterns were often complex, but the most admired were grid layouts (providing an interesting analogy with contemporary town planning). XENOPHON praised the regularity of trees in ranks and files in the royal PERSIAN ornamental orchards that he saw. Other planting patterns were concentric circles, with the perimeters planted in large olive trees to shut out the outside world, and smaller trees such as pomegranates, almonds or apples planted in rings inside. Sometimes exotic trees were planted as well. THEOPHRASTOS, a 4th-century BC plantsman, was obsessed with trying to make date palms (which never would fruit for him) grow in Greece.

A well, spring or cistern was a highly desirable feature. Not only did water add to the appeal of a garden, it was essential for the roses, myrtle, periwinkle and ivy that might be trained up the trees. Trees could also be underplanted with FLOWERS such as lilies, which

GARDENS: (a) formal garden in a Pompeian wall-painting.

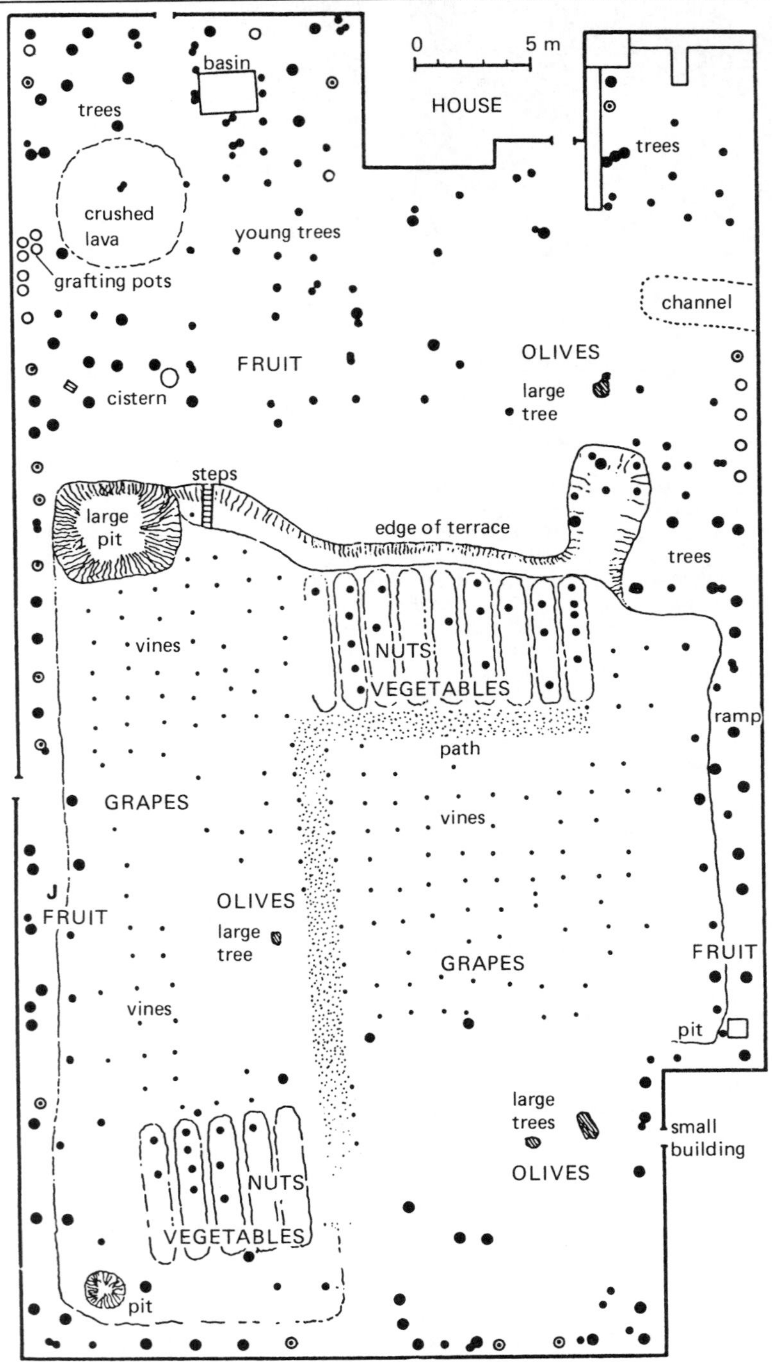

GARDENS: (b) in the special preservation conditions of Pompeii, it has been possible to excavate gardens and recover the planting patterns. A whole spectrum of garden types has been discovered ranging from small, functional vineyards behind taverns to elegant formal ornamental gardens. Plant species can be determined by the cavities left in the ground where the roots had grown, from which plaster casts are taken. Gardens like this one, relating to the House of the Ship Europa, can then be identified and reconstructed. From the finds we learn some of the activities which took place. Large numbers of olive stones and chicken and fish bones suggest that it was often used for dining.

would not survive the hot summer sun without protective shade. Though decorative, all these plants were picked to make the garlands worn on special occasions. Greeks loved flowers for their scent and beauty and are often depicted in art wearing and carrying them.

Roman gardens would have been more familiar to modern eyes. By the early imperial period, large private houses in a town such as Pompeii had gardens attached. Like their Greek counterparts, timber and fruit trees provided the backbone of the garden. Often trees had vines or other plants growing up them in a system of cultivation called the *arbustum*. Other kinds of restricted growth patterns such as cordons were developed by Roman gardeners as well. Like the Greeks, the Romans used circular plantings but preferred regular, grid-type patterns. One of the most favoured was the *quincunx*, a grid fixed onto a parallelogram rather than a square, so that lines of trees ran diagonally. Ornamental hedges and topiary were introduced by the Romans. With the Mediterranean united under imperial rule, many new plants and trees, as well as new varieties of old ones, spread across the empire. Exotic fruits like the peach and cherry served as both ornamental features and culinary delights. Roman gardens were also places to dine, walk, rest and linger. Planting patterns were elaborated by the wealthy with ornamental sculpture, sundials, large ceramic and stone planting pots, and sculptures (often copies of famous works of Greek art). Ponds with fish, fountains and aviaries with exotic birds might also feature. Gardens might incorporate shrines to suitable deities like Priapus or the Nymphs. As in Greece, gardens filled in odd bits of urban space as well as being attached to shrines and country houses.

Emperors built enormous gardens for their palaces, such as Hadrian's at Tivoli. These were imitated by lesser rulers across the empire. Excavations of king Herod's palace at Caesarea Maritima show that the same principles of planning and planting used in Roman Italy were adapted for the Palestinian climate, complete with terracing, statuary, flower pots and appropriate irrigation systems. Similarly, ornamental gardens attached to Roman villas in Britain have been found, as at Fishbourne. LF

See Hunt, J. D. (1992) *Garden History*; Jaschemski, W. F. (1989–93) *The Gardens of Pompeii*; Miller, N. F. and Gleason, K. L., eds. (1994) *The Archaeology of Garden and Field*.

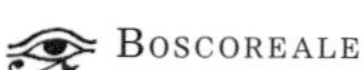 Boscoreale.

garum see fish sauces.

Gaugamela Site, in Iraq, of Alexander the Great's third major victory over the Persian empire in 331 BC, also called the battle of Arbela. Alexander came upon Darius' army after marching from Egypt through Mesopotamia. The Persian forces were made up of a very diverse collection of Darius' subjects, but outnumbered Alexander's forces. The battle took place on a broad plain, which gave the advantage to the Persians. It is not possible to reconstruct the details of the battle from the sources, but Alexander was victorious though, as at Issos, Darius himself escaped. He was murdered by his own subordinates 11 months later. Alexander's victory gave him control of the heart of the Persian empire, including the cities of Babylon and Susa and the royal palace at Persepolis. After Darius' death, Alexander was able to take the title of Great King. HB

See Arrian, *Anabasis* 3.8–15; Diodorus Siculus 17.56–61; Plutarch, *Alexander* 31–3; Quintus Curtius Rufus 4.12–16.

 Alexander: (b); battles (table).

Gaul In Latin *Gallia*, the Romans' name for much of their geographic empire in the European West, including northern Italy, France, Belgium, Luxembourg, and portions of the Netherlands, Germany and Switzerland. More generally used for regions beyond the Alps, the term also included northern Italy as far south as the Rubicon river (Gallia Cisalpina, 'this side of the Alps'). Before Julius Caesar's proconsulships in 58–49 BC, only Cisalpine Gaul and a coastal strip of transalpine territory (Gallia Transalpina, 'across the Alps', approximately equivalent to the later Gallia Narbonensis) were Roman provinces. Rome's initial involvement resulted from its alliance with the independent city-state of Massalia (Marseilles) and a need to protect the land route to Spain, especially after the second Punic war (218–201). From 125 to 121, Roman commanders, most notably Gnaeus Domitius Ahenobarbus, engaged Massalia's enemies at that city's request. Consequently, Rome became the master of this region, but Massalia remained independent. A new road from Italy to Spain, the Via Domitia, drew its name from Domitius, who remained to organize it. Transalpine Gaul was known simply as the 'province' (now Provence), while the rest of Celtic Europe (apart from the British Isles) was often called, disparagingly, Gallia Comata ('long-haired Gaul').

For more than a millennium before the Roman conquest, the dominant civilization in Gaul had been the successive Celtic Urnfield (c.1200 BC), Hallstatt (c.750) and La Tène (c.450) cultures, the latter still in place at the time of Caesar. The expansion of the Greeks into the western Mediterranean from the 7th century onwards, which accounted for the foundation of Massalia, and particularly the activity of traders up the Rhône, acquainted the region, or its élite at any rate, with some Greek ideas. These included coinage, whose inscriptions in native language were sometimes done in Greek letters. Large wine jars and other exquisite pottery, massive bronze cauldrons (notably that found at Vix in Burgundy, possibly of Laconian manufacture), and a variety of goods from Greek and Etruscan areas reached even the northernmost Celtic regions. These prestige goods represent diplomatic gift-giving, not the actual trade that might follow in the wake of diplomacy. Essentially, Celtic civilization was a tribal one and warlike. Because leaders of clans based their positions on personal prestige and ability in war, hostilities between the many different groups were endemic, as Caesar discovered both rapidly and constantly, though he was able to play this to his advantage at times.

From the late 2nd century to the time of Caesar, Transalpine Gaul remained an area of unrest, and Rome devoted attention to its stabilization. When Caesar became proconsul in 58 BC, he quickly added the rest of Gaul to the Roman world, employing

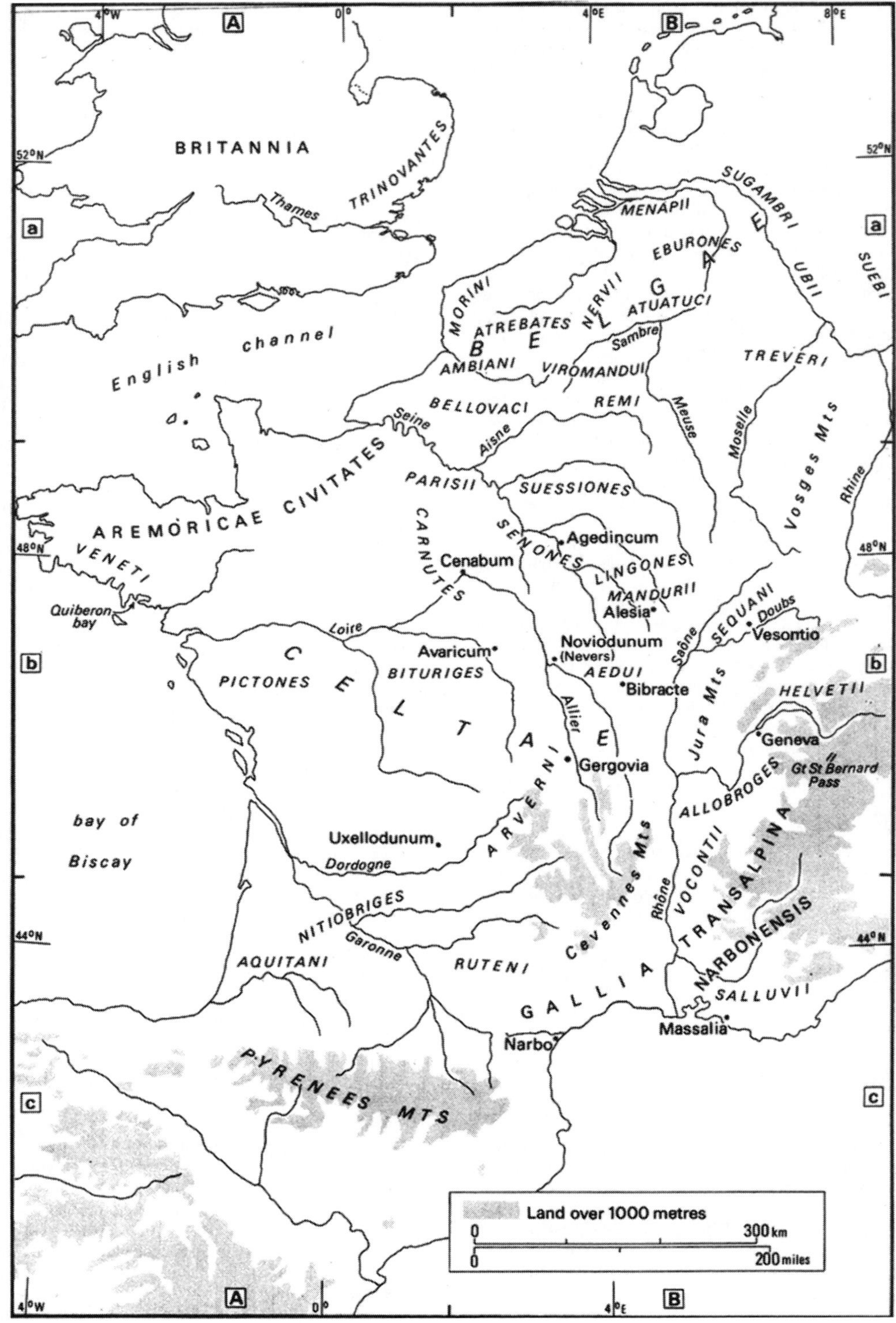

GAUL: (a) map of main Gallic peoples in the time of Caesar.

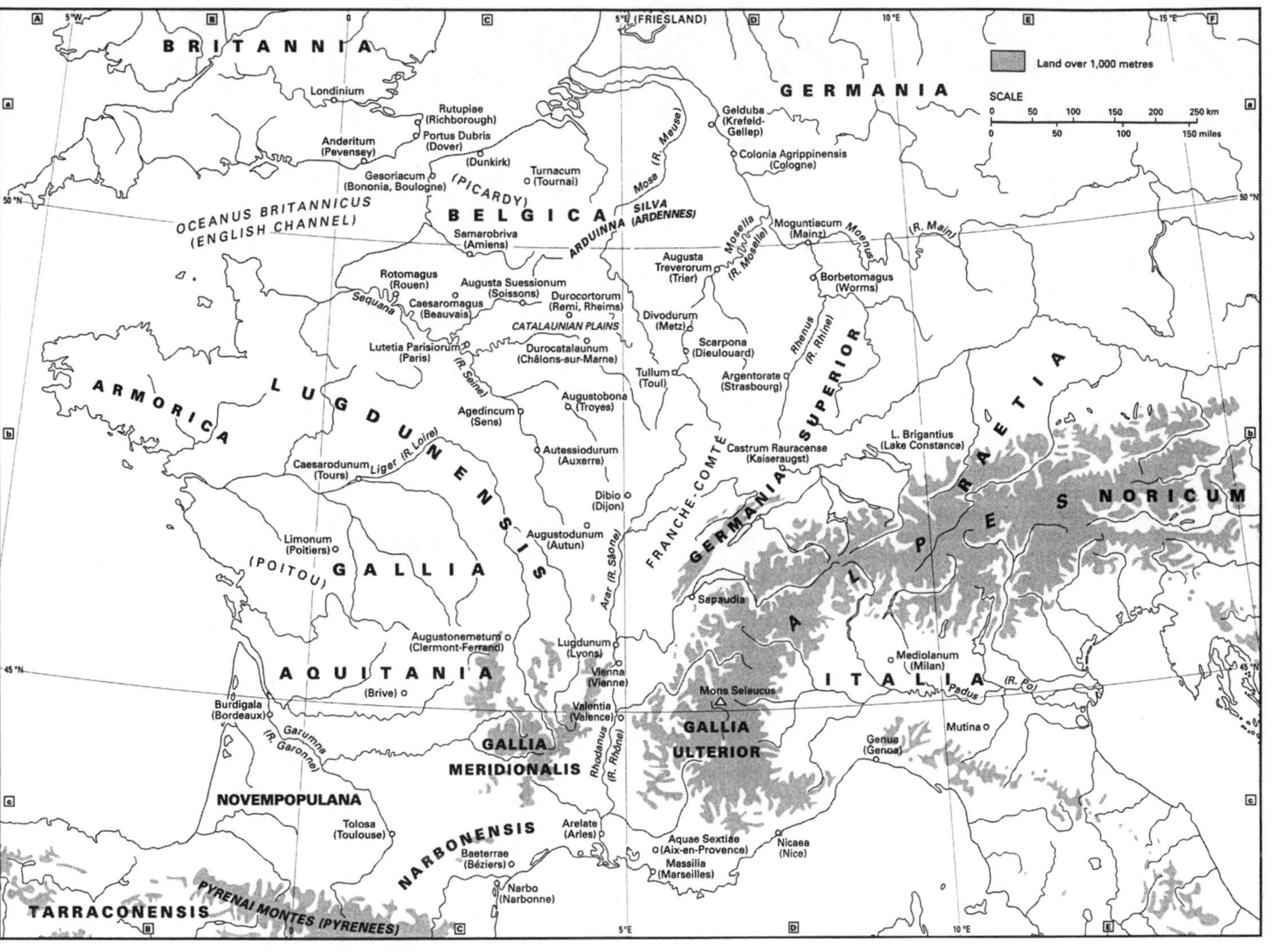

GAUL: (b) map of Roman Gaul and neighbouring provinces.

diplomacy, harshness and military successes. His death and the subsequent Roman civil wars slowed the region's organization until the reign of AUGUSTUS. The division of the territory into the three provinces of Aquitania, Lugdunensis, and Belgica (the 'Three Gauls') and the subdivision of these into individual *civitates* (smaller units, often reflecting pre-Roman tribal boundaries but centred on towns), as well as the foundation of COLONIES and the construction of roads and other infrastructure, all had their origin in the Augustan period. In many places, the native élite quickly adopted aspects of Roman ideals and culture, though the depth of this 'romanization' remains a question of some dispute. As emperor, CLAUDIUS argued that some inhabitants of Gaul had imbibed enough Roman culture to deserve places in the Roman SENATE, yet a few years later a revolt broke out. Led by Vindex, who was said to have had as many as 100,000 Gallic supporters, the uprising was a significant trigger for NERO's despair and the senate's withdrawal of support from the emperor. In an important sense, these events from successive reigns represent the Gallic attitude: on the one hand, wholesale enthusiasm for the benefits of Roman rule; on the other, deep-seated resentment of Roman domination. In any case, imperial culture and authority never quite ousted Gallic solidarity.

This mixed response continued into late antiquity. While Gaul was an important recruiting ground for soldiers, while its élite joined the imperial hierarchy, while elements of its culture made their way to Rome (e.g. EPONA), the Gallic population required little incentive to break ties. Partly because of the THIRD-CENTURY CRISIS and the consequent need to look to its own defence, the Gallic empire emerged in AD 259 as an independent entity with a succession of emperors (Postumus, Victorinus, Tetricus) who harboured little ambition to rule the entire Roman world. AURELIAN re-established central control in 273. In the 5th century, Gallic independence rose again. Several Gallic usurpers, with strong local support, attempted to gain the throne. At the same time, GOTHS, Burgundians, and FRANKS were given or simply took territory. While some, like SIDONIUS APOLLINARIS, mourned the loss of ties between Gaul and Rome, others sought employment with these new kingdoms. Aegidius, a Roman administrator who declined to step down, even established a short-lived kingdom centred at Soissons and passed it to his son Syagrius. The latter lost it to Clovis, king of the Franks, in 486, ending any semblance of Roman authority in northern Gaul. When Clovis expanded his kingdom to the rest of Gaul, except the areas under Visigothic rule, Roman political control of Gaul was entirely extinguished.

Rome's long-term impact on Gaul was significant. For more than a millennium after the collapse of Roman authority, Western CHRISTIANITY looked to Rome as its centre as it does, in part, to the present day. The modern languages of the region are descendants of Latin. Naturally, material remains from the Roman period survive to engage the attention of the archaeologist, the scholar and the tourist. JV

See Drinkwater, J.F. (1983) *Roman Gaul*; Ebel, C. (1976) *Transalpine Gaul*; Mathisen, R.W. (1993) *Roman Aristocrats in Barbarian Gaul*; Wells, P. S. (1980) *Culture Contact and Culture Change*; Woolf, G. (1998) *Becoming Roman*.

 CELTS; GERMANY AND GERMANS: (a); TEMPLES: (e).

Ge (Gaia) According to HESIOD's *Theogony*, Ge (*gê*) or Earth, together with Chaos, Eros (Desire) and Tartaros, is one of four primordial elements which simply exist. Hesiod describes her as both 'broad-breasted' and 'firm seat of all', epithets which indicate that her anthropomorphic characteristics were not complete. She created her mate Ouranos by parthenogenesis, the ability of female beings to reproduce without intervention of a male. By Ouranos, she gave birth to Kronos and the other Titans, then actively schemed to dethrone Ouranos and, from within herself, provided the metal sickle to castrate him. Later, she helped her daughter Rheia to devise the plot that ended the reign of Kronos. After the rule of ZEUS was established, Ge mated with Tartaros, gave birth to the monster Typhôeus and encouraged him to fight Zeus. Ge was always an instigator of change and evolution in society, though her role was usually more hidden than obvious. Earth is the material used to create Pandora, the first woman. For the Greeks, women thus shared with Ge her ability to produce change, conceived in part as violence towards men. Ge, as primordial female entity, is a source of life and death.

After the Olympic pantheon was securely established, the role of Ge diminished considerably. Although she was still worshipped at TEMPLES in her honour in the Greek *poleis*, PRIESTESSES of Ge did not enjoy many benefits, for her temples were rarely visited. RBC

Geertz, C. see CULTURE.

Gellius, Aulus c.AD 127–c.180 Roman author of the *Attic Nights* (*Noctes Atticae*). Gellius, possibly of AFRICAN origin, studied grammar, RHETORIC and PHILOSOPHY, the latter in 147 at Athens but also at Rome with Favorinus. Subsequently, Gellius devoted himself to scholarship. He owned a summer home at PRAENESTE, where on an evening walk he once contemplated the meanings of the preposition *pro*. He served as a judge and fathered children, but writes little about his relatives. A companion to the prominent, he knew many luminaries and was close to some, like Marcus Cornelius FRONTO and HERODES ATTICUS, yet was not, as they were, a friend of EMPERORS.

Gellius' habit of evening reading at Athens inspired his Latin title, but the collection represents a longer period of activity and was published in the 170s. Of 20 books, parts of the first and last and most of book 8 are lost. Nearly 400 discussions appear, sometimes portrayed as conversations within his circle and included for pleasure, education or utility. Gellius focuses on word usage, with a bias toward the archaic. The paragraphs, sentences and phrases quoted from earlier writers, Greek as well as Latin, contribute much to modern knowledge of authors whose works are lost. The *Attic Nights* was more popular in the Middle Ages and RENAISSANCE than subsequently. JV

See Aulus Gellius, *Attic Nights*, 3 vols., trs. J. C. Rolfe (1927); Holford-Strevens, L. (1988) *Aulus Gellius*.

gems and gem-cutting Engraved gems were used throughout the Greek and Roman world to make an impression into clay or beeswax, in effect acting as a personal signature and security device. They were also valued as protective charms and for their magical powers. From the classical period onwards Near Eastern cylinder seals, which were worn on necklaces or bracelets, were replaced by engraved gems set into finger rings. Such signet rings were used to seal letters, contracts, legal documents and other valuables. Seals were also used to secure vessels for food and drink, as PLINY THE ELDER (*Natural History* 33.26) disapprovingly notes. Documents and letters were secured with a cord, the ends of which were enclosed in wax or clay to which the signet ring would be applied. Sometimes a seal box was employed to keep the impression undamaged. Seals were unique to their owners, and the designs engraved on gems often held a very specific meaning. They could be personalized and linked to family or personal history: one of CAESAR's rings showed VENUS Genetrix, to whom he traced his family's origin. Deities, symbols and ANIMALS were other popular motifs.

Most engraved gems were made from semi-precious stones such as cornelian, red jasper, amethyst and agate, but much cheaper imitation gems were also produced from GLASS paste (*Natural History* 37.197). The popularity of types of precious stones changes over time and can contribute to the dating of engraved gems. Precious stones were valued for qualities such as their colour, hardness and origin (often INDIA), as well as their magical properties. Thus the wine-coloured amethyst was thought to be a charm against intoxication, while the magical qualities attributed to heliotrope, a greenish stone with small flecks of red, meant that it was often used for GNOSTIC gems (*Natural History* 37.165).

The production of engraved gems involved three stages: cutting the semi-precious stone, the actual engraving, and setting the stone in a ring. Gem-cutters were highly accomplished artists who in the Roman period often worked for the imperial court. Commonly, there are strong artistic links between the designs on gems and COINAGE, and it is possible that the same artists engraved gems and coin dies. A design was outlined on the stone, perhaps with the aid of a diamond-pointed tool (*Natural History* 37.60). The actual engraving was created using emery powder mixed with OIL and applied by friction. The tool is turned mechanically either by a bow-drill or, more commonly, by a wheel. The wheel's cutting edge appears to bite into the stone but in fact is not actually cutting it; the design is created by the action of the wheel rubbing the emery powder into the stone's surface. The cut design is finished with the diamond-pointed tool and polished with emery powder.

Engraved gems were collected (SUETONIUS, *Julius Caesar* 47) and often inherited. Thus the portrait of AUGUSTUS created by his gem engraver Dioskorides was used as a seal both by Augustus and by his successors (*Natural History* 37.8). HE

gender The most important principle of social organization in the classical world. The biological fact of whether you were born a girl or a boy determined the course of the rest of your life because, from birth, girls and boys were raised with very different expectations and as a result had very different life chances. Gender roles in classical antiquity were not shaped exactly as they are today in the modern West, but superficially they appear to work similarly. All societies in the classical world were fundamentally 'patriarchical' in that they were dominated by adult men, in particular wealthy men. Gender roles were interlinked with age, status and wealth. The values of rich, high-status men permeated social and political structures and institutions. On the other hand, this does not mean that WOMEN, children, SLAVES and people whose gender was not clearly 'male' or 'female' played no part in social and communal life.

One reason why ancient gender roles look similar to modern ones is that Greeks and Romans usually expressed gender as a male–female polarity both in written texts and in art. So, for example, in Athenian vase-painting women's skin is often depicted using added white while men are left dark. Greek and Latin have clearly defined words for 'man' (*anêr, vir*) and 'woman' (*gynê, mulier*) and for 'male', 'MASCULINE' (*arsên, masculus/virilis*) and 'female', 'FEMININE' (*thêlys, femina*). In Greek and Latin, as in most modern European languages, these male–female words were considered to be opposites. Frequently derivatives of these words took on positive and negative moral overtones along gendered lines. So in Greek *andreios*, 'manly' (derived from *anêr*), meant 'brave, courageous, virtuous'. Latin *virtus* (from *vir*) meant 'excellence, worth' and has become the English word 'VIRTUE'. In contrast, feminine words often had negative connotations. To call someone *femineus*, 'effeminate,' in Latin was an insult, and the Greek term *thêlys* (feminine) also carried the meanings of 'soft, weak, delicate'.

Moreover, such gendered oppositions were projected onto other aspects of the natural world. For example, Greeks regularly distinguished between TREES that were masculine (with wood that was hard, resistant and difficult to work) and those that were feminine (with wood that was smooth-grained, and easily worked) – the virtue of 'feminine' wood was that it could be easily dominated. These characterizations match the typologies of male and female bodies which abound in MEDICAL texts, from the Greek Hippocratic case studies to the Roman physician Galen. Men were perceived as hard, firm, hot and dry while women were wet, cold, soft and spongy. Even GODS and their sanctuaries might be gendered in this way: the sanctuaries of ARTEMIS at BRAURON in ATTICA and of Artemis Ortheia in SPARTA are both located in wet, boggy locations, and Artemis was a goddess closely associated with women and their transition to adulthood. The relationships between grammatical gender and social gender (i.e. gendered roles and ideals) were not straightforward, but sometimes the grammatical gender of crucial words might have socially gendered conceptual or ideological overtones. So both the Greek and the Latin words for the earth were feminine in grammatical gender, while in mythology and art the goddess Earth (Greek GE or *Gaia*, Latin *Tellus*) was depicted as a fecund woman.

At the most basic level, it is likely that far more baby girls than boys were exposed at birth as unwanted children. Slightly different birth RITUALS surrounded the birth of girls than of boys. In rich families, boys were EDUCATED to manage their own wealth and for careers in military and public life, while girls were groomed for MARRIAGE. In ÉLITE circles, this often meant that girls were also educated to more than basic standards of LITERACY and NUMERACY, since considerable responsibility for managing a large HOUSEHOLD might fall to a married woman. With the notable exception of Sparta, physical training and activity were usually seen as undesirable for girls, but essential for boys. Boys remained adolescents much longer than girls, who took on adult responsibilities with marriage. In most classical Greek cities, girls were married very young (aged 12–16) to men in their late twenties or thirties or even older. In Roman society, it seems there was often a smaller age gap between marriage partners, and it was not unusual for both men and women to marry in their twenties. However, the general trend in the ancient world for husbands to be older than wives highlighted gender differences and enhanced the dominance of men over women.

Officially, in Greek and Roman society only men held political power, undertook political action, and generally dominated public life. POLITICAL PARTICIPATION, LAWCOURTS, offices and positions of power were open only to men. The men in charge were, ideally, full masculine men; those whose gender identity was considered to be dubious because of their actions or their physique were sometimes excluded from political life. So, for example, there was considerable unease among Roman lawyers about whether a man without a penis, or one who had lost it, could be considered a man (*vir*) in the full legal sense. In the 4th century BC Athens Timotheos, a close friend of the orator DEMOSTHENES, was deprived of his CITIZENSHIP by the popular court because 20 years earlier he had regularly engaged in homoerotic sexual prostitution. Homoeroticism was not necessarily a challenge to Athenian masculinity, and a closely circumscribed range of homoerotic practices was a normal and reasonably acceptable part of the development of Greek men at particular stages in their lives, especially as boys and young men. However, PROSTITUTION – taking the role of a sexual subordinate and thereby feminizing oneself – was incompatible with the kinds of gender roles publicly acceptable for Athenian citizens. Because gender was so often expressed in the classical world as a stark male–female polarity, people whose personal gender identity or sexuality did not match the ideal types appear problematic in ancient sources. There is considerable evidence for homoerotic relationships between women, but men rarely mention them. Ideally, free men retained autonomous control of their own bodies and sexuality, but controlled women's sexuality and bodies, though this was not always the case in practice. This is an area where gender and status become entwined, because free men also controlled the bodies and the sexual activity of their male and female slaves. Effectively, personal autonomy was 'gendered' as free and male.

Women were legally subordinated to men and formally excluded from public life, in the narrow sense of the term. In most Greek cities engaging in public business, or even appearing in public, was not felt to be compatible with gendered ideals of good behaviour for women. This is not to say that all women adhered to these ideals, but the women who transgressed them by taking on wage labour or selling goods in the *AGORA* would have been regarded as low-status (regardless of their 'real' status) and probably fair game for exploitation by men. Athenian women had to get a close male relative to act on their behalf as a 'GUARDIAN' to undertake legal or financial transactions of any significance. It is likely that Athenian citizen women generally covered themselves completely when they went out in public places where they might be seen by men outside their own families. Although wealthy Roman women of high status were more active in public and economic life than the women of classical Greece, they were nonetheless barred from the institutions of law, politics, government and the army. There were no female senators, orators or emperors. Therefore much of the public SPACE of Greek and Roman CITIES was effectively 'out of bounds' for women, though areas such as the FOUNTAIN HOUSE on the edge of the Athenian Agora could be understood as a female preserve in otherwise male territory. Hence, women and men often lived separate lives, physically segregated from each other for much of the time; this, too, must have enhanced and emphasized the practice of gender distinction.

This is not to say that women were insignificant in Greek and Roman life – quite the contrary. In both Greece and Rome, women of citizen status were essential for both physical and political reproduction: citizen men needed wives of equal status to produce sons who would become citizens in turn. Perhaps the very exclusion of women from active participation in political and public life also encouraged the development of strong, feminine-gendered roles and activities. Men may have been quite marginal to some of these aspects of life, such as PREGNANCY AND CHILDBIRTH. Women may have dominated many aspects of domestic life, though we have little information surviving in written texts. Interestingly, some aspects of domestic life which we could consider female-gendered, such as shopping and interior decoration, were the preserve of men in the classical world. However, some religious cults and celebrations, such as the Thesmophoria, a Greek festival to DEMETER, excluded men altogether. Others, like the Roman mysteries of ISIS or early CHRISTIANITY, attracted as followers many women who felt excluded by traditional forms of Roman religion. Hence, public participation in religion was one area of life in which specifically feminine-gendered activity was very important, and women regularly held public positions as PRIESTESSES. (see also CHILDHOOD; HOMOSEXUALITY) LF

See Fantham, E. et al., eds. (1994) *Women in the Classical World*; Foxhall, L. and Salmon, J., eds. (1998) *Thinking Men* and *When Men were Men*.

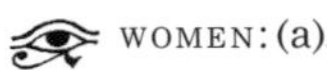 WOMEN: (a).

generalissimos The name sometimes given by modern scholars to supreme GENERALS, usually of barbarian extraction in part or whole, who gained ultimate authority and controlled EMPERORS in the 5th-century AD Western empire; earlier examples were more loyal to their emperors. The phenomenon was partly a consequence of the youth of emperors like HONORIUS and Valentinian III, partly a response to the military situation, and partly the result of strained relations between the Eastern and Western courts. Essentially, the Western Roman army no longer existed, except as barbarian units under native commanders who were rivals of each other. Experienced generals like STILICHO and Aëtius were able to employ shifting ALLIANCES with different peoples and their leaders to prevent any group from gaining complete supremacy. These alliances and their own activities laid generalissimos open to charges of collusion with the enemy, since every group was an enemy, and of seeking imperial power. Stilicho's opponents at court accused him constantly of allowing the Visigoths to escape defeat, when his policy was only to control Alaric, whose assistance he might later require. After Stilicho was assassinated in 408, no general capable of managing the complex alliances immediately emerged, a situation that allowed the Visigoths to lay siege to Rome twice before sacking it in 410. Although Constantius, later named co-emperor, experienced some success in the mid-410s, the Visigoths were able to negotiate their settlement in Aquitania. Aëtius, who had spent some years as a hostage among the Huns, employed the Visigoths successfully in the 430s and 440s, but broke Hunnic power when he defeated them in 451, capitalizing on their disarray after the death of Attila. Aëtius was eliminated in 454, and two years later Ricimer became the leading general and king-maker until 472. In 476, Odoacer completely dispensed with his puppet emperor Romulus Augustulus and ruled in his own right, but not as emperor. In northern Gaul, a different type of generalissimo emerged, as Aegidius and his son Syagrius carved out a kingdom which they shared with the Merovingian kings Childeric and Clovis from 456 until the latter eliminated Syagrius in 482. JV

See O'Flynn, J. F. (1983) *Generalissimos of the Western Roman Empire.*

 Stilicho.

generals

The Greek general (*stratêgos*) was, in many cases, an annually elected official responsible for the direction of military affairs. In Athens, the division of powers into religious, military and civil resulted in three archons, one of whom, the *polemarchos*, was the military leader. From 501 BC, the Athenians elected ten generals (*stratêgoi*), perhaps originally one from each of the Kleisthenic tribes. Later they seem to have been elected solely on the basis of perceived qualification. Unlike the archonship, which could be held only once (and was in any case determined by lot after 487), the *stratêgia* permitted unrestricted re-election. In other states and in federal states like the Boiotian, Aitolian and Achaian leagues, generalship was also an elected office whose holder was responsible for foreign policy and leadership in battle. The most famous Achaian *stratêgoi*, Aratos of Sikyon and Philopoimen, are well known on account of Polybios' *History* and Plutarch's *Lives*. A fairly extensive list of Aitolian generals and their origins can be constructed.

Not all were designated *stratêgoi*; sometimes the term *archôn* was used, as of the 4th-century Boiotarchs (leaders of the Boiotian league) and of Macedonian generals in the age of Philip and Alexander, who were regularly designated *archontes*. Infantry commanders were taxiarchs (*taxiarchoi*, leaders of a *taxis*), and cavalry officers hipparchs or ilarchs (*hipparchoi, ilarchoi*, the *ilê* being a smaller cavalry unit). When Alexander historians refer to *stratêgoi* they usually mean military overseers of conquered regions. In Ptolemaic Egypt, divided into roughly 40 administrative regions called nomes (*nomoi*), the *stratêgoi* were the heads of local administration and commanders of the armies there. The best known Ptolemaic *stratêgos* is Diophanes, from whose office we have numerous papyri dating to 222–218, during the reign of Ptolemy IV Philopator.

During the archaic and classical periods, professional generals were virtually unknown, though the 4th century saw the emergence of Greek *condottieri* in the service of other states, such as Iphikrates. The duties and qualities of generalship are spelled out in Onasander's work *On Generalship*. WH

See Fornara, C.W. (1971) *The Athenian Board of Generals from 501 to 404*; Grainger, J. D. (2000) *Aitolian Prosopographical Studies*; Hamel, D. (1998) *Athenian Generals*; Lewis, N. (1986) *Greeks in Ptolemaic Egypt.*

During the Roman Republic the command of troops was largely entrusted to the two highest levels of magistrates, the consuls and praetors, who alone exercised *imperium*, supreme power of command (excluding the temporary offices of dictator and *magister equitum*). The term commonly used for general was *dux* or 'leader', formalized in the later Roman empire into the rank of frontier commander-in-chief; from it comes the title 'duke'. The term *imperator*, used of a victorious general, begins with Lucius Aemilius Paullus, the victor in the third Macedonian war.

The restriction of major command to elected officials had its drawbacks. Because the consuls had equal authority, situations arose where armies were unwisely divided in two or commanded on alternating days by each consul. Generals were often not equipped with the military knowledge and leadership skills they required, since election to the higher offices of the *cursus honorum* resulted mainly from an extensive network of political alliances and the support of the *clientelae* of leading aristocratic families. After the *lex Villia annalis* of 180 BC, a law setting out the minimum ages for different magistrates, there was at least the possibility that consular generals had gained military experience as quaestors and had learned the art of command as praetors. Previously there was no orderly progression through the ranks; Publius Cornelius Scipio (Africanus), for example, had begun his military career in Spain as a private general (*privatus cum imperio*). The exercise of generalship by magistrates was not limited to the terms of their offices, since the practice of extending commands by *prorogatio* was possible, and indeed frequent. Hence they retained *imperium* as proconsuls or propraetors.

The generalship in the late 2nd and early 1st centuries BC underwent considerable change as non-elected officers gained the loyalty of their troops. Pompey, for example, was already one of Rome's greatest generals and the victor over Sertorius when he returned to Italy to demand the consulship even though he had not held the lower offices of the *cursus honorum*. The soldiers of the Roman army, after the reforms of Marius, expected upon demobilization grants of land in return for their service, and their loyalty to their general was often greater than to the senate and the state. In the imperial period, the emperors made every attempt to appoint as generals family members or men of proven loyalty. WH

genre Defined as a group of texts associated with each other by a common use of 'rules' and conventions. Ancient critics distinguish between different literary kinds, primarily according to the criterion of metre. The main divisions are *epos* (e.g. heroic EPIC, DIDACTIC, pastoral), ELEGY, melic and iambic poetry (the last three all forming subcategories of what is loosely referred to by modern critics as LYRIC), COMEDY and TRAGEDY. Also influential was the distinction drawn by PLATO (*Republic* 3.392–4) between narrative and dramatic form, to which modern theorists sometimes add lyric as a third 'mode'.

Particularly important to the understanding of classical (especially Roman) poetry is the concept of generic hierarchy, according to which (heroic) epic is generally recognized as the most important and serious kind of literature, while tragedy, didactic and lyric occupy an intermediate position, and elegy, EPIGRAM and SATIRE are assigned the lowest rank. Roman poets are intensely self-conscious about the placing of their chosen genre on this scale: a characteristic response (particularly in the Augustan period) is the *recusatio* or 'apology poem', in which epic is politely rejected in favour of a more lowly genre. Genres in prose writing are less clearly defined, though scholars often distinguish between broad categories such as HISTORIOGRAPHY, epistolography, BIOGRAPHY and the NOVEL. MG

See Conte, G. B. (1994) *Genres and Readers*.

gens see NAMES AND NAMING, ROMAN.

geography The subject matter and methods of geography are as diverse as those of history, for the two disciplines focus on processes in SPACE and TIME. Geographers acknowledge and try to incorporate the influence of the historical dimension on the subject of their study, while historians are becoming more aware of the influence of the spatial dimension on theirs. Geography is more general than history in its theory and methodology, and several of its methods can be usefully applied to ancient historical evidence.

The most commonly used of these are locational analysis methods, mainly gravity models and spatial interaction models, from the simple nearest-neighbour analysis to the complex computer simulation of non-linear simultaneous equations. These methods can at least reveal whether the distribution of sites or artefacts is random or patterned, and can at most employ mathematically formulated hypotheses to recreate the observed distribution.

Remote sensing techniques include magnetic survey, which measures changes in magnetic field intensity, and resistivity survey, which measures differential resistance to electrical currents passed through the earth. They are now regularly employed by archaeologists to explore sites before or instead of digging into them. These methods can reveal the location and dimensions of, for example, walls, ditches, pits, graves and rubbish tips. Other methods developed by earth scientists are sometimes used in ARCHAEOLOGY, e.g. microstratigraphy, from which details of past environments can be reconstructed. TER

See Butzer, K.W. (1982) *Archaeology as Human Ecology*; Carlstein, T. et al., eds. (1978) *Making Sense of Time*, 3 vols.; Rihll, T. E. and Wilson, A. G. (1991) Modelling settlement structures in ancient Greece, in J. Rich and A. Wallace-Hadrill, eds., *City and Country in Ancient Greece* 58–95.

geography, ancient Geographical understanding was important to Greeks and Romans, but their concept of *geographia* was both broader and looser than ours today, in particular embracing ethnography. For the most part, too, it was a literary genre in line with the nature of their EDUCATION, creatively blending the real and the imaginary. Objective concern for scientific or technical aspects, let alone training in them, was virtually confined to a few exceptional Greeks: it was they who coined the noun *geôgraphia* ('earth-description') in the 3rd century BC.

A strong sense of geography infuses the HOMERIC EPICS, in the Catalogue of Ships, on the Shield of ACHILLES and throughout ODYSSEUS' wanderings. Earth as a finite island-space encircled by boundless Ocean is likewise a Homeric vision that, despite repeated refutation, maintained a compelling hold throughout antiquity. Greeks' awareness of geography, and their appetite for it, grew with the COLONIZATION movement of the archaic period and the consequent interaction with other peoples overseas. In 6th-century Ionia, Anaximander and Hekataios led the way in creating the *periodos gês* ('circuit of the earth'), a type of work that aimed to describe the earth in an orderly, comprehensive scheme in prose or verse, sometimes accompanied by MAPS. No more than fragments of either author's path-breaking efforts survive, but it is clear that there developed an unflagging demand for such literature. It flourished in the hellenistic period, and culminated in the 2nd-century AD hexameter *Periêgêsis* of Dionysios, which Avienus translated and adapted for Latin readers in the 4th century. Both poems survive, as does the earliest work of this type in Latin, by Pomponius MELA, dating to the 40s AD.

In the 5th century BC HERODOTOS drew upon fresh knowledge of the PERSIAN EMPIRE, North AFRICA and the western MEDITERRANEAN to challenge the view that Ocean encircled what he newly termed the *oikoumenê*, literally the 'inhabited' world but signifying rather the known or familiar world. This concept leaves open the possibility that other parts of the earth may be inhabited, though the peoples there are unknown and have no contact with the *oikoumenê*. Except to the west, its boundaries are outer regions of empty, desert space. Despite its cogency, this alternative view did little to shift entrenched opinion. The report by one of ALEXANDER's admirals that the Caspian sea and Indian ocean were linked by water convinced ERATOSTHENES of the Homeric vision, and he was followed likewise by STRABO. Not until PTOLEMY in the 2nd century AD was there another firm restatement of Herodotos' view.

The Ionians typically envisaged the earth as a flattish, somewhat concave disc with a breadth three times its depth. The conception of earth as spherical and forming part of a solar system stemmed initially from PYTHAGOREAN theory and gained increasing acceptance. During the 4th century a layering of the globe by zones was first envisaged – Arctic, temperate, equatorial and Antarctic, divided by two tropics and an equator. Concurrent efforts to measure the globe's circumference confirmed that the *oikoumenê* was only small in relation to the whole, and reinforced speculation that other inhabited worlds cut off by sea or desert existed elsewhere – either, say, across the ATLANTIC (as imagined by PLATO) or south of the equator as a mirror image to Europe, Africa and Asia (hence names such as Antichthon, 'counter-world', and Antipodes). This latter scheme, favoured by ARISTOTLE, was extended by Krates of Mallos in the 2nd century BC, who proposed two more corresponding north–south worlds in the western hemisphere, bringing the total to four, each separated by branches of Ocean.

Greeks before Alexander had undertaken journeys for the express purpose of advancing geographical knowledge (among them Skylax and Ktesias, both in Persian service), but his expeditions surpassed all others in this respect and provided inexhaustible scientific and literary inspiration. Most notably, geography became a principal focus of interest at the MOUSEION in ALEXANDRIA, where Eratosthenes in the late 3rd century BC moulded it into a coherent rigorous discipline for the first time. His writings (only known to us at second hand) included calculations for establishing the circumference of the earth and instructions for mapping it. His methodology was sound, and he appreciated the need for precise physical and ASTRONOMICAL data. The difficulties of obtaining these, and of fixing longitude accurately (a problem not solved till the 18th century), weakened the results, though they still remained fundamental. His descriptive geographical writings, too, inspired a succession of Greek writers reacting in their different ways to the expansion of Roman power down to the time of AUGUSTUS – especially POLYBIUS, POSIDONIUS, DIODORUS SICULUS and above all STRABO, who rightly compares his work to a colossus. In 17 books, completed under TIBERIUS, Strabo offered a comprehensive 'chorography', a blend of geography and ethnography designed to justify and assist Roman imperial rule. Even so, his source materials are by no means all up to date, especially for more distant lands such as INDIA, and the work seems to have made little impact upon Roman readers.

Among leading Romans, JULIUS CAESAR remains exceptional for the degree of interest in geography and ethnography displayed by his *Gallic War*. After the Augustan period, Romans felt little urge to explore beyond the boundaries of their empire: strong incentives such as land hunger, commercial exploitation or missionary zeal were lacking. Geographical awareness was still seen as vital, as the ENCYCLOPEDIA of PLINY THE ELDER and the histories of AMMIANUS MARCELLINUS well demonstrate. But geography was valued mainly for its ability to entertain, to thrill, and to reinforce a sense of cultural superiority within a fixed framework of knowledge. It was seldom pursued as an ongoing quest to achieve a deeper, more accurate or sympathetic insight into peoples and places. RJAT

See Clarke, K. (1999) *Between Geography and History: hellenistic constructions of the Roman world*; Dicks, D. R. (1960) *The Geographical Fragments of Hipparchus*; Rawson, E. (1985) *Intellectual Life in the Late Roman Republic*; Romm, J. S. (1992) *The Edges of the Earth in Ancient Thought*.

 MAPS.

geometry see EUCLID.

Gerasa see JERASH.

Germanic wars In accomplishing the conquest of GAUL, JULIUS CAESAR made the river RHINE the limit of his ambition. For reasons of imperial security and personal aspirations, his adopted son and heir AUGUSTUS undertook a series of campaigns to incorporate GERMANY into the empire. Little was done before the 20s BC, except in connection with the organization of Gaul itself. The Romans did not yet hold the Alpine passes, which were still in the control of tribes who harassed troops moving through them or exacted tolls for passage. Caesar's forces were once pelted with boulders from above by natives who claimed that they had merely been gathering materials to build roads and bridges! To secure the movement of troops and supplies, in 25 BC Augustus sent an army which defeated the Salassi and gave Rome control of the Great St Bernard and Little St Bernard passes. A decade later, Augustus' two stepsons led a campaign to incorporate much of the region; TIBERIUS moved into the Rhine valley from Gaul and drove as far as the DANUBE, while Drusus came through the passes from the south. The result was, eventually, the organization of RAETIA and NORICUM.

With access to Gaul now guaranteed, Augustus turned his attention to Germany. Drusus was the principal commander from 12 BC until his death in 9 BC; he crossed the Rhine each year with varied success, reaching the Elbe in his last campaign. The following year, Tiberius was victorious against the Sugambri, creating an uneasy peace. Roman troops maintained a strong presence along the Rhine without occupying territory beyond the river in force, but that area was regarded as Roman. In AD 6, a new offensive targeted the MARCOMANNI in Bohemia; but this was quickly, though temporarily, halted because a revolt in ILLYRICUM required the transfer of troops to suppress it. After the attempt was renewed, a large army under Quinctilius Varus (who committed suicide) suffered a severe defeat across the Rhine in AD 9; the German leader Arminius had lured the Roman forces into an ambush that cost the empire three LEGIONS and Augustus his ambitious dreams. (Some said Augustus also regularly beat his head on a door, shouting to Varus for the legions' return: Suetonius, *Augustus* 23). Beyond efforts to recover the standards, no serious attempts to acquire territory were undertaken. Indeed, Augustus advised Tiberius to regard the river as a fixed boundary.

This frontier remained important, with a large military presence, but little more was accomplished until the Flavian period, when the *Decumates agri*, between the Rhine and the Neckar, were added. From the time of ANTONINUS PIUS to late antiquity, the Rhine (and Danubian) boundary was often under attack from outside the empire, and Roman armies frequently crossed the river(s) to pre-empt invasions or pursue retreating enemies. The wars of MARCUS AURELIUS and JULIAN are merely the best-known of many significant military engagements against the armies of Germanic peoples. JV

See Wells, C. M. (1972) *The German Policy of Augustus*.

Germanicus see AGRIPPINAE, THE; ASTROLOGY; NERO; TACITUS; TEUTOBURGIAN FOREST; TIBERIUS; TOURISM.

Germany and Germans The etymology of the Latin word *Germani* is unknown. No German would have called himself such, but by the name of his tribe. The first writer known to have distinguished the Germans from the CELTS is POSIDONIUS in the early 1st century BC. A generation later, CAESAR claims the RHINE as the boundary between the two peoples and depicts the Germans as far more primitive than the Gauls or Celts. He had his own political reasons for doing so, however, and ARCHAEOLOGY shows that the Rhine was not a cultural or ethnographic frontier. The original Germani may have been a group of Celtic or celticized tribes on the right bank whose name Caesar falsely extends to include all the peoples east of the river, including those who were not 'German' in the original sense but came to be regarded as archetypally such by later writers. Caesar himself knows of Germani on the left bank. Some of the right-bank Germani, like the Usipetes and Mattiaci, whose names appear to be Celtic, have quite different characteristics from the archetypal 'new' Germans. The latter include the warlike and migratory Suebi, whom Caesar fought, and the Chatti and Cherusci who were so prominent in the wars of the Augustan period. The initial *Ch* of their names is characteristically German.

Caesar was content to drive the Suebi out of GAUL. AUGUSTUS, however, set out to conquer Germany and was well on the way to doing so up to the river Elbe, until the loss of three legions under Quinctilius Varus in AD 9 forced the Romans back behind the Rhine. Extensive finds of Roman equipment and coins at Kalkriese near Osnabrück now suggest that the site of the Varian disaster was nearby. No attempt was made to reconquer permanently the lost territory. The tribes of northern Germany were thereafter left largely to their own devices, except for penetration by Roman TRADE, which led to the western tribes, the so-called Weser–Rhine Germans, assimilating certain features of Roman provincial culture. The more easterly Elbe Germans, and the peoples still further east, like the Burgundians, VANDALS and GOTHS, later so prominent, remained relatively untouched. Latin writers like TACITUS exaggerate both the grim and sombre nature of the land, all forests and marshes, and the primitive simplicity of the people, whose noble savagery Tacitus contrasts with Roman luxury and decadence.

Some Germans served in the Roman army, and the early emperors had a German bodyguard; from the late 3rd century AD onwards Rome relied increasingly on German recruits and even German commanders. The Germans fought mostly on foot, though Tacitus praises the Tencteri for their CAVALRY (*Germania* 32) and the Batavi supplied cavalry units to the Roman army. In traditional warfare the main infantry weapon was the lance, with swords for the ÉLITE only. The shield was round, commonly about 1 m (3 ft) in diameter, or rectangular, with a wood or wicker framework, LEATHER mountings, usually an IRON rim, and a prominent wooden or iron boss that could be thrust into an enemy's face. Only the chiefs wore ARMOUR; the rest fought naked or in trousers and cloak, and are invariably shown thus in Roman art. Even as late as the 6th century AD, commentators perceive the Germans as poorly equipped. Their tactics were primitive, and few leaders enjoyed absolute authority. The chieftain's retinue, the *comitatus* described by Tacitus (*Germania* 14) and still familiar to the audience of *Beowulf*, could only be maintained by successful violence and warfare.

The German homeland was southern Scandinavia and the north German plain extending from the Netherlands to Russia, with no elevation above 300 m (1,000 ft). It is drained by five major rivers, the Ems, Weser and Elbe into the North sea, the Oder and Vistula into the Baltic. German AGRICULTURE and husbandry were relatively primitive, though settled field systems developed in some areas during the early centuries AD. Metalwork was of a high standard, as were woodworking and TEXTILES. Imported goods, some originating as diplomatic gifts or booty rather than from trade, included bronze and SILVER vessels, Roman weapons, fine GLASSWARE, POTTERY, WINE and implements for serving wine. In return, the Romans imported SLAVES, hides, and perhaps textiles and women's hair for wigs and catapult cords. AMBER from the Baltic was highly prized. Roman COINAGE is found extensively beyond the frontier and may have served as currency, since the Germans did not strike their own. Evidence for religious belief and practice is obscure, but there was HUMAN SACRIFICE.

By the 2nd century AD, trade and cultural contacts on both the Rhine and the DANUBE had created a romanized FRONTIER society on both sides of the river. Beyond the middle Danube Roman-style buildings are found, presumably serving tribal leaders. Major cities grew up along both rivers, with Cologne (Colonia Claudia Ara Agrippinensium) outstanding for its wealth and romanized culture. But in the 160s and 170s German tribes along the Danube showed up weaknesses in the Roman defensive system, and from the middle of the 3rd century onwards the old frontier proved powerless to keep out German invaders. In the early 4th century TRIER became one of the imperial capitals, ideally placed to command the lower Rhine; but the gradual German takeover could not be stopped.

The German tribes involved in these invasions were not so much those that had long been in close contact with Rome, but those further east. The Goths, for instance, having emerged as a threat in the mid-3rd century, massively defeated a Roman army at ADRIANOPLE in 378, sacked Rome itself in 410, and in 418 established themselves in Aquitania, whence they were later expelled by the FRANKS. At the end of 406 the Vandals, ALANI and Suebi crossed the Rhine near Mainz: the Vandals ended up in AFRICA, taking CARTHAGE in 439. The Burgundi were settled in Savoy, an area of great strategic importance, in 437. By the end of the 5th century the German kingdoms in the West had replaced the Roman empire. (see p. 392) CMW

See Todd, M. (1992) *The Early Germans*.

FRONTIERS, ROMAN: (a)–(c); MARCOMANNIC WARS.

gerousia see EPHORS; SPARTA.

Geta see CARACALLA; JULIA DOMNA; SEVERUS, SEPTIMIUS;

EMPERORS, ROMAN: (a); SEVERUS, SEPTIMIUS: (a).

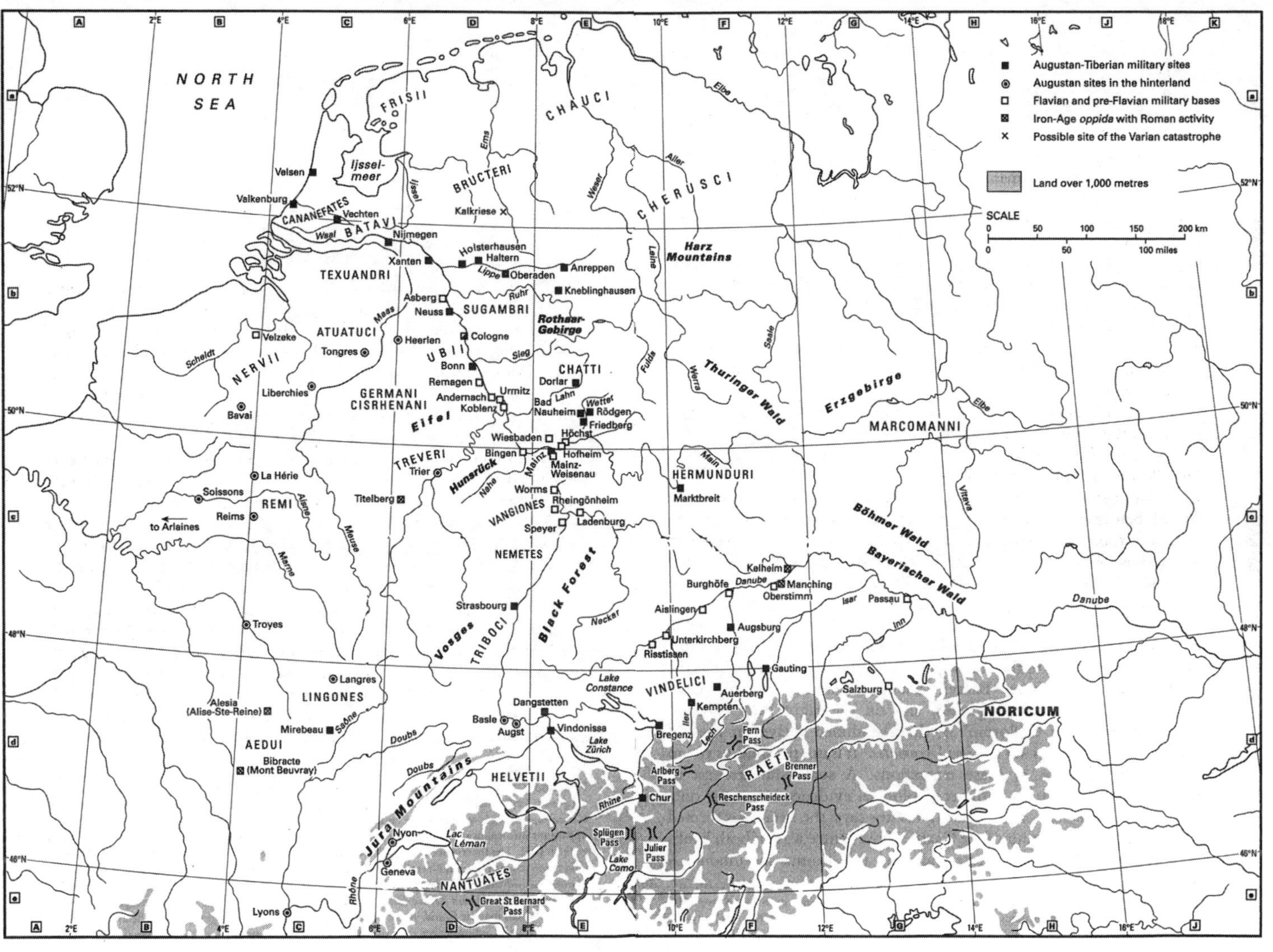

GERMANY AND GERMANS: (a) map of Roman Germany and principal early Germanic peoples.

GERMANY AND GERMANS: (b) Germanic peoples in the later Roman period and their initial encounters with the empire.

giants One of the most popular symbols used to represent barbaric enemies. In Greek MYTHOLOGY the giants (Greek and Latin *gigantes*) were the children of Earth and Sky. They were superhuman but subdivine in nature; they varied in name and number and were savage in behaviour, though their size was not an important element. They presented the final challenge to the divine order of the OLYMPIANS, whose success was prophesied to depend on the help of one mortal, HERAKLES. Some of the defeated giants were said to be buried under rocks and islands and to cause VOLCANIC eruptions.

By the 6th century BC Greek writers and artists narrated the battle of the gods and giants (*gigantomachia*), and in archaic and later ART the Gigantomachy became a popular theme in both public and private work. In SCULPTURE the battle lent itself to extended friezes and to more confined metopes. VASE-PAINTINGS provide a wide variety of compositions, including some adaptations of the design on the inside of the (lost) shield of PHEIDIAS' ATHENA Parthenos in the PARTHENON. Of missing treatments, the decorated robe occasionally presented to Athena on the ATHENIAN ACROPOLIS is the keenest loss. The figures of the giants were initially shown as warriors of normal size, equipped with HOPLITE weapons; then they were represented as primitive fighters dressed in ANIMAL skins and wielding trees and rocks; later they were given the serpent legs associated with other monsters.

In Roman art the battle of the gods and the giants is carved on SARCOPHAGI and may have funerary significance. BAS

Gibbon, Edward see HISTORIANS AND HISTORIOGRAPHY, MODERN.

gladiators Originally a south Italian entertainment, gladiatorial combat is first reported at Rome in 264 BC. By the early 2nd century, it was taken as symbolic of Roman military virtue, and gladiatorial displays (to promote such feelings) are recorded in SELEUKID SYRIA in specific imitation of contemporary displays at Rome. The great expansion of gladiatorial combat around the MEDITERRANEAN followed the emergence of monarchy under AUGUSTUS. Thereafter gladiatorial exhibitions became intimately connected with the celebration of the IMPERIAL CULT.

Gladiators themselves were often SLAVES put in the hands of *lanistae* for training. Others were free people who entered the *ludus* in search of gain and possibly excitement. The presence of free people of high status (senatorial and EQUESTRIAN) in gladiatorial troupes was restricted by decrees of the SENATE as early as the reign of Augustus. By the 2nd century AD an elaborate hierarchy had developed within the gladiatorial *ludi*, involving nine stages. A freshly recruited gladiator was a *novicius* until his (or very occasionally her) first fight as a *tiro*. A gladiator who survived the first fight (win or lose) became a *veteranus*. Later success led to admission to a *palus* of six grades, the highest ranking being the 'first' or *primus palus*. Gladiators of slave status could buy their freedom, and freemen could offer their services (for a fee) by agreeing to a form of technical enslavement for the duration of a display.

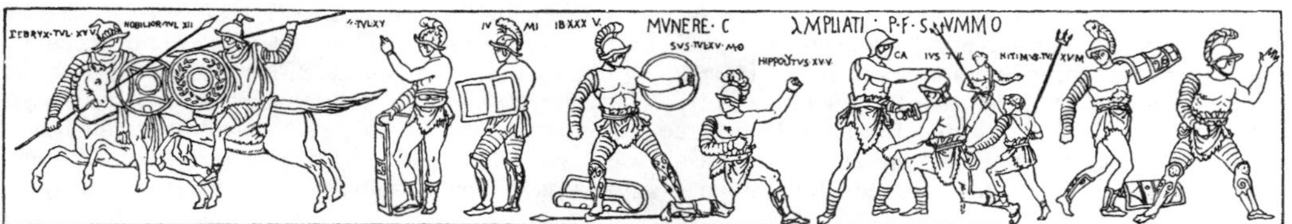

GLADIATORS: (a) Pompeian relief showing different pairings of gladiators, including a mounted combat (l.) and (r. of centre) a gladiator delivering the death blow to his defeated opponent.

Although enormous numbers of gladiators fought at imperial exhibitions at Rome, the average number of pairs in a provincial exhibition was not large, between 10 and 13 in the course of an afternoon. The pairs would fight individually, with the average bout expected to last between 10 and 15 minutes. Traditionally, gladiators with different armaments were matched against each other. The most popular pairing was between a *retiarius*, armed with a trident and net, and one of the various types armed with sword and shield. A bout would last until one gladiator raised a finger as a sign of surrender, and would be administered by two referees (whose task was chiefly to separate the contestants when the bout ended). The person responsible for the display (the *munerarius*) would then decide if the defeated gladiator should be allowed to live (the usual outcome) or should die. The death blow appears to have been administered off the floor of the AMPHITHEATRE. It was not uncommon for death to result from accident, as gladiators lost control during the bout. At no time does positive discourse on gladiatorial combat suggest a direct connection with death; study of death rates suggests about a 5 per cent fatality rate in any individual display. Gladiatorial combat should not be confused with two other forms of entertainment in the AMPHITHEATRE: wild beast hunts (pitting beast against beast, human against animal) and the execution of condemned prisoners.

Despite strong opposition from CHRISTIANITY, gladiatorial combats continued well after the conversion of CONSTANTINE. Nonetheless, the gradual disappearance of venues for gladiatorial display resulting from the transformation of the imperial cult, and the end of direct imperial support, spelled the end for gladiatorial combat. The last displays of gladiators may have occurred in the first half of the 5th century AD. DSP

See Köhne, E. and Ewigleben, C., eds. (2000) *Gladiators and Caesars* 31–74, 125–34.

 AMPHITHEATRES: (a)–(b).

GLADIATORS: (b) a *retiarius* (trident man) and a *myrmillo* (fish man) from a mosaic floor at Nennig, Germany.

glass and glass making The art of making glass was known by the Bronze Age Greeks, who appear to have learnt it from Egypt and the Near East. There was a lull in popularity after 1100 BC, but interest in glass production picked up again in the 9th century and continued through to Roman times. Archaic and classical Greeks used glass to make small flasks and bowls, or as inlays in larger work. Hellenistic glassmakers discovered the technique for blowing glass and used greater ornamentation with added gilt, cut decoration and a variety of colours.

The ingredients varied depending on the locality of the makers, but the basic recipe involved heating sand (silica), powdered limestone (calcium carbonate) and soda (sodium) to a liquid state and then manipulating it into the final product. A range of colours was produced by the addition of various minerals. Malachite (a green copper carbonate) creates a range from green to blue, while IRON oxides produce red or a bottle-green that is particularly seen in hellenistic and Roman glass. In the hellenistic period black glass was also produced using iron oxides. Cobalt created a blue colour, imitating *lapis lazuli*, manganese produced a purple visible in Egyptian glass, opaque white was made using a TIN oxide and yellow by adding a mixture of antimony and LEAD.

Beads are the most common surviving glass items. They appear in Bronze Age contexts in Greece, especially the Late Helladic period. Their popularity rose again in the hellenistic period, and we know of a glass bead factory on RHODES in the 3rd and early 2nd century BC. Their method of manufacture can be surmised from the shape of the air bubbles trapped in the cooling liquid. Moulded beads have spherical bubbles, while drawn beads have elliptical or tubular air bubbles. Spiral bubbles are produced when the glass is wound. Specific types of glass bead were made, such as 'eye beads' where a blob of coloured glass was added, or banding of colours could create an effect similar to agates.

Glass inlays could be either cut or moulded into shape and were made both cameo (with the background carved away) and intaglio (with the image either engraved or impressed into the glass) techniques. The ETRUSCANS set eye and coloured beads into GOLD JEWELLERY, while hellenistic and Roman tastes preferred their glass to imitate the colours of precious stones. As well as vases and bowls, complete items of jewellery were made from glass, and glass finger rings were particularly popular in hellenistic ALEXANDRIA. Roman glass rings often have impressed or moulded designs, and the Romans were also partial to glass bangles. Enamelling, or coating metal objects by dipping them into molten glass, is visible in 14th-century BC MYCENAEAN work, with other examples also dating to the 6th and 5th centuries BC. This technique again gained popularity in the hellenistic period, but was less common in Roman times, being restricted to the outer edges of the Roman empire.

The invention of glass blowing in the 1st century BC led to a revolution in the production of vessel glass, with a far wider range of forms produced in vast numbers in many separate centres, expanding from an initial focus in the Levant to the Western empire (notably in the Rhineland). Roman vessel glass reached a high level of sophistication, especially in the use of coloured glass, gilding, and cutting techniques. NJW

See Harden, D. B. et al. (1987) *Glass of the Caesars*; Newby, M. and Painter, K., eds. (1991) *Roman Glass: two centuries of art and invention*; Stern, E. M. and Schlick-Nolte, B. (1994) *Early Glass of the Ancient World 1600 BC–AD 50.*

glues (Greek *kolla*, Latin *gluten*) Glue was made from a variety of natural substances, including flour and PETROLEUM. In Egypt *kommi* (the origin of the word 'gum'), derived from the acacia plant, was used in preparing MUMMIES (Herodotos 2.86). The 4th-century BC accounts of the sanctuary of Apollo on DELOS include payments to workmen for 'glueing' broken silver and bronze vessels, though this could mean welding or soldering. Most often, however, the ancient sources refer to glue derived from animal bones and hides, which were available as by-products of PASTORALISM as well as urban BUTCHERY.

Making this substance was the unpleasant job of a 'glue-boiler' (Greek *kollepsos*; in Latin more simply *glutinarius*, 'glue-man'). The product, however, was in high demand for many purposes. Accounts from classical EPIDAUROS refer to individuals who contributed adhesive for new temple doors. Inscriptions and papyri refer to the use of glue in mending broken items. It was used in making furniture, armour and weapons, and Pliny discusses its application in wooden veneers. A superior sort of cement, 'stone-glue' (*lithokolla* in Greek), combining powdered marble with *taurokolla* ('bull glue'), was used in making JEWELLERY and MOSAICS.

Glue was particularly important in making BOOKS. While strips of PAPYRUS were made into sheets without glue, using their natural adhesive property, it was then necessary to glue the sheets together into rolls. This process is mentioned as early as the 4th century BC and is discussed much later by PLINY THE ELDER. Cicero mentions a specialist bookbinder called a 'gluer' (*glutinator*). DGJS

Gnosticism Collective name for religious sects which, by blending a variety of Christian, philosophical and mystical traditions, claimed special knowledge (*gnôsis*) of the divine. Since its origins, CHRISTIANITY has always been wary of mystical traditions that promised divine revelation. To the alarm of church leaders, such movements were successful in attracting Christians, provoking Irenaeus of LYONS (c.AD 140–200) to pen a massive polemic against them. His target was a mystical teacher at Rome called Valentinus, who had fused Christian ideas with others drawn from Greek PHILOSOPHY. Valentinus himself was building on earlier doctrines worked out by the Greek teacher Marcion. They believed in a cosmic conflict between good and evil, a dualism mirrored in humans by the spirit (which is good) and the flesh (which is evil). In humans, the spiritual element needs to be aroused through knowledge (*gnôsis*), by which means it can overcome the flesh.

A sensitive appraisal of what the Gnostics actually believed only became possible with the discovery of 4th-century Coptic PAPYRI at Nag Hammadi in Egypt in 1945. These provided several Gnostic texts, including gospels, apocalypses, dialogues and poems, many showing influences from Hermetic and Middle Platonic traditions. In light of these texts it has become clear that Gnosticism was not a united movement. Rather, it comprises several strands of thought, all seeking some form of mystical revelation of divine truth through self-knowledge. MDH

See Grant, R. M. (1997) *Irenaeus of Lyons*; Logan, A. H. B. (1996) *Gnostic Truth and Christian Heresy*; Pagels, E. (1979) *The Gnostic Gospels*; Robinson, J. M. (1977) *The Nag Hammadi Library in English*.

goats Animals that thrive in the dry and mountainous parts of the MEDITERRANEAN region even better than SHEEP, though they are sensitive to cold and damp conditions. In many parts of the classical world, goats were important flock ANIMALS for exploiting such marginal areas. They have a reputation for eating anything, but in fact they are fussier than sheep. Often kept in small flocks alongside sheep, goats were important providers of milk and MEAT. Their coarse, hairy fleeces were difficult to spin and weave, but were widely used for making sleeping pallets, tents, waterproof cloaks and saddlebags.

In art, the goat is often associated with the wild landscapes inhabited by DIONYSOS (the Roman BACCHUS), god of WINE, and his followers in MYTH. They were somewhat less common as a SACRIFICIAL animal than sheep, perhaps because of their associations with wild and untamed landscapes. LF

See Isager, S. and Skydsgaard, J. E. (1992) *Ancient Greek Agriculture* 89–91; Whittaker, C. R., ed. (1988) *Pastoral Economies in Classical Antiquity.*

God The Jewish concept of God developed out of competing religious traditions in the ancient Near East, and over time came to be influenced by Greek philosophical traditions. There are various designations in the BIBLE for the god of Israel (e.g. *el*, *elohim*, *YAHWEH*), and literary and archaeological evidence attest to many cultic sites (including Bethel, Gerizim and Shiloh) in the early history (10th–7th centuries BC). The similarities between these Israelite sites and other regional traditions are many, including the use of similar names and practices as the Canaanites, PHOENICIANS and BABYLONIANS. It is possible that the early God of Israel was represented with a female companion (*asherah*), but this may have been little more than a cult statue. From the 7th century BC, political moves sought to centralize the cult in Jerusalem alone, condemning the worship of other gods elsewhere, and to apply the many names to one god.

The literary picture found in the Bible presents this unified stage of the religion, but even then traces of the older cult tradition remain. Each nation was assigned an angel to watch over it, allowing for independent nations but under the watchful eye of god (based on Deuteronomy 32:8). This god displayed the characteristics of humans, evincing the emotions of love, care and anger, and also occasionally having human organs such as ears and eyes. In this respect the god was similar to that of the Greeks and Romans. However, the use of the word 'god' differed. For the Greeks and Romans god (*theos*) was an attribute and could be applied to humans and natural phenomena, whereas for the Jews the word god denoted a being, who himself had attributes. Thus, a Greek would tend to speak of an event or a person being a god (*theos*), while in Jewish tradition god would do or act (cf. 1 John 4:16, 'god is love'). The translation of the Old Testament into Greek, therefore, provided some original uses of the noun *theos* in Greek. Nevertheless, in Greek philosophy there developed a critique of the mythological conceptions of the Greek gods that led to a transcendent view of god in Platonic and Neoplatonic thought, a god that was ultimately unknowable. This philosophy had its influences on Alexandrian Jewish writers, notably the author of the Wisdom of Solomon (1st century BC) and Philo (1st century AD). Thus the human features and concern for humans by god were combined with transcendent philosophical notions. In due course this contributed to the debate over the nature of the Christian god, and the definition of the Trinity, which sought to combine earthly and transcendent facets of the deity. (see also monotheism) JKA

See Mettinger, T. N. D. (1988) *In Search of God*; Van der Toorn, K. et al., eds. (1999) *Dictionary of Deities and Demons in the Bible*.

gods and goddesses

The Greeks were polytheistic; for them, in Thales' words, everything was full of gods. The earliest Greek writings suggest that the gods were thought to be anthropomorphic, resembling humans in form but differing from them in a variety of essentials. Where humans were mortal and subject to weakness and ageing, the gods were deathless, were ever-youthful and, though not omnipotent, far exceeded humans in power. Where gods feasted on ambrosia and nectar, humans were 'bread eaters' and drinkers of wine, with blood flowing in their veins instead of divine *ichor*. When gods chose to reveal themselves openly to humans in an epiphany, they were awe-inducing, manifesting a superhuman form that was numinously beautiful and larger than life. Nevertheless, the gods also betrayed affinities with humans: theirs too was a social and hierarchical world, marked by envy, discord and, not uncommonly, amorality. Taken as a whole, the gods were popularly thought to reflect the totality of human experience, with individual deities presiding over selected spheres of it.

In Greek religion, the personalities of these deities were determined by a variety of factors: the name and genealogy of the deity, their local rites and sanctuaries, and their myths and iconography. The importance of this last feature can be seen, for instance, in Aelius Aristides' assertion that Athena appeared to him 'with her aegis and the beauty and size and the whole form of the Athena of Pheidias at Athens' (*Orations* 48.41). At the same time, the 'personalities' of the gods were far from uniform, and frequently it was a god's sheer power that was emphasized more than any personal aspect.

The origins of the Greek gods are diverse and reveal the influence of the ancient Near East, Indo-European culture, and the Minoan and Mycenaean civilizations. These influences, however, are difficult to trace, largely because of the Greek peoples' success in making them their own. By the 8th century BC, Greek religions had emerged with their own distinctive stamp, a fact attested by the widespread foundation of temples in this period. While conceptions of the gods were hardly uniform at this time, common features began to emerge as a result of the circulation of oral poetry, particularly that of Homer and Hesiod. The role of epic in producing a panhellenic religious sensibility is hard to overestimate, and Herodotos is not far wrong when he affirms that it was Homer and Hesiod who taught the Greeks the genealogies of the gods, assigned them their names, honours and skills, and showed their appearances (2.53).

As a consequence, it is easier to trace the gods' origins in myth. According to Hesiod, all the gods emerged from chaos. Prominent among them was Gaia (the earth, also known as Ge), from whom the ruling deities traced their descent. The first of these, Ouranos (the sky), is castrated by his son Kronos, who supplants him. Zeus, in turn, ousts Kronos and his siblings (the Titans) and, as head of his brothers and sisters (the Olympians), becomes the final and definitive ruler of the Greek gods, the 'father of gods and men'. He presides over Mt Olympos and the heavens, while his brothers Poseidon and Hades are granted control over the sea and the underworld respectively. Through his multiple marriages and liaisons Zeus is able to consolidate his rule and produce children both divine and heroic. The most important of these children and siblings constitute the Olympian pantheon, sometimes referred to as the 'Twelve' (the twelve on the Parthenon frieze are Zeus, Hera, Poseidon, Demeter, Athena, Dionysos, Apollo, Artemis, Hermes, Hephaistos, Aphrodite and Ares). This assemblage was not absolute, however, and other deities, like Hestia or Hades, are spoken of as residing on Mt Olympos when mythic narratives require it.

In addition to the Olympians, several other groups of divinities are often distinguished in Greek religion, one being the chthonic (*chthôn* = earth) deities, such as Hades and Persephone, who were associated with the underworld and the fertility of the earth. Divine abstractions and personifications comprise a second group; Hesiod, for instance, offers a detailed account of the various negative powers that emerge from Nyx (Night), which include, among others, Death, Sleep, Deceit, Fatigue, Old Age and Strife. Akin to the abstractions were collective deities, such as the Graces, Seasons and Muses. A final group of

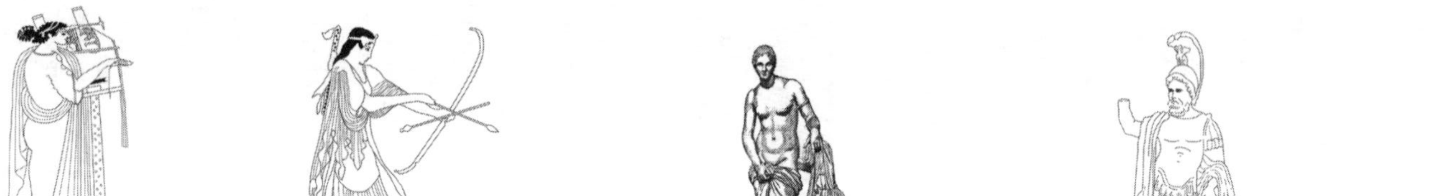

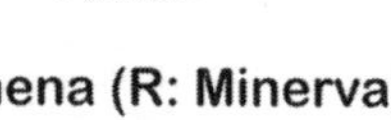

Apollo

God of music, culture prophecy, healing and illness. In later times associated with the sun.

Artemis (R: Diana)

Virgin goddess of hunting, twin sister of Apollo. Her cult was important to girls and women.

Aphrodite (R: Venus)

Goddess of love and sex. The depiction of her naked, emerging from bathing, was popular from the 4th c. BC through Roman times.

Ares (R: Mars)

God of war and violence. His cult was more important in Rome than in the Greek world.

Athena (R: Minerva)

Goddess of citadels wisdom, weaving and other crafts. Usually depicted wearing armour.

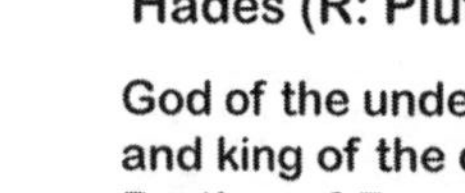

Demeter (R: Ceres)

Goddess of cereals, agriculture and the fertility of women.

Dionysos (R: Bacchus)

God of wine and wild parties. Often associated with wild places and creatures such as satyrs and maenads.

Hades (R: Pluto)

God of the underworld and king of the dead. Brother of Zeus and Poseidon.

Hephaistos (R: Vulcan)

God of metal working and similar crafts, and volcanoes. Portrayed as lame, riding a mule.

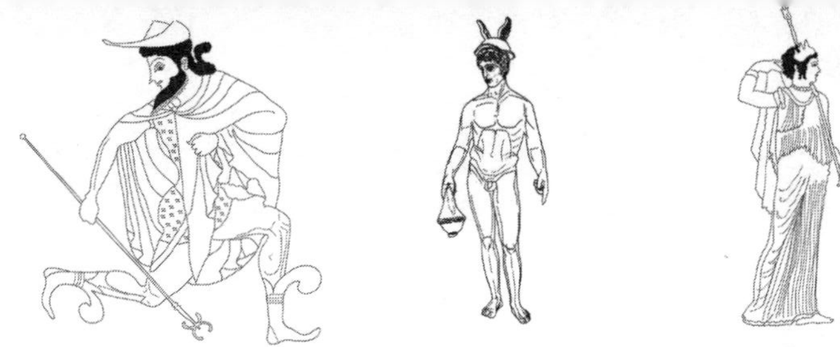

Hermes (R: Mercury)

The Greek god Hermes (L) wears winged sandals and carries a special staff (the caduceus). The Roman Mercury (R) wears a winged helmet.

Hera (R: Juno)

Goddess of marriage and wife of Zeus. Often shown covering (or perhaps uncovering) her face.

R: Janus

The Roman two-headed god of doorways and gates, who looked both forward and backward.

R: Mithras

Roman soldiers were particularly devoted to Mithras, supposedly an 'Eastern' god.

Nike (R: Victoria)

The winged goddess of victory often associated with Athena.

Pan

Goat-headed god of the woods and wilderness, protector of shepherds.

Poseidon (R: Neptune)

God of the sea and brother of Zeus and Hades. The trident he holds is a fish spear.

Zeus (R: Jupiter)

King of the gods, and god of storms and thunder, shown carrying a thunderbolt.

GODS AND GODDESSES: (a)–(b) deities of the Greco-Roman world. The Romans appropriated many Greek gods and assimilated their characteristics and mythology with gods of their own.

lesser divinities would include HEROES and *daimones*. The latter, though unnamed and largely undefined, were thought to be active in human affairs. The Greek words for happiness (*eudaimonia*) and misery (*dysdaimonia*) both point to the influential role of *daimones*.

These arbitrary divisions should not be taken to imply that Greek religion was in any way compartmentalized; there could be considerable overlap between these categories (for a 2nd-century AD attempt to classify the gods, see Artemidoros 2.34). Many of the Olympian deities also had chthonic manifestations, such as Zeus Meilichios or Demeter Chthonia. Nor should it be supposed that Greek religion was static. Gods native to one part of the Greek world could be introduced elsewhere, as when the cults of PAN and ASKLEPIOS were brought to Athens from ARKADIA and Epidauros respectively. In addition, the Greeks were generally open to the recognition of foreign gods. The PHRYGIAN goddess CYBELE, the 'Great Mother', was well established in the Greek world by the 5th century BC. In the hellenistic period, these tendencies accelerated with the diffusion of the cult of Tyche, and of Egyptian and ANATOLIAN deities such as ISIS and Sabazios. The period after ALEXANDER the Great also saw the emergence of the RULER-CULT, where divine honours were paid to kings and queens.

The Greeks reverenced their gods in a variety of ways. Animal SACRIFICE was the most characteristic feature, and frequently figured with other rituals such as PROCESSIONS, PRAYERS and libations. Given the *polis*-based nature of Greek religion, these cultic observances tended to be both public and corporate. So, too, were the widespread FESTIVALS, both local and panhellenic, that were established to honour the gods, including athletic competitions such as the OLYMPICS and the dramatic FESTIVALS of Athens.

Like the Greeks, the Romans were polytheistic and worshipped a great variety of deities. They differed from the Greeks, however, in not having a pantheon like the 'Twelve Olympians.' Moreover, if the Greek gods could be described as possessing 'personalities', this feature was far less characteristic of the Roman gods, chiefly because of the absence of divine genealogies, myths and, in early days, iconography. If divinities like JUPITER and MINERVA were thought to possess distinctive character traits which were expressed through epithets and a defining range of functions, there were many more deities who were defined by an exclusive function, abstract or concrete, such as Fides ('Good Faith') or Insitor ('Sower'). There were, in addition, spirits that were not defined at all and remained undifferentiated (*numina*). CHRISTIAN apologists later mocked the Romans' tendency to multiply divinities: AUGUSTINE (1) questioned the need for a crowd of supervising deities on a couple's wedding night, asking pointedly 'would not one god or goddess have sufficed?' (*De civitate Dei* 6.9).

The origins of many indigenous Roman gods are obscure owing to the scantiness of the sources. Sometimes only a god's name survives (e.g. Falacer); in other instances, information about the gods can be derived only from the festivals listed in the earliest calendars. In any case, it is unclear how many Roman gods were purely indigenous. One of the most distinctive features of the Romans' approach to the divine was their willingness to introduce new deities. Religious borrowings from the ETRUSCANS, SABINES and other neighbouring peoples appear to have taken place from the earliest days of Rome. Nevertheless, divinities such as Janus, Vesta, Quirinus, MARS, and Jupiter, JUNO and Minerva (the last three forming the CAPITOLINE TRIAD) were considered distinctively Roman from a very early date.

In the REPUBLIC, this process of borrowing continued in a variety of ways. One practice was *evocatio*, where the Romans formally summoned away the gods of their enemies by inviting them to come to Rome and receive a cult and temple (cf. Livy 5.21.1–7). More common was the formal introduction of a foreign deity in response to a crisis within Rome. Here, the priestly college of the *viri sacris faciundis* ('the men in charge of sacred acts') would, after consulting the SIBYLLINE ORACLES, recommend the induction of a foreign deity. The cults of CERES, Liber and Libera (496 BC), Apollo (431), Aesculapius (293), VENUS of Eryx (217) and Magna Mater (Cybele, 204) were all brought to Rome in this fashion. By far the most significant influence, however, was SYNCRETISM: the Romans, via the Etruscans and Magna Graecia, assimilated many of the Greek deities to their own gods. Thus Zeus was assimilated to Jupiter, Hera to Juno, Athena to Minerva, Hephaestus to Vulcan and so on. Many, though not all, of these gods came to be regarded as constituent of traditional religion in the later Republic (cf. Livy's account of the *lectisternium* at 22.10.19). By the 3rd century BC, temples had been established at Rome to the Roman counterparts of all the gods of the Greek pantheon. The situation of many of these temples outside the city boundary (*POMERIUM*) indicated their foreign origins, but others were placed inside because they were considered Roman gods who had simply not been formally recognized before.

When AUGUSTUS assumed power in 31 BC, he emphasized two of the Roman approaches to the divine. On the one hand, he advocated a staunch traditionalism, boasting of the many temples to Roman deities that he had either constructed or restored (*Res Gestae* 19–21). On the other, he just as clearly continued the process of religious innovation, as evidenced by his promotion of the IMPERIAL CULT. Although Rome was traditionally lacking in demigods (ROMULUS being a notable exception), Augustus drew upon myths of Romulus' divinization and features of eastern ruler-cults to introduce a new imperial practice which conferred divine honours upon humans. In Rome this resulted in the public worship of Augustus' *genius* ('divine spirit') during his lifetime, and his deification by the SENATE upon his death. This pattern, however, did not remain entirely consistent for subsequent emperors: some (CALIGULA and COMMODUS) claimed divine honours during their lives; and some (TIBERIUS, Caligula and NERO among others) were denied apotheosis upon their deaths.

The introduction of new deities to Rome continued throughout the imperial period. JUVENAL laments that 'the SYRIAN Orontes has long since emptied into the TIBER' (3.62–3), and there was certainly a notable migration of eastern religions to Rome. The god of the JEWS had been worshipped in Rome from the 2nd century BC, and the imperial period saw the emergence of a different type of MONOTHEISM in the form of CHRISTIANITY. It also witnessed the increasing popularity of Egyptian religion. The cults of Isis and Sarapis (or Serapis) were favoured by emperors such as VESPASIAN and DOMITIAN. Other deities, such as the PERSIAN god MITHRAS, were worshipped widely in the later empire. This diversity continued to characterize Roman religion until the ultimate triumph of Christianity.

The Romans regarded themselves as superior to other peoples in their reverence toward their gods (Cicero, *De natura deorum* 2.9). Although their modes of honouring the gods were largely similar to those of the Greeks, they were more punctilious and exacting in the performance of divine ceremonial and would, if necessary, repeat a ritual as often as was required to get it right. The Romans were also distinctive in having established priestly colleges, typically composed of prominent political figures, to supervise and direct divine procedure. JRCC

See Beard, M. et al. (1998) *Religions of Rome*; Bremmer, J. N. (1994) *Greek Religion*; Burkert, W. (1985) *Greek Religion*, North, J. A. (2000) *Roman Religion*; Sissa, G. and Detienne, M. (2000) *The Daily Life of the Greek Gods*; Turcan, R. (2000) *The Gods of Ancient Rome*.

 MITHRAS: (a)–(b); RELIGION: (a)–(b).

gold For PINDAR (*Olympian Ode* 7.1–4) a gold cup (*phialê*) was 'the peak of all possessions'. Gold was highly valued in ancient societies as it allowed its owner to display wealth. This was particularly true of the lavish gold dedications, including a krater made for the Lydian king Croesus and given by him to DELPHI. One of the ancient sources for gold cups was ETRURIA. Mentions of Greek gold plate in literature include the account of an Athenian called Demos trying to raise a loan against a gold cup which he had received as a gift from the Persian king (LYSIAS 19.25).

Little gold plate has survived because of looting. An exception is the gold cup found at OLYMPIA; the inscription records that it was dedicated by the Kypselid tyrants of CORINTH from spoils taken from the sack of Herakleia.

Gold was also widely used for JEWELLERY. Examples have been found in the cemeteries of Sindos in MACEDONIA, as well as the great burial mounds of the Crimea and southern Russia, such as the Great Bliznitza. One of the most remarkable pieces is a gold sword scabbard from the Chertomlyk kurgan, which appears to have come from the same die as another from the Five Brothers Tumuli.

Some of the workers in precious metals may have been SLAVES. For example, a CARIAN goldsmith, one of the slaves auctioned in the sale of the possessions confiscated from men convicted of mutilating the HERMS of Athens in 415 BC, fetched some 360 drachmas. Gold-working is likely to have taken place in most centres, though evidence rarely survives. A matrix for making gold jewellery has been found during the excavations of the Greek colony at Euesperides in CYRENAICA. DWJG

See Gill, D.W. J. (1996) Gold and silver, in J. Turner, ed., *The Dictionary of Art*, vol. 13, 568–71; Vickers, M. and Gill, D. (1994) *Artful Crafts*; Williams, D., ed. (1997) *The Art of the Greek Goldsmith*; Williams, D. and Ogden, J. (1994) *Greek Gold*.

golden age Humanity's primeval state, from which we have declined physically and morally. HESIOD sings of a golden 'race' (*genos*) of first mortals, created by Kronos (*Works and Days* 109–26). They were carefree and toiled not, while the earth rendered its fruits unstintingly. This race did not die of senility, but fell asleep while still vigorous; they have become tutelary spirits. Subsequent generations, created by ZEUS, have grown increasingly violent and impious. In wishing that he had been born either before or after the present iron race (174–5), Hesiod may intimate that the worsening trend could be reversed.

The association of Kronos with an era of peace belies Hesiod's cruel portrait of that god elsewhere, but coincides with the Roman tradition of a Saturnian paradise, located in Italy. OVID's golden *saeculum* (properly an 'age') is an Augustan reworking of Hesiod's myth (*Metamorphoses* 1.89–112), evoking an era innocent of greed and imperial ambition. Ovid's golden age happily knew nothing of LAW, NAVIGATION, commerce, AGRICULTURE or WAR. VIRGIL yearns for a return to this paradise, imperfectly mirrored in the pastoral Arcadia of his *Eclogues* and the rural Italy of his *Georgics*; he believed that a new golden age was imminent (*Eclogue* 4). JRH

See Hesiod, *Works and Days*; Ovid, *Metamorphoses*; Virgil, *Eclogues*.

GOLD: Pompeian painting of a Roman gold workshop. Note the minute balances and fine tools.

Gordian I, II, revolt of see Gordian III.

emperors, Roman: (a).

Gordian III (Marcus Antonius Gordianus) Son of Junius Balbus, a man of consular rank, and Maecia Faustina, daughter of Marcus Antonius Gordianus Sempronianus Romanus Africanus, born on 20 January AD 225 or 226. The senate, which had previously proclaimed Marcus Clodius Pupienus and Caelius Calvinus Balbinus as Augusti to lead resistance to Maximinus Thrax (235–8), named Gordian Caesar in February or March 238 to quell a disturbance led by associates of his grandfather and uncle, recently killed by troops loyal to Maximinus in North Africa.

Maximinus was murdered by his troops outside Aquileia in April, and members of the guard killed Pupienus and Balbinus a few weeks later, leaving the young Gordian as the only living person with a claim to the throne, to which he duly acceded. He was never more than a figurehead for a regime dominated by senior equestrian officials, led by Gaius Furius Sabinus Aquila Timesitheus, who took it as their task to reunite the governing class after the civil war of 238. This group was also faced with recovering Mesopotamia, which had been occupied by the Sassanians. Gordian, who married Timesitheus' daughter in 241, was taken to the East with the army, which drove the Persians from Mesopotamia in 243. At this point Timesitheus died, and it is not clear who ordered an invasion of Persian territory in the winter of 244. The army was defeated at Peroz Sapor, and Gordian was killed in the subsequent mutiny. He was succeeded by Philip the Arab, the praetorian prefect, who returned his body to Rome for burial, leaving an enormous tumulus constructed by the army after Gordian's death as a tomb on the border of Roman territory. DSP

Gorgias c.485–c.380 BC Sophist and rhetorician. A Sicilian from Leontini, Gorgias was a leading sophist, who specialized in teaching rhetoric. His method was probably based on the memorization of commonplace passages rather than a systematic handbook. He came to prominence as a member of the Leontinian embassy to Athens in 427, when his speaking stunned the assembly. This may have been due partly to a penchant for poetic vocabulary, but was mainly a result of his rhythmic, antithetical style, which was based on short, balanced clauses full of word-play – the so-called 'Gorgianic figures'. Only two works survive intact, the *Encomium of Helen* and *Defence of Palamedes*, both examples of how an ingenious orator could make the worse case seem the better. There are also fragments of a *Funeral Oration* and a treatise *On What is Not*, which was either a serious work of philosophy or more likely (given its paradoxical nature) a rhetorical parody. Gorgias himself suffers parody by Agathon in Plato's *Symposion* (194e–197e), but his importance is reflected by the dialogue named after him. His style influenced Antiphon and Thucydides, and especially his pupil Isokrates. Gorgias lectured throughout Greece, dying at Larisa in Thessaly. MJE

See Kerferd, G. B. (1981) *The Sophistic Movement.*

Gorgons see Medusa.

Gortyn code Among the eight Cretan cities with surviving legal inscriptions from the pre-hellenistic period, Gortyn's assemblage of 160 is exceptional. Much the largest of these is the great code of the mid-5th century BC. Virtually complete, it comprises 12 columns of Greek text cut onto the concave side of a curved wall, probably part of a lawcourt. The rationale of its creation and inscribing remains obscure. Some topics, such as inheritance and division of an estate (column 5), sale and pledge of property (6), marriage of an heiress (7–8), and adoption (10), are given a full set of lucid and systematic provisions. Other, briefer sections read as supplements or amendments to existing law on a variety of separate topics. Oddly, the last two columns, cut by a different hand, contain amendments to the code itself. Apart from a few lines on rape and forcible intercourse with a slave, 'criminal' law barely figures: the balance of preoccupations is overwhelmingly on relationships involving different legal statuses, on the transmission of property (especially on preventing it from leaching into female hands), and on ensuring the continuance of male lineages. Procedurally, juries being wholly absent, the roles of judges, witnesses and oaths are both prominent and informative. JKD

See Inscriptiones Creticae, IV.72; Willetts, R. F. (1967) *The Law Code of Gortyn*; Davies, J. K. (1996) Deconstructing Gortyn, in L. Foxhall and A. D. E. Lewis, eds., *Greek Law in its Political Setting* 33–56; (2005) The Gortyn laws, in D. Cohen and M. Gagarin, eds., *The Cambridge Companion to Ancient Greek Law* 305–27.

gospels see apocryphal gospels; Jesus; New Testament.

Gothic wars Conflicts between the Byzantine (Eastern Roman) empire and the Ostrogothic kingdom of Italy in the 6th century AD. The reconquest of Italy was central to the plans of the emperor Justinian (527–65) to restore the western Mediterranean lands to the Roman empire. Although there had been some tensions between the Gothic and Roman inhabitants of Italy, the region seems to have enjoyed stability, and even prosperity, under Ostrogothic rule. All this was to change with Justinian's war of reconquest.

The invasion launched in 536 at first was successful, not least because of the disunity of the Gothic opposition. Soon, however, the Goths regrouped and throughout the 540s and 550s maintained a vigorous resistance against the Byzantine forces. Only in 562 were the last Gothic strongholds crushed. Justinian's reconquest of Italy had been achieved, but at a bitter price. Over 25 years of continuous warfare had devastated Italy's cities and countryside. The effects were compounded by famine. Italy was left in a state of abject weakness, and so fell easy prey to the Lombards who invaded from across the Alps in 568. Without the resources to withstand this new assault, the region soon fragmented into rival Byzantine and Lombard territories. In this way, the unity of Italy, forged in the Roman Republic, was shattered, and the region would not be reunited until the 19th century. MDH

GORTYN CODE: part of the monumental 'Great Code' of Gortyn, originally inscribed on a temple, but now built into the Roman theatre.

See Heather, P. (1996) *The Goths*; Humphries, M. (2000) Italy, AD 425–605, in *CAH* 14, 525–51.

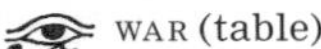 WAR (table).

Goths From the late 3rd century divided into the West (Visi-) and East (Ostro-) Goths, according to the Ostrogothic historian Jordanes, they originated in Scandinavia (Gotland) but migrated to the lower Danube in the 2nd and 3rd centuries AD. Archaeologically their roots lie in Greater Poland, with a recognized shift to the area between the DANUBE and Don rivers in the 3rd century. Ostrogothic lands lay between the Dniester and Dnieper rivers bordering the BLACK SEA; the Visigoths held the former Roman DACIA. Hunnic expansion in the 370s saw Ostrogothic subjection, Visigothic retreat and a request for land within the Roman empire. Allowed in, but starved and exploited, the Goths overwhelmed the Romans at ADRIANOPLE in AD 378, and various groupings (Greuthungi, Tervingi) sought out lands for themselves. THEODOSIUS I settled them in the Danube region and recruited many Goths to his armies. The Visigoths, however, subsequently plundered Greece and DALMATIA, then raided Italy between 398 and 410 under their king Alaric. In 410 they captured Rome before being granted lands in Provence and subsequently Spain, establishing there a kingdom. Visigoths assisted Rome in the decisive battle against Attila's HUNS. Visigothic Spain resisted Byzantine invasion but eventually fell to the Arabs in 711. Isidore of Seville provides the principal source for the kingdom.

After the Hunnic collapse in 454 an Ostrogothic kingdom was formed in Pannonia; from the 460s rival royal groups treated with CONSTANTINOPLE, and Ostrogothic unity was only created in the 480s. In 489 the Amal king THEODERIC moved westwards against Italy where he established a powerful kingdom, documented in the writings of Cassiodorus and Jordanes. Campaigns of building in northern cities, notably at the capital, RAVENNA, reflect Italy's stability under Theoderic. The kingdom eventually fell to Byzantium following the GOTHIC WARS of 536–55, documented by PROCOPIUS. NJC

See Heather, P. (1996) *The Goths*; Heather, P. and Matthews, J. (1994) *The Goths in the Fourth Century*.

 GERMANY AND GERMANS: (b).

gourmets Popular literature makes gluttons of Roman gourmets. We can blame the extravagant meal held by Trimalchio in PETRONIUS' *Satyrica*. Trimalchio's deliberately parodic meal consists of an *hors d'oeuvre* of OLIVES, dormice and sausage brought in on a bronze donkey; next, a serving of peahens' eggs containing a 'fat beccafico rolled up in spiced yoke of egg'; then an *entrée* based on the theme of the ZODIAC, with various servings matching the various signs; this is followed by roasts of MEAT; and so on. Romans were probably their own worst publicists. JUVENAL (*Satire* 4.23) mocks Marcus Gabius APICIUS, the most famous of Roman gourmets, who lived in the reigns of AUGUSTUS and TIBERIUS. SENECA records (*On Consolation to Helvia* 10.8–10) that after spending over 100 million *sestertii* on food and discovering he had little cash left, Apicius poisoned himself: no gourmet could be expected to survive on so little, he maintained. A cookbook survives, erroneously associated with his name.

The upper-class Roman meal must have provided plenty of opportunity for gourmets such as Apicius or Montanus (who could tell the provenance of an oyster from his first bite). The *cena*, or main evening meal, typically had an *hors d'oeuvre* of eggs, shellfish, dormice and olives, an *entrée* of up to seven servings (a roasted PIG, for example, as the main, accompanied by six smaller servings), and a dessert of snail, nuts, shellfish and FRUIT. The variety of foods that could be deployed in the *cena* can be gleaned from MARTIAL (*Epigrams* 13). Fish, meats, CHEESES and VEGETABLES were brought to Rome from the best Italian regions, while fruits and wines came from across the MEDITERRANEAN. The quality of the ingredients and their accompanying condiments, rather than the complexity of their preparation and serving, mark out the ancient gourmet's experience. PGT

See Gowers, E. (1993) *The Loaded Table.*

Gracchi A PLEBEIAN branch of the Sempronii, best known for two popular TRIBUNES of the later 2nd century BC. The line appears in the mid-3rd century with Tiberius Sempronius Gracchus, who occupied SARDINIA as consul in 238. His son (of the same name) died in the second PUNIC WAR (212). His grandson (again of the same name) was a great figure of the earlier 2nd century, conducting extensive campaigns in Sardinia and reaching the CENSORSHIP. He married CORNELIA, daughter of SCIPIO AFRICANUS, having 12 children by her. Only two sons survived to adulthood, becoming two of the most (in)famous figures of Republican history. The elder, yet another Tiberius Sempronius Gracchus, was elected tribune of the PLEBS for 133 BC. He proposed a land redistribution bill (a *lex agraria*), which aroused intense opposition from both the Roman and Italian ÉLITES. The unprecedented methods he employed (overthrowing an opposing tribune, attempting re-election) led to a breakdown of law and order in which he and his supporters were killed. His younger brother, Gaius, tribune in 123, won re-election for 122. He put through a very wide-ranging set of LAWS embracing provincial administration, the lawcourts, the army, land distribution and much else. Gaius also perished violently, in 121, after failing to be re-elected again. CICERO disapproved of the Gracchi for their popular politics, but conceded that Gaius was a superb ORATOR. Assessments of the Gracchi range from reforming idealists to violent demagogues. They were seen even in antiquity as marking the beginning of the end of the REPUBLIC. JRWP

See Plutarch, *Gaius and Tiberius Gracchus*, trs. R. Waterfield (1999); Stockton, D. (1979) *The Gracchi.*

grain see CEREALS.

granaries The best-attested structures specifically designed for the storage of grain were Roman. The basic requirements for preserving grain are that it be kept cool and free of moisture and vermin. Roman WAREHOUSES usually consisted of a series of small, elongated, rectangular rooms along a corridor or clustered around a courtyard, and could range in size from just a few rooms to several hundred on multiple levels. While it is sometimes difficult to distinguish granaries from general-purpose warehouses, or *horrea*, dedicated granaries often featured raised floors, suspended on wooden posts or short piers in order to keep the grain from becoming damp or overheating, to improve ventilation and to deter INSECTS and rodents. The walls were frequently 1 m or more (3–4 ft) in thickness to keep the grain cool; some had external braces to resist the powerful lateral pressure exerted by loose grain. Within granaries, grain could be stored loose, in sacks or in bins. Granaries shared with standard warehouses the usual features of elaborate LOCKING mechanisms on the doors and a limited number of entrances to the complex.

In the PROVINCES, Roman army FORTS almost always included granaries, usually near or adjoining the headquarters or close to one of the main gateways. These were built of both wood and STONE, but shared the same general design as civil granaries. Many such military granaries have been excavated in Britain and Germany, and most have the additional feature of external buttressing to support the walls. These buttresses suggest that grain was stored loose in bins on either side of a room with a central gangway running down the middle. Some late antique military *horrea*, such as the complex at Veldidena, were even fortified, complete with massive exterior walls and watchtowers at the corners of the building and at the midpoints of the side walls.

Pre-Roman granaries in the ancient world, particularly private or rural ones, can be difficult to identify. Grain often seems to have been preserved by the simple expedient of burying it in a pit in the ground, sometimes lined with wicker or straw. This type of storage pit was used throughout the MEDITERRANEAN world and at least as far north as BRITAIN. Small hoards of grain were also universally kept in clay pots. In Egypt, grain was kept in traditional beehive-shaped, or sometimes rectangular, buildings; grain was poured into an opening at the top and removed through another hatch at the base. In Greek cities, STOAS served as granaries. Most similar to Roman granaries were the magazines of hellenistic PERGAMON, which consisted of blocks of long, narrow rooms complete with raised floors. GSA

See Rickman, G. (1971) *Roman Granaries and Store Buildings.*

 WAREHOUSES: (a)–(b).

GRANARIES: reconstructed timber granary from the Roman fort at the Lunt in England. The raised floor is supported on numerous wooden posts. Note also the high loading bay for bringing supplies in by wagon.

Granikos River in north-west Asia Minor, the site of ALEXANDER the Great's first major victory over the Persian empire, in 334 BC. Soon after crossing the Hellespont, Alexander, whose army numbered about 50,000 of which about 6,000 were cavalry, was confronted by a probably somewhat smaller Persian force, raised by the local satraps and consisting, according to Arrian, of Greek mercenary infantry and non-Greek cavalry. The Persians drew up on the bank of the river Granikos, and, according to Arrian, Alexander led his troops through the river to attack them. Arrian's account echoes battle descriptions in the *Iliad*, concentrating on individual combats. Despite attacking from below, Alexander was victorious and suffered only light casualties. This victory gave Alexander control of all of Asia Minor. HB

See Arrian, *Anabasis* 1.13–16; Diodorus Siculus 17.18–21; Justin 11.6.8–13; Plutarch, *Alexander* 16.

 BATTLES (table).

Gratian see AUSONIUS; SYMMACHUS; THEMISTIUS; TRIER; VALENTINIAN I.

EMPERORS, ROMAN: (b); TETRARCHS: (b); THEODOSIUS I: (a).

Graupius, Mons see MONS GRAUPIUS.

Greece The term 'Greece', in discussions of antiquity, is generally used to denote roughly the area of the modern Greek state (southern Balkan peninsula, Aegean islands, Crete) together with the west coast of Asia Minor (including ancient Ionia). Depending on what period is in question, northern MACEDONIA (roughly the modern Greek province of Makedonía plus the former Yugoslav republic of Macedonia) may be included.

In ancient times, however, Greece had no defined boundaries in our sense. It also had a different name. *Hellas* (still the name of the state: in modern Greek: *Ellás* or *Elláda*) is mentioned in the earliest literature (Hesiod and Homer) as the homeland of the Achaians who sailed to Troy. Its extent is unclear; it may originally have denoted part of central Greece, as it occasionally does in later authors. By the time 12 states founded a sanctuary at NAUKRATIS in Egypt (early 6th century?) they could be referred to collectively as *Hellênes*; in Herodotos the sanctuary is called Panhellenion ('shrine of all the Hellenes'). By classical times the precise definition of Hellas could be a sensitive issue. The anonymous 4th-century geographer we call Pseudo-Skylax makes Hellas 'continuous' from Ambrakia (on the Adriatic coast) round the coast to Magnesia (on the east side of the peninsula) – it does not include Macedonia, perhaps for political reasons. Outside these limits he envisages a discontinuous Hellas comprising the hundreds of Hellenic cities on the coasts of the Mediterranean and BLACK SEA. The Greek-influenced part of Sicily and southern Italy (with an extent variously defined) became known as 'Great Greece' (*megalê Hellas*, e.g. Strabo 6.2.1); modern historians now use the Latin version of this name, MAGNA GRAECIA, to denote the area.

What holds *to Hellênikon*, 'the Hellenic (entity)', together was 'having the same blood and the same tongue, with common establishments and sacrifices for the gods, and customs of the same kind' (Herodotos 8.144). The Greeks, for example, recognized that their great families of dialects, such as Ionic, Doric and Aiolic, were closely related. They may have been less certain about the language of the Macedonians, but as the OLYMPIC GAMES were open to any Greek-speaker, the Macedonian kings, at least, were admitted. In modern terms, this is a case of constructing ETHNIC unity in terms of (possibly fictive) kinship, similar dialect, and common religion and customs.

The southern peninsula or PELOPONNESE (21,000 sq km, 8,100 sq miles) contained over 130 city-states including several of the most famous in archaic and classical Greece, such as SPARTA, CORINTH and ARGOS. Also here were three of the four great Panhellenic sanctuaries (OLYMPIA, Nemea, Isthmia) The fourth, DELPHI, lay north of the gulf of Corinth in central Greece (modern Stereá Ellás), a mostly mountainous area with few major states but many smaller ones, including the regional communities of (from west to east) Akarnania, Aitolia, Phokis, and West and East Lokris, all containing small city-states. Also on the eastern side of central Greece were BOIOTIA (main city Thebes) and ATTICA (containing ATHENS).

Approximately one-fifth of the area of modern Greece is made up of ISLANDS, the two largest being CRETE (13,000 sq km, 5,000 sq miles) and EUBOIA (3,600 sq km, 1,400 sq miles). The larger islands had powerful and prosperous cities, particularly in the late archaic period. Usually there was one city-state on each island (e.g. SAMOS, NAXOS, CHIOS), though Crete had many separate city-states and some medium-sized islands had several (four on Keos; six on Lesbos, the largest being Mytilene). The medium-sized islands, together with RHODES (which had a single *polis* only from the late 5th century) formed stepping-stones between Europe, North Africa and western Asia. They represent an archipelago unique in Europe, where both resources and distances were sufficient to favour strongly marked local civilizations from late prehistoric times.

Many of the islands are the eroded summits of mountain chains running generally north-west–south-east, the terminations of the Balkan ranges. This alignment reflects geological history: the North African tectonic plate is moving north-east and being subducted under the Balkans. Tectonic movements explain the frequency of EARTHQUAKES, the steepness of MOUNTAIN ranges, and the narrowness of valleys. In most parts of Greece, the characteristic geology is a mixture of older limestone (often converted into marble by pressure), later schists (easily eroded), younger interbedded marls and conglomerates, and more recent 'Neogene' (Pliocene–Miocene) deposits eroded from those rocks. The last, rather than the most recent alluvial valleys and coastal plains, provide some of the best-drained and most easily ploughed soils. A two-season Mediterranean climate is prevalent – mild and occasionally wet in winter, dry but not excessively hot (compared, for example, to inland Macedonia or inland Asia Minor) in summer. This is moderated by altitude, latitude (north Greece has a more Balkan climate) and longitude (prevailing winds make western Greece wetter than the east; western Asia Minor is similarly favoured). Geology and climate favour the southern Mediterranean uncultivated vegetation comprising

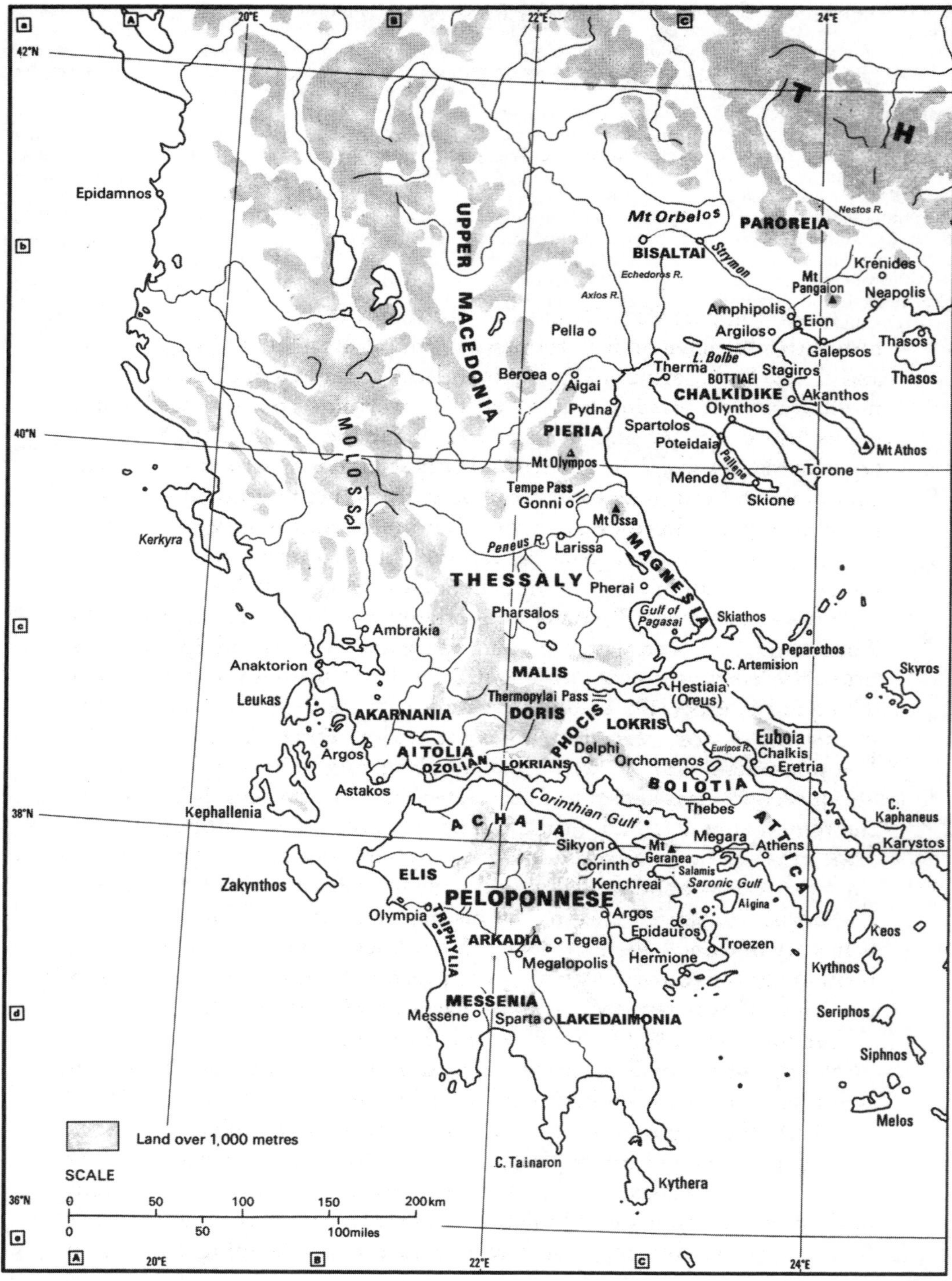

GREECE: map of mainland Greece in classical times.

upland forests (firs and pines), lowland scrub or *maquis* (a French term), woody aromatic plants (normally called by the Spanish term *gariga*), and grasses (steppe plants). They heavily influence Greek AGRICULTURE (with the 'Mediterranean triad'–vine, olive, and cereals) and the uses of the 'wild' landscape. Both landscapes are exploited by a PASTORAL (herding) economy that was extremely active until recently, with some communities practising long-distance TRANSHUMANCE.

In east-central and northern Greece there are extensive alluvial plains formed by the action of long rivers. The famously dissected Greek landscape, which favoured the development of local cultures, is mainly a feature of the south and the islands, though here too there are some substantial plains (such as the Eurotas valley around Sparta, the upland basins of eastern and western ARKADIA, and the Mesogeia of Attica). The world of the city-state (*POLIS*) was primarily a coastal one, since it gave access to varied resources, land-based and maritime, and thus offered a more than minimal livelihood and the possibility of relatively rapid and frequent seaborne EXCHANGE. Interaction between lowland and upland, with their different economic bases, was also important to the survival of Greek civic life. This is especially true in the Peloponnese, where, unusually, many successful city-states (*poleis*) were a fair distance from the sea (Sparta above all). COMMUNICATIONS were favoured by river valleys but enhanced by the dense network of ancient cart ROADS discovered recently. New work stresses the importance of extremely localized landscape diversity and of the 'connectivity' that allows specialized ecological micro-environments to interact to mutual benefit. (See also GREECE, MODERN) DGJS

See [British Admiralty] Naval Intelligence Division (1944–5), *Greece*, vol. 3; (1941) *Dodecanese*; Cary, M. (1949) *The Geographic Background of Greek and Roman History*; Grove, A.T. and Rackham, O. (2001) *The Nature of Mediterranean Europe: an ecological history*; Horden, P. and Purcell, N. (2000) *The Corrupting Sea: a study of Mediterranean history*; Pikoulas, Y. A. (1999) The road-network of Arkadia, in T.H. Nielsen and J. Roy, eds., *Defining Ancient Arkadia* 248–319.

ACHAIA, ROMAN: (a); AEGEAN SEA: (a)–(b).

Greece, modern To understand the ancient world, it can be helpful to examine the modern. In one sense, any investigation of the past is, to some extent, an examination of the present – of records or remains of the past whose status as evidence must be carefully assessed. More relevantly, the conditions we find around us may be used as the basis of arguments based on analogy. It is generally assumed, for example, that the CLIMATE of Greece is the same as in antiquity (allowing for recent changes apparently due to global warming), which provides first indications of what life and work were like then. The geology of modern Greece is broadly the same now as it was then, though in different places the sea level has either risen or fallen relative to the land (as a result of tectonic movements and the effects of EARTHQUAKES) while coastlines have both advanced (because of alluvial deposition by rivers) and retreated (because of local geomorphological changes). Land surfaces have undergone periods of deposition and erosion, so that earlier cultivated or settled landforms may have been washed away or covered by later soils; as with sea level, local circumstances vary and cannot be reduced to simple generalizations.

Argument by analogy comes to the fore when considering LAND use and AGRICULTURE, and even more in the study of social relationships. Social ANTHROPOLOGICAL studies of modern, pre-industrial or recently industrialized, Greek communities are sometimes used to suggest how ancient societies and economic systems worked. Despite the restructuring of Greek rural life by the Roman, Byzantine, Ottoman and in places Venetian empires, it remains true that the texture of pre-1950s rural life in Greek VILLAGES had many points of contact with ancient Greece. The widespread introduction of Christianity in late antiquity, however, has been a major factor in shaping modern Greek world-views in ways alien to ancient thought. Paradoxically, the Orthodox church may have preserved elements of classical culture in church traditions. This probably explains why, for example, the modern limits of INCEST, extending to second cousins (who are not allowed to marry), exactly matches the ancient limits of the extended FAMILY (*angchisteia*), within which relatives had specific obligations (e.g. BURIAL) and rights (e.g. INHERITANCE). However, argument from analogy must be used cautiously: for example, we cannot assume that Hesiod's or Xenophon's perspective on farming, or their aims, were the same as those of Greek PEASANT farmers in the recent past. Analogical argument is most useful in suggesting the limits of possible interpretations, and ruling out others, rather than offering a simple way to map the present onto the past. DGJS, LF

See Boulay, J. du (1974) *Portrait of a Greek Mountain Village*; Campbell, J.K. (1964) *Honour, Family, and Patronage*; Halstead, P. (1987) Traditional and ancient rural economy in Mediterranean Europe, *JHS* 107: 77–87; Forbes, H. (1996) The uses of the uncultivated landscape in modern Greece, in G. Shipley and J. Salmon, eds., *Human Landscapes in Classical Antiquity* 68–97; Grove, A.T. and Rackham, O. (2001) *The Nature of Mediterranean Europe*; Nixon, L. and Price, S. (2001) The diachronic analysis of pastoralism through comparative variables, *ABSA* 96: 395–424.

Greek Anthology A compendium of about 4,000 EPIGRAMS divided into 16 books. Epigrams are mostly short poems, many with a funerary character, written in elegiac couplets, though other types of verses are not excluded. The anthology includes works attributed to well-known authors such as ARCHILOCHOS, SIMONIDES or PLATO, but also contains many anonymous epigrams or epigrams written by minor poets.

The anthology stems from two previous anthologies: that of the Byzantine scholar Maximus Planudes (1255–1305) and the so-called *Palatine Anthology*. The latter takes its name from the Count of the Palatine, in whose library at Heidelberg (Germany) the manuscript was discovered in 1606. It had been assembled in the 10th century AD by Kephalas, who relied on anthologies collected during the ALEXANDRIAN and Roman periods. The first of these was Meleager's *Garland*, dated between 100 and 90 BC. Philip of Thessalonica compiled a *Garland* in AD 40 to supplement Meleager's. The third most important contribution is that of Agathias, who collected other epigrams in his *Cycle* by AD 570. Planudes based his anthology on the earlier work of Kephalas, but modified it extensively, by omitting poems but also adding new items, on the basis of his own criteria. This anthology enjoyed great popularity and was printed in 1484, shortly after the invention of the printing press. Planudes' anthology eclipsed that of Kephalas, which was preserved only by good fortune.

The poems of the *Anthology* range widely in quality, date, metre and origin. Among other varieties, there are erotic and satirical poems, votives and epitaphs, exercises in poetic forms, oracles, riddles and pattern poems as well as Christian epigrams. RBC

See Paton, W. R., trs. (1916–18) 5 vols.; Jay, P., trs. (1973) (selection).

Gregory of Nazianzus c.AD 329–89 One of the CAPPADOCIAN fathers, along with BASIL of Caesarea and Gregory of Nyssa. He was born into a wealthy family of the provincial Cappadocian aristocracy, son of the BISHOP of Nazianzus. He studied at ALEXANDRIA and Athens, where his friendship with Basil developed and he met the future emperor JULIAN. *Oration* 43, in honour of Basil, gives us a vivid glimpse of Athenian university life in the 350s.

On his return to Cappadocia, Gregory spent some time in monastic retreat with Basil in Pontos before reluctantly accepting ordination from his father (c.362). For the rest of his life, Gregory found it hard to resolve the tension between his desire for monastic seclusion and his involvement in the turbulent ecclesiastical politics of the day. In 371 he found himself bishop of Sasima, a godforsaken spot in rural Cappadocia, appointed by Basil as part of an ecclesiastical power struggle. Gregory did not take up residence there and never really forgave his close friend. In 379 he was invited to CONSTANTINOPLE to champion Nicene orthodoxy. The council of Constantinople of 381 recognized him as the city's bishop but he resigned soon after and retreated to Nazianzus, where he spent his remaining years combining pastoral duties with writing.

Gregory has been called the Christian DEMOSTHENES. Of 45 extant orations, among the most significant are his five *Theological Orations*, a comprehensive account of Trinitarian doctrine. About 400 of his poems survive, including an autobiographical work of almost 2,000 lines. (see also CHURCH COUNCILS) PMB

See Ruether, R. R. (1969) *Gregory of Nazianzus.*

grief The main cause of grief among ancient Greeks and Romans was DEATH – especially untimely death. Greeks in particular were inclined to be very demonstrative in their displays of grief. ACHILLES tears at his hair, throws dirt on himself, and cries out when he receives news of the death of his dear friend Patroklos, and his handmaidens beat their breasts (*Iliad* 18). Nearly destroyed by the death of his son HEKTOR, Priam refuses to eat, drink or sleep, and covers himself with dung (*Iliad* 24). Visual evidence for the physical expression of grief first appears in the Greek Bronze Age and becomes common in funerary art of the archaic period. Very often, however, the expression of grief was channelled and formalized, for instance in ritual songs of lament, both the *thrênos* and the more improvised *goös*; the lamentations which the women sing at Hektor's funeral (*Iliad* 24) are the earliest examples of these.

Many Greeks and Romans reflected on and wrote about the nature of grief. Krantor, a member of the ACADEMY in Athens in the late 4th century BC, composed a work *On Grief* which exerted a strong influence over the long tradition of consolation literature to which CICERO, SENECA, PLUTARCH and others contributed. Epitaphs on the thousands of surviving Greek and Latin tombstones illustrate the many ways in which grief was expressed and confronted. The evidence they provide for the depths of grief which Romans felt is especially extensive, as is the evidence from personal correspondence. MJ

See Alexiou, M. (1974) *The Ritual Lament in Greek Tradition*; Lattimore, R. (1962) *Themes in Greek and Latin Epitaphs.*

gromatici veteres see *AGRIMENSORES*; LAND SURVEYING, ROMAN.

Grote, C. see HISTORIANS AND HISTORIOGRAPHY, MODERN.

growth, economic There is considerable debate about whether the ancient economies of Greece and Rome experienced growth in the way it is understood by economists today. Growth is normally defined, in modern textbooks, as the process whereby a community increases its WEALTH in a manner that is sustained through time and generally linked to a *per capita* rise in production of goods and services. Aggregate increase in production is not true economic growth if it is simply the product of a commensurate increase in population, with *per capita* productivity remaining the same. The non-survival of detailed census records and historical documents on productivity constrains our ability to answer the question conclusively with respect to antiquity. Although attention has focused on both the Greek and Roman worlds, the evidence for growth seems stronger in the hellenistic period (c.300–30 BC) and especially in the late Roman REPUBLIC and early PRINCIPATE (c.200 BC–c.AD 200), when there is strong archaeological evidence for a rise in MEDITERRANEAN TRADE, urban MANUFACTURING and the non-agricultural sector of the ECONOMY. DJM

See Hitchner, R. B. (2005) The advantages of wealth and luxury: the case for economic growth in the Roman empire, in J. Manning and I. Morris, eds., *The Ancient Economy: evidence and models* 207–22; Millett, P. (2001) Productive to some purpose? The problem of ancient economic growth, in Mattingly and Salmon, *Economies beyond Agriculture* 17–48.

guardianship

In Greek antiquity, the institution of guardianship aimed at protecting those who were thought unable to protect themselves. At Athens, the law required that guardians take responsibility for children and WOMEN. In the case of children, the guardian (*epitropos*) would normally be their father. He was responsible for supplying food, home, clothes and EDUCATION to both male and female children. Male children no longer required a guardian after they came of age, but freeborn females needed a guardian (*kyrios*) throughout their lives. Before MARRIAGE this was usually a woman's father; after marriage it was often her husband, though women could have several potential guardians and play them off against each other. A woman's guardian would provide for her, give her hand in marriage and represent her in legal action.

A man usually stipulated a guardian or guardians for his children in his WILL. Frequently these would be relatives, but it was also possible to select non-relatives. Scholars believe that in the case of Athenian citizens at least one guardian would have to be another citizen. These men were responsible for maintaining both the children and their property until they came of age. This was seen as a serious responsibility, and maltreatment of an orphan (child without a father) was an offence which could be prosecuted by any Athenian. Similar concern for the vulnerable status of orphan children is expressed by PLATO, who recommends harsh penalties in his *Laws* for those who harm a ward. Often an Athenian ward would live with one of his guardians while his own property was let. The purpose of this was to secure an income from the estate that could be set against any expenses of his upbringing. Guardians were required to submit to the ward accounts of how they had dealt with any property when they handed it over at the end of their guardianship. Men could prosecute their guardians within five years of the end of the term of guardianship if they believed that their estate had been mismanaged.

At Athens, the archon was responsible for 'looking after' orphans. This probably means that he presided over all lawsuits involving them. It is also likely that he formalized the appointment of guardians named by fathers in their wills, and adjudicated cases where potential guardians were competing to take care of a ward. In the case where no guardian was stipulated by the father and no potential guardian came forward, scholars believe that the archon imposed the duty of guardianship on the man he deemed most appropriate.

Athenian women could not be without a guardian, though it seems that METIC women did not need one. If the guardian of a woman died, she would usually be passed to his heir. This could be her own son if he had reached the age of majority. Alternatively, she would return to her father's family. FMM

See Harrison, A. R. W. (1968) *The Law of Athens*.

Guardianship at Rome took two basic forms, *tutela* and *cura*. The form of guardianship known as *tutela* applied to minors until they came of age, and to women permanently. In the case of minors whose *paterfamilias* had died, the nearest agnate (relative through the male line) was generally, though not always, appointed guardian. If the child died, the tutor inherited the property. In instances where there was no agnate to act as tutor, the PRAETOR would appoint one. As long as the child was alive, the tutor was responsible for administering matters concerning the child's property. Boys were released from their tutors upon reaching adulthood at the age of 14.

In some of its forms, *cura* was an institution designed to look after the interests of lunatics and spendthrifts; little is known about this category. Better-documented guardianship of this type protected the interests of, originally, individuals between the attainment of adulthood and the age of 25 in the absence of a *paterfamilias* – in other words, those who were *sui iuris* (legally independent). Although these young adults were legally competent, a *curator* was required for the administration of most legal transactions. Rarely, a young adult was successful in an application for freedom from this restriction.

As legal precedent developed, guardians became liable for any fraudulent actions concerning the child's estate and could be sued for mismanagement. As a result, many guardians wished to be excused from their appointed roles, and a list of grounds was established so that they could legitimately do so. Also over time, much of the distinction between *cura* and *tutela* diminished, with tutors often maintaining their roles beyond their wards' attainment of adulthood and *curatores* exercising a general role, not merely the oversight of specific legal actions.

Roman WOMEN after the age of 12 retained their tutors. Although women were permitted to perform certain legal acts, they were not entitled to accept inheritances, make WILLS or MANUMIT SLAVES. The authorization to complete these transactions became a formality for guardians, since women had the ability to counter opposition. A woman could apply to a MAGISTRATE to change a guardian if the appointed individual was away or did not conform to the woman's opinion.

AUGUSTUS allowed for the release of a woman from her tutor if she performed her civic duty of begetting children (three for freeborn women, four for a freed slave). Women in general could not serve as tutors. There is evidence to suggest, however, that they could take interest in the property and affairs of their children if the father had authorized it. LAH

See Crook, J. A. (1967) *Law and Life of Rome, 90 BC–AD 212*; Evans Grubbs, J. (2002) *Woman and the Law in the Roman Empire*; Gardner, J. F. (1986) *Women in Roman Law and Society*; Johnston, D. (1999) *Roman Law in Context*.

gymnasia

The gymnasium probably took its name from the fact that boys and men engaged in physical exercises there in the nude (*gymnos*, 'naked'), since Greek athletics were practised without clothing. The facility developed during the archaic period, perhaps as a training place for citizens and young men, though no example of an early gymnasium has yet been excavated. The original purpose is debated. Some (e.g. Delorme) argue that the gymnasium was meant as a training area for HOPLITE soldiers, while others (e.g. Pleket) that it was meant as the preserve of the traditional ÉLITE. Certainly, the suitability of traditional Greek ATHLETICS for military preparedness, beyond simply levels of physical fitness, is dubious, even if the value system expressed by all athletes was especially martial. It is most probable that the gymnasium arose about the same time as athletic festivals, to provide a home for the competitive and individualistic ideology of the élite, an ideology displaced from the hoplite battlefield where individual values were suppressed.

Initially, the gymnasium was simply a large, open space with running facilities, where various athletic events could be practised, ideally with a supply of water and trees to provide some protection from the sun. The open space of the gymnasium was somehow defined, perhaps by a wall. Many gymnasia seem also to have an associated shrine (especially to Hermes or HERAKLES). During the classical period, many of the

Gymnasia, Greek: vase-painting illustrating some of the principal athletic activities that could be practised at the gymnasium.

characteristic structures associated with later gymnasia were gradually introduced. Typically they came to include a colonnaded track one *stadion* in length (c.192 m) called a *xystos* and another, open-air track called a *paradromis*. Beyond, in an open courtyard, was space enough for other events, such as discus and javelin. As at Olympia, the gymnasium came always to be associated with a palaestra, an area necessary for training in heavier combat events, particularly wrestling, boxing and the *pankration*. The exact relationship between the gymnasium and palaestra is debated, yet a gymnasium could not serve all athletic events without one; consequently, such a facility is necessary. This gymnasium–palaestra athletic complex also required changing and bathing rooms, as well as administrative offices.

The gymnasium also acquired cultural or educational spaces and in some cities, such as Athens in the 5th and 4th centuries BC, the gymnasia became centres of learning and philosophical debate (e.g. the Lyceum and the Academy). Especially in the expanded Greek world resulting from the conquests of Alexander the Great, the gymnasium came to be seen as a distinctly Hellenic institution and the centre of traditional Hellenic 'culture' (*paideia*, both intellectual and physical). As such, it could also acquire libraries, lecture-rooms, concert-halls and government offices, in addition to the necessary athletic facilities. The gymnasium now served as a centre of jealously guarded Greek identity in the larger non-Greek world. Writing under the Roman empire, Pausanias (10.4.1) famously lists the gymnasium alongside such essential amenities as an *agora* and a theatre for a community to be considered a proper *polis*.

The gymnasiarchal law from Beroia in Macedonia (mid-2nd century BC) provides detailed information concerning the administration and organization of a gymnasium in the hellenistic era. It was supervised by a gymnasiarch elected by the city council. It was his responsibility to see that the (often complex) rules of the gymnasium were obeyed, and he had the power to fine offenders. Olive oil was required in generous quantities as a prerequisite of athletic events, and this expense was typically undertaken as a liturgy by a wealthy member of the community. We see from this law the types of exercises and competitions undertaken by boys, youths and men. It also states that the lower classes were to be excluded from the gymnasium. MJC

See Delorme, J. (1960) *Gymnasion*; Gauthier, P. and Hatzopoulos, M. B. (1993) *La Loi gymnasiarchique de Beroia*; Pleket, H.W. (1976) Games, prizes, athletes and ideology, *Stadion* 1: 49–89; Raschke, W. J. (1988) *The Archaeology of the Olympics*.

The gymnasium was originally a Greek athletic facility. As a central institution in Greek society, it continued to flourish in Greek cities, including those in southern Italy, throughout the rise of the Roman Republic and under the empire. Perhaps under the influence of Roman building techniques and styles, Greek gymnasia under the empire often came also to include more complex bath buildings. Nevertheless, the gymnasium continued to be a centre of Greek culture and to play an important role in maintaining Greek identity.

Romans became acquainted with the gymnasium from their contact with the Greeks, first in southern Italy and then in the hellenistic East. Due perhaps to Rome's traditional lack of interest in, or hostility toward, Greek athletics, there seems to have been no gymnasium in Rome until the 1st century BC. Romans abroad, however, certainly did visit gymnasia and participate in gymnasium activities: Romans are known to have registered at gymnasia in Athens and DELOS as early as the 2nd century BC. Perhaps the SENATE resisted the establishment of a stereotypically Greek institution in Rome for the same reasons that it refused to allow the construction of a permanent THEATRE: such structures were believed to promote Greek licentiousness at the expense of traditional Roman values. The first gymnasium in Rome may have been connected with the baths of AGRIPPA (*thermae Agrippae*), a complex facility consisting of baths with an associated palaestra. The palaestra at POMPEII, beside the AMPHITHEATRE, seems to date to the reign of AUGUSTUS and may, like the facility built by Agrippa in the Campus Martius, reflect the imperial concern for the physical fitness of Roman and Italian youth. At any rate, the first explicitly attested gymnasium in Rome was built under NERO in AD 60 in the Campus Martius and was associated with his baths in the same area.

During the imperial period, gymnasia were found in most major cities of the empire. Inscriptions, especially from North AFRICA, refer to the gift of gymnasia, probably either meaning the sponsorship of athletic contests or the presentation of olive oil. MJC

See Ginouvès, R. (1962) *Balaneutike*; Yegül, F. (1992) *Baths and Bathing in Classical Antiquity* 6–29.

 ATHLETES AND ATHLETICS: (a)–(c); BALL GAMES.

Hades The Greek underworld, and its divine ruler. After the victory of the GODS over the Titans (HESIOD, *Theogony*), Hades received the underworld by lot as his share of the spoils of war, leaving the realms of sky and sea to his brothers ZEUS and POSEIDON respectively (*Iliad* 15; Apollodoros, books 1 and 3). Hades' wife was Persephone, the daughter of DEMETER, whose abduction by Hades is related in the *Homeric Hymn to Demeter*.

Ancient descriptions of Hades are offered in book 11 (*Nekuia*) of the *Odyssey* as well as by PLATO (*Republic* and *Phaedo*). In HOMER, Hades' kingdom is portrayed as dark and gloomy, inhabited by shadow-like souls. Its gate was guarded by a three-headed dog, Kerberos, its keys kept by Aiakos. Hades' home was on the farthest realm of Ocean, which was then thought to surround the earth, and beyond the physical boundary between the two worlds, the river Acheron and the lake Acherousia. Images of the MYTHOLOGY of death are abundant on 5th- and 4th-century vases, notably white-ground lekythoi and the works of the so-called Underworld Painter from Apulia in south Italy.

Hades' cult was not widespread in Greece but did exist in some areas, often under different names such as Plouton, Klymenos and Eubouleus. In many cases he had wider significance as god of the earth's produce, alongside his underground realm. EP

See Lindner, R. et al. (1988) Hades, in *LIMC* vol. 4, 367–94; Sourvinou-Inwood, C. (1995) *'Reading' Greek Death*.

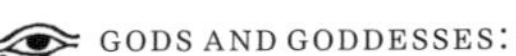
GODS AND GODDESSES: (a).

Hadrian (Publius Aelius Hadrianus) Emperor of Rome, AD 117–38. The son of a SENATOR, Hadrian was born at Italica in BAETICA in 76. After the death of his father in 85, he became the ward of TRAJAN. He

HADES: the Greek underworld, realm of Pluto, Persephone and their three-headed dog, Kerberos.

HADRIAN: coin portrait of Sabina, wife of Hadrian.

followed the well-established career pattern, holding a series of military tribunates in Italy, Moesia and GERMANY. These led to an imperial QUAESTORSHIP, senior military commands in the DACIAN WARS, a PRAETORSHIP and governorship of PANNONIA inferior in 105–6, and a suffect CONSULSHIP in 108. In 112 he was elected to an archonship in Athens, and embarked on a lifelong love of Athens and of Greek culture in general. He was appointed governor of SYRIA in 114 and designated consul for the second time in 117 (for 118).

Trajan died in CILICIA in August 117, unexpectedly naming Hadrian as his heir. The sources, especially the unreliable biographer of Hadrian, leave some implication that the adoption was false, but a careful emperor like Trajan would hardly have left this vital question open. It is a testament to Hadrian's skill and even ruthlessness, not to mention the usual public largesse, that he held onto power in spite of some senatorial opposition.

Hadrian is renowned as a careful and prudent emperor, if not innovative. He continued the considered financial policies of Trajan and was concerned more than most with the well-being of provincials, willing as he was to grant tax moratoriums. Considerable changes were made in jurisdiction; this, and the regularization of the *concilium principis* (the emperor's private committee made up of senators), continued the centralization of government seen under Trajan. This prudence extended to foreign affairs. Hadrian abandoned Trajan's ambitions in PARTHIA and the East, no doubt braving considerable senatorial opposition. The consolidation of PROVINCES such as Dacia and BRITAIN followed; especially important is the construction of HADRIAN'S WALL in northern Britain. His principate is notable for good order except in JUDAEA, which was reorganized after a revolt against his building of a temple to JUPITER Capitolinus in JERUSALEM (renamed Colonia Aelia Capitolina). Consolidation of the provinces is reflected in the increasing tendency after Hadrian for LEGIONS to recruit locally and to become more firmly attached to particular provinces.

Perhaps the most notable aspect of Hadrian's principate was its almost peripatetic nature. After coming to power, he stayed in Rome to confirm his position, then embarked on a tour of provinces which kept him away from the city for some seven years. GAUL, GERMANY, BRITAIN, Spain, ASIA Minor and Greece were visited in turn. A short spell in Rome in 127 was followed by a tour of AFRICA, a visit to Athens, and tours of CILICIA, SYRIA and Egypt in 130 (marked by the death of ANTINOUS, his constant companion and lover). From 131, despite the devastation of Antinous' death, Hadrian enjoyed life in Rome until his death in 138. His chosen successor, ANTONINUS PIUS, ensured Hadrian's burial in his mausoleum and his deification in the senate. (see also TIVOLI) CEPA

See Birley, A. (1997) *Hadrian: the restless emperor.*

 EMPERORS, ROMAN: (a); PANTHEON: (a)–(d); SCULPTURE: (d); TRAJAN.

Hadrian's Villa see ART; CARYATIDS; HOUSES, ROMAN; MOSAICS; TIVOLI; VILLAS.

Hadrian's wall The quintessential Roman FRONTIER in popular imagination, inspiring artists and poets (e.g. Frances Horovitz). The wall (80 Roman miles or 118 km long) was part of a complex series of military works spanning the isthmus between the Tyne and Solway estuaries in northern BRITAIN. Initially, a stone wall (3 m thick, over 4 m high) was built on the eastern half of the isthmus, continuing in the western sector as a turf wall (6 m wide, 4.2 m high) probably because of the shortage of limestone (for making lime mortar) in that area. The turf wall was all replaced in stone by the Severan period if not earlier (c.165–70?). To the north of the wall was dug a massive ditch (c.8 m broad, 3 m deep). Along the curtain were fortified gates (milecastles) every Roman mile (1,481 m), and towers (turrets) at intervals of

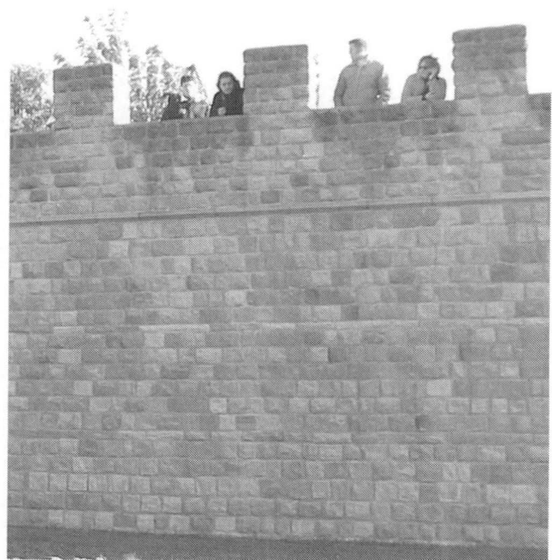

HADRIAN'S WALL: a reconstruction of the possible original appearance of the wall. There is considerable debate about the presence or not of crenellations, and about whether the wall was originally whitewashed to give it an even more striking visual impact.

one-third of a mile between them. Several changes of plan occurred during construction, starting with the decision to move most of the garrison posts up onto the wall from a road line a few miles to the south (known as the Stanegate). The addition of 12 forts (eventually 16) greatly increased the work of construction. So did the near-simultaneous decision to create an additional linear earthwork, comprising a flat-bottomed ditch between two mounds, known today as the Vallum. This earthwork restricted access to the wall from the south to a series of controlled gateways, and effectively created a militarized zone between the two linear features, along which a road (the Military Way) was later added. Additional elements of the frontier system included outpost forts along the routes into lowland Scotland and along the Cumbrian coast to the south-west (where evidence of mile-fortlets, towers and running ditches has been found).

Begun in AD 122, HADRIAN's grand project (and the emperor's own hand was probably behind this scheme) involved all three legions, the British fleet and no doubt many AUXILIARY units. Although the wall was abandoned in the early 140s, when the frontier was advanced into Scotland with the construction of the ANTONINE WALL, it was reactivated in the late 150s and 160s and saw major renewal work in the Severan period. Occupation can be shown to have extended well into the 4th century AD.

The function of the wall has been much discussed, starting from the statement by Hadrian's biographer that it served to divide Romans from BARBARIANS. This has generally been taken to imply that it served as a defensive shield for provincialized northern England against the tribes of Scotland. However, its original design with 80 gates, and the relative narrowness of the parapet walkway, will have made it difficult to use as a defensive line as such. The ostentation and scale of the engineering works, the large number of control points, the garrison based along it (up to 10,000), and the fact that the frontier works effectively faced both north and south suggest rather that it was designed to impress, intimidate and control indigenous communities on both sides of the frontier zone. DJM

See Bidwell, P. (1999) *Hadrian's Wall 1989–1999*; Breeze, D. and Dobson, B. (2000) *Hadrian's Wall*; Horovitz, F. (1983) *Snow Light, Water Light* (poems).

BRITANNIA; FORTS AND FORTRESSES, ROMAN: (c); FRONTIERS: (a)–(c).

hair and hairdressing

The ancient Greeks were very interested in varieties of hairdressing, for both men and women. In the Bronze Age, men are generally shown wearing their hair short, though men of the mainland MYCENAEAN culture sometimes wore it long. Beards were common on older men, but moustaches unusual. Women wore their hair long; in MINOAN culture it was often piled high on top of their heads.

In the archaic period only SLAVES, young boys, and women in mourning wore their hair short. Men tied their hair up with bands, around which the hair

(a) Young man with hair tied up in a band. He is just starting to grow a beard.

(b) Young woman with long hair held by diadem.

(c) Woman with hair tied up in *sakkos*.

GREEK HAIRSTYLES

(a) The short hairstyle of Augustus was widely emulated.

(b) By the 2nd C.AD, a longer 'Greek' hairstyle become fashionable under Hadrian.

(c) Early imperial woman with high pompadour.

(d) Later imperial woman with crown of braids.

ROMAN HAIRSTYLES

HAIR AND HAIRSTYLING: selected examples of Greek and Roman hairstyles.

could be rolled or plaited, sometimes with curls or waves on either side of the face. From the 6th century BC onward it became more popular for young men to cut their hair when they came of age. The exception to this rule was Sparta, where youths wore their hair short and grew it long upon reaching maturity. In the late 4th century Alexander the Great's distinctive hairstyle, visible in his official portraiture, encouraged a fashion for wavy, mane-like coiffures and clean-shaven faces. Beards were still worn by older men, but were far less common.

In the 7th and 6th centuries BC women wore their hair loose, spilling over their shoulders and down their backs; the front section was held back with hair-bands or, for those who could afford it, a metal diadem. Around 500 we see hair being gathered under a material covering, either a *sakkos* covering all the hair, with little wisps escaping, or a *sphendonê* covering less of the hair. This trend continued in the 5th and 4th centuries. The material was tied on with hair-bands; these could also be used without the material covering to produce a wide variety of 'up do's. The *sakkos and sphendonê* lost popularity in the hellenistic period. Hair was still worn up, but with added details of artificial curls and waves. Wigs and hairpieces were popular, as was dye, to cover grey hairs or to go blonde. NJW

Hairstyles, known especially from sculpture and coins, offer information about Roman fashion, social aspirations, and political beliefs. Fashion, for example, determines the shift from a woman's style involving not only a chignon of hair in the back but a huge pompadour of snail curls in the front, during the late 1st–early 2nd century AD, to a high crown of braids wound around the head in the first third of the 2nd century. Changes also indicate such social issues as a desire to emulate members of the court by appropriating popular hairstyles. Small boys in the time of Augustus often have the ruler's hairstyle, as do freed slaves whose desire for upward mobility finds expression in hair fashion. The emperor himself used hair to convey political messages; Augustus drew on the leonine hairstyle associated with Alexander the Great in order to suggest similarity to that ruler, as well as to draw on the ideas of physiognomic writers about the way character expressed itself through hair and facial features. The emperor Hadrian's full beard and longer hair, taken up by rulers until the first third of the 3rd century, signalled his interest in Greek culture. Roman men had normally been clean-shaven and short-haired, whereas Greeks were understood by Romans to be bearded. By his hair, Hadrian communicated philhellenism as well as his desire to be seen as cultivated and even perhaps as a philosopher. For women, such messages also could be borne by hairstyles, as when Augustus' wife Livia and his sister Octavia appeared in simple classical or traditionally Republican hairstyles.

For women, hair ornaments, pins and combs were, like mirrors, signs of womanliness. A number of funerary reliefs from Roman provinces show collections of objects clearly meant to signify womanliness; these include cosmetic jars and wool baskets, along with things used to care for women's hair. Such objects were not associated with manliness, and indicate the cultural value placed on women's physical attractiveness.

The hair depicted on some female portrait statues of the 1st to 4th centuries was apparently meant to show wigs. A few portraits lack the hair, which was to be set on later in the form of a wig; a few wig-sculptures have been found. In addition, pins, rats (hairnets), and extensions were used, as was hair-dye.

Stylists were called *tonsor* or *ornator* (male), *tonstrix* or *ornatrix* (female). They worked freelance (Martial, *Epigram* 2.17), as well as in houses where they were personal slaves or freed people. The poets and satirists speak of cruel and capricious mistresses slapping their hairdressing slaves and sticking them with pins (e.g. Juvenal, *Satire* 6.490–1). A number of reliefs, as on funerary monuments from Neumagen in 2nd–3rd century Gaul, show scenes of women having their hair done while attended by several womanservants. Such scenes often seem to be status-enhancing devices for the family that can afford women's leisure. Inscriptions, however, mention slaves, freedmen and freedwomen as barbers and hairdressers, whose occupations seem a source of identity or even pride for them (e.g. Lefkowitz and Fant 169–70). NBK

See Crawford, J. (1917) Capita desecta and marble coiffures, *Memoirs of the American Academy in Rome* 1: 103–19; Lefkowitz, M. and Fant, M. (1982) *Women's Life in Greece and Rome*.

 Alexander III: (a).

Halieis A small town on an excellent harbour (Pórto Chéli bay) near the southern tip of the Argolic peninsula, which came into being in the 7th century BC and was abandoned c.300 BC. Excavations have revealed city walls, a fortified *akropolis* with a small shrine (of Athena?), an orthogonal town plan (6th century) using halves of a 50 *plethra* square (a square with an area of c.500,000 sq ft, approximately 4.4 ha or 11 acres), a small, enclosed harbour, and an extramural sanctuary of Apollo (now submerged) with two temples and a race-course. A rise in sea level of over 5 m since the classical period has left the southern edge of the town underwater, with house plans and streets clearly visible from balloon photographs. The *agora* has not been located. The private houses are small but are revealing of the economic life of the occupants. One out of six houses accommodated a press bed.

The inhabitants of what was, at times at least, an independent *polis*, included refugees from Tiryns in the Argive plain (some 4th-century coins bear the legend *Tirynthioi*). Halieis was occupied at various times in the 5th century by Peloponnesian or Athenian forces (*IG* i^3 75, Athenian copy of inscribed treaty). The reasons for its abandonment, following a period when the occupied area had shrunk, are unknown. MHJ

See Boyd, T. and Rudolph, W. (1978) Excavations at Porto Cheli and vicinity, *Hesperia* 47: 338–55; Jameson, M. (1969) Excavations at Porto Cheli and vicinity, *Hesperia* 38: 311–42; (1974) The excavation of a drowned Greek temple, *Scientific American* 231: 110–19; (1982) The submerged sanctuary of Apollo at Halieis, *National Geographic Society Reports* 14: 363–7; Rudolph, W. (1979) Excavations at Porto Cheli and vicinity, *Hesperia* 48: 284–324.

 Peloponnese.

Halikarnassos (mod. Bodrum) A Greek city of CARIA in south-western Asia Minor, founded c.900 BC by colonists from Troizen, Halikarnassos was absorbed into the PERSIAN EMPIRE after CYRUS THE GREAT defeated the LYDIAN ruler Croesus. The city is perhaps most famous as the birthplace of the historian HERODOTOS and of the colourful queen Artemisia, who distinguished herself during the battle of SALAMIS, and as the home of the Mausoleum (tomb of MAUSOLUS), one of the Seven Wonders of the ancient world. Within the Persian empire Caria was attached administratively to Lydia (SARDIS), but in the 5th century Halikarnassos, with numerous other Carian cities, became a member of the Delian league; though first attested in the Tribute List of 453, the city may have joined already during the tyranny of Lygdamis. After the King's Peace (387/6) the city was again firmly under Persian control. The now separate satrapy of Caria was entrusted to the Hekatomnid dynasty of Mylasa, of which Halikarnassos became the administrative centre after its synoikism by Mausolus, who was culturally (but not politically) philhellenic. Captured by ALEXANDER the Great in 334/3, Halikarnassos was administered for a short period by Ada I, sister of Mausolus and widow of their brother Idrieus (or Hidrieus); she had been ousted by her youngest brother Pixodaros, and Alexander accepted her as his adoptive mother. Already in the age of the SUCCESSORS, the MACEDONIAN satrap was ruling again from Mylasa. Halikarnassos was controlled in turns by ANTIGONOS, LYSIMACHOS and the PTOLEMIES until finally coming under Roman control in 129 BC. WH

See Bean, G.E. (1980) *Turkey beyond the Maeander*; Hornblower, S. (1982) *Mausolus*.

 EAST GREECE.

Hallstatt Distinct cultural assemblage named after the site from which it was first recovered, the Iron Age cemetery at Hallstatt (Upper Austria). The term Hallstatt is also used to denote a geographical region, as well as a specific chronological period, c.750–450 BC.

The complexity in the social, political and economic systems of the initial Hallstatt period (Hallstatt C, c.750–600) marks a significant change from the preceding Urnfield culture of the late Bronze Age. Foremost, the grave goods recovered from the Iron Age inhumations in the zone ranging from Bohemia to the Upper DANUBE show the emergence of an élite class who are represented archaeologically by the presence of IRON swords, HORSE trappings, four-wheeled funerary wagons and vessels associated with feasting. The wealth of the recovered grave goods, some imported from the MEDITERRANEAN world, indicates the beginnings of a specialized economy that enabled TRADE with distant areas. In contrast to the largely agrarian ECONOMY of the preceding Bronze Age, the extensive exploitation of the SALT MINES of Hallstatt, in particular, indicate that a small percentage of the local population was no longer solely concerned with food production.

The emphasis on MANUFACTURE and trade developed further in Hallstatt D1 (c.600–530). This phase also marks the foundation of the Greek port of MARSEILLES (c.600) and may account for a shift in centres of power from Bohemia and the Upper Danube to the western Hallstatt zone of southern GERMANY and west of the RHÔNE. Certainly, the presence of imported goods in élite BURIALS from this area suggests increased trade with the Mediterranean world via the Greek COLONIES situated on the Rhône corridor. This acquisition of foreign goods by the western Hallstatt élite facilitated the expression of status and POWER that is also noted in the construction of hill FORTS at this time, a few of which are notably Grecian in style.

Hallstatt D2–3 (c.530–450) marks an intensification of power in the western Hallstatt zone which was facilitated by access to, and redistribution of, exotic goods from the south. The widespread abandonment of hill forts is evident, paralleled by a concentration of power in specific areas. A similar pattern is seen in the occurrence of rich burials, the majority directly associated with these newly consolidated centres of power. Increased trade with the southern Mediterranean is evident in the 'princely burials' that characterize this phase, in addition to the spatial patterning of major hill forts within the vicinity of RIVER systems that enabled trading relations between the north and the south. Hallstatt D2–3 also corresponds with the northward expansion of ETRUSCAN power. Items of Etruscan manufacture occur with some frequency in the western Hallstatt zone. This final phase of the Hallstatt period is reflective of a prestige goods economy, both dependent on, and facilitated by, trade with the Mediterranean world. MLM

See Cunliffe, B. (1997) *The Ancient Celts*; Wells, P. (1981) *The Emergence of an Iron Age Economy*.

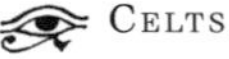 CELTS.

handicap see DISABILITY.

Hannibal 247–183/2 BC Carthaginian general, eldest son of Hamilcar Barca, who had fought the Romans in the first PUNIC WAR. When Hannibal was still a child, his father made him swear an oath never to have friendship with the Romans, and the inherited enmity lasted throughout Hannibal's life. He took up a command in Spain in 221, and by spring 218 had already begun his march across the ALPS to enter Italy in the autumn, with large forces of infantry and cavalry, as well as elephants. His astonishingly bold move appeared at first to have been successful: in spring 217 he defeated FLAMINIUS at Lake Trasimene, and in 216 overcame both consuls at CANNAE. The war did not continue in his favour, however; he was recalled to AFRICA in 203 with his ambitions unfulfilled, and was defeated in 202 by SCIPIO AFRICANUS at ZAMA.

Hannibal now turned his attentions to reforming the politics of CARTHAGE, reducing the power of the ÉLITE and arranging payment of the enormous indemnity imposed by the Romans. His political enemies complained to Rome, and he fled to ANTIOCHOS III of Syria. He urged Antiochos to go to war with Rome or give him an army, and tried to involve PHILIP V of Macedonia; but in 190 he was defeated at sea by the Rhodians, and his surrender was part of the peace deal struck between Rome and Antiochos.

He fled again to CRETE, then to Bithynia; in 183 or 182 king Prousias I of Bithynia was persuaded by Titus Quinctius FLAMININUS to give Hannibal up, and the great general anticipated his fate by taking poison. (see also HANNIBALIC WARS) CJS
See Cornelius Nepos, *Life of Hannibal*.

Hannibalic wars The Roman accounts of the causes of the second PUNIC WAR revolve around the SIEGE and capture by Hannibal of the town of SAGUNTUM, a Roman ally in Spain, in 219. POLYBIOS, however, looks back further to the Roman invasion of SARDINIA, at one time under Carthaginian influence. Whether or not Hannibal expected the capture of Saguntum to be taken by the Romans as a *casus belli* is less clear than his determination to anticipate retaliation. He did this by invading Italy in 218, via the ALPS, with a force of 50,000 infantry, 9,000 CAVALRY and 37 ELEPHANTS. During the crossing his force was reduced considerably through bad weather and skirmishes with the local tribes. He arrived in October 218.

The war began magnificently. In May 217 Hannibal was ravaging widely in ETRURIA, and he caught the consul FLAMINIUS in an ambush at Lake Trasimene; Roman casualties numbered 15,000. By 216 he was south of Rome in Campania and Apulia, and Quintus Fabius Cunctator had begun his careful policy of avoiding battle; but at CANNAE in Apulia both CONSULS (Gaius Terentius Varro and Lucius Aemilius Paullus) joined forces and were defeated by Hannibal, losing tens of thousands of men in a day of unremitting bloodshed. Of the prisoners who were spared, all the Italians were sent home; the Romans were kept.

This is the key to Hannibal's strategy: he hoped, by winning over the Italians, to leave Rome isolated and defenceless. Cannae brought him the support of southern Italy, but the Latins and the peoples of central Italy stayed loyal to the Romans, who successfully avoided another pitched battle for three years. Now Hannibal's major problems were the lack of support from CARTHAGE, where his political enemies vetoed the sending of further supplies, and his growing unpopularity in southern Italy because of his onerous demands for men and money. The Romans gradually recovered one city after another. In 212 they besieged CAPUA, and in the following year Hannibal tried to help by advancing on the walls of Rome itself, but the tactic was unsuccessful; Capua fell to Rome, and he was forced further south.

Meanwhile, the Romans were making progress in SICILY (thus depriving Hannibal of his contact with Carthage) and in Spain under Publius SCIPIO AFRICANUS. Hannibal's brother Hasdrubal tried to bring in reinforcements, but was defeated and killed in 207. Hannibal was now confined to Bruttium, and was further constrained when Scipio captured Lokroi Epizephyrioi in 205. Hannibal was finally recalled in 203 to defend Carthage as Scipio's forces came closer to the city; peace negotiations failed, and he was defeated in 202 at ZAMA.

The immediate consequence of the war was the devastation of Rome's only rival in the western MEDITERRANEAN; a huge indemnity was imposed by the Romans. In addition, Hannibal's attempt to involve PHILIP V of Macedonia in order to cause Rome problems on two fronts, though it had come to nothing, drew Rome further into the Greek world. Finally, the price of Roman victory for the allies of Rome that had backed Carthage was to see their lands confiscated and their status reduced, as Rome's predominance was further confirmed. CJS
See Lazenby, J. (1978) *Hannibal's War*.

 CARTHAGE AND CARTHAGINIANS: (a); WAR (table).

harbours The development of navigation in the eastern Mediterranean in the later 2nd millennium BC brought the need for manmade harbour facilities. The earliest securely dated examples are the riverside quays of Mesopotamia and Egypt, but some remains on the Levantine coast and in the Aegean are probably of this period.

After long disruption, maritime TRADE – the principal means of long-distance trade in antiquity – revived sufficiently to require harbour facilities in the 8th century BC. This was certainly the case in the LEVANT and probably in the Greek world, where the earliest major works are the mole and shipsheds of SAMOS, built by Polykrates c.530 BC. By then the development of fleets of warships also required bases and facilities. Other important harbours were those of CORINTH, soon ATHENS and later RHODES, the last refounded (408) at the best natural harbour on the island. In the classical period, most harbours exploited natural features such as bays and headlands (often providing a double harbour), with breakwaters providing extra protection; quays and FORTIFICATION walls were of ashlar masonry. In larger ports, military and commercial harbours were distinct wherever possible; but smaller cities had only simple facilities throughout antiquity. Ancient harbours were generally shallow compared with modern.

In the hellenistic period, increases in trade and in the size of ships required more large facilities (e.g. ALEXANDRIA, which introduced the monumental LIGHTHOUSE). From early Roman times, the exploitation of CONCRETE, which would set under water, enabled the construction of major harbour works not dependent on natural features, e.g. CAESAREA IN JUDAEA (Herod the Great, 20 BC) and Portus. The PHOENICIANS had met the challenge of inhospitable

HARBOURS: coin commemorating the construction of Rome's new harbour at Portus.

coasts by building harbour basins behind the shoreline, connected to the sea by a short canal, as at CARTHAGE. The Corinthians perhaps imitated this form (known at Carthage as the *kôthôn*) at their west port, Lechaion. Influence was probably two-way: at Carthage the shipsheds have Greek and Punic features. Rome lacked a good natural harbour, and in the Republican period depended for corn imports on the harbour of PUTEOLI, extended by Augustus. The ports at the mouth of the TIBER (OSTIA AND PORTUS) were built under Claudius and Trajan; goods were then shipped upriver on lighters. Roman emperors supported harbour construction and development in Italy and the provinces, notably Asia Minor, North Africa and the RHINE and DANUBE waterways. Their ventures were celebrated in coinage and inscriptions. The Roman fleet had its own bases, principally at Misenum and RAVENNA.

In classical times, Greek military harbours were normally within the city fortifications; their entrances, virtually city gates, were narrow and defended by towers and booms or chains. Some major inland cities were joined to their ports by long walls, notably Athens, Corinth and Megara. Silting was often a major problem, e.g. at EPHESOS; to deal with it, channels were set in breakwaters. In the Roman period we find arched breakwaters (e.g. Puteoli) and complex flushing channels (e.g. COSA).

The harbours of Athens and Rome were crucial for imports of grain; others served mainly export or transit trade. They were an important source of revenue from harbourage fees, from customs duties, and from the high level of economic activity and employment. This is well attested for PIRAEUS, and for Rhodes before Rome declared Delos a free port in 167 BC. Such ports had large numbers of foreign residents and visiting traders, leading to the establishment of foreign cults. Facilities would have included not only repair yards, workshops, warehouses and skilled workmen, but also inns and brothels. Plato saw the trading and financial activities of a port as dangerous for a city; Aristotle favoured a link with the sea. Many orators saw harbour and dockyard construction as important achievements for a state or ruler. DJB

See Blackman, D.J. (1982) Ancient harbours in the Mediterranean, *International Journal of Nautical Archaeology* 11: 79–104, 185–211; Shaw, J.W. (1972) Greek and Roman harbour works, in G. F. Bass, ed., *A History of Seafaring* 87–112.

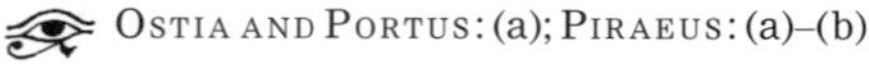
OSTIA AND PORTUS: (a); PIRAEUS: (a)–(b).

Hatra An independent ARAB city in MESOPOTAMIA, at the limits of Roman and PERSIAN political control. Hatra lay beside perennial springs in an otherwise arid part of Mesopotamia, some 50 km (30 miles) west of the Tigris. Inhabited by a population with an Aramaic-based culture, the city flourished from the 1st century AD to its destruction by the SASSANIANS c.240. CASSIUS DIO (76.12.2) records its wealth, doubtless derived from exploitation of caravan traffic stopping for water on the route between the Tigris and the cities of northern Mesopotamia. Hatra was besieged unsuccessfully by TRAJAN (117) and SEPTIMIUS SEVERUS (twice in 199–200). However, three Latin inscriptions imply the presence of a Roman garrison between c.235 and c.240, perhaps the result of an alliance caused by a common anxiety about growing Sassanian power, rather than of a final successful (but unrecorded) Roman reduction of the city.

The site has not been reoccupied since the Sassanian sack, and the topography is clearly visible in aerial photographs. Some 400 ha (1,000 acres) of dense urban occupation was contained within roughly circular walls. The winding streets seem to have developed organically rather than as the result of planning. A large rectangular walled area occupies the centre of the city, containing a number of sanctuaries including that of Hatra's sun god. ARCHITECTURE and ART at Hatra display strong influences from both the PARTHIAN empire and Roman SYRIA. NDP

See Kennedy, D. and Riley, D. (1990) *Rome's Desert Frontier from the Air*.

 SYRIA, ROMAN: (b).

hazard see BANDITRY; POISONS.

health Throughout antiquity, health or lack of health could be attributed to non-rational forces such as the supernatural. Amulets, charms and potions seem to have been used in abundance as one means of sustaining health. There was also a variety of popular healing shrines (and associated GODS) in Greece and Rome. The writings from the 5th century BC and later which survive as the HIPPOCRATIC CORPUS present a different picture. Their considerations of dietetics, which according to the Roman medical writer Celsus was one of three main branches of MEDICINE along with surgery and pharmacology, provide the beginnings of the day-to-day regulation of health. The maintenance of health required close co-operation between doctor and patient, avoidance on the patient's part of dangerous activities (e.g. excessive drinking) and careful observation on the doctor's part of the sorts of things liable to impact on patient health. These empirical Hippocratic ideas, despite the inevitable influence of theory (such as that relating to the humours) and of preconceived notions (such as 'opposites cure opposites'), remained of considerable significance for medical practice throughout antiquity. PGT

See Edelstein, L. (1967) *Ancient Medicine*; Lonie, I.M. (1977) *Medical History* 235–60.

heating Artificial heat for HOUSES (not only for cooking) is a primary need of any society – even in the Mediterranean, where part of each winter is always cold. Sources of heat were often portable, so living-rooms and kitchens did not necessarily have permanent fireplaces. (Sometimes the assumption that they did causes archaeologists to misinterpret floor-plans.) Early Greek cauldrons on tripod stands were designed to be placed over a fire, but most preserved examples come from sanctuaries and were designed as offerings rather than for use. More commonly, ceramic vessels such as braziers and chafing-dishes were filled with burning charcoal and used to warm rooms or prepare warm food and drink in KITCHENS and DINING ROOMS. Homer describes how Penelope's maids rake out the braziers onto the floor and pile them with new wood to give light and heat

(*Odyssey* 19.63–4). Heated water for bathing was something a hero could take for granted (*Odyssey* 8.249), and by the classical period there were hot as well as cold BATHS in Greek cities and sanctuaries. The Roman hypocaust, popularly taken today as a marker of Roman culture, required huge quantities of fuel as well as SLAVE labour. Hypocausts were therefore constructed mainly in rich houses, public BATHS, and GRANARIES. Even in houses with a hypocaust, some rooms were designed to be warmed by the sun (Pliny the Younger, *Letters* 2.17). DGJS

See Forbes, R. J. (1964–72) *Studies in Ancient Technology* 6. 1–100; Humphrey, J.W. et al. (1997) *Greek and Roman Technology: a sourcebook.*

Hecate see HEKATE.

Hector see HEKTOR.

Hekataios of Miletos see APOLLODOROS THE MYTHOGRAPHER; CELTS; GEOGRAPHY, ANCIENT; PROSE.

Hekate see FIRE; MOTHER GODDESSES.

Hektor TROJAN hero, Priam and Hekabe's eldest son, ANDROMACHE's husband. He is prominent in HOMER's *Iliad* and EURIPIDES' *Rhesus*, and his ghost looms in VIRGIL's *Aeneid* 2, but otherwise Hektor appears infrequently in ancient literature. In VASE-PAINTINGS and frescoes he is a fierce warrior (against AJAX, Menelaos, Patroklos and ACHILLES), a beloved husband and son (numerous portraits of his 'Farewell to Andromache', inspired by *Iliad* 6, and of the 'Mourning for Hektor'), or a corpse (in scenes where Achilles drags Hektor's body around the walls of TROY, and Priam subsequently ransoms it).

Hektor is unlike his playboy brother Paris, whom he upbraids in *Iliad* 3 and 6. His courage is most like that of Achilles; when Hektor slaughters Patroklos (*Iliad* 16) and dons the armour (of Achilles) that he has stripped from the corpse, he becomes a double for his chief enemy. But Hektor is finally no match for Achilles' inhuman rage. Their showdown, and Hektor's fateful death, occurs in *Iliad* 22. Though Achilles dishonours Hektor's corpse, Priam secures its return to Troy, and Hektor's funeral brings the *Iliad* to a close. So closely is Hektor identified with Troy that Homer's description of the flames of his pyre rising above Troy's walls is sufficient to indicate the city's doom.

Hektor is notable among heroes of Greek mythology for his devotion to his family and his general humaneness, all the more remarkable because he is not Greek but a foreigner. His concern for his wife and their infant son Astyanax, and his final terror before an unbeatable enemy, intimately link Hektor not only to the other players in the Trojan story but also to Homer's readership. JRH

See Garland, R. (1988) *The Greek Way of Death*; Touchefeu-Meynier, O. (1990) L'Humiliation d'Hector, *Métis* 5: 157–168; Touchefeu, O. and Karuskopf, I. (1988) Hector, in *LIMC* vol. 4, 482–98.

Helen of Troy Daughter of ZEUS and Leda or, according to another version, of Tyndareôs. She was famed for her godlike beauty, a feature inextricably connected with her fate and conduct in myth. She married Menelaos, the SPARTAN prince and brother of AGAMEMNON, and bore him a daughter, Hermione. Her marriage, however, was not long-lasting. She was seduced and abducted by the Trojan prince Paris when he visited Menelaos' palace at Sparta. Having acted under the guidance of APHRODITE, Paris married Helen as soon as they reached Trojan soil. The abduction of his wife triggered Menelaos' wrath, and he determined to restore his own and his family's pride by convincing his brother Agamemnon to take military action against the Trojan offenders. Thus, in myth, the Trojan war began as a joint expedition with other Greek forces to besiege the city of Ilion, with the aim of bringing Helen back to her homeland.

The playwright EURIPIDES allows the Trojan queen, Hekabe, to expose Helen's misconduct in his *Trojan Women*. The play contrasts Helen with Hektor's virtuous wife, ANDROMACHE. Yet Euripides' later *Helen* exonerates Helen by claiming that only her image went to Troy, while the real heroine waited out the war in Egypt with her virtue intact until she was rescued by Menelaos. EP

See Cladder, L. L. (1976) *Helen*; Kahil, L. (1988) Hélène, in *LIMC* vol. 4, 498–563.

Helena c.AD 250–c.327 Mother of CONSTANTINE, born at Drepanum in Bithynia of obscure origins. She became wife (concubine?) of Constantius Chlorus and gave birth to Constantine, but disappeared into the background when Constantius contracted a dynastic marriage with Theodora, stepdaughter of MAXIMIAN (293). Helena reappears as AUGUSTA c.324, together with Fausta, Constantine's wife. Her image as Augusta, wearing the diadem, appeared on coins with the legend *securitas reipublicae* ('safety of the republic') on the obverse. She was rumoured to be involved in the downfall of Fausta and Crispus, perhaps the reason behind her pilgrimage to JERUSALEM in 326. With Constantine she was responsible for founding and endowing the church of the Nativity in Bethlehem and the church on the Mount of Olives in Jerusalem. Also in association with her son, she founded the cemetery church of Saints Marcellinus and Peter in Rome. Some time after her return from Jerusalem, she constructed a large chapel in the Sessorian palace that, at some later date, became known as Santa Croce in Gerusalemme, reflecting the belief that she brought to it a relic of the True Cross. The legend that associates Helena with the discovery of the True Cross was current by the late 4th century (AMBROSE, *On the Death of Theodosius* 41–8), but the cult of Helena did not develop until the 8th century. MEH

See Eusebius, *Life of Constantine*, trs. with commentary, A. Cameron and S. Hall (1999); Brubaker, L. (1997) Memories of Helena, in E. James, ed., *Women, Men and Eunuchs: gender in Byzantium* 52–75; Drijvers, J.W. (1992) *Helena Augusta*.

 TETRARCHS: (b).

Heliogabalus see ELAGABALUS.

Helios see RHODES; SUN.

Hellanikos of Lesbos see EPHOROS; PELASGIANS; PROSE.

Hellas see GREECE.

Hellespont and Propontis (mod. Dardanelles) The narrow strait leading from the AEGEAN into the Sea of Marmara, divider of Europe and Asia. It was most famously crossed by XERXES and then by ALEXANDER the Great. FISHING was the staple activity of the cities on both shores. The name is connected with the myth of the Argonauts through Helle, who drowned after falling from the Ram with the Golden Fleece as it flew over the strait (*Hellês pontos* = Helle's sea).

The Propontis (Sea of Marmara) lies between the Hellespont and the Bosporos. Its maximum length is c.225 km (140 miles), its breadth c.64 km (40 miles). Although there is still discussion about whether the Greeks were able to pass through it before the 8th century BC, it seems that they could (as demonstrated by Tim Severin's expedition in 1984). Closer to the Asian side are several islands (the largest is Marmara), which provide excellent storm shelter. In the 7th century the peninsula of Kyzikos was probably an island as well. MEGARIAN colonies were established in the 7th century at Chalkedon (or Kalchedon), Astakos, Selymbria and Byzantion. The first three, founded before the fourth, enjoyed good HARBOURS, COPPER MINES and AGRICULTURAL hinterlands. Byzantion lacked an agricultural territory but was famous for its fisheries. The establishment of Propontine colonies before the Ionians colonized the BLACK SEA indicates that Byzantion and Chalkedon were the first step towards Pontic colonization. Kyzikos was known for its electrum COINAGE, which played an important part in international trade. After the city was incorporated in the Athenian maritime empire, its coins came to be used for this purpose by Athens. (see also BOSPORAN KINGDOM; CONSTANTINOPLE) GRT

See Boardman, J. (1999) *The Greeks Overseas*; Severin, T. (1985) *The Jason Voyage*; Tsetskhladze, G. R. and De Angelis, F., eds. (1994) *The Archaeology of Greek Colonization*.

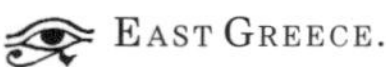 EAST GREECE.

helots (*heilôtai*) State serfs in the territory of ancient SPARTA. Their name may derive from the place-name Helos in southern LACONIA, or from the Greek verb *helein*, 'to capture'. The Spartans apparently believed that helots were the pre-existing inhabitants of the southern PELOPONNESE whom they, perhaps along with the other Lakedaimonians (who became the *perioikoi*, 'circumhabitants', of Sparta), had enslaved after invading the peninsula. Alternatively, helot status was created, or defined, after the Spartan conquest of MESSENIA, traditionally dated to the 8th century BC, or the suppression of a Messenian revolt in the mid-7th. THUCYDIDES says most helots were Messenian by ancestry and therefore they were all called Messenians, but this may obscure a process of identity-building that was going on throughout the 5th century.

Ancient writers recognized that helots were not harshly oppressed and had certain rights or expectations, unlike chattel SLAVES who could be sold. The most important statement to this effect, that they were 'between free people and slaves', is preserved in the 2nd-century AD lexicon of POLLUX but probably has an earlier origin. Their economic position was probably similar to that of share-croppers giving up a fixed proportion of their crops to individual Spartans, but they probably had a social structure akin to those of free communities, reproducing their families from generation to generation and inheriting (the use of) the same parcels of land. We know little, however, of the organization of their territory or the degree to which day-to-day control was exercised over them. They could not organize themselves into city-states, unlike the free *perioikoi*, who may even have exercised the function of control over helots in outlying areas. It remains to be proved whether the multi-roomed classical building excavated at Kopanáki in Messenia is a helot 'barracks'.

Helots may have internalized the values of their masters. Those in Laconia may not have shared the culture of the Messenian majority. They made up the bulk of the Lakedaimonian army, though not usually as heavy-armed soldiers. The threat of coercion was ever-present, manifested for example in annual declarations of war against them and (probably sporadic) lynchings by the Sparta *krypteia* or 'secrecy', participation in which may have been a rite of passage for Spartan SOLDIERS. When the army was on campaign, helots' families at home were effectively hostages for their menfolk's good behaviour.

Despite these obstacles, helots retained a common culture, unlike chattel slaves. This may explain why they periodically organized revolts against Sparta. The most famous of these (c.465 BC) lasted ten years and centred on their sacred mountain of Ithome. After the two-stage liberation of Messenia in the 4th century, most helots became free Messenians in a federal league whose capital city was Ithome, soon renamed Messene. In Laconia, however, the helot system lasted until the 2nd century BC. (see also REVOLUTION) DGJS

See Ducat, J. (1990) *Les Hilotes*; Luraghi, N. and Alcock, S. E., eds. (2003) *Helots and their Masters in Laconia and Messenia*.

Hephaistos (Hephaestus) see ATHENA; DIONYSOS; FIRE; GODS AND GODDESSES, GREEK; RELIGION, GREEK; TOOLS.

Hera The sister and wife of ZEUS and therefore the most powerful of the GODDESSES. Her realm is that of the good MARRIAGE, virtuous womanhood and childbirth. This last function she shares with her daughter Eileithuia. She represents the faithful wife, despite the many amorous escapades of her husband, to which she always reacts with profound jealousy and vindictiveness. The mythological tradition holds that she at first rejected a marriage to Zeus. When he transformed himself into a cuckoo, she took him into her lap, thus consummating the sexual union. Traditionally, their wedding night, spent in SAMOS, lasted for 300 years. Thereafter, Hera renewed her virginity annually by bathing in the springs of the Kanathos in ARGOS. Because of connections with her wedding and renewal of virginity, she was especially worshipped in ARGOS and Samos. The cow is regularly associated with the goddess, who is frequently called 'cow-eyed', and the usual SACRIFICES in her honour were white cows. The epithet most likely stems from a period when gods were not completely anthropomorphic, for it appears as well in Zeus's ability to transform himself and Hera's power to change her rivals into ANIMALS.

During the TROJAN WAR, Hera favoured the Greeks since she had been deeply offended by Paris' judgement in favour of APHRODITE. She demonstrates not only her insatiable hatred towards the Trojans but also her cunning, employing sex to distract Zeus from watching the battle. RBC

See Burkert, W. (1985) *Greek Religion*; Kossate-Diessmann, A. (1988) Hera, in *LIMC* vol. 4, 659–723.

 GODS AND GODDESSES: (a).

Heracles see HERAKLES.

Herakleitos fl. c.500 BC PRESOCRATIC PHILOSOPHER from EPHESOS in Asia Minor. His work survives in fragmentary form – around 125 short gnomic and oracular utterances preserved in later writers. Like other Milesian philosophers, he sought to give an account of the nature of the universe, and he shares with them the concern to describe a natural COSMOLOGY (his cosmology was later a profound influence on STOICISM). However, his version of monism, encapsulated in the famous dictum 'all things are one', also embraces a more general vision of a unity underlying all apparent duality and contradiction. For example, he asserts that night and day, life and death 'are one'. He also sees unity in constant processes of change and flux, emphasizing the latter in his equally famous assertion that 'it is impossible to step into the same river twice'.

The important notion of *logos* appears in a number of the fragments. It is a difficult word to translate (its meanings range from 'reason' to 'account' and even 'ratio'). Herakleitos distinguishes his own words from this *logos*, which instead appears to be both the source of the information that 'all is one' and also the cause and principle of this unity. By matching their reason with this principle, humans can achieve understanding. Both the riddling form and the explicit content of the fragments contrast the wisdom Herakleitos wishes to inspire and the polymathy of traditional sources of teaching such as HOMER and HESIOD. JIW

See Kahn, C. H. (1979) *The Art and Thought of Heraclitus*.

Herakles (Heracles) The most popular figure in Greek MYTH, legend and folklore, equated with the Romans' HERCULES. Herakles' status as HERO meant that he received invocations and SACRIFICES. It has long been debated whether he was based on an actual historical (Mycenaean?) leader, but the evidence suggests a figure who accumulated the traits of many mythological and historical characters. Born in THEBES of the union of ZEUS with a mortal woman, Alkmene, he became famous for his great achievements, both military and civilizing. He eventually went beyond the status of hero, being accepted into the pantheon on OLYMPOS for the help he gave the GODS against the GIANTS. PINDAR (*Nemean Odes* 3.22) called him a 'hero god' (*hêrôs theos*).

His career, from strangling snakes as a precocious baby in Thebes to painful death on Mt Oita, apotheosis, and marriage to Hebe, encompasses a variety of adventures. The most significant are his Labours (e.g. the Nemean lion, the Augean stables), eventually 12 in number, carried out in service to the lord of MYCENAE, Eurystheus. There are also incidental adventures and exploits that he carried out with others (e.g. the Argonauts). Herakles' lion-skin, his fights with monsters and his descent to the underworld (for Kerberos and for Alkestis) recall the MESOPOTAMIAN mythological figure Gilgamesh, who also wore skins, attacked giants and monsters, and was concerned with death.

Greed, anger, pride and lust were Herakles' failings. He is painted as antisocial, destructive and sacrilegious: he rustles CATTLE, murders Iphitos, kills his own children, steals APOLLO's tripod, and raises weapons against the gods. But he is also a benefactor of mankind, freeing them from natural and divinely motivated disasters ('clearing the jungle'). He is shown as lecherous and fond of food and drink, but is a 'culture-hero' in establishing the OLYMPIC GAMES, hot springs and healing shrines. He was champion of the Dorian Greeks and was used as a symbolic figure by cities and rulers (notably at SPARTA, where the kings and others claimed descent from Herakles).

In ART he is shown successively as an archer and a club-wielder, wearing the lion-skin won in his first labour – in both guises marked as an outsider, not a regular soldier. His exploits were the most popular in all forms of art, the best-known SCULPTURES being the metopes of the temple of Zeus at OLYMPIA. BAS

See Burkert, W. (1985) *Greek Religion*; Boardman, J. et al. (1988–90) Herakles, in *LIMC* vol. 4, 728–838 and vol. 5, 1–262.

heralds (Greek *kêrykes*) Heralds are first attested in the HOMERIC poems, where they serve the KINGS in discharging their public duties: maintaining order in ASSEMBLIES, making formal announcements and proclamations, and conveying messages. This last function seems to have been central to the figure, for heralds were under the protection of HERMES, who serves as divine herald in MYTH. Hermes was conceptually associated with borders, both establishing them – he is the Olympian projection of the boundary marker – and transgressing them. The herald moves freely between opposing sides during times of WAR and between independent states during peacetime. In DEMOCRATIC Athens of the classical period, heralds retained much of their ceremonial function and served in an official capacity at meetings of public bodies including the council, assembly, law-courts and board of generals, as well as serving the archons. Their chief function was to make public announcements, so it is not surprising that suitability for the position was determined by quality of voice. A focal point for the activity of the herald was the herald's stone in the AGORA, which seems to have served as a kind of podium for public proclamations. It was here that SOLON adopted the role of herald to deliver his poem on SALAMIS.

In Roman society the herald (*praeco*) seems to have played a role similar to the Greek *kêryx*, but seems to have had lower status. Also comparable were the high-ranking officials known as the *apparitores*, who attended MAGISTRATES in various official functions. CGB

Herculaneum City on the bay of Naples, destroyed during the eruption of Mt Vesuvius in AD 79. The site was discovered in 1709 by a workman who was

HERCULANEUM: general view towards Vesuvius, over the terraced sea-front villas of the ancient town.

digging a well. The city was explored through a series of innovative tunnelling techniques pioneered by the Swiss military engineer Karl Weber on behalf of the Bourbon kings of Naples. The buildings were mapped in plan, including the VILLA of the Papyri. The purpose of these early EXCAVATIONS was to fill the Royal Museum in Naples and create a major destination for aristocratic tourists; the finds from Herculaneum continue to astound visitors and include numerous bronze and MARBLE statues. However, after the discovery of Pompeii, Herculaneum was found to be hard to excavate and the suburbs of Naples expanded over the site itself in the late 19th and early 20th centuries. The site was opened up by area excavation from 1927, to reveal what we see today: HOUSES preserved to their first floor, a seat of the Augustales (priests of the IMPERIAL CULT), streets, BATHS, water-FOUNTAINS, a PALAESTRA and the THEATRE (the last still underground).

The preservation of Herculaneum is rather different from that of Pompeii, the city having been largely destroyed by a pyroclastic surge in the early part of the eruption sequences. The surge, moving rapidly at high temperature, carbonized wood and left it preserved for study at a later date. Significantly, one of the unique features from Herculaneum is our knowledge of wooden furniture, including BEDS, tables and *lararia*. The houses demonstrate the overall raising of the level of habitation, so that houses close to the walls could benefit from sea breezes and a maritime outlook.

The site is famous for its preserved PAPYRI, notably the texts of PHILODEMOS found at the Villa of the Papyri, and also a cache of documents in the town itself relating to the status of a woman known as Petronia Iusta. The latter sheds light on a legal case held in the FORUM of AUGUSTUS in Rome, and demonstrates the role of oral testimony by owners, SLAVES and ex-slaves of one HOUSEHOLD, as well as clarifying issues about the nature of slavery and freedom.

In the early 1980s, a group of 139 skeletons was found near the ancient sea-shore. All of these people died in the eruption of Vesuvius and the find demonstrated for the first time that the population was not evacuated prior to the town's destruction. For the study of ancient MEDICINE and social history, this is one of the most important finds from antiquity – for the reason that cultures which cremated bodies seldom provide archaeologists with skeletal remains. Study of the skeletons has revealed that, compared with the modern population of the USA, the people of Herculaneum were shorter in height, had better teeth and probably had a better diet, as well as experiencing similar incidences of spina bifida and other hereditary diseases.

Recently, the Villa of the Papyri has been partially cleared and conserved of volcanic materials, but the techniques used have been criticized in the media and are a subject of controversy. RL

See Deiss, J. J. D. (1968) *Herculaneum*; Mols, S. T. A. M. (1999) *Wooden Furniture in Herculaneum*; Pagano, M., ed. (2000) *Gli antichi Ercolanesi*; Parslow, C. C. (1995) *Rediscovering Antiquity: Karl Weber and the excavation of Herculaneum*; Wallace-Hadrill, A. (1994) *Houses and Society in Pompeii and Herculaneum*.

 MARKETS; WALL-PAINTING: (c).

Hercules In Roman culture, Hercules (known to the pre-Roman and ETRUSCAN peoples of Italy as Hercle) was both the strongman HERO of the Greeks and a divinity. Cults and TEMPLES dedicated to him existed in the city of Rome as early as the 4th century BC, coins represent him from the 3rd century BC onwards, and by the 2nd century, with the Roman conquest of Greece, a number of new temples, especially to Hercules Victor, were built.

Romans knew the stories of Hercules from Greek literature, and from plays such as PLAUTUS' *Amphitryo* and the *Hercules Furens* and *Hercules Oetaeus* of SENECA. OVID (*Metamorphoses* 9 and *Heroides* 9) and DIODORUS SICULUS (4.7–39) tell some of the god's stories, and myths appear as well in the *Bibliotheca* of APOLLODOROS THE MYTHOGRAPHER (2.61–166) and the *Fabulae* of Hyginus, demonstrating the enduring interest in Hercules. An example of his wide geographical dispersion can be seen in his combination in Spain and North Africa, during the Republic, with the Punic god Melkart as one of HANNIBAL's symbols. During the imperial period he was a favourite on religious monuments in GAUL and GERMANY.

The Romans of the later Republic and early empire emphasized certain elements drawn from Greek precedents when they represented Hercules: the assimilation of the ruler to the god, and the STOIC notion of the hero's struggle with his own failings. In the former category, one finds both a positive and a negative use of Hercules when MARK ANTONY takes on the god's imagery to convey his own strength and virtue and then AUGUSTUS and the writers associated with him turn this imagery against Antony. They do so by focusing on Antony's excess and lack of self-control, as well as his love for CLEOPATRA.

By the mid-2nd century AD, EMPERORS regularly associated themselves with Hercules on coins and in portraiture. The god signified victory and patronage of the army, and also represented the Stoic virtuous ruler. The most famous image is the bust of the emperor Commodus as Hercules, a lion-skin on his head and a club in his hand (Museo Conservatori, Rome). In this period, private individuals were combining famous Greek Hercules statue types with portrait heads to represent their own personal virtues on funerary statues and reliefs. Hercules appears often on sarcophagi in the 2nd and 3rd centuries; his strength and virtue, as well as his ability to return from the underworld unscathed, may have motivated this use. NBK

See Boardman, J. et al. (1988–90) Herakles, in *LIMC* vol. 4, 728–838 and vol. 5, 1–262; Brommer, F. (1986) *Labors of the Hero in Ancient Art and Literature*; Jongst, P. F. B. (1992) *The Twelve Labours of Hercules on Roman Sarcophagi*.

 Alexander III: (a).

heresy see Arianism; Athanasius; Augustine (1); Christianity; church councils; Eusebios; Manichaeism; schism; Tertullian.

heritage, classical Following the collapse of the Roman empire and the era generally termed the 'Dark Ages', the cultural, scientific and socio-political structures and achievements of the classical world began to resurface, chiefly in centres of learning such as monasteries and royal courts. By the Renaissance, scholars and artists were modelling themselves and their works on Greco-Roman precedents, a trend which continued into the 18th century (the 'Age of Enlightenment') and the 19th century, and is still keenly felt today in many areas of socio-cultural life. The influence of our Greek and Roman heritage has been reflected in the classically inspired architecture of many public buildings, houses and streets throughout the world. Buildings like the White House in Washington, DC, not only represent the classical architectural ideal but embody the concept of democracy, the system of government most closely linked (in the popular mind) with ancient Greece. However, other buildings using classical inspirations, such as the sports stadium at Nuremberg designed by Albert Speer, have been used to propagate different philosophies, such as fascism. Painters and sculptors, such as Flaxman, David, Ingres, Alma-Tadema and Canova, have long admired classical aesthetic ideals and incorporated them into their art works. Likewise, composers, especially of opera, and playwrights have drawn on the heritage of classical myth and literature to create dramas that have appealed to, and moved, contemporary audiences. Even modern popular culture draws upon the classical heritage in the shape of historic fiction, comic strips and films. LL-J

See Taplin, O. (1989) *Greek Fire*.

hermeneutics see Hermes.

Hermes Greek divinity, son of Zeus and Maia (the daughter of Atlas). Hermes' activities are associated with movement, mediation and exchange: he is messenger of the gods, protector of travellers (but also of highway robbers), guide of souls (*psychopompos*) into Hades, patron of trade – a mercantile function reflected in his Roman name Mercury – and god of interpretation. In that last capacity, he has given his name to the art of hermeneutics. In the Roman period, by assimilation with the Egyptian god Thoth, Hermes Trismegistos ('Thrice-greatest') was believed to be the revealer of a body of mystical, philosophical and magical writings thereafter known as *Hermetica*. But Hermes may deceive as well as instruct; he is akin to the trickster god found in other mythologies.

Hermes' Arkadian birth, remote from Mt Olympos, and his precocious childhood are recorded in the longer of two *Homeric Hymns* dedicated to him (6th century BC). There he is revealed as the inventor of the lyre, but also as a consummate liar and thief (of Apollo's cattle). Prometheus-like, he established animal sacrifices and gave fire to humans, but rather than angering Zeus (as Prometheus did), he amused his father by his mischievous deceptions, and Zeus accordingly admitted him to the company of Olympians. His accoutrements include a wand (Greek *kêrykeion*, Latin *caduceus*), golden sandals (usually depicted as winged) and a traveller's hat (*petasos*). Also among his emblems are herms, which served as distance and boundary markers. JRH

See Bonnefoy, Y., ed. (1991) *Greek and Egyptian Mythologies*; Burkert, W. (1985) *Greek Religion*; Copenhaver, B. P. (1992) *Hermetica*; Fowden, G. (1986) *The Egyptian Hermes*; Gantz, T. (1993) *Early Greek Myth*.

 gods and goddesses: (b); herms.

hermits Literally, someone who lives in the desert. Greek *erêmos* means both 'desert, uncultivated land' and 'deserted', 'lonely'. Some Christians retreated (Greek *anachôrein*, hence 'anchorite') to the desert in order to escape from the distractions of everyday life; they may have learned survival techniques from Egyptians who 'went up-country' (also *anachôrein*) from the Nile valley to avoid tax collectors. The chief role model for Christian 'solitaries' (Greek *monachoi*, the origin of 'monks') was Antony of Egypt, whose *Life*, ascribed to bishop Athanasius of Alexandria, influenced many 4th-century ascetics. The *Life* dates Antony's retreat to c.250, but the actual date may be nearer c.313; Jerome wrote a *Life of Paul the First Hermit*, a predecessor whom Antony buried with the help of two lions. Jerome himself spent some time in the Syrian desert (early 370s), in a hermitage unusually well provided with books: later tradition gave him a lion of his own. During the 4th century the Egyptian desert was said to have become overcrowded with those in retreat from the world and the tourists who came to admire these Desert Fathers (and a handful of Desert Mothers), and the Egyptian model was exported to countries with wetter climates, where ascetics were encouraged to create their personal deserts of austerity. But experience showed that solitude exposed hermits to assaults of temptation and demonic fantasies, and that most of them needed the support of a structured monastic community. Antony himself, after years of solitary combat with demons, became an abbot. GC

herms An English form of the name of the god Hermes when used of a partly iconic, quadrilateral image (in Greek simply a *Hermês*). The earliest surviving examples and illustrations, all of Athenian origin and from the 6th and 5th centuries BC, show a rectangular shaft surmounted by the bearded head of

HERMS: pillars ornamented with the head of Hermes and erect penis were a common form of Greek boundary marker.

the god. There is an erect PHALLUS at the appropriate position on the shaft and rectangular tenons (for arms?) at shoulder height. This is the only common type of aniconic or semi-iconic image to survive the archaic period.

Herms were the object of cult; some also served as halfway markers on ROADS, an innovation attributed to Hipparchos, son of the tyrant PEISISTRATOS. (While the conventional herm was an Athenian creation, there were roadside images of Hermes elsewhere.) At the entrance of HOUSES they were protective symbols. The latter function, rather than a concern with fertility or SEXUALITY, probably accounts for the aggressive phallus. The mutilation of many of these doorway herms one night in 415 BC, on the eve of the departure of the Athenians' great expedition to SICILY, was regarded as a subversive act (Thucydides 6.27.1).

By the later 5th century the phallus is reduced to a flaccid and perfunctory penis. Later the heads of other gods and of mortal persons may replace that of Hermes himself. By hellenistic times this is a common form for representing famous individuals, sometimes paired back to back. MHJ

See Furley, W. D. (1996) *Andokides and the Herms: a study of crisis in fifth-century Athenian religion*; Parker, R. (1996) *Athenian Religion: a history*; Siebert, G. (1990) Hermes, in *LIMC* vol. 5, 285–387.

 PHALLUS.

Heron of Alexandria (Hero of Alexandria) Greek mathematician (second half of 1st century AD), known as *mêchanikos* ('The Mechanician'), who wrote a dozen works on measurement and the practical applications of MATHEMATICS. Some survive only in ARABIC translation, or excerpts by later Greek and Arabic authors. Those on mensuration deal with the measurement and division of surfaces and three-dimensional bodies. On the applied side, he wrote on compressed-air devices (in *Pneumatika*), automatons (or 'miracle' machines, *thaumata*, often used in sacred contexts), the moving of large weights, PRESSES, instruments for measuring angles (such as the *dioptra*) and distances (an odometer), water-clocks (in a lost work), and mirrors. A work often quoted today is *Belopoiïka* (*On Making Catapults*; there was also a book, preserved in fragments, on the *cheiroballistra*, another piece of ARTILLERY). Although he builds on the work of hellenistic and MESOPOTAMIAN predecessors, he is proof that Greek SCIENCE was often concerned with practical applications in the service of public amenity. DGJS

See Irby-Massie, G. L. and Keyser, P. T. (2002) *Greek Science of the Hellenistic Era*; Lloyd, G. E. R. (1973) *Greek Science after Aristotle*; Marsden, E.W. (1971) *Greek and Roman Artillery: technical treatises* (trs. of *Belopoiïka*, *Cheiroballistra*); Thomas, I., trs. (1941) *Greek Mathematical Works*, vol. 2.

hero cult In Greece, a *hêrôs* was a semi-divine being. According to HESIOD (*Works and Days* 156–73) there had been a race of HEROES (*hêrôes*), living between the races of bronze and iron; but in the 1st millennium BC real men could also be heroized by being recognized, after their death, to have been more than mortal. Founders of cities and great ATHLETES were particularly likely to be heroized, but ORACLES could also pronounce that even quite obscure men had been heroes. Heroes received cult honours somewhat like those due to the GODS, involving ANIMAL SACRIFICE and votive offerings, but with huge variations. Cult often took place at the supposed site of the hero's TOMB. Some of these were real tombs; many were not.

The earliest example of heroic BURIAL rites like those described in HOMER (cremated ashes in a metal urn, weapons, mound, sacrifices) comes from Lefkandí on the island of Euboia, c.1000–950 BC. In the late 8th century such burials became quite common, and people also started visiting MYCENAEAN tombs and leaving dedications. Heroic scenes multiplied on vases, and Homer probably dates to these years. The archaic and classical idea of the hero probably crystallized by 700, then remained stable till the 4th century. Tomb inscriptions show that after 400 BC more and more of the dead were labelled as heroes, and even some living people received hero cult, as the bonds of egalitarian male CITIZENSHIP loosened. IM

See Antonaccio, C. (1995) *An Archaeology of Ancestors* (1995); Kearns, E. (1987) *The Heroes of Attica*; Morris, I. (2000) *Archaeology as Cultural History*.

 ACHILLES.

Herod the Great (Greek *Hêrôdês*) c.74–4 BC The son of an Idumaean JEW and a Nabataean ARAB. His gradual rise to power in Judaea from the mid-40s BC owed something to the patronage of the Hasmonaean ruler Hyrkanos, whom his father Antipater had served for many years. It was mostly brought about, however, by Roman politicians who found him a useful ally during the CIVIL WARS down to the battle of ACTIUM. Herod was appointed king of Judaea in 40 by the SENATE in Rome on the advice of MARK ANTONY, and won control of his domain in 37 with the aid of Roman LEGIONS.

Herod was rarely popular with his Jewish subjects. He protected himself from opposition by residing in secure fortresses like MASADA and controlling the populace through spies and terror. After the defeat of

Antony at Actium in 31, Herod persuaded OCTAVIAN that he would be as loyal to him as he had been to his enemy. Their relationship remained close until Herod's death, apart from a temporary lapse in 9 BC caused by his unauthorized invasion of Nabataean territory.

Relations with neighbouring states were constantly difficult for Herod, despite his attempts to engender friendship by ostentatious generosity and by dynastic marriages with the families of other petty rulers. Within his court he relied a great deal on his extensive family, a policy that turned sour as a result of his own suspicions, which led him to kill many of his relatives, including his Hasmonaean wife Mariamme (in 29 BC) and some of his sons.

The account of Herod's rule, in the detailed narrative preserved by Josephus in the *Antiquities of the Jews*, was based primarily on the work of Nikolaos of Damascus, Herod's court HISTORIAN, who naturally provided a favourable gloss in his interpretation of his master's policies. Josephus himself was more sceptical, and evidently also used other sources. MDG

See Josephus, *Jewish Antiquities* 15–17.205; Jones, A. H. M. (1967) *The Herods of Judaea*.

Herodas Hellenistic mimographer (author of mimes). Little can be said about the life of Herodas (sometimes spelt Herondas). It is not known where he was born, or where he lived. Neither are his dates certain, though it seems likely from references in his poems that he was writing in the middle of the 3rd century BC and was an approximate contemporary of THEOKRITOS and KALLIMACHOS.

Herodas was a composer of *mimiamboi*, poems which comprise the content of mime and the language and metre of the archaic *iambos*. His works are largely preserved on a single PAPYRUS containing some 700 readable lines. Eight of his mimes are more or less complete, while there are fragments of several more. The scenes of the mimes are everyday, including a SHOP, a school and a TEMPLE. The characters are common people, including a shoemaker, a pimp and a schoolmaster; the situations are often bawdy. The focus is not on plot but on character, and it seems likely that they were intended for performance by a single actor, skilled in representing different character traits, though this has been disputed by some scholars.

In the past, it was maintained that Herodas was an 'ancient realist', but recent research suggests he should be seen as a typical hellenistic POET, in that his work combines elements of different GENRES to create an original literary effect. FMM

See Cunningham, I. C. (1971) *Herodas, Mimiambi*; Rusten, J. and Cunningham, I. C., trs. (2002) (with Theophrastos' *Characters*, etc.).

Herodes Atticus c.AD 101–77 A wealthy Athenian, Lucius Vibullius Hipparchus Tiberius Claudius Atticus Herodes was the most famous and highly regarded SOPHIST of his time. His style of ORATORY recalled earlier rhetors whose elegance and restraint were not influenced by the more florid 'Asianic' oratory that developed in the 2nd century BC. He taught many pupils, including the future emperors MARCUS AURELIUS and Lucius Verus, and was a friend of HADRIAN and ANTONINUS PIUS. AULUS GELLIUS provides a Latin translation of one work, but beyond that only one speech of questionable authenticity survives. His public career included membership of the SENATE at Rome and a CONSULSHIP in 143, the same year that Marcus Cornelius FRONTO, another teacher of Marcus Aurelius and Lucius Verus, was a suffect consul.

Although Herodes modified his father's WILL bequeathing a *MINA* annually to each Athenian citizen, he employed his wealth to fund buildings at Athens, like the rebuilt Panathenaic STADIUM (renovated and reused for modern Olympic games) and a THEATRE, and gave BENEFACTIONS elsewhere. He quarrelled with rivals and with his native city, where opponents of his policies accused him of tyranny. He prosecuted Tiberius Claudius Demostratus during the reign of Antoninus Pius, and was himself on trial before Marcus Aurelius at Sirmium c.173, replying to Demostratus' charges of misconduct at Athens. The emperor solved the dilemma of ruling against a friend and teacher by punishing Herodes' co-accused freedmen instead. JV

See Philostratos, *Lives of the Sophists*; Bowersock, G.W. (1969) *Greek Sophists in the Roman Empire*.

ATHENS: (b).

HERODES ATTICUS: view of theatre he donated to the city of Athens.

Herodian (Herodianus) Almost nothing is known about Herodian, the author of an eight-book *History of the Empire after the Death of Marcus*, running from AD 180 to the accession of GORDIAN III in 238. A reference to the honesty of tax collectors in the reign of MAXIMINUS THRAX may suggest a connection with the equestrian bureaucracy in the 230s, the only possible indication of his status. Otherwise, it appears that he spent some time in Rome – he was almost certainly there in 238 – and that he had no intimate contacts with the SENATE. Unlike his contemporary CASSIUS DIO, he has little interest in senatorial affairs, and his portraits of emperors suggest that he knew them only through their public pronouncements. He was probably a native of ASIA Minor.

The first book of Herodian's history covers the reign of COMMODUS, the second the aftermath of Commodus' assassination down to Severus' arrival at Rome. In the third, Herodian covers the period from midsummer 193 to the death of SEPTIMIUS SEVERUS in 211, while the fourth treats the years 211–17, ending with Macrinus' campaign against the PARTHIANS. Book 5 is concerned with the rise and reign of ELAGABALUS, book 6 with SEVERUS ALEXANDER, and books 7–8 with the reign of Maximinus and his overthrow in the civil war of 238. The history of the early period, especially of conspiracies under Commodus, is quite badly done; as he gets closer to the end of the history, Herodian becomes increasingly reliable. The account of the civil war of 238 reveals a historian of genuine talent. DSP

See Whittaker, C. R., trs. (1969–70) 2 vols.

Herodotos c.484–c.428 BC The first Greek HISTORIAN. We have no certain information about his life. He was almost certainly born in HALIKARNASSOS in Asia Minor, but his place of death is disputed. Possibly in his youth he spent several years in SAMOS; he appears to have travelled over a considerable part of the eastern Mediterranean, and to have spent time in the Greek colony of Thourioi (in southern Italy) and in ATHENS. What survives of him is a single large work, the *Histories*. It is the earliest preserved work of Greek PROSE, and was almost certainly the earliest work that could be called a history. It was also by far the longest single work to have been written at that time. He took as his subject the deeds of Greeks and non-Greeks, starting with the first contacts between the Greek cities of Asia and the Lydians in the 6th century, and ending with the Greek victories over Xerxes' Persian invasion of 480–479.

The main narrative starts by introducing Croesus, king of LYDIA, who conquers the Greek cities of mainland Asia Minor and forces them to pay tribute to him. He in his turn is defeated by CYRUS, king of PERSIA and founder of its empire (book 1). Cyrus is succeeded by his son Kambyses, who adds EGYPT to the empire (2), and on his death DARIUS becomes king. The story of Darius' military campaigns (3–4) follows, then the IONIAN REVOLT (5–6), when a number of cities attempt to throw off Persian rule. This leads in turn to Darius' campaign against Athens and the defeat of his force at MARATHON (6). The climax of the narrative comes with XERXES' attempt to conquer the whole of Greece ten years later (7–9).

This structure is made more elaborate with some large digressions, including in book 1 brief histories of Lydia and Media, and in book 2 a long history of Egypt. Quite probably a further section on Assyria is missing from near the end of book 1. In the course of the first six books, quite a lot of information about the history of Greece is carefully slipped in. Herodotos is particularly interested in buildings, and these often act in the *Histories* as indicators of the greatness of the community or individual that built them. The effect of these digressions is twofold: by bringing in the Greek material he prepares the reader gradually for the conflict in the last three books, and by describing the strength and antiquity of the nations defeated by the Persians he magnifies the Greek achievement in conquering them. An alternative view is to see these digressions as the real heart of the work, containing as they do accounts of the 'great and wonderful achievements of the Greeks and BARBARIANS' (promised in the preface to book 1), and the story of the conflict as being there to provide a structure for them.

Herodotos' TRAVELS allowed him to learn about his subject from a variety of perspectives. He seems to have had access, probably indirectly, to 'official' versions of history in Persia and Egypt, as well as what he learnt from religious sanctuaries in Greece, where the dedications of Greek states and barbarian rulers would provide the basis for stories about them. He mentions a number of Greeks who spent time at the Persian court, who may have been his sources for some material. He often names a community as the source of his information, e.g. 'the Corinthians say'; this serves not only to indicate the breadth of his contacts, but also to distance him from what he reports – he does not necessarily believe everything he writes (7.152). ORAL TRADITIONS about the past are inevitably flexible, and it was perhaps only when Herodotos came to construct his work that these stories gathered from all over Greece could be turned into a consistent account.

He was very much a part of the Ionian intellectual tradition, and some of his ideas are similar to those of the HIPPOCRATIC writers and the SOPHISTS. The *Histories* include descriptions of the GEOGRAPHY and ethnography of much of the then known world, stretching from the Maghreb to India and from Ethiopia to southern Russia. Some of this is based on observation, some on what he has been told, and some probably on extrapolation from what he knows. In places his understanding of the shape of the world is schematic, with the oldest peoples furthest south and the youngest furthest north, and with customs more and more unusual the further they are from the centre of the world, that is, Greece.

His work was immediately popular, gaining for Herodotos the title 'father of history' in antiquity, and he was enormously influential on succeeding historians. His immediate successor, THUCYDIDES, while criticizing some points of detail, began his history at the point where Herodotos ended his. Although there have been attempts in modern times to discredit part or all of his work, the *Histories* have withstood the critical onslaught. What Herodotos wrote is by no means all true, but it is a thoroughly researched and elegantly presented account of what the Greek world of the 5th century BC believed about its past. HB

See Herodotos, trs. A. de Sélincourt (1996); Bakker, E. J. et al., eds. (2002) *Brill's Companion to Herodotus*; Boedeker, D., ed. (1987) *Herodotus and the Invention of History* (= *Arethusa* vol. 20); Derow, P. and Parker, R., eds. (2003) *Herodotus and his World*; Gould, J. (1989) *Herodotus*; Lateiner, D. (1989) *The Historical Method of Herodotus*; Pritchett, W. K. (1993) *The Liar School of Herodotus*.

heroes A *hêrôs*, 'hero', in ancient Greek was a demigod, a mortal worshipped after death as a semi-divine being with supernatural powers. Founders of new cities were heroized, and in rare cases other outstanding individuals might be honoured in the same way. The term 'hero' was also applied to a legendary 'race' of the past. Just as modern Greek folklore has stories about a vanished race of GIANTS which left behind the impressive classical ruins still visible everywhere, so ancient Greeks believed that the TOMBS, walls, and other remains of what we call MYCENAEAN civilization belonged to a distant age in which 'heroes' walked the earth. These heroes of legend, too, were regarded as demigods (HOMER, *Iliad* 12.23; HESIOD, *Works and Days* 160), and many received worship (HERO CULT) at grave-sites or hero shrines.

Throughout Greek history, prominent families claimed descent from legendary heroes. HERAKLES, the greatest hero of all, was most widely adopted as an ancestor, not only by several royal dynasties – including the SPARTAN – but also by many other upper-class families. Tellingly, PLATO mocked such claims because he found them banal and commonplace, not because he found them incredible (*Theaetetus* 175a–b; *Lysis* 205c–d). Despite their belief in genealogical connections of this kind, the Greeks insisted that there was a fundamental gap between the ancient heroes and themselves. The *Iliad* repeatedly contrasts the superhuman strength of its heroes with that of 'mortals as they are now'. Hesiod inserts the heroes as a distinct race after the golden, silver, bronze races and before the present, degenerate race of iron (*Works and Days* 156–73). A fragment of the lost EPIC poem *Kypria* adds that the heroes had been made extinct by the GODS to relieve the earth from the burden of overpopulation.

The Greeks knew a vast range of legends about the heroes, which were originally passed down in an ORAL TRADITION. This tradition may have reached back as far as the Mycenaean age, but clearly accumulated a great deal of material in the intervening centuries before taking the form in which it has come down to us. Out of a welter of local legends grew several major story-cycles, clustering around the Labours of HERAKLES, the wars against THEBES, and the TROJAN WAR. These were the subject of long EPIC poems (apart from Homer's *Iliad* and *Odyssey*, only fragments and summaries of the rest of the so-called Epic Cycle survive) as well as of shorter LYRIC songs, and later of Athenian TRAGEDIES. The essential historicity of the heroes and their great deeds was never doubted, but classical Greek HISTORIANS did question the accuracy of the details of heroic legend and drew a line between heroic tales and 'human' history (HERODOTOS 1.5, 3.122; THUCYDIDES 1.10, 21).

The significance of the heroes in Greek culture cannot be overestimated. Both in literature and in the visual arts, whatever the artists' message, the medium in which they chose to express it was, more often than not, the representation and retelling of heroic legend. HVW

See Hägg, R. (1999) *Ancient Greek Hero Cult*; Kearns, E. (1987) *The Heroes of Attica*.

 ACHILLES.

Heroninos This man, after whom the Heroninos archive is named, was the MANAGER (*phrontistês*) of a division of a large estate in the FAYÛM region of Egypt from c.AD 249 to 268. The archive, consisting of some 450 PAPYRUS documents, attests in a degree of detail unparalleled in the Roman world the management of this estate. It belonged to an ALEXANDRIAN aristocrat named Aurelius Appianus, and had a number of divisions centred around VILLAGES in the Fayûm. Most of the archive concerns the division at Theadelphia, for whose management Heroninos was responsible. The archive includes long monthly accounts of work done, expenditures and revenues connected with the cultivation of the division at Theadelphia, and correspondence from the central administration of the estate as well as from Heroninos and other managers. The archive indicates that the administration maintained central control over the estate's resources to keep down the costs of cultivating individual divisions. The Heroninos archive is one of the most significant collection of documents for Roman economic history. It provides information about the economic affairs of the provincial ÉLITE in Egypt during the 3rd century AD. It attests the level of sophistication that Roman landowners were able to achieve in the management of their estates, and so is at the centre of debate about the basic characteristics of the Roman ECONOMY. DPK

See Rathbone, D. (1991) *Economic Rationalism and Rural Society in Third-century AD Egypt*.

Hesiod The representative of mainland Greek EPIC poetry. Traditionally, Hesiod is dated at the end of the 8th century BC, perhaps in the period that lies between the composition of the *Iliad* and the *Odyssey*. As with many archaic poets, however, his date remains uncertain. Unlike HOMER, he tells us a little about himself in the poems, including the detail that his father was unsuccessful at the colony of Kyme and returned to BOIOTIAN Askra. Hesiod composed two epic works of very different character, *Theogony* and *Works and Days*. Some minor works were also attributed to him, among which *The Shield of Herakles* and the *Catalogue of Women* stand out. At the beginning of the *Theogony*, Hesiod describes a numinous encounter with the Muses of Mt Helikon, who initiated him into poetry and commanded him to celebrate the GODS through his singing.

The subject of *Theogony* is the origin and generations of the gods. It explains how all human realities have their source in the divine realm. For three generations, the gods dethroned their predecessors until ZEUS's reign was established. Ouranos, god of the first generation, was castrated by his son Kronos, who became the next ruler. Subsequently, Zeus defeated his father Kronos and the other Titans in battle (Titanomachia). The progressive movement from chaos to the rule of Zeus implies that the cosmic order guarantees JUSTICE. This succession of rulers of the universe is a common motif in MESOPOTAMIAN and other Near Eastern mythology, which therefore raises the question of Hesiod's source for these oriental influences, present in *Works and Days* as well.

Works and Days insists on the human responsibility for evil in the world. Unlike *Theogony*, it displays a pessimistic outlook on the human situation, progressively separated from the world of gods. The presence of evil is explained through the myths of Prometheus, Pandora and the Five Ages, which portray the decline of man. In this poem, Hesiod advises his brother Perses, with whom he was quarrelling because of their inheritance, to work hard since this is the only remedy for hunger and POVERTY. The advice on the correct way of life given by an older person to a younger one, usually a father to a son, constitutes a commonality in Egyptian and Mesopotamian DIDACTIC literature. The instruction to his brother on proper social, familiar and religious conduct can thus be seen as an oriental motif in Hesiod's poetry. *Works and Days* ends with descriptions of AGRICULTURAL and NAVIGATION activities and a list of the propitious and unpropitious days of the month. (see also AGRICULTURE; COSMOLOGY; CALENDARS; SUPERSTITION; WEATHER FORECASTING) RBC

See West, M. L., trs. (1988); (1966) *Hesiod, Theogony*; (1978) *Hesiod, Works and Days*.

Hestia see DEMETER; FIRE; GODS AND GODDESSES, GREEK; *POLIS*; VESTA; VIRGINITY.

Hesychios 5th- or 6th-century AD grammarian from ALEXANDRIA, and author of the most comprehensive surviving ancient Greek lexicon (*lexikon* in Greek). In its original form, the *Lexikon* covered both definitions of rare and difficult words from the whole field of classical Greek writing (EPIC, DRAMA, LYRIC, ORATORY, MEDICINE and HISTORIOGRAPHY), and proverbs with explanations of their origins. Like all later antique reference books, it relied very heavily on earlier works of the same kind, combined and supplemented as the author saw fit. Hesychios draws special attention to his use of the Hadrianic scholar Diogenianos, along with Aristarchos of Samothrace, Apion, Heliodoros and HERODIAN. As we now have it, his work has been both abbreviated and supplemented by other hands. The source references to specific authors and works, which he prided himself on including, have been removed, and a mass of extra classical and BIBLICAL vocabulary, and biblical names, has been added from various sources. Most entries now consist of only a few words; only a small minority are longer than five lines. Even so, the *Lexikon* remains an invaluable resource for understanding Greek dialects and correcting errors in our manuscript texts of the authors it quotes. MBT

See Latte, K., ed. (1954–6) *Hesychii Lexicon*, 2 vols.

Hibernia (Ireland) see CELTS; EXPLORATION; MIGRATIONS; RAVENNA COSMOGRAPHER; UTOPIAS.

hierarchies see CLASS; ÉLITES; PATRONAGE; PEASANTS; POLITICAL PARTICIPATION; POLITICAL SYSTEMS; SLAVERY; SOCIETY.

Hieronymos of Kardia c.360–260 BC Greek historian and politician. A follower of the SUCCESSOR Eumenes of Kardia, he survived him and also, thanks to his celebrated longevity, outlived other masters with whom he held influential positions: Antigonos I Monophthalmos, Demetrios I Poliorketes (who appointed him overseer of the cities in Boiotia) and Antigonos II Gonatas. His *Histories* or *The Events after Alexander the Great* seems to have covered at least the time until the death of Pyrrhos, but is almost completely lost. It has been argued that DIODORUS SICULUS used him for his account of the Successors (books 18–20), which would indicate Hieronymos' work to be quite reliable and not as biased as PAUSANIAS claims (1.9.8). KB

See FGrH 154; Hornblower, J. (1982) *Hieronymus of Cardia*; Landucci Gattinoni, F. (1997) *Duride di Samo*.

himation see *CHITÔN*; DRESS, GREEK; SCULPTURE, GREEK.

Himera Greek colony on the north coast of SICILY, founded by Syracusan exiles and settlers from Messina c.649 BC. It enjoyed a chequered history and was destroyed by the CARTHAGINIANS in 409. Like many Sicilian colonies, it was ruled by a TYRANT, Terillos, in the archaic period. He was driven out by Theron, tyrant of Akragas, in 483. This event triggered the first major war between SYRACUSE and the Carthaginian colonists of western Sicily, and illustrates the highly personalized nature of politics in archaic Sicily. Terillos was assisted by a Carthaginian guest-friend, Hamilcar, who invaded the territory of Himera, while Theron enlisted the support of his father-in-law, Gelon, tyrant of Syracuse. The Carthaginian army was decisively defeated at Himera in 480, and the victory of Theron and Gelon was marked by the construction of a new Doric TEMPLE in the city. By 461 Himera had regained its independence from Akragas, but it was abandoned after being sacked by Carthage in 409. A new city, Thermae Himeraeae, was founded 11 km (7 miles) to the west under Carthaginian rule, but was culturally and ethnically Greek. KL

See Diodorus 11.20–5, 48–52; Gabba, E. and Vallet, G. (1980) *Sicilia antica*, vol. 1.

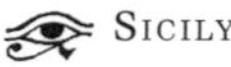 SICILY.

Hipparchia CYNIC PHILOSOPHER, born c.346 BC; a native of Maroneia in Thrace. She was the sister of Metrokles, also a philosopher, who studied with the Cynic Krates. DIOGENES LAËRTIUS tells us that she insisted on marrying Krates because she loved his philosophy. He is said to have responded that as his wife she would have to share the Cynic way of life. Hence she is said to have eschewed WEALTH and accompanied him on the open road, dressed as a man. They had a son named Pasikles.

Hipparchia is the only woman to appear in Diogenes Laërtius' *Lives of the Philosophers*, and it is from this work that much of our knowledge about her derives. She also features in an EPIGRAM by Antipater of Sidon and in the *SUDA*. Although the *Suda* maintains that she wrote philosophical discussions and essays, these do not survive and we can learn little of her philosophical thoughts from the surviving accounts. Instead, the accounts focus on her rejection of a woman's way of life (symbolized by her adoption of male clothes and neglect of WEAVING) in favour of a life of study and erudition. In Diogenes Laërtius, she defends her choice to the philosopher Theodoros, who censures her for stepping outside the bounds of correct behaviour for a woman. The *Suda* maintains that some of Hipparchia's writings were addressed to Theodoros. FMM

Hipparchos of Nikaia (Nicaea) Greek ASTRONOMER and MATHEMATICIAN (second half of 2nd century BC) who worked in RHODES, where he made many observations of the heavens. His surviving commentary on Eudoxos and ARATOS refines their accounts of the constellations on the basis of new data, and gives information about stellar risings and settings. His lost works are understood partly from PTOLEMY's use of them. He refined the theory of 'epicycles' (circles around which the SUN, MOON, and planets were said to revolve, while their centres themselves revolved in larger circular orbits about the earth) through the application of observed data. He determined the distance of the moon more accurately than his predecessors, and was able to predict eclipses of the sun and moon. Most famously, he may have invented latitude and longitude, and he identified the precession of the equinoxes (resulting from the pivoting round of the earth's axis every 25,800 years), a task that required accurate data gathered over a long period. Hipparchos was probably not the only Greek astronomer to draw on the long sequences of BABYLONIAN observations, now more accessible to Greeks after the creation of the hellenistic kingdoms. Although he overestimated the length of the precessional cycle as 36,000 years, his method was sound. He wrote a critique of ERATOSTHENES' geographical work, and researched CALENDARS, optics, arithmetic, PHYSICS, and ASTROLOGY. He stands at the point where Greek astronomy became less theoretical and more firmly founded on actual observation and mathematical prediction, but his methods for predicting celestial movements also gave a boost to astrology. DGJS, CLNR

See Dicks, D.R. (1960) *The Geographical Fragments of Hipparchos*; Neugebauer, O. (1975) *A History of Ancient Mathematical Astronomy*, vol. 1, 274–343.

Hippias (sophist) see ATHLETES AND ATHLETICS, GREEK; CHRONOLOGY; OLYMPIC GAMES; SOPHISTS.

Hippias (tyrant) see ATHENS; KLEOMENES I; MARATHON; PEISISTRATOS.

Hippocratic corpus The collection of about 60 medical treatises ascribed in antiquity, with varying degrees of controversy and commitment, to HIPPOKRATES, the founding figure of the Greek literary medical tradition. These are the earliest surviving Greek writings on MEDICINE, covering a broad spectrum of subjects: from ETHICS to embryology, dietetics to dentition, prognosis to pathology. This is done in a number of different ways – from the most theoretical to the most practical, with plenty of space in between for variation in both – and a range of styles from the florid to the frugal, the polished to the pithy. This diversity of form and doctrine clearly precludes the possibility of single authorship. Arguments were already beginning in the hellenistic period, when the corpus was being assembled, about which were genuine works of Hippokrates, which were the products of sons and pupils or might otherwise be described as in accordance with Hippocratic teaching, and which were simply spurious. These arguments have continued up to the present day. Scholars are becoming increasingly reconciled to the irresolvability of the issue: to not being able to attach Hippokrates' name to any of these texts with certainty, and to treating the whole collection in a more open manner.

The Hippocratic corpus may be a rather loose textual community, but it is a community nonetheless. With a few exceptions, such as the later anatomical treatise *On the Heart*, its constituent works were written between about 430 and 350 BC in the eastern MEDITERRANEAN. They are all participants in the process, the set of debates, through which the identity of Greek medicine as a specific *technê*, an acknowledged art, was forged. One text, *On the Art*, directly addresses the issues of the remit and function of medicine, stressing its value to society. The main lines of this definitional project are also clearly discernible in both the writings that attempt to prescribe the professional conduct of the physician (most famously the *Oath*, but also treatises such as *Decorum* and *Precepts*) and those that attempt to prescribe the type of knowledge requisite for the practice of medicine. The most forthright of the latter is *On Ancient Medicine*, as it argues that experience, not theoretical speculation, is the soundest basis for healing. This argument is directed against views such as those expressed in *On the Nature of Man*, that it is through understanding the elemental composition of the human being that an understanding of the causes of sickness and HEALTH will be achieved. The aim is to circumscribe a set of skills, body of knowledge, and mode of personal comportment distinct to medicine, that exists over and above everyday learning and activity. It is the territory thus established that is elaborated and explored, described and disputed by all these works. Their fascination thus lies both in their content and in the dynamic processes they reveal, the processes by which the Western medical tradition was first formed. REF

See Lloyd, G. E. R. (1978) *Hippocratic Writings*; Smith, W. D. (1985) *The Hippocratic Tradition*.

Hippokrates b.460/459 BC 'The father of Greek medicine', to whom the 60-odd works of the HIPPOCRATIC CORPUS were ascribed in antiquity, and about whom many stories were told. He was a descendant of the god ASKLEPIOS, and a pupil not only of his father but also of such famous men as Herodikos the physician, GORGIAS the SOPHIST and DEMOKRITOS the PHILOSOPHER. He travelled from his native Kos right across the Greek world, everywhere performing outstanding MEDICAL and moral deeds. He died at a ripe old age leaving scores of students to succeed him, most notable among whom were his sons.

Such is the stuff of his BIOGRAPHY as recounted in the classical world. This is less an account of a real life than the creation of a founding figure for the Greek literary medical tradition: a figure of divine descent, who combined healing, RHETORICAL and philosophical skills, was a virtuous and much-travelled philhellene (he reportedly refused to serve the king of PERSIA despite the vast reward he was offered), and passed on knowledge wherever he went. About Hippokrates the man, therefore, as about

Hippokrates the author, little is certain. He was an Ionian promulgator of medical ideas and therapeutic practices, of sufficient renown to be mentioned already by PLATO in the early 4th century BC (*Phaedrus* 270c–d; *Protagoras* 311b–c). He then became the authoritative guarantor, the powerful symbol, of a particular medical tradition, in which role he continues today. (see also DOCTORS) REF

See Jones, W. H. S. and Withington, E. R., trs. (1923–96) 4 vols.; Lloyd, G. E. R., ed. (1978) *Hippocratic Writings* (selected trs.); Pinault, J. R. (1992) *Hippocratic Lives and Legends*.

Hipponax see ARCHILOCHOS; LANGUAGES; LYRIC POETRY, GREEK; POETRY, GREEK; SCULPTURE, GREEK.

Hirpini see SAMNITES.

Hispalis see BAETICA.

Hispania The Roman name for the Iberian peninsula, called *Ibêria* by the Greeks. The original reason for Roman interest in Spain was the war against HANNIBAL (218–201 BC). Their original intention appears to have been to prevent reinforcements being sent to Hannibal in Italy from his bases in southern Spain. By the time the command was taken over by Publius SCIPIO in 210, however, this had been extended to include the removal of the CARTHAGINIANS altogether. That was achieved following the defeat of the Carthaginian armies at Baecula (208) and Ilipa (207). After the expulsion of the Carthaginians, the Romans controlled only that part of Spain which had been affected by the war: the eastern seaboard and the valley of the river Baetis (Guadalquivir). Although the next 30 years saw almost continuous fighting, chiefly against Iberian tribes of the north-east, the CELTIBERIANS in the north-eastern *meseta* and the LUSITANIANS in the west, there is little sign that this was co-ordinated. Although the area under Roman control increased in size, it did so only slowly. The region was divided into two provinces of Nearer and Further Spain (Hispania Citerior and Hispania Ulterior) in 197, after which elected MAGISTRATES (specifically PRAETORS) were sent to command the armies. The Romans, however, seem to have been more interested in winning victories over Spanish tribes than in establishing any organized administration. After the campaigns of Tiberius Sempronius Gracchus and Lucius Postumius Albinus in 180–178, TREATIES were arranged with the Celtiberians and probably with other tribes, as a result of which Roman TAXATION seems to have become more regular.

In the middle of the 2nd century, large-scale wars broke out in Celtiberia in the northern part of the *meseta* and in Lusitania, which resulted in a series of CONSULS being sent to Spain. The war against the Lusitanians was ended only by the assassination of their leader, VIRIATHUS, in 139. The Celtiberians were finally subdued by the capture of their main town, NUMANTIA, in 133.

In the 1st century BC, Spain was involved in the CIVIL WARS which afflicted the Roman world, first in the war with SERTORIUS, and then in the struggle between JULIUS CAESAR and the sons of POMPEY which was not resolved until Caesar defeated the Pompeians at MUNDA in 45. Not until the reign of AUGUSTUS was the military conquest of the peninsula

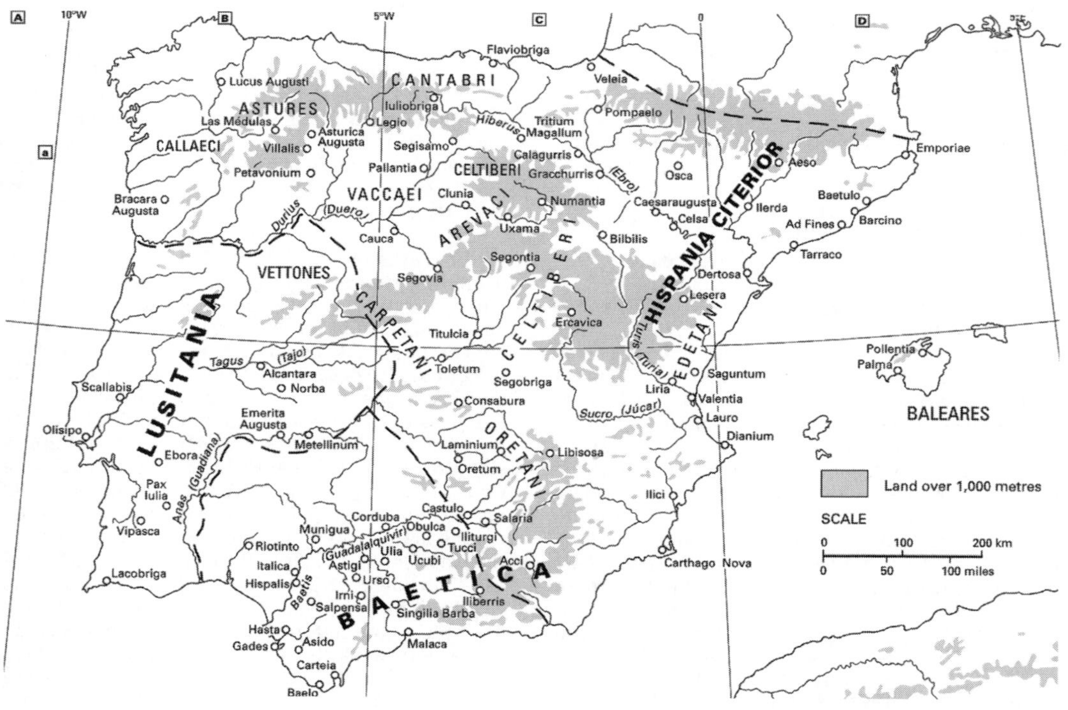

HISPANIA: map of Roman provinces.

completed. The last area, the Cantabrian mountains of the north-west, took from 26 to 16 BC to subdue, requiring the attention of Augustus himself in 26 and 25 and of his best general, Marcus AGRIPPA, in 19. It was probably after this that the peninsula was divided into three provinces: BAETICA, LUSITANIA and Tarraconensis (usually still called Hispania Citerior in inscriptions) with its capital at TARRACO. The provincial divisions instituted by Augustus continued to be used down to the time of DIOCLETIAN (AD 284–305), who subdivided Tarraconensis into three sections: Gallaecia, Tarraconensis and Carthaginensis.

It was not until the period of Julius Caesar and Augustus that full-scale, Roman-style foundations (*coloniae*) were established for the benefit of Roman legionary VETERANS. Some were founded upon already existing native towns (as at Tarraco), some on sites where there was only smaller-scale habitation previously, as at Emerita Augusta (Mérida). During the reign of Augustus and up to the overthrow of NERO in AD 68, native communities also began to model themselves on the Roman pattern, setting up public buildings including FORUMS, buildings for local government, TEMPLES and BATHS. Some acquired the status of *municipium*, by which the inhabitants gained the so-called LATIN right; this gave them privileges under Roman law and allowed the magistrates of the town to become Roman CITIZENS. This process was advanced rapidly during the reigns of the Flavian emperors, VESPASIAN (69–79), TITUS (79–81) and DOMITIAN (81–96). Vespasian granted the Latin right to all the communities of Spain.

The same period saw a progressive reduction in the number of Roman troops stationed in the peninsula. During the Cantabrian war under Augustus, the number of legions had risen to 7 or 8, but these had been reduced to 3 by the reign of his successor, TIBERIUS, and to 1 by the time of Galba's accession. From Vespasian's time to the end of the empire, the legionary force in Spain was limited to the Legion VII Gemina Felix, stationed at Legio (León) in the north. Both this legion and the other AUXILIARY units in Spain seem to have been recruited increasingly from the peninsula itself, and soldiers recruited from Spain served throughout the Roman world, from BRITAIN to SYRIA. From the time of Vespasian onwards, the amount of military activity in Spain itself was small and occasional, such as the expulsion of a Moorish attack from AFRICA in the 170s and raids by barbarians during the chaotic period of the later 3rd century. It seems probable that the Legion VII Gemina was split in the late 3rd or 4th century, one part being transferred to the *comitatenses*, the mobile army that accompanied the emperor. The remaining forces in Spain were further reduced by the removal of soldiers to fight in the civil war that followed the attempt by the usurper Constantine III to seize power from the emperor HONORIUS in 406. They were thus unable to provide very much resistance to the VANDALS, Suevi and ALANI who swept across the Pyrenees in 409.

The economy of Roman Spain was primarily AGRICULTURAL. In addition to food grown for local consumption, there was a considerable export TRADE, illustrated by the investigation of SHIPWRECKS and AMPHORAS found both in Spain and elsewhere in the Roman world. Particularly important are those from MONTE TESTACCIO in Rome, where emptied amphoras were dumped after reaching the city's docks. This hill, still some 50 m high, is composed mostly of the remains of amphoras which had carried OLIVE OIL from Baetica to Rome in the first three centuries AD. WINE from Baetica and Tarraconensis, while not highly regarded in Rome, was shipped in quantity from the 1st century BC to the mid-2nd century AD. Spain was also famous for the production of piquant FISH SAUCES, made especially from tuna and mackerel, of which the most renowned was known as *garum*. GLASS, fine POTTERY and esparto grass (for making ROPES and baskets) were also exported from Spain. JSR

See Keay, S. J. (1988) *Roman Spain*; Richardson, J. S. (1996) *The Romans in Spain*.

 CARTHAGE AND CARTHAGINIANS: (a); IBERIA (2); ROMAN EMPIRE: (a).

Historia Augusta As it now stands, the *Historia Augusta* is a collection of 30 BIOGRAPHIES of emperors and usurpers from AD 117 to 285. There is a gap in the manuscripts in which lives of emperors from 244 to 253 are lost, along with the bulk of the life of VALERIAN (r.253–60). In 1603, Isaac Casaubon produced an edition of this collection under the title *Scriptores historiae Augustae* (in effect 'writers of the histories of the emperors'), a title that stuck until the later 20th century. Casaubon used the plural because the manuscripts identify six separate authors in the collection, and at various points several of these authors are made to give details of their work in relationship to others, dating the collection as a whole to the early 4th century AD. There is now general, but not universal, consensus among modern scholars that this is an elaborate literary hoax. Most scholars hold, with the aid of electronic studies of the prose style, that a single author wrote the work under a series of assumed names at the very end of the 4th century or in the first decade of the 5th. There is as yet no consensus, among scholars who hold this view, as to why the author should have done what he did.

The quality of information conveyed by the author of the *Historia Augusta* is erratic. In writing the lives from HADRIAN to ELAGABALUS, he probably used a collection of imperial biographies written under Alexander SEVERUS by a senior SENATOR named Marius Maximus. There is significant disagreement on this point: some scholars hold that Marius was a poor biographer, and that the reliable information in these lives comes from a second, unknown writer. There is no question, however, that these lives preserve valuable information not otherwise available. In the lives from Alexander Severus to Carinus, there is much less reliable information, probably deriving from a historian who wrote a history of the 3rd century in Latin during or shortly after the reign of CONSTANTINE (possibly filtered through a history written by Nicomachus Flavianus in the late 4th century). References to Greek historians of the imperial period, such as Dexippus and HERODIAN, are probably taken by the author from his Latin sources (though on this point, too, there is debate).

Even allowing for the substantial elements of fiction in the later lives, the *Historia Augusta* remains an invaluable source of information about imperial history. The fictional sections as well offer insight

into many aspects of Roman life, and require attention from any student of Roman culture. DSP
See Syme, R. (1971) *Emperors and Biography.*

historians and historiography, ancient The writing of history can fairly be described as a Greek innovation. The earliest writer known to have used the term *historiê* ('enquiry') to describe his work was HERODOTOS, who wrote in the 430s BC. Detailed written records of historical events already existed in Egypt and the Near East, but they were official chronicles recording the military, religious and political deeds of the Egyptian, Assyrian and Babylonian kings. They were often inscribed on monuments built to celebrate royal victories, though 'handwritten' versions were kept in ARCHIVES. Herodotos' *historiê* (usually called *The Histories*) differed from such chronicles because it was not a state-authorized version of events but the result of his personal enquiries. It is structured around the activities and achievements of communities and political entities, rather than individual rulers. It shares this feature with contemporary Jewish historical writings, as reflected in the books of Kings, Ezra and Nehemiah, though the Jewish writers' need to offer a truthful account of God's actions on behalf of his people made these works significantly different in style and scope. Another important and distinctive aspect of Herodotos' work is his desire to explain how and why events occurred. His choice of a wide-ranging theme, and his open-minded search for ways to explain the complex connections between people and events, encourage him to reflect critically upon his diverse and sometimes conflicting sources of information.

Herodotos' near-contemporary THUCYDIDES wrote a history of the PELOPONNESIAN WAR (431–404 BC) which is similarly characterized by a strong compulsion to investigate and evaluate the causes of historical events, but he is more ruthless than Herodotos in rejecting unsatisfactory versions, and his focus is much narrower. Thucydides' authoritative narrative of political and military events in strict chronological order established a model for Greek and Roman historiography that was widely imitated. XENOPHON was one of several Greeks who wrote political histories that began where Thucydides left off. Historians who, like EPHOROS of Kyme, modelled themselves more on Herodotos gradually evolved the idea of a universal history covering all the significant peoples of the known world. This approach was partially adopted by POLYBIOS (c.200–118), whose *Histories* encompassed the political activities of Greeks, Romans and CARTHAGINIANS, and it was expanded by POSIDONIUS (c.135–51). It was in the 1st century BC, however, that works like the *Library of History* by DIODORUS SICULUS and the *Philippic History* of Pompeius Trogus (preserved in a summary by Justin) most effectively realized the concept.

The first example of Roman historiography imitated Greek models. FABIUS PICTOR was a Roman SENATOR who around 200 BC wrote an account, in Greek, of the first and second PUNIC WARS. Many other Roman aristocrats wrote narratives in Thucydidean style of recent political events, especially the wars in which they or their friends and patrons had distinguished themselves. JULIUS CAESAR's *Gallic War* and *Civil War* belong to this tradition. The focus of Latin historiography on the achievements of the senatorial aristocracy (and later the EMPERORS) is reflected in the surviving works of SALLUST, LIVY, TACITUS and AMMIANUS MARCELLINUS.

Jewish historiography was strongly influenced by the Greeks. From at least the 3rd century BC, Jews were writing histories of their own people in Greek, including an account of the MACCABAEAN rebellion by Jason of Cyrene. The most famous classical Jewish historian is JOSEPHUS, whose detailed account, *The Antiquities of the Jews*, was published in AD 93/4. It was intended primarily for a hellenized, PAGAN readership, but its most significant legacy was probably the model it provided for the development of CHRISTIAN historiography. EUSEBIOS of Caesarea (c.AD 260–339) was the first writer to attempt a systematic account of the history of the Christian CHURCH. He adopted a CHRONOLOGICAL framework, but substituted the struggle against heretics and the resistance to persecutors for the wars and political intrigues of traditional historiography. A key aspect of his work was his establishment of the historical continuity of the Christian apostolic tradition, which was independent of Roman political history. The distinction between ecclesiastical and political historiography was gradually lost, however, as the affairs of church and state became closely entwined. Political history of the Thucydidean kind still flourished, most notably in the writings of Ammianus Marcellinus and PROCOPIUS, though there was an increasing separation between Latin and Greek traditions as a result of the collapse of Roman imperial authority in the West. A pagan response to the christianization of history is exemplified by Zosimos, whose *New History*, written c.AD 500, sought to blame Christianity for the troubles of the Roman empire. This was a short-lived reaction, swamped by the rising tide of Christian orthodoxy.

There was considerable overlap in the arts and skills deployed by ORATORS and historians to persuade their audiences to accept their particular narrative as superior. Ancient commentators were aware of this. Given the general importance of public and private RHETORIC in Greek and Roman politics, it is not surprising that speeches figure prominently in classical historiography. In all likelihood, they rarely represent accurate reports or even summaries of what historical personages said; but they often convey key elements of the historian's own interpretation of events. Thucydides' work includes numerous speeches intended to offer insights into the mentality and values of the protagonists in the Peloponnesian war. Sallust uses speeches in his *Histories*, and in his *Jugurtha* and *Catiline*, to show how the moral and political values of the Roman aristocracy had declined from their earlier ideals. Tacitus took this a stage further, showing how the evolution of the PRINCIPATE into the worst form of tyrannical government was accompanied by increased public flattery (*adulatio*) of the emperor on the part of the aristocracy.

Thucydides, Xenophon, Polybios, Josephus, Tacitus and Ammianus were directly involved in some of the events they wrote about; but the feeling of an immediate link to the past is often missing from classical historiography. Much of it concerned recent events and was written by men who participated in them. Unfortunately, most of these accounts are completely lost or survive only in 'fragments' (short quotations or identifiable borrowings) and longer excerpts quoted by later writers, whose own works therefore lack the authority and immediacy of a contemporary source. Modern historians normally validate their interpretations of the past by referring to contemporary material; such references occur only sporadically in classical historiography. Quotations from original documents, and explicit reference to the sources of facts or interpretations, are scattered through the works of many surviving historians of classical antiquity; yet it is unlikely that many of them made systematic studies of archives or public documents. For the most part they were content to rely upon the factual accuracy of their predecessors' narratives, though the brief comments that some writers offer about their earlier sources often highlight shortcomings, particularly in terms of political bias, distortion and even outright falsification of events. These factors can sometimes make it very hard to establish the reliability of historians. We know, for example, that detailed histories of ALEXANDER the Great were written by several individuals who accompanied him during his conquest of the PERSIAN EMPIRE, including his companion and general PTOLEMY I and his engineer Aristoboulos; but all of these are now lost. Scholars have constructed elaborate theories about how closely they were followed by later writers such as Diodoros, PLUTARCH and ARRIAN. As can be seen, however, from their varied treatments of episodes like the burning of PERSEPOLIS in 330 BC (Diodoros 17.71–2; Curtius Rufus 5.7; Plutarch, *Alexander* 38; Arrian, *Anabasis* of Alexander 3.18.10–12; Athenaeus 13.576e), it is almost impossible to determine exactly what the original sources wrote and which of the later writers offers the most reliable version. PDeS

See Hammond, N. G. L. (1993) *Sources for Alexander the Great*; Hornblower, S., ed. (1994) *Greek Historiography*; Kraus, C. and Woodman, A. J. (1997) *Latin Historians*; Usher, S. (1969) *Historians of Greece and Rome*; Marincola, J. (2001) *Greek Historians*; Momigliano, A. D. (1990) *The Classical Foundations of Modern Historiography*; Rohrbacher, D. (2002) *The Historians of Late Antiquity*; Woodman, A. J. (1988) *Rhetoric in Classical Historiography*.

historians and historiography, modern The study of Greek and Roman history in modern times has benefited greatly from the enormous amount of work done since the RENAISSANCE to collect, edit and publish Greek and Latin texts, inscriptions and other written documents. Improved editions are published and more material continues to be discovered, especially as a result of archaeological excavations, but modern scholars still depend upon the work of philologists and antiquarians for most of their source material.

Edward Gibbon is one of the earliest examples of a historian who utilized this wide range of literary, EPIGRAPHIC and material evidence to study a major theme. His six-volume work *The Decline and Fall of the Roman Empire* was published between 1776 and 1788. Consciously aiming to blend the approaches of the antiquarian and the philosopher, Gibbon set himself the task of explaining the causes of what he saw as the decay of Roman civilization from its heyday in the late 2nd century AD to the fall of CONSTANTINOPLE in 1453. His personal identification with the values of the senatorial aristocracy encouraged him to comment with 'the grave and temperate irony' that he had learned from the philosopher Pascal on their defeat by the forces of barbarism and religion. He was criticized by several clerical scholars for his disrespectful and erroneous treatment of ecclesiastical history, but his *Vindication*, published in 1779, demonstrated that his analysis of the secular aspects of the rise of CHRISTIANITY was based on a thorough reading of the ancient sources. Gibbon's analysis remains a landmark in the historiography of the Roman empire.

The importance of adopting a critical, even sceptical, attitude to much of what is said in the ancient sources is one of the fundamental characteristics of modern historiography of the Greek and Roman world. A fine example of how fruitful this approach could be was the *History of Rome* by the Danish scholar B. G. Niebuhr, published in 1811–12. Niebuhr's application of source-criticism to the traditions about early Rome recorded by LIVY and others laid the foundation for much later work. George Grote's great 12-volume *History of Greece*, published between 1846 and 1856, was similar to Niebuhr's in its cautious approach to the sources and echoed Gibbon in its advocacy of a particular culture – in this case that of 5th-century Greece, especially Athens – as the apogee of a great civilization and an object lesson for contemporaries. One of his younger contemporaries, the philosopher John Stuart Mill, even argued that the Greek legacy of the democratic ideal was so intrinsic to Western society that the 'the battle of Marathon, even as an event in English history, is more important than the battle of Hastings'.

The fundamental contribution of Greek and Roman history to the development of Western civilization made it a subject of study and discussion for many of the great political and social thinkers of the 19th century. Both Karl MARX and Max Weber were well read in classical literature and history, and both began their studies of the modern political economy by attempting to characterize and explain the primary economic and social trends of classical antiquity. Marx's comments on the nature of the class struggle between rich and poor in the ancient world have attracted many adherents, especially in countries of the former Soviet bloc, though the most successful attempt to apply a Marxist mode of analysis to antiquity was *The Class Struggle in the Ancient Greek World* (1981) by the Oxford don Geoffrey de Ste Croix.

Weber advocated the use of theoretical models to create a scientific method of historical and social analysis. His prime concern was to understand the distinctive nature of Western capitalism, but his refinement of the concept of 'ideal types', which he applied to ancient history in his work of 1909 entitled *Agrarverhältnisse im Altertum* (usually translated as *Agrarian Sociology of Ancient Civilizations*), has had a major influence on the study of Greek and Roman history. A leading exponent of Weber's approach was the New Yorker Moses Finley, who drew on Weber, Marx and other social and anthropological theorists (such as Marcel Mauss) to formulate rigorous intellectual models that could be used to counter some of the inadequacies of the available ancient sources. Finley employed the 'ideal types' to characterize key features of ancient Greek society, economy and politics and provide a means of comparison with other pre-industrial cultures. In *The World of Odysseus* (1954) he showed how the application of this method could be used to explore the historical society that lay behind the HOMERIC EPICS. As lecturer and professor of ancient history at Cambridge (1955–79) he encouraged young scholars to explore diverse aspects of Greek and Roman civilization. His polemical analysis of the limits of Greek and Roman social and ECONOMIC development, entitled *The Ancient Economy* (1973), has been one of the most influential works on ancient history ever published.

Arguably the greatest of the 19th century's many distinguished scholars of Roman history was Theodor Mommsen. In his own lifetime he was best known for his three-volume *Römische Geschichte* (*History of Rome*, 1854–6), covering the period up to the victory of Julius Caesar in the CIVIL WARS. His posthumous reputation, however, was founded on his studies of Roman public and private LAW and his work as an editor of research collections. In 1858 Mommsen became the general editor of the Berlin Academy's vast project to produce a definitive collection of Latin EPIGRAPHY, the *Corpus inscriptionum Latinarum* (*CIL*). His devotion to this and to other collections of basic source material, like the *Monumenta Germaniae historica* (*MGH*), gave a tremendous boost to the study of ancient (and early medieval) history by making critical texts of histories, letters, laws, treaties, public decrees and many other documents widely accessible. The existence of copies of these collections in university libraries across the world has enabled the study of ancient history to become a truly international discipline.

The Italians had long claimed the Romans as the founders of their nation. This view was expounded in a thoroughly researched and systematic fashion by Gaetano De Sanctis, whose definitive, four-volume *Storia dei Romani* was published between 1907 and 1964. The history and institutions of the Roman empire were vigorously studied in countries that had once been Roman PROVINCES. In many cases the primary focus was on the province itself, such as France, where the energetic scholar Camille Jullian did much to highlight the importance of the combination of historical and archaeological research in his eight-volume *Histoire de la Gaule* (1908–26). In Britain the distinguished historian R. G. Collingwood produced a much smaller, but no less important study of *Roman Britain* (1932), drawing heavily on the evidence provided by Latin inscriptions, which he was editing for the eighth volume of *CIL*.

It was, however, the career and works of a scholar from the Ukraine, beyond the furthest reaches of Roman power, that most firmly established the centrality of archaeological evidence in discussions of Greek and Roman history. Michael I. Rostovtzeff was a schoolteacher's son from near Kiev who was fascinated by the material remains of classical antiquity, ranging from SCYTHIAN burial goods to Egyptian PAPYRI. Rostovtzeff moved to America in the 1920s and took charge of Yale University's EXCAVATIONS at the former frontier city of DURA EUROPUS on the Euphrates. He published a massively learned and profusely illustrated *Social and Economic History of the Roman Empire* in 1926 (2nd edn, 1957) and followed this up with his *Social and Economic History of the Hellenistic World* in 1941 (updated 1953). Although both works have been criticized for their bias towards the urban bourgeoisie, with whom Rostovtzeff closely identified, they nevertheless continue to inform and inspire generations of students and scholars with their brilliant use of the widest possible range of source material.

It is not surprising that many historians in the United States of America took a keen interest in the workings of the Roman REPUBLIC. Foremost among an influential school of political historians were T. Robert S. Broughton, who compiled an invaluable aid to research entitled *The Magistrates of the Roman Republic* (3 vols., 1951–86) and Lily Ross Taylor, who recognized the important similarities between the Roman and contemporary American political systems. Her painstaking analyses of *The Voting Districts of the Roman Republic* (1960) and *Roman Voting Assemblies* (1966) backed up her discussion of *Party Politics in the Age of Caesar* (1949), in which she used insights from the way American politicians achieved electoral success in a federal republic to interpret the politics of the late Republic.

The story of the transformation of the late Republican political system into a monarchy under the leadership of Julius Caesar's heir, AUGUSTUS, was expertly analysed by the New Zealand-born Oxford scholar Ronald Syme in *The Roman Revolution* (1939). Syme employed meticulous prosopographical research to underpin his discussion of the Augustan 'party'. He followed that up with a detailed analysis of the aims and methods of the imperial historian *Tacitus* (1958) that has inspired a host of other studies of Greek and Latin historians.

In the mid-19th century George Grote had helped to establish the new University College London. It soon became a centre for the study of ancient history. Several of the college's scholars have had a major influence on modern study of Greek and Roman history. They include Norman H. Baynes, who encouraged students of ancient history to extend their interests into what had been, since Gibbon, considered the inferior and degenerate Byzantine period. But it was the highly detailed and carefully researched work of another UCL professor, A. H. M. Jones, encompassed in his three-volume work, *The Later Roman Empire AD 284–602: a social, economic and administrative survey* (1964), that did most to make it possible for subsequent generations to explore further the history of what is now called late antiquity.

Perhaps the most influential scholar of classical history in the 20th century was Arnaldo Dante Momigliano, who came to England as a refugee from Fascist Italy and, after spells in Oxford and Bristol, became professor of ancient history at UCL in 1951. He had learned his method of rational inference based on close study of the ancient sources under the guidance of De Sanctis, and had developed a passionate interest in the search for intellectual and historical truths, partly inspired by the liberal historicism of Benedetto Croce. Croce argued that all history should be contemporary history, meaning that explanations of past events must take account of the meanings those events had for their contemporaries. Momigliano's primary concern was to elucidate the complex and fascinating development of historical writing from its ancient beginnings through to the modern era. His researches demonstrated how the work of all historians from HERODOTOS onwards can and must be understood in the context of both their own and their predecessors' intellectual, social, political and spiritual environment. In numerous books, essays and reviews Momigliano stressed that, especially when dealing with the classical world, the writing of good history requires constant reflection upon the efficacy of the methods and interpretations used to reconstruct events from the sources. PDeS

See (besides works cited above): Finley, M. I. (1975) *The Use and Abuse of History*; (1985) *Ancient History: evidence and models*; Momigliano, A. D. (1966) *Studies in Historiography*; (1977) *Essays in Ancient and Modern Historiography*; (1990) *The Classical Foundations of Modern Historiography*; (1994) *Studies on Modern Scholarship*.

Hittites see ANATOLIA; CILICIA; COMMAGENE; CUNEIFORM; MYCENAEANS.

hoards Concealed accumulations of artefacts, hoards may contain coins, valuables such as SILVERWARE and GOLD JEWELLERY, or the goods and tools of a travelling craftsman. Much of our knowledge of precious metal objects (such as silverware) and COINAGE depends on hoard finds, as most other metal artefacts were melted down and recycled in antiquity. Hoards often also contain objects of lesser value, such as POTTERY vessels and LEATHER purses to hold coins, or wooden chests to contain tableware. As so many hoards are chance finds made by metal detectors, such evidence is unfortunately often lost.

Objects were removed from circulation and deposited in hoards for a variety of reasons, but the two main possibilities are concealment with the intention of recovery and votive deposition. Hoards were concealed at times of crisis, unrest and WAR but, in the absence of a developed BANKING system, may also have been hidden temporarily to prevent opportunistic theft. It is often impossible to say why a hoard was not retrieved; for example, the owner may have died, or may have been unable to relocate the hoard. Samuel Pepys' 1667 account of the recovery of a hoard hidden by his wife and father only four months previously provides a salutary insight into the difficulties involved. In some cases, such as the drastic devaluations of currencies, it may simply not have been worthwhile to retrieve buried coins.

Votive deposits were not intended to be retrieved but were deposited as offerings to the GODS. Such votive hoards may contain unusual artefacts, such as religious items or weapons. In many cultures there was also a tradition of offering the weapons of defeated enemies to the gods. Votive hoards are commonly found in locations believed to be especially close to the spiritual world such as RIVERS, swamps, moors and lakes. There are also certain areas, such as East Anglia, where there appears to be a strong regional tradition of hoarding. In some cases, a combination of factors can be discerned. So-called 'Hacksilber' hoards (such as the famous British example from Traprain Law) contain silver vessels and other objects cut into small pieces. The objects are treated simply as bullion, perhaps indicating how the spoils of a raid were divided. The deposition of some of this material may nevertheless have served a RITUAL or votive purpose.

HOARDS: the late Roman silver hoard from Water Newton, England.

Coin hoards are dated by the coin with the latest minting date, but this only ever offers an earliest possible date (*terminus post quem*). High-value coinage may have a very long circulation life, and in periods of financial stress hoards often represent the best material available; such coins must predate the currency crisis against which the hoarder is reacting.

Hoards provide a spectacular insight into the lifestyle of ÉLITE families. Thus the early 5th-century Hoxne treasure, which was deposited in a large wooden chest, contained more than 14,000 coins and 200 gold and silver objects, in particular silverware and jewellery. HE

See Bland, R. and Johns, C. (1993) *The Hoxne Treasure*; Howgego, C. (1995) *Ancient History from Coins*.

holidays Public FESTIVALS (Greek *heortai*, Latin *feriae*) combining religious solemnity with joyous physical relaxation – even, in certain instances, the relaxation of social order. Holidays fell on fixed days, usually annually, often in tempo with the AGRICULTURAL seasons. Thus the Thesmophoria, DEMETER's November festival in Athens, anticipated the annual sowing, while the Anthesteria celebrated Dionysos and new WINE during Anthesterion (late February–early March), named, like other Greek months, after the major holiday occurring therein. Not surprisingly, public drunkenness featured prominently on this holiday, just as role reversal between masters and SLAVES, or men and women, characterized some other festivals (e.g. the Kronia in late July; compare the Roman Saturnalia in December). Presumably this licentiousness ultimately served social interests, as did attendance at the THEATRE, that most civic of activities central to Dionysos' feasts of the Lenaia (January) and Great Dionysia (March). Perhaps the Athenian holiday most closely connected to the city's honour and welfare was the Panathenaia (August).

Among Romans the principal calendrical distinction was between *fasti* and *nefasti*, i.e. days on which ordinary, especially legal, business was either permitted or forbidden. Thus it was a civic duty to rest from labour on the *feriae publicae*. These latter included agricultural festivals, of course, but also two clusters of holidays coinciding with the beginning (March) and end (October) of the military campaigning season. GAMES (*ludi*) were associated with many Roman holidays, as they were with the four-yearly or two-yearly 'agonistic' festivals of the Greeks (e.g. at OLYMPIA, DELPHI, CORINTH, and Nemea). JRH

See Burkert, W. (1985) *Greek Religion*; Parke, H.W. (1977) *Festivals of the Athenians*; Scullard, H. H. (1981) *Festivals and Ceremonies of the Roman Republic*.

Homer (*Homêros*) 8th-century BC EPIC POET. It would be hard to overestimate the importance of Homer, the first and greatest of the Greek epic poets. Yet the Greeks themselves knew nothing for certain about his life, and indeed some modern scholars have doubted his very existence. HERODOTOS placed him in the mid-9th century, but the evidence of the poems suggests a dating in the second half of the 8th, during the age of Greek COLONIZATION. The *Iliad*, with its focus in the BLACK SEA area, is usually placed c.750; the *Odyssey*, with its interest in the west, c.725. Homer was perhaps born in CHIOS, where the rhapsodes who called themselves the 'sons of Homer' (*Homêridai*) operated. The ancients believed him to be a blind, poverty-stricken, wandering minstrel, who died on the Cycladic island of Ios.

Of far greater importance than the poet are his poems, the *Iliad* and *Odyssey*. Other epics attributed to Homer, such as the *Battle of Mice and Frogs* (*Batrachomyomachia*) and the Homeric Hymns, are spurious. But the word 'his' immediately raises the 'Homeric question', which has been at the heart of Homeric studies since the late 18th century. Some hellenistic scholars already believed that the *Iliad* and *Odyssey* were the work of different poets. The view of these 'separatists' (*chôrizontes*) has been accepted by some modern scholars, who note differences in the language and society of the poems which they attribute to the *Odyssey* being composed a generation after the *Iliad*. 'Unitarian' scholars, on the other hand, emphasize the great difference in the subject matter of the poems, pointing out that the *Odyssey* was clearly designed as a sequel to the *Iliad*. But a far more probable explanation of these difficulties is that the poems are the product of a multiplicity of composers, especially since their language is an amalgam of dialects which are not even contemporaneous, and the society they depict is similarly a construct. The study by Milman Parry of the composition of epics in early 20th-century Yugoslavia demonstrated their essentially ORAL nature. By parallel, the Homeric poems were the product of shorter lays which had been sung for generations and were put together by, perhaps, a single editor.

Homer's own distinctive contribution then becomes a matter for investigation, but ARISTOTLE was on the right lines when he praised the artistic unity of the poems in the *Poetics* (8.3). We might note, for example, how the theme of the anger of ACHILLES runs through the *Iliad*. The poem begins with the old man Chryses coming to ransom his daughter Chryseis, and AGAMEMNON demanding as her replacement Achilles' concubine Briseïs. This causes their dispute and Achilles' angry withdrawal from the fighting. The poem ends with the old king Priam coming to ransom the body of his son Hektor, and the maturing of Achilles into a sympathetic hero. This theory then explains not only the apparent discrepancies and inconsistencies within the poems, but also its repetitive, 'formulaic' nature: nouns with epithets (such as 'swift-footed Achilles'), phrases, lines and indeed whole passages ('typical scenes', such as a hero donning his armour) are formulas which the poet can employ as an extempore aid to composition as he constructs his narrative. Throughout both poems the lines are written in dactylic hexameters.

The formulaic, oral nature of the poems also accounts for the range of historical periods reflected in them. Some elements are clearly relics of the Bronze Age, most notably armour such as Ajax's huge bronze tower-shield (*Iliad* 7.219–23), and take us back to the PALACE society of the MYCENAEAN period of c.1400–1200. The poems may even recall a real war, archaeologically attested, that ended with the destruction of TROY in the early 12th century. Most of the descriptions of social and ethical life, however, are indicative of the Iron Age, coinciding with the late Geometric period of Greek history in the 9th and 8th centuries. The *Odyssey*, in particular, telling of the long-drawn-out return of Odysseus from Troy to Ithaca, his encounters with dangers, monsters and exotic peoples, and his eventual recovery of his wife and lands, reflects a colonizing mentality in which Greek interest in the outside world is burgeoning.

It is probably no coincidence that the Homeric poems were composed in their extended form at the same time as the introduction of the PHOENICIAN alphabet into Greece. Whether Homer wrote the poems down himself (surely not, if he was blind) or dictated them to a scribe is of no consequence. But their complex unity is important, and indicates considered literary structure. Though oral in essence and sung to the accompaniment of the lyre, they are far too long for recital regularly in one session, and it is not easy to break the *Iliad* down into manageable portions that cohere. As they stand, they are the product of literary activity, and even if their compilation was the work of two men it may conveniently be assigned to Homer. A third possibility is that after Homer put the poems together they were memorized by the Homeridai and continued to be preserved orally, perhaps not being written down until as late as the 6th century. According to one tradition, the Athenian TYRANT PEISISTRATOS commissioned Onomakritos to put the text of the poems in order at that time. (If true, this may have been the point at which some Athenian elements found their way into the text; possibly, too, it was Onomakritos who divided each poem into 24 books.) But different oral and written versions nevertheless continued in existence, until the text as we have it was established by the scholars of hellenistic ALEXANDRIA.

The *Iliad* and *Odyssey*, along with the poems of HESIOD, were central to later Greek society, providing information about the GODS, setting examples of heroic conduct for male imitation and underlining proper and improper behaviour for WOMEN. They acted as a constant reference point and overshadowed later literature – even AESCHYLUS would say 'we are all eating crumbs from the great table of Homer'. It may be argued that Homer's achievement, even though he was the earliest author in Western literature, has never been surpassed. MJE

See Homer, *The Iliad*, trs. M. Hammond (1987); Homer, *The Odyssey*, trs. E.V. Rieu and D. C. H. Rieu (1991); Edwards, M.W. (1987) *Homer, Poet of the Iliad*; Finley, M. I. (1977) *The World of Odysseus*; Griffin, J. (1980) *Homer*; Schein, S.L. (1984) *The Mortal Hero*; McAuslan, I., and Walcot, P., eds. (1998) *Homer*; Morris, I. and Powell, B. (1997) *A New Companion to Homer*.

homicide see HUMAN SACRIFICE; MURDER.

homosexuality In modern terms, homosexuality is the sexual desire one individual has for another person of the same sex. From the ancient perspective, a man could have sexual desires for both men and women. In the Greek world, a desire for males can play out in pederasty, an *erastês* ('lover'), generally an older citizen, in a relationship with an *erômenos* ('loved one', 'beloved'), usually a freeborn adolescent. Homoerotic relations could also be employed in courtship rituals at the *SYMPOSIA*, where eligible bachelors substituted boys for young girls. An abusive relationship was not generally acceptable, and parents of youths taking part in such activities usually kept a watchful eye on the relationships. Cohen suggests that if an older male transgressed his relationship with a youth, the parents could charge him with *hybris* or insult, outrage or abuse. Athenian men engaging in PROSTITUTION, or in any passive sexual role, could potentially lose certain benefits that CITIZENSHIP offered, such as the right to address the ASSEMBLY. Legal statutes also technically protected young Athenian schoolboys by minimizing the potential for the development of sexual liaisons.

Traditionally, the writings of PLATO, XENOPHON and ARISTOTLE have been the basis for discussion of homoerotic relations between men in the Greek world. According to the literary sources, young men were ideally encouraged to dissuade any sexual advances or reciprocity of gifts. This was not necessarily the case in practice, as the material record shows. VASE-PAINTINGS frequently depict older males, usually bearded, absorbed in conversation with, handing over gifts to, and fondling their younger, clean-shaven suitors.

SPARTAN messes (*syssitia*) may have constituted another environment for males to consummate their sexual desires. Young men at the age of 20 were required to join the boot camps comprising only males. Spartan WOMEN also engaged in relations with both men and other women, as PLUTARCH suggests (*Lykourgos* 18).

HOMOSEXUALITY: the relationships between older and younger male (*erastês* and *erômenos*) were often idealized in Greek society.

Perhaps SAPPHO's relationships are those most often cited for homoerotic relations between women. She lived in the city of Mytilene on the island of LESBOS, whose women were known for intellectual prowess and beauty. Allusions in her poems to relations between women are fragmentary, but, when mentioned, appear to draw parallels with pederasty. The modern term 'lesbian' derives from this context and refers solely to same-sex relations between women. In antiquity, however, women (on Lesbos or elsewhere) could desire both men and women.

Similarly, one should not employ modern definitions of homosexuality, heterosexuality or bisexuality for the ancient Roman male. These words do not have correlative terms in Latin. A man or *vir* could have sex with another male, but what distinguished him from a 'non-man' (i.e. a SLAVE or a woman) was the sexual act itself (whether oral or anal): 'men' assumed the insertive role in penetration. Those who took on passive or penetrated roles (*pathici*) were considered 'non-men'; a freeborn male who chose to be part of such a relationship was still considered a 'man' as long as he assumed the dominant role. Foreign freeborn status was one avenue to a socially acceptable relationship. One noteworthy relationship was that between the emperor HADRIAN and ANTINOUS, a Bithynian of slave or possibly freeborn status. Hadrian clearly expressed sexual desire for both men and women, since he was married to Sabina. If Antinous was a slave, his relationship with Hadrian will have been deemed socially acceptable. If he was freeborn, the key was that he was not a Roman but a Bithynian.

To say that freeborn males did not engage in sexual relations with one another is erroneous, but they faced potential societal scorn and even legal penalties. For example, a freeborn male who had sexual relations with a freeborn Roman male, or indeed a freeborn Roman female, could be charged under the *lex Scantinia* for *stuprum*, shameful behaviour.

Pederastic relations between Roman males should not be regarded as inherently a consequence of Greek influence. It was perfectly acceptable for freeborn men to engage in sexual relations with their slaves or with prostitutes. Because of the slave's position in Roman law – that is, she or he was the property of the master – the master could do what he pleased with the slave and could not be legally penalized for engaging in sexual relations. Male prostitutes, *exoleti*, could be hired to perform either passive or aggressive roles in penetration. These males were usually past adolescence and typically belonged to a different master.

Roman literature provides suggestive evidence for women engaging in relationships with both men and women. For instance, SENECA THE ELDER refers to a man who killed his wife and the woman she was caught in bed with (*Controversiae* 1.2.23). MARTIAL makes reference to women who seek out both boys and girls for sexual gratification (1.90, 7.67). LAH

See Clarke, J. (1998) *Looking at Lovemaking*; Cohen, D. (1991) *Law, Sexuality and Society: the enforcement of morals in classical Athens*; Dover, K. (1978) *Greek Homosexuality*; Stewart, A. (1997) *Art, Desire and the Body in Ancient Greece*; Fantham, E. et al., eds. (1994) *Women in the Classical World*; Kilmer, M. (1997) Painters and pederasts: ancient art, sexuality and social history, in M. Golden and P. Toohey, eds., *Inventing Ancient Culture* 36–49; Williams, C. A. (1999) *Roman Homosexuality*; Winkler, J. (1990) *The Constraints of Desire*.

 ATHLETES AND ATHLETICS: (c).

honey (Greek *meli*, Latin *mel*) The product of the honey-bee, *Apis mellifera*. Since cane sugar was a costly eastern import, honey was the best available SWEETENER and source of dietary sugar. As such it was used in cookery and mixed to make sweet drinks. A mixture with water or milk was called *hydromeli* or *melikrêton*; a mixture with vinegar was *oxymeli*. Mixtures of honey with WINE made favourite aperitifs in classical Rome, under the names of *mulsum* and (when matured, with SPICES added) *conditum*. In these and other forms, honey was important in MEDICINE.

Honey was still gathered from the wild in classical Greece and Rome, as it had been in prehistoric Europe. BEEKEEPING, however, had already begun in Egypt in the 3rd millennium BC and was familiar in Greece (by 400 BC) and eventually in Roman Italy. Information on classical beekeeping comes not only from ARCHAEOLOGY but also from detailed written instructions by the farming authors VARRO and COLUMELLA and the poet VIRGIL. In myth, Aristaios was said to have shown the use of honey to humanity.

Honey was familiar as a light yellow liquid (not usually set or crystallized) which darkens and thickens with storage. It often had a smoky taste because smoke was used to drive the bees away while it was taken from the hive. It was well known that honey varied in flavour; the best was agreed to be that of Mt Hymettos in ATTICA, which had the aroma of thyme. AD

See Crane, E. (1999) *The World History of Beekeeping and Honey Hunting*.

Honorius (Flavius Honorius) AD 384–423 Western Roman emperor. On the death of his father THEODOSIUS I in 395, Honorius became emperor of the Western provinces while his brother Arcadius ruled in the East with a separate administration. Although the empire was still united in theory, this did not prevent rivalry between them; in particular, Honorius' supreme military commander, STILICHO, sought to influence affairs at Arcadius' court. The confrontations resulting from this rivalry were celebrated in polemical verse by the poet CLAUDIAN.

Honorius' reign was marked by constant military crisis leading to the territorial dismemberment of the Western empire. Invasions of ITALY by Gothic units of federate troops forced Honorius to move his court from MILAN to a more secure location at RAVENNA. Having caused much disruption in Italy, the Goths under ALARIC sacked Rome in 410; it was the first seizure of the city by barbarians (albeit barbarians serving in the Roman army) for eight centuries. In the aftermath, southern GAUL was given up to the Goths and north-western Spain to the VANDALS.

Honorius' regime was always weak. His inability to protect the empire from barbarian assault provoked a series of rebellions in BRITAIN (which he abandoned), Gaul and AFRICA. Following his death, the West was seized by the usurper John. Even at court, Honorius' government was dominated by others, above all by Stilicho until 408 and then by the patrician Constantius, who ultimately became co-emperor, until 421. MDH

See Claudian, 2 vols., trs. M. Platnauer (1922); Cameron, A. (1970) *Claudian*; Matthews, J. F. (1975) *Western Aristocracies and Imperial Court, AD 364–425*.

 THEODOSIUS I.

honour The high public regard in which a person is held, and HONOURS are the specific manifestations of that esteem. While the pursuit of honour was a noteworthy feature of ancient society at all points, it was particularly important in early Greek society, in which values were externalized; one's standing in society depended heavily on the general assessment of the community. In Greek the basic word for honour is *timê*, which refers broadly to the regard that is due to GODS as well as to one's superiors. In epic, *timê* properly belongs to KINGS (*Odyssey* 5.335) and safeguarding one's *timê* is necessary to maintaining one's position in society. In the world of the HOMERIC poems the warriors fight to win honour (*Iliad* 1.159), and the spoils of WAR (*geras*, 'prize', is the commonest term) are concrete manifestations of *timê*. In fact, the central conflict of the *Iliad* is built around a slight in the matter of *timê*: AGAMEMNON takes away Briseïs, ACHILLES' *geras*, and thus dishonours the hero (1.356). While Greek society is hardly static, concern for honour remained an important feature of social values, and *philotimia* (literally 'the love of *timê*) remains a salient characteristic of the ARISTOCRACY throughout Greco-Roman antiquity. The rich evidence for Athens of the classical period shows that *philotimia* resided in the zealous discharging of one's financial obligations to the state, especially in ways that were publicly conspicuous. There is a similar emphasis on the Roman concept of honour (*honos*), and the term is regularly used of public office (also in the plural, *honores*). CGB

See Fisher, N. R. E. (1992) *Hybris: a study in the values of honour and shame in ancient Greece*; Cairns, D. (1993) *Aidos: the psychology and ethics of honour and shame in ancient Greek literature*.

honours, public The award of various honours by Greek *POLEIS* (by means of a decree) to distinguished personalities, in return for, but also in anticipation of, services or BENEFACTIONS (material or other) to the community was a widespread institution in the Greek world. Their nature and scale depended on the benefaction(s) as well as the status of the honorand. Usually a foreigner received public praise and a crown, and was granted the title of benefactor (*euergetês*) and *proxenos* together with other privileges like the right to own land and a house in the territory of the awarding community. Bestowal of CITIZENSHIP was a higher and therefore rare HONOUR. In the classical period, citizens received a modest reward (e.g. a crown) for satisfactory performance of civic duties (like service on the council) but were not for that reason regarded as benefactors.

In the hellenistic period the institution was adopted to suit powerful individuals operating outside the *POLIS*. KINGS were often deified, and their officials were sometimes rewarded with the highest honours (including a statue) in order to recognize, demonstrate and encourage continuous benevolence towards the various cities. Citizens also had their share in the highest honours, reflecting their enhanced role in the survival of the *polis*. It was only in the late hellenistic period that bestowal of honours became a routine. IK

See Henry, A. S. (1983) *Honours and Privileges in Athenian Decrees*; Gauthier, P. (1985) *Les Cités grecques et leurs bienfaiteurs*; Herman, G. (1987) *Ritualised Friendship and the Greek City*; Veyne, P. (1990) *Bread and Circuses*.

hoplites Greek infantrymen of the *POLIS* (c.700–300 BC) were known as *hoplitai* because of their cumbersome gear (*hopla*): bronze breastplate, greaves, and helmet; double-grip, concave wooden shield; spear about 2.7 m (9 ft) long; and secondary short iron sword. The large shield, over 7 kg (15 lb) in weight and 1 m (3 ft) in diameter, explains the nature of hoplite fighting. The infantryman depended on the man next to him, to shield his own unprotected right side and maintain the cohesion of the entire phalanx. Military service now reinforced the solidarity of the citizenry. The shield's unique double grip allowed its weight to be held by the left arm alone, and its concave shape permitted the rear ranks to rest it on their shoulders as they pushed on ahead.

The weight of the panoply, ranging from 20 to 30 kg (50 to 70 lb), meant that hoplite battle would be short and decisive. Infantrymen massed into the columns of the phalanx and charged each other head-on. Soldiers sought cover in the array of shields, and victory through the sheer force generated by spearmen pushing against the backs of those ahead. On flat ground, hoplites in formation usually were invulnerable to mounted assault and the harassment of skirmishers. The battles of MARATHON (490 BC) and PLATAEA (479) are testaments to hoplite dominance over an array of foreign infantry, while KORONEIA (394) and LEUKTRA (371) illustrate the sheer brutality of such engagements between similarly equipped armies.

The hoplite's presence on the battlefield was a reflection of his free status in the *polis* community, and thus reinforced his privileged position as a yeoman farmer and voting citizen. Hoplite ASSEMBLIES alone decided when and where to fight, and sought such engagements to protect their own land and families. Originally hoplites, who provided their own weapons and ARMOUR and met strict property qualifications regulating military service, were little more than half the adult population of their city-states. Pitched and near-ritual infantry collisions during a summer day reflected their parochial interests in keeping warfare amateurish and non-disruptive to the agrarian population. (In Sparta, exceptionally, the hoplites were full-time soldiers who did not themselves farm.)

After the PERSIAN WARS, with the rise of the maritime Athenian empire of the 5th century BC, the limitations of hoplite warfare in an increasingly MEDITERRANEAN-wide theatre of operations became obvious. Fighting on land and sea required troops of all sorts: free and SLAVE, citizen and foreigner, conscript and MERCENARY. TAXATION and the growing importance of capital and SIEGECRAFT spelled the end of the primacy of shock battles between amateur farmers on plains. Gradually the hoplite lost his exclusivity, as Greek warfare became a dynamic enterprise designed to storm cities, destroy communities and acquire booty – a science divorced from cultural censure. With the rise of Macedonia, phalangites – their pikes extended to 5.5 m (18 ft) and defensive armour diminished to ensure greater mobility – became merely one contingent of a complex fighting force of CAVALRY, light infantry and missile troops. The ideal of hoplite warfare as an extension of civic agrarianism was lost, and with it the autonomy of the city-state itself. VDH

See Hanson, V. D. (2000) *The Western Way of War*; ed. (1991) *Hoplites*.

 ARMS AND ARMOUR: (a).

HOPLITES: the distinctive shield type (Theban) indicates that these warriors are from central Greece.

Horace (Quintus Horatius Flaccus) 65–8 BC POET. Owing in large part to the personal style of his poetry, we know considerably more about Horace's background and life than that of most ancient poets. He was born in Venusia in Apulia, of relatively humble stock: his father, he tells us in the autobiographical *Satire* 1.6, was a FREEDMAN but of sufficient means to have his son educated in Rome and Athens. In 43, Horace was appointed *tribunus militum* in the army of BRUTUS, but received a pardon after Brutus' defeat by MARK ANTONY and Octavian (the future AUGUSTUS) at PHILIPPI, whereupon he returned to Italy. Here he was introduced by his fellow-poets Varius and VIRGIL (apparently a close friend) to the literary patron MAECENAS. In due course, he became one of Maecenas' most highly favoured protégés, and enjoyed both his friendship and material support (the latter in the form, most notably, of a farm in the Sabine hills, to which Horace frequently refers in glowing terms). In the later years of his life, he attained a status something like that of poet laureate. The ancient *Life* of the poet, usually attributed to SUETONIUS, records that the *Carmen saeculare* (a hymn composed for performance at the Secular Games of 17) was directly commissioned by AUGUSTUS, at whose request the poet is also said to have embarked on the fourth book of *Odes* (a later addition to the original three-volume collection) and *Epistles* 2.1.

Horace's poetic output was extensive and varied. His earliest works, the *Epodes* and *Satires*, were composed during the period of the second TRIUMVIRATE and Octavian's rise to power. The former is a collection of 17 short poems in predominantly iambic metres. The majority adopt the aggressive tone traditionally associated with this metrical form: the subject matter ranges from attacks on ageing women, the social climber and the second-rate poet to more or less pessimistic reflections on contemporary politics and CIVIL WAR. The two books of *Sermones* or *Satires* (literally 'conversations'), published in c.35 and 30 BC – the second book contemporaneously with the *Epodes* – consist predominantly (though not exclusively) of moralizing diatribes, leavened by a strong note of witty humour and self-mockery. In the second book, the satiric message is frequently 'delegated' to other speakers, while the poet himself comes under attack more than once for his hypocrisy, inconsistency and other alleged vices. Horace's philosophical outlook in the *Satires* – as in the later *Epistles* – might be described as a loose, non-doctrinaire form of EPICUREANISM, with the emphasis on contentment with one's lot in life and the enjoyment of simple pleasures, together with a rejection of financial and political ambition.

Horace's most enduring reputation, as a lyric poet, was established by the three books of *Odes* (23 BC), to which a fourth was added in or after 13 BC. Although the *Satires* were more influential in antiquity, the poet's own prediction that the *Odes* would stand as 'a monument more enduring than bronze' (*Odes* 3.30.1) has proved true in the long run. The *Odes* are explicitly modelled on the work of the archaic and classical LYRIC poets (notably ALKAIOS, SAPPHO and PINDAR), but Horace gives his Greek exemplars a distinctly modern and Roman twist. Themes such as love, friendship and political life recur in Horatian as in Greek lyric, but are given in Horace's hands a new, quasi-philosophical colouring. The themes of contentment and peace of mind are prominent here, as in the *Satires*. Characteristic, too, are the ideals of moderation and enjoyment of life's fleeting pleasures (the famous phrase *carpe diem*, 'seize the day', is coined in *Odes* 1.11). The poems dealing with love can be seen in many cases as reacting against the passionate romanticism of CATULLUS and the elegists: Horace represents himself as a more realistic and resigned, less obsessive lover, prepared to take his pleasures where he may and to observe VENUS' 'cruel tricks' (1.33.12) with wry amusement. In his political poems (notably the so-called 'Roman odes', 3.1–6), Horace celebrates the ascendancy of Augustus and his programme of moral and religious reform while maintaining an air of studious – and sometimes perhaps critical – detachment. The *Odes* are further set apart from their Greek models by their intense stylistic refinement: Horace's metrical virtuosity is self-consciously displayed in the opening sequence of nine poems (the 'Parade Odes') in nine different metres. It is in the *Odes*, above all, that the *curiosa felicitas* ('studied felicity') for which he is praised by a character in PETRONIUS' *Satyrica* is to be observed. Deceptive simplicity of language, careful placement of words within the verse, and striking juxtapositions combine to produce an effect of concise and understated yet powerfully expressive eloquence.

Philosophical concerns come once again to the fore in the first book of *Epistles* (20 BC). This collection of verse letters to friends and acquaintances deals with a variety of subjects, but most prominent is the theme of philosophical retirement. (The epistolary form is used in several cases to emphasize the poet's distance – symbolic as well as literal – from the centre of things in Rome.) The two long epistles which make up the second book (c.3 BC) are concerned with literary matters. The *Epistle to the Pisones* or *Ars Poetica* (*Art of Poetry*) can be regarded as belonging to this group, but is sometimes treated as an independent DIDACTIC poem.

Like many of his contemporaries, Horace displays throughout his work an allegiance to the poetic principles – stylistic refinement, brevity, wit, recherché learning – associated with the name of KALLIMACHOS. The poet's commitment to Kallimachean canons of style is perhaps most evident in the studied elegance of the *Odes*, but can be detected even in the *Satires*, despite their self-consciously chatty manner (thus, Horace is critical of the prolixity of his otherwise admired predecessor Lucilius). In contrast to Catullus and the elegists, however, Horace sought in such poems as the 'Roman odes' to combine these poetic principles with a solemn and elevated mode of expression. Tension between 'public' and 'private' voices, between ideological engagement and playful lightness of touch, is a striking characteristic of the Horatian *corpus* as a whole. MG

See Horace, *Odes and Carmen saeculare*, trs. G. Lee (1998); Armstrong, D. (1989) *Horace*; Fraenkel, E. (1957) *Horace*; Rudd, N., trs. (1979) *The Satires of Horace and Persius*.

horoscopes see ASTROLOGY; ZODIAC.

horses and horsemanship The favoured riding animal of the ancient world, the horse, had a long history of domestication before the Greeks and Romans. Horses were bred and trained for CAVALRY use in war, for CHARIOT RACING and CIRCUSES (the use of chariots in WAR had declined by the end of the Bronze Age), and for normal riding. They were less commonly used as pack animals (mules and DONKEYS being more fit for that purpose).

In Greece from c.700–c.350 BC, horses were more commonly used for transport to battle, rather than as cavalry. Although armed riders were well established, it is clear from XENOPHON (an authority on horses who wrote a number of treatises on horsemanship and HUNTING) that they were not important in war. During the course of his expedition in PERSIA, however, he became aware of their potential in fighting the mounted PARTHIAN archers, famous for the 'Parthian shot' (shooting arrows while retreating). Certainly by the time of ALEXANDER the Great, cavalry formed an important part of Greek and Macedonian armies; at the time of Alexander's invasion of Asia in 334 BC, his cavalry is said by Arrian to have numbered 5,000.

Horses played an important role in Greek PROCESSIONS and spectacles. Chariot racing was a popular sport, central to sacred games such as those at

HORSES AND HORSEMANSHIP: north African mosaic depicting a Roman stud farm and, in the roundels, pairs of famous chariot horses.

OLYMPIA. Here, two- and four-horse CHARIOTS were raced by men of rich family. Indeed, horses and chariot racing were a symbol of WEALTH and status, and success in racing gave great renown.

In the Roman world, cavalry played an important role in battle but increasingly performed skirmishing roles, as well as reconnaissance. They came also to be used in relays as part of the *cursus publicus*, the imperial postal service established by AUGUSTUS and modelled on that of the Persians and PTOLEMIES.

The breeding of horses receives much attention from the Roman agricultural writers COLUMELLA and VARRO. The finest horses were bred for chariot racing and sacred games. Other fine horses were kept as breeding stock – especially for mules, which were important to the army's requirement for pack-animals. In agriculture, the horse had only a very small role to play. In Egyptian PAPYRI, our best source of evidence for everyday life in the ancient world, horses appear infrequently and usually only as riding animals for the wealthy, as military mounts, or for racing. They were valuable animals and expensive to maintain, so they were beyond the means of, and of little benefit to, ordinary farmers. Horses remained the preserve of the rich, and this is clear also from the treatises on horse breeding and horsemanship, from Xenophon to Columella and Varro. CEPA

See Clutton-Brock, J. (1992) *Horse Power: a history of the horse and the donkey in human societies*; Hyland, A. (1990) *Equus: the horse in the Roman world*.

 CAVALRY: (a)–(b).

Hostilius, Tullus The third KING of Rome, who traditionally reigned 672–641 BC. His first name is unique and his gentilicial name rare, so it is unlikely that he was invented by a later family seeking to legitimate its position. The sources state that he was the SENATE's choice after the death of NUMA, and he contrasts sharply with the religious and pacific second king in being noted for his military successes. His father was Latin and his mother SABINE (reflecting the two populations which had joined at Rome); he campaigned against Fidenae and VEII, and those Sabines who were still hostile. His major achievement was the subjugation of Alba Longa, finally decided by the duel between the Horatii and the Curiatii brothers. He is also given credit for building the CURIA Hostilia, the senate house of Rome. Rome's expanding territory and the development of the FORUM area in the 7th century are archaeologically attested, though this by no means proves the historicity of the king or of the ancient accounts. His death is variously reported; some sources have him die in a fire caused by a thunderbolt from heaven, as retribution for his wrongful celebration of certain religious rites; others make him the victim of his successor, Ancus Marcius. CJS

See Dionysios of Halikarnassos 3.1–35; Livy 1.22–31; Cornell, T. J. (1995) *The Beginnings of Rome*.

hotels

see INNS.

households

A fundamental social and political unit of classical Greek city-states. The Greek for household is *oikos* or *oikia*, words which can also mean 'house' (in a physical sense), 'estate', or even 'lineage', depending on the context. ARISTOTLE (*Politics* 1252b), writing political theory in the 4th century BC, conceptualized the household as based on two kinds of hierarchical relationship: husband to wife, and master to SLAVE. His analysis indicates that Greeks thought of households as including people other than family members, such as slaves. ANIMALS, property, land and businesses were also conceptually part of the household.

The senior male, generally the father of the family, acted as the *kyrios*, 'master' or 'head of household'. He served as the public representative of the household in economic, political and legal business, from which WOMEN were barred. One LAWCOURT speech (Demosthenes 47) provides an interesting example of a slave woman working as a nanny, who was freed by the father of the family (the *kyrios*). Thereafter for many years she lived elsewhere with a 'husband', but after he died she returned to dwell as a freedwoman in the household where she had once been a slave, apparently on intimate terms with the family. By that time the son of the original *kyrios*, the little boy she had once looked after, was grown up and acting as the *kyrios* himself. (see also FAMILY) LF

See Cox, C. A. (1998) *Household Interests: property, marriage strategies and family dynamics in ancient Athens*; Patterson, C. B. (1998) *The Family in Greek History*; Pomeroy, S. B. (1997) *Families in Classical and Hellenistic Greece*.

The Latin word *familia* does not mean 'family' in our sense of the word, and *domus* far from always means 'house'. In fact, the Romans did not have a word meaning family in our sense, probably because the basic unit in Rome was never just the nuclear family of mother, father and children. Rather, it was the entire household, comprising the male head of the household (*paterfamilias*), his wife (*materfamilias*), their children (*filii* and *filiae familias*), SLAVES, FREEDPERSONS and other dependants. The words *familia* and *domus* are both used to designate the household, though the two words are not quite interchangeable. *Domus* tends to mean the household both in the sense of the physical frame and all the members of the household; *familia* usually refers to the slaves of a household.

The Roman household was the foundation of society, the basis on which the state was built. People married to beget children (*liberorum creandorum causa*) who would grow up and become good Roman citizens and establish households of their own. A man could not establish a household of his own until the oldest male in direct ascending line (almost invariably his father or grandfather) had died. In principle, the power of the male head of the household was unlimited: he had *patria potestas* over wife, children and slaves as long as he lived, including the power of life and death (*ius vitae necisque*). This power also implied that his children and grandchildren were unable to obtain economic independence during his lifetime, precluding the establishment of any new household during the lifetime of a *paterfamilias*. Only upon his death would sons become independent heads of households. Another governing principle for the household was the deep sense of obligation and loyalty between its members, termed *pietas*. It is very important to emphasize that *pietas* was reciprocal: it was not owed only by children to their parents and by dependants to their master, but also the other way round. Therefore *pietas* contains, together with obligation, a very strong emotional feeling of attachment: Romans felt this obligation towards the other members of the households they lived in because they cared for them. The two principles of *patria potestas* and *pietas* obviously conflict. They share ground only in one respect, namely, with regard to the emphasis on a consciousness of preserving and protecting the family name and property over the generations.

Romans had a sentimental view of their historical past. Therefore, though there can be no doubt that the Roman household and state always remained strongly patriarchal and hierarchical, the old concept of *patria potestas* survived to a period where its reality had become obsolete. First, from about 200 BC MARRIAGE *sine manu* had been common. Unlike marriage *cum manu*, this implied that a bride was not legally transferred from her birth family to her husband's family but remained in the *patria potestas* of her father or grandfather, though she was also seen as very much a member of the household she had married into. Second, the DEMOGRAPHIC reality of Roman society should not be overlooked. Most people would have lost their fathers when they were about the age of 25, meaning that they became economically and legally independent, at the latest, at that age. Many would be orphaned much earlier and would be looked after, in economic terms, by a GUARDIAN. In the third place, because of DEATH and DIVORCE, remarriage was frequent, ensuring that many persons would be members of a household whose *paterfamilias* did not have *patria potestas* over them. Lastly, the right to 'power of life and death' is almost unheard of in later Republican and imperial times, perhaps with the exception of infant exposure that was practised throughout the history of Rome.

The more violent side of *patria potestas* is visible in the treatment of slaves. In contrast to the children of the household, slaves could be disciplined by being whipped. Excessive cruelty was checked by concern for one's reputation, but the sources frequently refer to VIOLENCE towards slaves as commonplace. Violence and the threat of violence were seen as natural ways to establish and maintain power relations. Slaves, in daily language often called the *familia*, might live in the *domus* of their master or mistress, or on his or her farm, but would still be considered members of the same household. Generally, slaves who lived under the same roof as their masters had a higher status than slaves working in the country, and were therefore treated better and less violently.

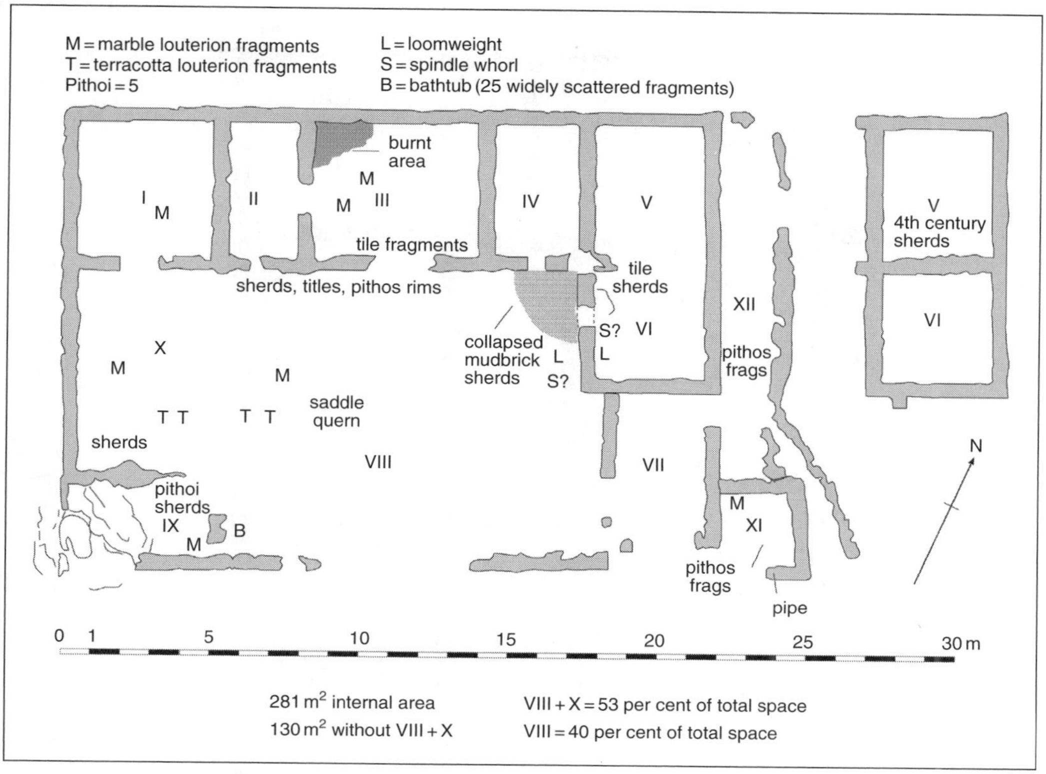

HOUSES, GREEK: (a) located north of Athens on a busy main road, the Dema House was probably the country house of a wealthy family in the late 5th century BC, perhaps abandoned because of the Spartan occupation of Dekeleia in 411. It is similar in layout to the urban houses found at Olynthos, with rooms off a large central courtyard. Although there were substantial storage facilities (indicated by the pithos fragments), there is no direct evidence of agricultural processing activities, and the range of material is similar to that found on urban sites.

Accordingly, their chances of being manumitted were higher. Upon MANUMISSION, slaves took the family name of their master or mistress and became Roman citizens; they remained members of the household as freedpersons. The connection between family name and household is important. The shared name naturally shows the extension of the power and influence of the master of a Roman household, but even more importantly reveals how far the sense of obligation and loyalty extended for members of the household. The expectations that parents and children had of each other are not surprising, but the inclusion of freedpersons of the household is extraordinary. Perhaps the BURIAL practice of households of a suitable size shows this most clearly: freedpersons and the descendants of freedpersons are usually mentioned explicitly among those who are to receive burial in the household TOMB. Likewise, freedpersons are naturally expected not only to continue the name of their former masters in the future, but also to preserve his memory through annual rites at the tomb. HSN

See Saller, R. (1994) *Patriarchy, Property, and Death in the Roman Family.*

houses

Despite the amount of textual material which survives from the Greek world, detailed descriptions of houses are rare. Our picture is mainly

HOUSES, GREEK: (b) reconstruction drawing of the Dema house.

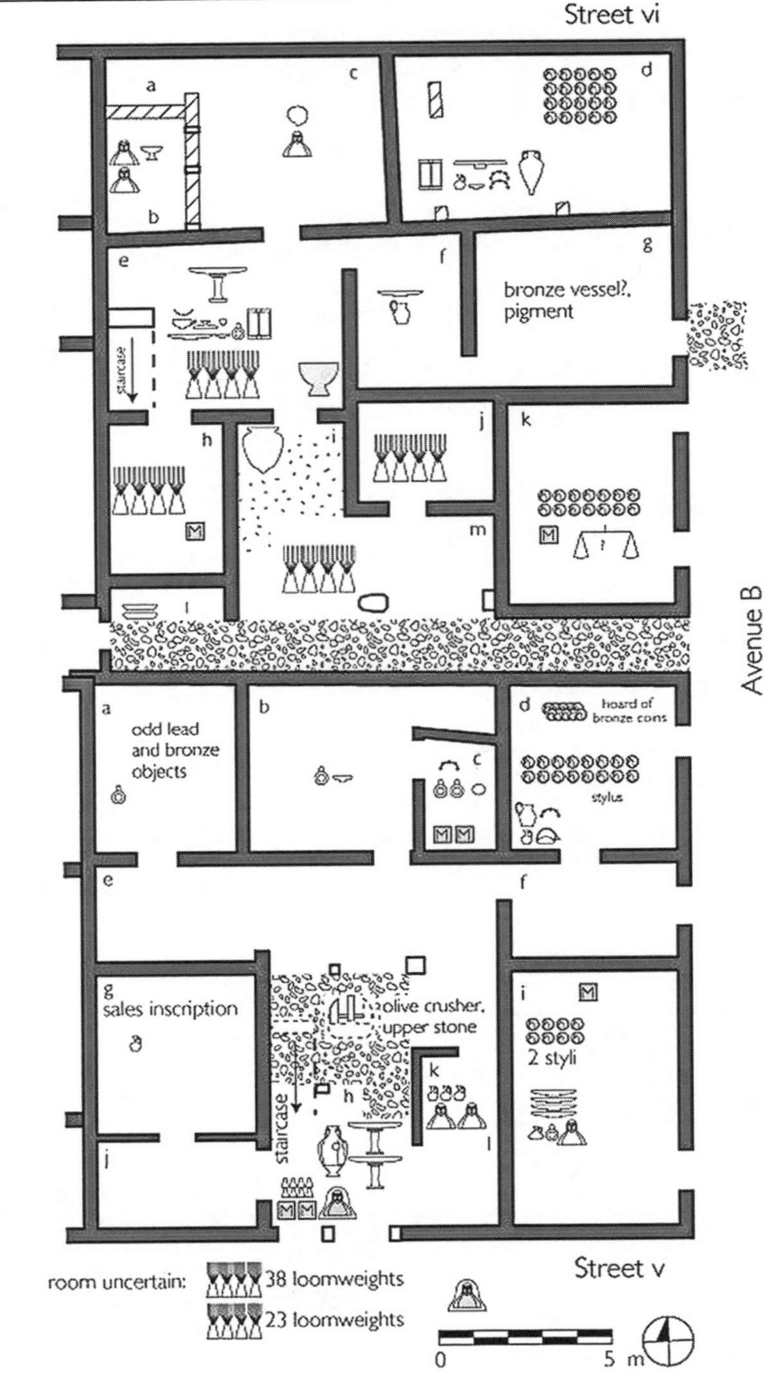

HOUSES, GREEK: (c) Olynthos, Houses Av9 and Av10. These two urban houses from Olynthos served as both domestic accommodation and as the location for shops and businesses. The southern house (Av10) has a large courtyard with double doors big enough for vehicles. The olive crushing stone found in the courtyard may indicate agricultural or industrial processing on a substantial scale, and there are three shops on the eastern side, with doors opening directly onto the street. The northern house (Av9) was apparently a textile factory as well as a house: the number of loomweights suggests at least four looms, which is too great for a single family's needs.

based on excavations, which usually reveal stone bases for mudbrick walls, now lost, together with architectural features such as column-bases, POTTERY and other household objects.

Between the 8th and 6th centuries there was considerable variation in house size and design. During the earlier part of the period, some houses were oval or apsidal, with a door at one end and a thatched roof (as at Nichoria in MESSENIA). Elsewhere, a square or rectangular shape was favoured, with a flat mud roof. Internal space was divided into a small number of rooms (as at Zagora on Andros). By the 6th century, the second pattern was dominant. A small range of architectural features and finds from these structures indicates that basic activities such as STORAGE and preparation of food, and production of cloth, were carried out in them.

Evidence from the late 6th to mid-5th centuries is scarce, but by the late 5th a distinctive house type had emerged which, with some variation, is found widely across the Greek world. Typically these structures covered 200–300 sq m and were square or rectangular with a flat or TILED ROOF. Each usually had only a single street entrance and a few small, high windows. Interior space was organized around an open court surfaced with plaster or with stone flags. The rooms were reached individually from here via a portico, the main ones being located to the north so that the low sun could warm the interior in winter. There was sometimes an upper storey, reached via a staircase in the court.

A widely used architectural typology divides these houses into three major forms, distinguished by differences in the portico surrounding the court. In the *prostas* house, first identified at Priene in ASIA Minor, a porch stands in front of the main room. In the *pastas* house, exemplified by the houses at OLYNTHOS, a longer portico shelters the entrances to several rooms. The third, slightly later type, the peristyle house, extends the columned portico around all four sides of the court.

Much of the domestic equipment is no longer preserved, and it is often difficult to reconstruct daily activity. Nevertheless, architectural features and finds recorded *in situ* offer a picture of some of the activities within. A variety of finds suggests that the court was used for a range of domestic activity. There was often a shaft here, giving access to a well or cistern below, which supplied the household water and sometimes a washbasin nearby. Commonly there was an interior bathroom with a terracotta bathtub, next to a large room with a hearth and a cooking area. Interior scenes on painted pottery give some indication of the decorative TEXTILES, wooden chairs, tables and chests that may have been present. Two parts of the house preserve more permanent decoration: the walls of the court sometimes had panels of red or yellow painted plaster, while similar decoration can also occur in one of the rooms, identified as the *andrôn* mentioned in textual sources as the location of the *SYMPOSION* or male drinking-party. Its decorative effect is sometimes increased by the presence of a MOSAIC floor, with an undecorated border marking off space reserved for the couches on which the revellers reclined.

The existence of the *andrôn* is one of the characteristics of classical Greek houses most frequently mentioned by ancient authors. Its link with the *symposion* has led to its being interpreted as a male area, contrasted with a corresponding female area called the *gynaikôn*. Thus scholars have pictured a household divided into separate men's and women's quarters. This, however, is not supported by the archaeological evidence. More probably *gynaikôn* refers to the remainder of the house, aside from the *andrôn*, that was used by the family as a whole.

The simplicity and homogeneity of these structures has been interpreted as a tangible sign of the egalitarian ideals of the democratic *POLIS*. This is not certain, however. By the mid-4th century, though some houses continued to resemble their 5th-century predecessors, there was a parallel trend towards progressively larger constructions, which by the 3rd century covered up to 2,000–3,000 sq m. Much of this area was occupied by unroofed courtyard space, but there was also an increase in the number of rooms and, in particular, apartments with mosaic floors. To accommodate this increase in size, such houses were built around two courts. Often the decorated rooms clustered around an ornate columned peristyle, while the domestic facilities were located around a second, simpler court (as at Eretria).

Limited evidence from Athens and Olynthos suggests that these kinds of housing were not available to all members of society, and that throughout the 5th to 3rd centuries some families lived in only two or three rooms and a small courtyard, with no colonnade and no *andrôn* or interior decoration.

These distinctive patterns of house design had been superseded by the middle of the 2nd century BC. The large double-courtyard structures were no longer built, and often the single court which remained had a decorative function, housing ornaments or a GARDEN, while domestic activities were carried out inside (as at DELOS). LCN

See Hoepfner, W. and Schwandner, E.-L. (1994) *Haus und Stadt im klassischen Griechenland*; Jones, J. E. et al. (1952) The Dema house in Attica, *ABSA* 57: 75–114; Nevett, L. C. (1999) *House and Society in the Ancient Greek World*; Shipley, G. (2004) 'Little boxes on the hillside': was there utopian town planning in ancient Greece? in M. H. Hansen, ed., *The Imaginary Polis* 335–403.

Ostentatious mansions, brashly decorated with elaborate WALL-PAINTINGS and MOSAICS, characterized the Roman world. Lavish expenditure on private houses was more marked under Rome than previously, especially in the late Republic when ARCHITECTURAL fashion was aggressively exploited to enhance PATRICIAN prestige. The sophisticated Roman house was a regional variant of the hellenistic house, a departure from the earlier vernacular traditions of Iron Age Italy which date to the orientalizing period (8th–6th centuries BC). The evolution of Rome's houses is illustrated by the contrast between the traces of 9th- or 8th-century BC TIMBER huts on the Palatine hill and the adjacent remains of the massive Domus Augustana, DOMITIAN's imperial residence from which the word 'PALACE' derives.

The house was designed for Roman social life, and included public areas – such as audience halls for receiving clients at the morning *salutatio* – as well as private ones. The Roman ARCHITECT was more concerned to impress the guest within the house than the passer-by. External façades could be anonymous, entrances could be marked by simple porches, but

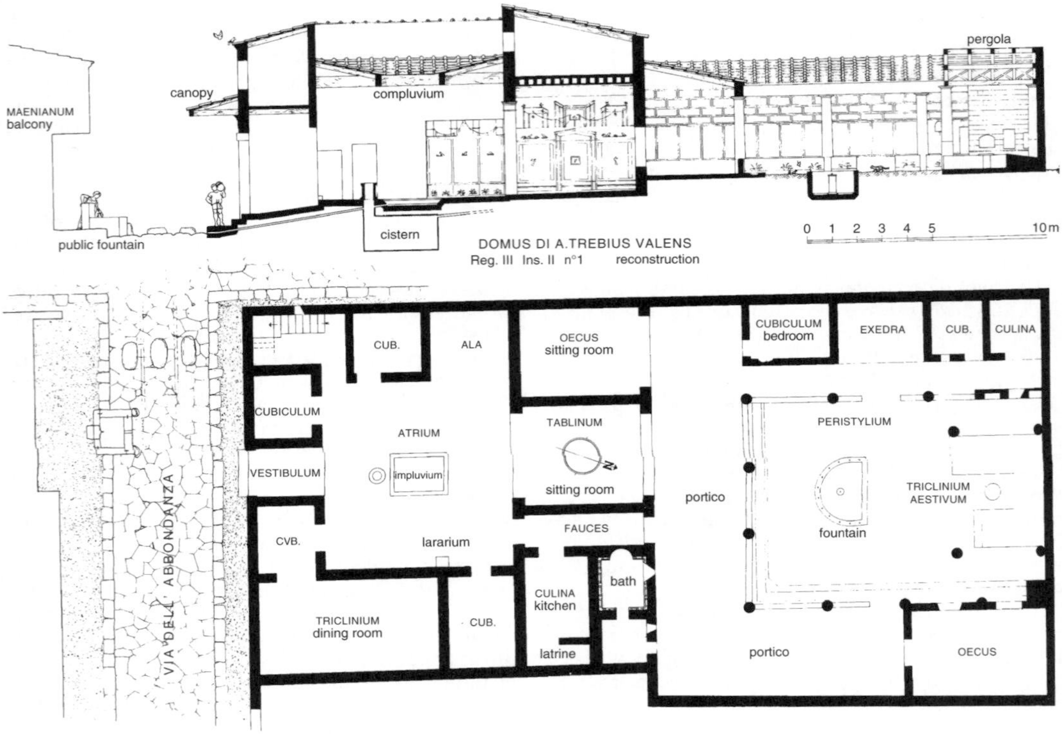

MAENIANUM
balcony
canopy
compluvium
pergola
public fountain
cistern
DOMUS DI A.TREBIUS VALENS
Reg. III Ins. II n°1 reconstruction
0 1 2 3 4 5 10m

CUB. ALA OECUS sitting room CUBICULUM bedroom EXEDRA CUB. CULINA
CUBICULUM ATRIUM TABLINUM PERISTYLIUM
VESTIBULUM impluvium sitting room portico TRICLINIUM AESTIVUM
CVB. lararium FAUCES fountain
bath
CULINA kitchen
TRICLINIUM dining room CUB. latrine portico OECUS
VIA DELL' ABBONDANZA

HOUSES, ROMAN: (a) plan and cross-section of a typical Pompeian atrium and peristyle house.

HOUSES, ROMAN: (b) atrium of the House of the Menander, Pompeii.

HOUSES, ROMAN: (c) peristyle of the House of the Vettii, Pompeii.

internal courtyards and GARDENS were increasingly used to establish striking views. The emphasis given to porticoes, corridors, forecourts and antechambers testifies to a hierarchical approach to space, where the privileged guest ascended to more intimate parts of the house. The essential facility here – found in all but the poorest houses – was the dining room. Arranged best to exploit available light, it frequently commanded views over formal gardens or courts. The main bedchambers were small but attached to suites of living rooms close to the reception areas. Service facilities were tucked away in the sides of the building. Separate rooms were not always provided for COOKING and TOILET activities. Domestic BATH-HOUSES were a rare facility though increasingly common in the later empire; but rooms heated with hypocaust floors were common in many regions.

Roman house design borrowed extensively from public architecture. Timber houses gave way to mudbrick-walled structures, which were in turn

HOUSES, ROMAN: (d) light and shade in a peristyle of the Oplontis villa at Torre Annunziata.

HOUSES, ROMAN: (e) the Via Biberatica, alongside Trajan's markets, gives a good impression of the exterior appearance of a Roman apartment house.

replaced by MASONRY and CONCRETE constructions, an architectural progression repeated in the formative phases of Roman settlements throughout the north-west provinces. Similarly, columns, ARCHES and apses were borrowed from public architecture to add *gravitas* to private spaces. Roman houses were less regular in layout than is sometimes assumed. HADRIAN'S VILLA at TIVOLI is a case in point. Although this building complex was designed around a number of key vistas with highly symmetrical elements, its overall plan lacks coherence.

Every community had its own building style, in which the standard elements of Roman house design were reinterpreted in local fashion. The Campanian *atrium*–peristyle house, described by VITRUVIUS and illustrated by examples buried by the eruption of Vesuvius in AD 79, is the most thoroughly documented. The House of the Faun at POMPEII is an elaborate example of the ideal type. A narrow entrance (*fauces*) opened onto an entrance hall (*atrium*), which was sometimes flanked by one or two wings (*alae*). The entrance hall was rarely entirely roofed over, and often contained a central basin (*impluvium*) for water catchment. From the archaic period the *atrium* was the focus of many household activities, including cooking and WEAVING, and the household shrine was usually located there. A reception room (*tablinum*) was frequently placed opposite the entrance. The introduction of a colonnaded GARDEN (*peristylium*) beyond these rooms is considered to have been inspired by Greek practice, and at Pompeii to date to the period after 180 BC. In the late Republic this formal garden, surrounded by the main rooms of the house including the main dining areas, replaced the hall as the centre of domestic life.

A separate tradition of Roman domestic architecture is evidenced by the multi-storied APARTMENT blocks of Rome and OSTIA, principally of 2nd-century AD date. This form of housing was made possible by developments in building techniques, in particular the use of cement, and was developed in response to urban overcrowding. Most people here lived in such accommodation. Although apartment blocks were generally of low status, and the higher the flat the poorer its quality, their tenants were not without social aspirations. Light was obtained not from courtyards within the buildings, but from large windows facing the street. Principal rooms – sometimes with mosaics and painted walls – were often located at the ends of buildings to exploit such lighting. Commonly the entrance hall had been reduced to little more than a corridor linking the more important rooms at either end, an arrangement illustrated by the Garden House at Ostia. These unheated buildings rarely had running water or private sewage.

Hellenistic-style courtyard houses were preferred in the Eastern empire. In these, a vestibule or corridor gave direct access to a central courtyard from which all major rooms were easily reached. Later courtyard houses often had one or two more magnificent reception rooms which opened onto a portico flanking the courtyard. This style of house was widely adopted in Italy in the later empire, notably at Ostia. Southern GAUL and Spain showed similarities to Italy. Here peristyle houses, sometimes prefaced by *impluviata atria*, were common. These building types were scarce in more northerly provinces, where the design of town houses owed much to the influence of both villas and commercial premises.

A building type well represented in urban and roadside settlements in the north-west provinces is the long 'strip building' set gable-end onto the street, with its shop to the front and living quarters – sometimes including one or two decorated reception rooms – behind. This building type is rare in Italy and the east, where single- or double-roomed commercial properties are more often found in rows around the edges of the larger town houses. DP

See Clarke, J. R. (1991) *The Houses of Roman Italy, 100 BC–AD 250*; Hales, S. (2003) *The Roman House and Social Identity*; Ward-Perkins, J. B. (1981) *Roman Imperial Architecture*.

 APARTMENT BUILDINGS; VILLAS: (a)–(b).

housework Few ancient authors deal directly with the ordinary daily tasks of washing, cleaning, cooking and running a household. This bias no doubt reflects the servile and female nature of much of this work. Advice to Greek husbands seeking wives stresses the importance of choosing one who can cook and clean. On Roman tombstones, housekeeping along with the production of children and textile manufacture is praised as one of the key female virtues. In Roman Egypt, we find MARRIAGE contracts that include housekeeping as one of the important duties of wives.

Few writers are interested in the practical mechanics of daily chores, despite their importance. References to housework tend to occur incidentally as part of other narratives. Activities such as doing laundry or fetching water provide a useful pretext for authors to locate their female characters outside the home and make them available for encounters with male protagonists. Some treatises offered advice on household management, but they were normally aimed at large estates operated by members of the wealthy ÉLITE and their usefulness for reconstructing the life of the majority is debatable. The wife in XENOPHON's *Oikonomikos* undertakes household duties not through necessity, but because it provides good exercise and improves her complexion (10.10–13). The spoilt wives of COLUMELLA's treatise on estate management are above housekeeping, and he advises handing over household management to the wife of the overseer (*On Agriculture* 12.9–10). She manages the house's resources, organizes storage, supervises the manufacture of clothing, preserves fruit and vegetables and oversees the cleaning. (See also COOKING; HOUSEHOLDS; SLAVES; WASHING; WOMEN) AJLB

human sacrifice Ritual slaying of a human as an offering to a divinity, usually to avert disaster in times of stress such as WAR, famine or plague. There are numerous examples of human sacrifice in Greek MYTHOLOGY. The theme of virgin sacrifice in time of war is particularly popular, for example the daughters of Erechtheus (Lykourgos, *Against Leokrates* 98–101). The GODS most frequently associated with human sacrifice are DIONYSOS and ARTEMIS. There is no evidence that human sacrifice was practised by the Greeks of the historical period, who viewed it as a practice of their remote past that had been mitigated or replaced by ANIMAL sacrifices, or as something practised by their BARBARIAN neighbours. Most modern scholars are sceptical as to whether the practice can be extrapolated back to some undefined period of Greek prehistory. The CARTHAGINIAN custom of sacrificing the firstborn child to Dionysos (BAAL HAMMON) is known from a number of Greek and Latin sources. There is some archaeological evidence for the rite, in the form of numerous *tophets* (specialized BURIAL grounds restricted to infant cremations) throughout the Punic west, which can be combined with the interpretation of dedicatory inscriptions on stelae from these sites. Human sacrifice might also include the ritual slaying of humans as an element of FUNERAL RITES. This might be an equivalent of the former Hindi custom of suttee (the burial of a female, presumably the wife, alongside a male), with which one might compare the double burial of a male and female in the Protogeometric *heroön* (so called) at Lefkandí Toúmba in Euboia; or it might involve the burial of retainers or SLAVES, such as the Skythian custom reported by Herodotos (4.71) or the 12 Trojans buried together with Patroklos (*Iliad* 18.333–7). LFS

See Brown, S. (1991) *Late Carthaginian Child Sacrifice and Sacrificial Monuments in their Mediterranean Context*; Hughes, D. D. (1991) *Human Sacrifice in Ancient Greece*.

Huns The Huns are first documented in Roman sources by AMMIANUS MARCELLINUS. He records their movements in eastern Europe in the 370s AD, when they conquered the Alan state and displaced the GOTHS from the BLACK SEA, thus precipitating major Germanic migrations within the Roman empire. The Huns formed one of a series of nomadic steppe tribes or confederacies; others later attacked the Byzantine empire, notably the Avars and Utrigurs – often erroneously called Huns by Byzantine sources (though such tribes perhaps encouraged the identification). Their origins are unclear, but they were perhaps displaced from central Asia by the Hsuing-nu recorded by Chinese historians. Fast horses and mounted archers were the key elements in their rapid expansion.

Between c.AD 400 and 435 the Huns occupied PANNONIA, the heartland for the 'empire' planned in the 440s by Attila, who advanced westwards towards GAUL, with numerous other campaigns and raids en route. The writings of the contemporary observer Priscus are invaluable in detailing Hunnic 'court' life, warfare and diplomacy under Attila. The Huns were finally repulsed by Aëtius' Roman–Franco-Gothic army at the Catalaunian Fields, forcing Attila's withdrawal. With Attila's death in 454, unified Hunnic power collapsed; many former subject tribes carved out kingdoms (as did the Ostrogoths in Pannonia), and varied Hunnic groups gained land as federates or entered Roman armies.

Key archaeological guides to the spread of the Huns and of Hunnic influence are the characteristic deep cauldrons ('stewpots') and instances of artificial skull deformation; the latter, however, appears to be a rite adopted by subjugated tribes, persisting after 450. Coin and metal hoards, plus a number of élite

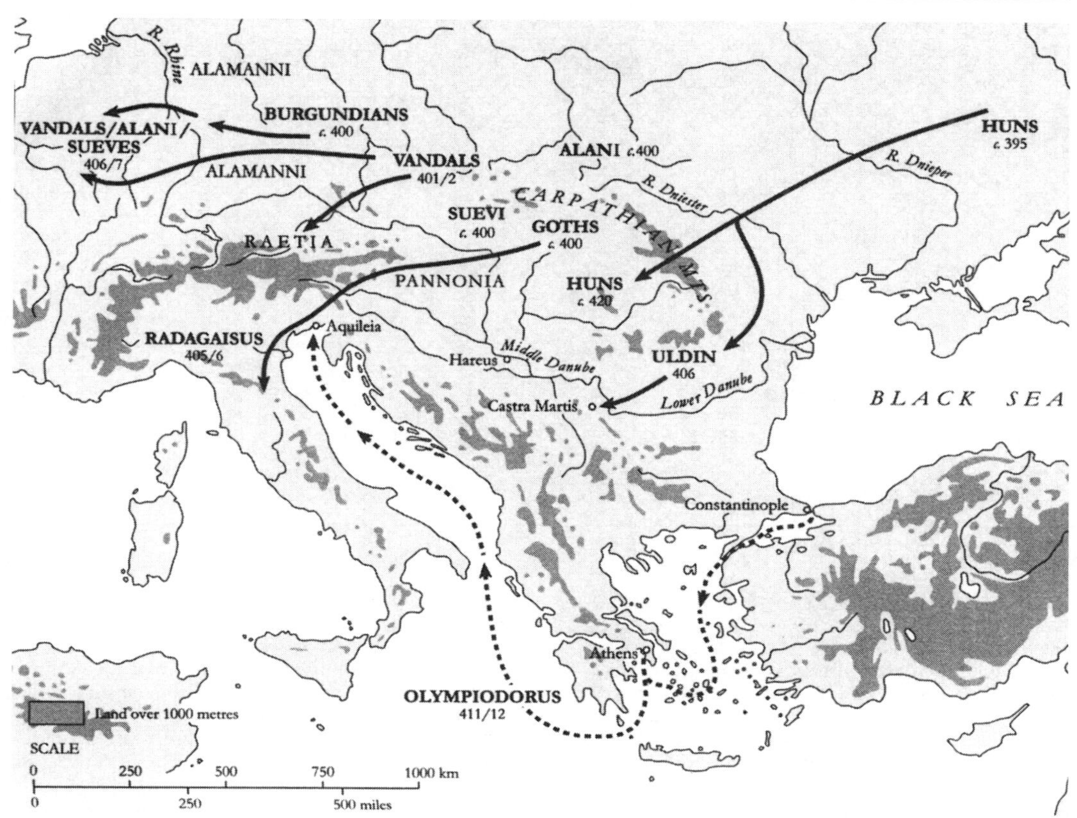

HUNS: map showing the impact of the westward migration of the Huns on Germanic peoples and on the Roman empire.

TOMBS in the middle Danube region, demonstrate Hunnic wealth. NJC

See Thompson, E. A. (1996) *The Huns*.

hunting In the archaic Greek period, ÉLITE men pursued stags and boars not just for the thrill of the hunt, but for food and in defence of themselves and their flocks. The heroic struggle between man and beast, and the dangers of hunting such ANIMALS, are reflected in legends such as those of ODYSSEUS slaying the Kalydonian boar (HOMER, *Odyssey* 19.418–58) or HERAKLES struggling with the Nemean lion. The use of the lion-hunt motif in MYCENAEAN and early Greek ART may also echo the importance of the Near Eastern royal lion hunt, so well attested in Assyria and Egypt. In the classical Greek world boars and deer were hunted on special occasions, but the usual quarry was the hare. A single hare was coursed by DOGS, with the hunters following on foot, often with nets. Hare hunting is a very common motif on vases, reflecting the popularity of the sport. Hunting was also seen as an important part of a young man's EDUCATION, in particular as preparation for WAR. The most detailed surviving account of Greek hunting techniques is XENOPHON's *Kynegetikos* (*Hunting Man*), which describes all aspects from the use of nets to breeds of hunting dogs.

Although hunting was still proclaimed to be a school of morals and martial arts, in the Roman world it became seen largely as sport and entertainment. However, there was still a hierarchy of esteem depending on the nature of the animal hunted, ranging from lions, boars, stags and hares to birds. Lion hunts were reserved by law for the emperor alone, and imperial propaganda was not slow to exploit the symbolism of the hunt. A series of medallions later incorporated into the ARCH of CONSTANTINE depicts the emperor HADRIAN hunting a lion, a boar and a bear. These scenes were paired with images of SACRIFICE, and thus symbolized the courage, manly virtue and piety of the emperor. The noble hunt of emperors such as Hadrian is often contrasted in literary sources with the mindless slaughter of effectively captive ANIMALS by 'tyrants' such as DOMITIAN and COMMODUS (PLINY THE YOUNGER, *Panegyricus* 81.1–3). Hunting as a symbol of heroism, and as an allegory for victory over death, is also a common motif on Roman SARCOPHAGI.

The hunting of boar, stag and hare was essentially an élite activity, often carried out on horseback in the Roman period. Servants and attendants were used to drive animals, catch them in nets and carry the dead animals home. A typical scene of such ARISTOCRATIC hunting for pleasure is depicted in a famous 4th-century hunting MOSAIC (the 'Small

HUNTING: professional hunters (*venatores*) employed in the Roman arena made public spectacle out of traditional élite pursuits. As this scene from the Hunting Baths, Lepcis Magna, shows, the action was not completely one-sided and some ferocious beasts established names (Rapidus) and reputations for themselves.

Hunt') from the rich villa in Piazza Armerina in Sicily. One of the central scenes shows the hunting party reclining for a picnic. The gentlemen are sheltered from the midday sun by an awning and stretch out on cushions. Servants supply food and drink while the horses are resting. The hunting net is slung over the branches of a nearby tree. The scene is something of a *topos* since it occurs in other media, including frescoes, sarcophagi, tapestries and silverware. Women generally did not hunt, though there are a few references to society ladies hunting (Juvenal, *Satires* 1.22–3). Hare hunting continued to be a popular sport in the Roman world and features prominently in another book on hunting, also called *Cynegeticus*, written by Arrian in the 2nd century AD. It details the aspects of the sport that had changed and developed since Xenophon's day. For example, in addition to the two main traditional breeds of dogs, the keen-scented Spartan hound used for tracking the prey and the heavier mastiffs used to bay it, Arrian describes Celtic hounds (*vertragi*), which were renowned for their speed. Such fast hunting dogs were a famous export of Britain (Strabo 4.5.2).

Wildfowling was a more humble and rustic form of hunting, generally more concerned with procuring food than with heroics or pleasure. It was usually carried out by specialized servants and required considerable experience as well as a calm hand. Captive birds and food were used as lures, and most birds were then caught with limed rods (Virgil, *Georgics* 1.307), though traps and snares were also employed. Some birds, such as thrushes, were especially valued as delicacies. Varro (*De re rustica* 3.5.8) reports that 5,000 thrushes (which had surely been bred in captivity) could fetch up to 60,000 *sestertii*. Other animals, such as hares (Varro 2.12.5) and deer, antelope and boar (Columella, *De re rustica* 9.1), were also kept in captivity, often in large game parks. These animals were bred for food but also for enjoyment. Thus the famous orator Quintus Hortensius used his game park to offer his friends a special form of 'mythological entertainment' (Varro 3.13.1–3). During a picnic the diners were entertained by 'Orpheus'. As he blew a horn, a wide range of animals, including deer and boar, appeared in response not to the charms of his music but to a well-known feeding signal.

A new style of hunting developed in the Roman world, as animals destined for the arena had to be caught alive. This was achieved by the use of nets and of travelling cages with sliding doors. Many animals no doubt died on their journey to Rome, adding to the enormous costs of putting on spectacles such as mock hunts and displays of wild animals. Nevertheless, these increasingly extravagant displays were an important way of gaining popularity in Rome. Thus Julius Caesar, on the occasion of his triumph in 46 BC, displayed elephants, 400 lions, Thessalian bulls and a giraffe (Cassius Dio 34.22–3). The enormous scale of such hunts (and presumably their devastating effect on local environments) is reflected in an altar to Diana from Cologne, which records that a certain Quintus Tarquitius caught 50 bears within a period of only six months. HE

See Anderson, J. K. (1985) *Hunting in the Ancient World*.

 PETS.

Hygieia see Asklepios.

hygiene By modern standards, life in the ancient world was decidedly lacking in hygiene. Cramped living conditions in cities, totally inadequate sewage systems, and water supply arrangements which excluded the private citizen were features common to most periods of Western history. In the absence of germ theory, disease was seen as the result of an imbalance of the constituent fluids of the body. Although external factors such as water supply and air could affect those fluids, there was no idea of water and air being able to cause disease without the intermediaries of the bodily fluids. Substances such as faeces were thought to be ritually powerful, and would sometimes be used in medical treatment. Surgical procedures would be performed without

WASHING either the patient or the medical practitioner. The concepts of POLLUTION and PURIFICATION are more common in RITUAL than medical contexts. For example, in cases of ritual pollution, which could be caused by contact with birth, death or blood-guilt, purification would be carried out by water or FIRE.

In the wider sense of 'the maintenance of health', however, hygiene was the central concern of medical practice. Treatises on health advised how to balance one's food and drink intake and one's exercise in relation to one's age, the CLIMATE, and the location of one's place of residence, in order to keep in a state of good health. HK

 BATHING: (a)–(b); PESTS.

hymns SONGS in metrical form, performed on various occasions and in particular to honour the GODS. The HOMERIC hymns are among the earliest examples of the genre and share common features of metre, language, mythological content as well as the nature of the deities they address. As Homeric hymns (unlike most other hymns) are written in the hexameter verse of epic poetry, they will not have been sung. Sometimes they purport to explain the origins of a cult (as in the *Homeric Hymn to Demeter*, which 'explains' the origin of the Eleusinian mysteries) or tell a characteristic story about the god (as in the *Homeric Hymn to Hermes*, in which the trickster Hermes successfully steals Apollo's cattle).

Although hymns did not originate as songs for gods, strictly speaking, most of them clearly adopted this form over time. They were composed in order to give honour (*timê*) and delight to divinity, and were often performed alongside other ritual acts such as SACRIFICE, an offering or even a procession. MUSIC was a usual supplement of hymns (two epigraphic examples survive with musical notation), which could be performed by CHORUSES or by solo singers. Their language was rich, full of praise for the divinity.

Hymns may contain PRAYERS in their structure, though this is not an inseparable and necessary combination, and they were not intended to ask a favour of a deity, as prayers generally were. Hymns regularly focus on the god's cultic epithets, special locations, powers and distinctive features and, like the Homeric hymns, may tell a story about the god. A hymn in the traditional sense was like a work of art in itself, an elegant and uplifting piece of POETRY designed to gratify the deity without necessarily expressing the need to request something from the divine recipient. EP, LF

See Bremer, J. M. (1981) Greek hymns, in H. S. Versnel, *Faith, Hope and Worship* 193–215; Pulleyn, S. (1997) *Prayer in Greek Religion*.

Hypatia d. AD 415 MATHEMATICIAN and NEOPLATONIST PHILOSOPHER and daughter of the Alexandrian mathematician Theon, who wrote extant works on PTOLEMY's treatises. Hypatia studied mathematics, including ASTRONOMY, with her father. She eventually surpassed her father in mathematics and studied philosophy, particularly Neoplatonism. After her education she began to teach, an unusual but not unprecedented occupation. Half a century earlier, Sosipatra held a chair of philosophy at PERGAMON and eclipsed her husband, Eustathios, while rivalling the great Aidesios (Aedesius) (Eunapius, *Lives of the Sophists* 6.6). Even earlier, Amphikleia, who married Iamblichos' son and studied with PLOTINUS, became a philosopher in her own right (Porphyry, *Life of Plotinus* 9).

Hypatia's teaching career included lectures on PLATO and ARISTOTLE; she also taught mathematics and astronomy, initially assisting her father as well as revising the third book of his *Commentary on the Almagest* of Ptolemy. Her own writings included commentaries on Diophantos' arithmetical works, on the canons of astronomy, and on Apollonios' *Conics*, none of which is extant. In Neoplatonic studies, she taught SYNESIUS, who held her in high regard, even after he had become a BISHOP. Provincial governors often visited her, as a leading citizen, soon after their arrival in the city.

Hypatia, who never married, was an accomplished ORATOR and widely respected for modesty, wisdom and political sense, but her popularity and influence attracted the attention of fanatical CHRISTIANS. In March 415, a mob instigated by the bishop Cyril attacked her and tore her to pieces. Her reputation remained strong, even casting a shadow over the great Isidoros a generation later. She remains a type even now, as is clear from the title of McAlister's book. JV

See Dzielska, M. (1995) *Hypatia of Alexandria*; McAlister, L. L. (1996) *Hypatia's Daughters: fifteen hundred years of women philosophers*.

Hyperboreans see SCYTHIA; UTOPIAS.

Hypereides see DEMOSTHENES; ORATORS, GREEK.

Hysiai A settlement, dependent on ARGOS in classical times, above a valley in the south-western part of Argive territory. Near here the Argives defeated the SPARTANS in a BATTLE usually dated (in modern works) to 669/8 BC and linked to the shadowy ruler Pheidon of Argos, as well as to the founding of the Spartan festival of Gymnopaidiai. It is a glaring example of how a tissue of speculative reconstruction (whose accuracy is not impossible) comes to be regarded as firm fact. The battle is mentioned only by PAUSANIAS (2.24.7), who dates it to the reign of the Athenian tyrant PEISISTRATOS (mid-6th century), though the date preserved in the medieval manuscript of Pausanias, '4th year of the 8th Olympiad', is (on a conventional reading) mid-8th-century. Scholars have assumed that Pausanias wrote '28th', giving a 7th-century date; but this is pure supposition, as is any link with Pheidon. Archaeological evidence may indicate that, if anything, the 8th century is a likelier time for Argos to have expanded its power westwards. Recent CHRONOLOGICAL research, however, suggests that the battle may belong to the very late archaic period. DGJS

See Foley, A. (1997) Pheidon of Argos, in J. M. Fossey, ed., *Argolo-Korinthiaka I* 15–28; Shaw, P.-J. (2003) *Discrepancies in Olympiad Dating*.

 PELOPONNESE.

I

iambic poetry see LYRIC POETRY; POETRY.

Iamblichos see BIOGRAPHY AND BIOGRAPHERS; HYPATIA; NEOPLATONISM.

Iazyges see PANNONIA.

Iberia (1) In the classical age, Iberia was situated the immediately to the north of the ARMENIAN plateau and south of the Caucasus mountains so that land with the ancestral capital at Harmozica (near mod. Tbilisi) straddled the middle valley of the Cyrus river (mod. Kura) in the heartland of the modern Georgian Republic. To the north of Iberia is the strategic Dariel gates, the gateway between the south Russian steppes and Transcaucasia (Armenia and Georgia). To the west of Iberia, lay Kolchis (Latin Colchis, Byzantine Lazica) in the valley of the river Phasis (mod. Rioni). The Kolchian port of Phasis (mod. Poli) linked Iberia to the sea borne commerce of the BLACK SEA.

The Iberians, who spoke dialects of Georgian, were prized as SOLDIERS. The GEOGRAPHER STRABO commented on Iberia's prosperity in TIMBER, metals, and the products of a pastoral way of life. In the early Iron Age, the Iberians prospered from the trade between Urartu centred on Lake Van and the Greek colonies on the Black sea. MITHRADATES VI of Pontos subjugated the Iberians and recruited them in a great numbers. In 66 BC POMPEY imposed Rome's hegemony over the Iberians.

In the Julio-Claudian age, the Iberians proved dutiful Roman allies against the kings of Armenia and the Arsakid kings of PARTHIA. In AD 35, at the behest of the emperor TIBERIUS (14–37), the Iberian king Pharsamenes intervened in Armenia. In the Roman–Parthian war of 54–66, NERO's general Gnaeus Domitius Corbulo deployed Iberian allies. From the Flavian age on, the Iberians were charged with guarding the Dariel gates. The SASSANID shahs of Persia, from SHAPUR I (240–70) on, contested Roman influence over Iberia, which had cultural links with the Iran. Persian shahs used it as a base in campaigns to secure ports on the Black sea. But in 523, king Tzath of Lazica converted to Orthodox CHRISTIANITY. From Lazica, Georgian-speaking missionaries arrived to convert the Iberians, who were henceforth linked to the Byzantine world. KH

Iberia (2) (Greek *Ibêria*) The western peninsula of Europe. In the Neolithic period, some Africans (Iberians) and Europeans (CELTS) invaded the region, creating in the north-west a CELTIBERIAN people that vigorously resisted domination, but the peninsula was always ethnically diverse. As early as the 11th century BC (traditional date; often redated to the 8th or 7th century), PHOENICIANS explored Tartessus (the Baetis river area; mod. Guadalquivir) and established a colony at Gades (Cádiz). Greek merchants arrived by the late 7th century; among the more important Greek (but also native and Roman) sites is Emporion (Empúries; Ampurias) founded by Massalia (MARSEILLES); its very name ('trading-place') indicates the importance of TRADE, especially in METALS. The Carthaginians added Spanish territory to their empire in the 3rd century under the leadership of Hamilcar Barca and HANNIBAL; the latter's siege of SAGUNTUM instigated the second PUNIC WAR and precipitated the arrival of Rome. (see also BAETICA; CARTHAGO NOVA; HISPANIA; LUSITANIA) JV

 HISPANIA.

Ibykos (Ibycus) see LYRIC POETRY, GREEK.

ice and icehouses In a MEDITERRANEAN summer, WINE and FRUIT could be chilled by plunging them into the water of a deep well or underground water tank; however, the only method of lowering the temperature of food and drink to near freezing point was to use ice. This was gathered as snow in mountain regions until late spring, transported to cities and kept in deep insulated pits. The use of these pits is reported as an invention of ALEXANDER the Great (ATHENAEUS 123f–124f.) but had perhaps already been practised in PERSIA or INDIA.

Ice and snow were used in ancient gastronomy as cooling agents and as mixers for wine. Ice was sometimes added directly to wine; it was also placed above a wine cup, either in a filter bag from which it gradually melted into the cup, or in a colander through which the wine could be poured. Snow was also used as a garnish on food (PLINY THE YOUNGER, *Letters* 1.15; *Apicius* 4.1.2). The safety of these practices depended on the cleanness of the ice or snow, which there was no way of assuring; hence the importance of an invention claimed by the Roman emperor NERO. He boiled water in containers which were then immediately chilled by placing them in ice. The result was more-or-less sterilized ice-cold water (*decocta*) to mix with wine. AD

See Geer, R. M. (1935) On the use of ice and snow for cooling drinks, *Classical Weekly* 29.8: 61–2; Gowers, E. (1994) Persius and the decoction of Nero, in J. Elsner and J. Masters, eds., *Reflections of Nero* 131–50.

identity A theoretical concept pertaining to the self-realization of an individual or collective group that is constructed in relation to the 'Other'. Identity is a comparative discourse that stresses the perceived differences between groups or individuals. As such, identity involves the process of 'exclusion', identifying the characteristics or traits that enable individuals or groups to distinguish themselves as different *vis-à-vis* others. In consequence, identity is an internal social construct that is propagated by,

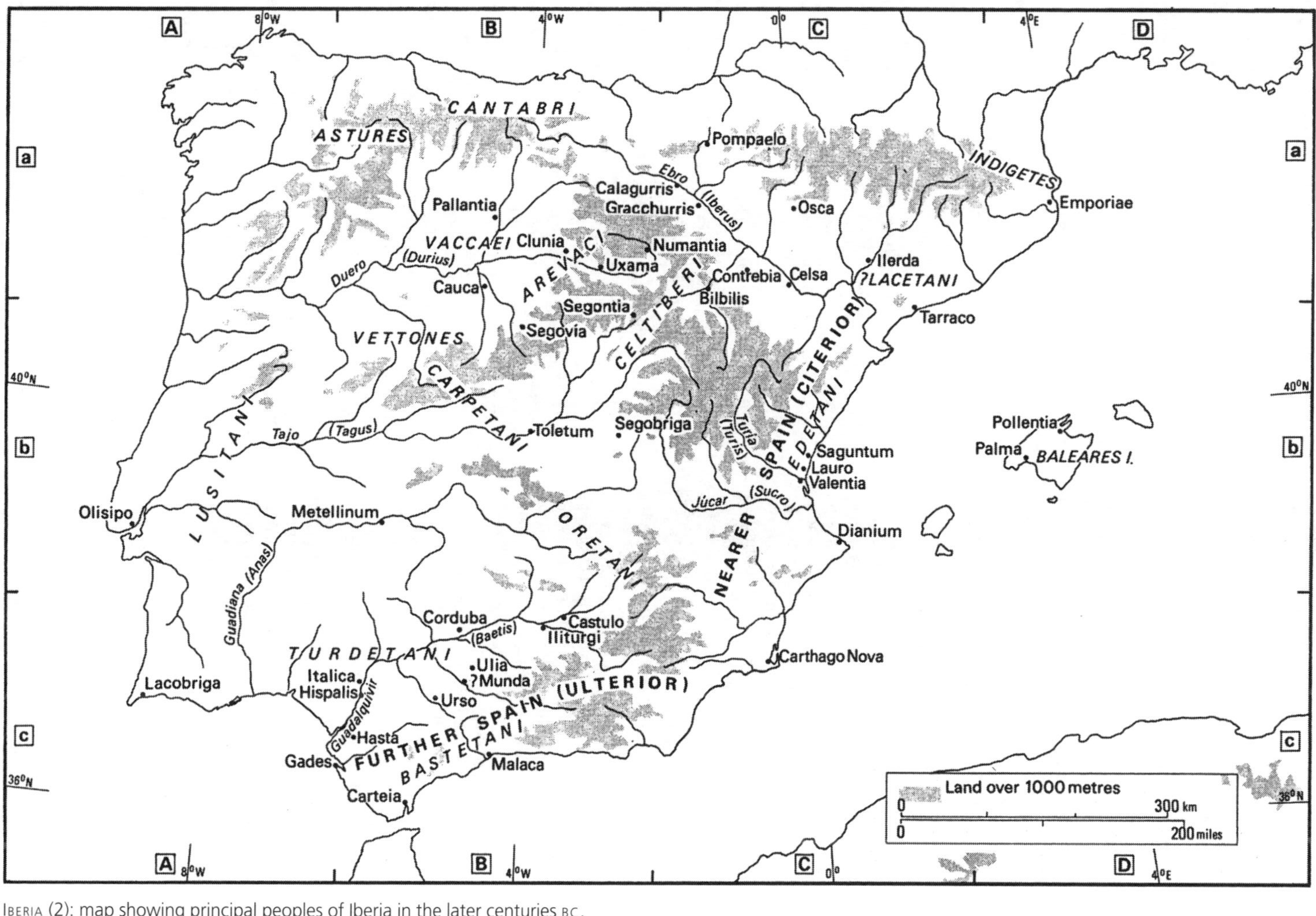

IBERIA (2): map showing principal peoples of Iberia in the later centuries BC.

and dependent on, interaction with other groups or individuals.

The majority of the earlier work on identity has concerned issues of gender. More recent research, however, has focused on identities of age, status, RELIGION, POLITICS, and ETHNICITY. Pluralism is a feature of any study of identity, since groups and individuals maintain multi-faceted roles within society. Within the social realm, identity is restricted by the context that fosters its construction. Since identity is culture-specific, its construction and maintenance are dependent on the contextual cultural boundaries within which it was formulated. Nevertheless, identities are not necessarily static, but can adapt in relation to the cultural environment that produces them. Identities of age and status, for example, are culture-specific yet require constant maintenance throughout the life-span of an individual. Thus, identities are often negotiable and are relative to circumstances, both external and internal.

The role of material culture in the construction, and signification, of cultural identity is at the forefront of scholarly research. Ethnographic studies, for example, have investigated how material culture is used to signify differences, and thus identities, between interactive communities, particularly in contexts where geographical boundaries are contested. In these instances, stylistic differences in material culture, in particular, become more pronounced when a culture is faced with the external threats of invasion or migration. Studies of this nature have had broad applications in the field of ARCHAEOLOGY.

In Roman provincial archaeology, an increased interest in the indigenous perspective, the main tenet of POST-COLONIALISM, has led scholars to focus on the way material culture can be utilized to negotiate identity, especially in contexts of unequal power relationships. The adoption and variant use of foreign material culture by a conquered group is no longer solely viewed as the outcome of cultural assimilation, but the means through which a subordinate group may negotiate with, or resist, domination in an imperial context.

Studies of identity in the classical world are rife with problems and provide material for much scholarly debate. An example is what it meant to be 'Roman'. Was it simply the adoption of Roman material culture and the practice of 'Roman' life-ways (a relative view of identity), or did one need to originate from Rome (an essentialist view)? The lack of a concrete definition for what it meant to be 'Roman' in imperial times, as well as the pluralistic nature of cultural identity and our own etic (outside) perspective, renders the reconstruction of past identities a difficult, yet fruitful, area of future research. MLM

See Huskinson, J., ed. (2000) *Experiencing Rome: culture, identity, and power in the Roman empire.*

ideology see AUGUSTUS; BARBARIANS; CHRISTIANITY; DIOCLETIAN; MARXISM; OTHER, THE; RACE; RACISM; ROME; STATE, THE.

Ilipa The battle of Ilipa in 206 BC was fought by SCIPIO AFRICANUS for the Romans and, for the Carthaginians, Mago and Hasdrubal, son of Gisgo, who had been responsible for the defeat and death of Scipio's father and uncle. Ilipa is thought to be modern Alcalá del Rio, 15 km (9 miles) north of Seville on the bank of the Guadalquivir. The armies were both large; Scipio had both Spanish allied infantry and Roman CAVALRY. The battle is famous for POLYBIOS' description of the astonishingly complicated manoeuvre that Scipio executed while marching towards the CARTHAGINIAN line. It had the effect of leaving the Spanish infantry in the centre, but allowing the right and left wings of infantry to overlap the Carthaginian line and the cavalry to attack from the side, where they did considerable damage. If the manoeuvre is properly understood, it is a remarkable testament to the drill skills of the Roman army. The tactic was robbed of its full impact, however, by a massive thunderstorm that halted the battle and temporarily let the Carthaginians off the hook. CJS

See Livy 28.12–13; Polybios 11.20–1; Lazenby, J. F. (1978) *Hannibal's War.*

illness The term is used in the SOCIOLOGY of MEDICINE in opposition to 'DISEASE', to designate the patient's experience: those symptoms which are found sufficiently disturbing that the patient or a family member calls in a DOCTOR to give a disease label to the condition. The point at which one decides that one feels ill is something which varies between individuals and societies. For example, in a society where it is expected that labour will be painful, or that arthritis will affect those in their thirties, no treatment may be sought. Those who remain able to carry out their normal activities may not regard as 'illness' symptoms which others, who find their normal activities impossible, choose to refer to a doctor or other practitioner. In modern medicine, one aspect of the role of the doctor is to translate the individual symptoms into a 'disease'. In ancient medicine, however, named diseases were used less frequently, and the doctor was instead expected to relate the symptoms to other aspects of the patient's life.

These distinctions can be clarified by the illnesses of the sophist AELIUS ARISTIDES (born AD 117), whose account of his own suffering makes him one of the few patients of antiquity to whose experience we have access. He graphically describes the pain he felt, and singles out among his symptoms difficulty in speaking, something crucial to a public speaker, which led him to consult a range of doctors and also to spend some years at the TEMPLE of ASKLEPIOS at PERGAMON. HK

Illyria and Illyrians A territory and its people occupying the region from the north-east coast of the ADRIATIC SEA to the DANUBE that later became the Roman PROVINCES of PANNONIA and DALMATIA. Mentioned occasionally by HERODOTOS, Illyria did not seriously enter the Greek consciousness, except as trading partners, until the rise of MACEDONIA, for Illyrian kings and soldiers were allied to PHILIP II and ALEXANDER (whose mother OLYMPIAS was an Illyrian princess). Subsequently, Illyrians regularly threatened Greek cities along the coast, either on their own or in alliance with the Macedonians, and engaged in PIRACY in the Adriatic. From 229 BC, when it intervened on behalf of Greek cities, Rome regularly undertook campaigns against Illyria. These only ended with the PANNONIAN WARS of AUGUSTUS and the establishment of Pannonia and Dalmatia; the region, of considerable strategic and some economic importance, was known to Romans as Illyricum.

The ethnic composition of the region was diverse and included CELTIC, Getic and THRACIAN elements. Various sources identify a large number of individual peoples; some may have been the same groups with different names at different times. Boundaries between peoples were not static geographically as a result of constant disputes and warfare and these presumably had an effect on composition and identity. Little is known, but much has been argued, about their languages and linguistic affiliations. ARCHAEOLOGY has been able to glean some information about their modes of life. JV

See Mócsy, A. (1974) *Pannonia and Upper Moesia*; Wilkes, J. J. (1969) *Dalmatia*.

 DALMATIA; DANUBE.

Illyricum see DALMATIA; ILLYRIA AND ILLYRIANS; PANNONIAN WAR.

immorality Forms of behaviour considered unacceptable within a given community. Issues concerning immorality typically focused on the wealthy freeborn élite who considered themselves the ones to set examples for other members of society to follow. The élite envisaged the poor as morally bankrupt; yet it seems that members within each particular status group had their own set of moral values.

In HOMERIC and classical Greece, individuals of wealth and high birth were not to bring shame (*aischron*) or failure upon themselves or upon their families. For the Greek PHILOSOPHERS immoral behaviour constituted the notion of self-advancement without regard for the interest of another. From this standpoint, immoral behaviour constituted theft, cowardice, cruelty and greed towards fellow-citizens. Immoral sexual behaviour comprised adultery, whereby a citizen seduced a fellow-citizen's wife, an unmarried daughter or widowed mother (Demosthenes 23.53–5).

For the Romans immoral behaviour centred on self-indulgence and could be expressed in terms of sexual practices and the over-consumption of material possessions. For example, in the late REPUBLIC, adultery was considered by some as one such form of sexual misbehaviour. To counter such behaviour and in effect enforce his own political agenda, AUGUSTUS promulgated laws on adultery, HOMOSEXUALITY and seduction in the *lex Iulia de adulteriis* of 18 BC to make such 'immoral' acts criminal offences. Despite his efforts, members of his own family, namely his daughter Julia, were guilty of lascivious behaviour. Augustus' MARRIAGE laws sought to increase the depleting numbers of the senatorial élite. Freeborn males, for instance, were prevented from marrying women with disreputable characters: these included PROSTITUTES, MIMES, and adulteresses.

Effeminacy or *mollitia* was another form of immoral sexual behaviour. When a man assumed both passive and excessive roles in sexual relations, he was viewed in the same light as a woman. In addition, effeminacy could be connected to the acquisition of foreign goods, particularly Greek or Asiatic unguents and clothing. The Roman moralists saw Greece as a catalyst for licentious behaviour permeating into Rome. The import of luxury goods, artistic styles and literature, all associated with effeminate behaviour, was viewed as a destabilization of traditional Roman cultural identity.

With JEWISH and CHRISTIAN value systems beginning to permeate into Roman culture in the late antique period, restraints on immorality began to appeal to the lower classes. Immoral behaviour included acts that displayed a lack of solidarity within the community and individual HOUSEHOLDS, as well as sexual infidelities. LAH

See Dover, K. J. (1974) *Greek Popular Morality in the Time of Plato and Aristotle*; Edwards, C. (1993) *The Politics of Immorality in Ancient Rome*; Veyne, P., ed. (1987) *A History of Private Life*.

immortality Humans are mortal and will die. The ancient conception of the GODS generally contrasted them with this human condition, making them immortal. Immortality, however, is to be distinguished from agelessness, another characteristic of ancient divinities. In MYTH, the goddess Dawn asked for her mortal lover Tithonos to be made immortal. This was granted. However, she forgot to ask that he be made ageless, so although he never died Tithonos continued to age, becoming more and more wizened.

Some PHILOSOPHERS argued that although humans may die, part of them (their SOUL, or some part of their soul) is immortal and does not die. In the *Phaedo*, PLATO presents SOCRATES offering a number of arguments to show that the soul is immortal. True philosophy, he says, is therefore in fact a preparation for death since it is concerned with purifying the soul and releasing it from bodily concerns. ARISTOTLE too, in the last book of the *Nicomachean Ethics*, argues that the best human life is one in which one emulates the activity of the gods and becomes immortal 'to the extent to which it is possible'. 'Becoming like god' became one of the regular definitions of the goal (*telos*) of a good human life.

Other philosophers, the EPICUREANS for example, set out to show that the soul is not immortal and that in fact the correct acceptance of human mortality was in fact an important step in the attainment of a good and peaceful life, free from unnecessary concerns. JIW

imperial cult The cult of the emperor and his family was practised throughout the Roman empire from the time of AUGUSTUS onwards. It is too easy to dismiss it as a way for the emperor to gain the loyalty of his subjects or a way for provincials to gain favour with the emperor. Instead, cults were largely established by provincials themselves in order to come to terms with a ruling power which was god-like. Like GODS, EMPERORS were invisible, in that they were unlikely to visit PROVINCES, and had the power of life or death over their subjects. It stands to reason, therefore, that provincials would want to mollify and objectify emperors in a similar way as they did gods. Just how emperors resembled gods varied. They could be honoured in the guise of a god, or as being god-like or, alternately, as divinely sent. Their spirit could also be venerated rather than themselves directly. To an extent, the cult of the emperor blurred these distinctions.

In general terms, there was a marked difference between the way the emperor was worshipped in the

Eastern and Western provinces of the empire. While the Greek provinces worshipped the living emperor, Western provinces tended to deify emperors after their deaths. In this part of the empire, including Rome itself, only the spirit of the living emperor was venerated. In Rome, people prayed to the genius of the emperor during meal times. There were also cults of the emperor's *lares* at the crossroads in Rome; these were generally organized by priests called Augustales. However, the emperor was only truly deified after his death and by a vote from the SENATE. Only misguided emperors, such as CALIGULA (GAIUS), claimed divinity in Rome during their lifetimes.

It is misleading to refer to cult of the emperor as though it comprised a definite set of practices. Instead, provincials could worship the emperor and his family in a variety of ways. They could erect TEMPLES, statues or inscriptions, just as they might honour the emperor through processions, SACRIFICES, BENEFACTIONS or through celebrating important anniversaries. Frequently, cities adapted traditional cults so as to include the worship of the emperor and his family. For example, the Ephesians venerated the emperor alongside their cult of Artemis by including busts of the imperial family in their traditional procession.

Imperial cult was organized on different levels. On the most basic level, the emperor could be worshipped by an individual or group of individuals. For example, a votive altar was found near HADRIAN'S WALL which was dedicated to CELTIC gods as well as the spirit of the emperor. More frequently, the cult of the emperor was organized on a civic level. This entailed, among other things, celebrating imperial anniversaries, organizing processions, erecting temples and statues for cities as a whole. The driving force behind imperial cult on this level was the ÉLITE which had the most to gain from the cult. By associating themselves with the ruling power, the status of the élite was increased and justified. Therefore, PRIESTHOODS of imperial cult were very prestigious. For this reason, the élite often advertised their tenure of such priesthoods, as Marcius Quadratus did on the stage building of the THEATRE at THUGGA. The élite also spent vast sums on buildings associated with imperial cult, which included temples or rooms in public buildings such as colonnades. A nice example can be found in EPHESOS where an élite erected a small, ornate temple to HADRIAN on Curetes Street. In addition, élites commissioned statues of emperors which were scattered throughout provincial cities. These could be monumental cult statues, as the statue of DOMITIAN from the temple of Domitian in Ephesos, or could be a part of a FOUNTAIN, such as the statue of TRAJAN also in Ephesos. Whatever form these statues took, they were instrumental in making the emperor's presence felt in cities. Statues were seen as the embodiment of the emperor and, as such, offered sanctuary for those who sought their protection. By the same token, it was an offence to deface a statue of an emperor in any way.

Imperial cult was also organized on a provincial level. These cults were practised by cities throughout a province and were instrumental in uniting provincials as they were frequently the only cults they practised together. Naturally enough, priesthoods of provincial cults were exceedingly important, the apogee of most political careers. The importance of provincial cults was underlined by the fact that, unlike civic cults, it was necessary to gain imperial consent. It was required for several reasons. In the first place, it was important for emperors to oversee large gatherings of provincials. In addition, giving or denying imperial approval increased the importance of these cults. For this reason, emperors frequently rejected requests to establish provincial cults, as TIBERIUS did when the citizens of Gytheion appealed to him. Cities vied with each other over the establishment of province-wide cults, as they conferred power over cities. A city which hosted a cult to the emperor practised by the whole province became more important than its neighbours. As such, an emperor who bestowed his approval on a provincial cult was showing favour to that city. So prestigious was the hosting of a provincial cult that ASIAN cities devised the title *neôkoros* to denote temples erected with imperial consent.

The cult of the emperor was also central to organizations which brought together people from different provinces. The Panhellenion, an institution established by Hadrian to unite all Greek cities, was cemented by imperial cult. Likewise, the cult of the emperor was crucial in linking the emperor to his soldiers. The army carried standards which were embossed with images of the emperor, as well as busts of the emperor which were placed inside camps. The majority of sacrifices and HOLIDAYS found in a military calendar from DURA EUROPUS were dedicated to the imperial family. As with all other imperial cults, these practices enabled soldiers to establish a relationship with their ruler. EACM

See Price, S. (1984) *Rituals and Power*.

imperialism, ancient

A discussion of imperialism in the Greek world must distinguish between the effective control of other states' foreign policies through military coercion – which the ancients call hegemony (*hêgemonia*), though modern political scientists (and many historians) use the term in a different way – and a true empire (*archê*), like that of the Athenians or that of ALEXANDER the Great, which was little more than a renovated and slightly enlarged version of the Achaemenid empire. Hegemony involved the direction of military resources (*dynamis*) against an external enemy (for example, SPARTAN and MACEDONIAN hegemonies in the wars against PERSIA), whereas *archê* employed *dynamis* for the purpose of subjecting other states, including members of an alliance (e.g. the Delian league), to their own power. If by 'empire' we mean the control and exploitation of foreign territory for the benefit of the imperial power, then few worthy examples present themselves in the course of a millennium of post-Bronze Age Greek history. Certain states – *POLEIS* ('city-states') and federal states or leagues – formed, either by bringing together scattered communities into a single political entity through a process we call *synoikismos*, or by the creation of representative government (as in the case of the leagues of BOIOTIA and THESSALY), but these represented the creation of 'states' that shared ethnicity and contiguous territory.

The creation of Spartan hegemony in the form of the 'PELOPONNESIAN league', which came to include states north of the Isthmus (most notably THEBES and MEGARA), marked a step towards imperialism, but it could be argued that the primary motive of the dominant state (the *hêgemôn*) was military security, facilitated by the control of the member states' foreign policies and the use of the league against the aggressive designs of non-members. A Hellenic alliance, created to resist the Persian invader in 480–479 BC, was a temporary accommodation without a formal constitution, though it recognized the military supremacy (*viz.* nominal leadership) of the Spartans. From the fractured remains of this alliance, which unravelled soon after the departure of XERXES' forces, the Athenians created the Delian league, which through its very organization (or constitution) laid the groundwork for the first true empire of Greek history. (Whatever sort of Bronze Age empires and thalassocracies – 'masteries of the sea' – are alluded to by the myths of AGAMEMNON and Minos need not be considered here.)

Through a series of bilateral treaties (each involving Athens and a member state) and by the assignment of military leadership to Athenian GENERALS and the collection of tribute (*phoros*) to Athenian collectors (*hellênotamiai*), the Delian league was from the very beginning the blueprint for the Athenian empire. Its relentless growth (and its suppression of rebellions and refusal to allow members to secede) during the period THUCYDIDES calls 'The Fifty Years' brought Athens to a level of wealth and power unprecedented in the Greek world. The empire was, however, threatened by over-extension (e.g. the Athenian involvement in Inaros' revolt in Egypt, 461–454 BC) and clashes with the Peloponnesian league. Internally, it provided member states with the benefits of Athenian LAW, security of TRADE and travel by sea and a common currency. But the benefits were more than balanced by a steady reduction in the number of autonomous allies who had been converted to tribute-paying subject states, no longer allowed to supply their own SHIPS and forced to accept Athenian military colonists (*klêrouchoi*) on expropriated lands. Furthermore, as conservative politicians in Athens were wont to point out, after making peace with Persia (the peace of Kallias, 449?), the *phoros* from the allies was being used for the beautification of Athens and the funding of public-works projects rather than for their original purpose. The naked imperialism of the Athenians is revealed by the speeches that Thucydides puts into the mouths of political leaders: it is for the powerful to do as they wish.

Destruction of the Athenian empire as a result of Sparta's victory in the PELOPONNESIAN WAR (431–404) left Sparta to try its hand at imperialism. But the result was an unmitigated disaster both for Greece as a whole and for the internal stability of the Spartan state. The Peloponnesian WAR and the demands of maintaining military control of the areas taken from Athens – Sparta had established political boards of ten called *dekarchiai* in various cities, supported by garrisons under Spartan *harmostai* – proved to be a drain on Sparta's already limited manpower; it demanded the use of newly enfranchised HELOTS (as *neodamôdeis*) and damaged the socioeconomic underpinnings of the state. Furthermore, it embroiled the Spartans in a seemingly endless series of wars in the first half of the 4th century. The Theban victory at LEUKTRA (371 BC) and the subsequent invasion of the Peloponnese, liberation of MESSENIA and establishment of Megalopolis emasculated Sparta and ended the state's ability (though not its desire) to re-establish its hegemony.

Weakness in the Greek world, brought on by the struggle for power on the part of Athens, Sparta and Thebes, allowed PHILIP II of MACEDONIA to acquire hegemony over the states to the south. This began as a gradual process which was fully realized by the Macedonian victory at CHAIRONEIA in 338 and the creation of the league of CORINTH, which recognized Philip as its *hêgemôn*, in the following year. Although Philip II was assassinated in 336, his son Alexander was able to use hegemony over Greece as the basis of his expedition against Persia. The Greek peace gave him stability in Europe during his absence and a supply of allied and MERCENARY soldiers. His conquest of the Persian empire was essentially complete when he made sacrifices at the mouth of the Indus in 325. But Alexander's empire proved to be a mixture of Greek states in the West, whose legal position (though often ignored by Alexander) was spelled out in the charter of the league of Corinth, and the former satrapies of the Persian empire which had now come under Macedonian rule. For the most part, Alexander retained existing structures, substituting Greco-Macedonian officials or, when he did retain barbarian rulers, securing the territories with garrisons and military overseers. Alexander's death led to the fragmentation of his empire as a result of the power struggle conducted by his SUCCESSORS (*Diadochoi*), who were unwilling to recognize the inept surviving members of the royal house or each other's claims to authority. By 280 the fragmentation into the so-called hellenistic kingdoms was complete, but the steady decline of the Greco-Macedonian 'empire' continued until the death of CLEOPATRA VII in 30 BC brought the hellenistic world to an end.

Imperialism was also a feature of Greek SICILY, where, since the early 5th century, various TYRANTS had built small empires that incorporated the smaller towns of the island. The extended periods of domination of the Sicilian towns, particularly by the tyrants of SYRACUSE (and especially from the time of DIONYSIOS I), can be explained both by the predominant size and power of Syracuse itself and the ever-present danger of the CARTHAGINIANS, who promoted their own commercial interests in the western MEDITERRRANEAN and championed the cause of their fellow-PHOENICIANS on the island. On occasions the tentacles of Sicilian imperialism extended as far as the Greek *poleis* of southern Italy. All this was, however, cut short by Roman expansion and the PUNIC WARS, which brought Sicily into the Roman orbit and eventually converted the island into its first *provincia*. WH

See Meiggs, R. (1972) *The Athenian Empire*; Wickersham, J. (1994) *Hegemony and Greek Historians*.

Rome was, from the earliest times, a military state, as is reflected in the national myth of its foundation by two sons of MARS and by the fact that the doors of the temple of JANUS, which remained open when the state was at WAR, were seldom closed. The highest elected MAGISTRATES, the CONSULS and, later, the PRAETORS (though initially the consuls were known as praetors), exercised *imperium* – the right to lead the army and to chastise, even with death, the disobedient. Consuls are thus invariably best known for their military exploits, especially when these, if they produced the requisite numbers of enemy dead, prisoners and booty, were rewarded with TRIUMPHS by the SENATE. Hence, the aspirations of the Roman aristocratic families, which vied for political office and influence, played no small part in promoting the Republic's innate sense of militarism. In the early Republican period wars and expansion arose from the basic need to defend the state against aggression by its neighbours, the SABINES, Volsci, Aequi and ETRUSCANS. The military successes of the 5th century BC were, however, partially undone by the Gallic sack of Rome in c.390, but expansion resumed and in 338 the Latin league was dismantled, with some former members receiving full, and others limited, CITIZENSHIP. Three bitter SAMNITE wars (343–341, 326–304, 298–290 BC) brought Roman power into southern Italy and a confrontation with PYRRHOS, whom the Tarentines had summoned to support their cause; after two initial 'pyrrhic victories' and a brief escapade in SICILY, Pyrrhos was driven from Italy in 272. The Romans now controlled virtually all Italy south of the Po. This set the stage for the seemingly inevitable clash with CARTHAGE in Sicily and the beginning of territorial acquisitions overseas.

Propaganda depicted Roman actions as defensive or pre-emptive, against enemies who had placed themselves in the wrong and allowed the Fetial priests to declare a *bellum iustum* ('just war'). And though it can be argued that the Romans were, in the early stages, not eager to annex foreign territory, not all of their military measures were defensive or reactive. The opportunities for military glory and plunder induced the senate to assign as *provinciae* (areas of responsibility or operations) regions that had not yet become PROVINCES in the modern sense of the word. Ultimately, the business class coveted the financial rewards that attended the annexation of territory, particularly the system of tax farming, which allowed administrators and syndicates to extort enormous sums from the provincials. Often, however, the costs of subduing and administering territories outweighed the benefits. Hence the primary motives of Roman imperialism during the Republic were national defence, aristocratic ambition and the opportunities for enrichment through plunder and taxation.

The PUNIC WARS (264–241, 218–201, 149–146 BC) brought under Roman control Sicily, CORSICA and SARDINIA, Spain and eventually North AFRICA. In Greece and the hellenistic East, there was greater reluctance to impose Roman rule, though ILLYRIAN PIRATES constituted a menace in the ADRIATIC and PHILIP V had made a pact with HANNIBAL for which the Roman people never forgave him (first MACEDONIAN WAR, 215–205). The second Macedonian war (200–196) ended with a settlement that guaranteed the autonomy of the various Greek states and weakened Macedonia's power. Allies and CLIENT KINGDOMS were supported as a means of keeping the more aggressive states in check, and Rome was content to play the role of puppet-master in the East. But the third Macedonian war (172–167), the revolt of Andriskos, and the ACHAIAN war between 149 and 146 resulted in further Roman victories, the deportation of numerous prisoners to Italy, and the imposition of direct Rome rule on Macedonia and Greece. Attalos III of PERGAMON bequeathed his kingdom to Rome in 133 (the province of Asia), and new PROVINCES were subsequently acquired as a result of POMPEY's victories over MITHRADATES (66–62) and the decline of the SELEUKID kingdom. The Seleukids had been dealt a blow by the peace of Apameia in 188, hard pressed by the growing power of PARTHIA, and crippled by dynastic strife. In the West, CAESAR conquered Gaul (58–49), during which time he launched an invasion of BRITAIN (not annexed to the empire until the time of CLAUDIUS), before plunging Rome into a civil war. His alliance with CLEOPATRA VII of Egypt had financial and military implications. At the time of his death he was planning an expedition against the Parthians, who, as it turned out, would not be forced to make territorial concessions to Rome until the time of the emperor TRAJAN. Egypt, casualty of the civil wars and of Caesar's untimely death, was incorporated into the Roman empire in 30 BC as a province under the personal control of the *princeps*, the last of the kingdoms of ALEXANDER'S SUCCESSORS to succumb to Rome.

Although the bulk of Roman imperial expansion was completed before the establishment of the PRINCIPATE, there were further additions under AUGUSTUS; for, though the periphery of the MEDITERRANEAN was now in Roman hands, the inland borders were more difficult to secure. Augustus thus added territories on the DANUBIAN frontier (including RAETIA, PANNONIA and Moesia), but Roman ventures beyond the RHINE proved disastrous (notably the defeat of Publius Quinctilius Varus in the Teutoburg forest in AD 9). In the East, Trajan (r. AD 97–117) at last avenged CRASSUS' disaster at CARRHAE (53 BC), and brought Rome's borders to the Euphrates. The East, however, remained unstable; in AD 224 the SASSANIAN Persians eclipsed Parthia and posed a more serious threat to an empire which was entering its most chaotic age.

The frontier regions brought increased military demands on the empire and permanent garrisons were established in the border provinces. The number of BARBARIANS, admitted into the empire and enrolled in the frontier armies (as *limitanei*), grew steadily, ironically for the purpose of keeping other barbarians out. All hopes of maintaining secure borders in the Danubian region were shattered at ADRIANOPLE (mod. Edirne) in 378, where the army of Valens was destroyed by the Visigoths.

Rome's empire endured until AD 476 in the West and until 1453 in the East, but the process of stagnation, decay and decline began not long after the empire was officially proclaimed. Internally, dynastic politics and the power of the PRAETORIAN GUARD weakened its leadership; the expense of imperialism in financial and military terms put a strain on manpower and brought the inevitable problems of heavy TAXATION and inflation; the borders were porous and the administration ponderous. Armies made and unmade emperors, most rapidly and shamelessly in the 3rd century, and the reforms of DIOCLETIAN that aimed to establish a new sense of direction and stability proved instead a blueprint for disintegration, slow but nevertheless steady. WH

See Harris, W.V. (1979) *War and Imperialism in Republican Rome, 327–70 BC*; Gruen, E. S. (1984) *The Hellenistic World and*

the Coming of Rome; Lintott, A.W. (1993) *Imperium Romanum: politics and administration* (1993); Jones, A. H. M. (1964) *The Later Roman Empire* 284–602.

imperialism, modern Defined in very general terms, imperialism is political control exercised by a dominant political unit over weaker ones for the primary benefit of the dominant (imperialist) power. Modern imperialist states, however, have justified their domination by claiming to bring civilization to the uncivilized and true religion to the infidel, or by tutoring the politically naïve in the arts of self-government. The concept of 'imperialism' was developed in the early 20th century by critical writers such as Hobson and Lenin.

Modern imperialism in a formal sense (the 'Age of Empires') spans the period from the Spanish and Portuguese empires of the 16th century to the end of the British empire in the mid-20th. This involved the acquisition (generally through conquest and colonization) of territories and peoples outside Europe by European powers, primarily for commercial exploitation, and was made possible by European technological superiority, which manifested itself most clearly in the military sphere. Nevertheless, at the beginning of this period, there was still a short period of expansion by the Ottoman empire into Europe; at the end of it, a Russian quasi-empire (the Soviet Union or USSR) developed through the steady conquest and occupation of adjacent territories that exhibited great ethnic and cultural diversity. Although not all ventures were financially rewarding, the mere fact of possessing overseas colonies became such a matter of pride to European powers that prestige outweighed financial gain in many cases. This was particularly true of the Germans, latecomers in the 'Scramble for Africa', or the partially lucrative and utterly brutal ventures of king Leopold of Belgium. Whereas Portuguese and Dutch imperialism had its origins with the creation of trading stations (factories) and were essentially seaborne empires, other European powers (notably the Spanish, French and British) were more heavily involved in claiming foreign territories as their own – one thinks of the famous Spanish *requiremiento* that preceded the appropriation of lands in the New World – and planting European populations there. Often, as in Australia, these were people regarded as the dregs of society. Usually, disease and death, exploitation and slavery, and forcible religious conversion followed; almost always the indigenous population was marginalized as socially and intellectually inferior. Today imperialism has a bad odour but continues to exist in a less structured way, in forms such as economic imperialism and military hegemony. The field of recent study has extended to the ways in which empire is represented in culture and ideology. (see also COLONIALISM) WH

See Porter, A. (1994) *European Imperialism*; Said, E. (1993) *Culture and Imperialism*.

incest Two distinct concepts apply to incest: sexual relations with kin and MARRIAGE to kin. In Attic law, there are no known legal sanctions against incest proper (incest was conceived of as a moral crime governed by unwritten laws), but legislation did restrict certain forms of kin marriage. In Roman law, *incestum* covered a broad range of sexual crimes including both marriage outside the permitted degrees and sexual relations with relatives. Under the Roman REPUBLIC, offenders could be punished by death, but in classical Greece the penalty in the worst cases was EXILE.

The Greeks were revolted by the idea of sexual relations with their closest kin. In his *Laws* PLATO informs us that Greeks readily abstained from sexual relations with a sibling, child or parent even if they found them attractive. His doctrine states 'these acts are absolutely unholy, an abomination in the sight of the gods, and nothing is more revolting' (*Laws* 838). Sophokles' OEDIPUS is so shocked at the revelation that he has committed incest with his mother that he blinds himself. The horror felt at incest meant that it was an ideal slur to use against a political opponent. At Athens, KIMON and ALCIBIADES were both accused of incest with their sisters, while at Rome CICERO insulted Publius CLODIUS Pulcher by levelling the same accusation at him.

However, sometimes there is a suggestion that incest can bring advantages. In one version of the myth, Thyestes fathers Aigisthos on his own daughter after an oracle tells him he will achieve revenge in this way. The implication is that a son born of a father–daughter relationship would have the greatest possible desire and duty to avenge his father, because of the link by blood on both sides. Although the Greeks expressed shock at such incestuous marriages, characterizing them as typical of BARBARIANS and TYRANTS, there was a strong tendency towards kin marriage throughout Greece. In Athens men often married their nieces and cousins and it was permitted to marry a half-sister by the same father. Kin marriage was even prescribed by law in the case of an heiress (*epiklêros*). Similar rules regarding heiresses applied in other Greek cities. In hellenistic and Roman Egypt the ruling PTOLEMIES indulged in full brother–sister marriage, and evidence suggests that commoners at this time often emulated their leaders. In Sparta a man could marry his half-sister by the same mother. Even ZEUS, king of the GODS, was married to his sister HERA.

In all these cases, kin marriage aimed at preserving the WEALTH and power of the FAMILY. The tendency to endogamy is much less pronounced in Rome. In the early Republic, marriage between even distant relatives was not acceptable. Later this was somewhat relaxed, though the Athenian ideal of uncle–niece marriage was not permitted until CLAUDIUS made it legal for himself to marry his brother's daughter. Even then it was still forbidden for men to marry their aunts, or their sisters' daughters. FMM

See Plato, *Laws*, trs. T. J. Saunders (1970).

India Despite earlier knowledge, Greek infiltration into India can be traced to ALEXANDER's conquest of Baktria and Sogdiana in c.327 BC. This set the stage for his Indian expedition (327–325), which eventually allowed him to cross the Indus; although he wanted to explore the Ganges, his men refused. Instead he travelled down the Indus to its mouth. Although hellenistic TRADE is known mainly from documents, Greek POTTERY and other archaeological finds are recorded from Taxila, PAKISTAN, where Alexander visited. His death in 323 BC saw the continuation of hellenistic culture through the Indo-Greek kingdoms of Baktria and Gandhara, which persisted into the early 1st century BC.

Trade was generally overland or from the mouth of the Indus via the Arabian gulf, exploiting pre-classical routes for similar goods, including SPICES. Central and southern India remained unknown to the Greeks. Around the late 2nd century BC they learned of the monsoons, after which it was possible to sail directly to India. However, the scale of Greek trade remained limited; it was not until 30 BC when AUGUSTUS annexed Egypt that it increased in volume and regularity.

India itself could supply spices, wild ANIMALS, pearls and semi-precious stones, while it served as an intermediary for items from further east, such as SILK from CHINA. Aromatics from south ARABIA and east Africa also circulated in the overall network. The *Periplus maris Erythraei*, a historical shipping document, provides a unique description of HARBOURS and their goods for the mid-1st century AD. Archaeologically the subject has been dominated by Wheeler's 1945 excavations at Arikamedu on the Coromandel coast of India, where Roman fine wares, AMPHORAS and GLASS suggested to him that the site was a colony for Roman traders who controlled and dominated the route. Recent Indian scholarship sees Arikamedu as a consumption centre for the local élite located there because of pre-existing trade patterns, and growing evidence indicates that Indians and Romans alike were active in the trade.

Indo-Roman trade can be traced across the Indian ocean, at sites such as Khor Rori (Oman) and Qana (Yemen). Recent excavations on the Red sea coast, particularly at Berenike and Myos Hormos in Egypt, have finds ranging from TEXTILES to pottery and stone originating from the Indian ocean and India. It seems that not only were goods exported, but that Indian communities resided along the route and on the Red sea. Emphasis has always been on the trade of the 1st century BC through the mid-1st century AD. While this was probably the most intense period it clearly continued into the 6th century. Roman coin hoards are common in India (gold and silver especially from the Flavian period, and bronze issues through the 5th), whether as bullion or currency is debated. RST

See Casson, L. (1989) *The Periplus Maris Erythraei*; Karttunen, K. (1997) *India and the Hellenistic World*; Narain, A. K. (2003) *The Indo-Greeks*; Ray, H.P. (1994) *The Winds of Change*; Sidebotham, S. E. (1986) *Roman Economic Policy in the Erythra Thalassa 30 BC–AD 217.*

 ALEXANDER III: (b); PERSIA AND PERSIANS.

individualism see CYNICISM; GYMNASIA; IDENTITY; KNOWLEDGE; SCIENCE; SOPHISTS.

industry Even in the so-called Dark Ages of Greece (c.1100–900 BC) and Geometric period (c.900–700) there was some labour specialization in the MANUFACTURE of metal and POTTERY. By the classical period, WORKSHOPS sometimes employed many SLAVES. The METIC Kephalos had 120 making shields during the PELOPONNESIAN WAR; DEMOSTHENES' father owned 32 or 33 making BEDS OR COUCHES and 20 making knives. These were probably exceptional. It has been estimated that at the height of Athenian pottery production there were at any one time some 500 workers, but the average workshop was small; excavated examples are often associated with domestic space. Women normally produced TEXTILES in the household. Larger numbers were employed in the MINES at LAURION, leased by the city to private contractors. NIKIAS alone owned 1,000 slaves and hired them out to others at a daily rate; but the establishments revealed by archaeology (ore-washeries, furnaces, MINING galleries) are on a much smaller scale. Only public building could, occasionally (as in Periklean Athens), compare with mining in the scale of total operations. Even then, craftsmen (slave and free, citizen and metic) were normally paid as individuals, though a system of contracts developed, probably more for convenience than for economic reasons. In the Roman world, mining continued to employ large numbers, though CRIMINALS were added to the slave labour force. There is evidence for a greatly increased scale of production in some respects, such as military equipment and BRICKS for new building techniques, but much remained in the hands of small establishments. Systematic attempts to increase output per worker are unknown. (see also TECHNOLOGY) JBS

See Burford, A. (1972) *Craftsmen in Greek and Roman Society*; Hopper, R.J. (1979) *Trade and Industry in Classical Greece*; Humphrey, J.W. et al. (1997) *Greek and Roman Technology: a sourcebook*; Mattingly and Salmon, *Economies beyond Agriculture*.

infanticide see CHILDHOOD; CONTRACEPTION; DEMOGRAPHY; DISABILITY; FAMILY, ROMAN.

infantry see ARMIES, ORGANIZATION OF; ARMS AND ARMOUR; LEGIONS; MERCENARIES.

inferiors see ARISTOCRACY; CLASS; ÉLITES; PATRONAGE; PEASANTS; SLAVES; SOCIETY.

inheritance In antiquity partible inheritance was the norm. The difficulty with this system is that a balance must be found between having too many children and having no children left alive to inherit. Various strategies were employed to overcome these problems. A man without children could adopt an heir, while a FAMILY with too many siblings could send sons away to colonize other lands. Alternatively, kin-marriage was a popular way of consolidating land.

At Athens the system preferred male heirs, and all sons inherited equal shares of their father's estate. When a man had sons, his daughters did not inherit, though some scholars argue that dowries can be seen as the daughters' share. If a man left only daughters, they became heiresses who were required by law to marry kin and produce a son to take over their father's estate. The preferred groom was the girl's paternal uncle. A man could not disinherit his legitimate children, and their claim on their inheritance was automatic. Other relatives had to go to court to claim their right to inherit. Only a man without sons could make a WILL. Women could not make wills.

There is much scholarly debate regarding the system of inheritance in Sparta. Some scholars, trusting the evidence of PLUTARCH, believe that there were strict state rules which did not allow estates to be divided or willed away. According to this theory only one son inherited his father's property. However, ARISTOTLE maintains that Spartans could bequeath their land. This and other contemporary sources suggest that there were no major differences between the Spartan system of inheritance and the system in other Greek states.

In the Roman world, if there was no will, sons and daughters, and after them the closest blood relatives, inherited equal shares of an estate. In early Rome wills were made only exceptionally, usually by men lacking children. Later, wills became prevalent. A woman could make a will with the consent of a male guardian. Wills were used to appoint an heir (or heirs), who would also function as executors since they were responsible for carrying out all individual bequests and legacies in the will. By the end of the REPUBLIC, the custom of making numerous bequests to persons outside the family had reached such levels that legislation was passed (the *lex Falcidia* of 40 BC) requiring that at least one-quarter of the estate remain with the heirs. A Roman *paterfamilias* could disinherit his children; however, the will was invalid unless they were specifically excluded. In addition, a law, probably from the latter part of the 1st century BC, allowed children to challenge a will by bringing an action of 'unduteous will'. FMM

See Champlin, E. (1991) *Final Judgments: duty and emotion in Roman wills 200 BC–AD 250*; Crook, J. A. (1967) *Law and Life of Rome*; Harrison, A. R.W. (1968) *The Law of Athens*; Lane Fox, R. (1985) Aspects of inheritance in the Greek world, in P. A. Cartledge and F. D. Harvey, eds., *Crux* 208–32.

INNS: (a) counter of an inn (*thermopolium*) at Pompeii.

INNS: (b) Pompeian picture depicting a scene in an inn.

initiation see ELEUSIS AND ELEUSINIAN MYSTERIES; FESTIVALS; MYSTERY RELIGIONS; RITUAL.

innovation see CONCRETE; ENGINEERING; SCIENCE; TECHNOLOGY.

inns With the expansion of trading routes in the classical Greek world and the subsequent increase in traffic, *pandokeia* or inns evolved to cater for those who were unfortunate enough to find themselves in a foreign town with no family, friends, or business associates to put them up. By the 5th century BC, inns were to be found along major ROADS, in towns, and especially around HARBOURS. Inn-keeping was a disreputable and predominantly a female profession. In ARISTOPHANES' *Frogs*, DIONYSOS consults HERAKLES about the best places to lodge in Hades, requesting a list of 'landladies with the fewest bedbugs'. Inns would have offered little more than a night's shelter, and rooms would rarely have been equipped with more than a pallet on which to sleep. In cold weather, the TRAVELLER would use his own cloak as a blanket, and as yet there is no evidence for latrines. In classical Greece, inns would have been distinct from taverns or *kapêleia* which would not have provided lodging, only WINE and food to be consumed on the premises and amphoras of wine sold for domestic consumption.

Several standards of inn were available along Roman highways or clustered about the main roads leading to a city's gates. Known as *hospitia*, *stabula*, *deversoria* or *caupones*, they provided food and accommodation for travellers, in addition to stabling and vehicle storage. PROSTITUTES would have been on hand to offer their services. As is the case with Greece, inns should not be confused with Roman *tabernae*. *Caupones* constituted the lowest category of establishment, a fact which the law recognized; as such, they were subject to special legislation, since a traveller on the road was completely at the mercy of their invariably dishonest owners. A guest at an inn whose belongings had been stolen was entitled to take legal action against the inn-keeper who was, in turn, legally responsible for the actions of his staff and servants.

Inns could be identified from the outside by painted signs or murals, and at night a lamp burned above the door. Known names were taken from the ANIMAL world (the Elephant, the Camel), the panoply of gods (the Diana, the Mercury and Apollo), or everyday objects (the Sword, the Wheel). A wall plaque from the Mercury and Apollo in LYON (Lugdunum) reads 'Here Mercury promises you wealth, Apollo health, and Septumanus' (presumably the inn-keeper) 'room and board'. CK-B

See Casson, L. (1974) *Travel in the Ancient World*; Kleberg, T. (1957) *Hôtels, restaurants et cabarets dans l'antiquité romain*.

inquiry In ancient PHILOSOPHY and SCIENCE inquiry has two main aspects: gathering empirical data and establishing theories based on these. Both features emerged in Greek thought before PLATO. HERODOTOS, for example, pioneered cultural anthropology when he accumulated data on ethnic groups, whereas PRESOCRATIC philosophers developed speculative theories about the nature and evolution of the world from only limited evidence. Plato established basic principles for inquiry. In recording Socrates' method of question and answer he identified a procedure for testing claims to moral KNOWLEDGE, while he himself saw MATHEMATICAL method as a means of establishing scientific and philosophical knowledge. In the *Republic*, for example, he demanded that the data of geometry, arithmetic, ASTRONOMY and harmonic science be systematized into theories built around fundamental concepts. For ARISTOTLE science was a form of inquiry that could integrate observations into a system of deductive reasoning about causes, while philosophy could develop theories that could be tested with reference to established views. Bold theorizing remained the goal of inquiry for the STOICS and EPICUREANS, as well as for major scientists like PTOLEMY and GALEN. However, the Epicureans considered some empirical data explicable by multiple theories and inaccessible to definitive explanation, while some SCEPTICS questioned the validity of both empirical data and theories, and advocated a programme of perpetual inquiry, analogous to the Socratic method. In MEDICINE, theoreticians (or rationalists), such as Galen, who developed theories about unobservable anatomical and physiological structures, attacked empiricists who practised therapy strictly on the basis of cumulative and unsytematized observations. RBT

insects According to ARISTOTLE, insects (*entoma*, singular *entomon*) were organisms with insections (*entomai*); his definition includes millipedes, scorpions, spiders, worms, and others not now considered insects. Scientific study, entomology, first appears in his works, mainly *Researches into Animals*, *Parts of Animals*, and *Generation of Animals* (usually known by their Latin names *Historia animalium*, *De partibus animalium*, and *De generatione animalium*). Later writers include THEOPHRASTOS, AELIAN, and PLINY THE ELDER. The last two are derivative and less scientific, reporting folklore and drawing dubious conclusions. Concepts of spontaneous generation and the lack of scientific equipment led Aristotle into errors corrected by modern study, but his work remains important.

Actual specimens are not especially common in the archaeological record, but insects regularly feature on works of art. Examples include images on seals and gems, from KNOSSOS and elsewhere, and on coinage, like BEES at EPHESOS and Hybla in SICILY. JEWELLERY could take the shape of insects, and VASE-PAINTINGS depict various creatures. In literature, some fables of AESOP draw moral themes from stories about insects, while organisms like dung-beetles and wasps provide sources of humour in plays of ARISTOPHANES. More generally, bees and ants were employed in similes and metaphors for industriousness, and epigrams on insects survive. Naturally, insects are occasionally considered pests, though the cicada was linked with the Muses and APOLLO by PLATO (*Phaedrus* 259c) and later writers. Butterflies and moths were regarded as human SOULS; *psychê* (Greek) and *anim(ul)a* (Latin) are words for both 'butterfly' and 'soul'. JV

See Davies, M. and Kathirithamby, J. (1986) *Greek Insects*.

insomnia For modern culture, insomnia has come to be a sign of something significant that resides deep within an individual psyche: sensitivity, psychological illness, creativity, grieving, childhood trauma, and so forth. It was usually far less complex a phenomenon for the ancients. JUVENAL is typical. He claims that modern Rome is so noisy that sleep in it is impossible – at least for those of insufficient means to escape this. People fall sick and die from lack of sleep, Juvenal claims (*Satire* 3.232–4). Insomnia occasionally can point to something of slightly greater psychological moment. It is often associated in Roman love ELEGY and in the Greek NOVEL with frustrated love. But sometimes this sleeplessness is as much the product of unsuccessful nocturnal wooing as it is of actual rejection (PROPERTIUS 1.16).

The condition was, naturally, an aspect of illness repeatedly noted in the writings of ancient physicians, but insomnia is never seen, of itself, as the key to the nature of an illness (a typical set of notes from the HIPPOCRATIC *Epidemics* 3.3: 'coma was present, aversion to food, despondency, sleeplessness, irritability . . .'). Nor was insomnia the subject of a literary work in the way that it can be today (no Sophoclean *Hercules Vigilans*, for example). Nor, one imagines, was insomnia a topic of conversation in any but the most banal of senses. PGT

instrumentum domesticum The modern Latin term used to describe a range of INSCRIPTIONS incised, stamped or painted on a range of portable artefacts from the ancient world. Examples include stamps and/or moulded marks on POTTERY vessels and AMPHORAS, GLASS, BRICKS and TILES, lead pipes, wooden barrels, etc.; control stamps on metal ingots and quarried STONE; metal tags and lead seals used in the transport of goods; and graffiti (often denoting ownership of personal artefacts). The definition normally excludes portable documents such as COINS, PAPYRI, OSTRAKA or writing tablets, as well as all inscriptions on stone. Much of the material simply provides evidence of the ability of people to write their own names on their possessions (though this is not without interest in itself), but some of these inscriptions are quite detailed and highly informative about the operation of ancient society and institutions. A good example is provided by the sets of painted inscriptions (*tituli picti*) on OLIVE OIL amphoras from Spain (the Dressel 20 type). This globular jar, average volume c.70 litres, reveals Roman procedures governing the bottling of olive oil at port sites along the navigable Guadalquivir river. The amphoras were first weighed empty; this figure was marked on the vessel, along with the name of the merchant who was to transport the oil overseas. In a third line, the weight of oil contained in the amphora was added. A fourth set of notations reveals the names and signatures of those responsible for carrying out and monitoring the weighing, as well as an indication of the actual farm from which the oil originated. DJM

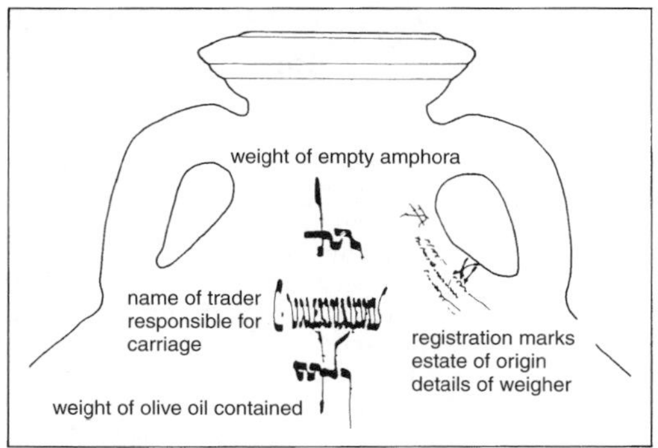

INSTRUMENTUM DOMESTICUM: painted inscriptions (*tituli picti*) on the neck and upper body of a Dressel 20 olive oil amphora from southern Spain.

See Harris, W.V. (1993) *The Inscribed Economy: production and distribution in the Roman empire in the light of instrumentum domesticum*.

insurance A form of protection whereby premiums are paid by an individual to compensate for any loss that may occur as a result of accident, death or other factors. Not all forms of insurance in the ancient world necessitated a premium. In Greece and Rome early forms of insurance were tied to maritime loans. Because of the great risk factor involved in the transportation of goods by sea, individuals would take out loans from a creditor, either a banker or specialized moneylender, to secure any loss that may occur as a result of a wreck. If a SHIPWRECK occurred, there was no obligation to repay the loan. In most cases, ships would arrive at their destinations safely and the borrower would pay back a premium, the amount of a loan plus interest. In the Greek world, the speeches of the 4th-century BC ORATOR DEMOSTHENES preserve the best evidence for maritime insurance (Demosthenes 34.6–7, 35.18). The *Digest* (45.1.122.1) records certain conditions that the Roman borrower was required to observe in order to receive a loan. For example, the voyage had to take place during a time of the year that was favourable for sailing. If the voyage took place otherwise and a wreck occurred, the borrower would have to pay the premium (Johnston, 96). Some scholars have debated whether or not the actual term insurance can apply to this particular form of negotiation. Millet believes that the term insurance is irrelevant, especially in view of the fact that most borrowers sailed along with their cargo. If the ship sank, the borrower went down with it and the concept of insurance became inapplicable (Millet 44–6).

Another form of protection against accidental loss is evident in the legal remedy known as *damnum infectum* or damage not done. This legal remedy pertained to situations when there was a potential threat to property. For instance, if your neighbour was building a chicken coop and you believed that the potential collapse of this coop could damage a wall on your property, you were at liberty to acquire a promise (*cautio*) from your neighbour. This promise ensured that the neighbour would be liable to compensate for any expenses if damage to your property occurred.

Roman funerary rites for FREEDMEN and SLAVES also inadvertently relate to insurance. FUNERAL CLUBS (*collegia funeratica*) ensured that the funerary rites of its members would be carried out. Typically, members met once a month to make payments to the club in return for the performance of rites upon their deaths. LAH

See Johnston, D. (1999) *Roman Law in Context*; Millett, P. (1983) Maritime loans and the structure of credit in fourth century Athens, in P. Garnsey, K. Hopkins, and C. R. Whittaker, eds., *Trade in the Ancient Economy* 36–52; Ste Croix, G. E. M. de (1974) Ancient Greek and Roman maritime loans, in H. Edey and B. S. Yamey, eds., *Debits, Credits, Finance and Profits* 41–59; Toynbee, J. M. C. (1971) *Death and Burial in the Roman World*.

intellectuals see LIBRARIES; MUSEUMS; ORATORS; PHILOSOPHY; PRESOCRATICS; SCIENCE; COMMENTATORS, TEXTUAL.

international relations The Greeks were but dimly aware that they formed a single cultural group, 'the Hellenes'. More usually, their primary point of identification and focus of patriotic loyalty was their *POLIS*. Relations between *poleis* were therefore as often as not unfriendly, and between neighbours downright hostile.

On the other hand, there were from an early date permanent friendly associations of Greek cities with a religious character, such as the DELPHIC amphiktiony in central Greece and the Panionian league of western Asia Minor. Common religious worship was the basis too of the panhellenic (all-Greek) ATHLETIC FESTIVALS organized into a regular cycle in the early 6th century: the OLYMPIC, Pythian, Isthmian and Nemean games.

Also beginning in the 6th century BC some attempt was made at establishing permanent multi-*polis* alliances of a political, or rather military, nature. The PELOPONNESIAN league is the best known of these, though it should be noted that its members were not allied to each other but swore to have the same friends and enemies as their common *hêgemôn* (leader), Sparta. Members might also, and did, fight against, as well as side by side, with each other. During the 5th century the league was successfully rivalled by the Athenians' naval alliance. It was typical of Greek international relations that these two power-blocs could not live in harmony. Some smaller Greek cities tried to preserve a position of neutrality between these feuding great powers, as they did later between the Macedonian and hellenistic monarchies of the last four centuries BC. But genuine neutrality was rarely a practical option.

The Romans organized these things very differently. At first they struggled with their fellow-Latins and non-Latin neighbours in central Italy very much like a Greek *polis*. But by the middle of the 3rd century they had come to dominate the entire Italian peninsula, and a key technique behind their remarkable empire was the spreading of Roman CITIZENSHIP to communities outside Rome through COLONIZATION as well as conquest.

Being legally minded, the Romans drew a distinction between *ius naturale* ('law of nature'), which might sanction the use of sheer brute force (as in the case of captive slaves), and the *ius gentium* ('law of peoples'): international relations fell within the purview of the latter. The Romans persuaded themselves, if not always their enemies, that they fought only defensive wars. High religious officials were appointed from among the political ÉLITE, whose function was to declare that war might legitimately be conducted. As long as the Romans were at war somewhere, the gates of the temple of JANUS in Rome were kept open. That they were closed only three times in hundreds of years tells its own tale about the Romans' implacable pursuit of their international aims through warfare.

Nevertheless, though it was founded on war and war was always kept available as an option just in case, the Romans' huge and immensely long-lived empire did usher in an unprecedented era of peace during the first centuries AD. It was a Roman peace (*pax Romana*), to be sure, peace on the Romans' terms. But it did have a remarkably universalizing outcome. In AD 212 every freeborn inhabitant of the empire was declared a Roman citizen – something utterly unimaginable in 5th-century BC Greece, where both Athens and Sparta jealously guarded their citizenship and (in the words of the Roman emperor CLAUDIUS, as reported by TACITUS) 'shut out those they had conquered on the grounds of their foreign birth'. (see also ATHENIAN EMPIRE; DIPLOMACY; FEDERALISM; POLITICAL SYSTEMS) PAC

intertextualism, intertextuality see APOLLONIOS OF RHODES; CRITICAL THEORY; POST-MODERNISM; STRUCTURALISM AND POST-STRUCTURALISM.

inventions Most elements of Greco-Roman TECHNOLOGY were already in place (inherited from prehistoric times), or adopted from 'barbarian' peoples absorbed during the expansion of empires. The intellectual atmosphere of Greece provided a genuine context for invention to take place as a conscious process distinct from accidental discovery. The Mouseion (sanctuary of the Muses), an institute founded at ALEXANDRIA by PTOLEMY I by 300 BC, demonstrated rulers' willingness to support research and development of MACHINES that would enhance their power, in contexts ranging from religious and social events (e.g. HERO's devices for opening temple doors or pouring liquids) to ARCHITECTURE and military ENGINEERING (e.g. cranes and CATAPULTS) and AGRICULTURE (water-lifting devices). Our knowledge of classical inventions is based primarily upon the survival of manuscripts (e.g. Hero's *Pneumatika*), while evidence for their application relies heavily on ARCHAEOLOGICAL discoveries (e.g. pumping equipment from MINES or SHIPWRECKS).

It is one thing to invent something; it is quite another for an invention to be applied. For example the water-powered rotary MILL consisted of diverse mechanisms that already existed – rotary millstones (Iberia?), geared transmission and a vertical waterwheel (Alexandria?) – but their combination was a genuine invention whose place and date remain unknown. Only through archaeological finds do we now know that it became an innovation found throughout the Roman empire. A modern stereotype praises Greek theory and invention rather than Roman practical application, and considers mechanical devices more significant than mundane inventions such as blown glass. (see also TECHNOLOGY) KG

See White, K. D. (1984) *Greek and Roman Technology*.

investment The possibility for growth in the Roman economy was constrained by a shortage of capital and the limited infrastructure of financial institutions to raise funds for business ventures. Much of the capital for investment was provided by private individuals, in particular members of the upper classes. Because they controlled a large portion of the empire's wealth, the investment strategies that upper class Romans followed affected all aspects of the Roman economy. Since AGRICULTURE dominated the Roman economy, it represented for many Romans the only feasible way to invest large amounts of capital. Concerned to gain financial security from their investments, Romans tended to regard land not as one investment alternative among many but as a permanent resource whose value was measured in its capacity to provide a stable income for the long term. To be sure, there were many other forms of investment, such as in commerce and industry, but they were generally much riskier than agriculture. This conception of the economic security gained from investing in agriculture informed many areas of Roman LAW and administration, from the management of the property belonging to orphans to the funding of state-sponsored ALIMENTARY programmes. The security that upper class Romans sought by investing in agriculture had important effects on their relationships between landowners and farm tenants and other labourers. This desire for security was a response to the dominant role of agriculture in the Roman economy, but it also diminished investment in commerce and industry and so impeded the development of these sectors of the economy. DPK

See Finley, M. I. (1999) *The Ancient Economy*; Kehoe, D. P. (1997) *Investment, Profit, and Tenancy*; Rathbone, D. (1991) *Economic Rationalism and Rural Society in Third-century AD Egypt*.

Ioannes Tzetzes see SCHOLARSHIP, BYZANTINE.

Ion of Chios Born on the island of CHIOS c.484–481 BC, by 465 he had moved to Athens, where he composed one of his most celebrated works, a prize-winning dithyrambic poem entitled *Aoios* ('Morning Star'); the opening lines were: 'We awaited the sky-wandering Morning Star, white-winged forerunner of the sun.' He was a successful writer of TRAGEDIES, winning first prize on at least one occasion, when he is said to have presented every Athenian citizen with a jar of Chian WINE. He was included by some ancient critics in the ranks of the five greatest tragedians, though not considered as good as his contemporaries SOPHOKLES and EURIPIDES. He also wrote several prose works. His *Epidêmiai* ('Visits') were memoirs of his encounters and conversations with famous men, including Sophokles, KIMON, PERIKLES and SOCRATES. He maintained close links with his birthplace and wrote an account of *The Foundation of Chios*, in which he claimed that Oinopion, the son of THESEUS, was the city's founder. In a philosophical treatise called the *Triagmoi* he argued that people's characters comprise a balance of three qualities: understanding, power and fortune. Ion attracted comment and admiration from other Greek POETS and dramatists, including ARISTOPHANES, who says of him in his play *Peace* (lines 836–7): 'Ion of Chios, who, hereabouts, some time ago, composed *The Morning Star*. And when he passed away, everyone immediately called him the Morning Star.' PDeS

See West, M. L. (1985) Ion of Chios, *BICS* 32: 71–8; Dover, K. (1986) Ion of Chios, in J. Boardman and C. E. Vaphopoulou-Richardson, eds., *Chios* 27–37.

Ionia see EAST GREECE; GREECE; HELLESPONT AND PROPONTIS; INTERNATIONAL RELATIONS; IONIAN REVOLT; MIGRATIONS; MILETOS; PERSIA AND PERSIANS; PRESOCRATICS; PROSE; SCIENCE.

Ionian islands Located in the ADRIATIC sea along the west coast of modern Greece and Albania, the ISLANDS served as a bridge between Italy and Greece and derived considerable economic benefit from their location. There are five major islands, which supported independent *poleis* in antiquity, and a considerable number of smaller islands.

The northernmost of the group is Korkyra (Latin Corcyra, mod. Corfu; the form 'Kerkyra' appears frequently in literary sources, especially in the ethnic name *Kerkyraios*, but 'Korkyra' seems to have been preferred on the island itself). It had a single *POLIS* whose chief city bore the same name as the island, but there were settlements, sanctuaries and at least one FORTRESS (held by oligarchs in 427–425 BC) scattered around the island. The *polis* was founded as a CORINTHIAN COLONY in the late 7th century BC (the exact date is disputed in the ancient sources), though some sources claim an earlier settlement by Eretrians from EUBOIA. Korkyraians played an important role in a number of events in Greek history. They fought the first recorded NAVAL battle (against the Corinthians, perhaps in 664 BC) and remained one of the greatest naval powers, second only to Athens, down to the PELOPONNESIAN WAR. Their dispute over Epidamnos (a Korkyraian colony) with their mother-city, Corinth, was a cause of the Peloponnesian war. The subsequent civil conflict in the *polis* became the subject of one of THUCYDIDES' most trenchant analyses of the consequences of war (3.69–84). APOLLO was the guardian deity.

Leukas was an artificial island, joined to the mainland originally by a narrow isthmus later cut by a canal. The *polis* was founded as a Corinthian colony under the tyrant Kypselos (so during 657/6–627/6). There was a separate HARBOUR, and a number of place-names are attested for settlements on the island and its *peraia* opposite. The *polis* began striking coins c.490 BC. Ithaca (Ithake) was famous as the home of ODYSSEUS, who was honoured as a god with cult, games (the Odysseia, attested in the late 3rd century BC), and depictions on coins. The goddess ATHENA, his patron and protector, was (unsurprisingly) the tutelary deity of the *polis*.

The territory of the island of Kephallenia was divided among no fewer than four *poleis*. One, Paleis, occupied the western part of the island. An extramural sanctuary, possibly dedicated to POSEIDON, has recently been discovered. Its COINAGE, in SILVER, began in the later 5th century BC. Kranioi occupied the southern part of the island (but not the western peninsula). The *polis* was pro-Athenian during the Peloponnesian war; refugees from MESSENIA were settled there by the Athenians but later expelled by the Spartans. Kranioi struck silver coins from the 5th century. Pronnoi occupied the south-eastern part of the island. POLYBIOS famously described the chief settlement as 'hard to besiege'. The *polis* began to strike silver and bronze coins about in the 4th or 3rd century BC. Finally, Same (*Samê*) occupied the north and north-east of the island. Same had two *akropoleis* according to LIVY, and the remains of settlements and FORTIFICATIONS have been identified in its territory. It struck silver coins from the 5th century.

Zakynthos was home to a single *polis* of the same name. A number of settlements are attested, including a place called Nellos held by oligarchs during a *stasis* in 373/2 BC. The *polis* struck silver coinage from the 5th century.

Smaller islands whose names are attested include the Paxoi islands, a small cluster of islets; Propaxos; Taphos; another small cluster of islands, possibly the Taphiai known from written sources; Karnos; and the Echinades islands. GR

See Gehrke, H.-J. and Wirbelauer, E. (2004) Akarnania and adjacent areas, in Hansen and Nielsen, *Inventory* 351–78; Talbert, R. J. A., ed. (2000) *Barrington Atlas of the Greek and Roman World*, map 54.

 GREECE.

Ionian revolt 499–494 BC Unsuccessful Greek uprising against Persian rule. According to HERODOTOS, our only significant source, the revolt was started using a man with a message tattooed on the back of his head: Herodotos' focus on the role of individuals probably over-emphasizes the role in the revolt of two tyrants of MILETOS, Histiaios and Aristagoras. It is impossible to establish precisely the causes and course of the revolt, but the outline is clear. Several Greek cities on the coast of Asia Minor were persuaded to eject the tyrants ruling them on behalf of the Persian king. Not all these cities were truly Ionian, and cities in CARIA and CYPRUS joined in. With the support of troops from Athens and Eretria, the Greeks achieved some successes, including an attack on SARDIS. Ultimately, the Persians regained control, defeated the Greek fleet at Lade, and besieged and captured Miletos. One response to this was the notorious tragic play *The Capture of Miletos*, written by the Athenian Phrynichos in 492. In the aftermath of the revolt, the Persians reorganized their administration of the Greek cities in a way more acceptable to them. DARIUS I's campaign against Eretria and Athens, which ended in Persian defeat at MARATHON in 490, can be seen as a final attempt to settle the region after the revolt. HB

See Herodotos 5.28–6.32; Murray, O. (1988) The Ionian revolt, in *CAH* 4, 461–90.

 WAR (table).

Ionian war see ATHENS; PELOPONNESIAN WAR.

Iphigeneia Usually identified as the daughter of AGAMEMNON, leader of the Greek expedition to Troy, and Helen's sister CLYTEMNESTRA, Iphigeneia is sacrificed to propitiate the wrath of the GODDESS ARTEMIS and to enable the Greek army to go to Troy. In the many variants of this panhellenic story,

Iphigeneia is sometimes rescued by Artemis, replaced by a beast or image of herself, then immortalized or transported to the land of the Taurians in the BLACK SEA to become Artemis' PRIESTESS. From there, in EURIPIDES' Attic version, she is rescued by her brother Orestes to become a priestess of Artemis' cult at Brauron (in ATTICA) and, after death, a heroine to whom sacrifices are offered on behalf of women who die in childbirth (her name means 'strong birth'). Her myth conflates various trends present in Greek myths of virgin SACRIFICE. As a prelude to battle virgin sacrifice generally guarantees military opportunity or success and may serve as a symbolic renunciation of SEXUALITY before battle. The girl's death as a (usually) voluntary victim is equated with that of men in war. In Attic cult, Iphigeneia's story is linked with other local myths, where a girl is nearly sacrificed to propitiate the wrath of Artemis over the killing of a wild bear. Girls celebrated in conjunction with these tales an initiatory ritual called the Arkteia, where they danced as bears and perhaps symbolically expiated their coming loss of virginity to a goddess who presided over both the wild state of youth and childbirth. HPF

Iphikrates Athenian GENERAL. Known in the tradition as the son of a cobbler, Iphikrates son of Timotheos rose to prominence when he developed the use of light-armed troops (*peltasts*). He used them effectively against Spartan HOPLITES during the Corinthian war, both at CORINTH in the late 390s and at Abydos in 389. Not a politician, he served as a general for at least 13 years between 389/8 (holding junior appointments before this) until 356/5. At that date he, along with the general TIMOTHEOS son of KONON, was discredited and deposed because he refused to pursue a naval engagement in heavy seas during the SOCIAL WAR. XENOPHON claims that his most brilliant victory was against a SYRACUSAN fleet at Kerkyra in 372 BC.

He was a great rival and enemy of Timotheos, and helped the politician Kallistratos prosecute him in 373/2. They later patched up their differences and Iphikrates' son married Timotheos' daughter. Iphikrates himself married either the daughter or sister of the Thracian king of the Odrysians, Kotys, after the King's Peace of 386. He was also adopted as a son by Amyntas of Macedonia and, when he was sent to Amphipolis in 368, drove out the pretender, Pausanias, at the request of the Macedonian queen. Claims that he was responsible for reforms in TACTICS and ARMOUR are sometimes doubted, but he was certainly one of the 4th-century breed of professional commanders whose services were let out for hire. LGM

See Aischines, *Oration* 2 (*The Embassy*); Demosthenes, *Oration* 23 (*Against Aristokrates*); Diodorus Siculus, books 14–16; Nepos, *Iphicrates*; Xenophon, *Hellenika*, books 4–6.

Ipsos, battle of Major engagement between Alexander's SUCCESSORS, fought in the spring of 301 BC on a great plain near the modern Turkish town of Sipsin in PHRYGIA. A coalition of forces had come together to oppose the ANTIGONID king Antigonos I Monophthalmos in 302, principally led by SELEUKOS and LYSIMACHOS. Antigonos had recalled his son DEMETRIOS from THRACE, and the four armies had wintered in Asia Minor: Antigonos at Dorylaion, Demetrios further north near the HELLESPONT, Seleukos in western CAPPADOCIA, and Lysimachos near Herakleia Pontica. With the coming of spring the armies marched, joined together, and met by Ipsos. Antigonos and Demetrios commanded 70,000 infantry, 10,000 cavalry, and 75 ELEPHANTS; Seleukos and Lysimachos, whose forces included troops supplied by Kassandros, had 64,000 infantry, perhaps 12,000 CAVALRY, and 400 or more elephants. The decisive action in the battle came when Demetrios, who commanded the cavalry, routed his mounted opponents but then pursued them too far, allowing Seleukos and Lysimachos to block him from reuniting with the main body of the army with a screen of elephants. Antigonos' troops were encircled and defeated; the king himself, 81 years old, died fighting. Demetrios escaped and fled to Greece. The battle marked the end of Antigonos' and Demetrios' hopes of reassembling ALEXANDER's empire under their sole authority. GR

See Billows, R. A. (1990) *Antigonos the One-eyed and the Creation of the Hellenistic State.*

 BATTLES (table).

Iran see AFGHANISTAN; AHURA-MAZDA; CUNEIFORM; CYRUS THE GREAT; ELAM; MIGRATIONS; MITHRADATES; MITHRAS AND MITHRAISM; PARTHIA AND PARTHIANS; PERSIAN EMPIRE; SELEUKID EMPIRE; ZOROASTER.

Ireland (Hibernia) see CELTS; EXPLORATION; MIGRATIONS; RAVENNA COSMOGRAPHER; UTOPIAS.

Irni City in the Roman province of Baetica, located to the south-east of Seville, essentially known for a copy of the Flavian municipal law found there in the early 1980s. It is the most complete copy of this document which presents invaluable evidence on the romanization of southern Spain. There is good reason to believe that all copies go back to a master document, a fragment of which is kept in the archaeological museum in Seville. The law embodied on the charter is highly Roman in form, and its provisions appear to assume that the workings of the town will operate in the same way as cities in Italy. The grant of the charter goes back to the emperor VESPASIAN and made available the LATIN right to the inhabitants, but neither the literary sources (PLINY THE ELDER) nor the fragments of the individual copies specify the reason for bestowing it. The fact that all copies of the law come from towns in Baetica suggests that it was only implemented in the most romanized province of Spain, and this makes it more plausible to assume that it was a reward for the progress made by the provincials towards a Roman style of living rather than an incentive to achieve this effect. Differences between the various copies show that cities were allowed to introduce modifications in accordance with local circumstances. One of the most striking features of the local government at Irni is that it had a municipal council of 63 members instead of the more regular complement of 100. MK

See Fear, A. T. (1996) *Rome and Baetica: urbanization in southern Spain c.50 BC–AD 150.*

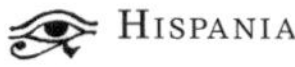

iron Among the commonest metals, iron ores occur in areas which are generally lacking in metals, including much of Greece and Italy. It was in use in Greece by the 11th century BC and in Italy by the 8th.

The iron used in antiquity was 'wrought iron' (an alloy containing c.0.5 per cent carbon) which cannot be cast but is forged at red heat. Though softer and more malleable than bronze, it is less brittle and can be joined by welding. This, and its greater accessibility, allowed the development of a wide range of artefacts, and it was used for many functional purposes for which bronze was too costly. The increased productivity which will have resulted from the widespread use of iron in many industries and crafts, especially in AGRICULTURE, will have had profound affects on the ancient economy.

Steel, an alloy of iron containing 0.5–1.5 per cent carbon, was available in limited quantities. It has markedly different properties to wrought iron, and rapid cooling of red hot steel (quenching) makes it extremely hard and brittle, too brittle for most purposes; fortunately this can be lessened by reheating it to a lower temperature (tempering).

We do not know how widely steel was used by the Greeks. In the Roman period the finest steel was imported from INDIA (Seric iron), but most was produced by carburization (the prolonged heating of iron in charcoal) which creates a casing of steel around a wrought iron core, a mixture which only needs quenching to maximize its physical advantages. However, the cost of steel probably limited its use to edged TOOLS and weapons. (see also METALLURGY) WHM

IRON: (a) vase-painting of Greek iron smelters at work, surrounded by representations of the tools of their trade.

IRON: (b) a Roman iron smithy.

Isaios (Isaeus) 4th-century BC Attic ORATOR. Very little is known about the long life of Isaios, and the ancient BIOGRAPHICAL tradition had no reliable information about his birthplace (perhaps Chalkis). He was reputedly taught by ISOKRATES, though the latter does not mention him in the list of his earliest students (15.93) and his style is much closer to that of LYSIAS, with whom he is compared (not entirely unfavourably) by Dionysios. Isaios probably taught DEMOSTHENES and may have written a rhetorical manual (*technê*), but he played no known part in Athenian political life. His importance is as a professional speechwriter (*logographos*), a member of the ancient canon of ten Attic orators. The Augustan critics pronounced 50 of the 64 speeches known to them as genuine, and it is clear from all 11 surviving speeches (dating from c.389), and a number of the fragments, that Isaios specialized in INHERITANCE cases. Various fragments, including that of a 12th speech datable to c.344/3, indicate that he also wrote a number of speeches on the related area of CITIZENSHIP rights. Isaios' speeches are vital, but far from straightforward, evidence for the intricacies of Athenian testamentary law: his purpose was to win the case, and to this end he used any chicanery he deemed necessary. He thereby gained a reputation for cleverness, and his at times highly complex arguments mark him out from Lysias, while the forcefulness of his attacks on the opposition (*diabolê*) presages the methods of the later members of the canon. MJE

See Forster, E. S., trs. (1927) *Isaeus*; Wyse, W. (1904) *The Speeches of Isaeus.*

Ischia see PITHEKOUSSAI.

Ishtar see MOTHER GODDESSES.

Isis Major goddess of the Egyptian pantheon, sister–wife of Osiris and mother of Horus. Her name may mean 'throne,' suggesting both her regal character and the posture assumed by a nursing mother. This maternal aspect was central to Isis' Greco-Roman cult, as were her roles as the guardian of marriage and guarantor of the fertility of crops. HERODOTOS identified Isis with DEMETER (2.59), and she began to be worshipped in the Greek world as early as the 4th century BC. Hellenized and syncretized versions of her cult became increasingly widespread and, by the time of the Roman principate, she was worshipped in various guises throughout the MEDITERRANEAN. Contemporary hymns in her

ISIS: wall-painting from Herculaneum depicting a temple of Isis (note the Egyptianized sphinxes). As with most other Roman temples, the religious ritual is held in the open, at an altar in front of the temple.

honour celebrate her as a culture-bringer and 'greatest of gods'. The mysteries of Isis proved to be especially influential, as is famously attested by the 11th book of Apuleius' *Metamorphoses*, where she restores Lucius to his human form and makes him one of her initiates.

The central myth associated with Isis concerns the murder of Osiris by Seth, and the quest of the grief-stricken Isis to find and restore Osiris' dismembered corpse. She is impregnated by his temporarily re-animated body, and gives birth to Horus, whom she protects from Seth. Horus finally defeats Seth and is initiated by Isis into his kingdom.

Representations of Isis often show a statuesque female holding a rattle (*sistrum*) and wearing a mantle with a characteristic knot at her chest (the 'Isiac knot'). JRCC

See Plutarch, *Moralia* 351–84; Turcan, R. (1996) *The Cults of the Roman Empire*.

islands While GEOGRAPHY does not determine history, it offers possibilities and limits. Under various material conditions, islands play an important role in social and cultural development. Because of their 'connectivity' they may become more prosperous than their limited resources would suggest. The MEDITERRANEAN contains a great variety of islands, which geographical authors liked to rank by size. Most large islands are in the AEGEAN, but not the largest (e.g. SARDINIA, SICILY, CYPRUS).

Particularly in the northern Mediterranean, islands provided stepping-stones to facilitate longer voyages. In early times, the existence of many varied ECOLOGICAL units close together may have fostered economic specialization and political experimentation, leading to rapid evolution of CITY-STATE forms. Compare, for example, the varying number of city-states on Keos (4), LESBOS (6), and CRETE (several dozen) as against SAMOS and CHIOS (1 each). In the archaic period the larger, prosperous island cities exercised regional hegemonies and were home to sophisticated ARISTOCRATIC cultures. Later the hellenistic city-state of RHODES, located at a junction of sea routes, rose to a peak of military and commercial power. Hellenistic and Roman EXPLORERS frequented the islands of the ATLANTIC, some of which were identified with the legendary Isles of the Blest. In mythological and UTOPIAN writings, islands can be other-worldly places. DGJS

See Broodbank, C. (2000) *An Island Archaeology of the Early Cyclades*; Horden, P. and Purcell, N. (1999) *The Corrupting Sea: a study of Mediterranean history*; Reger, G. (1997) Islands with one polis versus islands with several poleis, in M. H. Hansen, ed., *The Polis as an Urban Centre and as a Political Community* 450–92.

AEGEAN SEA: (a)–(b).

Isokrates 436–338 BC Speechwriter. Of the 25 speeches accepted by DIONYSIOS OF HALIKARNASSOS as genuinely Isokratean, 21 are extant (of which 6 were for the courts), as well as 9 letters. The speeches were not delivered by Isokrates (who considered himself to be weak at speaking), but were published as carefully revised and polished pamphlets. His themes were mostly political. In a number of speeches he called for WAR against the BARBARIAN in order to bring unity and prosperity to Greece, and to empty it of the rabble. In *Panêgyrikos* (written in 380 against the backdrop of the King's Peace of 386) this war is to be undertaken under the leadership of Athens and Sparta, though in fact the speech is a thinly veiled encomium of Athens. Later he looked to others to lead this war, especially PHILIP II of Macedonia in his *Philip* of 346. His desire was fulfilled after his death by the foundation of Philip's league of CORINTH in 337 and the subsequent Macedonian invasion of Asia, but he may ultimately have regretted his enthusiasm. One tradition says that he committed SUICIDE after Philip's victory in the battle of CHAIRONEIA, despite the fact that the last of his letters, if genuine, congratulates Philip on his success!

A student of GORGIAS, and perhaps also Prodikos of Keos, Teisias of SYRACUSE and the oligarch Theramenes of Athens, he was also a follower of SOCRATES. He began writing speeches after being financially ruined as a result of the PELOPONNESIAN WAR. While in *Antidôsis* he snipes at those who wrote forensic speeches, he began his professional career as a *logographos*, writing speeches for others in the courts. In the late 390s he established his school. Although in *Against the Sophists* (written at the time he opened the school) he attacks and distances himself from those who made money through teaching PHILOSOPHY and disputation, he remade his fortune by teaching RHETORIC and his own philosophical principles based on practical wisdom. Early rhetorical exercises, intended as 'display pieces', include *Busiris* and *Helen*, using mythical material. His pupils included the Athenian general TIMOTHEOS, as well as the HISTORIANS THEOPOMPOS, EPHOROS and Androtion, the orators Hypereides and ISAIOS, and the tragedians Asklepiades and Theodektas.

His style was distinctive and elegant, and his influence was felt even at Rome: CICERO in the *De oratore* calls him the Master of all Rhetoricians! His greatest speech was *Panêgyrikos*. In contrast, the *Panathênaïkos*, his last speech, written when he was 94 in open praise of Athens, lacks originality in theme and fluency in style. Grand claims are often made for his influence on the actions of Philip, particularly in regard to the peace with Athens in 346. Yet the idea of 'war against the barbarian' was not new in the 4th century, and Philip undoubtedly had his own agenda, in which his correspondent surely played little real part. LGM

See Norlin, G. and Van Hook, L., trs. (1928–45) 3 vols.; Dionysios of Halikarnassos, *Isocrates*; Pseudo-Plutarch, *Lives of the Ten Orators* 863e–839d; Kennedy, G. (1963) *The Art of Persuasion*; Too, Y. L. (1995) *The Rhetoric of Identity in Isocrates*.

Issos Site, in South-East Asia Minor, of ALEXANDER the Great's second major victory over the PERSIAN EMPIRE, in 333 BC. After conquering ANATOLIA, Alexander turned south towards SYRIA but then found that the Persian army, led by king DARIUS III, was to his rear. ARRIAN's description of the ensuing battle is based on that of Kallisthenes, which was criticized by POLYBIOS in some detail. The battle took place on a narrow plain between mountains and the sea, on the edge of the gulf of Alexandretta. The location meant that the Persians' greater numbers could not be used effectively. Alexander was able to break through their left wing using his cavalry, then wheel around to crush the centre, where Darius was stationed, which was being held in place by the Macedonian infantry. Darius escaped, but his mother, wife and children were captured; Alexander's courteous treatment of them became an important element in the mythology that built up around him. After the battle, Alexander was able to turn south through Syria to Egypt. HB

See Arrian, *Anabasis* 2.6–12; Diodorus Siculus 17.33–6; Plutarch, *Alexander* 20; Polybios 12.17–22.

 ALEXANDER III: (b); BATTLES (table).

Istanbul see CONSTANTINOPLE.

Italica see AMPHITHEATRES; BAETICA; HADRIAN.

Italy, Roman It was the first Roman emperor AUGUSTUS who incorporated Cisalpine GAUL – the Po–Adige plain – into Italia. Although it had been in popular usage since the 2nd century BC, Italia now became the official title for the whole peninsula, with the ALPS forming the northern boundary. Around the same time, Augustus also divided Italy into 11 regions. The precise reason is not known, but it may have been to do with facilitating CENSUS returns, and with the levying of taxes on legacies and sales, a measure introduced in AD 6. Though administratively very subordinate to Rome in the process of government, many elements of these regional divisions were still in existence 600 years later.

PLINY THE ELDER (*Natural History* 3.38–132) specifically uses these Augustan *regiones* as a framework for his description of the country, published in AD 77, while STRABO, MELA and PTOLEMY OF ALEXANDRIA also provide geographical accounts of Italy. All are at pains to stress the topographical and ethnic diversity of the peninsula, and it is clear that the regional divisions were largely based on tribal groupings. These in turn often reflect topographical factors, notably the contrast between Italy's mountainous backbone, the Apennines, and the fertile lowlands. Major RIVERS frequently served as boundaries, though not exclusively: the Arno for example, despite its size, lay within *regio* VII, rather than forming its northern limit.

Rome itself does not seem to have belonged to a *regio* and may have been regarded as a notional twelfth region. *Regio* I, incorporating Latium and Campania, stretched south-eastwards from it, across rich VOLCANIC lands. These were traversed by the Via Appia and the Via Latina, and by a CANAL through the Pomptine Marshes, travelled along by HORACE on a famous journey to Brindisi in 37 BC. Roman Italy's most fashionable area, it was AGRICULTURALLY bounteous, especially in fine WINE, OLIVE OIL and cereals, and supported such famous towns as POMPEII, HERCULANEUM and the great port of PUTEOLI (Rome's main harbour until supplanted by OSTIA in the 2nd century AD). It also became a popular holiday resort, as WALL-PAINTINGS, and the physical remains, of seaside VILLAS vividly attest. *Regio* II comprised Apulia and the Salentine peninsula (known in antiquity as Calabria, which today refers instead to Italy's 'toe'), a landscape of immense contrasts. Taranto and Brindisi remain important harbours, as they were in antiquity, but Horace describes the region as *siticulosa* (parched). Its agricultural reputation was thus mainly for SHEEP farming; but olives and vines grew well in the Tavoliere plain, an area where Luceria (Lucera) was a prominent settlement.

The 'toe' of the peninsula, the largely mountainous areas of Lucania and Bruttium, formed *Regio* III. The main cities were earlier Greek foundations like Rhegion (Reggio di Calabria) and Paestum, situated along the coast; the majority continued to flourish in the Roman period, not least as trading entrepôts. *Regio* IV was likewise largely mountainous. Roughly corresponding to the modern Abruzzi, it had no single agreed ancient name, partly because it was the focus of no fewer than nine major tribes, including the SABINES. Among its towns were Saepinum, Sulmo (Sulmona), Reate (Rieti) and Alba Fucens, which lay close to the Fucine lake, drained under CLAUDIUS. Flood management schemes were also a conspicuous feature of the flatlands that stretch northwards from Rieti.

Regio V was Picenum, the tribal area of the Praetuttii, dominated by the coastal city of Ancona. To its north and west lay *Regio* VI, UMBRIA and the Ager Gallicus; this is a hilly but fertile region, where towns like Iguvium (Gubbio), Asisium (Assisi) and Carsulae still retain abundant remains of their prosperous Roman past. By contrast, *Regio* VII, ETRURIA, did not exhibit much in urban vitality, despite its agricultural and mineral resources: many of the old Etruscan centres lapsed into obscurity. Centumcellae (Civitavecchia) did, however, develop into a significant port, though a place like Florentia (Florence) failed to grow into more than an average-sized town. Much of this may have been due to the economic and social attraction of Campania (*Regio* I), though Luna (Luni) was a successful foundation; this was because of its exploitation of the nearby

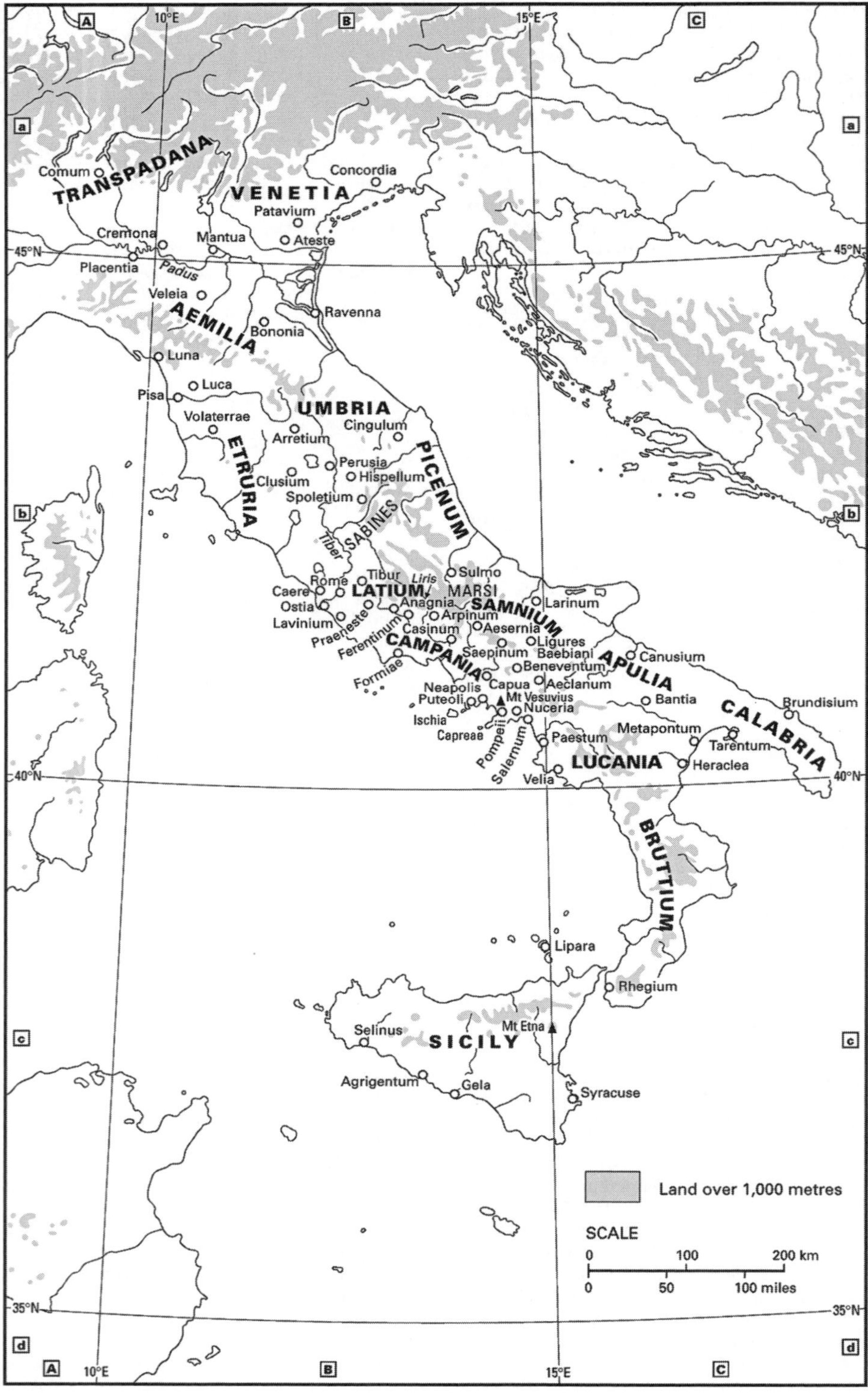

Italy, Roman: (a) the main subdivisions of Roman Italy and some of the principal sites.

Italy, Roman: (b) the Augustan regions of Italy.

Carrara marble quarries, a material in heavy demand especially from Augustan times.

The north was divided into four regions. The upland terrain of *Regio* IX, Liguria, meant that this was the poorest, despite Genua's (Genoa) fine, but underdeveloped port, and the Via Aurelia, a coastal road leading to Gallia Narbonensis and Spain. Most Romans preferred to travel along the Via Flaminia (refurbished by Augustus in 27 BC) into *Regio* VIII (Gallia Cispadana), where it had its junction with the Via Aemilia at Ariminium (Rimini). This major road skirted the western side of the Po plain, along which were a series of highly significant cities, such as Bononia (Bologna) and Mutina (Modena). Like *Regio* X (Venetia and Istria), this developed as a most prosperous region, especially through the cultivation of wheat, millet and wine, as well as the production of wool, for which Mutina and Parma were particularly renowned. Aquileia, as a hugely busy port at the head of the Adriatic, was to become one of the most populous cities of Italy, while Ravenna achieved the status of an Imperial capital in the early 5th century AD.

Regio XI, Gallia Transpadana, lay in the far northwest of Italy. Colonial foundations, for retired army veterans, at places like Augusta Praetoria (Aosta) and Augusta Taurinorum (Turin), together with cities like Comum (Como), the home of Pliny the Younger, attest the success of Augustus' policy of urbanization in newly acquired territory, a process perhaps aided by his novel administrative framework. Mediolanum (Milan), a pre-Roman foundation, likewise prospered in imperial times and also became an imperial capital in the late 3rd century. Henceforth, the north of Italy was to achieve a preeminence over the centre and south, the legacy of which remains to this day. TWP

See Horace, *Satires* 1.5; Pliny the Elder, *Natural History*, book 3; Strabo, books 5–6; Cornell, T. J. and Lomas K., eds. (1995) *Urban Society in Roman Italy*; Dyson, S. L. (1992) *Community and Society in Roman Italy*; Lomas, K. (1996) *Roman Italy 338 BC–AD 200: a sourcebook*; Potter, T.W. (1987) *Roman Italy*; Salmon, E.T. (1982) *The Making of Roman Italy*; Thomsen, R. (1947) *The Italic Regions*; various authors (1994) in *L'Italie d'Auguste à Dioclétien*.

 ETRURIA AND ETRUSCANS; LATINS; ROADS, ROMAN: (a); SAMNITES.

Ithaca see CORINTH; HOMER; IONIAN ISLANDS; ODYSSEUS.

Iulia see JULIA.

Iulii (Julii) An important *gens* in the late Roman Republic, though its origins lie deeper in the past. The family, especially its most prominent representative Gaius JULIUS CAESAR, advertised descent from Iulus, son of AENEAS, and from VENUS herself, but this is dubious and reflects a tendency for families to claim divine origins in a quest for political and social superiority. Early representatives, some bearing the *cognomen* Iullus, were prominent in MAGISTRACIES of the 5th century BC. The *gens* was PATRICIAN, but did not hold a CONSULSHIP between 267 and 157. Aided by MARIUS, who had married a Julia, the family boasted consuls in 102, 91 and 90, and Gaius Julius Caesar, the DICTATOR's father, was PRAETOR c.92. These magistracies brought the part of the *gens* with the *cognomen* Caesar back into public life, generally with the *populares* in the social and political struggles that followed, but a few individuals opposed Marius and his successors. Later, Julius Caesar and Gaius Julius Caesar Octavianus (AUGUSTUS) granted CITIZENSHIP to many communities whose citizens therefore employed the name Julius as their *gens*. The name, which also became a *praenomen*, thus remains common, though the family itself disappeared in the male line. JV

Iunii (Junii) A PLEBEIAN *gens* with a penchant for finding unnatural deaths. The best known branch had the cognomen BRUTUS. Lucius Junius Brutus was an assassin of TARQUINIUS SUPERBUS and one of the first CONSULS in 509 BC. According to legend, he inflicted capital punishment on his sons and died after a victory over the ETRUSCANS. The conspiracy against CAESAR included Marcus Junius Brutus and Decimus Junius Brutus. The former committed SUICIDE and the latter was executed on ANTONY'S orders. Lucius Junius Brutus Damasippus fought against SULLA at the Colline gate, was defeated and executed. Marcus Junius Brutus, father of the tyrannicide, was a legate of Marcus Aemilius Lepidus, the consul of 78 BC, who marched on Rome in 77. Brutus surrendered to POMPEY at Mutina after a promise of safe conduct, but was executed. Another branch, with the *cognomen* Silanus, was prominent in the late Republic and early empire. At least ten were exiled, executed, or committed suicide. Some descended from Augustus, including five children of Marcus Junius Silanus Torquatus, husband of Aemilia Lepida, a great-granddaughter of Augustus. They were eliminated late in CLAUDIUS' reign or under NERO, as AGRIPPINA and her son sought to remove rivals. JV

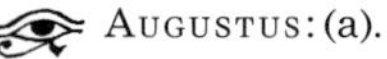

ivory Egypt and the Near East were the sources for the ivory imported to Greece and Italy. Egypt could obtain it from Ethiopia, Libya and Somalia, as well as using hippopotamus ivory, which does not appear to have been a popular export. Due to the nature of the material, it was used primarily for small-scale objects; inlays and plaques on FURNITURE or boxes, or items such as spoons or MUSICAL INSTRUMENTS, as well as small pieces of JEWELLERY (beads, bracelets and rings). It was used throughout antiquity as HAIR ornaments, for example combs or pins, where its smooth surface was valued for not damaging the hair. Pieces could be riveted together, or painted or even gilded, a practice that was utilized by MYCENAEAN Greeks. The MINOANS of Bronze Age CRETE used ivory for seals. The Egyptians were particularly fond of ivory for jewellery, while the PHOENICIANS used it for furniture decoration and may have had a hand in introducing ivory to 7th-century BC Greece, where it had its boom in popularity.

The best finds in Greece have been at the sanctuary of ARTEMIS Ortheia in SPARTA, where over 300 pieces dating to the second half of the 7th century BC were excavated. The collection includes numerous pinheads, beads, musical pipes, plectra, needles and seals. A significant number of the pieces were plaques, many of which seem to have come from fibulae (ancient safety pins). The images often reflect their Near Eastern trade route in the types of images and style of depiction, but the majority are in a distinctly Greek (Daidalic) style, similar to that of KOUROI AND KORAI. The amount of ivory dropped at the end of the 7th century, thought to be due to a closure of the Near Eastern trade route.

After the archaic period the Greeks' only significant use of ivory was in the extravagant chryselephantine (gold and ivory) cult statues, with the most famous being PHEIDIAS' ATHENA Parthenos in the Athenian PARTHENON, and ZEUS in his TEMPLE at OLYMPIA, where he was one of the Seven Wonders of the world. Ivory was used for the skin of the statues, with gold making up their clothes, hair, and other accoutrements. Being an organic material, the ivory required a humid atmosphere to maintain its lustre and to this end a shallow pool of water was placed in front of the statue. Ivory was still used in the Roman period, but the Romans appeared to have been more interested in it as a trade item. NJW

See Dawkins, R. M., ed. (1929) *The Sanctuary of Artemis Orthia at Sparta*; Ogden, J. (1982) *Jewellery of the Ancient World*.

İzmir see SMYRNA.

Janus Roman god of doorways and transitions. The noun *ianus* can mean simply 'gateway', and is related to the more common *ianua*, 'door'; the main features of the god Janus clearly reflect his origin as the personification of gates and doorways. He was normally depicted with a double face, presumably because, like a doorway, he looked both ways at once; in this guise he frequently appears on Republican coins from the late 3rd century onwards. As the god of beginnings, he gave his name to the month of January and was traditionally invoked first in every prayer. In MYTH also he appears at the beginning of things, as an archaic king of LATIUM who received SATURN on his arrival from Greece. As god of gateways, he was associated with the departure and return of armies on military campaigns; this was most famously expressed in the ritual of closing the doors of his temple in the forum during times of peace. Although this ritual was attributed to the archaic king NUMA, it is first definitely attested in 235 BC and was given new emphasis by AUGUSTUS; it became common in the imperial period. The cult of Janus was very ancient: he is given a place of honour in the archaic hymn of the Salii, and the old festival of the Agonalia was associated with him. He was primarily a deity of public cult and virtually never appears in private dedications. JBR

See Dumézil, G. (1970) *Archaic Roman Religion*.

 GODS AND GODDESSES: (b).

Jason see APOLLONIOS OF RHODES.

Jerash (anc. Gerasa in mod. Jordan) The city was probably founded as Antioch on the Chrysorhoas by Antiochos IV and was part of the Dekapolis, a loose confederation of ten cities in the region, whose exact nature is little understood. Captured by Alexander Jannaeus (103–76 BC), it remained in JEWISH hands until the Roman PROVINCE of SYRIA was established in 63 BC. In AD 106 Jerash became part of the Roman empire with the annexation of ARABIA Petraea. The wealth of Jerash was derived from the caravan trade, and the city greatly prospered in the 2nd century AD. After a decline, Jerash enjoyed a revival in the 5th and 6th centuries when many CHURCHES were constructed. The city was captured by both the PERSIANS (614) and the Arabs (635), after which it was gradually abandoned. Jerash was 85 ha (210 acres) in area and laid out on a grid plan, with an oval piazza as a caravanserai. The main TEMPLE to ARTEMIS was constructed in AD 161. The city also offered temples to ZEUS and DIONYSOS and at least two large BATH buildings and two THEATRES. A hippodrome was located outside the walls to the south; next to it, an ARCH was constructed to commemorate the visit of HADRIAN in AD 129/30. HD

See Browning, I. (1982) *Jerash and the Decapolis*.

 SYRIA, ROMAN: (b).

Jerome (Eusebius Hieronymus) c.AD 347–419/20 Born in Stridon on the DALMATIAN border and educated at Rome (c.360–6), Jerome spent time in TRIER and northern Italy in the late 360s. There he met Rufinus of AQUILEIA, and was attracted by the ascetic life. He undertook a pilgrimage to the East, staying first at ANTIOCH and then joining a cenobitic community in the desert of Syrian Chalcis (c.375). In this community he learned Hebrew and improved his Greek, resulting in a trilingual ability that informed his later scriptural translations and commentaries. After a dispute with other monks he left the community and returned to Antioch, where he was ordained. In 381 he attended the second council of Constantinople, called by THEODOSIUS I. Here he met Gregory of Nyssa and GREGORY OF NAZIANZUS. In 382 he went to the court of pope Damasus in Rome, where he worked as a secretary and supported Damasus' plans to revise the Latin text of the gospels.

While at Rome, he was sought out by a group of intellectual aristocratic women who were interested in the ascetic life. Jerome encouraged their way of life, which included guided study of the scriptures, celibacy, austerity in dress and diet, and seclusion. One of his most polemical letters on the value of the virgin life and ASCETICISM dates to this period (*Letter* 22, AD 384). On Damasus' death, and that of one of the young widow devotees who had taken to extreme asceticism, Jerome was expelled from Rome by those who disapproved of his 'antisocial' doctrines (385). He travelled again to the East, ending up in Bethlehem. Here, through the patronage of Paula and her daughter Eustochium (recipient of *Letter* 22), he set up a MONASTERY and convent. All three spent the rest of their lives there. Jerome died in 419/20.

Jerome's earliest writings, from his time in Chalcis, were translations of Greek theological works, particularly ORIGEN, into Latin. He also translated, and updated to 378, EUSEBIOS' *Chronicle* (380–1), and established his place in the ascetic community with his *Life of Paul, the First Hermit*. In Bethlehem he began (c.391) a translation of the Hebrew BIBLE into Latin, large parts of which were incorporated in to the Vulgate Bible in the 6th century. His output during the latter part of his life was prolific and diverse. He composed homilies, commentaries and exegeses on scripture, maintained correspondence (often in the form of polemic) with individuals across the Western empire, and wrote pamphlets on a range of topics. He was not afraid of controversy; in the 390s he changed his views on Origen and lost the friendship of Rufinus. Some of his adversaries, such as Helvidius (c.383) and Jovinian (393), are known only through Jerome's vociferous refutation of their views on the integrity of Mary, whom Jerome believed to be ever-Virgin. MEH

See Jerome, *Select Letters*, trs. F. A. Wright (1963); Davidson, I. (2000) Later theologians of the west, in P. F. Esler, ed., *The Early Christian World* 602–35; Kelly, J. N. D. (1975) *Jerome*.

Jerusalem Most important city in Jewish thought and prime site of Jewish temple cult. As Jerusalem has been continuously inhabited for the past 6,000 years, archaeological evidence is complicated and confused, and much of what we know from antiquity is derived from written sources more than ARCHAEOLOGY. Tradition has it that king David in the 10th century BC made Jerusalem his capital. It is likely that after the Assyrian conquest of northern Israel in 722 BC, and Jerusalem's avoidance of capture in 701, its position as the key city for JEWS was confirmed. HYMNS and psalms were written about the city, and traditions rapidly developed about its centrality and sanctity. In the Greek and early Roman period much of its importance is to be attributed to its twin political and religious function. The temple, destroyed by the BABYLONIANS in 586 BC and rebuilt under PERSIAN licence in the 4th century, served as a centre for religious devotion, such that even those not living in the city were required to send offerings and pay taxes to it. At the same time the high priest was viewed as a local governor and figure-head of the Jewish state. The central governing body, the Sanhedrin, presided in the city, perhaps on the model of Greek councils of elders, and was, until the destruction of the Temple by the Romans in AD 70, probably the main legislative body.

A move in the 160s BC to transform Jerusalem into a Greek *POLIS* was a possible cause of the Maccabaean revolt against such reforms, and led to partial independence for Jerusalem until it came under Roman control in 63 BC after a siege by POMPEY. The SELEUKID attempt to quell the Maccabaean revolt by the imposition of a Syrian cult in the Temple is indicative of the political importance of the cult. The territory of Jerusalem was greatly expanded in the era before Roman domination, and the importance of the Temple reinforced by a vast building programme under HEROD THE GREAT (37–4 BC), leading PLINY THE ELDER to describe it as 'the most outstanding city in the east' (*Natural History* 5.70). Increasing focus upon the city, including the belief that divine Wisdom resided there, presents the city-cult as a local cult for the Jewish god. A growing emphasis on Jerusalem as the centre of the world is similar to Greek ideas of the location of the world's navel at DELPHI.

Following a large-scale revolt against Roman rule, the city was captured and the temple destroyed in AD 70. Hopes for restoration of the cult continued, however, until a further revolt in 132–5 led to the banning of all Jews from the city and HADRIAN's building the city of Aelia Capitolina on the Temple Mount. In C.AD 361–3 the emperor JULIAN is said to have attempted to rebuild the Temple (perhaps as an anti-CHRISTIAN move) but failed to complete the project. The earliest extant map of the city is the 6th-century Madaba MOSAIC in modern Jordan, depicting Byzantine Jerusalem as a large walled city, with six gates and many towers. This continues the theme of the importance and centrality of the city, located as it is in the centre of the map. JKA

See Levine, L. I. (2003) *Jerusalem*.

 JUDAEA; TRIUMPHS, ROMAN: (b).

Jesus (4 BC?–AD 30?) A JEW from rural Galilee whose teaching and acts (particularly in healing the sick) brought notoriety and a large following both in his home region and in JUDAEA. Many aspects of his career and many of his reported sayings can be paralleled in the lives and words of contemporary charismatic Jews, but his unique impact on the history of late antiquity derived from the survival after his death of a religious movement which claimed his teachings as authoritative.

Precisely because the person of Jesus was central to the identity of early CHRISTIAN communities, which themselves rapidly developed novel and varied theological ideas, the traditions about his life were embroidered soon after his death, and the surviving gospel narratives contain many differences in detail. Nonetheless some BIOGRAPHICAL information can be accepted as almost certainly true, particularly when it does not fit well with later developments within the CHURCH and is therefore unlikely to be later invention. Thus it is nearly certain that Jesus was born in Galilee of humble parentage; that he had a large following, whom he taught; that he addressed himself almost exclusively to Jews rather than gentiles; that he was crucified by order of the Roman governor PONTIUS PILATE in JERUSALEM (precisely when is disputed) that his followers after his death believed that he was the Messiah (a term with somewhat fluid meaning in contemporary Jewish society).

In the eyes of the Roman state the career of Jesus was unimportant. TACITUS wrote simply that Judaea between AD 14 and 37 enjoyed peace (*Histories* 5.9.2). Josephus mentions Jesus briefly in the *Antiquities of the Jews* (18.63–4), but the passage in the extant manuscripts has been much interpolated by Christians. The real impact of Christianity on the religious life of the ancient world was to come only in the generations following Jesus' death. MDG

See Fredriksen, P. (1988) *From Jesus to Christ*; Sanders, P. (1985) *Jesus and Judaism*.

jewellery The use of jewellery for personal adornment was as important to the ancients as to modern society. Primarily the province of women, the main items of ancient jewellery were earrings, necklaces, bracelets and finger rings. Earrings were always made for pierced ears, and both stud and pendant versions were worn, with much variation in each period. Necklaces were worn either as chokers or hanging to the base of the neck, and more than one necklace could be worn at the same time. Bracelets could be worn on the wrist, elbow or as an armlet. Finger rings were always popular, and appear to have been the most socially acceptable item of jewellery for men. The natural world was the primary universal inspiration for motifs, both of flora (flowers, leaves, FRUIT, nuts, seeds), and fauna (ANIMAL heads, snakes, lions, BIRDS, and mythical beasts).

Jewellery had more uses than simple personal adornment. In the religious sphere it was given as a personal offering to a deity and made up part of the treasury goods of a sanctuary, as TEMPLE records demonstrate. It was used to ornament the cult statue itself, for example, the ATHENA Parthenos. Jewellery appears in grave goods, and can provide information as to the social standing of the deceased, as well as the living who were able to spare such wealth. At times jewellery had protective or apotropaic qualities, such as with amulets, often found in BURIALS, particularly of children, or again as votive offerings at sanctuaries. Amulets could also carry specific cultural significance, such as the *bulla*, an amulet worn by Roman children. Jewellery such as seals, used from the Bronze Age onward, were practical items. Seal rings were especially popular with Romans. Wreaths, the other socially acceptable item of jewellery for men, worn in FESTIVAL processions and awarded as prizes in ATHLETIC competitions, also appear in metallic forms and were often dedicated at sanctuaries where they appear on the inventory lists. The materials used for jewellery can trace the external contacts of each region and period.

A variety of metals were utilized, with GOLD the metal of choice. SILVER, COPPER and bronze were also used. LEAD was used for cheap imitation jewellery, with examples found among the votives at the archaic sanctuaries at SPARTA. Both ancient Greeks and Romans chose the materials for jewellery for more than pure appearance. Metals and stones were thought to have specific properties. Gold, for example, was thought to have purifying properties, and variations existed in each period and in different regions. The jewellery of the Greek Bronze Age was particularly impressive for its gold working. A prestige metal at this time, IRON was used for finger rings, as it was in the early Iron Age, where it could also be used for pins. Semi-precious stones were added decorative elements, such as pin-heads, or were jewellery items in their own right, such as seals, pendants and the ubiquitous bead. Gold, however, was the most popular material, and was utilized not only for specific jewellery items, but also as gilt decoration for clothing and FURNITURE. The most famous gold items are perhaps the 'death masks' of MYCENAE. Social rank appears to have been indicated by the wearing of multiple rings on the left hand, with several on a single finger. Bracelets, which were rare in this period, were also worn on the left arm. It has also been suggested that specifically religious jewellery may be visible with head-dresses, as worn by the 'priest-king' on the fresco at KNOSSOS.

Comparatively little jewellery survives from the early Iron Age and the archaic periods of Greece in comparison with other periods. In the orientalizing period (900–600 BC) hard stones were used for beads and inlay, with AMBER and rock crystal popular; however, the use of inlaid stones remained rare until the 4th century BC, and stones themselves were uncommon, except as seals. Gold itself was not readily available until after the PERSIAN WARS (c.479 BC), and Greek tastes preferred plain gold items without further embellishment.

In the hellenistic period, following ALEXANDER the Great's conquest of Persia and Egypt, areas where polychrome jewellery had always been popular, the use of coloured stones and GLASS as inlays increased. Flora and fauna continued to be the main inspiration for motifs but figures of deities such as APHRODITE and in particular EROS frequently occur as decorative embellishments. A new design, the 'HERAKLES knot', appears around this time, and is thought to have held amuletic qualities, appearing on all types of jewellery from diadems to rings. A new form of necklace, with links interlaced into a strap form, dates to this period also.

The Romans eventually adopted hellenistic tastes in jewellery but, officially at least, had previously disapproved of jewellery. 5th-century BC laws limited the amount of gold buried with the dead, and the *lex Oppia* of the 3rd century BC regulated the amount of gold a lady could wear. Gold rings were worn by men of certain classes of the Republic, such as SENATORS and EQUITES, and Romans began the tradition of giving engagement rings. CONSULS by the end of the 3rd century BC were using seal rings, and we also find rings with keys attached. The inhabitants of POMPEII, prior to the burial of their city, were especially fond of polychromy in their jewellery, and raw and uncut stones, such as emeralds and diamonds, appear in the material record. In the imperial period gold coins and medallions as finger ring bezels, necklace pendants and brooch fronts appear. (see also IVORY; SHELL) NJW

See Higgins, R. A. (1961) *Greek and Roman Jewellery*; Ogden, J. (1982) *Jewellery of the Ancient World*; Williams, D. and Ogden, J. (1994) *Greek Gold*.

Jews The early history of the Jews, known from the Hebrew BIBLE, is mainly the story of a people in the land of Israel, especially its capital, JERUSALEM. This national history continued in late antiquity, but Jews came also to settle in a wide diaspora in MESOPOTAMIA and (from hellenistic times) in the MEDITERRANEAN world, and the ethnic definition of Jewish identity was complicated by the acceptance into JUDAISM of gentile proselytes. Jewish history is particularly well known because much pertinent evidence has been preserved from antiquity by the continuous religious traditions of both Jews and CHRISTIANS. The writings of JOSEPHUS provide a detailed framework for this history. ARCHAEOLOGICAL discoveries, in particular the DEAD SEA SCROLLS, have filled some of the gaps in the record.

Jews developed a distinct ethnic identity at least by the middle of the 2nd millennium BC. The TEMPLE cult of the Jewish God in Jerusalem was unusual primarily because of the assumption (not always heeded) that Jews would not also worship other divinities. In other respects the kingdoms of Judah and Israel in the Iron Age were unremarkable. Despite varying degrees of power within the wider region, both kingdoms were at the mercy of the great empires of Mesopotamia and Egypt. In 586 BC Jerusalem was captured by the BABYLONIANS and the Temple destroyed. The resulting displacement to Babylon of many prisoners encouraged the development of a theology of exile. Despite official encouragement, only some exiles took the opportunity to return to Judah when the Babylonians were defeated by DARIUS in c.540 BC.

There is little evidence of contact between Jews and the Greek world before the conquests of ALEXANDER, but during the 3rd century BC the Jews integrated into the hellenistic world as easily as other native peoples of the Near East until an attempt in 167 BC by the SELEUKID king Antiochos IV Epiphanes to abolish the Jewish cult led to the revolt of the MACCABEES in which, according to the surviving accounts, Judaism was treated as antithetical to hellenism. However, the Maccabees themselves, once they had gained political power as the Hasmonaean dynasty, first as high priests, then from 104 BC as kings, were happy to adopt hellenistic literary and artistic modes and the Greek language.

Hasmonaean rule was ended in 37 BC by Roman interference. HEROD (37–34 BC) was installed as a CLIENT RULER, but his son Archelaos was deposed in AD 6. Direct rule by a Roman governor proved unsuccessful when the great revolt broke out in AD 66, ending with the destruction of the Jerusalem Temple by TITUS in 70. Further rebellions, in the diaspora in AD 116–17 and in Judaea in 132–5, were ruthlessly suppressed by the Roman state, and no more serious uprising by Jews are recorded after the defeat of BAR KOCHBA in 135. In the empire of the 4th century and after, the violent rhetoric of CHRISTIAN EMPERORS often masked lenient legislation, and at least by the time of THEODOSIUS I, the state gave formal recognition to the authority within Jewish society of the rabbinic patriarch.

The history of diaspora Jews began with the exile to Babylon in 586 BC, but little is known about the Babylonian Jews between the 6th century BC and the 3rd century AD, when the region became a centre of rabbinic study, eventually producing in c.AD 500 the Babylonian Talmud, the main text studied in later rabbinic Judaism. In the hellenistic period the Mediterranean diaspora was mostly confined to the eastern seaboard, Egypt, and, from the mid-1st century BC, the city of Rome. After AD 70 Jewish settlement spread to Spain, North Africa and, to a lesser extent, to northern Europe. Most diaspora Jews lived in distinct communities in cities, except in SYRIA and Egypt, where Jews were found in VILLAGES. The distinctive language of the Jews was Hebrew, but after AD 70 it was increasingly confined to religious use, alongside Greek and Aramaic.

Jewish religious practice and theology were very varied. Judaism was a way of life in which divine commands affected ETHICAL as much as RITUAL behaviour, but interpretation of those commands could take different forms. Thus pious Jews all accepted that the God whose Temple was in Jerusalem had made a covenant with Israel enshrined in the Torah (the first five books of the Hebrew Bible), but they disputed how Jews should behave as a result. For most Jews the prime focus for worship was the Jerusalem Temple, where the sacrificial cult was performed by a caste of priests, but a rival temple existed at Leontopolis in Egypt from the mid-2nd century BC, and the Dead sea sectarians seem to have regarded the Jerusalem cult as invalid. By the late hellenistic period distinctive types of Judaism were espoused by separate identifiable groups such as Pharisees, Sadducees and ESSENES.

Jews were often seen as marginal in the Greco-Roman world, both in their own eyes and in the eyes of others. After AD 135 rabbinic Jews at least paid little attention to the gentile world around them. Outsiders saw Jewish customs such as the sabbath, food taboos and male circumcision as bizarre, but hostility is mostly confined in the extant literature to animosity by Greeks and Egyptians to the Jews of Egypt, and to the context of the revolt of AD 66–70 and its aftermath. Despite such hostility it was possible for a Jew like Josephus to be a strong supporter of the Roman state while proudly affirming his status as a Jew. MDG

See Schäfer, P. (1995) *A History of the Jews in Antiquity*; Schürer, E. et al. (rev. edn, 1973) *The History of the Jewish People in the Age of Jesus Christ*, 3 vols.

jobs see CAREERS; EMPLOYMENT.

joinery see CARPENTRY.

Josephus Historian of the JEWS in Palestine in the 1st century AD. According to his autobiography (the *Life*) Joseph ben Mattathias was born in AD 37 of a priestly family, and received a good EDUCATION, which allowed him in AD 64 to lead a delegation to the emperor NERO and become familiar with Roman society. He became a commander of Jewish forces in Galilee at the start of the revolt against Rome in 66, but once captured he changed allegiance, moved to Rome where he became a ROMAN CITIZEN and adopted the Latin name Flavius Josephus. In Rome he wrote several works, all preserved in Greek, beginning with the *Jewish War*, the most important source for the Jewish revolt in AD 66–72. Both the *Jewish War* and his *Life*, written shortly before his death in c.100, aim to justify his own actions and to explain to a Jewish audience Rome's involvement, which included imparting blame on a small revolutionary minority of Jews, and not the Romans. In the *Life* he was in part responding to criticisms by his contemporary Justus of Tiberias. His second work was an extensive history of the Jews (the *Antiquities of the Jews*) from ancient Israel (largely an interpretative rewriting of the biblical historical accounts) through to the Jewish revolt. This serves as our main source for Jewish history from the time of ALEXANDER the Great to the fall of the JERUSALEM Temple (AD 70). Another work written towards the end of his life is *Against Apion*, an apologetic work refuting charges and criticisms made against Jews in some ancient Egyptian-Greek writers. These writers are mostly lost but for Josephus' extracts, and *Against Apion* is the first work of its kind employing systematic arguments in defence of a standpoint. It was to have a long heritage especially in CHRISTIANITY, where apologetic refutation of Jewish views became a literary tradition in antiquity from the 2nd century AD.

Josephus' writings are among the most extensive extant works of any hellenistic historian, and his technique is comparable to that of POLYBIOS and PLUTARCH. Like his Greek counterparts, he is interested in the role of 'fortune' in history, and ascribes divine providence a role in the success of Rome. Many of his sources can be seen to be biblical and Jewish, though he did make use of Nikolaos of Damascus and STRABO, and the style of THUCYDIDES is evident. For the Jewish war itself, he probably used his own first-hand experience along with reports by others and supplemented this with material from the diaries of VESPASIAN and TITUS. Josephus stands last in the line of Jewish writers in Greek in antiquity, though there may have been others which have not survived. Hebrew and Aramaic from the 2nd century AD on became the main literary language for Jews, and interest in

Josephus among Jews waned until the medieval period. The text of Josephus was preserved by CHRISTIANS, and this may account for the brief reference to JESUS in the text (the so-called *Testimonium Flavianum*), though the style and vocabulary there is in accord with Josephus' language elsewhere. JKA

See Thackeray, H.St J. et al., trs. (1926–65) 10 vols.; Bilde, P. (1988) *Flavius Josephus between Jerusalem and Rome*; Rajak, T. (2002) *Josephus*.

Jovian see JULIAN; SASSANIAN EMPIRE; THEMISTIUS; VALENTINIAN I.

EMPERORS, ROMAN: (b); TETRARCHS: (b).

Judaea The province of Yehud in the PERSIAN EMPIRE, renamed Judaea in the hellenistic period, comprised the city of JERUSALEM with its hinterland, which at times extended to the MEDITERRANEAN coast. Its political, economic and cultural history and the social structure of its JEWISH inhabitants were shaped by the role of the Temple.

Little can be said about the Persian period except that Judaean society was administered by high priests. Under PTOLEMAIC rule from 301 BC the region was subjected to more intensive economic exploitation. In 198 BC Judaea was brought under the sway of the Seleukids. The attack on the Temple cult by Antiochos IV Epiphanes in 167 BC provoked the revolt led by a family of priests, the MACCABEES, who in time established themselves as high priests and eventually became the royal dynasty of the Hasmonaeans. The Hasmonaeans became a regional power in the early 1st century but were brought under Roman control by POMPEY in 63 BC and removed altogether in 37, when Rome imposed HEROD as a CLIENT RULER. On Herod's death in 4 BC his son Archelaos was appointed ethnarch by AUGUSTUS, but in AD 6 direct Roman rule was imposed until the outbreak of revolt in AD 66, apart from a brief interlude (AD 41–4), when Herod's grandson Agrippa I was king.

The imposition of the CENSUS in AD 6 provoked an uprising, but, despite frequent minor disturbances subsequently, the Romans kept only a small garrison in the province. An attempt by Gaius CALIGULA to set up his statue in the Temple in AD 40 caused widespread opposition, but it was not violent, and the full scale provincial rebellion of 66 seems to have been unexpected. The rebels established an independent Jewish state in Jerusalem from 66 to 70. The ferocity of the final assault by TITUS in 70 owed much to the need of the new Flavian dynasty to win rapidly a prestigious victory; the Temple, and the social structure based upon it, were destroyed. After 70 Judaea was ruled by a praetorian legate. In 132 revolt broke out again under the leadership of BAR KOCHBA. His failure in 135 led to the incorporation of Judaea into the new province of SYRIA Palaestina and a prohibition against Jewish settlement in Jerusalem. (see p. 476) MDG

See Goodman, M. (1987) *The Ruling Class of Judaea: the origins of the Jewish revolt*; Schürer, E. et al. (rev. edn, 1973) *The History of the Jewish People in the Age of Jesus Christ (175 BC–AD 135)*.

SYRIA, ROMAN: (a)–(b).

Judaism As the religion of the Jews, Judaism is not as obvious a definition as it might appear. Judaism in antiquity was diverse, and can be identified in texts and inscriptions by Hebrew names, religious laws (circumcision, dietary laws etc.), or religious symbols (JERUSALEM Temple, one GOD etc.). Any individual Jew's attitude to these issues would have varied, and the very identity of Jews themselves remains an open question. While the perceived homeland for Jews was Judah, the district surrounding Jerusalem, they had, from perhaps as early as the 8th century BC, trading contacts abroad, both with the East and with the MEDITERRANEAN. A large Jewish population lived in BABYLON from the time of deportation in the 6th century BC. Soon after the foundation of ALEXANDRIA in the late 4th century BC a Jewish community rapidly arose there, so much so that by the time of the 1st century AD the Jewish writer PHILO could claim with evident exaggeration that there were a million Jews living in Alexandria. In the course of the ROMAN EMPIRE Jews are to be found in Italy, Asia Minor, southern France and Spain, as well as along the coast of North Africa. Such geographical diversity means that there was no central administration or religious authority, and the adoption of local practices according to local customs is likely. In politics the same would apply. The Jews in the East, for example, were not supportive of the JEWISH REVOLT against Rome in AD 66–70.

Comments in Greek and Roman authors on Jews can distort our picture of their place in Greco-Roman society. Classical authors identified Jews by their particular worship of god, and by their lifestyles in the observance of dietary laws and the sabbath, which sometimes they presented as 'unsociable'. But negative comments are comparatively rare, and often representative of more general Greek and Roman portrayal of foreigners. In reality Jews were regularly involved in Roman government, as they probably were in earlier Ptolemaic and SELEUKID affairs, where the evidence is sparser. Their position in Greek and Roman society is mirrored by Jewish writings of a thoroughly hellenistic nature, including many Jewish Greek HISTORIANS and even a Jewish tragedian, by the name of Ezekiel, who composed a TRAGEDY of the Exodus story (the *Exagôgê*). Such Greek writings could be seen as Jewish apologetic in the light of difficult social conditions and intellectual hostility. Jewish writers could have been trying to claim that their traditions were superior to the Greeks, and in particular were more ancient. However, it is also possible to view many of these writers as engaging in the same literary enterprises as their Greek neighbours, not so much writing as apologists but as thoroughly Greek literati. This does not mean that life was always easy for Jews. In Judah, the revolts of the Maccabees (160s BC), the first Roman revolt (AD 66–72) and the revolt of Bar Kochba (AD 132–5), along with disturbances in various places in the Mediterranean (AD 115–17), indicate dissatisfaction with foreign rule (something not unusual in the Roman empire). Expulsions from Rome and disturbances in Alexandria also suggest that in the hellenistic and early Roman periods Jews experienced treatment different from some of their neighbours. Nevertheless, after the revolt of Bar Kochba there were no Jewish

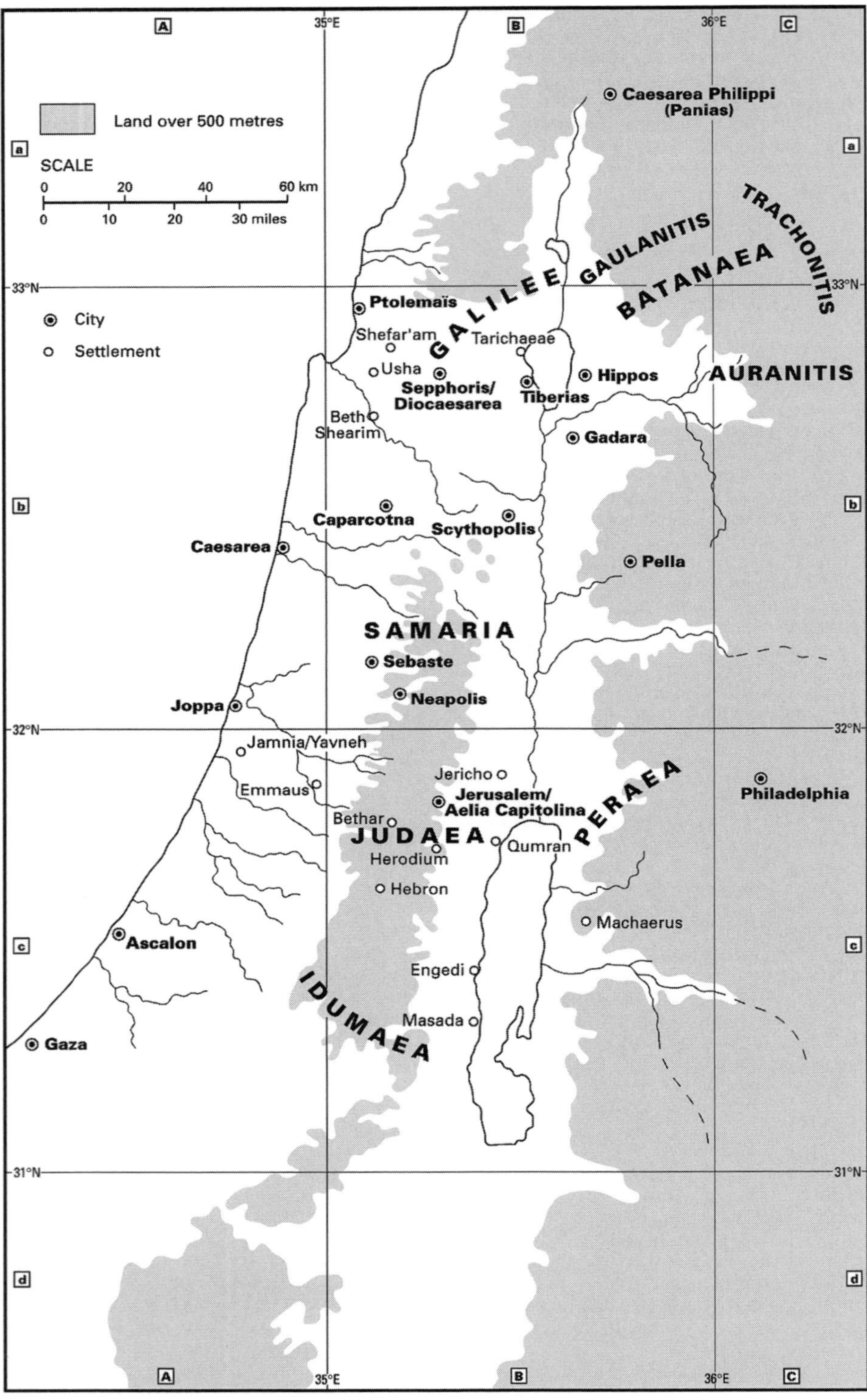

JUDAEA: map of Roman Judaea.

revolts until a small incident in Judaea under Gallus in the 4th century.

Many changes are to be seen in Jewish life and social organization in the period, often generated both by external events or influences and by internal reform. Under the PERSIAN EMPIRE an administrative system was established with a local governor in Judah, providing partial independence for the state. Some of the features of ancient Judaism arose in this period, the LAW CODES being given special prominence. As Jews settled in other regions local traditions and scholarship had their influence. This can be seen from the 3rd century AD in the art and ARCHITECTURE of synagogues, which were modelled on their neighbours. In Alexandria, and in due course elsewhere, the philosophical traditions contributed to Jewish philosophical writings (notably *Wisdom of Solomon* and Philo), and Jewish historiography took on Greek forms. Egyptian prayer houses (*proseuchai*) were adopted by Jews in 3rd-century BC Egypt, and probably developed over time into what we now understand as the synagogue. The Jewish meeting-place for study and communal affairs over time came to include PRAYER as one of its practices. This development began in Egypt and other Mediterranean sites (e.g. DELOS), and only later reached Jerusalem, perhaps after the destruction of the Temple in AD 70 when sacrificial rites could no longer be conducted there.

The destruction of the Jerusalem Temple by Rome, often seen as a turning-point in Jewish history, probably did not have immediate consequences, despite it being the central religious and administrative focus. Some people still believed in the restoration of the Temple cult, as had happened in the Persian period, and this became an important element of the liturgy and one factor behind the revolt of Bar Kochba against Rome in 132. After 135, and the exclusion of Jews from Jerusalem by HADRIAN, the need for reform grew stronger. The centre of Palestinian Jewish learning moved from Jerusalem to Galilee and to Babylonia, and in this nascent rabbinic movement an emphasis was placed on the Hebrew language. Nonetheless, it is likely that Greek still played a prominent role in Jewish scholarship, and a conventional distinction between rabbinic and hellenistic Judaism does not hold sway. Certainly, though we have no Jewish literature in Greek after JOSEPHUS (end of 1st century AD), Jewish inscriptions continue in Greek, suggesting that there may have been more literature no longer extant. We have evidence that Greek was still used in the synagogue in Rome in the 6th century, and medieval Jewish biblical texts and commentaries in Greek have survived.

The rise of CHRISTIANITY did not pose an immediate threat to Judaism, and Roman legislation was often much more favourable to Jews than to Christians. Until probably the 5th century AD Jews in Palestine had thriving communities, even if in c.430 the local Jewish leader there (the 'patriarch') seems to have been abolished by Roman authority. Elsewhere in the Roman empire Jews outnumbered Christians until the time of CONSTANTINE. Debate and dispute between Jews and Christians are attested, especially in Christian educational texts that portray dialogues between a Jew and a Christian. Such dialogues do reveal genuine contact and knowledge between the groups, and we know that some church fathers (JEROME and Origen) consulted Jewish scholars, a tradition that was to last into the Middle Ages. By this time Jews could be found throughout the Mediterranean, and contact between scholars led to a strong scholarly tradition in the Byzantine world. JKA

See Grabbe, L. L. (1994) *Judaism from Cyrus to Hadrian*; Schwartz, S. (2002) *Imperialism and Jewish Society, 200 BCE to 640 CE*.

Jugurtha King of Numidia (113–104 BC). Grandson of Masinissa, but outside the line of succession. His rise to power was rapid and ruthless, reflecting the dynamic nature of the emergent Numidian kingship and its relationship to its patron Rome. Jugurtha's valour at NUMANTIA gained the attention of SCIPIO AEMILIANUS, the destroyer of CARTHAGE. On Scipio's recommendation, Jugurtha was adopted by the reigning king Micipsa over the latter's two sons, Hiempsal and Adherbal. Following Micipsa's death (118) Jugurtha assassinated Hiempsal, and Adherbal fled to Rome. The SENATE sent a commission to Numidia and divided the kingdom, giving Jugurtha the western part and Adherbal the more developed eastern half. Soon afterward (112), Jugurtha besieged and killed Adherbal in his capital Cirta. The death of some Italian businessmen during the SIEGE drove Rome to WAR. For the next eight years, Jugurtha fought a successful guerrilla campaign against four successive Roman commanders as corruption and initial Roman reluctance to fight caused the war to drag on. Early in the conflict Jugurtha was invited to Rome to reveal his supporters among the senatorial ÉLITE, but after being silenced by a TRIBUNE, he assassinated a potential rival in Rome and fled the city. He was finally cornered and captured when Bocchus I of Mauretania was convinced by SULLA to betray him to MARIUS. He was executed following Marius' TRIUMPH. The war against Jugurtha was seen by SALLUST as the beginning of the end of the Republican OLIGARCHY. Jugurtha has also become a symbol of resistance to Roman rule. RBH

See Syme, R. (1964) *Sallust*.

Jugurthine war 112–104 BC This first war between Rome and the client AFRICAN kingdom of Numidia was seen by SALLUST as a conflict that exhibited the corruption of the senatorial oligarchy. It began with the assassination of king Adherbal by JUGURTHA following the siege of Cirta in 112. The war was fought reluctantly and unevenly by the Romans. The first Roman commander, Opimius, came to terms with Jugurtha (112) who was then summoned to Rome to defend himself. There, Jugurtha assassinated a potential rival in Rome and fled the city, leading to a renewal of the war. An incompetent campaign by Sextus Postumius Albinus in 110 led to an embarrassing Roman capitulation. This roused a furore in Rome and led to the appointment of Lucius METELLUS Numidicus in 109 to carry on the campaign. Though successful, he failed to bring the war to an end. In 107 Metellus' client and lieutenant, MARIUS, stood for the consulship claiming that he could end the war. Following his election, Marius raised a new army recruited for the first time from the urban *proletarii*. Marius sacked Capsa in a vigorous campaign, but it was not until Jugurtha was

JULIA: coin portrait.

JULIA DOMNA: coin portrait.

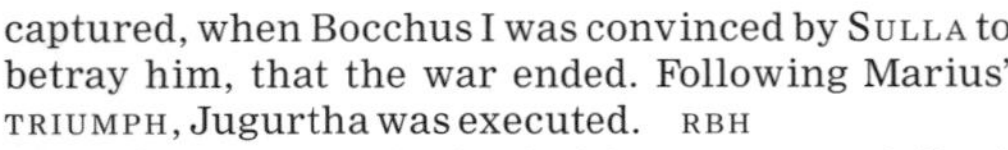

captured, when Bocchus I was convinced by SULLA to betray him, that the war ended. Following Marius' TRIUMPH, Jugurtha was executed. RBH

See Paul, G.M. (1984) *A Historical Commentary on Sallust's Bellum Jugurthinum*; Syme, R. (1964) *Sallust*.

Julia 39 BC–AD 14 The only child of Octavian (later AUGUSTUS). He immediately divorced her mother Scribonia to marry LIVIA, who reared Julia in the palace, teaching her to weave and spin in traditional style. In 25 BC Julia married her cousin Marcellus amid great dynastic hopes, but there were no surviving children by the time of his death in 23. In 21 Augustus married her to his minister, the 43-year-old AGRIPPA, with whom she had five children: Gaius, Lucius, Julia the Younger, Vipsania AGRIPPINA and (born after his father's death in 12 BC) Agrippa Postumus. In the following year she married her stepmother's elder son, TIBERIUS, but no child of the marriage had survived by the time he withdrew to RHODES in 6 BC. Julia figured in much of Augustus' dynastic and visual propaganda, often depicted with her sons Gaius and Lucius, whom her father adopted. Her role in the written histories, however, is dominated by her banishment in AD 2 for adultery. Historians are still divided on whether she was actually involved in treasonable schemes to overturn her ageing father, who insisted on show trials of her alleged lovers and publicized his own shame at her unchaste behaviour. He even forbade her to have young male guards or wine in her exile. On Augustus' death her allowance was stopped, and she starved to death at Rhegium (Reggio Calabria) in AD 14. SD

See Cassius Dio, book 55; Suetonius, *Life of Augustus*; Balsdon, J.P.V.D. (1962) *Roman Women*.

 AUGUSTUS: (a).

Julia Domna The second wife of the Roman emperor SEPTIMIUS SEVERUS. Of Syrian birth, she was the daughter of a Syrian (but Romanized) PRIEST named Julius Bassianus of Emesa, and was sister to Julia Maesa. It is reported by HERODIAN that her horoscope held that she would marry a king, and her name Domna means 'wife of a lord or king'. She was married to Septimius in AD 187, and quickly bore him two sons, Bassianus (later renamed Marcus Aurelius Antoninus, but more usually called CARACALLA) and Geta. Widely considered beautiful and cultured (she spoke fluent Greek and Aramaic, and learned Latin quickly), she is thought to have been included in a circle of learned men such as GALEN, and may have encouraged PHILOSTRATOS to write his *Life of APOLLONIOS OF TYANA*. She enjoyed great influence at court, but for a while at least lost influence over Septimius to his praetorian prefect Plautianus. Later sources accused Julia of promiscuity, even of incest with Caracalla, but while not impossible, it is likely that such rumours had Plautianus as their source. After the death of Septimius in 211, and his burial in YORK, Julia failed to reconcile her two sons. Geta, on the orders of Caracalla, was murdered and died in his mother's arms. Despite this, Julia remained loyal to Caracalla, but after his murder in 217, despite respectful treatment by the usurper Macrinus, Julia committed SUICIDE. CEPA

See Hemelrijk, E.A. (1999) *Matrona Docta: educated women in the Roman elite from Cornelia to Julia Domna*.

 SEVERUS, SEPTIMIUS.

Julia Mammaea Daughter of Julia Maesa and Julius Avitus Alexianus, niece of JULIA DOMNA. She was of equestrian Syrian descent and married a Syrian *eques*, Gessius Marcianus, but her most important family connections were with the imperial household. She was the mother of Gessius Bassianus Alexianus, who, on his formal adoption by ELAGABALUS as son and heir in AD 221, changed his name to Marcus Aurelius Alexander and took the title CAESAR. It was not long before the unstable Elagabalus became jealous of the favour which Alexander enjoyed, but his attempt to have him assassinated failed and resulted in Elagabalus' own murder. Alexander became emperor in 222 (Marcus Aurelius SEVERUS ALEXANDER). There is little doubt that his mother Julia was heavily involved in the events leading to his accession, and indeed she continued to dominate the young emperor, especially after the death of Julia Maesa. However, her power behind the throne and Alexander's position on it were acceptable, relations with the SENATE were good, and stability was maintained for a time. The army, deprived of its more warlike emperors, was dissatisfied, and ultimately moved against Severus Alexander, and in 235 both he and Julia Mammaea were murdered. CEPA

See Hemelrijk, E. A. (1999) *Matrona Docta: educated women in the Roman elite from Cornelia to Julia Domna*.

 SEVERUS, SEPTIMIUS.

Julian (the Apostate) (Flavius Claudius Iulianus) AD 331/2–63 Roman emperor from 360. Throughout his life Julian was surrounded by controversy, and it is ironic that the last member of the house of CONSTANTINE should also have been the last PAGAN emperor. After a traumatic youth, during which all his close male relatives were killed, Julian was made CAESAR in late 355 by Constantius II and given responsibility for the government of GAUL. Hitherto he had been a bookish lad, so his military successes on the RHINE frontier came as a startling surprise. He soon earned the devoted loyalty of the army in Gaul which, in 360, unilaterally made Julian emperor in opposition to Constantius. Civil war seemed inevitable, but Constantius' death in November 361 prevented open hostilities.

Now sole emperor, Julian announced his conversion from CHRISTIANITY to paganism (earning him the sobriquet of 'the Apostate' in Christian tradition) and embarked on a series of reforms aimed at restoring the old state cults. But his efforts, including anti-Christian measures which many pagans found indefensible, earned him widespread ridicule and contempt, and ended in failure. In 363, he embarked on his disastrous invasion of PERSIA. Outmanoeuvred by the Persians, Julian was forced into retreat. He was killed in a skirmish before reaching Roman territory, and in the following confusion his successor, Jovian, was forced to cede large territories to the Persians. To the Christians, Julian's catastrophic end seemed to be divine vengeance for his attempt to restore state paganism. MDH

See Ammianus Marcellinus 15.8–25.4; Julian, *Works*, 3 vols., trs. W. C. Wright (1913–23); Bowersock, G.W. (1978) *Julian the Apostate*; Lieu, S. N. C. (1989) *The Emperor Julian*; Smith, R. (1995) *Julian's Gods*.

 EMPERORS, ROMAN: (b); TETRARCHS: (b).

Julii see IULII.

Julius Caesar 100–44 BC Born into a PATRICIAN family on 13 July 100 BC, Julius Caesar experienced a precocious early career and became the most powerful man at Rome. A nephew of MARIUS, he was the son of Gaius Caesar, PRAETOR c.92, and Aurelia. After Marius and Cinna gained control of Rome in 87, Caesar was designated a PRIEST, a *flamen Dialis*, but never took it up since he was yet too young and SULLA later prevented it. He refused to divorce Cornelia, daughter of Cinna (and his wife since 84), at Sulla's command, and went into temporary hiding. In 80, Caesar began his military service in ASIA, winning a civic crown (*corona civica*), and in CILICIA in 78. After Sulla's death, he prosecuted Gnaeus Cornelius Dolabella for extortion, winning acclaim for ORATORY but losing the case. Captured by PIRATES on his way to study further at RHODES in 75, Caesar promised to return; once free, he assembled forces with which he captured and crucified them. He then expelled a detachment of Mithradates' forces from Asia and served with Marcus Antonius, father of the future triumvir MARK ANTONY. He returned to Rome in 73, having been named a *pontifex*. Elected military tribune in 72, he served as QUAESTOR in 69; Cornelia died before he left for Spain. At Rome in 67, he married Pompeia, granddaughter of Sulla, and was elected curator of the Via Appian. As curule AEDILE in 65, he sponsored splendid aedilician games, earning much popularity. During 63 he became *pontifex maximus* and spoke against the execution of CATILINE's supporters. While praetor in 62, he divorced Pompeia by messenger in the context of Clodius' sacrilege, stating that Caesar's wife must not only be innocent, but above suspicion (a remarkable statement from a man who once gave his mistress Servilia a pearl valued at 6 million *sestertii*). He was proconsul in Spain the following year.

In 60, the attempts of the ÉLITE *optimates* to forestal the ambitions of Caesar, CRASSUS and Pompey led these men to form a compact, which was cemented in 59 by Pompey's marriage to Julia, daughter of Caesar, who himself wedded Calpurnia (daughter of Piso, a party to the alliance and patron of PHILODEMOS). As consul in 59, Caesar, assisted by tribunes, resolved matters as arranged, ignoring the objections of his colleague Bibulus; this year was known in the streets as the 'consulship of Julius and Caesar'. He was given the two GAULS and ILLYRICUM as proconsular province for five years, later renewed for five more. During this decade, he incorporated Gaul into the Roman world by a series of brilliant campaigns combined with extensive use of alliance, threat and incentive. His attempts to add BRITAIN were unsuccessful. Caesar's dispatches won admirers, but also enemies fearing his intentions, and the bitter strife generated chaos at Rome. In 52 Pompey was named sole consul to restore order. Although Caesar had received permission to seek the consulship of 48 in absence (to avoid prosecution and thereby ineligibility), the *optimates* recanted and attempted to recall him. Responding to their

JULIUS CAESAR: coin portrait.

intransigence in the first days of 49, Caesar led his army across the Rubicon, marched to Rome, was named DICTATOR and was elected consul for 48.

Pompey fled across the Adriatic to Dyrrachium, where he broke Caesar's siege in July 48 only to be defeated at Pharsalus in Thessaly in August. Since his support in Spain had collapsed, Pompey eventually fled to Egypt, where he was killed by agents of Ptolemy XIII. Caesar, in pursuit, experienced difficulties at Alexandria, but overcame them and gave the throne to Cleopatra. Some time later, she bore a son, nicknamed Caesarion ('Little Caesar'). In the next period, Caesar was rarely at Rome, but occupied with remaining resistance. Dictator for a year in 47, he was consul each year thereafter, dictator for ten years beginning in 46, and for life in 44. He was granted many honours, including emblems of royalty and semi-divine status. After a public, but declined, offer of a diadem on 15 February 44, some 60 conspirators assassinated him on 15 March (the 'Ides of March') 44.

Not unsuitably for a Julian claiming descent from Venus, Caesar was deified. By his will, he adopted his grand-nephew Gaius Octavius (the future Augustus) and left legacies and property to the Roman people. At the funeral, Mark Antony stirred the populace against the conspirators. When renewed disturbances finally ended in 31, Gaius Julius Caesar Octavianus became sole master of Rome and Caesar's complete heir.

Despite the need to counter resistance, Caesar benefited Rome and its empire. His socio-political and economic reforms include colonies, additional quaestors and praetors, new LAWS and procedures on local government in Italy and of provinces, a law on bribery, changes to tax collection, cancellation of about 25 per cent of DEBT and a reduced number of individuals on the grain dole. At Rome, he began a new FORUM and temples to Venus Genetrix and Mars Ultor; elsewhere he gave attention to infrastructure like roads, the harbour at Ostia, and drainage of marshes and the Fucine lake. Caesar founded the first public library at Rome, and reformed the CALENDAR, effective 1 January 45 BC, from one based on a lunar cycle to a solar one. With later modifications, it is employed in the Western world today; the unmodified version is still used in Eastern Europe. From his pen, seven books on *The Gallic War*, a book for each year from 58 to 52 (completed to 50 by Aulus Hirtius), and three on *The Civil War* survive, creating a new genre and praised as 'pure and lucid brevity' by Cicero (*Brutus* 262). His lost *Anti-Cato*, written to counter Cicero's *Cato*, failed in its purpose.

Able to see new approaches, Caesar was an evolutionary, not a revolutionary. Until he crossed the Rubicon in 49, he conformed to established pattern in office-holding, given the changes of the 1st century BC, despite his ambition. His generalship was the most remarkable in antiquity, depending on a sure sense of timing and on diplomacy. He has been a subject for many literary and pictorial artists. JV

See Caesar, *The Conquest of Gaul* and *The Civil War*, trs. S. A. Handford, and J. F. Gardner (1982); Lucan, *The Civil War*; Cicero, various letters and treatises; Plutarch, *Caesar*; Suetonius, *Julius Caesar*; Gelzer, M. (1968) *Caesar*.

Augustus: (a).

Junii see Iunii.

Juno Roman goddess of Italic origin, Jupiter's chief consort, eventually conflated with Hera. In the 6th century BC Juno was allied with Jupiter and Minerva in the Capitoline triad. She was also identified with the Etruscan goddess Uni who, during Camillus' siege of Veii in 396 BC, was 'summoned' to a new TEMPLE on the Aventine by means of a solemn *evocatio* (Livy 5.21.3).

Juno was associated with motherhood, as is evident from her name (related to 'youth') and her various cults. As Juno Lucina ('Who brings to light') she presided over births and was honoured at the Matronalia on 1 March, originally the first day of the Roman calendar. By other titles Juno presided over other Calends: Sospita ('Saviour') on 1 February, a day marked by fertility rites; Moneta ('Who warns') on 1 June, a month evidently named after her; Regina ('queen') on 1 September; and Sororia ('Sisterly') on 1 October. Thus she was implicated in births, new moons and deliverance from mortal danger. In the last capacity, she saved Rome from nocturnal attack in 390 BC, when her consecrated geese awoke citizens to the threat of Gallic invasion (Livy 5.47.4). The warning goddess was thereafter honoured with a separate temple on the citadel, while retaining a throne in her husband's Capitoline shrine next door. When the temple of Juno Moneta later became the first Roman mint, her title was extended to the coining operation and to MONEY (*moneta*) itself. JRH

See Beard, M. et al. (1998) *Religions of Rome*; Bonnefoy, Y., ed. (1991) *Roman and European Mythologies*.

 GODS AND GODDESSES: (b).

Jupiter The chief GOD in the Roman pantheon. His name was usually spelt *Iuppiter*, compounded of *Iou* (from the root **dyeu*='day'; cf. the Greek Zeus and the Roman variant Jove) and *pater* (='father'). This etymology unites him more closely than any other Roman god to his Indo-European heritage. Like Zeus, Jupiter represented the day-sky, especially the atmospheric phenomena of thunder and lightning. More importantly, he was the supreme paternal figure, with many gods and heroes among his offspring. The Roman list of these largely corresponds to the roll-call of Zeus's children.

Among Jupiter's associations with other divinities we may identify two distinctively Roman groupings. With Mars and Quirinus he shared the distinction of having his own PRIEST, in his case the *flamen Dialis*. With Juno and Minerva, from the 6th century BC, he shared a temple on the Capitol. There the Roman SENATE and people assembled every 1 January around the new CONSULS; there, too, triumphant GENERALS deposited the most honourable spoils of WAR. Jupiter's Capitoline title reflected his national importance: Optimus Maximus ('Best and Greatest').

Jupiter's pre-eminence is reflected in the Roman CALENDAR. The Ides of each month were devoted to him, but three bore special significance. On 13 September, during the *ludi Romani*, the anniversary of the dedication of the Capitoline temple was observed. On 15 October, in the course of the *ludi Capitolini*, Jupiter *Feretrius* ('the Smiter'? at any rate, the guarantor of TREATIES) was honoured. On

13 November, during the *ludi Plebei*, the *Iovis epulum* ('Banquet of Jupiter') was celebrated by PLEBEIAN priests. JRH

See Beard, M. et al. (1998) *Religions of Rome*; Bonnefoy, Y., ed. (1991) *Roman and European Mythologies*; Dumézil, G. (1987) *Archaic Roman Religion*.

 CAPITOLIUM: (a)–(b); GODS AND GODDESSES: (b).

justice Athenian jurors (dikasts) every year swore an oath that they would give their verdicts 'according to the laws' and, in cases where there was no law, according to their 'most just judgement'. Some scholars have taken this to indicate that the laws were not comprehensive, but had perceived 'gaps', and that the dikastic oath gave litigants the opportunity to appeal to justice (*dikê*) independently of the law. The issue of conflict between the laws and justice was a topic broached in both TRAGEDY and PHILOSOPHY (as in the story of ANTIGONE defying the law of Kreon and burying Polyneikes); and ARISTOTLE (*Rhetoric*) recommends that litigants who find the law against them should appeal to the jurors, on the basis of their oath, to ignore the law in the interests of equity (*epieikeia*). But the speeches of the Attic orators suggest that in practice litigants did not appeal to the jurors' oath to support claims based on justice as opposed to the law. The law and justice (*dikê*) were treated as one, and the jurors' 'most just judgement' was regarded as being complementary to the law, which for the Athenians primarily meant the law-code of SOLON. At Rome, the business of justice (*iustitia*) was the work of professional jurists, whose close examination of legal rules and institutions (the so-called 'art' of law-finding) was designed to uncover their basic principles, which could then be applied in the making of new laws. MJE

See Johnstone, S. (1999) *Disputes and Democracy*.

Justinian (Flavius Petrus Sabbatius Iustinianus) C.AD 482–565 East Roman or Byzantine emperor from 527. Scion of a Balkan military clan, Justinian's early fortunes were intimately linked to those of his uncle Justin who, following a command in the imperial bodyguard, became emperor in 518. Under Justin's patronage Justinian held the consulship and even became joint emperor, and he succeeded to the throne in his own right without opposition.

On becoming emperor, Justinian immediately initiated such a vast enterprise of imperial restoration that he is often seen as the last great emperor of antiquity. He sought to reconquer for the empire the Western provinces that had been lost to Germanic kings in the 5th century. Success was mixed: North AFRICA and ITALY were retaken, the latter at the cost of long and debilitating GOTHIC WARS; in Spain only a coastal strip was retrieved, and no reconquest of GAUL was undertaken. Similar ambitions seem to have informed Justinian's projects at home. He revised the laws that formed the basis of imperial government, resulting in the issuing of his *Code*, *Digest*, *Institutes*, and *Novels*; and he embellished many cities with grand buildings, such as the church of Hagia Sophia (Holy Wisdom) in CONSTANTINOPLE.

Apart from the mixed success of the wars of reconquest, Justinian's reign was marred by other problems, such as outbreaks of plague, riots in Constantinople, relations between the emperor and the CHURCH that provoked more problems than they solved, and a court reputed to be dominated by the empress Theodora. Many of Justinian's failings became the focus of PROCOPIUS' notorious *Anekdota* (*Secret History*), a work that suggested to later generations that Justinian's grandiose ambitions concealed a weak man. Other verdicts have been more positive: Dante accorded Justinian's soul a place in the second sphere of Paradise. (see p. 482) MDH

See Evans, J. A. S. (1996) *The Age of Justinian*; Moorhead, J. (1994) *Justinian*.

Justinian, works of (*Code*, *Digest*, *Institutes*, *Novels*) Massive programme of legal compilation, collectively known since the 16th century as the *Corpus of Civil Law* (*Corpus iuris civilis*), undertaken at the behest of the East Roman or Byzantine emperor JUSTINIAN. Soon after his accession in 527, Justinian embarked on two enterprises: to reconquer the Western provinces of the Roman empire and to revise the laws. Both constituted integral parts of his scheme of imperial restoration: as he put it himself, 'the ruler of Rome ... may show himself as scrupulously regardful of justice as triumphant over his conquered foes' (*Institutes*, preface). Three major works were produced. (1) The *Justinianic Code* (*Codex Iustinianus*), a comprehensive collection in 12 books of imperial legal pronouncements by emperors from HADRIAN to Justinian, designed to replace the *THEODOSIAN CODE* produced a century earlier. (2) The *Digest* (or *Pandects*, from the Greek *pandektai*, 'all-encompassing'), a collection in 50 books of some 9,000 excerpts from the writings of Roman lawyers of the first four centuries. (3) The *Institutes*, a guide to the *Digest* in four books for students of law. In addition, Justinian continued to issue new legislation, known collectively as the *Novels* (*Novellae constitutiones*).

A striking feature of the enterprise is not only its scale but also the efficiency of the various commissions appointed to prosecute the task. Compilation of Justinian's new *Code* began in 528 and was completed in just over a year. Building on this success, another commission, headed by the expert lawyer Tribonian, was entrusted in December 530 with compiling the *Digest*; their work was published precisely three years later. This new work highlighted problems with the *Code*, so a second edition (the version that survives) was published in 534. In all these tasks, the commissioners were charged with ferreting out inconsistencies in the laws. One of Justinian's main intentions was to eradicate contradictions that had long been exploited by unscrupulous lawyers.

The *Code*, *Digest* and *Institutes* clearly looked back to the great achievements of Roman jurisprudence. In the *Novels* continuity with this tradition was maintained, but there were also hints of change. In particular, most of the *Novels* were issued in Greek, by now the vernacular of what was left of the Roman empire. As such, the *Novels* represent one of the cultural shifts between the later Roman empire and medieval Byzantium. Justinian's legislative activity thus marks both the culmination of the classical tradition of Roman law and its transformation at the dawn of the Middle Ages. Its significance, however, is broader than that. When manuscripts of the *Digest* were

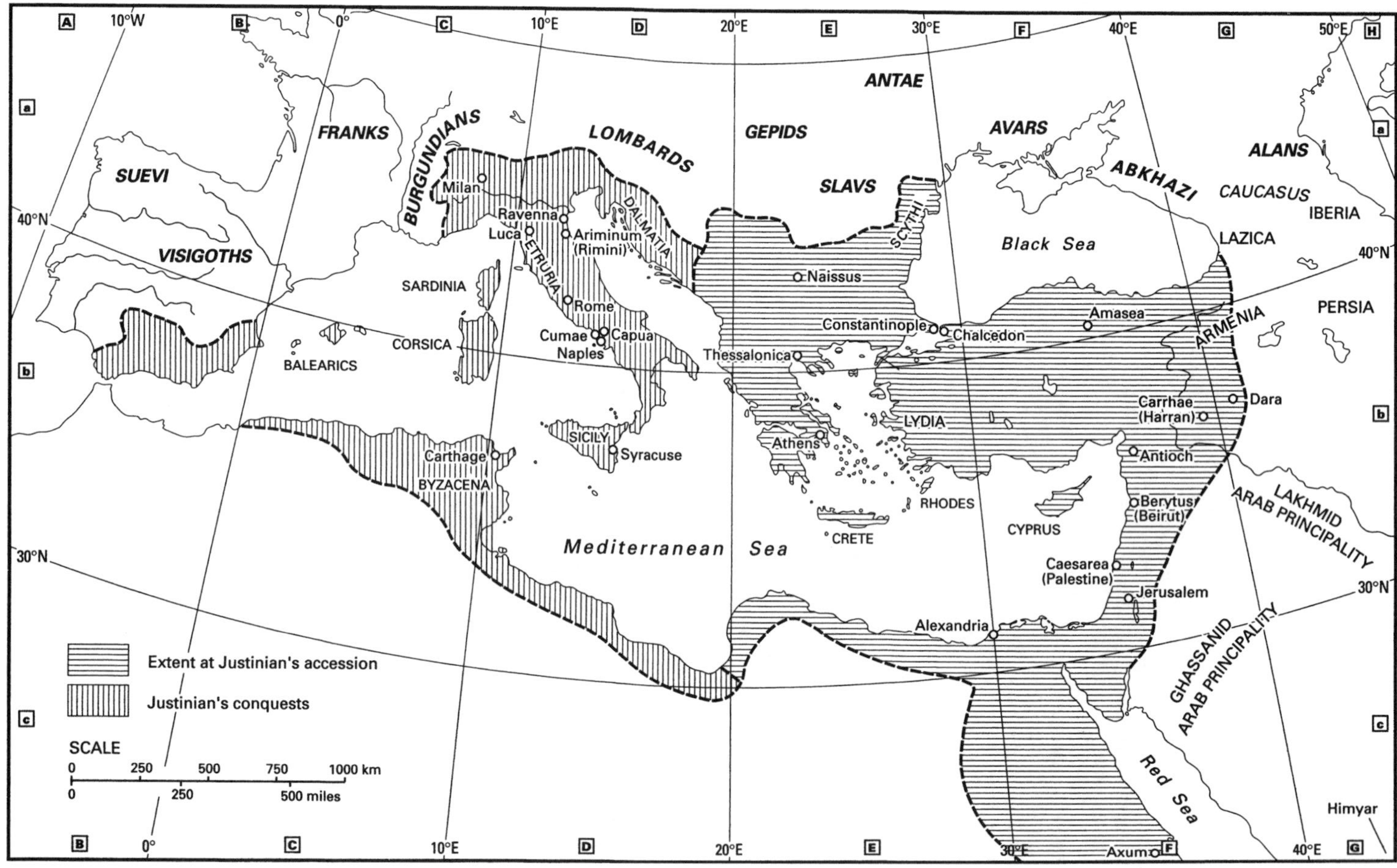

JUSTINIAN: map of the Byzantine empire under Justinian, showing his (re)conquests in the West.

rediscovered in 11th-century ITALY, they provided the impulse for the emergence of the first Western university at Bologna, thereby leading to that increased interest in the heritage of the ancient world that flowered as the RENAISSANCE. MDH

See The Digest of Justinian, 4 vols., trs. A. Watson (1985); *The Institutes of Justinian*, trs. P. Birks and G. McLeod (1987); Honoré, A. M. (1978) *Tribonian*; Liebs, D. (2000) Roman law, in *CAH* 14, 238–59.

Juvenal (Decimus Iulius Iuvenalis) b.AD 50–60; d. after 127 SATIRIC POET. Unlike his fellow-satirist HORACE, Juvenal tells us very little about himself; the ancient BIOGRAPHIES are – as often – unreliable, depending almost exclusively as they do on inferences drawn from the poems themselves. Juvenal is the addressee of three epigrams of MARTIAL (7.24, 7.91, 12.18), our only contemporary witness; his poems can be dated on internal criteria to the reigns of TRAJAN and HADRIAN. In view of the fact that the *Satires* lack any dedication to a patron, it seems probable that their author was of relatively high social status; but no further details of his life or background can be established with any degree of certainty.

The five books of *Satires* comprise a total of 16 poems, and focus on the vices and depravity of contemporary Rome. The most striking characteristic of Juvenal's style – particularly in the first two books – is the speaker's angry and indignant manner: in the programmatic first *Satire*, he proclaims that 'indignation makes [him] a poet' (*facit indignatio versum*, 1.79). He adopts the pose of a conservative, old-fashioned moralist, frequently contrasting the glory days of the past with the degeneracy of his own age, and deploring in particular the social ascendancy of foreigners, FREEDMEN and the *nouveaux riches*. At the same time, idealization of the past is itself undermined by passages such as the sardonic account of the GOLDEN AGE in the opening lines of *Satire* 6, and it is hard not to see the attack on excessive anger and vindictiveness in *Satire* 13 as self-conscious irony. Several critics have indeed suggested that the overt 'message' is often to be taken with a large pinch of salt, and the speaker himself to be regarded to some extent as an object of ridicule.

A second important programmatic claim made in the first *Satire* is the assertion that satire, unlike contemporary EPIC, is relevant: the poet complains that he cannot bear to listen to tedious MYTHOLOGICAL screeds while vice flaunts itself in the streets of Rome. The opposition between epic and satire is to some extent disingenuous, however: Juvenal, most of all the Roman satirists, makes constant capital of the fact that his poetry employs (as convention demanded) the same metre as that of the epic poets. Juvenal's diction is relatively elevated, and bathos and epic parody are among the most prominent sources of humour in the *Satires*: in poem 3, for example, a street-bully is incongruously described in language which recalls the grieving ACHILLES of *Iliad* 24.

Characteristic themes of Juvenal's poetry include the miseries of urban life (*Satire* 3), contemporary corruption of the patron–client relationship (*Satires* 1, 5, 7 and 9) and the vanity of human aspirations (*Satire* 10, perhaps Juvenal's most celebrated poem). The second book consists in its entirety of a single satire (6), an extended and outrageously comprehensive attack on women as, *inter alia*, sex-obsessed, vain, vindictive and superstitious. MG

See Juvenal, *The Satires*, trs. N. Rudd (1991); Braund, S. M. (1992) *Roman Verse Satire*; Coffey, M. (1976) *Roman Satire*.

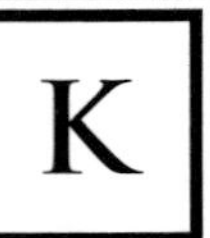

Kallikrates Son of Boïskos, citizen of the island of SAMOS, Kallikrates had a career as an important figure in the service of king PTOLEMY II of Egypt. He first appears as a dedicator of statues at OLYMPIA, perhaps c.279 BC. Soon thereafter he was appointed *nauarchos*, 'admiral', of the Ptolemaic fleet, and seems to have served in this capacity until c.257. He must have played an important role in the first Syrian war, but there is no direct evidence. During the CHREMONIDEAN WAR he and two brothers undertook an embassy to Olous on CRETE. Later, c.260, at the start of the second Syrian war, he was active in MILETOS with the enigmatic figure Ptolemaios the Son, who soon revolted from the king; Kallikrates cannot have been involved since he continued in Ptolemy II's service. In 269/8 he was appointed first priest of the new cult of Arsinoe-APHRODITE Euploia ('of fair-sailing') or Zephyritis ('of the zephyr', a fair wind) and built a temple for her in ALEXANDRIA. A team of HORSES he entered in the CHARIOT RACE at DELPHI won a dramatic victory. His career is commemorated in inscriptions from his home island of Samos, DELOS (by the League of the Islanders), and a number of other places in the AEGEAN world, as well as in three poems by Posidippos, two of which were only recently recovered. Nothing is known of his career before or after his service under the king. He is an example of an important historical figure of the early hellenistic period who is known only from documentary evidence. GR

See Bing, P. (2002–3) Posidippus and the admiral, *GRBS* 43: 243–66; Hauben, H. (1970) *Callicrates of Samos*.

Kallimachos Poet and literary scholar, born in CYRENE, in modern Libya, at the end of the 4th century BC who moved to ALEXANDRIA around 280. He began his work at the MOUSEION of Alexandria under the reign of Ptolemy II Philadelphos; it culminated under the third Ptolemy, Euergetes. At the Alexandrian library, he taught and worked with the most important POETS and critics of his time, such as APOLLONIOS OF RHODES, Aristophanes of Byzantium, and ERATOSTHENES. He repeatedly expresses his preference for shorter poems and sophisticated experimentation. The aesthetic approach that he championed made him not only one of the principal figures in hellenistic poetry, but also a great influence on Roman elegiac poets, among whom CATULLUS, HORACE, OVID, and PROPERTIUS often refer by name to Kallimachos or his poems.

His output was most likely immense, including both philological and literary works. The *SUDA* attributes more than 800 volumes to him, but very little of his verse production and none of his philological work has survived. Among the latter, the *Suda* mentions the *Pinakes* or catalogues of poets and their books, as well as several monographic studies about natural, cultural and mythical matters. His method for classifying authors and their works seems to have become a lasting model among the Alexandrian scholars. Especially unfortunate is the loss of his discourse *Against Praxiphanes*, which dealt with literary matters.

As a poet, Kallimachos was the teacher of a whole generation and a guide for the best poets in the following centuries. His literary concepts and programmes directed the preferences of the hellenistic poets. He wrote HYMNS in honour of the Olympic GODS in which he mimetically describes ritual acts. Probably none of his hymns were written for a specific religious occasion, but more as a mythological and literary exercise. These hymns also serve to justify the divine origins of royal power. He also composed *iambi*, SONGS, EPIGRAMS and a collection called the *Aitia* or *Causes* written in elegiac verse. This work, probably of more than 4,000 lines, explained the 'aetiology' or mythological causes of particular events, institutions and cultic practices. Kallimachos is also known for poems praising Berenike, wife of Ptolemy III Euergetes, including the *Lock of Berenike* and the *Victory of Berenike*. The last is an epinician poem written to commemorate queen Berenike's victory in the chariot competition at the Nemean GAMES. It also offers an aetiology for the institution of the games, specifying HERAKLES' defeat of the famous lion as the origin. In his poems, Kallimachos defies the convention that demanded each genre be composed in a specific dialect appropriate to the genre. By his time, Greek dialects had largely disappeared; this allowed him to develop his own literary language. RBC

See Nisetich, F. J., trs. (2001) *The Poems of Callimachus*; Cameron, A. (1995) *Callimachus and his Critics*; Hutchinson, G. O. (1988) *Hellenistic Poetry*.

Kallinos see ELEGY; LYRIC POETRY, GREEK; POETRY, GREEK.

Kallisthenes (historian) see ALEXANDER III; ISSOS; POLYBIOS.

Kambyses see BABYLON; CYRUS THE GREAT; PERSIAN EMPIRE.

Kappodokia see CAPPADOCIA.

Karanis Greco-Roman AGRICULTURAL community in the north-east FAYÛM in EGYPT. Karanis (Kom Aushim) is known principally from poorly recorded and published excavations by the University of Michigan (1926–35). Nevertheless, the dry preservation of organic materials such as PAPYRUS, wood and TEXTILES and the combination of documentary and archaeological evidence make it an important site for the study of daily life in a Roman rural community. The papyrus documents from Karanis have long been important evidence for historians studying the DEMOGRAPHY, ECONOMY and society of Roman Egypt.

The full extent of the site is not known, though excavations were carried out over an area c.1 × 0.75 km.

The only significant public buildings surviving were two Egyptian-plan stone TEMPLES of the early Roman period, one for the crocodile gods Pnepheros and Petesouchos. A BATH building was excavated in the 1970s by a French team, but most of the structures excavated in 1926–35 were mudbrick courtyard houses. The excavators' chronology of Karanis began with the earliest archaeological evidence of the 1st century BC, took in a period of expansion in the 1st–2nd century AD and ended in decline and abandonment by the 5th century AD. However, Karanis is mentioned in documents as early as the 3rd century BC, and renewed study of the ARCHAEOLOGY of the site (especially imported fine POTTERY and AMPHORAS) suggest it was occupied and perhaps prosperous until at least c.AD 525. NDP

See Alston, R. (1995) *Soldier and Society in Roman Egypt.*

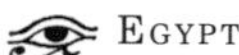 EGYPT.

Karia see CARIA.

Karneades see ACADEMY; PHILOSOPHY, ROMAN.

Kassandra see AJAX; APOLLO; CLYTEMNESTRA.

Kassandros see DEMETRIOS I; OLYMPIAS; SUCCESSORS.

Kassope see *AGORA*.

Keos see CITIES, GREEK; FIELD SURVEY; GREECE; ISLANDS.

Kephallenia see IONIAN ISLANDS.

Kerameikos A large region of north-west Athens that extended from the Agora to a point well beyond the city walls. The name derives from the ancient term for 'potters' quarter'. The area was demarcated by boundary stones, a number of which have been found *in situ*. The Themistoklean wall divides the region into two areas, conventionally known as the 'inner' and 'outer' Kerameikos. Set into the walls was one of the main entry points to Athens, the Dipylon (Double gate). Nearby is the Sacred gate, which is located on the road to Eleusis and was used for the procession to celebrate the Mysteries. The Eridanos river also flows out of the city at this point. Outside the walls is located the main cemetery of Athens. The earliest burials date from around 1200 BC. Tombs and burial plots lined the roads on the approach to the city. In addition to private burial plots, the cemetery contained a public tomb for the war dead. The elaborate civic rituals performed for those who died in the service of the state are described in detail by Thucydides (2.34). Within the walls, we find a region displaying a high variety of uses. Residential housing was mixed with industrial workshops. The Pompeion, the starting point of the Panathenaic procession, is located here. The area is home to the deme of Kerameis. AJLB

See Camp, J. (2001) *The Archaeology of Athens*; Knigge, U. (1991) *The Athenian Kerameikos*; Travlos, J. (1971) *Pictorial Dictionary of Ancient Athens.*

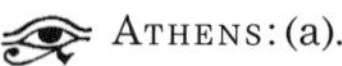 ATHENS: (a).

Kerkyra see CIVIL STRIFE; CORINTH; IONIAN ISLANDS.

keys see LOCKS.

Kilikia see CILICIA.

Kimon Athenian general and politician; son of Miltiades. Kimon led contingents of the Delian league against the PERSIANS, and in 476 BC he forced them out of Eion (in Macedonia). In Asia Minor he incorporated CARIA and LYCIA into the league, thus pushing the Persians into the interior. In c.466 he achieved a major victory over Persia at the Eurymedon river. Furthering Athens' particular interests, he forced Skyros to join the league and subdued THASOS after its revolt.

Kimon was a fervent supporter of friendship between Athens and Sparta, a policy that did not enjoy unanimous consent among Athens' leaders or the citizen body. Thus, when in 462 the Spartans dismissed Athenian troops that had been sent, on Kimon's proposal, to help them subdue the revolt of the HELOTS, there occurred a breach in Athenian relations with Sparta. Furthermore, Ephialtes introduced constitutional reforms at Athens, at the expense of the ARISTOCRATS of whom Kimon was the most outstanding representative, having put his wealth to political use. His attempt to upset these reforms led to his OSTRACISM in 461. He was recalled c.451, probably to negotiate a truce with Sparta (war having broken out a few years earlier). Shortly afterwards he was dispatched to CYPRUS to fight the Persians, and was killed at the battle of Kition. The same battle marked the temporary end of hostilities with Persia. IK

See Badian, E. (1993) *From Plataea to Potidaea*; Meiggs, R. (1972) *The Athenian Empire.*

kingship

In the classical age, Greek thinkers from HERODOTOS to ARISTOTLE considered kingship an earlier form of government characteristic of those peoples who had not evolved the rule of law (*eunomia*) and a constitution (*politeia*). Yet, Greek civic institutions evolved out of the monarchy described by HOMER. In turn, this Greek kingship of the Dark Age and Geometric period (c.1100–700 BC) was preceded by more sophisticated kingships of MINOAN CRETE and MYCENAEAN Greece in the Bronze Age. In the middle and late Bronze Age (2100–1400 BC), monarchs at KNOSSOS on the island of Crete established a bureaucratic kingship inspired, in part, by contemporary Near Eastern monarchies. The kings at Knossos imposed their naval hegemony in the AEGEAN SEA and so based their power on the revenues of sea-borne TRADE.

In the Mycenaean age (1600–1225 BC), kings under the title *wanax* or 'lord' (plural *wanakes*) ruled over kingdoms in central Greece and the PELOPONNESE, and, from 1400 BC on, in Crete. The Mycenaean (or ACHAIAN) *wanax* based his power on an aristocratic caste expert in CHARIOT warfare. From the revenues of commerce and PIRACY, each *wanax* staffed a BUREAUCRACY, bought Minoan prestige goods and constructed fortified PALACES. This kingship documented in the Linear B tablets disappeared with the collapse of the Mycenaean world.

In the second book of the *Iliad,* HOMER reveals a simpler kingship of the 8th century. Homer's king, styled *basileus* (plural *basileis*), reigned 'with force', and with the consent of the nobles – a body which gave rise to the *boulê* or COUNCIL of the Greek city-states (*POLIS*; plural *poleis*). The nation in arms voted on great matters such as PEACE and WAR, and so these gatherings were the origins of the ASSEMBLY (*ekklêsia*) of a city-state. Homeric kings lacked the means to forge a hereditary monarchy backed by a royal bureaucracy and army. In most cities the kingship was reduced to a set of elective offices monopolized by aristocrats who dominated the *boulê,* and therefore political life. The office of king was retained as an elective priesthood. Some aristocrats with popular backing seized power as tyrants, but tyrants ruled through civic institutions. Even successful tyrants such as Kypselos at CORINTH (c.657–625 BC) or PEISISTRATOS of Athens (546–526 BC) failed to establish dynasties. TYRANNY thus proved but a phase in the evolution from ARISTOCRACY to broader based governments as OLIGARCHY or DEMOCRACY.

Only in classical SPARTA did kings reign. Two hereditary kings, from the Agiad and Eurypontid houses, commanded Spartan armies, sat on the council of elders (*gerousia*), and presided over state SACRIFICES. Charismatic kings exercised considerable influence in Spartan society. The erratic, but brilliant, KLEOMENES I (c.525–490) extended Spartan political influence. King AGESILAOS II (399–360), architect of the Spartan hegemony, was a model for the later hellenistic kings.

After the classical age, kingship again became an effective government because of PHILIP II of Macedonia (359–336). Philip II transformed a Homeric kingship into a national monarchy by his reforms of the Macedonian army and society. His son ALEXANDER the Great (336–323) overthrew the PERSIAN EMPIRE, and so gained a great monarchy based on Near Eastern institutions. The civil wars following the death of Alexander the Great produced three important Macedonian monarchies. The Antigonid kings reigned in Macedonia after 279 as heirs to the kingship of Philip II. The PTOLEMIES in Egypt and the SELEUKIDS in Asia created dynastic states based on Greek officials and SOLDIERS. Each dynasty also drew upon the native regal traditions and sponsored RULER-CULTS.

Roman authors, even more than Greek, expressed distaste for kingship. In early Rome the king, or *rex,* was elective. His powers were comparable to those of his Greek counterpart described by Homer. Latin authors writing centuries later attributed Roman religious institutions or heroic conquest to the first four Latin or SABINE kings of Rome – ROMULUS (753–717 BC), Numa Pompilius (715–673), Tullus Hostilius (673–642), and Ancus Marcius (642–617). The last three legendary kings of Rome were of ETRUSCAN origin. The sixth king, SERVIUS TULLIUS (578–535), was credited with the organization of the centuriate assembly (*comitia centuriata*). The fifth and seventh, Lucius Tarquinius Priscus (616–585) and his son Lucius Tarquinius (531–510) respectively, perhaps sought to rule in the fashion of an Etruscan lord or *lucumo* (plural *lucumones*), and so provoked the aristocratic revolution that overthrew the monarchy and established the REPUBLIC (*res publica*) in 509 BC.

Under the Republic the powers of the ancient king, *rex,* were divided into *imperium,* the right to command armies, and *auspicium,* the right to consult the gods. A king priest, *rex sacrorum,* was retained, however, and the two annually elected CONSULS shared *imperium.* Given the dislike of kingship by the Roman SENATORIAL class, AUGUSTUS (27 BC–AD 14) cloaked the imperial power of the PRINCIPATE in Republican guise. KH

See Bilde, P. et al., eds. (1996) *Aspects of Hellenistic Kingship*; Braund, D. (1984) *Rome and the Friendly King: the character of the client kingship*; Carlier, P. (2000) Homeric and Macedonian kingship, in R. Brock and S. Hodkinson, eds., *Alternatives to Athens* 259–68; Cornell, T. J. (1995) *The Beginnings of Rome*; Fredricksmeyer, E. (2000) Alexander the Great and the kingship of Asia, in A.B. Bosworth and E.J. Baynham, eds., *Alexander the Great in Fact and Fiction* 136–66; Ogden, D. (1997) *The Crooked Kings of Ancient Greece.*

kinship

The closest bond of kinship in ancient Greece was through the male blood line. A father would expect to pass on his property to his sons, while sons were expected to perform burial rites for their fathers. They were both expected to be supportive of one another, especially in the face of an external enemy. In early times, the absence of centralized government and legal institutions meant it was important to have a strong network of blood kin. In HOMER'S *Odyssey,* ODYSSEUS' son Telemachos was at a disadvantage when faced by his mother's suitors because he was an only son born of an only son. The implication is that brothers and cousins would naturally be supportive of each other against external enemies. Daughters were also thought of as exceptionally loyal to their fathers, and their link to their original family home was not broken even by MARRIAGE. In addition, women formed exceptionally close relationships with their brothers. In MYTH, women are sometimes represented as favouring the cause of their father or brothers over that of their husband, or even their children. Althaia is said to have murdered her son because he killed her brothers. This representation suggests that at an ideological level the link between blood kin in the male line was felt to be stronger than links between maternal kin and kin through marriage.

Scholars have pointed out that, despite these ideals, Greeks did form close bonds with maternal kin and kin through marriage. Exogamous marriage (marriage outside the family) was an important way of gaining allies, and there is strong evidence of exceptionally good relations between a man and his mother's brother. At Athens maternal kin frequently provided support in the LAWCOURTS. Nevertheless, agnates (relatives in the male line) still maintained the strongest position in Athenian society; they dominate the order of intestate succession and were most frequently chosen as adopted heirs. Likewise, agnates were designated primary avengers of a murdered man. Our surviving examples of homicide cases confirm that it was usual for a father, son or brother to prosecute homicide in the lawcourts.

Larger kinship groups were also central to the organization of Greek society from the earliest times. Adult males belonged to kinship groups known as PHRATRIES (brotherhoods) which claimed descent from a common ancestor. Membership of phratries was usually hereditary, and adolescent boys were presented to the phratry members by their father and his kin at their coming of age. It was relatively common for phratry members to appear in court at Athens to support challenges to a man's CITIZENSHIP. In addition, it was common for a man to claim kinship with others from the same ethnic group (Ionian, Aiolian or Dorian) and cities frequently asked for help from other cities by appealing to common kinship along these lines. FMM

See Humphreys, S. C. (1978) *Anthropology and the Greeks*; Hunter, V. J. (1993) Agnatic kinship in Athenian law and Athenian family practice: its implications for women, in B. Halpern and D.W. Hobson, eds., *Law, Politics and Society in the Ancient Mediterranean World* 100–21; Lacey, W. K. (1968) *The Family in Classical Greece*.

Roman kinship can be divided into agnatic and cognate connections. *Cognatus* (masc.) and *cognata* (fem.) are general terms for any relative. Agnatic kinship, the basis of legal institutions such as INHERITANCE, was reckoned through the legitimate male line, so a man's grandchildren would be agnates if they were his son's children, but not if they were his daughter's. If his middle (gentile) name was Iunius, each son would be Iunius and each daughter Iunia, and the same would apply to his sons' children. A Roman woman did not change her name on MARRIAGE but she could either become part of the husband's family or remain legally in her birth family. In either case her children were part of her husband's and took his gentile name.

Certain legal procedures, such as the emancipation of children from the power of the *paterfamilias* or a woman's *coemptio* for making a WILL, extinguished agnatic links. A VESTAL VIRGIN had no legal kin, while those whose status had changed because of marriage or ADOPTION exchanged one agnatic network for another. In practice, however, people acknowledged the ties of affection and duty which bound them to all relatives. From the late Republican period, a Roman woman was unlikely to change families on marriage, but she was expected to make a will to ensure that her children (rather than her brothers and sisters, her agnates and therefore her heirs on intestacy) inherited from her on her death.

Romans probably lived in nuclear HOUSEHOLDS until the children grew up, but that did not change either the legal status of the children, who remained *in patria potestate* until the death of the father, or the workings of the extended family, which would have combined at FESTIVALS such as the Parentalia and life cycle events like weddings, baby namings and funeral rites.

Roman kinship was fairly open-ended. Earlier scholarship placed great emphasis on the legal rules for succession on intestacy (through the agnatic line) and the differential terms for relationships on the paternal and maternal side (a common linguistic feature) to draw restrictive conclusions about formal kinship – and even about ties of affection and obligation – which are not supported by evidence from the other ancient sources. The ORATOR CICERO and his friend ATTICUS showed equal concern for their mutual nephew young Quintus Cicero, son of Cicero's brother and Atticus' sister. Remarriage was common in Roman society and led to a proliferation of step- and half-relationships which were acknowledged as sources of support for political, business and emotional purposes. Adoption was sometimes used to give legal form to a cognate relationship, as with the adoption of PLINY the YOUNGER by his mother's childless brother, PLINY the ELDER. Modern studies of epitaphs have enhanced our understanding of Roman kinship ties. SD

See Bannon, C. J. (1997) *The Brothers of Romulus*; Bettini, M. (1988) *Anthropology and Roman Culture*; Dixon, S. (1992) *The Roman Family*; Hallett, J. (1984) *Fathers and Daughters in Roman Society*; Kertzer, D. I. and Saller, R. P. (1991) *The Family in Italy*.

kitchens and kitchen utensils Classical Greek HOUSES did not have kitchens as we know them. Facilities like running water and indoor plumbing did not exist. Few houses had their own wells, though many had cisterns which caught rain water from the roof for drinking, cooking and washing. If a house had no cistern or well, then water had to be carried from a communal well or FOUNTAIN HOUSE.

Fixed hearths were unusual, and when they appear in 'domestic' structures, this is usually an indication that the building has some special function (such as a tavern or restaurant) and was not simply a house, though a family is likely to have lived there as well. Most of the relatively complete houses which have been excavated show evidence of multiple cooking places. This suggests that cooking activities moved around the house seasonally, so that people prepared food in the open air of the courtyard in the hot summer, but switched to a cooking area under cover during the rainy winter months (preferably to a place where the cooking fire might also warm a room). Cooking fires were generally small (FUEL was a scarce resource in many parts of Greece), and frequently portable braziers were used, probably with CHARCOAL. Virtually no classical Greek houses had big ovens and in urban areas most BAKING was done commercially. However, there were portable ovens – clay domes under which small items could be baked – designed to fit on a little brazier or cooking fire.

KITCHENS AND KITCHEN UTENSILS: Roman cooking range from an apartment building in Ostia. Fuel was stored below the raised hearth base on which food was heated over small fires.

Most of the Greek cooking pots which survive are made of coarse, gritty POTTERY, specially designed to withstand heat. Few have a capacity of more than three litres. The preponderance of closed shapes suggests that much food was boiled or cooked as casseroles. Ceramic grills were probably used for small pieces of MEAT, FISH or POULTRY. There are also ceramic griddles and frying pans which would have been used for baking flat breads (like modern pitta bread) and roasting chick peas (and other legumes and CEREALS), as well ordinary frying. Although some metal containers and utensils may have been used, these rarely survive. Wooden utensils may have been common, but these virtually never survive at all. Small grindstones (saddle querns) for making flour from grain, and occasional stone pounders or mortars and pestles also appear.

These facilities indicate that the cooking which took place in Greek houses, especially in cities, was on a relatively small scale. The small size of cooking pots indicates that cooks did not expect to prepare meals for a large number of people at once. Almost no ANIMAL bones are found in these houses, suggesting that meat on the bone was rarely eaten at home. In wealthy households, cooking and food preparation was considered a menial task fit for SLAVES. Women and men did not generally eat together, and it is likely that large 'family meals' were not a feature of Greek domestic life.

In Roman towns we find kitchens that look much more familiar to us. These are much better documented, thanks in part to the survival of POMPEII. In wealthy households kitchens were much more elaborately equipped than Greek kitchens. Features such as sinks and permanent hearths appear more regularly, though portable braziers were still used, and few houses had big ovens. Water was supplied by wells and cisterns.

Many more metal utensils survive, such as spoons, forks, knives, cleavers, colanders and spits. Metal cauldrons and 'saucepans' feature alongside specialized coarse-ware pottery. These pots were, like their Greek counterparts, made of specially formulated ceramic, designed to cook food evenly and to withstand heat. Good quality cooking pots were sometimes traded over long distances. Closed shapes such as casseroles predominate but frying pans, griddles and dishes also appear. Roman HOUSEHOLDS might own a small rotary mill (unknown in classical Greece), but flour could also be bought commercially. More common was the mortarium, a heavy, shallow coarse ceramic vessel with big grits on the bottom surface used for grinding and pulverizing food with a pestle or pounder. Cooking techniques were similar to Greece, with much boiled food, but more elaborate dishes were also produced. Cooking and food preparation would have been done by slaves, and in these wealthy households, there might have been a considerable number of dedicated kitchen staff.

Animal bones are regularly found in Pompeian houses, usually in the GARDEN, suggesting that people regularly ate out of doors in fine weather. The wide range of bones from PIGS, SHEEP, GOATS, CATTLE, chickens, pigeons, quail and other birds, fish and shells from shellfish suggests that rich Romans regularly ate varied and elaborate meat and fish dishes. In addition, remains of a wide range of FRUITS and nuts (including grape, OLIVE, apple, pear, peach, pomegranate, hazel nut, walnut) suggest sumptuous meals compared with those of Greek city-dwellers. LF

Kleanthes see ZENO OF CITIUM.

Kleisthenes b. c.570, d. after 507 BC Born into the aristocratic family of the Alkmaionids, he laid the foundations for the Athenian DEMOCRACY of the classical era by introducing a series of constitutional reforms in 508/7 BC. In the place of the four ancient Ionic TRIBES into which the Athenians were divided, he created ten new tribes named after Athenian heroes. Each tribe was subdivided into three 'thirds' (*trittyes*); each *trittys* included a number of DEMES (communities) from the coast, the inland and the city respectively. The tribes formed the basis of the army and the council, whose membership was now increased to 500; each and every deme was represented in the council.

The 'deme' as an institution was Kleisthenes' own creation. Under his reforms pre-existing communities appointed their own leader (*dêmarchos*) annually; they assumed responsibility for their own affairs (like FESTIVALS), and had the right and the obligation to determine whether someone fulfilled the prerequisites of CITIZENSHIP. We can only speculate as to Kleisthenes' motives. Possibly he aimed at gaining political support, as in fact happened; but he may have also have borne in mind the pressing need to reorganize the army. On the other hand, it is not necessary to believe that he had foreseen every single result. Regardless of his motives, his reforms proved momentous in the long run: they ensured participation of the people in the affairs of the state. IK

See Andrewes, A. (1977) Kleisthenes' reform bill, *CQ* 27: 241–8; Osborne, R. (1996) *Greece in the Making*.

Kleomenes I One of the most influential, and controversial, kings of SPARTA (r. c.520–490 BC), under whom Spartan ambitions were restricted to the Greek mainland, where their power both peaked and began to be held in check. Kleomenes declined to help the Samians against their Persian rulers (c.515); the Spartans had had their fingers burned in SAMOS just before his reign. Similarly (in 499) he was dissuaded from helping the IONIAN REVOLT, apparently being anxious about taking Lakedaimonians too far from home. His most important achievement was to depose Hippias, TYRANT of Athens (510). A second intervention (508), when he briefly deposed the democrat KLEISTHENES in favour of Sparta's friends led by Isagoras, ended ignominiously when the Athenians trapped him on the ACROPOLIS and forced him to withdraw. In 504 he attempted to restore Isagoras but was prevented by Sparta's Corinthian allies and his co-king, Damaratos. In 494, Kleomenes won a great battle at Sepeia near ARGOS, after which he burned alive many Argives in a sacred wood; on this occasion he was acquitted by the Spartans of bribery (rather than impiety). Later, however, he was found to have bribed the DELPHIC ORACLE to declare Damaratos illegitimate, and while in PRISON he allegedly caused his own death by mutilation. Some believed he was touched with MADNESS; the Spartans told HERODOTOS it was because he drank unmixed WINE with his SKYTHIAN guest-friends. DGJS

See Herodotos, books 5–6; Cartledge, P. (2002) *Sparta and Lakonia*; Forrest, W. G. (1995) *A History of Sparta*.

Kleomenes III c.260–219 BC King of Sparta. In 241 Leonidas II overthrew the reformer AGIS IV and gave Agis' widow, Agiatis, to his own son Kleomenes, who reportedly learnt about the late king's ideals from her. As king from c.235 he reintroduced Agis' programme, professing to revive ancient LYKOURGAN values. Learning from Agis' failure to silence opposition, he had the EPHORS killed. To gain support, mainly from the rich, he cancelled DEBTS. To strengthen the citizen body, depleted and impoverished by generations of increasingly unequal landholding, he enrolled non-citizens and shared out public LAND. The revitalized Spartans extended their power over ARKADIA and the ARGOLID, but were defeated in 222/1 at SELLASIA by a MACEDONIAN–ACHAIAN alliance. Kleomenes fled to ALEXANDRIA, believing that Ptolemy IV would help him as Ptolemy III had; his hopes were dashed, and he died in a futile attempted coup.

POLYBIOS, an Arkadian in the Achaian league, predictably portrays Kleomenes as a TYRANT but praises his character. PLUTARCH, using pro-Spartan sources, approves of his reforms but exaggerates Sparta's social problems. Plutarch also gives women a leading role in events, dramatizing the deaths of Kleomenes, his relatives, and his followers to engage our sympathy. He compares Agis and Kleomenes with the GRACCHI – justifiably, for rather than socialistic revolutionaries, as some claim, all four were popular ARISTOCRATS seeking to revive their people's military fortunes. DGJS

See Plutarch, *Agis, Kleomenes, Aratos*; Polybios 2.45–70; Cartledge, P. and Spawforth, A. (1989) *Hellenistic and Roman Sparta*; Mitchison, N. (1931) *The Corn King and the Spring Queen* (novel).

Kleon Athenian politician, commonly considered as the demagogue and radical democrat *par excellence*. His entrance onto the Athenian political scene signalled the emergence of politicians who did not belong to the ARISTOCRACY, the so-called *nouveaux riches*. His origins (his father was a tanner) as well as his policies often became the target of ARISTOPHANES' scornful comments. The main features of his policy were continuation of the war against Sparta and the financial oppression of both allies and wealthy Athenians in order to meet war expenses. In 428 BC Kleon and his associates introduced a special war tax (*eisphora*), which burdened the richest of the Athenians. Under a special command he inflicted a major humiliation on the Lakedaimonians trapped at Sphakteria in 425 BC, bringing them to Athens in chains. His success rendered the people more receptive to his proposals and paved the way for a tightening of the tribute, proposed by his son-in-law Thoudippos. Towards rebellious allies Kleon was ruthless: on his proposal all male citizens of Skione (in Chalkidike) were executed (after his death) following their unsuccessful attempt to secede from the Delian league. In 422/1 BC Kleon campaigned in Chalkidike in order to coerce rebellious allies back into the league. A fatal lapse of judgement led to his death at Amphipolis, where the Spartan leader BRASIDAS was also killed. Soon afterwards a (short-lived) peace was agreed between Athens and Sparta. IK

See Connor, W. R. (1971) *The New Politicians of Fifth-century Athens*; Meiggs, R. (1972) *The Athenian Empire*.

Kleopatra see CLEOPATRA.

Klytaimnestra, Klytaimestra see CLYTEMNESTRA.

Knidos The first city of Knidos was probably sited about halfway along the Resadiye peninsula in the gulf of Kos in south-west Turkey, near the modern Turkish town of Datça (though this has been disputed). Knidos was founded in about 900 BC, traditionally by colonists from Sparta. It became one of the six cities of the Dorian *hexapolis* along with Kos, HALIKARNASSOS and the three cities of RHODES. In the archaic period Knidos sent colonists to SICILY and Lipari in the Aiolian islands, and had relations with NAUKRATIS in the NILE delta. Threatened by the growth of the PERSIAN EMPIRE in the 6th and 5th centuries (during which the Knidians vainly attempted to make their peninsula an island), Knidos joined the Delian league after the PERSIAN WARS but was drawn to the cause of Sparta after the PELOPONNESIAN WAR. In the 4th century it appears the city was moved to its present magnificent position on the Tekir promontory at the extreme western end of the peninsula. The new city lay both on the promontory and across the isthmus connecting it to the mainland. The possibilities of maritime trade were served by two splendid HARBOURS. The 'TRIREME harbour' lay north of the isthmus, and the main harbour, protected by artificial moles, lay to the south. During the hellenistic period Knidos came under Ptolemaic, then Rhodian influence and finally became a free city under Roman control in 129 BC.

There are substantial archaeological remains of the city, though systematic excavation has not yet been completed. There is a THEATRE and an *odeion*. Several TEMPLES included a round one on the hill above the harbours, which probably housed the 4th-century statue of the APHRODITE of Knidos, the first Greek female nude statue by the renowned sculptor PRAXITELES, which became one of the most famous sculptures of antiquity. The sanctuary of DEMETER produced the 4th-century seated statue of the goddess that is now in the British Museum. Extensive residential areas have been identified, including new excavations on the Tekir promontory itself. Outside the city walls, which also encircle a lofty ACROPOLIS, are extensive graveyards with distinctive precinct TOMBS. The famous Lion Tomb of Knidos lay several km east of the city and was the tomb of 12 people. The tomb would have been visible far out to sea and perhaps commemorated a military or naval battle. Its magnificent recumbent lion also resides in the British Museum. Knidos continued to be inhabited in CHRISTIAN times, and several CHURCHES were constructed from reused ancient blocks.

Famous Knidians included the ASTRONOMER Eudoxos, the polymath and geographer AGATHARCHIDES, Ktesias (a doctor at the 5th-century Persian court), and Sostratos, the ARCHITECT of the LIGHTHOUSE (Pharos) of ALEXANDRIA in Egypt. There was a flourishing medical school which rivalled that of Kos, and Knidian WINE was famed in antiquity. EER

See Bean, G.E. (1980) *Turkey beyond the Maeander.*

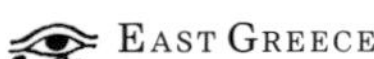 EAST GREECE.

knights see EQUESTRIANS.

knitting In antiquity, one way of achieving a 'knit' fabric was to loop thread with a single-eyed needle, a process known as nalbinding or single-needle knitting. The end product resulted in a stretchy fabric typically used for socks or small drawstring bags.

The earliest preserved examples of nalbinding, dating to the mid-3rd century AD, come from DURA EUROPUS in Syria and are now housed in the Yale University Art Museum. The three fragmentary pieces provide good evidence for variants in colour and decorative patterning. Two are knitted together with dyed wool threads to form bands of tan, red, grey, green and purple. The third example is made of undyed wool and has been stitched in an ovoid pattern.

Originating from Egypt, other preserved examples of nalbinding include woollen socks, also known as 'Coptic socks', dating between the 3rd and 4th centuries. These socks are ankle length and have a division for the big toe. Finds include socks for both adults and children. These socks vary in colour from solid red, brown, to purple, or they are interspersed with bands of blue, red, purple, or green. Some examples have been grafted or darned, indicating that they had been repaired. LAH

See Bellinger, L. and Pfister, R. (1945) *The Excavations at Dura Europus*, vol. 4, part 2: *the textiles*; Grass, M.N. (1955) The origins of the art of knitting, *Archaeology* 8.3: 184–90; Rutt, R. (1989) *A History of Hand Knitting*.

Knossos The most famous of the MINOAN PALACES. Its mythical role as the palace of king Minos led Arthur Evans to excavate the site in 1900. The palace, constructed c.1700 BC after the destruction of a predecessor, occupies the levelled top of a hill south of Irákleio. The central area was a large rectangular courtyard (53 × 28 m), oriented north–south, around which, on the slopes of the hill, were multi-storied wings. The ground west of the central court is taken up by storerooms whose exterior walls create the west façade of the palace. East of the courtyard is the residential quarter; built around a colonnaded staircase, this area has pier-and-door partitions, lightwells, colonnades, drains and frescoes. Above the storerooms on the west was a central area with broad flights of steps and a frescoed processional gateway leading to it. The area west of the central court, with pillar crypt, repositories and a tripartite arrangement of columns and entrances, was interpreted as a cult area by Evans. The Minoan approach to palace design appears utilitarian. Entrances lead visitors to the central court, the focus of the complex. The agglomerative design indicates that the various functions of the palace were not themselves taken into an overarching architectural scheme.

The palace was the centre of a large community which spread out around the central hill and was connected by road to a HARBOUR near Amnisos. Likewise the historical town of Knossos, north-west of the palace, was an important regional centre from the 9th century BC onwards, often in conflict with nearby Lyttos and GORTYN. In the hellenistic period, new sanctuaries, a cemetery and fortifications were added. Knossos was captured by the Romans in 67 BC and became a Roman colony 40 years later. Though eclipsed by Gortyn, it remained prosperous; the Roman period saw the building of the luxurious 'Villa Dionysos' and other élite houses. An earthquake around AD 350 may have caused the town's partial abandonment; late Roman churches were built outside the walls. AJ, DGJS

See Cadogan, G. et al., eds. (2004) *Knossos: palace, city, state*; Evely, D. et al., eds. (1994) *Knossos: a labyrinth of history*; Hood, S. and Smyth, D. (1981) *Archaeological Survey of the Knossos Area*; Sackett, L.H., ed. (1992) *Knossos from Greek City to Roman Colony*, 2 vols. (finds from 'Unexplored Mansion'); Sanders, I.F. (1982) *Roman Crete*.

 CRETE.

knowledge As the sure possession of accurate information concerning the world around us, knowledge would be easy enough to acquire, if only we could trust our most obvious sources of information, the senses. But how can we? They tell one person one thing (e.g. the wind is cold), another person something else (the wind is warm). When, then, can they be trusted? Among the Dogmatists of antiquity (i.e. PHILOSOPHERS who thought knowledge was possible) some said never, some said always, some said occasionally, with caution.

It seems odd to make a distrust of the senses the basis for claims to knowledge, but this is what PARMENIDES of Elea did. His bold account of reality was developed through the use of pure LOGIC instead of sense perception. PLATO was much influenced by Parmenides, and like him thought that knowledge was possible only when the mind operated without the interference of the senses. In Plato's case, this is not because he thought the senses were at fault: it is just that they have to operate on a shifting, unknowable world where there is, in effect, no truth to be had. The intellect, on the other hand, has access to the 'Forms', which are the stable, and therefore knowable principles underpinning the universe. Plato developed this theory in part with an eye on what he took to be the dangerous and contradictory position that the senses, along with judgements based on them, were always reliable. PROTAGORAS, famously, denied that we should be looking for a single, agreed truth about the world since truth is relative to the individual. If I perceive a wind to be warm or an action just, it really is so for me; this does not stop the wind from being cold (or the action unjust) for you, if that is how you see it.

Plato's theory of knowledge enjoyed a revival in the NEOPLATONISM of later antiquity, but to his immediate successors it seemed strange to deny the full reality of the perceived world. ARISTOTLE achieved a sort of compromise by making Forms into principles inherent in the perceptible world: the mind (he thought) was capable of extracting them from its sensory experience. The Dogmatists of the hellenistic era went further and maintained that sense impressions themselves were, at least some of the time, precise and reliable representations of the world. All that was needed was a 'criterion of truth' – a sure means by which reliable impressions could be sorted from the uncertain. The STOICS concluded that one should accept those impressions which were (1) true, as manifest in their being; (2) clear (i.e. clearly perceived); and (3) 'distinct' (i.e., markedly different from every possible false impression). Ironically, SCEPTICISM (which had become the official philosophy of the Platonic ACADEMY at this period) thrived on this definition of knowledge. It was easy to doubt that any impression could pass such a strict test. GB-S

See Everson, S., ed. (1990) *Epistemology*.

Kommagene see COMMAGENE.

Konon d. c.392 BC Athenian GENERAL. His first known appointment was in 414 BC, when he was stationed at Naupaktos. He is known to have served on the board of generals on four other occasions. Escaping the trial of the generals in 406 after Arginousai (he was given control of the fleet while the eight surviving generals were recalled), he went into voluntary EXILE after the debacle at AIGOSPOTAMOI.

Having fled to CYPRUS, Euagoras of SALAMIS is said to have introduced him to the PERSIAN satrap Pharnabazos, who made Konon admiral of his fleet in 397. He operated effectively along the coast of Asia Minor in the mid-390s, winning a significant victory against the Spartans at KNIDOS in 394 before moving the campaign into central Greece. He then persuaded Pharnabazos to fund the rebuilding of Athens' fleet and Long Walls. In 393/2, probably because of his Persian connections, he was sent as an ambassador to Tiribazos by the Athenians. Tiribazos, however, was pro-Spartan and Konon was imprisoned, though he later escaped and fled to Cyprus. LGM

See Cornelius Nepos, *Conon*; Diodorus Siculus, books 13–14; Lysias 19 (*On the Property of Aristophanes*); Thucydides 7.31.4–5; Xenophon, *Hellenika* 1–4.

Kopaïs, Lake Seasonal waters from Mts Parnassos and Helikon fed this large, shallow lake in western BOIOTIA (also known as the Kephisian lake). Sink-holes carried the overflow underground to the Euboian gulf and smaller lakes to the west. Lake Kopaïs covered an area of 240 sq km (90 sq miles) before it was drained at the end of the 19th century to create farmland. Settlement traces inside its western perimeter indicate that the level of the lake in classical antiquity was somewhat lower. A resource for FISHING, fowling and grazing on its marshy shores, the lake also yielded eels (a famous delicacy: ARISTOPHANES, *Acharnians* 880–90) and reeds for musical pipes.

Modern drainage has revealed the remains of ancient canals traversing the north shore of the lake, passing near Orchomenos. These were designed to carry the seasonal flood of the Kephisos and Melas streams directly into sink-holes, while ancient dykes reclaimed land from the perennial lake. Drainage engineering is attested in the later 4th century BC (STRABO 9.2.18), but it is probable that most of these works are Bronze Age. The largest areas reclaimed by these dykes surround the MYCENAEAN citadel at Gla, thought to be an administrative centre dependent on Orchomenos. The legendary wealth of Minyan Orchomenos may be based on this exploitation of the Kopaïs. The destructive potential of Kopaïc floodwaters is recalled in stories of HERAKLES blocking the sink-holes to inundate Orchomenos, enemy and rival to his native THEBES (DIODORUS 4.18.7; PAUSANIAS 9.38.6–8; POLYAINOS 1.3.5). MM

See Kalcyk, H. and Heinrich, B. (1989) The Munich Kopaïs project, in J.M. Fossey, ed., *Papers on Recent Work in Boiotian Archaeology and History* 55–71; Lauffer, S. (1986) *Kopais*.

 BOIOTIA.

korai see *KOUROI* AND *KORAI*.

Korinna see CORINNA.

Koroneia A town in west-central BOIOTIA, best known as the site of two battles. In 447 BC, when Athens controlled the area, various towns in Boiotia were seized by exiled oligarchs, among them CHAIRONEIA and Orchomenos. The Athenians sent a small army under the command of Tolmides, which recovered Chaironeia but on its return was attacked and defeated at Koroneia by the Boiotian army, aided by EUBOIAN, LOKRIAN and other allies. Tolmides himself was killed in this battle, which brought to an end a decade of Athenian domination that had begun with their victory at Oinophyta in 457.

In 394, soon after the start of the inconclusive Corinthian war, the Spartans under AGESILAOS II, returning to Sparta from Asia Minor, met in battle the Boiotians, whose allies now included the Athenians. The historian XENOPHON took part in this ferocious battle. Both right wings were victorious, the Thebans defeating the Spartan left and coming round behind the victorious Spartan right. The Spartans turned round to face them, but the Thebans broke through after bitter fighting, though Agesilaos claimed the victory. He subsequently continued his march, abandoning Boiotia as the Athenians had some 50 years earlier. MJE

 BATTLES (table).

Kos see ASKLEPIOS; HIPPOKRATES; SILK; SOCIAL WAR, GREEK; TEXTILES; WINE.

kosmos Meaning generally any ordering or arrangement, *kosmos* became rapidly applied to the world as a whole since the world itself seems to be arranged and ordered in some way (both the synchronic ordering of sky, water, land and so on and the diachronic ordering of night and day and the seasons). There is some debate in the ancient sources over who first used the word to describe the universe; PYTHAGORAS, PARMENIDES, and HESIOD were all offered as candidates.

There followed a vigorous philosophical debate over various cosmological questions. What were the basic stuffs out of which the *kosmos* is made? Did the apparent design of the *kosmos* provide evidence for the existence of a designer or some kind of natural teleology? Did the *kosmos* come into being and will it ever be destroyed? Is this *kosmos* unique or are there innumerable *kosmoi* both like and unlike our own?

On one side of the debate stands the Platonist–Aristotelian tradition, followed also by the STOICS. This holds that this *kosmos* is unique and exhibits certain features which rightly suggest that either the world as a whole (PLATO, the Stoics) or at least the natural species within it (Plato, ARISTOTLE, the Stoics) are as they are for some good. On the other side stands the atomist tradition of DEMOKRITOS and the EPICUREANS. On this view, this *kosmos* is only one among an infinite number and any teleological features are merely apparent; in fact the world is as it is merely as the result of mechanical collisions and interactions between ATOMS. JIW

See Furley, D. J. (1987) *The Greek Cosmologists*, vol. 1; Kahn, C. H. (1960) *Anaximander and the Origins of Greek Cosmology.*

Kounaxa see ARTAXERXES I, II, III; CYRUS THE YOUNGER; XENOPHON.

kouroi* and *korai These plural forms of the Greek word *kouros* ('boy') and *korê* ('girl') are terms used in modern scholarship to describe sculptural representations of adolescents in the archaic period. *Kouroi* date roughly from the end of the 7th to the end of the 5th centuries BC, while *korai* date from c.650–480 BC.

The *kouros* is a free-standing representation of a nude adolescent male, usually life-sized or larger, posed striding forward with his arms at his side. The statues are sculpted from STONE, or MARBLE by preference. Scholars disagree whether the proportions of the *kouroi* were taken directly from Egyptian canons, as it has been noted that no standard canon can be applied to the Greek statues. Patterns of symmetry are considered important and can be seen particularly in the depiction of HAIR, musculature and facial features. *Kouroi* were used variously as monuments on graves, as dedications to GODS, or as monuments of athletic victories, for example, at the OLYMPIC GAMES.

By contrast, the *korê* was usually under life-size. As it was not socially acceptable for women to appear naked in public, the *korê* was depicted clothed. Paint added detail to facial features, hair and especially clothing. She was usually more static in pose than the *kouros*, but had a wider range of poses available for her arms, which could be placed by her sides, with one lowered, holding a fold of her skirt, or in front of her body, sometimes holding an object such as a pomegranate. The purpose of the *korai* is less clear than that of the *kouros*, as *korai* could be dedicated at sanctuaries by men and appear as markers over male, as well as female, graves. (see also DRESS, GREEK) NJW

KOUROI AND *KORAI*: (a) *korê* statue, front and rear views.

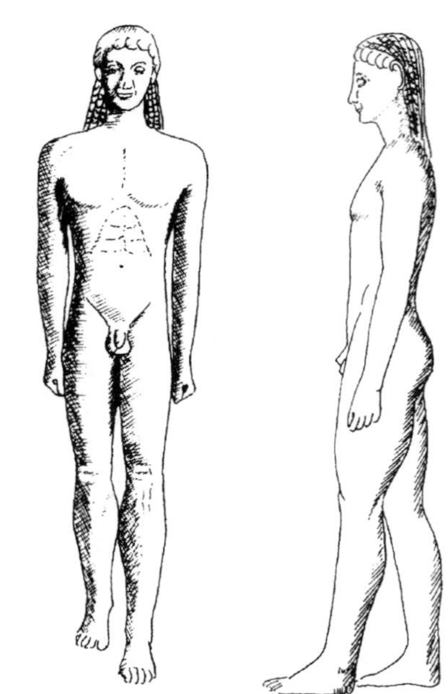

KOUROI AND *KORAI*: (b) *kouros* statue, front and side views. Both date to the late 7th century BC. Notice the stiff, block-like appearance and the two-dimensional character of these sculptures.

Krates of Mallos see COMMENTATORS, TEXTUAL; GEOGRAPHY, ANCIENT.

Kritias c.460–403 BC A leading member of the 'THIRTY Tyrants,' oligarchs who took control of Athens with Spartan aid in late 404. He is identified by several ancient sources as the most extreme exponent of authoritarian rule, modelled on Sparta. Although he belonged to one of the oldest and wealthiest Athenian families he was not prominent in politics before he proposed the recall of ALCIBIADES in 408. After Alcibiades' fall in 406 he went into exile in THESSALY. He returned in 404 as one of 30 men appointed to govern Athens according to ancestral laws. He may have proposed the execution of the prominent moderate Theramenes. He was killed fighting against pro-democratic Athenian exiles in 403. An admirer of the SOPHISTS, he had been a friend and, to some extent, a follower of SOCRATES, whom many Athenians blamed for the harshness of the Thirty. Kritias wrote poetry, including TRAGEDIES, SATYR plays and a poem in praise of the Spartan constitution, and prose, including descriptions of the constitutions of Athens, Sparta and other states, as well as a collection of aphorisms, one of which is: 'More men are good out of habit than by nature.' PDeS

See Ostwald, M. (1986) *From Popular Sovereignty to the Sovereignty of Law.*

Ktesiphon see CTESIPHON.

Kybele see CYBELE.

Kyklades see CYCLADES.

Kyme see CUMAE.

Kynoskephalai Site, in Thessaly, of a victory of the Romans under Titus Quinctius FLAMININUS over the Macedonian forces of Philip V in 197 BC. In 200, the Romans sent an army into Greece to support their allies against Macedonian aggression. The campaign is known as the second Macedonian war, in which little was achieved until Flamininus was put in command of Roman forces. He managed to win over several Greek cities from Philip through diplomacy. After failing to persuade Philip to accept terms, he harried him, and the two armies met at Kynoskephalai. On each side the right wing was successful, but at a crucial point in the conflict a Roman officer led a detachment of legionaries to attack the flank of the Macedonian infantry phalanx, which was unprotected. This manoeuvre turned the battle in the Romans' favour, and Philip was forced to flee. The battle demonstrated for the first time the superiority of the Roman manipular army over the Macedonian phalanx. After the battle Flamininus made peace with Philip, requiring him not to become involved in affairs outside Macedonia. After announcing the 'liberation of the Greeks', Flamininus withdrew all Roman troops from Greece. (see also ARMS AND ARMOUR) HB

See Livy 33.5–10; Polybios 18.18–27.

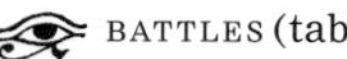 BATTLES (table).

Kyrene see CYRENE.

La Graufesenque see ECONOMY, ROMAN; SAMIAN WARE.

La Tène Iron Age site on the shore of Lake Neuchâtel (Switzerland), first identified in 1857, and the 'type-site' for the second Iron Age of western and central Europe (c.500–1 BC). La Tène is at once an enigma and a key site for the study of 'Celtic' art, technology and CHRONOLOGY.

This lakeside site first came to light when a series of TIMBER piles were exposed at the tip of Lake Neuchâtel, at a point overlooking the Thielle river. La Tène was at first interpreted as a VILLAGE of pile dwellings, but the range and quantity of the metal artefacts found in the lake mud around the piles (principally iron weapons, but also JEWELLERY and TOOLS) were such that the site was quickly reinterpreted as a weapons cache. The first EXCAVATIONS, undertaken between 1880 and 1900, demonstrated the presence of two BRIDGES or causeways, a palisade and a small number of possible timber dwellings. Human and ANIMAL remains were also found, along with TEXTILES, wickerwork and other rarely found organic materials preserved as a result of waterlogging. Numerous interpretations – ranging from arms deposit to marsh refuge – were hazarded for this enigmatic site, which did not appear to be a conventional settlement, but produced large numbers of deliberately mutilated weapons. From 1906, work carried out under the direction of Paul Vouga and William Wavre concentrated on the banks and bed of the Thielle, producing new groups of objects and evidence for further structures. Excavation ceased in 1917, and in 1923 Vouga summarized his findings in a monograph interpreting the site as a fortified emporium. It was not until the 1940s, when similar deposits of metal objects began to found in marshy contexts in Denmark and northern Germany, that more complex interpretations began to be put forward. After a detailed study of the swords and scabbards from La Tène, José de Navarro advanced the idea in the 1960s that La Tène was a votive site: the focus for a warrior-based cult involving the deposition of artefacts in water. Many archaeologists now accept the view that La Tène was a religious sanctuary, though others prefer to see it as a settlement.

Whatever the correct answer, the METALWORK found here has been of fundamental importance in Iron Age studies, furnishing a reference typology, a chronological framework and a name for the second (La Tène or 'Celtic') Iron Age. The majority of the finds from the site date to c.250–120 BC (La Tène C). Swords and scabbards, spearheads, *fibulae*, belt clasps, knives, *phalerae* and axes are the most commonly represented metalwork categories. Of these artefacts, the 166 swords and associated scabbards have been studied in the greatest depth, and were inventoried by de Navarro in 1972. JW

See Navarro, J. M. de (1972) *The Finds from the Site of La Tène*; Vouga, P. (1923) *La Tène*.

 CELTS.

labour

In the ancient world, labour was an undignified burden that everybody wished to escape, and an important status indicator was the extent to which freedom from labour could be achieved. For SLAVES it was impossible, and for the poor it was rare. The work of artisans and employees is routinely denigrated in our admittedly élite sources. No one wished to be defined solely by job or profession: 'What do you do?' was not a polite question for ancient society. Everything worthwhile in life came from leisure, which allowed SCHOLARSHIP, art and public service.

Labour relations were determined by a series of calculations that included factors such as status, skills and background. The distinction between freeman and slave is only one factor that determined labour activity, and not necessarily the decisive one. Inexpensive free labour was always cheaper than slave labour. Freemen and slaves were regularly employed in similar activities, and master and slave might work alongside each other on the same job. Further complicating this picture is the spectrum of relationships of dependency and obligation that fell between concepts of slavery and freedom. There were serf-like relationships such as those that existed for the Spartan HELOTS. Labour obligations could be created through formal contracts such as debt-bondage or social constructions such as PATRONAGE. Hellenistic contracts regularly employ terms that resemble systems of indenture.

The AGRICULTURAL cycle was the primary regulating mechanism of the ancient labour market. Even the smallest farms required additional labour at peak periods. Free wage-labour was also required by farms with large permanent servile labour-forces. Urban industrial MANUFACTURE was never conducted on a grand scale. The largest workforces rarely number more than a few hundred. Most manufacture of goods seems to have been performed by a WORKSHOP comprising an overseer and a few slaves or wage-labourers.

The contribution of women's labour to the HOUSEHOLD is hard to overestimate. Women generated income from, for example, wool-working, washing and MIDWIFERY. Other activities included the manufacture of domestic goods and assistance in farm duties, such as grape-picking, winnowing, and OIL-pressing. The evidence for female labour is more extensive from Rome where women are involved in a wide variety of commercial activities.

Discussion of labour as an abstract economic concept is not found in our sources. The evidence for extensive division in labour is debatable. Despite a large number of job titles, it is often unclear whether the same job was performed under several titles or whether these indicate fixed and exclusive professions. The creation of job titles may also be a function of genre. Writers were aware of the advantages that specialization offered in terms of quality (cf. XENOPHON, *Cyropaideia* 8.2.5), but seem oblivious to other advantages. Effectiveness tends to be valued more than efficiency. AJLB

See Brock, R. (1994) The labour of women in classical Athens, *CQ* 44: 336–46; Burford, A. (1993) *Land and Labor in the Greek World*; Cartledge, P. A. et al., eds. (2002) *Money, Labour and Land*; Finley, M. I. (1981) *Economy and Society in Ancient Greece*; Garnsey, P. D. A., ed. (1980) *Non-slave Labour in the Greco-Roman World*.

SLAVERY is attested from the earliest period of Roman history and certainly co-existed in varying ratios with non-slave labour. Whereas the use of hired labour in the VILLA economy was more cost-efficient than slavery, the choice between different types of workers was as much a matter of social standing, local/family tradition and availability of alternative solutions as of ECONOMIC RATIONALISM. Noteworthy are differences between PROVINCES: while the slave mode of production in AGRICULTURE is well attested in Italy and in some western provinces in the late Republic and early empire, there is almost no trace of it in Egypt. The villa economy developed into integrated enterprises, whose revenue also derived from the exploitation of natural resources, MANUFACTURE (garment, clay industries) and services (lodging, transportation of goods and persons). Both private and public sectors made constant use of temporary workers, day-labourers and skilled craftsmen, hired on a personal basis or through contractors. In larger enterprises (villas, MINES, mints) workers were organized into teams overseen by foremen subordinated to the MANAGER or owner. When access to special infrastructure (CANALS) or facilities (GRANARIES), or the use of means of production expensive to acquire (waterwheel, MILL), maintain (FISHPONDS, plough-oxen) or operate (KILN) was necessary, independent workers joined in temporary partnership.

Even though the ÉLITE affected a contemptuous attitude toward non-agricultural work, the overwhelming majority of the population was involved in some economic activity, not always connected with agriculture. EPIGRAPHIC evidence for TRADE is abundant and shows the diversity and specialization of trades for men and women. Chronic manpower shortages or, conversely, massive unemployment other than seasonal cannot be demonstrated, but evidence for labour unrest appears occasionally: strikes and RIOTS by BAKERS in 2nd-century AD EPHESOS necessitated the intervention of municipal and provincial authorities. Other similar cases amount to no more than isolated and short-lived incidents.

Although corvées (forced labour) were almost never exacted from TENANTS, FREEDMEN were compelled to perform certain tasks (*operae*) on behalf of former masters, but their obligations were strictly regulated. On the other hand, the imperial government increasingly imposed the performance of compulsory services upon provincials as part of their civic or fiscal obligations. Organized at the municipal or village level, such LITURGIES were first connected with the POSTAL service, TRANSPORT and billeting of troops and officials, but soon extended to tax collection, police duties, maintenance of ROADS and irrigation systems and exploitation of state mines, QUARRIES and factories.

Convicts condemned to hard labour were sent to imperial properties (estates, quarries, mines) and employed in public works: TRAJAN, writing to PLINY THE YOUNGER (*Letters* 10.32.2), asserted that people of that kind usually worked in BATHS, cleaned sewers and built roads. Considered respectively as a medium or mild form of punishment, on the same level as deportation and GLADIATORIAL GAMES or exile and imprisonment, condemnation *in metallum* ('to the mines', restricted to lower classes) or *in opus publicum* ('to public works') was meted out for a whole range of crimes (Paulus, *Sentences* 5.17–30b). Working conditions in these places ensured that condemnation was tantamount to capital punishment. JJA

See Aubert, J.-J. (1994) *Business Managers in Ancient Rome*; Carlsen, J. (1995) *Vilici and Roman Estate Managers until AD 284*; Dixon, S. (2000–1) How do you count them if they're not there? New perspectives on Roman cloth production, *Opuscula Romana* 25–6: 7–17; Joshel, S. R. (1992) *Work, Identity, and Legal Status at Rome*; Lewis, N. (1982) *The Compulsory Public Services of Roman Egypt*.

labour, unfree see DEBT-BONDAGE; HELOTS; LABOUR; SLAVERY.

Lacedaemon see LACONIA; SPARTA.

Laconia (Lakonia) A post-classical name (first found in Latin authors), now commonly used to denote the SPARTAN homeland in the south-eastern PELOPONNESE. At c.5,100 sq km (1,970 sq miles), Laconia is the largest region in the Peloponnese, though ARKADIA was said to have the largest population. Most of Laconia consists of the valley of the river Eurotas, running south to the sea, and the mountain ranges on either side. To the east is the complex of Mt Parnon, between Sparta and the Aegean sea. On the west stands the virtually impenetrable wall of Taÿgetos, which almost cuts Sparta off from MESSENIA and runs out into cape Tainaron (now Máni).

Sparta controlled the most fertile regions of Laconia, the upper and lower Eurotas valley, where its territory bordered those of its *perioikoi* or 'about-dwellers'. They lived in free but dependent towns, the most important of which (at least from the 4th century) was Sparta's chief port, Gytheion on the south coast. Central Laconia was usually approached from Arkadia in the north, or from Gytheion, but many other coastal perioikic cities conducted their own seaborne trade. The *perioikoi* supplied up to half Sparta's HOPLITE army, and exhibited a typical Greek social structure based on landholding; they owned chattel SLAVES and probably exploited HELOTS. The one-sided relationship between Sparta and Laconia was partly broken in the 3rd century with the dwindling of Spartan military power, then by the removal of the *perioikoi* by FLAMININUS in the early 2nd century. They now formed the 'league of the Lakedaimonians' independent of Sparta, later renamed the Eleutherolaconian ('Free Laconian') league, though Sparta remained economically dominant.

Laconia approximates to ancient *Lakedaimôn* (both an alternative name for Sparta and the geographical term for the Eurotas valley), and thus to the modern province of Lakonía. 'Laconia', however, is often used of all Spartan territory east of Taÿgetos, including the island of Kythera and the coastal district of Kynouria in the north-east, neither of which was in Lakedaimon. The entire territory controlled by Sparta, however, including all of Messenia until c.369 BC and coastal Messenia until c.338, is regularly called *Lakônikê*. DGJS

See Pausanias, book 3; Strabo, book 8; Cavanagh, W. G. et al. (1996–2002) *Continuity and Change in a Greek Rural Landscape: the Laconia survey*, 2 vols.; Shipley, G. (2004) Lakedaimon, in Hansen and Nielsen, *Inventory* 569–98.

 AEGEAN SEA: (a); PELOPONNESE.

Lactantius (Lucius Caecilius Firminianus Lactantius) c.AD 240–320 Professor of Latin RHETORIC at NICOMEDIA under DIOCLETIAN. His *Divine Institutes* was the first attempt to produce a systematic summary of CHRISTIAN thought in Latin. Of AFRICAN origin and a pupil of Arnobius, he was already an author before receiving the imperial summons to Nicomedia. JEROME remarks that Lactantius found his Latin talents underemployed in a Greek-speaking city and therefore turned to writing. He has been as much admired for the style and quality of his Latin, 'a river of Ciceronian eloquence' (Jerome, *Letters* 58), as patronized for the derivative and superficial quality of his thought and theology.

He was apparently a Christian by 303, when he resigned his professorship in response to the Diocletianic PERSECUTION. His first extant work, *On God's Design*, argues that the nature of man, in particular his endowment with reason, may be seen as evidence of God's providence. The *Divine Institutes* seek to expose the contradictions and flaws of PAGANISM and PHILOSOPHY before turning to the revelation of truth in the person of Christ. *On the Deaths of the Persecutors* takes great pleasure in describing the dreadful ends of persecutors from NERO onwards. Lactantius may be the author of the POEM *On the Phoenix*, which exploits the legend of this fabulous bird for Christian symbolic purposes. In extreme old age he became the tutor of CONSTANTINE's son, Crispus. PMB

See Creed, J. L. (1984) *Lactantius, De mortibus persecutorum*.

Lade see CHIOS; IONIAN REVOLT; MILETOS; NAVAL WARFARE, GREEK.

Lake Copais see KOPAÏS, LAKE.

Lake Regillus Site of an epic battle between Rome and the Latins (499 or 496 BC). The lake no longer exists, but the likely location is near modern Frascati in the territory of ancient Tusculum, some 16 km (10 miles) south-east of Rome. The Latins, led by Octav(i)us Mamilius of Tusculum, sought to restore the ousted king TARQUINIUS SUPERBUS. The infant REPUBLIC, led by the DICTATOR Aulus Postumius, was victorious. The war with the Latins, of which this was a part, ended in 493 with the treaty of Cassius (*foedus Cassianum*). The account in LIVY is strongly reminiscent of a HOMERIC battle, with clear echoes of the *Iliad*. Omitted by Livy (compare the version of DIONYSIOS OF HALIKARNASSOS) is any mention of the DIOSCURI. Famously, Castor and Pollux appeared in the battle, encouraging the struggling Romans, before reappearing in the Roman FORUM to announce the victory. Postumius vowed a TEMPLE to them during the battle. The columns which stand in the forum today belong to a later building, but foundations from the early 5th century survive, as does 6th-century evidence for the worship of the Dioscuri elsewhere in Latium. Postumius' descendants commemorated the victory on coins 400 years later. The tale gained new life in the Victorian age with Macaulay's *Lays of Ancient Rome*, which purport to reconstruct the Roman oral tradition. JRWP

See Dionysios of Halikarnassos 6.4–13, trs. E. Cary (1940); Livy, 2.19–20, trs. A. de Sélincourt (1960); Macaulay, T. B. (1842) *Lays of Ancient Rome*.

Lake Trasimene see BATTLES, ROMAN; CANNAE; FLAMINIUS; HANNIBAL; HANNIBALIC WAR; WAR.

Lakedaimon see LACONIA; SPARTA.

Lambaesis FORTRESS of the III Augusta LEGION, and main base of the Roman army in AFRICA, from the early 2nd century AD onwards. A separate town developed close by and was later the capital of the province of Numidia. The site has special significance in Roman ARMY studies, because of the extent of French excavations there in the late 19th and early 20th centuries, which exposed almost the complete plan of the fortress and recovered several thousand inscriptions, providing us with the names and other details of c.3,000 SOLDIERS who served here. Located in the high plains in central Algeria, the fortress succeeded a smaller auxiliary fort established here in the 80s AD to control the outlet of the major passes through the Aures massif from the desert beyond. The most visible standing monument is a huge four-way ARCH at the junction of the *via principalis* and *via praetoria* in front of the entrance to the headquarters building. The military parade ground associated with the fortress was also excavated in the 19th century, yielding fragments of a fascinating text, detailing the manoeuvres undertaken by the army on the occasion of the visit to the site by HADRIAN (*ILS* 2487; 9133–5). DJM

See Le Bohec, Y. (1989) *La Troisième légion auguste*.

 AFRICA, ROMAN.

Lamian war 323–322 BC A war in Greece after the death of ALEXANDER the Great. An alliance of Greeks and AITOLIANS, led by the Athenian Leosthenes, rose against Macedonian rule and, after initial successes, laid siege to Antipatros at Lamia in THESSALY. Unable to prevent the arrival of reinforcements for Antipatros from Asia Minor, the alliance was eventually defeated by sea (at Amorgos) and land (at Krannon in Thessaly). KB

See Schmitt, O. (1992) *Der lamische Krieg*; Shipley, G. (2000) *The Greek World after Alexander*.

 WAR (table).

lamps

Most extant Greek lamps were made from clay, though a SILVER lamp worth 38 drachmas was kept in the Pronaos on the ATHENIAN ACROPOLIS during the 430s BC. Although lamps were handmade in the early archaic period, by the late archaic period they were wheelmade and circular in shape. They consisted of a shallow circular reservoir for the OLIVE OIL, a spout through which a wick could be inserted, and sometimes a handle. By the hellenistic period lamps were often mouldmade.

The amount of light generated by the lamps was limited, and it is likely that they were set on stands to provide better illumination; the small amount of oil would only last two or three hours. Lamps were sometimes decorated in a black gloss, thus resembling other forms of plain Greek pottery.

Athenian clay lamps seem to have been exported in large numbers around the MEDITERRANEAN. A graffito scratched on the base of an Attic lamp, dated to the early 3rd century BC and excavated at Rhegium (Reggio di Calabria) showed that it was part of a batch of 285. The largest batch, from Athens itself, mentions 695 items. The prices seem to have been low, though the evidence is confusing. Two 4th-century BC examples from the Kerameikos at Athens carry the graffiti 'one hundred items for one drachma' and 'ten items for one drachma'. DWJG

See Bailey, D.M. (1975) *Catalogue of Lamps in the British Museum*, vol. 1; Gill, D.W. J. (1987) An Attic lamp in Reggio: the largest batch notation outside Athens, *OJA* 6: 212–15; Howland, R. H. (1958) *Greek Lamps and their Survivals*.

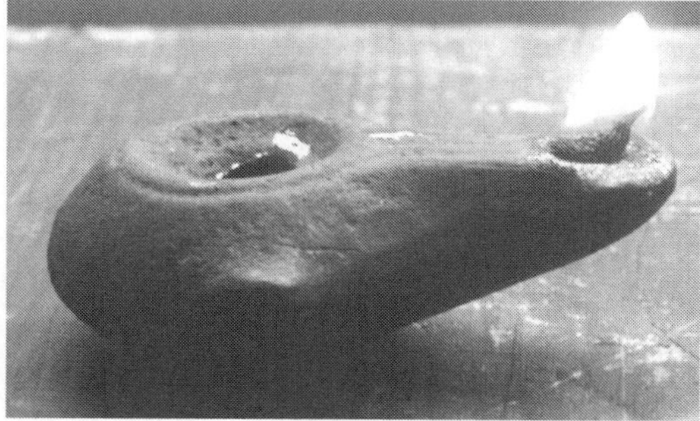

LAMPS: (a) the meagre light from a Roman lamp from Egypt.

LAMPS: (b) selection of Roman picture lamps.

Roman lamps, stylistically derived from hellenistic ones, were produced in metal, GLASS and especially POTTERY, the latter in most PROVINCES. Alongside torches and fire-baskets they were used for lighting in both the home and public places and were also important to religious ritual, as BURIAL furniture and votive objects at shrines. Fuelled primarily by OLIVE or other locally available OIL, their use equates to burning a food source and implies a degree of surplus and wealth. Closed lamps depended on a wick, while the less common open ones probably held an oil-soaked rag. In shape they are generally characterized by a round discus pierced for filling, with diametrically opposed nozzle(s) for the wick and handle(s), and base, frequently with a ring. The discus may be decorated with a range of motifs, including MYTHOLOGICAL, figurative, ARCHITECTURAL and floral or faunal themes.

Although some Roman ceramic lamps were wheelmade, the majority were made in moulds of various materials, including PLASTER or STONE; existing lamps were also used as a prototype. Some moulded lamps were stamped or signed by the maker or the firm. Fortis is a well-known lamp maker from the 'Firmalampen' WORKSHOPS of north Italy, whose distinctive elongate products with deep channels were copied throughout the north-west and north-east provinces from the late 1st to the 3rd centuries AD. Due to the long-established study of their form and marks, lamps provide useful evidence for dating and the long-distance transport of artefacts. RST

See Bailey, D. M. (1991) Lamps metal, lamps clay, *JRA* 4: 51–62.

land and property

The correct and efficient acquisition, cultivation, maintenance and disposal of land are issues that dominate Greek life. The vast majority of Greek states remained, both in reality and in their imagination, communities rooted in agrarian ideals and practice. The use and abuse of land were central concerns to most inhabitants.

Interests in land could take a variety of forms. Ownership seems to have been reasonably extensive, and those who were able to own land did so. Certain groups were sometimes formally excluded from ownership; in Athens, women and non-citizens were prohibited from owning property. However, practice varied throughout the Greek world. In Sparta, it was possible for women to inherit land, and even in Athens it was possible for non-citizens to be granted special rights to own property. Social controls supported the retention of interests in land. Strong censure attached to those who squandered and disposed of ancestral estates. Alongside these prejudices existed a number of myths that regarded the inalienability of land as a characteristic of a lost 'golden age'. It is difficult to determine whether such prohibitions on the sale of land ever existed. Certainly, by the classical period, such prohibitions had fallen into disuse and land was bought and sold in communities throughout the Greek world.

The practice of land ownership was aided by the tradition of partible inheritance, through which estates were divided equally between beneficiaries, ensuring that a maximum number of recipients retained a direct interest in land. The flaw in such a system was that continual division could reduce estates to a size that was no longer viable. This system contributed to a situation that saw landholding becoming gradually stratified, with an increasing gap between the sizes of large and small estates.

In addition to the acquisition of land through INHERITANCE and purchase, there was an extensive system of leasing. The concept of leasehold interest is attested from at least the 6th century BC. The largest concentration of leases for the classical period comes from ATTICA. However, examples are found in a number of other Greek city-states. In the hellenistic period leases are widely attested. They proved a particularly attractive way for corporate bodies such as city-states, TRIBES, DEMES and religious organizations to manage their assets. Their lease agreements were normally aimed towards wealthy members of the community and specified reasonably long periods of tenure. They often included specific instructions about land use and agricultural practice that were designed to assist in preserving the land's value. Although it is less well documented, leasing of property owned by private individuals was also reasonably common. Such arrangements were particularly important for those individuals, such as orphans, who were unable to manage their own estates. Within cities, the management of tenement blocks was organized through a system of short leases. Landlords often left the management of such blocks and the collection of rents to resident supervisors. Leasehold interests were also important in the exploitation of the resources located beneath the ground. The state normally reserved rights to mineral resources for itself. In Athens, leases for the SILVER MINING concessions were auctioned by public officials. Exploitation of the land through QUARRYING was also normally effected by setting up leases.

Real property provided the main security for loans. Except for a certain class of commercial trading transactions where the loan was secured on the future cargo ('bottomry loans'), loans set against moveable property or backed by guarantors were rare. In return for credit, it appears that lenders obtained ownership of the land. Borrowers retained possession and a right to redeem ownership on payment of the debt. A number of stone markers (*horoi*), placed to register interests in plots of land, survive.

Given the wide variety in CLIMATE and GEOGRAPHY, it is difficult to generalize about strategies for estate management. Analysis of patterns of land-holding in the classical period indicate a general preference for small scattered plots, and cropping arrangements which provided for a diversity of crops. What such practices lacked in efficiency they compensated for by minimizing risk of crop failure. As always there are exceptions. One of the most famous Athenian estates, the estate of Phainippos (Pseudo-Demosthenes 42) consisted of a continuous tract of land which seems to be largely given over to the cultivation of barley. After climate and geography, the third variable which affected management strategy was access to labour. Large estates could be run on SLAVE labour with an overseer (*epitropos*) appointed to manage daily affairs. Those who farmed the land themselves or with the assistance of only a few family members or slaves were dependent on access to casual LABOUR during periods of peak activity such as harvest. At such moments, assistance from neighbours and labour obtained from the services of the landless poor were crucial.

The conquests of ALEXANDER usher in a new stage in Greek land management. It is hard to find parallels in the classical Greek world that match the great SELEUKID and Ptolemaic estates in size or complexity of administration. Initially owners seem to have adopted modified versions of indigenous practices. However, gradually we can see the development of innovations that were designed to bring more land into cultivation and increase return on estate lands. AJLB

See Burford, A. (1993) *Land and Labor in the Greek World*; Finley, M.I. (1952) *Studies in Land and Credit in Ancient Athens, 500–200 BC*; Gallant, T.W. (1991) *Risk and Survival in Ancient Greece*; Harris, E. M. (1988) When is a sale not a sale? The riddle of Athenian terminology for real security revisited, *CQ* 38: 351–81; Hodkinson, S. (2000) *Property and Wealth in Classical Sparta*; Osborne, R. (1988) Social and economic implications of the leasing of land and property in classical and hellenistic Greece, *Chiron* 18: 279–323; Rostovtzeff, M. (1953) *The Social and Economic History of the Hellenistic World*.

A basic measure of wealth in the Roman world was land and property. In an economy dominated by AGRICULTURE, land provided for the Roman upper classes the most reliable way of investing wealth to achieve a stable income, and investment in land carried social prestige that other economic activities, such as commerce, did not. Roman landowners often built luxurious VILLAS on their estates, so that estates at the same time produced income and emphasized social status. Land was also significant for the Roman empire's finances. Agricultural land provided the basis for TAXATION in the Roman empire, while revenues from lands owned by the state, especially in Egypt and AFRICA, helped to supply Rome and later CONSTANTINOPLE with much needed foodstuffs.

Agricultural land fell into several juridical categories. Full rights of ownership under Roman LAW were limited to Italic land and provincial land classified as Italic. Other provincial land could be held privately, but the Roman people formally remained the ultimate owner. The Roman state maintained direct control over much of the land in the empire, and this land provided considerable revenues. Some state land formally belonged to the emperor, while other state or public land might be divided into various categories, such as royal land in Egypt.

Landed wealth was greatly stratified, with the bulk of land concentrated in relatively few hands. For example, the Roman SENATOR PLINY THE YOUNGER owned estates that were worth on the order of 17 million *sestertii* (Duncan-Jones 17–32). One set of his estates produced an annual rent of 400,000 *sestertii*. By contrast, the wealth of ordinary farmers in Egypt who paid taxes and performed crucial liturgies was on the order of several thousand *sestertii*. A recent investigation of agriculture at OXYRHYNCHOS in Egypt suggests the degree of stratification of land ownership in a Roman provincial city (Rowlandson). In the territory of Oxyrhynchos, with a population of about 125,000, only a few dozen individuals had holdings of 125 ha (309 acres) or more, and a somewhat larger number of families had holdings sufficient to allow them to live from rents. Most landowners had holdings barely large enough to provide a living for an individual family, and many people at the bottom end of the scale, especially villagers, supplemented their incomes by leasing in private land from other landowners or by cultivating state land.

The estates that members of the Roman ARISTOCRACY owned varied in their composition and organization from one province to another. In Italy, large estates, or *latifundia*, were typically agglomerations of smaller farms, which an individual landowner might acquire over the course of time. These estates were often not contiguous. Wealthy Romans, moreover, might own estates in several locations. Such estates might be exploited in a variety of ways. Beginning in the 2nd century BC, Roman landowners produced cash crops, in particular wheat, WINE, and OLIVE OIL, for the growing urban population of Rome and of other Italian cities. This effort led to some concentration of land and to the increased use of SLAVE labour. In the villa economy of late Republican and early imperial Italy, an estate might be managed by a slave bailiff, or *vilicus*, who would supervise the slave labour cultivating the land. The principal alternative method of exploiting estates was through tenancy. Roman landowners increasingly relied on farm tenancy in the early empire as a means of managing multiple and scattered holdings, but slaves provided labour on Roman estates throughout antiquity. Often slaves and tenants would be employed together on the same estate, with a central farm or farms cultivated by slaves under the management of a *vilicus*, and other farms leased out to tenants.

Other methods of organizing estates are attested in the PROVINCES, where it is apparent that slave labour was not used on the same scale as in Italy. Imperial estates in the Medjerda valley of northern Tunisia were cultivated by tenants, or *coloni*, who held perpetual leases over the land they cultivated and paid a share rent. Set above the *coloni* were middlemen (*conductores*), who leased from the state the right to collect the share rent from the *coloni* and used the labour of the *coloni* to cultivate additional land. In 3rd-century AD Egypt, an ARCHIVE of an estate MANAGER named HERONINOS reveals an altogether different method of organizing an estate. The estate of Aurelius Appianus in the FAYÛM region consisted of individual divisions organized around VILLAGES. Each division, in turn, encompassed numerous individual parcels, many of them quite small. The basic labour force for the estate of Appianus was provided by a relatively small number of permanent salaried workers, who were supplemented by a large number of workers hired on a daily basis. The central administration of the estate maintained control over important productive resources, such as livestock, and apportioned these resources among the various divisions. Some of the land of Appianus was leased out to tenants.

A much debated issue is whether Roman landowners managed their land 'rationally', in the sense of pursuing coherent long-term economic goals. On one side, M. I. Finley (1985) denied Roman landowners the ability to engage in anything but the most primitive long-term economic planning. But the recent investigation of the Heroninos archive by Rathbone indicates that Roman landowners were capable of implementing quite sophisticated methods of managing their estates. The managers of the estate of Appianus could calculate the relative profitability of various crops and manage resources in such a way as to keep under control the costs of producing these crops. But the scope for economic planning that sophisticated methods of accounting made possible was constrained by a largely agrarian economy with limited growth. DPK

See Duncan-Jones, R. (1982) *The Economy of the Roman Empire*; Finley, M. I. (1985) *The Ancient Economy*; Garnsey, P. and Saller, R. (1987) *The Roman Empire*; Rathbone, D. (1991) *Economic Rationalism and Rural Society in Third-century AD Egypt*; Rowlandson, J. (1996) *Landowners and Tenants in Roman Egypt*.

land surveying

The most lasting consequence of Greek land surveying was the creation of geometry (*geômetria*), literally 'land measurement'. The practical results of surveying are seen in the many town plans and the few divisions of agricultural land that have been recovered. Unfortunately no Greek treatises on the subject, inscribed MAPS, or surveying instruments have survived.

The Greeks used the methods developed by the Egyptians and continued by the Romans. Tools were rods, corded lines and a surveyor's cross with four plumb lines, the Roman *groma*. It seems likely that from the Egyptians they learnt to calculate the size of right-angled triangles and what we refer to as the theorem of PYTHAGORAS. The latter is implicit in the halving and doubling of squares, seen in rural land division in the Tauric Chersonesos and at Larisa in THESSALY, and in the town plan of HALIEIS in the ARGOLID. The most common land unit was the areal *plethron*, 100×100 feet (c.33×33 m). The settlements the Greeks established overseas from the 8th century BC required evenly divided agricultural and residential lots. Urban grids creating rectangular blocks, 100 or 120 feet wide, to be subdivided into roughly square HOUSE plots, were normal, and in some regions may also have prevailed in the countryside. The large squares of Thessalian and Crimean land division are rarer, or more rarely detected, in towns (Halieis, 6th century? RHODES, late 5th century). (see also TOWN PLANNING) MHJ

See Boyd, T. and Jameson, M. (1981) Urban and rural land division in ancient Greece, *Hesperia* 50: 327–42; Dilke, O. (1971) *The Roman Land Surveyors*.

Methods of Roman land survey were relatively sophisticated, involving precise measurements and the sighting and plotting of straight lines, right angles and squares. The most common surveying instrument was the *groma* (possibly derived through ETRUSCAN from *gnomon*, the Greek word for SUNDIAL). It consisted of a wooden pole set in a metal base; a horizontal cross was fitted to the top of the pole, possibly using an angle bracket, and to each of the four arms of the cross a plumb line was attached.

Surveyors measured and assessed land and established boundaries for central government, local communities and private individuals. They also assisted in the resolution of all types of land dispute. But their most important task was the division of land for allocation to new settlers, especially in the late REPUBLIC and early imperial period, when many colonies were set up, often for VETERAN soldiers. Surveyors established units of land measurement (*centuriae*) by plotting straight dividing lines (*limites*) in the form of roadways or balks, which intersected at right angles and produced a criss-cross pattern of squares or rectangles. It was common for *centuriae* to have sides

2,400 Roman feet long (c.709.68 m) and to contain 200 *iugera* (c.50.4 ha, 125 acres), though there were many variations of this. The two main *limites* were the *decumanus maximus* (often running east–west and up to 40 ft wide) and the *kardo maximus* (often running north–south and up to 20 ft wide), and their intersection marked the central point of the survey. On the basis of the original sighting, *centuriae* were designated to the right or left of the *decumanus maximus* and on the far or near side of the *kardo maximus*.

On the completion of land division, a MAP and other records were made in bronze, with details of the landholdings, and the topography and boundaries of the territory. These records were signed by the founder of the colony and retained there, while copies were lodged in the record office in Rome. A fragment of a surveyor's map has been recently discovered in Spain, marking *centuriae*, the river Ana (Guadiana), and the land of a neighbouring community, the Lacimurgenses. MARBLE tablets at Arausio (Orange) preserve aspects of a land survey carried out for TAXATION purposes, including *centuriae*, details of landholdings, and local topography.

In the early Republic, the large-scale demarcation of land for distribution to Roman citizens visibly demonstrated Rome's domination over defeated peoples. Later, changes in the pattern of landholding in rural Italy continued, as political leaders rewarded their soldiers and supporters. Aerial photography has evocatively illustrated how the great Roman field systems have left their mark to this day in the landscape of Europe and North AFRICA, and in Italy in the valley of the river Padus (Po) along the line of the Via Aemilia from Ariminum (Rimini) to Placentia (Piacenza). (see also *AGRIMENSORES*) JBC

See Campbell, B. (2000) *The Writings of the Roman Land Surveyors: introduction, text, translations and commentary*, vol. 1; Dilke, O. A.W. (1971) *The Roman Land Surveyors*.

landscape At its simplest, the natural world within which human societies live. A more complicated view is that the interrelationship of nature and people is what defines landscape, that the latter is the product of environment and human action or perception. The classical age is sometimes depicted as a world of cities, but Greco-Roman societies were acutely dependent on and conscious of the landscapes they inhabited, shaped and exploited. The importance of landscape was not simply economic, but also symbolic and psychological. For example, in their VILLAS and urban HOUSES, Roman ARISTOCRATS sought to tame nature by creating illusions of a rural idyll through carefully manicured GARDENS, FOUNTAINS/water features and interior decoration that evoked landscapes. However, Greek and Roman interest in NATURE and landscape should not be confused with modern ecological awareness of environment. The Greeks and Romans did not have a well-developed concept of the landscape as a whole. The point is most clearly illustrated by considering PLINY THE ELDER's *Natural History*, a vast ENCYCLOPEDIA that breaks the subject down into its smallest components, rather than reviewing all aspects of the environment in context. There was no consideration of the human impact on the landscape; for the ancients the environment was a divine realm populated by GODS, nymphs and spirits who controlled not only nature but the destiny of the human populations who occupied these physical spaces. The successful economic and practical exploitation of the landscape is, of course, a major preoccupation of Pliny's work. His philosophy to explain this, however, is concerned more with propitiation of these divine powers than with scientific understanding of landscapes and how they could be changed by human action. WARFARE was one means by which Pliny acknowledged the negative impact of people on the countryside, and the destruction of not only annual crops, but also orchards and vineyards, is a consistent theme of accounts of the bitterest wars of antiquity.

Landscapes of the Greek and Roman worlds have also been the subject of much scholarly attention in recent decades, in part as a by-product of the rise in FIELD SURVEY, but also reflecting a broadening in the scope of ancient historical enquiry. The Southern Argolid Survey is an example of a project with a particularly well-developed geoarchaeological component. Such studies can reconstruct the look of ancient landscapes, but also prompt reassessments of the contribution of humans in shaping them and of how this led to major changes over time. Parts of the ancient human landscapes still survive today: examples include the terraced hill-slopes of many regions, some at least of which are of great antiquity, and the regularly gridded layout of tens of thousands of square kilometres of the countryside – the long-term legacy of Roman LAND SURVEYS (centuriation). Areas of the landscape that are today considered marginal or wilderness are turning up evidence of dynamic exploitation in the past and it is clear that Greeks and Romans had very different views about the value of such wildscapes.

The Romans were also responsible for some major schemes of ENGINEERING that changed local environments completely, as in some of their major hydraulic schemes aimed at draining marshes and lakes and at controlling floodwaters. Mining landscapes are another important category of human-wrought transformation; arguably the most impressive example is the gigantic open-cast at Las Medulas in northwestern Spain, over 2 km ($1\frac{1}{4}$ miles) across and some hundreds of metres deep, with redeposited waste flows covering several further sq km. Human impacts on mining landscapes were exacerbated by the effects of POLLUTION from smelting activities. This point is brought home by the evidence of Greenland ice cores, where the Roman period stands out as the highest pre-industrial peak of atmospheric lead and copper pollution. The effects were far more dramatic at the major smelting sites. Recent work in Wadi Faynan, Jordan, has revealed a Roman copper mining operation that poisoned its environs to such an extent that the toxins are still at dangerous levels in the present-day environment. DJM

See Horden, P. and Purcell, N. (2000) *The Corrupting Sea: a study of Mediterranean history*; Shipley, G. and Salmon, J., eds. (1996) *Human Landscapes in Classical Antiquity*.

language and languages The modern view of classical civilization is built around two languages, ancient Greek and Latin. The Greeks believed that their language was autochthonous, but Greek is clearly descended from Indo-European, and Indo-European speakers seem to have moved into the Greek world some time before the MYCENAEAN age. This new language seems to have displaced an indigenous language (or languages), but traces of pre-Greek vocabulary remain in the lexicon of classical Greek. The Greek world is geographically disparate, and during the classical period Greeks inhabited not only mainland Greece, but the AEGEAN ISLANDS, the coast of Asia Minor, parts of north AFRICA and southern Italy. In this light it is hardly surprising that a number of dialects flourished, each with considerable variation in phonology, morphology and vocabulary. Although to the modern student ancient Greek is often synonymous with Attic Greek, in fact a standard version of Greek did not emerge until the later part of the hellenistic period, when *koinê* was used throughout much of the Greek-speaking world.

Although the Greeks themselves recognized differences among the various dialect groups, they nonetheless regarded themselves as speaking the same language. Despite considerable range of geography and variation in POLITICAL SYSTEMS, shared language was seen as the most conspicuous factor in defining ETHNICITY. HERODOTOS speaks of 'Greekness' (*to Hellênikon*) based on shared language, as well as shared blood, RELIGION and custom (8.144). The principal term for designating a non-Greek was *barbaros*, and its basic meaning was non-Greek-speaker. The Greek world was surrounded by *barbaroi*, and it is often difficult to determine what influence these other societies had on the language of their Greek neighbours. Although based on recognizable dialects, literary Greek, which constitutes the bulk of our evidence, is both formal and artificial; it provides little evidence for colloquial Greek as it was spoken in the marketplaces and streets. It is clear, however, that the Greeks traded with their neighbours, and commerce regularly finds a way of transcending linguistic boundaries. It would be very surprising if some Greeks did not have knowledge of other languages. Inscriptions occasionally preserve foreign words, and there is the striking example of Hipponax, a poet who lived on the coast of Asia Minor in the 6th century BC and seems regularly to have worked LYDIAN and PHRYGIAN words into his poems.

Latin began as the language of Latium, the region of which Rome is the most important centre, and, along with Faliscan, Umbrian, and OSCAN, Latin belongs to the Italic group of Indo-European languages. Having originally been spoken at Latium from c.800 BC, Latin came to be the dominant language of Italy, and later became the common tongue of the western MEDITERRANEAN world and as far as the Balkans to the east. The diffusion of Latin is a direct reflection of the growing influence of Rome, the city that dominated Italy politically and culturally. Considerable evidence survives which charts the development of Latin from the early legal and senatorial texts to the establishment after the middle of the 3rd century BC of a formal literary language, which is conventionally called classical Latin. The Romans themselves, however, spoke of *sermo urbanus*, a phrase which suggests both 'urbane speech' and 'speech of the city'. The city of Rome was synonymous with the cultural and linguistic achievement of early Italy. In sharp contrast to early Greece, where the literary language reflects the influence of a number of dialects and so a number of regions, other Italian dialects seem to have had little or no influence on the development of Latin literary culture.

The widespread use of Latin to the west seems to mirror the importance of Greek to the east, but the Romans were not linguistically insular. This was partly the result of the powerful influence of both Greek language and Greek culture on the Romans. Although Greece became a subject state in the 2nd century BC, the Romans found models for emulation in Greek culture as they sought to develop a high culture of their own. Despite the extraordinary achievements of many Roman writers, there remained an abiding sense of the inferiority of Latin. Few educated Romans would disagree with T. S. Eliot when he pronounced Greek 'a language which has never been surpassed as a vehicle for the fullest range and the finest shades of thought and feeling'. LUCRETIUS complained repeatedly of 'the poverty of our ancestral speech' (1.831ff.). However great the Roman literary achievement ultimately was, the Greeks on the whole took little interest in it; it remains a matter of controversy whether later Greek poets, such as NONNOS or Quintus, ever read VIRGIL or OVID.

Naturally the Roman empire, which incorporated territory from Britain to Mesopotamia, contained within it a great many other languages, some of local, others of more widespread, importance. For example, Punic was still spoken in North Africa at the time of AUGUSTINE (1), and Semitic languages, such as Aramaic and Syriac, were widespread in the LEVANT. In Europe, Latin never completely displaced native CELTIC and GERMANIC languages; indeed, use of the latter increased in late antiquity, as Germanic peoples established their own kingdoms in former imperial territory. CGB

Laodike see RULER-CULT; SYRIAN WARS, OF PTOLEMIES.

Laodikeian war see SYRIAN WARS, OF PTOLEMIES.

Lares see CHILDHOOD; DEATH; IMPERIAL CULT; RITUAL.

Lars Porsenna When TARQUINIUS SUPERBUS was expelled from Rome in 510 BC, he appealed for help to Lars Porsenna, king of Clusium. The standard accounts (e.g. Livy 2.9–14) represent this as the first test of the new REPUBLIC. In these versions, Horatius Cocles holds the BRIDGE across the TIBER against overwhelming forces, then swims the river in full armour; Gaius MUCIUS Scaevola, captured in an attempt to assassinate Porsenna, thrusts his right hand into a fire (hence earning the name Left-handed), declaring that hundreds of others will follow him against the ETRUSCAN king. Impressed by this display of fortitude, Porsenna diverted his attention to the Latin town of Aricia, where his son Arruns was defeated and killed by the Latins with the help of allies from CUMAE.

TACITUS (*Histories* 3.72) gives a variant tradition in which Porsenna receives the surrender of Rome, implying a far more successful campaign, presumably covered up by patriotic sources. This may be reflected in the fact that some sources date the beginning of the Republic to 507 BC, suggesting an interval of two years between the expulsion of Tarquinius Superbus and the foundation of the Republic. On the other hand, even if this brief intervention happened, Porsenna did not restore Superbus. CJS

See Cornell, T. J. (1995) *The Beginnings of Rome*.

latifundia see AGRICULTURE, ROMAN; LAND AND PROPERTY, ROMAN; SICILY; SLAVERY.

Latins The inhabitants of Latium, a region of c.2,500 sq km (970 sq miles), bordered by the TIBER to the north-west and Campania to the south-east. In legend, their origins stem from a combination of indigenous peoples, a very early Greek presence and the arrival of the Trojans with AENEAS, whose son Ascanius founded Alba Longa. Archaeologically, the Latins emerge as a distinct population around 1000 BC, with Rome and Alba Longa the main centres. Alba Longa remained the focal point of Latin worship, with the great annual festival of JUPITER Latiaris.

In the 6th century Rome extended its influence over its neighbours; at the battle of LAKE REGILLUS and again in 338 the Latin league failed to shake off Roman control. Latins owed a duty to supply soldiers for the Roman army, and had the right to marry Romans and inherit property at Rome; they could also take up CITIZENSHIP in another town by migration.

The alliance held through invasions by neighbouring peoples in the 5th and 4th centuries. After 338 the league was abolished; some Latins became full Roman citizens, others were citizens without the vote at Rome, still others were allowed alliance only with Rome. The success of the policy is attested by Latin loyalty in the HANNIBALIC and SOCIAL WARS. The mutual privileges, which characterized the Latin relationship with Rome, were granted to the colonies which Rome founded throughout Italy. Latium received full citizenship after the Social war, and the term became purely juridical (*ius Latii*) and was extended throughout the empire. CJS

See Sherwin-White, A. N. (1973) *The Roman Citizenship.*

COLONIZATION: (d).

Latium see ITALY, ROMAN; LATINS.

latrines see SANITATION; TOILETS.

Laurion (also spelt Laureion, in antiquity as now) Broadly a triangular region of land in south-eastern ATTICA, from the Pláka pass to the bottom of the peninsula, and also the name of the modern town on the east coast. The region is rich in mineral ores, and the spectacular landscape bears the scars and ruins of extensive and intensive MINING and materials-processing in antiquity and the 19th century. Visitors walking the hills and valleys should beware of ancient mine shafts, many of which are unmarked.

Laurion is one of the driest areas of the MEDITERRANEAN basin, and some of the most conspicuous ruins today were built to collect, distribute and recycle water, without which exploitation of the mineral wealth of the area would have been impossible. Some cisterns lined with hydraulic cement are still waterproof to a greater or lesser depth, more than two millenia after they were built. Water was needed for consumption by the workforce and for industrial processing of the SILVER ore prior to smelting.

The most famous monument in the area is the TEMPLE of POSEIDON at Sounion, on the southernmost tip of the Attic peninsula. At the foot of the cliff on which it stands are the remains of two shipsheds; the SHIPS stationed here were used to relay lookout information to Athens: Sounion is a brisk 8 hours' walk from the city. TER

See Conophagos, C. (1980) *Le Laurium antique*; Photos-Jones, E. and Jones, J. E. (1994) The building and industrial remains at Agrileza, Laurion, *ABSA* 89: 307–58.

ACHAIA, ROMAN.

lavatories see SANITATION; TOILETS.

law

It is difficult to generalize about Greek law. Certain features were shared by a number of city-states. For example, all communities seem to have recognized the importance of oaths, the sanctity of life and person, and a general notion of compensation for loss. They also seem to share a tendency to draw procedural or substantial distinctions according to sex or status. However beyond these general features, the form and substance of each legal system tended to be peculiar to each community.

Communities have long taken an interest in the supervision and regulation of disputes among their members. In our earliest literary example of a trial, the homicide trial on the shield of ACHILLES (*Iliad* 18.497–508), we see a community gathered together to resolve a homicide and negotiate the payment of blood money. The desire to obtain an effective resolution to disputes without relying on the whim or preferences of rulers or magistrates seems to have been one of the major factors in the growth of law. HESIOD in *Works and Days* expresses particular concern about 'crooked judgements' delivered by MAGISTRATES open to bribery and influence. The desire to prevent magistrates from abusing judicial procedure for financial or political gain is reflected in our earliest legal inscriptions, from Dreros in CRETE. Regulation of procedure is a feature shared by a number of other early legal inscriptions from Athens, CHIOS and Eretria. The rate of growth of law is difficult to estimate. A large number of states recorded legends about quasi-historical legislators (e.g. Drakon and SOLON at Athens, Zaleukos at Lokroi Epizephyrioi, and Charondas at Katane (Catana)) who establish complete LAW-CODES for their communities. However, it is difficult to sort the truth from highly embellished later fictions. Scholars debate whether legal systems grew in a piecemeal fashion or were developed complete as a code. It is probable that a combination of both these patterns was responsible for the development of Greek legal systems. Codification, when it happened, occurred partially and sporadically.

Each community's particular history and political development affected the shape of its law. The subject matter regulated by law and the procedure for regulation were both issues that varied from state to state. The Athenian legal system, for example, exhibits a number of features that could be regarded as 'democratic'. Its preference for large citizen juries (often numbering several hundred) appointed by lot, who judged a wide range of cases with minimal involvement from magistrates, accords strongly with a political ideology that valued the consensus of its citizens and gave them a high degree of competence in decision-making. The jury wielded considerable power. There was no appeal from its decisions. In a

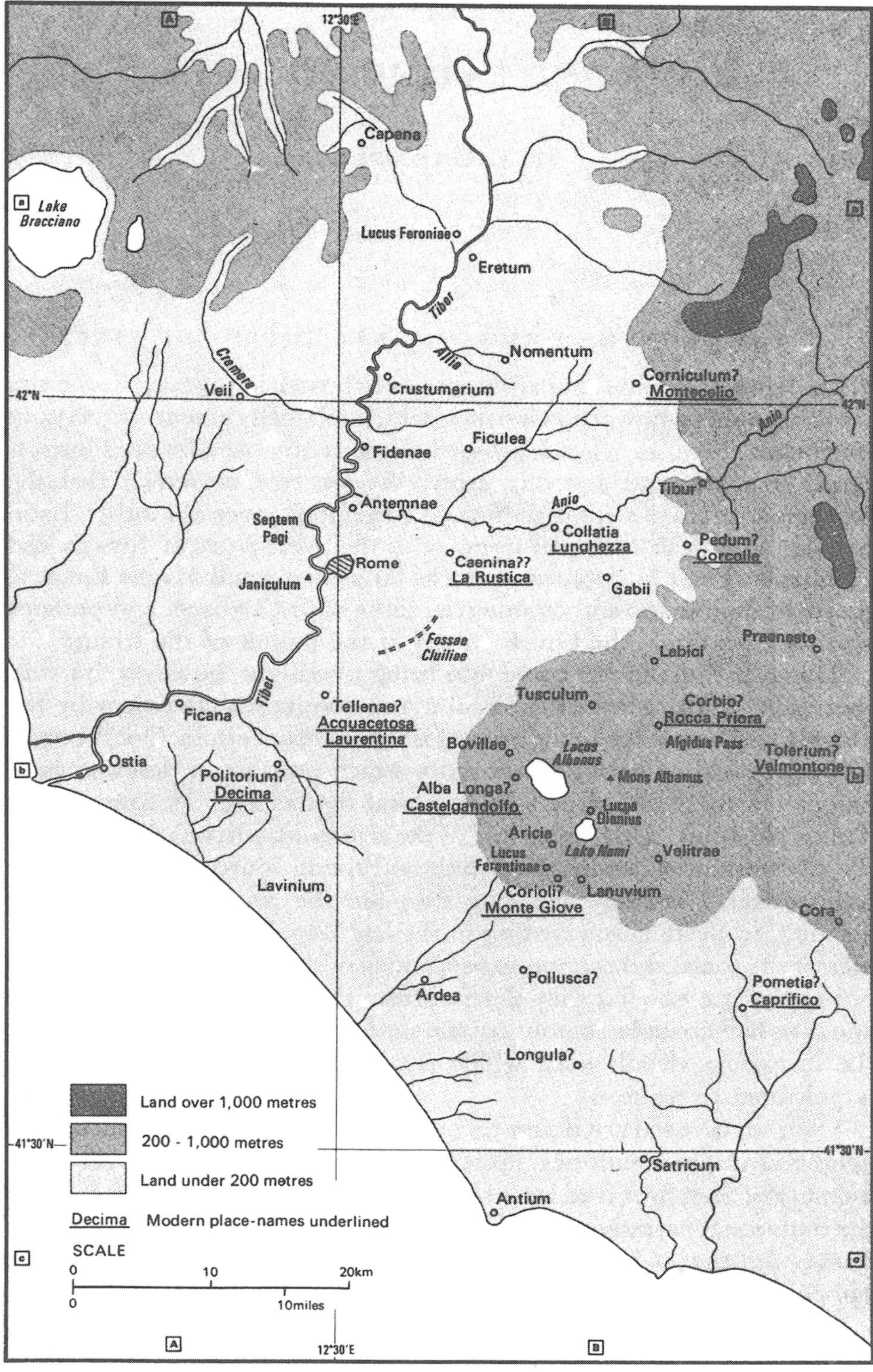

LATINS: map of ancient Latium.

large number of cases, the jury decided the punishment. Democratic explanations can also account for the court's resistance to professionalism and its desire to promote accessibility to the legal system. There were no state-appointed prosecutors in Athens. Trial lawyers did not exist. Instead, individuals were required to prosecute or defend cases themselves. However, there were a number of features to assist them in their action and increase participation in the courts. Laws were not written in excessively technical language. Over-legalistic arguments seem to have been frowned upon. There was a wide variety of procedures available to prosecute the same crime, allowing litigants to tailor their cases to their abilities. Arbitration was officially required for a number of cases so that the matter could be resolved without a trial. Speechwriters (*logographoi*), who could advise on legal issues and write the speech for their client to deliver in court, were available for hire. It was possible to bring along an associate (normally a relative or close friend) to deliver a speech alongside oneself. This desire to increase participation and protect the weak is confirmed by the decision to allow most serious crimes (homicide is the exception) to be prosecuted by 'anybody who wants'. In practice it is hard to find many examples of these public-spirited prosecutors. Most cases seem to be prosecuted by either the party directly affected or enemies hoping to wound an opponent.

We are particularly well informed about the Athenian legal system thanks to the survival of copies of over 100 LAWCOURT speeches, which were preserved as educational examples of forensic ORATORY by later scholars. Admittedly, this form of survival creates some problem in their use as evidence. The speeches are largely limited to the 4th century and come from a small number of speechwriters. The texts do not usually preserve the witnesses' statements or citations of the laws upon which the case was based. The clients tend to be an unrepresentative sample of wealthy members of the ÉLITE. We do not normally know the result of the case or the extent to which the speeches have been modified before publication. Despite these problems, the speeches provide an invaluable insight into Athenian legal procedure, the content and use of legislation, and the types of argumentation used to bolster a case. The requirement that speeches should seem believable and should persuade a large group of citizens have made them particularly interesting to social historians interested in popular morality and social mores. The lawcourt speeches are supplemented by a number of inscriptions. Perhaps the most famous is the reinscription of the homicide laws of Drakon that was undertaken during a revision of the laws begun in 410 BC.

COMEDY has been another important source for reconstructing the Athenian legal environment. One of the continuing themes in comedy is the litigiousness of Athenians. In the *Clouds*, a character jokes that he cannot recognize a MAP of Athens because he can't see the lawcourts (ARISTOPHANES, *Clouds* 207–9). Aristophanes' *Wasps* centres around the relationship between a father passionately devoted to attending the lawcourts and his son's attempts to wean him off this activity. This comedy's portrayal of the jury as impoverished old men, immune to pleas of JUSTICE and only driven by self-interest, reflects comic stereotypes rather than reality.

Evidence for legal systems outside Athens is sparse and patchy, and largely takes the form of inscriptions recording individual provisions. It is often difficult to reconstruct the wider legal framework in which these operated. Sparta and Gortyn are the classical Greek states whose legal systems we know best. For Sparta, our reliance on non-Spartan, often late, literary sources makes reconstruction difficult. The sources tend to romanticize their subject, and it is difficult to determine how many of the provisions they record were actually in use. They tend to describe extraordinary legal events such as the trials of kings and important officials. Apart from these events, most of the other legal material concerns status divisions in society and the Spartan system of education (the *agôgê*). Nevertheless, we do get a picture of a system for the administration of justice that stands in stark contrast to the Athenian. Our knowledge about Gortyn in Crete comes from the long legal inscription discovered there, the 'GORTYN CODE'. It details a comprehensive range of provisions relating to the FAMILY, INHERITANCE, property, mortgages, slavery and legal procedure.

The only rival for Athens in terms of legal sources is hellenistic Egypt. Here we find preserved on PAPYRUS a plethora of legal documents. MARRIAGE contracts, WILLS, financial documents and legal petitions survive in reasonable numbers. The PTOLEMIES instituted a legal system which recognized the Egyptian legal tradition as well as the legal traditions of Greece. In 275 BC, Ptolemy II Philadelphos set up a double network of specialized courts corresponding to the nationality of the litigants. In these courts, royal edicts had priority, but after that judges could impose either Greek or Pharaonic law, depending on the tradition of the litigants. AJLB

See Arnaoutoglou, I. (1998) *Ancient Greek Laws*; Christ, M. R. (1998) *The Litigious Athenian*; Gagarin, M. (1986) *Early Greek Law*; Hölkeskamp, K.-J. (1992) Written law in archaic Greece, *PCPS* 38: 87–117; MacDowell, D. M. (1986) *Spartan Law*; Maehler, H. and Geller, M., eds. (1995) *Legal Documents of the Hellenistic World*; Taubenschlag, R. (1955) *The Law of Greco-Roman Egypt in the Light of the Papyri, 332 BC–640 AD*; Todd, S. C. (1993) *The Shape of Athenian Law*; Willetts, R. F. (1967) *The Law Code of Gortyn*.

Roman law originally resembled law among other ancient peoples in having three main sources: statutes, the injunctions of magistrates, and longstanding custom. All three sources remained important in later periods. Statutes were initially defined as laws passed by the Roman people in ASSEMBLY, but in the empire decrees of the SENATE and legal pronouncements of EMPERORS were also treated as legislation. The annual edict of the urban PRAETOR, Rome's chief judicial magistrate, has particular importance for private law; but other MAGISTRATES, especially provincial governors, had similar edicts of their own. Custom and usage are prominent in many areas, but above all for constitutional law, since in all periods Rome lacked a written constitution.

Where the Romans differed from earlier peoples, and particularly from the Greeks, was in the intellectual consolidation of these sources into a more or less unified body of law (*ius*). This consolidation, at first centred on the law governing lawsuits between private persons, began in the later REPUBLIC with the emergence of the Roman jurists. Originally the jurists were ARISTOCRATIC patrons who, by virtue of their position, were familiar with the operation of Roman courts. Although they had no special legal education, they used their familiarity to dispense advice to clients who were, in turn, expected to provide political support. Already by the 2nd century BC, however, the small community of jurists had begun to publish technical legal commentaries. These legal writings formed a professional literature that rapidly acquired sophistication as the jurists refined their analytical techniques. In the following century the jurists became central to the judicial handling of private lawsuits; the jurists' opinions were accepted as authoritative in part because the central judicial system itself still was entirely lay, without legally trained judges or advocates.

During the first three centuries of the Roman empire, the 'classical' period of Roman law, the emperors generally sponsored and encouraged the jurists as they developed a coherent, rule-based form of judicial decision-making, more or less autonomous from the central government. This development was at first confined to private law, but by the mid-2nd century it spread to other areas, including administrative, tax, and criminal law. The greatest Roman jurists – Celsus, Julian, Scaevola, Papinian, ULPIAN and Paul deserve special mention – acquired not only immense legal authority but also a degree of access to power, though the Roman state itself never knew the rule of law in the modern sense.

Classical Roman jurisprudence is preserved mainly through the *Digest*, a collection of lightly edited excerpts from juristic writings. The *Digest*, which is over 800,000 words in length, was assembled on the order of the early Byzantine emperor JUSTINIAN, who promulgated it as law in AD 533. This work is undoubtedly the single most influential source in the Western legal tradition. Within the *Digest*, the intelligence of the jurists is on constant display as they analyse and debate, in intricate and sometimes wearisome detail, the institutions of Roman law. By and large, the style of the jurists was to set a hypothetical problem (sometimes suggested by a real case) that illustrated a significant question of law, and then to pronounce a decision on that question, often with a sketchy explanation of the ruling. This method is daunting to the inexperienced; but with time and patience one learns to work out the larger conceptual framework within which the jurists are operating. The jurists have little sympathy for highly abstract speculation, nor do they discuss jurisprudential method except in passing. Instead, they prefer to concentrate on the specific. This quality gives their law a considerable resilience and doctrinal flexibility, qualities that have long been esteemed as the sources of its power and endurance. During the first three centuries of the empire, the circle of eminent jurists at Rome was very small, probably fewer than 20 at any point in time. But the jurists were astonishingly productive; more than 300 'books' (PAPYRUS rolls) are attributed to the late classical jurist Ulpian alone, on an enormous range of subjects. Nearly three-fifths of the *Digest* is drawn from Ulpian and his equally productive contemporary Paul, both of whom, however, often cite earlier jurists.

During the early empire, legal knowledge gradually spread outward from the circle of jurists. Not until the 2nd century AD, however, did this spread result in a more systematic approach to legal education; and then the development took place, as it seems, mainly in the Eastern PROVINCES, where knowledge of Roman law became necessary as provincials were gradually granted ROMAN CITIZENSHIP. For us, at least, the central figure in the emergence of legal education is GAIUS, a jurist who seems not to have been recognized by the jurists at Rome. His works, which date to the mid-2nd century, may have been written in Beirut, where the first formal law school was organized in the following century. Of Gaius' works, by far the most significant is the *Institutes*, an elementary textbook that is the only work of classical jurisprudence surviving virtually intact; it also provided the basis for Justinian's *Institutes*. Probably for pedagogical purposes, Gaius imposed on Roman private law a powerful new dogmatic organization that is wholly unlike most juristic works in its clarity and simplicity. This organization, which was eventually reinterpreted as a statement of radical liberalism in private law, has remained characteristic of later legal systems that are strongly influenced by Roman law.

Although classical Roman law is strongly associated with juristic writings, their rulings were complemented, especially from the 2nd century on, by imperial rulings on questions of law. These decisions took several forms, but the most prominent was the rescript, a brief answer to a query put by a magistrate or a private citizen. The emperors may originally have intended these rescripts as nothing more than restatements of the law as it existed. However, because of their source, imperial rescripts rapidly acquired legislative force, and by the 2nd century important innovations were being effected through rescripts; jurists, serving as imperial secretaries, advised the emperors in their drafting. Imperial innovations often tend to expand the conceptual range of traditional Roman law. Rescripts were frequently collected in the later empire, but our major source for them is the second edition of Justinian's *Codex*, which was promulgated in 534. Imperial intervention also took the form of a new judicial system parallel to the traditional lay courts, but associated with magistrates and governors who were ultimately responsible to the emperor. This new system has a markedly more modern legal appearance than the older private law of the urban praetor. Above all, it permitted appeal from trial verdicts that litigants regarded as legally questionable.

By the early 3rd century the emperor and his judicial council, which often included prominent jurists, was regularly hearing important cases. For reasons that are unclear, the circle of eminent jurists at Rome dwindled to an end in 235 or so, just as the empire was plunged into political crisis. However, the legal revolution that the jurists had brought about was by this date strong enough to survive on its own, particularly in the law schools of the East, but also in the West. Most innovations now took place through numerous imperial rescripts or decrees, which were mainly directed toward administrative matters; but the emperors remained reasonably faithful to the substance of classical private law, even though the older procedure had by this time been abolished. Jurisprudence also continued, but often on a disappointingly pedestrian level, with a proliferation of works excerpted from classical writings. Still, the way was being prepared for the great codifying work of Justinian.

Beginning with the European rediscovery of the *Digest* in the late 11th century, Roman law has worked its way deeply into the fabric of the Western legal tradition. For this reason, objectivity about its benefits for the Romans themselves is today hard to obtain. The jurists, as legal professionals, were frequent targets of satire, and the Romans often treat their judicial system itself with aversion or contempt. Nonetheless, they seem generally proud of their law, and even generally aware of its enormous historical importance. Apart from any incidental benefits law may have offered in governance, the utility of Roman law lay, perhaps, less in its austere intellectual qualities than in the promise it offered of rule-based adjudication. As shared cultural values slipped away within a vast and diverse empire, the jurists offered the substitute of social integration through shared law. Simultaneously, however, the flexibility of their thinking permitted the jurists to accommodate many smaller social demands, thus obviating resort to the cumbersome legislative process. Ironically, then, the strength of Roman law was both its stability as an autonomous 'professional' discipline and its capacity to change in response to social needs. In the end, however, it is important not to overestimate the jurists' achievement. As an expression of Roman upper class culture, Roman law often appears rather hyper-developed in relation to the empire's crude social and economic institutions. Many hundreds of years would pass before the full potential of the Roman legal revolution was finally realized. BWF

See Buckland, W.W. (1964) *A Text-Book of Roman Law from Augustus to Justinian*; Crook, J. A. (1984) *The Law and Life of Rome*; Frier, B.W. (1985) *The Rise of the Roman Jurists*; Harries, J. and Wood, I., eds. (1993) *The Theodosian Code*; Honoré, T. (1994) *Emperors and Lawyers*; (1998) *Law in the Crisis of Empire 379–455 AD: the Theodosian dynasty and its quaestors*; Jolowicz, H. F. and Nicholas, B. (1972) *Historical Introduction to the Study of Roman Law*; Matthews, J. F. (2000) *Laying Down the Law: a study of the Theodosian Code*; Wolff, H. J. (1976) *Roman Law*.

law-codes From the later 7th century BC onwards, the growing complexity of life in many communities of MEDITERRANEAN Europe prompted the development of more detailed rules of public conduct. Such innovations were localized, spasmodic and highly varied, only much later occasionally becoming comprehensive enough to be called 'codes'. Format, content, validating authority and medium of transmission also showed wide variation, though no 'code' from the Greco-Roman world had quite so complex a history as that reflected in the Pentateuch of the OLD TESTAMENT. Likewise, few 'codes' from antiquity appear to have aimed for, still less attained, the degree of applicability and comprehensiveness with which the Code Napoléon or the German Civil Code are credited, though Athenian law after 399 may have been comparable in range (if less lucid). For convenience, the material may be loosely grouped into a series of 'movements'.

The first comprises the early codes attested in the literary tradition. These include the royal laws of Rome; the laws of 'Lykourgos' at Sparta, or of the western Greek lawgivers Zaleukos of Lokroi and Charondas of Katane; the 'laws' and customs of the CRETAN states; the work of Drakon and SOLON at Athens; and others. Our evidence comes indirectly, via reports in later HISTORIANS, ORATORS, PHILOSOPHERS and ANTIQUARIANS, and is of very dubious reliability, attributed to figures of sometimes uncertain historicity. Their provisions, moreover, are repeatedly said to have been divinely inspired, as when Numa held nocturnal communion with Egeria or Zaleukos was inspired by ATHENA. All sources report the Great Rhetra of Sparta as an oracle from APOLLO at DELPHI. That is not to deny the reality or durability of the customs and procedures encapsulated in these codes, for the creation of stability was a major theme of the tradition, emphatically so in respect of the wholly unwritten 'code' of classical Sparta. Rather, their formulations were ways of describing the processes of early state formation and of providing a charter myth to legitimate the results.

The documents cut on STONE and bronze which begin in the mid-7th century in Greece (but barely at all in Italy until much later) present a very different picture. Initially terse, later fuller, they all record specific provisions, mostly on a single topic such as the SACRIFICES to be made at a shrine, the duties of a MAGISTRACY, or the law about a particular procedure (e.g. ML 2 and 8). Longer and more systematic documents did come to exist, such as the transmitted portion of Drakon's code (ML 86) or the Roman TWELVE TABLES. Solon's systematization of Athenian law in the early 6th century was real enough, written on real objects, even if much interpolated matter has accrued in the attributed fragments. At least two other documents in this group may qualify in some sense as 'codes', the GORTYN CODE and the re-codification of Athenian law in 410–399. The former, however, was far from being a complete reformulation of all Gortynian law. The latter, though leaving substantial extant EPIGRAPHIC remains and reflected in two speeches (Andokides 1.71–89: LYSIAS 30), may never have been completed, yielding instead the intricate web of overlapping provisions and procedures which is visible in the 4th century.

By the later 5th century BC the roles of lawgiver, town-planner, colony-founder, and philosopher had converged sufficiently to generate a very different agenda, in the form of written descriptions of the ideal state, complete with ideal law-code. The clearest extant examples are PLATO's *Republic* and *Laws*, each purporting to provide a complete blueprint of how a state could so order itself as to maximize the *aretê* of its citizens. The genre, once created, was to have an endless progeny, but also seriously infected the literary tradition about the early lawgivers, as with the alleged influence of PYTHAGORAS on Zaleukos and Numa. Sadly, the extant fragments of the 24 books of THEOPHRASTOS' *Nomoi* leave undetermined whether his material was already infected.

Although the hellenistic kingdoms needed legal systems of some kind, and though Ptolemaic edicts went some way towards creating a code, the deep-rooted tradition, in Macedonia as in the LEVANT, of king as both judge and embodied law prevented any recognizable codification. The new royal city-foundations, however, must have been provided with law-codes of some kind. Regrettably, there is usable information only for ALEXANDRIA, which appears to have used a combination of Athenian and Rhodian law.

Although Greek cities continued to create new laws on specific subjects, from the 3rd century BC onwards Rome and Italy became the arena of most innovative work, both in extending the scope and detail of law and in its (re-)codification. One prime component of the latter came to be the edict of the urban PRAETOR, formally valid only for his year of office but informally transmitting a stable set of supplements to current statutory civil law. The process of gradual supplementation extended from the 2nd century BC until a definitive codified text was created c.AD 130 on HADRIAN's instructions. Meanwhile, two further processes aided the systematization of law. One comprised the drafting of formal laws, many due directly or indirectly to CAESAR or AUGUSTUS, which codified the law on specific topics (e.g. the *lex Aelia Sentia de manumissionibus*). The other was jurist-made 'law', which interacted with EMPERORS' edicts and rescripts to provide the vast mass of commentaries from which the codes of the late empire were compiled. However, this material itself came to need maps and guidebooks. Compilations of constitutions and *decreta* (decrees) were made by various jurists, as were two unofficial codifications of imperial laws by Gregorianus and Hermogenianus in the 290s. The *THEODOSIAN CODE* of 438 is the first imperially ordered codification, followed from 528 onwards by the *Codes*, *Digest*, *Institutes* and *Novels* of JUSTINIAN. JKD

See Adcock, F. E. (1927) Literary tradition and early Greek codemakers, *Cambridge Historical Journal* 2: 95–109; Camassa, G. (1996) *I Greci* 2.2, 561–76; Crawford, M. H. (1996) *Roman Statutes*; Dow, S. (1960) The Athenian calendar of sacrifices: the chronology of Nikomakhos' second term, *Historia* 9: 270–93; Effenterre, H. van and Ruzé, F. (1994) *Nomima*, 2 vols.; Fraser, P. M. (1972) *Ptolemaic Alexandria*, vol. 1; Gagarin, M. (1986) *Early Greek Law*; Harries, J. and Wood, I., eds. (1993) *The Theodosian Code*; Harrison, A. R.W. (1998) *The Law of Athens*, 2 vols.; Jolowicz, H. F. and Nicholas, B. (1972) *Historical Introduction to the Study of Roman Law*; Lenger, M.-T. (1964–90) *Corpus des ordonnances des Ptolémées*; Link, S. (1992) Die Gesetzgebung des Zaleukos im epizephyrischen Lokroi, *Klio* 74: 11–24; MacDowell, D. M. (1986) *Spartan Law*; Robertson, N. (1990) The laws of Athens, 410–399 BC, *JHS* 110: 43–75; Ruschenbusch, E. (1966) *Solonos Nomoi*; Szegedy-Maszak, A. (1981) *The Nomoi of Theophrastus*; Todd, S. C. (1993) *The Shape of Athenian Law*.

GORTYN CODE.

lawcourts

In ancient Athens the first law courts were tribunals located in the offices of individual MAGISTRATES, who would judge cases presented to them, in much the same fashion as the *dikastas* of the GORTYN code. There was no appeal against a magistrate's decision. The first courts composed of a body of jurors were connected with homicide. Under Drakon's homicide law, the *ephetai*, 51 men of WEALTH and distinction, judged cases of unintentional and lawful homicide at the Palladion and Delphinion respectively; the AREIOPAGOS, a council of ex-archons, judged cases of intentional homicide. But these bodies were aristocratic in nature.

The first popular lawcourt was created by SOLON (594 BC), who introduced the right of appeal against a magistrate's judicial decision. The appeal was heard by the *hêliaia*, a court composed of ordinary citizens; it was perhaps the ASSEMBLY (*ekklêsia*) sitting in a judicial capacity to judge cases of appeal. Probably the magistrate himself presided over the trial. The *hêliaia* not only had the right to overturn the magistrate's decision, but in some cases where it confirmed his decision it could impose an additional penalty, as in Solon's theft law. Under Ephialtes' reforms (462/1 BC) the *hêliaia* ceased to be a court of appeal and became a court of first instance, where cases automatically were referred for trial by the magistrate who initially received the charge. Except in cases involving very small claims, the magistrate lost his right to judge and was reduced to the administrative role of preparing the case for court by hearing the summons and conducting a preliminary hearing; he then presided over the trial. The growing litigation that resulted from these reforms led to the *hêliaia* being divided into smaller judicial panels (*dikastêria*). The Athenians adopted the practice of selecting at the beginning of the year 6,000 citizens, over 30 years of age, to swear the heliastic oath and serve as jurors (*dikastai*). Each juror was randomly assigned to a single court, such as the archon's court, for the year, and heard only cases before that particular court. On occasion the assembly could convene special courts of 1,000 or 1,500 drawn from the whole body of 6,000 jurors, but the smaller courts perhaps consisted of panels of 500.

Corruption led the Athenians to refine the selection process early in the 4th century. Jurors were no longer assigned to a single court, but were divided among ten panels, each designated by a letter (alpha to kappa). On a day courts were in session each jury panel was allotted to a particular court. In this period we hear of courts of 500 or multiples thereof.

In the 370s the system was revamped again, resulting in a complicated process of jury selection described in detail in Aristotle's *Constitution of the Athenians* (63–5). At the beginning of the year every juror selected for the year was given an identity ticket made of bronze, later of boxwood, bearing his name, his DEME name, and a letter (alpha to kappa). By 340 the court buildings were arranged in a complex, located in the north-east corner of the AGORA, that could be cordoned off; it had ten entrances, one for each tribe. On the morning of a court session, eligible jurors would present themselves before their tribal entrance. Their tickets were inserted into the lottery machines used to select the number of jurors needed to man the courts on that particular day. Not all jurors who showed up were selected, but each juror who was would then draw an acorn bearing a letter (lambda and above) corresponding to a court designated that morning by the same letter. Under this system no one knew in advance how panels would be composed, what cases they would try, or what court they would sit in. Even the magistrates responsible for bringing to trial the cases introduced to them were also assigned to courts at random. The archons oversaw the whole selection process, while the *thesmothêtai* determined the number of courts and jurors needed and the types of cases to be heard on any given day. Public suits required at least 501 jurors, private suits 201 or 401 depending on the size of the claim. Public trials lasted at most a day, but as many as four private suits could be heard by a single jury panel in a day.

To prevent pollution from contact with the accused killer in a confined space, homicide courts were open-air sites located at sacred shrines. Ordinary courts were roofed structures, like the Odeion, a music THEATRE which once served as the archon's court, or the Stoa Poikile (Painted STOA) and other colonnaded buildings that at times served as courts. Both open and enclosed courts allowed curious spectators, cordoned off from jurors and litigants, to stand and view proceedings. These were often noisy affairs, as onlookers or jurors seated on benches reacted to a litigant's statement, even interrupting him. Sometimes litigants encouraged bystanders and jurors to respond to questions put to them. Litigants would have supporters in the audience, with friends and relatives sitting close by the speaker's platform (*bêma*) from which litigants delivered their speeches and witnesses their testimony. Often litigants would call supporters forward to speak on their behalf, or parade wives and children before the jurors to elicit sympathy. But at the heart of proceedings were the litigants' speeches, whose length was measured by a water-clock (*klepsydra*). Each litigant had the same amount of time to give his account of events, introduce evidence such as witnesses and laws, argue his case, and in some private suits deliver a short rebuttal. After the speeches the jurors voted without discussion or instruction from the presiding magistrate. A simple majority determined the outcome. CC

See Boegehold, A. (1995) *The Lawcourts at Athens*; MacDowell, D. M. (1978) *The Law in Classical Athens*.

Two models lie behind most of the ways in which JUSTICE was administered at Rome: the arbitrator acceptable to both parties to a dispute, and the father of a family (*paterfamilias*) calling upon his friends to advise him in dealing with offences or CRIMES committed within his *familia*, which included his grown-up children and FREEDMEN as well as his SLAVES. In the vast majority of civil law cases the urban or peregrine PRAETOR remanded the disputants to a non-professional judge agreed on by the parties or, when there was disagreement, imposed by himself. In a few situations, particularly those involving the alleged use of VIOLENCE or armed gangs, a mini-jury of three to five 'recoverers' (*recuperatores*) was allotted. The parties could employ advocates. Most of the other forms of judicature followed the second pattern: for example, the provincial governor with his council, and under the empire the city and praetorian prefects with their assessors, the EMPEROR himself with his 'friends' (*amici Caesaris*) – a privy council – and the praetor or other judge presiding over the centumviral court which handled INHERITANCE and some other cases. The chief exception to these models was the use in the Republican period of the popular ASSEMBLIES to handle misdeeds with political implications, normally but not exclusively *perduellio*, a term covering a wide range of offences against the state. Lesser offences were handled by the *concilium plebis*, the more 'democratic' of the assemblies, where conviction resulted in a fine. Graver misdeeds came before the centuriate assembly (*comitia centuriata*), organized with a bias in favour of the wealthy, and here the penalty was capital in the Roman sense, that is to say in most cases tantamount to EXILE. The assembly courts are interesting in that they provide the only example of a Roman jurisdiction where a system of public prosecution was institutionalized. Prosecutions had to be initiated by a MAGISTRATE, in the historical period usually a TRIBUNE. Assembly prosecutions become much less frequent after Sulla's dictatorship (81–80 BC) and certainly did not outlast the Republic. They were cumbersome and from 149 BC an alternative simpler system of criminal justice grew up.

The new system, by 63 BC, consisted of seven permanent criminal courts (*quaestiones perpetuae*), dealing with extortion in the PROVINCES by officials (*repetundae*), misuse of public funds (*peculatus*), electoral corruption (*ambitus*), the forging of COINAGE and WILLS, treason (*maiestas*), MURDER with a weapon or by poisoning and breaches of the peace (*vis*). The emperor AUGUSTUS added an eighth to deal with ADULTERY; some other offences, like kidnapping and particularly heinous examples of assault, may have been dealt with by one or other of these courts. The language used of them suggests that they too were derived from the second model but with the crucial difference that the final decision was made by the council or jury, not by the president. These courts bear a certain resemblance to a modern criminal court with juries sitting under the direction of a judge and barristers appearing for plaintiff and defendant. This similarity is enhanced by the (edited) speeches which CICERO as counsel, usually for the defence, delivered, mainly before the courts concerned with homicide, breaches of the peace and extortion in the provinces. Their RHETORIC reminds the reader of a type of advocacy common until the 1930s on both sides of the Atlantic. It is therefore most important to emphasize the differences. First, there were separate courts for each crime. Admittedly, there was some overlap: carrying an offensive weapon was a crime under both the homicide law and the law dealing with breaches of the peace; conspiring to pervert the course of justice in a capital trial was in certain cases an offence under both the homicide law and the law relating to extortion in the provinces by officials. But rather than pursue someone successively in two courts (as happened to Milo in 52, convicted successively in the court dealing with breaches of the peace and the court dealing with electoral corruption), a prosecutor might include material not strictly relevant to the court in question. For example, the prosecutor in the trial of Aulus Cluentius in 66 accused him in the homicide court not only of murdering his stepfather but also of bribing a jury in 74 to convict the latter of attempting to murder Cluentius, though the homicide law's provisions in that field applied only to senators and Cluentius was a member of the EQUESTRIAN order. Second, there was no law of evidence; the president of the court (*quaesitor*) was not a legal expert but a career politician – a praetor for the more politically sensitive courts like those dealing with treason and electoral corruption, normally an ex-AEDILE for the murder and breach of the peace courts. His role was limited to ensuring that the legal requirements for the proper conduct of the trial were met. He had no power to rule on the interpretation of the law or to exclude irrelevant matter from advocates' speeches. Nor could he or the jury take into consideration mitigating circumstances by varying the penalty; for example, once convicted of homicide a defendant had to go into exile, whether or not there were extenuating circumstances. This flaw in the system led to the acquittal of guilty defendants. Prosecutions were always undertaken by individual citizens, usually either by ambitious politicians or by someone adversely affected by the behaviour of the defendant. Eligibility for jury service was confined to the equestrian order for most of the period between 123 and 81 BC, to the senatorial order between 81 and 70 BC and thereafter to a mix of the better-off citizens. Juries, though smaller than those in Athens, were larger than ours; the jury in a trial in 74 consisted of 34 senators. In 55 with a larger pool of jurors drawn from both the senatorial and the equestrian order the number was 75.

The permanent courts began in the 1st century AD to be replaced by the jurisdiction of the city prefect, later also by that of the praetorian prefect for the rest of Italy. They did not finally disappear until the 3rd century. The prefects' courts were felt to be less open to bribery, quicker and more impartial. To a limited extent they could show flexibility in imposing penalties. JDC

See Crook, J. A. (1967) *Law and Life of Rome*; (1995) *Legal Advocacy in the Roman World*; Jones, A. H. M. (1972) *The Criminal Courts of the Roman Republic and Principate*; Kelly, J. M. (1976) *Studies in the Civil Judicature of the Roman Republic*; Robinson, O. F. (1996) *The Criminal Law of Ancient Rome*.

lead Used for a wide range of purposes both on its own and alloyed with other metals (principally COPPER). It is relatively easy to smelt and can be easily worked into shape for a variety of functions: some utilize its softness (such as pipes for PLUMBING), others use its high density (e.g. weights, plumb-bobs or net sinkers). Most lead, however, was added to copper alloys to ensure that the molten alloy was as fluid as possible during casting. This was especially important when casting large and complex objects such as statues. Lead was regularly added to the alloys used for archaic and classical Greek statuary, and during the Roman empire considerable quantities of lead were added to most cast alloys used in the production of copper-alloy LAMPS, tableware, MUSICAL INSTRUMENTS and other products.

The Roman concern with the provision of water in towns led to the use of vast quantities of lead for pipes and cisterns. The lead would be cast into sheets which would be rolled up in to pipes and welded (the low melting point of lead, 327 °C, made this a simple process). The sections of pipe could then be joined together. The use of lead for pipes and PEWTER has generated some study of the possibility of lead poisoning and its effects, but the issue remains controversial. In antiquity, inhabitants were probably not generally aware of the toxic effects, though VITRUVIUS (8.6.10–11) discusses the quality of water flowing through different kinds of pipes.

Lead was, perhaps, most significant in the ancient world not as a metal in its own right but as a source of SILVER. Most lead ores contain some silver and this can be extracted by the cupellation process. Some of the lead produced may simply have been a by-product of the extraction of silver. DD

See Nriagu, J. O. (1983) *Lead and Lead Poisoning in Antiquity*.

 PLUMBING.

lead pipes see *INSTRUMENTUM DOMESTICUM*; LEAD; PLUMBING.

leadership see ARISTOCRACY; BISHOPS; COLONIZATION; ÉLITES; EMPERORS, ROMAN; GENERALS; OFFICERS, MILITARY; POLITICAL PARTICIPATION; PRIESTS AND PRIESTESSES; STRATEGY.

leather and leatherworking Deriving from the skins of ANIMALS such as GOATS, CATTLE and SHEEP, there is much historical and ARCHAEOLOGICAL evidence for the widespread use of leather in the classical world, including clothing, footwear, military equipment such as shields and ARMOUR, sails, tents and containers for liquids such as WINE and water. In order for skins to be made into leather it is necessary to subject them to a number of noxious processes designed to preserve them and render them impervious to the decaying actions of nature. Only a part of an animal skin is suitable to be made into leather. This is the corium, the middle layer of the three that make up the skin, the other two being the outer layer, the epidermis, and the inner layer of fatty tissue. The first part of the process involves the separation of the corium from the other two layers by scraping or soaking in water or an alkaline solution, or by the use of LIME.

Once this has been completed, the preservation process proper can begin. True tanning of hides involves the use of agents which produce tannin, the majority of those used by classical tanners being of vegetable origin. THEOPHRASTOS in his *Enquiry into Plants* and PLINY THE ELDER in his *Natural History* provide a great deal of information on the plant products used for this purpose, including oak galls, the roots of the sumach and lotus trees and the bark of the alder, among others. Before the actual tanning is carried out, the hide can be treated with an infusion of dung in order to make it swell. The tanning process then involved the skins being soaked in a tank containing a solution of the vegetable tanning agents.

Other methods of preservation included the use of OIL, which was rubbed into the hide, as referred to by HOMER in the *Iliad* (17.436) when describing the fight for the body of Patroklos, and smoke, where skins were hung over a fire or in a smoke-filled room, which treated the hides with aldehydes. Minerals such as SALT and alum were also used as preservatives for skins, as indicated by Pliny's referral to sails treated with ALUM in his *Natural History*. These latter

LEATHER AND LEATHER WORK: Greek vase painting of a leather-worker cutting out shoes.

methods, using oil, smoke and minerals, were not true tanning, and were not permanent, since their effects could be reversed through prolonged soaking in water. These processes can be combined, with the hide being treated with more than one method of preservation. Archaeological investigation has revealed tanneries in such places as POMPEII.

Following the preservation process, the leather was often decorated. This could be done by DYEING, though the leather was sometimes coloured during tanning as a result of a particular tanning agent used. Decorative patterns could also be burned, inscribed or beaten onto leather. MDM

See Forbes, R. J. (1966) *Studies in Ancient Technology*, vol. 5; Hodges, H. (1964) *Artifacts: an introduction to early materials and technology*.

 SHOES.

Lefkandí A major Bronze and early Iron Age site on the south-west coast of EUBOIA, on the Lelantine plain between Eretria and Chalkis. The main settlement is at Xerópolis, and there are five cemeteries, of which the richest is at Toúmba.

At Xerópolis there are late Neolithic and early Helladic II remains, but the main occupation dates from the end of the 3rd millennium BC, with the apparent arrival of an intrusive new population from ANATOLIA, until the Geometric period. During the middle Helladic period (earlier 2nd millennium BC) it was probably a large town of some importance and had close relations with THESSALY and BOIOTIA. The most important period of occupation is during the so-called Dark Ages, following the collapse of the Bronze Age palaces around 1200. During late Helladic IIIC (c.1200–1100) the site was home to an elaborate and fantastic pictorial pottery style. Around 1100 the site was briefly abandoned; the subsequent Submycenaean reoccupation may have been by new peoples. The most important and prosperous phase is during the Protogeometric period (10th–9th centuries), when Lefkandí was an important bronze-working centre and there is considerable evidence for trade with Thessaly, Macedonia (VERGINA), ATTICA and the east MEDITERRANEAN, especially CYPRUS. From around 900 the inhabitants began to put luxury trinkets – faience and GOLD JEWELLERY – in their TOMBS. The site was destroyed and abandoned around 700, possibly in the conflict between Eretria and Chalkis, the so-called Lelantine war.

At Toúmba a monumental apsidal building nearly 50 m long has been excavated. It was erected around 1000 BC and is the first significant post-Bronze Age building in Greece. After its abandonment, the building was used for the cremation BURIAL of an important man, apparently a warrior (perhaps the local chief), accompanied by a wealthy female inhumation and three or four HORSES. It was then covered with a large tumulus. The building is now generally known as the Heroön ('hero-shrine'), but an alternative interpretation is that it was a royal house converted into a burial place. (see also HUMAN SACRIFICE) LFS

See Popham, M. R. et al. (1979–) *Lefkandi*, 3 vols. (in progress); (1982) The hero of Lefkandi, *Antiquity* 56: 169–74.

legacies The modern European will is mostly concerned with the correct legal transfer of property to the direct descendants, usually children. The Roman WILL has the same concerns, but in addition it is characterized by the sharing out of portions from the estate to individuals other than the instituted heir or heirs. The recipients could be wives, children and relatives, but also SLAVES, FREEDMEN, friends and other individuals not connected to the deceased by blood. There was always the problem that the legacies might exhaust the estate so as to leave the heir nothing, and a number of laws tried to protect the heir from such developments. The *lex Furia testamentaria* (between 204 and 169 BC) set a limit on the size of the legacy allocated to one person, certain relatives excepted. The *lex Voconia* (169 BC) enacted that no person should take in the form of a legacy more than the heirs. Finally, the *lex Falcidia* (41 BC) laid down that a testator could not give more than three-fourths in legacies, and thus a fourth was secured to the heir.

Including a friend in a will was a mark of supreme honour, and omission could be regarded as a serious slight on the reputation of the individual thus excluded. The custom was to name a friend as a substitute heir, followed by the subsequent award of a legacy. Apart from land, slaves and personal belongings, special forms of legacies included the award of amounts of cash or small amounts of GOLD and SILVER, not in the form of worked metal, but as bullion. The size of most legacies was small compared to the overall size of the estate; it was the symbolic value that mattered most. CICERO records with evident satisfaction that he continued to receive legacies from friends at the time when he was in exile. His mention in their wills was a tribute to his political stature and a true comfort when his fortunes were low. An even stronger contrast with modern European wills was the Roman practice of leaving a legacy to high-powered or famous Romans. PLINY THE YOUNGER was extremely pleased that he and his friend TACITUS were mentioned together in the wills of the same people, and that they received similar amounts.

Naming the emperor in one's will as one of the legatees was a mark of honour under a good *princeps* and a mark of moral decay under a bad one. In his will AUGUSTUS recalled that in the previous 20 years he had received 1,400 million *sestertii* in inheritances and legacies. The imperial PALACE had a special department recording these legacies. No testament surviving on PAPYRUS or on stone actually names the emperor, which suggests that the concern was mostly a matter of the well-to-do living in Rome.

Some testators earmarked a specific legacy to their communities in the form of a posthumous BENEFACTION. The amount of money thus set aside could be used for the erection of a building, as a one-off gift, or to establish a foundation for the provision of an annual benefaction. MK

See Champlin, E. (1991) *Final Judgments*.

legions Sources for the early legion (POLYBIOS, LIVY, PLUTARCH) are a patchwork of useful and misleading detail. However, the term *legio* ('levy') referred at first to the whole army of Rome, 3,000 infantry and 300 cavalry drawn from three tribes. In the 6th century BC king SERVIUS TULLIUS supposedly reorganized men into five infantry classes based on wealth, so a legion of 4,000 infantry and 600 CAVALRY was created based on centuries of 100 men. During

LEGIONS: (a) a barbarian's perspective on the Roman army!

the Veian war (406–396 BC) the legion was expanded to 6,000 plus 1,800, then major reorganization, traditionally attributed to Furius Camillus, shaped the formation for almost the next 300 years. Legionaries (*legionarii*) were organized in 60-man centuries under centurions, paired in 'handfuls' (*manipuli*) of 120. The legion was drawn up behind a screen of light infantry (*leves*, *velites*) in distinct parallel lines of *manipuli*, designated, from front to back, *hastati* ('spearmen'), *principes* ('principal men') and *triarii* ('third' men). The pressures of the Pyrrhic, PUNIC and Iberian wars led to an increase in numbers of legions and to very high proportions of the citizen body being recruited at times of crisis. Thus by 362 BC the organization had been replicated into two 'legions', by 311 into four, two commanded by each CONSUL. Six tribunes served in each *legio*. Four or five legions operated during the first Punic war; four consular legions plus seven in 217–216; twenty legions in 214–203; reduced to six in 199. *Legionarii* normally served for six years but could be called up for a maximum of 16. Allied infantry seems to have adopted a similar legionary organization and to have drawn up in battle on the wings (*alae sociorum*) of the Roman legions.

Polybios provided the first reliable and coherent picture, writing in the 160s, of legionary strength, organization, service and equipment. Now there were ten *manipuli* each of *hastati* and *principes*, and ten centuries of *triarii*, giving 1,200, 1,200 and 600 respectively, plus a likely 1,200 *velites* and 300 cavalry, for an overall total of 4,500 men. There was a minimum property qualification but infantry and cavalry were paid expenses during service. As always before, the poorest people (*capite censi*, 'counted by head') were excluded. Theoretically each legion existed for a campaign season and with each call-up (*dilectus*) each body of men was numbered in sequence. In fact some were retained in existence for years in specific theatres. Individual soldiers served in different formations in different years, but the frequency and longevity of conflicts meant that a core of veteran individuals built up. MARIUS was the next credited 'reformer', learning from the JUGURTHINE WAR and under pressure from northern barbarians, though institutional changes occurred over the course of the 2nd century. The property qualification was lowered, then abolished, allowing in the *capite censi* manpower. The *velites* no longer appear under that title, but integral light infantry (*antesignani*) continued through the later Republic and beyond. A variety of animal standards was replaced at this time by a single eagle (*aquila*), the bird of JUPITER, for each legion. Most importantly for the future a new legionary subdivision appeared, the cohort (*cohors*), made up of three grouped *manipuli* (six centuries of 80 men). Already mentioned by Polybios, this became the tactical unit of manoeuvre and detachment. CAESAR generally thought in terms of numbers of *cohortes* rather than *legiones*, and never referred to *manipuli*. Yet the cohort took its centuries as a front-to-back slice of the old three lines, not six exclusively from one line; thus it was a microcosm of the legion.

During the CIVIL WARS the numbers of legions again grew, many being recruited by individual GENERALS bending the rules of 'citizen' recruitment. Legions moved between regions and were incorporated in victors' armies. They tended to retain their numbers and some started to take on *ad hoc* titles such as Martia, Equestris and Antiqua. Caesar's *Commentaries*, ANTONY's pre-Actium coins and a growing body of funerary inscriptions make it possible to trace the early histories of these formations. After ACTIUM there were up to 60 legions which were reduced down to 28, some new or reconstituted legions being entitled Augusta, amalgamations giving rise to the title 'Twin' (Gemina). ZODIAC animals were adopted as badges and carried as standards, usually reflecting the birth-sign of the supposed founder, Taurus for Caesar, Capricorn for Augustus. Numerals, titles and emblems continued through the PRINCIPATE.

The new establishment of Augustan legions became the basis for the army under the EMPERORS. Three were destroyed in the TEUTOBURGIAN FOREST in AD 9 (total 25); two added by CALIGULA (27); two by NERO (29); two were cashiered and two added in the civil war aftermath (29); one added and two lost under DOMITIAN (28); two added by TRAJAN (30); two(?) lost under HADRIAN (28), two added by MARCUS AURELIUS (30); three raised by Septimius SEVERUS (33). Having a stable number of legions was a distinct advantage to government in terms of recruitment, supply, economic budgeting and focused loyalty to the emperor (through pay, decorations, propaganda, ritual). Two inscriptions from Rome list the names and numerals of all the legions in clockwise geographical order, updated to include the Severan formations (*CIL* 6.3492). Dispositions around the empire were reviewed in detail by TACITUS (*Annals* 4.5) and CASSIUS DIO (55.23). Strong concentrations of legions were present in 1st-century AD GERMANY and SYRIA, but as a result of the Danubian wars of DOMITIAN, Trajan and Marcus, a greater number gravitated towards the DANUBE PROVINCES. For political reasons Domitian and his successors kept legions in separate bases. Severus divided provinces so that none had more than two legions under one governor. It was the *legionarii* as the armed element of the ROMAN CITIZENSHIP who could make and break emperors, especially in AD 68–9 and 193–7.

So much more is known about individual legions because they appear in literary and sub-literary sources. Their emblems and titles were used in official and private stone inscriptions, and stamped,

LEGIONS: (b) distribution of legions under Tiberius and under the Antonines [with Severan additions].

Province/region	Tiberius	Antonines [Severans]
Italy		[II Parthica]
Illyricum/Dalmatia	VII, XI	
Macedonia	IV Scythica, V Macedonica	
Spain	IV Macedonica, VI Victrix, X Gemina	1: VII Gemina
North Mediterranean provinces	**Total: 7**	**Total: 2**
Cappadocia		XII Fulminata, XV Apollinaris
Syria	III Gallica, VI Ferrata, X Fretensis, XII Fulminata	III Gallica, IV Scythica, XVI Flavia
Judaea		VI Ferrata, X Fretensis
Mesopotamia		[I Parthica, II Parthica]
Arabia		III Cyrenaica
Eastern Provinces	**Total: 4**	**Total: 10**
Egypt	III Cyrenaica, XXII Deiotariana	II Traiana
Africa	III Augusta?	III Augusta
Southern Provinces	**Total: 4**	**Total: 2**
Britain		II Augusta, VI Victrix, XX Valeria Victrix
Germania Superior	II Augusta, XIII Gemina, XIV Gemina, XVI	VIII Augusta, XXII Primigenia
Germania Inferior	I Germanica, V Alaudae, XX Valeria, XXI Rapax	I Minervia, XXX Ulpia,
Britain/Germany	**Total: 8**	**Total: 7**
Raetia		III Italica
Noricum		II Italica
Pannonia Superior	VIII Augusta, IX Hispana	I Adiutrix, X Gemina, XIV Gemina
Pannonia Inferior		
II Adiutrix		
Moesia Superior	XV Apollinaris	IV Flavia, VII Claudia,
Moesia Inferior		
I Italica, V Macedonica, XI Claudia		
Dacia		XIII Gemina
Danubian provinces	**Total: 3**	**Total: 12**
Total empire	**26**	**33**

carved, scratched and painted on quarry-faces, buildings, equipment, ceramics, tiles, metal ingots, etc., leaving a 'footprint' in the archaeological record. From the Augustan period onwards there is also the ARCHAEOLOGY of excavated military installations all along, and behind, the empire's frontiers. FORTRESSES were with few exceptions established along major waterways for supply. Fortress plans have been recovered in sufficient detail to elucidate evolving internal legionary organization from the 1st to the 4th centuries AD. The 1st- to 3rd-century legion had ten cohorts, the first in some places and times was made up of five or six double-strength centuries, the rest made up of six centuries of 80 men (total 4,800–5,280 men). There was one SENATORIAL legate of the emperor for each legion (EQUESTRIAN prefects in Egypt, and for new legions from the later 2nd century), plus one senatorial tribune, five equestrian tribunes, an equestrian camp prefect, and 59–60 centurions. The latter were ranked in seniority by their internal cohort title reflecting organization of the Republican *manipuli*: *centurio primus* (front) *pilus*, *pilus posterior* (behind), *princeps prior*, *princeps posterior*, *hastatus prior*, *hastatus posterior*. Integral to the legion were light infantry (*antesignani*, *lanchiarii*), artillerymen (*ballistarii*, *scorpiones*) and archers (*sagittarii*), in addition to 120 cavalry. Spread across the cohorts were numerous skilled technicians so that the legion could meet its own requirements for buildings and fortifications, military equipment, ceramics and other manufactures. LITERACY was also a valued skill for the army's 'ACCOUNTING' culture.

Service in the legions was set at 20 years and MARRIAGE during service was prohibited. Pay set by Augustus was raised successively by Domitian,

Severus and CARACALLA. Increasingly money sums were paid to men on honourable discharge rather than grants of land around VETERAN colonies. The ethnic intake to the legions changed over time, Italians making up a decreasing proportion in the face of localized recruitment from the empire's growing number of citizens. Although only citizens were allowed in, there were various loopholes exploited to maintain numbers of recruits, especially in the Eastern provinces. Except for new legions raised in Italy, Italian recruitment was negligible after Trajan. Only citizen troops were eligible for decorations (*dona militaria*) awarded for acts of valour.

After the Hadrianic period whole legions rarely moved from their bases, unless they were newly raised. However, throughout the principate legionary detachments (*vexillationes*), often consisting of one or more cohorts or paired detachments from two legions, were posted away from their parent formation. They contributed to field campaigns and to major building projects, and were moved around between governors and provinces very flexibly. During the 3rd century in particular these detachments were away for protracted periods, some eventually never returning to their old base but themselves becoming autonomous formations. During the 3rd and 4th centuries some old legions were renamed and new ones raised, particularly by the TETRARCHIC emperors (Iovia, Herculiana). At around 1,000 troops, the new legions were much smaller than those of the principate, to judge from subliterary evidence and late fortress sizes and internal plans. A practice of removing specialist troops from the old legions had also been continuing, so that separate units of legionary cavalry (*equites promoti*), *lanchiarii* and *ballistarii* are well attested. Thus in the late 4th- to early 5th-century list of military commands (*NOTITIA DIGNITATUM*) there were some 174 identifiable legionary formations both in the field armies and lower-status frontier units. Of the 33 Severan legions, 29 were still attested, some divided up into as many as six parts. These continued in existence in the 5th-century West until field armies melted away or frontier installations were overrun. In the Eastern provinces some identifiable legionary units survived through until at least the late 6th century (Augusta V Macedonica) and the first half of the 7th (Tetrarchic IV Parthica). JCNC

See Brewer, R. (2000) *Roman Fortresses and their Legions*; Keppie, L. (1984) *The Making of the Roman Army*.

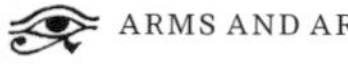 ARMS AND ARMOUR: (b).

leisure The crucial distinction between rich and poor in Roman society was the ability to control the use of one's body. SLAVES who technically had no control over the use of their persons had no capacity to choose when they would work, and when they would not. The same was true of the great majority of people in antiquity, who worked at the subsistence level. Their HOLIDAYS were formally set by the CITIES in which they lived, and the venues in which they could relax tended to be public – BATH houses, THEATRES and the like. The concept of leisure time, to be used at one's own discretion, and in private, was thus intimately linked with social status, and acquired significant moral aspects.

In Latin, the word for leisure was *otium*; in Greek it was *hêsychia*. In Roman thought *otium* was freedom from public life, a time that was ideally spent in cultural pursuits. Activities as varied as the composition of literary works or HUNTING could be ideal forms of *otium*. In Greek thought, *hêsychia* had somewhat different connotations, meaning to be at peace, to be still, or to be silent. These are meanings which reflect the face-to-face aspects of *POLIS* existence where the public person was supposed to be taking a physically active role in public life and to speak as needed in the public interest. In Greek PHILOSOPHY, *hêsychia* was to be used for moral improvement and contemplation. DSP

Lelantine war see EUBOIA; LEFKANDÍ.

Lemuria see ANCESTOR WORSHIP; FUNERAL RITES, ROMAN.

Leonidas Spartan king (r.490–480 BC) who died fighting at THERMOPYLAI. During the Karneia festival at Sparta, when the army would not muster, Leonidas took the initiative to defend the northern Greek pass from the PERSIAN invaders. His royal guard of 300 Spartiates was augmented on the march north by 7,000 allied HOPLITES. But after two days of hard fighting, the Persians found a way around Thermopylai and appeared at his rear. Leonidas choose to stay and delay the Persian advance to allow his surviving troops to retire. He died fighting with some 1,100 of his bodyguards and assorted allies; XERXES mutilated his body and placed his head on a stake.

Leonidas faced the largest Persian army of the war (somewhere between 100,000 and 200,000 infantrymen) and his men probably killed over 10,000 of the enemy. Nearly 3,000–4,000 Greeks may have died during the three-day resistance with Leonidas, more than all the Greek losses at MARATHON and PLATAEA put together. Leonidas' heroic stand was of psychological value to the squabbling Greeks and figured in the later rise of the Spartan mystique, in which he became in art and literature the epitome of the tough, no-nonsense, and, of course, dutiful warrior. Yet the massacre of a Spartan king and his bodyguard at Thermopylai marked the greatest defeat in the history of Greece and left the southern mainland open to the enemy. VDH

See Lazenby, J. F. (1993) *The Defence of Greece 490–479 BC*.

Lepcis Magna (mod. Lebda) One of the major towns of Roman AFRICA, its WEALTH in part based on large-scale OLIVE OIL production. The name is sometimes transliterated as Leptis, but local inscriptions use Lepcis (echoing the Libyphoenican *Lpqy*). The epithet Magna distinguished the town from LEPTIMINUS on the Lesser Syrtes. The town was favoured by Rome, achieving honorary promotions (*municipium*, AD 74–7; *colonia*, 109; *ius Italicum* status, 203). When the province of Tripolitana was constituted at the end of the 3rd century, Lepcis was its capital.

Early PHOENICIAN occupation of the 7th century BC has been detected in very limited work beneath the old FORUM, but most attention has focused on the fortunes of the city under Rome. The initial laying out of

LEPCIS MAGNA: (a) the theatre of AD 1–2, one of the earliest in Africa.

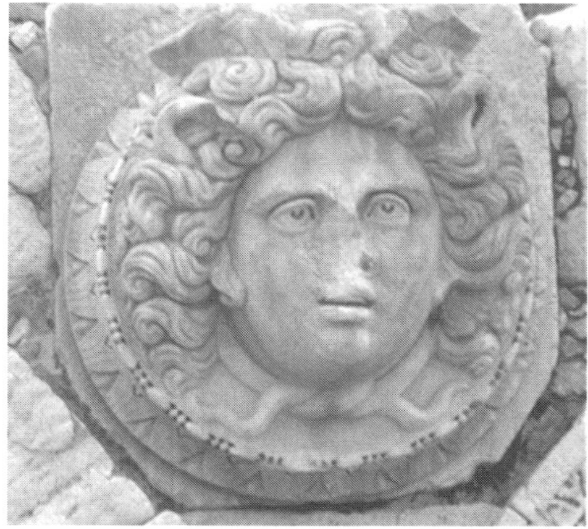

LEPCIS MAGNA: (b) fine marble head from the Severan forum, indicating presence of marble-workers from Asia Minor.

the 'old forum' and its surrounding *insulae* probably occurred in the 2nd–1st century BC, with new TEMPLES being added in the reign of AUGUSTUS. His reign also saw dramatic growth in the orthogonal street grid, incorporating a series of major monuments: the MARKET (8 BC), THEATRE (AD 1–2), and *chalcidicum* (AD 12). There are ARCHES of Tiberian date (recording the paving of the streets, AD 35–6) and the Flavian and Trajanic periods (commemorating urban promotions) and a great four-way arch dedicated to the Severan dynasty.

Lepcis has a very substantial set of urban inscriptions – up to the end of the 1st century AD frequently bilingual (neo-Punic and Latin), thereafter Latin. Many record the euergetism of local notables. ANNOBAL TAPAPIUS RUFUS paid for the market and theatre; Iddibal Caphada Aemilius donated the *chalcidicum*; Iddibal Tapapius a shrine to the *Di Augusti* in the theatre (AD 43); the forum was fully paved and given colonnades (AD 54) by G'y ben Hanno (Gaius Anno) and the civic BASILICA probably dates to the same period. An AMPHITHEATRE (AD 56) was constructed in an old quarry to the east of the town, and a portico on the western harbour mole was completed in AD 62. A temple to Magna Mater (CYBELE) was dedicated in the forum in AD 72 by Iddibal son of Balsillec, and an imposing temple to the Flavian EMPERORS was added (AD 93/4) to the west side of the harbour. The COUNCIL house (*curia*) was another late 1st–2nd century project. Under HADRIAN (AD 120) a citizen, Quintus Servilius Candidus, paid for the AQUEDUCT bringing water from the Wadi Caam and a series of public FOUNTAINS. The new WATER SUPPLY enabled the town to build one of the largest public BATHS complexes in the PROVINCES at that date. The town also had a magnificent CIRCUS, completed in AD 162.

The relative importance of the site can be gauged from its defended area. The total area enclosed by early earthwork defences is in the region of 425 ha (1,000 acres), of which perhaps two-thirds was reasonably densely built-up (280 ha, 660 acres). This makes it a very substantial town by ancient standards. The late Roman circuit enclosed 130 ha (325 acres) and the Byzantine defences a mere 38 ha (95 acres), soon reduced to 18 ha (45 acres).

The accession in AD 193 of a Lepcitanian as emperor, SEPTIMIUS SEVERUS, was followed by an extraordinary building programme, including a new forum/basilica complex, a colonnaded street, improvements to the harbour and a four-way arch. Despite this, the city declined in the later 3rd and 4th centuries. DJM

See Mattingly, D. J. (1995) *Tripolitania*; Vergara Caffarelli, E. and Caputo, G. (1966) *The Buried City*; Ward-Perkins, J. B. (1993) *The Severan Buildings of Lepcis Magna*.

 ANNOBAL TAPAPIUS RUFUS; BASILICAS; BATHS: (d); MARKET BUILDINGS: (b).

Lepidus see AEMILII; ANTONY, MARK; AUGUSTUS; CIVIL WARS, ROMAN; TRIUMVIRATES.

Leptiminus An important HARBOUR city in the Roman province of Byzacena (AFRICA) that has been the scene of important recent surveys and excavations. The site originated near the mid-1st millennium BC as a Punic *emporium* on the Tunisian coast to the south-east of CARTHAGE, c.35 km (22 miles) south of Hadrumetum (Sousse). It only briefly appears in our historical sources: for instance, as the landing point for HANNIBAL on his return to Africa en route to face SCIPIO AFRICANUS at ZAMA; by 111 BC it was one of seven free peoples (*populi liberi*) in the Roman province. It was caught up in the events of the civil war between CAESAR and the supporters of POMPEY in 46 BC, but rose rapidly thereafter, receiving its own mint under AUGUSTUS, and becoming a *colonia* in the reign of TRAJAN. The name is sometimes rendered Leptis Minor (to distinguish it from its eponymous neighbour, Leptis or LEPCIS MAGNA in Libya), but the correct styling appears to be Leptiminus. Because of a very shallow off-shore shelf, the town required an artificial harbour mole extending c.600 m (660 yards) out to sea. Recent research has emphasized productive and commercial activity at the city, especially in the mid-Roman period, when OLIVE OIL and FISH SAUCE appear to have been exported on a very considerable scale, using AMPHORAS manufactured in an extensive suburban zone. DJM

See Mattingly, D. J. et al. (2001) Leptiminus (Tunisia): a 'producer' city?, in Mattingly and Salmon, *Economies beyond Agriculture* 66–89.

 BURIAL, ROMAN: (b)–(c).

LEPTIMINUS: schematic plan of the city and its suburbs, based on field survey results.

Lesbos The largest AEGEAN island offshore from ANATOLIA, Lesbos was divided originally between six *poleis* (Mytilene, Methymna, Pyrrha, Arisbe, Antissa and Eresos). These settlements are said to have been established by Aiolian colonists from THESSALY and BOIOTIA (probably from the 10th century BC). The dialect spoken by the famous archaic lyric poets SAPPHO and ALKAIOS supports the suggested links to these two areas. A major feature of the archaic and classical culture, however, is the preservation of close cultural ties (which had existed from the Bronze Age) eastwards to Anatolia. In terms of ARCHITECTURE, locally produced ceramics and divinities, Lesbos is noticeably un-Greek in these early periods. It clearly formed a frontier area between the Aegean and Anatolia, and at some sites it is not until the classical period that more familiarly 'Hellenic' cultural features begin to assert themselves.

The island was famous for its WINE from the 7th century BC. Eresos produced the best variety, and in the west of the island near this city the hillsides are extensively terraced, with scattered farms of hellenistic and Roman date. Many impressive remains of similar date are scattered throughout the island, including a large pseudo-dipteral TEMPLE at Messa, sections of a long AQUEDUCT which brought water down to Mytilene from the slopes of the island's Mt Olympos, a well-preserved THEATRE at Mytilene, and fragments of fine late Roman HOUSES (also at Mytilene) including one with MOSAIC scenes from the comedies of MENANDER. NS

See Spencer, N. (1995) *A Gazetteer of Archaeological Sites in Lesbos*.

 AEGEAN SEA: (a).

Leto see APOLLO; ARTEMIS; MIDWIVES.

letters

Although letter-writing is an activity primarily associated with the Romans, a number of letters survive which are attributed to leading Greek literary figures, though it is unlikely that many (if any) of these are genuine. Letters survive under the names of ISOKRATES and DEMOSTHENES, but best known are the 13 letters ascribed to PLATO, all of which concern his activities in SICILY and his associates DION and DIONYSIOS I. *Letter* 7, addressed to Dion's friends, records events of Plato's life and contains a defence of his political ideals, as well as lamenting Dion's murder in 353. Letters like these may be classed as public and propagandist. Similarly, in the hellenistic and Roman periods official letters between cities, emperors, kings and high-ranking officials were published, mainly on inscriptions. Letters giving philosophical or moral advice (e.g. those of Epicurus) and consolation (Plutarch to his wife, *Moralia* 608a), and St Paul's *Epistles*, are other forms of public letter.

Private correspondence again is attested for leading figures such as Aristotle, though none survives until the 4th century AD, in the correspondence of the emperor Julian, the rhetorician Libanius, and Gregory of Nazianzus (the first of these to publish the letters himself). But a large repository of private correspondence between otherwise unknown individuals, such as soldiers writing home, is preserved in the papyri of Greco-Roman Egypt from the mid-3rd century BC onwards. MJE

See Harris, W.V. (1989) *Ancient Literacy*; Hunt, A.S. and Edgar, C., trs. (1952) *Select Papyri*, vol. 1; Welles, C.B. (1934) *Royal Correspondence in the Hellenistic Period* (includes translations).

In the Roman world letters (*epistulae*) represented a significant literary form as well as a means of personal communication. Often, these two aspects overlapped. The more personal aspect of letters can be seen in correspondence of Cicero (106–43 BC), which includes numerous letters to his friend Pomponius Atticus and to many other relations, friends, and members of upper class Roman society. The letters to Atticus contain frequent private jokes and allusions and so were not composed for publication, but were only collected and published after Cicero's death. Cicero's correspondence is an invaluable source for the political and cultural life of late Republican Rome.

By contrast, the published correspondence of Pliny the Younger (c.AD 61–113) is more literary in character. Pliny's correspondence includes nine books of letters written to various family connections and friends, and a tenth book of correspondence exchanged with the emperor Trajan. Pliny's letters were originally private communications, which Pliny carefully revised as he arranged them for publication. The influence of rhetorical principles is apparent. Pliny presents a picture of what he considers to be the most important values of aristocratic life, and he uses his own career and relationships as a model. Most of the letters are concerned with a single topic, and each book includes a selection of letters covering a range of subjects. Literary letters continued to be an important form of literature throughout antiquity. The rhetorician Fronto exchanged letters about style with the emperors Antoninus Pius, Marcus Aurelius and Lucius Verus. The correspondence of Symmachus portrays the political and cultural activities of a senator in late antique Rome. Christian writers, such as Cyprian, Sidonius Apollinaris, Jerome and Augustine (1) also published letters.

The didactic letter, which finds its roots in Greek philosophical writing, combines elements of personal communication with philosophical treatise. Thus Horace's *Epistles* are addressed to various contemporaries but impart a more general moral lesson. Seneca uses the form of a letter of admonition to his friend Lucilius as a rhetorical device for a broader discussion of Stoic ideals. Other examples of didactic letters include those written by church authorities, including the Epistles of the New Testament. Letters could be transformed into a purely literary genre; this is best illustrated by Ovid's *Heroides*, imaginary letters of mythological heroines.

The literary letter represents only one aspect of this form of communication significant for the student of antiquity. Much of our knowledge of Roman administration in the provinces comes from letters written by Roman emperors and other high ranking officials to magistrates or communities; these letters are preserved on inscriptions and papyri. Included among the papyri from Roman Egypt are numerous private letters, which reveal a great deal about the lives and values of the Greco-Egyptian population of that province. DPK

See Wilkinson, L.P. (1982) Cicero, and Browning, R. (1982) Oratory and epistolography, both in E.J. Kenney and W.V. Clausen, eds., *Cambridge History of Classical Literature*, vol. 2; Von Albrecht, M. (1997) *A History of Roman Literature*, vol. 1, 511–17.

 Sulpicia Lepidina.

Leukas see Ionian islands.

Leuktra Site, in Boiotia, of a Theban victory over a Spartan army in 371 BC. In the period after 378 Thebes had been strengthening its hold over the whole of Boiotia, and this was judged by the Spartans to be in breach of the terms of the King's Peace, originally agreed in 387/6. When the peace was being renegotiated in 371, the Thebans under Epameinondas refused to sign except on behalf of all Boiotia. When this was rejected, the Thebans withdrew from the negotiations and the Spartans under king Kleombrotos invaded Boiotia, in order to restore the autonomy of the Boiotian *poleis*. The Spartan army of about 11,000 men, of whom 700 were Spartiates, met the 7,000 Thebans and Boiotians under Epameinondas at Leuktra, south of Thespiai. In the battle the Theban left wing, which included the 'Sacred Band' under Pelopidas, was deepened and broke the Spartan right wing, where Kleombrotos was stationed; he himself was killed. The Spartan defeat allowed the Thebans to become dominant in central Greece, and they were able to take advantage of anti-Spartan feeling in the Peloponnese to invade it and liberate the Messenian helots. As a result, Sparta ceased to be a significant power in Greece. HB

See Diodorus Siculus 15.51–6; Xenophon, *Hellenica* 6.4.2–16.

 battles (table).

Levant One of the geographical terms used to refer to the body of land between the Mediterranean and the Euphrates river, bounded by Anatolia and the Taurus mountains to the north, and Egypt and the Sinai desert to the south. The name Levant goes back to the late 15th century AD and is, linguistically, the present participle of the French verb *lever*, 'to lift', used as a noun meaning 'East'. Although 'Levantine' is often used in a pejorative sense, designating activities seen as crooked or dishonest, 'Levant' seems once again to be gaining favour, especially among

ARCHAEOLOGISTS, but only in reference to the southern part of the Levant. The term 'northern Levant' is almost never used. The standard usage has become 'Syria and the southern Levant'. This north and south bipartite division of the Levant goes back to ancient times and is well documented in the archaeological and the historical record.

The southern Levant is essentially the ancient land of Canaan (from Hurrian *kinahhu*), a term used in ancient Near Eastern texts from at least the 18th century BC. Although its borders were flexible and seldom precisely defined in existing historical sources, ancient Canaan extended from El-Arish in the south to a point just north of Byblos in the north. Byblos was a Canaanite city; Ugarit (mod. Ras Shamra) to the north, was never considered one. This usage is still valid in hellenistic times. The coins from Beirut (2nd century BC), then called Laodikeia, bear the legend 'Laodikeia which is in Canaan' to distinguish it from 'Laodikeia on the sea' (STRABO 16.2.9), modern Latikia (just north of Ras Shamra).

From at least the time of the earliest surviving textual evidence, in the second half of the 3rd millennium BC, down to Roman times, the inhabitants of the southern Levant spoke different versions of a north-west Semitic language that can be called Canaanite. In the Iron Age the languages making up the Canaanite group included PHOENICIAN, Punic, Hebrew, Ammonite, Edomite and Moabite. Related north-west Semitic languages, that were not strictly speaking Canaanite, included Ugaritic and Aramaic. All these languages, except for Ugaritic, were written using the Canaanite linear ALPHABET, now attested in texts as early as the 16th century BC. This alphabet was eventually borrowed (and modified for their own specific needs) by the Greeks, LYDIANS, LYCIANS, CARIANS, ETRUSCANS and the Italic-speaking peoples of the Italian peninsula.

This reconstruction implies that the Iron Age Phoenicians (as they were known to the Greeks) were the descendants of the Bronze Age Canaanites (as they were known in Near Eastern texts). Both names seem to have originated as colour words, referring to the famous purple-dye industry of the area (the Greek being a translation of the Near Eastern name). This relationship is borne out by the continuity in language and onomastica and in human skeletal evidence (especially from the cemetery at Akhziv). In reality these are not national groups but inhabitants of city-states. There was a land of Canaan but it was populated by individuals who identified themselves by the names of their respective cities, as also in Iron Age Phoenicia, whose inhabitants considered themselves Sidonians, Tyrians or Arvadites. This is also the terminology found in HOMER.

The settlement history of the southern Levant, from Neolithic times, seems to have been dominated by a cyclic pattern of periods of urbanism interrupted by periods of semi-NOMADIC PASTORALISM. Urban collapse seems to have taken place, roughly speaking, at the end of the 4th, 3rd and 2nd millennia BC. A more stable urban environment existed to the north, in the land of SYRIA. The name 'Syria' is a hypocoristic form of Near Eastern 'Assyria' (correctly recognized by HERODOTOS 7.63). Greek usage of the toponym 'Syria' is rather confused. It can be used to refer to the entire Trans-Euphrates region, comprising the modern states of Syria, Lebanon, Israel and Jordan. This is actually the meaning of the terminology used by the inhabitants of ancient MESOPOTAMIA and PERSIA who, from their eastern perspective, referred to the 'land beyond the (Euphrates) river' (Akkadian *Eber nari*, Aramaic *Abar-nahara*). More often Syria designated an area approximately equivalent to modern Syria and to the ancient kingdom of the Aramaeans. This is why references to the 'kingdom of Aram' in the Hebrew BIBLE are translated by the SEPTUAGINT as 'Syria'.

This confused usage is probably what lies behind the terminology used by Herodotos, who refers to Syria and to the land of the Phoenicians that belongs to the Palestinian Syrians, as far as the city of Kadytis, modern Gaza (Herodotos 3.5). Palestine is the land of the ancient Philistines, who settled the coastal area, from Ekron (mod. Tel Miqne) to Gaza, following their defeat by Ramesses III in 1177 BC. Ancient Phoenicia is essentially modern Lebanon, and the name Lebanon is a survival of the ancient Semitic terminology, from the root *lbn*, 'to be white' (Hebrew *lebanon*). The reference is to the snow-capped peaks of Mt Lebanon (Arabic *Gabal al-Lubnan*), that rise to a height of 3,300 m (10,000 ft). It was, of course, most famous as a source of timber, especially the cedar tree that takes its scientific name, *Cedrus libani*, from the name of the mountain itself. Trade in timber from the cedars of Lebanon began in the late 4th millennium BC.

Between the Lebanon mountains, a chain running north–south for some 160 kms (100 miles), and the lower Anti-Lebanon mountains to the east, lies the fertile valley known as the Beqa' (Arabic *el-Biqa'*, 'the Valley'). At an elevation of some 1,100 m (3,600 ft), the valley was famous for its WINE and, in Roman times, for its great cult centre at BAALBEK, with its complex of temples dedicated to ZEUS/JUPITER, APHRODITE/VENUS and HERMES/MERCURY. JDM

See Bunnens, G., ed. (2000) *Essays on Syria in the Iron Age*; Markoe, G. E. (2000) *Phoenicians*.

lever see HERON OF ALEXANDRIA; MACHINES; MECHANICS; PHYSICS.

Lévi-Strauss, Claude see ANTHROPOLOGY; MYTH; SEMIOTICS; STRUCTURALISM AND POST-STRUCTURALISM.

Lezoux see SAMIAN WARE.

Libanius AD 314–c.393 A RHETORICIAN and intellectual, Libanius' extensive surviving works provide a major source for the social history of the 4th century AD. After an education in Athens, Libanius taught in CONSTANTINOPLE, Nicaea and NICOMEDIA in the 340s and early 350s. In 354 he returned permanently to his native Antioch. Libanius epitomized the civic patriotism which is one of the hallmarks of classical culture. One of his most famous speeches is a PANEGYRIC in honour of Antioch (*Oration* 11), and he acted as the city's spokesman in its quarrel with the emperor JULIAN. Shortly before his death he wrote to his fellow Antiochene AMMIANUS MARCELLINUS (this has been disputed), congratulating him on the success of his recently published *Histories*, which had brought renown to the city.

Some 1,600 letters attributed to Libanius survive, revealing a world of PATRONAGE and recommendation at work. His circle of correspondents embraced both CHRISTIAN and pagan, who shared at least a common *paideia*, if not a religion. While Libanius' own PAGANISM was not extremist, one of his most vivid passages is a denunciation of monks as a 'black-robed tribe, who eat more than elephants' (*Oration* 30.8); this is in a speech protesting the destruction of pagan shrines by Christian FANATICS. Although snobbish in some ways, many of his speeches show a concern for improving social conditions and combating injustice (e.g. *Orations* 45 and 50). Libanius was always preoccupied with his health. As a young man he was struck by lightning and suffered lifelong migraine as a result. PMB

See Norman, A. (1965) *Libanius' Autobiography*.

Liber see BACCHUS; CERES; GODS AND GODDESSES, ROMAN; PLEBEIANS; ROME.

libraries The earliest known public library was created in the 6th century BC by PEISISTRATOS at Athens, taken by XERXES when Athens was sacked during the PERSIAN WARS. The most famous ancient library was that of ALEXANDRIA, created by PTOLEMY I and intended to be more than a mere archive, as part of a wider complex which included the MOUSEION and GARDENS. In the 3rd century BC Ptolemy III wrote to various sovereigns asking to borrow their books. Unfortunately, he was not as good at returning them and gave up the bond of five talents paid to Athens when he kept the copies of the works of AESCHYLUS, SOPHOKLES and EURIPIDES that it had sent him. The library suffered in a fire in 47 BC during the war between Julius Caesar and Pompeian forces. Like the MOUSEION, it was heavily damaged by fire in the 270s, when ZENOBIA of PALMYRA attempted to retain control of Egypt, but a daughter library, long established at the SERAPEUM, survived until AD 391.

The main rival to the Alexandrian library was created at PERGAMON by Eumenes II in the 2nd century BC. When Alexandria sought to scupper its rival by refusing to export papyrus, Pergamon retaliated by turning the alternative, ANIMAL skins, into an art. It used skins of stillborn or newborn lambs and kids, and the resulting pure vellum was named after the city – Charta Pergamena – parchment.

At Rome, JULIUS CAESAR commissioned VARRO to collect the corpus of Greek and Latin literature. This project died with him, but Asinius Pollio established the first public library at Rome c.39 BC. AUGUSTUS also founded libraries, including one each for Latin and Greek on the Palatine. Later emperors frequently provided funds for libraries and their repair, and Rome eventually had 28 public libraries.

Private libraries were sometimes extensive. Philosophical schools, especially the LYCEUM, contained many volumes; other schools, of law and medicine, had specialist libraries, and some personal libraries were extensive. The best example comes from HERCULANEUM, where a large library of carbonized PAPYRI has been discovered in the Villa of the Papyri. The setting may have been a school of EPICUREAN PHILOSOPHY, possibly that of PHILODEMOS, and has yielded some new texts, including works of Philodemos himself.

Public libraries preserved and made texts available and attracted scholars. In praising Constantius for establishing a library and funding the copying of manuscripts, THEMISTIUS exuberantly boasts that CONSTANTINOPLE was now set to become a centre of learning (*Oration* 4.59d–61c). At libraries, scholars consulted texts and might have copies made. Libraries did not usually lend books, though scattered references hint at the occasional interlibrary loan. Opening hours could be restrictive: an inscription from the library of Pantainos at Athens reads (*SEG* 21.500): 'No book shall be taken out, since we have sworn this. Open just after dawn to midday.' NJW, JV

See Casson, L. (2001) *Libraries in the Ancient World*; Hoepfner, W., ed. (2002) *Antike Bibliotheken*; MacLeod, R., ed. (2001) *The Library of Alexandria*.

LIBRARIES: the columnar façade of the library of Celsus at Ephesos.

Libya The term used by ancient Greek authors for the whole of north AFRICA except Egypt. Ancient writers often call Libya the third continent and describe it as inferior to other two, namely Europe and Asia, because of its vast tracts of desert. Indeed, STRABO says Libya is like a leopard because it is a desert which is interspersed with settled regions. The full extent of the African continent was unknown in antiquity; ancient GEOGRAPHERS thought Libya ended with the Sahara and that the desert was bounded by an ocean.

Ancient authors tend to divide Libya into two regions, namely the coast and desert. The Libyan coast was the locus of cities and AGRICULTURE and was inhabited by Greeks and CARTHAGINIANS as well as indigenous Libyans. In contrast, the Libyan desert was sparsely inhabited; it was not only isolated from the rest of mankind and largely unknown, but was seen as dangerous and marginal. Ancient geographers thought the desert abounded with different kinds of deadly snakes. In addition, ancient writers say that mysterious phenomena occur in the desert, such as peculiar shapes, which gather in the sky and pursue people.

MOSAICS and literary sources indicate that Libya exported many wild ANIMALS for beast shows in Rome. In addition, many parts of Libya gained a lot of wealth through being an important source of grain and OLIVE OIL in the Roman period. Despite this, ancient writers continued to stereotypically view Libya as rugged and inhabited by NOMADS. EACM

See Mattingly, D. J. (1994) *Tripolitania*; Raven, S. (1993) *Rome in Africa*.

 COLONIZATION: (b).

Licinii An important Roman *gens*. One representative worked hard to benefit PLEBEIAN nobility. Traditionally, Gaius Licinius Stolo, TRIBUNE 376–367 BC with Lucius Sextius Lateranus as colleague, passed legislation that allowed the plebeians' own ÉLITE to become CONSULS and became one himself. The annalist Gaius Licinius Macer in the 1st century BC possibly exaggerated his other activities. The *cognomina* Crassus and Lucullus also appear. Publius Licinius Crassus passed laws against excessive display of luxury while tribune c.106 BC and against HUMAN SACRIFICE as consul in 97. His son Marcus Licinius CRASSUS was the wealthiest man at Rome. After an unorthodox early career, Crassus shared power with POMPEY and CAESAR in the 50s BC in a private arrangement, but died on campaign in the East. The careers of his son Publius Licinius Crassus and his grandson Marcus Licinius Crassus rose and fell with some regularity. Lucius Licinius Crassus is best known as CICERO's master and model for ORATORY, though he and Gnaeus Domitius Ahenobarbus as CENSORS in 92 BC forbade the teaching of RHETORIC in Latin, to stifle social and political mobility. Finally, Lucius Licinius Lucullus handed the Eastern command against MITHRADATES to Pompey, his long-time nemesis, in 66 BC. JV

Licinius (Caius Valerius Licinianus Licinius) c.AD 250–324/5 Eastern Roman emperor (308–24), Licinius first came to prominence as a general in GALERIUS' army, and in 308 he was appointed emperor with the task of bringing ITALY under Galerius' sway. Although he was unsuccessful, Licinius remained close to the centre of power, and in the aftermath of Galerius' death in 311 he quickly assumed power throughout the East. In 313, he travelled to Italy to make terms with the newly triumphant Western usurper CONSTANTINE, and together they promulgated the directive on religious toleration known erroneously as the Edict of Milan. This granted religious freedom to CHRISTIANS, and thus brought to an end the great PERSECUTION initiated by DIOCLETIAN. At first, Licinius treated the Christians kindly, but his capacity for toleration was compromised by his uneasy relationship with the ambitious Constantine. Already in 316 the two were at war, and Licinius was driven out of Europe, apart from THRACE. In 324, Constantine sought to achieve universal dominion and, using Licinius' renewed persecution of the Christians as a pretext, he invaded the Eastern empire. Licinius was routed first at Hadrianople in Thrace, and then at Chrysopolis near Chalcedon in ASIA Minor. By the end of September 324 he had been sent into internal exile at THESSALONIKE with the assurance that he would be spared. But by the spring of the following year, Licinius was dead, undoubtedly murdered at Constantine's orders. MDH

See Lactantius, *On the Deaths of the Persecutors*, trs. J. L. Creed (1984); Barnes, T. D. (1981) *Constantine and Eusebius*.

 EMPERORS, ROMAN: (b); TETRARCHS: (b).

lighthouses Long before the invention of purpose-built lighthouses HOMER (*Odyssey* 10.30) mentions simple FIRES on beaches to guide ships. Raised beacons could also be used, such as the two columns known to have guarded the entrance into the Athenian harbour PIRAEUS. The most famous lighthouse in the ancient world was the hellenistic Pharos of ALEXANDRIA, which rose to a height of 130 m (c.425 ft). Its design has to be reconstructed from hellenistic, Roman and medieval descriptions and depictions as well as from monumental MASONRY blocks recently discovered in Alexandria's harbour. The Pharos was a tower with three (quadrangular, octagonal and cylindrical) tiers, which was approached by a long ramp. A spiral staircase led to service rooms and enabled pack ANIMALS to bring firewood up to the third level. The monument was decorated with enormous statues of deities (ZEUS and POSEIDON) and of PTOLEMAIC rulers. The Pharos continued to serve as a lighthouse until AD 1303 when it was completely destroyed by an EARTHQUAKE. Other famous ancient lighthouses are known from CONSTANTINOPLE, OSTIA, Boulogne and Dover.

All ancient lighthouses were designed to warn and guide ships by marking shallows and harbour entrances. Some were placed directly onto the quay but others were constructed on heights (Capri) or on breakers (Portus). This function was initially

LIGHTHOUSES: (a) the four-stage lighthouse tower at Ostia, depicted on a Roman tombstone.

LIGHTHOUSES: (b) ships and lighthouse in a pavement from the Square of the Corporations at Ostia.

fulfilled during the day, and it is only from the Roman period onwards that lighthouses were regularly provided with fires to guide ships at night (PLINY THE ELDER, *Natural History* 36.12). HE

lighting An aspect of sophistication in the use of SPACE, exhibiting a wide diversity of applications. These range from indoor to outdoor space, from public to private, from sacred to secular, and assume different form through time and locality. The term 'lighting' describes both natural and artificial light; the first is another word for sunlight at different times of the day, and the second includes a variety of man-made means to obtain light, such as LAMPS, torches, candles, braziers, hearths and the like.

The way and extent to which ancient people manipulated light of either kind to adjust it to their needs reflect the level and type of their intervention in an important aspect of their natural environment. Considering that lighting is far from being a vital requirement for subsistence, the choice to use lighting should be viewed as a step towards an added luxury and complexity in living. The concern to invest in illumination is contingent on several parameters, such as a community's economic prosperity, availability of natural resources, sophistication and skill in TECHNOLOGY and/or ARCHITECTURE (for the manipulation of natural light), and diversity in patterns of living and social interaction at different times of the day or in different contexts.

The simplest way to take advantage of natural light is to restrict activity to the bright periods of the day, which fluctuated according to season and geographical location. This pattern of life appears to have been followed in Greece before the 7th century, judging from the surviving architectural remains and associated portable finds. Most activity took place in the open air with limited time spent indoors, perhaps during the darker hours of the day and particularly during the cold season. The extent to which light, in the strict sense, would have been a concern in this early period is not possible to assess, partly because of the perishable nature of the materials used for illumination (such as hearths or torches) and partly due to the absence of specially designed light-carriers of any sort from archaeological contexts of the period.

The latter kind of lighting device begins to appear, with increasing popularity, from the 7th century onwards, to develop fully by the classical period, when a two-way process may be observed. While artificial sources of light (particularly lamps) grow in variety and sophistication, there is a distinctive concern to make interior space 'visible' through illumination. The latter is achieved through the construction of more 'open' structures in terms of the number and type of apertures for the admission of natural light, as well as an increasing investment in sophisticated devices of artificial light. At the same time, light began to assume roles beyond that of practical necessity to illuminate space, particularly in sacred contexts. It is often loaded with metaphorical meaning and is manipulated in the ritual theatre of many cults. EP

See Parisinou, E. (2000) *The Light of the Gods*.

LAMPS: (a)–(b).

Liguria see ITALY, ROMAN.

Ligures Baebiani (mod. Macchia di Circello) Town in the central Apennines, located some 25 km (16 miles) north of Benevento. The community took its name from those Ligurians from the mountains north of Pisa who were transferred here in 180 BC to be settled on *ager publicus*, and from one of the pair of generals, Marcus Baebius Tamphilus and Publius Cornelius Cethegus, who had defeated them (Livy 40.38.1–9, 41.1–5). The related site of Ligures Corneliani has been identified near San Bartolomeo in Galdo, about 20 km (12 miles) north-east of Macchia. In 41 BC, part of the territory of Ligures Baebiani was assigned to VETERANS associated with the TRIUMVIRAL colony at neighbouring Beneventum. The community is perhaps best known for the ALIMENTARY Table dated to AD 101 (one of only two examples surviving, the other being from Veleia), which casts light on configurations of landholding in the territory at the time of TRAJAN.

Excavations at the site in the 1980s revealed the remains of a TEMPLE of late 2nd-century BC date, baths, part of the street grid and areas of housing, suggesting a community of modest scale. Similarities have been identified between POTTERY of Republican date discovered at Macchia and material from Liguria, reflecting the unusual history of the town. JRP

See Champlin, E. (1981) Owners and neighbours at Ligures Baebiani, *Chiron* 11: 239–64; Keppie, L. (1983) *Colonisation and Veteran Settlement in Italy, 47–14 BC*; Patterson, J. (1988) *Samnites, Ligurians and Romans*.

lime A common product in the Mediterranean world because of the prevalence of limestone and the usefulness of quicklime in AGRICULTURE and slaked lime in ARCHITECTURE. Disused examples of LIME-KILNS are common in Greece, often resembling small Mycenaean beehive or 'tholos' tombs. Those still in operation are often rectangular concrete structures and mechanized, though still fired with a succession of woody fuels (e.g. softwood followed by olive-stones) to give different grades of heat. Lumps of limestone or MARBLE are subjected to prolonged, intense heat to produce quicklime, then treated with water to give slaked lime. This brilliant white, pasty substance can be used to make PLASTER and whitewash. In ancient times it was the basis of lime plaster or STUCCO, on which WALL-PAINTINGS could be executed (Vitruvius 7.2–3). From hellenistic times it was used for making mortar and CONCRETE, and thus for WATERPROOFING buildings. A strongly alkaline substance, slaked lime was also used in treating LEATHER. Early modern travellers often blamed lime-burning for the destruction of sculptures and architectural pieces from ancient sites. At Corinth a number of heads of Roman statues were discovered next to a later lime-kiln; presumably the heads survived because they were awkward to break up for burning. DGJS

lime-kilns The only ancient description of a Roman lime-kiln comes from CATO (*On agriculture* 38), but this information can be supplemented from excavated examples. The kilns were periodic: the kiln was loaded, fired, cooled and unloaded, after which the cycle started again. A projection divided the kiln into two, the limestone being built up above the ledge with the fire in the lower part. This separated the fuel from the limestone, ensuring evenly burnt and clean lime, essential for good mortar and PLASTER. The kilns were often built into the side of a hill, or in a pit, so that they could be loaded and unloaded from the top, but fired from the bottom, again ensuring clean lime.

The size of kilns varied. Cato's kiln, 10 Roman feet (2.95 m) wide in diameter at the base, tapering to 3 feet (0.89 m) at the top, and 20 feet (5.90 m) high, had a capacity of about 27 cubic metres. Excavated examples range in volume from c.15 to c.120 cubic metres. The firing cycle for a middle-sized kiln would have taken c.20 days, using 1.5–3.5 tonnes of fuel for each cubic metre of lime produced. JDeL

See Dix, B. (1982) The manufacture of lime and its uses in the western Roman provinces, *OJA* 1: 331–45.

limes see FRONTIERS, ROMAN.

literacy

The oldest Egyptian PAPYRUS dates to around 3000 BC, and writing developed early in the Near East. But the earliest writing certainly in Greek is found on the Linear B tablets, discovered first in CRETE and then on the mainland, and perhaps dating back to the 14th century. These tablets are PALACE inventories, and there is no evidence of literary activity in the MYCENAEAN period other, perhaps, than a tantalizing reference to writing in HOMER's *Iliad* (6.168–70). It was, indeed, during Homer's time in the second half of the 8th century that the PHOENICIAN script was introduced into Greece; examples of writing are then found on pottery from all over the Greek world. They are often written retrograde (right-to-left) or even in *boustrophêdon* ('as the ox turns') style, i.e. in alternating lines from right to left and from left to right. There is also the problematic evidence of mythology: the legend of Kadmos includes the element that he taught the BOIOTIANS how to write with Phoenician letters. The alphabet developed over the course of the next two centuries and more; there were many local variants in archaic and early classical Greece, and it was not until 403 that the set of 24 letters was standardized in Athens.

The importation of papyrus from Phoenician Byblos (hence *biblos*, the Greek for 'book', or 'bible'), and, in Ionia, the alternative use of the skins of SHEEP and GOATS as writing materials, facilitated first the writing down of EPIC poetry and then the composition of LYRIC poetry from the 7th century. Nevertheless, there is little reason to believe that literacy, whether the ability to read or write, was ever widespread beyond a very basic level in what remained a predominantly oral culture. The evidence we have, in literature and from other sources, comes in scattered references and chance finds, and is mostly equivocal in its nature. For example, some Ionian MERCENARIES scrawled their names, and how they travelled up the NILE, on the statue of Rameses II at Abu Simbel in c.600; and HERODOTOS (6.27.2) describes the collapse of a school on CHIOS, killing 119 children, in 494. Schools existed elsewhere in Greece, at Astypalaia (Pausanias 6.9.6), Troizen (Plutarch, *Themistokles* 10.3), and Mykalessos (Thucydides 7.29.5), and school scenes appear in VASE-PAINTINGS, but this is evidence only for elementary education.

Possible evidence for mass adult literacy at Athens comes in the form of the political practice of OSTRACISM, perhaps introduced by KLEISTHENES in 508. This involved citizens writing the names of candidates for EXILE on sherds of POTTERY – but the discovery of pre-prepared batches of *ostraka*, written by a small number of individuals, raises doubts as to the reliability of the inferences we can draw from this process. Writing a candidate's name in any case only indicates a very basic level of literacy; it does not demonstrate that the voters could have gone home to read a papyrus, or to the *AGORA* to read the text of a decree. Indeed, the practice of setting up inscriptions does not in itself prove that the people could read them, since these stones had an important symbolic value as well. Some inscriptions seem purposely set up in high places so as not to be read. Another problem, common to inscriptions and literary texts, is that they were written without breaks between the words and with no punctuation; and long scrolls of papyrus did not make for easy reading. But some passages suggest that by the end of the 5th century the practice of reading (out aloud rather than to oneself) was becoming more popular, as in EURIPIDES' *Erechtheus* and ARISTOPHANES' *Frogs*, where DIONYSOS has read Euripides' *Andromeda*.

It is likely that literacy beyond the basic or functional level will have been achieved largely by men of the highest social levels. It was they who had the leisure time (*scholê*, hence 'school') to develop the skills acquired in elementary schooling, and in due course read and write literature. When Plato criticizes reliance on BOOKS in the *Phaedrus* (275d–e), he does so to promote the kind of dialectic taught at great expense in the ACADEMY. Similarly, his rival ISOKRATES composed political tracts for his wealthy students to read. DEMOSTHENES, who in the tradition could not afford Isokrates' fees after his INHERITANCE was embezzled by his guardians but in truth was still relatively wealthy, can attack AISCHINES for his background as the son of a schoolmaster and for reading out his mother's ritual texts (Demosthenes 18.258–9). But Aischines' family too, though impoverished by the PELOPONNESIAN WAR, was hardly poor. There was clearly a growing book trade in the late 5th and 4th centuries (cf. XENOPHON, *Anabasis* 7.5.12–14). It is doubtful, however, whether SOCRATES' claim that a text of Anaxagoras could be bought for one drachma 'at most' (Plato, *Apology* 26d) is indicative of a general interest in reading among the lower classes. Nevertheless, in Aristophanes' *Knights* even the lowly sausage-seller can just about read and write, while the SLAVE Demosthenes can read an ORACLE.

The spread of literacy will have varied in different times and circumstances, and it is not surprising, for instance, that private reading and the book trade took off in the vibrant society of 5th-century Athens. The military state of Sparta, on the other hand, had no need or desire for most of its citizens to be literate. In the hellenistic period, when it has been estimated (by Harris) that literacy reached a peak (though still at only 20–30 per cent), various cities made extensive state provision for elementary education, including Teos (all free boys), RHODES and MILETOS. Girls were educated at Teos and PERGAMON. The *Argonautika* of APOLLONIOS OF RHODES, like other hellenistic poetry, is very much a literary product, far removed in its composition from the earlier, primary, epic of Homer, and written in the intellectual milieu of a cosmopolitan city. The document-based administrative system of Greco-Roman Egypt required large numbers of people trained in functional (or 'craft') literacy (which is not the same as reading literature). But literacy did not confer status, and the use of slaves to do their reading and writing for them was a disincentive to citizens to acquire these skills themselves. MJE

See Harris, W.V. (1989) *Ancient Literacy*; Thomas, R. (1992) *Literacy and Orality in Ancient Greece*.

Sometime around 800 BC the Greek alphabet was invented, by a person or persons unknown. With the alphabet, the issue of literacy in the ancient world arose, since it became fairly easy for everybody to learn to read and write. Consequently, the extent and importance of literacy in the Greco-Roman world have been discussed intensely and with an almost ferocious interest by classical scholars for many years. In modern Western society literacy is deemed a necessity for personal success and prosperity, and the percentage of literate persons in a society is used as one of the parameters to measure its development and status. This notion is one of several that reveal how far the ideals and reality of ancient society were from modern Western society. Some of the questions addressed by scholars are how widespread the ability to read and write became, and what writing and reading were used for.

It is interesting to observe how much energy has been devoted to stipulate how many – or rather how few – throughout antiquity ever became fully literate in our sense of the word. (UNESCO defines literacy as a person's ability to read and write a shorter text in basic language about his or her everyday life.) The precise number of literate people in the ancient world will never be estimated precisely. To state that only a minority ever became able to read, and even fewer to read and write well, does not clearly enough reflect the importance of the written word in antiquity. Every student of Greece and Rome has noticed the impressive number of inscriptions still visible today (because they have been carved in stone). These inscriptions were normally put up by rulers and aristocrats to honour themselves and had enormous symbolic meaning. They should not necessarily be seen as sources of written information for the man and woman in the street. But ordinary people also put up inscriptions. Throughout the Roman empire thousands of epitaphs were set up to commemorate ordinary people with only a limited EDUCATION. Here too, the symbolic importance was considerable. But it is difficult to imagine that anybody would put up an epitaph to a relative in an underground and dark *columbarium* in Rome except for his or her own sake: nobody else would ever see it.

LITERACY: wall-painting from Pompeii showing people in the forum, reading temporary placards (painted?) making public announcements.

In POMPEII numerous graffiti show us how far down in society literacy went. Artisans and shop owners are, not surprisingly, frequently represented as scribblers of graffiti, but the PROSTITUTES and their customers in the brothels also seem to have been able to write. Although some clients – like today – may have been nice men from nice families with a good education, many others and the prostitutes themselves were not. How had these people learned to read and write? Only in a very few instances in antiquity was schooling of children subsidized by the state. The wealthy would be taught at home. As for others, itinerant teachers could set up temporary schools where they taught the freeborn of the lower classes for a fee; quite evidently, many took advantage of the opportunity. In addition, the value of slaves would increase significantly if they had a good education. Therefore the schooling of slaves was a good investment, in terms of possible resale. Not only the owner would prosper; the slave would benefit as well. In Rome, a slave could buy his or her freedom by saving his or her *peculium* and through work for others; literacy would provide more opportunities and was thus a good way out of slavery.

Pompeii's tragedy means that its graffiti have been preserved for us to try to understand. If Vesuvius had not erupted that August day in AD 79 all the parietal graffiti would have been lost and we would have been left with only the more lasting stone inscriptions put up by the educated ÉLITE. The preserved graffiti of Pompeii raise two interconnected issues. What materials were used for everyday writing, and how expensive were they? Both questions are important for understanding the spread of literacy. The extension of literacy to the unpropertied classes would have been impossible if writing materials were too expensive or not easily available. PAPYRUS was expensive and not always easily available; it is therefore normally considered the preferred writing material of the wealthy, and the extant letters of men like CICERO and PLINY were originally written on it. Besides papyrus, wooden tablets were widely used all over the empire. Reusable (and cheap) waxed wooden tablets (inscribed with a stylus) were used for everyday purposes like school exercises, letters and business documents. Thin wooden leaves inscribed with ink were used for letters.

The problem with these materials is that they are perishable and have only been preserved under special circumstances. The dry climate of Egypt provides an ideal environment for the preservation of papyrus. The huge amounts of papyri found in Egypt reveals that this material was not only used by the wealthy but also by the lower classes to record, for example, taxes paid, wills and contracts. Although far from all persons were literate, it is clear that the degree of literacy even in villages was high enough for administrative purposes. This meant both that government officials could count on written records to document the citizens' relations with the state, and that illiterate villagers could rely on knowing somebody who was both trustworthy and able to read sufficiently well to ensure the correctness of a document.

Egypt and Pompeii have always been considered to belong to particularly well-developed areas of the Roman empire and are therefore not seen as typical for the spread of literacy. Roman BRITAIN, on the other hand, is definitely regarded as much more backward and less developed. Therefore the discovery in the 1970s and 1980s of several hundred wooden tablets from VINDOLANDA has caused quite a sensation. These tablets contain records and letters relating to the military staff and their families stationed there and tell their correspondents (and modern students) about life in this outpost of the empire, very far from Rome. One letter is a birthday invitation from one woman to another. Another mentions that warm socks have been sent to a soldier probably suffering badly in the humid and cold British CLIMATE. These people were not particularly well educated. But they obviously found it natural to communicate with each other in writing.

Like archaic Greece, early Rome was not dependent on writing. At first, literacy developed slowly; in fact, the bulk of the written evidence stems from late Republican times and imperial times. For this reason, the picture of literacy in the ancient world will never be crystal clear or complete, and we will never understand exactly how widespread literacy was. Nevertheless, the evidence is convincing enough to show that, by the imperial period (and probably earlier), the ability to read and write was a natural part of peoples' lives in all status groups. HSN

See Beard, M. et al. (1991) *Literacy in the Roman World*; Bowman, A. K. (1998) *Life and Letters on the Roman Frontier*; Harris, W. V. (1989) *Ancient Literacy*.

 ADVERTISING; ALPHABETS; *INSTRUMENTUM DOMESTICUM*; SULPICIA LEPIDINA.

literary criticism The act of studying, analysing and evaluating a literary text. The process is governed by aesthetic and methodological principles and categories (literary theory); these in turn are derived from the act of critiquing concrete works. Consequently, literary criticism and literary theory imply each other. Literary criticism is based on abstract principles that relate to the tenets used to evaluate the nature and value of any given work of ART. This assumes, in consequence, that the study of literature, in spite of its specificity, is ruled by the same principles that apply to the analysis of any other art form.

Questions about the nature and interpretation of art, even the definition of art, are common to all cultures. In the Western world, critical debate about literature began with the Greeks, especially PLATO and ARISTOTLE. Plato expressed his ideas about literature mainly in the dialogues *Ion*, *Gorgias* and *Republic*. He was concerned about the MORALITY and spiritual values of the act of enjoying literature and the effect that literature had on its audience. He composed his treatments during a period of transition from an oral to a literate society. In that environment, he questioned the value of the old *paideia*, while not adhering to the new one completely. Aristotle's *Poetics* constitute the basis of Western literary theory and criticism. In his analysis, Aristotle emphasized the elements or characteristics that define a literary genre. Writing in response to Plato's understanding of literature, he too defines it as imitation but, unlike Plato, not as an imitation of an imitation of the ideal world. According to Aristotle, the historian writes what actually happened, but the artist that which could happen.

In the Roman world, the most important critics were HORACE and LONGINUS, though the latter was largely ignored until the 18th century. Horace wrote an *Ars poetica* (*Art of Poetry*), which set the standards for literary taste until the 18th century. His emphasis was not on the imitation of reality, but on imitation of other POETS. For him, the good poet is one who is able to treat an old subject in a new way, while a worthy piece of literature should achieve the double objective of education and pleasure. Longinus wrote a Greek treatise entitled *On the Sublime*, where he juxtaposes examples of the Greek, Latin and Hebrew literary traditions. He argues that sublime literary creation necessitates the natural virtues of talent and passion accompanied by learning, reflected in the use of tropes, word choice, and word order. Many other writers, like SENECA THE ELDER, QUINTILIAN and AULUS GELLIUS, among others, comment on the merits of a variety of literary works, but do not treat the theory of literary criticism in detail. RBC

See Russell, D. A. and Winterbottom, M., eds. (1972) *Ancient Literary Criticism: the principal texts in new translations*; Bresler, C. E. (1999) *Literary Criticism: an introduction to theory and practice*; Grube, G. M. A. (1968) *The Greek and Roman Critics*; Too, Y. L. (1998) *The Idea of Ancient Literary Criticism*.

literary theory see CRITICAL THEORY.

liturgies Citizens of Greek CITY-STATES did not regularly pay taxes. Instead, at Athens and elsewhere, wealthy citizens were required to perform *leitourgiai* ('people's works'), funding public events and amenities or meeting military and naval costs. XENOPHON, in *Oikonomikos* (*The Estate Manager*), outlines the duties of a rich landowner: performing lavish religious SACRIFICES, entertaining foreign friends, hosting one's fellow-citizens to keep political supporters happy, supplying horses to the CAVALRY, funding choruses at dramatic FESTIVALS (the *chorêgia*), organizing athletic teams, and paying the costs of a warship for a year (the *triêrarchia*). A lawsuit resulted if one man claimed that another was wealthier and should be called upon first, challenging him to accept the task or agree to a complete exchange (*antidosis*) of property.

Liturgies were not always resented, however, as public BENEFACTION brought popularity. The producer of a winning drama at Athens was allowed to dedicate a monument to his success in the city centre. In the hellenistic period, similar functions were often carried out by MAGISTRATES appointed from among the wealthy, who were expected to subsidize state expenditure and often received fulsome honours from the people in return. (see also TAXATION, GREEK) DGJS

See Davies, J.K. (1967) Demosthenes on liturgies, *JHS* 87: 33–40.

Livia (Livia Drusilla) 58 BC–AD 29 Married to Tiberius Claudius Nero in 43, and bore TIBERIUS in 42. Her DIVORCE in 39 BC and immediate remarriage to the already powerful Octavian (later AUGUSTUS) was scandalous because she was then expecting her second son, Drusus. The long but childless second marriage was a famously affectionate and successful partnership. Livia, like her sister-in-law Octavia, was publicly upheld as a model of Roman womanly virtue. Both women received great honours during Augustus' lifetime but Livia's surpassed all Roman female precedents on his death in AD 14 and the accession of her son Tiberius. Augustus' WILL gave her the title *Augusta*, appointment as chief PRIEST of Augustus' cult and adoption into the Julian family. SUETONIUS suggests that her influence, more tactfully exerted over her husband, alienated her emperor son, who withdrew to CAPRI in 27. Her popularity with the masses and the SENATE at Rome was enormous. Crowds gathered around the PALACE during her serious illness in 22, and her recovery was marked by a coin bearing a female image of the abstraction *salvs avgvsta* (Augustan/imperial health). From TACITUS' brief references to gossip, Robert Graves forged a powerful but historically ridiculous portrait of a Livia who poisoned her own grandchildren, her younger son and her ailing 77-year-old husband to secure the throne for Tiberius. Livia died in 29. She was deified by her great-grandson CLAUDIUS on his accession in 41. SD

See Cassius Dio, *Roman History* 57.3.12, 58.2; Suetonius, *Augustus*, *Tiberius*; Balsdon, J.P.V.D. (1962) *Roman Women*.

 AUGUSTUS: (a).

LIVIA: coin portrait.

Livii A *gens* at Rome in the Republican period, with different branches prominent at various times. In the 3rd and the early 2nd centuries BC, several representatives bear the *cognomen* Salinator. Another element in the family is characterized by the name Drusus, exemplified, among others, by two men named Marcus Livius Drusus, probably father and son. They were TRIBUNES in 122 and 91 BC respectively, and their policies caution historians against placing members of one family on the same side of all policy issues when other evidence is lacking. The tribune of 122 strongly opposed the idea of extending Roman CITIZENSHIP to the Italian allies and contributed to the fall of his fellow-tribune Gaius GRACCHUS who had proposed the measure. His namesake in 91 revived the Gracchan proposal with some modifications and was killed, as Gracchus had been.

LIVIA Drusilla, the wife of AUGUSTUS and the daughter of Marcus Livius Drusus Claudianus (a Claudius who had been adopted by a Livius, probably the tribune of 91), brought both of her names into the imperial family.

Manumitted SLAVES, like the playwright Lucius Livius Andronicus, and enfranchised Italians and their descendants, like the historian LIVY (Titus Livius), also carried the name. JV

Livius Andronicus see DRAMA, ROMAN; EPIC, ROMAN; POETRY, ROMAN.

Livy (Titus Livius) ?64 BC–AD ?17 Augustan HISTORIAN, author of a definitive history of Rome from its origins. The challenging years of the TRIUMVIRATE and early Augustan period (43–30 BC) inspired a number of meditations on Rome, its development and decline, and on the possibilities for its future, ranging from the UTOPIAN to the bleakly pessimistic. Livy's decision (made perhaps in the early 30s) to write a history of the Roman state from the fall of Troy to the present represents one of the most successful attempts to come to terms with the radical changes in the Roman world. His solution was similar to that of AUGUSTUS himself: he wrote Rome's history as a process of gradual development over time, of experimentation, of the interplay between tradition (the way of the ancestors, *mos maiorum*) and change, and of the difficult balance between charismatic leadership and the rights of the people as a whole. A concentration on Italy as well as Rome, and on the *plebs* as well as the ARISTOCRACY, marks the innovative nature of his project.

The history, called *Ab urbe condita* (*From the Founding of The City*), filled 142 books and covered events to 9 BC. This was probably not the stopping-point Livy originally planned (which has been variously estimated as earlier or later), but perhaps the point he had reached at his death. Books 1–120 – and perhaps the whole history – were probably published in groups of five; the surviving 35 (1–10, 21–45) narrate events through 167 BC. (We know the basic contents of the rest from late antique summaries, the *Periochae*.) Individual events are described in 'episodes,' which alternate with non-narrative material such as the record of trials, deaths or ritual activities; the history as a whole proceeds annalistically, articulated by yearly consular elections. Larger units, especially of five or ten books ('pentads' or 'decades'), are held together by repeated themes and images, dominant characters, the historian's own cross-references and other architectonic devices.

The history of Livian criticism has been marked by controversy, with scholarly consensus about his merits as a historian and as a thinker shifting according to the prevailing attitudes of the day. QUINTILIAN found him less authoritative than SALLUST; TACITUS used both men as models but gradually favoured a Sallustian approach. Dante spoke of 'Livy who does not err' (*Inferno* 28.12), while Machiavelli saw his history as a source of trenchant political analysis. Since the 19th century, however, scholars have tended to categorize his work as that of an 'armchair' or academic historian, and hence inferior in judgement and reliability to that of POLYBIOS or Tacitus, since unlike them Livy participated neither in politics nor in the military – though like them he came to Rome from the provinces (from Padua). Since the 1960s, influenced by new theories of historiography and literature, scholars have begun to evaluate Livy's historiographical technique on its own terms. They recognize that all history consists of events under a description, that is, of events which come to us already interpreted, whether by a historian, an archaeologist, or an ANTHROPOLOGIST. Even eyewitnesses will understand an event, and relay that understanding to others, differently (as recognized long ago: cf. THUCYDIDES 1.22). To an increasing number of cultural and literary historians, the primary value of ancient historical narrative lies in what it can tell us about the social, political, and intellectual assumptions and perceptions of the world it describes.

In his general *Preface* Livy engages the reader in his project, describing history – and his book – as a monument containing images which illustrate examples of every kind of behaviour. These examples are subjects for imitation or avoidance, and provide the medicine needed to cure social corruption. The reader, who is partly responsible for evaluating and wholly responsible for using them, is a citizen in a republic (*Preface* 9–10). Livy takes up Sallust's challenge to produce useful history, demonstrating ways of understanding the past in order to build the future. His role as guide causes him to intervene frequently in the narrative: sometimes he provides information similar to that in modern footnotes (for example, a variant in his sources, the physical traces believed to have been left by an ancient event, or the name of a historiographical authority). Sometimes he suggests how a story might be read, or discusses ways of finding and evaluating evidence. Reading Livy is not easy. His own authority can seem to undermine itself by the frequency with which he signals insecurity, conflict and debate among his sources, and by the almost comical despair with which he sometimes refuses to produce a definitive version of the past. Yet Livy is less interested in 'how it really was' than in how we read the past and what guidance it provides for contemporary MORAL and ETHICAL dilemmas; most importantly, he never minimizes the difficulty of history.

Style, for ancient as for modern critics, can be a means of interpretation, the author's voice and the form of his language a mirror of its content. Livy's style is tantalizingly varied, fashioned at once for utility – he writes in one way about exciting, moving events, in another about routine state business, in yet another way about legendary history, or about military manoeuvres – and for pleasure. He represents the beginning of imperial style, building on Sallust's jerky, mannered syntax and choice vocabulary, and anticipates developments in DECLAMATORY RHETORIC with its love of paradox, morbid psychology and intense emotion. But he was bred on the classicizing writers CAESAR and CICERO, together with the numerous (now lost) historians of the middle and late REPUBLIC. There is a delicate tension in his writing between the canonical and the experimental, perhaps reflecting his view of the world around him, in which tradition sat side by side with innovation and familiar names were filched for revolutionary concepts. CSK

See Chaplin, J. D. (2000) *Livy's Exemplary History*; Miles, G. (1995) *Livy: reconstructing early Rome*; Oakley, S. P. (1997) *A Commentary on Livy, Books VI–X*, vol. 1, introduction.

Lixus PHOENICIAN colony overlooking the Wadi Loukkos, 4 km (2.5 miles) inland from the Atlantic coast of Morocco. Like many Phoenician foundations, it possessed a good HARBOUR and dominated a fertile river valley. TRADE with the interior provided access to GOLD, COPPER, IRON, and LEAD. PLINY THE ELDER identified Lixus as the location of the Garden of the Hesperides and of a sanctuary of HERCULES (*Natural History* 5.2–4; 19.63). He and other ancient sources date its foundation to c.1100 BC. Archaeological evidence supports a later date, however. The earliest pottery belongs to the 7th–6th centuries BC and the first structures to the 4th century. The hellenistic and Roman phases of occupation are the most apparent.

EXCAVATIONS conducted by Spanish and French teams have revealed eight TEMPLES in a sanctuary that one is tempted to identify as that of Hercules-Melqart. The largest occupies 1,500 sq m. Several wealthy houses of the 2nd–3rd centuries AD have been excavated. Cemeteries, garum tanks and an amphitheatre have also been uncovered. The city was destroyed three times (100–50 BC; c.AD 40; c.AD 250); on each occasion it was rebuilt. CLAUDIUS elevated it to the status of a *colonia*. The town reached its largest extent in the 2nd–3rd centuries AD. It garrisoned the Cohors I Herculea in the 4th century and diminished in size afterwards. DLS

See various authors (1992) *Lixus: actes du colloque 1989*.

 CARTHAGE AND CARTHAGINIANS.

loans Among the many forms of loans in the ancient world were casual arrangements for the use of goods or money, negotiated among friends and family, and formal written agreements transacted with professional bankers or money-lenders. Loans for substantial sums normally required land as security. The largest exception to this general rule was a class of maritime trading loans where the loan was secured against the eventual cargo or sometimes the SHIP itself.

There was a variety of lending bodies. In Greece, collective institutions such PHRATRIES, DEMES and cult groups were prepared to lend small amounts to members at low interest rates. TEMPLES were a large source of credit, especially to wealthy borrowers. Banks and professional moneylenders were another source of credit. In Rome, credit could be obtained from wealthy landowners or professional bankers (*argentarii*).

Interest rates varied considerably. Size of loan, risk, and relationship to borrower all acted to determine the rate. For informal arrangements, the interest was often non-existent or negligible. More formal transactions attracted higher rates. Although no attempt was made in Athens legally to regulate interest rates, conventional usage seems to have regarded 12 per cent per annum as a reasonable interest rate. Highest rates were reserved for risky ventures such as trading ventures (up to 30 per cent or more) or small amounts borrowed for short periods (25 per cent per day is given in one source). On the other hand, Rome seems to have been more interventionist. At various times, different provisions were made to set interest rates. The TWELVE TABLES seem to contain a provision that prohibited interest rates above an annual rate of 100 per cent. It is unclear how successful these mechanisms were in controlling rates. AJLB

See Andreau, J. (1999) *Banking and Business in the Roman World*; Cohen, E. E. (1992) *Athenian Economy and Society*; Millett, P. (1991) *Lending and Borrowing in Ancient Athens*.

locks Apparently used relatively little in the classical Greek period, those locks which were used were of the simplest type of tumbler lock in which a tumbler (essentially a peg) dropped into a hole in the top of a bolt to prevent it being slid open. To open it, the tumbler was raised by means of a latch-lifter (the tip of which caught in a hole in the tumbler), so freeing the bolt which could then be slid by pulling a cord. The latch-lifter was a slightly curved rod, up-turned at its tip, with a flat handle. A more developed form of tumbler lock had paired tumblers which were raised by means of a T- or L-shaped key (lift-keys), the prongs of which were inserted into holes in the tumblers. Again the bolt was slid by a cord. The key holes for such locks were a vertical slot.

The most elaborate form of tumbler lock had a number of small tumblers that fell into holes which passed through the bolt. These tumblers were lifted by a key (slide key) which had teeth arranged in a pattern corresponding to the arrangement of the tumblers, a system which prevented the lock being opened by the wrong key. By pushing the teeth up into the holes in the underside of the bolt, the tumblers were raised clear of the bolt, which was then opened by sliding the key. By placing a spring above the tumblers to hold them in place and force them down, rather than relying on gravity, such locks could be adapted for use on portable objects such as caskets. The key-hole was L-shaped. This type of lock was the most popular form of lock used in the Roman period.

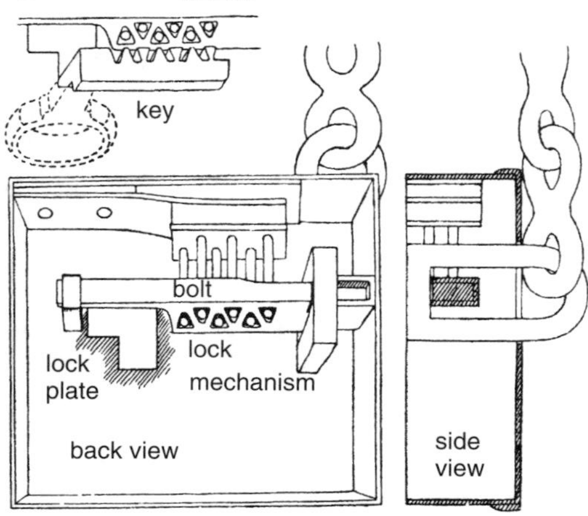

LOCKS: the more elaborate form of tumbler lock.

The most complex lock is the lever-lock, probably a Roman invention. It is derived from the tumbler lock, but used a single tumbler, pivoted at one end and held down by a spring. The lock was opened by turning the key, which had a flat plate (the bit) set at the end of a stem. As the key turned, the bit first lifted the tumbler and then caught in a notch, or against a projection, on the underside of the bolt, sliding it to one side and so opening the lock. To prevent the lock being opened by any other key, it had a series of wards which were matched by slits in the bit of the key. Keys for these locks are similar in appearance to modern keys.

Although lever locks usually took the form of padlocks, the commonest form of padlock consisted of a hollow case with a hole at one end, which received a bolt with a central spine that had two outward-curving springs riveted to its tip. When the bolt was pushed into the case the springs were compressed, only to spring out again once inside the case, so preventing the bolt being withdrawn. The lock was opened by inserting an L-shaped key into a slit in the rear end of the barrel. The bit of this key had a square hole in it that slipped over the springs on the bolt, compressing them against the spine and so allowing the bolt to be withdrawn. WHM

logic Shorthand for the Greek phrase 'art of reasoning' (*logikê technê*), 'logic' covers arguments in every sphere: from the courtroom to the philosophical debate, from the political arena to scientific theorizing. But Greek philosophers also invented what logic means today: formal logic, or the study of valid and invalid forms of argument independently of their content.

ARISTOTLE developed the most famous ancient system of formal logic. This is a sentential logic that involves identifying patterns of argument, or syllogisms, whose key terms are the quantities 'All' and 'Some'. In a syllogism a sequence of related propositions (e.g. All/Some persons are/are not Mortals) assert that all or some items do, or do not, have some property. A typical valid syllogism, with letters used as variables for classes, would be: All M is P; All S is M; therefore All S is P. M is the middle term that links S and P, as does 'men' in 'All men are mortal; all heroes are men; therefore all heroes are mortal'.

The other system, which was developed by the STOICS, was propositional logic. It identified argument forms that involved conditional (if . . . then), conjunctive (. . . and . . .), and disjunctive (either . . . or) statements in positive or negative form. A valid argument in propositional logic, with ordinal numbers used as variables for propositions, might be: If the first, then the second; but not the second; therefore not the first (e.g. 'If it is snowing, it is cold; it is not cold; therefore, it is not snowing'). Modern MATHEMATICAL logic has provided more elaborate rationales for both these ancient systems.

But schemes of formal logic formed only part of philosophical reasoning. Thus Aristotle, in addition to exploring deductive arguments in syllogistic form, identified induction (the drawing of conclusions from a set of examples), as well as 'dialectic' (valid reasoning based on agreed, but unproven, assumptions). He explored the latter in *The Topics*, while in the *Posterior Analytics* he formulated a theory of 'demonstrative science', i.e. SCIENCE founded on self-evident axioms. He also defined the field of modal logic, i.e. logic based on the related concepts of possibility, impossibility and necessity. Stoicism equally, though less elaborately, relied on other argument forms: e.g. the appeal to universally held principles (the 'common notions'), and analogies drawn from observations to establish theoretical claims.

Logic has a role not only in philosophy, but in all the significant forms of human discourse depicted in antiquity. It may be studied in disputes between characters in literature, in exercises in persuasion by orators, and in many informal argumentative contexts. In HOMER's *Iliad*, book 9, for example, ACHILLES concludes that since all human beings have the same fate (i.e. death), he himself has no reason to fight in the TROJAN WAR. This is a practical syllogism (it concludes with an action), a type of reasoning Aristotle later explored in his treatise on ETHICS. Again, Antigone in SOPHOKLES' play follows a religious principle (the dead should be buried) that she believes must override a man-made edict of the state (her brother should remain unburied). This is a piece of practical reasoning based on recognizing a hierarchy of rules derived from different sources of authority.

The techniques used by ORATORS in legal and political contexts were not always this elevated. In his *Art of Rhetoric* Aristotle drew on earlier practice to codify their techniques, an enterprise that CICERO later continued after his education in the Greek RHETORICAL tradition. Persuasion also involves appeals to the EMOTIONS, and here the SOPHIST Gorgias anticipated Aristotle in depicting its manipulative techniques.

The Sophists are famously, and somewhat unfairly, associated with specious forms of logic, designed and taught just to ensure victory in argument. They were mocked, and even accused of undermining morality, in ARISTOPHANES' *Clouds*, and had their philosophical limitations exposed in Plato's *Euthydemos*. Their fallacies were later inventoried in Aristotle's *Sophistical Refutations*. SOCRATES, despite Aristophanes' attempt to associate him with Sophistic logic, was committed to truth and moral excellence rather than argumentative victory. However, his refusal to claim KNOWLEDGE makes his method of inquiry (the *elenchos*) an unsystematic reaction to others' views, though some scholars believe that it relies on an implicit claim to knowledge. Socrates certainly identified the role of consistency and universality in ethical reasoning, and also reflected the long tradition of arguing from examples in demanding that moral knowledge conform to standards found in the specialized crafts to which he constantly referred. Plato, no innovator in logic, did offer important insights into the foundations of mathematics with his demand that such reasoning go beyond hypotheses and be based on knowledge of the content of mathematics. This was his paradigm of philosophical method.

In hellenistic thought there was, apart from Stoic logic, some innovation in the analysis of arguments based on empirical data, which were identified as 'signs' of entities that were not directly observable. The Epicureans and Stoics debated in this area, and the Epicurean PHILODEMOS, in his treatise *On Signs*, produced an important contribution to the history of the logic of scientific inquiry that reflected earlier Epicurean explorations. Also significant were debates between medical sects beginning in the late 1st century BC over the role of observation in connection with therapy. In the 2nd century AD Galen, who regarded a training in logic as essential for a physician, favoured an Aristotelian form of demonstration in the sciences rather than the reliance on data to the exclusion of theory that he deplored among certain contemporaries.

Finally, the SCEPTICS used logical techniques to argue against any commitment to claims to knowledge. Their arsenal of negative arguments was a logical *tour de force* designed to undermine the purpose of logic as an instrument of proof. But such nihilism was a side-show in a long tradition that saw logic as a constructive tool in philosophy, science, and practical affairs generally. RBT

See Kneale, W. and Kneale, M. (1978) *The Development of Logic*; Mueller, I. (1978) An introduction to Stoic logic, in J. Rist, ed., *The Stoics* 1–26; Smith, R. (1995) Logic, in J. Barnes, ed., *The Cambridge Companion to Aristotle* 27–65; Solmsen, F. (1975) *Intellectual Experiments of the Greek Enlightenment*.

Lokris Two regions in central Greece. West (Ozolian) Lokris stretched along the north coast of the Corinthian gulf from Naupaktos to Amphissa. East Lokris was known by various names (Opountian, Epiknemidian, Hypoknemidian) for parts or the whole, and reached from near THERMOPYLAI along the coast opposite EUBOIA to BOIOTIA. It is unclear why two geographically separated peoples shared the same name. Real connections were evident in the 5th century: East Lokrians founded a colony in the West Lokrian region at Naupaktos, before the place was taken by Athens and settled with MESSENIAN HELOTS c.460 BC. West Lokrians, along with neighbouring peoples in north-west Greece, were characterized by THUCYDIDES as primitive because they still regularly carried arms. The broad pattern is confirmed by a contemporary inscription which refers to PIRACY as accepted practice; they had not yet learned the *POLIS* habit. Despite the loss of Naupaktos, they fought alongside Athens under DEMOSTHENES during the PELOPONNESIAN WAR against their local enemies, who were Spartan allies; but East Lokris adhered to Sparta along with its Boiotian neighbours. Later both groups were found together, though that may be little more than coincidence. Both fought against Sparta during the Corinthian war. After LEUKTRA (371), both joined the first of EPAMEINONDAS' PELOPONNESIAN invasions. PHOKIANS subjected both to pressure in the third SACRED WAR. In the hellenistic period, West Lokris became part of the AITOLIAN LEAGUE, but the fate of the East Lokrians was more varied. Important excavations have taken place at the hellenistic town of Halai on the coast of East Lokris. JBS

See Coleman, J. E. et al. (1999) Halai, *Hesperia* 68: 285–341; Fossey, J. M. (1990) *The Ancient Topography of Opountian*

Lokris; Nielsen, T.H. (2004) East Lokris, in Hansen and Nielsen, *Inventory* 664–73.

 Greece.

Lombards The Lombards are first recorded by Tacitus (*Germania* 40) on the Lower Elbe in Lower Saxony. Their first aggressive action against Rome was a raid on Pannonia in c.AD 170, but the tribe did not otherwise participate in the empire's break-up. The Lombard migration in the 5th century towards Noricum/Pannonia is documented by the mid-7th-century *Origo gentis Langobardorum* (*Origin of the Lombards*) and the late 8th-century Lombard historian Paul the Deacon. A kingdom was established in Pannonia from 526 to 568, in which period the Lombards became allies of Byzantium, with troops serving in Persia and in the Byzantine-Gothic wars in Italy. In 569 they invaded Byzantine Italy, and despite not conquering the whole peninsula, they established a powerful kingdom based chiefly in the northern plains, with dukes established in the major cities, notably Cividale, Verona and Trento. Their capital lay first at Milan and, subsequently, Pavia. Larger semi-independent duchies were created at Spoleto and Benevento. As in Pannonia, archaeological evidence for the Lombards exists primarily in the form of cemeteries (notably Nocera Umbra, Castel Trosino and Trezzo sull'Adda); various place-names also record their settlement. The Lombards, initially pagan and Arian Christian, fully converted to orthodox Christianity in the late 7th century; extensive church and monastery building is attested in the 8th century and extant examples exist at Brescia, Cividale, Spoleto and Benevento. In addition, a series of law-codes were issued in Latin under the various kings between 650 and 756. The northern Lombard kingdom was conquered by Charlemagne in 774. However, independent Lombard rule persisted within the duchy (principality) of Benevento and in lesser principalities at Salerno and Capua into the 11th century. NJC

See Christie, N. (1995) *The Lombards*; Wickham, C. (1981) *Early Medieval Italy*.

London (Londinium) The principal city of Roman Britain. Hundreds of recent archaeological excavations, occasioned by office building, provide a detailed if fragmentary picture of London's evolution through the Roman period but few remains are now visible. No significant settlement existed before the Claudian conquest of AD 43. The main occupation dates after 47, by which time the strategic value of the site – where a tidal pool of the Thames formed a natural port at a bridging point – was evident. The Roman road network focused on this crossing. Londinium is first mentioned by Tacitus (*Annales* 14.32), who noted the site's vigour prior to destruction by Boudican rebels in AD 60. Archaeology confirms extensive suburban growth along the approach roads to the settlement. At this time London had no formal status, but the burial here of Julius Alpinus Classicianus, the procurator of the province appointed after the revolt, illustrates its importance. The settlement may possibly have been founded as a supply base for campaigns then underway to the north-west.

Timber quays were built along the waterfront adjacent to a ferry or bridge (on the site of the present London Bridge) in AD 63. This area was subsequently a busy port flanked by warehouses. London's main growth took place under the Flavians, and a major programme of public works continued over 50 years from c.70. Public buildings, including baths, temples and palaces, were built over riverside embankments. At the town centre a forum with a stone basilica replaced an earlier public open space surrounded by shops and stores. This was in turn replaced in the 2nd century by a massively enlarged complex. A fort built north-west of town in the late 1st century probably housed soldiers seconded to the governor and offices of provincial administration. Nearby was an amphitheatre, rebuilt c.120 to house up to 8,000 spectators.

The urban area, defined by bank and ditch, and enlarged more than once to cope with growth, was filled with houses, shops and workshops built of timber or mudbrick, often clad with weatherboarding. These were sometimes decorated with sophisticated wall-paintings and mosaics. From the 2nd century, especially after fire destroyed large parts of the town c.125, houses were more commonly stone-built. London's principal industries included tanning and baking. Glass and metalworking are also well attested. Water mills operated beside the Walbrook, a canalized stream which flowed into the Thames here.

London contracted massively in the late 2nd century, perhaps because of a decline in military-related commerce. The early 3rd century saw partial revival: a masonry town wall was erected and a monumental arch may have been part of a temple precinct built or restored at this time. Important discoveries from the later town include a temple of Mithras, a monumental public building – perhaps a palace – erected by the usurper Allectus in AD 293–4 and a large basilical building which may have been a 4th-century cathedral. Cemeteries, containing hundreds of thousands of graves, have been found outside the town gates. Some burials were accompanied by items of military dress of 4th–5th-century design. The city, much of which had already been given over to fields and gardens in previous phases of contraction, was largely abandoned in the 5th century. DP

See Milne, G. (1995) *English Heritage Book of Roman London*; Perring, D. (1991) *Roman London*; Watson, B., ed. (1998) *Roman London: recent archaeological work*.

 Britannia.

Longinus The name given to the author of a remarkable piece of literary criticism, entitled *On the Sublime*, which is usually dated to the 1st century AD. About two thirds of the original survives. The work aims to provide a proper treatment of the emotional element of literature (pathos), rather than relying on an analysis of dry rhetorical tropes. The question that 'Longinus' persistently asks is 'what are the characteristics of great literature'? Such works, he maintains in an almost Romantic fashion, have the capacity to transport. They do this, furthermore, in a universal manner. Great writers have access to a vigour and nobility of mind – or creativity,

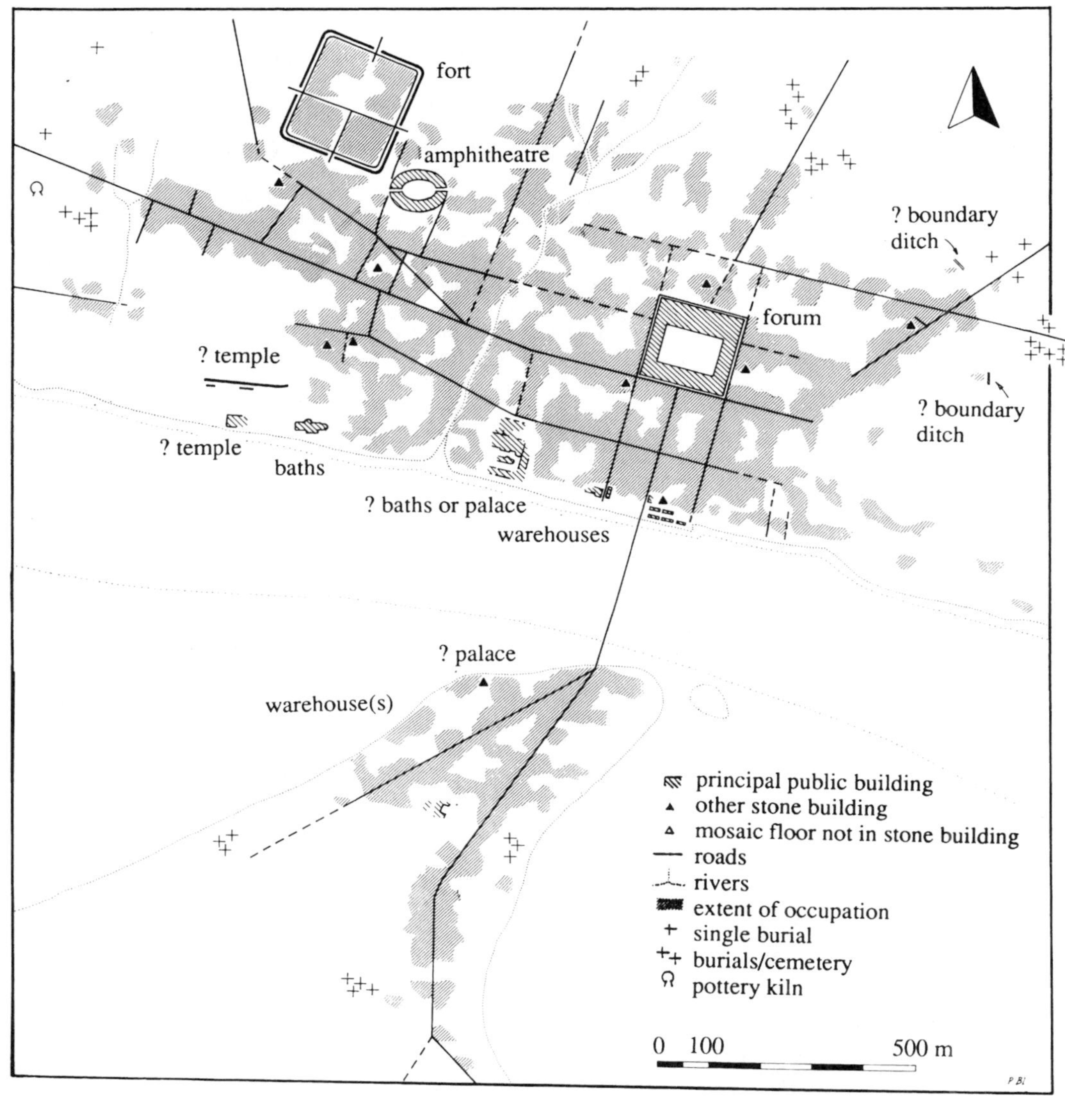

LONDON: plan of the city in the 2nd century AD.

as we would say – that, unromantically, is fed in part by the writer's own nature and in part by his training. In its close analysis of specific passages (drawn from EURIPIDES, SAPPHO or DEMOSTHENES) and authors (such as HOMER) combined with an insistence on feeling, the author rings curiously modern. He resembles most a cross between a Romantic critic and a 'New Critic'. Of all of the ancient literary critics Longinus speaks mostly and most sympathetically to modern audiences. PGT

See Fyfe, W. H. and Roberts, W. R., trs. (1960) (with Aristotle, *Poetics*, etc.).

Longobards see LOMBARDS.

Longus Some time in the 2nd or 3rd century AD, Longus wrote a much-loved NOVEL of four books entitled *Daphnis and Chloe*, or, more fully, *The Pastoral Story of Daphnis and Chloe*. (Its popularity is amply indicated by the more than 500 translations in the 18th and 19th centuries.) Longus is the most approachable of the ancient Greek novelists (the others are Xenophon of EPHESOS, Achilles Tatius and Heliodoros). The popularity of *Daphnis and Chloe* is the product primarily of its theme – the first love of innocents in an idyllic setting. Daphnis and Chloe are both abandoned children brought up by step-parents on the island of LESBOS as SHEPHERDS. As the novel progresses they gradually discover by precept and practice what love means for them emotionally and, of course, physically (such is the great plan of the god Love or EROS). The final union of the two young lovers is postponed by a variety of outlandish, if amusing, mishaps related to PIRACY, war and the attentions of rival suitors, all elements to be seen in other Greek novels. Their union (physically and emotionally) is in the end vouchsafed by MARRIAGE. This is provided furthermore with the blessing of their now-found true parents, ARISTOCRATS from the Lesbian capital of Mytilene. The tale is a simple one, but it is not without literary resource and reference. Ancient readers would have enjoyed the many references to earlier literary texts. PGT

See Gill, C., trs. (1989) Introduction and notes to Longus, *Daphnis and Chloe*, in B.P. Reardon, ed., *Collected Ancient Greek Novels* 285–348; Hägg, T. (1983) *The Novel in Antiquity* (1983); Winkler, J. (1990) *The Constraints of Desire*.

looms see WEAVING.

love The Greeks referred to 'love' in several ways, by using the terms *erôs* (meaning, to all intents and purposes, 'passion, destructive illicit love, sex'), *agapê* ('pure love that transcends sex') and *philia* ('companionship, passion, friendship, oneness'). The ancient Greek concept of love is clearly difficult to pin down and define. PHILOSOPHY promoted the ideal image of faithful (usually non-sexual) love, defined by the male pederastic love of an *erastês* ('lover') for an *erômenos* ('beloved'). These unbalanced relationships were supposedly characterized by mutual tenderness and love. By contrast, women were capable of returning their male lovers' passion and were referred to as exhibiting *anterôs* ('counter-desire'). Greek men clearly wanted faithful love, but when they actually did fall in love they considered themselves sick and tormented by a power beyond their control. They found love a god-sent affliction that lasted too long; they 'burn', 'ache', 'contort' and 'suffer' the pangs of love, which is often symbolized by the barbed arrows shot from the bow of the personification of love, EROS (Latin: Amor, Cupid) one of the oldest of the gods. Erotic literature and magic spells attest to the passion of love – but for whom? The Greeks did not necessarily connect love with MARRIAGE; wives were primarily considered as housekeepers and mothers, not inevitably as lovers. But that is not to dismiss the idea of marital love altogether. Even militaristic Homeric society produced its true-love romance in the partnership of ANDROMACHE and HEKTOR. The word *homonoia* means 'oneness of mind' and is often used by classical ORATORS and PHILOSOPHERS to refer to the love between a husband and wife. Nevertheless, *hetairai* (courtesans) were held superior to wives and often commanded a man's passions and love.

LOVE: Etruscan sarcophagus cover showing a married couple embracing tenderly in bed.

Unlike Greeks, the Romans preferred love without philosophy, but, like the Greeks, love (*amor*) was irrelevant to the success of a marriage. Love diminished one's ability for rational thought and was not something to be envied – themes that occur time and again in Latin erotic POETRY. There are, however, numerous attestations of positive Roman attitudes to love: POMPEY's devotion to his young wife Julia was renowned, though his critics regarded it as effeminate weakness. There is little doubt about ANTONY's deep love for CLEOPATRA (certainly as portrayed by PLUTARCH), even though his opponents saw his passion as a dangerous flaw. For to fall in love, to be spellbound by a woman, was to be in her power. The story of Dido and AENEAS well reflects Roman values, because it depicts the triumph of duty (and imperial conquest) over love. Familial love and a respect for ancestors, however, was highly regarded. Cicero's tender love for his daughter TULLIA (which outweighs any affection he had for his wife, whom he divorced after 30 years of marriage) is demonstrated at the time of her premature death, which broke the spirit of her father, who never fully recovered. LL-J

See Davidson, J. (1998) *Courtesans and Fishcakes*; Rawson, B. (1991) *Marriage, Divorce, and Children in Ancient Rome*.

SEX: (see PROSTITUTES).

Lucan (Marcus Annaeus Lucanus) AD 39–65 EPIC POET. Lucan was born in Corduba, Spain, but – like most young men of good family – educated in Rome and Athens. Like his uncle, the PHILOSOPHER SENECA THE YOUNGER, he was initially on good terms with the emperor NERO, his close contemporary. Having been appointed to the offices of *quaestor* and *augur*, he subsequently fell from favour and, in AD 65, joined the conspiracy to assassinate Nero led by Gaius Calpurnius Piso. When the conspiracy was discovered later the same year, he was compelled to commit SUICIDE.

Lucan's only surviving work (though the titles and some fragments of several others are preserved) is the *Civil War* (*De bello civili*) or *Pharsalia*, an epic in ten books, apparently unfinished at the time of his death. The subject is the war between CAESAR and POMPEY, culminating in the battle of PHARSALUS (48 BC). As it stands, the poem ends with the aftermath of the battle (the murder of Pompey and Caesar's liaison with CLEOPATRA in ALEXANDRIA). It has been speculated that the poet planned two further books (bringing the total to 12, to correspond with the 12 books of VIRGIL's *Aeneid*), and would perhaps have concluded his epic with the suicide of CATO after the battle of THAPSUS.

The *Civil War* is notable for the bleakness of its moral outlook. Of the three main protagonists, Caesar is portrayed as a power-hungry monster, Pompey as a weak has-been and Cato as a paradigm of almost superhuman virtue who is nevertheless powerless to resist the destruction of the REPUBLIC. Lucan (uniquely) jettisons the conventional supporting cast of GODS AND GODDESSES: the presiding deity of his poem is an arbitrary and apparently amoral abstraction, Fortuna. Highly RHETORICAL in style, and embellished with scenes of extreme and at times grotesque VIOLENCE, the *De bello civili* is a challenging and unsettling work which has found increasing favour with classicists in recent decades, but continues to excite considerable critical controversy. MG

See Lucan, *Civil War*, trs. S. M. Braund, (1992); Ahl, F. M. (1976) *Lucan*.

Lucania see ITALY, ROMAN.

Lucian A self-portrait in the *Dream* as 'a Syrian barbarian in speech' from a poor family was no doubt a clever way for Lucian to emphasize his achievement as a speaker of crystalline Greek and a successful sophist. Born at SAMOSATA on the banks of the Euphrates c.AD 120 he travelled widely, won reputation and wealth throughout the Roman empire and ended his life as civil servant in Egypt. This elusive author, given only a wretched derivative notice in the *SUDA*, sat uncomfortably between RHETORIC and PHILOSOPHY, accused of betrayal by the first and maltreatment by Dialogue, the son of the second, in the *Double Indictment*. Purporting to 'laugh at most things and taking nothing seriously' (*Menippus* 21), he turned the serio-comic upside down: instead of using humour for serious purpose, he often masks his humour under a pretence of seriousness.

The Lucianic corpus includes 86 titles, some spurious. It is characterized by a bewildering diversity of forms and styles, some of which confound generic distinctions. For Lucian wrote verse, a mock TRAGEDY in iambics and other metres, the *Gout*, and a hybrid mixture of iambics, hexameters and prose, *Zeus the Tragic Actor*. His prose pieces include 'curtain-raisers' (*prolaliai*) designed to humour the audience and commend the speaker (e.g *Herodotus or Aetion*); sophistic DECLAMATIONS (e.g. *Phalaris* 1 and 2); letters (*Peregrinus*); epideictic pieces such as the *Hall*; paradoxical (the *Fly*) or witty (the *Portraits*) praises; dialogues, either philosophical, parodying SOCRATIC refutations (*Zeus Refuted*) and PLATONIC banquet (the *Symposium or Lapiths*); or MYTHOLOGICAL, using the GODS for mocking naive anthropomorphism or more secular forms of authority. He may pose as a historian with *On the Syrian Goddess*, an imitation of HERODOTOS' language and style, and the *True Story*, a parody of Ktesias and Iamboulos explicitly presented as a metaliterary text; or as a critic of the inflated style, pedantic technicalities and excessive flattery of contemporary HISTORIOGRAPHY (*How to Write History*). He also wrote BIOGRAPHIES, either satirical as is the one discrediting Alexander of Abonuteichos, *The False Prophet*, or encomiastic, as is *Demonax*.

Under the guise of 'Free Speech, son of Truthful, grandson of Exposure', Diogenes, Menippos, Timon or Anacharsis, the perspicacious barbarian, Lucian – the inside outsider who defines himself as a 'hater of boasters, hater of fraud, hater of liars and hater of humbugs' (*Fisherman* 20) – deploys his caustic irony against those puffed up by wealth and power. He also debunks all kinds of pretenders, the ignorant book collectors, the hyper-Atticists 'who talk from a thousand years ago' (*Lexiphanes 20*), the charlatan sophists (*The Teacher of Rhetoric*), the sham philosophers (*Fisherman*) and the hunters of notoriety such as the CYNIC Peregrinos.

How should one gauge the *Comedy of Traditions* that parades his debt to the ancient masters of invective, ARCHILOCHOS and ARISTOPHANES? Probably as an attempt to take shelter from the present in a world of literary reminiscences, or, better, as a keen criticism of the contemporary social scene, written in the only language acceptable to those interested in literature: that is, the language of tradition. SS

See Branham, B. (1989) *Unruly Eloquence*; Jones, C. P. (1986) *Culture and Society in Lucian*.

Lucilla (Annia Aurelia Galeria Lucilla) AD 7 March 150–82 Empress, wife of Lucius Verus. One of 14 or 15 children, and the second daughter, born to the emperor MARCUS AURELIUS and Faustina, she was a granddaughter of the emperor ANTONIUS PIUS and FAUSTINA the Elder. Especially among the males, the family was of feeble constitution. Of eight boys, at least one stillborn, only one, the emperor COMMODUS, was still alive at Marcus Aurelius' death in 180 and merely one more, Marcus Annius Verus (AD 162–9) reached the age of six. The six girls fared better, with only Lucilla's older sister predeceasing her father (unless a putative seventh girl was born c.166) and the rest living long enough to marry, sometimes twice. Lucilla's name derives from her paternal grandmother and great-grandmother, both named Domitia Lucilla.

When his father-in-law died in 161, Marcus Aurelius chose Lucius Verus as co-emperor, betrothed him to Lucilla, and sent him, in 163, to take charge of the Eastern frontier. In c.164, Lucilla travelled to EPHESOS where she married Verus and became an Augusta. She was about 14 years old, with a husband nearly 20 years her senior. Lucilla and her husband returned to Rome in 166. Verus celebrated a TRIUMPH for his military successes against the PARTHIANS, but died while on route to the northern frontier in 169, of apoplexy. Lucilla had borne him a son and a daughter who both died young and a daughter who lived long enough to marry. Almost immediately, Lucilla was married against her will to Tiberius Claudius Pompeianus, an experienced governor and military commander trusted by Marcus Aurelius and nearing the age of 50; she was 19. During the marriage, she gave birth to a son, Aurelius Commodus Pompeianus. In 182, Lucilla formed a conspiracy, which included her married daughter, against her brother Commodus. The plot was unsuccessful, and she was first exiled to the island of CAPRI, but later executed. Her husband Pompeianus, who had retired to private life and was not implicated, was asked twice in 193, by Pertinax and Didius Julianus, to play a role in imperial administration, but was by then very old and unwell.

While she was married to Lucius Verus, Lucilla appears on COINAGE as an empress, with reverses depicting CYBELE and VENUS. She had also appeared on coins as a child. Coinage of her mother as empress, when Marcus Aurelius had been co-emperor with Antoninus Pius even before 161, depict Faustina with children of different number, ages and sexes. While the coins might simply represent Faustina's fertility, they are more easily understood, especially because the number rises from two to six, as family portraits depicting children born and still surviving at the time of minting. Several surviving portrait busts have been identified as representations of Lucilla. JV

See Historia Augusta, Marcus, Lucius Verus; Birley, A. R. (1986) *Marcus Aurelius.*

 TRAJAN.

Lucius Verus see ANTONINUS PIUS; EMPERORS, ROMAN; FRONTO; HERODES ATTICUS; LUCILLA; MARCUS AURELIUS; PARTHIAN WARS; POLYAINOS.

EMPERORS, ROMAN: (a); TRAJAN.

Lucretia A legendary rape victim of early Rome. The earliest account is LIVY 1.53.4–60; others include OVID in *Fasti* and CASSIUS DIO. In the legend, Sextus, son of TARQUINIUS SUPERBUS, entered the married Lucretia's bedroom, threatening murder if she did not sleep with him. Upon rejection, he proposed to place a dead SLAVE by her corpse, since adultery with a slave was a disgraceful crime. Lucretia yielded, but the next morning informed witnesses and executed herself as adulterous. This provoked Lucius Junius BRUTUS to revolt against Superbus and form a Republic.

Livy's Lucretia was a model of matronly virtue, a symbol of Rome and the immutability of law. However, her post-classical reputation has wavered. AUGUSTINE (1) damned Lucretia as adulterous or murderous (*City of God*). She was ridiculous or pure in Chaucer, Machiavelli and Shakespeare, and appealed to the erotic imagination of RENAISSANCE artists; Titian treated shockingly the moment before rape. Lucretia still provokes. Her resemblance to Livy's VERGINIA in the 5th century BC, killed by her father for refusing to submit to a *decemvir*, suggests that the writer was guided by sexual politics, not historical judgement. For feminists, Lucretia embodies women's conventional historical role as self-erasing; she is the space history conquers. SC

See Donaldson, I. (1982) *The Rapes of Lucretia*; Joshel, S. R. (1992) The body female and the body politic: Livy's Lucretia and Verginia, in A. Richlin, ed., *Pornography and Representation in Greece and Rome* 112–30.

Lucretius (Titus Lucretius Carus) c.97–55 BC Didactic POET. Nothing is known of Lucretius' life or background (the sensational details reported in the *Chronicle* of St JEROME, according to which the poet went mad after drinking a love-potion and subsequently committed SUICIDE, are now generally discredited). His only known work, the *De rerum natura* (*On the Nature of the Universe*), is a DIDACTIC poem in six books, dealing with the PHILOSOPHY of EPICURUS. Lucretius' focus is mainly on the physical aspects of the system, according to which the universe consists exclusively of ATOMS and empty space, and is immune from divine interference. Books 1 and 2 deal with the fundamental principles of atomic physics; 3 and 4 with human physiology (the nature of the SOUL and the senses, sleep, dreams and sex); 5 and 6 with the nature and origins of our world, including an assortment of celestial and terrestrial phenomena from lightning and earthquakes to magnetism and epidemic diseases.

Although the subject matter of the poem is – in modern terms – largely scientific, there is a clear, albeit largely implicit, emphasis throughout on ETHICS. Epicurus regarded fear of death and of the GODS as the two most serious obstacles to human happiness; and Lucretius structures his poem in such a way as to throw emphasis onto the abolition of these two sources of anxiety. The first half of the poem culminates in an extended argument for the mortality of the soul; death is simply the end of existence, and hence should not be a source of fear. The accounts of human physiology, COSMOLOGY and meteorology in the second half are designed to provide mechanistic explanations for phenomena traditionally regarded as manifestations of divine intervention.

The *De rerum natura* is a poetic masterpiece as well as a philosophical treatise. Lucretius responds with relish to the challenge presented by his technical subject matter, taking advantage of the Epicurean principle that sensory evidence should be our main criterion of truth. The poem abounds with passages of vivid description, and the extended simile, traditional in EPIC poetry, is effectively co-opted to serve as a vehicle for the development of 'scientific' analogies. Notable, too, is the prominence of military imagery. Lucretius presents an implicit challenge to the ethos of HOMERIC and ENNIAN epic, by representing Epicurus (especially in 1.62–79) as a conquering hero in the mould of HERAKLES, ALEXANDER the Great and the Roman generals. NATURE, too, is personified as the (feminine) power presiding over the 'battles' of the atoms, and – in combination with her alter ego, the symbolic figure of VENUS invoked in the opening lines of the poem – acts as a kind of challenge or alternative to the masculine warrior heroes of conventional epic. On the literal level, conversely, military activity is disparaged as a manifestation of futile ambition.

The reception of Lucretius' poem, with its rationalistic, materialist outlook, has varied greatly from the RENAISSANCE to the modern era. The *De rerum natura* has, at different periods, met with reactions ranging from enthusiastic acclaim to horror (at the author's alleged atheism) or disdain (at its supposedly prosaic subject matter). MG

See Lucretius, *De rerum natura*, text and translation W. H. D. Rouse, rev. M. F. Smith (1982); Gale, M. R. (2001) *Lucretius and the Didactic Epic*; Johnson, W. R. (2000) *Lucretius and the Modern World.*

Lucullus see ASIA, ROMAN; AVIARIES; CLODIUS.

ludi see ATHLETES AND ATHLETICS, ROMAN; CAPITOLINE TRIAD; DRAMA, ROMAN; EDUCATION, ROMAN; GAMES, ROMAN; GLADIATORS; HOLIDAYS; JUPITER; RITUAL, ROMAN; TRIUMPHS.

ludi saeculares see HORACE; LYRIC POETRY, ROMAN; MUSIC; PHILIP THE ARAB.

Lugdunum see LYON.

lumber see CARPENTRY; TIMBER.

Lupercalia see FESTIVALS, ROMAN; RITUALS, ROMAN.

Lusitania The name of the Roman PROVINCE, formed from part of the Republican province of Hispania Ulterior after the wars against the Cantabri and the Astures (27–16 BC), the remainder becoming the province of Baetica. The northern boundary was the river Durius (Douro), the southern the river Anas (Guadiana). The capital of the province was at Emerita Augusta (Mérida),which also formed the centre for one of the three judicial *conventus*, the others being based on Pax Iulia (Beja) and Scallabis (Santarem). It took its name from the group of CELTIC peoples known as the Lusitani, who had fought against the Romans under the leadership of VIRIATHUS in the mid-2nd century BC and who occupied much of the area. Although there were Roman towns in Lusitania, such as the *municipia* at Olisippo (Lisbon) and Conimbriga (Condeixa a Velha), it remained less urbanized than other areas, such as Baetica or the eastern coast, but the industries of metal MINING (especially SILVER) and FISHING were important. In the late empire, large-scale VILLAS were built, especially in the south of the province. After the Germanic invasions of AD 409, the area fell into the hands of the ALANI and by the later 5th century was divided between the Suevi and the Visigoths. JSR

See Alarcão, J. de (1988) *Roman Portugal*; Edmondson, J. C. (1987) *Two Industries in Roman Lusitania*; Richardson, J. S. (1996) *The Romans in Spain*.

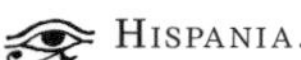 HISPANIA.

Lyceum (Lykeion) The name of the public GYMNASIUM where Aristotle lectured from 335 BC until shortly before his death in 322 (Aristotle had not been elected to headship of the Academy on PLATO's death). The Lyceum continued to be associated with PHILOSOPHICAL and SCIENTIFIC researches in the Aristotelian tradition after his death, when his mantle was assumed by his pupil THEOPHRASTOS (d.287 BC). Aristotelian philosophy was of a more empirical cast than that associated with Plato's Academy; Theophrastos sought, among other things, to plug the gaps left by Aristotle in his biological and physical researches with a series of works on plants, on minerals and on FIRE, as well as a short 'METAPHYSICS' and treatises on meteorology. Theophrastos also organized the systematic study of the history of ideas, or doxography, to which enterprise ultimately we owe much of our knowledge of early GREEK PHILOSOPHY. Theophrastos' successor Straton (d. c.265 BC) continued the tradition, adopting a powerfully all-embracing form of naturalism which rejected teleological explanations, as well as arguing for absolute concepts of space and time. After his death, ARISTOTELIANISM, and with it the Lyceum, lapsed into obscurity, until the revival of Aristotle's philosophy in the imperial period. RJH

See Lynch, J. (1971) *Aristotle's School*.

Lycia A mountainous region of south-west Asia Minor. Difficult communications with the interior of ANATOLIA, and a good supply of TIMBER for SHIPBUILDING and coastal harbourage, encouraged Lycia to look towards the sea and brought it into contact with Greece, especially RHODES. In origin the Lycians were probably descendants of ancient indigenous Anatolians. Politically, Lycia was probably a monarchy, becoming a league of cities in hellenistic times. Its language and culture were distinctive and often thought to be conservative, perhaps resulting from geographical isolation and HERODOTOS' tale that they traced lineage through the female line. However, once Lycia came into contact with Greece, civic life and culture developed along Greek lines and Lycian towns bore typical Greek hallmarks. The Lycian script was also largely derived from that of Greece, though the language itself is not yet fully understood.

Avoiding LYDIAN domination, Lycia was conquered for PERSIA by Harpagos (c.540 BC), who attacked the principal city of XANTHOS, on the region's only fertile plain. The Xanthians set fire to their city and families, and died fighting rather than be subject to Persia. This most famous act was repeated when Xanthos was again besieged by Brutus in the 1st century BC. In the mid-5th century, Lycia was freed of Persian control and became a tributary area of the Delian league. Subsequently, it was again ruled by Persian satraps until it was freed by ALEXANDER in 333 BC. It fell under Ptolemaic rule during the hellenistic period. AG

See Bryce, T. R. (1986) *The Lycians I*; Keen, A. G. (1998) *Dynastic Lycia*.

 ANATOLIA.

Lycurgus of Athens, Lykurgus of Sparta see LYKOURGOS OF ATHENS, LYKOURGOS OF SPARTA.

Lydia The kingdom of the Lydians (the Homeric 'Maeonians') was centred on western central Asia Minor in a basin of the upper Hermos, Caÿster and Maeander valleys. On a route from the Near East to the AEGEAN, this location was to prove important, especially to the Lydian capital, SARDIS, through which the Persian Royal Road and later Roman ROADS passed. The GOLD of the country was legendary. The Lydians adopted the Greek alphabet, and Lydian kings made rich dedications at Greek sanctuaries. HERODOTOS tells us that the Lydians were the first people to mint COINAGE (now dated to the mid-7th century BC), an invention which was soon taken up by the Asiatic Greeks.

When Gyges (687–652 BC) usurped the Heraclid king Kandaules to establish the dynasty of the Mermnadai, he tried to extend the Lydian kingdom westward to the Aegean coast. He moved down the three river valleys towards the Ionian cities of

SMYRNA, Kolophon and MILETOS, ports at the end of the eastern trade route. The incursions of the Kimmerians into Asia Minor halted Gyges' expansion. He was succeeded by Ardys, who repelled the Cimmerians and expanded Lydia east to the river Halys, though he and his successors failed to complete the expansion westwards and Greek cities such as Miletos repeatedly resisted capture. When Lydia's most famous king, Croesus (563–546) attacked PERSIA, having consulted the DELPHIC ORACLE, he brought about his own downfall and Persia took Lydia. Sardis was sacked in 499 during the IONIAN REVOLT. After two centuries of Persian rule, ALEXANDER took Sardis without a struggle in 334 BC. The city flourished until an EARTHQUAKE in AD 17. The rebuilt Sardis was a prosperous Roman town due to its strategic situation. AG

 ANATOLIA.

Lykia see LYCIA.

Lykophron Hellenistic tragedian and poet. Lykophron, son of Sokles, was a native of Chalkis in EUBOIA. He was born around 330–320 BC and went to ALEXANDRIA around 283, during the reign of Ptolemy II Philadelphos. There he was appointed to the LIBRARY to assemble the texts of the comic POETS. Presumably inspired by this task, he wrote a prose work about COMEDY which does not survive. The date of his death is uncertain, though OVID informs us that he was killed by an arrow.

Lykophron is included among the Tragic Pleiad, the seven pre-eminent tragedians of the time. As a poet he sought to emulate the style of AESCHYLUS. It is unclear how many tragedies he wrote (the Byzantine author Tzetses cites 46 or 64, while the *SUDA* lists only 20) and only four lines of one of his tragedies (the *Pelopidai*) survive. He also wrote a SATYR drama based on his former tutor, the PHILOSOPHER Menedemos, of which some fragments survive.

One whole work, ascribed to Lykophron by the *Suda*, remains extant. This is the *Alexandra*, a poem about the TROJAN WAR, composed in the form of a messenger's speech from TRAGEDY. The poem is famous for its obscure style and vocabulary, and many ancient grammarians wrote commentaries attempting to elucidate the difficulties. Much recent scholarly debate has focused on whether this work was actually composed by Lykophron at all, or by a later poet, perhaps of the same name. FMM

See Mair, A.W. and Mair, G. R., trs. (1921) (with Callimachus, *Hymns*, etc.); Mooney, G.W. (1921) *The Alexandra of Lycophron*.

Lykourgos of Athens c.390–c.325/4 BC Athenian statesman. A student of PLATO and ISOKRATES, Lykourgos rose to political prominence in the second half of the 4th century. He controlled Athenian state finances, either directly or through his friends, for twelve years from the mid-330s to the mid-320s. He may have held an official position, but the evidence is uncertain. He was largely responsible for Athens' economic recovery and a level of prosperity unknown since the end of the 5th century, with revenue growing to an average of 1,200 talents. He was also behind an ambitious public building programme, which included substantial additions to the fleet, as well as religious, political, military and financial reforms. Although he had held an aggressively anti-Macedonian stance during the war with PHILIP (he was one of the eight hostages demanded by ALEXANDER after the fall of THEBES), he advocated peace in the post-CHAIRONEIA period in order to establish financial security and regroup Athens' military and financial resources. Of the 15 speeches known to Pseudo-Plutarch, only one, *Against Leokrates*, has come down to us. LGM

See Pseudo-Plutarch, *The Lives of the Ten Orators*; Burtt, J. O., trs. (1954) *Minor Attic Orators*, vol. 2; Mitchel, F.W. (1973) Lykourgan Athens, in C. G. Boulter et al., eds., *Lectures in memory of Louise Taft Semple, 2nd Series* 163–214.

Lykourgos of Sparta Spartan lawgiver whose date and existence were debated even in antiquity. Different aspects of Spartan society should be distinguished. (1) Constitutional reforms embodied in the Great Rhetra, a seemingly genuine archaic text preserved in PLUTARCH's *Lykourgos*. These made Sparta a kind of early DEMOCRACY, and can plausibly be linked to a real lawgiver c.700–650 BC. (2) Peculiar social practices, some originating in pre-literate times, others evolving piecemeal later. (3) The famed austerity, which on archaeological evidence cannot be earlier than late archaic. Using Finley's tag, it may represent a mid-6th-century 'reinstitutionalization' of old customs with the aim of creating a successful military society. All these changes and more were attributed, impossibly, to the genius of one man, Lykourgos, who received divine honours as late as the hellenistic period. Conversely, if it suited one's purpose, one could dissociate anything one disliked from Lykourgos: KLEOMENES III claimed that the EPHORS were introduced after Lykourgos and could therefore be abolished. Lykourgos' wisdom was admired in Roman times; Plutarch's *Life*, like the earlier *Constitution of the Lakedaimonians* attributed to XENOPHON, makes him single-handedly responsible for Spartan 'good order', *eunomia*, in every aspect. Much of what is said about Lykourgos, however, conforms suspiciously to the narrative archetypes of folk-tale. DGJS

See Plutarch and (possibly) Xenophon, various works in R. J. A. Talbert, trs. (1988) *Plutarch on Sparta*; Finley, M. I. (1975, 1981), Sparta and Spartan society, in *The Use and Abuse of History*, reprinted in *Economy and Society in Ancient Greece*; Forrest, W. G. (1995) *A History of Sparta*.

Lyon (Colonia Copia Felix Munatia Lugdunum) A Roman colony founded by Lucius Munatius Plancus in 43 BC and for a brief time *civitas* of the Segusiavi. Under the empire, it was the capital of the province of Lugdunensis and the religious and administrative centre of the Three GAULS and GERMANIES. In the early empire (and again briefly in the reign of AURELIAN in the late 3rd century), it housed a mint and was on occasion an imperial seat. The city was situated on the colline known today as the Fourvière to the west of the confluence of the RHÔNE and Saône. The commercial port for the city was on an island off the Condate. An altar to Rome and AUGUSTUS was built in 12 BC at the confluence of the Rhône. Representatives from the Gallic provinces met annually in the city to affirm their allegiance to Rome. The city boasted cults to a range of Roman deities, a sanctuary to CYBELE and a CHRISTIAN community from at least the late 2nd century, reflecting the diversity of its population. It also contained the customary array of monuments including a FORUM, *capitolium*, THEATRE, Odeon, BATHS, CIRCUS and AQUEDUCTS. In the 2nd century some parts of the city south of Fourvière were abandoned. Under DIOCLETIAN it became the capital of the province of Lugdunensis Prima, but appears to have fallen into some decline in the 4th century, though it remained an important centre of ARISTOCRATIC culture into the 5th century. The city was seized by the Burgundians in 470–4. RBH

See Audin, A. (1979) *Lyon, miroir de Rome*; Burdy, J. (2002) *Les Aqueducs romains de Lyon*.

 GAUL: (b).

lyric poetry

A genre of poetry composed as early as EPIC, since HOMER mentions several types of lyric SONGS in his works. The conscious separation of epic and lyric took place, in the view of scholars, during the 7th century BC, when Eumelos of CORINTH was apparently the first poet who did not compose epic at all. The development of Greek lyric was strongly influenced by the peoples in Asia Minor, especially LYDIANS and PHRYGIANS who introduced the flute and the seven-chord lyre that were subsequently borrowed by the Greeks. These developments in MUSIC enriched poetry to a considerable extent. With the exception of four books of PINDAR'S poems and the ELEGIES of THEOGNIS, the corpus of Greek lyric is extant only in fragmentary state, either through quotation by other authors or on PAPYRI, whose continuous discovery permits even now an increasingly clear image of its nature. Early Greek lyric flourished during the archaic period and lasted through to classical times. The earliest author of extant poems is ARCHILOCHOS, while Pindar represents the end of the classical period. Subsequently, in hellenistic times, new lyric genres developed, including the epyllion and idyll. Both genres offer a larger narrative content than traditional lyric. KALLIMACHOS and THEOKRITOS are the best known representatives of this hellenistic poetry. Theokritos, Moschos and Bion are also known for their development of bucolic poetry. This last genre best characterizes the hellenistic poetry. Some manuscripts of minor hellenistic lyric compositions survive with musical notation included, permitting a glimpse into a little known and poorly understood area of study.

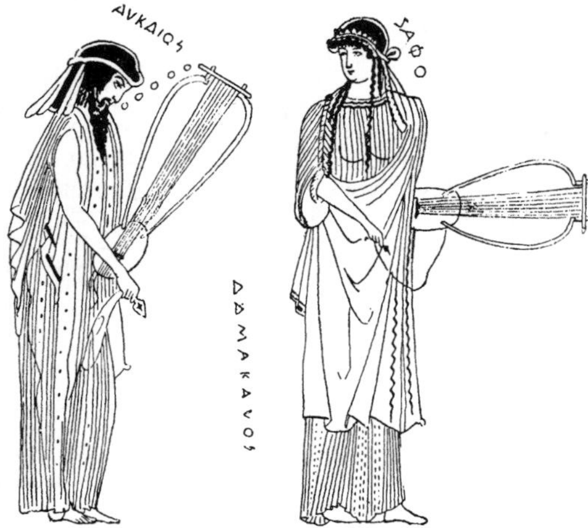

LYRIC POETRY: Sappho and Alkaios as depicted on later Athenian vases.

In modern scholarship, Greek lyric is divided into two major genres: choral (sung by a CHORUS) and monodic (either sung or recited by a single performer). Sub-genres are generated according to metre, dialect, god or place of performance. The dialect of the choral songs is Doric, that of monodic lyric is generally Ionic with strong Homeric influences and, in the case of SAPPHO and ALKAIOS, Lesbian.

Choral poetry was closely associated with RITUALS and was a sacral action. It was performed at the FESTIVAL of a GOD or HERO by a chorus of boys, girls, men or women depending on the nature of the god. DANCE was as well an important part of the performance. The subject of the choral song was usually local and specifically directed towards the needs of the community. The content was usually divided into three parts: an invocation to the god, the myth itself and the epilogue. Often it was performed by two semi-choruses which confronted each other in an *agôn* or competition resolved in a friendly and prearranged manner. The oldest representative of choral poetry is ALKMAN, who composed songs to be performed by choruses of young women. Pindar composed paeans, and his victory odes for the winners at the OLYMPIC GAMES and other sport competitions were probably also choral. The compositions of Stesichoros, who created a panhellenic lyric not associated with any specific festival, were most likely choral as well.

Monodic poetry was more personal and less ritualized. As much as the festival, the wedding and the funeral were the occasions for the performance of choral lyric, the monodic lyric found its natural place in the banquet or *SYMPOSION*. Some monodic poets were also composers of choral songs. For instance, Sappho composed numerous hymns and wedding songs to be performed by young women, but she also composed poetry dealing with the experiences of her circle of women. In both cases she used her own Lesbian dialect.

Although monody appears in several sub-genres, such as ELEGY, *iambos* and Lesbian monody, also known as melic, it presents some common themes, such as the separation between god and man and man's helplessness in the face of the god. Associated with these topics is the preoccupation with the limits of human actions, JUSTICE and true *aretê* or virtue. The fear of POVERTY and old age is also a common topic of lyric, and, naturally, love with its pains and pleasures. In elegy and in Sappho, love tends to be homoerotic, whereas in the *iambos* love or the scorn heaped on love is usually heterosexual in its context.

Representatives of elegy include Kallinos, Tyrtaios and SOLON. The general purpose of their elegies is to admonish the citizens on how to conduct themselves, either in WAR or in the political or private spheres. The iambographers were Archilochos, Hipponax and SEMONIDES. Iambic poetry laughs at particular individuals or groups, such as women. A second generation of elegiac poets is represented by Ibykos, Anakreon and SIMONIDES, precursors of classical ideas. The poets of this group were associated with the TYRANTS at whose courts they resided and composed poetry for their symposia. Their poetry was more elegant and refined in form and avoided the harshness of the quotidian. Lesbian monody is represented by Sappho and Alkaios. It differs from other monody in dialect, Lesbian instead of Ionic, and in the structure of the poems. Elegies were composed in a succession of elegiac distichs, constructed of a dactylic hexameter and a pentameter. *Iambos* employed iambic meters, also in a non-strophic sequence. Lesbian monody, on the other hand, is based on different types of stanzas of four verses. RBC

See Bowra, C. M. (1961) *Greek Lyric Poetry from Alcman to Simonides*; Campbell, D. (1967) *Greek Lyric Poetry*; Fränkel, H. (1975) *Early Greek Poetry and Philosophy*; Hutchinson, G. O. (2001) *Greek Lyric Poetry*; Mulroy, D. (1992) *Early Greek Lyric Poetry*; West, M. L., trs. (1993) *Greek Lyric Poetry*.

Among the genres of Roman literature, lyric is perhaps the most difficult to define. Whereas Greek lyric can be demarcated from other GENRES and categorized in terms of its metres and performance contexts, the same does not hold true for the Roman poets. In CATULLUS and STATIUS, for example, lyric metres are found alongside iambic, elegiac and/or hexameter verse. It is clear from references to reading and writing within the poems themselves (e.g. Catullus 1) that the notion of performance context is no longer applicable. References to the poem-as-song have become by this period purely conventional, and may be juxtaposed with poems framed as epistles, soliloquies or fragments of conversation. Definition in terms of subject matter is also problematic, given the considerable overlap with the related genres of EPIGRAM and ELEGY.

The distinctive character of Roman lyric is perhaps more clearly brought out by modern definitions of the lyric as 'a short poem of personal revelation, confession or complaint' (Miller). While it is important not to elide differences between ancient and modern lyric, the poetry of Catullus and HORACE does seem to convey a strong sense of authorial subjectivity, in contrast to the more collective character even of 'personal' lyric in archaic and classical Greece.

The one Roman poet who can be unambiguously categorized as lyric (since he uses the label himself) is Horace, whose four books of *Odes* are composed mainly in the stanzaic metres known as Sapphic, Alcaic and Asclepiad. Many of Horace's characteristic themes – the shortness of life, WINE and women, political troubles – have precedents in Greek lyric, though the Augustan poet gives his traditional subject matter a distinctively 'modern' twist.

Horace boasts in *Odes* 3.30 that he has been 'the first to draw down Aeolian song into Italian rhythms' (i.e. to adapt lyric metres to the Latin language), conspicuously ignoring the polymetric poems (1–60) of Catullus, at least some of which must be regarded as lyric on any definition. Poems 11 and 51 employ the Sapphic stanza (the latter is in part a translation of SAPPHO fr. 31); other poems in this part of the collection employ a variety of lyric and iambic metres. Still more than Horace, Catullus conveys in his shorter poems a very strong (if ultimately artificial) impression of individual subjectivity: we seem to be presented with a fragmentary but coherent picture of the poet's emotions, loves and enmities, and his experience of the world around him. In this sense, Catullus might with some justification be regarded as the founder of the lyric genre in the modern sense.

Under the empire, Horace's virtuoso adaptation of Greek metres and themes seems to have found few emulators. Statius' *Silvae*, a collection of occasional poems on a range of themes, defies generic classification. Statius' favourite metre is the hexameter, but several poems employ the Catullan hendecasyllable, and Horace's use of stanzaic metres is emulated in 4.5 and 4.7. Themes include encomia of the emperor Domitian, celebration of such events as weddings and birthdays, consolatory poems addressed to bereaved friends or patrons, and descriptions of buildings or *objets d'art*.

Other 'personal' lyric poets writing between the 1st century BC and the 4th century AD are little more than names to us, though meagre fragments have in some cases survived. Catullus' predecessor Laevius (fl. c.90 BC) was a forerunner of the 'new poets', whose style is characterized by bold experimentation. Under the empire, Caesius Bassus and Passennus Paulus are singled out for praise by, respectively, QUINTILIAN (10.1.96) and PLINY THE YOUNGER (*Letters* 9.22), but virtually nothing of their work has come down to us. Choral lyric is represented among the fragmentary remains of Republican TRAGEDY, and in the tragedies of the younger SENECA (whose intense exploration of emotional extremes at the expense of dramatic action renders him, for Johnson (150–1) an inherently 'lyrical' poet). The *Carmen saeculare* of Horace was also, it appears, composed for choral performance at AUGUSTUS' Secular Games. Mention should be made, finally, of the SONGS (*cantica*) which punctuate the COMEDIES of PLAUTUS and (much more infrequently) TERENCE.

In late antiquity, the classical lyric tradition was given new impetus by CHRISTIAN poets – notably PRUDENTIUS (AD 348–after 405) – who drew on the style and language of both the PAGAN HYMN and the psalms. Prudentius' *Cathêmerinon* (*The Daily Round*, a collection of twelve hymns) and *Peristephanon* (*Crowns of Glory*, a group of longer poems in lyric metre, celebrating the heroism of the MARTYRS) display something of the metrical variety of Horace's *Odes*, while his use of biblical *exempla* might be seen as analogous to Horace's characteristically allusive references to classical MYTHOLOGY. Though probably not originally intended for liturgical performance, extracts from Prudentius' poems were subsequently so employed, and became an established part of church liturgy. MG

See Johnson, W. R. (1982) *The Idea of Lyric*; Miller, P. A. (1994) *Lyric Texts and Lyric Consciousness*.

Lysander d.395 BC Spartan statesman and commander. Although a Spartiate of uncertain status (perhaps from a poor family), Lysander rose to prominence at the end of the 5th century. Having befriended Cyrus the Younger, and with the resources made available to him by this friendship, as supreme commander of the Spartan navy he built up the fleet and brought the PELOPONNESIAN WAR to a victorious outcome. Following victories at Notion in 406 and

Aigospotamoi in 405, he forced the Athenians to surrender in 404. He supported the oligarchic coup of that year at Athens and the installation of The Thirty, as well as setting up oligarchies (so-called 'decarchies') in a number of cities of what had been the Athenian empire. His imperialistic ambitions received a check when Pausanias, one of the Spartan kings, intervened to end the Athenian civil war which resulted in the downfall of the Thirty. By about 402 official Spartan support had been withdrawn for his decarchies.

Possibly also about 403, Lysander tried to bring about the end of hereditary monarchy at Spartan in favour of elective kingship (with the hope of being the first elected king) by bribing the oracles at Delphi, Dodona and Siwah. Failing in this, he threw himself into the succession crisis of 400 on the death of king Agis, and had his protégé and lover, Agesilaos (the brother of the king), placed on the throne over Agis' son, Leotychidas (who was rumoured to be the son of the Athenian Alcibiades).

Lysander then persuaded Agesilaos to support his own imperialistic dreams and to lead the Spartan campaign against Persia in 396. Agesilaos, however, would not tolerate being Lysander's puppet: the two fell out, and Lysander was despatched to the Hellespont in disgrace. By 395 and the outbreak of the Corinthian war, Lysander was back in Sparta. He led the Spartan army at Haliartos against the Thebans, where he died. An ambitious, clever and capable commander, he was deified by the Samians where a short-lived cult was established in his honour. LGM

See Diodorus Siculus, books 13–14; Plutarch, *Lysander*; Xenophon, *Hellenika* 1–3.

Lysias c.459/8 (or mid-440s)–c.380 BC Attic orator. Lysias was born in Athens, but as the son of a Sicilian he was a metic, not an Athenian citizen. His father, Kephalos, was a wealthy friend of Perikles, and the family house in Piraeus is the setting for Plato's *Republic*; Lysias also features in the *Phaedrus*. With his brother Polemarchos, Lysias settled in the panhellenic colony of Thourioi, where he studied rhetoric (reputedly under Teisias). He returned to Athens in 412/1 after the Sicilian disaster. Polemarchos was subsequently executed by the Thirty and much of the family wealth was confiscated, but Lysias escaped and supported the democrats in exile. For this he was temporarily rewarded with citizenship by the decree of Thrasyboulos, which was quickly annulled. Impoverished by the confiscation and by his contribution to the democratic cause, Lysias took up the career of a professional speechwriter (*logographos*). He made a name for himself by personally prosecuting Eratosthenes, one of the Thirty, whom he accuses of being responsible for his brother's death. The fragments of the *Hippotherses* are from a connected case in which Lysias seeks to recover his property sold by the Thirty.

The corpus of Lysias' works contains 34 speeches (though not all are genuine), and we know the titles of about 130 more. In the Augustan period, however, 425 speeches existed under his name, of which 233 were regarded as genuine by Dionysios and Caecilius. This voluminous output reflects Lysias' reputation for being one of the finest logographers, and indicates that unlike Isaios, who specialized in inheritance disputes, Lysias wrote speeches for a wide range of cases in both public and private suits. Unfortunately, few of the private speeches survive, but speeches 1 (a defence pleading justifiable homicide), 10 (an action for defamation), and 32 (the prosecution of an allegedly dishonest guardian) are fine examples of his talents in this sphere. A number of the public speeches were delivered at the scrutiny (*dokimasia*) of men connected with the regimes of the Four Hundred and the Thirty. The *Funeral Speech* (if genuine) and *Olympic Speech* are examples of epideictic ('display') oratory; while the speech *On the Ancestral Constitution* is deliberative (political).

Lysias' success as a logographer was based on three main factors. The first was his plain, simple style, for which he was singled out by later critics and rhetoricians as the main representative of pure Attic Greek; he avoids stylistic affectations and the arousing of pathos. The second was his ability to construct a persuasive, vivid narrative, full of claims made with apparently artless simplicity that are, on mature reflection, highly contentious. Third, his narratives served to characterize his client, and to a lesser extent his opponents and other figures involved in the case. This *êthopoiïa* (cf. Dionysios, *Lysias* 8) meant not so much a personal characterization (though this is certainly evident, for example, in speeches 1 and 16), but constructing for the client a persona suited to the case, with the moral qualities that would win over the jury. Lysias was a master of narrative and characterization, unsurpassed even by Demosthenes. MJE

See Lamb, W. R. M., trs. (1930); Carey, C. (1989) *Lysias, Selected Speeches*; Edwards, M. J. and Usher, S. (1985) *Greek Orators*, vol. 1: *Antiphon and Lysias*.

Lysimachos (son of Agathokles) c.355–281 BC One of Alexander the Great's Successors. Lysimachos belonged to an important Macedonian family from Pella that was prominent under Philip II and Alexander. His father was a Thessalian recruited by Philip. One brother, Alkimachos, held military commands early in Alexander's reign; another, Philippos, was one of Alexander's pages; a third, Autodikos, was a *sômatophylax* (bodyguard) of Philip. Although Lysimachos himself was a bodyguard of Alexander, he held no significant commands during the latter's reign. In the division of the empire at Alexander's death, he received Thrace. Although he became king in 306, he did not play a major role in the wars of the Successors. His principal achievements were the foundation of Lysimacheia and the reassertion of Macedonian authority in Thrace. In 302, he and Seleukos I defeated Antigonos Monophthalmos at Ipsos. Lysimachos received as his share of Antigonos' kingdom Anatolia north of the Tauros mountains. His kingdom reached its maximum extent in 285 when he annexed Macedonia after helping to expel Demetrios I. Rivalry between his eldest son, Agathokles, and the sons of Arsinoë, daughter of Ptolemy I, resulted in the execution of Agathokles and the flight of his supporters to Seleukos. Lysimachos was killed in 281 at the battle of Koroupedion, defending his kingdom against Seleukos. Descendants of his son by Arsinoë, Ptolemaios, ruled Telmessos in Caria until the early 2nd century BC. SMB

See Lund, H. S. (1992) *Lysimachus*.

Lysippos b.380s BC The earliest evidence of his work as a SCULPTOR may be a signed statue base from Akraiphia (BOIOTIA), dated 372–362 BC. Inscriptions suggest that he worked at OLYMPIA, THEBES, CORINTH, MEGARA, and RHODES, while his hand has been attributed stylistically to sculptures particularly from Sikyon, Thespiai, Dion, Athens and Taras. He became the court sculptor for ALEXANDER and afterwards served SELEUKOS. His career spanned most of the 4th century BC.

He worked exclusively in bronze, and on the human male form. Examples of his work are all Roman MARBLE copies with the exception of one contemporary replica of the figure of Agias (erected 337–332). His early style, in the 360s, was one of idealistic conservatism, with solid, self-contained figures. In the 340s he produced more individual representations that conveyed a sense of restless idleness or inner tension. This was achieved by a new proportion canon incorporating smaller heads, slimmer bodies and less frontal poses to give figures greater height, epitomized by *Apoxyomenos* (*The Body-Scraper*). Some of his works were on a colossal scale, such as his HERAKLES type. He had an interest in allegory and psychological narrative and produced numerous ATHLETE types and portraits. The Agias figure is said to represent the first portrait rendered in a Greek victory dedication. His heaven-gazing Alexander became the archetype for later rulers who claimed superhuman and divine qualities. TH

See Ridgway, B. S. (1997) *Fourth-century Style in Greek Sculpture*.

Maccabees, revolt of In 167 BC the SELEUKID king Antiochos IV Epiphanes brought to an end the Jewish cult in JERUSALEM. He replaced the ancient RITUAL with an altar to Olympian ZEUS, described in a contemporary passage in the biblical book of Daniel (11.31; 12.11) as 'the abomination of desolation'. Jews were forbidden to practise their ancestral customs, especially the sabbath and circumcision. The outrage provoked an uprising led by a family of priestly origin, chief among them Judas, called Maccabaeus. The rebels succeeded through guerrilla warfare in capturing the Temple and restoring worship of the JEWISH God. Political independence does not seem to have been attempted.

The two main extant narratives, both preserved as part of the SEPTUAGINT, blame the desecration of the Temple on the excessive zeal for hellenizing shown by the high priests who controlled the cult in the 170s. The truth of this explanation is uncertain. *I Maccabees*, a dynastic history composed to justify the power of the Hasmonaeans, the dynasty established by the Maccabaean family, enhanced their reputation by denigrating their predecessors as high priests. *II Maccabees* is a religious text written in praise of piety and MARTYRDOM. Both writers naturally followed the standard characteristic of Jewish HISTORIOGRAPHY to explain misfortune by reference to the sins of Jewish leaders. The increased hellenization of the Jerusalem ARISTOCRACY in the 170s is not in doubt (though it was not yet far advanced), but it is not clear how this led to the attack on the Temple cult by Antiochos.

The actions of Antiochos may be explained without reference to the attitude of the Jews. In 169 BC Antiochos began a campaign to conquer Egypt. After astonishing successes, the attempt was thwarted in 167 through Roman intervention. Antiochos, left with a large army to pay, was tempted by the wealth of the Jerusalem Temple and avoided accusations of sacrilege by declaring the Jewish cult impious: much of the anti-Jewish slander found in Greek authors may derive from Antiochos' propaganda. If the attack on the Temple was the product of political opportunism rather than ideological opposition to Judaism, this would explain the willingness of later Seleukids to countenance the reinstated Jewish cult. MDG

See Bickerman, E. J. (1979) *The God of the Maccabees*; Tcherikover, V. A. (1959) *Hellenistic Civilization and the Jews*.

Macedonia, ancient The CLIMATE of Macedonia is characterized by heavy rains during the summer, while the winter is very cold. The coastal plain was extremely fertile; the mountains offered excellent pasture and were rich in TIMBER and metals. Initially confined to the lower valleys of the Haliakmon and Axios rivers, from 650 BC onwards the Macedonian state progressively expanded. In the 4th century, in the reigns of PHILIP II (359–336) and ALEXANDER III (336–323), it reached as far east as the river Strymon and Chalkidike. It was geographically divided into Lower Macedonia (Pieria, Bottiaia, Amphaxitis) and the Upper, mountainous, part (Tymphaia, Elimiotis, Orestis, Lynkos, Pelagonia). The capital lay first at Aigai (now VERGINA) but moved in c.400 BC to PELLA.

The ethnic affiliation of the Macedonians, as well as their language, has been a hotly disputed matter; most scholars now tend to consider them as Greek-speakers using an idiosyncratic dialect. In the 5th century BC Amyntas I and Alexander I established contacts with the southern Greek mainland; Archelaos (413–399) became the patron of artists and writers. Archaeological finds, especially those of the TOMB at Vergina, show that Macedonian art was flourishing in the 4th century, contrary to Athenian views that portrayed Macedonians as BARBARIANS.

Macedonia was a monarchical 'federal' state, comprising by the late 5th century BC different entities: civic territories, *sympoliteiai* ('joint polities') and groups of VILLAGES (*ethnê*). It was ruled by a king (until 323 from the Temenid or Argead dynasty) who held political, military, judicial and religious authority. His political power was to a certain extent curtailed by a council (*synedrion*) consisting of noble and wealthy landowners. These local ARISTOCRATS often laid claim to the throne. The instability was only enhanced by invasions of northern tribes; states from the Greek mainland also tried to capitalize on these problems. This situation was brought to an end by Philip, who progressively turned Macedonia into the dominant state in the eastern MEDITERRANEAN.

Under the Temenid kings the Macedonians abandoned semi-nomadic life; instead they lived on AGRICULTURE while Macedonia was progressively urbanized. Philip accelerated this process, building new *POLEIS* and transferring entire populations; more *poleis* were built in the hellenistic period. The ECONOMY was largely 'royal': timber and metals belonged to the king, and taxes were probably paid on arable land. In Alexander's time Macedonia was turned into an empire. As a result it came into unprecedented financial prosperity. Kassandros assumed power in 316 and reigned until 297. After a period of upheaval the Antigonid DEMETRIOS I POLIORKETES became king in 294, establishing a dynasty that after 277 remained uninterruptedly on the throne until its defeat by the Romans at PYDNA in 168 BC. Macedonia was then divided into four confederations and in 146 BC it became a Roman province. IK

See Mee, C. and Spawforth, A. (2001) *Greece: an Oxford archaeological guide*; Hammond, N. G. L. (1972) *A History of Macedonia*, vol. 1; Shipley, G. (2000) *The Greek World after Alexander*.

 GREECE.

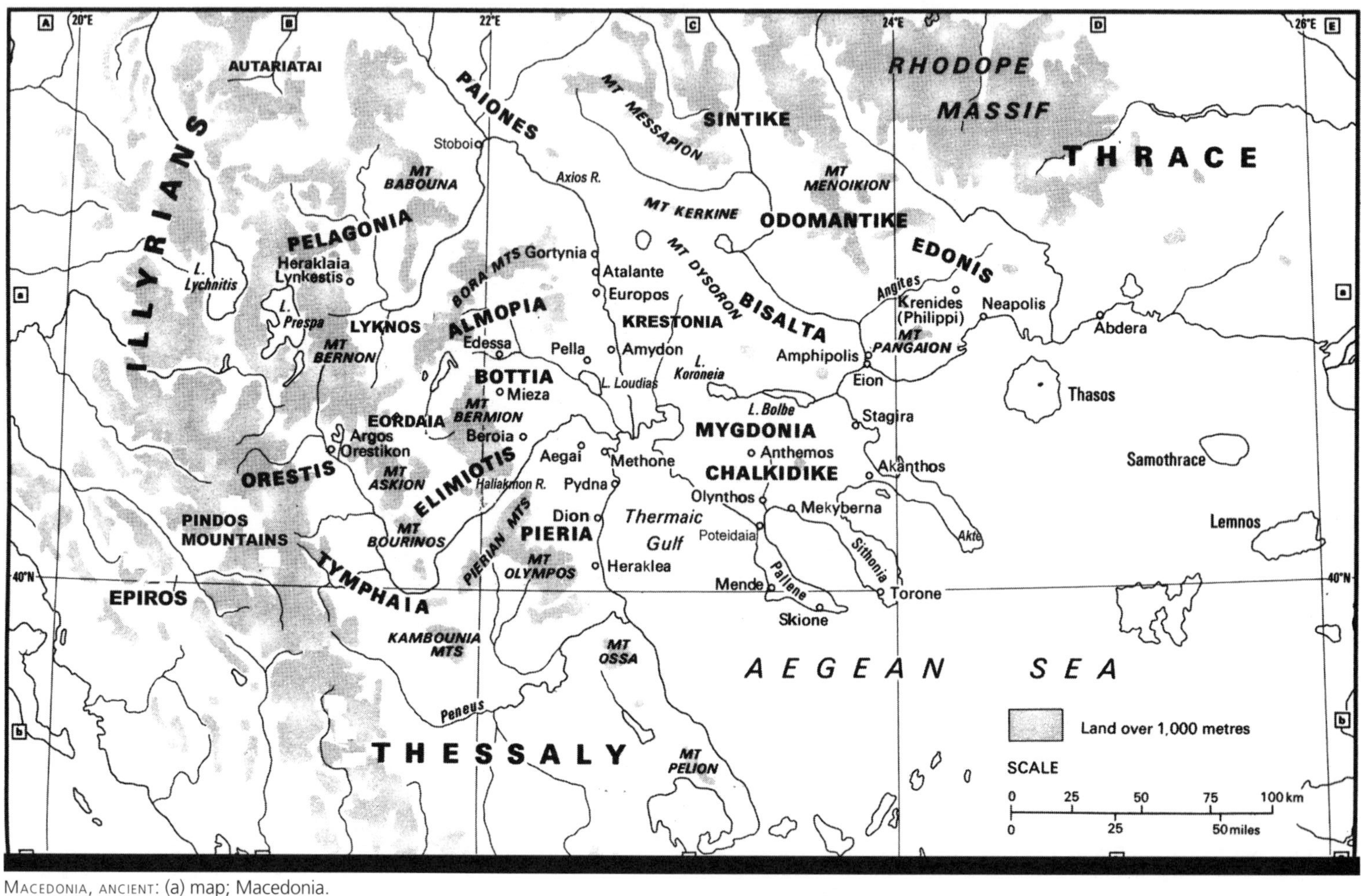

MACEDONIA, ANCIENT: (a) map; Macedonia.

MACEDONIA, ANCIENT: (b) the family of Alexander and Antigonid rulers of Macedonia.

Date	Ruler	Relationship to other rulers
360/59–336	Philip II	
336–323	Alexander III (the Great)	s. Philip II
323–317	Philip III Arrhidaios	s. Philip II
323–310	Alexander IV	s. Alexander III
317–316	Olympias	mother of Alexander III
315–297	Kassandros (king from 305)	s. Antipatros (regent)
297	Philip IV	s. Kassandros
297–294	Antipatros and Alexander V	ss. Kassandros
294–288	Demetrios I Poliorketes ('Besieger')	s. Antigonos I Monophthalmos
288/7–285	Pyrrhos of Epeiros	
287–281	Lysimachos	
281–279	Ptolemaios Keraunos ('Thunderbolt')	s. Ptolemy I
c.277–239	Antigonos II Gonatas	s. Demetrios I
239–229	Demetrios II	s. Antigonos II
c.229–222	Antigonos III Doson	nephew of Antigonos II
222–179	Philip V	s. Demetrios II
179–168	Perseus	s. Philip V

Key: s. = son of. Strictly speaking, Antigonos II should be Antigonos I, and Antigonos III should be Antigonos II, but the numbering given above is conventional (Antigonos I Monophthalmos was never king in Macedonia).

Macedonian empire see ALEXANDER III; PHILIP II.

Macedonian wars, Roman Three wars in the Balkans waged by Rome against the hellenistic kingdom of Macedonia (214–167 BC). The so-called 'first Macedonian war' (never formally declared), was a continuation of earlier Roman campaigns across the ADRIATIC (first and second Illyrian wars, 229 and 219). PHILIP V of Macedonia campaigned in the same region (important to Macedonian border interests) during the Greek SOCIAL WAR (220–217). Discovery of a treaty between Philip and HANNIBAL in 215 raised Roman fears of a 'second front' in the second PUNIC WAR. However, Philip lacked the necessary naval power to invade Italy, and the Carthaginians never provided sufficient support. Marcus Valerius Laevinus allied Rome with the Aitolian league c.211, effectively reopening the Social war. This took the war to Philip with a minimal investment of Roman manpower, but the Aitolians grew disaffected, making peace with Philip in 206. Rome agreed terms (mostly concerning ILLYRIA) at Phoinike in EPIRUS in 205 and withdrew.

The cessation of hostilities (205–200) is often perceived as a holding operation, enabling Rome to defeat Carthage, before returning for revenge on Philip for siding with Hannibal. Philip's activity in the east in 201, and appeals to Rome by RHODES and Attalos of PERGAMON, led to a Roman ultimatum that Philip cease to attack 'the Greeks'. Philip ignored it. Rome crossed the Adriatic in force late in 200 (the second Macedonian war). Titus Quinctius FLAMININUS defeated Philip at Kynoskephalai in Thessaly in 197. Rome withdrew in 194, after Flamininus had declared the 'freedom of the Greeks' to general rejoicing in 196.

An uneasy peace followed. Disputes within the ACHAIAN LEAGUE, recounted by POLYBIOS (contemporary and an Achaian), illustrate the uncertainty of what exactly Rome's gift of 'freedom' entailed. Macedonian ambition was reinvigorated with the accession of Philip's son Perseus in 179. By late 172 war (the 'third') was declared against Perseus. AEMILIUS PAULLUS defeated him at PYDNA in 168. Perseus was paraded in TRIUMPH at Rome (dying later in captivity). The peninsula was transformed: Macedonia was reduced to four independent republics (later becoming a PROVINCE); Epirus was savagely plundered; Illyria was declared 'free' and divided into three; the leading men of Aitolia were massacred; and 1,000 hostages were taken from the Achaian league to Rome – Polybios among them. So much for 'freedom'. The quantity of booty transported back to Rome meant that from 167 Roman CITIZENS ceased to pay tax (*tributum*). JRWP

See Plutarch, *Flamininus*, *Aemilius Paullus*, trs. B. Perrin (1921); Polybios, trs. W. R. Paton (1922); Derow, P. S. (1989) in *CAH* 8, ch. 9; Errington, R. M. (1989) in *CAH* 8, ch. 4, 8.

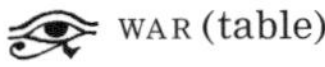

machines Most work in the ancient world used ENERGY from the muscles of humans and animals, and their power was normally applied directly by means of simple tools rather than compound machines. From the 17th century AD, English definitions of 'machine' have emphasized 'several parts each with a definite function and together performing certain

MACHINES: Roman crane for raising columns, powered by human treadmill.

kinds of work' (*Concise Oxford Dictionary*, 1991), but broader meanings still embody the rather suspicious notion of 'contrivance' that lies behind the Latin *machina* or Greek *mêchanê*. Cotterell and Kamminga (74) define the purpose of a machine as 'to perform a particular task in a more convenient way than could be done through muscular power alone', and stress that this is achieved by making the work involved physiologically more convenient, rather than by reducing it.

Ancient machines present interesting problems of classification; Drachmann organized his comments on the ancient manuscript evidence in terms of the 'five powers' defined in Hero's *Mechanics*, book 2. These were the winch or capstan, the lever, the pulley, the wedge and the SCREW; Drachmann added toothed wheels and 'sundries' (hot air, steam, windpower). Capstans were used extensively in cranes (with pulleys) and CATAPULTS. Simple levers were converted into powerful machines by the addition of weights or screws for pressing OLIVES and grapes, and counterweighted levers were common as well-sweeps (equivalent to the modern *shaduf*). Pulleys were very widely used to facilitate lifting, including five-sheaved compound devices on large cranes, but wedges were not readily adaptable to machines.

Hero's fifth power, the screw, was a genuine 'engineering solution' to the problem of transmitting linear power from a capstan to a rotating toothed wheel; it also provided a strong and easily adjustable means of applying pressure in oil or WINE presses. ARCHIMEDES may well have invented the 'water-snail', a hollow cylinder with an internal screw-like spiral compartment that raised water when rotated. Toothed wheels occurred primarily in small machines such as ASTRONOMICAL and surgical instruments. Designs for geared lifting-machines remained theoretical because of friction problems and the shape of cogs, but toothed wheels at 90° worked well in mechanical MILLS powered by water or ANIMALS. Like the Archimedean 'water-snail', use of the water-mill with 'Vitruvian' gearing survived into the 20th century AD virtually unchanged.

In contrast to Drachmann's approach, Schürmann classified machines according to their functional settings: WAR, AGRICULTURE, heavy TRANSPORT, ceremonial meals, RELIGION, public time-measurement, and precision instruments. This approach elucidates the application of considerable technical complexity to seemingly fruitless purposes, such as mechanical singing birds or automatic temple doors. KG

See Cotterell, B. and Kamminga, J. (1990) *Mechanics of Pre-industrial Technology*; Drachmann, A.G. (1963) *The Mechanical Technology of Greek and Roman Antiquity*; Price, D.J. de Solla (1974) *Gears from the Greeks*; Schürmann, A. (1991) *Griechische Mechanik und antike Gesellschaft*.

 PRESSES: (a).

Macrinus see HERODIAN, JULIA DOMNA; PARTHIAN WAR.

 EMPERORS, ROMAN: (a).

Macrobius (Ambrosius Theodosius Macrobius) Early to mid-5th-century AD SENATOR, imperial official and author of philosophical treatises. Little is known of Macrobius' life apart from his senatorial status (identified in the manuscripts of his works) and his tenure of the praetorian prefecture of ITALY in 430. He clearly belongs to that same literary élite which included members of the families of the senators SYMMACHUS and Nicomachus Flavianus, and which was concerned with the literary heritage of Rome just as its political greatness was in decline.

He produced three works which are testimony to his learning. Least known is his comparision of Greek and Latin verbs, now preserved only in fragments. More famous is his *Saturnalia*, written in the form of learned discussions by late pagan luminaries of the senate, such as Symmachus, and scholars such as Servius, the famous commentator on VIRGIL. His most celebrated work, however, is the commentary on CICERO's *Dream of Scipio*. It eschews the more customary grammatical and historical concerns of many late antique commentaries in favour of a philosophical approach, dominated by NEOPLATONISM. The work was immensely popular in the Middle Ages, precisely because of its philosophical content, and for centuries it was the Latin West's most importance source for Neoplatonic doctrines. MDH

See Macrobius, *Commentary on the Dream of Scipio*, trs. W.H. Stahl (1952); *Saturnalia*, trs. P.V. Davies (1969); Cameron, A. (1966) The date and identity of Macrobius, *JRS* 56: 25–38.

madness In early Greek literature, madness seems to be understood as a punishment from the GODS. This appears to be the tradition in the dramatic versions of the troubles of HEROES such as Pentheus (in EURIPIDES' *Bacchae*), HERAKLES (in Euripides' *Hercules Furens*), Ajax (in SOPHOKLES' *Ajax*), and Orestes (in AESCHYLUS' *ORESTEIA* and Euripides' *Orestes*). Madmen, however, are not common in popular literature. The abundant medical literature from the 5th and later centuries BC presents a more generous picture. In the HIPPOCRATIC text *On the Sacred Disease*, madness is linked to physiological imbalance, rather than divine interference: epilepsy is the result of an excess of phlegm in the brain, madness the result of a similar excess of yellow bile. Treatment is dietetic and medicinal. This tradition of attributing the origins of madness to corporeal problems is also evident in the romantic (but very influential) Pseudo-Aristotelian, *Problema* 30.1. Mania is the product of an overheating of black bile, depression of its cooling. Subsequent medical writers tended to focus on physiology (and some, like Caelius Aurelianus (5th century AD), vehemently deny spiritual elements in madness), and produced remarkable aetiologies or impressive distinctions. For Asklepiades of Bithynia, incoming information is likened to atoms and when the canals of perception are blocked, as it were, madness can result. Aretaios of CAPPADOCIA (2nd century AD) prefers to give a description. He associates, above all, three conditions with 'madness': *phrenitis* (a condition resembling mania, but accompanied by fever), mania and melancholia (which both lack fever). The distinction is not unlike that between schizophrenia and manic-depression. PGT

See Jackson, S.W. (1987) *Melancholia and Depression*; Pigeaud, J. (1981) *La Maladie de l'âme*; Toohey, P. G. (2003) *Melancholy, Love, and Time.*

Maecenas (Gaius Maecenas) c.70–8 BC Literary patron and ally of AUGUSTUS. Among Octavian's closest adherents during his rise to power, Maecenas became under the PRINCIPATE a kind of unofficial minister for the arts, encouraging and supporting promising young POETS. His 'circle' included VIRGIL, HORACE and PROPERTIUS, all three of whom dedicate poems to him; Horace offers a glowing (if arguably somewhat ironic) account of his character in *Satires* 1.9.

Maecenas' background was aristocratic (both Horace and Propertius address him as the 'offspring of ETRUSCAN kings'), and his wealth enormous; yet he never rose above EQUESTRIAN status, declining throughout his life to stand for public office. For the poets, his ambiguous status endows him with great symbolic importance. At once powerful and (superficially) restrained in his ambitions, he represents (especially in the second book of Propertius and the works of Horace) both political authority and the life of leisure (*otium*) to which the Augustan poets generally aspire. He can be addressed either as a personal friend or as an intermediary between the writer and Augustus. In the latter role, he is a key figure in the *recusatio* (poem of refusal), in which the writer politely declines the *princeps*' putative desire for an epic in his honour.

In addition to his role as patron, Maecenas was himself also a writer of both verse and prose. The few surviving fragments of the former are strongly reminiscent of CATULLUS; his poetry was – perhaps not unjustly – criticized in antiquity for its affected style. MG

magic Traditionally, a variety of practices outside the bounds of established religion, but now usually regarded as part of a broad continuum of belief system(s). Ancient writers distinguish magic from religion primarily on the basis of practitioners' efforts to manipulate, rather than to supplicate, the supernatural realm; magic was used to compel, not to persuade. Magicians employed such diverse means as CURSES, binding spells, secret words and formulas, potions and necromancy, among others. A person's perspective played an important role; supporters of a man like APOLLONIUS OF TYANA proclaimed that he performed his feats with the genuine assistance of the divine, while detractors castigated him as a magician or sorcerer. Similarly, an individual who employed magic might readily despise and accuse others who used the same techniques.

Evidence for the use of magic is widespread. In addition to frequent references in literature, hundreds of amulets have survived. Several examples, presumably worn around the torso, offer formulas and the imperative 'Digest, digest', and others graphically depict sexual intercourse, with invocations to appropriate deities to grant their bearers' wishes. For curse tablets, the preferred (but not the only) medium was a sheet of lead inscribed with the curse, which could be used to bind the tongues of opponents in legal proceedings, hamper competition in business or the horse races, and seek the return of stolen goods, sometimes to the victim, sometimes to the deity invoked (especially at BATH and Uley in Britain). Typically, ritual was involved, and tablets were deposited under a target's doorsill, in graves, temples, wells or springs, and elsewhere. Often, they are not gentle; an example from Gaul asks that an opponent's legal counsel's tongue be as lifeless and cold as the dead puppy buried with the tablet, and that the counsel be as unable to defend his client as the puppy's mother had been to defend it.

Magical papyri are another source of information. In addition to so-called recipes, which offer, for example, formulas and instructions, lists of ingredients for potions, many specific examples with the names of individuals survive. Useful for understanding the practice of magic, they also allow a glance into the lives of ordinary people. One common type is the erotic spell, made by one person to bind another to himself or herself, or to separate an individual from his or her current lover. They were written by (or for) both males and females to secure both males and females as lovers; the majority are men seeking women, but all possible combinations occur. A typical example has a male asking a ghost and/or a deity to ensure that the target female should not engage in any sexual activity until she comes to him. Sometimes, she is not to eat or drink either, and on occasion a lock of hair or nail cuttings are deposited with the spell to ensure correct identification. Most often the stated goal is sex, less often marriage, children and lifelong love.

Belief in the utility of magic was widespread even in educated circles and among many religious groups. LIBANIUS discovered a dead chameleon deliberately hidden in his classroom that had prevented him from delivering his lessons, and sufficient evidence survives to indicate that JEWS and CHRISTIANS frequently had recourse to magic. As early as the TWELVE TABLES, the use of magic was banned (specifically, charming a neighbour's crops). Trials occurred with some frequency, notably in the case of APULEIUS, but were most dangerous for the accused when property or the state, including its officials, were alleged targets. By and large, however, many persons practised magic with reasonable impunity, except when someone chose to make an issue of it. JV

See Theokritos, *Idyll* 2 (*The Sorceress*); Ankarloo, B. and Clark, S., eds. (1999) *Witchcraft and Magic in Europe: ancient Greece and Rome*; Betz, H. D., ed. (1986) *The Greek Magical Papyri in Translation*; Dickie, M.W. (2001) *Magic and Magicians in the Greco-Roman World*; Faraone, C. M. (1999)

Ancient Greek Love Magic; Gager, J. G. (1992) *Curse Tablets and Binding Spells from the Ancient World*; Graf, F. (1997) *Magic in the Ancient World*.

curses: (a)–(b).

magistrates Officials responsible for specific duties and appointed on a regular, often annual, or *ad hoc* basis in both the Greek and Roman worlds. The regularly elected officials at Rome were not accountable to the citizen body in the way that Athenian magistrates were in the democracy.

In most Greek cities magistrates had replaced the kings of the archaic period. Magistracies could be an individual office or a board of officials, the latter being one way of diluting power. The larger and more complex the community, the more magistracies are usually found: 700 officials were appointed each year to run democratic Athens. Responsibilities were wide-ranging and some offices highly specialized: the *agoranomoi* in Athens oversaw the sale of goods in the market, and the *astynomoi*, among other duties, had to make sure that sewage was not deposited too close to the city and that dead bodies were removed from the street.

In the Greek world magistrates were appointed by lot or by election. Lot, frequently associated with more democratic constitutions, also operated in oligarchies. The decision to elect to some magistracies and not others recognized that certain positions could not be left to chance (e.g. the generalship at Athens). Qualification for magistracies was always restricted to citizens and often depended on property qualification, particularly in an oligarchy.

In the hellenistic era, magistrates were often 'friends' of a king. The 'friends' enjoyed the more important offices in the hellenistic kingdoms, but for the most part lesser magistracies in many Greek cities were unaffected by the diffusion of kingship. The 'friends' were rewarded frequently by the kings with land and wealth.

Unlike in Greek cities, at Rome there was a strict hierarchy of magistrates, the *cursus honorum*. Some magistracies were appointed regularly (most every year, e.g. consuls) while others were created only occasionally or under particular circumstances (e.g. dictator); magistracy was an honour and not salaried.

At the top of the ladder of the annually appointed positions were the two consuls, then the praetors, curule aediles, quaestors, tribunes of the plebs and aediles of the plebs. Every four (later five) years, censors were elected and served for 18 months. Among the extraordinary magistracies were dictator, *interrex* and *magister equitum*, none of which was elected.

Those magistrates with *imperium*, the right to issue commands in war and to execute laws, were distinguished by the possession of *fasces* carried by special attendants called lictors. Magistracies with *imperium* (notably consuls, praetors, dictators and military tribunes with consular power) were distinct from those without. The tribunes of the plebs who enjoyed the power of veto against elections, laws and *senatus consulta* were able to limit the *imperium* of the magistrates.

Membership of the senate was largely dependent on reaching the quaestorship after Sulla's reforms. The fact that the number of magistracies decreased as one climbed the *cursus honorum* meant there was considerable competition among the élite for the magistracies, a factor that characterized politics in the late Republic. GJO

Magna Graecia 'Great Greece' was the name given to Sicily and southern Italy by the Romans, who thought of the area as a foreign land full of Greek cities. Even after the Roman conquest during the 3rd century BC, the region remained heavily hellenized. Post-Roman (Byzantine) and early modern influxes of Greek-speakers mean that Greek is still spoken in a few parts of the region, and there are still many Greek place-names and personal names. LF

Magna Mater see bulls; drama, Roman; gods and goddesses, Roman; Lepcis Magna; Phrygia.

Magnentius see Proba.

Tetrarchs: (b); Theodosius I: (a).

Magnesia, battle of The decisive engagement for the Romans against Antiochos III was fought near Magnesia-by-Sipylos late in 190 BC (Livy says winter was approaching). It followed the expulsion of Antiochos from Greece, where he had been at the Aitolian league's invitation and as champion of the 'freedom of the Greeks' against the Romans. The Seleukids had been defeated in a naval battle near Myonnesos, and thus abandoned any attempt at barring a crossing of the Hellespont. Lucius Cornelius Scipio, consul for 190, commanded the Roman forces, but though he had with him his older brother Publius (the victor over Hannibal) the famous Africanus had fallen ill and was at Elaia on the Hellespont. Surviving accounts are based on Polybios, who had used Rhodian and Pergamene sources: not surprisingly, Eumenes II and his brother Attalos figure prominently and are credited with much of the battle's success. After sending slingers, archers and javelinmen to throw the enemy's scythed chariots into confusion, Eumenes' cavalry rolled up the Seleukid left wing, which was already collapsing into flight. The Romans on the left, which lacked the protection of auxiliaries (relying instead on the presence of the Phrygios river), were initially put to flight but were soon rallied. With the help of 200 cavalry under Attalos, they drove the Seleukid army back with great slaughter. Livy's numbers for the dead, 50,000 infantry and 2,000 cavalrymen, are grossly exaggerated: Antiochos' entire army comprised 60,000 infantry and 12,000 cavalry. The Seleukid defeat forced Antiochos to sue for terms which resulted in the peace of Apameia (188 BC). WH

See Bar-Kochva, B. (1976) *The Seleucid Army*; Gruen, E. S. (1984) *The Hellenistic World and the Coming of Rome*.

Magnus Maximus see Ausonius; Symmachus; Trier.

Theodosius I: (a).

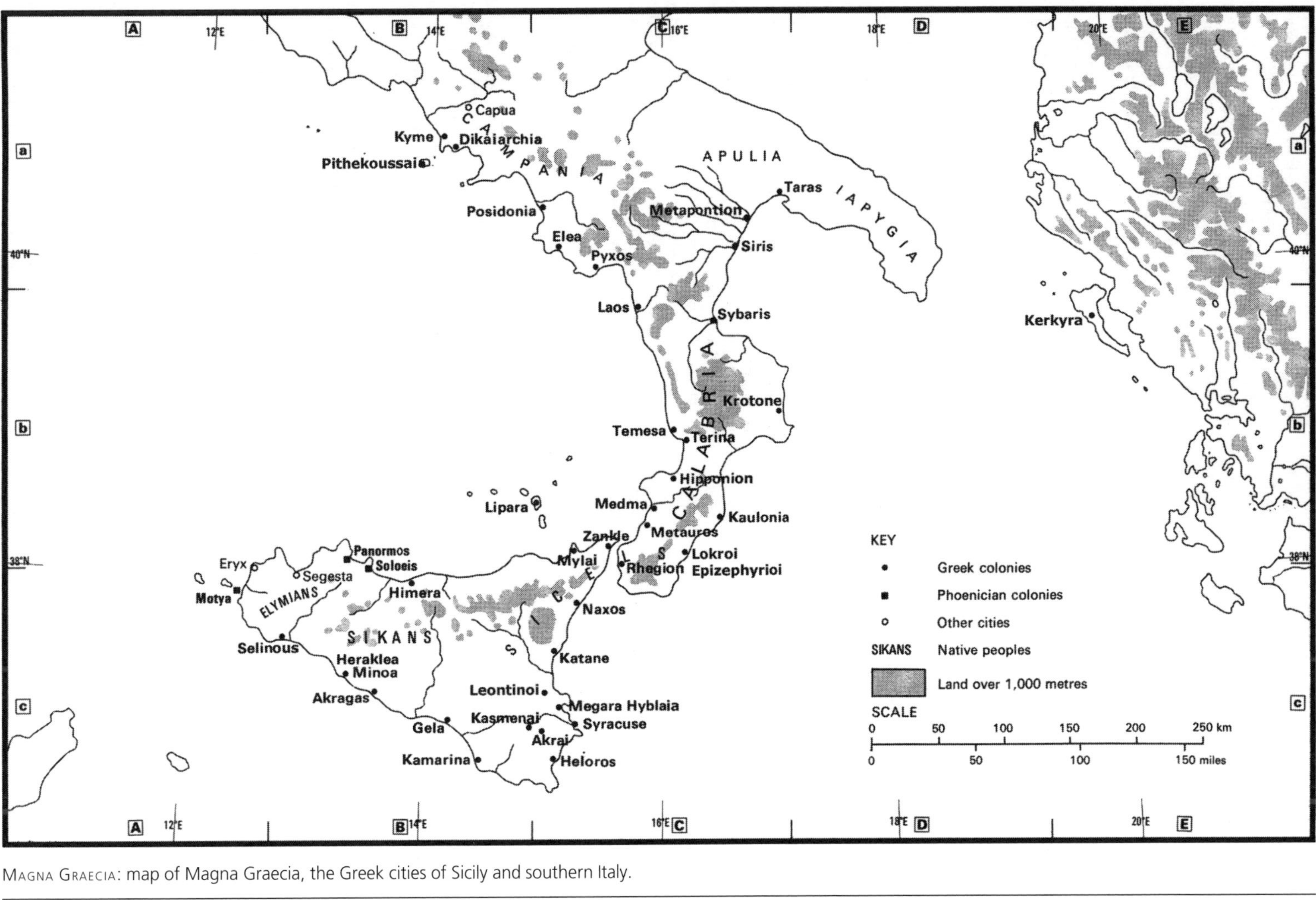

Magna Graecia: map of Magna Graecia, the Greek cities of Sicily and southern Italy.

Mago pre-146 BC A CARTHAGINIAN who wrote extensively on AGRICULTURE. His work was highly esteemed by the Romans, even though the Carthaginians were Rome's long-standing enemies. The Roman agricultural writers VARRO and COLUMELLA quote him frequently, and the latter praises him as the 'father of rural crafts'. 28 volumes of his writings were translated from Punic into Latin by senatorial decree following the Roman destruction of Carthage in which most Punic books were destroyed. Substantial excerpts had been earlier translated into Greek by Dionysios of Utica. Despite widespread admiration in ancient times, no text of Mago survives today except for a few quotations by Roman authors. It is clear from these that his wide-ranging expertise covered such topics as vine cultivation, recipes for making WINE, planting OLIVES, growing and preserving pomegranates, BEEKEEPING, mules, and the qualities to look for in CATTLE. Like other classical writers on agriculture, he seems to have taken a strong moral line about the virtues of rural life: 'one who has bought land should sell his house in the city'. His advice relates to the dry conditions of his North AFRICAN homeland, and Greeks and Romans plainly realized this when adapting it to their own countryside. Mago's work offers us a glimpse of a vast and important documentary tradition in the Punic and Phoenician languages, now largely lost and beyond our reach. LF

Maiden Castle see BRITANNIA.

Majorian see SIDONIUS APOLLINARIS.

managers The ancient economy being mostly based on AGRICULTURE, farm managers are better known than those in charge of workshops, stores and other types of facilities. Managerial units were always limited in size, which did not exclude employment of up to several dozens of workers, thus requiring some degree of supervision and co-ordination. The rules of sound management were discussed in treatises on *oikonomia* (*oikos* designating the HOUSEHOLD) and *agricultura* or *res rusticae*, going back to a tradition represented in Greek by HESIOD, XENOPHON and Pseudo-Aristotle, and preserved in Latin in works of CATO, VARRO, COLUMELLA and Palladius. Owners were advised to take part personally in the management of their estates, while relying to some extent upon a trustworthy SLAVE (*oikonomos*, *epitropos*). Threats, combined with various kinds of economic and social incentives, were deemed instrumental in implementing the main lines of management policy: a quest for self-sufficiency, stability of income and safekeeping of the capital. Nevertheless, some managers happened to be creative. When PERIKLES inherited an estate in the mid-5th century BC, he entrusted it to a servant named Euangelos, who sold the produce in bulk and bought from the MARKET all commodities necessary for the household, to the dismay of Perikles' relatives (PLUTARCH, *Perikles* 16.3–6). In the same way, some unidentified managers of the estate belonging to the descendants of Laches in 2nd-century AD Tebtynis (FAYÛM) devised a highly successful system of crop rotation to increase production.

Because of the nature of the evidence, managers are much better known in the hellenistic and Roman periods. In the late Republic, the Roman PRAETOR developed through his edict a sophisticated legal system of indirect agency, with various levels of liability for the principal and of independence for the agent (*Digest* 14 and 15). One important consequence was the enhancement of the position of slaves in business. As these are more readily identifiable in the capacity of agents in inscriptions than their freeborn counterparts, the social and economic profile of managers may be somewhat distorted. As slaves promoted to a privileged position, perhaps looking forward to eventual MANUMISSION, it is likely that they were able to secure social peace between manpower and employers. Free of the aristocratic prejudice against non-agricultural work, a show of dynamism, creativity and discipline was their best bet for social promotion. Masters and their slave managers had a shared interest in the latter's success, so that the legal and social distance between them was less significant. A lack of regulation opened the way to managerial positions for women and youngsters (*Digest* 14.3.7.1 and 14.3.8).

PAPYRI from Egypt reveal that from the 3rd century BC to late antiquity, large estates were managed by freeborn administrators organized in a many-tiered hierarchic structure, with managerial units at the village level and regional headquarters. By contrast with Italy and some western provinces, evidence for diversification (with a non-agricultural sector attached to a VILLA) is almost non-existent. Managers of urban facilities are even more elusive despite the large number of documents that have survived from midsize towns such as OXYRHYNCHOS. Non-agricultural production did not generate the kind of detailed accounts, inventories and contracts of hire and lease commonly found in connection with the management of large estates. JJA

See Aubert, J.-J. (1994) *Business Managers in Ancient Rome*; Finley, M.I. (1985) *The Ancient Economy*; Rathbone, D.W. (1991) *Economic Rationalism and Rural Society in Third-century AD Egypt*.

Manetho Egyptian priest and author (late 4th and first half of 3rd century BC) from Sebennytos in the Delta. Manetho served PTOLEMIES I and II, and collaborated with the Athenian exegete Timotheos in the development of the Sarapis cult. Surviving fragments of his work indicate that he was literate in Egyptian and Greek.

His numerous writings were devoted to correcting Greek misconceptions of Egypt. The most important was *Aigyptiaka*, a history in three books based on Egyptian sources. Book 1 treated the history from the origin of the GODS to the end of the first Intermediate period, book 2 the Middle and New Kingdoms, book 3 the third Intermediate, Saite and Persian periods. The work was little read in antiquity and only fragments survive, principally as excerpts in JOSEPHUS' *Against Apion* and Eusebios' *Chronicle*. Nevertheless, Manetho's king-list underlies all modern histories of Egypt.

His works on Egyptian religion and thought include *The Sacred Book*, *Epitome of Physical Doctrines*, *On Festivals*, *On Ancient Ritual and Religion*, and *On the Making of Kyphi* (a form of incense). The few fragments suggest that he offered rationalistic interpretations of Egyptian religious phenomena. Like his contemporary BEROSSOS, Manetho belonged to the group of native élite figures whose collaboration was vital to Alexander's Successors in ruling their new kingdoms. SMB

See Redford, D.B. (1986) *Pharaonic King-lists, Annals and Day-books.*

Manichaeism Sub-Christian religion of Persian origin. The roots of Manichaeism lie in the idiosyncratic fusion of Christian doctrines of salvation and Persian mysticism by the Mesopotamian visionary Mani (216–76). According to Mani, the universe consisted of particles of light which were good, trapped within evil matter. Manichaean communities consisted of an extreme ascetic 'elect', whose duty it was to release these particles through rational meditation, supported by 'hearers', who provided for their every need. In time, Mani aroused the animosity of the Zoroastrian priesthood of the Persian empire, and under the orders of king Varahran I he was tried and executed. Nevertheless, his followers, fired with missionary zeal, saw to it that the cult spread outwards from Mesopotamia. Manichaean communities are attested in many Roman provinces around the Mediterranean by the beginning of the 4th century. Among the more famous adherents to Manichaeism was Augustine (1), the advancement of whose career was fostered by networks of Manichaean communities in Carthage, Rome and Milan. The expansion of Manichaeism in the empire was countered by sporadic persecutions. The first occurred under Diocletian, who saw the religion as a pernicious Persian influence in the empire. Later, Christian emperors persecuted Manichaeans as heretics. Yet failure in the Mediterranean was balanced by success elsewhere. Missionaries preached Mani's doctrines along the Silk Road leading from Persia to China, where Manichaean communities endured into the Middle Ages. MDH

See Lane Fox, R. (1986) *Pagans and Christians*; Lieu, S.N.C. (1992) *Manichaeism in the Later Roman Empire and Medieval China.*

Mantineia One of the larger city-states of Arkadia, dominating the centre of the eastern Arkadian plain. The town is notable for the roughly elliptical plan of its early 4th-century fortifications. It was also the site of two important battles. In 418 BC Spartans won a victory over the Argives, Mantineians and Athenians. In 421 BC the peace of Nikias between Athens and Sparta and the end of the 30 years peace between Argos and Sparta led to political upheaval in the Peloponnese. The Eleians and Mantineians, who had a number of grievances against the Spartans, joined a defensive alliance with Argos, and Alcibiades persuaded the Athenians to join them. After the Spartans threatened to attack Argos, a small Athenian force was sent to the Peloponnese. They combined with the Mantineians and Argives to try to win over Tegea to their alliance. This caused the Spartans to advance against them, and the two sides met in Mantineian territory. The Spartans were victorious, and soon afterwards negotiated a peace treaty with the Argives. Thucydides describes the battle in considerable detail, despite its relative unimportance, and his account provides valuable information about hoplite battles in the classical period. Sparta infamously dispersed Mantineia into separate villages (385 BC).

In 362 BC Mantineia witnessed an inconclusive battle between pro- and anti-Theban forces in the Peloponnese. The Thebans under Epameinondas invaded the Peloponnese to support members of the Arkadian league grouped around Tegea, against other Arkadians sympathetic to Mantineia, who were in turn supported by the Spartans and Athenians. In the battle Epameinondas employed the usual Boiotian tactic of deepening his forces on the left wing, and thus breaking through the opponent's right, which was here made up of the Spartans. The Boiotian and Thessalian cavalry used a similar formation. Epameinondas' forces had the better of the fighting, but after he himself had been killed, they failed to press home their advantage. With the death of Epameinondas, effective Theban involvement in the Peloponnese ceased. Xenophon chose the battle as the end-point of his history of Greece, emphasizing the confusion of the result. HB

See Diodorus Siculus 15.85–7; Thucydides 5.64–75; Xenophon, *Hellenika* 7.5.18–27; Hodkinson, S. and Hodkinson, H. (1981) Mantineia and the Mantinike, *ABSA* 76: 239–96.

 battles (table); Peloponnese.

manufacturing

The objects used in the Greek world were often produced in small workshops. The evidence for such manufacture is both literary and archaeological, and workshops are sometimes represented on Athenian red-figured pottery. Demosthenes (27.9) discussed the two workshops (*ergastêria*) owned by his father: one producing swords which employed 32 or 33 slaves and the other an establishment making couches (*klinai*) with 20 slaves. The exotic nature of the furniture was emphasized by the presence of ivory in the assets, presumably used for inlay. Some textile manufacture was the preserve of men; Xenophon (*Memorabilia* 2.7.6) has Socrates refer to two separate cloak workshops owned by Dameas of Kollytos and Menon. A possible late 4th-century textile workshop, suggested by loom-weights recovered from many of the rooms, has been identified in a building just inside the Dipylon gate at Athens. The gender of those working in such workshops is not always clear, and evidence suggests that both men and women were involved. Aischines (1.97) refers to an *ergastêrion* of 9 or 10 men working as leatherworkers, perhaps shoemakers. An example of a 5th-century shoemaker's establishment – apparently owned by somebody called Simon whose name was found inscribed on the base of a drinking cup – was excavated just to the south-west corner of the Athenian Agora. Finds included iron hobnails and bone rings which would have served as eyelets.

Several bronze-working establishments have been found in Athens. A bronze-working foundry dating to the 2nd century BC was located in a house on the western slope of the Areiopagos. Further workshops were located in the valley that extends southwestwards from the Agora towards the Pnyx. Some of these workshops are likely to have been producing bronze implements and weapons.

Items made from clay were an important aspect of manufacture. Terracotta figures were made by *koroplastai* for dedication in sanctuaries, or to be placed in graves as funerary offerings. These were usually mouldmade. A pottery workshop excavated during

MANUFACTURING: Roman coppersmith's workshop, shown in a relief from Naples.

the construction of the Athens Metro Station at Agios Ioannis has suggested that it might have been located to produce pottery to be used in the adjacent cemetery. Several deposits in the Athenian Agora associated with the cleaning up of the area after the Persian destruction appear to contain pots from several pottery workshops which appear to have been located in the area. DWJG

See Hopper, R. J. (1979) *Trade and Industry in Classical Greece*; Knigge, U. (1991) *The Athenian Kerameikos*; Mattusch, C. C. (1977) Bronze- and iron-working in the area of the Athenian agora, *Hesperia* 46: 340–79; (1988) *Greek Bronze Statuary: from the beginnings through the fifth century* BC; Parlama, L. and Stampolidis, N. C. (2000) *Athens: the city beneath the city*; Richter, G. M. A. (1966) *The Furniture of the Greeks, Etruscans, and Romans*; Vickers, M. (1999) *Images on Textiles*.

As in the Greek world, much manufacturing activity in the Roman world was carried out in the domestic sphere or in small WORKSHOPS. There is an absence of evidence of 'factory' production in the Roman world. Finley memorably commented on the fact that even the largest POTTERY manufacturers were 'not even little Wedgwoods'. However, there are indications that the overall scale of manufacturing rose considerably during the hey-day of the empire. This can be traced both in the abundant evidence of large-scale production and distribution of manufactured goods across the Roman world and in the EPIGRAPHIC testimony of an increase in the range of craft specializations. At Rome there are at least 180 separate professions listed, of which about half involve manufacturing; POMPEII provides also evidence of many professions. The typical workshop was an enterprise involving less than ten people, though a few larger manufactories are attested. What distinguished Roman production was not the scale of individual enterprises but the aggregate impact of large numbers of small units. A second distinctive aspect is the degree of job specialization that was developed in some workshops. For instance, the production of moulded *terra sigillata* pottery involved several separate stages of work, often carried out by different individuals, all of whom could contribute individual stamps to the finished vessel: mould maker, bowl former, foot turner, bowl finisher. This comes as close as one can find to production line assembly in a pre-industrial society.

The status of workers in manufacturing was varied, from SLAVES, to FREEDMEN or FREEDWOMEN, to freeborn. Although Roman ARISTOCRATS looked down on manual work, many of these craftspeople were evidently proud of their skills and celebrated their trades on funerary memorials.

The Roman ARMY was a major manufacturer of a wide variety of goods as part of its MILITARY SUPPLY system. FORTS AND FORTRESSES normally included workshops for metal- and leatherworking, both of which were essential for the production and maintenance of ARMS AND ARMOUR, vehicles and horse-trappings. Examples of specialized military potteries are known, as at Holt in Britain, where the XXth legion based at Chester produced a range of pottery, BRICK and TILE. State armouries and weaving centres (*gynaecea*) are also attested in textual documents, though these are unlikely to have been anything more than large manufactories. DJM

See Brewster, E. H. (1917) *Roman Craftsmen and Tradesmen of the Early Empire*; Loane, H. J. (1938) *Industry and Commerce of the City of Rome*; Peacock, D. P. S. (1982) *Pottery in the Roman World*.

HOUSES, GREEK: (c); IRON: (a)–(b); PERFUME; SCULPTURE: (a); WORKSHOPS.

manumission Literally means 'letting go from the hand' and refers to the emancipation of a SLAVE by his former master. The subject of the manumission of Greek slaves has drawn very little scholarly attention in comparison to that of Roman slaves. The Greek slave in general was not granted full CITIZENSHIP with his freedom; he achieved only METIC status. Only special circumstances, such as services rendered, warranted the granting of full citizenship to former slaves. In return for his freedom, a Greek slave may have needed to perform services for his former master, a practice similar to one performed by slaves in Rome.

A great deal more can be said on manumission in Rome. Slaves who worked in proximity to their masters stood a better chance for manumission and probably carried on working relations with their master after their freedom was granted. There were several forms of formal manumission: manumission *testamento* (freedom gained according to the will of the master), manumission *vindicta* (freedom gained according to the wand; proclaimed before a MAGISTRATE), and manumission *censu* (freedom gained before CENSORS when registering as citizens). In return for the slave's freedom under the manumission *testamento*, the patron ensured himself a luxurious funeral and continual maintenance of the family TOMB, as the slave was legally bound to carry out these obligations. It was usually beneficial for a patron to let his slaves know of their placement in the will, since the master who did so stood to gain better service from the slave in this world as well as in the next.

A master could also free his slave in his own lifetime by manumission *vindicta*. In the presence of an administrative official, the master would pronounce words of freedom (*eum liberum addico*, 'I adjudge that he is free') and touch the head of the slave with a wand or *vindicta*. Since this form of manumission took place while the patron was alive, he thereby increased the number of his clients. As mentioned, a slave who worked in close proximity to his master would also continue work relations after manumission. As *clientes* (clients), the freedmen created further prestige for the patron.

In addition to these forms of manumission, a female slave could gain her freedom either by marrying her patron or if her slave companion paid for her freedom. The master could also manumit a slave couple together. Finally, a slave could buy his or her freedom from the master by offering *peculium* (the money granted to a slave by his master). Slaves manumitted informally, that is, not according to the law, were not recognized as citizens. LAH

See Davies, J. K. (1971) *Athenian Propertied Families 600–300 BC*; Duff, A. M. (1928) *Freedmen in the Early Empire*; Joshel, S. (1992) *Work, Identity and Legal Status at Rome*; Treggiari, S. (1969) *Roman Freedmen during the Late Republic*; Weaver, P. R. C. (1972) *Familia Caesaris*.

manure The use of natural manure in AGRICULTURE, universal in the Mediterranean, is not a response to over-farming as is sometimes suggested. Like fallowing and crop rotation, it is a time-honoured way to balance inputs and outputs, replacing nutrients taken out of the soil by growing crops. Another way is to cultivate nitrogen-rich plants such as beans and vetch, recognized (e.g. by Pliny the Elder, *Natural History* 17.50–7) as improving the soil. Natural fertilizers can be divided into composted vegetable matter and animal dung produced by animal husbandry (see PASTORALISM), most commonly from SHEEP and GOATS. Vegetable matter from kitchen waste, or the by-products of crops (e.g. OLIVE-pressing), were recognized sources of nutrients for the soil. Human WASTE (both liquid and solid) was collected in both Greek and Roman cities and recycled on the land. Animal dung would be spread on the fields after the harvest for autumn sowing, or before the winter ploughing. THEOPHRASTOS, CATO THE ELDER, VARRO and PLINY THE ELDER discuss the relative merits of dung from different animals (and from humans), though they disagree on certain points. In reality, particularly on smaller farms, the full range of options would not be available. There is more than a little superstition in the ancient sources. Pliny says a west wind and a waning moon increase the effectiveness of manure, and insists that this does not mean a particular time of year. Both smallholders and managers of larger estates, however, recognized that manuring was indispensable to the long-term health of the land. Its ubiquity has been invoked to explain the thin 'background scatter' of ceramic material (potsherds and tile fragments) found on FIELD SURVEYS, on the reasonable supposition that material from farmyard middens will have been spread across the land, though this has been much debated in recent years. In parts of the Mediterranean where birds such as doves were 'farmed' in aviaries, their droppings were an additional source of fertilizer. In some parts of the ancient world dung was used as FUEL. DGJS

See Alcock, S. E. et al. (1994) Intensive survey, agricultural practice and the classical landscape of Greece, in I. Morris, ed., *Classical Greece* 137–70; Humphrey, J. W. et al. (1997) *Greek and Roman Technology: a sourcebook*.

manuscripts see BOOKS; COMMENTATORS, TEXTUAL; CYRIAC OF ANCONA; DEAD SEA SCROLLS; LIBRARIES; PAPYROLOGY; RENAISSANCE; SCOLARSHIP, ANCIENT; SCHOLARSHIP, BYZANTINE; SCHOLARSHIP, ISLAMIC; SCHOLIA; TEXTUAL CRITICISM; TRANSMISSION.

maps Many kinds of maps – in the broad sense of graphic representations that facilitate spatial understanding – were produced by Greeks and Romans from early times. What, if anything, they derived from forerunners elsewhere (BABYLONIAN, Egyptian, ETRUSCAN) is obscure. Their variety of representations stays disparate, however, because a common concept of 'map' failed to develop. Our standard term has no equivalent: *gês periodos* or *pinax* in Greek, *charta*, *forma*, *mappa*, *tabula* in Latin, can denote much besides a map. There never were 'general purpose' maps, nor mass production. Although maps with specific aims were made, altogether they featured little among the means which Greeks and Romans (even at the highest level) typically employed to organize and record their surroundings. Thus there were no atlases, much less a discipline of cartography (the term is a 19th-century neologism). This is not to overlook the remarkable succession of Greek scientists who addressed projection, the problem of representing the earth's curvature on a flat surface. The culmination of their work is PTOLEMY's *Geography* of the mid-2nd century AD, where co-ordinates (not all accurate) and instructions are given for drawing a world map and 26 regional ones: whether Ptolemy circulated such maps himself, however, is uncertain.

Without doubt the cartographic data most frequently assembled by Greeks and Romans were names of settlements and the distances between them along recognized routes: from this, lists termed *itineraria* were compiled for land journeys, and

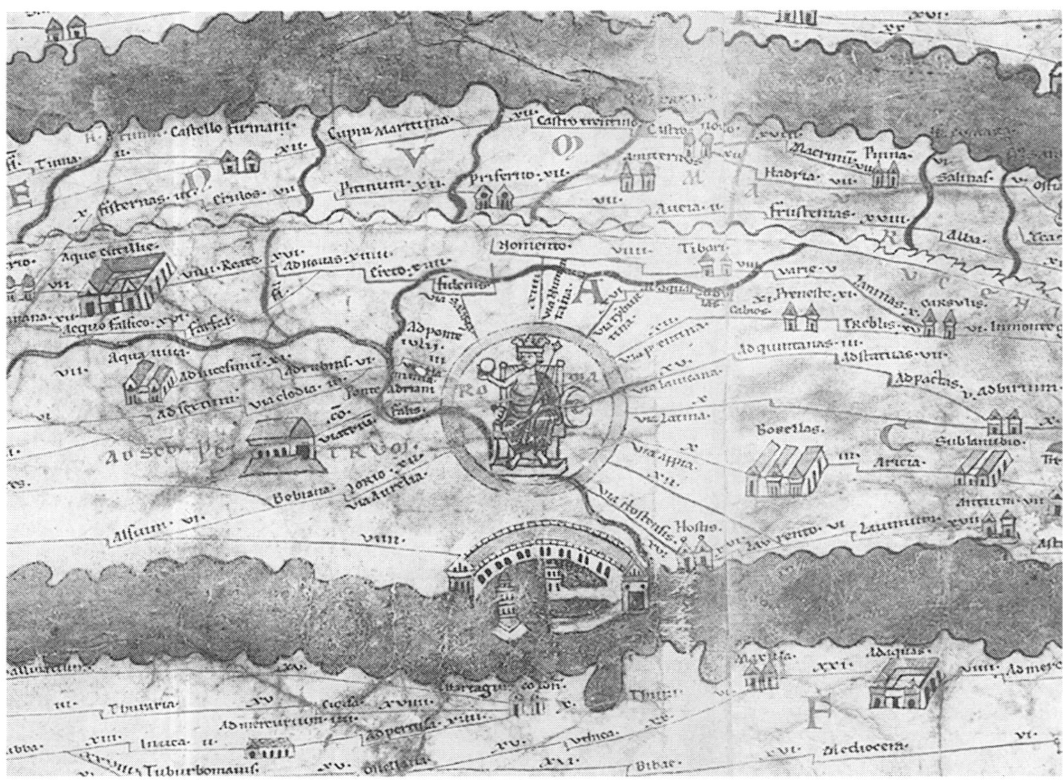

MAPS: detail from the *Tabula Peutingeriana* map, centred on Rome and Ostia.

periploi for sea voyages. If developed into maps, these could only offer a linear representation of space. There is no knowing how often even this was done, though it did happen, as in the *Peutinger Table*.

At the local level, large-scale maps or plans certainly were made. The practice was most widespread in Ptolemaic Egypt and at Rome. Professional surveyors (*agrimensores*) who divided up the cultivable land of Roman communities mention in their handbooks that they were required to leave a bronze map of their work on site and deposit a copy in Rome. Of such bronzes, one small fragment found in Spain in the 1980s alone survives. But the much better preserved Marble plans of the Flavian period for the territory of Arausio (Gaul) are similar. Corresponding activity in cities by *mensores aedificiorum*, who made plans at a standard scale of about 1:240, is thinly documented. But their painstaking work is reflected in the huge (235 sq m) Severan marble plan of Rome, of which about 10 per cent is known. Oriented south-east, its purpose was propagandistic, not practical.

One or more Caesars supposedly commissioned empire-wide surveys, but this is hard to credit; maps of regions were not made. There were attempts, however, originating in 6th-century BC Ionia, to make small-scale representations of the world on both globes and flat surfaces. There are few clues to what these looked like, so that modern reconstructions should be viewed sceptically. Most controversial is the nature of the world map commissioned by Agrippa during the reign of Augustus for display in Rome: it may even have been more text than map. RJAT

See Brodersen, K. (1995) *Terra Cognita*; Harley, J.B. and Wood, D. (1997) Mapmaking, in *Encyclopaedia of the History of Science, Technology, and Medicine in Non-western Cultures* 549–54; Woodward, D., eds. (1987) *The History of Cartography*, vol. 1, pt 2.

Marathon In Athenian eyes, the battle of Marathon had an almost mythical status. In 490 BC, the Athenian hoplite forces along with the Plataeans had met the army of the Persian king Darius I in the plain of Marathon, after it had landed on the coast of Attica from the island of Euboia. For the Athenians, the battle symbolized an important chapter in the idea of resistance to tyranny and the emergence of democracy, partly because Darius had apparently wanted to reinstate Hippias as tyrant of Athens. The story of the Athenian success has a number of legendary features. While the Persian dead apparently numbered 6,400, the Athenians allegedly lost only 192 men: the idea of the success of few against many is a keynote of the tradition. The story went that the runner Pheidippides (or Philippides) was sent as a messenger to take the news of victory to Athens, running the first 'marathon', and then ran all the way to Sparta to summon help. The Spartans, delayed by religious scruples, arrived too late. The

Athenian 'Marathon-fighters' and their general, Miltiades, were treated as heroes, while both HERAKLES and Pan were believed to have had roles in the events. The dead were buried in a mound on the battlefield itself, and the survivors were proud to remember their role. Marathon was portrayed alongside mythical battles on the STOA Poikile commissioned by Miltiades' son KIMON in the 460s BC, and even in the Roman empire its mention evoked the glorious past of Athens. ED

See Herodotos, *Histories* 6.

 BATTLES (table); PERSIAN WARS.

marble Geologically, marble is a limestone metamorphosed into a crystalline rock. Marbles derived from pure limestone consist simply of recrystallized calcite. However, impurities in the rock give certain marbles their characteristic appearance and colour. Many modern stonemasons follow ancient practice in applying the term marble (Latin *marmor*) to denote any rock which can be easily polished; this includes granites, porphyries and unmetamorphosed limestones.

In the 3rd millennium BC the white marbles of the Greek islands were used for Cycladic figurines, normally 20–50 cm, though some life-size examples are known. The MINOANS employed coloured marbles and other polishable stones for vases and FURNITURE and in ARCHITECTURE for facings and column bases. The MYCENAEANS also used coloured marbles including green porphyry from LACONIA and *rosso antico* (from the Mani peninsula) for furniture and in architectural decoration. Neither the Minoans nor the Mycenaeans used marble as a building stone or for SCULPTURE. The fine white marbles of Greece, the Greek islands (THASOS, NAXOS) and Asia Minor (Prokonnesos, EPHESOS) were widely used for architecture and sculpture from the 7th century BC onwards. The luminous white marble from Paros, known as *lychnites* (PLINY THE ELDER, *Natural History* 36.14) was particularly prized for sculpture. In ATTICA the fine-grained Pentelic marble from Mt Pentelikon was used in the PARTHENON and other 5th-century buildings, as well as the white and grey Hymettan from Mt Hymettos to the east of Athens. Coloured marbles were not generally used by the Greeks until the hellenistic period, when they were used especially in interior decoration.

In Rome in the later 2nd and 1st centuries BC white marble from Greece was occasionally used for TEMPLE building (e.g. temple of HERCULES Victor in the FORUM Boarium). Coloured marbles from Greece

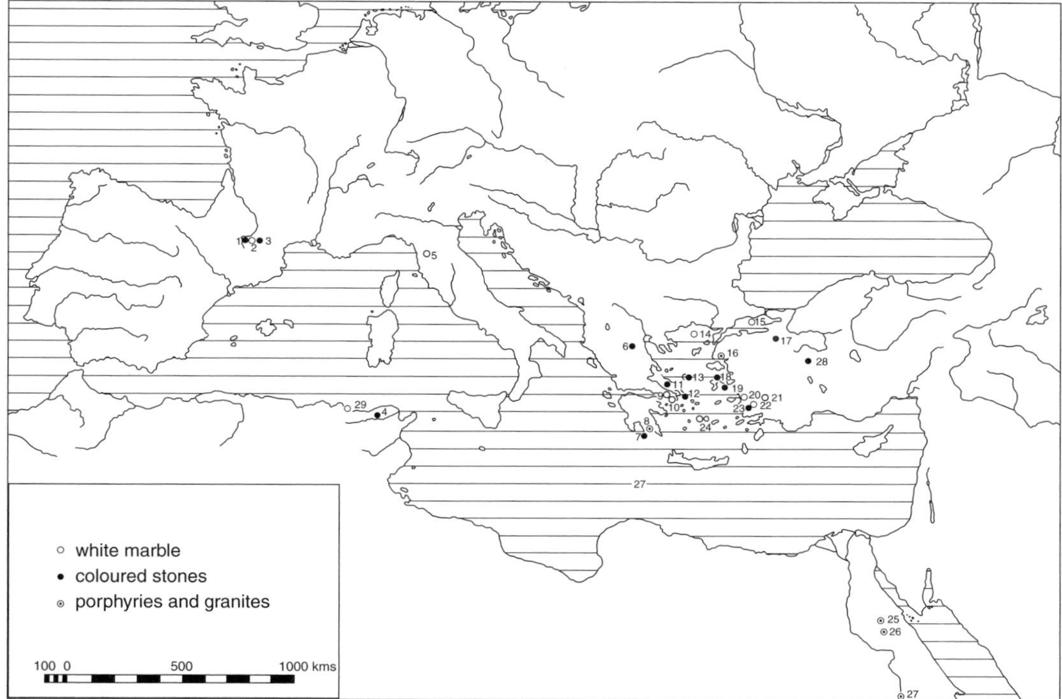

MARBLE: map of the principal sources of decorative stones in the Roman world. 1. Campan; 2. St Beat; 3. St Girons; 4. Simitthus (Chemtou); 5. Luna (Carrara); 6. Thessaly; 7. Cape Taenaros; 8. Krokeai; 9. Mt Pentelikon; 10. Mt Hymettos; 11. Chalkis; 12. Karystos; 13. Skyros; 14. Thasos; 15. Prokonnesos; 16. Troad; 17. Vezirken; 18.=Chios; 19. Teos; 20. Ephesos; 21. Aphrodisias; 22. Herakleia under Latmos; 23. Iasos; 24. Paros; 25. Mons Claudianus (Gebel Dokan); 26. Mons Porphyrites (Gebel Fatireh); 27. Syene (Aswan); 28. Dokimeion; 29. Cap de Garde.

and Numidia were increasingly brought into Rome by prominent individuals, mainly for the decoration of their private homes (e.g. Mamurra and Marcus Lepidus: Pliny, *Natural History* 36.48–50), though sometimes also in more public contexts (Marcus Aemilius Scaurus in his temporary THEATRE in 58 BC: Pliny, *Natural History* 36.113–15). The famous QUARRIES at Luna (CARRARA) were not opened commercially until the middle of the 1st century BC. Augustus employed white (especially Luna) and coloured marbles extensively in his programme of rebuilding the city of Rome (particularly in his forum). Marble was commonly used for columns and wall veneer, and sometimes for construction. A wide variety of coloured marbles was in use in the 1st to the 3rd centuries AD. For statuary the Romans used Luna marble, most of the Greek marbles and some coloured marbles, particularly *giallo antico* from Numidia and *pavonazzetto* from DOKIMEION. By the later 1st century AD a flourishing TRANSPORT system for marble had developed, first of all meeting the emperor's needs in Rome and then broadening out throughout the empire, with many of the main quarries under some kind of imperial control. HD

See De Nuccio, M. and Ungaro, L., eds. (2002) *I marmi colorati della Roma*; Dodge, H. and Ward-Perkins, B., eds. (1992) *Marble in Antiquity*.

 SARCOPHAGI.

Marcelli Principal branch of the PLEBEIAN CLAUDII (perhaps distantly related to the PATRICIAN Claudii). The family belonged to the Arnensis TRIBE. PLUTARCH suggests that the *cognomen* means 'martial'. Marcus is the regular *praenomen*. Both the first known Marcellus, DICTATOR in 327 BC, and the greatest, Marcus Claudius Marcellus (CONSUL 222), met with patrician opposition. The latter was one of Rome's great GENERALS. He won the coveted *spolia opima* (for a commander who kills the opposing commander) and a TRIUMPH against the Gauls in 222; active against Hannibal after CANNAE, he recovered SICILY for Rome, capturing and plundering SYRACUSE in 211; consul for the fifth time in 208, he was killed in an ambush. Marcellus and his descendants were the principal patrons of the Sicilians. The line is difficult to trace in the 2nd century. Marcelli were consuls in 51, 50 and 49 (all anti-Caesarian), but thereafter the family fades away, dying out with AUGUSTUS' nephew and potential successor, whose early death in 23 was mourned by VIRGIL and PROPERTIUS. A minor branch, the Marcelli Aesernini, survived marginally longer (the name perhaps recalling a Marcellus' resistance at Aesernia during the SOCIAL WAR). JRWP

See Plutarch, *Marcellus*, trs. I. Scott-Kilvert in *Makers of Rome* (1965).

Marcellus (Marcus Claudius Marcellus) b. 42 BC Son of AUGUSTUS' sister Octavia by her first marriage to Gaius Claudius Marcellus (CONSUL 50 BC). Augustus, who lacked a son but hoped to found a dynasty, turned first to Marcellus. He was marked out as the eventual successor by marriage to Augustus' daughter Julia (25 BC) and admission to the SENATE with the rank of PRAETOR and the right to stand for the consulship ten years early (24 BC). In 23 he held his first MAGISTRACY, the AEDILESHIP, giving magnificent games. During Augustus' illness early in that year, the emperor passed his ring to AGRIPPA, his friend and effective deputy: Marcellus was not yet old enough for the succession. However, the advancement of Marcellus was probably resented by Agrippa, and the sources report tension between them. In the event, Marcellus died in late 23. He was the first to be buried in Augustus' Mausoleum, and the emperor built the THEATRE of Marcellus in his name. PROPERTIUS composed a lament for his death (3.18) and VIRGIL poignantly made him the culmination of the procession of future Romans shown to AENEAS in the underworld (*Aeneid* 6.860–86). JWR

 AUGUSTUS: (a).

Marcian see CHRISTIANITY; CONSTANTINOPLE; PULCHERIA.

 THEODOSIUS I: (a).

Marcii A PLEBEIAN *gens* at Rome during the Republic and early empire, drawing its name from Ancus Marcius, fourth king of Rome, who is credited with the founding of OSTIA. In the early period, one member of the family was a champion of the plebeians. Gaius Marcius Rutilus, CONSUL four times (357, 352, 344 and 342 BC), was the first plebeian DICTATOR (356) and CENSOR (351). He may have organized fortifications at Ostia, and, when dictator, drove off an ETRUSCAN invasion. He was awarded a TRIUMPH despite PATRICIAN opposition.

The *cognomina* Rex and Philippus appear regularly. Quintus Marcius Rex, PRAETOR in 144 BC, built the Marcian AQUEDUCT. Another Quintus Marcius Rex, consul for 68, returned from a proconsulship in CILICIA and used his *imperium* against CATILINE while waiting in vain for the award of a triumph. Lucius Marcius Philippus, consul in 91, opposed CITIZENSHIP for the Italians. His son, Lucius Marcius Philippus, consul in 56, was the second husband of Atia, mother of AUGUSTUS. A second Lucius Marcius Philippus, son of the previous, married his stepmother's sister and thus became his father's brother-in-law. His daughter Marcia was an associate of LIVIA. JV

Marcionism see CHURCH, THE.

Marcomannic war Fought between Romans and the Marcomanni, AD 167–80. The first phase (167–71), of barbarian invasions along the middle DANUBE, began in 167 with a LOMBARD invasion of PANNONIA, expelled by MARCUS AURELIUS who moved to the Danube in 168. Continued warfare led to an unsuccessful Roman spring offensive into Iazygia in 170. Then the Quadi and Marcomanni invaded Pannonia and NORICUM, entered north Italy and besieged AQUILEIA. At the same time, the Costobocci broke through Moesia and THRACE to Greece where they sacked ELEUSIS. The second phase (171–3), of repelling the invaders, began in 171. After defeating and expelling the invaders of 170, Marcus made peace with some barbarians at Carnuntum. Roman

Marcomannic war: the column of Marcus Aurelius in the Campus Martius presents an illustrated history of the war.

Marcus Aurelius: equestrian statue, now displayed on the Capitoline Hill, Rome.

captives were returned, and some barbarians were settled in the empire, others incorporated into the army. In 172 the main Roman counterstroke began with the invasion of Marcomannia and Quadia (events depicted on the column of Marcus Aurelius). The Asding Vandals allied with the Romans and fought against Costobocci. The third phase of the wars (173–80) saw a series of Roman offensives intended to occupy the region, and in 175 permanent forts were constructed across the Danube. In 177 Marcus left the Danube to deal with the revolt of Avidius Cassius and to declare his son Commodus Augustus. After Marcus' death in 180, Commodus carried out limited campaigning on Danube, then negotiated peace with Quadi and Marcomanni. HWE

See Birley, A. R. (1993) *Marcus Aurelius*.

 Dalmatia (a); war (table).

Marcus Aurelius (Marcus Annius Catilius Severus) AD 121–80 Son of Marcus Annius Verus and Domitia Lucilla, born on 26 April AD 121. On 17 March 136 he was betrothed to Ceionia Fabia, the daughter of Lucius Aelius Caesar, Hadrian's heir designate, and changed his name to Marcus Annius Verus. After Aelius' death he was adopted by the new heir designate, the future emperor Antoninus Pius, taking the name Marcus Aelius Aurelius Verus. In 145 he married Faustina, daughter of Antoninus, and was clearly designated as Antoninus' successor in 147 with grants of tribunician power, *imperium proconsulare* and the right to speak fifth in meetings of the senate.

Marcus succeeded upon the death of Antoninus, and honoured what appears to have been Hadrian's original desire by adopting his half-brother, Lucius Ceionius Commodus (the biological son of Lucius Aelius Caesar) and promoting him to the rank of Augustus as Lucius Aurelius Verus. Lucius had been betrothed to Marcus' daughter, Lucilla, and the two were married at Ephesos in 163, where Lucius was providing symbolic leadership for the Roman army engaged in resisting a Parthian invasion of the Eastern provinces, launched almost as soon as Marcus had taken the throne. The Parthians were defeated, and their capital at Ctesiphon sacked, in 165. Subsequently, a serious epidemic struck the empire; it has been estimated that 10 per cent of the empire's population died in the next few years. Lucius himself fell victim in 167.

As plague ravaged the empire, the Germanic tribes north of the Danube began to take a more aggressive stance. In the winter of 169, a German army besieged Marcus in Aquileia, and he spent most of the next decade in the Balkans, directing the operations of various generals. In 175 he left the Danube to suppress a revolt led by Avidius Cassius, appointed *corrector* of the Eastern provinces. The motivation for the revolt is not clear, and it fizzled out very rapidly when Avidius was assassinated by his own men within a few weeks. After returning to Rome in 176/7, Marcus left again for the Danubian provinces, threatened by fresh German invasion, in 178. He died near Sirmium on 17 March 180.

His contemporaries regarded Marcus as a truly great emperor, with a reputation as an extremely hard worker and fair judge. His private diary, the *Meditations*, not written, unlike many imperial memoirs, for publication, confirms the picture in other sources of a man deeply concerned with justice. In general terms his stewardship of the empire followed in the tradition of his immediate predecessors; he did not annex new territories after his victories in the East, and sought no significant territorial gains in the course of the northern wars. The record of his wars suggests that he made competent appointments to high office, and his correspondence, as preserved in the corpus of FRONTO and public documents, shows a great respect for tradition. While it might be possible to criticize Marcus' conservatism in light of later developments, it is testimony to his skill as an administrator that he made the government work. DSP

See Birley, A. R. (1987) *Marcus Aurelius.*

 EMPERORS, ROMAN: (a); MARCOMANNIC WARS; TRAJAN.

Marius (Gaius Marius) c.157–86 BC A *novus homo* from Arpinum (like CICERO), Marius played a pivotal role in the military and political transformations leading from REPUBLIC to empire. He is a difficult figure to evaluate: many of the original accounts (now lost) were written by his opponents, and he became the stereotype of the uneducated soldier statesman. Additionally, his background – Italian not Roman, equestrian not senatorial – repeatedly places him in opposition to various senatorial groups. Five successive consulships (104–100), to protect Rome against the northern threat of the Cimbri and Teutones, after his success against JUGURTHA in AFRICA (as CONSUL, 107), provided a unique opportunity for military reform. This laid the foundations for the professional Roman army (not all directly attributable to Marius). But his actions also strengthened ties between army and commander, weakening those between army and state. Marius' alliances with the popular TRIBUNES Saturninus (104–100) and Publius Sulpicius (88), the former to maintain his position and reward his troops, the latter to transfer the command against MITHRADATES from SULLA to Marius, foreshadowed later political practice. Both tribunes lost their lives: Saturninus' demagoguery forced Marius himself to depose him; Sulpicius fell when, in the aftermath of the SOCIAL WAR, Sulla marched on Rome, outlawing him and Marius. When Sulla went east, Marius in turn marched on Rome, supposedly massacring his opponents. Marius died 13 January 86, during his record seventh consulship. JRWP

See Plutarch, *Marius*, trs. R. Waterfield (1999); Evans, R. J. (1994) *Gaius Marius.*

Mark Antony see ANTONY, MARK.

market buildings Structures designed for the exchange of commodities. Although ancient commerce regularly took place in locales without permanent facilities, market buildings were built in many urban centres in antiquity. Greek cities generally contained an *AGORA* which served commercial interests, as well as those of LAW, politics and religion. The STOA, a long and narrow colonnade, was the typical building in Greece for market activities from the 5th century BC. The Stoa of Attalos in the Agora at Athens (c.135 BC) contained two levels of colonnades with 21 rooms at the back; the city probably rented rooms to merchants. 'Peristyle' (colonnaded) markets developed in the 3rd century BC, as at MILETOS.

MARKET BUILDINGS: (a) the great vaulted hall of Trajan's markets in Rome, the centrepiece of a purpose-built shopping mall.

The Roman FORUM fulfilled the same functions as the Greek *agora*. No standard design for the Roman market building existed; preserved examples are circular (POMPEII, LEPCIS MAGNA), rectilinear (OSTIA), and apsidal (THAMUGADI). Their size varies but most market buildings accommodated 10–25 shops; each was a room with counters for butchery or the display of merchandise. At Rome, the more elaborate markets of TRAJAN resemble a modern shopping mall with their multiple floors of one- or two-room shops positioned over the length of a vaulted hallway. Built into the side of a hill with BRICK and CONCRETE, streets on three levels provided access to the markets. Some 150 shops are visible today. DLS

See Frayn, J. M. (1993) *Markets and Fairs in Roman Italy.*

 ARCHITECTURE: (d).

marketing see ADVERTISING; see also SHOPPING.

markets Exchange centres. Two basic types of markets existed: daily and periodic. Daily markets operated in large towns, often within permanent MARKET BUILDINGS. Periodic markets served smaller towns and countrysides at fixed intervals from once to several times per month. They probably did not have permanent facilities. Fairs, associated with religious FESTIVALS and other occasions, are best regarded as infrequent supplements to daily and periodic markets.

Many ancient towns had markets located in the main place of assembly, the *AGORA* (Greece) or FORUM (Rome). Both served as the hub of LAW, POLITICS, RELIGION and commerce in their towns, but in larger cities non-commercial activities dominated. Commercial transactions moved to specialized market buildings nearby, whose size varies, but most accommodated 10 or more shops. The North Market of the 3rd century BC at MILETOS provides a good

MARKET BUILDINGS: (b) the colonnaded market square with central kiosks (*tholoi*) at Lepcis Magna, dating to 8–7 BC in its original form.

MARKETS: much market activity utilized temporary stalls in public spaces, such as forums – as here in a painting from Herculaneum.

example of an early market building. Portable wooden stalls and tables were probably typical in temporary markets.

Whether daily or periodic, markets united town and countryside by providing a place for the distribution of goods from one to the other. They sold a variety of foodstuffs and commodities: MEAT, FISH, POULTRY, game, grain, VEGETABLES, WINE, OIL, TEXTILES, wool, building materials, POTTERY, FURNITURE and AGRICULTURAL equipment. Even land and SLAVES could be purchased here; all these commodities suggest the presence of both upper and lower class individuals in marketplaces. It was common for large towns to contain specialized market districts for standard items: thus Rome had a *forum boarium* (CATTLE market), *forum holitorium* (vegetable market), etc.

Town officials (*agoranomoi*, AEDILES) had responsibility for managing markets. They posted the times of markets in public spaces, as is evident from inscribed market CALENDARS which attest the dates of periodic markets in 26 towns in central Italy in the 1st century AD. Officials also supervised transactions. Markets contained WEIGHTS AND MEASURES of various sizes to guarantee the accuracy of dealings, examples of which have been found in the Agora in Athens.

Rural markets functioned differently from urban ones. It was here, ancient authors indicate, that landowners sought to hire surplus LABOUR. Authorities monitored rural markets as the congregation of individuals here contained the potential for unrest (Shaw). Senatorial permission was required to institute periodic markets in the Roman world, not just in the provinces (*CIL* 8.270) but also in Italy (PLINY THE YOUNGER, *Letters* 5.4, 5.13). The emperor CLAUDIUS even requested permission from the SENATE to hold markets on his estates (Suetonius, *Claudius* 12.2).

In addition to its more tangible definition as a physical location, the word 'market' connotes the more abstract notion of the exchange of a single commodity, for example, the 'WINE market', 'OLIVE OIL market', 'SLAVE market' and others. DLS

See Frayn, J.M. (1993) *Markets and Fairs in Roman Italy*; Shaw, B.D. (1981) Rural markets in North Africa and the political economy of the Roman empire, *Ant Af* 17: 37–83.

 CALENDARS: (b).

Marmor Parium see PARIAN MARBLE.

marriage

Pandora was the first woman and the first bride, and it has been argued that the verb *didômi*, 'to give', from which Pandora's name is derived (having the meaning 'all gifts'), reflects the notion that the bride was originally a 'free gift' that came to the groom's home bearing more gifts. Certainly, the HOMERIC bride brought gifts to her new *oikos*, an act which formalized a marriage and legitimized the children of the union. In Homeric EPIC, a man could also 'marry' a girl by winning her in a competition or by stealing her as booty. Marriage in archaic SPARTA was, apparently, very different to other Greek practices: wife-sharing and selective breeding were, allegedly, common practices in the Spartans' quest for the production of strong warriors. But because data from the Homeric and archaic periods are so sparse, much of our information about marriage is based on Athenian practices of the 5th and 4th centuries BC. In Athens, a girl married around the age of 14, presumably to guarantee her virginity and fertility. A prospective groom, on the other hand, was about 30 when he first married. A girl was obliged to marry whomever her *kyrios* (male guardian) decided upon; his choice of groom was conditioned by political and socio-economic factors, since a well-made marriage could consolidate family wealth.

There was no set precedent for a legal marriage, as marriage was held to be a private arrangement between two families, a process of transfer organized chiefly by the bride's *kyrios*. However, most marriages followed some form of set order: marriage negotiations began with the *enguê*, an oral agreement between the bride's *kyrios* and the groom (or his family). The *kyrios* entrusted the bride-to-be to the man for the purpose of producing children, and a formal exchange of words seems to have used, with an AGRICULTURAL metaphor encouraging the groom to 'plough' the bride for the purpose of begetting children. A dowry was agreed upon and then *ekdosis*, the second part of the marriage transaction, was free to proceed. The *ekdosis* was the transfer of the bride to her husband's household, an important element of the marriage transfer, since a bride was required to renounce her ties to her paternal *oikos* and to be adopted instead into her marital *oikos*. Her father gave up his role as *kyrios*, and her new husband assumed that role. The wedding rites themselves marked three phases in the bride's transformation into a wife: separation from her *oikos*, transition to a new home, and her integration into her new roles as daughter and wife within a new *oikos*. To correspond with these three phases, a bride went through a triple transformation from a *parthenos*, a virgin, to a *nymphê*, a bride, and finally to a *gynê*, an adult woman with a child.

MARRIAGE: (a) the reception of the bride at the house of her husband, with music and torchlight, is illustrated on this painted cup in Berlin.

There was no legal wedding ceremony to speak of, though a series of domestic rituals were placed together (in a somewhat *ad hoc* manner) to encompass the period between *enguê* and *ekdosis*. The ceremonies took between three and five days, and were a time of feasting and display. The first day's wedding rituals included the bathing of the bride in sacred water and the offering of TEXTILES to ARTEMIS, acts which prepared the bride for her transformation into a wife. The next day was probably celebrated in the home of the bride's *kyrios*, where a huge bridal feast was prepared. This was one of the few public events women were permitted to attend, though men and women sat at different tables. The bride's face and figure were completely VEILED and it was at some point during the feast that the bridal veil was lifted – temporarily – so that the assembled guests could look at her face. The ritual unveiling, or *anakalyptêria*, was just one of several unveilings endured by the bride throughout the wedding ceremonies; it is incorrect to think that there was one climactic unveiling. At the end of the feast the bride and groom left the *kyrios*' house and travelled by night in a torch-lit procession to the groom's family home. The bride was then showered with ritual *katachysmata* (nuts, seeds and FRUIT), a rite performed to guarantee her future fertility, and was welcomed to the family hearth as another stage of the *anakalyptêria* was enacted. The couple entered the bridal chamber (*thalamos*) as the guests sang wedding songs. It was here that the bride gave up her virginity to her husband who symbolically removed her 'internal veil', her hymen. The final day of the wedding ceremony was called the *epaulia*, a ceremony of gift-giving accompanied by songs that emphasized the transition of the bride to her new status.

Athenian marriages, as occurred in the Homeric period, were usually accompanied by the gifts of property or money. In Athens the bridal dowry was intended to support the wife and any children she might have, though the giving of a dowry was not a legal requirement. A woman's consent to marriage was not required either, and in many of the wedding ceremonies the bride was little more than a fetish to be admired, viewed and led about. A woman was not permitted to marry a direct ascendant or descendant, nor her brother or half-brother by the same mother (though marriage to a half-brother by the same father was allowed). From 451/0 BC marriage between an

MARRIAGE: (b) relief carving of an élite Roman marriage ceremony, accompanied by the sacrifice of an ox. The figure of Eros between the couple, seen to r. of the scene, denotes the hope of children from the union.

Athenian citizen and a foreigner was outlawed. Bigamy was illegal, though a man could take a concubine as well as a wife (children born to the concubine were regarded as illegitimate). DIVORCE was easily achieved: a husband could send his wife back to her paternal *oikos*, allowing her *kyrios* to farm her out to another husband. It was not unusual for a woman to have had two or more marriages. LL-J

See Blundell, S. (1995) *Women in Ancient Greece* (1995); Llewellyn-Jones, L. (2003) *Aphrodite's Tortoise*; Oakley, J. and Sinos, R. (1993) *The Wedding in Ancient Athens*.

With few exceptions (such as LATINS), proper marriage (*nuptiae iustae*) was between Roman CITIZENS and traditionally contracted for the purpose of producing legitimate issue. The technical basis of Roman marriage was the desire of both parties to be married (*affectio maritalis*) and their consent (and that of their fathers) was required, but that of a young girl was in practice assumed. Other factors (age, close kinship) affected the legal capacity for marriage. Roman law gave great power to the father to arrange and even to end a match, but custom assigned a major role to the mother and other relatives of the bride and groom. Dowry was a normal feature but not a legal requirement of marriage, which was an essentially private institution.

Few love matches based on individual choice are known to us, but they may have been the norm in the proletariat. For those with property, marriage was viewed as a union of families with implications for future generations – important considerations for the peasantry, bankers and the political ÉLITES of Roman Italy. Roman citizens throughout the empire were subject to the same laws, but probably followed local custom, at least until the 3rd century AD, when virtually all free Roman subjects gained citizenship and such institutions as Egyptian brother–sister marriage became problematic. Age differentials between partners and the typical age at first marriage varied across the social spectrum, with élite girls marrying at quite young ages – even sometimes below the legal limit of 12. 'Abduction marriage' also occurred, in which, with the assistance of his friends, a man would kidnap the woman of his choice, virtually forcing her parents to accept him as a son-in-law.

Traditionally, the *univira* ('one-husband woman') passed as a girl from her father's power to her husband's *manus* and died before her husband. By late Republican times, the term meant a widow who declined to remarry and many women – like CORNELIA, mother of the GRACCHI – were praised for meeting this ideal, which continued to be celebrated in tombstones and literature. Remarriage, however, was the norm after DIVORCE and also on the death of a spouse. Childbirth could be fatal to some women, while others – married sometimes to much older men – could be widowed at an early age. Divorce, rare or unknown in early Rome, had become unremarkable by the last century of the Republic. Children might therefore have contact with a range of step- and half-relations. The fact that stepmothers usually lived with their stepchildren might explain traditional suspicion of them, in spite of the many examples of benevolent stepmothers. Some men (e.g. Octavian's stepfather Philippus) took stepchildren into their homes and were praised for being good surrogate fathers to their stepchildren.

SLAVE 'marriage' (*contubernium*) was never recognized at law but enjoyed some effective recognition, as did the unions of soldiers (often with non-Romans), whose marriages were invalidated from the time of AUGUSTUS, but possibly legally permitted from the time of SEPTIMIUS SEVERUS two centuries later. People tended to marry within their own social group, but marriages did occur between masters or mistresses and their freed slaves and, in spite of Augustan legislation penalizing slave–free unions, freeborn women 'married' the élite slaves of the imperial family. Epitaphs record unions formed within slavery and continued after one partner was freed and then bought out the other, together with children where possible.

A Roman woman retained her own family (gentile) name after marriage. But she could either remain legally a member of her birth family (and therefore still in the power of her father, or independent – *sui iuris* – if he were dead or had 'emancipated' her) or become a member of her husband's family, passing from the *potestas* ('power') of her father to the *manus* ('hand') of her husband or father-in-law. If she remained a legal member of her own family, her property (apart from the dowry, which her husband owned for the duration of the marriage) was distinct from that of her husband. Substantial gifts between husband and wife were legally void from 204 BC (the *lex Cincia*). If the wife passed into her husband's *manus*, all her property and any which she acquired during the marriage passed into the common holdings of his family and she had no right to inherit on intestacy from her own blood relations, who ceased to be her legal kin (*agnati*). Whichever form of marriage she had chosen – or her father had chosen for her – the children were part of her husband's family, were in his (or his father's) paternal power and were his rightful heirs. There is no standard Latin expression for the two basic types of marriage. By the late Republic, for reasons not clear to modern scholars, the dominant preference had changed from the merged to the separate system of marriage. *Confarreatio*, an elaborate and indissoluble form of sacral '*manus* marriage' practised by certain PATRICIANS in early Rome, had fallen entirely into disuse, which made it difficult to fill certain PRIESTHOODS (Tacitus, *Annals* 4.16).

Although Roman marriages were not based on romance, there was an expectation and ideal of love, harmony (*concordia*) and loyalty during the marriage. These values are exalted in tombstones, especially those from husbands to wives, celebrating marriages of '*x* years without a complaint (*sine ulla querela*)', and inspirational stories of touching devotion enjoyed wide circulation. Slave epitaphs to spouses (sometimes called *contubernales*) used the same terminology. Engagements were generally brief but probably accompanied by romantic rituals, and such diverse authors as CICERO, STATIUS and PLINY THE YOUNGER all employed the extravagant language of Latin love poetry in writing to their wives. SD

See Evans-Grubbs, J. (1989) Abduction marriage in antiquity: a law of Constantine and its social context, *JRS* 79: 59–83; Rawson, B., ed. (1991) *Marriage, Divorce and Children in Ancient Rome*; Treggiari, S.M. (1991) *Roman Marriage*.

Mars Roman war god, of Italic origin. His name is of uncertain etymology, sometimes appearing as Mavors. With JUPITER and Quirinus, Mars may have belonged to an archaic Roman triad of gods (cf. Dumézil). He was served by his own priest, the *flamen martialis*. Mars was eventually identified with Ares, but always played a paternal role peculiar to his Roman identity as the father of ROMULUS and, hence, the nation. Some scholars have made Mars do double duty as an agrarian god, but in rites like the *suovetaurilia* he was probably invoked merely apotropaically, as a protector of fields and herds from external threats (cf. CATO, *De agricultura* 141).

March was named for Mars and was punctuated with his ceremonies. 19 March was *Quinquatrus* ('fifth day' after the Ides), official opening of the military campaigning season. On other days in March, the Salii danced in his processions. The Ides of October, too, were devoted to Mars, with horse races in the Campus Martius, which was used in Republican times for army exercises. Before AUGUSTUS, Mars' principal Roman TEMPLES were outside the *POMERIUM*, in the Campus Martius and on the Via Appia, while his sacred shields and spears were housed within the city walls in the Regia. In 2 BC Augustus consecrated a temple to Mars Ultor ('Avenger') in the new imperial FORUM, marking the war god's role in Augustus' victory at PHILIPPI. JRH

See Beard, M., North, J. and Price, S. (1998) *Religions of Rome*; Bonnefoy, Y., ed. (1991) *Roman and European Mythologies*; Dumézil, G. (1987) *Archaic Roman Religion*.

 GODS AND GODDESSES: (a).

Marseilles (anc. Massalia, Massilia) A Greek COLONY to the east of the RHÔNE delta in France, founded c.600 BC by the city of Phokaia in Asia Minor. Marseilles itself established a network of coastal colonies, and its location made it both a centre of MEDITERRANEAN TRADE and a commercial gateway to the interior of GAUL. Excavations of its deep-water HARBOUR, the Vieux-Port, confirm the importance of the city as a major port from the archaic period through late antiquity. Marseilles played an important mediating role between the peoples of Gaul and the ROMAN REPUBLIC, with whom it was long allied. The city was defended throughout antiquity by substantial circuit walls built in the mid-2nd century BC. The walls did not resist, however, the prolonged SIEGE of CAESAR, who ceded much of its hinterland to Arles (49 BC). Despite the reduction in territory, and the emergence of Arles as the primary gateway to Gaul, Marseilles remained an important port city, to judge from the recent discovery of wooden tablets mentioning the *quadragesima Galliarum* indicating its right to collect *portorium*. Marseilles exported WINE in the Roman period and was famous as a cultural and intellectual centre. The city flourished in late antiquity, in contrast to other Provençal cities. RBH

See Loseby, S.T. (1992) Marseille: a late-antique success story, *JRS* 82: 165–85.

 GAUL: (b).

marshes see ARKADIA; CANALS; RAVENNA; SPINA; TARRACINA; WETLANDS.

Marsi see SOCIAL WAR, ROMAN.

Martial (Marcus Valerius Martialis) c.AD 40–104 From Bilbilis in north-east Spain, where he retired after a career at Rome as the foremost Latin epigrammatist under four successive EMPERORS (TITUS, DOMITIAN, Nerva and TRAJAN). Fifteen books of his EPIGRAMS survive. The earliest, *Liber spectaculorum* (*The Book of Spectacles*), survives only in excerpts in medieval collections and is incomplete. It was composed to celebrate the spectacles at the inauguration of the Colosseum under Titus in AD 80, and is strongly PANEGYRIC in tone. Two further volumes on unified themes appeared in 84/5 and are traditionally numbered out of chronological order: book 13, *Xenia*

('Guest-gifts'), comprising 127 epigrams, mostly individual couplets describing edible gifts; and book 14, *Apophoreta* ('Gifts to take away'), comprising 223 of these 'gift-tag verses' to accompany a wide range of items, mostly inedible. From AD 86 to 96 Martial published 11 volumes of miscellaneous epigrams, usually timed to coincide with the Saturnalia FESTIVAL in December. Book 12 was composed in Bilbilis under the reign of Trajan. Five of the books (1, 2, 8, 9, 12) contain prefatory material in prose that was not necessarily composed to introduce the published volume as a whole; the preface to book 12 shows Martial already disenchanted with provincial life. Book 10 has not survived in its original form; under Trajan Martial revised it by eliminating those epigrams that conveyed extravagant compliments to Domitian. Book 11, hastily compiled when Nerva became emperor, contains a preponderance of obscenity, which Martial excuses on the grounds that Nerva's accession presages a freer atmosphere (Nerva himself composed obscene verse). Book 8 had been intentionally lacking in obscenity, to conform to Domitian's strict moral programme in his office as CENSOR.

In his epigrams Martial commonly sets up a situation at the beginning that results in an unexpected dénouement at the end, or uses a question-and-answer format. He adopted from contemporary Greek epigram the tendency towards a witty and pointed conclusion, and stamped the genre with the characteristics of brevity and wit that still identify it today. Even the congratulatory poems of the *Liber spectaculorum* manifest the same pointed style that is particularly associated with the satiric element in Martial's *oeuvre*. His addressees include a range of identifiable contemporary figures, though he defends himself against charges of defamation on the grounds that his attacks are aimed exclusively at fictitious persons. He moulds the repertoire of Greek epigram into a vivid (if partially unverifiable) portrait of the physical and social fabric of Flavian Rome, a foil and complement to that of his contemporary STATIUS. His preferred metre is elegiac couplets, his diction peppered with colloquialisms and Graecisms. Few of his epigrams exceed twelve lines. Ever since the RENAISSANCE his work has been widely translated and adapted in all the major European literatures. KMC

See Martial, *Epigrams*, trs. D. R. Shackleton Bailey, 3 vols. (1993); Boyle, A. J. and Sullivan, J. P., eds. (1996) *Martial in English*; Sullivan, J. P. (1991) *Martial: the unexpected classic*.

Martin, St c.AD 316–97 Bishop of Tours and Gallic saint. Born in PANNONIA but raised in northern Italy, Martin served in the Roman army in GAUL for about 25 years. He became a monk c.356 and was influenced by Hilary, bishop of Poitiers. When Hilary was exiled, Martin travelled widely, but his attempt to found a monastery outside MILAN was unsuccessful. Hilary's return provided Martin with an opportunity to establish a monastery at Ligugé near Poiters. Bishop of Tours from 371 until his death, he was buried in a small church at the outskirts of the city. His tomb immediately became the centre of a cult and attracted pilgrims from Gaul and elsewhere seeking the miracles his relics were said to perform. Bishop Perpetuus built a new church of St Martin late in the 5th century. A century later, Gregory of Tours raised the profile of St Martin considerably. He became the quintessential Gallic saint, but his supremacy was threatened by occasional Merovingian favour toward the cult of St Denys at Paris.

Traditionally, Martin converted Gaul to CHRISTIANITY, focusing on the rural areas. According to his BIOGRAPHERS, he performed many miracles and established CHURCHES and monasteries wherever he found pagan shrines, after overturning them. Ninian, the missionary of northern BRITAIN, visited Martin and may have adopted some of his methods. JV

See Sulpicius Severus, *Life of St Martin*; Gregory of Tours, *The Miracles of the Bishop St Martin*; Van Dam, R. (1993) *Saints and Their Miracles in Late Antique Gaul*.

martyrs Someone who witnesses (Greek *martyromai*) to his or her faith in God by choosing to endure death rather than recant. Some CHRISTIAN martyrs offered SOCRATES as an example because, according to PLATO (*Apology*, *Crito*), he accepted a death penalty rather than renounce what he believed to be a god-given mission. The DELPHIC ORACLE said that he was the wisest of the Greeks, and his much-resented challenges to those who claimed to be wise showed that his wisdom lay in realizing his own human ignorance. But that is an exceptional case. Because polytheism could easily accommodate previously unknown gods, it was only JEWS and Christians who risked martyrdom by denying the authority of any gods other than the One God. Jewish MONOTHEISM was generally respected because it was ancient, but the book of Maccabees records the death of Jewish martyrs when Antiochos Epiphanes tried (167 BC) to suppress their religion. Under the Roman occupation, other Jews died because they would not tolerate Roman political and military symbols which they saw as idolatrous. Christian martyrs died for refusing to acknowledge the Greco-Roman gods, even by token worship such as a pinch of incense on the altar. This refusal was interpreted as a rejection of the society in which they lived, and some of them suffered the extreme forms of public punishment applied to rebels or to criminals of the lower social classes. Those who were willing to die, but survived torture or were not in fact executed, were called confessors, and had great spiritual authority. Some Christian martyrs were thrown to the lions, or to other wild ANIMALS, in the arena (*ad bestias*); some were burned alive (*crematio*) or variously tortured in the course of interrogation or execution. Christians regarded their endurance of bodily suffering as a demonstration of God's power. Records of their trials and detailed accounts of their death, called martyr-acts (from Latin *acta*), were read to commemorate their 'birthdays' as martyrs. The texts called, by modern scholars, *Acts of the Pagan Martyrs* commemorate the courage of ALEXANDRIAN Greeks defending not their religion, but the rights of their city, against menacing Roman emperors.

Relics (Latin *reliqua*, remains) of the bodies or clothing of Christian martyrs were believed to be charged with spiritual power and able to heal illness. The shrine or TOMB of a martyr also had a protective power like that ascribed to the tomb of a hero, with the important difference that the hero was understood to be dead, whereas the martyr was believed to be alive in union with God. In the 4th century AD Christian BISHOPS used the cult of martyrs, much as heroes were used in archaic Greece, to establish a new Christian history for their cities by the building of shrines and of CHURCHES containing relics. In the 5th century, some resolute pagans were martyred – usually by lynching, as in the notorious case of the PHILOSOPHER HYPATIA – for their refusal to abandon the traditional religion. GC

Marx, Karl (1818–83) Generated major impacts in socio-economic history and theory. Born in TRIER to a prominent Jewish family, Marx was the product of the social and legal constraints imposed on the Jewish community. In order not to face reprisals, Marx's father converted himself and his children to Christianity. Marx's deep interest in classical studies commenced in his early schooldays and continued into university. In the 1830s he began to study jurisprudence at the University of Bonn. His studies eventually drew him towards philosophy as he began to critique Roman law from a philosophical standpoint. In Berlin he completed his doctoral dissertation, 'The Difference between Democritean and the Epicurean Philosophy of Nature' (1841). In the years that followed, scattered frequently throughout Marx's works and correspondences are references to Greek and Roman literature, PHILOSOPHY and culture. Marx collaborated with Engels to write the *Communist Manifesto* (1848), which highlighted class conflicts as they related to the production and possession of goods. A source of class conflict arose in the Roman REPUBLIC, for example, when wealthy landowners exploited their forced SLAVE LABOUR to reap AGRICULTURAL profits. LAH

See Ste Croix, G. E. M. de (1975) Karl Marx and the history of classical antiquity, *Arethusa* 8: 7–41.

Marxism Karl MARX (d.1883) was himself trained as a classical scholar and wrote his doctoral dissertation on the ATOMIST theories of DEMOKRITOS and EPICURUS (1841, published 1928). Throughout his adult life he continued to read classical texts – in the original, as he proudly told Engels; and it is arguable that at least ARISTOTLE had an important influence on his own theories of ECONOMY, society, culture and politics. But he was of course above all else a student – and critic – of modern capitalism, not primarily interested in the ancient world for its own sake. Moreover, his voluminous writings were never reduced to a strict system by Marx himself, and there have been almost as many 'marxisms' during and after his lifetime as there have been different forms of CHRISTIANITY.

Marx gave primacy in historical explanation to material factors. In one summation of his theory (preface to *Critique of Political Economy*, 1859) he outlined a scheme whereby increases in productive capacity necessarily imposed strains on the prevailing social relations and led to the emergence of a new MODE OF PRODUCTION or social formation. But in the notebooks known as the *Grundrisse* ('First Sketches', 1857–8), which were preparatory to *Das Kapital* (vol. 1, 1867; vols. 2–4 published posthumously), he characterized all pre-capitalist societies as essentially static in economic terms.

The central concern of Marx's intellectual and practical activity was CLASS conflict, and he regarded class struggle as the key to understanding all human history. But he never provided a definitive account of what he understood by class, and he applied the term to the ancient world in different ways. Sometimes the struggle was said by him to be between 'freeman and slave', though strictly that is a distinction of legal status, and not all freemen by any means owned SLAVES. Elsewhere he gave it as one between 'debtors and creditors', that is, a struggle within the free and indeed citizen population. Historians of Greece and Rome wishing to apply Marxist theory and insight have therefore had to evolve their own definitions and applications.

Some Marxists, sticking quite closely to Marx's original economic preoccupation and emphasis, have privileged exploitation of LABOUR (especially servile labour) as the key to historical change. How the rich got and stayed rich in class-based Greek and Roman SOCIETIES is for them the principal question to answer. Others, while generally emphasizing that ideas and institutions depend on a society's underlying relations of production, would not argue that economic relations and interests determine all aspects of culture, from morality and the arts to EDUCATION and law. Nor does their interest in ideology encompass only the ideas deployed by ruling classes to preserve their hegemony. By uncovering evidence of class conflict in canonical works of literature, which they see as having been crucially shaped by tensions and evasions having their roots in the contradictions of exploitative social relations, they have contributed significantly to a new interest in the material conditions of artistic production.

Many Marxists, finally, have become increasingly sensitive to analyses of forms of oppression besides the narrowly economic, above all that of WOMEN and other marginalized 'outsiders' (as seen from the point of view of the dominant male citizen group). PAC

See Ste Croix, G. E. M. de (1981, corr. repr. 1983) *The Class Struggle in the Ancient Greek World*.

Marzabotto A modern village in north Italy near an ETRUSCAN site, perhaps Misa or Misna, 27 km (17 miles) south of Bologna (Felsina) along the Reno. Founded c.500 BC at a site with little trace of Villanovan and earlier settlement, the town was planned on a rectangular grid. Street alignment coincides with a TEMPLE complex on a plateau in the north-west corner. The main road is 16.4 m (50 ft) wide and runs north to south; three streets, 5.6 m (17 ft) wide, cross at right angles, with tertiary roads between. The northernmost secondary road passes the foot of the plateau. Water and drainage systems were complex and well designed. Industrial areas occur in the city centre, reflecting the town's economic rather than military importance. Iron work predominated, and a potters' quarter lay at the north end of the main road. Cemeteries, with cremation BURIALS, were located in the north and the south-east. Finds include local bronze brooches, bracelets and statuettes, gold JEWELLERY from southern Etruria, and imported Attic vases.

By the beginning of the 4th century BC, Marzabotto was under attack from GAULS, perhaps the Boii, who resided at Marzabotto briefly. A Gallic cemetery yielded iron swords and other LA TÈNE goods, while small huts at the town centre contained La Tène brooches and armbands. The abandoned city, partly washed away by the Reno, was never rebuilt, offering a unique picture of Etruscan town-planning at a specific period. JV

See Haynes, S. (2000) *Etruscan Civilization*; Scullard, H. H. (1967) *The Etruscan Cities and Rome.*

Masada A large isolated rock outcrop on the west side of the Dead sea, flat-topped with precipitous sides. The principal occupation belongs to the 2nd century BC to the 2nd century AD, providing scholars with superb examples of architecture and artefacts (Roman and rebel coins, everyday objects and, preserved in the arid conditions, important TEXTILES and PAPYRI), as well as the best-known and preserved SIEGE in Roman history.

Major occupation began in the Hasmonaean period, but the evidence was largely obliterated by the extensive work of HEROD THE GREAT. Early in his reign, Herod developed the site, creating a luxurious and secure retreat with FORTIFICATIONS, water supply, stores, a synagogue, BATHS, a PALACE and VILLA. Most are detailed by JOSEPHUS (*Jewish War* 7.285–303); judging by extensive modern excavation, he was not personally familiar with the site. Especially notable is the villa, set on three levels down the cliff promontory at the north end. As in Herod's construction work at CAESAREA MARITIMA and Jericho, Roman influence is prominent in the character of buildings and architecture, including mosaics and frescoes.

After Herod's death a Roman garrison was installed, but the fortress fell to the rebels in the first Jewish revolt in AD 66. Josephus describes the subsequent Roman siege (*Jewish War* 7.275–407). The governor of Judaea, Flavius Silva, invested the site with a large force (c.7,500 men), which constructed a long wall of circumvallation, towers, a series of camps, and a siege ramp. The rebels are reported to have committed mass SUICIDE to evade capture. A garrison was subsequently reinstalled. DLK

See Yadin, Y. (1966) *Masada.*

 JUDAEA; SIEGES AND SIEGE WARFARE.

MASADA: view of the great Roman siege ramp against the sheer cliffs of the hilltop fortress of Masada. In the foreground are the remains of one of the camps built by the besieging army.

masculinity A mode of behaviour or means of representation assigned to the male gender. Factors such as biological SEX as well as status, age, class and wealth contribute to conceptions of masculinity. For instance, in Greek society, ÉLITE men were perceived as fit and brave, whether it be through military prowess or ATHLETIC competition. Images of what constituted fit and brave changed over time on the basis of political ideology. For the Romans, masculinity embodied the *paterfamilias*, or head of the HOUSEHOLD. This role gave him the legal right to hold power, *potestas*, over members of his family. Status designations also played a key role in defining masculinity. The Romans used, for example, generally two words for man, *vir* and *homo*. *Vir* usually applied to an aristocratic man who was praiseworthy (*virtus*), whereas *homo* described a man engaged in hostile or violent contexts. Customarily, élite Roman males looked back at their illustrious ancestors as role models; however, this changed in the late empire, when soldiers began to assume responsibility as *viri* because of their ability to administer control over the populace. LAH

See Foxhall, L. and Salmon, J., eds. (1998) *When Men were Men* and *Thinking Men*; Gleason, M.W. (1995) *Making Men.*

Masinissa c.238–148 BC First and most significant king of Numidia, who succeeded (c.207) his father, Gaia, as king of the Massyli, a tribe located to the south of Constantine in eastern Algeria. Brought up in CARTHAGE, he fought in the Carthaginian campaign in Spain in the second PUNIC WAR. He eventually went over (c.206) to the Roman side. After defeating his rival Syphax, king of the Masaesyli, Masinissa annexed the eastern half of Syphax's territory, which when combined with the territory of the Massyli formed the core of the kingdom henceforth identified as Numidia. Masinissa joined SCIPIO AFRICANUS at the battle of ZAMA where HANNIBAL was defeated (202). Honoured by the Romans as a hellenistic monarch, and granted the ornaments of a Roman TRIUMPH, Masinissa was formally awarded his former Punic territory east of Carthage. He is credited with transforming Numidia into a hellenistic state. Language and religious practices were Punic. He promoted urbanization and AGRICULTURE and thus laid the basis for the later Roman province of Numidia. The Medracen, a royal tumulus, just north of the Aures mountains in Algeria, thought to have been built by Masinissa or his father, reflects the fusion of African, Punic, and MEDITERRANEAN traditions. As a CLIENT of Rome, he provided grain to Roman troops while on campaign in MACEDONIA. Masinissa's encroachment on the territory of Carthage furnished Rome with a pretext for beginning the third Punic war. Masinissa is a landmark figure in the history of North AFRICA. RBH

See Brett, M. and Fentress, E. (1996) *The Berbers*; Camps, G. (1960) *Massinissa* (= *Libyca* VII).

masks One of the common paraphernalia of cult practice in classical antiquity and a standard medium for impersonation in ancient THEATRE. Masks, often complemented by other forms of disguise, were used to conceal the identity of their wearers in order to perform specific ritual or other roles under different identities. They were made of a range of mainly soft materials, such as cloth, LEATHER, wax and cork, but also wood and clay.

MASKS: Greek Old Comedy made much of grotesque masks and huge phallic appendages, as illustrated in this scene from a vase.

Masks are known to have been worn in the worship of DIONYSOS in Greece by groups representing followers of the god. By the 6th century, their ritual performances had already been transformed into a primitive type of DRAMA, played by SATYR-like creatures who also wore masks. At that time, a mask was nothing more than a simple linen cloth which covered the face, quite different from its 5th-century counterparts, which tended to conceal the whole head and often had hair attached to them. Dionysos himself often appears as a mask, probably symbolizing the duality of his nature, made up of a human and a divine part. Masks were also used in the cult of ARTEMIS Ortheia at SPARTA and the cult of DEMETER.

In the Roman world, theatre masks often had exaggerated features. In Republican times, realistic masks in the likeness of ancestors, generally of wax, were worn at FUNERALS of prominent Roman ARISTOCRATS to commemorate their heritage and recall their virtues. EP

See Henrichs, A. (1993) He has the god in him: human and divine in the modern perceptions of Dionysus, in T. Carpenter and C. A. Faraone, eds., *Masks of Dionysus* 36–9; Walton, M. J. (1980) *Greek Theatre Practice*.

ACTORS AND ACTRESSES: (a)–(b).

masonry styles The Greeks and Romans used a wide range of different types of masonry for construction; these varied chronologically but also geographically. An important early masonry style used in Greece from MYCENAEAN times (e.g. at Mycenae) and in Italy from the 6th to 5th centuries BC (e.g. Arpino) involved the use of polygonal STONES, sometimes on a very large scale (called Cyclopean). From the 7th to 6th centuries BC ashlar masonry (*opus quadratum*) began to be used, as QUARRYING and stone-working skills advanced. This employed blocks of stone cut to a rectangular shape of more of less uniform size and laid in horizontal courses. Sometimes the blocks were laid alternately as headers (short side forming face of wall) and stretchers (long side forming face of wall), with the headers bonding into the wall and adding greater stability. The use of this type of masonry depended on good quality stone being available locally. The Greeks usually clamped the blocks together using bronze clamps set in LEAD (to stop corrosion). The Romans often laid the stones dry and relied on the skilled stone dressing to create friction between the stones and hence a kind of adhesion.

In the 3rd century BC the use of CONCRETE developed on the bay of Naples and a range of masonry styles developed in conjunction with this. In the Roman PROVINCES where true concrete could rarely be made, a mortared rubble masonry developed, particularly in areas where the building stone was of poor quality. This employed a good quality LIME mortar laid with rubble with a facing made of small, often rather roughly dressed stones in neat rows; this type of masonry is found all over the empire but particularly in the north-western provinces (where it is often referred to by the French term *petit appareil*), the Balkans, Greece and ASIA Minor. By the later 2nd century it was often combined with 5 or 6 courses of fired brick which were laid through the thickness of the wall and acted as bonding courses; modern scholars sometimes use the term *opus mixtum* for this. A variation is *opus vittatum* (a wholly modern term and a technique more common in the later Roman period) where 1 or 2 courses of small stones alternate with one course of fired brick.

In North AFRICA a particularly distinctive type of masonry style is also used, *opus africanum*. This technique had Punic origins; it was used for the construction of the Carthaginian period houses preserved on the slopes of the Byrsa hill at CARTHAGE. It is made up of vertical chains of large roughly dressed blocks, placed one on top of the other, with upright blocks alternating with horizontal ones. This forms a framework of supporting elements; the areas in between were filled with rubble mortared together. Good examples can be seen at Timgad (THAUMUGADI), Djemila and Dougga (THUGGA), but it occurs all over Africa Proconsularis. HD

See Adam, J.-P. (1994) *Roman Building: materials and techniques*.

TEMPLES, ROMAN: (d).

masons The work of the mason included the selection, shaping and placing of ARCHITECTURAL STONE, the majority tending to be procured from local sources. However, stone was transported around the classical world, depending on the demands of different building projects. Much of this material was desired for decorative effects (e.g. the red Egyptian granite columns at Heliopolis (BAALBEK)), but other properties, such as density, may also be wanted in stones not necessarily available locally. Certain QUARRIES were prized for certain products and produced rough versions of such items (such as Corinthian column capitals) for transportation. The mason at the construction site then completed them. (There are examples at POMPEII of just such unfinished column capitals in different stages of final dressing at a construction site.)

Masons were a necessary part of any complement of builders on a construction project. As with other workers they comprised a mixture of SLAVES, FREEDMEN and freeborn. It can be imagined that work for all but the most skilled would have been very precarious, and that masons travelled widely, seeking and fulfilling commissions. Masons did not belong to the writing élite, and direct historical evidence for them is thus very limited. Evidence for the more successful masons comes to us through markers, such as tombstones, though the symbols and tools of the successful mason can easily be confused with those of other stone workers such as SCULPTORS. Many of these tools are the same as those used today. PJEM

Massalia (Massilia) see MARSEILLES.

Mastarna see SERVIUS TULLIUS.

mathematicians The earliest mathematicians are shadowy figures known only through reports in later writers; only in the hellenistic period do professional mathematicians appear, usually dependent on the PATRONAGE of hellenistic kings. The earliest mathematician whose writings survive is EUCLID, whose principal work, the *Elements* in 13 books, summed up and systematized the work of his predecessors, and covered plane geometry, number theory, irrational numbers and solid geometry. Even in antiquity little was known about him (he is occasionally confused with Eukleides of Megara, the pupil of SOCRATES); anecdotes of dubious historical value associate him with ALEXANDRIA and the early PTOLEMIES. He was, however, used by ARCHIMEDES, who died in the Roman sack of SYRACUSE in 211 BC. Ancient sources are mostly interested in Archimedes as an ASTRONOMER and ENGINEER (and especially the ingenious machines he devised for the defence of Syracuse). Substantial surviving mathematical works reveal him to have been a mathematician of genius, who used Eudoxos' 'method of exhaustion' to solve the kind of problem for which we would now use integral calculus, and extended mathematical methods to the study of floating bodies and the centre of gravity of various figures. The third mathematician whose work survives to any extent is APOLLONIOS OF PERGE, who seems to be later than Archimedes, and was probably working around 200 BC. Like Euclid's *Elements*, his *Conics* is largely a crystallization of earlier work rather than innovative MATHEMATICS. It deals with the figures created by cutting cones with a plane, namely the parabola, hyperbola and ellipse. RW

See Dijksterhuis, E. J. (1987) *Archimedes*; Heath, T. L. (1926) *Euclid, The Thirteen Books of the Elements*.

mathematics Long before the Greeks took an interest in it, mathematics had developed elsewhere. Of their near neighbours, the cultures of Egypt and MESOPOTAMIA had both developed sophisticated ways of manipulating numbers and figures and exploring the relationships between them. Indeed, Greek writers (e.g. HERODOTOS 2.109) assert that geometry was invented in Egypt and imported from there into Greece (though surviving Egyptian evidence does not support the view that the detail, rather than the concept, of mathematics was transferred to Greece from Egypt). In addition, there was in all cultures undoubtedly a widespread knowledge of practical mathematics among craftsmen and traders. For example, instances of the relationship between the sides of a right-angled triangle will have been well known to builders and surveyors long before the so-called theorem of PYTHAGORAS provided a formal proof of the relationship in its general form. The distinctive contribution of the Greeks to mathematics was the formal proof and the construction of mathematical systems deriving quite complex propositions from the simplest axioms possible. Unfortunately, no Greek mathematics from before EUCLID survives, apart from a few theorems that seem to have been modified to put them into Euclidean form. Much of our information on the early history of mathematics comes from late authors like Proclus and Simplicius (perhaps relying on Eudemos), so that the stages by which this process took place, and the reasons for it, remain unclear. It was only in geometry that Greek mathematics developed in this distinctive way. Although there are some hints that a parallel development of arithmetic (or perhaps more accurately number theory) had begun by the 4th century BC, little trace of it has survived.

The decisive change in the nature of geometry took place in the 5th and 4th centuries BC, though its details are obscure. The central concern of mathematics at the time seems to have been the solution of certain problems of how to construct figures. Of these the most famous were the squaring of the circle (constructing a square equal in area to a given circle) and the duplication of the cube (constructing a cube with twice the volume of a given cube). (The latter is sometimes referred to as the 'Delian Problem' from a legend that it originated when the people of DELOS, when they consulted an ORACLE about how to avert a plague, were told to double the size of the altar of APOLLO.) These problems of construction threw up more fundamental mathematical problems. One of these was how to handle infinitesimals. This arises from the fact that any finite magnitude can be divided an infinite number of times. For example, no matter how close the sides of an inscribed polygon come to the circumference of a given circle, another polygon can always be drawn between the circle and the first polygon; so no inscribed polygon, however many sides it has, can ever coincide with the circle. Another was the difficulties posed by irrational numbers, which probably originated in the discovery that the ratio of the side of a square to its diagonal is $1 : \sqrt{2}$ so that they are not commensurable – i.e. the relationship of one to the other cannot be expressed as a ratio of integers. Of the mathematicians of this period working on these problems, perhaps one of the most important is Hippokrates of CHIOS (late 5th century), who reduced the problem of duplicating the cube to one of finding two means in continuous proportion. His work on the quadrature of lunes was probably an early attempt at making a start on the squaring of the circle, and he was said to have been the first to put together a set of geometrical theorems in a logical order. Another is Theaitetos (d.369 BC), who produced a general theory of irrationals. A third is Eudoxos of KNIDOS (4th century BC), who in the so-called 'method of exhaustion' devised a mathematical strategy for evading the problems of infinitesimals and infinite divisibility. He was also responsible for a theory of proportion that would include commensurable and incommensurable magnitudes.

The first surviving mathematical work is the *Elements* of Euclid (probably late 4th or early 3rd century BC). This summed up (and therefore made obsolete) the work of his predecessors, creating out of it a coherent system of geometry in which a whole range of theorems were ordered in relation to one another and derived from the minimum number of axioms achievable. This work became the foundation of all subsequent geometry. Following Euclid, ARCHIMEDES (d.212/11 BC) greatly increased knowledge of the geometry of various planes and bodies bounded by curves, mostly by the ingenious application of the 'method of exhaustion'. He created new branches of mathematics by applying the principles of geometry to mechanics and hydrostatics. Apollonios of Perge (late 3rd or early 2nd century BC) summed up and extended the geometry of conic sections (parabola, hyperbola, ellipse). Later geometers such as Pappos (4th century AD) added little that was original to geometry.

In no other branch of mathematics apart from geometry was the concept of formal proof developed. A kind of algebra is found in Diophantos' *Arithmêtika*. In the surviving manuscripts a form of symbolic notation is used (though it is by no means certain that this is original to Diophantos). Solutions are found to a number of equations, including indeterminate and quadratic equations (though negative roots are ignored). The work is in the form of a series of worked examples, however, and no proofs are offered. Similarly Heron of Alexandria demonstrates the ability to solve quadratic and other equations (perhaps using something similar to the formula used today), but does not go beyond simple manipulation of numbers. The work of Greek astronomers, especially Ptolemy of Alexandria, shows familiarity with, and capacity to handle, the principal trigonometrical functions, and Ptolemy produced a *Table of Chords* which is the equivalent of a modern sine table. RW

See Heath, T. L. (1921) *A History of Greek Mathematics*.

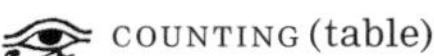 counting (table).

matriarchy A form of social organization where a female is the head of the family and familial descent is traced through the female line. It can also refer to women who wield some form of political authority. Influenced by Darwin's theories of evolution, the Swiss anthropologist J. J. Bachofen postulated a theory on the evolution of kinship systems in his 1861 work, *Das Mutterrecht* (*Mother Right*). His interest lay in Greek mythological and historical sources, especially those referring to Lycian heritage and Amazon pursuits of motherhood, as well as pre-classical Athenian Great Goddess cults. Bachofen posited that social life began in the prehistoric period when women were subject to the sexual whims of men. A sexual liberation resulted through women's participation in religion. Society thus was centred on women, who were honoured as incarnations of the Great Goddess, associated with life, death, and rebirth. Proponents of the matriarchal myth, including Marija Gimbutas and others, believe that during this period men and women lived together peacefully. Eventually, men altered this situation by introducing the notion of procreation into religion. As a result they began ascending into religious roles, which in part led to a patriarchal organization of society. Matriarchal rule is a largely hypothetical proposition, but it is evident that goddess worship was widespread in the Mediterranean and Europe. LAH

See Bachofen, J. J. (1992 (1861)) *Myth, Religion, and Mother Right*; Eller, C. (2000) *The Myth of Matriarchal Prehistory*; Gimbutas, M. A. (1990) *The Goddesses and Gods of Old Europe, 6500–3500 BC*.

matter (Greek *hylê*, Latin *materia* or *silva*) Constituent stuff of a thing or the world. The question of what the world is made of exercised Greek philosophers from the 6th century BC onwards, but Aristotle in the 4th century first introduced a word meaning 'matter'. From carpentry he borrowed *hylê*, literally 'wood', to mean the raw material of which anything is constituted. The 'matter' of a sword is iron and so is that of a ploughshare, even though the same 'matter' is shaped differently in each for different purposes.

Aristotle proposed a thought experiment in his *Metaphysics* (7.3), attempting to understand the most fundamental matter common to all things. Take any ordinary object. It has shape, colour, smell, texture and so forth. Underlying these characteristics must be some property common to all, and this would be the ultimate, basic matter of the object. To find this, subtract the smell, colour, weight, shape, hardness and so on. Is anything left? Perhaps something a bit like air remains. Carry on until every last property has gone, and whatever still remains must be pure, basic matter. And what is left? Nothing At All, Aristotle ruefully admits! This left him with a problem. Perhaps basic matter is not after all devoid of properties, but possesses distinctive powers which it confers on the things made of it. In *Physics* 2.1, Aristotle allows that there is some truth in this. If a statue gets solidity, colour and other characteristics from its bronze, and the bronze gets its properties from its constituent metals of tin and copper, these too presumably get their properties from whatever they consist of, and so on down the line. Continuing in this way, will we not eventually get down to the irreducibly basic stuffs from which everything else is built up?

Aristotle saw that this was the path by which the Presocratic philosophers had searched for fundamental matter. Their regular answer, he continues, was that at root everything consists of one or more of four items: earth, water, air, fire. These 'four elements' were first listed jointly as the world's ingredients by Empedokles. He was followed in this by Plato, Aristotle, the Stoics, and in fact most thinkers until the 17th century (though they differed from him in holding that the 'elements' were themselves analysable into even more basic principles). All were agreed that the world's structure consists of these four stuffs, organized into layers: earth, partly covered with water, and above them air and the fiery heavens, towards which any fire we create down here naturally moves as if heading off to join it. It was easy to believe that all familiar objects are formed from bits of these four huge reservoirs of matter. Human beings, for example, evidently consist of all four: earth gives us our solidity and fire our vital warmth, while the fact that we have to drink and breathe apparently proves we consist of water and air too.

An alternative approach to matter was the atomic theory of Demokritos and Epicurus, which postulated that the world was made of conglomerations of particles. DNS

See Sorabji, R. (1988) *Matter, Space, and Motion*.

Mauretania see Africa and the Africans; Africa, Roman; Caesarea (Mauretania); Roman empire; *Tabula Banasitana*.

Mausolus (Maussollos) 377–353 BC Ruler of Caria, a member of the indigenous Hekatomnid dynasty, who were promoted to satrapal power in

Caria by the PERSIANS in the 4th century (though doubts have been expressed about their status). Mausolus ruled Caria with Artemisia, his wife and sister, having moved his court to HALIKARNASSOS from the Lelegian city of Mylasa. Caria itself being of partly Greek population, Mausolus' rule evidenced both cultures. Documents were inscribed in Greek, and though the forms of his decrees follow Greek patterns they have a local spin. For example, an inscription honouring the citizens of KNOSSOS confers *proxenia* on the whole citizen body of the Knossians, a nonsense in Greek terms. Similarly, the Mausoleum, the TOMB built by Artemisia on Mausolus' death (which was to become one of the SEVEN WONDERS of the ancient world), had both Greek and oriental features.

Mausolus' control extended as far as Knossos, Pamphylia and Pisidia. In the late 360s Mausolus was involved in the satraps' revolt, though he had returned to the Persian fold by 361/0. Furthermore, in the early 350s he was following Persian policy and supporting the Athenian allies in their revolt from the second Athenian confederacy during the SOCIAL WAR, though DEMOSTHENES is probably exaggerating his role. After his death, Artemisia ruled alone. LGM

See Demosthenes 15 (*The Liberty of the Rhodians*); Diodorus Siculus 15.90.3, 16.7.3, 36.2; Strabo 13.1.59, 14.2.16; Hornblower, S. (1982) *Mausolus*.

Maxentius see CONSTANTINE; GALERIUS; MAXIMIAN; MILVIAN BRIDGE, BATTLE OF; TETRARCHS.

 TETRARCHS: (b).

Maximian (Marcus Aurelius Valerius Maximianus) c.AD 240–310 Born in Sirmium of peasant family, Maximian rose through the ranks of the military under AURELIAN and Probus to the position of general. DIOCLETIAN named him CAESAR in 285. In 286, he campaigned against the Bacaudae in GAUL and was raised to AUGUSTUS, with responsibility for ITALY, AFRICA, Spain, Gaul and BRITAIN. In 288 and 292 he was engaged on the lower RHINE and in RAETIA. Constantius became his Caesar in 293 and operated in Britain until 296, while Maximian was busy on the Rhine frontier. In 296 Maximian dealt with a revolt of Quinquegentanei and other Mauritanian tribes in Africa. Two years after he and Diocletian celebrated their *vicennalia* at Rome in 303, he abdicated, reluctantly, with Diocletian in 305. He came out of retirement when his son Maxentius was declared emperor in 306. In support of his son, Maximian established an alliance with CONSTANTINE, recognizing his title of Augustus and marrying his daughter Fausta to him, and forced Severus (Augustus in the West) to abdicate. While Constantine did not aid Maxentius against attacks by Severus and GALERIUS, he did shelter Maximian after he had a quarrel with his son (308). The conference at Carnuntum (308) required that Maximian again retire but he could not resist power. In 310 he was captured by Constantine at MARSEILLES, was forced to commit SUICIDE and suffered *damnatio memoriae* (erasure of all commemoration). MEH

See Jones, A. H. M. (1986) *The Later Roman Empire*; Williams, S. (1997) *Diocletian and the Roman Recovery*.

EMPERORS, ROMAN: (b); TETRARCHS: (a)–(b).

Maximinus (Daia) see CONSTANTINE; GALERIUS.

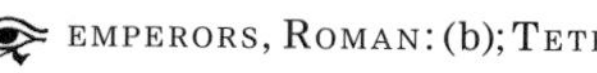 EMPERORS, ROMAN: (b); TETRARCHS: (b).

Maximinus Thrax Roman EMPEROR, AD 235–8. Gaius Julius Maximinus was supposedly a THRACIAN PEASANT (hence 'Thrax'), serving as a private soldier, when SEPTIMIUS SEVERUS promoted him to the rank of centurion because of his great strength. In 233 he was *praefectus* of MESOPOTAMIA before returning to the West with SEVERUS ALEXANDER. In 235 Severus Alexander was murdered and Maximinus acclaimed emperor, on the RHINE. He continued Severus' planned campaign against the Alamanni, before moving to the DANUBE to campaign against the Dacians and Sarmatians. He remained on the Danube until 238. His absence from Rome as well as his low birth led to tensions with the SENATE. At the same time, plots within the army induced Maximinus to double military pay (already increased under Septimius Severus and CARACALLA). The subsequent financial crisis led to various emergency measures, including the melting down of statues and confiscation of TEMPLE treasuries. This led in spring 238 to the acclamation of the proconsul of AFRICA, Marcus Antonius Gordianus, as emperor. He was quickly defeated by troops from Numidia, but not before Gaul and Italy had accepted him. The senate then declared Pupienus and Balbinus emperors in Italy. Dacia, Spain, the Balkans and ASIA Minor remained loyal to Maximinus, who immediately marched from the Danube into Italy, provoking an attack by the Carpi on the Danube. Maximinus' troops became bogged down in the SIEGE of AQUILEIA, and he was soon murdered by soldiers of Legion II Parthica on 10 May 238. (see also GORDIAN III) HWE

EMPERORS, ROMAN: (a).

Maximus Planudes see *GREEK ANTHOLOGY*; SCHOLARSHIP, BYZANTINE.

Maximus, Pupienus

 EMPERORS, ROMAN: (a).

meals In classical Greece there were some who took one meal a day, some two. The one meal was *deipnon*, which was taken in the evening and sometimes extended into a *SYMPOSION* or drinking-party. The other was *ariston*, often translated 'breakfast' but taken about noon. The dietary author Diokles of Karystos advises those making a journey in summer to pause for *ariston* and to take a siesta. The principal Roman meal was *cena*, which, in Greek fashion, was taken in the evening. It was said that *cena* used to be an early afternoon meal followed by *vesperna* or supper. Romans ate more frequently than Greeks. The Roman *ientaculum* or breakfast was bread and perhaps CHEESE; *prandium* or lunch was bread, cold MEAT, salad, FRUIT and WINE. Other terms are found: Greek *akratisma* was a nip of wine and a bite of food at the beginning of the day; Latin *merenda* was an afternoon snack.

A typical full Greek meal consisted of cereal staple (Greek *sitos*) with relishes (*opsa*). PHILOSOPHERS from SOCRATES onwards urged that the staple, not the relish, must be emphasized: to do otherwise was gluttony. This main course might be preceded by an aperitif and hors d'oeuvres, and would be followed by wine (mixed with water) and dessert. A full Roman meal had a similar structure, but Romans drank wine with the main course and did not always dilute it. The traditional Roman staple was *puls*, porridge or gruel; an alternative Greek staple was *maza*, barley mash. In both Greece and Rome, wheat bread was preferred by people who had the choice. Relish was whatever helped the bread on its way: in simple meals, a splash of OLIVE OIL, a bite of cheese, salad, cooked VEGETABLES or legume soup; in lavish entertaining, a wide range of FISH, seafood and meat dishes. Fresh fruits and salad vegetables were taken as hors d'oeuvres; sweet cakes, cheese and HONEY, dried fruits and nuts were typical desserts.

Leisured people reclined to eat. In classical Greece, respectable women did not recline with men. Except in the nuclear family, men and women dined in separate circles, in different rooms or at different times. Women who went out to dinner with men were assumed to be *hetairai* or sexually promiscuous. The ideal of classical Greek dining was equality: those who were not equal, from philosophers to *parasitoi*, paid for their presence by amusing the rest. In Roman dining, following ETRUSCAN practice, the sexes reclined together to dine. The ideal of classical Roman dining was the reciprocal relationship between host and guests, a relationship symbolized in the place allocated to each diner. AD

See Dalby, A. (1996) *Siren Feasts*; (2003) *Food in the Ancient World from A to Z*; Davidson, J. (1997) *Courtesans and Fishcakes*; Garnsey, P. (1999) *Food and Society in Classical Antiquity*; Nielsen, I. and Nielsen, H. S., eds. (1998) *Meals in a Social Context*; Slater, W. J., ed. (1991) *Dining in a Classical Context*; Wilkins, J., Harvey, D. and Dobbs, M., eds. (1995) *Food in Antiquity*.

 DINING ROOMS: (a)–(b); POTTERY, GREEK.

measurement The role of measurement in everyday life was not as all-pervasive as now, but even the invention of COINAGE that can be divided and subdivided, and the standardization of civic WEIGHTS AND MEASURES, imply that most people used arithmetic regularly. Yet Greeks and Romans also used sophisticated measuring techniques. Despite not having arabic numerals or the decimal point, they could perform complex calculations in writing. Present TIME was structured through the CALENDAR, SUNDIALS, and clocks, largely for the purpose of co-ordinating public activities (such as trials and assemblies) rather than private life, let alone industrial efficiency. From the 5th century BC, historical CHRONOLOGY began to be calculated systematically.

Regular land division was practised from early times. The grid-planning of archaic COLONIES reveals a concern for proportionality – to each his due – like the numerically 'rational' divisions of the citizen body adopted by reformers like SOLON and KLEISTHENES. The 6th-century tunnel of Eupalinos in SAMOS, town plans such as that of PIRAEUS, and orthogonal farm plots in the Crimea all reveal that Greeks could carry out LAND SURVEYING accurately over considerable distances. TEMPLES such as the PARTHENON sometimes embody measurements and proportions of a level of accuracy even a modern surveyor would admire.

The pre-Greek empires of the Near East set an example in the measurement of distances. The Persian Royal ROAD from Susa to Sardis had stages totalling 450 *parasangai* (Herodotos 5.52–3). The figure is suspiciously round, but Herodotos' interest is in the time it takes to travel the road, so he converts it to 13,500 *stadia* (c.2,500 km, 1,550 miles) and reckons 90 days. ALEXANDER took *bêmatistai*, 'pacers', with him into Asia so that he could know how far he had come. In Roman times, milestones were routinely set up along many major roads to aid the traveller.

Sea distances were quite accurately expressed. The Greek navigational text known as the *periplous* of Pseudo-Skylax (4th century BC) contains hundreds of distances, given either in days and nights or in *stadia*. It reckons the voyage from Chalkis via Mykonos to Samos as 2,370 *stadia* (c.430 km, c.270 miles), that from cape Malea via Crete to the mainland opposite Rhodes as 4,270 *stadia* (c.780 km, c.480 miles). The figures are roughly correct, but the real point is not accuracy but the fact that attempts were being made to unify the world mathematically. In 3rd-century Alexandria, ERATOSTHENES calculated the circumference of the earth (on sound principles) as 252,000 *stadia* (c.46,000 km, c.29,000 miles) and ARISTARCHOS (less soundly) the distance of the MOON.

Measuring the earth (literally 'geo-metry', *geômetria*) was a blend of cosmological reasoning and practicality. The advance of SCIENCE in the hellenistic period, driven both by a love of theorizing and by a colonialist mentality, were passed on to Romans who took surveying to new lengths (see *GROMATICI*). VITRUVIUS preserves an outline of many Greek treatises that gave detailed technical measurements, such as on catapults (book 10), and adds what may be more recent, Roman quantitative data, such as on lead pipes (book 8). STRABO (2.5.6), building upon his predecessors and writing at the moment when Rome had unified the world politically, calculates the dimensions of the inhabited portion of the globe (70,000 *stadia* by less than 30,000), but stresses that this is only a small portion of the earth. DGJS

 WEIGHTS AND MEASURES: (a).

meat Sparingly eaten, the status of meat was all the greater; hence its ubiquity in the imaginary HOMERIC society. It was regarded as a nourishing and strengthening food, ideal for ATHLETES.

In Greece domestic ANIMALS (PIG, SHEEP, GOAT, chicken, goose) were sacrificed to a GOD when slaughtered. Fat was burnt; the tongue was reserved for the officiating priest. Trade in sausages, offal and salt meat (note the sausage-seller in ARISTOPHANES' *Knights*) ensured that an animal went a long way; it is untrue that Greeks only ate meat immediately after SACRIFICE. In Rome there was no fixed link between slaughter and sacrifice but it is uncertain whether meat was more prominent in the diet. Oxen were sacrificed for special occasions and public FESTIVALS; however, Greeks and Romans ate beef seldom, and saw beef-eaters as greedy and stupid. Large game (such as boar and hare) was a luxury, but wild birds were widely available. Members of some sects were VEGETARIAN, or refused certain items such as the brain; otherwise practically all edible parts, except fat, were eaten.

Greek *mageiros* ('butcher, cook') has religious overtones: he supplied the animal, sacrificed it and prepared the feast (see MENANDER's *Bad-tempered Man*). Latin *macellarius*, 'butcher', is named for the covered MARKETS (*macella*), where meat was sold. Meat was roasted or stewed: Roman recipes demanded elaborate SPICING. AD

See Corbier, M. (1988–9) The ambiguous status of meat in ancient Rome, *Food and Foodways* 3: 223–64; Frayn, J. M. (1995) The Roman meat trade, in J. Wilkins et al., eds., *Food in Antiquity* 107–14; Frost, F. (1999) Sausage and meat preservation in antiquity, *GRBS* 40: 241–52.

 BUTCHERY: (a)–(b).

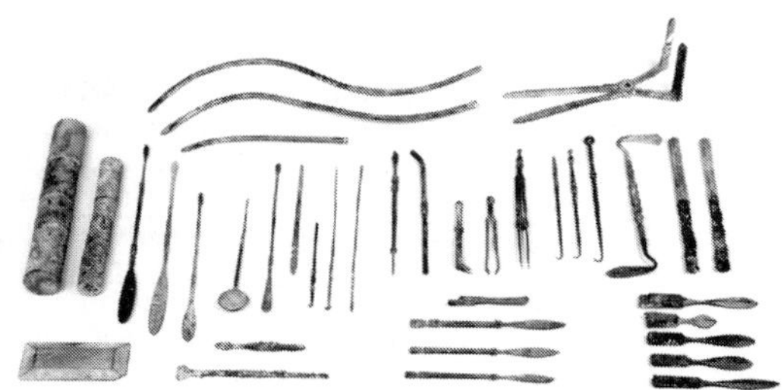

MEDICINE: collection of Roman surgical instruments.

mechanics The study of force on objects and their resulting movement, mechanics combined both theoretical and practical knowledge in antiquity. Ancient mechanics differed from modern mechanics in that it allowed for the tendency of an object to return to and occupy its natural position as defined by Aristotelian terms. In his attempt to formulate mathematical laws for physical dynamics, ARISTOTLE established mechanics as a specialized discipline. *Mechanics*, a PERIPATETIC work probably written soon after Aristotle's death, reflects the nature of the field; it outlines the theoretical concept of the lever and its application in such devices as oars and tooth-extractors. Many theorists contributed to the development of theoretical mechanics, notably ARCHIMEDES, Heron of Alexandria and PHILO OF BYZANTION. The most insightful volume on mechanics, however, is the 4th-century AD compendium (*Mathematical Collection*) written by PAPPOS OF ALEXANDRIA. The author, apparently intending to create an all-encompassing handbook, extensively quotes his predecessors. Pappos clearly describes how mechanics involves both intellectual knowledge and hands-on experience; one must be a geometer, MATHEMATICIAN, ASTRONOMER and PHYSICIST as well as a metalworker, ARCHITECT, carpenter and painter. In this way, mechanics in antiquity had much in common with MEDICINE; both were considered a SCIENCE and an art. TJA

medicine Greek and Roman medicine was used as the basis of medical training until almost the present day. Although 6th-century BC PHILOSOPHERS had discussed the constituents of the human body, ancient medicine begins with the treatises associated with the name of HIPPOKRATES, known as the 'HIPPOCRATIC CORPUS'. This group of texts includes material from possibly the late 5th century until the 1st century BC. It has been disputed whether anything in it was in fact written by Hippokrates, a DOCTOR mentioned by PLATO as a contemporary. Historically, the treatises most associated with the name of Hippokrates are the *Aphorisms*, a list of pithy sayings which could be memorized and recalled in any situation, and books 1 and 3 of the *Epidemics*, collections of case histories which have been acclaimed as evidence of the ancient doctor's ability to observe and note down the significant features of DISEASE. The term 'doctor' is a rather misleading translation of the Greek *iatros*, which may be more appropriately translated as 'healer', thus avoiding the implication that there was a medical profession in the sense we know it today. There was no recognized programme of training for ancient doctors, no qualifications and no way of proving competence other than by success in particular cases.

The Hippocratic corpus contains one document which has been particularly influential in later medical history. This is known as 'the Oath', and it sets out a code of ETHICS for at least a limited group of healers in the ancient world. Some of its clauses concern the need to keep medical knowledge away from lay people, as the doctor is required to swear by APOLLO, ASKLEPIOS and Hygeia (Health) to respect his teacher and to transmit the knowledge he has been given only to fellow healers or apprentices. Others concern the proper use not only of medical knowledge but also of the personal information a doctor may acquire in the course of his work; for example, the doctor swears to use medicine only to help the sick – not giving lethal drugs on request – and to respect anything patients tell him in confidence. Still other clauses involve maintaining the sort of lifestyle which increases patients' trust, and the avoidance of sexual contact with patients or members of their HOUSEHOLD, whether free or SLAVE. The medicine we know from surviving texts was in competition not only with other groups offering healing underpinned by different theoretical systems, but also with the popular medicine known to us from writers such as PLINY THE ELDER and from magical texts and PAPYRI. The ethics of the Oath represent one way doctors could try to increase patients' confidence in their healing powers, while adding to the feeling of solidarity within a particular local group of healers.

The lack of any institutionalization of medicine meant that persuasion played a central part, as a further means of gaining the confidence of clients. The theories of Greek and Roman medicine about the nature of the body and how it works can be seen as part of the process of persuading the patient to entrust himself or herself to a doctor. Explaining the puzzling experiences being undergone by the patient could even go some way towards making the patient feel better. Most medical theories were based on the idea that the body is made up of a number of fluids. The dominant theory, most fully expressed in the late 2nd century AD in the voluminous works of GALEN (physician to the gladiators of PERGAMON and subsequently to MARCUS AURELIUS), argued for four of these 'humours', but some healers claimed that there were only two or three. Disease was the result of an imbalance of these substances in the body. Four-humour theory related the four constituent fluids – black bile, yellow bile, blood and phlegm – to the four seasons, the four winds and the four elements, so that blood was associated with spring, and was hot and wet. In Galenic medicine, four organs were added to the theory: black bile was associated with the spleen, blood with the heart (though it was made in the liver), phlegm with the brain and yellow bile with the liver. In Galenic physiology, blood was thought to be produced by the liver from *chylos*, the partially digested food that travelled to the liver from the stomach. Blood was then attracted to parts of the body needing nutriment. The theory would then suggest the most appropriate therapies, so that a disease due to an excess of the hot and wet humour needed cooling and drying remedies.

Most therapy took the form of a modification of the regimen, usually involving adjustments to the individual's pattern of diet or exercise, so that the production of humours within the body could be altered. Since humours were also affected by external factors such as the prevailing wind, it was necessary for medicine to consider all aspects of the individual's lifestyle before prescribing treatment. DRUGS and surgery were options to be considered if changes to the regimen were not enough. Other therapies included enemas and purgatives, salves and ointments, and painkillers. Several treatises from the Hippocratic corpus concern the important area of the treatment of wounds and injuries, and advise on how to set broken bones and treat dislocations. Blood-letting, performed by opening a vein in an arm or leg or by applying heated metal, GLASS, or horn cups to the skin, played an increasingly important role in ancient medicine, since it was thought to remove excess blood or other surplus humours.

Humoural medicine was not the only possible medical approach to disease. Some writers preferred medical systems based on the idea that the body was constructed from 'atoms', and believed all disease was due to blockages in the pores. 'Methodist' medicine, a variation which began with Asklepiades of Bithynia in the 1st century BC and developed further in the 1st century AD, was an easily taught system which held that all diseases were the result of constriction, looseness or a mixture of the two conditions. Methodist doctors favoured gentle remedies such as baths, massage and 'passive exercise', in which the patient used a swing or went riding.

These medical theories were based on observation of the external qualities of the body, rather than on knowledge of the inside. The treatises on prognosis in the Hippocratic corpus and by Galen demonstrate how detailed observation of the appearance of the patient was combined with questioning to discover how far this deviated from what was normal for a particular individual. In hellenistic ALEXANDRIA, systematic human dissection – and, perhaps, vivisection – was practised for the first time by Herophilos and Erasistratos. This development was made possible by royal PATRONAGE, the absence of taboos on touching the corpse shown in the Egyptian practice of mummification and the availability of a subject population to serve as the object of medical enquiry. However, with the exception of 'accidental dissection' when an injury made it possible to see inside the body, human dissection did not continue; it was argued that examination of the dead was of no use in helping the living. Galen dissected only ANIMALS, including PIGS, GOATS, the Barbary ape and even the heart of an ELEPHANT. These dissections meant that some of his beliefs about the human body were based on features only present in animals.

In the Roman world in particular, medicine was used as an idiom through which to criticize aspects of society. Almost all doctors were of Greek origin, and writers such as CATO and Pliny claimed that dangerous Greek theoretical medicine had taken over from practical, traditional and allegedly more effective Roman herbal medicine. The distinction which may be more relevant here than Greek–Roman is urban–rural. Most people lived outside the cities of the ancient world, and for them there would not have been any choice between healers applying different theories of medicine. Writers of the early Roman empire also argued that apparently new diseases were the result of decadent behaviour and an influx of luxury foods from around the world.

The efficacy of ancient medicine is not easy to determine. Some of the drugs used would have been effective, but it was difficult to identify plants correctly. The use of WINE or vinegar to wash wounds would have had antiseptic effects, but other substances used as antiseptics, such as mercury, and LEAD and COPPER salts, would have killed not only bacteria but also healthy tissue cells. Since many conditions are in any case self-limiting, medicine may have claimed the credit where time was, in fact, the real healer. (see also EPIDEMICS) HK

See King, H. (2001) *Greek and Roman Medicine.*

Mediolanum see MILAN.

medism and medizers see BOIOTIA; PERSIAN WARS; THEBES; THESSALY.

Mediterranean sea Although the name means, literally, the 'midland sea', the Mediterranean is actually an extension of the ATLANTIC. It stretches from the straits of Gibraltar (the Pillars of HERCULES in antiquity) to the Levantine coast, a distance of some 3,500 km (2,200 miles). From north to south, from southern Europe to northern AFRICA, its maximum width is just under 800 km (500 miles). The Hellespont (Dardanelles), Propontis (sea of Marmara), Bosporos and BLACK SEA are actually extensions of the Mediterranean, bringing the total area of the sea to almost 3 million sq km (1.16 million sq miles), an area large enough to contain the world's eighth largest country (Argentina). A deep sea, with relatively high saline levels but little affected by tides, the Mediterranean is, however, a volatile and geologically unstable region, punctuated regularly by EARTHQUAKES and VOLCANIC eruptions. Hence, the Greek sea-god POSEIDON was also known as the 'earth-shaker'.

Apart from the Black sea, the Mediterranean is subdivided into lesser seas, some more clearly demarcated than others: the AEGEAN, situated between the Greek peninsula and the Turkish coast; the ADRIATIC, between the Balkans and Italy; the Ionian sea, just to the south; and the Tyrrhenian sea, between Italy and the western islands of SICILY, SARDINIA and CORSICA.

The impact of the sea on CLIMATE, and consequently on travel, settlement and culture, cannot be underestimated. Ringed by mountains, the sea provided at the same time the avenues of travel and TRADE, while also confining much of the population to its shores by the uncertainty and danger of its waters. The latter were soon overcome by necessity and enterprise. Already in the Bronze Age, settlers, merchants and their goods had dispersed throughout much of the Mediterranean; in the Iron Age, PHOENICIANS sailed to the southern coasts of France and Spain, and beyond the straits into the Atlantic. The extent of their settlement was rivalled by that of the Greeks, whose colonies were more substantial than the Phoenician *emporia*. This resulted in the creation, in the region of southern Italy and Sicily, of a densely populated and prosperous area known as MAGNA GRAECIA. By the end of the pre-Christian era the ROMAN EMPIRE completely enclosed what came to be called *mare nostrum* ('our sea'), not as the result of a desire to create a thalassocracy or 'rule by sea' (as was the case with Athens in the Aegean) but by relentless annexation of the littoral states.

The Mediterranean lacks the variety of marine life of some other inland seas, and deep-sea fishes are scarce on account of the excessive salt and low oxygen levels. But like the Black sea, which below a depth of 150–200 m (500–660 ft) cannot support life, the Mediterranean nevertheless provides a valuable supplement in fishes and shellfish to the agricultural produce of surrounding lands, which were affected by lengthy periods of summer drought. WH

See Bradford, E. (1971) *Mediterranean: portrait of a sea*; Braudel, F. (2001) *The Mediterranean in the Ancient World*; Horden, P. and Purcell, N. (2000) *The Corrupting Sea: a study of Mediterranean history.*

Medusa Female monster, one of three Gorgons. Medusa was mortal, Sthenno and Euryale immortal, but all were of horrific appearance, turning beholders to stone. Polydektes set Perseus the 'impossible' task of fetching Medusa's head; with ATHENA and Hermes' help, however – they supplied winged sandals, a cap of invisibility, a sickle (*harpê*) and a bag for carrying the head – Perseus beheaded Medusa while she slept. From her severed neck sprang the warrior Chrysaor and the winged horse Pegasos. The head continued to have its petrifying power, which Perseus employed in gaining revenge on Polydektes before handing it over to Athena, who put it in the centre of her shield (HESIOD, *Theogony* 270–82, APOLLODOROS 2.4.1–2, OVID, *Metamorphoses* 4.604–5.249). Perseus seems to have been connected with the young warrior's initiation at MYCENAE, and the myth may have its origins in this ritual (Jameson). Oriental influence is apparent in elements of the story, and the Gorgons' iconography is borrowed from the MESOPOTAMIAN Lamashtu. Popular decorative motifs in archaic art, Gorgons appear as women with monstrous heads, snakes for hair, tongue hanging out of ravening mouth; the Gorgoneion's use as a shield motif reflects Athena's appropriation of Medusa's head. Medusa herself appears flanked by Chrysaor and Pegasos on the east pediment of the 6th-century temple of ARTEMIS on Kerkyra (Corfu). Over the 5th century Gorgons lose their hideous aspect and are hardly found at all in art after the 4th century BC. EJS

MEDUSA: the snake-haired Gorgon was a common motif in ancient art and material culture.

See Jameson, M. H. (1990) Perseus, the hero of Mykenai, in R. Hägg and G. Nordquist, eds., *Celebrations of Death and Divinity in the Bronze Age* 213–23; Vernant, J.-P. (1991) *Mortals and Immortals.*

Megara Central Greek city. Its territory (*Megaris*, the Megarid), lying between ATTICA and Corinth and with BOIOTIA to the north, was unimpressive, but it enjoyed access to the Corinthian and Saronic gulfs. Megarians founded colonies both to the east (including Byzantion and as far as the BLACK SEA) and the west (Megara Hyblaia in Sicily). Theagenes was among the earliest Greek tyrants. He 'slaughtered the flocks of the wealthy' (ARISTOTLE), and gave support to his son-in-law Kylon in his attempt on the Athenian TYRANNY, perhaps in order to assist Megara's claim in the ultimately unsuccessful dispute with Athens over SALAMIS. The poetry of THEOGNIS reflects bitterly the disputing claims of WEALTH and birth as archaic society changed. Megara's fate was to suffer from more powerful neighbours. Already a Spartan ally by the late 5th century, it did much to start the so-called first Peloponnesian war in the 450s by going over to Athens for protection against Corinthian aggression. A change in the reverse direction brought the war to an end, when the Megarians allowed the Spartans to pass through their territory to invade Attica. The infamous Megarian Decrees passed by Athens may not have played as important a role in the origins of the PELOPONNESIAN WAR in 431 as some have thought. Athens regularly invaded Megara in the initial phase of the war, but an attempt by democrats to betray the city to Athens failed. The Megarian stance in the 4th century is unclear: ISOKRATES records its enjoyment of the benefits of peace, but it fought against PHILIP II at CHAIRONEIA. JBS

See Goette, H. R. (2001) *Athens, Attica and the Megarid: an archaeological guide*; Legon, R. P. (1981) *Megara*; (2004) Megaris, Corinthia and Sikyonia, in Hansen and Nielsen, *Inventory* 462–71.

 PELOPONNESE.

megaron see CHIOS; MYCENAE.

Mela (Pomponius Mela) His *De chorographia* or *De situ orbis* is the earliest surviving GEOGRAPHICAL work in Latin. Brief and superficial, it remained popular through to modern times. Mela mentions that his birthplace was southern Spain and that he completed his three books soon after an emperor's triumphant return from Britain (thus CALIGULA or CLAUDIUS in the early 40s). He first divides the world into eastern (ASIA) and western (Europe, AFRICA) hemispheres, with five CLIMATIC zones from north to south. After a rapid overview of the three continents, he next adopts the format of a *periplous* ('circular voyage') to proceed (in book 1) eastwards along the African coast of the MEDITERRANEAN, and then north through Asia Minor to the BLACK SEA. In book 2 he proceeds thence through Greece and Italy to return to Gades, before doubling back to give attention to the islands of these inland seas. In book 3 he moves north from Gades to take in the ATLANTIC coasts of Spain and GAUL, followed by the remote edges of Europe, Asia and Africa, until he regains his starting-point in a great arc, having thus breathlessly encompassed the entire *oikoumenê* surrounded by Ocean. Seemingly no more than an armchair traveller, Mela wrote to please others like himself, offering them the expected references to marvels and MYTHOLOGY. He shows no special concern to reflect accurate current information. His sources are hard to identify; he and PLINY THE ELDER (who cites him) probably used some in common. RJAT

See Romer, F. E. (1997) *Pomponius Mela's Description of the World.*

Melania, Elder and Younger An early female ASCETIC, Melania the Elder (c.AD 342–c.410) came from an aristocratic family. Widowed at 22, she left her son, Valerius Publicola, in Rome and departed on pilgrimage to the Holy Land (c.372), where she spent 20 years, founding a convent on the Mount of Olives. She returned to Rome (400), visited Paulinus of Nola and supported her homonymous granddaughter in the pursuit of the ascetic life. Melania the Younger (c.383–439), the subject of a hagiographic *Vita* by Gerontius (written c.440), was drawn to the ascetic life from a young age but made to marry by her parents. After the early deaths of two children she persuaded her husband, Valerius Pinianus, to join her in acts of renunciation, and the couple began to divest themselves of property against the wishes of their families, their SLAVES and the SENATE. The couple left Rome c.407 for SICILY, AFRICA (411), where they met AUGUSTINE (1), and finally JERUSALEM (418). For 14 years Melania spent part of the year living in a cell on the Mount of Olives, undertaking increasingly extreme deprivations, until c.431 she moved to a MONASTERY she had constructed there. She remained in it until her death, apart from a visit to CONSTANTINOPLE to see, and convert, her maternal uncle Volusianus. MEH

See Palladius, *Lausiac History*, trs. R. Meyer (1965); Paulinus of Nola, *Letters*; Clark, E. A. (1984) *The Life of Melania the Younger.*

Melkart see HERCULES.

Melos Renowned in the prehistoric period as a source of OBSIDIAN, Melos (151 sq km, 58 sq miles) was the site of an important MINOAN settlement at Phylakopí. The island was said to have been colonized by the Lakedaimonians in the 12th century BC. The Melians struck coins from the late 6th century BC (perhaps starting c.515). They refused to submit to the PERSIANS in 490 and supplied troops and SHIPS to the Greeks ten years later. They did not join the Delian league, and during the PELOPONNESIAN WAR contributed money to the Spartan war fund. In 416/15 they were besieged by the Athenians in an episode made famous by THUCYDIDES' dialogue between them and the Athenians (5.84–116), in which the Melians called upon claims of JUSTICE and the support of the GODS while the Athenians argued strict power politics. Ultimately defeated, the Melians were killed or expelled and the island repopulated with 500 Athenian colonists. The Spartans allowed the survivors to return after 405. Diagoras, condemned to death in Athens in 416/15 as an atheist (*atheos*), was a Melian. After 338 Melos became part of the league of CORINTH. One of the very few documents preserved from that league is an arbitration of a dispute between Melos and the neighbouring island Kimolos over the possession of three small islets. Melos was often home to PIRATES (this was true also after antiquity). The island is poorly attested in later times. A good deal about settlement patterns over the long term is known thanks to the extensive survey of the 1970s, a classic study of the relationship between a *POLIS* centre and its territory. GR

See Reger, G. (2004) Melos, in Hansen and Nielsen, *Inventory* 758–60; Renfrew, C. and Wagstaff, M., eds. (1982) *An Island Polity.*

 AEGEAN: (a)–(b).

Memphis see ALEXANDRIA; EGYPT; SYRIAN WARS, OF PTOLEMIES.

men In earlier periods of Athenian history a man (*anêr*) is defined by his ability to serve in the army or take part in amateur ATHLETIC competitions. Later, with the onset of DEMOCRACY, an Athenian man is also characterized by his ability to speak in public and to administer his right to VOTE. A man could only become a CITIZEN if he himself was born into a citizen family. Within the family, he exercised legal GUARDIANSHIP over a woman within the HOUSEHOLD or *oikos*. This means that he essentially had control of a woman's property with the exception of her clothes and JEWELLERY. Within the physical setting of the household, men had a room set aside specifically for their use: in the *andrôn* they would recline, dine, and entertain. SPARTAN youths became men at the age of 20, when they were able to join the messes or *syssitia*. MARRIAGE was permitted, with however, only limited access to WOMEN until the age of 30. To be a man in Spartan society was synonymous with having ability as a warrior.

Archaic art and literature reveal that men expressed grief and sadness at funerals. However, in the classical period men became more obliged to restrain their emotions because of changes in the way masculinity was perceived. Men were further segregated from women during the mourning process, and it became the women who were responsible for openly mourning the dead.

The Romans defined men (*viri*) as adult freeborn citizens, and it is apparent that not all males were considered men. In literature *homines* usually refers to men of disrepute or of lower social standing. Male SLAVES, young freeborn males who had not yet matured into adulthood and males of lower social standing were not men. For a freeborn youth at the age of 15 or 16, the donning of the *toga virilis*, the TOGA of manhood, marked his entrance into the world of men. As freeborn citizens, men were able to exercise power over other individuals. From a legal standpoint, a man in his familial role was *paterfamilias* or legal head of the family who exerted his *potestas* or power over his children. After AUGUSTUS, the ideal of who actually wielded power began to change, coinciding with a changing concept of MASCULINITY. Traditionally, the freeborn ÉLITE held power and made important political decisions; however, Roman soldiers began to assume these roles, undermining the traditional definition of men or *viri*. LAH

See Foxhall, L. and Salmon, J., eds. (1998) *When Men were Men*; Hallett, J. P. and Skinner, M. B., eds. (1997) *Roman Sexualities*; Pomeroy, S. B. (1997) *Families in Classical and Hellenistic Greece*.

Menander c.342–292 BC Writer of gentle NEW COMEDY based on misunderstandings in human relationships. His plays were lost for centuries, but through adaptations by the Roman playwrights PLAUTUS and TERENCE, whose works were known to SHAKESPEARE and Molière, Menander has had an important influence on the development of modern European comedy. He is, in this respect, rather more significant than ARISTOPHANES. One could define Aristophanes' comedy as the comedy of the *polis* and Menander's, who, by contrast, avoids politics and concentrates on the family, as the comedy of the *oikos*.

The 20th century brought the rediscovery of a substantial number of Menander's texts. Some fragments turned up (1844) in the binding of a book from St Catherine's monastery on Mt Sinai, but the two major discoveries are from ancient copies surviving in the dry climate of Egypt, the Cairo codex (1905) and the Bodmer codex (1958; 1969). Yet another PAPYRUS, almost contemporary with Menander himself, had been shredded and used to wrap a mummy (it was retrieved by Sorbonne papyrologists in 1964).

A statue was erected to Menander in the THEATRE of DIONYSOS at Athens and a large number of later portraits survive. He is depicted as a handsome man, though he is sometimes given a squint. His plays continued to be performed, both at Athens and beyond: scenes from them have been found in MOSAICS, or on frescoes, on Mytilene (dating from the 3rd century AD), in modern Bulgaria, at EPHESOS and at POMPEII. Both Greek and Roman scholars praised his work: QUINTILIAN, in particular, admired his realism. The number of papyri found in Egypt is an indication of his popularity there – only HOMER and EURIPIDES have provided more finds, and new fragments of Menander continue to come to light.

Menander created some memorable and appealing characters, for example the misanthrope, Knemon, in the *Dyskolos*, the only play to survive complete. The *Dyskolos* is introduced by the god PAN speaking a prologue. There is also the lively, intelligent and compassionate girl Habrotonon (*Epitrepontes*) and the rash but remorseful soldier Polemon (*Perikeiromene*). Why these texts disappeared remains a mystery not unlike that described in Umberto Eco's *The Name of the Rose*. The plots often contain love affairs, seductions and illegitimate infants, which may have offended the early CHRISTIANS, more so, apparently, than the outrageous obscenities to be found in Aristophanes. There may also have been prejudice against Menander's 4th-century, rather than classical, Greek. Or was it just bad luck that the plays were lost?

Modern scholarship has perhaps viewed Menander too much as the product of an age of lost Greek glory (the period just after ALEXANDER the Great). However, it is now beginning to be recognized that there was considerable cultural continuity between the 5th and the 4th centuries BC and Menander has started at last to be studied in his own right. In fact, as a fragment from *Dis exapaton*, the play on which Plautus based his *Bacchides*, shows (the papyrus was published in 1968), Plautus made major changes to his model and created plays with a very different mood. Scholars remain divided as to Menander's merits, however, making him an interesting if controversial figure in ancient Greek literature. Some would describe his plays as repetitious, some others as subtle, situation comedies.

Approaches to his plays have, in the past, been given direction by a recognition that Menander took up established stereotypes such as the soldier and the *hetaira* ('call-girl' is one attempt at a translation) from the comedies written immediately before him, sometimes referred to as MIDDLE COMEDY. The latter is much more fragmentary, however, than Menander, and therefore any conclusions about its content, and in particular its techniques of characterization, must be provisional. Attention has rightly turned to what Menander does with these stock characters. The standardized MASK conveniently worn in ancient drama is used to create an impression which may then be overturned, encouraging the feeling that one should get to know people before judging them.

Menander's characters have been vividly brought to life by archaeological discoveries in recent years on the beautiful but remote Aiolian ISLAND of Lipari off the northern coast of SICILY. Hundreds of replica masks and statuettes in terracotta have been found, dating from Menander's time and displaying the costumes and gestures that were used by ACTORS performing his plays.

The literary stereotypes represented by many of Menander's characters also reflect in some way the people of Menander's world. When social norms are taken into account, such as the situation of women and SLAVES in Athens in the 4th century BC, subtle studies in characterization emerge which are given individuality by a delicate and skilful exploitation of language. Expect a smile rather than a laugh with Menander, but always a thoughtful portrayal of human nature. AMH

See Menander, *Aspis to Epitrepontes*, 3 vols., trs. W. G. Arnott (1979–2000); Menander, *Samia*, ed., trs. D.M. Bain, (1985); Menander: *the plays and fragments*, trs. with notes by M. Balme, intro. by P. Brown (2001); Menander, *The Bad-tempered Man* (*Dyskolos*), ed., trs., intro. and comm. S. Ireland (1995); Handley, E.W., ed. (1965) *The Dyskolos of Menander*; Arnott, W.G. (1975) *Menander, Plautus, Terence*; Goldberg, S. M. (1980) *The Making of Menander's Comedy*; Walton, J. M. and Arnott, P. D. (1996) *Menander and the Making of Comedy*; Zagagi, N. (1994) *The Comedy of Menander*.

Menelaos (Menelaus) see AGAMEMNON; HELEN OF TROY.

mental illness The mind–body dualism which has been part of our cultural inheritance since Descartes was of course unknown in the ancient world. This meant that 'mental' illness was not a separate category. Mental symptoms, like physical symptoms, could be caused either by divine forces, or by internal disturbances of bodily fluids. Physical pressure arising from the presence of too much of one humour could cause what we would interpret as 'mental' symptoms. Thus, for example, melancholy, in which the patient withdrew from society and became taciturn and sad, was thought to be caused by an excess of black bile. Women in whom a surplus of blood failed to leave the body through menstruation could suffer from visions and come to desire death if the blood settled in the region of the diaphragm, one of the alternative 'seats of consciousness' proposed by ancient MEDICINE. Women were seen as particularly liable to mental disturbances; in religious terms, they were more open to DEMONIC invasion, while in medical terms their need to menstruate was thought to indicate a body always fighting to reach the sort of balance only really possible for a male. HK

mercenaries As a general rule, mercenaries were rarer in times of economic stability and consensual government, ubiquitous during social upheaval and entrenched autocracy. Thus, for much of the first three centuries of the city-state (700–400 BC), Greek mercenaries were employed by local TYRANTS as bodyguards or used overseas by Egyptians and PERSIANS as élite corps. Civic HOPLITE militias were usually more numerous and superior fighters. Thus, bought troops in Greece proper were largely restricted to specialized auxiliary contingents such as RHODIAN slingers, CRETAN and Skythian archers, THRACIAN peltasts and THESSALIAN horsemen who could enhance, but not replace, heavy infantry.

The three-decade turmoil of the PELOPONNESIAN WAR revealed the limitations of hoplites when battle was prolonged and entered theatres beyond flat plains. Both sides found their citizen manpower reservoirs inadequate for total war, and so hired – often at as much as a drachma per day – rowers and specialized troops on the open market. In the aftermath of the war, the successful march of the 10,000 through Asia accelerated the use of mercenaries. It was now clear that Greek hoplites could be successful overseas if they were protected by light, missile and mounted troops. Thousands of potential needy recruits, especially from the central PELOPONNESE, were eager for work, men who either could not or would not fit within the old rigid social and political culture of the classical *POLIS*. The stereotype in literature of mercenaries as itinerant, brutal, grasping thugs displays the widespread civic prejudice of the very class who hired them.

The flexibility of mercenaries who could train year around and master specialized equipment made their use even more common by the time of PHILIP II and ALEXANDER. Most city-states had conceded that civic militias and old taboos against property and income taxes hampered defence, and Greece as a whole began to invest human and material capital into hired armies as never before. The Greeks naturally feared the rise of Macedonian professionalism as the fruition of this evolution: crack troops, with novel weaponry, and allegiance to the highest bidder.

Alexander's theft of the imperial treasuries of Persia unleashed enough bullion to fuel a mercenary explosion that would last for centuries until the coming of the citizen militias of Republican Italy. The SUCCESSORS fielded purchased armies that could reach in size 100,000 and more. The hellenistic city-states usually employed Macedonian and Greek recruits to form the phalanx proper. It is nevertheless accurate to call these local phalangites mercenaries, since they were hired on a contractual basis, had no true political liberties, were not always of uniform ethnic and linguistic affiliation, and would cease fighting when money vanished.

Under the Roman Republican system, mercenaries originally were limited to horsemen and missile troops who formed foreign AUXILIARIES. Such contingents increased under the empire, and Spain, GERMANY and GAUL became favourite recruiting grounds. While it is true that the bulk of the Roman infantry was civic-inspired and remained pre-eminent for nearly a thousand years, by the later empire the legionaries for all practical purposes were paid professionals whose willingness to fight depended entirely on the amount of pay they could exact. (see also XENOPHON) VDH

See Griffith, G.T. (1935) *Mercenaries of the Hellenistic World*; Parke, H.W. (1933) *Greek Mercenary Soldiers*; Pritchett, W. K. (1971) *The Greek State at War*, vol. 1.

Mercury Roman GOD, patron of merchants. The name is connected with the noun *merx*, 'commodity', and the verb *mercari*, 'to buy'. According to tradition, a TEMPLE was dedicated to Mercury in Rome on the south-western slope of the Aventine on 15 May 495 BC, in association with a college of merchants. It is generally thought that Mercury was an adaptation, perhaps mediated by the ETRUSCAN god Turms, of the Greek Hermes, whose more complex character the early Romans simplified by emphasizing his mercantile side. The iconography of Mercury from an early date depicts him with the standard attributes of the Greek god, the broad-rimmed traveller's hat and the *caduceus*. The foundation day of the temple became a merchants' festival (OVID, *Fasti* 5.663–92), and Mercuriales, presumably associations of merchants, are attested both in Rome and in other Italian cities. In classical Latin literature, Mercury assumed much of the mythological role of Hermes, appearing as the intermediary between gods and mortals and between the living and the dead. Although evidence of his cult is found sporadically throughout the empire, outside Italy it became popular only in the GALLIC and GERMANIC PROVINCES, where he was identified with important local gods. Dedications to Mercury are very frequent in these regions, and often give him local epithets (e.g. Arvernus) or associate him with other native deities, notably the goddess Rosmerta. JBR

See Dumézil, G. (1970) *Archaic Roman Religion*.

GODS AND GODDESSES: (b).

Meroë City in the central Sudan and capital of the kingdom of Kush. Meroë was located on the east bank

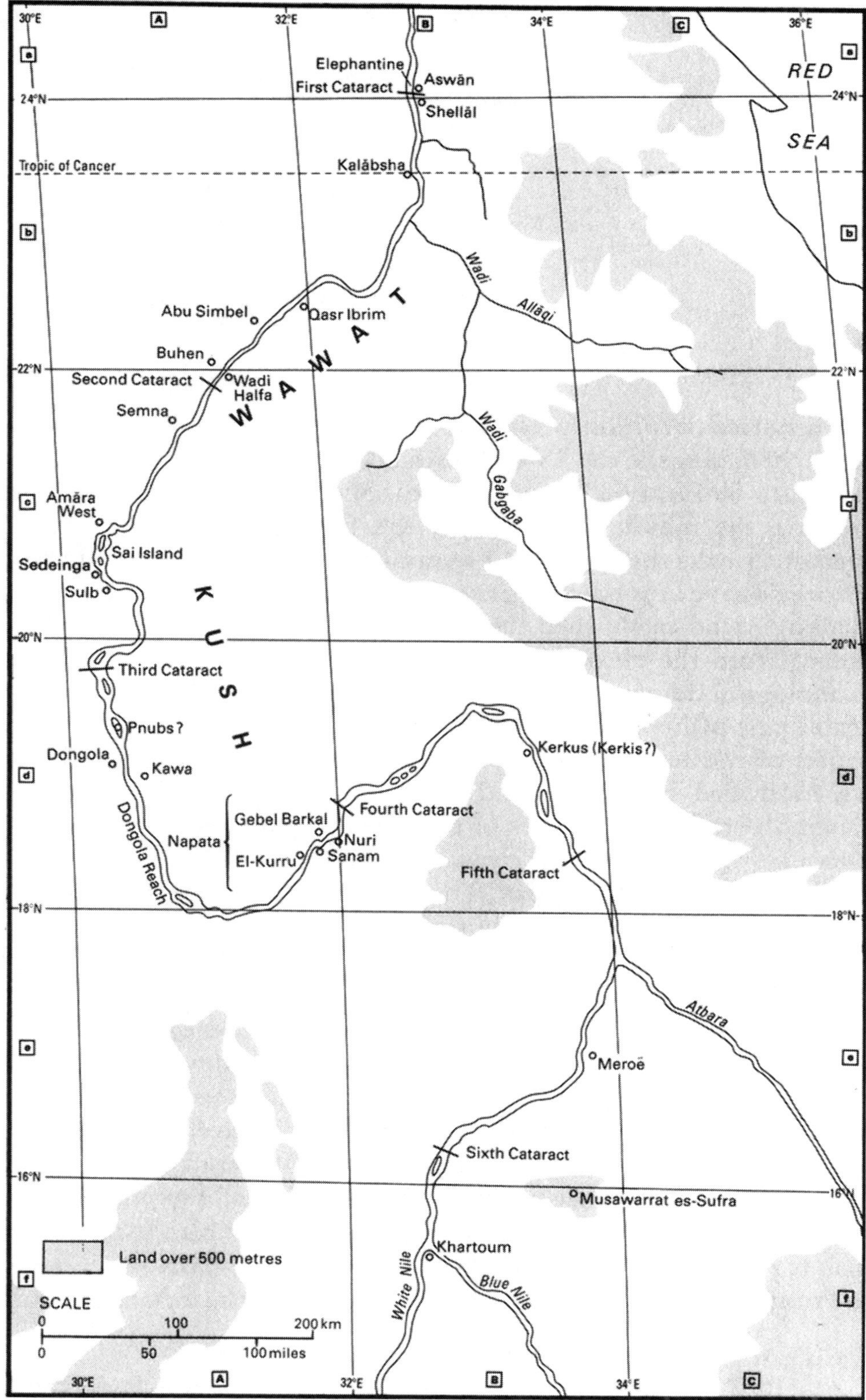

Meroë: map showing location of the kingdom of Meroë (Kush) on the Upper Nile.

of the Nile, just south of the junction of the Nile and Atbara rivers. Despite its ancient fame, the site was first identified by James Bruce in 1772. Because of the lack of written sources, its history is based on archaeological evidence. Though founded in the 8th century BC, it became the principal royal residence only in the 6th century. It survived attacks by Persia, Ptolemaic Egypt and Rome and remained the capital of Kush until the mid-4th century AD, when Kush succumbed to attacks by Noba raiders and the kingdom of Axum in modern Ethiopia.

The most famous monuments of Meroë are the pyramids in which the rulers of Kush were buried. The heart of the city, however, consisted of the huge Egyptian-style temple of the royal palace and other government buildings. The great slagheaps scattered over the site suggested to some that the city's prosperity rested on its role as a centre of iron manufacturing. More recent research indicates that its wealth was actually based on control of the trade routes that brought African goods such as gold, ivory, animal products, hardwoods and slaves to Egypt in exchange for Greek luxury goods. SMB

See Edwards, D. N. (1996) *The Archaeology of the Meroitic State*; (2004) *The Nubian Past: an archaeology of the Sudan*, ch. 6; Wellbsy, D. A. (1996) *The Kingdom of Kush*.

Mesopotamia Region of the Seleukid and Parthian kingdoms, province of the Roman empire, between the Tigris and Euphrates, including parts of modern Iraq, Turkey and Syria. Literally (in Greek) 'between the rivers', Mesopotamia was the home of sophisticated civilizations for centuries before Alexander the Great's conquest. It was bounded to the south and west by the Euphrates, to the north and east by the Tigris and the Armenian mountains, and in the extreme south-east by the confluence of the rivers above the mouth of the Persian (Arabian) gulf. Urban settlement concentrated in two areas, the south-east (Babylon, Seleukeia-on-the-Tigris, the Parthian capital Ctesiphon) and the north (the Roman provinces of Osrhoene and Mesopotamia, including Edessa, Amida and Nisibis). Other cities lay along the fertile valleys of the rivers. Travel west to east, peaceful and warlike, was mostly along the valley of the Euphrates or along the Tigris and across the cities of the north. These were well-trodden routes of communication within the Seleukid empire and axes of east–west trade. In centuries of warfare between Rome and Persia cities on these axes (Edessa, Nisibis, Dura Europus) became the scenes of conflict as armies sought to capture them and push on into the enemy's heartland.

Mesopotamia was an important part of the Seleukid and, subsequently, Parthian kingdoms. The Romans never controlled all of it (except very briefly after Trajan's campaign of AD 113–17), and the Roman province called Mesopotamia (established in the Severan period) was only a small part of the geographical region, centred on northern cities such as Amida and Nisibis. NDP

Sassanian empire; Syria, Roman: (b).

Messalina (Valeria Messalina, or Messallina) Descended on both sides from Octavian's sister Octavia, she was about 20 years old when she married

Messalina: coin portrait.

her 50-year-old relative, the emperor Claudius, in AD 39 or 40. She bore him two children, Claudia Octavia and Britannicus (41 and 40). Beyond this basic information, the record is overwhelmed with the spectacular circumstances of her downfall in AD 48. The historiographic tradition, dominated by Tacitus, is hostile to her and to Claudius, who is characterized as weak and uxorious. Her excessive influence over him is blamed for the secret palace trials that often resulted in executions. Her motives are represented as the 'typically feminine' ones of greed and jealousy.

Her semi-public 'marriage' to the consul-designate Gaius Iunius Silius in AD 48 led to their condemnation for treason, and Messalina was executed. Claudius subsequently married his niece Agrippina, whose son eclipsed Britannicus and succeeded to the throne as Nero in 54, later causing the deaths of both Britannicus and Octavia (whom he had married and divorced).

For women of the imperial family, charges of treason and adultery often elided, but the judicial purges following Messalina's death left her with an extraordinary reputation for rampant promiscuity, culminating in Juvenal's satiric depiction of her in willing competition with common prostitutes (*Satire* 6.114–35). The florid tradition, so thin on facts, impedes serious historical reconstruction of her life and actions. SD

See Cassius Dio, *Roman History*, book 61; Suetonius, *Life of Claudius*; Balsdon, J. P. V. D. (1962) *Roman Women*.

 Augustus: (a).

Messenia The south-western Peloponnese, roughly modern Messinía (3,800 sq km, 1,500 sq miles); called *Messênê* in archaic and classical sources, but from about the 3rd century BC *Messênia*. Mountains divide the two principal plains from a third on the west coast. Internal travel is easy, and Messenia is accessible by land from the north and north-east, but separated from Laconia by Mt Taÿgetos. Its fertility tempted the Spartans to seize it in the 8th or 7th century BC, making most Messenians into helots. Sparta tolerated no independent cities, and archaeological data suggest that the normal Greek scatter of outlying farmsteads did not develop. Sparta exercised control partly through dependent city-states of *perioikoi* like those of LACONIA. Central Messenia was liberated by the Thebans in 369, the coastal areas by Philip II in 338. A new capital city arose after 369; initially named Ithome after the nearby mountain with its sanctuary of Zeus Ithomatas, it was soon known as Messene. It has the finest surviving fortifications in Greece; excavation of the town centre has uncovered spectacular buildings and numerous inscriptions. Post-liberation Messenia may have been FEDERAL, though Messene, the most powerful city, appears to have dominated the others. One of the most interesting aspects of Messenian history is how the Messenians after liberation retold their early history and revisited local cults whose memory they had kept alive during Spartan rule. DGJS

See Pausanias, book 4; Alcock, S. E. (2002) *Archaeologies of the Greek Past*, ch. 4; Davis, J. L., ed. (1998) *Sandy Pylos*; Shipley, G. (2004), Messenia, in Hansen and Nielsen, *Inventory* 548–68.

 AEGEAN SEA: (a); PELOPONNESE.

Messenian wars The two main stages in Sparta's conquest of MESSENIA, the region to its west. The details and dates, however, are hazy. Pausanias, in book 4 of his *Tour of Greece* (2nd century AD), narrates the mythological history of Messenia before its subjugation by Sparta. In his account the Messenian leader Aristodemos leads vain resistance in the first Messenian war (now conventionally dated c.735–710 BC). The hero of the second Messenian war (or 'first Messenian revolt', usually put in the mid-7th century) is Aristomenes. He wins a famous victory, is then defeated by using underhand means, is captured but escapes certain death with divine help, withstands a siege at Mt Eira for 11 years, and is forced to abandon Messenia only when – by the will of fate – a furious rainstorm causes his guards to desert their posts. In the aftermath, some Messenians escape to Zankle in Italy, which becomes Messana ('New Messene') – but this is securely dated to the 490s. There are tortuous arguments about the chronology of the second Messenian war, which some scholars date c.500 rather than c.650. The story of Messenia's heroic resistance may have been 'written up' only after its liberation in the 4th century, but it is now accepted that the Messenians may well have preserved reasonably accurate memories of their past – particularly if that past was more recent than we usually suppose. DGJS

See Alcock, S. E. (2002) *Archaeologies of the Greek Past*, ch. 4; Cartledge, P. A. (2002) *Sparta and Lakonia*, chs. 8–9; Shaw, P.-J. (2003) *Discrepancies in Olympiad Dating*; Ogden, D. (2004) *Aristomenes of Messene*.

 WAR (table).

metallurgy The classical civilizations of the MEDITERRANEAN world were based on the use of metals. Precious metals such as GOLD and SILVER were used to produce the COINAGE which paid for the armies and navies that conquered the new empires, while IRON was used to manufacture the swords, spears and ARMOUR used in the wars of conquest. COPPER and its alloys were used to produce small denomination coins for the first market economies. An understanding of these civilizations must include a study of the production and use of these metals.

Pure metals are very rare in nature. Gold is the only metal used at this time that occurs in the metallic state. All the other metals occur as ores: these are usually the oxides, carbonates and sulphides of the metals. The ores can occur as beds in sedimentary rock or as veins intruding into other rock. The ores are rarely homogeneous and contain other metal ores and a variety of other minerals. Prospecting for ores was made easier as many are brightly coloured (e.g. the green of the copper ore malachite). Most early MINES consisted of simple pits to dig out the ore, though in a few ancient mines the seams of ore were pursued deep into the ground. Some Greek and Roman mines show increased use of complex technology such as the ARCHIMEDES SCREW or wheels to pump water out of the mines. During this period iron

METALLURGY: huge slag heaps derived from Roman copper working at Khirbet Faynan in the Jordanian desert. Recent research shows this was one of the most heavily polluted landscapes yet known from classical antiquity.

tools came to replace the stone tools which had been used as picks and hammers. The Athenian silver mines at Laurion and the Roman mines in various locations in Spain show an intensity of mining activity rarely seen in earlier periods. Long tunnels were dug in order to follow the seams of ore and numerous shafts were dug to ensure a sufficient flow of air for the miners.

Once the ore was mined from the ground it was processed and smelted in order to obtain the pure metal. The processing of ore was carried out in order to remove some of the unwanted minerals which contained no metal (e.g. silica). This could be achieved by hand sorting, crushing the rock and sometimes by washing. As metal ores are denser than ordinary rock, washing would retain ores while the lighter rock would be washed away. Such washing floors have been found near the Athenian silver mines. The processed ore was usually smelted in a furnace. Charcoal was used to produce a reducing atmosphere and a high temperature. The impurities in the ore and any remaining silica were removed in slags (essentially iron-rich glass) which were liquid at high temperatures and so could be 'tapped' from the furnace. Many ancient smelting sites are dominated by enormous dumps of such slag. The smelted metal was usually molten as well and could be tapped separately into ingots. Copper ingots were often circular while lead ingots ('pigs') were rectangular. Lead pigs often had inscriptions cast into them while other copper and silver ingots may have had stamped inscriptions. Iron was the exception as it was usually smelted at a much lower temperature than its melting point. The product of iron smelting was a 'bloom' which was then forged into a bar ready for further working into artefacts.

Most ancient metals were worked into shape by two basic processes: smithing and casting (as iron was not heated up to its melting point it was never cast). Smithing was used to hammer ingot metal into the desired shape. This technique was used in the manufacture of basic items such as wire and sheet, as well as complex artefacts such as bowls and brooches, and was used widely to achieve detailed decorative schemes such as those on tableware. Detailed decoration and complex shapes could also be achieved by casting molten metal into moulds. The distinctive statues of the Greek and Roman civilizations were produced by casting into large moulds.

The scale of some ancient mining and metalworking processes will have had a considerable impact on the environment. The diversion of rivers, erosion of land, accumulation of spoil and slag heaps and the felling of timber (especially for fuel for smelting) will have despoiled large areas.

While mines were usually state property and convicts and slaves were used as miners, there are records which show that freeborn individuals were also engaged in mining. The right to mine was often leased to individuals. Many small mines, such as those which consisted of a single shallow pit, may even have been worked without the attention of state officials. Evidence for iron mining or working appears on almost every excavated site in the north-western provinces of the Roman empire. Those engaged in mining or metalworking need not have been full-time specialists. They may have mined or smithed on a seasonal basis to supplement agricultural production.

Ancient attitudes to metallurgy were not always based on rigorous science or the most efficient methods. These attitudes are not simply 'primitive' but show a complex system of belief which must be considered alongside the scientific study of metallurgy. The earth was often seen as a female entity and ores were in one sense her 'offspring'. Pliny writes that miners 'penetrate her inner parts' (*Natural History* 33.1), that minerals 'do not come quickly to birth' (33.1), and records that a mine abandoned might replenish itself 'just as a miscarriage seems to make some women more prolific' (33.49).

It is clear that once the metal was produced it was often seen as more than simply a material to be used for a utilitarian purpose. The diversity of copper alloys used in the Roman period, in particular the ways in which broadly similar artefacts often had significantly different compositions, shows that production was shaped by traditional knowledge and the use of recipes. Recipes also hint at the symbolic dimensions of some metal artefacts. Spiral finger rings were made from brass while spiral earrings were made from bronze. There is no utilitarian reason for this difference and it may point to a symbolic view of the different copper alloys and how they could or could not be used.

Even an item which appears unproblematic, such as a nail, may have had complex layers of meaning attached to it. Roman nails were used in explicitly religious contexts, such as those hammered into the walls of the Capitoline temple to Jupiter every year to prevent plague (Livy 7.3.3–9). DD

See Tylecote, R. F. (1987) *The Early History of Metallurgy in Europe.*

 iron: (a)–(b).

metaphysics The term 'metaphysics' (from the Greek *meta ta physika*) means 'after' or 'beyond' what is natural, and was used as the title of Aristotle's treatise, the *Metaphysics*. Its meaning depends on the relation established between a theory and what is defined as natural. Thus Parmenides, who initiated metaphysics with his theory of an unchanging being, undermined the validity of the natural world as the realm of change. Plato, by contrast, restricted immutability to objective ideas (or Forms) that were distinguished from, and helped explain, the natural world. In his *Symposium*, for example, the unstable beauty of an individual person is distinguished from, but better understood, in relation to the Form of Beauty that, unlike a particular instance of beauty, is unchanging, and thus eternally beautiful. The Platonic version of metaphysics also carried a prescription to acquire knowledge of Forms through a rigorous education based on mathematics and geometry, and designed to develop intellectual powers leading to an understanding of the Forms. This kind of metaphysical thought and inquiry continued in Neoplatonism, where the hierarchical relation of the Forms to the world, and the procedures for acquiring knowledge of them, were elaborated by thinkers such as Plotinus and Proclus. It also entered Christian philosophy, notably in the writings of St Augustine (1).

Aristotle's metaphysics partly replicated Platonism in its vision of unchanging entities beyond the natural world: that is, the heavenly bodies that move eternally through the agency of the divine 'unmoved mover' in a physically unchanging realm (the *aithêr*), in contrast to other bodies that undergo change. But he also used metaphysics to analyse and understand the natural world through a theory of being applicable to complex organic structures. The forms of such substances are eternal because the Aristotelian world has no beginning (e.g. the species Horse has not come into being nor will it ever change), but Platonism is, as it were, brought to earth through a metaphysics that regards forms as immanent in the world and, in particular, understands organisms as substances with definable properties and relations, and a place in biological and zoological hierarchies. Such a descriptive and analytical form of metaphysics contrasts sharply with the otherworldly Platonism, which, to modern eyes, has often seemed speculative and scientifically irrelevant.

The hellenistic schools of STOICISM and EPICUREANISM offered a materialistic metaphysics in which primary bodies (ATOMS for the Epicureans; spiritualized matter for the Stoics) underwent evolutionary processes, and thus explained the structure and evolution of the natural world. In one sense, these philosophers revived the materialism of the PRESOCRATICS whose metaphysics also involved identifying the elements of the physical world, but they did so in a sophisticated way that ensured that the analysis of complex phenomena was not simply a reduction of complexes to elementary bodies.

Anti-metaphysical thought in antiquity is represented by the SCEPTICS. Their critique of sense experience and theory meant that they challenged metaphysical speculation by systematically undermining the positive explanatory constructions that most Greek philosophers developed and used to positive effect. RBT

Metapontum (Greek *Metapontion*; mod. Metaponto) Located on the instep of ITALY, between Tarentum and Siris, Metapontum was founded according to tradition by ACHAIAN colonists from Sybaris along with Achaians from the mainland (STRABO 6.1.15). The first signs of settlement date to around 690 BC and record a mixture of Greek and indigenous POTTERY and HOUSES with native characteristics, suggesting not a solely Greek community but a mixture of Greeks and Italian natives. Around 600 BC, however, there are clear signs of URBANIZATION and distinctly Greek buildings appear, suggesting perhaps an influx of Greek settlers.

Metapontum was set on a fertile plain between two rivers, and its AGRICULTURAL wealth was symbolized in the ear of barley stamped on its COINAGE. After strife broke out in Kroton against the ruling Pythagoreans there in 510, PYTHAGORAS fled to Metapontum where he died and was buried. Despite the setback, the Pythagoreans regained control and extended their influence to other Greek cities of southern Italy. Metapontum may have fallen under the control of Kroton during the first half of the 5th century, but by the second half of the century it was allied with the Spartan colony of Taras. In 413 the city supported the Athenians' invasion of SICILY, providing SHIPS and javelin throwers. In 280 Metapontum, with other Greek cities of southern Italy, joined PYRRHOS in war against Rome. After Pyrrhos' withdrawal it became an ally of Rome (272) until the invasion of HANNIBAL, whom it supported in 212. CC

See Carter, J. C. (1990) Metapontum: land, wealth and population, in J.-P. Descoeudres, ed., *Greek Colonists and Native Populations* 405–41; Dunbabin, T. J. (1948) *The Western Greeks*; Osborne, R. (1996) *Greece in the Making*.

 MAGNA GRAECIA.

Metelli Important family of the later REPUBLIC and principal branch of the PLEBEIAN Caecilii, probably belonging to the Arnensis TRIBE. Lucius Caecilius Metellus Denter was first to hold the consulship (284 BC). His son, also Lucius, defeated the CARTHAGINIANS at Panhormus (Palermo) in the first PUNIC WAR (250). The ELEPHANTS which he captured and transported to Rome were the first ever seen in the city; thereafter, the animal was associated with the family. At its height in the later 2nd century, the family's *cognomina* in this period map Roman IMPERIALISM: Macedonicus, Baliaricus, Delmaticus, Numidicus and Creticus. Between 123 and 102 the sons of Quintus Caecilius Metellus Macedonicus and Lucius Caecilius Metellus Calvus (brothers and CONSULS) obtained six consulships, five TRIUMPHS and four CENSORSHIPS. Despite another seven consuls, the family's dominance was never the same. Celer was the husband of CLODIA (CATULLUS' Lesbia). The last, Pius Scipio, adopted into the family, commanded the Pompeian centre at PHARSALUS (48 BC), falling at THAPSUS (46). Delmaticus' daughter was the wife of SULLA; Creticus' daughter (both simply Caecilia Metella) married CRASSUS' elder son and is commemorated by a monumental TOMB on the Via Appia, Byron's 'stern round tower of other days'. JRWP

metics (*metoikoi*) Resident aliens of a Greek CITY. In the case of Athens foreigners (*xenoi*) could visit and remain for a certain period of time (perhaps a month) without legal formality. Beyond that, they were required to register. In order to take up permanent residency a foreigner had to find an Athenian sponsor who would register him as a metic in his DEME. It was an indictable offence for a metic not to have a sponsor; the penalty was enslavement. Metics were required to pay a special tax (*metoikion*), which amounted to 12 drachmas a year for males and 6 for independent females. Wealthy metics could be called upon to contribute LITURGIES (except the trierarchy) and pay the property tax (*eisphora*). Metics were also liable for military service and could be found serving as HOPLITES in the army or as rowers in the NAVY.

Unless given a special grant by the Athenian ASSEMBLY, a metic could not own land or house in ATTICA and was thus forced to rent from citizens. This restriction may have had the effect of forcing metics to concentrate in areas of MANUFACTURING, TRADE and BANKING. Though free, metics had no rights of political participation, but had legal rights to prosecute and defend themselves in court. Cases involving metics were either heard in the polemarch's court or passed on by him to other MAGISTRATES for trial. Only in exceptional circumstances was a metic granted CITIZENSHIP by the assembly. CC

See Whitehead, D. (1977) *The Ideology of the Athenian Metic*.

metope see ARCHITECTURE, GREEK; ORDERS, ARCHITECTURAL; PARTHENON; TEMPLES, GREEK.

metre The study of metre is one important component in any understanding of how ancient writers manipulated their language to achieve sounds and other effects in an effort to leave an impression on their audiences. Language has a natural rhythm, and the term metre generally denotes a regular pattern imposed on the natural rhythm of language within the context of a literary work. Most commonly, metre is found in poetry and music, but not exclusively; it appears in PROSE as well, particularly in oratory. The rhythm of both the Greek and Latin languages was produced by the alternation of long (–) and short (˘) syllables (not long and short vowels). Therefore, Greek and Latin metre is said to be quantitative, that is, it is based on the quantity of the syllable. The study of the rules for determining the long or short quantity of a syllable, as well as which syllables are to be counted at all, is called prosody.

In Greek there are two basic types of metres: the stichic and the strophic. Stichic metres are repeated line after line for an undetermined number of verses. Strophic metres are also called lyric metres. Within a poem a whole strophe (stanza) is repeated a number of times. Traditionally, stichic metres are divided into what are called feet. A foot is a combination of two or three syllables that is repeated within the metre. The basic feet are the iambic: ˘ –, trochaic: – ˘, dactylic: – ˘ ˘, and anapaestic ˘ ˘ –. The most common stichic metres are the dactylic hexameter (the metre of epic poetry), elegiac couplet (built by a hexameter and a pentameter; used extensively for elegy), iambic trimeter (the most common metre for DRAMA), and the iambic and trochaic tetrameters (also used for drama). Best-known representatives of strophic metres are those created by the Lesbian poets SAPPHO and ALKAIOS, from whom they receive the names of Sapphic and Alcaic stanzas.

Roman metres were adopted and adapted from Greek metres as early as the beginning of the Latin literary tradition in the third century BC. Only the so-called saturnian verse is a native Italian metre independent of Greek influence. To poets influenced by Greek metres, the saturnian (apparently based on word accent, not syllable quantity) sounded rude and primitive. In general, Roman writers employed the same metres as the Greeks for similar types of poetry. In both cultures, a variety of less common and sometimes complex metres were employed by poets. RBC

See Devine, A. M. and Stephens L. D. (1984) *Language and Metre: resolution, Porson's Bridge, and their prosodic basis*; Maas, P. (1962) *Greek Metre*; Raven D. S. (1962) *Greek Metre: an introduction*; (1965) *Latin Metre: an introduction*; West, M. L. (1987) *Introduction to Greek Metre*.

metrology see MEASUREMENT; WEIGHTS AND MEASURES.

Michael Psellos see SCHOLARSHIP, BYZANTINE.

Middle Comedy see COMEDY 2: MIDDLE AND NEW COMEDY.

midwives Women in the ancient world gave birth at home, surrounded by family and neighbours. They had their own ideas about how to help; PLINY THE ELDER mentions amulets, including placing the right foot of a hyena on a woman in labour, and tying a snake's discarded skin on her thigh. In his *Gynaecology*, the 2nd-century AD writer SORANUS does not discourage such methods, because they may help the woman to feel better. However, he recommends as the ideal midwife a woman who is physically strong, sober, free from superstition, literate, and trained in diet, surgery and DRUGS. This paragon of virtue is, however, little more than an ideal. Midwifery was rarely a profession; even in the later Roman empire we read of a midwife whose 'day job' was as a barmaid. More commonly, a woman would gain a local reputation and would be called in to help, and in particular to cut the cord, if needed. Parallels with simple societies all over the world suggest that traditional midwives can be highly skilled, capable of turning a child *in utero* if it presents in positions other than the straightforward head-first.

Midwives did not necessarily need to have given birth. ARTEMIS, the GODDESS most associated with birth after helping her mother Leto deliver her own twin APOLLO, remained forever virgin. The Roman writer Hyginus tells a story about an Athenian called Agnodike whom he claims as 'the first midwife'; like Artemis, she is a young, unmarried woman. (see also PREGNANCY AND CHILDBIRTH) HK

migrations The movement of populations across vast landmasses. Throughout history, humankind has been a migratory species, which from the earliest period down to the modern era has moved across and colonized the face of the earth. Such migrations occurred in classical antiquity too, both within and beyond its geographical limits. According to THUCYDIDES (1.12), for example, the period after the TROJAN WAR saw the invasion of mainland Greece by the 'Dorians', thus forcing much of the original population to flee across the AEGEAN to the Ionian coast of Asia Minor. There are problems with this narrative, however. The linguistic and archaeological evidence for such migrations is either slight or ambiguous, and it has been argued that Thucydides' account was primarily an attempt to provide an explanation for the variation of dialects and socio-political structures found in Greece in his own day.

We are better informed about migrations from the classical period onwards. CELTS from central Europe expanded westwards into BRITAIN and Ireland, south into ITALY, and eastwards into the Balkans and even further afield into central Asia Minor. Later, at the end of the 2nd century BC, the migration of the Germanic Cimbri and Teutones into southern GAUL and northern Italy was halted only by Roman military action. In the 1st century BC too, JULIUS CAESAR records the movement of the Celtic Helvetii within Gaul. Above all, however, mass migrations of populations from central Europe, southern Scandinavia and the western Eurasian steppe are associated with the events that brought about the end of the Roman empire in Western Europe between the 3rd and 6th centuries AD. Although the impact of such groups is particularly well attested in the Roman world, it is clear that migrations affected other regions. The HUNS, for example, are known to have launched incursions through the Caucasus into Iran in the 5th century. Further east the CHINESE EMPIRE suffered periodic attacks from central Eurasian nomads.

The interpretation of migrations is fraught with difficulties. It is not fully understood why such migrations occurred, though CLIMATIC CHANGES, sociopolitical metamorphosis, economic motives and pressure from other migrant groups have all been cited. Nor can the exact numbers of such supposed migrants be ascertained. A more serious obstacle to interpreting migrations is that they have often been used to explain, or justify, ethnic divisions (real or supposed) in later ages. This was not only the case in the ancient world, as with Thucydides' account of the 'Dorian' migrations. In the modern era too, the study of historical migrations was often driven by nationalist political agendas. This was particularly apparent in the emerging interest in early Germanic *Völkerwanderung* ('people wanderings') that coincided with the rise of a German national consciousness in the 19th century. Such approaches assumed that migrating populations retained a certain ethnic purity and cultural integrity (Geary); the reality, however, seems to be that populations on the move underwent ongoing cultural, ethnic and political redefinition. MDH

See Geary, P. J. (2002) *The Myth of Nations*; Todd, M. (2001) *Migrants and Invaders*.

 GERMANY AND GERMANS: (b); HUNS.

Milan (anc. Mediolanum) Milan was created as a Latin colony in 222 BC following defeat of the Insubres tribe (Livy 5.34.9). It became a *municipium* in 89 BC, but only rose to *colonia* status under HADRIAN. It formed the centre for *regio* XI, Liguria, lying at the crossroads for roads leading from the busy Alpine passes, and exploiting the rich Po plains of north Italy. In AD 284, following the THIRD-CENTURY CRISES, the imperial capital shifted here from Rome, allowing the Western emperor to be closer to the northern frontiers. This initiated extensive building campaigns within the city and heightened exploitation of the surrounding countryside. Ausonius (*Ordo urbium nobilium* 7) lists Milan as the seventh largest city in the empire, reflecting this expansion. CONSTANTINE and LICINIUS here issued their so-called Edict which gave CHRISTIANITY its supreme religious hand. Milan subsequently became a major focus for the new state religion, with St AMBROSE a powerful protagonist, rivalling the BISHOP of Rome for power and influence. In 402 the emperor HONORIUS moved his court to RAVENNA. Although Milan did not decline dramatically in consequence, it suffered through the attacks of Alaric in the 400s. Later, in the course of the GOTHIC WARS (AD 535–55), the Ostrogoths are recorded as massacring the whole male population and selling the women and children off as slaves to the Burgundians. With the LOMBARD invasion, the archbishop of Milan moved to Genoa (until the 640s). Though Milan was the Lombard capital from c. AD 580 to 610, its unwieldy size prompted the transfer of court to nearby Pavia. NJC

See Sena Chiesa, G., ed. (1990) *Milano capitale dell'impero romano 286–402 d. C.*

 CITIES: (b).

Miletos City in Ionia, favourably located on a peninsula where the Maeander valley, giving access deep into western Asia Minor, meets the Aegean. A very early settlement, Miletos came into contact with Greece in the MINOAN and MYCENAEAN periods before being founded (in myth) by Neleus and becoming one of the greatest of the Ionian cities. HERODOTOS tells us that the Ionian colonists killed the CARIANS who lived at Miletos and married their womenfolk. The peninsula's fine HARBOURS gave Miletos a maritime aspect; it grew wealthy, with a reputation for high-quality wool. The city's main sanctuary was the Apolline oracle of the Branchidai at DIDYMA, 16 km (10 miles) to the south.

Miletos flourished in the archaic period under the TYRANT Thrasyboulos and founded many colonies, particularly in the BLACK SEA (e.g. Olbia, Kyzikos and Sinope). Many of Greece's great early thinkers were Milesians, including THALES, Anaximander and Anaximenes. Miletos had resisted LYDIA but came under PERSIAN control only to lead the IONIAN REVOLT (499–494 BC). The revolt was quashed and Miletos and Didyma sacked, following a sea battle at the nearby island of Lade. Although it lost much influence as a result, Miletos re-emerged as a wealthy trading city in the hellenistic and Roman periods. Miletos initially resisted ALEXANDER in 334 BC and became part of the SELEUKID kingdom on his death. As part of the Attalid kingdom of PERGAMON, it passed to Rome in 133 BC.

The site of Miletos has been excavated since the late 19th century. Its rebuilding after the Ionian revolt (probably in the mid-5th century) was a notable example of developed Greek TOWN PLANNING, with house blocks laid out differently in different zones and spaces reserved for public use. The noted town planner Hippodamos came from Miletos, though he was not responsible for the planning of his home town. Many of the hellenistic urban structures were on a grand scale, including lengthy STOAS framing a rectangular *AGORA*. AG

See Gorman, V. B. (2000) *Miletos, the Ornament of Ionia*; Greaves, A. M. (2002) *Miletos*.

 COUNCILS: (a); EAST GREECE; THEATRES: (a).

mills and milling Grinding grain into flour was one of the most time-consuming domestic tasks in ancient society. Between the classical period and the end of the Roman period substantial advances were made in milling technology that produced – except for the windmill – all the main types of mill that remained in use until the Industrial Revolution. The Neolithic saddle-quern was still used in archaic Greece – a stone pushed back and forth over a saddle-shaped slab by an operator kneeling behind the mill. During the 5th century BC this was supplanted by the 'Olynthian' or hopper-rubber quern, with a flat lower stone, usually grooved in a herring-bone pattern, and a rectangular upper stone moved back and forth by a wooden lever, with a hopper in the upper face of the stone and a grooved slot allowing the grain to be fed through. This was used in some areas until the 1st century BC, but the rotary quern, enabling more efficient grinding, made its appearance by the 3rd century BC, and became the standard tool for domestic milling into the Middle Ages.

The switch to rotary motion opened up new possibilities for greater output and for the use of non-human

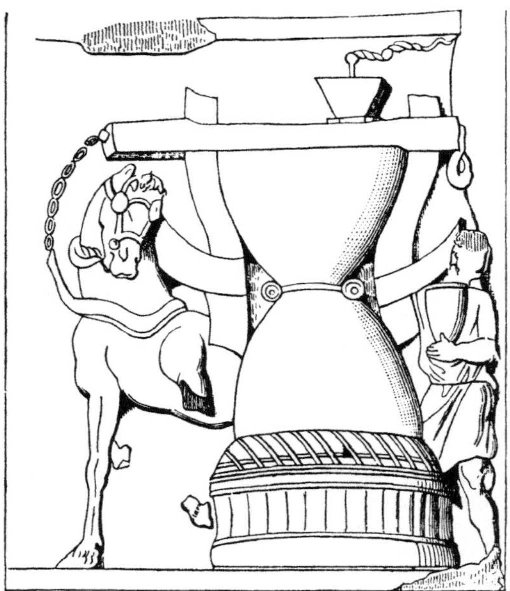

MILLS AND MILLING: (a) relief carving of Roman animal powered grain mill.

MILLS AND MILLING: (b) olive crushing mill with lunate stones (*trapetum*) from Pompeii.

power sources. Technological developments went hand-in-hand with the growing specialization of labour and the rise of the professional BAKER. The first ANIMAL-driven mills appear in the 3rd century BC, consisting of a conical lower stone (*meta*) and an hourglass-shaped upper stone (*catillus*), the upper part of which acted as a hopper for grain. They were turned by a HORSE or DONKEY harnessed to a wooden turning rig; smaller versions could be turned by SLAVES or hired labour. Such mills were used into late antiquity; they are found in rural VILLAS, but also in urban bakeries. WATER MILLS further encouraged the specialization of labour, leading to a distinction between baker (*pistor*) and miller (*molendinarius*) by the 2nd century AD. Water mills used discoid millstones similar to large hand querns without a handle socket; their diameters generally range between 0.6 and 1.3 m (24 to 51 inches). Originally designed with a steep grinding profile like those of animal mills, over time both water millstones and hand querns became flatter as it was realized that centrifugal force was sufficient to propel the ground flour to the circumference of the stone without the aid of gravity. From the 2nd century AD onwards grinding surfaces tend to be dressed, except in lava millstones. Technological crossover between water mills and animal-driven mills may have resulted in another kind of animal-driven mill, for which there is some evidence especially from north-west Europe. Its reconstruction is still debated, but it seems to have used disc-shaped millstones like those of water mills, but turned by animals harnessed to a turning rig that powered the stones by a geared drive. If so, it would be the ancestor of a type of animal mill common from the medieval period until the 19th century. AIW

See Curtis, R. I. (2000) *Ancient Food Technology*; Moritz, L. A. (1958) *Grain Mills and Flour in Classical Antiquity*.

 BARBEGAL.

Milo see ATHLETES AND ATHLETICS, GREEK; see also CLODIUS; PUBLIC ORDER, ROMAN.

Milvian bridge, battle of The Milvian bridge carried the Via Flaminia over the TIBER and was the site of the battle between CONSTANTINE and Maxentius (28 October AD 312). Having crossed the river on a bridge of boats, Maxentius' army was defeated, and Maxentius himself drowned. The victory gave Constantine control of the Western empire and is presented, by Christian writers, as the triumph of CHRISTIANITY over PAGANISM. In the *Ecclesiastical History*, written c.324, EUSEBIOS presents an image of Maxentius that recalled the destruction of Pharaoh in the Red Sea from the OLD TESTAMENT. According to LACTANTIUS, writing not long after the event, Constantine was told in a dream to mark his soldiers' shields with the heavenly sign of God (some form of chi-rho) and thus he was victorious. The dream, preceded by a vision, is central to Eusebios' narrative of the early part of Constantine's campaign against Maxentius in the *Life of Constantine*, written c.337, and claims to be reported by Constantine himself: at midday Constantine saw a cross of light above the sun, with the words 'by this conquer' attached. This was followed by a dream in which God urged him to use the sign as protection. Constantine ordered his army to march under the sign of the *labarum* (chi-rho). Maxentius is said (among other crimes in the invective against him) to have consulted the SIBYLLINE oracles and both to have taken war to the enemy to avenge his father and to have been reluctant to fight. MEH

See Eusebius, *Life of Constantine*, trs. A. Cameron and S. Hall (1999); *Ecclesiastical History*; Lactantius, *De Mortibus Persecutorum*, ed. and trs. J. L. Creed (1984).

mime *Mimos* was the word given to an imitative semi-dance performance and to its performer. In classical Greece, XENOPHON tells of a mime of Ariadne and DIONYSOS performed at a private dinner party to the accompaniment of MUSIC and narration. By the hellenistic era the mimes become the property of the legitimate THEATRE, taking the form of frivolous, often vulgar, quasi-dance-dramas. The Romans had an ancient performance tradition of unmasked clowns (many of whom bore Greek names) improvising sketches at the annual Floralia. Soon professional mime companies were established, with men and women performing skits loaded with sexual innuendo and farce. Although only fragments survive, mime scripts, written by the likes of Laberius, Matius and Decimus, tended to employ stock situations: adultery, disguise, the escape of criminals and rags-to-riches stories are the staple diet of mime scenarios. In addition, other non-dramatic literary texts (some of which were of a very high quality) could be performed as mimes: OVID's ELEGIES were certainly staged, as were VIRGIL's versions of the stories of Turnus and Dido. The nature of mime allowed actors to lampoon or criticize the state and prominent individuals. Some actors become imperial confidants and even lovers; JUSTINIAN actually made a mime actress, Theodora, his empress. Mime actresses were particularly popular, and female performers like Dionysia and Arbuscula achieved both notoriety and great wealth. Elements of the ancient mime were later found in the Renaissance *commedia dell'arte*. LL-J

See Beachman, R.C. (1991) *The Roman Theatre and its Audience*.

Mimnermos see ELEGY.

mina (Greek *mna*, Latin *mina*) Originally a Near Eastern measure, in Greece this was both a unit of WEIGHT (c.500 g) and a sum of currency – in both cases one-60th of a talent. Its monetary value is thus normally 100 drachmas, but varies with the value of the drachma. Thus 1 Attic *mna* equals only 70 Aiginetan drachmas; and by the late hellenistic period it was necessary for the market regulations of Athens to define the 'trading (*emporikê*) *mna*' as 138 new-style drachmas (*IG* II^2 1013). In both guises the *mna* seems to carry prestige value, and though less familiar to modern readers it occurs nearly as often as the drachma does in Greek sources and documents. HERODOTOS (2.168) tells us that the Egyptian pharaoh's bodyguards received 5 *mnai* of bread, 2 *mnai* of beef and 4 cups of wine per day, and that the regular ransom for prisoners in Peloponnesian warfare was 2 *mnai* (6.79). HERODES ATTICUS' father left 1 *mna* per year to each Athenian citizen. Rates of interest could be stated in terms of drachmas per *mna* per month (1 drachma at this rate is 12 per cent per annum), and the value of one's estate was often stated in *mnai*. Judicial penalties at Athens could be expressed in *mnai*, and in 420 BC the Eleians fined the Spartans 2,000 *mnai* (2 per man) for breaking the Olympic truce (Thucydides 5.49). DGJS

See Austin, M. M. (1981) *The Hellenistic World*, no. 111 (market regulations).

mind and body The question of how much of human behaviour can be explained by the body alone is not one systematically explored before SOCRATES. Earlier Greek thought posits, in addition to the body, a *psychê* (soul) or *daimôn* which represents something like its animating force; but details of its nature and capacities are left vague. Even those who (like PYTHAGORAS, or certain religious sects) supposed the SOUL to be immortal did not automatically assume that it carried with it the capacity for perception or consciousness. Empedokles followed the Pythagoreans in his belief that a person's *daimôn* could be reincarnated; but he must have excluded even thought from its characterization, since he explained this as a process which occurs in the blood.

Against this background, Socrates was intrigued to hear that Anaxagoras had placed at the heart of his view of the cosmos a clearly defined distinction between an incorporeal Mind (*Nous*) and the material world which it organizes. Could this model be applied to an understanding of human nature? Socrates was disappointed, on reading Anaxagoras' book, to discover that his was a 'mind' that did very little thinking. But inspired by what he failed to find in Anaxagoras, Socrates started to argue precisely that the *psychê* by which a human was animated must be characterized and distinguished from the body by its ability to think. He reasoned that our bodies give us the means of doing things, but only our thoughts and decisions can explain why we do them. Since our actions are determined by our decisions, he concluded that our reasoning is what animates us – in other words, that the *psychê* could not be an impersonal force of animation, but must be a mind.

Crucial though this distinction between body and mind was, not everyone agreed that it was the end of the story: somewhere one had to fit in perception and EMOTION. Some people suggested that these were functions of the body; others (including Socrates) argued that they were products of the mind operating within the body. The CYNICS and, later, the STOICS sided with Socrates in explaining emotions in particular as characteristics of certain beliefs. (To desire something, for example, is to believe it beneficial.) But PLATO and ARISTOTLE focused on the fact that emotion could sometimes pull against belief – for example when I desire things I know to be bad for me. Both of them came to see emotions as intermediaries between mind and body: existing alongside the mind as part of a composite soul, but particularly sensitive to the needs of the body.

Plato thought that the mind, and perhaps even the sensitive parts of the soul (i.e. perception and emotion), were incorporeal and immortal, and could exist independently of the body. But this raised a new question: how, exactly, something incorporeal could interact with the physical body at all. Aristotle's concerns about this led him to deny the soul's independence: to think, or to feel anger, involve physical processes as much as WEAVING or building a house. For him, then, the soul represented the way in which a body functions, and was no more separable from it than the shape of a statue is separable from the metal out of which it is made. (Correlatively, he believed that it made no sense to talk about a body without a soul: a corpse is something quite different from a living body.) Aristotle insisted that the soul remained in charge even so; but some of his followers developed his view to the more radical position that all of its functions are merely manifestations of physical processes – dependent on the body, not in charge of it. This seemed to many people obviously wrong: thought in particular seems largely independent of the body. The obvious solution was to make the soul a distinct material entity – which is what, in the hellenistic era, the Stoics and EPICUREANS did. Each constituted their soul from the finest form of MATTER available to their physical systems. By pervading the grosser matter of the body, they argued, the mind which lay at its centre could send commands to and receive feedback from the furthest reach of every limb. For the Epicureans, this meant that the soul was a network of extremely fine atoms. For the Stoics it was *pneuma* or 'breath' – something which had the added advantage of sharing god's nature and so explaining the mind's natural ability to think about the world as structured by god.

In the Platonist revival of later antiquity, the mind became once again something non-material – a lower manifestation of divine intellect. Perception and emotion are registered in an intermediate body of ethereal matter which the mind acquires as a 'cloak' or 'vehicle'. Wrapped in this, the mind is capable of interaction with the physical world, and of further descent into a succession of 'earthy' bodies (NEOPLATONISTS believed in transmigration). CHRISTIAN philosophers were much influenced by this model, though their thought took some distinctive turns of its own. Most, for example, came to think that individual minds are created at the moment of conception, and are uniquely associated with the body for whose care they are created – a fact which precludes their reincarnation, despite their incorporeality and immortality. The only aspect of Christian thinking in this area which achieved the status of dogma is a corollary of this model: the belief in the resurrection of the body. According to this (at least on a literal interpretation), each individual mind will at the end of time draw together into a glorious and permanent reconstitution the matter which had composed its temporal body. In this way, individuals would achieve eternal life as the unified individual, body and mind, they were originally created to be. GB-S

See Annas, J. (1992) *Hellenistic Philosophy of Mind*; Claus, D. B. (1981) *Toward the Soul*; Everson, S., ed. (1991) *Psychology*.

Minerva Roman goddess of ETRUSCAN or perhaps Faliscan origin. Her name (related to 'remembrance') suggests that she had associations with intellectual and artistic pursuits before ever being assimilated to the Greek goddess ATHENA. This is confirmed by the *fasti* (calendar) of PRAENESTE, where 19 March is dedicated to Minerva as the 'day of artisans'. In Rome, too, that same day, known as *Quinquatrus*, originally observed for Mars' sake, was gradually expropriated by Minerva and became the first of a 'five-day' festival (19–23 March). This rivalry between Minerva and Mars was natural – Minerva (like Athena) was also a goddess of WAR. Already by the 6th century BC she and JUNO may have displaced Mars and Quirinus in a new divine Triad (JUPITER remaining the constant), worshipped on the CAPITOLINE. Minerva also had temples on the Aventine and Caelian hills. The former, located outside the *POMERIUM*, was dedicated in the inaugural year of the first PUNIC WAR (264 BC); the latter contained a cult statue of Minerva presumably captured during the siege of Falerii in 241.

Though a goddess of venerable Italic heritage, Minerva sometimes suffered in Roman estimation because of her conflation with the pre-eminent deity of the Athenians, cultural rivals of the Romans. Thus we find VIRGIL describing her coolly in the *Aeneid*, by contrast with his warm-blooded portrait of VENUS. JRH

See Beard, M., North, J. and Price, S. (1998) *Religions of Rome*; Bonnefoy, Y., ed. (1991) *Roman and European Mythologies*; Dumézil, G. (1987) *Archaic Roman Religion*.

 GODS AND GODDESSES: (a)–(b).

mines Ancient mines typically follow the mineral wherever it goes from the original discovery site at the surface. Most mines were opencast, but in deep mines shafts may go down as much as 340 m (1,120 ft) from the surface, and individual galleries may be over a mile long. In the well-developed area of the LAURION in southern ATTIKA, the combined length of the galleries is said to be some 140 km (90 miles). The mine shafts and galleries are at least large enough to allow cramped passage by one person, or at most large enough to extract the lode without causing collapse. The chief factors determining the extent of a mine over space are the presence of ore and breathable air, and the absence of water flooding the working face. Some shafts were dug solely to improve ventilation, and others were carefully refilled for the same purpose. On ore-fields where long experience could guide prospectors, exploratory shafts were sometimes sunk or galleries cut in the hope of finding new lodes underground.

Stone hammers, metal chisels and hammers, and fire-setting were the main tools and techniques used in antiquity. Hushing and hydraulicking used the power of water to wash away waste material at some opencast sites (PLINY THE ELDER, *Natural History* 33.74–7). Antlers, BONE, wood and skins were used to make picks, scoops, shovels, sieves and sluices, and iron-headed battering rams might be used on occasion (*Natural History* 33.71). Ore was moved around on wooden sledges, in leather buckets, or in rush or wickerwork baskets.

The income generated from precious metal mines could be considerable. Athens, for example, built the fleet which defeated XERXES at SALAMIS from

MINES: Corinthian ceramic plaque showing underground mine.

SILVER mine revenue. PHILIP II transformed the Macedonian army with revenue from GOLD and silver mines which reputedly yielded to him 1,000 talents per year. Some 7 per cent of the total Roman state income under the Flavians came from the gold fields of north-west Spain alone.

Exhaustion of viable deposits, insurmountable technical problems within a mine, and changes in socio-economic conditions led to the downsizing and abandonment of workings. Laurion was worked from MYCENAEAN times, saw its hey-day in the 5th and 4th centuries BC and was worked only sporadically thereafter. The major mines of the Roman empire were at their peak in the 1st and 2nd centuries AD, production was disrupted in the 3rd, and was resumed at some sites on a reduced scale in the 4th.

It was not just metals that were mined. Laurion miners seeking silver ore would extract yellow ochre instead if they found it (VITRUVIUS 7.7.1). Extraction of earths such as ochre presented different problems to miners, as soft rocks of this kind are more liable to collapse and suffocate the workforce than are most metal-ore bearing rocks (THEOPHRASTOS, *On Stones* 52).

There was some extraction of coal in BRITAIN, the range and extent of which is currently under investigation. It was apparently carried out as opencast workings of outcrops, in areas where wood and charcoal were difficult to obtain in the quantities required by local consumers of these preferred fuels. (see also MINING) TER

See Edmondson, J. (1989) Mining in the later Roman empire and beyond: continuity or disruption?, *JRS* 79: 84–102; Shepherd, R. (1993) *Ancient Mining*.

mining The Greeks and Romans dug in the earth to find and extract metals, earths and stones. Many of the substances they sought, and the areas they exploited, were sought and exploited by succeeding generations, and a few are still in production today, e.g. Rio Tinto, about 50 km (30 miles) north-west of Sevilla, Spain. Many of their tools and techniques remained essentially unchanged until the 19th century, when technological improvements enabled cost-effective extraction of lower-grade ores in the same fields and reworking of ancient slags, as at LAURION, about 40 km (25 miles) south of Athens.

Mineral-rich areas typically contain a variety of useful minerals, not just one, and each mineral might be exploited for more than one type of product. For example, malachite (copper carbonate) could be transformed into metallic COPPER, or a green pigment, or an effective antibacterial wound dressing. This is reflected in language, for the English word 'metal' and Latin *metallum* are derived from the Greek verb *metallaô*, 'to search for other things'; but there is no ancient Greek equivalent for our noun 'metal'. The search for precious minerals took the ancients to some very remote and inhospitable areas, where extravagant and dangerous methods might be developed and deployed to find and extract, for example, GOLD (Pliny, *Natural History* 33.66–77). The ancient philosophical distinction between 'things mined' (*ta metalleuomena*) and 'things dug' (*ta orykta*), normally translated as 'metals' and 'fossils' respectively, does not correspond to modern classification of minerals, nor does it reflect the difference between opencast and deep mine extraction methods.

Besides metal ores, many special or rare earths were mined, such as cinnabar, a red sand, which provided the best scarlet colour in antiquity and was also the main ore for mercury, obtained from it by distillation. Others include sulphur and Pozzolana, a volcanic ash which transformed Roman CONCRETE into an immensely strong, waterproof and fire-resistant building material.

Mining was intrinsically dangerous and unpleasant, and SLAVES constituted the great majority of the labour force. Sources testify to the appalling conditions under which miners sometimes worked. A greater number worked above ground than below it, however, processing the mined material in light, space and fresh air.

Ancient surface works and debris offer a lasting impression of the scale and effort of ancient exploitation of the earth's mineral resources. With ancient technologies it was possible and cost-effective to extract silver, for example, from an ore in which it

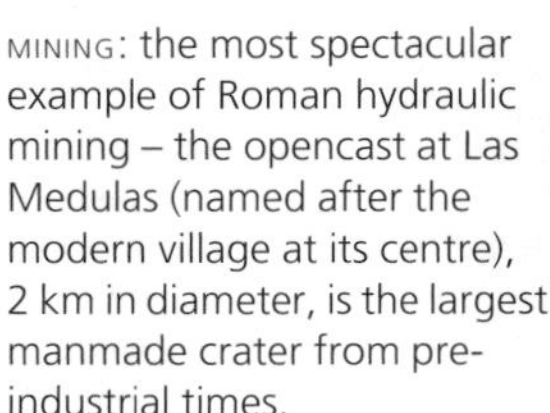

MINING: the most spectacular example of Roman hydraulic mining – the opencast at Las Medulas (named after the modern village at its centre), 2 km in diameter, is the largest manmade crater from pre-industrial times.

occurred at as little as 150 ppm. That is to say, if a million kilos of such an ore were mined and perfectly processed, the end product would be 150 kilos of silver and 999,850 kilos of waste. Even more material is required to process the ore (FUEL and LEAD). It is estimated that the IBERIANS, PHOENICIANS, Greeks and Romans who successively worked the Rio Tinto area produced some 7 million tonnes of slag through smelting about 2 million tonnes of argento-jarosite ore. (see also MINES) TER

See Craddock, P.T. (1995) *Early Metal Mining and Production*; Healy, J.F. (1978) *Mining and Metallurgy in the Greek and Roman World*.

Minoans The term 'Minoan', coined by Arthur Evans during his excavations at KNOSSOS, is used to describe the Bronze Age culture of CRETE. The name derives from the legendary king Minos of Knossos, whom Thucydides (1.4) among others regards as a historical figure. The 3rd millennium BC, or early Minoan period, is identified by the presence of large amounts of painted POTTERY including wares similar to those of the Cyclades. The mottled Vasiliki ware is particularly distinctive. Architectural development is seen at two sites in east Crete, Myrtos, a small VILLAGE, and Vasiliki, usually described as a VILLA. The Minoans of this period buried their dead in large communal TOMBS which were rectangular in plan in the north. The tombs in the Mesara plain were circular and may have been prototypes for later tholos tombs.

The greatest visible change at the start of the middle Minoan period (2000–1700 BC), are the PALACE complexes. Remains of early palaces are known from Knossos, Phaistos and Mallia. These are constructed of ashlar masonry and must have required trained workers to build. At Knossos and Phaistos they are associated with grain storage facilities. Similar techniques were also used for other buildings such as those in *Quartier Mu* at Mallia. At this time both pictographic and Linear A scripts come into use. A special group of scribes used this script for palace record-keeping. The pottery of the period includes the famous Kamares style, characteristic of the palace centres. During this period chamber tombs are first seen. These 'protopalatial' centres were destroyed, probably by EARTHQUAKE, c.1750 BC. They were rebuilt on a grander plan at the end of the period c.1700.

The main features of the 'neopalatial' period, 1700–1450, are the great palaces of the island. These multi-storied structures centred on a rectangular central court are found at Knossos, Phaistos, Mallia and Kato Zakro. All of the palaces have elaborate storerooms and residential quarters. Ashlar masonry, tapered columns and wooden beams are used throughout. Light-wells and drains made the residences habitable, while shrines were also situated in these buildings. These architectural elements are characteristic of Minoan buildings on Crete and also occur in sites like Akrotiri on THERA.

Minoan art of the period includes the frescoes that decorated the palace walls. Scenes of nature, processions, boxing and bull-leaping are common. The pottery of this late Minoan period has parallels with the frescoes: marine and vegetal motifs predominate on very well made wares. The palaces were centres of artistic and technical activities, and evidence of metal and GEM working shops have been found. The picture emerges of an élite which patronized art and dominated MANUFACTURE and overseas TRADE, all concentrated in the palaces. Art and information from Cretan peak sanctuaries show that Minoan religion stressed a female figure associated with a male attendant. BULL imagery is frequent, particularly the famous 'horns of consecration' used as architectural ornaments.

The destruction of the Minoan palaces is dated to the late 15th century BC. Palace Style pottery and a change in record-keeping from Linear A to Linear B (a script of early Greek rather than Cretan), along with the destruction of the palaces except for Knossos, indicate the conquest of Crete by mainlanders. Minoan civilization survives until the end of the Bronze Age, c.1050 BC, in a form strongly influenced by MYCENAEAN culture. AJ

See Cadogan, G. (1976) *Palaces of Minoan Crete*; Hamilakis, Y., ed. (2002) *Labyrinth Revisited: rethinking Minoan archaeology*; Higgins, R. (1967) *Minoan and Mycenaean Art*; Krzyszkowska, O. and Nixon, L., eds. (1983) *Minoan Society*; MacGillivray, J. A. (2000) *Minotaur: Sir Arthur Evans and the archaeology of the Minoan myth*.

Minucii A PLEBEIAN *gens* at Rome, with some reputation for dealing with food supply. Several members of this family became prominent in the Roman REPUBLIC. The most important was Marcus Minucius Rufus, CONSUL in 221 BC, appointed *magister equitum* of the DICTATOR Quintus Fabius Maximus Cunctator in 217. After he attacked HANNIBAL against the wishes of Fabius, he was made co-dictator or given the powers of a dictator, which justified his action after the fact. He died at CANNAE in 216. More than two centuries earlier, Lucius Minucius Esquilinus Augurinus in 439 BC dealt with a famine and an attempt at revolution by Spurius Maelius. A column and statue in his honour later stood at the Porta Trigemina or Minucia. Marcus Minucius Rufus, consul for 110 BC, built the Porticus Minucia in 106 to celebrate a TRIUMPH earned for his activities as proconsul in MACEDONIA. This Porticus was used for grain distributions beginning in the reign of the emperor CLAUDIUS, whose knowledge of early Roman history probably contributed to the choice of location.

Marcus Minucius Felix, an AFRICAN, bore the name but was probably not a descendant. He wrote the *Octavius*, a justification of CHRISTIANITY, c.AD 225. JV

Minucius Felix see CHRISTIANITY; MINUCII.

Mithradates (or Mithridates) VI Eupator Long-lived king of Pontos in northern ASIA Minor (r. c.120–65 BC). From the early 3rd century an Iranian dynasty of kings, aligned with the SELEUKIDS, had built up a kingdom in Pontos, where Greek cities and non-Greek villages coexisted. After seizing power in 120, Mithradates VI extended his power to the lands north of the Black sea. In the 100s and 90s he took over neighbouring regions of Asia Minor, leading to his first clash with the Romans, who supported the king of CAPPADOCIA. Defeating them four times in one year (89), he seized the whole of the Roman province of Asia, thus extending his power to the shores of the Aegean. He made himself notorious by killing the Roman commissioner, Manius Aquillius, by pouring molten gold down his throat. His image as a monstrous enemy of Rome was crystallized when, in 88, he persuaded Greek cites throughout Asia Minor to murder all resident Italians, with their relatives, on an appointed day. Tens of thousands certainly perished. The atrocity indicates the unpopularity of Rome and its representatives, especially among propertied Greeks on whom the cost of Roman administration chiefly fell. During the decades that followed, the cities paid the price many times over.

Although Mithradates' siege of RHODES was unsuccessful, many Greek states joined his cause. Surprisingly they included democratic Athens, which had been staunchly pro-Roman for a century. The Athenians elected a pro-Mithradates politician as general, perhaps wishing to ensure that the king spared their commercial interests in the Aegean and Black sea. Many were unhappy at this betrayal of Rome, but this did not spare the city. SULLA's two-year siege ended in spring 85 with massacres that merely added to the numbers already dead from starvation. The city was plundered, the democracy abolished. Soon afterwards, Sulla roundly defeated Mithradates in Boiotia but allowed him to keep his kingdom on payment of an indemnity and the surrender of nearly all his fleet.

Opposition to Mithradates grew in Asia Minor, and his rule grew crueller. On the other side, Sulla dealt harshly with cities in Asia that had supported Mithradates. A second treaty (also in 85) did not end the danger Mithradates posed to Rome; neither did the brief second Mithradatic war (83–81), fought in Asia Minor. Mithradates continued to make military preparations, and his attempt to seize Bithynia in 73 led to a third and final conflict lasting ten years. This had turned in favour of Rome by 71, yet Mithradates revived again, winning victories and recovering his homeland by 67. Finally, at Rome in 66, POMPEY (with CICERO's support) was awarded the prestigious and controversial command against Mithradates over the heads of existing commanders. With vast resources at his disposal, Pompey defeated Mithradates within months. The old king's final attempt to rebuild his forces in the Crimea was frustrated by his son Pharnakes, whereupon he ordered a Celtic officer to kill him with a sword. It was said he could not use POISON because, as a precaution against assassination, he had inured himself to its effects since his early days by continually taking small quantities.

Over the last three decades of his 57-year reign, Mithradates represented a serious threat to Roman power in the East. Resistance ended with him, and he remained a legendary enemy to whom superhuman capacities were attributed. DGJS

See Appian, book 12 (*Mithradatic War*); Justin, books 37–8; Cassius Dio, books 36–7; Cicero, *Pro Flacco*, *Pro Murena*, and *Pro lege Manilia* (*On the Command of Gnaeus Pompeius*); Plutarch, *Sulla*, *Lucullus*, and *Pompey*; Hind, J. G. F. (1994) Mithridates, in *CAH* 9, 129–64; McGing, B. (1986) *The Foreign Policy of Mithridates VI Eupator*.

Mithras and Mithraism A religion (and its principal deity) widespread in the Roman empire, particularly in the 2nd and 3rd centuries AD. The name Mithras and some aspects of the cult (e.g. the use of some Persian words in ritual) suggest a connection with the Iranian deity Mitra, associated with the sun, with the struggle against darkness and evil and with oaths and contracts.

Much past scholarship, notably the work of Franz Cumont, regarded Roman Mithraism as a religion that had spread from Iran across the Eastern Roman empire and that, as a consequence, owed much to Iranian antecedents in its theology and ritual. Recent scholarship tends to the view that Roman Mithraism was an independent development within the multicultural context of the Roman empire, drawing, perhaps superficially, on the vocabulary of the Iranian cult. Central features of the Roman cult, such as its exclusiveness and the bull-slaying iconography, are not found in the Iranian version. There is relatively little evidence of the worship of Mithras in the Eastern provinces, diminishing the plausibility of transmission from the East (though the famous Mithraeum at DURA EUROPUS is a well documented example, and another has been discovered recently near Apameia in Syria). Most evidence comes from ITALY and the Balkan provinces, and the cosmopolitan religious environments of ROME and OSTIA may have seen the initial development of Mithraism in Roman form in the later 1st century AD. However, recent arguments for Cappadocian origins are also attractive.

Mithraism was a MYSTERY RELIGION with initiation by secret ritual. Some light is shed on this and other ritual aspects of the religion by ancient literary sources (some CHRISTIAN and hostile) but ARCHAEOLOGY, ART and inscriptions provide the best evidence. Mithraic meeting-places (*mithraea*) tend to be relatively small and numerous in major urban centres; Ostia had at least 17. The *mithraea* are often cave-like and in some inscriptions (especially from Italy) they are described as *spelaea* ('caves'). They frequently have fixed benches for ritual meals and other furnishings such as altars and cult images (mostly relief SCULPTURE). Ritual and theology may vary from one small community of worshippers to another. Iconography shows variation, but the central image of Mithras slaying a BULL recurs, along with other elements which have been used in more or less successful attempts to reconstruct Mithraic theology (the god's birth from a rock, Mithras firing an arrow at a rock which spouts water, ASTROLOGICAL images, and recurring figures such as the torch-bearers Cautes and Cautopates).

Adherents of Mithras were exclusively male and mostly from lower down the Roman social spectrum. Soldiers are particularly well represented and may have been responsible for much of Mithraism's spread. However, minor administrative officials, FREEDMEN and SLAVES are also prominent. The association of the original Iranian deity with oaths and contracts may have been appropriate to individuals whose lives predisposed them to loyalty and obedience. SENATORIAL adherents are only found in a few very late inscriptions of the later 4th-century PAGAN revival in Rome. Mithraism was never a Roman official state cult, but was tolerated, if not actively encouraged. Acceptance was made easier by the fact that Mithras often was identified with SOL INVICTUS ('the Unconquered Sun'), a recipient of official cult from the Severan period onwards. NDP

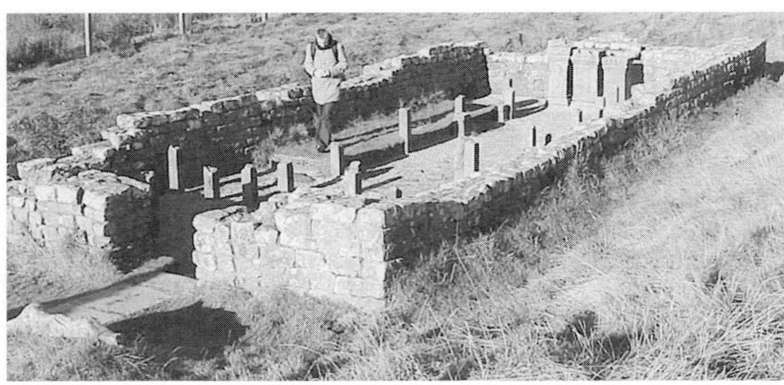

Mithras and Mithraism: (a) view of the temple (Mithraeum) at Carrawburgh on Hadrian's wall.

Mithras and Mithraism: (b) reconstruction drawing of the interior of the Mithraeum at Carnuntum, showing subterranean setting, raised benches for devotees and positions of statues and relief sculpture associated with the cult.

See Beck, R. (1988) The Mysteries of Mithras: a new account of the Genesis, *JRS* 88: 115–28; Clauss, M. (2000) *The Roman Cult of Mithras*, trs. R. Gordon.

 gods and goddesses: (b).

mna see *mina*.

modes of production A technical term originating within Marxist theory and history. The concept refers to the prevailing form of labour relation through which food and other material goods are produced. In the theory's crudest form (derived from Engels' interpretation of Marx rather than Marx himself) all human history is seen as a succession of stages characterized by the prevailing mode of production. Each stage yields to a higher, that is more productive, stage as a result of class struggles. More sophisticated versions of the theory, also Marxist in orientation, note that in all human societies above the most economically primitive level more than one mode of production co-exists. They prefer therefore to speak of 'social formations', which are the resultant of this productive co-existence.

In Marxist historiography Greece and Rome are commonly understood to have been slave societies, characterized by a mode of production in which exploited slave labour yields the greatest quantity of 'surplus value' – that portion of the value created by the slaves' labour which the slave owners appropriate without giving back to the slaves an equivalent economic or non-economic return. However, slavery on this conception need not account for either the majority of labourers or the majority of the total productive output. Peasant farmers may well have been responsible for the larger part of the value produced in the society overall. Yet the chief form in which surplus value was extracted was slavery (in its various forms), and it was thus slavery that was the basis for the leisure and power of the dominant social class.

Considerable disagreement remains over just when and how slavery took hold in earnest as the primary mode of production for large landowners in classical antiquity, and – at the other end of the chronological spectrum – over when and how it was superseded by feudal labour relations. Within that time-span, too, important differences may be noted between Greece and Rome, for example, regarding the extent of slave labour in agriculture as opposed to household services. Many questions in this sensitive area remain open and keenly debated. (see also agriculture; class; economy; Marxism; peasants; slavery) pac

Momigliano, A. D. see biography and biographers; historians and historiography, modern.

Mommsen, T. see HISTORIANS AND HISTORIOGRAPHY, MODERN.

monasteries By the 3rd century AD, some CHRISTIANS had chosen to pursue spiritual life in solitude, living austerely as HERMITS (monks, anchorites) particularly in the semi-desert areas of Palestine, SYRIA and Egypt. At the start of the 4th century St ANTHONY of Egypt devised the *laura*, a loose association of hermits who would leave their huts or caves at intervals and gather for communal acts of worship. About a century later, St Euthymios brought a similar development to Palestine. Another monastic pattern is evident by the mid-4th century, when St Pachomios in Egypt and St BASIL in ANATOLIA established Coenobitic monasteries, wherein monks (or nuns, in separate establishments) gave up personal property and lived together, following a prescribed routine of spiritual and domestic life. This required ARCHITECTURE consisting typically of a walled enclosure for rooms serving domestic purposes (cells, storerooms, washing facilities, WORKSHOPS and a refectory for communal meals) as well as the freestanding main CHURCH (*katholikon*). The earliest such monasteries were in the remote areas favoured by hermits, but by the 5th century they are found in rural areas throughout the Byzantine empire and also within towns. Coenobitic monasticism eventually became the norm, often accommodating individuals drawn to the hermit life by allowing them to live in caves or huts apart from the monastic complex. Most monasteries depended for their income on the donations (particularly of land) of patrons, often not themselves members of the monastic community. (see also ASCETICISM) LR

See Chitty, D. J. (1966) *The Desert a City*; Walters, C. C. (1974) *Monastic Archaeology in Egypt*.

money In the early classical world, barter prevailed. Greek authors claimed their SILVER currency was derived from exchange based on iron spits. Roman authors stressed the use of CATTLE (*pecora*, the origin of *pecunia*, 'money') and bronze ingots (*aes rude*). The Greeks learned to coin money from the LYDIANS, who had minted ELECTRUM coins in the late 7th century BC. In the 6th century, Greek cities adopted SILVER currency as the medium of exchange by striking denominations based on a drachma (*drachmê*). In the 5th century, the Athenians imposed their currency and so monetized AEGEAN markets. SICILIAN Greeks devised fiduciary bronze COINAGES. ALEXANDER the Great (336–323 BC) and the hellenistic kings extended the use of coined money (struck in GOLD, silver and COPPER) across the Near East.

In 310 BC the Roman REPUBLIC struck its first silver coins, inspired from Greek prototypes, to be used in tandem with cast Italic bronze coins. Rome's silver *denarius* became the TRADE coin of the MEDITERRANEAN world in the 2nd century BC. AUGUSTUS (27 BC–AD 14) added a gold denomination, the *aureus*, against which the *denarius* and its base metal fractions were struck. After 235, the imperial government met rising fiscal obligations by debasing the silver coinage into a fiduciary currency of billon (an alloy of 25 per cent or less silver), and so compromised markets and exchange rates. Currency reforms between DIOCLETIAN (284–305) and Anastasius I (491–518) built a new currency based on the gold *solidus* and so assured the monetary stability of the Byzantine empire. KH

 COINAGE (tables).

money supply

Between 700 and 300 BC, the supply of specie in the Greek world expanded due to mining and commerce. But, as the SOLONIAN property classifications at Athens indicate, negotiable commodities (grain, OIL and WINE) were reckoned as part of the money supply. Furthermore, credit doubled or tripled the money supply.

The best indications of money supply are the revenues and expenditures of Athens. In 432 BC Athens had reserves in GOLD and SILVER totalling 9,000 talents or the equivalent of 54 million drachmas. The drachma was reckoned as a HOPLITE's daily wage; a third of this sum (2 *obols*) as daily subsistence. Athens spent annually 800 talents (4.8 million drachmas) on the fleet. In 483–410 BC Athens built 1,500 TRIREMES at a price of 15,000 talents (90 million drachmas). Known building costs of 447–425 BC totalled 8,000 talents (48 million drachmas). Such expenditures were premised on the widespread availability of money. In the hellenistic age, the money supply expanded dramatically. ALEXANDER the Great is reported to have captured Persian reserves totalling 216,500 talents (over 1.2 billion drachmas), 24 times the Athenian reserve.

Numismatists have employed statistical formulas to estimate the output of COINAGES based on die studies, but there is little agreement on the number of coins produced from a set of ancient dies (with estimates ranging from 10,000 to 40,000). Save for coinages of limited size, it is difficult to count the number of dies employed so that the great coinages indicative of money supply are beyond reckoning. KH

The money supply effectively consisted of the coin in circulation. There was no paper money, and Roman credit is most naturally understood as a way of making the COINAGE work harder, rather than as a separate element in the money supply. In terms of value, as opposed to numbers, the precious metal coinage formed the most important component of the money supply. From the time of the second PUNIC WAR SILVER was struck in substantial quantities, whereas GOLD was significant only from 46 BC onwards. Base metal coinages were important for the way in which coinage was used from day to day, but counted for less in terms of total value.

No mint records survive, let alone any estimate of the total volume of coinage in circulation at any one time. An estimate of the size of a particular issue of coins may be based on the original number of dies used to strike it, which may itself be extrapolated from the number of dies observed by modern study. Hoards give some idea of the range of issues available at the time they were deposited, and also of the extent to which earlier issues had already been lost from circulation by then. Thus die-studies and hoards offer a basis from which to quantify the money supply. Scholarly opinion is divided about the accuracy and usefulness of the results of such calculations.

Regardless of the merits of absolute quantification, the concept of the money supply has proved useful in a number of ways. It has directed attention to important questions such as the sources and patterns of use of the metals for coining, and the scale of the export of the coin. It has also been a key component in economic analyses, for example, of the development of TRADE in the early empire, and of the inflation which affected the Roman empire from the later 3rd century AD onwards. CH

See Duncan-Jones, R. (1994) *Money and Government in the Roman Empire*; Howgego, C. (1992) The supply and use of money in the Roman world, 200 BC to AD 300, *JRS* 82: 1–31.

money-lending Moneychangers, who operated banks or 'tables' (the Greek for 'table' is *trapeza*, the Latin *mensa*) and customarily leased their rights from the governing authorities, offered credit and LOANS in the ancient world. In the late archaic and classical periods, the range and complexity of lending and credit increased with rising commerce and civic activities, notably building programmes and the construction of fleets. Interest rates on loans fluctuated according to the season and the risk of investment, but rates of 8–12 per cent were the norm of most short-term loans from the late classical to early Roman imperial ages. Money-lending remained a bilateral agreement that stipulated repayment of the principal and interest by the borrower within a fixed period. Bills of exchange fundamental to modern BANKING were never devised.

In the 2nd century BC Rome emerged as the banking centre of the MEDITERRANEAN economy. Companies (*societates*) which bid on state contracts also lent money to provincials at scandalously high interest rates. The ensuing abuses contributed to anti-Roman sentiment. In 89 BC, the Greeks of Asia welcomed MITHRADATES VI as their liberator from Roman moneylenders and tax farmers.

At Rome, money-lending bankers (*argentarii*) distinct from the humble moneychangers (*nummularii*) emerged in the 2nd and 1st centuries BC. They engaged in deposit and loans for speculation in commodity markets or government contracts. The range and scale of such activities are revealed by the archive of Marcus Caecilius Iucundus, recovered at POMPEII. In the imperial age, money-lending and stable interest rates contributed to the prosperity of cities and could endow many of their activities and social amenities. KH

Monica c.AD 331–87 Mother of AUGUSTINE (1), of North AFRICAN origin. Monica is known only from the writings of her son and thus the portrait presented, while full of detail, is highly subjective. She was a CHRISTIAN married to the PAGAN Patricius. She appears to have been an influential woman, both in terms of dealing with her husband's abuse and in persistently caring for her son's spiritual welfare, especially when he flirted with MANICHAEISM. It may be the focus of Monica, or the self-absorption of her son, but his two siblings seem to feature little in their mother's life. Despite Augustine's attempt to avoid it at the age of 28, Monica followed him first to Rome in 383, thence to MILAN, and was instrumental in Augustine's conversion and baptism by AMBROSE. She was also part of the community of young men who retired to Cassiciacum after that conversion to study spiritual matters. Here she played the role of the uneducated Christian whose faith revealed knowledge more valuable than that of the philosophers. At OSTIA, mother and son shared an emotional and mystical conversation on the life of the blessed just before she died. MEH

See Augustine, *Confessions*, trs. H. Chadwick (1991); Atkinson, C.W. (1985) 'Your servant, my mother': the figure of Monica in the ideology of Christian motherhood, in C. Atkinson et al., eds., *Immaculate and Powerful* 139–72; Brown, P. (1969) *Augustine of Hippo*.

monotheism Belief in a single deity. One of the earliest references to the Jewish GOD in classical literature is THEOPHRASTOS' (372–288/7 BC) recognition of Jewish conversation about 'the deity' (*to theion*) (Diodorus Siculus 40.3.1–3), which implies Theophrastos' identification of the Jewish god with the one highest being of the PRESOCRATICS. It is not surprising that a PHILOSOPHER identified such monotheism, for ancient monotheism was not as exclusivist as is often thought, and was based more on historical and political foundations than philosophical. Jewish monotheism has counterparts in Babylonian and Greek RELIGION, where it never became such an issue. As late as the 6th century, portions of the book Isaiah were championing monotheism but in the real political terms of an anti-BABYLON stance, hence anti-Babylonian gods. The origins of Israelite religion lie in the pantheons of the Canaanite religions; over the course of centuries, perhaps from the 9th to the 6th centuries BC, one God came to dominance. The many descriptions and titles for the Jewish God in the OLD TESTAMENT probably reflect older cultic traditions. In the Greco-Roman period there was still no consistency. The literature reflects preferences for different divine titles (e.g. god most high, god of heaven). The existence of divine intermediaries or angels, a belief in a spirit world, and the emphasis upon the figure of Wisdom and the *logos* suggest an accommodation towards a polytheistic understanding. In JUDAISM such figures were never allowed to be superior to God. Although some Jewish and, later, CHRISTIAN refusal to recognize local shrines did take place, there is evidence of Jews making votive offerings to other gods (e.g. to PAN in Upper Egypt), and many Jews and Christians were probably in practice less exclusivist than the literature sometimes implies. Much late antique philosophy, especially NEOPLATONISM, was also basically monotheistic while allowing for lower level divinities. JKA

See Grabbe, L. L. (2000) *Judaic Religion in the Second Temple Period*.

Mons Claudianus Roman QUARRY in the eastern desert of Egypt, possibly linked administratively to nearby Mons Porphyrites, and the source of the grey granite or MARBLE used in imperial building projects in Rome, most importantly the monolithic columns of the PANTHEON porch. Quarrying took place from the early imperial period to at least the reign of CARACALLA, but most intensively during the reigns of TRAJAN and HADRIAN. Major EXCAVATION and survey carried out from 1987 to 1993 on the Roman FORT and quarry fields has yielded considerable knowledge of the techniques used in quarrying and the TRANSPORT of products, as well as the lifestyle of the inhabitants. Of crucial importance is the discovery of some 9,000 ostraca, potsherds on which writing has been preserved. These documents, written in Greek, preserve valuable information on the day-to-day running of the quarries and the nature of the resident garrison, and supplement the archaeological evidence (largely of flora and fauna, but including WINE AMPHORAS) for the diet and lifestyle of the inhabitants. This has helped to overturn the picture of life in the quarry settlements painted by literary evidence. Mons Claudianus was not worked by SLAVES, but rather by well-paid, skilled workers (possibly paid on an empire-wide scale), who, along with the soldiers of the garrison, enjoyed a rich and varied diet of foods and wines, often imported from long distances. A complex system of supply connected Mons Claudianus to the Red sea and the NILE valley; this also supported the transport of quarry products to the Nile, and thence to Rome. CEPA

See Maxfield, V. (1999) Stone quarrying in the Eastern Desert with particular reference to Mons Claudianus and Mons Porphyrites, in Mattingly and Salmon, *Economies beyond Agriculture* 143–70; Peacock, D. P. S. and Maxfield, V. (1997) *Survey and Excavation at Mons Claudianus*, vol. 1: *Topography and Quarries*.

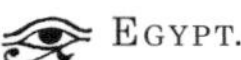 EGYPT.

Mons Graupius Battle between a Roman army commanded by governor AGRICOLA and a confederacy of Caledonian tribes at the 'Graupian Mount' in the Highlands of Scotland in the late summer of AD 83 (or 84). The exact location of the battle is unknown, and various locations have been suggested along the eastern flanks of the Highlands between the estuary of the Tay and the Moray firth. The overwhelming victory gained by the Roman forces at Mons Graupius was the culminating point of Agricola's conquest of northern Britain. The battle 'at the very limit of the natural world' forms the dramatic climax of the *Agricola* of TACITUS. His account is notable for the speech ascribed to the Caledonian leader, Calgacus: 'Robbery, butchery, rapine, the liars call empire; they create a desert and call it peace' (ch. 30).

The battle was fought by Gallic, German and British auxiliaries on the Roman side without the active participation of the legionaries. The occupation of Mons Graupius by the Caledonian force ensured a stiff fight for the advancing Roman forces. An attempted flanking movement by the Caledonians was met by a counter-attack by the Roman cavalry, resulting in massive slaughter. Tacitus estimates 10,000 Caledonian dead as against 360 of the Romans. Although this victory seemed to herald the complete conquest of Britain, a change in policy led rather to a progressive disengagement from Scotland soon afterwards. By the beginning of the 2nd century, Roman forces had retreated to the Tyne–Solway line. CMF

See Tacitus, *Agricola*; Maxwell, G. (1990) *A Battle Lost*.

Mons Porphyrites see MONS CLAUDIANUS; TRADE, ROMAN.

Montanism see CHURCH COUNCILS; TERTULLIAN.

Monte Testaccio The Italian name for a literal mountain of potsherds (50 m high, 1 km in circumference) that dominated the main HARBOUR quarter of the city of Rome. It is made up almost entirely of fragments of AMPHORAS used in the transport of OLIVE OIL as part of the FOOD SUPPLY (*annona*) of the city. Evidently it represents the result of the deliberate discarding, over a period of c.250 years, of c.50–70 million amphoras after their contents were transferred into larger storage receptacles in the main oil WAREHOUSE complex (the *Horrea Galbana*). Liberal sprinklings of LIME were used to keep the stench down. The bulk of the pottery mountain comprises the Dressel 20 amphora type from Baetica (southern Spain), many of which were stamped and adorned with painted inscriptions (*tituli picti*) which give details of aspects of the MANUFACTURE of the amphoras and the production and TRANSPORT of the oil. These provide some of the most remarkable data on the logistics of the imperial FOOD SUPPLY system, on the measures taken by the state to combat fraud and on the scale of the Roman ECONOMY. By the 3rd century, there was an increasing component of AFRICAN oil amphoras being dumped, from important oil exporting cities like LEPCIS MAGNA and LEPTIMINUS. (see also *INSTRUMENTUM DOMESTICUM*) DJM

MONTE TESTACCIO: the hill of broken potsherds.

See Mattingly, D. J. and Aldrete, G. (2000) The feeding of imperial Rome, in J. Coulston and H. Dodge, eds., *Ancient Rome* 142–65; Rodriguez-Almeida, E. (1984) *Il Monte Testaccio*.

 *INSTRUMENTUM DOMESTICUM*.

monumentality see ARCHITECTURE; TEMPLES.

moon The moon, the second brightest celestial object after the SUN, lights up the night sky, and the cycle of its phases, the 'synodic month' of 29.5 days, is one of the most obvious of the celestial cycles. Many cities in classical Greece employed CALENDARS based upon the lunar phase cycle. The appearance of the first sliver of the new moon in the evening sky marked the beginning of a new month. The Greeks divided the month into three periods of ten days known as 'decades', whereas the Romans used a division into three non-equal parts marked by the calends, nones and ides (*kalendae*, *nonae* and *idus*).

Lunar calendars must be kept in step with the solar year by observing seasonally correlated events, whether terrestrial or ASTRONOMICAL, and occasionally adding or missing out months as required – a process known as intercalation. However, following the discovery of the Metonic cycle in the 5th century BC, such empirical practices could be replaced by a set of mechanical rules. Meton's scheme did not catch on everywhere, and more crude and subjective schemes of intercalation persisted in the Roman world until they were eventually superseded in the Roman world by the solar-based Julian calendar. Nonetheless, Meton's discovery is a development that epitomizes the move towards a logical and MATHEMATICAL way of understanding nature, and to an abstract concept of time, that developed in ancient Greece and prevails in the Western world today. CLNR

 ZODIAC: (a).

Moors (Mauri) see AFRICA AND AFRICANS; HISPANIA.

morality Denotes a mode of behaviour or character that conforms with societal expectations of what is good or right. In HOMERIC Greece, the notion of morality revolves around honour. Individuals of WEALTH and high birth acted in such a way so as not to bring shame or failure (*aischron*) upon themselves or upon their families, not according to what was morally right. For these men, only publicized success in their endeavours mattered, not good intentions. For example, if a battle was lost it was to no avail to point out that someone 'did the best they could' (*Iliad* 13.222). This also coheres with the idea that a Homeric character behaves in accordance with what is morally right precisely because he is concerned more with how he appears to others, not because of any abstract concept of morality itself.

In the classical period issues concerning morality mainly appear in ETHICAL or moral philosophical doctrines, especially those of PLATO and ARISTOTLE. Here, discussions of moral goodness, duties, obligations and values pervade. Most importantly in these discussions, the question arises whether there is any reason to be moral at all. For example, Plato in his *Republic* equated 'the good' with elements of the SOUL, elements that also appear in society. The soul embodies three main virtues: wisdom (corresponding to the ruling part of the soul), courage (corresponding to the spirit or the enforcing part of the soul) and moderation (corresponding to appetite or productive part of the soul). JUSTICE occurs only when the parts of the soul are in harmony with each other. This means that when individuals act in accordance with reason, they subsequently do what is right with respect to goodness, or excellence (*aretê*).

In contrast, certain SOPHISTS, like PROTAGORAS, believed that virtue or excellence is not innate but rather is something that could be taught to an individual. For Aristotle, the Doctrine of the Mean serves as a guideline for moral behaviour in that individuals should avoid excess and paucity (*Nicomachean Ethics* 2.2). Other sources that pertain especially to morality occur in epitaphs, speeches and plays. Unlike the Romans, the Greeks did not look to their distant past to set precedents for moral behaviour.

The Romans did look back in time for models of exemplary behaviour. Morality was tied to the *mos maiorum* or customs or morals of the ancestors. As opposed to looking at Greek philosophical texts for models of appropriate behaviour, the Romans looked to figures in their mythological or historical past. Historical sources, for instance, refer to *exempla*, images that offer the reader a precedent-setting pattern for moral behaviour. One such instance appears in the account of LUCRETIA, who was known for beauty and domestic ability. At Livy 1.58 the virtuous Lucretia is an *exemplum* of the model Roman wife, as she is depicted spinning, an action symbolic of her role in the HOUSEHOLD and of her chastity. Subsequently, by taking her own life after Sextus TARQUINIUS rapes her, she embodies chastity (*pudicitia*), the idea of how adulterous women should not behave. Morality, manifest in terms such as VIRTUE (*virtus*) and piety (*pietas*), went hand in hand with the duties found in the Roman state (*res Romana*) that wealthy, freeborn males had to perform. For example, one of the moral duties of the citizen was to marry. Before the 2nd century AD, the moral code allowed young men to engage in SEXUAL activities with PROSTITUTES or mistresses before they married. A moral revival of sorts is evident in the age of AUGUSTUS. The emperor sought to revitalize the moral environment by curbing the sexual behaviour of the upper classes. The *lex Papia Poppaea*, the result of two legislations, one in 18 BC, the other in AD 9, penalized individuals who did not beget children, by denying the right to INHERITANCES; at the same time the law made provisions for those who did. FREEDWOMEN gained more opportunities for marriage outside their social standing, with the exception of marriage to SENATORS. In keeping with moral issues, freeborn males were prevented from marrying women with disreputable characters; these included PROSTITUTES, MIMES and adultresses. Augustus also promulgated laws on ADULTERY, HOMOSEXUALITY and seduction in the *lex Iulia de adulteriis* of 18 BC. Other emperors, such as DOMITIAN, sought to maintain some degree of moral order by forcing men to marry their mistresses and to prevent POETS from using obscenities in their works. After the 2nd century AD, an effort was made to curtail the sexual pursuits of young male Romans prior to marriage. Moreover with the popularity of STOICISM, marriage became more than just civic duty. Under Stoic precepts married couples were obligated to be dutiful companions to one another. Emperors in the 3rd and 4th centuries also took part in enforcing morality by decrees. The SEVERI, for example, legislated against abortion and made it illegal for husbands to have adulterous affairs. In the late antique period JEWISH and CHRISTIAN morals began to permeate Roman culture. The various systems of morality associated with these religions appealed particularly to the lower classes. LAH

See Boer, W. Den (1979) *Private Morality in Greece and Rome*; Dover, K. J. (1974) *Greek Popular Morality in the time of Plato and Aristotle*; Edwards, C. (1993) *The Politics of Immorality in Ancient Rome*; Fantham, E. et al., eds. (1994) *Women in the Classical World*; Ferguson, J. (1958) *Moral Values in the Ancient World*; Veyne, P., ed. (1987) *A History of Private Life*.

mosaics Although the origin of the word 'mosaic' is uncertain, the term has come to mean a design

MOSAICS: (a) pebble mosaic from Corinth, 3rd century BC.

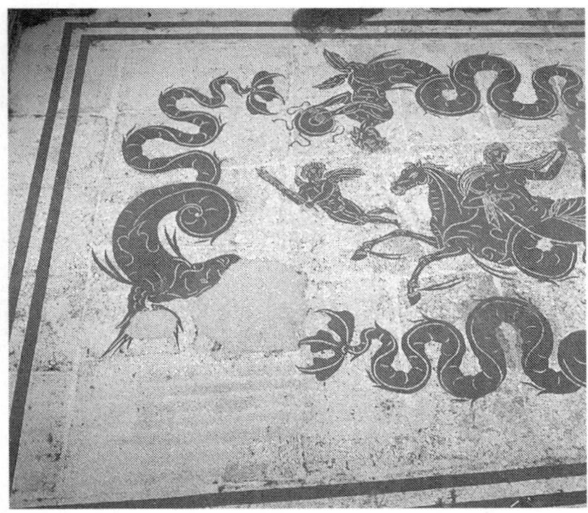

MOSAICS: (b) black and white mosaic with nautical theme from baths of Neptune in Ostia, 2nd century AD.

constructed from small pieces of a variety of man-made and natural substances, held together with some form of mortar. Mosaics may decorate floors, walls or ceilings, and they usually form an integral feature of their ARCHITECTURAL context.

The earliest mosaics were probably the Greek pebble pavements, some of which date before the mid-1st millennium BC. These plain floors soon came to include simple geometric and floral ornaments, which were usually executed in black and white. By the late 5th century BC the first figural mosaics appear, with light figures on a dark ground, showing affinities with Greek VASE-PAINTING. Examples of these early figural mosaics have been found at Olynthos, Pella and elsewhere in northern Greece. The 4th-century BC temple of ZEUS at OLYMPIA seems to have been the focus of a further innovation in mosaic art. The mosaic at this TEMPLE had stones which were cut in order to fit them more closely together. These cut stones were the first *tesserae*, and this development was crucial for the later history of mosaic art. The cutting of stones meant that they could be ground in order to bring out their various colours, and this enabled mosaicists to create polychrome compositions. Excellent examples of these early polychrome mosaics have been discovered in HOUSES on the island of DELOS. These mosaics date from the first half of the 2nd century BC and represent the emergence of a hellenistic style. The mosaics commonly include large areas of relatively coarse decoration, and smaller areas with elaborate polychrome pictures known as *emblemata* ('inserts').

The art of mosaic spread from the eastern MEDITERRANEAN to Rome as part of a general expansion of hellenistic luxury goods. An example of this hellenistic style in a Roman context is the ALEXANDER mosaic found at the House of the Faun in POMPEII, and dating from the late 2nd century BC. This is an example of a highly elaborate and luxurious mosaic, with an extremely large and detailed *emblema*. The majority of mosaics, however, were much simpler, with little difference in quality between the *emblema* and the surrounding ornamental zones.

By the 1st century BC, mosaic had become extremely popular as a floor covering in Italy, and there was a demand for less expensive designs. This resulted in the increased popularity of black and white designs. Dramatic lines and figures characterized this particularly Roman form of mosaic art. Black and white mosaics retained their popularity throughout Italy until the 3rd century, though polychrome mosaics still appeared in luxury dwellings, such as HADRIAN'S VILLA at TIVOLI. Although black and white forms were predominant in Italy, this was not the case in other PROVINCES. In Roman BRITAIN, for example, mosaics were usually polychrome, using local materials for *tesserae*. By the 3rd and 4th centuries mosaic was widespread throughout the empire, and provinces such as Britain, France, Spain and North AFRICA are rich with examples. In a number of cases there is evidence for local schools of mosaicists, often producing mosaics of a very high standard of workmanship.

Throughout the history of the art form, mosaics have been integral to the design and use of the architecture of which they were a part. In particular, the subject matter of mosaics was often carefully chosen in order to suit the functions of various rooms within both public and private buildings. At a simple level, certain subjects were considered appropriate for buildings or rooms with specific functions. For example, BATHS in Rome and Pompeii were decorated with aquatic scenes. Geometric designs were also often carefully positioned in order to enhance architectural design and to complement other forms of interior decor. Geometric patterns could effectively draw attention to specific architectural features, and could also help to encourage certain patterns of movement within a building. At a more sophisticated level, mosaics could include quite complex figural scenes. The rich *emblema* designs, such as the Alexander mosaic, were placed in important reception and dining areas, and could include scenes from MYTHOLOGY or representations of prestigious activities such as HUNTING. Mosaics helped to define certain areas of buildings as prestigious, and could convey important messages about the wealth and status of the owner.

By the 4th century, there are many examples of sophisticated compositions throughout the provinces. In Britain, a number of mosaics with mythological scenes have been discovered in 4th-century villas.

MOSAICS: (c) polychrome geometric mosaics from house at Thuburbo Maius, Tunisia.

MOSAICS: (d) polychrome figural mosaic from Piazza Armerina in Sicily, 4th century AD.

In North Africa, numerous impressive mosaics have survived, including scenes of hunting, the CIRCUS and the AMPHITHEATRE. The villa at Piazza Armerina in SICILY has a particularly extensive range of pavements, ranging from striking mythological compositions to hunting scenes and representations of everyday activities. The mosaics were thoroughly integrated within their architectural setting, and communicated powerful social messages both to members of the HOUSEHOLD and to visitors to the villa. It is this rich repertoire of 4th-century mosaic art that set the stage for further developments in the 5th century and beyond. By the early medieval period mosaic was exploited for the decoration of Christian CHURCHES, and glittering wall and ceiling mosaics were skilfully employed to create divine spaces.

In all periods, mosaics must be seen as integral to their architectural setting, as defining and enhancing space. In order to understand the significance of their imagery it is clearly necessary to consider the architectural and social context of which they were such an integral part. SAS

See Dunbabin, K. M. D. (1999) *Mosaics of the Greek and Roman Worlds.*

ANIMALS; BIRDS: (a); VILLAS: (a).

Moschos see LYRIC POETRY, GREEK; PASTORAL POETRY.

mother goddesses General designation for a type of deity worshipped throughout the MEDITERRANEAN world. Mother goddesses are associated with the fertility of plants and ANIMALS and, less commonly, the nurture of infants. They are thought to have been pervasive throughout the ancient Near East, as well as in the MINOAN and MYCENAEAN worlds (Gimbutas). Their influence is further supposed to underlie the representations of many of the goddesses of Greece and Rome such as Gaia, Rhea, Hekate, DEMETER (CERES) with her daughter Kore or Persephone (Proserpina), HERA (JUNO) and Bellona. Of the Olympians, the goddess APHRODITE is the most representative figure. Not only do her explicit associations with SEXUALITY and fertility suggest this connection, but also her involvement in myth and ritual with the dying-and-rising god Adonis. The myth relates that Adonis, the child of the incestuous union between Myrrha and her father Cinyras, becomes Aphrodite's lover. Warned by her not to go HUNTING, he disobeys and is gored in the groin by a wild boar. He dies and, from his blood, flowers arise. The features of Adonis' life and death formed the basis of the Adoneia rituals, where quick-growing plants were planted in potsherds on the rooftops. When the green plants withered in the sun, the women lamented the passing of Adonis. These myths and rituals are characteristic in their association of a mother goddess with a younger male consort who dies at a young age and is mourned by her, a pattern also evident in the accounts of the PHRYGIAN goddess CYBELE and in the Near Eastern figures of Ishtar and Tammuz.

In addition to the myths associated with mother goddesses, there are extensive material remains of female figurines that have been interpreted as various types of mother goddess. Dating from as early as the Neolithic period, these figures have been excavated throughout the Mediterranean basin and in northern Europe. Their frequency and their apparent emphasis on the female sexual organs have led some scholars to argue that they are representations of a 'great' goddess who was the embodiment of the processes of life, death and rebirth. This supposition has, in turn, given rise to the view that many of these ancient societies were once dominated by women, MATRIARCHATES that only slowly gave way to the dominance of males and to the dominion of male sky gods (Gimbutas).

As the above examples suggest, the designation 'mother goddess' is not without its usefulness. Nevertheless, recent critical discussion has begun to question the assumptions about the pervasiveness and importance of mother goddess figures in the ancient Mediterranean. Proponents of a universal 'great' goddess have been faulted for misreading the material evidence and for an uncritical use of comparative sources (Roller). They have, in addition, been criticized for inventing matriarchal myths of their own (Loraux). JRCC

See Gimbutas, M. (1989) *The Language of the Goddess*; Loraux, N. (1992) What is a goddess?, in P. Schmitt Pantel, *A History of Women* 11–44; Roller, L. (1998) *The Mother of the Gods*.

motion In Greek thought motion (i.e. locomotion, or change of place) was first analysed by ZENO THE ELEATIC, who supported PARMENIDES' theory of unchanging being by arguing that motion was impossible. Previously motion was assumed to be uncaused, or to be caused by a dominant mover (e.g. Anaxagoras' 'Mind'). PLATO framed later debate by arguing that something in motion was either self-moving or moved by something external. ARISTOTLE reacted by positing an 'unmoved mover' (an external mover that was not self-moved) as a divine source of motion in an eternal universe, leaving self-motion (the circular motions of the *aithêr* of the heavens; the rectilinear motion of other elements) ultimately dependent on this stable source. In hellenistic philosophy, the STOICS attributed purposive self-motion to their primal matter (Fire) to explain a cyclical repetition of the universe, while the EPICUREANS posited ATOMS falling in space, and combining through an unpredictable movement (a 'swerve') that was neither self-motion nor externally imposed. Both schools also confronted the thorny problem of whether human action, which, if free, should involve self-motion, was determined by an external cause. John Philoponus (6th century AD) analysed the motion of projectiles as the result of an inherent motion (impetus) derived from the mover. Ancient theories of motion can be contrasted with Newton's concept of inertia, i.e. motion as continuous unless impeded – a theory that eliminates the search for a mover entirely. RBT

See Gill, M. L. and Lennox, J. G. (1994) *Self-motion*; Sorabji, R. (1988) *Matter, Space, and Motion*.

Motya (mod. Mozia) An island of c.45 ha (111 acres) just off the west coast of SICILY, to which it was joined by an artificial causeway, now submerged. Colonized by PHOENICIANS at the end of the 8th century BC, it became, with Panormus and Soloeis, one of the three principal settlements of CARTHAGINIAN Sicily. DIONYSIOS I of SYRACUSE violently sacked Motya in 397 BC after a SIEGE; the city was replaced by Lilybaeum (Marsala) as the principal Carthaginian stronghold in western Sicily. Subsequent hellenistic occupation down into the 3rd century was insignificant, but does include a peristyle house with a fine black and white pebble MOSAIC. There is an impressive girdle of surviving defences; also noteworthy are remains of two sanctuaries – one has yielded evidence of burnt HUMAN baby and animal SACRIFICE, in honour of the Carthaginian goddess TANIT (*tophet*) – and an artificial, land-locked HARBOUR. A striking MARBLE statue of a charioteer, a masterpiece of western Greek SCULPTURE fashioned in a precocious style about 460 BC, was found on Motya in 1979; it had presumably been looted from some Sicilian Greek city. Along with Kerkouane (Tunisia), Motya is a type-site for the study of Punic ARCHAEOLOGY in the central MEDITERRANEAN, lacking substantial Roman or later overlay. Joseph Whitaker (1850–1936), a wealthy British wine entrepreneur and amateur archaeologist of the first rank, bought the island and conducted the first serious research there; his book remains a classic. RJAW

See Isserlin, B. S. J. and du Plat Taylor, J. (1974) *Motya* I; Moscati, S., ed. (1988) *The Phoenicians*; Whitaker, J. I. S. (1921) *Motya*.

 SICILY.

mountains The Greeks and Romans regarded mountains with a mixture of awe and respect. In many parts of the MEDITERRANEAN world they contributed significantly to the development of territorial space, especially in defining the extent of ancient city-states. The use of mountain passes for travel was common but weather, brigandage and ambush could make them dangerous places. The most famous and highest mountain in Greece is OLYMPOS (2,918 m, 9,568 ft), located on the border of THESSALY and MACEDONIA. In MYTHOLOGY, the snow-peaked and cloud-covered Olympos was the location of ZEUS' magnificent palace and home to the Olympian gods. Ida (*Idê*), the highest peak on Crete (2,456 m, 8,058 ft), also figured in Greek mythology as the birthplace of Zeus. Among the mountains of central Greece, the most famous was Parnassos (2,457 m, 8,200 ft) whose craggy mass overlooked the oracular sanctuary of APOLLO at DELPHI. In the Roman world, the massive range of the ALPS (highest point: Mt Blanc; 4,807 m, 15,771 ft) provided a natural boundary for Republican Italy. The range took on a legendary quality when HANNIBAL and his army unexpectedly crossed into Italy through a still-debated Alpine pass. In Italy itself, the much less mighty Apennine mountains (highest point: Mt Corno; 2,914 m, 9,560 ft) were home to many hill towns and the source of the main RIVERS of Italy. TJA

Mouseion see ALEXANDRIA; COMMENTATORS, TEXTUAL; INVENTIONS; LIBRARIES; MUSEUMS; TECHNOLOGY.

Mucii A PLEBEIAN *gens* at Rome, associated with expertise in the law. The *cognomen* first appears in the late 6th century BC. In legend, Gaius Mucius (Scaevola) gained access to Lars Porsenna, who had occupied Rome, but failed to kill his target. To show disdain for physical pain, he placed his right hand in a fire; he was afterwards known as Scaevola, from a word for the left hand (*scaeva*), 'left-handed'. Possibly, the legend developed to explain the name, since *scaevola* also describes an amulet worn by children. Publius Mucius Scaevola, the CONSUL of 133, learned jurisprudence from his father, who had been consul in 175, and firmly established the family's pre-eminence in legal scholarship and was an ORATOR as well. As *pontifex maximus*, he published the *annales maximi*, the pontifical chronicle of Rome's early history. His son, Quintus Mucius Scaevola, consul in 95 and called 'Pontifex' to distinguish him from the man below, published the first systematic treatment of civil law and surpassed his father as an orator. An older, related, contemporary who had the same name, Quintus Mucius Scaevola, consul in 117 and called 'Augur', was also a well-known lawyer. He lived long enough to be one of CICERO's teachers. JV

mudbrick see AL MINA; FORTIFICATION, GREEK; HOUSES, ROMAN; KARANIS; LONDON; VILLAS.

mules see DONKEYS AND MULES.

mummies Mummification was the process by which dead bodies were preserved in Egyptian mortuary practice – the prevention of decay was important. It is likely that the practice developed as a natural extension of the process of desiccation, but developed over time and acquired many more ritual components. Our best evidence for the process (apart from material remains) is a portion of HERODOTOS' description of Egypt. He notes that there were three processes; WEALTH and social status determined which one was used. Typically, the process required the removal of internal organs and the desiccation of the body, the most efficient method being the use of dry natron. The body would be treated with various unguents and coated in resin, before being wrapped in resin-soaked bandages. AMULETS and other decorations were commonly used.

By the Greco-Roman period, the process of mummification had undergone changes, including the use of cartonnage to cover the entire mummy. Frequently portraits of the deceased would be attached to the body, as well as mummy labels, which served as a means of identifying the body. The practice of mummification remained specialized, and we know of guilds of embalmers and mortuary specialists (*nekrotaphoi*) from ARCHIVES of PAPYRI. We also have isolated documents that preserve details of the unguents used, the ritual processes, and the cost of burial (which could be substantial).

Although the practice of mummification is clearly Egyptian, in the Greco-Roman period we see the inclusion of Greco-Roman iconography and ritual in burial practice. It is clear that Greek and Roman individuals and, interestingly, CHRISTIANS were mummified alongside their Egyptian counterparts. (see also MUMMY PORTRAITS) CEPA

See Andrews, C. (1998) *Egyptian Mummies*; Brier, B. (1994) *Egyptian Mummies*; Grajetski, W. (2003) *Burial Customs in Ancient Egypt*.

mummy portraits Remarkable painted representations of inhabitants of Egypt included with mummy BURIALS, primarily in the FAYÛM, but also elsewhere. Executed on various materials, including wood, cartonnage and linen, portraits were painted in tempera, encaustic or both. Gilded depictions were also employed, as was painted plaster designed as part of a coffin lid. Portraits on wood were bound to the mummy with the wrappings, while linen shrouds, sometimes full-length, were attached to the exterior. In general, CAT scans of the mummies, and reconstructions based on them, confirm age, sex, and facial features of the images, though pictures occasionally suggest a younger person than the mummy itself. Despite a modern suggestion that portraits were done as an individual neared death, a recent portrait or a painting made after death are more plausible sources.

While Egyptian burial traditions developed through a long history, mummy portraits are from the period of Roman Egypt, primarily the mid-1st century to the early 3rd century AD. Some examples of later date appear, especially at Antinoöpolis. The

MUMMY PORTRAITS: encaustic portrait of a young woman from Hawara, Egypt, c.AD 55–65.

images depict individuals of high status, who are sometimes named, but their precise identity in the complex social structure of Roman Egypt is uncertain. A positive or negative relationship to Roman CITIZENSHIP is possible, since the use of portraits declined rapidly after the *constitutio Antoniniana*, an extension of citizenship to most inhabitants of the empire during the reign of CARACALLA. JV

See Doxiadis, E. (1995) *The Mysterious Fayum Portraits*; Walker, S., ed. (2000) *Ancient Faces*.

 PORTRAITURE.

Munda The last battle of the Caesarian civil war, fought in 45 BC, near the Spanish city of Urso (mod. Osuna). In September 46 Caesar had celebrated four TRIUMPHS for his victories in GAUL, ASIA Minor, Egypt and AFRICA, but the two sons of POMPEY, Gnaeus and Sextus, along with Titus Labienus, had raised a large army and wrested control of much of Spain from Caesar's commanders. In the winter of 46–45 Caesar led an army of 80 legionary cohorts and 8,000 CAVALRY against them. The Roman core of the Pompeian army comprised 13 LEGIONS, though none would have been at full strength. Occupying rising ground they stoutly resisted Caesar's attacks and nearly defeated him. Their determination may have been due to the fact that many of them had been spared by Caesar after previous battles, but could not expect clemency again. Caesar's ally, the Mauretanian king Bogud, played a key role in the battle, threatening the Pompeian camp with his forces and causing Labienus to move part of the Pompeian left wing to protect it. Other Pompeians interpreted this as the beginning of a retreat, which became a general rout with losses of 30,000. This virtually ended military opposition to Caesar. Labienus and other leading Pompeians fell in the battle. Gnaeus Pompeius fled, but was soon captured and killed; his brother Sextus survived, but Spain was back under Caesar's control. PDeS

See Appian, *Civil Wars* 103–5; [Caesar] *Spanish War* 28–32; Cassius Dio 43.36–9; Plutarch, *Caesar* 56.

 HISPANIA.

murder

In early Greek society, as represented in HOMER, homicide was not regulated by law but was left to family members to avenge. The result was that the killer either fled into EXILE to avoid being killed himself, or came to some kind of accommodation with the family by paying blood money. No distinction was drawn between intentional and unintentional homicide, nor was consideration given to any extenuating circumstances. Legal procedures were introduced to regulate homicide, once a community felt the need to make such distinctions and avoid the religious POLLUTION that could follow from the killing of an accused murderer, who might have taken sanctuary at a shrine to plead his innocence or the lawfulness of the killing. Despite state intervention, homicide did not become a criminal offence prosecuted by the state but remained a private suit, left to the family to initiate and prosecute in COURT.

Little is known of early homicide law outside Athens. Drakon (621) is credited with introducing Athens' homicide laws, which in the 5th century were believed to be the oldest laws in Athens and to have changed little since they were first introduced. In 409/8 his laws were republished (*IG* I^{3} 104), and they remained in effect throughout the 4th century. Athenian law distinguished three degrees of homicide: intentional, unintentional, and lawful. Intentional homicide was the most serious, was tried by the AREIOPAGOS, and was punished with death or permanent exile. It covered both premeditated and unpremeditated murder, such as killing in a fit of rage. The law was not concerned with the amount of time taken to formulate the killing but with the intent of the act at the moment it was committed. If one's actions intended to cause harm and death resulted, the homicide was considered intentional. At some point intentional wounding and death by poisoning came to be tried by the Areiopagos; these were punished as severely as intentional homicide. This suggests that intentional wounding represented the Athenian equivalent of attempted murder. Unintentional homicide was tried by the *EPHETAI* at the Palladion and was punished with exile; the convicted killer could return when granted a pardon by the family of the deceased. The killings of non-citizens were also tried at the Palladion, but no distinction was drawn between intentional and unintentional homicide; consequently any killing of a foreigner or SLAVE, regardless of intent, was only punished with temporary exile. Planning of homicide was also tried at the Palladion; the person convicted of planning a homicide was treated as equally guilty with the one who carried out the killing, and was punished according to whether the homicide was intentional or unintentional. The planning of unintentional homicide covered cases of negligence, and was thus punished with temporary exile. Lawful homicide, which included killing a burglar, killing an ADULTERER caught in the act, or accidental killing in ATHLETIC competition, was tried by the *ephetai* at the Delphinion. If the jury ruled that the killing was lawful, there was no penalty. CC

See Gagarin, M. (1986) *Early Greek Law*; MacDowell, D. M. (1963) *Athenian Homicide Law in the Age of the Orators*.

King NUMA is credited by the etymologist Festus with the earliest Roman murder law. It proscribed 'one who killed a free person by stealth' as a *parricida* (parricide), a formulation like English murder: the taking of life 'with malice aforethought'. The resemblance ends there. By the mid-Republic, *parricidium* refers to killing a parent. Either the term became specialized or Festus must be taken to mean that the ordinary murderer was to be treated as a parricide. Parricide, the killing of ascendants – parents and grandparents – was an exceptional crime marked by its punishment; after ritual humiliations, the parricide was sealed in a sack with a cock, a monkey and a snake and tossed into the TIBER. It was the subject of a late Republican law which extended the group of potential victims even to PATRONS.

MAGISTRATES for *parricidium*, a public CRIME, are recorded in the 5th-century BC TWELVE TABLES. Only in the early 2nd century BC do temporary murder courts appear. The acquisition of an empire was a catalyst for permanent criminal courts, *quaestiones*; corruption by provincial governors received the first. Murder was granted a permanent standing court by SULLA in 81 BC. A Cornelian law *de sicariis et veneficiis* (on assassins and poisoners) created a tripartite court for assassins, poisoners, and SENATORS who murdered by legal corruption. Parricide was distinct, but tried in the same courts, as was attempted murder. Charges in these courts – open to citizens throughout the empire – were brought privately. EMPERORS eroded their authority, and in the 3rd century the senate became the supreme criminal court. Jurists applied the Cornelian law to malefactors including arsonists, SHIPWRECKERS, those who castrated and those who underwent abortions.

In the modern world, at a rhetorical level at least, murder is the same act whatever the circumstances or status of those involved. This contrasts with Rome, where there was arguably no murder at all, simply the murderous: parricides, poisoners, assassins. Victims of legally defined murder, traditionally excluding SLAVES and children, were a more restricted group than in most modern societies. Although the empire extended the classes of individuals whose lives were protected by law, judicial practice appears to have stressed adult male citizens as victims. Only in CHRISTIAN sources and late antique legal texts is a more abstract concept of murder, *homicidium*, invoked.

Murder's social place can be detected in forensic speeches, those from cases – especially Cicero's – and RHETORICAL exercises, *declamationes*, including those written by SENECA THE ELDER and Pseudo-Quintilian. Murder emerges as a practice of women, slaves, Greeks, the sexually voracious and politically ambitious against the virtuous Roman male; the fondness for counter-accusations of murder means that 'murderers' appear on either side. Proof lay in disclosing the opponents' vicious character. The paradigm of Roman murder is poisoning, which distils murder's un-Roman SECRECY and indirectness and was particularly identified with women. TACITUS and SUETONIUS record female poisoners at the emperors' courts. (see also LAWCOURTS) SC

See Cicero, *Murder Trials*, trs. M. Grant (1975); Robinson, O. F. (1995) *The Criminal Law of Ancient Rome*.

museums The word 'museum' comes from the Greek *mouseion*, literally a house for the Muses, the GODDESSES who inspired POETRY, MUSIC and literature. The most famous museum was that at ALEXANDRIA founded in the 3rd century BC by PTOLEMY Soter as part of a cultural project that also included the great LIBRARY. The two made up a prototype university, where scholars, such as ARCHIMEDES and KALLIMACHOS, were invited to study and whose research was funded by the state. The Mouseion (Museum) housed ART (in the form of statues of thinkers), scientific equipment and curiosities such as ELEPHANTS' trunks, but it also had botanical and zoological GARDENS and possibly an observatory. It was headed by a priest of the Muses, called an *epistatês*, and like any other cult centre, the Mouseion had GAMES, FESTIVALS and literary competitions. The Mouseion was destroyed in the 3rd century AD, but recovered: HYPATIA's father Theon in the late 4th century AD is its last known member.

While not strictly defined as museums, collections of valued objects for the public did exist before Alexandria's Mouseion. Greek temples held votive offerings which were prized for more than their sheer monetary value. The Romans were avid collectors of paintings and SCULPTURE from throughout the empire, often taken as booty. This artistic appreciation extended to the general populace, as is clear from a story reported by the elder PLINY (*Natural History* 34.62): when the emperor TIBERIUS put the *Apoxyomenos* in his bedroom, the uproar was such that the statue was returned to public view. (see also ZOOS) NJW

See Alexander, E. P. (1996) *Museums in Motion*.

music Greeks brought music to all significant public occasions, most elaborately at major FESTIVALS and GAMES, more simply to conduct routine religious rituals, to celebrate weddings, to lament the dead or to brace themselves for WAR. The EPIC chants and LYRIC songs of travelling MUSICIANS gave entertainment, but served also to create, preserve and disseminate the traditions and values which gave Greeks their shared identity. Children's social EDUCATION revolved around poetic recitation, singing and playing instruments; adults sang and played as guests at *SYMPOSIA*. The ethical and political influence of such music-making, for good or ill, was recognized and tirelessly discussed by PHILOSOPHERS. Music had larger, more mysterious powers too. It captivated even the GODS; it created ecstatic frenzy or trance; it was an instrument of magic and healing. Not all music was high-minded or publicly meaningful. Work-songs and folk-songs were everywhere; SHEPHERDS piped; women sang at their looms; riotous revellers capered with instruments in the streets; and hired pipe-girls (*aulêtrides*) played seductively at *SYMPOSIA*, where sometimes impresarios laid on lavish musical cabarets with pipes and lyres, songs and dances, even miniature balletic dramas (Xenophon, *Symposion*).

Religion supplied the context, though not always the content, of most public music. All but the simplest performances were also competitive, a fact that stimulated rapid developments in the art. Dithyramb, with its circle-dancing, singing, 50-strong male chorus accompanied by a piper, was little known in Athens before the late 6th century, but in the 5th

MUSIC: a Greek music lesson. A pupil, with his elderly slave minder (*paidagôgos*) sitting behind him, plays the *aulos* (double-reeded double flute) accompanied by his teacher on the lyre.

became the focus of major contests between choruses representing Athenian tribes. With such numbers of performers, all amateurs except the piper, this seems an unlikely vehicle for radical musical experiment; yet dithyramb became the standard-bearer of the avant-garde, its 'incomprehensible' complexities attracting fierce denunciations from conservatives. Smaller groups sang the CHORUSES of DRAMA (another competitive genre), again with pipe accompaniment. Girls' choruses sang and danced everywhere for ARTEMIS and other GODDESSES. Choruses sometimes travelled long distances to compete at major festivals, such as those at Helikon and DELOS.

Festivals included soloists' competitions too, providing showcases for professional virtuosi. At DELPHI, contests for *kitharôidoi* (singers accompanying themselves on the *kithara*) began in the 7th century; contests for singers to the pipes (*aulôidoi*) and for pure instrumentalists (*kitharistai, aulêtai*) were added in the 6th. The pieces they performed, called *nomoi*, were ambitious and substantial, demanding skill and stamina. We hear of a melodramatic 'tone-poem' in five movements for a solo piper; and when Timotheos performed his colourful kitharoidic *nomos*, the *Persians*, he must have sung and played continuously for some 40 minutes.

Even when purely instrumental, Greek music was based on song. Its essentials were melody and rhythm. Choruses sang in unison or octaves; there was no 'harmony' in our sense. But accompaniment (despite modern claims to the contrary) did not always just duplicate the melody. Pipers added a variable drone, sounded notes alien to the tune to create dissonance and resolution, and wove decorative embroideries. On lyres, several strings were strummed together to emphasize rhythm. Accompaniments were in principle secondary to singing, but we hear bitter complaints about instrumentalists who grabbed the limelight with their noisy elaborations; accompaniments were often extemporized by the accompanists themselves, rather than determined in advance by the composer (e.g. PLATO, *Laws* 812d). Even large-scale productions standardly involved only one instrumentalist; the best were in great demand.

Early melodies had a narrow compass, and used scales from which, by later standards, certain notes were missing. Specimens of this antique (essentially pentatonic) style, attributed to the semi-legendary piper Olympos, survived into the 4th century, admired for their simple nobility. But a seven- or eight-note octave, and access to notes beyond it, were normal from the 7th century or shortly afterwards. Regional traditions developed melodies based on different scale-patterns, along with characteristic rhythms, pitch-ranges and turns of melodic phrase; these complexes of idiosyncrasies gave 'Ionian', 'Dorian', 'Aiolian' music and the rest their special aesthetic flavourings, and the 'ethical' properties that so fascinated philosophers. (Later the names were attached to scale-forms, *harmoniai*, alone, distant ancestors of the medieval Church modes.) Some scale-systems were 'diatonic', akin to our own; others ('enharmonic', 'chromatic') used intervals that fall into the cracks of a modern keyboard, including some as small as a quarter-tone. In early times each kind of *nomos* and each choral genre held to its own scalar and rhythmic forms and melodic conventions. 5th-century 'musical revolutionaries' such as Phrynis, Melanippides and Timotheos, besides greatly increasing music's complexity and expressiveness, breached all these barriers, abandoning formal structures and modulating freely between rhythmic and melodic schemes.

Most poetry composed before 400 BC was song. POETS composed their own music, performed their own solo lyrics and *nomoi* and commonly directed the performance of their own choral works. The poetry, music, DANCE and spectacle of PINDAR's odes or the lyrics of drama were conceived together, as facets of a unified but multidimensional artefact.

In most cases only the words remain. Musical notations existed from the 4th century, perhaps earlier, but were not used to 'publish' compositions; we know little of their history and purposes. Nevertheless some scores survive; explanations in Greek theoretical treatises allow us to interpret their symbols, both melodic (based on forms of the ALPHABET) and rhythmic (differently coded). Most are fragmentary, and of hellenistic or later date; the earliest is a broken scrap of a chorus from EURIPIDES' *Orestes* (conceivably the music is Euripides' own). Complete or nearly complete specimens include two splendid Athenian paeans sung at Delphi in 127 BC; two little songs from the 1st century AD; three pieces by the Cretan Mesomedes, court composer for HADRIAN; and a CHRISTIAN hymn from the late 3rd century. All are intelligible to modern ears as music, though only the paeans are self-evidently remnants of a sophisticated art. The others are relatively slight.

From the late 5th century, theorists sought to grasp music's nature intellectually, and to analyse musical structures in a scientific manner. Aristoxenos' analyses, devised around 320 BC, provided the basis on which most educated Greeks and Romans later understood their music. A different, MATHEMATICAL approach, pioneered by PYTHAGOREANS, linked music with wider concerns. Its principles accounted for 'harmonious' relations wherever they existed; bodily health, virtue of soul, even the orderly movements of the heavens were analysed and understood as 'musical'. Such tempting speculations reappear repeatedly from Plato to BOËTHIUS, and again in the RENAISSANCE.

Music was always part of Roman life, especially in ritual, but developed artistically only under Greek cultural influence. Greek-inspired Roman dramas included songs and pipe-music. Other musical entertainments of Greek origin, especially 'PANTOMIME', were elaborated from the first century BC in characteristically Roman ways, becoming spectacular shows with virtuosic singers and dancers and groups of instrumentalists. Concerts were mounted on a scale unknown in Greece. SENECA (*Letters* 84.9) depicts a THEATRE's corridors swarming with singers, its below-stage area with brass players and its stage with other instrumentalists, and marvels at the united ensemble of these massive and diverse forces.

Musical skills were especially desirable in young Roman women; but upper class Romans of both sexes were enthusiastic amateurs, playing and singing in their homes. Wealthy households kept musicians (SLAVES or FREEDMEN) in their service, to entertain guests (Cicero, *In Defence of Caelius* 15.35) and teach their children. The choir of 27 girls and 27 boys which HORACE trained for the *ludi saeculares* ('secular games') of 17 BC must already have had solid musical grounding; Livy (27.37) records a comparable performance by 27 Roman girls nearly two centuries earlier.

The Romans, then, were not an unmusical people, though their religious pipe-music and the massed brass of military displays were perhaps their only native contributions to the art. Hellenic musical erudition pervades their literature. VITRUVIUS applies Aristoxenian musical theory to theatre construction; QUINTILIAN champions musical education for prospective ORATORS; PLINY analyses the nightingale's song in terms of sophisticated pipe-technique; poets write eloquently of music's beauty and power. Practical skills and potted musical theory were on schools' curricula throughout the empire. Roman schizophrenia about this 'noble art', however, was more acute even than Greek; even its most admired theatrical practitioners were reckoned disreputable, at best lacking *gravitas* and at worst downright IMMORAL.

As Rome's empire expanded, it encountered a host of non-Greek practices, from LYDIAN harp-playing to CELTIC war-dances. Many reached the capital, either attached to cults (the Egyptian cult of ISIS, for example), or along with captive slaves imported as exotic entertainers. SYRIAN *ambubaiae*, girl-dancers playing harps, percussion and the *ambub* or *abub* (a small pipe), had a particular vogue in the CIRCUS. At this popular level, Rome was awash with music from everywhere; but the status of serious 'art' belonged to the Greek tradition alone. AB

See Anderson, W. D. (1994) *Music and Musicians in Ancient Greece*; Barker, A. (1984–9) *Greek Musical Writings*; Henderson, I. (1957) Ancient Greek music, and Scott, J. E. (1957) Roman music, in *The New Oxford History of Music*; West, M. L. (1992) *Ancient Greek Music*; Wille, G. (1967) *Musica Romana*. Recordings: Ensemble Kérylos (1994) *Musique de l'antiquité grecque*; De Organographia (1995) *Music of the Ancient Greeks*.

 EDUCATION: (a).

musical instruments Ancient MEDITERRANEAN and Near Eastern civilizations possessed lyres, harps, zithers, lutes, reed-pipes, panpipes, flutes, trumpets and percussion instruments of every description. The Greeks knew them all, but their musical culture revolved around members of just two families which they developed in ways peculiar to themselves, lyres and the pipes called *auloi*.

All lyres have a soundbox and two arms, attached in roughly the plane of the flat front. The arms are joined by a crossbar, from which strings are stretched across the box, raised from its surface by a bridge. On Greek lyres, unlike many Near Eastern versions, the crossbar makes a right angle with the strings. This arrangement has no musical advantages (rather the reverse), but is essential to the instruments' elegant symmetry. Early lyres had only three or four gut strings, tuned by devices on the crossbar. The classical norm was seven; from the late 5th century some professionals' instruments had a dozen.

Two species of lyre, called *lyra* and *kithara*, dominated the scene from the 7th century. The small *lyra*, described in the Homeric *Hymn to Hermes*, figured mainly in amateur music-making and in EDUCATION. Its soundbox was a tortoiseshell, with hide stretched over the opening; its arms were curved horns, or wood shaped to resemble them. A variant was the *barbitos*, with a similar soundbox but very long, slender arms and deeper pitch; it is linked to DIONYSOS and his satyrs, revelry and drinking.

The magnificent *kithara*, emblem of APOLLO, was massively built of wood, sometimes adorned with GOLD or IVORY, a professional's instrument, designed for public competition and display. The soundbox had a flat base and a bulging back. Its straight sides tilted outwards, continuing into arms shaped like bulls' horns. On these stood upright rectangular members, between which ran the crossbar, tipped with disks. The structure was supported by brackets of complex, perhaps symbolic design inside the curve of the arms. A smaller variant appears in 5th-century PAINTINGS, sometimes in women's hands. Its modest size and curved base recall Geometric depictions of their common ancestor, the *phorminx* of EPIC.

Lyres were sometimes finger-plucked, but usually the right hand held a large plectrum and swept it across the strings; the left hand's fingers damped those not intended to sound. The effect was rhythmic and ringing, rather than melodic. Lyre-players sat, stood, even DANCED while playing. Kitharists stood, supporting the instrument between body and left arm, and by a cloth band tied to the instrument and looped round the left wrist.

No other stringed instruments achieved comparable status. Some, like the obscure *nablas* and the *pandoura* (a small, three-stringed lute), were curiosities from abroad. Harps were more familiar, but were regarded as 'eastern' and not publicly used. They had up to 20 strings, plucked without a plectrum by the fingers of both hands. Paintings (none before the late 5th century) show lavishly decorated instruments, often played by seated women in settings suggesting MARRIAGE or peaceful domesticity; female harpists performed also at men's *SYMPOSIA*.

Auloi were not flutes, despite time-honoured mistranslations. Their double-reed mouthpiece gave a colourful tone between those of an oboe and a bagpipe. The pipes, of wood, BONE or ivory, often included separate, bulbous sections next to the reed, socketed into the main, cylindrical tube in which finger-holes were pierced.

An aulete normally played two pipes simultaneously, sometimes supporting the cheek muscles with a special strap, the *phorbeia*. How the paired pipes functioned in performance is uncertain; most probably each supplied some notes of the tune, and while not so occupied provided an accompanying drone. Most varieties had pipes of equal length. A notable exception was the *elymos* or PHRYGIAN *aulos*, used especially in the cult of CYBELE; its longer, left-hand pipe ended in an upturned bell made of horn. From about 400 BC, some *auloi* had far more finger-holes than unaided fingers could manage, closed when not needed by metal collars.

The versatile, emotional *auloi* had special affinities with Dionysos, but found roles everywhere from solemn ceremonial to uninhibited revelry. They accompanied DRAMA and dithyramb; professional soloists wove vivid sound-pictures of lamenting Gorgons, or Apollo's fight with the Python (complete with battle-sounds and trumpetings, and the dying monster's hissings). Their irrational emotive power provoked PHILOSOPHERS' suspicion ('not a moral instrument', said ARISTOTLE); but they were enormously popular. Other wind instruments were unimportant. A long, straight, cylindrical trumpet (*salpinx*) was used for signalling, not music. Country people had simple flutes and a panpipe (*syrinx*), originally rectangular, with pipes plugged to appropriate lengths with wax; the 'wing-shaped' type is hellenistic and Roman.

Rome inherited all Greece's instruments, its native *tibiae* converging with Greek *auloi*. It popularized the 'water-organ' (*hydraulis*), an organ with hydrostatically controlled air pressure, invented by Ktesibios, an ingenious 3rd-century ALEXANDRIAN Greek. This was eventually replaced with a waterless, bellows-blown version, sometimes of prodigious power. Rome also developed new forms of lyre, and adopted the percussion instruments of Greek cult – cymbals, hand-drums and *krotala* (wooden clappers used also in informal dancing) – along with imports from further east: *sistra*, gongs and bells.

More peculiarly Roman were the brass (more properly bronze) instruments of its military and ceremonial music: *tuba*, *bucina*, *cornu* and *lituus*. The straight *tuba*, some 140 cm ($4\frac{1}{2}$ ft) long, was akin to the Greek *salpinx* but with a gently conical bore. The *bucina* was short and curved, a simple horn. The 3 m (10 ft) semicircular tube of the *cornu* had its bell facing forward above the player's head, while a crossbar rested on his shoulder and was grasped in his left hand. The strident *lituus* had a straight, conical tube of about 80 cm (30 inches), with a curiously upturned bell; it seems to be related to the CELTIC *carnyx*, though its name may be ETRUSCAN. In the massed trumpetings of these instruments, the Romans developed the only one of their musical arts that was genuinely independent of Greek models. AB

See Anderson, W. D. (1994) *Music and Musicians in Ancient Greece*; Maas, M. and Sachs, C. (1977) *The History of Musical Instruments*; Snyder, J. M. (1989) *Stringed Instruments of Ancient Greece*.

 LYRIC POETRY; PROCESSIONS.

musicians Ancient cultures always needed specialist musicians. Early SPARTA retained eminent professionals to organize FESTIVALS, compose, perform, train and accompany CHORUSES. Athenian DRAMA and dithyramb demanded chorus-trainers, solo singers and virtuoso pipers, paid as a public duty by wealthy citizens. Outside the civic context, KINGS and ARISTOCRATS kept musicians in their retinues; POET-composers like PINDAR and BACCHYLIDES lived partly on private commissions. Humbler practitioners included schoolteachers and instrumental hacks; pipe-girls (*aulêtrides*) hired for *SYMPOSIA* were generally SLAVES.

Major musicians travelled to festivals everywhere, seeking employment and prize-money, facing tough journeys, shabby lodgings, disputes with rivals and employers (Athenaeus 347f.), sometimes real dangers (Herodotos 1.23). From the 3rd century musicians' 'guilds' negotiated rather securer arrangements. Adulation of international stars was tempered with contempt; 'not like a musician', comments ARRIAN (*Anabasis* 4.16) on a kitharist's courageous death.

Buskers thronging Rome's streets and taverns were usually foreign. So were musicians of the THEATRE and CIRCUS, often slaves or freedmen but occasionally achieving great wealth and fame (e.g. Horace, *Satires* 1.2 and 1.3, on Tigellius). The spectacle of NERO singing in competitive festivals was embarrassingly un-Roman. Acceptably Roman niches existed outside the entertainment industry. Priestly ARVALS chanted, Salii played, sang and cavorted; public SACRIFICES required reliable pipers (*tibicines*), later lyre-players (*fidicines*) too; brass-players (*aenatores*) had special status in the army. Associations (*collegia*) of these 'official' musicians, suppressed when the REPUBLIC fell, reappeared (along with expanded Greek 'guilds') under AUGUSTUS. AB

See West, M. L. (1992) *Ancient Greek Music*.

MUSICIANS: female water organ player and trumpeter performing at gladiatorial games, as depicted on mosaic from Nennig, Germany.

Mycenae The mythical FORTRESS of AGAMEMNON and one of several late Bronze Age citadels on the Greek mainland – the one that has given its name to the MYCENAEAN culture. First excavated by Heinrich Schliemann in the 1870s, it occupies a hill on the eastern edge of the north Argive plain in a strong defensive position. Mycenae was occupied in the 16th century BC, as shown by the shaft graves of Grave Circles A and B. The Cyclopean walls of the citadel and the Lion gate reached their full extent by 1200 BC. At the centre of the citadel is the PALACE proper. A three-room *megaron* ('Great Hall') complex with a throne room and circular hearth was its focus; it was accessed by a large multi-flight staircase to the south, which led to an open courtyard west of the central *megaron*. The lower citadel was occupied by storerooms and residences. The largest areas are east and south of the palace. The southern residential area also contains the late Bronze Age shrine of Mycenae with its frescoes and figurines. Outside the citadel, the settlement areas lay to the north and west along the Panagía ridge. There is a group of HOUSES (including the House of the OIL merchant') southwest of the citadel. Nine tholos TOMBS (including the famous 'Treasury of Atreus') and several chamber tomb cemeteries are scattered around the citadel. There is evidence for destruction of the citadel around 1200 BC, but Mycenae was occupied after the Bronze Age. The men of Mycenae fought Xerxes in 480–479 during a period of independence from ARGOS, but the Argives destroyed the city about a decade later. They refounded it as a fortified dependency in the 3rd century but it declined in the 2nd, though it was apparently still inhabited in Pausanias' day. Though Mycenae features strongly in Homer, later myths elevate Argos to greater prominence. AJ

See Klein, N. L. (1997) Excavation of the Greek temples at Mycenae, *ABSA* 92: 247–322; the *Well-built Mycenae* series of booklets gives an overview of the site.

Mycenaeans The term 'Mycenaean' is attached to the late Bronze Age culture of mainland Greece, as a result of Heinrich Schliemann's descriptions of the remains of the Bronze Age citadel of MYCENAE in the 1870s. The Mycenaean period is divided into various subphases but dates approximately from 1600 to 1050 BC.

The shaft grave burials at Mycenae dating from the 16th and 15th centuries indicate a wealthy society with links to the MINOAN culture of CRETE. The centuries following the shaft grave period saw the construction of large citadels in different areas of Greece. These FORTRESSES were built in a rough Cyclopean style and were centres of government, as shown by the presence of PALACES within them. Not all Mycenaean palaces were fortified (e.g. Pylos), nor do all fortresses have fully developed palaces (e.g. Gla in BOIOTIA, associated with the drainage works of the KOPAÏC basin). Around the citadels and settlement, elaborate tholos TOMBS were constructed to receive the remains of the upper classes, while more modest chamber-tomb cemeteries were used by others. The remains of highways and dams are found near some citadels.

The citadels functioned as economic and political centres, as the Linear B texts recovered from all of them show. These texts, using an ideogrammatic-syllabic script to write a form of early Greek, indicate that the palaces were concerned with the storage and distribution of various commodities. They also show the class structure of Mycenaean society from the *wanax* (ruler) down to SLAVES. Deities are mentioned, and shrines such as that found at the citadel at Mycenae indicate the religious importance of the citadels. That the rulers were also artistic patrons is indicated by the Minoan stylistic elements of the frescoes and other arts.

The predominant art form that survives is POTTERY. Mycenaean pottery is well made, with distinctive motifs allowing very detailed stylistic chronologies to be built up. The fact that this pottery was traded to CYPRUS, the LEVANT and Egypt also links it to the better-known Egyptian chronology. The pottery distribution, Bronze Age SHIPWRECKS and probable mentions in Hittite archives give a sense of the scope of Mycenaean maritime activity. Mycenaean remains have also been found in south Italy and SICILY, while trade with the north is indicated by Baltic AMBER.

In the mid-15th century BC the island of CRETE was conquered by Mycenaeans. This expansion of Mycenaean power is visible in the pottery, art and Linear B texts found at sites like KNOSSOS. We can date the height of Mycenaean power to the early 13th century, but by c.1250 there is evidence for destruction at some sites in the PELOPONNESE. Increased fortification work at Athens, Mycenae and Tiryns indicates an attempt to defend against some threat. Evidence from Athens and the Argolid indicates a general collapse of the society about 1200. Nevertheless we have continued occupations in ATTICA, Tiryns, Achaia and Cyprus. The exact causes of these destructions are debated, as are the reasons for the collapse of the society. Most theories associate this with the general disruptions of the eastern MEDITERRANEAN area in the 12th century BC.

The Mycenaeans, however, did not entirely disappear. The material culture of the mainland retains Mycenaean elements down to the 11th century BC. This sub-Mycenaean period comes to an end with the Protogeometric phase of the early Iron Age. AJ

See Chadwick, J. (1976) *The Mycenaean World*; Dickinson, O. T. P. K. (1977) *The Origins of Mycenaean Civilisation*; Higgins, R. (1967) *Minoan and Mycenaean Art*; Hooker, J.T. (1976) *Mycenaean Greece*; Hope Simpson, R. (1981) *Mycenaean Greece*.

Mykale, battle of see PERSIAN WARS, GREEK; XERXES.

Mylai Town on the north coast of SICILY (now Milazzo), site of several notable sea and land battles. The most famous is that of 260 BC in which the Romans under Gaius Duilius defeated the CARTHAGINIAN fleet. It was on this occasion, according to Polybios (1.22–3), that the Romans used a device known as the 'raven' (*korax* in Greek), which let fall a gangway that pinned itself to the deck of an enemy ship. With its help the Romans, despite their slow and ill-equipped warships, captured or destroyed 50 out of 130 Carthaginian vessels. In 36 BC, Mylai was the location of Marcus Agrippa's naval victory over Sextus Pompeius (the son of POMPEY), who had used Sicily as a base from which to blockade Italy as part of his campaign against Octavian (the future AUGUSTUS). DGJS

 SICILY.

mystery religions A general designation used to describe a number of secret cults that flourished throughout the Greco-Roman world. While generalization about the mysteries inevitably produces distortions, one can say that their defining feature was the initiation ('to initiate' in Greek is *muein*) of an individual (the *mystês*). The secret, ritual proceedings open to initiates were described as *mystêria*, which gave rise to the above designation.

The most celebrated of these mysteries were the rites associated with DEMETER and Persephone at ELEUSIS in ATTICA, which endured for a millennium (7th century BC to AD 395). They were open to the public; those who wished to could become initiated – only barbarians and murderers were forbidden. Unusually for a Greek TEMPLE, the actual celebrations took place inside the temple – the Telesterion – which could accommodate more than 3,000 *mystai*. The rites practised there appear to have consisted of three interrelated features: 'things performed' (*drômena*), 'things said' (*legomena*) and 'things shown' (*deiknumena*). Although the specifics remain obscure, they may have included the exhibition of an ear of grain, the 'appearance' of Persephone, and the proclamation of the birth of a divine child. These rites were thought to secure salvation for the initiate, resulting in health and prosperity in this life and the promise of a blessed existence in the next.

Besides the Eleusinian Mysteries, there were mysteries associated with DIONYSOS (and/or ORPHEUS), the Kabeiroi (Cabiri), CYBELE, MITHRAS and ISIS. Book 11 of APULEIUS' *Metamorphosis* offers a famous, if cryptic, account of Lucius' initiation into the mysteries of Isis. JRCC

See Burkert, W. (1987) *Ancient Mystery Cults.*

 MITHRAS: (a)–(b).

myth In ancient Greek *mythos* could signify any utterance by mouth. Like its Latin counterpart *fabula*, it most commonly meant a traditional narrative about GODS or HEROES, or an account of the origins of everything from the COSMOS to local customs. Already in the 5th century BC the traditional *mythoi* were being distinguished from factual accounts (*logoi*) of historical events (cf. HERODOTOS 2.23.1); ever after, *mythos* has been tainted with the connotation of falsehood. But the ancients rarely doubted that myths possessed meaning, especially allegorical, while many ancients and some moderns, from Euhemeros to Heinrich Schliemann, have still maintained the value – though rarely the face value – of myths as history. Since the 18th century, however, the 'science of myth' ('mythology', a hybrid coinage whose modern signification would have baffled Herodotos) has neither dismissed myths as jejune nor naively trusted their documentary value, but has proposed what other anthropological, cultural or psychological meanings they may contain (see below).

Classical myths were sometimes universal, more often national, but usually local, in focus. The accounts contained in HESIOD's *Theogony* of how the world and the gods came to be are cosmic in scope; they also most obviously betray Near Eastern and Indo-European influences. These stories have become the special concern of modern comparative mythologists, who usually propose cultural diffusion to explain the striking similarities between Greek and non-Greek cosmologies. Many classical myths, however, even those about exotic tribes such as the AMAZONS, are more chauvinistic in nature, serving to define classical culture by marking a distinction between Greeks (or Romans) and BARBARIANS. The majority of Greek myths are associated with specific geographical sites in the Greek-speaking world, whether cities (e.g. the Athenian tales of THESEUS or the THEBAN stories of the House of Kadmos), shrines (e.g. APOLLO's DELPHI or DEMETER's ELEUSIS), or topographical features (e.g. various RIVERS, springs, grottoes and glades, with their presiding gods, nymphs, fauns, etc.). Even panhellenic myths about the wanderings of DIONYSOS or HERAKLES comprise many specifically local traditions. We know less about the contents or local connections of properly Roman myths because the Italian gods were so early assimilated to the Greek pantheon. Still, it is often in Roman guise that the original Greek myths are most familiar to us, e.g. from OVID's *Metamorphoses*, which was Western Europe's principal sourcebook for ancient myth throughout the Middle Ages and RENAISSANCE, though his versions of the Greek stories are often eccentric.

The etymology of *mythos* ('utterance') indicates an oral prehistory for most myths, before they became literary phenomena. In reality, our knowledge of classical myths depends almost entirely upon written versions. These may sometimes be corroborated by ancient visual representations, while in a few instances presumably mythical episodes have been preserved for which we have no literary evidence, and whose narrative significance may therefore only be guessed (cf. an Attic red-figure cup, c.480 BC, depicting a serpent's disgorging of Jason, a scene not attested in literature). For the main, although a distinction between the story itself and the storyteller, or between a basic myth and its many versions, is often rightly made, there is in fact no myth without its narrator. The latter may be bard or academician, TRAGEDIAN or ENCYCLOPEDIST, purveyor of traditional tales or – one sometimes suspects – inventor of new ones. Even the inventor, however, professes merely to be handing on a traditional story. Myths, then, may be paradoxically defined as anonymous stories of immemorial antiquity that are nonetheless tied to time and place by particular narrators, who have their eye upon an actual audience (e.g. those in attendance at the THEATRE of Dionysos) and have often composed for a specific occasion (e.g. a religious FESTIVAL).

We may cite another ancient signification of *mythos*. For ARISTOTLE, it meant 'plot', the kind of action that unfolds in a play (*Poetics* 50a4). This reminds us that ancient myth is more than simply a gallery of divine or heroic personalities (or, for that matter, a collection of Jungian archetypes). The old stories are both determinate and dynamic. They are to be distinguished from fairy or folk-tales which happened 'once upon a time', for they usually claim to have occurred in actual history, such as during the TROJAN WAR. They are dynamic in that they concern inter-generational rivalries, domestic and social relations, and the active governance – or mismanagement – of the city and the cosmos.

But a plot, for all its intricacies, may still be easily summarized, and the Aristotelian usage portends the encyclopedic, especially genealogical, treatment of myth common in the hellenistic and imperial periods, which sacrificed specificity and significance for scope. Vast but cursive handbooks like APOLLODOROS' *Bibliothêkê* (c.1st or 2nd cent. AD), or even the infinitely more artful *Metamorphoses* of Ovid, are instances of this tendency to record and chronologically harmonize as many myths as possible. The reflex is actually as old as the *Catalogue of Women* ascribed to Hesiod, but is usually associated with the later mythographers. When myth lost its moorings in bardic narrative or theatrical representation, it submitted itself thus to pattern, but only with some loss of poetic vitality. Indeed, a general shift in Greek literature from verse to prose, beginning in the 5th century BC, may be taken to mark the termination of myth's natural life. Afterwards myths could still be told and even invented (e.g. by the allegorical poets of late antiquity), but they could not hide their artificiality.

While the encyclopedists strove to compile, the STOIC allegorists and the Euhemerists of the hellenistic period strained to salvage the old stories through respectful but ingenious reinterpretation. But the historians and, more influentially, PLATO had forestalled them. In Plato's estimation, the time-honoured tales of HOMER and Hesiod were simply lies (though Plato himself valued the educative function of a noble lie, and so fashioned his own philosophically correct 'myths', such as those of Er and Atlantis). The early church fathers followed Plato's lead by denouncing pagan myths as deceptions – devilish ones at that – and for a millennium and a half European art and literature resorted to myth, usually in its Roman form, only for art's sake, or occasionally as the foundation for elaborate allegories. Only in modern times have various theoreticians begun to reinvest these stories with a certain veracity. A few influential schools of mythical interpretation are sketched below; it is a mark of modern interdisciplinarity that the names of most current scholars, including those mentioned, cannot usually be identified with one approach alone.

What may be termed the 'modern allegorical school' regards myth as a function of language. It is associated with the 19th-century Sanskrit scholar F. Max Müller, and is still employed by comparative mythologists because of its dependence upon theories of linguistic growth and diffusion. This school assumes the task of rediscovering the original referents that lie behind mythical names and stories, usually natural phenomena (e.g. meteorological) or basic social structures (e.g. Georges Dumézil's proposed tripartite division of Indo-European cultures into priests, warriors and farmers, or stockbreeders). Allegory in this sense is seen not as an imposition of meaning but the recovery of pristine significations that have been lost over time.

The anthropological school, represented by the Cambridge 'myth-ritualists' such as J. G. Frazer and Jane Harrison in the late 19th and early 20th centuries, and today by scholars such as Jean-Pierre Vernant and Walter Burkert, ties many myths to archaic sanctuaries, festivals and RITUALS – initiatory, matrimonial, fertility, funerary – whose liturgical customs may predate the stories that evolved to explain them.

The psychoanalysts, heirs to Sigmund Freud (including Philip Slater and Richard Caldwell), understand myth as a reflection of unconscious drives and phobias that have surfaced in the ancient narratives. Myths thus correspond at a cultural level to personal dreams, and as Freud undertook to interpret the latter, so may the old stories be explained with reference to symbolism, displacement, projection, and the other tools of psychoanalysis. OEDIPUS serves as this school's most famous case study. Carl Jung, formerly Freud's pupil and latterly the inventor of archetypes, such as that of the divine child or the mother, which presumably lie beneath all myths, has had an enormous popular influence.

The structuralist school, founded by Claude Lévi-Strauss (cf. also Pierre Vidal-Naquet and Marcel Detienne), proposes a formal structure behind many myths that has less to do with the specific details of plot or characterization, and more with intellectual and cultural categories (such as the 'binary opposition' between nature and culture, or civilized and uncivilized). A case is made, for example, that many myths concern not particular locations and practices as such, but the borders, and tensions, between regions and categories. Thus monster tales mark the distinction between civilization and the ANIMAL world, and many heroic myths concern the sometimes porous frontier between humanity and divinity. JRH

See Bonnefoy, Y., ed. (1991) *Mythologies*; Burkert, W. (1987) *Greek Religion*; Detienne, M. (1986) *The Creation of Mythology*; Dowden, K. (1992) *The Uses of Greek Mythology*; Edmunds, L., ed. (1990) *Approaches to Greek Myth*; Gantz, T. (1993) *Early Greek Myth: a guide to literary and artistic sources*; Graf, F. (1993) *Greek Mythology: an introduction*; Kirk, G. S. (1974) *The Nature of Greek Myths*; Vernant, J.-P. (1980) *Myth and Society in Ancient Greece*.

Mytilene see CLERUCHS, CLERUCHY; ELECTRUM; LESBOS; POST (MAIL); SAPPHO.

N

Nabataea Old Testament and Assyrian sources locate the origins of Nabaioth or Nabatu in north-eastern ARABIA. In 312 BC the historical Nabataeans appear for the first time far to the west, centred in the mountains of Edom, south-east of the Dead sea. In that year, ANTIGONOS I launched an unsuccessful attack on PETRA. Later, Nabataeans are found in the Negev and Sinai, down into the Hedjaz and as far north as the Hauran. A king-list, beginning with Aretas I in c.170 BC can be traced through nine successors, followed by men with by the Greek title *stratêgos*. Nabataea retained its autonomy in the face of SELEUKIDS and PTOLEMIES and occupied Damascus for a few years after c.96 BC. The Nabataeans were besieging JERUSALEM in 66 BC when Roman forces first arrived, but, thereafter, its KINGS were gradually forced into degrees of vassalage. The peak of their prosperity, based on trade, and development came under Aretas IV (9 BC–AD 40). In AD 106 the kingdom was annexed and became the province of Arabia, with Bostra as capital.

Although classical writers are often unflattering, Nabataea remained an extensive kingdom for at least four centuries and developed a remarkable mixed culture. Their written language, known from more than 4,000 inscriptions, a handful of PAPYRI and coins, was Aramaic. They worshipped deities such as Dushares and Allat. The form and decoration of monumental buildings was heavily hellenistic. The elaborate rock-cut tombs of Petra are well known but others have been found at Hegra. Familiar, too, is their fine, decorated pottery. These nomadic people became extensively sedentarized and developed not just agricultural settlements but an important urban civilization. Traces of farms and villages abound, often marked by clever systems of water harvesting and storage. In addition to Petra, a major town with a large population, other towns also emerged, Bostra in the Hauran and Auara (Humeima) in the Hisma. DLK

See Bowersock, G.W. (1983) *Roman Arabia*.

 PETRA.

Nabis Last king of SPARTA (r.207–192 BC), successor to the regent Machanidas. Probably ruling alone, he revived the political programme of KLEOMENES III while rebuilding Sparta's power. Unlike Kleomenes, however, he felt the need for a personal guard and adopted the luxurious trappings of contemporary monarchy, which may partly explain why anti-Spartan sources portray him as a TYRANT. He gave citizenship to 'slaves' – probably meaning HELOTS – and seems to have developed commerce in Sparta, where archaeology reveals an increase in craft production and a fashion for elaborate tombs. For a time he cultivated the Romans, but then accepted from their enemy PHILIP V the city of Argos, where he cancelled debts and redistributed land. After Philip's defeat (197), the Roman general FLAMININUS invaded Laconia on the pretext of liberating Argos. Sparta lost territory, and Nabis was assassinated while attempting to retake it. Sparta's perioikic system was broken up and the city was enrolled in the ACHAIAN LEAGUE, ending its independent history. Sparta had briefly resurfaced as a threat to other states, but the issues are clouded by our sources' prejudices. Reform programmes are open to multiple interpretations; like others, that of Nabis seems to have had pragmatic aims and to have provoked opposition from propertied interests. DGJS

See Livy, book 34; Polybios, book 13.

Naevius see DRAMA, ROMAN; ENNIUS; EPIC; POETRY, ROMAN.

nails Metal spikes primarily used for joining pieces of wood. Although bronze nails were used occasionally, they were too expensive and brittle for general use, and it was not until IRON became both widespread and cheap in the Roman period that nails became common. Even then wooden pegs ('treenails') were probably preferred for fastening major structural timbers.

Although a variety of nails existed, the great majority were of one type, tapering square-sectioned spikes, varying in length from c.5 cm to c.30 cm, with a flat or pyramidal head. Of the million or more nails buried in the Flavian legionary fortress at Inchtuthil, Scotland, only 28 were not of this type.

The widespread use of iron nails must have fundamentally altered methods of BUILDING construction, as they enabled TIMBER buildings to be erected rapidly and made possible the widespread use of plank cladding, which was nailed in place. The use of nails will also have had profound effects in other areas; for example, the use of horseshoes, which were almost a necessity on metalled roads, was only possible when they could be nailed in place.

A number of specialized forms of nail existed. The commonest had flat triangular heads which were driven into wood, making them invisible from a distance; others include hob-nails, fiddle-shaped horseshoe nails, and nails with large flat or domed heads which were used by upholsterers. WHM

names and naming

The Amphidromia was a ceremony held between five and ten days after a child's birth, at which the infant was given a name. The chosen name would invariably reflect the child's place in the wider family. The first-born son would usually adopt his paternal grandfather's name; the second-born son would take up his maternal grandfather's; fewer guidelines existed for daughters. A child would normally receive only one name. To distinguish an individual, the father's name (patronymic), or for women, the husband's name, was added: Perikles, the 5th-century Athenian leader, was *Periklês Xanthippou*, or Perikles [son] of Xanthippos. One's name was often qualified further by an adjective denoting an origin, a place or perhaps a deme or a tribe. In Athens, a citizen was identified by name, patronymic and deme: Lykourgos son of Lykophron, of Boutadai (*Lykourgos Lykophronos Boutadês*). But abroad, most Greeks would have been identified by their name and an ethnic, denoting origin or citizenship: Protagoras of Abdera.

The earliest literary examples of Greek nomenclature appear in the epic poems of Homer: Achilles son of Peleus (*Achilleus Pêlêidês*) or Ajax son of Telamon (*Aias Telamônios*). The patronymics ending *-idês* often developed as names in their own right, for example Euboulides, Leonides, and Philonides. But the names of the Homeric heroes were not that popular in antiquity: Odysseus and Achilles, for example, are 'practically non-existent' among Greek names. The form of such names (ending in Greek *-eus*) is much more common in Linear B documents of the Mycenaean period. It was not until the later Roman imperial period that heroic names became more widely used.

Greek names come in all forms, derived from simple or compound nouns or adjectives or created by the addition of a prefix or a suffix to a noun or adjective. Many words provide a quality or concept which the name reflects: from *pyrrhos* (adj. = red) Pyrrhos, Pyrrhichos and Pyrrhinos; from *lykos* (noun = wolf) Lykos and Lykiskos; from *myrtos* (noun = myrtle) Myrta, Myrtilos and Myrton.

The gods were probably the most popular inspiration for names. 'Theophoric' names refer to a divinity and are among the most common names found in the Greek world. Such names can derive from a single god, so from Dionysos we have Dionysios (masc.; probably the most popular Greek name in antiquity) and Dionysia (fem.), from Aphrodite Aphrodisios (masc.) and Aphrodisia (fem.), and from Athena Athenaios (masc.) and Athenaia (fem.). On occasion two gods can be combined to create a name, e.g. Hermaphroditos. The name of a god more often provides the stem for a compound word to which a suffix (e.g. Apollonios, Apollonia, Apollonides) or specific notions can be added (giving = -doros: Apollodoros; fame = -phanes: Apollophanes). Zeus (stem Dio-), the king of the gods, provides numerous compound names: Diogeiton, Diogenes, Diodotos, Diodoros, Diokles, Diokleia, Diokleides, Diophanes, Diophantos and Diophilos. In later Greek history, the introduction of personal names reflected the increased worship of foreign gods. The Egyptian divinities Serapis and Isis provide, for example, Serapion, Isidoros and Isigenes from the 3rd century BC on. Isis-derived names reach their height of popularity by the 1st century BC.

Different attributes, derived from the meaning of the noun or adjective, could be described in a name. Arete may have been a virtuous woman or Eukleia famous. In fact, names often tell us a great deal about desirable associations. Horses were expensive to maintain and became a sign of great wealth. Is it any surprise that numerous horsey names (Hipp- or -ippos) are known? Hippias, Hippodamos, Hippokleides, Hippokrates, Hipponikos, Kleippos, Leukippos, Menippos, just to name a few.

Aristophanes, the Athenian playwright, had great fun in selecting or inventing names for his characters: the playboy son of Strepsiades in the *Clouds* was Pheidippides, another horsey name. But often we find individuals in the Greek world apparently burdened by names with negative characteristics. Kopria (from *kopros*, 'dung') and Simaitha (from *simos*, 'snub-nosed') have less savoury associations.

It is difficult to distinguish status from names alone. Thrace, the origin of many slaves, provides names such as Thraix and Thraissa. Such evidence might suggest but does not confirm that an individual was a slave. Other evidence might be needed to confirm a servile status.

In the Roman period, many people in the Greek world adapted their names to the patterns of nomenclature that had developed in Italy. So Greeks with Roman citizenship adopted the Roman *tria nomina*, often transliterating the Roman *praenomen* and *nomen* while retaining their Greek name as a *cognomen*. So the philosopher from Pergamon, Kratippos, granted Roman citizenship by Julius Caesar on the suggestion of Cicero, became Marcus Tullius Kratippos. Some Greeks took on Roman names without any adjustment to their own civic identity. The varied forms of Greek names typical of the Roman period had been simplified by the Christian era when individuals were usually known by one name alone.

Thousands of different Greek names are known from antiquity. Many are peculiar to certain regions or cities of Greece and some appear only once. Therefore a name not only identifies an individual but it can often indicate where someone has come from. Individuals named Orop(o)- are only found in or around the city of Oropos in central Greece; Kaikosthenes (from the river Kaikos on Lesbos) is peculiar to Mytilene. Names then can be peculiar to a specific geographic region. Omoloichos is a popular name in Boiotia, Balakros is typically Macedonian.

The *Lexicon of Greek Personal Names*, an onomastic lexicon of Greek names organized by region, gives all known instances of a name based on literary, epigraphical and numismatic evidence and is an indispensable tool for those interested in pursuing Greek names. GJO

See Fraser, P. M. and Matthews, E., eds. (1989–) *The Lexicon of Greek Personal Names*; Matthews, E. and Hornblower, S., eds. (2000) *Greek Personal Names*.

Marcus Tullius Cicero and Gaius Iulius Caesar exemplify the Romans' distinctive system of three names (*tria nomina*). However, this pattern was only dominant from the 1st to the 3rd centuries AD, and even then only for men. Roman men of the early Republic shared with the Etruscans and the Italic peoples of peninsular Italy a system of two names: a personal forename (*praenomen*), e.g. Gaius, and an adjectival clan (*gens*) name, frequently derived from an ancestor's personal name or geographical origin and inherited through the male line by both sons and daughters, e.g. Iulius or Iulia. That this clan designation was generally known simply as 'the' name (*nomen*) indicates its priority in an individual's nomenclature. While there was a wide variety of *nomina*, the number of *praenomina* in regular use was sufficiently small

(17 account for 99 per cent of instances) for them to be reduced to a series of standard abbreviations, the most common being A(ulus), C. (for Gaius), Cn. (for Gnaeus), D(ecimus), L(ucius), M(arcus), P(ublius), Q(uintus), S(extus), Ti(berius), and T(itus). (Note also M.' for Manius.) Predating the differentiation of C and G in the Latin alphabet, the abbreviations for Gaius and Gnaeus demonstrate the antiquity of the system. Indeed, the etymology of most *praenomina* was generally opaque to Romans by the classical period. Formal contexts required the male citizen to add his 'filiation' (father's *praenomen* in the genitive; on occasion even that of grandfather and great grandfather) and voting TRIBE, e.g. M. Tullius M(arci) f(ilius) Cor(nelia tribu). It was to this sequence that the final element of the classic *tria nomina*, the *cognomen* (extra name), was first appended by families of the Roman ÉLITE to differentiate one branch from the wider *gens*. *Cognomina* seem to have begun as individual nicknames, often with pejorative meanings, e.g. Cicero is 'Chickpea' and Strabo 'Squinty'. Notable exploits might earn individuals additional celebratory epithets that might in turn become extra inherited *cognomina*, such as 'Africanus' for SCIPIO the vanquisher of HANNIBAL.

Children were formally named at a ritual purification ceremony (*lustratio*) on the eighth day after birth for girls, the ninth for boys. In Republican Rome tradition was valued over individuality and each family employed a very small selection of *praenomina*, the eldest son commonly taking that of his father. Accordingly, the orator Cicero shared the same *tria nomina* with both his father and his son. The predictability of the system has made it a valuable resource for those tracing the genealogies of leading men of the Republic. Although it was the individuating name, the lack of distinctiveness of the *praenomen* meant that it was rarely used alone outside the household. Depending on context and the level of familiarity, a man might be referred to by any one of the three elements of his name, or a combination of two of them, but in speech rarely by all three. In contrast, women generally lacked both *praenomina* and *cognomina* and were known simply by their *nomina* (e.g. Claudia, Iulia), which remained unchanged on MARRIAGE, and they were distinguished as daughter or wife of *X* as necessary – though within families informal epithets such as *secunda* and *tertia* (second, third) or *maior* and *minor* (elder, younger) might be employed.

The peculiarity of the Roman naming system made the single names of SLAVES and foreign provincials (e.g. Greeks) stand out by contrast. It was, however, the assimilation of large numbers of these two groups into the Roman citizen body that transformed Roman name-giving practices from the 1st century BC. On being freed, slaves usually took the master's *praenomen* and *nomen* and retained their existing single name in the final position otherwise occupied by an aristocrat's family *cognomen*. In recognition of the origin of their new identity, slaves substituted *lib.* (*libertus* or *liberta*) for the freeborn person's *f.* (*filius* or *filia*) after the ex-master's *praenomen*, so that the full name of Cicero's famous secretary, Tiro, will have been written *M. Tullius M. lib. Tiro*. Enfranchised foreigners similarly converted their single names into *cognomina* and frequently adopted the *praenomen* and *nomen* of the sponsor through whose agency they received the CITIZENSHIP or, from the 1st century AD, of the EMPEROR who granted it. As a result the *nomina* of the leading families of the Republic and then the emperors become widely disseminated in the urban population and throughout the Roman PROVINCES. Moreover this population was dominated by Romans who considered the *cognomen* rather than the *praenomen* their principal individuating name. As an individuating name the *cognomen* offered parents much greater flexibility and choice in naming their offspring than did the *praenomen*. It allowed not only the importation or retention of exotic names but also the coining of new names from ordinary vocabulary words so as to project a specific identity (Maximus, Valens, Constans). This afforded an opportunity to commemorate the hitherto neglected maternal line (e.g. by naming a son Iulianus after a mother Iulia). Women undoubtedly benefited from the shift, since it became increasingly common for them to receive personal *cognomina* in parallel with their male siblings. The personal *cognomen* could also still indicate family relationship by the use of variations upon a common theme (e.g. Maximus, Maximinus, Maximianus, Maxentius and their feminine equivalents). These factors led to the widespread adoption of a personal *cognomen* by established Roman families and the fossilization and general redundancy of the *praenomen*. Nevertheless the *praenomen* did not automatically cease to act as the individuating name, especially in cases of homonymity between father and son, such as the emperor VESPASIAN and his son TITUS (both Titus Flavius Vespasianus) – Titus' younger brother (Titus Flavius Domitianus) was differentiated by his *cognomen*. By the early 4th century AD the *praenomen* had fallen out of general use, so that for most Romans the naming system was once again one of two names: the *nomen* and *cognomen*.

Meanwhile, however, the function of the *nomen* had undergone significant developments. After the extension of Roman citizenship to nearly all free inhabitants of the empire in AD 212, the consequent ubiquity of the then emperor's *nomen*, Aurelius, undermined its function in distinguishing clans and for many Romans rendered it little more than a badge certifying citizen status. In response, beginning under the TETRARCHY but becoming firmly established under CONSTANTINE and his successors, those from humble backgrounds entering military or other imperial service adopted the habit of swapping their original *nomen* for that of the imperial family ('Flavius' from Constantine onwards). Thus by the mid-5th century the Roman world was predominantly divided between humble Aurelii and privileged Flavii. As for the personal *cognomina*, the spread of citizenship over the vast majority of the provincial population further broadened the range in general use. Furthermore the increasing CHRISTIANIZATION of society popularized a whole new set of names taken from scripture, while the worship of saints injected new significance into traditional names that sometimes had overtly PAGAN etymologies, such as Dionysius (Denis) and Martinus (Martin). RWBS

See Salway, R.W.B. (1994) What's in a name? A survey of Roman onomastic practice from c.700 BC to AD 700, *JRS* 84: 124–45.

Narcissus (Narkissos) Son of the river GOD Kephissos and nymph Leiriope. The fullest version of his life is offered by OVID (*Metamorphoses* 3.342–510). In the myth, his beauty is as notorious as his solitary nature and pride, all of which eventually bring about his tragic end at an early age.

The nymph Echo was possessed by love for Narcissus, strongly wishing sexual union with him. The young man, however, rejected her love. In despair, Echo transforms, from a young and beautiful woman, into a voice (i.e. the sound of her echo). Narcissus' excessive pride in resisting union with a divinity had been experienced in the past by other nymphs and was not meant to be left unpunished. The goddess of retribution, Nemesis, devised for Narcissus a suffering similar to that that he had inflicted, even unwittingly to an extent, on others.

Narcissus fell victim to an unreal and unrequited love, the love of his own reflection in the water of a pool. This love was as passionate as the one he had once inspired in Echo. Yet, it was equally condemned never to prosper and eventually led to his utter delusion and loss of any sense of logic and control over his desire. The end of Narcissus as a human came as an inevitable consequence, through his magical transformation, in a way not unlike Echo, from a young and handsome boy into a white and yellow flower with his name. EP

See Rafn, B. (1992) Narkissos, in *LIMC* vol. 6, 703–11.

nationalism A term closely linked to the rise of the nation-state in the 19th century; it would therefore be anachronistic to apply it to the ancient world, even though some theorists of nationalism consider the nation to be a perennial feature of mankind. The major difference lies in the definition of CITIZENSHIP. Classical Greece was made up of CITY-STATES with their own separate identities, and local identity always overrode any national concerns, except in times of crisis, for example in the face of PERSIAN invasion. Rome developed from a small city-state into an empire, and over time citizenship was acquired by growing numbers of non-Romans, but these became citizens of a city, not of a nation. Nationalism can also be defined as a state of mind, an act of consciousness, which is characterized by a feeling of collective identity and the promotion of this identity. Both Greece and Rome developed a strong sense of self-identity, especially in encounters with other ethnic and cultural groups, but ETHNICITY is a more appropriate tool than nationalism to understand this process. It is tempting to identify indigenous 'resistance' to Roman culture, or the breaking away of parts of the Roman empire in periods of crisis, as inspired by a sense of peripheral nationalism. The argument of cultural resistance to Rome is controversial since it can only be traced in surviving items of material culture and comes with no written ideology, while the temporary independence of PROVINCES was more determined by Roman failure than by feelings of nationalism. MK

natural history The study of plants and ANIMALS. In antiquity, the original meaning of the word *historia* (an 'inquiry' into things particularly worthy of note) had a greater impact on the collection of data than in the modern discipline of natural history. Thus, there was a tendency to record unusual or surprising facts rather than mundane or ordinary information. The study of natural history engaged intellectuals whose interests could be wide-ranging; they included HISTORIANS, PHILOSOPHERS and physicians. It may be possible to see the pursuit of natural history among the PRESOCRATIC philosophers, especially in descriptions such as that offered by Anaximander, who theorizes that the origins of animals and humans may be found in a kind of primordial slime heated by the SUN. A more developed enquiry, however, is evident in 5th-century Athens. One of the first contributors to the field of natural history was the historian HERODOTOS who not only includes detailed accounts of the wonders found in INDIA as reported to him by other explorers, but also offers significant descriptions of his own personal encounters in Egypt. Among his many interests, ARISTOTLE had a keen eye for the natural world, and devoted much of his writing to recording his findings. Several texts of Aristotle, including the *History of Animals* and *On the Parts of the Animals*, contain masses of zoological and botanical information. The underlying organization of material in his research offers the first systematic analysis of the inhabitants of the natural world. Using the vital or internal heat of a living creature as a criterion, Aristotle created a system of classification that is still applicable today. The accuracy and detail with which Aristotle approached his subject is remarkable. His description of a placenta in the dogfish is only one well-known example; observation and confirmation of his account did not occur until the 19th century. For Aristotle, however, the real interest in collecting this kind of information was that it could then be used to prove the existence of an orderly and patterned universe. Discerning this made it possible to approach true knowledge of the universe. In this sense, the study of natural history was very closely related to philosophical concerns. Handbooks and ENCYCLOPEDIAS, popular especially in the hellenistic and Roman periods, offered another aspect of ancient natural history. Herbal manuals, such as that prepared by Dioscorides for medicinal uses, or vast encyclopedias, best represented by PLINY THE ELDER's work entitled *Historia Naturalis* (*Natural History*), are also sources of ancient natural history. In contrast to the lofty aims set forth by Aristotle, these works were meant both to provide useful information and to entertain the reader. TJA

See French, R. (1994) *Ancient Natural History*.

nature, Nature The Greek term *physis* and the Roman term *natura*, both of which embrace the meaning of 'nature', can refer to the sum total of what is in the world – that which is material and which humans have not created. The study of nature, as stands to reason, could therefore involve an examination of such diverse topics as CLIMATE, constellations, GEOGRAPHY, EARTHQUAKES, mineralogy, PHYSICS, botany, MEDICINE and so forth. Nature thus could be the object of study for scientists. It was also appropriated by PHILOSOPHERS of various types. Earlier Greek thought (that of the SOPHISTS in the 5th century) highlighted an opposition between *nomos* (convention or law) and *physis*: did ethical norms exist by nature (*physis*) or by norm (*nomos*)? STOIC LOGIC (from the 3rd century BC onwards) saw nature (*natura*) as a basic, semi-divine pattern or organizational principle within the universe. Human behaviour, through the application of reason, should bring itself into line with *natura*. The sentimental ideal of Nature, perhaps best associated with the Romantic movement in Western culture, is not something to be found in ancient literature or art. Locale rather than LANDSCAPE seems to have interested the ancients. Their depiction of nature is often admiring (as is evident in VIRGIL's *Eclogues* or *Georgics* or in the abundant and often beautiful Roman WALL-PAINTINGS) but it is seldom sentimental. PGT

See Guthrie, W. K. C. (1971) *A History of Greek Philosophy*, vol. 3; Sambursky, S. (1959) *Physics of the Stoics*; Soutar, G. (1939) *Nature in Greek Poetry*.

Naukratis Greek city of Egypt (mod. Kom Ge'if, 83 km or 52 miles south-east of Alexandria), founded in the mid-7th century BC by Milesians in the Saite nome (west Delta) as a trading station. It received exclusive HARBOUR rights for Greek trade under Amasis (c.560 BC) and enjoyed a long period of prosperity. Pseudo-Aristotle, *Oikonomika* 2, tells how Kleomenes, ALEXANDER's finance chief in Egypt (and a native of Naukratis), took bribes not to remove the city's market (*emporion*) to the newly founded ALEXANDRIA, then moved it anyway. Under the PTOLEMIES Naukratis was one of just three cities (Alexandria and Ptolemaïs in Upper Egypt are the others) in Egypt with Greek political institutions, but its history in this period is poorly known. Despite its Hellenic status and its many cults derived from the Ionian foundation, the population and cults of the city were in considerable part Egyptian. Again poorly known in the Roman period, Naukratis seems not to have had a council until SEVERUS. It had throughout the hellenistic and Roman periods a vigorous Greek agonistic and cultural life, producing numerous writers and scholars including ATHENAEUS, Philistos, Polycharmos, Charon, Chairemon, Julius Pollux and Lykeas.

The remains of Naukratis are poorly preserved but have been the object of several campaigns of EXCAVATIONS, from Petrie's work in the 1880s to an American expedition almost a century later. The remains of many sanctuaries were excavated in the 19th century, but little of the domestic or artisanal parts of the city. RSB

See Coulson, W. D. E. and Leonard, jr., A. (1981) *Cities of the Delta* 1: *Naukratis*.

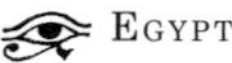 EGYPT.

naval tactics and weapons Ancient naval warfare was never about the control of the open sea. Ancient ships, especially warships, could not stay at sea for more than a few days at a time. Whenever possible crews of warships put into shore at least once a day for rest, water and food. Hence, fleets needed to operate between secure beaches, or, preferably, harbours.

Ancient warships were designed to use the ram as their principal weapon. It could pierce or collapse the hull of an enemy vessel, causing it to become awash; the light, un-ballasted design of ancient warships meant that they rarely sank outright. The best way to position a ship for ramming involved rowing through the opposing line and sailing round enemy ships to ram at an acute angle from the side or rear. These two stages were called the *diekplous* and the *periplous* and required the application of superior speed, manoeuvrability and seamanship to be effective. A variation was to use the ram or the projecting beams alongside a ship's prow (Greek *epôtides*) to break the oars and oarboxes of an enemy ship. The RHODIANS favoured this tactic, for which their favourite three-level warship, the *triêmiolia*, was well suited. Thus, in the battle of Side in 190, the Rhodians defeated the forces of king Antiochos III under the command of HANNIBAL through their superior seamanship (Livy 37.23–4).

The manoeuvring skills needed for ramming tactics were not easily acquired. Ramming often resulted in a warship becoming entangled with its victim, leaving it vulnerable to attack from other vessels. Fleets with inexperienced or depleted crews often resorted to grappling and boarding. As vessels neared each other, marines on the fighting decks and, on larger ships, in wooden towers, would launch volleys of arrows and slingshots to clear away opponents prior to boarding. Grapnels, known as 'iron hands', and heavy weights called 'dolphins' were employed when ships were close enough.

The use of torsion CATAPULTS is first attested in a naval battle between the fleets of DEMETRIOS I POLIORKETES and PTOLEMY I Soter at Cypriot Salamis in 306. DIODOROS (20.49.4) says that Demetrios put stone-throwing catapults on the main decks of his ships, along with arrow-shooting catapults on their prows. Occasionally commanders experimented with innovative weapons like flaming baskets attached to the prow, or even containers of snakes hurled onto an opponent's deck to distract the helmsman. PDeS

See Rice, E. E. (1991) The Rhodian navy in the hellenistic age, in W. R. Roberts and J. Sweetman, eds., *New Interpretations in Naval History* 29–50; Strauss, B. S. (2004) Classical naval battles and sieges, and de Souza, P. (2004) Hellenistic naval and siege warfare, both in P. Sabin et al., eds., *The Cambridge History of Greek and Roman Warfare*, vol. 1.

naval warfare, Greek Since most of the Greek population lived within a short distance of the sea, the main avenue of communication and trade, it was natural for the Hellenes to promote seafaring and, ultimately, naval warfare. THUCYDIDES assumes that the power of the legendary king Minos of CRETE was based on thalassocracy or 'rule of the sea', thus indicating that in 5th-century Athens control of the sea was regarded as an important instrument of power. In this regard, he was influenced by the experience of the Athenian empire, but it soon became clear that Sparta too would have to challenge for supremacy at sea to extend its hegemony beyond the PELOPONNESIAN league.

The political consequences of maintaining a large navy can be seen in Athens, where the task of defending the empire fell heavily on the lowest class (*thêtes*). Their livelihood depended in no small way on the fleet and they lent their enthusiastic political support to those radical democrats whose policies maximized the use of the navy. Payment for SAILORS varied according to time and place, but in the late stages of the PELOPONNESIAN WAR, an Athenian rower earned three *obols* (or half a drachma) per day.

In Athens the direction of the fleet was placed in the hands of the annually elected *stratêgoi* ('generals'); the office of *nauarchos* (which we might translate as 'admiral') was created by the Spartans, but its incumbents were not necessarily experienced in the naval arts – one Spartan navarch, Kallikratidas, was knocked overboard during a battle and drowned because he could not swim.

The first naval battles of consequence in the Greek world were fought during the wars with PERSIA. The defeat of the Greeks at Lade in 494/3 sealed the fate of the Ionian rebels, but an overwhelming victory in the narrows between SALAMIS and the Attic coast in summer 480 was the decisive turning point of the PERSIAN WAR. The destruction of XERXES' fleet, comprising mainly PHOENICIANS and subjected Ionians, not only impelled the Great King's hurried retreat to Asia, but provided the impetus and the means for Greek domination of the AEGEAN. In consequence, a new defensive alliance against Persia known as the Delian league developed. This, in turn and by degrees, was transformed into the Athenian empire. During this period, an allied naval victory (combined with a land offensive) at the Eurymedon river in south-western Asia Minor brought an end to any serious threat from Persia – or so it was thought, until the loss of a substantial portion of the Athenian fleet on the NILE reversed the balance somewhat.

The Peloponnesian war also saw its share of significant naval engagements, most of them in its final phase. At Arginousai, an Athenian victory over the Spartans resulted in a political fiasco when the Athenian assembly illegally put on trial the victorious generals ('admirals') for their failure – in fact, they were prevented by a storm – to rescue the Athenian survivors. A decisive victory at AIGOSPOTAMOI put an end to Athens' ability to resist and was followed a blockade of the Athenian port at PIRAEUS.

Sparta's own thalassocracy lasted only from Aigospotamoi to the battle of KNIDOS (394) where the Athenian Konon, with a fleet funded by Persian money, defeated that of AGESILAOS' brother-in-law Peisandros (Peisander). The 4th century saw no truly decisive sea-battles until 322 – ALEXANDER the Great had chosen to disband his fleet rather than risk a setback at sea – when the Macedonian admiral Kleitos 'the White' defeated the Athenians near Amorgos and thus helped to bring to an end the Lamian war. The most important naval engagements of the hellenistic East were fought at Salamis (306), Kos (261?), Andros (246/5?), Myonnesos (190) and, of course, ACTIUM (31). WH

See Casson, L. (1991) *The Ancient Mariners*; Morrison, J. S. and Coates, J. F. (1986) *The Athenian Trireme*; Tarn, W.W. (1930) *Hellenistic Military and Naval Developments*.

navies

A navy can be defined as comprising one or more fleets of state-owned and/or operated warships, supported by public HARBOUR facilities for docking and maintenance. These naval resources are used for the projection of military power in pursuit of the political objectives of that state.

The earliest Greek warships probably developed in the 8th century BC and were distinguished from other vessels by their elongated shape, accommodating from 30 to 100 oarsmen, their high sides, the presence of a ram and a fighting deck. It is clear from HOMERIC EPIC and early Greek VASE-PAINTING that ships were used for raiding and warfare in the 8th and 7th centuries BC, but it is most likely that no Greek state had a proper navy before the late 6th century BC. In the archaic period warships belonged to individuals, such as the ship loaned to Telemachos by Noëmon in the *Odyssey* (2.386–92). Privately owned warships persisted until the late 5th century BC, but the establishment of the TRIREME as the principal warship made the operation of such vessels very expensive.

An entire navy of triremes required huge resources of money and manpower. By the early 5th century several Greek city-states in Asia Minor had significant fleets, supplied and largely financed by the PERSIAN king. In the Ionian revolt, 353 triremes were defeated by 600 vessels from PHOENICIA and CILICIA. The Persian invasion of Greece in 480 BC saw over 1,000 of the Great King's ships deployed against about 300 triremes assembled from mainland Greek states, especially Athens and CORINTH. The 200 Athenian triremes had been built recently, following the discovery of a rich vein of SILVER in the public mines in 483 BC.

By combining its resources with those of the Delian league states from 478 to 404 BC, Athens commanded the largest naval forces in the Greek world. At their height the Athenians operated several large fleets

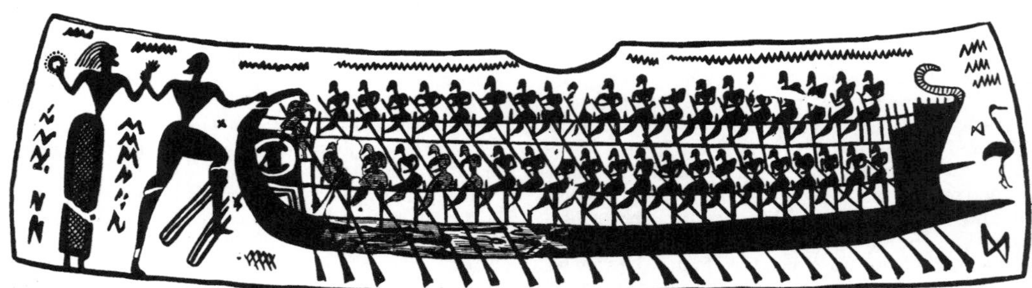

NAVIES: this Geometric painting illustrates the fact that ancient naval warfare became dominated by fast, manoeuvrable ships equipped with rams and powered by banks of rowers (but note that the idea of a navy as such was a later development).

simultaneously, an exceptional naval achievement which they could not repeat in the 4th century. During the early hellenistic period some very large fleets were assembled. Early ANTIGONID, SELEUKID and PTOLEMAIC kings could employ huge resources from the remains of ALEXANDER the Great's empire, but their successors were unable to match them in naval power.

A small number of large warships were built, powered by hundreds or even thousands of oarsmen, but these slow and cumbersome polyremes were only of limited use in sea battles. Their principal purpose was perhaps to act as artillery platforms and assault ships in attacks on coastal cities and harbours. The very largest, apparently built to enhance the prestige of individual monarchs, were never used in combat. Smaller ships were also regularly deployed in fleets, especially the type known as the *lembos*, often used to harry larger ships and prevent them from manoeuvring into position to ram their opponents.

Ships' captains and officers often came from citizen families, but naval service was not held in high regard among Greek aristocracies. Only the RHODIANS seem to have accorded it as much prestige as land-based warfare. Crews were usually recruited from MERCENARIES or poorer citizens and sometimes included SLAVES. Most would not have been strong swimmers and were as likely to die from drowning as from wounds or injuries. Control of an accessible shoreline was, therefore, important. Oarsmen were more likely to be captured with their ships than the marines whose duty it was to defend them. (see also SAILORS) PDeS

See de Souza, P. (1998) Towards thalassocracy? Archaic Greek naval developments, in N. Fisher and H. van Wees, eds., *Archaic Greece* 271–94; Gabrielsen, V. (1994) *Financing the Athenian Fleet*; (1997) *The Naval Aristocracy of Hellenistic Rhodes*; Rice, E. E. (1991) The Rhodian navy in the hellenistic age, in W. R. Roberts and J. Sweetman, eds., *New Interpretations in Naval History* 29–50.

In spite of a literary tradition portraying Romans as landlubbers uninterested in seafaring, they apparently recognized the importance of naval power as early as the 4th century BC when they founded a series of maritime colonies and established an annual board of officials known as *duumviri navales*. Even so, the Romans long resisted a permanent standing navy, presumably because they knew the high expenses involved. Throughout their wars with CARTHAGE, MACEDONIA and SYRIA, they preferred to raise *ad hoc* fleets to meet the demands of their foreign entanglements until events of the 1st century BC (notably the wars with MITHRADATES and the PIRATES) demanded the constant maintenance of a fleet.

Throughout their history, the Romans relied on their fleets for transporting troops, supporting land campaigns and protecting coastal settlements. They were not renowned for their skill in naval manoeuvres. Historians like LIVY and POLYBIOS contribute to this impression by repeatedly stressing the skill of their marines in deck fighting and by their invention of devices, like the *corvus* or boarding bridge, to counter the superior seafaring skills of their enemies. In spite of this, casualty totals often show that Roman navies neutralized more ships by ramming than by capture and reveal that when possible, ramming, not boarding, was the preferred method of destroying an enemy. This said, Roman marines were excellent deck fighters. Presumably because of the costs involved, the Romans initially relied on small to medium-sized warships and eventually adopted the Hellenic-style quinquereme (Greek *pentêrês*) as their main ship of the line. Following the successful siege of SYRACUSE (213–212 BC), they employed CATAPULTS on their warships and, like other hellenistic navies, engaged in naval SIEGE warfare (at Utica, in 203 BC, for example).

After defeating ANTONY and CLEOPATRA at ACTIUM in 31 BC, AUGUSTUS emerged as the sole naval power of the MEDITERRANEAN basin. He thereafter decommissioned most of the larger ships in the fleets he controlled and adopted the smaller TRIREME as the preferred ship of the line. Regular fleet stations were established at Forum Iulii (mod. Fréjus), RAVENNA, Misenum, ALEXANDRIA and Seleukeia-in-Pieria. Later EMPERORS relied on their standing fleets for the transport of dignitaries, soldiers and orders. They also seem to have considered their navy a form of insurance by establishing stations at the borders of the empire: on the north coast of AFRICA, in BRITAIN, in the BLACK SEA and on the DANUBE and RHINE RIVERS. Although the station at Forum Iulii seems to have been disbanded before the end of the 1st century AD, the other stations continued until the time of CONSTANTINE I, when the fleets were reorganized and divided into smaller squadrons. After the naval defeat of LICINIUS in AD 324, triremes ceased to be the main ships of the imperial fleets, and a 6th-century treatise on naval strategy fails even to mention ramming manoeuvres as a topic for discussion. WMM

See Casson, L. (1995) *Ships and Seamanship in the Ancient World*; Starr, C. G. (1993) *The Roman Imperial Navy*.

 SHIPS AND SHIPBUILDING: (a)–(b).

navigation The art of taking a SHIP or watercraft from one geographical location to another. The presence of island OBSIDIAN on mainland sites demonstrates successful navigation in the MEDITERRANEAN from at least the 10th millennium BC. Early navigation was probably carried out in small paddled vessels and, by the 3rd millennium, included watercraft propelled by both oars and sails. Successful voyages always depended upon favourable weather and a marked increase in storm frequencies from November to March explains ancient warnings against sailing at these times. In the general absence of navigational charts and instruments, the captain's knowledge of local conditions, landmarks, and weather signs was critically important. We possess some geographical accounts, called *periploi*, that record sequences of HARBOURS and landmarks, but the information they provide was no substitute for a knowledgeable captain. Voyages could be short hops along a coast or extended journeys beyond the sight of land with navigation aided by the stars and by prevailing winds that blew at certain times of the year. Navigation was made possible by oars, paddles, sails, anchors, tow lines (vessels could be towed through windless or difficult waters) and sounding weights, often fitted with beeswax so that the bottom consistency could be tested. Large, navigable rivers like the

NILE, Euphrates, RHINE, RHÔNE and DANUBE were also heavily used. WMM

See Casson, L. (1995) *Ships and Seamanship in the Ancient World.*

 ASTRONOMY.

Naxos The largest of the Cyclades (430 sq km, 170 sq miles), the island of Naxos was inhabited in the Bronze and Iron Ages. The chief habitation site, at modern Chóra, became the *POLIS* centre, but VILLAGES or other subordinated settlements persisted throughout the island. ARISTOTLE tells us that in the archaic period wealthy Naxians preferred to live in villages. In the archaic period, the Naxians competed with their neighbours the Parians for control of the central AEGEAN, fighting several wars; enmity, or at least distrust, persisted into hellenistic times. Lygdamis became tyrant of Naxos in the later 6th century with the help of PEISISTRATOS; under his patronage was erected the great TEMPLE of APOLLO Delios, whose ruins still dominate the HARBOUR. Important Naxian dedications on DELOS included a series of MARBLE lions and a colossus. The Naxians coined in SILVER from c.600 BC. Recent work has discovered many new sanctuaries, including that to the chief god, DIONYSOS. The island was famous for its high-quality marble. A target of PERSIAN aggression in the IONIAN REVOLT, the Naxians resisted successfully in 499 but were conquered in 490 and had their temples burned. In 477 they joined the Delian league as contributors of SHIPS; THUCYDIDES notes their unsuccessful rebellion in c.475–470 as a stage in the transformation of league to empire. Five hundred Athenian colonists (*klêrouchoi*) were settled on the island after the revolt (c.453–448). Allied with Sparta in the later stages of the PELOPONNESIAN WAR and afterwards, they joined the second Athenian confederacy in the 370s after a siege in 376 by Chabrias. Later, in the hellenistic period, they belonged to the league of the Islanders, an instrument of dynastic policy in the Aegean. The island is poorly attested during Roman imperial times. GR

See Reger, G. (2004) Naxos, in Hansen and Nielsen, *Inventory* 760–3.

 AEGEAN: (a)–(b).

Neaira A PROSTITUTE who attempted to pass herself off as an Athenian CITIZEN wife. Born in the 390s BC, Neaira was brought up as a prostitute by a 'madam' named Nikarete at CORINTH. She was taken to Athens while still a child and at an early age she was bought from Nikarete by two men – Timanoridas and Eukrates. She eventually earned enough money through prostitution to buy her own freedom, with the help of her owners and clients. She arrived in Athens with her lover Phrynion in 373 BC. Scandal forced her to flee to MEGARA in 372, but she returned to Athens in 371 with a man named Stephanos. She and Stephanos lived together in Athens as a married couple, Neaira passing herself off as a citizen wife. The charade was played out so convincingly and with so much confidence that her illegitimate daughter, Phano, married a man who became *archôn basileus*, one of Athens' most public figures. Neaira was prosecuted in court in the 340s by APOLLODOROS (the orator) and Theomnestos for falsely claiming Athenian citizenship. The surviving speech by Apollodoros sheds much light on Athenian social life and values (especially the perceived roles of WOMEN). It also indicates an internal political struggle in Athens during the period of MACEDONIAN threat. Apollodoros' speeches have survived under the name of DEMOSTHENES, to whom they were falsely ascribed in antiquity. LL-J

See Carey, C. (1992) *Apollodoros, Against Neaira: [Demosthenes] 59*; Kapparis, K. A. (1999) *Apollodoros' Against Neaira.*

Nemesis see NARCISSUS; PERSONIFICATION; TIBULLUS.

Neoplatonism A school of PHILOSOPHY that developed in ALEXANDRIA in the 3rd century AD. PLOTINUS is regarded as the founder of the school, though the shadowy figure of Ammonius Saccas, Plotinus' teacher at Alexandria, seems to have been very influential in its development. Other important figures in the development and spread of Neoplatonism were Porphyry (AD 234–305), Plotinus' biographer and literary executor, Iamblichos (c.245–325), and Proklos (Proclus, 412–85). Neoplatonism (new-Platonism) was a radical development of the METAPHYSICS of PLATO. Porphyry tells us that Plotinus' writings are 'full of concealed STOIC and PERIPATETIC doctrines. ARISTOTLE's *Metaphysics*, in particular, is concentrated in them' (*Life of Plotinus* 14). Neoplatonism, then, was a synthesis of the ideas of PLATONISTS, Stoics and Aristotelians, uniquely and originally blended by Plotinus to produce a coherent philosophical doctrine. His essential doctrines, the *Enneads*, collected and edited by Porphyry, were developed and expanded by the later members of the school so that Neoplatonism became the dominant philosophy in the ancient world for over 200 years after Plotinus' death.

The backbone of Neoplatonic metaphysics is the triad of the One, Nous and World Soul. The One is at the highest level. It is a perfect unity which overflows (a process referred to as emanation) to produce the diversity of Nous (the intelligible world of Plato's Forms). Nous in turn produces World Soul and from this level individual souls emerge and inhabit bodies in the material world. Through a rigorous asceticism a soul can return to the highest level and to unity with the One.

Neoplatonism was strongly influential in the development of CHRISTIAN philosophy from St AUGUSTINE (1) through to the Middle Ages and beyond. KM

See Wallis, R.T. (1972) *Neoplatonism.*

Neopythagoreanism This modern term designates the revival of PYTHAGOREAN beliefs and practices which lasted from the hellenistic period until the 3rd century AD. Texts which claimed to be from the hand of Pythagoras himself began to appear around the middle of the 3rd century BC; the degree to which these reflect original Pythagorean doctrine and can be used as evidence for the study of Pythagoreanism is a subject of considerable debate. From the 1st century AD the influence of Pythagoreanism showed itself in various ways. Some shamanistic figures reflected its ascetic and mystical side; the most famous of these was APOLLONIOS OF TYANA, who was credited with the performance of miracles. Others took up Pythagorean number-mysticism, going so far as to associate different numbers with the various Olympian gods. The most profound influence from Neopythagoreanism, however, was on contemporary PLATONISM. This influence can be seen as early as Eudoros of ALEXANDRIA (late 1st century BC), who held the Pythagorean belief that all matter is the product of 'the One'. More important is Noumenios (Numenius) of APAMEIA, who called himself a Pythagorean but is generally viewed as the most significant Platonist of the 2nd century AD. PLOTINUS, the founder of Neoplatonism, both developed and reacted against Noumenios' Pythagorean-inspired teachings about god and reality, as did Plotinus' followers. MJ

See Dillon, J. (1977) *The Middle Platonists, 80 BC to AD 22*; O'Meara, D. J. (1989) *Pythagoras Revived*.

Nepos (Cornelius Nepos) ?110–?24 BC Roman author and polymath. The end of the Republic was particularly fruitful in antiquarian research, which perhaps provided a refuge from crisis by grounding the crumbling Roman state in a scholarly knowledge of its own history, languages, geography and religious rites. Nepos, who came to Rome from Transpadane GAUL, contributed to this project a series of innovative, learned books – now known largely through quotations in later authors – aimed at a middlebrow audience. Among them are the *Chronica*, a synchronism of Greek and Roman culture and history; *Exempla* (models of behaviour drawn from historical figures); BIOGRAPHIES of distinguished men, of which those on the elder CATO, ATTICUS, and foreign generals survive; love poems; and a geographical work perhaps concentrating on marvels. He knew CICERO and other literary figures; CATULLUS dedicated a poetic collection to him, praising Nepos' learning and literary labour. Opinion is divided on the nature of Nepos' contribution to Latin literature. What survives is written in a plain, repetitive style that has earned Nepos a place in the schools since the RENAISSANCE and a widespread reputation as a mediocre intellect. But his works explore important timely issues, such as the benefits of history and the relationship between military success and political control, while his attempts to make current intellectual concerns accessible to the Greekless reader, and to synthesize Rome's Latin and Greek heritage, make him an important figure for understanding the contemporary literary and social milieu. CSK

See Horsfall, N. (1989) *Cornelius Nepos: a selection*; Wiseman, T. P. (1979) *Clio's Cosmetics*.

Neptune Roman god of the sea (originally of fresh water), of immemorial Italic antiquity. The etymology of his name is uncertain. In later times Neptune was identified with POSEIDON, though he inherited relatively little of the latter's mythology or cult. If Poseidon was honoured for mastering a third of the KOSMOS, Neptune merited neither his own *flamen* (priest) nor his own TEMPLE at Rome. Even his literary office is limited: he appears majestically in the opening scene of VIRGIL's *Aeneid* (1.124–56), but otherwise retires for the greater part of that poem, hardly matching Poseidon's intrusiveness in HOMER's *Odyssey*.

Neptune's early functions as a fresh-water deity, however, are quite distinctive. His festival on 23 July, the Neptunalia, was antique and remained a popular holiday for its outdoor recreations. The god presided over the day in the company of the female abstractions Salacia and Venilia, who may have represented gushing and still waters. The extant evidence for the feast suggests that Neptune's importance lay in the conservation of water during summer drought. At the very first public *lectisternium* (banquet of the gods), celebrated in 399 BC, Neptune occupied a place on the couch beside MERCURY (Livy 5.13.6), who may have been the original patron of maritime (and all other) commerce. It could be a sign of growing hellenization that, by the *lectisternium* of 217, Neptune was partnered with MINERVA instead, perhaps reflecting the closeness of Poseidon's cult with that of ATHENA. JRH

See Bonnefoy, Y., ed. (1991) *Roman and European Mythologies*; Dumézil, G. (1987) *Archaic Roman Religion*.

 GODS AND GODDESSES: (b); TEMPLES: (a).

Nero (Lucius Domitius Ahenobarbus) AD 37–68 Roman emperor. Last of a famous line (SUETONIUS found many anecdotes against the 'Brassbeards'), he was son of the CONSUL of AD 32 and, vitally, of AGRIPPINA the Younger, grandchild of AUGUSTUS and daughter of Germanicus. Her claim to imperial power made him a claimant too, and soon after her MARRIAGE to CLAUDIUS he was ADOPTED (50) and became Nero Claudius Caesar Drusus Germanicus; he took the TOGA of manhood early and was betrothed to Claudius' daughter Octavia. Three years older than the emperor's son Britannicus, he was the only possible successor until Britannicus came of age. When Claudius died in October 54, Nero was proclaimed emperor and Britannicus did not survive.

In his first five years Nero's position, because of other claimants, was weak, and his advisers SENECA and Burrus showed that the only way to security was to court the SENATE and People, outbidding his mother's untraditional and extra-senatorial power. By killing Agrippina (59) Nero freed himself from all three. He did not want to rule tyrannically but to be popular and to use the PRINCIPATE as a means to the expression of his taste for POETRY and MUSIC, ART and ARCHITECTURE (note his fine COINAGE).

Revolt in BRITAIN (60–1) and Judaea (66–73) and war with PARTHIA (54–63), like the fire at Rome (64), were costly. Nero's financial demands alienated provincial ÉLITES and his elimination of rivals antagonized the ARISTOCRACY. The Pisonian conspirators (65) were disgruntled courtiers, the military men who died in 66 more weighty. During his reign, the armies were not always promptly paid, but did not rebel, though governors were not as loyal. The revolt of Vindex, governor of GAUL (68), involved 20,000 Gauls and also included Galba, governor of Tarraconensis; Nero, thinking himself deserted, killed himself. Better men, Seneca, PETRONIUS, and LUCAN, besides many CHRISTIANS killed after the fire, had already paid for Nero's overestimate of the theatrical element in his job and for his inevitable insecurity. BML

See Boethius, A. (1960) *The Golden House of Nero*; Griffin, M. T. (1984) *Nero*; MacDowall, D. (1979) *The Western Coinages of Nero*.

AUGUSTUS: (a); EMPERORS, ROMAN: (a)–(b).

Nerva see *ALIMENTA*; FORUMS; FRONTINUS; MARTIAL; PLINY THE YOUNGER; TRAJAN.

EMPERORS, ROMAN: (a); TRAJAN: (a).

New Comedy see COMEDY 2: MIDDLE AND NEW COMEDY.

New Testament A collection of 27 writings, mostly composed in the last decades of the 1st century AD. Although it is hazardous to generalize about a diverse body of material, most of the works are concerned to convey to readers the meaning and significance of the life, death and resurrection of Jesus of Nazareth. There are important differences between how these ideas are articulated, but this figure is presented as, in some sense, definitive for humanity and indeed the universe. The fact that four different accounts of Jesus' life were accepted as authoritative by the early CHURCH and included in the canon of the New Testament, though perplexing for some modern readers and providing ammunition for early critics of CHRISTIANITY (notably Porphyry, who made much of obvious contradictions) demonstrates that, despite its exclusive claims about Jesus (John 3.16; Acts 4.12; 2 Corinthians 6.14–7:1), early Christianity was, within limits, surprisingly pluralist. It is telling that harmonies of the gospels, such as the *Diatesseron* of Tatian, did not become widely accepted.

Different genres are found in the New Testament: in addition to four lives of Jesus, it includes letters (most notably those of PAUL), a history (*Acts of the Apostles*) and an apocalypse (*Revelation*). A variety of other literary forms can be discerned within these compositions; most are variations of those common in the 1st century (such as the anecdote or *chreia*), though some are quite distinctive (such as the PARABLE – few examples of non-Christian parables predate the New Testament).

All the books of the New Testament were written in *koinê* Greek, the common language of the eastern MEDITERRANEAN, but for many authors Greek was probably not their first language. Despite evident passion, conviction and material of enduring literary merit (e.g. 1 Corinthians 13, the so-called 'Hymn to Love'), the New Testament writings are not, in terms of style, very accomplished. For example, Mark's gospel is a compelling, breathless narrative but its Greek is poor and its narrative clearly unsatisfactory to many early readers. Some found it necessary to append additional verses after its abrupt ending at 16.8, while Matthew and Luke felt the need to produce expansions and corrections of the entire gospel. On some occasions, the poor style makes it difficult to grasp what exactly was intended to be conveyed, as even the New Testament itself concedes in reference to one of the most prominent but most often impenetrable authors, the apostle Paul (in 2 Peter 3.16 his letters are described as 'difficult to understand').

Who wrote the New Testament is a matter of critical debate. Although many books name their author or were attributed to specific individuals soon after they were composed, the authorship of others has been contested from the outset. Some theologians in the early church, such as Theodore of Mopsuestia, vigorously disputed the authenticity of the letter of James, maintaining that it could not have been written by the brother of Jesus (the leader of the JERUSALEM church: Galatians 2.9 and Acts 15) as was traditionally assumed. With the advent of historical critical scholarship, questions have been raised about the authorship of an even wider range of New Testament books. For example, the majority of scholars now doubt that the apostle Paul wrote the Pastoral epistles (1 and 2 Timothy and Titus) despite the claims made by the letters themselves. It is now generally thought that differences from the undisputed Pauline epistles in vocabulary, syntax, style, chronology and theology indicate that that they were produced a generation or so after the apostle's death.

The process by which the early church distinguished which books should be regarded as authoritative and included in the canon of the New Testament is difficult to describe with any certainty. Except in the case of Revelation (see 22.18–19), it is not evident that any of the books were written with the clear intention that they should be considered sacred literature, despite the importance of their subject matter and an awareness, on the part of some authors, that their writings were of significance to more than their intended audience (see Colossians 4.16). For the earliest Christians, 'scripture' referred to the Hebrew BIBLE (or more accurately, a Greek rendering of it) and in particular the Law and the Prophets (e.g. Matthew 5.17, Luke 24.27, Acts 28.23), not the New Testament – the JEWISH canon was itself still in a state of flux in the 1st century (4 Ezra 14.45), and the New Testament can quote or allude to a wider range of Jewish literature (see Jude 14). There was a clear interest in passing on definitive traditions about the life, passion and resurrection of Jesus from early in the life of the church (1 Corinthians 11.23, 15.3ff.), but it is only in the mid-2nd century that Christian writings begin to be clearly equated with 'scripture' (Justin, *First Apology* 67) and that we see the first steps towards the formalization of a Christian canon. This development was at least in part a response to the promulgation of a rival, expurgated collection of Christian writings by the radical dualist Marcion. It was not until ATHANASIUS of ALEXANDRIA (39th *Festal Letter*, AD 367) that we have the first canonical list identical to that accepted by most Christian churches today. However, the contents of the late 2nd-century Muratorian canon indicates that canonical lists in circulation before Athanasius' letter largely resembled it (the Muratorian canon does not include 1 and 2 Peter and Hebrews, and includes the apocalypse of Peter and the Wisdom of Solomon).

For the student of classical civilization the writings of the New Testament are important not just because of what they tell us about the practices and beliefs that eventually came, with the conversion of CONSTANTINE, to dominate the later Roman empire. They also give us an unrivalled picture of the empire from the perspective of the ruled, and consequently provide us with an invaluable source for studying the religious, political and social history of the eastern Mediterranean in the 1st century. The main human protagonist of the New Testament was, after all, executed on a Roman cross. JM

See Cook, J. G. (2002) *The Interpretation of the New Testament in Greco-Roman Paganism*; Duling, D. (2002) *The New Testament*, trs. L.W. Barnard (1997); McDonald, L. (1995) *The Formation of the Christian Biblical Canon*.

Nicias see NIKIAS.

Nicomedia (Nikomedeia, mod. İsmit) Hellenistic and Roman city, capital of the hellenistic kingdom and Roman province of Bithynia. The site lies close to the southern (Asian) shore of the sea of Marmara (Propontis), some 90 km (55 miles) east-south-east of Istanbul. The city was founded in 264 BC by Nikomedes I of Bithynia as his royal capital. The city is particularly well documented as a provincial capital, for it was PLINY THE YOUNGER's base during his term as governor there in AD 110–12, and the affairs of Nicomedia figure prominently in book 10 of his *Letters*. Similarly the speeches of the contemporary Bithynian orator DIO CHRYSOSTOM mention the city frequently. These sources illustrate the continued importance of local politics and the attention paid to civic prestige and rivalry (often manifested in ambitious public building projects) in Greek communities in the Roman empire.

Nicomedia gained much of its importance from its port and its location on the main overland route from Europe, across the Bosporos, and thence to the Eastern provinces of the Roman empire. It was a significant place of transit for armies, TRAVELLERS and traders. In the later empire it was a military (particularly naval) base, sacked by the GOTHS in AD 256. Its role as an Eastern imperial capital under DIOCLETIAN was eclipsed by the establishment of CONSTANTINOPLE.

Little of the ancient city is visible today, except some fragments of late Roman walls, public buildings and AQUEDUCTS, though Pliny's *Letters* make it clear that in his day Nicomedia had a full and fine range of public structures. NDP

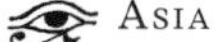 ASIA.

Nike Personification of *nikê*, victory (Latin: Victoria). Nike's only mythology is a brief appearance in HESIOD (*Theogony* 383–4) as daughter of the Titan Pallas and the river Styx. The early 6th-century sculptor Archermos of CHIOS was reputedly the first to represent Victory with wings (scholiast on ARISTOPHANES, *Birds* 573), which remains the dominant iconographic type, a popular figure for temple akroteria as well as free-standing sculpture; like EROS, Nike often multiplies (pl. Nikai). Before the 1st century BC she was worshipped as an aspect of other gods, primarily ATHENA, rather than as an independent deity. Athena Nike had an altar on the ATHENIAN ACROPOLIS from c.566 BC and a temple from c.410, which PAUSANIAS (1.22.4) calls the temple of 'Wingless Victory'; the balustrade depicts (winged) Victories leading BULLS to sacrifice, pouring libations, one fastening her sandal. PHEIDIAS' chryselephantine statues of Athena Parthenos and OLYMPIAN ZEUS each had a small Nike on their outstretched right hand. Paionios' Nike at Olympia (c.420 BC) stood on a high pedestal, enhancing the impression of flight; similarly, the hellenistic Nike of Samothrace seems just to have alighted, drapery still swirling. Nike's presence may signify not only a city's military victory, but also an individual's success in ATHLETIC or DRAMATIC contests. She is particularly popular on vases of the classical period, holding out a garland to crown the victor, or equipped with jug, phiale or censer to officiate at a celebratory ritual; in more military vein she may carry weapons or decorate a trophy. EJS

See Goulaki-Voutira, A. et al. (1992) Nike, in *LIMC* vol. 6, 850–904.

 ARCHITECTURE: (b); GODS AND GODDESSES: (b).

Nikias c.469–413 BC Athenian politician and GENERAL. His public position derived from SILVER-MINING property at LAURION and from the LABOUR of a huge SLAVE workforce there (reportedly 1,000, the largest known from classical Greece). It allowed him to invest in ostentatious public spectacles and BENEFACTIONS, both as *chorêgos* at dramatic FESTIVALS and as leader of a sacred embassy to DELOS, probably in 418/17. His gifts to Delian APOLLO, recorded in 4th-century inventories, undoubtedly conveyed political messages but also reflected an intense conservative piety which set him apart from Athenian fashions and gave him a profile of caution, decency and trustworthiness.

Public confidence accordingly gave him repeated tenure as general from 428/7 (maybe earlier) until his death. He led several minor expeditions in the Aegean in the 420s, but was no fierce militarist; his caution over Pylos in 425 allowed KLEON to supersede him but also made him the obvious peacemaker with Sparta, especially for the 'Peace of Nikias' in spring 421. Politically challenged by the upstart ALCIBIADES, he could not prevent the conflict at MANTINEIA in 418, but apparently joined Alcibiades in murky manoeuvres which secured Hyperbolos' OSTRACISM in 417. Still one of Athens' leading active generals, he was appointed, against his better judgement, to the SICILIAN EXPEDITION in summer 415. THUCYDIDES' narrative in books 6–7 depicts a tragic figure, initial success being followed by isolation, illness, defeat, retreat, surrender and execution. JKD

See Plutarch, *Life of Nikias*; Thucydides 4.27–8; 5.12–20; 6–7 *passim*.

Nikomedeia see NICOMEDIA.

Nile Major RIVER in Africa, originating in the mountains of Uganda and flowing to the MEDITERRANEAN. Early exploration reached little further than the kingdom of MEROË, so the Nile's source and the explanation for its flood in the summer months remained a mystery. Two explanations stand out as more accurate than others: Anaxagoras considered the flood to be caused by melting snow, and, later, Diogenes mentions the Mountains of the Moon, which supplied two major lakes, possibly Lakes Victoria and Albert. HERODOTOS described Egypt as the 'gift of the river' (2.5), as it was the annual flood, and the silts that flood water deposited, which was responsible for Egypt's fertility. The flood not only punctuated the agricultural year but also generated furious bureaucratic activity: land measurement and registration, censuses of livestock and other documentation relevant to the land economy. The height of the flood was crucial. For fiscal purposes, the prospective height of the flood was estimated using Nilometers, often found in TEMPLES or important locations such as Elephantine, and tax rates were set accordingly. STRABO, PLINY THE ELDER, and AELIUS ARISTIDES variously record that the ideal height was 16 cubits (c.24 ft), much less meant famine, and more meant that the fields were not properly drained to receive seed. The number 16 is clearly of significance, for at religious FESTIVALS celebrating the flood, offerings of 16 various items of produce were made (*P. Oxy.* IX.1211). The Nile was celebrated in many MOSAICS of the Roman period, the most important being the Nile mosaic at Palestrina (PRAENESTE). CEPA

See Bowman, A. K. (1996) *Egypt after the Pharaohs.*

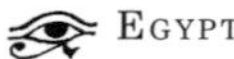 EGYPT.

Nîmes see AMPHITHEATRES; ARCHITECTURE, ROMAN; FORTIFICATIONS, ROMAN.

Ninian see MARTIN, ST.

Nisibis Hellenistic, Roman and SASSANIAN city in MESOPOTAMIA (mod. Turkey). The city of Nisibis (Nusaybin) was founded as a SELEUKID military colony as Antioch in Mygdonia, probably by SELEUKOS I Nikator. Like EDESSA, it lay on the strategically important northern route between the Euphrates and Tigris, and hence between the eastern and western parts of the Seleukid kingdom. It was brought under long-term Roman control by SEPTIMIUS SEVERUS, probably by AD 194, and became the capital of the Roman province of Mesopotamia, had the title of colony, and was a base for Severus' PARTHIAN WARS, with a legion perhaps stationed in or near the city.

Its location on the eastern frontier of Roman Mesopotamia made it a key FORTRESS through the later 3rd and 4th centuries AD, occupied and besieged successively by the Sassanian PERSIANS and Romans. It was finally surrendered to the Persians in 363, after JULIAN's defeat, against the wishes of its Syriac CHRISTIAN population. AMMIANUS MARCELLINUS (25.7–9) describes the poignant scenes as the citizens were evacuated, many to Edessa. Subsequently Nisibis served as a fortress and advanced base for the Persians, playing a prominent part in PROCOPIUS' account of the wars of the 6th century AD. The site has been continuously occupied since then and the topography and ARCHAEOLOGY of the ancient city are not known well. Ammianus Marcellinus supplies a few details of the city's defences in his day, and fragments (notably the 4th-century CHURCH of Mar Ya'qub) of the ancient city are visible. NDP

See Lightfoot, C. S. (1988) Fact and fiction: the third siege of Nisibis, *Historia* 37: 105–25.

 SYRIA, ROMAN: (b).

nomads For Greeks and Romans nomadic (from Greek *nomos*, pasture) tribes had a lifestyle antithetical to their own. Nomads were good horsemen who had no permanent settlements and wandered around taking all their possessions with them. They drank undiluted WINE and their main diet was milk and MEAT. Some of them, such as the SCYTHIANS, were cannibals (Herodotos 4.106). The main nomadic groups confronting the Greco-Roman world were Scythians, LIBYAN and ARABIAN nomads. The information given by ancient authors about these tribes is often exaggerated, failing to differentiate between nomadic and semi-nomadic peoples. Descriptions of the nomadic way of life are given from a thoroughly Hellenic standpoint, even giving Greek names to the nomads' gods and telling fantastic tales about the origins of these peoples (Herodotos 4.1–42). Greeks often enjoyed close trading and cultural links with nomads, who provided SLAVES, cattle, animal skins and other products in exchange for wine, luxurious clay and metal vessels and golden JEWELLERY. In the northern BLACK SEA, Greek cities were under pressure from the Scythians, paying them tribute and producing luxurious objects for the nomadic élite. The Romans spent much time defending their territories from nomadic attack. GRT

See Davis-Kimball, J., Bashilov, V. A. and Yablonsky, L. T. (1995) *Nomads of the Eurasian Steppes in the Early Iron Age*; Genito, B., ed. (1994) *The Archaeology of the Steppes.*

nomen see NAMES AND NAMING, ROMAN.

Nonnos fl. AD 450–70 Purportedly a CHRISTIAN, Nonnos of Panopolis is one of classical antiquity's great mythographers, a successor to the hellenistic writers of the KALLIMACHEAN school. He is the main surviving exponent of an elaborate style of Greek metre used for EPIC POETRY which developed throughout the Roman imperial period. His best-known work is an enormous epic poem entitled *Dionysiaka*. It was Nonnos' intention to surpass the work of HOMER, and, at 48 books long, the *Dionysiaka* is the size of the *Iliad* and the *Odyssey* combined. It tells of the birth of DIONYSOS and how the young god fought for a place in the Olympian pantheon. He meets with hostility from HERA, who plays her familiar role as wicked stepmother. The central section of the poem (books 13–40) deals with Dionysos' war against the INDIANS. But scattered throughout the epic are many digressions telling the stories of other deities and heroes. The last book, for example (influenced by the genre of the novel), concentrates on the tension between ARTEMIS and her nymph, Aura, in which Dionysos plays the less than heroic role of rapist. Nonnos' other extant work is a hexameter reworking of the Gospel of St John, probably written before the *Dionysiaka*. LL-J

See Hopkinson, N., ed. (1994) *Studies in the Dionysiaca of Nonnos.*

Noricum The Roman PROVINCE of Noricum and the CELTIC kingdom, *regnum Noricum*, that preceded it covered the eastern ALPS, approximating to central and eastern Austria. Rome's first contact with this area dates from the 180s BC (Livy 39.22), when the Norici were beginning to consolidate their hegemony over other Celtic settlers and over the earlier Venetic and ILLYRIAN population. By the late 2nd century BC Roman traders had settled permanently in the capital Noreia on the Magdalensberg near Klagenfurt, the site of major EXCAVATIONS. MINING was important. Norican IRON was like steel and much prized. Imports included OIL and WINE, POTTERY, lamps, and GLASS and bronze vessels.

Noricum came peacefully under direct Roman rule c.15 BC, with an equestrian governor and an

AUXILIARY garrison, and under CLAUDIUS the capital was transferred to Virunum in the Drava valley. Close TRADE and cultural relations were maintained with northern Italy, and urban life developed rapidly, Claudius alone granting five communities municipal status. In the late 160s, however, the Marcomanni and Quadi burst across the DANUBE and Noricum was heavily plundered. The newly raised Legion II Italica was assigned to the province, which remained in the front line thereafter. In the 4th century Noricum seems relatively impoverished, but CHRISTIANITY gained a firm foothold and towards the end of the century numerous PAGAN shrines were destroyed. In the 5th century Roman rule collapsed, settlements (even Virunum) were abandoned, and the area came wholly under German control. CMW

See Alföldy, G. (1974) *Noricum*.

 DALMATIA; DANUBE.

Notitia Dignitatum A Latin list of offices of the late Roman empire. It is divided into two parallel sections, reflecting the division of the empire into Eastern and Western administrations after 395. Each part outlines the officials, including provincial governors and military officers, and their staffs. This includes a list of all the PROVINCES in the empire with the ranks of their governors, a complete army list, and graphic representations of the responsibilities of the various officials (including shield patterns for field army regiments). The extant version is probably a Western working copy, since the Eastern part is heavily abbreviated, but this is not easy to reconcile with the lavish decorations in the surviving manuscripts. The dating is controversial, though the Eastern part is generally agreed to date to c.395. The Western part reflects the dominance of STILICHO as senior Western *magister equitum*, but has been variously dated between 408 and 423. The dating is complicated by the inconsistencies between sections of the Western part, which do not appear to have been kept up to date equally; more attention has been paid to military than to civil administration. A typical problem is the list of troops still deployed in BRITAIN, after the probable abandonment of the province. HWE

See Goodburn, R. and Bartholomew, P. (1976) *Aspects of the Notitia Dignitatum*.

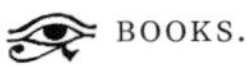 BOOKS.

novels Although several extended fictional prose narratives survive from antiquity, they were not originally classified within a single (indeed, any) genre. The 9th-century Byzantine scholar Photios (Photius), however, spoke of the Greek 'romances' in common, and today five Greek and two Latin specimens comprise the usual scholarly canon of the ancient novel. Often excluded are short stories like Pseudo-Lucian's *Ass* (though it resembles, on a smaller scale, APULEIUS' novel), and biographies of historical persons, like PHILOSTRATOS' *Life of Apollonios of Tyana*, that are largely fictional but pretend to veracity. Cases have been made, however, for including much of the Lucianic *oeuvre*, Philostratos, various CHRISTIAN saints' lives, or the *Alexander Romance* within the canon.

Among the Greek novels are Chariton's *Chaireas and Kallirhoë* (late 1st century AD?), the *Ephesian Story* by Xenophon (of Ephesos? first half of 2nd century AD?), Achilles Tatius' *Leukippe and Kleitophon* (second half of 2nd century AD?), Longus' *Daphnis and Chloë* (late 2nd or early 3rd century AD?), and Heliodorus' *Ethiopian Story* (early 3rd or late 4th century AD?). Achilles Tatius and Longus are called SOPHISTS in the manuscripts, befitting their Atticizing, RHETORICAL style. Heliodoros, according to the church historian Socrates Scholasticus, became a BISHOP. This is historically dubious but reminds us that Christian authors, too, produced novelistic works: compare the Pseudo-Clementine *Recognitions* (Greek), or JEROME's *Life of St Paul the First Hermit* (Latin), both 4th century.

In Latin, the *Satyricon* by PETRONIUS (normally identified with the 'Arbiter' of NERO's court) and Apuleius' *Metamorphoses* or *Golden Ass* (mid-2nd century AD) are typically classified as novels. The former has not survived in its mammoth entirety; the lengthy fragments contain discrete – hardly discreet – tales, such as the notorious *Trimalchio's Dinner*, originally forming part of an episodic whole. Petronius' stories belong to the tradition of Menippean SATIRE, and probably also owe a debt to the erotic 'Milesian tales' (surviving only fragmentarily) invented by Aristeides (c.100 BC). Apuleius explicitly acknowledges this Milesian tradition (*Metamorphoses* 1.1).

The novels probably appealed to a literarily sophisticated rather than a popular (or, as has sometimes been suggested, primarily female) audience. While they narrate outrageous incidents aplenty (kidnappings, pirate raids, enslavements, faked deaths), the novelists consciously echo, sometimes to the point of parody, the classics, especially HOMER's *Odyssey*. The outrageous twists of fate recall Greek TRAGEDY, the stereotypical characterizations NEW COMEDY, the conversational style PLATO's dialogues. Perhaps the closest kinship is to the descriptive narrative set pieces and invented speeches of the ancient historians. Indeed, the *SUDA* (10th century) labels Xenophon (like his more famous namesake) a *historikos*. Above all, the novels resemble each other. They are erotic adventures that begin with violent separation, usually of two young lovers (a boy and girl in their early or mid-teens or, in Petronius' case, heroes of the same sex), and end with joyous reunion. In Apuleius the separation is more ridiculous and the reunion more psychologically profound than usual: the hero loses his human form, becoming an ass, but finally regains not merely his own identity but union with divinity. JRH

See Hansen, W., ed. (1998) *Anthology of Ancient Greek Popular Literature*; Reardon, B. P., ed. (1989) *Collected Ancient Greek Novels*; Tatum, J., ed. (1994) *The Search for the Ancient Novel*.

novels, historical The vogue for historical fiction set in the ancient world began in the mid-19th century with orientalist works by authors such as Gustave Flaubert (*Salammbô*, 1862; *The Temptation of St Antony*, 1874). Rejecting Flaubert's sensuality and fuelled by classical learning and CHRISTIAN zeal, in 1880 Lew Wallace, an ex-general of the American civil war, published his novel *Ben-Hur: A Tale of Christ*, the heroic and highly moral story of a JEWISH prince whose life runs concurrently to that of JESUS Christ.

Ben-Hur was an enormous success and quickly opened the way for the publication of more ancient world stories in America and Europe. In 1896, for example, a Polish author, Henry Sienkiewicz, published *Quo Vadis*?, a vivid account of Christian–PAGAN conflict in imperial Rome (particularly memorable for its depiction of a vile NERO). The Christian agenda set by Wallace and Sienkiewicz was still strong in mid-20th-century writing. Lloyd Douglas, an American, published *The Robe* in 1942 (the title refers to the garment worn by Christ at his crucifixion). The protagonist of the story is a young Roman soldier, Marcellus, who wins the robe in a dice game at the foot of the cross and begins a quest to find the truth about Jesus. To date the book has sold over 6 million copies. The high moral tone of these novels made them particularly appealing to Hollywood producers, and all three books were turned into successful films.

The high water mark of great historical fiction was set with the publication of Robert Graves' *I, Claudius* (1934) and *Claudius the God* (1935). These 'autobiographical' novels of the Roman emperor CLAUDIUS represent, for many critics, the apex of fiction writing. As a classicist, Graves' novels are noted for their academic research, but instead of offering a dry history, he presented them as Claudius' own words, and thus gives the reader a purely subjective viewpoint on the proceedings and characters. Mary Renault's travels in Greece resulted in the publication of her brilliant historical reconstructions of ancient Greece, including *The Last of the Wine*, *The King Must Die*, *The Mask of Apollo*, *Fire from Heaven*, *The Persian Boy*, and *The Praise Singer* (published between 1953 and 1981). Renault was a lesbian author who showed a talent for using passing references to people and events in historical records to create complex characters and plots, and for presenting HOMOSEXUALITY in a positive – and unthreatening – light, as part of the continuum of human SEXUALITY. Her strong grasp of ancient history helped her to depict in vivid detail an era that many readers found fascinating but knew little about. Renault continued writing fiction until shortly before her death from cancer in 1982. Today the genre of ancient historical fiction is more popular than ever. Leading authors in the field include Lindsey Davis, Colleen McCullough, Steven Pressfield, Steven Saylor and Gore Vidal. LL-J

See Dick, B. (1972) *The Hellenism of Mary Renault*; Firla, I. (2001) *Robert Graves' Historical Novels*.

nudity Attitudes toward nudity in ART varied in the classical world according to the gender and status of the person without clothing and the circumstances in which the nudity was to be imagined occurring. From the earliest days of Greek art, nudity was normal for images of male GODS and HEROES, warriors and ATHLETES who exercised unclothed. For mortals, to be nude was to resemble the gods and the heroes of legend and myth and thus to take on heroic status. Nudity is a kind of costume that may reveal more about beliefs than everyday practices in all parts of Greece (Bonfante).

The heroic male nude had a smooth muscular body whose pose and attributes indicated self-control. Even when nude men, presumably from the Athenian élite, cavort on late 6th–early 5th-century vases with PROSTITUTES whose bodies are often flabby and contorted, the youths retain their idealized bodies. In contrast, vases with scenes from burlesque or comedy show short, fat, bow-legged men with enormous genitals; their nudity was created by costume and padding to show their low status and underline the crude humour of their lines in the show (Winkler).

Female nudity was rare in early Greek art except for images of entertainers and prostitutes. A few vases show what may be RITUAL nudity at the temple of ARTEMIS at Brauron, but it was not until the early 5th century that vase-painting depicted the rape of Kassandra, whose nudity indicated her physical and, more particularly, sexual vulnerability (Cohen).

Although small statuettes had long shown nude goddesses, the famous mid-4th-century MARBLE statue of APHRODITE by PRAXITELES, displayed at her sanctuary at KNIDOS, was the first monumental example of a nude goddess. Rather than stressing the heroic nudity of the gods, athletes, and warriors of Greek art, however, the statues of Aphrodite all share features that seem to fight against the goddess's grandeur. They represent her as if at her bath or just emerging from the water, and in many cases the position of her hands suggests a failed attempt at covering her nudity.

Nudity in Roman art has a great deal to do with the appreciation, collecting, and copying of Greek art. Not only did Greek statues decorate public and private spaces, but EMPERORS from AUGUSTUS on frequently combined the bodies of famous Greek statues of nude gods or heroes with their own portrait heads. This custom also gained popularity during the imperial period among prosperous men and women who chose to be represented in the guise of nude gods and heroes in their tombs (Wrede). In doing so, the person depicted could borrow both virtues and heroism and also appear knowledgeable about Greek art and culture.

Roman erotic art and the mythological scenes on luxury goods, WALL-PAINTINGS, and SARCOPHAGI gained much from Greek art too. Using Greek myths and artistic traditions as their starting-point, Roman artists (like ETRUSCAN artists before them) regularly showed gods and heroes nude, but they avoided showing mortals in this way in daily life scenes. Once more one can say that nudity is a costume, but in the Roman world it is part of a different set of scenarios. The divine or heroic qualities that attached to the nude figure in Greek culture come into the Roman world mediated by the desire of patrons to appear cultivated and knowledgeable. NBK

See Bonfante, L. (1989) Nudity as a costume in classical art, *AJA* 93: 543–70; Clark, K. (1956) *The Nude*; Cohen, B. (1993) The anatomy of Kassandra's rape, *Source* 12.2: 37–46; Winkler, J. (1990) Phallos politikos, *Differences* 1.2: 29–45; Wrede, H. (1981) *Consecratio in formam deorum*.

Numa The second KING of Rome, who traditionally reigned 715–673 BC. Numa Pompilius was of SABINE descent (from Cures) and renowned in tradition for his religious reforms at Rome. Among his introductions were the *pontifices* (the major priests of Rome), the VESTAL VIRGINS, the palace or Regia and the CALENDAR. PLUTARCH pairs him with the equally mysterious SPARTAN lawgiver LYKOURGOS. Legends grew up around him, such as his claim to be in communion with a goddess Egeria (he regularly spent the night with her in a sacred grove), and his connection with Pythagoras, which had to be discarded in antiquity upon the realization that the traditional chronology put him two centuries before the Greek philosopher. He died aged 80; a famous story related that in 181 BC his tomb was accidentally discovered, together with certain books of Pythagoras, which were destroyed. He was of sufficient interest and fame for several Roman families to claim that they were related to him. CJS

See Livy 1.18–21; Plutarch, *Life of Numa*; Cornell, T. J. (1995) *The Beginnings of Rome*.

Numantia A Celtiberian city at Garray, near Soria, in the upper part of the valley of the Durius (Douro). It was the main city of the Celtiberian people called the Arevaci, and formed the major centre of resistance against Rome during the Celtiberian wars of the second half of the 2nd century BC. In 153 BC the consul Quintus Fulvius Nobilior, who had been sent to fight the Celtiberians after a dispute over the town of Segeda, failed to capture Numantia, as did a series of Roman consuls who followed him, notably Marcus Marcellus (152), Quintus Pompeius (140) and Marcus Popillius Laenas (139–138). In 137, yet another consul, Gaius Hostilius Mancinus, was trapped with his army and compelled to surrender. Eventually Publius Scipio Aemilianus was elected consul in 134 and, after training his army, which consisted largely of volunteer soldiers, undertook a full-scale siege. The Numantines, after a prolonged and heroic resistance, were defeated, and the city sacked with large loss of life. The remains of Scipio's siege works were identified and excavated early in the 20th century by the German archaeologist Adolf Schulten. JSR

See Richardson, J. S. (1986) *Hispaniae*; Schulten, A. (1914–31) *Numantia*.

 Iberia (2).

numen A Latin word denoting divine power. Derived from the same root as the verb *nuto*, 'to nod', it probably first indicated a nod of the head as an expression of will. Scholars earlier in this century argued that the word originally denoted the impersonal divine forces inherent in particular objects or locations, forces only later personified as deities. More recent scholars have largely discredited this theory by noting, among other points, that in Republican usage *numen* is always an attribute of a specific entity; its original meaning thus seems to have been 'the expressed will of a deity'. Cicero occasionally uses it metaphorically of the senate or the Roman people, while at the end of the 1st century BC it was applied to the emperor Augustus. Its utility in this context lay in the fact that it allowed people to emphasize his exceptional and quasi-divine power without attributing to him outright divinity. An altar to the *numen* of Augustus was dedicated in Rome c.AD 6, while a similar altar in Narbo (Narbonne), dedicated in AD 12/13, served as the focus of a civic cult. Thereafter, dedications to the imperial *numen* are common throughout the Gallic provinces, and occur sporadically elsewhere. In literary texts from the Augustan period onwards the word is often used by metonymy to mean 'deity'. JBR

See Dumézil, G. (1970) *Archaic Roman Religion*; Fishwick, D. (1987–92) *The Imperial Cult in the Latin West*.

numeracy Plato (*Laws* 7.818e–820e) complained of the neglect of mathematics in Greek education, and commended the Egyptian practice whereby children learned arithmetic and geometry through play from the earliest age. Certainly, traditional Greek education involved little mathematics. By the hellenistic period the influence of Plato and other philosophers had helped to establish the concept that mathematics was a good thing for the young to learn, sharpening the mind and accustoming it to rigorous argument. It is hard, however, to assess to what extent education included any mathematics beyond the most elementary level. Both arithmetic and geometry are regularly referred to as part of normal education; an inscription of the 2nd century BC from Magnesia in Asia Minor records that arithmetic was one of the subjects on which pupils were examined. Writers on education regularly pay lip service to the importance of mathematics; Quintilian says 'without geometry there can be no orator' – though he makes minimal provision for it in his syllabus (1.10.49). Nevertheless, education remained firmly literary, and it is hard to find any evidence that anyone (apart from professionals) knew much mathematics beyond the first couple of books of Euclid's *Elements*. Complex arithmetical and geometrical procedures were, however, part of the trade of surveyors, architects, astrologers, businessmen and financiers, and there is evidence of the existence of formulas and reference tables for use by such people. They were also used in schools, though perhaps as part of technical, rather than general, education. RW

See Dilke, O. A.W. (1987) *Mathematics and Measurement*.

Numerianus

Emperors, Roman: (b).

Numidia see Africa and Africans; Africa, Roman; Jugurtha; Masinissa.

numismatics see coinage.

nuraghi The modern Sardinian and non-Indo-European word *nuraghe* (pl. *–i*) denotes a tronco-conical dry-stone tower with an interior chamber covered by a false dome; a complex *nuraghe* consists of one such tower surrounded for the purposes of active defence by one or more circuits of linked towers. This class of field monument is unique to Sardinia, where around 8,000 specimens are known. Still a distinctive feature of the island's modern landscape, they are the hallmark of the nuragic civilization which flourished between c.1800 and 238 BC, when Sardinia passed to Rome. On present evidence, it seems unlikely that any new *nuraghi* were built after the end of the local late Bronze Age, c.900. Decisive arguments against Mycenaean influence have emerged from detailed comparison of the structural mechanics of *nuraghi* and Aegean tholoi. Refined architectural achievements, such as the magnificent pentalobate Nuraghe Arrubiu (14th century), the elegant sanctuary erected before 1200 over the 'sacred' spring at Su Tempiesu, and many more, make it difficult to regard Sardinia as a culturally inferior party to exchanges with the Aegean and the Levant. It is entirely reasonable to define the society that could commission and execute the major nuragic building programmes as firmly aristocratic by the 12th–11th centuries at the latest, to credit it with the inception by then of the brilliant nuragic series of BRONZE FIGURINES, and to digest the inevitable conclusion: the indigenous Bronze Age communities of Sardinia evolved faster and further than their contemporaries on the Italian mainland and in SICILY. DR

See Balmuth, M. S., ed. (1987) *Nuragic Sardinia and the Mycenaean World*; Trump, D. (1990) *Nuraghe Noeddos and the Bonu Ighinu Valley*.

nurses and nursing In our culture it is assumed that nursing the sick – soothing them, washing them, making them comfortable and giving them the treatment prescribed by a DOCTOR – is an inherently female role, because we associate it with caring and gentle qualities which we label 'feminine'. However, in the ancient world nursing could be an appropriate expression of a commander's care for the troops under his control. More generally, because HEALTH was seen as a personal matter of regulating one's lifestyle according to variables such as age, season and location, DISEASE represented a failure to exercise the necessary self-control. Since women were thought unable even to control their own bodies, they were the least likely people to be allowed to care for the sick. When we do read of women looking after sick family members, as in Athenian LAWCOURT speeches such as Apollodoros' *Against NEAIRA*, they are presented as something to be feared: they can take advantage of a sick man's weakness in order to persuade him to do what they want. If one was ill in the ancient world, one might therefore have preferred to be cared for by a man rather than submit to women. Furthermore, ancient doctors, already struggling with competition from other types of healer, much preferred to carry out in person those functions we would associate with 'nursing' care. If other people helped, then they would perhaps want a share of the credit when the patient recovered. (see also WETNURSES) HK

nymphaea see AQUEDUCTS; FOUNTAINS AND FOUNTAIN HOUSES, ROMAN.

oaths These were sworn in a variety of contexts in the classical world: by litigants; commercial and private contractors; doctors (the Hippocratic oath); parties to marriage; state representatives such as those signing treaties; other officials and jurors; conspirators (e.g. Sallust, *Catiline* 44); Roman soldiers in their oath of allegiance (*sacramentum*); and citizens in general affirming their allegiance to the emperor. The force of an oath was strengthened by invoking a god (or gods) as witness and adding a curse. Greek deities regularly called on included Zeus, Poseidon, Herakles, and (by women) Artemis. The Romans invoked Jupiter, Hercules, Pollux, and (women) Castor. Further strengthening was provided when the oath was taken in a sanctuary or accompanied by sympathetic magic (e.g. the use of voodoo dolls) or sacrifice. Oath-taking was therefore central to both public and private piety, and the punishment called on for oath-breakers might be the destruction of the perjurer and his entire family (cf. Andokides 1.96). The Spartans attributed their defeat at Pylos in 425 BC and other defeats to the breaking of oaths (Thucydides 7.18.2).

In Athenian law, the challenge to swear an oath (*horkos*) could lead to the settlement of a dispute, and women (who could not act as witnesses in court) might swear an evidentiary oath. Aristotle classes oaths among the non-artificial proofs (*Rhetoric* 1.15.2) – proofs that were simply used by the speaker (the other types were witness statements, laws, contracts and torture evidence), in contrast to artificial proofs discovered by the art of rhetoric. In Roman law the *iusiurandum* was used extensively: in most actions, for instance, one party might exact from the other an oath that he was acting in good faith (*iusiurandum calumniae*). MJE

obol

 coinage (table).

obsidian A dark, extremely hard, volcanic glass, used since prehistoric times to make sharp cutting and piercing tools. The main sources in the Mediterranean are in Anatolia and on the Cycladic island of Melos; it also occurs in Sardinia and the Aiolian islands (e.g. Lipari) off Sicily. It was a prized commodity, but correspondingly expensive and rare with increasing distance from a source and therefore likely to be replaced with flint and chert. It may be the *obsianum* that was used in making gems and statuettes (Pliny, *Natural History* 36.67.196–7) and for testing the genuineness of gemstones (37.76.200). DGJS

occupations see careers; clubs, Roman; employment; labour; shops and shopping; women; workshops.

Octavian see Augustus.

Odysseus King of the island of Ithaca, one of the Ionian islands. He came from the family of the Kephalidai and is generally known as son of Laërtes and Antikleia; yet his real father was Sisyphos, the son of Aiolos. Odysseus married the Spartan

Odysseus: incidents such as the encounter with the Sirens were frequently illustrated in ancient art, as on this vase now in the British Museum.

princess Penelope, whose loyalty to her husband is legendary in myth.

In HOMER's *Iliad* Odysseus figures prominently as the wise adviser of the Achaians. He is endowed with exceptional physical and military prowess when it comes to action. He masterminded the fall of Troy, aided by the goddess ATHENA, through the shrewd device of the legendary wooden horse. Yet he often displays unnecessary cruelty to the enemy, notably when he demands the SACRIFICE of the Trojan princess Polyxena.

For this and other acts, such as the blinding of POSEIDON's son the Cyclops, Odysseus, along with other leading Achaians, receives divine retribution, a fate that the Trojan prophetess Kassandra revealed to AGAMEMNON (AESCHYLUS, *Agamemnon*). His punishment is to undergo a long and painful string of adventures during his return trip to Ithaca from Troy; these are the central theme of Homer's *Odyssey*. Cunning intelligence is a prominent feature of the hero in the poem, enabling him to outwit his enemies, whether human, monstrous or divine. Once back home, guided by Athena, his divine patron, he begins new struggles to re-establish both his royal and his family status after his long absence. This is achieved through a carefully constructed plan, based on a process of disguise which eventually leads to recognition. EP

See Touchefeu-Meynier, O. (1992) Odysseus, in *LIMC* vol. 6, 943–70.

Oea see AEMILIA PUDENTILLA.

Oedipus (Oidipous) Hero known from tragic DRAMA, particularly the works of SOPHOKLES (*Oedipus tyrannos* and *Oedipus at Colonus*). Originally from the family of the Labdakidai, rulers of THEBES, Oedipus was adopted by the king and queen of Corinth, Polybos and Merope, after his natural father Laios had him exposed on Mt Kithairon because of a DELPHIC ORACLE promising that his child was fated to kill his father and commit other dreadful crimes.

Oedipus' quest for his real parents leads him back to Delphi. He soon attempts to flee the terrible fate pronounced by APOLLO. After unknowingly killing Laios at a crossroads, he solves the riddle of the monstrous sphinx who is threatening Thebes and wins the kingship and the hand of his mother Jocasta in marriage. After producing four incestuous children, Oedipus eventually discovers the crimes that he has unwittingly committed, and blinds himself. In later years he is exiled, curses his sons Eteokles and Polyneikes for their mistreatment of their father, and, accompanied by his faithful daughter ANTIGONE, eventually finds heroic burial in Athens. This story inspired the psychoanalyst Sigmund Freud to develop his famous 'Oedipus complex' as well as numerous later dramatic versions of the story. EP

See Edmunds, L. (1985) *Oedipus*.

Oenanthe see OINANTHE.

Oenophyta see OINOPHYTA.

officers, military In ancient Greek and Roman ARMIES, general officers were invariably elected officials, KINGS or local ARISTOCRATS in charge of territorial levies. They were thus responsible for general STRATEGY, moral leadership and exhortation before battle. But the control of fine tactics, that is, the leadership of the smaller units during the actual fighting was assigned to commoners, often professional SOLDIERS, on the basis of merit, valour or seniority. The ancient historians focus on the larger unit commanders and tend to ignore the chain of command which translated the generals' orders into the actions of the individual soldier. Thus the Spartans employed *polemarchoi*, *lochagoi*, *pentêkostêres* and *enômotarchai* in succession, though these officers are scarcely identified by name. In the MACEDONIAN army the direction of smaller groups, as we know from the authors of military manuals, was entrusted to the *dekadarchês* (literally 'leader of 10', but actually of 16), *dimoirités* and *dekastatêros*. The last was named not for the number of men he led but for the pay he received; the significance of *dimoirités* is less certain, though some have taken it to mean 'a double-pay man'.

In Rome the most vital officers among the ranks were undoubtedly the centurions, of whom there were six per cohort of the post-Marian LEGION, except for the first cohort, which had only five. The centurions of each cohort were ranked according to seniority, but the centurions of the first cohort constituted an élite group whose titles in ascending order were *hastatus posterior*, *princeps posterior*, *hastatus*, *princeps*, and *primus pilus*. The centurion was promoted from the ranks and the office represented the highest that most common soldiers could hope to attain. The prospects of promotion were dimmed somewhat during the empire when many centurions were selected from the PRAETORIANS, over the heads of the common soldiers, and given substantially higher pay. During the empire centurions were also elected by the troops, generally to the detriment of military efficiency. WH

Oia see OEA.

Oidipous see OEDIPUS.

oikist see COLONIZATION.

oils Highly valued commodities in the ancient world, oils fulfilled a range of uses: cooking medium, culinary ingredient, marinade, table dressing, medicine for humans and ANIMALS, LAMP fuel, 'SOAP', body lotion, and base for PERFUMES and unguents. Oil seeds were first crushed and then pressed, or in other cases placed in boiling water and the oil floated off. Oil (especially OLIVE OIL) could be stored, if kept dark and cool in sealed AMPHORAS, and was therefore a form of HOUSEHOLD wealth. Both pure oils and perfumed oils were traded.

Olive oil was undoubtedly the most ubiquitous and economically the most important of the oils of the classical world. It was produced in most of the lands adjacent to the MEDITERRANEAN coast; as an essential and indispensable food item, it was distributed throughout the Greek and Roman world. The boundaries of olive cultivation are among geographical features often noted by ancient TRAVELLERS.

Classical authors noted that in northern Europe, in regions where classical influence was weak, butter

OILS: a valuable commodity in the ancient world, probably sold here as perfumed oil.

and animal fats took some of the roles played by olive oil in the south. Greeks and Romans knew of a range of other oils. Oils from flax (linseed oil) and sesame had been important in the ancient Near East south of the usual range of the olive, and retained economic significance there, as did clarified butter (ghee). Radish seed oil first came to prominence in hellenistic times. Oils with more local and specialized uses included those of the castor oil plant, Egyptian balsam (zachum oil), safflower seed, bitter almonds, sweet almonds, colocynth seed and terebinth fruit. Castor oil was used as fuel and medicine; its flavour was too strong for food use. Linseed oil can be and was used in food, but it rapidly goes rancid when stored. Sesame, safflower, colocynth and radish seed oils were useful as fuel and in food. Zachum oil was a good base for perfumes. Butter was relatively unfamiliar in classical lands; animal fats had few uses, and none of the other sources of modern cheap food oils (rapeseed or colza, peanut, oil palm, sunflower) was available in the classical world.

In PTOLEMAIC Egypt oil production was highly regulated, indicating the economic importance of the commodity. The diversity of products mentioned in PAPYRI reflects the relatively low level of olive cultivation in Egypt. The production of oils from animal fats was specifically forbidden. Egypt, being on the usual route for importing oriental SPICES to the Mediterranean, was a centre of manufacture for perfumed oils, to which myrrh, balsam of Mecca, spikenard, malabathron, cinnamon, amomum, costus and other costly exotics lent their aromas. The edict of DIOCLETIAN that gives maximum prices for products regularly purchased by the Roman army around AD 300 specifies three grades of olive oil and radish seed oil. At the beginning of the Byzantine period, Alexander Trallianus listed no fewer than 29 types of oil that might be used in medicinal prescriptions. AD, DJM

See Sandy, D.B. (1989) *The Production and Use of Vegetable Oils in Ptolemaic Egypt.*

 PRESSES: (a)–(b).

Oinanthe Courtesan at the Ptolemaic court. Her name, 'Wineflower', may be an assumed one. Originally from SAMOS, she migrated to ALEXANDRIA under Ptolemy III Euergetes (r.246–222 BC) and probably became his mistress. Her son AGATHOKLES and daughter Agathokleia (perhaps by different husbands) became minister and mistress, respectively, to Ptolemy IV Philopator (r.222–205). It is alleged, but unproven, that Oinanthe and Agathokleia exercised official powers. Upon Philopator's death, Agathokles claimed that the king had entrusted the care of the young Ptolemy V Epiphanes (r.204–180) to the two women. POLYBIOS, though purportedly avoiding sensationalism, describes in some detail how, when her son fell from power two years later, the whole family was gruesomely lynched by the Alexandrian mob. Oinanthe's story, though hedged around with uncertainty and rumour, illustrates how courtesans could wield influence at court in competition with the royal family; but such power as they enjoyed was derivative and at best conditional. It also offers an example of courtesan status inherited across three generations. DGJS

See Justin, 30.2; Polybios, books 14–15; Ogden, D. (1999) *Polygamy, Prostitutes and Death.*

Oinophyta This town in BOIOTIA leaves little impression on the historical record, other than as the scene of a famous battle in 457 BC. Two months after their defeat at Tanagra, the Athenians under Myronides were victorious at Oinophyta over the Boiotians, and this began a decade of Athenian control of the area (except THEBES) until they were defeated at KORONEIA. It was probably after Oinophyta that the Athenians restored a monument commemorating an earlier victory (c.506) over the Boiotians and Chalkidians. The money acquired from ransoming the prisoners had paid for a bronze CHARIOT, which was taken to Susa after the PERSIAN sack of Athens in 480 (cf. Herodotos 5.77). MJE

 BATTLES (table).

old age Some Greeks and Romans lived long enough to be called old. Some POETS felt prematurely old in their 30s, but old age was generally held to commence around age 60. No stricter age limit need be expected, especially as there were no general institutionalized schemes of retirement or pensions. About 7 per cent of people would have been over 60 at any one time. A very select few even survived to be centenarians. The human life span has not increased dramatically over the past two millennia, it is just that a greater proportion of people now survive into old age.

For some, old age was not an unhappy or unaccomplished time. We know of many Greeks and Romans – politicians, writers, PHILOSOPHERS – admired for their active old age. Literature provides a host of images, positive and negative. PLATO and CICERO attributed old age's negative features to people's dissipated youth and stressed the boons of ageing, not least in the political sphere. This is revealing. Old age did not automatically confer the respect and authority that some (namely the old) felt it deserved. In DEMOCRATIC Athens age did not bring power. In Rome, most authority, EMPERORS (young or old) apart, tended to lie with SENATORS in their 40s and 50s. SPARTA alone operated along gerontocratic lines: members of the *gerousia* had to be at least 60 years old. But even there effective rule lay with younger EPHORS, and ARISTOTLE noted the risks in giving power to men subject to the potential liabilities of old age. Certainly old age's negative repercussions were noted, most memorably by JUVENAL.

Literature focuses on upper class males. Elderly females tended to be stereotyped as sex-crazed witches or ALCOHOLICS. Besides being unpleasant, this points to marginalization. Past reproducing, old women might be dismissed as non-functioning members of society. For the poorer classes, old age must have been singularly unenviable. Children were expected to look after parents in old age; this was allegedly one motivation for having children. Without willing children, a destitute and lonely old age ensued. If a person's failing health led to inability to be self-supporting, then, in the absence of effective medication, dependence may have been short-lived anyway. The key was not how old, but how active or useful. Cicero's words are timeless (*On Old Age* 38): 'Old age will only be respected if it fights for itself, maintains its rights, avoids dependence on anyone, and asserts control over its own to the last breath.'

On the other hand, in antiquity old age was less of a 'problem', at least for men, than it appears to be today. Old age then was not seen formally as a distinctive stage of the life cycle. In the absence of wage-labour and retirement, most people were expected to go on doing whatever they had always done until they dropped. Old age, with all the negative features it might entail, was still regarded as part of the natural course of adult life. TGP

See Parkin, T. G. (2003) *Old Age in the Roman World*; Richardson, B. E. (1933) *Old Age among the Ancient Greeks*.

Old Oligarch Preserved with the minor works of XENOPHON is a curious pamphlet about 5th-century BC Athenian DEMOCRACY, entitled *Athênaiôn politeia* (*Constitution of the Athenians*). Its author was an oligarch – though neither 'old' nor, probably, an Athenian citizen – who had good 'insider' information, surely in the main through visits to Athens. The work was probably written before c.415 BC, a few years before democracy was temporarily superseded. The author does not approve of democracy, but he sees that it is popular, that it works, and that it will prove very hard to overthrow. He warns fellow oligarchs against precipitate action. The tone is often ironic and cynical, even when he is praising the Athenian system. All governments aim to satisfy their supporters, and he cannot blame the Athenian people for embracing one that looks after them so well. Political freedom means more to them than good government and order. In Athens you may not with impunity strike a foreigner or SLAVE in the street (here the oligarchic attitude comes through), since even they have rights. Athens' power depends ultimately on the fleet, and it is the common people, not the upper classes, who man the SHIPS. At times the author's show of fairness breaks down. Democracies cannot be trusted to uphold TREATIES (he says), and the people can always pass the buck if agreed policy has suddenly to be ditched. This, he assures us, cannot happen under oligarchy. He fails to see how a man of his class could prefer to work with a democratic system – unless it was easier there to make one's pile and get away with it. With all its faults, the pamphlet is a fascinating contemporary exposé of the democratic and oligarchic minds. HBM

Old Testament The books forming a collection spanning many centuries of Hebrew and a little Aramaic literature. In addition to these books found in the Jewish and Protestant canons, the APOCRYPHAL or deutero-canonical books are also often reckoned within the 'Old Testament'. These latter derive from the Greco-Roman period, preserved and, many originally composed, in Greek. Occasional Greek words in Hebrew in the Old Testament indicate some linguistic contact with Greeks, and ARCHAEOLOGY attests to trade between Israel and Greece from as early as the 7th century BC. Although many of the Old Testament books were composed in the classical period, they rarely provide any evidence for Greco-Roman history. The book of Daniel, whose narrative is set in the BABYLONIAN period (6th century BC) but was written during the persecution of JEWS in JERUSALEM by Antiochos IV Epiphanes (168–164 BC), alludes to hellenistic history. It divides world history into four empires, Babylonia, Media, PERSIA and Greece – a sequence found in the historian Ktesias in the 4th century BC, POLYBIOS in the 2nd and the little-known historian Aemilius Sura. Daniel predicts the death of the king of 'Greece', Antiochos IV, as the end of the fourth empire. Like other books in the Old Testament (Esther and the apocryphal 3 Maccabees) Daniel can be seen as a court tale, comparable to that found in HERODOTOS or Ktesias. The tale of the persecution by Antiochos IV, and the relations of Jews and Greeks, are also recorded in the historical works 1 and 2 Maccabees in the *Apocrypha*. They provide rare insights into Seleukid relations, and into Roman governance of the East.

The literary forms attested in the Old Testament are as diverse as any in the ancient world, paralleled by much in Greco-Roman culture. While we cannot call, for example, the book of Job TRAGEDY as such, it shares much of the agony over the human condition and the uncertainty of divine action. We can also find national sagas (Genesis), history (1 and 2 Samuel), love poetry (Song of Songs), proverbs (Proverbs), sceptical literature (Ecclesiastes) and NOVELS (Judith). The books of the *Apocrypha* are directly influenced by Greek literature. 1 and 2 Maccabees draw upon the HISTORIOGRAPHICAL tradition; the Wisdom of Solomon, a philosophical treatise on the Jewish figure of Wisdom, reflects the philosophical climate of 1st-century BC ALEXANDRIA and prefigures many NEOPLATONIC ideas; the book of Judith is an example of an ancient novel. These later books' technique of drawing upon earlier biblical books and at times making direct reference to older stories is indicative of the developing commentary tradition in JUDAISM. This is comparable to the rise in hellenistic commentaries in Alexandria, which themselves might also have had an influence on later Jewish biblical commentaries. JKA

oligarchy Greek word meaning 'rule by the few', a small group of usually affluent people. Oligarchy was one of the three forms of government used by the Greeks, the others being monarchy and DEMOCRACY. Its conceptualization is much influenced by its opposite number democracy, which advocated the political participation of all adult male citizens. Opponents of democracy either favoured a less radical form of democracy, one by which the poorest two citizen classes were excluded, or the strict enforcement of CENSUS criteria, limiting citizenship rights to the 5,000 or 3,000 most wealthy individuals. A good illustration of ÉLITE dissatisfaction with the democratic government towards the end of the 5th century can be found in the *Athênaiôn politeia* (*Constitution of the Athenians*) wrongly attributed to XENOPHON, usually known as 'the OLD OLIGARCH'. Exacerbated by a prolonged war with SPARTA, the champion of oligarchies, existing resentment was translated into action during the short-lived oligarchic regimes of the FOUR HUNDRED and the Five Thousand. Athens' military defeat resulted in the oligarchic coup by the THIRTY, during which regime more than 1,500 Athenians lost their lives. The political reversal, however, was short-lived: the democrats secured a victory in 403 and called for an amnesty, which they kept to religiously. After these events, oligarchy became a discredited term in Athens. After PHILIP II of Macedonia had put an end to the independent city-state, oligarchy was rarely heard of again, though hellenistic democracy, the usual form of government for Greek city-states, was not as radical as in classical Athens. When the Romans conquered Greece, however, a more oligarchic system of government was revived. MK

See Herodotos 3.80–4; Ostwald, M. (2000) *Oligarchia*.

olive, olive oil The cultivated olive tree (*Olea europaea* L. *sativa*) was one of the mainstays of the ancient agrarian ECONOMY, being rated 'first among trees' by COLUMELLA. Olive cultivation is closely contingent with the climatic and environmental limits of the MEDITERRANEAN itself; though more tolerant of low rainfall than either the grapevine or wheat, it is highly susceptible to frost damage. As an evergreen tree, it is a constant in the landscape through the seasons. The tree is also celebrated for its longevity and its ability to regenerate (as was the case of the tree on the ATHENIAN ACROPOLIS burned in the PERSIAN sack). Many olives are centuries old, though productivity has sometimes to be restored by the drastic action of cutting back to the rootstock. It is no surprise therefore to find that the olive occupied a special place in society as well as the economy in this zone. The tree is also known for its quirkiness – it has an inherent tendency towards biennial fruiting, leading to an irregular pattern of harvest yields, and it can take time to arrive at mature production, making the establishment of new orchards an investment for the next generation. No wonder it has also long been associated with PEACE.

It appears to have been first cultivated by the early Bronze Age in the eastern Mediterranean and the empirical knowledge of its propagation and cultivation spread from there to the west. Olive oil is believed to have been a significant element of the economy of MINOAN and MYCENAEAN civilizations, and regional and personal fortunes continued to be made from olive orchards and the oil trade throughout the Greek, hellenistic and Roman periods. The Roman period probably marks the apogee of inter-regional TRADE in olive oil, with Spain and North AFRICA in particular witnessing a 'boom' in production.

Olives are harvested across the late autumn and winter months, and the oil is pressed out of the milled or crushed fruit. When first picked from the tree, olives are inedibly bitter and must be treated or

OLIVE, OLIVE OIL: (a) olive harvesting with sticks, as illustrated on a British Museum vase.

OLIVE, OLIVE OIL: (b) and as still practised in Tunisia – olives, leaves and twigs fly in all directions as the tree is cudgelled.

preserved for eating. The distinction between green and black olives relates to the stage of maturity of the fruit; the former will eventually turn to the latter if left on the tree. Both olives and olive oil are highly nutritional food sources and their distinctive flavour has long been valued in cooking. Olive oil was not simply a comestible, but fulfilled a wide range of other uses in society – as lighting FUEL, as a base for PERFUMES and unguents, as 'SOAP', as a skin moisturizer and massage OIL. The by-products of its manufacture were equally practical: the desiccated pulp left after pressing was valued as solid FUEL, FERTILIZER and ANIMAL feed; the black liquid residue (*amurca*) was used as, among other things, insecticide, moth-proofer, wood-preserver, sealant, lubricant and animal tonic. (see also PRESSES) DJM

See Mattingly, D. J. (1996) First fruit? The olive in the Roman world, in G. Shipley and J. Salmon, eds., *Human Landscapes in Classical Antiquity* 213–53.

 *INSTRUMENTUM DOMESTICUM*; MILLS AND MILLING: (b); PRESSES: (a)–(b); RURAL SETTLEMENT.

Olympia Ancient cult site in ELIS in the north-western PELOPONNESE, birthplace of the OLYMPIC

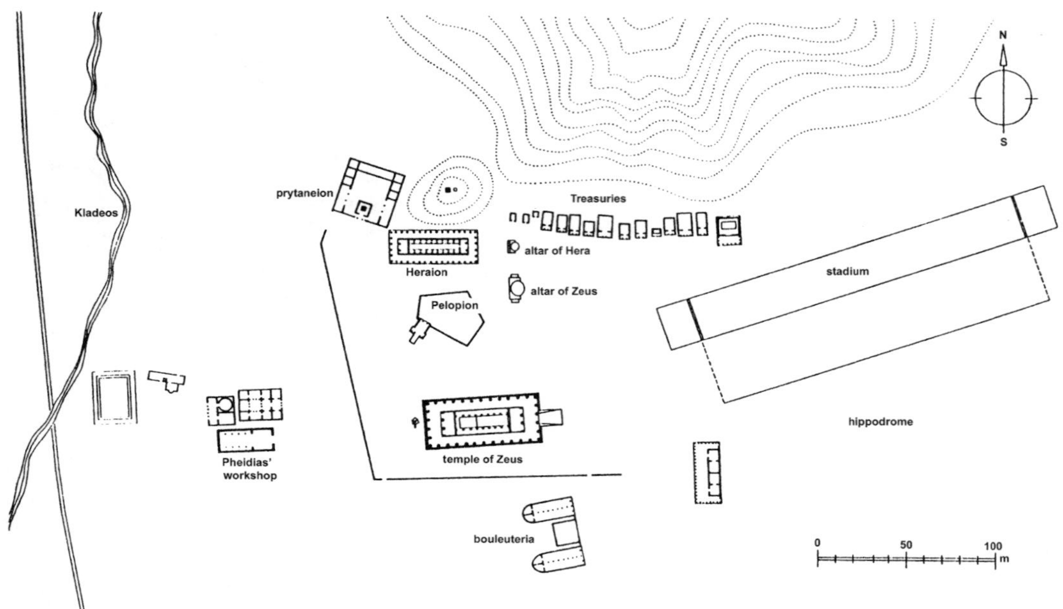

OLYMPIA: general plan, showing main temples, treasuries and the stadium.

GAMES. These took place every four years from (traditionally) 776 BC to AD 393 to honour ZEUS Olympios, the chief patron god of the major sanctuary at the site. The ATHLETIC contests at Olympia were the oldest of four such panhellenic (national) encounters, alongside the Pythian games at DELPHI, the Isthmian at CORINTH and the games at Nemea. All were integrated into religious FESTIVALS.

Occupation at the site of the sanctuary began as early as the 3rd millennium BC, but its religious character cannot be traced before the late MYCENAEAN period. Remains of SACRIFICES to Zeus go back to the 10th century BC in the area of the Altis, the sacred wood in the sanctuary. In the same area stood the first stadium in the late 6th century, opening towards the altar of Zeus and thus reflecting the religious significance of the games. By the 4th century BC the games had already been established in their own right, which necessitated moving the stadium outside the walls of the sanctuary. Further athletic grounds were laid out south-east of the Altis (the Hippodrome) and to its west (a GYMNASIUM and PALAESTRA). BATH buildings facilitated the preparation of athletes in the western area of the site from the classical period onwards. The temple of the god was a work of the Eleian ARCHITECT Libon, and was constructed in 456 BC. It was famous for the colossal image of the god that it housed, a chryselephantine statue ('of gold and ivory') by the renowned sculptor PHEIDIAS. Other sacred buildings and enclosures included the archaic temple of HERA, the sacred *temenos* of the local hero Pelops (the Pelopion), a temple dedicated to the Mother of the Gods CYBELE, and a long series of treasure buildings (*thêsauroi*), of a type similar to those at Delphi, to store valuables.

Excavations were begun in May 1829 by French archaeologists and continued from 1875 by the Germans. Systematic archaeological investigation did not begin before 1936, under the auspices of the German Institute of Archaeology, which has continued work until the present day together with the Greek Archaeological Service. EP

See Morgan, C. A. (1990) *Athletes and Oracles*; Yalouris, A. and Yalouris, N. (1987) *Olympia*.

 EARTHQUAKES; PELOPONNESE.

Olympias Daughter of Neoptolemos the Molossian; fourth wife of PHILIP II, king of Macedonia, and mother of ALEXANDER III. Perhaps she was partly responsible for Alexander's aspirations to divinity. A forerunner of the formidable QUEENS of the hellenistic era, she became notorious for her ambition and violent temper.

She did not take easily Philip's seventh marriage. Thus, when he was assassinated in 336 BC she became the prime suspect and put to death Philip's last wife as well as their child. After Alexander's death in 323, she became involved in the power struggle among the SUCCESSORS. In an effort to outweigh the regent Antipatros' influence on the chiliarch Perdikkas (the dominant Successor at that time), she offered Perdikkas her daughter Kleopatra in marriage (Antipatros had offered him his daughter Nikaia). When Kassandros (Antipatros' son) challenged the appointment of Polyperchon to the regency of Macedonia, Olympias sided with Polyperchon and together they attacked the puppet king Philip III Arrhidaios (half-brother of Alexander) and his wife EURYDIKE (3). Olympias put both to death and unleashed a witch-hunt against Kassandros' brothers and followers, but he proved stronger and Olympias was executed by his army in 316. IK

See Hammond, N. G. L. and Griffith, G. T. (1979) *A History of Macedonia*, vol. 2.

Olympic games The oldest and most famous ATHLETIC competitions (*agônes*) in the ancient Greek and Roman world. The games were held at the sanctuary of ZEUS, in a precinct known as the Altis beside the river Alpheios at OLYMPIA. Traditionally the first games were held in 776 BC. They continued every four years until AD 393, when they were forbidden by the CHRISTIAN emperor THEODOSIUS I. In the following centuries the site was largely forgotten, destroyed by EARTHQUAKES and buried by flooding of the Alpheios and its tributary, the Kladeos. The Altis, in fact, sits in the flood plain at the junction of these two rivers and the hill of Kronos. The site was gradually buried under c.4 m (13 ft) of silt and not rediscovered until the late 18th century. The rediscovery and excavations of Olympia further inspired the British doctor W. P. Brookes and French nobleman Pierre de Coubertin in their quest to revive the Olympic games for the modern age. The first modern games took place at Athens in 1896.

The origin of the games belongs to the realm of MYTH, though historical and archaeological investigations have provided further information. The traditional date, 776 BC, derives from the victory-lists composed around 400 BC by Hippias of Elis, who records that Koroibos was the first to win the *stadion* race. The Olympics are far older than any of the other great periodic games. The Pythian games for APOLLO at DELPHI date to 586, the Isthmian for POSEIDON to 582, and the Nemean for ZEUS to 573. Yet we need not doubt the early appeal of athletic competitions. HOMER's descriptions of the funeral games for Patroklos (*Iliad* 23) and the games at Phaiakia (Phaeacia) in which ODYSSEUS competes (*Odyssey* 8) provide evidence for Greek interest in ATHLETIC competitions by the early archaic age at the latest. Indeed, myth suggests that the games at Olympia were far older. PINDAR, in his first *Olympian Ode*, explains that they were founded by Pelops to celebrate his victory over Oinomaos in the CHARIOT RACE for the hand of Hippodamia, though elsewhere he states that HERAKLES founded the games (*Olympian* 10).

Hippias' lists of victors do not survive, but modern historians have reconstructed them in part. The early lists are dominated by Dorian Greeks from the Peloponnese, especially SPARTANS, but the games themselves were properly panhellenic, that is, open to all (and only) Greeks. For much of their early history, the sanctuary and games were controlled by nearby Elis. The Olympic truce, announced by HERALDS known as *spondophoroi*, was meant to allow safe passage for athletes and spectators travelling to Olympia for the celebration of the games. Athletes and their trainers arrived about a month in advance for a mandatory training period, probably held at Elis, under the supervision of the *hellanodikai* (literally, 'judges of the Greeks'). In part, this supervisory period allowed the *hellanodikai* to verify the ages of the competitors, since boys competed against boys and men against men. Before the games began, competitors were inspected, a process known as the *dokimasia*. Other athletic festivals that adopted the Olympic rules were known as 'isolympic'.

Unlike many other agonistic festivals, which included MUSICAL and poetic competitions, Olympia at first held only athletic and equestrian events, though competitions for heralds and trumpeters came to be included later. Early festivals seem to have lasted four days; this was extended to five in the hellenistic period and six under the Roman empire. The festivities seem to have opened with the swearing of an OATH to Zeus, probably followed by the competition for heralds and trumpeters. Religious rites for Pelops, a procession and a great sacrifice to Zeus were held on the third day. The athletic events were held in the stadium, just east of the Altis. The classical stadium was 1 *stadion* or 600 Olympic feet in length (c.192 m, 210 yards), and had banks on all sides for spectators to stand (there were no seats). It is estimated that about 40,000 people were able to watch. Athletes entered the stadium from the Altis, through a tunnel under the embankment on the west side. The earliest and most prestigious athletic event was the *stadion* race, in which the athletes ran the length of the stadium towards the Altis. The stadium of the archaic period was a simple, open space and ended inside the Altis, reinforcing the religious association of the games. Other running events included the *diaulos* (2 *stadia* in length), *dolichos* (24 *stadia*), and *hoplitodromos* (a race in HOPLITE ARMOUR). A starting mechanism, the *hysplêx*, ensured a fair start. Other athletic events included the *pentathlon* (javelin, discus, jump, foot race and wrestling) and the so-called heavy events: wrestling, boxing and the *pankration*. Victors were awarded an olive wreath.

Equestrian events were held in the hippodrome, a large, open space to the south of the stadium. The remains of the hippodrome are lost, swept away by the Alpheios river. It is estimated that the hippodrome was over 600 m (660 yards) in length, perhaps as much as 1,050 m (1,150 yards). A number of equestrian races were held, usually on the second day: the *tethrippon* (four-horse chariot race), *kelês* (horse-race), *apênê* (mule-cart race), *kalpê* (mares' race) and *synôris* (two-horse chariot race). The owners of the horses, rather than the jockeys or charioteers, were considered to be the victors. One woman, a Spartan princess named Kyniska (sister of AGESILAOS), won an equestrian victory. Otherwise, women did not compete, though they seem to have been permitted to watch. Young women, however, could compete in the four-yearly games of HERA (Heraia), held at Olympia, which included a shortened *stadion* foot-race organized by women of different ages. MJC

See Golden, M. (1998) *Sport and Society in Ancient Greece*; Lee, H. (2001) *The Program and Schedule of the Ancient Olympic Games*; Raschke, W. J., ed. (1988) *The Archaeology of the Olympics*.

Olynthos City on the Chalkidike peninsula in northern Greece. Literary sources show that it played a dominant role in the politics of the area, leading two successive confederacies of Chalkidian cities and fighting off attacks by Athens, Sparta and Macedonia. The city finally fell to PHILIP II in 348 BC, and DEMOSTHENES says it was completely obliterated.

The remains of the ancient city occupy two flat-topped hills and spill onto the plain below. Four major campaigns of excavation were carried out by the American School of Classical Studies in the 1920s and 1930s, led by D. M. Robinson. He established that after a brief phase of Neolithic occupation the main episode of settlement began at around 1000 BC and lasted until the 4th century BC, with limited reoccupation in Byzantine times. Although his original aim was to locate some of the main public buildings, he found only ancillary structures, including a FOUNTAIN HOUSE and mint. Nevertheless, he was able to reconstruct the rectilinear grid pattern of the streets, and the line of the defensive walls. The importance of the site, however, lies in the large numbers of early 4th-century HOUSES excavated on the north hill and recorded in detail, which offer an unparalleled picture of domestic life in a late classical city. (see also TOWN PLANNING) LCN

See Cahill, N. (2002) *Household and City Organization at Olynthus*; Gude, M. (1933) *A History of Olynthus*; Robinson, D. M. et al. (1929–52) *Excavations at Olynthus*, 14 vols.

 GREECE; HOUSES, GREEK: (c).

Opimii A PLEBEIAN *gens* at Rome, few of whose members reached the consulship. One member of the family, Lucius Opimius, as PRAETOR in 125 BC defeated Fregellae, which had revolted, but did not celebrate a TRIUMPH. He used a *senatus consultum ultimum* to rid Rome of Gaius GRACCHUS and his supporters when he was CONSUL in 121. Opimius was acquitted of charges after this incident, but in 109 was sent into exile for actions regarding JUGURTHA. He was buried at Dyrrachium. His consulship became known for the high quality of the WINES made during it. In the *Satyricon* of PETRONIUS (34.6), TRIMALCHIO boasts about serving Falernian wine of Opimian vintage, which he calls 100 years old. In fact, the wine was older, though its true age depends on the dramatic date of the work. PLINY THE ELDER reports that wine made in 121 BC was still available when he was writing, in the 50s–70s AD (*Natural History* 14.6.55–7). It was not consumed on its own, but used to flavour and spice newer vintages. JV

Oplontis The *PEUTINGER TABLE* (a Roman map or itinerary) locates Oplontis (mod. Torre Annunziata) between POMPEII and HERCULANEUM. EXCAVATIONS along the ancient shoreline have revealed a grand VILLA destroyed by Vesuvius in AD 79. Built in the mid-1st century BC, the *villa maritima* expanded for over 130 m (430 ft) along the sea. Its central axis stretched through the atrium and interior GARDEN to a large reception hall that enjoyed a back view onto park-like grounds lined with trees, shrubs and statuary. Second Style painting of false doors and views of colonnades and sanctuaries adorned the walls of the atrium and nearby rooms. Subsequent additions and renovations were in the Third and Fourth Styles, offering a study of changing styles and subjects in aristocratic artistic taste.

The west wing housed residential and reception spaces, a BATH suite and kitchen. To the east was an internal peristyle painted with diagonal black and white stripes, signifying the servile staff's storage, work and living spaces. Further east, a large pool lined with trees and statuary created the feel of a Greek GYMNASIUM. Along its west and south sides, intricate suites of rooms recall the complex ARCHITECTURAL planning of NERO's Golden House in Rome (AD 64–9). EPIGRAPHIC evidence attributes this villa to the family of Nero's second wife, POPPAEA Sabina. Although the south-east corner contains wine-press facilities, the villa was primarily a *locus amoenus*, a place of charming fiction, where plantings, paintings, MOSAICS and SCULPTURE reconciled raw nature with elegant scenes of civilization for the studied enjoyment of reposing Romans. PWF

See Clarke, J.R. (1991) *The Houses of Roman Italy, 100 BC–AD 250*; Varone, A. (2002) Villa of Poppea at Oplontis, in F. Coarelli, ed., *Pompeii* 360–77.

 HOUSES, ROMAN: (d); WALL-PAINTING: (b).

optimates see ÉLITES; PLEBEIANS.

oracles A term with multiple significance, generally connoting the response of a GOD (or deified HERO) to a question posed by an individual about a present or future situation. 'Oracle' is regularly used to refer to the shrine or sanctuary of a god whose PROPHECIES were sought, but it may also allude to the human vehicle through whom the god spoke (the prophet or prophetess). Ancient oracles offered prestigious advice to those who consulted them on private or public matters. Questions of the former kind ranged from childbirth and sea voyages to MARRIAGE and other aspects of private life. States consulted oracles before important political decisions and military undertakings, such as a war or founding a COLONIAL settlement abroad, but also in cases of natural disaster and ritual POLLUTION. Specialized oracles existed too, offering advice on health matters, notably at the sanctuaries of healing deities, such as ASKLEPIOS at Epidauros and Amphiaraos at Oropos.

In both Greek and Roman contexts, oracles were delivered orally but recorded in order to be interpreted for the enquirer by special groups of religious personnel. Such was the case at DELPHI, where the cryptic utterances of Pythia, the virgin priestess of APOLLO, were written down by 'the prophets'. At the oracle of ZEUS at DODONA on EPIRUS, the Selloi or Helloi seem to have performed a similar function. At the sanctuaries of healing divinities, the response from the god came to the enquirer in a DREAM, which often required interpretation. Apollo was the god of prophecy *par excellence*. His oracular sanctuaries attracted people from all over Greece and abroad to Delphi and to DIDYMA, Klaros and MILETOS, the last three all in Ionia.

At Delphi, the prophetess or Pythia delivered the oracles in a form unintelligible to the common enquirer, usually a reflection of the ecstatic state of divine possession she experienced during the prophetic process. PLUTARCH reveals interesting insights into the oracular process at the site, where he himself served as a PRIEST in the late 1st and early 2nd centuries AD. Late descriptions of the oracular process refer to the Pythia eating leaves of laurel, a plant believed to carry prophetic properties, or sitting on the sacred tripod of Apollo. Methods of divination practised elsewhere relied on reading a variety of signs generated by natural phenomena and the elements, or interpreting the behaviour of victims during SACRIFICE and similar evidence. Standard rituals surrounding the central act of prophecy included PRAYERS, sacrifice and other offerings to the deity.

Public confidence in the effectiveness of oracles was shaken in the 5th century BC, partly because of the criticism traditional religious practice endured from the Sophists. The advent of Christianity put an official end to paganism in Greece, including prophecy and the places where it was practised. EP

See Parker, R. (2000) Greek states and Greek oracles, in R. Buxton, ed., *Oxford Readings in Greek Religion* 76–108; Price, S. (1985) Delphi and divination, in P. E. Easterling and J.V. Muir, eds., *Greek Religion and Society* 128–54 (repr. 2000).

oral tradition Ancient Greece was predominantly an oral society, where the percentage of people who were able to read and write beyond a basic level was small. This orality manifests itself in both literature and various day-to-day activities. The most obvious literary example of oral composition and transmission is the epic poetry of Homer and Hesiod. The formulaic nature of their hexameter verse facilitated spontaneous composition and memorization, and the poems were transmitted orally for centuries before they were written down. This kind of extempore composition continued later in poetry written for *symposia*, but the introduction of the alphabet in the 8th century naturally encouraged written composition, though even then the lyric poetry that was one of its first products was meant to be listened to rather than read. Oral tradition was also crucial for the preservation of historical information down to the 5th century BC. Herodotos on his travels consulted people before records, then recited his story to the Athenians. The notorious factual errors in the texts of the Attic orators (notably at Andokides 3.3–12, repeated at Aischines 2.172–6) are due to faulty and biased oral family recollections. Oratory, while it became one of the most influential literary genres, was nevertheless first and foremost an oral affair: politicians and litigants were expected to speak without a text. The importance of written literature clearly increased during the 5th and 4th centuries, but the element of performance remained crucial.

Apart from literature, the oral nature of Greek society as a whole is highly visible in, for example, legal affairs. Written documents and contracts were deeply distrusted, and the only area of Athenian law where contracts were required was in disputes involving maritime trade. But even here the role of witnesses was central (though paradoxically, in the 4th century, witness testimony was produced in written form and read out by the clerk, without cross-examination); and in all forms of contract, such as marriage or loans, witnesses were present. A defendant named Euphiletos, accused of the homicide of one Eratosthenes, goes to great lengths to demonstrate that when he killed his wife's lover (as was permitted by law under certain circumstances) he did so in front of witnesses (Lysias 1.23–4, 37–42). Again, there were no birth certificates in Athens; to demonstrate his citizenship (as was periodically required during the 4th century in revisions of the deme registers) a man needed to produce witnesses to the status of his parents, and prove that his father had accepted him as his own when a baby and subsequently enrolled him in the requisite groupings, such as deme and phratry.

Roman society generally placed much greater emphasis on the written word, as the many documents from Roman Egypt indicate. Though accurate comparative statistics are elusive, levels of literacy were typically higher in the Roman world; as a result, scholars have paid much less attention to orality in Roman society. But the practice of having an educated slave (*anagnôstês* in Greek) to give literary recitations is one area where the influence of orality persisted. Family histories handed down to succeeding generations along with the masks worn at funerals are another example. For the most part, authors dictated their works to slaves who did the actual writing; this oral process was undoubtedly helpful for incorporating prose rhythm, but the emphasis was primarily on the written text, often even in the realm of rhetoric. MJE

See MacKay, E. A., ed. (1999) *Signs of Orality*; Thomas, R. (1992) *Literacy and Orality in Ancient Greece*; Watson, J., ed. (2001) *Speaking Volumes*.

Oramazda see Ahura-Mazda.

orators

The main flowering of Greek oratory came in Athens in the late 5th and 4th centuries BC. Most, but not all (Lysias, Isaios, Deinarchos), of the best practitioners were Athenians, and their works were categorized in the great libraries of Alexandria and Pergamon. It was perhaps due to an Alexandrian scholar that the canon of ten Attic orators was formed, but another candidate as founder is Kaikilios (Caecilius) of Kale Akte in the Augustan period, who wrote a work *On the Style of the Ten Orators*. Kaikilios' contemporary Dionysios did not accept this canon, and lists only six of its members as worthy of imitation (*On Imitation* 5). He wrote essays on these (replacing his earlier choice of Lykourgos with Isaios), later adding an essay on Deinarchos. Five is the number given by Quintilian (10.1.76–80, but ten at 12.10.20ff.) and Dio Chrysostom (18.11).

Who Kaikilios' ten were, precisely, is unclear. They may not have been the same as those who had become canonical by the 2nd century AD, when Hermogenes (*On Ideas* 2.11) gives the list as Lysias, Isaios, Hypereides, Isokrates, Deinarchos, Aischines, Antiphon, Lykourgos, Andokides and Demosthenes. The same names feature in the *Lives of the Ten Orators* wrongly attributed to Plutarch. These are the orators under whose names the speeches have come down to us in manuscripts and papyri (Hypereides survives only on papyrus), though some of these speeches were clearly written by other orators, such as Apollodoros. MJE

See Edwards, M. J. (1994) *The Attic Orators*; Usher, S. (1999) *Greek Oratory*.

From the late Republic until late antiquity, oratory occupied an important place in the exercise of politics in the Roman world. By the 1st century BC, training in Greek rhetorical principles formed a central part of élite education, and the ability to speak well in public was an essential element in political success. Hence many great politicians of the late Republic were also accomplished orators. Cicero, for example, first came to prominence through his oratorical abilities. Even if the advent of the principate meant that freedom of speech was restricted, oratory remained an integral part of élite education. Orators' talents now were often deployed to praise ruling emperors, and successful orators could achieve star status. In the 2nd century AD, men such as DIO CHRYSOSTOM ('Golden-mouthed') of Prusa and AELIUS ARISTIDES performed their speeches in various cities around the empire, and commanded the ears of emperors. Two centuries later, the pagan THEMISTIUS' oratorical talents allowed him to remain a prominent figure at the courts of several successive emperors, regardless of their stance on the religious conflicts of the age. That the speeches of so many orators survive is testimony to the success of the genre. Indeed, orators themselves collected and circulated editions of their speeches in an effort to enhance their reputations. Yet some speeches are not what they might seem: Cicero, for example, published six speeches against Gaius Verres, the corrupt former governor of Sicily; only one, however, was delivered at VERRES' actual trial in 70 BC. (see also RHETORIC, ROMAN) MDH

oratory

The practice of public speaking, oratory, was central to Greek culture and society, and the ability to address persuasively an assembly, LAWCOURT or other public gathering was a key skill. Our earliest literature, the Homeric EPICS, contains numerous examples of the HEROES making public pronouncements. In the work of HISTORIANS the narrative of events is regularly punctuated by speeches. These literary creations reflect the reality of public life, especially in DEMOCRACIES. Oratory became increasingly important at Athens during the 5th century BC as the impetus towards radical democracy grew. Leading politicians such as THEMISTOKLES and PERIKLES (famous for *bons mots* such as 'AIGINA, the sty in the eye of PIRAEUS') were accomplished speakers. Tuition in speaking was available from the SOPHISTS, notably GORGIAS, but it was recognized that the best political, or deliberative, oratory was spontaneous. No transcripts of political speeches survive until the 4th century.

It is with judicial, or 'forensic', oratory that the picture changes, beginning with Antiphon in the last quarter of the 5th century. Spontaneity was prized in the lawcourt too, and litigants were expected to speak without a written text, but inexperienced speakers were able to consult professional speechwriters (*logographoi*) who would give them a speech to memorize. The writers then published the speeches to advertise their ability, and a new literary genre was born. One of the most important logographers of the 4th century was LYSIAS, but oratory reached its peak with the speeches, both forensic and deliberative, of DEMOSTHENES. Troubled times (in this case the Macedonian threat) produce great speakers, but none greater than Athens' finest patriot. A few examples also survive of a third type of oratory, the epideictic ('display') funeral orations given by a prominent figure in honour of those who had fallen in war.

The Macedonian conquest of Greece inevitably led to a decline in deliberative oratory, as the freedom to debate major policy issues in the assembly was restricted during periods of dictatorship or external rule, and particularly after the Roman conquest. While the courts continued to function, no speeches are preserved from the hellenistic period. What certainly did flourish now (though again nothing extensive survives) was the study of oratory, or RHETORIC, which already had a long history going back to the 5th-century sophists and had reached its own peak with ARISTOTLE'S *Rhetoric*. Hellenistic scholars made increasingly intricate studies of rhetoric, and alongside these grew the practice of DECLAMATION (*meletê*), speeches on imaginary themes which became central to Greco-Roman EDUCATION. These *meletai*, especially in Asia Minor (at RHODES and PERGAMON), became increasingly exuberant and florid. Their so-called Asianist style eventually sparked a reaction at Rome in the later 1st century BC, to be followed in the 2nd century AD by the Attic revival known as the SECOND SOPHISTIC.

One other setting deserves mention here, Greco-Roman Egypt, from where PAPYRI survive containing the transcripts of Greek speeches delivered in trials. They are not the works of master orators, but are practical examples of oratory in that period. MJE

See Kennedy, G. A. (1963) *The Art of Persuasion in Greece.*

In Roman rhetorical handbooks three categories or genres of oratory were distinguished, according to the context in which orations were performed. (1) Deliberative oratory, used by speakers in political debates in the SENATE and other assemblies. (2) Forensic oratory, used by advocates in the lawcourts. (3) Epideictic oratory, a wide-ranging category that encompassed speeches in praise or blame of a particular individual. These categories show the influence of Greek rhetorical ideas on Roman practice, though public speaking – such as in political debates and at aristocratic FUNERALS – must have been well established since the beginnings of the Roman Republic.

The last two centuries of the Republic saw the flourishing of deliberative and forensic oratory, both of which reached their apogee in the speeches of CICERO. A 'new man' (*novus homo*) from outside the traditional senatorial aristocracy, Cicero made his name through oratory, first through forensic speeches (notably those delivered when he prosecuted Gaius VERRES, the governor of SICILY, on charges of extortion in 70 BC), and later through his political orations (such as his contributions to the debate on the CATILINARIAN conspiracy in 63). With oratory so central to the political and legal operations of the Republic, a thorough training in RHETORIC became a central part of ÉLITE EDUCATION. Cicero himself wrote treatises on the theory and practice of rhetoric.

Under the PRINCIPATE, deliberative and forensic oratory must have declined as political and legal debate fell under the increasingly close scrutiny of the emperor. Epideictic oratory flourished, however, particularly in the form of speeches in praise of the emperor, such as PLINY THE YOUNGER'S *Panegyric* on TRAJAN (AD 100), or the many eulogies delivered in honour of numerous late antique emperors. Thus, in spite of the portentous warnings of TACITUS' *Dialogue on Oratory* that public speaking was falling into decline under the emperors, rhetoric and oratory remained the cornerstone of élite education down to the end of antiquity. Indeed, with the rise of CHRISTIANITY, oratory found a new outlet in the sermons delivered by BISHOPS to the faithful.

The central importance of oratory in Roman education reflected the complex rules attached to

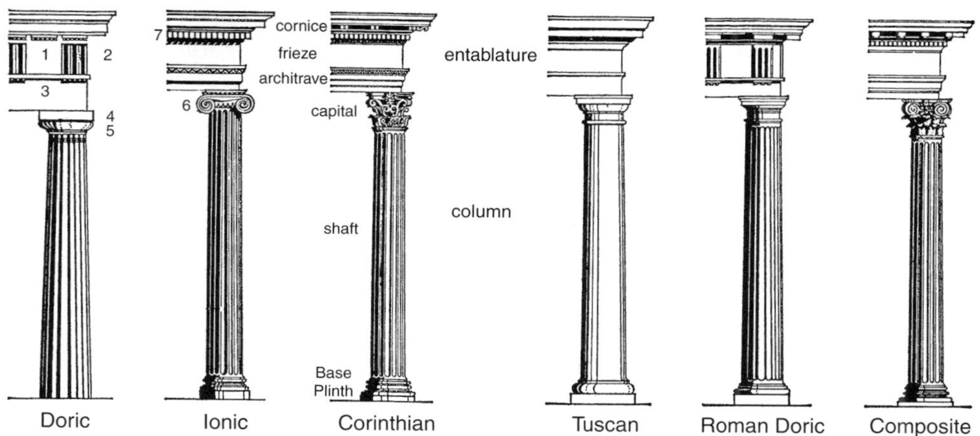

ORDERS, ARCHITECTURAL: (a) the main orders of classical architecture and their principal components. Note also 1. metope; 2. triglyph; 3. guttae; 4. abacus; 5. echinus; 6. volute; 7. dentils.

the composition and delivery of speeches. An oration was meant to be formally structured, with various rhetorical devices (e.g. juxtaposition of words, wit) deployed to make the argument of speeches all the more persuasive. In addition, the performance of speeches was circumscribed by rules relating to modulations of the voice and gestures made by the orator. Through the manner of their delivery, then, orators could add emphasis to their arguments. Thus, when Gaius GRACCHUS, while making speeches in the Roman forum, physically turned his back on the senate to address the people (PLUTARCH, *Gaius Gracchus* 5), he made an emphatic statement of popular appeal before even uttering a word. MDH

See Cicero, *On the Ideal Orator*, trs. J. M. May and J. Wisse (2001); Aldrete, G. (1999) *Gestures and Acclamations in Ancient Rome*; Clarke, M. L. (1996) *Rhetoric at Rome*; Dominik, W. J., ed. (1997) *Roman Eloquence*; Nixon, C. E.V. and Rodgers, B. S. (1994) *In Praise of Later Roman Emperors*.

orchestra see DRAMA, GREEK; THEATRES; see also PANTOMIME.

orders, architectural The principal orders of Greek ARCHITECTURE in the 6th and 5th centuries BC were the Doric and the Ionic. Doric, distinguished by its plain 'cushion' capital and the triglyphs and metopes which make up the frieze, developed in stone in the 6th century, with possible forerunners in TIMBER. Doric columns, which are fluted, rise from the stylobate without bases. The Ionic has a pair of volutes on either side, linked in developed Ionic by egg-and-dart decoration. Ionic was inspired by orientalizing motifs, but the transfer to monumental architecture seems to have been a Greek idea. The entablature of Ionic consists of dentils immediately above the plain architrave in the Ionic homelands, but in mainland Greece, a sculptured frieze replaced the dentils. The base of the Ionic column varies: the 'mainland' variant is more compact than the taller 'eastern' version.

In the late 5th century BC in mainland Greece, Doric and Ionic were joined by Corinthian, allegedly designed by PHEIDIAS' pupil Kallimachos when he saw an acanthus plant growing round the base of a grave monument at CORINTH. The developed Corinthian capital is decorated with two rows of acanthus leaves at the base and with volutes (smaller than Ionic) springing from all four corners. It was

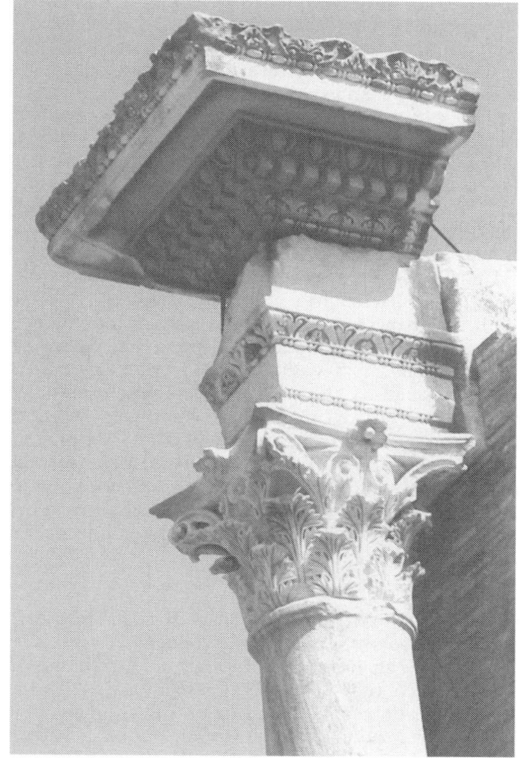

ORDERS, ARCHITECTURAL: (b) the Corinthian order of the Forum Baths at Ostia.

slow to appear on exteriors, but became Rome's most popular order into late antiquity.

Rome added two orders, as well as a version of Doric. The Tuscan, perhaps borrowed from the ETRUSCANS, has a narrow decorative band near the top of the column shaft, which is plain rather than fluted. When employed with triglyphs and metopes it is called 'Roman Doric'; in the more elaborate version, the normally austere and plain 'cushion' of the capital is decorated with a continuous ring of egg and dart. The other original contribution of Rome is the Composite order, a combination of the prominent volutes of Ionic with the acanthus leaves of Corinthian. RJAW

See Barletta, B. (2002) *The Origins of the Greek Architectural Orders*; Onians, J. (1988) *Bearers of Meaning: the classical orders in antiquity, the Middle Ages, and the Renaissance.*

 ARCHITECTURE: (a)–(d).

ores Few of the metals used in antiquity were readily available in nature as metals (GOLD is one of the exceptions). The IRON, COPPER and other metals used were obtained by extracting metal from rocks. Most rocks contain small quantities of metal, and where the proportion of metal is sufficiently high the rocks are usually known as ores. Importantly, a rock can be classed as an ore if it contains a high enough level of a desired metal and the appropriate TECHNOLOGICAL, social and economic setting exists to allow people to exploit it. The status of the same ore body may change over time as technologies, social conditions and economies change.

The ores for non-ferrous metals (i.e. copper, TIN, lead, SILVER and gold) generally occur in mountainous areas, such as Spain, the ALPS, Greece and ASIA Minor. These ores are denser than most other rocks and many are brightly coloured. The ores are often found as thin veins in the 'country rock' or as 'placer' deposits in sediments downstream from the veins. Many of the more valuable non-ferrous ore bodies were worked by the state, e.g. the silver MINES at LAURION. Iron ores are found more widely than non-ferrous ores, are common in lowland regions, and often occur as relatively large ore bodies. In some cases iron ores were exploited on a large scale as state enterprises, but in other cases small iron ore deposits were worked on an occasional basis for purely local needs. DD

Oresteia A trilogy of three tragedies (*Agamemnon*, *Libation Bearers*, *Eumenides*) produced at Athens by AESCHYLUS in 458 BC in conjunction with the SATYR play *Proteus* (now lost). The *Oresteia* deals with the disastrous homecoming of AGAMEMNON and its aftermath: the murder of Agamemnon upon his return from Troy at the hands of his wife CLYTEMNESTRA and her lover Aigisthos (*Agamemnon*); the eventual deaths of Clytemnestra and Aigisthos at the hands of Agamemnon's son Orestes (*Libation Bearers*); the hounding of Orestes by the Furies of the dead Clytemnestra; and his acquittal at Athens before the court of the Areiopagos – founded, in this version of the myth, for this very purpose (*Eumenides*).

The myth is treated at some length in HOMER's *Odyssey*, where it serves as a complex foil for the return of ODYSSEUS, and in PINDAR's *Pythian Ode* 11 (474 BC?). In Aeschylus' treatment it provides the occasion for a profound meditation on the nature of the GODS, vengeance, and the administration of JUSTICE, with particular relevance to the Athens of Aeschylus' day. As the sole trilogy to survive intact, the *Oresteia* offers valuable insights into Aeschylus' dramatic methods.

Agamemnon portrays a society caught up in a seemingly inextricable web of MURDER, vengeance and betrayal. Through the meditations of the CHORUS, Aeschylus involves the audience in a nightmarish world of vengeance killings, where each tainted act of 'justice' (*dikê*) leads to an equally tainted response. The unwholesomeness of this world is brought out through a series of images, particularly that of the burgeoning of EVIL, as new desecrations repeatedly blossom to fulfilment. More troubling still is the fact that the GODS themselves are implicated, as sponsors of a retributive justice that drives each avenger to commit a new act of sacrilege. This theme is brought to the fore through the image of the corrupt SACRIFICE, which becomes a metaphor for the tainted justice that dominates the play. Also prominent is the image of the net, symbolizing the confounding (and conflicting) obligations and imperatives in which the various figures find themselves enmeshed. The title character appears on stage for only some 200 lines; instead, the focus is on Clytemnestra, whose sinister presence comes to symbolize the primitive lust for blood vengeance that haunts the House of Atreus.

The confusion of *Agamemnon* is brought to a head in *Libation Bearers* with the murder of Clytemnestra. The impossible position in which the youthful Orestes finds himself – compelled to slaughter his own mother or face the wrath of his father's vengeful spirit – vividly illustrates the inherent contradictions of the blood feud.

A resolution is achieved with Orestes' acquittal before the court of the Areiopagos (*Eumenides*). On the human level, the primitive blood vengeance of *Agamemnon* is replaced by a *POLIS*-based system of trial by jury. The redemption of the old order is symbolized, on the divine level, by the subordination of the Furies – portrayed as the physical embodiment of the older system of retributive justice – to the authority of the OLYMPIAN deities and the *polis*. An important element of the redeemed order is the subordination of the female to the male, presented as a triumph of rationalism over primitive blood lust.

The trilogy's conclusion is usually read as a celebration of the enlightened political and legal mechanisms of contemporary Athens. Debate continues on whether, and how, *Eumenides* may comment on the curtailment of the Areiopagos' authority by Ephialtes in 462/1. Moreover, several scholars have noted that the sophistic arguments by which APOLLO obtains Orestes' acquittal offer a curious charter for the new *polis*-based system. The *Oresteia* informs several works of SOPHOKLES and EURIPIDES. In modern times, it has provided the basis for various MARXIST and feminist interpretations of ancient society. JP

See Collard, C. (2002) *Aeschylus, Oresteia*; Conacher, D.J. (1987) *Aeschylus' Oresteia*; Goldhill, S. (1992) *Aeschylus, The Oresteia*.

oriental cults see CYBELE; GODS AND GODDESSES; ISIS; MITHRAS AND MITHRAISM; SOL INVICTUS.

orientalism, modern The concept of orientalism has been shaped over centuries by 'westerners'; it challenges the very notion of how the West has come to view the East, mainly from a 'superior' viewpoint. The concept has been given academic kudos by Edward Said's study *Orientalism*, in which he highlights common misconceptions regarding the orient. He chastises Western historical, social and religious studies of the Middle East and North Africa, and accuses Western civilization of being inherently biased against the East, a concept he traces back to the first performance of AESCHYLUS' tragedy *Persians* in 472 BC. Here, as in later European and American works, oriental cultures and RELIGIONS, when compared to their Western counterparts, are painted as exotic, different, traditional, sensual and fanatic. Said describes orientalism as a means through which the West comes to terms with the orient. This is based on the orient's special place in Western experience; orientalism has helped to define the West. Said describes the desire for knowledge about the orient as having been spawned from the desire to colonialize the East effectively, not to decipher the complex nature of a society which is inherently different. By comprehending the orient as intrinsically different, the West justified a position of ownership. The most common classification for orientalism is an academic one: those who teach, write about or research the orient, regardless of whether they are ANTHROPOLOGISTS, SOCIOLOGISTS or historians, are orientalists, and what they say or do is orientalism. LL-J

See Hall, E. (1989) *Inventing the Barbarian*; Said, E. (1978) *Orientalism*.

Origen see CHRISTIAN PHILOSOPHY; CHRISTIANITY; CHURCH COUNCILS; EGYPT; EUSEBIOS; JEROME.

Oromazda see AHURA-MAZDA.

Orontes river see AL MINA; ANTIOCH; PHOENICIA AND PHOENICIANS.

Orosius The presbyter Paulus Orosius is best remembered for his *History against the Pagans*, composed at the request of AUGUSTINE (1). It is a compilation of world history from the Flood to AD 416, written against the backdrop of the sack of Rome in 410 and concerned to refute the pagan argument that CHRISTIANITY was responsible for this disaster.

Orosius was born in Spain, probably at Braga c.375–80, and as a young priest experienced the various barbarian incursions into Spain in 409. He went to AFRICA and sought the favour of Augustine by presenting him with a pamphlet on Spanish heretics. Augustine warded off this eager young zealot against heresy by sending him to question JEROME at Bethlehem. While in the Holy Land he met BISHOP John of JERUSALEM in 415 but failed to sway him from his support for Pelagius. Orosius returned with relics from the newly discovered tomb of St Stephen, which he deposited in Minorca. Returning to Hippo, he composed the *Apology against the Pelagians*, a work in two parts containing a personal defence against accusations of blasphemy made by John and an exposition and refutation of Pelagian doctrines. PMB

See Hunt, E. D. (1982) *Holy Land Pilgrimage in the Later Roman Empire*.

Orpheus The origins of Orpheus have been much debated. In particular, there has been controversy as to whether he was an actual historical figure. Whether real or mythical, Orpheus is certainly mentioned in mid-6th-century BC writings, and occurs even earlier in art.

Throughout the classical world, Orpheus assumed many roles. The Greeks regarded him as a great POET and spiritual leader. Throughout his existence, he has also been seen as a gifted MUSICIAN, with the power to charm nature. He is perhaps most famous, however, for his devotion to his wife EURYDICE. In the famous love story, she is poisoned by a snake and dies. He uses his musical gifts to persuade the powers of the underworld to allow her to return to the living. He is successful, and she is allowed to return on the understanding that Orpheus does not look back as she follows him out of HADES. Unfortunately, he cannot stop himself from taking a glance over his shoulder, and she is lost forever. Because Orpheus continues his mourning and refuses to remarry, he is torn to pieces by THRACIAN women. His head floats out to sea, still singing laments for the lost Eurydice.

The many aspects of Orpheus' character have encouraged continued reinterpretation of the MYTH throughout the ages. The Greeks were particularly concerned with his spiritual powers, while the Romans tended to focus on the love story of Orpheus and Eurydice, as exemplified in the work

ORPHEUS: the lyre-playing Orpheus surrounded by wild beasts in a replica of the Woodchester Great Mosaic Pavement.

of VIRGIL and OVID. By the later Roman period his spiritual powers were once again admired, and he came to play an important role in NEOPLATONIC thought. He can also be seen as an allegorical figure in early CHRISTIAN contexts, and remained a popular figure throughout the medieval period and beyond. SAS

orphism Ancient MYSTERY cult founded by the mythical figure Orpheus. The latter was known as a SINGER and MUSICIAN, POET and prophet, who after his death received divine honours. He is renowned in myth for descending to the underworld to bring back his dead wife, having cast a spell with his music on Kerberos, the three-headed monster guarding the gates of HADES.

Orpheus was believed to have written a *Theogony* as well as books and instructions for rituals, which included purifications and initiations (PLATO, *Republic* 364b–365a). These aimed at a happy life after death, promising punishment to wrongdoers and the uninitiated. VEGETARIANISM, ASCETICISM and the belief that the human BODY was the tomb of human SOUL, which could only be released after death, seem to have been some of the instructions and beliefs of the Orphic devotees as they appear in the texts of Plato and EURIPIDES.

A PAPYRUS from Derveni, THRACE (the mythical birthplace of Orpheus) together with EPIGRAPHIC testimonia from the BLACK SEA, south Italy, THESSALY and CRETE, suggest strong links between the 'Orphics' (as the devotees of the cult described themselves) and BACCHIC cult and rites, but also connections with the mysteries at ELEUSIS, Samothrace and Phlya. Affinities have often been noted between orphism and modern MONOTHEISTIC religions with respect to their aim and voluntary initiation, as well as their beliefs about the AFTERLIFE, sins and transmigration of the soul. EP

See Parker, R. (1995) Early Orphism, in A. Powell, ed., *The Greek World* 483–510; West, M. L. (1983) *The Orphic Poems*.

Oscans The Oscans appear to have been very early settlers in Campania, and were also known as Opici. They were overwhelmed by the invasions of peoples known as Sabelli from the Apennine region. Presumably they survived and were absorbed into that composite population. The name Oscan remained to describe the LANGUAGES spoken across large areas of non-Roman Italy (Osco-Umbrian or Sabellic). The value of the tradition of the Oscans or Opici as the indigenous inhabitants of southern Italy (they may also be the same as or related to the Aurunci of Campania and the Ausones of south Italy and SICILY) is difficult to gauge, though the extent and success of the Sabellan expansion can be seen by the fact that their migrations continued through the 5th and 4th centuries BC. The term ceases to be an ethnic designation in the archaic period. Oscan was spoken in some form throughout central and southern Italy (ENNIUS spoke it, and Atellan farces were composed in it), until it began to be superseded by Latin after the SOCIAL WAR. Although it disappears as a language for official purposes, it was still spoken at POMPEII before the destruction of the city and may have survived even longer in the countryside. CJS

See Dench, E. (1995) *From Barbarians to New Men*; Pulgram, E. (1958) *The Tongues of Italy*.

Osiris see ISIS; PLUTARCH.

Ostia and Portus Ostia was a city located at the mouth of the TIBER river, c.35 km (c.22 miles) downstream from Rome. According to legend, it was founded by king Ancus Marcius. The city's main functions were always linked to the sea and commerce, with the area first gaining importance due to the trade in SALT extracted from nearby lagoons.

Much maritime trade bound for Rome came through Ostia, though the exposed anchorage was vulnerable both to storms and to PIRATES (an entire fleet was ravaged by pirates in 67 BC). By the end of the REPUBLIC, and especially after the establishment of the grain dole, hundreds of thousands of tons of foodstuffs alone annually passed through Ostia bound for the capital, in addition to vast quantities of other goods and materials, such as imported MARBLES. Ostia's physical and social infrastructure grew to accommodate this trade and included extensive WAREHOUSE complexes, APARTMENT BUILDINGS, TEMPLES, a THEATRE, and merchant organizations and offices. There was an array of *collegia* (guilds) of various types of dockworkers, SAILORS and craftsmen associated with maritime commerce. These workers were necessary, since large ships did not go directly to Rome but were offloaded at the mouth of the Tiber, their cargoes being transferred by lighters to Ostian warehouses and eventually sent up the Tiber to Rome in barges.

In the early empire, the emperor CLAUDIUS had a new, more sheltered harbour excavated at a site 4 km (2.5 miles) north of Ostia. Known as Portus, it was replete with warehouses, wharves, a mole, a LIGHTHOUSE and a harbour basin over 1,000 m wide, and was connected to Ostia and the Tiber by CANALS. The new harbour was still not immune to storms, as evidenced by the sinking of 200 ships in AD 62, which led the emperor TRAJAN to add a hexagonal inner harbour 600 m in diameter. The construction of Portus, made possible by the use of a special aquatic cement, constituted a gigantic public works project employing thousands of workers, covering an area of over 130 ha (320 acres), and vividly demonstrating the political importance of providing a reliable FOOD SUPPLY to the capital city.

By the 5th century AD, trade to Rome was drying up while the Tiber river was silting, with the consequence that Ostia was largely abandoned. The swampy, malaria-ridden site was not overbuilt, so that today its EXCAVATIONS reveal one of the best-preserved Roman cities in Italy, which has offered important information and insights into Roman commercial activity. Portus similarly declined in antiquity, but the site has not been as fully excavated, today lying partially under the Fiumicino airport. (see also TRANSPORT) GSA

See Descoeudres, J-P., ed. (2001) *Ostia: port et porte de la Rome antique*; Gallina Zevi, A. and Claridge, A., eds. (1996) *'Roman Ostia' Revisited*; Hermansen, G. (1982) *Ostia*; Meiggs, R. (1973) *Roman Ostia*.

 APARTMENTS; HARBOURS; ITALY ROMAN: (a); LIGHTHOUSES: (a)–(b); WAREHOUSES: (b).

ostracism A method used to exile individual politicians in Athens. In 488/7 BC, threatened with a PERSIAN invasion, Athens devised (or first used) an

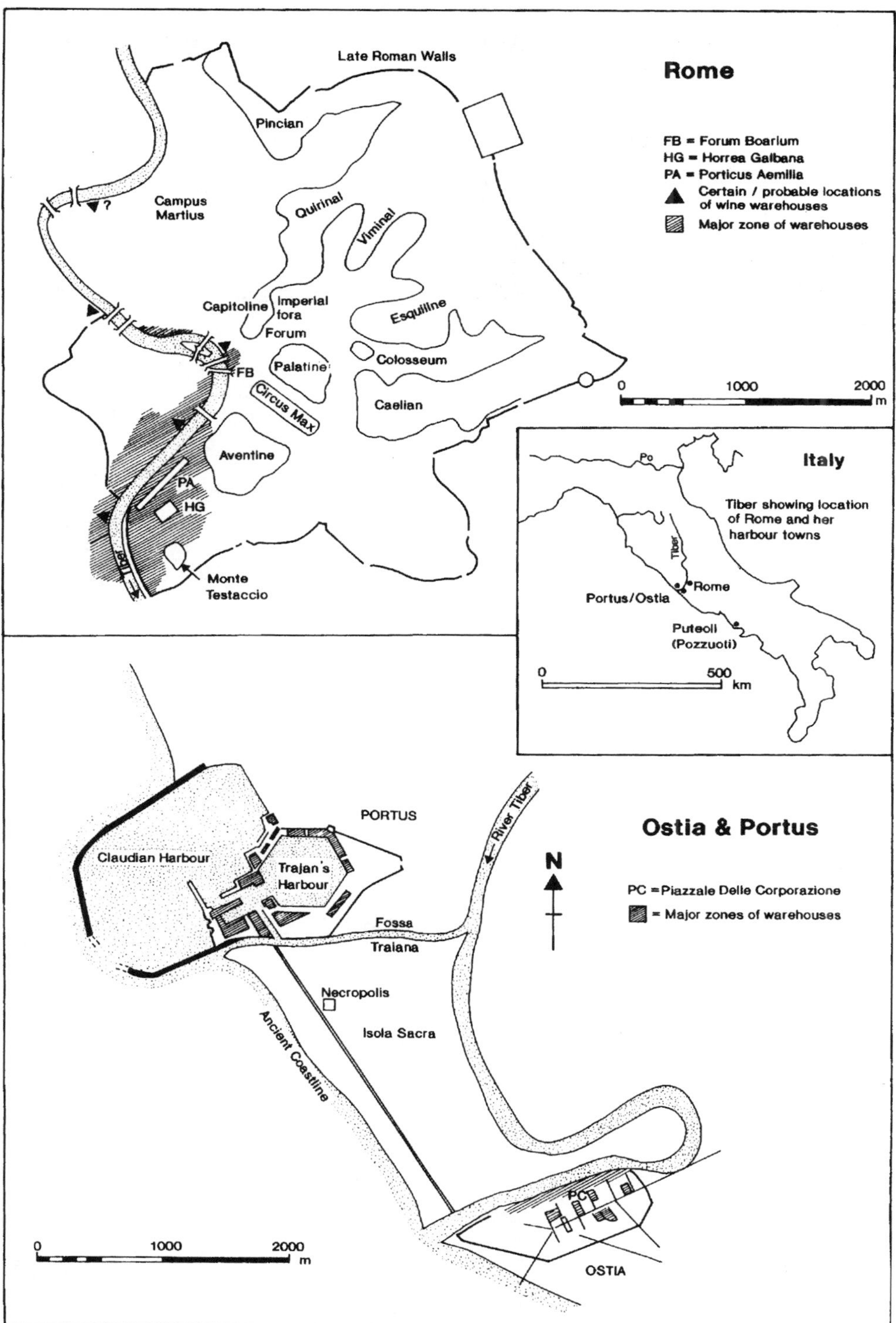

Ostia and Portus: (a) plan of harbour facilities at the ports of Rome and in the Aventine district of the city of Rome itself.

Ostia and Portus: (b) typical apartment block, with shops on ground floor.

effective method for dealing with ambitious individuals who might prove to be traitors. It remained effective for two generations, evolving into a useful means of resolving political deadlock. The citizens could decide to hold an ostracism in any year. They voted in the Agora by inscribing on a piece of pottery (*ostrakon*) the name of their chosen victim. If more than 6,000 valid votes were cast, the man with the highest score had to go into exile for ten years. He did not lose his political rights or property. Four men were expelled before Xerxes invaded Greece in 480, and only four more thereafter. Just one man made a successful comeback after returning from exile. The system was obviously effective in curbing ambition, and did not need to be used much. Voters sometimes added comments on their potsherd, while a few made their point clear by drawing a caricature. In the 480s, Kallias son of Kratias 'the Persian' is illustrated by a Persian archer. Other men are called 'traitor', 'accursed', 'adulterer' and 'owner of racehorses'. 'Long hair' may imply oligarchic tendencies or a love for Sparta. Ganging up against one man can be proved to have happened at least as early as 472, when many pre-prepared votes against Themistokles were distributed by his enemies and helped ensure his exile. Finally the practice became an open scandal, when in 416 Alcibiades and Phaiax ganged up against the demagogue Hyperbolos – 'for such as him ostracism was not designed'. Ostracism was never used again, and other legal controls on politicians had to be developed. HBM

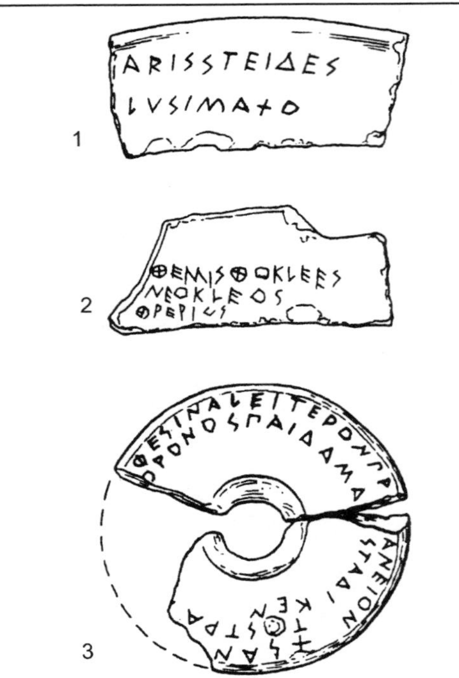

ostracism: scratched on broken pieces of pottery (*ostraka*) are the names of political leaders from classical Athens whom individual voters proposed for ten-year exile. The practice implies widespread literacy to a certain level; the variations in spelling partly reflect 5th-century Attic practice and partly the absence of standardized, 'dictionary' forms at this time. (1) Arissteides Lysimacho, which we would spell 'Aristeides Lysimachou' = Aristeides son of Lysimachos. (2) Themisthoklees Neokleos Phrerios, which we would spell 'Themistokles Neokleous Phrearrhios' = Themistokles son of Neokles, from the deme Phrearrhiai. (3) 'Chsan[thippos' (which we would write Xanthippos) 'son of Arriph]ron'. His deme name is not given, but he is the father of Perikles and is known to have been ostracized in 484 BC. The voter has inscribed an elegant two-line elegiac couplet, to the effect that Xanthippos 'is the biggest wrongdoer among all those cursed politicians' – a familiar complaint today.

Ostrogoths see Goths.

other, the Classics has borrowed the concept of the other from the French term *altérité*, a concept used in 20th-century discussions of identity, especially in the fields of psychoanalysis and the social sciences. In the field of classics, the concept of the other is most frequently applied to discussions of how the Greeks – or smaller individual groups – defined themselves by means of distinguishing themselves from what they were not, that is, the other. This modern concept of the other seems particularly relevant to discussions of the Greeks, because the concept of polarity is highly important within the traditional structures of Greek thought. Modern scholarship most frequently engages with the concept in relations to the sometimes overlapping categories of mortals versus immortals, humans versus animals, men versus women, and Greeks versus barbarians. The definition of selves against other peoples is not the only circumstance in which a sense of ethnic identity may arise: for example, some concept of being Greek seems to have pre-existed the idea that being a Greek (Hellenic) was a matter of not being a barbarian. But it is undoubtedly true that, in the decades after the Persian wars, the particular 5th-century Athenian self-image of democracy, freedom and moderation was formed by the identification of the (Persian) barbarian with the 'opposite' qualities of despotism and excess. ED

See Cartledge, P. (1993), *The Greeks: a portrait of self and others*; Lloyd, G. E. R. (1966) *Polarity and Analogy*.

Otho (Marcus Salvius Otho) AD 32–69 Roman SENATOR and member of a PATRICIAN family which had enjoyed the PATRONAGE of the emperor CLAUDIUS. Otho was married to POPPAEA SABINA, but later divorced her; she subsequently married NERO, with whom Otho had been friends. Otho was sent to the province of Lusitania as its governor in 58, where he remained in semi-exile until, as SUETONIUS has it, he could revenge himself on Nero by declaring his support for Galba after Nero's death. His desire to be Galba's heir was foiled and complicated still further upon the declaration of Vitellius on 2 January 69 and the latter's subsequent march on Rome. Otho organized a conspiracy among the PRAETORIANS and was hailed emperor on 15 January 69 (after the assassination of Galba), enjoying the support of LEGIONS in AFRICA, Egypt, SYRIA and the DANUBIAN region, which could not reach Italy quickly. With the forces available, he opposed Vitellius' RHINE legions and succeeded in some minor engagements, but a decisive victory eluded him. Eventually Otho's forces were decisively defeated at Bedracium, and Otho, acknowledging defeat, committed SUICIDE. CEPA

See Wellesley, K. (2000) *The Year of the Four Emperors*.

 AUGUSTUS: (a); EMPERORS, ROMAN: (a).

ovations An official celebration of a military victory at Rome, at a lower level than a TRIUMPH. The earliest recorded celebrant was Publius Postumius in 503 BC, and about 30 are recorded in the *Fasti*. The right to celebrate an ovation might be granted to a GENERAL when circumstances did not merit a triumph. According to AULUS GELLIUS (5.6.21), this could occur when a war had not begun with the proper rites or was not a just war, when the enemy defeated was too humble or unsuitable (like SLAVES or PIRATES) or when surrender gave a bloodless victory. In practice, no war was ever considered unjust, and a second general at a single victory might also be permitted to celebrate an ovation. The general, dressed in a purple-bordered TOGA, entered the city on foot or horseback (not on a CHARIOT), did not carry a sceptre, was wreathed with myrtle (not laurel), and did not need the accompaniment of his soldiers. Flutes rather than trumpets provided the music as he made his way to the temple of JUPITER on the CAPITOLINE, where he performed the sacrifice of a BULL. JV

See Pais, E. (1920) *Fasti triumphales populi Romani*; Versnel, H. S. (1970) *Triumphus*.

Ovid (Publius Ovidius Naso) 43 BC–AD 17 POET. Ovid was born to an EQUESTRIAN family at Sulmo in the Abruzzo region of central Italy. As he tells us himself in the autobiographical poem *Tristia* 4.10, he was educated in Rome, and embarked briefly upon a political career, which, however, he soon abandoned in order to devote himself exclusively to poetry.

Ovid's prolific output can be roughly grouped under three headings: love poetry; MYTHOLOGICAL poetry; poems from exile. With the exception of his *magnum opus*, the *Metamorphoses*, all are written in the elegiac couplet, though generic classification is difficult, since the manipulation of generic conventions is a characteristic feature of his work. We know that he also wrote a tragedy, the *Medea*, which won a high reputation in antiquity but has not survived; and a DIDACTIC poem on cosmetics, the *Medicamina faciei femineae*, of which a 100-line fragment is extant.

Under the heading 'love poetry' can be placed the three books of *Amores* (*Loves*), and the didactic *Ars amatoria* (*Art of Love*) and *Remedia amoris* (*Cures for Love*). Ovid's characteristically flippant humour and irreverent wit is much in evidence in all three works. The *Amores* allude frequently to earlier poets (especially PROPERTIUS), often in such a way as to send up the conventions of the GENRE. Thus, whereas Propertius, for example, proclaims that it is glorious to die of love, Ovid hopes to expire in the middle of the sexual act (*Amores* 2.10.35–6). The *Ars amatoria* similarly deflates the serious pretensions of the didactic genre, employing LUCRETIAN and (especially) VIRGILIAN language for advice on the arts of seduction. Conversely, elegiac language and convention are employed in such a way as to undermine the love poet's traditional pose of sincerity (the pupil is advised, for instance, to look pale and thin, so that everyone can see he's in love). The cynical tone already apparent in the *Amores* is taken to extremes here: the instructions offered to the pupil are based on the assumption that both lover and mistress are out for what they can get, and that the lover's objective is to get his chosen partner into bed while parting with as little cash as possible. Here again, Ovid plays on elegiac convention: the rapacious, extravagant mistress and the poor but faithful poet are stock figures of the genre. Yet the latter, Ovid implies, is actually every bit as duplicitous and manipulative as the former.

To the category of mythological poetry belong the *Heroides* (*Letters from Heroines*), the *Metamorphoses* and the *Fasti*. In the first collection, Ovid gives familiar love stories – such as the myths of Dido and Aeneas, or Medea and Jason – an ingeniously innovative twist by presenting them exclusively from the point of view of the abandoned heroine. The poet's interest in female character and psychology is – like much else in his poetry – a trait inherited from the ALEXANDRIAN and Neoteric poets (such as KALLIMACHOS and CATULLUS). The *Metamorphoses*, a hexameter poem in 15 books, is a kind of ENCYCLOPEDIA of Greek and Roman mythology, notionally unified by the theme of transformation. While the metre and grandiose scale of the work (which begins with the creation of the world and concludes with events of the poet's own day) are appropriate to an epic, the style of the poem is itself highly metamorphic, shifting constantly between COMEDY and TRAGEDY, between the martial and the erotic, between the stylistic registers of EPIC and ELEGY or PASTORAL. Striking, too, is the ingenious variety of ways in which the transitions between stories are contrived: the very multiplicity and episodic character of Ovid's poem pull against the idea of epic unity suggested by the chronological framework. The *Fasti* (an unfinished six-book poem on the religious FESTIVALS of the Roman year) similarly defies generic categorization. Sometimes regarded as a didactic poem, it has perhaps most in common with KALLIMACHOS' (now fragmentary) four-book elegiac poem, the *Aitia*.

In AD 8, at about the time that he was completing the composition of the *Metamorphoses*, Ovid was banished from Rome to Tomis (Constanza) on the BLACK SEA.

Here, despite persistent appeals both to AUGUSTUS and to his successor TIBERIUS, the poet was to pass the remaining ten years of his life. The reasons for his banishment are mysterious and are likely to remain so, despite intense scholarly controversy and much speculation. The poet himself identifies his crime in *Tristia* 2.207 as 'a poem and a mistake'. The poem was evidently the *Ars amatoria*, whose cheerfully amoral attitude towards extramarital relationships appears to have given offence. We can only guess what the 'mistake' may have been, though it is perhaps no accident that Ovid's banishment coincided with that of Augustus' granddaughter Julia.

Exile did not, however, put an end to Ovid's poetic output, which continued with five books of *Tristia* (*Sorrows*), four of *Epistulae ex Ponto* (*Letters from the Black Sea*) and the invective *Ibis*. Long disparaged as uninspired, maudlin and repetitive, the exile poetry has been to some extent rehabilitated in recent years, as critics have begun to detect the continuing presence of Ovid's characteristic irreverence and defiant humour, even in appeals for clemency directed to the emperor. In the single long poem that forms book 2 of the *Tristia*, for example, the poet devotes considerable space to the absurd argument that the *Ars amatoria* is in no way exceptional, since all poetry – even such apparent pillars of respectability as ENNIUS' *Annales* and Virgil's *Aeneid* – is concerned to a greater or lesser extent with passionate and illicit love affairs.

Ovid's poetry – particularly the *Metamorphoses* – enjoyed immediate and lasting popularity. Though occasionally dismissed as trivial or excessively RHETORICAL, his work has been continuously read and reinterpreted, from the allegorical and moralizing interpretations of the Middle Ages to late 20th-century appropriations of the poet as a forerunner of the parodic and self-reflexively ironic style of postmodern fiction. MG

See Ovid, *Metamorphoses*, trs. A. D. Melville (1986); Ovid, *The Love Poems*, trs. Melville (1990); Ovid, *Sorrows of an Exile (Tristia)*, trs. Melville (1992); Hardie, P. R., ed. (2002) *The Cambridge Companion to Ovid*; Mack, S. (1988) *Ovid*.

oxen see CATTLE; DRAUGHT ANIMALS; TRANSPORT; WHEELED VEHICLES.

Oxyrhynchos (mod. al Bahnasa) City in middle Egypt, metropolis of its administrative division, the Oxyrhynchite nome. It had a population estimated at c.30,000. Little remains of the city archaeologically; early EXCAVATIONS are poorly recorded and were focused on the recovery of PAPYRI. However, it had a THEATRE, which seated c.12,000, one of the largest outside Rome. Its importance lies in the number of papyri recovered, making it one of the most highly documented sites of the ancient world. Few papyri date from the PTOLEMAIC period, but nearly all come from the Roman and Byzantine periods. They provide a rich picture of life in the city. Works of Greek literature are common among the papyri, HOMER being the most popular, showing that Greek EDUCATION was important. Indeed the city was strongly hellenized, as demonstrated by a few archaeological remains and from buildings mentioned in the papyri, though there are definite traces of traditional Egyptian religion as well. The city was also Roman, as shown not least by an important ARCHIVE of documents from the 3rd century AD concerning a corn dole, probably modelled on that of Rome. Documentary texts from Oxyrhynchos offer an unparalleled view of how a provincial city was administered and, with other evidence, suggest that cities in Egypt were not all that different from those elsewhere in the empire. Oxyrhynchos remained important into the Byzantine period, when it became a CHRISTIAN centre with a BISHOP and a large number of CHURCHES. From this point, Christian literature dominates the literary papyrological record. CEPA

See Alston, R. (2000) *The City in Roman and Byzantine Egypt*.

 EGYPT.

Oxyrhynchos historian A continuator of THUCYDIDES. The so-called Oxyrhynchos historian wrote about events in Greece from 410 BC, where Thucydides' work ended, to 396. The work now remains only in fragments discovered among PAPYRI at OXYRHYNCHOS in Egypt (the first of which was found in 1906). The (presumably male) author's identity is unknown, though many scholars have favoured an identification with THEOPOMPOS (Kratippos is another possibility).

He has a rather dry style but also an eye for detail, and arranges his material in summers and winters as Thucydides does. The principal importance of the text is as a counter-balance to XENOPHON's more literary account of events. Not only does the Oxyrhynchos historian provide a strong alternative tradition for events such as the battle of Notion, but he also agrees with the account of DIODORUS SICULUS at several points, making it likely that he was Diodorus' ultimate source (through EPHOROS) for this period. As a consequence, the text greatly strengthens Diodorus' claim for attention on matters where he and Xenophon disagree. The work also features a number of digressions, the most significant of which provides important details for the FEDERAL constitution of BOIOTIA. LGM

See Bruce, I. A. F. (1967) *Historical Commentary on the Hellenica Oxyrhynchia*; McKechnie, P. R. and Kern, S. J. (1988) *Hellenica Oxyrhynchia* (includes trs.).

P

pack animals see CAMELS; DONKEYS AND MULES; TRANSPORT.

paganism A term widely used for the traditional religion of Greece and Rome, especially in contrast to CHRISTIANITY. It is now recognized as unsatisfactory, because it is a (disparaging) Christian description of non-Christians, and groups together people who would have described themselves simply as worshippers of the GODS. Latin *paganus* probably means 'someone who lives in a *pagus*' (village, i.e. the backwoods), or it may be army slang for a civilian, applied to someone who is not a 'soldier of Christ'. But there is no generally accepted alternative. Those who worshipped the traditional gods had many gods and many religious practices in common, but they did not have a common creed or sacred text or agreed list of deities. Christian legislation in the 4th century against traditional religion did not give it a name, but focused on SACRIFICE, the most widespread form of honour to the gods. Many modern writers use 'polytheist', but not all Greeks and Romans were polytheists: some PHILOSOPHERS were henotheists, that is, they held that the many gods are manifestations of one god (whereas MONOTHEISTS hold that there is only one god). In the early Christian centuries, some Greeks used 'Hellene' for those who followed traditional Greek culture and religion, but Greek Christians objected that they too spoke Greek and had a Greek EDUCATION, and there is no equivalent term for Latin-speakers. The problem of what word to use conveys the deeper problem of what to say about Greek and Roman religion. GC

pageants see FESTIVALS; PROCESSIONS.

pagus see PAGANISM; VILLAGE.

painting This became one of the major art forms in the Greek world during the 5th and 4th centuries BC. From literary evidence and echoes in other media (notably VASE-PAINTING and MOSAIC) we learn that artists such as Kimon of Kleonai, Apollodoros, Zeuxis, Parrhasios, Apelles and Protogenes made successive advances towards the achievement of illusionism. By the mid-4th century the archaic convention of stylized figures, rendered in a combination of outline and flat colour-washes, had given way to naturalistic compositions showing a mastery of foreshortening and chiaroscuro. The so-called ALEXANDER mosaic at POMPEII, based on a late 4th-century painting of a multi-figure battle-scene, illustrates the virtuosity that was attained. The subjects of classical paintings were mostly MYTHOLOGICAL, historical or allegorical, to which painters of the hellenistic period added still life, genre scenes and ultimately peopled landscapes. Much of the output of this golden age was on wooden panels, and we hear of a developing art market in which pictures were sold for vast sums and artists acquired wealth and fame. In the Roman period, while panel-paintings continued to be produced, more prestige seems to have attached to WALL-PAINTINGS in the fresco technique. The elder PLINY deprecates this fashion, which took painting out of the public domain, but ironically the preservation of painted PLASTER in HOUSES and TOMBS means that we can study ancient frescoes first-hand when all the great panel-pictures have long since perished. RJL

See Ling, R. (1991) *Roman Painting*.

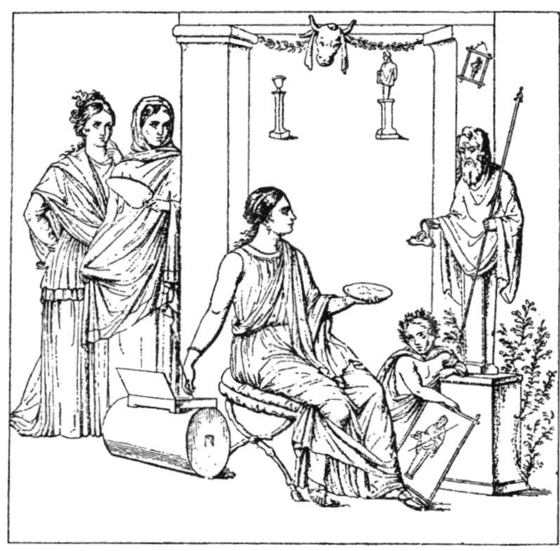

PAINTING: an anonymous female artist at work, as depicted in a painting from Pompeii.

 MUMMY PORTRAITS; PORTRAITURE; WALL-PAINTING: (a)–(c).

Pakistan The modern state of Pakistan embraces most of the Punjab, the lower Indus valley, and the highlands south of AFGHANISTAN (anc. Arachosia and eastern Gedrosia). In the north, it borders on north-eastern Afghanistan (anc. Baktria). For Greeks and Romans, the whole region was the gateway to the Indian subcontinent. Thus, when ancient writers (and older archaeological works) refer to INDIA and Indians, they sometimes mean Pakistan and its ancient inhabitants. Some historians use 'Ancient Indian North-West' for the culture region.

The Indus valley was a theatre of war during ALEXANDER's expedition. His capture of the rock of Aornos (mod. Pir-Sar?) is told by Arrian (*Anabasis* 4.28–30), and Gedrosia was the scene of his ill-advised desert march in 325 BC. SELEUKOS I was forced to give up much of Pakistan and eastern Afghanistan – Gandhara, Gedrosia, Paropamisadai (south-east

Afghanistan), and part of Arachosia – to Chandragupta ('Sandrakottos' in Greek; r. c.324/321–300/297), founder of the Mauryan empire of northern India.

Major sites of classical interest in northern Pakistan include the great Buddhist city of Taxila, on the Silk Road (30 km north-west of Rawalpindi), replanned on Greek lines in the early 2nd century BC. The town with the Sanskrit name Pushkalāvatī (mod. Charsadda, 28 km north-east of Peshawar), probably Arrian's 'Peukelaotis', was the capital of the Gandharan culture, and thus of the kingdom to which king Aśoka (r. c.268–c.232) introduced Buddhism. He set out his moral tenets in rock-cut edicts, such as the famous Greek–Aramaic bilingual example from Kandahar (Afghanistan). Buddhist Gandharan art became an impressive fusion of local, Baktrian, Parthian and Roman styles. DGJS

See Allchin, B. and Allchin, R. (1982) *The Rise of Civilisation in India and Pakistan*; Arora, U. P. (1996) *Greeks on India*; Burstein, S. M. (1985) *The Hellenistic Age*, no. 50 (Aśoka edict); Marshall, J. H. (1960) *Buddhist Art of Gandhara*.

palaces In the Bronze Age MEDITERRANEAN area, first MINOAN complexes in CRETE and then Mycenaean palaces in mainland Greece at MYCENAE, Tiryns, THEBES and Pylos indicate the administrative and residential centres of monarchs. They then disappear until the rise of the MACEDONIAN kings in the 4th century BC: both the palaces at VERGINA (Aigai) and at PELLA, birthplace of ALEXANDER the Great, have been excavated. The Vergina palace consists of a peristyle court with rooms on all four sides and a grandiose entrance in the east wing. One circular chamber on the ground floor, with elaborate black and white pebble MOSAIC, may have been used for audiences. Six other rooms were equipped for feasting; private quarters were to the north, with the best views over the surrounding countryside. A smaller peristyle court to the west, added later, provided service quarters. That at Pella was much bigger (6 ha, 15 acres) and was arranged around at least three interior courts. For the palace at ALEXANDRIA, enlarged by successive PTOLEMIES, literary sources speak of administrative blocks and a separate suite for feasting; one room, the *megiston* ('biggest'), had a dais and could hold a huge crowd. Banqueting halls adorned with many columns were popular in the Alexandrian palace and may have inspired the Roman BASILICA.

In Palestine, HEROD THE GREAT built a series of spectacular palaces, some in cities (JERUSALEM, a seaside palace at CAESAREA MARITIMA) or just outside (the Second and Third Winter palace at Jericho), others in remote locations (the desert FORTRESSES of MASADA and Herodion). All offer columnar halls, GARDENS, running water, BATHS, sumptuous private quarters and official reception rooms – features copied in the palaces of Roman emperors.

AUGUSTUS' dwelling on the Palatine, spacious and comfortable, did not manifest the megalomaniac tendencies of some successors. The Domus Aurea (Golden House) of NERO (between AD 64 and 68) occupied a vast area (140 ha, 350 acres) in the heart of Rome; this feature (MARTIAL called it 'a piece of countryside in the City') caused a greater sensation than its lavish decoration. It was demolished or obliterated by Nero's successors. DOMITIAN built the definitive imperial palace on the Palatine, the Domus Augustana, completed c.AD 92. Its grandeur was unparalleled, with polychrome MARBLES from across the Roman world. This palace remained the principal home of emperors into late antiquity, supplemented by other palaces (e.g. Domitian's at Castel Gandolfo, HADRIAN's near TIVOLI).

The Domus Augustana was the model for imperial palaces in the late 3rd century, when new provincial capitals were created. Substantial fragments of late Roman palaces survive at TRIER, Sirmium, THESSALONIKE and elsewhere, quite apart from rural retreats (Split in Croatia, built by DIOCLETIAN, and Gamzigrad in Serbia, constructed for GALERIUS). Some late Roman palaces incorporated CIRCUSES, as in the VILLA built by Maxentius on the Via Appia; and impressive mausolea were another frequent feature (Split, Gamzigrad, Maxentius' Via Appia villa).

The word 'palace' is sometimes used for spacious and sumptuous residences owned by non-royal individuals, whether urban (the 'Palace of the Columns' at Ptolemaïs in Libya) or rural (the villa near Piazza Armerina in SICILY). Such buildings in antiquity would have been styled *domus* or *villae*, not *palatia*. RJAW

See MacKay, A. G. (1975) *Houses, Villas and Palaces in the Roman World*; Nielsen, I. (1994) *Hellenistic Palaces*; Roller, D.W. (1998) *The Building Programme of Herod the Great*.

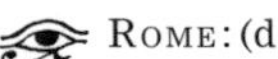

ROME: (d).

palaestra Originally the palaestra (Greek *palaistra*) was the area set aside for wrestling and other physical exercise within the groves of a Greek GYMNASIUM. By the hellenistic period the palaestra took the form of a square or rectangular court surrounded by colonnades on all four sides, off which opened rooms of various kinds. According to the Roman ARCHITECT VITRUVIUS, writing in the late 1st century BC, these included rooms for the ATHLETES to oil and sand themselves, a room for boxing practice with a punch-bag, and a suite of hot and cold bathing rooms; the main hall in the centre of one side was the *ephebeum*, set aside for the young men (*On Architecture* 5.11.1–2). Buildings which broadly fit this description, though without the hot BATHS, have been found at a number of Greek sites including OLYMPIA and Priene. Since Vitruvius also includes halls (*exhedrae*) for intellectual pursuits in his palaestra, some modern authorities believe he was describing a gymnasium and have labelled some of these buildings accordingly. The distinction should, however, be between the overall educational institution (the gymnasium) and the area within it devoted to physical development (the palaestra).

The palaestra followed a different line of development in connection with Roman-style baths in central Italy. The original context of the Greek gymnasium was lost, and the palaestra became merely an adjunct to the baths themselves, as can be seen in the Stabian Baths at POMPEII. The essential function as an area for physical exercise was, however, retained together with the basic architectural form. JDeL

Palatine hill see CIRCUS MAXIMUS; HOUSES, ROMAN; PALACES; ROME.

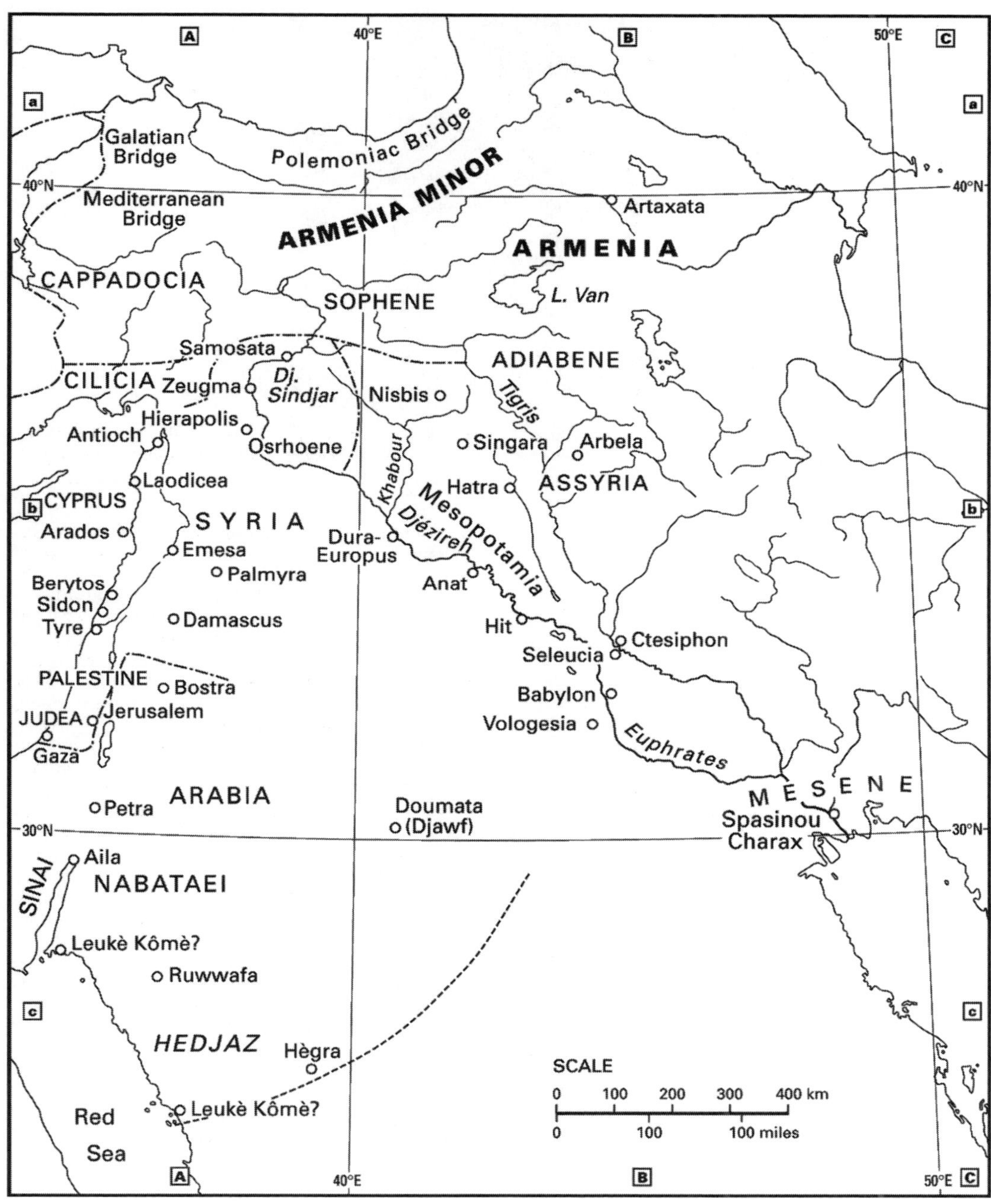

PALMYRA: (a) map of the Roman East, showing position of Palmyra in the Syrian desert.

Palestine see JOSEPHUS; JUDAISM; LEVANT; PHOENICIA AND PHOENICIANS.

Palestrina see PRAENESTE.

Pallas see ATHENA; NIKE; see also SLAVERY, ROMAN.

Palmyra At the largest oasis of the Syrian desert lies Palmyra (semitic Tadmor), about 240 km (150 miles) from both the MEDITERRANEAN and the river Euphrates. AGRICULTURE was extensive on the steppe to the north-west, but copious springs permitted intensive cultivation around the town. In the Roman period it achieved prosperity from servicing TRADE.

Palmyra: (b) general view of ruins of ancient Palmyra.

In 41 BC, the attempted raid by Mark Antony first indicated a rich prize. Incorporated into Syria by the reign of Tiberius (AD 14–37), a Roman garrison was installed and roads built. Hadrian, the first emperor to visit, added Hadriane to its name. The city was subsequently made a *colonia* (by Septimius Severus?). Roman military disasters led to the rise of the Palmyran and Roman aristocrat, Septimius Odenathus, with the titles *dux* and *corrector*. After his assassination in 267, his wife Zenobia, in the name of her younger son Vaballathus, briefly seized much of the Roman East. Their defeat by Aurelian culminated in a sack in 273. The city survived but in rapid decline.

Inscriptions appear as early as 44 BC. Many are bilingual (a few trilingual with Latin). Greek is usually inscribed first (including the famous Tax Law) and became a rich source of loan words. The great colonnaded street, the *agora*, the arch and the tetrapylon are distinctively Greco-Roman and the calendar employed the Seleukid era. Deities are mostly Semitic; the temple of Bel (AD 32) is classical in concept and decoration but embodies features integral to Semitic worship. Other structures are less certain: the theatre is not only late but minute (nine rows of seats) and was never completed. Conversely the art is distinctive and, even though its subjects wear Greco-Roman garments, their rigid, frontal representation is Mesopotamian or Parthian. Rich Palmyrans lived in peristyle houses; the poor in mud-brick ones. In death many were laid in the tower tombs which remain a distinctive landmark and a rich source of sculpture, inscriptions and funerary artefacts. DLK

See Browning, I. (1979) *Palmyra*; Colledge, M. A. R. (1976) *The Art of Palmyra*.

Syria, Roman: (a)–(b).

Pamphylia see Apollonios of Perge; Cassius Dio; Mausolus; Plancia Magna.

Pan Woodland shepherd god, whose cult originated in Arkadia. Hermes is named his father in *Homeric Hymn* 19, where his mother is called simply the daughter of mortal Dryops, whose flocks Hermes tended while wooing the maid. She was later identified variously as Kallisto and even Penelope. The Romans merged Pan with their rural god Faunus.

Pan has a goat's horns, ears, beard, legs and hooves, and frequently an erect phallus; in many respects he resembles a satyr. Not surprisingly, he is occasionally depicted in Dionysos' retinue, and some authors speak of many Pans, as there are many satyrs (and fauns). Pan's failed pursuit of women such as Syrinx or Echo generally led to their metamorphosis into, for example, his pipe or scattered voices. More often Pan is to be found in the company of herders and nymphs, playing the *syrinx* ('panpipes') which he invented. Like Dionysos, he is credited with a form of daimonic possession, namely panic, which derives its name from him. Though a god of the wild, Pan was worshipped in Athens, too, where he had a grotto shrine from 490 BC, in thanksgiving for his supposed aid to the Greeks at Marathon (Herodotos 6.105).

A late tradition transformed Pan into the unlikely deity of philosophers, one god under many titles, thanks to an etymology of his name, 'All'. Plutarch reports an eerie oracle heard during the reign of Tiberius, announcing that 'Great Pan is dead' (*Moralia* 419b–d). The later Christian author Eusebios interpreted this as heralding the death of all pagan gods (*Praeparatio evangelica* 5.17). JRH

See Bonnefoy, Y., ed. (1991) *Greek and Egyptian Mythologies*; Gantz, T. (1993) *Early Greek Myth*.

gods and goddesses: (b).

panegyrists The term panegyrists refers to a group of imperial Latin orators whose speeches in praise of contemporary Roman emperors have been transmitted to us under the title *XII Panegyrici Latini*. Most of these panegyrists date from the late 3rd or early 4th centuries AD, though Pliny the Younger's panegyric of the emperor Trajan sits at the head of the collection as a classical model for subsequent productions. The combined panegyrics provide important information about the troubled history of the later Roman empire, and give insight into the culture of later Roman schools, especially in GAUL. In particular they attest to a strong sense of continuity with earlier Roman history that is to serve as a source of confidence in a period racked by civil war, religious controversy, barbarian invasion and depopulation. The practice of delivering a speech of praise on an occasion of celebration or mourning was widespread in antiquity. Read in this context, the late Latin panegyrics can be interpreted not just as adulation of powerful leaders, but also as an expression of communal values, anxieties and aspirations. Although delivered by professional orators, they may also have served to inform the audience of the emperor's programmes and aims. TNH

See MacCormack, S. (1981) *Art and Ceremony in Late Antiquity*; Nixon, C.E.V. and Rodgers, B.S. (1994) *In Praise of Later Roman Emperors* (text, trs., comm.).

Pannonia The Roman PROVINCE of Pannonia corresponded to south-western Hungary, part of eastern Austria and the northern part of the former Yugoslavia. The population was partly CELTIC, especially in the west and north, partly ILLYRIAN. The first Roman incursion was in 119 BC, but only the Roman conquest in 13–9 BC brought political unity to an area that had never previously enjoyed it. In the 1st century AD, Pannonia had a governor of consular rank and a strong legionary garrison with numerous AUXILIARY units. TRAJAN divided it into two, Pannonia Superior, based on Carnuntum, facing the GERMANS, and Inferior from Aquincum (Budapest) southwards, facing the Sarmatian Iazyges.

Augustus settled VETERANS in the area, and there were early colonies at Emona (Ljubljana) and Savaria (Szombathely). POTTERY finds also suggest early Roman settlement around Lake Balaton. The DANUBE soon became an important trade and supply route, but rather surprisingly there is no evidence for systematic garrisoning of the river before Flavian times. Despite damage in the MARCOMANNIC WARS of the 160s and 170s the province enjoyed renewed prosperity in the early 3rd century, with evidence of immigration from elsewhere, especially SYRIA, but it suffered in the civil wars following the fall of the Severan dynasty in 235. Thereafter its strategic importance is underlined by the fact that Sirmium (Sremska Mitrovica) became an imperial capital in the later empire, when the area proved a fertile recruiting ground for the army and provided several emperors. CMW

See Mócsy, A. (1974) *Pannonia and Upper Moesia*.

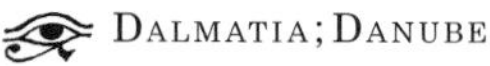 DALMATIA; DANUBE.

Pannonian war Military campaigns between the deaths of JULIUS CAESAR (44 BC) and AUGUSTUS (AD 14) to achieve the conquest and control of PANNONIA, a part of ILLYRICUM. Lying between the middle DANUBE and the ADRIATIC SEA, and bounded on the west by Italy and NORICUM, Pannonia had long been an area of interest to Rome: partly for its mineral resources, partly for the dangers it posed to Italy and MACEDONIA. Despite occasional Roman interventions from the late 3rd century BC, serious attempts at annexation and pacification had never occurred. Augustus (as Octavian) inherited Caesar's designs and began a series of successful campaigns in 35 BC. Two years later, after a revolt had been pacified, the area, particularly around the Save and Drave RIVERS, came under Roman control. Difficult, ultimately successful, WARS under Marcus AGRIPPA and TIBERIUS from 13 to 11, in response to another revolt, brought Roman control, at times more nominal than real, to the Danube itself. When Augustus launched war against the Marcomanni north of the Danube in AD 6 under the command of Tiberius, a large-scale revolt broke out in Pannonia itself, requiring Tiberius' return to combat the rebellion. By AD 9, the task was complete, and Illyricum was divided into two provinces, Pannonia and DALMATIA. Given its strategic location, Pannonia naturally saw further wars, especially the MARCOMANNIC WARS of MARCUS AURELIUS, but also the internal struggles of the THIRD-CENTURY CRISIS and the inroads of peoples across the Danube from the late 4th century. JV

See Mócsy, A. (1974) *Pannonia and Upper Moesia*.

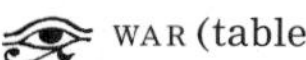 WAR (table).

Pantheon Roman TEMPLE built by HADRIAN between AD 118 and 128 in the Campus Martius in Rome. Replacing an original completed by AGRIPPA in 25 BC, Hadrian's Pantheon was a new building, even if the original builder's name appears alone in the dedicatory inscription. The façade has a portico of columns and triangular pediment tacked uncomfortably onto the circular *cella*. The superb lines of the CONCRETE DOME are accentuated by five rings of coffers. Painted and decorated in antiquity, the coffers provided rhythm and variety to the dome, at 43 m (142 ft) in interior diameter, the largest manmade dome until modern times. The geometry is simple: the building's diameter is identical to its height. The circular drum wall has recessed niches and projecting *aediculae* intended to avoid any single visual focus to distract from the impact of the dome.

The Pantheon embodies the principal characteristics that define the Roman contribution to ARCHITECTURE: the use of polychrome MARBLES and granites for COLUMNS, floor paving and wall veneers; mastery of brick-faced concrete in its 6 m (20 ft) thick walls, with relieving ARCHES and dead recesses; mastery too in the pouring of 5,000 tons of concrete. The Pantheon is an eloquent essay in the creation of interior space, and in the lighting of that space by a single opening at the summit.

Used principally as a temple, CASSIUS DIO states that the emperor employed it occasionally as an audience chamber. Thanks to preservation as a CHURCH and comparatively few alterations, the Pantheon is a rare Roman structure which can be experienced in something approaching its original condition. More than any other Roman building it has inspired countless imitations and adaptations since it was built. (see pp. 642–3) RJAW

See MacDonald, W. L. (1976) *The Pantheon*; Ward-Perkins, J. B. (1981) *Roman Imperial Architecture*.

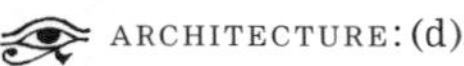 ARCHITECTURE: (d).

pantheon see GODS AND GODDESSES; RELIGION.

pantomime Although the form of DANCE known as pantomime, which may be translated 'imitation of

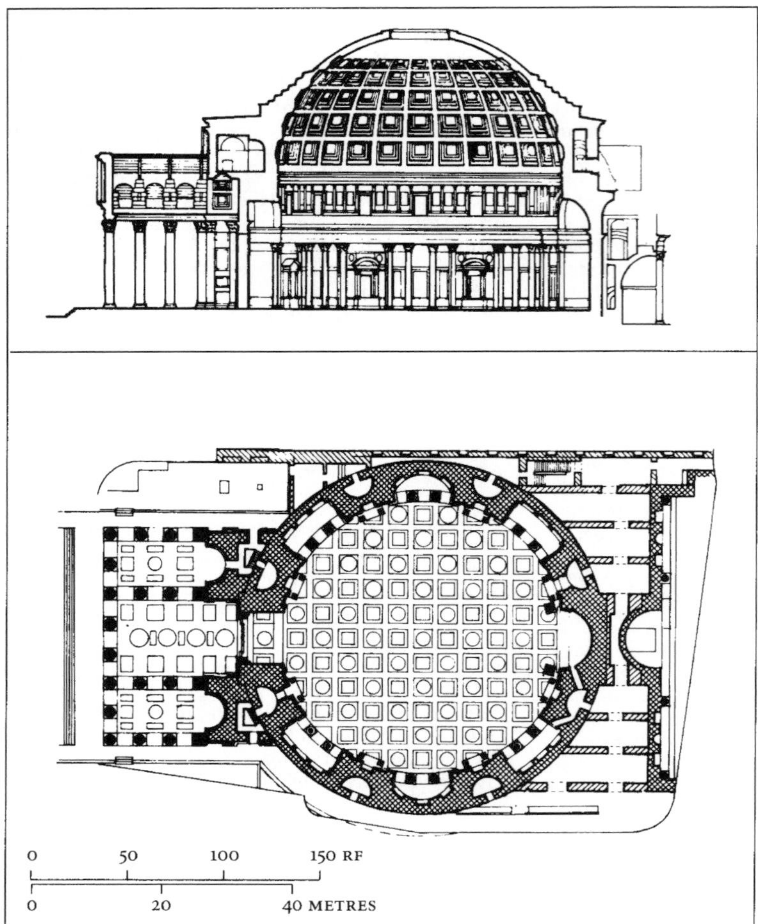

PANTHEON: (a) cross-section and plan of the Pantheon of Hadrian.

PANTHEON: (b) exterior view of the Pantheon, showing pedimental rectangular porch and the dome-topped drum of the cella.

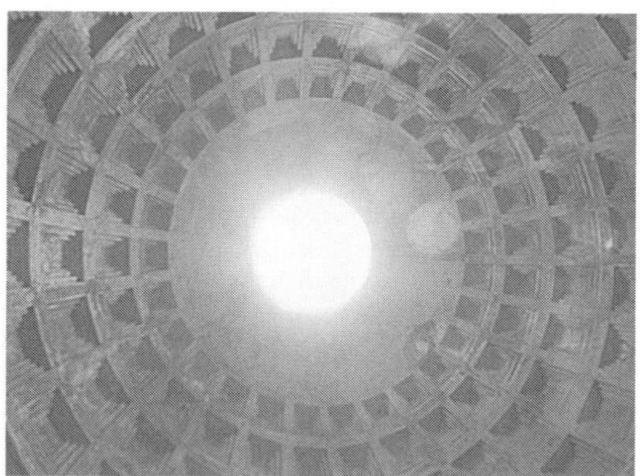

PANTHEON: (c) view of the interior of the dome, with central opening (*oculus*).

PANTHEON: (d) decoration of the interior of the drum, with *aediculae* (colonnaded niches).

everything', had deep roots in traditions of performance in the Greek world, it took its classical form at Rome during the reign of AUGUSTUS. At that time there were two leading proponents: Pylades, who danced mythological themes, and Bathyllus, whose performances were of a more erotic nature. The style of Pylades won through, and in the Greek world pantomime might also be described as 'Italian dance' or 'rhythmic tragic dance'. So popular did pantomime become that it was even admitted to Greek agonistic festivals – the only new art form to be so recognized.

The components of performance were the dancer, who wore an ankle-length silk robe and used a series of closed-mouthed masks to dance the story, a CHORUS and an orchestra. The orchestra could include flautists (*scabilarii*), who beat time with clappers attached to their feet, a variety of percussion instruments, and at times a citharist and even an organ. The chorus sang a libretto to which the dancer performed, using his body and hand gestures to illustrate the action and indicate the emotions of the various characters. The style of the dance was intended to arouse the passions of the audience, and preferred stories tended to be those with strong emotional content.

In the early empire it appears that pantomime dancers were male, but by the late empire, and into the Byzantine period, there were female dancers, who would not use masks. Successful dancers of both sexes rivalled charioteers in their popularity and had devoted followings, which ensured the survival of their art well into the 6th century AD, despite the strenuous disapproval of the leaders of the CHRISTIAN church. DSP

paper see PAPYRI; SCHOLARSHIP, BYZANTINE; SCHOLARSHIP, ISLAMIC.

Pappos of Alexandria MATHEMATICIAN, ASTRONOMER and GEOGRAPHER who flourished c.AD 320. Although the *SUDA* dates him to the reign of THEODOSIUS I (379–95), Pappos refers to a solar eclipse of 18 October 320 as a recent event in his *Commentary on the Almagest* of PTOLEMY. He was therefore active earlier in the 4th century. The dedication of books 7 and 8 of his *Synagôgê* (*Collection*) to his son Hermodoros offers the only information about his family circumstances.

His surviving writings provide a wealth of information about mathematics and geometry in the ancient world, and are therefore highly useful to the historians of these fields. In particular, the *Synagôgê* is a handbook to the works of other practitioners, many no longer extant. Pappos often adds explanations and proofs of his own. Book 1 and much of book 2 do not survive, but book 7 discusses a puzzle called 'Pappos' problem' since René Descartes' *Des matières de la géometrie* (1637). Pappos also wrote on the *Elements* of EUCLID; a commentary on book 10 extant in an Arabic translation is likely, but not certainly, part of this work. On Ptolemy's *Almagest*, treatments of books 5 (lacunose) and 6 survive in Greek. The *Geography* in Armenian by Moses of Khorene was either a translation of a work of Pappos or is heavily based on one. Various sources refer to other, but lost, writings on mathematics, geometry and geography. JV

See Cuomo, S. (2000) *Pappus of Alexandria and the Mathematics of Late Antiquity.*

papyrology The discipline devoted to the reading and interpretation of texts found on PAPYRUS and a variety of other materials including parchment, clay and stone (ostraca; in the case of stone, only texts written in ink), and wood (tablets, with or without waxed writing surfaces). The term has referred mostly to the study of Greek and Latin texts, but other scripts from Egyptian hieroglyphs to Arabic have been found on papyrus. In recent decades the barriers between those disciplines based on Egyptian scripts (especially Demotic and Coptic) and Greco-Roman ones have started to fall, though language training remains the main basis for disciplinary differentiation. The number of papyri, ostraca and tablets found outside Egypt has grown markedly in recent years, including notably Greek and Aramaic texts from the areas of the Euphrates and the Dead sea, Latin ostraca from Bu Njem in Libya, and Latin writing tablets from VINDOLANDA on the northern frontier in BRITAIN. These have demanded the technical skills of papyrology but have drawn it away from the Egyptian-centred character it has had since the 19th century.

Within the dominant Greek papyrology of Egypt, a distinction between literary and documentary studies has long prevailed. Literary papyrology has concerned itself with the editing and criticism of papyrus manuscripts of known works of ancient literature and with the editing and study of previously unknown texts, the latter probably the aspect with the greatest appeal to classicists. Documentary texts – in a broad sense, ranging from private letters to imperial edicts – have served as a feeder for political, administrative, social and economic history. In a peculiar limbo have stood the 'sub-literary' papyri like school exercises. The intellectual directions of the post-war period have begun to break down this divide also: interests like the history of the book, cultural studies, and the *Annales* approach to history have all brought literary papyri into view as artefacts rather than disembodied texts, and at the same time asked questions about the EDUCATION and culture of those who produced documents. Magical papyri, also often classed as 'sub-literary', have generated a new wave of studies that treat them both as artefacts and as the crucial texts that they are.

The study of papyri goes back to the discovery of the EPICUREAN library of HERCULANEUM in the 18th century; documents started to trickle into European collections in the late 18th and early 19th centuries. Systematic study of papyri and a sense of papyrology as a field start in the 1880s, particularly with Ulrich Wilcken (Germany) and Carl Wessely (Austria). Important discoveries of authors and works not surviving in the medieval manuscript tradition (e.g. MENANDER, Hypereides, HERODAS, the Aristotelian *Constitution of Athens*) and of large masses of documents (particularly in the FAYÛM) in the late 19th century gave an enormous spur to collecting, excavating and editing. EXCAVATIONS yielded large quantities of new material, especially from the British work at OXYRHYNCHOS, and systematic buying by national and international consortia enlarged university and library collections. By the 1920s the field was systematically organized and provided with reference tools, with every century from the 3rd BC to the 8th AD adequately represented in the published texts. International congresses (now triennial) began in 1930; a formal association was founded after the Second World War. Coptic studies were stimulated by the editing of the 'GNOSTIC' codices found at Nag Hammadi, though that impetus has had only modest effects on the study of Coptic documents. Demotic papyrology has emerged as a specialty in its own right in recent years, with increasingly close ties to Greek papyrology.

For the practitioner, papyrology shares some characteristics with EPIGRAPHY: a need for a good command of the relevant languages (in the case of documentary Greek, *koinê* in various registers rather than the classical language); a large body of textual material to be controlled and used for parallels; a sprawling mass of technical knowledge of chronology, geography, vocabulary and institutions; and a large specialist bibliography. To these it adds palaeographical expertise, for the texts are written in a great variety of hands used over a millennium for various types of texts. Formal book hands are relatively easy to read, but informal and cursive styles are harder, sometimes impenetrable except by the aid of parallel texts. In such cases, reading practically requires the difficult art of projecting oneself into the mind of the writer. A good knowledge of palaeography is also essential for dating texts in cases where no explicit chronological indications are provided by the contents. These hurdles have kept papyrology, particularly documentary, largely the preserve of specialists. The technical character of specialist work and papyrology's identification with Egypt – so alien to the classicizing canon entrenched in the field of Greek and Latin literature – have led papyrology to seem of secondary interest to many classicists. The result has been a precarious institutional base.

At present two trends are extending papyrology on different axes. One is the application of its techniques, tools and results to the newly discovered bodies of material from places outside Egypt and to the larger historical problems of classical studies – in short, horizontal or spatial diversification. The other is the increased linkage of Egypt-centred papyrology to Egyptology and Coptology – that is, vertical or chronological connection. These directions have different implications for the institutional and organizational bases of the discipline, the one integrating papyrology synchronically more fully into classical studies, the other connecting it to a more diachronic approach to the history of the ancient and medieval Near East. A third direction of development is the integration of papyrology and ARCHAEOLOGY, partly a result of interest in setting the papyri in a full cultural context, partly of the fact that in an era when the antiquities market is more strictly policed, newly available papyri increasingly must come from controlled excavations. This development has implications for both of the other two trends; but, despite hopes, the archaeological context is not always very informative for the texts. RSB

See Bagnall, R.S. (1995) *Reading Papyri, Writing Ancient History*; van Minnen, P. (1993) The century of papyrology (1892–1992), *BASP* 30: 5–18; Youtie, H.C. (1963) The papyrologist: artificer of fact, *GRBS* 4: 19–32.

papyrus The principal writing material of the classical world, derived from a reed-like Egyptian plant, always a virtual Egyptian monopoly. It was slow to displace clay, wood, skins and other materials outside Egypt, but for books it was standard from classical Greece until the end of antiquity, even after the roll gave way to the codex in late antiquity. Public and private documents continued to use a large range of supports, especially the more readily reusable wood, but papyrus dominated at least the Eastern part of the Roman empire. Replaced in medieval times by parchment and eventually paper, papyrus first came back to European attention with the discovery of carbonized book rolls at HERCULANEUM in the 18th century. The trickle of finds in Egypt in the early 19th century accelerated in its closing decades and the start of the 20th century. So far, 30,000 have been published, with many more awaiting publication. Papyri are our main source for the text of some authors (e.g. MENANDER, Hypereides) and texts (e.g. the Aristotelian *Constitution of Athens*), but early hopes that most of the missing works of classical Greek literature would be recovered have not been fulfilled: other than fragments, only one missing drama of SOPHOCLES, for example, and that a satyr play (the *Ichneutai*). About 95 per cent of published papyri are documents, letters and other everyday texts, a rich source of material for administrative, social, economic and cultural history. The discovery of papyri in the Near East outside Egypt has accelerated in recent years. Greek texts dominate the surviving material (the survival of the most recent), but considerable numbers in Hieratic and Demotic (Egyptian), Coptic, Latin, Persian, Arabic and Aramaic also remain. RSB

See Bagnall, R. S. (1995) *Reading Papyri, Writing Ancient History*; Lewis, N. (1974) *Papyrus in Classical Antiquity*; Turner, E. G. (1980) *Greek Papyri*.

parables Aristotle defines the *parabolê* ('comparison') as a sub-class of proof in rhetoric (*Rhetoric* 2.20). Like the fable, it is an invented example, but one that lacks fabulous elements such as talking animals. Unlike the fable, it should be plausibly analogous to a historical situation. Aristotle's chosen instances are 'Socratic parables', such as the following: to select a governor by lot is like putting at the helm of a ship not the sailor who is well trained but the sailor on whom the lot falls (cf. Plato, *Republic* 551c). From this example it appears that parables are more than simple comparisons. They must be applied to circumstances beyond the merely poetic, such as the ethical, religious or forensic. The longer and more colourful epic similes that are found throughout Homer and Virgil are not, therefore, parables, perhaps because they paint a picture but do not prove a point.

On the other hand, while some of Jesus' Parables of the Kingdom resemble Aristotle's examples in their succinctness, the typical gospel parable hardly matches the classical definition in either brevity or transparency. For example, the parable of the Sower and the Seed (Matthew 13.1–23) is an extended narrative that requires careful interpretation from Jesus and is intended, he says, to illuminate the divine mystery for some but obfuscate it for others. Such a parable is difficult to distinguish from a separate classical genre, invented allegory. JRH

See Crossan, J. D. (1992) Parable, in D. N. Freedman, ed., *The Anchor Bible Dictionary*.

parades see drama, Greek; festivals; processions; triumphs.

paradoxes The Greek word *paradoxon* was used in antiquity to denote anything surprising or 'contrary to expectation'. As such, paradoxes had a particular interest for philosophers: if you find something 'paradoxical', it shows either that your expectations are wrong (and need correction), or else that it simply isn't true. Aristotle tended to side with seriously held expectations (which he called *endoxa* – the opposite of *paradoxa*). As a matter of method, he supposed that the closer a philosophical explanation came to justifying them, the more likely it was to be right. For others, paradoxes highlighted the gap between our everyday assumptions and the true nature of things. The wilfully paradoxical style of Herakleitos, for example, seems designed to shake us out of our intellectual complacency; and some of Socrates' more challenging ethical statements can be counted as paradoxes – notably his assertion that 'no one deliberately does wrong'. That people liked to be surprised and intrigued is demonstrated by the popularity, especially in the hellenistic period, of 'paradoxographical' works – reports of amazing phenomena (including everything from stalactites to two-headed children). The Stoics went out of their way to advertise their ethical theory in a series of (what they themselves called) 'paradoxes': 'Only the wise man is rich', 'All misdeeds are equally bad', and so on. The serious aspect of this was their belief that if you really understood the world, you would never find anything (whether stalactite or ethical doctrine) 'paradoxical'.

In modern parlance, a 'paradox' is an argument whose conclusion seems absurd or obviously wrong. The term is applied, for example, to the arguments devised by Zeno the Eleatic in defence of his teacher Parmenides. When Parmenides was ridiculed for denying the reality of change and movement, Zeno tried to show that a 'common sense' belief in these things was worse than amusing – it was self-contradictory. If you believe in movement, for example, you will believe that someone can cross a stadium; but you will also believe that they must first make it halfway across; and before that, halfway to that point . . . and so on until an infinite number of prior steps have been generated. Conclusion: if you believe that someone can cross a stadium, you should also believe that they can never get started. Similar challenges to common sense were offered by the logical puzzles known as 'sophisms'. The Liar Argument, for example, aims to disprove the principle that every assertion must be either true or false. It does so by offering a counter-example: if I say 'I am now lying', is my assertion true? (If it is, it isn't; if it isn't, it is.) Some of these arguments are easily dealt with (If this is your dog, and it is a father, it must be your father . . .); but the tougher ones had an important role to play as test cases in the development of logic. And if a philosopher's logical system was not robust enough to solve or avoid them, why should we believe that it could support his deductions about the nature of the universe? GB-S

See Barnes, J. (1999) in K. Algra et al., eds., *The Cambridge History of Hellenistic Philosophy* 157–76; Hansen, W. (1996) *Phlegon of Tralles' Book of Marvels* (trs.).

parasites see actors and actresses; Comedy, New; Comedy, Old; see also pests and pest control.

parchment see Dead Sea scrolls; libraries; papyrus; *Peutinger Table*.

Parentalia see ancestor worship; death; festivals, Roman; funeral rites, Roman; kinship, Roman; rituals, Roman.

Parian Marble A marble inscription (also known as Marmor Parium), set up in the 3rd century BC on the Aegean island of Paros, which records the dates of various political, military, mythical, religious and literary events. The stone survives now in two pieces. One, discovered in 1897, is located on Paros; the other is in the Ashmolean Museum, Oxford. The Oxford fragment has a complicated history, which reflects the growing interest in Greek culture in 17th-century England. It was brought to London in 1627, and formed part of Lord Arundel's pioneering collection of antiquities. The upper half was destroyed when it was built into a fireplace; the lower half was saved by the diarist John Evelyn.

The Parian Marble's original purpose and creator are not known. All 128 lines of text list kinds of events dated by a relative chronology and (where available) by Athenian archon, working back in terms of the years before the monument's creation, which is dated to 264/3 BC by the eponymous archon of Paros and Athens. For example, 'from the time when . . . Socrates the philosopher died, having lived for 70 years, 137 years, when Laches was the archon at Athens' refers back to the archon-year 400/399 BC. Some of the earliest events are what we would call mythical, for example the AMAZONS attacking Athens (1256/5 BC). Others are more tantalizing, such as the Greek expedition against Troy (1218/17 BC). Unlike the Parian marble, ancient writers (such as DIODOROS SICULUS) usually resolved chronological problems not only by referring to Athenian archon years but also to the specific year within an OLYMPIAD cycle. GJO

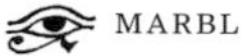 MARBLE.

Paris (Alexander) see AGAMEMNON; HELEN OF TROY; HERA.

Parmenides b.515–510 BC The most important PRESOCRATIC PHILOSOPHER. He was born in Elea, south Italy. He wrote in EPIC verse form and about 200 lines (not all continuous) of one poem survive. Most are quoted by Simplicius, a 6th-century AD commentator on ARISTOTLE. Parmenides' followers, known as the Eleatics, were ZENO (famous for his paradoxes) and Melissos. Parmenides' poem takes the form of an introductory account of a revelation of the truth by an unnamed GODDESS to a young traveller who passes through 'the gates of Night and Day' (mentioned earlier in HESIOD's *Theogony*). She tells him first 'a trustworthy thought about Truth', then 'a deceitful account of the beliefs or opinions of mortals'. Truth is about 'what is'. Belief is about 'what is and is not'. One surviving fragment consists of 60 consecutive lines, which contain the earliest connected philosophical argument in classical (and Western) tradition. Here Parmenides claims that there is an exclusive distinction between 'being' and 'not-being'. To say of something that 'it is not' is to say nothing intelligible about it. Hence only statements about being make sense. So to say a bird is not a dog is to attribute non-being to the bird. Therefore, all being is one, and homogeneous. No rational account can be given of differentiation or of change. Parmenides' argument is severely limiting since within its terms it is virtually impossible to communicate anything intelligible about the perceptible world. Subsequent philosophers aimed to find ways of transcending or circumventing it so as to explain the nature of the physical world, plurality and change. It could be claimed that Parmenides initiated the whole tradition of Greek METAPHYSICS and epistemology. DJF

See Gallop, D. (1984) *Parmenides: Fragments*; Guthrie, W. K. C. (1965) *History of Greek Philosophy*, vol. 2; Kirk, G. S. et al. (1983) *The Presocratic Philosophers*.

Paros One of the largest of the Cyclades (196 sq km, 76 sq miles), the island of Paros was inhabited in the Bronze and Iron Ages. Settlements have been discovered at Paroikía (the modern chief town) and at a number of other places such as Koukounariés. It has been suggested that in the Geometric period the ISLAND may have begun to develop more than one *POLIS*, but by the time it emerges into the light of history it is unified under the authority of a single *polis*, which issued coins starting c.600 BC. Somewhat earlier, it was the mother-city of THASOS (c.680 BC). The POET ARCHILOCHOS, later honoured with a sanctuary where some of his poetry has been preserved on inscriptions, participated in the early stages of the colony's foundation, and his poetry provides important evidence for the event. Paros competed with NAXOS for supremacy in the central AEGEAN, leading to several wars between them. Paros was a target of the PERSIANS in the events that led to the IONIAN REVOLT, but on the Persian side in the subsequent wars, and THEMISTOKLES forced the Parians to pay tribute. After the Persian wars they joined the Delian league. In the 4th century Paros belonged to the second Athenian confederacy and may have been the object of an attempt to end bitter local factionalism by the league's *synedrion* (governing body); its citizens founded a colony at Pharos in the ADRIATIC in 385/4. Paros was famous throughout antiquity for its high-quality MARBLE, and had many sanctuaries, including a notable Delion (shrine of Delian Apollo). The Parians belonged to the League of Islanders in the hellenistic period. Evidence for the island in later times is poor. GR

See Reger, G. (2004) Paros, in Hansen and Nielsen, *Inventory* 764–8.

 AEGEAN: (a)–(b).

Parthenon TEMPLE dedicated to ATHENA Parthenos, patron GODDESS of Athens. It is situated at the most prominent spot of the sanctuary of the goddess in the upper city, the ACROPOLIS. Most of the surviving ARCHITECTURAL remains at the site date to the years of the generalship of PERIKLES, who was responsible for its building. Its dates of construction are known from the so-called 'building inscriptions', which begin in the year 447 BC and record payments for the QUARRYING and transportation of MARBLE for the new temple. The Periklean Parthenon was structurally complete, with the pedimental SCULPTURES in place, by 432. The project benefited financially from the common fund of the Greek defensive alliance (or ATHENIAN EMPIRE), which was kept in Athens, the leader of the alliance.

As part of a substantial building programme on the Acropolis, the Parthenon was erected as a thanksgiving to the patron goddess of Athena for having kept her city safe and victorious during the PERSIAN WARS (490–479). It was built at the site of an old temple to the goddess (known as *archaios neôs*) which had been destroyed by the Persians during their invasion of Athens in 480.

The Periklean Parthenon was entirely made of marble extracted from Mt Pentelikon in Attica, and was designed by the ARCHITECTS Iktinos and Kallikrates. The temple is peripteral (i.e. surrounded by a colonnade on all four sides). Its ORDER is Doric combined with Ionic elements, notably the Ionic frieze and the interior columns of the back room of the temple. Oblong in shape, it has eight columns across the short sides of the *peristasis* (surrounding

PARTHENON: (a) general view of east façade of temple.

PARTHENON: (b) view of interior of cella of temple.

colonnade) and 17 on the long sides. Inside the colonnade, the main structure (*naos*) was divided into two parts, each entered independently through a short porch. The eastern part was the main cult room which housed the chryselephantine ('gold and ivory') cult statue of Athena Parthenos by the sculptor PHEIDIAS. The smaller, western part (*opisthodomos*) functioned as a treasury.

An impressive programme of architectural sculptures adorned the Parthenon, completed by a large number of leading artists of the time under the supervision of Pheidias. These included a Doric frieze of metopes and triglyphs around the top of the outside of the temple, above the colonnade; an Ionic frieze around the top of the *naos* inside the colonnade, not properly visible from the outside; and two pedimental compositions crowning the top of the short sides (east and west). Iconographic themes were inspired by the local history and mythology of Athens. Many fragments of these sculptures were removed piecemeal by visitors during Ottoman rule in Greece and reside in other countries. The much larger quantities removed for Lord ELGIN'S COLLECTION, and now deposited in the British Museum, remain the subject of heated controversy over whether they should be returned to Greece.

The later history of the Parthenon was marked by the invasions of the GOTHIC Herulians in AD 267 and its subsequent conversion into a CHRISTIAN CHURCH and a mosque (AD 1450s–1460s) by the Christians and the Turks respectively. The monument came into its present ruined state after an explosion of Turkish ammunition then housed in the Parthenon, during the siege of the town by the Venetians in 1687. EP

See Beard, M. (2003) *The Parthenon*; Hurwit, J. M. (1999) *The Athenian Acropolis*.

 ACROPOLIS, ATHENIAN: (a)–(c); TEMPLES: (b).

Parthia and Parthians The Parthian empire took its name from Parthava, a satrapy of the Achaemenid and SELEUKID empires south-east of the Caspian sea. By the 3rd century BC, it had been occupied by a NOMADIC people, the Parni, whose dynasty took its name of Arsakidai from king Arsakes, and dated from the year of his accession, 247. These new 'Parthians' threw off Seleukid control and extended their own. After a setback when ANTIOCHOS THE GREAT recovered his eastern satrapies (212–206), their advance continued. The principal architect of empire was Mithradates I (176–138/7) whose reign culminated in the seizure of Media (148 or soon after) and BABYLONIA (141) and the capture of the Seleukid king Demetrios II (140). Less than half a century later (c.96), a Parthian envoy met the Roman governor SULLA on the Euphrates. Within a generation, Parthia and Rome had divided the Seleukid empire between them, with everything east of the Euphrates going to Parthia. During the next three centuries, Rome advanced eastwards and Parthia eventually lost much of MESOPOTAMIA and struggled to retain control of Babylonia and even Adiabene just beyond the Tigris.

The Parthian empire remained large and powerful for these three centuries. During that period, along with Rome and distant CHINA, it was one of the three great empires of classical antiquity. At its height it extended from the Euphrates to Afghanistan, Central Asia to the Indian ocean. Although its origins lay on the Iranian plateau, the economic and cultural heartland was in the west, in Babylonia and the adjacent highlands of the Zagros mountains. Most of the great cities lay there, both those of the Achaemenid and earlier periods and, most importantly, the great new hellenistic city Seleukeia, one of the largest and richest of the ancient world. The economic base of Parthian power rested largely in the rich arable lands of Babylonia. Extensive deserts in eastern Iran further emphasized the western tilt. TRADE was important, both the caravan trade from the east and that by sea up the Persian gulf. It is no accident that PALMYRA, the great caravan city of Roman SYRIA, maintained trading posts in the Parthian empire.

The Parni had been iranized as rulers of Parthava; later, as rulers of an empire, they absorbed features of hellenism, the dominant cultural force in western Asia. They used Greek for administration, DIPLOMACY and culture, employing it even on their coins. Their Greek subjects, through whom much of Parthian history was transmitted to the West and

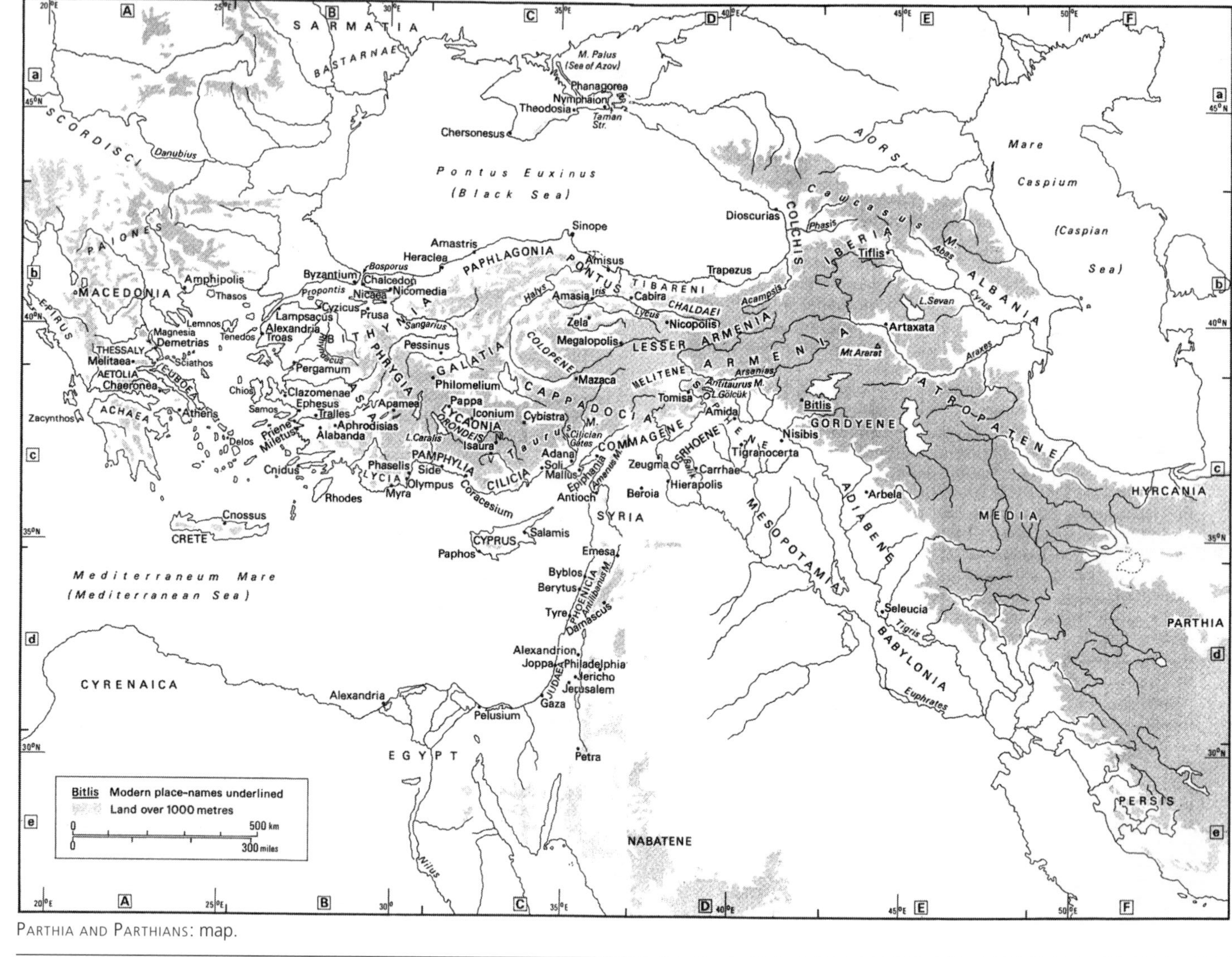

PARTHIA AND PARTHIANS: map.

preserved, were prominent in government. Greek architecture was influential, as was Greek SCIENCE and even entertainment: notoriously, Orodes II (c.56–c.38 BC), was watching EURIPIDES' *Bacchae* in 53 when the head of CRASSUS was brought to him at Seleukeia, the winter counterpart to the summer capital at Ekbatana.

Greek cities enjoyed considerable autonomy. Elsewhere, the Arsakid ruler was King of Kings, presiding over an empire with powerful fiefdoms in the hands of kings with substantial independence. Best known are the rulers of Seistan, the Surenas, and the SASSANIDS of Persis. The former, one of seven great Parthian families outside the dynasty, organized the defeat of Crassus and reappeared over the coming centuries as warlords and king-makers. The Sassanids, having retained much independence, overthrew the Arsakids in AD 224 and established themselves as Great Kings of a new Iranian empire. Marriage alliances failed to curb powerful vassals; rather it added complexity to the fratricidal squabbles of the royal family.

From the late 1st century BC, Arsakid power seems in slow decline, bludgeoned in the west by Rome and racked by repeated civil wars. Control was further weakened by the absence of a strong central army. The royal forces were slender, and wars depended on contingents provided by vassals. The core was aristocratic armoured CAVALRY and mounted archers, in sharp contrast with Rome's short-term governors and a huge standing army, mainly heavy infantry. Relations with Rome, punctuated by dangerous wars, were nevertheless generally stable. Diplomatic contacts are attested, not least personal meetings on the Euphrates. Likewise Parthia was in diplomatic contact with China. Less predictable were nomadic peoples of central Asia: Roman writers report wars, but the best-known are great raids by a Sarmatian tribe, the ALANI; one passed through into Roman territory and involved the governor and author ARRIAN.

The philhellenism of the early Arsakids was marked by willingness to send princes to Rome as hostages, whose return to Parthia was seldom successful. An insight into Parthian taste is provided by the complaint that one returned hostage did not share the aristocratic taste for HUNTING and HORSEMANSHIP. In AD 10 the ruling family was replaced by a more Iranian branch, then ruling Atropatene. The change brought immediate results: the suppression of a great revolt by Seleukeia and the creation of new winter capitals at Vologesia and CTESIPHON. Culturally, greater emphasis was given to Iranian Mazdaism in religion, and their art and architecture emerged as distinctively 'Parthian', essentially Mesopotamian but certainly with little now of hellenism. Characteristic of the latter, in monumental terms, is the great vaulted hall of Parthian PALACES. A further impetus to indigenous traditions came when, ironically, the Romans sacked Seleukeia in 114 and 164, destroying that great Hellenic centre.

There is no Parthian literature; most of what is known comes through Roman sources such as Justin, JOSEPHUS, TACITUS and CASSIUS DIO. There are a few inscriptions. Art shows a mixture of hellenism and older native tradition, which extended beyond Mesopotamia to the rigid frontal pose of figures in the SCULPTURE and PAINTINGS of Hatra, Palmyra and even in the depiction of Roman officers at DURA EUROPUS. In the heartlands of the west, characteristic objects of popular art are the figurines – some typically Hellenic, others Parthian rider gods, yet others heavy-hipped nude females – which belong to an indigenous art of the east. Costume is the long robes of the east and loose baggy pants. Native figures appear with long hair, bearded and with striking moustache. DLK

See Colledge, M. A. R. (1967) *The Parthians*; (1977) *Parthian Art*; Kennedy, D. L. (1996) Parthia and Rome: eastern perspectives, in D. L. Kennedy, ed., *The Roman Army in the East* 67–90; Yarshater, E., ed. (1983) *The Cambridge History of Iran*, vol. 3.

Parthian wars For three centuries Rome and Parthia faced one another across the Euphrates' bend and in northern MESOPOTAMIA; each protagonist had the capacity to inflict great damage. The initial contempt of SULLA at his meeting with a Parthian envoy on the Euphrates in the 90s BC was transformed by the annihilation of CRASSUS' army at CARRHAE in 53 BC and the subsequent Parthian invasion of SYRIA. There was further conflict under AUGUSTUS and CLAUDIUS but no serious warfare until NERO. The major wars were those of TRAJAN (113–17), MARCUS AURELIUS and Lucius Verus (162–5), SEPTIMIUS SEVERUS (195–6; 198–9), CARACALLA (216–18) and Macrinus (218).

Until the 2nd century AD, warfare was confined largely to ARMENIA and the Euphrates' bend. Parthia never emulated its early successes; its occasional victories must be set against a long-term advance by Rome. From Trajan onwards, Rome thrust aggressively east and south-east, capturing CTESIPHON and other great cities of BABYLONIA, and progressively shifting its sphere of direct control eastwards, finally annexing Osrhoene and creating a province of Mesopotamia. From Trajan, emperors normally conducted the wars in person, adopting victory titles – Parthicus (Maximus) and Adiabenicus (Maximus) – and taking acclamations for wars waged in the sphere of ALEXANDER, whom Trajan and Caracalla were consciously imitating. Emperors paraded their successes in art: the cuirass of the Prima Porta statue of Augustus, the coins struck by Trajan, and the great victory arch of Severus in the Roman FORUM. DLK

See Kennedy, D. L., ed. (1996) *The Roman Army in the East*; Kennedy, D. L. and Riley, D. N. (1990) *Rome's Desert Frontier*.

WAR (table).

parties see ALCOHOL AND ALCOHOLISM; DINING; *SYMPOSIA*.

partnerships see *PUBLICANI*.

Pasion see APOLLODOROS THE ORATOR; WEALTH.

past The past was generally regarded as better than the present. In almost every aspect of life, citizens considered that they were living in a period of decline from a long-gone GOLDEN AGE. In the past, politicians were invariably more honest, EMPERORS more spectacular, and GENERALS more dashing and glamorous. This attitude encouraged people to recreate the past in HISTORY and MYTH, and to preserve its physical remains. A number of factors assisted this generally positive attitude towards the past. People's knowledge of it tended to be limited to events within only a few generations of their own time. Studies of historical allusions tend to show that, apart from a cluster of a few famous events, ancient authors tend not to use non-recent history without providing an explanatory gloss. Reality became quickly subsumed in a hazy warm glow.

Moreover, there was little to create a sense of progress in the present. Technological change was slow and generally small-scale, and when it occurred it tended to enjoy a limited circulation among members of the élite. The ancient world lacks any equivalent of the Industrial Revolution. Even the most spectacular machines of the hellenistic period were considered poor imitations of the wonders produced by Hephaistos and Daidalos. Other aspects of progress passed unnoticed. The period of the Roman empire is a period of long-term economic growth for the Mediterranean. However, owing to an absence of the necessary conceptual tools for theoretical economics, this was never fully appreciated. Of course, the actions of some individuals (most notably ALEXANDER the Great and AUGUSTUS) could reverse this sense of decline. Even here, however, their reigns are described as a return to the 'golden age' rather than a new stage of existence. The best that the FUTURE could offer was the past. AJLB

See Boardman, J. (2002) *The Archaeology of Nostalgia: how the Greeks re-created their mythical past*; Bowie, E. L. (1970) The Greeks and their past in the Second Sophistic, *P&P* 46: 3–41.

pastoral poetry As the name suggests, pastoral or bucolic poetry is principally concerned with dialogues between herdsmen in a pleasant rustic setting. The creation of the GENRE is traditionally attributed to THEOKRITOS of SYRACUSE (early 3rd century BC), whose *Idylls* include a number of rural sketches of this type. Theokritos may have derived his inspiration in part from the folk traditions of his native SICILY; his pastoral poems are, nevertheless, highly sophisticated literary creations and present what is very clearly a city-dweller's view of country life. The rustic characters are depicted with a combination of nostalgic idealism and urbane superiority; though they are in many cases figures of fun, the poet's loving portrayal of their simple lifestyle simultaneously suggests a hankering after lost innocence. Typically, two herdsmen encounter each other in a delightful spot (for which modern critics often use the Latin phrase *locus amoenus*) in the heat of the day, and engage in conversation and/or in a competitive exchange of SONGS. The exchange may take the form of an 'amoebaean' or alternating dialogue, in which the second speaker's words imitate and cap those of the first speaker. Typical subjects include the beauties of NATURE, the pleasures of music-making, and the loves and rivalries of the rustic characters.

Theokritos' successors in the genre include Moschos and Bion (2nd century BC), and the Roman poets VIRGIL, Calpurnius Siculus and the anonymous author of the so-called Einsiedeln Eclogues (both mid-1st century AD), and Nemesianus (late 3rd century AD). Of these, the most innovative and influential was Virgil, whose *Eclogues* (a collection of ten pastoral poems, published between about 42 and 37 BC) contain much close imitation of Theokritos, but also much that is wholly Virgilian. Whereas Theokritos' pastorals are set in (idealized versions of) real Greek or south Italian localities, Virgil's setting is a fantastic blend of Greece and rural Italy, the forerunner of the Arcadia of RENAISSANCE poetry. Yet the dreamy idealism of the *Eclogues* is strikingly juxtaposed with allusions to the socio-political realities of the poet's own day, particularly in poems 1 and 9 (whose theme is the upheavals brought about by the land confiscations following the battle of PHILIPPI) and in the 'messianic' *Eclogue* 4 (which anticipates the birth of a 'wonder-child', perhaps to be identified as the anticipated offspring of the short-lived marriage between MARK ANTONY and OCTAVIAN's sister Octavia). Figures from the real contemporary world intrude several times into the pastoral setting: the herdsmen in poem 3 mention Virgil's patron Pollio and his literary rivals Bavius and Maevius; the poet and statesman GALLUS appears in *Eclogues* 6 and 10; and the 'young god' praised by Tityrus in poem 1 is usually identified by critics as Octavian. Characteristic of the *Eclogues* generally is a mysterious, riddling quality which perhaps owes something to *Idylls* 1 (with its enigmatic narrative of the death of Daphnis) and 7 (a work which has been interpreted since antiquity as a *poème à clef*), but is otherwise distinctively different from the more direct style of Theokritos' vignettes. MG

See Gutzwiller, K. J. (1991) *Theocritus' Pastoral Analogies*; Rosenmeyer, T. G. (1973) *The Green Cabinet*.

pastoralism The raising of ANIMALS, also called animal husbandry. Pastoralism was the second most important means of food production in the classical world after AGRICULTURE. Animals were raised for their 'primary product', meat, and their 'secondary products', milk, clothing, traction, manure and transportation. The most common domesticated animals were SHEEP, GOATS, CATTLE, HORSES, DONKEYS, PIGS and dogs. Since the initial domestication of animals occurred in the eastern MEDITERRANEAN c.8000–7000 BC and this knowledge spread across the Mediterranean to northern Europe by c.2500, pastoralism was by the classical period widespread and thoroughly integrated in the ancient ECONOMY.

Raising animals can take several forms; two types of pastoralism are well attested in classical antiquity. Small-scale husbandry involved the raising of a limited number of animals in a single location throughout the year. It was regularly practised on farms, and in VILLAGES and towns. TRANSHUMANCE, the seasonal movement of flocks between upland and lowland pastures, was also pervasive. Due to the proximity of MOUNTAIN and plain in the Mediterranean, such movement may require only a few hours' walk. In vertical transhumance, SHEPHERDS ordinarily move animals to the uplands in the summer and the lowlands in the winter to take advantage of both environments. 'Inverse transhumance', a variant of the vertical type, refers to movement in the opposite direction. Two other types of pastoralism have been recognized in Mediterranean history but were of little consequence in the classical period. 'True' nomadic pastoralism, the movements of peoples and flocks with no fixed homes, and horizontal transhumance, the seasonal movement of millions of animals over hundreds of kilometres, were rare or did not exist in the classical Mediterranean.

Pastoralism in the classical Mediterranean was characterized by its close relationship to agricultural production. Transhumant pastoralists needed to trade for wheat and other crops, which formed a large portion of their diet. Agriculturalists needed manure, traction, threshing and surplus labour at harvest times. Thus, pastoralists timed their movements to arrive in agricultural zones shortly before the crops were ripe. They provided assistance in gathering the harvest in return for grain and other goods. In addition, they allowed their flocks to graze on stubble and to fertilize the fields.

Animal husbandry in classical Greece is generally thought to have been practised with small herds (c.50–100 animals) and over short distances. With the exception of some cross-border arrangements, seasonal transhumance was restricted within *polis* boundaries. Nonetheless, herds could still produce profit through the sale of wool, CHEESE and animals intended for SACRIFICE at religious festivals. They also provided insurance, in the form of 'grain on the hoof', against crop failure.

The Roman world exhibited more variety in pastoral systems. Subsistence farmers practised small-scale husbandry. Large landowners may have owned substantial flocks; one estate owner, Caecilius Isodorus, reportedly had 257,000 sheep. The agricultural writers VARRO (*On Agriculture* book 2) and COLUMELLA (books 6–7) describe techniques for raising individual species that pertain mainly to these wealthy landowners. Transhumant pastoralists passed back and forth across the empire's borders during annual migrations between winter and summer pastures. We get a sense of the economic activities of these pastoralists from a list of items taxed by the Roman empire at a frontier customs station in Algeria. Two-thirds of the goods on the Zarai tariff derive from the pastoral economy. They include sheep, goats, pigs, horses, mules, donkeys and a variety of secondary products including blankets, tunics, cloth and glue (*CIL* 8.4508). Other items are agricultural products which the pastoralists transported from one region to another, no doubt at a profit (dates from the Sahara, WINE and FISH SAUCE from the north).

Although pastoralism played an important role in the ancient economy, Greek and Roman authors gave pastoralists a bad reputation (Shaw). The Roman historian SALLUST, for example, connected the origin of the word 'nomad' with

> the Gaetulians and Libyans who inhabited Africa in the beginning, rough and uncivilized peoples who ate raw flesh and wild plants like animals. They followed neither law, nor custom, nor anyone's rule; roaming and rambling, they stopped only where night obliged them. (*Jugurthine War* 18.1–2)

The pastoralist in the eyes of Sallust was a savage, lawless wanderer, the antithesis of civilized city-dwellers, the educated class from which most ancient authors originated. That largely accounts for the negative stereotype of the pastoralist in Greek and Roman thought. HOMER (on the Cyclopes; *Odyssey* 9), HERODOTOS (on Scythians and Africans; *Histories* 4) and other authors express similar opinions.

Archaeological interest in pastoralism has increased in recent years with the recognition that although pastoral groups often build smaller and less permanent settlements than sedentary communities, they are not invisible. Studies of seeds and BONES have shown that agriculture preceded pastoralism, thus contradicting the views of ancient authors who regarded pastoralists as a primitive, pre-agricultural society. Through ETHNOARCHAEOLOGY, the study of modern cultures and artefacts for insights about the past, archaeologists have progressed beyond the initial question 'did transhumance exist?' to more complex problems such as 'how can evidence of pastoralism be recognized?' and 'how did pastoral systems feature in the economic strategies of subsistence farmers, large landlords, and states?' (Chang; Barker and Grant). DLS

See Columella 6, 7; Herodotos 4; Homer *Odyssey* 9; Varro, *On Agriculture* 2; Barker, G. and Grant, A. (1991) Ancient and modern pastoralism in central Italy, *PBSR* 59: 15–88; Chang, C. (1994) Sheep for the ancestors: ethnoarchaeology and the study of ancient pastoralism, in P. N. Kardulias, ed. *Beyond the Site* 353–71; Shaw, B. D. (1982–3) Eaters of flesh, drinkers of milk: the ancient Mediterranean ideology of the pastoral nomad, *Ancient Society* 13–14: 5–31; Whittaker, C. R., ed. (1988) *Pastoral Economies in Classical Antiquity.*

patricians The highest level of ARISTOCRACY at Rome, in contrast to PLEBEIANS. In the legendary period of Rome, a social and political class called the '*patres*' or patricians, of obscure origins but limited to a select group of *gentes* and their descendants, emerged. They are not descendants of the original SENATORS or the families of a single ethnic group, since the patricians include *gentes* of Latin, Sabine or ETRUSCAN origin who joined the city at different points. The major priesthoods at Rome were limited to members of patrician *gentes*, and patrician status was probably defined by the right to hold these religious offices. In the regal period, the patricians appointed the *interrex* between reigns and granted the auspices to the new KING, but could not become kings themselves. The elimination of the last king was a patrician attempt to reassert themselves against a tyrant who had limited their power by appealing to a wider populace. Conflict between patricians and other groups continues to feature in early Republican history. In general, patricians attempted to control the state through their hold on CONSULSHIPS and priesthoods, and they were conservative in their willingness to accept change. After the rise of the plebeian class threatened their primacy, they were forced over a period of time to allow others to share rule without becoming patricians. On occasion, a branch of a patrician *gens* chose to become plebeian. Important patrician families include the Caecilii, CLAUDII, CORNELII, FABII, JULII, Servilii and others. JV

See Cornell, T. J. (1995) *The Beginnings of Rome.*

patron–client relations see FREEDMEN AND FREEDWOMEN; PATRONAGE.

patronage Greek and Roman society was both heavily stratified, and many forms of dependence tied people to their superiors in wealth, power and status, patronage being one of them. In classical Greece, patronage played a minor part in the formation of social relationships. This does not mean, however, that patronage as such did not exist. The politician KIMON, who dominated Athenian politics in the second quarter of the 5th century BC, has been frequently identified as a prototype of patronage on the scale of Roman republican ARISTOCRATS. He opened up his fields and GARDENS to any CITIZEN and allowed them to take whatever they needed. He invited many people for dinner, and he walked around the city accompanied by a number of youths who handed out small numbers of coins to whoever was in need. In addition, he donated clothes to the ill-clothed and helped out with BURIAL expenses. Kimon was the Greek aristocrat *par excellence*, but this kind of behaviour was severely curtailed in the period of the radical DEMOCRACY which started with the revolution of 462, by which time Kimon had been OSTRACIZED.

At Rome, patronage was thought to have been invented by ROMULUS, who assigned all PLEBEIANS to a PATRICIAN patron. Whatever the merits of this belief, patronage was a long-standing component of Roman social relations. It may have originated with the people from the lowest strata of society feeling the need for protection, creating a tie of dependency which later developed into a system. There are three characteristics which mark off patronage from other forms of dependent relationships. Patronage is a social relationship which is reciprocal, involving exchanges of services over time between two parties. It is a personal relationship as opposed to a commercial one, and it is essentially asymmetrical, that is, between parties that are of different status. It might be added that patronage is structured as a permanent relationship, implying a flow of exchanges over time, rather than an incidental teaming up of two individuals. Bonds of patronage could be and were passed over from father to son. A client was expected to provide support to his patron in the political and forensic arena and to join him on his walks through the city as an entourage, the number of clients serving as a visible testimony to the patron's influence and power. In general terms, the dependant (*cliens*) was required to pay his respects to his patron at all times. This is most clearly exemplified in the social institution of the *salutatio*, the morning-call to a patron's house. One should imagine crowds of dependants setting out at sunrise dressed in their finest TOGAS to visit their patrons. In the late 2nd century Gaius GRACCHUS was the first to introduce the custom of admitting clients on a hierarchical basis, a practice which provoked extreme dissatisfaction. In return for their loyalty clients received legal guidance and support where necessary. In the literature the most frequently recorded support is financial. Clients who paid their respects to their patrons during the morning-call received a sum of money. This was not a token sum, but an amount sufficient to feed a man for a day. In addition we hear of items of considerable value being given to clients, such as clothes (especially the toga, at the same time a necessary item for paying homage to one's patron and the product of that relationship), SILVER plate, bullion and even land.

The correspondence of CICERO and PLINY THE YOUNGER offers a good perspective on how the system worked as a means of entering politics for young ambitious SENATORS. They made use of an extended network which was founded on the exchange of favours and wrote letters of recommendation to promote their protégés. The net return was the advertisement of the favour, thus adding considerable prestige to its bestower. The perspective of the client is largely absent from this kind of evidence, and Cicero does not even appear to have shown a great interest in his relationships with social inferiors. This absence is alleviated to some degree by the literary sources from the PRINCIPATE, though they have to be treated with due caution as historical evidence. From the viewpoint of the client, as described by MARTIAL and JUVENAL, the system of patronage was a series of humiliating experiences. It was especially the practice of the *salutatio* which received a lot of criticism. Typically, after his return to his native Spain Martial imagines his friend Juvenal climbing the hills of Rome to visit a patron. In other poems the social differences between patron and client have been removed. If the pyramid of patronage extends from the top down to the lowest subject, we should expect clients to pay their respects to patrons who are themselves away calling on their patrons, and Martial draws from this circumstance the inescapable conclusion that when patron and client are engaged in the same humiliating business they are essentially equal.

In the principate patronage was no longer merely based on lineage, political reputation and wealth, but with the onset of one-man rule it came to include proximity to the EMPEROR. This could lead to circumstances where senators were forced to pay their respects on those lower in social status but higher in political power. The senators who sought the political support of SEJANUS, himself a Roman knight, are labelled clients in the historical sources. SENECA sketches a particularly upsetting incident in which the former senatorial owner of an imperial FREEDMAN was snubbed as he was queuing up outside the freedman's house, and was not even admitted among the group of most-respected clients.

Patronage was deeply embedded in Roman society, though its range is not always clear from the sources, due to a tendency to cast patronage in the guise of a more positive relationship, such as *amicitia*, friendship. Cicero observed that some people considered it tantamount to death to accept a patron or to be called a client, and a century later Seneca testifies to the survival of these sentiments. Other evidence suggests that patronage was a social system enveloping the majority of Roman citizens. MK

See Saller, R.P. (1982) *Personal Patronage under the Early Empire*; Wallace-Hadrill, A., ed. (1989) *Patronage in Ancient Society*.

Paul, St d. c.AD 64 Apostolic CHRISTIAN missionary leader and author, supposedly MARTYRED at Rome under NERO. Paul was born as Saul into a hellenized JEWISH family with ROMAN CITIZENSHIP rights at Tarsus in south-eastern ASIA Minor. He was educated in JERUSALEM at the scribal schools run by the Pharisees, where he developed a deep knowledge of Jewish law. He became passionately loyal to the Pharisaic ideology of complete obedience to God's law, and it was in this capacity that he undertook to eradicate those groups which had begun to recognize the Galilean JESUS as the Messiah. At first he was active in Jerusalem, where he was involved in the condemnation of Stephen, the leader of the city's Christian sect. Later, he sought out more renegades at Damascus, but on his way there he underwent a mystical experience which resulted in his conversion to CHRISTIANITY and his assumption of the name Paul.

Paul's background guided his relationship with the young church organization in Jerusalem. In particular, his urbane hellenism gave him a very different world-view from the largely Aramaic-speaking group which had grown up around Jesus in Galilee. Paul soon fell out with some of the more traditional Jewish elements in the CHURCH: his advocacy of a mission to the Gentiles went against their views that Jesus' message was solely for the Jews, who had always been God's chosen people. But Paul persisted in his determination to bring the gospel to non-Jews, and under his direction the early church made its quantum leap from a rural sect to a religion of the Greek cities of the eastern MEDITERRANEAN. To this end, Paul undertook extensive travels through Asia Minor and Greece, and corresponded with young church communities as far away as Rome. Such relentless proselytism provoked the wrath of Jewish leaders, resulting in Paul's arrest by the Roman authorities. Playing the trump card of his Roman citizenship, he demanded the right to appeal to the emperor himself, and so was dispatched to Rome. The account of his activities given in the *Acts of the Apostles* breaks off with his arrival in Rome, but numerous APOCRYPHAL stories recount his activities there up to his death in the Neronian persecution.

Paul's travels and writings reveal a strong interest in the development of church organization, a theme which also underpins (albeit in rather exaggerated terms) the pro-Pauline narrative of the *Acts of the Apostles*. His epistles are concerned with the direction of Christian mission, the proper conduct of worship, and social order, particularly MARRIAGE and sexual relations. Much of this effort was driven by Paul's concern to determine the identity of the Christian community, of which he himself, drawing on his twin heritage of Judaism and hellenism, had a particular vision. MDH

See Acts of the Apostles; Pauline epistles (New Testament); Esler, P. F. (1987) *Community and Gospel in Luke–Acts*; Hengel, M. (1991) *The Pre-Christian Paul*; Meeks, W. (1983) *The First Urban Christians*; Murphy-O'Connor, J. (1996) *Paul*; Sanders, E. P. (1991) *Paul*.

Paulus see LAW, ROMAN.

Pausanias In the mid-2nd century AD, Pausanias travelled around much of the southern Greek mainland, the Roman PROVINCE of ACHAIA, and described what he saw in his *Periêgêsis tês Hellados*, his 'guide' or 'description' of Greece. Pausanias might not have presented so unusual a figure if not for the fact that the *Periêgêsis*, probably completed by c.AD 180, has survived largely intact. The work thus represents the most complete example from a body of contemporary periegetic literature now largely lost to us.

The *Periêgêsis* is organized in ten books, most of which treat a single region (ELIS, with the famed sanctuary at OLYMPIA, comprises two books). He starts with ATTICA (book 1), and moves in roughly clockwise fashion around the PELOPONNESE (through the Corinthia, LACONIA, MESSENIA, Elis, ACHAIA, and ARKADIA), before ending (in books 9 and 10) in BOIOTIA and PHOKIS and Ozolian LOKRIS. Within each region, Pausanias tends to follow a systematic course, moving repeatedly from border to centre and back again, before passing on to the next area. As he goes, Pausanias enumerates and describes sights or 'things seen' (*theôrêmata*), including sanctuaries, urban centres, art works, votives, sacred groves, TOMBS, and remarkable natural phenomena. Woven through each book are also mythic tales, historical accounts and local traditions (*logoi*).

Pausanias' systematic movements, apparently ENCYCLOPEDIC coverage, and seemingly neutral and careful reportage have encouraged the orthodox view (and use) of him as an antique equivalent of a modern-day *Baedeker* or a *Blue Guide*. The *Periêgêsis* was long carried out into the field and read 'on site'; its influence on later perspectives of Greece, both touristic and scholarly, is undeniable. Yet Pausanias states, on more than one occasion, that he will pick out for mention only the things that 'deserve to be recorded', and it is clear that the *Periêgêsis* has strong emphases and deliberate omissions. Pausanias spends most time describing cities and sanctuaries, almost completely ignoring features of the rural countryside. The cultic landscape of Greece is particularly stressed, Pausanias himself participating along the way in certain rituals (which he often feels constrained not to describe). In company with many contemporary authors of the 'SECOND SOPHISTIC', he demonstrates a strong classicizing bias in his reporting, though he by no means entirely disregards his own imperial age.

Pausanias himself originated from western ASIA Minor, not from Achaia, and just how he should be described – as TRAVELLER, TOURIST, or pilgrim – has been the subject of much recent debate, as has his attitude to Rome and imperial rule. Today most would agree that the *Periêgêsis*, with its concern for the Greek past as sedimented in its rituals and monuments, is deeply engaged with the construction of Greek identities within the empire. SEA

See Alcock, S. E. and Elsner, J., eds. (2000) *Pausanias*; Arafat, K. (1996) *Pausanias' Greece*; Elsner, J. (1992) Pausanias: a Greek pilgrim in the Roman world, *P&P* 135: 3–29; Habicht, C. (1998) *Pausanias' Guide to Ancient Greece*.

Pausanias (king of Sparta) As a member of the Agiad family he ruled SPARTA between 445–426 and 408–395 BC. Initially ruling as a minor after the exile in 445 of his father, Pleistoanax, he ceased to be king when his father was recalled but acceded again on Pleistoanax' death. Thanks to his lenient treatment of Athens at the end of the PELOPONNESIAN WAR, which recalls his father's aborted invasion of Attica 40 years earlier, democracy was restored and Athens became Sparta's ally. For this he was tried but acquitted. After missing a rendezvous in Boiotia with LYSANDER, and the latter's subsequent death in battle, Pausanias was condemned and left Sparta – the third successive member of his family to be exiled. At Tegea he wrote the first known prose work by a Spartan. This lost book attacked his enemies and advocated a return to the supposed laws of LYKOURGOS. It was probably the source of important information in surviving writers, complementing the eye-witness account of XENOPHON, but it may have reinforced the inaccurate, idealized image of Sparta that has bedevilled historians ever since. DGJS

See Xenophon, *Hellenica* 2.4, 3.5; David, E. (1979) The pamphlet of Pausanias, *P&P* 34: 94–116.

Pausanias the regent Spartan regent 480–c.470 BC. Acting as regent for Pleistarchos, son of LEONIDAS who died at THERMOPYLAI in 480, Pausanias was put in command of the Greek forces at PLATAEA, where he led them to victory. HERODOTOS presents him as a particularly honourable man. THUCYDIDES provides details of his subsequent career, with a far more hostile presentation. In 478 he led the Greek naval campaign against CYPRUS and Byzantium, but became alienated from some of the allies and was recalled to Sparta. There he was tried and acquitted on various charges, including collaboration with the PERSIANS. He then returned to the HELLESPONT in a private capacity and was again recalled to Sparta and imprisoned for a short while. Eventually the Spartan EPHORS became convinced that he was conspiring with the Persians. When he took sanctuary from them in the TEMPLE of ATHENA Chalkioikos, they had him walled up inside it until he starved to death. He was buried in the precinct of the temple on the instruction of the DELPHIC ORACLE. HB

See Herodotos 9.76–82; Thucydides 1.94–5, 128–34.

peace The Greek word for peace, *eirênê*, was first used in vernacular language to describe a state of peace without wars (perhaps the result of a peace treaty), but not as a technical term to denote a peace treaty. The word became part of the official language of peace treaties in the 4th century. It was first applied to the King's Peace (387/6), whose terms were incorporated in all subsequent 4th-century peace treaties and formed the underlying principles of what the Greeks called 'Common Peace'. In the 5th century, treaties were called truces (*spondai*) and were of limited duration, implying that WAR was the normal state of affairs. Both the Thirty Years' Peace, which concluded the first Peloponnesian war (446/5), and the peace of NIKIAS (421), which was to last 50 years, were called truces and were bilateral agreements between Sparta and Athens. The King's Peace, which ended the Corinthian war, called for two things that would shape the very notion of what constituted peace. First, all Greek states were to be free and autonomous; second, the treaty was a multilateral agreement made between all Greeks and applying to all Greeks equally. Moreover, the King's Peace had no time limit, implying that peace rather than war was now the expected norm. Such were the principles of the Common Peace advocated by Andokides (3.10–17), who delineates clearly the differences between the unequal truce that ended the Peloponnesian war (404) and a peace that treats all equally.

In Roman thinking, *pax*, like *eirênê*, referred to the absence of war rather than to a peace treaty (for which the proper term was *foedus*). Closing the doors of the temple of Janus at Rome signified that the Republic was at peace, a condition notoriously achieved (other than under the legendary king Numa) only in 235 BC. It was next done under Augustus, and then oftener under later emperors, more frequently as propaganda than as a reflection of true peace in the entire empire. Concomitantly, Pax appears as a PERSONIFICATION around the time of Augustus, who developed the ideology of the 'Augustan peace' (*Pax Augusta*) in monuments such as the ARA PACIS. Vespasian added a temple of Pax in AD 75. Virgil's well-known verses, that it was Rome's destiny 'to add tradition to peace, to be merciful to the conquered, and to bring down the proud by war' (*Aeneid* 6.852–3), encapsulate the Augustan attitude perfectly. Tacitus' acerbic comment on Roman rule, put in the mouth of the British rebel Calgacus – 'they make a desert and call it peace' (*Agricola* 30) – is probably to be read as a critique of Roman decadence rather than of empire. Other writers, such as AELIUS ARISTIDES in *Oration* 26, offer a more positive view on the benefits of peace and the state of the empire. The notion of *pax Romana* (Roman peace) regularly appears as a reverse legend on coins, but its use to characterize the period from 30 BC to AD 180 is a later construct employed by historians. CC, DGJS

See Ryder, T. T. B. (1965) *Koine Eirene*.

peasant uprisings While native revolts against imperial or hegemonic authority were widespread in the ancient world, PEASANT uprisings are not as well known, partly because the ÉLITE were reluctant to acknowledge them. Peasant uprisings threatened the social fabric, but revolts against imperial or hegemonic authority were attacks against the state, an institution rather than a social class; naturally, both motivations might lie behind some disturbances. Peasants involved in uprisings are often castigated as bandits (because they robbed landowners) and characterized as ignorant rustics (more a social than a descriptive label). Leaders might be shepherds and ploughmen, but also dispossessed or even disgruntled landowners. Their precise aims are not always clear, but the burden of taxation was often a factor. In some cases, such as the Bagaudae (or Bacaudae), one result (not necessarily the intent) was that landowners became the SLAVES of their slaves. A relatively mild form of uprising was *anachôrêsis*, a withdrawal by tenant-farmers until their grievances were settled, a practice best known from hellenistic and Roman Egypt. Its frequency, there and elsewhere, is unknown. Sources often hint at peasant disturbances in the ancient world, but usually provide very little detail.

Somewhat better known, and perhaps more significant, are uprisings in western Europe and AFRICA. About AD 186, an army deserter named Maternus gathered a significant force of the disaffected; it plundered GAUL and Spain before turning to Italy, intending to replace Commodus with Maternus himself as emperor. Evidently, initial social aims graduated to a political purpose as the movement gained confidence. A disaffected peasantry was endemic in the 3rd century in Gaul and Spain (and presumably elsewhere), even before the emergence of the Bagaudae, a term of uncertain origin employed for peasant uprisings from the late 3rd to the 5th centuries. MAXIMIAN engaged and defeated them: so his panegyrists proclaim, while simultaneously voicing embarrassment at the nature of his military achievements. Generally speaking, the Bagaudae operated from areas where the empire no longer maintained complete authority, such as Armorica. Disturbances continued through the 4th century; in the 5th, the Bagaudae once again afflicted large portions of western Europe, wreaking much havoc. By this time, Rome's authority had declined considerably, and 'Bagaudae' may be a generic term for inhabitants without state authority whose activities caused upheaval.

In Africa, Donatism contributed to disturbances in the late 4th and early 5th centuries. In general terms, Donatism was more popular among the peasantry and other lower classes, while the landowning classes adhered to orthodox CHRISTIANITY. Bands of the rural lower classes, known as the Circumcellions, attacked and plundered the property of the wealthy, as well as cities. Although the Circumcellions and Donatism are linked, it is not clear whether religious dispute or peasant disaffection was the incipient cause; most likely, each fed on the other. JV

See Drinkwater, J. (1992) The Bacaudae of fifth-century Gaul, in J. Drinkwater and H. Elton, eds., *Fifth-century Gaul* 208–17; Thompson, E. A. (1952) Peasant revolts in late Roman Gaul and Spain, *P&P* 2: 11–23.

peasants Generally defined as small-scale farmers functioning as a sub-sector of a hierarchical, politically complex society. They can be identified in a wide range of societies from ancient times to the present. In the study of classical antiquity, the peasants of classical Greece and Republican Rome have generally been regarded as modest but self-sufficient, independent HOUSEHOLDS, farming their own land using family LABOUR. This is probably an idealistic oversimplification. There is little secure information about peasants in the ancient world for they were, as Erich Wolf aptly dubbed them, 'the people without history'. Certainly it is clear from ancient texts that there were many farmers who were 'peasants', though ancient writers were not very interested in their way of life. Archaeological survey has revealed the activities of farmers in ancient Mediterranean countrysides, but it is often difficult to attribute these to any particular group and it is likely that peasants would have left only a faint imprint on the archaeological record. The reality for most peasants is likely to have been a permanent struggle to make ends meet in the face of the threat of frequent crop failure. We know from legal sources and from the documentary PAPYRI of Greco-Roman Egypt that many peasants were permanently encumbered by DEBT. Many may not have owned the land they worked. Even the better-off who did may have had long-term ties of obligation or PATRONAGE to wealthier people. The peasant-citizens of classical Athens appear to have been fortunate compared to most small-scale farmers known from classical antiquity. LF

See Garnsey, P. (1998) Where did Italian peasants live?, in P. Garnsey, *Cities, Peasants and Food in Classical Antiquity* 107–33 (ed. with addenda by W. Scheidel); Wolf, E. (1982) *Europe and the People without History*.

pederasty see ATHLETES AND ATHLETICS, ROMAN; BODY, THE; HOMOSEXUALITY; SEXUALITY.

pediment see ARCHITECTURE, GREEK; PANTHEON; PARTHENON; SCULPTURE; TEMPLES.

peer polity interaction An approach to understanding social and political change in certain circumstances. It seeks in particular to explain the mutual interactions of relatively small, politically independent entities ('polities') which are at similar levels of social and political formation and of roughly equal size and power ('peers'). This approach aims at avoiding the hierarchical features of diffusionist and core–periphery models of cultural and social change. Polities typically occupy a relatively circumscribed geographical region and share the same civilization – social, political, cultural, and religious structures, and language. Change can occur through a variety of mechanisms including 'competitive emulation', in which different polities seek to outdo each other in some competitive sphere (e.g. the construction of TEMPLES); 'symbolic entrainment', in which symbolic systems are adopted by neighbouring polities (e.g. writing systems); and 'transmission of innovation', in which new ideas, including non-symbolic ones, are adopted widely by members of the peer polity system (e.g. technological innovations). Analysis within this framework places special emphasis on the role of ÉLITES: how and where they interact, and how the actions of élites in one polity affect the actions of élites in others. Peer polity interaction has been deployed especially as a way to explain rapid change among the *poleis* of archaic Greece, which meet the conditions of the theory particularly well. GR

See Renfrew, C. and Cherry, J. F., eds. (1986) *Peer Polity Interaction and Socio-political Change*.

Peiraios see PIRAEUS.

Peisistratos TYRANT of ATHENS, claiming descent from the Neleids of Pylos and from Peisistratos, archon of 669/8 BC (traditional date). As a military officer (562/1), though perhaps not polemarch (archon in charge of war), he gained fame in a war against MEGARA, which he converted into popular support. He formed a faction of supporters called the 'hillmen' to rival the aristocratic factions of Lykourgos (the 'plainsmen') and Megakles ('coastmen'), and in the year 561/0 he staged a coup. Wounding himself, and then pretending to need protection from his enemies, he persuaded the Athenians to vote him a bodyguard of club-bearers, which he used to seize the ACROPOLIS and make himself tyrant. His reign was only short-lived, as Megakles and Lykourgos combined forces to drive him out. But Megakles, who began to lose ground in the aristocratic rivalry that still continued, offered to return Peisistratos to power, an arrangement sealed through a dynastic marriage. Peisistratos' supporters, who had dressed a woman named Phyê in ARMOUR and placed her in a CHARIOT, began circulating the rumour that ATHENA herself was leading Peisistratos' return. The ruse worked, but the second tyranny was equally short-lived. Peisistratos' failure to consummate his marriage with Megakles' daughter led to renewed hostilities and a second EXILE, which lasted ten years, sufficient time to raise money to hire mercenaries. In 546/5 he landed at MARATHON and defeated Athenian forces at Pallene and remained in power until his death in 528/7, succeeded by his son Hippias who ruled until 510. Peisistratos ruled moderately, without changing the existing laws or offices of state. He was credited with introducing local administration of justice across Attica, as well as farming subsidies, but the tyranny was increasingly unstable. Hippias' rule was undermined first by the assassination of his brother Hipparchos (by Harmodios and Aristogeiton, the renowned 'tyrannicides', in 514), then by the machinations of other aristocrats, notably the ALKMAIONIDAI. Intentionally or not, the Peisistratids prepared the ground for the democratic reforms of Kleisthenes. (see also *SKOLIA*; TYRANNY) CC

See Aristotle, *Athenian Constitution*; Herodotos.

Pelagianism see AUGUSTINE (1); OROSIUS.

Pelasgians A mythical people whom HOMER in his 'Catalogue of Ships' describes as allies of the TROJANS. Their name has come to be associated with the indigenous (apparently pre-Greek) inhabitants of the AEGEAN area and even Magna Graecia; the name Pelasgia was sometimes indiscriminately applied to Greece in general. They are attested early in the Hellespontine region, Lemnos and CRETE; later we find traces of them in Lower Macedonia (i.e. near the Strymon), the ARGOLID and ARKADIA. Their name apparently meant 'uncivilized' and it came to designate indigenous *Urvolk* ('original people') of the Aegean. The hero Pelasgos is thought to have been autochthonous – born from the earth and still living in the land of his birth. HERODOTOS, who mentions them on numerous occasions, is nevertheless confused about their identity, speaking at one time of the Athenians as being of Pelasgic origin (because they claimed to be indigenous and unchanged) and on another of the BARBARIAN speech of the Pelasgians. Modern scholars have suggested various 'racial' origins, making them Semites, ILLYRIANS or even founders of the MYCENAEAN civilization. The 5th-century historian Hellanikos believed that the Pelasgians were expelled from Greece and settled in Italy, where they were known as the Tyrsenoi, i.e. ETRUSCANS. Today, when the term is not studiously avoided, 'Pelasgians' is used to denote pre-Hellenic peoples, though there is considerable scholarly debate about the period (or periods) when Greek-speakers appeared in Greece. WH

See Myres, J. (1907) A history of the Pelasgian theory, *JHS* 27: 170–225; Sourvinou-Inwood, C. (2003) Herodotos (and others) on Pelasgians, in P. Derow and R. Parker, eds., *Herodotus and his World* 103–44.

Pella The new royal capital in place of Aigai (mod. VERGINA) developed by king Archelaos of Macedonia at the end of the 5th century BC. It was ideally situated on major land routes leading east, west and north, and was located beside the Lydias river, which was then navigable to the sea. It grew into the largest city in Macedonia. The Athenian tragic poet EURIPIDES, who worked at Archelaos' court, died there in 406, and ALEXANDER the Great may have been born there in 356.

Archaeological excavation has revealed early cemeteries and the grid-plan of the city. Impressive houses in the lower town were adorned with the finest pebble MOSAICS ever produced in 4th-century Greece (still visible on the site). The adjacent *AGORA* area has produced rich finds. The recently excavated royal PALACE on the hill behind, which is probably not the original palace of Archelaos, is still being studied and will tell much about Macedonian royal life in the hellenistic period. It is clear that Pella was a hugely sophisticated city that was hellenized to a high degree in its lifestyle and culture.

The city fell to the Roman general Lucius AEMILIUS PAULLUS after the battle of PYDNA in 168 BC, whereupon Macedonia became a province of Rome. Pella gradually declined in importance relative to the coastal city of THESSALONIKE. EER

See Ginouvès, R. (1993) *Macedonia*; Petsas, P. (1978) *Pella*.

Pelopidas c.410–364 BC Theban statesman and general, the key events in whose life have been chronicled in PLUTARCH's *Life*, as well as in the very brief *Life* by CORNELIUS NEPOS. These writers credit Pelopidas with strong military capabilities and leadership skills. In about 382, when the Spartans seized the citadel of Kadmeia at THEBES, Pelopidas went into EXILE in Athens. With a party of fellow-exiles, he returned in 379 to drive out the Spartan garrison and to overthrow the oligarchic government at Thebes. After the success of this enterprise, he became Boiotarch at Thebes (378) and leader of the sacred band. He led this élite company of 300 Theban troops at the Theban victories at Tegyra (375) and LEUKTRA (371). In 369 he was sent north to drive out the tyrant Alexander of Pherai in THESSALY. On his second expedition to Thessaly in 368, he was imprisoned by Alexander, but was later rescued by EPAMEINONDAS. He finally defeated Alexander at Kynoskephalai (364), but was himself killed in the battle, allegedly while trying to attack Alexander single-handedly. FMM

See Georgiadou, A. (1997) *Plutarch's Pelopidas*; Scott-Kilvert, I., trs. (1973) *The Age of Alexander*.

Peloponnese (Peloponnesos, 'island of Pelops') Peninsula divided from mainland Greece by the isthmus of CORINTH. It was not the earliest part of Greece to be inhabited, but for the last three millennia BC the most characteristic features of successive cultures in Greek lands either originated or were partly developed here. STRABO called the Peloponnese the *akropolis* of Greece. Mountain chains form three headlands which point southwards from the central heights and are divided by gulfs; the eastern Cape, Malea, was notoriously difficult. Much of the interior is too high to enable OLIVES to survive. A fourth headland, the ARGOLID, is separated from ATTICA by the Saronic gulf, while the deep indentation of the Corinthian gulf cuts the peninsula off from central Greece: the Isthmus is some 6 km (4 miles) wide. Plains in the Argolid, LACONIA and MESSENIA provide the agricultural resources which enabled the development of successive cultures: broadly, the early Helladic in the 3rd millennium, the MYCENAEAN in the 2nd, and the archaic and classical in the 1st. There are smaller, enclosed plains in the higher central regions (ARKADIA), larger alluvial plains in the north-west (Elis), and a narrow coastal shelf in the north (ACHAIA). It remains unclear how significant the arrival of new peoples was in the establishment of new features. There was destruction on many sites towards the end of early Helladic and again at the end of Mycenaean, and the decipherment of the Linear B script has demonstrated that the PALACE BUREAUCRACY in the Mycenaean world was conducted in a form of Greek. How much earlier the language was spoken in the peninsula is uncertain, though many place-names, including Corinth (*Korinthos*), have a non-Greek origin.

After the collapse of the Mycenaean world, there are signs of co-operation among various inhabitants of the peninsula in the cult of ZEUS at OLYMPIA in the 9th century BC. By the late 8th the idea of the *POLIS*, the defining feature of Greek culture, had taken shape at Argos, Sparta, Corinth and (on a lesser scale) elsewhere; a similar development in Messenia was probably suppressed by the Spartan conquest. The *polis* took longer to establish itself in the central mountainous area of ARKADIA and in the north-west, but it had done so soon after the PERSIAN WARS.

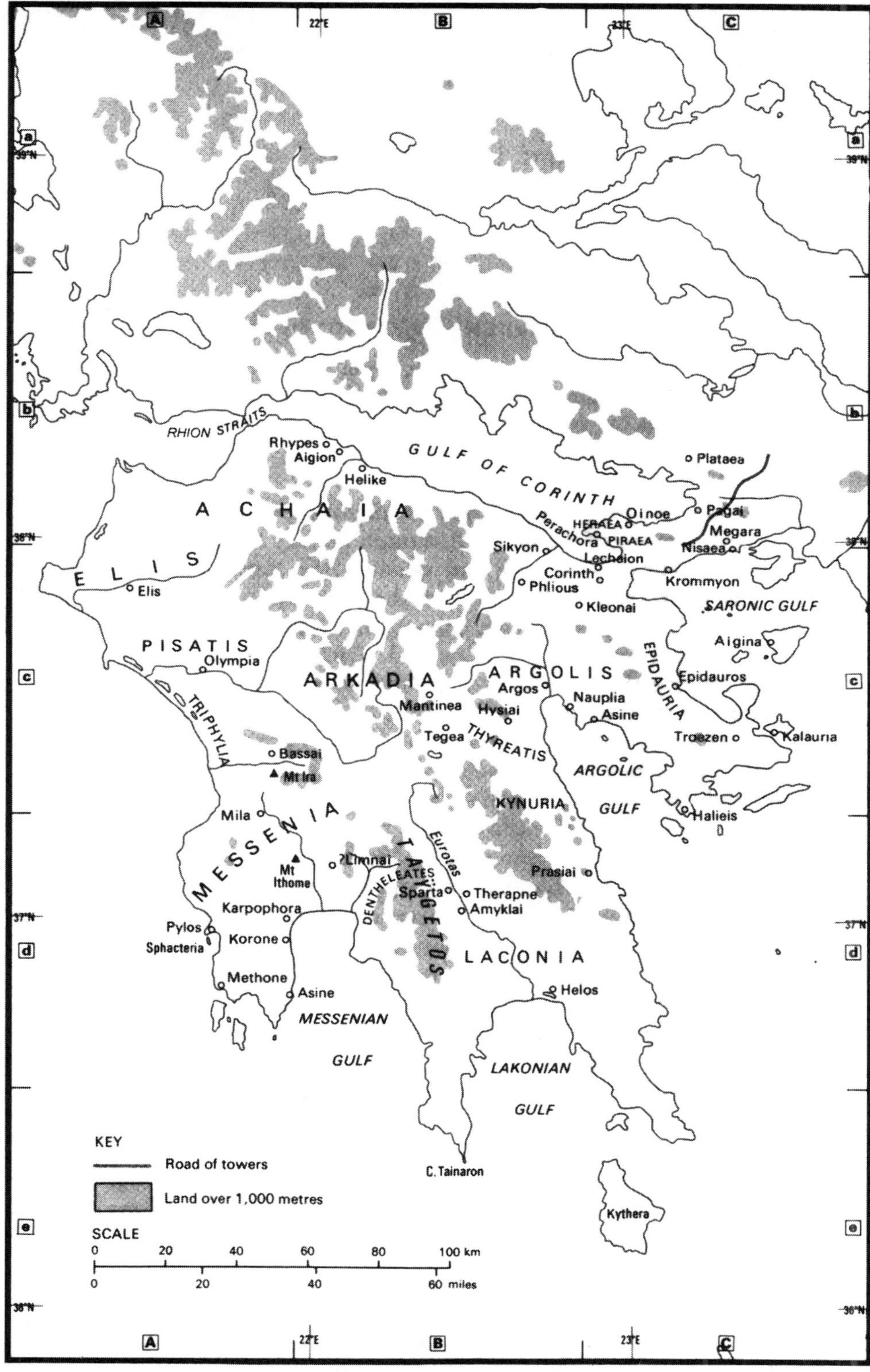

PELOPONNESE: map.

Sparta headed an alliance of many cities from c.550, but never secured the allegiance of the whole peninsula: at least Argos remained hostile, and others usually stood aside, especially ACHAIA in the north. In the 5th and early 4th centuries, Sparta controlled most cities through compliant OLIGARCHIES, but after Sparta's defeat at LEUKTRA (371) there were strong, and closely linked, movements for independence and democracy. The last great cities of the Peloponnese, Messene and Megalopolis, were founded at this point with Theban help; but divisions between and within the various cities led to difficulties which PHILIP II of Macedonia could exploit. Few Peloponnesian cities fought at CHAIRONEIA. In the 3rd century the federal state of the ACHAIAN LEAGUE brought a measure of unity and successfully resisted both Macedonian and Spartan attempts to dominate the peninsula. Despite the efforts of PHILOPOIMEN, 'the last of the Greeks' (PLUTARCH), the Achaian league was unable to maintain a satisfactory relationship with Rome. JBS

See Pausanias, books 2–8; Strabo, book 8; Baladié, R. (1980) *Le Péloponnèse de Strabon*; Hägg, R., ed. (2002) *Peloponnesian Sanctuaries and Cults*.

 GREECE.

Peloponnesian 'league' see ALLIANCES; IMPERIALISM, GREEK; INTERNATIONAL RELATIONS; SPARTA; THUCYDIDES; TREATIES.

Peloponnesian war 431–404 BC Fought between Athens and Sparta and their respective allies, the Peloponnesian war is so named and identified thanks to its HISTORIAN, THUCYDIDES. The very name itself is not the least of his achievements. For Thucydides was an Athenian, so that from his point of view it was the war against the Peloponnesians. But from a Spartan standpoint it was 'the Athenian war', a phrase used by Thucydides himself. Besides, by no means all contemporaries and participants agreed with Thucydides that it had been a single, 27-year war. In 421 a formal peace had been sworn, after which declared hostilities did not resume until 414, so that on a straightforward view between 431 and 404 there were two wars not one. Some modern scholars, by contrast, have taken a more extended chronological view even than Thucydides. Between 460 and 445 the same antagonists had fought each other for very much the same reasons as they did between 431 and 404, and the peace concluded in 445 was not much more stable than that of 421. So, these scholars ask, why not extend 'the Peloponnesian war' back to 460?

Nevertheless, Thucydides' war, 'the' Peloponnesian war, is a construct hard to dislodge or to explode entirely. What was at stake in it was POWER: both the power of Sparta and Athens over their respective alliances, that is, the Peloponnesian league and the Athenians' naval empire, and also the relative power of the two alliance blocs. If we follow Thucydides' own typically complex interpretation, making due allowance for possible Athenian bias, it was the Spartans who began the conflict in 431 because the growth of Athenian power was beginning seriously to destabilize their hold over the Peloponnesian league. They depended on their domination of the league for security against their economically vital HELOT underclass at home, and for prestige and influence abroad.

The two alliances were fundamentally different in military character, Sparta's being land-based and Athens' essentially naval. Sparta's initial strategy of invading ATTICA annually by land soon proved futile, despite the unexpected bonus of the plague at Athens, since Athens did not depend for economic survival exclusively on its home agricultural territory. Paradoxically, Athens caused far more difficulty for Sparta by establishing a base for raiding in Sparta's home territory, at Pylos in MESSENIA, in 425.

Stalemate and exhaustion led to the peace of 421, but the balance shifted decisively in Sparta's favour with the disastrous failure of Athens's attempt to conquer some large part of SICILY (415–413). Further paradox ensued when during the final phase of the war (413–404), known either as the Ionian or Dekeleian war, Sparta received massive injections of PERSIAN money and became Athens' equal at sea. Eventual victory for Sparta was secured in summer 405. Under LYSANDER the Spartan fleet gained control of the Hellespont (Dardanelles) and thereby choked off Athens's chief food lifeline – the supply of seaborne wheat from the rich black-earth soil around the north shore of the BLACK SEA. Starvation quickly ensued at Athens, which surrendered unconditionally in spring 404 and made peace on Sparta's terms. Those terms included the end of the ATHENIAN EMPIRE, the destruction of the walls round the port of PIRAEUS and of those linking Piraeus to the city of Athens, and the replacement of the DEMOCRACY by a narrow, dogmatically pro-Spartan junta later known as the THIRTY Tyrants. PAC

See Thucydides, *Histories* (on 431–411); Xenophon, *Hellenika* (later stages of war); Hornblower, S. (2002) *The Greek World: 479–323 BC*, chs. 9, 13–14; Kagan, D. (1969) *The Outbreak of the Peloponnesian War*; (1974) *The Archidamian War*; (1981) *The Peace of Nicias and the Sicilian Expedition*; (1987) *The Fall of the Athenian Empire*; Powell, A. (2001) The Peloponnesian war, 431–404, in A. Powell, ed., *Athens and Sparta*, ch. 5; de Ste Croix, G. E. M. (1972) *The Origins of the Peloponnesian War*.

 WAR (table).

peltasts see ARMIES, ORGANIZATION OF, GREEK; ARMS AND ARMOUR, GREEK; IPHIKRATES; MERCENARIES; TACTICS, MILITARY, GREEK.

Penates see RITUAL, ROMAN.

Perachora see CORAL.

perfume Beginning in the MYCENAEAN period, perfumes exerted a magical attraction for the Greeks. Held to be of divine origin, perfumes were essential in cult worship: after ANIMAL offerings, rare perfumed substances, such as myrrh, were burned as incense to please the GODS. In the same way, births, MARRIAGES, and deaths were accompanied by perfumed fumigations. Perfumes (or, more properly, perfumed OILS) played a major role during funerals, since the dead were wrapped in perfumed shrouds and buried with precious perfume receptacles and sweet smelling plants, such as roses, lilies and violets – probably symbols of eternal life. In addition to these

PERFUME: Pompeian wall-painting depicting production and sale of perfume. 1. Extraction of high quality olive oil in a wedge press (wedges are hammered between planks in a frame to depress baskets of pulped olives); 2. Oil is mixed with crushed flowers or other scent-giving materials, being mixed in the pestle; 3. Customer in the shop sampling perfume on the back of her wrist; 4. The accompanying slave appears to be carrying the money.

rituals, the Greeks considered bodily hygiene and physical beauty hallmarks of a civilized society. HIPPOKRATES thus recommends sage- or cumin-based remedies, administered in the form of fumigations, rub-downs and baths, to be used to keep the body in a state of health. Following their ablutions at the GYMNASIA, men perfumed their bodies (iris and marjoram oils being particularly popular). During *SYMPOSIA*, guests' feet were washed as a sign of hospitality, after which they were offered wreaths of flowers, perfumed WINES and rose-scented or clove-oil ointments. In the stadium, ATHLETES smeared their bodies with oil, which they removed afterwards with strigils.

Women adorned and embellished themselves with a wide variety of perfumed oils, keeping the precious commodities in delicate and beautifully decorated perfume containers (such as an *alabastron* or *aryballos*). By the 4th century BC, the Greeks began to adopt heavier scents, like frankincense and myrrh, once reserved for the gods, as fashionable perfumes. Benozin, cinnamon, sandalwood, castoreum, musk and civet are increasingly attested from this period. Under the influence of Greece, the Romans were enthusiastic in their use of perfumes, often employing them excessively. Perfumes were extensively used in religious cults and funerary rituals, where frankincense, myrrh, costus and musk become indispensable. EMPERORS were trendsetters in the conspicuous consumption of perfumes: NERO is supposed to have burnt a whole year's worth of myrrh in one day when he cremated the body of his wife, POPPAEA. But perfumes were also used abundantly in daily life, especially for washing. In the BATHS, everyone aspired to use perfumes of some kind; due to this demand, the Romans were responsible for spreading the use of *sapo*, a foamy paste made from GOAT-fat and soapwort ashes, the ancestor of soap. By perpetuating and developing Greeks customs, the Romans helped maintain the ancient TRADE routes which brought the raw perfume products from INDIA, ARABIA and AFRICA. These raw materials were used by the Romans to prepare ointments, toilet waters, perfumes, scented pills and powders. To store these substances, the Romans employed a variety of containers, often replacing the traditional ceramic and stone vessels with glass bottles, which allowed greater diversity of shape and colour. LL-J

See Dalby, A. (2000) *Empire of Pleasures*; (2002) *Dangerous Tastes*.

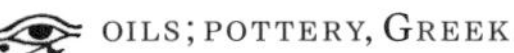 OILS; POTTERY, GREEK.

Pergamon A mountain citadel in north-west Asia Minor (mod. Turkey). Pergamon entered the mainstream of Greek history in the early 3rd century BC when it became the treasury of king LYSIMACHOS, who deposited considerable funds there under the control of a local general named Philetairos. Philetairos gained control of the funds and administered Pergamon from c.302 BC under SELEUKID suzerainty. His campaigns against the Gauls who invaded Asia Minor helped establish Pergamon as an independent state. Greater independence was achieved under his nephew Eumenes I (r.263–241). Their descendants, the 'Attalid' dynasty, claimed descent from Telephos (a son of HERAKLES) and ruled the surrounding area until 133 BC, taking the royal title from around 240. They transformed Pergamon into a glittering city that rivalled other hellenistic capitals in wealth and sophistication. Perennial conflicts with the Gauls, notably under Attalos I (r.241–197), were commemorated by the sculptures of Gauls fighting Greeks such as the famous 'Dying Gaul' (only a later copy survives). Attalos was a major player in Rome's wars against Macedonia, at one point defending Piraeus against Philip V; this led to civic honours at Athens and Attalid dedications of sculpture on the Athenian Acropolis. His son Eumenes II (r.197–159) gained control of much of northern Asia Minor as a result of Rome's victory over the Seleukid ANTIOCHOS III in 188. Attalos II (r.158–138) was the dedicator of the stoa of Attalos in Athens.

The *AKROPOLIS* area was adorned with splendid buildings, among them PALACES, the sanctuary of ATHENA, the Great Altar of ZEUS, and a LIBRARY to compete with the famous library of ALEXANDRIA. Some of the most famous works of Greek SCULPTURE came from the Great Altar (now in Berlin) and the various dedications made to commemorate Attalid military victories. Extensive excavation of the *akropolis* and civic and religious areas has yielded much vital information about Pergamene life. The lower town housed a famous healing sanctuary of ASKLEPIOS.

In the mid-2nd century the Attalids' relationship with Rome was more problematic. For uncertain reasons, in 133 BC Attalos III bequeathed his kingdom to Rome. Pergamon continued to flourish as a city, and was adorned by new temples under Roman emperors. It remained an important intellectual centre until late antiquity. EER

See Hansen, E.V. (1971) *The Attalids of Pergamon*; Radt, W. (1988) *Pergamon*; Shipley, G. (2000) *The Greek World after Alexander* 312–19.

 ASIA.

PERGAMON: (a) the Attalid dynasty of Pergamon.

Date	Ruler	Relationship to other rulers
283–263	Philetairos (not king)	
263–241	Eumenes I (not formally king)	nephew of Philetairos
241–197	Attalos I Soter	cousin and adopted s. Eumenes
197–159/8	Eumenes II Soter	s. Attalos I
159/8–139/8	Attalos II	s. Attalos I
139/8–133	Attalos III	s. Eumenes II
[133–129	Aristonikos ('Eumenes III')]	

Key: s. = son of.

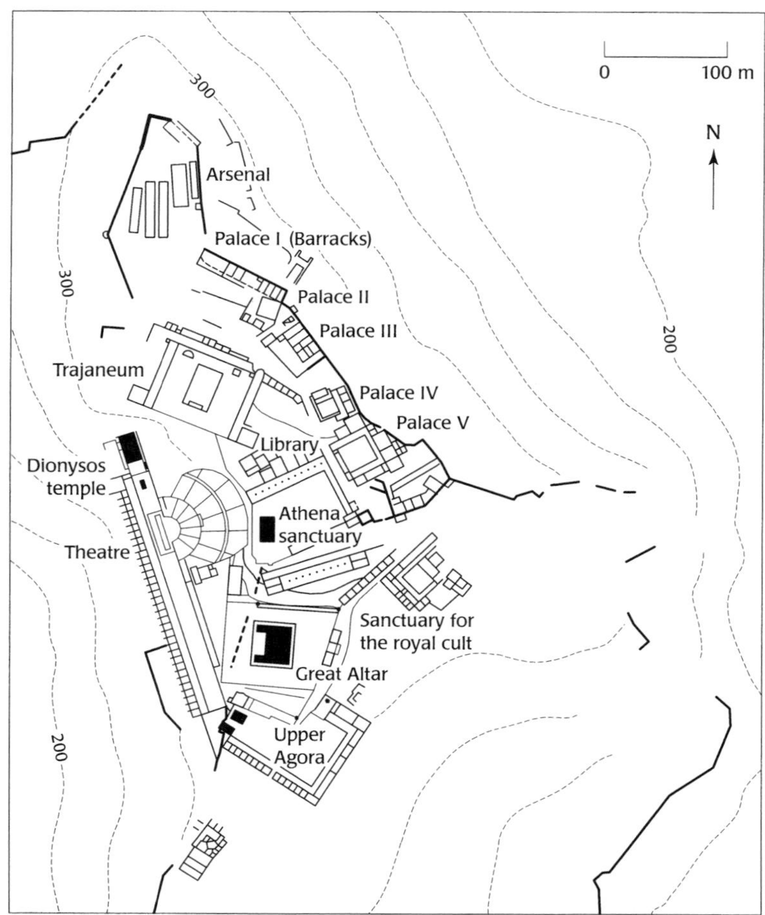

PERGAMON: (b) plan.

Perikles c.500–428 BC Athenian politician and GENERAL, born into a distinguished family (his father, Xanthippos, was OSTRACIZED in 484). Perikles became a dominant figure in Athens from the 450s until his death in 428. He was an effective general, a persuasive orator and an expert in managing the democratic system and keeping the people in check. With friends in both SCIENCE and the arts, he inaugurated an ambitious building programme on the ACROPOLIS, in the lower city and in ATTICA whose impact can still be felt as one views the PARTHENON. His steady consolidation of Athens' military and financial strength, in particular his transformation of a free anti-Persian alliance of Greek states into an ATHENIAN EMPIRE, met with opposition at home. The deadlock was broken when his main enemy, Thucydides son of Melesias, was ostracized. That left Perikles supreme, but his authority even earlier is shown by the fact that only two *ostraka* are known to have been cast against him whereas hundreds survive with Thucydides' name. When war with a jealous Sparta broke out in 431, Perikles adopted the cautious policy of evacuating the Attic countryside each summer and relying on the walls and fleet of Athens for survival. This was not entirely popular, and Perikles for the first time nearly lost power. He did not survive long, and having lost two sons in the famous plague of 430/29 he left no dynasty. His son by his mistress ASPASIA was legitimized by the ASSEMBLY, but he too left no heir and the family died out. Perikles was much lampooned on the comic stage, but this is a tribute to his role in history; the historian THUCYDIDES had the greatest admiration for him. He had made Athens 'the school of Greece' (2.40), and under him the government was 'the rule of one man' (2.65) rather than plain DEMOCRACY. HBM

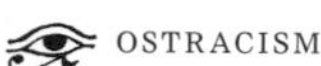 OSTRACISM.

Peripatetics Followers of ARISTOTLE, so named from the walkway (*peripatos*) in the LYCEUM where Aristotle taught. The first two heads of the school after Aristotle, THEOPHRASTOS and Strato (Straton; head c.287–269 BC), and other associates and pupils of Aristotle such as Dikaiarchos and Eudemos (late 4th century BC), developed Aristotle's researches, Strato concentrating on investigation of the natural world. Peripatetics were particularly active in the genre of BIOGRAPHICAL writing. With the predominance of ALEXANDRIA as a centre of research, the Lyceum went into decline; it probably ceased to exist as an institution when SULLA sacked Athens in 86 BC. The 1st century BC, however, saw a renewed interest in the study of Aristotle's own writings: Nikolaos of Damascus (b. c.64 BC), court philosopher to HEROD the Great, compiled a summary, and a series of commentators, of whom the first was Andronikos (precise dates uncertain), elucidated the texts. Andronikos produced the first collected edition of Aristotle's works. The extent to which he intervened in the details of the text is uncertain. Other commentators include Boëthos (1st century BC), Aspasios (c.AD 100–150) and above all Alexander of APHRODISIAS (fl. c.AD 200), of whose earliest works a substantial proportion survives. Subsequently, with the notable exception of THEMISTIUS (c.AD 317–88), Aristotle's works were studied, and commentaries on them written, chiefly in the NEOPLATONIST school. (see also ARISTOTELIANISM) RWS

See Gottschalk, H. B. (1987) Aristotelian philosophy in the Roman world, in *ANRW* II.36.2: 1079–174; Lynch, J. P. (1972) *Aristotle's School*; Sharples, R.W. (1999) The Peripatetic school, in D. J. Furley, ed., *From Aristotle to Augustine* 147–87.

peristyle see ARCHITECTURE, GREEK; DINING ROOMS, ROMAN; GARDENS AND GARDENING; HOUSES; MARKET BUILDINGS; VILLAS.

Perpetua (Vibia Perpetua) d.AD 203 MARTYRED at CARTHAGE in 203 with Felicitas, and four male catechumens. She is known from the *Passion of Perpetua and Felicitas* which claims to include, within a narrative framework by an unknown hand, Perpetua's own account of her imprisonment, her trial and the divinely inspired visions she experienced while incarcerated. She is described as well educated, married, and nursing a baby son at the time of her arrest. Her husband is never mentioned. Family pressure to renounce CHRISTIANITY came from her father. She appears indifferent to pleas to pity his old age and the needs of her son, who is eventually handed over to the father. She has four visions. In the first she climbs a ladder, lined with sharp weapons, to a garden where she is given milk to drink by an old man; she and her companions interpret this to mean that they will suffer death in the arena. The next two visions concern her deceased brother Dinocrates, first suffering and then relieved. Finally, Perpetua sees herself as a man defeating an Egyptian; she understands this to mean she will fight the devil and emerge victorious. Perpetua and Felicitas were martyred by being stripped naked, clad in netting and sent to fight a mad heifer. Only wounded, they had to be finished off by the sword. If the *Passion* does include Perpetua's own writing, it is the only first-person account of a martyr's experience, and the earliest surviving female Christian writing before the 4th century. MEH

See Kraemer, R. and Lander, S.L. (2000) Perpetua and Felicitas, in P. Esler, ed., *The Early Christian World* 1048–68; Musurillo, H. (1972) *The Acts of the Christian Martyrs*; Shaw, B. (1993) The passion of Perpetua, in *P&P* 139: 3–45.

persecutions The suppressions of a religious movements. Although most usually associated with the measures taken against CHRISTIANITY by the Romans, there were other persecutions in antiquity. In 186 BC, the Roman SENATE ordered the suppression of the cult of Bacchus in southern ITALY. In the imperial period, harsh measures were taken against MANICHAEISM and DRUIDISM. In late antiquity, the Christians themselves proved energetic in taking violent action against PAGANS, JEWS and even other Christians.

In most cases, persecution was provoked by a combination of socio-political and religious motives, in that cults were suppressed because they were seen to threaten both the cosmic and the social order. Nevertheless, persecution in the Roman world tended to be local rather than universal in character. For example, the persecutions in Rome under NERO, in Bithynia under TRAJAN and in LYON under MARCUS AURELIUS were localized. Only with the outbreak of persecution under Decius (249–51) was there empire-wide action against Christianity, a trend which reached its climax in the great persecution begun by DIOCLETIAN in 303. Yet even in these persecutions, the implementation of anti-Christian measures varied from province to province. Under the Christian empire, pagans, Jews and heretics suffered restrictions imposed by law, but state-led persecution did not occur. The state was more concerned to maintain the social order, and so sought to discourage local Christian communities from persecuting their religious enemies. MDH

See Lane Fox, R. (1986) *Pagans and Christians*.

Persephone see DEMETER; ELEUSIS; FLOWERS; GODS AND GODDESSES, GREEK; HADES; MOTHER GODDESSES; MYSTERY RELIGIONS.

Persepolis (Old Persian *Parsa*) The Greek name of the royal city of the Achaemenid kings, founded by DARIUS I. The PALACE complex, built on an artificially raised terrace 18 m (60 ft) high, included palaces of Darius I, XERXES and ARTAXERXES III, a throne hall (Apadana) and treasury of Darius I, and the One-hundred-column Hall. The ROOFS of the throne halls were supported by 20 m (66 ft) high columns and had ceilings made of cedar wood. Stone reliefs decorating the doorways and staircases show the king enthroned or in PROCESSION, while others depict the royal hero in combat with lions and mythical beasts. Reliefs carved on the northern and eastern staircases of the Apadana depict delegations of the peoples of the empire bringing gifts to the king, including vessels, cups, weapons and JEWELLERY crafted in Achaemenid court style. The central panel of the staircase, now removed, shows an audience scene with the king seated on the throne and the heir to the throne standing behind him. The royal guest, standing in front of two incense burners, respectfully bows before the king. The architecture of Persepolis, built in the distinctive Achaemenid style, incorporates artistic elements from Egypt, Assyria, Babylonia, Media and the Greek world.

Since the Persian kings migrated between several royal residences throughout the empire, it has been suggested that Persepolis may only have been a royal ceremonial centre. Textual evidence, however, demonstrates that the city was the administrative centre of Persis, and was continuously occupied by officials and members of the royal family. MB

See Roaf, M. (1983) *Sculptures and Sculptors at Persepolis*; Root, M. C. (1979) *The King and Kingship in Achaemenid Art*.

 PERSIA AND PERSIANS.

Perseus (hero) see MEDUSA.

Perseus (king of Macedonia) see ANTIGONIDS; MACEDONIAN WARS; PYDNA

Persia and Persians The ancient region of Parsa (Old Persian) or Persis (Greek) corresponds to modern Fars. In antiquity, the region is best known for three successive PERSIAN EMPIRES: the Achaemenid (mid-6th century–330 BC), the PARTHIAN (late 2nd century BC–early 3rd AD) and the SASSANIAN, which emerged in the early 3rd century AD and provided a persistent threat to the late Roman empire. The Achaemenid empire takes its name from Achaemenes, the ancestor from whom the Persian kings, at least from DARIUS I (522–486 BC) onwards, traced their descent. For historians of the Greco-Roman world, the Achaemenid empire is most famous for its clashes with the Greek world, notably the Persian wars of the early 5th century BC, and ALEXANDER the Great's final destruction of the empire in 330. Later traditions of these conflicts continued to be highly significant and emotive. The PERSIAN WARS were used as a foil against which classical Athens could assert the self-image with which we are all familiar today: restrained, promoting DEMOCRATIC ideals, and the rightful leader of an empire. In hellenistic and Roman thought, the 'Persian' empire was conceptualized as the first major player in theories of a sequence of succession of empires. The ethnocentric, 'orientalizing' figures of Persia and Persians developed in classical antiquity represent the beginnings of a long tradition of Western stereotypes of Eastern decadence, menace and exoticism that have been maintained in modern Western ideologies.

Persian expansion begins with CYRUS THE GREAT (559–530 BC). Stories of his miraculous early years circulated in antiquity. So threatening were the portents of his birth that there were orders to kill the newborn child, but he was rescued, was reared by a herdsman and lived to fulfil the portents. Such stories mark out his perceived importance, and can be compared with the stories of ROMULUS and Moses. Cyrus first defeated Astyages of the neighbouring kingdom of Media. Then, in the 540s BC, he defeated Croesus of LYDIA, sacking the Lydian capital of SARDIS. It was when Cyrus took over Croesus' kingdom, which took in the west of Asia Minor (mod. Turkey), that the Ionian Greeks of the eastern Aegean first encountered the Persians directly. After his conquest of Babylonia, the empire extended over much of the Near and Middle East, from the LEVANT to the north-west border of INDIA. By the reign of Darius I, who planned the mass expedition to the Greek mainland that eventually took place under XERXES (480–479 BC), the empire also included Egypt, north-western India and THRACE.

Greek sources make much of the defeat of Xerxes in the Persian wars, and XENOPHON in the *Cyropaedia* goes so far as to imagine that a Persian decline set in on the death of Cyrus the Great. It should, however, be remembered that it was with Persian aid that Athens was finally beaten by Sparta in the PELOPONNESIAN WAR in 404, and that Alexander's success in 330 was by no means a foregone conclusion. When viewed from a less hellenocentric perspective, Greek success in driving back the Persians in the eastern Mediterranean in the first half of the 5th century was short-lived. We hear periodically of power struggles and court intrigue in the Persian court, as well as of revolts in the Persian empire, especially of those during the reign of Darius I; these included the Ionian revolt, which ended in disaster in 494. While these revolts represent temporary acute crises, the Achaemenid dynasty and Persian domination were long-lasting. The structure of the empire was sophisticated. The territory under Persian domination was divided up into a number of administrative areas called satrapies, each with a capital headed by a satrap. Taxes were collected in the capital of each satrapy, part being forwarded to the Persian kingdom itself and part retained for the use of the satrap. Efficient communications through the empire were enabled by roads with staging posts used by royal messengers. The Persians effectively redeployed local administrative systems, employed local manpower within the army, and cultivated relationships with local élites.

For most readers, the most accessible source for the history of the Achaemenid empire and its contacts with the Greek world is HERODOTOS' *Histories* (430s BC), which depict the Persian wars as the end of centuries of conflict between East and West. Xenophon's *Anabasis* is an account of the author's participation in the abortive campaign of the younger CYRUS against his older brother Artaxerxes II in 401 BC, while his *Cyropaedia* (*Education of Cyrus*, meaning Cyrus the Great) is an ethical exploration of KINGSHIP. Unfortunately, these literary sources, along with AESCHYLUS' tragedy *The Persians* and the *Persika* by Ktesias, a Greek doctor at the court of Artaxerxes II (405–359), are problematic as evidence for the Persian empire and Persian customs. We have texts of the Persians themselves (most notably Darius' Behistun inscription regarding his accession), largely administrative texts (particularly from Persepolis, Babylonia and Egypt), and limited archaeological evidence. This evidence can sometimes be used to confirm details in Greek sources. However, one problem is that the Greek literary sources are different in kind from the sources from the Persian empire. Moreover, only rarely do we find references to the same event in both sets of sources. In addition, while Greek sources may contain some accurate details, these details are interpreted through Greek frameworks of thought, and the meaning may therefore be changed beyond recognition. For example, Persian texts portray the king's deeds and the empire itself as part of the universal scheme for happiness of the creator god AHURA-MAZDA. The king's absolutism is thus portrayed in very favourable terms. Within the Greek sources, however, the king becomes a despot indulging his basest desires, his imperial subjects grovelling at his feet in an unseemly display of servitude that shows up the freedom of the Greeks. (see pp. 664–5) ED

See Herodotos, *Histories*; Kuhrt, A. (1995) *The Ancient Near East*, vol. 2; (1987–94) *Achaemenid History*, vols. 1–8.

Persian empire The Persian, or 'Achaemenid', empire was founded by CYRUS THE GREAT (559–530 BC). It was ruled by the Achaemenid dynasty (named after its eponymous founder Achaemenes) until the death of Darius III in 330. The multicultural and multilingual empire stretched from LIBYA and Egypt to the Indus river, from the Caucasus and the borders of the Russian and central Asian steppes to the Persian gulf.

Within three decades Cyrus conquered the kingdoms of Media, Lydia and Babylon, the regions of east and south-east Iran, as well as Baktria. Kambyses II (530–522) took Egypt and Nubia, and DARIUS I (522–486) added THRACE and Macedonia as well as INDIAN territory. After Athens' and Eretria's involvement in the IONIAN REVOLT he ordered a punitive campaign against these cities in 490, followed by a Persian invasion under XERXES in 480–479, in which the Persians sacked Athens but withdrew from Greece after their defeat at SALAMIS and PLATAEA.

Each land in the empire was administered by a Persian satrap (the term means 'protector of the realm'), paid annual tribute to the king, and levied troops as required. Royal Roads provided an efficient infrastructure throughout the empire; swift communication between centre and periphery benefited administration, TRADE and the army. As absolute ruler the king was supported by members of the Persian nobility who held influential positions at court in a system of meritocracy, including a complex process of reciprocal gift-giving. MB

See Cuyler Young, T. (1988) in *CAH* 4, ch. 1.

 PERSIA AND PERSIANS.

Persian wars, Greek c.546–331 BC Intermittent conflict between some Greek states and the Achaemenid empire. From a Persian perspective, the conflict with Greek states was a matter of trying to stabilize and pacify the north-west frontier of their empire. The Persians first came into contact with the Greeks of Asia Minor after CYRUS THE GREAT'S conquest of LYDIA in the mid-540s. Those cities had been tributary to the Lydians, and although some supported Cyrus against the Lydians, the mainland cities of Asia Minor and some of the ISLANDS soon came fully under Persian control. In the next few decades many Greek cities (including an embassy from Athens) offered earth and water as symbols of submission to Persia, but the AEGEAN region was not formally absorbed into the empire's administrative system. After the failure of the IONIAN REVOLT in 499–494 DARIUS attempted to extend Persian influence further west, with an expedition in 492 led by Mardonius, which was wrecked by storms. Another expedition, in 490, destroyed NAXOS and parts of EUBOIA before being defeated by the Athenians and Plataeans at MARATHON. Ten years later XERXES attempted to gain control of the whole of Greece with a large invasion by land and sea. After defeating a small force of Spartans and PHOKIANS at THERMOPYLAI, Xerxes' army devastated much of central Greece, and sacked the city of Athens. His fleet, meanwhile, was damaged by storms and was then defeated by a Greek fleet in the straits between the island of SALAMIS and ATTICA. At this point Xerxes himself returned to Asia, probably in response to a rebellion in Babylonia. In 479 the army he had left to pacify the remaining areas of Greece under the command of Mardonius was defeated by a Greek army. At the same time the Greek naval force was taking the opportunity to liberate the cities in Asia Minor from Persian control, and this led to a series of Persian defeats from Mykale in 479 to Eurymedon c.466.

Eurymedon coincided with the assassination of Xerxes, and his successors appear to have pursued a less aggressive policy. For the next 130 years Persian influence on the Greek states was maintained by promises of financial support and threats of military intervention. It is possible that a peace TREATY was signed between Athens and Persia in 449 BC, the so-called peace of Kallias; if so, it did not prevent negotiations between Sparta and Persia during the PELOPONNESIAN WAR, or Persian support for groups aiming to seize power in cities allied to the Athenians. Sparta's victory over Athens in the Peloponnesian war was made possible only through

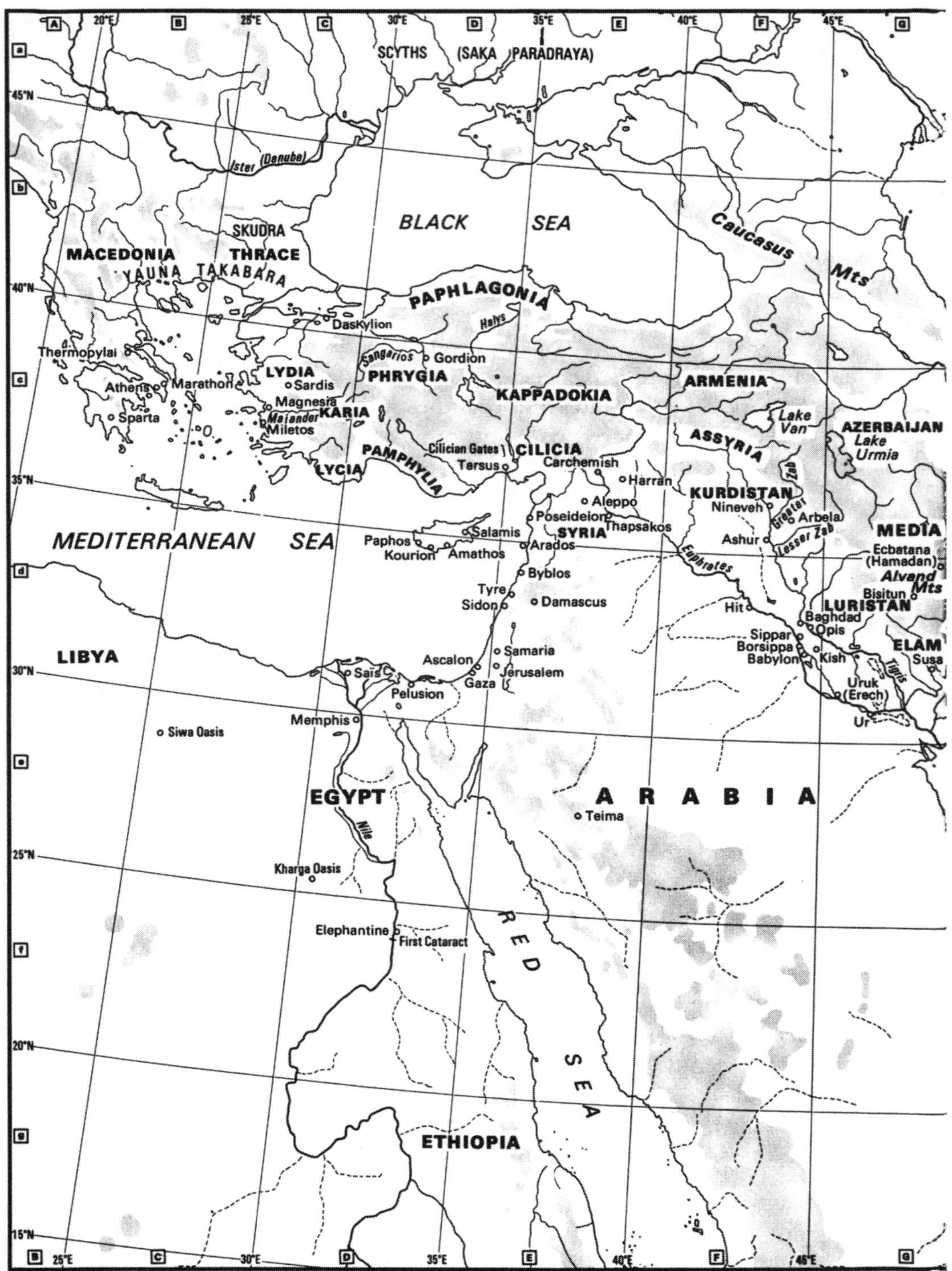

PERSIA AND PERSIANS: map showing Persian empire in 5th century BC.

KAZAKHSTAN
ARAL SEA
Jaxartes
(Syr Darya)
MASSAGETAE
SAKA HAUMAVARGA
CASPIAN SEA
Oxus
(Amu Darya)
CHORASMIA
Kyropolis
FERGHANA
SAKA TIGRAKHAUDA
SOGDIANA
Aï-Khanoum
Pamirs
Merv
MARGIANA
Balkh
BAKTRIA
HYRCANIA
Mt Demavand
Tehran
PARTHIA
AFGHANISTAN
Hindu Kush
Himalayas
ARIA
Peshawar
GANDARA
DRANGIANA
PUNJAB
ARACHOSIA
Kandahar
Zagros Mts
Dahan-i Ghulaman
KHUZISTAN
SATTAGYDIA?
Multan
Helmand
SEISTAN
Pasargadae
Anshan
Persepolis
Indus
PARSA
PERSIAN GULF
CARMANIA
INDIA
GEDROSIA
SIND
Land over 1,000 metres
SCALE
0 200 400 600 800 1000km
0 200 400 600miles

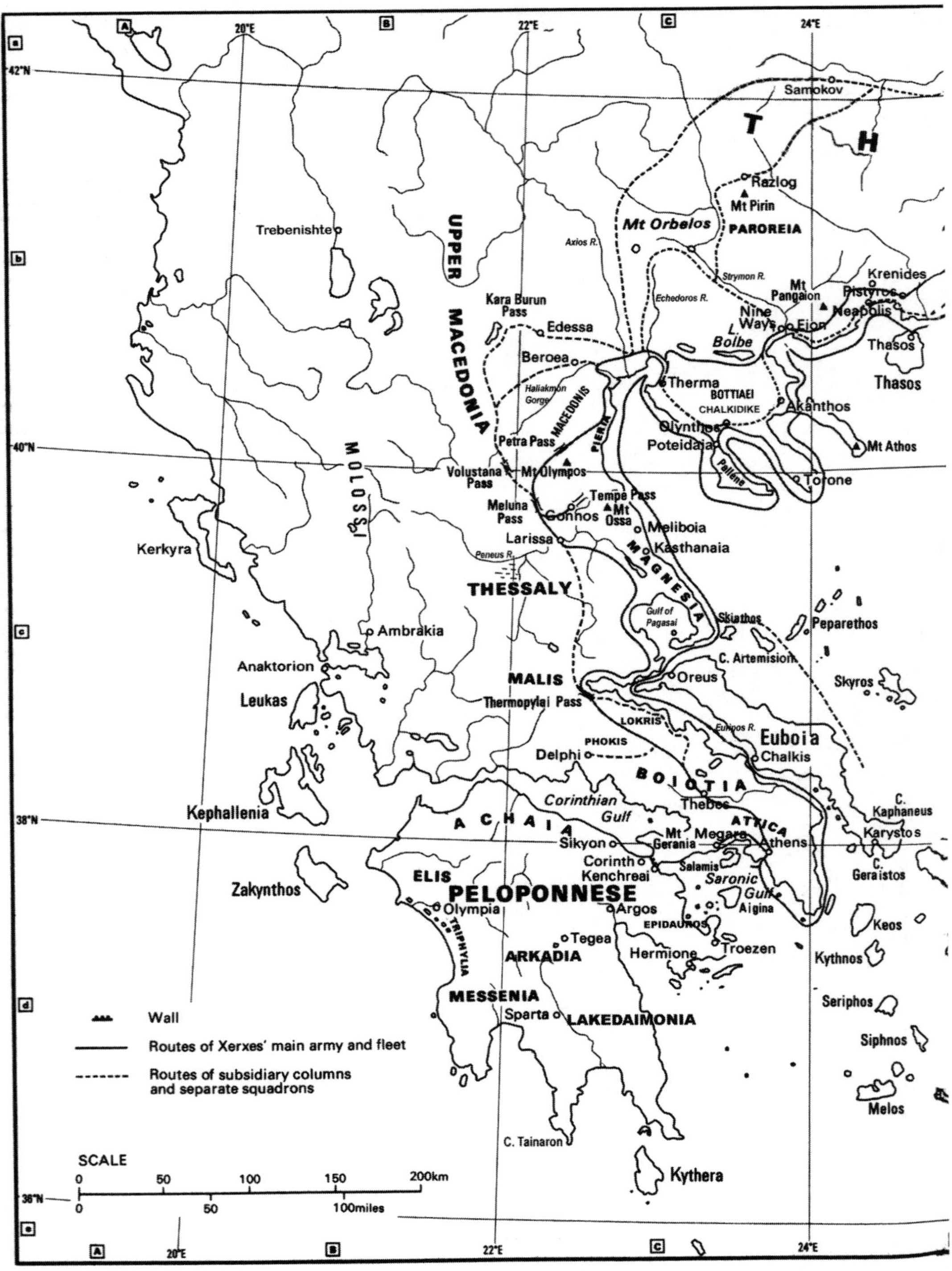

PERSIAN WARS, GREEK: map showing routes of advance of forces of Xerxes.

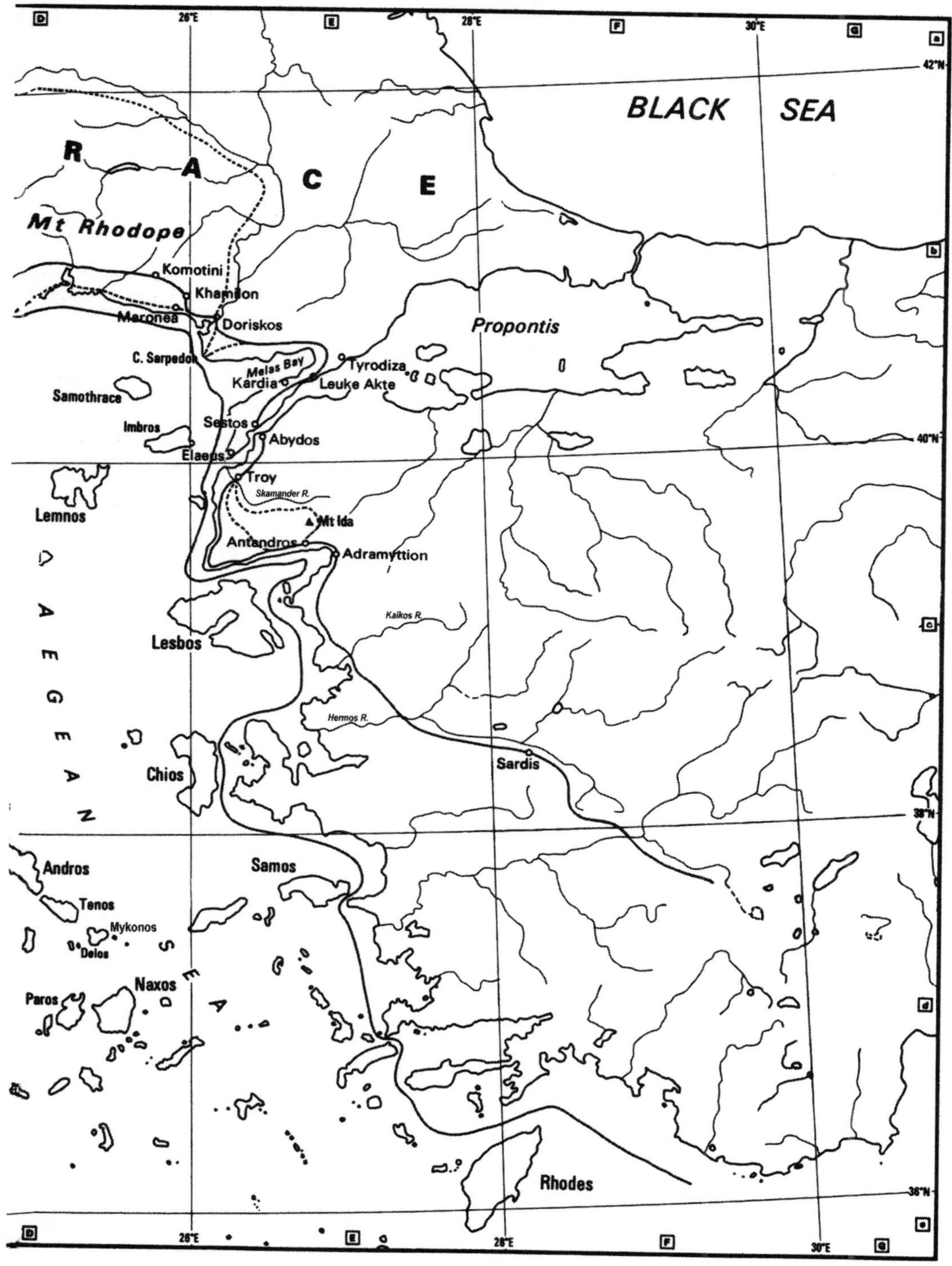
BLACK SEA
Propontis
Mt Rhodope
Komotini
Khamilon
Maronea
Doriskos
C. Sarpedon
Melas Bay
Kardia
Tyrodiza
Leuke Akte
Samothrace
Imbros
Sestos
Abydos
Elaeus
Troy
Skamander R.
Mt Ida
Lemnos
Antandros
Adramyttion
Kaikos R.
Lesbos
Hermos R.
Chios
Sardis
Andros
Samos
Tenos
Mykonos
Delos
Naxos
Paros
Rhodes
AEGEAN SEA
26°E
28°E
30°E
42°N
40°N
38°N
36°N

Persian intervention, but Sparta's failure to return the cities of Asia Minor to Persian control soon led to a breakdown in relations. In 396 AGESILAOS led a Spartan army into the PERSIAN EMPIRE, but was forced to withdraw due to difficulties in mainland Greece, fomented with Persian support. By 387/6 Persia had regained control of the Greek cities in Asia Minor, and was able to interfere openly in the organization of the rest of Greece through the agency of Sparta, in accordance with the terms of a series of treaties known as 'the King's Peace'. The influence of Persia remained strong in ALEXANDER the Great's invasion of the empire in 334. Through his military skill, and despite the fact that the empire was still powerful, he was able to defeat the Persians in three major land battles (GRANIKOS, ISSOS and GAUGAMELA). After the assassination of the then ruler, Darius III, he had himself crowned as Persian king. Far from being the inevitable result of Persian decline (for which there is no evidence), Alexander's conquest came as a surprise.

The Greek, particularly the Athenian, perspective on these events was different. HERODOTOS presents the victory over Xerxes as the culmination of hostilities between Greeks and non-Greeks. The Athenians proclaimed themselves saviours of Greece for their roles at Marathon and Salamis. In 5th-century art and literature, Persians are caricatured as effeminate BARBARIANS, and the idea of a panhellenic crusade against them becomes a regular theme for Athenian rhetoricians in the 4th century, in particular ISOKRATES. In all these areas the Persians are presented as the 'OTHER', and this has distorted subsequent assessments of the significance of the conflict.

The rhetoric of the sources must not hide the fact that there was a large number of Greeks fighting on the side of the Persians, both in Xerxes' army and fleet of 480–479 and in Darius III's army in 334–331. Greek cities and individuals were prepared frequently to turn to Persia for assistance in their quarrels with other Greeks, and the courts of the Persian king and his satraps were often the first destination of EXILES from the cities. When Agesilaos at the start of his campaign against Persia attempted to sacrifice at Aulis, in imitation of AGAMEMNON on his way to TROY, he was prevented by the BOIOTIANS. Rather than being a conflict between East and West, as Herodotos and writers to the present day have presented it, the Persian wars may be seen as one of a number of disputes within the eastern Mediterranean world, in which the Greeks themselves were divided. HB

See Arrian, *Anabasis of Alexander* 1–3; Herodotos; Burn, A. R. (1984) *Persia and the Greeks*; Cook, J. M. (1983) *The Persian Empire*; Davies, J. K., ed. (1988) *CAH* 4; Hall, E. (1993) Asia unmanned: images of victory in classical Athens, in J. Rich and G. Shipley, eds., *War and Society in the Greek World* 106–33; Kuhrt, A. (1995) *The Ancient Near East*, vol. 2, ch. 13.

WAR (table).

Persian wars, Roman The successive Roman invasions of the PARTHIAN empire in the Severan period and the humiliating sack of its winter capitals, CTESIPHON and Seleukeia, ended abruptly with the transition to the SASSANID dynasty in what thereafter was termed PERSIA. Ardashir I inflicted defeat on SEVERUS ALEXANDER, and his son SHAPUR I defeated GORDIAN III and Valerian, who was taken captive. For the first time since the late Republic, the Eastern provinces were invaded, and from ASIA Minor to Palestine, cities sacked. Most stunning was the capture of ANTIOCH itself and the enslavement of its population.

The 4th century saw restoration of the frontier and its extension by Rome to and beyond the upper Tigris. The defeat and death of JULIAN (363) brought about a forced peace. The new frontier ran through northern MESOPOTAMIA, new FORTRESSES were constructed and warfare was often a matter of protracted SIEGES and struggles for such places as Amida and Dara. ARMENIA again became a bone of serious contention until the powers divided it between them in 387.

The last generation of Sassanian Persia was again one of great danger. Persian armies entered Syria, sacked Antioch and invaded both Asia Minor and EGYPT, aiming at occupation rather than plunder. Heraclius, however, turned the tide, invaded the Iranian heartland and forced a peace. Soon after, the exhausted protagonists were assailed by the forces of Islam: Persia was overthrown entirely and Rome lost North AFRICA and SYRIA. (see also PARTHIAN WARS) DLK

See Dodgeon, M. H. and Lieu, S. N. C., eds. (1991) *The Roman Eastern Frontier and the Persian Wars AD 226–363*; Kennedy, D. L. and Riley, D. N. (1990) *Rome's Desert Frontier.*

SYRIA, ROMAN: (b); WAR (table).

Persius (Aulus Persius Flaccus) AD 34–62 Author of six difficult and often bitter satires, published as a *libellus* (small book) during the reign of the emperor NERO (AD 54–68). The first satire derides the popularity of mythological poetry and asks for something more relevant – moral SATIRE. The second attacks those who look for good fortune from the GODS rather than acting morally. The third, using medical language, examines the link between vice and spiritual ill-health. The fourth urges Alcibiades to seek out self-knowledge rather than popular acclaim. The fifth eulogizes Persius' teacher and moralizes on human enslavement to materiality. The sixth satire urges humans to live within their material allotment in life. Persius' teacher was the STOIC PHILOSOPHER, Lucius Annaeus Cornutus (the subject of *Satire* 5, who became his posthumous editor). Persius' concern for moderation, self-control and right behaviour mirrors the Stoic tradition of which Cornutus was an exemplar. The difficulties of Persius' poetry – evident above all as an apparent confusion of voices, a density of imagery, and a prevalence of vivid and realistic pictures that are very hard to link to the poem as a whole – embody and vivify powerfully the seriousness and depth of feeling which underlies both his craft and his poetry. PGT

See Persius, *The Satires*, trs. G. Lee (1987); Clausen, W. V. (1992) *Persius*; Dessen, C. S. (1968) *Iunctura Callidus Acri*; Hooley, D. (1997) *The Knotted Thong*.

personification The embodiment in anthropomorphic form of abstract ideas, personification figures in the literature, ART and RELIGION of the Greeks and Romans. In HOMER we find personified Ate ('Madness'), Phobos and Deimos ('Fear'), Eris

('Strife') and the Litai ('Prayers'), as well as Sleep and Death, all given human form. In Hesiod, more graphically still, we find such figures as 'Fate' (Momos, Ker or even Nemesis), 'Justice' (Dike), 'Peace' (Eirene) and so on, all represented in corporeal form. In later Greek literature, perhaps due to a rationalizing tendency in Greek culture generally, these figures are less common, except perhaps in Aristophanic comedy where we find the embodiment of such abstractions as 'Wealth' (Ploutos), 'Poverty' (Penia), the 'People' (Demos) and 'Just Argument' and 'Unjust Argument' (Dikaios and Adikos Logos). In Greek, from early on, there are also personifications of such figures as Geras ('Old Age'), Harmonia ('Harmony'), Himeros ('Desire'), Peitho ('Persuasion') and Themis ('Law'). Greek religion seems to have been no more immune to this anthropomorphizing tendency than literature or art. Pausanias mentions that at Athens there were altars to Eleos ('Pity'), Aidos ('Shame'), Pheme ('Renown') and Horme ('Violence' or 'Impulse'). There were cults to other comparable personifications in other Greek cities. In the later years of Greek culture Fortune (Tyche) was added to this list.

Roman culture, always a more superstitious one than that of Greece, developed over time a noteworthy roster of divine personifications. Cicero (*On the Nature of the Gods* 2.23) produces a remarkable list of figures: Fides ('Faith'), Mens ('Mind'), Virtus ('Virtue'), Honos ('Honour'), Ops ('Abundance'), Salus ('Health'), Concordia ('Concordia'), Libertas ('Liberty') and Victoria ('Victory'). The introduction of the cults to these figures, it is said, is often linked to specific, relevant historical events (Concordia followed the accord that came in 367 BC in the wake of the Licinian laws). Roman literature of the classical period appears to be chary of the excessive use of personifications. Virgil, for example, shows us Iustitia ('Justice'), Fides ('Faith' or 'Trust'), and Fama ('Renown' or 'Rumour'). The deeper that we read in Roman literature, however, the more common becomes the inclusion of personified and eventually allegorized types. So, in Ovid's *Metamorphoses* we encounter Invidia ('Envy'), Fames ('Hunger') and Fama. In later writers of epic, such as Statius (in his *Thebaid*), personified and allegorized types can come to play a key role in the very action of the poem; figures such as the Furies and Pietas ('Piety') come to clash with one another in the climactic duel of the poem between the Theban brothers, Eteocles and Polyneices. Perhaps, as the endpoint of this long tradition, we could cite Prudentius' *Pyschomachia*, in which the Christian vices and virtues, personified, are set in traditional epic combat against one another. PGT

See Feeney, D. (2000) *The Gods in Epic*; Whitman, J. (1987) *Allegory: the dynamics of an ancient and medieval technique.*

Pertinax see Lucilla; Severus, Septimius.

Emperors, Roman: (a).

Pescennius Niger (Gaius Pescennius Niger Iustus) Roman emperor, AD 193–4; short-lived rival to Septimius Severus. Little is known of his earlier career. Cassius Dio (the principal source along with Herodian and a very fictional *Life* in the *Historia Augusta*) indicates that he was an Italian of equestrian background, had been successful in wars in Dacia in the reign of Commodus, and was made governor of Syria by Commodus due to his unremarkable character. Herodian, in contrast, presents him as quite capable.

In AD 193 demonstrators in Rome called on Niger to return from Syria to save the city from the then emperor, Didius Iulianus. Niger was proclaimed emperor by his troops in Antioch. Herodian notes his popularity in Antioch and in Syria in general, and he won the support of other Eastern provincial governors. Meanwhile Septimius Severus was also proclaimed emperor in Pannonia, marched on Rome and deposed Iulianus. Late in 193 Severus' army outflanked Niger's base at Byzantium, defeating Niger's subordinate Asellius Aemilianus (proconsul of Asia) in Asia Minor. A further defeat near Nicaea forced Niger to retreat east to fortify the passes of the Taurus mountains between Severus' forces and Syria, and caused defections among allied provinces and cities. After a final defeat at Issos, Niger fled to Antioch and beyond (heading to Parthian territory, according to Dio) but was caught and killed. Byzantium continued to hold out against Severus after Niger's death. Severus punished Niger's supporters (including the city of Antioch, demoted in status) and rewarded his opponents (Antioch's rival Laodikeia). NDP

See Birley, A. R. (1988) *Septimius Severus.*

Emperors, Roman: (a).

pests and pest control Despite the absence of a pharmaceutical industry in the ancient world, some degree of pest control was achievable by natural means. Agricultural habitats were undoubtedly richer in species than today's chemical-sprayed fields, and a balance between insects, birds, rodents and other potential 'pests' would normally be maintained by natural competition. Aristotle, for example, observes that woodpeckers feed on grubs in the bark of trees. Theophrastos refers to worms or grubs (*skôlêkes*) attacking plants such as medlars, olives and wheat; he believes them to be born from rotten wood, and notes that they will not penetrate an olive-tree if wet weather follows the rising of Arcturus in September. Gnats (*knipes*) attack trees (including oaks and figs) and certain vegetables such as pulses; bitter and juicy plants, says Theophrastos, are less subject to these pests, while gnats can be deterred from fig-trees by pinning crabs to the trees. An element of superstition is sometimes apparent, as when Columella cites the practice of keeping seeds in a basket covered in a hyena's skin, presumably to deter pests. It is not likely that hyena-skins were widely available in Italy.

Stored foods could be treated directly in various ways, and granaries and grain-pits could be impregnated with insecticides or made airtight. Coriander is noted as a flavouring, preservative, medication and insect repellent. Olive oil was regarded as an insecticide; Pliny the Elder also recommends various minerals, herbs, spices and even preparations of dung; and Cato the Elder prescribes concoctions of *amurca* (the toxic, watery residue of olive-oil pressing) to deter rodents from granaries and caterpillars from vines. In beekeeping, smoke was used against pests. Bay-leaves may have been used against clothes-moths,

PESTS: fumigation of textiles in a Greek household.

as in modern Greece – presumably many common practices go unrecorded in the literature. DGJS

See Humphrey, J.W. et al. (1997) *Greek and Roman Technology: a sourcebook*; Panagiotakopulu, E. et al. (1995) Natural insecticides and insect repellents in antiquity, *JAS* 22: 705–10.

Petra Located in a valley between steep mountains south-east of the Dead sea, Petra (its Greek name; Selah in Aramaic; both mean 'rock') has protection and an aura of mystery. In addition to north and south approaches, a route leads west to the Wadi Araba, but the principal entrance is along the Siq, a narrow gorge coming from Wadi Musa to the east. Petra first appears as the NABATAEAN capital in 312 BC, when it was attacked by ANTIGONOS I. Its principal development took place under Aretas IV (9 BC–AD 40). After Roman annexation, it remained a major city, and was granted the titles *metropolis* under TRAJAN, Hadriane by HADRIAN, and *colonia* by ELAGABALUS. In CHRISTIAN times it was a major BISHOPRIC.

Petra and its ruins were 'rediscovered' by Burckhardt in 1812. Best known are rock tombs beginning outside the Siq but mainly found after exiting the gorge. Cut from the living rock and decorated in hellenistic baroque style, they attest to cultural pretensions, craftsmanship and external influences. Unlike lesser examples at Hegra, these have no inscriptions and were presumably for royal and aristocratic inhabitants. One was for an early Roman governor of ARABIA. Other features and free-standing structures include Roman ARCHES, the AQUEDUCT through the Siq (one of several elaborate WATER SUPPLY facilities), the THEATRE, FORTIFICATION walls, BATHS, housing, religious 'high places' and POTTERY KILNS. Major excavations have focused on religious structures: Qasr Bint Faroun (Dushares, the principal deity), temple of

PETRA: the 'monastery', rock-cut tomb of the 1st century BC.

the Winged Lions (dedicated to Allat), a large 'southern temple', and a large Byzantine CHURCH with an important cache of carbonized PAPYRI. DLK

See Browning, I. (1977) *Petra*; McKenzie, J. (1990) *The Architecture of Petra*; Markoe, G. (2003) *Petra: lost city of the Nabataeans*.

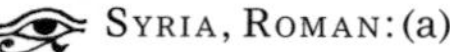 SYRIA, ROMAN: (a).

Petrarch (Francesco Petrarca) AD 1304–74 Born in Arezzo of a Florentine family that moved in 1311 to Avignon, where his father worked in the papal curia, the young Petrarch studied law in Montpellier and Bologna before returning to Avignon on the death of his father. Soon afterward, he devoted himself to philological and literary activity, and gained the patronage of the influential Colonna family, on whose behalf he worked and travelled extensively. In 1353 he moved to Milan, and thereafter lived in the Veneto region until his death.

Today Petrarch is best known for his collection of vernacular poems, which he named (with false modesty) the *Rerum vulgarium fragmenta* ('fragments of vulgar matters'), better known simply as the *Canzoniere*. The work's 366 poems are centred on his beloved Laura's effects on his life, poetry and thought; these poems were of the greatest importance to European literature of several subsequent centuries. But these vernacular writings were not representative of Petrarch's work, which was almost entirely composed in Latin. Some of his work was philological, such as his editions of Ciceronian texts he had discovered on his travels. Others were epistolary (heavily influenced by CICERO). Many were historiographical and philosophical; of the latter, most famous is his *Secretum*, in the form of an interior dialogue with St AUGUSTINE (1). His unfinished epic poem in Latin, *Africa*, led to his coronation as poet laureate in 1341. GF

See Foster, K. (1984) *Petrarch: poet and humanist*; Mann, N. (1984) *Petrarch*.

petroleum products Though not as ubiquitous as now, petroleum (Greek *asphaltos*, Latin *bitumen*) was known in the ancient world and used for a variety of purposes. Liquid, viscous and solid forms were known and used for WATERPROOFING, building materials and adhesive. In MEDICINE it was thought effective (often mixed with other substances) for cataract, leprosy, gout, epilepsy, toothache, cough, dysentery, diarrhoea and fever, among other ailments. The material was collected in different ways, depending on location and accessibility. Most oozed out of deposits near the surface, but some was collected by myrtle branches dipped into pools of water in Zakynthos (Herodotos 4.195) or, at the Dead sea, in coagulated lumps (Tacitus, *Histories* 5.6). In PERSIA it might be drawn out of a well with an animal skin (Herodotos 6.119).

PLINY THE ELDER offers the best description of the places where bitumen was found and its different varieties (*Natural History* 35.50.178–82; cf. Strabo 16.1.15). Solid forms were found near Sidon, viscous in the Dead sea and on Sicily. Zakynthos, Apollonia and, above all, Mesopotamia provided liquid forms, including one usually called *naphtha*. This was highly flammable and was used instead of OLIVE OIL for LAMPS; Babylonian natives treated ALEXANDER to a light show one evening, when they sprinkled the street with *naphtha* and set it on fire (Plutarch, *Alexander* 35). Pliny regarded it as too flammable to be of any practical use. JV

Petronius As Petronius Arbiter, the well-known author of a 'novel', the *Satyrica*, or *Satyricon* as it is best known. It is usually said to have been composed during the reign of NERO (AD 54–68) and may have originally been as long as 20 books. Fragments of books 14–16 survive. Book 15, *Cena Trimalchionis* (*Trimalchio's Dinner*), survives nearly complete (and has influenced writers like F. Scott Fitzgerald in *The Great Gatsby*). The plot of the *Satyricon* (loosely inspired by the *Odyssey* and that poem's structuring theme of the wrath of POSEIDON) seems to be built around the wandering (driven not by Poseidon but by PRIAPUS) of the down-at-heel Encolpius and his young lover Giton, in a low-life southern Italian setting. The key organizational motif seems to be the impotence of Encolpius. As it stands, the fragments seem to parody exemplars as various as PLATO's *Symposium* (so the *Cena Trimalchionis*), the Greek NOVEL (so Encolpius' and Giton's affair) and traditional EPIC (Encolpius as ODYSSEUS, and the 'epic' poetry on the fall of Troy and the CIVIL WAR). The work, with its blend of narrative, poetic inserts and short pointed tales, is sometimes said to be an example of Menippean SATIRE. Petronius Arbiter is usually identified with a SENATOR and courtier of Nero named Petronius, who is described as *arbiter elegantiae*. The death of the latter in 66, through a SUICIDE enforced by the emperor, is described by TACITUS at *Annals* 16.18. The *Satyricon* has a fine film version made by Fellini. PGT

See Sullivan, J.P. (1986) *The Satyricon; The Apocolocyntosis* (trs.); (1968) *The Satyricon of Petronius*; Staler, N.W. (1989) *Reading Petronius*.

pets Keeping ANIMALS as pets is a fashion inherited from ancient times. The favourite was the dog, which existed in many varieties. A longhaired lapdog from Malta seems to have been a particular favourite, in a similar way to the small dogs beloved of 'it-girls' today. Working dogs were common, minding and protecting flocks with SHEPHERDS and also protecting homes. HUNTING with dogs was a

PETS: the dogs on leashes here were probably kept for hunting, not strictly as pets.

popular ARISTOCRATIC pastime for both Greeks and Romans, and discussions by XENOPHON (*On Hunting*), VARRO (*On Agriculture* 2.9) and HORACE (*Epodes* 6.5) on the breeding of dogs have survived. The attachment felt by owners for their dogs is attested by epitaphs (*Anthologia Latina* 1176; 1512); the emperor HADRIAN had tombstones set up over the graves of his favourite dogs.

Other pets included monkeys, BIRDS and even fish. Birds were kept for their song or their ability to mimic human speech. OVID (*Amores* 2.6) and CATULLUS (2 and 3) both wrote poems about their lovers' birds, and the ORATOR Hortensius is said to have wept when his pet flatfish died.

Cats gained popularity comparatively late, except in Egypt where they were a sacred animal. HERODOTOS (2.66–7) relates that when a cat died a natural death all the house's inhabitants were required to shave off their eyebrows (for a dog, they shaved their whole bodies). The corpses were embalmed and mummified at Bubastis, and have been found in EXCAVATIONS. NJW

Peutinger Table Uniquely large, sophisticated and important Roman map. The surviving copy, today in Vienna, is named after its owner in the early 16th century, Konrad Peutinger; 'table' is from the Latin *tabula*, 'map'. This copy was made on parchment in the 12th century and comprises a roll of 11 sheets which end-to-end measure c.6.70 × 0.34 m (22 ft × 13 in). At least one further left-hand sheet is lost (so that Britain, Spain and western North Africa are largely missing).

In all likelihood the original, centred upon Rome, spanned the known world from the Atlantic to Sri Lanka and achieved its present form in the 4th century AD. Some earlier, outdated elements are retained, however, and several later copyists' additions and adjustments can also be identified. In accordance with the map's curious shape, the north–south dimension is severely collapsed, and the west–east elongated, giving pride of place to land rather than sea, and to Italy and the Mediterranean region in particular. Regardless of such deliberate variations in scale, the map incorporates a remarkable quantity of geographic information. Rivers and lakes are named and coloured in green; MOUNTAIN ranges likewise mostly in brown. Many seas, islands, regions and peoples are named, as are cultural features marked with a range of pictorial symbols (including HARBOUR, LIGHTHOUSE, spa). Principal settlements are graded, and distances between them recorded stage by stage in Roman miles or other local units. One of the map's distinctive concerns is to display land routes: altogether about 2,700 names of cities or road stations appear, making a major contribution to modern mapping of the Roman world. Even so, it remains unclear how innovative the original map was, which experts created it with what purposes or setting uppermost in their minds, and from what forerunners or other source materials it derives. RJAT

See Weber, E. (1976) *Tabula Peutingeriana* (facsimile); Gautier Dalché, P. (2003) La trasmissione medievale e rinascimentale della Tabula Peutingeriana, in F. Prontera, ed., *Tabula Peutingeriana* 43–52; Talbert, R. (2004) Cartography and taste in Peutinger's Roman map, in R. Talbert and K. Brodersen, eds., *Space in the Roman World* 113–41.

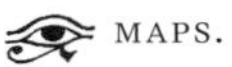 MAPS.

pewter The name given to the alloy of TIN and LEAD used to manufacture vessels (though alloys of the same composition were also used as solder). The use of pewter for casting plates, dishes and jugs begins in the 1st century AD but only becomes common in the 3rd century. Most pewter artefacts are concentrated in the west and especially in BRITAIN (one of the principal sources of tin). Britain has also produced most of the evidence for casting pewter in the form of limestone moulds. Limestone would not be a suitable material for casting copper alloys but is well suited for casting pewter because of its low melting temperature.

The chemical analysis of pewter artefacts shows a wide variety in the proportions of tin and lead used. In some cases the pewter is of very good quality and the proportion of lead very low, but in some cases up to 60 per cent lead was used. Lead in pewter could contaminate the drinks and food contained in such vessels; it is not clear whether people were generally aware of the toxic effects of lead at this time, though Vitruvius (8.6.10–11) seems to make the link. In the medieval period, guilds attempted to regulate the alloys used to manufacture pewter vessels and minimize the proportion of lead in artefacts used to store and serve food and drinks. DD

Phaedrus see FABLES.

phalanx see ARMS AND ARMOUR, GREEK; HOPLITES; TACTICS, MILITARY, GREEK.

phallus Image of the penis, usually erect. The phallus is generally a symbol of fertility and regeneration, a ubiquitous feature in Greek and Roman RELIGION and ART. In ritual the phallus is particularly associated with DIONYSOS: a giant phallus was carried in the processions of the Attic Rural Dionysia (ARISTOPHANES, *Acharnians* 241–79), and of the Roman Liberalia (VARRO in Augustine, *City of God* 7.21), both FESTIVALS concerned with AGRICULTURAL fertility. The phallus may also have been the sacred

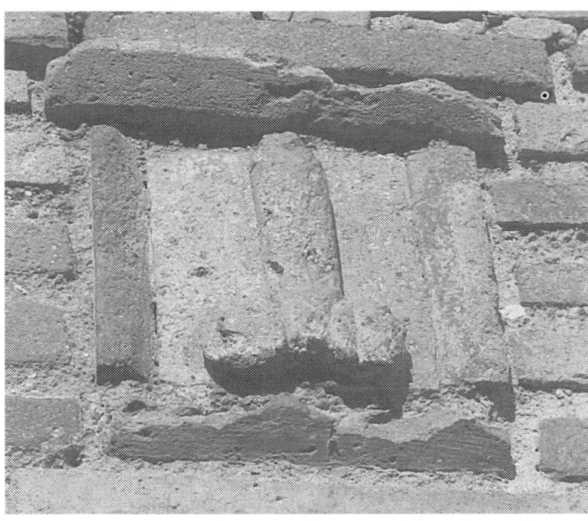

PHALLUS: as a good luck symbol, depictions of the phallus are frequently to be seen in the ancient world, as here on the walls of a house in Pompeii.

object revealed in Dionysiac mysteries: the Villa of the Mysteries mural (POMPEII) shows a woman unveiling a phallus in a winnowing basket. In DRAMA oversize phalli were a standard part of the costume of COMEDY and SATYR plays, emphasizing the bawdy nature of the genres but also a reminder of comedy's supposed origins in songs to accompany phallic processions (ARISTOTLE, *Poetics* 1449a11). The phallus' power gives it an apotropaic function, often employed as a protective device to ward off the evil eye. SCULPTURAL phalli would have been ubiquitous as part of HERMS, which marked and protected the dangerous areas of boundaries and crossroads. Statues of the ithyphallic PRIAPUS guarded the fertility of Roman GARDENS and HOUSEHOLDS (HORACE, *Satire* 1.8). The phallus appeared independently in wall-carvings, or in the form of bronze *tintinnabula* (chimes) intended to hang in an open courtyard. EJS

See Johns, C. (1982) *Sex or Symbol?*; Keuls, E. (1985) *The Reign of the Phallus.*

 HERMS; MASKS; PRIAPUS.

Pharsalus (Greek Pharsalos) A city of THESSALY and the site of important battles. From its *akropolis* on a hill, Pharsalus looked over a fertile plain intersected by the road from Larissa, the leading city of Thessaly, to central Greece. Because of the political competition between leading families, the city was at times disunified, to its detriment. In 364 BC at nearby KYNOSKEPHALAI, PELOPIDAS of THEBES defeated Alexander, the tyrant of Pherai who was attempting to expand into BOIOTIA and within Thessaly. Pharsalus was an early supporter of PHILIP II of Macedonia, and enjoyed prosperity and security in his reign and that of his son ALEXANDER, but paid a heavy price when it joined other Greek states in an attempt to overthrow Macedonian domination after Alexander's death in 323. In 197, during Rome's second MACEDONIAN WAR, Titus Quinctius FLAMININUS defeated PHILIP V at Kynoskephalai, thereby liberating Greece from Macedonian control.

The most famous battle at Pharsalus was the victory of JULIUS CAESAR over POMPEY in 48 BC. When the civil war broke out in 49, Pompey initially fled to Dyrrachium. After denying Caesar's attempt to blockade him, he took refuge at Pharsalus. On 9 August, Pompey pitched his forces against those of Caesar and was seriously defeated. He managed to escape personally, but was killed as he entered Egypt. This battle, near the Greek city which had seen the recovery of freedom from TYRANNY a century and a half earlier, now became the symbol for the loss of Roman freedom and a new tyranny. JV

Pheidias Athenian sculptor of the classical period, credited with several masterpieces in Athens and elsewhere. PLINY THE ELDER records that Pheidias began his career as a painter (*Natural History* 35.54), but his major artistic engagement was the overall supervision of the SCULPTURES of the PARTHENON, part of the major rebuilding of the ATHENIAN ACROPOLIS initiated by Pheidias' friend, PERIKLES. The extent to which Pheidias actually worked on the sculptures of the Parthenon is not clear, but Plutarch (in *Perikles*) states that he accepted the contract for the chryselephantine (GOLD and IVORY) statue of Athena Parthenos (PAUSANIAS 1.24.5). It was in connection with this statue that Pheidias stood trial in Athens having fallen victim to jealousy, as Plutarch remarks.

Pheidias worked in a variety of materials including MARBLE, wood, bronze, gold and ivory. Among his greatest works, the sources mention an over-life-size chryselephantine statue of ZEUS at OLYMPIA in ELIS. In Athens he made bronze statues of Athena Promachos and Lemnia Athena, an APHRODITE Ourania and a bronze APOLLO. For the PLATAEANS, he made a gilded wooden statue of Areia Athena; at Thebes, statues of Athena and Hermes Pronaoi. Also famous was his AMAZON for the Artemision at EPHESOS. EP

See Harrison, E.B. (1996) Pheidias, in O. Palagia and J.J. Pollitt, eds., *Personal Styles in Greek Sculpture* 16–65; Palagia, O. (1996) Pheidias, in *The Dictionary of Art*, vol. 24, 592–4.

Philadelphia see APOLLONIOS THE *DIOIKÊTÊS*; ARSINOË II PHILADELPHOS.

Philetairos of Pergamon see PERGAMON.

Philetas Hellenistic POET and grammarian. Philetas (sometimes spelt Philitas), son of Telephos, was born in Kos in the latter part of the 4th century BC. He was tutor to Ptolemy II Philadelphos, also born in Kos (309/8), as well as to other well-known Alexandrian poets and grammarians including Zenodotos and perhaps THEOKRITOS. He went to ALEXANDRIA c.297/6, but seems to have returned to Kos in the 290s and to have died there in the 280s. The people of Kos are said to have erected a statue in his honour.

The *SUDA* tells us that Philetas composed EPIGRAMS and ELEGIES, as well as being a grammatical critic. Of these works (which remain only in fragments), his elegies were most admired in antiquity and he was included in the Canon of Elegists. The elegies were a source of inspiration for Roman poets, especially PROPERTIUS, who aimed to imitate Philetas' style. His critical work, on the other hand, did not find such favour. His *Miscellanea*, in which he offered explanations of rare words in HOMER, various dialects and technical terms, was much criticized by ARISTARCHOS. FMM

See Spanoudakis, K. (2002) *Philitas of Cos.*

Philip II c.383–336 BC King of Macedonia (r.359–336). In his reign Macedonia was transformed into the dominant state in the eastern MEDITERRANEAN, reaching as far as the HELLESPONT and controlling most of the Greek mainland. To achieve this Philip had to tackle several issues. Financial prosperity was brought about by systematic exploitation of the state's resources in metals and TIMBER as well as by the building of ROADS, enlargement of existing cities, foundation of new ones, and population transfers. In this manner Philip also secured his territorial conquests. He proved remarkably resourceful in the techniques he applied to control nobles who could challenge his position: their children were brought to court to be educated, becoming his hostages as well as his future followers. Additionally, he elevated to the status of Companion (*hetairos*) other Greeks as well as foreigners, reducing the power of the old nobility.

PHILIP II: the reconstructed face of Philip of Macedonia, based on the human remains found in the tomb at Vergína.

Philip reorganized the army, introducing a permanent heavy infantry force and the phalanx formation; it was equipped with a javelin 5 m long (the *sarissa*), which rendered it invincible when in close ranks. Progressively, he increased substantially the number of infantrymen as well as the CAVALRY; numbers were combined with exhaustive training and adoption of novel TACTICS. Combining these military reforms with DIPLOMACY, he managed to bring Macedonia's northern neighbours (ILLYRIANS and Paionians) under control.

In 357 and 356, strategic positions on the North AEGEAN coast fell into Philip's hands: Amphipolis, PYDNA and Poteidaia. These conquests transgressed Athenian interests in the area, and thereafter DEMOSTHENES did not stop urging the Athenians (and the other Greeks) to fight Philip. Having secured the northern border, Philip turned his attention to the south. In 352, taking advantage of internal strife, he secured leadership of the THESSALIAN *koinon*. In the next few years he operated again in the north; in 348 he annexed the CHALKIDIKE peninsula; Athenian help for OLYNTHOS arrived too late.

Conflict between THEBES and PHOKIS over control of DELPHI (the 'third SACRED WAR') gave Philip the opportunity to intervene and gain a seat in the Amphiktionic league in 346. Fearing that Philip would cross THERMOPYLAI, the Athenians (allies of Phokis) acceded to the 'peace of Philokrates'. After prolonged warfare, in 341 Philip annexed most of Thrace. The uneasy peace with Athens lasted until 340. When Athens interfered in Philip's operations in the Thracian Chersonese, he declared war. The issue was settled in 338 at CHAIRONEIA, where he defeated Athens and THEBES; his lenient treatment of Athens is notable. In 337/6 he established the league of CORINTH, comprising almost all Greek states (except SPARTA); a common peace was thus achieved under his leadership. However, his plans to campaign against Persia were cut short by his assassination in 336. The invasion of the Persian empire had barely begun; it was left to his son, ALEXANDER the Great, to resume it.

The probable cremation burial of Philip was excavated in the 1970s in a rich tomb at VERGINA, and his facial features spectacularly reconstructed using forensic techniques. (see also OLYMPIAS) IK

See Cawkwell, G. L. (1978) *Philip of Macedon*; Hammond, N. G. L. and Griffith, G. T. (1979) *A History of Macedonia*, vol. 2; Prag, A. J. N.W. et al. (1984) The skull from tomb II at Vergina, *JHS* 104: 60–78.

 MACEDONIA: (b).

Philip III Arrhidaios see EURYDIKE (3); OLYMPIAS; SUCCESSORS.

Philip V 238–179 BC Son of Demetrios II and Phthia-Chryseis, Philip ascended to the Macedonian throne in 221 after the death of Antigonos Doson. His attention was drawn at first to problems in ILLYRIA and to a conflict with the AITOLIAN LEAGUE, but he also intervened in CARIA, where he had a claim to authority deriving from Antigonos Doson's campaign there in 227. In 215 he struck an alliance with the CARTHAGINIANS, then at war with Rome, which set the stage for later mistrust and conflict. The Romans allied with the Aitolians, and the two sides fought (with relatively little direct Roman involvement) until 206/5, when the Aitolians abandoned the Romans to make peace with Philip. At this point Philip's attention turned to the AEGEAN and Asia Minor; he sponsored the Aitolian Dikaiarchos in raiding Aegean ISLANDS. In 203 he and ANTIOCHOS III negotiated a 'secret treaty' to divide between them the holdings of the PTOLEMIES; the historicity of this agreement has been challenged, but more recent opinion is inclined to accept it as genuine. Philip's operations led Greek cities to protest to the Romans, who first attempted to impose a settlement and then declared war. The ACHAIANS and Aitolians sided with Rome in 199, but Philip was able to hold his own until the arrival in Greece in 198 of Titus Quinctius FLAMININUS, who defeated Philip decisively at KYNOSKEPHALAI in June 197. The subsequent peace treaty required Philip to leave the Greek cities alone and pay the Romans an indemnity of 1,000 talents. For the remainder of his reign, Philip concentrated on improving the economic conditions of Macedonia, with an eye toward restoring its ability to support an army. He maintained peaceful relations with Rome until his death. His son Perseus succeeded him as king. GR

See Walbank, F.W. (1967) *Philip V of Macedon*.

Philip the Arab (Marcus Iulius Philippus) c.AD 204–49 Roman emperor, AD 244–9, born in Shahba (renamed Philippopolis) in south-west SYRIA. Little is known of his career until he rose to prominence as praetorian prefect under GORDIAN III, during the campaign against the PERSIANS. On Gordian's death, Philip was proclaimed emperor by the troops (244), negotiated PEACE with the Persians and returned to Rome. He made his ten-year-old son, Marcus Iulius Severus Philippus, AUGUSTUS in 246/7. In 248 he celebrated the Secular games at Rome with lavish display. During his reign, signs typical of the period came to the fore. He had to deal with incursions on the northern frontier (246) and trouble from the Carpi in Dacia (247). In 248 Pacatianus was acclaimed emperor by troops in PANNONIA, and the GOTHS seized the opportunity to invade. Philip sent Decius, an experienced Pannonian soldier and urban prefect, to deal with the situation. In a manner characteristic of the period, Decius' success led to his proclamation as emperor by his troops. He marched on ITALY, defeated and killed Philip at Verona in 249.

Much of Philip's history is contentious. His low birth is stressed by the *HISTORIA AUGUSTA*, while Eutropius claims he was the son of an ARAB chief. The *Historia Augusta* also implicates him in the death of Gordian, though this may be spurious. Philip's portrait style is distinctive in its militaristic 'designer stubble' look. MEH

See Bowersock, G. (1983) *Roman Arabia*.

 EMPERORS, ROMAN: (b).

Philippi (Philippoi) A city in eastern Macedonia on the Via Egnatia, the Roman road from the ADRIATIC SEA to Byzantium. Originally known to the Greeks as Krenides and occupied by THRACIANS, it was refounded in 360 BC by Thasians and called Daton. Only four years later, in 356, PHILIP II of Macedonia refounded it yet again, as his centre for the gold mines in the area, and named it after himself.

The town is known mainly for two reasons. Philippi was the site of the last great battles of the civil war between the successors and the assassins of JULIUS CAESAR in 42 BC. The conspirators and their forces, led by Marcus Iunius BRUTUS and Gaius Cassius Longinus, met the forces of the TRIUMVIRS, under ANTONY's command (Octavian was ill). When his camp was captured during the first battle, Cassius committed SUICIDE. Brutus did not commit suicide until after he lost the second battle, on 23 October. Antony established a colony of VETERANS at Philippi, and Octavian sent more there after the battle of ACTIUM. Despite the fame of these battles and their consequences for the Roman state, Philippi never developed the symbolic value that PHARSALUS did. Nearly a century after these battles, Philippi was the first city in Europe to hear CHRISTIAN missionaries, as PAUL and Silas travelled from ASIA Minor into Greece c.AD 50. A letter written by Paul to the inhabitants of Philippi was included in the NEW TESTAMENT. JV

Philo (Philon) of Byzantion c.200 BC Author of works in Greek on MATHEMATICS and, more famously, TECHNOLOGY. Preserved portions of his *Mechanical Collection*, a set of technological studies, include *Belopoiïka* (*On Making Catapults*), *Pneumatika* on wind-driven devices, and *Poliorkêtika* on SIEGE technology. Among the ARTILLERY designs he describes is a catapult invented by his predecessor Ktesibios, powered by bronze springs and compressed air. The *Belopoiïka* is also famous for the account of how ENGINEERS improved catapults through careful EXPERIMENTATION. They discovered that the key to projectile power was the diameter of the ring in which the coiled spring was held; thus 'not everything can be accomplished by the theoretical methods of pure mechanics, but much is to be found by experiment'. This rebuts the stereotype that Greek scientists remained in the abstract world of non-utilitarian speculation. Philon also points out explicitly the role of royal patronage in the advancement of technology at Ptolemaic Alexandria. His *SEVEN WONDERS of the World* includes a description of the Colossus of Rhodes. DGJS

See Marsden, E.W. (1971) *Greek and Roman Artillery: technical treatises* (includes trs. of *Belopoiïka*); Stewart, A. (1990) *Greek Sculpture*, vol. 1 (trs. of *Seven Wonders*).

Philo Judaeus c.20 BC–c.AD 50 Philo of ALEXANDRIA was a politician and leader of the Jewish community in Alexandria, and an original PHILOSOPHER whose writings exercised a strong influence among CHRISTIAN theologians of later generations. He was a member of the most influential JEWISH family in Alexandria. His political career is known almost entirely from his own, highly coloured account of his role as spokesman of a delegation sent to Rome in AD 40 by the Alexandrian Jews. The purpose of the mission was to protest to Gaius CALIGULA about the forcible erection of statues of the emperor in synagogues (*The Embassy to Gaius*) and about the anti-Jewish pogroms of AD 38 (described by Philo in *Against Flaccus*). One passing reference in JOSEPHUS' *Antiquities* (18.259–60) does nothing more than confirm Philo's participation and his reputation as a philosopher.

Philo's voluminous philosophical writings, composed in erudite Greek, show a close familiarity with a range of Greek philosophical ideas, especially those of PLATO and the STOICS, and with the SEPTUAGINT translation of the Hebrew BIBLE. His books attempt to demonstrate that the underlying message of the Hebrew scriptures, especially the Pentateuch, is actually identical to that of GREEK PHILOSOPHY. This aim is achieved primarily through a complex but coherent system of allegorical interpretation of the Bible, which he may have invented.

Philo employed four distinct literary genres in expounding his philosophy. (1) A few of his writings are purely philosophical treatises, making only rare allusions to Jewish sources (e.g. *On the Eternity of the World* and *On Providence*). (2) A much longer series, grouped together under the rubric *Expositio legis* ('exposition of law'), tries to demonstrate how the biographies of the patriarchs and the COSMOLOGY of Genesis refer allegorically to ETHICAL teachings. These works, probably intended for a gentile audience, give in each case a summary of the biblical narrative before the allegorical interpretation is advanced. (3) By contrast, the treatises grouped together in *Legum allegoria* ('allegory of laws') are so abstract and confused, presupposing a readership fully conversant with both Philo's method and the text of the Pentateuch, that they must have been aimed at Jews. (4) Much less difficult to follow are the *Quaestiones et solutiones* on Genesis and Exodus, extant only in part and only in Armenian translation. In this work Philo poses exegetical issues, to be solved first in literal fashion and then by allegory.

This huge output was widely cited by CHRISTIANS at least from the time of Clement of Alexandria, and by the 4th century AD Philo was sometimes believed to have been a Christian; but it is unknown how many

of his Jewish contemporaries appreciated his philosophical approach to Judaism. None of the other extant Jewish Greek writings share his consistent allegorical technique, and he seems to have been ignored by the Jewish tradition preserved by the rabbis. The extent of his influence, if any, on Josephus is debated. The enthusiastic adoption of his works by Christians, compared to their lack of interest in most other Jewish Greek authors, may suggest that his philosophy was unusual or even unique. MDG
See Sandmel, S. (1979) *Philo of Alexandria.*

Philodemos 110–40/35 BC PHILOSOPHER and POET from Gadara. Around 75 BC, after his EDUCATION under Zeno of Sidon in the EPICUREAN school at Athens, Philodemos moved to Italy. There he met his future patron, Lucius Calpurnius Piso, and, in company with the Epicurean Siro, who ran his own school in Naples, became active in a circle of writers sympathetic to Epicureanism – Siro's old pupil VIRGIL among them. All that we know of his philosophy comes from the charred remains of a LIBRARY preserved under the volcanic mud at nearby HERCULANEUM. (It is not fantastic to suppose that the VILLA in which it was found had belonged to Piso, and that the library was Philodemos' own.) To date, some 30 philosophical works have come to light, the most original being those in which he discusses MUSIC and literary theory, attacking critics who thought that POETRY should be judged solely on the propriety of its subject matter, or solely on the skill of its execution. (The two, he thought, were inseparable.) His own poetry, as the surviving EPIGRAMS attest, owed much to KALLIMACHOS, Asclepiades and Meleager, and in its turn influenced a number of Latin poets, notably HORACE. GB-S
See Gigante, M. (1995) *Philodemus in Italy*; Sider, D. (1997) *The Epigrams of Philodemus.*

philology, comparative Comparative linguistics, as comparative philology is more commonly called, is a branch of historical linguistics, which studies the development of LANGUAGES over time. Central to this field is the fact that languages are related genetically and descend from older languages, which in many cases have passed out of existence. Latin and Greek, along with older languages such as Sanskrit, Armenian and Germanic, are descended from a parent language, for which no direct evidence exists. This language has been called Proto-Indo-European (often simply Indo-European), and has been reconstructed through detailed comparative analysis of its descendants. Although the focus has been chiefly on technical features of language, scholars have often moved beyond the narrowly linguistic and used the results of comparative studies to shed light on aspects of the history and society of both the parent culture and its descendants. It has also been argued that some features of ancient POETRY, in particular metre and formulas, reflect the Indo-European heritage. Though hampered by the necessity to focus on written texts, comparativists have done much to show how the phonology and morphology of Greek and Latin developed (especially in relation to Sanskrit), and the working out of detailed phonological rules has been vital for etymology. It is striking, for example, to observe that the Greek word *thymos* – 'spirit' or 'passion' in its earliest occurrences – is cognate with Sanskrit *dhumah* and Latin *fumus*, both of which mean 'smoke', 'vapour'. This linguistic point strengthens the argument that the Greeks connected the stuff of consciousness with breath or vapour. CGB
See Sihler, A. L. (1995) *New Comparative Grammar of Greek and Latin*; Watkins, C. (1995) *How to Kill a Dragon.*

Philon of Byzantion see PHILO (PHILON) OF BYZANTION.

Philopoimen (Philopoemen) 252–182 BC Elected GENERAL of the ACHAIAN LEAGUE on multiple occasions, subject of two BIOGRAPHIES, one by PLUTARCH and another by POLYBIOS (now lost). Philopoimen reformed the Achaian army by introducing heavier ARMOUR, the solid shield and the long javelin, and trained the infantry to use them. Thus Achaia was able to break free from Macedonia (leader of the Hellenic league of which Achaia had been a member). Furthermore, under Philopoimen's guidance it could choose to take sides with Rome in the wars against PHILIP V as well as against ANTIOCHOS III.

Employing the reformed army, Philopoimen adopted an expansionist policy that culminated in the incorporation of Sparta into the Achaian league in 192 BC. He demolished Sparta's walls, abolished its institutions (including the EDUCATION system or *agôgê*), and installed a regime favourable to Achaia. This policy caused continuous unrest and tension with Rome, since it upset the Roman policy of equilibrium of power in the Greek world. Philopoimen, on the other hand, steadfastly asserted Achaia's independence of action in the PELOPONNESE and refused to allow Roman intervention. Thus he came to be called the 'last of the Greeks'. He died in the course of MESSENE's revolt from the league, while being held in captivity by the Messenians (poisoned, according to Polybios' doubtful narrative). IK
See Plutarch, *Philopoimen*; Errington, R.M. (1969) *Philopoemen.*

philosophical schools Although the early PYTHAGOREANS had already formed a cultic sect, it was only in the 4th century BC that rival philosophical schools emerged, many of them 'SOCRATIC' in inspiration. Thereafter most PHILOSOPHERS professed membership of this or that school, defined primarily by allegiance to the teachings of its founder.

PLATO's ACADEMY and ARISTOTLE's LYCEUM became major education and research centres, though their legal and institutional standing remains obscure. Both were named after groves in suburban Athens where their public activities were conducted. The STOICS similarly were named after the Athenian public STOA where they met. Although classes and discussions were undoubtedly held on private premises too, a high public profile was crucial both for consolidating a school's identity and for attracting the prospective students who flocked to Athens in the three centuries down to 86 BC. Only the politically minimalist EPICUREAN school, based in its 'Garden' outside the Athenian city wall, avoided the public gaze.

Minor schools came and went, but by the imperial age PLATONISM, ARISTOTELIANISM, Stoicism and Epicureanism jointly constituted the philosophical canon, with a full philosophical education ideally including study under a teacher in each. In AD 176 the philosopher-emperor Marcus Aurelius established chairs of all four philosophies at Athens. However, Athens had long since lost its status as undisputed centre of the philosophical world, and much teaching continued in local schools scattered around the empire. DNS

See Glucker, J. (1978) *Antiochus and the Late Academy.*

philosophy

From the 6th century BC to the 6th century AD, PHILOSOPHERS were among the dominant intellectuals of the Greek-speaking world, and during that time the foundations for all subsequent Western philosophy were laid. Rarely regarded as a detached academic discipline, philosophy frequently carried high political prestige, and its modes of discourse came to infect disciplines as diverse as MEDICINE, RHETORIC, ASTROLOGY, HISTORY, grammar and LAW. While its absolutely pivotal figures were Socrates in the 5th century BC and Plato and Aristotle in the 4th, almost equal originality and importance should be attached to the Presocratics and Sophists of the 6th and 5th centuries, the Stoics, Epicureans and Sceptics of the hellenistic age, and the many Aristotelian and (especially) Platonist philosophers who wrote under the Roman empire.

Ancient philosophy is conventionally held to start with Thales in the mid-6th century BC, though the Greeks themselves frequently made Homer (c.700 BC) its true originator. Officially it is often regarded as ending in AD 529, when the Christian emperor Justinian is thought to have banned the teaching of PAGAN philosophy at Athens, though in fact its cessation was more gradual than that.

The first phase, occupying most of the 6th and 5th centuries BC, is conventionally known as Presocratic philosophy. Its earliest practitioners – Thales, Anaximander, Anaximenes – came from Miletos in the east Mediterranean, while some other leading figures, such as Pythagoras, Parmenides and Empedokles, operated in Sicily or southern Italy. The dominant concern was to explain the origin and regularities of the physical world and the place of the human SOUL within it. The period also produced such rebels as the Eleatic philosophers – Parmenides, Zeno of Elea, and Melissos – whose radical monism used pure reasoning to undermine belief in the physical world. The theory of ATOMISM, developed by Leukippos and Demokritos, is sometimes regarded as the most important single outcome of the Presocratic period, but in the ancient world itself Parmenides' impact was much more far-reaching.

The term 'Presocratic' reflects the traditional view that Socrates (469–399 BC) was the first philosopher to shift the focus away from the natural world to human values. In fact, however, this shift to a large extent coincides with the concerns of his contemporaries the Sophists, who professed to teach the fundamentals of political and social success and consequently were also much concerned with moral issues. But the figure of Socrates became, and has remained, so powerful an icon for the life of moral self-scrutiny that it is his name that is used to mark this watershed in the history of philosophy. Following his death, many schools looked back to him as the living embodiment of philosophy and sought to rediscover in philosophical theory the principles of his life and thought.

Socrates and the Sophists made Athens the philosophical centre of the Greek world. There, in the 4th century, the two greatest philosophers of antiquity, Plato and Aristotle, lived and taught. Originally a pupil of Socrates, Plato eventually set up his own school, at the Athenian grove called the Academy. His published dialogues are literary masterpieces as well as philosophical classics, and develop, albeit unsystematically, a global philosophy which embraces ETHICS, POLITICS, PHYSICS, METAPHYSICS, epistemology, aesthetics and psychology. His more celebrated doctrines include his theory of transcendent 'Forms', the immortality of the soul, and the world's intelligent creation.

The Academy's most eminent alumnus was Aristotle, whose own school, the Lyceum, came for a time to compete with the Academy as an educational centre. His highly technical but also often provisional and exploratory school treatises may not have been intended for publication and became widely known only around the late 1st century BC. The main philosophical treatises among them (leaving aside his important zoological works) include seminal studies in all the areas covered by Plato, plus LOGIC, a discipline which he pioneered. His world-view is fundamentally teleological: both physical processes and human lives are structured by their natural goals. Aristotle's treatises are, along with Plato's dialogues, among the leading classics of Western philosophy.

Down to the late 4th century BC, philosophy was widely seen as a search for global understanding; hence in the major schools its activities could include, for example, biological and historical research. In the ensuing hellenistic age, however, a geographical split helped to isolate philosophy more sharply as a self-contained discipline. While Alexandria, with its comprehensive LIBRARY and royal PATRONAGE, became the centre of scientific, literary and historical research, the philosophical schools at Athens concentrated on areas which correspond more closely to philosophy as it has since come to be understood. The following features were to characterize philosophy not only in the hellenistic age but for the remainder of antiquity.

The three main parts of philosophy were usually labelled 'physics' (a primarily speculative discipline, concerned with such concepts as causation, change, space, time, god and MATTER), 'logic' (which sometimes included theory of KNOWLEDGE), and 'ethics'. Ethics was agreed to be the ultimate focus of philosophy, which itself became a systematized route to personal virtue and happiness. There was also a strong spiritual dimension. One's religious beliefs – that is, the way one rationalized and elaborated one's own (normally pagan) beliefs and practices concerning the divine – were themselves an integral part of both physics and ethics, never a mere adjunct of philosophy.

In the hellenistic age, one of the two dominant philosophical creeds was Stoicism, founded by Zeno of Citium around 300 BC, though its most important exponent was Zeno's second successor Chrysippos. Stoicism treats the world as if it is a play scripted in minute detail by a divine intelligence, our goal being to understand our allotted role and co-operate fully with the cosmic plan. Epicureanism, founded by Epicurus a few years earlier, is diametrically opposed, offering a route to enjoyment of a life which has no god-given purpose, in a world consisting ultimately of mere inanimate ATOMS and their motions. A powerful contemporary force was scepticism. This operated largely through the Academy (which in this period became a critical rather than a doctrinal school) and also, starting from the last decades of the hellenistic era, through Pyrrhonism – a movement which in time adopted the actual title 'Sceptics' (literally 'inquirers').

The really crucial watershed belongs half a century before the end of the hellenistic age, in the early 80s BC. Political and military upheavals at Athens drove most of the philosophers into exile at cultural havens such as Alexandria and Rome. The philosophical schools of Athens never fully recovered, so that this decentralization amounted to a permanent redrawing of the philosophical map. Philosophy could now no longer be, for most of its adherents, a living activity within the Athenian school founded by Plato, Aristotle, Zeno or Epicurus. Instead it was a subject pursued in small study groups led by professional teachers scattered around the Greco-Roman world. It was as if the history of philosophy had now come to an end, so that the job was to seek the correct interpretation of the 'ancients' by close study of their texts. Hence a huge part of the philosophical activity of late antiquity went into the composition of commentaries on philosophical classics.

In this final 'imperial' era of ancient philosophy (so called because it more or less coincides with the era of the Roman empire), the hellenistic creeds were gradually eclipsed by the revival of doctrinal PLATONISM. This based itself on the close study of Plato's text, out of which it developed a massively elaborate metaphysical scheme. Aristotle, usually regarded as an ally by these Platonists, became himself the focus of many commentaries. Despite its formal concern with recovering the wisdom of the ancients, however, this age produced many highly original thinkers, the greatest of whom was the NEOPLATONIST PLOTINUS.

A huge body of ancient philosophical texts, albeit a minute proportion of those circulating in antiquity, has come down to us. These are somewhat weighted towards those philosophers – above all Plato, Aristotle and the Neoplatonists – who were of most immediate interest to the Christian culture that preserved them throughout the Middle Ages. Some further ancient philosophical writings have been recovered through translations into Arabic and other languages, or on excavated scraps of PAPYRUS. For the vast majority of ancient philosophers, however, our knowledge of them depends on other writers' reports of their words and ideas.

Ancient Greek philosophy was principally pagan, and was finally eclipsed by Christianity in the 6th century AD. But it was so comprehensively annexed by its conqueror that it came, through Christianity, to dominate medieval and RENAISSANCE philosophy. Despite the suppression and distortion that its contributions have suffered over two millennia, it remains a seminal influence on any modern conspectus of what philosophy is and can be. DNS, DJF

See Algra, K. et al., eds. (1999) *The Cambridge History of Hellenistic Philosophy*; Armstrong, A.H., ed. (1967) *The Cambridge History of Later Greek and Early Medieval Philosophy*; Guthrie, W.K.C. (1962–81) *A History of Greek Philosophy*, 6 vols.; Sedley, D., ed. (2003) *The Cambridge Companion to Greek and Roman Philosophy*; Zeyl, D., ed. (1997) *Encyclopedia of Ancient Philosophy*.

Roman tradition made NUMA Pompilius, the legendary second king of Rome (trad. 715–673 BC), a pupil of PYTHAGORAS. This association had a long and popular career, even though it was challenged by writers like CICERO and LIVY on the grounds of its impossible chronology. The discovery of 'Numa's coffin' in 181 BC, and the subsequent public burning of supposedly Pythagorean books found within, may suggest a general official antipathy to philosophy at the time, as may the expulsion of PHILOSOPHERS and RHETORS in 161. However, these public actions against philosophers at Rome may be the product of a belated reactionary, and somewhat token, attempt to stem an increasing tide of hellenistic culture flowing into Rome, rather than a sign of animosity towards philosophy in particular. Indeed, in 155 an Athenian EMBASSY came to Rome consisting of the heads of three major philosophical schools: the ACADEMIC Karneades, the STOIC Diogenes and the PERIPATETIC Kritolaos. This visit seems to have sparked considerable interest, but also considerable nervousness, especially on the part of the stern moralist CATO, because of Karneades' ability to argue the cases both for and against any proposition with equal cogency. The great popularity of Karneades' lectures, and their endorsement by the presence of leading citizens in the audience, point to widespread popular enthusiasm for Greek philosophy at Rome. In fact, for a considerable period already the EDUCATION of the children of the Roman ÉLITE had been in the hands of Greek teachers. The expulsion of the EPICUREAN philosophers Alkaios and Philiskos in (probably) 154 for 'introducing pleasures' should perhaps be taken as evidence of increasingly sophisticated Roman assessments of the moral value of the different Greek schools, rather than as evidence of continuing official opposition to philosophy as a whole.

In the 140s BC the Stoic philosopher Panaitios moved to Rome; he lived alternately there and at Athens until he succeeded Antipater as head of the school in 129. Panaitios was one of the entourage of Publius Cornelius SCIPIO AEMILIANUS, and his influence on the thinking of the Roman political élite was considerable. Stoicism, with its emphasis on fate, virtue as the highest good, and the duty of the citizen to become involved in politics, was as if tailor-made to become the dominant philosophy of Rome. Panaitios had a particular focus on politics and practical ETHICS that further popularized the system among Romans. He softened the impractical severity of the earlier Stoic ethical code of 'living virtuously', in which virtue may seem impossible to achieve for anyone other than the ideal Stoic philosopher. Instead he gave greater emphasis to 'living in accordance with one's natural propensities'. By moving the focus from abstract ethical concerns to practical ethical actions, he broadened the appeal of the system, placing more emphasis on the moral worth of ordinary people and their practical moral and ethical development. His systemization of rules of conduct, and his model of public service that places heavier burdens of public duty on those of wealth and talent, provided a philosophical underpinning for paternalistic Roman ARISTOCRATIC government.

Panaitios' most famous pupil, POSIDONIUS, established his school at RHODES, and this became the chief centre for Stoic philosophy. Although he was a member of at least one embassy to Rome, he had less direct contact with the city than had Panaitios, but was highly influential especially through leading Romans such as Cicero, who studied under him. Posidonius' range of writing was vast, encompassing subjects as diverse as ethics, GEOGRAPHY, ANTHROPOLOGY, history, zoology and natural history. His influence was powerful in his own day and for centuries to come, especially outside the Stoic school, though it is heavily exaggerated by modern 'pan-Posidonianism' which tends to see his influence almost everywhere in Roman literature. Although he followed the orthodox Stoic division of philosophy into PHYSICS, ethics and LOGIC, he saw logic not simply as a tool of philosophy but as an integral part of an organic philosophical whole, with physics as the flesh and blood, ethics as the soul, and logic as the bones. In ethics he reacted against Chrysippos' analysis of the passions as arising from false judgements of the rational faculty of the SOUL, and argued that they were caused by the irrational faculties of the soul. His physical enquiries were famous, especially in ASTRONOMY and meteorology, and his explanation of how the tides are connected with the motions of the MOON remained scientific orthodoxy until Newton. Perhaps his most remarkable work was the lost *On Ocean*, which ranged from geography and astronomy to climatology and anthropology. Among important later Roman Stoics were Epictetus, SENECA and MARCUS AURELIUS.

The Stoics' main rivals in Roman philosophy were the Epicureans. Although the two schools came close together in certain areas, in others they were fundamentally different, especially in theology, physics and ethics. The Epicureans argued that the gods did not take any part in human affairs and did not direct the world in any way. For them, there was no fate or predestination. In physics Epicurus introduced an element of randomness: an uncaused and unpredictable swerve of atoms that broke any chain of physical causation, freeing the world from any physical determinism and providing humans with FREE WILL. For the Epicureans, traditional religion was impiety; the cause of all human psychological and societal ills was the fear of the gods and the consequent fear of death, which they saw as fostered by *religio* (false religion or SUPERSTITION). Epicurus advised his followers to refrain from taking part in public life (contrast the Stoic encouragement of involvement in public affairs). In a Roman context this, along with Epicurean theology and their ethical theory of pleasure as the end (contrast virtue as the Stoic end), could make the system appear highly 'un-Roman'. However, Epicureanism had an early popularity at Rome – Cicero describes, perhaps rather exaggeratedly, the writings of a certain Gaius Amafinius and his imitators taking all Italy by storm – and continued in popularity well into the imperial period. Several important political figures, such as JULIUS CAESAR and Gaius Cassius, had strong Epicurean leanings.

The Epicurean PHILODEMOS of Gadara came to Rome c.75 BC under the patronage of Lucius Calpurnius Piso Caesoninus, who perhaps owned the VILLA at HERCULANEUM where Philodemos set up his school. Philodemos was a successful and admired POET as well as a philosopher, and among his pupils were the poets VIRGIL, Varius Rufus and Plotius Tucca. Philodemos' LIBRARY, containing about a thousand PAPYRUS rolls of his own philosophical works and those of Epicurus, was preserved by being buried during the eruption of Vesuvius in AD 79, in a charred but often legible state. His works are of considerable scope, from rhetoric and ethics to theology, poetics and MUSIC, in which he was particularly interested.

The other main Roman exponent of Epicureanism was the poet LUCRETIUS (c.94–55 BC). His *De rerum natura* (*On the Nature of the Universe*) is a poem in six books of EPIC hexameters on Epicurean physics, cosmology and ethics. It stands as one of the greatest achievements of Latin POETRY, and was powerfully influential on the work of Virgil and later Latin poets. Although his philosophy is essentially orthodox Epicureanism (his main source was probably the first 15 books of Epicurus' *On Nature*), his choice of poetry as his DIDACTIC medium, and his use of highly charged mythological language and imagery, mark a departure from the approach of his contemporary Philodemos (who rejected poetry as a didactic medium) and from that of Epicurus himself (who considered poetry to be one of the things responsible for spreading superstition and recommended his followers to avoid it). Lucretius' achievement was to produce a blend of philosophy and poetry, and so to make attractive and pleasurable a philosophy that, as he says, many people may find unpalatable.

In his youth, Cicero studied under various teachers of philosophy both at Athens and at Rhodes, including the Epicureans Zeno and Phaidros, the Stoic Posidonius, and the Academics Philo of Larissa and Antiochos of Askalon. His continuing interest in philosophy during his political career is shown by his patronage of the Stoic Diodotos, who lived in Cicero's own house, but his main period of philosophical writing came during his retirement from politics under Caesar's dictatorship. Cicero set out to provide Romans with their own philosophical literature and, since philosophy had been done mostly in Greek, during this vast task he forged the Latin philosophical vocabulary. In the course of a few years he produced a remarkable series of philosophical works including *On the Nature of the Gods*, *On Divination*, *Academica*, and *On Duties*, in which he surveyed the systems of the main Greek schools of philosophy, presenting them in a digestible form for a Roman readership. Personally Cicero leant towards the SCEPTICAL wing of the Academy, though he displays considerable sympathy for the Stoics, especially Stoic ethics; he has a marked distaste for the Epicureans. AUGUSTINE (1) was 'converted' to philosophy by reading Cicero's exhortation to philosophy, the *Hortensius*. Of Roman philosophy it was Cicero's philosophical works above all that became influential in the Middle Ages and eventually informed the syllabus of RENAISSANCE and Enlightenment philosophy.

In the 3rd century AD, Platonic philosophy was revived by PLOTINUS, whose *Enneads* may be regarded as one of Rome's greatest contributions to philosophy. Although his language was Greek, his name is Roman and he taught at Rome from the age of 40. NEOPLATONISM, thought of in antiquity as simply Platonism, became with its syncretizing tendency the dominant philosophy of later antiquity. Plotinus' pupil Porphyry produced a synthesis of Platonism with ARISTOTLE's logic and was influential on many later thinkers, especially on Augustine, whose Neoplatonism produced a transformation in Western CHRISTIANITY. GLC

See Griffin, M. and Barnes, J., eds. (1989) *Philosophia Togata*; Long, A. A. and Sedley, D. N. (1987) *The Hellenistic Philosophers*.

Philostratos Except for the short dialogue on *Nero*, two *dialexeis* and the second book of the *Imagines*, the surviving works attributed to three Philostrati by the baffling notice of the *SUDA* were written by Philostratos the Elder (c.AD 160–244), a sophist from a Lemnian family of sophists, who settled in Athens. They offer an illuminating glimpse into the culture of the time. The *Heroïkos*, a dialogue between a PHOENICIAN and a vine-dresser on HEROES and heroic cult, blends pastoral fiction with correction and supplementation of HOMER. The *Gymnastikos* associates antiquarian erudition and contemporary interest in ATHLETICS. The *Imagines* (Greek title *Eikones*), purporting to describe an existing collection of paintings in Naples, demonstrates the capacity of RHETORIC to beget images and the ORATOR's command of MYTH and literature. *In Honour of Apollonios of Tyana*, undertaken at the suggestion of the empress JULIA DOMNA, is a masterpiece of PAGAN hagiography as well as a manifesto for hellenism. It claims to rely on authentic oral and written testimonies and to give an accurate account of the life of this famous PHILOSOPHER who was turned into a rival of JESUS Christ by the late pagans. Mainly, however, it is a wonderful TRAVEL romance that leads its hero to all the canonical sites of rhetorical GEOGRAPHY. With his *Lives of the Sophists* in two books, Philostratos invented the 'SECOND SOPHISTIC', anchoring the rhetoric of the empire in the classical age of Greece. This series of BIOGRAPHIES of various lengths offers, through a mosaic of anecdotes, a fairly reliable portrait of the masters of epideictic ORATORY. SS

See Anderson, G. (1986) *Philostratus*.

Phocion see PHOKION.

Phocis see PHOKIS.

Phoenicia and Phoenicians In the BIBLE, the Phoenicians are called *can'ani* and their land Canaan, referring to the coastal plain north of Israel (Genesis), though the term is used sometimes to refer just to the area around Tyre (Isaiah). Other biblical references, contemporary Assyrian documents and HOMER refer to the Phoenicians by their cities of origin, or sometimes they are all called Sidonians. Classical historians use the terms Phoenician, Punic and Carthaginian somewhat indiscriminately, though generally Carthaginian refers to an inhabitant of CARTHAGE, while Punic is used to describe the other Phoenicians of North Africa. In modern writing, the term Phoenician specifies the Phoenicians of the eastern MEDITERRANEAN and Phoenician homeland, while Punic refers to the Phoenicians of the western Mediterranean who lived within the sphere of influence of Carthage.

The Phoenician homeland was AGRICULTURALLY extremely fertile, and its forests were famous for their cedars, pines and cypresses. Bears, panthers and wolves made excellent game, while fish salting and purple dye production from murex SHELL provided successful sea-based industries. IRON and lignite were mined in the hills above the coast.

Phoenician settlements tended to be built on small promontories that dominated a bay or small inlet, which provided HARBOUR anchorage and protection to SHIPS from winds and storms. The principal cities of the Phoenician homeland, including Byblos, Berytos (Beirut), Sarepta, Sidon, Akko and Akhziv, are examples of this. Tyre and Arvad were founded on easily defensible offshore islands. Many of the Phoenician colonies in the Mediterranean have similar characteristics. Phoenicians rarely settled inland or away from easy shipping access.

Phoenicia developed as a series of independent political units organized into city-states, rather than a politically unified country. Each city had a hereditary monarchy, though the KING's powers were restricted by a strong merchant OLIGARCHY. The kings also had priestly duties. In fact, Phoenician religion fascinated ancient authors largely because of the *molk* rite, or the practice of child immolation. Literary evidence suggests that in the Phoenician homeland it was the children of patriarchs and kings who were burnt as sacrifice to the deities Baal or Tanit during times of conflict in the interest of the state. In the later colonies of the western Mediterranean, however, the practice seems to have occurred on a much wider scale. The ritual took place in the *tophet*, which in the western colonies is a sacred open-air enclosure on the edge of the colonial centres.

The settlements were particularly competitive with regard to TRADE, and the Phoenicians' reputation as the traders of the ancient world goes back to the Bronze Age, when their cities became the principal intermediaries in trade between the Syrian states and Egypt. Byblos furnished the royal houses of Egypt and MESOPOTAMIA with cedar wood for building.

During the Bronze Age, the land of the Phoenicians covered the coastal territory of Syria and Palestine, extending from the Orontes river in the northeastern Mediterranean to the Egyptian frontier. Around 1200 BC, however, invasion and incursion by Israelite, Philistine and Aramaean tribes reduced the Phoenician territory to a narrow coastal fringe. With the loss of nearly three-quarters of their territory, the Phoenicians turned to the sea for their commercial endeavours. In the 10th century BC, king Hiram I of Tyre (969–936) gained control of the trade routes of the Asian continent. Jointly with king Solomon of Israel, he built a merchant fleet on the Red sea to bring back GOLD, SILVER, IVORY and precious stones from the distant land of Ophir, thought to be Sudan, Somalia, ARABIA, or possibly in the Indian ocean.

During the 9th century BC, the Phoenician city-states began to establish settlements elsewhere in the Mediterranean to facilitate their long-distance trade. Tyre founded the colony of Kition on CYPRUS, securing access to the island's COPPER resources. Phoenician imports from this time have been found in Greece at sites such as KNOSSOS and Lefkandí, attesting to some form of EXCHANGE. During the following centuries, the Phoenicians established settlements in western SICILY, SARDINIA, Malta, North

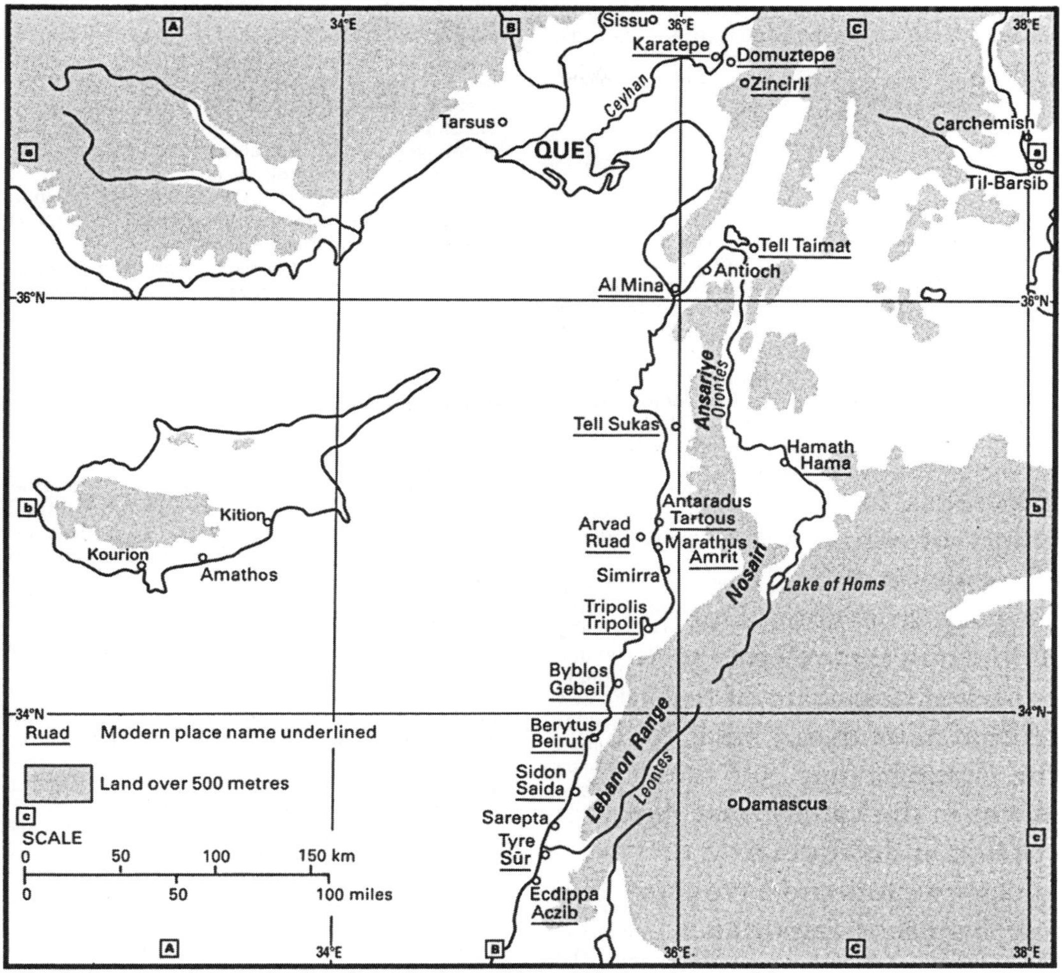

Phoenicia and Phoenicians: (a) map.

Phoenicia and Phoenicians: (b) Carthaginian face beads depicting Phoenician racial types.

Africa and Spain. Many of these colonial sites were located on promontories or offshore islands with good harbours and communication routes. Silver and other precious metals seem to be the primary interests of these Phoenicians. In exchange, they offered decorated pieces of ivory, gold and silver JEWELLERY, silver bowls and bronze jugs, COSMETIC and unguent containers, TEXTILES and GLASS beads. There is evidence that Greeks and Phoenicians worked side by side in their maritime commercial enterprises, as suggested in the *Odyssey* (13.272–86; 14.288–97). In addition, it is presumed that Greek knowledge of potential settlement sites in the western Mediterranean was based upon knowledge shared by Phoenician traders.

The growing power of the Assyrian empire made control of the Phoenician cities a key factor in the politics of the Near East during the 8th and 7th centuries BC. Their strategic position and political and economic importance conditioned, to a considerable extent, the balance of power between Assyria and Egypt. The Assyrian monarchs therefore had a great interest in controlling the Phoenician ports and their commercial networks. By the middle of the 7th century, the city-states of the Phoenician homeland had been subjugated by the Assyrian empire.

The diaspora settlements turned to Carthage, the first Phoenician settlement in the western Mediterranean, for leadership. Thus the 6th century BC saw the rise of Carthage as a power base in the Mediterranean. TH

See Aubet, M. E. (2001) *The Phoenicians and the West.*

 CARTHAGE AND CARTHAGINIANS: (a); COLONIZATION: (a)–(c).

Phokion (Phocion) c.402–318 BC Athenian GENERAL and politician. PLUTARCH presents him as a model of virtue and moderation, but this conceals an ambiguous political attitude. For the greater part of his long career, decorated with numerous generalships, our information is meagre. Although he had enjoyed some success as a military commander, he assumed prominence only after Athens' defeat by PHILIP II at CHAIRONEIA in 338. He became a 'Friend' of Philip and ALEXANDER and forged bonds with members of the Macedonian court, which in Athenian eyes was at once useful and suspect. It appears that the OLIGARCHIC regime established in Athens by the Macedonian regent Antipatros in 322/1 had his approval.

The trademark of Phokion's policy was passivity, which in his last years bordered on treason. Defying the will of the Athenians, Phokion proved criminally negligent when he allowed Nikanor (the Macedonian garrison commander at Mounychia) enough time to get hold of the PIRAEUS, despite orders by the new regent to evacuate Mounychia. Phokion arranged for negotiations between the two conflicting Macedonian sides, but in the end he was regarded as a traitor by all – Macedonians and Athenians – and was put to death by the *dêmos* in 318. (see also SUCCESSORS) IK

See Plutarch, *Phocion*; Bearzot, C. (1990) *Focione*; Tritle, L. (1988) *Phocion the Good.*

Phokis Region in central Greece, west of BOIOTIA. DELPHI was in Phokian territory, and its panhellenic significance seriously distorted Phokian affairs. The important city of Krisa, on the Corinthian (called by THUCYDIDES the Krisaian) gulf, was accused of interfering in the affairs of the sanctuary and was destroyed by THESSALY, Athens and Sikyon in the first SACRED WAR (early 6th century BC). Thereafter there was no major *POLIS* in Phokis, and the landscape was characterized by small settlements with a mainly PASTORAL economy. The remaining *poleis* combined to win some success against Thessaly, but suffered destruction by the PERSIANS in 480. An attempt to recover control of Delphi in the mid-5th century was supported by Athens, but a subsequent alliance with Sparta seems to have remained intact until the 370s, when Kleombrotos marched from Phokis to his defeat at LEUKTRA (371). Iason of Pherai briefly threatened, but Phokis was subjected by THEBES in time to participate in EPAMEINONDAS' first invasion of the PELOPONNESE (370). Phokians did not, however, join his final invasion in 362. After further Boiotian attempts to subject them, they seized Delphi and its treasures and raised an army of MERCENARIES. They won some success in the third sacred war against both Boiotia and PHILIP II of Macedonia, whom they defeated at first, only to suffer in turn at the battle of Crocus Field. Philip had the corpses of 6,000 who had fallen, and perhaps 3,000 prisoners, thrown into the sea as 'temple-robbers', and reparations were imposed which were still being paid at the time of CHAIRONEIA (338); how much this story owed to propaganda and how much to truth is unclear. In the hellenistic period, the Phokians adopted a tighter FEDERAL structure than before, defending themselves against Alexander's SUCCESSORS and helping to repel the Gauls' assault on Delphi. They suffered AITOLIAN rule in the mid-3rd century, freeing themselves only to be dominated by Macedonia and Rome. JBS

See Fossey, J. M. (1986) *The Ancient Topography of Eastern Phokis*; McInerney, J. (1999) *The Folds of Parnassos: land and ethnicity in ancient Phokis.*

 BOIOTIA.

Photios (Photius) see SCHOLARSHIP, BYZANTINE.

phratries Social groupings with membership based on descent through the male line. This institution comes to be identified particularly with Ionian states, though there were some non-Ionian phratries. The earliest literary references to phratries are in HOMER.

Our best evidence for the composition and working of phratries comes from Athens. We know the names of nine; estimates suggest that there were at least 30. Almost all citizens were members of a phratry. Phratries provided an opportunity for feasting; *epibda*, the day after a phratry's annual FESTIVAL (the *apatouria*) becomes a euphemism for a hangover. Phratry rituals helped to monitor and control claims about the legitimacy of children, whose enrolment at the *apatouria* gave fathers an opportunity to declare their legitimacy publicly. The acceptance of children by the phratry was strong evidence of the veracity of these claims. Phratry members are often found as witnesses to familial and social relationships in legal cases. AJLB

See Jones, N. F. (1987) *Public Organization in Greece*; (1999) *The Associations of Classical Athens*; Lambert, S. D. (1998) *The Phratries of Attica*; Parker, R. (1996) *Athenian Religion.*

Phrygia and Phrygians In classical antiquity, an amorphous territory and its people occupying the fertile highlands of ANATOLIA. The Phrygians were originally invaders from the Balkans who for a time controlled the region from Gordion. The extent of their influence can be measured by the presence of rock-cut monuments that often depict a door. Their last king, Midas, lost his kingdom to the Kimmerians in (traditionally) 696 BC. Subsequently, political independence was rare, since LYDIAN, PERSIAN, SELEUKID, ATTALID and Roman domination followed. In the late empire, DIOCLETIAN created a Roman province named Phrygia; it was subdivided into two by CONSTANTINE.

Despite influxes of Macedonians, Galatians and others, the native population held to its cultural traditions and beliefs with some tenacity, and the (Indo-European) Phrygian language survived into the Byzantine period. 'Old' Phrygian inscriptions, in the 8th–3rd centuries BC, were written in an ALPHABET adapted from Greek and Semitic models. 'New' Phrygian reappears in the 1st–3rd centuries AD, now employing the Greek alphabet. Phrygian religion incorporated Anatolian deities, like the mother goddesses and Mên. Its fame depended primarily on CYBELE or the Magna Mater, whose primary sanctuary stood at Pessinos. This cult was officially brought to Rome in the late 3rd century BC, but worship was carefully regulated and controlled because of its licentiousness and its castrated priests, the *galli*. The Phrygians held to a strict MORALITY that made the region receptive to JUDAISM and CHRISTIANITY. JV

See Mellink, M. (1991) The native kingdoms of Anatolia, in *CAH* 3.2, 619–75; Roller, L. (1999) *In Search of God the Mother.*

 ANATOLIA.

Phrynichos see IONIAN REVOLT; TRAGEDY.

Phylarchos see POLYBIOS.

physics The word physics comes from the Latin term *physica* and Greek *physikê* (a feminine singular noun), which itself derives from Greek *physis*, best defined as the nature of a thing. In his attempt to explain why certain behaviours exist or how the character of something comes to be, ARISTOTLE uses *physis* to refer to the essential property of a thing. Hence, a physicist is someone who investigates natural things and natural changes. The realm of concern for an ancient physicist is therefore much broader than what is understood by the discipline today. Nonetheless the main interests of a modern physicist – principles of matter, energy, MOTION and force – engaged the ancients, in both practical and theoretical ways. The questions of MATTER and force first attracted the attention of the PRESOCRATIC PHILOSOPHERS in the 5th century BC, EMPEDOKLES' notions of four elements and the actions of Love and Strife being the most influential through to the 17th century. Aristotle, in the 4th century, was deeply concerned with many aspects of physics. He poses a clear set of questions concerning the action of force on a object in *Problems* 32–4, where he ponders what causes a moving body to come to a standstill; he attempts to determine whether an item which is thrown responds either to its own internal nature or to an exterior force acting upon it. He explains dynamics in an account of terrestrial and celestial movement, where he outlines the natural and unnatural motion of the four earthly elements (earth, air, fire and water) and the heavenly *aithêr* (*On the Heavens* 270b20–5). In *Mechanics* 1–4, Aristotle outlines the principle of the balance; later ARCHIMEDES would state the law of the lever in a more convincing manner (*Plane Equilibriums* 1). In perhaps one of the greatest misconceptions of ancient science, Aristotle incorrectly claimed that a heavier body falls faster than a lighter one (e.g. *On the Heavens* 273b30–274a2, 290a1–2; *Physics* 216a13–16). His error, identified in part by Philoponos in the 6th century, lay in his assumption that the medium of air through which an object travelled acted as a force on the falling object. Many of these kinds of questions remained unanswered in the Roman period, as seen by SENECA's queries about the forces visible in the everyday world (*Natural Questions* 2.9.2–3). The existence of technical treatises such as Archimedes' *On Floating Bodies* or VITRUVIUS' popular account of the discovery of water displacement (*On Architecture* 9) demonstrates that sophisticated knowledge of other aspects of physics, such as hydrostatics, had been developed. Moreover, the related field of MECHANICS relied on such knowledge, and the prevalence of machines such as looms, olive PRESSES and building cranes shows that physics could be put to practical application. TJA

See Aristotle, *Physics*, trs. R. Waterfield and D. Bostock (1999); Rihll, T. E. (1999) *Greek Science.*

Picenum see ITALY, ROMAN; POMPEY; SPARTACUS.

pigeons see AVIARIES; POULTRY.

pigments For the pigments used in ancient PAINTING and DYEING we have invaluable information from VITRUVIUS and PLINY, to which can be added the evidence derived from modern scientific analyses of surviving material. Most of our information relates to WALL-PAINTING executed on PLASTER in the fresco technique. Here the basic colours were obtained from earth pigments: red and yellow ochre, green earth, and chalk white. Blue was artificially produced by baking a mixture of copper, soda and sand; being very coarse, it was sometimes mixed with, or applied over, white to ensure its adherence. Black was carbon, obtained from burning resin, brushwood or wine-lees. All these 'plain' pigments (*colores austeri*) painters held in stock, while the 'rich' pigments (*colores floridi*) had to be supplied by special arrangement. Chief among the rich pigments was cinnabar (mercuric sulphide), a brilliant red pigment obtained from Spain, which cost nearly ten times as much as the best red ochre (from SINOPE on the BLACK SEA). It tended to go black when exposed to light, and had to be protected by waxing, which contributed to its costliness. It was invariably reserved for *de luxe* decorations in important rooms. Organic dyes, such as Tyrian purple and various colouring matters extracted from plants, were used primarily for colouring TEXTILES but are occasionally attested in wall-painting. Vitruvius gives elaborate instructions for preparing them as suspensions in milk or honey which were then mixed with chalk to produce a suitable 'powder paint'. RJL

pigs Versatile and prolific producers of MEAT in many parts of the classical world. They were smaller, more bristly and hairy, and probably more athletic than modern pigs. Ancient farmers, like modern ones, exploited the capacity of pigs for thriving on scraps and waste products. In antiquity pigs were often fed on agricultural by-products such as grape pressings (from WINE-making). Hence, CATO's (*On Agriculture* 11.1) ideal vineyard includes a swineherd, though he does not specify the number of pigs. In areas of extensive FOREST such as central Italy and the central PELOPONNESE in Greece, pigs could be left to roam semi-wild in the forests, foraging for acorns, chestnuts and other wild nuts and FRUITS. According to VARRO (*On Agriculture* 2.4.20–1) a swineherd would train his pigs to come to the sound of his horn, so that he could assemble them in the forest quickly and efficiently.

Pigs breed all year round and were generally butchered young. They were a very important source of meat in the classical world, and pork was often preserved for storage. Cato (*On Agriculture* 162) and COLUMELLA (*On Agriculture* 12.55) provide instructions for making salt pork, ham, bacon and sausages. Suckling pig was a special treat served in the Saturnalia, a Roman FESTIVAL which corresponds to our Christmas. In Greece, suckling pigs were frequently used as SACRIFICIAL ANIMALS, especially in cults of DEMETER. LF

See Isager, S. and Skydsgaard, J. E. (1992) *Ancient Greek Agriculture*; Whittaker, C. R., ed. (1988) *Pastoral Economies in Classical Antiquity*.

Pindar Arguably the greatest of the canonical nine LYRIC POETS of early Greece. He was born in Kynoskephalai in BOIOTIA c.518 BC, and the date of his death is placed c.446. He seems to have belonged to a distinguished ARISTOCRATIC family, and his surviving poetry offers a striking glimpse into the world of the ruling élite in the 5th century BC. Throughout his career Pindar received commissions from most parts of the Greek world, and thus the world-view implicit in his poems is truly panhellenic. In this light, he constitutes an important complement to the tragic poets, with whom he is often contrasted, for their world is very much that of DEMOCRATIC Athens.

In antiquity, scholars working in ALEXANDRIA gathered Pindar's poetry together into 17 books. Of these 11 were focused on the worship of the GODS: HYMNS, paeans (songs to APOLLO), two books of dithyrambs (celebrations of DIONYSOS), three books of *partheneia* (maiden-songs) and two books of *hyporchêmata* (DANCING songs). The remaining six books contained poems that were addressed to men: encomia (poems of praise), *thrênoi* (poems of mourning) and four books of epinicians (celebrations of ATHLETIC victory). Although numerous fragments provide some sense of the full range of Pindar's poetry, only the epinicians survive more or less complete. These poems were composed at the request of wealthy patrons to celebrate and commemorate victory in various competitions held at the four panhellenic athletic FESTIVALS, celebrated at OLYMPIA, DELPHI (the Pythian games), Nemea and Isthmia. The odes seem to have been intended to be performed either shortly after the victory at the festival itself, or some time later after the victor had returned to his native city. It is commonly assumed that the odes were sung by a CHORUS, but there is good evidence to suggest that some poems at least were delivered by a solo singer.

While the corpus of epinicians exhibits considerable range and variation, general patterns can nonetheless be discerned. The longer odes regularly fall into three sections, the first and last of which concern the victor and his successes (a catalogue of victories is a common feature), with the central section devoted to a MYTHIC narrative. The opening typically involves a striking rhetorical flourish, announcing the victor and setting his achievement within the context of the victory celebration. Descriptions of the actual victory are rare; Pindar is more interested in focusing on the transfiguring power of victory, as it reveals the inherited excellence of the victor and his family. He is also concerned to set the victory within the larger context of Greek RELIGION and the dispensation of the gods. For modern readers the mythic narratives constitute the most compelling aspect of Pindar's odes. In sharp contrast to the more discursive manner of EPIC, Pindar presents MYTHS impressionistically and elliptically, focusing on the narrative moments that are most suited to his purpose. Again unlike the more objective narrative of epic, Pindar clearly articulates the moral import of myth. CGB

See Pindar, 2 vols., trs. W. H. Race (1997).

Piraeus (Peiraieus) Port of Athens, 7 km ($4\frac{1}{2}$ miles) south-west of the city. On the west side of a rocky peninsula lies the main HARBOUR, Kantharos (the modern harbour), which was mainly devoted to commerce. On the east side two small harbours, Zea (now Pasalimáni or Zéa) and Mounychia (now Mikrolímano) had the main naval facilities, protected by breakwaters with entrances closable by chains (some remains still visible in Mounychia). THEMISTOKLES first recognized the port's quality, persuading the Athenians (493/2) to transfer their fleet there from the open bay of Phaleron, and starting its fortification. This was completed after the PERSIAN WARS; in 458/7 KIMON linked Piraeus to Athens by the Long Walls; a Middle Wall (c.446) reduced the area fortified. The grid plan of Piraeus is ascribed by ARISTOTLE to Hippodamos (c.450). Traces of housing on this grid, mainly hellenistic and Roman, have been found in excavations in residential areas. Other finds include remains of three of the five STOAS which lined Kantharos on north-east and east, and boundary stones of this *emporion* and of the *agora*, which has not been found but lay near Zea.

In 404 the Spartans destroyed the FORTIFICATIONS and the THIRTY sold the shipsheds for scrap, but the walls were rebuilt by KONON after 394. Most visible remains of walls and gates date from this reconstruction. The shipsheds were rebuilt more slowly to house the expanding fleet; from the mid-4th century they occupied the entire shorelines of Zea (196 shipsheds), Mounychia (82) and the south part of Kantharos (94). Remains have been excavated on Zea (in 1885) and recently on Zea and Mounychia. How these numbers were fitted in is still debated. The Arsenal of Philon, built 347–330 according to specifications which survive (*IG* II^2 1668), has finally been found just north-west of Zea. The sanctuary of ARTEMIS Mounychia and the Asklepieion have been located. The earlier THEATRE, on the west slope of Mounychia hill in the sanctuary of DIONYSOS, is not preserved, but the later theatre (c.200 BC) is visible west of Zea harbour.

During the 5th and 4th centuries Piraeus was very prosperous, with many resident aliens leading to the establishment of foreign cults. Base of the Athenian fleet and of resistance to the Thirty, its population was, according to Aristotle, more DEMOCRATIC than that of Athens; not a separate city, it had features which distinguished it from other *dêmoi* of Athens. After Athens' defeat in 322 BC a Macedonian garrison was installed on Mounychia hill; the Piraeus was finally liberated in 229. It continued to function as a port, serving as Roman fleet base in 200 BC, but lost its commercial pre-eminence to ALEXANDRIA, RHODES and DELOS, and its population declined. It was taken and burnt by SULLA in 87/6 BC; important bronze statues of APOLLO, Artemis and ATHENA, discovered in 1959 packed for shipment, must have been caught in that fire. Little was visible to PAUSANIAS when he visited, but EXCAVATION has revealed much

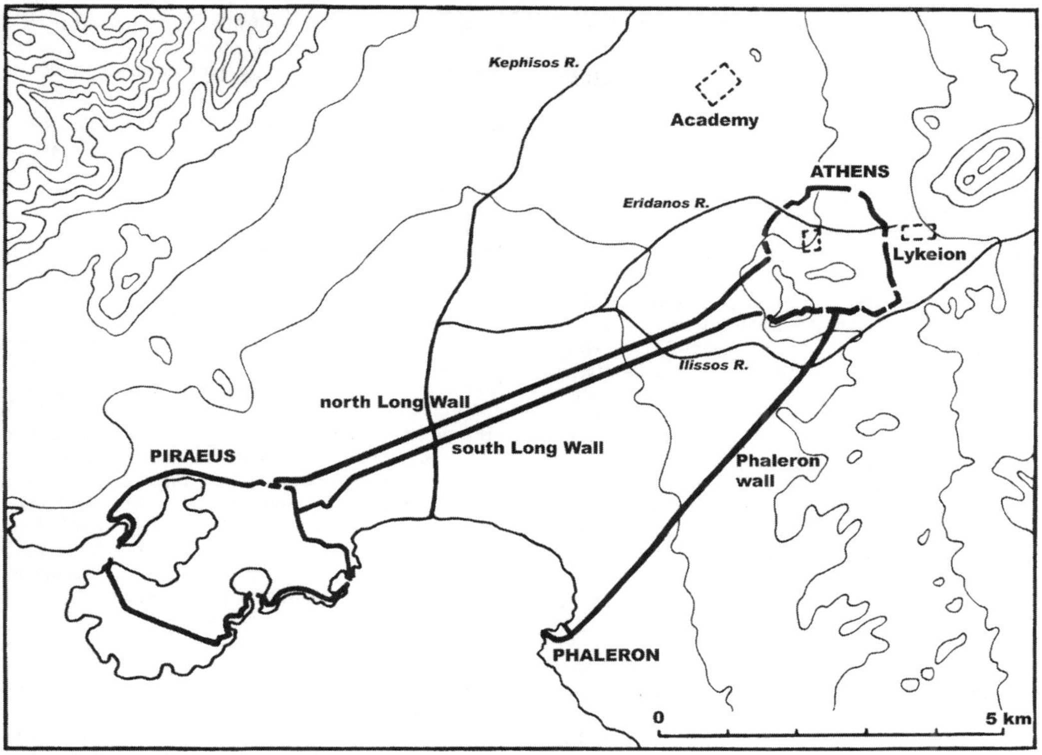

Kephisos R.
Academy
ATHENS
Eridanos R.
Lykeion
Ilissos R.
north Long Wall
south Long Wall
PIRAEUS
Phaleron wall
PHALERON
0
5 km

PIRAEUS: (a) map showing relation of Athens, Piraeus and the Long Walls.

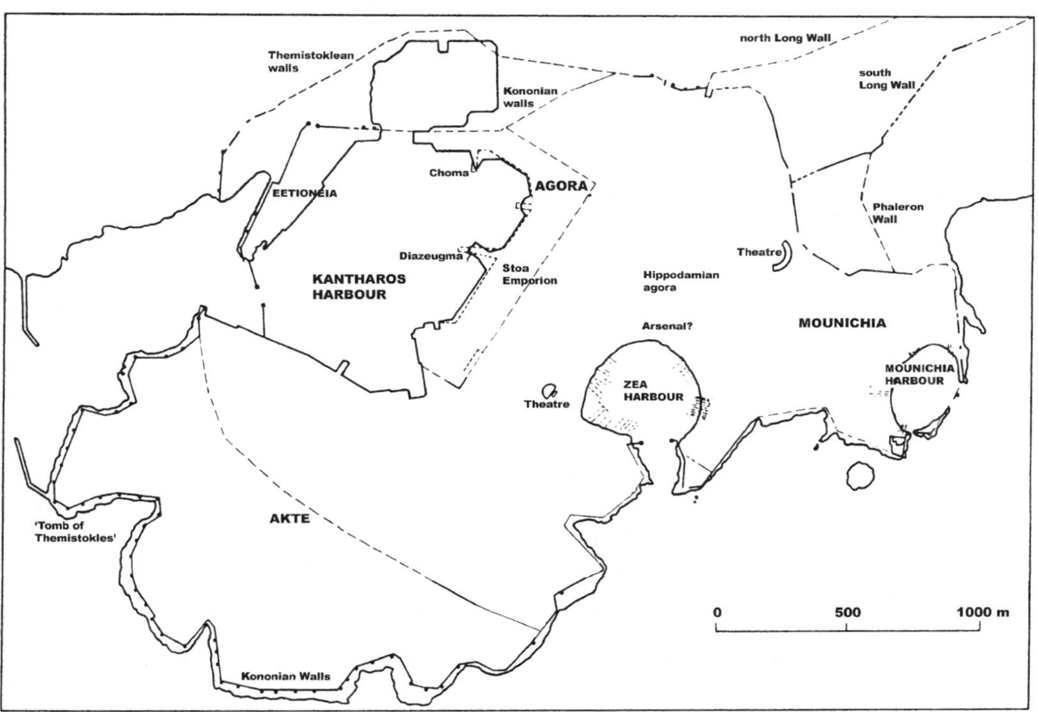

PIRAEUS: (b) detailed plan of the harbour areas of ancient Piraeus.

evidence of Roman housing. Piraeus is last mentioned during ALARIC's invasion (AD 396). DJB

See von Eickstedt, K.-V. (1991) *Beiträge zur Topographie des antiken Piräus*; Garland, R. (2001) *The Piraeus*.

 AEGEAN SEA: (a).

pirates and piracy The Homeric poems are the earliest evidence for piracy in the classical world. They display an ambivalent attitude towards pirates, particularly in the *Odyssey*. In the archaic period there was no great distinction between piracy and warfare in the MEDITERRANEAN. It was only in the 5th and 4th centuries BC that the scale of inter-state warfare increased to a point where the two could be distinguished, though they continued to be closely related. The almost constant warfare of the classical and hellenistic periods tended to encourage piracy at its margins. Greek and Latin words for pirate and BANDIT are often identical (Greek *lêistês* and *peiratês*, Latin *latro* and *praedo*; Greek *katapontistês* and Latin *pirata* are only used of seaborne robbers), but the greater mobility afforded by the use of SHIPS distinguished piracy from other forms of armed robbery.

While attacks were occasionally made on ships at sea, in many cases pirates directed their attention to the land, particularly in the AEGEAN, where the numerous ISLANDS and coastal cities provided them with ample opportunity to plunder property and seize captives for ransom, or for sale as SLAVES. In hellenistic and later literature the separation of young lovers as the result of abduction by pirates became a popular romantic plot device (e.g. Achilles Tatius, *Kleitophon and Leukippe*). There was considerable overlap between unprovoked piratical attacks and the seizure of goods and persons in reprisal for injuries of insults (Greek *sylê*). Some communities, notably the AITOLIANS, were criticized for their abuse of this customary right (e.g. POLYBIOS 4.3–6). The reputation which certain peoples, such as the Aitolians, the CRETANS or the CILICIANS acquired as pirates was, however, due in part to the use of the terms 'pirates' and 'piracy' as pejorative labels by their political opponents in order to illegitimize them. In the political rhetoric of the classical world, 'pirates' often appears to be the victors' term for the vanquished.

The suppression of piracy required the control of territory in order to deprive would-be pirates of secure bases from which to operate. This could only be achieved through close co-operation between states or the imposition of control by an imperial authority. The Athenians undertook some measures to limit piracy in the 5th and 4th centuries BC, as did the RHODIANS in the hellenistic period. They acted primarily to protect their own commercial interests, but were enthusiastically praised for their achievements by later writers. As the Romans conquered more and more of the Mediterranean region, other states began looking to them for action. The Romans launched some strikes against those held to be responsible for piracy during the 1st century BC, most notably in POMPEY the Great's campaign against the Cilicians in 67 BC. It was only after the army and navy of the emperors had secured control of the entire Mediterranean coastline, however, that piratical activity was reduced to a minimum. When the Roman empire began to fragment in the 5th century AD, piracy became widespread once more. PDeS

See Souza, P. de (1999) *Piracy in the Greco-Roman World*.

pitch see AMPHORAS; SHIPS AND SHIPBUILDING; SIEGE AND SIEGE WARFARE; WATERPROOFING; see also MUSIC; MUSICAL INSTRUMENTS; RHETORIC, ROMAN; SOUND AND ACOUSTICS.

Pithekoussai Ancient writers (STRABO, LIVY) and modern ARCHAEOLOGY agree in defining the first western Greeks as EUBOIANS, and their first western base as Pithekoussai (Ischia island, bay of Naples). The component sites investigated there by Giorgio Buchner since 1952 amount to a vast centre of production and distribution, active for half a century from c.750 BC and uniquely well connected for its time and place. Expatriate potters from Euboia and CORINTH exploited the island's clay beds for both the local and the export markets. IRON (from Elba) and the constituent elements of bronze were imported and worked – the latter to make Italian types of fibula (for Italian wives?). A few LEVANTINE residents, indicated EPIGRAPHICALLY, may have been specialist gold-workers. Pithekoussai has produced Europe's first literary allusion – to Nestor's cup – inscribed on a RHODIAN kotyle perhaps used at a *SYMPOSIUM* before it was interred c.720. While the story of Euboian Pithekoussai undoubtedly constitutes the first chapter in the history of western Greek COLONIZATION, it may also be read as the last chapter of a long story of earlier east–west exchanges, involving SARDINIA and the Levant (especially CYPRUS), that in its earlier stages was hardly Greek at all. An 8th-century Greek farmstead 12 km (7.5 miles) from the *akropolis* may mean that Pithekoussai was a surprisingly early 'real' colony (*apoikia*), with a formally organized *chôra* (territory). Or it may represent a serious attempt to attain maximum self-suffiency for a large trading settlement (*emporion*) in AGRICULTURAL circumstances that were far from ideal. DR

See Buchner, G. and Ridgway, D. (1993) *Pithekoussai I*; d'Agostino, B. and Ridgway, D., eds. (1994) *Apoikia*; Ridgway, D. (1992) *The First Western Greeks*.

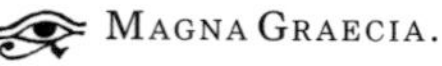 MAGNA GRAECIA.

plagues see CORSICA; EPIDEMICS; MARCUS AURELIUS; JUSTINIAN; METALLURGY; PERIKLES; PROCOPIUS; STORAGE; THIRD-CENTURY CRISIS; THUCYDIDES.

Plancia Magna Inhabitant of the city of Perge in Pamphylia, Asia Minor, in the 2nd century AD, during the reign of the emperor HADRIAN. She is known to us entirely from the numerous inscriptions found in Perge documenting her civic activities and BENEFACTIONS. Even by the standards of ÉLITE WOMEN of Roman times, she appears remarkable. Her most impressive donation is the monumental southern gate of the city in the form of a courtyard and triple ARCH faced in MARBLE and lavishly decorated with statues of GODS, HEROES and members of the imperial family. Inscriptions in Greek and Latin proclaim the work as her donation. Among the mythical city founders are statue bases inscribed 'city-founder Marcus Plancius Varus, father of Plancia Magna' and 'city-founder Gaius Plancius Varus the Pergean, brother of Plancia Magna'. This is the reverse of the normal Greco-Roman convention, where women are identified by the names of their father and brothers, and supports the view that Plancia was a very ambitious and powerful woman, as well as a wealthy one. Plancia held a number of important priesthoods in the city, served as gymnasiarch (head of the GYMNASIUM, the school for the young men of the city), and even served as *dêmiourgos*, chief MAGISTRATE of the city, after whom the year was named. LF

See Boatwright, M.T. (1991) Plancia Magna of Perge, in S. B. Pomeroy, ed., *Women's History and Ancient History* 249–72.

plants From the beginning of farming in the Neolithic period, human knowledge of the plant world may be divided into two categories: plants that are cultivated, and those found in the wild. Since the early Neolithic (9000–6000 BC in the eastern MEDITERRANEAN) the number of plants actively cultivated in any region has tended to increase, for three reasons: humans have gradually learned the necessary skills; additional uses for plants have been discovered or devised; and plants have been spread by farmers and gardeners beyond the region where they were taken into cultivation. Skills needed include gathering and planting of seed, division of roots, planting of cuttings (vines, OLIVES and others), grafting (apples, pears, cherries and others), assistance with pollination (dates, FIGS, sycamore figs) and an understanding of the seasonal behaviour of each kind so as to propagate at the best time and protect young plants when they need it. The number of different plants used in the wild may or may not tend to increase: new discoveries may supplement inherited knowledge, but some plants may cease to be used. Human food is one major application of cultivated and wild plants. There are many others, notably ANIMAL fodder, BUILDING materials, human and veterinary MEDICINE, POISONS, DRUGS, incenses, COSMETICS, fabric and DYEING.

Ancient knowledge of plants is set out most systematically by THEOPHRASTOS in *History of Plants* (usually *Enquiry into Plants* in recent work) and *Causes of Plants* (these traditional titles might be better rendered in English 'Study of Plants' and 'Physiology of Plants'), compiled just before 300 BC. He and his assistants dealt both with wild plants and with cultivated kinds. Their informants included the 'root-cutters' (*rhizotomoi*), the traditional experts in Greece on the medicinal uses of wild plants. Although classification was a crucial step in Theophrastos' work, he attempted no total classification comparable to that of modern botanical taxonomy. Instead, in these texts, plants are placed in multiple sets according to various criteria, anatomical, physiological and pharmacological. The looser structure of PLINY THE ELDER's survey of plants in the *Natural History*, compiled in the 60s AD, is based largely on the uses of plants to humanity. Pliny draws from Theophrastos (largely unacknowledged) and from many authorities now lost. Other systematic surveys of plants by ancient authors are much more limited in their aims, dealing either with farming and gardening (notably works by VARRO, COLUMELLA and Gargilius Martialis) or with the identification and use of medicinal plants (works by Dioskourides and Pseudo-Apuleius). AD

See Pliny, *Natural History*, vols. 4–6 trs. H. Rackham and W. H. S. Jones (1945–51); vol. 7, 2nd edn with index by A. C. Andrews (1980); Theophrastus, *Enquiry into Plants*, 2 vols., trs. A. Hort (1916–26); *De causis plantarum*, 3 vols., trs. B. Einarson and G. K. K. Link (1976–90); Raven, J. E. (2000) *Plants and Plant Lore in Ancient Greece*; White, K. D. (1970) *Roman Farming*; Zohary, D. and Hopf, M. (1993) *Domestication of Plants in the Old World*.

Planudes, Maximus see *GREEK ANTHOLOGY*; SCHOLARSHIP, BYZANTINE.

plaster and plastering The term 'plaster' is applied generically to hard materials used (1) to provide a protective coating on ARCHITECTURAL surfaces, (2) to make moulds and casts. In ancient Egypt the availability of gypsum and the shortage of limestone for LIME-BURNING meant that both functions were performed by gypsum-plaster. But this material, which sets quickly and takes sharp impressions, is best suited to moulding; and in Greece and Italy the preferred material for architectural surfacing was the less friable and more damp-resistant plaster based on lime. Plastering was increasingly exploited for decorative purposes, giving buildings of brick and other low-prestige materials the appearance of MARBLE. In interior decoration it provided a foundation for mural painting. By the late hellenistic period preparing this foundation had become a fine art, for which VITRUVIUS gives elaborate prescriptions, with up to seven coats of diminishing thickness, each applied before its predecessor was dry. In the lower coats the lime was mixed with sand, in the upper coats with finer materials, such as powdered marble, which produced the gleaming whiteness favoured at the time. The purpose of the multiple layers was to create a homogeneous mass which retained its moisture long enough to allow painting in the fresco technique. The presence of the sand and marble powder helped the plaster to 'breathe', thus releasing the lime-impregnated water which reacted with carbon dioxide in the air to form the crystalline web of calcium carbonate which bound the pigments to the wall. RJL

Plataea, battle of Town in Boiotia, and site of a Greek victory over a PERSIAN army in 479 BC. After the Persian defeat at SALAMIS, their general Mardonius and his army wintered in THESSALY. In the spring they advanced to Athens, in preparation for an invasion of the PELOPONNESE. When, in the high summer, the Greek forces advanced from the Peloponnese, Mardonius retired to BOIOTIA in order not to be trapped in ATTICA. HERODOTOS gives the Greek numbers as 38,700 heavily armed troops and 69,500 auxiliaries, and the Persian as 350,000 – including 50,000 Greeks. The figures for the Persian side are generally reckoned to be too great. The two armies met in the territory of Plataea, and faced each other for 11 days without a full engagement before the Greek forces moved to avoid Persian CAVALRY raids. Mardonius took this as an opportunity to attack, and engaged the Spartan and Tegean contingents. The Athenians were attacked at the same time by Greeks fighting for Mardonius. After a fierce struggle, the Persians were heavily defeated and Mardonius killed. Herodotos' account of the battle emphasizes rivalries between the Greek *poleis* fighting against the Persians; it also introduces references to battles fought in the same area in the 'heroic age', against the Herakleidai and the Amazons. (see also EPHOROS). HB

See Herodotos 9.25–85.

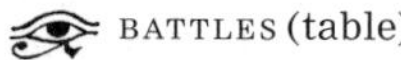 BATTLES (table).

Plato 427–347 BC Greek PHILOSOPHER. Plato was born in Athens to an aristocratic family. He had two brothers, Adeimantos and Glaukon, and one sister, Potone. His parents were Ariston and Periktione, whose political sympathies lay with the ARISTOCRACY. When Plato's father died, however, his mother took as husband a man called Pyrilampes, a democrat. As a boy, Plato was presumably exposed to both OLIGARCHIC and DEMOCRATIC influences. The PELOPONNESIAN WAR (431–404), fought between Athens and SPARTA (a democracy and oligarchy respectively) and their various allies, overshadowed his youth and clearly left a lasting impression on him. He witnessed the democracy's mismanagement of Athenian affairs until 411, when it was replaced briefly by an oligarchy, and then saw the restored democracy lose the war against Sparta. Convinced of a democracy's inability to govern effectively, he turned with optimism to the oligarchs who took control in 404. Two of these oligarchs, Charmides and Kritias, were uncles of Plato. In the *Seventh Letter* Plato tells us that he was asked to join them but that when he saw these oligarchs (the THIRTY Tyrants, as they became known) behave even worse than the democrats he turned aside from practical politics. The Thirty slaughtered their former opponents, confiscated their property and, significantly for Plato, attempted to implicate the philosopher SOCRATES in their misdeeds. Plato had by this time become greatly impressed by the teachings of Socrates. When he saw the restored democracy put Socrates to death in 399, he seems to have become totally disillusioned with the prospect of either oligarchs or democrats ruling a state successfully. He began to form the conviction that states could not be governed properly until philosophers became rulers or rulers became philosophers.

What he did immediately after Socrates' death is not clear. The tradition contains stories about stays in MEGARA and further afield in Egypt. Later, and less certain, are stories about visits to PHOENICIA and PERSIA. It is quite likely that his earliest dialogues were written in the period just after Socrates' death. He made his first trip to Italy in 387, where he met the PYTHAGOREAN Archytas and was greatly influenced by his beliefs. He moved on to SYRACUSE in SICILY, to the court of the TYRANT DIONYSIOS I. It is said that Plato annoyed the tyrant with his views on the nature of ruling, with the result that Dionysios had him sold into SLAVERY. He is said to have been ransomed at AIGINA before returning to Athens. Plato makes no mention of any of this in any of his letters. Back in Athens, Plato founded his school, the ACADEMY, and remained teaching there for the next 20 years. The dream of the philosopher-ruler, though, still drove him, and he returned to Syracuse in 368, on the death of Dionysios I, in an attempt to turn the young Dionysios II into such a ruler. Dionysios, however, did not take to philosophy and Plato returned to Athens. Four years later he made a final visit to Syracuse at the prompting of Dionysios himself, who it seems had now begun to take philosophy seriously; Plato reluctantly returned because he still hoped to create a philosopher-ruler. However, the project failed again, either because of the rigour of the instruction imposed by Plato on the young man or because of Plato's friendship with political exiles from Syracuse. Plato, it seems, had difficulty in getting back to Athens, since he was kept a virtual prisoner by Dionysios. He finally made it back to the Academy in 360 and never left Athens again. He died in 347 and was buried in the grounds of the Academy.

Plato presents his philosophy in dialogue form. The dialogues, especially the early and middle ones, show Socrates engaged in disputation with various opponents. Often the focus seems to be on the method of argumentation rather than upon the desire to produce dogmatic views. Plato himself does not appear in any of the dialogues but uses Socrates as his mouthpiece, leaving us with the 'Socratic problem' of where the philosophy of the historical Socrates ends and Plato's begins. The views presented in the dialogues centre on the theory of Forms. This theory seems to have developed from a number of influences. Chief among them was Socrates, who is depicted in Plato's early dialogues as seeking objective general definitions of various terms such as piety (see *Euthyphro*), courage (*Laches*) or friendship (*Lysis*). Plato was clearly interested in the idea that general objective KNOWLEDGE existed somewhere, independent and unchanging. This was the knowledge that philosopher-rulers needed if they were to govern successfully. But where did it exist? Plato was searching for a METAPHYSIC that gave a home to such entities or Forms, as he would later call them. Plato began to believe in a reality that contained all that we perceive in this sensible world but, unlike this world, contained them in their archetypal state, perfect and unchanging. The world of sense that we inhabit only exists through participation in physical, moral and MATHEMATICAL Forms. The PYTHAGOREANS also influenced Plato with their belief in the transmigration of SOULS. He began to see the soul as something which originally belonged to the same metaphysical level as the Forms but had become trapped in the body in the sensible world.

In the dialogue *Parmenides*, however, Plato presents a severe criticism of the theory of Forms, questioning its ability to explain satisfactorily the content of the world of the senses. The theory, however, seems not to have been rejected in the dialogues written after *Parmenides*. There is also the view that the philosophy presented in the dialogues does not contain Plato's true beliefs at all, but rather shows methods of philosophizing. ARISTOTLE, and other pupils of the Academy, support this view when they mention a highly mathematical philosophy that was taught in the Academy, but never written down lest it get into the wrong hands.

Plato was perhaps the greatest philosopher of all time. He has excited both admiration and hostility. No one could deny that his ideas greatly shaped the Western philosophical tradition, whether one agrees with A. N. Whitehead, who considered that all Western philosophy was simply footnotes to Plato, or with Nietzsche, who insisted that Plato had perverted the entire development of Western philosophy. (see also DIALECTIC; PLATONISM) KM

See Cooper, J., ed. (1997) *Plato, Complete Works*; Hare, R. M. (1982) *Plato*; Jackson, R. (2001) *Plato*; Kraut, R., ed. (1992) *The Cambridge Companion to Plato*.

Platonism The term Platonism refers to the system of ideas developed by PLATO. Our chief source for them is the dialogues written by Plato himself. At the heart of his PHILOSOPHY is the theory of Forms. Plato refers to the Forms as perfect, unchanging archetypes of all that is present in the sensible world around us. Everything in this world, physical, moral or MATHEMATICAL, has a perfect and permanent Form, which exists at a higher METAPHYSICAL level. Our sensible world subsists only through participation in these Forms, and as a result we exist on a lower level of existence and everything here is subject to TIME and mortality. Only the SOULS of human beings, if properly trained, have the capacity to transcend this world and regain the metaphysical level of the Forms. Platonism is not a neatly packaged set of philosophical doctrines. The theory of Forms is not laid out systematically in any of the dialogues, and Plato himself subjects it to severe criticism, but ultimately he does not appear to reject it. Some critics think the philosophical tenets in the dialogues do not represent Plato's most developed philosophical views, which they argue are to be found in the 'unwritten teaching' confined to Plato's school, the ACADEMY.

Platonism has had a profound influence on the subsequent development of Western philosophy. Many of the central themes in the Western philosophical tradition – the struggle between reason and the appetites, the need for the soul to purify itself of the BODY and the belief in a permanent, non-corporeal, destination for the purified soul – can be found in Plato's dialogues. The word 'platonic' itself, meaning non-sexual (describing love), has achieved common currency. (see also NEOPLATONISM) KM

Plautus (Titus Maccius Plautus) fl. c.195–184 BC Comic playwright. Plautus remains for us a somewhat mysterious figure: even the form of his name is uncertain, and the version conventionally accepted may have originated as a nickname (Maccius Plautus means something like 'Flat-Foot of the Clowns'). The few BIOGRAPHICAL details retailed by ancient sources are suspiciously reminiscent of the playwright's own comic plots, and should probably be dismissed as fiction.

Plautus was a prolific and successful author. 21 plays survive, but many more were attributed to him in antiquity. (AULUS GELLIUS tells us that his name was attached to as many as 130 COMEDIES, but that the authenticity of most of these was disputed.) Among the most highly regarded and widely read (or, occasionally, performed) in modern times are the *Pseudolus*, *The Braggart Soldier* (*Miles gloriosus*), *The Brothers Menaechmus* (*Menaechmi*, the model for SHAKESPEARE's *Comedy of Errors*) and *Amphitruo* (exceptionally among Plautus' plays, a mythological burlesque on the conception of the hero HERCULES).

Most – if not all – of the surviving plays are loose adaptations of Greek originals, and employ the stereotyped plots and characters typical of New COMEDY. Plautus' most memorable characters are his clever, unscrupulous SLAVES (Pseudolus in the play of the same name, and Palaestrio in the *Braggart Soldier*, are characteristic examples). Their conventional role is to aid the youthful hero in winning his beloved (usually a courtesan, who sometimes turns out to be freeborn), while gleefully outwitting the young man's stingy old father and/or the girl's pimp. The slave character often acts as a kind of stand-in for the playwright, directing the action of the play from within, and will frequently draw attention to this role by means of direct address to the audience.

Plautus' plots are, in general, somewhat loosely constructed, and narrative logic is often sacrificed for the sake of immediate effect. Humour is, however, achieved on many levels, from broad knockabout to sophisticated verbal and metatheatrical play. Particularly characteristic of Plautine comedy are verbal effects such as puns, neologisms and *double entendres*, and the playfully incongruous intrusion of Italian–Roman elements into the supposedly Greek setting of the plays. Common, too, are asides addressed to the audience and temporary rupture of the dramatic illusion (references, for instance, to costumes and role-playing, or to the ACTORS as actors). Plautus' verbal and metrical virtuosity is displayed above all in the SONGS (*cantica*) which punctuate and diversify the dramatic action.

The characteristic mood of Plautine comedy might best be summed up as a temporary suspension or inversion of the values ordinarily prevalent in Roman society. Patriarchal authority is regularly overthrown; youth, love and – above all – the labyrinthine deceits of the cunning slave are, for once, triumphant. MG

See Nixon, P. (1916–38) *Plautus*, 5 vols., text and trs.; Anderson, W. S. (1993) *Barbarian Play*; Moore, T. J. (1998) *The Theater of Plautus*.

plebeians A segment of Roman society, in contrast to PATRICIANS. The word is related to PLEBS, often used to describe the lower classes, but the plebeians had their own ARISTOCRACY that became part of the ruling ÉLITE after a series of struggles in the 5th to 3rd centuries BC. Early in the REPUBLIC, the poorer segments of Roman society formed a plebeian class that created an ASSEMBLY and officials (*concilium plebis*, TRIBUNES, AEDILES), claimed the right to pass legislation (plebiscites), established an official archive and worshipped their own triad (Liber, Libera, CERES), like the patricians (JUPITER, JUNO, MINERVA). In consequence, two political structures co-existed disharmoniously. Although the early CONSULS included non-patricians, these were probably clients who had not yet joined the plebeians. As patricians gradually eliminated them from political influence, they became plebeians and began to agitate for political rights, employing secession as a tactic. In one sense, the development of Rome's complex political structure was an amalgamation of two entities, a little at a time, but plebeians never gained the right to hold all the ancient PRIESTHOODS. The initial conflict involved the treatment of debtors. Soon, plebeians agitated for the codification of law, resulting in the TWELVE TABLES in 449 BC. The Licinian-Sextian legislation of 367 BC restored the consulship, which had given way to the consular tribunate, and made plebeians eligible to hold it. The final stage occurred in 287 when the DICTATOR Quintus Hortensius mandated that plebiscites were binding on the entire population. JV

See Cornell, T. J. (1995) *The Beginnings of Rome*.

plebs The urban plebs was the subset of the PLEBEIAN order who lived in the city of Rome. Because of this, plebeians played a significant part in politics and were the recipients of special BENEFACTIONS and privileges. On the other hand, many of them were chronically underemployed, ill-housed, and endured squalid living conditions. When VOTING, the urban plebs was scattered by wealth among the centuries of the *comitia centuriata*, but in the *concilia plebis* and *comitia tributa* it was grouped into four urban tribes. Because casting a vote was contingent on being physically present at Rome, the urban plebs had greater opportunity to participate in ELECTIONS than its rural counterparts. The amount of political power plebeians exercised through voting is disputed, but their importance was magnified by their symbolic identity as representatives of all Roman citizens, a role which had clearly emerged by the late REPUBLIC. At public events and spectacles, the applause, shouts and jeers of the urban plebs were closely scrutinized by politicians like CICERO, who famously stated that 'the opinion and feeling of the Roman people regarding public matters can be most plainly expressed at *contiones*, ASSEMBLIES, and at GAMES and GLADIATOR shows' (*pro Sestio* 106). In turn, the urban plebs received numerous benefactions, ranging from distributions of foodstuffs, most notably the monthly grain dole, to being plied with a series of ever more elaborate and impressive public entertainments. In the early empire the formal political power of the plebs was reduced, but the acclamations of the urban plebs at public events became even more important as a source of legitimacy for the EMPEROR. The plebs continued in this role until Rome's population declined and, more significantly, the emperor left the city, though the urban populace of new imperial capitals such as CONSTANTINOPLE then assumed similar roles. GSA

See Aldrete, G. (1999) *Gestures and Acclamations in Ancient Rome*; Brunt, P.A. (1966) The Roman mob, *P&P* 35: 3–27; Malkin, I. and Rubinsohn, Z.W., eds. (1995) *Leaders and Masses in the Roman World*; Millar, F. (1998) *The Crowd in Rome in the Late Republic*; Yavetz, Z. (1988) *Plebs and Princeps.*

Pleistoanax King of SPARTA, from the Agiad family (r.459–408/7 BC). He acceded, initially as a minor, upon the death of his father's cousin Pleistarchos, and reigned in all for 50 years. He was in exile, however, for 18 of those, being prosecuted in 445 for cutting short an invasion of Attica (Thucydides 1.114, 2.21, 5.16); it was alleged that PERIKLES bribed him. He returned in 427/6 with the support of the Delphic oracle (again amid accusations of bribery), remaining king until his death. He was thus, following the death of ARCHIDAMOS II, the senior king during much of the PELOPONNESIAN WAR. True to his earlier conciliatory policy towards Athens, he was the author of the peace of NIKIAS (421). AGIS II, however, became the more prominent commander after his victory at Mantineia (418). DGJS

Pliny the Elder (Gaius Plinius Secundus) AD 23/4–79 Roman encyclopedist and natural historian. Born in northern Italy and raised in an EQUESTRIAN family, he was probably educated in Rome. After completing his military service in 57 or 58, he avoided the public spotlight for the next ten years or so, perhaps because of the political climate under the emperor NERO. Pliny's writing career took off during this time. Under the Flavians, Pliny's fortunes substantially improved and he was appointed fleet commander at Misenum. On 24 August AD 79, while attempting to rescue victims from the eruption of Mt Vesuvius, he was overwhelmed by intense volcanic fumes. A vivid letter written by his nephew PLINY THE YOUNGER (*Letters* 6.16) describes how his uncle persisted in recording the natural phenomenon even until his final moments.

Pliny's surviving work, an ENCYCLOPEDIA called *Historia naturalis* (*Natural History*) represents only a small portion of his total output. His nephew records (*Letters* 3.5) how his uncle used all spare time for research, working by lamplight in the evenings and even while sunning himself during the summer. Pliny's remarkable energies resulted in numerous books on a wide range of topics including Roman history, RHETORIC, linguistics and the use of javelins on horseback. The famous encyclopedia, drawn on heavily by medieval scholars such as Solinus and Bede, provides a wealth of information about Roman life in the 1st century AD. Pliny himself alleges that he amassed 20,000 facts by consulting 2,000 volumes written by 100 authors. In fact he under-represents his efforts, since nearly 500 authors are cited by name. Pliny carries on a well-established hellenistic tradition of handbook writing (e.g. POSIDONIUS and VARRO) despite his claim that he is embarking on an entirely new kind of project. His originality lies in the breadth of material researched, including ASTRONOMY, GEOGRAPHY, zoology, botany, MEDICINE, pharmacy, CHEMISTRY, minerals and metals, ART and ARCHITECTURE.

Pliny offers little distinction between explanations that are based on folklore, MYTH and rational science; descriptions based on his own personal experience seem more credible. For example, the account of lightning and thunder (2.135–46) provides many facts that Pliny himself may have observed (e.g. that thunder occurs less frequently in the winter, and that lightning is visible before thunder is heard) and even more details that seem implausible (e.g. that lightning does not strike laurel bushes, and that a person dies from a lightning strike only when turned around by the force). The comprehensive nature of Pliny's work has led to modern charges that the natural historian approached his work with an uncritical and unscientific mind. Pliny's interest in describing marvellous and unusual subjects (e.g. the one-legged hopping Monocoli, 7.23, or the dolphin that swam with men on its back, 9.26) speaks to his aim of creating a work that will attract a large audience. It is not his aim to create a carefully constructed, theoretical explanation of the world. The importance of his contribution to the development of ancient SCIENCE is his ability to observe, record and disseminate his findings. TJA

See Beagon, M. (1992) *Roman Nature: the thought of Pliny the Elder*; French, R. (1994) *Ancient Natural History*; Healy, J. (1999) *Pliny the Elder on Science and Technology*; (1991) *Pliny the Elder, Natural History: a selection.*

Pliny the Younger (Gaius Plinius Caecilius Secundus) c.AD 61/2–c.113 Orator and Roman SENATOR whose career spanned the reigns of DOMITIAN (81–96), Nerva (96–8) and TRAJAN (98–117). His published correspondence provides an important source for the political and social values of imperial Rome.

Born in Comum, Pliny was one of numerous senators who came from the municipal ARISTOCRACY of northern Italy and the western PROVINCES during this period. His parents died when he was young, but he was adopted by PLINY THE ELDER, his maternal uncle, an EQUESTRIAN. The first of his family to enter the senate, Pliny pursued a career in LAW and administration rather than in military affairs. After serving as PRAETOR (in 93), prefect of the military treasury (94–6), and prefect of the treasury of SATURN (the public treasury, c.98–100), he became suffect CONSUL on 1 September 100. He then served as curator of the TIBER and the sewers of the city of Rome (c.104–c.107) and was also an augur. His final and probably most significant post was as a special imperial governor of the province of Bithynia and Pontus, from 111 apparently until his death in 113. A leading member of the Roman bar, Pliny tried civil cases, in particular in the centumviral court, which heard cases involving testamentary law. He also took part in public trials in the senate, assisting in the successful prosecution of several Roman officials accused of corrupt administration in the provinces, and defending several others accused of the same offence.

Pliny's published correspondence consists of nine books of letters to various friends, family members, and members of upper class Roman society, as well as a tenth book of correspondence exchanged with the emperor Trajan. The correspondence in the nine books deals with events between the death of Domitian in 96 until some time around 108 or 109. The letters in the nine books are carefully wrought literary pieces in which Pliny presents a portrait of himself in the many activities, both political and social, that were central to a Roman senator's sense of identity. Pliny's letters thus provide critical evidence for such issues as the situation of Roman aristocratic WOMEN, the relationships between upper class Romans and their slaves and freedmen, the appropriate uses of wealth by upper class Romans, and the place of literature and literary studies in upper class life. In addition, Pliny's letters also provide crucial information for Roman economic history. The letters offer relatively little information about key political developments under Trajan, but Pliny does comment on his own conduct under Domitian, which he was at pains to justify. For Pliny, as for TACITUS (*Agricola* 4), the senate's participation in the execution (in 93) of a group of senators known for their adherence to STOIC PHILOSOPHY represented an outrageous example of Domitian's tyranny. Pliny sought to demonstrate that he remained a loyal friend of these Stoic senators both under Domitian, when such friendship proved dangerous, and after Domitian's death, when Pliny's refusal to bow to efforts to forget the injustices of the previous regime could have threatened his own career.

The majority of the letters in the tenth book of Pliny's correspondence were exchanged when Pliny was governor of Bithynia–Pontus, and this book is primarily significant for the light it sheds on Roman provincial administration. Bithynia–Pontus was a troubled province when Pliny took it over with special instructions to investigate the finances of the cities. In carrying out this assignment, he frequently consulted the emperor about matters of administrative policy. Of particular interest is an exchange of letters (10.96–7) occasioned by Pliny's investigation of CHRISTIANS.

Pliny devoted much of his time to literary activities, reading works written by friends, writing poetry and revising his own speeches for publication. One such speech was the one he delivered in the senate against a fellow senator, Publicius Certus, whom he believed to have acted unjustly in the prosecution of the Stoic senators in 93. Pliny's only surviving speech is his PANEGYRIC of the emperor Trajan, which Pliny delivered upon assuming the consulship. It is significant because it recounts what Pliny, and presumably other senators, saw as the essential virtues of a good emperor. DPK

See Fantham, E. (1996) *Roman Literary Culture*; Sherwin-White, A. N. (1985) *The Letters of Pliny*.

Plotinus AD 205–70 Greek PHILOSOPHER, regarded as the founder of NEOPLATONISM. He was born at Lykopolis (Assiut) in Upper Egypt. Although his name is Roman, his language was Greek. Porphyry, his most famous pupil, tells us that Plotinus 'seemed ashamed of being in the body. As a result of this state of mind he could never bear to talk about his race or his parents or his native country' (*Life of Plotinus* 1).

What we know about Plotinus comes mainly from a short biography by Porphyry. Plotinus' pursuit of PHILOSOPHY first took him to ALEXANDRIA, where he studied under Ammonius Saccas. After an abortive attempt to study eastern philosophy, he settled in Rome at the age of 40 and set up a school. Here he lived and taught until shortly before his death. His writings were collected and arranged by Porphyry: a total of 54 treatises divided into six groups of nine, hence the title *Enneads* (*Nines*).

Although Plotinus claimed to be a PLATONIST pure and simple, the *Enneads* betray strong ARISTOTELIAN and STOIC influences. They teach us that everything emanates from the One, the highest principle in the universe. From the One comes Nous (Intellect) and then in turn World Soul and individual SOULS, which enter BODIES in the material world. These souls have freely descended into bodies, attracted by carnal pleasures. As a mystic, Plotinus believed that the soul, if it obeyed reason and ignored bodily desires, could reascend the ladder of existence and ultimately experience reunification with the One, even while in the body. Porphyry notes that Plotinus experienced this reintegration on at least four occasions. His PAGAN METAPHYSIC was tremendously influential in the development of CHRISTIAN philosophy and the whole notion of salvation. KM

See Armstrong, A. H. (1966–89) *Plotinus*: *The Enneads*, 7 vols.; Gerson, L., ed. (1996) *The Cambridge Companion to Plotinus*; O'Meara, D. (1993) *Plotinus*.

plumbing Greek water-pipes were mainly of terracotta, with flanged joints sealed with mortar; larger, long-distance pipelines of STONE blocks were built in a similar way. Metal pipes were used for the hellenistic inverted siphon at PERGAMON. These are largely public systems; domestic plumbing was minimal.

Although in the Roman period terracotta pipelines remained in widespread use throughout the East, domestic plumbing increasingly used pipes made of LEAD (*plumbum*, hence our 'plumbing') from the 1st century BC. Pipes were made by pouring lead into a shallow mould to create a sheet. This was wrapped around a wooden core and the joint soldered. The core was then removed, giving the pipe a lightly

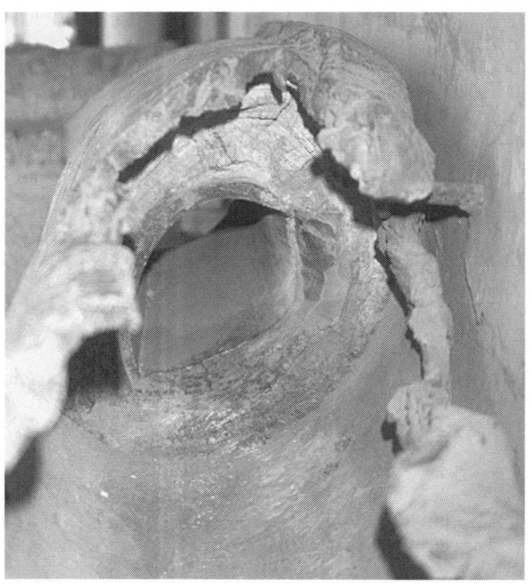

PLUMBING: the thick build-up of lime-scale on the inside of this Roman lead pipe, seen in cross-section, may have protected its users from the worst effects of lead poisoning!

ovoid section with the joint at the top. VITRUVIUS (10.6) and FRONTINUS give details of common sizes used at Rome, with standard perimeter measurements or cross-sectional areas. Excavated examples, however, rarely conform to these. Names stamped on numerous pipes from Rome and its environs mainly record the recipients of the water, but sometimes the plumber or water officials. Experiments have shown that Roman pipes could withstand pressures of up to 20 atmospheres before bursting. The outlet pipes and stopcocks of reservoir cisterns at Rusicade (Algeria) operated under a static water head of 11 m (36 ft). Taps were usually bronze (occasionally MARBLE), similar to modern stopcocks but without the screw thread; they are probably an invention of the 2nd or 1st century BC. (see also FOUNTAINS AND FOUNTAIN HOUSES; TOILETS; WATER SUPPLY) AIW

See Bruun, C. (1991) *The Water Supply of Ancient Rome.*

Plutarch C.AD 45–120 Plutarch spent most of his life in the small town of Chaironeia, where his family was well established. He had also close ties with Athens, where he studied RHETORIC and PHILOSOPHY and later acquired citizen rights, and with DELPHI, where he held various offices including a PRIESTHOOD. Like many upper class Greeks, he travelled to ASIA Minor, Egypt and Italy. Connected with Greek notables and Roman CONSULS and governors, and honoured by the EMPERORS TRAJAN and HADRIAN, he was granted ROMAN CITIZENSHIP with equestrian status. Widely read, he had broad interests and wrote for an ÉLITE thoroughly conversant with Hellenic culture.

The so-called Lamprias catalogue of his works, probably dating from the 3rd or 4th century AD, includes 227 titles. What survives is impressive: 48 *Lives* and over 70 works usually referred to by their Latin title *Moralia*, 'moral (writings)', a name both accurate (since Plutarch's influence rested largely on his popular ETHICAL works) and misleading (it does not convey the extraordinary diversity of the corpus).

As a BIOGRAPHER, Plutarch dealt almost exclusively with statesmen and GENERALS. Before the *Parallel Lives*, he wrote isolated biographies such as *Aratos*, expressly composed for the instruction of the subject's descendants, and *Artaxerxes*, the only Plutarchean life devoted to a BARBARIAN ruler. Plutarch also inaugurated the *Lives of the Caesars*, a series of imperial biographies running from AUGUSTUS to Vitellius, of which only *Galba* and *Otho* survive. The 46 *Parallel Lives*, written between C.AD 96 and his death, remain his greatest achievement. Each pair matches a Greek man with a Roman (in one case, two Spartans and two Roman brothers). Plutarch's 'noble Grecians' are mostly Athenian (10 out of 23) and belong for the most part (15 examples) to the classical period, from the PERSIAN WARS to the death of ALEXANDER. Excepting the two mythical kings, ROMULUS and NUMA, all his Romans belong to the Republican period, with a preponderance towards the late REPUBLIC from the GRACCHI to MARK ANTONY (13 examples). Comparison between Greeks and Romans was already to be found in NEPOS, VARRO and VALERIUS MAXIMUS. Some pairs, such as *Alexander–Caesar* and *Demosthenes–Cicero*, seem to be traditional. Most were invented by Plutarch on the basis of similarities in external circumstances (Romulus founded Rome, Theseus created Athens as a unified city-state), character (PERIKLES and Fabius both exemplified a dignified self-control) or abilities (SERTORIUS and the SUCCESSOR Eumenes were both commanders of superior craft). Chronology is usually discarded: *Philopoimen–Flaminius* is the only pair of contemporaries.

Plutarch's comparative method is mostly visible in the *synkrisis* (systematic comparison) that concludes most of the pairs with arguments in favour of the two subjects in turn. It implicitly permeates the whole narrative as well. This is not to be explained by Plutarch's political agenda, as an attempt to promote a better understanding between the conquerors and the conquered (by demonstrating to the Romans that the Greeks were able statesmen and warriors, and to the Greeks that the Romans were civilized). Rather, he has a moral and artistic purpose: the juxtaposition helps to illustrate the universal validity of moral laws and keeps the reader alert. In these cradle-to-grave accounts, chronological considerations are often subordinated to thematic, since the biographer, as opposed to the 'pragmatic' historian, is only interested in the deeds and words of his heroes as evidence for their psychological dispositions and moral qualities. For the *Lives*, as paradigms of virtue or – exceptionally – cautionary tales about vices, are intended to contribute to the moral improvement of the readers by exploring ethical truths and teaching them how to become 'more zealous spectators and imitators of better lives' (*Demetrios* 1.6). This explains why the narrator systematically plays down the weaknesses of his subjects and imposes on them the same moral assumptions, a denial of history that may account for the lasting popularity of the *Lives* and the homogeneous 'classical antiquity' they constructed.

The *Moralia* include example of many literary genres and topics. There are sophistic declamations on historical or moral themes, which weigh the role of fortune and virtue in Alexander's conquests or Rome's universal empire, or compare women's virtue to that of men. There are *Problems* or *Questions* on philosophical, antiquarian or scientific topics, *Table Talks* adapting the genre of the questions to a *symposiac* setting, *Advices* on health, politics or conjugal life, *Consolations* for the death of a beloved child, collections of exemplary deeds and sayings, and of course treatises and dialogues. The treatises sometimes address an anonymous interlocutor. When the addressee is named, the topic is often chosen aptly: *On Exile* is dedicated to an exile, *On Brotherly Love* to two brothers. They deal with philosophy: to elucidate some problematic passage of Plato, as in *The Generation of the Soul in the Timaeus*, to vigorously polemicize against the Epicurean Kolotes, or to convict the Stoics of *Self-contradictions*. They deal with ethics (*On Tranquillity of Mind*, *Harmful Scrupulousness*), religion (*On Isis and Osiris*), education (*On Reading the Poets*) and literary criticism (*The Malice of Herodotos*). The dialogues depart from their Platonic model in many ways: in their diversity of topics, in their chronological setting (the archaic age for the *Banquet of the Seven Sages*, mythical times for the *Gryllos*), or in combining philosophical discussion with the narrative of a love affair (*A Book of Love*) or historical event (*Socrates' Sign*). They also privilege long speeches, and give some place to their author as participant or even principal speaker.

However, there is an essential unity between the *Moralia* and the *Lives*, due to the language and even more to the persona of their author. The language is rich in images, examples, anecdotes and quotations, yet free from classicizing mannerisms. The person is rather complex: a declared Platonist, yet humane and tolerant; a believer, who nevertheless attempts to reconcile religion and reason by reading myths allegorically and attributing symbolic value to ritual; a Roman citizen who is also a Greek, viscerally attached to his city-state. SS

See Duff, T. (1999) *Plutarch's Lives*; Jones, C. P. (1971) *Plutarch and Rome*; Pelling, C. (2002) *Plutarch and History*; Russell, D. A. (2002) *Plutarch*.

Pnyx see assemblies, Greek; manufacturing, Greek.

poetesses With the exception of Sappho, poetesses in the ancient world are, in general, poorly known: only some names and a very small number of fragments survive. From the Greek world, the tradition about Corinna of Tanagra records her criticism of Myrtis, a contemporary of Pindar, for her attempt, as a woman, to compete with him, but no fragments of Myrtis' work are extant. Only some few verses of Telesilla of Argos have survived, and we possess some fragments by Praxilla of Sikyon of a hymn to Adonis, a possible dithyramb and some sympotic poems. Perhaps all of them are parodies. A few fragments of Erinna are also extant.

In the Roman world, the number of known poetesses is even smaller and includes two female poets called Sulpicia. One was a contemporary of Tibullus (1st century BC), the other of Martial (1st century AD). Six poems by the earlier Sulpicia are preserved within the *Corpus Tibullianum*. They are short and beautiful love poems addressed to her lover Cerinthus. Given the exceptionality of a woman writer, many scholars have suspected an impersonation, perhaps by a young Tibullus or another poet of his circle. In the 4th century AD, Faltonia Betitia Proba wrote Christian poetry; her *Cento*, a pastiche of verses from Virgil, is extant. RBC

See Churchill, L. J. (2002) *Women Writing in Latin*; Lightman, M. (2000) *Biographical Dictionary of Ancient Greek and Roman Women*; Rayor, D. J. (1991) *Sappho's Lyre: archaic lyric and women poets of ancient Greece*.

 lyric poetry.

poetry

Greek poetry, which itself borrowed from other early Mediterranean and Indo-European traditions, developed and shaped for the Greco-Roman world a number of important literary genres composed and often performed in verse: epic; various genres of lyric poetry designed to be sung on a great variety of occasions by individual voices or choral groups; drama, including tragedy, satyr play, and Old Comedy and New Comedy; and epigram, which flourished above all in the hellenistic period. The evolution of each genre is variously conditioned by the social and geographical context to which the poems responded, the occasions on which they were performed, the nature of literary patronage, the choice of metre, and the influence of previous poetry in a particular genre.

Our earliest preserved poems, the epics of 'Homer' and Hesiod, probably date from around the late 8th–early 7th centuries BC. The Homeric poems may have taken a written form close to what has come down to us as late as the 6th century in Athens. Although both later epic (Homeric hymns and Hesiod) and archaic lyric bear the marks of oral tradition, the *Iliad* and the *Odyssey* alone seem to have been composed largely within it. The Homeric poems aimed at a panhellenic audience and drew on Greek myths about gods and heroes that date back as early as the Mycenaean period on the Greek mainland. The preserved tradition seems to have crystallized in Asia Minor or on islands in the vicinity. We remain uncertain as to the audience for which these hexameter poems were composed and sung or chanted to the accompaniment of a lyre. Within the Homeric poems themselves, bards sing relatively short poems for aristocratic audiences. Poems on the scale of the *Iliad* and *Odyssey*, however, may have been composed for elaborate public festivals.

The somewhat later Epic Cycle poems, for which we have only fragmentary evidence, touched on Theban myths and cosmological themes, but above all developed narratives preceding and following the Trojan war that were not addressed in the two great Homeric poems. Other lost 5th-century post-Cyclic epics offered a range of mythical narratives drawn from, for example, Thebes (Antimachos' *Thebais*), the labours of Herakles (Panyassis' *Herakleia*) or historical narratives such as Choirilos of Samos' *Persika*. Later panegyrical epics celebrated the achievements of Alexander the Great and his

Successors. The *Homeric Hymns*, short, largely archaic, poems attributed to Homer that often served as preludes (*prooimia*) to the recitation of major epics, celebrated various Greek deities and narrated their births, important exploits, attributes and cults.

Hesiod's *Theogony*, an elaborate Hymn to Zeus, offered a version of the birth and evolution of the divine universe that became canonical. His *Works and Days* drew on a tradition of wisdom literature that descends from Egypt and other Near Eastern traditions, just as the *Theogony* adapts earlier Near Eastern cosmological traditions. The poem offers myths about the origins of the human race, and didactic advice on proper farming and social and religious conduct. His fragmentary poems address a range of other topics, including genealogical tales about the mothers of famous heroes in his *Catalogues of Women*.

Epic was revived as a literary form for a reading public in the hellenistic period. The surviving *Argonautika* of Apollonios of Rhodes, which narrated the adventures of Jason in his search for the Golden Fleece, revised the Homeric tradition to suit a sophisticated, self-conscious, and equally panhellenic audience. The learned didactic poems, such as Nicander of Kolophon's 2nd-century bc *Theriaka* on snakes, or Aratos of Soloi's 3rd-century bc *Phainomena* on astronomy, revived the Hesiodic tradition of the *Works and Days* but focused as much on style and elegance as content. The pagan Greek epic tradition continued to evolve at a considerably later period in, for example, Quintus Smyrnaeus' 3rd-century ad *Posthomerica*, the 4th-century ad epics of Claudian such as the unfinished *De raptu Proserpinae* (*The Rape of Proserpina*), and the *Dionysiaka* of Nonnos (5th century ad). The poems of Homer and Hesiod were immensely influential in antiquity and formed the basis of Greek education for many centuries.

Various lyric poetic traditions certainly predate the Homeric poems, which refer to lamentations (*thrênoi*), marriage songs (*epithalamia*) and paeans. Others, such as maiden songs (*partheneia*), dithyrambs for Dionysos, processional songs (*prosôdia*), *epinikia* (songs celebrating athletic victories) or military exhortations in elegiac metres (Tyrtaios, Solon, Simonides) seem to have played an important role in the civic community of the *polis* (city-state) that emerged sometime in the 8th–7th centuries throughout the Greek world, and served to educate and link citizens to their communities. Monody (song for a single voice accompanied by the lyre) tended to be sung for informal groups of friends in private *symposia* or cults, and originated largely in eastern Greece. This poetry often featured erotic themes, wine and song, or invective towards outsiders, and tended to use local dialects suited to an intimate audience. Poems sung or recited in elegiac metre, which alternated one dactylic hexameter line with a dactylic pentameter line, touched on erotic themes, proper symposiastic behaviour, the perils of aristocratic life, military exhortations and historical narratives. The historical narratives were often designed for a larger, more heterogeneous group of citizens.

Choral poetry, which was both sung and danced, had strong associations with western and central Greece; it often focused on relations between men and gods in a public, ritual context. Its general thrust was encomiastic, though it took care to moderate its celebration of human achievement in order to diffuse human or divine envy. Its eclectic language had a strong Doric colouring. Poets from around the mid-7th to the mid-5th centuries by and large served their own communities, and could often be involved in unstable and oppressive local politics (Archilochos, Hipponax, Kallinos, Tyrtaios, Solon, Stesichoros, Sappho, Alkaios). Later poets, however, such as Ibykos, Anakreon, Simonides, Pindar and Bacchylides, travelled to the courts of tyrants and could work for fees. Sappho, Alkman and Pindar composed *partheneia* to celebrate choruses of young women on the verge of marriage. Wedding songs, dithyrambs (also performed at Athens' dramatic festivals), lamentations, lengthy poems on mythological themes (especially by Stesichoros) and a variety of praise poems, above all hymns and victory songs, are prominent among them. The performance of public choral lyric began to decline in the 4th century bc, though dithyrambs, hymns and paeans to military or secular leaders continued to be composed and performed during the hellenistic period, sometimes as part of ruler cults.

Among the various archaic poems that come down to us, *iamboi* (poems in iambic or trochaic metre) by Archilochos, Hipponax, and Semonides may have been recited rather than sung. They were often focused on food, sex and excrement, and mercilessly abused individual enemies or groups such as wives. Archilochos, however, composed poetry on a larger range of themes, and the Athenian lawgiver Solon used iambic metre to lay out and defend his political programme.

Although archaic poetry is often composed in the first person, we cannot assume that the contradictory information that we can extrapolate from the poems represents reality in any direct fashion. For example, the works of the group of elegiac poems, composed over a substantial time period, that come down to us under the name of Theognis probably represent the perspective of aristocratic fellow symposiasts dissatisfied with the emerging *polis*, rather than a single individual voice. The playful symposiastic poetry found in the corpus of 'Anakreon' again represents a persona more than a person.

The dramatic poetry of tragedy, satyr play and comedy, which began to develop in late 6th-century Athens, drew eclectically on various traditions: local festal traditions of performance in masks and costumes, Greek mime traditions, dithyramb for Dionysos, the narrative poems of Stesichoros, local laments for cultic heroes throughout Greece, Dorian choral and other lyric poetry, the myths of epic, emerging rhetorical and philosophical writing (including Solon's poetry) and, in the case of Old Comedy, iambic blame traditions. Dramatic poetry was initially designed for an enormous democratic audience, who viewed the plays in large outdoor theatres and adapted myths from the entire Greek world to explore issues that mixed familial and public conflicts. Tragedy developed iambic trimeters as the preeminent metre for dramatic dialogue and speeches (*rhêseis*). Drama's singing and dancing chorus, and its actors, both drew on a range of pre-existing lyric traditions as well as developing new metres (e.g. dochmiacs) that served to capture peaks of tragic suffering and anxiety. Although Greek tragedy and New Comedy continued to be composed for initial performance in Athens, both tragedy and New Comedy were adapted and performed at new festivals throughout the Greek world by hellenistic authors and professional actors. A fragment of the *Alexandra* of LYKOPHRON, a lengthy prophecy of Kassandra, suggests that tragedy could even take new forms during this period. The works of AESCHYLUS, SOPHOKLES and EURIPIDES became canonical by the 4th century BC, and their achievements were never surpassed. Euripides, the most controversial of the three in the 5th century, became far the most popular and influential thereafter. The bawdy and highly political Old Comedy of ARISTOPHANES and others gave way in the mid- to later 4th century to the New Comedy of MENANDER and other poets, who developed plots that focused on family life and romantic and bourgeois social themes. The later reception of Greek tragedy in the West was heavily shaped by ARISTOTLE's discussion of the genre in his *Poetics*.

During the hellenistic period, literary forms were transformed to become virtually new genres. Sophisticated descendants of mime drew on the characterization, situation, and sometimes on the sex, food and vituperation found in comedy. Of these, HERODAS' *Mimiamboi*, short vignettes depicting urban low life, and the eclectic *Idylls* (largely in hexameters) of THEOKRITOS, written in Doric dialect, survive. Although his corpus includes poetry praising the PTOLEMAIC monarchs, mini-epic poems, and urban vignettes, Theokritos' rural songs depicting life in the countryside in essence founded a tradition of bucolic or PASTORAL poetry that became popular in Rome in later centuries. The learned 3rd-century poet KALLIMACHOS, situated at the Ptolemaic MOUSEION or LIBRARY at Alexandria in Egypt, wrote, among a wide range of poems, learned and sophisticated hymns, a four-book elegiac poem (*Aitia* or *Causes*), 13 *Iamboi* that mix themes from archaic iambic, and the mini-epic *Hekale*. The last depicts the story of THESEUS' encounter with an elderly woman who entertains him on his way to slay the Marathonian BULL. The elegiac metre continued to be used for a wide range of themes, including victory odes and longer narratives. The polished epigram or inscriptional poem in elegiacs, however – used for epitaphs, dedications, or victory monuments as well as for symposiastic themes (wine and love) – underwent a dramatic development during the 3rd century BC. It could now be published in the form of carefully crafted anthologies, such as the *Garland* of Meleagros (Meleager) of Gadara (c.100 BC). HPF

See Easterling, P.E. and Knox, B.M.W., eds. (1985) *Greek Literature*; Taplin, O., ed. (2000) *Literature in the Greek and Roman Worlds: a new perspective*.

Roman poetry is conventionally said to begin in the middle of the 3rd century BC with Livius Andronicus' translation of the *Odyssey*. The poet was probably a freed SLAVE of Greek or south Italian origins; his translation employed what appears to have been a native Italian metre, the Saturnian. Although his successors soon turned from direct translation or adaptation of Greek originals to the composition of poems based more loosely on models drawn from the Greek literary canon, the dual source of Roman poetry – which combined from the outset native Italian and Hellenic elements – was to exert an enduring influence over its subsequent development. From ENNIUS onwards, Roman writers began to employ Greek rather than native METRES. Ennius opens his *Annales* (fr. 1) with an ostentatious invocation of the Greek Muses rather than the native Camenae (minor local deities to whom Livius, and probably his EPIC successor Naevius, had appealed for inspiration). The tragedians (Ennius, Pacuvius, Accius) and comic playwrights (PLAUTUS, TERENCE) of the 2nd century BC – the heyday of Roman drama – made extensive use of Greek models: the majority of the surviving plays and fragments can be identified as loose adaptations of specific source-texts. But it is quite misleading to refer to the Latin plays as 'translations'. The playwrights clearly felt no scruples about the introduction of new material, and the tone and emphases of the Greek originals seem often to have been significantly altered in order to appeal more directly to the interests of the Roman audience. Plautus, in particular, finds a fertile source of humour in the incongruous combination of Greek and Roman elements in the settings of his comedies.

Later poets continue to pay lip service to the Greek poets who were conventionally regarded as the founders of the various genres – even when they engage just as closely or more closely with Roman predecessors. VIRGIL, for example, refers to his DIDACTIC poem, the *Georgics*, as a 'Hesiodic song' (*Georgics* 2.176); LUCRETIUS, whose influence on the form and themes of the work is at least as important as that of HESIOD, is invoked only implicitly and never mentioned by name. Like many poets of the late Republic and early empire, Virgil displays considerable ambivalence about his relationship with his Greek models: expressions of modest acknowledgement can be found alongside proud assertions that the poet has outdone the Greeks on their own territory, conquering new 'provinces' of literature for Rome just as its generals had conquered new territories in the physical world. Characteristically, this combination of respect and rivalry emerges in the close imitation of (specific or generic) Greek models, combined with the careful adaptation and reworking of the original to reflect specifically Roman concerns. Virgil's *Aeneid* is not only a tissue of verbal echoes of HOMER's *Iliad* and *Odyssey* and the *Argonautika* of APOLLONIOS OF RHODES, but closely follows the three Greek archetypes in its structure, in the depiction of its characters and in its language, imagery and style. Yet, at the same time, Virgil's hero is an exemplar of characteristically Roman virtues. The experiences he undergoes – though modelled on those of ODYSSEUS, Jason and the heroes of the *Iliad* – simultaneously recall, in different ways, very recent events in the Roman world, and illustrate prominent aspects of the ideology of the Augustan period.

A second factor of considerable importance for the development of Roman poetry was the relationship between poets and their patrons. Until the 1st century BC, most poets – with the notable exception of the aristocratic Lucilius – seem to have been of relatively low social status. For this reason, it was vitally important to secure the support of a patron or patrons, who would help the poet to disseminate his work and ensure that it found an audience among the educated élite who naturally formed the 'market' for literary texts. The traditional *quid pro quo* received by the patron was a poem dedicated to his exploits, particularly in the military arena. From the 1st century onwards, poetry seems to have been regarded as a more respectable profession, and many of the surviving works of the late Republican and imperial periods were composed by members of the EQUESTRIAN or SENATORIAL classes. The traditional relationship between poet and patron continues to manifest itself, however, in the form of elaborate dedications and a persistent element of encomium common to many GENRES of Roman poetry. Related to these traditions is a prominent concern, particularly in the poetry of the late Republic and the Augustan period, with generic hierarchy. Epic – the established vehicle for praise of a patron's exploits – had traditionally been considered the most serious and important form of verse composition. During the last decades of the Republic, however, the poetic principles advocated by the hellenistic poet KALLIMACHOS are increasingly espoused by his Roman successors. This – simply put – amounted to a preference for small-scale poems on 'lighter' themes, composed with minute care and attention to detail. The concomitant rejection of epic by most surviving poets of this era (Virgil, of course, being the triumphant exception) is marked by the prevalence of the type of poem known as a *recusatio* or 'refusal poem'. Here the poet politely declines to celebrate his patron's glorious deeds, usually on the grounds that his Muse will not inspire him to compose poetry of a suitably elevated kind.

Characteristic of this period, too, is a tendency (again influenced by Kallimachos and his fellow-Alexandrians) towards generic experimentation. The rhetorician QUINTILIAN (*Institutio oratoria* 10.1.93) famously claimed verse SATIRE as the one genre 'wholly our own' (i.e. not based on a Greek model). Similar claims could be made, however, for the short-lived but clearly defined genre of love elegy, which begins with GALLUS in the mid-1st century BC and dies an early death with the *Amores* of OVID at the end of the century. Ovid's *Heroides*, *Ars amatoria* and *Remedia amoris* were also, in different ways, experimental works, while the *Metamorphoses* notoriously defies generic classification.

The most influential work of the Augustan period was undoubtedly Virgil's *Aeneid*, which immediately became a school text and was almost universally regarded as the greatest work of Latin literature. Partly for this reason, no doubt, the literature of the earlier empire is characterized by a strong sense of belatedness or 'anxiety of influence'. Post-Virgilian epic – notably LUCAN's *De bello civili* (*On the Civil War*) and STATIUS' *Thebaid* – is intensely concerned to establish its credentials in relation to the masterwork, much as Roman poetry as a whole is concerned to negotiate its position with respect to the earlier achievements of the Greeks. Virgilian allusion is also prominent in works of other genres, such as the *Satires* of JUVENAL. The poetry of this period displays, too, an increased tendency towards RHETORICAL display and an interest in the exotic or grotesque (notable especially in Lucan's epic and the TRAGEDIES of SENECA). These 'baroque' or 'anti-classical' features have until quite recently been regarded with distaste by modern critics. As a result, so-called 'Silver Latin' poetry has traditionally been relegated to the status of a kind of 'poor relation' to the literary 'greats' of the late Republic and the Augustan period.

The literature of the later 2nd and 3rd centuries AD is dominated by prose writing, and little poetry of note seems to have been produced. Such works as survive from this period (notably the pastoral and didactic poems of Nemesianus from the later 3rd century) are characterized, on the whole, by their classicism rather than their innovativeness. But from the mid-4th century onwards, poets found new inspiration, derived particularly from the desire to produce a CHRISTIAN literature fit to compare with that of the PAGAN past. The names of PRUDENTIUS and Paulinus of Nola stand out in this connection. Both poets employ classical forms (hexameter verse; Horatian lyric metres) in combination with new, Christian themes (HYMNS in honour of saints and MARTYRS; sin and redemption). Equally innovative, in the rather different sphere of court poetry, are the PANEGYRICS of CLAUDIAN (which strikingly rework the conventions of Virgilian and post-Virgilian epic) and the multifarious poetic works of AUSONIUS.

It is, of course, impossible to sum up in a few words the poetic production of an entire culture spanning a period of some 700 years. With all due caveats, however, we may characterize Roman poetry as a whole as a form, or set of forms, notable for their densely allusive quality; for their highly self-conscious concern with the poet's place in society and relationship with his (or, in the exceptional case of Sulpicia, her) literary predecessors; and for the interplay between tradition and originality, whereby genres in most cases hundreds of years old are constantly reworked and reinvented as vehicles for contemporary concerns and preoccupations. MG

See Braund, S. M. (2002) *Latin Literature*; Conte, G. B. (1994) *Latin Literature*, trs. J. B. Solodow; Kenney, E. J., ed. (1982) *The Cambridge History of Classical Literature*, vol. 2.

poets Our word 'poet' comes from Greek *poiêtês*, literally 'maker', from the verb *poiëô* ('I make'). It is first attested with the meaning of poet in HERODOTOS (5th century BC), though the use of *poiêô* to describe the activity of a poet is first attested in SOLON (6th century). The choice of this word is perhaps associated with the spread of writing as means of composition. Previously, the terms employed in Greek are associated with the oral production and transmission of poetry. These include designations like *aoidos* ('singer') and *rhapsôdos* ('song-stitcher'), which refers to the activity of 'stitching' different SONGS together into a longer poetic creation. The metaphor that underlies this image is that of poetic creation as WEAVING. This metaphor is still employed in such words as 'text' from the past participle of Latin *texo* ('I weave').

The Latin word *poeta* is borrowed from *poiêtês*. The original Latin term, however, was *vates* ('seer'). This word alludes to the equivalence, also present in Greece, of the PROPHET and the poet, understood as 'master of truth'. This implies a divine sanction and inspiration for poetry, criticized as early as PLATO in *Ion*. Nevertheless, poets were very self-conscious of their ART and role in society, and from very early times they named and described themselves in their works. RBC

See Detienne, M. (1996) *The Masters of Truth in Archaic Greece*; Nagy, G. (1996) *Poetry as Performance*.

 LYRIC POETRY.

poisons The Greek *pharmakon* means both healing DRUG and poison, which is understandable when many of the substances used as medicinal drugs were fatal if used in larger doses. The idea that those who cure disease can also cause harm is seen in GREEK RELIGION, in the attribution of plague to the 'arrows of APOLLO' and the belief that ARTEMIS can help women in labour but can also inflict sterility on those who do not honour her. In the mortal world, DOCTORS – particularly Greek doctors at Rome – were often suspected of being able to poison their patients. Roman writers tell us that some Eastern rulers, such as Mithradates, deliberately took small amounts of poison to make themselves immune to poisoning attempts. Fears of poisoning flourished above all in the Julio-Claudian court. CALIGULA is said to have owned a chest full of different types, and CLAUDIUS was alleged to have been poisoned by his wife AGRIPPINA, aided by the interesting combination of a famous female poisoner, Locusta, and a doctor, Xenophon (Suetonius, *Nero* 33–4; Tacitus, *Annals* 13.14). After an unsuccessful attempt was made on her life, Tacitus' Agrippina showed another side of women's knowledge of *pharmaka*: not only had she already taken antidotes to stop poison affecting her, but she also treated herself for her wounds (Tacitus, *Annals* 12.66–7; 14.5–6). We may conclude that the use of poison as a method of MURDER, being indirect and invisible, was generally associated with enemies of the state, debased Eastern monarchies and women. HK

Polanyi, K. see RATIONALITY, ECONOMIC; TRADE, GREEK.

policing see AEDILES; CRIME AND CRIMINALS.

polis 'City' and 'city-state' are traditional designations for what the Greeks called a *polis*, the form of community that dominated the eastern MEDITERRANEAN world from c.750 BC to c.AD 550. The word has two basic meanings, settlement and community. As a settlement, a *polis* consisted of HOUSES; as a community, it was made up of human beings. Not every settlement or community was a *polis*. In the sense of settlement, a *polis* was primarily a nucleated settlement; in the sense of community, it was a self-governing community. *Polis* thus means both 'city' and 'state'. The word is often used in both senses simultaneously, so an apt rendering is 'city-state'. The two senses (city and state) are virtually inseparable. An urban centre was only a *polis* if it was also the political centre of a state. Conversely, *polis* in the sense of state was applied almost exclusively to a small political community consisting of a city with its hinterland. In archaic sources *polis* sometimes means 'stronghold' or 'hilltop settlement'. Keywords derived from '*polis*' include *politês* (citizen) and *politeia* (citizenship or constitution).

A *polis* was a micro-state consisting of a settlement and its immediate hinterland (*chôra* or *gê*), and, in the sense of state, can denote the city and its hinterland together. The territory often covered less than 100 sq km (39 sq miles), rarely over 1,000 sq km (390 sq miles). Most *poleis* had fewer than 10,000 inhabitants (e.g. Plataiai (Plataea), DELPHI, Siphnos), large *poleis* between 10,000 and 100,000 (e.g. CORINTH, MEGARA, Eretria), the largest few over 100,000 (Athens, CYRENE, SYRACUSE, Akragas, Taras, later ALEXANDRIA and ANTIOCH). The population was divided into CITIZENS (*politai*), free foreigners (often called *metoikoi*, 'metics', literally 'migrants') and SLAVES. A large part of the population – sometimes the majority – lived in the city. The rest lived in the hinterland, either nucleated in VILLAGES or dispersed on farmsteads. As in other city-state cultures in pre-modern human history, the degree of URBANIZATION was far higher than in other societies. The town with its hinterland was an economic and social community of the members of all HOUSEHOLDS (*oikiai*), metics as well as citizens, free and slave, young as well as old. Although the *polis* was a male society as a political and as a military organization, women played important roles in the rites and cults of their household and of the *polis*.

As a state, the *polis* was the community of adult male citizens involved in political institutions, whether they lived in the town or the country, but not their wives and children, free foreigners, or slaves. Citizens were only a minority of the population, in small *poleis* sometimes less than 1,000. Many Greeks believed that the ideal *polis* had 10,000 citizens, but few did. In a small *polis*, all citizens knew one another; larger *poleis* were too populous to be 'face-to-face societies', as has sometimes been claimed.

The *polis* was self-governing but not necessarily independent. The Greeks distinguished between *poleis* with and without *autonomia*, which in the classical period denoted independence but in the hellenistic period self-government ('autonomy' in the modern, watered-down sense). Conquered city-states often retained their status of *poleis* and became dependent; examples include the perioikic *poleis* of LACONIA and MESSENIA, dominated by Sparta (some conquered, others perhaps founded by Sparta itself). Other dependent *poleis* were the result of alliances and federations, such as the so-called Delian league which became the Athenian empire. From c.500 BC an increasing number of *poleis* united in federations, still *poleis*, but no longer independent. The oldest known federations are the Lokrian and Phokian, both attested c.500 BC. In the 4th century, at least a third of all *poleis* in Hellas (GREECE) had become member states of a regional federation. In the hellenistic and Roman periods, almost all *poleis* were dependent.

As principally a community of citizens, the *polis* par excellence was democratic. From the 4th century BC the concept of *polis* is increasingly associated with DEMOCRACY. However, even OLIGARCHIC *poleis* had a popular assembly (with restricted powers), and even Greek TYRANTS convened assemblies of citizens. Democratic or not, the *polis* had some political institutions in which all citizens (though only they) were entitled to participate. In the archaic period, constitutions were monarchical (kingship, tyranny) or oligarchic (aristocracy, oligarchy). During the 6th century, democracy began to emerge as an alternative form of government. During the 5th and 4th centuries, it became dominant, and by the hellenistic period almost all *poleis* were democracies, though their *autonomia* (no longer independence, just self-government) often depended on royal approval. In the Roman period, democracy was replaced by oligarchy; the council (*boulê*) eclipsed the assembly (*ekklêsia*) as the main decision-making body, and upper class citizens monopolized all important magistracies.

Greek city-state culture reveals a clear divide between ethnic and political identity. Greeks in one *polis* shared language and culture with those in other *poleis* and recognized each other as belonging to the same people; but politically they considered themselves citizens of their own *polis* as opposed to another. This is reflected in how they named themselves. When citizens from different *poleis* were together, they used a form of their *polis*' name as a kind of surname. Hippodamos Milesios, for example, means 'Hippodamos from Miletos'. The Greeks seem to have been unique in history in using surnames that both referred to a place and indicated a political status. The *polis*' name was not that of the town or the country, but its citizens. Although the settlement we know as Athens had the name *Athênai*, in political contexts it was called *hoi Athênaioi* (the Athenians) or *Athênaiôn ho dêmos* (the people of the Athenians).

Diplomatic relations between *poleis* were not maintained by permanent AMBASSADORS but by envoys (*presbeis*) sent out, whenever needed, to negotiate, for example, a truce or alliance. A network of personal relations between prominent persons in different *poleis* was developed through formal guest-friendship (*xenia*). This was later institutionalized as *proxenia*, whereby *polis* A would appoint a citizen of *polis* B as *proxenos* (host and protector) to look after its own citizens when they visited *polis* B.

There were some 1,500 Hellenic *poleis*, about 800 in Hellas including the ISLANDS and the west coast of Asia Minor, the rest founded as colonies along the Mediterranean and BLACK SEA coasts or in the Near East. Almost all *poleis* lay near or by the sea. Most developed or were founded c.750–200 BC, but as late as c.AD 500 many were still essentially city-states, not just cities. Thus the Hellenic city-state culture persisted for 1,200 years, a span of time surpassed only by the MESOPOTAMIAN city-states. During the early Roman empire, the Greek-speaking city provided the primary form of identity for perhaps 30 million people.

It is still debated whether the *polis* emerged in Hellas before the beginning of the COLONIZATION period c.750 BC, or took shape in the colonies and was copied in Hellas. It seems, however, to have emerged almost simultaneously in both places. But colonists had to set up a new self-governing community with an urban centre from scratch. The *polis* must soon have reached its mature form in the colonies, but the development was slower in Hellas. There, the first *poleis* emerged along the coasts of the AEGEAN, partly in Asia Minor (where the oldest identifiable *poleis* are MILETOS and SMYRNA) and partly in mainland Greece (where Eretria, Athens, ARGOS, Corinth and others can be traced back to the 8th century). The first *poleis* in written sources are Sparta, THASOS and Dreros (in CRETE).

Some *poleis* began as small settlements and grew to become walled towns. Elsewhere, a cluster of villages might merge. Other *poleis* were formed by a formal act of migration or synoikism (*synoikismos*), with people moving to a central place. Alternatively, colonists went abroad to found a *polis*. Regardless of origin, many *poleis* had an *AKROPOLIS* or citadel, sometimes reserved for TEMPLES and other public buildings but sometimes used for habitation. Every *polis* was divided into (1) publicly owned areas used for walls, streets, HARBOURS, MARKETS and monumental ARCHITECTURE, and (2) privately owned areas with family houses, mostly fairly simple. Houses were originally built according to no master plan, but in the archaic period many *poleis* adopted centralized TOWN PLANNING. Rectangular blocks were framed by streets and subdivided into plots of equal size. Standardized terrace houses were often constructed on these plots, as at Olynthos in Chalkidike. Another famous example of grid-planning is the PIRAEUS, the port of Athens, laid out c.450 BC by Hippodamos of Miletos. This form of town-planning is often called 'Hippodamian', though he did not invent it: on SICILY it can be traced back to c.700 BC.

By the 4th century, a defence circuit had become an essential aspect of most towns. The walls typically contained enough open spaces for the entire rural population, in case the enemy occupied the countryside. But whereas in medieval towns the sharp division between city and country began at the gates, Greek city walls were for defence only. In wartime the gates were guarded, but in peacetime people could get in and out even at night. The walls did not become a barrier between town and country.

Apart from city walls, monumental political architecture began to appear only in the 4th century. By then, virtually every *polis* had a *prytaneion* where the chief MAGISTRATES hosted prominent guests and an eternal flame on an altar of Hestia symbolized the life of the *polis*. There was a council house or town hall (*bouleutêrion*) in which the council (*boulê*) met, as well as *archeia*, offices for magistrates and boards (*archai*). Purpose-built LAWCOURTS (*dikastêria*) are rare; public buildings erected for other purposes were often used. Few *poleis* had a separate meeting-place for the ASSEMBLY, which often took place in an open-air THEATRE.

The most urgent need of the *polis* as a habitation centre was a sufficient supply of fresh water. Many *poleis* were adorned with one or more public FOUNTAIN houses where people could supplement the water drawn from wells in their own home. As a centre of public cult the *polis*, especially the *akropolis*, housed a number of religious sanctuaries. Other sanctuaries were suburban or extra-urban, the latter serving almost as a demarcation of the *polis*' territory. Sanctuaries of ATHENA, APOLLO and APHRODITE are typically inside the walls, those of ZEUS, DEMETER, HERA and POSEIDON often in the countryside.

The *polis* economy was characterized by a considerable division of LABOUR, and inhabitants satisfied an essential part of daily needs by buying locally produced or imported goods. Many city-dwellers had farms within walking distance from their homes; they were usually not subsistence farmers, but produced crops for market. The economic centres were the marketplace (*AGORA*) and the harbour (*limên*). In archaic towns, the *agora* was simply an open square marked by boundary stones (*horoi*). From the classical period, the *agora* was often adorned with one or more STOAS, some of which housed SHOPS. The right to own landed property was confined to citizens, yet – except in Sparta and perhaps some other *poleis* – foreigners and slaves took part in TRADE and crafts alongside citizens, often on the same footing. To a large extent, the *polis* involved itself in the economic life of the people only to collect taxes and to ensure that a citizen could get his daily BREAD at a manageable price.

As a centre of EDUCATION and entertainment, the *polis* was the place for private schools (there were no state schools). Education of adults was often connected with public GYMNASIA, though these were primarily for SPORT and military training. Early gymnasia were usually outside the *polis*, but in the late classical and hellenistic periods were built inside the walls. They became perhaps the most important public building, housing what was now a central institution of the *polis*: the *ephêbeia*, the education and military training of young citizens. Civic entertainments, often connected with major religious FESTIVALS, were centred on sporting competitions and theatrical performances. Sport took place in a PALAESTRA (a wrestling-hall), *stadion* (running-track) or *hippodromos* (horse-racing track). Dramas were performed in a theatre sacred to DIONYSOS. These various types of building became monumentalized in the late 5th and 4th centuries.

Each *polis* had its own army; armies of leagues or federations were composed of contingents from member *poleis*. The core of a city's armed forces was the heavy-armed infantry, the HOPLITES. In some *poleis*, citizenship was restricted to current and former hoplites. It has often been suggested that the emergence of the hoplite phalanx c.750 BC was closely connected with the rise of the *polis*. In the classical and hellenistic periods, however, the identification of hoplites with citizens gradually lapsed.

RELIGION, it is sometimes said, was the dominant aspect of *polis* life, and '*polis* religion' is even used to describe Greek religion in general. Certainly, every communal activity was accompanied by religious acts. An assembly meeting in Athens, for example, opened with a SACRIFICE, a PRAYER and a curse. Most *poleis* had a specific patron god or goddess. Gods and heroes were worshipped by the whole community in connection with large festivals organized by the *polis* and attended by all inhabitants (not just citizens). Religion, however, was only one aspect of *polis* life; the focal point was the political community of citizens. Modern political institutions are often seen as a framework through which the state organizes all military, religious, economic, social and cultural matters. The Greeks took a different view: participation in political life was a value in itself, and political institutions were not a frame of the *polis* but its core. (see also FEDERALISM) MHH

See Hansen, M. H. et al. (1993–2003) *Acts of the Copenhagen Polis Centre 1–6*, especially M. H. Hansen, *Polis and City-state* (1998); (1994–2003) *Papers of the Copenhagen Polis Centre 1–7*; Hansen and Nielsen, *Inventory*.

political participation

The level of participation by the citizen body of a given community depended on the type of political constitution it had. In the early history of the Greek CITY-STATE (750–650 BC), when many communities were ARISTOCRACIES, participation was limited to families who claimed noble descent. Their members alone could hold office, sit on the governing council, and perhaps attend the ASSEMBLY. In OLIGARCHIES, which came to replace aristocracies in many places, either after reform or following a TYRANNY, the franchise was more broadly held and participation was based on a certain level of property ownership. In SPARTA, all male citizens were entitled when they came of age at 20 to attend the assembly, vote on issues placed before them, and elect certain officials. The EPHORS were elected from the whole assembly; membership of the governing council (*gerousia*), though elected, was restricted to those over 60 from noble families. SOLON's constitution, which divided ATHENS' citizen body into four property classes, had similar restrictions. Only those from the top property class (500-bushel men) could be elected archons and then sit on the council of the AREIOPAGOS, while those from the lowest class (*thêtes*) were eligible only to attend the assembly. In DEMOCRACIES, such property restrictions were largely removed or simply ignored.

In Athens after the democracy was introduced (508), the Areiopagos still remained a council of ex-archons who sat for life, but the archonship was progressively opened up to the lower property classes; the same was true of other public offices. Limited tenure of a year for holding office, ineligibility in most cases to hold the same office twice, and collegiality of boards of ten for most offices ensured that power rotated more widely among the citizen body. The introduction of pay, first to attend the courts as jurors, then to hold office and finally even to attend the assembly, encouraged wider participation by the poor. Despite these efforts, however, outside the courts and the assembly, participation in Athens seems to have been limited to the upper three classes, the men of sufficient wealth and leisure to serve in office for a full year.

Participation was restricted in other ways in Athens. Only male citizens who had come of age and finished their military training at 20 could attend the assembly and vote; only male citizens over 30 could sit as jurors or hold office. Citizen WOMEN were completely excluded. Citizens who were public debtors were denied political and legal rights until they paid their DEBT. Non-citizen males, regardless of age or length of residency, had no political rights; they had legal rights which gave them access to the courts, but the right to sit as jurors was reserved for citizens. Those few METICS who were granted CITIZENSHIP still could not hold office, but their sons could, provided they were born of an Athenian mother. CC

The Roman REPUBLIC was a form of DEMOCRACY. Therefore the main way in which citizens were expected to take part in political life was by exercising their right to VOTE on the passage of legislation and the election of MAGISTRATES. The structure of the three main voting ASSEMBLIES – *comitia centuriata*, *comitia tributa* and *concilium plebis* – had the practical effect of weighting the votes of the wealthy more than those of the poor, and of the old more than the young. To cast a vote, one had to be physically present at Rome, and the voting process was more or less an all-day affair. Another form of political participation was to attend and take part in public assemblies known as *contiones*, which were convened to debate issues, often as a preparatory step before a vote. Therefore, while all citizens technically had the right to vote and express opinions on state policy, in reality only those in or near the city of Rome who had the inclination or motivation, as well as sufficient leisure, actually participated in a given vote or debate.

Other ways in which average citizens could have an effect on politics were through such means as graffiti, attendance at trials and public demonstrations.

In the empire, the major change occurred in AD 14, when the EMPEROR TIBERIUS transferred the election of magistrates from the assemblies to the SENATE. This was apparently the end to most direct involvement of the citizens in politics, but really it marked a shift in emphasis from formal methods of participation to more informal ones. The urban plebs played important roles at religious and secular ceremonies at Rome. Additionally, public entertainments became settings which regularly brought ruler and ruled into direct contact with one another. Here the people could, and did, express their opinions to, make demands of, and even directly criticize the EMPEROR, with the expectation that he would be receptive to these comments. There are numerous examples of emperors acceding to the people's requests. Such crowds served as the symbolic representatives of the entire citizen body, and their acclamations were a significant factor in establishing the legitimacy of an emperor. The identification of the CIRCUS, in particular, as the new arena of political participation is reflected in the ARCHITECTURE of the later empire. Each imperial PALACE was inevitably constructed with an adjoining hippodrome, to provide a site for imperial interactions with a group of citizens. GSA

See Bollinger, T. (1969) *Theatralis Licentia*; Nicolet, C. (1980) *The World of the Citizen in Republican Rome*; Taylor, L. R. (1966) *Roman Voting Assemblies*.

political systems

Our term 'political' is derived from the Greek *POLIS*, a word that is very hard to translate exactly. The traditional rendering 'city-state' was designed to convey the idea that – in theory, anyhow – the *polis* was a sovereign, autonomous political entity, like the city-states of medieval Italy, for example, or Singapore today. On the other hand, by no means all *poleis* had a properly urban 'city' centre. Even if they did (as in the most conspicuously exceptional case of Athens), the relationship between town and country was one of symbiosis and co-operation, not exploitation and antagonism. For the *polis* was normally a fundamentally agrarian unit, dependent economically on its farmland; and the territory of a *polis* was co-extensive with the land owned individually and collectively by its citizens. In fact, so tight was the connection between *polis* and landholding that legal ownership of a *polis*' land was on principle restricted to its citizens. The vital importance of CITIZENSHIP, which was confined to adult males, is well conveyed by the ancient phrase 'men are the *polis*'. Hence perhaps the most useful modern translation of *polis* is 'citizen-state'.

In ARISTOTLE's day (384–322 BC) there were well over 1,000 such *poleis* in an area extending from the straits of Gibraltar in the west to the far eastern end of the BLACK SEA. The conquests of ALEXANDER the Great (336–323) extended the range of the *polis* even further east, up to modern AFGHANISTAN. In the hellenistic world, however, the *polis* typically was a small and subordinate component of a large territorial monarchy or empire rather than a sovereign entity. Aristotle, like his teacher PLATO, divided all Greek political systems into three broad generic categories: rule by one, rule by some, rule by all. Using their general schema, but without necessarily following them in all their moral judgements, we may thus identify the following broad systems of rule: monarchy (both constitutional and illegitimate), OLIGARCHY and DEMOCRACY.

The earliest form of regime authentically attested in Greece were the highly centralized and bureaucratized monarchies of the late Bronze Age or MYCENAEAN period (c.1500–1150). The fictional Homeric poems betray some traces of this Mycenaean system, but the characteristic form of rule assumed in the world of the EPIC was a far more limited monarchy, in which kings ruled by might rather than right and were subject to challenge as well as check from their fellow 'kings' or aristocrats. The word *dêmos* ('people') was freely used by HOMER to mean the common people as opposed to the 'kings'. It had no strictly political content since the *polis* or citizen-state was not yet born, or at any rate not yet consistently recognized in the context of the epic.

The earliest form of *polis* seems to have appeared by 700 BC. It was ruled by ARISTOCRATS who claimed their title in virtue of alleged direct descent from a GOD or HERO. During the 7th century some cities produced written laws laying down the terms on which the aristocrats were to rule, for their own benefit as much as that of the common citizenry. At Dreros on CRETE, for example, the highest officials bound themselves not to rule more than once within a ten-year period. Other cities produced the first illegitimate monarchs, known as TYRANTS (*tyrannoi*, a word of non-Greek origin), who responded to a variety of internal and external pressures, political, economic, ethnic or military, by seizing sole power. Their rule was not, however, necessarily tyrannical in the modern sense, that is despotic. Some, such as PEISISTRATOS of Athens, could even present themselves as 'constitutional' rulers, for the most part abiding by the existing rules. The tyrants' main function, in the longer perspective, seems to have been to open up positions of power and responsibility to others besides scions of the traditional aristocratic families.

Normally, the kind of regime that succeeded a tyranny was some form of oligarchy. Literally meaning 'the rule of a few', oligarchy in practice meant the rule of the few richest. Athens, untypical in this as in so many ways, passed from tyranny not to oligarchy but an early form of DEMOCRACY, thanks, on the one hand, to the 'constitutionalism' of Peisistratos and, on the other, to the imaginative reform bill proposed in 508 by the progressive aristocrat KLEISTHENES. However, although oligarchies and democracies gave different answers to the question 'who should rule?', they agreed for the most part that citizen self-rule should be effected through a small or very small COUNCIL (*boulê*), a more or less authoritative ASSEMBLY (*ekklêsia*) of fully qualified citizens, and boards of annual magistrates chosen either by election (in an oligarchy) or by lot (in a democracy). Overall numbers of citizens were normally very low; the average or typical *polis* may have numbered as few as 500–2,000 citizens. There was thus very great scope for direct personal involvement at most levels of government. Such involvement was furthermore encouraged, or necessitated, by the fact that *poleis* did not have governments as we understand them, based on parties, and lacked most of the apparatus of the modern STATE.

Ancient Greek political systems were therefore direct, not representative, and for the most part republican, not monarchical – until the hellenistic period ushered in by Alexander. Greek Sicily provided one major exception. Here tyranny was the rule from the 6th century onwards, partly because of the Greek inhabitants' geopolitical situation. As colonists they were faced with both large numbers of subordinated natives and rival colonists from Phoenicia who had the support of another Phoenician colony, Carthage.

One final difference from the political systems familiar to us today is worth stressing. The Greeks did not recognize the doctrine of the separation of the powers (legislative, executive and judicial) of government. The same citizens ruled in the courts as in the assembly and council – either the rich few (*oligoi*) or the poor many (*dêmos*), depending on whether the constitution was formally an oligarchy or a democracy. (see also political theory) PAC

From its foundation in 753 BC, Rome was a city-state ruled by a king. Through his divine power or *imperium* the king was responsible for managing military, religious and political affairs. He was usually accompanied by twelve lictors bearing the *fasces*, or axe bound within a bundle of sticks, that symbolized this *imperium*. The king was by no means an absolute ruler. He required the support of the 'fathers' (*patres*) of the privileged families of Rome, who were organized into an advisory board, perhaps originally comprising 100 Roman citizens, known as the senate.

The Romans expelled their last king, Tarquin the Proud, in 509 BC, and subsequently founded the Republic. Under the Republican system, three main divisions existed: the elected magistrates, the popular assemblies and the senate. Originally, in order to be appointed to the senate, an individual was required to be patrician. In contrast, those who were not patricians fell into the category of plebeians. Tensions between these two groups typically ran high, because the plebeians felt they were not adequately represented in government and occasionally pressed for change. As a consequence of a revolt, they acquired, for example, the right to elect tribunes, who in turn had the ability to veto any senatorial law. Later, the right to sit in the senate was extended to the plebeians. The senate prepared legislation to be forwarded to the assemblies and also handled financial, diplomatic and religious affairs. It also issued decrees known as *senatus consulta*, which did not have the same force as law but more often than not decided matters.

The Roman political system was also made up of four popular assemblies. The earliest popular assembly in Rome was the curiate assembly (*comitia curiata*), consisting of thirty wards (*curiae*). As Rome expanded, this assembly began to lose importance. Its function was primarily ceremonial, as it was the legislative body that conferred *imperium* on both consuls and praetors. More responsibility fell upon the centuriate assembly (*comitia centuriata*), which met in the Campus Martius and was summoned by a magistrate holding *imperium*. The voting units consisted of 193 centuries, originally based on a man's age and property class. This assembly had the power to declare both war and peace, and to appoint high magistrates; it functioned as a court of appeal for cases dealing with capital punishment. The senate ultimately approved these decisions and appointments. The assembly of tribes (*comitia tributa*), which met in the Roman forum, comprised voters divided into 35 tribal units. Summoned by consuls, praetors or tribunes, this assembly met to vote on laws and also acted as an appeals court. Finally, there was the plebeian assembly (*concilium plebis*), which also met at the forum. Made up of plebeians only, this assembly elected the tribunes and also voted on legal measures, known as *plebiscita*, that were binding on all citizens.

The elected magistrates made up the executive branch of Roman government. The offices of this branch were collegial in nature in that they were at least held by two men. When an individual pursued political office, he had to follow a particular route known as the *cursus honorum* ('sequence of honours'). The first office held was that of quaestor, then aedile, praetor, consul and censor. During the empire, other titles were added to these. Typically a term of office lasted for one year and other offices could be held in addition to the magistracy (e.g. priesthoods). Quaestors served as financial officers and administrative assistants, and were in charge of the treasury (*aerarium*). There were two types of aediles, plebeian and curule. The two had similar functions, in that they were responsible for maintaining festivals, games, temples, the grain supply and markets. The praetors were the key to the administration of civil law. For instance, they could issue edicts, an important source of Roman law. Consuls worked in close proximity with the senate. Elected by the centuriate assembly, each consul had the power to veto the other, creating a system of checks and balances. The consuls, with their *auctoritas* or ruling power, would lead the Roman armies during war and exercised control over state religion. They convened the senate as well as the curiate and centuriate assemblies. The censors were elected every five years to hold office for 18 months. They had to conduct the census, register the citizens and review the membership of the senate. They also had the ability to control public morals, and supervised contracts concerning the use of public land and the building of new monuments. The censor held the highest rank in the *cursus honorum* during the Republic; his position, however, was eventually turned over to the emperor.

During the late Republic, military commanders (*imperatores*) began to raise armies which allied themselves to these leaders more than to Rome. These military commanders, including such men as Sulla, Pompey, Julius Caesar, Mark Antony and Octavian, were known for their intimidating actions against the senate.

In the imperial period, the senate's power became more symbolic. Real governing power was in the hands of the emperor. Octavian, the first emperor, later given the title Augustus by the senate, was given broad powers to reform the Republic. He is considered the first emperor, but he never proclaimed himself absolute ruler. LAH

See Braund, D. C., ed. (1988) *The Administration of the Roman Empire* (241 BC–AD 193); Cornell, T. J. (1995) *The Beginnings of Rome*; Wells, C. (1992) *The Roman Empire*.

 demes (fig. and table); ostracism.

political theory Political thinking is apparent in the earliest preserved Greek literature, the EPIC poems of HOMER and the DIDACTIC poetry of HESIOD, which may be dated to c.700 BC or shortly thereafter. Much LYRIC and ELEGIAC poetry of the 7th and 6th centuries is concerned with political matters, including the distribution of political power between the ÉLITE and the mass of the citizens, and within the élite themselves. But political theory in the strict sense, abstract theorizing from first principles, is a development of the 5th century in Greece, provoked by – and typically in opposition to – the rise of DEMOCRACY particularly in Athens. From Athens, in the hellenistic period, Greek political theory in its various major forms – STOIC, EPICUREAN, CYNIC, ACADEMIC, PERIPATETIC – passed along with so much other Greek high culture to the conquering Romans. CICERO was to Republican Rome what SENECA was to Rome of the early EMPERORS: each absorbed and transmuted Greek political theory to suit their own times and temperaments.

The first examples of political theory proper are to be found in the history of HERODOTOS and the political pamphlet attributed to the 'OLD OLIGARCH'. In Herodotos' imaginary Persian debate (3.80–2) three PERSIAN nobles solemnly discuss the merits and demerits of DEMOCRACY (rule by all), ARISTOCRACY (rule by the best 'some') and monarchy (rule by the best 'one'). The context dictates that monarchy (spoken for by the future Great King, DARIUS I) should win, but it is the pro-democracy speech that sets the terms and the tone of the debate. The pro-democracy speaker is, however, scrupulous to avoid using the word *dêmokratia*, since that could be construed negatively – as by the 'Old Oligarch' – as meaning 'dictatorship of the proletariat'. Instead, he advocates *isonomia*, equality of status under the laws. This was an ideal to which oligarchs too might formally aspire, but here it is given an unequivocally democratic spin: decision-making by all, offices to be selected by lot, all officials so selected to be accountable.

Both pro-aristocratic and pro-monarchist speakers can see no merit in the rule of all the people, since the masses are in their view congenitally stupid and fickle and, because of their poverty and lack of EDUCATION and breeding, ignorant into the bargain. But they differ from each other regarding the respective merits of aristocracy (rule of the best because most virtuous and wise – or rule by competing factions, with a tendency to degenerate into oligarchy?) and monarchy (rule of the one best and wisest – or rule by a megalomaniac prone to despotism?). The political theory of PLATO and ARISTOTLE, though infinitely more sophisticated and finely tuned, nevertheless remains rooted in this fundamentally tripartite conception. In so far as Plato moves beyond the high utopian theory of the *Republic* and its philosopher-kings to pragmatic political recommendations for real people in the *Laws*, the form of rule that he ultimately advocates is a special kind of aristocracy, though he gives the idea of a mixed regime an extended hearing. Aristotle likewise approves the idea of a balance between the extremes of radical democracy and ultra-oligarchy, but his pragmatic ideal is also some form of aristocracy.

Hellenistic philosophies offered both something old (Academic, Peripatetic) and something new and more specifically attuned to an age of impersonality and disempowerment (Stoic, Epicurean, Cynic). None of them was remotely democratic in inspiration or application. The Roman theorists, typically eclectic and practical, followed mainly in the tradition of rule by those who really knew how to rule themselves and were capable of sorting out the morally significant from the morally indifferent; in other words, the tradition of the Stoic sage.

Rome began as, and in many crucial institutional respects remained, a kind of citizen-state. The Latin equivalent of Greek *polis* was *res publica*, literally 'the matter of the *populus* (or People)', and the Roman People was made up of Roman citizens (*cives Romani*). But although official doctrine held that 'the safety of the People was the supreme law' (*salus populi suprema lex*), the People was not expected to rule as such. Elaborate VOTING arrangements for the chief magistracies (PRAETORSHIP, CONSULSHIP) were designed to ensure that only the votes of the rich minority really counted. All magistrates were automatically members of the SENATE, a body without legally enshrined executive power but so endowed with symbolic and moral authority that its word was as good as law, so far as even the top magistrates were concerned. In the circumstances, it would have been odd if Roman political theorists had given more credence to democracy than their Greek mentors.

Cicero was so wedded to the notion of the sanctity of private property that in *De officiis* (*On Duties*) he propounded the novel doctrine that the state had come into existence precisely in order to protect it. But he was theorizing towards the end of an extended period of acute political instability, in which confiscated property was one of the major prizes of the political game. Seneca, adviser to an emperor, lived in stabler times but was more constrained than Cicero to find virtue in the political status quo: his ideal ruler was a prince-emperor who tempered his mundane autocracy with Stoic self-mastery. But if the influence of all ancient political theory on political practice was usually rather tenuous, in Seneca's case the mere mention of the name of his emperor addressee will be sufficient to indicate its futility here – NERO. PAC

See Cartledge, P. (2000) Greek political thought: the historical context, in C. J. Rowe and M. Schofield, eds., *The Cambridge History of Greek and Roman Political Thought* 11–22; Hansen, M. H. (1989) *Was Athens a Democracy?*; Matthews, J. (1985) *Political Life and Culture in Late Roman Society*; Millar, F. (2002) *The Roman Republic in Political Thought*.

pollution, environmental Ancient cities were highly polluted. Greeks and Romans seem to be mostly concerned with ensuring that bodies did not contaminate their cities. The prohibition against intramural BURIAL, however, stemmed from a fear of ritual POLLUTION rather than hygiene. Romans did take some measures to ensure the hygiene of their city. They prided themselves on their Cloaca Maxima (main sewer) and outlawed the disposal of human waste and bodies in cities. However, as stepping-stones across the streets of POMPEII testify, ancient cities were somewhat noxious. In the first place, sewage was drained into RIVERS such as the TIBER, which periodically flooded. Furthermore, despite legal measures, it seems clear that human corpses littered Athens and Rome. ANIMAL and human excrement must have been a problem despite Rome's public TOILETS. These *foricae* were often associated with public BATHS or APARTMENT blocks, and were more common in cities with larger populations. In Pompeii, most latrines consisted of pits located in or near kitchens. In ancient cities, the use of chamber pots was common, as was the disposal of their contents on streets. In ancient cities, the disposal of human excreta was facilitated by their use in AGRICULTURAL processes. Specialists collected human waste from houses and sold it on to farmers. In addition, urine was collected in large vats placed near FULLERS, who used the contents to treat cloth. This combination of waste and the absence of a cleaning force meant that ancient cities were inevitably polluted. EACM

See Hope, V. and Marshall, E. (2000) *Death and Disease in the Ancient City.*

pollution, ritual A state of defilement affecting individuals and communities as well as inanimate objects. Ancient literature presents pollution (*miasma* in Greek) as a kind of ritual dirt which inhibits the smooth functioning of human life. The only way to restore the latter is through the ritual of PURIFICATION.

Pollution may be connected with inevitable states of the human body at different stages of life, notably at birth (both for child and mother), death, illness or sexual intercourse. Many of these states are temporary, often transitional. Pollution is manifested through a range of visible signs, such as bodily discharge and scars, as well as signs of loss of life. Another type of pollution may be caused by actions or behaviours contrary to generally accepted social rules, as with homicide, distortion of the truth or law, impiety and similar offences. In this case, polluted individuals or communities do not display consistent signs of their 'disease'. The latter may at times be the cause of sufferings inflicted by divine agents of retribution for their actions, notably the FURIES (Greek *Erinyes*). Polluted individuals were deemed to be contagious to their friends, relatives and society at large. Legal provision for their banishment from the 'healthy' life of the city or a HOUSEHOLD was often made. Well-known examples of polluted individuals from tragic DRAMA include Orestes after the murder of his mother (AESCHYLUS, *Eumenides*) and OEDIPUS king of THEBES (SOPHOKLES, *Oedipus the King*). EP

See Parker, R. (1983) *Miasma.*

Pollux (Iulius Pollux) 2nd-century AD ORATOR and scholar from NAUKRATIS. A pupil of HERODES ATTICUS, Pollux had a controversial career as an epideictic orator, in which he rose to hold the imperial chair of RHETORIC at Athens. PHILOSTRATOS gives him a brief biography in his *Lives of the Sophists*, in which he is allowed to have had a mellifluous style but said to have been incapable of real oratorical heights. LUCIAN attacks him for stylistic affectation and rhetorical showmanship in his *Guide to Orators* (41). His eight-book *Onomastikon*, dedicated to the emperor COMMODUS, survives in epitomized form (but with the dedicatory letters at the book beginnings intact). A thesaurus of terms, organized by topic, it presents lists of 'words that are synonymous and therefore interchangeable, and the words that can be used to signify a given thing': for instance, 23 ways of saying 'bad-tempered' and 39 distinguishing epithets for varieties of GOD. Topics covered include MUSIC, DRAMA, RELIGION, LAW, the arts and crafts, ARCHITECTURE, navigation, cookery and many more, with a good deal of discursive matter worked in along the way. Particularly interesting are the accounts of the Athenian constitution in book 8 (through the vocabulary of courts, MAGISTRATES and public procedures), and of theatrical antiquities in book 4 (including the *ekkyklêma*, a wheeled platform, the *mêchanê*, a crane, and most famously the different varieties of mask used in TRAGEDY and COMEDY). MBT

See Bethe, E., ed. (1900–37) *Lexicographi Graeci*, 3 vols.

Polyainos (Polyaenus). Macedonian rhetorician (born c.AD 100) who in later life authored a collection of stratagems (*Stratêgika*), ostensibly to aid the emperors MARCUS AURELIUS and Lucius Verus in the PARTHIAN WAR of 162. Polyainos and FRONTINUS (*Stratêgêmata*) are our only extant examples of a lost rich tradition of military compendia, which sought to glean examples of astute generalship from mythology and from Greek, hellenistic, Roman and BARBARIAN experience. Critics rightly note the hastiness of the collection, the artificiality of Polyainos' stilted Greek prose, his gullibility in using earlier sources, and his general lack of historical sense. He often misquotes or misrepresents information taken out of context from earlier unnamed tactical writers and HISTORIANS. Nevertheless, his work contains many fascinating trivia found nowhere else, and he is cited far more frequently by military historians than warnings about his unreliability would suggest.

Polyainos' GENRE is not history, but rather the military handbook of examples and adages that involve trickery and deception. As hellenistic and Roman warfare put greater emphasis on SCIENCE and technique than on sheer numbers and infantry courage, the ideal of generalship evolved into an art of winning wars without great losses and expenditure – a skill imminently teachable through a proper course of instruction and exempla. If Polyainos' didactic purposes are kept in mind, and if we remember that the employment of ruses was far less common in actual classical infantry practice than his collection suggests, then his *Stratêgika* is an often fascinating source of 500 years of Greek and Roman generalship. VDH

See Krentz, P. and Wheeler, E.L., eds. (1994) *Polyaenus, Stratagems of War*, text and trs., 2 vols.

Polybios c.200–c.118 BC Greek historian, the main source for Rome's rise to supremacy. The son of Lykortas, an eminent Achaian politician from Megalopolis, he had already served as CAVALRY commander of the ACHAIAN LEAGUE when in 167 BC, following the third MACEDONIAN WAR, he was among 1,000 Achaians accused of disloyalty to Rome and detained in Italy until 150 BC. As a friend of Publius SCIPIO AEMILIANUS, he enjoyed preferential treatment and in 151 accompanied him to Spain and AFRICA, returning to Italy through the ALPS in search of HANNIBAL's route. He was with Scipio at CARTHAGE, and after its fall made an exploratory voyage in the ATLANTIC. In 146/5 he acted as mediator following the Achaian war. Polybios later visited SARDIS and ALEXANDRIA and probably attended Scipio at NUMANTIA in 133; he subsequently wrote a monograph on the Numantine war. This and other early publications – a biography of PHILOPOIMEN, a book on *Tactics*, and a monograph on the habitability of the equatorial regions – are all lost.

Polybios' main work, the *Histories*, which eventually contained 40 books though originally planned as 30, was conceived and partly written at Rome, but finished later. It aimed at showing how, in almost 53 years (220–167), Rome had conquered virtually the whole inhabited world. Rome's success lay in its outstanding military efficiency and excellent constitution, both analysed in book 6. Two introductory books covered the years from the outbreak of the first PUNIC WAR in 264; the main narrative began in 220, where Aratos' *Memoirs* ended. From 217, in Polybios' eyes, history had become 'an organic whole', which called for a 'universal history'. This universality Polybios expressed through a chronology based on flexible Olympiad years and by treating events annually under Italy, SICILY, Spain, Greece and Macedonia, Africa, Asia and Egypt, normally in that order. Two Olympiad years were assigned to each book, but that number varied to match the importance of the contents.

To describe the kind of history he wrote, dealing primarily with military and political events, Polybios devised the term 'pragmatic history' (*pragmatikê historia*). He relied chiefly on personal memories and those of eye-witnesses, but also used written sources: for books 1 and 2 ARATOS OF SIKYON, Phylarchos and, for Roman events, FABIUS PICTOR and Philinos. For his main history he used a wide range of authors and informants, few of whom can now be firmly identified. His purpose was to provide a moral training by describing how historical characters faced the vicissitudes of fortune, but also to instruct politicians and generals in their craft, a procedure which required emphasizing the causes and results of each action. This he regarded as essential if his *Histories* were to help present and future readers. Following tradition, he introduced speeches into his text at critical points; his claim that these record what was actually said is not invariably sustainable. He asserts a utilitarian view of history against a popular school which employed meretricious and sensational writing to entertain the reader, a fault for which he criticizes Phylarchos. Polybios' claim to write truthfully and impartially is largely justified, though occasionally prejudice against Achaian enemies like AITOLIA warps his judgement, and his self-righteous criticism of forerunners like Kallisthenes, TIMAIOS (attacked at length in book 12) and Phylarchos, and of contemporaries like Zeno of Rhodes, is unattractive.

When precisely Polybios wrote and published his *Histories* is conjectural. At some date after 146 he decided to extend his work to 40 books to take in the years 167–146/5 and so enable readers to judge Rome's rule. An additional reason for the extension was to publicize Polybios' own role in events of which he 'not only witnessed most but took part in and directed some' (3.4.12) and also to glorify his friend Scipio. He describes the final years of the extended period as a time of 'disturbance and trouble', to be approached as if it were a new work. How Polybios intended his readers to judge Rome remains controversial. His comments on Roman conduct towards other states and rulers between 167 and the late 150s are often quite cynical. Yet when he reaches the third Macedonian, third Punic and Achaian wars he strongly condemns Rome's enemies and their leaders. In relating Greek debates on the justice of Roman action against Carthage in the third Punic war, he expresses no personal view and his alignment has been variously interpreted. It is, however, unlikely that he was in principle opposed to a policy closely identified with Scipio Aemilianus.

Book 6 contains a detailed account, mostly now lost, of the Roman state in the broadest sense. In what survives, Polybios outlines its adoption of a balanced combination of KINGSHIP, ARISTOCRACY and DEMOCRACY. This he sees as having enabled Rome to evade the tendency to corruption inherent in each of these separate political forms, which normally followed each other in a cycle of alternating good and corrupt constitutional types: kingship, TYRANNY, aristocracy, oligarchy, democracy, mob-rule, ending up in monarchy, and so back to kingship. Directly or indirectly, Polybios' account of both the 'mixed constitution' and the cyclical development has greatly influenced statesmen, historians and political theorists since the RENAISSANCE.

Books 1–5 survive intact and books 6–18 in a substantial collection of fragments (known by the Latin name *excerpta antiqua*). For the rest we rely mainly on what survives from a collection of excerpts made for Constantine VII Porphyrogenitus in the 10th century (when books 17, 19, 26, 37 and 40 were already lost), supplemented from ATHENAEUS, STRABO, the *SUDA* and other late sources. Some of the substance of the lost narrative figures in LIVY, books 21–45, and also in DIODORUS, in various lives of PLUTARCH and in APPIAN. But neither his style, based on the *koinê*, nor his theme had much appeal under the empire. Our present text was largely reconstructed by I. Casaubon (1609) and J. Schweighaeuser (1789–95). FWW

See Büttner-Wobst, T. (1889–1904) (text); Eckstein, A. M. (1995) *Moral Vision in the Histories of Polybius*; Paton, W. R. (1922–7) (text and trs.); Scott-Kilvert, I. (1979) *Polybius and the Rise of the Roman Empire* (trs.); Walbank, F.W. (1957–79) *A Historical Commentary on Polybius*, 3 vols.; (1972) *Polybius*; (1985) *Selected Papers*; (2002) *Polybius, Rome and the Hellenistic World*.

Polykleitos (Polyclitus) Sculptor, Argive (Sikyonian according to PLINY, *Natural History* 34.55), active c.450s–410 BC. No original works of his survive, but they were much copied in the imperial period. Three bases signed with his name have been found at OLYMPIA.

Polykleitos worked in bronze, preferring male subjects, particularly HEROES and ATHLETES, though Pliny says his *Astragalizontes* (*Boys Playing Knucklebones*) was 'generally considered to be the most perfect work of art in existence'. He made an Amazon for EPHESOS, portraits, and statues of divinities which are said to have included a chryselephantine (GOLD and IVORY) cult statue for the Argive Heraion, though a later Polykleitos may be intended.

Polykleitos' most innovative and influential work was the *Doryphoros* (*Spear-bearer*), an athletic nude male (possibly ACHILLES) known from over 50 copies. Posed between standing and walking, with chiastically relaxed and tense limbs (the right arm and left leg relaxed, the left arm and right leg tense), it established new balance and proportions for the male body, reflecting contemporary interest in geometry and anatomy. The *Doryphoros* was probably the embodiment of principles explained in Polykleitos'

Canon, the first known sculptural treatise, of which only fragments survive. His other athlete statues included the *Diadoumenos*, which showed a victorious athlete tying a fillet round his head and was famous for its cost, 100 talents. Polykleitos' advances were lasting and were continued initially by his pupils. His influence became pervasive, culminating in LYSIPPOS' new norm for male proportions in the mid-4th century. KWA

See Borbein, A.H. (1996) Polykleitos, in O. Palagia and J. J. Pollitt, eds., *Personal Styles in Greek Sculpture* 66–90; Moon, W. G., ed. (1995) *Polykleitos, the Doryphoros and Tradition*.

Polyperchon see SUCCESSORS.

polytheism see GODS AND GODDESSES; MARTYRS; MONOTHEISM; PAGANISM.

pomerium The sacred boundary of Rome (and other cities), differing in location from both the city wall and the actual inhabited area, though it coincided in some places. Some types of auspices could only be performed within the *pomerium*. Delineated by boundary stones (*cippi*), the region within the *pomerium* was prohibited to men under arms, except by special permission, as in the case of TRIUMPHS. Even the centuriate ASSEMBLY, based on a military premise, met outside the boundary, at the Campus Martius.

The ancient sources vary considerably in their treatments of the origins and expansions of the *pomerium*, and scholars have failed to reach agreement on most points. While some sources credit the establishment of the circuit to ROMULUS, the *pomerium* was most likely laid out by SERVIUS TULLIUS, employing an ETRUSCAN ritual. The area included four regions, Suburana, Esquilina, Collina and Palatina, which were also the districts of the four urban TRIBES. Both SULLA and JULIUS CAESAR enlarged the *pomerium*. Although TACITUS (*Annals* 12.23) credits AUGUSTUS with a further expansion, the emperor does not mention any enlargement in his account of his own achievements. CLAUDIUS, who included the Aventine for the first time, and VESPASIAN both extended the *pomerium*, but boundary markers from the reign of HADRIAN are restorations rather than indications of further enlargement. While AURELIAN (AD 270–5) was responsible for the Aurelian wall, he probably did not augment the *pomerium*, despite the claim in some sources that he did. JV

See Cornell, T. J. (1995) *The Beginnings of Rome*, 202–3.

Pompeii (city) Ancient city on the bay of Naples, destroyed by the eruption of Vesuvius (PLINY THE YOUNGER, *Letters* 6.16, 6.20). EXCAVATIONS at the site began in the 18th century and have continued to the present day. These have revealed extensive destruction due to a series of pyroclastic surges through the day and night of 24 August AD 79 and subsequent attempts by the inhabitants to recover possessions. The city revealed demonstrates that it was extensively damaged by the EARTHQUAKE of AD 62 (SENECA, *Natural Questions* 6), estimated to have been 6–7 on the Richter scale. Hence, what we see today is a city undergoing reconstruction following an earthquake and subsequently destroyed through volcanic events. The notion that in Pompeii we may see normal daily life or a time-capsule snapshot has been discredited – we see a city destroyed, with artefactual evidence disrupted on its destruction and subsequently through attempts to recover possessions.

The period after the earthquake was one of gradual recovery. Few public buildings had been completely repaired by 79 – the notable exceptions being the AMPHITHEATRE and the TEMPLE of ISIS. The latter was repaired by the son of a FREEDMAN, who gained entry onto the town council at the age of six – a further sign that this period was a time of emergency measures. This is further indicated by the presence in the city of Suedius Clemens, a TRIBUNE sent by the emperor Vespasian from Rome, who restored property divisions, including that of the *POMERIUM*. The plan to restore the FORUM and its associated building was ambitious and still to be completed in 79. From this period few inscriptions refer to those involved in the reconstruction, simply because the buildings were not completed. Other areas of construction included the partially built central BATHS, even though there is evidence that the AQUEDUCT and water system were not operating as before. What does survive from this period are electoral notices painted on the outer walls of HOUSES, urging support for key candidates in annual ELECTIONS to junior and senior magistracies (AEDILES and duumvirs). This evidence demonstrates links of PATRONAGE to individuals (both male and female), and to groups such as the FULLERS, fruit sellers or goldsmiths and suggests that the social institutions associated with political life were active.

Excavations have revealed settlement and a street plan back to the 6th century BC, with many buildings from the AD 79 destruction dating back to the 2nd or even the 3rd centuries BC. Following the SOCIAL WAR, VETERANS from SULLA's forces were settled in the city. In the period immediately following, we find the amphitheatre and small THEATRE constructed, alongside a new temple of VENUS associated with the name of the colony: Colonia Cornelia Veneria Pompeianorum. The reshaping of public buildings is symptomatic of the conflict associated with the arrival of the veterans. However, the cultural change may not have been marked, since the city had already many forms of ARCHITECTURE associated with Roman colonies: forum, BASILICA, baths and theatre. The forum, often cited as a classic in terms of 'Roman' architecture, was actually produced by an OSCAN-speaking allied town. In the absence of direct evidence for a separate community of veterans, it would be logical to assume that these newcomers took over property from dispossessed inhabitants.

A further significant phase of development of the forum occurred in the early 1st century AD. Streets into the Piazza area were blocked off by buildings on the eastern side. These included the largest public building, a *porticus* dedicated to Concordia Augusta, built by Eumachia, a PRIESTESS. Other buildings associated with the IMPERIAL CULT were dedicated to the Genius of Augustus and to Fortuna Augusta. The latter encloses dedications by minor magistrates, often FREEDMEN, known as *magistri* or *ministri Augusti*. This phase of the city saw the remodelling of the theatre and the temple of APOLLO. From this period of renewal, there is evidence of key families, e.g. the Holconii, as well as links to patrons beyond the town. It is notable that STRABO, writing within this period, considered Vesuvius an extinct volcano. He also accounts for the early history of the city and suggests that it had been a SAMNITE town. This

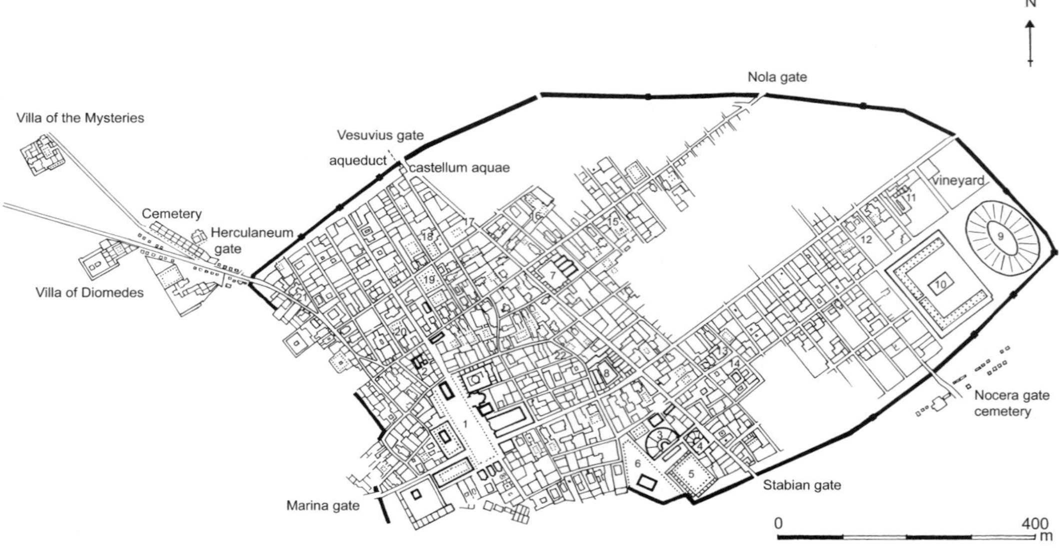

Pompeii: (a) plan of excavated area of the ancient city: 1. Forum (for detailed plan of this area see forums; 2. Forum baths; 3. Theatre; 4. Odeion; 5. Gladiators' barracks; 6. Triangular forum; 7. Central baths; 8. Stabian baths; 9. Amphitheatre; 10. Great Palaestra; 11. House of Julia Felix; 12. House of Loreius Tiburtinus; 13. House of the Cryptoporticus; 14. House of the Menander; 15. House of the Centenary; 16. House of the Silver Wedding; 17. House of the Golden Cupids; 18. House of the Vettii; 19. House of the Faun; 20. House of the Tragic Poet; 21. House of the Surgeon; 22. Brothel/inns.

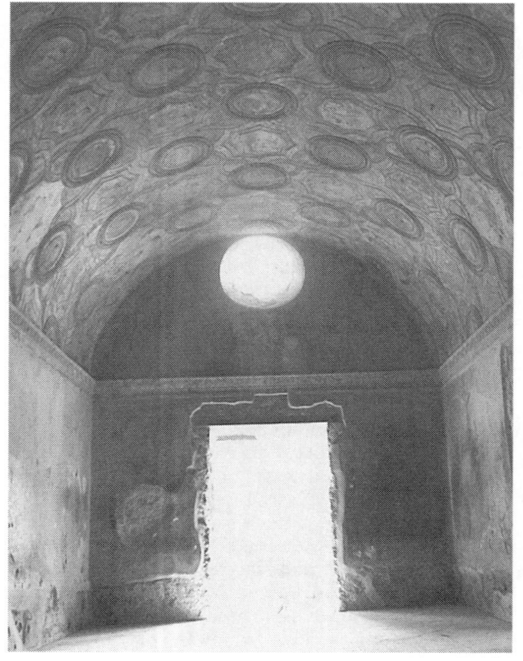

Pompeii: (b) preserved vault with stucco relief in the Stabian baths.

Pompeii: (c) Pompeian street with a 2-storey house (rear) and public fountain (foreground).

creative ethnic origin has been taken literally and associated with the most simple building and styles of painting and construction. The association is now largely avoided, but excavations have revealed earlier peoples mentioned by Strabo, including an ETRUSCAN presence.

Even though there was much disruption after the earthquake of 62, there is a greater level of evidence within the archaeological record for the writing of social and economic history than at similar sites (e.g. OSTIA). However, it needs to be recognized that the level of recording of archaeological evidence was haphazard even in the 1950s and 1960s. Many artefacts were simply not recorded and it is difficult to pin down the context (i.e. a room within the house) for many artefacts in store, or on display in museums. However, for economic historians the architecture of certain key activities (e.g. BAKING or fulling) reveals the place in the city of production and services (e.g. eating and drinking). In the absence of key artefactual evidence, historians have utilized literary texts to interpret the site. The addition of formal methods of spatial analysis drawn from GEOGRAPHY has enhanced the understanding of the city form and zoning of activities (Laurence). There was no social segregation of population according to socio-economic zones, and the activities of the most prosperous were not separated from those of the most plebeian. The survival of wax tablets from two key ARCHIVES of documents found in the Murecine Inn provides unique information for BANKING and the loaning of money within the city and around the bay of Naples.

The fabric of Pompeii reveals the nature of urban living and particularly of housing. This might vary from a large property within a single city block (*insula*) to that of a small single-room SHOP with living space above in a block that was divided up for the purpose of rental. However, it needs to be recognized that the eruption destroyed most of the information relating to upper floors of these two-storey buildings. All reconstructions of the houses are partial and limited for the most part to the ground floor. These interpretations are informed by the discussion of the atrium-peristyle house found in VITRUVIUS (*On Architecture*) and other key texts that have been seen as a semiotic language for the description of house-form and an explanation of its structure. It is at the level of the house that environmental ARCHAEOLOGY has made a major contribution to understanding the urban environment. The study of tree roots, pollen, INSECT remains, molluscs and other plant remains has made possible the reconstruction of planting patterns in GARDENS. This has included productive plots as well as decorative SCULPTURE in the gardens of the élite. The houses contain the basis for our understanding of decorative style in the 1st century AD. The frescoes on walls reveal a range of attitudes to MYTHOLOGY and LANDSCAPE. The conjunction of the WALL-PAINTINGS with floor MOSAICS provides one of the few opportunities to examine three-dimensional stylistic conventions from the Roman world. There is also considerable information for the study of gender and SEXUALITY of all classes: the deployment of erotic scenes, graffiti and the physical settings for PROSTITUTION. More striking are the masses of artefacts and their associations: there are more objects preserved at Pompeii than anywhere else in the Roman empire, and 80 per cent of all known Roman GLASS was excavated from the Vesuvian sites of Herculaneum and Pompeii. These finds have seldom been the subject of study and for the most part their archaeological contexts cannot be reconstructed with certainty. The range of materials, from simple AMPHORAS to surgical instruments or AGRICULTURAL TOOLS to the ARMOUR of GLADIATORS, reveals a range of TECHNOLOGIES for life and RITUAL.

Pompeii and its discovery had an important impact on European culture and the classical tradition in the West. The impact of the discovery had a profound effect on artistic style and contemporary material culture: much FURNITURE and interior colours (notably blue) in the 18th century originated from visits to Pompeii. Numerous poems, operas, accounts of personal experiences and early photographs were published in the 18th and the 19th centuries, culminating in Bulwer-Lytton's *The Last Days of Pompeii*, later made into a film, and as recently as the 1980s a TV mini-series. In the 20th century, the association between destruction and resurrection of the site was to establish Pompeii as a reference point for Western culture (for example in Freud's writings on psychoanalysis). RL

See Allison, P. (1997) Artefact distribution and spatial function in Pompeian houses, in B. Rawson and P. Weaver, eds., *The Roman Family in Italy* 321–54; Dobbins, J. (1994) Problems of chronology, decoration and urban design in the forum at Pompeii, *AJA* 98: 629–94; Clarke, J. (1998) *Looking at Lovemaking*; Ciarello, A. and De Carolis, E. (1999) *Pompeii: life in a Roman town*; Coarelli, F., ed. (2002) *Pompeii*; Cooley, A. E. (2003) *Pompeii*; Fulford, M. and Wallace-Hadrill, A. (1999) Towards a history of pre-Roman Pompeii, *PRBS* 67: 37–144; Jashemski, W. (1979, 1993) *The Gardens of Pompeii*; Laurence, R. (1994) *Roman Pompeii*; Laurence, R. and Wallace-Hadrill, A. (1997) *Domestic Space in the Roman World*; Leppman, W. (1968) *Pompeii in Fact and Fiction*; Mouritsen, H. (1988) *Elections, Magistrates and Municipal Élite*; Nappo, S. (1998) *Pompeii*; Siggurdson, H. et al. (1985) The eruption of Vesuvius in AD 79, *National Geographic Research* 1: 332–87; Wallace-Hadrill, A. (1994) *Houses and Society in Pompeii and Herculaneum*.

BATHS: (c); FOUNTAINS AND FOUNTAIN HOUSES: (b); HOUSES, ROMAN: (a)–(c); WORKSHOPS.

Pompeii (family) PLEBEIAN family of the late REPUBLIC; POMPEY the Great is the best known representative. Their TRIBE was the Clustumina. The name probably has the same etymological root as the town in Campania, but there are no direct links between the family and the place. The family rose to prominence with Quintus Pompeius, CONSUL in 141 BC and a *novus homo*; he went on to be CENSOR. There were three lines, the Rufi, the Bithynici and that of Pompey. The first two are closely related, but the connection between these and the third is obscure. The third line stands out: Gnaeus Pompeius Strabo, his son Pompey, and Pompey's two sons, Gnaeus and Sextus. Strabo, by his opposition to SULLA (his troops killed a distant relative, Quintus Pompeius Rufus, sent to replace him), offered a foretaste of the methods which Pompey himself and CAESAR would employ. Pompey's career began under Sulla, earning him the sobriquet *adulescens carnifex* ('teenage executioner'), and was marked by a series of extraordinary commands. Consul in 70 without holding previous office, he went on, in the 60s, vastly to extend

Rome's empire in the East. Coming into conflict increasingly with Julius Caesar and embroiled in senatorial politicking, he led the opposition when Caesar crossed the Rubicon in 49 BC and was murdered in Egypt, fleeing after defeat at PHARSALUS in 48. Pompey's sons, and Sextus in particular, sought in vain to continue the struggle against first Caesar and then the TRIUMVIRS; their father's name became synonymous with the 'free' Republic. JRWP

See Plutarch, *Pompey*, trs. R. Waterfield (1999); Seager, R. (1979) *Pompey*.

Pompey (Gnaeus Pompeius Magnus) 106–48 BC Known usually by the English version of his name, he was the dominant political figure of the late Roman Republic. CIVIL WAR, and Pompey's own talents and ruthlessness, enabled him to rise to pre-eminence by wholly exceptional means, not even entering the SENATE until his CONSULSHIP. When SULLA returned to Italy in 83, the young Pompey raised an army of three legions, recruiting initially from his father's VETERANS and clients in Picenum. This led Sulla to employ him as a commander, sending him to crush opposition in SICILY and AFRICA. These exploits earned him the *cognomen* Magnus ('Great') and a TRIUMPH, grudgingly conceded by Sulla and unprecedented for one who had held no office. After Sulla's death, the weakened senatorial government was obliged to call on Pompey to help suppress Lepidus' revolt and then to send him to Spain against SERTORIUS (77). After initial setbacks, Sertorius' assassination enabled Pompey to crush the rebellion there, and on his return he was rewarded with another triumph and the consulship of 70. As consul, with his colleague CRASSUS, he endeared himself to the people by carrying a LAW restoring to the TRIBUNES the powers Sulla had taken from them. Laws passed by tribunes granted Pompey great commands against the PIRATES (67) and MITHRADATES (66). He rapidly defeated these enemies, annexed SYRIA and reorganized the East, returning in 62 to a spectacular triumph.

Senatorial opposition obstructed the ratification of Pompey's Eastern settlement and his wish to reward his veterans with land. As a result, CAESAR reconciled Pompey to Crassus and, as consul in 59, forced through these and other controversial laws with their backing. Caesar's reward was the GALLIC command, which he used to make conquests rivalling Pompey's. Now married to Caesar's daughter Julia, Pompey remained in Rome, at odds with Crassus and harassed by the demagogue CLODIUS. In 57 a corn crisis led to his being put in charge of the corn supply, and in 56 Pompey, Caesar and Crassus renewed their alliance at Luca. Pompey became consul again with Crassus in 55 and took a five-year command in Spain but remained at Rome, governing his PROVINCE through legates. The deaths of Julia (54) and Crassus (53) weakened his ties with Caesar. Mounting anarchy at Rome culminated in Milo's killing of Clodius (52), and the senate was obliged to turn to Pompey. Appointed sole consul, he restored order through trials and legislation, obtained an extension of his own command and for Caesar the right to stand for the consulship in absence. Pompey's rapprochement with the senatorial conservatives led in 51–50 to a breach with Caesar. The sticking point was Caesar's claim to retain troops until he assumed the consulship. The fundamental issue was personal dignity: 'Caesar could not brook a superior, nor Pompey an equal' (LUCAN 1.125–6).

When Caesar invaded Italy in 49, Pompey lacked the forces to face him and withdrew to MACEDONIA to mobilize. After Caesar crossed in 48, Pompey was successful in initial manoeuvres at Dyrrachium, but accepted pitched battle at PHARSALUS and was crushingly defeated. He fled to Egypt, but was killed on landing. JWR

See Greenhalgh, P. (1980) *Pompey: the Roman Alexander*; (1981) *Pompey: the republican prince*; Leach, J. (1978) *Pompey*; Seager, R. (2002) *Pompey*.

 AUGUSTUS: (a).

Pontius Pilate Governor of JUDAEA probably from AD 26 to 36, Pilate is best known as the man who condemned JESUS to crucifixion. An inscription from CAESAREA MARITIMA accords him the military title of *praefectus Iudaeae*. His greed and cruelty are described in some detail by his contemporary PHILO, quoting (*Embassy to Gaius* 302) king Agrippa I, who knew him in Judaea. Many of his unsavoury actions are reported by JOSEPHUS. The precise dates of his long governorship are disputed, but the length of his tenure was probably a result of the retirement to CAPRI of the emperor TIBERIUS and his refusal to take decisions about provincial administration.

Pilate's rule was punctuated by unrest provoked by Pilate himself. His actions were tactless at best, perhaps malicious. There was mass opposition when he ordered his soldiers to bring into Jerusalem military standards bearing the emperor's image and votive shields inscribed with the emperor's name, and when he took sacred money from the Temple treasury for the erection of an AQUEDUCT for the city. To some extent Pilate may simply have misunderstood Jewish taboos. Eventually he was sent to Rome to answer for a massacre of Samaritans who had congregated on Mt Gerizim. Despite later speculation by CHRISTIAN writers, his fate after he left Judaea is unknown. MDG

Pontos (Pontus) see ANTINOUS; MITHRADATES (MITHRIDATES) VI EUPATOR; PLINY THE YOUNGER; STRABO (STRABÔN).

Poppaea Sabina Daughter of Titus Ollius, a QUAESTOR and member of a distinguished SENATORIAL family. Poppaea's first husband was Rufrius Crispinus, a PRAETORIAN prefect during the reign of CLAUDIUS. Her second was the future emperor OTHO. During this marriage she became the enamoured of the emperor NERO, whom she married subsequently. Poppaea became an important and influential figure at Nero's court. Our sources, principally SUETONIUS and TACITUS, imply her complicity in the death of Nero's mother, AGRIPPINA (thus precipitating, along with the deaths of SENECA and Burrus, the sharp decline in Nero's rule), and in the banishment and execution of Nero's second wife, Octavia, on fictitious charges of ADULTERY. In AD 63, Poppaea gave birth to a daughter named Claudia Augusta, who died aged four months. Suetonius notes that Nero loved Poppaea greatly, but it may be testament to his character, and perhaps hers, that Nero kicked her to death (though she was pregnant again) after she had complained that he had come home late after attending races. In life, the honour of the title Augusta was conferred on Poppaea, and in death she received a public funeral and divine honours. CEPA

See Griffin, M. (1984) *Nero*.

populares see ÉLITES.

population, size of see DEMOGRAPHY.

Populonia see ETRURIA AND ETRUSCANS.

Porcii see CATO THE ELDER; CATO THE YOUNGER.

pornography Sexually explicit material was prevalent and highly visible throughout the Greek and Roman worlds. Street corners in Athens were often adorned with a statue representing the god HERMES sporting an erect penis. Drinking vessels regularly displayed scenes of comic bestiality and masturbation. Sex manuals describing positions for intercourse were in wide circulation. Roman WALL-PAINTINGS depicting intercourse were common and were displayed to passing viewers. A large number of lamps depict scenes of copulation. There seems to have been little or no effort to screen these images from viewers on the basis of age or sex. Men, women and children were regularly exposed to images that would be subject to legal or social sanction in many cultures today.

A considerable amount of this material presents individuals (esp. women and youths) as passive sexual objects. Little attention is paid to the sex object's desires or pleasure. Scenes of RAPE are common. Mythological rapes tend to be less explicit than depictions of earthly ones. On Attic vases designed for the *SYMPOSIA*, we have a number of scenes where women are being coerced into performing sexual acts through violence. Greek and Latin literature often delights in recounting male fantasies of pursuit and sexual conquest. AJLB

See Clarke, J. R. (1998) *Looking at Lovemaking*; Keuls, E. C. (1985) *The Reign of the Phallus*; Montserrat, D. (1996) *Sex and Society in Graeco-Roman Egypt*; Richlin, A., ed. (1992) *Pornography and Representation in Greece and Rome*.

Porsenna see LARS PORSENNA.

portraiture

PLINY THE ELDER (*Natural History* 35.153) says Lysistratos (c. mid-4th century BC) introduced 'likenesses' (*similitudines*) and was the first to take a portrait (*imago*) from a living face. Previous practice had been 'to make as handsome a face as possible', an exception being the portrait of the notoriously ugly Hipponax (c.540; *Natural History* 36.11–12).

During the archaic period, interest grew in showing individuality in sculpture, e.g. the Rampin Rider (c.550). Some statues have inscribed names, including the KOUROS Kroisos (c.530), three statues from the Samian Geneleos group (c.560–550), or Chares, ruler of Teichioussa in CARIA, placed on the sacred way to DIDYMA (c.575). All these, however individual they may appear, are in the style of their time. The vase-painter Exekias (c.540) wrote 'Amasos' beside a depiction of an ETHIOPIAN, presumably referring to his fellow potter-painter Amasis, with African features alluding to his Egyptian descent. It is a generic representation, not a portrait. The captioned depictions of each other by late 6th-century vase-painters are in the style of the period.

PORTRAITURE: painting of a young couple from Pompeii.

From the classical period, portraiture develops on coins, GEMS and, primarily, in SCULPTURE. Arguably the first genuine portrait is the tyrannicides group (477/6), often copied and perhaps itself copying the original group (soon after 510), stolen by the PERSIANS (Pliny, *Natural History* 34.17; Pausanias 1.8.5). The tyrannicides are named in an inscription, and differentiated by age. AESCHYLUS' fragmentary *Isthmiastai* (c.460) mentions SATYRS holding lifelike images (*eikones*) of themselves, and the contemporary portrait of THEMISTOKLES, preserved as a Roman herm, displays a realism which contrasts with the idealizing of most contemporary sculpture. This appears in the portrait of PERIKLES, perhaps by Kresilas (Pliny, *Natural History* 34.74), preserved only as a bust in a Roman copy. Pliny calls this Perikles 'Olympian', suggesting exactly the idealized features it bears, in the spirit of the PARTHENON sculptures. Its individuality lies in the helmet, worn, according to PLUTARCH (*Perikles* 3.2), because artists were unwilling to show Perikles' unusually shaped head. Plutarch adds (*Perikles* 31.4) Perikles' depiction in the Amazonomachy of the ATHENA Parthenos' shield, alongside the artist, Pheidias. Both were recognizable only from the side, indicating that portraits were considered inappropriate in a sacred context. They occur, however, in the secular STOA Poikile, where Pheidias' brother, Panainos, painted prominent Greeks and Persians at the battle of MARATHON. Later classical portraits become less idealizing, with more interest in suggesting character. Thus Roman works believed to be copies of the statues of Aeschylus, SOPHOKLES and EURIPIDES erected in Athens c.330 show individual features within a type appropriate to a tragedian.

The later 4th century ushers in the hellenistic age, heralded by Alexander the Great's careful control of his image. This included appointing his personal portraitists, Apelles (painter), Lysippos (sculptor) and Pyrgoteles (gem-cutter). Hellenistic rulers manipulated their images in the succeeding centuries. Non-royal portraits became more realistic, e.g. the Demosthenes created c.280 and known from over 40 copies, and the creation in the 2nd century of the blind Homer, replacing earlier, less naturalistic types. From the late hellenistic period, Roman Republican portraits adopt similar realism. KWA

See Richter, G. M. A., rev. R. R. R. Smith (1983) *The Portraits of the Greeks*; Walker, S. (1995) *Greek and Roman Portraits.*

Roman portraiture is particularly noted for its high level of verism (truth), exemplified, for example, in the meticulous recording of facial infelicities. The origins of this stylistic preference are obscure. A possible prototype may be found in the ancestral portraits displayed in the homes of noble families. Moreover, in funeral processions it was customary for young nobles to wear masks of the ancestors whom they most resembled. In a later development, an actor wearing a mask played the part of the deceased. Both practices cannot be understood if the mask was not intended to proclaim a close physical likeness. This does not explain why Romans had no problems with displaying the less appealing side of the human anatomy, especially in the portraits of their most revered representatives. Roman nobles consciously represented themselves in art as men whose features clearly bear the signs of their weighty public responsibilities and service to the state. The challenge of expressing weightiness and a serious disposition could have been easily met in ways which avoided the almost obsessive attachment to the requirements of verism. The predisposition to represent individuals in art as they were in real life may derive from a deeply ingrained cultural expectation which declared falsehood and lying to be un-Roman characteristics, and which considered external beauty to be less important than the cardinal virtues of hard work, courage and dedication. The same attachment to ultraverism which was common to noble families characterizes the portraits of freedman families on their funerary monuments from the late Republic onwards. The celebration of traditional Roman virtues had spread to newly enfranchised citizens who proudly displayed their freshly acquired Romanness.

From the 2nd century BC onwards some aspiring political leaders adopted the more idealizing Greek style of representation. The portrait busts of Pompey which show him in the guise of a Roman Alexander the Great are a prime example. The hellenizing trend made a lasting impact on the shape of Roman portraiture, and in the principate it was routinely followed by other strata in society, such as ex-slaves, most of whom came from a Hellenic background. Yet it did not succeed in eclipsing the Roman fondness for lifelike representation. Obviously, some concessions were made to the requirements of extreme verism, as when the portraits of Sulla do not feature his well-known facial blemishes and the balding Julius Caesar only has a receding hairline. Augustus blended an idealizing programme with a modesty of presentation, but no portraits of him have survived that show him as the ageing emperor, and probably none were made. Verism, again, was a requirement for emperors of more modest origins, such as Vespasian, but even the portraits of Nero, one of the most enthusiastic Julio-Claudian supporters of Hellenic culture, do not attempt to hide his chubbiness. Even though Nero and Domitian are occasionally represented as bearded, it was not until the time of Hadrian that the full beard made its entrance in Roman portraiture. This was an expression of his attachment to Greek culture. MK

See Walker, S. (1995) *Greek and Roman Portraits.*

 mummy portraits.

Portus see Ostia and Portus.

Poseidippos see comedy 2: Middle and New Comedy.

Poseidon Greek god of the sea, earthquakes, horsemen and horse races. Son of Kronos and Rhea, and brother of Zeus and Hades. His share of the world was assigned by lot between him and his brothers after their victory against the Titans. He received the realm of the sea, leaving to Zeus and Hades the sky and underworld respectively.

Poseidon is one of the most senior gods in the *Iliad* along with Zeus and Hera. In the Trojan war he supports the Achaians, yet causes endless wanderings for Odysseus on his way home from Troy after the latter blinds his son, the Cyclops Polyphemos. Poseidon's relationship with Polyphemos and other earth-born monsters is a typical aspect of his persona which probably goes back to his capacities before he took over the realm of the sea. This is suggested by his name, the first part of which contains the Greek term for 'consort' (*posis*) with *da* probably alluding to *gê* (earth). This relationship with the earth is further reflected in his Homeric title 'earth-shaker'.

The trident is his most striking attribute in ancient imagery, as is the golden chariot which he drives together with his wife, Amphitrite. Poseidon was popular as protector of fishermen and seafarers and was worshipped at coastal places such as capes, peninsulas and islands. Athena defeated him in a contest for the control of Attica. His sanctuaries at Isthmia (near Corinth), Sounion (Attica) and Tainaron are among the best known, and many functioned as places of refuge for slaves. EP

See Simon, E. (1994) Poseidon, in *LIMC* vol. 7, 446–79.

gods and goddesses: (b).

Posidippos see epigrams; Kallikrates.

Posidonius (Poseidonios) 135–51 BC Stoic philosopher. Originally from Apameia, Posidonius studied in Athens with the Stoic Panaitios (Panaetius) but later became a naturalized citizen of Rhodes. There, he enjoyed some political prominence: he was elected to the prytany (one of the most important offices) and in 87/6 served on the Rhodian embassy to Rome. His intellectual fame drew Cicero to his lectures in the early 70s, and Pompey twice took an opportunity to visit him in the 60s. The thematic scope of his work was huge: his many writings, all now lost, contained contributions to fields such as ANTHROPOLOGY, GEOGRAPHY, meteorology and ASTRONOMY as well as the standard topics in LOGIC, PHYSICS and ETHICS. Many of these interests converged in his massive *History*, a work 52 books long – though it covered a period of no more than 60 years from 146 BC.

Stoicism, from its foundation by ZENO OF CITIUM, looked back to the philosophy of SOCRATES, which had been corrupted, as some thought, by PLATO. Posidonius, however, worked in a tradition, inherited through Panaitios, that had started to see in Plato and his immediate followers important links between Socrates and Zeno. This fact colours a lot of Posidonius' thought. The very range of his interests, and the prominence he gave to the empirical SCIENCES, might already suggest comparison with Plato's pupil ARISTOTLE. More importantly, there are echoes of Plato himself in his insistence that such studies were only the starting point for the philosopher, whose real aim was an understanding of the fundamental causes at work in the universe. Only in his discussion of human psychology, however, can Posidonius be accused of diverging in any important respect from his Stoic predecessors. For while they argued that EMOTIONS were forms of belief ('fear', for example, the belief that something dangerous was at hand; 'desire' the belief that something is beneficial), Posidonius thought Plato right to suppose that they involved independent activities of the SOUL which could even conflict with belief (so that we sometimes fear things we know cannot hurt us). His agreement with the 'divine' Plato on this score has led some people to think of Posidonius as a 'Platonist'; but the truth is that he reworks Plato as much as he rethinks Stoicism. Plato's own followers, for example, generally supposed that he had distinguished between good and bad emotions, but Posidonius insisted that all emotion was evil, and happiness possible only once we are freed from the excessive attachment to material wellbeing which it implies. If details of Posidonius' psychology were 'Platonic', the wider ethical system into which it fitted was thoroughly Stoic after all.

Posidonius was read much more than he was followed by subsequent Stoics, who were interested most in ethics, and preferred the ethics of Panaitios and Chrysippos. His reputation remained high and his influence significant. Cicero never tires of dropping his name. Another pupil, Athenaios, founded the Pneumatist school of MEDICINE. STRABO relied heavily on his work, and VITRUVIUS, SENECA and GALEN variously acknowledge their debt to him. GB-S

See Kidd, I. G. (1999) *Posidonius*, vol. 3: *The Translation of the Fragments*.

post (mail) The classical world never developed a postal system to deliver letters and packages. As a consequence, letters, messages and parcels sent between private individuals were taken by private messenger. Correspondence for public purposes like DIPLOMACY often travelled with AMBASSADORS or other representatives of states. Messages did not always move with equal speed. For example, a SHIP carrying the message that the Athenian ASSEMBLY had voted to kill the males and enslave the women and children of Mytilene was caught just in time by a second vessel sent the next day, after the assembly changed its mind.

The Roman imperial administration developed a system for the delivery of official dispatches. The service provided changes of HORSES at regular intervals for a messenger who retained the message from beginning to end; it was not designed to pass a message from hand to hand, as in a modern postal or courier system. The post was theoretically limited to official dispatches and representatives, but EMPERORS and governors could grant use to private individuals. From the time of CONSTANTINE, BISHOPS travelling to CHURCH COUNCILS often employed the system, a privilege roundly criticized by some non-Christian writers as a waste of state resources.

People who travelled from one place to another often carried large packets of letters from the place of origin to individuals resident along the way and at the destination. CICERO, LIBANIUS and others often refer to the carriers of their letters. Many recipients of mail in the ancient world received their correspondence in this fashion. JV

post-colonialism A theoretical model that seeks to identify the 'discrepant experience' of subordinate cultures. As its main objective, post-colonial theory examines the cultural politics of colonization: the hegemonic processes by which direct control over foreign peoples was maintained. A primary focus of post-colonial theory is the interaction between ruler and subordinate, 'discourses' that determine, as well as sustain, hegemony.

Although post-colonial theory originally emerged as the study of decolonized cultures previously subject to Western imperialism, its recent application to the study of the Roman empire has been significant in furthering our understanding of the 'native experience'. Foremost, a post-colonial perspective dictates a shift in emphasis from Rome to its 'colonial' margins. Thus, there is a greater tendency for recent research to focus on the peripheral regions of the empire and to embrace the regional diversity that is noted as a result of local conditions and responses. This emphasis on colonialism, rather than the imperial agenda of Rome, enables research to identify the situated 'discourses' that contributed to the active history of Rome's PROVINCES. In consequence, a salient feature of post-colonial study is the active role of the indigenous populations in the formation of their own culture. From a post-colonial perspective, and in direct contrast to traditional models whereby subjugated populations were 'given a civilization', the adoption and variant use of Roman material culture by indigenous peoples were means of negotiating with, as well as resisting, imperial domination. MLM

See Webster, J. and Cooper, N., eds. (1996) *Roman Imperialism: post-colonial perspectives*.

post-modernism Post-modernism is best characterized as an attitude or approach towards literary or discursive sources that treats with profound scepticism the claim that such texts represent with accuracy 'reality', 'real life', or authorial intention. Such scepticism is extended to the interpreters of texts, as well as the texts themselves and their creators.

Post-modernism, when embodied as a heuristic method, is to be seen in literary studies. It can be extended into PHILOSOPHY (it was born there, above all in the work of Jacques Derrida), history (so Michel Foucault), cultural studies (Foucault again) and psychology (Jacques Lacan). It has had influence, as is to be expected, in fields outside literary studies, such as ARCHAEOLOGY. Because post-modern scepticism focuses on the modes by which the signifier (e.g. a word) becomes disconnected from the signified (the thing a word refers to) – an insight drawn ultimately from linguistics and Ferdinand de Saussure – the critic (or writer) tends to look for discontinuity, fragmentation and self-referentiality in a particular text. Post-modernism is therefore the enemy of unity and authorial intention, and has often been accused of relativism, because of its scepticism about the transmissibility of KNOWLEDGE. It has been associated with ethical nihilism and, particularly, with the POST-STRUCTURALIST schools of DECONSTRUCTION and INTERTEXTUALISM. The post-modern moment peaked in the 1990s and is currently being undermined, above all, by a type of criticism associated with the cognitive sciences. This criticism looks for certainties in the psychological continuities and sureties offered by a 'chemical' of Darwinian, or materialist, understanding of psychology, humans, their cultures and their texts. PGT

post-structuralism see STRUCTURALISM AND POST-STRUCTURALISM.

pottery

As baked clay is virtually indestructible, Greek pottery has survived in great quantities and provides useful material for understanding its production, use and distribution, and its place in social and economic life. Scenes painted on the pots also give some help, though there is little information to be derived from written sources.

The composition of clays differs from region to region in Greece. This has two consequences: some regions produced better pottery than others, and modern study of clays enables pots to be traced back to their source of production. Potters' shops are found in most Greek areas: the mainland, the islands, the Asia Minor seaboard, south Italy and SICILY. Most were doubtless family businesses, small-scale and working only seasonally. In larger cities the potteries were more numerous and more productive, for both local and foreign demand. But no WORKSHOP was very sophisticated. What was needed was a good source of clay, wood for burning in the KILN, and water for help in fashioning the clay. For shaping pots, different methods were used: hands alone for small pots or for building up larger ones by sections or coils; paddle and anvil for thin-sided cooking pots;

POTTERY, GREEK: many shapes in classical Greek pottery were used in the *symposion*. Kraters (a, b) were for mixing wine with water. The amphorae (g, h) held wine, while the hydria (i), with three handles, contained water. Jugs like the oinochoe (j) were used for pouring wine into cups. The skyphos (c) is the most common type of cup, while the kylix (d, e) and the kantharos (f) are less common and are usually restricted to sanctuaries and urban sites, though they are also sometimes found in graves. The lekythos (k), for holding oil, is specifically associated with funerary ritual and graves. The aryballos (l) contained oil or perfumed oil for use by athletes in the gymnasium.

slow turntables and fast wheels for finer pottery, with a boy to turn the wheel. Some pottery was made in moulds, and in the hellenistic period mould-made bowls were one of the commonest forms of fine pottery.

Pots were required for the storage and TRANSPORT of liquid and foodstuffs, for drinking and eating, for fetching water from the FOUNTAIN or the well, for mixing ingredients, for COOKING, for preserving. The potters fashioned their own particular shapes, which varied from area to area, but they also borrowed ideas from nature and from forms in other materials: gourds, baskets, leather containers, and wood, metal and stone objects. In a few centres we find the names of the men who made and/or painted the pots, but it was essentially an anonymous craft. It was also a dirty job, of low status, carried out in poor conditions; many workers are likely to have been immigrants or SLAVES.

Once shaped, most pots received some decoration. This could be incised or impressed patterns, relief designs pressed or rolled onto the soft clay, or various attachments in the form of floral designs, humans or ANIMALS. The commonest form of decoration, however, was the application of paint, a suspension of settled clay with some additional ingredients which could be fired black. The decorative designs varied in different areas and from one period to another. The basic patterns were geometric, floral, and human or animal. In many centres the paint was applied by itself in silhouette, but later the combination of paint, incision and added colours became popular, to enliven the inner features of the figures. The subjects of the figured compositions centred on death, the GODS, fantasy and everyday life.

The firing of finished pots could be carried out on open bonfires, but kilns were the usual method. These were of the cylindrical, up-draught type with an arched stoking hole which led to the wood-burning firing chamber; this had a pierced floor to enable the heat to reach the pots. The process, which was tricky and liable to hazards, consisted of three stages: oxidizing, reducing and re-oxidizing. The finished articles had a clay-coloured body and typically a shiny black coat of paint.

The selling of finished pots was done from the potters' shops, or in some cases potters went round with their DONKEYS trading their wares. Most business was local, but for bigger centres there were sales to be made to merchants who had (potential) customers further away. The evidence we have for the prices of pots (literature, inscriptions and graffiti on the pots themselves) suggests that they were very cheap. Even large, figure-decorated pots fetched only a few obols.

The contexts in which one would expect to find pottery are basically three. There are those concerned with everyday life, both public and private (less well preserved because subject to daily breakage). Cooking pots and coarse wares, as well as the finer shapes such as drinking cups and PERFUME bottles, were in high demand. The second context is the sanctuary where the faithful deposited their offerings, for favours received or help requested. The quality of these offerings ranges from the highest to the lowest. The third context is that of the TOMB where the pots are usually found whole or at least in good condition. Here again they are usually private and cheap offerings made to the dead by the family members. Unlike some of their neighbours (THRACIANS, SCYTHIANS, ETRUSCANS), it was not the practice among classical Greeks to deposit expensive items such as SILVER and GOLD in graves. In most of these three contexts the pottery was of local manufacture, but Athens and CORINTH commanded a wider distribution, and their products are found in all corners of the Greek world.

Study of the clay, shape and decoration enables pottery to be traced back to its source of production. It is thus possible to build up a picture of the direction and volume of the more widely traded pottery. It is unlikely that the SHIPS that carried pottery counted much of it as their major cargo, the exception being those being shipped for their contents, particularly the large transport jars (AMPHORAS) that carried such commodities as WINE and FISH. Cargoes were mixed, and would have included consignments of pottery alongside more expensive articles such as TIMBER, corn and slaves. Athenian black-figure and red-figure vases of the archaic and classical periods, which were the most widely distributed of all fine wares, has been found in most areas of Greece and Italy and also in Egypt, PERSIA and south Russia. BAS

See Cook, R. M. (1972) *Greek Painted Pottery*; Jones, R. E. (1986) *Greek and Related Pottery*; Sparkes, B. A. (1991) *Greek Pottery*.

Roman pottery served many functions, from STORAGE, TRANSPORT, COOKING and serving to eating, drinking and RITUAL: various vessel forms were made to meet these needs. A standard repertoire exists throughout the empire, with regional variations arising from such factors as indigenous culture and CLIMATE. In hellenized PROVINCES continuity in diet and culinary practices meant continuity in vessel forms. In areas such as the CELTIC west, however, the introduction of the Roman way of life saw a radical change; the influx into BRITAIN of the jug for pouring WINE or OIL is one example. Despite similarities in ceramics between regions, it was widely exchanged. In prestige terms, pottery was secondary to GLASS and metal, and some ceramic forms imitate these materials.

Types are defined by the association between vessel shape and clay fabrics. Normally function is implicit, though vessels were frequently put to the

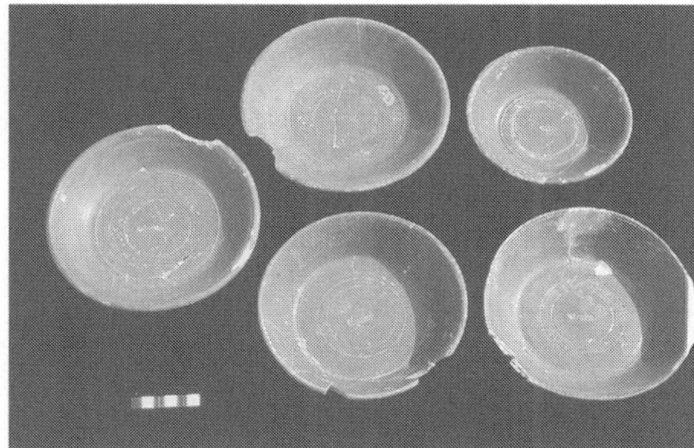

POTTERY, ROMAN: (a) Italian fineware dishes (form Dragendorff 18) exported to the central Sahara in the 1st century AD.

POTTERY, ROMAN: (b) Italian wine amphoras from the bay of Naples area.

purpose needed; for example, table wares used for cooking are evidenced by soot deposits on some specimens. Reuse for different purposes was typical: AMPHORAS were used for transport of water or other secondary products, or as drains or coffins.

Amphoras, in use from the Bronze Age but readily available to all segments of society only from the hellenistic period, represent a specialized type. The transport container of antiquity, they were used for long-distance conveyance of liquid commodities, particularly goods necessary to the Roman way of life. Although a diverse range of products was transported, the most common were wine (and by-products, e.g. *defrutum* syrup, or inferior wine known as vinegar), olive oil and FISH products (e.g. garum). Product identification was tied to vessel shape, as with coloured wine bottles or cola bottles today. Manufacture of amphoras was normally linked to the regions or estates producing their contents, and thus to the SUBSISTENCE economy. Their widespread distribution relates primarily to their contents, not to them as objects in their own right. Some vessels (e.g. the imperial products of the Guadalquivir valley in Spain containing olive oil) carried detailed inscriptions, known as *tituli picti* (a Latin term) or *dipinti* (Italian). These provide information on the empty weight of the vessel, weight of contents, date, and details of the estate, as well as export control, including where and by whom. Throughout the imperial period, stamps (especially on the handle) were more common than inscriptions and named their maker, WORKSHOP or estate. Amphoras ranged in size and capacity, but oil vessels carried up to 80 litres (18 UK gallons) which, together with their own weight, made them unwieldy. This helps explain the characteristic long spikes on Roman amphoras, which served as a third handle for carrying or pouring and facilitated layered, top-to-bottom storage in ships' holds. Through time their efficiency increased, and many late Roman and Byzantine amphoras are smaller, with thinner walls and weighing less.

Sealants or stoppers protected contents during transport and maintained freshness. Stoppers are occasionally found *in situ*, particularly from wreck sites. Typically they comprise bedding, in a range of materials from cork to organic material, or sherds and vessels, covered by mortar or pozzolana. They were removed by pulling on string wrapped under them, somewhat like a ring-pull top today. Some were stamped by the estate or merchant.

Another specialized vessel type, the *dolium*, is occasionally found on shipwrecks, but its main purpose was for fermentation or liquid storage on the farm or at commercial outlets. *Dolia* were most common in the MEDITERRANEAN and Near East; complete vessels can often be seen dotted around sites such as POMPEII.

Domestic vessels were used for cooking, serving and eating. Cooking wares vary somewhat from province to province, depending on dietary habits, but cooking pots and casseroles were universal. Special clays that could withstand constant heating and cooling were desirable. The best contain volcanic inclusions, but other densely packed aplastic fragments such as sand and SHELL are also suitable. Cooking pots made from volcanic clays have the widest distribution, though in limited numbers, as they were frequently produced on a small scale as a means of supplementing income in areas of poor subsistence potential. Cooking vessels made on the Italian island of Pantelleria, west of SICILY, are one example, occurring around the Mediterranean littoral from Spain to Tripolitania.

A variety of open (cups, bowls, dishes, lids) and closed vessels (jars, flagons, jugs) were used for serving, eating and domestic storage. A particularly distinctive vessel is the *mortarium*, a spouted bowl with an abrasive inside surface formed by pressing stones or other fragments into the vessel wall before the clay was dried. *Mortaria* were then used for grinding, in the same way as a mortar (with pestle), most likely for both dry and liquid foodstuffs. With a long hellenistic tradition, they were never common in the Roman Mediterranean (their function fulfilled by stone vessels) but were abundant in the north-west provinces. Production sites are known throughout GAUL, the Rhineland and especially Britain, where they became particularly common. Like amphoras, through the 3rd century AD they were frequently stamped, in this case on the rim flanking both sides of the spout. Single-handled closed vessels (flagons, jugs) were produced throughout the empire for storing and serving oil, wine and other liquid commodities. As a class they owe their inspiration to contemporary metal vessels. In south Gaul some flagons may have been used as kettles, as suggested by deposits of fur on the inside. In Egypt and the LEVANT a specialized vessel within this class has a spout on the side, rather than the rim, and frequently a strainer over the opening at the neck. This may facilitate water cooling, as well as protecting the contents from INSECTS.

Many types could be made in either coarse-ware fabrics or as better quality vessels (finewares), depending on the affluence of the household or the occasion. Though tending to be fine, the latter designation comes not only from the clay but also from overall appearance, which is well-finished, normally slipped (a liquid of fine clay suspended in water) and frequently decorated in other ways, including rouletting, moulding or appliqué. In addition to Italian and Gaulish sigillata, numerous other provincial red-slip industries existed. A range was produced in the eastern Mediterranean, from ASIA Minor (established by Italian potters) to SYRIA, most of it widely distributed. African Red Slip ware, from modern-day Tunisia, was current between the 1st and 7th centuries AD and dominated the Mediterranean between the 4th and 6th centuries. A wide range of provincial slipped wares (both light and dark coloured) was manufactured throughout the empire and occasionally alongside sigillata (e.g. in Gaul). Glazed wares were uncommon in the Roman world, though they were occasionally imported into the Eastern empire from MESOPOTAMIA and were produced on a small scale in many provinces. The better known and more widely distributed of early Roman workshops are from Asia Minor, Tarsus, Italy and south Gaul. Slightly more common were glazed vessels produced in northern Italy and PANNONIA (including *mortaria*) during the 4th and early 5th centuries. Finewares travelled extensively, frequently alongside amphora-borne products.

Vessels used for RITUAL are difficult to identify. Normally the association between vessel and context rather than the vessel type is significant, such as the use of ordinary bowls for burning aromatics in shrines or TEMPLES, or pots as part of burial furniture. 'Pilgrim-flasks', miniature flat vessels for carrying holy liquids, were manufactured specifically for ritual in both PTOLEMAIC and later Egypt. Vessels offering a blessing of the Egyptian saint Menas were produced during the CHRISTIAN era for his shrine near ALEXANDRIA, but have been found as far south as Aksum in ETHIOPIA.

Production occurred in every province, and the scale and complexity of workshops varied from sporadic vessels made in association with the HOUSEHOLD, such as the Pantellerian wares, or through large workshops manufacturing vast quantities, such as those making Gaulish SAMIAN. Different technologies were maintained as appropriate to the different types of vessels and workshops, rather than a single technology being employed. Handmade pottery fired in a bonfire (e.g. Pantellerian wares) was produced throughout the Roman period, though the vast majority was made on a wheel and fired in a permanent KILN. Some potteries, such as those for amphoras, were specialized, but more frequently a range of types was produced together. Other ceramics sometimes produced alongside pottery include building materials and LAMPS. The introduction of Romanized pottery into a province often came on the heels of the army, who may initially have required specialist potters soon replaced by local craftsmen.

Serious and consistent scholarship on Roman pottery was under way by the mid-19th century and has accrued an immense database. Initially seen as objects of art, special interest was taken in stamped pieces. Dressel's 1899 study of the amphora inscriptions from MONTE TESTACCIO in Rome, a vast man-made mound of carefully arranged sherd waste, still provides the foundation for amphora typology.

As the most prolific and durable of cultural finds, many types are well dated from years of study in tandem with stratigraphic sequences and other datable finds, and pottery normally provides the best dating evidence for archaeological sites. While dating evidence from the West is somewhat more refined due to EXCAVATION of short-lived military sites, such as the FORTRESS at Oberaden on the German *limes* occupied c.11–8 BC, excavation in the East is gradually altering this imbalance.

Pottery can also be used to address functional and social issues, particularly by recording the distribution of vessel types throughout excavated areas. Identification of pottery shops, such as that found at SARDIS, is an unusually clear-cut example. To the Romans pottery was very much about eating, drinking, cultural identity and display. The acquisition of imported goods had much to do with the latter category, with certain wines, for example, more highly regarded. Recent work has focused on the identification of ethnic groups through pottery: for instance, locally made braziers (small portable stoves) on the ANTONINE WALL indicate the presence of North Africans associated with the 20th legion (Swan).

The ability to provenance pottery makes it ideal for charting movement of goods and, implicitly, contacts throughout the empire. Sourcing is established through identification of production sites, distribution of types and scientific analysis of clay, for which both geological and chemical methods are available. The geological technique of thin-section enables clay fabrics to be viewed under polarized light so that aplastic inclusions in the clay fabric can be precisely identified and compared with the geology of proposed source areas. It is an efficient method for investigating coarsely tempered fabrics. In contrast, chemical analyses, such as neutron activation or inductively coupled emission spectrometry, focus on major and minor elements and are more suitable for investigating clay. The Italian sigillata centres have been successfully distinguished from each other by another method, x-ray fluorescence. Since the mid-1970s, quantification has become a standard tool for recording pottery, and this allows a picture of the relative importance of different source areas to be established. In this way, pottery makes a major contribution to general ECONOMIC studies, illuminating the mechanics of PRODUCTION and charting exchange on a local, regional and inter-regional level. RST

See Greene, K. (1992) *Interpreting the Past: Roman pottery*; Hayes, J.W. (1997) *Handbook of Mediterranean Roman Pottery*; Peacock, D. P. S. (1982) *Pottery in the Roman World*; Peacock, D. P. S. and Williams, D. F. (1986) *Amphorae and the Roman Economy*; Swan, V. G. (1999) The twentieth legion and the history of the Antonine wall reconsidered, *PSAS* 129: 399–480.

 MONTE TESTACCIO.

poultry The domestic fowl of the classical world was probably descended from the bantam breeds of INDIA and may have reached Greece, in perhaps the 5th century BC, via PERSIA (hence, ARISTOPHANES, *Birds* 485 calls it 'the Persian bird'). Some of the most prized strains were Greek, such as the Tanagran, Chalkidian and Rhodian. The island of DELOS became particularly associated with developing poultry-rearing as part of profitable farming. The Roman writers on AGRICULTURE give details on the creation and management of hen-houses. Poultry were reared both for their eggs and for the table, though the agronomists seem to concentrate more on production for eating. Eggs formed a regular part of the first course at dinner and were much used to bind sauces. They were also preserved over winter in chaff or in brine. Pullets and capons were favourites, normally boiled rather than roasted. In addition to chickens farmyards regularly included African guinea fowl, ducks, geese (*foie gras* was known to the Greeks but was particularly championed as a delicacy in the 1st century BC: PLINY THE ELDER, *Natural History* 10.52), pigeons and doves. Peacocks, pheasants and even ostrich (a favourite of the emperor ELAGABALUS) were reared for the tables of the rich. JJP

See Columella 8; Palladius 1.23–30; Varro, *On Agriculture* 3; White, K. D. (1970) *Roman Farming*.

poverty From the standpoint of Greek MORALITY, individuals became destitute as a result of their own actions. Therefore, one could avoid or ultimately rise above poverty. Those who became impoverished were seen as bringing about shame within the community. Those who remained impoverished, however, were typically drawn towards CRIME and were thus considered morally inferior. The CYNICS, flourishing in the 3rd century BC, took a somewhat different stance, in that they advocated a life of poverty, a viewpoint taken up by future Cynics and CHRISTIANS living in the 1st and 2nd centuries AD.

Poverty for the Romans, according to Veyne, was a relative term whereby those who were considered to be poor were those who simply were not very rich. Poverty became synonymous with a virtuous existence for certain Roman authors such as HORACE. He considered himself to be living in poverty since he owned VILLAS at Sabine and TIVOLI only. Poverty was thus used metaphorically to convey an idea of modest living.

JEWS and CHRISTIANS sought to alleviate poverty within their communities. If an individual was in need, other community members took it upon themselves to provide, in the form of a donation or EMPLOYMENT. These cultures focused on moral obligation and compassion to care for the poor. LAH

See Dover, K. J. (1974) *Greek Popular Morality in the Time of Plato and Aristotle*; Veyne, P., ed. (1987) *A History of Private Life*.

power A much-debated sociological concept and one that defies easy summation, not least because definitions may vary according to the bases of power addressed (WEALTH, status, knowledge, force), the form of power (coercion, control, influence) and the locale of application of that power (individual or communal, political or economic spheres). Yet the ability of individuals and states to impact on the behaviour of others and to induce consequences was fundamental to the structure of ancient societies. The exercise of power concerns how X can get Y to do something they would not otherwise do. In analysing the power dynamics of such situations we need to consider a range of factors: the operation of power (intentional actions and effects and unintentional actions and effects), as well as the agents, actors and victims of power. The negotiation of power between individuals and within and between social groupings can be recognized as a fundamental aspect of human relationships.

An alternative approach, and one that helps outline a particular characteristic of power, is to compare it with force. Force is a finite, physical commodity, as the Spartans had to accept after LEUKTRA or as AUGUSTUS recognized when he mourned the loss of three legions in AD 9. Although it can be employed to ensure compliance, it is also consumed in the process. Power, on the other hand, is subtler. As it acts mainly at the psychological level, it can produce a result with no diminution of the force that lies behind it. It may also be noted that power elicits responses, rather than directly causing effects. However defined, it is clear that power is a key concept to explain how any society functions, especially when it is appreciated that power is not just a repressive tool of social control but can also operate in a creative and productive manner.

Ancient concepts of power are numerous. For the Roman world, *imperium* was the key expression of power in society from early times. This was an absolute power to command and to be obeyed, rather than to be negotiated with. During Republican times, the exercise of *imperium* was carefully circumscribed in time and space – GENERALS were appointed to specific campaigns or PROVINCES for strictly limited periods (hence the problems set in train by CAESAR overstaying his period of office in GAUL or bringing his army south of the Rubicon). The EMPERORS got round this restriction by legitimizing their own *imperium* to be held continuously and without geographical limit, even in the city of Rome itself. Thus, the vaguely defined titular power of the emperor (*tribunicia potestas*, *imperium maius*) masks the true magnitude of his authoritarian power. In aristocratic circles, the power of the father (*patria potestas*) in a traditional Roman FAMILY was also absolute, even if it was rarely fully deployed, for this power drew its strength from the exceptionality of a father killing his own offspring. DJM

See Foucault, M. (1980) *Power/Knowledge*; Luttwak, E. (1976) *The Grand Strategy of the Roman Empire*.

pozzolana see CONCRETE; MINING; POTTERY, ROMAN; VOLCANOES.

Pozzuoli see PUTEOLI.

Praeneste (mod. Palestrina) One of the most powerful and wealthy of the LATIN towns. Built on a hillside overlooking the plain of Latium, it was in a commanding position. Its archaic phase is represented by the wealthiest BURIALS found in Latium hitherto, with astonishingly wealthy GOLD offerings, some from Syria and PHOENICIA. Many of these are clearly similar to offerings found in CERVETERI, suggesting a close link between the two sites. In the 5th and 4th centuries BC, Praeneste fought the repeated incursions into Latin territory by Volscians and Aequians, but also resisted Roman domination until the defeat of the Latins in 336. Praeneste commanded several small settlements, and its territory was confiscated by the Romans. Praeneste preserved its own citizenship down to 90, when it became a *municipium* and declared for MARIUS. It was sacked by SULLA in 82, and a VETERAN colony was imposed.

Dominating the site is the massive sanctuary of FORTUNA Primigenia. Scholars dispute whether it had been begun before Sulla's time or was entirely his creation, but the former view is gaining ground. This sanctuary rises up the steep hillside on a series of magnificent terraces, and was venerated into the 4th century AD for its famous ORACLE, consulted by drawing lots of slips of wood with obscure texts on them (Praeneste is thought to have had a slightly unusual dialect of Latin). CJS

 LATINS.

praetorian guard The initial purpose of the praetorian guard, when AUGUSTUS established it, was to serve as the imperial bodyguard, both at Rome and when the emperor was on campaign. Praetorians also protected other members of the imperial family, served in ceremonial capacities, were seconded for various special purposes and assisted other urban security forces when necessary. Their commander was EQUESTRIAN, appointed by the emperor himself; some, such as SEJANUS, gained great influence. Guardsmen were recruited almost exclusively within Italy; the guard comprised, eventually, 10 cohorts of 500 men each, who were fully fledged soldiers but drew higher pay than legionaries. As the primary military force at and around Rome, it was often involved in accessions, even raising candidates to the throne against senatorial wishes (e.g. CLAUDIUS). Frequently, a donative of 15,000 *sestertii* or more per man was paid, or promised, by a candidate or emperor, to gain or retain loyalty.

The guard's nature changed under SEPTIMIUS SEVERUS, who made service in the body a reward for loyal soldiers from the LEGIONS. In the later empire, further changes occurred; the praetorians regularly travelled with the emperor on campaigns as his primary personal troops, and the praetorian prefect was, in effect, the second in command to the emperor himself. Later, the development of regional prefectures meant that there were usually several prefects, each serving as the emperor's regional vice-ruler and usually remaining in his territory even when the emperor was elsewhere. When several CAESARS and AUGUSTI were in power, each had a prefect assigned to him. JV

PRAETORIAN GUARD: tombstone of a praetorian guardsman, Lucius Septimius Valerinus.

praetors Roman MAGISTRATES elected annually by the *comitia centuriata*, who fulfilled important judicial and administrative roles in the state. Originally *praetor* (pl. *praetores*) seems to have been the title of the chief magistrate, but by 367 BC this function was given to the two CONSULS and the praetor had been differentiated as the holder of a form of full civil and military *imperium* which was, however, subordinate to the authority of the consuls. The original praetorship, the post of *praetor urbanus*, was concerned with administration and LAW in the city of Rome. This was joined in the 240s by a second praetorship, the post of *praetor inter peregrinos* ('concerning foreigners'), charged either with mediating law cases involving foreigners or with serving as an additional military commander, perhaps both. The need for magistrates to govern the PROVINCES of Rome's expanding empire resulted in a rapid increase in the number of praetors: to four in 227 BC, six in 197, eight in 80, and 16 by the end of the REPUBLIC. In the empire this was trimmed back to 12, and the duties of praetors were reduced to primarily judicial functions, in which role they nevertheless remained influential. Ultimately, the most prominent job of the *praetor urbanus* became the supervision and funding of public entertainments. GSA

See Brennan, T. C. (2000) *The Praetorship in the Roman Republic*; Lintott, A. (1999) *The Constitution of the Roman Republic.*

Praxilla see POETESSES.

Praxiteles Athenian sculptor, active c.375–330 BC. Perhaps the son of the sculptor Kephisodotos; his own sons were sculptors, and his family became very wealthy. Over 100 sources, anecdotes and inscriptions show that he produced bronze and MARBLE works in about equal numbers. He was famous especially for marble, reviving its popularity for freestanding statues. His work encompassed cult statues, personifications, portraits and architectural sculpture, including (according to VITRUVIUS but not PLINY THE ELDER), part of the Mausoleum at HALIKARNASSOS.

No proven original by Praxiteles survives, but several candidates, e.g. the HERMES and DIONYSOS in OLYMPIA attributed to him by PAUSANIAS (but perhaps by a descendant of the same name), give some idea of his style. His male statues are often of sinuous young men with soft musculature, a type he applied to APOLLO, whom he depicts in several guises, e.g. Sauroktonos or Lizard-slayer.

Praxiteles' most famous work was the APHRODITE of KNIDOS, preserved in several copies. It shows Aphrodite (supposedly modelled on Praxiteles' mistress Phryne) naked, just before or after a bath, one hand modestly in front of her. Female NUDITY, unprecedented in monumental art, was particularly striking for a GODDESS, as a hellenistic EPIGRAM showed: 'Paris saw me naked, Anchises and Adonis too. Three alone that I know of – so how did Praxiteles contrive it?' The effect was heightened by elaborate polychromy, which Praxiteles' preference for marble allowed him to develop, collaborating with the painter Nikias. KWA

See Ajootian, A. (1996) Praxiteles, in O. Palagia and J. J. Pollitt, *Personal Styles in Greek Sculpture* 91–129; Havelock, C. M. (1995) *The Aphrodite of Knidos and her Successors.*

prayer A common RITUAL act (*euchê* in Greek) seeking to establish contact with a deity before or alongside other rituals such as a SACRIFICE, a VOW, a libation or another offering. The first substantial examples of Greek prayers appear in HOMER, and are often made up of distinct constituent parts. These include an invocation to the deity by name, patronymic (father's name) or a prominent feature of their persona or operations. This is often followed by the setting of the context for the request (the so-called argument), which often reminds the god of past services or pious actions by the person praying. Last comes the request revealing the purpose of the prayer.

The length and verbal elaboration of a prayer vary according to the person performing it and the occasion. In its simplest form it would include an invocation and a request. Prayers were normally spoken aloud and were often combined with appropriate posture (upward gaze, outstretched arms). Prayers to the gods of the underworld were performed differently, with respect not only to content but also to the accompanying ritual acts. Kneeling down for a prayer was not usual, as imagery in ART confirms. Ancient prayers could be enacted in public in the context of a religious occasion, such as a FESTIVAL, or in private space, particularly when they concerned personal wishes. EP

See Pulleyn, S. (1997) *Prayer in Greek Religion*; Versnel, H. S. (1981) Religious mentality in ancient prayer, in *Faith, Hope and Worship* 1–64.

prediction see ASTROLOGY; ASTRONOMY; BIBLE; DOCTORS; ETRURIA AND ETRUSCANS; HIPPARCHOS OF NIKAIA; ORACLES; PROPHECY; ROADS, ROMAN; SCIENTIFIC INSTRUMENTS; WEATHER FORECASTING.

pregnancy and childbirth In Greek and Roman medicine, the most fertile time of the menstrual cycle was believed to be when a period was just ending, so that the womb was open to receive semen, but not so full of blood that it would be overpowered and poured out again. Our 'fertile period', around the middle of the cycle, was seen as the time when a woman's womb was most firmly closed. There was also a tradition that women knew when they had conceived because they felt the mouth of the womb close to retain the male seed. After this had occurred, those who believed in the 'two-seed' theory, according to which both the man and the woman contributed seed, thought that the seeds mingled in the womb, their relative strengths and quantities determining both the sex of the unborn child and its physical resemblance to its parents. ARISTOTLE, however, argued that the mother contributes only the blood which forms the raw material of the child, the father providing its 'form'.

During pregnancy, a woman was believed to have cravings (Greek *kissai*, Latin *picae*). A woman carrying a girl would have a more difficult pregnancy, the sex of the foetus being obvious from her poor colour and swollen legs. The cessation of menstruation in pregnancy was thought to be due to the diversion of blood to form, and then nourish, the foetus. Some believed that females were carried on the colder, left side of the womb, males on the right.

There were different views on how long an embryo took to form in the womb. Some argued that the body had all its necessary parts seven days from conception. Another view was that a male foetus was formed in 30 days, a female in 42, with the lochial discharge after childbirth lasting for the same periods. It was widely believed that a child born in the seventh month was more likely to live than one born in the eighth month, and pregnancies lasting up to 11 months were possible. In the inscriptions from the temple of ASKLEPIOS at Epidauros, pregnancies of two or five years long are seen as possible, particularly when a woman has sought help from the god in becoming pregnant, but has forgotten to ask for the child to be delivered (presumably, such women were crediting the deity after a temple visit, even when conception occurred much later). In medical texts, it was claimed that birth was initiated by the foetus trying to get out, and its movements were thought to cause labour pains. Childbirth could be attended by women from the family or neighbourhood or, particularly if it did not proceed normally, by physicians, who could if necessary remove a dead foetus from the womb. Traction hooks and knives would be employed; examples have been found at POMPEII. Childbirth was perceived as a dangerous experience; the assistance of GODDESSES such as ARTEMIS and Eileithuia was sought, and amulets were often worn. The medical writer SORANUS, while regarding these as ineffective, advises against their removal, accepting that they serve to reassure women in labour. (see also MIDWIVES) HK

Presocratic philosophy The early trends of thought from which Western PHILOSOPHY arose had as their object an explanation of the nature and origin of the cosmos. Not that there had previously been a lack of interest in these questions, but earlier accounts tended to trace the growth of the universe to its present state by the gradual accretion of components 'born' from those already in place. Thales of Miletos challenged this model with his radical suggestion that everything in the physical world could be explained as a product of, in the sense of being made out of, a single substance. This opened the way for the study of the cosmos as a unified, evolving organism, not just a more or less stable collection of disparate objects. Where ASTRONOMERS had previously been content to record the movements and appearance of heavenly bodies, for example, philosophers now attempted to explain them in terms of the universe as a whole. In the terrestrial realm, altogether new fields of investigation opened up, and theories proliferated on everything from the formation of land masses to the origins of life.

Most important for understanding the evolution of philosophy is the concomitant interest taken by Presocratics in the nature and limits of the evidence for the world they were studying. Thales' follower Anaximander criticized his claim that everything was made from water on the grounds that a watery universe could not possibly sustain the obvious presence of (for example) fire. He himself went on to account for the cosmos in terms of opposing qualities which arose in equal proportions from some 'indefinite' substance (the *apeiron*). But here is the crucial question: what are qualities? Anaximenes (also from Miletos) argued that they could not be thought of as objective features of the world unerringly recognized by us; they merely describe what it feels like for us when we encounter different objects. (Objects themselves he thought of as made of air, compressed more or less, and feeling different to us according to how dense or rarefied it is.) This insight had important ramifications. If the 'qualities' I perceive are not really 'out there', then (1) my senses give me only an indirect indication of what the cosmos is like; and (2) they do not give me privileged information about it. I might experience something as cold that you experience as warm – and neither of us would be wrong. This insight is the starting-point for Herakleitos' view that the senses tie us into a limited and partial view of the world. The road looks as if it goes up to me, and so it does; but it also goes down. A true understanding of the world would transcend any particular perspective in space or time: the truth about the cosmos is the sum of all possible, all opposing, perspectives.

The earliest Presocratics all came from towns in eastern Ionia, since the 8th century the intellectual centre of the Hellenic world, but their debates were taken up in the western colonies. PARMENIDES of Elea solved the problem of the senses' partiality by dispensing with their evidence altogether, constructing a picture of what exists based on reason alone. Perhaps the most important thing reason tells us, according to him, is that the substance out of which the cosmos is made could not change its nature. If the world is made of water, for example, and water is different from earth, then earth could only come about by a kind of magical substitution for the water that had been there. (If earth and water are not really different, then there was not really any change after all.) Parmenides concluded that there exists only one thing, unchanging and undifferentiated. This was a conclusion that few were ready to accept. One might have to treat the evidence of the senses with caution, but they provide our one opportunity for contact with the physical world, and their evidence needed to be explained, not dismissed. (The interest evident at this period in the PHYSICS of perception is no coincidence.) Change and diversity could be explained after all if one supposed that the cosmos was made not from one, but from a plurality of substances which could be mixed in different ways. Empedokles of Akragas described a cosmos built by forces of combination (Love) and separation (Strife) operating on four basic 'roots': earth, air, fire and water. (An artist, similarly, can paint anything he wants with colours from a very limited palette.) Anaxagoras of Klazomenai supposed that there were an infinite number of basic substances ('seeds'), which, under the direction of divine Nous (Mind), interpenetrate each other and fill the entire universe, becoming thicker or thinner in different places at different times. (Bone, for example, is rather 'thicker' where my leg now is, and thinner where it was a minute ago.) Leukippos and DEMOKRITOS posited an infinite stock of atoms (*atoma*, 'uncuttable' units of matter). As they move about in perpetual motion they combine and recombine to form the complex structures familiar to us.

Amidst all this attention to cosmic issues, there is little systematic ETHICAL theory to be found. Demokritos was unusual in spelling out (and at length) the human consequences of his physics: since humans are purely material objects, liable as everything else to dissolution, his advice was to 'be cheerful' while you live. Others found room for discussion of the individual as part of their cosmic philosophy. PYTHAGORAS and his school were especially noted for their work on MUSICAL harmony, in terms of which they viewed the structure of the cosmos at large; but they incorporated into this model a view of the individual SOUL as a 'divine', immortal entity subject to reincarnation. Their ritual observances (codified in the so-called *akousmata*, which famously included abstention from beans) seem meant to 'purify' the soul and improve its future lot. But ETHICS only really came into its own with the SOPHISTIC movement of the 5th century, when 'relativists' such as PROTAGORAS scandalized popular opinion by arguing that what is right or good (like what is 'warm') can only mean what seems right to you – and that everyone's opinion on the matter is equally valid. SOCRATES was fatally prejudiced by his association with this movement, though according to PLATO, at least, his intention in engaging with these issues had been to re-establish ethical certainty. And it was Plato's attempt to pursue Socrates' project by appropriating earlier, Presocratic, themes for an ethics-led inquiry into nature that formed the basis for philosophy as the Western world came to know it. GB-S

See McKirahan, R. D. (1994) *Philosophy before Socrates*; Long, A. A., ed. (1999) *The Cambridge Companion to Early Greek Philosophy*.

presses Used for a variety of purposes in the ancient world, from OIL and WINE production through to cloth pressing. Technology and design varied considerably, though often radically different machines can be shown to have existed contemporaneously, with simpler designs continuing in use alongside technologically more advanced ones (PLINY, *Natural History* 18.74). Wine making and OLIVE OIL production accounted for the largest numbers of presses, with much regional variation in design and scale. An important point to grasp is that production of wine and oil did not necessarily require a press, and subsistence farmers have in many periods of history managed without. The presence of a press may conversely be a good indication that surplus production is intended. Presses made use of five main mechanical devices outlined by HERON: the lever, the screw, the wedge, the pulley and the windlass. The earliest 'presses' were modified versions of Egyptian 'torsion' machines, designed to squeeze liquid out of a pulped commodity held inside an animal skin that was being twisted (often on a frame). By the later Bronze Age in the AEGEAN, lever presses were in use. These involved long beams, pivoted in the wall of a building, with pulped olives or grapes placed beneath and the free end manipulated by human brawn (and later by the addition of weights). The lever press continued to evolve technologically throughout the Roman period, with the use of windlasses to draw down the free end of the beam, and the addition of large counterweight blocks that could be lifted off the floor by means of the windlass mechanism and pulley blocks. Some of the largest Roman presses were designed for processing very large quantities of oil and wine in a single load (as much as a tonne of pulped fruit). If operated at full capacity through a pressing season of several weeks, it is clear that yields in excess of 10,000 litres (2,200 UK gallons) from a single large olive press were possible in the best years.

The screw press was introduced from the 1st century BC or AD, both as a direct screw mechanism and

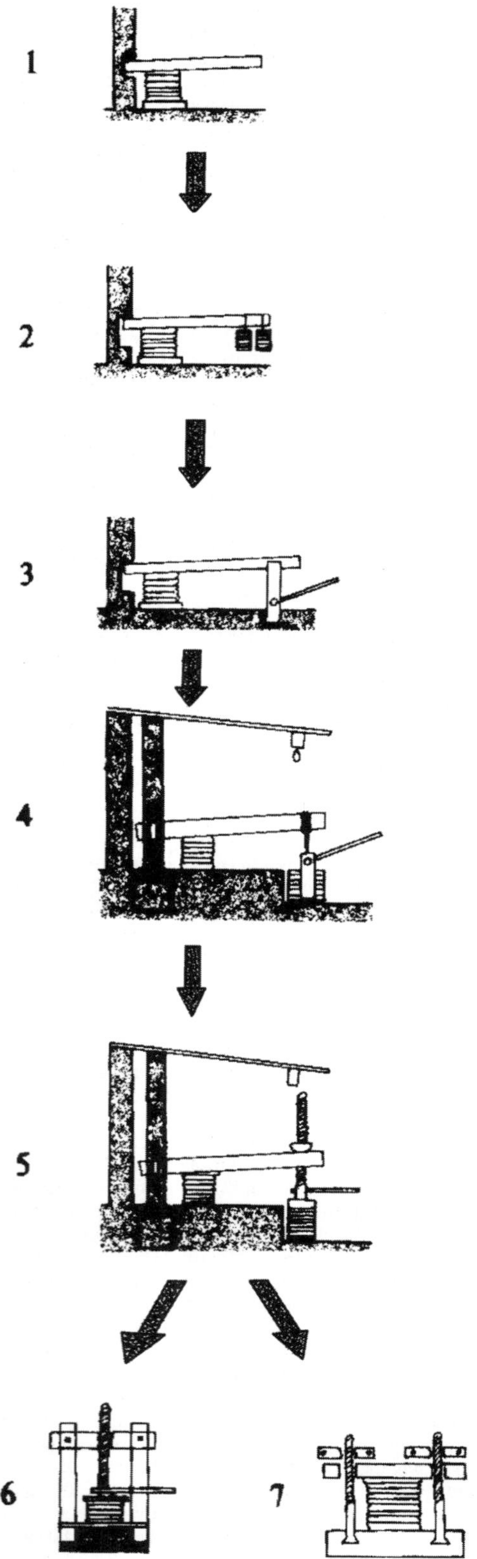

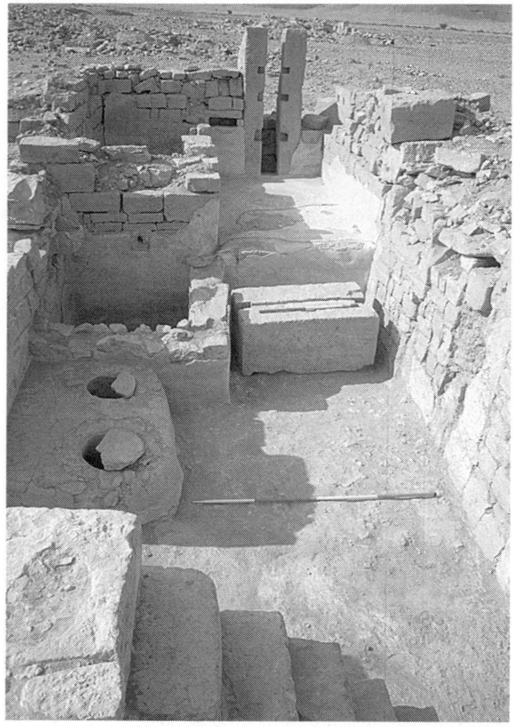

PRESSES: (b) excavated olive press in the Libyan pre-desert. Note the large stone uprights for securing the head of the press, the counterweight block with setting for windlass mechanism and the triple separation vats.

as a replacement for the windlass in some lever presses. However, the diffusion of screw presses of all sorts was not widespread in Roman times, and in many areas lever-and-windlass presses continued to be the most common type, demonstrating the greater practicality (and possibly the larger capacity) of that technology.

The wedge press was a more specialized type of machine, used for the production of small quantities of very high-quality oils needed in PERFUME production. They involved a rigid vertical frame with moveable horizontal planks set in grooves in the uprights. The planks could be forced apart by the insertion of wedges between them, exerting great pressure on baskets of pulped olives placed below the lowest plank.

PRESSES: (a) technological evolution of ancient presses, from simple lever (1), to lever and weight (2), lever and fixed windlass (3), lever and counterweight with windlass (4), lever and counterweight with screw (5), single direct screw (6), double direct screw (7). In reality, things did not evolve in such a neat linear fashion and many different technologies can be found in simultaneous use, often conditioned by local preferences.

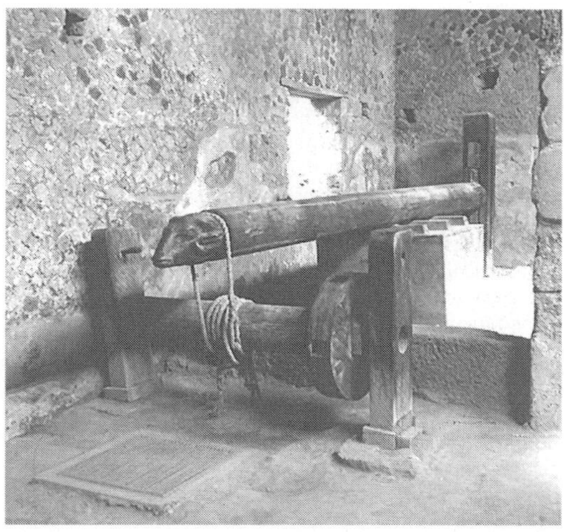

PRESSES: (c) reconstructed wine press from the Villa of the Mysteries, Pompeii.

An important distinction to be drawn between presses, in addition to the scale of the individual elements, concerns the number of separate presses provided at a single establishment. In some regions of the ancient world, and especially during the Roman empire, we can trace the evolution of multiple press farms, or wineries (Italy and southern Gaul) and oileries (North Africa and Spain). DJM

See Mattingly, D. J. (1996) First fruit? The olive in the Roman world, in G. Shipley and J. Salmon, eds., *Human Landscapes in Classical Antiquity* 213–53; Rossiter, J. J. (1978) *Roman Farm Buildings in Italy*.

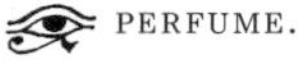 PERFUME.

Priam see GRIEF; HEKTOR; HOMER.

Priapus and *Priapea* Ithyphallic god of SEXUALITY and fertility, a general averter of evils. His cult was closely associated with the north-western coast of ASIA Minor, especially Lampsakos, where it may have originated. Possible representations of Priapus appear on Attic red-figure vases of the 5th century BC, but the earliest definite reference is the title of a lost comedy of the following century. In Greek texts of the early 3rd century BC he makes his first appearance as the guardian of GARDENS who threatens to punish by penetration any would-be thieves. This becomes the typical treatment of Priapus in Latin literature, especially the anonymous collection of 80 witty and obscene short poems known as *Priapea*. There are only a few references to Priapus in MYTH. He is said to be the son of DIONYSOS by APHRODITE (Diodorus Siculus 4.6.1) or a nymph (Strabo 13.1.12). OVID tells an aetiological story to explain the otherwise unattested SACRIFICE of an ass to the god (*Fasti* 1.391–440; 6.319–48). His cult centred on small shrines, or more commonly on statues in gardens and vineyards. Examples from the imperial period usually depict him lifting his robe to expose his erect phallus. He received sacrifices of FISH and small

PRIAPUS: the Roman ithyphallic god weighing up his assets greets visitors to the House of the Vettii at Pompeii.

ANIMALS, more commonly offerings of FRUIT, FLOWERS, and WINE. His cult spread throughout the Greco-Roman world, in part through his assimilation to local ithyphallic gods. JBR

See Parker, W. H. (1988) *Priapea*.

prices The prices for all sorts of goods and services are preserved from MYCENAEAN times to the end of antiquity in literary texts, on pots and other containers, on inscriptions and in PAPYRI. Most such prices are of limited value for the study of the ECONOMY because they appear as isolated data, or because insufficient information is recorded about the good or service purchased to compare prices over time. The chief exceptions come from two places. First, the island of DELOS in the first half of the hellenistic period, where a series of prices is preserved on inscribed accounts of the sanctuary. Second, Egypt, particularly under the ROMAN EMPIRE, where thousands of documentary papyri include prices. In these cases, and arguably a few others, prices for comparable goods and services over time can be studied to reveal long-term price trends and can be treated as evidence of economic change. Prices can, however, be deployed in response to non-economic questions about the Greek and Roman world. For example, high prices for food during SIEGES offer insight into the conditions imposed by warfare. High prices for 'luxury goods' (a contested and difficult concept) suggest something about the demand for exotica and the mechanisms whereby some goods were designated as markers of status. Notions of 'typical prices' for staple goods like grains may represent the sense that ordinary people had about what was a 'fair' price for a necessity. The mechanisms by which prices were set included barter; traditional notions of exchange value; state intervention; and market interactions locally, regionally and over long distances. Theoretical discussions of price-setting mechanisms appear occasionally in ancient sources, most notably in Aristotle's treatment of the 'just price' in the *Nicomachean Ethics*. Xenophon in his *Ways and Means* (*Poroi*) has a brief but intriguing discussion of supply and demand, and a lively sense of the ways to manipulate prices appears in the advice offered in the second book of the Pseudo-Aristotelian *Oikonomika*. GR

See Reger, G. (1994) *Regionalism and Change in the Economy of Independent Delos*.

 ADVERTISING.

Priene see HOUSES, GREEK; PALAESTRAS.

priests and priestesses

A category of religious personnel, including both men and women. Our information about priests in ancient Greece derives mainly from textual evidence. Of special interest are inscriptions recording sacred regulations, or programmes of religious FESTIVALS, which make special mention of priests of different GODS AND GODDESSES who were to assume leading roles in the performance of various RITUAL acts within religious festivals. Such roles included the collection of raw materials and ingredients for SACRIFICES and other offerings, the collection of money for religious rites, and other aspects of the administration and policing of festivals. In return, priests received payment for their service, along with perquisites from public sacrifices which are often recorded in public documents. They received goods in kind, in the form of portions of other offerings for the gods made at their sanctuary. In addition, they received honours, presiding over major religious occasions of the state along with other state officials of high rank. They enjoyed privileges, such as special seats set apart for them in THEATRES, as at the theatre of Dionysos Eleuthereus in Athens.

Priests and priestesses (*hiereis* and *hiereiai* respectively in Greek) were above all public officials appointed by the state, usually for a fixed period of time. They could be elected to their office, be selected by lot from among the citizen body of a city, or could assume the priesthood as a hereditary prerogative of their extended family (*genos*). Hereditary priesthoods appear to have been remnants of early ARISTOCRATIC rule, which also carried religious authority. Some priestly offices were held for life, as in the case of Pythia at Delphi and probably also the priests who interpreted her prophetic utterances. Specific restrictions are sometimes associated with priestly office, particularly pertaining to sexual purity, age limitations and dietary prohibitions.

Priests resided in or close to the sanctuary they served and performed a range of duties depending on the size of the sanctuary and the nature of deity worshipped. Some of their routine tasks were the maintenance of good order in the sacred buildings of a sanctuary, including the treasures and ritual objects kept in them, and contacts with pilgrims or other worshippers. They took part in processions within festivals and oversaw the smooth running of public sacrifices with the subsequent fair distribution of MEAT to the participants. Priests also administered the finances of a sanctuary. In the last two areas of responsibility, priests were aided by several other categories of religious personnel who specialized in various functions: for example, the rendering of accounts of sacred property, the organization of festivals, the upkeep of sacred laws, the performance of rituals and routine tasks in sacred buildings. EP

See Bruit Zaidman, L. and Schmitt Pantel, P. (1992) *Religion in the Ancient Greek City*; Burkert, W. (1985) *Greek Religion*; Price, S. (1999) *Religions of the Ancient Greeks*.

The word 'priest' is a somewhat misleading term for the various religious functionaries of Rome. Their organization and institutions were not distinct from those of the state, nor did they have a monopoly on interactions with the divine world. With very few exceptions, priesthoods were not full-time positions or associated with specific deities. The typical structure was instead an association or college responsible for either a particular body of ritual techniques or, less commonly, a specific ritual. Most priesthoods were held for life and open only to men; the only important priestesses were the Vestals. The major priesthoods were prestigious positions, held by the leading men of the state in conjunction with normal political careers. Their chief function was to provide the SENATE with expert advice on religious questions; the senate made the actual decisions and so constituted the true locus of religious authority. It was only under Augustus that this was concentrated under the control of an individual.

The two most important priestly colleges were the AUGURS and the pontiffs (*pontifex*, pl. *pontifices*). The former were responsible for augury, though MAGISTRATES rather than augurs actually took the auspices. The college consisted originally of three PATRICIANS but eventually included PLEBEIANS and grew in number to 16. The pontiffs, who underwent a similar development, had general oversight over the rites of public cult; they also had expertise in TOMB LAW and ADOPTIONS, on which they advised private individuals. Their head was the *pontifex maximus*, a position later held by all Roman emperors down to Gratian. Attached to the pontifical college were several archaic priesthoods with unusual features: the Vestals, *rex sacrorum* and *flamines*. The *rex sacrorum*, 'king of sacred rites', conducted rites originally performed by the Roman kings and could hold no other office. The 15 *flamines* were priests assigned to individual deities; the three 'greater' *flamines* were those of Jupiter (*flamen Dialis*), Mars and Quirinus. The *flamen Dialis*, in particular, was subject to numerous ritual prescriptions which, until relaxed by Augustus, made it difficult for him to pursue a normal political career.

The *quindecimviri sacris faciundis*, '15 men for performing rites', constituted the other major college. Their chief duty was the consultation of the Sibylline books, an ancient collection of ritual prescriptions. In the earlier REPUBLIC the *fetiales*, responsible for the religious aspects of declaring WAR and making TREATIES, perhaps had an equally high rank. Minor colleges had more specific functions: the Salii, for example, performed archaic ritual military DANCES on specified occasions. The introduction of new cults could entail the establishment of new priesthoods; some, like the *galli* of the Great Mother (CYBELE), were originally restricted to non-Romans. The most important new priesthoods of the imperial period were those of the deified EMPERORS, modelled either on the flaminate and/or on the lesser priestly colleges. At the same time, the traditional priesthoods, while retaining their prestige, apparently played a less important role in public life. JBR

See Beard, M. and North, J., eds. (1990) *Pagan Priests*.

 BACCHUS; SACRIFICE: (a), (c), (d).

***princeps* and principate** The first EMPEROR, AUGUSTUS, adopted the title *princeps*, 'leader', to describe his position; it occurs several times in his own account of his achievements, the *RES GESTAE* (13, 30, 32). Subsequently it became the term in general use for the ruling emperor, and its derivative, *principatus* ('principate') was used for the reign. It neatly suited the image which Augustus sought to project by representing himself as working within the tradition of the *principes viri* ('leading men') of the Republican period. The characteristics of such a man are set out by CICERO (*On the Orator* 3.63) as 'an author of public policy, a leader in ruling the state, and a leader in offering opinions and in making speeches in the senate, before the assemblies of citizens, and in the courts'. Such men exerted control, even when not holding a MAGISTRACY, through their influence and the respect they inspired for their views (their *auctoritas*, a key idea which Augustus made central to his concept of the role of the ruler; see *Res Gestae* 34.2). The influence of a *princeps* is frequently contrasted with *dominatio*, the arbitrary decision-making which was characteristic of the relationship between master and SLAVE. What was expected of the *princeps* was neatly summed up by PLINY THE YOUNGER for a senatorial audience as 'the Emperor thinks of himself as one of us' (*Panegyric* 2.4). JJP

See Millar, F. and Segal, E., eds. (1990) *Caesar Augustus*.

 EMPERORS, ROMAN: (a)–(b).

prisons Imprisonment was not a form of punishment much employed by either the Greeks or the Romans. It seems to have been used at Athens for certain public debtors (Demosthenes 24.134–5), but the best-known example of imprisonment is probably that of SOCRATES, who was imprisoned while awaiting execution after his trial for impiety. This indicates its regular use as a means of detention before and after trials. The Athenian prison (*desmôtêrion*) was run by the officials called the Eleven, who had the power to arrest persons accused of crimes such as theft. Similarly, imprisonment was not a penalty in Roman law, at least in theory; and the public prison at Rome (*carcer*) was mainly used for the brief detention of convicted criminals before execution. Quintus Pleminius, however, seems to have been incarcerated for nearly a decade at the start of the 2nd century BC after his conviction for atrocities committed against the Lokrians. The prison was also used by MAGISTRATES as one of the measures they could take (*coercitio*) against disobedience of their orders. As in Athens, a man accused of a criminal offence could be held before his trial pending investigations, but not always in the prison. The CATILINARIAN conspirators, for example, were detained in the houses of leading citizens (Sallust, *Catiline* 47). Further, the rich would have workhouses (*ergastula*) where SLAVES and debtors could be imprisoned and also (in the Republic) thieves, who effectively became the slaves of the men from whom they had stolen. MJE

Proba On the usual view of her identity, Faltonia Betitia Proba (identified only as Proba in the manuscript tradition) is the earliest known female CHRISTIAN author of a complete and extant work, a *Cento (Patch-work)*, and one of the earliest Latin Christian POETS of either sex. Linked by birth and marriage to the greatest families at Rome, she was the wife of Clodius Celsinus Adelphius and the mother of Clodius Hermogenianus Olybrius and Faltonius Probus Alypius. The *Cento*'s preface records earlier compositions about wars, and a remark in a medieval manuscript states that she chronicled the conflict between CONSTANTINE and the usurper Magnentius; one of the two needs emendation, either to Constantius or Maxentius (possibly Maximian). No longer extant, the latter work was perhaps an historical epic like those of CLAUDIAN. Alternatively, Proba is sometimes identified as Faltonia Betitia Proba's grand-daughter Anicia Faltonia Proba. The most recent view suggests that the grandmother had died by c.AD 350.

The date of the *Cento* depends on the identity of its author. It is usually ascribed to the late 350s or early 360s, but sometimes to the 380s (by those who suggest the grand-daughter as author); naturally, the latter date and authorship gains some support if the grandmother died by 350, but a publication date in the 340s may not be impossible. The *Cento*'s 694 verses, compiled entirely from lines and partial lines from VIRGIL's poems, are a selective retelling of the BIBLE, primarily stories from Genesis, including Creation, and the life of JESUS. Proba's approach encourages a conclusion that she shared the perspective of a conservative ARISTOCRATIC class and opposed the renunciation of traditional family and social values by Christian women. Some manuscripts preserve a scribe's dedication of a copy to an Eastern emperor, probably Theodosius II, whose wife Eudocia compiled a Greek *Cento* of her own and may have been inspired by Proba's. In the West, Proba's *Cento* was a popular teaching tool for many centuries. JV

See Barnes, T. D. (2006) An urban prefect and his wife, *CQ* 56; Clark, E. A. and Hatch, D. F. (1981) *The Golden Bough, The Oaken Cross: the Virgilian Cento of Faltonia Betitia Proba*; Shanzer, D. (1986) The Anonymous Carmen contra paganos and the date and identity of the centonist Proba, *Revue des Études Augustiniennes* 32: 232–48.

Probus see AURELIAN; MAXIMIAN;

 EMPERORS, ROMAN: (b).

PROCESSIONS: religious parades made for great street theatre in the ancient world, well illustrated by this torch-lit Bacchic scene, with music, dance, colourful costumes and exotic animals.

processions Movements of a group towards ritual goals. A procession (*pompê* in Greek) may form part of a religious FESTIVAL enacted in public SPACE, but can also be performed in the context of a more private ritual among members of a HOUSEHOLD (*oikos*) and their relatives. The ritual end of a procession could coincide with a SACRIFICE, a PURIFICATION or an offering to a god, as well as a more personal ritual act such as an initiation or funeral. Shared features include the participation of people of all ages and social status, including women, children and elders, as well as citizens and SLAVES. Many fulfilled precise ritual roles, which took a more formal form in public processions. Among these roles were PRIESTS AND PRIESTESSES, MUSICIANS, state officials, and carriers of sacred objects or utensils. HYMNS and PRAYERS or (for private processions) SONGS were further typical features. Public processions could be directed towards or away from the civic centre, traversing civic and sacred SPACE, normally ending up at a sacred location.

A procession could take place at different times of the day depending on the occasion. Some nocturnal processions were famed in antiquity, such as that during the celebration of the ELEUSINIAN MYSTERIES. EP

See Burkert, W. (1985) *Greek Religion*; Graf, F. (1996) Pompai in Greece: some considerations about space and ritual in the Greek polis, in R. Hägg, ed., *The Role of Religion in the Early Greek Polis* 55–65.

proconsul see ASIA, ROMAN; CONSULS; EMPERORS, ROMAN; GENERALS, ROMAN.

Procopius 6th-century AD Greek historian, major witness to the reign of the Eastern Roman or Byzantine emperor JUSTINIAN. Procopius was born in CAESAREA MARITIMA in Palestine and, in 527, was appointed as an adviser to Justinian's dynamic general Belisarius. As Procopius himself asserted, this made him an eyewitness to many of the events he narrated (*History of the Wars* 1.1.3), such as the assaults on VANDAL North AFRICA and Ostrogothic ITALY and the outbreak of plague at Constantinople in 542. His writings seem to have been produced before 555 – though precise dating has provoked considerable debate.

Procopius wrote three works of startlingly different character. His *History of the Wars*, which dealt with Justinian's conquests, was self-consciously written in the language and style of the historians of the classical past, most notably THUCYDIDES. On the *History of the Wars* has rested Procopius' reputation as a 'great' historian. Yet this subjective evaluation has often led scholars to decry the character (and sometimes deny his authorship) of his other works: open PANEGYRIC of Justinian's architectural programme in *Buildings*, and vicious invective against members of the court in *Anekdota* (better known in English as *Secret History*). Each, however, in its own way, provides a compelling portrait of Justinian's reign. The challenge for modern scholars is to formulate a view of both the historian and his emperor that leaves room for the various facets revealed in Procopius' different works. MDH

See Procopius, *History of the Wars*, *Buildings*, *Anekdota*, 7 vols., trs. H. B. Dewing (1914–40); Cameron, A. (1985) *Procopius and the Sixth Century*.

procurators An agent for some upper class individual, usually a paid employee, FREEDMAN or freeborn, in charge of administering parts or all of his principal's HOUSEHOLD and/or property and of representing him in court. Acting upon a general mandate or the assumption of later ratification, the procurator had a separate juristic personality and was held solely accountable for his acts, insofar as negligence or fraud on his part was involved. When Roman nobles started expanding their economic interests far from home, procurators proved to be efficient and sometimes ruthless middlemen. The city of Salamis on Cyprus ran into serious financial crisis because BRUTUS' procurators insisted on collecting exorbitant compound interest on a loan (CICERO, *Letters to Atticus* 5.21; 6.1–3). Personal loyalty to employer, self-interest and unlimited duration of tenure were the foundations of an administrative system adopted in the public sector by JULIUS CAESAR. He put his personal staff and dependants in charge of the mint and the fiscal administration, threatening to do the same for the government of the city of Rome (SUETONIUS, *Julius Caesar* 76.3; 79.3). During the early PRINCIPATE, imperial freedmen and members of the EQUESTRIAN order took over most of the imperial government at Rome and across the empire. Landed properties and MINES, tax collection, public finances and mints, GLADIATORIAL GAMES, water and FOOD SUPPLY, and even minor PROVINCES were entrusted to them. A differential pay structure, and the variously desirable nature of the tasks, caused equestrian procuratorships to be arranged into a fixed career path open to ranking military OFFICERS and leading up to the major prefectures. JJA

See Aubert, J.-J. (1994) *Business Managers in Ancient Rome.*

 EQUESTRIANS (table).

production and surplus The ancient world was a pre-modern agrarian economy geared to the self-sufficient production of foodstuffs, cloth and other essentials of everyday life. Environmental and geographical constraints could limit production in some areas while surplus production was extracted in others; the latter process promoted MARKET exchange and commodity movement of other necessities and items of perceived cultural value produced elsewhere. Although governments in the ancient world did not generally intervene in the production of food and other commodities, they frequently procured and distributed AGRICULTURAL goods to meet the demands of large urban populations and the military. This had the effect of generating substantial productive surpluses in grain, OIL, MEAT, WINE and other agricultural and non-agricultural goods. In cases where this occurred in antiquity (in parts of the Roman empire, for example), such production may have constituted, for the most part, growth in the aggregate as opposed to per capita. Production in the non-agricultural sector formed a much smaller percentage of the ancient economy, but under the Roman empire there is some evidence for growth in MANUFACTURING, ranging from household production to specialized workshops and cottage industry, to meet growing demand. (see also GROWTH, ECONOMIC) RBH

See Finley, M. I. (1985) *The Ancient Economy*; Garnsey, P. (1999) *Food and Society in Classical Antiquity*; Horden, P. and Purcell, N. (2000) *The Corrupting Sea: a study of Mediterranean history.*

progress Ancient ideas of the development of human culture have traditionally been analysed into two distinct threads. One, usually labelled the primitivist view, is a seemingly pessimistic idea that humanity has suffered a gradual decline from a former perfect blessed state. This is often expressed in terms of a decline through successively worsening ages, or races, associated with metals that mark the moral value of each. Thus in HESIOD's *Works and Days*, where we find the idea first expressed schematically in Greek literature, the first race of humanity was a golden race of perfect piety who lived a life of endless leisure, in an eternal spring when all crops grew spontaneously and no work of any kind was necessary. The next race was of silver, the next of bronze and the last, our own, of iron. Each stage of increasing moral decadence is paralleled by the increasing hardness of each metal and accompanied by a decline in the fertility of the earth that makes work more necessary.

The other main thread, the progressivist or anti-primitivist view, argues that the first humans led a miserable violent life 'like wild beasts', with no technology, arts or human culture of any kind. Either these had to be developed gradually, by the application of human ingenuity using trial and error over time and driven by necessity, or arts were granted to humanity, either as gifts of the gods or by human or quasi-divine culture-heroes like Prometheus. Often the early humans were imagined to have been not clearly differentiated from wild animals either physically or behaviourally. Although there is little evidence of a fully evolutionary theory of the origin of species in ancient thought, the evolution of human culture is often linked to the physical evolution of modern humans from a former beast-like state.

Inevitably however, such a neat dichotomy obscures the complexity of ancient theories of culture history. Already in *Works and Days* we see in the Hesiod's advice to his brother Perses that progress may possibly be achieved, if only painfully and through unremitting toil. Indeed it is difficult to see what purpose a GOLDEN AGE would serve if it were impossible one day to regain it. Similarly in progressivist accounts, progress and decline may be seen as parallel processes: we may progress technologically while declining morally, for instance. Technological and moral progress may proceed in tandem up to a certain point in the past, but after that, increasing civilization may lead to moral regress. Arts and technologies that were developed to meet a pressing need by our ancestors, leading lives of poverty and toil in a harsh, unfriendly world, may, now that their use has led to leisure and plenty, be debilitating for their descendants. Moral and spiritual progress, then, may actually be a return to an earlier and purer state. Equally, arts and technologies may progress but in the wrong direction: METALLURGY led to the development of AGRICULTURE and associated arts of peace, but also WAR. GLC

See Blundell, S. (1986) *The Origins of Civilization in Greek and Roman Thought*; Edelstein, L. (1967) *The Idea of Progress in Classical Antiquity*; Lovejoy, A. O. and Boas, G. (1935) *Primitivism and Related Ideas in Antiquity.*

Prokonnesos see MARBLE.

Propertius (Sextus Propertius) c.50–10 BC Elegiac POET, born (so he implies in poem 4.1) at or near Assisi in Umbria, to a wealthy land-owning family. Although his inheritance was somewhat diminished in the land confiscations of 41–40 BC, he seems to have retained sufficient property to ensure his financial independence and EQUESTRIAN status. Like most young men with literary ambitions, he apparently spent most of his adult life in Rome. There he came into contact with the literary patron MAECENAS, to whom the second book of *Elegies* is (implicitly) dedicated. The date of his death cannot be established with certainty, but falls some time after 16 BC (the latest datable reference in his poetry).

Propertius' first three books of *Elegies* purport – like the love elegies of Gallus, TIBULLUS and

Ovid – to trace the stormy relationship between the poet and his beautiful, domineering but inevitably unfaithful mistress, Cynthia. Many of the characters and situations depicted in the poems are conventional, and we should beware of assuming that they are in any sense autobiographical. In Propertius' hands, the genre takes on a markedly double-edged irony. The poet combines a defiantly rebellious attitude towards authority (including the newly established authority of Augustus) with the persistent employment of self-deflating hyperbole and outrageously extravagant mythological comparisons. Thus it is rarely clear whether we are being invited to laugh at, or to sympathize with, the lover's plight. The fourth book is a highly innovative collection of poems explicitly modelled on the aetiological elegy of Kallimachos. The theme of love remains prominent, however, and several of the poems are, strikingly, presented as a whole or in part from the perspective of female characters. MG

See Propertius, *The Poems*, trs. G. Lee, (1994); Hubbard, M. (1974) *Propertius*; Lyne, R. O. A. M. (1980) *The Latin Love Poets*; Wyke, M. (2002) *The Roman Mistress*.

prophecy The craft of the seer in ancient societies, which revealed the will of the gods in connection with past, present and future situations. Prophecy was a form of divination and could be delivered to those who sought it, usually but not exclusively in the context of a sanctuary. It was a form of 'active' religious experience generated by individual or collective preference, which intended to establish communication with the divine in a form different from that of traditional ritual (sacrifice, prayer, procession, votive offering). This active element of prophecy is reflected in the etymology of the word: *pro-phêmi* in Greek means 'I speak forth', 'I proclaim'.

Prophets were believed to be the mouthpiece of gods, and as such were well-respected members of the community. Their utterances (*chrêsmoi* in Greek) were thought to be the product of possession by a god, and prophets or prophetesses often exhibited signs of divine mania (becoming *entheos*) in their attempt to convey divine messages to humans. The Greek term for prophet, *mantis* (from *mainomai*, 'I rant' or 'I rage'), points to the notion of a prophetic fit which the god's vehicle underwent during the process. Similar prophetic behaviour is suggested by the Latin term *vates* (prophet).

Oracular divination is generally considered as one of the forms of subjective divination suggesting direct contact with the god. Further practices showing the god's apparition – drawing lots or rolling dice – were followed at some oracles. Inductive divination, on the other hand, was not dependent on direct divine communication and was represented by practices such as astrology or interpretation of dreams. The wide range in the manner of divination at different places and periods serves as a mirror of the dramatic cult variations of the polytheistic system, a particularly distinctive feature of the Roman empire. Personal preference was clearly one of the main factors for the practice of some oracles or divination procedures, but what really determined the popularity of the latter was their antiquity. Some of the most ancient oracles of the Greek world, such as Delphi, Didyma and Claros, continued to flourish in the early Roman empire. By contrast, certain types of oracle, such as the lot oracles, were not considered so reliable, as Cicero's criticism of them shows (*On Divination* 2.41, 86–7).

The role of prophets and oracles in shaping politics was pivotal in both ancient Greece and Rome. Although only indirectly connected with politics, the value of prophecy lay in its validation of politics and its agents. Oracles, like ancient religious cult and rituals, assisted in the maintenance of both the social and political state of affairs by confirming the integration of the latter in the area of divine order.

Some of the earliest prophetic texts found in the history of Herodotos were allegedly produced by figures such as Orpheus, Bakis and the Sibyl, but their reliability is often doubted by modern historians. Extant collections of prophecies of a later date include the Sibylline and Chaldaean oracles. EP

See Potter, D. S. (1994) *Prophets and Emperors*.

Propontis see Hellespont and Propontis.

propraetors see generals, Roman; praetors; Sardinia.

prose Greek literary prose developed long after poetry, since the oral composition required in preliterate society lent itself to poetry by virtue of its metrical patterns. The earliest prose writers were the Ionian chroniclers and philosophers of the 6th and 5th centuries. The former, who were called *logographoi* and included such figures as Hekataios of Miletos, wrote a form of proto-history and geography. Their works are lost, but consisted of surveys into mythical and genealogical topics, regional and local histories (such as Hellanikos' *Atthis*), and chronologies. The philosophers, such as the Milesians Thales, Anaximander and Anaximenes, were involved in speculation about the origins of the universe and the single substance that was its material principle. Their writings are again mostly lost, and the earliest extant prose work is the history of Herodotos, written in Ionic Greek. By the late 5th century the Attic dialect had become the standard: the rhetorical works of the Sicilian Gorgias are written in Attic, and we have a number of speeches by the Attic orators from that period. Other prose being written at the time included history (Thucydides), medical literature (the Hippocratic corpus), and political theory (the so-called Old Oligarch's pamphlet on the Athenian constitution). Attic prose reached its zenith during the 4th century, when the older, 'Grand' style of authors such as Thucydides was replaced by the 'Plain' style of Lysias and the mixed, 'Middle' style of authors such as Plato and Isokrates. Plato, indeed, was one of the finest Greek prose writers, surpassed only by Demosthenes. The supremacy of Attic gave way in the hellenistic period to the far less subtle 'common' Greek dialect (*koinê*), which was based on Attic and whose influence is already discernible in Xenophon. Greek prose was also heavily influenced from the 3rd century by the florid style called 'Asianist'. A reaction set in during the late 1st century at Rome, as in the works of the literary critic and historian Dionysios of Halikarnassos. The 2nd century AD saw the Attic revival called the Second Sophistic, among whose finest exponents was Lucian. The novel, too, flourished in that period.

Latin prose in part, at least, originated in the religious records of the pontiffs (*Annales*), which served as the basis of later Roman historiography; and other early influences included public speech and Roman law. Little survives before the 1st century BC, when two forms dominate. ORATORY, central to Roman politics, reached its peak in the works of CICERO; history found expert exponents in the plain style of CAESAR and the more elaborate LIVY. Post-Ciceronian prose tended to be more epigrammatic in style, most notably in the historical works of TACITUS and the philosophical prose of the younger SENECA. The influence of the rhetorical schools was also marked, as authors learned their trade by practising DECLAMATION; the letter-writing of PLINY THE YOUNGER is an example here. QUINTILIAN reacted against the artificiality of this form of writing, promoting a return to Ciceronian style.

Prose literature in the ancient world, like poetry, was primarily written to be read aloud. This in turn meant that rhythm was an important aspect of composition, and the endings of cola and sentences, known as *clausulae*, were of particular significance. Rhythm can be analysed on the basis of metrical patterns, though ARISTOTLE (*Rhetoric* 3.8) warns that prose should be 'rhythmical but not metrical, or it will be a poem'. Demosthenes favoured the *clausula* – – – *x* (three long syllables followed by either a long or a short) and avoided successions of more than two short syllables. Cicero, on the other hand, preferred *clausulae* composed of the metrical foot known as the cretic (long, short, long: – ˘ –) followed by a ditrochee (– ˘ – *x*), or a double cretic, or a cretic followed by a trochee (– ˘) or spondee (– –). He regularly resolves long syllables into two shorts, producing successions of three short syllables, in the so-called *esse videatur* rhythm (–˘˘˘ – *x*). Livy avoided the latter, but his prose is full of poetic rhythms, a practice picked up by Tacitus, the opening sentence of whose *Annals* follows the metrical pattern of a hexameter verse. MJE

See Broadhead, H. D. (1922) *Latin Prose Rhythm*; McCabe, D. F. (1981) *The Prose-rhythm of Demosthenes.*

prostitutes and prostitution Famously called 'the world's oldest profession', prostitution has a very long antiquity. However, there is no mention of prostitution in the earliest Greek sources, the HOMERIC poems, though this does not mean that prostitution did not appear in Greece at a very early age. CORINTH, with its busy port and cult centre for the worship of APHRODITE, was associated with a lively prostitution scene from at least the middle archaic period; it had the reputation of being the red-light city of ancient Greece. Prostitution was legal in Athens as long as it was not practised by an Athenian CITIZEN wife or daughter. Indeed, SOLON is credited with establishing Athens' first brothels. The city had many public brothels, largely staffed by SLAVES, though the main red-light district was located in the Kerameikos near the city's graveyard, gates and drains. The *POLIS* farmed out the right to collect taxes from prostitution to enterprising individuals. Prostitutes tended either to be slaves (female or male) or metics. Prostitution was divided up between the common *pornai* (streetwalkers and brothel whores) and *hetairai* (literally 'companions'),

PROSTITUTES AND PROSTITUTION: one of the brothels at Pompeii, its squalid and tiny cubicles contrasting with the sumptuous furnishings depicted in idealized scenes of love-making in a series of tableau decorating the walls of this lobby area.

accomplished courtesans well beyond the pocket of the average Athenian male. In between these two poles there was a group of prostitutes who worked as entertainers, DANCERS, acrobats and *aulos*-players, who attended *SYMPOSIA* and could be called upon to perform SEX with assembled male guests.

Forbidden to marry a citizen, a *hetaira* could hope to captivate one by her wit and beauty. If a slave, a *pornê* could aspire to win the purchase of her freedom, as indeed happened to the prostitute named NEAIRA. It is this tension between the perceived avarice of *hetairai* and the ruinous infatuation which they inspired in their clients that provides the conventional themes for much Greek literature. Classical literature delights in showing beautiful, clever and witty *hetairai* such as Phrynê, Laïs, Theodote and ASPASIA, courtesans who achieved considerable notoriety both in their own time and in later traditions. But it must be remembered that whatever power they gained came from their ability to be recognized by the powerful men with whom they consorted.

Textual evidence suggests that *pornai* were readily identifiable by their semi-naked appearances in public, hanging around outside brothels. They also wore make-up and flower-patterned, transparent dresses. *Hetairai*, however, are difficult to distinguish in the art works from 'respectable' women. They frequently wear veils and concealing robes. Indeed, according to some ancient sources, it was more difficult to get a glimpse of a great *hetaira* than it was to see a man's wife. Male prostitution was also a feature of Greek life, but the stigma it attracted to any boy who put himself into prostitution was great: he was debarred from holding any public or religious office. Nevertheless, male prostitution seems to have thrived in Athens.

The Romans were as pragmatic about sex as the Greeks. Women were routinely sold into prostitution or chose the life themselves because it could be lucrative – the emperor CALIGULA actually added a tax to prostitution to raise money for the state. Laws forbade women from turning to prostitution if they were the daughters of *EQUITES* (the merchant class). Usually only the lowest economic classes chose, or were forced into, the life of prostitution and took the title *meretrix*, *lupa*, or *scortum*, the most common Latin terms for 'prostitute'. Roman laws about prostitution were inconsistent and often ambiguous, though there was a certain tolerance of the system (and of the women who practised it) until the rise of the CHRISTIAN CHURCH, when the first consistent efforts were made to suppress it. Women who were neither PATRICIANS nor slaves, but relied on other means of income (for example, ACTRESSES, MIMES, MUSICIANS and dancers) were free to sell sexual services without registration or TAXATION. Male prostitutes (also called *scorta*) were also numerous in Rome, but were not regulated by the state.

Brothels (*lupanaria*) run by pimps (*lenones*) were found throughout the empire. They were usually staffed by slaves and, to judge from the graffiti found within them, were frequented by slaves and the poor. In the brothels of POMPEII, erotic scenes of idealized lovemaking contrast markedly with the explicit and sometimes violent language of the graffiti scrawled on the walls of the tiny cubicles. The red-light districts of Rome were located in the Subura, near the CIRCUS MAXIMUS, and underneath the ARCHES of the Coliseum. The women who plied their trade in these areas were known as *noctilucae* (night moths), *ambulatrices* (strollers), *busturiae* (grave watchers) and *diobiloriae* (two-bit whores). Prostitutes were routinely found in BATH houses and at THEATRES. Female employees of inns and taverns were grouped with prostitutes by law, as were actresses, who were forbidden from marrying citizens. Some sources suggest that Roman prostitutes were easy to identify by their dress, and that they were forced to wear the TOGA. This, however, is debatable. It is clear that sex workers were found everywhere throughout the Roman empire, though few name their jobs on their tombstones. An exception is the gravestone of Vibia Calybeni, who classifies herself as 'a free-woman madam'.

'Sacred prostitution' is also attested in classical societies, though the term itself is a modern one and somewhat misleading. According to ancient understanding, some TEMPLE personnel would dedicate their sexual services (and sometimes their income) to a deity, but 'sacred prostitution' should not be thought of as an institution in its own right. At the temple of Aphrodite at Corinth, STRABO (8.6.20) tells that there were 1,000 prostitutes in service to the goddess, but he may be referring to the number of prostitutes located in the city, not necessarily to any 'formal' temple staff. (see also SEXUALITY) LL-J

See Dalby, A. (2002) Levels of concealment: the dress of hetairai and pornai in Greek texts, in L. Llewellyn-Jones, ed., *Women's Dress in the Ancient Greek World* 111–24; Davidson, J. (1997) *Courtesans and Fishcakes*; McGinn, T. (1998) *Prostitution, Sexuality and the Law in Ancient Rome*; Williams, C. A. (1999) *Roman Homosexuality*.

Protagoras c.490–420 BC The leading SOPHIST PHILOSOPHER of his day, from the city of Abdera. Protagoras visited Athens on several occasions and was closely associated with PERIKLES and his circle. Perikles is even reported to have asked him to write the constitution for the Athenian colony of Thourioi. A professional educator, he is famous (or notorious) for his focus on techniques of argument and for training students to be able to argue both sides of any question. He is associated with the ability 'to make the weaker argument the stronger', the sort of training parodied by ARISTOPHANES in the *Clouds*. This, along with his relativistic approach to truth and his agnosticism, may have resulted, as ancient tradition asserts, in his condemnation for impiety and flight from Athens.

Two other sayings attributed to Protagoras illustrate his thinking. One, that 'man is the measure of all things', may be interpreted in two ways. The first is that truth is always only subjective – whatever anyone believes will be true. This is refuted by DEMOKRITOS, and by PLATO in the *Theaitetos*: if all beliefs are true, then the belief that 'all beliefs are true' is false must also be true. It is a self-refuting argument. Second, it may be a statement of relativism: anything that anyone believes will be true for the person who believes it. Another saying illustrates his agnosticism: 'Concerning the gods, I am unable to know either that they exist or that they do not exist or what form they have. For there are many obstacles to knowledge: the obscurity of the matter and the brevity of human life.' GLC

See Guthrie, W. K. C. (1969) *A History of Greek Philosophy*, vol. 3; Kerferd, G. B. (1981) *The Sophistic Movement*.

provinces and provincial government, Roman A province is a MAGISTRATE'S 'job', originally without territorial sense. Then peoples and tracts of land outside Italy (SICILY, SARDINIA, SPAIN) needed special appointees. SULLA (81 BC) made the numbers of CONSULS and PRAETORS (10) and of provinces match: each of the dozen governed a province after their magistracy. As Rome expanded, provinces multiplied by acquisition; under the empire smaller areas such as JUDAEA were assigned to knights instead of senatorial governors. Subdivision, for example, under SEPTIMIUS SEVERUS and DIOCLETIAN, increased numbers from the 3rd century on.

Military control and dispensing JUSTICE were a governor's prime duties; generally he issued an edict on entry to his province to publicize the legal principles of his government. Many governors succumbed to various temptations, particularly corruption and sadism. Efforts at control, from the *lex Calpurnia* of 149 BC, increased in severity, until CAESAR imposed death for VIOLENCE (59). His *lex Julia* subsisted throughout the empire, modified by AUGUSTUS' speedier (but not surer) methods of trial by SENATORIAL commission (4 BC).

It is disputed whether widening CITIZENSHIP and provincial participation in senatorial and equestrian service led to improvements. The contribution of provinces to the imperial chest and army made them important, but the Italy–provinces antithesis took long to die; only in the 4th-century Verona List was Italy classified as a province. BML

See Lintott, A. (1993) *Imperium Romanum*.

ROMAN EMPIRE: (a)–(b).

Prudentius (Aurelius Prudentius Clemens) AD 348–c.407 The most important CHRISTIAN Latin POET of late antiquity, he was born in Spain and received a

PROVINCES AND PROVINCIAL GOVERNMENT, ROMAN: (a) the Roman provinces in AD 50.

Province	Governor	Rank	
Sicilia	Proconsul	ex-Praetor	
Corsica–Sardinia	Proconsul	ex-Praetor	
Hispania Tarraconensis	Leg. Aug. p.p	ex-Consul	
Baetica	Proconsul	ex-Praetor	
Lusitania	Leg. Aug. p.p	ex-Praetor	
Gallia Narbonensis	Proconsul	ex-Praetor	
Aquitania	Leg. Aug. p.p	ex-Praetor	
Gallia Lugdunensis	Leg. Aug. p.p	ex-Praetor	
Gallia Belgica	Leg. Aug. p.p	ex-Praetor	
Germania Superior *Germania Inferior*	Leg. Aug. p.p Leg. Aug. p.p	ex-Consul ex-Consul	Technically military commands rather than provinces until late 1st century AD
Alpes Maritimae	Procurator	Eques	
Alpes Cottiae	Procurator	Eques	
Alpes Poeninae	Procurator	Eques	
Britannia	Leg. Aug. p.p	ex-Consul	
Raetia	Procurator	Eques	
Noricum	Procurator	Eques	
Pannonia	Leg. Aug. p.p	ex-Consul	
Dalmatia	Leg. Aug. p.p	ex-Consul	
Moesia	Leg. Aug. p.p	ex-Consul	
Thracia	Procurator	Eques	
Macedonia	Proconsul	ex-Praetor	
Achaea	Proconsul	ex-Praetor	
Asia	Proconsul	ex-Consul	
Bithynia–Pontus	Proconsul	ex-Praetor	
Galatia	Leg. Aug. p.p	ex-Praetor	
Cappadocia	Leg. Aug. p.p	ex-Praetor	
Lycia–Pamphylia	Leg. Aug. p.p	ex-Praetor	
Cyprus	Proconsul	ex-Praetor	
Syria	Leg. Aug. p.p	ex-Consul	
Judaea	Procurator	Eques	
Aegyptus	Praefectus	Eques	
Creta-Cyrene	Proconsul	ex-Praetor	
Africa Proconsularis	Proconsul	ex-Consul	
Numidia	Leg. Aug. p.p	ex-Praetor	Technically military command
Mauretania Caesariensis	Procurator	Eques	
Mauretania Tingitana	Procurator	Eques	

Key: italics indicate imperial provinces; Leg. Aug. p.p. = Legatus Augusti pro praetore.

traditional EDUCATION before entering state service. He held several positions and eventually took a position at the imperial court, but details are unknown. He visited Rome at least once, but spent the last years of his life in Spain.

Much of Prudentius' poetry concerns the growing cult of MARTYRS, following the lead of Damasus and AMBROSE, bishops of Rome and MILAN respectively. His martyrs were mainly Spanish, but Lawrence (Rome) and others appear. Some poems are hymns, though not written for liturgical use. His most well-known poem is *Contra Symmachum* (*Against Symmachus*), a long work in two books. It argues against the several attempts, most famously in 384, by SYMMACHUS and other non-Christian SENATORS to have the Altar of Victory and state subsidies for

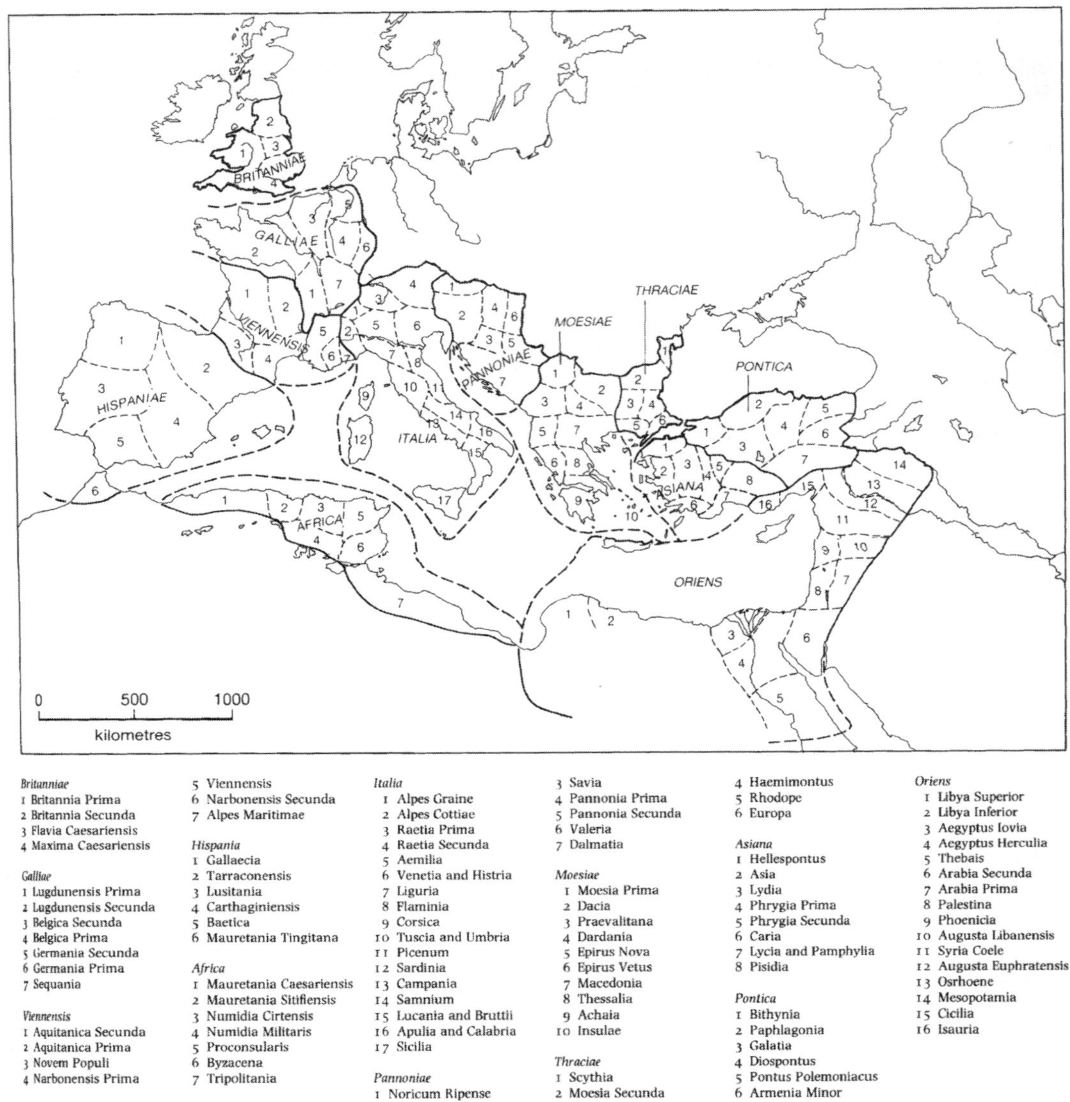

PROVINCES AND PROVINCIAL GOVERNMENT, ROMAN: (b) map of Late Roman provinces and dioceses.

traditional cults restored. The poem shows evidence of reworkings and was revised for these various occasions. Other poems include *Peristephanon* (*Crowns of Glory*), *Cathemerinon* (*Daily Round*) and *Psychomachia* (*Battle for the Soul*).

Literary parallels reveal that Prudentius knew the poems of contemporaries, as well as classical Latin poetry. His skill is evident in the variety of metres he employs. Less clearly, but arguably, non-Christian poets like CLAUDIAN knew his writings. Not surprisingly, he became a model for later Christian poetry, and his works were popular in the Middle Ages. JV

See Palmer, A.-M. (1989) *Prudentius on the Martyrs*; Thomson, H. J. (1949–53) *Prudentius* (text, trs.).

prytany Best known as an Athenian chronological and political term, signifying one-tenth of the year in which the 50 members of the council (*boulê*) from each of the ten post-Kleisthenic tribes in turn performed administrative and executive tasks as presidents (*prytaneis*) for both council and assembly. This roughly month-long period was known as a *prytaneia*, and ranged from 34 to 39 days due to the imprecision of the Athenian lunisolar CALENDAR.

Each day, a chairman (*epistatês*) from the 50 *prytaneis* was chosen by lot to assume formal executive duties of the Athenian state for a continuous 24-hour tenure in the AGORA. Because the office was not repeated, as many as half the citizens may have served as *epistatês* at some time.

The term *prytanis* itself is a generic and ancient usage to denote simply a MAGISTRATE, and *prytaneia* ('prytany') his tenure of office. While, outside Athens, state officials were known as *prytaneis* throughout the Greek world down to hellenistic times, the intricate combination of assigning offices by lot and by tribe to match a particular period in the year seems to be uniquely an Athenian democratic idea. It reflects both confidence in the average citizen and the fear of accumulated power in the hands of any one person. VDH

See Rhodes, P. J. (1972) *The Athenian Boule.*

Psellos, Michael see SCHOLARSHIP, BYZANTINE.

Psyche see APULEIUS.

Ptolemies MACEDONIAN dynasty which ruled Egypt 323–30 BC. PTOLEMY I Soter acquired Egypt as his satrapy at the death of ALEXANDER the Great, dislodged Kleomenes of NAUKRATIS, declared himself king in 305 and founded the longest-lasting of the hellenistic kingdoms. The kingdom ended with the death of CLEOPATRA VII following the arrival of OCTAVIAN in Egypt after ACTIUM. The earlier Ptolemies controlled CYPRUS, CYRENAICA, Palestine, much of the coast of Asia Minor, most of the AEGEAN islands and part of the north Aegean coast, mainly due to a powerful fleet and abundant financial resources. The concerted actions of PHILIP V of Macedonia and the SELEUKID king ANTIOCHOS III deprived the young Ptolemy V Epiphanes of the possessions in the Aegean, Asia Minor and Palestine (204–197), but Cyrene and Cyprus were lost only in the 1st century BC.

Despite fighting many wars – at least seven with the Seleukids, mainly over Palestine, and others elsewhere – the Ptolemies boasted few military kings of note (none approaching the stature of Antiochos III), and much of their warfare was unsuccessful. Only Roman intervention and PATRONAGE preserved the kingdom from Antiochos IV's aggression and kept

PTOLEMIES: the Ptolemaic dynasty.

Date	Ruler	Relationship to other rulers
305–283	Ptolemy I Soter ('Saviour'; governor from 323)	
285–246	Ptolemy II Philadelphos ('Sister-friend')	s. Ptolemy I
246–221	Ptolemy III Euergetes ('Benefactor')	s. Ptolemy II
221–204	Ptolemy IV Philopator ('Father-friend')	s. Ptolemy III
204–180	Ptolemy V Epiphanes ('(God) Manifest')	s. Ptolemy IV
180–145	Ptolemy VI Philometor ('Mother-friend')	s. Ptolemy V
170–163	[1]Ptolemy VIII Euergetes II Physkon ('Potbelly')	s. Ptolemy V
170–164	[1]Kleopatra II	d. Ptolemy V
163–116	[2]Kleopatra II	
145	Ptolemy VII Neos Philopator (with Ptolemy VI, and briefly after the latter's death)	s. Ptolemy VI
145–116	[2]Ptolemy VIII	
116–101	Kleopatra III	d. Ptolemy VI, wife of Ptolemy VIII
116–107	[1]Ptolemy IX Soter II Lathyros ('the Bean')	s. Ptolemy VIII, Kleopatra III
107–88	Ptolemy X Alexander I	s. Ptolemy VIII
101–88	[1]Kleopatra Berenike	d. Ptolemy IX
88–81	[2]Ptolemy IX	
80	[2]Kleopatra Berenike	
80	Ptolemy XI Alexander II	s. Ptolemy X
80–58	[1]Ptolemy XII Neos Dionysos Auletes ('the Piper')	s. Ptolemy IX
58–55	Berenike IV (at first with her sister Kleopatra Tryphaina)	d. Ptolemy IX
56–55	Archelaos	husband of Berenike IV
55–51	[2]Ptolemy XII	
51–47	Ptolemy XIII	s. Ptolemy XI
51–30	Kleopatra VII Philopator	d. Ptolemy XI
47–44	Ptolemy XIV	s. Ptolemy XI

Key: s. = son of; d. = daughter of; [1] first period of rule. [2] second period of rule.

Egypt independent through most of the succeeding century and a quarter. But Egypt's grain production and other resources (not including SILVER, crucially) gave the Ptolemies the scope for widespread patronage and intervention. Much money was spent on developing ALEXANDRIA as the leading city of the hellenistic world (in competition with ANTIOCH and PERGAMON) and on patronage of POETS, scholars, scientists and artists, above all in the Alexandrian MOUSEION and its LIBRARY. RSB

See Bevan, E. (1927) *A History of Egypt under the Ptolemaic Dynasty*; Hölbl, G. (2001) *A History of the Ptolemaic Empire*.

Ptolemy I c.367/6–283/2 BC Founder of the PTOLEMAIC dynasty and historian of ALEXANDER the Great. Born about 367/6, Ptolemy was Alexander's older contemporary and youthful friend. In the first part of the expedition to Asia, he was a minor figure, becoming a bodyguard in 330 and one of the inner circle in the last years. From the caucus at BABYLON in 323 he emerged with Egypt as his satrapy; Perdikkas died trying to dislodge him in 320. Taking the title of king in 305 after the repulse of ANTIGONOS' invasion of Egypt, he ruled until his death in 283/2. With prudent opportunism, and no unnecessary risks, he acquired CYRENAICA, CYPRUS, Palestine and bases in the AEGEAN. His son by BERENIKE, Ptolemy II Philadelphos, succeeded him. His posthumous cult termed him Soter, 'saviour'; the basis for this is disputed.

Ptolemy's narrative of Alexander's career was (with Aristoboulos' account) one of the twin bases of ARRIAN's history and has been much venerated in modern times, but is hardly cited in antiquity apart from by Arrian. Its date and context are unknown, but praise of Alexander, flattery of the MACEDONIANS, exaggeration of his own role and denigration of his competitors suggest that it was an early production, for self-justifying use in the struggle over the succession to Alexander's empire. RSB

See Bosworth, A. B. (1988) *From Arrian to Alexander*; Ellis, W. M. (1994) *Ptolemy of Egypt*.

Ptolemy of Alexandria Greek writer on GEOGRAPHY, ASTRONOMY, and ASTROLOGY under the Roman empire, also known as Claudius Ptolemy or Claudius Ptolemaeus. Between AD 146 and c.170 he wrote lengthy treatises that remained fundamental for over a millennium in Islamic culture as well as Western. His most famous work on astronomy is known as *Almagest*, a name derived from the Arabic version of its Greek title, *Megistê syntaxis* (*Greatest Treatise*). It deals with all aspects of astronomy and the underlying geometrical models. Ptolemy adopts and refines the earlier theory of epicycles to explain the apparent movements of heavenly bodies. His *Geography* covers the known world, listing places and their coordinates. Although latitude and longitude had been invented earlier, perhaps by HIPPARCHOS, Ptolemy may have been the first to use them systematically as a reference system. The work was accompanied by a map, of which derivative versions are extant. Inaccuracies in his treatises are often due to faulty data supplied to him. His *Tetrabiblos* ('Four-book') gave a mathematical basis to astrology, a discipline to which astronomy was, if anything, subordinate at that time. His other surviving works cover planets, SUNDIALS, optics, harmonics and other subjects. Recent scholarship has upgraded Ptolemy from a pedestrian compiler into a truly innovative researcher. DGJS

See Robbins, F.E., trs. (1940) *Ptolemy, Tetrabiblos*; Stevenson, E. L., trs. (1932) *Geography of Claudius Ptolemy* (not always accurate); Toomer, G. J., trs. (1984) *Ptolemy's Almagest*.

public order

The Greek states did not have police forces in the modern sense, but they appointed a range of officials to keep public order in different situations. In the Ionian states in all periods 'city MAGISTRATES' (*astynomoi*) kept the streets and sanctuaries secure and free from obstructions, and enforced sumptuary laws – the CYNIC Krates was punished for wearing linen (DIOGENES LAËRTIUS 6.90). A 2nd-century AD inscription (*SEG* 13.521) records the duties of the *astynomoi* at PERGAMON, set in a law of the 2nd century BC. At Athens there were ten such officials, five in the city and five in PIRAEUS, appointed annually by lot. There were likewise ten market overseers (*agoranomoi*) and ten weights and measures magistrates (*metronomoi*). The officials responsible for the all-important corn trade (*sitophylakes*) numbered at first five in the city and five in Piraeus, later 20 and 15 respectively.

The Athenians also had a board of officials appointed by lot to deal with certain forms of criminal activity, the Eleven. Their duty was to arrest and imprison common CRIMINALS (*kakourgoi*) such as thieves and muggers. If they caught a criminal red-handed (*ep' autophôrôi*) and he confessed, the Eleven were empowered to execute him without trial. Otherwise, they were responsible for carrying out executions after trial. Athenian officials could call on the assistance of public SLAVES. After the PERSIAN WARS and down into the early 4th century these comprised a corps of 300 Scythian archers, whose main function was to keep order in the ASSEMBLY, COUNCIL and LAWCOURTS.

Criminal activity and small-scale disturbances were, however, primarily a private matter, dealt with by citizens with the help of their friends and relatives. In this form of self-help procedure, neighbours and passers-by were also expected to intervene. It was only when the problem became a threat to the community as a whole that the state itself became involved, as in the religious scandal of the Mysteries and HERMS in 415 BC, when the council ordered the GENERALS to call the citizens to arms (Andokides 1.45). A peculiar form of public order was kept at SPARTA by a notorious secret force of citizen youths, called the *krypteia*, which was used, perhaps sporadically, to terrorize the HELOTS. MJE

See Aristotle, *Constitution of Athens* 50.2–52.1; Hunter, V. J. (1994) *Policing Athens*; Lintott, A.W. (1982) *Violence, Civil Strife and Revolution in the Classical City 750–330* BC.

Discussion of Roman attitudes towards public order must begin with Rome's lack of anything resembling a modern police force whose purpose is the maintenance of public order, protection of the populace, and prevention, detection, investigation and punishment of crime. Rome had an elaborate LAW code and MAGISTRATES with the power to make judicial decisions and inflict punishment, but most of the duties of a police force rested with private initiative. Since most private conflicts were not a major concern of the state, KINSHIP and PATRONAGE systems played important roles in settling these disputes. The attention of the state focused on actions perceived to constitute a threat to the broader political or social order. Complicating matters in the REPUBLIC was the prohibition of military forces within the boundaries of the city; thus the most obvious recourse for quelling RIOTS, calling in the troops, was unavailable.

During the Republic, urban concerns including general order in the city were the responsibility of the AEDILES and other minor officials; however, they lacked effective means of enforcement. Higher level magistrates, such as PRAETORS and CONSULS, were granted *imperium*, which enabled them to fine, punish or even kill citizens, and had staffs including lictors, who may have been used to enforce their judgements. But even they mainly acted on cases which were brought before them by private initiative. Large-scale urban VIOLENCE became more acute during the upheavals of the late Republic, due to the use of gangs by politicians as well as the increase in focal points for outbreaks of violence, such as the many sensational trials of this period. Organized violence, instigated by figures such as CLODIUS and Milo, was greater than could be suppressed by senatorial appeals to citizens for help. Troops were therefore used within the city to deter violence, for example at the trial of Milo in 52 BC, and to suppress riots.

During the empire, the most significant development was the existence, in or near the city, of the nine PRAETORIAN cohorts. While their primary duty was to act as the EMPEROR's bodyguard, the presence of these soldiers served as a deterrent. In addition, there was the new post of city prefect, who had at his disposal the three urban cohorts and whose duties included the suppression of riots. Finally, there were the *vigiles*, a body of FIRE-FIGHTERS whose presence may also have served a deterrent function. All of these institutions were in place by the middle years of TIBERIUS' reign. Also alleviating some tensions was the establishment of public spectacles as accepted arenas, at which the people could express their will and make demands of the emperor. In the PROVINCES, most issues of public order and interpersonal crime were left to individuals and local authorities. BANDITRY and PIRACY, however, were major problems in the ancient world, and the military was often employed in attempts to apprehend them. GSA

See Nippel, W. (1995) *Public Order in Ancient Rome*; Vanderbroeck, P. (1987) *Popular Leadership and Collective Behaviour in the Late Roman Republic.*

publicani The companies (*societates*) in Rome of rich investors, who bid for state contracts (*publica*), such as the supply of arms, the provision of other services and, above all, the right to collect various TAXES. Rome, like other pre-industrial societies, did not have the mechanisms to provide these services centrally. The contracts were let regularly by the CENSORS. They were bid for by groups of partners (*socii*); but the actual contract was made with just one or more individuals (*manceps, mancipes*) from the partnership, who had to provide security in the form of land. Roman law never fully evolved the concept of giving a company a legal personality distinct from that of its individual members; but the privileges granted to the companies of the *publicani* amounted to the same thing, to enable them to function over time with changing membership. SENATORS by tradition were excluded from being *socii*, but found indirect ways of investing in the companies. The companies created networks of representatives in the PROVINCES down to the lowly and often despised local collectors, such as Zacchaeus and other 'publicans and sinners' vividly described in the NEW TESTAMENT (Matthew 9.9–13, Luke 19.1ff.)

The origins of this system lay in the early Roman REPUBLIC, and at the start the most profitable areas were probably the supply of ARMS and equipment to the Roman ARMIES. But as the empire expanded, so the opportunities from taxation increased greatly, and the heyday of the *publicani* was in the last two centuries BC; an inscription from ASIA details the complexities for collecting import–export taxes in that province. Through their networks the companies also acted as kinds of public BANKS enabling individuals, such as governors, to have access to state funds in their provinces without an actual transfer of coins. The key roles played by the *publicani* in the running of the empire are illustrated in CICERO's speeches against the corrupt governor VERRES, and the first part of his speech in favour of POMPEY's command against MITHRADATES.

Of course, the *socii* were motivated by the potentially huge profits, and were thus dogged by accusations of corruption. 'Wherever there was a *publicanus*, there was no law and no freedom for the subjects', claimed LIVY (45.18.4). In theory provincial governors were there to restrain the *publicani*. In practice, such was their influence at Rome and their potential power to make or break careers that few governors were prepared to challenge them seriously. As a result in part of the resentment thus created, the system of *publicani* was gradually replaced in many areas in the early imperial period. JJP

See Badian, E. (1983) *Publicans and Sinners.*

Pulcheria 19 January AD 399–July 453 Daughter of Arcadius and Eudoxia, Aelia Pulcheria lost her mother to childbirth on 6 October 404. She and her siblings then came under the care of the eunuch Antiochus. Pulcheria excelled at her studies and was later praised for skill in speaking and writing both Greek and Latin. When Arcadius died on 1 May 408, Pulcheria was the oldest of his surviving children. Her younger brother Theodosius II, named AUGUSTUS on 10 January 402, now became sole emperor in the East. At the age of 13, after a dispute with Antiochus, Pulcheria convinced Theodosius to dismiss him and took charge of the family's upbringing and her brother's EDUCATION. She was known as the emperor's GUARDIAN, even replacing officials on occasion. In keeping with her piety, the PALACE took on a monastic ambience, as the children sang antiphons at canonical hours and fasted twice a week. By her 14th birthday, she had declared herself a virgin dedicated to God and imposed the vow on her sisters, partly from piety, partly to avoid dynastic complications. She had also begun her philanthropy, founding MONASTERIES, CHURCHES, and housing for the poor. Not undeservedly, she was proclaimed Augusta on 4 July 414, but continued to work through her brother.

When Theodosius married Aelia Eudocia on 7 June 421, Pulcheria moved to residences of her own and lost some influence. Eudocia's education gave her the ability to counter Pulcheria's arguments, a capacity exploited by courtiers. Pulcheria was still able to procure Theodosius' signature easily, for a story circulated that he had signed unread a document presented by his sister granting her the right to sell his wife into slavery. By the late 420s, Pulcheria was a devotee of the cult of the Virgin Mary. This resulted in discord, for Theodosius supported Nestorius, BISHOP of CONSTANTINOPLE, who attempted to diminish the cult of the Virgin. Nestorius was charged with heresy and lost his position when Theodosius was forced to yield to Pulcheria's greater support. Eudocia gained much influence when she returned from a pilgrimage to JERUSALEM bearing relics in 439. At the instigation of Chrysaphius, she convinced Theodosius that Pulcheria's choice of an ASCETIC life precluded the exercise of worldly power. To avoid consecration as a deaconess, Pulcheria retired to a private existence outside the city. Soon Chrysaphius accused Eudocia of ADULTERY, and she returned to Palestine for the rest of her life. Nevertheless, Pulcheria did not return to favour until Chrysaphius was exiled in spring 450. On 28 July 450 Theodosius died from injuries suffered in falling from a horse. About a month later, Pulcheria married Marcian, a military officer who promised to respect her vow of virginity, and crowned him emperor on 25 November. The couple attempted to restore unity within Christianity by summoning the council of Chalcedon in 451. Pulcheria died in July 453, leaving her remaining wealth to the poor. She was buried in the mausoleum of CONSTANTINE, near her relatives. More than any emperor or empress before her, Pulcheria exemplifies a unity of Christianity and political power within a single person. JV

See Holum, K. G. (1982) *Theodosian Empresses.*

THEODOSIUS I.

pulleys see ENERGY; ENGINEERING; MACHINES; PRESSES; WATER SUPPLY.

Punic wars 264–146 BC The three great wars in the struggle for power between Rome and CARTHAGE in North AFRICA. They are called Punic from the Latin *Poenus* ('Phoenician', 'Punic', or 'Carthaginian'), since Carthage (Tunis) was a PHOENICIAN foundation. Other names for the wars existed, e.g. Sicilian (for the first war) and HANNIBALIC (for the second), but the victors write history. Despite good early relations (POLYBIOS 3.22–6 records several TREATIES), Roman expansion brought the two powers into opposition. A request to Rome for help, from the Oscan city of Messana, resulted in Roman forces crossing into SICILY, where Carthaginian and Greek interests had clashed since the 6th century BC, and precipitated the first Punic war (264–241). After a heavily NAVAL conflict, including a failed Roman invasion of North Africa, Hamilcar (father of HANNIBAL) sued for terms in 241. Sicily was ceded to Rome (SYRACUSE remained under Rome's ally, Hieron II), becoming the first Roman province. Relations worsened when Rome opportunistically seized Sardinia in 238.

A revival of Carthaginian imperialism in Spain, under first Hamilcar and finally Hannibal, led to the second war (218–201). The exact chain of cause and responsibility remains one of the great historical debates. The Roman ultimatum was followed by Hannibal's famous march across the ALPS into Italy and a series of devastating Roman defeats (Trebia, 218; Trasimene, 217; CANNAE, 216). Roman reserves of manpower, the refusal of many Italians to revolt and a Carthaginian failure to provide adequate naval support or reinforcements ultimately doomed Hannibal to failure. Quintus Fabius Maximus Verrucosus' policy of avoiding battle (hence his nickname Cunctator, 'the Delayer') destroyed Hannibal's initial advantage and SCIPIO AFRICANUS, after victory in Spain, invaded Africa (204). Hannibal was recalled, and Scipio defeated him at ZAMA (202). Carthage sued for peace, paying an indemnity of 10,000 talents.

An uneasy 50-year peace followed. Carthage's rapid economic recovery caused suspicion. Provocation of Carthage by Rome's Numidian ally MASINISSA raised tensions, as did CATO THE ELDER's repeated cry *Carthago delenda est* ('Carthage must be destroyed'). Carthaginian retaliation against Masinissa in 150 provided the pretext, and Rome declared war. The third Punic war (149–146) ended when Carthage was razed to the ground by Publius Cornelius SCIPIO AEMILIANUS (Africanus the younger). The story that SALT was ploughed into the ground is a late invention. Carthaginian territory now became the PROVINCE of Africa.

The three wars were fundamental to the evolution of Roman IMPERIALISM, both practically and ideologically. They expanded Roman horizons beyond the Italian peninsula, transforming Rome's position within Italy and leaving it the dominant power in the MEDITERRANEAN basin. JRWP

See Livy, trs. A. de Sélincourt (1965); Polybius, trs. W. R. Paton (1922); Goldsworthy, A. (2000) *The Punic Wars*; Lazenby, J. F. (1978) *Hannibal's War*; (1996) *The First Punic War.*

CARTHAGE AND CARTHAGINIANS: (a).

punishment Various concepts lay behind Greek and Roman punishment, including revenge, recompense, deterrence, appeasement of the GODS and the assertion of the state's authority. Although the earliest law-codes were notorious for their harshness, later legislators took into account the severity of the offence, the intention of the offender and the status of offender and victim.

A range of punishments was used, some of which seem harsh by today's standards. Execution was common – and terrible. Victims might be thrown down a pit (the *barathron* at Athens) or cavern (the Kaiadas at Sparta), hurled off cliffs (the Tarpeian rock at Rome), hanged (at Sparta), crucified with death caused by exposure (called *apotympanismos* at Athens), or ordered to drink hemlock (an agonizing death, despite PLATO's sanitized account of SOCRATES' end). Other penalties might accompany the execution. When, for example, Archeptolemos and Antiphon were executed as traitors in 411 BC, their bodies were denied BURIAL in ATTICA, their property confiscated, their houses razed to the ground and their families disfranchised.

An effective alternative to execution, given the high value placed on CITIZENSHIP and membership of a community, was EXILE; CICERO's misery when out of Italy was abject. Those accused of intentional homicide at Athens could withdraw into voluntary EXILE during their trial (on pain of death if they ever returned), suffering confiscation of property as well. But exile was used as a penalty in its own right (again on pain of death for illegal return) and, after due process, served as a means of removing political rivals (e.g. OSTRACISM in 5th-century Athens).

A less severe, though still heavy, penalty was loss of citizen rights (Greek *atimia*, Latin *infamia*). This could involve losing the right to speak in the Athenian ASSEMBLY or, at Rome, the removal of one's SENATE membership by the CENSORS. On occasion, as at Athens when an appeal against removal from a DEME register was unsuccessful, a free man might even be sold into slavery. A thief in the Roman REPUBLIC could be placed under the control of the victim.

Detention in PRISON was not used regularly in Greece or Republican Rome, but under the PRINCIPATE convicts might be condemned to the MINES, public works or the GLADIATORIAL arena. Flogging, though employed elsewhere in Greece, was associated at Athens with TYRANNICAL behaviour and was reserved for SLAVES. It was widespread in the Roman world, especially in the army, and until the early 2nd century BC MAGISTRATES had the right to flog citizens for disobedience (their symbols of power, the *fasces*, which comprised rods and axes, were connected with flogging and execution). Financial penalties were imposed both to recompense a victim and (in public suits at Athens) as a fine to be paid to the state (vast in the cases of Miltiades in 489 and DEMOSTHENES in 324).

The last word in punishments goes to the Romans. The penalty in the Republic for parricide was drowning in the sea in a sack with a dog, a cock, an ape and a viper. While it was a capital offence to pass under the litter of the VESTAL VIRGINS, their punishment for unchastity was to be entombed alive. (see also TORTURE) MJE

See Crook, J. A. (1967) *Law and Life of Rome*; Todd, S. C. (1993) *The Shape of Athenian Law.*

 EDUCATION: (b); OSTRACISM.

Punjab see ALEXANDER III.

Pupienus Maximus

 EMPERORS, ROMAN: (a).

purification The process by which ritual dirt (*miasma*) is eliminated in order to regain a new pure status. Purification (*katharsis* in Greek) is a ritual process performing a distinct social function. Its purpose is to reintegrate formerly polluted, and therefore socially dysfunctional, individuals into the 'healthy' social group, both on a public and a private level. In its simplest sense, it was a requirement for everyone wishing to come into contact with the divine.

Purification was achieved through a ritual process which varied with respect to the media used (purifiers). Its central act usually involved the symbolic contact of a specially chosen purifier with the polluted person or object. In its simplest form, it was restricted to ritual cleansing with water before a SACRIFICE, PRAYER, consultation of an ORACLE or initiation. Ritual bathing in seawater was common practice at some FESTIVALS. FIRE in its pure form, or as an agent in fumigation, was used for purifications as early as HOMER; it appears in ODYSSEUS' cleansing of his PALACE after the killing of the suitors (*Odyssey*, book 22). Similar use of fire appears to have been made at some initiation rituals, as well as rituals of birth (the so-called *amphidromia*) and death (the funeral pyre). Certain plants were believed to carry purificatory qualities, such as laurel (an attribute of APOLLO, who presided over purifications) and OLIVE. EP

See Parker, R. (1983) *Miasma.*

purple A colour made by mixing blue and red, with many different shades such as puce, violet and fuchsia. It was probably the most prestigious colour in the ancient world, and clothes dyed purple were the equivalent of a black Armani suit today. The most sought after purple dye, known as 'Tyrian purple', was derived from certain species of MEDITERRANEAN shellfish, *Murex trunculus*, *Murex brandaris* and *Purpura haemostoma*. The colours obtained from the dye ranged from a scarlet red to a deep blue-violet, depending on which species of shellfish was used. The dye was produced by removing the shellfish from their shells and then fermenting them with SALT and urine in a vat for about three days. The material to be dyed was then immersed in the vat (PLINY THE ELDER, *Natural History* 9.133). There were alternatives to Tyrian purple, such as the pomegranate flower (*Natural History* 13.113) and certain species of lichen (THEOPHRASTOS, *Enquiry into Plants* 4.6.5; Pliny, *Natural History* 26.103, 22.66).

The amount of raw material and time needed to produce Tyrian purple led to its acquiring prestige, as indicated by the epithets 'royal' and 'imperial'. Numerous references in literary sources refer to purple TEXTILES as indicators of high status (e.g. Homer, *Odyssey* 4.135, 6.53; Aeschylus, *Agamemnon* 958–63). In the Roman period clothes dyed with 'Tyrian purple' were used to signify rank, and were worn by CONSULS, noble boys, SENATORS, *EQUITES*, PRIESTS performing sacrifices and those celebrating TRIUMPHS (Pliny, *Natural History* 9.127). MDM

Puteoli (mod. Pozzuoli) City in Campania, founded in 530 BC by political exiles from SAMOS under the name of Dikaiarcheia ('Just Government'). In 338 it fell into Roman hands, and in 194 a military colony was settled close to the site of Dikaiarcheia. In 37 OCTAVIAN and AGRIPPA established a military port, the Portus Iulius, the better to co-ordinate their war against Sextus Pompey. This position it quickly lost to Misenum. In the early PRINCIPATE Puteoli was the main HARBOUR for the arrival of the grain fleet from ALEXANDRIA. Problems caused by seismic activity forced EMPERORS to look for a more suitable harbour closer to Rome, and from the time of CLAUDIUS they began to build a new harbour at OSTIA. After TRAJAN expanded the harbour at Ostia, Puteoli lost its prominent position and slipped into gradual decay. Wax tablets found in Murecine (near POMPEII) vividly illustrate the breadth of Puteoli's commercial activities. It was a cosmopolitan city, with a strong contingent of foreigners from all over the MEDITERRANEAN. It housed the only TEMPLE of the ARAB god Dusares built in the West. It is commonly accepted that, even though the town is not mentioned by name, it is the setting for PETRONIUS' *Cena Trimalchionis (Trimalchio's Dinner)*, and inscriptions testify to the strength in numbers of wealthy FREEDMEN involved in the IMPERIAL CULT (over 200). The site has revealed an extraordinary Republican inscription listing the regulations for a commercial company of undertakers and, more disturbingly, the existence of a torture and execution service for SLAVES operated by the same undertakers.

Because of continuous occupation and a lack of systematic excavation, many details of ancient Puteoli are unknown and many remains cannot be identified. A few temples survive, as well as the outline of a stadium north-west of the city along the Via Domitiana. Construction of the great BATHS, the so-called Tempio di Nettuno, began in the early 2nd century AD, with a restoration in the Severan period. They stood a little west of two AMPHITHEATRES, which were themselves just north of a FORUM area separated from the coast by the old colony. The smaller amphitheatre was built no later than the Augustan period. The larger complex was built under the Flavians and is the most impressive monument to survive. Of great interest is the Macellum, the MARKET BUILDING of Flavian date that still stands. This large square building had SHOPS facing both inwards and outwards on all its four sides and contained a shrine and a latrine, as well as a circular pavilion in its quadrangle. A variety of evidence, including inscriptions and pictorial representations on glass vases, attests to many more public buildings, including a temple of SERAPIS, but precise locations and appearance are often uncertain. MK, JV

See Frederiksen, M. (1984) *Campania*.

 ITALY: (a).

Pydna An old Greek colony on the Macedonian coast, not far from the old capital, Aigai (modern VERGÍNA). Here, after three years' inconclusive campaigning by the Romans against king Perseus, Lucius AEMILIUS PAULLUS finally engaged the enemy in 168 BC near Perseus' main base and supply centre. After the battle Perseus attempted to rally but soon fled; he was captured and sent to Italy to live his life out in captivity. Paullus, with the usual senatorial board, settled MACEDONIA and ILLYRIA, ending their monarchies. Macedonia was broken up into four republics, divided economically and politically from each other and left too weak for their own defence against BARBARIANS. Within 20 years, Rome had to intervene to crush a rising in favour of restoring the monarchy, and Macedonia became a PROVINCE. Pydna, as POLYBIOS saw, was a watershed in Roman history. Rome was left indisputably supreme in the East, and king Antiochos IV of Syria was unceremoniously ordered out of Egypt after the battle; he had to give up all idea of a takeover.

Seen in perspective, Pydna had long represented the soft underbelly of the Macedonian kingdom. It lay dangerously near the old capital. In 432 BC, in support of a pretender, Athens had attacked it but failed to take the town and had to make peace with Perdikkas II. Between c.430 and 413, however, Athens continued to use Pydna's close neighbour Methone as a base for operations against Macedonia. PHILIP II learned the lesson. Early in his reign, between 357 and 354, he prised Methone and Pydna out of Athenian alliance and integrated them finally into his kingdom. From there he moved steadily to supremacy in Greece, and his son ALEXANDER went on to conquer the known world. How much of this did the Romans know, or reflect on, when Pydna became, in turn, their watershed? HBM

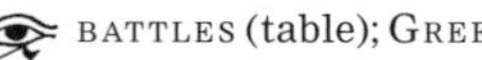 BATTLES (table); GREECE: (a).

pygmies In classical literature and art, pygmies (from *pygmê*, 'fist') exemplified an alternative and inferior people, often with a burlesque or apotropaic intent. Stories concerning pygmies go back to HOMER (*Iliad* 3.2–6), where the Greeks and Trojans are likened to the pygmies, who are said to live by the streams of Ocean, fighting against the cranes migrating from the winter rains. Later they are located at the edge of the known world, usually in equatorial Africa or INDIA. The war of small humans versus large BIRDS is most likely derived from a foreign folk-tale.

By the 6th century BC the Greeks had some knowledge of African pygmies through direct or indirect contact with Egyptians. HERODOTOS (2.32.6) describes the small men eye-witnesses saw as 'smaller than common . . . and black' (their colour is otherwise rarely mentioned) and (4.43) as 'small men wearing palm-leaf clothing'. ARISTOTLE (*History of Animals* 8.597a7) uses the term 'pygmies' and says they lived in caves and rode dwarf HORSES.

In Greek ART the battle of the pygmies and cranes is shown as a parody of the heroic world, the pygmies dressed in ANIMAL skins and wielding sticks and slings. On an early Athenian black-figure volute crater of c.570 BC (the François Vase), the pygmies are painted as small men without any deformities. On Athenian red-figure pottery of the 5th century, and in later art it was common to represent pygmies as dwarfs, substituting the type of pathological figure known in Athens and elsewhere for the ethnically different features of the exotic and unknown pygmy. BAS

Pylos, battle of see NIKIAS; OATHS; PELOPONNESIAN WAR.

Pyrrhos 319/18–272 BC The first cousin of ALEXANDER the Great and claiming descent from ACHILLES, Pyrrhos had one of the most mercurial careers among hellenistic monarchs. At the age of two, he was hurried away from the PALACE of the Molossian kings in EPIRUS to neighbouring ILLYRIA. He briefly returned to the Molossian throne, but by 302 he was in exile again, joined his brother-in-law DEMETRIOS POLIORKETES and then went on to ALEXANDRIA, to the court of PTOLEMY, who restored him to the Molossian throne in 296.

Pyrrhos gained the sobriquet 'Eagle' in his campaigns to defend and establish the Epirot league against the other SUCCESSORS of Alexander. He then turned his attention to Italy. Tarentum invited him to liberate from Rome the Greeks of southern Italy, and Pyrrhos arrived in 280. He defeated the Romans, at great cost to his own army, at Heraclea and at Ausculum, after which he is reported to have said 'If we win one more battle against the Romans, we shall be utterly ruined'; hence the phrase 'Pyrrhic victory'. For a while he was within a few kilometres of the walls of Rome, but he was hampered by lack of support from the Italian Greeks and in 278 in turned to SICILY, attacking the CARTHAGINIANS. Again initial Greek support faded away. Back in Italy he was defeated at Beneventum in 275, whereupon he returned to Epirus.

His last adventure was to attempt to conquer Macedonia and Greece. He invaded the PELOPONNESE and besieged SPARTA, where ANTIGONOS Gonatas turned the tide against him. He was killed in ARGOS late in 272 while trying to evacuate the city, struck down by a roof-tile thrown by an old woman and clumsily decapitated by a soldier. CJS

See Plutarch, *Pyrrhos.*

Pythagoras and Pythagoreanism Born on SAMOS in the mid-6th century BC, Pythagoras migrated to Kroton in SICILY about 530. He is a PHILOSOPHER around whom many myths, legends and mysteries grew up in antiquity. The philosophical school he founded had many of the characteristics of a MYSTERY cult, with secret rites, secret doctrines and initiations. His doctrines were transmitted orally in *akousmata* and *symbola*, series of oracular sayings. He was considered divine even in his own lifetime – he had a golden thigh and possessed the ability to be in two places at once – and his word was considered by his followers to have absolute authority: 'he himself said it'. Pythagoras was said to have received his divine wisdom from Egyptian and BABYLONIAN wise men, and he became the prototype of the seer or sage whose WISDOM was greater than human.

No works of Pythagoras are extant; the earliest evidence is in the system of Philolaos in the late 5th century BC. PLATO's appropriation of Pythagorean doctrine, in *Timaeus* and *Phaedo* especially, has led to much uncertainty over the form of early Pythagoreanism, but recently it has been shown that much of the Pythagoreanism of later antiquity was in fact Plato's own creation. There is, and was in antiquity, considerable argument over what constituted Pythagorean doctrine and over which member of the school discovered what part of the system. Various mystical cults and schools of thought, especially ORPHISM, tended to be regarded as 'Pythagorean'.

Pythagoras is perhaps most famous for the doctrine of the transmigration of SOULS. The universe is a divine, immortal, living being ruled by harmony, and the human being shares a part of this divine harmony and immortality: the soul. The soul is immortal, then, but is trapped within the corrupting body until it is transplanted into another body after death. It can either ascend or descend through the scale of creation until it finally reaches perfection. The Pythagorean ethical project is to bring the soul into harmony with the harmony of the cosmos; since the body corrupts the soul within it and disrupts its harmony, their ethical emphasis is on PURIFICATION. Pythagoras himself was said by his followers to be the only human to be able to remember all his past lives and experiences, and the members of the school would train themselves in memory exercises so as to be able to emulate this feat.

Pythagoras' greatest achievements were in MATHEMATICS. Besides the famous theorem that bears his name, he is credited with the discovery of the numerical ratios of MUSICAL consonances (2 : 1, 3 : 2 and 4 : 3) representing the octave, the fifth and the fourth. These were illustrated in the *tetraktys*, a triangle of ten dots – ten being the perfect number. The *tetraktys* was considered divine by the Pythagoreans, oaths were sworn by it, and it was invested with huge significance as the representation of the order and harmony of the cosmos itself. Attempts to link Pythagorean mathematics closely to Greek TOWN PLANNING, however, rest on late, unreliable sources. GLC

See Burkert, W. (1972) *Lore and Science in Ancient Pythagoreanism*; Kahn, C.H. (2001) *Pythagoras and the Pythagoreans.*

Quadi see MARCOMANNIC WAR; MARCUS AURELIUS; NORICUM; VALENTINIAN I.

quaestors The quaestorship was a MAGISTRACY at Rome, usually held by younger men. Early in the REPUBLIC, each CONSUL appointed a *quaestor* to assist him, but later they were elected. As the state required more officials, including PRAETORS and governors, the number of quaestors increased in necessary stages, to a total of 20 in the time of SULLA. Most quaestors were allocated to the staffs of magistrates and governors, but some were assigned to food and water supply offices and other duties. Generally, quaestors managed the financial accounts of their superiors, but could be asked to perform other duties, including the command of military units. Occasionally, supreme command might fall into their hands, in the absence of a superior magistrate. For example, CICERO, unwilling to wait for the appointment and arrival of a successor, left his province of CILICIA to a quaestor he himself regarded as unsuitable for the task (*Letters to Atticus* 6.3.1).

Before Sulla, quaestors were young men in their late twenties who had been military tribunes or had held a minor elected office. By the late 2nd century BC, the quaestorship regularly ensured enrolment in the SENATE at the next CENSUS. Sulla enacted changes to the *cursus honorum*, including the quaestorship: he fixed the minimum age at 30, established the quaestorship as a prerequisite for a praetorship and made senate enrolment automatic. Quaestors were designated under the empire and retained some tasks in senatorial provinces, but many appointments were honorary, designed to promote young men of promise, and carried few duties. JV

 SENATE (table).

quarries and quarrying The whole subject of ancient quarries has been relatively neglected until the last three decades. It involves consideration not only of the location of quarries but also the techniques used to work STONE; the nature of the stone and how techniques might have to be adapted; and the TRANSPORT problems that might be encountered. Traditionally, the Egyptians are credited with developing the quarrying expertise which forms the basis of Greek quarrying from the 7th century BC, though recent work has suggested that Near Eastern cultures may also have been using similar techniques.

Quarrying techniques varied little throughout the Greek and Roman periods, and indeed remained broadly the same down to the 19th century. The most common method of quarrying was the isolation of blocks by trenches using a quarry hammer. Metal or wooden wedges were then used to split the blocks from the parent rock. It is quite obvious that, as today, ancient quarrymen knew and capitalized on the fact that it was easier to split off stone according to the naturally occurring beds or planes. This has important implications for the later use of the block, for example, cutting it up into veneering slabs. Essentially there are three breaking characteristics of stone which need to be exploited: bedding planes, other natural features which do not follow the bedding (e.g. faults) and grain. Each of these affects the way in which the stone can be worked, and the more work required, the more wastage is involved, hence, the more expensive the stone. Open quarrying was preferred on grounds of ease and expense. However, if the good-quality material ran out above ground, underground workings might be opened, as in the Parian MARBLE quarries (on the Cycladic island of Paros) and the limestone 'La Pyramide' quarries near Glanum (southern France). In the limestone quarries at BAALBEK are found two of the largest cut stones (the larger, the Hajar el Hibla – Stone of the Pregnant Woman – is 21.72 m or just over 71 ft long, and weighs an estimated 1,200 tons).

The major difference between Greek and Roman quarrying was the scale of exploitation. Greek extraction involved the stone essentially quarried on demand, usually from the nearest source. To judge from the contemporary records of the building of the PARTHENON (constructed of Pentelic MARBLE), stone was ordered literally block by block, one explanation why it could take a long time for structures to be completely finished. Roman quarrying was carried out on a more modular basis. This can be seen clearly with the exploitation of decorative stones in particular. A system of accountancy was developed in some quarries from the middle of the 1st century AD. Inscriptions were carved on blocks indicating the area of extraction and the personnel involved. Often objects were roughed out in the quarry before their

QUARRIES AND QUARRYING: Roman stone quarry in Tunisia, with the striations on its walls indicating the extraction of stone in a series of level beds.

export. In the classical Greek period quarries probably belonged to and were administered by the nearest town. In the Roman period there was much more diversity in ownership. Some marble and granite quarries were owned by the EMPEROR and administered by his representatives. Quarrying was a skilled activity, but convicts and SLAVES could form part of the LABOUR force, presumably carrying out the unskilled tasks. (see also MONS CLAUDIANUS) HD

See Dworakowska, A. (1975) *Quarries in Ancient Greece*; (1983) *Quarries in Roman Provinces*.

 MARBLE.

queens There were few queen-regnants in classical antiquity. Consequently the word 'queen' as understood in modern English is not totally applicable to the ancient sources. While Greek had the word *basilis* (later *basilissa*) and Latin *regina* for queen, the words have a limited meaning and are usually employed for women ruling alone in foreign lands: the mythic Dido is therefore called *regina*. More generally, classical texts call 'queens' by the more conventional titles 'king's wife' or 'king's mother'. While a woman like CLEOPATRA VII held the prime ruling position in her own right, this situation was unusual; women were generally debarred from holding the position of monarch. But this did not mean that royal women were denied access to power. Proximity to the king enabled a queen to exert considerable influence: Atossa, the wife of the PERSIAN KING DARIUS I, for example, supposedly pestered him to invade Greece. The heyday of royal female power came in the hellenistic period, largely due to the political prestige created by OLYMPIAS, the mother of ALEXANDER the Great who, following her son's death, briefly established herself as sole ruler of MACEDONIA. The royal women of the PTOLEMAIC household were particularly ambitious for personal power. It can be argued that in the early years of the dynasty, ARSINOË II and Berenike II shared power with their brother-husbands and were accorded high honours; later on, Ptolemaic women began to squabble openly for absolute power. Cleopatra II, for example, wrested the throne away from her brother-husband, Ptolemy VIII (170–116 BC), but had to settle for an uncomfortable stalemate when she was forced to reinstate him as king and to share her throne with both Ptolemy and his second wife, Cleopatra III. In turn, Cleopatra III held sway during the reigns of her two weak sons, Ptolemy IX (116–80) and Ptolemy X (107–88). During her 'reign' she did much to bolster her political and religious image and attempted to bestow legitimacy on her queenship.

The women of the SELEUKID dynasty were equally feisty. Cleopatra Thea (Cleopatra II's sister) was certainly driven by personal ambition and to secure her power she is reputed to have murdered her son, Demetrios II (146–139). Her nieces, Cleopatra Thea, Cleopatra Selene and Cleopatra IV, all Ptolemaic princesses, became queens of SYRIA and, because of their personal rivalries and dynastic ambitions, brought Syria into civil war and helped the demise of the Seleukid royal line. The Romans had many dealings with the vassal queens dotted throughout their empire. The Hasmonaean dynasty of Judaea, for example, included several powerful royal women: Mariamme I, Salome II and the infamous Herodias. Berenike (b. AD 28), the wife of king Herod of Chalkis, later became the mistress of the emperor TITUS and lived with him openly as a common-law wife. ZENOBIA, ruler of PALMYRA, modelled herself on Cleopatra VII and rose up against Roman rule in AD 270. LL-J

See Macurdy, G. (1937) *Vassal Queens*; Odgen, D. (1999) *Polygamy, Prostitutes and Death*.

questions and answers The mid-5th-century BC SOPHIST PROTAGORAS boasted that he was equally good at giving speeches and at question and answer, apparently two ways of giving public demonstrations of knowledge and verbal skill. The latter presumably involved either the audience posing questions to the SOPHIST or speakers asking questions of one another. Despite the virtues of the SOCRATIC *elenchos*, asking questions in order to fox one's opponent regularly seems to have disreputable associations in the 5th century: witness ARISTOPHANES' *Clouds* (e.g. 1179ff.) and the routines of the eristic brothers in PLATO's *Euthydemos*. ARISTOTLE's *Topics*, perhaps designed as a course of lectures in DIALECTIC in Plato's ACADEMY, details techniques for a formal competition in which one player chooses to attack or defend a proposition and the other, by asking questions, has to force him into contradiction. In the *Sophistical Refutations* Aristotle classified the fallacy-type 'multiple questions' (e.g. 'Have you stopped beating your wife?'), the solution of which played an important role in defining the proposition and hence in the development of LOGIC. The sophistic contests also survived in the tradition of 'problems' or 'questions', where authorities were asked to answer difficult questions, often traditional, from any learned realm, such as Homeric interpretation, natural science or grammar. Such 'problems' sessions often also served as learned entertainments, and served authors such as PLUTARCH, ATHENAEUS and AULUS GELLIUS as a literary conceit. Finally, question and answer became a formal didactic framework, with students learning set answers to set questions. This practice is recorded in handbooks of 'questions' (*erôtêmata*), especially in grammar, and in the CHRISTIAN 'catechism'. CA

Quinctii see FLAMININI.

Quintilian (Marcus Fabius Quintilianus) AD ?35 – ?96 Rhetorician and educator. Born in Spain, Quintilian was the first holder of the first publicly financed chair of Greek and Latin RHETORIC at Rome. Best known for his *Institutio oratoria*, a massive compendium on the training of ORATORS, he was also the author of a lost treatise *De causis corruptae eloquentiae* (*On the Causes of the Corruption of Eloquence*). Because of his prestige, unauthorized or pseudonymous works circulated under his name during his lifetime and later. Chief among these were the so-called major and minor DECLAMATIONS – ironically enough, since he strongly objected to the unreality of the declamatory tradition. His *Institutio oratoria* is distinctive among ancient rhetorical handbooks for treating the EDUCATION of the orator from infancy through adulthood, for its presentation of lore about the performance of oratory, for its critical judgements of earlier POETS and orators, and for its attempt to adapt the CICERONIAN ideals of broad education and social responsibility to drastically altered circumstances. Quintilian went so far as to claim that the ideal orator was a *Romanus sapiens* ('intelligent Roman'), someone who combined the wisdom of the Greek philosophical tradition with the pragmatic versatility of the Roman politician. This move places him squarely in the tradition of Roman cultural imperialists and won him the respect of later humanists, especially in the RENAISSANCE and the 18th century. TNH

See Butler, H. E., ed. (1920), *The Institutio Oratoria of Quintilian* (text and trs., 4 vols.); Habinek, T. (1987) Greeks and Romans in book 12 of Quintilian, *Ramus* 16: 192–202.

Quintillus

EMPERORS, ROMAN: (b)

Quirinus see CAPITOLINE TRIAD; GODS AND GODDESSES, ROMAN; JUPITER; MARS; MINERVA; PRIESTS AND PRIESTESSES, ROMAN.

R

race There was no concept of race, nor was there a word for race, in antiquity. Like the concept of, and the appearance of, the ideological term 'nationalism', it was the product of the theorizations that attended on the birth of the nation state in the 19th century. Ideology, in the sense of complex theoretical ideas used to support the edifice of political power in the nation state, is largely absent from the ancient world. 'Race' is part of this ideological panoply, and is best regarded as a set of more or less bogus theories of heredity designed to justify the claim of a specific group to a particular geographical area. The notion of race is both inclusive (encouraging a sense of belonging among the chosen) and exclusive (designed to keep out those seen as disruptive of the integrity of the 'nation'). Having said that, however, it would be incorrect to maintain that the Greeks and the Romans had no sense of the 'otherness' of particular groups. Rather, this sense of otherness was not used for ideological ends. It is easiest to use a term such as 'ethnocentrism' when discussing Greeks and Romans and their attitude to the 'OTHER'. Greeks and Romans clearly distinguished themselves from one another (often with attendant animus) and from BARBARIANS (non-Greek or non-Latin speakers). The distinctions here were primarily cultural, however, and might or might not overlap with skin colour (the product, in their eyes, of how far north or south one lived). (see also ETHNICITY AND IDENTITY; IDENTITY) PGT

See Balsdon, J. P. V. D. (1979) *Romans and Aliens*; Sherwin-White, A. N. (1967) *Racial Prejudice in Imperial Rome.*

racism The Greeks and Romans cannot be said to have been racist in the sense of having operated with an ideology of pseudo-biological, permanent inequality based on classification by somatic types (whites at the top and BLACKS at the bottom). That was a 19th-century invention. In the later 5th century BC, the Greeks discussed whether differences between peoples were attributable to nature, or to culture and environment. They largely favoured the latter view. Greeks and Romans did exhibit ethnocentrism – cultural prejudice – in their assumption that judging other cultures through the frameworks of their own was valid, and in their frequent assumption that their own culture was superior to that of others. For both Greeks and Romans, belief in the significance of races, in the sense of perceived common descent from a GOD or HERO, was an important aspect of IDENTITY. Such descent groups, however, frequently asserted links between peoples from disparate parts of the known world, sometimes for transparently opportunistic reasons. Martin Bernal's central thesis is that the modern academic discipline of classics is rooted in a racist denial of the Semitic and African roots of classical civilization. This idea is flawed on a number of levels: Bernal equates Egyptian with black African; conflates cultural interchange, influence and genetic origins; and ignores the important influences of other non-Greek peoples, such as the BABYLONIANS and Sumerians. ED

See Bernal, M. (1987) *Black Athena: the Afroasiatic roots of classical civilization*, vol. 1; Lefkowitz, M. and Rogers, G. M., eds. (1996) *Black Athena Revisited*.

Raetia The Raeti of the central ALPS were subdued in the celebrated campaign of 15 BC led by AUGUSTUS' stepsons TIBERIUS and Drusus (Horace, *Odes* 4.4, 4.14). The original PROVINCE embraced Raetia, Vindelicia and the Vallis Poenina (the upper valley of the RHÔNE), until the last was split off, probably under CLAUDIUS. By the end of Augustus' reign, the province no longer had a legionary garrison, and its governors were of equestrian rank, including a former centurion. Not until AD 179, with the establishment of a legionary base at Regensburg (Castra Regina) on the DANUBE, did it rate a governor of senatorial rank. The capital was Augsburg (Augusta Vindelicorum).

Raetia was threaded by ROADS of great strategic and commercial importance, crossing the Alpine passes such as the Furka, Splügen, Septimer, Maloja-Julier, Reschenscheideck and Brenner. Of these the most important was the Via Claudia Augusta crossing the Reschenscheideck into the upper valley of the Inn and thence into the valley of the Lech, leading to Augsburg and thence to the Danube. Other major routes ran east–west between Salzburg (Iuvavum) and AUGST (Augusta Raurica) via Kempten (Cambodunum) and Bregenz (Brigantium), and from Salzburg to Augsburg and across the Danube at Aislingen. The Danube was an important TRADE and supply route, guarded by FORTS from TIBERIUS' reign onwards. The northern part of the province, corresponding to Upper Bavaria, became extremely prosperous, until it suffered heavily in the Alamannic invasions from the second half of the 3rd century onwards. CMW

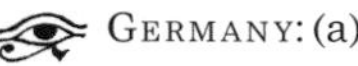
GERMANY: (a).

rams, battering The Greeks believed that the battering ram (*krios*) – long known to the BABYLONIANS, Assyrians and PERSIANS – was invented by Artemon during the Athenian assault against SAMOS (440 BC). By the time of the PELOPONNESIAN WAR, rams, along with mining and mounds, were the chief method of breaching a city's walls. Models rapidly evolved from the very simple – a wooden beam with bronze head and ROPES – to sophisticated designs involving roofed and wheeled enclosures. These provided a platform for the stock, allowed the use of a larger metal ram, and shielded operators from the usual Greek counter-measures: setting fire to the wooden frame, dropping weights on the ram-head, using grappling hooks to catch the stock and slam it against the wall, hanging cushions and padding on the citadel walls, and strewing obstacles before likely points of assault. The invention of ARTILLERY and torsion CATAPULTS in the 4th century BC swung the advantage back to the attacker, since covering fire could allow the ram to operate more safely and aid its assault on MASONRY walls and wooden gates.

By Roman times, with greater use of mound-building techniques, and the common use of torsion catapults, scaling ladders and large, mobile SIEGE towers, rams (*arietes*) were used primarily against the wooden gates of a citadel and were but one weapon in the sophisticated arsenal of Roman siegecraft. VDH

See Winter, F. (1971) *Greek Fortifications*.

rape Not a specific offence in Roman law, rape, as a category of violent assault (*vis*), could be punished as a crime, or pursued in a civil suit for insult (*de iniuriis*), in which damages would be determined by the status of the woman – or girl, man or boy – involved and the degree of offence. Various forms of sexual (or other) harassment and enticement also fell under the law on insult. The law hardened over time. CHRISTIAN laws imposed severe penalties on the rapist or seducer, but also penalized the victim unless she proved she had resisted. Rape (in its current English meaning) should be distinguished from *raptus*, abduction. This was an institutionalized means employed by a young man, helped by friends, of forcing MARRIAGE by kidnapping and raping his preferred bride, on the assumption that she and her parents would have to accept marriage as the only face-saving possibility.

The victim of rape is often of less concern to the ancient sources than the implications of the act for her male connections. The legendary Roman heroine LUCRETIA killed herself after telling her husband and relations to avenge her rape by the ETRUSCAN prince Tarquin. The young PLEBEIAN girl VERGINIA was murdered by her own father to prevent her violation by the PATRICIAN Appius Claudius. These traditional stories are passed on by the historian LIVY, who represents the women as political symbols triggering revolution rather than as wronged individuals.

Rape of a free boy or girl was a serious matter, but did not deprive the raped boy of civic rights. Illicit sex was regarded as polluting a woman and making her useless to the family in the marriage exchange. This is probably why SOLON, who banned the sale of free Athenians in 594 BC, made an exception of unmarried citizen girls who had been raped (or seduced). Their male relatives could legally sell them into slavery. Stories of rape victims – male and female – hanging themselves suggest that the shame of rape to the victim was extreme. Scholars are now suspicious of RHETORICAL claims that rape of a married woman was considered a lesser offence in Attic law than her seduction.

Rape of SLAVES had no real meaning in either Greek or Roman society. The male owner had unrestricted sexual rights over male and female slaves of any age, and could offer them to guests and friends. Rape would be an offence only against their owners. SD

See Cohen, D. (1991) *Law, Sexuality and Norms in Classical Athens*; Deacy, S. and Pierce, K. F., eds. (1997) *Rape in Antiquity*; Dixon, S. (1982) Women and rape in Roman law, *Arbejdsnotat* 3/82, Women's Research Centre in Social Science, Copenhagen 27–47; Evans-Grubbs, J. (1989) Abduction marriage in antiquity: a law of Constantine and its social context, *JRS* 79: 59–83.

rationality, economic Moses Finley, drawing on the work of Max Weber and Karl Polanyi, contended that economic rationality in the modern sense of the term was absent from the ancient ECONOMY, which he regarded as entirely different in its nature and structure from its modern counterpart. Others have argued for a more robust ancient economy, susceptible to analysis in terms of neo-classical economic theories. They have claimed that, within the context of the economic options available in the ancient world, rationality in matters of investment, in accounting practices and management skills and in the organization of both AGRICULTURAL and non-agricultural production (commerce and MANUFACTURING) was not wholly dissimilar to modern economic decision-making behaviour. The opportunities for economic rationality on the part of the individual were probably greatest under the Roman empire, as even smallholders in PROVINCES such as AFRICA appear willing to take INVESTMENT risks beyond the requirements of security. (see also GROWTH, ECONOMIC) RBH

See Finley, M. I. (1985) *The Ancient Economy*; Mattingly, D. J. and Salmon, J. (2001) The productive past, in Mattingly and Salmon, *Economies beyond Agriculture* 3–14; Rathbone, D. (1991) *Economic Rationalism and Rural Society in Third-century* AD *Egypt*.

rationality, philosophical see LOGIC; PHILOSOPHY.

Ravenna AUGUSTUS selected the port of Ravenna, Classe, as the fleet base for the eastern MEDITERRANEAN. Set in marshy land near the north-west ADRIATIC seaboard of Italy, it is revealed by later Roman sources such as SIDONIUS APOLLINARIS as a rather unhealthy spot, though the city was a favoured GLADIATOR training centre. Ravenna functioned as a small colony for much of the imperial period. The decisive rise in its fortune came with the relocation of the imperial capital from MILAN under HONORIUS in 402. Its marshes were seen as a vital source of security, combined with the communications potential of Classe. Subsequently retained as a royal capital by Odoacer (476–93) and the Ostrogoths (493–538), and as the seat of the Byzantine governor-general (until 751), Ravenna saw unrivalled urban growth in the 5th and 6th centuries. Numerous state buildings (PALACES, CIRCUS, mint, BATHS), plus CHURCHES and MONASTERIES were established. Most prominent survivals are the major BASILICAS constructed under the Ostrogothic king THEODERIC, notably San Vitale, Sant'Apollinare Nuovo (the palace church) and Sant'Apollinare in Classe, each richly adorned with MOSAICS and marblework. The Byzantines reconsecrated the ARIAN GOTHIC churches and added additional mosaics. With the LOMBARD invasion of 568, building activity greatly diminished. Excavations at the port of Classe have revealed sustained trade activity until the mid-7th century, followed by rapid decline and abandonment of the port facilities. Following its loss of capital status after 751, Charlemagne in the late 8th century robbed various churches and palaces of their marblework, though the city retained much symbolic and ecclesiastical significance. NJC

 CITIES: (b); ITALY: (a).

Ravenna cosmographer An unnamed monk c.AD 700 at Ravenna, who drew up a list of about 5,000 geographical names, from INDIA to Ireland, sloppily compiled in the format of an itinerary. Three late medieval Latin manuscripts survive. The work (in five books) was once thought to be a translation from Greek. The author divides the world into 12 southern and 12 northern zones, and lists settlements, RIVERS and islands, moving from east to west, as well as including a *periplous* of the MEDITERRANEAN. He often garbles names, places them in the wrong category, fails to differentiate settlements by size, and seldom indicates distances. He disclaims any personal experience as a TRAVELLER, but draws upon a wide range of identifiable sources (including PTOLEMY and the PEUTINGER TABLE), though maybe only at second hand and not always by name. He also incorporates much that is imaginary. The BIBLE and CHRISTIAN writers are his main inspiration, not least when he discusses the location of Paradise in his introduction. His avowed purpose is the laudable one of preserving a vision of the world once known to the Romans (hence the title *Cosmographia*) in a disturbed period when it was shrinking and irrevocably fragmented. The work has special value for the Iberian peninsula and the British Isles, where the relevant sheet of the Peutinger Table is lost. (see also GEOGRAPHY, ANCIENT; MAPS) RJAT

See Jones, B. and Mattingly, D. J. (1990) *An Atlas of Roman Britain*; Lozovsky, N. (2000) *'The Earth is Our Book'*; Schnetz, J. (1990) *Itineraria Romana*, vol. 2.

Reate see ITALY, ROMAN.

rebellions and revolts see BOUDICA; IONIAN REVOLT; JUDAEA; PEASANT UPRISINGS; VERCINGETORIX.

reciprocity see EXCHANGE.

recitations We know little about authors giving recitations in the Greek world, though competitions seem to have provided a venue. For example, HESIOD writes of winning a tripod for his poetry at a competition held in Chalkis (*Works and Days* 656–9), while there is a less reliable tradition of HERODOTOS performing in a contest at OLYMPIA. There is much more evidence for the Roman world: recitations of poetry, PROSE and DRAMA to invited audiences were part of the intellectual and social life of the early imperial upper classes. This activity was sponsored by the EMPERORS, and was one aspect of the promotion of Rome as an intellectual capital to rival classical Athens and Ptolemaic ALEXANDRIA. AUGUSTUS is said to have made a point of attending recitations, while CLAUDIUS' compositions were read for him and NERO and DOMITIAN read their own. HADRIAN created the Athenaeum as a centre for recitations and lectures. Although some Roman writers poke fun at boring recitations, we should try to imagine the dramatic atmosphere of more exciting occasions. Augustus' sister Octavia is said to have fainted from grief when she heard VIRGIL recite lines from his *Aeneid* concerning her newly dead son Marcellus. PLINY THE YOUNGER pragmatically paid some of his SLAVES to applaud him on more formal occasions, while his wife Calpurnia provided invisible support from behind a curtain. ED

See Friedländer, L. (1909) Belles-lettres: poetry and artistic prose, in *Roman Life and Manners under the Early Empire*, vol. 3, 1–83.

records, public

The consensually governed states of classical Greece kept an enormous variety of civic records on display. Their ubiquity and breadth is in marked contrast to other eastern MEDITERRANEAN societies, where public decrees were rarer and confined mostly to dynastic, theocratic or royal proclamations from on high. While almost any medium was used – stone, bronze, lead, wood, clay, PAPYRUS – as a general rule more important records were copied onto permanent surfaces and publicly displayed in the *AGORA*, sanctuaries and cemeteries. Thus inscriptions on imperishable bronze and stone were often in some way religious in nature, detailing public SACRIFICES and RITUALS, or votive offerings to particular deities. In theory, all inscribed public records were copies of originals, mostly on papyrus, that were stored as official documents in specially constructed state ARCHIVES or in TEMPLES and private offices.

The rise of imperial Athenian DEMOCRACY, where busy, informed citizens made law, demanded accountability and could precipitately inflict fines, EXILE or execution, led to an explosion in public record-keeping. Thousands of inscriptions, many intricately lettered, brightly coloured, and on large stones, appeared to keep the populace apprised of government policy, and implicitly to remind the citizens at large of the importance of their civic participation. While perhaps no more than 20–30 per cent of the resident population of any Greek city-state was fully literate, the common oral recitation of written texts, the ability of most to recognize some names and numbers, and the symbolic value of civic documents themselves all ensured the growth of public record-keeping.

The factors determining which documents were copied on permanent surfaces, displayed publicly or kept in perpetuity are complex. Items most commonly deemed worth the time and expense of setting up elaborate inscribed copies included votives (e.g. the first-fruits at ELEUSIS, 422 BC), religious practices (e.g. public curses at Teos, 470), financial matters (e.g. the Athenian Tribute Lists, 454/3–432/1), confiscations (e.g. the property of the Hermokopidai, 414), treaties (e.g. between ARGOS, KNOSSOS and Tylissos, 450), legal codes (e.g. the civil laws of GORTYN, 450), city foundations (e.g. CYRENE, 7th century), contracts and building expenditures (e.g. the PARTHENON accounts, 434), HONOURS and BENEFACTIONS (e.g. the assassins of Phrynichos, 409), casualty lists (e.g. the dead of the Erechtheid tribe, 460/59) and war commemorations (e.g. the Athenian portico at DELPHI, 479). All these were seen as vital information for the citizenry at large.

By hellenistic times both the nature and number of Greek public records had changed dramatically. The monetization of the ECONOMY, increases in population, and the enormous growth in TAXATION created a BUREAUCRACY of record-keepers, clerks, and accountants. There was much greater demand for archives to house the new information on papyrus, as private data outgrew publicly inspired documents. The gradual reliance on written records rather than oral recall in legal, legislative and executive transactions also required authoritative texts – even as the decline of consensual government meant that publicly displayed records were increasingly commemorative and honorific, rather than reflections of the work of a truly autonomous and deliberative citizenry. VDH

See Klaffenbach, G. (1960) *Bemerkungen zur griechischen Urkundewesen*; Thomas, R. (1980) *Oral Tradition and Written Record in Classical Athens*.

Record-keeping practices at Rome were a haphazard mixture of tradition and attempts at organization, which resulted in a number of different archival sites and officials whose duties sometimes overlapped. In the REPUBLIC, the main place where important state documents was kept was the state treasury, the *aerarium*, located in the TEMPLE of SATURN complex. The QUAESTORS, the magistrates in charge of financial affairs, seem to have used the treasury as a kind of headquarters for their activities, and it is reasonable to assume that they would have generated vital registers concerning state expenditures. Once this financial ARCHIVE was established, it became a general repository for other significant state documents as well. The resolutions of the SENATE were deposited here, and in fact were not considered valid until they had been filed at the *aerarium*. Space will have been very limited, and in 78 BC a special building, the *tabularium*, was constructed to serve as the main archive for official documents. The *tabularium* was a multi-storey structure at the north-west end of the FORUM, built into the slope of the Capitoline hill. Various other sites became the traditional repositories of certain specific records. TREATIES were stored at the temple of Fides, CENSUS results pertaining to *EQUITES* were placed in the *atrium libertatis*, and some other financial information relating to the census was kept in the temple of the Nymphs.

The senate maintained an account of its proceedings, known as the *acta*, though how detailed and accessible they were and where they were stored is unclear. JULIUS CAESAR made public the *acta* of the senate; AUGUSTUS revoked this. In the empire, some records may have been kept by the EMPERORS' personal staff, but the *tabularium* continued to be used, as evidenced by the appointment of three *curatores tabularum publicarum* in AD 16 to restore and organize the archives. Official records were at least partially available to individuals for consultation, since authors such as SUETONIUS and TACITUS were able to examine them. The periodic census of citizens also produced considerable amounts of information. Local magistrates were responsible for taking the census in their jurisdictions and forwarding the results to Rome. The Romans produced detailed MAPS and documents relating to land ownership throughout the empire, and copies of such cadastral inventories were also to be sent to Rome. Provincial governors, cities and the military all kept records of their own. Another essential form of public records was the CALENDARS, or *fasti*, listing HOLIDAYS, MARKET days and days with restrictions on conducting legal and political activity. These were frequently painted on public buildings. GSA

See Nicolet, C. (1991) *Space, Geography, and Politics in the Early Roman Empire*; Posner, E. (1972) *Archives in the Ancient World*.

refugees In the classical world many people were forced to flee their homes and seek refuge with others because of natural disasters, such as floods, FIRES, EARTHQUAKES, VOLCANIC eruptions, droughts and famines. There were no organizations devoted to refugees, but they benefited from widespread customary practices of hospitality and the almost universally acknowledged duty to aid the destitute. Religious sanctuaries would provide shelter and sustenance, particularly if their PRIESTS were wealthy citizens, and much was done by EMPERORS, KINGS and local rulers. After the fire of AD 64 in Rome NERO opened public buildings and GARDENS to provide temporary accommodation for the homeless, and established a relief fund with compulsory donations (Tacitus, *Annals* 15.39; Suetonius, *Nero* 38). Warfare created many refugees, often forcing country-dwellers to seek shelter in fortified towns and cities, though ruthless commanders might expel the most vulnerable (Aeneas Tacticus 10.10). In AD 359 AMMIANUS MARCELLINUS encountered a young boy in MESOPOTAMIA whose mother had abandoned him as she fled the invading PERSIANS. His noble birth secured him an armed escort to NISIBIS (Ammianus 18.6.10–11). Non-combatants could be evacuated in anticipation of an attack, as the PLATAEANS were in 431 BC (Thucydides 2.6). Inhabitants of captured cities might be allowed to take some money and clothing with them, as at Poteidaia in 429 BC (Thucydides 2.70). They could usually expect shelter from neighbouring cities, though in 335 all Greeks were forbidden to shelter survivors of the sack of THEBES as a punishment for Theban medism (support for the Persians) in 480. PDeS

refuse see SANITATION; WASTE.

religion

A cultural phenomenon present in almost every society, ancient and modern. Religion, in its broadest sense, as a set of human ideological attitudes and practices seeking to establish communication with the supernatural, should be viewed as inseparable from its creative forces in the social, political and intellectual spheres. In the ancient Greek world, the concept of religion is firmly integrated into the socio-political structure of the city-state (*polis*), the basic civic unit. Religion helped to define and to justify the nature and aims of a *POLIS* in the physically segmented territory of the Greek landscape. Every *polis* paid honours to its own local divinities, often quite distinct from those worshipped in neighbouring city-states (*poleis*). It had its own patron GODS who, alongside other local deities, were primarily responsible for the safekeeping of their city-states. Typical epithets of gods acting in this capacity for particular states include Polieus or (for goddesses) Polias, Poliouchos, Phratrios, Patroös and others. In return, the *polis* made religion a central element in its ideological framework and an indispensable part of every activity that concerned the state. Manifestations of religious worship of various kinds not only accompanied ordinary civic business, such as the sittings of the ASSEMBLY (*ekklêsia*) and the people's courts, but was also part of important military undertakings and political decisions. With respect to the latter, advice from the gods was obtained through ORACLES, which were perceived as the ultimate guides on vital state issues in times of crisis.

RELIGION: (a) simple rustic cult statue of Dionysos fashioned on a wooden pole, as depicted on a painted vase in Museo Archeologico, Naples.

Religious FESTIVALS were a standard feature of Greek religion and a regular occasion for worshipping the gods at different times each year. They were celebrated on a local and panhellenic ('of all the Greeks') scale, the latter referring to those which attracted pilgrims from all over the Greek world to worship major deities. The existence of divinities acknowledged by all the Greeks constitutes one feature of a common cultural map which, albeit allowing room for local diversity, went beyond local fragmentation. Religion held a definite place in the self-perception of the Greeks as an essentially unified cultural group, as asserted by the Athenians in HERODOTOS (8.144). Here, the TEMPLES of the gods and mode of worship are mentioned alongside common language, blood and ancestry as unmistakable signs of the collective identity of being Greek.

In contrast to 'public' religion, the concept of 'private' religion is less well defined. It is generally used to describe a more personal engagement with the divine. In its simplest form, this may consist of a PRAYER by an individual, or consultation of an oracle on a private matter. It may also apply to religious customs centring around a HOUSEHOLD (*oikos*) on occasions such as a wedding, birth or funeral. The special functions of the domestic hearth constituted perhaps one of the most distinctive aspects of Greek private religion, where the practical met the divine. This ensured that every *oikos*, as a social unit, conformed to the generally accepted religious structures, both practical and ideological.

Greek religion was based on a polytheistic system, like most PAGAN religions of ancient times. It lacked a clear theoretical framework of the form known in modern theological systems. No central creed or dogma existed, thus eliminating concepts present in modern religions, notably sin and heresy. Instead of sacred books, there were stories (so-called MYTHS) about the divine, transmitted from generation to generation principally by means of POETRY. The Greek religious system evolved around a range of divine figures of varying status, including gods and minor divinities as well as HEROES. Our image of the Greek gods is owed to HOMER, who first describes the basic divine group or pantheon as anthropomorphic and structured as a family unit. Every god, male or female, is responsible for different realms, controlling natural elements and particular aspects of the mortal world. ZEUS is found at the head of the divine hierarchy, and possesses supreme power over both gods and mortals. He and his fellow Olympians (the name alludes to their mythical place of residence, Mt Olympos) constituted the main body of the Greek pantheon, which comprised twelve members: the goddesses HERA, ATHENA, APHRODITE, ARTEMIS and DEMETER, and the gods POSEIDON, APOLLO, HERMES, Hephaistos, Ares and DIONYSOS, as well as Zeus. An altar dedicated to the Twelve Gods in the Athenian AGORA by the PEISISTRATIDS in the 6th century BC confirms Homer's presentation of the basic form of the Greek pantheon. HESIOD's *Theogony* illustrates another aspect of the mythical history of the Twelve Olympians, describing their divine origins and monstrous predecessors, the Titans. Hesiod offers glimpses of ancient stories surrounding the gods' struggle to establish themselves as the supreme power in the world. Tragic DRAMA, on the other hand, sheds more light on the less intelligible side of divine behaviour, insofar as their relationships and contacts with humans are concerned. It also explores the role of minor divinities and DEMONIC creatures who interfere with the lives of mortals.

In all three literary genres, the character of the Greek pantheon presents great consistency. Greek gods are subject neither to the passing of time nor to death, despite their human-like appearance. They remain eternally young and indestructible. Their special nature and functions are reflected in both their physical traits and the objects with which they are associated, known as 'attributes'. As father of the gods with supreme power over mortals, natural elements and the gods, Zeus alone possesses the weapon of the thunderbolt. Most goddesses were imagined as beautiful, but none was as beautiful as Aphrodite, goddess of sexual love. Athena's military nature and close association with her father Zeus are reflected by her attributes, such as the set of bronze weapons that she wears. Apollo, on the other hand, is distinguished by his youthful and ATHLETIC bodily stature and attributes such as the laurel, which alludes to his PURIFICATORY and PROPHETIC powers.

Despite the gods' human-like external features, they inspire awe and fear in humans: partly because of their extraordinary powers and their ability to use it in any way they wish, but above all due to their obscure nature and operations, which at most times mortals could not comprehend. This is particularly discernible in the Homeric poems and tragic drama, where we see gods interfering in human action, most times uninvited and with a partiality towards their favourite mortals. Their fickle patterns of association with humans, in terms of bestowing or withdrawing support, are highlighted in poetry, with strong colours underlining the vulnerability of human nature. Greek gods were not benevolent figures driven by the aim to help humanity at all costs, neither did they require their worshippers to follow such rules. Unlike in modern theological systems, gods' behaviour is neither consistent nor morally correct. This should be viewed within the framework of a general fluidity regarding absolute religious truths and beliefs, and acceptable moral behaviour, inherent in the ideological structure of Greek religion. No sacred books existed to define the precise nature and intentions of the gods and what they expect from humans. Gods act with pride, in a manner quite like powerful mortals, both towards each other and towards their weak, mortal lookalikes. They take their superior status for granted, and act with the right of might. To humans, the gods' will is unpredictable and hard to interpret. To bridge this unequal relationship between man and the divine, exceptionally gifted individuals known as prophets undertook the role of mediators. Their role was to foresee and interpret the gods' wishes or attitudes by reading natural signs, believed to be sent from the gods, in the form of omens.

Gods demanded to be acknowledged in public through a range of practices which were thought appropriate. These are known as RITUALS and varied widely with respect to duration, scope, the number and status of people involved, and the time of the day or year in which they took place. Most important was SACRIFICE, which appears to have been the essential mode of thanksgiving to the gods. Among other rituals, one may mention prayers, libations, processions and purifications, all seeking to establish a relationship with the gods for the benefit of humans. Reciprocity was a vital rule in contact with the divine. The gods must receive their due, through the right rituals, in order to respond to human requests. A second major issue in terms of human relationships with the gods has to do with the acknowledgement of mortal limits and restrictions. Excess, in the form of over-reaching pride, arrogance or strong confidence in one's mortal self (known as *hybris*), could be a severe offence to the gods, provoking harsh punishment.

Minor divinities, demonic figures and heroes also received worship through ritual, following modes which best suited the special nature of each divinity. These were particularly venerated on a local scale; this is particularly true of PERSONIFICATIONS of natural elements, nature deities, and heroic figures whose origins or actions were often closely associated with specific locations. In the case of heroes, their cult usually post-dates their mortal lives, since their status is upgraded to that of divinity at, or immediately after, their death. Many cults of non-Olympian divinities appear to be particularly associated with the earth (in this connection the usual Greek word is *chthôn*, 'land'), rather than the sky, which was the realm of the Olympians. These links are expressed in ORAL TRADITIONS about these gods, who are hence called chthonic. Chthonic gods were venerated through their own distinctive rituals, such as special types of sacrifice and libation.

Stories about the gods, their lives and their relationships were preserved in the collective memory of the Greeks for many centuries. Myths generally followed narratives known from early poetry, such as Homer and Hesiod. By the end of the 6th century BC, doubts began to be expressed with regard to the validity of these myths and the messages they conveyed. XENOPHANES was among the first critics of traditional religion who found weaknesses in the moral aspect of Greek gods and the attribution of anthropomorphic features to them. The latter issue was picked up and illustrated further by ARISTOTLE in the 4th century. The former was expanded by PLATO, who was deeply interested in wider moral issues such as piety and holiness. Plato was an uncompromising critic of MYTHOLOGY, in its old-fashioned form shaped by archaic EPIC and DIDACTIC poetry. These radical trends against traditional religion at times went as far as complete denial of the gods and open admittance of atheism. Such attitudes may be evaluated against the broader context of the rise of PHILOSOPHICAL thought and SCIENCE, which reached new levels in the 5th century. The challenges to the existing religious system were usually followed by alternative suggestions about the beginning (*archê*) of the world by groups such as natural philosophers and SOPHISTS, culminating in highly influential figures such as SOCRATES. A further facet of the broader religious debate seems to have been the introduction of new gods added to the list of the basic pantheon. This phenomenon intensifies from the 5th century onwards, with a range of gods imported from places like Egypt, THRACE and Ionia.

Despite the cracks in the traditional religious system and the external borrowings, it continued, in one form or another, until and beyond the coming of the Romans, who embraced and expanded Greek pagan beliefs and forms. These forms did not completely disappear before the spread of CHRISTIANITY, which began forcibly to uproot pagan traditions, customs and beliefs and, eventually to shake the broader sociopolitical systems that these religions represented. EP

See Bremmer, J. N. (1994) *Greek Religion*; Bruit Zaidman, L. and Schmitt Pantel, P. (1992) *Religion in the Ancient Greek City*; Easterling, P. E. and Muir, J.V., eds. (1985) *Greek Religion and Society*; Price, S. (1999) *Religions of the Ancient Greeks*; Sourvinou-Inwood, C. (2000) What is polis religion?, in R. Buxton, ed., *Oxford Readings in Greek Religion* 13–37.

Our sources for traditional Roman religion are uneven and problematic. Since it was a religion of RITUAL rather than doctrine, it had no sacred scriptures of the sort familiar from other traditions, to contain its essential beliefs. Even our knowledge of the ritual depends on works at several removes, because the great collections of priestly prescriptions are lost, apart from brief references, as are the antiquarian writings of Roman scholars like VARRO. Hence for major literary sources we rely on material like the PHILOSOPHICAL dialogues of CICERO, the historical data compiled by LIVY, OVID'S POETIC exposition of the Roman CALENDAR in his *Fasti* (only the first six months survive), and the citations of Republican scholarship by CHRISTIAN polemicists like AUGUSTINE (1) or late antique scholars like

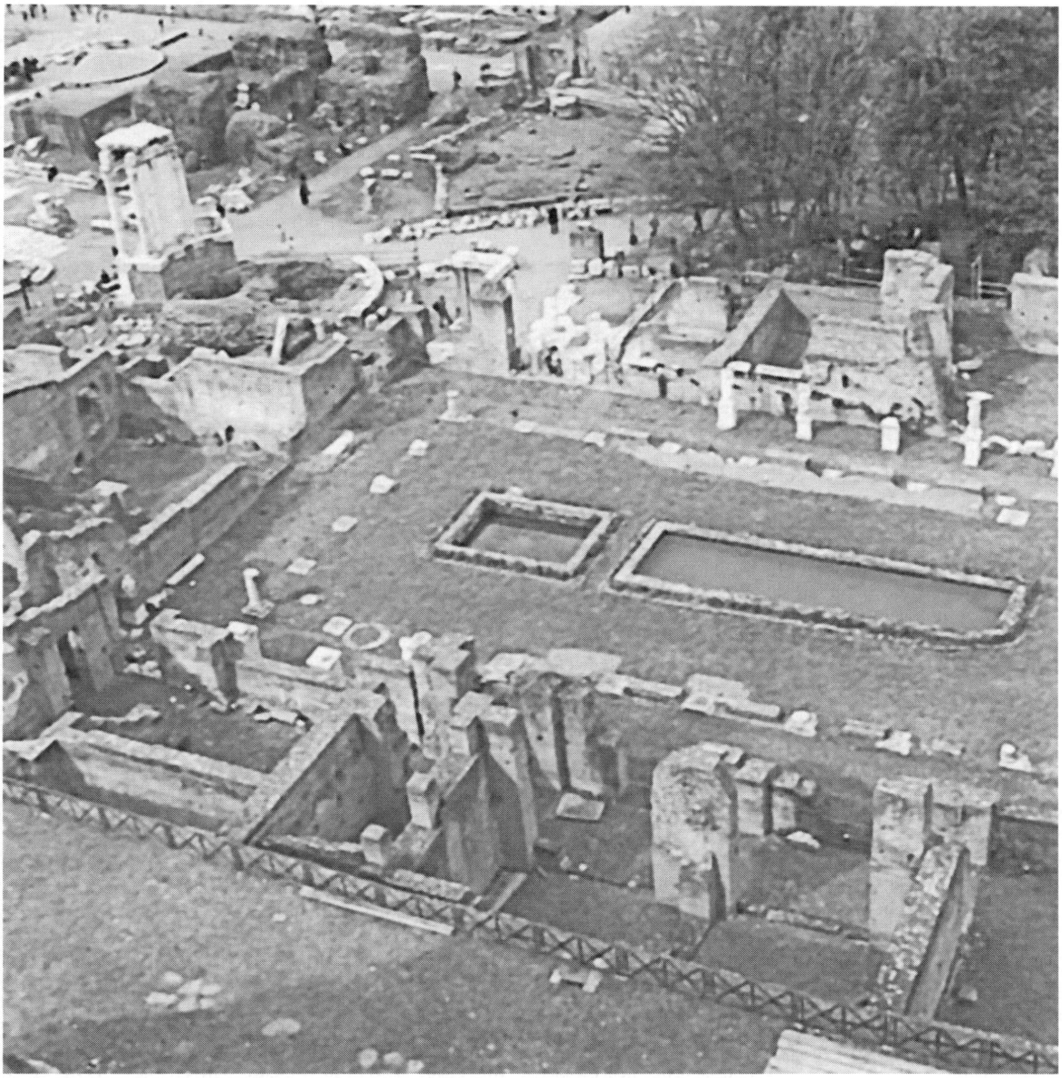

RELIGION: (b) general view of the temple of Vesta and the House of the Vestal Virgins by the forum in Rome.

Macrobius. ARCHAEOLOGY is a significant source of information for all periods, particularly the archaic, for which the literary evidence is late and unreliable. Inscriptions, an equally important source, are few (though informative) for earlier periods, abundant from the reign of AUGUSTUS onwards. Particularly valuable are the numerous copies of the calendar (which allow a reasonably full knowledge of the religious year), the detailed records of the ARVAL BRETHREN, and the huge range of votive dedications.

The earliest strata of Roman religious tradition reveal connections with those of other Indo-European speakers; thus the name of the Roman sky-god JUPITER is cognate with Greek 'ZEUS' and Vedic 'Dyaus' (the form *Diovis-pater*, 'Father Jove', is inferred though not attested). Dumézil has argued cogently that the threefold structure of Indo-European society (religious and legal authority, military power and AGRICULTURAL production) informs both the most archaic rites and the legends about early Roman KINGS and heroes; in his view the latter take the place of a Roman divine MYTHOLOGY, which is otherwise strikingly absent. Roman religious tradition is even more closely cognate with those of other Italic-speaking peoples, with which it shares certain deities (e.g. Jupiter, MARS, JUNO, CERES), organizational structures (e.g. priestly colleges) and ritual forms (e.g. the *lustrum*). From an early date, however, Roman religion was subject to influences from non-Italic peoples, notably ETRUSCANS and Greeks. The extent of Etruscan influence is debated, but obviously lies behind such important institutions as the CAPITOLINE TRIAD of Jupiter, Juno and MINERVA. Greek influence was more constant, resulting not only in the adoption of Greek gods (HERCULES, Castor and Pollux, APOLLO) but also in the reinterpretation of traditional deities (e.g. VENUS as Aphrodite). Down to the early 2nd century BC official Roman religion remained strikingly absorptive, with the adoption of new rites and the founding of new cults for an increasing range of Italic and Greek deities. This innovative tendency reached a peak in the critical years of the second PUNIC WAR, most strikingly with the installation of the PHRYGIAN cult of CYBELE. In the 180s BC, however, Roman authorities clamped down on a popular and secretive cult of BACCHUS, and for the next two centuries showed a tendency to distrust the more exotic religious traditions with which the expansion of their empire had brought them into contact.

The repression of the Bacchic cult also illuminates one of the key features of Roman religion, the intermingling of religious and civic structures. The fundamental principle was that if the Romans fulfilled their collective obligations to their gods, the latter would grant them prosperity. Hence in Rome there were no separate 'church' and 'state'; rather, community affairs in both the human and the divine spheres were managed by the same ÉLITE. Although a range of private cults existed, these were subsidiary to public cult. Likewise, religious activity was not the product of individual belief, but rather an aspect of Roman identity. The emphasis therefore lay not on personal assent to a set of doctrines, but rather on the correct performance of prescribed rituals by representatives of the community. Since the cult of Bacchus embodied a new type of religious orientation, one that bypassed the political community and centred on a voluntary body of devotees, it posed a threat to the traditional system. But another source of change, less obvious and more gradual, had already begun: the expansion of Roman CITIZENSHIP. Although this encouraged the spread of specifically Roman cults in Italy, it also meant that there were communities of Roman citizens whose public cults were not identical with those in Rome itself. The peoples of other Italian towns did not abandon their local traditions on becoming Romans.

The late Republic has often been seen as a period of decline for Roman religion, when the élite, influenced by Greek PHILOSOPHY, paid only lip-service to Roman traditions and the authorities either neglected public cult or exploited it for political gain. This view is now widely rejected. What modern observers consider exploitation, the Romans themselves may have regarded as the legitimate intermingling of religious and political concerns. Moreover, while some of the data cited as evidence for religious decline represent genuine cases of disruption and neglect, others are better interpreted as adjustments to the system. Old rites were altered or gradually abandoned to fit new circumstances, while new ones appeared. Such adjustments were presumably a constant feature of Roman religion, but our evidence is such that we are more aware of them in the late republic than in earlier periods. Moreover, it suited Augustus that the writers of his day portray the preceding period as one of decline, since this provided support for his claim to have effected a religious restoration. It was largely under the guise of this restoration that Augustus wrought his most significant changes in Roman religion, by incorporating the new figure of the *princeps* into traditional structures. This took various forms: the EMPEROR became the chief religious official, a model of piety towards the gods as well as the focus of divine favour towards Rome, and a quasi-divine figure in his own right.

In the imperial period 'Roman religion' became an increasingly elastic concept. Roman cults spread throughout the Western empire, though in the East the Greek tradition remained dominant. CAESAR and Augustus founded numerous colonies of Roman citizens, who not only established cults of traditional Roman deities but also replicated Roman PRIESTHOODS and religious organization. But non-Roman provincials also adopted Roman cults as a sign of their identification with the ruling power. The most important of these was IMPERIAL CULT. This was in no sense a single institution, but took many different forms: there was not so much a common imperial cult as a general tendency to incorporate the emperor, his house and his deified predecessors into local religious practice. Although authorities in Rome exercised a certain control over these cults, particularly those organized on a regional basis, some of them were Roman only insofar as they focused on the Roman emperor.

But Romans also came to participate in a range of other cults during the imperial period. This was true not only in Rome itself, where cults that had initially met with official resistance (such as that of ISIS and SERAPIS) gradually became important features of the religious landscape. It was true also and especially in the PROVINCES, where the spread of Roman citizenship to peoples with other traditions made it increasingly unclear what cults counted as Roman. Local deities were worshipped under Roman names, such as MERCURY in GAUL or SATURN in AFRICA, and might even assume various attributes of their Roman counterparts, yet they did not thereby lose their local identity. Religious organization also became more varied. Although the sorts of civic cults characteristic of Republican Rome remained widespread and popular, they were joined by a range of private associations and individual pursuits. Cults with restricted membership and their own hierarchies became more common and were no longer necessarily viewed as threats. That of MITHRAS even drew its membership largely from the military and the imperial bureaucracy.

At the same time as these developments rendered 'Roman' religion increasingly diffuse, there was a growing tendency to mark off certain types of religiosity as officially unacceptable. Beginning in the late Republic, some of these began to be grouped together and conceptualized as a perversion of true religion, i.e. 'magic'; by the 2nd century AD, MAGIC was being treated as a capital offence in Roman law. Likewise, Roman authorities defined adherence to Christianity, and later MANICHAEISM, as punishable behaviour. This trend towards a legal distinction between 'good' and 'bad' religion was accelerated by CONSTANTINE's decision to patronize Christianity, which as a MONOTHEISM concerned with correct belief had a strong tradition of excluding unacceptable forms of religion. By the end of the 4th century AD Christianity had become, at least officially, the exclusive religion of the Roman empire. JBR

See Beard, M. et al. (1998) *Religions of Rome*; Dumézil, G. (1970) *Archaic Roman Religion*; Liebeschuetz, J. H. W. G. (1979) *Continuity and Change in Roman Religion*; MacMullen, R. (1981) *Paganism in the Roman Empire*; Turcan, R. (1988) *Religion romaine*.

 GODS AND GODDESSES: (a)–(b); SACRIFICE: (a)–(d).

Renaissance A term used to describe a cultural vision that was born in the Italian peninsula and spread to other parts of Europe. This vision was based on a perceived overthrow of intellectual and aesthetic values in favour of ones founded upon the imitation of classical antiquity, particularly ancient Rome.

The notion of the Renaissance as a historical period rather than simply a cultural vision was born in the mid-19th century, particularly through Jacob Burckhardt's *Die Cultur der Renaissance in Italien* (1860). This work's influence was pervasive, especially in its claims regarding the period's development of notions such as human individuality, the universal (or indeed 'Renaissance') man, and an anthropocentric rather than theocentric cosmos. Such claims must be understood, for most (if not all) of the period, as representing the views of an extremely limited cultural élite – this Renaissance was not a mass movement or an integral part of popular culture.

The Renaissance has no obvious chronological signposts, but can be said to take its origins within the activities of 14th-century humanists, most notably Francesco Petrarca (PETRARCH) and his circle. Among these humanists and their followers, there developed a sense that culture and civilization had declined after the fall of the Roman empire. Since the humanists had brought to light hitherto ignored manuscripts of great antiquity (most of them, ironically, Carolingian rather than classical), they felt themselves best equipped to introduce these classical models to their otherwise ignorant contemporaries. The period of the Renaissance may be said to end, depending on location, anywhere from the mid-16th to the mid-17th century. Throughout this time, Italian scholars and artists were of the greatest influence.

The fascination of Renaissance scholars with classical models led them to embark on widespread searches for manuscripts of ancient texts, to which they applied their formidable skills of collation, editing and critical analysis. Many classical texts that had hitherto been ignored or were considered lost came to light during this period. The most famous example of Renaissance philology, however, is Lorenzo Valla's study of the *Donation of Constantine*, which he proved, on textual grounds, to be a forgery.

Perhaps the greatest scientific developments were in the areas of astronomy (notably Nicolaus Copernicus) and optics. The latter developed alongside what may be the most widely admired legacy of the Renaissance: its art and architecture, and the fascination of its artists with classical models and their penchant for newly developed rules and techniques of perspective. From the generation of Giotto onward, it became accepted to create pictures with the effect of depth. By the early 1400s, Filippo Brunelleschi developed mathematical formulas and techniques in order to create the illusion of three dimensions on a two-dimensional surface. Some of the more famous 15th-century works featuring the effect of perspective are by Masaccio, Donatello, Piero della Francesca and Andrea Mantegna. Many of these works use classical architecture or architectural forms in their backgrounds. Renaissance architecture was heavily influenced by the revival of interest in ancient Roman architecture; Brunelleschi's Ospedale degli Innocenti in Florence – often called 'the first Renaissance building' – used Corinthian columns and proportions associated with Roman buildings. GF

See Burckhardt, J. (1860) *Die Cultur der Renaissance in Italien* (*The Civilization of the Renaissance in Italy*, 2002); Campbell, G. (2003) *The Oxford Dictionary of the Renaissance*.

Republic, Roman The greatest problem for understanding the first two or three hundred years of the Republic was the late beginning of Roman historical writing, but, in broadest terms, the themes of the earliest years of the Republic seem clear. The expulsion of the last KING, TARQUINIUS SUPERBUS, at the end of the 6th century BC, and the establishment of a working relationship with the Latins, seem undeniable. The latter was Rome's salvation through a century and more of invasion from the peoples of the Apennines and, most humiliatingly, the sack of the capital city by the GAULS. Nonetheless, Rome had been able in 396 to defeat and sack the neighbouring ETRUSCAN town of VEII, and through the 4th century Rome's control over its Latin neighbours strengthened. The keys to Roman success at this time must have been the combination of a large population, which provided soldiers for the army, and the willingness of Rome to extend the privileges of CITIZENSHIP beyond its borders. As the 4th century progressed, Rome began the practice of sending out colonies granted LATIN or citizen status, which guarded Rome's expanding empire and carried Roman customs of URBANIZATION, ARCHITECTURE and politics into Italy. By the 2nd century BC, there were colonies throughout the peninsula from the Po valley all the way to the south.

This was not achieved without internal difficulties. The fault line along which this disunity ran was the distinction between the PATRICIANS, who arrogated to themselves political and religious office and power, and the PLEBEIANS, who sought to gain the same rights. The plebeians were able to gather large-scale popular support, for instance in the Secessions of the Plebs in 494, 449 and 287 BC, when the urban population of Rome left the city and camped on one of the hills outside the city boundary. In due course, patrician control weakened in all essential aspects of politics and religion, though that did not make Rome any the less weighted towards the wealthy classes. It was always a struggle to enter Republican politics without a powerful family background or a powerful PATRON.

The 3rd century saw the beginnings of Rome's dramatic expansion towards a MEDITERRANEAN empire. The military burden sustained by Rome through the 3rd and 2nd century deserves to be noted; no other Western society has maintained so heavy a burden of regular service by so high a proportion of its male population. The SAMNITE WARS gave Rome some control in central Italy, and were followed swiftly by the first PUNIC WAR and Roman intervention in southern Italy and SICILY. When HANNIBAL invaded in 218, southern Italy supported him but the LATINS and others stayed loyal. Victory in 202 removed Rome's major threat in the western Mediterranean, and attention focused immediately on the eastern Mediterranean, the kingdoms of PHILIP V of Macedonia and ANTIOCHOS III of Asia Minor.

By the later 2nd century, Rome had risen to be the unchallenged power in the Mediterranean. Such achievements naturally had consequences for Italy. In the first place, the empire was beginning to provide a previously unknown degree of financial prosperity through legitimate taxes and the opportunities for extortion. This wealth flowed mostly to Rome, which was being improved with civic amenities, public buildings and private display as befitted the capital city; but some found its way to the cities and ÉLITES of Italy. Italian traders appeared in the empire, and all over the peninsula cities developed their urban features and private luxury increased. At the same time, a profound change occurred in AGRICULTURE, with the development of increasingly intensive and slave-based agricultural techniques – the SLAVES another by-product of empire.

The changes accelerated the crisis of the late Republic, which was the result of a number of interlinked factors. One aspect was the demand of the Italians for proper recognition, which led to the SOCIAL WAR of 91–89, after which all Italians were granted Roman citizenship. This inevitably changed radically the sense in which politics at Rome could claim to be linked to the people. Another aspect was the demand by the city population of Rome, and by the discharged VETERANS of the army, for land outside the overcrowded and unhealthy city. Before the Social war this land was often confiscated from Italians, which was a grievance in itself. After the war it became even more difficult to meet this demand, leading to tensions in the city itself. A third aspect is the development of an increasingly professional army, bound to long-serving generals like MARIUS, SULLA, POMPEY and CAESAR. These men were immensely enriched by their campaigns in the east and GAUL, and extremely vulnerable to their political opponents at home. Each took it upon himself at one stage or another to march on Rome to demand his due. In the end, with Pompey and Caesar implacably opposed to each other, a CIVIL WAR was inevitable; it led to the victory of Caesar in 49 and establishment of a kind of monarchy. After Caesar's assassination in 44 by a BRUTUS who claimed to be descended from the first CONSUL, it took just over ten years for the main players to be reduced to one man: OCTAVIAN, later named AUGUSTUS. On defeating Mark ANTONY at ACTIUM in 31, he became the ruler of Italy and its empire, pursuing with a combination of judgement and good fortune 40 years of a reign that finally laid to rest the ghost of the Republic. CJS

See Beard, M. and Crawford, M. (1985) *Rome in the Late Republic*; *CAH* 7.2 to 9; Cornell, T. J. (1995) *The Beginnings of Rome*.

republics The word 'republic' is a Latin term (*res publica*, 'the public matter') and defines the constitution of the ROMAN REPUBLIC, a system of government preceded by a monarchy and followed by an imperial dynasty. It avoided such constitutional extremes by maintaining the rule of LAW, by allowing some popular participation, and by rotating key offices among an ÉLITE. It thus resembled ARISTOTLE'S 'polity' (*politeia*) or mixed constitution, which, like the system depicted in PLATO'S *Laws*, was designed to ensure social stability by avoiding either autocracy or populism. The Roman Republic was praised by the historian POLYBIOS, and rationalized by CICERO, who incorporated STOIC ideas of natural law as a further justification of its principles. Its theory and practice were espoused in the late 18th century in the American Revolution against the British crown. By contrast, the best-known ancient political constitution, Plato's *Republic* (a loose translation of the work's Greek title, *Politeia*), envisaged rule by a dominant intellectual class whose philosophical education allowed access to absolute moral truth; this supposedly ensured rulers who would provide just government. This UTOPIAN vision was expressed in more extreme terms by ZENO the Stoic, in an imaginary republic consisting only of philosophical sages. Heirs to this speculative 'republicanism', based not on law but on the character and training of the rulers, are theorists such as Thomas More in his *Utopia*. RBT

See von Fritz, K. (1940) *The Theory of the Mixed Constitution in Antiquity*; Rowe, C. and Schofield, M. (2000) *The Cambridge History of Greek and Roman Political Thought*.

Res Gestae The usual short form of *Res gestae divi Augusti* ('achievements of the deified Augustus'), the account of his accomplishments left by AUGUSTUS at his death in AD 14. It was read in the SENATE, and, as he had instructed, inscribed on two bronze pillars in front of his Mausoleum. Copies may have been set up widely in the PROVINCES. A nearly complete copy survives, with accompanying Greek translation, from Ancyra (mod. Ankara), the capital of the province of Galatia. Fragments of two other copies survive, also from Galatia.

The document has affinities with the inscribed records (*elogia*) of the careers of other notable Romans, but is on a much larger scale and throughout stresses the unique number and magnitude of Augustus' achievements. The bulk of the work lists his military and civil honours, his expenditures, principally for the benefit of the Roman people, and his achievements in WAR and DIPLOMACY, summarized in the preamble's claim that he 'subjected the globe to the empire of the Roman people'.

Throughout Augustus displays a masterly economy with the truth. His rivals are never named. The opening summary of his early career glosses over his shifts of allegiance, and the co-author of the proscriptions declares that in the civil wars 'I spared the lives of all citizens who asked for mercy'. He says nothing of the division of the provinces in 27 BC which secured his control of the army, and maintains that subsequently his primacy was based not on official power (*potestas*), but on his personal authority (*auctoritas*). JWR

See Brunt, P. A. and Moore, J. M. (1967) *Res gestae divi Augusti*.

Res Gestae: the opening lines of the 'biography' of Augustus, copied onto the walls of a temple in Ankara, Turkey.

research see ACADEMY; ARISTOTLE; EXPERIMENTATION; INVENTIONS; LIBRARIES; LYCEUM; MUSEUMS; NATURAL HISTORY; PHILOSOPHICAL SCHOOLS; PLINY THE ELDER; SCHOLARSHIP, ANCIENT; SCIENCE; TECHNOLOGY.

resin In the Greek and Roman world aromatic resins from various sources were variously used in food, MEDICINE, RELIGION and industry. Pine resin, from Aleppo pine and Scotch pine, was widely found. The terebinth tree (*Pistacia atlantica*) is native to the Near East. Mastic comes from a lentisk tree (*P. lentiscus var. chia*) found on the Greek island of CHIOS. Storax came from the Syrian tree *Styrax officinalis*. Balsam of Mecca came from plantations of *Commiphora opobalsamum* in Palestine. Other resins were imported at high cost in the eastern SPICE trade: frankincense and myrrh from southern ARABIA, bdellium (*Commiphora mukul*) from south-eastern Iran.

Frankincense, myrrh, bdellium and storax were burnt as incense. Myrrh, storax and balsam of Mecca served in medicines and unguents. Mastic was a medicine and a chewing gum. WINES aromatized with myrrh, terebinth and mastic were drunk as aperitifs. Pine and terebinth resins served to fumigate and WATERPROOF earthenware vats for maturing wine. The flavour was enhanced, and the product stabilized, with bouquets of resin suspended in the fermenting wine (which would now be called retsina).

Trade in resins antedated the classical period and continued later. Half a ton of terebinth resin went down in a SHIPWRECK in the mid-2nd millennium BC at Ulu Burun in south-western ANATOLIA. Mastic was one of the spices that Columbus was most anxious to discover in the 'Indies'. AD

See Beek, G.W. van (1960) Frankincense and myrrh, *Biblical Archaeologist* 23: 69–95; Dalby, A. (2000) Mastic for beginners, *Petits propos culinaires* 65: 38–45; Groom, N. (1981) *Frankincense and Myrrh*; Mills, J. and White, R. (1989) The identity of the resins from the late Bronze Age shipwreck at Ulu Burun (Kas), *Archaeometry* 31: 37–44.

revolution Dissension by some members of a society, which either attempts to or successfully overthrows or drastically changes the government. Most violent changes in the Greek and Roman worlds derived less from popular ideologically motivated uprisings, on the model of the French Revolution, than from power struggles among different factions for political control of the state. Examples are the CIVIL WARS during the late Roman REPUBLIC, ending in the establishment of the PRINCIPATE by OCTAVIAN, or the struggles among the OLIGARCHS in Greek city-states. In Greece, external forces could play an important role in determining the outcome of a revolution, such as the widespread use of MERCENARIES by TYRANTS. They could also spark them, as in the case of Athenian and Spartan encouragement of DEMOCRATIC and oligarchic factions within other states before the PELOPONNESIAN WAR. Closer to true, broadly supported, democratic revolutions were the expulsion of tyrants such as that of the PEISISTRATID family from Athens in 510 BC and, at Rome, that of the TARQUINS, in the same year according to tradition, which marked the transition from monarchy to Republic. Revolutions of the oppressed were relatively infrequent, usually unsuccessful, but often bitter when they occurred. This is true of the many revolutions of the HELOTS against SPARTA and the SLAVE revolts at Rome, most notably the one led by SPARTACUS in 73 BC. (see also CIVIL STRIFE; VIOLENCE) GSA

See Lintott, A. (1982) *Violence, Civil Strife, and Revolution in the Classical City 750–330 BC*.

Rhaetia see RAETIA.

rhetor see ORATORS; ORATORY; RHETORIC; SOPHISTS.

rhetoric

Defined as influential and finely crafted speech, rhetoric is as old as Greek literature (no doubt much antedating written Greek). ACHILLES in HOMER's *Iliad* is not only a great warrior but a powerful speaker. In book 1, the goddess ATHENA urges him to lash his opponent, AGAMEMNON, with words as an alternative to dispatching him with a sword. Speech here becomes a worthy stand-in for the use of deadly force in defence of a hero's honour. Many an archaic figure (e.g. Solon of Athens) was famous for his ability in public speaking. The self-conscious study of rhetoric as a craft (*technê*) is, however, an artefact of the cultural and political innovations of the 5th century BC. Although the earliest attested teachers of rhetoric (Korax, Teisias and Gorgias) were natives of Sicily, the rhetorical craft flourished especially in democratic Athens. The histories of Athenian democracy and Greek rhetoric are closely conjoined from the mid-5th to late 4th centuries, and Athenian orators established themselves as enduring exemplars of rhetorical excellence.

Athenian democracy was predicated on persuasive speech to mass audiences (in the citizen assembly and the people's courts). Given the institutional structure of assembly and courtroom (vigorous debate followed by binding decision of the listeners), the politician or litigant who spoke most persuasively was the most successful. The high-stakes game of Athenian public life fed a growing market for training in speaking: wealthy young Athenian aristocrats who hoped to make a name for themselves in politics sought out men who could teach them the necessary skills. This market was initially met by certain of the so-called sophists, including Gorgias and Thrasymachos of Chalkedon. Plato's dialogue *Gorgias* offers a hostile portrait of the relationship between an ambitious Athenian student and his teachers in the art of speaking well. According to Plato, the student learned only how to enslave himself by seeking to please a mass audience, and to harm others by deploying his ill-gotten public influence in self-aggrandizement. Early rhetoricians typically publicized their wares by the publication of handbooks (*technai*), but also by public performance of display pieces (*epideixeis*) on paradoxical subjects like 'the virtuousness of Helen'. Sophistic education emphasized argument from probability, antithesis, and elaborate verbal effects; it was predicated on a psychology that equated persuasion by speech with enchantment, desire (*erôs*) and force. The sophists were, rightly or not, reputed to eschew all moral considerations and to teach their students how to 'make the worse argument defeat the better'. This charge was levelled at the philosopher Socrates, first comically by Aristophanes (in the *Clouds*, a parody of sophistic education), then in deadly earnest by legal adversaries in 399.

Our best evidence for the practical employment of rhetoric in late 5th- and 4th-century Athens is the corpus of speeches by Attic orators preserved by hellenistic scholars as models of eloquence. These include the early set-piece orations (*Tetralogies*) of Andokides, the display speeches of Isokrates (see below), and several assembly speeches by Demosthenes. But most preserved classical speeches take the form of forensic orations, written by prominent Athenian politicians like Demosthenes and Aischines or by professional speechwriters (*logographoi*) like the metic Lysias. The rhetorical corpus offers insight into the complex relationship between the Athenian *rhêtôr* and his mass audience. Hyper-sophisticated verbal pyrotechnics ('Gorgianic figures') are notable by their absence; the Athenian audience of jurymen or assemblymen demanded diction that was more down-to-earth and arguments that had at least the semblance of plausibility. Central to classical Athenian rhetoric was the self-representation of the speaker. He sought to demonstrate to his listeners that his own attitudes and way of life conformed to Athenian democratic values and that his opponent was an enemy of the people – his life an affront to common standards of patriotism, liberality, political equality, moderation and modesty. Prominent politicians faced the added burden of demonstrating why their voices deserved special attention in public assemblies, and why their opponents should be disqualified as public advisers. The tension between rhetorical claims to be 'ordinary' (just like other Athenians) and 'extraordinary' (outstanding in capacity to advise and to lead the state) helps to make Attic oratory enduringly fascinating and an excellent source for social history.

The burgeoning reputations of famous public speakers, and Plato's attacks on rhetoric as corrupting to individual soul and body politic alike, left professional teachers of rhetoric in a tight spot. Isokrates, whose weak voice and lack of audacity prevented him (or so he claimed) from speaking in public, took up the challenge of promoting and defending the study of rhetoric as morally uplifting and culturally valuable. In a number of brilliant *epideixeis* (especially *Against the Sophists* and *Areiopagitikos*) he claimed to teach his students not merely the craft of persuasion or artful prose, but a method of clearly expressing to others (in speech or in writing) whatever was most in need of expression – and was therefore invariably avoided in the discourses of those false rhetoricians he derided as sophists or sycophants. Isokrates promoted a commitment to 'Hellenic' values, an aristocratic sensibility that would transcend the narrowly Athenocentric concerns of the working orators and even the pervasive Greek prejudice against hellenized dynasts. He thus offered a cultural role for rhetoric that was in one sense very expansive. Anyone who mastered his lessons in expressive (Greek) speech could be regarded as a fully fledged member of a graceful, cosmopolitan, morally serious society of like-minded souls. Yet this society was also forthrightly élitist: the audience was no longer the mass of ordinary citizens that composed the Athenian *dêmos*, but an aristocratic society of those who could afford to spend time in advanced training and could pay the master-teachers' fees.

In the late 4th century Aristotle offered a somewhat similar (in terms of intended audience) but much more systematic discussion in his *Art of Rhetoric*. Here, rhetorical reasoning was carefully distinguished both from formal logic and 'persuasion by any means'. Aristotle analysed the relationship between speaker and audience, emphasizing the need to pay close attention to the attitudes and predilections of the latter. He offered a detailed discussion of stylistics, the individual parts of a speech, the use of metaphor, the relationship between individual character and expression, and techniques of delivery. Aristotle's and Isokrates' projects serve as a bridge from political and forensic rhetoric in democratic Athens to the long history of rhetoric in the hellenistic, imperial Roman and Byzantine eras.

After the 4th century, Greek rhetoric was increasingly sundered from politics. Intellectual studies failed to transcend Aristotle; what little is left suggests an increasingly arid focus on stylistic details.

But the teaching of rhetoric as eloquence continued unabated. Wealthy students learned the many and various techniques of refined expression that were regarded as essential to success in an aristocratic Greek society that increasingly embraced persons whose ancestors were not native Greek speakers. Isokrates' expansive Hellenic vision of a culture predicated on skilful expression was, in some sense, fulfilled. The evidence is especially good for the era of the 2nd century AD (the 'SECOND SOPHISTIC'), when many new schools of Greek rhetoric were established throughout the Eastern Roman empire. Public competitions in declamation by travelling *rhêtores* became popular spectacles. Rather than a means to political ends, rhetoric became a simulacrum of politics. We may recall book 1 of the *Iliad*: like Achilles restrained by Athena, the imperial Greek male was debarred by Roman authority from proving his manhood through deadly force. And so he sought to emulate the Homeric hero's skill with words. In an age when the traditional political and military conduits to extraordinary deeds and public acclaim were mostly closed, the rhetorical competition was a primary arena for the forging of reputations through public competition, and remained so well into the Byzantine era. JO

See Ober, J. (1989) *Mass and Elite in Democratic Athens*; Rubinstein, L. (2001) *Litigation and Cooperation: supporting speakers in the courts of classical Athens*; Woodman, A. J. (1988) *Rhetoric in Classical Historiography*; Worthington, I., ed. (1994) *Persuasion: Greek rhetoric in action*.

The art of persuasion was a relatively late feature in the development at Rome. Although speeches and ORATORY were a part of Roman politics and the LAWCOURTS from early times, special training and attention to techniques arrived after the beginning of Greek influence, in the 2nd century BC. For some time, teachers and training were almost exclusively Greek, with Roman students applying their new skills to Latin speeches on their own initiative. As late as 92 BC, CENSORS forbade schools of Latin rhetoric, citing departure from custom, though Greek rhetoricians continued to teach. As the education of CICERO illustrates, training in Roman rhetoric was possible by private arrangement with skilled practitioners. When, in the late 90s, Cicero lived at the house of Lucius Licinius Crassus, an eminent orator and one of the censors of 92, he studied his mentor's methods and trained under teachers employed by his host, at least some of them Greek. His practice speeches were mostly in Greek, for only in that language could his teachers critique him. He met Marcus Antonius (grandfather of Mark ANTONY), another outstanding orator, but, because Crassus forbade him, did not visit Plotius Gallus, the first Latin rhetorician.

Cicero calls Marcus Cornelius Cethegus (CONSUL 204 BC) the first eloquent Roman, but considers Marcus Porcius CATO (censor 184) the first orator who reveals Greek rhetorical techniques, though in a somewhat crude manner. After him, orators singled out for their achievements, with increasing attention to technique, include Servius Sulpicius Galba (consul 144), who employed pathos, Marcus Aemilius Lepidus Porcina (consul 137), with an emphasis on wit and periodic sentences, followed by Gaius Papirius Carbo, the first to practice oratorical exercises, and Tiberius GRACCHUS and his brother Gaius. The latter introduced physical movement during delivery and a level of emotion that required him to position a SLAVE nearby, with a musical pipe to remind him, when necessary, to moderate his pitch. In the 1st century BC, the greatest orator was Marcus Tullius Cicero himself. His greatest rival, but later his friend, was Quintus Hortensius Hortalus.

As early as the 5th century BC, Greek oratory had been divided into three types, judicial, deliberative and epideictic. Judicial and deliberative oratory were the first to make their mark at Rome. The lawcourts provided many opportunities for oratory, and, like Cicero, many young men made their first impression in that environment. After the legal system changed in the PRINCIPATE, judicial oratory remained a prominent feature. In the schools, boys would practice by composing *controversiae*, where a law and imagined circumstances, often unusual, were set as topics. Speeches in the political arena belong to deliberative oratory, delivered to recommend action or oppose it. Late in the 1st century BC and thereafter, as the opportunities for political debate declined, students and others might deliver deliberative speeches in an artificial environment, often called *suasoriae*. Epideictic oratory was the application of praise and blame. Little practised outside the schools in the Republican period except in FUNERAL speeches, epideictic oratory became endemic under the principate. PANEGYRICS, the speech of gratitude (*actio gratiarum*) for a consulship, orations to greet the arrival (*adventus*) of a governor, and other forms of public rhetoric fall into this category, as do exhibitions of oratory for no purpose other than to display rhetorical technique. Skilled practitioners sought to impress audiences on such themes as *Eulogy of a Gnat* or *In Praise of Hair*, both topics addressed by DIO CHRYSOSTOM. Speeches of all types practised in the schools or other artificial environments are usually called DECLAMATIONS.

Although Latin oratory continued, most surviving speeches from the principate are Greek. Latin rhetoric, in the Republic, had diverged somewhat from Greek rhetorical theory, but converged again with Greek theory in the 1st century AD. TACITUS' *Dialogue on Orators* addresses this, suggesting that the changes represent a decline, though possibly better technique had resulted. About the same time, QUINTILIAN wrote *On the Education of an Orator*, emphasizing a complete education designed to produce 'a good man skilled in speaking', reflecting the Roman view that rhetorical skill was most valuable in a man of good moral fibre and not an end in itself. The same theme had already been evident in the pronouncements of Cato the Elder and Cicero, but featured less prominently in Greek theorists of rhetoric.

A considerable body of ancient work on Latin rhetoric is extant. The earliest is the *De inventione* (*On Invention*) written by Cicero, probably during his schooldays, and left incomplete. Book 1 discusses the parts of an oration, while book 2 treats the three kinds of oratory. A work of slightly later date is the *Rhetorica ad Herennium* (*Rhetoric to Herennius*), a more complete treatment, written by an unknown hand and addressed to a Gaius Herennius who cannot be identified. In 55, Cicero composed *De oratore* (*On the Orator*) as a dialogue between several outstanding orators, who discuss both elements of rhetoric and the qualities required by orators. Some years later, in the mid-40s, Cicero's *Brutus* outlined the history of rhetoric at Rome, while his *Orator* covers much of the same ground as *De oratore*. Many of Cicero's own speeches survive in whole or in part. Early in the 1st century AD, Seneca the Elder collected a large number of themes and treatments into his *Controversiae* and *Suasoriae*, many of which survive, and offer some critique as well. These works provide the best evidence for rhetoric as practised in the early imperial period, in combination with two collections of declamations preserved under the name of Quintilian, but possibly not his work. Tacitus and Quintilian wrote on rhetoric, as has been observed, and Aulus Gellius, a generation later, preserves portions of speeches of bygone days and comments on them. Other than Pliny the Younger's *Panegyric* on the emperor Trajan, few Latin speeches of imperial date survive in their entirety until the panegyrics of the late 3rd and the 4th centuries AD. Other Latin writers treated rhetoric, but their works are minimally extant. JV

See Kennedy, G. (1972) *The Art of Rhetoric in the Roman World 300 BC–AD 300.*

Rhine The river Rhine (anc. Rhenus) has at all times been one of the great highways of Europe. Rising high in the Raetian Alps, where the Furka pass links the upper valley of the Rhine with that of the Rhône, it flows into the Bodensee and thence westwards to Basel, where it turns north on its long journey to the North sea. Its total length is 1,320 km (825 miles). The name is Indo-European and first appears in Caesar's *Gallic War*, book 1, where Caesar claims that the Rhine is the boundary between the Celts (or Gauls) and the Germans. Archaeology, however, suggests that it was never a linguistic or cultural boundary: it was the Romans who made it a frontier.

The Rhine and its major tributaries like the Moselle were important trade and supply routes throughout the Roman period. Guilds of shippers are attested, it was paramount for army supply, and the Romans maintained a fleet of patrol vessels with headquarters at Cologne (Colonia Claudia Ara Agrippinensium). They dug canals and built dykes to improve navigation, including a channel linking the lower Rhine with the Zuider Zee to give access to the Frisian coast. Ships from the mouth of the Rhine carried military supplies and civilian trade to Britain. From the reign of Augustus the left bank of the river was the site of several legionary bases, under whose stimulus towns grew up, of which Cologne was the greatest. Most of the major cities along the Rhine today trace their origin to Roman times. CMW

Germany and the Germans: (a).

Rhodes (Rhodos) The largest island of the Dodecanese in the south-east Aegean, Rhodes hosted Minoan settlements and Mycenaean colonies in the 2nd millennium BC. When the Dorian Greeks arrived in the so-called Dark Ages, habitation centred on three cities, Ialysos, Kameiros and Lindos. These grew into prosperous, independent city-states during the archaic and classical periods.

In 408/7 BC, the three cities synoikized and founded a new federal capital, also called Rhodos, at the northern tip of the island in Ialysian territory. The reasons for the synoikism are not certain, but the new city was ideally placed for trade between east and west, and commercial interests were served by the development of five harbours. Rhodes gained control of several Dodecanese islands and areas of the mainland opposite (the *peraia*).

Wealthy and influential, Rhodes remained independent from the main hellenistic empires during the 3rd century, though it was much influenced by the vicissitudes of international politics and the growing power of Rome. Finally Rhodes became an uneasy ally of Rome in 164, with no further autonomous foreign policy. Civic and intellectual life continued to flourish. Rhodes was an important centre of Stoic philosophy, and several Romans (including Cicero) studied there. One of the most famous statues of all antiquity was the Colossus (Kolossos) of Rhodes, a 33 m (108 ft) tall bronze statue of the city's patron god Helios, erected to commemorate its escape from a siege in 305/4 BC and felled by an earthquake 80 years later. (see also Philon of Byzantion; Seven Wonders) EER

See Berthold, R.M. (1984) *Rhodes in the Hellenistic Age*; Gabrielsen, V. (1997) *The Naval Aristocracy of Hellenistic Rhodes*; Gabrielsen, V., ed. (1999) *Hellenistic Rhodes*; Mee, C. (1982) *Rhodes in the Bronze Age*.

 Aegean sea: (a).

Rhône Originating in a source in the Swiss Alps through Lake Geneva, the river Rhône (anc. Rhodanus) is fed by the Saône (Arar) at Lyon (Lugdunum). It traverses some 900 km (550 miles) before debouching into the Mediterranean. Recent scientific and archaeological research indicates that the river was hydrologically stable, for the most part, between the 3rd century BC and 4th century AD, though there appears to have been heavy flooding on the upper Rhône in the Julio-Claudian period. Sedimentation in the Rhône delta was a contributing factor in Marius' decision to dig a canal (*fossa Mariana*) from the Grand Rhône to a point near Fos on the coast. The river constituted a major commercial and communications route between the Mediterranean, the lower Rhône valley and central Gaul, particularly after the foundation of Marseilles (Massalia) in the 6th century BC. In the Roman period a number of Roman cities were established on or near its banks, most notably Arles (Arelate), Avignon (Avennio), Orange (Aurasio), Vienne (Vienna), Valence (Valentia) and Lyon. Heavy trade and inland transport on the river was controlled by an association known as *nautae Rhodanici et Ararici* (*CIL* 13.1688 and elsewhere) centred on Arles and Lyon. Trade declined along the upper Rhône in late antiquity but remained active along the lower Rhône and centred on Arles. RBH

Gaul: (b).

Ricimer see generalissimos.

riots Type of protest, including both actual violence and the threat of violence, to make known grievances and express opinions. Riots were often spontaneous forms of collective behaviour. In some periods, such

RIOTS: schematic drawing of a famous Pompeian wall-painting depicting the historic riot of AD 59 in and around the town's amphitheatre, between local men and visiting spectators from Nola.

as in imperial Rome, they constituted an almost tacitly recognized form of social protest. They were frequently characterized by symbolic actions, such as burning a hated politician's house to protest his policies, breaking a lictor's *fasces* as a sign of disrespect for authority, pelting the EMPEROR with bread during a grain shortage, and mass chanting of demands. Causes of riots were many, but they often began at public spectacles where large numbers of people were gathered. The riots at the funeral of JULIUS CAESAR, which resulted in the burning of the SENATE house, are a case in point, as is the fighting that broke out at the POMPEII AMPHITHEATRE in AD 59. Riots seem to have been more characteristic of large cities in the Roman world, though they were not unknown in Greece, particularly during the hellenistic period. Perhaps the most destructive ancient riot was the *Nika* riot at CONSTANTINOPLE in AD 532, which began in the hippodrome, resulted in days of rioting and the burning of much of the city, and was only quelled by the army massacring thousands of people. It derived its name from the racing factions' habitual shouts of *nika* ('victory'). (see also CIVIL STRIFE; REVOLUTION) GSA

See Lintott, A. (1982) *Violence, Civil Strife, and Revolution in the Classical City 750–330 BC*; Nippel, W. (1995) *Public Order in Ancient Rome*; Vanderbroeck, P. (1987) *Popular Leadership and Collective Behavior in the Late Roman Republic.*

risk see BANKING; MONEY LENDING; SHIPS AND SHIPBUILDING; TRADE; TRANSPORT.

rites of passage Rituals which mark and validate crucial stages of transition in a person's life. These are radical and permanent changes of status, such as the passage from life to death or the coming to life at birth, as well as transitions of age, social status or religious experience. Rituals of passage are not exclusive traits of ancient societies, as anthropological studies have shown. Their type and duration vary enormously and, in ancient societies, participation in some of them was subject to social status in forms such as CITIZENSHIP and wealth. A distinct feature of such rituals is their preparatory character for the attainment of a future, usually non-reversible, role or aim at the end of the transition.

Depending on the type of transition, and particularly in cases of birth and death, the issue of RITUAL POLLUTION was taken seriously into account. To avert pollution, various PURIFICATORY procedures were integrated into the rites accompanying such transitions. In transitions of the social status of age, the candidates often underwent a process of a segregation from everyday life that transformed them from their previous identity, in order to be reintroduced effectively into society under a new status. As such, one may mention a variety of rites for adolescents, both girls and boys, or processes of initiation in religious cults, such as the ancient MYSTERIES. EP

See Bruit Zaidman, L. and Schmitt Pantel, P. (1989) *Religion in the Ancient Greek City*; Van Gennep, A. (1960) *The Rites of Passage.*

ritual

A system of practices and behaviours employed in different cultures to fulfil specific aims on behalf of the community. Almost everywhere, rituals consist of representational behaviour in the form of symbolic acts which are intelligible to the people of a particular community. RELIGION was a major domain of human life which made extensive use of rituals with the goal of establishing regular and effective communication with the divine. In the context of ancient societies, the true meaning of rituals is sometimes very hard for the modern student to decipher. They functioned as a language which was so deeply embedded in its immediate social and political background that, even if the latter is partially known to us, we may still not be able to assess precisely the entire frame of ideological cues associated with ritual acts.

A range of ritual practices is known to have formed part of ancient Greek cults. Vase representations and textual evidence, and particularly the so-called sacred CALENDARS, offer valuable glimpses into procedures, requirements and dates of many rituals which usually formed part of religious festivals. Their nature and structure varied depending on chronological period and locality, as well as the type and popularity of the divinity worshipped. Ritual was a public demonstration of worship, and the very act was a way of 'acknowledging the GODS' (*nomizein tous theous*). As such, its role was vital for the promotion of many functions of the Greek city-state (*polis*), in connection with the state's aims of safeguarding and preserving the lives and interests of its people under divine patronage. Religious ritual literally framed the everyday operations of basic civic institutions, such as court sessions, the people's ASSEMBLIES, ELECTION procedures for MAGISTRATES and other actions. It added lustre and purpose to basic state functions, and above all contributed significantly to the perception of the state's role and concern for the people on the part of the citizens themselves. Religious ritual culminated in the celebration of FESTIVALS that

RITUAL: shrine to the domestic gods (*lararium*) from the House of the Menander at Pompeii. Such shrines were the focus of much domestic ritual activity in Roman households.

contained a series of ritual acts of varying nature and duration. It engaged a large number of people from the civic community, including men and women, different age groups, citizens, foreigners and even SLAVES. State officials were primarily responsible for organizing public rituals and for appointing religious personnel for them. At the same time, most of them were involved in the festivities of the ritual proper, along with the rest of participants, who were called to perform religious roles often quite distinct from their actual roles and status in real life. However, this 'anomaly' found its ultimate justification in the essential purpose of religious ritual, of which everyone was aware: to delight and propitiate the gods for the collective good. Some of these roles included the exclusive participation of women in some festivals (notably in honour of DEMETER), their free access to a wide range of public rituals (such as PRIESTHOODS), and the participation of slaves along with citizens.

Ritual behaviour, as a means of social communication highlighting common identity and culture, also served the more private needs of communal life. Different ritual actions were standard components of a range of major events or phases in the life of the members of a HOUSEHOLD (*oikos*), such as a wedding, birth or death. Routine worship of the gods within a household centred around the domestic hearth. Further rituals encompassed age transitions or transitions of status, such as coming of age for girls and boys in different states and the registration of young men in the catalogues of their districts (known as DEMES in Athens) or their *polis*. Major collective undertakings, such as WAR, HUNTING, AGRICULTURAL activities, the founding of a colony or the aversion of a natural disaster, were framed by appropriate sets of ritual acts.

Ordinary rituals comprised a basic range of acts that were practised on a panhellenic scale. These included PRAYERS, libations (*spondai*), offerings of first-fruits (*aparchai*), PROCESSIONS (*pompai*), ritual meals, SACRIFICES (*thysiai*), PURIFICATION and supplication. More complex ritual processes took place on special religious occasions. For instance, initiation (*myêsis*) was part of the MYSTERY CULTS that reached their peak of popularity in the 5th century BC, or of special rituals associated with foreign cults, many of which arrived in Greece by the same time. The sacrificial ritual was perhaps the most distinctively Greek way of offering the gods their due. Sacrifice essentially consisted of the ritual slaughter of one or more ANIMAL victims. It was preceded by prayers, procession and acts to purify the victims, and was concluded with the consumption of the cooked MEAT of the victim by those performing and those attending the ritual. The part of the animal to be offered to the gods was left on the altar to burn completely; the rest of the meat was distributed among the participating officials, priests and people according to established rules. Chthonic divinities including HEROES received a different type of sacrifice known as a holocaust (*holokauston*,'wholly burnt'). Here the entire victim was left to burn completely on a lower altar (known as an *eschara*) after its blood had been collected in a hole in the ground. Bloodless sacrifices were also practised, by consecrating natural products at the altar of a god. These were offerings of different sorts, such as cakes, FRUITS, VEGETABLES, grains or cooked meals.

The setting of Greek ritual was generally simple, but varied as much as the acts themselves. Religious places could be as simple as an open-air altar, or could take the more complex form of a sanctuary, TEMPLE or graveside. Alternatively, they could display more spatial flexibility, extending to secular SPACE, public or private. This was quite common, for instance, with festivals, which comprised long sequences of ritual events often lasting several days, and with more secular rituals like weddings. EP

See Bremmer, J. N. (1994) *Greek Religion*; Bruit Zaidman, L. and Schmitt Pantel, P. (1989) *Religion in the Ancient Greek City*; Burkert, W. (1985) *Greek Religion*.

The basic rituals of the Romans were in essence the same as those found in other MEDITERRANEAN traditions. They centred on the presentation of offerings, and on communication to and from the GODS – PRAYER and divination. The former took many different forms. A worshipper might burn incense, place FLOWERS or cakes on an altar, or make a libation (pour a liquid, usually WINE, onto an altar or the ground). The most important offering was the SACRIFICE of an ANIMAL, for which Roman tradition specified a fairly strict format. Typically, it began with the procession of the participants and victims to the altar, where the sacrificer, his TOGA draped over his head, made a preliminary offering of wine and incense. He then said a prayer dedicating the animal to the god, while pouring wine on its forehead and sprinkling a special salted flour on its back. At this point specialist attendants (not the sacrificer himself) slaughtered the animal and the sacrificer inspected the organs to determine whether the offering was acceptable to the god. The attendants prepared the organs, which were burnt on the altar, and the rest of the flesh was made available for human consumption; most sacrifices concluded with a banquet.

Roman prayers included, as a minimum, an invocation, specifying the deity by name and epithet, and a request for a particular benefit. In many cases this was accompanied by an offering, apparently with the idea that a gift would make the deity more disposed to grant the request. Prayers in which an offering was promised at a later date were called VOWS, and developed a quasi-contractual form: if the god granted the request, the person was obliged to fulfil the promise. Vows played a significant role in both public and private cult. The typically Roman form of divination was the taking of auspices. Romans also made use of the ETRUSCAN tradition of haruspicy, divination from inspecting the organs of sacrificed animals, for which they employed Etruscan specialists.

Ritual was generally not a major feature of private life. Although the Romans believed that in ancient times auspices were taken before private as well as public enterprises, by the historical period this practice had disappeared. Unlike in many other cultures, religious ceremonies did not mark the major transitions of life: birth, coming of age, MARRIAGE and death. Weddings, for example, involved a number of ritualized elements, such as the flame-red veil worn by the bride, the joining of hands by bride and groom, and the procession escorting the bride to her new home; but they were generally not religious occasions. The major contexts for private ritual were instead domestic cult and the cult of the dead. In Republican times the former centred on the hearth (VESTA) and the protectors of the storeroom, the Penates, to whom the head of the HOUSEHOLD offered food and drink during the main meal. Houses of the imperial period often included small shrines to the Lares and the *genius* (divine alter ego) of the head of the household, at which members of the household might make small offerings. People would likewise bring offerings of flowers and food to the graves of family members and patrons, both on particular anniversaries and especially during the Parentalia of 13–21 February. Otherwise, the most common occasions for religious ritual in private life were *ad hoc*. Inscribed dedications to a wide range of deities indicate the frequency with which private individuals made vows for recovery from illness, safe childbirth, successful journeys and other matters of HEALTH and prosperity.

In contrast, ritual was a pervasive feature of public life. Public officials took the auspices before BATTLES, ASSEMBLIES of the people and meetings of the SENATE; unfavourable signs would necessitate a postponement. Officials were also responsible for public vows. Some were annual, such as those on 1 January for the well-being of the state and, later, on 3 January for that of the EMPEROR. Others were irregular: in Republican times it was a common response to crisis for an official to vow a public cult for a new deity. The dedication of a new TEMPLE had its own precise ritual: a MAGISTRATE grasped the door-post and repeated without slip or hesitation a formula dictated by a pontiff (*pontifex*), one of the PRIESTS of Rome. Once established, most public cults consisted of prescribed prayers and sacrifices on an annual basis. Some also involved performances or contests (*ludi*), such as plays or mimes, CHARIOT RACES and eventually GLADIATORIAL combats or wild beast hunts. These major spectacles often included other elements, such as sacrifices or elaborate processions of public officials and deities, represented by statues or symbols. Another complex public ritual was the *lustrum*, a ceremony of purification. In this the presiding figures, together with the means of purification, usually sacrificial victims, went in a circular procession around the people or place to be purified; it was normally accompanied by MUSIC and ended with a sacrifice. The Roman calendar also contained a number of archaic rituals with odd and poorly understood features. The Lupercalia, for example, began with the sacrifice of GOATS and a dog in an ancient cave, after which the members of a special priestly college, naked except for goatskin girdles, ran around the Palatine striking WOMEN with goatskin thongs.

Although the same basic rituals were common to both private and public life, public rituals were much more extensive and complex, distinguished by a meticulous concern for form and correctness of detail. This was also a characteristic of the Roman legal tradition, with which the ritual tradition had much in common. The importance of precise and correct ritual explains the need for bodies of experts, the priests in their colleges, who were responsible for maintaining this mass of detailed prescriptions. JBR

See Ogilvie, R. M. (1969) *The Romans and their Gods in the Age of Augustus*; Ryberg, I. S. (1955) *Rites of the Roman State Religion in Art*; Scullard, H. H. (1981) *Festivals and Ceremonies of the Roman Republic.*

 SACRIFICE: (b)–(c).

rivers A highly utilized natural resource in the Greek and Roman world. Although there are few major river systems in Greece, many cities such as Athens and Sparta had their origins alongside small waterways. In contrast, the GEOGRAPHY of the Roman world is distinguished by numerous major rivers, such as the Po (Padus in Latin) and RHÔNE (Rhodanus). Many Roman cities were located on major rivers, including the city of Rome itself, which lay on the banks of the Tiber (Tiberis). As is typical in antiquity, the turbulent and unpredictable nature of rivers led to a widespread belief in river gods. The EPIC poets (such as Hesiod, *Theogony* 362–70) describe how rivers were the offspring of Okeanos, the personification of the body of water encircling the earth. Many rivers figured prominently in MYTHOLOGY. The Skamandros (Scamander) near TROY became a combatant against ACHILLES (Homer, *Iliad* 21.211–382). The water of the Alpheios, the largest river in the PELOPONNESE, was fabled to flow under the sea, rising in the fountain of Arethousa (Arethusa) in SICILY (STRABO 6.2.4). The most notorious of all mythological rivers is the Styx, whose ferryman, Charon, transported the souls of the dead across its waters to HADES, never to return to the land of the living. Reverence for river gods continued well into the Roman period, when striking images of river deities appear, such as that of the DANUBE on TRAJAN'S COLUMN.

As in modern times, rivers linked distant regions, facilitating TRADE and communication. The Tiber was critical in the movement of goods from the HARBOUR at OSTIA to the city of Rome; barges laden with imported goods plied its waters, bound for the riverbank WAREHOUSES. Many rivers were difficult to navigate because of strong currents or variable water levels. In Italy, the water hazards of the Po hindered river traffic further inland than Turin. The Bagradas (mod. Medjerda) made possible the transport of MARBLE from QUARRIES in central Tunisia to the coast, albeit only in the rainy winter months. Several rivers are particularly significant as boundary markers. The longest river in Greece, the Acheloös, served as the frontier between AITOLIA and Akarnania. Similarly, the north-eastern limit of the ROMAN EMPIRE was largely determined by the line of the RHINE and Danube. Rivers provided water, for both drinking and irrigation. The annual inundation of the NILE valley provided not only ample moisture but also fertile silt; both were necessary for producing abundant crops. In the Roman period, the energy potential of rivers was exploited, resulting in water-driven grain MILLS; several archaeological examples are known, including the BARBEGAL mill in France and the Simitthus mill in Tunisia. TJA

roads

To build roads in Greece is often desperately difficult. Especially in central Greece and the PELOPONNESE, all land journeys of medium or long distance, and many short ones, require the traveller to negotiate passes, sometimes very steep. Neighbouring cities were often separated by passes; difficulty of communication was one reason for the rise of distinct *poleis*. By contrast, roads in plains encroached on precious agricultural land: they might be dusty in summer and made impassable by mud in winter. Even as late as the period of the Turkish occupation, a paved road (mod. Greek *kalderími*: there is a good example above the stadium at DELPHI) might be wide enough to carry wagon traffic, but often there was room only for pack ANIMALS. Literary sources may reveal ancient routes, but to identify and date preserved road surfaces is a more difficult task, with which little progress has been made. Even the extent to which classical Greeks felt the need for roads is unclear.

Communications within a city's territory were important. PEISISTRATOS' grandson of the same name established an altar in the ATHENIAN AGORA as the centre of the Attic road network; earlier, the tyrant's son Hipparchos placed inscribed stones at the halfway points between various places in ATTICA and the city. Xenokles was praised in 321/0 BC for providing a stone BRIDGE at ELEUSIS for the safety of the inhabitants and the farmers. A 5th-century milestone is known from THASOS. Since Greeks often lived in nucleated settlements and farmed land some way off, roads of a sort, perhaps even wagon roads, were needed in cultivated territory. The heaviest weights carried were blocks of STONE (sometimes pulled by as many as 38 pairs of oxen). Significantly, the accounts for the PARTHENON refer to the construction of a road to move MARBLE.

Roads in cities were of doubtful quality, and even close to the Athenian Agora they might be muddy. *Koprologoi* ('dung-collectors') performed an important role. Five *hodopoioi* (road-makers) kept them in repair, but excavation suggests that the surfaces were not paved, but at best made of packed earth and gravel. The Panathenaic Way in Athens has only a short paved section; the remainder is packed pebbles. Even when SMYRNA was magnificently built and given paved roads in the late 4th century, they had no sewers. Excavated roads in cities normally range between 3 and 5 m (10 and 16 ft) wide; gradients often reach 15 per cent, twice as steep as is usual now.

Individuals often travelled from one city to another, for example, to visit panhellenic sanctuaries or to sell goods; but the normal method was to go on foot, or at best on (or walking beside) beasts of burden. The importance of roads between cities should not be exaggerated. Cities were often economically nearly self-sufficient. Land transport was probably expensive; that may have been partly because there were few good roads, but it is only in the second half of the 20th century that the inherent difficulties of the Greek LANDSCAPE have been effectively conquered. Brigands were not unknown. Built roads between cities were as likely to facilitate access for an enemy as to assist the arrival of anything desirable; there might be little incentive to build them. There are few references to the use of wagons in the supply trains of Greek armies; some occur in XENOPHON, but in contexts which suggest PERSIAN rather than Greek practice. HERODOTOS was impressed by the Persian road system precisely because of its contrast with Greece.

Especially in mountain passes on routes between cities where the land was not exploited for AGRICULTURE, road surfaces might be rudimentary if they were made at all. There was no lack of engineering skill: already c.600 BC Periandros (Periander), tyrant of Corinth, built a specialized road to transport SHIPS across the Corinthian isthmus. This was the *diolkos* ('drag-way'), a paved surface with large squared blocks and cut grooves for wagon wheels; in the 5th century it carried triremes. Nothing remotely similar has been found elsewhere. There may often have been no built surface to a road: early modern travellers in Greece, such as Leake, often used 'roads' that were stream beds, and a similar practice is likely enough in antiquity. Such 'roads' were often impassable in winter. Many passes certainly used in the classical period show no sign of anything better than paths.

The earliest form of engineering for wagon roads was probably the cutting of ruts in the native rock to guide cart-wheels, improving traction and giving stability. Ruts are usually impossible to date, but some are associated with settlements not known to have been occupied after the classical period. They occur in many places, including between Eleusis and MEGARA and between Sparta and MESSENIA over Mt Taÿgetos. Ruts in a given stretch of road have the same gauge over considerable distances. Gauges differ somewhat from one case to another, but there seems to have been a standard of around 1.40 m (55 inches). The depth may be as much as 0.40 m (16 inches) in the roughest terrain; they tend to be concentrated precisely there, where they could make important contributions to stability. Where the

roads, Roman: (a) map of principal roads in Italy.

ROADS, ROMAN: (b) the Via Praenestina, south-east of Rome, is typical of many Italian roads for its hard-wearing surface of basaltic (*selce*) slabs.

ROADS, ROMAN: (c) roads within towns were often well paved, as here at Pompeii (though the stepping stones indicate that the road surface was probably not kept very clean).

natural rock was more amenable it was left unimproved, so that ruts only occur intermittently and usually away from cultivated land. There seems to have been a dense network of these cart-roads in the southern Peloponnese, perhaps reflecting Spartan power as head of the Peloponnesian league, or the economic and military aspirations of individual *poleis*.

Fully paved road surfaces can often be found, but most are Turkish; no example certainly of classical date is known. The pass used in antiquity between Tegea and the Argolid, one of the main roads in the Peloponnese, provides significant evidence. It takes a direct route, far shorter than the modern road or railway. There are two paved surfaces. The Turkish *kalderími* to the south, known as the Stairway of the Bey, systematically uses zigzags and steps to diminish the gradient. An earlier surface, in a different technique, employs fewer zigzags and thus has a steeper gradient – sometimes 25 per cent or more – which is countered for wagon traffic by cross-ramps. The earliest (classical?) road in this spot, upon which PAN appeared to Pheidippides, may have been the stream bed itself. PAUSANIAS characterizes the road here as very good for carriages; yet for a 19th-century traveller it was one of the wildest, bleakest paths in all Greece. JBS

See Pikoulas, Y. A. (1999) The road-network of Arkadia, in T. H. Nielsen and J. Roy, eds., *Defining Ancient Arkadia* 248–319; Pritchett, W. K. (1980–92) *Studies in Ancient Greek Topography*, vols. 3–8.

The GEOGRAPHY of the Roman empire depended on an integrated system of sea, river and road TRANSPORT. The last in many ways created new routes and configurations of geography, which allowed for the expansion of Rome, first across Italy and then across the adjacent land masses of Spain and GAUL beyond the sea-based transport systems of the MEDITERRANEAN. Roads were intimately connected to the very concept of a Roman empire and IMPERIALISM. The end result across the empire was a total of more than 100,000 km (60,000 miles) of roads.

Roads were constructed either by the state, the local town, or by private individuals. Legally a road had to be wide enough to drive a WHEELED VEHICLE (Justinian, *Digest* 8.1.13). Initially, many of the routes incorporated earlier roads, but were formulated into long-distance routes, for example, the Via Latina or the Via Salaria. The decision to construct the first long-distance road was made in the late 4th century BC by APPIUS CLAUDIUS (Livy 9.29). This road, known as the Via Appia, was to connect Rome to CAPUA via a coastal route through the Pomptine marshes. The project included land drainage and facilitated the foundation of colonies at sites such as TARRACINA and Minturnae, and in itself was the first major public work beyond the vicinity of Rome. It is clear that the road was not paved when it was laid out (Livy 10.23; 10.47). Funds for paving roads were acquired from fines placed on those infringing the *lex Licinia*. The quality of road surfaces varied greatly from simple compacted clay, to compacted gravel, to the most sophisticated paved surfaces made from hard-wearing basalt rocks. Later paving and repair were matters for the state, often funded by the emperor, and the Via Appia was even in late antiquity the subject of repair and renewal by the GOTHIC king THEODERIC. Other major roads in Italy followed, for example, the Via Flaminia linking Rome to its colony at Rimini in 220 BC. The road system provided a link between those citizens living in colonies at a distance and the city of Rome itself, which permitted the extension of Roman CITIZENSHIP across SPACE to places at a distance from the capital.

This system of roads and communications that had been established in Italy was extended into the PROVINCES. In Gallia Narbonensis the Via Domitia (the south coast road to Spain) was built in the 2nd century BC. The system extended throughout the provinces by the early 1st century AD. In many ways, the roads created a geography for the empire. All public roads were measured, with inscribed markers up to 3 m (10 ft) high every mile recording distances and who had built or restored the road. These milestones date from the 3rd century BC through to the Gothic king Theoderic. They provide an indication of the repairs undertaken and the need to renew the road (e.g. Via Appia, *CIL* 10.6812–73). In the 1st and 2nd centuries AD, we find an emphasis on the paving of roads for carriages at a cost of about 22 *sestertii* per foot (*ILS* 5875). The high cost of paving did not prevent it from becoming widespread across Italy and being extended to local roads built by towns or villages (*CIL* 5.1008; 10.3913) or by key local figures such as *duumviri* or *augustales* (*CIL* 5.2116; 10.1064). Most roads in the provinces were not paved but were surfaced with compacted gravel.

The design of Roman roads was intended to create an all-weather route that was clearly defined. The ENGINEERING of the route did not simply involve a straight line, as is popularly supposed, but frequently followed ridges and contours to avoid river crossings and valleys. Where BRIDGES were required, they were built, and in some cases tunnels were dug, to create new routes that redefined the physical geography. The system for maintaining roads was apparently established by the late 1st century BC, with a *curator* in charge of the major routes (Cicero, *Letters to Atticus* 1.1.2). JULIUS CAESAR strengthened his political position by spending vast sums of his own money as *curator* of the Via Appia (Plutarch, *Caesar* 5). The system was reformed by AUGUSTUS. Initially, in 27 BC, encouragement was given to SENATORS to repair roads, but this failed to produce effective repairs, apart from Augustus' overhaul of the Via Flaminia. Subsequently, public funds or those of the emperors were utilized for repairs. Further reform was undertaken in 20 BC, when Augustus established the golden milestone in Rome. From this date on, *curatores* were drawn from the ex-PRAETORS and attended to the repair and construction of roads in Italy. Repairs were subcontracted, and were the subject of corruption. The LABOUR for road repairs was often provided by convicts in both Italy and the provinces, but the *possessores* of adjacent lands also made a major contribution (*Digest* 49.18.4; *ILS* 5875). There was a strict definition of a repair to a road: it restored the structure to its former condition; for example, paving was to be replaced by paving as opposed to gravel, and the width of the road was not to be changed (*Digest* 43.11.1).

The purpose of road building has been debated, and recently there has been a significant move away from the orthodoxy of the 1970s that road building and improvement had no significant impact on the economy of the Roman empire. It has been argued that significant gains were made in terms of time, allowing goods and people to travel further in a single day. There is a clearly identified preference for property in places with easy road access (Varro, *On Agriculture* 1.16; Pliny the Elder, *Natural History* 18.26). It is notable that roads such as the Via Claudia Augusta linked river systems together – the Po to the Danube – and we should regard roads, RIVERS and CANALS and the sea as a complementary network of communications. The system of measured distance allowed for the prediction of journey times and the ability to communicate via letters between two persons on the move (e.g. Cicero, *Letters to Atticus* 5.2, 5.3). Further evidence of the intersection of time and distance can be found in the *Antonine Itineraries* and the *RAVENNA COSMOGRAPHY*, which cover the whole empire. Roads were a major feature of the LANDSCAPE of the Roman empire, as well as one of the objects of greatest expenditure by the state. The commemorative ARCHES (such as that of Augustus at Rimini) and the milestones promoted an image of the emperor as the restorer of roads and order to the world, whether it be Augustus or the emperors of late antiquity.

After antiquity, many of the major routes across Europe were based on the roads of the Roman empire (for example, the Via Flaminia in Italy, or Ermine Street in England). The excavation of sections of Roman roads was an influence on later road builders, most notably Thomas Telford in the 18th century. The imagery of the Roman road SURVEYOR providing new routes was an image reinvented in Fascist Italy with the building of the Appia Nova and other routes. The intention to include a section of the Via Appia within the continuously proposed and reproposed archaeological park in Rome points up this road's cultural significance. Milestones from the Via Appia had been reused in Michelangelo's entrance to the Campidoglio. The Via Appia is also featured in numerous films set in antiquity. Roman roads are thus a significant part of the cultural landscape of the classical tradition. RL

See Adams, C. and Laurence, R., eds. (2001) *Travel and Geography in the Roman Empire*; Chevallier, R. (1976) *Roman Roads*; Davies, H. (2002) *Roads in Roman Britain*; Laurence, R. (1999) *The Roads of Roman Italy*.

 EPIGRAPHY, ROMAN: (c).

Roma Roman goddess (*Dea Roma*), both a personification of Rome and a deification of the power of the Roman state and its people. In early Greek legend, *Rhômê* is a Trojan refugee who accompanies AENEAS to Italy. Fed up with wandering, she precipitates the founding of the city named after her by inciting her fellow women EXILES to burn the Trojans' ships. She is later said to marry Latinus (or Aeneas). Her connection with the cult of Roma, however, is debated.

Worship of Roma, originating in Asia Minor in the 2nd century BC, displayed some features of hellenistic ruler cults and proliferated in the wake of Rome's military successes. TEMPLES and statues were erected in Roma's honour, and sacrifices and offerings were regularly performed by her (usually male) officiants. Her festival, the *Rhômaia*, featured ATHLETIC, MUSICAL and dramatic competitions. While the cult was popular in the Greek East, it was slow to come to Rome and the Western PROVINCES, and did not begin to assume prominence until the early empire. Under AUGUSTUS, Roma was deployed as a political and religious symbol designed, like the IMPERIAL CULT, to unify the empire. It is only with HADRIAN that a temple, priesthood and cult of Roma actually become established in Rome.

In iconography, Roma assimilates features of ATHENA and the AMAZONS, usually appearing as a stately, armed and helmeted figure (as on the *Gemma Augustea*). JRCC

See Beard, M. et al. (1998) *Religions of Rome*; Mellor, R. (1981) The goddess Roma, *ANRW* II.17.2: 950–1030.

Roman empire One of the largest and longest-lived empires in human history, the very attributes of which make it hard to generalize about. The empire was a multi-faceted institution and changed hugely over time. It can be defined variously in terms of its chronology, its geography, its system of government, its people and its culture. Only CHINA can match it for scale and beat it for longevity in the pre-industrial ages. At its height in the 2nd century AD the Roman empire approached 4 million sq km (1.5 million sq miles) in area, stretching from the ATLANTIC to the Euphrates, from Scotland to the Sahara. It encompassed all the lands bordering the MEDITERRANEAN and all the Mediterranean ISLANDS (the only time in history that this has been achieved), as well as much of central and western Europe up to, and in places beyond, the great river systems of the RHINE and DANUBE. The population of this vast territory was also large (a common estimate is c.60 million people by the mid-2nd century AD – a huge total for a pre-industrial society) and was culturally and ethnically very diverse. The impact of Rome on the development of Western civilization was immense, not least because the Romans succeeded, by dint of conquest, to the Greek CITY-STATES, the empires of ALEXANDER and CARTHAGE, and parts of the PERSIAN–PARTHIAN state. The culture and society of Rome built on this heritage and, for instance, much of what was rediscovered in the RENAISSANCE of Greek art and ARCHITECTURE was mediated by its transmission via Roman copies and imitations.

The evolution of the Roman empire was a long process, but is generally seen as a product of its wars of expansion outside Italy from the mid-3rd century BC onwards. The PUNIC WARS with Carthage were the crucial test of the early phase, but eventually brought about a string of overseas territories (SARDINIA, SICILY, HISPANIA and later part of North AFRICA). The 2nd century BC saw the rapid widening of overseas conflicts to other hellenistic kingdoms of the eastern Mediterranean. Military success over MACEDONIA and SYRIA were to bring in undreamed of wealth for the embellishment of the city and to the commanders sent to the East. The expansionism was in part driven by the ambitions of Rome's leading men, straining the Republican system of government to breaking point. The subjugation and provincialization of the eastern Mediterranean was completed in the 1st century, in part by POMPEY the Great. In the West, JULIUS CAESAR was responsible for the major addition of GAUL to the European territory and for enlarging the African territory at the expense of the Numidian kingdom. When the REPUBLIC disintegrated into CIVIL WAR, the empire endured and grew. The concluding act of the civil wars in 30 BC was the addition of Ptolemaic Egypt, marking the start of a long phase of expansionism on behalf of the first EMPEROR (*princeps*) AUGUSTUS. The fiction of the restored Republic is reflected in the division of PROVINCES between those nominally under the control of the SENATE and those whose GOVERNORS were appointed directly by the emperor (mainly those with military garrisons). Although Augustus allegedly counselled his successor TIBERIUS to keep the empire within its then established limits, having endured major setbacks in his attempt to conquer and hold territory well beyond the Rhine in GERMANY, several later emperors were responsible for significant advances of imperial territory. CLAUDIUS added BRITAIN and Mauretania; VESPASIAN annexed numerous client kingdoms and pushed frontiers forward in several provinces; TRAJAN conquered DACIA, ARABIA and briefly MESOPOTAMIA; and SEPTIMIUS SEVERUS advanced frontiers and again established provinces beyond the Euphrates.

In the early period, the expansion of the empire was both territorial and hegemonical, with many peoples beyond the directly controlled territory acknowledging Roman suzerainty through TREATIES. The POETS of the Augustan age spoke of an empire without limits (*imperium sine fine*), reflecting the self-confidence and acquisitiveness of the time. Augustus famously sent reconnaissance missions up the NILE to Sudan, into the Arabian peninsula, down the Red sea towards INDIA and across the Sahara to the land of the GARAMANTES. The military insecurity of later emperors (who could not allow potential rivals to accrue too much military glory) acted as a major brake on expansionism, while logistical practicalities promoted the solidification of FRONTIERS. By the later 2nd century AD, the empire was already being forced onto the defensive by neighbouring peoples, who were attracted by its wealth and growing wise in the Roman way of WARFARE. Despite the well-documented collapse of the Western provinces by the 5th century, the Eastern Byzantine empire had a long afterlife, only ended by its final overthrow by the Turks in 1453.

The creation of the Roman empire depended on the Romans' remarkable propensity for warfare and on their permissive attitude to the expansion of their citizen body through assimilation of subjugated enemies. The latter tendency had two important effects. First, it allowed the Roman ARMY to grow massively in size over time, creating a numerical advantage in terms of potential recruitment over rivals. Despite a series of catastrophic defeats by HANNIBAL in the late 3rd century BC, the ability of the Roman state to raise further armies was a critical factor in its eventual victory. Second, the absorption of other peoples into the empire, and the opening up of avenues for their élite classes to participate more fully in its political and economic opportunities, fuelled further expansion to satisfy the developing aspirations of these people. Had the Roman state continued to be dominated by a narrow oligarchy of Latin descent, it is unlikely that it would have prospered or endured as it did. By the 2nd century many SENATORS came from provinces outside Italy, culminating in 193 when a man of Punic descent, Septimius Severus, became Roman emperor. Many modern empires have proved far less successful at integrating the ruling order of their subjugated peoples into their system of government and society. Nonetheless, this should not blind us to the significance of resistance to the Roman empire, both external and internal.

ROMAN EMPIRE: (a) population of the Roman empire.

Area		AD 14		AD 164	
	(1000 km^2)	Est. population (millions)	Density (per km^2)	Est. population (millions)	Density (per km^2)
Greek East					
Greece	267	2.8	10.5	3	11.2
Anatolia	547	8.2	15	9.2	16.8
Greater Syria	109	4.3	39.4	4.8	44
Cyprus	9.5	0.2	21.2	0.2	21.1
Egypt	28	4.5	160.7	5	178.6
Cyrenaica	15	0.4	26.7	0.6	40
Annexations				0.2	
Total	**975.5**	**20.4**	**20.9**	**23.1**	
Latin West					
Italy	250	7	28	7.6	30.4
Sicily	26	0.6	23.1	0.6	23.1
Sardinia/Corsica	33	0.5	15.2	0.5	15.2
North Africa	400	3.5	8.8	6.5	16.3
Iberia	590	5	8.5	7.5	12.7
Gaul/Germany	635	5.8	9.1	9	14.2
Danube	430	2.7	6.3	4	9.3
Britain				2.5	
Total		**25.1**	**10.6**	**38.2**	
Roman empire		**45.5**	**13.6**	**61.4**	

Adapted from B. Frier in *CAH* vol. 11, 812, 814.

The cultural and linguistic fabric of the empire was extremely heterogeneous, given that it was composed of literally hundreds of earlier states, tribes and peoples. Paradoxically, modern scholarship on the Roman provinces has been built around a tradition of study that emphasizes the degree of sameness achieved, summed up by the term 'romanization', though this is increasingly seen as a flawed concept. While there are common characteristics of Roman GOVERNMENT and SOCIETY, there is increasing interest in the way in which the empire embraced and assimilated diversity. There were numerous fault lines running through the empire; the division between an Eastern empire where the *lingua franca* was Greek, and a Western one where Latin predominated, is the most obvious. But most regions remained strongly polyglot throughout the Roman period. In parts of North Africa, for instance, the Punic language of Carthage was still the dominant dialect, even if now transcribed with the Latin alphabet; in rural districts particularly, LIBYAN (Berber) was widely spoken and written. The Eastern provinces were even more diverse, and apart from Greek and Latin there was a strong tradition of written Hebrew, Syriac, Aramaic, Arabic, Palmyrene, Nabataean and so on. The practice of RELIGION was another area of huge regional diversity, and although there are well-documented instances of cults spreading from one province to another, encouraged by the polytheistic tendencies of the Roman state, the regional mix often reflected considerable continuity of pre-existing practices. Even in the use of material culture we can detect major differences between provinces and peoples, though certain groups, such as the army, stand out as developing a more widespread communal IDENTITY. However, there were myriad possibilities for the construction of a 'Roman identity' across the provinces, and these reflected the multiple understandings that its subjects could form of the nature of the Roman empire itself. (see pp. 764–5) DJM

See CAH vols. 7–14 (1989–2005); Goodman, M. (1997) *The Roman World 44 BC–AD 180*; Harris, W.V. (1979) *War and Imperialism in Republican Rome*; Lintott, A. (1993) *Imperium Romanum: politics and administration*; Wells, C. (1992) *The Roman Empire*.

 PROVINCES AND PROVINCIAL GOVERNMENT, ROMAN (fig. and table).

romance see NOVELS; SEXUALITY.

Rome The city of Rome was the political capital and ideological centre of a geographic and political empire that eventually incorporated much of Europe, ASIA Minor, the Middle East and North AFRICA. According to later legends, it was founded in 753 BC by ROMULUS AND REMUS, whose ancestry included AENEAS and the GODDESS VENUS. Initially a VILLAGE like many others, Rome was not the first settlement at the site; ARCHAEOLOGICAL evidence, naturally difficult to

ROMAN EMPIRE: (b) the Western provinces in the mid-2nd century.

ROMAN EMPIRE: (c) the Eastern provinces in the mid-2nd century.

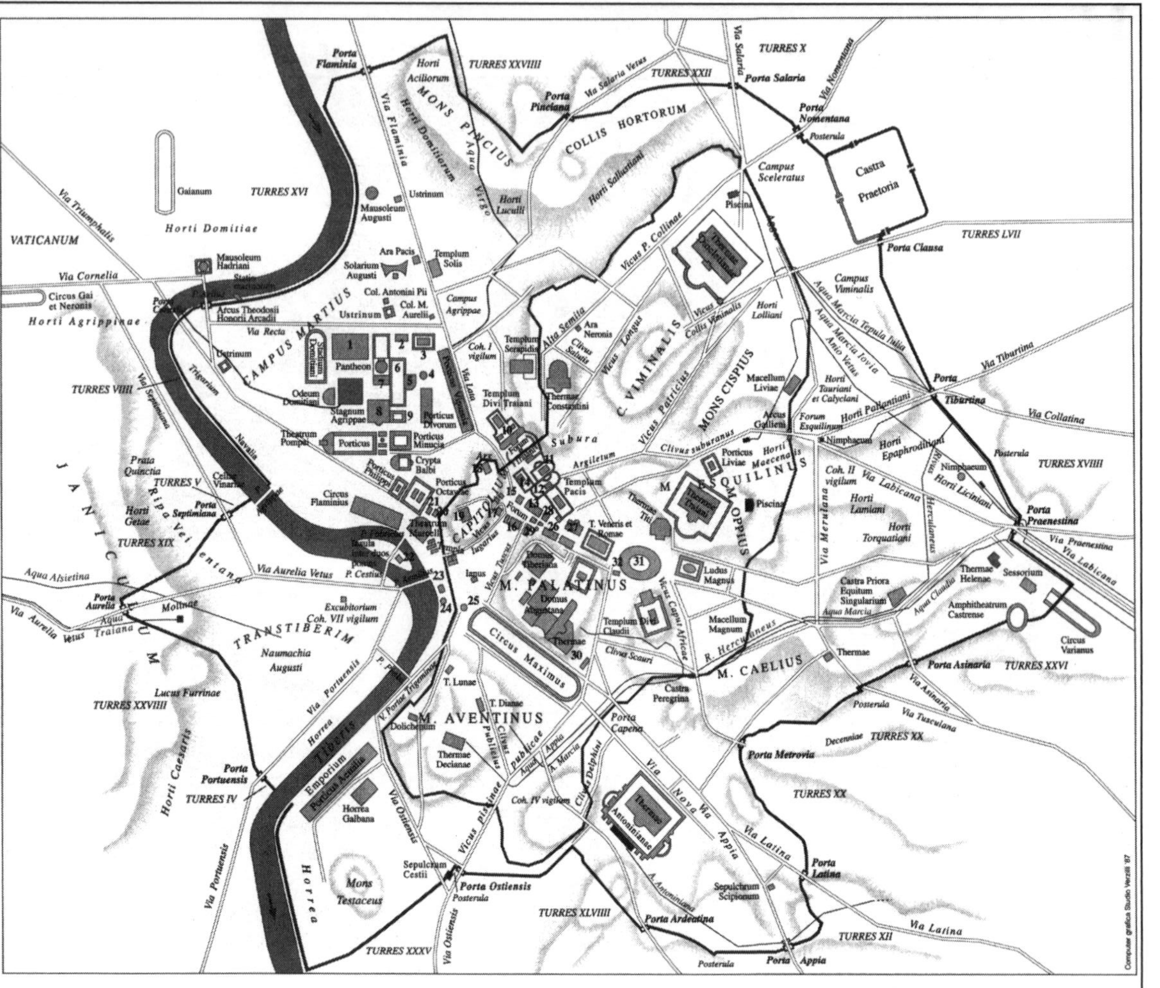

Rome: (a) plan of ancient Rome, showing major monuments, the hills, roads, the Aurelianic walls (outer circuit) and the Servian walls (inner). Key to most significant numbered structures: 1. baths of Nero; 3. temple of Hadrian; 6. Saepta; 7. basilica of Neptune; 8. baths of Agrippa; 9. Diribitorium; 10. Trajan's column; 11. forum of Augustus; 12. Forum Transitorium; 13. Basilica Paulli; 14. forum of Caesar; 15. Curia; 16. Basilica Julia; 17. temple of Vespasian; 18. temple of Juno Moneta; 19. Capitoline temple; 21. temple of Apollo Sosianus; 22. temple of Aesculapius; 23. temple of Portunus; 24. temple of Hercules; 26. House of the Vestals and temple of Vesta; 27. Basilica Nova; 28. temple of Antoninus and Faustina; 29. temple of Castor; 30. Septizodium (or Septizonium); 31. Colosseum; 32. arch of Constantine

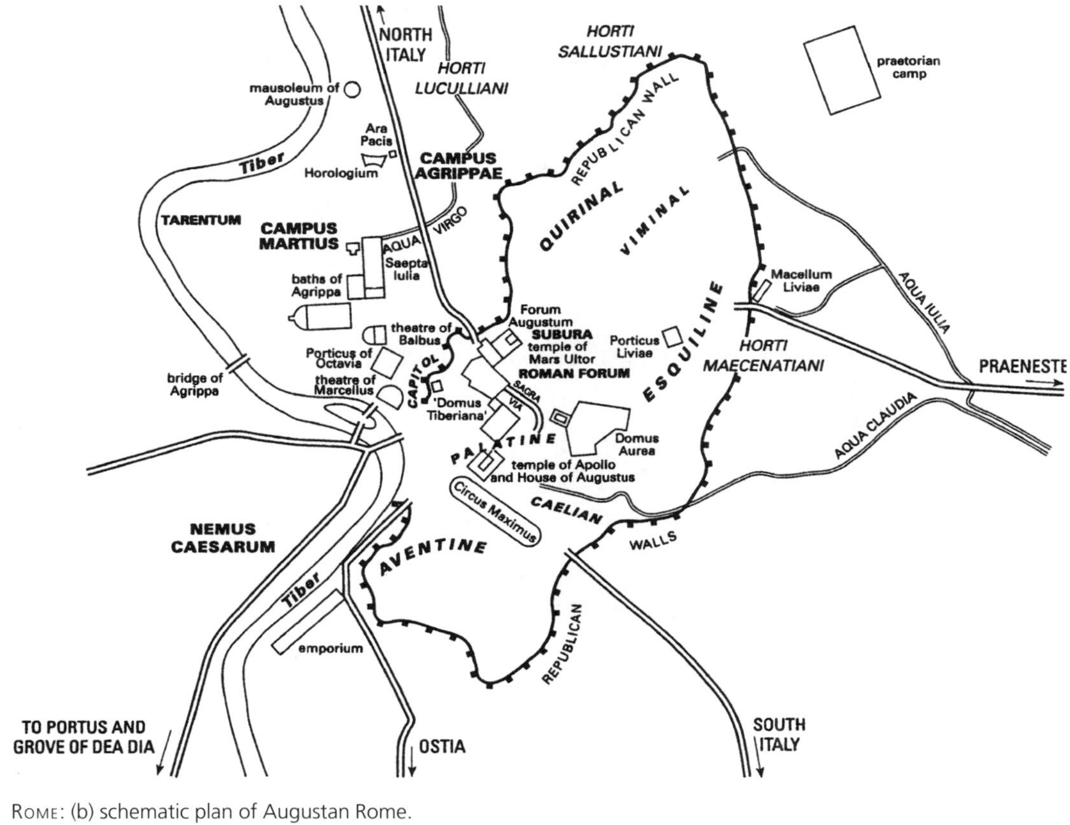

Rome: (b) schematic plan of Augustan Rome.

obtain from a living city, indicates previous habitation going back some centuries. Under some influence from Etruria and the Etruscans when it was governed by kings (753–509 bc), Rome became a Republic with the election of consuls in 509. Especially from the 4th century onwards but beginning earlier, Rome's influence expanded rapidly, first within Italy and subsequently throughout the Mediterranean world. To govern all this territory, the Romans developed a system of provinces with governors. After the rise to power of Julius Caesar and Augustus (49 bc–ad 14), Rome and its geographical empire were transformed into an imperial system in political terms. Its last Western emperor was Romulus Augustulus, deposed by Odoacer, the *de facto* ruler of the West, in ad 476. By then, the empire's East had long been governed from a second capital, Constantinople, which survived, though with authority over regularly decreasing territory, until it fell to the Ottoman empire in 1453.

Ancient Rome was located at a natural crossing of the Tiber river about 30 km (19 miles) upstream from the coast, on and around a series of hills. These include the Capitoline, Palatine, Aventine, Esquiline and Caelian hills, which may previously have held separate villages. In time, the urban area extended far beyond the original territory. Because the city was a place of peace, citizens in military array would marshal at the Campus Martius, outside the *pomerium*, a boundary with religious implications, probably delineated by Servius Tullius and later extended on occasion. The Capitol housed the temple of the Capitoline triad, Jupiter, Juno and Minerva, the city's main deities. On the Aventine, the plebeians built their own temple to their three deities, Ceres, Liber and Libera. Other shrines and temples were located on these hills and throughout the city. The Roman forum, the city's central political and commercial region, lay between the Palatine and Capitoline hills. Other markets and commercial areas included the Forum Boarium, a cattle market at the Tiber, and the harbour nearby, as well as the Subura, particularly in later times the location of taverns, cookhouses and similar enterprises.

Because low-lying areas of the city were situated on marshland, drainage works completed early in Rome's history permitted building activity and habitation on reclaimed land. As an example, the Cloaca Maxima, a sewer and drainage system for the forum area, was in origin the project of a Tarquin king. The wealthy owned extensive plots with large, elaborate town-houses. Evidence from later periods suggests that many other inhabitants lived in small units within apartment blocks up to five storeys high, the *insulae*, whose dangers of fire and other calamities Juvenal describes so well. Artisans and shopkeepers often resided within their places of business. In general, the streets among the houses,

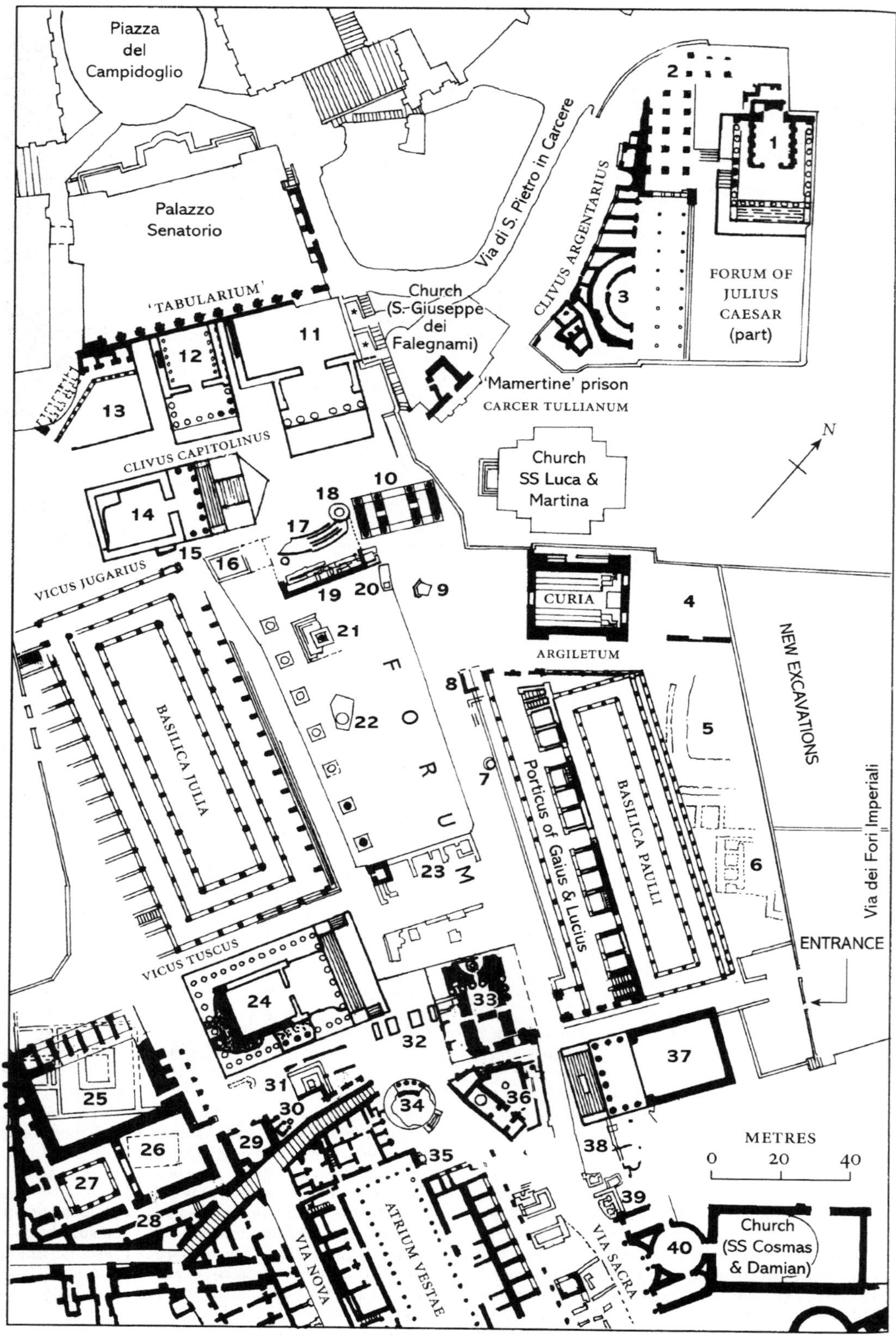
Piazza del Campidoglio
Palazzo Senatorio
'TABULARIUM'
Via di S. Pietro in Carcere
CLIVUS ARGENTARIUS
FORUM OF JULIUS CAESAR (part)
Church (S. Giuseppe dei Falegnami)
'Mamertine' prison
CARCER TULLIANUM
Church SS Luca & Martina
N
CLIVUS CAPITOLINUS
VICUS JUGARIUS
CURIA
ARGILETUM
NEW EXCAVATIONS
FORUM
BASILICA JULIA
Porticus of Gaius & Lucius
BASILICA PAULLI
Via dei Fori Imperiali
ENTRANCE
VICUS TUSCUS
METRES
0 20 40
Church (SS Cosmas & Damian)
VIA NOVA
ATRIUM VESTAE
VIA SACRA
1
2
3
4
5
6
7
8
9
10
11
12
13
14
15
16
17
18
19
20
21
22
23
24
25
26
27
28
29
30
31
32
33
34
35
36
37
38
39
40

ROME: (d) view of Domitianic palace, the Domus Augustana on the Palatine.

businesses, public buildings and open spaces were laid out in a haphazard arrangement defined by the urban topography: the hills, the low-lying areas and the winding course of the Tiber. When areas were demolished by fire or other circumstances, new streets sometimes followed a more regular plan. Streets generally bustled with humans during the day and vehicular traffic at night, with all the attendant noises of each. Rubbish was often tossed into the streets and presented various dangers, like lack of SANITATION, obstruction and physical harm from debris tossed from upper floors of buildings. Laws and regulations required property owners to keep streets unobstructed. Other legislation regulated many aspects of urban activity, from the illegality of flinging dung, to a ban against fighting in the streets, to the prohibition against throwing out dead ANIMALS and skins. In the larger city of the late Republic and imperial periods, a small army of public SLAVES, under the supervision of officials or MAGISTRATES, fought constantly to maintain some sanitation, cleanliness and safety by removing garbage, cleaning drainage systems and sewers, and repairing streets. The numerous funerary monuments and CATACOMBS lining the ROADS outside the city testify to the prohibition against BURIAL within the city boundaries, other than in exceptional circumstances.

WATER and FOOD were vital, and the state in both Republican and imperial times ensured availability. The first AQUEDUCT, the Aqua Appia, was begun in 312 BC, when Appius Claudius was CENSOR; many others followed. Water was directed to FOUNTAINS, public buildings and sanitation. Only surplus supply reached private hands, usually at a price and primarily to private BATHING establishments and FULLERS; some leading citizens might receive a grant of public water for private use. From the time of Augustus, water supply was supervised by a *curator aquarum* (supervisor of the water supply). Jurisdiction for

ROME: (c) detailed plan of the forum area. Key to numbered structures: 1. temple of Venus Genetrix; 2. 'Basilica Argentaria'; 7. shrine of Venus Cloacina; 8. arch of Janus (?); 9. Lapis Niger; 10. arch of Septimius Severus; 11. temple of Concordia Augusta; 12. temple of Vespasian and Titus; 13. precinct of the 'harmonious gods'; 14. temple of Saturn; 17. Caesarian *rostra*; 19. Augustan *rostra*; 21. column of Phocas; 23. late antique *rostra*; 24. temple of Castor; 25–27. Domitianic forehall of palace (later Santa Maria Antiqua church); 28. ramp to Palatine; 30–1 shrine of Juturna and Lacus Juturnae; 32. arch of Augustus; 33. temple of Caesar; 34. temple of Vesta; 36. Regia; 37. temple of deified Antoninus and Faustina; 40. 'temple of Romulus'.

ROME: (e) arch of Constantine – in part put together from reused materials from earlier arches and monuments.

the major contracts for public works of all types, including aqueducts and other waterworks, rested with the censors elected every five years in the Republican period, and between censorships with the aediles. In 123 BC, Gaius GRACCHUS began the practice of subsidizing grain prices to some inhabitants of Rome. During the next century, grain was often provided free to eligible citizens, whose number climbed to 150,000 by the late 1st century BC, when eligibility was restricted somewhat. To provide grain and to ensure that sufficient food was available, the state exacted tax revenues from some areas, including SICILY and North Africa, in measures of grain, and purchased additional quantities; up to a million tons per year was unloaded at Rome's docks to feed the city's human and animal inhabitants. Since SHIPPING was a hazardous commercial venture, some EMPERORS, especially CLAUDIUS, offered special privileges for ship-owners to encourage new investment in ships and shipping. Two generations earlier, Augustus had created a new administrative role, the *praefectus annonae* (prefect of the grain supply), to co-ordinate the purchase of grain and its shipment to Rome.

Entertainment was also a concern to public officials. In addition to places like the THEATRE of Marcellus, where the public could view theatrical performances, Rome offered several venues for HORSE-racing, GLADIATORIAL combat, and other spectacles, including mock NAVAL WARFARE on occasion. The CIRCUS MAXIMUS and the Flavian AMPHITHEATRE or Colosseum were the largest, with seating and standing room capacities of 150,000 and 50,000 respectively. Admission was generally inexpensive and sometimes free. Games and entertainments were provided by private individuals as well as the state, for the wealthy sought acclaim for their expenditures on games to celebrate their magistracies, especially when ELECTION to further office was a goal, or to commemorate deceased family members.

According to tradition, Servius Tullius divided Rome into four districts. By the late 1st century BC, the population had become vast; estimates vary from 600,000 to 1,250,000 inhabitants. Naturally, administrative problems increased, and the city was divided into 14 regions. As emperor, Augustus established various security forces, in contrast to Republican times, when security was haphazard. The new forces include the PRAETORIAN GUARD, charged mainly with the protection of emperors and their families, but also available against RIOTS and for crowd control; the urban cohorts, essentially a rudimentary police force; and the night watch (*vigiles*), whose primary duty was FIRE-FIGHTING, though they would assist other security forces in emergencies. Each unit had a prefect and, except for the praetorian guard, a devolved command structure and a presence in the regions of the city. At the broadest level, Rome was under the jurisdiction of the SENATE during the Republic, with judicial responsibilities under the control of the urban PRAETOR. In imperial times, a prefect of the city was established; its incumbent gained increasing powers and eventually became the primary government official in the city.

Rome was at the centre of ideology for many inhabitants of the empire. For example, in the 2nd century AD, AELIUS ARISTIDES composed a speech, *To Rome*, that elevates the city far beyond an imperial capital. Reflecting a similar perspective, JEROME, at Bethlehem early in the 5th century AD nearly fell to pieces in despair when ALARIC's Goths sacked Rome in 410; he laments in several letters that the end of the world must surely soon follow the sack of the central city of his world. Much earlier, the sack of Rome by the GAULS, traditionally dated 390 BC, generated ever afterwards a sense of insecurity whenever possible threats arose, like that presented by the Cimbri and Teutones, who reached northern Italy at the end of the 2nd century BC. Rome's position at the centre of ideology and its role as the political capital were equally important factors when it was chosen as the pre-eminent city of CHRISTIANITY: first for the empire as a whole, later for the West only, as Constantinople became the religious capital of the East. JV

See Cornell, T. J. (1995) *The Beginnings of Rome*; Coulston, J. C. and Dodge, H., eds. (2000) *Ancient Rome: the archaeology of the eternal city*; Lançon, B. (2000) *Rome in Late Antiquity*; Robinson, O. F. (1992) *Ancient Rome: city planning and administration*.

 CHURCHES: (b)–(c); CITIES: (b).

Romulus and Remus Legendary founders of Rome, twin sons of Rhea Silvia. Forcibly designated a VESTAL VIRGIN when her uncle Amulius deposed her father Numitor as king of Alba Longa, she was impregnated by MARS. Her twins were tossed into a flooded TIBER, but were beached by the receding water. A wolf adopted and suckled them, and later the shepherd Faustulus brought them to his wife Larentia. During their career as CATTLE thieves, Remus was captured in a raid on Amulius' herd. Told of his origins by Faustulus, Romulus and his band worked with resistance forces to restore Numitor and rescue his brother. They founded a city at the spot where they had landed as infants. Each wanted it named after himself and sought divine signs in support, unfortunately extending the argument. Romulus killed Remus then or perhaps later, when Remus spitefully leapt over the partially built foundations. Romulus continued to found his city, traditionally dated 753 BC, and became its first ruler. Rome was originally no more than Romulus, his men and a few individuals from the local area, but soon expanded to include Sabines and others.

The legend has many elements which are clearly unhistorical, and scholars have speculated at length on the origins of the story and its constituent elements. The wolf suckling infants was an enduring image of the origins of Rome, especially on COINAGE, even as late as the 4th century AD. Like Aeneas and Dido, Romulus and Remus became the subject of art, both literary and pictorial. JV

See Livy, book 1.

roofs and roofing materials Evidence for roofing styles comes from a variety of sources. Rarely does a roof itself survive from antiquity, but depictions on MOSAICS and WALL-PAINTINGS show the range of types available. A further form of evidence is SARCOPHAGI, which, as houses of the dead, can have depictions of roofs on their lids. A variety of roofing methods was used. The choice depends on cost, status, cultural preferences, the strength of the building and available materials. Thatched roofs were used throughout the classical period and tended to be used for the lowest status buildings. Shingles are wooden tiles, which tend to be shaped and put together in a pattern reminiscent of fish-scales.

Fired clay roofing is usually pitched at 20°, where the TILES are held in place by their own dead weight and do not usually require securing by NAILS. They are bedded in mortar, and the roof becomes a solid mass, though accidents from falling tiles are known from TOMB inscriptions. Three main styles were used. The Sicilian style was most favoured by the Romans and is prevalent in the western MEDITERRANEAN and North AFRICA, gradually spreading eastwards. The Corinthian and Laconian styles remained the favourites in the eastern Mediterranean, enjoying a resurgence with the rise of CONSTANTINOPLE.

Stone tiles can be in the same style as shingle roofs, or in higher-status cases can emulate fired clay tiles. Stone tiles were usually local, but imported stone tiles are known. Roofs of mortar and clay, either flat or domed, are also known. PJEM

See Brodribb, G. (1987) *Roman Brick and Tile*; Hellmann, M.-C. (2002) *L'Architecture grecque*, vol. 1: *Les Principes de construction* 278–326.

rope Made from the fibres of several different plants. In the classical world, flax and hemp were the most common, but nettles and bark fibre (often of the lime, *Tilia* spp.) were occasionally used. CATO also describes making long, heavy-duty ropes from twisted LEATHER. Rope-making appears as a specialist occupation in 4th-century Athens. Rope was essential for SHIPBUILDING and making rigging, in construction, TRANSPORT and haulage, in OLIVE and WINE PRESSES, SIEGE machinery, cranes and other MACHINES, and in many other jobs. It was expensive compared with today, and rope appears on the ATTIC *STÊLAI* among the confiscated property auctioned off by the Athenian state. LF

Rostovtzeff, M. I. see HISTORIANS AND HISTORIOGRAPHY, MODERN.

rubbish see SANITATION; WASTE.

Rufus fl. c. AD 100 A prominent physician and prolific author in the rationalist tradition of classical MEDICINE. Rufus was born in EPHESOS, also studied and practised in ALEXANDRIA, and probably even reached Rome at some stage in his career. He wrote a great number of medical works, of which only a handful survive despite the evident esteem in which he was held in both the Roman, and then the Islamic, worlds. Rufus' extant *oeuvre* includes the anatomical treatise *On the Naming of the Parts of the Human Being*; pathological tracts on the affections of the bladder and kidneys, and of the seminal vessels and genitals (*gonorrhoia* and *saturiasis*); and the diagnostic aid *On Medical Interrogation*, which advises on what questions to ask a patient in order to gain the fullest possible understanding of their condition. Extracts from several other works, mainly on DISEASES and dietetics, are incorporated in both Byzantine and Arabic medical ENCYCLOPEDIAS, most extensively in the *Medical Collections* of Oribasius. Rufus emerges from these texts as a less strident self-promoter than many of his colleagues, a man who draws fully and freely on the rich tradition of rationalist medicine as he articulates his own vision of the healing art. REF

ruler-cult The worship of rulers, whether still living or dead, as GODS. Its origin is probably to be sought in certain forms of heroic HONOURS accorded by the Greeks in the classical period. These honours included BURIAL in the *AGORA* and the establishment of an altar and SACRIFICE. City-founders and 'great men', like the Thasian ATHLETE Theagenes, were often accorded these honours. Cult is reported in the 4th century for successful military leaders like the Spartans AGESILAOS on THASOS (he refused) and LYSANDER on SAMOS (a cult that may have been posthumous). In the 330s a statue of PHILIP II of Macedonia was erected in the sanctuary of ZEUS at Eresos on LESBOS. ALEXANDER the Great represented something of a turning-point, since he clearly wished to be regarded as a god, though it remains uncertain whether actual cult was established for him while he lived. He did receive cult after his death.

In the hellenistic period, Greek *poleis* regularly awarded cult to rulers who had provided civic benefits. For example, cult was granted at Iasos in CARIA to ANTIOCHOS III and his wife Laodike in recognition of aid they provided after an EARTHQUAKE. Such cult was related to, and derived many of its elements from, the *isotheoi timai*, 'honours equal to those of the gods', accorded to rulers and others by Greek *poleis*. But rulers themselves also promoted dynastic cults; the best attested are those of the SELEUKIDS, who had priests of the dynastic cult in each satrapy of the empire. The cult of the PTOLEMIES started as posthumous worship of PTOLEMY I Soter but soon expanded to include the living ruler and his consort as the *theoi adelphoi* ('sibling gods') Ptolemy II Philadelphos and ARSINOË II. The Macedonian kings, in contrast, seem not to have established ruler-cult.

In the Roman world, the earliest example of worship accorded an individual seems to be that of Gaius Marcellus, for whom a festival was established at SYRACUSE after its capture from the CARTHAGINIANS. But the prototype for cult of successful Roman military figures was provided by that of Titus Quinctius FLAMININUS, for whom Chalkis in EUBOIA voted divine honours in 191 BC; other cities in Greece soon followed suit. Many notable figures of the 1st century BC received similar honours, including SULLA and POMPEY. Lesser figures also received honours, like Gaius Marcius Censorinus, for whom GAMES were instituted after his death at Mylasa in Caria. Like Alexander, JULIUS CAESAR marked an important new development. In a series of decrees starting in 46 BC the SENATE accorded him more and more honours associated with the gods. He was (almost certainly) granted the title 'god', *divus*, in the first acts of 46, and brought into close association (but not identification) with JUPITER. After Caesar's death Octavian worked to promote a cult of Divus Iulius throughout the empire. In 29, for example, he granted EPHESOS and Nikaia in Asia Minor the right to establish sanctuaries devoted to ROMA (Rome) and Divus Iulius. He seems to have been cautious, however, about making explicit claims to his own divinity (despite some efforts to identify himself with APOLLO). In effect, Octavian (as AUGUSTUS) worked out a policy, largely followed by his successors, that stopped short of direct worship of the emperor in Rome but permitted such worship in the PROVINCES.

Augustus accepted a broad range of *isotheoi timai* and associated himself with worship of the goddess Roma and various other 'abstract' deities. This arrangement (to which the 3rd-century AD historian CASSIUS DIO attests) fitted with the 'constitutional' situation of the empire, which rendered direct cult to the living emperor impossible, at least in the capital. However, private cult did flourish in various guises in Italy and Rome, as well as in the provinces. Imperial cult is first attested in the west in GAUL, in 12 (or 10) BC at Lugdunum; other places soon followed. Augustus himself was declared a god on 17 September AD 14, soon after his death, and not long afterwards the first request arrived from Spain to construct a temple for Divus Augustus. His worship became the paramount element of the subsequent cult. Imperial cult came to be connected with temples erected for that purpose all over the empire. A famous example, with a copy of Augustus' *RES GESTAE* inscribed on it, stands still today in Ankara. These were equipped, as usual in ancient cult, with priests and set ritual. A few notorious figures like the emperor Gaius (CALIGULA) demanded worship while living, but for the most part the Augustan model was followed, with the senate determining after an emperor's death whether he belonged with the gods or not. SENECA has left us a biting parody of the deification of CLAUDIUS in his *Apocolocyntosis divi Claudii* or 'Pumpkinification of the divine Claudius'. Emperor-worship helped provide a mechanism for binding together the empire, whose RELIGIOUS diversity was truly extraordinary, and for assuring loyalty to the reigning emperor. The Jews worked out with the Roman state a condominium which allowed them to honour the emperor without actual worship. Refusal by CHRISTIANS to make sacrifice to the imperial cult was taken as a mark of disloyalty, and became a factor in some cases of PERSECUTION. GR

See Fishwick, D. (1987–92) *The Imperial Cult in the Latin West*, 2 vols.; Gradel, I. (2002) *Emperor Worship and Roman Religion*; Price, S. R. F. (1984) *Rituals and Power*; Small, A., ed. (1996) *Subject and Ruler*.

rural settlement The essential complement to ancient URBANIZATION. Despite the importance given to towns in ancient writings, the majority of people in most periods and regions of the classical world dwelt in smaller settlements in the countryside, varying from isolated huts to substantial VILLAGES. The ancient sources are generally far less detailed about the nature of these settlements, but archaeological FIELD SURVEY in recent decades has added much new information about this hitherto neglected area. The study of rural settlement patterns is important for several reasons. First, it can inform us of the lifestyle and economic orientation of the 'silent majority' of the ancient world. Second, it is of the greatest interest to explore how rural settlement within a given area changed over time. Far from being an unchanging backdrop to the urban arena, rural history reveals radically different regional trajectories of settlement and ECONOMY, and major changes over time at the local level. Third, the hierarchy of ancient settlement from towns to hovels also mirrors the structure of society and informs our view of how political and socio-economic relations were played out. Finally, for the Roman period at least, the rural LANDSCAPE is now known to have been far more densely occupied and 'busy' than was previously believed possible of the ancient world.

Despite the increasing weight of archaeological discoveries of rural sites around many towns, the predominant view of the Greek world is that most citizens of a *POLIS* lived for at least part of the time in

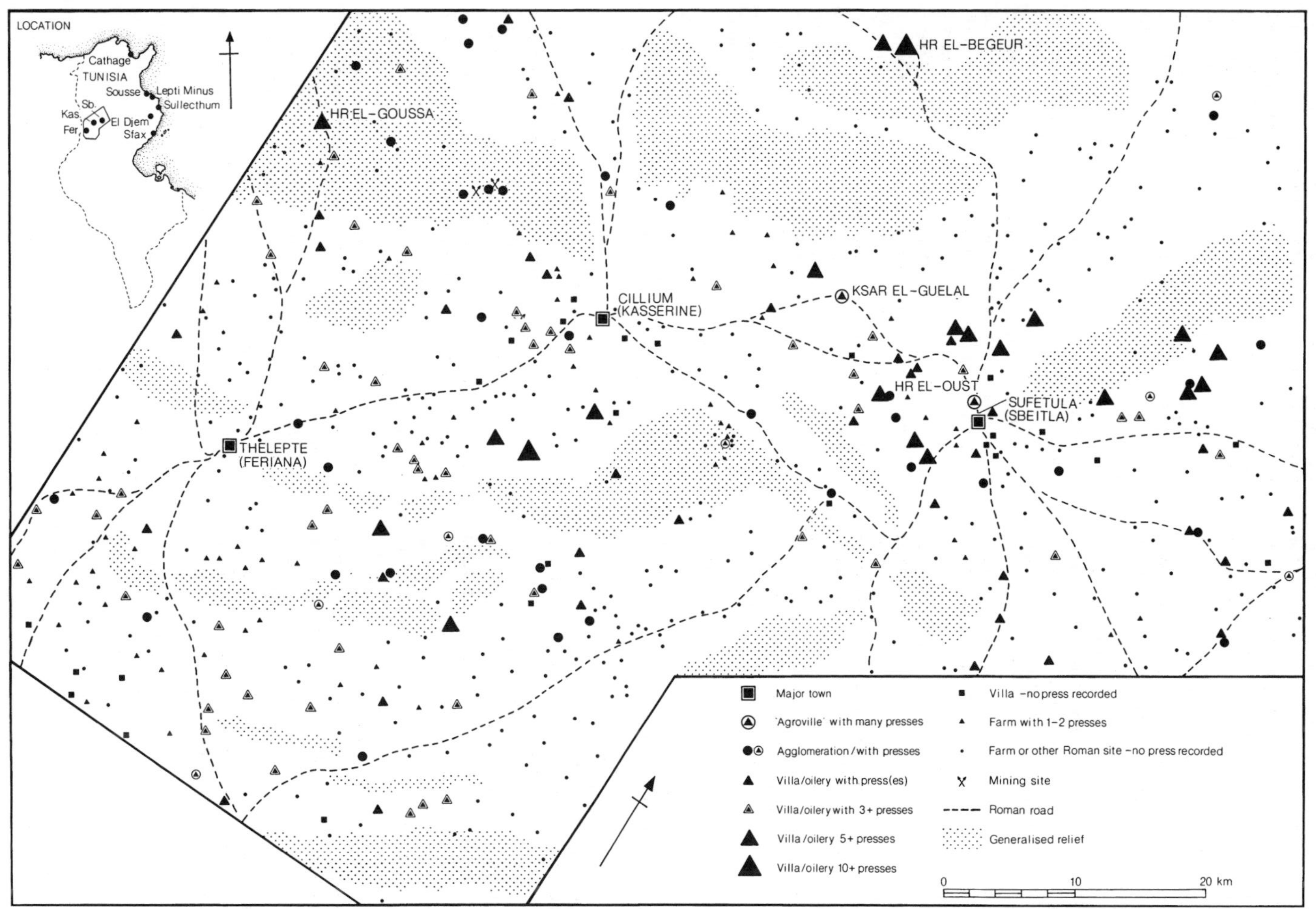

RURAL SETTLEMENT: map of the High Steppe of central Tunisia, showing the high numbers of farms and villas with olive presses in this region of somewhat specialized production.

TOWNS. The plough-zone scatters of POTTERY sherds and building debris are sometimes interpreted as representing seasonally occupied farmsteads, barns and sheds. More EXCAVATIONS of smaller rural sites are needed, in order to distinguish more clearly the functions they performed. The evidence of well-preserved patterns of field systems and associated farms in the Crimea suggests that some at least of the survey evidence from elsewhere in the Greek world may eventually need reappraisal. The role of the village in Greek rural settlement is similarly in need of review; recent work suggests that villages were not a prominent feature of the classical Greek landscape.

In the Roman world the organization of rural settlement was often dependent on urban-based systems of territorial control, with many villages (*vici*) and districts (*pagi*) being defined in relation to a particular town. Attention has focused on determining the legal status of provincial lands. Although there is evidence in many regions of an initial pattern of land allotment to numerous smallholders, over time this tended to get submerged by the evolution of large estates, whether owned by the state, the imperial house or private individuals. The administration of imperial estates has been one particular focus of interest, the search for a typical 'slave estate' in Italy another. The estate model can be detected in the archaeological record more easily than the precise type of labour involved, though Settefinestre in Italy is rightly celebrated as the clearest example of a major SLAVE-run estate. Much rural settlement evidence supports the view that there was a clear settlement hierarchy in many areas, with wealthier sites often involved in relations of dominance over the lower-order settlements. One significant aspect is the presence of élite sites generally referred to as VILLAS, marked out by their scale, design and use of luxury materials (such as MARBLE and MOSAICS). However, the modern definition of a villa varies considerably. In Britain, for example, it is used to refer to almost any rural dwelling constructed in what might be called Roman style. It is clear that the richer sites have often existed side by side with simpler and more utilitarian farms and farmsteads, echoing the sort of economic relations that are hinted at in our primary source material. To take the case of Britain again, villas co-existed in many areas with traditional roundhouses of Iron Age type.

In some areas of the ancient world, the Roman period marked a sharp transition from PASTORALISM to agricultural exploitation of the landscape. This is perhaps most clearly attested in parts of Roman AFRICA. The rural settlement patterns that evolved reflect the economic organization of society and production. In central Tunisia, for example, a distinct regional specialization of OLIVE OIL production is attested by the numerous large-scale PRESSES. In the region of Sufetula (Sbeitla), for instance, over 350 olive presses have been recorded (with over 70 sites containing four or more presses and being categorized as oileries). Sites with only one press are interpreted as farms; some simple sites without presses, but often with small enclosures, are identified as farmsteads. In addition, there is a sprinkling of more luxurious villas, of small urban sites with a highly visible agricultural function (known by the French term *agrovilles*), and of other villages. The complexity of these rural landscapes when examined in detail is striking.

Some areas of the ancient world appear to have been marginal, or marginalized by their treatment by the political authorities. The contrast between the military zone and the civil zone in BRITANNIA is particularly marked, villas being common in the south and east but extremely rare in northern Britain. The exploitation of the desert zones to the east and south of the MEDITERRANEAN can be read as a point of intersection of different systems of land exploitation (pastoral and sedentary AGRICULTURAL) and different social groups. In a similar way, comparison of rural settlement patterns across frontiers, as along the RHINE in GERMANY and the Low Countries, has revealed significant differences developing over time between those inside and those outside the empire.

A major obstacle to improved understanding of rural sites is the lack of excavation at a representative sample. In many areas, even the villas are very poorly explored at present and humbler structures, such as oil or wine presses, barns, storage cellars and animal stalls, have rarely been subject to detailed investigation. The lack of any modern excavation of a large-scale oilery in Africa, for example, remains a major gap in knowledge. DJM

See Alcock, S. E. (1993) *Graecia Capta: the landscapes of Roman Greece*; Barker, G. and Lloyd, J. (1991) *Roman Landscapes*; Dyson, S. L. (2003) *The Roman Countryside*; Greene, K. (1986) *The Archaeology of the Roman Economy*; Hansen, M. H. (2004) The concept of the consumption city applied to the Greek polis, in T. H. Nielsen, ed., *Once Again: studies in the ancient Greek polis* 9–47, esp. 26–30 (villages); Hitchner, R. B. et al. (1990) The Kasserine Archaeological survey 1987, *AntAf* 26: 231–60; Kehoe, D. (1988) *The Economics of Agriculture on Imperial Estates of Roman North Africa*; Mattingly, D. J. (1988) Oil for export, *JRA* 1: 33–55; Rossiter, J. (1978) *Roman Farm Buildings in Italy*; Shipley, G. (2002) Hidden landscapes: Greek field survey data and hellenistic history, in D. Ogden, ed., *The Hellenistic World* 177–98.

FIELD SURVEY: (a)–(b).

S

Sabines Inhabitants of the area north-east of Rome towards the Apennines; they are connected to the Sabelli who overwhelmed the Oscans, perhaps one subset of that wider group. Archaeologically, their culture differs little from Latin culture, which has made it impossible to detect their presence at Rome itself, despite the fact that one key aspect of their early history is the incorporation of some Sabines into the city. Romulus is said to have orchestrated the seizure of Sabine women at a festival; the women then persuaded their fathers and brothers to join the Roman foundation rather than destroy it. Hence for a while Romulus had a Sabine (Titus Tatius) as co-regent. The story perhaps reflects the later co-existence with some Sabines: late in the 6th century, the followers of Attus Clausus came to Rome, were admitted to the patriciate, received land and became the Claudii. Others remained hostile; there are incursions through the 5th century and a final defeat by Manius Curius Dentatus. Incorporation as citizens without the vote followed in 290, and full citizenship in 268. Later, the area became popular as a quiet agricultural area, where the poet Horace had a farm, which Maecenas had given to him and which he describes with fondness in his poetry. CJS

See Dench, E. (1995) *From Barbarians to New Men.*

 Italy, Roman: (a).

Sabratha see theatres, Roman.

sacred wars, Greek Fought for the control of the sanctuary of Apollo at Delphi. The sanctuary was allegedly put in the care of the Pylaian amphiktiony after the first sacred war (c.595–590 BC), though the historicity of this war has been doubted as a product of 4th-century BC propagandists. The second sacred war (449) receives only a brief notice in Thucydides, who says the Spartans seized the sanctuary from the Phokians and gave it back to the Delphians, but then the Athenians took it back and restored it to Phokian control.

The importance of the third (355–346) and fourth (339–338) sacred wars lies in the fact that they legitimated Philip II of Macedonia's entry into southern Greece. War first broke out when the Phokians, provoked by the Thebans in the amphiktionic council which governed Delphi, seized Delphi and appropriated funds in order to pay mercenaries. In 346 Philip forced the Phokians to surrender: their cities were razed, their votes on the amphiktiony were transferred to Philip, and they were required to pay reparations. But war was declared again in 339 after further jostlings for power in the council, and Thebes and Athens were ranged against Philip, who conducted the war on behalf of the amphiktiony. It ended in Philip's victory at Chaironeia in 338. LGM

See Buckler, J. (1989) *Philip II and the Sacred War*; Forrest, W. G. (1956) The first sacred war, *BCH* 80: 33–52; Robertson, N. (1978) The myth of the first sacred war, *CQ* 28: 38–73.

 war (table).

sacrifice Central act of Greek and Roman religious ritual, an offering to gods, heroes or the dead. Blood sacrifice, the ritual killing of animals, was the major form. 'Bloodless sacrifices' of cakes, wine, incense, oil or honey were also made, especially in daily household ritual. A sacrifice might be performed as part of a public festival or in private observance by an individual or family, and might vary in scale from a single goat to the hundred cattle involved in a hecatomb (*hekatombaion*). Sacrifices were made on a wide variety of occasions: before a journey or a battle, in thanks for protection received, in propitiation of a potentially hostile deity, and in rites of passage, purification or expiation. Choice of victim was determined by the deity involved and by economic factors, though the animal always had to be without blemish. The most common victims were sheep, goats, pigs and cattle, the cheapest being a piglet, the most expensive an ox. A few cults demanded fish, fowl or more rarely wild animals, dogs or horses. Whether myths of human sacrifice reflect actual practice is a subject of considerable modern debate.

Greek animal sacrifice had three main stages: preparation, slaughter, and distribution of the meat. First, the animal was led to the altar in procession. Participants washed their hands and took a handful of barley from a basket. Water was sprinkled on the victim's brow, prompting the nod of 'willingness'. Hair cut from the victim was burnt on the altar fire and barley was scattered, while a prayer was said specifying the return expected. Second, the victim's

sacrifice: (a) Greek vase-painting depicting the sacrifice of a goat kid to Dionysos at an altar with an attached offering table.

throat was cut, larger animals having previously been stunned with an axe-blow. The blood was caught in a bowl and poured over the altar. At the moment of death, women raised the *ololygê* (ritual cry). In the third stage the god's portion (the thigh bones wrapped in fat) was burnt on the altar fire with wine and incense, the scented smoke communicating between human and divine worlds. The entrails were inspected for omens, then roasted on skewers and shared out among the immediate participants. The remaining meat was cut into equal portions, boiled and distributed to a wider circle of participants, usually in the context of a communal feast, though occasionally the meat was taken away for consumption at home.

This standard 'Olympian' sacrifice is traditionally distinguished from a 'chthonian' variety, made primarily to heroes and the dead. In this version the victim is dark in colour and is killed with its head down over a pit or low hearth; libations are wine-less, and the animal is not eaten but burnt whole (a 'holocaust'). Such variations certainly do occur, but there seems to be no systematic application of the distinction. PAUSANIAS (8.18.7) records an exceptional sacrifice in honour of ARTEMIS Laphria at Patrai, where both domesticated and wild animals were thrown into the flames while still alive. Some followers of DIONYSOS practised *ômophagia*, the eating of raw flesh, a complete inversion of 'proper' civic sacrifice. HESIOD's *aition* (explanation) for the origin of sacrifice, in which Prometheus tricks ZEUS into accepting the poorer portion of bones and fat, suggests unease with the human–divine relationship that sacrifice implies (*Theogony* 535–64). The moral legitimacy of life-taking is raised by the Athenian Bouphonia ritual: after sacrificing an ox the PRIEST fled, and the sacrificial knife was tried for murder and then cast into the sea.

Roman sacrifice usually consisted of four stages: *praefatio*, *immolatio*, slaughtering and banquet. First, participants and victim were purified before processing to the altar, where an offering of incense and wine was performed on a portable hearth. Then wine and salted flour (*mola salsa*) were sprinkled over the victim and the sacrificial knife passed over its back while a prayer was said, marking ritual transference to divine possession. Several professionals might be involved in the slaughter: a *popa* to stun the animal, a *cultrarius* to slit its throat, and a *victimarius* to butcher it. The presiding figure inspected the victim's *exta* (peritoneum, liver, gall bladder, lungs, heart); good condition meant that the deity accepted the sacrifice. To prevent ill-omened sounds being heard, a flute player (*tibicen*) might be employed, and the officiator would keep his head covered with his TOGA. After the slaughter, the victim was beheaded and the *exta* boiled or grilled on spits, then made over to the god by being burnt, basted with *mola salsa* and wine. The rest of the victim could now be claimed by the human participants; some or all of the meat was consumed there and then in a sacrificial banquet, while any surplus was sold in butchers' shops.

Some public sacrifices were performed according to the 'Greek rite'. The main differences seem to be that the presiding figure might have his head uncovered, that *immolatio* hairs cut from victim's brow were burnt and crowns offered, and the *exta* were called by their Greek name, *splanchna*. An

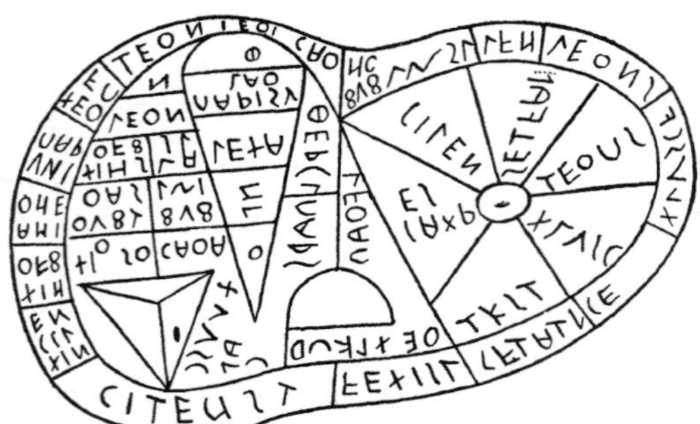

SACRIFICE: (b) model of a liver engraved in Etruscan to aid reading of sacrificial organs.

'ETRUSCAN rite' is also attested, in which the inspection of the vital organs (*haruspicatio*) allowed for divination. Certain AGRICULTURAL festivals were celebrated with a *suovetaurilia*, a combined sacrifice of a pig (*sus*), sheep (*ovis*) and ox (*taurus*), also made at the conclusion of some military campaigns. Some cults of the imperial period were marked by variations on the basic ritual, e.g. the *taurobolium* and *criobolium*, where a worshipper stood in a pit beneath the ox or ram being slaughtered so as to be bathed in the blood.

Sacrifice has attracted a variety of anthropological interpretations. Some emphasize its origins among prehistoric hunters and see it as a dramatization of violent killing and its associated guilt, or more generally as a legitimation of the life-taking involved in eating meat. Others place emphasis on the role of sacrifice in articulating the hierarchy between gods, humans and animals. Greek and Roman sacrifice certainly established hierarchies among mortals: the feast following a public sacrifice could be on very grand scale, demonstrating the munificence of the financing liturgist or patron, and participation was a sign of social inclusion. Unwillingness to participate in public sacrifice marked out the ORPHICS and PYTHAGOREANS, and later JEWS and CHRISTIANS, as outside the social norm. EJS

See Burkert, W. (1983) *Homo Necans*; Hughes, D. D. (1991) *Human Sacrifice in Ancient Greece*; Rosivach, V. J. (1994) *The System of Public Sacrifice in Fourth-century Athens.*

Saguntum An Iberian city on the eastern coast of Spain, 25 km (16 miles) north-east of Valencia, now called Sagunto. The Iberian name was probably *Arsê*, which appears on its COINAGE. The city lies on a high ridge on the landward side of the route up the MEDITERRANEAN coast. Its situation meant that when in 220/19 BC HANNIBAL was preparing to move his forces along the coast towards the Pyrenees on the way to invading Italy, he had to secure this point. It is probably for the same reason that the Romans had at some earlier moment made an alliance with the Saguntines. However, when the Saguntines appealed for help from the Roman SENATE, the reaction was to send messages to Hannibal telling him not to touch Saguntum, but not to dispatch forces to ensure that he did not. Consequently Hannibal attacked Saguntum in 219,

SACRIFICE: (c) Roman relief from the Basilica Ulpia in Rome, showing the inspection of the internal organs of an ox in front of the Capitoline temple.

SACRIFICE: (d) In a scene from his column Trajan leads a sacrifice in preparation for the crossing of the Danube at the start of the second Dacian war.

capturing it after an eight-month SIEGE. The city was recaptured (though perhaps only temporarily) by the Romans in 212, and remained an allied town probably through the Republican period. By the time of AUGUSTUS, it had achieved the status of a *municipium* and developed a set of Roman buildings, including a FORUM perched on the top of the ridge and a THEATRE set into its side. EXCAVATION has revealed that its port continued active into the late imperial period, though it never became an important place, probably because of its proximity to Valentia (Valencia). JSR

See Richardson, J. S. (1986) *Hispaniae.*

 HISPANIA.

sailors There is very little direct evidence of the lives of ordinary seamen in the classical world, so we have to rely almost entirely upon literary and artistic depictions. The most important member of a ship's crew was the helmsman (Greek *kybernêtês*, Latin *gubernator*), who operated the steering oars in person or, on larger ships, supervised their operation. He would be in command of the ship's personnel, but was subordinate to a trierarch on a naval ship, or to the owner of a merchant vessel (Greek *nauklêros*, Latin *navicularius*). A typical merchant ship would have, in addition to the helmsman, an administrative officer (Greek *toicharchos*) who took care of cargo and passengers, a prow officer (Greek *prôreus*, Latin *proreta*), a carpenter (Greek *naupêgos*, Latin *faber*) and a few ordinary sailors (Greek *nautai*, Latin *nautae*). Naval ships would also have a rowing master (Greek *keleustês*, Latin *celeusta*, *pausarius*), who supervised the oarsmen (e.g. Xenophon, *Oikonomikos* 21.3); some carried a DOCTOR. The sources present typical sailors as scantily clad or nude, and comment on their coarse behaviour and language (e.g. DIO CHRYSOSTOM, *Orations* 32.9; 72.1, 6). Officers were usually freeborn, but many merchant sailors were of servile status or origin. The crews of naval vessels were mostly free conscripts or MERCENARIES, but sometimes SLAVE oarsmen were hired (e.g. Thucydides 7.13). In times of crisis large numbers of slaves were used to man fleets (e.g. Xenophon, *Hellenika* 1.6.24; Livy 24.11; 26.35–6; Cassius Dio 48.49). PDeS

See Casson, L. (1971, 1995) *Ships and Seamanship in the Ancient World.*

NAVIES; SHIPS AND SHIPBUILDING: (b).

Saint (St) Albans see BRITANNIA.

saints Holy men and women considered to possess a special closeness to the divine. Those venerated for sainthood achieved it largely by means of suffering for their beliefs as MARTYRS or by renouncing the world as ASCETICS. These ideas are found in ancient religions other than CHRISTIANITY. JUDAISM, for example, could boast ascetics and martyrs, while PAGAN philosophical movements, such as the NEOPLATONISTS, sought closeness to the gods through self-denial. It was Christianity, however, that developed these ideals most systematically, thus providing a model of sainthood for the medieval and modern eras. PERSECUTIONS provided the church with martyrs, whose lives were embroidered with miraculous events. After burial, these martyrs continued to show their sainthood by miracles at their TOMBS, which were seen as conduits through which divine power acted on earth. Relics, whether the corporeal remains of martyrs or items (such as clothing) which they had touched, were also venerated as having special powers. After the end of the persecutions, which robbed the church of its supply of martyrs, sanctity was more likely to be found in those who followed lifestyles of extreme asceticism. The prototype was provided by the Egyptian hermit ANTONY (AD 251–356), but asceticism could also bestow the aura of sainthood and spiritual authority on figures more active in public life, such as BISHOPS. As with martyrs, the tombs and relics of ascetics became focuses of the cult of saints. MDH

See Anderson, G. (1994) *Sage, Saint and Sophist*; Brown, P. (1981) *The Cult of the Saints.*

Salamis, battle of An ISLAND just off ATTICA, Salamis was in 480 the site of a famous sea battle fought between the Greeks and Persian forces of XERXES. Although a number of Greek peoples sent SHIPS, the Athenians, who supplied half of the total fleet, claimed the major role in the defeat, which led to the Persian withdrawal from mainland Greece. HERODOTOS' narrative of the battle suggests the tensions and disputes on the Greek side, particularly among the Peloponnesians, who wished to flee and defend the isthmus of Corinth. Ancient accounts draw on a number of themes familiar from Greek (particularly Athenian) treatment of the PERSIAN WARS as a whole. For example, they emphasize the huge size of the Persian fleet, as opposed to the comparatively small Greek fleet, but the orderliness and team effort of the Greek fleet wins out. There is also some characteristic gender-role reversal: the best and bravest Persian captain is the HALIKARNASSIAN woman Artemisia. For the Athenians, Salamis was of great political and ideological importance. THEMISTOKLES had built up the fleet from funds from the LAURION MINES. Subsequently, he interpreted as ships the 'wooden walls' that a gloomy DELPHIC ORACLE suggested would be the sole salvation of Athens from the Persian invasion. In traditional thought, Salamis, as Athens' first great naval success, paved the way for the Athenians' sea empire and the 'radical' DEMOCRACY, which gave a political role to the thetes, the lowest, ship-rowing, property class. ED

See Aeschylus, *Persians*; Herodotos, *Histories* 7–8.

Sallust (Gaius Sallustius Crispus) ?86–?35 BC Late Republican historian of Roman society and POLITICS. The monographs of Sallust on the CATILINARIAN conspiracy (64–62 BC) and the JUGURTHINE WAR (118–105 BC) are the earliest works of history in Latin to survive complete (Caesar's *Commentaries* belong to a different GENRE). Sallust inherited a well-developed tradition which included POLYBIOS (in Greek), the Elder CATO and Sisenna together with the 1st-century narrative historians (the 'annalists'). Each helped form the mode of Roman HISTORIOGRAPHY; but it is Sallust whose imprint on that mode we can best appreciate. His writing, withdrawn and disillusioned, mirrors his world: sharp, bitter, characterized by façade and deceit. His style is mannered, abrupt, unbalanced. Eschewing canonical political terms, he prefers archaizing or innovative, often poetic vocabulary which highlights the kinship of history and EPIC.

Sallust, who was for a short time a politician and military governor of AFRICA, saw the writing of history as a complement to the doing of it, regarding his own literary contribution as a kind of political action. In this he is followed by LIVY and TACITUS, who adopt, to varying degrees, his dyspeptic voice. Fascinated by *virtus*, the quintessential Roman quality of 'excellence' as expressed primarily in WAR and politics, Sallust explores its manifestations in complex, flawed personalities such as Catiline, JUGURTHA, MARIUS, SULLA and POMPEY. Roman historiography, for Sallust, is the record of decline. If it is to be useful, however, it must help arrest that decline: hence his emphasis, which is THUCYDIDEAN at heart, on the political analysis of causes and character.

The topics of Sallust's monographs were remarkable, he claims, both for their impact on Roman society and for their intrinsic excitement. Each work contains speeches, composed by the historian to illuminate character or to dissect motivation; these are carefully arranged in narratives packed with vivid descriptions of battles and political turmoil. Sallust exploits the reader's expectations and emotions by sudden shifts of perspective, either within the narrative (so, in the *Jugurthine War*, the scene often moves from the fighting in Africa to Rome, where citizens and readers alike react with joy or fear) or in digressions, an important tool for analysis and comment. In the preface to the *War of Catiline* Sallust discusses the development of political systems and how history preserves memory; he marks the monograph's centre with a discussion of politics, situating Catiline's abortive coup in the socio-political upheavals of the 1st century. The *Jugurthine War* contains both historical and political digressions, together with ethno-geographical excursuses in which, through comparison and contrast, Sallust investigates Rome's relations with outsiders. The remains of at least three such digressions in Sallust's last (now fragmentary) work, the *Histories*, suggest that he continued to ponder issues of national identity throughout his life. His influence on later historians and thinkers was considerable, especially in late antiquity and the early RENAISSANCE, where Bruni and Politian took him as a model. CSK

See Sallust, *The Jugurthine War; The Conspiracy of Catiline*, trs. S. A. Handford (1963); Kraus, C. S. and Woodman, A. J. (1997) *Latin Historians*; Syme, R. (2002) *Sallust* (new foreword by R. Mellor).

Salonica see THESSALONIKE.

salt Familiar in classical times in the forms both of sea salt and of rock salt. There were salt MINES; in several Roman PROVINCES, including BRITAIN, an industry of salt production developed with the use of artificial salt pans. A necessity in human nutrition and an important preservative, salt was traded to regions where it was not available locally.

Salt was the single most important added substance in food conservation, sometimes in solid form, sometimes as brine. A good deal of the FISH in the classical diet had been salted for distribution and storage. Brine was a medium in which CHEESE was kept; brine was added to must in the making of certain WINES. Cheese and fish were washed before eating to remove undesired excess salt.

Pure salt was in use in cooking; we hear of it sprinkled on sacrificial meat, and of its use to flavour fish. 'We shared salt' serves in Greek as a shorthand implying the sharing of a meal and the establishment of friendship and mutual obligation. In Latin, *sal*, 'salt', is used metaphorically for 'wit, good sense'. In spite of these indications of the importance of salt in food, evidence of its presence at MEALS is very limited, until we take account of various combined forms in which it was used, including thyme salt, cumin salt, brine and vinegar brine.

By far the commonest salt compound, in the texts and in archaeological evidence, is fermented FISH SAUCE or *garum*. Familiar in the MEDITERRANEAN world from the 5th century BC to the end of antiquity, fish sauce was the commonest way to incorporate salt in all kinds of cooked dishes. The literary evidence is amply supported by finds of AMPHORAS that once contained the product and by excavations of salteries, from Portugal and Spain to the Crimea, where fish sauce was manufactured. Recipes, probably Roman in date, are given in the Byzantine text *Geoponika* 'Farming'. Various fish and parts of fish (innards of mackerel and tunny being the preferred ingredients) were mixed with plentiful salt and allowed to stand in the sun for several weeks, after which a liquid (whence the alternative Latin name *liquamen*) was allowed to flow off. Apicius makes it clear that fish sauce was the normal way to add salt in cooking: scarcely any recipes call for solid salt. AD

See Curtis, R. I. (1991) *Garum and Salsamenta*; De Brisay, K.W. and Evans, K. A., eds. (1975) *Salt: the study of an ancient industry*; Hocquet, J.-C., and Hocquet, J. (1985–7) The history of a food product: salt in Europe, *Food and Foodways* 1: 425–47; Kurlansky, M. (2002) *Salt: a world history*.

samian ware Red-gloss tableware produced throughout GAUL between the 1st and 3rd centuries AD. The term is employed only in Britain and derives from antiquarian use of the elder PLINY's list of production centres of both eastern and western red-slipped wares, of which he names Samos as one; con tinental scholars refer to samian as *terra sigillata*. Current knowledge of the industry is based upon detailed research dating from the late 18th century, when the German scholar Dragendorff introduced a typology still commonly in use. The vessels were produced on a large scale and distributed widely, consisting of a limited range of forms (mostly cups, bowls and platters) used for drinking, eating and serving.

The ware was produced in three shifting geographic regions, which overlapped chronologically; each region was represented by a number of WORKSHOPS. South Gaul was the earliest of these centres, active for export between c.AD 15 and 100, with the largest and most important workshop at La Graufesenque near Millau. Initially influenced by ARRETINE potters and vessels, soon the industry created a distinctive style, of classical motifs simplified through Gaulish execution. Although production for a local market continued at La Graufesenque, by the turn of the century the focus of production had shifted to central Gaul near Clermont-Ferrand; of centres here, Lezoux dominated the export market by AD 120. The central Gaulish potteries remained important throughout the 2nd century AD, but during this same period numerous centres sprang up in east Gaul, in the Argonne, and in the Moselle and RHINE valleys, at places such as TRIER and Rheinzabern that contributed significantly to export from the mid-2nd century. Production in central and east Gaul ceased around the mid-3rd century. There were other western centres but even the largest, in Spain, was essentially for the local market.

Samian vessels are classified as plain or decorated, all of which are well dated. Plain vessels were generally made on a wheel, aided by modelling tools or templates, sometimes with sparse barbotine (clay applied as icing), rouletted or occasionally applied decoration. Elaborate, densely arranged relief decoration was produced by throwing the vessel in a ceramic mould, itself impressed by a punch or poinçon (for the individual motifs), roulette and stylus. The glossy surface was then achieved by dipping the part-dried vessel into slip (clay of liquid consistency, in this case illite-rich). Uniform quality was assured by the sophisticated KILN, which channelled air through tubes rather than being free-flowing as in other Roman kilns.

Although not every vessel was marked, different names stamped or inscribed on the mould and the vessel illustrate specialized division of LABOUR, while less common graffiti refer to the owner of the mould rather than the maker, indicating they were not always the same. The organization of firing was equally complex. Tallies incised on vessels from La Graufesenque show that up to 30,000 vessels could be fired together, representing the output of as many as ten potters or workshops in a single load. The movements of stamps, moulds and (by implication) potters all help build up a picture of the industry. RST

See Bémont, C. and Jacob, J.-P., eds. (1986) *La Terre sigillée gallo-romaine*; Webster, P. (1995) *Roman Samian Pottery in Britain*.

 POTTERY, ROMAN: (a).

Samnite wars 343–290 BC The three wars between Rome and the Samnites which determined control of central Italy. The Samnite peoples were a (military) federation of Oscan-speaking tribes inhabiting the southern central Apennines, notable for ethnic solidarity. The first war (343–341) broke out, despite a treaty in 354, when Rome responded to a Campanian appeal for help against the Samnites. It ended with the treaty's renewal, but its historicity is questionable (it appears only in LIVY). More significant was the revolt of the Latins which followed (341–338). The resolution of this dissolved many other tribal groups in the region and led to the evolution of fresh tools of Roman imperialism, notably the Latin colony. The foundation of the colony of Fregellae in 328 provoked the second war (327–304). Although Rome suffered a humiliating reverse at the CAUDINE FORKS in 321, the Samnites, increasingly surrounded by allies of Rome, sued for peace in 304. The third war (298–290) saw the decisive battle of Sentinum in 295, perhaps the largest in Italy thus far, at which Quintus Fabius Maximus Rullianus defeated a coalition of Gauls and Samnites. By 290 the Samnites surrendered, becoming allies (*socii*) of Rome. The wars (and the accounts of them) played a crucial role, not merely in the extension of Roman control across the peninsula, but also in the evolution of Roman identity and imperial ideology. JRWP

See Livy, books 7–10, trs. B. Radice (1982); Cornell, T. J. (1995) *The Beginnings of Rome*; Dench, E. (1995) *From Barbarians to New Men*; Salmon, E.T. (1967) *Samnium and the Samnites*.

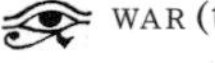 WAR (table).

Samnites OSCAN-speaking people of the central Apennines. The term is used by ancient sources to refer to an alliance of Pentri, Caraceni, Caudini and Hirpini (or sometimes to the Pentri alone) who occupied much of the modern region of Molise. Expansion by the Romans southwards in the mid-4th century BC brought them into conflict with the Samnites in a series of major wars (343–290 BC). The Samnites were eventually defeated, but not before inflicting major reverses on the Romans (e.g. at the Caudine Forks in 321). Brutal repressive measures taken against the Samnites by SULLA after the SOCIAL WAR led to heavy casualties.

The Samnites were often viewed by Romans as 'rustic mountain-dwellers' (e.g. LIVY 9.13.7) and their celebrated toughness and austerity were reflected in legends linking them with the SPARTANS. They came to be seen as exemplars of traditional virtue (e.g. HORACE, *Odes* 3.6.37–44). Their landscape was characterized by hillforts, VILLAGES and rural sanctuaries; many of the latter (notably at Pietrabbondante) were monumentalized in hellenistic style during the 2nd century BC, probably using the profits of commercial activity in the Greek east by leading Samnites. JRP

See Barker, G. (1995) *A Mediterranean Valley*; Dench, E. (1995) *From Barbarians to New Men*; Oakley, S. P. (1995) *The Hillforts of the Samnites*; Salmon, E.T. (1967) *Samnium and the Samnites*.

Samnium see ITALY, ROMAN.

Samos Mountainous ISLAND (490 sq km, 190 sq miles) in the eastern AEGEAN, with a city of the same name. Samos was considered fertile but its arable land was limited, so the Samians regularly farmed the nearby coast of Asia Minor. The ancient city (mod. Pythagóreio, formerly Tigáni) lay in the south-east lowlands, the sanctuary of the patron goddess, Hera (the Heraion) c.8 km (5 miles) west. Upland forests provided timber for ships, and in the archaic period Samos often dominated smaller islands. Seafaring, both TRADE and PIRACY, made a landed élite still richer. Soon after 800 BC the Samians built for Hera one of the first stone temples in Greece. Competition for power between leading families culminated in the tyranny of Polykrates (c.550–522), who patronized famous artists, poets, and architects. Herodotos describes the harbour mole, the city walls, and the tunnel (with water-pipe) built by Eupalinos of Megara through the *AKROPOLIS*; these all survive and may date to Polykrates' reign, like the huge male *kouros* statue found at the Heraion. After the Persian wars Samos, with its large fleet, joined the Athenian alliance. When Samos later rebelled, it took Perikles two years to subdue it.

Social divisions may explain the frequency of both civil strife (notably during the PELOPONNESIAN WAR, when radical DEMOCRACY briefly prevailed) and emigration (for example, in early colonial ventures to Africa and the western Mediterranean). At various periods a distinctive élite culture produced artists, writers and thinkers, particularly in archaic times and among émigrés to 3rd-century Alexandria. After c.400 BC Samos' freedom was usually short-lived; most notoriously, the Athenians colonized the island for over 40 years (365–322). Leading men, however, could bargain with great powers, exploiting the island's strategic value to secure their own position at home against political rivals. PTOLEMAIC rule in the early 3rd century helped the élite rebuild the

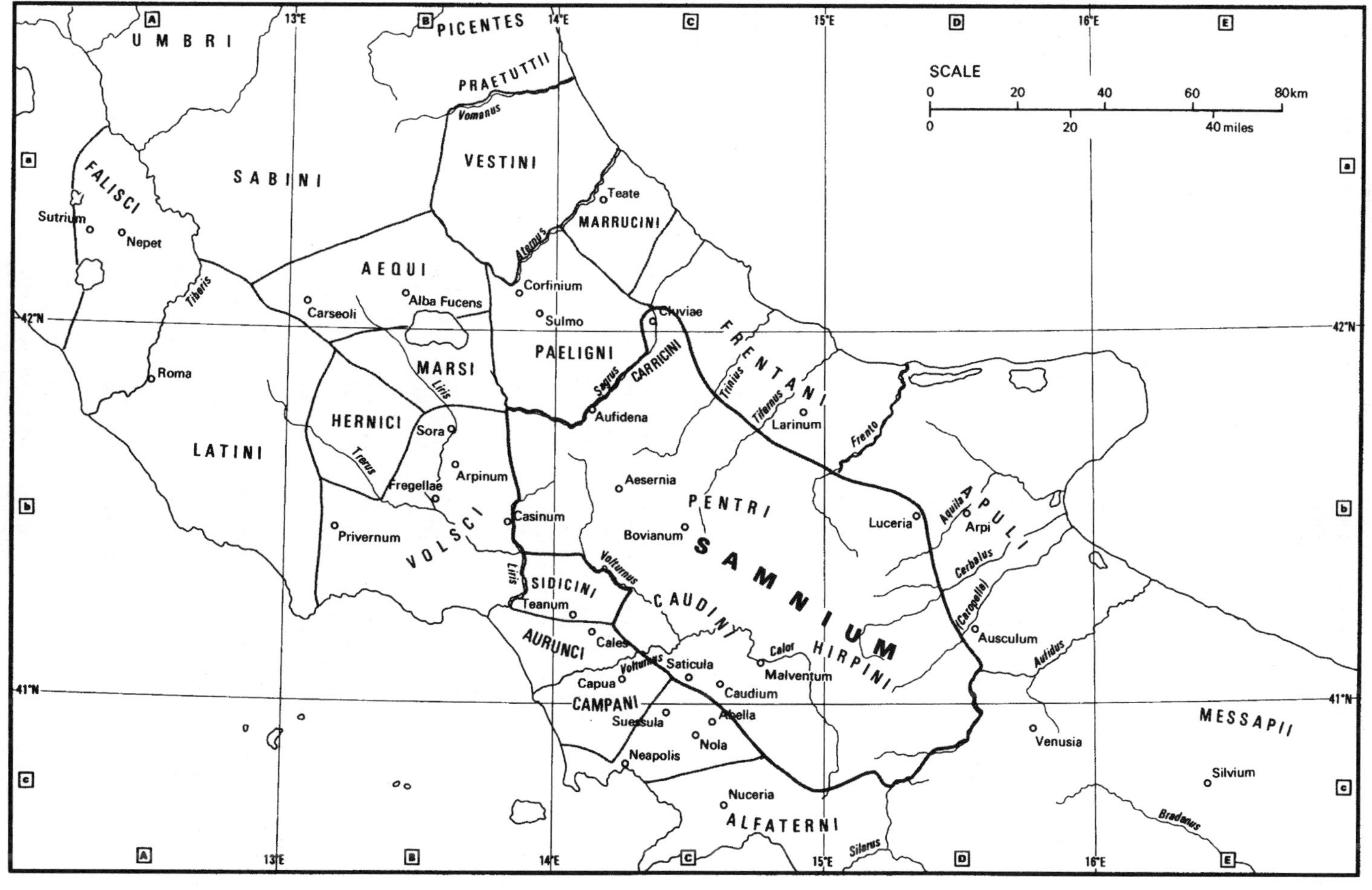

SAMNITES: map showing the Samnite heartlands in relation to other peoples of central Italy.

town, erecting fine houses and adding new monuments to the Heraion. Strategically less significant in Roman times, Samos served as a retreat for aristocrats like Tiberius and Livia. The expansion of settlement into the west of the island may indicate either a change in the *polis* or increased agricultural activity, or both. DGJS

See Shipley, G. (1987) *A History of Samos*; excavation reports in *Samos* volumes of the German Archaeological Institute.

 Aegean sea: (a)–(b).

Samosata This large and important city (in mod. Turkey) was founded on the west bank of the Euphrates, at a location whose huge Bronze Age tell and Hittite relief attest to ancient settlement. Its relative remoteness made exploration difficult, and modern excavation was limited and remains largely unpublished. The entire town now lies beneath the Atatürk Dam. Assyrian records refer to a town and kingdom of Kummuh, apparently the predecessor of Samosata, but it was sacked and foundered, not reappearing until the emergence of the kingdom of Commagene in the 2nd century BC. Named perhaps for king Samos (c.130–c.100 BC), it developed rapidly; indeed, in 38 Antiochos I (c.69–c.36) withstood a siege by Mark Antony who allowed himself to be bought off (Plutarch, *Antony* 34.2–4).

'Fortified by nature' according to Strabo (16.2.3), the city probably received its walls in this period. They enclosed an extensive irregular area of c.230 ha (570 acres) on a river terrace which included the tell. Despite the strongly hellenistic character of the culture favoured by the kings, the walls are unexpectedly and strikingly Roman. For much of their length they are faced in *opus reticulatum*, an architectural style fashionable in central Italy but seldom found around the eastern Mediterranean. *Opus reticulatum* is also found in the walls of the large structure excavated on the tell. Mosaics were laid down in the rooms, and the excavators have identified it as the palace of the Commagenian kings. Herod the Great's use of the technique in his villa at Jericho implies that these allied rulers of the Roman empire consciously adopted Roman practices. The city became part of Roman Syria during brief annexations of the kingdom by Tiberius and Gaius (Caligula). In AD 72 it passed into permanent Roman control. One of Syria's legions was established there, and it remained a major fortress city on or close to the frontier. More widely, Samosata lay at the nexus of routes, from Melitene, Garmaniceia, Zeugma and Edessa, that converged on this important river crossing.

Unlike at Zeugma 75 km (47 miles) downstream, surprisingly little material evidence survives from this period – only a handful of inscriptions and a few mosaics. The cemeteries are less impressive, but there are extensive traces of a major aqueduct from the Kahta Çay, a tributary of the Euphrates 25 km (16 miles) upstream. The town is frequently mentioned in Greco-Roman literary sources and named in inscriptions from as far away as Britain, but is seldom noted by either of its famous literary sons, Lucian (2nd century AD) and Paul (3rd century AD). In the 2nd and 3rd centuries, coins bearing its name were struck. It is on the list of cities sacked by the Persian king, Shapur I, around 256. It evidently recovered, still a place of significance in the pages of Ammianus Marcellinus and frequently mentioned as a bishopric. A victim of Roman–Persian warfare, Samosata declined slowly, changing hands frequently as Byzantine, Arab, Armenian and Turk fought over the region. It was reduced eventually to a modest fortress, then to the village of modern times set on the edge of a great, buried ruinfield. (see also Parthian wars; Persian wars, Roman; masonry styles) DLK

 Commagene; Syria, Roman: (a).

Samothrace see Cyriac of Ancona; orphism.

Samosata: the prehistoric tell by the Euphrates dominates the Roman town and legionary fortress.

sandals see FOOTWEAR.

sanitation Preserved public notices forbidding urination or defecation suggest that approaches to sanitation were sometimes informal, and attitudes towards hygiene more relaxed than today. Nevertheless, increasing urban populations required more sophisticated facilities for waste management, and in most cities waste water was carried through drains beneath the streets.

ARISTOPHANES mentions the use of chamber pots in classical Athens. Excavated 4th-century HOUSES from OLYNTHOS include terracotta urinals and even a terracotta TOILET seat. Most sophisticated are the facilities in houses from DELOS, dating to the 3rd or 2nd century BC onwards. A specialized room inside the street door has a stone-flagged floor in which a channel was set, running along one or more walls. Originally a wooden bench ran above, with one or more holes over which the occupants would sit. The waste was carried away into the street sewer by water flowing in the channel beneath.

Similar arrangements were used in the Roman world. Private houses often incorporate lavatories, and there was a trend towards large public facilities, which can still be seen at sites like EPHESOS. These are similar in construction to the private ones at Delos, but more elaborate and larger, with adjacent stone, rather than wooden, seats which could provide space for up to 40 or 50 individuals at a time. This suggests that Roman conceptions of privacy were very different from our own. (see also BATHING; BATHS; TOILETS; WATER SUPPLY) LCN

See Crouch, D. (1993) *Water Management in Ancient Greek Cities*; Neudecker, R. (1994) *Die Pracht der Latrine.*

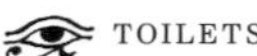 TOILETS.

Santorini see THERA.

Sappho Lived c.590 BC, in MYTILENE, the most important city on the ISLAND of LESBOS. She is, with ALKAIOS, representative of Lesbian melic POETRY. They were contemporaries and it is likely, judging from a fragment of Alkaios, that they knew each other's literary pursuits. Like Alkaios, her ARISTOCRATIC family was also sent into exile, and Sappho spent several years in SICILY. One of her brothers was involved in maritime trading. He fell in love with a *hetaira* who apparently brought him to bankruptcy, and his sister composed poems praying to APHRODITE to intervene and end the affair. Sappho, who describes herself in her poems as being dark, small and not very pretty, was married and had one daughter to whom she composed poems. Seemingly, this daughter died young and Sappho composed a lament for her BURIAL; only a few lines have survived. In spite of her aristocratic background, educating girls may have been for Sappho a source of income. She sometimes mentions her modest economic situation; for example, one fragment mentions that she cannot afford to buy a LYDIAN headband for her daughter. Lesbos is very close to Asia Minor, and during Sappho's time the Lydian empire was at its peak. Consequently, in Sappho's poems Lydia is synonymous with power, luxury and wealth.

She composed two different types of poems. On the one hand, she composed CHORAL poems to be sung by the girls under her care for all festive occasions. Especially famous in antiquity were the wedding songs or *epithalamia*. A long fragment about a mythical wedding, that of Hektor and ANDROMACHE, has survived. Other fragments of wedding songs present a popular flavour. In them she describes the bride as a ripe apple, ready to be picked by the husband. The groom is presented in the most favourable terms, as huge as a GOD, and Sappho encourages the CARPENTERS to raise the beams, so he might enter the house. Wedding songs traditionally included a lament about the daughter leaving the mother's house and a fictitious confrontation with the men. One fragment describes the bride as a hyacinth trampled on the mountains, representing the normal expression of the girls' anxiety towards their MARRIAGE and first encounter with SEXUALITY.

The other group of poems are those in which Sappho expresses her own feelings, mostly directed towards one girl of her circle. Homosocial groups were common in archaic Greece, as a place where young persons received their EDUCATION. Affections would develop among the members of the group, or between a member and the leader. The girls of Sappho's circle belonged to good families of Lesbos and Ionia, and were trained for marriage and a 'happy' life. This included their ability to produce song and poetry, which were used as a means of internalizing the rules of proper behaviour. A basic cultic organization lay behind these groups. Young women worshipped together and celebrated FESTIVALS together, mostly dedicated to Aphrodite. The cult to Aphrodite symbolizes the readiness of the girls to leave childhood behind and be married, which was considered their transition into adulthood. As we see from the many weddings songs for which Sappho was famous, marriage was never questioned and was accepted as a natural stage in life.

In several of her poems, Sappho shows desire for a particular girl, or her jealousy towards a girl who does not return her love. One famous poem is a PRAYER directed to Aphrodite to change a girl's mind. Another, translated into Latin by CATULLUS, talks about Sappho's emotions – described purely as physical reactions – when a groom is seated in front of his future bride. Sappho's was not the only group of girls in the island. In one fragment she complains about a girl who has abandoned her for Andromeda; we know the name of another rival, Gorgo. These groups were supposed to instil in the young girls a love of beauty and refinement, and contempt for rusticity.

Sappho's style is direct and elegant. She used EPIC language to express a world that had nothing to do with epic. Thus, she developed a new style that soon became traditional. Her influence in antiquity was immense and began early. Her poetry was appreciated by both HERODOTOS and PLATO and was often a topic in COMEDY. She was seen in classical times either as educator of youth or corrupter. In spite of the polemic, ALEXANDRIAN scholars edited her works in nine books. One of these contained her poems in 'Sapphic ode'. This is a poem composed in several four-line stanzas, each with three 'sapphic' hendecasyllables (lines of 11 syllables) and a fourth line of five syllables. In Rome, Catullus imitated and translated her, and HORACE imitated her topics and metrical forms. RBC

See Greene, E. (1996) *Reading Sappho*; Hutchinson, G. O. (2001) *Greek Lyric Poetry: a commentary on selected larger pieces*; Lightman, M. (2000) *Biographical Dictionary of Ancient Greek and Roman Women*; Mulroy, D. (1992) *Early Greek Lyric Poetry*; Rayor, D. J. (1991) *Sappho's Lyre*; Reynolds, M. (2001) *The Sappho Companion*; West, M. L., trs. (1993) *Greek Lyric Poetry*; Wilson, L. H. (1996) *Sappho's Sweetbitter Songs*.

 LYRIC POETRY.

Sarapeum see SERAPEUM.

Sarapis (Serapis) see EGYPT; GODS AND GODDESSES, ROMAN; RELIGION; SERAPEUM.

sarcophagi The term sarcophagus is derived from the Greek for 'flesh-eater' (JUVENAL, *Satires* 10.171). It was known in antiquity that certain kinds of STONE, as well as the addition of chalk, led to the almost complete destruction of the body (PLINY THE ELDER, *Natural History* 37.131). The concept sits uneasily with the view that sarcophagi were viewed as final and secure resting places. Their use is linked to a preference for inhumation rather than cremation, and thus fluctuates throughout antiquity. Greek and ETRUSCAN sarcophagi are known, the latter often showing a husband and wife reclining for a funerary banquet. In the Roman period, especially from the 2nd century AD onwards, decorated sarcophagi were made of MARBLE and usually imported from ASIA Minor and Greece. Frequently, designs were only roughly carved at the QUARRIES and then finished by a local WORKSHOP. Carved marble sarcophagi were viewed at funerals and during visits to the cemetery, and are often decorated with sophisticated scenes. Designs range from MYTHOLOGY to scenes of daily life, and can often be understood as allegories on the theme of transformation and death. Thus the story of Endymion, a mortal youth loved by the goddess Selene, equates sleep and death, while HUNTING and battle scenes elevate the deceased into the heroic sphere. Scenes of daily life, especially weddings, may remind the viewer of happier times or point to missed opportunities. Sarcophagi are often decorated with garlands, giving them the appearance of miniature shrines. HE

See Walker, S. (1985) *Memorials to the Roman Dead*.

SARCOPHAGI: elaborate marble sarcophagi from Istanbul (anc. Constantinople).

Sardinia At 24,000 sq km (9,300 sq miles), Sardinia has the second largest surface area of any MEDITERRANEAN island. From the 6th millennium BC, the distinctive artistic and technological achievements of its flourishing and outward-looking prehistoric communities were clearly conditioned by the availability of abundant natural resources: obsidian, metals, grain and wool. Their presence in the centre of the Mediterranean ensured seaborne interest from the outside world from the earliest times. Whatever the extent of this interest at any stage, the cultural matrix of Sardinia remained obstinately home-grown. Pope Gregory the Great's complaint in the 6th century AD that the Sardinians 'worshipped stones' was probably occasioned by the survival of an originally prehistoric rite involving the use of standing stones for cult purposes.

Sardinian prehistory culminates in the unique NURAGIC civilization (c.1800 BC onwards). MYCENAEAN contact is attested from the 14th century; it led to peaceful cohabitation with Mycenaean residents, in circumstances that produced the earliest evidence (pre-1200) for worked IRON in the central Mediterranean. During the 11th to 9th centuries, a significant degree of east–west exchange was maintained by complementary METALLURGICAL interests in Sardinia and the LEVANT, especially CYPRUS. Thus it is that a nuragic village, Sant'Imbenia on the coast near Alghero, has yielded some of the earliest EUBOIAN Geometric pottery, which is directly associated with metallurgical activity that on present evidence appears to be PHOENICIAN.

Actual Phoenician colonies, at least at Nora, Sulcis and Tharros, were actively involved in pan-Mediterranean exchanges by the 8th century. By the 6th, problems at home caused all the western Phoenician foundations to depend increasingly on the greatest of their number, CARTHAGE in North Africa. For Sardinia, the adjectival change from 'Phoenician' to 'Punic' signifies a brusque transition from peaceful TRADING, industry and settlement to military occupation, which was designed to promote maximum exploitation of the island's AGRICULTURAL and mineral resources in the period between the decline of Etruscan seapower and the rise of Rome. But the latter was inexorable, and conflict with the commercial imperialism of Carthage finally exploded into the first PUNIC WAR (264–241).

Carthage ceded Sardinia to Rome in 238. The natives under their redoubtable leader Hampsicora revolted in 215, with Carthaginian support; the uprising was ruthlessly suppressed, as were the desperate and unaided insurrections of 177. Under Rome, Sardinia functioned as a place of political exile, and as a source of grain and woollen clothing for the army. In 54, CICERO successfully defended SULLA's unsavoury stepson Marcus Scaurus, propraetor in Sardinia, against local charges of extortion. Elsewhere in the Roman world, inscriptions show that the island's perennial status as a granary is matched by the Sardinian origin of many 'Roman' soldiers and sailors. At home, the effects of

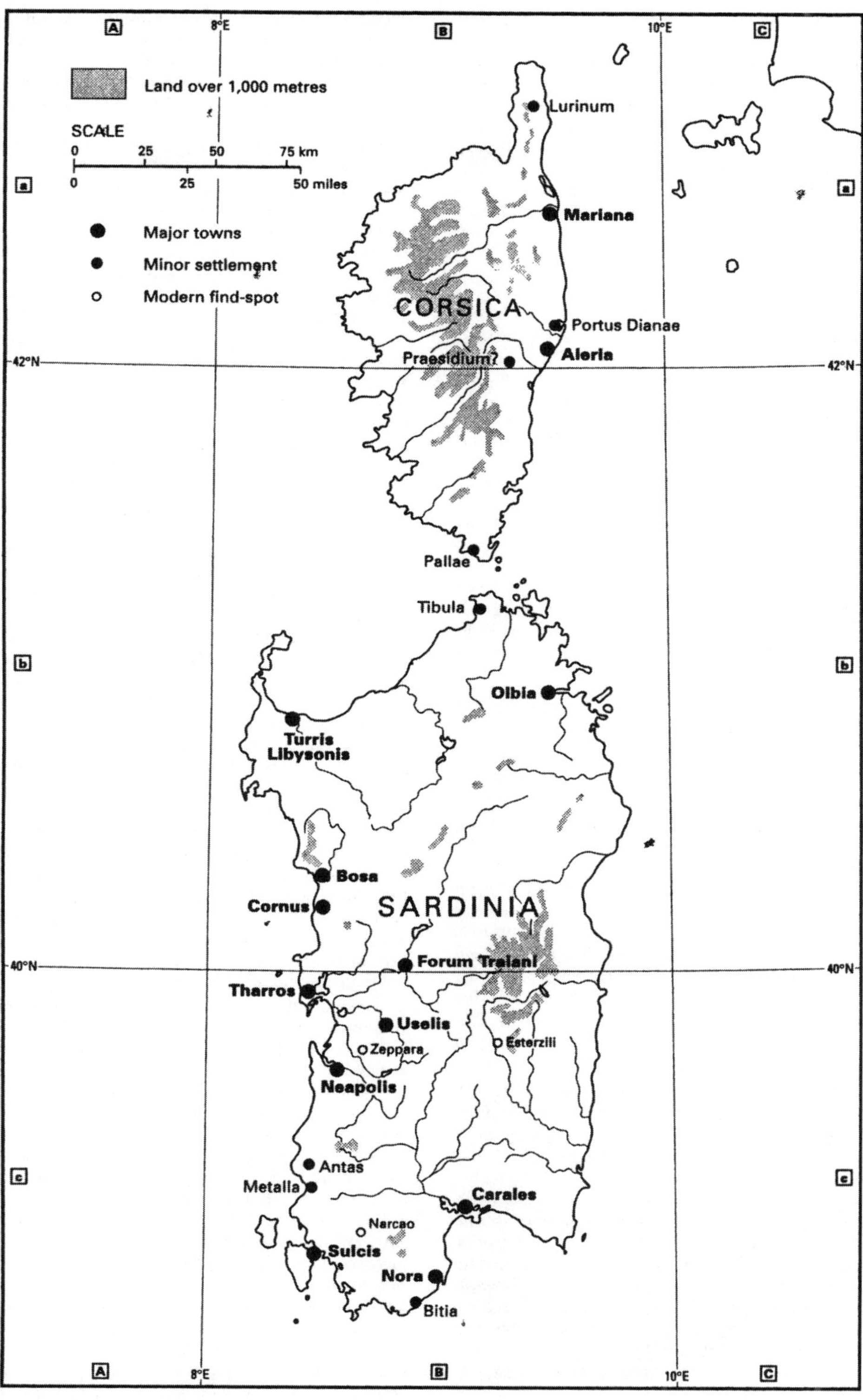

SARDINIA: map of Sardinia and Corsica.

romanization never extended far beyond the urban and coastal areas. The highland clans of the interior were the perpetual bane of the Roman administration; their activities are vividly documented in the Esterzili Decree of AD 69. They and their nuragic forebears are clearly responsible for Sardinia's status as the only region of modern Italy that was not impregnated by classicism. DR

See Balmuth, M. S. and Tykot, R. H., eds. (1998) *Sardinian and Aegean Chronology*; Tykot, R. H. and Andrews, T. K., eds. (1992) *Sardinia in the Mediterranean*; Van Dommelen, P. (1998) *On Colonial Grounds*.

Sardis Capital city of the kingdom of LYDIA (c.680–546 BC), located 100 km (62 miles) due east of SMYRNA. Neolithic and Bronze Age remains have been found, but MINOAN and MYCENAEAN items are scant. Later Greek tradition knew a Heraclid dynasty that ruled Sardis for 22 generations. The last Heraclid, Kandaules, was murdered by Gyges, who married his widow, proclaimed himself king c.680 and established the Mermnad dynasty. This was fated to endure five generations, according to the DELPHIC oracle (Herodotos 1.13). Croesus, the fifth ruler, was overthrown by CYRUS the Great of PERSIA in 546. Sardis became capital of the satrapy of Sparda and was the western terminus of the great Royal Road from Sousa (Herodotos 5.52–3). Burned during the IONIAN REVOLT (499–494), the city was conquered in 334 by ALEXANDER, who reportedly restored ancient Lydian laws and customs.

After Attalos III bequeathed his kingdom of Pergamon to the Roman people in 133, Sardis became part of the PROVINCE of ASIA. Both HADRIAN and MARCUS AURELIUS visited the city. After provincial reorganization under DIOCLETIAN, it was the centre of a judicial district that encompassed both Lydia and PHRYGIA. The city was conquered by the Arabs in AD 716.

Under Mermnad rule, Sardis became the cultural centre of the eastern MEDITERRANEAN world. Lydian luxury, fashions, PERFUME, MUSIC and POETRY became famous throughout the Greek world. Sardis was known for its TEMPLE of CYBELE (later replaced by one dedicated to ARTEMIS), its massive fortification wall, its HORSES and cavalry, but especially for its great wealth – the legendary gold of Croesus. The Lydians' resources in precious metal encouraged them to strike the world's first COINS. JDM

See Hanfmann, G. M. A., ed. (1983) *Sardis from Prehistoric to Roman Times*; Ramage, A. and Craddock, P. (2000) *King Croesus' Gold*.

 EAST GREECE.

Sassanian empire The PERSIAN successor to the PARTHIAN empire, named after Sasan, a founder whose precise relationship to the dynasty cannot be determined. The Sassanids unseated the Arsakid Parthians in the 220s AD. Papak, the local king of Persis, apparently revolted against Parthian authority c.205, when the Arsakids were preoccupied by SEPTIMIUS SEVERUS' invasion of MESOPOTAMIA. About 20 years later, Papak's son Ardashir (fathered by Sasan in some accounts, however) ended effective Parthian rule. From the late 220s and essentially until the Arab conquest, periods of hostility and relative peace between the Roman (Byzantine) and Persian empires alternated at irregular intervals, with Armenia a regular point of contention.

The sources do not always allow certainty on dates of accessions and relationships between rulers and their successors, though the broad outlines are clear enough. The Sassanids claimed to be the descendants of the Achaemenid Persians. This was equally true in religion: the dynasty subscribed to ZOROASTRIANISM. This developed into something approaching an organized state religion – with a view of orthodoxy and heresy mirroring that of CHRISTIANITY – that was very powerful whenever the leadership could impose its authority. MANICHAEISM, encouraged by SHAPUR I (c.240–c.272), became a byword for heresy in later periods. JEWS, in general, seemed to have been a legally permitted minority, and from the time of Yazdagird I (399–421), Christians enjoyed a similar status most of the time.

Other than Ardashir, the most important Sassanian kings were Shapur I, Shapur II (309–79) and Chosroës I (531–79). Under Shapur I, the Sassanian empire reached its greatest extent, reaching as far as the Indus river and (briefly) the MEDITERRANEAN. During the late 240s and 250s, Shapur's forces captured Antioch at least once and drove into the Lebanon valley. In the late 250s, he captured the emperor VALERIAN, but the PALMYRENES Odenathus and ZENOBIA soon dispossessed him of his Roman acquisitions. In the east, his sovereignty depended more on fealty than on direct control in some areas, which his successors were unable to retain. Shapur had Mani at his court for some time, and was attracted by the new Manichaean religion; for what purpose cannot be determined.

Shapur II was, quite literally, 'born to the purple'. After the death of his predecessor Hormizd II (302–9), court intrigue ended in the selection of the very young Shapur as successor; some sources claim that the royal diadem had been placed on his mother's womb even before his birth in 302. His long rule generated a stability that the short, disputed reigns of his immediate predecessors (and successors) did not. Perhaps partly for that reason, the 4th century saw great and regular enmity between the Roman and Persian empires. Christians in Persia were regularly persecuted on grounds of suspect loyalty, and from the late 330s to the 370s military campaigns by one side or both were an almost annual event. Despite several sieges, Shapur was unable to capture NISIBIS, but Amida fell to him in 359. The failure of JULIAN's campaign and his death in 363 forced Jovian to make peace; the Persians received much territory, including Nisibis. Shapur II's reign also saw further developments in Zoroastrian orthodoxy and in religious organization.

The last great king, Chosroës I, restructured society in a number of ways and brought the Sassanians to their apogee. He instituted a new tax system and made changes to the structure of the army. Both reforms reduced the power of the feudal families, and helped to centralize power and the economy. In religion, he reformed the clergy and probably gathered together the material for the current form of the *Avesta* (the sacred writings of Zoroastrianism). Following his death, the suppressed aristocracy generated problems for his weaker successors, contributing to the kingdom's

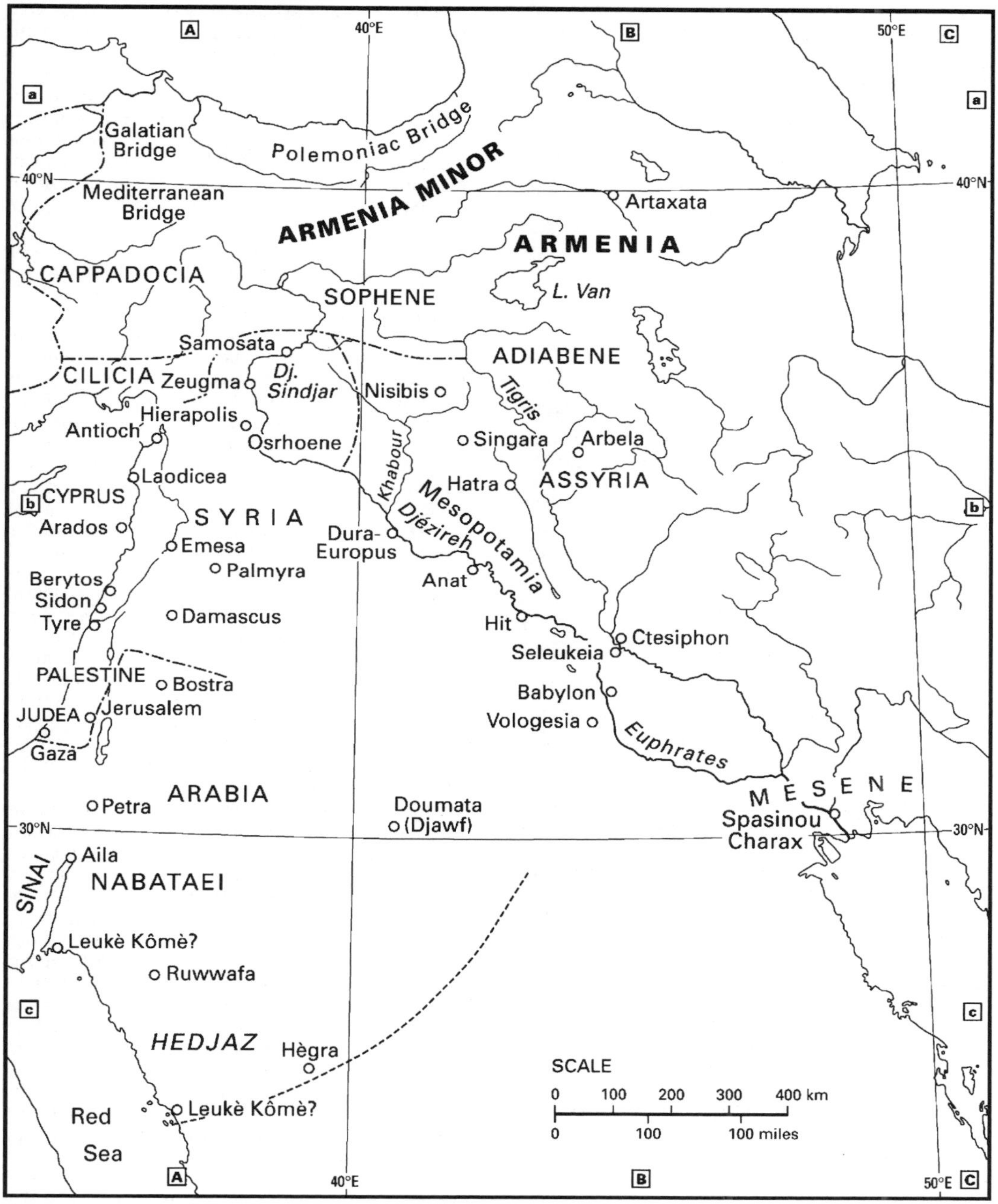

Sassanian empire: (a) map of Sassanian heartlands in Mesopotamia.

decline. In 642, the Sassanian army was defeated by the Arabs, effectively ending Sassanid rule. The last king, Yazdagird III, fled to the east, but was eventually captured by his unwilling host and put to death in 651. (see p. 788) JV

See Christensen, A. (1944) *L'Iran sous les Sassanides*; Dodgeon, M. H. and Lieu, S. N. C. (1991) *The Roman Eastern Frontier and the Persian Wars* AD *226–363*; Frye, R. N. (1984) *The History of Ancient Iran*; Greatrex, G. and Lieu, S. N. C. (2002) *The Roman Eastern Frontier and the Persian Wars*, vol. 2: *363–628* AD.

 Persia and Persians.

satire A quintessentially Roman literary genre (Quintilian 10.1.93), whose original characteristics

SASSANIAN EMPIRE: (b) the Sassanid dynasty.

Sassanid kings	Dates AD
Papak	208–222
Shapur	222
Ardashir	223–240
Shapur I	240–272
Hormizd Ardashir	272–273
Varahran (Vahram) I	273–276
Varahran II	276–293
Varahran III	293
Narseh	293–302
Hormizd II	302–309
Shapur II	309–379
Ardashir II	379–383
Shapur III	383–388
Varahran IV	388–399
Yazdagird I	399–421
Varahran V	421–439
Yazdagird II	439–457
Hormizd III	457–459
Peroz I	459–484
Valash	484–488
Kavad I (first reign)	488–496
Zamasp	496–498
Kavad I (second reign)	498–531
Khusro I (Chosroes)	531–579
Hormizd IV	579–590
Khusro II (first reign)	590
Varahran Chobin	590–591
Khusro II (second reign)	591–628
Kavad II	628
Ardashir III	628–629
Shahrvaraz	629
Khusro III	630
Boran	630–631
Peroz II, Hormizd V, Khusro IV	631–632
Yazdagird III	632–651

Some dates approximate or disputed; names are sometimes spelled differently.

are unrelated to the English genre. The name *satura* means something close to 'full', and may have been taken from the term *lanx satura*, a plate stuffed with food, or from *satura*, a term for a sausage and stuffing mixture. The Roman genre of *satura* was 'stuffed' – full, that is, of a variety of different thematic elements. In practice, this free-for-all Roman genre might be characterized by the English term farrago (see Juvenal 1.86). Its earliest exemplar, ENNIUS (239–169 BC), makes this clear. He wrote a large amount of satire (no longer extant). It was not satirical in our sense, but a mix of moralizing, censure, dialogue and authorial monologue. Moral censure, or perhaps moralizing, seems to have become one abiding trait of the genre. Lucilius (180–103 BC) was the father of the genre. He wrote 30 books of this form of poetry, in which moral censure seems to have played a prominent role but was blended with an authorial persona that has been described as the 'rollicking adventurer'. VARRO (116–27 BC), the next major practitioner, seems to have practised a variant, Menippean satire, a mix of prose and verse. In this version, PHILOSOPHY seems to have overlaid moral censure but the farrago was maintained. He wrote 150 books of this sort of material. HORACE (65–8 BC) wrote two books of *Satires* (or *sermones*). The often violent politics of his era may account for moral censure being displaced by moralizing of a STOIC or EPICUREAN type. The blend is as various as might be expected: autobiography, moralizing and LITERARY CRITICISM, ETIQUETTE, gastronomy and travel figure, among other things.

During the reign of NERO (AD 54–68), PERSIUS (34–62) wrote six difficult satires, all based firmly within the ambit of Stoic philosophy. The censure, though not directed towards live characters (unlike that of Lucilius), is constant. The farrago is less wild but still evident; Persius treats topics such as literary criticism, vice and sickness, public popularity, the morality of SACRIFICE, virtue and living within one's means. The last of the extant satirists in verse is JUVENAL (b. between AD 45 and 65, d. after 127), who left 16 satires in which moral censure and black humour mingle in a manner that resembles modern satire. Juvenal's targets are all dead, a safer practice in imperial Rome. The farrago element is no less apparent. His various topics or polemics include attacks on mythological poetry (*Satire* 1), HOMOSEXUALITY (2, 9), life in Rome (3), imperial decision-making (4), the client's life (5), WOMEN (6), the problems with PATRONAGE (7), gastronomy (11), friendship (12), children (14), Egyptians (15) and the soldier's life (16).

Satire remained essentially a genre based in poetry. There survive some prose texts, however, which resemble this Roman tradition of the *satura*. SENECA wrote a parody of the emperor CLAUDIUS called the *Apocolocyntosis* ('pumpkinification'). PETRONIUS' prose EPIC, the *Satyrica*, may also be considered in this light. Some dialogues of LUCIAN (b. AD 120) share in this spirit of parodic censure and breadth of theme. PGT

See Freudenburg, K. (2001) *Satires of Rome*.

satrap see ALEXANDER; PERSIA AND PERSIANS; PERSIAN EMPIRE.

Satricum (mod. Borgo le Ferriere) A settlement located 30 km (19 miles) south-east of Rome. It was captured in 488 BC by the Volsci, who stayed there until 346, when it was destroyed, rebuilt and resettled with Roman colonists. More than 200 trench graves that do not reflect native styles in Latium have been discovered in the south-west necropolis. After 346 Satricum is only mentioned in connection with the TEMPLE of Mater Matuta, a GODDESS primarily concerned with newborn babies; it was her main sanctuary. Rediscovered in 1896, the sanctuary has revealed a number of terracotta antefixes, among which feature those of a warrior and a bearded god.

Satricum is now otherwise famous for the discovery, by a team of Dutch archaeologists, of an archaic Latin inscription, the so-called Lapis Satricanus. The stone is dedicated to Mamers (MARS), but was discovered in the foundations of the temple of Mater Matuta. While the temple dates to the beginning of the 5th century BC, the inscription evidently predates its reuse as building material. Its main historical significance lies in the fact that it mentions a Publius Valerius, perhaps to be identified with Publius Valerius Publicola, one of the leading Roman politicians after the expulsion of the last ETRUSCAN king. Another salient feature is that it is dedicated by Valerius' *sodales* ('companions'), who are taken to be a group of armed supporters. Their presence at Satricum remains unexplained. None of the literary sources credits Valerius with military operations in the south. MK

See Stibbe, C. M. et al. (1980) *Lapis Satricanus.*

 LATINS.

Saturn (Saturnus) Roman god, notable for his FESTIVAL, the Saturnalia. His cult was deeply hellenized by the historical period, but its antiquity is demonstrated by the invocation of Saturn in the ancient hymn of the Salii, and by the inclusion of his festival in the earliest form of the Roman religious CALENDAR. His original nature is obscure, but the timing of his festival between those of two AGRICULTURAL deities suggests that his significance was similar. The ancient etymology that derived his name from *satus*, 'sowing', is unlikely for linguistic reasons. Saturn was early on identified with the Greek god Kronos; the cult statue in his TEMPLE in the FORUM (which also housed the state treasury) depicted him like Kronos with a veiled head and a sickle, while his SACRIFICES were performed 'in the Greek rite'. The Saturnalia began on 17 December with a public sacrifice and banquet, and lasted for (usually) seven days of feasting, drinking and social laxity presided over by a 'Saturnalian king'. Business was suspended, and public GAMBLING sanctioned. SLAVES ate with or were even served by their masters, and small gifts were exchanged. In Latin literature, Saturn appears as the father of JUPITER and also as the king who ruled Italy in the GOLDEN AGE. Outside Rome his cult was limited, though in AFRICA, where he was identified with the great Punic god BAAL, it was one of the most popular. JBR

See Versnel, H. S. (1993) *Transition and Reversal in Myth and Ritual.*

Saturnalia see HOLIDAYS; PIGS; SATURN.

satyr plays see AESCHYLUS; DRAMA, GREEK; EURIPIDES; PHALLUS; POETRY, GREEK; SOPHOKLES; TRAGEDY.

satyrs Mythical creatures, male in gender and of a mixed nature, made up of a human and an animal part. The latter consisted of features of a goat with a horse's tail. They are frequently represented in ART, particularly Attic VASE-PAINTING, as inseparable companions of the Greek god DIONYSOS, often alongside the god's female mythical followers, the maenads. They usually appear as part of a larger Dionysiac group (*thiasos*) which also includes maenads in scenes of revelry and orgiastic DANCING. Some of their typical activities are drinking WINE, pursuing females and parading in procession. Their excessive sexual appetite and their addiction to wine are prominent features of satyrs in both myth and art.

Their connection with the cult of Dionysos, and their association with dances and SONGS in his honour, made their shape particularly suitable for performances at Athenian festivals of Dionysos, notably the Great Dionysia and the Lenaia. Furthermore, satyr plays, a sort of COMEDY which in Athens traditionally accompanied TRAGEDIES, were performed by CHORUSES of men dressed and MASKED as satyrs. Satyr-like figures also appeared outside dramatic performances, as part of the ritual THEATRE of some festivals of Dionysos. EP

See Carpenter, T. H. (1997) *Dionysian Iconography in Fifth-century Athens.*

savings see BANKING; ECONOMY, GREEK.

scandals As today, scandals, which abounded in classical antiquity, tended to involve sex or politics and notable individuals. Scandal-mongering was a pastime indulged in by rich and poor at taverns, barber's shops, dinner parties and BATH houses. One scandal that rocked Athenian society was the attack on the HERMS (phallic images of Hermes) by a group of vandals on the eve of the Athenian fleet's departure for Sicily in 415 BC. It was considered an inauspicious omen, especially when accusations were also made that the ELEUSINIAN mysteries had been profaned. The scandal resulted in ALCIBIADES' arrest. The profanation of the mysteries was also the subject of the Roman scandal of the Bona Dea, a religious rite exclusively held for women, which in 62 BC was infiltrated by a man, Publius CLODIUS Pulcher, disguised in female dress. The scandal was made even more acute by the fact that the celebration was held in the home of JULIUS CAESAR, then *pontifex maximus*, with his wife, Pompeia, and his mother, Aurelia, placed in charge of the rituals. Caesar divorced Pompeia over the scandal, claiming that Caesar's wife had to be above suspicion. Imperial scandals continued apace, especially under the Julio-Claudian emperors. They range in detail from the sexual shenanigans of Julia the Elder, on the steps of the FORUM, to the pornographic library of TIBERIUS and the alleged incestuous relationship between NERO and his mother. LL-J

See Blond, A. (2000) *A Scandalous History of the Roman Emperors.*

scepticism, religious Despite PLATO's assertion that 'all mankind, Greeks and non-Greeks alike, believe in the existence of gods' (*Laws* 886a), it is evident that in classical antiquity, some did not. Diagoras of Melos (c.420 BC), for example, on discovering that his prayer for the safe return of a manuscript was not answered, denied that the GODS existed. He proceeded to boil up his turnips using a wooden statue of HERAKLES as fuel, and was condemned to death – a high price for his lack of conviction. Not many people, however, could be labelled atheists in any modern sense of the term, as few denied the existence of a METAPHYSICAL reality that transcended the empirical world – even if, as with the EPICUREANS or the CYNICS, their belief in 'gods' was of the most attenuated kind and they were dubious of traditional claims that the gods had dealings with humans. Indeed, those labelled atheists (*atheoi*, 'godless', in Greek) denied the gods of popular belief and, more specifically, the rites associated with their worship – not the divine *per se*. Hence the accusation that the early CHRISTIANS were atheists (e.g. Athenagoras, *Embassy* 4). Advocates of philosophical Scepticism, a movement born in the hellenistic period but finding its most famous flowering in the work of Sextus Empiricus (c.AD 200), argued that it was necessary to suspend judgement on such issues, as humans could not know anything for certain. The SCEPTICS' championing of custom (in place of knowledge) meant that they were not necessarily hostile to the practice of conventional religion, whatever that might be.

Scepticism was not restricted to the Greek and Roman traditions in antiquity. For example, there is also a sceptical tradition within JUDAISM, represented by the book of Ecclesiastes, in which God's ways (in particular God's justice) are deemed so inscrutable that humans are advised that the only sensible course of action is to eat, drink and enjoy yourself (8.15). JM

See Athenagoras, *Embassy for the Christians* (trs. J. Crehan, 1956); Thrower, J. (1980) *The Alternative Tradition*.

sceptics Many ancient PHILOSOPHERS expressed pessimism regarding the attainability of KNOWLEDGE or challenged the reliability of everyday experience of the world. But scepticism, the systematic rejection of knowledge claims across the full philosophical spectrum, began only in the early hellenistic age. Pyrrhon was a guru figure, who wrote nothing but profoundly influenced others by his extraordinary calm. One tradition attributed this to his cognitive detachment, and Pyrrhonist scepticism resulted. After a quiet start, the movement gained prominence in the 1st century BC, when Ainesidemos refounded it. It is well represented in the surviving writings of Sextus Empiricus (2nd century AD), by whose day 'Sceptics' (lit. 'inquirers') had become an alternative name of the school.

A second sceptical movement was the 'New ACADEMY'. PLATO's hellenistic followers read his SOCRATIC dialogues as models of open-ended debate in which knowledge claims were systematically demolished. They made it their business to inflict the same treatment on their contemporaries.

Both schools proclaimed 'suspension of judgement' as the outcome of their arguments. Ainesidemos' ten 'modes' of suspension systematically undermine knowledge claims. Judgements inevitably depended on individuals' perspectives, they argued, and no privileged viewpoint was available from which arbitration might be attempted. (see also SCEPTICISM, RELIGIOUS) DNS

See Burnyeat, M. F., ed. (1983) *The Skeptical Tradition*.

schism A division in the CHURCH arising primarily from disagreements about practice. The earliest schisms seem to have been provoked by disputes about CHRISTIAN conduct during times of PERSECUTION. For example, during Decius' persecution (250–1), many succumbed to imperial pressure and lapsed from their faith, some even going so far as to offer sacrifice to PAGAN GODS. After the persecution, many of these lapsed Christians sought readmission to the church, only to face protests from hard-liners who had resisted efforts to make them deny Christ. In Rome this resulted in the election of rival BISHOPS, as the hard-liners elected Novatian in opposition to the moderate Cornelius (251–3).

Similar problems afflicted the AFRICAN church after the DIOCLETIANIC persecution. In CARTHAGE, bishop Caecilius found himself opposed by Donatus, a bishop from Numidia, over the conduct of the Carthaginian clergy during the persecution. The dispute came to the attention of the newly converted CONSTANTINE, for whom the ideology of ecclesiastical unity was inseparable from that of imperial unity. He sought unsuccessfully to resolve the dispute at CHURCH COUNCILS in Rome (313) and Arles (314). The schism continued to divide the African church until the early 5th century when, with the agreement of bishop AUGUSTINE (1) of Hippo, the state sought to effect unity by the bloody suppression of the schismatics.

For Constantine and his successors, schism and heresy alike undermined ecclesiastical unity and demanded severe counter-measures. As a result, the distinction between heresy and schism began to break down, and schisms often occurred within the context of doctrinal debates. For example, the church of ANTIOCH was divided throughout the 4th century in a dispute which often involved the protagonists of the controversy over Christological doctrine. Similarly, bishop Lucifer of Cagliari (d. c.371), in a move which recalled that of Donatist hard-liners, initiated a schism with those whom he considered to have caved in to heretical doctrines. In the 6th century, the efforts of the emperor JUSTINIAN (527–65) to have certain doctrines condemned as heretical initiated the schism of the Three Chapters, as churchmen in Rome and northern ITALY debated the propriety of allowing an emperor to browbeat bishops in doctrinal matters. The development of the church as a powerful social and political institution plainly exacerbated the problem of schism. In 498, for example, Symmachus and Laurentius were elected as rival popes at Rome. They represented differing parties within the church which reflected not only different political allegiances to the Ostrogothic government at RAVENNA, but also different dynastic affiliations within the Roman ARISTOCRACY.

For all the division and disruption which they caused, schisms could be long-lasting. The Donatist church flourished for over a century, while Novatian and Luciferian sects remained active in CONSTANTINOPLE in the mid-5th century. Like heresy, schism is a constant reminder of the essentially diverse character of early Christianity. MDH

See Frend, W. H. C. (1971) *The Donatist Church*; Greenslade, S. L. (1964) *Schism in the Early Church*; Moorhead, J. (1992) *Theoderic in Italy*; (1994) *Justinian*; Urbainczyk, T. (1997) *Socrates of Constantinople*.

scholarship, ancient Both Greeks and Romans accorded a high status to the investigation and description of the cultural heritage. The full apparatus of what a modern observer would recognize as 'scholarship' is not found before the early 3rd century BC, but remoter beginnings can be traced. Both the geographer-ethnographer-historians of the late 6th and early 5th centuries and the SOPHISTS of the succeeding half-century can be seen as appropriating the POETS' traditional guardianship of knowledge about the PAST and other lands and of the skills of language, and converting it into a newly detached and analytical project of inquiry, categorization and systematic record. A further stage is marked by the development of the philosophical schools of 4th-century Athens, particularly ARISTOTLE'S LYCEUM, with its research and publication in such fields as constitutional, MUSICAL and literary history. The decisive point is reached with the revolutionary cultural project of the PTOLEMIES in ALEXANDRIA at the beginning of the 3rd century, when scholars were provided with an institutional home (the MOUSEION) and an unprecedentedly rich research archive (the LIBRARY), as well as a new sense of the Greek cultural heritage as a coherent whole to be collected, catalogued and analysed. The great monuments of this era of scholarship include KALLIMACHOS' *catalogue raisonné* of the whole of Greek literature in his *Pinakes*, the Homeric studies of Zenodotos, Aristophanes of Byzantium and Aristarchos, and a mass of antiquarian and lexicographic works by these and other scholars. Theoretical grammar was also developed, culminating in the work of Dionysios Thrax (though STOIC philosophers outside Alexandria also made important contributions).

In due course, other centres of scholarly activity developed, most notably in PERGAMON. The process was accelerated in the mid-2nd century when persecution by Ptolemy VIII Euergetes II Physkon (r.170–163, 145–116) prompted an intellectual diaspora. At about the same time, scholarly interests began to stir in Latin, as part of the grand appropriation of Greek culture practised by Rome over the last two centuries BC. Lucius Ateius' work in the fields of antiquarian research, literary study and language paved the way for the greatest of all Roman scholars, Marcus Terentius VARRO, with his *Human and Divine Antiquities*, *On the Latin Language* and *On Poets*. AUGUSTUS' foundation of the Palatine library gave Rome an archive to rival those of Alexandria and Pergamon, and scholarly activity continued with new variations by such figures as the elder PLINY and AULUS GELLIUS. As previously in Greece, so too in Rome scholarly work, particularly on language and literature, became an indispensable resource for the schools of grammar and RHETORIC that formed the backbone of ÉLITE EDUCATION.

Relatively few of the great works of ancient scholarship now survive in their original form (more in Latin than in Greek). Much is known to us only from late antique summaries and reworkings, above all from the notes known as *SCHOLIA*, found in the margins of medieval manuscripts. MBT

See Pfeiffer, R. (1968) *History of Classical Scholarship*; Reynolds, L. and Wilson, N. (1991) *Scribes and Scholars.*

scholarship, Byzantine To a considerable extent, the effect of Byzantine scholarship was the preservation of the classical Greek heritage. In addition to copying texts, much work was devoted to collection and exposition of material that had not been read or studied much, partly because of CHRISTIANITY'S disregard for it.

While the 7th and 8th centuries, often called a dark age, exhibit a dearth of scholarship, some individuals kept alive a tradition of knowledge. Grammatical and lexical work continued to reflect the educational enterprise, and much of what survives from this period falls into that category. In the 9th century, scholarship revived, accompanied by two important developments, the availability of paper to replace PAPYRUS (parchment was also used) and the invention of a minuscule script. Renewed Byzantine interest in secular, especially scientific and philosophical, works of the past coincides with the 'translation movement' in ISLAMIC SCHOLARSHIP; some interrelationship – perhaps simply the interest in acquiring manuscripts of Greek authors – is almost certainly to be surmised. One key difference is evident: Byzantine scholarship maintained an enthusiasm for literature and history. Two important early figures are Leo the Philosopher (c.790–c.869), one of whose students knew enough EUCLID to surprise an Arab caliph, and Photios (Photius, c.810–c.893), twice patriarch. The latter compiled a *Lexikon* (of which the only complete manuscript was discovered as recently as 1959), the *Amphilochia* (short essays) and the work known as *Bibliotheke* ('Library'). Primarily an account of his private reading, the *Bibliotheke* describes the content of individual works in 280 chapters or *Codices* of varying length with Photios' own comments. It is often regarded as a record of what texts were available to an avid reader.

In the 10th century, the emperor Constantine Porphyrogenitus' (912–59) patronage of schools and education was significant. Himself an author, he sponsored ENCYCLOPEDIAS of MEDICINE, veterinary science, zoology and agriculture. He planned an encyclopedia of human activity in 53 parts, but this was perhaps never completed. Surviving portions reveal that the technique was to string together excerpts from earlier writers, primarily historians; they preserve the known portions of several authors. The *SUDA* also belongs to this period.

Subsequently, a richer tradition of scholarship developed, especially in the circle of Michael Psellos (b.1018), professor of philosophy at Constantinople, who studied, wrote about, and taught a wide range of philosophy, from PLATO and NEOPLATONISM to Chaldaean theurgy. Equally adept at literature, he was, not surprisingly, accused of heresy. In 1082 his student and successor John Italos (also known as Longibardos) was banned from teaching and ordered to live in a monastery. Such were the dangers of espousing views considered heterodox that some writers subsequently cited pagan authors anonymously. In the 1070s, John Xiphilinos produced his epitome of CASSIUS DIO.

The 12th century represents a second renewal and produced writers as diverse as Anna Comnena (*Alexiad*), Zonaras (a world history to 1118), Gregory of Corinth (works on syntax and style), John Tzetzes (treatments of classical authors) and Eustathios (commentaries on HOMER). Many scholars of this period, and earlier, were churchmen, and almost all had access to works no longer extant today. Their writings offer information, and many fragments of classical authors, that are otherwise unknown.

After the Fourth Crusade captured and sacked Constantinople in 1204, Byzantine scholarship fell into steep decline, with a brief revival beginning late in the century. Maximus Planudes (c.1255–c.1305) concentrated on poetry and produced new texts, but was competent in other fields, including science and mathematics; he compiled a version of the *Greek Anthology*. His contemporary Demetrios Triklinios produced texts of many authors, such as the fabulist Babrius, HESIOD, PINDAR and ARISTOPHANES. His texts of AESCHYLUS and EURIPIDES are in places fundamental for the modern textual critic, for he edited plays not regularly read in the schools. Theodoros Metochites (1270–1332) was a commentator on ARISTOTLE and an essayist on various authors and topics. Subsequently, Byzantine scholarship declined, though scholars continued to produce material.

From a modern perspective, Byzantine scholars were hampered by Christianity's restrictions, but it is unlikely that they shared this view. They were capable of original thought, but their originality does not accord with modern tastes. Nevertheless, as products of their own environment assessed on their own terms, some Byzantine scholars were highly competent men. JV

See Wilson, N. G. (1983) *Scholars of Byzantium*.

scholarship, classical The term 'classical' (*classicus*, meaning 'from the highest citizen grade') goes back to the 1st-century AD scholar FRONTO, describing authors whose literary style was most worthy of imitation. While 'classic' describes anything that is among the best of its kind ('a classic car'), 'classical' usually refers to a past period regarded as the culmination of what preceded it and a starting-point for later output (as in 'classical music'). In ancient contexts, 'classical' is either a broad term for ancient Greek and Roman cultures over the millennium and a half of their development, or a specific CHRONOLOGICAL term for the 5th and 4th centuries BC in Greece.

Apart from their physical remains, everything we know about classical cultures derives from ancient writings copied and recopied down the centuries (TRANSMISSION), and therefore surviving mostly in late medieval manuscripts. Ancient, Byzantine–medieval, and Islamic SCHOLARSHIP are treated in adjacent entries. Modern classical scholarship starts with the collecting of manuscripts from Western Europe by Italian 'humanists' during the Italian RENAISSANCE, when the study of ancient Latin as part of formal education was revived. In a reaction against the prestige accorded to ARISTOTLE and his legacy in medieval times, the humanists reopened a wider range of Latin works to study. Eventually, particularly from the 15th century and the fall of Constantinople, Greek works found their way to the West and began to be studied (though often in Latin translations).

Like their predecessors in Ptolemaic ALEXANDRIA (3rd–1st centuries BC), scholars began by comparing differences between manuscripts of older works in order to establish the 'correct' reading through TEXTUAL CRITICISM. The invention of movable-type printing in 1454 led to wider dissemination of classical works (by ERASMUS and others) and ensured their preservation. The 16th century saw the first collections of authors who survived only in 'fragments' (quotations in other authors). Textual criticism gathered pace in the second half of the century, with particular attention paid to Roman history and law as well as the first collections of inscriptions. Comprehensive reconstructions of chronology were made, notably by Joseph Scaliger (1540–1609).

In the 17th and 18th centuries the Low Countries were a centre of scholarship. EPIGRAPHY and archaeology began to provide new sources of evidence through collectors of antiquities from abroad and, later, under the impetus of the first excavations at HERCULANEUM. At the same time, the classics were starting to lose their universal status, as scientific thinking grew and modern languages developed their own literatures. On the textual front, the idea gained credence that ancient texts could be analysed by the same scientific criteria as natural phenomena, and their assertions thereby challenged.

In German-speaking states, however, classical studies were restored to the centre of education. Radical reassessments, such as the art-historical studies of the flamboyant J. J. Winckelmann (1717–68), put the chronology of sculptural styles on a new footing and enshrined the notion that most ancient art was mythological in content. By the 19th century, German scholars and their institutions had pride of place in the 'science' of antiquity, *Altertumswissenschaft*, along with distinguished practitioners in other European countries and increasingly the USA. Later in the century, early social ANTHROPOLOGY fostered a new interest in non-western belief systems, reflected in Frazer's *Golden Bough* and his compendious edition of PAUSANIAS, and in the work of Jane Harrison on ancient RELIGION. New universities and, in England, reforms to the curricula of old universities, increased the standing of classical specialists, opened academic posts to non-clerics, and made classical disciplines available to a wider public through translations and COMMENTARIES. The mid-19th century also saw the beginnings of scientific archaeology. Schliemann's discoveries at TROY, and those of Evans in CRETE, demonstrated the existence of advanced cultures in the pre-literate Mediterranean, radically renewing views of early history. With the foundation of western archaeological missions in Mediterranean lands, and the creation of governmental departments of antiquities and local museums, an interest in material evidence for the ancient world came to the fore.

The 20th century was a time of radical change in scholarship. Classics no longer dealt almost exclusively in a canon of revered texts studied in the original languages. Popular publishing of 'pocket edition' translations increased, while mass-circulation colour printing and cinema played their parts in popularizing and refashioning ancient material culture and famous events. The new disciplines of sociology and economic history began to influence how Greek and Roman history were studied, particularly in Germany and the USA. The first steps were taken towards 'women's history', and research-level books began to include translated quotations. In France, geographical history and the *ANNALES* SCHOOL proved influential, though anglophone scholars made limited use of their techniques until after the Second World War. Ancient HISTORIANS in the UK at this time became rather drily focused on political history until explicit theoretical analysis became popular in the 1960s and 1970s. This revolutionized not only history but the study of literature, archaeology, art, philosophy, and languages. New areas of research such as reception and GENDER emerged in the later decades of the century.

In the early 21st century, while humanities are under pressure at universities, the public's interest in the ancient world never ceases to grow, fuelled by television and semi-popular magazines. Scholarship reacts to new challenges by redefining its activities, reaching out to a wider audience, and revisiting earlier conclusions. Work on ancient and medieval texts continues: not only do tens of thousands of PAPYRI await study and publication, but the texts of some ancient works are still being improved as methods of evaluating alternative readings become even more rigorous, partly with the help of computer technology. While EXCAVATION is increasingly costly, archaeological FIELD SURVEY has become a productive source of new data, and new methods of analysing and presenting material finds are continually developed. The internet may yet prove the most important innovation in classical scholarship, facilitating the transfer and manipulation of information almost without limit. DGJS

See Burstein, S. M., et al. (1997) *Ancient History: recent work and new directions*; (2002) *Current Issues and the Study of Ancient History*; Grummond, N.T. de, ed. (1996) *An Encyclopedia of the History of Classical Archaeology*, 2 vols; Lloyd-Jones, H. (1982) *Blood for the Ghosts;* Momigliano, A. D. (1994) *Studies on Modern Scholarship*; Pfeiffer, R. (1976) *History of Classical Scholarship: from 1300 to 1850*; Reynolds, L. D. and Wilson, N. G. (1991) *Scribes and Scholars*; Sauer, E.W., ed. (2004) *Archaeology and Ancient History*; Todd, R. B., ed. (2004) *Dictionary of British Classicists*, 3 vols; Wilamowitz-Moellendorff, U. von (1982) *History of Classical Scholarship*.

scholarship, Islamic With reference to classical civilization, primarily the 'translation movement' of the 8th–10th centuries AD and its effects. The use of paper (learned from CHINA) contributed by making writing materials less expensive. In the mid-8th century, the new 'Abbasid dynasty, which founded Baghdad as a capital, required strategies to differentiate it from the Ummayids of Damascus and to further secure Mesopotamian support. The second caliph, al-Mansur (754–75), portrayed himself as the successor of the SASSANIDS. These Persian kings had been ZOROASTRIAN, which held that all knowledge was contained in its sacred literature or was derived from it. Much had been lost, according to its legends, when ALEXANDER captured PERSIAN libraries, had the volumes translated into Greek and destroyed the originals. The Sassanids, especially SHAPUR I (240–71) and Chosroës I (531–78), employed ASTROLOGY in their ideologies and commissioned Pahlavi versions of Greek works in this and related fields. This translation culture – CHRISTIANS who had retained Greek for liturgical, among other reasons, did much of the work – continued after the ARAB conquests of the mid-7th century. As Pahlavi declined, translations into Syriac (previously under way) and Arabic, directly from Greek or from Pahlavi, made Greek works accessible to new generations. In emulation of the Sassanids, al-Mansur put astrology and Zoroastrian desire to reclaim knowledge into his ideology and commissioned Greek works in Arabic, from Greek, Syriac and Pahlavi originals. His successors and their courts also sponsored translations, now most often directly from Greek, and patronized the academic community, sometimes with different goals. For example, al-Mamun (813–33) castigated Byzantine negativity towards secular literature, and employed his own patronage of Greek scholarship as propaganda against the enemy empire.

As original Arabic scholarship developed, new translations diminished and the movement slowed by the end of the 10th century. Although it had begun largely with Greek astrology, ASTRONOMY, geometry and MATHEMATICS, from the outset works in other areas were also turned into Arabic. The most important fields were MEDICINE (primarily GALEN) and PHILOSOPHY, but include agriculture, botany, falconry, GEOGRAPHY, grammar, magic, meteorology, mineralogy, MUSIC, optics, pharmacology and zoology. Literature, especially poetry, and history were not often translated, though exceptions may be found. For the classical scholar, these translations are often instrumental in establishing the correct versions of texts, and some works are extant only in Arabic.

In philosophy, ARISTOTLE and his successors and commentators took pride of place. NEOPLATONIC works were often thought to be Aristotle's, but of PLATO mainly the *Republic* and *Timaeus* were popular. Schools of ARISTOTELIANISM developed in Baghdad and elsewhere, with Avicenna, Averroes, al-Kindi and al-Farabi the best known philosophers. Their work is very much responsible for knowledge of Aristotle in the mediaeval West; some writings of Thomas Aquinas were, in turn, translated into Arabic. Naturally, names and works of many other Islamic scholars are known, but of general interest is Ibn an-Nadim, whose *Fihrist* is, among other things, a compendium of Arabic scholarship and an account of books, including translations (with comments on translators), available to him. JV

See Dodge, B. (1970) *The Fihrist of Ibn al-Nadim*, trs., 2 vols.; Gutas, D. (1998) *Greek Thought, Arabic Culture*; Rosenthal, F. (1975) *The Classical Heritage in Islam*, trs. E. Marmorstein and J. Marmorstein.

scholia The Greek term 'scholia' is applied to notes on the texts of Greek and Latin authors. They range from brief one-word explanations of individual words (often called 'glosses') to continuous exegetical commentaries. In antiquity such works were published independently, but at some point scribes began the practice of incorporating scholia into editions of the relevant author. The scholia were now written around the text, often in a smaller, less formal hand. Scholia typically represent the detritus of ancient learning, and in many cases are extremely valuable for preserving the ancient understanding and evaluation of a text, sometimes going back to early hellenistic ALEXANDRIA (3rd century BC) or the Roman Republican period. The processes that have led to the formation of most collections of scholia are quite obscure, and it is often difficult to determine the reliability of the material preserved. In most cases what survives seems to represent successive stages of excerption and abbreviation. The guiding principles of selection, however, seem to have been the desire to elucidate the text at hand, and often the scholia constitute a priceless assemblage of information on a wide range of topics. At the most basic level scholia shed light on the words of the text, offering the ancient understanding of the meaning of rare words (this can be the reflection of reasoned scholarly opinion or simply wild guesses), and in some cases providing information relevant to the assessment of textual problems. At other times scholia illuminate the mythical or historical background, preserving material from sources that are otherwise lost. CGB

schools Establishments for organized education. Early education seems to have occurred on an *ad hoc* basis to provide training for individuals in specific skills. The first appearance of organized schools occurs in the early classical period in the eastern AEGEAN, by which stage it already seems quite sophisticated. HERODOTOS (*Histories* 6.27) records 119 children killed by the collapse of a school building on CHIOS in 496 BC. Thereafter, references to schools are common in literature, as are depictions of pupils and teachers in the visual arts. Even so, more precise details about organized schooling in the Greek and Roman world are often lacking. Formal education was provided primarily for male children, but it is still uncertain how much was undertaken within the family home and how much outside it. It is especially difficult to identify school buildings in the archaeological record. Such buildings presumably existed, but perhaps only for advanced education, such as that organized by religious or philosophical groups. For example, PLATO's ACADEMY outside the Dipylon gate of Athens boasted groves and rooms for instruction and discussion. Also buildings such as GYMNASIA fulfilled some function in physical education. Otherwise it would appear that many classes met in venues not built as schools: rooms simply commandeered for the purpose, TEMPLE porches, and, as suggested by a fresco from POMPEII, porticoes by the *AGORA* and FORUM. MDH

See Harris, W.V. (1989) *Ancient Literacy*; Marrou, H. I. (1956) *A History of Education in Antiquity.*

 EDUCATION: (a)–(b).

schools, philosophical see PHILOSOPHICAL SCHOOLS.

science In antiquity there was no single word equivalent to the modern term 'science'. Indeed, much of what is meant by science today is not evident in the Greek or Roman world. One reason is that there was no clear distinction between superstition (by today's standards) and science. The 'scientists' of antiquity, better termed natural PHILOSOPHERS, differed greatly from those of the modern world. One important distinction is that many learned their field on their own or in informal teaching arrangements. A second difference is that their scientific pursuits often occupied only a fraction of their time. Concepts such as EXPERIMENTATION, controls or universal mathematical laws, seen as essential in scientific thinking today, are found only on the sidelines. Furthermore, the division of scientific disciplines into familiar categories such as PHYSICS, MATHEMATICS, CHEMISTRY, biology and ASTRONOMY did not occur until early modern times. As a result, attempts to identify science in antiquity often fall short because we are tempted to judge achievements of the past by modern measures and definitions of science. Nevertheless, important advances were made in efforts especially to understand and often to manipulate the world in which the ancients lived; it is in activity of this kind that we may locate ancient science.

It is a generally accepted belief that Thales, an intellectual who lived in MILETOS during the 6th century BC, had a foundational role in the early stages of Greek science. Hailing from Ionia in Asia Minor, Thales and other early thinkers lived at the crossroads of Greek and Near Eastern civilizations. This region, probably home also to the epic poet HOMER, is renowned for its revolutionary ways of thinking. In ways still not entirely understood, Ionia served to foster the transmission of pre-scientific ideas from Egypt and MESOPOTAMIA to the Greek world. Other factors in the development of scientific thinking clearly had a part as well, including a change in the socio-political environment, seen in the rise of the *POLIS*, and an overall increase in WEALTH, productivity and TRADE between Greeks and non-Greeks. The outcome was a greater sense of individualism and more time to contemplate abstract ideas. What resulted was a new way of looking at the world, one that rejected the traditional beliefs in the GODS as explanatory forces in everyday events.

The development of science throughout antiquity is often characterized by its 'agonistic' (competitive) quality; the ancient scientists did not so much stand on each other shoulders as compete to push their own ideas into prominence. There is, however, a sense that a scholarly community existed in which dialogue and discussion took place. Among the PRESOCRATICS, for example, each contributor who ponders the question of what is the ultimate stuff of reality seems to respond directly to an earlier supposition. Thales initially stipulated that water was the ultimate stuff of reality. His fellow Milesians, Anaximander and Anaximenes, could reject his claims and put forth their own explanations of the *apeiron* ('the unlimited') or air. These kinds of claims, known to later natural philosophers such as PLATO and ARISTOTLE, would later be dismissed and eventually rejected. Likewise, any attempt to argue for the existence or impossibility of change, a problem debated by 5th-century thinkers such as HERAKLEITOS and PARMENIDES, continued to catch the attention of later scientists, notably Aristotle, who denied the possibility of the PARADOXES proposed by ZENO THE ELEATIC.

An important relationship in the development of scientific thinking is that of teacher and student. The sequence of students descended from SOCRATES and his teachings – Plato, Aristotle and THEOPHRASTOS – reveals a typical pattern: each tried to improve significantly upon his predecessor's teaching by promoting entirely different, but related, theories. Aristotle did not accept Plato's theory of forms, but could only successfully propose a different theory by being thoroughly aware of his teacher's claims. Thus he could claim that reality was based entirely on sensory perception. Similarly, Theophrastos was not prepared to accept fully Aristotle's teleological view of the universe, nor was he satisfied with the idea that the world consisted of only four elements mixed in varying amounts. At times, a disciple might inherit a basic set of principles that could then be worked out more carefully. Such is the case with ZENO OF CITIUM, the founder of STOIC philosophy, and his successor Chrysippos. The latter outlined as precisely as possible what was meant by the binding force of *pneuma* ('breath') and its presence in the continuum of matter.

In many cases preliminary advances in science were accepted rather than passed over. The work of earlier thinkers could thus be seen as springboards from which later scientists could jump. For example, LUCRETIUS offers the fullest account of EPICUREAN natural philosophy, while incorporating a significant amount of his own thought. GALEN accepts the majority of HIPPOCRATIC MEDICINE and adds what he had learned from his vast experience as a physician. PTOLEMY acknowledges the astronomical theories of the epicycle and eccentric motion put forth by APOLLONIOS OF PERGE, using both as major components of his own explication of heavenly movements.

Although one outcome of science was the elimination of divine explanations in favour of 'rational' systems of belief, it must be pointed out that this did not occur in a progressively linear manner. Science had many functions, some of which served to counter any movements towards advances as understood by moderns. Although the Presocratics attempted to replace religious beliefs with scientific postulations, their proposals cannot be accepted by today's scholars as any more or less rational than the descriptions found in Homer or HESIOD. Plato used science to demonstrate his ETHICAL beliefs; his efforts to explain the world ultimately rely on divine forces. Aristotle, too, employs science in his quest to explain the regular patterning observable in nature; his lasting contribution is the ability to analyse and then organize his findings in a systematic manner. As a part of ethical beliefs and philosophical doctrine, science could be utilized to provide freedom from the unknown (thereby achieving *ataraxia*, the state of living without mental pain); this is the premise of both the Epicureans and the Stoics who were not inherently interested in the natural world for its own sake. The thorough collection of information for pragmatic or DIDACTIC purposes, in the manner of POSIDONIUS, VARRO, and PLINY THE ELDER, is a further application of science.

What is important about the development of science in antiquity is not so much the actual advances that were made. It is the ways in which ideas were exchanged and formulated by a great number of thinkers that are especially noteworthy. To be sure, the scientific discoveries of the ancients in fields such as pneumatics, hydrostatics and optics are impressive. Although there is considerable controversy as to whether such developments should be seen as a continuous progression from ancient to modern times, it is fair to say that our scientific way of looking at the world owes a great deal to the ancient forerunners. TJA

See Clagett, M. (1955) *Greek Science in Antiquity*; Lindberg, D. C. (1992) *The Beginnings of Western Science*; Lloyd, G. E. R. (1970) *Early Greek Science: Thales to Aristotle*; (1973) *Greek Science after Aristotle*; Rihll, T. E. (1999) *Greek Science*; Shipley, G. (2000) *The Greek World after Alexander*, ch. 9; Tuplin, C. J. and Rihll, eds. (2002) *Science and Mathematics in Ancient Greek Culture*.

scientific instruments In antiquity scientific instruments served three purposes: to measure, record or predict. Among the earliest described is the *gnomon*, a simple rod device used to track the motion of the SUN. The majority of scientific instruments trace their origins to the hellenistic period. The most famous is the Antikythera Mechanism, an elaborately geared bronze object discovered on an ancient SHIPWRECK in 1900. This device, datable to the earlier part of the 1st century BC, is often identified as a precursor to the computer. It had an ASTRONOMICAL or calendrical function, and although its full abilities await further study it is clear that it was capable of very complex calculations and projections. Other instruments also demonstrate a sophisticated ability to observe and record the heavens. PTOLEMY OF ALEXANDRIA describes the construction and use of the armillary astrolabe to observe the MOON and to chart over 1,000 stars on a spherical model of the heavens. ARCHIMEDES' invention of a mechanical planetarium was a vast improvement on earlier models of the movement of the planets, moon and sun. In a few cases, what may be seen by modern eyes as scientific instruments were merely practical devices. SUNDIALS, fixed and portable, provided one means by which to measure time. Another method was the water-clock, a sophisticated version of which, the in-flow *klepsydra*, was attributed in antiquity to Ktesibios. Other scientific instruments include surveying tools such as levels (*chôrobatês*), instruments that divided land into squares and rectangles (*groma*), and optical sighting devices similar to the modern theodolite (*dioptra*). Land and sea travel could be measured by different kinds of odometers as described by VITRUVIUS and Hero; the instruments relied on geared mechanisms that converted forward motion into units of length. TJA

See Yalouris, N. (1990) The shipwreck of Antikythera, in J.-P. Descoeudres, ed., *Eumousia* 135–6.

Scipio Aemilianus (Publius Cornelius Scipio Aemilianus Africanus) 185/4–129 BC One of Rome's greatest GENERALS and statesmen. Son of Lucius AEMILIUS PAULLUS, and adopted by the son of SCIPIO AFRICANUS (the conqueror of HANNIBAL), he was born to greatness. He was friendly with the historian and statesman POLYBIOS and the STOIC PHILOSOPHER Panaitios. CICERO ranked him as one of the chief Roman orators. On two occasions he served the state well in a crisis. In 148 BC, when Roman generals were performing badly against CARTHAGE in the third PUNIC WAR, Scipio was made CONSUL by popular acclaim at an unusually young age, and was appointed to end the war. He must have had strong support in the SENATE. With efficiency and ruthlessness he ended the conflict and razed Carthage to the ground. Soon after returning to Rome, he went on a prestigious tour of inspection in the east with two colleagues. He then became CENSOR, but was prevented by his colleague from making effective use of his office to reform and revitalize Roman life. In 135 he was elected consul for the second time, with the duty of ending Roman humiliation and lack of success against the Celtiberian rebels in Spain. Again he showed his ruthless instincts in hunting the enemy down and gaining victory. NUMANTIA was razed to the ground, and Rome had no more trouble in Spain for a long time. On his return to Rome, he found the state dangerously divided over the agrarian reform of his brother-in-law Tiberius GRACCHUS. Scipio sided with the conservative reaction and lost much popularity. When the last king of PERGAMON in Asia Minor, Attalos III, died childless in 133 and left his kingdom to Rome, a rebel pretender, Aristonikos, arose. It became clear that Rome would have to claim its inheritance by force. Scipio wanted this command, but a TRIBUNE's proposal to this effect was massively defeated and one of the consuls of 131 was sent instead. Scipio's last service to Rome was to try to mediate between the Italian allies and the land commissioners of Gracchus, but death took him suddenly in 129 before he achieved much. A sense of disappointment and lack of fulfilment hangs over his whole career. HBM

See Astin, A. E. (1967) *Scipio Aemilianus*.

Scipio Africanus (Publius Cornelius Scipio Africanus) 236–183 BC 'A greater than Napoleon' is the title of Liddell Hart's biography. Legends (of divine inspiration, even of divine parentage) grew up rapidly around HANNIBAL's conqueror. The son and nephew of leading GENERALS of the early second PUNIC WAR, he married the daughter of Lucius Aemilius Paullus (killed at CANNAE). SCIPIO AEMILIANUS (the destroyer of CARTHAGE) was his grandson by ADOPTION (and patron of the historian POLYBIOS, one source of the favourable tradition). Scipio appears in 'heroic cameos' at the disastrous battles of Ticinus (saving his father's life) and Cannae (rallying the survivors). Appointed in 210, following the deaths of his father and uncle, to command in Spain (unprecedented for one so young), he utterly defeated the Carthaginian forces, notably at the battles of Baecula (208) and Ilipa (206). He was elected consul in 205, and a fierce debate ensued over whether Rome should invade AFRICA. Scipio did so in 204. After a prolonged campaign and abortive peace negotiations, he defeated Hannibal at the battle of ZAMA in 202, ending the second Punic war. He succeeded where others had failed by virtue of his tactical skill and innovation, first demonstrated at Baecula. He TRIUMPHED, receiving the *cognomen* Africanus. Despite holding the CENSORSHIP (199) and a second consulship (194), his later career was less spectacular. He died in voluntary EXILE after accusations of embezzlement, probably politically motivated. JRWP

See Scullard, H. H. (1970) *Scipio Africanus*.

screws The screw was the last simple machine developed, after the lever, wheel, wedge and pulley. Unlike modern screws that function both as mechanical devices and as FASTENERS, only the mechanical properties of screws were exploited in antiquity. To judge from ancient descriptions of the intricate procedures necessary to make screws, it is not altogether surprising that their application was limited. Screws were used primarily as labour-saving devices, either for moving water or for AGRI-CULTURAL purposes. According to ancient tradition, ARCHIMEDES of SYRACUSE invented the screw in the 3rd century BC after he visited Egypt and witnessed inefficient water-raising devices. His new machine, a wooden cylinder enclosing an endless screw, was able to move water easily for irrigation or MINING. DIODORUS SICULUS praises the machine, but offers little explanation of how it worked. VITRUVIUS provides a detailed account of its design and construction, though the problem of operating it is explained more fully by PHILO OF BYZANTION, who reveals that the machine is worked by treading on the wooden barrel rather than by using a crank. The second main function of the screw was its application for OIL and WINE presses. PLINY THE ELDER records that vertically mounted screws had been adopted for presses 100 years earlier. He also mentions later refinements to the length of screw that provided more efficient presses. Finally, Oribasius describes a device for setting fractured bones that relied on the screw. TJA

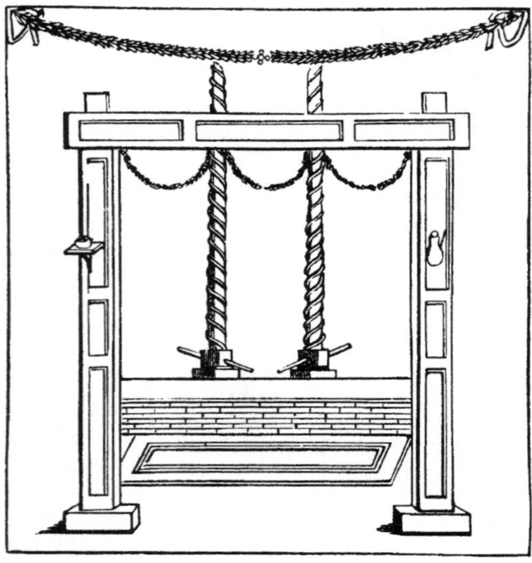

SCREWS: a twin screw direct cloth press, depicted in a Pompeian wall-painting, 1st century AD.

 PRESSES: (a).

scribes see BOOKS; LITERACY; SCHOLIA; TEXTUAL CRITICISM; TRANSMISSION.

sculpture

The history of Greek sculpture generally begins with the relief and free-standing carved STONE works of the mid-7th century BC. Before this, sculpture in stone was rare, the most famous exception being the Bronze Age Lion gate of MYCENAE. During the earliest centuries of the first millennium BC, small terracotta animal FIGURINES were produced, as well as human, animal and mythological creature forms in IVORY and bronze under the influence of craftsmen from the Near East.

Monumental carving in stone appeared c.660 BC in East Greece and was heavily influenced by contemporary Egyptian representations of free-standing, frontal figures with arms generally at the side. Like their Egyptian prototypes, the Greek sculptures were meant to be viewed frontally, as they are roughly hewn on the back, and in profile their widths are narrow; they stare straight ahead. They also follow the Egyptian canon of figural proportions. The style is often called Daedalic, after the mythological Greek sculptor. The earliest examples of this style are of female figures. Hair is often formalized as knobs, ridges and grooves, while other features are very stylized, with limited indication of the human shape underneath garments. The female form wears traditional DRESS, either the Doric *peplos* or Ionic *chitôn* with *himation*. Patterns on these TEXTILES are represented by incision and paint. The feet are parallel. The earliest extant male figure dates to the last quarter of the 7th century. The form is NUDE and has one foot advanced, usually the left, but the weight is evenly distributed across both feet. These figures are referred to as *kouros* and *korê* forms (pl. *KOUROI* and *KORAI*). Both types served as sanctuary dedications and as grave markers, where they recalled idealized youth and values such as beauty or ATHLETICISM of

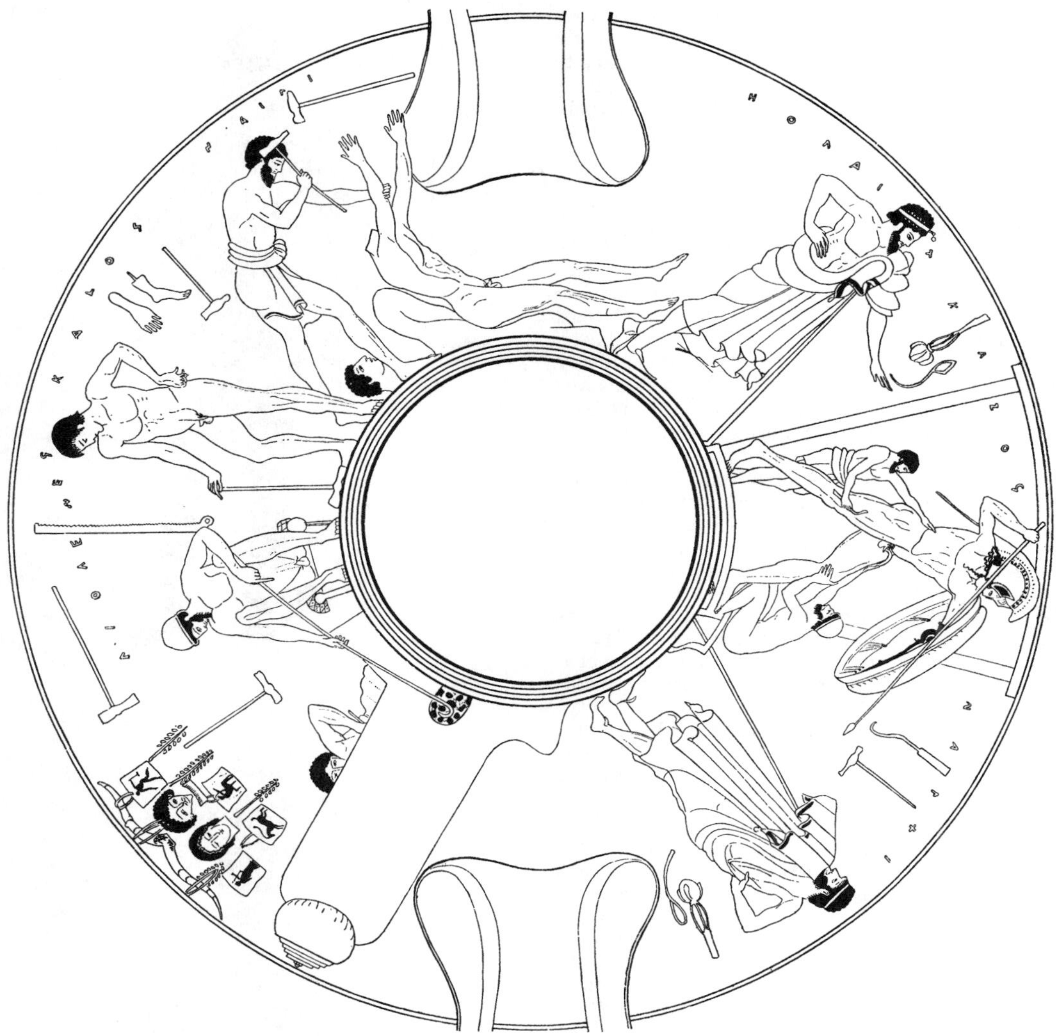

SCULPTURE: (a) vase-painting of a foundry, showing stages in assembly and finishing of bronze statues.

the deceased. During the 7th century, there was an increasing emphasis on anatomical details, which during the 6th century shifted to a more realistic representation of the human form. The mouth was depicted with a smile, to imbue a sense of life and symbolize the *aretê* ('excellence') of the person represented. Eyes were large and almond-shaped, and sometimes inlaid. The male forms became more muscular, particularly in the abdomen, while the drapery of the female figures developed along more realistic representations of hanging fabric folds, implying the shape of the figure underneath the garment.

At the beginning of the 5th century BC, a breakthrough in the representation of realistic poses was achieved, in the outline of the human form, by abandoning symmetry in favour of a curve. In the case of standing figures, this was achieved by the representation of the shift in weight balance when the feet are not side by side; the leg carrying more weight will have a lower hip and shoulder. The first example of this is the Kritian Boy (c.480). With the introduction of this method, poses became more free and expressive. There was no more need for the figures to be frontal as they could be represented in motion realistically. Thus throughout the 5th century, there was an increasing emphasis on the tectonics of the body. Drapery contours emphasized the form underneath the fabric, the folds of which were almost corrugated. Figures were represented as ideals but in realistic manners. Bronze became the preferred free-standing medium for artists to work in, though few such works survive, such as the DELPHI charioteer and the ZEUS or POSEIDON from Artemision, because bronze was often melted down and reused. Our knowledge of many of these comes from MARBLE copies of Roman date.

Sculptural narrative had developed during the early 6th century, in the context of TEMPLE pedimental sculptures and friezes, with themes often relating to the power of the gods. The earliest example is from the ARTEMIS temple on Kerkyra (Corfu). Military and political victories a century later resulted in more political symbolism in ARCHITECTURAL art, with characterization and narrative used to explore emotion and motion. Portraits of identifiable individuals appear. Popular themes of this period included HEROES, such as the Tyrannicides, Harmodios and Aristogeiton. The sculptures from the temple of Zeus at OLYMPIA, carved between 470 and 456, provide an excellent example of sculptural symbolism and style of the time. The east pediment depicts the moment before the chariot race between Pelops and Oinomaos, while the west pediment shows the fight between the Lapiths and Centaurs at the wedding of the Lapith king Peirithoös. One is a myth of local significance, while the other reflects the struggle of Greek civilization over barbarism, another popular theme at the time. The choices of sculptural themes are thus political, patriotic and partisan. The art itself is carved to fit the space, and the figures are imbued with a sense of realism, such as the bulging veins of a centaur's hand or the sagging flesh of the seer at the face. Expression is conveyed in the body and pose of the figures, not just the face. Yet there is an austerity and simplicity of expression and representation, such as with the idealized APOLLO, that has given rise to the identification of this phase of sculpture as the Severe Style.

Sculpture of the later 5th century further emphasized the ideal, sometimes to the extent that the pose of the figure would be impossible in reality, as with Myron's mid-century *Diskobolos* ('discus-thrower'). POLYKLEITOS' *Canon* outlined a framework for achieving balanced idealism within sculpture, from the proportions between head, torso and legs to the crossed symmetry of tension and relaxation, as depicted by his *Doryphoros* ('spear-bearer'). Such balance was the idealistic achievement, rather than musculature under stress or on display. Drapery, too, became overly idealistic to such an extent that the impression is of wet, clinging cloth. This High Classical period is exemplified in the architectural sculptures of the PARTHENON, where drapery clings tightly to the figures, who are all depicted in their idealized youth. As at Olympia, the imagery has both local and more wide-reaching significance. The pediments tell tales relevant to Athenian MYTHOLOGY, history and supremacy: the depiction of the birth of ATHENA overlooks her city, while her triumph over Poseidon in a contest to be the protector of the city faces the Propylaia, the entrance to the ACROPOLIS, to remind all who enter the citadel of Athens' naval supremacy. The metopes reflect the continued triumph of the civilized over the uncivilized, as metaphors for Greek victories over the PERSIANS and Athens' imperialistic power over the other Greek city-states: they depict the battle of the gods against the giants, that of the Lapiths against the centaurs, an Amazonomachy and tales from the TROJAN WAR. The famous frieze, representing the annual Panathenaic procession and the folding of Athena's *peplos*, or the myth of the SACRIFICE of the daughters of Erechtheus to save Athens, has a more local significance.

By the 4th century, the hyper-idealized images of the previous century gave way to a much more

(b)

(c)

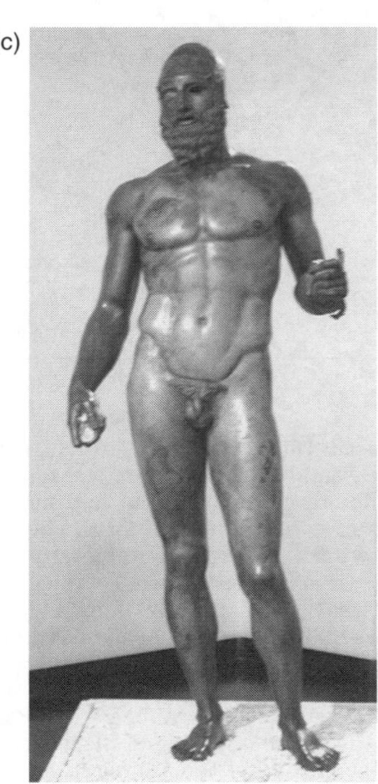

SCULPTURE: (b)–(c) Greek bronze statues of the 5th century BC found in a shipwreck off the coast of Reggio Calabria (anc. Rhegion), southern Italy.

naturalistic style through proportional and representational innovations. PRAXITELES improved upon Polykleitos' proportions by elongating figures and posing them in a pronounced sinuous 'S', giving the figures a sense of naturalistic ease. He also introduced the female nude as a sculptural art form. PORTRAITURE became more prominent during this time, as individual features were favoured over idealized youthful representations. PHILOSOPHERS, ORATORS, HISTORIANS and other public figures were often the subjects of early portraits. Funerary sculptures increasingly depicted individuals and interpersonal relationships, rather than images of generic idealism. The representation of gods became more akin to real men. LYSIPPOS served as the sculptor to the court of ALEXANDER the Great. These stylistic developments affected the interpretations of civic art to the viewer, creating an individual experience, illustrated by the art of the temples at Bassai and Tegea.

After Alexander's territorial conquests, there followed a period of mobility among craftsmen, as Greek culture was diffused around the hellenistic world. Yet the hellenistic kingdoms also developed their own individual sculptural styles. The SELEUKID style was one of violent action and movements, characterized by the altar at PERGAMON. Art of the PTOLEMAIC kingdom, particularly of ALEXANDRIA, by contrast appears much more calm, perhaps to be in keeping with the intellectual, philosophical and scholarly reputation of its capital city. Alexandrian rulers were depicted in a royal-divine style, not quite as idealized as images of the GODS and therefore with expressions of concern, but still with a sense of aloofness from their subjects. Sculpture on the Greek mainland maintained the natural and traditional motifs and styles characteristic of the 4th century, particularly through the continuation of philosopher portraits; these famous people are depicted with individualizing realism. Art of the hellenistic world explored methods of expression, pain and age through undulating surfaces and textural contrasts created by deep carving. TH

See Osborne, R. (1998) *Archaic and Classical Greek Art*; Pollitt, J. (1972) *Art and Experience in Classical Greece*; Smith, R. R. R. (1991) *Hellenistic Sculpture*.

KOUROI AND *KORAI*: (a)–(b).

The richness of Roman sculpture comes not only from its diverse media, MARBLES white and coloured, limestone, sandstone, and basalt, bronze, SILVER, and GOLD, terracotta and PLASTER. It comes as well from the incredible range of genres, subjects and styles. This diversity led to puzzlement and disparagement by scholars and connoisseurs, for whom the apparently consistent evolution of Greek sculpture provided a model that Roman sculpture never emulated.

The Romans made sculpture for an array of functions. In the 3rd century BC they had already begun to make portraits in bronze, stone and terracotta. These were mainly of ÉLITE men, perhaps related to the ancient death MASKS of wax, described by POLYBIOS as part of state funerals and kept in the houses of descendants (6.53). The tradition of portraiture in sculpture came at least in part from hellenistic Greece and from the ETRUSCANS (some of whom were the makers of objects for Romans). By the 1st century BC, however, the Romans had developed portraiture into a vehicle for Romans of every social stratum who could afford the expense. Portraits in three dimensions, in bronze and stone as well as terracotta, were used both for funerary purposes and as public commemorations of great deeds, benefactions or political power. Even the families of freed SLAVES could have portraits of themselves, in the form of reliefs or of statues, decorating their TOMBS.

SCULPTURE: (d) the so-called Canopus at Hadrian's Villa near Tivoli, showing the architectural and garden setting of the sculptural groups collected by the emperor.

Portraiture took the form of single and grouped free-standing statuary, busts and reliefs. It is found in all these forms in almost all parts and periods of the Roman empire. Style and materials change according to local preference as well as the differing needs of patrons and differing fashions. Thus, an elaborately coiffed female portrait of c.AD 90 (Museo Capitolino, Rome), probably representing a lady of the imperial court at Rome, takes the form of a marble bust that may have been intended for insertion into a separate, draped statue. Its function is unknown. It can be compared with a female portrait head from Rome, with the same kind of HAIRSTYLE, which tops a body in the form of a famous hellenistic Greek statue of the nude goddess VENUS (Museo Capitolino, Rome). Such statues in the form of divinities seem to have been popular at the time among prosperous freed slaves as tomb monuments. A contemporary bronze head of a woman with a similar hairdo and inlaid SHELL eyes comes from Ampurias in Spain (Museo Arqueológico, Barcelona). Its style is quite different from that of portraits at Rome: the volumes simpler, the surfaces less mobile. The basic unit of the female head with the same fashionable hairstyle was used by people from different social strata and geographical locations, but with some variation in the materials, styles and monument types they preferred.

Roman sculptors executed literally hundreds of copies or versions of Greek free-standing statues, especially in the later Republic and the first two centuries AD, in order to satisfy the appetite of wealthy Roman art collectors. Ever since the conquest of Greece and Asia Minor in the 2nd century BC, Romans had been collecting Greek art in the form of original works, replicas and adaptations, including miniatures and those in new materials such as gold or silver. Whether such statues were copied with the aid of machines or not, they often provide our only ideas about what many Greek statues, such as the *Doryphoros* of POLYKLEITOS, known from literary sources, might have looked like. These statues were displayed in private HOUSES, public GARDENS, and public buildings both secular and religious.

Stone and cast bronze ARCHITECTURAL sculpture, both in the round and in relief, came in many shapes and forms and occurs on almost every spot on a building. In the imperial FORUM of the emperor AUGUSTUS, constructed at the end of the 1st century BC, for example, a colossal statue of MARS the Avenger stood in the temple complex dedicated to him. On the triangular pediment above the temple porch were statues of Mars and other deities in marble. Free-standing statues appeared in the colonnades that led to the temple, and the attic above the colonnades was decorated with CARYATIDS (female figures used in place of columns) which replicated the classical ones on the Erechtheion at Athens. All these uses of sculpture would have been unsurprising to a Greek of the 5th century BC, and give evidence of Augustus' interest in Athens and in showing himself a traditionalist.

Compared with this kind of architectural sculpture, that of the forum of TRAJAN, dated between AD 100 and 110, would have seemed innovative to that same Greek observer. In the centre of a plaza stood an equestrian statue of the emperor. In structures around the plaza there may have been large reliefs showing him in battle and in triumph. The temple probably had the usual architectural sculpture, but in front of it stood an extraordinary site for sculpture, the 30 m (100 ft) high COLUMN of Trajan. Winding round the column were reliefs showing the emperor's victories over the DACIANS. Both the architectural structure and the format are rarities, but the Romans used both several times at least. Innovative use of public architectural sculpture characterizes Roman art as much as does self-conscious traditionalism.

The sculpture made for the state in Rome reveals a diversity of styles that has to do not only with chronological change, but with differences in genre and function. A general movement from more classicizing and more naturalistic to more abstract seems to occur at an uneven pace from the 1st century BC to the 4th century AD. But the unevenness of the changes has led scholars to ask why Roman styles take hold in certain periods. For example, under the emperors Augustus (27 BC–AD 14), HADRIAN (117–38) and Gallienus (253–68), far separated in time, evocations of classical 5th-century Athenian art are extremely common, whereas in the time of VESPASIAN (69–79) many artists seem to produce work with a powerful sense of deep space and a concern for the wrinkles and irregularities of the face. Reasons may include (among others) the taste of the emperor, or the ability of certain styles to suggest political values such as Republican or democratic government or to associate a ruler with an earlier one.

Breaking apart schematic descriptions of the history of Roman style depends, first, on a sense of the styles that go with specific sculptural genres and even with certain kinds of subjects; second, on a sense of the different tastes and traditions of Rome's various social strata. The examples in the preceding paragraph assumed the hegemony of the bronze and marble sculpture, especially portraits, made for the imperial house. The complexity comes when the rest of Roman art is brought into focus. Thus, the forum of Trajan has great panel reliefs (now cut up and immured in the arch of CONSTANTINE in Rome) with monumental figures that fill the space and make use of the proportions and poses well known from Greek sculpture. In the same complex, the style of the column of Trajan makes use of relatively small figures, clustered in land- and city-scapes, arranged in deep space, and taking poses that seem appropriate to digging trenches and loading boats as well as to making speeches or dying tragically. Style differences can emerge even on the same monument, as is the case with the column base of ANTONINUS PIUS, dated to about AD 161 (Vatican Museums, Rome). On the front of the base the relief places monumental figures, real and allegorical, in an open space devoid of naturalistic landscape, to show the apotheosis of the emperor and empress. On the sides, however, two reliefs show the ceremonial HORSE races that were part of the funeral GAMES to celebrate the deceased emperor. The figures here are small, with large heads and unclassical proportions; they ride around a space that is seen in bird's eye view, as from above, but the figures themselves appear as if seen head-on. The style is clearly unlike that of the front of the monument, but whether two different sculptors were responsible, or whether styles were chosen for differing subjects but executed by the same hand, is unknown. What is certain is that the style of the races is the one that became dominant from the later 3rd century onward.

Style differences also result from social differences in Rome. The élite often favoured a style that, perhaps for reasons of skill and economics, perhaps for reasons of taste and status, seldom appeared on monuments made for people lower in the social hierarchy. The most vivid examples of such differences can be seen in the funerary monuments of working people. In the Isola Sacra cemetery at the port city of OSTIA, a number of reliefs were found still attached to their tomb façades; often made of inexpensive painted terracotta, they depict people at work (e.g. relief of a MIDWIFE, Museo Ostiense, Ostia). The style is usually flat, rather than modelled with rounded or curving forms. The figures are normally somewhat squat and compact, their faces barely detailed, and there is far more emphasis on the objects with which they work than on their portraits. The majority of these reliefs seem to date to the mid-2nd century AD, but they share a number of features with earlier and later reliefs made for the same social and economic strata. This suggests that certain WORKSHOPS may have catered to specific groups of people over several generations, and that together artists and patrons maintained a style-preference that helped to identify social position.

Just as social location matters to the look of Roman sculpture, so does geographical location. In many areas of the vast Roman empire, sculptural genres, monument types and styles differed greatly from what one would have seen in the city of Rome. From metropolitan areas with long-standing hellenized traditions, such as Athens, EPHESOS or Tarragona (TARRACO), comes sculpture not unlike that of the city of Rome, but away from these areas the differences can be striking. Along the ANTONINE WALL in Scotland, the stone markers with reliefs that identified the LEGIONS and the amount of military construction they did suggest the hands of soldiers or of local artisans untrained in hellenizing traditions (Hunterian Museum, Glasgow). Dated to the early 140s AD, the reliefs have a flat and gawky quality even when they use the same compositions and poses as are found in the great panel reliefs of Trajan discussed above. At ADAMKLISSI near the battlefields of Dacia, reliefs commemorated Trajan's victories with monumental figures whose proportions are elongated and whose style seems flat and rubbery (Museum, Tropaeum Traiani). In Asia Minor, however, in a small but prosperous city such as APHRODISIAS, sculpture that decorated the great Sebasteion (erected in honour of the imperial house, probably in the 50s AD) used a style familiar to that area. Classicizing, with flowing three-dimensional drapery and heroic musculature on the men, the forms in the Aphrodisias reliefs have more in common with the art of metropolitan Rome than with the battle monument at Adamklissi. And finally, the sunken reliefs from the small temple of Dendur in Egypt (Metropolitan Museum of Art, New York), carved in honour of Augustus, are utterly traditional in their use of pharaonic style. The figures appear with bodies frontal and heads in profile, striding and gesturing as if on their way to the pyramids at Giza. Such wide differences in sculptural typology and style have to do not only with social and political needs and functions, and with personal taste and ability to pay, but with local traditions that remained alive and unchallenged by a specifically Roman brand of imperialism. NBK

See Brendel, O. J. (1979) *Prolegomena to the Study of Roman Art*; Kleiner, D. E. E. (1992) *Roman Sculpture*; Rockwell, P. (1993) *The Art of Stoneworking*; Vogel, L. (1973) *The Column of Antoninus Pius*.

Scythia and Scythians Tribes called Scythians (*Skythai* in Greek) occupied the coastal region and hinterland from north of the DANUBE across the northern shores of the BLACK SEA to the north Caucasus, settling the rich valleys and plains between the rivers Danube, Dniester, Bug, Dnieper and Don, and most of southern Ukraine. They had migrated from northern Siberia at the beginning of the 7th century BC into the north Pontic steppes previously controlled by the Kimmerians, whom they pursued through both the Caucasus and THRACE to Asia Minor and ANATOLIA. The Scythians were one of many groups recorded by classical authors as living in Scythia. The term 'Scythian' embraces different and often opposed groups ethnically related: Alazones, Callippidae, Geloni, Budini and others. Not all were NOMADS. The 'Royal Scythians' were the most valiant and numerous Scythian tribe, and deemed all other Scythians to be their slaves (Herodotos 4.20). In the middle of the 7th century BC the Scythians went to the Near East, following the footsteps of the Kimmerians and overthrowing the Medes, Assyria, Urartu and so on. HERODOTOS (1.104) says the Scythians became masters of Asia. At the end of the 7th or the beginning of the 6th century, they returned through the Caucasus to the steppes of the northern Pontos. Only at the end of the 6th century, after victory in the Scythian–Persian war, was north Pontic Scythia finally formed, consolidated in two centres: on the lower Dnieper, not far from the Greek colony Olbia, and in the Crimean steppes close to the BOSPORAN KINGDOM. The 4th century was a time of prosperity. Under king Atheas the boundaries of the Scythian kingdom reached the Danube, leading to a conflict with PHILIP II that ended with Atheas' death in 339. Nevertheless, in 331 the Scythians were capable of inflicting defeat on Zopyrion, general of ALEXANDER the Great's army. Sarmatian migration from the river Don towards the Crimea in the 3rd century forced them to give up much of their territory and concentrate in the western Crimea, with a capital at Scythian Neapolis (situated within modern Simferopol). The city was abandoned in the 3rd century AD, in the final eclipse of the Scythians and their state.

SCYTHIA AND SCYTHIANS: famed in antiquity as archers.

Scythian territory was not highly urbanized, and the characteristic ARCHAEOLOGICAL site is the burial tumulus, though there are a few fortified settlements. Scythian art belongs to a nomadic culture. It is known as Scythian Animal Style, and is expressed mainly in small objects – dress, weapons and horse harnesses – made from GOLD, bronze, BONE, wood and various TEXTILES. Initially, Scythian culture was much influenced by the Animal Style of the Asian steppes, the best examples of which are found in the frozen sites of Siberia. From the Near East the Scythians returned with art heavily influenced by what they had seen there. From the 5th century BC, the Greek cities of the northern Black sea were a meeting place of Scythian and Hellenic cultures, which combined to create the unique Scythian-Greek art. Greek craftsmen in the north Pontic colonies produced highly artistic golden and SILVER JEWELLERY and vessels for the Scythian élite, adapting their work to the tastes and demands of the latter. GRT

See Boardman, J. (1994) *The Diffusion of Classical Art in Antiquity*; Piotrovsky, B. et al. (1987) *Scythian Art*; Rolle, R. (1989) *The World of the Scythians*.

 AMAZONS; BLACK SEA.

Second Sophistic (*deutera sophistikê*) The collective term for practitioners of Greek oratory in the Roman empire, invented by PHILOSTRATOS in his *Lives of the Sophists*. Although he begins the movement with AISCHINES, scholars generally limit it to the late 1st and 2nd centuries AD. Some modern treatments include 4th-century AD orators like Himerius, LIBANIUS and THEMISTIUS; others argue for a 'Third Sophistic' instead. Philostratos considered sophists both those orators who were adept at philosophy and those who were outstanding rhetors; a long-standing debate about the definitions of 'philosopher', 'sophist' and 'rhetor' lies behind his choice. In regard to style, the Second Sophistic tended to 'Atticize' after the 'Asianic' oratory of the previous period.

Philostratos' sophists were typically wealthy and famous men who consorted with the powerful, including even the emperor. They regularly benefited their own cities by undertaking LITURGIES and embassies. Rivalries were frequent, as they sought to outdo each other in fame and influence. The best-known individuals are AELIAN, AELIUS ARISTIDES, DIO CHRYSOSTOM, Favorinus ('a Gaul who spoke Greek' – one of his own paradoxes about himself; the others are 'a eunuch prosecuted for adultery' and 'a man who quarrelled with the emperor and lived'), HERODES ATTICUS, LUCIAN (not treated by Philostratos), PAUSANIAS and POLLUX. (see also ORATORY, GREEK; PROSE; RHETORIC, GREEK). JV

See Anderson, G. (1993) *The Second Sophistic*; Bowersock, G.W. (1969) *Greek Sophists in the Roman Empire*; Kennedy, G. A. (1994) *A New History of Classical Rhetoric*.

secrecy An important concept in antiquity. Naturally, perpetrators of crimes sought to keep their activities private. Presumably, adulterers and philanderers attempted to hide activities from spouses, families and other associates, though ELEGIAC poets and others boast of illicit liaisons. Financial dealings were sometimes matters of privacy; for example, Roman SENATORS, on principle not permitted to derive income from business, nevertheless invested in many companies fronted by *EQUITES*.

Many political decisions emerged from private meetings, and uprisings and conspiracies required secrecy. Leaks were not insurmountable, for JULIUS CAESAR ignored warnings and lost his life. An army's ability to surprise opponents depended on concealment of its own activity, but also on espionage and disinformation. Ingenious methods were employed to send covert messages, treated by AENEAS TACTICUS, among others. Apart from codes known only to sender and recipient, messages could be tattooed into a skull after shaving the hair (Herodotos 5.35) or slipped into the carcass of a rabbit, carried by, ostensibly, a hunter (Herodotos 1.123–4).

MYSTERY RELIGIONS kept their practices hidden, and, in late antiquity, PAGANS often found it necessary to conceal their beliefs. Some forms of divination were illegal, and anyone who sought the identity of an EMPEROR's successor was well advised to consult the gods in secret. Inevitably, informers were a constant danger, though a formalized system of secret police never existed. Both the SPARTAN *krypteia* and the late antique *agentes in rebus*, often translated 'secret service' and 'SECRET POLICE', are best regarded as special agents who occasionally operated under cover. JV

secret police Agents who covertly gather information against internal enemies for the government. As befits their name, evidence for such organizations is scanty and ambiguous. The best-attested examples are from the Roman empire. A universally despised figure in the literature of the early empire was the *delator* (informer), who made a career of denouncing fellow citizens to the EMPEROR with accusations of treason or disloyalty (e.g. Tacitus, *Annals* 1.74, 3.66). Informers found ready employment under emperors such as NERO and DOMITIAN who actively persecuted and put to death members of the SENATE based on such denunciations, but more moderate emperors such as HADRIAN also appear to have used spies to investigate even their friends (*HISTORIA AUGUSTA*, *Hadrian* 11.4–6). By the 2nd century AD, a formal intelligence-gathering agency seems to have been established. Officially, the *frumentarii* were soldiers, serving as couriers between the capital and the PROVINCES, whose name implies that they were also involved with the FOOD SUPPLY. Ancient sources suggest that in reality they served as spies for the emperor and even carried out assassinations. The notoriety and hostility they incurred caused them to be disbanded under DIOCLETIAN, though their duties were assumed in the later empire by a new organization whose members were known as *agentes in rebus*. (see also SECRECY) GSA

See Austin, N. J. E. and Rankov, N. B. (1995) *Exploratio: military and political intelligence in the Roman world*.

Sejanus (Lucius Aelius Seianus) d. AD 31 Ambitious praetorian prefect. Born to an EQUESTRIAN family in the town of Volsinii (Bolsena) in ETRURIA, he was appointed co-prefect of the PRAETORIAN GUARD along with his father. Under TIBERIUS, he became sole prefect and received a number of indications of the emperor's favour. He gained power as Tiberius' confidant, particularly after the death of the emperor's son Drusus (in whose death Sejanus was suspected of having played a role). He was responsible for establishing the praetorian camp at Rome, and used his influence to have a number of his enemies accused of treason and executed. He supposedly won Tiberius' complete trust when he threw himself over the emperor to protect him from falling rocks in the dining room or grotto at Sperlonga. After Tiberius' withdrawal to the island of CAPRI in AD 27, Sejanus was effectively left in charge of Rome and vigorously attempted to expand his power, aid his supporters and eliminate his enemies. Eventually Tiberius realized that Sejanus was less interested in serving the emperor than in promoting himself, and in October 31 a long, rambling letter from Tiberius denouncing Sejanus was read aloud in the SENATE. Sejanus was quickly arrested and executed along with his family. GSA

See Hennig, D. (1975) *L. Aelius Seianus*; Seager, R. (1972) *Tiberius*; Shotter, D. (1992) *Tiberius Caesar*; Syme, R. (1958) *Tacitus*.

Seleukeia-on-the-Euphrates see ZEUGMA.

Seleukid empire When ALEXANDER the Great died in 323 BC, he had conquered a vast empire but had not yet succeeded in organizing it. The realm was soon shattered by insurrections, and divided up between the SUCCESSORS. One of the GENERALS, SELEUKOS (later king Seleukos I Nikator) reconquered from his rivals a huge swathe of the empire stretching from Asia Minor via SYRIA and BABYLONIA to Iran and central Asia, and secured it for himself and the dynasty he founded, known as the SELEUKIDS.

There is continuing debate among historians about whether the Seleukid empire was westward- or eastward-looking. It is undeniable that, in organizing their empire, Seleukos and his son and successor, Antiochos I Soter, continued and adapted the practices of their Achaemenid Persian predecessors. Like them, they used local peoples in the army and in local BUREAUCRACY, continued the Achaemenids' colonizing policy and used several 'royal capitals' (Seleukeia-on-the-Tigris, ANTIOCH, SARDIS). While much of the evidence for Seleukid activity comes from Greek sources, especially inscriptions, and from the western parts of the empire, some scholars now consider that the core of Seleukid power, and the chief focus of their dynastic interests, lay in MESOPOTAMIA and the Iranian plateau. The dynasty nevertheless engaged relentlessly in power politics with the other great post-Alexander kingdoms, forming ALLIANCES often cemented (temporarily in some cases) by dynastic intermarriage. One locus of long-standing conflict was Koile (Hollow) SYRIA (roughly modern Lebanon and Israel), the object of the lengthy series of SYRIAN WARS with the PTOLEMIES.

The second half of the 3rd century saw the hiving off of large territories in the east, where independent kingdoms were established by processes still not well understood. After a period of difficulties the empire enjoyed a marked revival, especially in the east, under ANTIOCHOS III (223–187), who succeeded in reconquering most of what used to belong to the founders of the dynasty. His later conflict with Rome, however, marked a turning-point in the history of the empire. Defeat at Magnesia, followed by the peace settlement of APAMEIA (188), forced him to give up western Asia Minor.

SELEUKIDS: the Seleukid dynasty.

Date	Ruler	Relationship to other rulers
305–281	Seleukos I Nikator ('Victor'; secure from 312)	
281–261	Antiochos I Soter (co-ruler from 294 or 293)	s.Seleukos I
261–246	Antiochos II Theos ('the God')	s.Antiochos I
246–226/5	Seleukos II Kallinikos ('the Glorious Victor')	s.Antiochos II
226/5–223	Seleukos III	s.Seleukos II
223–187	Antiochos III Megas ('the Great')	s.Seleukos II
187–175	Seleukos IV Philopator	s.Antiochos III
175–164	Antiochos IV Epiphanes	s.Antiochos III
164–162	Antiochos V Eupator ('the Good Father')	s.Antiochos IV
162–150	Demetrios I Soter	s.Seleukos IV
150–145	Alexander Balas (Epiphanes)	's.' Antiochos IV
145–140	[1]Demetrios II Nikator	s.Demetrios I
145–142	Antiochos VI Epiphanes	s.Alexander Balas, Kleopatra Thea
142–139/8	Diodotos ['Tryphon', pretender]	
139/8–129	Antiochos VII Sidetes	s.Demetrios I
129–126/5	[2]Demetrios II Nikator	
126/5–123	Kleopatra Thea ('the Goddess')	wife of Demetrios II
126/5–96	Antiochos VIII Grypos	s.Demetrios II
126	Seleukos V	s.Demetrios II
114/13–95	Antiochos IX Philopator Kyzikenos ('of Kyzikos')	s.Antiochos VII
95	Seleukos VI	s.Antiochos VIII
95	Antiochos X Eusebes ('the Pious') Philopator	s.Antiochos IX
95–88	Demetrios III Philopator Soter (at Damascus)	s.Antiochos VIII
95	Antiochos XI Epiphanes Philadelphos (in Cilicia; twin of Philip I)	s.Antiochos VIII
95–84/3	Philip I (in Cilicia)	s.Antiochos VIII
87	Antiochos XII Dionysos (at Damascus)	s.Antiochos VIII
84/3	Philip II	s.Philip I
69–64/3	Antiochos XIII Philadelphos Asiatikos	s.Antiochos IX

Key: s. = son of; [1,2] = first, second periods of rule.

The 2nd century also saw the emergence, in eastern Iran and AFGHANISTAN, of the PARTHIANS, who ultimately conquered the whole Iranian plateau. In 141 they seized Seleukeia-on-the-Tigris (the Seleukid 'capital' in Mesopotamia), stripping the Seleukids of the rich heart of their kingdom. From the later 2nd century, complex dynastic struggles, as well as the further advance of the Parthians and the interference of Rome, led to the decline of the empire, eventually reduced to a rump kingdom centred on Syria. POMPEY's annexation of Syria in 64 BC marked the end of more than 250 years of Seleukid rule.

The Seleukid era, dated retrospectively from the beginning of Seleukos' reign in 312, continued to be used throughout the Middle East as the most common dating system well into the Middle Ages. KB, GR

See Bevan, E. R. (1902) *The House of Seleucus*, 2 vols.; Grainger, J. D. (1997) *A Seleukid Prosopography and Gazetteer*; Kuhrt, A. and Sherwin-White, S., eds. (1987) *Hellenism in the East*; Rostovtzeff, M. (1951) *The Social and Economic History of the Hellenistic World*; Sherwin-White, S. and Kuhrt, A. (1993) *From Samarkhand to Sardis*; Shipley, G. (2000) *The Greek World after Alexander*, ch. 8; Will, E. (1979–82) *Histoire politique du monde hellénistique*; *CAH* 7.1, chs. 6 (D. Musti) and 11 (H. Heinen), and vol. 8, ch. 10 (C. Habicht).

Seleukids The name given to the descendants of SELEUKOS I who ruled the largest, eastern part of ALEXANDER's empire from 312 BC. Many of the kings bore the name Seleukos or Antiochos. Seleukos I is credited with superhuman capacities (Appian, *Syrian Wars* 55–8), though this may reflect later royal propaganda or RULER-CULT. Otherwise we know little or nothing of the individual personalities of the kings, though their varying strategic abilities can sometimes be inferred. Most prominent are Seleukos I, ANTIOCHOS III, and – mainly because of his unfortunate, perhaps mishandled, relationship with the JEWS – Antiochos IV. The dynasty controlled a shrunken territory by the time the last king, Philip II, was defeated in 64/3 BC by POMPEY, who organized Syria into a territory under Roman control. (see also MACCABEES; SELEUKID EMPIRE; SYRIAN WARS) GR, DGJS [table (p. 803) by KB]

Seleukos I ?358 or ?354–281 BC A Macedonian nobleman who served ALEXANDER the Great in secondary capacities but rose to become one of the winners in the struggle between Alexander's SUCCESSORS to control his empire after his death. He participated in affairs following Alexander's death, notably as (probably) one of the assassins of the regent Perdikkas. In 320, in the settlement at Triparadeisos, he was awarded the satrapy of BABYLON, but he lost it in 315 and took refuge with PTOLEMY in Egypt. Restored to Babylon in 312, he campaigned in the east as far as INDIA, where Chandragupta defeated him; nevertheless, he secured much of PERSIA, Media and Baktria. In 301 he combined with LYSIMACHOS to defeat the army of Antigonos Monophthalmos (founder of the ANTIGONID dynasty) at IPSOS. In the subsequent division of territory Seleukos received SYRIA and MESOPOTAMIA. By his victory at Kouroupedion near SARDIS in early 281 he obtained control of much of Asia Minor, which had been ruled by Lysimachos, who was killed in the battle. A few months later, however, as he was advancing into THRACE, Seleukos (now in his seventies) was murdered by Ptolemy Keraunos, an estranged son of Ptolemy I.

Seleukos was married to the Persian noblewoman Apama in the mass wedding sponsored by Alexander in 324 at Sousa. Their son was Antiochos I. Apama seems to have died before 298, when Seleukos married STRATONIKE, the daughter of DEMETRIOS I POLIORKETES. In 293 or 292 Seleukos gave her over to Antiochos (who is said to have been pining away with love for his stepmother) and sent him to be vice-regent in the east.

Seleukos was a skilled GENERAL and administrator, arguably one of the two most successful of Alexander's Successors in the long term. He founded many cities in Syria and Asia Minor, most notably ANTIOCH (named after his father, another Antiochos). (see also SELEUKID EMPIRE; SELEUKIDS) GR

See Grainger, J. D. (1990), *Seleukos Nikator*.

Seleukos II see ANTIOCHOS III; SELEUKIDS.

Seleukos III Kallinikos see ANTIOCHOS III; SELEUKIDS.

Sellasia, battle of 222 BC Fought near the SPARTAN perioikic town of Sellasia in northern Laconia, in the valley of the river Oinous (mod. Kelephína). The combined forces of ANTIGONOS III of Macedonia and the ACHAIAN LEAGUE, led by ARATOS OF SIKYON, defeated the Spartans under KLEOMENES III, who had learned that Ptolemy III of Egypt was withdrawing his financial support. The anti-Spartan allies had 28,000 foot-soldiers and 1,200 cavalry; Kleomenes 20,000 Lakedaimonians, allies and mercenaries including cavalry. Kleomenes occupied an excellent position, but after several days' stand-off Antigonos attacked, perhaps rashly. An enterprising initiative by the young PHILOPOIMEN turned the battle in the allies' favour. The Spartans missed the chance of a telling response, and the huge Macedonian phalanx and its *sarissa* (long thrusting-spear) proved decisive. Victory allowed Antigonos to become the first invader to capture Sparta. He annulled Kleomenes' reforms and dealt the latest telling blow (not the final one) to Spartan independence. Sellasia did not bring peace to the PELOPONNESE. Years of turmoil followed between Sparta and the Achaians, only temporarily ended by Sparta's forced enrolment in the league in 192. DGJS

See Polybios 2. 63–71; Morgan, J. D. (1981) Sellasia revisited, *AJA* 85: 328–30; Pritchett, W. K. (1965) *Studies in Ancient Greek Topography* 1, 59–70.

semiotics Semiology, as semiotics is also termed, is the study or the science of signs (*sêmata* in Greek). Messages or texts, according to semioticians, are systems of signs (which can be lexical or graphic – made up of words or images) and gain their effects through the constant interplay between these signs. So it is that signs, meaningless in themselves, interact to produce systems of signification. A restaurant menu, for example, has elements or signs that may remain constant, but its signification or system can be filled differently, according to time of day and the type of restaurant. These sign-produced systems, like languages themselves, are therefore culture-specific. Semioticians tend to look for patterns and systems, and these closely resemble those made famous by such STRUCTURALISTS as Claude Lévi-Strauss. They can be seen in such diverse cultural products as kinship, MYTH, grammar and even advertising (Barthes).

There is an abundance of ancient technical literature that is overtly semiotic. The study of signs is evident in work on dreams (ARISTOTLE, *On Interpretation through Dreams*; Artemidoros, *The Interpretation of Dreams*), divination (CICERO, *On Divination*) and natural sign systems such as star systems (ARATOS, *Phainomena*) or in MEDICINE (GALEN, for example, described his symptomatology as a careful study of signs).

Interest in semiotics, in classics at least, has waned since the 1980s and has been replaced by a variety of post-structuralist critical modes. Semiotics saw its system-building as being in some way hard-wired into the brain, a concept opposed by the post-structuralists. It probably has its best legacy in work on non-verbal communication. (see also CRITICAL THEORY) PGT

See Barthes, R. (1967) *Elements of Semiology*; Eco, U. (1976) *A Theory of Semiotics*; Felson-Rubin, N., ed. (1983) *Semiotics and Classical Studies*; Jorio, A. de (2000) *Gesture in Naples and Gesture in Classical Antiquity*; Lateiner, D. (1995) *The Sardonic Smile*.

Semonides Greek lyric poet of the mid-7th century BC. Semonides was born on SAMOS but, in ancient tradition, was thought to have founded a colony on nearby Amorgos in 693; he is usually therefore called Semonides of Amorgos, though in ancient sources his name is often Simonides. He belongs to the canon of iambic poets established by ALEXANDRIAN scholars. Because of confusion with SIMONIDES of Keos, he is also said by some ancient sources to have written ELEGIES; this is now doubted. Few fragments are extant, and it is difficult to assess him as a poet.

Semonides does not draw on personal experience, but employs traditional themes; his poems lack the passion and honesty of his contemporary ARCHILOCHOS. He had a pessimistic outlook on life, describing it as short, hard and plagued by sickness and empty hope. He is best known for his poem against women (fr. 7), which contains strong echoes of HESIOD and AESOPIC fables. Supposedly, Semonides warns men against marrying the wrong wife. Ten kinds of women – born from the sow, fox, dog, earth, sea, mule, weasel, mare, ape and bee – exist, and only men who marry bee-women, who are chaste and hard working, and remain at home, can consider themselves fortunate. Others cannot, since women are the worst EVIL for men. For the modern scholar, the poem offers useful insight into male expectations of women during the archaic period. RBC

See West, M. L., trs. (1993) *Greek Lyric Poetry*; Fränkel, H. (1975) *Early Greek Poetry and Philosophy*; Podlecki, A. J. (1984) *The Early Greek Poets and their Times*.

Sempronii see GRACCHI.

senate and senators, Roman For CICERO (*pro Sestio* 137) the senate was the 'everlasting council' (*consilium sempiternum*) of Rome, set up to be 'the guardian, leader, and defender of the state'. Tradition represented its origins in the body which first the KINGS and subsequently the MAGISTRATES in the REPUBLIC gathered together to advise them. This role was reflected in the fact that only a magistrate could call a meeting of the senate. He introduced, sometimes with a speech of his own, the issue or proposal on which he wished to consult the senate and then asked the senators, normally in order of seniority, for their views, which they were required to give. The magistrate then framed the motion to be voted on. If this was passed and was not vetoed either by a CONSUL or a TRIBUNE, the presiding magistrate was responsible along with a selected group of senators for drafting the actual 'consulted opinion of the senate' (*senatus consultum*, often abbreviated as *s.c.*).

As Rome expanded, so the complexity of issues to be decided grew greater and the senate was the only standing institution in which the necessary detailed discussion could take place. Since in theory a senate meeting could be called at any time, the requirement was introduced in the 2nd century BC for senators to reside in Rome unless given permission to be absent. Magistrates needed support and, when by the end of the 4th century BC the senate had come to consist largely of ex-magistrates with all their experience, it was the obvious place for them to turn. For a Greek observer, POLYBIOS (6.11–18), by the middle of the 2nd century the senate's influence was paramount in issues of state finance, the maintenance of order in Italy, and in receiving and sending embassies, along with effective control of magistrates in decisions over which PROVINCES they were to have and for how long. For Cicero, the senate was at the heart of the Republican system and challenges to its authority were threats to the very fabric of the state. His views have bewitched much modern scholarship. In reality, however, the Republic had no written constitution; the senate's authority was based on custom and precedent and was always open to challenge. Indeed, the history of the Republic can be seen a continuous debate and endless tension between the various potential sources of power: the magistrates, the senate and the ASSEMBLIES.

Under the principate the senate had to develop a working relationship with the EMPEROR. The emperor had the power to convene the senate, to attend its meetings (sitting between the consuls) and to present issues to it. This created a dilemma for senators, neatly summed up in the question that one of them asked the emperor TIBERIUS: 'Will you vote first or last? If first, I shall have your lead to follow; if last, I am afraid of unwisely voting against you' (Tacitus, *Annals* 1.74). Although emperors might seek to promote effective debate, their effective control of PATRONAGE undermined their efforts. From the time of HADRIAN, an emperor's speech to the senate became cited by jurists as a source of LAW in its own right. Yet the imperial period also saw real increases in the senate's powers. From AD 14 magisterial ELECTIONS were held by the senate. Its decisions came to have the force of law, and it functioned as a court. Recognition by the senate remained a key moment in legitimizing a new emperor.

The traditional figure for the size of the senate for much of the Republic was 300. This was increased by SULLA in 81 BC to 500–600. The kings and the early

SENATE AND SENATORS, ROMAN: (a) the Roman forum, with arch of Severus (l.) and the 4th-century rebuilt senate house (r.).

SENATE AND SENATORS, ROMAN: (b) interior of the senate house, with original late Roman floor and surviving steps for seating down sides of chamber.

consuls had simply recruited whoever they wished. But this changed radically with the *lex Ovinia*, passed sometime between 339 and 318 BC, when the task of selecting the senators was undertaken by the CENSORS who were sworn 'to enrol the best men of all ranks'. This came to be interpreted as a requirement to enrol the holders of most of the magistracies, provided they were of good character. Free birth and wealth at least at the level of the equestrian order (400,000 *sestertii*) were also essential. Sulla refined the system by making entry to the senate automatic on holding the QUAESTORSHIP. After the civil wars AUGUSTUS fixed the senate's size at 600 and introduced a new higher wealth qualification of 1 million *sestertii*. This helped to define for the first time a separate senatorial class. Only senators and their sons had the right to wear the distinctive *latus clavus* (a broad purple stripe on the tunic). The wives of senators had the right to be carried in covered chairs when they went out. Senators and their families had certain protections from prosecution for some civil charges, and the right to be treated differently from others when found guilty in court themselves.

According to Cicero, 'entry to the highest order was open to all citizens through industry and merit' (*pro Sestio* 137). He himself was a clear example of this, as he came from a non-senatorial background. Although candidates for office and the senate emphasized, when they could, their descent from previous holders of the magistracies, there was a constant need to replace families that had died out. A steady flow of new men from non-senatorial backgrounds was therefore essential. In the last two centuries of the Republic, the rich gentry of the towns of Italy increasingly sought careers in the Roman senate. Emperors used their patronage to introduce new talent by granting the right to wear the *latus clavus* to men of non-senatorial background, and even by promoting men directly into the senate by the process known as 'adlection'. Increasingly the provincial élites were drawn in, and by the end of the 2nd century AD they predominated in the senate. Senators remained an exclusive club of the super-rich long

SENATE AND SENATORS, ROMAN: career paths and employment c. AD 100.

Prospective senators	
Freeborn citizens meeting property qualification of 1 million *sestertii*	
Sons of senators	
Introductory level (mostly of one year term)	
Adoption of *latus clavus* – toga of senatorial class	Aged c.18
Year as *vigintivir*: minor administrative post with mint, with responsibilities for roads, legal affairs, etc.	20 per year
Service as military tribune (*tribunus laticlavus*)	20–25 normally available, though might be held for more than a year
Some senators substituted work in courts at Rome	Variable
Quaestor or financial officer	Aged 24–25, 18 per year (8 in Rome, 10 in provinces)
Tribune of plebs or aedile (not necessary for patrician)	10 tribunes and 6 aediles each year
Praetor (normally held 5 or more years after quaestorship)	At age c.30. Ultimately 18 per year, but only 8 under Augustus.
Upper levels (various posts were open to ex-praetors)	
legati proconsulis (assistants to provincial governors)	(14 per year – rank unspecified)
curator viarum	1 ex-praetor
iuridici	2 ex-praetors
praefectus aerarii Saturni	1 ex-praetor
praefectus aerarii militaris	1 ex-praetor
Consulship or suffect consulship	Theoretically not before age 42, though patricians from 32 and imperial family/heirs earlier. Suffect consulships swelled: number available from 2/year to c.8/year. AD 190 record year with 25
curator Tiberis, curator operum publicum, curator aquarum	3 ex-consuls
Proconsulship (provincial governor)	8 ex-praetors, 2 ex-consuls
legatus Augusti pro praetore (provincial governor)	6 ex-praetors, 2 ex-consuls
legatus legionis (legionary commanders)	28–30 posts, rank varied
praefectus alimentorum	1 ex-consul
ad hoc appointments as special legates, *curator urbis, censitor, comes*	Number and rank varied
praefectus urbi	1 ex-consul

Though senators were regularly employed in provincial administration and other posts, there was no such thing as a standard career pattern.

after their real influence on affairs had gone. Their excesses appalled AMMIANUS MARCELLINUS from Syrian ANTIOCH in the 4th century, who describes their gilded, but useless, lives with biting satire (14.6; 28.4). JJP

See Hopkins, K. (1983) *Death and Renewal*; Lintott, A. (1999) *The Constitution of the Roman Republic*; Talbert, R. J. A. (1984) *The Senate of Imperial Rome*; Wiseman, T. P. (1971) *New Men in the Roman Senate 139 BC–14 AD*.

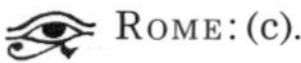 ROME: (c).

senatus consulta The *senatus consultum* (*s.c.*) was advice given by the SENATE to the MAGISTRATES, recorded and deposited in the treasury and having the force of law if acted upon. Often the decree was published in inscriptions outside Rome; several examples translated into Greek have been found. They treat an enormous range of issues: the *s.c. de Bacchanalibus* of 188 BC, which limited DIONYSIAC celebrations in Italy; treaties with Greek states such as the *s.c. de agro Pergameno*, concerning land which had come to Rome through the bequest of king Attalos III in 133 and was soon pressed for tax; the *s.c.* passed to grant JULIUS CAESAR the right to be buried inside the *POMERIUM* of Rome. A special form, the *senatus consultum ultimum*, was perhaps first declared in 121 BC and accepted by the CONSUL Opimius against Gaius GRACCHUS. Opimius interpreted this call by the senate to defend the REPUBLIC as justifying the murder of Gracchus. CICERO took a similar line in the CATILINARIAN affair. In both cases it came to a matter of LAW whether the illegality involved in killing a citizen without trial was justified. *Senatus consulta* continued to be an important aspect of the functioning and authority of the senate well into the imperial period. CJS

See Sherk, R. K. (1969) *Roman Documents from the Greek East*; Talbert, R. J. A. (1984) *The Senate of Imperial Rome*.

Seneca the Elder (Lucius Annaeus Seneca) c.50 BC–AD 40 Memoirist and historian. Seneca is best known for his *Controversiae* and *Suasoriae*, remnants of a larger work that sought to legitimize the study and practice of DECLAMATION in the Roman world. His writings inform us of the set topics or themes of declamation, the approaches taken (with varying degrees of success) by practising declaimers, and memorable sayings or *sententiae* composed on the spot in the context of declamatory competition. Although declamation is often regarded as a school practice, Seneca's declaimers are by and large adults, many of whom achieved political and/or artistic prominence in the early PRINCIPATE. His privileging of declamation stands in contrast to the late Republican, chiefly Ciceronian, emphasis on political ORATORY; it is perhaps for this reason that declamations on the life and death of CICERO are well represented in the collection. While Seneca's works provide important insight into the intellectual and social formation of ÉLITE males at Rome and supply us with many sensational anecdotes, they describe a practice that remained controversial throughout Roman history. Seneca was perhaps most successful in promoting the interests of his sons: although he was born in Spain, all three of his sons rose to high positions in Roman politics. TNH

See Winterbottom, M., ed. (1974) *The Elder Seneca, Declamations* (text and trs., 2 vols.); Bloomer, W. M. (1997) *Latinity and Literary Society at Rome*.

Seneca the Younger (Lucius Annaeus Seneca) ?4 BC–AD 65 STOIC PHILOSOPHER and TRAGEDIAN. Seneca, son of SENECA THE ELDER, was born in Corduba, Spain, and was educated in Rome where – after a brief spell in Egypt – he embarked on a political and forensic career. Banished to Corsica by CLAUDIUS in AD 41, he was recalled in 49 through the agency of AGRIPPINA, mother of the future emperor NERO, to whom he was appointed tutor. Seneca remained on good terms with Nero during the early years of the latter's reign, and took on the unofficial but influential role of political adviser. By 62, however, the emperor's favour was on the wane, and Seneca gradually withdrew from public life to devote himself to writing and philosophical study. He was accused in 65 of involvement in the conspiracy headed by Gaius Calpurnius Piso, and forced to take his own life. His elaborately staged SUICIDE is memorably described by TACITUS (*Annals* 15.62–4).

Seneca's extant prose works (we have titles of several more that have not survived) are united by an overriding concern with practical ETHICS. The 12 books of essays known collectively as the *Dialogi*, together with the seven-book *De beneficiis* (*On Beneficence*) and the *De clementia* (*On Clemency*; originally in three books, though only the first and part of the second survive), are devoted mainly to ethical questions. The *Moral Letters*, addressed to a younger friend, Lucilius, are in effect more informal exercises in philosophical exhortation, employing the chance occurrences of daily life as points of departure for reflection on a variety of moral issues. The *Natural Questions* – a work in seven books, dating, like the *Moral Letters*, from the period of Seneca's retirement from public life – is principally concerned with the workings of the physical world; but Seneca finds opportunities for moral exhortation here too. In these works, he is consistent in his adherence to Stoic theories of virtue and wisdom, while maintaining a tolerant and undogmatic attitude towards philosophers of rival schools, whose writings are not infrequently cited with approval.

In addition to the philosophical works, Seneca's output included an amusing SATIRE of the 'Menippean' type on the deification of the emperor Claudius, the *Apocolocyntosis* or 'Pumpkinification'. He wrote nine tragedies, among which *Medea*, *Phaedra* and *Thyestes* are perhaps the most highly regarded (a tenth, *Octavia*, is almost certainly not by Seneca, though transmitted under his name). Seneca's subject matter is drawn from Greek myth (most of the plays rework EURIPIDEAN or SOPHOKLEAN models), though his memorable portrayals of TYRANNY and the lust for power must have appeared highly topical to contemporary audiences. The tragedies are notable for their powerfully RHETORICAL, if rather static, character, and for their graphic descriptions of violence and overwhelming emotion. It remains an open and hotly debated question whether the tragedies are suited to full stage performance. Many scholars believe that they were originally intended for recitation. Also controversial is the relationship between Senecan drama and Stoic philosophy. While the conflict between reason and passion is central to both, the apparent triumph of such bloodthirsty characters as Atreus (in *Thyestes*) and Medea renders any straightforwardly Stoic reading highly problematic.

Seneca's philosophical works remained popular throughout antiquity, and became so again in the later Middle Ages and RENAISSANCE. The tragedies, on the other hand, were largely neglected until the 14th century, but thereafter exerted a formative influence on Renaissance and Jacobean drama. MG

See Boyle, A. J. (1997) *Tragic Seneca*; Griffin, M. (1976) *Seneca*.

Septimius Severus see SEVERUS, SEPTIMIUS.

Septuagint The translation into Greek of Jewish scriptures produced between the 3rd century BC and 1st century AD. The term originally referred to the translation of the first five books of the BIBLE (the Pentateuch). It then came to denote the translations of all the Hebrew and Aramaic books, along with some Jewish works originally composed in Greek (and partially forming what is now known as the *APOCRYPHA*). The translations, probably made by JEWS in Egypt, indicate a need at that time for the scriptures to be read in Greek in the liturgy, and show the existence of a Jewish literary class working in Greek, not only in Hebrew and Aramaic. Although, for many Jews in the Greco-Roman world, this was their BIBLE, Greek and Roman writers do not seem to have taken note of it until its eventual adoption by CHRISTIANITY. Consequently, knowledge of JUDAISM in Greco-Roman authors is based on accounts by Jewish authors or personal experience. The Septuagint does occasionally refer to 'Greeks' in a negative tone, perhaps following SELEUKID persecution of Jews under Antiochos IV in the 160s BC. JKA

See Jobes, K. H. and Silva, M. (2000) *Invitation to the Septuagint*.

Serapeum (Greek Sarapeion, Latin Sarapeum) The TEMPLE of Serapis (or Sarapis), in the south-west quarter of ancient ALEXANDRIA, was built by Ptolemy III Euergetes (246–221 BC), though it may have been a replacement for an earlier Ptolemaic shrine. The Greco-Roman cult was based on an Egyptian version, centred at Memphis, that combined aspects of the Osiris and the Apis-bull cults (as well as their names). A primary feature was healing, through incubation, oracles and dream-interpretation, and the temples attracted many visitors from Egypt and elsewhere. While the details remain obscure, the Ptolemies adopted and transformed the cult in the late 4th and 3rd centuries BC to suit their political need for a divine patron. In time, the worship of Serapis spread throughout the Greco-Roman world, where it was sometimes assimilated to ZEUS and associated with Roman emperors. Despite its ubiquity, the cult never achieved the prominence that ISIS attained outside Egypt.

Set in a porticoed court, Ptolemy III's temple remained in use until it was destroyed in a fire in AD 181. Subsequently the court was enlarged and a new, imposing, hexastyle temple was built on a lofty podium in the Roman manner, with columns of red Aswan granite. This was probably finished c.AD 215. It contained a huge statue of Serapis, and was widely regarded as the most beautiful temple in antiquity. In association with the LIBRARY (even holding a subsidiary collection) and MOUSEION of Alexandria, the Serapeum contributed to the city's repute as a centre of learning and culture.

In the 380s, Maternus Cynegius, a fanatical CHRISTIAN prefect of the East, encouraged the destruction of statues and temples everywhere. Not surprisingly, Theophilus, BISHOP of Alexandria, stirred up frenzy, and non-Christians attacked Christians, who defended themselves with the assistance of military forces. To defuse the situation, the emperor THEODOSIUS ordered statues in the city, as a source of conflict, to be destroyed, and hermits and monks were installed at temples to prevent renewed use. The Serapeum itself was taken down 391. For both Christians and adherents of traditional cults, the destruction of the Serapeum came to symbolize victory and defeat, respectively, in the struggle between CHRISTIANITY and PAGANISM. JV, RJAW

See Empereur, J.-Y. (1998) *Alexandria Rediscovered* 89–109; McKenzie, J. S., Gibson, S. and Reyes, A.T. (2004) Reconstructing the Serapeum in Alexandria from the archaeological evidence, *JRS* 94: 73–121; Wild, R. A. (1984) The known Isis–Sarapis sanctuaries from the Roman period, *ANRW* II.17.4: 1739–851 (at 1756–8).

Serapis (Sarapis) see EGYPT; GODS AND GODDESSES, ROMAN; RELIGION; SERAPEUM.

serfs see HELOTS; LABOUR; PEASANTS.

Sertorius Quintus Sertorius served under Quintus Servilius Caepio and Gaius MARIUS in the wars against the Cimbri and Teutones (106–101 BC), and also as TRIBUNE of the soldiers under Titus Didius in HISPANIA Citerior from 97 to 93 BC. When Cinna was expelled from Rome in 87, Sertorius fled with him, returning in the march on the capital by Cinna and Marius later in the same year. In 83 he was PRAETOR, and, after assisting the Marians in their attempt to prevent Sulla's march through Italy, he left for his province of Hispania Citerior. After Sulla captured Rome from the supporters of Marius in 82, Sertorius was expelled from Spain by the praetor sent from Rome to replace him. Managing to return in 80 when invited by a dissident group of LUSITANIANS, he was able, relying partly on his good relations with local Spanish communities, to frustrate the attempts of a series of Roman commanders to dislodge him. He is said to have made contact not only with PIRATES, who were able to provide him with NAVAL support, but also with Mithradates V of Pontos, who attempted to make an alliance. Neither Quintus Metellus Pius (sent to Hispania Ulterior in 79) nor the young POMPEY (sent to Hispania Citerior in 77 to help Metellus) were able to regain control of the peninsula, though from 76 onwards Sertorius was increasingly less successful. In 72 he was assassinated by Marcus Perperna, who had joined him with substantial forces in 77 after the collapse of the revolt of Marcus Lepidus, and this resulted in the collapse of his cause. JSR

See Plutarch, *Life of Sertorius*; Spann, P. O. (1987) *Quintus Sertorius and the Legacy of Sulla*.

Servilii see PATRICIANS.

Servius Tullius One of the most enigmatic of the seven kings of Rome. He was the sixth to reign, traditionally from 578 to 535 BC. Said to be the son of a servant woman in the house of the TARQUINII, he was seen with a tongue of flame playing around his head when still a baby. Another tradition, which the emperor CLAUDIUS espoused, held that he was the same person as the ETRUSCAN adventurer Mastarna. The latter is depicted in a 4th-century painting in the François TOMB at Vulci with his leader Caeles Vibenna, who, in the view of some, settled at Rome and gave his name to the Caelian hill.

Servius is credited with reforms that put him in the mould of Athenian reformers like SOLON and KLEISTHENES. The sources give him a popular aspect that contrasts sharply with the tyranny that was to follow. He is said to have introduced the CENSUS (and the centuriate ASSEMBLY) and reformed the Roman TRIBAL system and the army. The 4th-century circuit wall around the city was attributed to him (though there are 6th-century portions). His close connection with the goddess FORTUNA in the sources fits in with the 6th-century phases of a TEMPLE, perhaps to Fortuna, under Sant' Omobono at Rome. Servius died gruesomely at the hands of his daughter Tullia and son-in-law TARQUINIUS SUPERBUS. CJS

See Livy 1.39–48; Dionysios of Halikarnassos 4.1–40; Cornell, T. J. (1995) *The Beginnings of Rome*.

sesterce(s), ***sestertius, -i, sestertium, -a*** see COINAGE (tables).

Seven Wonders A list of seven 'sights' (*theamata*), important documents of art and ARCHITECTURE, is first attested in the 2nd century BC, for example in Antipatros of Sidon (*Palatine Anthology* 9.58). It comprises the pyramids of Egypt, the city walls of BABYLON, the hanging gardens of Semiramis there, the TEMPLE of ARTEMIS at EPHESOS, the statue of ZEUS at OLYMPIA, the MAUSOLEUM of HALIKARNASSOS, and the colossus of RHODES. The concept was developed in references to single 'wonders' (*thaumata*) and in complete lists of seven, sometimes drawn up to celebrate an 'eighth' wonder such as the COLOSSEUM in Rome (MARTIAL, *Spectacula* 1) or St Basil's hospital (in GREGORY OF NAZIANZUS).

Later lists keep the number seven, but not always the same wonders. A rhetorical treatise, purporting to be a guidebook to the seven wonders for the armchair traveller, and attributed to the engineer PHILO OF BYZANTIUM, still refers to the seven of the old canon. Other wonders, however, like the Pharos (LIGHTHOUSE) of ALEXANDRIA, Egyptian Thebes, the labyrinth of Memphis, and the temple of Zeus at Kyzikos, are first counted among them in PLINY's list (*Natural History* 36.75ff.). The altar of horns at DELOS appears first in Martial (see above), CYRUS' PALACE at Ekbaṭana first in Ampelius (*Liber memorialis* 8), and the Asklepieion of PERGAMON and the Capitol of Rome first in *Palatine Anthology* 9.656.

CHRISTIAN authors replace pagan sanctuaries with Noah's ark and Solomon's temple, or add the church of Hagia Sophia in CONSTANTINOPLE, eventually listing up to 16 wonders to accommodate both traditional and new marvels. RENAISSANCE and later authors revert to the old canon, often replacing the city walls of Babylon with the Pharos of Alexandria. KB

See Clayton, P.A. and Price, M.J., eds. (1988) *The Seven Wonders of the Ancient World*; Brodersen, K. (2001) *Die sieben Weltwunder*.

Severus

 EMPERORS, ROMAN: (b); TETRARCHS: (b).

Severus, Alexander AD 208–35 Bassianus Alexianus, the future emperor Alexander Severus, was born at Arce in Phoenicia on 1 October AD 208, the son of Gessius Marcianus and JULIA MAMMAEA. He was the grandnephew of JULIA DOMNA, wife of SEPTIMIUS SEVERUS. He accompanied his cousin ELAGABALUS to Rome in 219, and, when he received the *toga virilis* on 26 June 221, was adopted by Elagabalus as Marcus Aurelius Alexander and given the rank of CAESAR. He was proclaimed emperor in the praetorian camp, during the coup d'état in which Elagabalus was murdered on 13 March 222, and recognized by the SENATE the next day as the emperor Marcus Aurelius Severus Alexander. The new name proclaimed his attachment to the dynasty founded by Septimius Severus.

Although the reign of Alexander was remembered in later Latin tradition as a heyday of senatorial privilege and imperial restraint, there is little contemporary evidence to support this view. Alexander had limited control of the government, which was left in the hands of court favourites (including the famous jurist ULPIAN) and dominated by his mother. There were signs (including the murder of Ulpian by the guard in 224) of military discontent throughout the reign. The antipathy of the army grew in the wake of Alexander's ineffectual campaign against the new SASSANID dynasty in PERSIA in 231, and in 235 he was murdered in a mutiny at Mainz.

The rise of the Sassanians was the most important event in Alexander's reign. His belated support for the former Arsakid rulers of Persia placed Rome in an adversarial relationship with the Sassanids, whose first two kings, Ardashir and SHAPUR, would be implacable and deadly foes of the Roman empire for nearly fifty years. DSP

 EMPERORS, ROMAN: (a); SEVERUS, SEPTIMIUS.

Severus, Septimius (Lucius Septimius Severus) AD 145–211 Second son of Fulvia Pia and an EQUESTRIAN named Publius Septimius Geta, born at LEPCIS MAGNA on 11 April AD 145. Despite Roman names, Severus' parents were Punic, and he is said to have spoken with a pronounced accent. Severus' grandfather was a patron of the poet STATIUS, and two uncles were SENATORS, one suffect consul in 153, the other in 160. Family influence secured Severus the QUAESTORSHIP in 170 and admission to the senate. He married twice, first Paccia Marciana from Lepcis, and, after her death, JULIA DOMNA, of the royal family of Emesa. In 190 he was appointed governor of PANNONIA Superior and was still there when COMMODUS was murdered on New Year's Eve, 192.

After the murder of Pertinax in 193 he forged a coalition of DANUBIAN governors to support him in a coup d'état against Didius Julianus. Proclaimed emperor by his troops on 9 April, he invaded Italy in May, occupying Rome on 9 June after Julianus' death. Meanwhile, Clodius Albinus in BRITAIN and PESCENNIUS NIGER had been proclaimed by their LEGIONS. Severus allied with Albinus, whom he recognized as CAESAR, and shared the consulship of 194 with him. He had already moved forces to the East, and, by the end of April 194, defeated Niger. Afterwards, Severus adopted himself into the family of MARCUS AURELIUS, a move designed, along with the PARTHIAN WAR, to secure legitimacy for his intended hereditary dynasty. It shocked senatorial opinion, but Severus would brook no opposition, ordering large-scale executions.

In 195 Severus invaded the PARTHIAN empire, perhaps to punish it for supporting Niger. He declared war on Albinus in late 195, defeating him at Lyon on 19 February 197. Later that year, he invaded Parthia again, sacking CTESIPHON in the autumn of 198. He annexed the PROVINCE of MESOPOTAMIA, creating a new frontier on the Tigris that shaped Roman relations with Parthia and PERSIA into the 4th century. Severus remained in the East until 202. In 203 he left Rome for North AFRICA and began a massive building programme designed to make Lepcis a worthy birthplace. In 204 he returned to Rome where he celebrated the 900th anniversary of the city's foundation.

Throughout these years, much day-to-day administration was left to a relative, Plautianus, the new praetorian prefect, whose daughter married the emperor's eldest son CARACALLA. Antipathy between son-in-law and father-in-law flared up in 205, resulting in the execution of the latter. Severus remained in ITALY only three more years; in this period he decided to make his younger son, Geta, co-emperor with Caracalla. In 208 Severus left Rome to campaign in northern Britain. He died at YORK on 4 February 211.

Severus based his power on the army and allegedly advised his sons to look to the soldiers above all else. His most significant reforms included doubling military pay, eliminating the long-standing (if symbolic) ban on legitimate marriage by serving soldiers and creating three new legions, two for Mesopotamia,

Severus, Septimius: stemma of the Severan dynasty.

one based at Alba. His powerful personality, and tendency to extremely brutal repressive measures, left senators like Cassius Dio in fear, and his style of autocratic government was a stark contrast with the Antonine age. By changing the style of imperial administration, linking the security of the emperor to the loyalty of the soldiers, and redefining the Eastern frontier, he shaped the development of the empire for the next century. DSP

See Birley, A. R. (1999) *Septimius Severus: the African emperor.*

 emperors, Roman; senate and senators, Roman: (a).

Seville see Baetica.

sewers see bathing; fountains and fountain houses, Roman; Rome; sanitation.

sex Two definitions can apply. The first refers to the act of reproduction or gratification resulting from the attraction of two individuals. Individuals undertake either 'active' or 'passive' roles. Men (*viri*) assume the active roles because of their anatomical makeup: the penis allows for the active role of penetration whether it is vaginal, oral or anal. Women and any males who receive the act are often held to take on passive sexual roles. Other forms of gratification such as kissing, fondling, biting and hitting do not constitute specific power or gender roles.

In the second instance, sex refers to the division between male and female, whether plant, animal or human. In the ancient world the biological designation of the sex of an individual was determined simply by a visual examination of the genitalia. Plants were not so easy to sex. For example, the Greeks identified plants as male or female in terms of how citizens could dominate them. Plants classified as masculine are metaphorically treated as barbarians, while female plants are envisaged as those that can be tamed or conquered. Philosophers, such as Aristotle, debated the credibility of the categorization of plants according to sex (*Generation of Animals* 731a). LAH

sex: erotic picture from the brothel in Pompeii (see prostitutes). The lavish furnishings and the ornate bed belie the sordid reality of small cells with narrow concrete bed bases.

See Foxhall, L. (1998) Natural sex: the attribution of sex and gender to plants in Greece, in L. Foxhall and J. Salmon, eds.,

Thinking Men 57–70; Foxhall, L. and Salmon, J., eds. (1998) *When Men Were Men*; Hallett, J.P. and Skinner, M.B., eds. (1997) *Roman Sexualities*.

 HOMOSEXUALITY.

sexuality When we consider Greek and Roman sexuality, we must also necessarily discuss the theories that have developed since the mid-1970s about why Greek and Roman sexualities look the way they do. It is not enough just to state which types of sexual practice were considered normal or even expected in different societies. We must include the cultural and political framework of these societies in order to understand ancient sexual practice and ideals.

Dover made it clear that the sexual morals of the Greeks were not identical with the ones prevalent in modern Western society. What we would term HOMOSEXUALITY was therefore to be seen as an accepted phase in a Greek man's development. Foucault claimed that sexuality did not even exist until the 18th century and was an invention that came with the understanding of the individual as individual; the latter claim is widely discussed among classicists. It seems probable, however, that the invention of sexuality lies at some point in the 1st century AD, when people painfully realized their selves. At this time people begin to suffer from love-sickness, and romantic love, in our sense of the word – between a man and a woman (Foucault was only interested in male sexuality) – became the most popular theme in the Greek novels.

In modern Western society, sexuality is seen as something defining a person's identity. One is attracted either to males or females (or to both). A person attracted to persons of the same sex as himself or herself is homosexual, and a person attracted to others of the opposite sex heterosexual. This distinction would not have made sense in antiquity, where heterosexuality and homosexuality did not exist. Furthermore, nowadays we usually think of sexuality as something happening between, usually, two people. This would have not been understood in antiquity either: sexuality was something someone did to somebody else.

The important sexual distinction in both Greece and Rome was between activity and passivity. To be sexually active was to penetrate somebody vaginally, anally or orally. Thus, in effect, the active person could only be an adult citizen male who through his sexuality could exercise his power over WOMEN, boys, foreigners and SLAVES. Biological sex plays no role here. Moreover, ancient sources are most interested in upper class males; we therefore know most about this group, and have to search harder to find evidence for everybody else. For Greece we are limited even further, because almost all written and much of the archaeological evidence comes from Athens. Greek *poleis* were not identical, neither were their sexual mores. In Athens the literary evidence and painted POTTERY show that it was normal for adult men to have sexual and emotional relationships with boys. Women were looked at with contempt. They were uneducated, kept indoors much of the time and married very early, at about 14 years old, to men frequently as much as 20 years older.

Scholars have frequently discussed how far the sexual relationship between an older man (the *erastês*, 'lover') and his younger boyfriend (the *erômenos*, 'beloved') went. Did the boy actually submit to being penetrated anally by his older lover? In all probability he did. The boy would, of course, be considered womanish because of his passive sexual attitude, but his future manliness would not suffer. Only an adult man who suffered penetration was looked down upon. He lost his citizen rights. Some scholars believe that the reason why pederasty was institutionalized as it was in Athens was that access to women was, to say the least, limited. Equally, however, scholars have addressed the issue of how far the ideal of confinement of Athenian women was from reality. Women who were kept indoors could only go out to attend funerals or to participate in religious FESTIVALS. Most women, however, had to work and could not afford to sit at home in seclusion; as a consequence, they would also meet men. In terms of sexual activity, the seduction of a married woman was considered a more serious offence than RAPE, because seduction implied her co-operation and also planning on the part of the adulterer. Rape, by contrast, was seen as an impulsive act! Therefore, the man whose property the woman was, as his wife, suffered much more from her seduction than her rape. The woman's feelings were not taken into consideration at all, nor was her role as sexual partner taken seriously. A decent woman did not take initiatives, only PROSTITUTES and *hetairai* did. Indeed, a sexually active woman was seen as monstrous: she could not be sexually active, since that required the ability to penetrate.

In Rome, too, sexuality was seen as a reflection of the hierarchy of power in society. The significant difference between Greece and Rome is that women are much more visible and held in much more respect in Rome than in Greece. But sexuality nevertheless was still seen as the penetrating activity of the man in power. PLAUTUS mentions (*Poenulus*) that everybody except freeborn girls and boys and wives was fair game. At the end of the REPUBLIC, homosexual affairs or relationships between men became fashionable in the upper classes, but that does not necessarily mean that some were therefore homosexual. In principle all men married, whether their sexual preferences were for males or for females. The crucial issue for the Romans was whether a man was sexually very active with many lovers of whichever gender, or whether he lived in moderation. It was simply assumed that a very sexually active man had both male and female lovers. For most modern people who first read CATULLUS and the AUGUSTAN elegiacs it comes as a surprise to realize that, besides their beloved mistresses, these poets also were very preoccupied with boys. Only OVID declares that he definitely preferred women.

While references to men's homosexual relationships are very frequent in Roman literature, women's homosexual relationships are hardly ever mentioned, except in strongly pejorative contexts. There are two obvious reasons for this. First, it was seen as abominable; second, men did not find this an interesting topic to write about. One further aspect of ancient sexuality is the almost total lack of privacy in all spheres of life. People were probably not embarrassed at having sex when slaves were present.

In the middle of the 1st century AD a new concern for the individual appears. Consequently we also see a new interest in individuals' sexual relationships, now seen as strongly emotional relationships as well, not merely something to alleviate lust. It became popular to fall in love and to waste away from lovesickness if the feelings were not reciprocal. Likewise, young lovers – now only heterosexual – could prefer death if their families prevented their relationship. In MEDICAL literature, conditions of consumption are described, but often turn out to be caused by unrequited love.

With CHRISTIANITY came the ideal of worldly abstinence, including sexual renunciation, but Christians did not invent ASCETICISM; rather, they simply made it all-pervading. All through pagan antiquity, moderation in bodily desires had been the ideal. A man who gave in to lust or one who could not tolerate hunger, thirst or pain was looked down upon. But while the pagans considered moderation a means to strengthen the individual person, the Christians saw abstemiousness as the only way to salvation. Likewise pagans had never claimed that anybody should live in total sexual renunciation. That, however, became the ideal of the Christians, though in practice sexual activity continued to occur. HSN

See Dover, K. J. (1978) *Greek Homosexuality*; Foucault, M. (1978) *The History of Sexuality*; Golden, M. and Toohey, P., eds. (2003) *Sex and Difference in Ancient Rome*.

Shakespeare, William 1564–1616 England's most famous dramatist. He received a classical education in Stratford-upon-Avon, becoming proficient (like many Elizabethan schoolboys) in Latin and Greek. His formative years served his theatrical career well, and he frequently turned to classical sources for the settings or inspiration for his plays. He was aided by the publication of several classical texts into English in the Elizabethan period, including, most importantly, Sir Thomas North's 1579 English translation of PLUTARCH's *Parallel Lives*. North's Plutarch was Shakespeare's primary source for his 'Roman plays': *Julius Caesar* (1599), *Timon of Athens* (1604–8), *Antony and Cleopatra* (1607) and *Coriolanus* (1608). OVID was also a major source, especially the *Metamorphoses*, which was a central influence upon several of the plays: *Titus Andronicus* (1588, also incorporating elements from SENECA's *Thyestes*), *The Winter's Tale* (1609), and *A Midsummer Night's Dream* (1595), which is set in Athens and contains the Ovidian story of Pyramus and Thisbe. George Chapman's influential English translation of the *Iliad* aided Shakespeare's creation of *Troilus and Cressida* (1602). Shakespeare's early farce *A Comedy of Errors* (1592) is an amalgamation of several Plautine comedies. He also drew on the Greek romance *Apollonius of Tyre* as the source for *Pericles* (1607–8). In addition to the stage works, Ovid's *Metamorphoses* is also the source for the poem *Venus and Adonis* (1593), while LIVY provides the inspiration for *The Rape of Lucrece* (1594). LL-J

See Martindale, C. (1994) *Shakespeare and the Uses of Antiquity*.

Shapur I (Sapor, Shabuhr) d. c.272 No ruler of the PARTHIAN and PERSIAN EMPIRES was more dangerous to Rome than Shapur I. Already active under his father Ardashir, the first SASSANID dynast, his assaults on the Roman East reached new heights after he came to power as King of Kings in c.AD 242. Shapur is known mainly from Roman sources, but an extraordinary addition is the great trilingual inscription at Naqs-i-Rustam recording his achievements in a text known as the *Res gestae divi Saporis*.

Shapur reigned alone for some 30 years. His armies overran ARMENIA and drove out the Arsakid rulers who survived there. In campaigns against the Roman empire, his forces inflicted defeat on GORDIAN III in 242–4 and compelled his successor PHILIP THE ARAB to make a humiliating peace. In the 250s, his military forces entered SYRIA (defeating a Roman army at Barballisos) and MESOPOTAMIA, and crossed into ASIA Minor. The *Res gestae* provides a long list of places captured, including legionary bases at Satala, Zeugma and Raphanaia and great cities from DURA EUROPUS to ANTIOCH. In 260 he crushed the army brought in from Europe and captured the emperor VALERIAN, as well as cities across Asia Minor; prisoners were transported and settled in his empire. Subsequently, the PALMYRENE Odenathus repelled some of his forces, and when Shapur died he had just witnessed AURELIAN's restoration of control.

Shapur was a great builder, employing captives to construct and settle the new towns that spread out in the vicinity of Seleukeia-CTESIPHON. He evidently had some interest in MANICHAEISM and retained its founder Mani at his court for a period. (see also THIRD-CENTURY CRISIS) DLK

See Dodgeon, M. H. and Lieu, S. N. C., eds. (1991) *The Roman Eastern Frontier and the Persian Wars AD 226–363*; Yarshater, E., ed. (1983) *The Cambridge History of Iran*, vol. 3.

sheep Probably the most numerous and important flock ANIMALS in the classical world. From the BONES alone, MEDITERRANEAN sheep are often difficult to distinguish anatomically from GOATS. They are much more economical to keep in Mediterranean landscapes than CATTLE. Most Greek and Roman sheep were small and rugged, with long legs suitable for coping with rugged terrain, and capable of surviving on a diet of agricultural by-products such as chaff, bean husks, tree prunings, weeds and thistles. Generally they were all-purpose animals, used for milk, MEAT, wool and hides. Most will have had wool that was coarse and hairy compared to modern sheep. However, Greek and Roman farmers bred many local varieties of sheep, some kept for specific purposes such as high-quality milk or wool. Wealthy farmers were more likely to keep flocks of specialist breeds, such as the Tarentine and other breeds known for their fine wool (Demosthenes 47.52; Columella, *On Agriculture* 7.3–5; Varro, *On Agriculture* 2.2.18).

Generally flocks were probably quite small (under 20 animals) and kept as part of a mixed farm that also included arable and tree crops. CATO's ideal OLIVE grove also included a flock of 100 sheep and a SHEPHERD (*On Agriculture* 10.1–2). Many flocks probably contained a mixture of sheep and goats. There is only limited evidence for specialist TRANSHUMANT PASTORALISM, or for the maintenance of large flocks, before imperial Roman times. LF

See Isager, S. and Skydsgaard, J. E. (1992) *Ancient Greek Agriculture* 91–2; Whittaker, C. R., ed. (1988) *Pastoral Economies in Classical Antiquity*.

shell Marine shells were used by the earliest inhabitants of the MEDITERRANEAN as decoration and also in TRADE. Palaeolithic inhabitants of Greece perforated them for ease of wear. Spondylus shells found in Neolithic contexts in the DANUBE area point to trade links with Greece, where they were again used as ornamentation. The MINOANS of Bronze Age CRETE seem to have been particularly fond of seashells; shell beads have been found in pre-palatial contexts (c.3000 BC), and stone vessels from the first PALACE period (c.2000 BC) have been found with shell inlays. Hundreds of shells have been excavated at the religious site at Atsipadhes in the south of Crete, where presumably they were dedicated as votive offerings. Shells are also among the repertoire of the distinctive 'marine-style' of POTTERY dating to Late Minoan IB (c.1500 BC), especially the argonaut with its twisty shell and emerging tentacles. Tritons, with a similar twisting shell, also appear and seem to cross over to the MYCENAEAN repertoire with examples of the whorl shell motif present in Late Helladic II vases (c.1500–1400 BC), thought to be an iconographical combination of triton and *murex* shells.

The *murex* shellfish is most commonly associated with the PHOENICIANS, as the purple dye it produced was an integral part of their trading repertoire. *Murex* have also been found on the shores of the island of Kythera, just south of the PELOPONNESE. The 'wool' of the *Pinna nobilis* shellfish was used by classical Greeks to make very fine, transparent and gold tinted scarves.

While the by-products of shells are known in Greece, shells themselves were not especially popular. Large tridacna shells, decorated with floral and animal designs, coming from the Red sea and dating to c.650–600 BC, have been found in many places: AIGINA, SMYRNA, the islands of SAMOS, RHODES, Kos and PAROS, the Greek city of NAUKRATIS in Egypt, at CYRENE and in ETRURIA. Boardman, however, has noted that these appear to have been TOURIST novelties.

The Romans appear to have been more interested in marine shells, with gold imitations appearing as earrings and pendants. A cowrie shell set in gold and worn as a pendant survives; cowries are thought to have had fertility significance, particularly for the Egyptians.

Pearls, while not shells, are created from secretions of molluscs, especially the oyster. The most prized pearls came from Ceylon, with the golden-brown pearls of BRITAIN rating second best. Other sources include the Malabar coast, the Ganges and, considerably inferior, the Persian gulf. Freshwater pearls were also produced by mussels in various parts of Europe. Pearls first appear in necklaces found in the Near East dating to the 5th or 4th centuries BC, and became popular in hellenistic and Roman JEWELLERY, especially in necklaces and earrings. Mother-of-pearl was a common, cheaper alternative. NJW

See Boardman, J. (1980) *The Greeks Overseas*; Ogden, J. (1982) *Jewellery of the Ancient World*.

shepherds Generally, people of low status in the ancient world. Often they worked as SLAVES for wealthy landowners. Most looked after flocks of SHEEP and GOATS. Sometimes they managed herds of PIGS, or more rarely, CATTLE. Sheep and goats will only eat if they are not too hot, so in the sultry MEDITERRANEAN summer, shepherds had to take them to graze early in the morning and in the evening when it was cooler. Because ancient fields generally did not have fences or hedges, and flocks were, in any case, often grazing in the wilderness, the shepherd had to stay with his animals to make sure they did not stray. At night, his job was to protect the flock to ensure that the sheep were not attacked by jackals, foxes or wolves. Many shepherds were accompanied by dogs, which served not as herding dogs, but as guard dogs to attack enemies, human or animal.

Specialist shepherds spent much of their lives in wild and inhospitable places far from the comforts of city life, hence shepherding was considered a highly undesirable occupation, almost synonymous with being a BANDIT. For this reason, ancient sources provide little information about their activities. SOPHOKLES (*Oedipus the King* 1241–51) portrays shepherds from two different cities meeting in the no-man's land of Mt Kithairon, where one handed over the baby OEDIPUS to the other. An inscription (*IG* v.2.3) from the temple of ATHENA Alea in Tegea, in the central PELOPONNESE, gives the price per ANIMAL per night for keeping animals on TEMPLE land. These sources suggest that there were at least some TRANSHUMANT shepherds who moved flocks seasonally between the cooler pastures of the high mountains in summer to the winter grazing of the coastal lowlands. However, it is difficult to be certain how common this practice was in classical Greece. Also, few flocks were probably larger than 50 animals because diseases that can be controlled in modern times regularly devastated flocks in antiquity.

The evidence for the Roman world is more abundant. Specialist shepherds and swineherds regularly looked after relatively large flocks of 100 or more animals. Sometimes flocks were attached to large farms specializing in CEREALS, vines and other tree crops owned by rich men. Sheep and goats could make use of vegetation growing under trees, leaves from prunings and 'waste products' such as stubble and chaff. However there is some evidence for transhumant flocks as well.

Because the job of the shepherd was to guard his flock, keep them safe and lead them to good grazing, the figure of the shepherd became an important symbol of KINGSHIP throughout the Near East and Mediterranean region from very early times. A hymn to the Assyrian king Assurbanipal (668–631 BC) proclaims: 'May Shamash, king of heaven and earth, elevate you to shepherdship over the four regions . . . Place in his hand the weapon of war and battle, give him the blackheaded people that he may rule as their shepherd' (Kuhrt 507–8). In the biblical Psalms, king David is similarly celebrated as the shepherd who became the king and the shepherd of his people. The CHRISTIAN image of JESUS as the Good Shepherd has featured in Western art, music and literature up to the present day. All of these images owe their origin to the humble people who protected their animals at the margins of ancient civilization. LF

See Kuhrt, A. (1995) *The Ancient Near East*; Whittaker, C. R., ed. (1988) *Pastoral Economies in Classical Antiquity*.

ships and shipbuilding Following traditional shipbuilding terminology, ships are large sea-going

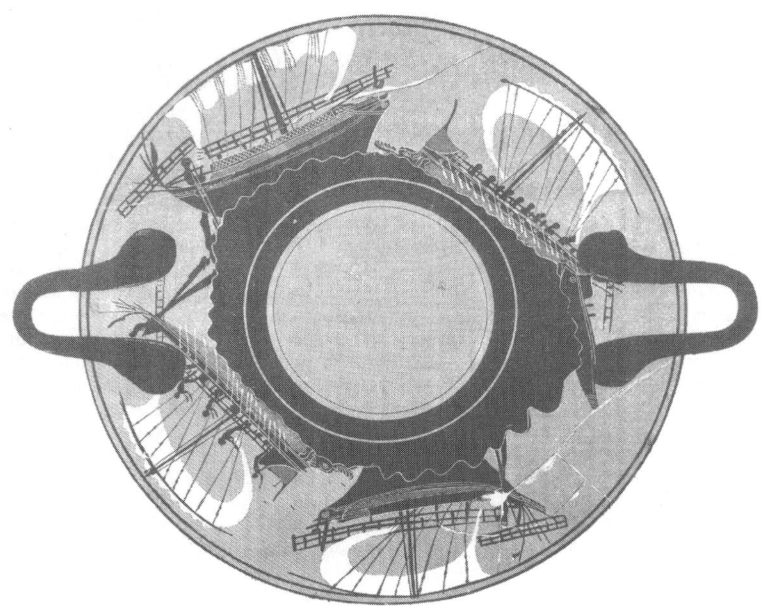
SHIPS AND SHIPBUILDING: (a) base of Greek vase showing two oared warships and two more round hulled merchant ships.

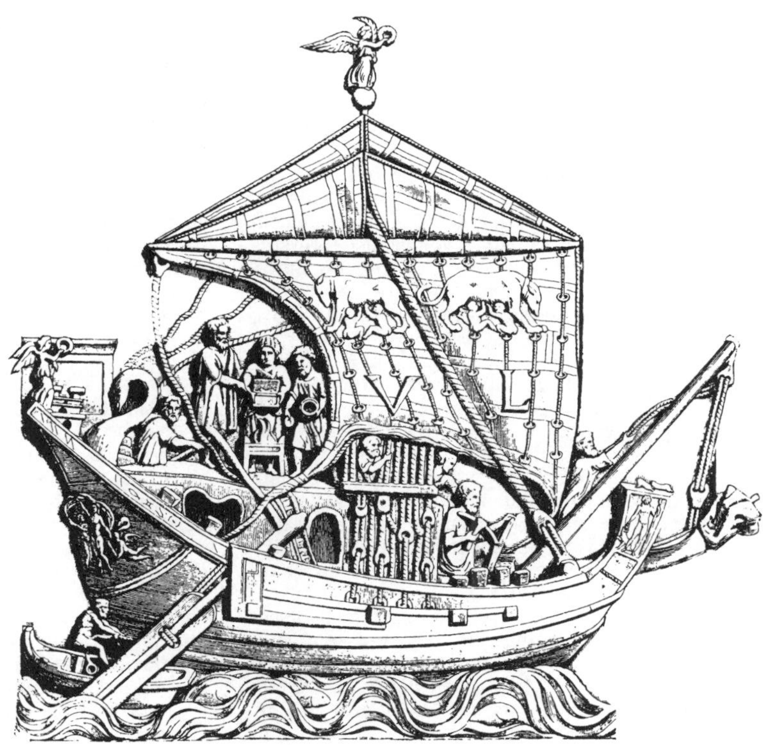

SHIPS AND SHIPBUILDING: (b) typical Roman merchant ship, with side mounted steering oar. Note the decorative touches at prow, stern, masthead and on the sails.

vessels driven by square sails arranged on three to five masts. In classical antiquity, however, the term 'ship' defines a smaller range of sea-going vessels and is used in opposition to 'boat' which signifies a group of still smaller, open vessels not intended for sea voyages. Greeks and Romans divided ships into two categories – 'round' and 'long' – depending upon their hull shapes and whether they were driven primarily by sails or by oars. Round ships or merchantmen were built mainly for bulk TRANSPORT, and were less suitable than long ships or galleys in areas where unpredictable winds and frequent calms made sailing difficult. Both round and long ships were used for warfare and TRADE, and we find a large number of different designs among each general category. Our body of evidence derives from a growing number of documented SHIPWRECKS, from ancient literature, inscriptions and PAPYRI, and from artistic depictions found on POTTERY, coins, WALL-PAINTINGS and SCULPTURE.

Ships developed in slightly different ways in different parts of the MEDITERRANEAN based upon the local requirements for seafaring and weather conditions. Designs included long canoes (early Bronze Age AEGEAN), substantial RIVER craft reinforced with rope trusses (Bronze Age Egypt), rounded sail-driven cargo carriers (Bronze Age LEVANT), and sleek galleys powered by 20 and 30 oars (MYCENAEAN Greece). HOMER refers to both 20- and 50-oared galleys, and ships appropriate for the larger size appear on ceramic mixing bowls of the 8th century BC with rowers set at two distinct levels. Prior to the 6th century, galleys might serve the dual purposes of trading and raiding, but by the reign of Kambyses (530–522) single-purpose warships like TRIREMES (*triêreis*) were built in large numbers and added to most major fleets. These ships were propelled by rowers arrayed along each side, in three files set at three different levels.

In general, warships were built to be fast and manoeuvrable. From the 6th century onward, they carried a powerful offensive weapon at the bow in the form of a waterline ram. Before this period, the elongated rams depicted on Greek galleys seem to have functioned more as reinforced cutwaters and deterrents to frontal attacks than as functional offensive weapons. Following the introduction of the trireme, however, warships engaged in regular combat with their rams, which were obviously expected to deliver and withstand the jarring forces of the ramming manoeuvre. During the 4th and 3rd centuries when NAVAL WARFARE increasingly involved sieges, much larger warships were built with five (*pentêreis*, 'quinqueremes'), ten (*dekêreis*), and even more files of oarsmen, set along each side at two and three levels. These 'big hulls' used their mass to crush in their enemies' bows, smash through HARBOUR barriers and even attack city walls (Philo, *Poliorketika* D 29). Big and beamy, they carried troops of deck soldiers, artillery weapons and lofty siege towers. Such ships were expensive to build, man and maintain, but were made possible by the PERSIAN wealth liberated by ALEXANDER's campaigns. Once this windfall was spent, however, naval commanders generally reverted to the more economical galleys like the triremes and quinqueremes favoured by Rome and CARTHAGE for their NAVIES.

Round ships or merchantmen were primarily used as bulk transports. Judging from preserved wreck evidence, their sizes remained fairly constant throughout antiquity and can be broken down into three major categories. Ships carrying less than 75 tonnes of cargo (up to c.1,500 AMPHORAS) were most common in all periods from the 5th century BC to the 12th century AD. Ships carrying 75–200 tonnes (c.1,500–3,000 amphoras) appear from the 1st century BC to the 3rd century AD. Those carrying more than 200 tonnes (one ship carried more than 6,000 amphoras) date mostly to the late REPUBLICAN period.

Remains dating back to the Bronze Age reveal that the Greek terms *gomphoi* and *harmoniai* refer to fasteners (pegs or dowels, and tenons) used to join a ship's hull planks in a technique called 'shell first' or 'edge-joined' construction. The shipwright started with the keel, or bottom-most timber, and joined each successive plank to its neighbour by means of closely spaced tenons set in rectangular slots, or mortises, cut into the adjacent edges of each plank to be joined. A line of tenons, which resembled thick tongue depressors, were inserted into the mortises of the fixed plank and lined up with matching mortises in the edge of the unattached plank. The new plank was then pushed toward the fixed plank, which caused the tenons to slide firmly into their slots. Once the two planks were firmly joined edge-to-edge, the tenons (now embedded in their slots) were further locked into place by a wooden dowel or peg, drilled through the tenon from outside the hull. Plank by plank, the sides of the hull were built up with thousands of these interlocking fasteners, resulting in a seaworthy hull that did not rely on interior frames for strength. This labour-intensive process was the preferred method of shipbuilding in the Mediterranean until the medieval period. Some merchant hulls of the 7th–6th centuries BC (and later), however, reveal that hull planks and interior timbers could also be laced to one another, joined with fibrous cords passed through carefully cut slots.

Successful shipbuilding and maintenance, whether for mercantile purposes or for WAR, required access to natural resources like TIMBER, pitch, pine tar, beeswax, hemp, flax, papyrus, COPPER, TIN, IRON and LEAD. Silver fir, pine and cedar were particularly prized as shipbuilding timbers; oak was used for keel planks because of its strength and resilience to wear. Pitch, tar and wax were liberally used as waterproofing agents and hemp, flax and papyrus were used for cordage, sails and caulking materials. Copper was used for tacks, nails and spikes as were bronze and iron. Lead was used for shipboard piping (found in bilge pumps) and for sheathing and patches placed on the hull. WMM

See Casson, L. (1995) *Ships and Seamanship in the Ancient World*; Garlan, Y. (1974) *Recherches de poliorcétique grecque* (trs. of Philo, *Poliorketika*); Steffy, J.R. (1994) *Wooden Shipbuilding and the Interpretation of Shipwrecks.*

shipwrecks The invention of the aqualung at the end of the Second World War stimulated, from about 1950 onwards, the increasingly intensive study of the off-shore sea beds of the MEDITERRANEAN and other seas and the discovery of numerous wrecks from the classical period (well over 1,000 from the Mediterranean itself). The results have transformed our knowledge of ancient SHIPS and our understanding of TRADE in the ancient world. The vast majority of wrecks located were cargo vessels, not warships. They varied enormously in size. A few were perhaps 400 tonnes or more (the 1st-century BC wreck of Madrague de Giens, which carried up to 7,000 AMPHORAS of Caecuban WINE from Italy), but most were much smaller vessels. Their cargoes included grain, MARBLE COLUMNS, SARCOPHAGI, metal ingots and POTTERY of all sorts. By far the largest number, however, contained amphoras, the pottery bulk-carriers of wine, OIL, FISH SAUCE and other products. The discovery of these amphora wrecks stimulated in turn the search for the centres of production

SHIPWRECK: macabre Geometric vase painting scene of drowned sailors by their upturned boat.

SHOES: cobblers at work in a painting from Herculaneum.

of the amphoras and the mapping of their distribution on land. As a result, scholars have been able to recreate in detail, for example, the trade in wine from Thasos and Rhodes in classical Greece, the trade in Italian wine from the late 2nd century BC onwards, particularly with Gaul, the export of olive oil from the Guadalquivir valley of southern Spain, and the North African olive oil trade of the 2nd century AD onwards. Many of the small ships were most suited to acting as 'tramps', shuttling back and forth along short-haul coastal routes. Further, many of the cargoes were clearly mixed, made up of part-loads. This helps to explain how low-cost products, such as pottery and lamps, could be transported economically large distances by 'piggybacking' on other cargoes. The number of wrecks belonging to the period 200 BC to AD 200 exceeds by a huge extent those of any other period, not just in antiquity but down to the modern era, and is important testimony to the vitality and scale of ECONOMIC activity stimulated by the growth of the Roman empire. JJP

See Casson, L. (1994) *Ships and Seafaring in Ancient Times*; Gibbins, D. (2001) Shipwrecks and hellenistic trade, in Z. H. Archibald et al., eds., *Hellenistic Economies* 273–312; Parker, A. J. (1992) *Ancient Shipwrecks of the Mediterranean and the Roman Provinces*; Peacock, D. P. S. and Williams, D. F. (1986) *Amphorae and the Roman Economy*.

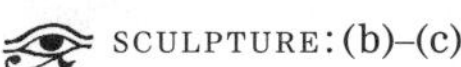
SCULPTURE: (b)–(c).

shoes Greeks used a wide variety of shoes from dainty slippers to calf-length boots. These ranged from purely functional wear to elegant status symbols. Basic shoes were made from wool or untanned LEATHER, while more expensive items were made from soft oriental leathers. Soles were made from vegetable fibres, cork, wood or leather, depending on the shoe and status of the owner. More exclusive shoes could be dyed, typically yellow, green, white or red, and could be adorned with precious metals.

It can be difficult to understand the terminology used for shoes since the same words can be used for different shoes. *Sandalia* can either be slippers or sandals, while *kothornoi* are either sandals, walking shoes or boots. Greeks used several kinds of sandals. *Hypodêmata* consisted of a sole and laces tied over and around the heel. *Amyklai*, a more elegant variety, were dyed red and were worn by men. *Krêpides* were perhaps the commonest form of sandal and were worn by both sexes; these were open shoes with laces that started from the gap between the first two toes and went halfway up the calf. More expensive *krêpides* had dyed soles and were decorated with precious metals. *Sandalia* were more exclusive sandals or slippers, frequently red and intricately decorated. Other types of slippers include the elegant *blautê*, a light-soled and elegantly adorned shoe worn by both genders. The *sykchas* was a rather less intricate shoe, normally for everyday wear. More functional shoes, adapted for use in wet or muddy countries, include the *arbylê*, a thick-soled shoe which covered the ankle. *Embades*, either functional or elegant boots, were laced in the front and had thick soles.

While the basic term for shoes in the Greek world was *pedila*, Romans referred to their shoes as *calceamenta*. Roman shoes were in many cases similar to Greek, though sandals may have been less common. Like Greeks, Romans used shoes as a means of demonstrating status. The commonest Roman shoe was the *calceus*, which was a leather shoe dyed different colours depending on the gender and status of the wearer. Luxury shoes included *babylonicae*, which were made of soft leather and did not have soles. These could be richly adorned and needed to be worn with *sandalia* to protect them. More basic shoes included the *soccus* and *socculus*, which were wooden-soled and were closed in the upper parts by strips of leather or wood; the same terms were also used for socks and slippers. The poor, when they wore shoes, used *carpatinae* (or *carbatinae*) of raw leather tied around the foot and ankles with laces. They could also wear an inexpensive boot called the *pero*, made of untanned leather. These were also worn by soldiers. More frequently, soldiers wore *caligae*, which were sturdier boots and were often open-toed. Officers and emperors wore *campagi* which were fur-lined, calf-length boots richly decorated with precious materials. EACM

 FOOTWEAR; LEATHER AND LEATHERWORKING.

shops and shopping Important features of both Greek and Roman urban society. ARISTOPHANES' comedies (e.g. *Acharnians*) make many references to everyday items bought with cash, and writers such as Lysias and Demosthenes refer to men of all classes spending time socializing in shops. Although much buying and selling involved temporary stalls in large open MARKETS (such as the *AGORA* and FORUM), over

SHOPS AND SHOPPING: (a) a Roman wine merchant displays his wares.

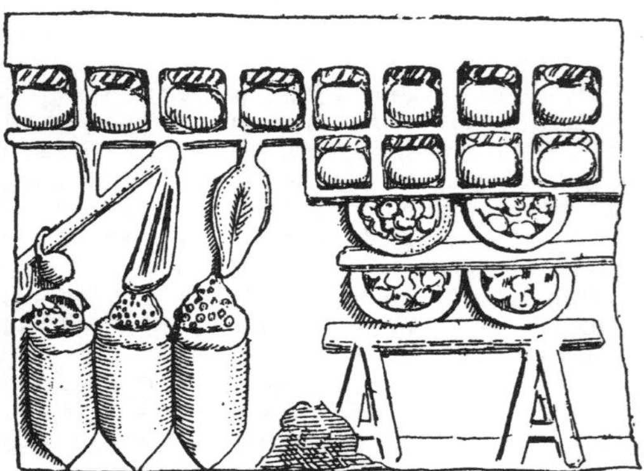

SHOPS AND SHOPPING: (b) displays of produce were frequently spread out onto the pavements in front of Roman shops.

time increasing numbers of permanent shops appeared in STOAS fronting onto marketplaces. Aristophanes' *Assembly Women* (391 BC) refers to a stoa where barley is sold, and from the 4th century on stoas were built with increasing frequency. Many, like the Stoa of Attalos at ATHENS, may have been intended partly as commercial premises.

Many shops, however, were located in the front of HOUSES, as at OLYNTHOS. Increasingly, therefore, shops began to appear along the main thoroughfares. This is particularly clear at well-preserved Roman towns such as POMPEII and OSTIA, where the economic value of the prime road frontages was exploited, whereas far fewer shops were located along minor roads. Most of these shops consisted of a single rectangular chamber, with a wide doorway (closed at night by wooden shutters) and a brick or stone-built counter looking out onto the street and passing trade. From preserved representations of shops at Ostia, we know that there was a wide range of specialized premises and that goods for sale were piled on the counter, hung from the ceiling, and arranged on temporary wooden stands that intruded out onto the pavement. (DOMITIAN evidently tried to ban the encroachment of shop displays into already congested streets.) As can still be seen in traditional Arab souks, much of the activity actually took place in the open air in front of the shop. Certain types of up-market shops, however, did make some interior space available for customers to come in and sit in comfort to inspect the wares; these include PERFUME shops, TEXTILE and clothing sellers, and WINE merchants. The rear of many shops served as both stockroom and living space for the shopkeeper, who may have had a small bedroom on a mezzanine floor overhead.

Many shops doubled as WORKSHOPS, with artisans working inside to the rear of the counter at the street entrance. Although shops and workshops were generally run by people of lower status (sometimes SLAVES or FREEDMEN), there were connecting doors between some Pompeian shops and wealthy HOUSES, indicating economic ties between the urban ÉLITE and commercial premises. Leases also indicate the ownership of shops by the rich and rental to their would-be retailers. In larger cities, shops were sometimes incorporated into larger market complexes, somewhat equivalent to modern shopping malls. The most impressive is TRAJAN's market in Rome, comprising over 150 separate shops on five main levels and a large central hall.

The experience of shopping was probably rather different in the Greek and Roman worlds, in part reflecting differences in the status and freedom of WOMEN. Although both Greek and Roman playwrights make much of the dramatic possibilities of slaves being sent to do the HOUSEHOLD shopping, in Roman times we have better evidence for women shopkeepers and women customers. From Pompeii, for instance, we have representations of wealthy women customers, accompanied by slaves, testing PERFUME. What is most striking about Roman shops is the high degree of specialization that was reached in major cities – attested by archaeological remains, literary sources and EPIGRAPHY alike. From a system based on periodic markets and fairs, many ancient cities developed a recognizably 'modern' pattern of permanent shops open daily. DWJG, DJM

See Camp, J. M. (1993) *The Athenian Agora: an ancient shopping center*; Laurence, R. (1994) *Roman Pompeii: space and society*; Lewis, S. (1995) Barbers' shops and perfume shops, in A. Powell, ed., *The Greek World* 432–41.

BUTCHERY: (a); MARKET BUILDINGS: (a); TEXTILES.

Sibylline oracles Traditions concerning a female prophet, the Sibyl (*sibylla*), extend as far back as the 5th century BC. She was perceived as similar to other prophets like Bakis and Musaios, figures independent of major prophetic shrines. By the end of the hellenistic period, traditions about numerous Sibyls had developed; these were catalogued by VARRO in his *Human and Divine Antiquities*.

ORACLES attributed to Sibyls took several forms. The most famous was the collection at Rome, owned and supervised by the PRIESTS known as *quindecimviri sacris faciundis*. It contained lists of prodigies and prescriptions for cult to ward off ritual POLLUTION. Other oracles, represented in two collections compiled in the 5th–7th centuries, take form of *ex eventu* PROPHECY and preserve texts written from the late hellenistic period to the Arab conquest of ALEXANDRIA.

According to a tradition preserved by Varro (including the story of the Cumaean Sibyl's interviews with Tarquinius Priscus), Rome acquired its original collection at the end of the regal period. Impossible to confirm, there is no reason to doubt that the Roman collection was early. As Rome's power expanded, interest in Sibyls increased, leading to the explosion in traditions about Sibyls around the Mediterranean. The connection with Rome also made *ex eventu* prophecy in the sibylline style a vehicle for the expression of Christian doctrine by the beginning of the 2nd century AD. The link between the Sibyl and Christ grew with time, and a Christian tradition of Sibylline prophecy remained strong into the Middle Ages, represented by a wide variety of prose oracles attributed to the Tiburtine Sibyl (from Tibur, mod. Tivoli). DSP

Sicilian expedition War between Syracuse and Athens, 415–413 BC. Athens had established interests in the western Mediterranean and had fought an earlier war against Syracuse in 427–424. The events of 415–413 also interconnect with the Peloponnesian war, setting Athens against Syracuse, an ally of Athens' enemies Corinth and Sparta. The cause was a war between the Sicilian cities of Selinous and Segesta, which broke out in 416. Syracuse gave support to Selinous, and Segesta appealed to Athens. Despite initial caution, Athens gathered a force of 250 ships and 25,000 troops under the leadership of Nikias and Alcibiades. The departure of the fleet was marred by the desecration of the herms, in which Alcibiades was implicated. He was recalled to Athens to stand trial but fled into exile, while the Athenian force spent 415 seeking support from other Sicilian cities. Meanwhile, Syracuse strengthened its fortifications and received troops from Greece under the command of the Spartan general Gylippos in 414. Athens also received reinforcements and the war resolved into a struggle for control of Syracuse, with both sides competing for control of the harbour and the heights of Epipolai, and constructing siege works. Late in 413, the Athenian force was depleted by an epidemic and tried to retreat, but was massacred by the Syracusans. 7,000 survivors were imprisoned in a quarry, where many died, and the remainder were sold into slavery, with only a handful escaping and returning to Athens. KL

See Diodorus 13.1–14.70; Plutarch, *Life of Nicias*, *Life of Alcibiades*; Thucydides, *Histories*, books 6–7.

Sicily Thucydides (6.2) names three native peoples as occupying Sicily when the Greeks arrived: *Sikanoi* in central Sicily, *Sikeloi* in the east, and *Elymoi* in the west. Archaeologically their identification has proved elusive: the cultural entities of pre-Greek Sicily are complex. From c.735 BC, when Naxos was founded by émigrés from Chalkis in Euboia, until 580, when Akragas (mod. Agrigento) was settled as a daughter colony of Gela, the colonization movement (there were a dozen major foundations) was at its height. It was especially active on the south and east coasts; only Leontinoi (mod. Lentini), a colony of Naxos, was settled substantially inland. The west coast of the island received Phoenician settlements at the same time, the principal three being Motya, Panormos (mod. Palermo) and Soloeis (mod. Solanto).

The wealth and prosperity of archaic Sicily in the 6th century BC are witnessed above all by impressive temple-building programmes in the major Greek cities, such as Syracuse and Selinous. The first coinage, in silver, also appears c.550. Many leading cities at this time were ruled by tyrants, for whom major building works were a *sine qua non*. In time, Greek civilization spread throughout the island, so that it is easy to forget that places like Segesta, with its magnificent 5th-century unfinished Greek temple, or Morgantina, where a very complete idea of a hellenistic Sicilian Greek town can be obtained, were never formal Greek colonies. By that time (the 3rd century BC) the Sikel language, which by the 6th century had adopted the Greek alphabet in its few written pronouncements, was in decline.

The growing power of Carthage in the central Mediterranean, which had extended the Carthaginian sphere of influence into a wider area of western Sicily, eventually brought Carthage into conflict with Rome. The Romans took much of Sicily into their fold at the end of the first Punic war (241), when the fledgling province became 'the first such jewel in our imperial crown' (Cicero, *Against Verres II*, 2.1.2). Only the kingdom of Syracuse in south-east Sicily, under its benevolent ruler Hieron II (c.260–216), was allowed to remain independent – an early case of 'client kingship', a device that Rome was later to use often when absorbing into the empire a newly conquered territory. The island became united as a single province only in 211. Syracuse had fallen by force the year before, four years after Hieron's death.

The province of Sicilia was ruled by a governor (praetor). Cities were left largely to their own devices; provided that they paid the imposed taxes, in the form of a grain tithe (only eight cities were singled out for exemption as a special favour), Rome interfered little. As a result, the cultural romanization of Sicily was slow during the Republic. Gaius Verres (73–71), the governor prosecuted by Cicero for extortion, needed interpreters to conduct business, as Greek, not Latin, was still the dominant language. So far from suffering from punitive taxation, Sicily seems to have flourished under the Republic, as agriculture expanded to meet the demands of the new masters. Sicilian wheat soon became vital to Rome's food needs, and large landed estates (*latifundia*), especially concerned with stock-raising and grazing, grew up in some parts of the island. They were run largely by slaves, whose poor working conditions prompted serious slave rebellions between 135 and 132 and between 104 and 100.

In imperial times Sicily continued to prosper. Augustus founded six veteran *coloniae*, and gave Latin rights to a handful of other communities. Grain continued to be Sicily's most important export commodity, though the island had to cede first place to Africa and Egypt in terms of sheer output. Other exports included wine, timber, wool and sulphur. *Latifundia*, including large imperial estates, remained an important feature of some parts of the landscape, but there was more rural village settlement now, especially as many of the old hill-towns of the interior were gradually abandoned in favour of less inconvenient places to live. Coastal cities by contrast flourished. The prosperity of the countryside in the 4th century AD is

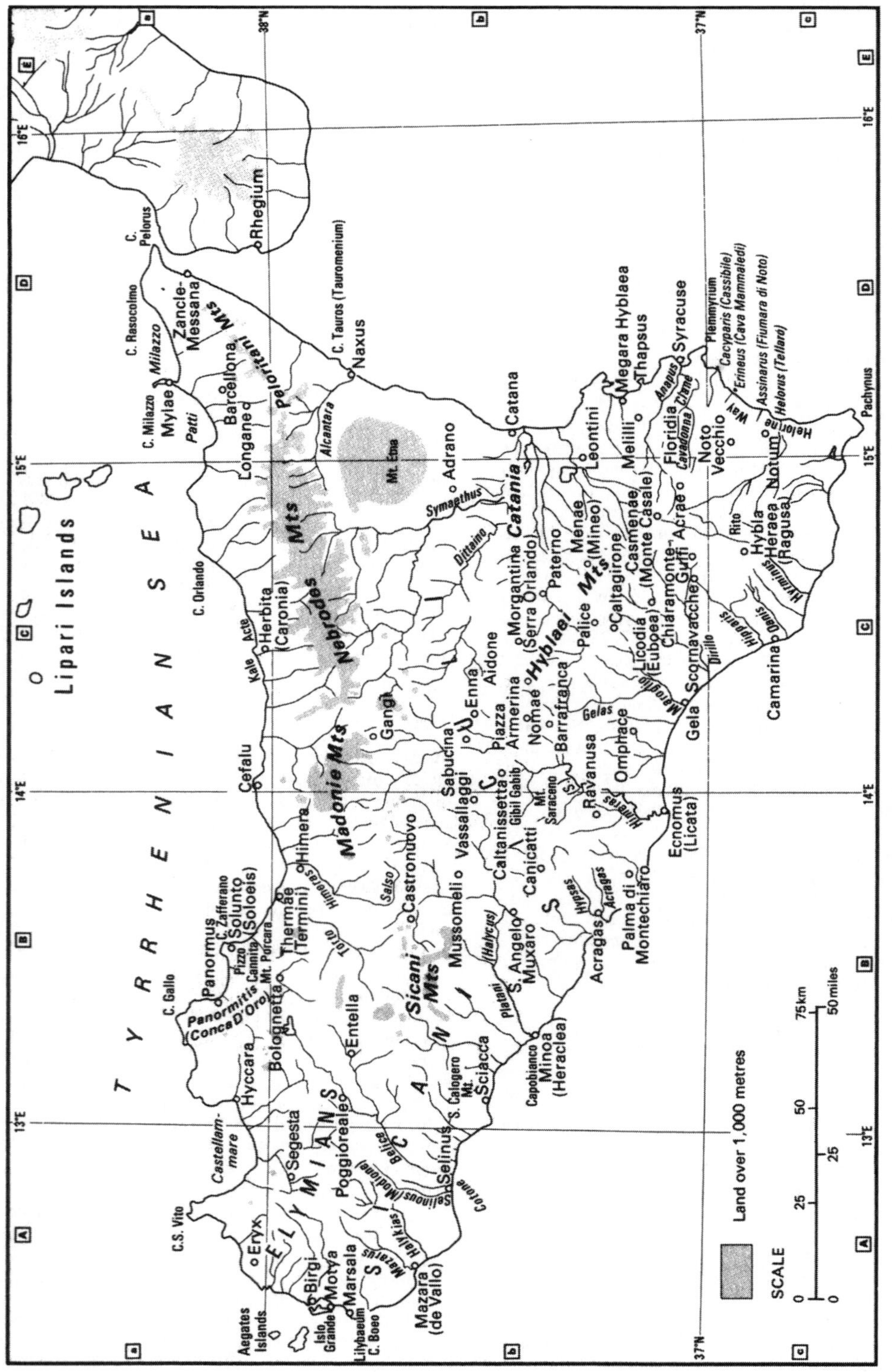
TYRRHENIAN SEA
Lipari Islands
ELYMIANS
SICANS
SICELS
Land over 1,000 metres
SCALE
0 25 50 75km
0 25 50 miles
Aegates Islands
Isola Grande
Lilybaeum
C. Boeo
C.S. Vito
Eryx
Birgi
Motya
Marsala
Mazara (de Vallo)
Mazarus
Halykias
Selinous (Modione)
Cotone
Selinus
Poggioreale
Belice
Segesta
Castellammare
Hyccara
C. Gallo
Panormitis (Conca D'Oro)
Panormus
Bolognetta
Entella
Mt. Porcara
Pizzo Cannita
C. Zafferano
Solunto (Soloeis)
Thermae (Termini)
Torto
Himeras
Himera
Sicani Mts
S. Calogero Mt.
Sciacca
Capobianco
Minoa (Heraclea)
Platani
(Halycus)
S. Angelo Muxaro
Mussomeli
Castronuovo
Salso
Madonie Mts
Cefalu
Gangi
Vassallaggi
Sabucina
Caltanissetta
Gibil Gabib
Canicatti
Mt. Saraceno
Ravanusa
Hypsas
Acragas
Palma di Montechiaro
Ecnomus (Licata)
Himeras
Enna
Piazza Armerina
Nomae
Barrafranca
Gelas
Omphace
Gela
Maroglio
Kale Acte
Herbita (Caronia)
Nebrodes Mts
C. Orlando
Aidone
Morgantina (Serra Orlando)
Hyblaei Mts
Palice
Paterno
Menae (Mineo)
Caltagirone
Licodia (Euboea)
Chiaramonte Gulfi
Scornavacche
Dirillo
Hipparis
Camarina
Oanis
Hyrminus
Hybla Heraea (Ragusa)
Rito
Acrae
Casmenae (Monte Casale)
Dittaino
Symaethus
Catania
Adrano
Mt. Etna
Alcantara
C. Milazzo
Mylae
Milazzo
Patti
Longane
Barcellona
C. Rasocolmo
Zancle-Messana
Peloritani Mts
C. Pelorus
Rhegium
C. Tauros (Tauromenium)
Naxus
Catana
Leontini
Melilli
Megara Hyblaea
Thapsus
Floridia
Cavadonna
Anapus
Cyane
Syracuse
Plemmyrium
Cacyparis (Cassibile)
Erineus (Cava Mammaledi)
Assinarus (Fiumara di Noto)
Helorus (Tellaro)
Noto Vecchio
Helorine Way
Notum
Pachynus
13°E
14°E
15°E
16°E
37°N
38°N

SICILY: map.

suggested by luxury VILLAS with MOSAICS, such as those of Patti Marina, Caddeddi on the Tellaro, and above all Piazza Armerina, the most sumptuous of all known late Roman villas anywhere in the empire. Latin now co-existed with Greek, especially in the cities, but much of the island remained Greek at heart down into the late empire. RJAW

See Dunbabin, T. J. (1948) *The Western Greeks*; Leighton, R. (1998) *Sicily before History*; Pugliese Carratelli, G., ed. (1996) *The Western Greeks*; Rutter, N. K. (1997) *Greek Coinages of Southern Italy and Sicily*; Sjøqvist, E. (1973) *Sicily and the Greeks*; Wilson, R. J. A. (1990) *Sicily under the Roman Empire*; (1983) *Piazza Armerina*.

MAGNA GRAECIA.

Siculus Flaccus see *AGRIMENSORES*; ROADS, ROMAN.

Sidon see PHOENICIA AND PHOENICIANS.

Sidonius Apollinaris (Gaius Sollius [Modestus?] Apollinaris Sidonius) c.AD 430–c.484 Gallic ARISTOCRAT, politician, writer, and BISHOP. Sidonius Apollinaris was born in southern GAUL into a distinguished aristocratic family. He maintained such advantageous connections throughout his life: his father-in-law, for example, was the ephemeral Western emperor Eparchius Avitus (455–6). Sidonius showed himself adept at negotiating the complex political vicissitudes of his age by attaching himself to a number of emperors. In all cases, he sealed his alliance with these emperors by composing PANEGYRICS in their honour. For his pains, he received political promotion. He served in some minor capacity under Majorian (457–61), an impressive achievement given that Majorian had defeated and replaced Avitus and that, at first, Sidonius was bitterly opposed to him. More impressively he was appointed in 468 to the urban prefecture of Rome by Anthemius (467–72). It was probably around this time that he achieved the elevated social rank of 'patrician'. Throughout his career, Sidonius was a vigorous representative of Gallic cities in the crises attending the collapse of Roman rule in Gaul. In this context he was elected bishop of Clermont in the Auvergne, and the chief event of his episcopate was the defence of the city against Visigothic attacks. Sidonius himself narrated his career in panegyrics, POEMS and letters that provide a striking portrait of aristocratic mentalities at the twilight of the Roman empire. MDH

See Sidonius, *Poems and Letters*, trs. W. B. Anderson, 2 vols. (1936); Harries, J. (1994) *Sidonius Apollinaris and the Fall of Rome*.

siege and siege warfare The ability to capture FORTRESSES and fortified towns was, for most of classical antiquity as in other eras, the ultimate proof of military superiority. Yet it was rarely thought as glorious as victory in pitched battle. Material resources, logistics and technical expertise were more essential than individual skill or bravery, and the besieger was more manager than warrior. In this as in other matters, the Romans followed traditions established by the Greeks, while the Greeks made systematic in their own terms the practices learned from their materially advanced eastern neighbours.

It is symptomatic of Dark Age conditions that Homeric EPIC told the story of a great siege. Yet the siege of TROY itself was usually incidental to the action of the *Iliad*, and in the end Troy was taken only by a marvellous trick. The TROJAN WAR legend preserves a Bronze Age tradition of siege narrative, represented by the Akkado-Hittite story of the siege of Syrian Urshu and by Thutmose III's account of the siege of Megiddo. Between the 11th and 6th centuries BC, Greeks could experience warfare on this scale only abroad. Around the AEGEAN the sudden raid, usually seaborne, was the chief threat to settlements.

The Greeks learnt by experience the ancient techniques of siege from the kingdoms of western Asia. Soon after 600 the LYDIANS surmounted the defences of Old SMYRNA by raising an earth ramp against its walls. The PERSIANS did the same against Phokaia and other Ionian towns in 544 (Herodotos 1.162–9). Such ramps allowed shielded rams on trucks to approach walls, while other shielded vehicles, 'tortoises', protected SOLDIERS building the ramp. Undermining, by burning the wooden props in a tunnel dug beneath a wall, was another ancient technique used by the Persians against Cypriot and Ionian towns during the IONIAN REVOLT. A Persian siege ramp at Old Paphos on CYPRUS was undermined by the defenders.

The Athenians, building their Aegean empire, were the first Greeks to acquire a reputation for besieging fortifications (Thucydides 1.102.2). Under 5th-century conditions towns were rarely taken by assault, more often by betrayal from within or by starving out the inhabitants. The Athenian siege of SAMOS in 440–439, involving a NAVAL blockade and circumvallation by land, lasted nine months and was notable for its great expense, and for being the first reported Greek use of rams and tortoises (DIODORUS 12.28). A double wall of circumvallation enabled the Peloponnesians to take PLATAEA in 427 after a two-year siege.

Siege warfare encouraged ingenuity. Thucydides describes counter-rams used at Plataea and a crude flame-thrower used at Delion. Incendiary devices, employed by attackers and defenders, usually consisted of fire-arrows and pitch-soaked bundles of brushwood thrown against exposed woodwork (true 'Greek fire', a naphtha compound, was an invention of the Middle Ages). AENEAS TACTICUS' 4th-century BC treatise describes many devices and practical counter-measures.

Developments on SICILY brought into general use the major devices of siegecraft. With improvements, these remained standard for Greek, CARTHAGINIAN and later Roman armies. In 409 BC the Carthaginians employed mobile siege towers with gangways for storming the battlements of Selinous, and DIONYSIOS I introduced bolt-shooting CATAPULTS at the siege of MOTYA in 397. Torsion springs of twisted horsehair later replaced oversize bows on catapults. By the time of ALEXANDER's campaigns in Asia these were capable of throwing stone balls heavy enough to batter walls, as at Tyre in 333–332.

In 305–304, monumental efforts devoted to the siege of RHODES earned DEMETRIOS the nickname Poliorketes, 'The Besieger' (Diodorus 20.87–99). He repeatedly attacked Rhodes by sea and by land, using SHIPS transformed into floating battle towers with catapults, huge rams brought up on land and the nine-story siege-tower Helepolis, 'City-taker', armour-plated and housing catapults on each level.

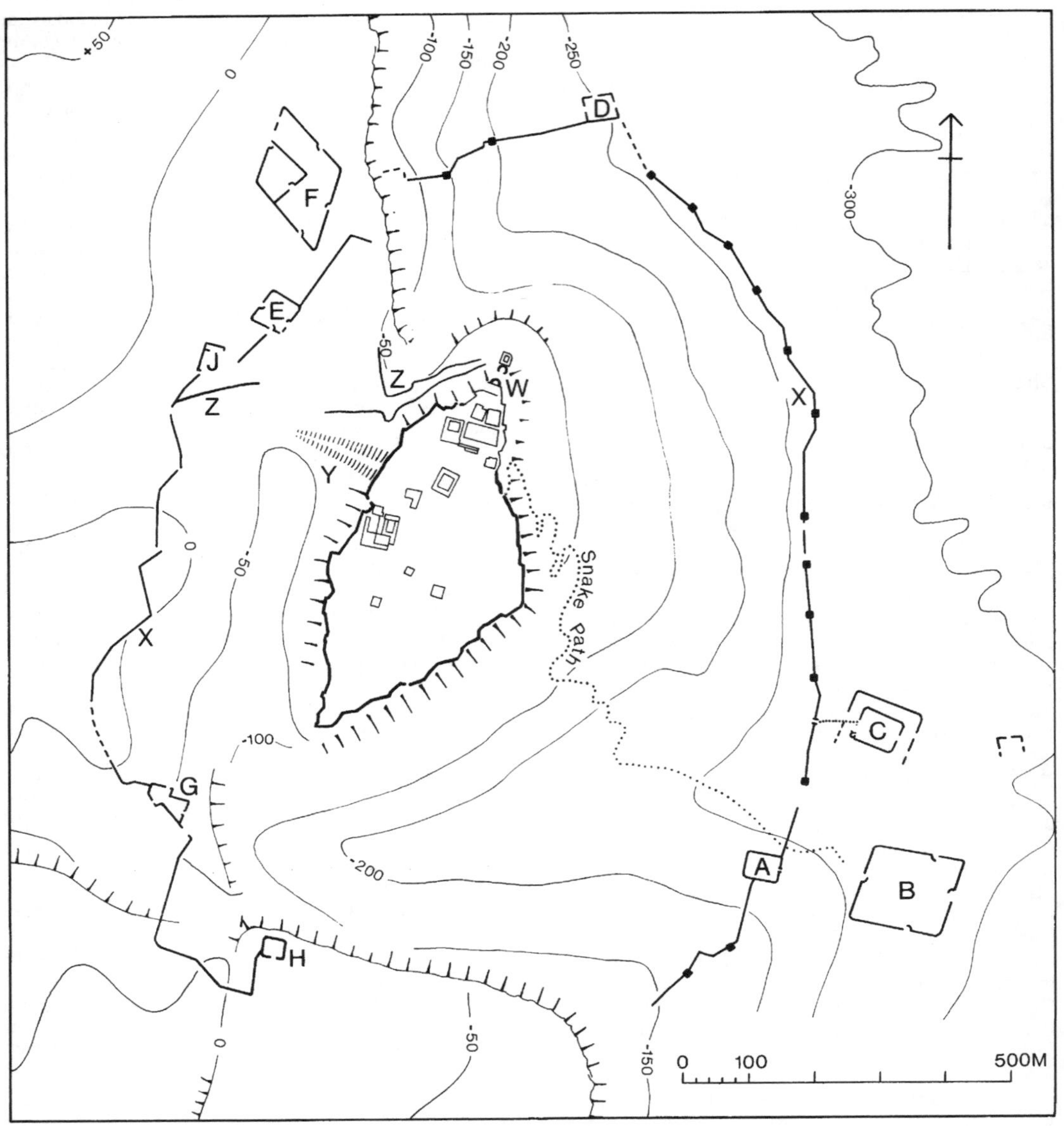

SIEGES AND SIEGE WARFARE: plan of the Roman siege works around the fortress of Masada, last refuge of the Jewish rebels in AD 73. The Roman army built a series of camps around the base of the hill (A–H), connected by a continuous circumvallation. The construction of the siege ramp (Y) eventually allowed them to breach the defences, precipitating the mass suicide of the defenders.

His machines broke down sections of wall, and his troops nearly succeeded in overrunning the defenders, but the Rhodians were able to run Demetrios' naval blockade and bring in supplies from their allies. Although vastly outnumbered, they could sustain their forces and provide their catapults with sufficient ammunition to batter Demetrios' machines. The siege became the focus of conflict between the technical and logistical resources of vast armed forces. It was ended by negotiation, proving that a well-supplied defence could withstand even the greatest of siege forces. The outcome depended upon the cost of continuing the siege.

Roman armies became proficient in Greek and Carthaginian techniques of siege warfare during the PUNIC WARS of the 3rd century BC. Marcellus' siege of SYRACUSE (213–211) exemplifies the tenacity of Roman siegecraft. Fortifications perfected under the tyrant Dionysios and his successors made Syracuse more challenging to assault than Rhodes, and the mechanical ingenuity of ARCHIMEDES made the destructive capacity of the defender's machinery famous. Failing in initial assaults, Marcellus maintained a long siege which succeeded by preventing the resupply of the defenders and by capturing strategic outer defences by stealth (PLUTARCH, *Marcellus* 14–19; Livy 25.24–31).

Skill in building fortified encampments served the Romans well in their works of circumvallation. Substantial remains of these are to be seen at NUMANTIA in Spain, where an eight-month siege broke Iberian resistance to Rome in 133 BC, and at MASADA in Israel, where the first Jewish revolt was brought to a close in AD 73 in an assault after six months' preparation. The siege-ramp constructed against the towering rock of Masada demonstrates, like the energetic attacks on JERUSALEM in AD 70, that even the Romans preferred to try an assault before relying on a prolonged siege (JOSEPHUS, *Jewish War*, books 5–7). The principles of siege-work and city fortification remained much the same in the later empire as under the hellenistic monarchies, but attackers and defenders were chiefly rival Roman armies. GERMANIC armies did not rely on siege warfare to undermine Roman power. MM

See Connolly, P. (1981) *Greece and Rome at War*; Garlan, Y. (1974) *Recherches de poliorcétique grecque*; Marsden, E.W. (1969) *Greek and Roman Artillery: historical development*; Whitehead, D., ed. (2001) *Aineias the Tactician, How to Survive under Siege*.

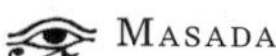 MASADA.

Sikyon see ACHAIAN LEAGUE.

Silenos see DRAMA, GREEK.

Silius Italicus (Titus Catius Silius Italicus) AD 26–101 had a successful career under NERO in the LAWCOURTS, was CONSUL in 68 and became proconsul of ASIA. Having gained considerable wealth, he retired to take up POETRY. He was obsessed with VIRGIL; apart from the many busts of the poet that he owned, he restored Virgil's TOMB near Naples. He held fashionable literary parties, and was known to MARTIAL and PLINY THE YOUNGER.

His epic poem *Punica* in 17 books was not highly regarded by Pliny, who regards it as showing more signs of careful working than of genius. The narrative is largely, though not slavishly, based on LIVY, and the verse is heavily influenced by Virgil. Silius' choice of subject matter made the *Punica* a bridge between the *Aeneid* and LUCAN's *Pharsalia*. It shows a careful structure, with the battle of CANNAE (books 8–10) at the centre of the work. Silius explores the lengthy campaign fought by HANNIBAL in Italy, and the action is motivated by the intervention of the GODS. Each major figure on the CARTHAGINIAN and Roman sides is carefully delineated. Hannibal gains our respect for his courage, ambition and ultimately tragic failure. Fabius, the cautious hero of the earlier part of the war, is superseded by SCIPIO AFRICANUS. Despite two laudatory references to DOMITIAN (himself an epic poet in his youth), there is a tone of paradox and pessimism. Hannibal's victories bring out Rome's true greatness, in particular after Cannae, while the anticipated result of Scipio's successes is the beginning of the decline of Rome, as individual glory overtakes the communal welfare. CJS

See Duff, J. D. (1933–9) (trs.); Ahl, F. et al. (1986) Silius Italicus, *ANRW* II.32.4: 2492–561.

silk A fabric spun from the cocoons of moths. In the classical world it was known in two forms, both of them costly and luxurious. Ancient sources do not juxtapose these two forms or treat them as comparable. Wild silk fabrics (Latin *bombycina*, *Coa*) were made from the cocoons of the moth *Lasiocampa otus*. This method had been devised by a woman from the Greek island of Kos, Pamphile, daughter of Plates. The industry developed on that island and its neighbour Amorgos at some date preceding the writing of ARISTOTLE's *History of Animals*, where it is described. A similar form of wild silk came also from islands in the Persian gulf. Throughout classical times, from ARISTOPHANES' *Lysistrata* to APULEIUS' *Metamorphoses*, shifts and shawls made of wild silk are treated poetically as revealing, semi-transparent and sensuous garments for beautiful women.

CHINESE silk fabrics (Latin *Serica*) were made from the cocoons of the domesticated Chinese silk moth, *Bombyx mori*. Chinese silk was probably not familiar in the ancient west until after the opening in 125 BC of the trade route across central Asia now known as the 'Silk Road'. In later classical texts *Serica* develop a reputation similar to that of *bombycina*. However, no ancient author is aware that this exotic imported fabric, just like *bombycina*, is woven from cocoons, with the single exception of PAUSANIAS, who describes the manufacture accurately (*Guide to Greece* 6.26.6–7). About AD 550 the Chinese silk moth was naturalized at CONSTANTINOPLE. AD

silphium An umbelliferous plant that grew wild in CYRENAICA (similar plants were found in SYRIA and PERSIA). It had a broad root and a stalk, which resembled fennel, while its leaves resembled either

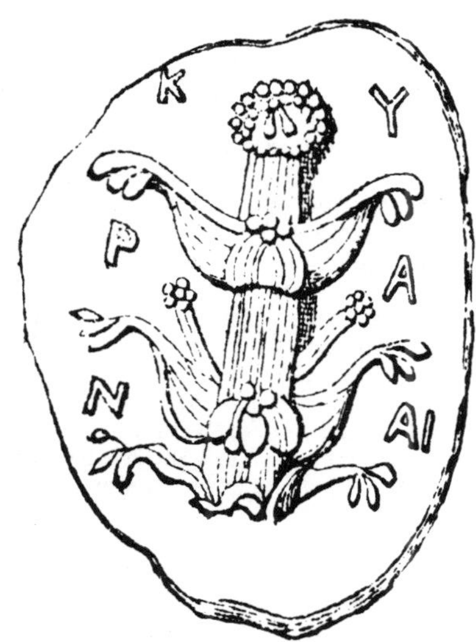

SILPHIUM: (a) as depicted on a coin of Cyrene.

SILPHIUM: (b) this Greek vase-painting scene is generally interpreted as showing the weighing of silphium for export.

parsley or fennel. Various parts of the plant were exploited, including the stalk, roots and leaves; in addition, juice was extracted from the roots. Silphium was used as a condiment and a luxury food, as well as a DRUG. It was prescribed for prolapsed anuses, for the delivery of stillborn children, for sore throats, for the removal of warts, for bringing on menstruation and for epilepsy and lumbago. It was also thought to aid digestion. When used as a condiment, it was grated over food; it was said to have had a pungent flavour. Silphium was also eaten either roasted or boiled, and its root was preserved in vinegar. Since it was so prized, silphium was an important source of revenue for the Cyrenaicans, who believed that it came into being after a downpour of rain seven years before the foundation of Cyrene. In the Roman period, silphium became increasingly scarce and valuable. By the 1st century AD it had become largely extinct, probably because of over-exploitation. Roman *publicani* caused a lot of damage by allowing SHEEP to graze on land in which silphium grew. Although PLINY THE ELDER says the last stalk of silphium was sent to NERO, the plant still existed in the time of SYNESIUS, writing in the 5th century AD. However, it appears to be extinct today. EACM

Silvanus Roman god of forests, herding and HUNTING. As his name suggests (*silva* is Latin for 'woodland'), he is 'lord of the woodlands' and the embodiment of trees and shrubs. His cult probably originated in rural Italy, and literary sources appear to trace his worship back to the beginnings of Rome (Livy 2.7.2–3; Propertius 4.4.5ff.). However reliable or unreliable these accounts may be, by the 2nd century AD his was a popular and widespread cult in the empire; some 1,100 inscriptions mention Silvanus. Despite its popularity, the cult was not public and had no official sanction in terms of state FESTIVALS, PRIESTHOODS or holy days. As the inscriptions attest, the great majority of Silvanus' devotees were not ARISTOCRATS, but commoners, FREEDMEN and SLAVES. His appeal to them seems to have been twofold. First, to many of his worshippers he was a humble rural figure who evoked the joys of rural life. Second, he was the protector of FAMILY, home and property and thus served as the guardian of a family's fortune.

Representations of Silvanus typically show a hairy, unkempt, male figure, either nude or clothed, holding a pruning hook (*falx*). He is also frequently depicted holding a pine bough or wearing a crown of pine branches, with a dog seated at his feet. In myth, he figures rarely. He has no genealogy, and appears in one version of the myth of Cyparissus, where he kills Cyparissus' stag (Servius on *Georgics* 1.20). JRCC

See Dorcey, P. F. (1992) *The Cult of Silvanus.*

silver Widely used by classical civilizations as a means of currency and for the manufacture of JEWELLERY and tableware. The rich hoards of silver tableware characteristic of the later Roman empire, such as the Sevso treasure, demonstrate the lavish use of this precious metal by some sections of ancient society.

Silver was often alloyed with other metals. It could be diluted by the addition of COPPER and yet retain a silvery appearance. In this way the silver coins of the Roman empire were progressively debased. Silver was often added to GOLD, but some copper would also have to be added to prevent loss of the golden colour.

The silver MINES of the classical civilizations were rarely silver mines as such. Silver can be smelted from its ores, but these ores are not common. LEAD ores are, however, relatively common and regularly contain silver. Most ancient silver mines were actually lead mines, such as the Athenian mines at LAURION. The lead smelted at Laurion contained around 0.2 per cent silver, which could be separated from the lead by the process of cupellation. The lead was melted and oxidized in a blast of air; this form of lead oxide is called litharge. The litharge was easily removed (the hearths at Laurion had clay linings which would react with it to form a slag), leaving the unoxidized, metallic silver. Cupellation was never able to separate all the silver from lead, so it was unlikely to be carried out on lead containing less than 0.02 per cent silver. (see also SILVERWARE, GREEK, ROMAN) DD

Silver Age literature see POETRY, ROMAN.

silverware

In literary sources, Greek silverware regularly appears in the hands of symposiasts, as the means of securing a loan, or even as an item of inheritance. However, because of problems of survival its rightful place in the material culture of the Greek world has been supplanted by POTTERY.

Inventories of precious items, often recording the weight, were frequently inscribed on *stêlai* (upright stone slabs) placed in Greek sanctuaries. One reason for this may have been to stop the embezzlement of dedications. Some of the most complete lists are associated with the various TEMPLES and cult sites on the ATHENIAN ACROPOLIS. A particularly large piece of silver plate was the krater made by Theodoros of SAMOS and dedicated at DELPHI by Croesus; it was said to have the capacity of 600 AMPHORAS (Herodotos 1.51). Sometimes silver plate fell into disrepair and had to be mended, like the handle which had to be reattached to a krater by the silversmith Aristarchos on DELOS (*IG* XI.2.161, A102). On the Athenian Acropolis, Nikokrates of Kolonos seems to have been active over some 20 years reworking some of the precious metal dedications. The sanctuary inscriptions also suggest that silver plate was made to a round number of units (though not always in drachmas). *Phialai* (cups) regularly have the recorded weight of 100 drachmas, a weight that corresponds with an extant silver example from the burial mounds at Duvanli in modern Bulgaria.

As silver could be melted down and reworked, few extant pieces of Greek silver plate have survived. Exceptions include pieces such as the gilded silver *phiale* in the Rogozen hoard from THRACE, one of 165 silver items. This particular piece was decorated with a relief of HERAKLES and Auge. Silver cups and a *kantharos*, decorated in a gold-figured technique that evokes contemporary Athenian red-figured pottery, were found at Duvanli. Similarly decorated silver cups were found in the Seven Brothers' (Semibratny) tumuli in southern Russia. An unusual janiform head-vase, dating to the 4th century BC, appears to come from the Pithom hoard in Egypt. Elaborate silver *rhyta* (drinking-horns) include examples from Duvanli and from Borovo in Thrace, and one from the Tuch el-Karamus hoard in Egypt.

Some inscribed pieces show that they had been carried off as booty from sanctuaries. For example, a silver *phiale*, originally dedicated to MEGARIAN Athena, was discovered in a 4th-century BC TOMB at Kozani in MACEDONIA. A similar piece from a Sarmatian tomb in the Kuban had originally been dedicated in the Greek sanctuary of Apollo at Kolchian Phasis on the Black sea. DWJG

See Bothmer, D. von (1984) A Greek and Roman treasury, *Bulletin of the Metropolitan Museum of Art* 42.1; Cook, B. F., ed. (1989) *The Rogozen Treasure*; Gill, D.W. J. (1996) Ancient Greece VIII. Metalwork 1. Gold and silver, in *The Dictionary of Art* 13: 568–71; Harris, D. (1996) *The Treasures of the Parthenon and the Erechtheion*; Oliver, A., jr. (1977) *Silver for the Gods*; Strong, D. E. (1966) *Greek and Roman Gold and Silver Plate*; Vickers, M. and Gill, D. (1994) *Artful Crafts*.

Silver plate was of enormous importance in the domestic, political and economic life of the Roman empire. Dining was an important social occasion in the Roman world, and silver vessels, as well as those made from rare materials such as rock crystal, indicated high status and wealth. Table silver was usually divided into *argentum escarium* or eating silver (dishes, plates and bowls) and *argentum potorium* or drinking silver (jugs, cups and ladles). Other silver objects associated with dining are containers for SALT and pepper, and spoons. In addition to objects actually used for dining, silverware could be exhibited in the *triclinium* or other public areas of the house. Such show pieces (*emblemata*) often have medallions with busts in the centre of the dish, and could be displayed on special stands. Many HOUSEHOLDS also had domestic silver in the form of candlesticks, boxes and mirrors.

Silver plate was used in religious ceremonies as libation vessels, as containers for sacrificial WINE, and for serving sacrificial MEAT. Many temple treasuries contained large quantities of silver plate. In the later Roman empire, silver dishes were highly valued in the CHRISTIAN church. In some cases Christian symbols or inscriptions were engraved onto dishes, but there are examples where PAGAN and Christian imagery intermingle, reflecting the changing beliefs of the Roman élite at this time. Silver vessels were traded widely, but could also be given as diplomatic gifts by the emperor (TACITUS, *Germania* 5). Fragments of such vessels have been discovered in rich 'native' pre-Roman burials in BRITAIN, GERMANY and Denmark. In the later Roman empire, silver dishes were distributed (as *largitio* dishes) on the occasion of imperial anniversaries.

Most of our knowledge of Roman silver is derived from hoard finds. These contained much of the portable wealth belonging to élite families, and in some cases to early Christian communities. They appear to have been hidden during times of unrest and crisis. Famous examples include the Hildesheim treasure in Germany and the Mildenhall and Water Newton hoards in Britain. One of the few 1st-century hoards was discovered underneath the bath-suite of the Casa del Menandro in POMPEII; it consisted of

118 pieces, which had been wrapped in cloth and placed inside a wooden box.

The value of silver plate was defined not just by the raw material and its weight, which is often recorded in inscriptions, but also by its decoration. Most silver plate was produced by SLAVES or FREEDMEN, who appear to have worked with a high degree of specialization. Certain firms enjoyed a particularly good reputation (PLINY, *Natural History* 33.139). Special prices were paid for antiques attributed to famous, often Greek, craftsmen (Pliny, *Natural History* 33.47) and for signed pieces (SENECA, *Dialogues* 9.1.7). The flourishing market for collector's pieces (see also Pliny, *Natural History* 33.53; 33.55) led to forgeries (MARTIAL, *Epigrams* 8.34) and copying. A famous example is a Roman period hoard from Mit Rahinet near Memphis, which contained plaster casts of hellenistic silver vessels. HE

See Kent, J. P. C. and Painter, K. S., eds. (1977) *Wealth of the Roman World* AD *300–700*; Painter, K.W. (2001) *Insula of the Menander at Pompeii*, vol. 4: *The Silver Treasure*; Strong, D. E. (1966) *Greek and Roman Gold and Silver Plate.*

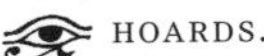 HOARDS.

Simonides Born on Keos 557 BC, died in SICILY 468 BC. Simonides was included by ALEXANDRIAN scholars in the canon of the nine lyricists, though he alone is not ascribed a specific number of books. He was a prolific author, known for versatility, and was said to have composed 'songs of laments, praise, paeans in honour of APOLLO, TRAGEDIES and others'. No tragic fragments survive; his alleged tragedies were perhaps dithyrambs with elements of dialogue. In antiquity, he was regarded mainly as an epigrammatist, and many extant EPIGRAMS were, in consequence, attributed to him at some point. Other than the poem for his friend, the seer Megistias who died at THERMOPYLAI (quoted by Herodotos 7.228), the authorship of most items under his name remains questionable. Papyri published in 1992 added many new fragments to those previously known, including part of a long elegiac poem celebrating the battle of Plataea.

Simonides was possibly the first to compose epinician poetry. If correct, this view harmonizes with the generally innovative character of his poetry, which coincides with the transformation from the archaic to the classical periods. In many ways, he was a precursor of the SOPHISTS, commenting on the human situation under the new economic and political structures of his time. The sophist PROTAGORAS, in a PLATONIC dialogue (*Protagoras* 339), quotes some of Simonides' lines on the meaning of goodness.

Simonides associated with tyrants in THESSALY and Sicily, and the PEISISTRATIDS at Athens, all centres of political power and economic well-being. After the assassination of Hipparchos, he remained in Athens and became an admirer of DEMOCRACY. He had a reputation for being a lover of money and was the first poet to receive money from patrons in exchange for poetry. This reflects both the economic changes of the times and the social gap between patron and poet. (see also SEMONIDES, who is sometimes confused with Simonides) RBC

See Boedeker, D. and Sider, D., eds. (2001) *The New Simonides*; Fränkel, H. (1975) *Early Greek Poetry and Philosophy*; Podlecki, A. J. (1984) *The Early Greek Poets and their Times*; West, M. L., trs. (1993) *Greek Lyric Poetry.*

singers In the Greco-Roman world singers often performed in CHORUSES: we know that 27 boys and 27 girls sang HORACE's *Secular Hymn* at the Secular ('hundred-yearly') Festival of 17 BC. Individual singers were sometimes itinerant. Arion, the legendary archaic singer from Methymna, allegedly rode to safety on a dolphin's back to escape sailors who plotted to kill him for the large sum of money he had made from a tour of Italy and SICILY. Solo singers were also a feature of the courts and great houses of the Greeks and Romans. The rhapsodes Phemios and Demodokos in HOMER's *Odyssey* are fictional examples of this phenomenon. In the hellenistic age, Glauke of CHIOS was a singer-songwriter in the court of Ptolemy II in Egypt. She was of such legendary beauty that even a ram and a gander were supposed to have fallen in love with her. In the late REPUBLIC, Tigellius Sardus, the favourite of JULIUS CAESAR, was pilloried by Horace (*Satires* 1.2 and 1.3) for his tedious and unsolicited performances. The emperor NERO scandalously loved to sing publicly at NAPLES and Rome, shocking Roman moralists, who did not consider professional ACTING, singing or DANCING worthy of upper class or imperial dignity. Nero took seriously the exacting regime expected of professional singers, involving attention to diet, purges, and lying with a slab of lead on his chest, but his voice was nevertheless said to be feeble and husky. (see also SONGS AND SINGING) ED

See Baudot, A. (1973) *Musiciens romains de l'antiquité.*

Sinope City situated on the southern coast of the Black sea, birthplace of the PHILOSOPHERS Diogenes the CYNIC and Timotheos Patrion, the poet Diphilos, and the historian Baton. It was founded by MILETOS in the late 7th century BC on a peninsula with two HARBOURS. Its location made Sinope the most important trading place in the BLACK SEA, not least for offering the shortest crossing to the Crimea. The surrounding hills were noted for their TIMBER, and the seas for their tuna catch. In almost every settlement around the Black sea, thousands of fragments of Sinopean AMPHORAS and amphora stamps and hundreds of Sinopean coins are known. Sinopean cinnabar was famous as a trading commodity. In c.437 BC PERIKLES overthrew a TYRANT, leaving behind him many Athenian settlers (Plutarch, *Perikles* 20). For a short time it was occupied by the PERSIAN satrap Datames, but it maintained its freedom under ALEXANDER the Great and his Successors. In about 183 BC it became the capital of the Pontic empire of Pharnakes I. At the time of STRABO it had imposing buildings, a MARKET, GYMNASIUM and FORTIFICATION walls (12.3.11). In the Roman period there was a Roman colony here. GRT

See Robinson, D. M. (1906) *Ancient Sinope.*

Siwa see ALEXANDRIA; AMMON; EGYPT.

skolia Short poems of two to four lines (with some exceptions), performed by the guests at banquets. The name *skolion* refers to the zig-zagging order in which these guests, seated or reclining around the table, recited their poems. To determine the sequence, they passed a myrtle branch from guest to guest. ATHENAEUS (694c) offers a collection of 25; others are known from different sources. The oldest are dated to the 6th century BC, the rest to the 5th. They are usually composed in Attic dialect, but use the metres of LESBIAN poetry. The general view is that these poems were recited, not sung, during the banquet. The topics are those typical of sympotic poetry: food, drink and love, combined with praises and exempla of mythical and historical characters, or a discussion of what constitutes a good friend. In spite of the generally aristocratic character of the banquet, our collection of *skolia* includes several in praise of Harmodios and Aristogeiton, who killed the tyrant Hippias' brother Hipparchos in 514 BC and became the alleged fathers of DEMOCRACY. RBC

Skythia see SCYTHIA.

slavery Both Greece and Rome were slave-owning societies, and both used slaves to perform all manner of tasks in public and private life. Slaves were legally recognized as chattels and were owned by their masters. They were typically acquired through warfare, kidnapping and PIRACY, or breeding. In both classical Athens and Roman Italy slaves formed a significant proportion of the population, estimated at a quarter to one-third of the populace.

Slaves were an integral part of the AEGEAN world from the earliest times, as references in the Bronze Age Linear B tablets indicate. Large numbers of these slaves were women and children, many probably situated in the PALACES as domestic workers. During the 8th and 7th centuries BC many poorer farmers fell into personal debt and became obligated, even enslaved to their wealthy landowners. Debt bondage of the small landholder became such a serious issue at Athens that SOLON abolished the practice shortly after 600. The loss of this cheap labour force may have been one reason why the Athenians turned to the use of slavery. But not all city-states used an outside source of slaves. The serf-like HELOTS at SPARTA were defined as 'between free and slave'. They were forced to work the land and in return were allowed minimal rights, such as MARRIAGE and protection from eviction. Nevertheless, helot revolts were constant threat, and as a result Spartan males became the best-trained HOPLITES in Greece by engaging in constant warfare against their subjugated populations.

In classical Athens, slaves were prevalent in even modest *oikoi* (HOUSEHOLDS). Domestic tasks could include food preparation, TEXTILE manufacturing, child-care, personal grooming and even extend to sexual services for the master of the house. Domestic slaves also carried out many exterior tasks, such as water collection and marketing, since these were not deemed acceptable activities for freeborn women. Outside the home, slaves worked in MANUFACTURING and crafts, either directly for their masters or as hired labour. Others worked in AGRICULTURE, but the Greeks did not employ large numbers of slaves on huge estates as the Romans did.

Public (*dêmosioi*) slaves enjoyed higher status and typically greater independence. Since they were owned by the city-state they lived on their own. They could be clerks, coin testers, assistants to MAGISTRATES, or even the public executioner. In Athens after the PERSIAN WARS, a special group of 300 SCYTHIAN slaves trained as archers was employed as a rudimentary police force. They kept order in the LAWCOURTS and ASSEMBLIES, but had no authority to investigate or arrest citizens. Other slaves were associated with TEMPLES, belonging to the GOD or GODDESS of a particular shrine.

The most frequently used term for a slave was *doulos* (fem. *doulê*) as opposed to *eleutheros*, a freeborn citizen of a *POLIS*. It was generally felt that slaves should be BARBARIANS (i.e. not Greeks), yet the practice of Greek owning Greek never disappeared in classical times. In fact, frequent warfare between city-states often resulted in the enslavement of women and children. Males from captured cities were typically executed, but the women and children posed less risk and were easier to integrate into servitude. With the loss of their community these individuals were marginalized, making their enslavement psychologically easier. The same policy worked for enslaving barbarians as well. The fact that they were not Greek made their servitude acceptable, since they were defined as 'the other' from the outset. These ideas form the basis for the discussion on the attitudes towards slavery in the classical world which can be found in ARISTOTLE's *Politics* (1.2.2–3). He states that slaves are by their innate character servile, and refers to them as living instruments or tools to be used by the master. To justify this use of another human being, Aristotle states that their subordinate character makes a slave fit to be governed by another person. Furthermore, it is advantageous for these inferior individuals to be slaves since they have no FREE WILL or real intellectual abilities. This makes their servitude a justifiable act and a cultural, not a racial, prejudice.

Slave owning was also an integral aspect of Roman society. From the earliest times, slaves worked and lived alongside their masters in households, on domestic and agricultural tasks. Warfare or debt slavery were the most common sources of slaves. The term *servus* (fem. *serva*) was applied to a slave, as opposed to *ingenuus* (fem. *ingenua*), a freeborn citizen.

SLAVERY: Roman bronze tag identifying a runaway slave: 'Hold me, lest I escape, and take me back to my master Viventius on the estate of Callistus.'

As the Romans conquered Italy, they captured both prisoners and large parcels of land, which became concentrated in the hands of ARISTOCRATIC families. These were organized into estates (*latifundia*) which were primarily dependent on slave labour for large-scale agricultural production. The subsequent conquest of the MEDITERRANEAN world brought increasingly large numbers of slaves to Italy and to the rest of the Roman world. Slaves were desirable since they were cheap, easily obtained and on the whole reliable, as opposed to the free tenants who were increasingly conscripted to serve in the army. Indeed, heavy reliance on slave labour enabled the Romans to draft a high percentage of their male population into the military. The large concentration of slaves on the large estates of the Roman world created a constant threat of revolt, and Rome experienced several such risings. The worst broke out in SICILY in 136 BC; its eventual suppression five years later resulted in the crucifixion of thousands of slaves. Another led by the GLADIATOR SPARTACUS occurred in Campania in 73 BC and was a serious threat to all Italy. Thousands of slaves joined the revolt, until their number grew to around 70,000 men. It took Rome two years and eventually ten legions to conquer this well-armed and determined group.

The dramatic increase in wealth of the patricians of the late Republic and imperial periods resulted in huge slave families, often numbering hundreds. The first emperors owned and employed large numbers of slaves and freed slaves, known collectively as the *familia Caesaris*, to carry out routine bureaucratic tasks. Many EMPERORS felt that they could trust their slaves or freedmen more than the SENATORIAL class or even EQUESTRIANS. Some of these were able to use their influence to amass great sums of money, such as the administrators Pallas and Narcissus, who during the reign of CLAUDIUS were able to acquire millions of *sestertii*.

Throughout the classical world, it was the general view that the owner had the right to punish slaves. Beatings were a regular occurrence; even executions could take place. Harsh treatment stemmed from a belief in the slave's lack of intelligence or free will, and corporal punishment was not only acceptable but reinforced the slave's status as separate from the citizen community. A good example of this practice is the obligatory torturing of slaves to obtain evidence in legal cases. TORTURE was necessary to ensure the veracity of the information, since slaves had no moral capacity and were not bound by the same principles as free men. Slaves had no direct legal recourse against their masters, and even in the Roman empire, when some laws were enacted to control the punishments by masters (usually to restrict executions), these were done more to restrain the masters than for humanitarian reasons. Notably, slavery did not end with the conversion of the empire to CHRISTIANITY in the 4th century.

The treatment of slaves had much to do with their personal skills and their relationship with their master. Amenable and LITERATE individuals could expect to work in a household as personal servants or domestic workers. Ambitious slaves were often set up in business, either working alongside their masters or independently. In the Roman world they were often allowed to keep part of their earnings (*peculium*), which they could spend or save in order to purchase their freedom later. Obedient slaves were allowed to set up their own families, and while these existed at the indulgence of the master, numerous servile funerary inscriptions attest to the importance of these family bonds in the Roman world. MANUMISSION was the ultimate reward for loyalty, and the Romans were liberal with the numbers they freed. FREEDMEN, *liberti* (fem. *libertae*), faced some social restrictions and were still bound to their former masters, yet they were considered Roman citizens. In Athens, manumitted slaves became METICS (free foreigners); only under exceptional circumstances were they granted citizenship.

Slaves who were aggressive or CRIMINALS would most likely end up as heavy labourers, agricultural workers or, in the Roman world, street cleaners or BATH stokers. These slaves were much less fortunate. Their lives were filled with toil, their diet was poor, and they had few or no amenities. In both the Greek and the Roman world, the worst fate befell those sent to the MINES: the work was backbreaking, dangerous and usually fatal. MJC

See Bradley, K. (1987) *Slaves and Masters in the Roman Empire*; Finley, M., ed. (1987) *Classical Slavery*; Wiedemann, T. (1987) *Slavery*.

Smyrna Old Smyrna (mod. Bayrakli) was located a few km north of post-Alexandrian Smyrna (mod. İzmir). Ancient Smyrna was one of the twelve Aeolian towns of Asia Minor, but became Ionian when it was captured treacherously by the city of Kolophon (Herodotos 1.149–50). Little is known of prehistoric Smyrna. The Greek (Aeolic) settlement of Smyrna begins c.1000 BC. Prehistoric and early Greek settlements were on a peninsula, separated from the hinterland by a defensive wall. The city was damaged by an earthquake c.700, but then experienced a major urban expansion, including a series of TEMPLES dedicated to ATHENA. After a LYDIAN sack, under Alyattes (c.600), the city lay abandoned for some 200 years. According to tradition, ALEXANDER the Great founded the new city of Smyrna in 334.

Hellenistic and Roman Smyrna is known mainly from literary sources. It was regarded as the fairest Ionian city, and according to LUCIAN of SAMOSATA it produced the most beautiful women. AELIUS ARISTIDES, who made his home there, has left descriptions of the city in the 2nd century AD, extolling 'the profusion and splendour of its buildings – GYMNASIA, city-squares, THEATRES, walls, HARBOURS, enormous BATHS, several fine racecourses, innumerable FOUNTAINS, (and) sunlit streets' (Cadoux). Little of this can be identified today, though some remains were still visible to the author of a poetic stone inscription dated AD 1222. Much was destroyed by Tamerlane in his ferocious sack of 1402, further damage being caused by a disastrous fire in 1922. JDM

See Cadoux, C. J. (1938) *Ancient Smyrna*.

soap There is little information available to suggest that soap was commonly used in bathing and washing clothes in the classical world, though there is evidence that it existed. According to PLINY THE ELDER (*Natural history* 28.51.191) the substance *sapo* was invented in the Gallic provinces and was used as a red hair-dye. He states that it was made from suet or animal fat and ash, and that the substance came in either a thick or a liquid form. The best soap was made with beech ash. According to Pliny and MARTIAL (14.26), it was the GERMANS (specifically the Chatti in Martial's account) that were most in favour of dyeing their hair red with the substance.

Instead of soap, the Romans tended to use OILS in bathing, some of them scented. Essentially they would sweat in the BATHS, rub oil on their bodies, and remove the oil and dirt with a strigil. Sometimes scented oils would be used during cleansing or afterwards as a perfume.

Although SLAVES or family members may have washed clothes, *fullones* (FULLERS) were also responsible for washing woollen garments as well as newly dyed materials. For cleaning woollen materials, they used urine and fuller's earth (Pliny, *Natural History* 28.18.66; 35.57). PAB

social mobility see FREEDMEN AND FREEDWOMEN; SOCIETY, GREEK; SOCIETY, ROMAN.

social occasions see DINING.

social stratification see ÉLITES; SOCIETY, GREEK; SOCIETY, ROMAN.

Social war The name 'social war' (deriving from Latin *socius*, 'ally') refers to various wars involving alliances, notably two in Greek history and one in Roman.

The first is the revolt that brought to an end the second Athenian confederacy (357–355 BC). Founded in 378 in response to Spartan aggression, the Athenians' new alliance was styled in sharp contrast to their 5th-century empire. The 'charter' of the new confederation (Tod 123) specified that members would not pay tribute, have their constitution imposed from without, or be garrisoned. Disaffected by Athenian leadership and encouraged by MAUSOLUS, satrapal ruler of CARIA, the allied states of CHIOS, RHODES, Kos and Byzantion began the revolt from Athens in 357. Worried especially by Byzantion's position on its grain route, the Athenians responded by diplomatic efforts in THRACE. They sent the generals Chares and Chabrias to Chios, where Chabrias was killed in a naval battle, and they imposed garrisons (Tod 156). Following Chares' defeat at Embata in the HELLESPONT (356), and ARTAXERXES III's threat to bring in the PERSIANS on the side of the rebellious allies, Athens gave up the conflict (355). Chios, Kos and Rhodes were allowed to withdraw from the league, and Byzantion became fully autonomous.

The other notable 'Social war' in Greece was that of 220–217 between the Aitolians and Philip V of Macedonia, whose allies included the Achaians. It led to the Romans' second intervention in Balkans in 219, and was ended by the peace of Naupaktos. According to Polybios (5.103–6), the peace conference was the occasion when the affairs of Greece, Italy and Africa were first indissolubly linked and Rome began to be the arbiter of eastern affairs. JDD, DGJS

See Cawkwell, G. (1962) Notes on the Social War, *CM* 23: 34–49 [4th-century war]; Walbank, F.W. (1984), in *CAH* 7.1, ch. 12.8 [3rd-century war].

War (91–89 BC) between Rome and the Italian allies (*socii*), ending in the extension of Roman CITIZENSHIP to the whole of Italy, also known as the Marsic (the *Marsi* were first to revolt) or Italic war. The war has been the subject of recent historical revisionism. Traditionally it has been seen as the culmination of the Roman conquest of Italy, and in particular of a series of events beginning with the land reforms of Tiberius GRACCHUS (133 BC). Suggestions that the unification of Italy was inevitable, or that the Italians primarily sought Roman citizenship, have now been rightly challenged. Italian grievances were a consequence of the growth of empire. They arose from the changing economic structure of the peninsula, the burden of military service, the lack of participation in the decisions of empire, and a general resentment of increasingly harsh treatment as subjects rather than allies. The failure of measures proposed by the TRIBUNE Marcus Livius Drusus, and his assassination in late 91, sparked open war. Most of the fighting was over by late 89. The allies had long experience of the Roman army, but Roman reserves were considerable and commanders such as MARIUS and SULLA highly experienced. A series of laws between 90 and 88 granted the citizenship to most Italians, thereby conciliating the main complaints. However, the SAMNITES in particular did not lay down their arms, were drawn into the subsequent civil war between Sulla and Cinna, and were finally defeated at the Colline gate in 82. The traditional view that the allies simply wanted Roman citizenship is complicated by the creation, by late 91, of a federal capital called Italica in direct opposition to Rome. The year 89 nonetheless marked a watershed in the history of the peninsula. The extension of citizenship led to the political and cultural transformation of Italy with, for example, the spread of Roman institutions such as *municipia*. Many of the pre-existing cultural differences between the peoples of Italy seem to fade away from this moment. JRWP

See Appian, *The Civil Wars*, trs. J. Carter (1996); Brunt, P. A. (1978) *Social Conflicts in the Roman Republic*; Gabba, E. (1994) Rome and Italy: the Social war, *CAH* 9, 104–28; Mouritsen, H. (1998) *Italian Unification*.

societies see CLUBS; FRATERNITY.

society

There was no such thing as Greek society, but rather a plurality of sometimes radically different Greek societies. The two best known are Athens and Sparta, which – as PERIKLES (in THUCYDIDES' portrayal) and others were fond of pointing out – were in some ways diametrically opposite. All Greek cities, however, agreed in drawing three sharp boundary lines among their inhabitants: one on grounds of legal status, between the free and the unfree; a second on grounds of political status, between citizens and non-citizens; and a third on grounds of GENDER, between the spheres of life and activities judged appropriate for MEN and WOMEN.

People who were counted merely as means to a higher end, and who were thought incapable or unworthy of legal or psychological autonomy and independence, were rated below the level of the ideal, politically active adult male citizens. The latter collectively formed the most important part of the *koinon* ('commonwealth') or *koinônia* ('community'). Thus the unfree, foreigners (Greek as well as non-Greek), and all women (with the partial exception of some PRIESTESSES) were excluded from active political CITIZENSHIP in the public sphere. The private sphere, moreover, was generally regarded instrumentally, as a means rather than an end in itself, the supreme end being communal political activity.

Yet although Greek cities might agree on the overriding importance of politics, as against economic or other activity in the private sphere, they did not agree on the best way of shaping citizens towards the desired end. In education (*paideia*), for example, Athens and Sparta represented very different points of view. The Spartans devised a comprehensive, minutely detailed and closely supervised educational programme (*agôgê*) that was compulsory for all would-be male citizens from the age of seven upwards. The Athenians did not require Athenian children legally to attend school at all. On the other hand, such Athenian schools as there were taught cultural pursuits – LITERACY, NUMERACY, MUSIC – no less than physical EDUCATION, whereas the Spartans, without entirely neglecting higher culture, very firmly privileged the physical. The chief aim of the Spartan educational programme as a whole was turning out exemplary SOLDIERS.

Athenian girls, if formally educated at all, were educated at home, chiefly to perform key domestic tasks such as cooking and WEAVING. Spartan girls, on the other hand, were given some sort of public and physical education like their brothers, but were expressly not trained to perform domestic tasks. When they were married, those would be carried out for them by unfree HELOT women. In general, although both Athenian and Spartan girls were raised with a view to becoming wives and mothers, a Spartan wife's domestic life was typically much more sharply differentiated from her husband's than that of her Athenian counterpart. This was because for most Athenian men their home was attached to their principal means of livelihood, their farm; but all Spartan men were deliberately denied any private economic occupation, since all had just the one, public occupation, that of citizen-soldier.

In all Greek cities, unfree men and women made up a significant part of society – symbolically and psychologically if not necessarily numerically. Most chattel SLAVES in Greece were of non-Greek origin, the largest concentrations occurring in Athens and CHIOS. ARISTOTLE in the *Politics* writes of the ideal *oikos* (HOUSEHOLD) as containing both free and unfree persons, but actually by no means all Greeks could afford to own even one slave. Nevertheless being Greek meant, ideologically speaking, being free, and freedom was defined by opposition to real servitude. The Spartans, as often, differed from most Greeks in their slave-holding regime. Their servile population of helots were ethnic Greeks, enslaved through conquest and collectively subjects of the Spartan *polis*. Unlike chattel slaves elsewhere, they enjoyed some sort of FAMILY life and other privileges. But they also suffered the unique stigma of having WAR declared upon them annually, which licensed Spartans to kill them with impunity.

All Greeks drew a distinction between Greek foreigners (*xenoi*) and non-Greek foreigners (*barbaroi*) – except the Spartans, who lumped both categories together and periodically conducted expulsions of them (*xenêlasiai*). Very few non-Spartans were ever granted Spartan citizenship, though before the hellenistic period that practice was not common in other Greek cities either. Not all foreigners were equally unwelcome in Sparta; some ÉLITE Spartans like other Greeks maintained a special kind of friendship (*xenia*) with their peers abroad, non-Greek as well as Greek. In about 70 cities the formal status of resident alien (usually called *metoikos*) is attested. Most metics would be Greeks, either political or economic migrants. Though legally free, they suffered a second-class status marked by the necessity to pay a poll tax. *Barbaroi* who were permanently resident in a Greek city were typically either slaves or ex-slaves. Athens, and especially its port city of PIRAEUS, were in this regard by far the most cosmopolitan of *poleis*. PAC

See Jameson, M. H. (1977–8) Agriculture and slavery in classical Athens, *CJ* 73: 122–45; Millett, P. (2000) The economy, in R. Osborne, ed., *Classical Greece* 23–51, and other chapters in the same volume.

The bases upon which Roman society was defined varied enormously over time. In the earliest period, definitions derived from the idealized structure of the *familia* in which the *paterfamilias* (the ascendant living male) possessed absolute *potestas* over all members of the group, whether related to him by blood or not. This included wives of his children who had entered into a *manus* MARRIAGE, and SLAVES. In public life, the dominant group in society constituted the *patres*, or ARISTOCRACY, who dominated public life through bonds of PATRONAGE over groups of *clientes*. This aspect of early society was preserved into the 5th century BC, when the duties of *clientes* were codified in the TWELVE TABLES, and the PATRICIANS, an aristocracy based upon blood relationship, dominated public life. All citizens who were not patrician were classified as PLEBEIAN.

By the time that the Twelve Tables were composed, the family model of Roman society was already showing signs of severe stress. Before the end of the 6th century, a new form of social division had been introduced in conjunction with the (re)organization of the hoplite army, or LEGION. In this scheme, Romans were assigned to *classes* according to wealth. The theory behind this division was that three basic services could be expected of the citizen: tax paying, VOTING and military service. Power was granted to groups in accordance with their ability to perform these services. The uneven division of the five classes into 194 'centuries' (*centuriae*) illustrates this principle. The first *classis*, which included the CAVALRY (*equites*) and heavily armed INFANTRY, constituted 80 centuries. The bulk of the population, however, the *proletarii*, whose function was defined as producing children, were relegated to a single century.

In the course of the 5th century, a further division of the Roman people according to location became significant; this was the tribal organization. By the end of the 4th century there were 35 TRIBES. Their significance is reflected in Roman nomenclature, as a Roman's full NAME included a *praenomen*, patronymic, tribal affiliation and *cognomen* (if the family had one). In the later Republic and early empire, as Roman society expanded, the most significant divisions were based upon status within the community as defined by wealth and birth. The most fundamental divisions were between SLAVES and free, and between citizen and non-citizen. Within the community of free Romans, the dominant class included members of the SENATORIAL order, the EQUESTRIAN order, members of municipal councils and, in the post-Augustan period, VETERANS. By the end of the 1st century AD, Roman law created a distinction between members of these classes, the *honestiores*, and all other free Romans, the *humiliores*, giving the former group significant protections before the law that the other lacked.

In the course of the 3rd and 4th centuries, while the divisions between slave and free, *honestiores* and *humiliores*, remained fundamental, the structure of the upper class was altered by the centralization of authority around the imperial palace, and rank was linked to a person's status within the imperial government. DSP

sociology The scientific study of the beliefs, values and organizations of societies. Max Weber (1864–1920) was responsible for establishing this discipline. Weber, the product of a bourgeois German family residing in Berlin, studied both Roman and German legal history and wrote dissertations in both fields. Influenced by the works and direction of the legal historian Theodor Mommsen, Weber completed his second dissertation on Roman land use, *Die römische Agrargeschichte*. In this work, he showed how the economic productivity of AGRICULTURAL land relied upon the correlation between political and social factors, namely constitutional and civil law. Weber recognized that, more often than not, traditional historical approaches were grounded in the historian's own value systems. Weber manoeuvred around this by stating that potentially subjective claims needed to be supported objectively with as many pieces of supporting evidence as possible. Weber's studies focused on more than newly discovered facts about individuals or events. Rather, his analyses revealed the internal make-up of a specific society whereby certain characteristics, that is, individuals, events, and cultures, represent an 'ideal type'. After establishing the 'ideal type' he would compare it to other contemporary, not modern, societies to demonstrate what specific characteristics were common to all. Then the historian needed to seek causal explanations for the presence of these characteristics. LAH

See Love, J. R. (1991) *Antiquity and Capitalism: Max Weber and the sociological foundations of Roman civilization*; Weber, M. (1924) *The Agrarian Sociology of Ancient Civilizations*, trs. R. I. Frank (1976).

Socrates 469–399 BC Greek PHILOSOPHER. Socrates was born in Athens, the son of Sophroniskos and Phainarete from the DEME of Alopeke. He was father to three boys, of whom we know next to nothing. We have first-hand accounts of what his life was like from PLATO and XENOPHON, and a caricature of him in ARISTOPHANES' COMEDY *Clouds*. Plato and Xenophon basically present the same Socrates, but Plato's superior skill as a writer has produced a more sophisticated and colourful portrait than the one created by Xenophon and it is, by and large, Plato's account that has become the accepted one. Xenophon's account, however, has lately been undergoing something of a resurgence. Aristophanes' portrayal is, not surprisingly, exaggerated and misleading. The 'Socratic problem' concerns the attempt to extract the historical Socrates from these various literary representations. Socrates is reported to have been fairly ugly and most of the time unkempt. He spent his time wandering around the training grounds and the AGORA of Athens, discussing PHILOSOPHY with anyone prepared to engage with him. He fought for Athens in the PELOPONNESIAN WAR (431–404) at Poteidaia, Delion and Amphipolis. Plato's *Symposium* supplies brief vivid sketches of him on campaign at Poteidaia and in the Athenian retreat from Delion. In the aftermath of Athens' defeat in the Peloponnesian war, Socrates was brought up on charges of corrupting the young and believing in new GODS of his own creation. After a trial, recorded for us by Plato in the *Apology*, he was sentenced to death. He eschewed chances to escape his punishment, claiming that he had lived by Athens' laws his entire life and would not now desert them. He died by drinking hemlock.

Socrates did not belong to any philosophical school. From the outset he showed little interest in the material philosophy of the Ionian tradition, preferring instead to focus on ETHICAL philosophy and the requirements for excellent human conduct. In Plato's early dialogues, questions about human behaviour and correct conduct in search of excellence are paramount for Socrates. In his view the proper understanding of the excellences (virtues) such as courage, piety and justice is central to any kind of useful and meaningful dialogue, and therefore has important implications for our practical ethical behaviour. Knowledge of these excellences will make us excellent human beings, hence another of his sayings: 'KNOWLEDGE is virtue' (excellence). However, when Socrates asked acknowledged experts for this knowledge, i.e. for general objective definitions of the various excellences, they were not able to supply them. He therefore set off on a crusade against sham knowledge, which brought him into conflict with the established order at Athens. He compared himself to a gadfly, which stung the collective Athenian conscience. When Chairophon, a devoted friend of his, brought back from the DELPHIC ORACLE the message that Socrates was the wisest of all men, this was further corroboration for him that the admission of ignorance was the first step to wisdom. Socrates famously said that he was wise because he knew that he did not know. He claimed to be like a midwife who gave birth to knowledge but did not possess any himself, which is often referred to as Socratic irony. The historical Socrates, who wrote nothing himself, is probably best captured in the early dialogues of Plato. Here, in a process of question and answer, he is seen breaking down the viewpoint of his interlocutors (using the Socratic *elenchos*, 'test'), before going on to establish that they do not know what excellence is or whether or not it can be taught. The middle and late Platonic dialogues, where the character Socrates philosophizes on the basis of the theory of Forms, are the creation of Plato and go well beyond the philosophy of the historical Socrates. Where the historical Socrates finishes and Plato begins, however, is another aspect of the 'Socratic problem'.

Socrates had a widespread influence. He made a profound impression on Plato. His insistence on objective knowledge, which set him apart from the subjectivity of the SOPHISTS, helped shape Plato's metaphysical world of the Forms. Reshaped through Neoplatonism, this is turn strongly influenced the metaphysical aspect of CHRISTIAN philosophy. Socrates' way of life, his ambivalence towards material possessions and money, and his shabby appearance were linked in the ancient tradition to the beginnings of CYNICISM, of Hedonism and later of STOICISM, though it is generally accepted that this link involved a certain amount of distortion and artificiality. That said, the historical Socrates became for these schools the archetypal philosopher. As a result, he has had a profound effect on the development of western philosophy in general. KM

See Plato, *Early Socratic Dialogues*, ed., trs. T. J. Saunders (1987); Xenophon, *Conversations of Socrates*, trs. H. Tredennick and R. Waterfield (1990); Guthrie, W. K. C. (1971) *Socrates*; Vlastos, G. (1991) *Socrates*.

Sol Invictus The god of the 'Unconquered Sun', popular in the Roman empire during the 3rd century AD. Solar cults and deities were common in many of the cultures that surrounded the ancient MEDITERRANEAN. Although scholars debate whether the Romans had an indigenous sun god, the cult of Sol was active in Rome by the time of the second PUNIC WAR. Even so, the form Sol Invictus is heavily laden with eastern influences, especially in a form associated with the LEVANTINE deity Baal. The cult of Sol Invictus was introduced to Rome by the Syrian-born emperor ELAGABALUS (218–22) but declined after his violent death. Despite this false start, it remained popular in the empire because of its capacity for association with other gods, and in the form of Sol Invictus MITHRAS was worshipped widely by the troops. The military emperor AURELIAN (270–5) reintroduced the cult to the imperial capital, where he built a TEMPLE and established a PRIESTHOOD. After Aurelian's death, the cult remained popular, both with the emperors and their subjects. Even the youthful CONSTANTINE was an adherent of Sol Invictus, but after his conversion the cult suffered a sustained attack by CHRISTIANITY. Indeed, as part of the conflict, the date of the main annual festival of the cult, 25 December, was adopted by the CHURCH for the rival feast of Christ's birth. MDH

See Halsberghe, G. H. (1972) *The Cult of Sol Invictus*; Hutton, R. (1996) *The Stations of the Sun*.

soldiers In theory the Greeks employed a wide assortment of heavy infantry, skirmishers, archers, slingers, rowers, marines and CAVALRY. However, during the primacy of the early *polis* (700–500 BC), military utility often was pre-empted by political and cultural concerns. Thus amateur HOPLITE infantrymen were usually used restrictively in pitched battles to decide entire wars, the primacy of the agrarian citizen in the political life of the city-state being ratified on the battlefield. Both ARISTOCRATIC horsemen and poorer missile troops were ineffective against massed spearmen, once war was defined by an exclusive engagement of hoplites.

By the 5th century the advantages of sea-power, the decline in agrarian exclusivity, and the natural advantages of light-armed troops became unmistakable, and the Greek battlefield became the domain of a variety of forces. All this necessitated enormous expenditures and the introduction of property and income taxes. State pay was common for all Greek soldiers by the mid-5th century. Ethical restraint against the free use of capital, SCIENCE and MERCENARIES vanished, unleashing the full Greek genius for costly military experimentation. Hence, after PHILIP II and ALEXANDER the Great a Greek army was characteristically multifaceted: phalangites at its core, other infantry and cavalry on the wings, slingers and archers to the rear. The entire corps was now often supplied and transported by sea, and equipped with ARTILLERY and SIEGE engines. It was one of the great paradoxes of the hellenistic age that the Greek armies of the later SUCCESSOR kingdoms fell to Roman Republican militiamen, whose military service was inseparable from their political franchise. In that sense, the LEGIONS were more Hellenic than the Greek-speaking armies they defeated. VDH

See Hanson, V. D. (2000) *The Western Way of War*; Pritchett, W. K. (1971–91) *The Greek State at War*, vols. 1–5.

Solon Athenian political reformer and poet, early 6th century BC. Appointed archon and mediator in Athens (594) to deal with a looming political crisis, Solon introduced a package of reforms. Some of his POETRY explaining and justifying his activity is extant, though the precise nature of his reforms is debated.

Solon's changes opened up POLITICAL PARTICIPATION to non-aristocrats, offered greater legal protection to the lower classes and provided a level of economic stability to the poor. First he cancelled all outstanding debts and returned all land unencumbered to those who worked it, perhaps creating private ownership for the first time. He also made debt slavery illegal, guaranteeing the personal freedom of all Athenians. Next he abolished all of Draco's law-code except his homicide laws. Two legal innovations were most significant: first, the right to appeal against a MAGISTRATE's judicial decision before a popular lawcourt (*hêliaia*) composed of ordinary citizens; second, the creation of the public suit (*graphê*) which allowed a third party to prosecute on behalf of the disadvantaged. The former reform began the erosion of the magistrate's power; the latter created criminal offences that affected the entire community. Finally, by dividing the citizen population into four property classes, Solon reformed the political system. Now political participation was based on WEALTH and not birth: level of wealth determined level of participation. Those belonging to the top property class, 500-bushel men (*pentakosiomedimnoi*), could hold the highest offices. The next two classes, *hippeis* ('horse-men' = 300-bushel men) and *zeugitai* ('yoke-men' = 200-bushel men) could occupy more minor posts. Even the lowest class, the thetes (*thêtes*), had entitlements: they could attend the ASSEMBLY. Solon's reforms, which aimed at preventing TYRANNY, satisfied no one. The ARISTOCRATS resented the loss of their political monopoly; the poor, who were demanding complete redistribution of land, felt the reforms were insufficient. CC

See Aristotle, *Athenian Constitution*; Lattimore, R. (1960) *Greek Lyrics*; Foxhall, L. (1997) A view from the top: evaluating the Solonian property classes, in L. G. Mitchell and P. J. Rhodes, eds, *The Development of the Polis in Archaic Greece* 113–36.

songs and singing Choral and – more rarely – solo singing was a central part of life for the ancient Greeks and Romans, but we do not really know what their songs sounded like. The words of a few popular songs survive, such as the millers' song about Pittakos, tyrant of LESBOS. Songs were a feature of *SYMPOSIA* and Roman dinner-parties, and used to mark occasions such as weddings and ATHLETIC victories. Songs and HYMNS were used extensively in ritual contexts. Best-known examples include the Greek paean, a generic name for a choral song sung in battle, after victory, or in thanksgiving, and the songs of the Roman PRIESTHOODS of the ARVAL BRETHREN and the Salii. We should not forget that POETRY was often sung or chanted to musical accompaniment. This is best attested for the Greek world (e. g. the HOMERIC poems, LYRIC poetry, the CHORUSES of COMEDY and TRAGEDY), though there are some indications that Roman poetry was also sometimes chanted or spoken to music. Belief in the power of song (for good or evil) is widely attested in the Greco-Roman world, most famously in the myth of the Sirens. For the Roman upper classes, singing as or like a professional could occasion censure, and the early CHRISTIANS wondered about the moral propriety of singing, especially on the part of WOMEN. (see also SINGERS) ED

See Friedländer, L. (1908) Music, in *Roman Life and Manners under the Early Empire*, vol. 2; West, M. L. (1992) *Ancient Greek Music*.

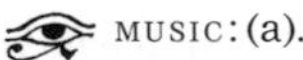 MUSIC: (a).

Sophists Travelling teachers of higher EDUCATION. The 5th century BC saw PHILOSOPHY gradually turning its attention away from the physical world, and the principle(s) which might explain it, to man himself. There was increased interest in the variety of human nature and human behaviour and it was in these circumstances that the Sophists arose. They came from many different places and travelled widely in the Greek world. Often referred to collectively, they were very much individual teachers who provided instruction on quite diverse topics. They should not be regarded as a school; they were not part of an organization nor did they avail themselves of any common philosophical doctrine. The general skill they offered to teach was that of getting on in life, and they went from city to city teaching their skills for a fee. As Athens became wealthier, it naturally became more attractive to such people. It was particularly desirable in a DEMOCRACY, such as at Athens, to be able to argue effectively in the ASSEMBLY. Consequently the most important skill taught by the Sophists was effective public speaking, RHETORIC.

Unfortunately, we have only fragments from the teachings of the Sophists. Their writings are, by and large, lost, and we are forced to recreate their views from the works of often hostile contemporaries, such as ARISTOPHANES, ARISTOTLE, XENOPHON and in particular PLATO. One Sophistic method of teaching was to make people argue both sides of a case (*dissoi logoi*, 'double words'). This led to the accusation that they did not care which side won, and that they could make the worse cause appear the better. The Sophists were accused of not knowing the difference between right and wrong, or, if they knew, not caring about it. In addition, they were viewed as relativist in their ETHICAL approach. They did not acknowledge objective absolute standards. This could be read into the famous statement of perhaps the best known of the Sophists, PROTAGORAS of Abdera, who said that 'Man is the measure of all things'. Plato was particularly critical of this stance. Their approach sought to deny the presence of objective unchanging standards, and in Plato's opinion this destroyed the possibility of real KNOWLEDGE. Protagoras' dictum could be interpreted as meaning that whatever an individual thinks is ethical is ethical as long as that individual continues to believe it.

In the Greek world which had fought the PERSIAN WARS (490, 480–479 BC) and was also to fight a massive interstate conflict (the PELOPONNESIAN WAR of 431–404), ethical issues were of paramount importance, especially to a city like Athens which had begun to create its own empire that verged on tyranny at times. Sophistic teaching was therefore a hot topic in Athens, and many embraced the sophists' teachings on subjectivity and the importance of nature over convention as justification for empire building. This tone is well captured by Plato in the 'might is right' attitude espoused by the sophists Thrasymachos in the *Republic* and Kallikles in the *Gorgias*. These characters are highly critical of a MORALITY that is dependent on a social contract, which, they suggest, is simply a matter of convention, put in place by the weaker to keep the stronger in check.

Not all Athenians embraced the teachings of the Sophists. Many conservative Athenians saw them as a corrupting force, damaging the state with their smart teachings, not caring what happened to it as they were mostly foreigners. The power of the *dissoi logoi* is ridiculed by the comic writer Aristophanes in his play *Clouds*. Behind the laughter, however, one detects a serious charge against the Sophists in terms of their ability to destroy the moral fabric of society. In addition the Sophists taught mainly the sons of the wealthy and were therefore regarded as supporters of OLIGARCHY and consequently undemocratic. It did not help them that Athens' chief rival SPARTA also embraced an oligarchic constitution.

The Sophists as a group have to some extent received a bad press, mainly because of the current state of our sources concerning their teachings. The sort of word play that we find in *Clouds* has given rise to the modern term sophistry as meaning something tricky and inherently hollow. This should be redressed. In general the Sophists were regarded with suspicion by the establishment as corrupters of the people. Some may have been, many were not. There were remarkable men among them: Protagoras, Hippias of Elis, Prodikos of Keos and GORGIAS of Leontinoi. They taught people to be critical and tolerant. They advanced ideas about the equality of rich and poor, man and woman, Greek and barbarian and about the unnaturalness of SLAVERY. Plato may have felt that Socrates' confusion with the Sophists was in part responsible for his death, but the reality is that they helped create a climate of opinion in Athens where ideas could be freely discussed and where someone like Socrates could be listened to. KM

See Kerferd, G. B. (1981) *The Sophistic Movement*; Romilly, J. de (1992) *The Great Sophists in Periclean Athens*, trs. J. Lloyd.

Sophokles c.495–406/5 BC Greek tragedian, the son of Sophilos, a wealthy manufacturer from the Athenian DEME of Kolonos. We are somewhat better informed about Sophokles' life than those of other 5th-century literary figures, in large part due to his participation in public affairs. He was elected to the board of state treasurers (*hellênotamiai*) in 443/2 and served as one of the ten Athenian GENERALS during the Samian war (probably 441/0). A second term as general, with NIKIAS, is less well attested. In 420/19 he served as Athens' official representative at the induction of the GOD ASKLEPIOS, by hosting the god (in the form of a sacred snake) until a proper shrine could be built. In 413 he was one of the ten commissioners (*probouloi*) appointed to oversee state affairs in the aftermath of the failed SICILIAN EXPEDITION. According to an anecdote in ARISTOTLE, he later claimed to have supported the establishment of the Four Hundred only *faute de mieux*. He also served as PRIEST of the HERO Halon. Upon his death, Sophokles himself was honoured as a hero, with the title Dexion ('the Greeter').

These facts suggest an individual of some wealth, influence and popularity, an impression that is confirmed by references to his friendship with PERIKLES and other literary and intellectual figures, including HERODOTOS. Tradition recalls Sophokles as an affable individual who was handsome and accomplished as a youth and, as an adult, given to the pleasures of MUSIC, WINE and young men. A fragment of the memoirs of his contemporary Ion of CHIOS (ATHENAEUS 13.603ff.) preserves an engaging picture of him in conversation. The ancient *Life* sums up his character with the comment that 'such was the charm of his personality that he was loved everywhere and by everyone'. This observation is supported by the evidence of Old COMEDY, where Sophokles during his lifetime was often accorded sympathetic treatment – a rare thing for any POET, but particularly one engaged in contemporary politics.

Sophokles' first production was in 468. He is said to have composed over 120 plays (approximately 30 tetralogies), to have been victorious on as many as 24 occasions and never to have fared worse than second place. Seven complete plays survive: *Ajax*, *Women of Trachis* (both early works), *Antigone* (c.442–441?), *Oedipus the King* (c.429–425?), *Electra* (c.420–410), *Philoktetes* (409), and *Oedipus at Kolonos* (produced posthumously in 401). We also have a substantial portion of the SATYR play *Trackers*, dealing with the theft of the CATTLE of APOLLO by the infant Hermes.

Sophokles is credited with having introduced a number of innovations in the tragic art, including the use of a third ACTOR, scene painting, and an increase in the size of the CHORUS from 12 to 15 members. He is also cited as the first playwright not to act in his own productions. Many of these claims are questionable, but reference to a prose treatise under his name entitled *On the Chorus* suggests an interest in the technical elements of his craft, an impression that is confirmed by the plays themselves.

The hallmark of Sophoklean TRAGEDY is the focus on a central tragic figure whose presence dominates the play, even when he/she is not on stage, and whose decisions drive the course of the action. Like the HOMERIC ACHILLES, Sophokles' heroes operate according to a rigid code of personal honour and, like Achilles, either bring about or augment their own suffering through their utter refusal to engage in practical compromise. While the unyielding idealism of these heroes arouses our admiration, they remain distant and not altogether sympathetic figures, particularly in their habit of dividing the world rigidly between friend and foe.

The larger vision that informs the plays is no less uncompromising. Sophokles' works consistently focus upon the physical and mental anguish of the hero: Ajax, who dies humiliated and betrayed by his fellow Greeks; the death agonies of HERAKLES; the despairing Antigone's lonely SUICIDE; the ruined OEDIPUS of *Oedipus the King*; Elektra, isolated and embittered; the wounded and abandoned Philoktetes; the blind and universally shunned protagonist of *Oedipus at Kolonos*. At the same time, however – and in stark contrast to EURIPIDES' practice – the plays affirm the presence of a divine order which oversees human affairs and offers assurance that the painful events being witnessed are not random or senseless. The world presented by Sophokles is, as a result, far from comforting. Like Homer's *Iliad*, these works acknowledge suffering as part of the fabric of human existence. Yet this suffering is accorded a fundamental dignity by its location within a divine scheme, however obscure or problematic that scheme might appear to the mortals on stage. In the words of Herakles' son Hyllos, at the conclusion of *Women of Trachis*, 'There is nothing here that is not ZEUS.'

Sophokles' plays are also marked by their dynamic plot construction. The mature works, in particular, present dramas of personal conflict, as the lesser characters attempt, without success, to alter or stymie the hero's resolution. Consistently, the action is driven by decisions that the characters take in the course of their interactions with others. This brings Sophokles' characters vividly to the fore and lends the plays an immediacy and realism unmatched in AESCHYLUS or even Euripides. In this, as in many other features of his works – their diction, the rhythms of the characters' speech, the use of RHETORIC, the imagery – Sophokles' genius is revealed in his ability to combine an elevated style appropriate to the genre with a naturalism and immediacy that draw the audience into the world of the play.

Sophokles' works also yield interesting insights into the development of Athenian tragedy. While the early *Ajax* and *Women of Trachis* display certain affinities with Aeschylean drama, *Philoktetes* and *Oedipus at Colonus* reflect an increasing interest in theatricality and a number of 'Euripidean' features. JP

See Ehrenberg, V. (1954) *Sophocles and Pericles*; Knox, B. M. W. (1964) *The Heroic Temper*; Segal, C. P. (1981) *Tragedy and Civilization*; (1993) *Oedipus Tyrannus*.

Soranus fl. c. AD 98–138 Noted medical author and practitioner, a leading representative of the Methodic sect of classical MEDICINE. Soranus followed the well-worn path for ambitious physicians in the Roman empire, from his native city in Asia Minor (Ephesos), to Alexandria – a great centre of medical learning – to Rome, the imperial capital itself, where he flourished in the reigns of Trajan and Hadrian. Little remains of his substantial and wide-ranging literary output. The *Gynaecology* is the best-preserved work, though fragments on fractures and bandaging (perhaps from a larger work *On Surgery*), and Caelius Aurelianus' later Latin rendering of his treatises on acute and chronic diseases, also survive along with a range of more attenuated remnants and references. In the *Gynaecology*, Soranus rejects previous approaches to the subject in favour of organizing his material around the person and purview of the midwife. He describes first what the midwife needs to be, then what she needs to know – about the female reproductive organs and their functions, about childbirth and the care of the newborn, and about the diseases of women as treated by regimen, drugs and surgery – in order to conform to his ideal. Despite the increasing dominance of Galenism in the later empire, it was Soranus' work, and its later Latin versions, that proved to be the most influential of its kind, in both East and West. REF

See Soranus, *Gynecology*, trs. O. Temkin (1956); Hanson, A. E. and Green, M. H. (1994) Soranus of Ephesus: methodicorum princeps, *ANRW* II.37.2: 968–1075.

Sosibios see Agathokles and Sosibios.

Souda see *Suda*.

soul, the In the Greek philosophical tradition, the soul (*psychê*) is best understood simply as a life force. In general, anything that lives is alive by virtue of its soul, whether it is a plant, ant, horse or human. In Homer the soul is described in terms of air or breath, and is depicted as existing after the death of the material body, continuing to carry something of the personality of the dead person. Among the Presocratics there is no uniform depiction of the soul. Socrates seems to have considered the soul synonymous with reason, but it is not clear that he thought of it as immortal. Plato, adapting and adopting Pythagorean and Orphic teachings, greatly developed the nature of the soul and emphasized its immortality. He regarded it as the most important part of the body–soul compound; it can survive the death of the material body and, if properly prepared, can avoid a process of reincarnation into another body. Plato's philosophy is centred on the purification of the soul in order to separate oneself permanently from the material body. In the dialogue *Phaedo*, the soul is regarded as a uniform entity and we are presented with arguments for its immortality as a whole. In the *Republic*, however, we come across an advanced psychology where we have a threefold division within the soul itself, into reason, spirit and the appetites, where only the part that is reason appears to be immortal. If spirit sides with reason and allows it to control the appetites, then the soul can permanently free itself from the tyranny of body. A famous myth from the *Republic* has Er, a soldier fallen in battle, journey with other disembodied souls and witness the transmigration of souls and their various reincarnations. Plato, however, never really deals satisfactorily with the problem of the immaterial soul operating on a material body. Aristotle, a scientist as much as a philosopher, grounds the soul on a biological framework and presents it as having powers or faculties. Aristotle tries to avoid Plato's problem of the immaterial acting on the material by describing the soul as the form of body, and emphasizing that soul and body are not two different substances but two different aspects of a single entity. In addition, Aristotle seems to make only a tenuous claim for the immortality of the highest part of the soul, which is reason, and only the active part of reason at that.

Epicureans and Stoics also saw reason as the dominant element in the soul but, as materialists, they had a different view of its nature. Epicurus considered that it was made up of very fine atoms of different kinds. As these atoms disperse on death, there is no possibility of an afterlife for the soul. Survival of the soul after death is also difficult for the Stoics, who thought of it as a mixture of fire and air that breaks up on the death of the body. They have no account of the soul outside the body, nor did such a thing concern them. KM

See Bremmer, J. (1983) *The Early Greek Concept of the Soul*.

sound and acoustics Sounds are not things, yet we perceive them. They have puzzling properties, especially since Greek always represents them metaphorically. What, in reality, constitutes a sound's 'sharpness', 'heaviness', 'brightness' or 'density'? The main achievements of Greek scientific acoustics were a working account of sound's physical nature and an analysis of one attribute, pitch, which allowed its variations to be expressed mathematically.

Archytas, Plato, Aristotle and others argued that sounds are movements transmitted through air from an impact. More vigorous agencies – shorter strings, for instance – generate speedier movements; swifter movements make higher pitches. Earlier Pythagoreans had shown that pitch and string-length are related in astonishingly neat mathematical ways: half the length sounds an octave above the whole, two-thirds a perfect fifth above, and so on. Interpreting these results, the scientists argued that a note one octave above another was a movement twice as swift; alternatively, the impacts generating it succeeded one another twice as rapidly. Such accounts remained the norm, underpinning mathematical analyses of pitch-relations in musical systems, though dissident voices, notably Theophrastos, attacked the whole programme of quantification. Their qualitative theories seem strange, but reflected more faithfully the metaphors embedded in the language.

Academics and Peripatetics speculated inconclusively about the physiology and psychology of hearing, and offered rudimentary explanations of differences in timbre and volume. But experimental technique hampered progress (though Ptolemy gives meticulous descriptions of 'laboratory' instruments); and acoustics never attained the sophistication of the major Greek sciences. AB

See Barker, A. (1989) *Greek Musical Writings*.

Sounion see Attica; forts and fortresses, Greek; Laurion.

space How a society defines space reveals a great deal about the society. Thanks to recent research, we can now see a detailed picture of the conceptualization and use of space in the ancient world, at different scales: imperial and colonial LANDSCAPES, urban and rural territories, and public and private spaces. Nevertheless, key issues remain unresolved.

Concepts of GEOGRAPHICAL space and MEASUREMENT mirrored opportunities to alter space. Geography and COSMOLOGY evolved in tandem with early Greek EXPLORATION and COLONIZATION, developed further in the SELEUKID and PTOLEMAIC kingdoms, and culminated in a Roman world-view enshrined in the compendious geographical and historical handbooks of the early principate (e.g. STRABO, DIODORUS SICULUS, LIVY, PLINY THE ELDER). Each new hegemonic power would intervene in urban and rural environments to make its power visible and reward its friends. Early Greek grid-planned colonies, for example, over-wrote the physical and mental landscapes of indigenous populations. Foundations of cities by ALEXANDER and the Seleukids 'exported' the *POLIS* but also laid it on top of older landscapes. Claims about the adaptability of the *polis*, and the 'fusion' of Greek and non-Greek urban form (as at AI KHANUM), must be weighed against the fact of conquest. The spread of Roman power in Italy, then further afield, gave opportunities for creating new landscapes using veteran colonies, centuriation and redistribution – even in Old Greece (e.g. around Dyme and Corinth).

In a more local setting, the town–country relationship has been variously characterized. For some observers the CONSUMER CITY model, in which the interests of town and country are opposed, explains much. For others, a two-way model of economic flows seems preferable. From an ecological point of view, we could even dissolve the town–country boundary altogether. Archaeological FIELD SURVEY highlights the inter-dependency of town and country, raising the questions of where boundaries really lie and whether urban expansion is necessarily good or bad for town or country. Some cities draw in population, perhaps leading to the blurring of existing mental maps of rural space. In hellenistic Greece, for example, some rural cults were neglected. Roman rule brought a revival of rural cults, even as urban populations expanded. If this reflected a shift in cultural power to the owners of expanding estates, was it too high a price to pay for *pax Romana*?

Movement through both countryside and town could be controlled by modifying space. The newly identified network of built ROADS in southern Greece may reflect either Spartan power or the aspirations of several *poleis*. Rome's power over Italy and its provinces was expressed by building highways. Greek towns regulated the uses of public space, but did not have separate 'civic spaces' to which only citizens were admitted. In hellenistic centres, control over *polis* space was partially surrendered to outside powers, as Macedonian rulers reshaped the centres of cities outside their domains, by offering to build spectacular amenities and monuments that even the Athenians could not refuse. The similarity between the Roman military camp and the Roman town encapsulates the notion of romanization through the reworking of space.

Public and private spaces, in houses and towns, have been active areas of research. Traditionally, studies of ARCHITECTURAL space have focused on the identification of room function, materials and techniques employed in construction, and the nature of interior décor. For example, in POMPEII scholars have attempted to assign labels to rooms in both public and private buildings using Vitruvius as a guide; his typology has even been taken as applying to Greek HOUSE layouts from earlier centuries. In ROME, archaeologists have devoted much time to the detailed analysis of construction techniques used in public architecture, through empirical study and the analysis of literary sources. For Greece, the modest exterior and interior decoration of town houses down to the 5th century (e.g. around the ATHENIAN AGORA) contrasts with the start of élite ostentation in the 4th, leading to the grand peristyle houses of hellenistic towns such as DELOS. A change in civic values, according to which the rich were not supposed to flaunt their wealth, has been posited. Until recently the interpretation of room functions in Greek houses was simplistic; but whereas archaeologists used to map the archetypal functions of an *andrôn* (men's space) onto the main dining room, it is now acknowledged that rooms have multiple uses. Even *andrônes* may mean different things depending on the *polis* and the social context.

Similarly in the case of Roman HOUSES, particularly in Pompeii, HERCULANEUM and OSTIA, it has been demonstrated that the assignment of room function is in many cases a fruitless exercise, given the complexity of domestic life. More critical readings of literary sources, and detailed examination of interior décor and material culture, reveal that domestic space was inherently flexible, allowing the master (*dominus*) or mistress (*domina*) to carry out a wide range of public and private activities. Houses were designed to accommodate the full spectrum of social responsibilities including the reception of clients, the housing of slaves and the entertainment of social equals. In many cases a room may have been used for several purposes depending on what was required at a given time. Interior décor, including furniture, was used to create a particular ambience and encourage preferred patterns of movement.

It is obviously difficult to apply such detailed techniques of analysis to those regions of the empire where the survival of buildings is far less substantial. For example, in BRITAIN archaeologists only have a basic ground plan, occasionally some MOSAICS or fragments of WALL-PAINTING, and possibly some associated material culture if the excavation has been carried out in recent years. In spite of these problems much headway has been made in broadening our understanding of architectural space in Britain. Public buildings are now understood as part of the urban landscape, rather than as individual structures. Similarly, Romano-British VILLAS have been examined in relation to the broader social context in which they were constructed and used, and interior décor is seen as central to the definition of social status and the use of space.

While most studies have focused on the public and private structures of the Republic and early empire, more recently the architectural developments of late antiquity have received more attention. Audience chambers and other imperial forms were adopted in domestic contexts, and space was used to frame the formal, highly structured social events that were important features of social life. Studies of late Roman houses in France and North Africa clearly demonstrate the importance of architectural design to social life, and many developments foreshadow the appearance of Christian forms of architecture in the early medieval period.

At all scales – domestic, urban, and regional – an understanding of space in the ancient world depends crucially on the integration of written and archaeological evidence. (see also LAND SURVEYING; TOWN PLANNING) SAS, DGJS

See Hansen, M. H. (1997) Public space or civic space? in *The Polis as an Urban Centre and as a Political Community* 12–17; Horden, P. and Purcell, N. (2000) *The Corrupting Sea: a study of Mediterranean history*; Jameson, M. H. (1990) Private space and the Greek city, in O. Murray and S. Price, eds., *The Greek City* 171–95; Laurence, R. and Wallace-Hadrill, A., eds. (1997) *Domestic Space in the Roman World*; Nicolet, C. (1991) *Space, Geography, and Politics in the Early Roman Empire*; Scott, S. (2000) *Art and Society in Fourth-century Britain: villa mosaics in context*; Talbert, R. J. A. and Brodersen, K., eds. (2004) *Space in the Roman World*; Westgate, R. C. (2000) Space and decoration in hellenistic houses, *ABSA* 95: 391–426.

Spain see HISPANIA.

Sparta The second best-known Greek CITY-STATE, located in the south-east PELOPONNESE, Sparta exemplifies the principle that it is wrong to generalize from Athens (the state we know most about) to other communities. Not only was Sparta a very different society, but it produced almost no writers (except for noted poets like ALKMAN and TYRTAIOS), so that nearly all the literary evidence comes from elsewhere. Sparta was held up by both admirers and detractors (in ancient times and often since) as an exemplar of particular political and philosophical principles; but its culture of SECRECY meant that facts were hard to come by. Much of our evidence is late, above all from PLUTARCH; but he refracts his sources through a lens characteristic of his own class, time and place – just as other writers (from latest to earliest Polybios, Xenophon, Thucydides and Herodotos) each had their own take upon the evidence available to them.

Unusually among leading Greek states, Sparta lay some 35 km (22 miles) from the sea, in the upper Eurotas valley. It was the chief town of the region we call LACONIA. Sparta was also called Lakedaimon, the name of the valley, Homer's 'hollow Lakedaimon'. Until it lost power and territory between 369 and 195 BC, Sparta ruled both Laconia and MESSENIA. The male Spartans (*Spartiatai*, anglicized as 'Spartiates') were citizens of the central town. The free inhabitants of the smaller towns of Laconia and Messenia were *perioikoi*, 'circumhabitants', with no formal say in Spartan decision-making. Spartans and *perioikoi* together made up the Lakedaimonians (or Lacedaemonians). Most literary sources (such as Thucydides), and all formal documents such as treaties, use 'Lakedaimonians', which translators nearly always, but misleadingly, render as 'Spartans'; often the *perioikoi* are also meant.

The economy was dependent, to a degree unique in Greece, upon the coercive extraction of agricultural surpluses from a semi-free population, the HELOTS. From this source the Spartans drew their monthly contributions in kind to their army messes or dining-clubs (*syssitia*), membership of which was a condition of citizenship. Our sources claim that helot farms were assigned as *klêroi* (plots) to individual Spartiates. This, like many elements of the Spartan way of life, was thought to derive from the reforms of LYKOURGOS. In reality, much that was attributed to this perhaps legendary man was a relatively recent enactment or wholly fictitious. Interminable debate surrounds the sources' assertion that Spartans held equal *klêroi* from the state (possibly called 'the ancient portion', though that may denote the helot tribute); the claim may have been invented for political reasons in the hellenistic period. Recent analysis suggests that the traditional picture of Sparta as austere and egalitarian is essentially false. It is clear, as early as Herodotos, that there were rich and poor Spartans.

Sparta was unique in having a dual KINGSHIP, whose origins are obscure. Heirs to the throne did not undergo the severe 'upbringing' (*agôgê*) imposed

SPARTA: (a) the acropolis of ancient Sparta. The walls visible are those of a Byzantine church.

SPARTA: (b) sanctuary of Artemis Ortheia.

SPARTA: (c) the Spartan kings from mid-6th century BC.

Agiads	Eurypontids
c.560 Anaxandridas	
	c.550 Ariston
c.520 Kleomenes I (s.) (1st s. of Anaxandridas by wife #2; not displaced by Dorieus, 1st s. of wife #1, born after K.; plots Damaratos' deposition, later goes mad and kills himself)	
	c.515 Damaratos (deposed, goes to Persia) 491 Leotychidas II (cousin; great-g-s of Hippokratidas) (wins battle of Mykale but goes into exile c.477 to avoid trial, remains king in name)
490 Leonidas I (half-bro.) (not much younger than Kleomenes; d. Thermopylai)	
480 Pleistarchos (s.) (father's bro. Kleombrotos prob. regent but d. 480; then Kleombr.'s s. Pausanias #1, victor of Plataia, regent till 460s when tried, starves)	
	469 Archidamos II (g-s) [c.16, *OPW* 142 n.] (d. natural causes)
459 Pleistoanax (s. of Pausanias #1) (initially father's bro. Nikomedes is regent; P. exiled 445–427/6 for withdrawal from Attica; P.'s s. Pausanias #2 then regent)	
	427 Agis II (s.) (d. natural causes)
409 Pausanias #2 (s.) [c.37, *OPW* 143] (tried for withdrawal from Haliartos; flees to Tegea 395)	
	400 Agesilaos II (bro.) [44] (Lysander fixes succession; d. old age)
395 Agesipolis I (s.) [little more than a boy, Plut. *Lys.* 20] (d. besieging Olynthos)	
380 Kleombrotos I (bro.) (d. at Leuktra)	
371 Agesipolis II (s.) (d. without heir)	
370 Kleomenes II (bro.) (little known)	
	360 Archidamos III (s.) [c.40] (d. fighting in Italy)
	338 Agis III (s.) (d. fighting Macedonians)
	330 Eudamidas I (bro.) (little known)
309 Areus I (g-s) (d. fighting Macedonians at Corinth) [calls parents 'king Akrotatos (#1) and queen Chilonis', *Syll.*^{3} 430]	

SPARTA: (c) the Spartan kings from mid-6th century BC (cont.)

Agiads	Eurypontids
	c.305 Archidamos IV (s.) (little known; d. fighting Demetrios I at Mantineia) c.275 Eudamidas II (s.) (little known)
265 Akrotatos #2 (s.) (d. fighting Macedonians at Megalopolis)	
262 Areus II (s.) (infant; gt-uncle Leonidas is regent)	
254–c.243, c.241–c.235 Leonidas II (s. of Kleonymos and g-s of Kleomenes II) [c.62; regent since 262]	
	c.244 Agis IV (s.) (executed)
242 Kleombrotos II (s.-in-law) (rules briefly when Leonidas is exiled, then he in turn goes into exile)	
	241 Eudamidas III (s.) [infant, dies young, doubtfully poisoned]
c.235–222 Kleomenes III (s. of Leonidas) [c.25] (goes into exile in Egypt 222, d. in coup attempt there)	
	c.228 Archidamos V (uncle) (recalled by Kleomenes but murdered by K.'s enemies – or on his orders)
	227–222 Eukleidas (AGIAD; bro. Kleomenes III) (d. at Sellasia)
219–215 Agesipolis III (g-s Kleombrotos II) Then sole rulers Lykourgos, early 210s; Machanidas, c.212–207; Nabis, 207–192	

Adapted from *Oxford Classical Dictionary*, 3rd edn; more details from *Kleine Pauly* encyclopedia; *OPW* = G. E. M. de Ste. Croix (1972) *The Origins of the Peloponnesian War*; *Syll.* = W. Dittenberger, ed. (1915–24) *Sylloge inscriptionum graecarum*, 3rd edn.
The first item in parentheses denotes relationship to previous ruler.
Key: bro. = brother; g-s = grandson; s. = son; d. = died; # = no. Age at accession in brackets, where known.

upon other boys, though their main function was to lead the army. Their power was limited by the COUNCIL (*gerousia*) of 28 elders, the citizen assembly, and five EPHORS (*ephoroi*, 'overseers') elected annually. This still left room for initiative, and a charismatic and long-lived ruler such as AGESILAOS could impose his vision of Spartan policy by manipulating political alliances. Networks of friendship and patronage were woven into the fabric of life. Each mess was a dining-club with about 15 members, elected for life. New members were identified through homoerotic friendship between a young candidate and a man about ten years older; since he would himself have been selected in this way, each mess was built on cross-generational solidarity and unshakeable loyalties. The strength of male fellow-feeling may have reflected, or promoted, problematic relationships with WOMEN. This may be illustrated by Sparta's peculiar MARRIAGE rites – the bride shaven-headed (to resemble a boy?), the groom capturing her (as if on a hunt?) – and by the requirement that the man sleep with his companions, rarely (it is claimed) seeing his wife in daylight. There must be an element of exaggeration in these stereotypes, but it is true that Spartan women, unlike Athenian, led a partly public life: they took exercise, inherited LAND and property, and sometimes (notably in the hellenistic period) wielded considerable political influence. The notorious Spartan 'oliganthropy' (shortage of population), however, has a social rather than biological origin, the result not of in-breeding but of demoting from citizenship men who could not pay their dues.

The Spartans' origins and the so-called Dorian invasion are obscure, as is the process by which Laconia was unified. Conquest of Messenia was followed by setbacks and a more egalitarian style of empire, the so-called PELOPONNESIAN LEAGUE (really 'the Lakedaimonians and their allies', supported by individual treaties between the Lakedaimonians and other states). Joint leadership of Greece in the Persian wars sealed Sparta's reputation as a formidable land power. Victory over Athens in the 'Peloponnesian' war, however, exposed the contradictions in society and the difficulty for such a conservative state in attempting to be a naval empire. Defeat by the Thebans at LEUKTRA (371) led to invasion by EPAMEINONDAS, the partial liberation of Messenia, and the foundations of Messene and Megalopolis as fortresses to hem Sparta in. PHILIP II of Macedonia removed more territory. Under AREUS I (309–265), who adopted the trappings of hellenistic monarchy and minted Sparta's first coins, the city interacted more with the outside world. In the mid-3rd century, AGIS IV and KLEOMENES III attempted to revive Spartan power in the Peloponnese, based on internal reforms and an appeal to an imagined past of egalitarianism and austerity. Kleomenes was defeated by an Achaian–Macedonian alliance. After a brief resurgence under NABIS, the Romans under FLAMININUS liberated the *perioikoi* c.195 BC, and Sparta became a modest provincial town. The open-textured settlement noted by Thucydides was unified in the hellenistic period, perhaps by migration from the countryside. The town was embellished with fine buildings, particularly under the Romans. It became a place of cultural pilgrimage for Greek and Roman élites, accelerating the idealization of its image. The archaeology of the town, its cult places, and its countryside is increasingly well understood and gives a more rounded picture than the often tendentious and controversial written sources. The greatest progress, however, has been in the reassessing the sources and acknowledging the power of stereotypes.

Sparta, though conformist, was never the homogeneous society portrayed by the stereotypes. To pretend otherwise does an injustice to the Spartans, who were not the only Greeks who lived off dependants. They lived in a political society, with all the internal conflict that implies. (see also LABOUR; MESSENIAN WARS) DGJS

See Herodotos; Pausanias, book 3; Plutarch, *Lykourgos, Agesilaos, Lysander, Agis–Kleomenes*; Polybios; Thucydides; Xenophon (including *Constitution of the Lakedaimonians* attributed to him); Cartledge, P. A. (2002) *Sparta and Lakonia*; Cartledge, P. A. and Spawforth, A. (2002) *Hellenistic and Roman Sparta*; Forrest, W. G. (1995) *A History of Sparta*; Hodkinson, S. (2000) *Property and Wealth in Classical Sparta*; Lazenby, J. F. (1985) *The Spartan Army*; Pomeroy, S. B. (2002) *Spartan Women*; Rawson, E. (1969) *The Spartan Tradition in European Thought*; Talbert, R. J. A. (2000) *Plutarch on Sparta*; Whitby, M., ed. (2002) *Sparta*.

 PELOPONNESE.

Spartacus A THRACIAN and, according to APPIAN, a VETERAN of the Roman army, who had been sold as a GLADIATOR. In 73 BC Spartacus and some comrades rebelled and fled from the gladiator school in CAPRI to Mt Vesuvius, gathering men as they went. Small Roman forces were sent to subjugate the uprising, but were defeated. Spartacus' 'army', continually growing in number, is estimated at between 70,000 and 120,000 men. Facing two LEGIONS of Roman forces, Spartacus and his second-in-command, Crixus, apparently divided forces. Crixus was defeated and killed by one legion. However, Spartacus smashed both legions, and in a battle at Picenum he was triumphant once more. The Romans sent out six more legions under Licinius CRASSUS, who in a series of smaller clashes trounced the SLAVE army at every turn. Spartacus seems to have attempted to turn the war into more of a guerrilla fight, but Crassus kept him closed in. When Spartacus tried to make it to the sea and SICILY with his slave army, Crassus threw him back again. Closed in, Spartacus finally engaged Crassus head-on, and was defeated and killed, though his body was not afterwards discovered.

Spartacus was adopted as an official folk-hero by the Soviet regimes of the 20th century. The 1960 American film *Spartacus* created a fictionalized account of the rebellion, successfully capturing the inhumanity of slavery, the brutality of the arena and the oppression of the Roman regime. It presents the most important slave revolt in Roman history as a personal freedom-fight against oppression. LL-J

See Shaw, B. D. (2001) *Spartacus and the Slave Wars*.

Sperlonga The emperor TIBERIUS built a VILLA by the sea between Rome and Naples, next to which were a series of caves (*speluncae*, hence the modern place-name). Little of Tiberius' building remains, but the caves yielded up thousands of MARBLE SCULPTURE fragments during the excavations that began in 1957. These pieces have been reassembled to show the dazzling complex made for the emperor between about AD 4 and 26.

The cave opened behind a large pool; two smaller caves extended the space at the rear, and all contained sculptural groups connected to the story of ODYSSEUS' wanderings. Groups of statues include a warrior supporting the limp body of a wounded youth (the 'Pasquino group') and the theft of the Palladium (a wooden image of Athena) by Odysseus and Diomedes. In the centre of the circular pool was the dramatic tableau of Odysseus' ship before Scylla, and in the small cave at the rear the space was nearly filled by a giant reclining Polyphemos whose one eye was about to be blinded by Odysseus and his men. The theatricality of the complex, light and shadow playing on sculpture and moving water alike, must have been astounding. And as if to make a distant view as spectacular as a near one, the cave itself was surmounted by a huge polychrome statue of Ganymede being abducted by ZEUS as the Eagle.

Numerous questions remain about Sperlonga, one of the most interesting being the artists' names inscribed on the sculpture. Hagesandros, Athanadoros and Polydoros, all of RHODES, who made the famous hellenistic Laokoön sculpture group, are named on the Scylla group's ship. It may be, then, that the Sperlonga sculpture was copied from hellenistic originals. NBK

See Andreae, B. and Conticello, B. (1974) *Die Skulpturen von Sperlonga*; Stewart, A. F. (1990) *Greek Sculpture*.

spices Botanical materials used like today as condiments, but also for COSMETIC (especially PERFUMES), medicinal (e.g. antidotes, DRUGS, charms) and ritual (religious, funerary, official) purposes. Associated with commodities of special value, many of which were imported from the east (from cinnamon and nutmeg to pepper, frankincense and myrrh), European varieties such as basil and dill were also considered spices.

Most of our knowledge of spices during the classical period comes from documents: plays, historical, geographical and medical texts, and cookbooks all contribute. HIPPOKRATES is the first classical author to mention pepper, c.400 BC. In the hellenistic world it was used mostly for medicinal purposes. Only from the imperial period was the culinary use of spices widespread. Many of the spices traded in the classical world had an ancient tradition: in Egypt myrrh was known even before Queen Hatshepsut set sail to Punt (probably modern Eritrea or Somalia) for it in the 15th century BC. The best quality myrrh came from northern Somalia, the Yemeni mountains and east to Dohar.

Due to the indirect nature of much of the trade, knowledge of spices and their sources was often confused. Cinnamon and cassia (a qualitative difference in antiquity) were erroneously attributed to south ARABIA or east Africa for this reason, when in Roman times they actually came from south-east Asia and southern CHINA. The writer of the *Periplus maris Erythraei*, however, realized that *malabathron* (cinnamon-leaf) ultimately derived from China. Its earliest ARCHAEOLOGICAL occurrence is in the 7th century BC at the sanctuary of HERA on SAMOS.

Archaeological finds of spices are geographically limited and depend on suitable conditions for preservation. A unique find comes from Berenike on the Red sea coast of Egypt, where 7.55 kg of pepper has been excavated in a 1st-century AD context. Found in the large Indian jar in which it travelled, it is the black pepper of southern India rather than the long pepper of the north which, according to PLINY, was more than three times as expensive. The quantity of pepper at Berenike suggests that it was fairly common. Although recorded throughout the eastern desert of Egypt, elsewhere pepper is rarely preserved, found only at the German sites of Oberaden (8 peppercorns) and Straubing (52).

Indirect archaeological evidence for pepper and other spices comes from the *Horrea piperataria* on the Sacra Via in Rome, established by DOMITIAN and used for storing, and possibly selling, oriental spices and pepper. Pepper-pots (*peperatoria*), such as the silver ones buried with other treasure at Hoxne in Suffolk (eastern England) at the turn of the 4th century AD, attest to its continuing export. Its continuing value is demonstrated by ALARIC, who at the siege of Rome demanded c.35,000 pounds of GOLD and SILVER and 3,000 pounds of pepper. RST

See Cappers, R.T.J. (1999) Archaeobotanical evidence of Roman trade with India, in H.P. Ray, ed., *Archaeology of Seafaring* 51–69; Dalby, A. (2000) *Dangerous Tastes*; Miller, J.I. (1969) *The Spice Trade of the Roman Empire*.

spies and spying The most common Greek word for a spy was *kataskopos*; its Latin equivalent was *speculator*. Ancient military and political leaders regularly made use of irregular forces or individuals operating covertly to obtain information. They might be current or former soldiers, enemy deserters, or independent operatives with no specific military status, including SLAVES and WOMEN. Spies might disguise themselves as soldiers, camp followers, civilian refugees or even slaves. Their preferred hunting grounds included MARKETS and taverns frequented by military personnel. If discovered their likely fate was execution, unless they could be induced to betray their former employers. Exceptionally, the Greek spies who were captured while gathering information on PERSIAN preparations for the invasion of Greece in the 480s BC were given a full tour and then released on the orders of XERXES, to go home and impress upon their superiors the overwhelming might of his forces. Spies were regularly deployed in frontier zones. Hostile relations between the Roman and Persian empires from the late 3rd to the early 7th century AD encouraged both sides to use undercover operatives to obtain military and political information. Suspicion and caution might cause a spy's information to be treated as untrustworthy without independent corroboration, but there is no evidence of any moral objection to using it. Contrasting attitudes to spies are seen in the case of the Trojan Dolon, captured and killed by ODYSSEUS and Diomedes, who are themselves on a spying mission (Homer, *Iliad* 10.248–464). PDeS

See Austin, N.J.E. and Rankov, N.B. (1995) *Exploratio: military and political intelligence in the Roman world from the second Punic war to the battle of Adrianople*; Richmond, J. (1998) Spies in ancient Greece, *G&R* 45: 1–18.

Spina An ETRUSCAN port at the southern branch of the river Po. Now inland because of subsequent silting of the delta, its precise location was unknown until aerial photography revealed it in 1956, though two associated necropoleis were discovered in 1922 and 1954 during drainage works. Sources ascribe the foundation near the end of the 6th century BC variously to Greeks or ETRUSCANS, but both groups were present from an early stage at a port that opened up new markets for Greek POTTERY. Large quantities of Attic and other Greek vases have been found at Spina and its associated cemeteries. The presence of similar goods at Felsina (Bologna) and elsewhere in the region indicates that Spina was a hub of Greek trade with northern Italy, as well as a consumer. Other products, including metalwork from Magna Graecia and northern Etruscan bronzes, reveal the extent of Spina's trading network in Italy and the ADRIATIC.

Because of marshes, Spina was largely built on piles and wooden platforms, with a rectangular grid of canals providing the main thoroughfares of a town that occupied more than 300 ha (740 acres). A wide canal to the Adriatic sea served as HARBOUR, in a manner reminiscent of a wide central street at MARZABOTTO. To protect trade, Spina became a naval power in the Adriatic. The city maintained good relations with its Greek partners by establishing a treasury at DELPHI. JV

See Haynes, S. (2000) *Etruscan Civilization*; Scullard, H.H. (1967) *The Etruscan Cities and Rome*.

 ITALY, ROMAN: (b).

spinning The process of twisting animal or vegetable fibres so that they form a relatively unbreakable thread. Although this can be done with the fingers alone, thread spun using a counterweight (spindle whorl) is stronger, and can more easily be spun to a consistent thickness. In classical antiquity, the spinning-wheel was unknown and all spinning was done

SPINNING: depictions from Greek vase-paintings of women spinning.

using a drop spindle. This consists of a stick with a notch or hook in the top and a spindle whorl stuck on the bottom. A short length of thread or yarn is attached to the stick and wrapped around the hook or notch. The wool to be spun is held in the secondary (i.e. normally left) hand, usually on a distaff tucked under the arm. A length of wool of about 40 cm (16 inches) is roughly teased out into a long, thin roll and held tightly with the left thumb and first finger close to the spindle. The spindle is twirled hard and allowed to swing freely; the spinner then runs her left thumb and finger up the roll of wool. The force of the whirling spindle twists the roll of wool into a new thread attached to the existing thread. The spinner then winds the new thread around the spindle, and begins the process again. The advantage of a drop spindle is that the spinner can work while walking around, looking after children or animals. It is also quick and easy to pick up and put down. Clay spindle whorls readily drop off spindles, which is perhaps why archaeologists regularly find them in odd places. LF

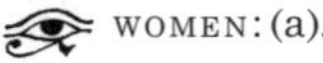 WOMEN: (a).

Split see DIOCLETIAN; PALACES.

sport The English word 'sport' covers a vast range of physical activity, from personal training regimes for promoting good health to children's games, and further to professional team sports such as cricket and football (both sorts), athletics, and other vehicles for mass entertainment. The rise of professional women's leagues, such as the WUSA or WNBA in the United States, has underscored the further role of professional athletics as a vehicle for the promotion of social equity, as did the breaking of the colour barrier by black athletes in the United States during the 1950s and, in the 1990s, in South Africa. At the same time, international events such as the football World Cup and the Olympics have enhanced the role of professional, or pseudo-amateur, sport on the stage of international politics.

The state of sport at the opening of the third millennium AD offers some parallels to classical antiquity, especially in its imperial Roman phase. Both Greek and Latin could distinguish between physical exercise for personal improvement – *sômaskia* in Greek, *exercitatio* in Latin – and exercise for competitive purposes, for which the primary words in Greek were formed from *agôn* ('contest') or *athlon* ('prize'); Latin terminology here consisted largely of loan words from Greek. Both languages, however, also grouped both sorts of activity together with formulations based on the verb *gymnazô* 'to train naked' in Greek or *ludo* 'play' in Latin.

The problem of definition in antiquity derived from the connection between physical training and warfare. Citizens who were expected to play a role in the defence of their state were expected to keep themselves in shape, and there was an implicit connection between the discipline required for proper physical training and proper membership in a civic community. It is of considerable interest that, as in the modern word before the late 20th century, little provision was made for women to participate in any form of training on a par with men. Only classical SPARTA required girls to exercise, and games involving women, usually footraces, were rarities. This is a reflection of the fact that women were seen as playing a role in society that was distinct from that of men.

Competitive sports were primarily seen as a way for men to demonstrate their personal prowess, with the result that team sports were very rare. In our earliest accounts of ATHLETICS, offered in the HOMERIC poems, skill in the games was seen as a complement to martial excellence and a class marker (only ARISTOCRATS could be good athletes). With the rise of international festivals in the Greek world, there was some democratization of athletic glory, as it reflected upon an entire city, creating space for men of less than aristocratic lineage to gain status. In the hellenistic and Roman periods, cities competed to host games that would reflect upon their standing by attracting famous athletes, and athletes themselves obtained ever greater standing in society. Competition for civic standing through the hosting of games can be seen as a substitute for war. The opportunity to rise to a position of wealth and social standing (including significant exemptions from civic duties and taxes) led to an extremely high degree of professionalism and the formation of international athletic synods. These associations were recognized by the Roman imperial government as playing an important role in the organization of festivals. DSP

stadium see ATHLETES AND ATHLETICS; OLYMPIA.

state, the The State (capital S), in the modern sense of a semi-autonomous entity composed of the government, civil service, judiciary and police, was not a strongly marked feature of classical civilization in its original forms. Sparta, up to a point, is the only real exception to the rule that the State did not exist in full force before the hellenistic monarchies in Greek history, and before the establishment of the PRINCIPATE by AUGUSTUS (partly on hellenistic lines) in Roman history. The Greek *polis* and the Roman *res publica* were both, rather, citizen-states. That is, both in their ideology and in their practice they stressed the primacy of personal and direct participation in political decision-making and the overriding value of communal political life. The vital characteristic of citizen politics, according to ARISTOTLE, their greatest analyst, was that citizens both ruled and were ruled, turn and turn about. In circumstances such as these, the State was unlikely to arise, or at any rate to experience a significantly great development. (see also CITY-STATE; *POLIS*; POLITICAL SYSTEMS, POLITICAL THEORY) PAC

See Aristotle, *Politics*.

Statius (Publius Papinius Statius) C.AD 50–96 Latin poet from Naples. At Rome he was associated with the court of DOMITIAN, the last of the Flavian EMPERORS. For Domitian and for a range of private patrons, Statius composed honorific poems that he subsequently published in four books of *Silvae*. A fifth book, published posthumously, includes a famous address to Sleep (5.4) that is short, introspective in tone, and utterly unlike the rest of the *Silvae*. The longer virtuoso pieces, born of a tradition of extemporization, convey a vivid impression of Flavian society. In a prose preface to each of the first four books, Statius justifies himself for publishing these extempore compositions alongside the serious endeavour of EPIC, represented by the 12 books of his *Thebaid*, on the Greek myth of the 'seven against Thebes'. This poem is widely regarded as the most brilliant representative of post-VIRGILIAN EPIC poetry, stamped by learning, imagination and powerful use of language. Statius subsequently completed just one book of the *Achilleid*, on the life of ACHILLES, a poem characterized by sophisticated erudition and irreverent, Ovidian wit. Whereas his epics were popular in the Middle Ages (the *Thebaid* was beloved of Dante and Boccaccio, the *Achilleid* of Chaucer), the *Silvae* only just survived into the RENAISSANCE, preserved in a single manuscript. KMC

See Statius, *Silvae, Thebaid, Achilleid*, trs. D.R. Shackleton Bailey, 3 vols., 2003; *Thebaid*, trs. A.D. Melville (1992); Hardie, A. (1983) *Statius and the Silvae*; Hardie, P.R. (1993) *The Epic Successors of Virgil.*

status see CITIZENSHIP; ÉLITES; SOCIETY.

Stesichoros see LYRIC POETRY, GREEK; POETRY, GREEK.

Stilicho AD 394–408 Roman general, the dominant *magister militum* in the West between 394 and 408. Flavius Stilicho had a court and military upbringing, as his father was an officer in a CAVALRY regiment. From 395 he employed the Latin POET CLAUDIAN, whose works provide much evidence for the period. Stilicho's early career is unknown, but in 383 the EMPEROR THEODOSIUS I sent him on a diplomatic mission to PERSIA. On his return, he married Serena, Theodosius' niece. This led to rapid promotion, and (with Timasius) he commanded Theodosius' 394 expedition against Eugenius. On Theodosius' death he was accepted as GUARDIAN of Honorius and quickly dominated the Western empire, but was vigorously opposed by the Eastern court, first under Rufinus, then Eutropius. During the early years of his dominance Stilicho was faced with a revolt in AFRICA by Gildo (397–8). He also had to deal with ALARIC's GOTHS, fighting inconclusive battles in Greece in 395 and 397 and in Italy at Verona and Pollentia in 402. From 405 the empire came under greater strain, with the invasion of Italy by Radagaisus in 405–6, the crossing of the RHINE in 406 and the usurpation in BRITAIN, GAUL and Spain under Constantine III (407–11). These crises, as well as tension with the Eastern empire, which declared him a public enemy in 407, strengthened opposition to Stilicho. He was murdered in 408 as the result of a PALACE coup led by the *magister officiorum*, Olympius. HWE

See Cameron, A. (1970) *Claudian*; Matthews, J.F. (1975) *Western Aristocracies and Imperial Court.*

 THEODOSIUS I:

stoa A distinctively Greek ARCHITECTURAL type, in the form of an oblong portico fronted by a colonnade. The latter could be double or, rarely, triple, thus widening the interior space of the building. Series of rooms often replaced the single back wall in stoas, which could be free-standing as independent

STILICHO: ivory diptych of Stilicho, his wife, Serena, and son Eucherius.

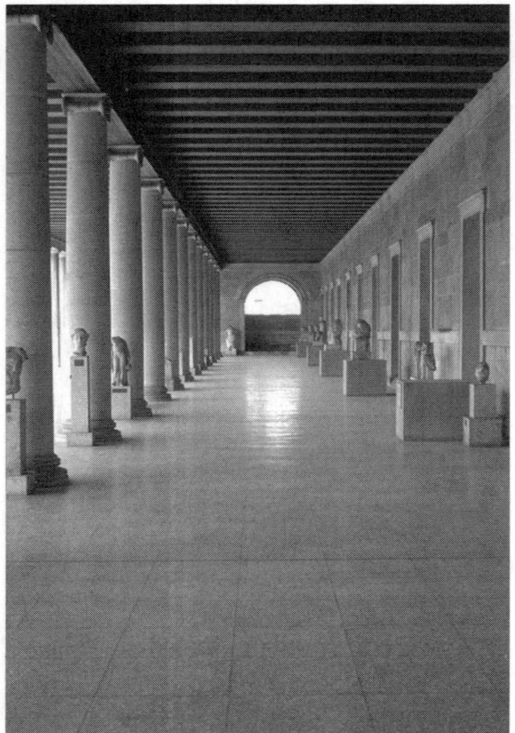

STOAS: (a) the inner corridor of the reconstructed Stoa of Attalos, Athens.

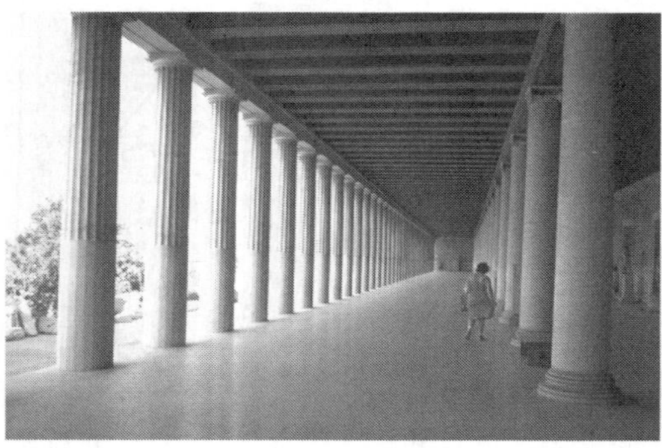

STOAS: (b) the outer corridor and columnar façade of the Stoa of Attalos.

buildings. Alternatively, they could line the boundary walls of sanctuaries or civic SPACE forming a court area. It was not uncommon for them to 'lean' on other types of building as a kind of extension. Stoas could be higher than the ground-floor level, with particular preference for additional storeys being shown from the late 4th century BC onwards. The Doric style is the architectural ORDER most often encountered on stoas and related structures. Stoas first appear as part of a continuous architectural tradition in the 7th century BC, but the type was not unknown in the architecture of the Bronze Age.

Stoas were useful for structuring space. Because of their oblong and open shape they could accommodate a variety of functions, depending on the wider architectural contexts in which they were used. For example, they could house SHOPS, LAWCOURTS and civic offices. They could be short-term lodgings, dining rooms and storerooms, or could offer ample room for the display of paintings or public documents. In the simplest of functions they offered shelter from the weather and were suitable places for rest, social interaction and EDUCATION. The STOIC PHILOSOPHERS derived their name from this architectural form. EP

See Coulton, J. J. (1976) *The Architectural Development of the Greek Stoa*.

👁 AGORA, ATHENIAN: (c).

Stoicism The Greek philosophical system founded by ZENO OF CITIUM c.300 BC and developed by him and his successors, notably Chrysippos (late 3rd century), into the dominant philosophy of the hellenistic age. It continued to flourish in the early Roman empire in the writings of SENECA, Epictetus and MARCUS AURELIUS. It was divided into PHYSICS, LOGIC and ETHICS.

The world is MATTER permeated by a rational god and hence is supremely good. Any impression of imperfection arises from misleadingly viewing its parts (including ourselves) in isolation, as if one were to consider the interests of the foot in isolation from the whole body. Personal happiness may be achieved by replicating that perfect cosmic rationality in oneself, discovering and enacting one's own 'fated' role.

'Logic' includes both logic in its modern sense (in which the Stoics excelled) and theory of KNOWLEDGE. Certainty is founded on ordinary sensory encounters, thanks to the providential availability of self-certifying sense-impressions.

In Stoic ethics, *oikeiôsis*, our natural 'appropriation' first of ourselves and later of those around us, makes other-concern integral to human nature. Conventionally prized items like honour and health are commended by nature and should be pursued, but not for their own sake. Rather, learning to choose rationally between them is a step towards our real goal of 'living in agreement with nature'. What can eventually bring virtue and happiness is the rational coherence of one's choices, not the attainment of their objects. DNS

See Long, A. A. and Sedley, D. N. (1987) *The Hellenistic Philosophers*; Sandbach, F. H. (1975) *The Stoics*.

stone An important material in both the Greek and Roman periods, stone was not only for building but also for decoration, SCULPTURE and vases. The stone varied greatly in structure, hardness, and the ease with which it could be extracted from the mass and cut to shape. Generally speaking, stone was not transported any great distance unless it was unusual and therefore highly prized, such as certain MARBLES and other decorative stones. Some cities, such as Athens, had a marble quarry (Mt Pentelikon) in close proximity and therefore made great use of the stone. Other Greek sites, such as DELPHI and OLYMPIA, had to make do with the local stones, and marble was only brought in for very specific purposes. In the vicinity of Rome the commonest stones were the soft volcanic tufas, for example the yellowish, soft Grotta Oscura (quarried near VEII and used in the construction of the Servian wall) and the blue-grey, hard peperino (*Lapis Albanus*, quarried in the Alban hills). When several sources of stone were available locally, stones were used according to their qualities or appearance: for example, hard volcanic stones for paving as the *selce* blocks for ROAD surfaces in central Italy. HD

See Dworakowska, A. (1975) *Quarries in Ancient Greece*; (1983) *Quarries in Roman Provinces.*

stone tools see FLINT AND CHERT; OBSIDIAN.

storage A crucial requirement for farmers in the classical past. Food products such as CEREALS, legumes, dried FIGS, OIL and WINE can all be stored for several years, though their quality may deteriorate. In the arid parts of the MEDITERRANEAN region, crops may fail as often as one year in five. Crop failure is unpredictable, and may be caused by human catastrophes such as invading armies, as well as by natural events such as drought or plagues of locusts. Storing surplus food allowed individual households and communities to survive such disasters.

There is considerable archaeological evidence for storage facilities at every level of society throughout the ancient world. In Bronze Age Greece, PALACES contained vast storage facilities, such as the ranks of enormous storage jars (*pithoi*) in the 'Magazines' of the palace of KNOSSOS. Roman VILLAS specializing in wine or oil production, and owned by rich proprietors, had substantial storage facilities. At the other end of the scale, excavated country HOUSES in Attica and the more modest Roman houses and SHOPS in POMPEII were equipped with a few large *pithoi*. Such jars were used for liquids (wine, oil, FISH SAUCE or honey) and cereals or legumes.

Classical texts and images document storage facilities other than ceramic vessels. Wooden chests were often used for storing grain: in the famous 5th-century BC PARTHENON frieze from Athens, DEMETER, the goddess of cereals and farming, sits on one. The Roman writers CATO and COLUMELLA have many tips on preserving food. (see also WAREHOUSES) LF

See Forbes, H. A. and Foxhall, L. (1995) Ethnoarchaeology and storage in the ancient Mediterranean, in J. Wilkins et al., eds., *Food in Antiquity* 69–85.

 WAREHOUSES: (b).

Strabo (Strabôn) Greek author of the most important geographical work surviving from antiquity. Born c.64 BC to an aristocratic family from Amaseia in Pontos (north-east Asia Minor), Strabo in early adulthood studied at Rome, which he was to visit several times. There he made the acquaintance of POSIDONIUS. Around his early forties he spent several years in ALEXANDRIA, where he probably conducted most of the research into earlier authors that informs his work. His first publication was a universal history, now lost. The vast *Geography* (c.400,000 words in English translation) was completed later. References to datable events suggest he had drafted most of it by 3/2 BC but revised it only in Tiberius' reign (AD 14 onwards). The latest events he mentions are in the early 20s AD, when he was over 80. A new manuscript of the work, discovered in the late 19th century, has clarified many details of the text.

Books 1–2 deal with the theory of geography and mathematical aspects of the discipline, giving a detailed but not always well-founded critique of ERATOSTHENES and Posidonius. With book 3 we begin systematic description. Strabo follows earlier navigational writers in starting at Gibraltar and moving along the north Mediterranean via Spain (book 3), Gaul (with a detour to Britain), and the Alps (book 4) to Italy and Sicily (5–6). With book 7, however, he turns inland to complete his account of northern Europe. This brings him to Thrace and Macedonia (preserved only in summaries). Greece and its islands receive three books (8–10), his own homeland of Asia Minor no fewer than four books (11–14). The work closes with India and Parthia (book 15), the Middle East (16), and North Africa (17, including a famous description of Alexandria).

The problem of separating eye-witness description from information derived from earlier sources arises often. In describing the PELOPONNESE, Strabo devotes much space to topography described by Homer and Attic tragedians, or recounting historical events relevant to particular places. Thus

> Epidauros was once called Epikauros, and Aristotle says Karians once occupied it as they did Hermion, but when the sons of Herakles returned [from the Trojan war] Ionians from the Attic *tetrapolis* [league of four cities] who had followed the Herakleidai to Argos settled here with these Karians. This *polis* is far from obscure, especially because of the presence of Asklepios, who is believed to cure all kinds of diseases. His temple is always full of sick people and of the dedicated tablets on which their treatments are written up, as at Kos and Trikka. (Strabo, *Geography* 8.6.15)

Here, typically, he explains the fame of a Greek place by citing legends, but also indicates how its fame is manifested in his own day. Because he uses hellenistic GEOGRAPHERS extensively, such as Artemidoros, he is sometimes accused of retailing outdated information; but in areas he has visited, such as the Peloponnese, he is aware of recent change. He is far less interested in the LANDSCAPE and its management than a modern geographer would be, often illustrating land use by quotations from long-dead poets. There are surprises, however, such as the calculated height of Acrocorinth (the citadel of CORINTH).

Strabo's work has often served literary scholars as a source of quotations from lost authors, while historians and archaeologists have mined it for information about particular places. This has obscured the work's overall architecture and literary intentions. Strabo admits he is better travelled in the Eastern Roman empire than in the West, but the prominence of Greece and Asia Minor is not simply due to this. Those areas were the heartland of the civilized world for Greeks and Romans. They were also the core of history for a Greek writer, as well as for Romans who admired Greek culture. Strabo's work is not simply a systematic spatial description. Although, like POLYBIOS, he admired Roman government and mixed easily with Romans, Strabo gives pride of place to the collective history of the Greek city-states. Again like

Polybios, he embodies in his work a reassessment of the world at a turning-point, when it had come definitively under the sway of a single superpower following the Roman civil wars. If his scheme is Roman, its presentation is distinctively Greek. DGJS

See Strabo, *Geography*, 8 vols. (needs updating in places), trs. H. L. Jones (1917–32); Clarke, K. (1999) *Between Geography and History: hellenistic constructions of the Roman world*; Dueck, D. (2000) *Strabo of Amasia*; Nicolet, C. (1991) *Space, Geography, and Politics in the Early Roman Empire*.

strategy, military Clausewitz defined strategy as the art of employing BATTLES to gain the object of WAR, a view that has in more recent times been considered too restrictive in that it regards battle as the sole means of achieving that object. There is a certain amount of truth in this, since strategy requires the formation of accurate estimates of manpower and resources, terrain and logistics, and the exploitation of psychological, moral and ethical factors. On a large scale, it is often referred to as 'grand strategy', which is itself the attempt to implement policy. But strategy is essentially the domain of the GENERAL (*stratêgos* in Greek) and its aim is to produce military results, though once it has established the conditions for military action it yields to the execution of the plan, which we call TACTICS. Perhaps the most important single element of strategy is deception (combined with speed). The aims of strategy are to overcome one's enemy with the least amount of danger or loss to oneself, to concentrate overwhelming force against the enemy's point of weakness, and to do so with speed and SECRECY in order to prevent the enemy from changing his front and to gain psychological advantage through surprise. Such an approach does, however, assume that the objectives of war can best be attained through decisive victory on the battlefield. The aim of defensive strategy – like the grand strategy of PERIKLES at the outbreak of the PELOPONNESIAN WAR or the strategy of Fabius Maximus in the HANNIBALIC WAR – is to avoid decisive battle, to frustrate and outlast an opponent in a war of attrition. But defensive strategists demand sacrifices from their own people, and thus render them susceptible to the psychological warfare of their opponents. WH

See Alexander, B. (2002) *How Wars are Won*; Liddell Hart, B. H. (1954) *Strategy*.

Stratonike Daughter of DEMETRIOS I POLIORKETES, second wife of king SELEUKOS I Nikator, and mother of Phila. In 294 BC Seleukos joined her in a new MARRIAGE with his son, Antiochos I, whom he appointed joint king and ruler of the eastern satrapies and who succeeded him on his death as king of the whole realm. Among the couple's children were the future kings Seleukos II Kallinikos and Antiochos II, as well as Apame, who married Magas of CYRENE. The story of the lovesick prince who is eventually allowed to marry his stepmother (cf. the myth of Hippolytos) has appealed to literary authors from the hellenistic to the modern worlds. KB

See Brodersen, K. (1985) Der liebeskranke Königssohn, *Athenaeum* 73: 459–69; Grainger, J. (1990) *Seleukos Nikator*.

strigil see BATHING; PERFUMES; SOAP.

string One of the world's most important inventions. Although it can be made by simply twisting fibres with the fingers, it was generally made on a drop spindle. In classical antiquity most string was probably made of coarse flax fibres (less refined than those used for making linen thread for clothing), though hemp, nettles and other plant fibres could also have been used. One of the most important uses of string was for making nets, and netting needles made of bone occasionally survive in the archaeological record. (see also SPINNING) LF

structuralism and post-structuralism As a perspective, structuralism looks for the system behind a particular text or group of texts. Most famously, this can be seen in the work of Claude Lévi-Strauss on MYTH. He found patterns and 'explanations' in myth that allowed, in his case, South American natives to find their place in the systems of polar opposites, to be seen as nature and culture (and as the human and the divine, the raw and the cooked, and so forth). Parisian scholars such as Jean-Pierre Vernant and Pierre Vidal-Naquet first introduced structuralism to classics through their influential studies of Athenian TRAGEDY and COMEDY within the context of religious FESTIVALS. Occasionally, the practice of 'intertextualism' is seen as an offshoot of structuralism. Here, a particular text is studied as a member of a literary or generic system (understood through the tracing of allusion). Intended or unintended verbal recollection of one text by another (e.g. Valerius Flaccus of VIRGIL) can create new and deeper levels of meaning in the later text. Intertextualism, however, could as easily be seen as the product of post-structuralism, for example deconstruction, as of structuralism. Deconstruction, made famous by the French philosopher Jacques Derrida, demonstrates, at the simplest level, that meaning is not 'out there' but is inherent in writing itself (the signifier), and that meaning has an unstable relationship with 'reality' (the signified). Meaning resides in the signifiers themselves, whose meaning depends on other signifiers (so Valerius Flaccus draws 'meaning' from Virgil, who draws 'meaning' from APOLLONIOS OF RHODES, and so on). Simplified, this has meant that, increasingly, critics have attempted to discern how apparent or intended meaning has been made unstable by literary generic forces, or by mythological, 'subconscious', or even historical ones. PGT

stucco The term 'stucco' is used to distinguish PLASTER based on LIME (calcium oxide) from *gesso*, based on calcined gypsum (a hemihydrate of calcium sulphate). Its normal function in Greece and Rome was to provide a protective and attractive coating for walls, but it was also modelled in imitation of ARCHITECTURAL ornament. It was used, for example, to add fluting and Corinthian capitals to columns of plain brickwork. Its most notable role was in the creation of a surface decoration in relief on internal walls and ceilings. This form of decoration began during the 1st century BC by imitating wooden ceiling-coffers, which then, under the liberating influence of vaults, dissolved into networks of richly framed panels containing vegetal ornaments and figures. Normally stuccoes were entirely free of COLOUR, relying on the whiteness of the plaster and the subtle play of light and shade to offset the polychromy of

WALL-PAINTINGS. In many cases, however, the background was painted so that the white reliefs stood out cameo-like within fields of blue, red or purple. In the finest works, such as the vaults of the Farnesina VILLA in Rome (c.20 BC), an exceptional delicacy was achieved. Executed by hand in the damp plaster, stucco reliefs were a luxury which could be afforded only by well-off clients, and were often reserved for the most important rooms of a house, or the most pretentious mausolea in a necropolis. They largely passed from fashion after the early 3rd century AD. RJL

subsistence The amount a farmer needs to produce to survive even if things go horribly wrong, rather than just enough to get by for a single year. Most farmers in antiquity probably aimed to grow sufficient food to store or sell a surplus beyond their immediate needs, though they may not often have achieved this aim. How much food a city or a HOUSEHOLD needed to produce for 'subsistence' is therefore notoriously difficult to calculate from the few unreliable figures that survive in ancient sources. Ancient farmers may have estimated household consumption of CEREALS at about 150–200 kg (330–440 lb) per person per year, so 200,000 tonnes of wheat per year would have been needed to feed the city of Rome around the time of AUGUSTUS. LF

See Garnsey, P. (1988) *Famine and Food Supply in the Graeco-Roman World*.

Successors of Alexander (Greek *diadochoi*) The men who served with ALEXANDER (and many also with his father PHILIP II) and were left to decide what to do with his great empire when he died young at BABYLON on 10 June 323 BC. The nominal heirs were Philip III Arrhidaios, who apparently suffered from physical or mental deficiencies, and Alexander IV, born to Rhoxane after Alexander's death. At first, different men were given different parts of the kingdom to administer under the general authority of Perdikkas, who was serving as regent. After Perdikkas was killed in 321, Antipatros emerged briefly as the most important figure, but his death in 319, just after he had made Polyperchon the new regent instead of his own son Kassandros (Cassander), led to further quarrels.

A key figure in these years, though the only non-Macedonian Diadoch, is Alexander's former secretary, Eumenes of Kardia, put in charge of northern Asia Minor in 323. The others later turned upon him, and as a result he never wielded great power; but by clever tactics, and by proclaiming his loyalty to Alexander's legitimate heirs, he avoided capture and his division of the Macedonian army remained loyal. In 316, however, Antigonos Monophthalmos ('One-eyed') captured him and put him to death.

Antigonos, his son DEMETRIOS (I), PTOLEMY (I), Polyperchon, Kassandros and LYSIMACHOS were the most important figures through the rest of the 4th century, together with SELEUKOS after his restoration to Babylon in 312. Ptolemy remained permanently in charge of Egypt and founded the dynasty of the PTOLEMIES. The two 'legitimate' claimants to the Macedonian throne, and rightful heirs of Alexander, were assassinated in 317 and 310, and most of the successors took the title of king between 306 and 304. Polyperchon, however, died in obscurity, having lost out to Kassandros, who ruled Macedonia from 316. For some of the Successors, notably Antigonos, the aim continued to be the reconstitution of Alexander's empire under one man. The battle of IPSOS (301), however, marked the end of Antigonos' efforts, and thereafter the struggles were more about consolidation of power over limited territory. Lysimachos was probably the largest beneficiary of Antigonos' defeat. Kassandros' death in 297 triggered further fighting. As late as 281, Lysimachos was defeated by the remaining contenders and killed, and shortly afterwards the equally elderly Seleukos was assassinated.

More than 40 years had passed since Alexander's death. By now the configuration of the hellenistic world was largely determined, except for control of Macedonia, which had changed hands between Antigonos, OLYMPIAS (Alexander's mother), Kassandros, and Demetrios, but finally fell to Antigonos II Gonatas (son of Demetrios) in 277.

The struggles of the Successors form the chief political theme of the first half-century of the post-Alexander era. We are, however, poorly informed about many of the details after the end of DIODORUS' connected narrative in 302. GR, DGJS

See Diodorus Siculus, books 18–19; Plutarch, *Demetrios* and *Eumenes*; Green, P. (1990) *From Alexander to Actium*; Shipley, G. (2000) *The Greek World after Alexander*.

 AFGHANISTAN; MACEDONIA; PERGAMON; PTOLEMIES; SELEUKIDS (all with tables).

Suda The largest and most wide-ranging Byzantine reference work to survive intact, dating from c.AD 1000. The name means 'stronghold' (cf. perhaps the description of a modern reference work as a 'powerhouse of knowledge'); the alternative attribution to an individual named Suidas is a long-standing mistake. Although now most frequently cited for its potted BIOGRAPHIES of writers and intellectuals (mainly taken over from an epitome of the *Onomatologos* of HESYCHIOS of MILETOS), its overall range is broad enough to make it into a kind of historical ENCYCLOPEDIA. In entries ranging from bare synonyms to articles of several pages (e.g. JESUS, HOMER, Adam and PYTHAGORAS), it offers also explanations of difficult or obscure words and grammatical forms, proverbs ('gardens of Adonis', 'go shake another oak tree'), places, institutions (Apatouria, AREIOPAGOS, OSTRACISM), and philosophical terms and concepts (SOUL, syllogism, TIME). In keeping with the aim of aiding the reading of educated literature, both PAGAN and CHRISTIAN, the focus is almost wholly classical and biblical. Christianizing comments occasionally obtrude, for instance when it is asserted that the satirist LUCIAN was torn apart by dogs and 'will inherit the eternal fire with Satan' for his blasphemous attacks on Christianity. As a compilation from a wide range of earlier handbooks, commentaries and reference works, the *Suda* is of very variable reliability; but it presents a mass of information about the Greek language and ancient culture not otherwise preserved. MBT

See Adler, A., ed. (1928–38) *Suidae Lexicon*, 5 vols.; trs. in progress at *Suda On Line* (website).

Suebi see GALLIC WARS; GERMANY AND GERMANS.

Suetonius (Gaius Suetonius Tranquillus) A native of Hippo Regius in North AFRICA who held a number of senior secretarial positions under the emperors TRAJAN and HADRIAN. The basic information about his career comes from a badly damaged inscription. His most senior position was the important post of *ab epistulis Latinis*, or secretary responsible for the emperor's correspondence in Latin. The *Historia Augusta* tells us that he was dismissed by Hadrian in AD 121, the same year that Hadrian dismissed Suetonius' patron, the praetorian prefect Septicius Clarus, to whom Suetonius had dedicated what is now his most famous work, *The Lives of the Twelve Caesars*.

Glimpses of Suetonius' earlier career appear in the letters of the younger PLINY, who obtained for him a military tribunate in BRITAIN (which Suetonius declined) in 101. Suetonius was probably 31 at the time and already embarked on a literary career, having discovered that he lacked the confidence to be an ORATOR. He did, however, join Pliny's staff when the latter was appointed governor of Bithynia in 109.

Suetonius' literary interests were of a distinctively antiquarian sort. A list of his works compiled from citations in other authors and from the *SUDA* shows that he treated subjects as diverse as the lives of famous courtesans, weather signs, the Roman year, spectacles and public offices. He is best known for the *Lives of the Twelve Caesars* and *Concerning Famous Men*, a work that offered short BIOGRAPHIES of something like one hundred Romans of various occupations, grouped by category. Selections from this work, including that on grammarians and a part of that on RHETORICIANS survive, as do the substance of several of his lives of POETS, including TERENCE, VIRGIL, HORACE, TIBULLUS, PERSIUS and LUCAN. In these lives Suetonius reveals wide reading in Latin literature, and, as befits the antiquarian style, he quotes sources verbatim.

The Lives of the Twelve Caesars is a much more ambitious work, though odd in that the first six lives from JULIUS CAESAR to NERO contain a wealth of documentary material, while the last six are much less well informed. The stylistic disjuncture has led some scholars to posit that the Julio-Claudian lives were written when Suetonius had access to material that he would afterwards lose; another explanation is that he wrote the last six lives first – a reasonable assumption in that they are closer in style to Suetonius' other work. The decision to begin the work with Julius Caesar is significant, reflecting a very different view of the Julio-Claudian house than that which had been current under the Julio-Claudians themselves, who considered AUGUSTUS the first in the line of succession. The lives themselves are arranged according to a strict pattern, beginning with the subject's ancestry, his birth and his career before becoming emperor. After the subject of the biography became emperor, his actions and personal characteristics are dealt with thematically rather than chronologically. Each life ends with an account of the subject's death. This style was adopted by later biographers in the Latin tradition. DSP

See Suetonius, *The Twelve Caesars*, trs. R. Graves (1979); Wallace-Hadrill, A. (1983) *Suetonius*.

suicide The concept of suicide is as difficult to pin down in antiquity as it is in modern times. The act of suicide involves the taking of one's own life actively, instead of leaving this to old age, illness, accident or other individuals. This is the simplest way to think of suicide. But more still is expected from suicide; more, that is, than a mere act of self-killing. One expects suicide to be freely chosen, and to represent an end in itself. So a suicide compelled by external circumstances (for example, by the demands of emperors such as TIBERIUS or NERO) is little more than *de facto* execution. A suicide, furthermore, that is driven by mental illness (as is no doubt the case for the HOMERIC hero, AJAX) represents the playing out of the course of an illness, rather than of suicide (no end in itself). Durkheim's famous definition could well be compared: 'any death which is the direct or indirect result of a positive or negative act accomplished by the victim himself, which he knows should produce this result'. Because choice and intention are uncommon in real-life suicide, it follows that successful suicide is infrequently depicted in ancient literature. At any rate, PHILOSOPHERS such as PLATO and ARISTOTLE tended to look down on suicide. It had its heyday with the STOIC philosophers (and models in the deaths of SENECA THE YOUNGER and CATO) who, though disapproving of suicide in most cases, viewed it with favour when it was chosen instead of a path of dishonour. PGT

See van Hoof, A. J. L. (1990) *From Autothanasia to Suicide*.

Suidas see *SUDA*.

Sulis Native goddess of healing and retribution, venerated at the thermal waters of BATH (Aquae Sulis), who was conflated with the healing aspect of MINERVA after the Roman conquest of BRITAIN. Offerings of CELTIC coins dating to the late Iron Age suggest the importance of this divinity in pre-conquest ritual. However, not until the construction of the associated BATH and TEMPLE complex in Flavian times (c.AD 60–75) does the cult gain religious significance, attracting a wide range of pilgrims from within the empire.

Votive offerings and CURSE tablets recovered from the sacred spring at Bath attest to the needs of the local community. The majority of the curse tablets address the theft of personal property, while anatomical models, like the IVORY carving of a pair of breasts, relate to health issues. Gifts to the goddess include JEWELLERY and coins, some of which show evidence for RITUAL 'killing'.

The cult of Sulis Minerva is one of a few cases within the empire where the native deity retains its supremacy and character despite its equation with a Roman counterpart. For example, native symbolism is evident in the male MEDUSA head on the temple pediment, variously interpreted as either a native water or solar deity, while the solar aspect of the native cult is noted in other dedications, particularly to MARS Loucetius, a Treveran deity whose epithet means 'brilliant', and to the Suleviae, who, along with Sulis, share an etymological link to the sun. MLM

See Green, M. (1997) *The Gods of the Celts*.

BATH; CURSES: (a)–(b).

Sulla (Lucius Cornelius Sulla) c.138–78 BC Born into a PATRICIAN family which had not reached the CONSULSHIP since 277, Sulla entered public life only when he came into funds, and Gaius MARIUS (consul

107) required him as QUAESTOR. As a CAVALRY commander and the DIPLOMAT in AFRICA who convinced Bocchus to surrender his son-in-law and ally JUGURTHA to Marius, Sulla was invaluable. Subsequently, he accompanied Marius against the Cimbri and Teutones (104–103). Sulla obtained his PRAETORSHIP (97) at the second attempt, probably because he was still associated with Marius, who had been discredited in 100. He went to ANATOLIA, where he installed Ariobarzanes in CAPPADOCIA and belittled a PARTHIAN AMBASSADOR by the seating arrangements at their meeting. An abortive prosecution on his return may have been due to Marius, who claimed the east as his new sphere; they were at loggerheads when the SOCIAL WAR broke out (91). Sulla was successful in the south and became consul (88), marrying a Metella. When MITHRADATES VI invaded ASIA, Sulla received the command. Crushing opposition from Marius and the TRIBUNE Sulpicius, he took his army east, twice defeating Mithradates and sacking ATHENS. On returning (83), he extinguished Marian resistance with massacre and confiscation, and as DICTATOR (81) he debilitated the tribunate and systematically reconstituted the state under SENATORIAL control. Believing himself favoured by the GODS, he took the *cognomen* Felix. After inaugurating his constitution as consul (80) he retired, leaving too many discontents for permanent stability. Attempts at change began immediately, but his arrangements did not break down until 49. His 22 books of memoirs influenced historians. BML

See Badian, E. (1970) *Lucius Sulla: the deadly reformer*; Brennan, T. (1992) Sulla in the nineties, *Chiron* 22: 103–58; Keaveney, A. (1982) *Sulla: the last republican*.

sulphur This substance occurs naturally in some parts of the Mediterranean region, especially in the vicinity of hot springs and VOLCANOES such as the peninsula of Methana in the Saronic gulf, Mt Vesuvius near POMPEII, and Mt Etna in SICILY. Sulphur and its compounds, including copper sulphate and Epsom salts, were known and exploited in classical antiquity as fumigants and fungicides, and were used in FULLING (for bleaching) and some industrial processes. LF

Sulpicia Lepidina Wife of FLAVIUS CERIALIS, Roman commanding OFFICER of an AUXILIARY unit based at VINDOLANDA in northern England in the late 1st century AD. Her claim to fame comes in the form of her private correspondence with her friend Claudia Severa, married to another commander at a neighbouring FORT. Among their LETTERS is the invitation from Severa inviting Lepidina to her birthday party. The excavations at Vindolanda, coupled with the evidence from the writing-tablets, reveal that the commanding officer was in residence with his wife and young FAMILY and living in reasonable comfort. One tablet appears to be a household inventory, listing everything from large serving dishes to egg cups! A woman like Lepidina will have had an important role to play in the domestic management of the HOUSEHOLD and its SLAVES. However, life for WOMEN on the FRONTIER must have been quite isolated and lonely at this stage in the development of its infrastructure. There is an urgency in several of the letters referring to anticipated visits between Lepidina and Severa: 'Farewell my sister, my dearest and most longed-for soul'. DJM

See Bowman, A. (1994) *Life and Letters on the Roman Frontier*.

Sulpicii Long-lived PATRICIAN clan of the REPUBLIC (a *gens minor*). The *praenomen* Servius is common. The family plays no part in the foundation myths of the Republic, appearing with Servius Sulpicius Camerinus, consul in 500 BC – *cognomen* and date suggest a link with the Latin town of Cameria, destroyed by Rome in 501. The Camerini endured almost two centuries. The family tree is difficult to trace in the mid-Republic, various *cognomina* appearing for only a generation or two. The principal line from the 3rd century is the Sulpicii Galbae, initially associated with the Sulpicii Gali. Pre-eminent

SULPICIA LEPIDINA: the famous 'birthday party invitation' sent to Sulpicia Lepidina by her friend Claudia Severa.

among the early Galbae was Publius Sulpicius Galba Maximus, commander in the first and second MACEDONIAN WARS. The last great scion of this house was the emperor Galba (AD 69). The Sulpicii Rufi resurfaced in the late Republic, though whether the tribune Publius Sulpicius (Rufus?), who supported MARIUS against SULLA (88 BC), belonged to this family is uncertain. Servius Sulpicius Rufus (consul 51 BC) was the greatest jurist of the Roman Republic. CICERO's *Ninth Philippic* contains a eulogy. The six elegies (in the TIBULLAN corpus) by Sulpicia, perhaps the jurist's granddaughter, are the only surviving poems by a woman from this period. JRWP

sun The sun influenced philosophical thought and religious beliefs in the classical world, as well as the conduct of everyday life, in two different though not wholly distinct ways. First, it was a means of determining the time of year and the time of day. Some of the earliest Greek CALENDARS – the *parapêgmata* that were developed in the 5th century BC – used the sun indirectly to reckon the days of the year, by tracking the appearance and disappearance of various stars and constellations in the dawn and dusk sky. But it was the Romans who replaced lunar calendars, which became especially problematic when the process of intercalation became dogged by political interference, by introducing a truly solar calendar. The Julian calendar is remarkable not only for its accuracy (to within about 3 days in every 400 years) but for introducing a year divided into 12 'months' that were, in fact, completely independent of the MOON. For determining the hour of the day, SUNDIALS were commonplace in both the Greek and Roman worlds.

Second, the sun was an object of direct worship. This is best known in the context of MITHRAISM which, though present in hellenistic Greece, spread most spectacularly through the Roman empire in the 2nd century AD, and came to present one of the most serious PAGAN challenges to early CHRISTIANITY. In Greece, Mithras became identified with Helios and APOLLO. In the Roman empire, he was identified with SOL INVICTUS (the 'unconquered sun').

It is probable that indigenous solar rituals (for example, marking the solstices, and possibly even the equinoxes and mid-quarter days) strongly influenced the development of the Roman and, subsequently, of the Christian calendar. CLNR

 ZODIAC: (a).

SUNDIAL: a Roman example from Pompeii.

sundials Measuring time was not a priority in everyday life in the ancient world. As the daylight time was divided into 12 parts, the length of an hour varied with the seasons. To establish a rough estimate of the time of day, a measure of the length of one's shadow could be used. Another way to refer to a specific time of day was 'when the *agora* is filled' (e.g. Herodotos 4.181).

Herodotos (2.91) claims that, like the division of the day into twelfths, sundials were introduced into the Greek world from BABYLON. They used a pointer (gnomon) to cast a shadow on a flat, spherical or conical surface marked to indicate the hours. Their wider use is not attested until the 3rd century BC, when the MATHEMATICAL theory for the lines on the surface had been developed. From then on, several hundred sundials are preserved, mainly in stone. They vary in size from very small, portable objects to the massive sundial, with an obelisk as its gnomon, which AUGUSTUS ordered to be built on the Campus Martius in Rome.

For measuring spans of time, e.g. in a LAWCOURT, the time-related movement of a steady stream of liquid into or out of a vessel (*klepsydra*, 'water-stealer') was used. This developed into a clock, described by VITRUVIUS (9.8). KB

See Buchner, E. (1982) *Die Sonnenuhr des Augustus*; Gibbs, S. (1976) *Greek and Roman Sundials*.

superstition As religious belief or practice founded on fear or ignorance, superstition appears first in HESIOD's *Works and Days*, in a list of instructions to his brother Perses (705–828). Some of these are RITUAL PURIFICATIONS. Others are health precautions: 'do not urinate in springs', 'do not wash in a woman's bath-water'. Most, however, would count as superstitions – for example, 'never put the ladle on the wine bowl, for that brings bad luck' – and especially the section on lucky and unlucky ('stepmother') days for various tasks, in which the 1st, 4th and 7th are holy, the 13th bad for sowing. PYTHAGOREAN number symbolism had some rational basis (four for justice, ten as perfect), but most of the later Pythagorean 'rules' did not, such as 'do not gaze in a mirror beside a lamp', 'once you have left your house, do not look back, for the Furies come after you', or 'put on your right shoe first' (see Iamblichos, *Protrepticus* 21; DIOGENES LAËRTIUS 8.17). The left was unlucky for the northward-looking Greeks, lucky for the Romans who had the rising sun on their left (*sinister*) side. In the Roman Republic, political and military procedures were dominated by auspices and omens, especially concerning the entrails of sacrificial ANIMALS, the flight and cries of BIRDS and the eating habits of the sacred chickens. Long rituals were conducted with precision, and any slip meant starting again. Politicians often blatantly manipulated such practices, which the EPICUREAN poet LUCRETIUS aimed to expose by rational explanations, so overcoming the EVIL done by superstitious beliefs (1.110). The main superstitions in the Roman empire were concerned with ASTROLOGY. MRW

supply, military The logistical support for ancient ARMIES, whether on campaign or stationed in garrison, was a matter of the highest concern. In the case of Sparta, an entire society, with its subservient HELOTS and *perioikoi*, was created to service the needs of the military. The ROMAN EMPIRE provides an example of the potentially large scale and sophistication of ancient supply systems. With a standing army of c.500,000 men, widely dispersed around the empire and many in economically less well-developed PROVINCES, the *annona militaris*, as the supply system was known, operated through a series of measures: direct requisitioning (including goods collected as tax or tribute), military production (of foodstuffs and a range of manufactured goods) and purchase (whether on the open market or through contracts). Military supply contracts were at the heart of the system, with many army units dispatching personnel across provincial boundaries (and even across the imperial frontiers) to broker contracts. For example, a unit based in MOESIA in the early 2nd century dispatched soldiers to GAUL to buy clothing, others to get CATTLE from the Balkans and some even across the DANUBE to secure 'annona grain'. A writing tablet found in Holland confirms that personnel involved with military supply purchased cattle well beyond the Roman frontier.

Archaeological evidence supports the idea that military contracts were important. Food preparation bowls (*mortaria*) from Colchester in southern England are predominantly found within 100 km (c.60 miles) of the KILNS, with the notable exception of concentrations along the FORTS of HADRIAN'S WALL and the ANTONINE WALL. Similarly, the distribution of stamped oil-AMPHORAS from Spain in the Rhineland reveals a pattern of relationships between individual forts and particular kiln sites which suggests that contracts were brokered by individual units, rather than centrally for the RHINE FRONTIER army as a whole.

The merchants (*negotiatores* and *conductores*) who tendered for military contracts are well attested in the EPIGRAPHIC record, congregating strongly on the main routes of military supply, for instance along the RHÔNE, Saône, Mosel and Rhine axes in Gaul. Military consignments evidently travelled across provincial boundaries tax-free, in some cases with TRANSPORT costs also covered, and as such acted as a subsidy for the movement of other goods. The VINDOLANDA tablets include several documents dealing with the procurement of military supplies, by people who were probably attached to the garrison in an official capacity. In one example, a man called Octavius writes about a complicated set of deals involving separate purchases of sinew, hides and grain.

The army's consumption of animals was huge: cavalry HORSES and baggage ANIMALS, sacrificial victims, MEAT for the military DIET, LEATHER and hides. DRAUGHT ANIMALS were commonly requisitioned, generally being subject to compulsory purchase after veterinary inspection. Some cavalry horses may have been specially bred, just as the state had some armouries and clothing manufactories under its direct control, and much MANUFACTURING was undertaken directly by military units. The larger units, especially the LEGIONS, had lands assigned to them for production of part of their food needs and other resources, such as grazing and TIMBER. Most forts included WORKSHOPS for METALWORKING and tanning, and POTTERIES and tileries under military control are well attested. But whatever the desire to attain self-sufficiency, archaeological evidence is unequivocal that most army units were big importers of foodstuffs and manufactured goods, and provided a significant stimulus to inter-provincial TRADE. DJM

See Davies, R. (1989) *Service in the Roman Army*; Whittaker, C. R. (1994) *Frontiers of the Roman Empire*.

surpluses see GROWTH, ECONOMIC; PRODUCTION; SUBSISTENCE.

sweets and sweeteners The major sweeteners used in Greek and Roman cookery were HONEY and grape syrup (must concentrated by boiling). A sweet flavour, often combined with the bitterness of lovage and the heat of black pepper, was required in many of the complex sauces served with meat in Roman cuisine. Cakes and sweetmeats served at dessert and offered at SACRIFICES were typically honey-soaked, like those of the modern MEDITERRANEAN, and will have been extremely sweet.

Must is a sweet juice which begins to ferment into WINE almost as soon as it flows from the wine press. Immediate boiling concentrates the sugar, producing a more effective sweetener; it also makes the substance more stable. Grape syrup at various concentrations was known as *hepsêma* and *siraion* in Greek, *defrutum* and *sapa* in Latin. Date syrup was more familiar in the LEVANT, where dates fruit readily. Dried dates, dried FIGS and raisins are much sweeter than the corresponding fresh FRUITS and were significant sources of dietary sugar in solid form.

Cane sugar (Greek *sakchar*, borrowed from Prakrit *sakkhara*) was a great rarity, imported from INDIA and sufficiently costly to be reserved for medicinal rather than culinary use. The sugar cane, first grown in New Guinea several thousand years ago, had become an important crop in India by hellenistic times. Granulated sugar was available by the 1st century AD; it is described by Dioskorides as 'a sort of crystallized honey, found in India and Arabia ... not unlike salt in its texture, and it can be crunched between the teeth like salt'. AD

swimming For the Greeks and Romans, swimming was not just a matter of necessity or enjoyment: it was laden with cultural values. Among Greeks and

SWIMMING: scene of Greek women bathing from a vase in the Louvre.

Romans, the ability to swim was regarded as being as basic as reading: the allegations that ALEXANDER the Great and the emperor CALIGULA could not swim are treated as remarkable. Both Greeks and Romans boasted of legendary feats of swimmers, some more believable than others, such as the HELOT divers who brought food to the Spartans stranded on the island of Sphakteria in 425 during the PELOPONNESIAN WAR. The Greeks assumed that BARBARIANS could not swim: the disproportionate Persian losses in the battle of SALAMIS were attributed to the Persians' inability to swim to safety. This Greek belief may be based on an ethnocentric contrast between the ideal of the Greek stripped, athletic body and perceptions of 'barbarian' laziness and physical indulgence. For the Romans, boasts of swimming in ice-cold torrents were used to prove manly austerity, but swimming could also be linked with decadent behaviour at seaside and riverbank pick-up joints, such as Baiae on the bay of Naples. AUGUSTUS' friend MAECENAS was said to have built the first heated swimming-pool in Rome, but in practice swimming-pools within BATH complexes were generally too small and shallow to allow serious swimming to take place. ED

See Couch, H. (1934) Swimming among the Greeks and barbarians, *CJ* 29: 609–12; Sanders, H. (1924) Swimming among the Greeks and Romans, *CJ* 20: 566–8; Hall, E. (1994) Drowning by nomes: the Greeks, swimming, and Timotheus' *Persians*, in H. A. Khan, ed., *The Birth of the European identity*, 44–80.

sycophant see RHETORIC, GREEK.

Syme, R. see HISTORIANS AND HISTORIOGRAPHY, MODERN.

Symmachus (Quintus Aurelius Symmachus) c.AD 345–402 Senatorial ARISTOCRAT of Rome, defender of the pagan tradition and author of many orations and letters. Scion of an important senatorial family, Symmachus came to prominence as a representative of the SENATE to the imperial court. His first mission was in 369–70, when he delivered PANEGYRICS on Valentinian I and Gratian at TRIER. Under these emperors he had a successful administrative career, culminating with the proconsulship of AFRICA in 373–4. He was prefect of Rome in 384–5 under Valentinian II. During tenure of this post, he became embroiled in a dispute with bishop AMBROSE of MILAN over the removal of the altar of Victory from the senate house in Rome. After Valentinian II's expulsion from ITALY (387), Symmachus delivered a panegyric on the usurper Magnus Maximus. Although he did this as representative of the senate, he found himself abandoned by his peers a year later when THEODOSIUS I invaded and displaced Maximus. His position looked precarious, but he was pardoned, and in 391 he was honoured with the CONSULSHIP. During the usurpation of Eugenius (392–4), however, he remained neutral, unlike other pagan senators.

Of his works, the vast collection of Symmachus' letters provides a unique insight into the lifestyles of late Roman aristocrats. They are only occasionally concerned with affairs of state; otherwise they reveal much about the cultural interests of 4th-century senators and the workings of PATRONAGE among the imperial ÉLITE. MDH

See Barrow, R. H. (1973) *Prefect and Emperor*; Matthews, J. F. (1975) *Western Aristocracies and Imperial Court, AD 364–425.*

symposia The term symposium (*symposion*) is commonly, and wrongly, used of any private drinking-party in classical Greece. The symposium proper was a highly regulated, élitist, men-only affair. Ideally it took place in a room called the *andrôn* or 'men's room' of a house, though such dining rooms are ubiquitous in sanctuaries and secular buildings alike. These 'dining rooms' are normally identified by their off-centre doorway (an arrangement which allowed for the most efficient accommodation of couches) and a raised platform around the edge of the room on which the couches stood. In buildings where only one room, or suite of rooms, was decorated, the *andrôn* tends to be this room; it could have painted walls and a MOSAIC floor if the owner was wealthy.

Taking place after the dinner plates had been cleared away, the serious business of drinking began. Presided over by the *symposiarchos*, guests reclined on their couches and drank WINE mixed with water in a *kratêr*, an essential part of the sympotic furniture. Wine was served to the symposiasts by SLAVES, who could also entertain the guests by playing MUSICAL INSTRUMENTS, DANCING or providing sexual favours. Symposiasts might also recite POETRY or play games such as *kottabos*, which involved spinning a *kylix* (the cup of preference) around the forefinger before skilfully flicking the wine dregs at a target floating in a dish of water, or perhaps at the object of the player's affection on the other side of the room. CK-B

See Murray, O., ed. (1990) *Sympotica: a symposium on the symposion.*

syncretism In the traditional definition, syncretism is the merger, or mixing, of two disparate cultures to produce a hybrid form. Within the confines of classical scholarship, syncretism is generally understood as the merger of foreign cultures with that of Rome, or the fusion of cultures to create the hellenistic world in ASIA Minor and the Near East.

Evidence for syncretism in the classical world is primarily noted in, but not limited to, the conflation of belief systems. An oft-cited example is the perceived emergence of Romano-Celtic religion in GAUL and BRITAIN after the Roman conquest. Much

SYMPOSIA: Greek revellers playing the game of *kottabos*, which involved flicking the dregs in their wine cups at a target.

research has focused on the numerous inscriptions that equate a native deity with a Roman counterpart, suggesting that they are indicative of a syncretistic religion. Traditionally, this EPIGRAPHIC merger of foreign and Roman GODS was thought to result from similarities in belief systems that enabled the conflation of indigenous belief with that of Rome. Recent scholarship has questioned the validity of this assumption, suggesting that equations of this nature are not viable acts of syncretism, since the majority of these conflations appear to be Roman-led. They may reflect not a religious merger but the translation of native deities into Roman form.

This line of enquiry is in keeping with theological debates on syncretism. From a theological perspective, incompatibility between beliefs is a fundamental aspect of the syncretistic process and moderates the extent to which two different belief systems will attain cohesion. Thus, syncretism necessitates the reinterpretation of belief to enable conflations to occur. From a POST-COLONIAL perspective, for example, the epigraphic name-pairings of foreign and Roman deities do not reflect a merger of religious systems, but the imposition of Roman belief resulting from differences in POWER.

The concept of unequal power relationships is a salient feature in a theological approach to syncretism. Issues of dominance and subordination are viewed not as deterrents to syncretism, but as mechanisms that affect its development, since the dominant religion will influence subsequent equations. It does not naturally follow, however, that asymmetries in power limit the process of syncretism to the ruling hierarchy. Syncretism can also be utilized by the lower classes of society as a means of resisting the dominant view. Consequently, syncretism is a dialogue that can operate as a positive construct and empower the segments of society that utilize it. MLM

See Gort, D. et al. (1989) *Dialogue and Syncretism*.

Synesius AD 370–413 A writer, ORATOR and BISHOP from CYRENE. He was born into one of the most prominent families of Cyrene, which he emphasizes by saying he was descended from the city's founder, Battos. In his youth, he studied in ALEXANDRIA; under the tutelage of HYPATIA, he became a NEOPLATONIST. Later, he was made one of the *curiales* of the city and was sent on an embassy to CONSTANTINOPLE to plead for tax relief for LIBYA. He was made bishop of Ptolemaïs in AD 411, a post he only took up after six months' deliberation. Although he was a conscientious bishop, Synesius was never a fully convinced CHRISTIAN. He believed that the resurrection was symbolic, and he did not follow Christian dogma where it conflicted with his PHILOSOPHICAL views. One is also struck by the number of references to PAGAN GODS in his letters, though this may be due to literary convention.

Synesius' letters, which contain innumerable references to Greek literature, give us a glimpse of the literary world of his day. They also give an invaluable insight into a series of skirmishes fought between Cyrenaicans and a Libyan tribe, the Ausurians, who invaded the province from 405 to 412. Synesius organized local defences, setting up a militia to patrol the country and later, as bishop of Ptolemaïs, establishing the defence of that city.

Apart from his letters, Synesius' most-read works include *Dion*, in which he lambasts both ASCETIC Christian monks and pagan beliefs, and *De providentia* (*On Providence*), written in praise of Aurelian, a high official at Constantinople. EACM

See Bregman, J. (1982) *Synesius of Cyrene*; Liebeschuetz, J. H. W. G. (1990) *Barbarians and Bishops*.

synoikism (synoecism) see IMPERIALISM, GREEK; *POLIS*.

Syracuse (Syrakousai) The leading ancient city of SICILY, founded c.734 BC by CORINTHIANS. Large and elaborately decorated TEMPLES to APOLLO, Olympian ZEUS and ATHENA, as well as an Ionic temple, indicate the city's prosperity in archaic times. Its government was an aristocratic land-owning ÉLITE, but in 485 Gelon of Gela made himself TYRANT of Syracuse. His brother and successor, Hieron I, consolidated Syracusan pre-eminence over south-eastern Sicily, and encouraged learning and culture: AESCHYLUS, SIMONIDES and PINDAR all came to grace his court. After the battle of Himera against the Carthaginians in 480, Hieron rebuilt the temple of Athena in stone. After his death, Syracuse became a DEMOCRACY in 466, ruled through an ASSEMBLY and a council (*boulê*) and headed by annually elected *stratêgoi* ('generals'). The city's influence declined, however, as a result of internal struggles and wars against Akragas (Agrigento) and the Sikels of Sicily. A later resurgence attracted Athens, whose expedition (415–413) ended in total disaster.

By 405 democracy had given way to tyranny under DIONYSIOS I. He preserved the democratic constitution, fortified Syracuse with a great girdle of walls 27 km (17 miles) long – the longest in the Greek world – extended Syracusan hegemony to include much of central and eastern Sicily and even parts of southern Italy, and fought four wars against Carthage. His son, Dionysios II, was forced out of Syracuse in 357. The ensuing years of anarchy only came to an end after the intervention of the Corinthian TIMOLEON in 344. The oligarchy established by the latter was overthrown in 317/16 by AGATHOKLES, styled initially *stratêgos* but a tyrant in all but name; later he changed his title to *basileus* ('king'). A period of Syracusan decline after his death in 289 was reversed by Hieron II, who enjoyed a long, prosperous and peaceful rule as *basileus* (c.270–216). His building programme included the great THEATRE, a grandiose STOA and a gigantic altar to Zeus Eleutherios, 200 m (218 yds) long – the largest altar ever erected by Greeks.

Rome respected Hieron's kingdom when Sicily became a PROVINCE. Once his successor, Hieronymos, sided with Carthage, however, Syracuse's fate was sealed. After a siege (213–211) the city fell to Marcus Claudius Marcellus, despite the efforts of ARCHIMEDES, who designed new defensive devices. Incorporated into the province, Syracuse retained pre-eminence as the capital of Sicily and seat of its governor. A tax-paying community under the REPUBLIC, it was 'a fine sight whether approached by land or by sea' (CICERO, *Against Verres 2*, 4.52.117). Under AUGUSTUS, in 21 BC, Syracuse became a *colonia*, with an influx of retired legionary settlers, a new public square, a monumental ARCH, the first phase of the AMPHITHEATRE, and possibly the Galermi AQUEDUCT. A 2nd-century theatre–temple complex (the 'Gymnasium') is the only substantial surviving public building of mid-imperial date. The city's continuing size in late antiquity is demonstrated by the substantial CATACOMBS (C.AD 200–600) which ring the city on its north side. (see also SICILIAN EXPEDITION) RJAW

See Wescoat, B. D., ed. (1989) *Syracuse*; Wilson, R. J. A. (1990) *Sicily under the Roman Empire*.

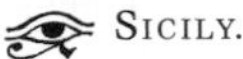 SICILY.

Syria, hellenistic see COMMAGENE; SELEUKIDS.

Syria, Roman The PROVINCE of Syria was first organized by POMPEY in 64 BC from the remnants of the SELEUKID kingdom, which had been broken up by PARTHIAN attacks and civil wars since the 2nd century. There was a core of Seleukid northern Syria (cities such as ANTIOCH and APAMEIA), autonomous cities (e.g. Tyre) and autonomous kingdoms in the south (e.g. Emesa in southern Syria, Ituraea in modern Lebanon). In the north, the Euphrates provided a RIVER frontier with the Parthian empire. The frontiers in the south were less well defined, often fading into desert. The province remained somewhat fragmented for decades, disrupted by Parthian attacks and by the local impact of the Roman civil wars of the 40s and 30s BC.

AUGUSTUS retained the basic form of Pompey's Syria, with both directly controlled territories and semi-autonomous CLIENT kingdoms. However, the military importance of the Parthian frontier was recognized, and a garrison of four legions, with a comparable number of AUXILIARY troops, was installed. Roman governors of Syria were appointed by the emperor as imperial legates. The governor (legate) of Syria had civil duties, such as the administration of justice, but also commanded the garrison in time of war and conducted diplomacy with the Parthians and client rulers. He had to have initiative (Rome was too far away to consult in a crisis) but also had to be trustworthy. For these reasons, the legateship of Syria became an extremely important and prestigious position for Roman SENATORS. Antioch was the legate's base, the provincial capital and *de facto* capital of the Eastern empire. The emperor himself often visited when touring the East or preparing military campaigns, as did members of the imperial household (AGRIPPA, GERMANICUS).

Throughout the 1st century AD the Romans took direct control of the client kingdoms. By the end of the century Roman Syria was a province entirely under formal Roman control, bounded by the provinces of CAPPADOCIA and CILICIA to the north and JUDAEA to the south. To the east the Euphrates was still a major boundary, with some expansion into the desert to the south, so the formerly independent city of PALMYRA now lay within the Roman province. Expansion to the east, into ARABIA and MESOPOTAMIA, under TRAJAN and the Severans meant that by the early 3rd century Syria was no longer a frontier province. Nevertheless, warfare further east still had a substantial impact, as Roman armies gathered here and, on occasion, PERSIAN penetration of the frontier provinces led to Syria itself becoming a battleground. This happened twice in the 250s, when the SASSANID king SHAPUR I overran the territory as far as Antioch. In the subsequent power vacuum the rulers of Palmyra seized control of much of the Eastern empire (including Syria), until AURELIAN restored Roman power in 272–3. A series of Persian attacks in the 6th century penetrated into Syria, but it remained politically part of the Eastern Roman (Byzantine) empire until 636, when it was conquered by Arab armies.

Culturally, Roman Syria was complex. Only around Berytos (mod. Beirut) was there significant settlement by Latin-speaking Western Romans, specifically legionary VETERANS in the reign of AUGUSTUS. The Greek language was widespread, as were the descendants of hellenistic (Greco-MACEDONIAN) colonists. Civic life in cities such as Antioch tended to follow the norms of the Greek eastern Mediterranean in areas as diverse as local politics, ART and ARCHITECTURE. However, the indigenous (pre-hellenistic) cultures of the region remained important throughout the Roman period. For example, the pre-Greek form of settlement in 'VILLAGES' (Greek *kômai*; the word 'village' does not do justice to the diversity of such nucleated rural settlements) remained typical outside the immediate vicinities of the cities, especially in southern Syria and the middle Euphrates valley. Linguistically, these indigenous cultures were based on dialects of Aramaic; one of these, Syriac, became the basis of an important literary (especially CHRISTIAN) culture from the 4th century AD. The art and architecture of the province sometimes falls into the mainstream of the Greco-Roman East, but often displays the influences of both indigenous and Iranian forms. Of particular note are the figured WALL-PAINTINGS from DURA EUROPUS and the distinctive sculptural styles of Palmyra.

Discussion of the economy of Roman Syria (one of the wealthiest provinces of the empire) tends to emphasize TRADE. Certainly, trade involving Syria was important to the Roman state as a whole and to individual communities. Revenue was raised by the repeated levying of CUSTOMS dues upon traders passing from the east to the MEDITERRANEAN, at the imperial frontier, at provincial boundaries and the limits of city territories. Doubtless some communities on well-trodden routes (Palmyra, Dura Europus and Seleukeia–ZEUGMA are obvious examples) derived a substantial proportion of their revenues in this way, particularly when the traded commodities were high-value luxury goods. Evidence for the administration of these customs boundaries exists in the form of inscriptions, most notably the civic customs tariff from Palmyra, which lists the taxes levied on a wide range of commodities. Inscriptions identifying Syrians as traders are found in some numbers throughout the Roman world; archaeologically, however, this trade is difficult to detect. Many of the goods they dealt in were perishable. AMPHORAS that contained perishable goods and fine table POTTERY, which may have been traded along the same routes and can act as a 'marker' for perishable goods, have not been as intensively studied as elsewhere in the Roman empire. As in any other Roman province, AGRICULTURAL production formed the basis of the wealth for most communities, and ARCHAEOLOGY has provided evidence for this aspect of life in the province. Syria was the location of pioneering French projects in aerial and

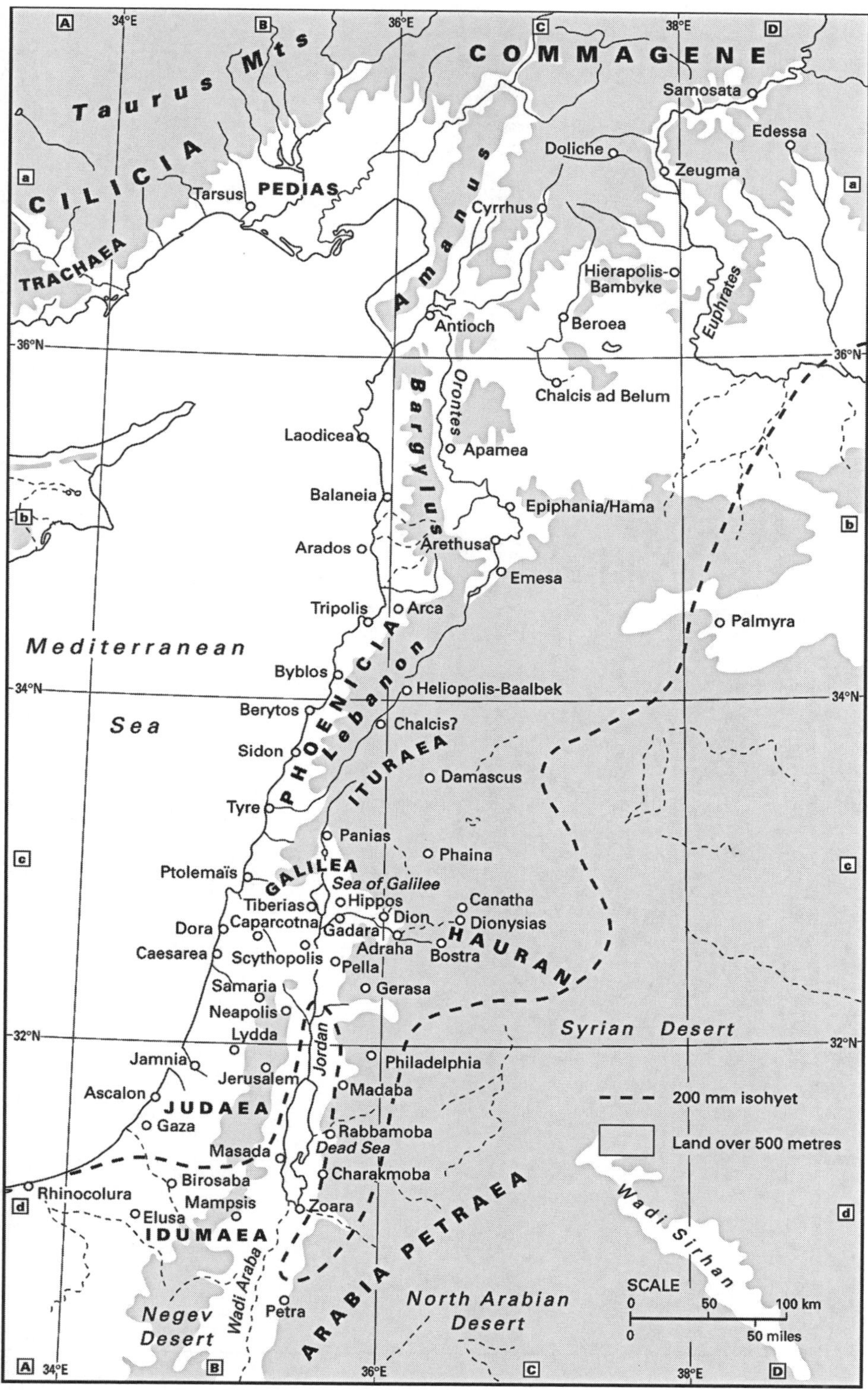

SYRIA, ROMAN: (a) map of Syria and Arabia.

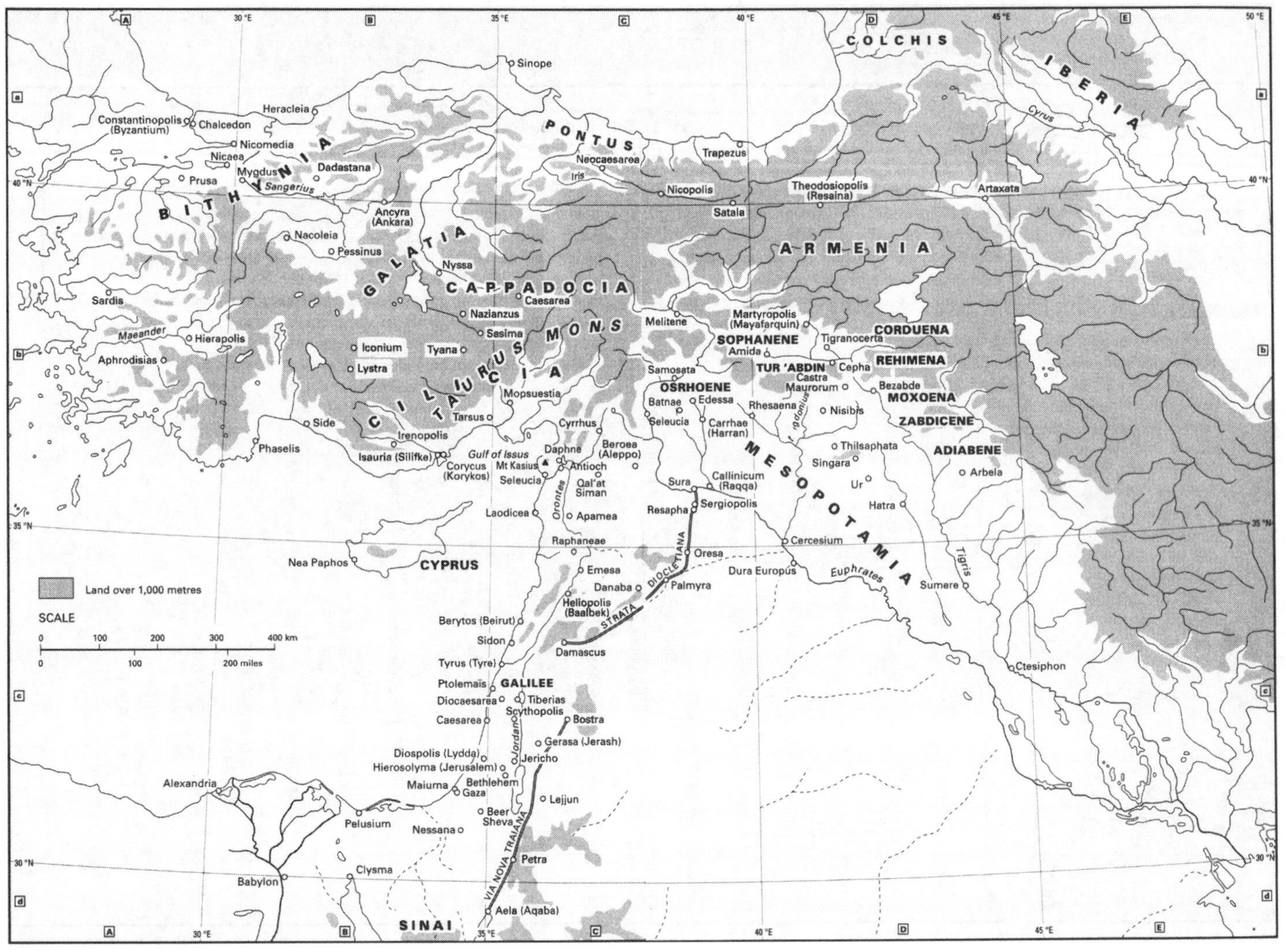

SYRIA, ROMAN: (b) the East in the late Roman period.

ground-based rural survey. More recent work has included a major survey in the Hauran and a re-evaluation of Tchalenko's work in the Bélus massif of northern Syria. NDP

See Kennedy, D. (1996) Syria, *CAH* 10, 703–36; Millar, F. (1993) *The Roman Near East, 31 BC–AD 337.*

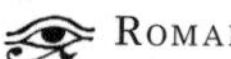 ROMAN EMPIRE: (b).

Syrian wars, of Ptolemies A series of wars, all except the last in the 3rd century BC, fought by the PTOLEMIES against the SELEUKIDS for control of the strategically important area of Koile (Coele) Syria ('Hollow Syria'). Although the territory was annexed by PTOLEMY I Soter in 320 BC, SELEUKOS I Nikator claimed it as his reward for defeating Antigonos Monophthalmos at IPSOS in 301. Seleukos did not press his claim, in part because Ptolemy had given him refuge in 315 and helped him recover his satrapy of BABYLONIA after the battle of Gaza in 312, but the struggle was taken up by the successors of Soter and Nikator. Firm dates for the earliest wars are difficult to establish, but the wars can be broken down as follows. The first (late 270s), apparently precipitated by the alliance of the Seleukid king Antiochos I Soter with Magas of CYRENE, and second (c.260–253) were fought by Ptolemy II Philadelphos, who attempted to establish peace with the Seleukids by marrying his daughter Berenike to Antiochos II Theos (who agreed to repudiate his first wife, Laodike). The third Syrian, or Laodikeian, war (246–241) was a consequence of this arrangement. The fourth Syrian war (219–217) saw native Egyptian forces of Ptolemy IV defeat ANTIOCHOS III at Rhaphia in 217, but this was avenged in a fifth war (202–195), when the now mature Seleukid ruler overcame the forces of the boy-king Ptolemy V Epiphanes, who subsequently married Antiochos' daughter Cleopatra (I). In the sixth and final war (169–168), Cleopatra's brother Antiochos IV brought his army to Memphis after defeating Ptolemy VI Philometor but was confronted by a Roman SENATORIAL delegation. The leader of the Roman embassy, Gaius Popillius Laenas, threatened Antiochos with war if he did not withdraw from Egypt. Polybios records that Popillius drew a circle in the sand, requiring the king to stay inside it until he had answered the ultimatum – a clear indication of how the geopolitical realities had changed. There were no more Syrian wars. WH

T

Tabula Banasitana Inscribed bronze plaque found in 1957 at Banasa, Mauretania (Sidi Ali bou Jenoun, Morocco), now in the Antiquities Museum, Rabat. Its three Latin texts document how a native tribal leader in this FRONTIER province successfully petitioned for ROMAN CITIZENSHIP, and the reasons given for granting it. Two grants of citizenship are recorded: c.AD 168 to Iulianus, chief of the Zegrenses, his wife Ziddina, and their children; then in 177 to Faggura, wife of Aurelius Iulianus (the same man or possibly his son), and their children. The Latin names of Iulianus and the children demonstrate a pre-existing aspiration to Roman culture and the tablet's elegant production reflects the beneficiaries' pride in the grant. The first two documents are letters from the EMPERORS to the provincial governors, demonstrating the importance of the governors' sponsorship (*suffragium*) of the petitions. The last document reproduces, uniquely, an authenticated copy of the entry in the central register (*commentarius*) of those awarded citizenship by imperial grant, certified by the names and seals of 12 witnesses – a snapshot of the emperors' advisory council (*consilium principis*) on that day. This confirms a continued liability to both the law of the tribe and all TAXES collected by Rome. RWBS

See Gascou, J., ed. (1982) *Inscriptions antiques du Maroc*, vol. 2, no. 94 (critical edition and photograph); Lewis, N. and Reinhold, M., eds. (1990) *Roman Civilization: selected readings*, vol. 2, 57–8 (trs.); Williams, W. (1975) Formal and historical aspects of two new documents of Marcus Aurelius, *ZPE* 17: 37–78.

Tabula Peuteringiana see PEUTINGER TABLE.

Tacitus (Cornelius Tacitus) AD ?56–?118 HISTORIAN, ORATOR and CONSUL. 'Austere' – 'cynical' – 'pessimistic' – 'brooding' – 'violent' – 'brilliant': some adjectives commonly applied to the intellect and imagination of Cornelius Tacitus. But attempts to divine the real man behind and within his content and style have been baffled. The voice, at once conspiratorial and aloof, defies easy interpretation. Little is known about his life: even his *praenomen* is uncertain. We have some dates. A successful SENATORIAL career, including a PRIESTHOOD, possibly the rank of *quaestor Augusti* (personally responsible to the emperor), and a CONSULSHIP (97), ended with the proconsulship of ASIA (112–13). He married the daughter of Gaius Julius AGRICOLA, governor of BRITAIN; Agricola was from Gallia Narbonensis, and it is often assumed that Tacitus was as well.

The life experiences of historians had a special relevance to their conception of style and content. Tacitus' career, it would seem, is no exception. Working always from the perspective of an insider, he constructs an ideal audience, the *prudentes*, or 'wise' readers, versus the *stulti*, the stupid ones who are taken in by appearances. His world comprises a series of concentric circles: an outer ring of barbarians, on the threshold of Roman *imperium*, neither wholly inside nor wholly out, tantalizingly exotic, often morally superior, yet still 'other'; a middle group of crowds, soldiers or urban populace, dangerous, venal and necessary; and an inner circle of ARISTOCRATS, senators and military commanders, driven by traditional Roman values of glory and prestige but now turned inward on themselves, burdened with the consciousness of Republican history and picking their way over the hot coals of a terrifying present. This universe centres claustrophobically on the EMPERORS, who manipulate an elaborate system of deceit, subterfuge, double-speak and horror, and who ceaselessly read the countenances and actions of their subjects. These, in turn, must read the emperor, in whose absolute power meaning lies, a reading that is neither neutral nor optional. Misinterpretation means death.

Tacitus seems to have modelled not only his style but perhaps his literary development on his two great predecessors, SALLUST and LIVY. Like Sallust, he begins with monographs: a biography of his father-in-law, an ethnography of GERMANY (both published in 98), and a neo-Ciceronian dialogue on the decline of political oratory (c.102). Next, around 109, comes an account of the Flavian dynasty (the *Histories*) beginning with the power struggles of the Year of the Four Emperors (69); only the first four and a quarter books (of an original 12?) are preserved. Opening with the announcement that AD 69 was nearly Rome's last year, the preface to *Histories* 1 bills the forthcoming narrative as one 'rich with disaster' and illustrative of divine revenge; on display too, the historian promises, are examples of admirable, even heroic behaviour. History for Tacitus is here like Livy's: a compelling record of human actions that offers moral instruction. Like Livy, too, Tacitus settles on annalistic history, the yearly record of the Roman state, articulated by consuls. His last work (originally in 18 books?) begins with the death of AUGUSTUS, and is titled in the manuscript *Ab excessu divi Augusti* ('from the death of the deified Augustus'); we know it as *Annals*. Most consider this last work Tacitus' best. Certainly, in it he perfects his skill at vivid and nasty characterization, at the interweaving of military and political narratives, and at the concentrated analysis of hypocrisy, both political and domestic. The starting-point has been criticized; but Cornelius Tacitus understood the importance of origins. To penetrate the PRINCIPATE one must return to the point at which it became an inheritance. The backward progression of *Histories* and *Annals* betrays the historian's fascination with cause.

Annals are an ideal mode for expressing the disjunction between the Republican forms 'preserved' or 'restored' by Augustus and the imperial content that gradually – and designedly – crept into the mechanisms of the state. *Annals* 4 opens thus: 'When

Gaius Asinius and Gaius Antistius were consuls it was Tiberius' ninth year . . .'. Such a conjunction of consular and regnal dates is senseless. Rome's annual MAGISTRACIES were multiple – no one man could hold sole power in any given office – and limited (in theory) to a single year, whereas imperial power is temporally unlimited and admits of no partnership. In the *Annals* the historian thus inscribes a duality into the very form of his narrative. The same duality is found in the person of the writer himself. Senatorial rank and Republican offices persisted under the empire; but like the yearly consular elections, were increasingly seen – and felt – to be a sham. Writing Roman history from the inside, Tacitus constantly faces the gap between form and content. It shows in his manner of expression: imbalance, contradiction, epigrammatic cruelty, dizzying variety, novel and archaic vocabulary, free, often inventive metaphor, and above all surprise and ambiguity combine to make his one of the most exciting and difficult of all Latin styles. But it is personalities that are at the heart of all his work. They are what we most remember: the brave but modest Agricola; the fiercely independent Calgacus; the Catonian Maternus; Aper, the brilliant devil's advocate; NERO's savagely inadequate successors; the masked TIBERIUS; the coldly controlling LIVIA; the wrong but romantic Germanicus; CLAUDIUS, the idiot-savant; the uncontrolled, gluttonous MESSALINA; the murderous actor Nero; SENECA, the cartoon character.

The *Histories*, together with *Annals* 11–16 and *Annals* 1–6, barely survived the medieval period, each being preserved in a single manuscript. The monographs did not fare much better. Since their rediscovery by RENAISSANCE humanists, however, they have been influential in such varying spheres as French classical theatre, Enlightenment philosophy and 20th-century eastern European politics. Tacitus' style, together with his pervasive consciousness of living in a decadent, post-classical world, makes him particularly attractive to our own, post-modern society. CSK

See Bartsch, S. (1994) *Actors in the Audience*; Martin, R. (1981) *Tacitus*; Syme, R. (1958) *Tacitus*; Woodman, A. J. (1998) *Tacitus Reviewed*.

Tacitus (emperor)

EMPERORS, ROMAN: (b).

tactics, military

The arrangement and use of troops on the field of battle proper (*taktika*) fall into three distinct periods in Greek history. For many of the wars of the earlier city-states (700–500 BC), battle was nearly without tactics. The predominately agrarian character of the citizen militias tended to define WAR as a single collision between phalanxes of heavily armed infantry – a decisive engagement where causalities were limited, victory and defeat clear-cut, and damage to the surrounding countryside and civilian population limited. GENERALS fought in the front rank, and their tactical options were exhausted with pre-battle placement of particular contingents along the battle line and the choice of terrain. Fleets were rare, sea battles essentially non-existent. Armies were challenged to fight by formal notification, and occasionally coerced to action by the ravaging of crops. Battle itself was not much longer than half an hour or so; pursuit was rare.

The PERSIAN (480–479 BC) and PELOPONNESIAN (431–404 BC) WARS changed all that, and revealed the tactical limitations of HOPLITE armies when faced with forces that did not share the same protocols of warfare, and fought in theatres of war and on terrain that were far removed from flat plains. Athens turned to its fleet, and soon developed sophisticated methods of defensive – the *kyklos* or circling of SHIPS – and offensive manoeuvres: attacking through (*diekplous*) or around (*periplous*) an enemy line of ships to achieve ease in ramming. In contrast, the Spartans sought to improve on the simple collision of hoplite battle, by mastering outflanking movements on the right wing, made possible by the superior drill and training of their professional corps. THUCYDIDES' magnificent description of MANTINEIA (418) reveals how such tactical competence might shatter an enemy line and change the entire course of a battle. At the battle of Delion (424) the THEBAN general Pagondas first employed reserves, massed phalanxes deeper than the standard eight shields, and used horsemen for more than just preliminary skirmishing. KLEON, BRASIDAS and Demosthenes during the Archidamian war (431–421) experimented with light-armed troops to attack hoplites, through manipulation of terrain, darkness and sheer surprise. None sought decisive confrontation through traditional hoplite pitched battles.

EPAMEINONDAS (d.362) is often considered the father of Greek infantry tactics. In fact, none of his 'discoveries' – a deepened phalanx, the use of superior troops on the left, the oblique order of march, incorporation of élite units, and the combined use of horsemen – was novel *per se*. Rather, his originality lay in combining these previously known tactical options into a unified battle plan, one uniquely suited to his phalanx of dour Theban agrarians who had a reputation in antiquity for physical prowess and infantry ferocity. His victories at LEUKTRA and Mantineia proved that an innovative heavy infantry might still alone clear a battlefield of the enemy. Other 4th-century reactionaries were more abstract. PLATO and ARISTOTLE, for example, speculated on ways of preserving the hoplite supremacy within the city-state, ranging from using infantry in expanded roles on the borders to the incorporation of stockades and FORTIFICATIONS into the old civic idea of a hoplite militia defence.

Nevertheless, throughout the 4th century most generals worried not so much about the tactical possibilities of infantry employment as about learning the new uses of ARTILLERY, missile troops, peltasts and CAVALRY, both for the attack on and the defence of fortified positions. Utilitarian PHILOSOPHERS and rhetoricians reflected this growing tactical renaissance, as they sought to apply dialectic and induction to generalship (*stratêgika*), the arrangement of troops (*taktika*) and weapons training (*hoplomachia*). War was no longer a question of bravery or a reflection of values, but simply an art (*technê*), teachable like any other. XENOPHON (428–354), author of monographs such as *The Cavalry Commander* and *On Horsemanship*, is the best example of this mixture of battlefield experience and philosophical training. His contemporary, the pragmatic AENEAS THE TACTICIAN, follows in the same utilitarian tradition.

Aeneas' apparently vast *Military Preparations* is lost, but an extant monograph about survival under SIEGE covers everything from the mundane (e.g. passwords, reveille, codes, tunnelling, fire-signals) to the broader employment of MERCENARIES, sorties and plans of evacuation.

PHILIP II and ALEXANDER sought to combine infantry innovation with light-armed, missile and mounted troops to form a true symphony of forces. Battle became longer, as much as several hours in duration. The general – nearly always mounted – now had a host of options and different troops at his command, which allowed much smaller Macedonian armies to create havoc on particular spots in the enemy's battle line, through which poured heavy cavalry and infantry, causing psychological terror and general collapse. Perhaps Alexander's greatest tactical contribution was the idea of rapid and unceasing pursuit, as part of his overall aim of destroying the enemy outright on the battlefield. Until this date, battle tactics had not been closely integrated with larger strategic issues. But Alexander saw troop arrangement as merely a part of grand STRATEGY; his aim was not to win on the battlefield, but to destroy both materially and spiritually the enemy's will to resist. Battle would then logically lead to the invaded party surrendering its territory and its very culture to Macedonian control.

In that regard, Alexander reinvented entirely the notion of Greek tactics, which in the 4th century had evolved from, but not replaced, the original emphasis on formal infantry engagements to resolve border disputes. The purpose of Greek battle had been to limit casualties and resolve disagreement through simple and often economic use of force. With the decline of the agrarian city-state in the 4th century, however, Greeks enhanced decisive battle with AUXILIARY troops to make fighting longer and more elaborate – but not necessarily all-destructive. Under the Macedonians, the west at last applied its full scientific and rational arsenal to the battlefield, as part of a larger effort to destroy a culture, rather than defeat an enemy. Tactics at last now fully served strategy. VDH

See Anderson, J. K. (1970) *Military Theory and Practice in the Age of Xenophon*; Delbrück, H. (1975) *History of the Art of War*, vol. 1; Hanson, V. D. (1989) *The Western Way of War*.

Battle tactics in the REPUBLICAN period are best described by POLYBIOS. The initial skirmishing was begun by the CAVALRY and light-armed troops (*velites*), who screened the lines of the heavy infantry of the LEGION. The last formed up in three 'lines' (each six or three men deep), which comprised the various 120-man maniples (*manipuli*, literally 'handfuls') of the *hastati*, *principes* and *triarii*. Before settling down to close combat with the sword, the first lines would discharge their javelins (*pila*, singular *pilum*). Between each maniple of the first line was a space roughly large enough to contain a maniple, and behind each of these spaces, in the second line, were the maniples of the *principes*. The *triarii* were similarly arranged, being located behind the spaces in the second line. Hence the individual maniples could exert pressure on a rigid opposing line and then fall back into the open space and allow the maniples of the *principes* to move forward to the attack. Against a more fluid enemy formation, like that of the Gauls, the gaps would be filled by portions of the enemy line that pushed forward, but the effect would be to disrupt the continuity of the enemy force. In the event of both the *hastati* and *principes* tiring, their maniples could fall back behind the line of the *triarii*, who continued to use the thrusting spear (*hasta*), and would presumably extend their line into a solid formation similar to the Greek HOPLITE line.

The maniples existed before and after the Romans reformed the army and made the cohort the basic organizational unit. The oval shield (*scutum*) allowed better protection to the body than the circular *clipeus*. Together these two features gave the Roman line an elasticity for both offensive and defensive actions. For an offensive against the Macedonian phalanx, the maniple was particularly effective. It allowed smaller groups of men to penetrate gaps that developed among the hedge of *sarissai* (Macedonian pikes, 5.5–7 m or 18–24 ft long) and make a close-up attack on the insufficiently protected phalangites, who were employing both hands to wield the *sarissa*. And, in such situations, the Spanish sword adopted by the legionaries proved to be an effective instrument of death and dismemberment. (see also ARMIES, ORGANIZATION OF, ROMAN) WH

See Goldsworthy, A. (2000) *Roman Warfare*.

talent see MONEY SUPPLY, GREEK; WEIGHTS AND MEASURES.

Tanagra see BOIOTIA; FIGURINES, TERRACOTTA; OINOPHYTA, BATTLE OF.

Tanit Main goddess of CARTHAGE, equivalent of PHOENICIAN Astarte. Tanit was a MOTHER GODDESS, connected to fertility and also the heavens; BAAL HAMMON, the primary god of Carthage, is her companion. An inscription recently discovered at Sarepta in Lebanon provides the first evidence of her cult in the 7th century BC, but inhabitants of Punic colonies in North AFRICA, SARDINIA, SICILY, Spain, the

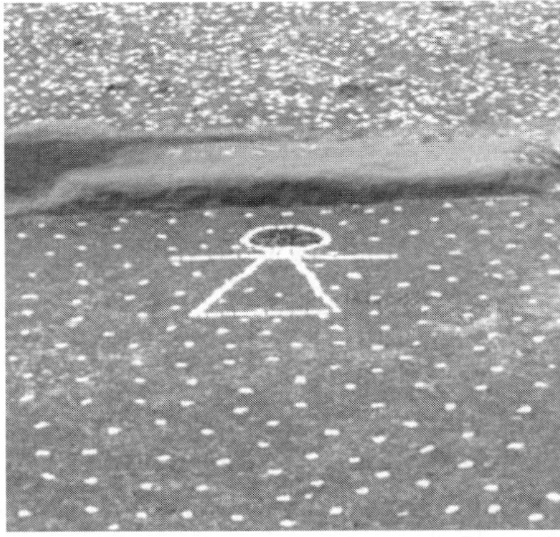

TANIT: symbol of the goddess in a Carthaginian tessellated floor at Kerkouane, Tunisia.

Balearic islands and Malta left more ample testimony to her veneration. Her worship is particularly evident from the 5th to 2nd centuries BC in Carthage. Later, syncretized with JUNO Caelestis of Carthage, she continued to be worshipped under the Roman empire.

The evidence relating to Tanit is complex and imperfectly understood. Her name (TNT in Phoenician) may instead be spelled 'Tinnit'. Inscriptions from the *tophet*, a sanctuary found in Carthage and Punic colonies, refer to her as 'Tanit face of Baal' (TNT PN BL or 'Tanit pene Baal'), though the meaning is not clear. Many archaeologists believe that Carthaginians sacrificed children to Tanit and Baal Hammon in the *tophet*, though there is not universal agreement about this conclusion. Finally, a schematic drawing of a female figure consisting of a circle atop a horizontal line above a trapezoid may represent the goddess. Thousands of these figures appear on stelae, coins, amulets and other objects and are commonly called the 'sign of Tanit'. DLS

Tarentum see FLAMININUS; METAPONTUM; PYRRHOS.

Tarquinia The modern town at Tarquinii, chief city of ETRURIA and legendary home of TARQUINIUS PRISCUS and TARQUINIUS SUPERBUS, kings of early Rome. Known as Tarch(u)na in Etruscan, the city was founded by Tarchon, brother or son of the eponymous hero Tyrrhenus. Legends tell of Tages, who revealed the arts of divination, and of the CORINTHIAN Demaratos, who immigrated to Tarquinii, married an Etruscan woman and fathered Lucumo, Rome's Tarquinius Priscus. Archaeological finds confirm early contact with Greece. Relations with Egypt are evident from the Bocchoris tomb, named after the pharaoh of that name (c.718–712 BC), whose cartouche appears on a faience vase, an early example of orientalizing features in Etruria. Greek and Villanovan elements decorate other artefacts. Paintings from chamber tombs depict scenes of Etruscan life, and inscriptions record names of individuals and families who held MAGISTRACIES, providing a picture of civic administration. More evidence comes from the *Elogia Tarquiniensia*, fragmentary Latin inscriptions of early imperial date outlining achievements of prominent citizens and their ancestors.

Located on a plateau about 100 km (c.60 miles) from Rome and 8 km (5 miles) inland, the city lost some commercial importance to Caere (CERVETERI) and Vulci from the mid-7th century onwards, but remained significant. In the 4th century, Rome's expansion within Italy generated enough hostility for Tarquinii to build a wall. The city's independence declined for the next centuries. It became a Roman *municipium* in 90 BC, its inhabitants becoming Roman citizens. JV

See Haynes, S. (2000) *Etruscan Civilization*; Scullard, H. H. (1967) *The Etruscan Cities and Rome*.

ETRURIA AND ETRUSCANS.

Tarquinius Priscus A legendary ETRUSCAN son of the Demaratos who fled Corinth after the rise to power of the TYRANT Kypselos. Tarquinius Priscus moved to Rome (changing his name from Lucumo), became KING in what the sources represent as a peaceful manner and ruled 616–579 BC. He is credited with military success and building works that are often also associated with TARQUINIUS SUPERBUS. The mobility of the élite between cities in central Italy is reflected in this story. He does not represent the beginning of an Etruscan domination of Rome, rather the adoption of some Etruscan practices and characteristics at Rome and elsewhere. He was alleged to have commissioned the master craftsman Vulca from VEII to decorate his new TEMPLE of JUPITER Optimus Maximus on the CAPITOLINE (finished by Superbus). This may relate to the story that Demaratos introduced various artistic and ARCHITECTURAL innovations to Italy. Tarquinius was allegedly murdered by the sons of Ancus Marcius, but was succeeded by Servius Tullius because of the intervention of Priscus' wife, Tanaquil. CJS

See Dionysios of Halikarnassos 3.46–4.7; Livy 1.34–41; Cornell, T. J. (1995) *The Beginnings of Rome*.

Tarquinius Superbus Son or grandson of TARQUINIUS PRISCUS, and seventh and last king of Rome (534–510 BC). He is credited with a series of military successes that cohere with the apparent strength of Rome at the end of the 6th century. He is also said to have completed many major building works, such as the great storm drain (Cloaca Maxima) and the TEMPLE of JUPITER Optimus Maximus on the CAPITOLINE. His expulsion from Rome, as the result of a conspiracy led by Marcus Junius BRUTUS, encouraged the sources to draw a picture of a reign similar to that of the worst Greek TYRANTS. His extravagant building works placed enormous stress on the Roman population, and his lifestyle was cruel and given to excess. The final crime was his son's rape of the modest LUCRETIA, wife of his cousin Tarquinius Collatinus. Superbus made strenuous attempts to return to power, but eventually sought refuge with Aristodemus of CUMAE in Campania. While there are several points of convergence between the sources and the ARCHAEOLOGICAL evidence for the power and splendour of the city of Rome by this date, the distortions introduced by the hellenizing style of the sources have made it extremely difficult to isolate a genuine historical account. CJS

See Dionysios of Halikarnassos 4.41–85; Livy 1.49–60; Cornell, T. J. (1995) *The Beginnings of Rome*.

Tarracina Ancient city (mod. Terracina), also known as Anxur, that in the literary tradition fell within the orbit of Roman power by the beginning of the 4th century BC. A Roman colony composed of 300 settlers was founded adjacent to the ancient sanctuary in 329 BC. It was one of a series of maritime colonies on the Pontine coast. With the construction of the Via Appia across the Pontine plain (312 BC), Tarracina was closely connected to Rome and a place passed by travellers. The addition of a CANAL (Decennovius) across the marshes speeded up the journey time. Port facilities were vital for the city's development, as the closest port to Rome prior to the building of OSTIA. There was state expenditure on the building of HARBOUR facilities in the 2nd century BC, and further development in the late 1st and 2nd centuries AD created a large artificial harbour. During the TRIUMVIRATE (43–33 BC), VETERANS were settled in the area. It is possible today to view the considerable archaeological remains of the city: polygonal walls, harbour moles, the Via Appia running through the city, the forum repaved in the Augustan age and the surviving remains of TEMPLES, as well as the famous sanctuaries of Feronia (the so-called temple of JUPITER Anxur). The continued importance of Terracina in late antiquity is pointed up by the GOTHIC king THEODERIC's restoration of the Via Appia and the Decennovius. RL

See Coarelli, F. (1982) *Lazio* 308–22; Christie, N. and Rushforth, A. (1988) Urban fortification and defensive strategy in fifth and sixth century Italy: the case of Terracina, *JRA* 1: 73–88.

Tarraco and Tarraconensis (mod. Tarragona) The capital of the Roman province of HISPANIA Citerior, which was often called Tarraconensis for this reason. It may be the site of the Iberian city that issued coins with the name *Cese* and was adopted by Publius and Gnaeus Scipio as their base in Spain, soon after the first arrival of Roman troops in the peninsula in 218 BC. The FORTIFICATIONS erected by the Scipios can still be seen around the upper town. It remained an important base through the Republican period, and was given the status of *colonia* by JULIUS CAESAR, with the name Colonia Iulia Urbs Triumphalis. Tarraco was also the centre of one of the seven judicial *conventus* of the province. In the late 1st century AD a magnificent complex was built in the upper town to accommodate provincial assemblies, with a TEMPLE, FORUM and CIRCUS. The remains of this and of the AMPHITHEATRE, THEATRE and forum of the *colonia* are still visible. In the reign of the emperor VALERIAN, the BISHOP of Tarraco, Fructuosus, and his two deacons were MARTYRED, and the early CHRISTIAN cemetery reveals a strong and wealthy Christian community through the 4th and 5th centuries. It remained under Roman control, to a variable extent, down to AD 476, when it was absorbed into the Visigothic kingdom. JSR

See Keay, S. J. (1988) *Roman Spain*; Richardson, J. S. (1966) *The Romans in Spain*.

HISPANIA.

taxation

While death was universal and perennial in the classical Greek world, taxes were selective and intermittent. The methods by which states obtained resources from their inhabitants varied considerably. A collection of these methods was made by a student of the PERIPATETIC school (Pseudo-Aristotle, *Oikonomika*, book 2). Among the more novel suggestions are taxes on long hair, and extorting protection money from the owners of sacred crocodiles. More commonly, states raised funds through the management of assets such as land and MINES which could be rented out, and the imposition of indirect taxes. Tolls and sales taxes were effective means of revenue-raising for commercial centres like Athens and CORINTH. Imperial powers could establish monopolies in certain key commodities. Fines and property confiscation also contributed to state funds.

There was a certain reluctance to impose regular direct taxation calculated as a percentage of WEALTH. Such impositions were regarded as degrading and were associated with TYRANNICAL rule. Low state expenditure was probably a factor behind the ability to dispense with direct taxation. Public welfare was limited and the burden of many social services was carried by individuals, not the state. Unlike, for example, Rome, most Greek states did not have the costly burden of maintaining a standing army. The large fleet controlled by Athens in the 5th century BC is the exception rather than the rule. Its maintenance required the development of an elaborate system of tribute collection and financial recording. It is noticeable that the large-scale hostilities of the PELOPONNESIAN WAR placed financial burdens on Athens and Sparta that both struggled to meet. Fiscal planning was fairly rudimentary, and Greek cities tended to be reactive rather than proactive in making their financial arrangements.

The tax burden in Athens fell almost exclusively on the wealthy and the foreign. Complaints about tax burdens are not found outside the ÉLITE. The main financial burden on them came in the form of the LITURGY (*leitourgia*, 'work for the people'). Through their sponsorship of these public works, the élite citizens were able to demonstrate their patriotism and curry favour with the populace. Many individuals spent more money than the bare minimum that was required. Liturgies seem to have been borne with reasonable tolerance.

In times of emergency, a levy (*eisphora*) could be made on the basis of a resident's declared wealth. The property threshold for the tax and its rate were determined by the people's ASSEMBLY. Although the number of men liable for these taxes exceeded those normally liable for liturgies, it did not extend to the poorest sections of the city. The system was reorganized in the year 378/7 BC when those liable were arranged into 100 partnerships or 'symmories' (*symmoriai*). The richest three members of each partnership were required to advance the whole assessment for the partnership, and reimbursed themselves from the other members.

Foreigners who wished to remain resident in Athens were liable for the metic tax (*metoikion*), a fixed annual payment of 12 *drachmas* for men, 6 for women. Foreigners, if they wanted to trade in the AGORA, had to pay a fee. One of the honours that could be bestowed upon non-citizens was 'equality of taxation' (*isoteleia*) with Athenian citizens. Fees were also payable by certain professions. For example, PROSTITUTES who wished to ply their trade in Athens were liable to pay an annual sum. Certain goods also attracted taxes. However, our knowledge of indirect taxation is largely limited to chance finds, and our picture of this area is patchy. Indirect taxes were normally farmed out to contractors, who competed at auction for the right to collect taxes. Andokides recounts how he broke up a syndicate that had formed to keep the auction price low (*On the Mysteries* 133–4).

More complex and systematic tax arrangements existed in the hellenistic period. Taxation on land and produce either through rent or tithes constituted the most important form of state revenue. Commodities such as SALT and water could attract high taxes. Tax concessions became one of the tools of government, and were a highly prized honour. PTOLEMAIC Egypt with its strict control of the ECONOMY seems to have been the most heavily taxing of the hellenistic kingdoms. AJLB

See Archibald, Z. H. et al., eds. (2001) *Hellenistic Economies*; Finley, M. I. (1981) *Economy and Society in Ancient Greece*; Gabrielsen, V. (1994) *Financing the Athenian Fleet*; Niku, M. (2002) Aspects of the taxation of foreign residents in hellenistic Athens, *Arctos* 36: 41–57; Rostovtzeff, M. (1953) *The Social and Economic History of the Hellenistic World*; Samons, L. J. (2000) *Empire of the Owl: Athenian imperial finance*; Thomsen, R. (1964) *Eisphora: a study of direct taxation in ancient Athens*; Wilson, P. (2000) *The Athenian Institution of the Khoregia: the chorus, the city and the stage*.

The imperial system of taxation was the result of historical development. A scheme originally devised to fulfil the needs of a growing, though numerically limited, urban community was adjusted progressively, and somewhat chaotically, to provide eventually for the military and economic welfare, or mere survival, of an enormous empire. Rome exploited the resources of the PROVINCES through an all too thin layer of non-professional administrators who relied on private contractors (*publicani*), military personnel and municipal liturgists. The Roman government took note, however, of differences in the nature and availability of such resources between areas. It tried to incorporate the pre-Roman fiscal traditions and institutions (e.g. the PTOLEMAIC system) of each area, rather than impose a unified system all over the empire. Moreover, the system of taxation does not seem to have been thoroughly reformed between the mid-Republican period and the end of the 3rd century AD, and even then the DIOCLETIANIC reform took over many features of the previous system.

Before 167 BC Roman CITIZENS were required to make occasional, theoretically refundable, contributions (*stipendium*, *tributum*) to supplement, when necessary, various forms of state income. These forms included (1) war booty and indemnities, (2) provincial taxes and (3) *vectigalia* derived from (a) indirect taxes, such as *portoria* (CUSTOMS dues) and the *vicesima libertatis* (tax on MANUMISSION), and (b) the exploitation of state properties (such as land, MINES, and QUARRIES) and monopolies (taxes on SALT, minium [red lead, vermilion] and SILPHIUM). As the territories subjected to Rome expanded, Roman citizens in Italy, Roman colonies, and other communities enjoying the *ius Italicum* were exempted from paying the *tributum*. This took the form of either a land tax (*tributum soli*) or a poll tax (*tributum capitis*), both assessed on the basis of the CENSUS. The land tax, better attested, was paid in money or in kind, as a fixed sum (or quantity, the *stipendium*) or a percentage of the harvest (e.g. *decuma*, 'tithe', but smaller for grain than for fruits). The poll tax was levied in the provinces on adult non-citizens, from the age of 14 (men) or 12 (women) to c.65. Exemptions were granted to various categories of persons (e.g. ATHLETES, PRIESTS, PHILOSOPHERS). During the PRINCIPATE and later, other taxes were levied on trades and occupations, INHERITANCE, the sale of SLAVES, and almost everything else, either on a regular or occasional basis.

Roman and provincial wealth was assessed through general and local censuses, originally held every four or five years by the CENSORS (during the Republican period), every 14 years in Egypt, or on an irregular basis in other places, where the operation was performed by the provincial government or by minor officials (senatorial or EQUESTRIAN *censitores*). The census return (*forma censualis*) listed details about the location, extent and nature of landed property (cultivated or not); about the origin, age and special skill of each slave and free resident; and about other forms of property such as FISHPONDS and HARBOURS. Censuses were introduced in the provinces by AUGUSTUS and AGRIPPA. Their purpose was to inventory all human and material resources, to allow for an equitable distribution of *tributum* among cities and territories.

Little is known about methods of collection outside Egypt. From the Republican period until the early 3rd century AD, collection was farmed out by the censors, then by imperial PROCURATORS or the prefect of the treasury, to companies of PUBLICANS (*socii, publicani*). A company was represented by an agent (*manceps*, *redemptor* or *conductor*) and by elected central and regional administrators (*magistri* and *promagistri*) at the head of a numerous, hierarchically organized staff (*familia publicanorum*). *Vectigalia* were collected at *stationes* managed by *vilici* (bailiffs). From the 1st century AD imperial procurators supervised the publicans; little by little, they took over the whole process while retaining the same organizational model at the bottom. Collection of taxes in kind carried its own problems, such as the necessity of maintaining public GRANARIES, the varying quality and risk of decay of the products, and the logistics of distribution to beneficiaries (the army, or the populations of large cities). For that reason, taxes due in kind were sometimes collected in money (by *adaeratio*).

In Egypt, tax farmers were assisted or superseded by town and village liturgists, on whom provincial and local authorities kept maximum pressure to meet the government's expectations. Even though taxes were rather low by modern standards, taxpayers regularly seem to have had a hard time fulfilling their obligations, and took to flight (by *anachôrêsis*) out of desperation. In that case, the community was responsible and had to make good their unpaid share.

Public revenues went to local and central treasuries (*aerarium*, *fiscus*, *patrimonium*, or *res privata*), from which the government used them according to the will of the SENATE, the EMPEROR, or the finance departments of the imperial, provincial or municipal administrations. The main expenditure was the army, but the imperial administration, the food supply (*annona*) and the construction and maintenance of public ROADS and buildings were costly as well. Certain taxes were earmarked from the start. Such was the case, for instance, with the *vicesima hereditatium* created by Augustus in AD 6 to be specifically allocated to the retirement fund of army VETERANS.

Viewed as a necessity by the government and as a plague by taxpayers, taxation had overall positive side-effects for the entire population of the empire. It forced small farmers to produce marketable surpluses, and contributed to the monetization of the outer provinces, where the army was stationed. JJA

See Brunt, P. A. (1990) *Roman Imperial Themes*; Duncan-Jones, R. (1990) *Structure and Scale in the Roman Economy*; (1994) *Money and Government in the Roman Empire*; Harl, K. W. (1996) *Coinage in the Roman Economy, 300 BC to AD 700*.

technology Just as 'INVENTION' implies a conscious action different from discovery, the Greek origins of *technologia* denote systematic, informed knowledge distinct from purely practical competence. In contexts such as ARCHITECTURE or TRANSPORT, the term 'technology' has become synonymous with 'ENGINEERING' in modern scholarly usage. It is also, however, applicable to a wider range of activities – such as AGRICULTURE, metallurgy and METALWORKING, or ceramic production – whose technical complexity lies in their processes rather than in engineered machinery, tools or structures. The Greek word *technê* translates better as German *Kunst*, which embodies both art and craft, than any single English word. Used in combination (*mêchanikê technê*), and despite the associations with artfulness and trickery implicit in *mêchanê*, it embraced everything mechanical, including devices based upon MATHEMATICS, such as SURVEYING instruments.

Opinions about classical technology frequently involve invidious comparisons between Greece and Rome, labelling the Greeks as theoretical scientists rather than practical technologists, the Romans as adapting the principles of the Greeks' 'temple toys' to large-scale beneficial applications. This distinction is quite unfair. First, none of the MACHINES used widely in WAR, architecture, irrigation and drainage throughout the Roman EMPIRE derived from the curious devices, designed for religious or secular ceremonial occasions, that feature in HERON's *Pneumatika*. Second, the texts composed in ALEXANDRIA also included extensive studies of mathematical and technical aspects of devices such as cranes and presses. (It is a very modern error to dismiss as 'toys' items that helped to cement the social and ritual fabric of ancient statehood.) The considerable overlaps between SCIENCE, MECHANICS and technology in the ancient world were reflected by the MOUSEION (Museum) at Alexandria, whose range of scholars included grammarians and PHILOSOPHERS in addition to medical, GEOGRAPHICAL and ASTRONOMICAL specialists. The potential for interaction among small bands of scholars in centres of this kind must have resembled that of England's Royal Society in the 17th century AD.

Modern development economists would categorize most classical technology as 'low' or 'intermediate', and would praise classical engineers for using renewable energy sources such as water power, and readily available raw materials that allowed easy maintenance. The absence of special materials and precision components, and the lack of legal patents, encouraged technology transfer between ECONOMIC sectors (e.g. from military to civil) and between geographical regions. Military conquest followed by garrisoning was undoubtedly instrumental in the diffusion of technical knowledge. The labour-intensive nature of classical technology provided employment (albeit complicated by the existence of slavery), both in urban construction projects and rural industries. The COMMUNICATIONS infrastructure established for strategic and administrative purposes grew dramatically during the expansion of the Roman empire, and allowed material goods such as ceramics or TEXTILES to be traded, rather than produced on a self-sufficient domestic basis. Substantial TRADE took place on land as well as along the MEDITERRANEAN seaways originally established through Greek and Punic COLONIZATION.

Thus classical technology may be judged (in modern terms) as 'appropriate', for it met the needs of its time without making extravagant demands upon resources. ARCHAEOLOGY shows that a number of newly developed machines, techniques and processes really were applied very widely. MINES in Wales or Spain possessed water-lifting devices like those described by Alexandrian 'scientists' and VITRUVIUS. Water-MILLS could be found from HADRIAN'S WALL to the LEVANT. Blown GLASS and ceramic table-wares with lustrous slips were made in numerous production centres and distributed to most categories of settlements (including many outside the Roman empire). However, non-technical factors such as military security, political unification and monetary integration must be given as much emphasis as technology itself. They facilitated the spread of Greco-Roman civilization throughout the Mediterranean region, and extended it to the formerly 'barbarian' areas to the north.

Most general histories of technology comment upon the absence of 'progress' in classical antiquity, an observation reinforced by influential ancient historians such as Finley. However, Finley's criticism of the failure to exploit water power has proved to be unfounded. Many Roman mills are now known, but most result from archaeological discoveries; what was lacking were the kinds of contemporary documentary sources that would refer to mills. Milling also illustrates the concept of the 'technology shelf', a range of devices of increasing complexity – from manual rotary querns to mechanical, animal-powered or water-powered mills – from which appropriate forms could be selected according to the power sources available and the scale of food processing required. As long as it is recognized that modern views about progress are conditioned by the experience of economic 'take-off' that accompanied the Industrial Revolution, it is possible to acknowledge the existence of extensive applied technology in the ancient world without having to explain why it did not lead to exponential GROWTH.

Thus, a clear perception of Greek and Roman technology requires a broad view that can give credit to the achievements of mechanical engineers and inventors as well as to theoretical scientists – irrespective of modern judgements about 'usefulness', speed of development or scale of application. Likewise, political and economic development must be seen as playing an essential, reciprocal role in the application of technology. Finally, a definition that will be helpful in understanding the classical world must be sufficiently broad to include technology that would be classed today as 'low' (e.g. the availability and degree of specialization of iron farming tools; the use of wheels, moulds and kilns in POTTERY production), 'intermediate' (e.g. mechanical mills and pumps; harnessing systems for heavy traction; domestic WATER SUPPLY and heating) or 'high' (large-scale concrete vaulting; ASTRONOMICAL and SURVEYING instruments with precision gearing). The assessment of technology must always take account of its context, and judgement should have regard to appropriateness rather than sophistication. KG

See Finley, M. I. (1965) Technical innovation and economic progress in the ancient world, *EHR* 18: 29–45; Greene, K. (1990) Perspectives on Roman technology, *OJA* 9.2: 209–19; (1994) Technology and innovation in context, *JRA* 7: 22–33; Oleson, J. P. (1986) *Bronze Age, Greek and Roman Technology: a select, annotated bibliography*; White, K. D. (1984) *Greek and*

Roman Technology; Wikander, Ö. (1985), Archaeological evidence for early water-mills, *History of Technology* 10: 151–79.

 MACHINES; PRESSES: (a).

Telesilla see POETESSES.

Tell Soukas see AL MINA.

Tellus see ARA PACIS; CERES.

temples

The use of monumental buildings recognizable as temples begins to appear in Greece in the 8th century BC. The basic design consisted of a room (the cella or *naos*) on a wide base (stylobate), usually surrounded by a line of columns, the colonnade. An extra room at the entrance (*pronaos*) or rear (*opisthodomos*) could be added, as could extra columns either just outside the entrance at the *pronaos* or inside the cella, or as an extra row in the colonnade.

The origins of the Greek temple may lie in the massive ARCHITECTURE of Egypt, and also in a cultural memory of MYCENAEAN halls. The method of construction was post-and-lintel, with no use of the ARCH. The columns were therefore necessary to support the weight of the ROOF and the decorative entablature between columns and roof. Early temples, such as the temple of HERA on SAMOS (8th century) were overly massive, as the ARCHITECTS appear to have underestimated the strength of their building materials. During the archaic period, wood was gradually replaced by STONE as a building material; when available, MARBLE was the stone of choice. In areas such as the colonies in southern Italy and SICILY, where marble was not readily to hand, limestone was used, sometimes with a marble STUCCO over the top, as in the temple of Hera at Paestum (mid-6th century). Roofs appears to have been of wood, with clay tiles in common use from the mid-7th century.

Two main types of design are recognized, the Doric and Ionic ORDERS. Variations attributed to each order appear mainly in the fashioning of the columns and the entablature. The Doric order generally appeared in mainland Greece and in the Italian colonies. The columns rested directly on the stylobate, without bases. They were fluted, and topped with a simple capital. The entablature, above the columns and below the roof, consisted of an architrave; above that was a repeating horizontal line of metopes and triglyphs. Triglyphs are thought to have originally been the ends of the wooden beams extending from end to end, but became a sculptured decoration of vertical grooves in the stone. Metopes (*metôpa*, singular *metôpon*, in Greek), the 'blank' areas in between, allowed space for decoration.

The Ionic order was less minimalist. As the name suggests, the order began life on the Ionian coast among the east Greek colonies; it also appeared on the AEGEAN ISLANDS. The columns had more fluting than their Doric counterparts, and the ridges of the flutes were flattened. Influences from the Near East can be seen in details such as the volute capitals and the bases upon which the columns rested – ideas that seem to have been borrowed from Near Eastern FURNITURE, like the floral decoration that appears on the capitals and entablature. Rather than triglyphs and metopes, Ionic temples had a continuous decorative area, the frieze.

The two orders did not remain discrete. Blending is visible, for example, on the PARTHENON (c.447–432), where the overall Doric style is mixed with an Ionic frieze along the outer wall of the central building, behind the colonnade. The temple of APOLLO at Bassai had a Doric exterior dating to c.450, and the innovation of a Corinthian capital – a more ornate capital, with stylized acanthus leaves – in the otherwise Ionic interior (c.400).

Temple design also included optical 'refinements' to make the construction more pleasing to the human eye. These include *entasis*, the outward curve of the column shafts, which prevented the illusion that the columns were curving in. The columns were also tapered towards the top, so as not to look top-heavy, and were slanted slightly inward. The

TEMPLES, GREEK: (a) Paestum, temple of Hera.

TEMPLES, GREEK: (b) colonnade and interior wall of cella of the Parthenon.

stylobate and entablature were slightly convex, partially to encourage the run of rainwater from the stylobate, partially so they did not appear to sag in the middle. The Parthenon is usually noted for the use of refinements, but they existed earlier; for example, extremes of *entasis* are visible on the temple of Hera at Paestum.

Decoration, in the form of paint and SCULPTURE, covered much of the temple structure. The main areas of decoration were the pediments, with their triangular fields at either end of the temple, and the metopes and friezes, where painted sculpture quickly took over from purely painted scenes. Often the scenes depicted were of local import, such as the race between Oinomaos and Pelops on the eastern pediment of the temple of ZEUS at OLYMPIA (c.470–457), or the birth of Athena and her fight with POSEIDON for patronage of Athens on the east and west pediments, respectively, of the Parthenon. Some mythological stories were of universal (Greek) appeal, such as the battle of the Greeks against the Amazons (Parthenon; Apollo's temple at Bassai), that between the Lapiths and Centaurs (Parthenon; Bassai; temple of Hephaistos in Athens, c.449–448), and the labours of HERAKLES (temple of Zeus at Olympia; Athenian treasury at DELPHI, c.490–480). Decoration also appeared on the roof. Acroteria at the apex and corners of each gable, and also guttering outlets, could take the form of monsters, *nikai* (winged personifications of victory) or floral motifs. On such temples as the Erechtheion on the Athenian ACROPOLIS (c.421–405), CARYATIDS (statues of women) could act as columns, though this is rare.

TEMPLES, ROMAN: (c) a typical Roman temple with colonnaded porch and pediment, Sufetula, Tunisia.

TEMPLES, ROMAN: (d) side view of the high podium and porch of a similar temple at Thugga, Tunisia.

TEMPLES, ROMAN: (e) a reconstructed temple of 'Romano-Celtic' type, characteristic of northern Gaul and Britain.

The cult statue – the ultimate piece of decoration, and to the ancients the entire reason for the temple – was housed inside the cella. This is particularly notable with PHEIDIAS' monumental chryselephantine (GOLD and IVORY) statues: Zeus at Olympia (c.438–420), one of the Seven Wonders of the world, and Athena Parthenos (c.447–438), whose image we can reconstruct from copies and descriptions. PRAXITELES' cult statue of APHRODITE, bought by the people of KNIDOS (c.350), also became a tourist attraction in its own right. NJW

See Boardman, J. (1996) *Greek Art*; Grinnell, I. H. (1943) *Greek Temples.*

Temples were one of the most prominent architectural landmarks in the ancient city, and today they provide the most visible remains of Roman civilization. However, temples were much more than impressive physical structures: they were expressions of political power and of Roman virtues (piety, honour, virtue itself). Since temples were often vowed and dedicated by conquering GENERALS, they were a visible sign of the prestige urbanism in which the Roman ÉLITE engaged. Their ideological importance is well illustrated by the fact that they were frequently used as the backdrop for forensic speeches. This allowed the speaker to expose the criminal behaviour of his opponent by contrasting it with the venerability of the temple and the cult it housed. The SENATE meeting that decided the fate of the CATILINARIAN conspirators took place in the temple of CONCORD. On a less dramatic scale, the entire municipal council of the city of VEII assembled in the temple of VENUS Genetrix at Rome, the divine ancestor of JULIUS CAESAR, to pay tribute to an imperial FREEDMAN.

Besides serving as places of worship, Roman temples acted as BANKS or places to store money and bullion. The most famous example of this is the temple of SATURN in Rome, where the state treasury was kept. Temples served as meeting-places for people with various occupations, such as the temple of MERCURY for merchants and that of HERCULES Musarum for POETS. They served as offices for Roman state officials: the QUAESTORS resided in the temple of Saturn, the CONSULS in that of Castor, and the plebeian AEDILES in that of CERES. Temples also served as repositories for works of ART. In 211 BC the Roman general Marcus Claudius Marcellus returned after his decisive defeat of SYRACUSE. With him came a vast booty of hellenistic artefacts. He opened his TRIUMPH impressively, with an allegorical painting of Syracuse made prisoner. After using their paintings in the procession, triumphant generals often exhibited them in the temples of the GODS to whom the victories were pledged, where they joined other artworks brought back as booty.

Not every religious site in Rome was a temple. Originally, the word *templum* indicated any place that was circumscribed and separated by the AUGURS from the rest of the land using a certain solemn formula. The space was always intended to serve religious purposes, but chiefly for taking the auspices. The temple was consecrated by the augurs and then by the *pontifices* (pontiffs); not until inauguration and consecration had taken place could religious rites be performed or senate meetings be held in it. It was necessary, then, for a temple to be sanctioned by the gods, and where this had not been obtained a place was not a temple. VARRO (in AULUS GELLIUS 14.7.7) considers the ceremony performed by the augurs as essential to a temple, since the pontiffs also consecrated other sanctuaries that were not temples. Thus the sanctuary of VESTA on the FORUM Romanum was not a *templum* but an *aedes sacra*. The various meeting-places of the Roman senate, such as the CURIA Iulia built by Julius Caesar, required consecration by the augurs before valid decisions could be made in them.

The most important features of the Roman temple were axiality, elevation and frontality. The temple building was placed near the back of the rectangular area, centred on an axis running back from the sanctuary entrance. It was placed on a relatively high podium of STONE or CONCRETE, and was usually set at the back of the sanctuary, approached by a flight of steps, and entered only from the front. Its entrance was often towards the west, the side which was at the same time faced by the image of the god, so that people offering PRAYERS or SACRIFICES at the altar looked east. In the earliest times there appear to have been very few temples at Rome; we may therefore suppose that most places of worship among the earliest Romans were simple altars or shrines. The earliest Roman temples were strongly influenced by the ETRUSCAN style of temple building. The materials were wood (for the columns), mud-brick (for the cella) and TILE for the ROOFS. The roofs were decorated with colourful revetments of terracotta along the cornices. Brightly painted terracotta statues were placed alongside the roofs or in the pediments. Such temples had two rows of columns in the foremost inner area, and three units (*cellae*) at the back. Examples are the JUPITER temple on the CAPITOLIUM, built in the late 6th century BC.

From the 4th century onwards, perhaps inspired by their contacts with the Greeks living in southern Italy, the Romans started to build temples in stone. This allowed higher walls, and the heavier superstructure required that columns be closer together. In general, the adoption of Greek materials and techniques led to the assimilation of Greek proportions and dimensions. Despite strong Greek influence, most surviving Roman temples show a mixture of Greek and indigenous features, worked out in a style clearly of local origin. The earliest surviving specimen of this kind is temple A on the Largo Argentina in Rome, which probably dates to the 4th century. MARBLE was introduced into temple ARCHITECTURE for the first time in 146 BC, at the temple of Jupiter Stator at the CIRCUS FLAMINIUS. After this, the one major innovation that the Romans introduced to temple architecture was that of poured CONCRETE, which made possible vaulted structures with DOMES, one of the prime later examples being the PANTHEON. Outside Rome, monumental temple complexes were built from the 2nd century BC onwards, such as the majestic sanctuary of Fortuna Primigenia at PRAENESTE, dedicated to a goddess of birth but also serving as an oracular shrine. In contrast to Greek sanctuaries, Roman temples owned no vast stretches of land. The only exception is the temple of DIANA Tifatina, located near Capua, on which SULLA bestowed huge properties after his victory over Norbanus in 83 BC. MK

See Barton, I. M., ed. (1989) *Roman Public Buildings* 67–76; Gros, P. (1996) *L'Architecture romaine* 1: *Les Monuments publics* 122–206; Kähler, H. (1970) *Der römische Tempel*.

 ARCHITECTURE: (a)–(d); CAPITOLIUM: (a)–(b); DELPHI.; PANTHEON: (a)–(d); PARTHENON: (b).

tenants and tenancy In Anglo-American common law, tenancy is a property relationship whereby, in the usual case, a tenant receives possession of real property from a landlord; their relationship originates in a lease. In classical Roman LAW, by contrast, tenancy is primarily a contractual relationship (its technical name is *locatio conductio rei*) in which a landlord provides a tenant with the use and enjoyment, but not the actual physical possession, of property. In both systems, however, there are two main types of tenant: the tenant of a dwelling (*inquilinus*) and the tenant of a farm (*colonus*). Lease of commercial premises is a sub-type of farm lease. Roman tenancy had important antecedents in Greek law, and at Rome the social practice also arose very early. However, only in the later Roman REPUBLIC did the Roman jurists begin working out the legal rules for lease. This law applied in principle to all tenants; but the jurists thought typically of wealthier tenants who had better access to legal remedies. Parties concluded a lease through an informal agreement between themselves. Although this agreement could involve special arrangements, the jurists developed elaborate default rules determining what the parties were entitled to do when something went wrong during the term of the lease. In the case of urban lease, for example, the jurists ruled on when the landlord could justifiably expel the tenant from the dwelling, and what the tenant could claim when enjoyment of the leasehold was impaired. Within the Roman context, these rules are reasonably well balanced between the interests of the two parties.

Farm lease, involving the exploitation of LAND, is considerably more important because it is an ECONOMIC relationship. The jurists sought to protect the financial interests of both parties by specifying what each must provide to equip the farm, and by imposing largely commonsensical duties. The tenant had to pay the cash rent, cultivate diligently and maintain the farm in good condition. The landlord had to defend the tenant's control of the farm, compensate for some improvements and (remarkably) abate the rent when it was unavoidable and catastrophic crop losses occurred. The result was a coherent and powerful body of law, intended to secure the landlord a continuing and reliable income while protecting the tenant from oppression. However, Roman law did not entirely succeed in its aims, as is shown by increasingly frequent legal and literary references to arrears in rent payment and the difficulty in finding suitable tenants. Many tenants, less wealthy than those the jurists commonly describe, were sharecropping PEASANTS who at times farmed, not by contract, but on grant from the owner (*precarium*). Payment in kind was also common on imperial estates, especially in the PROVINCES. In the late empire, through a process that remains obscure, tenants such as these became tied to the land through an institution known as the COLONATE, often mentioned in tax and administrative legislation, which has been thought to foreshadow early medieval forms of landholding. BWF

See Frier, B. W. (1980) *Landlords and Tenants in Imperial Rome*.

Terence (Publius Terentius Afer) ?184–159 BC Comic playwright, author of six COMEDIES, first staged between 166 and 160 BC. Terence was born (according to the ancient life attributed to SUETONIUS) in CARTHAGE, and came to Rome as a SLAVE of one Terentius Lucanus, who soon set him free on account of his literary talents. Terence became a protégé of such powerful nobles as SCIPIO AEMILIANUS and Gaius Laelius. His last play, *The Brothers* (*Adelphoe*), was commissioned by Scipio and his brother for performance at their father's funeral games in 160. The earlier plays are *The Girl from Andros* (*Andria*, 166 BC), *The Mother-in-law* (*Hecyra*, 165), *The Self-tormentor* (*Heautontimoroumenos*, 163), *The Eunuch* (*Eunuchus*, 161) and *Phormio* (161).

Like his predecessor PLAUTUS, Terence based his plays on Greek originals, though he seems to have followed his models (especially MENANDER, the source for four of the plays) more closely. The stereotyped characters and typical scenarios of Greek New Comedy recur. Typically, the improvident young hero in love with an (apparently) unsuitable woman is aided by the clever slave or parasite in winning his heart's desire; relationships between fathers and sons are another recurrent theme. Despite a general similarity in scenario and plot-structure, however,

Plautus and Terence differ markedly in the style and character of their comedy. The slapstick and metatheatrical aspects of Plautine drama are significantly reduced in Terence, who gives correspondingly greater attention to characterization and elaborate plotting. The comic inversions characteristic of Plautus are modified, too, by a renewed interest – inherited from Menandrian comedy – in the ARISTOTELIAN values of moderation and the avoidance of excess. Terence's writing is notable for its naturalistic yet refined style (for which he was praised in antiquity by both CICERO and JULIUS CAESAR); again, there is a strong contrast with Plautus' verbal exuberance.

While perhaps less uproariously funny than Plautus, Terence's more subtle and sympathetic portrayal of human relationships has its own appeal. His plays appear to have met with a mixed reception in antiquity. Both the original performance of *Hecyra* and a subsequent revival (as the playwright himself tells us in the prologue to a third production) had to be abandoned when the audience's attention was diverted by the superior attractions of tightrope walkers and GLADIATORS. Caesar's complimentary remarks on Terence's style are somewhat undercut by complaints about his lack of comic power. *Eunuchus*, on the other hand, was a triumphant success, and Terence's plays were still being performed on stage in the late REPUBLIC. Their early adoption as school texts (read, however, more for their elegant Latinity and 'improving' moral sentiments than for their comic genius) ensured their preservation through late antiquity and the Middle Ages into the modern era. MG

See Terence, *The Comedies*, trs. B. Radice (1976); Goldberg, S. M. (1986) *Understanding Terence*.

Tertullian (Quintus Septimius Florens Tertullianus) c.AD 160–c.240 Little is known about Tertullian's early life, except that he came from or near CARTHAGE and was clearly educated, perhaps in the law. According to JEROME, he was the son of a centurion. At some stage in the 190s he converted to CHRISTIANITY; he was married to a Christian. In later life he converted to Montanism, and in the last decades of his life he became ever more rigorous in his practice of Christianity. According to AUGUSTINE (1), Tertullian was one of the first Christians to write in Latin; he is credited with bringing legalistic vocabulary into Christian discourse, particularly with respect to judgement, reward and punishment. Before this, Christian writings had been in Greek. Tertullian's writings are traditionally divided into three categories (apologetic; doctrinal and polemical; moral and ethical), but these belie the complexity of his work and create somewhat arbitrary divisions. His earliest works (late 190s) were certainly apologetic: *To the Nations* and *Apology* defended the Christian way of life against the most extreme Roman propaganda (accusations of incest and cannibalism) and argued for religious toleration. They also contain one of the earliest descriptions of Christian worship. The next period (c.200–6) offers moral and ethical works that addressed, in increasingly puritanical tones, the ideal Christian life. These include *On Shows*, which condemned all kinds of public entertainments and forbade Christians from attending them, and *On the Apparel of Women* and *To His Wife*, which offer interesting detail on female appearance and the idealized role of a Christian wife in Carthage. *On Patience*, *On Penitence* and *On Prayer* also date from this time. *On Baptism*, written to refute the work of GNOSTICS, was the first Christian work on the subject. His efforts against Gnosticism continued in a number of treatises addressing scripture, tradition (*Prescription against the Heretics*), the nature of Christ (*On the Flesh of Christ*), the soul and a refutation of heresy (*On the Soul*), and resurrection of the body and life after death (*On the Resurrection of the Flesh*). From 207 Tertullian's work was aimed at the dualist heresies of Valentinian and Marcion (5 books); the influence of Montanism is increasingly evident. Perhaps from this period is *On the Pallium* (date disputed), a short pamphlet that stresses the differences that should exist between the way Christians and PAGANS live their lives; it centres around an item of dress. Tertullian rejected the Roman TOGA as the garment of the state, and of Roman civic values and honours. In its place he suggested the *pallium*, a simple everyday garment but one associated with philosophers.

The final period of his work contained *Against Praxeas* (c.212), a treatise that gave definition to the Trinity and developed a vocabulary for the relationships between Father, Son and Spirit (using terms such as *trinitas*, *tres personae*, and *una substantia*). Tertullian's formula meant that the West was not so engrossed by the controversies over the nature of Christ that consumed the East after ARIUS in the 4th century. Other works of the Montanist years include *Exhortation to Chastity* and *On the Veiling of Virgins*; both demanded increasingly rigorous practice, presenting remarriage as tantamount to bigamy and insisting that women be veiled at all times, not just in church. *On the Soldier's Crown* (*De corona militis*) suggested that Christianity was incompatible with Roman military service. His last works included *To Scapula* (212), addressed to a governor of AFRICA who persisted in PERSECUTING Christians; this recalls much of the *Apology*, while also threatening divine retribution. Another late work, *On Idolatry*, is against all idolatrous practice. *On Modesty* (*De pudicitia*) was written in response to a ruling (perhaps by Callistus, BISHOP of Rome 217–22) that sins such as adultery, fornication and murder could be redeemed by penitence; Tertullian denied that even the highest churchmen could forgive such sins. This last treatise became central to the debate on penitence in the early CHURCH.

Tertullian's work was highly influential, not only on the development of later Christian doctrine and practice in the West, but also as a witness to the life of Christians in North Africa. As the first significant Christian author to write in Latin, his terminology has had a long-lasting effect. Despite his Montanism, he was clearly known by patristic writers and features in Jerome's *Lives of Illustrious Men*. The *Apology* was one of the earliest early Christian works to be printed, in 1483. MEH

See Barnes, T. D. (1971) *Tertullian*; Wright, D. (2000) Tertullian, in P. Esler, ed., *The Early Christian World*, vol. 2, 1027–47.

Tetrarchs The four simultaneous rulers of the TETRARCHY, one of DIOCLETIAN's measures to reform the Roman empire at the end of the 3rd century AD. Widespread military problems required frequent

TETRARCHS: (a) relief carving of the four Tetrarchs showing many details of late Roman élite dress.

delegation of authority and resources, but also led to frequent usurpations and civil wars. The diversion of resources from the FRONTIERS to fight civil wars in turn led to more frontier crises. The Tetrarchy was Diocletian's attempt to break this cycle. Its creation depended on recognizing that the empire was too large for a single EMPEROR. Diocletian therefore formalized a system of multiple rulers. He began by appointing MAXIMIAN as CAESAR in 285, creating both a subordinate and an heir. Diocletian took primary responsibility for the East, Maximian for the West. Maximian was soon (286) elevated to the status of AUGUSTUS, though clearly still junior to Diocletian (the pair were often referred to as HERCULES and JUPITER respectively). In 293, the system was expanded to involve four rulers – the Tetrarchs. Two Caesars were appointed, subordinate to their Augusti, with GALERIUS serving in the East, Constantius I in the West. This system continued until 305, when Diocletian retired and compelled Maximian to retire with him. The cycle of civil wars had been broken and Roman dominance restored on the frontiers. The stability achieved by the Tetrarchy played a large part in this.

After the retirement of the senior Augusti in 305, the Caesars were promoted to Augusti and two new Caesars appointed: Severus in the West, Maximinus Daia in the east. Diocletian had been able to make these appointments through the force of his personality, assisted by his lack of male heirs. However, the settlement of 305 meant that Maxentius, son of Maximian, and CONSTANTINE, son of Constantius I, were both excluded. When Constantius I died in 306, his troops acclaimed Constantine. Galerius responded by raising Severus to the status of Augustus. Encouraged by this, Maxentius appealed to the praetorian guard in Rome and seized power; his father Maximian soon returned from retirement to support him. Conflict had been avoided for now, but in 307 Severus tried unsuccessfully to defeat Constantine and Maxentius and was killed.

Thus, without Diocletian to keep the participants in order, the Tetrarchy quickly collapsed. Usurpers, like Alexander in AFRICA, also began to appear. In 308 Galerius forced Diocletian to emerge from retirement to broker a settlement at Carnuntum, where he rejected Galerius' attempt to restore him to power. The final result of the conference was to accept four Augusti – Galerius, Constantine, Maximinus and a new appointee, LICINIUS – the Second Tetrarchy. Although peace was decreed between the four rulers, it could not be effective without a strong hand at the top. A series of civil wars between 308 and 313 reduced the Augusti to Constantine in the West, Licinius in the East; Constantine ruled alone from 324. HWE

See Williams, S. (1985) *Diocletian and the Roman Recovery*.

Teutoburgian forest The *saltus Teutoburgiensis* was the place beyond the river RHINE where a Roman army of three legions with auxiliaries (up to 20,000 troops), commanded by Publius Quinctilius Varus, was destroyed in AD 9 by GERMAN TRIBES under Arminius. In one of the signal disasters of Roman military history, Varus was duped into making a long march across difficult country in foul weather – his army encumbered with baggage and non-combatants – while supposedly friendly German leaders gathered their forces for increasingly determined attacks on the exhausted and hungry column. Over three days, Roman organization broke down, Varus committed SUICIDE and the army disintegrated into small last stands and hopeless flight. Some soldiers escaped; most were killed. Prisoners were taken: some for torture and SACRIFICE, some for SLAVERY, others for ransom. Germanicus' army visited the site in AD 15, gathered the skeletal remains and raised a monument. Some captured military standards were recovered piecemeal into the reign of CLAUDIUS, but the legions were never reformed and their numbers (XVII–XIX) were never repeated. The defeat contributed to the Roman decision not to conquer Germany between Rhine and Elbe. Archaeological finds scattered over a large area at Kalkriese (near Osnabrück, Germany) may represent part of the route along which Varus' army was defeated. They include human and pack-animal remains, coins, weaponry, TOOLS and JEWELLERY of appropriate date. JCNC

See Cassius Dio 56.18–22; Florus 2.30; Tacitus, *Annals* 1.61–2; Velleius Paterculus 2.117–19; Schlüter, W. (1999) The battle of the Teutoburg forest, in J. D. Creighton and R. J. A. Wilson, eds., *Roman Germany* 125–59.

textiles Because of their fragile make-up, textiles often appear in a disintegrated state when excavated by archaeologists. However, when present because of favourable climate and environment, mainly in desert conditions, they survive quite well. Examples include those found at DURA EUROPUS in Syria, while especially from late Roman Egypt we have elaborately decorated woven textiles used in both robes and wall-hangings, of which substantial portions

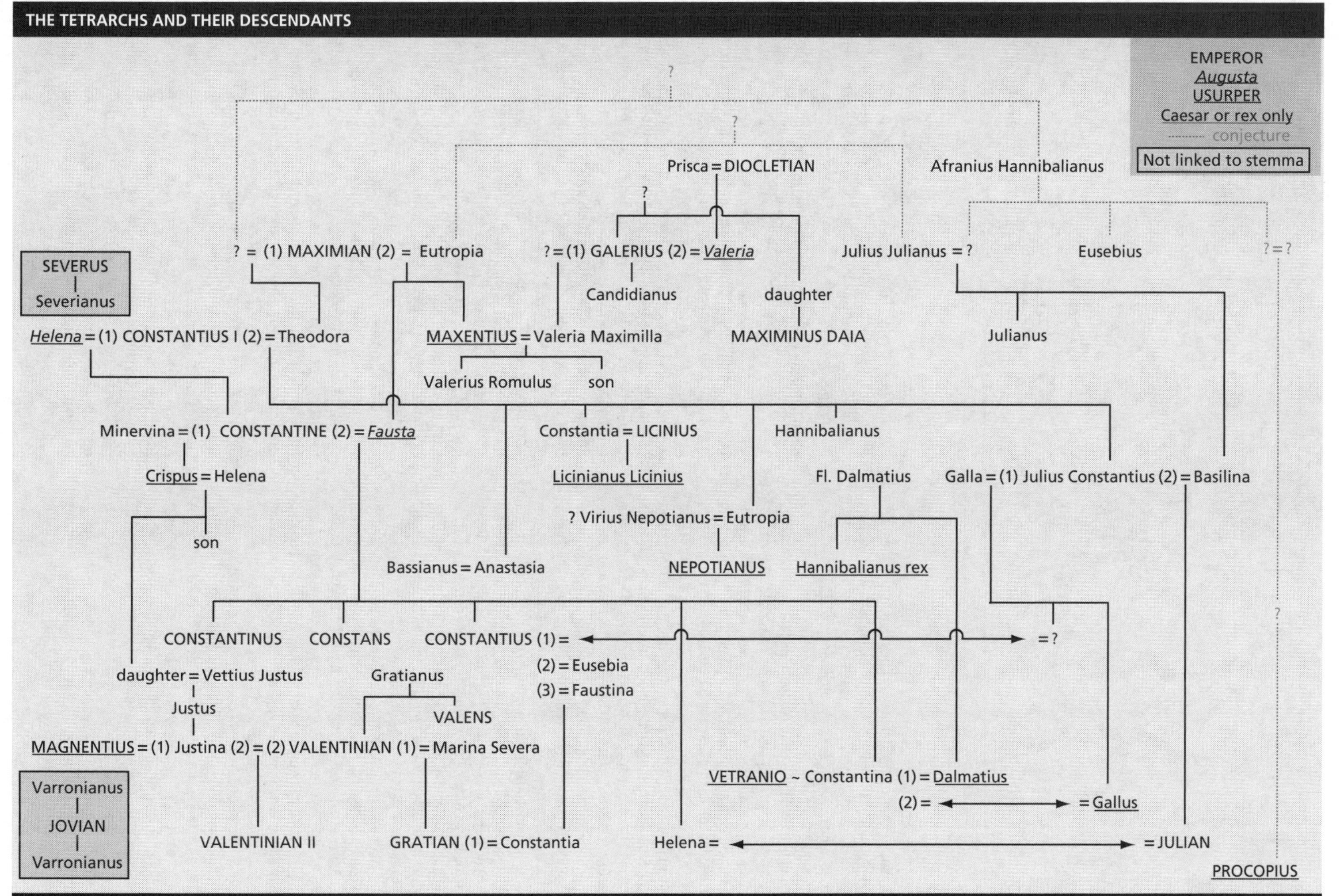

TETRARCHS: (b) stemma of the Tetrarchs and their descendants.

TEXTILES: sale of textiles in a well-appointed boutique, in a relief from Florence.

survive. Popular fabrics in antiquity included linen, wool, hemp, SILK and cotton. 'Experimental' materials used by the Romans were rabbit and GOAT hair, mallow and asbestos. These textiles could be fashioned into a variety of forms: clothing, blankets, bags and tapestries.

The presence of even a minute quantity of thread or fibre allows for interpretations of mode of manufacture, trade and social status. By examining a particular weave, one can learn whether the piece was made in a domestic or a professional context. Analyses of textiles can provide information on TRADE and agricultural practices. Silks, for example, were obtained from CHINA, INDIA and the AEGEAN island of Kos. Colour and fibre composition in wool can inform the researcher where a particular breed of SHEEP came from.

Cloth production entailed assembling the raw product, spinning, weaving, dyeing and fulling. First, the product had to be removed or harvested from its original source. This was usually achieved in the summer months. Wool was sheared and combed. Flax and hemp, harvested by hand, were submerged in a stream or pond and hung up to dry; the dried stalks were then beaten and combed. Little is known about the initial preparatory stages for cottons or silks. The second processing stage was SPINNING.

The final stages of production involved WEAVING, DYEING and FULLING. Threads could be woven on vertical warp-weighted looms, two-beam looms or tablets. Flax and hemp were typically dyed after spinning, whereas wool was dyed before. Dyes could be made of vegetal materials, as well as INSECTS and shellfish. Fabric colours were important status indicators. Cloth in its last processing phase was sent to the fullery, where it was placed in a tub filled with a solution of urine, water and/or fuller's earth, then trodden, rinsed, and hung to dry. While it was still slightly damp, the nap of wool cloth was raised with a spiked board, then cropped to create a smooth finish. Cloth could be bleached by placing it over a semicircular cage, inside which stood a pot of burning SULPHUR. The fuller also cleaned stained garments. LAH

See Barber, E. J.W. (1991) *Prehistoric Textiles*; Bellinger, L. and Pfister, R. (1945) *The Excavations at Dura Europus*, vol. 4, part 2: *the textiles*; Jenkins, D., ed. (2003) *The Cambridge History of Western Textiles*, ch. 3; Mattingly and Salmon, *Economies Beyond Agriculture*; Rutschowscaya, M.-H. (1990) *Coptic Fabrics*; Wild, J. P. (1970) *Textile Manufacture in the Northern Roman Provinces*; (1988) *Textiles in Archaeology*.

 DRESS, GREEK: (a); SPINNING; WEAVING.

textual criticism The practice of textual criticism has long been a central concern of classical scholarship. It is the attempt to restore the texts of ancient authors to their original form. An inevitable feature of surviving ancient texts is that they have undergone a process of corruption. Manuscripts were copied by hand; accordingly, errors were introduced at various stages. Obvious mechanical errors, such as misreading or omission, were compounded by difficulties posed by changing fashions in handwriting and by physical damage to manuscripts. Every text has its own history, and the state of preservation varies enormously; problems must be addressed on an individual basis. In this light, it is hardly surprising that many scholars would prefer to practise textual criticism rather than talk generally about it.

It is true that textual criticism is a pragmatic business, but the main lines can be set out. The first task is to survey the evidence for the text. In most cases, this involves cataloguing a series of medieval manuscripts, the products of the long process of TRANSMISSION; these are now housed in libraries and museums. Although a number of extant manuscripts date from the 5th century AD, most were written between the 8th or 9th centuries and the beginning of the RENAISSANCE. Often the so-called primary tradition of manuscripts can be supplemented by PAPYRI and by what is regularly called the secondary or indirect tradition – quotations preserved in other ancient authors. Papyrus texts rarely survive in a good state, but they are much older than the medieval manuscripts and may preserve features of ancient editions. The secondary tradition can shed light on many passages: these texts have been transmitted independently, and so have not been corrupted in the same way as the tradition of the primary author. Quotations can be unreliable, however, especially because of the ancient tendency to quote from memory.

Manuscript evidence can vary enormously in both quantity and quality. An editor of HOMER, for example, relies on a large number of manuscripts, as well as numerous papyri and a rich secondary tradition. The sheer abundance of textual evidence for the Homeric poems can seem overwhelming, but this situation is preferable to that of, for example, the surviving plays of AESCHYLUS, which depend largely on a single, manifestly corrupt, manuscript. Texts that were popular in the medieval period, such as the works of HORACE and Ovid's *Metamorphoses*, are represented by a large number of manuscripts; but early evidence is often lacking, and the interrelationship of these manuscripts is often highly problematic. In sharp contrast, for VIRGIL there are a number of carefully produced, early codices from the 4th and 5th centuries. Popularity with medieval readers is regularly a guarantee of survival, but medieval tastes often seem at variance with modern sensibilities. LUCAN and STATIUS, for example – both POETS with more than their share of modern detractors – were widely read, and a broadly based manuscript tradition attests to their popularity. CATULLUS, on the other hand, a central figure for modern Latinists, was all but unknown in the Middle Ages. His survival came about by the chance discovery of a single manuscript that came to light in Verona around 1300.

Once the range of material has been established, it is necessary to examine the contents of the extant manuscripts. This is done by 'collating' manuscripts to isolate variants, which can be used to determine the interrelationship of the surviving copies. All manuscripts must have been copied from an exemplar; therefore it is possible, in many cases, to establish a genetic relationship among them. This insight lies behind one of the most influential approaches to textual criticism, what is often called the stemmatic method. It has long been recognized that a manuscript that is a copy of an earlier, extant manuscript is intrinsically less valuable as a witness for the text. The chief criterion for assessing the relationship between manuscripts is the presence of shared errors. While certain errors can arise independently, it is argued that a concentration of errors, especially errors that are unusual in some way, in two manuscripts indicates that one was copied from the other. In principle this may sound straightforward, but in practice the case can often be difficult to make. That one of the two manuscripts for the alphabetic plays of EURIPIDES is directly dependent on the other was not proved decisively until it was determined that a physical blemish in the paper of one was reproduced as an unnecessary punctuation mark in the other! Stemmatic criticism argues that one can illustrate affiliation among manuscripts by constructing a *stemma codicum*, a sort of family tree that plots the descent of manuscripts from an original exemplar, the 'archetype' of the tradition. In theory at least, that archetype can be understood to be the original text, uncorrupted by scribes. Through judicious assessment of the evidence, the critic can move up the stemma towards the archetype.

Stemmatic criticism is useful in illustrating aspects of transmission, but rests on problematic assumptions. The most obvious is that every scribe uses only one exemplar – a 'closed' transmission. It is clear, however, that scribes regularly checked their copy against others, making corrections and importing variants as they saw fit. This process is called contamination. 'Contaminated' manuscripts are part of an 'open' transmission, which in fact seems to be the most common type. Accordingly, the attempt to establish a stemma is often frustrated by the character of the tradition; many derivative manuscripts can be identified, but variants must be considered on an individual basis. The editor must employ a variety of philological skills – in particular a sensitivity to the language and the author's style – to assess readings and choose those most likely to reflect the original text. Moreover, it is also clear that the true text is not always to be found among the primary and secondary evidence. Those same philological skills can determine that in one passage, though transmitted unanimously, a reading is suspect; in another, that none of the variants is plausible. In many cases the corruption can be remedied through conjectural 'emendation', a correction proposed by a modern scholar; but there are passages in which the correct text remains deeply uncertain.

In this light, it is impossible to produce a definitive text of most ancient authors. Many decisions crucial to the enterprise require judgement, and no scholar's judgement will persuade every reader on every point. For this reason it is customary to produce 'critical editions' of texts. The text incorporating the editor's choice of readings is accompanied by a scholarly 'apparatus' (or *apparatus criticus*) that informs readers of the state of the evidence in significant cases, and enables them to view the text with an informed and critical eye. Issues of text often bear significantly on interpretation, so textual criticism is not just a preoccupation of editors but a necessary aspect of the serious study of Greek and Latin texts. CGB

See Reynolds, L. D. and Wilson, N. G. (1991) *Scribes and Scholars*; West, M. L. (1973) *Textual Criticism and Editorial Technique*.

Thales see COSMOLOGY; PHILOSOPHY, GREEK; PRESOCRATIC PHILOSOPHY; SCIENCE.

Thamugadi see TIMGAD.

Thapsus A PHOENICIAN foundation, identified with the extended ruins of Ras Dimas on the north-east coast of AFRICA (mod. Tunisia). In Punic its name means 'passage' or 'ford'. It sided with Rome in the third PUNIC WAR, and is among the *oppida libera* or 'free cities' in the region of Byzacium mentioned by PLINY THE ELDER. It was the site of JULIUS CAESAR's victory over the Pompeians and king Juba in 46 BC. The city struck coins under TIBERIUS, and became a colony (*CIL* 9.5087) and flourishing port in the imperial period. It was later incorporated into the late Roman PROVINCE of Byzacena, and was a titular see in the ecclesiastical province of the same name. Its only known BISHOP, Vigilius, was a participant in the council at CARTHAGE in 484 convoked by the VANDAL king, Huneric, who subsequently exiled him. (Vigilius was the author of some treatises against ARIANISM and Eutychianism.) Remnants of a mole, FORTIFICATIONS, AMPHITHEATRE, large cisterns, a BATH or GYMNASIUM with MOSAICS, and a Punic necropolis have been found. RBH

Thasos A green and mountainous island, in the northern Aegean opposite the mouth of the river Nestos, with a city of the same name. In antiquity, it was rich in gold mines and timber and famed for its wine. Famous Thasians included the poet Archilochos and the painter Polygnotos. The island had a renowned school of sculpture during the 7th and 6th centuries BC.

Thasos was colonized in the early 7th century BC by Parians, probably attracted by the gold. During the 7th century the colonists conquered the Thracians on the mainland opposite, and set up colonies and mines there. At this period, Thasos flourished because of the wealth derived from mining and trade, and built up a strong navy. After the defeat of the Persians, Thasos joined the Delian league and became a democracy. In 465 it seceded from the league because of a dispute with Athens over the mines on the mainland. The Athenians defeated the Thasians in a sea battle, and besieged the town for three years until it capitulated. Athenian rule continued until 411 when Thasos rebelled and went over to the Spartans. In 404, all those still loyal to Athens were slaughtered by the Spartan general Lysander. Nevertheless, in 369 Thasos joined the second Athenian league. The island was seized by Philip II of Macedonia in 340, and remained Macedonian until liberated by the Romans in 196. FMM

See Graham, A. J. (2000) Thasos: the topography of the ancient city, *ABSA* 95: 301–27; Lazaridis, D. (1973) *Thasos and its Peraia*; Wynne-Thomas, R. J. L. (1978) *Legacy of Thasos*.

 Chalkidike.

Theadelphia see Heroninos.

theatre, modern Classical drama is now being performed on the professional and amateur stages with greater frequency than at any time since classical antiquity. Performances fall into roughly two areas: those using translations of the classical texts (though sometimes plays are performed in ancient Greek or, more rarely, Latin), and those using reworkings or versions of ancient plays or stories. The former category includes Peter Hall's National Theatre productions of Aeschylus' *Oresteia* (1981; translated by Tony Harrison) and Euripides' *Bakchai* (2002; translated by Colin Teevan). The latter is represented by John Barton's epic drama cycles *The Greeks* (1980) and *Tantalus* (2000), reworkings of well-known tragedies and mythic stories. The timeless qualities of Greek drama and myths act as an inspiration for many theatre practitioners, who utilize the universal themes of tragedy and, indeed, comedy to highlight modern preoccupations. Thus, for example, in 1993 Peter Sellars directed a production of *The Persians*, setting the ancient tragedy in the contemporary Middle East to reflect the politico-cultural hostility of the Gulf war. Recent sites for Greek tragedies have included Bosnia and Northern Ireland, two locations imbued with the political and social tensions which are so well reflected in the ancient texts. Katie Mitchell's 1999 production of Ted Hughes' *Oresteia* had a Balkan setting of the early 1950s, though it incorporated state-of-the-art technology including video screens and video cameras.

One important theme emerging in modern productions is multiculturalism: many plays are translated into a variety of languages and are performed worldwide, sometimes incorporating 'traditional' theatrical conventions. Tadashi Suzuki's versions of *Bakchai* in 1981 and *Trojan Women* in 1985, as well as Yukio Ninagawa's 1992 production of Euripides' *Medea*, drew heavily on Japanese kabuki theatre conventions. Ariane Mnouchkine's epic play cycle (1992), combining Euripides' *Iphigeneia at Aulis* and the *Oresteia*, called *Les Atrides*, incorporated Japanese *kabuki* and *noh* and Indian *kathakali* performance styles. Some playwrights have used classical stories and reset them in different periods: Eugene O'Neill's 1931 transplantation of the *Oresteia* to New England at the end of the American civil war, in his play *Mourning becomes Electra*, highlighted the claustrophobia and pent-up passions of family relationships. In 1944 the French dramatist Jean Anouilh gained critical and public acclaim with *Antigone*, a version of Sophokles' classical drama, because of its thinly disguised attack on the Nazis and on the Vichy government. Classical drama and themes have also proved popular with modern opera composers. Richard Strauss' *Electra* (1909), *Die ägyptische Helena* (1928) and *Die Liebe der Danae* (1952) are operas whose libretti either closely follow the ancient texts, or else play with the themes of the well-known classical myths. Benjamin Britten turned to classical stories on several occasions, though he rejected using Greek tragedy as his texts; his *Rape of Lucretia* (1946) draws instead on Livy. Likewise, Michael Tippett's *King Priam* (1962) is taken from Homer's *Iliad*. LL-J

See Hall, E. et al. (2001) *Medea in Performance 1500–2000*; Hardwick, L. (2000) *Translating Words, Translating Cultures*; Wiles, D. (2000) *Greek Theatre Performance*.

theatres

In the Greek world, theatres were used for the performance of tragedies, comedies and dithyrambic choruses. At Athens performances were first based in the Agora, with wooden scaffolding as seating around the performance area, which archaeology, not surprisingly, has been unable to uncover. However, the collapse of the scaffolding at the end of the 6th century BC led to the removal of performances to the sacred area of Dionysos Eleuthereus on the southern slope of the Acropolis.

The theatre was made up of several distinct areas. The auditorium (*theatron*, 'viewing-place'), where the spectators sat, originally had wooden benches to sit on, though people could also sit or stand on the bare hillside. Eventually stone seating arrangements replaced the wood, with special seats in the front centre for important citizens.

The orchestra (*orchêstra*, 'dancing-place') was the original performance area. Scholars disagree about the canonical shape of this area, particularly for the theatre of Dionysos at Athens, but it would appear that a circular orchestra was not the norm until the 4th century BC. The excavators of the theatre at Isthmia were able to reconstruct the shape of its orchestra from water channels, and found that it was roughly quadrilateral with straight bench seating on three sides. Other theatres, such as those at Rhamnous, Ikaria, Tegea and Morgantina, all had straight rows surrounding the orchestra, supporting

THEATRES: (a) the hellenistic/Roman theatre at Miletos.

the idea that the performance area was a quadrilateral rather than a circle. Those at ARGOS and Thorikos combined straight and curved elements. Although some scholars continue to refer to the Athenian orchestra as circular, more likely it was originally quadrilateral.

In the 5th century BC, the orchestra at Athens was pushed back into the seating area, which in turn was cut further into the hillside in order to create more space for the scene building – the *skênê*. This may originally have been little more than a tent for one or two ACTORS to rest in and to store properties. The development of this tent into a proper building, with access to an upper level, doors, windows and other features, is not visible in the archaeological record. Rather, scholars have used the texts of the plays to interpret the surroundings in which they were presented. AESCHYLUS' plays up to c.463 BC do not seem to require any scenic structures, while the *ORESTEIA* (458) requires a building behind it. Stone foundations exist for a STOA (portico building, dated roughly late 5th–early 4th century) which faced the TEMPLE of Dionysos south of the theatre and presented a stone wall to the auditorium. Slits in this wall would be able to support beams for holding scenery; however, the exact nature of the layout is unclear, as the rest of the theatre structure continued to be made from wood. *Paraskênia* (side walls) and *skênographiai* (painted scenes, generally thought to have been on wooden panels) also date to the 5th century.

The presence of a stage is again debated by scholars. The early *skênê* may well have included a platform that was raised slightly higher than the orchestra, with evidence from the plays suggesting that it increased in height in the late 5th century. VITRUVIUS (5.7.2) mentions a high stage in Greek theatres, but this is thought to be a later development; as the importance of the chorus diminished over the 4th century, so the level of the raised platform increased. Entrances and exits were made via ramps on either side of the orchestra; these were called *eisodoi* ('entrances') by the ancients, but are usually referred to as *parodoi* ('side-entrances') by scholars. In the centre of the orchestra was an altar. Hellenistic innovations include the addition of a *proskênion*, a one-storey porch which stood forward from the *skênê* building and appears to have been added to earlier theatres.

The theatre at Epidauros is the best preserved of the Greek theatres. PAUSANIAS (2.27.5) notes that it was built by Polykleitos the younger and was part of the sanctuary of the healing god ASKLEPIOS. It has been dated c.350 BC, and is therefore 200 years into Greek theatre building experience. The stone auditorium was sunk into the hillside, allowing it to be symmetrical, and is separated into sections with walkways for ease of access to seats. The orchestra is circular and, as the auditorium is slightly more than a semicircle, some seats on the outer edges had impeded views of the stage area.

A vital part of the theatre experience was the costumes of the actors. They wore bodysuits as a base under the main outfit. Comedy actors appear to have gone barefoot, but tragic actors wore long boots. As all actors were male, the bodysuits of female characters were suitably padded, and comedy actors always had extra padding on their bottoms and stomachs, as can be seen on Corinthian vases of the mid-7th to

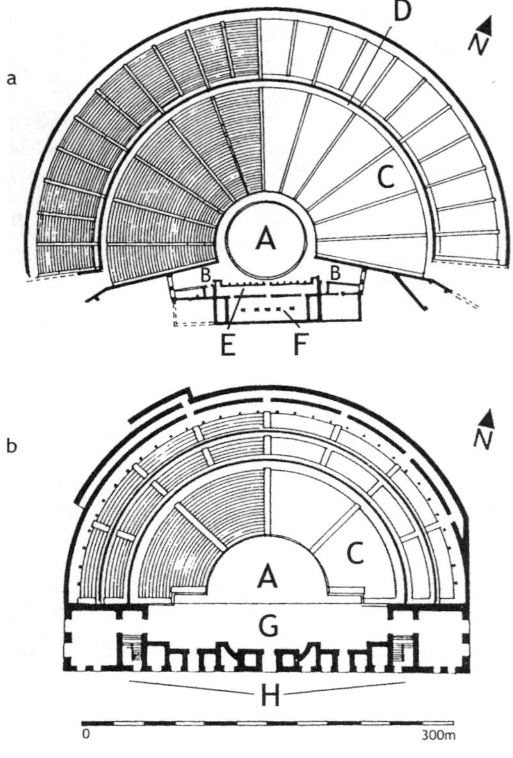

THEATRES: (b) comparative plans of Greek and Roman theatres. A = *orchestra*; B = *parados*; C = *cuneus*; D = *diazoma* or *praecintio*; E = *proscaenium*; F = *scene*; G = *pulpitum*; H = *scaenae frons*.

mid-6th centuries BC. Comedy actors had cloth PHALLUSES, even if they were playing female roles (in which case the phallus was hidden under the long skirt), and these were often rolled up for ease of performance. Phalluses were also worn by actors in the chorus of a satyr play. Attic vases dating to the late 5th century include depictions of a type of loincloth to which their (considerably smaller) phalluses and horse-tails were attached. Comedy choruses, too, are depicted on Attic vases from the second half of the 6th century and through the 5th century.

An essential part of the costume was the MASKS worn by the actors. These were more like headpieces, as they included hair and covered the whole head. They served to identify the character, allowing actors to swap between roles, and had large mouth-holes through which the actors spoke. NJW

See Gebhard, E. R. (1973) *The Theater at Isthmia*; Lawrence, A.W. (1962) *Greek Architecture*; Sommerstein, A. H. (2002) *Greek Drama and Dramatists*.

Although the Roman theatre, like Roman DRAMA, was Greek in origin, its design differs in several aspects (VITRUVIUS, books 5–6). As a result of advances in building technology in the 3rd to 1st centuries BC, the use of vaulted substructures became more common. This meant that the theatre no longer required a hillside for its construction (though obviously hillsides could cut down on construction costs, and were still employed wherever possible) and the auditorium or *cavea* was usually semicircular in shape. As the action of performances no longer took place in the orchestra, a permanent stage building was always constructed. The stage or *pulpitum* projected much further than the *proskênion* of the Greek theatre, reducing the *orchestra* to a semicircle. The *orchestra* itself became part of the auditorium (Vitruvius 6.2), the paving often incorporating broader steps to accommodate movable VIP seating. The back wall of the stage building (the *scaenae frons*) rose usually to the height of, and was attached to, the *cavea* to create an enclosed building. It was often elaborately decorated with statues and MARBLE columns on several storeys.

In Rome in the REPUBLIC permanent theatres were banned by senatorial decree. In 154 BC the construction of a permanent theatre in Rome by the CENSORS was blocked by the SENATE under

THEATRES: (c) detail of the reconstructed stage building (*scaenae frons*) at Sabratha, Libya.

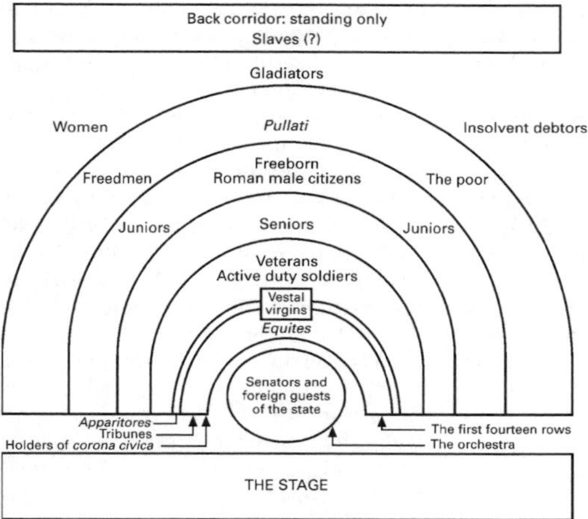

THEATRES: (d) schematic diagram of seating allocation within the Roman theatre, showing social hierarchy.

the CONSUL Publius Cornelius Scipio Nasica. From then on, spectators were apparently barred from remaining seated during performances (VALERIUS MAXIMUS, *Memorabilia* 2.4.2). From this time by law (presumably before this by custom) all theatres built at Rome were temporary wooden structures, demolished after the conclusion of the FESTIVAL for which they were erected. Early on, these could be little more than extended seating from the steps of a temple, but they became increasingly sumptuous in the late Republic. Marcus Aemilius Scaurus erected a magnificent temporary theatre during his AEDILESHIP of 58 BC, with marble columns and gilded decoration (PLINY THE ELDER, *Natural History* 36.113). TACITUS (*Annals* 14.20–1) remarked that in the end it proved more economical to build a permanent theatre than to go to the expense of these temporary structures which were demolished each year. The first permanent theatre in Rome was built by POMPEY the Great on the Campus Martius and dedicated in 55 BC. At the time, he described it as a monumental stairway to the temple of VENUS Victrix. TERTULLIAN (*On Shows* 10) actually says that Pompey built the temple in order to elude the senate's ban. The plan of Pompey's theatre is known from the *forma urbis Romae* (*Plan of Rome*; early 3rd century AD), and some of the substructures are preserved in the cellars of later buildings on the Campus Martius. It was built of Roman CONCRETE faced with *opus reticulatum*. It had a semicircular orchestra and *cavea*. From the *forma urbis* it appears to have a low, wide stage. Pompey's theatre was followed by the theatre of Balbus in 19 BC and the theatre of Marcellus, dedicated in 13 or 11 BC.

The earliest theatres in Italy were those built by the Greek colonies in the south and in SICILY. The majority date between the late 4th and 2nd centuries BC, though many were remodelled in the Roman imperial period. Theatre buildings are found all over the empire, but their form can vary quite considerably. Particularly well-preserved examples are at Merida in Spain (Augustan), Orange in the south of France (1st century AD), Sabratha in LIBYA and Aspendos in southern Turkey (both mid-2nd century AD). All have semicircular auditoriums and surviving stage buildings (those at Merida and Sabratha have been re-erected) and are built partly against a hillside and partly on substructures. In the north-western PROVINCES, theatres tended to be of a simpler form, often resting against a hillside or earth banks (e.g. LYON). A development particularly characteristic of this area is a combined form of AMPHITHEATRE and theatre (e.g. Les Arènes, Paris).

In Greece and ASIA Minor, most Greek-period theatres were adapted, many retaining their greater than semicircular plan but provided with a Roman style of stage building, as at EPHESOS and the theatre of DIONYSOS in Athens. Of course, many new structures were also built. A particularly fine theatre, built up completely on substructures, was constructed in the 2nd century AD at Bostra, provincial capital of ARABIA. Vitruvius (5.9) recommends a colonnade or portico behind the stage building (a *porticus post scaenam*). One example of this arrangement was at LEPCIS MAGNA, where the portico surrounds a TEMPLE dedicated to the *Dii Augusti*, the deified members of the imperial family. These areas were multipurpose, and might be used for props and equipment for the performance, or for the audience to promenade in during intervals. At POMPEII, where such an arrangement was associated with the Large Theatre, the area was being used as a training ground for GLADIATORS at the time of the eruption in AD 79. From the mid-1st century BC, awnings were customarily used to cover the seating of temporary theatre structures in Rome (LUCRETIUS 4.75–83). This practice became common in the permanent theatre. Physical evidence for their use survives in the form of corbels for masts which projected around the outside of the *cavea* (e.g. at Aspendos). Interestingly, at Orange similar corbels are placed on the exterior of the stage building and were presumably part of the set-up covering the stage. Many theatres, particularly in the Eastern empire, were adapted in the later Roman period to stage gladiatorial combats (e.g. XANTHOS, CORINTH, Perge) and aquatic displays (e.g. ARGOS, OSTIA). HD

See Bieber, M. (1961) *The History of the Greek and Roman Theater*; Gros, P. (1996) *L'Architecture romaine* 1: *Les Monuments publics* 272–307.

DRAMA: (a)–(c); GAMES, ROMAN; HERODES ATTICUS.

Thebes (Thêbai, mod. Thíves) The chief city of BOIOTIA in the classical period, Thebes lay at a convergence of routes in eastern Boiotia. Its foundation was attributed to the PHOENICIAN Kadmos, giving the *AKROPOLIS* of the city its name of Kadmeia. The legendary walls and seven gates of the Kadmeia were attributed to the sons of Antiope, Amphion and Zethos, who named the city after Thebe, a sister of Antiope. The Kadmeian legacy made Thebes the birthplace of DIONYSOS and later OEDIPUS. HERAKLES was born here to Alkmene, a Perseid. The wars of the descendants of Oedipus brought an end to the Kadmeian dynasty at Thebes before the TROJAN WAR (PAUSANIAS, 9.5 and 9.9, summarizes EPIC sources). Excavated portions of an extensive MYCENAEAN PALACE on the Kadmeia (under modern Thíves) have yielded Linear B tablets, a large collection of Near Eastern seals in a lapidary WORKSHOP, and evidence that the palace was destroyed by c.1200 BC. Monumental chamber TOMBS have been excavated beside the Kadmeia.

According to tradition, Boiotian Thebes was resettled after the Trojan war (Thucydides 1.12.3, 3.61.2). At the head of a Boiotian league, Thebes opposed THESSALIAN and Athenian interference in Boiotia in the later 6th century. The medism of Thebes' ruling OLIGARCHY during XERXES' invasion put the city into eclipse for most of the 5th century, but alliance with Sparta against Athens during the PELOPONNESIAN WAR strengthened its authority. With Athenian support, Thebes opposed Sparta during the Corinthian war (395–386). Spartan efforts to control it led to the occupation of the Kadmeia by a Spartan garrison (382). A Theban uprising against Sparta (379) established a moderate DEMOCRACY that aggressively reasserted Theban leadership over Boiotia, and victory over Sparta at LEUKTRA inaugurated a decade of Theban hegemony in Greece (371–362). Led by EPAMEINONDAS (d. 362) and PELOPIDAS (d. 364), the Thebans liberated a large part of MESSENIA from Sparta, exerted influence in Thessaly and Macedonia, and briefly took the lead in diplomacy with Persia. The third SACRED WAR (356–346) against PHOKIS proved costly to Theban prestige. Macedonian influence compelled the Thebans to ally with Athens against PHILIP II, with disastrous consequences at the battle of CHAIRONEIA (338). A Theban uprising against a Macedonian garrison was crushed by ALEXANDER, who destroyed the city and divided its territory among neighbouring states (335).

Thebes was rebuilt by Kassandros (316), but was no longer the capital of the Boiotian league. Thebes sided with Rome in the third MACEDONIAN WAR, but opposed Rome during the ACHAIAN and MITHRADATIC WARS, suffering under the settlements imposed by Mummius (146) and SULLA (86). Only the Kadmeia was inhabited in the time of the Antonine emperors.

Physical remains of classical Thebes are sparse, largely because of the extraction of building materials for the medieval town. Fragments of 4th-century BC and hellenistic city walls remain, and the foundations of the temple of Ismenian APOLLO stand southwest of the Kadmeia. (see also FEDERALISM) MM

See Buckler, J. (1980) *The Theban Hegemony*; Demand, N. (1982) *Thebes in the Fifth Century*; Symeonoglou, S. (1985) *The Topography of Thebes from the Bronze Age to Modern Times.*

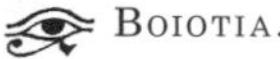 BOIOTIA.

Thebes (Egypt) see AMON-RA; SEVEN WONDERS.

Themistius (Themistios) c.AD 317–88 PHILOSOPHER, orator and SENATOR at CONSTANTINOPLE. Born in Paphlagonia, Themistius studied RHETORIC and PHILOSOPHY at Neocaesarea and Constantinople. Unlike NEOPLATONISTS, he preferred Aristotelian philosophy and wrote *Paraphrases* of several of ARISTOTLE's works. After teaching elsewhere, Themistius moved to Constantinople c.347. He was added to the Eastern senate by the emperor Constantius in 355, became its leading spokesperson, and in 357 was charged with enlarging it to 2,000 members. His first of many PANEGYRICS was presented to Constantius in 347 at Ancyra (mod. Ankara). He delivered speeches at different places to several emperors, including Constantius, Jovian, Valens, Gratian and THEODOSIUS. Themistius counsels emperors in the direction of moderation and humanity toward their subjects and toward invaders like the GOTHS; he often praises a minor policy or action when it reflects his own views, or in order to elicit stronger imperial responses in the same direction. His political career reached its peak when he became prefect of Constantinople in 384, and the successes in the 350s and 380s led to attempts to discredit him as a philosopher. He answered critics in several orations that survive, as do speeches on other topics. Although he was not CHRISTIAN, he held that the concept of hellenism represented cultural rather than religious values, and did not strongly support JULIAN's attempt to restore traditional religion. JV

See Heather, P. and Moncur, D. (2002) *Politics, Philosophy, and Empire in the Fourth Century: selected orations of Themistius*; Penella, R. J. (1999) *The Private Orations of Themistius*; Vanderspoel, J. (1995) *Themistius and the Imperial Court.*

Themistokles c.524–c.459 BC Athenian politician and GENERAL. Like KLEISTHENES a generation earlier, his importance for Athenian history is equalled only by his elusiveness. The biographical tradition in PLUTARCH's *Life* and elsewhere is distorted both by his later years as a PERSIAN protégé and by a cultural debate about 'untrained' intelligence, for which he was a symbolic figure.

He is first securely known as elected archon for 493/2, when his initial steps towards fortifying PIRAEUS foreshadowed his later redirection of Athenian policy seawards. In 483/2 he persuaded the city not to distribute a windfall dividend from the LAURION SILVER MINES among the citizens but to build warships; this allowed Athens to provide over half the Greek fleet in 480. During that, his supreme year, he totally masterminded Athenian action. He led a force to block the pass at THESSALIAN Tempe; commanded the fleet at Artemision; persuaded a frightened citizenry to adopt an active NAVAL interpretation of a 'wooden walls' ORACLE from DELPHI; manipulated PELOPONNESIAN allies into accepting a naval engagement at SALAMIS; and inveigled the Persians into entering the narrow channel there, with fatal results for them.

Absent from the PLATAEA campaign, he re-emerged in winter 479/8 to drive the rebuilding of Athens' city wall and to oppose Spartan moves against pro-Persian regimes. However, his huge prestige, still unchallenged at OLYMPIA in summer 476, faded rapidly, allowing his OSTRACISM by the Athenians (probably in 472) and his persecution by the Spartans. He avoided the latter only by a dramatic flight (narrated in uncharacteristically HERODOTEAN style by THUCYDIDES 1.135–8) via north-west Greece to Asia Minor, whence he sought and obtained the protection of the Persian king until he died, aged 65. Thucydides admired him unreservedly for his intelligence, but for others (including Herodotos) the contrast with ARISTEIDES 'the just' was irresistible. JKD

See Plutarch, *Themistokles*, trs. I. Scott-Kilvert (1960) (in *The Rise and Fall of Athens*); Lenardon, R. J. (1978) *The Saga of Themistocles*; Podlecki, A. J. (1975) *The Life of Themistocles.*

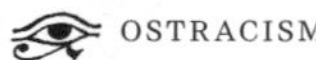 OSTRACISM.

Theocritus see THEOKRITOS.

Theoderic (Flavius Theodericus) C.AD 453/4–526 Ostrogothic king of ITALY from 493. Theoderic was born into the Amal family, which led the Goths based in PANNONIA. Following a period as a hostage at CONSTANTINOPLE (461–71), Theoderic returned to the Pannonian Goths, succeeded his father in 474, and set about forging a unified group – the Ostrogoths – from his Pannonian followers and other Gothic groups in the northern Balkans. The next decade was dominated by difficult relations with the imperial government at Constantinople, from whom he repeatedly sought land for his men and high honours for himself. In 489 the Eastern emperor, Zeno, sought to deflect the Ostrogothic problem by commissioning Theoderic to invade Italy to exact vengeance from Odoacer, who had deposed the last Western emperor in 476. The campaign was successful, and after four years Theoderic established himself as king in Italy. Thereafter, he implemented a successful policy that sought to integrate the Gothic and Roman populations into the administration of the kingdom. This was no meagre achievement, and the success of the policy is largely attributable to the king's personality. To his Gothic subjects he remained first and foremost a warlord, under whom successful campaigns extended the kingdom into the Balkans and southern GAUL. To the Roman population he was a devotee of Roman traditions who, despite his adherence to ARIANISM, did not persecute CATHOLIC CHRISTIANS, as had happened in VANDAL AFRICA. The later years of the reign saw a deterioration of Roman–Gothic cooperation, largely as a consequence of souring relations with Constantinople. With the deaths of prominent SENATORS and churchmen, Theoderic's reign ended ominously, foreshadowing the conflicts of the Gothic wars that were to tear ancient Italy apart in the 6th century. MDH

See Cassiodorus, *Variae*, trs. S. J. B. Barnish (1992); Heather, P. (1996) *The Goths*; Moorhead, J. (1992) *Theoderic in Italy.*

Theodosian Code (*Codex Theodosianus*) Compendium of late Roman legislation covering the period from CONSTANTINE (AD 306–37) to AD 437. The *Code* takes its name from the Eastern Roman emperor Theodosius II (408–50), who commissioned it in 429. It was designed to complement two earlier compendia, compiled by the lawyers Gregorius and Hermogenianus under the emperor DIOCLETIAN (284–305). Together with those collections and the writings of earlier Roman jurists, the *Code* was intended to contribute to yet another volume (never completed) that would provide a comprehensive guide to Roman law. Compiled by two successive committees of legal experts, it drew together imperial edicts and laws intended for general application. The work was completed in 437, and the *Code* was proclaimed amid much pomp and circumstance at CONSTANTINOPLE. Similar celebrations greeted its arrival in Rome the following year. Thus publication of the *Code* reaffirmed the unity of the empire at a time when it was under serious pressure.

The published *Code* included some 3,500 laws. These were arranged into 16 books, of which the first five survive only in mutilated form and must be reconstructed with the help of later law-codes. Within each book, the laws were organized under titles into thematic groups (e.g. in book 16, which deals with matters relating to the CHURCH, the first two titles are 'On the catholic faith' and 'On bishops'). Although the compilation is voluminous, the *Code* clearly does not record all imperial legislation produced in the period it covers. Inscriptions have been found bearing the texts of laws that have not made their way into the *Code*. Moreover, the laws included were subject to editing. This can be observed by comparing the versions of laws in the *Code* with those preserved in inscriptions or in other collections, such as the *Sirmondian Constitutions* (a collection of 21 laws of the 4th and 5th centuries, dealing with ecclesiastical matters and named after their 17th-century editor, Jacques Sirmond). In addition, new legislation (termed *novellae*, novels) continued to be generated after the *Code*'s promulgation.

The impact of the *Theodosian Code* was considerable. In the early medieval West, it formed the basis of legal codes issued in the Visigothic and Burgundian kingdoms. Moreover, it is an important source for social and administrative history of the late empire (albeit from the perspective of highlighting problems encountered by the state). Since each law was dated by the emperor who issued it, the *Code* is also an important source for plotting the movements of late Roman emperors and their itinerant courts. Even so, interpretation and use are rendered difficult by the means of its compilation and the history of its survival. MDH

See Barnes, T. D. (2001) Foregrounding the Theodosian code, *JRA* 14: 671–85; Harries, J. (1999) *Law and Empire in Late Antiquity*; Harries, J. and Wood, I., eds. (1993) *The Theodosian Code*; Matthews, J. F. (2000) *Laying Down the Law*; Pharr, C. et al. (1952) *The Theodosian Code and Novels and the Sirmondian Constitutions.*

Theodosius I (Flavius Theodosius) C.AD 346–95 Roman emperor from 379. Scion of a Spanish military clan, Theodosius became emperor following the battle of ADRIANOPLE (9 August 378), when the Balkan provinces were at the mercy of GOTHIC warbands. Through a successful policy that combined military strategy with diplomacy, he brought the Goths to treaty arrangements in 382. Although the Goths undertook to provide troops for the Roman army, the status of the Goths as self-governing communities on Roman soil presaged the dismemberment of the Western empire in the 5th century. After 382, much of Theodosius' energy was taken up with maintaining the unity of the empire in the face of challenges thrown up by Western usurpers. At the same time, he was deeply involved in asserting the supremacy of CHRISTIANITY as the religion of the Roman state. In 381, for example, he sought to bring the ARIAN controversy to an end by convening a CHURCH COUNCIL (later designated the Second Ecumenical Council) at CONSTANTINOPLE. His measures against PAGANISM were harsh, too, and in 391/2

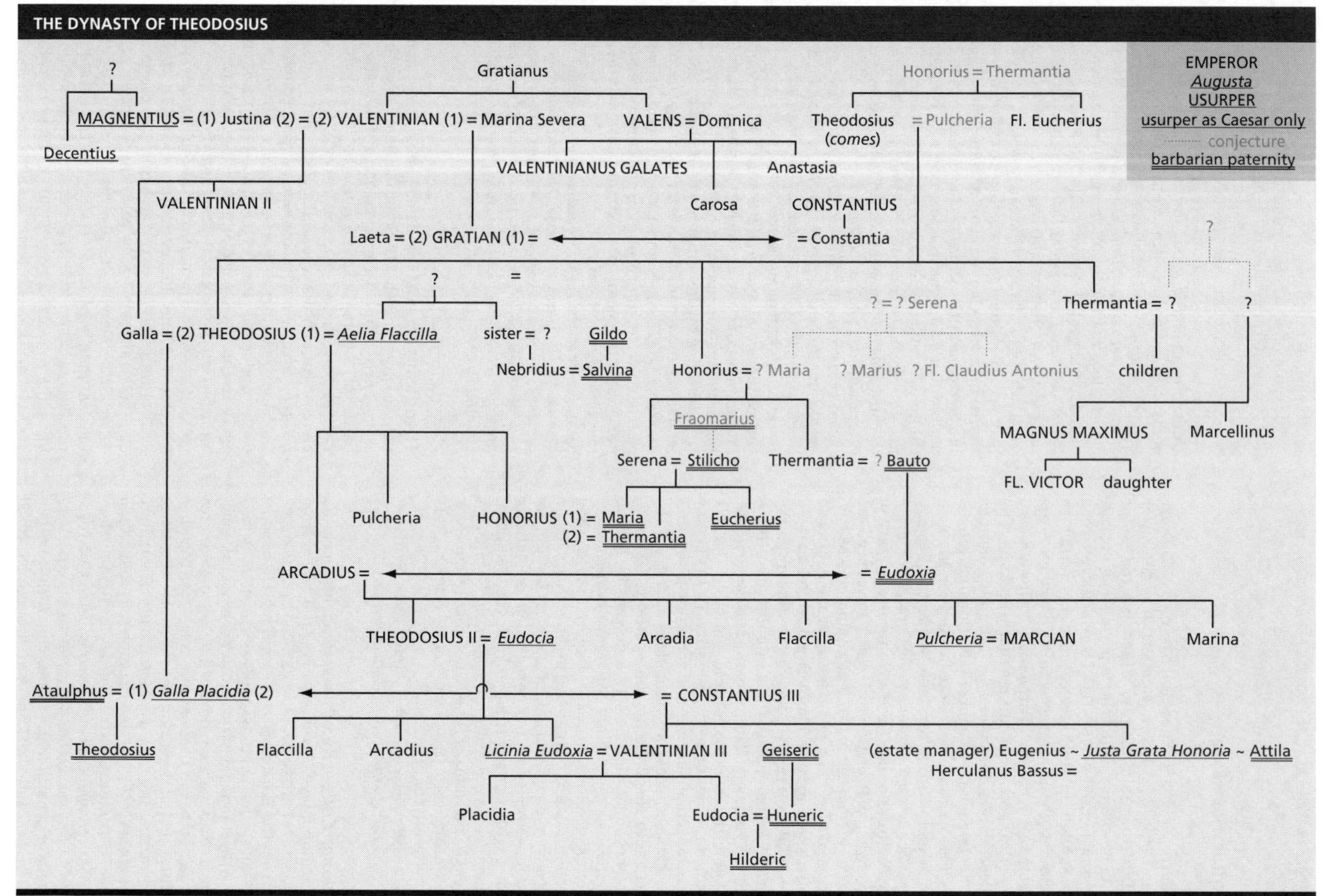

THEODOSIUS: stemma of the Theodosian family.

he effectively outlawed pagan cult. Much of this activity was centred around a stormy relationship with bishop AMBROSE of MILAN, who became Theodosius' spiritual impresario, even compelling the emperor to perform public penance. In terms of the fragmentation of the empire, and the increasing influence of the church and barbarian peoples, Theodosius' reign is clearly a watershed. MDH

See McLynn, N. (1994) *Ambrose of Milan*; Williams, S. and Friell, G. (1994) *Theodosius: the empire at bay.*

Theodosius II see CONSTANTINOPLE; FRANKS; GALLA PLACIDIA; PULCHERIA; *THEODOSIAN CODE.*

Theognis and the *Theognidea* The sole Greek LYRIC poet and poetry extant in a direct manuscript tradition. The poet gives his name as Theognis of MEGARA; however, it is not known whether it is Greek Megara or its colony in SICILY. There is no agreement about his date either, with suggestions varying from 640 to 544 BC. The manuscripts contain a collection of ELEGIAC poems of varied authorship known as the Theognidean corpus. The poems are meant to instruct Kyrnos, Theognis' young lover, in the traditional virtues. They are generally short, composed to be recited at banquets. They reflect on contemporary events in a negative manner and present a reactionary philosophy of life. Theognis belonged to the old aristocracy who saw the rise of new wealthy classes as a threat. In his poems, he expresses resentment and hatred towards them and sees corruption everywhere. He advises Kyrnos to associate with the 'good' or noble and stay away from the 'bad', against whom only deceit would work. RBC

See Gerber, D. E., trs. (1999) *Greek Elegiac Poetry*; West, M. L., trs. (1993) *Greek Lyric Poetry*; Fränkel, H. (1975) *Early Greek Poetry and Philosophy*; Podlecki, A. J. (1984) *The Early Greek Poets and their Times.*

Theokritos Hellenistic poet, born c.300 BC in SYRACUSE. An ancient EPIGRAM says that his parents were Praxagoras and Philinna. Around 270 he went to ALEXANDRIA, where he worked at the court of Ptolemy II Philadelphos. Little else is known about his life, but it is likely that he spent some time on the island of Kos. His date of death is unknown, but scholars speculate that he died c.260.

Of the surviving *Idylls* (*eidyllia*, 'little pictures') 30 are ascribed to Theokritos, along with several fragments: eight of the idylls are generally acknowledged to be spurious. Of the epigrams 25 are attributed to him, at least some of which are thought to be authentic. It is uncertain how much of his output has been lost. Although he wrote in a variety of styles and across several poetic GENRES, he is best known for innovative bucolic poems, the progenitors of PASTORAL POETRY. They are in the Doric dialect and feature rich descriptions of cowherds and SHEPHERDESSES in rural settings, though some refer at the same time to Ptolemy and reflect the court circles in which Theokritos moved. Like many other hellenistic POETS, his poetry combined old forms with new ideas. Theokritos was a contemporary of KALLIMACHOS, to whom he alludes in some of his poems. He was influenced by other hellenistic poets, especially PHILETAS, and has been much imitated by later poets, including VIRGIL and Spenser. FMM

See Theocritus, *Idylls*, trs. A. Verity and R. Hunter (2002); Gutzwiller, K. J. (1991) *Theocritus' Pastoral Analogies.*

Theophrastos 371–287 BC Follower of Aristotle and prolific author, who is happy proof that originality is not the only measure of philosophical greatness. Indeed, after his early education in Eresos (Lesbos) and a short period with PLATO in Athens, we know hardly anything about Theophrastos' life and work that does not reflect in some way his association with ARISTOTLE. His real name was Tyrtamos; it was Aristotle who called him Theophrastos (in token of his 'divine eloquence'). His boyfriend was Aristotle's son Nikomachos; he shared Aristotle's foppish taste in clothes. He also shared Aristotle's ENCYCLOPEDIC interests. The ancient catalogue of his works runs to some 225 titles, covering LOGIC, PHYSICS, ETHICS, politics, EDUCATION, RHETORIC and the history of PHILOSOPHY. As one of Aristotle's more conservative followers, he was a natural candidate to take over his school (at the LYCEUM in Athens) when Aristotle retired to Chalkis in 323. There his popularity as a teacher was as great as his research was prolific: 2,000 people are said to have attended his lectures. He was succeeded, on his death, by Straton (Strato) of Lampsakos.

If Theophrastos did not develop a distinctive philosophical system of his own, he was by no means uncritical in his reception of Aristotle's philosophy. On the contrary, he was astute in identifying difficulties in it, and actually dispensed with some of Aristotle's more distinctive doctrines. He had no use for the 'fifth substance' of which Aristotle believed the heavenly bodies were made. Where Aristotle thought that the ultimate source of change and movement was the 'first unmoved mover', a divinity existing beyond the heavens, Theophrastos seems to have argued that they could be explained by the animate nature of heaven itself. Other areas of thought he developed far beyond their beginnings in Aristotle. He made important innovations in logic, and turned the history of philosophy into an independent discipline, writing numerous studies of earlier philosophers as well as a lengthy survey cataloguing philosophical beliefs about the natural world (the *Physikai doxai*, an important sourcebook for subsequent historians of philosophy). By applying to the plant world Aristotle's model for classifying ANIMALS and explaining their workings, Theophrastos invented the systematic study of botany.

The botanical works survive. For the rest we have a handful of fragments, extracts and shorter studies. One of the most endearing and influential of the latter is the *Characters*, a series of caricatures illustrating various personality traits (such as loquacity, or SUPERSTITION). The purpose of the work remains unclear. As a study of behaviour, it might have been meant as a contribution to ethics; as a study of characterization, it could be read as a contribution to rhetoric or poetics. It has certainly influenced many writers over the centuries, starting, it has been suggested, with the comic poet MENANDER – himself one of Theophrastos' pupils. GB-S

See Theophrastus, *Characters*, trs. J. Rusten and I. C. Cunningham (2003); *De Causis Plantarum*, 3 vols., trs. B. Einarson and G. K. K. Link (1976–90); *Enquiry into Plants*, 2 vols., trs. A. Hort (1916–26); Fortenbaugh, W.W. et al., eds.

(1993) *Theophrastus of Eresus: sources for his life, writings, thought and influence*, 2 vols. (fragments); Fortenbaugh, W.W., ed. (1984) *Theophrastus of Eresus: on his life and work*.

Theopompos 387/77–c.320 BC Greek HISTORIAN. As a young man he was exiled, with his father, from CHIOS for *lakônismos* (being pro-Spartan). In 333/2 he was allowed to return by ALEXANDER the Great, but after the latter's death was exiled again. Eventually he stayed at the court of PTOLEMY I. Trained as a rhetorician (by ISOKRATES) and a political pamphleteer, he became best known as an important historian. His works, however, survive only in fragments. We know of his *Epitome of Herodotos* in 2 books, 12 books of *Hellenika* (*Greek History*) starting, like XENOPHON, where THUCYDIDES stops in 411 BC and detailing events until 394. Theopompos' main work, his *Philippika* (or *Philippikai historiai*) in 58 books, presents 'the actions of Greeks and barbarians' with many an excursus, but with PHILIP II of Macedonia at the account's centre. He was apparently an adherent of the Spartans and of ARISTOCRATIC governments, and, like EPHOROS, an important exponent of RHETORICAL historiography. He was widely read in hellenistic and Roman times, and is praised by Dionysios of Halikarnassos for his truthfulness and scholarship. Pompeius Trogus gave his own world history the title *Philippica*, a reference to Theopompos. KB

See FGrH 115; Connor, W. R. (1968) *Theopompus and Fifth-century Athens*; Flower, M. A. (1994) *Theopompus of Chios*; Pédech, P. (1989) *Trois historiens méconnus*; Shrimpton, G. S. (1991) *Theopompus the Historian*.

theoric fund At certain times, money was provided to all Athenian citizens for the expenses of attending FESTIVALS (for decorous garb, offerings, and especially admission to the THEATRE during the Dionysia). It came from the theoric fund (*ta theôrika*, 'for spectacles'), beginning not later than the 350s BC. Earlier public doles at Athens may also have served this purpose; some sources appear to confuse 5th-century distributions and salaries with the later practice. The amount given was originally 1 drachma according to Philochoros, later commonly 5 drachmas. The frequency of distribution depended upon the availability of surplus state revenue. This distribution was extremely popular ('the glue of democracy' according to Demades), but controversial when decisions had to be made between it and funding the military. On this account the Athenians were criticized for becoming more interested in festivals than in military affairs. MM

See Buchanan, J. J. (1962) *Theorika*; Hansen, M. H. (1999) *The Athenian Democracy in the Age of Demosthenes*; Rhodes, P. J. (1981) *A Commentary on the Aristotelian Athenaion Politeia* 514–16.

theory (modern) see ANTHROPOLOGY; CORE–PERIPHERY; CRITICAL THEORY; ETHNICITY AND IDENTITY; FEMINISM; IDENTITY; LITERARY CRITICISM; MARXISM; MODES OF PRODUCTION; POST-COLONIALISM; POLITICAL THEORY; SEMIOTICS; SOCIOLOGY; STRUCTURALISM AND POST-STRUCTURALISM.

Thera The ISLAND of Thera (mod. Santoríni) skirts the eastern edge of the flooded caldera of a VOLCANO. Smaller islands ring the caldera; the largest, Therasia, may have been an independent *POLIS* for part at least of the hellenistic period. The small islands in the middle of the caldera were born of later eruptions, some in antiquity, others afterwards. The island was an important outpost of MINOAN civilization until c.1628/7 BC, when the volcano erupted explosively and buried the Minoan settlement at modern Akrotíri. There, excavators have found a fully preserved city, an 'Aegean Pompeii', with HOUSES, personal effects and splendid frescoes, but no bodies – the inhabitants evidently had enough warning to flee. Later colonized by Sparta, Thera came under the control of a single *polis* in the archaic period. Its colonization of CYRENE in North AFRICA c.631 BC is well documented by HERODOTOS and by inscriptions found at the colony (later sources add details or different interpretations); the episode is often treated as a paradigm for archaic COLONIZATION. The island was hostile to Athens early in the course of the PELOPONNESIAN WAR but paid tribute too. It is not certain whether the Theraians joined the second Athenian confederacy. In the hellenistic period the island fell under the control of the PTOLEMIES and hosted a garrison that left behind important EPIGRAPHICAL records. Most of the impressive physical remains at the settlement of Thera belong to the hellenistic period, and the settlement of this date was the object of a pioneering archaeological study directed in the late 19th century directed by F. Hiller von Gaertringen. GR

See Reger, G. (2004) Thera, in Hansen and Nielsen, *Inventory* 782–4.

 AEGEAN SEA: (b).

Thermon (Thermos) The symbolic centre of AITOLIA in north-west Greece. During the hellenistic period Thermon, with its shrine of APOLLO overlooking Lake Trichonis, was the venue for meetings of the annual assembly of the powerful AITOLIAN LEAGUE, and the place where the league displayed its inscribed decisions. The Apollo temple, however, had existed at least since the late 7th century BC and overlay late Bronze Age structures. The site, which had the character of a sanctuary complex rather than a fully fledged city-state, boasted a grand monument to the league's links with Ptolemaic Egypt but was twice plundered by PHILIP V of MACEDONIA. It was rebuilt with strong FORTIFICATIONS, but its decline may have begun after the league's loss of power in the mid-2nd century BC, since by the 1st-century BC BURIALS were taking place on the sites of public buildings. Thermon is notable among Greek sites in having become important in the hellenistic period but failed to maintain its role as a central place under Roman rule. DGJS

See Scholten, J. B. (1997) *The Politics of Plunder: Aitolians and their koinon in the early hellenistic era*.

Thermopylai A narrow pass between the mountains and the sea on the east coast of central Greece, the site of several important battles. In 480 BC the Greeks who did not submit to XERXES chose the pass as the place to prevent his advance into central Greece. It was the only means of access from THESSALY to the south, and the topography would prevent the PERSIANS from taking advantage of their superior numbers. An advance force of around 10,000 men, mostly from places close to Thermopylai, was sent under the Spartan king LEONIDAS, in the expectation that the rest of the Spartan army would join them. The existence of a track by-passing the Greek camp was only discovered on arrival and weakened Leonidas' position. Greek resistance lasted until the track was shown to the Persians, after which Leonidas dismissed all the troops except 700 Thespians, 400 THEBANS and 300 Spartans. In fighting to delay the Persian advance further, almost all the Thespians and Spartans were killed, along with Leonidas. The story of his self-sacrifice quickly became part of the mythology of the PERSIAN WARS.

In 279 BC Brennos led one of a number of Gaulish raids into Greece, and was repelled at Thermopylai by a large army drawn from all over the Greek world and led by the Athenians. The GAULS subsequently outflanked the Greeks using the same track that the Persians used in 480. The account of Brennos' campaign, recorded by PAUSANIAS, closely parallels HERODOTOS' account of Xerxes' actions.

In 191 BC ANTIOCHOS III was supported by some factions within AITOLIA, who had encouraged him to enter Greece the previous autumn, but was defeated by a Roman army under Manius Acilius Glabrio and Marcus Porcius CATO, who led his troops around the track used by the Persians in 480. Antiochos withdrew to Asia Minor, where he was defeated at Magnesia the following year. HB

See Herodotos 7.201–33; Livy 36.15–19; Pausanias 10.20–3; Plutarch, *Cato Maior* 13.

 PERSIAN WARS, GREEK.

Theseus The Athenian HERO *par excellence*, son of the Athenian king Aigeus and Aithra, princess of Troizen. Mythical traditions describe his exceptional courage and strength as a child and teenager in Troizen, where he grew up away from his father. Later he made his way to Athens, marking the beginnings of his permanent association with ATTICA.

Theseus' name is linked to a series of major exploits, notably clearing the Attic countryside of brigands and similar dangers. Upon his arrival at Athens, he successfully overcame traps and conspiracies against him devised by Medea, wife of Aigeus at the time, and by the Pallantidai, his father's relatives. The latter, who had their eye on the throne, felt severely threatened by the presence of Theseus, the king's natural son.

THESEUS: the hero finds his métier and his Minotaur.

As a young prince in Athens, Theseus continued to serve his city through his labours. The most prominent was indisputably his killing of the monster Minotaur on CRETE, which saved the Athenians from a cruel tribute that they had long been paying to Minos, the island's mythical king. But at Naxos, on his return voyage to Athens, Theseus abandoned the king's daughter Ariadne, who had assisted him.

As king, Theseus is credited with unifying the scattered rural communities in Attica (the so-called SYNOIKISM), as well as with refounding the Isthmian games and with other constitutional and social reforms. Among his most significant labours during this period was his participation with HERAKLES in a victorious campaign to the land of AMAZONS in the Pontos area. EP

Thesmophoria see DEMETER; HOLIDAYS; WOMEN, GREEK.

Thessalonike (Salonica) This city on the Thermaic gulf was founded in 315 BC by Kassandros (Cassander), ruler of MACEDONIA, and named after his wife, a half-sister of ALEXANDER the Great. Macedonia became part of the Roman empire in the late 2nd century BC, with Thessalonike the provincial capital from 146. At the start of the 4th century AD, the city was the residence of the TETRARCH Galerius, and by mid-century the prefecture of Illyricum had moved there from Sirmium (whence probably came also Thessalonike's patron saint, Demetrios). For most of the Byzantine period, Thessalonike was second in importance only to CONSTANTINOPLE. Famous visitors included CICERO, who was exiled there in 58 BC, and St Paul, who preached in its synagogue in AD 50/1.

The FORTIFICATIONS of Kassandros' city were rebuilt and extended in several phases in Roman and Byzantine times. Substantial remains of the walls enclose a roughly trapezoid area, with an ACROPOLIS to the north. The lower town, sloping gently towards the sea, is laid out on a grid plan, probably of hellenistic origin; behind it the irregular upper town rises steeply. Extensive remains of the Greek and Roman *AGORA* have been excavated in the centre of the lower town. To the east of this are parts of the grand building complex of Galerius: a triumphal ARCH, PALACE, hippodrome and his intended mausoleum (the rotunda, a church since the late 4th century). Above the *agora*, the church of St Demetrios was built in the mid-5th century (reconstructed after a fire in 1917). The Acheiropoietos BASILICA nearby, and Hosios David in the upper town, are also 5th-century foundations. LR

See Vacalopoulos, A. (1963) *History of Thessaloniki.*

Thessaly The northern Greek state of Thessaly comprised two vast plains, divided by hills and bounded by high mountains on all sides. Although not part of Thessaly proper, the mountain regions were home to communities of *perioikoi* ('dwellers round about') and for the most part remained under Thessalian control. Thessaly itself was divided into

Thessaly: map.

four regions (*tetrades*): Thessaliotis, Hestiaiotis, Pelasgiotis and Phthiotis. At the end of the 7th century these were united into a loose semi-political organization, whose principal purpose was joint military action and whose commander-in-chief was known as the *tagos*.

Thessaly first became prominent in the 6th century, perhaps as a result of involvement in the first Sacred war (though the authenticity of this war is sometimes doubted), but certainly because of its important role in the amphiktiony at Anthela, which was later transferred to Delphi. During Xerxes' preparations for the Persian wars, the Aleuadai, a prominent aristocratic family in Thessaly, medized to further their own interests. The rest of Thessaly was forced to join the Persians only after the Greeks decided to abandon the defence of Tempe in favour of a position further south. In the 4th century, after the state was almost torn apart by factional fighting, Thessalian influence waxed anew under Iason of Pherai, who united the country into a coherent political force. He was beginning to extend his influence into southern Greece when he was assassinated in 370. In the mid-4th century, control of the Thessalian league passed to Philip II of Macedonia. The opportunity for greatness had passed, though the Thessalian league operated successfully under Roman rule. LGM

See Herodotos, *Histories* 7.6; Xenophon, *Hellenika* 6.1.2–19, 4.20–37; Westlake, H. D. (1969) *Thessaly in the Fourth Century* BC.

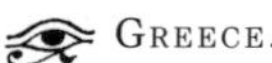 Greece.

third-century crisis Traditionally, the name given to the period from the death of Severus Alexander (AD 235) to the accession of Diocletian (284), characterized by a large number of short-lived emperors; incursions across all frontiers; civil war; economic decline, evidenced by a collapse in silver currency and desertion of agricultural land; withdrawal of the *curiales* from civic responsibilities; and crises such as plague, famine and population decline. The power of the military was enhanced by the need to react to hostile neighbours, and by its assumed right to proclaim its candidate emperor and replace him once he ceased to serve their purposes. Senators lost power, as emperors, no longer made at Rome, tended to promote men like themselves to positions of authority. Increased army size created an economic burden. Pressure for army pay hastened the debasement of coinage, with the result that not only much of army pay but also taxes reverted to payment in kind. Main external threats came from the Sassanians in the east, who captured the emperor Valerian (253–60), and from Germanic tribes in the north and west. The reasons behind these incursions are unclear; they were periodic and did not involve huge numbers. However, 'crisis' was not universal. While there is a sense of acceleration of processes already set in train under the Severans, there was also a flowering of local cultures in some areas. Short-term but successful independent kingdoms were established in Palmyra (267–73) and Gaul (258–74). Continued urban growth and economic prosperity through the oil trade were marked particularly in North Africa. MEH

Thirty, the The board of 30 Athenians who imposed oligarchy on Athens following the surrender to Sparta in 404 are sometimes known as 'the Thirty Tyrants' because of their authoritarian rule. Led by Kritias son of Kallaischros, they included statesmen exiled by the DEMOCRACY, some having participated in the government of the FOUR HUNDRED (e.g. THERAMENES). Appointed under pressure from the Spartan LYSANDER, their charge was to 'compile the ancestral laws' (Xenophon, *Hellenika* 2.3.2) to conform with anti-democratic, pro-Spartan ideals. They limited citizenship to 3,000 select Athenians, and arrested and executed or drove into exile many other Athenians and prominent metics (e.g. the family of Lysias; see Lysias, 12). They attempted, unsuccessfully, to implicate SOCRATES in their regime. Theramenes criticized their extreme policies but was put to death on Kritias' orders. After eight months of rule, exiles led by THRASYBOULOS defeated the Thirty in battle at Mounychia, where Kritias died. When the Spartans intervened and reconciled Athenian factions later in 403, the remnants of the Thirty were allowed to withdraw to ELEUSIS. Their enclave finally fell in 401. MM

See Krentz, P. (1982) *The Thirty at Athens*; Munn, M. (2000) *Athens in the Age of Socrates*.

tholoi As a building type, the round, conical-roofed tholos is thought to have derived its unique shape from temporary dining-tents or huts of the pre-classical period. Limestone triglyphs and metopes from an early 6th-century tholos have been discovered at DELPHI, though its existence is only attested through the reuse of its blocks in the late 6th-century treasury of the Sikyonians; its original location has not yet been identified, and it should not be confused with the ornate 4th-century MARBLE tholos which forms part of the Marmária site to the south-east of the main sanctuary site. This lost tholos is considered to have been among the earliest known round buildings built above ground (as opposed to Bronze Age so-called tholos TOMBS, which may also have inspired the construction of circular buildings). A plain tholos erected in the ATHENIAN AGORA around 470 BC served as the dining room for citizens involved in the city's administration and, presumably due to the shape of its roof, was known as the *skias* or sunhat!

The Roman traveller PAUSANIAS was not particularly impressed when he visited the magnificent ornate tholos at Epidauros, simply saying that it was 'a circular building of white marble, called tholos, which is worth seeing' (2.27.3). Unfortunately for us, he failed to mention the function of the mysterious 'labyrinth' of concentric passages and blocked doorways discovered under the floor. CK-B

See Pausanias, *Guide to Greece*; École Française d'Athènes (1991) *Guide de Delphes: le site*; Lawrence, A.W. (1967) *Greek Architecture*.

AGORA, ATHENIAN: (a); MARKETS.

Thrace and Thracians Mentioned in Homer (*Iliad* 6.130, 9.5, 14.227, 21.390, 10.434–5; *Odyssey* 8.361), the Thracians were agricultural tribes who occupied an extensive area stretching from the western BLACK SEA to the AEGEAN and the trans-Danubian lands, bordering the Troad and ILLYRIANS and MACEDONIANS. Thrace possessed some very large, fertile plains (especially the Danubian plain), contained many FORESTS, whose TIMBER the Greeks valued greatly for SHIPBUILDING, and was rich in FISH and game. Some parts were fairly well endowed with precious metals and IRON and COPPER ores; GOLD and SILVER were mined in Aegean Thrace.

The Greeks first bestowed the designations Thrace and Thracians; the origin of the name is not clear. There were many Thracian tribes, including the Triballians, Dardanians, and the mountain peoples of Haimos and Rhodope. The Thracians who lived south-east of DACIA, the Getae, formed a large group consisting of several tribes who occupied a vast territory on both banks of the DANUBE. In Dobrudja, with the assimilation by the Dacians of the Getae and Thracians from the second half of the 6th century BC, a Getic–Dacian culture was formed.

Before the period of confrontation with Rome, the Thracians were a warlike, essentially non-urbanized people, ruled by various dynasties. In the classical period the king of the Odrysai (Odrysians) was dominant until the middle of the 4th century BC when this kingdom collapsed and PHILIP II of Macedonia invaded Thrace, founding cities including Philippopolis (mod. Plovdiv). Thrace fell to Lysimachos after the death of ALEXANDER the Great. It was one of Rome's most important Danubian PROVINCES, protecting the lines of communication from Macedonia via Byzantium to Bithynia and Asia Minor. Thracians were reputed excellent soldiers. Later the GOTHS passed through the province, destroying everything in their path. Barbarian ravaging of Thrace continued in the 4th and 5th centuries AD, and from the 6th century the area was under Byzantine influence.

Thracian tribes were advanced in METALWORKING. After the colonization of western Pontos by the Greeks, the Thracians became customers for some fine Greek imports. Furthermore, Greeks worked for the Thracian kings and nobility, creating an ÉLITE culture and participating actively in the construction of the royal city of Seuthopolis and of royal and élite TOMBS. The best-known tombs with murals by a Greek artist are at Kazanluk and Sveshtari. Recent EXCAVATION in the Shipka area has brought to light several dozen new rich tombs decorated with murals. Current investigation of a Greek *emporion* of the classical period, Pistiros (not far from Plovdiv), shows that Greek craftsmen and traders lived in the hinterland under the control of the Thracian king. Between c.513 and 479 BC Thrace was held by the PERSIANS.

THRACE AND THRACIANS: distinctive dress styles and *pelta*-shaped shields identify Thracians in Greek vase-paintings.

Thus the area was exposed to both Greek and Persian influence, each apparent to differing degrees in different areas. The influence on its culture of the Scythian Animal Style was also quite strong. The relationship between the Odrysian kings and the Greek cities on the Thracian Black sea coast was based on tribute and gift-giving, very well demonstrated by ancient authors (Thucydides 2.97; Xenophon, *Anabasis* 7.3.15–20, 26–32) and the Rogozen treasure. GRT

See Archibald, Z. H. (1998) *The Odrysian Kingdom of Thrace*; Boardman, J. (1994) *The Diffusion of Classical Art in Antiquity*; Bouzek, J., Domaradzki, M. and Archibald, Z. H., eds. (1996) *Pistiros I*; Fol, A. and Marazov, I. (1977) *Thrace and the Thracians*; Hoddinott, R. F. (1987) *The Thracians*; Isaac, B. (1986) *The Greek Settlements in Thrace until the Macedonian Conquest*.

Thrasyboulos Champion of the democratic restoration in Athens of 403 BC, Thrasyboulos of the DEME Steiria represented the spirit of Athenian imperial DEMOCRACY from the PELOPONNESIAN to the Corinthian war. XENOPHON, whose personal loyalties were opposed to his, reports three important speeches by him (*Hellenika* 2.4.13–17, 2.4.40–2, and 3.5.16). A close supporter of ALCIBIADES, Thrasyboulos held generalships in the north AEGEAN and HELLESPONT from 411 until he fell from favour after Alcibiades' second EXILE in 407. Following the surrender of Athens in 404, he was condemned as an enemy of the regime of the THIRTY, fled to THEBES and organized a movement of Athenian exiles. Seizing Phyle in the winter of 404/3 with 70 followers, he fought off assaults by forces of the Thirty and led his growing following to PIRAEUS, defeating the Thirty in the battle of Mounychia. Following the reconciliation of 403, he proposed the enfranchisement of all who fought against the Thirty, but his motion was defeated in court by Archinos. By the outbreak of the Corinthian war in 395, he was the leading statesman in the movement to unite Athens, Thebes, CORINTH and ARGOS against Sparta. His reputation suffered, however, from the Spartan victory at the battle of Corinth in 394. In 390 he led a naval expedition to Ionia, the Hellespont and Byzantium, in an ambitious attempt to restore Athenian maritime supremacy in those areas. Preparing to assault RHODES in 389, he was killed in a skirmish at Aspendos in Pamphylia. MM

See Cawkwell, G. L. (1976) The imperialism of Thrasybulus, *CQ* 26: 270–7; Seager, R. (1967) Thrasybulus, Conon and Athenian imperialism, 396–386 BC, *JHS* 87: 95–115; Strauss, B. (1986) *Athens after the Peloponnesian War*.

Thucydides Son of Oloros, Thucydides the Athenian was the author of a well-known history of the PELOPONNESIAN WAR, a work often and not unreasonably regarded as our finest example of ancient HISTORIOGRAPHY. Little is known of his life. He was born c.460–455 to a family with ancestral holdings in THRACE, and died sometime after 404. Having survived the plague that struck Athens in 430–427 (he describes the progress of symptoms in clinical detail, influenced by HIPPOCRATIC writing), Thucydides served as one of Athens' ten elected GENERALS in 424. His failure to defend the strategic northern port city of Amphipolis against the Spartan BRASIDAS led to his EXILE; he returned to Athens only after the Athenian surrender 20 years later. He presumably enjoyed an EDUCATION suited to his family's ÉLITE status. His conceptual vocabulary demonstrates a keen awareness of major contemporary intellectual currents, especially the SOPHISTS' concern for language, the power of persuasive speech, and the relationship between customary behaviour and innate human nature. Where he can be checked, his descriptions of events are generally accurate though, as with all historians, his emphases and interpretations are his own.

Thucydides claims that he began work on his history at the outbreak of what he calls 'the 27-year war' and he mentions the war's end, but his opus, preserved in eight books, was never completed. It stops with a description of events of 410, virtually in mid-sentence. Despite much scholarly debate, there is no consensus on the question of composition. Some sections (e.g. 2.65, the highly positive assessment of PERIKLES' political leadership) were clearly composed in light of much later events, but the extent of rewriting remains uncertain, as does the question of whether Thucydides changed his mind about the causes or meaning of the conflict. The incomplete history was continued by XENOPHON (as well as by the anonymous OXYRHYNCHOS HISTORIAN and other 4th-century historians). It influenced many later historians (including PROCOPIUS in the 6th century AD) but remains unique in style and intellectual aspiration.

Thucydides was very aware of his predecessors in the enterprise of describing the past, both POETS (especially HOMER) and prose writers (especially HERODOTOS). In a methodological introduction he seeks to demonstrate that the events he describes were greater than all previous Greek wars. He also draws a sharp distinction between his own text and earlier works, written to please a listening audience and which sought to 'win their way into the realm of the fabulous'. By contrast, Thucydides asserts that his own work will not afford much pleasure to listeners. He is right – the Greek in many passages is so rebarbative as to be incomprehensible except to a very careful reader. Thucydides' history is thus among the first surviving Greek texts that seems specifically to be composed for readers rather than listeners. It is also DIDACTIC, tacitly offering the careful reader an impartial understanding of events superior to that of most of the wars' actual participants.

The methodological introduction features a brief and hypothetical synopsis of early Greek civilization. In this section, known as the 'Archaeology', Thucydides establishes key principles regarding the operations of POWER and human nature. Central among them are the assumptions that imperial power is a force of civilization and predicated upon three elements: security (in the form of city walls), a mobile striking force (a large navy) and deep financial reserves. The state commanding these resources will naturally compel the obedience of weaker states. The citizens of those weaker states may accept a subordinate position for as long as they regard their own interests to be furthered (especially via suppression of PIRACY) by the international regime guaranteed by the hegemon. The Peloponnesian war is figured by Thucydides as a confrontation between Athens – a bold, aggressive, wealthy, democratic, imperial, naval power – and Sparta, a stable, cautious, oligarchic land power, and hegemon of a league of Peloponnesian states. The war's underlying cause – which Thucydides specifically contrasts with various overt provocations – was Sparta's fear that the dynamic growth of Athens' empire might undermine the Peloponnesian league. Among Thucydides' many historiographic innovations is his confident assertion that a 27-year period, which included long periods without overt hostilities between the principals, should be understood as a single war.

Thucydides' history offers a careful year-by-year description of the war's major events, based on eyewitness accounts. It offers a sophisticated analysis of the relationship between internal political organization (especially Athenian DEMOCRACY) and national capacity to project power in the international arena. Through the literary device of speeches (often in pairs), Thucydides explores themes of democratic decision-making, charismatic leadership, the corrosive effect on state policy of self-interested groups, and the complex relationship between domestic ideals (especially the Athenian focus on freedom, equality and individual dignity) and the much harsher realities of inter-state relations. The speeches (by historical individuals such as Perikles of Athens and Archidamos of Sparta, and by nameless state representatives such as 'the Corinthians') may have been loosely based on genuine originals, but were designed by Thucydides to grant the reader a clear understanding of factors and trends that remained obscure to most of his contemporaries. He advertises his work as 'a possession for all time' that grants the reader both an accurate knowledge of a particular past and a secure grasp on motive forces lying behind the human affairs of any era.

While Thucydides is often regarded as the father of scientific, secular history, much of the impact of his text arises from his explorations of moral psychology and national character. His Athenians are as remarkable for their devotion to democratic freedom at home as for their capacity to act as a collective tyrant toward their subjects. The close correlation between Athenian freedom and imperial expansionism, and the sharp challenge offered to a democratic culture by the need to restrain expansionist impulses, find a corollary in the increasingly naked hypocrisy of Sparta's role as defender of freedom for the Greek states. These issues are explored in the 'Melian dialogue' of book 5. Here the oligarchic rulers of the island *POLIS* of MELOS argue that they should resist Athenian invasion in hopes of succour from justice-preserving divinities or Sparta. Their Athenian interlocutors reassert the basic lesson about power first defined in the so-called 'Archaeology' (*archaiologia*; 1.1–23, where Thucydides outlines early Greek history): the strong will seek to do whatever they can, whereas the weak may find that their own interests are best served by submission. Unconvinced, the Melians resist and are slaughtered. Thucydides' account of Athens' destruction of Melos leads directly to a discussion of the fateful Athenian decision to invade SICILY. This in turn precipitates the 'greatest event of the war', the utter destruction of the Athenian expeditionary force. While seldom making overt moral pronouncements, the history invites the reader to form moral judgements.

Among the most striking elements of Thucydides' prose style, along with austerity, the syntactical complexity of certain passages, and a frequent resort to verbal abstractions, is his reliance on antitheses. Especially prominent is the contrast between *logoi* (speeches, discourse) and *erga* (brute facts, deeds). He consistently asserts the priority of *erga* over *logoi*, demonstrating time and again the folly of the general human (and specifically democratic Athenian) tendency to imagine that public speech can bring about conditions that will render brute facts irrelevant. It is, for example, the Athenians' ignorance about the realities of Sicilian demographics, politics and resources that leads them to accept the blithe assurances of self-seeking politicians, that the expedition must lead to either the conquest of the island or a safe return after a memorable trip abroad. Book 7 counterpoises in vivid detail, the harsh, unimagined alternative of failure. Of course the reader eventually realizes that Thucydides himself failed in the realm of military *erga*, and that his reputation rests entirely on the persuasive power of his own difficult and rewarding *logos*. JO

See Thucydides, *The Peloponnesian War*, trs. R. Warner (1972); Cawkwell, G. L. (1997) *Thucydides and the Peloponnesian War*; Hornblower, S. (1987) *Thucydides*; (1991–6) *A Commentary on Thucydides*, 2 vols. (in progress).

Thucydides (son of Melesias) see PERIKLES.

Thugga (Dougga) A Numidian and later Roman town in AFRICA Proconsularis (mod. Tunisia), on the road from CARTHAGE to Theveste (mod. Tébessa in Algeria). Little is known of the pre-Roman phase, but the winding streets of the central quarter are a legacy from that period, and a fine mausoleum of the 2nd century BC survives, built for an unknown prince by the Numidian ARCHITECT Atban. British determination to remove the inscription to the British Museum entailed the demolition of the monument – a shameful act of colonial ARCHAEOLOGY; the tomb has since been restored. Thugga was an unusual double settlement, comprising both native community (governed by *suffetes*) and a Roman *pagus* (initially dependent on Carthage). These co-existed until they were united by SEPTIMIUS SEVERUS (AD 205), when Thugga became a *municipium*; 50 years later the town was promoted to colonial rank. Long before gaining Roman status, the town was already displaying its *Romanitas* with such structures as a Capitoline TEMPLE (166/7), a THEATRE (168/9) and other public buildings. The ruins of Thugga are among the most extensive in North Africa, and include two sets of BATHS, a small Byzantine FORT enclosing the former FORUM, and temples of Caelestis (between 222 and 235) and of SATURN (195). The latter is of Romano-African type, in which shrines open off one side of an open courtyard – probably a legacy of Punic temple ARCHITECTURE. Most of the MOSAICS from numerous private houses have been removed to the Bardo Museum in Tunis. Survey work in the territory has added much to knowledge of Thugga's hinterland. RJAW

 AFRICA, ROMAN; BURIAL, ROMAN: (e).

Tiber (Tiberinus, Tiberis, Thybris) The most important river of central Italy, which extends 403 km

(250 miles) from its source below Monte Fumaiolo (north of Arezzo) to where it flows into the Tyrrhenian sea at OSTIA. Rome itself was located at the first crossing-point of the river. Like other rivers in central Italy, it tended to have an erratic flow, meagre in summer but torrential and silt-laden in winter and spring (PLINY THE ELDER, *Natural History* 3.5.53). This led to serious problems of flooding at Rome, despite efforts which included dredging the river, the institution of a board of curators of the Tiber channel by AUGUSTUS (Suetonius, *Augustus* 30, 37), and an abortive scheme to reroute some of the tributaries flowing into the river (Tacitus, *Annals* 1.76, 79).

Despite these difficulties, the Tiber was a route of major commercial importance. In archaic times, it allowed access from the inland cities to the salt pans at the coast. Later, it had a major role in supplying Rome with food and other supplies both from inland and from overseas. AGRICULTURAL produce from the upper part of the valley was transported downstream to Rome (PLINY THE YOUNGER, *Letters* 5.6.12), as were wood, building STONE and BRICKS (STRABO 5.3.7). Goods coming in the opposite direction were either taken directly upriver, or transferred on to smaller boats known as *naves codicariae* at Ostia or Portus to complete their journey upriver. JRP

Tiberius (Tiberius Claudius Nero) 42 BC–AD 37 Roman emperor, who was from the branch of the PATRICIAN CLAUDII that had not held the CONSULSHIP since 202 BC. Tiberius' father, an adherent of ANTONY, gave up his wife LIVIA to OCTAVIAN (38 BC), who had divorced Scribonia, a relative of Sextus Pompey, after she gave birth to JULIA. Tiberius began (in 27) as an officer in Spain, ARMENIA (where he crowned a Roman nominee in 19), the ALPS and the Balkans, taking over from Marcus AGRIPPA. Previously married to Agrippa's daughter, he also took Agrippa's widow Julia (Scribonia's daughter) in 11, and when his brother was killed in GERMANY in 9 he transferred there. Tribunician power (6 BC) made him Augustus' partner, but he retired to RHODES in anger at irregular advancement demanded for his stepsons Gaius and Lucius Caesar. Their deaths returned him to power and to ADOPTION by Augustus (AD 4). Further service in Balkans and Germany followed, and advancement to near-equal power with Augustus (13), whose death left him in full control. SENATORS who had thought him finished suspected his demand for their participation in government, but at the age of 56 he was expected soon to yield to his popular adopted son Germanicus. The deaths of Germanicus (AD 19) and of his own son Drusus Caesar (AD 23) reopened the succession question and led to struggles between his minister SEJANUS and Germanicus' family, and to the political trials that blackened Tiberius' name. Parsimony due to shortage of funds already evident in Augustus' later years, and caution in Germany, intensified his unpopularity. BML

See Levick, B. (1976) *Tiberius the Politician*.

AUGUSTUS: (a); EMPERORS, ROMAN: (a).

Tibullus (Albius Tibullus) c.55–18 BC Elegiac POET. The date of Tibullus' birth cannot be established with certainty, but he was probably a slightly older contemporary of his fellow-elegist PROPERTIUS. We can be fairly certain (on the basis of his poetry, supplemented by the brief and somewhat suspect biographical notice transmitted in the manuscripts) that he was of EQUESTRIAN rank and belonged to the circle of poets under the patronage of Marcus Valerius Messalla Corvinus, whom he perhaps accompanied on military campaigns in Aquitania and the east. His death, shortly after that of VIRGIL, is lamented in a contemporary EPIGRAM by Domitius Marsus and by OVID in *Amores* 3.9.

Tibullus follows elegiac convention in depicting himself as the impoverished yet devoted lover of a fascinating but faithless mistress (Delia in book 1, succeeded in book 2 by the still more rapacious Nemesis). Unlike his fellow elegists, however, Tibullus also writes of his love for a boy, Marathus (who falls in turn for the proud Pholoë, producing an intriguingly complex emotional triangle). Recurrent themes of the elegies are the condemnation of WAR and luxurious living, both contrasted in several poems with the simplicity and peace of rural life: Tibullus draws here on the traditions of PASTORAL poetry, though the lover's idealization of rustic life is repeatedly undercut and dismissed as an unrealizable fantasy. The anti-war sentiments of the love poems also clash with Tibullus' celebration of the military exploits of Messalla (the addressee or subject of several poems in books 1 and 2).

A third book of (mainly) elegiac poems transmitted along with Tibullus 1 and 2 is probably to be attributed to other poets of Messalla's circle (among whom Sulpicia is notable as one of the few female poets of antiquity whose works are extant). MG

See Tibullus, *Elegies*, text and trs., G. Lee (1990); Lyne, R. O. A. M. (1980) *The Latin Love Poets*.

Tibur see TIVOLI.

tiles In the ancient world, ROOFS and floors were often constructed with tiles made of terracotta or stone. Handmade tiles from the Greek Bronze Age period are associated with monumental structures (e.g. the house of tiles at Lerna), but it is difficult to discern whether the surviving pieces are roof or floor tiles. In the archaic period, we see the development of mould-formed, interlocking, specialized roof tiles that are slipped and used on high-status public buildings (e.g. the early TEMPLE of APOLLO at CORINTH). After the archaic period, roofing tiles simplify into a few forms: ridge tiles; curved or faceted cover tiles (known by the Latin name *imbrices*); large, flat, flanged tiles (Latin *tegulae*); and a curved pan tile. They develop into three main styles: Laconian, Corinthian and Sicilian. The Laconian comprises curved pan tile and curved *imbrex*, the Corinthian comprises *tegula* and faceted *imbrex*, and the Sicilian comprises semicircular cover tiles and *tegulae*. Variants of these, and different styles, also exist. As the use of ceramic roof tiles spread, they were less likely to receive special finishes, but the practice does sporadically continue (e.g. African red slip *imbrices* are reported from early Roman CARTHAGE). A more specialized use of tile is the square, mould-made series depicting geometric and figured images, known from early Christian churches in modern-day Tunisia, where they were used to decorate ceilings and possibly also walls.

They are also found in eastern Algeria, and occasionally in GAUL and Spain. PJEM

See Brodribb, G. (1987) *Roman Brick and Tile*; Cacan de Bissy, A. and Petit, J., eds. (1982) *De Carthage à Kairouan* 187–9; Hellmann, M.-C. (2002) *L'Architecture grecque*, vol. 1: *Les Principes de construction* 278–326.

Timaios c.350–260 BC Greek historian. After AGATHOKLES' conquest of Tauromenion (Taormina) c.315, Timaios was exiled to Athens, where he wrote historical works of which only fragments survive. He was the author of a list of OLYMPIAN victors, Spartan EPHORS, Athenian archons and Argive PRIESTESSES of HERA, establishing the Olympiad (the four-yearly interval between Olympic games) as the basic unit in CHRONOLOGY. His major work, the *Sicilian History* in 38 books (used by DIODORUS and others), covered events in the western MEDITERRANEAN from the mythical past up to Agathokles' death in 289/8. It was followed by an account of the Roman war against PYRRHOS and events up to 264, the date POLYBIOS uses as the starting-point for his own history. Apparently biased in favour of the western Greeks and aristocratic governments, and highly critical of most of his predecessors (hence the witty epithet *epitimaios*, 'blamer', applied to him), his own work was criticized by Polybios (especially in the latter's book 12) for its lack of reliability and historical method. Timaios remains, however, the most important historian between EPHOROS and Polybios. KB

See FGrH 566; Brown, T. S. (1958) *Timaeus of Tauromenium*; Pearson, L. (1987) *The Greek Historians of the West*; Schepens, G. (1994) Politics and belief in Timaeus of Tauromenium, *Ancient Society* 25: 249–78; Walbank, F.W. (1968–9) The historians of Greek Sicily, *Kokalos* 14–15: 476–98.

timber The ancient world had a huge appetite for timber, especially in periods of urban growth. Timber buildings frequently employed unseasoned timber from young trees (especially oak), but various methods of preparing seasoned timbers were practised. Pine was preferred for the longer timbers needed in ROOF construction and SHIPBUILDING. Local sources, usually from managed woodlands, were exploited for most uses. STRABO's description implies that even the city of Rome had little need to go beyond the TIBER basin for its main needs, though he describes how Rome exploited forests near Pisa and Genoa.

Specialist supplies could, however, be imported long distances to obtain larger structural timbers needed for public buildings and the specialist woods used in FURNITURE making. These included cedars from Lebanon, oak from the Ardennes and Corsica, firs from the Vosges and Jura, and pine, maple and birch from various sources. Such supplies were generally moved by water, and from the early 2nd century BC Rome's timber merchants were established in the HARBOUR below the Aventine.

PLINY THE ELDER describes the arrival in Rome of the largest tree seen in the city: a 37 m (120 ft) larch from the Raetian ALPS. DIOCLETIAN's Price Edict of AD 301 regulated the sale of these larger structural timbers, with $4\frac{1}{2}$ m (5 yards) of 45 cm square (18 × 18 inches) pine costing as much as 50,000 *denarii*, compared to 250 *denarii* for $6\frac{1}{2}$ m (7 yards) of oak or ash only 23 cm (9 inches) square. (see also CARPENTRY; FORESTS AND FORESTRY) DP

See Meiggs, R. (1982) *Trees and Timber in the Ancient Mediterranean World*.

 CHARCOAL.

time An object of study to ancient PHILOSOPHERS from PARMENIDES onwards. Parmenides argued that time cannot exist, because the same object cannot have opposing qualities. Time changes one thing into another; for example, something hot becomes cold. Since things cannot have differing properties, time, like change, cannot exist. Furthermore, at the root of his philosophy is the premise that that which is, is and must be. It follows that the present is, but the PAST, by definition, is not – just as the FUTURE is not. Therefore, only the present exists. Parmenides, like PLATO after him, argued that time only exists in our sensory world, whereas in the real world (which Plato sees as the perfect version of our world) time and change do not occur.

LUCRETIUS, the Roman EPICUREAN philosopher, is influenced by this conception of time. According to him, time is an imperceptible concept, which has been invented in order to gauge the unfolding of events. It is change that makes us aware of the passage of time, and it is only through change that we have a concept of past, present and future. The purpose of time is purely to measure change.

The outbreak of the PERSIAN WARS in the early 5th century BC changed the way people investigated time. The need to know how the war came to happen and how it was won led HERODOTOS to investigate past events. This meant articulating a causal relationship between the past and present, as well as charting an established account of past occurrences. The exploration of time is also central to Greek TRAGEDY, which developed simultaneously. Tragic time is clearly located in the present, while the past is brought in to explain the present. Typically, what occurs in the present will pave the way for a change in situation; in this way tragedies chart the future. So, like history, tragedy explores causation, namely how the present has come to being and how it contributes to the future.

Romans did not necessarily characterize the past in strictly CHRONOLOGICAL terms. They viewed the past as incorrupt, and the present as a deviation from that ideal. However, the past was indistinct and not located in a specific time and place. It was a generic formulation of Roman ideals laid out in temporal terms, which existed only as a counterpart of the present. (see also CALENDARS; TIME-KEEPING) EACM

See Romilly, J. de (1968) *Time in Greek Tragedy*.

time-keeping Greeks and Romans both divided each day into 12 equal sections, the first beginning at sunrise and the last ending at sunset. HERODOTOS (2.109.3) attributes this to the BABYLONIANS; the Egyptians may also have contributed to the adoption of this practice. In the early period, there is some evidence that more unscientific methods were used for the reckoning of time (ARISTOPHANES and MENANDER refer to meal times set by the length of the hungry person's shadow, and confusion arises in both instances). Water could be used to mark off time in some contexts; the *klepsydra*, a pot with a hole in the bottom to let out water into another pot, was used to regulate the length of speeches in the lawcourts at Athens.

SUNDIALS become more common in the 3rd century BC and afterwards, though often in official rather than private contexts: for instance, the sundial from Catina set up in the Roman FORUM in 264. Time at Rome had previously been announced publicly by an assistant of the CONSUL, who marked the hours by the passage of the sun with reference to various monuments (PLINY THE ELDER, *Natural History* 7.60). The Catina clock, inaccurate with regard to the seasons at Rome, and Scipio Nasica's water-clock of 159, were new ways of measuring public time. At night, the stars could be scrutinized.

The lengthiest discussion of the topic is in VITRUVIUS (*On Architecture* 9.7–8). While it is relatively straightforward to devise a method of marking fixed periods of time, it was harder in the ancient system to keep 12 equal periods of time across the seasons, since the length of the day changes. Some method was necessary to take account of seasonal variation. Clocks that use water, sand or weights are effective in the absence of sunlight, and sundials can be adjusted for this purpose and are widely found. POMPEII, in particular, has produced a wide variety in public and private settings. Such elaborate instruments are vitiated, however, if the CALENDAR is allowed to fall out of line with the process of the year, as happened in the 190s at Rome where spring months came round in the actual autumn.

One of the most famous and largest sundials was in Rome: the Horologium of AUGUSTUS, the gnomon of which was an obelisk taken from Egypt and set up in the Campus Martius. There may have been some relationship between the obelisk and the nearby ARA PACIS, but it seems only to mark out the meridian, not the more elaborate divisions that were once claimed for it. CJS

See Bickerman, E. J. (1980) *Chronology of the Ancient World*; Gibbs, S. L. (1976) *Greek and Roman Sundials*.

 SUNDIALS.

Timgad (anc. Thamugadi) A Roman town in Numidia (mod. Algeria), 32 km (20 miles) east of the legionary fortress of LAMBAESIS. Founded in AD 100 by TRAJAN as a settlement (*colonia*) for retired soldiers, the original town covered 12.5 ha (30 acres) and was surrounded by a defensive walled circuit. It was designed on a very regular grid, with streets intersecting at right angles to form square blocks (*insulae*) of buildings. This neat regularity of layout, a classic example of Roman town-planning, and the fact that the ancient town has been laid bare in its entirety – one of the very few such examples in the Roman empire – have given Timgad a special prominence in Roman ARCHAEOLOGY. The excavations were essentially clearance operations, and we know little about the development of the town apart from what can be gleaned from inscriptions. At its centre lies the FORUM, together with the BASILICA and council chamber (*curia*). Elsewhere are a THEATRE, two MARKETS, fourteen public BATHS and a public LIBRARY,

TIMGAD: the forum of the Roman colony of Thamugadi (mod. Timgad), established AD 100.

identifiable by a 3rd-century inscription. The last is one of few such structures recognized with certainty in the ancient world. An enormous Capitoline TEMPLE was built outside the original nucleus in the second half of the 2nd century, when the city expanded beyond its original size and the defensive walls were dismantled and largely built over; whether provision for it was included elsewhere in the original settlement is disputed. Among the numerous private HOUSES, the bigger ones with central peristyles (mostly in the west and south quarters) nearly all had a piped WATER SUPPLY, at any rate by the later empire. Their MOSAICS, with strikingly detailed floral and ornamental patterns, show a distinctive style unmatched elsewhere in North AFRICA. They belong mainly to the 3rd and the first half of the 4th century, when the city was at the peak of its prosperity. The houses in the north-east quarter were less well appointed. A dozen FULLING establishments have been identified here, so cloth production must have been a significant local industry, to add to bronze-working and the handling of AGRICULTURAL produce from the fertile surrounding territory. In the 4th century, Thamugadi was a centre of the Donatist schism which rent early African CHRISTIANITY. What are claimed as separate Donatist and CATHOLIC 'cathedrals', along with six other CHURCHES and three chapels, have been identified on the western outskirts. In the VANDAL period Berber raiders sacked Thamugadi. Although the Byzantines built a FORT outside the town to the south in 539/40, among the best preserved of its type in North Africa, there is little sign of Byzantine urban regeneration, and no evidence that any part of the town site was occupied much beyond c.600. Two inscriptions are particularly memorable. A threshold to a bath is inscribed 'Wash well; it is good to have washed', accompanied by two pairs of sandals, one facing inwards, the other outwards. A step in the forum is scratched with the proclamation 'Hunting, bathing, gambling, laughing, that is what life's all about'. RJAW

See Courtois, C. (1951) *Timgad, Antique Thamugadi*; Fentress, E.W. B. (1979) *Numidia and the Roman Army*.

Timoleon Briefly TYRANT of CORINTH in the 360s BC, but best known for suppressing tyranny in SICILY. Little is known about his early career. He arrived in Sicily in 344 after Syracusan exiles from the regime of Dionysios II appealed for assistance from Corinth. Timoleon was nominated but initially given no military support, though an army was provided after his successful landing in Sicily. He recruited a MERCENARY army and landed at Tauromenion, defeated the tyrant of Leontinoi and captured SYRACUSE, exiling Dionysios to Corinth. A CARTHAGINIAN invasion in support of the remaining tyrants was repelled, and a treaty limiting Carthaginian influence to western Sicily was imposed. Timoleon expelled the remaining tyrants and encouraged new settlers from Greece to repopulate Sicily. He introduced DEMOCRATIC reforms at Syracuse, but nevertheless remained *stratêgos autokratôr* for several years. He retired from office due to blindness and died c.335–330. His regime was marked by an economic and cultural revival, and sources all take a highly favourable line towards him, despite his own tyranny and apparent involvement in his brother's assassination during his rise to power. KL

See Diodorus 16.65–90; Plutarch, *Life of Timoleon*; Talbert, R. (1974) *Timoleon and the Revival of Greek Sicily, 344–317 BC*.

Timotheos Athenian GENERAL (d.354 BC), born in the late 5th century (probably not later than 414/13) into a wealthy though not necessarily aristocratic family; son of the 5th-century general KONON. Timotheos is first known to have served in public office as general in 378. In his campaigns, he brought a number of new allies from the north-west into the second Athenian confederacy. Being responsible for a resumption of hostilities in 374, he was deposed from office in the following year and charged with treason after failing to act upon orders, though he had not been given the resources to do so. Iason, TYRANT of Pherai in THESSALY, and Alketas, king of the Molossians, spoke in Timotheos' defence and he was acquitted.

As well as involvement in other campaigns in the northern AEGEAN, Timotheos was sent to support the revolt by the PERSIAN satrap Ariobarzanes in 368, with orders not to violate Athens' treaty with the king of Persia. Timotheos' assistance was oblique, taking SAMOS, which had a Persian garrison. Charged with bribery in 356 during the SOCIAL WAR, he died in EXILE. He is credited with many tactical ruses and administrative ingenuity. LGM

See Diodorus Siculus, *Library of History* 15–16 (*passim*); Nepos, *Timotheus*; Polyainos 3.10.

Timotheos (poet) see MUSIC.

tin A widely used non-ferrous metal in the classical world. It was rarely used on its own but was an important ingredient in bronzes, PEWTER and solder. Tin ORES are not widely found, and the only significant sources were in BRITAIN and Spain. The ores are found as pebbles of tin oxide in 'placer deposits', i.e. in stream sediments downstream of the veins of ore. The smelting of tin ore to produce metallic tin is a very simple process and requires only modest temperatures and reducing conditions (especially compared to the smelting of IRON ores). Tin smelting would not produce large quantities of waste materials (such as slags), and so has not been recognized archaeologically. Tin ingots have been recovered from around the coasts of western Europe. Few of these ingots were stamped, and in many cases it is not possible to be certain when they were produced.

Tin was a minor but important component in COPPER ALLOYS. The copper alloy used throughout classical and hellenistic Greece was a bronze containing 5 to 8 per cent tin. This alloy (and other copper alloys containing tin) continued to be used to the end of the Roman empire and beyond. Very large quantities of tin were required to form these bronzes.

The same alloy that was used to make pewter (a tin–LEAD alloy) was also used to make solders. A tin–lead alloy containing 60 per cent tin (and 40 per cent lead) has a melting point of 187° C and can be used to join pieces of copper alloy and even lead to each other. A tin–lead alloy containing 40 per cent tin (and 60 per cent lead) melts over a temperature range (187–240° C) and so can be wiped over a join as the solder solidifies. DD

Tiryns see ARGOS AND THE ARGOLID; MYCENAEANS; PALACES.

Titus (Titus Flavius Vespasianus) 30 December AD 39–13 September 81 The elder son of VESPASIAN, whom he succeeded as EMPEROR in June AD 79. Born in Rome, educated in the imperial court, he accompanied Vespasian on his JEWISH campaign and was left in charge to capture JERUSALEM and destroy the Temple in 70. He returned to Rome to play a key role in the consolidation of the Flavian dynasty as heir apparent. He shared seven CONSULSHIPS, the CENSORSHIP and the powers of a TRIBUNE with his father and, quite exceptionally, was PRAETORIAN prefect. He caused some scandal by his relationship with Berenike, the much-married sister of the oriental king Agrippa II, and stirred up hatred by his involvement in the execution of alleged plotters against Vespasian. His reign in his own right was noted for the destruction of POMPEII and HERCULANEUM by Vesuvius on 24 August 79. Titus took personal control of the relief effort. The Colosseum was inaugurated with lavish games in 80. Titus died unexpectedly of natural causes (though there were the inevitable stories of poisoning). His reputation as 'the darling and delight of the human race' (Suetonius, *Titus* 1) owes much to the brevity of his reign and was probably created as a stick with which to beat his successor, DOMITIAN. The ARCH erected in Titus' memory is one of the most pictured remains of classical Rome. JJP

See Cassius Dio 66.17–26; Josephus, *Jewish War*; Suetonius, *Titus*; Jones, B.W. (1984) *The Emperor Titus*; Mozart, *La clemenza di Tito*.

 EPIGRAPHY, ROMAN: (a); TRIUMPHS, ROMAN: (a)–(b); VESPASIAN.

Tivoli (anc. Tibur) Originally a powerful Latin town 30 km (18 miles) east of Rome, holding a strategic position on the river Anio. Although defeated by Rome in 338 BC, Tibur remained nominally independent until after the SOCIAL WAR. It was a common place of imprisonment and exile for Rome's enemies, most notably the Numidian chief Syphax (203 BC) and queen ZENOBIA of PALMYRA (AD 273).

Tibur's most notable remains are the two Republican TEMPLES on the acropolis overlooking the Anio; the circular temple of the Sybil provided the model for the Bank of England's 'Tivoli Corner'. Just outside the town walls is the large, terraced sanctuary of HERCULES Victor, an ancient local cult later exported to Rome and much favoured by AUGUSTUS.

The territory of Tibur was famous for three things: its FRUIT; the travertine QUARRIES which supplied Rome with some of its finest building STONE, used for example in the façade of the Colosseum; and the summer VILLAS of the Roman élite, including those of Calpurnius Piso (consul 58 BC) and Quintilius Varus (consul 13 BC). The most famous was built by the emperor HADRIAN; covering 120 ha (300 acres), it was larger than the town itself and included many quasi-urban amenities such as BATHS and THEATRES. Hadrian is also said to have incorporated representations of famous monuments of the empire, including the Canopus CANAL and the SERAPEUM of ALEXANDRIA. The ruins of Hadrian's Villa provided the inspiration for modern Tivoli's most famous attraction, the RENAISSANCE gardens of the Villa d'Este designed by the ANTIQUARIAN Pirro Ligorio. JDeL

See Coarelli, F. (1982) *Lazio*.

 LATINS; SCULPTURE: (d).

toga A semicircular woollen cloth worn mainly by Roman men. In the 6th century BC it was no longer than a cloak, but it became longer and more voluminous, until it reached 7 m long in the 1st and 2nd centuries AD and became increasingly difficult to wear. It was worn in a variety of styles. The basic method of draping involved having one-third of the cloth hanging forward over the left shoulder, then passing behind the wearer's back, under the right arm and flipped over the left shoulder, or draped over the left arm. Folds at the front could be used as a pocket, and the material at the back could be pulled over the head.

The standard toga, worn after the ceremony to mark the attainment of manhood, was the *toga virilis* or *toga pura*. This was left the natural colour of the wool. The *toga praetexta* had a purple border on the straight edge and was worn by upper class men under the age of 17, young women before they married, officials, PRIESTS and judges. The *toga candida* was whitened with chalk and worn by candidates (hence *candidati*) for public office. The *toga pulla* was of a black or dark colour and was worn when in mourning, while the *toga picta*, which was purple with gold embroidery, was TRIUMPHAL wear which later came to be the official outfit of the EMPEROR and CONSULS. NJW

TOGA: a cumbersome and distinctive garment of male attire.

See Symons, D. J. (1987) *Costume of Ancient Rome*.

DRESS, ROMAN: (a).

toilets Greek cities lacked public toilets. Domestic toilets consisted of a urinal and excretion space connected to a drain or sited over a cesspit, and sometimes equipped with a terracotta seat, as at OLYNTHOS. Chamber pots were also probably used. In the Roman world, *foricae* or multi-seater public latrines are a source of modern fascination, as they reveal a culture of communal defecation alien to us. We know men used them; there is no direct evidence as to whether women did. Public latrines had a STONE or wooden bench pierced with numerous keyhole-shaped apertures, set over a channel around three sides of a room. After excretion, one cleaned oneself with a communally shared (!) sponge on a stick thrust through an aperture in the front of the bench; the sponge was rinsed in a channel in front of the seats. Latrines were also equipped with a basin for WASHING hands. They were flushed by overflow from FOUNTAINS or by outflow from public BATHS. Domestic latrines were of similar design, though usually with one to four seats, if there was sufficient piped water available to flush them; otherwise, a tiled splashback and an open hole below the latrine seat indicate that they were flushed with a bucket or jar. AIW

TOILETS: a well-preserved multi-seater latrine at Thugga, Tunisia.

See Crouch, D. (1993) *Water Management in Ancient Greek Cities*; Wilson, A. I. (2000 [2001]) Incurring the wrath of Mars: sanitation and hygiene in Roman North Africa, in G. C. M. Jansen, ed., *Cura Aquarum in Sicilia* 307–12.

tombs Most ancient cultures used monumental tombs to express high social status, but in very varied ways, depending on local power structures. For instance, in 5th-century Athens large STONE tombs were set up at public expense for the war dead and small ones for AMBASSADORS, while private monumental tombs were very rare indeed. This pattern was probably linked to Athenian civic egalitarianism, but broke down at the end of the 5th century, as wealthy Athenians began to imitate the symbolism of the state war tombs in their private *peribolos* ('enclosure') tombs. These tombs had carefully built stone walls, relief and free-standing SCULPTURES and inscriptions. The shift in the use of tombs was probably linked to major sociological changes and the emergence of a more assertive ARISTOCRACY.

In Republican Rome, on the other hand, tomb building was linked to larger conflicts within the aristocracy over the value of Greek culture. Indigenous Roman tomb building had been very restrained since the 6th century, but by 100 BC some noblemen were imitating hellenistic tomb ARCHITECTURE and building very large stone tombs along the ROADS outside the main cities in Italy. Roman tomb building was as tightly linked to changing power structures as Athenian, and AUGUSTUS' reduction of aristocratic display after 30 BC had a major impact. Lavish tombs first disappeared from Rome itself, where Augustus' mausoleum redefined display after 28 BC, and then

TOMBS: (a) prominent and individualistic tomb monuments were a feature of road frontages approaching many towns, as here at Pompeii.

TOMBS: (b) the religious aspects of tombs are reflected in the temple-like appearance of this group from Ghirza, Libya.

from provincial cities too. By the 60s AD, PETRONIUS could even use the desire for a lavish tomb as a sign of bad taste. IM

See Fedak, J. (1990) *Monumental Tombs of the Hellenistic Age*; Kurtz, D.C. (1971) *Greek Burial Customs*; Morris, I. (1992) *Death-ritual and Social Structure in Classical Antiquity*; Toynbee, J.M.C. (1971) *Death and Burial in the Roman World*.

 ARCHITECTS; BURIAL, ROMAN: (a); PETRA.

tools In the classical world almost all tools were made of IRON, a metal which is far more plentiful than the COPPER and TIN required to make bronze. As a result many more tools, including a far wider range of specialized types, were available in the Iron Age than in earlier periods. Almost all tools in both the Greek and Roman periods were made of wrought iron, a relatively soft metal. Steel was expensive, and its use was largely confined to a limited range of high-quality, edged tools. The fact that iron artefacts were forged individually, rather than cast, probably aided the relatively rapid evolution of more specialized forms; an example is the wide range of smiths' tongs found in the Roman world. But this was not always the case. Most Roman axes, for example, are of one basic type, varying only in their size, and more specialized forms for felling, CARPENTRY and other purposes did not develop until the Middle Ages. Clearly the rule applied in the classical world, as in other periods, that if the number of tools a craftsman possessed was limited by cost or availability, it was better to have a tool that could be used for several related functions with reasonable efficiency, rather than one that was highly efficient for one task and almost useless for all others.

We know less about Greek tools than Roman, partly because less emphasis has been placed on their study, partly because soil conditions are generally unfavourable to their preservation, and partly because the Greeks did not normally deposit tools in TOMBS or even sanctuaries, both of which are major sources of artefacts. It is also probable that the metal was more valuable in Greece than in Italy and western Europe and so was more thoroughly recycled.

Fortunately, for the later archaic and classical periods in the Greek world we have the evidence of vase-paintings which illustrate some of the tools used in

TOOLS: relief sculpture of a Roman cutler's shop.

key crafts. These include smithing (often shown in scenes associated with HEPHAISTOS), sculpting (both in wood and STONE), carpentry, and such unexpected scenes as a cobbler's shop. Most of the tools shown indicate that the basic forms familiar today had already evolved, though they still remained relatively simple in design. In many of these scenes, the workmen are shown crouched down with their work resting on the ground, unlike similar scenes in Roman SCULPTURE where the craftsmen usually stand or are seated at benches. With the ending of the figured vase tradition our evidence is more restricted. While it is likely that many of the important tool types, such as the carpenter's plane, that we find in the early Roman period (e.g. at POMPEII) were developed in the hellenistic period, we currently lack the evidence to prove this.

Even in the Roman period, there are large areas, particularly in the Eastern PROVINCES and North AFRICA, where we have little information on tools. Fortunately, such evidence as we do have suggests that most were similar to those found in the West. The amount of material which has survived in the Western provinces (the area where most studies have been undertaken) is formidably large. One reason is that the early imperial army was very well equipped, and, for various reasons, discarded large amounts of equipment, particularly on the GERMAN and BRITISH FRONTIERS. Another reason is that in all of the 'CELTIC' areas the Iron Age custom of depositing votive hoards of metalwork reappeared at intervals in the Roman period. As a result we know of many hundreds of tool types covering all of the major crafts and industries, including blacksmithing and METALWORKING, CARPENTRY, stoneworking, AGRICULTURE and LEATHERWORKING, as well as a wide range of domestic tools. Although it is difficult to make a detailed comparison with Greek tools, there can be little doubt that the range of types was considerably greater, and that there was a marked increase in tool specialization. It seems clear that iron was relatively cheap in the Roman period; the large amount used in utilitarian objects, such as plough coulters, indicates this.

The quantity of material which has survived from the Roman period makes us less dependent on pictorial representations than for the Greek period. But while tools are rarely shown on pottery – with the partial exception of smiths' tools and occasional smithing scenes (as in an appliqué from Corbridge, England) – we have a number of relief sculptures, usually funerary, and some frescoes from the area around Vesuvius, that show craftsmen at work. In the main these merely serve to place known tool types in their context, but occasionally they provide evidence of new types. Thus the famous fresco from the House of the Vettii at Pompeii showing *amorini* (cupids) working metal illustrates not only a wide variety of rare tools including anvils, but uniquely shows the use of a blowpipe to heat a crucible. Similarly, a relief from AQUILEIA provides the only evidence that the Roman smith used double bellows to provide a continuous blast of air to his hearth.

Despite the large number of tools that have survived from the Roman period, there are clearly still gaps in our knowledge. For example, we cannot have the full range of smiths' tools, for in some cases it would have been almost impossible to produce existing artefacts using only the surviving tool types. Nor is it clear whether we have the basic toolkit of the ancient sculptor, for while the use of rasps and claws is often taken for granted we still lack the tools themselves. WHM

 IRON: (a)–(b).

torches see FIRE; LAMPS; LIGHTING.

torture (Greek *basanos*, Latin *quaestio*) The Athenians did not normally subject free Greeks to torture, but SLAVES were tortured to secure confessions or evidence against others. During the inquiry in LESBOS into the disappearance of the Athenian Herodes, a free man and a slave were tortured (Antiphon 5.29). But in judicial proceedings the evidence of slaves was only admissible if secured under torture which, in turn, had to be performed with the consent of both litigant parties. Hence one side would make a formal challenge (*proklêsis*) to the other; but none of the 42 recorded challenges was accepted, at least in part because slaves were valuable commodities whom their masters would not wish to see damaged. Therefore, though torture is classed by ARISTOTLE (*Rhetoric*) as a non-technical proof (along with laws, witness statements, oaths and contracts), in the ORATORS it always in fact serves as the basis for commonplace, rational argument either extolling the virtues of the process or emphasizing its unreliability, given that the slave will say anything to be free from pain.

A similar reluctance to torture citizens was felt under the Roman REPUBLIC, but the situation changed during the PRINCIPATE. Slaves were tortured, but could not give evidence against their masters except in certain circumstances such as treason (e.g. the CATILINARIAN conspirators) and sacrilege. AUGUSTUS, with his emphasis on MARRIAGE and MORALITY, extended these to include ADULTERY, though he then had the slaves sold to himself or the state. The way for an apprehensive master to prevent his slave being tortured was to free him first, and this practice may have led to the torture of lowborn free men under TIBERIUS. Further, the increasing despotism of the EMPERORS meant that men of all ranks were potential victims of torture as conspirators, though this was by no means a new phenomenon: ALEXANDER notoriously tortured his general Philotas in 330 BC and executed him for conspiracy. The official line was that torture was unreliable and was only to be used when no other evidence could be found (ANTONINUS PIUS' rule for pecuniary suits). MARCUS AURELIUS exempted members of the highest class from torture (treason excepted). But the reality was probably different, and by the late empire it seems that torture of lower class citizens had become common practice. (See also PUNISHMENT) MJE

See Crook, J. A. (1967) *Law and Life of Rome*; Todd, S. C. (1993) *The Shape of Athenian Law*.

tourism Travel for pleasure or other personal motives (e.g. RELIGIOUS or scholarly) is attested among the Greeks from the archaic period onward. HOMER'S ODYSSEUS, though a reluctant sightseer, may be regarded as the prototypical tourist, since he 'saw the cities of many people and learned their customs' (*Odyssey* 1.3). Later commentators identified his exotic way-stops with actual MEDITERRANEAN sites. Some Homeric locales would later become tourist destinations (e.g. Troy, piously visited by ALEXANDER the Great and JULIUS CAESAR).

SOLON of Athens (6th century BC) spent a decade visiting the antiquities of Egypt and Asia Minor (Herodotos 1.30). In the next century, HERODOTOS himself travelled to Egypt on research. In hellenistic and Roman times, tourists benefited from travel guides, such as STRABO'S *Geographia* and PAUSANIAS' *Description of Greece* (1st and 2nd centuries AD respectively). Religious sanctuaries and healing spas were destinations of choice, while Egypt continued to lure visitors.

From the 1st century BC the Romans began earnestly to suppress maritime PIRACY, so that under the empire long-distance travel was safer than before, though never worry-free – consider that plot device of ancient NOVELS, kidnapping by pirates. Famous

Roman tourists included the inquisitive CICERO and the restless HADRIAN. Germanicus played the tourist in AD 19, travelling to Egypt in casual (Greek) clothing and without imperial permission (Tacitus, *Annals* 2.59). Much later, CHRISTIAN pilgrimages to biblical sites became increasingly common, and detailed itineraries such as those of the Spanish tourist EGERIA (between AD 381 and 384) have survived. JRH

See Casson, L. (1994) *Travel in the Ancient World.*

town planning A 3rd-century BC description of central Greek towns (attributed to Herakleides the Critic) states that Athens 'is all dry, not well watered, and badly segmented because of its antiquity'. A contrast is implied with newer cities, often laid out on the grid-plan system that has come to be seen as the hallmark of Greek town planning.

The same contrast between older, unplanned cities and modern, grid-planned layouts is implied when ARISTOTLE (*Politics*, book 7) states rather cryptically that 'the placement of private dwellings is thought more pleasant and more useful for most activities if it is well segmented' (by streets) 'and is done in the more modern, Hippodamian manner'. In book 2 he informs us that Hippodamos was a citizen of MILETOS who 'both discovered the division of city-states' (probably referring to his theory of social classes) 'and cut up the Piraeus' (again meaning by streets). Hippodamos was evidently both theorist and practising town planner. PIRAEUS was laid out in the mid-5th century; STRABO says that the same man built the city of RHODES at the end of the century. If, as a young man, Hippodamos also saw Miletos rebuilt on rectangular lines after the PERSIAN WARS, or even assisted in its planning, he had a long, but not impossibly long, career. He has also been linked to the planning of the Greek colony of Thourioi in Italy, founded in the 440s (its rectangular layout is described by DIODOROS), though all we know for sure is that he went to live there.

Hippodamos was in fact giving new expression, and perhaps new theoretical underpinning, to an old idea. Greek new towns in SICILY and Italy from the 7th century had parallel streets with elongated blocks of (usually) equal house plots between them. The HOUSES were usually separate rather than contiguous; terrace housing, similar to that of late 19th- and early 20th-century Britain, was perhaps first used at the 5th-century Piraeus. The German word *Typenhaus* ('model house') has become a standard term for Greek terrace housing, which is sometimes claimed to be inherently egalitarian, even democratic, but it is more likely that considerations of technical convenience and economy lie behind its form.

Both in the early colonies and in Hippodamos' more developed form, new Greek towns were characterized by spaces reserved for public buildings such as temples and MARKETPLACES (*AGORAI*). In the hellenistic period, ALEXANDER and the SUCCESSOR dynasties deployed their colossal wealth to benefit cities within their domains, displaying their power through architectural intervention in the civic arena. Greek town planning was introduced to the LEVANT and western Asia, where we see both archetypal Hellenic constructions and fusions of Greek and non-Greek, as at DURA EUROPUS, where the Greek-style *agora* and other schemes were never completed. In general, open spaces became increasingly monumental. At Miletos and Athens, for example, marketplaces were rectangular and surrounded on three or four sides by colonnades (*STOAS*), probably used for administrative offices or élite SHOPS. Aesthetic considerations now seem to take precedence over traditional orientations partly based on astronomical

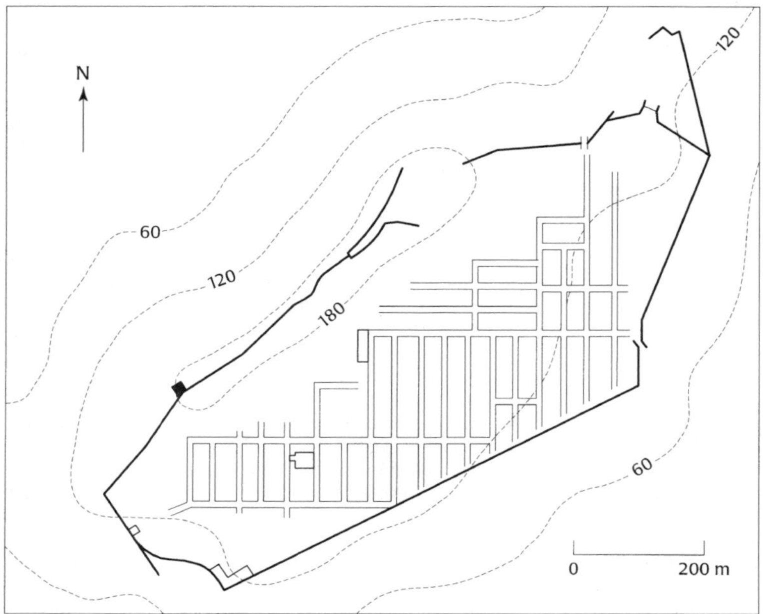

TOWN PLANNING: (a) plan of Goritsa, with its typically Greek orthogonal street grid (though note the different modules employed).

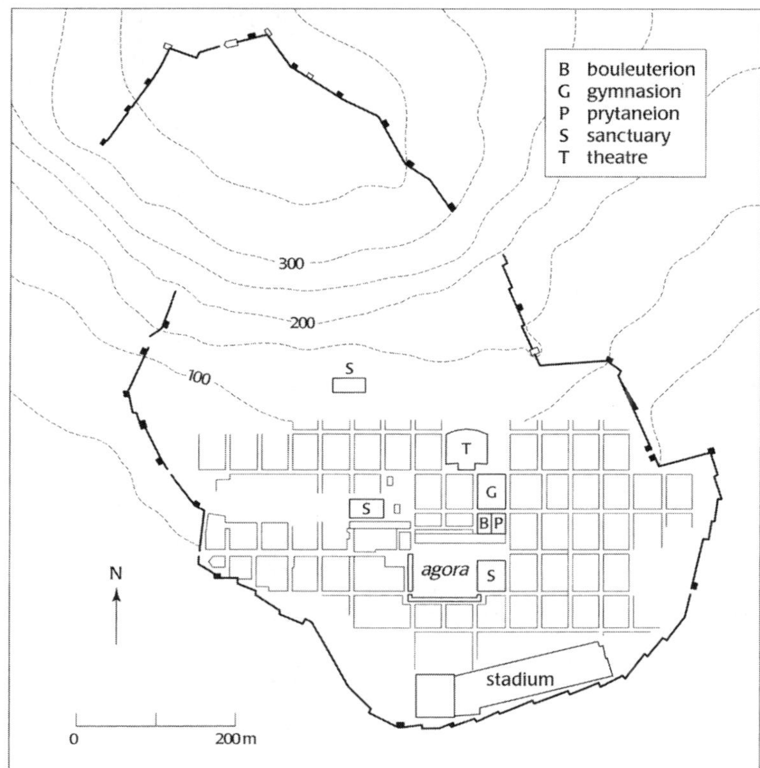

TOWN PLANNING: (b) Priene has a street grid based on squarer *insulae* (more commonly a feature of Roman towns), in part because of the difficulty of this sloping site.

TOWN PLANNING: (c) not all Roman towns were planned on rigid rectilinear grids, as this fragment of the marble map of Rome (the *forma urbis*) illustrates – though also demonstrating that even on irregular sites the Romans had the skill to survey accurately their built environment.

phenomena. Aristotle and VITRUVIUS devote space to the best orientations for temples and streets, but give weight to utility (especially wind direction) and aesthetics rather than to town layouts expressing political or philosophical ideas.

Roman town planning is simpler, at least in the sense that, once Roman culture became dominant in Italy, new towns and colonies were being built at the behest of a single central authority and generally followed a standard model, with slight variations. Typically, these towns had a regular, gridded layout based on rectangular or square blocks (*insulae*). The main north–south street was defined as the *kardo*, the main east–west street as the *decumanus*. One of the best examples is the site of TIMGAD. At the centre of a town was a complex of monumental public buildings, often focused around the FORUM. Many town plans reveal evidence for successive phases of expansion, marked by changes in the alignment of the road grid, as is visible at POMPEII. Even at Timgad, the town quickly outgrew its neat, gridded core, though here the arrangement of the outlying quarters was much more haphazard.

Pre-existing Roman towns often reveal greater complexity and less regularity in layout. Paradoxically, the evolution of ancient ROME produced one of the least regular layouts because of the hilly site and localized development along a series of roads converging on the area of the forum and the Tiber crossing. This is clear from fragments of a marble map of the city produced in the 3rd century AD, though the production of such a map (at a scale of c.1: 300) is itself testimony to Roman skill in urban planning. However, no one would claim that Rome was not a 'planned' city: urban development was governed by complex religious beliefs (the maintenance of a sacred boundary or *pomerium*) and subject to specific laws, for instance proscribing burial within cities. Some guiding principles of Roman town planning are also outlined by VITRUVIUS, though differences between towns suggest that these were not universally observed. Urban magistrates and provincial governors had specific responsibilities in relation to planned developments in towns (a process that could be highly contentious, to judge from the correspondence between PLINY THE YOUNGER and TRAJAN and from the *Orations* of Dio Chrysostom, all relating to disputes in BITHYNIA). (See also ARCHITECTURE; FORTIFICATION; FORUM; HOUSES) DGJS, DJM

See (on Greek) Austin, M. M. (1980) *The Hellenistic World*, no. 83; Hansen, M. H. and Fischer-Hansen, T. (1994) Monumental political architecture in archaic and classical Greek poleis, in D. Whitehead, ed., *From Political Architecture to Stephanus Byzantius* 23–90; Owens, E. J. (1991) *The City in the Greek and Roman World*; Wycherley, R. E. (1962) *How the Greeks Built Cities*; (on Roman) Perring, D. (1991) Spatial organisation and social change in Roman towns, in J. Rich and A. Wallace-Hadrill, eds., *City and Country in the Ancient World* 273–93; Robinson, O. F. (1992) *Ancient Rome: city planning and administration*; Stambaugh, J. E. (1988) *The Ancient Roman City*.

ALEXANDRIA; CITIES: (a); PERGAMON.

toys For the ancients, toys were an essential part of childhood. Babies could have rattles and feeders in the shape of ANIMALS such as PIGS. The most popular toys include knucklebones and miniature FIGURINES. Human figurines have been found in BURIALS and sanctuaries; while they may have had other functions, they often appear to have served as dolls. Primarily depicting women, they could have moveable arms and legs attached to the body with pins. They are modelled with rounded chests indicating breasts, so the young girls were playing with adult versions of themselves rather than babies.

Other miniature items include FURNITURE and animals, wheeled HORSES being especially popular. In Athens, children were given a miniature vase (*choê*) when they turned three, in which they could join in the WINE-drinking on the second day of the Anthesteria FESTIVAL. Visual evidence tells us of less common toys such as tops, yo-yos, hoops, seesaws, swings and miniature CHARIOTS. Literature mentions kites, rocking horses and boats. These toys were often handmade: ARISTOPHANES (*Clouds* 878–81) refers to the carving of wooden toys, including frogs made out of pomegranates.

Toys could also be miniature versions of adult tools. A collection of toys found in an Egyptian town dating to AD 154–214 included a toy weaver's comb and a miniature scribal writing-stand. Epigrams record the dedication of toys by both boys and girls on reaching adulthood. (see also BOARD GAMES) NJW

CHILDHOOD: (b).

trade

The exchange of commodities between two Greek states, or with a non-Greek people. Trade forms the link between producers and consumers, though some restrict it to 'the purchase and movement of goods without the knowledge or identification of a future purchaser' (Snodgrass, in Garnsey et al. 26). Karl Polanyi's anthropological models for trade have been widely used, though they are not without problems. Polanyi's definition, drawn from 'primitivist' societies, includes categories such as 'gift trade' or 'market trade'.

The mode of trade can involve overland or maritime activity. Trade can embrace contact between different *poleis*, or it can be more local, the hinterland of a *polis* supplying the needs of a main urban community. The directional commercial trade of raw materials and foodstuffs on a regular basis might be indicated by grain to Athens, and mirrored by the export of low-cost Attic painted POTTERY to places such as ETRURIA. Greek trade also has an extended definition to include the dispersal of Greek artefacts – pottery and gemstones, for example, recognized in the archaeological record – around the countries bordering the MEDITERRANEAN, BLACK SEA, and beyond. Trade does not necessarily require an exchange of coin or bullion.

Ancient trade is likely to have been dominated by the major staples such as grain, as well as the movement of WINE and OLIVE OIL. Alongside such commodities would have been cargoes of metals, TIMBER and SLAVES. Such cargoes are unlikely to be easily detected in the archaeological record, though the scale can be surmised from the presence of transport AMPHORAS. Large urban populations are unlikely to have been supported by their territories and would have relied on imported grain. Thus Athens would have imported perhaps some 290,000–580,000 *medimnoi* (11,500–23,000 tonnes) of grain to support its population in a non-famine year. No doubt such important trade is reflected in the Greek luxury items, such as gilded silver cups, IVORY objects and JEWELLERY, which regularly turn up in élite graves in the grain-producing areas along the north coast of the Black sea. Some trade consisted of less essential items, which no doubt helped to maintain ÉLITE values. For examples, racehorses from the northern ADRIATIC were transported to the Greek mainland (e.g. Euripides, *Hippolytos* 231, 1131). A hint at this luxury trade can be derived from Kritias (cited at Athenaeus 1.28b–c) who recorded the movement of Etruscan gold cups to Athens.

The taste for MARBLE statuary in the sanctuaries, and indeed cemeteries, of the Greek world encouraged the movement of marble from the Greek islands. For example, a colossal archaic marble *kouros*, dating to the early 6th century BC, was dedicated by the Naxians in the sanctuary of APOLLO on DELOS. The statue, perhaps originally weighing c.23 tonnes with a base of c.34 tonnes, appears to have been made from Naxian marble. Indeed, the associated inscription makes a virtue of the fact that both base and statue were made from the same marble. The base is unlikely to have fitted into an oared ship; this might suggest that during the archaic period, there was specialized movement of such luxury materials. Other early examples of the movement of Naxian marble include the Nikandre *korê* also dedicated on Delos. The movement of marble for major construction projects includes the construction of the Siphnian treasury at DELPHI (Herodotos 3.57), the pedimental sculpture for the temple of Apollo at Delphi built with the aid of the ALKMAIONIDAI (Herodotos 5.62), and the pedimental sculpture of the temple of ZEUS at OLYMPIA. Such transport of heavy materials is not considered as trade by some definitions.

The trade of a *polis* was not necessarily conducted by members of that community or by its citizens. At Athens, for example, there is a reference to a PHOENICIAN merchantman tied up in the PIRAEUS (Xenophon, *Oikonomikos* 8.11–14). Commercial graffiti scratched on the undersides of Attic pottery are invaluable here. They show that Phoenicians and Etruscans, as well as Greeks, were involved in the distribution of pottery. Traders include Kolaios of SAMOS, known from HERODOTOS (4.152), who dedicated a bronze cauldron decorated with griffins in the sanctuary of HERA on his home island. This dedication, worth 6 talents, was a tithe of the proceeds of the expedition. Another archaic trader mentioned by Herodotos (4.152) was Sostratos of AIGINA, perhaps to be identified with the trader who dedicated a STONE anchor to Aiginetan Apollo in the Etruscan HARBOUR town of Gravisca. An insight into the arrangements for late archaic trade is provided by the letter cut on a lead tablet found on the island of Berezan near the colony of Olbia in the Black sea (Austin and Vidal-Naquet, no. 41).

SHIPWRECKS have demonstrated that cargoes were usually mixed. Many contained transport amphoras, presumably for wine or olive oil, though some may have contained solids like olives. In the late 5th-century BC Porticello shipwreck from the straits of Messina, lead ingots and SILVER nuggets were found, as well as remains of a life-size bronze statue (perhaps of a PHILOSOPHER). The 4th-century Kyrenia shipwreck off CYPRUS was found to contain 11 types of transport amphora (including RHODIAN and Samian) and a consignment of almonds. Wrecks from the hellenistic period (3rd–1st centuries BC) demonstrate the increasing volume and inter-connectedness of Mediterranean trade in this period, while PAPYRI from PTOLEMAIC EGYPT document active importation of Greek commodities from the Aegean, particularly through the middleman state of RHODES.

The EUBOIANS have been widely linked with early Greek trade, partly through the widespread distribution of Euboian pottery. In particular they have been linked with the establishment of the Greek trading centre at Al Mina, at the mouth of the river Orontes on the eastern seaboard of the Mediterranean. Excavations have revealed a number of WAREHOUSES which were in use from the 8th century. In the western Mediterranean, one of the earliest centres for trade seems to have been the settlement of PITHEKOUSSAI on the island of Ischia in the bay of Naples. One of the activities on the island may have been the smelting and working of IRON from Elba; some iron slag comes from 8th-century contexts.

A further commercial centre, which again did not have the status of a colony, was the Greek settlement at NAUKRATIS in Egypt. Although Herodotos (2.178) seems to suggest that the settlement was established during the reign of the philhellene pharaoh Amasis (570–526), the archaeological evidence seems to point to activity from the late 7th century. The trade through Naukratis in the 4th century is well illustrated by the *stêlai* (one recently discovered in the sea) dating to the reign of Nektanebis I (380) – originally read as Nektanebo I (380–362) – which gave a tithe to the Egyptian goddess Neith. The link between Egypt and the Greek world is emphasized by the presence of Egyptian bronzes in the sanctuary of Hera on the island of Samos, perhaps dedicated by Samian shippers on their return. Contact between Amasis and Polykrates of Samos is also recorded in Herodotos.

The movement of Greek objects beyond the Greek world is a well-recognized phenomenon. Essentially it marks trade with the barbarian peoples, as well as a growth in the desire for non-Greeks to adopt Greek culture. Greek (as well as Etruscan) objects regularly turn up in France and central Europe. This reflects both transalpine trade, as well as the use of the RHÔNE, which had presumably been opened up with the establishment of the Greek colony at Massalia (MARSEILLES). Such Greek material as finds its way inland includes the enormous bronze krater (Laconian?), as well as Attic black-figured pottery, found in a HALLSTATT period grave at Vix in Burgundy, near the source of the Seine. From the later LA TÈNE period comes Greek material from contexts at Somme-Bionne in France as well as in the Heuneburg cemetery in Austria. The distribution of transport amphoras up the Rhône seems to have gone alongside the movement of Greek *SYMPOSIUM* pottery, and this may indicate the adoption of wine-drinking by non-Greeks. This trade with the Greeks has been linked to changes in European society, and it has been suggested that central Europe may have been supplying slaves to feed demand by Greek communities. (see also CONSUMER CITY; CONSUMERS; ECONOMY; GROWTH, ECONOMIC; MANUFACTURING; PRODUCTION; SURPLUSES) DWJG

See Arafat, K. and Morgan, C. (1994) Athens, Etruria and the Heuneburg, in I. Morris, ed., *Classical Greece* 108–34; Austin, M. (1970) *Greece and Egypt in the Archaic Age*; Austin, M. M. and Vidal-Naquet, P. (1977) *Economic and Social History of Ancient Greece*; Boardman, J. (1999) *The Greeks Overseas*; Finley, M. I. (1999) *The Ancient Economy*; Garnsey, P. et al., eds. (1983) *Trade in the Ancient Economy*; Gill, D.W. J. (1991) Pots and trade: spacefillers or objets d'art?, *JHS* 111: 29–47; Hopper, R. J. (1979) *Trade and Industry in Classical Greece*; Humphreys, S. C. (1978) *Anthropology and the Greeks*; Johnston, A.W. (1979) *Trademarks on Greek Vases*; Meijer, F. and van Nijf, O. (1992) *Trade, Transport and Society in the Ancient World*; Möller, A. (2000) *Naukratis: trade in archaic Greece*; Nash, D. (1985) Celtic territorial expansion and the Mediterranean world, in T. C. Champion and J.V. S. Megaw, eds., *Settlement and Society* 45–67; Osborne, R. G. (1996) Pots, trade and the archaic Greek economy, *Antiquity* 70: 31–44; Ridgway, D. (1992) *The First Western Greeks*; Wells, P. S. (1980) *Culture Contact and Culture Change*; Archibald, Z. H. et al., eds. (2001) *Hellenistic Economies*.

ROAD and maritime networks, and an efficient monetary system, as well as an expansive empire, contributed to the growing trade in the Roman world. Goods circulating throughout the empire included building materials, food and manufactured goods. Merchandise could be bartered, but with the implementation of an effective monetary system trade became more fully developed.

Rome's trade routes extended as far as North AFRICA and CHINA. Food was the most important item in terms of production, consumption and trade. Perishable goods such as eggs, dairy, MEAT, POULTRY, FRUITS and VEGETABLES were most likely produced and sold locally, while other foodstuffs such as OLIVE OIL, GRAIN, SALT and FISH could be TRANSPORTED over longer distances. The population needed to be fed; therefore grain from SICILY, and eventually Egypt and North AFRICA, began to be imported into the city of Rome and to the other PROVINCES. Olive oil for food, FUEL and COSMETICS made its way from Spain and North Africa to Italy. WINE, a component of the Roman DIET, was produced primarily in Campania, Latium and ETRURIA and exported mainly to Spain and GAUL. In northern Italy and southern Gaul, wine was transported in wooden barrels. Barrels could also store FISH SAUCE (*garum*) or salt.

For the most part goods such as wine, oil and fish were stored in AMPHORAS, clay transportation vessels that could be stacked on their sides or stood upright. Amphoras from SHIPWRECKS and archaeological sites provide important information regarding trade. For example, MONTE TESTACCIO, located outside ROME near the TIBER river, is a site 1 km in circumference and 50 m (165 ft) high, comprising mainly Spanish amphora sherds. The quantity of sherds at this site presupposes that c.23 million kg (c.23,000 tonnes) of olive oil had passed through this port. Many of the sherds are inscribed in black ink with the names of traders, as well as the weight and content of the goods the amphoras contained. ARCHAEOLOGISTS posit that this marks the site where ships docked and unloaded cargo to be distributed in Rome. Other pottery goods include COOKING, coarse wares and some fine wares that were either produced locally or imported and exported through trade. For example, most fine wares were traded between Gaul, Italy, Spain and North Africa. Pottery such as *terra sigillata*, a kind of red-gloss POTTERY, was exported from southern Gaul.

Building and decorative materials such as limestone and MARBLE were popular trade goods. Limestone could be quarried locally in certain areas of the empire. Marble, however, especially in the age of the emperor AUGUSTUS, was the stone of choice in the capital and outlying towns and cities. The marble of choice up to the 2nd century AD was the Italian CARRARA (ancient Luna) stone, still quarried and exported today. Other stones and marbles came from Greece (PAROS), PHRYGIA, and Egypt (Mons Porphyrites, MONS CLAUDIANUS).

Precious metals predominantly from Spain, such as GOLD, SILVER, COPPER, IRON and TIN, were mined and exported into centres for further production. For example, the town of CAPUA in Campania was known for its silver and copper goods. Luxury goods such as PAPYRUS, IVORY, SPICES and precious stones were also prevalent. For example, Egypt exported papyrus, North Africa and ARABIA incense, the Baltic AMBER, and SCYTHIA emeralds. Cardamom, cinnamon, turmeric, sesame and the most popular SPICE in the Roman empire, PEPPER, all came from INDIA. SILK, in both raw and processed forms, came from China. GLASS was extensively traded, with ALEXANDRIA, SYRIA, CYPRUS and RHODES the major centres. With the Syrian invention of glassblowing, glass production and trade became more widespread. Centres sprang up in Rome, PUTEOLI, AQUILEIA and Cologne. Glass vessels could either hold liquid for transportation or be sold on their own. TEXTILES were another valued trade commodity. Sheared wool from SHEEP could be imported, the best reputedly being from MILETOS, while Italian sources included Apulia and Calabria.

Trade in ANIMALS became increasingly popular, especially when beast HUNTS became a frequent spectacle in AMPHITHEATRES. Animals such as lions and leopards came from North Africa or ASIA. Domesticated animals were raised and exported to supply the Roman military and farms. CAMELS from

TRADE, ROMAN: transhipment of goods from a sea-going vessel onto a river barge (*codicarius*) at Ostia.

North Africa and the Middle East were used as pack animals in the army. HORSES, rarely used on farms, were imported from southern Italy and Spain for the CAVALRY. During the late Republic, humans could be traded like animals and were considered valuable commodities. Either obtained through war or by marauding pirates, SLAVES were sold to estate owners seeking labour to work their properties. POMPEY stopped one aspect of this practice in the 1st century BC by eliminating piracy in the MEDITERRANEAN.

Individuals and a BUREAUCRATIC system were necessary to maintain control over the transportation of goods. Traders were typically individuals of lower status, but most traders probably acted as middlemen for the ÉLITE. CUSTOMS DUTIES (*portaria*) were levied on imported and exported goods; instituted by the emperor Augustus, they ranged from 2.5 to 25 per cent. Some goods, however, received exemptions, most notably animals, transportation vehicles, military gear, and property belonging to the emperor.

Theories concerning the impact of trade in the Roman empire are complicated at best. Moses Finley asserted that trade did not have a major impact on the social and economic development of the Roman empire. This was due, in his opinion, to the fact that areas in the Mediterranean were capable of producing their own staple goods; to the high costs inherent in the importing and exporting of goods; and to the desire of traders to upgrade their social status through profit. If goods were moved, they did so because the emperor took steps to ensure that staples and goods met the needs of the city of Rome and of the Roman army distributed over parts of the empire. Keith Hopkins and Kevin Greene have challenged Finley's thesis by focusing their attentions on widespread agricultural production and the archaeological evidence, namely coin finds and pottery production such as amphoras and fine wares. They argue that trade, if anything, intensified, especially during the 1st century AD. (see also CONSUMER CITY; CONSUMERS; ECONOMY; GROWTH, ECONOMIC; MANUFACTURING; PRODUCTION; SURPLUSES) LAH

See Casson, L. (1986) *Ancient Trade and Society*; Duncan-Jones, R. (1990) *Structure and Scale in the Roman Economy*; Garnsey, P. et al., eds. (1983) *Trade in the Ancient Economy*; Greene, K. (1986) *The Archaeology of the Roman Economy*; Mattingly and Salmon, *Economies beyond Agriculture*; Parkins, H. and Smith, C., eds. (1998) *Trade, Traders and the Ancient City*; Whittaker, C. R. (1993) *Land, City and Trade in the Roman Empire*.

 *INSTRUMENTUM DOMESTICUM*; MONTE TESTACCIO.

trademarks see *INSTRUMENTUM DOMESTICUM*; MONTE TESTACCIO.

tragedy As a literary form, tragedy originated in Greece, underwent its most critical period of development in classical Athens, and spread from there, first to the entire Greek world, and then, from the 3rd century BC, to the Roman world.

The early history and development of tragedy are hard to reconstruct. The most plausible interpretation of the name, *tragôidia* or 'goat-song', is 'song delivered at the sacrifice of a goat'. At Athens, tragedy was performed in honour of the god DIONYSOS. Yet even if victorious poets carried off a sacrificial GOAT as a prize in early 'tragic' contests for Dionysos – visual evidence of pre-tragic choral performances in masks and costumes offer possible precedents – the institutionalization of Attic tragedy in the last quarter of the 6th century remains unexplained. ARISTOTLE plausibly argues that tragedy was developed by leaders of the dithyramb and evolved slowly from improvisational beginnings, marked by minimal plots and ridiculous diction, into a dignified art (*Poetics* 4.1449a 12–21). The dithyramb, a choral performance on mythological subjects, was linked with Dionysos from at least the 7th century; dithyrambic contests were presented alongside tragic contests at Athens' chief Dionysiac festival, the City Dionysia. Early tragedy apparently involved dramatic interchanges between a CHORUS and a single ACTOR. Attic tradition identified the first actor to add prologue and speech to a choral performance as Thespis. AESCHYLUS reportedly increased the number of actors to two, diminished the choral portion of tragedy and gave the leading role to speech. SOPHOKLES added the third actor and scene painting. The Greek word for actor, *hypokritês*, meaning 'answerer' or 'interpreter', supports the hypothesis that DRAMA developed by defining a new role for choral leaders. Since the lyric poetry of tragedy retains a trace of Doric dialect, it seems likely that an increasingly powerful Athens, which apparently had no important poetic traditions of its own until the 6th century, imported and transformed a non-Athenian choral tradition in order to develop its own claim to literary glory through drama.

Evidence from the northern PELOPONNESE suggests that 6th-century TYRANTS attempted to consolidate their power by promoting choral performances in honour of Dionysos, a god of WINE and fertility traditionally popular with the masses. Under the tyrant Periandros of CORINTH, the poet Arion reportedly made important contributions to the development of the dithyramb (Herodotos 1.23) and the 'tragic mode'. Kleisthenes, tyrant of Sikyon, transferred to Dionysos 'tragic choruses' memorializing the sufferings of an aristocratic cult hero, Adrastos (Herodotos 5.67). Both tyrants were linked by marriage to the Athenian ARISTOCRACY. The Attic tyrant, Peisistratos (and/or his sons), who otherwise patronized poetry, may have introduced or enhanced the festival of the City Dionysia in order to consolidate a political base among the non-aristocratic rural and urban populace. Early Athenian DEMOCRACY (first established in 508/7) either followed in the tyrant's wake for the same reasons or perhaps itself established the tragic competitions.

Tragic poets, then, seem gradually to have transformed choral performances into the alternation of choral odes and spoken scenes (prologue, episodes and *exodos*) familiar in classical drama. Tragedy shed the original, satyr-play-like crudity attributed to its early phases by Aristotle, adopting fully worked-out plots and a spoken metre closer to ordinary speech, the iambic trimeter. The famous early Attic statesman SOLON composed poems on social and political themes that re-emerge in Aeschylean tragedy and probably influenced this choice of METRE. The dialogue (*stichomythia*) and formal debates (*agônes*) of tragedy developed in conjunction with the traditions of ASSEMBLY and LAWCOURTS, while pervasive metaphors drawn from RITUAL, as well as the aetiological foundation myths that close some plays, linked tragedy to its religious and social context. The HOMERIC *Iliad* and *Odyssey*, which had been recited in the Athenian Panathenaic festival from the mid-6th century, had an equally important influence on the content and plot structure of the emerging genre. Aristotle attributes to HOMER the development of the most sophisticated form of tragic plot, in which events selected from myth contribute to the unfolding of a single unified action or *praxis* (e.g. the *Iliad* revolves around the wrath of ACHILLES, not the Trojan war in its entirety). Tragic poets drew much from Homer, but frequently borrowed plots from lesser EPIC poems. Some early tragedians experimented with historical drama, but the outrage that greeted the early tragedian Phrynichos' *Sack of Miletos*, a play that brought Athens' own troubles too close to home, put a damper on this development (despite Aeschylus' successful *Persians*). Entirely fictitious plots emerged only in the 4th century. Not surprisingly, tragic plots that ended in disaster were often drawn from the heroic mythical traditions of Athens' enemies THEBES and SPARTA, while those with more positive outcomes revolved around local HEROES or figures worshipped in Attic hero cult.

Tragedy puts the mythical past and its aristocratic protagonists in dialogue with a chorus representing a more communal perspective and traditional wisdom. Tragic heroes struggle to act and advance the plot, while the meditative chorus examines human action in relation to past, future and non-human realities. Through tensions developed between family and city, men and women, citizen and foreigner, or leaders and community, traditional myths are reshaped to address intractable issues central to contemporary Attic democracy and its ideology. Tragic representation of divinity, moral conflict, and the authority of language and tradition is influenced by changes in PHILOSOPHY, especially the controversial teachings of the SOPHISTS. The tragic encounter between powerful, nearly incomprehensible gods and humans aspiring to secular authority over their world repeatedly comes to an ambiguous conclusion for which mortals nevertheless take responsibility. Despite a growing interest in the psychology of individuals, tragic characterization remains more conditioned by political ideology, myth and plot. Without underestimating the emotional, aesthetic and ritual power of tragedy, its concern with a broad range of cultural and religious ideas and controversies probably explains its early panhellenic appeal, as well as its appropriation by Roman, later European and other world cultures. (see also EURIPIDES). HPF

Trajan (Marcus Ulpius Traianus) AD 56–117 Roman emperor. The son of a distinguished SENATOR of consular rank who held a number of important provincial commands, Trajan entered public life in 77 as a legionary tribune and prosecuted a successful military career, with a CONSULSHIP in 91 and a provincial command as *legatus Augusti* in PANNONIA. In 97 the emperor Nerva formally adopted Trajan as his heir. He took the names Nerva Caesar and some imperial powers, namely *proconsulare imperium maius* and the tribunician powers. In 98 Trajan shared the consulship with Nerva, who died shortly afterwards.

Trajan's reign saw the full realization of the imperial system. A new way of choosing an emperor – adoption of the best candidate – was found, and Trajan came to be recognized as the ideal emperor within the system created by AUGUSTUS. He was Optimus Princeps ('the Greatest Emperor'), popular in his own lifetime and venerated after his death. Trajan embarked on an ambitious policy of centralization of government, a tightening up of administration and bureaucracy, and efficient but fair imposition of TAXATION. The centralization of provincial government is evidenced by the letters exchanged between Trajan and PLINY THE YOUNGER, governor of Bithynia–Pontus. But Trajan is more famous for his successful wars, particularly the DACIAN WARS, with his victories celebrated not only by TRIUMPHS but also by the construction of TRAJAN'S COLUMN and the assumption of the epithet Dacicus. Further campaigns in PARTHIA, triumphs and the epithet Parthicus assured Trajan's reputation as a conqueror. In 117, shortly after the Parthian war, Trajan fell ill and died. He was succeeded by HADRIAN, his adopted son and appointed heir. CEPA

See Bennett, J. (1997) *Trajan*.

BATHS: (a); SACRIFICE: (d).

Trajan's column The largely intact honorific column which stands amid the ruins of Trajan's forum in Rome. Dedicated in AD 113, it originally stood in a colonnaded court flanked by two LIBRARIES, adjoining the Basilica Ulpia. The Luna–CARRARA MARBLE column consists of a pedestal topped by a shaft of drums, with an internal spiral staircase lit by 40 slit-windows. A Doric capital supports a balcony and a plinth for a lost statue of Trajan (overall height 38 m, 125 ft).

The pedestal is covered in veristic (true-to-life) reliefs of captured barbarian equipment. A door and dedicatory inscription (*CIL* 6.960) are positioned on its south-east side. A 200 m (220 yd) long, sculpted helical frieze depicting Trajan's DACIAN WARS (AD 101–2, 105–6) winds round and up the shaft. Scenes of imperial speeches, SACRIFICE and army marching, camp construction and battle, barbarian retreat and submission are strung together formulaically. A few actual locations and events are interspersed: the DANUBE BRIDGE at Drobeta (Turnu Severin), the capture of Dacian treasure, the suicide of king DECEBALUS. Significant scenes are placed on vertical axes, to be seen from specific viewpoints and to aid the observer's comprehension.

The column was multi-functional. It honoured Trajan and his army, explained the funding of the forum complex with barbarian treasure, marked the height of hill cut back for the building project, acted as a viewing platform over Trajan's Rome, and housed Trajan's ashes after 117. JCNC

See Coarelli, F. (2000) *The Column of Trajan*; Lepper, F. and Frere, S. (1988) *Trajan's Column*.

COLUMNS, MONUMENTAL: (a); DACIAN WARS.

transhumants Migratory SHEPHERDS, also called PASTORALISTS or pastoral NOMADS. Transhumants raised ANIMALS for their 'primary product' – MEAT – and their 'secondary products' – milk, clothing,

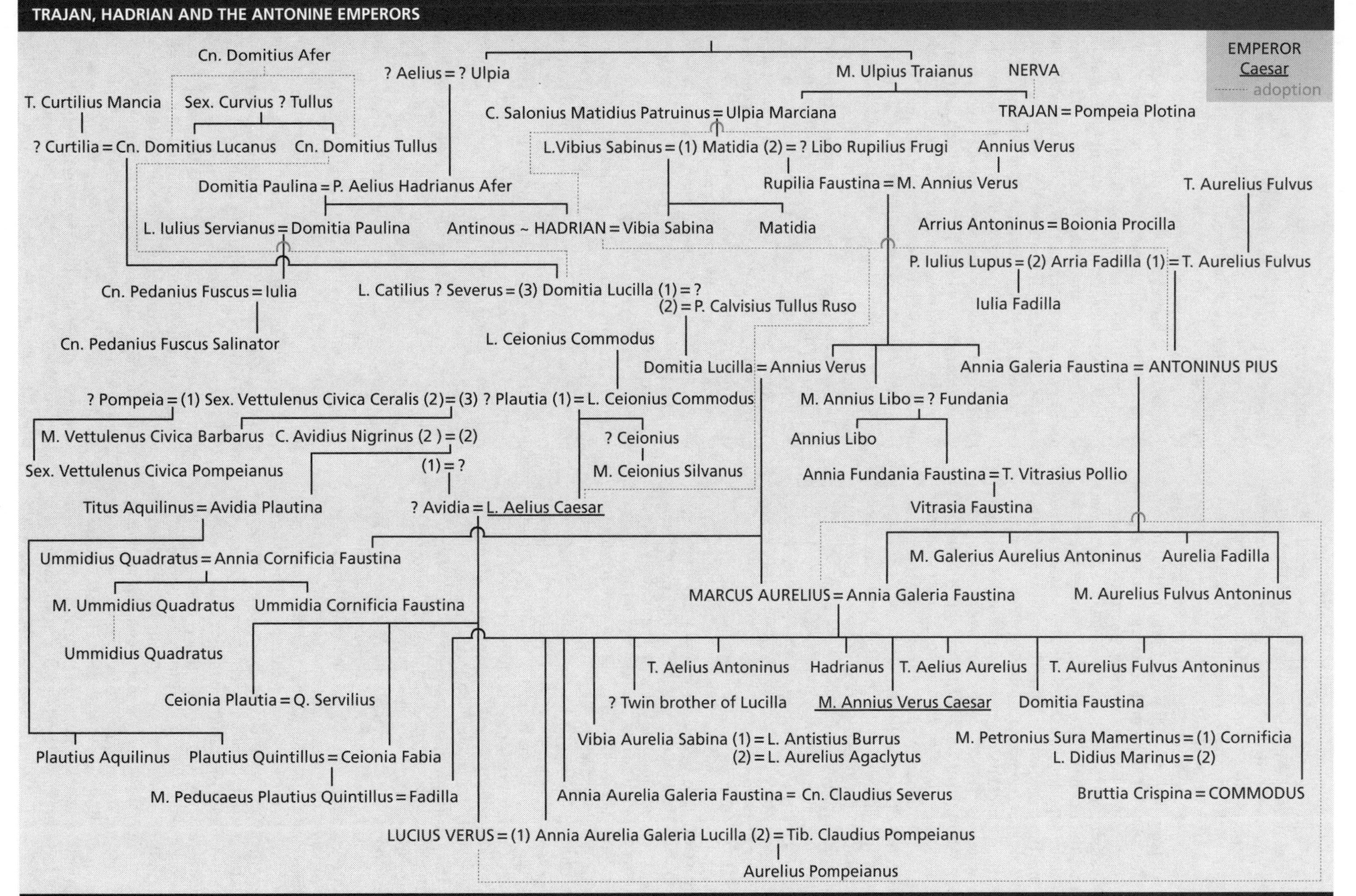

TRAJAN: stemma showing the relations between the Antonine emperors.

traction, MANURE and TRANSPORTATION. In the classical period, transhumants moved flocks between upland and lowland pastures. When animals graze in the uplands in the summer and the lowlands in the winter, the practice is known as 'vertical transhumance'. 'Inverse transhumance', a variant of the vertical type, refers to movement in the opposite direction at these times. Transhumants had close relationships with settled AGRICULTURALISTS. They exchanged primary and secondary products, goods imported from other regions and their own labour in return for wheat, barley and other agricultural produce. Greek and Roman writers regularly stereotyped transhumants as savage, lawless wanderers since they did not belong to civilized urban society.

Two other types of transhumance have been recognized in MEDITERRANEAN history, but were of little consequence in the classical period. 'True' nomadic pastoralism concerns the movements of peoples and flocks with no fixed homes. It has rarely been common throughout the Mediterranean. Horizontal transhumance refers to the seasonal movement of millions of animals over hundreds of kilometres. Although the *Dogana delle pecore* in medieval southern Italy was a form of horizontal transhumance, most authorities agree that this type of pastoralism did not exist in the classical Mediterranean. DLS

See Shaw, B. D. (1982–3) Eaters of flesh, drinkers of milk: the ancient Mediterranean ideology of the pastoral nomad, *Ancient Society* 13–14: 5–31; Whittaker, C. R., ed. (1988) *Pastoral Economies in Classical Antiquity*.

transmission The process by which ancient texts survived into the modern world. Accordingly, transmission is closely associated with the history of our printed texts in antiquity. It is now generally agreed that the HOMERIC poems and the other early examples of Greek POETRY were the products of an oral tradition, but at some point in the archaic period the recently invented ALPHABET was first used to record poems and so preserve them for posterity. The earliest medium for writing seems to have been a roll of sheets made from the PAPYRUS plant. During the Roman period, the papyrus roll was replaced by the codex, the precursor of the modern book. References to written texts are surprisingly rare in the early period, but there is the story that HERAKLEITOS deposited his 'book' in the temple of ARTEMIS for safe keeping, and in the classical period there are references to reading and booksellers at Athens. An important event for the transmission of Greek texts was the founding of the MOUSEION and LIBRARY at ALEXANDRIA in the early 3rd century BC. There, texts of the central works of Greek literature were gathered, and authoritative editions were produced. These editions set the standard for much of later antiquity, determining Roman as well as Greek practice, and they served as exemplars for copies made for use throughout the ancient world. In an age before the printing press, anyone who wanted a text had to have it copied from an existing exemplar. Extant ancient texts have survived through the labour of generations of scribes, and many works of ancient literature have undergone a period of transmission of more than 2,000 years. The extant manuscripts contain errors introduced in the process of manual copying, but they also bear witness to the continuing interest in a wide range of ancient texts. (see also COMMENTATORS; TEXTUAL CRITICISM) CGB

Transpadana see ITALY, ROMAN.

transport From the earliest Greek colonists to the CHRISTIAN pilgrims of the later Roman empire, people in antiquity showed a high level of mobility, and resources were carried to the ends of the MEDITERRANEAN and beyond. Compared to modern experiences, however, land and sea transport was slow, inefficient and expensive, but scholars may have exaggerated the contrasts with other pre-industrial periods. Ancient transport technology was more than adequate to the demands made on it by contemporary society. Much of the accepted wisdom on the nature of ancient transport has been based on literary texts. They may not give much technical detail, but have the advantage of offering insights into the lived experiences of ancient travel – varying from the mild discomforts suffered during a journey from Rome to Brindisi (HORACE, *Satires* 1.5), to the SHIPWRECK experienced by St PAUL on his way to Rome (Acts 27). Knowledge of the technical aspects of ancient transport has benefited substantially from recent advances in ARCHAEOLOGY.

Greek ROADS in general do not appear to have been very good. There were exceptions, such as roads leading towards larger cities or major sanctuaries, but even these were not always accessible to large vehicles. Networks of cart-roads seem, however, to have criss-crossed the SPARTAN-dominated PELOPONNESE from the archaic period on. Major road systems, such as the Persian Royal Road from SARDIS to Sousa, could not have been maintained by the competitive and continually warring Greek city-states.

The Romans are deservedly famous for their elaborate system of well-built highways. Appearing as straight lines in the landscape, often slightly elevated above it, and with BRIDGES crossing rivers and deep ravines, they remain striking symbols of Roman power. It has been estimated that by the end of the 4th century AD more than 85,000 km (53,000 miles) of roads connected even the most remote PROVINCE to the imperial centre. Built by MAGISTRATES and EMPERORS, whose names were commemorated on the numerous milestones, these roads were not designed to boost TRADE and commerce. Their main purpose was to provide an all-weather surface for the boots of the Roman legionaries.

Pack animals were widely used for the transport of goods. DONKEYS AND MULES may not have been fast, but they were sure-footed and were particularly suited to the mountainous landscapes of the Mediterranean region. The transport of heavy goods depended on vehicles pulled by oxen. There is little evidence for the types of vehicles used in ancient Greece apart from chariots used in WAR or competitions, but a building account from ELEUSIS shows that up to 47 teams of oxen could be used to pull one wagon carrying heavy building material (*IG* ii^2 1673). Roman sources provide the names for a wide variety of vehicles, from two-wheeled chariots to large coaches, and paintings and reliefs (mainly from Roman GAUL) provide additional visual evidence. HORSES were less used as draught animals than in other pre-industrial periods. This was not so much due to inefficient harness systems that would throttle the horses as to the fact that ancient horses were much smaller than modern. Nevertheless, the fact remains that land transport was relatively slow and expensive.

It is not surprising, therefore, that transport by sea or RIVER was often preferred. Knowledge of ancient seafaring has increased dramatically over the last half-century as a result of the development of underwater archaeology, with more than 1,000 known ancient shipwrecks located in the Mediterranean, the majority dated to the period 200 BC–AD 200. Their number is not only an index of increased maritime traffic, but also a poignant illustration of the dangers of the sea.

There has been much scholarly interest in the oared SHIPS of ancient Greece, which has even resulted in the modern reconstruction of a Greek TRIREME. Such ships were essentially battleships, using a ramming technique to sink their opponents. They were less well suited for transporting commercial cargoes. However, a Greek trading ship of c.300 BC, known as the Kyrenia wreck, was found off the coast of CYPRUS. Its contents show that it was used for small-scale coastal TRADE.

The Romans adapted oared warships by adding boarding-bridges, but we are best informed about the Roman round ships that were used as freighters. The most common size appears to have been around 150 tonnes, but vessels of 350–500 tonnes were also frequent. In the imperial period super-freighters appeared, designed for transporting grain to the capital. They could be over 1,000 tonnes; not until the 18th century would ships of this size reappear. In contrast to later practice, ancient naval architects started by building the hull: planks were attached to the keel using a technique known as mortise-and-tenon, and the internal frame and decks were added later. This method was expensive in terms of manpower and raw material, but may have produced sturdier ships. Ancient ships usually carried one square main sail and in some cases additional mizzens and topsails. Although they could sail closer to the wind than has often been thought, speedy voyages were possible only with back winds. The journey from Rome to ALEXANDRIA could be done in less than 10 days (though 20 may have been average) due to the prevailing summer winds from the north-west or north-north-west, but the return journey required a long detour and took at least twice as long. Excavations of ancient shipwrecks indicate that the most common cargo was AMPHORAS filled with WINE, OIL, or FISH SAUCE. Shipwrecks have been found carrying other goods as well, including works of ART and building materials, but shipwrecked grain-traders have proven much harder to find. OvN

See Casson, L. (1991) *The Ancient Mariners*; Chevallier, R. (1976) *Roman Roads*; Greene, K. (1986) *The Archaeology of the Roman Economy*; White, K.D. (1986) *Greek and Roman Technology.*

 TRADE, ROMAN; WHEELED VEHICLES: (b).

trash see SANITATION; WASTE DISPOSAL.

Trasimene, Lake see BATTLES, ROMAN; CANNAE; FLAMINIUS; HANNIBAL; HANNIBALIC WAR; WAR.

travellers

From the end of the 'Dark Ages' (c.1000–c.800 BC), votive objects at Greek sanctuaries, such as the Heraion on SAMOS, tell of contacts between the Greeks and foreign peoples, particularly in the Near East and Egypt. Tales nested within HOMER's *Odyssey* indicate occasions for long-distance travel: the aristocrat who spends his early adult years amassing a fortune on the seas; hard-nosed PHOENICIAN traders willing to accommodate passengers, or other traders, in return for payment; persons displaced after capture by PIRATES (or traders) and sold. The swineherd Eumaios says one does not invite a wandering stranger to stay permanently unless he has some skill that benefits the people: a seer, doctor, woodworker or singer. The MEDITERRANEAN world depended crucially on long-distance contacts. Emigration to a COLONY was another reason to embark on a voyage. Many Greek mercenaries went abroad in the archaic period, like those who served an Egyptian master and left graffiti on a colossus at Abu Simbel (ML 7), or Alkaios' brother who served Nebuchadnezzar. Greek craftsmen were employed by the early Persian kings to decorate their PALACE at Persepolis. By the late archaic and classical periods, we find intellectuals both visiting, and receiving visits from, their counterparts in the east. Thales of MILETOS, statesman and cosmologist, may have had access to Babylonian ASTRONOMICAL data. The doctor Ktesias, who resided at the court of ARTAXERXES II, wrote books on PERSIA and INDIA and a GEOGRAPHY of the world. Storytellers like HERODOTOS appear to have undertaken journeys for the sake of interest, adding to a growing genre of travel literature that also included NAVIGATIONAL works (*periploi*) enumerating the coasts of the Mediterranean and BLACK SEA in sequence. Herodotos' work, however, surpasses all others in its breadth of detail about non-Greek peoples. On a smaller scale, XENOPHON's *Anabasis*, arising from his service as a mercenary, does the same for parts of the Persian empire.

Within the Greek homeland, land journeys were undertaken for TRADE and during military campaigns. The network of cart ROADS recently discovered in the Peloponnese may have served both purposes. Other road users included those travelling to religious FESTIVALS, and the *theôroi* ('observers') sent by one state to another's festival. In the hellenistic period, *theôroi* also denoted envoys sent out by major sanctuaries in advance of a festival. In response, cities all across the Greek world appointed ceremonial 'envoy receivers' (*theôrodokoi*). Travel related to international competitions in ATHLETIC and other skills, as well as by actors such as the Artists of DIONYSOS, increased in volume in the hellenistic period and began to approximate to modern TOURISM. It was, however, largely an ÉLITE activity, except perhaps in the case of individuals seeking cures at healing sanctuaries. It was in the Roman period that tourism developed features more akin to pilgrimage. (see also EXPLORATION; MAPS) DGJS

See Casson, L. (1974) *Travel in the Ancient World*; Dillon, M. (1997) *Pilgrims and Pilgrimage in Ancient Greece.*

Most journeys comprised relatively short trips to and from daily LABOUR in the fields, to weekly MARKETS in nearby towns, or to religious sanctuaries on holy FESTIVALS. Longer journeys were regularly made by TRANSHUMANT herdsmen between winter and summer pastures, and by merchants engaged in international TRADE. However, the literary record is dominated by ARISTOCRATIC travel between Rome and various country estates, or abroad to postings in provincial government, or for cultural purposes, such as study in Athens. In the 2nd century AD, PAUSANIAS provided the cultural TOURIST with a guide to mainland Greece; but this was not the only destination, as Roman-period graffiti left on Egyptian monuments demonstrate. Outside the ÉLITE, most long-distance journeys were probably undertaken on a less than voluntary basis: for example, by messengers carrying letters on public and private business, soldiers being deployed to new units, economic migrants, imported SLAVES, and even exotic ANIMALS destined for the arena.

In the REPUBLIC, citizens had to travel to Rome to VOTE. Under the empire, petitioners had to seek out the imperial court wherever it might be. Within the PROVINCES, the administration of justice necessitated governors' peregrination around an assize circuit. In the absence of scale MAPS, those planning a journey could rely on publicly displayed lists of distances for routes within the region, and perhaps also to Rome. A sufficient travelling public existed for a body of itinerary literature to develop, describing routes between all the major centres in the Roman world. One attempt to represent this information as a route diagram survives in the shape of the *TABULA PEUTINGERIANA*. Itinerary collections allowed the traveller to choose the route that was likely to offer the best facilities in terms of food, accommodation, BATHING and entertainment. Once on the road, milestones enumerating the distance to or from the road's terminus allowed travellers to monitor progress. The threat of brigandage, even in the most peaceable provinces, meant that reaching the safety of a settlement by nightfall was a real anxiety.

Although the Roman road network facilitated WHEELED traffic, a cart without suspension is not a comfortable option. Thus foot, DONKEY and horseback remained the principal modes of travel. Limited to the hours of daylight, overland travel varied in speed not only according to the terrain but also the season; the jurists reckoned 20 Roman miles per day reasonably achievable. Land travel was regularly supplemented by taking boats where waterways were navigable. Although passage on a deep-water SHIP was a fast option for long journeys through the Mediterranean, these vessels were limited to the fair-weather sailing season (c.April–October) and the risk of SHIPWRECK was not insignificant. However, lighter craft that hugged the coast and put ashore every evening offered TRANSPORT all year round.

Under the empire, a system of transport for public officials was established that developed into an elaborate network of staging posts and inns, whose use was regulated by permit. Its working is illustrated by annotations on an itinerary of AD 333 that carefully record whether a place was for a change of animals (*mutatio*) or a stopover (*mansio*). This trip from Burdigala (Bordeaux) to CONSTANTINOPLE was extended to Palestine, foreshadowing the late antique boom in Christian pilgrimage. RWBS

See Adams, C. and Laurence, R., eds. (2001) *Travel and Geography in the Roman World*; Casson, L. (1974) *Travel in the Ancient World*.

 WHEELED VEHICLES: (a).

treaties The earliest Greek treaties borrowed from the models of personal FRIENDSHIPS (often using 'personalized' friendship terminology), and were often bilateral alliances where both partners agreed to balanced and corresponding conditions. A development of this pattern was independent treaties made with one leading state, which then convened the allies in common council. The PELOPONNESIAN league, formed in the 6th century BC by SPARTA, was just such an organization and retained its integrity until the 4th century.

In addition, there were peace treaties, which could either be 'for all time' or have a limited tenure. In the 4th century, common peace agreements were sworn, whereby it was agreed that all states should be free and autonomous, though the ambiguity of 'autonomy' quickly became a device for exploitation and manipulation. The league of CORINTH, formed in 337 between PHILIP II of Macedonia and the Greek states, combined features of both the common peace treaty and the league.

In Italy, Rome itself had from an early date headed a league bound together by treaty. Military treaties also embraced the Italian allies. Treaties were extended to other states who surrendered themselves to Rome's authority, such as the AITOLIANS in 189 BC, but these were lopsided arrangements, with the burden of obligation placed on Rome's partner. LGM

See Gruen, E. S. (1984) *The Hellenistic World and the Coming of Rome*; Larsen, J. A. O. (1955) *Representative Government in Greek and Roman History*; Ryder, T. T. B. (1965) *Koine Eirene*.

Trebonius Gallus see VALERIAN.

EMPERORS, ROMAN: (b).

trees, cultivated Trees were cultivated for economic and, in some cases, aesthetic reasons. The plane (*Platanus orientalis*) and manna ash (*Fraxinus ornus*), without significant practical uses, spread westwards across the MEDITERRANEAN region, with human encouragement, during the 1st millennium BC. The plane was planted along roads at sites where TRAVELLERS would welcome shade.

Most cultivated trees were planted for their FRUIT. Cultivated varieties of the FIG, OLIVE, apple and pear were grown in orchards in Greece and Italy well before the end of the prehistoric period; date palms were cultivated across much of North AFRICA and the Near East by that time. Sweet chestnuts, walnuts and cultivated plum varieties followed later; the spread of cultivated cherry varieties came during the last few centuries BC.

The plane, manna ash and sweet chestnut can be large and striking trees when mature, but of all the species named it was the olive that made the greatest impact on the appearance of the landscape. Readily propagated from cuttings, it was eventually very widely grown in suitable locations across the Mediterranean region. Large systems of terraces were gradually created so that olives could be planted and irrigated on otherwise unproductive hillsides. Individual olive trees are not large, but their distinctive foliage makes them unmistakable. They may live for many hundreds of years. AD

See Bottema, S. (2000) The Holocene history of walnut, sweet chestnut, manna-ash and plane tree in the eastern Mediterranean, *Pallas* 52: 35–59; Zohary, D. and Hopf, M. (1993) *Domestication of Plants in the Old World*.

 OLIVE: (a)–(b).

tribes

The Greeks had various ways of conceptualizing social, political and/or religious groupings other than the *POLIS*, within the *polis*, and on a larger scale than the *polis*. To describe the first and last types of groupings, the word most commonly used was *ethnos* ('people', 'group'; plural *ethnê*). The 'tribal state', a unit with a VILLAGE type pattern of settlement, was an alternative to the *polis* model of social and territorial organization. Examples include the Akarnanians, AITOLIANS and various peoples of northern Greece, though such states also contained *poleis*. In the 5th century BC, conflict between the Spartans and Athenians during the PELOPONNESIAN WAR was construed in terms of the opposing behavioural characteristics of Dorians (a descent group believed to include the Spartans and their allies) and Ionians (the Athenians and their eastern Greek allies, who celebrated their supposed common ancestry in an annual FESTIVAL). We hear most about 'FEDERAL states', such as the Aitolians and ACHAIANS, from the 4th century onwards. *Ethnê* in this sense were groups of individual *poleis*, or a combination of *poleis* and smaller *ethnê*, committed to collective action by solemn agreement and common cults.

Within the *polis*, 'tribal' organization was common. We know most about the *phylai* (another word translated by 'tribes') of Athens, originally four, but ten after KLEISTHENES' reform of 508/7 BC. Each of the ten *phylai* performed the cult of its eponymous HERO, while they functioned also as military, political and administrative sections. ED

See Alty, J. H. M. (1982) Dorians and Ionians, *JHS* 102: 1–14; Ehrenberg, V. (1969) *The Greek State*; Jones, N. (1987) *Public Organization in Ancient Greece*; Larsen, J. (1968) *Greek Federal States*; Nielsen, T. H. (1996) Arkadia: city-ethnics and tribalism, in M. H. Hansen, ed., *Introduction to an Inventory of Poleis* 117–63.

Units of civic organization, to which every Roman citizen belonged. The original three tribes, the Ramnes, Tities and Luceres, each subdivided into 10 *curiae* (which survived in the obscure curiate ASSEMBLY), were replaced by the reforms of SERVIUS TULLIUS (6th century BC). All Roman territory within Italy was assigned to a tribe, and a citizen's tribe was determined by the location of his property. There were four urban tribes. By 495 BC there were 17 rural tribes, but as Roman territory expanded so did the number, rising to 31 by 241 BC. After this date, new territory was added to the existing 35, so that tribes became split across several regions. A proposal to create additional tribes after the SOCIAL WAR, to accommodate new citizens, was not adopted. Tribes were the basis for TAXATION, troop levies and the CENSUS. Lesser MAGISTRATES were elected in the tribal assembly (*comitia tributa*). The PLEBEIAN assembly (*concilium plebis*), which had a legislative role, was organized by tribes, as was, by 218 BC, the other main assembly (*comitia centuriata*), though less directly and privileging the rich. A citizen's tribe, in abbreviated form, constituted part of his official name. The tribes had a fixed order for certain purposes, which we can partially reconstruct. In alphabetical order, the urban tribes were *Collina*, *Esquilina*, *Palatina*, and *Suburana*. The rural were *Aemilia*, *Aniensis*, *Arnensis*, *Camilia*, *Claudia*, *Clustumina*, *Cornelia*, *Fabia*, *Falerna*, *Galeria*, *Horatia*, *Lemonia*, *Maecia*, *Menenia*, *Oufentina*, *Papiria*, *Poblilia*, *Pollia*, *Pomptina*, *Pupina*, *Quirina*, *Romilia*, *Sabatina*, *Scaptia*, *Sergia*, *Stellatina*, *Teretina*, *Tromentina*, *Velina*, *Voltinia* and *Voturia*. Many early tribes share the names of PATRICIAN clans; the later ones are geographical. JRWP

See Cornell, T. J. (1995) *The Beginnings of Rome*; Taylor, L. R. (1960) *The Voting Districts of the Roman Republic*.

tribunes *Tribuni plebis* (or *plebi*), tribunes of the people, at Rome. After a PATRICIAN uprising expelled the last king, a debt crisis in 494 BC led to the formation of the PLEBEIAN class, which elected tribunes as officers, with AEDILES as assistants, and created a separate political structure. Tribunes, originally meant to assist individuals against unfair oppression, could act with impunity because their persons were sacrosanct. To achieve their objectives, plebeians seceded, withdrawing services until the patricians yielded, a tactic repeated as necessary in the first centuries of the Republic. Tribunes passed legislation in their assembly, and after 287 these plebiscites had the force of law on all citizens. In the late Republic, tribunes like Tiberius GRACCHUS and Lucius Appuleius Saturninus often harnessed the unruly power of the urban plebs against the established order, sometimes as clients of reform-minded ARISTOCRATS. In reaction, SULLA reduced their powers, but these were soon restored. EMPERORS held tribunician power as one basis of their authority.

For about 80 years in the 5th and 4th centuries, the CONSULSHIP was replaced by the consular tribunate, probably a patrician attempt to usurp the name and powers. Three to six were elected annually, and the MAGISTRACY was open to plebeians but held mainly by patricians.

Military tribunes (*tribuni militum*) were elected officers, six per legion, mainly younger men beginning political careers. Tenure of this tribunate or election to a board became a prerequisite for other magistracies. Treasury tribunes (*tribuni aerarii*) collected and distributed the tax to pay soldiers, and served as judges. JV

See Cornell, T. J. (1995) *The Beginnings of Rome*.

Trier (Augusta Trevorum; French, Trèves) City on the RIVER Moselle, and important 4th-century AD imperial residence. Roman rule displaced the principal settlement of the Treveri from the Tetelbierg (Luxembourg) to this crossing-point of the Moselle. The nucleus of the street grid was laid out under AUGUSTUS, and CLAUDIUS raised the town, which was the seat of the *procurator* of Belgica and the two Germanies, to the status of *colonia*. During the 2nd century the city was furnished with a range of public

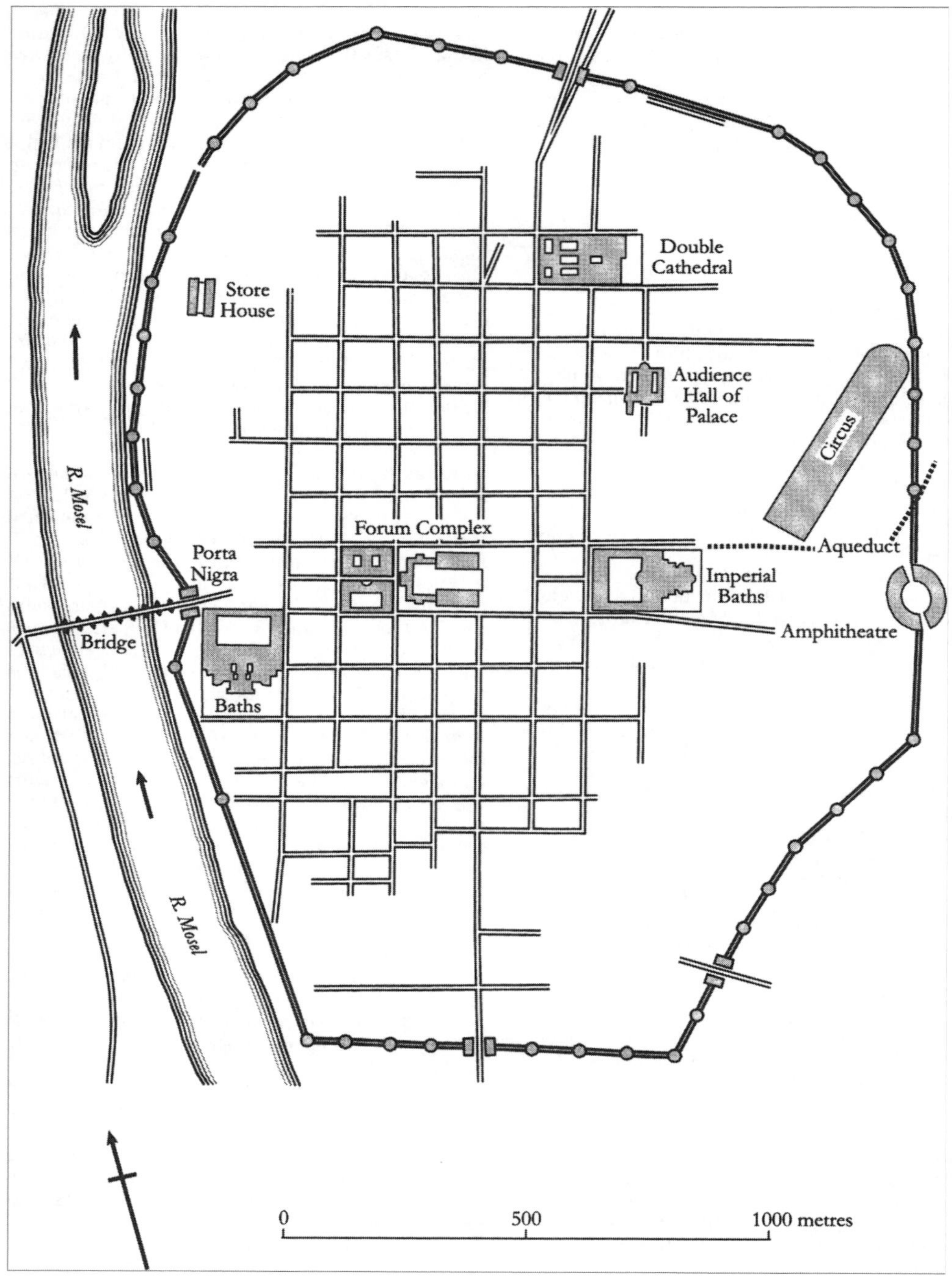

TRIER: town plan of Augusta Trevorum.

buildings exceptional in the Three GAULS: a FORUM–temple complex; the large 'Viehmarkt' BATHS and the even larger 'Barbarathermen' baths; and a third (also very impressive) public baths, found in 1987 but not widely known (though now open to the public). In addition, the public buildings of this period included a replacement Moselle BRIDGE that still survives, a large earth and stone AMPHITHEATRE, a CIRCUS, three major TEMPLES, and a temple district (the Altbachtal). In the late 2nd century, walls enclosing 285 ha (704 acres) were built; the imposing north gate, the 'Porta Nigra', survives. EPIGRAPHIC and SCULPTURAL evidence points to wealth from AGRICULTURE and the military supply route to the Rhine. Of increasing importance in the 3rd century, Trier became an imperial residence under CONSTANTINE I, was much used by VALENTINIAN I, Gratian and Magnus Maximus, and was headquarters for important officials and factories. An imperial quarter constructed in the north-eastern part of the city included the Constantinian 'Basilika' (audience hall), the 'Kaiserthermen' (unfinished imperial baths, later remodelled), and the large double cathedral. The city lost its administrative importance at the end of the 4th century and was repeatedly sacked in the 5th. ASEC

See Kuhnen, H.-P., ed. (2001) *Das römische Trier*; Wightman, E. M. (1985) *Gallia Belgica*.

CITIES: (b); GAUL: (b); GERMANY AND THE GERMANS: (a).

trierarchy see LITURGIES; METICS; TAXATION, GREEK.

Trimalchio A central character of PETRONIUS' novel, *Satyricon*, he is the eponymous host of the central characters of the work (Encolpius and his companions). The dinner is the best example of one of Petronius' plot devices; Encolpius is simply present to witness certain events and to narrate them, for Trimalchio is certainly the star. He represents the archetypal self-made man: enormous WEALTH generated in a less than noble manner, huge pretensions, extreme vulgarity, conspicuous consumption on an absurd scale, obsequious behaviour in his inclusion among the *Augustales* (priests of the imperial cult), and poor education. On one level, Trimalchio represents everything a traditional, wealthy Roman citizen would despise, illustrating the normal social and hierarchical disregard for men of freed status and for those engaged in any form of moneymaking outside traditional AGRICULTURE and landholding. On another level, he assumes the position of a great comic character, more than just a target for Petronius' satire. For the most important question which can be posed at the level of social history is the extent to which Trimalchio can be held typical of individuals of his social position. Any answer is difficult and controversial. Is it possible to cut through the satire to reveal a real or believable character? Perhaps it is. Many freedmen became exceedingly wealthy and successful. Trimalchio, for all the absurd glamour, is a rich trader and landowner who spreads his interests and risks in a rational manner. All might be summed up in the identity of his household gods: Gain, Luck and Profit. CEPA

See Petronius, *Satyricon*, trs. J. P. Sullivan (1965); Smith, M. S. (1975) *Cena Trimalchionis*.

Tripolitania see AFRICA, ROMAN.

trireme The best known of all ancient warship designs. Meaning 'three-fitted', the term (Greek *triêrês*, Latin *triremis*) implies an arrangement of oarsmen in three files along each side of the vessel. Invented, perhaps, during the 8th century BC in PHOENICIA, triremes were not built in large numbers until the 6th century, when the PERSIAN king Kambyses (530–522) built up a large fleet in the coastal cities of Phoenicia, CYPRUS and Ionia. From this time, triremes became the preferred warship in most major NAVIES because of their agility, speed and excellence in manoeuvre-and-ram warfare. Although the ship existed in different designs and changed over time, we know most about Athenian triremes of the 4th century, when speed and agility were the vessel's hallmarks. Preserved slipways indicate a length of c.37 m (c.120 ft) and a maximum width of 6 m (20 ft). Detailed records from the period indicate a full crew numbered 200, including 170 oarsmen, ten marines, four archers, a captain, helmsman, bow lookout, purser, boatswain, flute player, CARPENTER and deckhands. THUCYDIDES, a squadron commander who knew first-hand how they worked, provides our best details of trireme warfare. The vessel's main offensive weapon was its ram, made of high-grade bronze and mounted on the bow at the waterline. Warfare between triremes involved speed and agility, with squadrons manoeuvring to ram each other, shatter the enemy's oars and drive his vessels ashore. Triremes continued in use into the 3rd or 4th century AD, until ramming warfare fell from favour. WMM

See Morrison, J. S. et al. (2000) *The Athenian Trireme*.

triumphs, Roman Official celebrations of victories, beginning in Rome's ETRUSCAN period. After

TRIUMPHS, ROMAN: (a) the arch of Titus, the emperor riding in his triumphal chariot.

TRIUMPHS, ROMAN: (b) the arch of Titus, procession through streets of Rome of treasures from Jerusalem.

TRIUMPHS, ROMAN: (c) Roman triumphs, 753–19 BC.

Date	No. of triumphs	Enemies defeated
753–700	2 (+?)	Antemnates?, Caeninenses
699–650	(+?) } c.5 missing	?
649–600	1 (+?)	Sabini, Veientes
599–550	6	Etrusci (4), Latini, Sabini
549–500	9	Sabini (7), Tarquinii, Veientes (2), Volsci
499–450	12 (+2 missing)	Aequi (3), Hernici, Latini, Medullini, Sabini (2), Veientes (2), Volsci (5),
449–400	9	Aequi, Falerii, Fidenates, Sabini, Veientes (3), Volsci (2)
399–350	18	Aequi (2), Etrusci (2), Galli (6), Hernici (3), Praenestini, Privernates, Tiburtes (2), Veientes, Volsci (2)
349–300	28	Aequi (2), Anagnini, Atinates (2), Apuli, Aurunci, Caleni, Campani, Etrusci (3), Heruli, Lanuvini, Latini (2), Marsi, Palaeopolitani, Pedani, Privernates, Samnites (12), Satricini, Sidicini, Sorani, Tiburtes, Veliterni, Volsci
299–250	41 (+c.8 missing)	Brutti (6), Carthago (11), Corsi, Cossura, Etrusci (3), Galli, Hiero *rex* Sicilia, *rex* Pyrrhus, Lucani (6), Messapii, Nequinates, Picentes, Regini, Sallentini (3), Samnites (13), Sardi (2), Sarsinates (2), Siculi (2), Tarentini (3), Volsinienses (2), Volsones, Vulcientes
249–200	15 (+c.10 missing)	Carthago (++), Corsi, Falisci, Galli (4), Germani, Illyrii, Ligures (3), Sardi (3), Siculi
199–150	26 (+c.14 missing)	Aetoli, Apuani, Celtiberi/Iberi (7), Cephalenes, Corsi, Delmatae, Eleates, Galli (5), Histriani, Illyrii, Ligures (6), Lusitani, Macedonia (3), *rex* Antiochus (3), *rex* Perseus (2), Sardinia
149–100	18 (+c.14 missing)	Allobroges, Arverni (2), Asia, Baliares, Delmatae, [Carthago], Galli, Hispania, Iapydes, Ligures (3), Macedonia, Numidia (*rex* Jugurtha), Salluvii (2), Sardinia (2), Scordisci (2), Thracia (2), Vocontii (2),
99–50	10 (+c.17 missing)	Albania, Allobroges, Armenia, Asia, Cappadocia, Celtiberi, Cilicia, Creta, Hispania Ulterior, Iudaea, Lusitani (2), Paphlagonia, Picentes, pirates, Pontus, *rex* Mithradates, *piratae*, Syria, Scythia
49–19	24 (+c.13 missing)	Africa (4), Alpes, Corsica, Gallia (3), Getae, Hispania (4), Illyricum, Iudaea, Macedonia, Parthia (2), Sicilia, Taurus (*mons*), Thracia
Total	219 (+75–80 missing)	
Overall total	c.300 triumphs × min. 5,000 dead	
753–19 BC	1.5 million ++ enemy dead	

See *Fasti Triumphales*, *Inscriptiones Italiae* 13, f.1 for detail.

waiting outside the *POMERIUM* (sacred boundary) in order to retain *imperium*, a GENERAL awarded a triumph entered through a Porta Triumphalis on a laurelled CHARIOT, enhanced with a phallus underneath and drawn by four horses. With his face painted red, he wore purple garments embroidered with gold, a laurel wreath and a gold amulet, and carried a sceptre and laurel branch. A state SLAVE held a gold wreath over him and repeated the words, 'Look behind you; remember that you are a man.' Spoils, prisoners and white BULLS preceded the chariot, while laurel-wreathed soldiers followed, singing satirical songs. The parade ended at the temple of JUPITER on the CAPITOLINE, where the general presented his clothing and accessories, then sacrificed the bulls.

Although the word *triumphus* derives from shouts invoking divine epiphany in ASIA Minor, a general was not fully Jupiter or king, despite appearances. His clothing and accessories, recreations of official garments of the Etruscan kings, normally decorated the statue of Jupiter and were also borrowed by the magistrate celebrating the *ludi Romani*. Camillus (396 BC) caused offence by using white horses, a divine privilege. POMPEY's use of ELEPHANTS sparked laughter because the team was wider than the gate: it was unharnessed, led through and reharnessed.

A general not awarded a triumph might choose to celebrate a 'triumph on Mount Alba', without official sanction but recorded in the *Fasti*. First performed by Gaius Papirius Maso (231 BC), the procedures were not appreciably different. Later, only emperors and their families triumphed, with HONORIUS in AD 403 the last recorded example. JV

See Pais, E. (1920) *Fasti triumphales populi Romae*; Versnel, H. S. (1970) *Triumphus*.

triumvirates Literally, 'three men' (*triumviri* or *tresviri*), originally used to designate several annually elected boards of three officers of Rome, drawn from the college known collectively as the *vigintisexviri*, '26 men' (reduced to *vigintiviri*, '20 men', in the imperial period), which also supplied several boards with more than three members. Important boards of three included the *tresviri monetales*, the 'three moneyers' who supervised the mint, more colourfully known as *tresviri aere argento auro flando feriundo*, 'three men for melting and striking bronze, silver and gold'. The *tresviri capitales*, responsible for PRISONS, executions and security at night, were sometimes called *tresviri nocturni*. Three-man boards were a regular feature of towns throughout Italy.

A more familiar triumvirate is the agreement between Mark ANTONY, Marcus Aemilius Lepidus and Gaius Octavius (Octavian, later AUGUSTUS) to divide the empire among themselves for a five-year period from 27 November 43 BC. An official legal enactment designated them *tresviri rei publicae constituendae*, 'three men for establishing the state', in effect a triple DICTATORSHIP with virtually unlimited powers of life and death, as well as the opportunity to be free of SENATORIAL, electoral or any other interference. For this reason, their proscriptions of opponents without trial were fully legal, if unpleasant. In their quests for individual supremacy, the triumvirs did not always co-operate, but after they chose to retain their positions beyond the initial expiry date (31 December 38) the triumvirate was renewed for five more years. Not long into the second term, Lepidus was deposed and not replaced.

The completely private agreement made between CAESAR, CRASSUS and POMPEY in 60 BC had no legal standing and should not be considered a triumvirate, though it is often erroneously referred to as the 'First Triumvirate' (that of 43 BC supposedly being the Second). JV

Trojan war The term defines the period of ten years during which, according to myth, the united Achaian (Greek) forces under the leadership of the PELOPONNESIAN king AGAMEMNON besieged the city of TROY. Much of our knowledge about the Trojan war derives from the *Iliad*, an EPIC poem traditionally believed to have been composed by HOMER, a figure whose historical existence has been widely disputed. The historicity of the Trojan war itself has been a further matter of controversy among scholars for many years, and there is as yet no satisfactory answer to the questions of whether, when, precisely where or how it happened.

The *Iliad*, a product of oral tradition as a kind of POETRY suitable for recitation on public occasions, focuses its narrative on the events of a few days during the last year of the war, with only brief references to its earlier phases. It offers details about the military leaders and chief warriors of both sides (e.g. ACHILLES, AJAX, HEKTOR, ODYSSEUS), highlighting their interaction, character and exploits on the battlefield. We learn about the cause of the war and how this relates to the expectations and beliefs of the warriors, offering substantial glimpses into the nature, culture, moral beliefs and religious behaviour of early Greek society. However, the epic story is far from providing a realistic or historical account in any sense, considering the godlike qualities and natures of the HEROES and, perhaps most importantly, the direct interference of the supernatural in human action in a way perceivable by mortals. Stories that detail the return of the Greek heroes from the Trojan war and the survival of a few Trojans in exile are preserved in Homer's *Odyssey*, in the lost poems of the Epic Cycle preserved largely in summary, and in a few TRAGEDIES. (see also AENEAS; ANDROMACHE; HELEN) EP

See Foxhall, L. and Davies, J. K., eds. (1984) *The Trojan War*.

ACHILLES; ODYSSEUS.

trophies, military

Trophies (*tropaia*) are associated with the earliest battles recorded in Greek history. Originally, a crude image of ZEUS or POSEIDON – depending on whether the battle was fought on land or at sea – was fashioned out of wood, preferably using the nearest living oak-tree, and dedicated by the victors on the battlefield. A small representative assortment of captured weapons and armour decorated the image, as part of the votive offering to the god in his role as the 'turner' (*tropaios*). Ostensibly, the winners offered thanks for the critical appearance of deities at the 'turn' (*tropê*), the place where they had helped to turn the enemy. Sometimes after minor engagements, crude shrines or simply piles of stones without human shapes were constructed and covered with war spoils, often on remote borders

TROPHIES, MILITARY: (a) detail of Roman relief sculpture showing a battlefield trophy and barbarian captives.

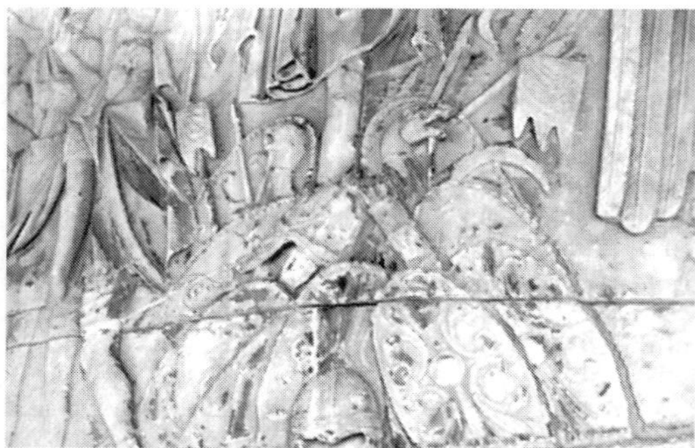

TROPHIES, MILITARY: (b) detail of military trophy on Trajan's column, showing heaped arms and armour and trumpets.

where public access and viewing would have been rare. Scholars disagree about whether trophies evolved from tree-worship, rituals of HUNTING and the chase, efforts to deter dangerous war spirits (all improbable), or (most likely) simple thank-offerings for victory.

By classical times, trophies became an integral part of the formal protocols of Greek warfare. Along with heralds, sacrifice, pre-battle speeches and other post-mortem accords, they helped to define WAR and often limited it to single battle occasions. Such gaudy displays of battle prowess were always seen as valuable propaganda, adding to the humiliation of the defeated. The right to erect a trophy fell to the legal victors, as indicated by their possession of the battlefield and the corpses of the fallen. In that sense, trophies marked a formal closure to battle, and were valuable panhellenic diplomatic tools to solemnize the clear winners and losers of military engagements. In theory, trophies were to be neither violated nor repaired, but allowed to decay naturally. The sanctity of the practice is clear from the few occasions when we hear of complaints of sacrilege or illegality: some city-states have tried to repair or alter old trophies; a defeated army has pulled down the victor's trophy; or both sides have claimed victory and thus erected duplicate trophies.

After the PERSIAN WARS and increasingly in the 4th century, permanent commemorative battle dedications – such as the Athenian monuments at MARATHON or the round MARBLE pillar of the THEBANS at LEUKTRA – were also referred to as 'trophies'. Such advertisements of victory were far more impressive than earlier *ad hoc* piles of weapons or decorated trees, often appearing as permanent small towers, TEMPLES and shrines decorated in elaborate sculpted relief. They could be erected in local or panhellenic sanctuaries, on the battlefield or even at the home of the victor. Such lasting dedications reflect the steady evolution of Greek warfare away from its origins as temporary border squabbling among neighbours to more serious efforts at conquest and permanent subjugation. VDH

See Janssen, A. J. (1957) *Het antieke tropaion*; Pritchett, W. K. (1974) *The Greek State at War*, vol. 2.

Roman celebrations of victory became highly ritualized, and the iconographic language built on Greek and hellenistic antecedents to create an internationally recognized visual vocabulary for use both on and off the battlefield. The city of Rome was notable for the number of TEMPLES that were dedicated to GODS in respect of particular military victories and stashed full of the spoils of victories. Major BATTLES were also sometimes marked by monuments on or close to the site of the engagement. A basic distinction can be made between temporary battlefield displays of captured materials (normally piled around and hung from a tree whose branches had been lopped short) and permanent memorials known as *tropaea* or *trophaea*. The latter were frequently decorated with artworks, often setting in stone images of the tree draped with ARMS AND ARMOUR collected from the field; but such monuments came also to include representations of the victors, scenes of fighting and representations of dead and captured enemies (the latter often shown chained to the central trophy tree). Such imagery became enshrined in Roman triumphalism later, embellishing not only formal trophies, as at ADAMKLISSI, but also a range of other civic structures, such as monumental ARCHES. In a sense TRAJAN'S FORUM in Rome can be read as a vast victory monument, with its colossal statues of captured DACIANS set off by relief panels of the emperor in the thick of battle, and the COLUMN celebrating victory in the DACIAN WARS (through its ornate base drawing on trophy imagery and its spiral reliefs). NAVAL BATTLES were often commemorated with a particular style of monument, incorporating the rams (*rostra*) taken from captured enemy ships (as at ACTIUM). Trophies were not simply architectural curiosities: they remained active sites of commemoration, and the ritual and religious aspects of such structures were as important as their function as symbols of Roman military might. DJM

See Picard, G. C. (1957) *Les Trophées romains*.

Troy The site which is now thought to have been ancient Troy (mod. Hissarlik in Turkey), was first identified by Heinrich Schliemann on the basis of descriptions given in the Homeric poems. Hissarlik

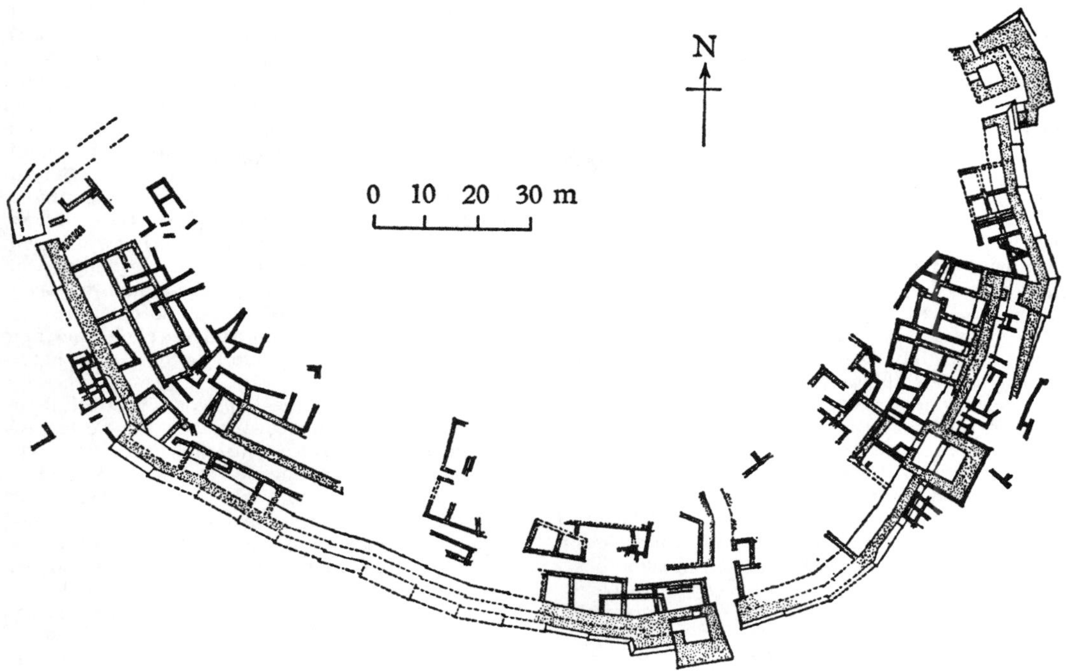

TROY: plan of the Phase VII settlement, thought by many to be contemporary with the mythical Trojan war.

is a defensible mound strategically located on a bay (now silted up) between two rivers, overlooking the Dardanelles. When Schliemann excavated, he identified nine archaeological levels and believed the second of these (which he called Troy II), with its fine treasures and buildings, to be the ruins of HOMER's Troy.

Troy II is now known to be almost 1,000 years earlier than the period Homer was describing. Imported MYCENAEAN POTTERY first appears in the later settlement of Troy VI. The relatively disappointing settlement of Troy VIIA, which shows signs of having been besieged, sacked and burned in the later 13th century BC, appears to correspond in date, if not description, to the Homeric city.

The site was resettled by the Greeks c.700 BC (period Troy VIII). They named it Ilion (the Greek name of Troy) and it was a prosperous, though not large, town that derived much fame from its earlier history. When ALEXANDER crossed the HELLESPONT in 334 to begin his war on Persia, he visited Ilion and made dedications in the TEMPLE of ATHENA and at the supposed tombs of ACHILLES and Patroklos; he also exempted the city from TAXATION. The hellenistic and Roman city of Ilion (Troy IX) continued to prosper. It was visited by JULIUS CAESAR, and later became the seat of a BISHOPRIC until finally fading away c.AD 400. (see also TROJAN WAR) AG

See Blegen, C.W. (1963) *Troy and the Trojans*.

 ANATOLIA.

Tullia c.79–45 BC The first child of CICERO's marriage to Terentia, she is well known to us from Cicero's letters (hers do not survive) and PLUTARCH's *Cicero*. Cicero appears to have been much closer to her than to his son, Marcus. She first appears as a little girl in the earliest surviving letters. At the age of, perhaps, 11 she was engaged to Gaius Calpurnius Piso Frugi, who died in 57. Her second marriage in 56, to Furius Crassipes, is obscure; it ended in DIVORCE in 51. She met Cicero at Brundisium on his return from exile on her birthday, 5 August 57. She was married again in late 50, to Publius Cornelius Dolabella. Cicero's letters (he was governor in CILICIA at the time) refer to possible husbands, but Terentia and Tullia had been given considerable freedom and their decision caught Cicero by surprise. However, divorce was being discussed by early 48 (Dolabella was notoriously unfaithful). Tullia bore him two sons, in 49 and 45, but both died in infancy. The divorce was not completed until late 46; Dolabella was in favour with CAESAR, and Cicero remained on good terms with him. Tullia never recovered from the second pregnancy, and died in February 45. Cicero was devastated, spending an unusually long period in mourning by the standards of the time. He wrote a famous *Self-consolation* (now lost) and proposed to build a shrine to her memory. JRWP

See Cicero, *Letters to Atticus*, trs. D.R. Shackleton Bailey (1978); Plutarch, *Cicero*, trs. B. Perrin (1921).

Twelve Tables (*lex* [or more correctly *leges*] *duodecim tabularum*) A set of early Roman legal provisions originally inscribed on twelve bronze or possibly wooden tablets. According to the traditions, it was the work of a board of ten (*decemviri*) who promulgated the first ten tables in 451, and a second board which promulgated the last two in 450. The legislation was a response by the ÉLITE to popular demand for accessible and ascertainable law, and was partly based on material collected from Athens by their commissioners. Most scholars reject the second board but accept an element of truth in the rest of the story. The tables may well have been a response to some kind of social upheaval in the mid-5th century, though the content may also suggest an element of self-regulation by the élite. Again, there are a few curious parallels with Athenian legislation, and in any case some Greek influence on 5th-century Roman legislation is to be expected. Only fragments of the Tables survive: these cover legal procedure, assault and battery, theft, rules governing slavery, damage to property, the casting of spells, unlawful killing, funeral regulations, the prohibition of MARRIAGE between PATRICIANS and PLEBEIANS and some other matters. The fragments are not necessarily a representative sample of the original text, but the virtual absence of constitutional rules, as of any distinction between private and public law, is striking and probably significant. The Romans valued the Twelve Tables as a symbol of the central importance they attributed to LAW, though as an actual instrument they were almost completely obsolete by the late REPUBLIC. For modern historians they provide a unique insight into society in archaic Rome. JDC

See Cornell, T. J. (1995) *The Beginnings of Rome*; Crawford, M. H., ed. (1996) *Roman Statutes*, vol. 2; Watson, A. (1975) *Rome of the Twelve Tables*.

Tyche see FORTUNA.

tyranny A political phenomenon representing a stage in the political evolution of many Greek CITY-STATES from narrow ARISTOCRACIES to broader forms of government, such as OLIGARCHY in CORINTH or DEMOCRACY in Athens. Tyrants were often men of aristocratic origins who exploited the growing resentment against the ruling élite to seize power and rule above the constitution. The first tyrants were almost always well received. Only in the second or third generation of a dynasty did tyranny fall into disfavour. The first tyrant, Kypselos of Corinth (650), was on his mother's side a member of the Bakchiadai, a family renowned for its noble birth, wealth and oppressive behaviour. DELPHIC ORACLES predicting Kypselos' overthrow of the Bakchiadai, and folk tales describing his miraculous escape as a baby from their hands, indicate the popularity of his tyranny (HERODOTOS 5.92). One oracle notes how he will bring justice to Corinth, suggesting that he promised to correct injustices and bring greater equality to the citizens. Other sources indicate that his kind treatment of debtors while in public office won him sufficient popularity to stage a coup and drive the Bakchiadai into EXILE. We are told that he confiscated Bakchiad property to distribute among the poor and ruled mildly, enjoying the goodwill of the Corinthians and needing no bodyguard, which indicates his popularity with the HOPLITE class. The pattern of using high office to garner support for a bid at tyranny was repeated by others. At nearby Sikyon, Orthagoras used his position as military officer to make himself tyrant (630) and establish the Orthagorid tyranny, which lasted a hundred years. At Athens, PEISISTRATOS' military accomplishments in the war against MEGARA won him enough popular support to secure a bodyguard for his first bid at tyranny (561/0).

After the initial purge, Kypselos ruled Corinth for 30 years, to be succeeded by his son Periandros (Periander), who ruled until his death (585). The tyranny came to an abrupt end with Periandros' nephew, deposed after only two years (583). Periandros was a figure of international stature: he was called upon to arbitrate disputes between Athens and Mytilene (610), and was friends with Thrasyboulos, tyrant of MILETOS, and with Alyattes, king of LYDIA. But he is characterized in later sources such as Herodotos and ARISTOTLE as the tyrannical type, a brutish figure who used various methods to suppress opposition: removing outstanding personalities, banning all forms of ASSEMBLY, employing SPIES, and embarking on building programmes and WARS to keep the poor busy. Some of these tactics may have been more characteristic of the later SICILIAN tyrants like Hieron of SYRACUSE (478–467) than of earlier tyrants like Periandros, though he did aggressively expand Corinth's control over north-western Greece. What is true is that the early tyrants were great TOWN PLANNERS, whose building programmes led to real URBANIZATION, with TEMPLES built, HARBOURS improved, and ROADS paved. They were also great patrons of the arts, who reorganized religious FESTIVALS and attracted POETS to their courts. CC

See Salmon, J. (1997) Lopping off those heads? Tyrants, politics and the polis, in L. G. Mitchell and P. J. Rhodes, eds., *The Development of the Polis in Archaic Greece* 60–73; Sancisi-Weerdenburg, H., ed. (2000) *Peisistratos and the Tyranny*.

Tyre see PHOENICIA.

Tyrtaios see LYRIC POETRY, GREEK; POETRY, GREEK; SPARTA.

Tzetzes, Ioannes see SCHOLARSHIP, BYZANTINE.

Ulpian (Gnaeus (?) Domitius Ulpianus) d. AD 223/4 In some ways the most important of the Roman jurists. His family came from Tyre and he retained a pride in his home town which was mutual, to judge from an inscription published in 1988. Little is known for certain about his official career, except that the emperor ALEXANDER SEVERUS (222–35) first made him prefect in charge of the corn supply (*praefectus annonae*) and subsequently praetorian prefect. He was murdered by his mutinous troops.

Ulpian's bureaucratic career began probably as secretary in charge of petitions (*a libellis*) under the emperor SEPTIMIUS SEVERUS. Most of his writing was done during the sole reign of the latter's son, CARACALLA (211–17). His two major works are a commentary on the praetor's edict in 81 books and a commentary on Masurius Sabinus and the civil law in 51 books. Ulpian's subsequent celebrity is partly fortuitous; 40–41 per cent of Justinian's *Digest* consists of often long quotations from his works, and as the *Digest* was the chief medium by which Roman law was transmitted to the high medieval and modern periods, Ulpian – excerpted, edited and sometimes forged – becomes our chief source for it. Yet his works have real merit: they are scholarly, comprehensive and written in understandable Latin. They were presumably aimed at the new citizens created by the Antonine constitution (c.212) for whom Latin was not their first language. These qualities doubtless commended his work to later practitioners of law – he is prominent in the scanty PAPYRUS and pre-Justinianic sources – as well as to the (Greek) editors of the *Digest*. Ulpian's speed of production explains his weaknesses: heavy dependence on earlier jurists, repetitiousness and banality of style. (see also JUSTINIAN, WORKS OF) JDC

See Honoré, T. (1982) *Ulpian*.

Ulysses see ODYSSEUS.

Umbrians People of north central Italy, described by PLINY as 'the oldest race of Italy' (*Natural History* 3.112). The Umbrian language was closely related to OSCAN; a major ritual document in that language from Iguvium (mod. Gubbio) has been preserved. The Umbrians occupied the area east of the TIBER and north of SABINE territory. They were brought under Roman control in a series of campaigns during the first half of the 3rd century BC, colonies being established at Narnia (Narni) in 299 and Spoletium (Spoleto) in 241. The building of the Via Flaminia in 220 provided a further impetus to romanization. Some Umbrians joined the insurgents in the SOCIAL WAR, but only at a late stage. The topography of Umbria is varied, and includes fertile plains in the lower reaches of the Tiber, known for VILLA estates and brickworks, upland basins and high mountains. Traditional Umbrian settlement seems to have combined hillforts (e.g. at Colfiorito), mountain sanctuaries (e.g. at Monte Ansciano above Gubbio), often identified by votive deposits of bronze FIGURINES, and lowland VILLAGES. By the early imperial period, the area was characterized by a series of flourishing towns, many of which continued to be inhabited into medieval and modern times. (see also ITALY, ROMAN) JRP

See Harris, W.V. (1971) *Rome in Etruria and Umbria*; Malone, C. and Stoddart, S., eds. (1994) *Territory, Time and State*.

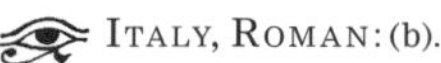 ITALY, ROMAN: (b).

underwater archaeology see ALEXANDRIA; ARCHAEOLOGY; BRUNDISIUM; CAESAREA MARITIMA; SHIPWRECKS; TRANSPORT.

unemployment Like employment, unemployment is largely a capitalist concept; nonetheless the fear, and experience, of a lack of employment can be attested in antiquity. LABOUR was very differently composed from that of modern industrial societies, given the ancient mix of freeborn, SLAVES, freed slaves and various degrees of dependent labour. In the Greek world, the economy was fundamentally based on AGRICULTURE, though there are suggestions that a majority of people lived in towns and walked or rode out to tend their fields. Wage labour was probably less common than self-employment, at least among citizens, and the sources refer to men as landless rather than unemployed. Apparent references to men 'without work' (*apergoi*) are rare and hard to interpret with confidence; possibly they denote the disabled or those too old to work, since one 3rd-century BC inscription from Samos (*SEG* 27.545) clearly implies that an *apergos* can be a landowner (*geouchos*) with produce to sell. In the Roman empire, the majority of the population was rural-based and engaged in AGRICULTURE, but for the urban populace the value of a trade or skill is evident from the emphasis placed on this on many humble tombstones. Unemployment then as now was more likely to afflict the unskilled, especially economic migrants from the countryside seeking work in areas subject to seasonal and economic downturns (the construction industry, dock-workers and porters). Much has been written about the 'idle plebs' of the city of Rome, who allegedly lived on state handouts and free BREAD and eased the monotony of their lives by attending lavish GAMES and entertainments laid on for their diversion. This image is false: there is ample evidence to show that successive Roman EMPERORS were highly concerned to ensure that there was work available for the poor in Roman society. VESPASIAN's reported lack of interest in labour-saving devices for use in the construction industry at Rome is a case in point (Suetonius, *Vespasian* 18). DJM, DGJS

urbanization An important concept of historical and sociological enquiry, though its meaning can be variously understood as the shifting DEMOGRAPHIC balance between rural and urban communities, or the study of the changing character and morphology of urban centres. In the context of the Greco-Roman world, we might understand urbanization as the means by which we can discriminate between the different urban traditions of ancient societies and trace the wider adoption of new ideas and forms of urban communities. Key questions to ask of any urban society are what makes a site 'urban', and how we are to understand the processes by which the structures and institutions that define 'towns' evolved.

In the Greek world, the concept of the *POLIS* was fundamental, though the function of the *polis* as an independent political entity was to some extent as significant as its physical form (ARISTOTLE, *Politics* 1). Both philosophical discussions of the nature of the town and the development over time of characteristic urban buildings and spaces, such as *AGORAI*, STOAS and TEMPLES, helped to give more concrete shape to a specifically Greek urban form. Although this shows regional diversity, the close links between physical form and political functions enhanced certain characteristics, and a degree of orthogonal TOWN PLANNING became common in new foundations. Early Greek COLONIZATION exported both idea and form, and this was enhanced by the foundation of hellenized cities across the PERSIAN and Egyptian territories conquered by ALEXANDER.

Roman urbanization developed its own traditions, reflecting the character of Rome's own urban constitution. The significance lies in the extent of the empire and the scale of urban development achieved. In the Western empire, this involved some areas with only limited proto-urban development before incorporation.

Studies of ancient urbanization remain focused on the physical attributes of towns, and more theoretical models to explain their social function are needed to complement these approaches. DJM

See Adams, P. and Wrigley, E. (1978) *Towns in Societies*; Cornell, T. and Lomas, K. (1995) *Urban Society in Roman Italy*; Hansen, M. H. (1998) *Polis and City-state*; Ward-Perkins, J. B. (1974) *Cities of Ancient Greece and Italy.*

 CITIES: (a)–(b); TOWN PLANNING: (a), (c).

Urfa see EDESSA.

usurpers see ALARIC; CARAUSIUS; DIOCLETIAN; GALLA PLACIDIA; GAUL; HISPANIA; HONORIUS; JULIA DOMNA; LONDON; MARCUS AURELIUS; PROBA; SYMMACHUS; TETRARCHS; THEODOSIUS I; VALERIAN.

usury see BANKING; MONEYLENDING.

Utica A PHOENICIAN, Punic and Roman city, 33 km (21 miles) north-east of Tunis in Tunisia. Utica was traditionally founded in 1101 BC and held to be the oldest Phoenician settlement in AFRICA, but this date is not supported by ARCHAEOLOGICAL evidence: the earliest BURIALS uncovered are of the 8th century BC. Utica was an important port, but the topography has changed because of silting, and it now lies 11 km (7 miles) inland. A major city within the CARTHAGINIAN empire, it was a target for invading armies, being conquered by AGATHOKLES OF SYRACUSE in 308 and besieged by SCIPIO AFRICANUS in 204. Because the city sided with the Numidian king MASINISSA in 149, Utica was rewarded on the fall of Carthage three years later: it was made a 'free city' and named capital of the new PROVINCE of Africa. POMPEY used it as his base during his campaign against the supporters of MARIUS in 81, and the city remained loyal to Pompey against JULIUS CAESAR. CATO THE YOUNGER committed suicide here in 46. Its political importance declined with the refoundation of Carthage under AUGUSTUS, when Utica received Latin rights, but it was raised to colonial rank under HADRIAN, and the number and size of its public buildings (including BATHS, a THEATRE, an AMPHITHEATRE and a CIRCUS) indicate that it remained a flourishing city. The principal visible remains are an excavated quarter of wealthy town houses, mostly of late Republican and early imperial date, with MOSAIC and MARBLE floors; and a sector of the Phoenicio-Carthaginian necropolis. (see also PUNIC WARS) RJAW

Lézine, A. (1968) *Carthage, Utique.*

utopias and utopianism The word (ambiguously *outopia* or *eutopia*, 'no place' or 'good place') was coined by Sir Thomas More in 1516 for his imaginary ideal island civilization. It may also reasonably be used for ancient ideal societies, since More consciously followed an ancient tradition that combines two closely connected strands of Greek thought. One is the 'republic' genre of political writing, best represented by PLATO's *Republic* (actually entitled *Politeia*, 'constitution', in Greek), in which political ideas are examined by the construction of an imaginary ideal *POLIS*. The second is the ancient tradition of constructing imaginary blessed lands and blessed islands, situated either far away from the MEDITERRANEAN (the 'centre' of the world) at the 'edges of the earth' or on an imaginary cultural boundary between the Greek and 'barbarian' worlds. These blessed lands tend to have very close conceptual similarities to both the GOLDEN AGE view of prehistory first found in HESIOD's *Works and Days*, in which the first age of humanity is seen as the ideal, and to ancient conceptions of 'paradise' such as the Elysian Fields and the Isles of the Blessed where HEROES and the virtuous go after death. It seems that often in ancient thought the farther away one travels, the farther back in time one goes, until the river Ocean is reached where the primeval chaos of creation still reigns. Hence the placing of such blessed lands at 'sacred extremes'. Such utopian lands, at sacred extremes or on cultural boundaries, are of considerable number and variety and include, among others, those of the Hyperboreans, ETHIOPIANS, the Isles of the Blessed themselves, INDIA, the Fortunate Isles, Scythia, BRITAIN, Ireland and Ultima Thule. In HOMER's *Odyssey*, various lands and islands of varied utopian characteristics are visited, from Scheria – the land of the Phaiakians (Phaeacians) – to the island of the savage Cyclopes who, though they live in a paradisiacal island, exhibit no noble tendencies.

The combination of the republic genre of political literature with the blessed lands or blessed islands tradition is perhaps best expressed by Plato's imaginary, lost, ideal island republic of ATLANTIS (situated in Ocean beyond the impassable gates of HERAKLES) in his dialogues *Timaeus* and *Critias*. ARISTOPHANES in the *Birds* situates his ideal republic of BIRDS, Cloudcuckooland, at another sacred extreme – in the sky. The tradition is carried on in Iamboulos' Island of the Sun (in the Indian ocean) and Euhemeros' Panchaia (off the southern coast of India), and is satirized by LUCIAN in *A True Story*. In medieval literature are found the wondrous land of Prester John in the east, and the Garden of Eden, again located in the far east. In modern literature the Atlantian tradition was revived by More, and later by Sir Francis Bacon in his *New Atlantis*.

Few if any ancient utopias are really intended as blueprints for an ideal society. Rather they come into being more as distorting mirrors in which to view Greek society and to examine its defects. Very frequently, therefore, they are, as Shakespeare puts it in *The Tempest*, constructed 'by contraries': in their various differing ways they are 'not-Greece'. GLC

See Clay, D. and Purvis, A. (1999) *Four Island Utopias*; Ferguson, J. (1975) *Utopias of the Classical World*; Romm, J. S. (1992) *The Edges of the Earth in Ancient Thought*.

vacations see TOURISM.

Valens see VALENTINIAN I.

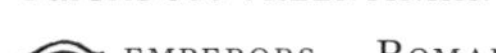 EMPERORS, ROMAN: (b); TETRARCHS: (b); THEODOSIUS I: (a).

Valentinian I (Flavius Valentinianus) AD 321–75 Roman emperor from AD 364, he was a PANNONIAN army officer. Exiled by JULIAN because of his CHRISTIANITY, he was soon recalled by Jovian. On Jovian's death in 364 he was acclaimed emperor at Nicaea. He quickly appointed his brother Valens as AUGUSTUS for the East, and ruled the West himself. Until 375, Valentinian's court was based at TRIER. Much of his time was spent fighting the Alamanni (including the victory at Solicinium in 368) and erecting FORTIFICATIONS on the RHINE. Expeditions under the elder Theodosius were sent to BRITAIN and AFRICA to deal with problems there. During his reign Gaul benefited tremendously, in terms of greater security and political opportunity, exemplified by the appointment of AUSONIUS as tutor to Valentinian's eldest son, Gratian. In 375 Valentinian moved to Pannonia to fight against the Quadi. After a successful campaign, he died of a stroke during peace negotiations with the Quadi in 375. Valentinian's non-military concerns were limited. He avoided ecclesiastical controversy and never visited Rome. He was notorious for a bad temper, a concern for regulations and his maneating bears, Goldflake and Innocence. HWE

See Matthews, J. F. (1989) *The Roman Empire of Ammianus.*

Valentinian II see SYMMACHUS.

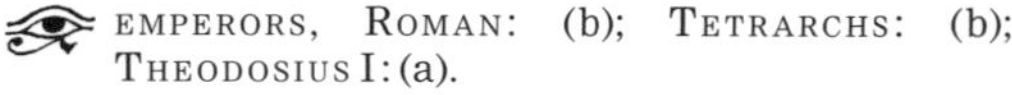 EMPERORS, ROMAN: (b); TETRARCHS: (b); THEODOSIUS I: (a).

Valentinian III see GALLA PLACIDIA; GENERALISSIMOS; VANDALS.

 THEODOSIUS I: (a).

Valerian (Publius Licinianus Valerianus) Emperor AD 253–60. Little is known of his early career, but Valerian came from an aristocratic family and rose to CENSOR under Decius. As commander of troops in RAETIA he supported Trebonius Gallus against the usurper Aemilian (253). Gallus died before his arrival, and Valerian's army proclaimed him emperor (aged 60). Valerian marched to Rome, where he and his son, GALLIENUS, were accepted as joint AUGUSTI. His reign saw trouble from the FRANKS on the RHINE, the Alamanni on the DANUBE, Saxons in the north, and GOTHS and PERSIANS on the Eastern frontiers. Valerian left Gallienus in charge of the West while he went East to deal with the Goths in ASIA Minor (253–6). In 259 he was forced to face the Persians, who under SHAPUR I had invaded ARMENIA, CAPPADOCIA and SYRIA. With an army weakened by plague, Valerian was captured by the Persians at EDESSA (260). The humiliation of the defeated Roman emperor can still be seen in the rock monuments at Bishapur and Naqs-i-Rustam. Valerian died in captivity, and his flayed skin decorated a Persian temple.

Valerian, like his predecessor Decius, was one of the last emperors to have had a senatorial career. He also followed Decius in his PERSECUTION of CHRISTIANS. He had the foresight to see that a single emperor was no longer sufficient to deal with the problems of the empire in the 3rd century. MEH

See Watson, A. (1999) *Aurelian and the Third Century*; Williams, S. (1997) *Diocletian and the Roman Recovery.*

Valerius Flaccus see EPIC; STRUCTURALISM AND POST-STRUCTURALISM.

Valerius Maximus Author of *Nine Books of Memorable Sayings and Deeds* who wrote in the reign of TIBERIUS. Internal evidence reveals that he accompanied Sextus Pompeius when the latter was governor of ASIA in AD 25, that he survived the death of Sextus in 29, and that he was still writing after the conspiracy of SEJANUS, whom he condemns, in 31. His claims to modest status need to be treated with caution: he had senatorial friends and a solid RHETORICAL education.

Valerius' work is organized by institutions and personal qualities. Book 1 deals with religion, book 2 with 'ancient institutions,' books 3–8 with good qualities and book 9 with evil. The typical organization of a section within a book opens with examples culled from Roman history, followed by examples from the history of non-Roman peoples. The bulk of these examples are drawn from CICERO and LIVY, with occasional excursions into the works of VARRO, Coelius Antipater, Trogus and possibly some Greek sources.

Valerius' work is intended as a guide to proper living for members of the aristocracy. It is decidedly hostile to heroes of the *popularis* cause in the REPUBLIC, and favourable to defenders of the ARISTOCRACY, a view that may be compared with that of Valerius' contemporary VELLEIUS PATERCULUS. The *Memorable Sayings and Deeds* was widely read in antiquity and the Middle Ages, as a source for historical *exempla* about the Romans and other peoples of the classical MEDITERRANEAN. DSP

See Bloomer, W. M. (1992) *Valerius Maximus and the Rhetoric of the New Nobility.*

Vandals Having fully emerged in AD 406, together with the ALANI and Suevi, Vandals crossed the frozen RHINE to wreak havoc within GAUL and subsequently within SPAIN. They were removed from here by the arrival of the Visigoths, who themselves established a kingdom in Spain. The Vandals sought territory in AFRICA and succeeded in occupying the former

Roman PROVINCES between 429 and 439, establishing their capital at CARTHAGE. Their fleet later secured the BALEARICS, CORSICA and SARDINIA. Prominent was the long-lived Vandal king Gaiseric. Under his initiative, from the 440s Vandal fleets undertook numerous raids against the coasts of Italy, SICILY and Greece, culminating in the capture of Rome in 455, where they removed much treasure and the princess Eudocia, daughter of Valentinian III. Abortive or failed Roman assaults on Vandal Africa occurred in 465 and 470, but it was only much later, under the Eastern Roman (Byzantine) emperor JUSTINIAN (r.527–65) and in the campaigns of 532–3 by his general Belisarius, that the Vandal state was defeated, as recorded in PROCOPIUS' *Wars*.

The Vandals largely maintained Roman towns and VILLAS, as revealed by EXCAVATIONS (e.g. Carthage, Cherchel) and FIELD SURVEY. CHURCH building is attested, though the contemporary historian Victor of Vita documents conflicts between ARIAN Vandals and orthodox natives. Archaeologically, there is little specific 'Vandal' material culture and very few Vandal burials have been identified, suggesting a cultural *rapprochement*. Most significantly, the Vandal presence does not appear to have greatly disrupted production and export in North Africa of POTTERY, AMPHORAS and their WINE and OIL cargoes. NJC

See Courtois, C. (1955) *Les Vandals et l'Afrique*; Humphrey, J. H. (1980) Vandal and Byzantine Carthage: some new archaeological problems, in J. G. Pedley, ed., *New Light on Ancient Carthage* 85–120.

 GERMANY AND GERMANS: (b).

Varro (Marcus Terentius Varro) 116–27 BC A prolific author, unrivalled among Romans. Born at Reate, he studied at Rome with the philologist Lucius Aelius Stilo, who wrote on PLAUTUS' comedies, and at Athens with the ACADEMIC PHILOSOPHER Antiochos of Askalon. He enjoyed a public career, reaching the PRAETORSHIP, and fought for POMPEIAN forces in Spain. CAESAR restored him to favour and appointed him director of his planned LIBRARY, but ANTONY later proscribed him. He escaped death, but his libraries were plundered. After the CIVIL WARS he devoted his remaining life to peaceful study. According to AULUS GELLIUS, Varro had compiled 490 books by his 77th birthday.

Some of his output is extant. Of his work *On the Latin Language* in 25 books, much of books 5–10 survives; the work was a lengthy treatment of Latin, discussing words, grammar and syntax. Also still extant are the three books *On Agriculture*. In the first book, Varro discusses some of the more general aspects of AGRICULTURE, while book 2 treats the topics of CATTLE and SHEEP and book 3 offers the author's thoughts on the farming of smaller farm animals like BIRDS and BEES, among others.

Fragments of many works appear in quotations by other writers, and a selection of the 55 works known by title reveals Varro's breadth and scope as a scholar. He wrote 90 books of *Menippean Satires*, a curious but not uncommon literary form, offering PROSE essays interspersed with humour and POETRY. His 41 books *On Human and Divine Antiquities*, especially the 16 books on matters divine, provided AUGUSTINE (1) in the early 5th century AD with much of the material that he critiques and satirizes in his *City of God*. Varro authored 76 books of *Dialogues* on a variety of philosophical and social topics, including chastity and the upbringing of children. The *Hebdomades* or *Pictures* presented the BIOGRAPHIES of famous Greeks and Romans, with 700 illustrations, while the 9 books *On the Disciplines* discussed the essential liberal arts. In the area of HISTORICAL research, Varro composed *On the Life of the Roman People*, treating topics of social history, and *On the Origin of the Roman People*, which discussed and offered a CHRONOLOGY for the early period of the Roman state. *On Civil Law* was a treatment of matters of LAW and legal interpretation. In addition, he wrote works on the arts, like *On the Origins of the Stage* and *On the Comedies of Plautus*.

The breadth of Varro's work is impressive, treating many aspects of life and culture at Rome. Although he was not always correct, he provides much of the raw material used by scholars to understand details relating to the ancient world. The traditional dates for many events, such as the foundation of Rome in 753 BC (in our calendar), are Varronian. JV

See Varro, *De lingua Latina* trs. R.G. Kent (1938); *On Agriculture* (with Cato), trs. W. D. Hooper and H. B. Ash (1954).

vase-painting The term 'vase-painting' usually refers to Greek decorative painting on POTTERY that includes geometric and floral designs and figure compositions. After some generations of geometric designs in the early centuries of the first millennium BC, painters depicted ANIMAL and figure scenes. In the 8th century, some large Athenian funerary vases carried complex scenes of *prothesis* (laying out the dead) and *ekphora* (transporting the dead to the cemetery). Before the end of the 8th century, mainly in CORINTH, the Geometric style and technique of drawing gave way to techniques that owed much to the influence of eastern METALWORK. This period, mainly c.725–625, is called orientalizing. The figures were now fuller than in Geometric; there were new elements of florals, ANIMALS (e.g. lions) and monsters (e.g. chimaeras), and stories from MYTH began to monopolize the subject matter. Also, the technique was more complex: instead of the plain silhouette of Geometric, contours and inner markings were incised, and red and white colours added. This 'black-figure' technique was adopted in Athens, and by the close of the 7th century the Athenian potters and painters were producing high-quality pieces with well-made shapes and diverse myths. During the 6th century the drawing displayed a precise technique, with jet-black figures against a vivid orange background. Around 530 a new technique was invented, a reversal of the black-figure; in this new 'red-figure' technique the figures were reserved with inner markings in black, and the background painted black. Athens' production was beyond compare, and it was not until Athenian and local potters and painters began working in SICILY and south Italy in the later 5th century that Athens had any rivals in this technique. Another technique practised in the 5th century was 'white-ground', with the figures in outline on the white, the nearest approximation to the lost monumental PAINTINGS that are known only from literary references and descriptions. The white-ground technique was used mainly for oil-bottles (*lêkythoi*) made specially for the TOMB. Vase-painting

VASE-PAINTING: famous scene showing the interior of a Greek vase-painting workshop. The image hints at ancient connoisseurship (with Athena presiding as judge whilst Nikai, personified Victories, crown individual artists) although this could reflect vase-painters' view of their own importance. Note the manner in which the artists held their brushes (in the fist, rather than between fingers) and also the presence of a woman painter at the r. side of the scene.

continued in hellenistic times, particularly in Greek Italy and ALEXANDRIA. In the middle and late hellenistic period, red-slipped pottery and mouldmade relief-decorated wares (e.g.'Megarian bowls') became more common. A notable exception is the ceremonial Panathenaic amphoras filled with oil, which were still being awarded as prizes for the games in Athens during the Roman period.

Although a few vases carry the names of painters, the craft was basically anonymous, but modern connoisseurship has shown that it is possible to group together pots painted by one man, even without knowledge of his name. Hence, alongside the names of such painters as Exekias and Douris, we have modern names such as the Gorgon Painter, Berlin Painter and Nausikaa Painter.

In Athenian black- and red-figure the subject matter continues to favour myths, and much of our understanding of myths, and of their political and social significance, derives from scenes on vases. Incidents from everyday life become more common from the 6th century, such as *SYMPOSIA*, ATHLETICS, and boudoir scenes, and once again they help students to appreciate the social and religious background of the city. Figured vases have been found locally, in domestic and religious contexts and alongside the dead. They were also exported within and beyond the MEDITERRANEAN. BAS

See Cook, R. M. (1972) *Greek Painted Pottery*; Sparkes, B. A. (1996) *The Red and the Black*; Williams, D. (1985) *Greek Vases*.

 ATHENA.

vegetables An important component of most people's diets in the classical world. However, many of the vegetables we associate with modern Mediterranean cooking were unknown in the classical world. Chief among these are tomatoes, peppers, potatoes, most varieties of green bean, okra and possibly eggplant (aubergine).

Some vegetables which Greeks and Romans ate are familiar today, including leeks, broad beans and globe artichokes. However, the classical varieties of others would look very inferior to modern consumers. Root vegetables such as beet and carrot were tough and fibrous, and both were used more for their edible leaves than for their roots in antiquity. Radishes, grown for their pungent, spicy roots, were chewy and would have needed considerable processing before eating. Similarly, celery was grown for its leaves, not the stalks, which would have been inedible in Greek and Roman varieties. CATO provides numerous recipes for cabbage, all of which entail boiling it for hours, probably because the leaves were leathery and strongly flavoured. Cucumbers and some marrows were probably very bitter and most palatable when pickled. The bulbs of onions and garlic are likely to have been small compared to modern varieties. There were also some plants eaten as vegetables which would be totally unfamiliar in most of modern temperate Europe and North America. For example, black nightshade (*Solanum nigrum*) was boiled and eaten like spinach, and the flowers of marrows (squashes) were consumed as well as the FRUITS. Vegetables such as rocket and chicory, which we would use in salads today, were probably also eaten as boiled greens. LF

See Cato, *De re rustica*; Theophrastos, *Causes of Plants*, *Enquiry into Plants*.

 SHOPS AND SHOPPING: (b).

VEGETABLES: common vegetables in the classical world.

Modern name	Botanical name	Description and uses
asparagus	?	Several different plants were called 'asparagus' (literally meaning 'unsown') in antiquity, and one of them was spiny. None seem to be the plant we now call asparagus (*Asparagus officinalis*).
beetroot and leaf beet (Swiss chard)	*Beta vulgaris*	used mostly for its leaves, roots were tough and chewy
broad beans (fava beans)	*Vicia faba*	used green and dried
cabbage and kale	*Brassica oleracea*	used tough leaves after long boiling and flowering shoots like sprouting broccoli
carrot	*Daucus carota*	leaves probably used more than roots as boiled vegetable
celery	*Apium graveolens*	used leaf celery only – no crisp stalks like modern varieties, similar to parsley
chickpeas	*Cicer arietinum*	mostly used dried, in storage, particularly impervious to attack by pests
chicory	*Cichorium intybus*	leaves used as boiled greens
cucumber	*Cucumis sativus*	spiny and probably very bitter and may have needed soaking or pickling before use
fennel	*Foeniculum vulgare*	leaves used, swollen rooted varieties probably did not exist
garlic	*Allium sativum*	bulbs (cloves) and leaves used
globe artichoke	*Cynara scolymus*	as now, immature flower heads boiled
leek	*Allium ampeloprasum*	leaves and stems used, probably tougher and chewier than modern varieties
lentils	*Lens culinaris*	used dried
lettuce	*Lactuca sativa*	chewy and tough by modern standards
marrows, pumpkins, squashes	*Cucurbita* spp.	most modern varieties originated in America, but at least one type of marrow/squash was known
mushrooms	many species	gathered wild
onions	*Allium cepa*	bulbs probably smaller and leaves may have been used more often
parsley	*Petroselinum crispum*	leaves used, similar to celery
peas	*Pisum sativum*	used green and dried
radish	*Raphanus sativus*	leaves and roots eaten, probably usually cooked
rocket	*Eruca sativa*	probably mostly used as boiled greens, though could be eaten fresh
salsify	*Tragoporgon porrifolias*	roots peeled and boiled, young leaves edible raw
scorzonera	*Scornozera hispanica*	roots peeled and boiled
sorrel	*Rumex acetosa*	leaves eaten as boiled greens
spinach	*Spinacea oleracea*	leaves eaten as boiled greens
turnip	*Brassica rupa*	leaves may have been used more than the tough roots
wild greens (dandelion, black nightshade, good King Henry etc.)	*Taraxacum officinale, Solanum nigrum, Chenopodium bonus-henricus*	gathered from the wild, in fallow fields or as crop weeds and used as boiled greens

Vegetables absent from the classical world:
aubergine (eggplant) (probably until late Roman times, may have been brought in by the Arabs); Jerusalem artichoke (American); Lima beans (American); parsnip (native of northern Europe); peppers (American); potatoes (American); runner beans/string beans (American); sweet corn (American); tomatoes (American).

vegetarianism Ancient attitudes to meat-eating and ANIMALS are best expressed by the NEOPLATONIST PHILOSOPHER Porphyry in his pro-vegetarian survey of ancient ideas, *On Abstinence from Animal Food* (3rd century AD). Arguments over the nature of the relationship between humans and animals, and whether it is right to kill and eat them, can be traced in philosophy back to PYTHAGORAS in the 6th century BC, and in popular thought at least to the moralizing treatment of HESIOD's myth of the ages (from *Works and Days*) found in AESOP's *Fables* (6th century BC?).

Pythagoras, Empedokles and some later PLATONISTS argued against eating animals, at least partly because of the possibility of human SOULS transmigrating into animal bodies. For Empedokles the first age of humanity was dominated by love and marked by vegetarianism, by a lack of animal SACRIFICE, and consequently by harmony between humans and animals. Later philosophers, however – ARISTOTLE in particular – denied animals the power of reason, and thus placed them outside human justice. The STOICS agreed, and further insisted that animals actually existed for the purpose of serving humans; the sole purpose of animals such as the PIG was to be killed and eaten.

In Aesop again, the GOLDEN AGE was one of harmony between humans and animals. In the *Phainomena* by ARATOS OF SOLOI, the first killing and eating of animals marks the departure of Justice from the world. In the culture-history of the influential PERIPATETIC philosopher Dikaiarchos, the killing of animals ends the golden age and also begins the killing of humans; so begins WARFARE. GLC

See Porphyry, *On Abstinence from Killing Animals*, ed. and trs. G. Clark (2001); Dombrowski, D. (1984) *The Philosophy of Vegetarianism*; Wilkins, J. et al., eds. (1999) *Food in Antiquity*.

Vegetius (Flavius Vegetius Renatus) A Christian *vir inlustris* and *comes*, a high-ranking official, who composed the only complete handbook of Roman military science to survive. The work was written between AD 383 and 450, and book 1 is dedicated to an emperor, who then commissioned books 2–4. If praise of the emperor's personal military skills in book 3 is not pure flattery, THEODOSIUS I (379–95) is the only reasonable candidate, though others have been proposed. Publius Flavius Vegetius Renatus, a horse breeder, who wrote on diseases of horses and cattle (*Digesta artis mulomedicinae*), is almost certainly the same man.

The military work names several sources, including CATO THE ELDER, FRONTINUS, Paternus and enactments of the emperors TRAJAN and HADRIAN. For later material, the author drew on personal knowledge or BUREAUCRATIC handbooks. The work offers much information about the workings of the Roman ARMY, but this material was not sorted into a coherency useful for the modern student of the Roman military. Since Vegetius intended only to correct perceived faults in the system, his military is a theoretical amalgam of current procedures and the best practices from ancient Rome, when the state successfully defended itself and even expanded. The work is not unlike a treatise *On Military Matters* probably presented to the emperor Valens in 367. Each seems to be an attempt by a literate bureaucrat to scour previous literature for old solutions to apply to current problems. JV

See Vegetius, *Epitome of Military Science*, trs. N. P. Milner (1993).

Veii An ETRUSCAN city north of the TIBER about 16 km (10 miles) from Rome, Veii was built, like Caere (CERVETERI) and TARQUINIA (Tarquinii), on a defensible plateau. Evidence for Villanovan occupation is extensive, including individual settlements and several cemeteries. In the 6th century BC, Veii was known for its artistic output, particularly statuary. One artist, Vulca, received a commission from TARQUINIUS PRISCUS to sculpt a terracotta statue of JUPITER for the CAPITOLINE temple; he also made a statue of HERCULES at Rome. His workshop, if not he himself, sculpted many statues discovered at Veii's most famous sanctuary, the Portonaccio or temple of APOLLO, used for the cult of MINERVA in Roman times. The town's streets radiated from a centre nearer the north end of the plateau, with roads leading in different directions to neighbouring cities. Drainage systems in the valleys north of Veii, and waterworks on the citadel, testify to Etruscan engineering skill.

Veii's proximity to Rome dictated its history. During the 6th and 5th centuries BC, relations were cordial, though wall segments at key positions were built after 450. In 396, after a long siege, Rome sacked and annexed Veii, distributing its citizens into four new rural TRIBES. Veii's sanctuaries nevertheless remained places of worship. Until the 2nd century BC, the city retained some importance as a market town. It became the *municipium Augustum Veiens* c.2 BC, but declined during the imperial period. JV

See Haynes, S. (2000) *Etruscan Civilization*; Scullard, H. H. (1967) *The Etruscan Cities and Rome*.

 ETRURIA AND ETRUSCANS.

veiling Greek women routinely veiled their heads and sometimes their faces (evidence suggests that even SPARTAN women used veils). Veiling was part of a Greek ideology that required women to be socially invisible; by placing herself beneath a veil a woman was symbolically separated from society. The earliest attestations for veiling occur in HOMER, where the veil is the preserve of GODDESSES and royal women. However, by the classical period (in ATHENS) women of varying social strata are shown veiled with their mantles (*himatia*). In the 4th century BC a new type of veil appears. Called a *tegidion* (literally 'little roof'), it covered a woman's face, leaving only her eyes exposed. This type of veil is frequently found in hellenistic sources, but was particularly popular in ALEXANDRIA. Greek men also veiled themselves in *himatia* when their honour was at risk; this often occurs at times of crisis, when in mourning or when angry or shamed. The veil was also worn by Roman men as a mark of piety; a fold of the TOGA was pulled over the head during PRAYERS or SACRIFICE. A Roman woman veiled herself with a section of her *stola*; veiling was a hallmark of the *matrona*. Greek and Roman brides wore distinctive red-yellow veils, which Latin sources call the *flammeum*. LL-J

See Cairns, D. L. (2002) The meaning of the veil in ancient Greek culture, in L. Llewellyn-Jones, ed., *Women's Dress in the Ancient Greek World* 73–93; Llewellyn-Jones, L. (2003) *Aphrodite's Tortoise*.

Veleia Town in northern Italy, mod. Velleia near Lugagnago Val d'Arda, 30 km (19 miles) south of

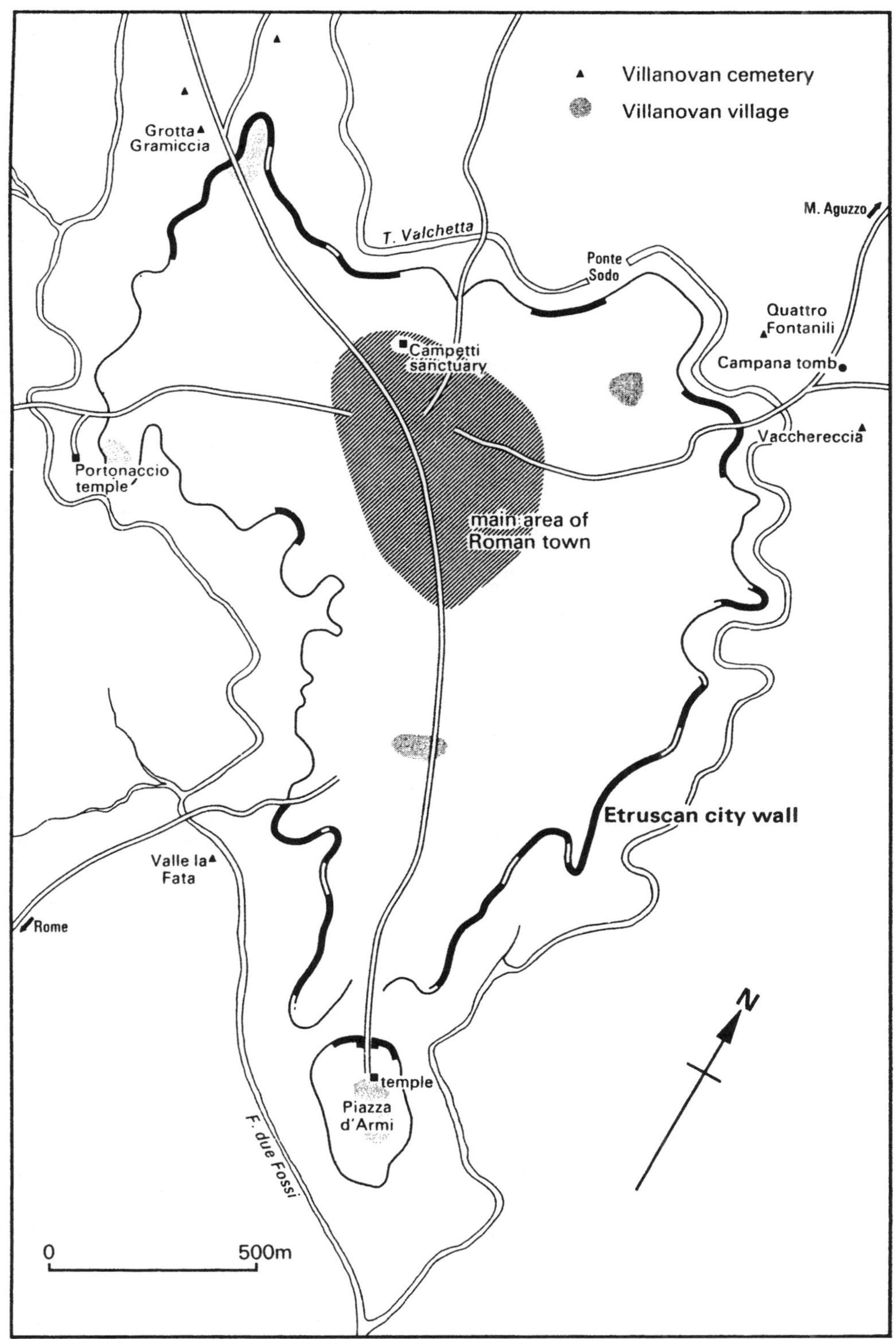

Veii: plan of the Etruscan city, showing location of main areas of preceding Villanovan activity.

Piacenza. The hilly landscape around Veleia was occupied by the Ligurians prior to the Roman conquest. The town's development seems to have taken place largely in the AUGUSTAN period, perhaps at the initiative of Lucius Calpurnius Piso (CONSUL 15 BC). Excavations at the site have revealed a well-preserved FORUM, a BATH complex and an area of housing. Along the south side of the forum lay the BASILICA, which produced a series of statues of members of the Julio-Claudian imperial family and of Piso himself. Two bronze documents were found here. The first, the *lex de Gallia Cisalpina*, lays out regulations for civil law in Cisalpine GAUL. The second, the Trajanic ALIMENTARY Table, records the arrangements for two schemes to support 300 poor children of the district. It allows us to reconstruct the agrarian history of the territory of Veleia, which extended as far as those of Luca and Libarna on the other side of the Apennines.

Veleia was noted for the longevity of its inhabitants, one of whom is said to have lived to the age of 150 (PLINY THE ELDER, *Natural History* 7.163). This information may be due as much to the low level of LITERACY among the population as to the healthy location of the city. JRP

Velleius Paterculus (20/19 BC–?c.AD 33) SENATORIAL historian of EQUESTRIAN origin (Aeclanum, Capua) who served in the East as military TRIBUNE partly under Gaius Caesar (d. AD 4). As *praefectus equitum* and legionary legate, he fought under TIBERIUS in the Balkans and GERMANY (AD 4–12), becoming QUAESTOR in AD 6. With his brother, and supported by both EMPERORS, he was among the first PRAETORS elected by the senate (for 15). He is not known to have held further posts, but probably in 30 he published patriotic histories in two books, of which part of the first and the second survive. He dedicated them to M. Vinicius (consul 30), under whose father he had served. The work slants history in favour of the ruling dynasty and current favourites, echoing official language, betraying apologetic tenseness over the role of Tiberius' minister SEJANUS (who shares features with SALLUST'S CATILINE), and intimating unease over the future. The bias of the work has been lambasted, but its content and style deserve the attention they are receiving. BML

See Sumner, G.V. (1970) The truth about Velleius Paterculus: prolegomena, *HSCP* 74: 257–97; Syme, R. (1984) Mendacity in Velleius, in *Roman Papers*, vol. 3, 1090–104; Woodman, A. J. (1977, 1983) *Velleius Paterculus, Historia Romana*.

Veneti see NORICUM.

Venetia see ITALY, ROMAN.

Venus Roman GODDESS of LOVE and erotic desire. The unattested noun *venus* probably originally denoted the charming quality of a religious supplication (*veneratio*) that allowed the worshipper to obtain divine favour (*venia*). At some early date this quality was anthropomorphized as a goddess, who by the 4th century BC was identified with Greek APHRODITE. There is no evidence for a public cult of Venus in Rome until the beginning of the 3rd century. Thereafter her importance rapidly increased, as her mythic role as the mother of AENEAS caused her to be regarded as the ancestral goddess of the Roman people. She was strongly associated with female SEXUALITY; one of her epithets was Verticordia, which Roman writers understood to mean 'turning the hearts of women to chastity', and her FESTIVALS were celebrated by both PROSTITUTES and matrons. In the 1st century BC, political leaders increasingly exploited her role as ancestress of the Roman people. SULLA boasted of her favour, and POMPEY built a temple to Venus Victrix. CAESAR, whose family traced their ancestry to AENEAS' son Iulus, claimed a special kinship with her and dedicated a temple to Venus Genetrix, 'the Ancestress'. HADRIAN'S massive temple to Venus and Roma further emphasized her political role. The widespread popularity of her cult, however, depended more on her associations with love and sexuality. Dedications are common throughout the Western empire, and numerous representations of the goddess have been found in all regions. JBR

See Dumézil, G. (1970) *Archaic Roman Religion*; Staples, A. (1998) *From Good Goddess to Vestal Virgins*.

Vercingetorix King of the Arverni, a Gallic tribe, and general of the confederation against JULIUS CAESAR in 52 BC. For several years, the CELTIC tribesmen that constituted his army kept Caesar at bay. Vercingetorix was an able leader, and adopted the policy of retreating to heavy, natural FORTIFICATIONS and burning the Gallic towns to keep Roman soldiers from living off the land. Caesar and his chief lieutenant, Labienus, lost in several engagements. Ultimately, however, Vercingetorix's army was surrounded by Caesar's while penned into the hilltop FORTRESS of Alesia in GAUL. They slowly starved as they watched Caesar build a palisade of stakes around their refuge and another around the Roman army as a defence against other Gauls who came to reinforce Vercingetorix and raise the SIEGE. The Romans kept up the siege for over a year, forcing Vercingetorix and his starving men to surrender. The warrior king was led captive back to Rome and imprisoned for several years, before finally being led in chains as a foreign captive in Caesar's military TRIUMPH of 46. After this ostentatious display of captured booty, he was ritually strangled. His career shows how dangerous the Gallic nations were to Rome, though once conquered, they quickly yielded to foreign rule. He is remembered today in France as a symbol of national freedom. LL-J

See Harmand, J. (1984) *Vercingetorix*.

Vergil see VIRGIL.

Vergina Located at the foot of the Pierian mountains, overlooking the Haliakmon river and the Emathian plain, stands Vergína, ancient Aigai, capital of MACEDONIA. During the 8th and 7th centuries BC the site was occupied by the ILLYRIANS, whose graves have been found in the great cemetery that stretches northward from the city to the river. Around 650, Vergina was taken by the Macedonians under the first king of the Argead dynasty, Perdikkas I, who established his capital there. Archelaos (c.413–399) transferred the capital to PELLA, though Aigai remained the sacred burial ground of the kings and the location of important royal ceremonies.

Recent excavations have uncovered in the western part of the city a large PALACE, consisting of a Doric peristyle surrounded by rooms. Constructed in the second half of the 4th century, it forms the central part of a complex comprising an *AGORA* and THEATRE, the site of PHILIP II's assassination in 336. In the cemetery buried under tumuli (earthen mounds) are stone chamber TOMBS dating from the 4th century and the hellenistic period. Under the 'Great Tumulus' were discovered four such tombs, one of which may be the tomb of Philip. Its façade is decorated with Doric columns and a Doric frieze, above which stands a painted course depicting a HUNTING scene. Inside the main chamber, a MARBLE SARCOPHAGUS contained a golden chest, in which were found the charred bones of the deceased. FORENSIC reconstruction has plausibly identified them as the remains of Philip himself. Next to the sarcophagus lay the remains of a ceremonial COUCH and small IVORY heads carved in relief, perhaps depicting images of the royal family. CC

See Andronicos, M. (1984) *Vergina*; Ellis, J. R. (1986) *Philip II and Macedonian Imperialism*; Pedley, J. G. (2002) *Greek Art and Archaeology.*

 PHILIP II; MACEDONIA: (a).

Verginia In 450 BC at Rome, Verginia died at the hands of her father, Verginius. He killed her to preserve her modesty by preventing her from falling into the lustful hands of Appius Claudius, head of the decemvirs. The story is told by both LIVY (3.44–9) and DIONYSIOS OF HALIKARNASSOS (11.28–38) in the context of the struggle by the PLEBEIANS of Rome for greater political freedom from the PATRICIANS. The historical kernel of the story is that the decemvirs, commissioned by the SENATE to write down the laws as a concession to plebeian demands, failed to satisfy these demands and were forced to give way to the more radical reformers Valerius and Horatius. But over time this kernel had been embellished and romanticized in Roman tradition. A second decemvirate was set up to complete the codification of the TWELVE TABLES, headed by the tyrannical figure Appius, who acted as tyrant by demanding the sexual favours of a citizen's daughter. Thus Verginia became a second LUCRETIA, whose rape and death led to the expulsion of the last Roman king. In early accounts (DIODORUS 12.24), Verginius and Verginia are anonymous figures of patrician background. In the embellished versions of Livy and Dionysios, they are plebeians and Verginia is betrothed to Icilius, the first TRIBUNE, whose office had been suspended under the decemvirs. Livy's sources presented 'the story as a paradigm of a *causa liberalis* as defined in the Twelve Tables' (Ogilvie). Livy himself retains the legal aspects in a confused fashion, but concentrates on the episode's drama. CC

See Ogilvie, R. M. (1965) *A Commentary on Livy, Books 1–5.*

vermin see PESTS AND PEST CONTROL; WAREHOUSES.

Verona List see PROVINCES AND PROVINCIAL GOVERNMENT.

Verres Gaius Verres gained political prominence at Rome as a supporter of SULLA. His father may have been raised to SENATORIAL rank by Sulla, and although Verres initially opposed Sulla during the CIVIL WARS, he soon changed sides. He had a track record of corruption as legate in the province of CILICIA and as *praetor urbanus* (74 BC), but became notorious due to his behaviour as governor of SICILY (73–71). As an AGRICULTURALLY wealthy PROVINCE, and a major producer of grain for Rome, Sicily provided rich pickings for an extortionate governor. Verres conducted a reign of terror, robbing and assaulting Roman tax-collectors, looting valuables from TEMPLES and private individuals, and extorting money from both Italian and Sicilian landowners. His main targets were those with small and medium-sized estates, and he seems to have avoided antagonizing the large landowners; but his depredations were widespread, and of the major Sicilian cities only Messina, which reached an agreement with him, escaped his impositions. His governorship is documented by CICERO, who prosecuted him for extortion on his return to Rome in 70. Verres went into exile at Massalia (MARSEILLES) and never returned to Rome. KL

See Cicero, *Verrines*; Wilson, R. J. A. (1990) *Sicily under the Roman Empire.*

Verulamium see BOUDICA; BRITANNIA; BRITISH ISLES AND BRITONS; CAMULODUNUM.

Vespasian (Titus Flavius Vespasianus) 17 November AD 9–23 June 79 Vespasian was acclaimed EMPEROR of Rome on 1 July 69 by the troops at ALEXANDRIA in Egypt, in his 60th year. He ruled for a decade, during which stability was restored after the chaos of the 'Year of the Four Emperors', and handed on the empire peacefully to his sons, TITUS and DOMITIAN, to rule in their turn.

Vespasian and his elder brother were the first in their family to undertake SENATORIAL careers. Vespasian, indeed, trumpeted the 'mediocrity' of his family in order to present himself as a representative of the gentry of the Italian towns, who had come to dominate the SENATE in the early empire. He affected the bluff, no-nonsense values of that class in order to contrast with the exotic tastes of emperors like NERO. The Flavii came from Reate (mod. Rieti) and their fortunes were based on moneylending, shrewd MARRIAGES, and connections in the PALACE (Antonia, mother of CLAUDIUS). Beginning his career under TIBERIUS, Vespasian rose steadily. On CLAUDIUS' invasion of BRITAIN, he was responsible for the capture of the Isle of Wight. Out of favour for a time, he re-emerged in the 60s and was appointed by Nero to deal with the JEWISH revolt in 66. From his vantage-point in the East he was able to pick his own moment to bid for the empire. The victory was won by his subordinates before he himself returned to Rome in 70.

His relatively uneventful reign included the restoration of the imperial finances through increased TAXATION, and the building of the Flavian AMPHITHEATRE, the Colosseum. All emperors have witty sayings ascribed to them; Vespasian's are more enduring than most, such as 'It does not stink' (on the money raised by his tax on the urine used in DYEING and FULLING); 'Alas, I think I am becoming a god' (while dying); and 'An emperor should die standing up' (his last words). JJP

See Cassius Dio, books 65–6; Suetonius, *Vespasian*; Tacitus, *Histories*; Levick, B. (1993) *The Emperor Vespasian.*

 EMPERORS, ROMAN: (a).

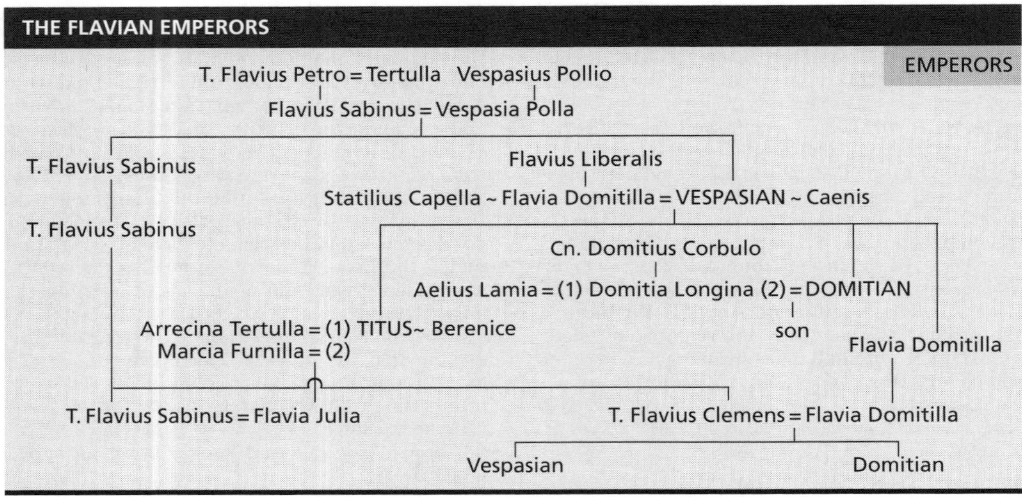

VESPASIAN: stemma of the Flavian dynasty.

Vesta Roman goddess of the hearth fire. Her cult, also attested in other parts of LATIUM, was of great antiquity, traditionally attributed to ROMULUS or NUMA. The ancient association of her name with that of the Greek goddess Hestia may be correct. Vesta was worshipped in both domestic and civic cult. Her public shrine, a circular building in the FORUM, housed no cult statue but rather a sacred fire that was never allowed to go out; its permanence was one of the great symbols of Rome's eternity. The shrine also included a secret inner sanctum containing, among other things, the public PENATES and the palladium, a wooden image of Athena supposedly brought from Troy. The cult was maintained by a priestly college, the VESTAL VIRGINS. Their chief regular duties were tending the sacred fire and preparing the salted grain (*mola salsa*) used in public sacrifices; hence the Vestalia on 9 June became a holiday for BAKERS and MILLERS. The cult endured until the end of the 4th century AD. JBR

See Dumézil, G. (1970) *Archaic Roman Religion*.

 RELIGION: (b).

Vestal virgins Virgin priestesses of VESTA. LIVY relates that Rhea Silvia, mother of ROMULUS, was a Vestal (1.3), and their PRIESTHOOD was said to have been instituted by NUMA (PLUTARCH, *Numa* 10). In historical times there were six Vestals, who constituted the only female priesthood in Rome. They were selected – usually from SENATORIAL families – by the *pontifex maximus* when they were aged between six and ten. Their period of service was 30 years, during which time they were required to remain virgins, though they might marry thereafter. Unchastity was punished by entombing the offender alive, a punishment otherwise unprecedented in Roman ritual. There were executions of Vestals in 216 and 114 BC; the last recorded instance was under DOMITIAN. Lesser offences, such as allowing the undying fire to go out, were punished by a flogging from the *pontifex maximus*.

Vestals were distinguished by their DRESS. In certain respects – the long dress (*stola*) and bands around the head (*vittae*) – they resembled the traditional Roman matron, but in others, notably the HAIRSTYLE, they suggested a bride. Their legal status was also distinctive: their person was sacred, they were emancipated from their father's tutelage (*patria potestas*), and they were permitted to write WILLS. JRCC

See Aulus Gellius 1.12; Beard, M. (1980) The sexual status of Vestal virgins, *JRS* 70: 12–27; Staples, A. (1998) *From Good Goddess to Vestal Virgins*.

veterans Most Greek states of the archaic and classical periods called upon their citizens to do military service as circumstances demanded. The Romans instituted a system of conscription, which generally required 16 years' military service. Veterans often served another four years in a special veterans' regiment (*vexillum veteranorum*). During the REPUBLIC it was common for veterans to be settled on expropriated land in conquered territories, but there were drawbacks to this system. Many veterans, in receipt of or in expectation of land, displayed greater loyalty to their GENERALS than to the STATE. Hence, in 60 BC, the SENATE was reluctant to ratify land grants made by POMPEY to his veterans; there were also problems with the locals in whose lands the veterans were settled. AUGUSTUS required 20 years' military service, after which discharged veterans received a cash bonus. The length of service soon rose to 25 or 26 years. But veterans continued to be settled in *coloniae* in the PROVINCES. Thus, like the CLERUCHS of the ATHENIAN EMPIRE or the MERCENARIES deposited in military colonies (*katoikiai*) in the empires of ALEXANDER and his SUCCESSORS, veterans provided a military reserve in times of need. In battle they could be a steadying influence on less experienced troops, but in the camp they were often disruptive, if not seditious. Although conditions of service were different in Greek and hellenistic armies, the Argyraspids, veterans of the wars of Alexander and his early Successors, were not far different from SOLDIERS like Spurius Ligustinus, a long-serving centurion described by Livy 42.34. WH

See Keppie, L. (1984) *The Making of the Roman Army*; Webster, G. (1979) *The Imperial Roman Army.*

Vienne see RHÔNE.

villages Smaller nucleated rural settlements, 'villages' by modern analogy, were common throughout the ancient world, with statuses like *kômê* in the Greek world and *vicus* or *pagus* in the Latin-speaking world. These categories encompassed a much wider range of communities than 'village', including substantial settlements that we might call 'small towns' even if they lacked formal CITY status. Likewise, just as we might call a small *polis* a village in geographical terms, the Greeks could call a place both *polis* and *kômê* to indicate its small size. Classical Greece, however, contained relatively few middle-sized settlements of this kind (Hansen). Sometimes village communities lay within the territories and control of Greco-Roman cities and were administrative sub-units of *polis* territory; the DEMES (*dêmoi*) of Attica are a good example. Others were independent communities, in regions where cities were fewer and/or less important. Southern SYRIA, JUDAEA and Egypt are areas where villages remained an important settlement category outside the direct control of Greco-Roman cities.

Classical Greek authors use 'village' terminology more frequently of foreign (especially eastern) settlements, and generally more often in the hellenistic and Roman periods than earlier. Village communities of the Roman–Byzantine East are well documented. Asia Minor has provided a wealth of EPIGRAPHIC evidence for sophisticated internal organization (see especially *SEG* 38.1462 from Oinoanda, dated AD 125, trs. in Mitchell 1990), with village magistrates employing titles such as *dêmarchos*. Inscriptions from southern Syria show similar internal complexity. Roman–Byzantine *kômê* sites on the limestone massif east of Antioch have survived particularly well. Village sites in Egypt, like KARANIS in the FAYÛM, offer both PAPYROLOGICAL evidence of administration and ARCHAEOLOGICAL evidence of daily life. The eastern communities labelled village (modern) and/or *kômê* (ancient) are extremely diverse. Most were primarily AGRICULTURAL; some had public buildings (BATHS at Sergilla, TEMPLES at Karanis); most were unplanned, but some (Androna in eastern Syria) provide evidence of regular TOWN PLANNING. Some (notably in Egypt) were survivals of pre-Greco-Roman settlement patterns; others (Androna) developed during the hellenistic, Roman and Byzantine periods.

Villages in the Roman empire were not exclusively an Eastern phenomenon. Communities spanning the range of small town to village are well documented in Western provinces like GAUL and BRITAIN. In Britain villages (as opposed to 'small towns') were largely a phenomenon of the later ROMAN EMPIRE, often associated with later imperial changes in land tenure. In some cases (Kingscote, Gloucestershire) they developed around focal VILLA sites, perhaps housing dependants of the owner. Elsewhere (Catsgore, Gloucestershire) they appear as independent communities with relatively homogeneous houses for peasants or tenants. NDP

See Hanley, R. (2000) *Villages in Roman Britain*; Hansen, M. H. (1995) Kome, in M. H. Hansen and K. Raaflaub, eds., *Studies in the Ancient Greek Polis* 45–81; Mitchell, S. (1990) Festivals, games, and civic life in Roman Asia Minor, *JRS* 80: 183–93; (1993) *Anatolia* 176–97; Osborne, R. (1987) *Classical Landscape with Figures*.

villas The villa was a country or suburban house, usually but not invariably a farm, which used ARCHITECTURAL motifs of Greco-Roman inspiration to display status. Roman sources recognize the existence of a hierarchy of RURAL SETTLEMENT, which in addition to villas also included huts (*tuguria*) and other buildings (*aedificia*). There is no precise ARCHAEOLOGICAL definition of a villa, though it is unusual for Roman farmhouses with STONE walls, painted wall-plaster and tiled roofs not to be described as such. In Roman BRITAIN, where over 1,500 so-defined villa sites have provisionally been identified, these make up c.15 per cent of rural settlement sites.

The villa was a favourite subject in Roman literature, in which the country residence was a source of rural pleasures, such as HUNTING and gentleman farming; a place of retreat from the pressures of urban life where friends and guests could be received; a source of social power through the dependency of local tenants and clients; and the centre of a productive estate managed for profit.

Wealth and status derived from the ownership of property, and the social and economic life of the Roman ÉLITE required an involvement in both town and country affairs. Although the rural landscapes of Italy and Greece had long been populated by small farmsteads, villa development was essentially a product of the introduction of urban values into the countryside. There was a close relationship between villa and urban architecture and between the process of URBANIZATION and the spread of villa life. Villas were more frequent around administratively important centres than in more remote areas, and their distribution reflects social considerations more than economic. The need for a high-status country mansion was more evidently a feature of Italian urban society than it had been in the earlier hellenistic world. In the Greek-speaking East, villas were generally a Roman introduction, and mostly comparatively late.

The development of villa estates in Italy and the Western provinces was much encouraged by imperial growth in the 2nd and 1st centuries BC. The investment of profits in land, the ready availability of SLAVE LABOUR, and the creation of new markets for certain classes of rural produce (notably WINE and OIL) promoted the development of large country estates. It was increasingly common for members of the élite to own a multiplicity of villas. The scattered nature of landholding added emphasis to the need for bailiffs and slave labour (or, later, sharecroppers) to work the estates.

The writings of VARRO and COLUMELLA, among others, define a variety of villa types. Some were exclusively places for luxurious living and entertaining (especially suburban and maritime villas). More commonly the villa was also a place of agricultural activity where the decorated reception and living quarters (the 'urban part', *pars urbana*) were set

VILLAS: (a) mosaic depiction of villa estate from Tabarka, Tunisia.

VILLAS: (b) reconstruction of a winged corridor villa at Mehring, Germany.

VILLAS: (c) general view of the well-preserved Vesuvian villa at La Regina, Boscoreale.

alongside a working farm (the *pars rustica*). In some cases, farm buildings stood alone and, though of impressive scale, were not attached to a luxurious residence; these were working estates, more probably under the management of a bailiff (*vilicus*).

The very smallest villas, which could include half-timbered and mudbrick structures, consisted of a single range of six or seven rooms distinguished only by modestly painted walls. In contrast suburban and maritime villas – such as Oplontis, the Villa of Mysteries outside POMPEII, or HADRIAN's villa at TIVOLI – were among the most palatial of Roman houses. These were usually set over an elevated platform on rising ground, with a southerly or easterly aspect. Views over water, especially the sea, were also preferred. Buildings were planned to exploit such views to the full, with colonnaded verandas laid out along the principal façades of the house, whose plan was also adapted to present well-lit corner rooms.

Villas of the late Republic and early empire were frequently built around a central circulation and reception space, including a hall (*atrium*) and colonnaded court (*peristylium*), similar to contemporary townhouses. Porticoes and peristyles were given greater prominence after the SOCIAL WAR, when most of the grander villas were built. Many of these early villas did not survive the 2nd century AD. Villas also flourished in the later Roman period, especially the 4th and 5th centuries, when greater emphasis was given to the group of principal reception rooms opening onto one or more formal courtyards (as at Piazza Armerina in SICILY).

At many sites in the north-western PROVINCES, free-standing building ranges were set around two or three sides of a courtyard. In some instances an outer courtyard provided space for further structures. The main house, usually set at the far end of the inner court, contained the principal living quarters. This building was frequently fronted by a colonnade and flanked by a pair of projecting pavilions, a building type known as a 'winged-corridor villa'. Such houses typically contained about 8–12 rooms, though several were considerably larger. Outbuildings could include bath-houses, wine and oil-presses, barns, workshops, sleeping quarters for slaves, and subsidiary houses. In Britain, many villa sites also included lofty aisled halls, which were used as barns and workshops and sometimes provided additional accommodation.

At Anthée (near Namur, Belgium), 20 separate buildings were arranged around the outer courtyard. A large workforce would have been housed and employed here. Some sites were provided with two or three separate bath-houses, suggesting that these were separately reserved for different social groups dependent on the estate. There has been speculation that divided inheritances may have seen some villas subdivided into different households.

The close relationship between villas and urban civilization was to mean that where urbanism faltered and failed, in late antiquity, this was also the case for the surrounding villas. Although some structures were later adapted or built over to form medieval farmsteads and villages, there is little archaeological evidence for continuity of occupation on most excavated sites. DP

See Percival, J. (1976) *The Roman Villa*; Smith, J.T. (1997) *Roman Villas: a study in social structure.*

Boscoreale; rural settlement; field survey: (b).

Vindolanda Roman name for a fort at Chesterholm in northern England, initially constructed in the Flavian period (c.AD 90) on an east–west road (the Stanegate) that preceded Hadrian's wall across the Tyne–Solway isthmus. This site was not totally abandoned when the wall was constructed 3 km (2 miles) to the north, but went through several further phases of military occupation from the AD 120s to 400, accompanied by the growth of a substantial civil community (*vicus*). Extensively excavated since the 1930s, the site is one of the best places to appreciate the aspect and lifestyle of a Roman frontier outpost. Beneath and to the west of the well-preserved stone forts, with typical playing-card plan, exploratory trenches have revealed traces of a sequence of turf-and-timber forts dating to c.80–120. The first fort was occupied from the early 80s until c.92, when it seems to have been enlarged to at least 3.24 ha (8 acres). This second fort went through at least four main structural phases until it was abandoned in the 120s, prior to the construction of the first stone fort. The garrison in the earliest phase appears to have been the 1st Tungrian cohort, followed later by the 9th Batavian cohort, both units being originally recruited from people in the lower Rhine region. There are indications that the garrison situation was highly fluid, with troops frequently out-stationed; men of the 3rd Batavian cohort may also have been based at Vindolanda for part of the period.

Due to unusual environmental and hydrological conditions, the preservation of organic materials in these pre-Hadrianic levels is exceptional, revealing not only many details of the construction of timber and wattle-and-daub buildings, but also well-preserved bracken floor-covering and an astonishing range of everyday artefacts. The finds include a remarkable archive of wooden writing tablets, many being thin, postcard-sized slivers of beech, alder or oak, written upon in ink. Several thousand have been found, ranging from small fragments to complete documents of several linked tablets, with over 250 substantial texts so far reconstructed. There are also numerous wax stylus tablets, but these are harder to decipher. The tablets provide a vivid window onto Roman garrison life: from duty and strength rosters to military reports (one describes the 'wretched little Brits'), requests for leave and for advancement, accounts of food held or disbursed by the quartermaster, private correspondence relating to the commanding officer and his family (e.g. Flavius Cerialis), lists of domestic equipment, and letters between soldiers and their friends and families. One letter-writer complains that the recipient is a 'neglectful man, who has sent me not even one letter'. Another mentions a present of sandals, socks and underpants. Another alludes to complicated wheeler-dealing in military supplies. Perhaps most evocative of all is the plaintive plea from an outposted band of soldiers who write to check whether they can all return to the comforts of the fort, failing which they request that they be sent more beer! DJM

See Birley, A. (2002) *Garrison Life at Vindolanda*; Bowman, A. (1994) *Life and Letters on the Roman Frontier.*

 Sulpicia Lepidina.

vine Vinifera species of grapes (*Vitis vinifera sativa*) were known to the Mycenaean Greeks, but only with the advent of the *polis* did such domesticated cultivars, which produce larger and better fruits, become truly ubiquitous. The classical Greeks planted vineyards from the Black sea to Crete, and from southern Italy to northern Asia Minor. Along with olives and grains, they became part of the great triad of Greek agronomy, an agricultural diversity that helped to make the ancient rural household self-sufficient and the city-state prosperous. Vines could grow well in difficult terrain and on poor soils, were resistant to extremities of temperature and humidity, and provided the farmer with in-season fresh fruit and juices, storable raisins and non-perishable wine. The spring prunings can be used as fuel or mulch, and the leaves in cooking.

The wide variety of soil and weather conditions in Greece and Italy allowed for regional specialization, and the Aegean islands, the bay of Naples and Campania gained a Mediterranean-wide reputation for premium vintages. Greek and Roman agricultural writers developed a keen appreciation of the combination of climate, soil and vine species necessary to produce premium grapes, and their treatises attest to the mastery of viticulture from the arts of trellising, fertilization, pruning and pest management to the intricacies of pressing and processing. The Greeks and Romans saw viticulture as emblematic of their culture at large, whose stable populations, sturdy yeomen and fiercely independent rural communities were the natural dividends of the time, patience, expertise and investment necessary to grow good grapes. VDH

See Amouretti, M.-C. and Brun, J.-P., eds. (1993) *La Production du vin et de l'huile en Méditerranée.*

violence Public violence was a regular feature of Greek and Roman societies. The public killing of

ANIMALS either for SACRIFICE or for entertainment, the public punishment of children and SLAVES, the public execution of convicts and prisoners of war, the spectacle of armed men fighting, perhaps to the death, are seldom seen any more in the countries of western Europe and North America. Yet they are all sights that could readily have been seen in the Greek and Roman world. The violence seems ubiquitous. Greek MYTHS, both divine and heroic, often centre on acts of violence. ZEUS and the OLYMPIANS, for example, forcefully replaced Kronos and the Titans, as Kronos had previously overthrown Ouranos. Heroic myths are equally violent, frequently involving warfare, itself an immediate experience for many Greek and Roman men, whose civic duty it was to serve in the army in times of war. The fighting was face-to-face and brutal. Greek ATHLETICS, especially the combat sports (boxing, wrestling and *pankration*) were often bloody and occasionally fatal; Romans regularly saw men and animals killed for pleasure in public spectacles. The scale only increased over time: AUGUSTUS claimed that he compelled 10,000 GLADIATORS to fight and killed 3,500 animals during his long reign. TRAJAN reached these numbers in just one extended celebration. Indeed, many modern scholars have had some difficulty reconciling the apparent contradiction between Greece and Rome as civilizing forces on the one hand, and their willingness to condone and even enjoy such public violence on the other. Yet it was not long ago that modern western countries tolerated, even enjoyed, public executions, and there still exists violence in sport and cruelty to animals. Moreover, to apply modern values to the ancient Greeks and Romans would be to misunderstand their motivations.

The Greeks and Romans tended to regard animals, which were deemed to be without reason, and outsiders, who were without rights, as legitimate objects of violence. Thus animals could be beaten, and slaves had to be TORTURED to exact reliable evidence from them for legal purposes. Roman gladiatorial *munera* and wild-beast fights (*venationes*) are the most obvious examples of ancient violence. These spectacles often included public executions as part of the show. But where modern readers see cruelty to animals and humans alike, the Romans saw expedient punishment and the elimination of a threat to society. Wild animals, however admirable, were a threat to human society as predators. Condemned men, BARBARIAN enemies or dropouts from society, such as early CHRISTIANS, were equally dangerous threats to the established order, and so were justifiably killed.

Many modern ANTHROPOLOGISTS and SOCIOLOGISTS have assumed that human violence is a universal feature of humanity. Some suggest that violent aggression is an instinctive impulse in human nature, while others instead see the predilection to violent acts as socially determined. R. Girard, in a classic study, linked violence to the sacred, and Burkert theorizes that the sacrifice of animals was a ritualized remembrance of our Palaeolithic prehistory as hunters. MJC

See Burkert, W. (1983) *Homo Necans*; Girard, R. (1977) *Violence and the Sacred*; Kyle, D. G. (1998) *Spectacles of Death in Ancient Rome*; Lintott, A. (1968) *Violence in Republican Rome*; Riches, D., ed. (1986) *The Anthropology of Violence*; Wistrand, M. (1992) *Entertainment and Violence in Republican Rome*.

Virgil (or Vergil; Publius Vergilius Maro) 70–19 BC Latin POET whose life spanned the events that led from the destruction of the Roman REPUBLIC to the establishment of the principate under Octavian (later AUGUSTUS). Virgil was one of the leading members of the generation of Latin poets who created a canon of works that could claim a status equal to that of the Greek classics. He was born in Andes, a VILLAGE near Mantua, and all of his works display a profound sense of attachment to Italian localities as well as to the city of Rome. The ancient lives record that his father's farm was confiscated in the land settlements that followed the Caesarians' victory over the tyrannicides at the battle of PHILIPPI in 42, an experience that may be reflected in *Eclogues* 1 and 9. Educated at CREMONA and MILAN, he was later associated with an EPICUREAN community near Naples. In antiquity a number of works, collected in the *Appendix Vergiliana*, were ascribed to the young poet, but almost all are certainly spurious. After the publication of his first major work, the *Eclogues*, composed probably in 42–39/8, he entered the circle of MAECENAS, Octavian's right-hand man, the dedicatee of the *Georgics*, composed probably in 36–30. The last ten years of his life were devoted to the *Aeneid*, which was left unfinished when he died at Brundisium on 20 September 19 after a journey to Greece. Augustus is said to have overruled his dying wish that the poem be burned, and it was edited for publication by Virgil's friends Varius Rufus and Plotius Tucca. He was buried at Naples.

The *Eclogues* are a group of ten pastoral poems of between 63 and 111 lines, modelled on the poems of the hellenistic bucolic poet THEOKRITOS. The book contains an alternation of dramatic poems, in which fictional herdsmen converse and exchange SONGS, and poems in which the poet himself introduces PASTORAL themes. In these exquisitely crafted and self-consciously riddling pieces, Virgil shows himself heir to the 'neoteric' school of poets of the generation of CATULLUS. But far from simply being specimens of an Alexandrian art for art's sake, the *Eclogues* also reflect the troubled events of the years following the assassination of JULIUS CAESAR. In addition to references to the land confiscations, the songs in *Eclogue* 5 on the death and apotheosis of Daphnis probably relate to the apotheosis of Julius Caesar. The oracular *Eclogue* 4, sometimes known as the 'Messianic *Eclogue*' because CHRISTIAN centuries believed it to contain a prophecy of the birth of Christ, uses the myth of the GOLDEN AGE to articulate hopes for a new beginning after the CIVIL WARS. In *Eclogues* 6 and 10 Virgil introduces into the fictional pastoral world his friend GALLUS, the first of the Latin love elegists.

Virgil's *Georgics* is a DIDACTIC poem on farming in four books (1 on field crops; 2 on trees and vines; 3 on large ANIMALS; 4 on BEES). The ultimate model is HESIOD's *Works and Days*, but Virgil draws largely on later Alexandrian didactic poems and on his Latin predecessor LUCRETIUS, as well as on KALLIMACHOS' *Aitia* and on VARRO's prose AGRICULTURAL treatise, *On Agriculture*. Neither a practical manual for smallholders nor a purely literary exercise, the poem uses man's relation to the agricultural and to the wider natural world to air themes of both contemporary and more universal interest. A Roman nostalgia for a simpler and more virtuous life in the countryside suggests an alternative to the chaotic impiety of the civil wars that ended with the defeat of ANTONY and CLEOPATRA in 31 at ACTIUM by Octavian, who appears in the *Georgics* as a saviour figure. The poem's themes are drawn together at the end, in a long mythological passage that narrates the miraculous regeneration by Aristaeus of the bees he had lost after causing the death of EURYDIKE (1). Her ultimately unsuccessful return from the Underworld through the power of ORPHEUS' MUSIC is told to Aristaeus by Proteus.

The *Aeneid* is an epic poem in 12 books on the wanderings and battles of the Trojan hero AENEAS, ancestor of Julius Caesar and Augustus. The narrative runs from the time of his flight from the sacked city of TROY, with his father and son and the GODS of Troy, to his foundation of a Trojan settlement in Italy and killing of an Italian enemy Turnus, rival for the hand of the Italian princess Lavinia. The poem's legendary subject tells of the origins of Rome, and allusively sketches out a future history in which the race descended from the defeated Trojans will come to rule the world. The poem also manifests a literary imperialism through its rewriting of HOMER's *Odyssey* (in the wanderings of Aeneas in the first half of the *Aeneid*) and *Iliad* (in the war in Italy in the second) as the national EPIC of the Romans. But far from being a simple vehicle of nationalist and dynastic panegyric, the *Aeneid* dwells equally on the pains and sorrows both of Aeneas and his people and of those, like Dido and Turnus, who obstruct or oppose the god-given destiny of the Trojan exiles. Many modern readers respond more readily to the tragic and pessimistic qualities of the poem.

All three works are in hexameters. In hindsight they seem to form a natural progression from a humble to the grandest GENRE, symbolizing the developmental stages of society: pastoral, agricultural, martial and urban. The resulting 'myth' of the poet's career was acted out by later poets such as Spenser and Milton. From the time of Virgil's death his poems formed the centre of the Roman, and later the medieval and RENAISSANCE, European canon. In particular, his influence was decisive for the later history of pastoral and epic poetry. PRH

See Brooks, O. (1964) *Virgil*; Griffin, J. (1986) *Virgil*; Martindale, C. (1984) *Virgil and his Influence*.

virginity In Homer, a *parthenos* is a young woman who does not yet have the social status of a wife but may already have a child. In later Greek literature, *parthenos*, like Latin *virgo*, refers to someone who has not had sexual intercourse, almost invariably a female. Male virginity was not a concern until the early CHRISTIAN centuries. A female virgin's first intercourse was often described as 'spoiling' or 'corrupting' her, even if it was with her husband and even though many medical writers thought that postpubertal virginity was a health risk. Some advocated first intercourse as a remedy for menarche later than the 14th year. The underlying theory was that intercourse relaxed channels within the female body, allowing menstrual blood to be shed instead of causing dangerous pressure. Other medical writers, especially the gynaecologist SORANUS (1st–2nd centuries AD), were aware that puberty is not the same as being physically ready to have children and recommended delaying marriage to eighteen. But both Greeks and Romans were concerned that a bride should be virgin on her first MARRIAGE, to remove any doubt about the legitimacy of her children. PLUTARCH says that this is why Roman law set 12 as the age when a MARRIAGE is legally valid.

The Greek and Roman pantheon included virgin goddesses, notably ARTEMIS–DIANA, huntress and protector of young creatures, and ATHENA–MINERVA, warrior and intellectual. Neither provided a role model for women, or expected women (or men) to remain virgin in her service. In the *Hippolytos* of EURIPIDES, exclusive devotion to Artemis is an offence against APHRODITE. Hestia–VESTA, also a virgin goddess, symbolized the unmarried daughter who has not left her father's house and represents its hearth fire. She is not a major figure in Greek cult, whereas the VESTAL VIRGINS at Rome have no known parallel in Greek or Roman tradition. They served Vesta for 30 years, beginning when they were aged 6–10, and could in theory marry when their term ended. Some cults required a virgin PRIESTESS, but either she would serve for a fixed term before marriage, or a post-menopausal woman would symbolize virginity, as in the case of the Pythia at DELPHI, who could not be possessed by anyone but APOLLO.

The Christian church did not have the problem that service to one god excluded another. It gave support and prestige to women (and men) who chose to remain virgin. St PAUL said that the unmarried could concentrate on pleasing God, whereas the married had to think about spouses and house-holding. Christian literature increasingly emphasized the theme that virginity guards against corruption. Many writers insisted that physical virginity is not enough, arguing that the virgin dedicated to God must also avoid corruption by sensual thoughts and experiences. They found it offensive (and unreliable) that 'virginity tests' were used as a proof of chastity. From the 4th century on, the virginity of Mary, mother of Jesus, became a model of physical and spiritual integrity. GC

Viriathus Leader of the LUSITANIANS in Spain during their wars against the Romans in the 2nd century BC. He is said to have begun life as a SHEPHERD, and to have escaped from the slaughter of many Lusitanians by Servius Sulpicius Galba, the Roman commander in HISPANIA Ulterior, in 150. He became the leader of the Lusitanians in 147. After defeating two Roman PRAETORS in 147 and 146, he was temporarily checked by the CONSUL of 145, Quintus Fabius Maximus Aemilianus, in a battle in 144. After making contact with the CELTIBERIANS in the north, he won further victories against Roman armies in 142 and 141, which led to a peace being concluded. This, however, was rejected by the SENATE. The consul who had arranged for the negotiations to fail, Gnaeus Servilius Caepio, succeeded at last in dealing with Viriathus, but only by bribing three of his Lusitanian associates to assassinate him in 140. JSR

See Appian, *Iberian Wars*, 60.251–75.322.

virtue The exhibition of moral excellence, variously defined in different social and cultural contexts. The English word 'virtue' comes from the Latin *virtus*, which the Romans associated with the Greek concept of *aretê* ('goodness'). The earliest descriptions of *aretê*, from HOMER to PINDAR, see it as an

ARISTOCRATIC quality, dependent on birth and wealth, and associated with military and political accomplishments. The classical period saw debate on the nature of *aretê* that distanced it from its aristocratic origins. A capacity for *aretê* enabled a citizen to serve his community to the best of his ability. PHILOSOPHERS also investigated the concept, formulating notions such as the four cardinal virtues (prudence, justice, temperance and fortitude).

A similar trajectory was followed by the Roman concept of *virtus*. This term, which was cognate with *vir* (man), had connotations of manliness and courage and seems to have originated as an aristocratic quality, won through serving the state in politics or WAR. Modifications of the concept occurred under the pressure of ideas from Greek thought. Similarly, the challenge to aristocratic power in the late REPUBLIC led to a redefinition of the relationship of *virtus* to birth (SALLUST, *Jugurthine War* 85.38). Even so, virtue remained a desirable quality for the political ÉLITE, as emphasis on the virtues of Roman EMPERORS suggests. In late antiquity, the debate on virtue continued within a CHRISTIAN framework, so that 'theological' concepts such as faith, hope and charity joined the classical formulations. MDH

See Ferguson, J. (1958) *Moral Values in the Ancient World*.

Visigoths see ALARIC; GOTHS.

Vitellius see OTHO.

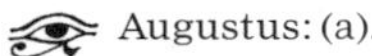 Augustus: (a).

Vitruvius An ARCHITECT and military ENGINEER known to JULIUS CAESAR. Some scholars have attempted to identify him with Mamurra, Caesar's *praefectus fabrum*, though there is insufficient evidence to support this. He was put in charge of the building and repair of war engines by AUGUSTUS, who treated him so generously that, free from all financial anxieties, he was able to devote himself to writing a treatise in ten books *On Architecture*, the only ancient work of this type still extant. In a fulsome tribute to Augustus he praises the emperor's interest in the provision of public buildings 'so that the majesty of the empire should find expression in the outstanding dignity of its public buildings' (book 1, pref. 2).

Vitruvius claims to have organized the muddled commentaries of previous writers (4, pref. 1). He deals with the general qualities needed in an architect and the principles of TOWN PLANNING (book 1); typical building materials and methods of construction (2); ORDERS of TEMPLE architecture, including rules of proportion (3–4); other public buildings, notably THEATRES (with a digression on harmony), BATHS, the PALAESTRA and HARBOURS (5); domestic buildings (6); interior decorations – pavements, STUCCO, WALL-PAINTING (7); WATER SUPPLY and the building of AQUEDUCTS (8); geometry, measurement and ASTRONOMY (9); and MACHINES for civil and military purposes (10). His purpose is partly didactic: 'I expounded to you' (the emperor) 'our profession and its qualities and the studies through which an architect should improve himself' (3, pref. 4; cf. 6, pref. 7). The work also serves to illustrate and emphasize the importance of architecture and engineering as respectable, professional subjects. He is keen that untrained men should not swagger around pretending to be architects (10, pref. 2). He intended *On Architecture* to be comprehensive. His ideal architect, in line with the non-specialist approach in the ancient world, would be a man of wide learning and experienced not only in draughtsmanship and MATHEMATICS, but also in history, PHILOSOPHY, MUSIC, MEDICINE, LAW and ASTRONOMY.

Vitruvius uses personal observation and experience, but draws heavily on the work of earlier Greek architects, notably Hermogenes (c.200 BC), and preserves important details from many lost Greek authors, particularly of the hellenistic period. He has curiously little to say about contemporary building projects in Rome, and is rather old-fashioned, emphasizing the value of traditional building materials and warning against excessive boldness in architectural method.

Little is known about Vitruvius' own architectural work. He designed and oversaw the construction of a BASILICA at Fanum Fortunae (Fano) in Umbria (5.1.6), and perhaps supervised other buildings in this Augustan colony, in which he displays a special interest. In fact, Vitruvius' fame rests on the *On Architecture*, which was already being used by PLINY THE ELDER in the later 1st century AD, and was very influential in the RENAISSANCE and afterwards. JBC

See Vitruvius, 2 vols., trs. F. Granger (1983–5); McKay, A. G. (1978) *Vitruvius*; Rowland, I. D. and Howe, T. N., eds. (1999) *Vitruvius, Ten Books on Architecture*.

volcanoes Unpredictable and powerful, volcanoes were a source of amazement and fear in antiquity. The earliest mythological explanations of their causes were soon replaced by more rational accounts, albeit strange-sounding to most people today. The substantial volcanic activity of southern Italy and SICILY may have influenced the PRESOCRATICS: the PYTHAGOREANS believed that a central fire existed within the earth, and Empedokles jumped into the crater of Mt Etna in an attempt to display godlike qualities. Speculation about volcanoes took a new direction when ARISTOTLE (*Meteorology* 3.8) described how winds, heated by the SUN and moving below the surface of the earth, could erupt forth in a fiery display. Roman scientists and observers continued to ponder the cause of volcanoes. In his description of what made Etna erupt, LUCRETIUS sustained the main elements of Aristotle's theory. Yet clearly this was not sufficient explanation for all: PLINY THE ELDER suffocated while attempting to observe at close proximity the eruption of Mt Vesuvius.

Two of the most famous eruptions in the MEDITERRANEAN world had devastating consequences. The eruption at THERA (mod. Santoríni) in c.1650 BC may have contributed to the end of MINOAN civilization. In Italy in AD 79, Vesuvius' blow-out buried several Roman towns including POMPEII, HERCULANEUM and Oplontis. For the ordinary Greek or Roman, however, the dangers of volcanoes were greatly outweighed by their considerable benefits. Fertile volcanic soil could be extensively cultivated, and sandy volcanic ash, known by the Italian term *pozzolana*, formed an essential ingredient in the manufacture of strong, waterproof cement. TJA

Volsci see CORIOLANUS; IMPERIALISM, ROMAN; PRAENESTE; SATRICUM.

Volterra see ETRURIA AND THE ETRUSCANS.

Volubilis see AFRICA, ROMAN.

Volusianus

EMPERORS, ROMAN: (b).

voting In the modern world the right to cast a vote is regarded as a fundamental characteristic of a working DEMOCRACY. In the ancient world voting was not primarily associated with a democratic form of government, and in the birthplace of democracy, Athens, selecting a suitable MAGISTRATE from a pool of candidates by drawing lots was viewed as more democratic than voting. In Athens, voting was used in the COUNCIL, ASSEMBLY, and LAWCOURTS, normally by show of hands in the council and assembly but by ballot in the courts (pebbles being dropped into urns). In SPARTA, where the political influence of the assembly was limited, voting took the form of acclamation. The ELECTION method designed for the Spartan council of elders involved a hidden panel of judges who tried to estimate the volume of applause given to each contestant by the assembly, a practice deemed childish by ARISTOTLE. Democracy survived in the hellenistic period, but probably with greater use of election than the lot. In Greek cities of the Roman period, however, there was a fossilized democracy in which candidates for office were selected and screened beforehand by the council, then presented to the assembly for approval.

In Rome, all adult male citizens had the right to vote to elect magistrates, make LAWS and declare WAR. A public meeting preceded the voting procedure, during which candidates were introduced or the matter in hand discussed. Then the crowd was told to disperse and to take up their positions in groups behind a rope. When called, the voters proceeded over raised gangways to cast their votes. Votes were always cast in assigned groups, and it was the majority of individual votes within the group that carried the group. A majority of groups decided the general vote on the proposal or the candidate. The lot decided which group was to vote first and the order in which the votes were announced. The first candidates to achieve a simple majority were declared elected. Originally each voter was asked orally for his vote by one of the officials, who put a mark against the name or decision. In an effort to contain intimidation and bribery, the secret ballot was introduced from 139 BC onwards, and from then on the voter marked his assent or dissent, or the name of the candidate whom he chose to support, on a wax tablet with a stylus. The tablets were subsequently assembled and then counted. For elections the chosen spot was the Campus Martius, where CAESAR planned a huge building, the Saepta Iulia, to house the election process. The building was eventually completed under the emperor AUGUSTUS by his trusted lieutenant AGRIPPA. Voting in assemblies continued into the PRINCIPATE, even though their political influence had faded. The elections of magistrates which took place in some cities in the Roman West, for example, POMPEII, were firmly controlled by the ÉLITE, in that actual voting behaviour was governed by localized PATRONAGE networks. Elections to the office of *duumvir* (the highest civic magistracy in most towns) went uncontested, since no more than two candidates stood for the two positions that were available. MK

See Staveley, E. S. (1972) *Greek and Roman Voting and Elections*.

vows Expressions of a wish, desire, voluntary promise or dedication. In classical antiquity, vows are generally associated with religious aspects of life. Like PRAYERS, vows were made aloud and in front of witnesses, cultivating the reciprocal relationship of the ancient community with their GODS. Vows and prayers share linguistic affinities in their address to the gods, and this link is also expressed by their shared name in Greek, *euchê*. Etymological cognates of the Latin word for a vow (*votum*, from the verb *vovere*), notably *ex voto* and *votivus*, evidently relate a vow to make an offering to the gods to the outcome itself, the object dedicated. Both a vow and an offering were regular expressions of gratitude to, and acknowledgement of, the divine, but they could also be exceptional promises made to the gods at critical moments. Formal, public vows were taken regularly by Roman MAGISTRATES at the beginning of every year, or for the health and safety of the EMPERORS.

A further interesting connotation of the ancient concept of a vow is revealed by the etymological link between the Latin *votum* and the English verb 'to vote'. In this case, casting a vote resembles the act of expressing a vow or wish, whose fulfilment is expected at the end of the process. EP

See Eisenhut, W. (1974) Votum, in *RE* Suppl. 14: 964–73; Orlin, M. E. (1997) *Temples, Religion and Politics in the Roman Republic*; Versnel, H. S. (1981) *Faith, Hope and Worship*.

EPIGRAPHY, ROMAN: (b).

Vulcan see GODS AND GODDESSES, ROMAN.

wall-painting The art of wall-painting was already well established in Egypt and the AEGEAN during the 2nd millennium BC. In classical Greece the most famous murals were those of Polygnotos and Mikon in various public buildings in Athens and DELPHI (second quarter of 5th century BC). These grand multi-figure MYTHOLOGICAL and historical compositions no longer survive, but can be visualized from the descriptions of PAUSANIAS and from echoes in contemporary VASE-PAINTINGS. They were evidently executed on wooden hoardings, with COLOURS applied over a white primer. The more characteristic support for wall-painting in Greece and Rome (as in the Bronze Age Aegean) was PLASTER. Painting on plaster was normally in the fresco technique, which was brought to new levels of sophistication during the late hellenistic period, with polychrome decorations burnished to achieve a surface-sheen.

Decorative fashions in wall-painting can be traced in detail from the 2nd century BC to the late 1st century AD, thanks to the hundreds of frescoes preserved at POMPEII and HERCULANEUM. The so-called Pompeian First Style, a version of a style found throughout the hellenistic world, used not only colour but relief, working the plaster in imitation of blocks of drafted masonry which were then painted to suggest exotic stones. The Second Style, which evolved around 100 BC, reproduced ARCHITECTURE by purely pictorial means, using shading and perspective to construct grand colonnaded edifices which opened the wall in illusions of space. The Third Style, introduced under AUGUSTUS, closed the wall once more. Architectural forms were reduced to insubstantial framing devices, and emphasis was placed on broad areas of colour tricked out with miniaturist ornament. A major innovation of this phase was the central picture, generally a scene from Greek

WALL-PAINTING: (a) example of Second Style from the Oplontis Villa.

WALL-PAINTING: (b) example of Fourth Style from Herculaneum.

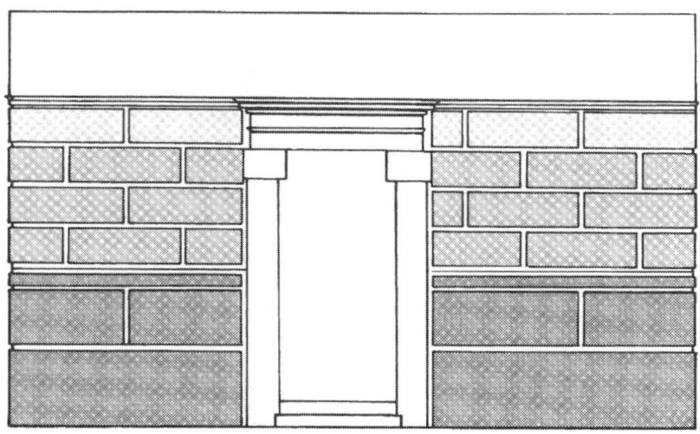

First 'Masonry'

Second 'Architectural'

Third 'Closed'

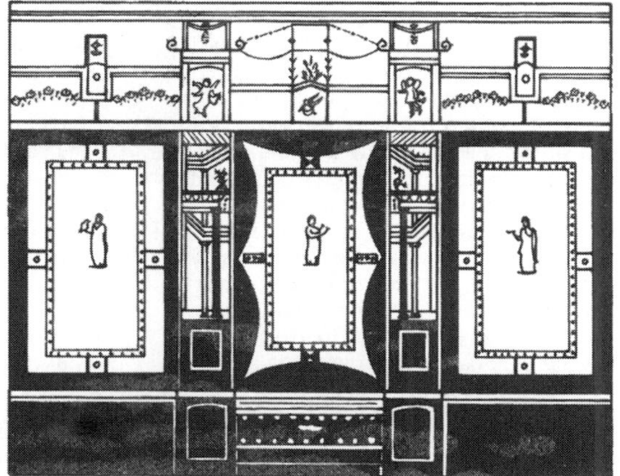

Fourth 'Fantastic'

WALL-PAINTING: (c) the four styles of wall-painting, as defined from discoveries at Pompeii and Herculaneum.

myth loosely based on an 'old master' panel-picture. In the Fourth Style, which emerged in the mid-1st century AD, the flimsy pavilions of the Third Style were retained but with a new sense of space which lent itself to the creation of a soaring fantasy ARCHITECTURE, golden yellow in colour and populated by small figures and ANIMALS.

After Pompeii there were various fashions of architectural wall-painting, but some of the more interesting paintings were those applied on ceilings, where the ubiquitous cross-vaults engendered designs which stressed the diagonals. In the 3rd century AD, a desire for cheaper effects led to the popularity of simple systems of panels framed by red and green lines on a white ground. Even before this, architectural schemes with figure paintings had never been the exclusive mode of decoration. They were at the top of a hierarchy, reserved for the best rooms, while less richly coloured schemes containing landscapes, still lifes and other minor subjects were relegated to lesser rooms. These variations, for which decorators probably operated a sliding scale of costs, are of great interest for the light they shed on the relative importance of rooms and the way space was organized in ROMAN HOUSES. RJL

See Ling, R. (1991) *Roman Painting*.

war A dominant fact of life throughout classical antiquity, though some societies, such as SPARTA and ROME, made a particular art form of it.

Relatively few 'manuals' on the Greek approach to war survive (see XENOPHON; AENEAS TACTICUS), but warfare and its effects are recurrent themes of Greek historical writings and literature. Literary depictions are not always an accurate depiction of reality. At the time of HOMER's evocation of heroic war in the *Iliad*, the Greek world was already starting to embrace a radically different style of fighting, involving the armoured infantry phalanx (so-called HOPLITES), with an emphasis on thrusting weapons over missiles and relatively low casualties. Much warfare involved local struggles between neighbouring CITY-STATES, with male citizens called up to fight. The history of the Greek *poleis* can be traced as a shifting pattern of ALLIANCES, campaigns and TREATIES, with two dominant powers emerging. The Spartan hoplites, leaders of the PELOPONNESIAN LEAGUE, were supreme in land warfare in the later 6th to early 4th centuries BC. Being few in number, however, and having constructed their society in a way that precluded major expansion of the citizen body, they paradoxically became more reluctant to engage in continuous warfare. Athens in the 5th century, on the other hand, developed the capability of its NAVY, allowing it to carry war overseas and construct an AEGEAN empire. The main PELOPONNESIAN WAR (431–404) was the ultimate trial of strength of these contrasting styles, with the Athenians acknowledging Spartan dominance on land by retreating inside their FORTIFICATIONS and relying on their sea power to maintain supplies for the city and to harass Spartan interests. The war also brought light-armed troops into greater prominence, often men from less urbanized areas of Greece, such as Thrace and Crete, who fought in alliance with the leading powers and gave them greater tactical flexibility. Only when Sparta invested heavily in naval power too was the impasse broken, with the collapse of the ATHENIAN EMPIRE.

The sudden decline of Sparta a generation later was followed by the emergence of Macedonia as the dominant power in Greece in the mid-4th century. The 4th and 3rd centuries saw the increased integration of MERCENARY soldiering with the military arm of the *polis*. Leaders such as AGESILAOS, IPHIKRATES and KONON could combine a career in the service of their *polis* with spells in the service of the highest bidder, usually a non-Greek power. Within democratic Athens, GENERALS were now often military specialists, distinct from the orators who advanced policy debates. Another development of the Peloponnesian war and 4th century was SIEGE warfare, leading to more elaborate fortifications. The momentous conquests of ALEXANDER, after he irrupted deep into the PERSIAN EMPIRE, were based in part on the addition of a more powerful CAVALRY arm onto a variant of the traditional phalanx. The 40-year wars of Alexander's SUCCESSORS saw the Macedonian army fragmented into separate parts, which became effectively mobile military machines not necessarily tied to any region; in order to be a king it was almost more important to have an army than a territory. The ANTIGONID, PTOLEMAIC and SELEUKID dynasties that were now established engaged in frequent clashes (notably the SYRIAN WARS), with BATTLES often involving very large multi-ethnic contingents, even sometimes supported by elephants. The scale of hellenistic warfare also entailed widespread settlement of time-served VETERANS, either superimposed on existing Greek cities or planted in new localities in Egypt and western Asia – effectively a new Greco-Macedonian COLONIZATION movement. The Greek *poleis* of the homeland retained little autonomy in defence and attack; military service was now closely bound up with service in a king's army, though there were periodic revolts against Macedonian domination, particularly spearheaded by the ACHAEAN LEAGUE. Whether the Successor kingdoms wore themselves out by mutual hostilities, or whether the Roman LEGION was simply decisively better than the Macedonian phalanx, Rome made inexorable progress towards total domination of the eastern Mediterranean from the late 3rd century onwards.

Late hellenistic treatises on warfare survive by the Greek authors Asklepiodotos (a pupil of POSIDONIUS) and Onasander (a 1st-century AD PHILOSOPHER). While the former emphasizes the theoretical composition of the phalanx, preserving some interesting historical nuggets, the latter, addressed to a Roman general, is more concerned with the character of the good commander and with military psychology as well as stratagems. The last is also the concern of the Greek author POLYAINOS (2nd century AD).

War was at the very heart of Roman society and politics, with many institutions constructed around militaristic ideals. Military service was initially required of all eligible CITIZENS and demanded of allies, while the Roman ÉLITE competed for the honour of leading the armies into battle. Throughout long stretches of the regal period and the REPUBLIC, they waged campaigns on an annual basis – an extraordinary martial commitment in a basically agrarian society. They also devised means of spreading their militaristic view of the world, and of growing their military strength, by the assimilation of defeated opponents into their citizen body or as allies providing troops.

From the 4th century BC the Romans enjoyed increasing success in war and conquered the other peoples and communities of the Italian peninsula. From the 3rd century, they launched themselves onto the MEDITERRANEAN stage with their epic struggles with CARTHAGE. By the 2nd century they were established as an imperial power, gradually subduing the hellenistic kingdoms of the east and the Gallic peoples of northern Italy and western Europe. Under the PRINCIPATE, the army became a large, professional standing force, recruited from across the PROVINCES, though expansionist warfare was increasingly rare after the reign of AUGUSTUS. Nonetheless, though the army and warfare were increasingly made more marginal within Roman society, Rome was still a notably militaristic state in late antiquity, drawing its leaders and emperors from the militarized sector of society. The relative lack of military zeal in the core PROVINCES of the empire was to lead in time to the *en bloc* recruitment of BARBARIANS to guard the FRONTIER regions – with the unsurprising result that poachers turned gamekeepers turned overlords!

Many of Rome's erstwhile enemies tried to explain Rome's success in war, generally focusing on the organization and training of the army (POLYBIOS, JOSEPHUS). Although the nature of Roman warfare changed over time, with tactical, organizational and technological shifts in the army, certain basic tenets remained consistent and characteristic. The Romans fought as a disciplined unit, with a strong emphasis on heavily armoured infantry – the LEGIONS (developed with greater tactical flexibility from Greek and ETRUSCAN use of the phalanx). The mobility that the infantry lacked was provided by allied (AUXILIARY) troops, often organized as cavalry, ARCHERS and light-armed skirmishers. The legions worked best when able to engage at close quarters with less well-armoured troops, though the real slaughter would generally follow when the enemy attempted to disengage and flee the field. Surviving military treatises (e.g. VEGETIUS, ARRIAN) demonstrate the Roman predilection for doing things by the book, a much-imitated facet in the modern age.

Military campaigns were designed to be attritional – the army advanced slowly and provocatively, burning and pillaging as it went in an effort to bring its enemies to a pitched battle. When the enemy retreated within fortifications, the Romans were excellent SIEGE-makers. One of the lessons learnt by Rome from its early (less illustrious) wars was the understanding that it could lose a battle (or several) but still win the war. The steady growth of the Roman citizen body and allied states during the later centuries BC allowed Rome to sustain catastrophic defeats, such as those inflicted by HANNIBAL at CANNAE and Lake Trasimene, yet still to refuse to surrender and simply to raise another and another army. No other ancient state (and few in any age) operated in this way.

The nature of the principate, characterized by the precarious security of the ruling dynast if he allowed potential rivals to accrue military glory, accounts in large measure for the changing face of war after Augustus. Expansionist wars were now rarely undertaken, unless commanded by the emperor himself or a trusted kinsman. The brief participation of CLAUDIUS in the final stages of the invasion of Britain in AD 43 represents one extreme of a spectrum that also saw outstanding generals such as TRAJAN leading conquests in DACIA and the East. Successful generals from outside the imperial household had a habit of dying mysteriously (AGRICOLA), being forced to commit suicide (CORBULO) or, occasionally, ascending to the purple (VESPASIAN, SEPTIMIUS SEVERUS). If expansionist war was more carefully rationed over time, the size of the empire necessitated increasing vigilance along its frontiers and more defensive actions. There were few emperors who eschewed military experience altogether (ANTONINUS PIUS), and even the philosopher emperor MARCUS AURELIUS took the field. In general, military credentials became increasingly necessary for a ruling emperor.

The Roman celebration of major victories as TRIUMPHS, with elaborate processions through the streets of Rome, was a strong incentive for GENERALS ruthlessly to pursue any advantage gained. A battle that ended a war and claimed more than 5,000 dead from the enemy ranks might be voted this honour by the people (though the tradition effectively died with the Republic, as after 19 BC only members of the imperial household were allowed them). This again served to divorce the bulk of the traditional Roman élite under the principate from their military heritage. The human implications of the more than 100 triumphs celebrated by the Romans over their enemies in the Republic and early principate give pause for thought about the demographic impact of Roman war. Occasionally Roman excesses were meted out on civilian communities of civilized nations – as in the sack of CORINTH and Carthage in 146 BC. Such incidents did little to persuade besieged rebels, such as the Jewish defenders of MASADA, to surrender themselves to Roman clemency.

There was no equivalent of the Geneva Convention in ancient warfare, though each age had its own customs. Plundering property, destroying crops, and enslaving captives were all considered legitimate tactics of much ancient warfare. In the Greek world, the granting of truces to the defeated side after a battle, to allow them to bury their dead and withdraw, was commonplace. For much of its history, Rome employed a legal fiction of only fighting defensive wars, though with a hair-trigger interpretation of what constituted a threat to its strategic interests. Pre-emptive strikes and engineered conflicts (through Roman breach of past treaties) became Roman trademarks during the later Republican period. Indeed, the Romans were notorious for setting aside the normal rules of war when it suited them – as when they reneged on the terms of surrender agreed at the CAUDINE FORKS in SAMNIUM. However, the crucifixion inflicted on the defeated remnants of SPARTACUS' slave revolt of 73–71 BC was unusually ferocious, and indicates both the severity of the rebellion and the fact that Rome placed SLAVES outside the normal rules of war. Although charges of atrocities were often raised against enemies of Rome (especially those classed as 'barbarians' by Roman writers), Roman military monuments such as TRAJAN'S COLUMN candidly depict Rome's own attacks on civilians. DJM, DGJS

WAR: the major wars of the classical world.

Dates	Greek world	Dates	Roman world
BC			
c.734–680	Lelantine war		
730–710?	first Messenian war		
650–620?	second Messenian war		
595–586	first sacred war		
499–494	Ionian revolt		
490	first Persian war		
480–479	second Persian war	486–425	intermittent wars with Hernici, Aequi, Volsci and Veii
461–451	first Peloponnesian war		
431–404	second Peloponnesian war	405–396	siege of Veii
395–386	Corinthian war	388–385	war with Aequi, Latins, Volsci and Hernici
357–355	Social war		
356–352	second sacred war	343–341	first Samnite war
334–323	campaigns of Alexander the Great	328–304	second Samnite war
323–322	Lamian war		
		298–290	third Samnite war
274–271	first Syrian war	280–275	war with Pyrrhus
267–262	Chremonidean war	264–241	first Punic war
260–253	second Syrian war		
246–241	third Syrian war		
		229–228, 219	first and second Illyrian wars
219–217	fourth Syrian war		
		218–201	second Punic war
214–205	first Macedonian war of Rome		
212–205	Parthian war of Antiochus III		
203–200	fifth Syrian war	202–191	conquest of Cisalpine Gaul
200–197	second Macedonian war of Rome		
		197–133	wars in Spain (Celtiberian, Lusitanian and Numantian wars)
		192–188	Syrian war with Antiochus
171–167	third Macedonian war of Rome		
170–168	sixth Syrian war		
148–146	fourth Macedonian war of Rome		
		149–146	third Punic war
		135–132	Sicilian slave war
		124–121	war in Transalpine Gaul
		112–106	Jugurthan war
		105–101	war with Cimbri and Teutones
		91–88	Social war

WAR: the major wars of the classical world (cont.)

Dates	Greek world	Dates	Roman world
88–85, 83–82, 74–63	first, second and third Mithradatic wars of Rome		
		72–71	slave revolt of Spartacus
		58–49	Gallic wars of Caesar
		55–51	war with Parthians
		49–45, 42, 36–35	civil war
		32–30	Octavian vs Antony and Cleopatra
		29–27	war in Spain
		12–9	Pannonian war
AD		4–5	conquest of Germany to Elbe
		6–9	Pannonian and German revolts
		17–24	Tacfarinan revolt
		43–83	invasion of Britain
		55–66	Armenian/Parthian wars
		66–73	Jewish revolt
		68–9	civil war
		86–92	Danubian wars
		101–6	Dacian wars
		114–17	Parthian war
		115–17	Jewish revolt
		132–5	Bar-Kochba's revolt
		162–6	Parthian war
		168–75, 178–80	Germanic wars along Danube
		193–6	civil war
		194–8	Parthian war
		208–11	British war
		230–8	Persian war
		235–84	numerous civil wars and Germanic invasions
		252–60, 283, 296–7	Persian wars
		267–73	secession and war with Palmyra
		312–24	rise of Constantine (sporadic civil war)
		325–78	numerous wars with Persia and Germanic peoples
		361–3	Persian war of Julian
		367–82	wars with Goths
		367, 372	revolts in Britain, Africa
		395–411	wars with Alaric the Visigoth
		406–end of Western empire	major barbarian invasions of Western empire; constant war and civil war
		447–51	wars with Attila the Hun

See Garlan, Y. (1982) *War in the Ancient World*; Gilliver, K. (1999) *The Roman Art of War*; Goldsworthy, A. (2000) *Roman Warfare*; Pritchett, W. K. (1971–91) *The Greek State at War*, 5 vols.; Rich, J. and Shipley, G., eds. (1993) *War and Society in the Greek World* and *War and Society in the Roman World*.

 BATTLES (table); TRIUMPHS (table).

warehouses The general Latin term for warehouses was *horrea*. The standard Roman *horreum* consisted of a series of long, narrow, rectangular, adjoining rooms either arranged along a corridor or around a courtyard. Additionally, ventilation windows were small and placed high on the walls, and the entrances to the storage complex were both few and surprisingly narrow, suggesting that intensive use was made of human porters rather than ANIMALS and carts. Warehouses designed specifically for the storage of grain often had raised floors. Security was another factor which influenced warehouse design. Doorframes reveal that a variety of elaborate bolts and locking systems were used to deter intruders. Sophisticated LOCKS have been identified not only on the main entrances to the complex, but on individual rooms and at stairways leading to upper levels. The single biggest known warehouse was the *horrea Galbana* in Rome, whose ground floor alone contained over 140 rooms and covered 21,000 sq m (225,000 sq ft). The 4th-century AD regionary catalogue of Rome lists 290 *horrea* distributed throughout all 14 regions of the city. The larger warehouses involved in the FOOD SUPPLY of the city of Rome were clustered along the banks of the TIBER in the Emporium district near the Aventine hill and at Rome's port of OSTIA. Provincial warehouses and GRANARIES, such as those at LEPCIS MAGNA or CAESAREA MARITIMA, are similar in basic form to those found at Rome and Ostia.

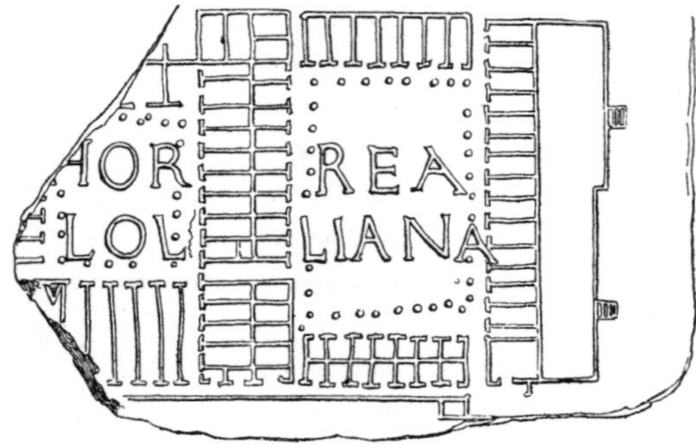

WAREHOUSES: (a) drawing of a fragment of the marble map of Rome showing a major warehouse complex (*horrea Lolliana*) by the Tiber.

WAREHOUSES: (b) large storage jars (*dolia*) set in the floor of a warehouse at Ostia.

Four warehouses at Ostia feature very large earthenware jars (*dolia*) embedded up to the neck in the ground. These could have been used to store liquids such as OLIVE OIL or WINE, and the largest of these buildings, the Magazzino Annonario, contains over 1,000 *dolia* with a cumulative capacity of over 90,000 litres (20,000 UK gallons). Many of the great warehouse complexes were originally built and operated by wealthy individuals or families. Extant contracts demonstrate that subdivisions of these warehouses, or even single rooms, could be rented out to individuals for storage. Paralleling the state's increasing control over other aspects of the food supply system, during the empire the ownership of most major warehouses seems gradually to have passed into imperial hands.

The typical Roman elongated storage room had precedents in the pre-Roman eastern MEDITERRANEAN. Such rooms are found at the lower level of MINOAN PALACES as at KNOSSOS, at the great granary at Harappa in the Indus valley and at the TEMPLE complex of Marduk in BABYLON (where the rooms are even grouped around a courtyard). In Greek cities, the standard multi-purpose building constructed around HARBOURS and MARKET areas was the STOA, a long, covered colonnade usually with a row of small rooms down one side. Stoa complexes such as the five stoas found at the Emporion at PIRAEUS, the HARBOUR of Athens, would have served analogous functions to Roman *horrea*. By the terms of the tax law of 374/3 BC, grain collected as taxes was to be stored in the Aiakeion (not securely identified) at Athens. The specific design of Roman *horrea* is strikingly similar to the so-called arsenals at hellenistic PERGAMON, which appear to have been a series of long, rectangular storage rooms with raised floors. GSA

See Patrich, J. (1996) Warehouses and granaries in Caesarea Maritima, in A. Raban and K. Holum, eds., *Caesarea Maritima* 146–76; Rickman, G. (1971) *Roman Granaries and Store Buildings*; Stroud, R. S. (1998) *The Athenian Grain-tax Law of 374/3 BC*.

washing Both the Greeks and Romans developed sophisticated public BATHS for bathing, but less is known about how they washed at home. Besides 'Nestor's bath' from the PALACE at Pylos, STONE or clay bathtubs occur in domestic bathrooms in Late Helladic IIIA Dimini (THESSALY), and on Greek, Punic and Republican Roman sites; they were generally short hip-baths in which the bather sat while water was poured over him or her. The Greeks also used a stone or terracotta basin or *loutron*, resembling a modern birdbath, for domestic ablutions; it was usually placed in the courtyard next to the wellhead or cistern mouth. SLAVES might also bring their masters or mistresses water for washing in a bowl or basin (PETRONIUS, *Satyricon* 27. 5–6; Dionisotti). In the Mediterranean OLIVE OIL was the main cleansing agent. SOAP, a CELTIC invention, was used only in northern Europe.

Clothes were washed by beating or trampling them in streams (*Odyssey* 6.85–98) or FOUNTAINS. In the Roman world, garments would usually be taken to professional FULLERS for cleaning. Almost nothing is known about the washing of dishes or KITCHEN UTENSILS, though two Greek terracotta figurines from Athens show women washing dishes in a *loutron*. Dishwashing was also probably done, without detergents, in the various stone basins found in many domestic contexts; such sinks are found in the SHOPS and bars of OSTIA and POMPEII. AIW

See Crouch, D. P. (1993) *Water Management in Ancient Greek Cities*; Dionisotti, A. C. (1982) From Ausonius' schooldays? A schoolbook and its relatives, *JRS* 72: 83–125.

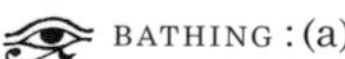 BATHING : (a).

waste disposal The growth of cities in the Greek and Roman worlds necessitated the disposal of unprecedented quantities of waste – sewage, domestic and industrial refuse – produced by nucleated urban populations. Greek urban drainage systems were patchy; although a large drain was built at Athens in the 5th century BC, in parts of the city houses still discharged water directly into the street in the 4th century (ARISTOTLE, *Constitution of Athens* 50.1). Streets at EUESPERIDES lacked drains, and domestic refuse was thrown out into them; they were periodically resurfaced so that their level rose some 1.5 m (5 ft) over 350 years. Other towns, however, developed complex and integrated drainage networks, with drains from buildings discharging into street drains that then fed into main collector drains. A trend towards regular TOWN PLANNING facilitated such networks, as with the rebuilding on a grid plan of MILETOS after 479, or the construction of the new quarter at Olynthos in 432, and they became commoner in the hellenistic period.

Roman drainage systems did not introduce new elements, but applied existing technology on a wider scale. A large number of new urban foundations, especially colonies, provided opportunities to plan a drainage network in conjunction with a regular street plan from the outset; as a result, some of the most complete and impressive Roman drainage systems are found in colonies, such as TIMGAD and Cologne. But retrofitting street drains to a town originally built without them was difficult, and neither POMPEII nor Alba Fucens received a complete under-street drainage network. Instead, the streets themselves served as drains, with raised sidewalks and stepping stones at intervals to keep pedestrians clear of the muck. Responsibility for maintaining drains and keeping streets clean rested with the AEDILES (city MAGISTRATES); the work might be performed by public SLAVES, or, as at ANTIOCH, was an obligation laid on shopkeepers in return for the right to trade. The link between central authority and the installation and functioning of civic drainage networks is underscored by the fact that in Western Europe many drainage systems fell out of use during the early Middle Ages, classical drainage technology persisting largely in MONASTERIES. In areas without under-street drains, soakaways and cesspits were used.

For the disposal of solid wastes, Greek cities had *koprologoi*, who emptied domestic cesspits for a fee and sold the ordure to farmers as fertilizer. In Roman cities, *stercorarii* served the same function, and their importance is shown by the fact that their carts were the only vehicles exempted from the ban on traffic in the city of Rome during the hours of darkness. Refuse was dumped in dungheaps, usually outside the city gates. At Rome, the size of the population and the scale of the problem of waste disposal must have necessitated a permanent workforce, whether state-maintained or composed of private contractors engaged by the aediles. AIW

See Dupré Raventós, X. and Remolà, J.-A., eds. (2000) *Sordes Urbis*; Wilson, A. I. (2000) Drainage and sanitation, in Ö. Wikander, *Ancient Water Technology* 151–79.

water mills The water mill represents one of the earliest uses of natural forces to perform mechanical work. Invented in the 3rd century BC, it was in widespread use for MILLING across the Roman world by the 1st century AD. Several different designs were known. Vertically wheeled mills (the preferred type in Europe) were driven by water striking paddles as it flowed under the wheel ('undershot'), or delivered from a chute to fill buckets on the top of the wheel ('overshot'). A cogwheel transmitted the drive via right-angle gearing to a vertical spindle passing through the lower millstone, which drove the upper millstone by an iron cross-bar (rynd). Some very large installations are known, notably the 2nd-century AD factory with 16 overshot wheels at BARBEGAL (France) and the Janiculum series in Rome, in existence certainly from the 3rd century AD.

The horizontal mill, however, needed no gearing, as the waterwheel was mounted on the lower part of the mill spindle. Horizontal mills in the Middle East were driven by a jet of water exiting under pressure from the base of a tall cylindrical reservoir and striking angled blades on the wheel. In North AFRICA, two highly sophisticated 4th-century turbine mills are known from Chemtou and Testour, each with three wheels running fully submerged in a rotating column of water. AIW

See Lewis, M. J. T. (1997) *Millstone and Hammer*; Wikander, Ö. (2000) The water-mill, in Ö. Wikander, *Handbook of Ancient Water Technology* 371–400; Wilson, A. I. (2002) Machines, power and the ancient economy, *JRS* 92: 1–32.

 BARBEGAL.

water supply The acquisition of water to support a settled population was a major preoccupation in the ancient MEDITERRANEAN world, and increasingly sophisticated techniques were adopted to support larger and larger urban populations. Natural springs attracted settlement, and might be used with a minimum of artificial enhancement, such as the construction of a catch-basin. Wells allowed access to groundwater where this occurred not too far below the surface; wells of up to 60 m (200 ft) and deeper are known from the Greek and Roman world. Water would be lifted out using a jar or bucket on a ROPE and pulley, or by a water-lifting device such as the shaduf or the *saqqiya* (animal-driven wheel with pots lashed to the rim). Rainwater was collected from ROOFS and courtyards and stored in cisterns, which were

WATER SUPPLY: the water distribution tank (*castellum aquae*) at Nîmes. Water feeds a series of pipes set at different levels in the side of the reservoir, to prioritize distribution and allow opening and closing of supply to different facilities.

covered, often underground, reservoirs lined with cement or some other form of WATERPROOFING. Domestic cisterns were almost ubiquitous around the ancient Mediterranean, and the larger roofed and paved spaces associated with public buildings (TEMPLES, and even FORA and THEATRES) were also used as catchment areas for cisterns. If local water sources were insufficient, water might be conveyed from a more distant source by means of AQUEDUCTS. In some areas, such as Egypt, water was lifted out of rivers by machines such as shadufs, *saqqiyas*, *norias* and the ARCHIMEDES SCREW, and collected in reservoirs before distribution through an urban piping network.

In the case of Roman aqueduct- and river-fed distribution networks, water was delivered primarily to public FOUNTAINS, public BATHS and private and commercial users who paid a fee. The ÉLITE might have water piped to their houses, but the majority of the urban population would rely for their water supply on wells and cisterns. The poor, whose dwellings might lack these amenities, would be especially reliant on public fountains. In the drier parts of the Roman empire, large reservoir cisterns on the aqueduct distribution networks created a storage buffer, allowing night-time aqueduct delivery to be stored for daytime use. Such reservoir cisterns are particularly associated with public baths, and seem to be a way of accommodating the heavy water demands of these establishments without detrimentally affecting daytime delivery to public fountains.

Water quality varied considerably according to the source. Aqueducts and their distribution networks often included settling tanks, and sometimes also filter systems. Large storage reservoirs tended to have cascades at the inlet to aerate the water. Rainwater collected in cisterns would become stagnant, but underground storage kept it cool and reduced the growth of organisms. Ancient writers recognized that water quality was improved by boiling; and the practice of drinking WINE mixed with water was probably intended as much to add a mild antiseptic that disguised the flavour of the water as it was to reduce the strength of the wine. AIW

See Hodge, A.T. (1992) *Roman Aqueducts and Water Supply*; Wikander, Ö., ed. (2000) *Handbook of Ancient Water Technology*; Wilson, A.I. (1998) Water supply in ancient Carthage, in *Carthage papers* (*JRA* Supplement 28), 65–102.

 AQUEDUCTS: (a)–(b).

waterproofing Bitumen was one of the first substances to be used as a waterproofing material. It was used in the ancient Near East for waterproofing bathrooms, and the pitch lakes on the Greek island of Zakynthos were exploited through the classical period. Clay might also be used for lining cisterns and channels to make them watertight, as in archaic Rome, but at an early date artificial waterproofing materials were also developed. In the PHOENICIAN and Punic worlds cisterns were lined with a grey-blue lime mortar to which wood ash (charcoal lumps and finely combusted particulates) had been added; this technique persisted under Roman rule. In ATTICA during the 5th century BC, cisterns at the LAURION ore-washeries were lined with a lime plaster whose impermeability was due to a high litharge content. In the Roman world, a standard waterproofing material for hydraulic structures (cisterns, AQUEDUCTS) was a LIME mortar mixed with finely crushed terracotta, often, but incorrectly, called *opus signinum* in modern literature. This characteristically pink cement is a very effective and durable waterproof material owing to alumino-silicates in the terracotta, which react with the lime mortar to create an impermeable compound. AIW

See Forbes, R. J. (1964) *Studies in Ancient Technology*, vol. 1.

wealth The foundation for status, rank and power in the stratified societies of the classical world. Status and rank were not entirely based upon wealth (other factors such as birth and family connections might also be significant), but it was crucial for sustaining them. The most secure form of wealth was land, the primary means of production, and in Greek and Roman society the wealthiest people were generally the biggest landowners. Those who made their money by other means, such as MINING or SHIPPING, usually invested it in land. There were certainly 'self-made' men. The banker Pasion and his son Apollodoros started as SLAVES of foreign origin in Athens in the 4th century BC but earned a huge fortune through BANKING, MONEYLENDING and money changing. Eventually they were awarded Athenian CITIZENSHIP for their services to the city, and Apollodoros presents himself in his speeches as a rich landowner (Demosthenes 53). In the Roman world, slaves and FREEDMEN regularly documented their rise to prosperity on their tombstones. However, most wealthy people inherited their wealth. CICERO and PLINY THE YOUNGER, both born into wealthy families, tell us a great deal in their letters about how they used and managed their wealth. Often they did not use their money for the kinds of productive activities that would be most common today, such as investing in a business. A particularly important use of wealth in ancient societies was for display. The younger Pliny spent considerable amounts of money on benefactions in his home town of Comum to enhance his reputation, including building a LIBRARY, paying part of a teacher's salary and providing for needy children. LF

See Davies, J. K. (1981) *Wealth and the Power of Wealth in Classical Athens.*

weather forecasting Without the use of modern scientific methods, weather forecasting for the Greeks and Romans was a matter of observation. Predicting the weather was highly important for AGRICULTURE and sailing, and this is reflected in literature. HESIOD, in his 8th-century BC *Works and Days*, used the stars as a guide, the appearance of certain constellations signalling the appropriate moment for particular tasks. The rising of the Pleiades, for example, signals the time to begin harvesting, while their setting indicates the time to plough (383–4). The Romans also used ASTRONOMY as a weather guide. This is explicitly stated by VIRGIL (1st century BC) in book 1 of his *Georgics* (231–58). He relates the layout of the heavens and the constellations, and claims that their uniformity of movement over the annual cycle allows humans to foretell changes in the weather, the seasons and the appropriate times for agricultural duties and safe seafaring. PLINY THE ELDER (1st century AD), in book 18 of his *Natural History*, modifies this slightly. He notes that any astronomical reading needs to be tempered first by common sense (a farmer should start his spring chores when the west wind actually blows, not when it should blow: 18.238) and second by a thorough knowledge of the vagaries of local conditions (18.226).

Observations of wildlife, especially BIRDS, acted as another guide to the coming weather. Hesiod notes that the cry of the crane indicates the coming of winter (448–51), and Virgil observes that swallows flit around pools when it is about to rain (*Georgics* 1.377). However, as Pliny comments (18.209) such signs are not always concrete: the reappearance of migratory birds or butterflies is not proof positive that cold weather has finished. Both Romans and Greeks believed that the weather was ultimately controlled by the GODS, and, as Hesiod notes (*Works and Days* 483–4), the whims of the gods are not for mortals to understand. NJW

weaving The interlacing of threads on a loom to create fabrics made of wool, linen, SILK and even cotton. Looms in Greece and Rome were typically vertical and warp-weighted. Propped against a wall, the loom was made up of two vertical timbers with a horizontal beam at the top. Warp threads were then attached to the horizontal beam. Half of these threads were attached to a shed rod at the bottom of the loom, separating even- from odd-numbered warp threads. The other half were attached to loom-weights of stone or terracotta that hung behind the loom. A gap, or shed, was then created that allowed the weft thread to be woven through. A heddle-rod, with the rear warp threads attached to it, allowed the odd-numbered warp threads to be brought forward and backward, in order for the weft thread to be woven in one movement. The weaver, standing, then beat the weft thread into the cloth using a weaving sword inserted into the shed.

As early as the 1st century AD, vertical two-beam looms began to replace the vertical warp-weighted loom, both in Italy and the Roman PROVINCES. The warp threads were held in place between an upper and a lower cloth beam. The weaver, seated, would beat the weft in a downward motion with a wooden comb. This loom was used primarily to fashion tapestries. With the increased used of silk in the late antique period, the horizontal loom also appeared on the scene.

A final form of weaving did not require a loom-frame and was used to create bands of fabric. For example, tablet-weaving involves weaving with tablets of BONE or bronze to create twisted cords. Each tablet had small holes punched into each corner, with warp threads passing through the individual holes. The weaver, holding several tablets in the hand, turned each tablet either forward or backward to twist the threads into a cord. The weft simply held the cords together.

Unfortunately, archaeological evidence for actual looms is lacking. Greek VASE-PAINTINGS provide a few representations of the warp-weighted loom;

WEAVING: vase-painting depicting Penelope, the put-upon wife of Odysseus, at her loom.

Roman WALL-PAINTINGS, illuminated manuscripts and tombstones depict the two-beam loom. Archaeologists rely primarily on loom-weights to determine whether weaving activity existed at a site. Also, when cloth is preserved, TEXTILE analysis can supply important clues about weaving methods.

For the most part, WOMEN did the weaving both in Greek and Roman societies; however, MEN are known to have participated as well. Weaving was also a popular metaphor used to describe political and conjugal relationships in Greek and Latin MYTH. LAH

See Barber, E. J.W. (1991) *Prehistoric Textiles*; Scheid, J. and Svenbro, J. (1996) *The Craft of Zeus*; Wild, J. P. (1970) *Textile Manufacture in the Northern Roman Provinces.*

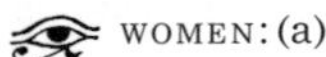 WOMEN: (a).

Weber, Max see HISTORIANS AND HISTORIOGRAPHY, MODERN; SOCIOLOGY.

weddings see MARRIAGE.

wedges see CARPENTRY; MACHINES; PRESSES; QUARRIES AND QUARRYING.

weights and measures At a very early date, measures were needed because of INHERITANCE and market exchange. Dividing a farm between heirs meant assessing its size. Grain could only be sold, bartered, or paid as tax in identifiable amounts. Early societies might use a day's ploughing as their land-measure, and gourds or animal skins as units of capacity.

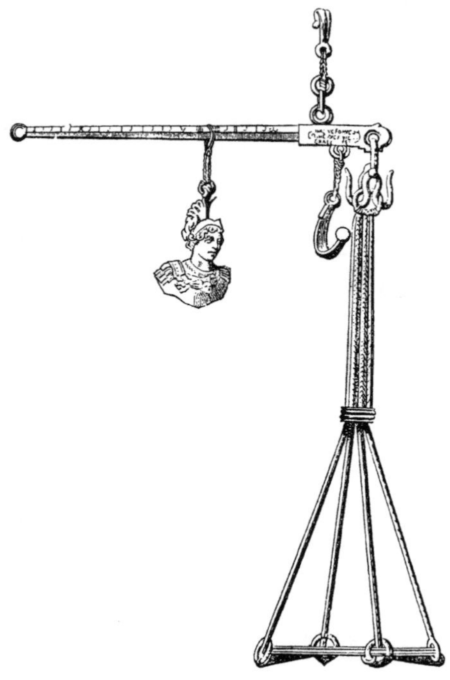

WEIGHTS AND MEASURES: (a) Roman steelyard balance from Pompeii.

WEIGHTS AND MEASURES: (b) relief showing balance in use.

Advances in theory and TECHNOLOGY led to the introduction of geometry, literally 'earth-measurement', and the production of containers for measuring capacity, as well as weights and balances. The main developments were already current in Egypt, Babylon and MINOAN CRETE many centuries before the classical period, and measures were evidently influenced by these sources. Primitive features could persist nonetheless. Rome under the empire still had subjects whose tax unit was the ox-hide, and sometimes included ploughing-units in the terminology of land taxation. Measurement of land by sowing-units, reflecting its productive capacity and obviating the need for precise measurement, was also a persistent practice.

The earliest measures were essentially local. A single measuring vessel or set of weights might be accepted throughout a single VILLAGE or town whether or not it represented a standard used anywhere else. Differing local standards were characteristic of classical Greece with its small political units, though there could be moves towards standardization where political or trading units became larger. Localization was nevertheless a natural condition of pre-industrial society, and local variants in measure almost certainly remained widespread within larger states as well. Partly in order to make TAXATION more efficient, great powers such as PERSIA, Rome and the hellenistic kingdoms imposed standard measures wherever they could, without being able to eliminate local differences.

The standard large Greek unit was the talent (*talanton*), with the *MINA* as $\frac{1}{60}$ talent and the drachma, familiar as a coin, as $\frac{1}{6000}$ talent. Widespread archaeological evidence from early Greece suggests a talent of c.29.28 kg (c.64 lb 7 oz in UK measures), and a *mina* of c.0.488 kg (c.17.2 oz) (Petruso 1992). The Attic talent in Priscian, of $83\frac{1}{3}$ Roman pounds, c.26.9 kg (c.59 lb 3 oz), is quite close to GALEN's equivalence of 80 pounds or 25.8 kg (c.56 lb 12 oz). Attic coin-weights of the late classical period imply a similar talent of c.25.95 kg (c.57 lb 1 oz). The talent in the heavier Aeginetan standard was c.36.6 kg (c.81 lb 8 oz), together with lighter PTOLEMAIC, RHODIAN and cistophoric (2nd-century PERGAMON) standards.

Coin standards could change through economic pressure, and did not always reflect the weights used for other purposes.

The Greek *stadion* was a unit of 600 feet or 400 cubits. Building dimensions and metrological reliefs suggest that the foot in the classical period could range from 0.296 m (11.65 inches) to 0.320 m (12.60 inches), 0.327 m (12.87 inches) or even 0.345 m (13.58 inches), implying *stadia* from 177.6 m (194 yards 8 inches) to 207.0 m (226 yards 14 inches). The foot in POLYBIOS, like the Roman foot, is evidently 0.2957 m (11.64 inches), since $8\frac{1}{3}$ *stadia* equal the Roman mile (1,478.5 m, 4,850 ft).

The large capacity unit was the *medimnos*, made up of 48 *choinikes* or 96 *xestai*. Several sources give the Attic *medimnos* as 6 Italic *modii*, 51.7 litres (11.4 UK gallons). The corresponding *choinix* measures 1.077 litres, the *xestês* 0.539 litres. But despite standardized terminology, local variants existed in the Greek world even in Galen's time.

Archaeological evidence supports the coherent system for weight, length and capacity shown in Roman metrological writings. The *sextarius* held $1\frac{2}{3}$ pounds of WINE, while the volume of 16 *sextarii* or 1 Italic *modius* equalled $\frac{1}{3}$ of a cubic foot. Surviving weights and coins point to a pound of 0.3228 kg (c.11.4 oz UK). And evidence from surviving measures and from LAND SURVEY makes the foot c.0.2957 m (11.64 inches). Converging definitions of capacity measure show that these co-ordinates support each other: the Italic *modius* of 16 *sextarii* holds $26\frac{2}{3}$ pounds

WEIGHTS AND MEASURES: ancient weights and measures, with ancient and modern equivalences.

Greece				
Weight				
talent	*mina*	drachma	obol	metric (Attic measure)
1	160	6,000	36,000	25.95 kg
Liquid capacity				
metretes	*chous*	*xestes*	*kotule*	metric (Attic)
1	12	72	144	38.78 litres
Dry capacity				
medimnos	*choenix*	*xestes*	*kotule*	metric (Attic)
1	48	96	192	51.71 litres
Length				
stadion	*plethron*	cubit	foot	metric
1	6	400	600	177.4–207 m
Square measure				
plethron	foot	metric		
1	10,000	874.4–1190 sq m		

Rome					
Weight					
pound	*uncia*	*scripulum*	*siliqua*	metric	
1	12	288	1728	0.3228 kg	
Liquid capacity					
amphora	*congius*	*sextarius*	*cyathus*	metric	
1	8	48	576	25.86 litres	
Dry capacity					
modius	*sextarius*	*hemina*	*cyathus*	metric (*modius Italicus*)	
1	16	32	192	8.6185 litres	
Length					
mile	*passus*	foot	metric		
1	1,000	5,000	1478.5 m		
Square measure					
centuria	*heredium*	*iugerum*	*actus*	foot	metric
1	100	200	400	5,760,000	503,646 sq m

of wine, therefore 8.608 kg or litres (nearly 2 UK gallons); it also measured $\frac{1}{3}$ of a cubic foot, therefore 8.6185 litres.

The Italic *modius* was not the only standard of capacity. The larger *kastrensis* measure co-existed with it under the PRINCIPATE, and is seen in metrological texts and in surviving metal measures as a unit 35–50 per cent larger. In DIOCLETIAN's Price Edict of AD 301, the *modius kastrensis* (here probably 12.93 litres, c.3 UK gallons) is used in preference to Italic measure in almost all cases. Some other ambiguities in capacity measure reflect the choice between levelling off grain at the top of the measuring vessel and heaping it up above the rim, which could increase volume by $\frac{1}{9}$ or more.

Many local measures evidently existed in the provinces of the Roman empire, of which explicit survivals are probably only a small part. Hyginus mentions a foot $\frac{1}{8}$ larger than the *pes monetalis* in GERMANY among the Tungri (0.3327 m, 13.10 inches), called the *pes Drusianus*, and a foot $\frac{1}{24}$ larger than the *pes monetalis* in Cyrenaica, the Ptolemaic foot of 0.308 m (12.13 inches). In Egypt, the most prominent grain measure was an *artaba* of $4\frac{1}{2}$ Italic *modii* (38.78 litres, 8.5 UK gallons), apparently used for taxation. Land there was measured by the *aroura* or plough-unit of 100 Egyptian cubits squared (2,767 sq m, 3,300 sq yards), or by a 96-cubit equivalent (2,550 sq m, 3,050 sq yards) approximating to the Roman *iugerum* of 2,518 sq m (3,012 sq yards). RPD-J

See Dekoulakoi-Sideris, I. (1990) A metrological relief from Salamis, *AJA* 94: 445–51; Duncan-Jones, R. P. (1982) *Economy of the Roman Empire*; (1994) *Money and Government in the Roman Empire*; (1976) The choenix, the artaba and the modius, *ZPE* 21: 43–52; (1976) The size of the modius castrensis, *ZPE* 21: 53–62; (1979) Variations in Egyptian grain-measure, *Chiron* 9: 347–75; (1980) Length-units in Roman town planning, *Britannia* 11: 127–33; Hultsch, F., ed. (1864–6) *Metrologicorum scriptorum reliquiae* (original texts); Kula, W. (1986) *Measures and Men*; Lang, M. (1964) *The Athenian Agora* 10; Mørkholm, O. (1991) *Early Hellenistic Coinage*; Morrison, J. (1991) Ancient Greek measures of length in nautical contexts, *Antiquity* 65: 298–305; Petruso, K. M. (1992) *Keos Excavations* 8.

 FOOD SUPPLY, ROMAN.

wells see WATER SUPPLY.

wetlands The important ECOLOGICAL role of wetlands was not recognized in antiquity, and little effort was made to preserve swamps and marshes associated with RIVERS, lakes and other bodies of water. Nevertheless, wetlands played a role in both the Greek and Roman worlds whose reality is demonstrated by the early development of many cities close to such areas. By the 5th century BC, HIPPOCRATIC writers were well aware of the impact of environment on HEALTH, noting that inhabitants of wet, low-lying regions were more sickly and full of phlegm and bile (see the Hippocratic *Airs, Waters, Places*). This knowledge passed to the Romans, as is evident in the many recommendations to avoid swampy areas. VITRUVIUS comments on the importance of choosing healthful, non-marshy sites for cities (1.4.1). VARRO argues against constructing farmhouses near marshes because of the disease-bearing INSECTS that breed there (*On Agriculture* 1.12.2). COLUMELLA describes the poisonous gases emitted from marshes during hot seasons (*On Agriculture* 1.5.6). One method of dealing with unpleasant, foul-smelling and often malarial wetlands was to drain them. JULIUS CAESAR intended to do this at the Pomptine marshes near Rome (Suetonius, *Julius Caesar* 44.2). The most impressive wetland reclamation project was the draining of the marsh beneath the hills of Rome, generally attributed to TARQUINIUS PRISCUS early in the 6th century BC; the drained land later served as the grounds for the Roman FORUM. The most famous inhabitant of a marsh was the Hydra, a fearsome, many-headed mythological beast slain by HERAKLES, which lived in the Lernaian marsh on the plain of ARGOS. TJA

See Borca, F. (2000) Towns and marshes in the ancient world, in V. M. Hope and E. Marshall, eds., *Death and Disease in the Ancient City* 74–84.

wetnurses We know little about wetnursing in ancient Greece, but the word for a child-nurse, *titthê*, implies that the NURSE was expected to breastfeed the child in her care. PLUTARCH insists in the *Moralia* that mother's milk is best, while FAVORINUS worries that the use of a foreign SLAVE as a wetnurse will transmit a bad moral character to the child. Complaints like these, taken with epitaphs praising women who breastfed their own children, suggest that in fact wetnursing was very common, if not the norm, at all levels of Roman society. SORANUS' *Gynaecology* gives detailed instructions on how to select a suitable woman: she must avoid ALCOHOL and sex while employed. These restrictions are repeated in contracts of employment that survive from Egypt. Being a wetnurse was a job taken by a slave or by free-born, poor women. Even slave children could be allocated a wetnurse if their mother died, if they were found after being exposed, or if the mother was weak or otherwise unable to breastfeed. Keith Bradley has argued that the use of a wetnurse acted to distance parent from child, a psychologically shrewd move in a society with high infant mortality. However, it may also have occurred because women wanted to preserve their figure or, as lactation was known to have a CONTRACEPTIVE effect, because they wanted more children. Ties between nurse and nurseling could last for many years, and in many cases the wetnurse went on to be the nurse throughout CHILDHOOD. HK

See Bradley, K. R. (1986) Wet-nursing at Rome, in B. Rawson, ed., *The Family in Ancient Rome* 201–29.

wheat see CEREALS.

wheel, the see CARPENTRY; POTTERY; SCREW; TECHNOLOGY.

wheeled vehicles Carts drawn by oxen or mules, and HORSE-drawn chariots, were important means of transportation in the ancient world. Little is known about Greek vehicles, as few material remains have survived. CHARIOTS were introduced from the LEVANT at least in the MYCENAEAN period. Drawn by one or two horses, they carried at most two standing persons. They were designed for fast travelling, especially in warfare, and in CHARIOT RACES at Greek FESTIVALS. Heavy vehicles with two or four wheels

WHEELED VEHICLES: (a) four-wheeled horse drawn carriage (*carruca*).

WHEELED VEHICLES: (b) reconstruction of Roman cart from Cologne.

WHEELED VEHICLES: (c) two-wheeled dray cart.

were used for the TRANSPORT of goods that were too heavy or bulky for pack animals. The larger four-wheeled vehicles were unwieldy, especially on the bad ROADS of ancient Greece. Oxen were more often used as draught animals than were horses, less because of inefficient harnessing systems than because ancient horses were physically much smaller than modern.

We are relatively well informed about Roman vehicles, as many literary and artistic representations – particularly from Roman GAUL – inform us about a wide variety of vehicles. They range from two-wheeled vehicles such as the *essedum*, a luxurious vehicle in use by state officials, to the large *raeda*, drawn by two or four horses. Archaeological finds from northern Greece have made it possible to reconstruct a Roman coach of the 2nd century AD. These vehicles could be fairly comfortable: they had excellent suspension, and their frontal axis could be turned, which made them easy to manoeuvre. OVN

See Spruytte, J. (1983) *Early Harness Systems*; White, K. D. (1984) *Greek and Roman Technology*.

wills By law, no Athenian father with a living son could write a will. Upon the father's death, the property devolved automatically to the son. If there was more than one son, they would share the property equally, either in common or separately, after dividing it; there was no primogeniture. Daughters received their share of the estate in the form of a dowry upon MARRIAGE. A son could not be disinherited, neither could a daughter be deprived of the position of *epiklêros*. In the first part of the 6th century a law introduced by SOLON permitted a man without sons to adopt one by will, the ADOPTION taking effect only after his death. This established the notion that precedence be given to the wishes of the deceased individual over the claims of other family members. The primary concern of society was the survival of the *oikos*, and the use of a will was only required in the absence of a successor. The adopted heir was usually a relative in any case. The written document could easily be forged and was therefore considered suspect; the Greeks preferred to rely on the testimonies of witnesses.

In earliest Rome, the curial ASSEMBLY met twice a year to review cases involving citizens without heirs, displaying the same correspondence between the making of a will and adoption as was prevalent in Athens. The law of the TWELVE TABLES allowed CITIZENS to dispose of their property directly and to make use of legacies. In the 4th century BC, citizens were also allowed to adopt and MANUMIT by will. Children were normally considered to be automatic heirs, but Roman law did give the testator the freedom to disinherit, though it had to be done explicitly.

There was a strong cultural expectation that the head of the household produce a will, though there was never any formal legal requirement that it had to be a written document. The will was perceived to be a yardstick for measuring the social life of the deceased, and it mattered how he rewarded his relatives and friends. There was an additional notion that a will revealed people's true nature. In short, the reading of the will was a key factor in the politics of reputation, not only for the deceased but also for those forming part of his social network. Upper class Romans were in the habit of revising their wills regularly, to respond to new circumstances or simply because they changed their minds. From the reign of AUGUSTUS onwards it became customary to add supplements, last-minute changes. These codicils could do anything but name an heir. A codicil could be used as an outlet for bottled-up frustrations and concerns, and it thus gained importance for being able to convey the truest sentiments of the deceased which could not be entrusted to a will. When forced to commit SUICIDE by Nero, PETRONIUS added to his will a list of the emperor's sexual debaucheries. In the same period, the outspokenness of the codicil was shaped into a new literary subgenre by Fabricius Veiento for his attack on SENATORS and PRIESTS. MK

See Champlin, E. (1991) *Final Judgments*.

Winckelmann, J. see ARCHAEOLOGY.

wind Both divine and rational explanations for the cause of wind occur in antiquity; the puzzling phenomenon of objects moving because of an unseen force provoked many theories. For some, the winds were thought of as GODS: at times benevolent, as in HESIOD's catalogue of winds (*Theogony* 378–80) and ACHILLES' prayer for winds to blow on Patroklos' funeral pyre (*Iliad* 23.194–214); at other times hostile, like the bag of winds encountered by Odysseus (*Odyssey* 10.1–55). Although many different wind-gods were recognized, the most common were Boreas or Aquilo (the north wind), Zephyrus or Favonius (west), Notus or Auster (south) and Eurus or Vulturnus (east). Scientific explanations included ARISTOTLE's claim that wind resulted from the sun's heat and the subsequent evaporation of the earth's moisture (*Meteorology* 1.3). LUCRETIUS, a proponent of EPICUREAN science, suggested that invisible wind particles moved through the sea, land and sky (1.50). Many artefacts and monuments are associated with wind, including a SUNDIAL with the names of 12 winds found near Rome, a windrose carved into a stone pavement at Dougga (THUGGA) and several MOSAICS showing personifications of wind. The famous Tower of the Winds, built in Athens in about the late 2nd century BC, depicts eight wind deities in relief SCULPTURE. The exterior of this building, described by VITRUVIUS (1.6), incorporated a weathervane and sundial. Somewhat perplexingly, the use of wind power other than for sailing was not developed until the medieval period; the only reference to a wind-driven machine is HERON OF ALEXANDRIA's description of an organ pump (*Pneumatics* 1.43). TJA

wine One of the defining characteristics of the classical world was wine and wine-drinking – a symbol of what it was to be civilized. Wine was part of culture from the earliest times – in MYCENAEAN Greece, for example, or later in the poems of HOMER. Its survival in Western Europe after the collapse of the ROMAN EMPIRE was partly the result of the Christian CHURCH's need for wine for the communion, and partly of the continuing desire of the new BARBARIAN masters to represent themselves as heirs of classical culture. The descriptions of vineyards in SIDONIUS APOLLINARIS and Venantius Fortunatus, in the 5th and 6th centuries AD, are as vivid as anything in VIRGIL or PLINY. Wherever they settled, the Greeks and Romans sought to introduce viticulture, as, for example, in the Greek colonies in southern France and Spain and the expansion into France and BRITAIN that swiftly followed the Roman conquest.

While, in the earlier civilizations of MESOPOTAMIA and dynastic Egypt, wine was the preserve of the ruling ÉLITES, in the Greco-Roman world everybody drank wine. There was little alternative. Spirits were unknown, and while BEER was widely drunk in the Middle East, Egypt and the CELTIC countries of northern Europe, it never had the cultural cachet associated with wine. There were those, like DEMOSTHENES (it was claimed), who drank only water, but this was frequently seen as misanthropic behaviour. Wine was the key to socializing. Among the élites there was the ritual of the dinner party – the *symposion* in Greece, the *convivium* in the Roman world – while the population as a whole drank in the taverns and bars found throughout ancient cities and towns. Stroll down practically any street in POMPEII and you will soon encounter the local bar. Furthermore, it was not just what one drank, but how one drank, that was important. The civilized

WINE: (a) fermenting vessels (*dolia*) set in the court of Roman villa at Boscoreale.

WINE: (b) relief carving showing activity of Roman wine merchant, including filling of amphoras from *dolia*.

WINE: (c) Roman wine shop in Gaul, with different sizes of jugs.

way was to mix the wine with water. Drinking wine neat was seen as inspiring MADNESS, and was the characteristic of the barbarian. It even played a role in the definition of gender – it was assumed that WOMEN were constitutionally addicted to wine. Wine was everywhere. It played a key role in the ritual of libation in Greco-Roman religious practice. The effects of wine fascinated DOCTORS, and it was much used in MEDICINE. The rich imagery of the VINE and wine was at the heart of ancient POETRY and the iconography of painting, SCULPTURE and MOSAICS.

Most wine, then as now, was drunk young ('new' wine was defined legally as under one year old). Wine would usually be produced locally, to be consumed by the peasant producer, or transported only as far as the neighbouring town or the town houses of the rich estate-owners. But from quite early on in Greece and in Italy, there also grew up a long-distance trade in wines produced in vineyards with easy access to the sea. Inscriptions from the island of THASOS show how in the 5th century BC the state was conscious of its role as a leading producer of wine, and of the need to regulate production to preserve its reputation. The trade in the wines of Italy, France, Spain and elsewhere was to become a major factor in the economy of the Roman empire.

DNA studies hold out the prospect that we may eventually be able to identify ancient grape types with some certainty. The classical writers on AGRICULTURE detail the very varied way in which vines were grown. The growing of vines up trees was much more widespread than in the modern period, and was characteristic of the vineyards which produced all the best wines of Roman Italy. The process of making the wine often resulted in a product high in ALCOHOL, which needed clarification or even straining before being drunk. Frequent references to collecting grapes late, to drying grapes, and to the addition on occasion of boiled must, suggest a preference for sweet wines. Red and white wines were produced, along with what is described as 'amber', which possibly refers to white wine which has been maderized, a form of oxidation. The white form of great wines such as Falernian was the most prized. Although connoisseurs clearly expressed a preference for pure wines, all sorts of additives, such as herbs, were put in wine, frequently to disguise the fact that it was turning rapidly to vinegar. The addition of sea SALT to wine was a noted characteristic of the wines of the island of Kos in the AEGEAN. Interest in particular vintages seems to have grown up in Roman Italy rather than Greece, along with the practice of ageing wines for very long periods; Falernian was supposedly at its best between 15 and 20 years old. The storing of AMPHORAS of wine next to the fireplace or under the roof-tiles, where they would be heated by the sun, was a way of accelerating that ageing process.

In Greece the most noted wines came, in particular, from the islands of the Aegean such as THASOS, LESBOS, CHIOS, and later Kos and RHODES, along with those from the north, such as Mende in CHALCIDIKE. In Roman Italy, early favourites, such as Alban, Caecuban, Falernian and Surrentine, all came from the areas of southern Latium and Campania, where the Roman rich had their country estates. They later gained rivals from the east and north-east coasts of Italy, and by the middle of the 1st century from the estates of southern Spain and Gaul. JJP

See Davidson, J. (1997) *Courtesans and Fishcakes*; Murray, O. and Tecuşan, M., eds. (1995) *In Vino Veritas*; Unwin, T. (1991) *Wine and the Vine*.

 ADVERTISING; SHOPS AND SHOPPING: (b).

wisdom The synthesis of morality and knowledge essential to the good conduct of life. Three types of wisdom can be discerned in Greek. *Sophia* is the most accurate form of intellectual knowledge, particularly associated with PHILOSOPHY (*philosophia*, 'love of *sophia*'). Yet the operation of *sophia* was dependent on the application of 'understanding' (*synesis*) and 'practical sense' (*phronêsis*). Wisdom was specifically a human attribute, and from as early as HOMER it is associated with the proper and moral guidance of affairs, such as government.

Since the earliest times, the Greeks had also been acutely aware of the wisdom of foreign peoples, particularly the Iranians, INDIANS and EGYPTIANS. The conquests of ALEXANDER the Great (336–323 BC) permitted the interaction of Greek and foreign conceptions of wisdom, in a manner that was to have important ramifications for the subsequent development of Western civilization. On the one hand, Greek ideas of wisdom were disseminated: witness SENECA's assertion that 'wisdom' (Latin *sapientia*) 'is the perfect good of the human mind, while philosophy is the love and desire for wisdom' (*Letters* 89.4). Meanwhile, other intellectual traditions, particularly religious ones, assimilated and manipulated Greek *sophia*.

Nowhere was this more apparent than in JUDAISM. The JEWS had a long tradition concerning wisdom, which was associated with the operation of and obedience to divine law, and was the preserve of God's chosen people. Hellenistic Jewish literature, such as the *Wisdom of Solomon*, shows how profound was the influence of Judaism's broader cultural milieu. Wisdom often appears personified in this literature. This was nothing new, in that Sophia appears in ARISTOPHANES (*Birds* 1320), while the inhabitants of hellenistic cities, such as EPHESOS, could erect statues of Sophia and other personifications.

The appearance of Sophia in Jewish literature was not an isolated phenomenon. She became a central figure in GNOSTIC and MANICHAEAN MYTH, while from its beginnings CHRISTIANITY was concerned to stamp its own identity on the nature of wisdom. For the CHURCH, of course, Christ's teachings had revealed the only true wisdom, which was not of this world and so could not be achieved through earthly philosophy (1 Corinthians 2.6–8). AUGUSTINE (1), through his dalliances with philosophy and Manichaeism, was well placed to pass judgement on different claims to wisdom. His affirmation of the exclusivity of Christian wisdom was uncompromising: 'there are not many wisdoms, but one wisdom' (*City of God* 11.10). Yet Augustine's assertion must be seen in the context of his lifelong attachment to NEOPLATONISM. His ideas reflect a masterly synthesis of biblical, classical and hellenistic speculations on wisdom. Just as PAGANS, Jews, Gnostics and Manichaeans were able to personify wisdom, so too were Christians: witness the great church dedicated by the emperor JUSTINIAN (527–65) to Holy Wisdom (Hagia Sophia) at CONSTANTINOPLE. Through this apotheosis, ancient wisdom was handed down to medieval and modern civilization. MDH

See Guthrie, W. K. C. (1962–81) *A History of Greek Philosophy*, 6 vols.; Kee, H. C. (1995) *Who are the People of God?*; Momigliano, A. (1971) *Alien Wisdom*.

women

Our sources give us limited access to the lives of Greek women at any period. In the archaic period, we have only POETRY and material remains. In the classical period, the range of sources written by MEN increases. Only in the hellenistic period, however, do we begin to have more extensive access to the lives of ordinary women in the form of LETTERS (some by women) written on PAPYRUS from Greek and Roman Egypt, inscriptions on stone honouring female civic donors and MAGISTRATES, and monuments perhaps erected by women themselves. The voices of women are few. Among women POETS of antiquity, we have little preserved from the famous SAPPHO of LESBOS (7th century BC) and a few poems or fragments from the later (largely hellenistic) poets CORINNA, ERINNA, Nossis, Anyte and Moiro. Women studied at the philosophical schools of PLATO and EPICURUS, or practised CYNIC PHILOSOPHY (HIPPARCHIA, married to the Cynic Krates); the scholarly HYPATIA headed a NEOPLATONIC philosophical school at ALEXANDRIA in the 4th–5th centuries AD. Some treatises attributed to female PYTHAGOREAN PHILOSOPHERS like Theano may date from the 4th century BC or later. The Athenian statesman PERIKLES' mistress, the hetaira ASPASIA, was said to have ghost-written his speeches and composed a treatise on HOUSEHOLD management. By the hellenistic period, a few women had begun to enter professions as obstetricians (Hagnodike) and painters (e.g. the famous Laia or Lala of Kyzikos).

At all periods, the primary role of respectable women was to reproduce the families of their husbands (as wife) or fathers (as an 'heiress' or *epiklêros* who could be married off to male relatives to produce heirs for her paternal line). Wives and unmarried women cared for children, worked wool, made clothing, and supervised and guarded the household and its SLAVES. Even SPARTAN women, who perhaps did not perform these household duties, engaged in

WOMEN: (a) life and work for respectable women, as depicted on this Greek vase painting, were expected to be largely focused on the domestic sphere. How true this was for all sectors of society is more open to debate.

WOMEN: (b) a wealthy Roman woman attended by her female servants, in a relief from Germany.

ATHLETIC exercise in order to produce better children for their highly militarized state. Poorer women sold goods in the marketplace, shopped, and worked in the fields; but middle and upper class women, especially of child-bearing age, were meant to spend most of their time in the HOUSE and, in classical Athens, may even have been segregated to some extent in special women's quarters, if our sources are to be believed. Few women are likely to have been literate until the hellenistic period, which saw the establishment of some SCHOOLS for girls.

The emerging city-states of Greece had increasingly regulated MARRIAGE and the lives of Greek women. Athens, for example, in 451 passed a CITIZENSHIP law that deprived of their citizenship all children (including those of concubines) except those with two citizen parents. Growing legislation on ADULTERY and RAPE also reflects a concern to insure the legitimacy of children.

Although Spartan and some other Greek women could own property, women in DEMOCRATIC Athens were legal minors, who could do little more than the week's shopping without the consent of a male guardian. Throughout the Greek world, women were generally barred from any significant participation in politics, though their indirect influence may have been greater in the case of ARISTOCRATIC women not living in DEMOCRACIES. In hellenistic Egypt, however, the PTOLEMAIC queens were active rulers, whether in conjunction with their husbands or even on their own (the famous CLEOPATRA). Ideal and reality did not always correspond, of course, and we have evidence that women discreetly visited neighbours and had considerably informal influence on family affairs and finances, including WILLS.

In Athens, respectable women's names were not supposed to be mentioned publicly unless they were dead. PERIKLES' famous funeral oration of 431 advises widows that for them the best reputation consisted in being talked of least, whether in praise or blame (THUCYDIDES 2.45.2). Spartan women, however, were famous for their public reinforcement of civic ideology (PLUTARCH, *Sayings of Spartan Women*). Moreover, at all periods and ages, Greek women played an active role in RELIGION both inside and outside the house. Girls participated in CHORUSES in honour of deities and in various initiatory rites. At Athens, the young Arrephoroi helped WEAVE the robe for the statue of the goddess ATHENA and performed secret RITUALS on the ACROPOLIS. Other unmarried girls performed RITUALS and DANCED as 'bears' for ARTEMIS at BRAURON. Throughout Greece, women organized and ran their own all-female rituals for DEMETER, such as the Thesmophoria, and served as PRIESTESSES for many other GODDESSES. Women participated in many other local and civic FESTIVALS and officiated at ecstatic rituals for the WINE god DIONYSOS. From the 4th century onwards, however, inscriptions indicate that women who were menstruating, or had recently engaged in sex or delivered children, were excluded from some cults; other cults were exclusive to men. Women played a major role in the BURIAL and cult of the dead. Indeed, in the archaic period their role in death ritual was so assertive that most city-states passed legislation that relegated mourning largely to the private sphere and deprived women of their role as hired mourners in aristocratic funerals. At Athens, women could wail at prescribed points in state funerals, but they could not give public lamentations for the heroic dead as in HOMER's *Iliad*.

Despite their general exclusion from political life, women played an exceptionally important role in the imaginative life of Greek culture. Archaic statues of unmarried maidens, the *KORAI*, adorned graves and the Attic ACROPOLIS, and images of women in family contexts appear on grave *stêlai*. Greek VASE-PAINTINGS show women in many domestic and public contexts (wedding vases were probably made for brides), and express considerable interest in the sexual lives of courtesans and PROSTITUTES, who also received attention in literature on the Greek *SYMPOSION* or drinking party. The mythical defeat of the all-female race of AMAZONS pointedly adorned the friezes of TEMPLES and public buildings. Nude statues of the goddess APHRODITE made their debut in the 4th century. Women were apparently appreciative viewers of public as well as private ART, especially at religious sites.

The epics of Homer laud the virtues of the faithful Penelope, while only discreetly criticizing the infamous HELEN. Homer's aristocratic wives are present at, and have considerable interest in, the court life presided over by their husbands. In the *Odyssey*'s utopian Scheria, women even adjudicate quarrels for their male favourites. The archaic poet HESIOD, by contrast, links the creation of the first woman (Pandora) with the fall of man from a GOLDEN AGE existence. Attic DRAMA creates heroines who seem to act in a fashion more autonomous, public and heroic than women were ideally meant to in life – though we do not know whether women were present at the dramatic festivals to see them. Heroic virgins in TRAGEDY make noble sacrifices to family, city or state; older mothers can offer men sage advice; but wives often complain about their lot and, like Medea or CLYTEMNESTRA, go so far as to kill their children or husbands. Comic heroines like Lysistrata organize a sex strike for peace, or put the playwright EURIPIDES on trial for misogyny. Literature after the 4th century, such as epic, MIME, NEW COMEDY, and EPIGRAM, instead expresses more interest in the lives of ordinary women and in female victims of sexual passion. (The fragments of Sappho alone, from an earlier period, dwell extensively on female homoerotic relations.)

Medical and biological texts express extensive interest in the female body and reproduction. In the classical period, the HIPPOCRATIC DOCTORS practised a humoural MEDICINE that aimed to preserve HEALTH through a proper balance of bodily fluids. They attempted to explain menstruation by postulating that because women were wetter than men and exercised less, they needed to eliminate fluid on a regular basis. As the dissection of humans was not performed until the hellenistic period, the Hippocratics thought that a woman's womb was not firmly attached in place. Unreleased menses, or a dry and hence mobile womb, could cause a range of female ills including MADNESS. Hippocratic doctors thus logically prescribed marriage, intercourse and pregnancy as a cure for these gynaecological ills. Moreover, although the Hippocratic doctors believed that conception resulted from the mixing of male and female seeds drawn from all over the bodies of both partners, ARISTOTLE, whose biological treatises argue directly for the inferiority of the female body, believed that menstrual blood provided matter for the generative male seed to quicken and form. The conception of a female child was in his view a 'natural mutilation'.

The philosophical followers of SOCRATES, Plato and XENOPHON, argue, respectively, that some properly trained women could in the ideal state become rulers and philosopher kings (Plato, *Republic*, book 5), and that husbands should train their wives to manage the household with philosophical awareness (Xenophon, *Oikonomikos*). Aristotle, by contrast, affirms women's inability to assume full moral and political adulthood. Hellenistic philosophical and later treatises followed him in advocating conventional roles for women, though by the 2nd century AD PLUTARCH advocated a more companionable marriage and a philosophical education for wives (*Advice to the Bride and Groom*). HPF

Roman upper class males are responsible for almost all the information we have about Roman women. Not surprisingly, these writers were primarily interested in themselves and their own narrow world. Consequently, our sources for understanding the living conditions of women and their role in society are biased not only by the male perspective but also by their interests. Women did not usually fight WARS or rule the state, but ideally were chaste daughters, wives and mothers. Therefore the descriptions of them in the sources tend to be somewhat stereotypical. If women could not be described as chaste mothers, they were instead evil seductresses or scheming power-mongers, rather than the sensible women they usually were, fulfilling their roles as mothers, wives, educators, MIDWIVES, WETNURSES, ACTRESSES, politicians, PHILOSOPHERS, literary figures, greengrocers, purple-dyers and BENEFACTRESSES. It has become commonplace to describe the female sex as the eternal other in relation to the 'normal' male sex, and this is true also for ancient Rome, where male was the norm. In the past, many studies have simply enumerated everything women could not do or could not be in Roman society. A more positive approach is a focus on what they actually could do and did; in other words, a consideration of the real women, not abstract concepts.

Women had no POLITICAL rights, could not vote and could not be elected as MAGISTRATES. This condition they shared with most people in Rome. The only persons with recognized and usable political rights were MEN of the ARISTOCRACY. Women did, however, play a prominent role in politics throughout the history of Rome, both in a mythologically ideal and in a very concrete way. A woman could be a passive ideal (like LUCRETIA or VERGINIA), expected to exemplify the morals and ideals of the state and happily sacrifice her life for these ideals. She could play an active role in politics, either through the men in her life (CORNELIA, mother of the GRACCHI) or in her own right, like Servilia who, after the assassination of her lover and friend JULIUS CAESAR by her son BRUTUS, chaired political meetings – almost a shadow cabinet – during the political crisis following the murder. The politically active woman was open to criticism, while the passive one was idealized. LIVIA (AUGUSTUS' wife) succeeded in combining a seemingly virtuous and old-fashioned behaviour with a very active political agenda. This combination made her extremely powerful and influential in politics for half a century.

In principle, Roman men considered women to be frail and weak of mind, which meant that they should not have anything to do with business transactions. Therefore women would always require a legal GUARDIAN (a *tutor*). The reality was different from the legality. CICERO would publicly support the concept of female weakness, only to rely at home on his wife Terentia's handling of their finances and to discuss PHILOSOPHY and politics with his daughter TULLIA. Women did indeed control their own finances and appointed their own tutors – frequently FREEDMEN – who would never interfere with their dispositions.

Women's participation in religion tends to be underestimated by modern scholars, but it played an enormous role. Basically, it is not an exaggeration to state that the men went out and won the wars with the help of the women, who stayed home and performed important religious duties by praying, SACRIFICING and living chaste lives. Some of the disasters of the second PUNIC WAR were believed to have been mitigated by the women's donation of GOLD and their offering of PRAYERS to JUNO. This, of course, also meant that women could be seen as responsible for a threatening crisis.

In all aspects of life, a Roman woman was judged by her SEXUALITY or the lack of it. A woman who behaved too independently was always considered promiscuous. CLODIA, wife of Metellus, is a good example: Cicero could publicly question her morals and call her a whore and a PROSTITUTE because her behaviour, in his opinion, came dangerously close to that of a man. She probably did have many lovers, but so did a great many people among the upper classes during the late Republic. Privately, Cicero did not object to her attitudes in the least, but was happy to receive information on the political situation in Rome from her.

Roman women married already when they were in their teens, and their husbands would usually be 10 to 15 years older. Women who reached the age of MARRIAGE could statistically expect to survive until they were about 45 years old. During that time they would give birth, on average, to six children, but would also lose three of them. These are very harsh living conditions, and they inevitably had a huge impact on women's emotional life. Without taking this into account, we can never get a full understanding of women's lives and experiences. Ideally, a woman was only married to one man and remained faithful to his memory if widowed. The technical term for such a woman was *univira* (a one man's woman). Reality was different. DIVORCES and remarriages were frequent, and, by the terms of Augustan legislation, it became illegal to remain unmarried. Nevertheless, the chaste (*pudica* or *casta*) *univira* remained a highly praised ideal, though in real life chastity was not normally a virtue that a husband would emphasize. Strangely enough, however, modern scholars have adopted the idea of the chaste Roman wife as reality, and it is now widely claimed that Romans of all status groups held this ideal. That may well be, but the sources employed by scholars to support their claim – namely, tombstones dedicated by husbands to wives – hardly ever mention these ideals. Among the almost 40,000 epitaphs published from the city of Rome, only a handful mention wifely chastity as a virtue.

All Roman women in pagan times married. To remain unmarried was not an option until CHRISTIANITY developed its anti-familial emphasis on sexual renunciation and ASCETICISM around AD 400. Many, particularly aristocratic, Christian women preferred a life of severe asceticism. They either took the veil and remained virgins of the CHURCH, or made a promise of chastity after becoming widows. It is frequently stated that the popularity of asceticism among Christian women is to be seen as a reaction to the oppression pagan Roman women experienced. That is difficult to understand, however, for most pagan women seem to have been quite independent and thus hardly needed a radical statement like asceticism to obtain freedom from male dominance.

Marriage was also seen as the most important way of creating alliances between FAMILIES and of transferring property. In the ruling classes, these alliances would usually be political, but, among the majority of the working population, marriage partners would typically be found within the same trade or craft. For the owner of a WORKSHOP, it was important that both husband and wife could work side by side to increase the family's income. Roman women were not homemakers, but were required to work along with their husbands. Consequently, children could be a problem. Many newborn children, from both the upper and the working classes, were sent away from home to be raised by WETNURSES. The job of the wetnurse was very important because she, not the child's mother, fed and raised the child during the important first years of its life. Since infant mortality was very high, we rather frequently find tombstones put up to children by their wetnurses.

Another very important job for some Roman women was that of MIDWIFE. The midwife would not only assist women in labour but also diagnose and cure women's DISEASES. Like most crafts at that time, midwives generally learned through apprenticeship. Some midwives, however, were literate and able to read textbooks on gynaecology and obstetrics. SORANUS of EPHESOS wrote one such textbook around AD 100. His advice is very modern and sensible, and a midwife who followed his teachings would be able to save the lives of many mothers and children. The midwife had responsibility for examining the newborn child for congenital weaknesses. If the child were not deemed worth rearing, it would be killed. Children who for some reason were unwanted could be exposed and were often later picked up and reared by someone else. Girls were deemed more useless and, due to the dowry they had to be paid upon marriage, also more expensive than boys; they were therefore more frequently exposed. How often exposure took place cannot even be guessed at, but it was socially accepted and did happen.

The lives of individual midwives and wetnurses are only very infrequently referred to in the literary texts. They did not, like most other Romans, belong to the upper classes. Our best source of information about the lives of ordinary women comes from epitaphs where they are either commemorate or themselves commemorate relatives. Most frequently we see them here as daughters and mothers, but many are also mentioned with some indication of job – like midwife or wetnurse – or as PATRONS (*patronae*) of their own FREEDPERSONS or SLAVES.

Women are visible in all parts of Roman society in many different roles. The view may be blurred by the gender and class bias of the sources, but it is possible, nevertheless, to get a clear picture of Roman women and their lives. HSN

See Fantham, E. et al., eds. (1994) *Women in the Classical World*.

woodcutting see FORESTS AND FORESTRY; FUEL.

woodworking see CARPENTRY.

workshops Craft production in the classical world was carried out in workshops of varying sizes and at different scales of production, as well as in the domestic sphere. These workshops could take the form of whole HOUSES, or combinations of houses, containing well-laid-out and well-constructed production equipment; or single rooms in houses containing such equipment; or sheds or lean-tos built near or against houses, again with production equipment. It is possible to identify workshops in the ARCHAEOLOGICAL record from the remains of the production equipment they contained, as well as from remains of the materials used and the products made. Of course, this depends on the nature of the production activity, since some products, equipment and materials survive better in the archaeological record than others. Evidence of workshops can also be provided by the literary sources. The evidence of these workshops can be used to assess the organization and scale of ancient production, using such criteria as the nature of the equipment and the use of space for production in relation to other activities. Production organized on a larger scale had a large, clearly defined production space with well-made equipment. Smaller-scale

WORKSHOPS: distribution of workshops in Pompeii, illustrating the existence of many small to medium enterprises.

production had a smaller production area, with less well-constructed equipment that may have been used for other activities. The people working in these workshops included SLAVES as well as free craftspeople; in fact it has been argued that 'what counted for most was the workers, not the plant' (Burford 78).

In classical and hellenistic Greece, there is evidence for potters' workshops in Athens and CORINTH. An 'Industrial District' north-west of the AREIOPAGOS in Athens contained a number of different workshops, including some involved in STONE working and terracotta and bronze production. In ancient Greek literary sources we hear of workshops MANUFACTURING FURNITURE and knives, in which over 50 slaves worked (DEMOSTHENES 27.9). In another workshop, slaves ground DRUGS or colours, perhaps producing dyestuffs or paint. In another case, a man employed slaves to make sails in the house in which he lived (Demosthenes 48.12–13). Another man had three workshops which produced and sold PERFUME, in which slaves made up at least part of the workforce (Hypereides, *Against Athenogenes*). Workshop scenes are depicted on painted POTTERY and gravestones.

There is also evidence of Roman workshops, some organized on a much larger scale than their classical Greek counterparts. In POMPEII, for instance, a number of workshops have been found. These included TEXTILE workshops such as FULLERIES, DYEWORKS, and SPINNING and WEAVING shops. Most Roman FORTS had an area devoted to the manufacture of equipment and other necessities of army life, but the military also purchased items made by workshops located in the civilian communities outside the forts themselves. At Rome and elsewhere, inscriptions and other evidence point to a high degree of specialized labour within individual enterprises when the number of workers permitted. Nevertheless, the typical establishment involved fewer than ten people. Large-scale output was generally achieved as the aggregate production of many small workshops, even in the POTTERY industry, where some very large enterprises are known. MDM

See Arafat, K. and Morgan, C. (1989) Pots and potters in Athens and Corinth, *OJA* 8.3: 311–46; Burford, A. (1972) *Craftsmen in Greek and Roman Society*; Finley, M. I. (1973) *Studies in Land and Credit in Ancient Athens, 500–200 BC*; Moeller, W. O. (1976) *The Wool Trade of Ancient Pompeii*; Young, R. S. (1951) An industrial district of ancient Athens, *Hesperia* 20: 135–288.

 GOLD; PERFUME; SCULPTURE: (a).

world systems analysis see CORE–PERIPHERY.

worry (Greek *meletê*, Latin *cura*) A characteristic of an AGRICULTURAL society such as classical Greece and Rome, where independent yeomen comprised the majority of the population and autonomous communities were often a harvest away from real hunger. Such rural anxieties were superimposed on society at large in a variety of literary, political, religious, military and artistic ways. The concern to preserve the annual harvest explains much of the classical Greek reliance on short, decisive warfare as practised by amateur heavy infantry militias, who were bothered by absences away from their crops and the possible ravaging of farmland by enemy invaders. The terror of formal collision of agrarian armies was assuaged through pre-battle speeches, ANIMAL SACRIFICES and drinking. Early Greek and Roman legal codes resonate with agrarian tension, and thus were aimed at protecting fruit-trees and vines, sources of irrigation water, and crops from theft and roaming animals. Religious FESTIVALS in honour of DEMETER and CERES reflect the larger social uncertainties over soil fertility and successful crop propagation – it was never assured that each new season the seeds would germinate or the blossoms develop into fruit. In literature, a variety of farmers – HESIOD, XENOPHON's Ischomachos (in *Oikonomikos*), ARISTOPHANES' Dikaiopolis (in *Acharnians*), the folk of AELIAN's and Alkiphron's epistles, and VIRGIL's rustics – appear as cantankerous, worrisome and near-paranoid. They are conservative: loyal to time-honoured agricultural practices and social customs that had proven records of crop successes, they alone ensured agrarian continuity. VDH

See Hanson, V. D. (1995) *The Other Greeks: the agrarian roots of western civilization*.

writing In 494 BC, 120 boys died when the roof collapsed at a SCHOOL on CHIOS. There was one survivor. HERODOTOS, in this earliest reference to formal schooling in the Greek world, tells us that the ill-fated students had been learning letters (6.27). Writing pervades both Greek and Roman society. Much of public and private life would have required contact with writing. But LITERACY is a broad term, and only a small number may have enjoyed highly developed skills of both reading and writing. The victims of the Chios disaster are likely to have been in the minority. Formal EDUCATION was the preserve of the wealthy. Any community which could boast writing skills among 20–30 per cent of its population would probably have been exceptional in the classical period, and unusual in hellenistic times. GENDER also affected reading and writing skills: boys, not girls, were the victims at Chios.

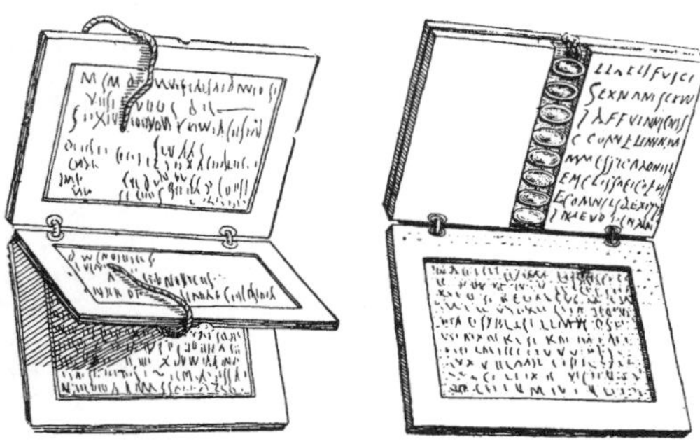

WRITING: triple-leaf wax writing tablets were often used for legal documents, with copies being witnessed and sealed (upper r.).

Evidence for writing survives painted or scratched on pieces of POTTERY, inscribed on STONE or bronze, or scratched onto LEAD tablets. The abundance of PAPYRI from Egypt and the ink writing tablets from VINDOLANDA (England) illustrate the extensive use of perishable materials for writing. Scenes showing written materials in an educational environment are preserved in Greek VASE-PAINTINGS. The earliest evidence of Greek writing appears in the late 8th century BC, and the ORAL nature of written Greek is particularly dominant in the archaic and early classical periods.

The evidence for OSTRACISM at Athens in the first few decades of the 5th century suggests that many citizens enjoyed basic reading skills, but not all could necessarily have written the name of the politician they wished to expel; archaeologists have found batches of *ostraka* all written by the same person, perhaps for handing out to those unable to write. By the late classical period, writing was part of daily life for most people in the Greek world, and writing could be found on public display in many communities in the form of inscriptions, even if they were only tombstones recording the names of the deceased, or dedications to GODS.

Under the Roman empire, certain groups may have had more access to writing materials and education. Some SOLDIERS, for instance, seem to have picked up Latin in addition to their own language. The Vindolanda tablets reveal that soldiers who came from the area of what is now Belgium and the Netherlands were using written letters to communicate to friends and family. At POMPEII we have a unique insight into the use of writing in a townscape. Graffiti decorate the walls of many buildings and ADVERTISE, for example, the virtues or vices of local politicians or SLAVE girls. The evidence of the graffiti here suggests that many residents could read. Even if not all people could write, the diffusion of written materials in the Greek and Roman world is the legacy of a literate society. GJO

See Bowman, A.K. (1994) *Life and Letters on the Roman Frontier*; Harris, W.V. (1989) *Ancient Literacy*; Thomas, R. (1992) *Literacy and Orality in Ancient Greece*.

 ALPHABETS; SULPICIA LEPIDINA.

X

Xanthos The chief city of LYCIA, known already to HOMER. It was famous for its resistance to Harpagos, the general of CYRUS THE GREAT, and the self-immolation of its population (545 BC); this sacrifice is said to have been repeated in 42 BC when the city was besieged by BRUTUS. Xanthos was restored and repopulated soon after the Persian sack, and indeed the destruction was apparently not as wholesale as HERODOTOS says. In the middle of the 4th century, Xanthos and Lycia came under the control of the Hekatomnids of CARIA. The city had a major sanctuary of LETO, and was noted for its tombs (of which the so-called 'Lion Tomb' is thought to be that of the first PERSIAN dynast of the city) and for the Nereid monument (now in the British Museum). Xanthos is also noted for its major EPIGRAPHIC finds, including trilingual inscriptions dating from the time of the PELOPONNESIAN WAR and the mid-4th century. WH

See Keen, A. G. (1998) *Dynastic Lycia*.

 ANATOLIA.

Xenophanes fl. c.550 BC PRESOCRATIC PHILOSOPHER and POET from Kolophon in Ionia. Sometimes hailed in antiquity as the founder of the 'Italian' branch of philosophy, he had a profound influence on PARMENIDES. Fragments of a number of works survive, including *SYMPOSIUM* poetry. His philosophical views, also in verse, criticize conventional theology and offer an alternative, rational theological view. First, he censures the poets for their depiction of GODS acting immorally. Second, he seems impressed by the fact that different nations each depict their gods in their own image and offers the following *reductio ad absurdum*: 'If horses had hands they would draw the form of the gods like horses . . .'. Rejecting traditional anthropomorphism, Xenophanes instead offers a picture of a god which can move everything by thought (so has no need to locomote, which is 'unfitting' for a divinity) and all of which sees, all of which hears.

Xenophanes was also interested in epistemology. He was pessimistic about man's chances of attaining sure and confirmed knowledge, but nevertheless recommended constant enquiry as a route to better approximations to the truth. The fact that fossils of sea creatures had been discovered far inland led him to conclude that the sea periodically advances and retreats. A similar rationalist and empiricist trend can be seen in his other COSMOLOGICAL pronouncements. He stressed, for example, that Iris, the rainbow, is 'a cloud'. JIW

See Lesher, J. (1992) *Xenophanes of Colophon: fragments*; Broadie, S. (1999) Rational theology, in A. A. Long, ed., *The Cambridge Companion to Early Greek Philosophy* 205–24; Lesher, J. (1999) Early interest in knowledge, in A. A. Long, ed., *The Cambridge Companion to Early Greek Philosophy* 225–49.

Xenophon c.430–c.350 BC Athenian HISTORIAN, PHILOSOPHER and professional SOLDIER, all of whose known works survive. Xenophon is important for the political and intellectual history of the late 5th and 4th centuries. Not only a chronicler of his age, he had first-hand knowledge of several key events of his lifetime, and knew personally some of its most important figures. Although not a thinker of the first order, few from antiquity can match his range and originality.

Born into a wealthy family during the early years of the PELOPONNESIAN WAR, Xenophon was from the Attic DEME of Erchia (also ISOKRATES' deme). In all likelihood a knight (*hippeus*), he probably saw combat late in the war. In his early years at Athens, he became associated with the circle of individuals who admired SOCRATES. His ÉLITE background, association with Socrates and eye-witness awareness in the relevant portions of his *Hellenika* encourage the view that he was involved in the government of the THIRTY Tyrants immediately following the war (404–403). In the spring of 401 he joined the Greek MERCENARY contingent of the army of CYRUS THE YOUNGER, who was attempting to wrest the PERSIAN throne from his brother ARTAXERXES II. Following Cyrus' death at the battle of Kounaxa (Cunaxa), and the later abduction and murder of the commanders of the Greeks, Xenophon emerged as an important leader, helping the Ten Thousand march back from BABYLONIA to the Greek world. He served briefly as a mercenary under Seuthes, king of THRACE. When the mercenaries were absorbed into a Spartan army operating in ASIA Minor, Xenophon was as well, and he remained there for the next five years.

It was during this period of increased Spartan involvement in Asia that Xenophon came to know the Spartan king AGESILAOS. With the outbreak of the Corinthian war, Agesilaos returned to Greece, and Xenophon with him. He seems to have witnessed first-hand the battle of KORONEIA (394). Either because of his presence in the Spartan ranks at Koroneia or because of his service with Cyrus, or perhaps both, he was exiled from Athens during this period. Thanks to his Spartan connections, he was granted an estate at Skillous near OLYMPIA, where he lived until Spartan control of the northern PELOPONNESE collapsed after the battle of LEUKTRA in 371. Although a return to Athens cannot be ruled out (his exile was at some point revoked), the Corinthian orientation of the later books of the *Hellenika* have suggested to some that he lived out his last years in that city. He was married and had two sons, one of whom (Gryllos) was killed in combat before the battle of MANTINEIA (361). Xenophon died soon after 355.

Xenophon wrote important works of history and philosophy, as well as technical treatises. His *Hellenika* is a history of the Greek world from 411 to 361. It is in some sense intended as a continuation of

Thucydides' history of the Peloponnesian war, picking up where, roughly speaking, the earlier work stops. Written in at least two different stages of Xenophon's career (early and late), it focuses on the expansion and collapse of Spartan power. It has been criticized for major omissions due to pro-Spartan and anti-Theban bias; a moralizing tendency that obscures historical explanation; and reliance on the divine at a crucial juncture in the narrative (5.4.1). A more sympathetic view sees the work as a departure from the type of war monograph pioneered by Thucydides, and a move towards history centred on *exempla* or paradigms, especially examples of good leadership (see esp. 5.1.3–4); in this regard it anticipates later Greek historiography. One also sees in it a significant panhellenic component which is challenged by a sense of pessimism in its final pages, with the Greek world beset by confusion and disorder.

The *Anabasis* is Xenophon's memoirs of his march 'up-country' (*anabasis* means 'ascent') and return with the Ten Thousand Greek soldiers under Cyrus. It illustrates the increasing importance of the mercenary, and sheds light on the workings of the Achaemenid empire. It, too, contains elements of biography and autobiography, as well as a panhellenic perspective. The *Constitution of the Spartans* (*Lakedaimoniôn politeia*) is also important and, together with passages from the *Hellenika*, provides an unparalleled 'insider's' view of Spartan society. *Agesilaos* is a treatment of the Spartan king, and probably the first true biography in Greek literature.

A number of works have Socrates as the central figure: *Apology*, *Symposium*, *Memorabilia* and *Oikonomikos*. In general they present a Socrates who is much more interested in practical issues of day-to-day living than the man we see in Plato, in topics ranging from self-control to the ordering of the household. His piety is also a common theme (esp. *Memorabilia* 1.1), as is an effort to distance him from the events of the Thirty. Texts especially illustrative of Xenophon's views are the choice of Herakles and a very un-Socratic treatment of the design of the universe (*Memorabilia* 2.1.21ff., 1.4). Taken together, these works provide important testimony about Socrates separate from that of Plato. *Cyropaedia* (*Kyrou paideia*, *Education of Cyrus*) is an idealized account of the life of Cyrus the Great, especially his training to be a leader of men; it is a full-scale treatment of ideal leadership, and is important for the evolution of the ancient novel. The combination of interest in Socrates and Cyrus is paralleled in Cynic works, among them those of Antisthenes. *Hieron* is a dialogue between that tyrant and the poet Simonides, and concerns tyranny.

Xenophon's technical treatises are *Revenues*, *The Cavalry Commander*, *On Horsemanship* and *On Hunting*. *Revenues* (*Poroi*) is especially important: written shortly after the Social war (355), it demonstrates a conception of revenue generation almost unparalleled in the ancient world. It is a prime example of the technical works whose frequency increased in the 4th century (like that of Aeneas Tacticus).

A work entitled *Constitution of the Athenians* (*Athênaiôn politeia*, often called *The Old Oligarch*) was also included in the works of Xenophon in antiquity, but is usually thought not to be by him. JDD

See many accessible translations, including the complete works in the Loeb Classical Library; Anderson, J. K. (1974) *Xenophon*; Higgins, W. E. (1972) *Xenophon the Athenian*; Tuplin, C., ed. (2004) *Xenophon and his World*.

Xerxes (Khshayarshan) Persian king (r.486–465 BC), son of Darius I and Atossa, who is best known in the Western historical tradition for his attempt to force the mainland Greeks to submit to Persian rule. His expedition to Greece was partly successful: some states, such as Thessaly and Thebes, did submit through medism while others, such as Argos, claimed neutrality. The Spartans and Athenians, who had famously refused to submit, were prominent in fighting Xerxes' army in 480/79 in the sea battles of Artemision and Salamis and the land battles of Thermopylai, Plataea and Mykale. Xerxes himself was forced to retreat after being defeated in the battle of Salamis, and his subordinate Mardonios was beaten back after Mykale. While we know something of Khshayarshan's projected persona from the Persepolis texts, the colourful character of Xerxes is best known from 5th-century Greek accounts, most notably Aeschylus' *Persians* and Herodotos' *Histories*. Greek accounts dwell on the excessive aspects of Xerxes in contrast with the more moderate Darius I: the wealth of his palace, his cruelty, and his hybristic interference in the order of nature – he cuts through land to make the Athos canal, and whips the Hellespont when it destroys his bridge. These accounts should be read as Greek attempts to explain the failure of Xerxes' expedition within the traditional moral framework of *hybris*. Xerxes was murdered in 465 in a palace incident, along with his son. ED

See Kuhrt, A. (1995) *The Ancient Near East c.3000–330 BC*, vol. 2.

Persian wars, Greek.

Y

Yahweh Of the many names used of the GOD of Israel in antiquity, Yahweh became the most important and the only one used in cultic contexts. Its origins are unclear; it is not attested in other religions of the region, but by the later stages of the composition of the BIBLE it had become the paramount name of God. We find, in inscriptions from the 7th century BC onwards, a predominance of personal names formed with Yahweh, indicating that it had by this period become predominant. In a 4th-century Jewish colony at Elephantine in Egypt a form Yhw continued, often in combination with names of other gods (e.g. *'ntyhw*, 'Anath-Yahwe'), reflecting an earlier tradition of various local gods with the name Yahweh. In JEWISH tradition, the name came to be understood as symbolic of divine presence (cf. Exodus 3.14), perhaps through its formal association with the verb 'to be' in Hebrew, and of the enduring nature of god 'who was, and is, and ever shall be'. It was translated into Greek in the SEPTUAGINT of Exodus 3 by 'the one who is', and this was taken by the Jewish PHILOSOPHER PHILO JUDAEUS as denoting philosophical immutability. A Greek form of the name is found as IAO on a 4th-century BC coin and in one early Greek biblical manuscript, but the Greek *kyrios* ('lord') was generally used. IAO was, however, adopted into MAGIC and can be found in many magical texts – not all necessarily Jewish, given the syncretistic nature of such works. JKA

York (anc. Eboracum) An important Roman centre in northern England. Established as a legionary FORTRESS in the late 1st century AD, it later developed into the provincial capital of BRITANNIA Inferior. The town, on the opposite bank of the river Ouse to the fortress, was eventually promoted to the rank of *colonia*. As the closest legionary base to HADRIAN'S WALL, York retained its military importance into the 4th century. After the withdrawal of the Legion IX Hispana (to be lost on another FRONTIER) in the early 2nd century, it housed the Legion VI Victrix. Major EXCAVATIONS here have revealed important details of the fortress, the town and particularly the everyday life of the population.

The historical importance of the site lies in the coincidental deaths there of two EMPERORS and in what followed. SEPTIMIUS SEVERUS used York as the base from which to launch campaigns deep into Scotland from 208 to 211. When he died in 211, his elder son CARACALLA concluded peace with unseemly haste, in order to get back to Rome and settle scores with his brother Geta. In 306, the death of the Western AUGUSTUS, Constantius Chlorus, led to the proclamation as emperor of his son, CONSTANTINE, by the army, which was wintering at York after campaigning against the Picts. Again, this was a defining moment in imperial history, wrecking the TETRARCHIC system set up by DIOCLETIAN and sparking renewed civil war, before Constantine's final victory over LICINIUS in 324. DJM

See Ottaway, P. (2000) *Roman York*.

BRITANNIA.

Z

Zakynthos see IONIAN ISLANDS; PETROLEUM PRODUCTS; WATERPROOFING.

Zama (Zama Regia or Zama Maior, Colonia Aelia Hadriana Augusta Zama Regia) Almost certainly to be identified with modern Jama, 30 km (19 miles) north of Mactar in central Tunisia. It was perhaps here that SCIPIO AFRICANUS defeated HANNIBAL in 202 BC. A royal seat of the Numidian king Juba, Zama was identified by SALLUST as an *urbs magna* ('great city'), though it may have suffered during the war with JUGURTHA (*Jugurthine War* 56.1, 57.1). Zama contained a community of Roman citizens, probably *negotiatores* ('businessmen'), before its seizure by JULIUS CAESAR at the end of the civil war in Africa ([Hirtius], *African War* 97.1). The city became a colony under HADRIAN, and was later a seat of a BISHOPRIC. RBH

Zarathustra see ZOROASTER.

Zeno (Zenon) of Citium 334–262 BC The founder of STOICISM. A PHOENICIAN by birth and a merchant by trade, Zeno was converted to PHILOSOPHY by a description of SOCRATES in XENOPHON's *Memorabilia*. He went on to study with contemporary thinkers in the Socratic tradition, notably Polemo (PLATO's successor; the Greek form of his name is Polemon) and Krates the CYNIC. His mature philosophy, which he taught at Athens in the Painted STOA (hence 'Stoic'), shares with the Cynics the position that happiness is entirely a function of mental attitude: only the belief that your circumstances are bad can make you unhappy. The virtuous live 'according to NATURE', welcoming everything that happens in the understanding that it is part of the unfolding life of the cosmos. They are, in consequence, 'indifferent' to their material circumstances. (In his *Republic*, for example, Zeno notoriously employed Cynic arguments to show that an ideally happy community would be uninterested in the conventional trappings of civilization.) Despite this, Zeno thought it right that our everyday choices should be based on 'preferences' determined by our natures as human beings (according to a model that owes much to Polemo). We do normally try to be healthy, for example, and even pursue pleasure: Zeno himself was partial to FIGS and sunbathing. It is just that our happiness is unaffected by the outcome. Zeno's LOGIC and PHYSICS bolstered the conclusion of his ETHICS by showing that nature is governed by FATE – inexorable laws of CAUSE and effect. What happens is inevitable, so one's only hope is to enjoy it! On Zeno's death, leadership of his school passed in turn to his pupils Kleanthes and Chrysippos. GB-S

See Long, A.A. and Sedley, D.N. (1987) *The Hellenistic Philosophers*; Sharples, R.W. (1996) *Stoics, Epicureans and Sceptics*.

Zeno (Zenon) the Eleatic b.490–485 BC A pupil of PARMENIDES and fellow-citizen of Elea in southern Italy. Zeno sought to defend Parmenides' claims that change and plurality are unreal, by showing that the common-sense beliefs in change and plurality are paradoxical and incoherent. All or most of his arguments were in the form of antinomies, deriving pairs of apparently incompatible conclusions from these common-sense beliefs – for instance, that if there are many things they must be both finite and infinite in number, and both sizeless and infinitely large. His most influential arguments, reported in ARISTOTLE's *Physics* (6.2, 6.9 and 8.8), are PARADOXES involving MOTION. Of these the most famous is now known as 'ACHILLES and the tortoise'. Zeno argues that if a fast runner such as Achilles gives a slow-moving tortoise a head start in a race, he can never catch up. Before he can catch up, Achilles must first run to the tortoise's starting-point (*A*); but by the time he reaches *A* the tortoise has moved on a little distance, to *B*; now Achilles must run to *B*, but by the time he reaches it the tortoise has again moved on a little way, to *C*: when Achilles reaches *C*, the tortoise has moved on to *D* – and so on *ad infinitum*. No matter how many times Achilles repeats this process, he is always one stage behind the tortoise and so – apparently – can never catch up with it. Zeno's paradoxes continue to inspire and provoke both philosophers and mathematicians. RLJ

See Barnes, J. (1979) *The Presocratic Philosophers*; Kirk, G.S., Raven, J.E. and Schofield, M. (1983) *The Presocratic Philosophers*.

Zenobia Ruler of PALMYRA C.AD 267–72, whose exploits generated much legend. After the assassination of her husband, Odenathus, Zenobia governed the Near East as regent for their son, Vaballathus. Odenathus claimed to be an agent on Rome's behalf, but Zenobia transformed Palmyrene hegemony into an empire and expanded into Roman ARABIA and EGYPT. Mints at ANTIOCH and ALEXANDRIA issued two-headed COINS portraying Vaballathus on the obverse and AURELIAN on the reverse. While coin legends were at first cautious, later Alexandrian issues proclaimed full imperial status for Vaballathus and Zenobia. These increasing claims reflected the growing conflict between Palmyra and Rome. After retaking Egypt, Aurelian in 272 moved against Palmyra, which capitulated after a SIEGE. Zenobia was captured alive during an attempt to escape to PERSIA. Although Aurelian was generous to Palmyra, it revolted in 273 and was besieged and captured again.

Sources report Zenobia's fate variously. Some state that she died on the journey to Rome, others that she graced Aurelian's TRIUMPH in 274 and was executed, and still others that she lived near Rome in retirement after the triumph. Nothing is known of Vaballathus. Zenobia's descendants, possibly through daughters, were living in Italy a century later. Like other female rulers, she was viewed with a mixture of admiration and disgust. She herself encouraged comparison with Cleopatra, whom she surpassed in chastity at least: Zenobia never engaged in sexual intercourse, except when she was absolutely certain that she was not already pregnant. JV

See Stoneman, R. (1992) *Palmyra and its Empire*; Watson, A. (1999) *Aurelian and the Third Century.*

Zenon Archive see Apollonios the *dioikêtês*; archives.

Zeugma Town at a crossing of the upper Euphrates, where the river turns east from the westernmost part of its course, in modern Turkey. The name, which means a join (from *zeugnumi*, to join X to Y) or span (bridge), is entirely appropriate: the city consisted of two settlements, Apameia on the east bank (or north, given the river's flow here) and Seleukeia on the west (south). Both were founded c.300 BC by Seleukos I Nikator, who named them to honour himself and his Iranian wife Apama; he also built a bridge. The colloquial name Zeugma celebrates their marriage, but also the linking of Syria and Mesopotamia, of west and east. The region, inhabited previously, thrived particularly through the hellenistic and Roman periods until the Persian wars of the 3rd century AD, when Zeugma ceased to house a legion. The city survived the Islamic conquest, remaining a bishopric until at least 1048, but disappears from the record subsequently.

Until recently, Zeugma was usually identified with Birecik, a few kilometres to the south. In 1917, Franz Cumont argued for Belkis, and in 1976 Jörg Wagner discovered there some roof-tiles bearing the rare stamp *Legio IIII Scythica* (which had headquarters at Zeugma). As yet, no inscription gives the name of Seleukeia, Apameia or Zeugma, but scholars generally accept the identification. Little archaeological work had been done until the late 20th century, when the imminent construction of a dam downstream counselled immediate rescue excavation. The finds, of pottery, coins, glass, gemstones, metalwork, mosaics, inscriptions and works of art, as well as remains of buildings, streets, water supply and more, have been spectacular. They reveal a city of considerable size, importance and wealth. Work continues, but parts of the site are now under water, raising the possibility of permanent destruction and making recovery more difficult. JV

See Kennedy, D. et al. (1998) *The Twin Towns of Zeugma on the Euphrates*; Wagner, J. (1976) *Seleukeia am Euphrat/Zeugma.*

Zeus King of the gods (Latin Jupiter). Indo-European origins can be seen in Zeus' name, derived from a root meaning 'day', '(clear) sky'. The succession myth in Hesiod's *Theogony* has close parallels in Hittite and Mesopotamian myth. With help from Rhea, Zeus deposes his father Kronos, who had himself deposed Ouranos. Thereafter Zeus establishes order, overcoming challenges from the Giants and Typhon and allotting particular spheres of influence to the gods. Marriages to Metis, Themis and Hera, and liaisons with various mortal women, produce numerous offspring. Ganymede is Zeus' only homosexual beloved. In Homer Zeus is 'father and king of gods and men', his main domain the upholding of justice at both cosmic and human levels. He is especial protector of kings, strangers and suppliants. The 'will of Zeus' is often indistinguishable from 'fate'. Epithets such as 'cloud-gathering' and 'delighting in thunder' emphasize his association with weather, reflected in the frequent choice of mountain-tops as his primary place of worship.

Zeus' main panhellenic sanctuary was at Olympia, where the quadrennial festival involved a huge sacrifice to Zeus Olympios, followed by the games. The smaller sanctuary at Nemea also hosted quadrennial games. At Dodona, Zeus' oracle answered enquiries through the sound of the wind in an oak tree and the flight of doves, or via ecstatic priestesses, the drawing of lots or hydromancy (divination by water vessels). Although often called Polieus, Zeus had only a few *polis* festivals and no major temple on a city's *akropolis*. At Athens, the Dipolieia festival focused on the strange ritual of the Bouphonia, while the Diasia honoured Zeus Meilichios ('of propitiation'), represented in the form of a snake, who received holocausts or bloodless offerings. On a smaller scale, Zeus Agoraios ('of the *agora*') oversaw the community's political and commercial life, Zeus Phratrios or Patrôios was a patron of phratries and clans, Zeus Herkeios protected individual households, and across all groupings Zeus was the primary *sôtêr* ('saviour') in times of crisis.

In art Zeus is a mature, bearded male figure, his most common attribute the thunderbolt. In the archaic period he strides; in the classical and later periods he is more often seated, holding a sceptre, as in Pheidias' cult statue at Olympia. He appears in many scenes, from the Gigantomachy to pursuits of mortals, in the latter case depicted in appropriate animal form. His appearances as a bull to Europa, and as a swan to Leda, are among the more popular depictions. EJS

See Arafat, K.W. (1990) *Classical Zeus*; Dowden, K. (2005) *Zeus*; Lloyd-Jones, H. (1983) *The Justice of Zeus.*

Athena; drama: (b); earthquakes; gods and goddesses: (b).

zodiac A band of the night sky 8° on either side of the ecliptic, the imaginary line depicting the Sun's apparent path through the heavens. The zodiac is divided into a dozen 30° segments, each named from a constellation in the sector and representing approximately one month. The cycle starts at the spring equinox, when Aries, the first sign of the zodiac, appears at the ecliptic. Taurus, Gemini, Cancer, Leo, Virgo, Libra, Scorpio, Sagittarius, Capricorn, Aquarius and Pisces follow. The zodiac was used primarily for astrology, which plotted locations of the known planets into the zodiac and interpreted their impact. The early history is obscure, but the zodiac was probably developed in Mesopotamia in the late 6th or early 5th century BC to lend greater precision to the observations of astronomers. The earliest uses on record are 464 BC in general terms, and late in the 5th century BC for horoscopes. After an early practice of dividing each sign into beginning, middle and end, overlapping partitions developed. The 36 decans, adopted from Egypt, partitioned them into three segments of 10° each. Five

ZODIAC: (a) miniature from a 9th-century AD manuscript of Ptolemy. In the centre is a representation of the chariot of the sun, surrounded by 12 nude females representing hours (day/night distinguished by white/black), with the next circle of 12 figures representing the months of the year and the outer ring the signs of the zodiac. The day and hour of transition from one sign of the zodiac to another can be deduced from the inscriptions.

ZODIAC: (b) relief from Argos depicting 12 signs of the zodiac, seven planets and the moon.

unequally spaced terms were also used, while dodecatemories, applied variously by different writers, sectioned each sign into 12 parts.

Beyond astrology, the zodiac was used for other purposes. Although writers do not agree on details, the GEOGRAPHY of the known world was sometimes allocated to signs of the zodiac, as were parts of the body. The zodiac was also an important element in religions with a COSMOLOGICAL element, like MITHRAISM. JV

See Barton, T. (1994) *Ancient Astrology*.

Zonaras see CASSIUS DIO; SCHOLARSHIP, BYZANTINE.

zoos The connection between royal power and the ability to collect ANIMALS was probably imprinted upon the classical consciousness by the *paradeisoi* (HUNTING parks) of the PERSIAN kings. Here, exotic animals were collected so that they could be hunted by the king or other high-status individuals. In the hellenistic period, we hear of zoos in the context of royal power. Ptolemy II Euergetes, for instance, seems to have had a very well-stocked one. Their inhabitants might be put on display at royal FESTIVALS.

Evidence for zoos in the Roman world is better than for the Greek. Roman ARISTOCRATS developed breeding areas (*roboraria* or *leporaria*) on their estates in the Republican period. The early terms developed as descriptions of the structures, *roboraria* because they were made of oak, *leporarium* connected with the breeding of rabbits. By the end of the 1st century BC, they had been extended to other animals: VARRO refers to a *leporarium* that housed wild boars (*On Farming* 3.8). These breeding facilities were connected with the gastronomic demands of the Roman aristocratic dinner table, and discussion is found in combination with other structures designed to provide luxury foods – FISH PONDS and apiaries. In the imperial period, *vivaria* as breeding grounds, or specialized hunting parks, are supplemented by *vivaria* for exotic animals to be used at imperial spectacles. NERO's Golden House included a menagerie, and there is solid evidence for an imperial ELEPHANT farm near Laurentum, as well as separate *vivaria* for herbivores and 'fierce' animals outside Rome. DSP

Zoroaster (Zôroastrês in Greek; Iranian Zarathustra or Zarathushtra, 'camel-driver') An Iranian religious prophet. He is credited with introducing a new theology based upon the worship of Ahura-Mazda ('Lord Wisdom'), a creator GOD responsible for the universe in all its aspects, including EVIL. To account for evil, Zoroaster introduced a dualism based upon the twin children of Ahura-Mazda, *Spenta Mainyu* ('Beneficient Spirit') and *Angra Mainyu* ('Hostile Spirit'), who chose *asha* ('truth') and *druj* ('lie') respectively. In the battle between good and evil, mankind must make right choices, bringing about the Last Judgement, with a torrent of FIRE like a river of molten metal. Similarities to early JEWISH and CHRISTIAN eschatologies (theologies of 'last things') have generated endless scholarly debate. The teachings survive as a series of short HYMNS to Ahura-Mazda, supposedly composed by Zoroaster himself but probably the product of an ORAL transmission not written down before the 5th century AD. These poetic hymns, the *Gathas*, consist of 17 compositions (numbers 28–34, 43–51, 53) in an archaic East Iranian language (Avestan) within a corpus of 72 works forming the liturgy of daily worship, known collectively as the *Yasna*.

Greek literary tradition put Zoroaster 258 years before ALEXANDER the Great, making it possible to suggest a teacher–pupil relationship between Zoroaster and PYTHAGORAS. Arguably, Zoroaster had a profound impact upon PRESOCRATIC PHILOSOPHY. His patron, Kavi Vistaspa, was identified as Vistaspa, father of DARIUS I, or as Darius' teacher in the theology of Zoroaster.

Following the conversion of Darius I, Achaemenid rulers apparently worked with the Magi to turn Zoroastrianism into a syncretic, polytheistic, imperial religion. The drinking of *haoma* (Indian *soma*), a hallucinogenic substance (perhaps derived from mushrooms), seems to be part of pre-Zoroastrian Iranian religion re-introduced by the Magi, along with other deities and ritual practices (including fire altars). JDM

See Insler, S. (1975) *The Gathas of Zarathustra: text, translation, commentary*; Boyce, M. (1982) *A History of Zoroastrianism*; West, M. L. (1971) *Early Greek Philosophy and the Orient*.

Sources and Acknowledgements for figures

Additional Abbreviations

Initials follow author abbreviations (see p. vi above). DMW *is D. Miles-Williams.*

Amiet, *Art in the Ancient World* = Amiet, P. et al. (1981) *Art in the Ancient World: a handbook of styles and forms* (trs.).

Blümner, *Technologie* 1–4 = Blümner, H. (1877–1912) *Technologie und terminologie der Gewerbe und Künste bei Griechen und Römern*, 4 vols.

British Museum 1928 = *A Guide to the Department of Greek and Roman Antiquities in the British Museum.*

British Museum 1929 = *A Guide to the Exhibition Illustrating Greek and Roman Life.*

CAH = *Cambridge Ancient History*, Cambridge, 2nd edn.

Cohen 1880–92 = Cohen, H. (1880–92) *Description historique des monnaies frappées sous l'empire romain communement appelées médailles impériales*, 9 vols.

Daremberg–Saglio 1–5 = Daremberg, C. and Saglio, E. (1877–1919) *Dictionnaire des antiquités grecques et romaines d'après les textes et monuments*, 5 vols.

ACCULTURATION: Simon James drawing; ACHAIA, ROMAN: *CAH* 11, map 8; ACHILLES: DMW drawing after a vase in the British Museum; ACROPOLIS, ATHENIAN: (a)–(b) DGJS photos; (c) after *CAH* 5, 216; ACTORS AND ACTRESSES: (a) Daremberg–Saglio 4.1, 436; (b) Daremberg–Saglio 1.2, 1116; ADVERTISING: DJM photo; AEGEAN SEA: (a) *CAH* 3.3, 114; (b) *CAH* 3.3, 250; AENEAS: Daremberg–Saglio 1.1, 106; AFGHANISTAN: DGJS table; AFRICA AND AFRICANS: Daremberg–Saglio 1.1, fig. 169; AFRICA, ROMAN: *CAH* 11, 516; AGORA, ATHENIAN: (a) after *CAH* 5, 212; (b) LF photo; (c) DJM photo; AGRICULTURE: (a) British Museum 1929, 167; (b) DJM/Society for Libyan Studies; AGRIPPINAE, THE: Cohen 1880–92; ALEXANDER III ('THE GREAT'): (a) Daremberg–Saglio 1.1, 181; (b) *CAH* 6, 792–3; ALEXANDRIA: DGJS, *Greek World after Alexander* 216; ALPHABETS: Peter Haarer table; AMAZONS: Daremberg–Saglio 1.1, 222; AMON–RA: Daremberg–Saglio 1.1, 232; AMPHITHEATRE: (a) DSP and DJM, *Life, Death and Entertainment in the Roman World* 229; (b) Cohen 1880–92; AMPHORA: (a) DMW from roughs provided by Ian Whitbread; (b) DJM; ANATOLIA: *CAH* 3.2, 620; ANIMALS: DJM photo; ANNOBAL TAPAPIUS RUFUS: DJM photo; ANTONY, MARK: Cohen 1880–92; APARTMENT BUILDINGS: DJM photo; AQUEDUCTS: (a)–(b) DJM photo; ARA PACIS: DJM photo; ARABIA AND ARABS: *CAH* 14, 690; ARCHES, MONUMENTAL: after Daremberg–Saglio 1.1, 394; ARCHITECTS: after Daremberg–Saglio 2.2, 1250; ARCHITECTURE: (a)–(e) RJAW photos; ARCHITECTURE, MODERN: MJG photo; ARMIES, ORGANIZATION OF: after H. Johnson, *Roman Forts* 29; ARMS AND ARMOUR: (a) *CAH* 3.3, 341; (b)–(c) DJM photos; (d) M. Bishop and JCNC, *Roman Military Equipment* 27; (e) S. James, *Excavations at Dura-Europos, Final Report VII, the Arms and Armour, and other Military Equipment*; ARTILLERY: DJM photo; ASIA, ROMAN: *CAH* 10, map 16; ASTRONOMY: DMW after a photo by J. N. Coldstream, An astronomical graffito from Pithekoussai, *PP* 288, 221–2; ATHENA: British Museum 1928, 195; ATHENIAN EMPIRE: (a) LF after *CAH* 6, 2 and RJAT, *Atlas of Classical History* 44; (b) *CAH* 5, 1–2; ATHENS: (a) LF plan; (b) *CAH* 14, 723; ATHLETES AND ATHLETICS: (a) Daremberg–Saglio 4.2, 1055; (b) Daremberg–Saglio 3.2, 759; (c) Daremberg–Saglio 1.1, 649; AUGUSTUS: (a) JV stemma; (b) A. Claridge, *Rome: an Oxford archaeological guide* 158 (drawing Sheila Gibson); AUXILIARIES: DJM photo; BAALBEK: Simon James photo; BABYLON: *CAH* 3.2, 104; BACCHUS: Daremberg–Saglio 3.2, 1486; BAKERS: DJM photo; BAKING: A. Mau, *Pompeii: its life and art* 388; BALL GAMES: DMW after a vase in the Ashmolean Museum, Oxford; BARBEGAL: DJM photo; BASILICAS: DJM photo; BATH: DJM photo; BATHING: (a) Daremberg–Saglio 1.1, 649–50; (b) HD in DSP and DJM, *Life, Death and Entertainment in the Roman World* 247; BATHS: (a),(c) HD in DSP and DJM, *Life, Death and*

Entertainment in the Roman World 245, 250; (b),(d) DJM photos; BATTLES: HB table; BENEFACTORS AND BENEFACTION: Daremberg–Saglio 1.2, 14443; BIRDS: (a)–(b) DJM photos; BLACK SEA: *CAH* 9, 134; BLACKS: after *CAH* 3.2, 483; BOIOTIA: *CAH* 3.3, 296; BONE: DMW/LF after R. M. Dawkins, *The Sanctuary of Artemis Orthia*, pl. 173; BOOKS: Daremberg–Saglio 3.2, 1180; BOSCOREALE: after W. Jashemski in E. B. Macdougall, *Ancient Roman Villa Gardens*; BRAURON: LF photo; BREAD: Blümner, *Technologie* 1, 90; BRIDGES: DJM photo; BRITANNIA: *CAH* 11, 560; BRITISH ISLES AND BRITONS: from S. James, *The Atlantic Celts* 1999, 101; BURIAL: (a)–(f) DJM photos; BUTCHERY: (a) Daremberg–Saglio 1.2, 1159; (b) Daremberg–Saglio 3.2, 1740; CALENDARS: (a) GJO table; (b) from *CAH* 7.2, 575; CAPITOLIUM: (a) *CAH* 7.2, 252; (b) Daremberg–Saglio 1.2, 904; CARAUSIUS: (a)–(b) Cohen 1880–92; CARPENTRY: Daremberg–Saglio 5, 334; CARTHAGE AND CARTHAGINIANS: (a) *CAH* 7.2, 488–89; (b) DJM photo; CARYATIDS: (a) Daremberg–Saglio 1.2, 930; (b) DJM photo; CAVALRY: (a) Daremberg–Saglio 2.1, 765; (b) DJM photo; CELTS: *CAH* 6, 406; CENSUSES: DJM table, after P. Brunt, *Italian Manpower* 13–14; *CAH* 7.2, 137; CEREALS: LF table; CHALKIDIKE: *CAH* 3.3, 114; CHARCOAL: LF photo; CHARIOT RACING: Daremberg–Saglio 1.2, 1190; CHARIOTS: (a) Daremberg–Saglio 1.2, 1640; (b) Daremberg–Saglio 1.2, 1198; CHILD ABUSE: DMW after a vase in the Museo Civico Archeologico, Bologna; CHILDHOOD: (a)–(b) British Museum 1929, 196; CHOREGIC MONUMENTS: DGJS photo; CHORUS: Daremberg–Saglio 1.2, 1123; CHRISTIANITY: NJC photo; CHURCHES: (a) NJC photo; (b) *CAH* 14, 920; (c) after V. F. Nicolai et al., *The Christian Catacombs of Rome* 28; CIRCUS BUILDINGS: DSP and DJM, *Life, Death and Entertainment in the Roman World* 238; CITIES: (a) DGJS, *Greek World after Alexander* 93; (b) *CAH* 13, 374, fig. 2; COINAGE: (a)–(b): CH tables; COLONIZATION: (a) *CAH* 3.3, 84; (b) *CAH* 3.3, 86; (c) *CAH* 3.3, 87; (d) *CAH* 7.2, 390; COLUMNS, MONUMENTAL: Cohen 1880–92; COMEDY 2: MIDDLE AND NEW COMEDY: Daremberg–Saglio 1.2, 1422; COMMAGENE: DJM photo; CONCRETE: after JDeL in F. Sear, *Roman Architecture* 74; CONSTANTINE I ('THE GREAT'): DJM photo; CONSTANTINOPLE: LR plan; CORINTH: (a)–(b) after C. K. Williams and N. Bookidis, *Corinth XX: the centenary 1896–1996*, (a) xxviii; (b) xxv; COUNCILS: (a) *CAH* 7.1, 378; (b) DJM photo; COUNTING: RW table; CRETE: *CAH* 3.3, 224, *CAH* 3.1, 772; CURSES: from R. Tomlin, in *The Temple of Sulis Minerva at Bath, 2: the finds from the sacred spring* 122–23; CYPRUS: *CAH* 3.3, 58; CYRENE AND CYRENAICA: *CAH* 10, 620; DACIAN WARS: DJM photo; DALMATIA: *CAH* 13, 96–7; DANCE: (a) *CAH* 3.3, 460; (b) Daremberg–Saglio 2.1, 848; DANUBE: *CAH* 10, 546–7; DECEBALUS: DJM photo; DELPHI: *CAH* 5, 194; DEMES: (a) from R. Osborne, *Greece in the Making* 297; (b) LF table; DINING: Daremberg–Saglio 1.2, 1279; DINING ROOMS: DJM after sketches by Pedar Foss; DOMES: (a) DJM photo; (b) RJAW photo; DRAMA: (a) DMW drawing; (b)–(c) from M. Bieber, *The History of the Greek and Roman Theatre* 484, 775; DRAUGHT ANIMALS: DJM photo; DRESS, GREEK: Daremberg–Saglio 4.1, 286–90, 1174–5; DRESS, ROMAN: (a) DAI neg. no. 29.172; (b) Daremberg–Saglio 2.1, 274; DURA EUROPUS: S. James, *Excavations at Dura-Europos, Final Report VII: the arms and armour, and other military equipment*; EARTHQUAKES: DJM photo; EAST GREECE: *CAH* 4, 462; ECONOMY: DJM photo; EDUCATION: (a) Daremberg–Saglio 2.1, 468; (b) Daremberg–Saglio 3.2, 1380; EGYPT: *CAH* 10, 678; ELEPHANTS: *CAH* 6, 831; ELEUSIS AND ELEUSINIAN MYSTERIES: Daremberg–Saglio 2.1, 545; EMPERORS, ROMAN: coin images from Cohen 1880–92; EPIGRAPHY, GREEK: (a)–(c) GJO photographs; EPIGRAPHY, ROMAN: (a) DJM; (b)–(e) LK, *Understanding Roman Inscriptions* (b) 96; (c) 65; (d) 83; (e) 129; EQUESTRIANS: DJM tables; ETRURIA AND ETRUSCANS: *CAH* 4, 678; FASTENING: DMW after D. Ridgway, *Pithekoussai*; FAUSTINA: (a)–(b) Cohen 1880–92; FESTIVALS, GREEK: Daremberg–Saglio 1.2, 1066; FIELD SURVEY: after TWP, *Changing Landscape of South Etruria*; FISH AND FISHING: DJM photo; FISH SAUCES: DJM photo; FLOWERS: Blümner, *Technologie* 1, 309; FOOD SUPPLY: DJM photo; FOOTWEAR: after M. Bishop and JCNC, *Roman Military Equipment* 101; FORTIFICATION: (a)–(c) DGJS photos; (d) DJM photo; FORTS AND FORTRESSES, ROMAN: (a) Simon James drawing – © British Museum; (b)–(c) DJM photos; FORUMS: RL, *Roman Pompeii* 33; FOUNTAINS AND FOUNTAIN HOUSES: (a) Daremberg–Saglio 2.2, 1230; (b) DJM photo; FRONTIERS: (a)–(c) DJM photos; FULLING: (a)–(b) A. Mau, *Pompeii: its life and art* 394; (c) DJM photo; FUNERAL RITES: (a) Daremberg–Saglio 2.2, 1374; (b) Daremberg–Saglio 2.2, 1392; FURNITURE: (a) Blümner, *Technologie*

2, 343; (b) Daremberg–Saglio 3.2, 1724; GAMBLING: Daremberg–Saglio 5, 127; GAMES: DSP and DJM, *Life, Death and Entertainment in the Roman World* 206; GARAMANTES: (a)–(b) DJM photos; GARDENS AND GARDENING: (a) Daremberg–Saglio 3.1, 288; (b) KG, *Archaeology of the Roman Economy* 97; GAUL: (a) *CAH* 9, 382; (b) *CAH* 13, 52–3; GERMANY AND GERMANS: (a) after *CAH* 10, map 9; (b) *CAH* 13, 462; GLADIATORS: (a) British Museum 1929, 63; (b) DJM photo; GODS AND GODDESSES: (a)–(b) DMW after Greek vases in Boston, Copenhagen, London, British Museum, Palermo, Basel, Tarquinia, Florence, Karlsruhe; after Amiet, *Art in the Ancient World* 510, no. 121, 503, no. 84; Daremberg–Saglio 5, 731; GOLD: Daremberg–Saglio 3.2, 1735; GORTYN CODE: JKD in L. Foxhall and A. D. E. Lewis, *Justifications not Justice* 38–9; GRANARIES: DJM photo; GREECE: *CAH* 6, 2; GYMNASIA: Daremberg–Saglio 2.2, 1701; HADES: Daremberg–Saglio 3.1, 508; HADRIAN: Cohen 1880–92; HADRIAN'S WALL: DJM photo; HAIR AND HAIRSTYLING: Daremberg–Saglio 1.2, 1361, 1368–9; HARBOURS: Daremberg–Saglio 5.1, 18; HERCULANEUM: DJM photo; HERMS: Blümner, *Technologie* 2, 340; HERODES ATTICUS: DJM photo; HISPANIA: *CAH* 11, map 3; HOARDS: © British Museum; HOMOSEXUALITY: DMW after a vase in the Ashmolean Museum, Oxford; HOPLITES: *CAH* 3.3, 455; HORSES AND HORSEMANSHIP: Daremberg–Saglio 2.1, 793; HOUSES, GREEK: (a) LF; (b) *CAH* 5, 201; (c) NC, *Household and City Organization at Olynthus*, fig. 25; HOUSES, ROMAN: (a) J.-P. Adam, *Roman Building: materials and techniques* 302; (b)–(e) DJM photos; HUNS: *CAH* 13, 501; HUNTING: DJM photo; IBERIA AND IBERIANS (2): *CAH* 9, 216; INNS: (a) DJM photo; (b) Daremberg–Saglio 1.2, 973; *INSTRUMENTUM DOMESTICUM*: DJM after D. Peacock and D. Williams, *Amphorae and the Roman Economy* 14; IRON: (a) Blümner, *Technologie* 4, 364; b) Daremberg–Saglio 2.2, 1091; ISIS: Daremberg–Saglio 3.1, 583; ITALY, ROMAN: (a) *CAH* 11, 404; (b) TWP, *Roman Italy* 15; JUDAEA: *CAH* 11, 666; JULIA: Cohen 1880–92; JULIA DOMNA: Cohen 1880–92; JULIUS CAESAR: Cohen 1880–92; JUSTINIAN: *CAH* 14, 68; KITCHENS *AND* KITCHEN UTENSILS: DJM photo; *KOUROI* AND *KORAI*: *kouros*, National Museum, Athens, Amiet, *Art in the Ancient World* 371, no. 155; *kore*, Louvre, Amiet, *Art in the Ancient World* 369, no. 143; LAMPS: (a)–(b) DJM photo; LATINS: *CAH* 7.2, map 2; LEATHER AND LEATHER WORKING: Blümner, *Technologie* 1, 287; LEGIONS: (a) DJM photo; (b) DJM table; LEPCIS MAGNA: (a)–(b) DJM photos; LEPTIMINUS: David Stone plan; LIBRARIES: DGJS photo; LIGHTHOUSES: (a) Daremberg–Saglio 4.1, 599; (b) DJM photo; LITERACY: A. Mau, *Pompeii: its life and art* 56; LIVIA: Cohen 1880–92; LOCKS: after British Museum 1929, 140; LONDON: DP, *Roman London* 67; LOVE: Daremberg–Saglio 2.1, 838; LYRIC POETRY: Daremberg–Saglio 3.2, 394; MACEDONIA, ANCIENT: (a) *CAH* 6, 724; (b) DGJS table; MACHINES: Blümner, *Technologie* 3, 126–7; MAGNA GRAECIA: *CAH* 3.3, 96; MANUFACTURING: Blümner, *Technologie* 4, 250; MAPS: RJAT photo; MARBLE: HD map; MARCOMANNIC WARS: DJM photo; MARCUS AURELIUS: DJM photo; MARKET BUILDINGS: (a)–(b) DJM photos; MARKETS: Blümner, *Technologie* 4, 252; MARRIAGE: (a) Daremberg–Saglio 3.2, 1654; (b) Daremberg–Saglio 2.1, 838; MASADA: DJM photo; MASKS: Daremberg–Saglio 3.1, 220; MEDICINE: © British Museum; MEDUSA: DMW after a vase in the Louvre, Paris; MEROË: *CAH* 3.2, 678; MESSALINA: Cohen 1880–92; METALLURGY: DJM photo; MILLS AND MILLING: Daremberg–Saglio 3.2, 1961; MINES: Daremberg–Saglio 3.2, 1853; MINING: DJM photo; MITHRAS: (a) DJM photo; (b) Daremberg–Saglio 3.2, 1950; MONTE TESTACCIO: DJM photo; MOSAICS: (a)–(c) DJM photos; (d) RJAW photo; MUMMY PORTRAITS: © British Museum; MUSIC: DMW after a vase in the British Museum; MUSICIANS: DJM photo; NAVIES: Daremberg–Saglio 4.1, 26; ODYSSEUS: Daremberg–Saglio 4.2, 1354; OILS: Blümner, *Technologie* 1, 335; OLIVE, OLIVE OIL: (a) Blümner, *Technologie* 1, 333; (b) DJM photo; OLYMPIA: after *CAH* 5, 194; ORDERS, ARCHITECTURAL: after *Penguin Dictionary of Architecture*, 3rd edn, 230–31; ORPHEUS: DJM photo; OSTIA AND PORTUS: DJM map; OSTRACISM: after *CAH* 4, 337; PAINTING: Blümner, *Technologie* 3, 226; PALMYRA: Simon James photo; PANTHEON: (a) A. Claridge, *Rome: an Oxford archaeological guide* 202; (b)–(d) DJM photos; PARTHENON: (a)–(b) DGJS photos; PARTHIA AND PARTHIANS: *CAH* 9, 230–31; PELOPONNESE: *CAH* 3.3, 322; PERFUME: Blümner, *Technologie* 1, 363; PERGAMON: (a) DGJS, *The Greek World after Alexander* 97; (b) DGJS table; PERSIA AND PERSIANS: *CAH* 4, 2–3; PERSIAN WARS, GREEK: *CAH* 4, 528–9; PESTS: DMW drawing from Attic vase; PETRA: DJM photo; PETS: Daremberg–Saglio 1.1, 698; PHALLUS: DJM photo; PHILIP II: © University of Manchester; PHOENICIA AND PHOENICIANS: (a) *CAH* 3.2, 462; (b) after *CAH*

3.2, 483; PIRAEUS: (a) after *CAH* 5, 208; (b) after DJB, Ancient harbours, *International Journal of Nautical Archaeology* 11.3, fig. 3; PLUMBING: DJM photo; POMPEII (CITY): (a) adapted from RJAT, *Atlas of Classical History* 116; (b)–(c) DJM photos; PORTRAITURE: Daremberg–Saglio 3.1, 408; POTTERY, GREEK: LF after R. Osborne, *Greek Art* 114–15; POTTERY, ROMAN: (a)–(b) DJM photos; PRAETORIAN GUARD: Simon James drawing; PRESSES: (a) DJM, *Africa Romana* 11, 591; (b)–(c) DJM photos; PRIAPUS: DJM photo; PROCESSIONS: Daremberg–Saglio 1.1, 599; PROSTITUTES AND PROSTITUTION: DJM photo; PROVINCES AND PROVINCIAL GOVERNMENT, ROMAN: (a) DJM table; (b) from B. Jones and DJM, *Atlas of Roman Britain* 149; PTOLEMIES: DGJS table; QUARRIES AND QUARRYING: DJM photo; RELIGION: (a) Daremberg–Saglio 1.1, 626; (b) DJM photo; *RES GESTAE*: DJM photo; RIOTS: A. Mau, *Pompeii: its life and art* 221; RITUAL: DJM photo; ROADS, ROMAN: (a) *CAH* 9, 42; (b)–(c) DJM photos; ROMAN EMPIRE: *CAH* 11, map 1; ROME: (a) © Studio Verzelli; (b) *CAH* 10, 786; (c) A. Claridge, *Rome: an Oxford archaeological guide* 60; (d)–(e) DJM photos; RURAL SETTLEMENT: DJM in *JRA* 1, 46; SACRIFICE: (a) Daremberg–Saglio 1.1, 349; (b) Daremberg–Saglio 2.1, 298; (c) A. Claridge, *Rome: an Oxford archaeological guide* 238; (d) DJM photo; SAMNITES: *CAH* 7.2, map 5; SAMOSATA: DJM photo; SARCOPHAGUS: DJM photo; SARDINIA: *CAH* 10, 444; SASSANIAN EMPIRE: (a) *CAH* 13, 440; (b) JV table; SCREWS: Blümner, *Technologie* 1, 188; SCULPTURE: (a) Blümner, *Technologie* 4, 330; (b)–(c) LF photo; (d) DJM photo; SCYTHIA AND SCYTHIANS: *CAH* 4, 425; SELEUKIDS: KB table; SENATE AND SENATORS, ROMAN: DJM photos; SEVERUS, SEPTIMIUS: JV stemma; SEX: DJM photo; SHIPS AND SHIPBUILDING: (a) Daremberg–Saglio 4.1, 35; (b) Daremberg–Saglio 4.1, 40; SHIPWRECKS: *CAH* 3.1, 791; SHOES: Blümner, *Technologie* 1, 289; SHOPS AND SHOPPING: (a)–(b) Daremberg–Saglio 5, 9; SICILY: *CAH* 5, 148; SIEGES AND SIEGE WARFARE: D. Kennedy and D. Riley, *Rome's Desert Frontier from the Air* 98; SILPHIUM: (a) Daremberg–Saglio 1.1, 232; (b) Daremberg–Saglio 3.2, 1222; SLAVERY: British Museum 1929, 14; SPARTA: (a)–(b) LF photos; (c) DGJS table; SPINNING: Blümner, *Technologie* 1, 132; STILICHO: Daremberg–Saglio 2.1, 274; STOAS: (a)–(b) DGJS photos; SULPICIA LEPIDINA: © British Museum; SUNDIALS: DJM photo; SWIMMING: Daremberg–Saglio 1.1, 651; *SYMPOSIA*: Daremberg–Saglio 1.2, 850; SYRIA, ROMAN: (a) *CAH* 11, 636; (b) *CAH* 13, 440–41; TANIT: DJM photo; TEMPLES: (a) DJM photo; (b) DGJS photo; (c)–(e) DJM photos; TETRARCHS: (a) NJC photo; (b) JV stemma; TEXTILES: Daremberg–Saglio 3.2, 1739; THEATRES: (a) DGJS photo; (b) DSP and DJM, *Life, Death and Entertainment in the Roman World* 211; (c) DJM photo; (d) *CAH* 11, 389; THEODOSIUS I: JV stemma; THESEUS: Daremberg–Saglio 3.2, 883; THESSALY: *CAH* 6, 744; THRACE AND THRACIANS: *CAH* 4, 425; TIMGAD: DJM photo; TOGA: DJM photo; TOILETS: DJM photo; TOMBS: (a)–(b) DJM photos; TOOLS: Blümner, *Technologie* 4, 371; TOWN PLANNING: (a) DGJS, *Greek World after Alexander* 94; (b) DGJS, *Greek World after Alexander* 90; (c) DJM photo; TRADE: DJM photo; TRAJAN: JV stemma; TRIER: *CAH* 13, 385; TRIUMPHS: (a)–(b) DJM photos; (c) DJM table; TROPHIES, MILITARY: (a) Daremberg–Saglio 5, 516; (b) DJM photo; TROY: *CAH* 1.2, 412; VASE-PAINTING: Blümner, *Technologie* 2, 85; VEGETABLES: LF table; VEII: *CAH* 7.2, 296; VESPASIAN: JV stemma; VILLAS: (a)–(c) DJM photos; WALL-PAINTING: DJM photos; WAR: DJM/JV table; WAREHOUSES: (a) Daremberg–Saglio 3.1, 269; (b) DJM photo; WATER SUPPLY: DJM photo; WEAVING: DMW after a vase in Chiusi; WEIGHTS AND MEASURES: (a) Daremberg–Saglio 3.2, 1228; (b) British Museum 1929, 156; (c) RPD-J table; WHEELED VEHICLES: (a), (c) Daremberg–Saglio 1.2, 928–9; (b) OVN image; WINE: (a) DJM photo; (b)–(c) Daremberg–Saglio 5, 896; WOMEN: (a) Daremberg–Saglio 2.2, 1708; (b) DJM photo; WORKSHOPS: RL, *Roman Pompeii: space and society* 66; WRITING: Daremberg–Saglio 5, 2; ZODIAC: (a)–(b) Daremberg–Saglio 5, 1052, 1051.